SIXTH EDITION

ART HISTORY

MARILYN
STOKSTAD

MICHAEL W.
COTHREN

This sixth edition of **ART HISTORY** *is dedicated
to the memory of Marilyn Stokstad (1929–2016) who
conceived and created the first edition, published in 1995.*

Pearson

Editor-in-Chief: Sarah Touborg
Sponsoring Editor: Helen Ronan
Product Marketing Manager: Jeremy Intal
Product Marketing Assistant: Frank Alarcon
Executive Field Marketer: Wendy Albert
Project Management Team Lead: Melissa Feimer
Content Producer: Barbara Cappuccio
Senior Producer, REVEL: Rich Barnes
Digital Imaging Technician: Corin Skidds

This book was designed and produced by
Laurence King Publishing Ltd., London
www.laurenceking.com

Editorial Manager: Kara Hattersley-Smith
Senior Editor: Sophie Wise
Production Manager: Simon Walsh
Designer: Ian Hunt
Picture Researchers: Katharina Gruber and Julia Ruxton

Cover image: Miriam Schapiro, *Personal Appearance #3*, 1973.
Acrylic and fabric on canvas, 60 × 50″(152.4 × 127 cm). Private collection.

Acknowledgments of third party content appear on page 1180, which constitutes an extension of this copyright page.

Library of Congress Cataloging-in-Publication Data
Names: Stokstad, Marilyn, 1929-2016, author. | Cothren, Michael Watt, author.
Title: Art History / Marilyn Stokstad, Michael W. Cothren.
Description: Sixth edition. | Upper Saddle River : Pearson, [2018] |
Includes
    bibliographical references and index.
Identifiers: LCCN 2016034108| ISBN 9780134475882 (combined volume) | ISBN 0134475887 (combined volume) |
    ISBN 9780134479279 (student edition volume 1) | ISBN 0134479270 (student edition volume 1) |
    ISBN 9780134479262 (student edition volume 2) | ISBN 0134479262 (student edition volume 2)
Subjects: LCSH: Art--History--Textbooks.
Classification: LCC N5300 .S923 2018 | DDC 709--dc23
LC record available at https://lccn.loc.gov/2016034108

2 17

Student Edition Combined Volume
ISBN-10:   0-13-447588-7
ISBN-13: 978-0-13-447588-2

Books a la Carte Combined Volume
ISBN-10:   0-13-447589-5
ISBN-13: 978-0-13-447589-9

Brief Contents

Contents

29 Arts of Africa from the Sixteenth Century to the Present   894

30 European and American Art, 1715–1840   920

31 Mid- to Late Nineteenth-Century Art in Europe and the United States   978

Letter from the Author

Dear Colleagues,

When Marilyn Stokstad wrote the first edition of *Art History* in the early 1990s, it represented an historical advance in the conception and teaching of the history of art. The discipline had recently gone through a period of crisis and creativity that challenged the assumptions behind the survey course and questioned the canon of works that had long been its foundation. We all rethought what we were doing, and this soul searching made us better teachers—more honest and relevant, more passionate and inclusive. With characteristic energy and intelligence, Marilyn stepped up to the task of conceiving and creating a new survey book for a new generation of students ready to reap the benefits of this refined notion of art history. From the beginning, she made it global in scope, inclusive in coverage, warm and welcoming in tone. Marilyn highlighted the role of women in the history of art both by increasing the number of women artists and by expanding the range of art to focus on media and genres that had traditionally engaged female artists and patrons.

It was an honor to become part of her project almost a decade ago, and it is my sad responsibility to acknowledge her passing, just as this sixth edition went to press. To me, she was more than a brilliant art historian; she was a loyal and compassionate colleague, a great friend. The warmth and trust with which she welcomed me into the writing of *Art History* was one of the great experiences of my professional life. I will truly miss her, and I will work faithfully to continue her legacy as this book moves into the future. I promised her I would.

After all, reconsidering and refining what we do never ceases. Like art, learning and teaching change as we and our culture change, responsive to new objectives and new understandings. Opportunities for growth sometimes emerge in unexpected situations. One day, while I was inching through sluggish suburban traffic with my daughter Emma—a gifted teacher—I confessed my disappointment about my survey students' struggle with mastering basic information. "Why," I asked rhetorically, "is it so difficult for them to learn these facts?" Emma's unexpected answer shifted the question and reframed the discussion. "Dad," she said, "you are focusing on the wrong aspect of your teaching. What are you trying to accomplish by asking your students to learn those facts? Clarify your objectives first, then question whether your assessment is actually the best way to encourage its accomplishment."

Emma's question inspired me to pause and reflect on what it is we seek to accomplish in art history survey courses. One of my primary goals has been encouraging

my students to slow down and spend extended time studying the illustrations of the works of art, what I call "slow looking." I thought memorizing the IDs would accomplish this. But I have grown to realize that there are more effective ways to make this happen, especially in the new online REVEL format that is transforming this textbook into an interactive learning experience. REVEL is more like a classroom than a book. It is based on the premise that students will focus more effectively on a series of changing formats tailored to the content being presented. When I piloted REVEL in my survey classroom last Fall, I discovered that my students were "slow looking" while taking advantage of interactive REVEL features such as the pan/zoom figures (which allow them to zoom in on details) and the architectural panoramas (which allow them to explore the interacting spaces of architectural interiors from multiple viewpoints). I doubted my students would take advantage of these opportunities while doing "assigned reading," but I was wrong. The first week of class a student's hand shot up to ask if I could explain a detail she had seen when using the pan/zoom. Within the same week, another student shared his surprise at the small size of a work of art discovered when clicking on the pan/zoom's scale feature. In three decades of teaching art history survey, never had a student brought to class an observation or question about scale, even though measurements were included in captions. I love books, I really do, but in my experience REVEL is a more effective teaching resource.

I urge you to continue thinking with me about how the study of art history can be meaningful and nourishing for students. Our discipline originated in dialogue and is founded on the desire to talk with each other about why works of art matter and why they affect us so deeply. I would love to hear from you—mcothre1@swarthmore.edu.

Warm regards,

Michael

What's New

WHY USE THIS NEW EDITION?

Art history—what a fascinating and fluid discipline,which evolves as the latest research becomes available for debate and consideration. The sixth edition of *Art History* has been revised to reflect such new discoveries, recent research, and fresh interpretive perspectives, and also to address the changing needs of the audience—both students and educators. With these goals in mind and by incorporating feedback from our many users and reviewers, we have sought to make this edition an improvement in sensitivity, readability, and accessibility without losing anything in comprehensiveness, in scholarly precision, or in its ability to engage readers.

To facilitate student learning and understanding of art history, the sixth edition is centered on six key Learning Objectives. These overarching goals helped steer and shape this revision with their emphasis on the fundamental reasons we teach art history to undergraduates, and they have been repeated at the beginning of each chapter, tailored to the subject matter in that section of the book so that the student will be continually reminded of the goals and objectives of the study of art history.

LEARNING OBJECTIVES FOR *ART HISTORY*

1. Identify the visual hallmarks of regional and period styles for formal, technical, and expressive qualities.

2. Interpret the meaning of works of art from diverse cultures, periods, and locations based on their themes, subjects, and symbols.

3. Relate artists and works of art to their cultural, economic, and political contexts.

4. Apply the vocabulary and concepts used to discuss works of art, artists, and art history.

5. Interpret art using appropriate art historical methods, such as observation and inductive reasoning.

6. Select visual and textual evidence to support an argument or interpretation.

DESIGNING *ART HISTORY* IN REVEL

One of the principal objectives of the current edition has been to advance the transformation of the traditional narrative into an interactive learning experience in REVEL. REVEL is conceived to promote learning in a digital platform that is engaging and meaningful to today's student. Along with traditional narrative text passages, features such as pan/zoom images, videos, architectural panoramas, and audio text are integrated to better explain and present concepts key to understanding the history of art.

- **Pan/zooms** appear with a simple click for most of the figures, allowing students to zoom in and examine details with stunning clarity and resolution, and then return to the overall view of the work of art, so they can relate these details to the whole.

- The pan/zooms' **scale feature** opens a window where works of art appear next to a scaled human figure (or for small works a scaled human hand), giving students an instant sense of the size of what they are studying. Since all works of art are scaled in a fundamental sense to the size of human creators and viewers (rather than to an arbitrary measuring system),

this intuitive communication of size is more instructive for students than the specific measurements found in the captions.

- There are three kinds of **writing prompts** in each chapter. All are keyed to specific works of art and appear in conjunction with figures that illustrate the works. **Journaling** prompts focus on building skills of visual analysis; **Shared Writing** responses relate the material in the chapter to today's world; and **Writing Space** prompts encourage students to engage in cross-cultural thinking, often across chapters.

NEW TO THIS EDITION OF REVEL

- **3D animations of architectural and art historical techniques** depict and explain processes and methods that are difficult for students to grasp simply through narrative text.

- **New panoramas from global sites** sourced from 360Cities have been integrated, bringing students into the setting of major buildings and monuments such as the Taj Mahal and Great Zimbabwe.

- **Each and every Closer Look** has been transformed into a REVEL video presentation, where students are guided through a detailed examination of the work, coordinated with the interpretive material about style, subject matter, and cultural context as it unfolds.

SOME ADDITIONAL CONTENT HIGHLIGHTS OF THE NEW EDITION

- **Global coverage has been deepened** with the addition of new works of art and revised discussions that incorporate new scholarship. This is especially true in the cases of South and Southeast Asia, as well as Africa—the chapters addressing these areas have been significantly reworked and expanded.

- **Chapter 33 on contemporary art** has been rethought, reorganized, and reworked for greater clarity and timeliness. Numerous new works have been incorporated.

- Throughout, **images have been updated** whenever new and improved images were available or works of art have been cleaned or restored.

- The **language used to characterize works of art**—especially those that attempt to capture the lifelike appearance of the natural world—has been **refined and clarified** to bring greater precision and nuance.

- In response to readers' requests, **discussion of many major monuments** has been revised and expanded.

- **New works have been added** to the discussion in many chapters to enhance and enrich what is said in the text. These include the Standard of Ur, the Great Mosque of Damascus, a painting from the tomb of Nebamun, the Ardabil Carpet, the burial mask of Pakal the Great, Mesa Verde, Kim Hongdo's scene of roof tiling, Imogen Cunningham's *Two Callas*, and the works of many additional contemporary artists. In addition, the following artists are now discussed through new, and more representative, works: Zhao Mengfu, Rosalba Carriera, Antonio Canova, Georgia O'Keeffe, Vladimir Tatlin, Paula Modersohn-Becker, Suzuki Harunobu, and Mary Cassatt.

Acknowledgments and Gratitude

Art History, originally written by Marilyn Stokstad and first published by Harry N. Abrams, Inc. and Prentice Hall, Inc. in 1995, has relied, each time it has been revised, on the contributions of colleagues. Their work is reflected here, and they deserve enduring gratitude since this sixth edition represents the cumulative efforts of the distinguished group of scholars and educators who contributed to the previous five editions. The work of Stephen Addiss, Chutsing Li, Marylin M. Rhie, and Christopher D. Roy for the original book has been updated by David Binkley and Patricia Darish (Africa); Claudia Brown and Robert Mowry (China and Korea); Patricia Graham (Japan); Rick Asher (South and Southeast Asia); D. Fairchild Ruggles (Islamic); Claudia Brittenham (Americas); Sara Orel and Carol Ivory (Pacific cultures); and Bradford R. Collins, David Cateforis, Patrick Frank, and Joy Sperling (Modern). For this sixth edition, Robert DeCaroli reworked the chapters on South and Southeast Asia; Susan Kart extensively rethought and revised the chapters on African art; and Virginia Spivey did the same for the final chapter, "The International Scene since the 1950s".

Words can hardly express the depth of my own gratitude to Marilyn Stokstad, who welcomed me in 2008 with enthusiasm and trust into the collaborative adventure of revising this historic textbook, conceived for students in the 21st century. We worked together on *Art History* since the fourth edition, and with her passing in 2016 as this sixth edition was going to press, I have lost a treasured colleague.

Marilyn would want me to thank her University of Kansas colleagues Sally Cornelison, Susan Craig, Susan Earle, Charles Eldredge, Kris Ercums, Sherry Fowler, Stephen Goddard, Saralyn Reece Hardy, Marsha Haufler, Marni Kessler, Amy McNair, John Pulz, Linda Stone Ferrier, and John Younger for their help and advice; and also her friends Katherine Giele and Katherine Stannard, William Crowe, David Bergeron, and Geraldo de Sousa for their sympathy and encouragement. Very special thanks go to Marilyn's sister, Karen Leider, and her niece, Anna Leider, without whose enduring support, this book would not have seen the light of day.

At Pearson, I have collaborated closely with two gifted and dedicated editors, Sarah Touborg and Helen Ronan, whose almost daily support in so many ways was at the center of Marilyn's and my work for years. I cannot imagine working on this project without them. Also working with me at Pearson were Barbara Cappuccio, Joe Scordato, Melissa Feimer, Cory Skidds, Victoria Engros, and Claire Ptaschinski. At Laurence King Publishing, Sophie Wise, Kara Hattersley-Smith, Julia Ruxton, Katharina Gruber, and Simon Walsh oversaw the production of this new edition. Much appreciation also goes to Wendy Albert, Marketing Manager extraordinaire, as well as the entire Social Sciences and Arts team at Pearson. My work has been greatly facilitated by the research assistance and creative ideas of Fletcher Coleman, Andrew Finegold, Moses Hanson-Harding, and Zoe Wray, who helped with previous editions. I also have been supported by a host of colleagues at Swarthmore College. Generations of students challenged me to hone my pedagogical skills and steady my focus on what is at stake in telling the history of art. My colleagues in the Art Department—especially Stacy Bomento, Syd Carpenter, June Cianfrana, Randall Exon, Logan Grider, Laura Holzman, Constance Hungerford, Brian Meunier, Thomas Morton, Derek Burdette, Patricia Reilly, and Tomoko Sakomura—have answered questions, shared insights on works in their areas of expertise, and offered unending encouragement and support. I am so lucky to work with them.

Many art historians have provided assistance, often at a moment's notice, and I am especially grateful to Betina Bergman, Claudia Brown, Elizabeth Brown, Brigitte Buettner, David Cateforis, Madeline Caviness, Sarah Costello, Cynthia Kristan-Graham, Joyce de Vries, Cheri Falkenstien-Doyle, Sharon Gerstel, Kevin Glowaki, Ed Gyllenhaal, Julie Hochstrasser, Vida J. Hull, Penny Jolly, Padma Kaimal, Barbara Kellum, Alison Kettering, Benton Kidd, Ann Kuttner, Anne Leader, Steven LeBlanc, Cary Liu, Elizabeth Marlowe, Samuel Morse, Thomas Morton, Kathleen Nolan, David Shapiro, Mary Shepard, Larry Silver, David Simon, Donna Sadler, Jeffrey Smith, Mark Tucker, and Tarynn Witten.

I am fortunate to have the support of many friends especially John Brendler, David Eldridge, Fiona Harrison, Stephen Lehmann, Mary Marissen, Denis Ott, Bruce and Carolyn Stephens, and Rick and Karen Taylor.

My preparation for this work runs deep. My parents, Mildred and Wat Cothren, showered me with unconditional love and made significant sacrifices to support my education, from pre-school through graduate school. Sara Shymanski, elementary school librarian at St. Martin's Episcopal School in Metairie, Louisiana, gave me courage through her example and loving encouragement to pursue unexpected passions for history, art, and the search to make them meaningful in both past and present. Françoise Celly, my painting professor during a semester abroad in Aix-en-Provence, sent me to study the Romanesque sculpture of Autun, initiating my journey toward a career in art history. At Vanderbilt University, Ljubica Popovich fostered this new interest by unlocking the mysteries of Byzantine art. My extraordinary daughters Emma and Nora remain a constant inspiration. I am so grateful for their delight in my passion for art's history, and for their dedication to keeping me from taking myself too seriously. But deepest gratitude is reserved for Susan Lowry, my wife and soul-mate, who brings joy to my life on a daily basis. She is not only patient and supportive during the long distractions of my work on this book; she provides help in countless ways. The greatest accomplishment of my life in art history occurred on the day I met her in graduate school at Columbia University in 1973.

It seems fitting in this sixth edition of *Art History*, dedicated to the memory of the scholar who created it, to conclude with the statement that ended Marilyn's "Preface" for the first edition in 1995, since it captures in her inimitable style my own thoughts as well. "As each of us develops a genuine appreciation of the arts, we come to see them as the ultimate expression of human faith and integrity as well as creativity. I have tried here to capture that creativity, courage, and vision in such a way as to engage and enrich even those encountering art history for the very first time. If I have done that, I will feel richly rewarded."

Michael W. Cothren
Sedona, AZ, and Philadelphia, PA

IN GRATITUDE: As its predecessors did, this sixth edition of *Art History* benefited from the reflections and assessments of a distinguished team of scholars and educators. The authors and Pearson are grateful to the following academic reviewers for their numerous insights and suggestions for improvement: Victor Coonin, Rhodes College; Sarah Blick, Kenyon College; Elizabeth Adan, California Polytechnic State University, San Luis Obispo; Sara Orel, Truman State University; Carolyn E. Tate, Texas Tech University; April Morris, University of Alabama; Catherine Pagani, University of Alabama; Jennie Klein, Ohio University; Rebecca Stone, Emory University; Tanja Jones, University of Alabama; Keri Watson, University of Central Florida; Stephany Rimland, Harper College; Elizabeth Sutton, University of Northern Iowa; Elizabeth Carlson, Lawrence University; Laura Crary, Presbyterian College; Camille Serchuk, Southern Connecticut State University; Lydia Host, Bishop State Community College; K.C. Williams, Northwest Florida State College; Elissa Graff, Lincoln Memorial University; Ute Wachsmann-Linnan, Columbia College; Amy Johnson, Otterbein University; Lisa Alembik, Georgia Perimeter College; Virginia Dacosta, West Chester University; Megan Levacy, Georgia Perimeter College; Victor Martinez, Monmouth College, Julia Sienkewicz, Duquesne University; Jamie Ratliff, University of Minnesota Duluth; Maureen McGuire, Full Sail University; Heather Vinson, University of West Georgia.

This edition has continued to benefit from the assistance and advice of scores of other teachers and scholars who generously answered questions, gave recommendations on organization and priorities, and provided specialized critiques during the course of work on previous editions.

We are grateful for the detailed critiques from the following readers across the country who were of invaluable assistance during work on the third, fourth, and fifth editions:

Craig Adcock, University of Iowa; Charles M. Adelman, University of Northern Iowa; Fred C. Albertson, University of Memphis; Kimberly Allen-Kattus, Northern Kentucky University; Frances Altvater, College of William and Mary; Kirk Ambrose, University of Colorado, Boulder; Michael Amy, Rochester Institute of Technology; Lisa Aronson, Skidmore College; Susan Jane Baker, University of Houston; Jennifer L. Ball, Brooklyn College, CUNY; Samantha Baskind, Cleveland State University; Tracey Boswell, Johnson County Community College; Mary Brantl, St. Edward's University; Jane H. Brown, University of Arkansas at Little Rock; Denise Budd, Bergen Community College; Stephen Caffey, Texas A&M University; Anne Chapin, Brevard College; Michelle Moseley Christian, Virginia Tech; Charlotte Lowry Collins, Southeastern Louisiana University; Sarah Kielt Costello, University of Houston; Roger J. Crum, University of Dayton; Brian A. Curran, Penn State University; Cindy B. Damschroder, University of Cincinnati; Michael T. Davis, Mount Holyoke College; Juilee Decker, Georgetown College; Laurinda Dixon, Syracuse University; Rachael Z. DeLue, Princeton University; Anne Derbes, Hood College; Sheila Dillon, Duke University; Caroline Downing, State University of New York at Potsdam; Laura Dufresne, Winthrop University; Suzanne Eberle, Kendall College of Art & Design of Ferris State University; April Eisman, Iowa State University; Dan Ewing, Barry University; Allen Farber, State University of New York at Oneonta; Arne Flaten, Coastal Carolina University; William Ganis, Wells College; John Garton, Cleveland Institute of Art; Richard Gay, University of North Carolina, Pembroke; Regina Gee, Montana State University; Sharon Gerstel, University of California, Los Angeles; Rosi Gilday, University of Wisconsin, Oshkosh; Kevin Glowacki, Texas A&M University; Amy Golahny, Lycoming College; Steve Goldberg, Hamilton College; Bertha Gutman, Delaware County Community College; Deborah Haynes, University of Colorado, Boulder; Mimi Hellman, Skidmore College; Julie Hochstrasser, University of Iowa; Eva Hoffman, Tufts University; Eunice D. Howe, University of Southern California; Phillip Jacks, George Washington University; Kimberly Jones, University of Texas, Austin; Evelyn Kain, Ripon College; Nancy Kelker, Middle Tennessee State University; Barbara Kellum, Smith College; Patricia Kennedy, Ocean County College; Jennie Klein, Ohio University; Katie Kresser, Seattle Pacific University; Cynthia Kristan-Graham, Auburn University; Barbara Platten Lash, Northern Virginia Community College; Paul Lavy, University of Hawaii at Manoa; William R. Levin, Centre College; Susan Libby, Rollins College; Henry Luttikhuizen, Calvin College; Lynn Mackenzie, College of DuPage; Elisa C. Mandell, California State University, Fullerton; Elizabeth Mansfield, New York University; Pamela Margerm, Kean University; Elizabeth Marlowe, Colgate University; Marguerite Mayhall, Kean University; Katherine A. McIver, University of Alabama at Birmingham; Dennis McNamara, Triton College; Gustav Medicus, Kent State University; Lynn Metcalf, St. Cloud State University; Janine Mileaf, Swarthmore College; Jo-Ann Morgan, Coastal Carolina University; Eleanor Moseman, Colorado State University; Johanna D. Movassat, San Jose State University; Sheila Muller, University of Utah; Beth A. Mulvaney, Meredith College; Dorothy Munger, Delaware Community College; Jacqueline Marie Musacchio, Wellesley College; Bonnie Noble, University of North Carolina at Charlotte; Elizabeth Olton, University of Texas at San Antonio; Leisha O'Quinn, Oklahoma State University; Lynn Ostling, Santa Rosa Junior College; David Parrish, Purdue University; Willow Partington,

Hudson Valley Community College; Martin Patrick, Illinois State University; Ariel Plotek, Clemson University; Patricia V. Podzorski, University of Memphis; Albert Reischuck, Kent State University; Margaret Richardson, George Mason University; James Rubin, Stony Brook University; Jeffrey Ruda, University of California, Davis; Tomoko Sakomura, Swarthmore College; Donna Sandrock, Santa Ana College; Erika Schneider, Framingham State University; Michael Schwartz, Augusta State University; Diane Scillia, Kent State University; Joshua A. Shannon, University of Maryland; David Shapiro; Karen Shelby, Baruch College; Susan Sidlauskas, Rutgers University; Jeffrey Chipps Smith, University of Texas, Austin; Royce W. Smith, Wichita State University; Stephanie Smith, Youngstown State University; Stephen Smithers, Indiana State University; Janet Snyder, West Virginia University; Richard Sundt, University of Oregon; Laurie Sylwester, Columbia College (Sonora); Carolyn Tate, Texas Tech University; Rita Tekippe, University of West Georgia; James Terry, Stephens College; Tilottama Tharoor, New York University; Sarah Thompson, Rochester Institute of Technology; Michael Tinkler, Hobart and William Smith Colleges; Amelia Trevelyan, University of North Carolina at Pembroke; Rebecca Turner, Savannah College of Art and Design; Julie Tysver, Greenville Technical College; Mary Jo Watson, University of Oklahoma; Reid Wood, Lorain County Community College; Jerelyn Woodard, University of Houston; Linda Woodward, LSC Montgomery.

Our thanks also to additional expert readers including: Susan Cahan, Yale University; David Craven, University of New Mexico; Marian Feldman, University of California, Berkeley; Dorothy Johnson, University of Iowa; Genevra Kornbluth, University of Maryland; Patricia Mainardi, City University of New York; Clemente Marconi, Columbia University; Tod Marder, Rutgers University; Mary Miller, Yale University; Elizabeth Penton, Durham Technical Community College; Catherine B. Scallen, Case Western University; Kim Shelton, University of California, Berkeley.

Many people reviewed the original edition of *Art History* and have continued to assist with its revision. Every chapter was read by one or more specialists. For work on the original book and assistance with subsequent editions thanks go to: Barbara Abou-el-Haj, SUNY Binghamton; Roger Aiken, Creighton University; Molly Aitken; Anthony Alofsin, University of Texas, Austin; Christiane Andersson, Bucknell University; Kathryn Arnold; Julie Aronson, Cincinnati Art Museum; Michael Auerbach, Vanderbilt University; Larry Beck; Evelyn Bell, San Jose State University; Janetta Rebold Benton, Pace University; Janet Berlo, University of Rochester; Sarah Blick, Kenyon College; Jonathan Bloom, Boston College; Suzaan Boettger; Judith Bookbinder, Boston College; Marta Braun, Ryerson University; Elizabeth Broun, Smithsonian American Art Museum; Glen R. Brown, Kansas State University; Maria Elena Buszek, Kansas City Art Institute; Robert G. Calkins; Annmarie Weyl Carr; April Clagget, Keene State College; William W. Clark, Queens College, CUNY; John Clarke, University of Texas, Austin; Jaqueline Clipsham; Ralph T. Coe; Robert Cohon, The Nelson-Atkins Museum of Art; Alessandra Comini; James D'Emilio, University of South Florida; Walter Denny, University of Massachusetts, Amherst; Jerrilyn Dodds, City College, CUNY; Lois Drewer, Index of Christian Art; Joseph Dye, Virginia Museum of Art; James Farmer, Virginia Commonwealth University; Grace Flam, Salt Lake City Community College; Mary D. Garrard; Paula Gerson, Florida State University; Walter S. Gibson; Dorothy Glass; Oleg Grabar; Randall Griffey, Amherst College; Cynthia Hahn, Florida State University; Sharon Hill, Virginia Commonwealth University; John Hoopes, University of Kansas; Reinhild Janzen, Washburn University; Wendy Kindred, University of Maine at Fort Kent; Alan T. Kohl, Minneapolis College of Art; Ruth Kolarik, Colorado College; Carol H. Krinsky, New York University; Aileen Laing, Sweet Briar College; Janet LeBlanc, Clemson University; Charles Little, The Metropolitan Museum of Art; Laureen Reu Liu, McHenry County College; Loretta Lorance; Brian Madigan, Wayne State University; Janice Mann, Bucknell University; Judith Mann, St. Louis Art Museum; Richard Mann, San Francisco State University; James Martin; Elizabeth Parker McLachlan; Tamara Mikailova, St. Petersburg, Russia, and Macalester College; Anta Montet-White; Anne E. Morganstern, Ohio State University; Winslow Myers, Bancroft School; Lawrence Nees, University of Delaware; Amy Ogata, Cleveland Institute of Art; Judith Oliver, Colgate University; Edward Olszewski, Case Western Reserve University; Sara Jane Pearman; John G. Pedley, University of Michigan; Michael Plante, Tulane University; Eloise Quiñones-Keber, Baruch College and the Graduate Center, CUNY; Virginia Raguin, College of the Holy Cross; Nancy H. Ramage, Ithaca College; Ann M. Roberts, Lake Forest College; Lisa Robertson, The Cleveland Museum of Art; Barry Rubin; Charles Sack, Parsons, Kansas; Jan Schall, The Nelson-Atkins Museum of Art; Tom Shaw, Kean College; Pamela Sheingorn, Baruch College, CUNY; Raechell Smith, Kansas City Art Institute; Lauren Soth; Anne R. Stanton, University of Missouri, Columbia; Michael Stoughton; Thomas Sullivan, OSB, Benedictine College (Conception Abbey); Pamela Trimpe, University of Iowa; Richard Turnbull, Fashion Institute of Technology; Elizabeth Valdez del Alamo, Montclair State College; Lisa Vergara; Monica Visoná, University of Kentucky; Roger Ward, Norton Museum of Art; Mark Weil, St. Louis; David Wilkins; Marcilene Wittmer, University of Miami.

Use Notes

The various features of this book reinforce each other, helping you to become comfortable with terminology and concepts that are specific to art history.

Starter Kit and Introduction   The Starter Kit is a very concise primer of basic concepts and tools. The Introduction explores the way they are used to come to an understanding of the history of art.

Captions   There are two kinds of captions in this book: short and long. Short captions include information specific to the work of art or architecture illustrated:

 artist (when known)

 title or descriptive name of work

 date

 original location (if moved to a museum or other site)

 material or materials a work is made of

 size (height before width) in feet and inches, with meters and centimeters in parentheses

 present location

The order of these elements varies, depending on the type of work illustrated. Dimensions are not given for architecture, for most wall paintings, or for most architectural sculpture. Some captions have one or more lines of small print below the identification section of the caption that gives museum or collection information. This is rarely required reading; its inclusion is often a requirement for gaining permission to reproduce the work.

Some longer captions also include information that complements the discussion of a work in the main text.

Definitions of Terms   You will encounter the basic terms of art history in three places:

 In the text, where words appearing in boldface type are defined, or glossed, at their first use.

 In features on technique and other subjects, where labeled drawings and diagrams visually reinforce the use of terms.

 The glossary contains all the words in boldface type in the text and features.

Maps   At the beginning of most chapters you will find a map with all the places mentioned in the chapter.

Other In-Chapter Features   Throughout the chapters is special material set off from the main text that complements, explains, or extends the chapter narrative.

"Art and its Contexts" features tell you more about selected works or issues from the chapter. "Closer Look" features help you learn more about specific aspects of important works. "Elements of Architecture" features clarify specific architectural features, often explaining engineering principles or building technology. "Technique" features outline how certain types of art are created.

Bibliography   The bibliography lists books in English, organized by general works and by chapter, that are basic to the study of art history today, as well as books cited in the text.

Learning Objectives   At the beginning of each chapter is a list of its key learning objectives: what the authors hope you will learn by studying the chapter.

Think About It   These critical thinking questions appear at the end of each chapter and help you assess your mastery of the learning objectives by thinking through and applying what you have learned.

Dates, Abbreviations, and Other Conventions   This book uses the designations BCE and CE, abbreviations for "Before the Common Era" and "Common Era," instead of BC ("Before Christ") and AD ("Anno Domini," "the year of our Lord"). The first century BCE is the period from 99 BCE to 1 BCE; the first century CE is from the year 1 CE to 99 CE. Similarly, the second century BCE is the period from 199 BCE to 100 BCE; the second century CE extends from 100 CE to 199 CE.

Circa   ("about") is used with approximate dates, abbreviated to "c." This indicates that an exact date (or date range) is not yet verified.

An illustration is called a "figure," abbreviated as "fig." Thus, figure 6–7 is the seventh numbered illustration in Chapter 6, and figure Intro–3 is the third figure in the Introduction. There are two types of figures: photographs of artworks or models, and line drawings. Drawings are used when a work cannot be photographed or when a diagram or simple drawing is the clearest way to illustrate aspects of an object or a place.

When introducing artists, we use the words *active* and *documented* with dates, in addition to "b." (for "born") and "d." (for "died"). "Active" means that an artist worked during the years given. "Documented" means that documents link the person to that date.

Accents are used for words in French, German, Italian, and Spanish only. With few exceptions, names of cultural institutions in Western European countries are given in the form used in that country.

Titles of Works of Art   It was only over the last 500 years that paintings and works of sculpture created in Europe and North America were given formal titles, either by the artist or by critics and art historians. Such formal titles are printed in italics. At other times, and in other traditions and cultures in which single titles are not important or even recognized, the descriptive titles used here are not italicized. Most often formal titles are given in English, but if a non-English title is commonly used for the work (as in FIG. 31–17, Manet's *Luncheon on the Grass*), that title (*Le déjeuner sur l'herbe*) will appear in parentheses after the English title. In all cases, titles of works that are particularly important in a chapter are shown in all capital letters and bold type.

Starter Kit

Art history focuses on the visual arts—painting, drawing, sculpture, prints, photography, ceramics, metalwork, architecture, and more. This Starter Kit addresses the basic, underlying information and concepts of art history; you can use it as a quick reference guide to the vocabulary used to classify and describe art objects. Understanding these terms is indispensable because you will encounter them again and again in reading, talking, and writing about art.

Let us begin with the basic properties of art. A work of art is a material object having both *form* and *content*. It is often described and categorized according to its *style* and *medium*.

FORM

Referring to purely visual aspects of art and architecture, the term *form* encompasses qualities of *line*, *shape*, *color*, *light*, *texture*, *space*, *mass*, *volume*, and *composition*. These qualities are known as *formal elements*. When art historians use the term *formal*, they mean "relating to form."

Line and **shape** are attributes of form. Line is an element—usually drawn or painted—the length of which is so much greater than the width that we perceive it as having only length. Line can be actual (when the line is visible), or it can be implied (when the movement of the viewer's eyes over the surface of a work follows a path encouraged by the artist). Shape, on the other hand, is the two-dimensional, or flat, area defined by the borders of an enclosing *outline* or *contour*. Shape can be *geometric*, *biomorphic* (suggesting living things; sometimes called *organic*), *closed*, or *open*. The *outline* or *contour* of a three-dimensional object can also be perceived as line.

Color has several attributes. These include *hue*, *value*, and *saturation*.

Hue is what we think of when we hear the word *color*; the terms are interchangeable. We perceive hues as a result of differing wavelengths of electromagnetic energy. The visible spectrum, which can be seen in a rainbow, runs from red through violet. When the ends of the spectrum are connected through the hue red-violet, the result may be diagrammed as a color wheel. The primary hues (numbered 1 in the diagram) are red, yellow, and blue. They are known as primaries because all other colors are made by combining these hues. Orange, green, and violet result from the mixture of two primaries and are known as secondary hues (numbered 2). Intermediate hues, or tertiaries (numbered 3), result from the mixture of a primary and a secondary. Complementary colors are the two colors directly opposite one another on the color wheel, such as red and green. Red, orange, and yellow are regarded as warm colors and appear to advance toward us. Blue, green, and violet, which seem to recede, are called cool colors. Black and white are considered neutrals, not colors but, in terms of light, black is understood as the absence of color and white as the mixture of all colors.

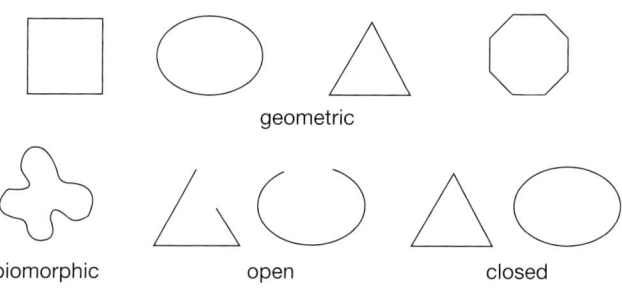

geometric

biomorphic   open   closed

Shape

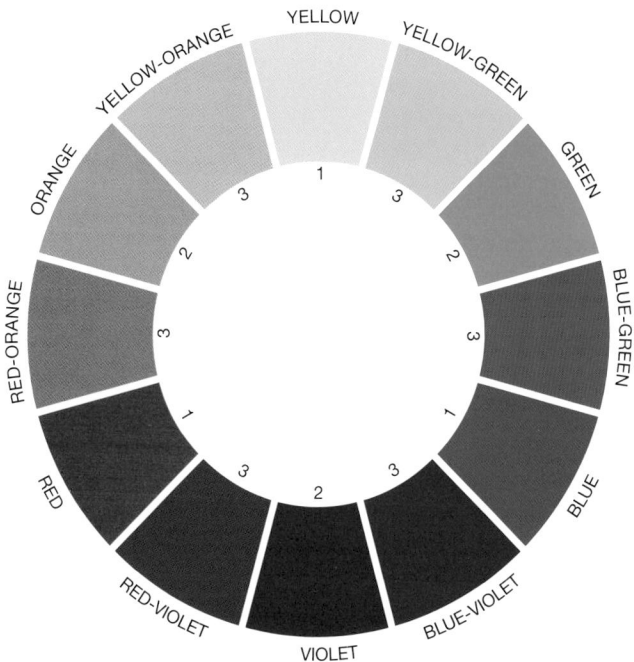

Value is the relative degree of lightness or darkness of a given color and is created by the amount of light reflected from an object's surface. A dark green has a deeper value than a light green, for example. In black-and-white reproductions of colored objects, you see only value, and some artworks—for example, a drawing made with black ink—possess only value, not hue or saturation.

Value scale from white to black.

+ WHITE   PURE HUE   + BLACK

Value variation in red.

Saturation, also sometimes referred to as *intensity*, is a color's quality of brightness or dullness. A color described as highly saturated looks vivid and pure; a hue of low saturation looks muddy or grayed.

PURE HUE   DULLED   PURE HUE

Intensity scale from bright to dull.

Texture, another attribute of form, is the tactile (or touch-perceived) quality of a surface. It is described by words such as *smooth, polished, rough, prickly, grainy,* or *oily*. Texture takes two forms: the texture of the actual surface of the work of art and the implied (illusionistically described) surface of objects represented in the work of art.

Technique

PICTORIAL DEVICES FOR DEPICTING RECESSION IN SPACE

overlapping

In overlapping, partially covered elements are meant to be seen as located behind those covering them.

diminution

In diminution of scale, successively smaller elements are perceived as being progressively farther away than the largest ones.

vertical perspective

Vertical perspective stacks elements, with the higher ones intended to be perceived as deeper in space.

atmospheric perspective

Through atmospheric perspective, objects in the far distance (often in bluish-gray hues) have less clarity than nearer objects. The sky becomes paler as it approaches the horizon.

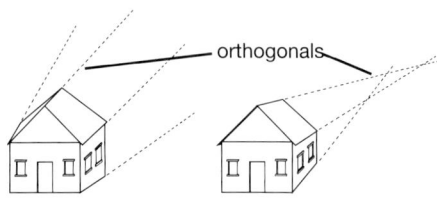

orthogonals

divergent perspective

In divergent or reverse perspective, forms widen slightly and imaginary lines called orthogonals diverge as they recede in space.

intuitive perspective

Intuitive perspective takes the opposite approach from divergent perspective. Forms become narrower and orthogonals converge the farther they are from the viewer, approximating the optical experience of spatial recession.

one-point   two-point

vanishing point   horizon line   vanishing point

linear perspective

Linear perspective (also called scientific, mathematical, one-point and Renaissance perspective) is a rationalization or standardization of intuitive perspective that was developed in fifteenth-century Italy. It uses mathematical formulas to construct images in which all elements are shaped by, or arranged along, orthogonals that converge in one or more vanishing points on a horizon line.

Space is what contains forms. It may be actual and three-dimensional, as it is with sculpture and architecture, or it may be fictional, represented illusionistically in two dimensions, as when artists represent recession into the distance on a flat surface—such as a wall or a canvas—by using various systems of *perspective*.

Mass and **volume** are properties of three-dimensional things. Mass is solid matter—whether sculpture or architecture—that takes up space. Volume is enclosed or defined space and may be either solid or hollow. Like space, mass and volume may be illusionistically represented on a two-dimensional surface, such as in a painting or a photograph.

Composition is the organization, or arrangement, of forms in a work of art. Shapes and colors may be repeated or varied, balanced symmetrically or asymmetrically; they may be stable or dynamic. The possibilities are nearly endless, and the artist's choices depend both on the time and place where the work was created and the objectives of individual artists. Pictorial depth (spatial recession) is a specialized aspect of composition in which the three-dimensional world is represented on a flat surface, or *picture plane*. The area "behind" the picture plane is called the *picture space* and conventionally contains three "zones": *foreground*, *middle ground*, and *background*.

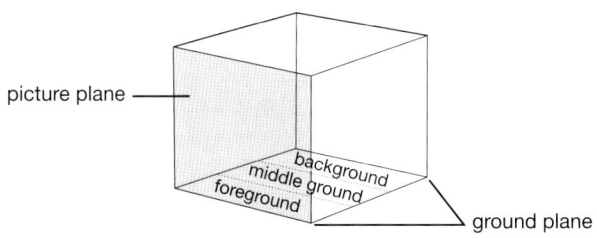

Various techniques for conveying a sense of pictorial depth have been devised by artists in different cultures and at different times (see "Pictorial Devices for Depicting Recession in Space" opposite). In some European art, the use of various systems of perspective has sought to create highly convincing illusions of recession into space. At other times and in other cultures, indications of recession have been suppressed or avoided in order to emphasize surface rather than space.

CONTENT

Content includes *subject matter*, but not all works of art have subject matter. Many buildings, paintings, sculptures, and other art objects include no recognizable references to things in nature nor to any story or historical situation, focusing instead on lines, colors, masses, volumes, and other formal elements. However, all works of art—even those without recognizable subject matter—have content, or meaning, insofar as they seek to communicate ideas,

convey feelings, or affirm the beliefs and values of their makers, their patrons, and usually the people who originally viewed or used them.

Content may derive from the social, political, religious, and economic *contexts* in which a work was created, the *intention* of the artist, and the *reception* of the work by beholders (the audience). Art historians, applying different methods of *interpretation*, often arrive at different conclusions regarding the content of a work of art, and single works of art can contain more than one meaning because they are occasionally directed at more than one audience.

The study of subject matter is called *iconography* (literally, "the writing of images") and includes the identification of *symbols*—images that take on meaning through association, resemblance, or convention.

STYLE

Expressed very broadly, *style* is the combination of form and composition that makes a work distinctive. *Stylistic analysis* is one of art history's most developed practices, because it is how art historians recognize the work of an individual artist or the characteristic manner of groups of artists working in a particular time or place. Some of the most commonly used terms to discuss *artistic styles* include *period style*, *regional style*, *personal style*, *representational style*, *abstract style*, *linear style*, and *painterly style*.

Period style refers to the common traits of works of art and architecture from a particular historical era. It is good practice not to use the words "style" and "period" interchangeably. Style is the sum of many influences and characteristics, including the period of its creation. An example of proper usage is "an American house from the Colonial period built in the Georgian style."

Regional style refers to stylistic traits that persist in a geographic region. An art historian whose specialty is medieval art can recognize Spanish style through many successive medieval periods and can distinguish individual objects created in medieval Spain from other medieval objects that were created in, for example, Italy.

Personal style refers to stylistic traits associated with an individual artist.

Representational styles are those that describe the appearance of recognizable subject matter in ways that make it seem lifelike.

> **Realism** and **naturalism** are terms that some people use interchangeably to characterize artists' attempts to represent the observable world in a manner that appears to describe its visual appearance accurately. When capitalized, Realism refers to a specific period style (see Chapter 31).

Idealization strives to create images of physical perfection according to the prevailing values or tastes of a culture. An artist may work in a representational style and idealize it to capture an underlying value or expressive effect.

Illusionism refers to a highly detailed style that seeks to create a convincing illusion of physical reality by describing its visual appearance meticulously.

Abstract styles depart from mimicking lifelike appearance to capture the essence of a form. An abstract artist may work from nature or from a memory image of nature's forms and colors, which are simplified, stylized, perfected, distorted, elaborated, or otherwise transformed to achieve a desired expressive effect.

Nonrepresentational (or nonobjective) is a term used for works of art that do not aim to mimic lifelike appearances.

Expressionism refers to styles in which the artist exaggerates aspects of form to draw out the beholder's subjective response or to project the artist's own subjective feelings.

Linear describes both styles and techniques. In linear styles artists use line as the primary means of definition. But linear paintings can also incorporate *modeling*—creating an illusion of three-dimensional substance through shading, usually executed so that brushstrokes nearly disappear.

Painterly describes a style of representation in which vigorous, evident brushstrokes dominate, and outlines, shadows, and highlights are brushed in freely.

MEDIUM AND TECHNIQUE

Medium (plural, *media*) refers to the material or materials from which a work of art is made. Literally anything can be used to make a work of art, including not only traditional materials like paint, ink, and stone, but also rubbish, food, and the earth itself.

Technique is the process that transforms media into a work of art. Various techniques are explained throughout this book in "Technique" features. Two-dimensional media and techniques include painting, drawing, printmaking, and photography. Three-dimensional media and techniques are sculpture (using, for example, stone, wood, clay, or metal), architecture, and small-scale arts (such as jewelry, containers, or vessels) in media such as ceramics, metal, or wood.

Painting includes wall painting and fresco, illumination (the decoration of books with paintings), panel painting (painting on wood panels), painting on canvas, and handscroll and hanging scroll painting. The paint in these examples is pigment mixed with a liquid vehicle, or binder. Some art historians also consider pictorial media such as mosaic and stained glass—where the pigment is arranged in solid form—as a type of painting.

Graphic arts are those that involve the application of lines and strokes to a two-dimensional surface or support, most often paper. Drawing is a graphic art, as are the various forms of printmaking. Drawings may be sketches (quick visual notes, often made in preparation for larger drawings or paintings); studies (more carefully drawn analyses of details or entire compositions); cartoons (full-scale drawings made in preparation for work in another medium, such as fresco, stained glass, or tapestry); or complete artworks in themselves. Drawings can be made with ink, charcoal, crayon, or pencil. Prints, unlike drawings, are made in multiple copies. The various forms of printmaking include woodcut, the intaglio processes (engraving, etching, drypoint), and lithography.

Photography (literally, "light writing") is a medium that involves the rendering of optical images through a recording of light effects. Photographic images are typically recorded by a camera.

Sculpture is three-dimensional art that is carved, modeled, cast, or assembled. Carved sculpture is subtractive in the sense that the image is created by taking away material. Wood, stone, and ivory are common materials used to create carved sculptures. Modeled sculpture is considered additive, meaning that the object is built up from a material, such as clay, that is soft enough to be molded and shaped. Metal sculpture is usually cast or is assembled by welding or a similar means of permanent joining.

Sculpture is either free-standing (that is, surrounded by space) or pictorial relief. Relief sculpture projects from the background surface of the same piece of material. High-relief sculpture projects far from its background; low-relief sculpture is only slightly raised; and sunken relief, found mainly in ancient Egyptian art, is carved into the surface, with the highest part of the relief being the flat surface.

Ephemeral arts include processions, ceremonies, and ritual dances (often with décor, costumes, or masks); performance art; earthworks; cinema and video art; and some forms of digital or computer art. All impose a temporal limitation—the artwork is viewable for a finite period of time and then disappears forever, is in a constant state of change, or must be replayed to be experienced again.

Architecture creates enclosures for human activity or habitation. It is three-dimensional, highly spatial, functional, and closely bound with developments in technology and materials. Since it is difficult to capture in a photograph, several types of schematic drawings are commonly used to enable the visualization of a building:

Plans depict a structure's masses and voids, presenting a view from above of the building's footprint as if it had been sliced horizontally at about waist height.

Plan: Philadelphia, Vanna Venturi House

Sections reveal the interior of a building as if it had been cut vertically from top to bottom.

Section: Rome, Sta. Costanza

Isometric drawings show buildings from oblique angles either seen from above ("bird's-eye view") to reveal their basic three-dimensional forms (often cut away so we can peek inside) or from below ("worm's-eye view") to represent the arrangement of interior spaces and the upward projection of structural elements.

Isometric cutaway from above: Ravenna, San Vitale

Isometric projection from below: Istanbul, Hagia Sophia

Introduction

Learning Objectives

I.a Explain the cultural foundations of the diverse ways art has been defined and characterized.

I.b Distinguish four ways art historians investigate works of art.

I.c Identify the components of the four-part method of art historical investigation that leads to the historical interpretation of a work of art.

The title of this book seems clear. It defines a field of academic study and scholarly research that has achieved a secure place in college and university curricula across North America. But *Art History* couples two words—even two worlds—that are less well focused when separated. What is art? In what sense does it have a history? Students of art and its history should pause and engage, even if briefly, with these large questions before beginning the journey surveyed in the following chapters.

What is Art?

What are the cultural foundations of the diverse ways art has been defined and characterized?

Artists, critics, art historians, and the general public all grapple with this thorny question. The *Random House Dictionary* defines "art" as "the quality, production, expression, or realm of what is beautiful, or of more than ordinary significance." Others have characterized "art" as something human-made that combines creative imagination and technical skill and satisfies an innate desire for order and harmony—perhaps a human hunger for the beautiful. This seems relatively straightforward until we start to look at modern and contemporary art, where there has been a heated and extended debate concerning "What is art?" The focus is often far from questions of transcendent beauty, ordered design, or technical skill; it centers instead on the conceptual meaning of a work for an elite target audience or the attempt to pose challenging questions or unsettle deep-seated cultural ideas.

The works of art discussed in this book represent a privileged subset of artifacts produced by past and present cultures. They were usually meant to be preserved, and they are currently considered worthy of conservation and display. The determination of which artifacts are exceptional—which are works of art—evolves through the actions, opinions, and selections of artists, patrons, governments, collectors, archaeologists, museums, art historians, and others. Labeling objects as art is usually meant to signal that they transcended or now transcend in some profound way their practical function, often embodying cherished cultural ideas or asserting foundational values. Sometimes it can also mean they are considered beautiful, well designed, and made with loving care, but this is not always the case. We will discover that at various times and places, the complex notion of what art is has little to do with standards of skill or beauty. Some critics and historians argue broadly that works of art are tendentious embodiments of power and privilege, hardly sublime expressions of beauty or truth. After all, art can be unsettling as well as soothing, challenging as well as reassuring, whether made in the present or surviving from the past.

Increasingly, we are realizing that our judgments about what constitutes art—as well as what constitutes beauty—are conditioned by our own education and experience. Whether acquired at home, in classrooms, in museums, at the movies, or on the Internet, our responses to art are learned behaviors influenced by class, gender, race, geography, and economic status as well as education. Even art historians find that their definitions of what constitutes art—and what constitutes artistic quality—evolve with additional research and understanding. Exploring works by twentieth-century painter Mark Rothko and nineteenth-century quilt-makers Martha Knowles and Henrietta Thomas demonstrates how definitions of art and artistic value are subject to change over time.

vision." In part because they are carefully crafted by an established artist who provided these kinds of intellectual justifications for their character and appearance, Rothko's abstract paintings are broadly considered works of art and are treasured possessions of major museums across the globe.

Works of art, however, do not always have to be created by individuals who perceive themselves as artists. Nor are all works produced for an art market surrounded by critics and collectors ready to explain, exhibit, and disperse them, ideally to prestigious museums. Such is the case with this quilt (**FIG. Intro-2**) made by Martha Knowles and Henrietta Thomas a century before Rothko's painting. Their work is similarly composed of blocks of color, and, like Rothko, they produced their visual effect by arranging these flat chromatic shapes carefully and regularly on a rectangular field. But this quilt was not meant to hang on the wall of an art museum. It is the social product of a friendship, intended as an intimate

Rothko's painting **NO. 3/NO. 13 (MAGENTA, BLACK, GREEN ON ORANGE)** (**FIG. Intro-1**), is a well-known example of the sort of abstract painting that was considered the epitome of artistic sophistication by the mid-twentieth-century New York art establishment. It was created by an artist who meant it to be a work of art. It was acquired by the Museum of Modern Art in New York, and its position on the walls of that museum is a sure sign of its acceptance as art by a powerful cultural institution. However, outside the context of the American artists, dealers, critics, and collectors who made up Rothko's art world, such paintings were often received with skepticism. They were seen by many as incomprehensible—lacking both technical skill and recognizable subject matter, two criteria that were part of the general public's definition of art at the time. Abstract paintings inspired a popular retort: "That's not art; my child could do it!" Interestingly enough, Rothko saw in the childlike character of his own paintings one of the qualities that made them works of art. Children, he said, "put forms, figures, and views into pictorial arrangements, employing out of necessity most of the rules of optical **perspective** and geometry but without the knowledge that they are employing them." He characterized his own art as childlike, as "an attempt to recapture the freshness and naiveté of childish

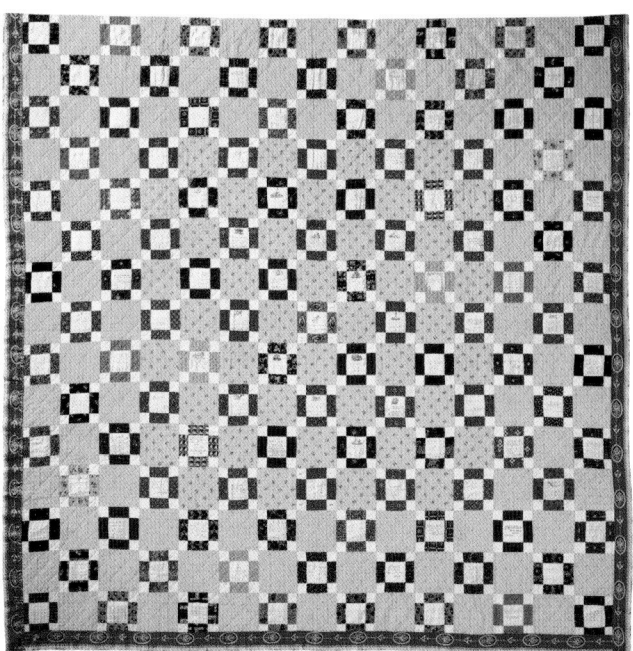

INTRO-2 Martha Knowles and Henrietta Thomas **MY SWEET SISTER EMMA**
1843. Cotton quilt, 8'11" × 9'1" (2.72 × 2.77 m). International Quilt Studies Center and Museum, University of Nebraska, Lincoln.

gift presented to a loved one for use in her home. An inscription on the quilt itself makes this clear: "From M.A. Knowles to her Sweet Sister Emma, 1843." Thousands of such friendship quilts were made by women during the middle years of the nineteenth century for use on beds, either to provide warmth or as a covering spread. Whereas quilts were sometimes displayed to a broad and enthusiastic audience of producers and admirers at competitions held at state and county fairs, they were not collected by art museums or revered by artists until relatively recently.

In 1971 at the Whitney Museum in New York—an establishment bastion of the art world of which Rothko had been a part—art historians Jonathan Holstein and Gail van der Hoof mounted an exhibition entitled "Abstract Design in American Quilts," demonstrating the artistic affinity we have already noted in comparing the way Knowles and Thomas, like Rothko, create abstract patterns with fields of color. Quilts were later accepted—or perhaps **appropriated**—as works of art and hung on the walls of a New York art museum because of their visual similarities with the avant-garde, abstract works of art created by elite New York artists.

Art historian Patricia Mainardi took the case for quilts one significant step further in a pioneering article of 1973 published in *The Feminist Art Journal*. Entitled "Quilts: The Great American Art," her argument was rooted not only in the aesthetic affinity of quilts with the esteemed work of contemporary abstract painters, but also in a political conviction that the definition of art had to be broadened. What was at stake here was historical veracity. Mainardi began, "Women have always made art. But for most women, the arts highest valued by male society have been closed to them for just that reason. They have put their creativity instead into the needlework arts, which exist in fantastic variety wherever there are women, and which in fact are a universal female art, transcending race, class, and national borders." She argued for the inclusion of quilts within the history of art to give deserved attention to the work of women artists who had been excluded from discussion because they created textiles and because they worked outside the male-dominated professional structures of the art world—because they

were women. Quilts now hang as works of art on the walls of museums and appear with regularity in books that survey the history of art.

As these two examples demonstrate, definitions of art are rooted in cultural systems of value that are subject to change. And as they change, the list of works considered by art historians is periodically revised. Determining what to study is a persistent part of the art historian's task.

Architecture

This book contains much more than paintings and textiles. Within these pages you will also encounter sculpture, vessels, books, churches, jewelry, tombs, chairs, temples, photographs, houses, and more. But as with Rothko's *No. 3/No. 13 (Magenta, Black, Green on Orange)* (SEE FIG. Intro-1) and Knowles and Thomas's *My Sweet Sister Emma* (SEE FIG. Intro-2), criteria have been used to determine which works are selected for inclusion in a book titled *Art History*. Architecture—which includes churches, tombs, temples, and houses, as well as many other kinds of buildings—presents an interesting case.

Buildings meet functional human needs by enclosing human habitation or activity. Many works of architecture, however, are considered "exceptional" because they transcend functional demands by manifesting distinguished architectural design or because they embody in important ways the values and goals of the culture that built them. Such buildings are usually produced by architects influenced, like painters, by great works and traditions from the past. In some cases they harmonize with, or react to, their natural or urban surroundings. For such reasons, they are discussed in books on the history of art.

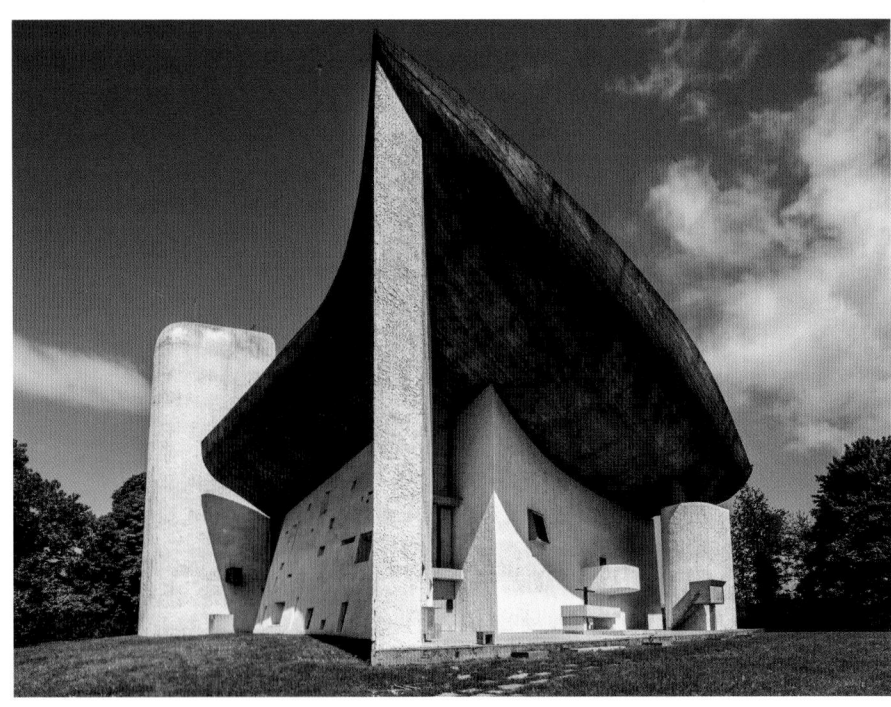

INTRO-3 Le Corbusier
NÔTRE-DAME-DU-HAUT
Ronchamp, France. 1950–1955.

Typical of such buildings is the church of Nôtre-Dame-du-Haut in Ronchamp, France, designed and constructed between 1950 and 1955 by Swiss architect Charles-Edouard Jeanneret, better known by his pseudonym, Le Corbusier (**FIG. Intro-3**). This building is the product of a significant historical moment, rich in international cultural meaning. A pilgrimage church on this site had been destroyed during World War II, and the creation here of a new church symbolized the end of a devastating war, embodying hopes for a brighter global future. Le Corbusier's design—drawing on sources that ranged from Algerian mosques to imperial Roman villas, from crab shells to airplane wings—is sculptural as well as architectural. Built at the crest of a hill, it soars toward the sky but at the same time seems solidly anchored in the earth. And its coordination with the curves of the natural landscape creates an outdoor setting for religious ceremonies (to the right in the figure) to supplement the spaces of the church interior. In fact, this building is so renowned today as a monument of modern architecture that the bus-loads of pilgrims who arrive at the site are mainly architects and devotees of architectural history.

What is Art History?

What are four ways art historians investigate works of art?

There are many ways to study or appreciate works of art. Art history represents one specific approach, with its own goals and its own methods of assessment and interpretation. Simply put, art historians seek to understand the meaning of art from the past within its original cultural contexts, both from the point of view of its producers—artists, architects, and patrons—as well as from the point of view of its consumers—those who formed its original audience. Coming to an understanding of the cultural meaning of a work of art requires detailed and patient investigation on many levels, especially with art that was produced long ago and in societies distinct from our own. This is a scholarly rather than an intuitive exercise. In art history, the work of art is seen as an embodiment of the values, goals, and aspirations of its time and place of origin. It is a part of culture.

Art historians use a variety of theoretical perspectives and interpretive strategies to do their work. But as a place to begin, the work of art historians can be divided into four types of investigation:

1. assessment of physical properties,
2. analysis of visual or formal structure,
3. identification of subject matter or conventional symbolism, and
4. integration within cultural context.

Assessing Physical Properties

Of the methods used by art historians to study works of art, this is the most objective, but it requires close access to the work itself. Physical properties include shape, size, materials, and technique. For instance, many pictures are rectangular (SEE FIG. Intro-1), but some are round (see **FIG. C** in "Closer Look" on page xxvii). Paintings as large as Rothko's require us to stand back if we want to take in the whole image, whereas some paintings (see **FIG. A** in "Closer Look" on page xxvi) are so small that we are drawn up close to examine their detail. Rothko's painting and Knowles and Thomas's quilt are both rectangles of similar size, but they are distinguished by the materials from which they are made—oil paint on canvas versus cotton fabric joined by stitching. In art history books, most physical properties can only be understood from descriptions in captions, but when we are in the presence of the work of art itself, size and shape may be the first thing we notice. To fully understand **medium** and technique, however, it may be necessary to employ methods of scientific analysis or documentary research to figure out the details of the practices of artists at the time when and place where the work was created.

Analyzing Formal Structure

Art historians explore the visual character that artists give their works—using the materials and the techniques chosen to create them—in a process called **formal analysis**. On the most basic level, it is divided into two parts:

*   assessing the individual visual elements or formal vocabulary that make up pictorial or sculptural communication, and

*   discovering the overall arrangement, organization, or structure of an image, a design system that art historians often refer to as **composition**.

THE ELEMENTS OF VISUAL EXPRESSION Artists control and vary the visual character of works of art to give their subjects and ideas meaning and expression, vibrancy and persuasion, challenge or delight (see "Closer Look" on pages xxvi–xxvii). For example, the motifs, objects, figures, and environments in paintings can be sharply defined by line (SEE FIGS. Intro-2, Intro-4), or they can be suggested by a sketchier definition (SEE FIGS. Intro-1, Intro-5). Painters can simulate the appearance of three-dimensional form through **modeling** or shading (SEE FIG. Intro-4 and **FIG. C** in "Closer Look" on page xxvii), that is, by imitating the way light from a single source will highlight one side of a solid while leaving the other side in shadow. Alternatively, artists can avoid any strong sense of three-dimensionality by emphasizing patterns on a surface rather than forms in space (SEE FIG. Intro-1 and **FIG. A** in "Closer Look" on page xxvi).

A Closer Look

VISUAL ELEMENTS OF PICTORIAL EXPRESSION: LINE, LIGHT, FORM, AND COLOR

LINE

A. CARPET PAGE FROM THE LINDISFARNE GOSPELS

From Lindisfarne, England. c. 715–720. Ink and tempera on vellum, 13⅜ × 9⁷⁄₁₆″ (34 × 24 cm). The British Library, London.

Credit: © The British Library Board (Cotton Nero D. IV, f.26v)

Every element in this complicated painting is sharply outlined by abrupt changes between light and dark or between one color and another; there are no gradual or shaded transitions. Since the picture was created in part with pen and ink, the linearity is a logical extension of medium and technique. And although line itself is a "flattening" or two-dimensionalizing element in pictures, a complex and consistent system of overlapping gives the linear animal forms a sense of shallow but carefully worked-out three-dimensional relationships to one another.

LIGHT

B. Georges de la Tour **THE EDUCATION OF THE VIRGIN**

c. 1650. Oil on canvas, 33″ × 39½″ (83.8 × 100.4 cm). The Frick Collection, New York. Purchased by the Frick Collection 1948. (1948.1.155).

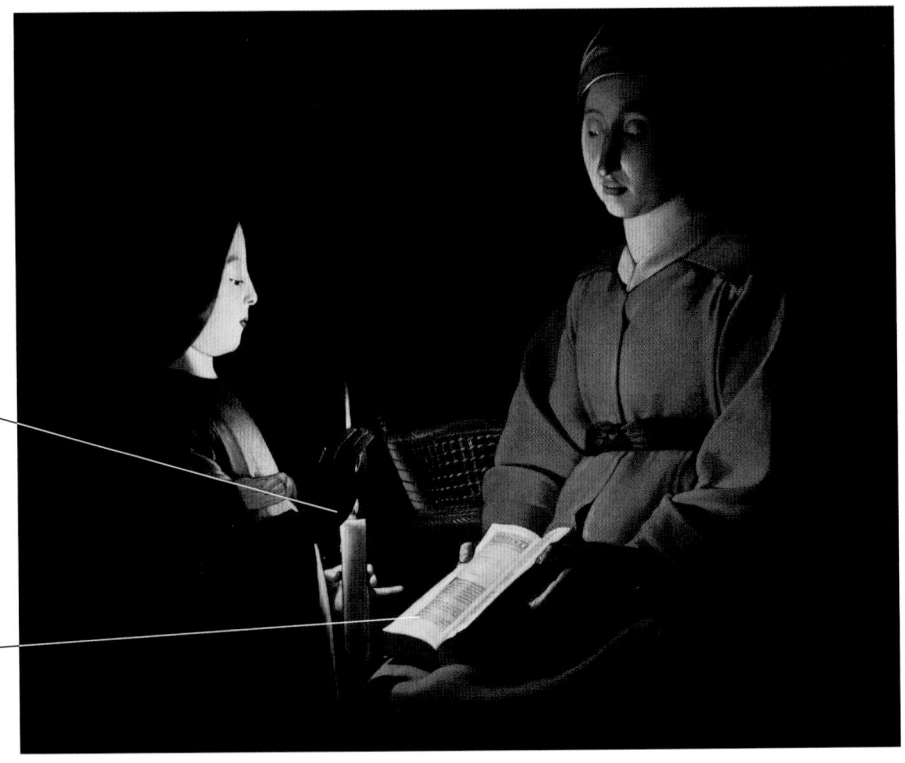

The source of illumination is a candle depicted within the painting. The young girl's raised right hand shields its flame, allowing the artist to demonstrate his virtuosity in painting the translucency of human flesh.

Since the candle's flame is partially concealed, its luminous intensity is not allowed to distract from those aspects of the painting most brilliantly illuminated by it—the face of the girl and the book she is reading.

FORM

C. Michelangelo
THE HOLY FAMILY (DONI TONDO)

c. 1503. Oil and tempera on panel, diameter 3′11¼″ (1.2 m). Galleria degli Uffizi, Florence.

Credit: © Studio Fotografico Quattrone, Florence

The complex overlapping of their highly three-dimensionalized bodies conveys the somewhat contorted positions and spatial relationship of these three figures.

Through the use of modeling or shading—a gradual transition from lights to darks—Michelangelo imitates the way solid forms are illuminated from a single light source—the side closest to the light source is bright while the other side is cast in shadow—and gives a sense of three-dimensional form to his figures.

In a technique called **foreshortening**, the carefully calculated angle of the Virgin's elbow makes it seem to project out toward the viewer.

The actual three-dimensional projection of the sculpted heads in medallions around the frame—designed for this painting by Michelangelo himself—heightens the illusion of three-dimensionality in the figures painted on its flat surface.

Junayd chose to flood every aspect of his painting with light, as if everything in it were illuminated from all sides at once. As a result, the emphasis here is on jewel-like color. The vibrant tonalities and dazzling detail of the dreamy landscape are not only more important than the simulation of three-dimensional forms within a space, they actually upstage the human drama taking place against a patterned, tipped-up ground in the lower third of the picture.

COLOR

D. Junayd **HUMAY AND HUMAYUN**

From a manuscript of the Divan of Kwaju Kirmani. Made in Baghdad, Iraq. 1396. Color, ink, and gold on paper, 12⅝ × 9⁷⁄₁₆″ (32 × 24 cm). The British Library, London.

Credit: © The British Library Board (Add. 18113, f.23)

XXVIII Introduction

INTRO-4 Raphael **MADONNA OF THE GOLDFINCH (MADONNA DEL CARDELLINO)**
1506. Oil on panel, 42 × 29½" (106.7 × 74.9 cm).
Galleria degli Uffizi, Florence.

The vibrant colors of this important work were revealed in the course of a careful, ten-year restoration, completed in 2008.

Credit: © Studio Fotografico Quattrone, Florence. Courtesy of the Ministero Beni e Att. Culturali

In addition to revealing the solid substance of forms through modeling, dramatic lighting can also guide viewers' attention to specific areas of a picture see **FIG. B** in "Closer Look" on page xxvi), or it can be lavished on every aspect of a picture to reveal all its detail and highlight the vibrancy of its color (see **FIG. D** in "Closer Look" on page xxvii). Color itself can be muted or intensified, depending on the mood artists want to create or the tastes and expectations of their audiences.

Thus, artists communicate with their viewers by making choices in the way they use and emphasize the elements of visual expression, and art historical analysis seeks to reveal how these choices bring meaning to a work of art. For example, in two paintings of women with children (SEE FIGS. Intro-4, Intro-5), Raphael and Renoir work with the same visual elements of line, form, light, and color in the creation of their images, but they employ these shared elements to different expressive ends. Raphael concentrates on line to clearly differentiate each element of his picture as a separate form. Careful modeling describes these outlined forms as substantial solids surrounded by space. This gives his subjects a sense of clarity, stability, and grandeur. Renoir, on the other hand, focuses on the flickering of light and the play of color as he minimizes the sense of three-dimensionality in individual forms. This gives his image a more ephemeral, casual sense. Art historians pay close attention to such variations in the use of visual elements—the building blocks of artistic expression—and use visual analysis to characterize the expressive effect of a particular work, a particular artist, or a general period defined by place and date.

COMPOSITION When art historians analyze composition, they focus not on the individual elements of visual expression but on the overall arrangement and organizing design or structure of a work of art. In Raphael's **MADONNA OF THE GOLDFINCH** (FIG. Intro-4), for example, the group of figures has been arranged in a triangular shape and placed at the center of the picture. Raphael emphasized this central focus by opening the clouds to reveal a patch of blue in the middle of the sky and by flanking the figural group with lacelike trees. Since the Madonna is at the center and the two boys are divided between the two sides of the triangle, roughly—though not precisely—equidistant from the center of the painting, this is a bilaterally symmetrical composition: on either side of an implied vertical line at the center of the picture, there are equivalent forms on left and right, matched and balanced in a mirrored correspondence. Art historians refer to such an implied line—around which the elements of a picture are organized—as an **axis**. Raphael's painting has not only a vertical, but also a horizontal axis, indicated by a line of demarcation between light and dark—as well as between degrees of color saturation—in the landscape. The belt of the Madonna's dress is aligned with this horizontal axis, and this correspondence, taken with the coordination of her head with the blue patch in the sky, relates her harmoniously to the natural world in which she sits, lending a sense of stability, order, and balance to the picture as a whole.

The main axis in Renoir's painting of **MME. CHARPEN-TIER AND HER CHILDREN** (**FIG. Intro–5**) is neither vertical nor horizontal, but diagonal, running from the upper right to the lower left corner of the painting. All major elements of the composition are aligned along this axis—dog, children, mother, and the table and chair that represent the most complex and detailed aspect of the setting. The upper left and lower right corners of the painting balance each other on either side of the diagonal axis as relatively simple fields of neutral tone, setting off and framing the main subjects between them. The resulting arrangement is not bilaterally symmetrical, but blatantly asymmetrical, with the large figural mass pushed into the left side of the picture. And unlike Raphael's composition, where the spatial relationship of the figures and their environment is mapped by the measured placement of elements that become increasingly smaller in scale and fuzzier in definition as they recede into the background, the relationship of Renoir's figures to their spatial environment is less clearly defined as they recede into the background along the dramatic diagonal axis. Nothing distracts us from the bold informality of this family gathering.

Both Raphael and Renoir arrange their figures carefully and purposefully, but they use distinctive compositional systems that communicate different notions of the way these figures interact with each other and the world around them. Art historians pay special attention to how pictures are arranged, because composition is one of the principal ways artists give their paintings expressive meaning.

Identifying Subject Matter

Art historians have traditionally sought subject matter and meaning in works of art with a system of analysis that was outlined by Erwin Panofsky (1892–1968), an influential German scholar who was expelled from his academic position by the Nazis in 1933 and spent the rest of his career of research and teaching in the United States. Panofsky proposed that when we seek to understand the subject of a work of art, we derive meaning initially in two ways:

- First we perceive what he called "natural subject matter" by recognizing forms and situations that we know from our own experience.

- Then we use what he called "**iconography**" to identify the conventional meanings associated with forms and figures as bearers of narrative or symbolic content, often specific to a particular time and place.

Some artworks, like Rothko's abstractions and Knowles and Thomas's quilt, do not contain subjects drawn from the world around us, from stories, or from conventional symbolism, but Panofsky's scheme remains a standard method of investigating meaning in works of art that present narrative subjects, portray specific people or places, or embody cultural values with iconic imagery or allegory.

NATURAL SUBJECT MATTER We recognize some things in works of visual art simply by virtue of living in a world similar to that represented by the artist. For example, in the two paintings by Raphael and Renoir just examined (**SEE FIGS. Intro–4, Intro–5**), we immediately recognize the principal human figures in both as a woman and two children—boys in the case of Raphael's painting, girls in Renoir's. We can also make a general identification of the animals: a bird in the hand of Raphael's boys, and a pet dog under one of Renoir's girls. And natural

INTRO–5 Auguste Renoir
MME. CHARPENTIER AND HER CHILDREN
1878. Oil on canvas, 60½ × 74⅞" (153.7 × 190.2 cm). Metropolitan Museum of Art, New York.

subject matter can extend from an identification of figures to an understanding of the expressive significance of their postures and facial features. We might see in the boy who snuggles between the knees of the woman in Raphael's painting, placing his own foot on top of hers, an anxious child seeking the security of physical contact with a trusted caretaker—perhaps his mother—in response to fear of the bird he reaches out to touch. Many of us have seen insecure children take this very pose in response to potentially unsettling encounters.

The closer the work of art is in both time and place to our own situation temporally and geographically, the easier it sometimes is to identify what is represented. However, it's not always that simple. Although Renoir painted his picture almost 140 years ago in France, the furniture in the background still looks familiar, as does the book in the hand of Raphael's Madonna, painted five centuries before our time. But the object hanging from the belt of the scantily clad boy at the left in Raphael's painting will require identification for most of us. Iconographic investigation is necessary to understand the function of this form.

ICONOGRAPHY   Some subjects are associated with conventional meanings established at a specific time or place, some of the human figures portrayed in works of art have specific identities, and some of the objects or forms have symbolic or allegorical meanings in addition to their natural subject matter. Discovering these conventional meanings of art's subject matter is called iconography (see "Closer Look" opposite).

For example, the woman accompanied in the outdoors by two boys in Raphael's *Madonna of the Goldfinch* (SEE FIG. INTRO-4) would have been immediately recognized by members of its intended early sixteenth-century Florentine audience as the Virgin Mary. Viewers would have identified the naked boy standing between her knees as her son Jesus and the boy holding the bird as Jesus's cousin John the Baptist, sheathed in the animal skin garment that he would wear in the wilderness and equipped with a shallow cup attached to his belt, ready to be used in baptisms. Such attributes of clothing and equipment are often critical in making iconographic identifications. The goldfinch in the Baptist's hand was at this time and place a symbol of Christ's death on the cross, an allegorical implication that makes the Christ Child's retreat into secure contact with his mother—already noted on the level of natural subject matter—understandable in relation to a specific story. The comprehension of conventional meanings in this painting would have been almost automatic among those for whom it was painted, but for us, separated by time and place, some research is necessary to recover associations that are no longer part of our everyday world.

Although it may not initially seem as unfamiliar, the subject matter of Renoir's 1878 portrait of *Mme.* *Charpentier and her Children* (SEE FIG. INTRO-5) is in fact even more obscure. There are those in twenty-first-century American culture for whom the figures and symbols in Raphael's painting are still recognizable and meaningful, but Marguérite-Louise Charpentier died in 1904, and no one living today would be able to identify her based on the likeness Renoir presumably gave to her face in this family portrait commissioned by her husband, the wealthy and influential publisher Georges Charpentier. We need the painting's title to make that identification. And Mme. Charpentier is outfitted here in a gown created by English designer Charles Frederick Worth, the dominant figure in late nineteenth-century Parisian high fashion. Her clothing was a clear attribute of her wealth for those who recognized its source; most of us need to investigate to uncover its meaning. But a greater surprise awaits the student who pursues further research on her children. Although they clearly seem to our eyes to represent two daughters, the child closest to Mme. Charpentier is actually her son Paul, who at age 3, following standard Parisian bourgeois practice, has not yet had his first haircut and still wears clothing comparable to that of his older sister Georgette, perched on the family dog. It is not unusual in art history to encounter situations where our initial conclusions on the level of natural subject matter will need to be revised after some iconographic research.

Integration within Cultural Context

Natural subject matter and iconography were only two of three steps proposed by Panofsky for coming to an understanding of the meaning of works of art. The third step he labeled "**iconology**." Its aim is to interpret the work of art as an embodiment of its cultural situation, to place it within broad social, political, religious, and intellectual contexts. Such integration into history requires more than identifying subject matter or conventional symbols; it requires a deep understanding of the beliefs and principles or goals and values that underlie a work of art's cultural situation as well as the position of an artist and patron within it.

In the "Closer Look" on iconography, the subject matter of two **still life** paintings (pictures of inanimate objects and fruits or flowers taken out of their natural contexts) is identified and elucidated, but to truly understand these two works as bearers of cultural meaning, more knowledge of the broader context and specific goals of artists and audiences is required. For example, the fact that Zhu Da (1626–1705) became a painter was rooted more in the political than the artistic history of China at the middle of the seventeenth century. As a member of the imperial family of the Ming dynasty, his life of privilege was disrupted when the Ming were overthrown during the Manchu conquest of China in 1644. Fleeing for his life, he sought refuge in a Buddhist monastery, where he wrote poetry and painted.

A Closer Look
ICONOGRAPHY

These grapes sit on an imported, Italian silver *tazza*, a luxury object that may commemorate northern European prosperity and trade. This particular object recurs in several of Peeters's other still lifes.

An image of the artist herself appears on the reflective surface of this pewter tankard, one of the ways that she signed her paintings and promoted her career.

Luscious fruits and flowers celebrate the abundance of nature, but because these fruits of the earth will eventually fade, even rot, they could be moralizing references to the transience of earthly existence.

These coins, including one minted in 1608–1609, help focus the dating of this painting. The highlighting of money within a still life could reference the wealth of the owner—or it could subtly allude to the value the artist has crafted here in paint.

Detailed renderings of insects showcased Peeters's virtuosity as a painter, but they also may have symbolized the vulnerability of the worldly beauty of flowers and fruit to destruction and decay.

This knife—which appears in several of Peeters's still lifes—is of a type that is associated with wedding gifts.

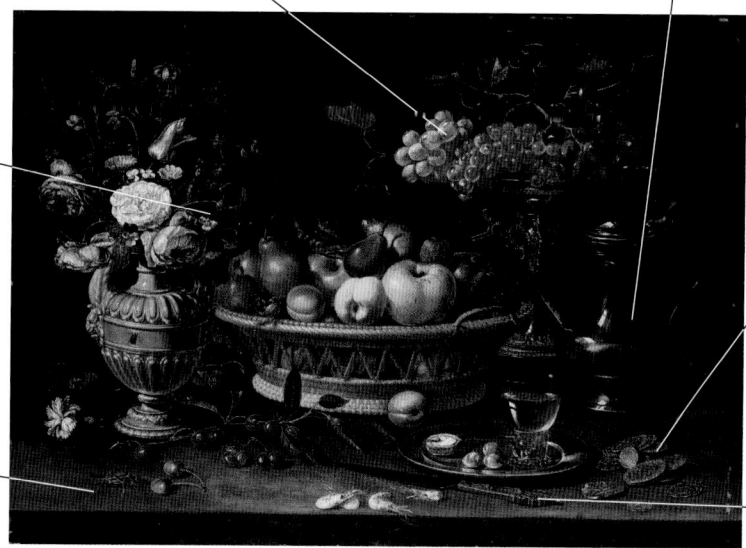

A. Clara Peeters **STILL LIFE WITH FRUIT AND FLOWERS**
c. 1612. Oil on copper, 25⅕ × 35″ (64 × 89 cm). Ashmolean Museum, Oxford.

Credit: Bridgeman Images

Quince is an unusual subject in Chinese painting, but the fruit seems to have carried personal significance for Zhu Da. One of his friends was known as the Daoist of Quince Mountain, a site in Hunan Province that was also the subject of a work by one of his favorite authors, Tang poet Li Bai.

The artist's signature reads "Bada Shanren painted this," using a familiar pseudonym in a formula and calligraphic style that the artist ceased using in 1695.

This red block is a seal with an inscription drawn from a Confucian text: "Teaching is half of learning." This was imprinted on the work by the artist as an aspect of his signature, a symbol of his identity within the picture, just as the reflection and inscribed knife identify Clara Peeters as the painter of her still life.

B. Zhu Da (Bada Shanren) **QUINCE (MUGUA)**
1690. Album leaf mounted as a hanging scroll; ink and colors on paper, 7⅞ × 5¾″ (20 × 14.6 cm). Princeton University Art Museum.

Credit: © 2016. University Art Museum/Art Resource/Scala, Florence. Photo: Bruce M. White.

Almost 40 years later, in the aftermath of a nervous break-down (that could have been staged to avoid retribution for his family background), Zhu Da abandoned his monastic life and developed a career as a professional painter, adopting a series of descriptive pseudonyms—most notably Bada Shanren ("mountain man of eight greatnesses") by which he is most often known today. His paintings are at times saturated with veiled political commentary; at times they seek to accommodate the expectations of collectors to assure their marketability; and in paintings like FIGURE B, the artist seems to hark back to the contemplative, abstract, and spontaneous paintings associated with great Zen masters such as Muqi (c. 1201–after 1269), whose calligraphic pictures of isolated fruits seem almost like acts of devotion or detached contemplations on natural forms, rather than the works of a professional painter.

Clara Peeters's still life (see FIG. A in "Closer Look" on page xxxi), on the other hand, fits into a developing Northern European painting tradition within which she was an established and successful professional, specializing in portrayals of food, flowers, fruit, and reflective objects. Still-life paintings in this tradition could be jubilant celebrations of the abundance of the natural world and the wealth of luxury objects available in the prosperous mercantile society of the Netherlands. Or they could be moralizing **vanitas** paintings, warning of the ephemeral meaning of those worldly possessions or even of life itself. But this painting has also been interpreted in a more personal way. Because the type of knife that sits in the foreground near the edge of the table was a popular wedding gift and is inscribed with the artist's own name, some have suggested that this still life could have celebrated Peeters's marriage. Or this could simply be a witty way to sign her picture. It certainly could be personal and at the same time participate in the broader cultural meaning of still-life paintings.

INTRO-6 Rogier van der Weyden **CRUCIFIXION WITH THE VIRGIN AND ST. JOHN THE EVANGELIST**
c. 1460. Oil on oak panels, 71 × 73″ (1.8 × 1.85 m). John G. Johnson Collection, Philadelphia Museum of Art.

Mixtures of private and public meanings have been proposed for Zhu Da's paintings as well. Some have seen his picture of quince as part of a series of allegorical self-portraits that extend across his career as a painter. Art historians frequently discover multiple meanings when interpreting single works. Art often represents complex cultural and personal situations.

A Case Study: Rogier van der Weyden's Philadelphia *Crucifixion*

How does the four-part art historical method lead to an art historical interpretation of a specific work of art?

The basic, four-part method of art historical investigation and interpretation just outlined and explored may become clearer when its extended use is traced in relation to one specific work of art. A particularly revealing subject for such a case study is a seminal and somewhat perplexing painting now in the Philadelphia Museum of Art—the **CRUCIFIXION WITH THE VIRGIN AND ST. JOHN THE EVANGELIST** (**FIG. Intro–6**) by the Flemish artist Rogier van der Weyden (c. 1400–1464) (see Chapter 19). Each of the four levels of art historical inquiry reveals important information about this painting—information that has been used by art historians to reconstruct its relationship to its artist, its audience, and its broader cultural setting. The resulting interpretation is rich, but also complex. An investigation this extensive will not be possible for all the works of art in the following chapters, where the text will focus only on one or two facets of more expansive research. Because of the amount and complexity of information involved in a thorough art historical interpretation, it is sometimes only in a second reading that we can follow the subtleties of its argument, after a first reading has provided a basic familiarity with the work of art, its conventional subjects, and its general context.

Physical Properties

Perhaps the most striking aspect of this painting's physical appearance is its division into two separate tall rectangular panels, joined by a frame to form a coherent, almost square composition. These are oak panels, prepared with chalk to form a smooth surface on which to paint with mineral pigments suspended in oil. A technical investigation of the painting in 1981 used infrared reflectography to reveal a very sketchy underdrawing beneath the surface of the paint, indicating that this painting is almost entirely the work of Rogier van der Weyden himself. Famous and prosperous artists of this time and place employed many assistants to work in large production workshops, and

they would make detailed underdrawings to ensure that assistants replicated the **style** of the master. But in cases where the masters themselves intended to execute the work, only sketchy compositional outlines were needed. In addition, modern technical investigation of Rogier's painting used **dendrochronology** (the dating of wood based on the patterns of the growth rings) to date the oak panels and consequently the painting itself, now securely situated near the end of the artist's career, c. 1460.

The most recent restoration of the painting—during the early 1990s by Mark Tucker, senior conservator at the Philadelphia Museum of Art—returned it, as close as possible, to what experts currently believe was its original fifteenth-century appearance (see "De-restoring and Restoring Rogier van der Weyden's *Crucifixion*" on page xxxiv). This project included extensive technical analysis of almost every aspect of the picture, during which a critical clue emerged, one that may lead to a sharper understanding of its original use. X-rays revealed dowel holes and plugs running in a horizontal line about one-fourth of the way up from the bottom across the entire expanse of the two-panel painting. Tucker's convincing research suggested that the dowels would have attached these two panels to the backs of wooden boxes or to carved tracery to form a complex work of art that combined sculpture and painting and was hung over the altar in a fifteenth-century church. Recently, Tucker worked collaboratively with art historian Griet Steyaert to identify two paintings that were originally on the reverse of these two panels, demonstrating that the Philadelphia **diptych** (two-panel painting) formed part of the exterior of the wings of the original **polyptych** (multiple-panel painting), visible only when it was closed (SEE FIGS. 19–13, 19–14 for views of another polyptych altarpiece with wings open and closed).

Formal Structure

The visual organization of this two-part painting emphasizes both connection and separation. It is at the same time one painting and two. Continuing across both panels are the strip of midnight blue sky and the stone wall that constricts space within the picture to a shallow corridor, pushing the figures into the foreground and close to the viewer. The shallow strip of mossy ground under the two-figure group in the left panel continues its sloping descent into the right panel, as does the hem of the Virgin's ice-blue garment. We look into this scene as if through a window with a mullion down the middle and assume that the world on the left continues behind this central strip of frame into the right side.

On the other hand, strong visual forces isolate the figures within their respective panels, setting up a system of "compare and contrast" that seems to be at the heart of

RECOVERING THE PAST
DE-RESTORING AND RESTORING ROGIER VAN DER WEYDEN'S *CRUCIFIXION*

Ever since Rogier van der Weyden's strikingly asymmetrical, two-panel rendering of the *Crucifixion* (SEE FIG. Intro-6) was purchased by Philadelphia lawyer John G. Johnson in 1906 for his spectacular collection of European paintings, it has been recognized not only as one of the greatest works by this master of fifteenth-century Flemish painting, but also as one of the most important European paintings in North America. Soon after the Johnson Collection became part of the Philadelphia Museum of Art in 1933, however, this painting's visual character was significantly transformed. In 1941, the museum employed freelance restorer David Rosen to work on the painting. Deciding that Rogier's work had been seriously marred by later overpainting and disfigured by the discoloration of old varnish, Rosen subjected the painting to a thorough cleaning. He also removed the strip of dark blue paint forming the sky above the wall at the top—identifying it as an eighteenth-century restoration—and replaced it with gold leaf to conform with remnants of gold in this area that he thought were surviving fragments of the original background. Rosen's restoration of Rogier's painting was uncritically accepted for almost half a century, and the gold background became a major factor in the interpretations of art historians as distinguished as Erwin Panofsky and Meyer Schapiro.

In 1990, in preparation for a new installation of the work, Rogier's painting received a thorough technical analysis by Mark Tucker, the museum's senior conservator. There were two startling discoveries:

- The dark blue strip that had run across the top of the picture before Rosen's intervention was actually original to the painting. Remnants of paint left behind in 1941 proved to be the same azurite blue that also appears in the clothing of the Virgin, and in no instance did the traces of gold discovered in 1941 run under aspects of the original paint surface. Rosen had removed Rogier's original midnight blue sky.

- What Rosen had interpreted as disfiguring varnish streaking the wall and darkening the brilliant cloths of honor hanging over it were actually Rogier's careful painting of lichens and water stains on the stone and his overpainting on the fabric that had originally transformed a vermillion undercoat into deep crimson cloth.

In meticulous work during 1992–1993, Tucker cautiously restored the painting based on the evidence he had uncovered. Neither the lost lichens and water stains nor the toning crimson overpainting of the hangings were replaced, but a coat of blue-black paint was laid over Rosen's gold leaf at the top of the panels, taking care to apply the new layer in such a way that should a later generation decide to return to the gold leaf sky, the midnight tonalities could be easily removed. That seems an unlikely prospect. The painting as exhibited today comes as close as possible to the original appearance of Rogier's *Crucifixion*. At least we think so for now.

the painting's design. The striking red cloths that hang over the wall are centered directly behind the figures on each side, forming internal frames that highlight them as separate groups and focus our attention back and forth between them rather than on the pictorial elements that unite their environments. As we begin to compare the two sides, it becomes increasingly clear that the relationship between figures and environment is quite distinct on each side of the divide.

The dead figure of Christ on the cross, elevated to the very top of the picture, is strictly centered within his panel, as well as against the cloth that hangs directly behind him. The grid of masonry blocks and creases in the cloth emphasizes his rectilinear integration into a system of balanced, rigid regularity. His head is aligned with the cap of the wall, his flesh largely contained within the area defined by the cloth. His elbows mark the juncture of the wall with the edge of the hanging, and his feet extend just to the end of the cloth, where his toes substitute for the border of fringe they overlap. The environment is almost as balanced. The strip of dark sky at the top is equivalent in size to the strip of mossy earth at the bottom

of the picture, and both are visually bisected by centered horizontals—the cross bar at the top and the alignment of bone and skull at the bottom. A few disruptions to this stable, rectilinear, symmetrical order draw the viewer's attention to the panel at the left: the downward fall of the head of Christ, the visual weight of the skull, the downturn of the fluttering loin cloth, and the tip of the Virgin's gown that transgresses over the barrier to move in from the other side.

John and Mary merge on the left into a single figural mass that could be inscribed into a half-circle. Although set against a rectilinear grid background comparable to that behind Jesus, they contrast with, rather than conform to, the regular sense of order. Their curving outlines offer unsettling unsteadiness, as if they are toppling to the ground, jutting into the other side of the frame. This instability is reinforced by their postures. The projection of Mary's knee in relation to the angle of her torso reveals that she is collapsing into a curve, and the crumpled mass of drapery circling underneath her only underlines her lack of support. John reaches out to catch her, but he has not yet made contact with her body. He strikes a stance of strident instability without even touching the ground, and he looks blankly out into space with an unfocused expression, distracted from, rather than concentrating on, the task at hand. Perhaps he will come to his senses and grab her. But will he be able to catch her in time, and even then support her, given his unstable posture? The moment is tense; the outcome is unclear. But we are moving into the realm of natural subject matter. The poignancy of this concentrated portrayal seems to demand it.

Iconography

The subject of this painting is among the most familiar themes in the history of European art. The dead Jesus has been crucified on the cross, and two of his closest associates—his mother and John, one of his disciples—mourn his loss. Although easily recognizable, the austere and asymmetrical presentation is unexpected.

More usual is an earlier painting of this subject by the same artist, **CRUCIFIXION TRIPTYCH WITH DONORS AND SAINTS** (**FIG. Intro–7**), where Rogier situates the crucified Christ at the center of a symmetrical arrangement, the undisputed axial focus of the composition. The scene unfolds here in an expansive landscape with a wider cast of participants, each of whom takes a place with symmetrical decorum on either side of the cross. Most crucifixions follow some variation on this pattern, so Rogier's two-panel portrayal (SEE FIG. Intro–6)—in which the cross is asymmetrically placed and the two figures near it are relegated to a separately framed and severely restricted space—requires some explanation, as does the mysterious,

dark world beyond the wall and the artificial backdrop of the textile hangings.

This scene is not only austere and subdued, it is also sharply focused, and the focus relates it to a specific moment in the story that Rogier decided to represent. The Christian Bible contains four accounts of Jesus's crucifixion, one in each of the four Gospels. Rogier took two verses in John's account as his painting's text (John 19:26–27), cited here in the Douai-Reims literal English translation (1582, 1609) of the Latin Vulgate Bible that was used by Western European Christians during the fifteenth century:

> When Jesus therefore had seen his mother and the disciple standing whom he loved, he saith to his mother: Woman, behold thy son. After that, he saith to the disciple: Behold thy mother. And from that hour, the disciple took her to his own.

Even the textual source uses conventions that need explanation, specifically the way the disciple John is consistently referred to in this Gospel as "the disciple whom Jesus loved." Rogier's painting, therefore, seems to focus on Jesus's call for a newly expanded relationship between his mother and a beloved follower. More specifically, he has projected us slightly forward in time to the moment when John needs to respond to that call—Jesus has died; John is now in charge.

There are, however, other conventional iconographic associations with the crucifixion that Rogier has folded into this spare portrayal. Fifteenth-century viewers would have understood the skull and femur that lie at the base of the cross as the bones of Adam—the first man in the

INTRO–7 Rogier van der Weyden **CRUCIFIXION TRIPTYCH WITH DONORS AND SAINTS**
c. 1440. Oil on wooden panels, 39¾ × 55″ (101 × 140 cm). Kunsthistorisches Museum, Vienna.

Credit: ©
KHM-Museumsverband

Hebrew Bible account of creation—on whose grave Jesus's crucifixion was believed to have taken place. This juxtaposition embodied the Christian belief that Christ's sacrifice on the cross redeemed believers from the death that Adam's original sin had brought to human existence.

Mary's swoon would have evoked another theological idea, the *co-passio*, in which Mary's anguish while witnessing Jesus's suffering and death was seen as a parallel passion of mother with son, both critical for human salvation. Their connection in this painting is underlined visually by the similar bending of their knees, inclination of their heads, and closing of their eyes. They even seem to resemble each other in facial likeness, especially when compared to John.

Cultural Context

In 1981 art historian Penny Howell Jolly published an interpretation of Rogier's Philadelphia *Crucifixion* as the product of a broad personal and cultural context. In addition to building on the work of earlier art historians, she pursued two productive lines of investigation to explain the rationale for this unusually austere presentation:

- the prospect that Rogier was influenced by the work of another artist, and

- the possibility that the painting was produced in a context that called for a special mode of visual presentation and a particular iconographic focus.

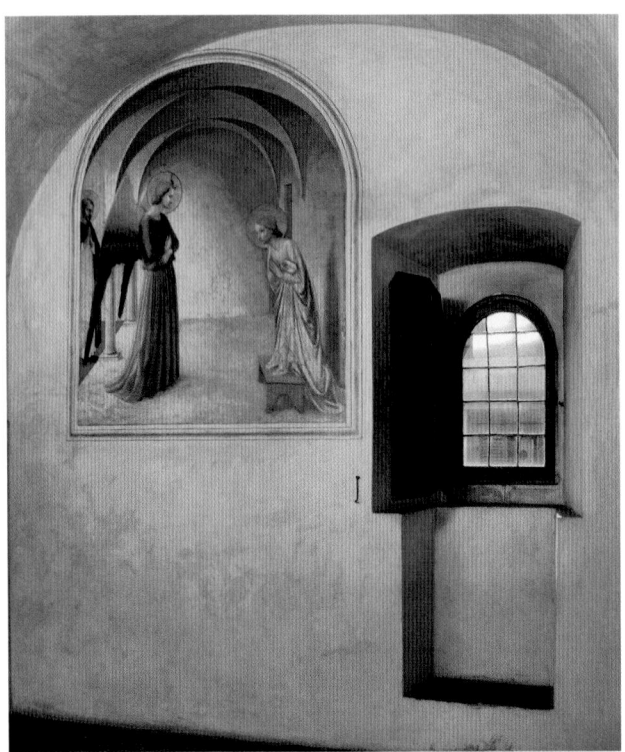

INTRO–8 VIEW OF A MONK'S CELL IN THE MONASTERY OF SAN MARCO, FLORENCE

Including Fra Angelico's fresco of the *Annunciation*. c. 1438–1445.

Credit: © Studio Fotografico Quattrone, Florence

INTRO–9 Fra Angelico **MOCKING OF CHRIST WITH THE VIRGIN MARY AND ST. DOMINIC**

Monastery of San Marco, Florence. c. 1441–1445.

Credit: © 2016 Photo Scala, Florence - courtesy of the Ministero Beni e Att. Culturali

FRA ANGELICO AT SAN MARCO We know very little about the life of Rogier van der Weyden, but we do know that in 1450, when he was already established as one of the principal painters in northern Europe, he made a pilgrimage to Rome. Either on his way to Rome or during his return journey home, he stopped in Florence and saw the **altarpiece**, and presumably also the frescos, that Fra Angelico (c. 1400–1455) and his workshop had painted during the 1440s at the monastery of San Marco. The evidence of Rogier's contact with Fra Angelico's work is found in a work Rogier painted after he returned home based on a panel of the San Marco altarpiece. For the Philadelphia *Crucifixion*, however, it was Fra Angelico's devotional frescos on the walls of the monks' individual rooms (or cells) that seem to have had the greatest impact (**FIG. Intro-8**). Jolly compared the Philadelphia *Crucifixion* with a scene of the Mocking of Christ at San Marco to demonstrate the connection (**FIG. Intro-9**). Fra Angelico presented the sacred figures with a quiet austerity that recalls Rogier's unusual composition. More specific parallels are the use of an expansive stone wall to restrict narrative space to a shallow foreground corridor, the description of the world beyond that wall as a dark sky that contrasts with the brilliantly illuminated foreground, and the use of a draped cloth of honor to draw attention to a narrative vignette from the life of Jesus, to separate it out as an object of devotion.

THE CARTHUSIANS Having established a possible connection between Rogier's painting and frescos by Fra Angelico that he likely saw during his pilgrimage to Rome in 1450, Jolly reconstructed a specific context of patronage and meaning within Rogier's own world in Flanders that could explain why the paintings of Fra Angelico would have had such an impact on him at this particular moment in his career.

During the years around 1450, Rogier developed a personal and professional relationship with the monastic order of the Carthusians, and especially with the Belgian Charterhouse (or Carthusian monastery) of Hérrines, where his oldest son was invested as a monk in 1450. Rogier gave money to Hérrines, and texts document his donation of a painting to its chapel of St. Catherine. Jolly suggested that the Philadelphia *Crucifixion* could be that painting. Its subdued colors and narrative austerity are consistent with Carthusian aesthetic attitudes, and the walled setting of the scene recalls the enclosed gardens that were attached to the individual dormitory rooms of Carthusian monks. The reference in this painting to the *co-passio* of the Virgin provides supporting evidence, since this theological idea was central to Carthusian thought and devotion. The *co-passio* was even reflected in the monks' own initiation rites, during which they re-enacted and sought identification with both Christ's sacrifice on the cross and the Virgin's parallel suffering.

In Jolly's interpretation, the religious framework of a Carthusian setting for the painting emerges as a personal framework for the artist himself, since this *Crucifixion* seems to be associated with important moments in his own life—his religious pilgrimage to Rome in 1450 and the initiation of his oldest son as a Carthusian monk at about the same time. The sense of loss and separation that Rogier evoked in his portrayal of a poignant moment in the life of St. John (**FIG. Intro–10**) could have been especially meaningful to the artist himself at the time this work was painted.

ART HISTORY: A CONTINUING PROJECT The final word has not been spoken in the interpretation of Rogier's Philadelphia *Crucifixion*. Mark Tucker's recent work on the physical evidence points toward it having been part of a large sculptured altarpiece. Even if this rules out the prospect that it is the **panel painting** Rogier donated to

INTRO–10 DETAIL OF FIG. INTRO–6 SHOWING PART OF THE LEFT WING

Credit: © 2004. Photo The Phildelphia Museum of Art/Scala, Florence

Hérrines, it does not negate the relationship Jolly drew with Fra Angelico, nor the Carthusian context she outlined. It simply reminds us that our understanding of works such as this will evolve when new evidence about them emerges.

As the history of art unfolds in this book, it will be important to keep two things in mind as you read about individual works of art and their broader cultural contexts. Art historical interpretations are built on extended research comparable to what we have just surveyed for Rogier van der Weyden's Philadelphia *Crucifixion*. But the work of interpretation is never complete. Art history is a continuing project, a work perpetually in progress.

Think About It

1   Analyze the composition of one painting illustrated in this Introduction.

2   Characterize the difference between natural subject matter and iconography, focusing your discussion on a specific work of art.

3   What are the four separate steps proposed here for art historians to interpret works of art? Characterize

the cultural analysis in step four by showing how it expands our understanding of one of the still lifes in the second "Closer Look."

4   What aspect of the case study of Rogier van der Weyden's Philadelphia *Crucifixion* was most interesting to you? Why? How did it affect your understanding of what you will learn in this course?

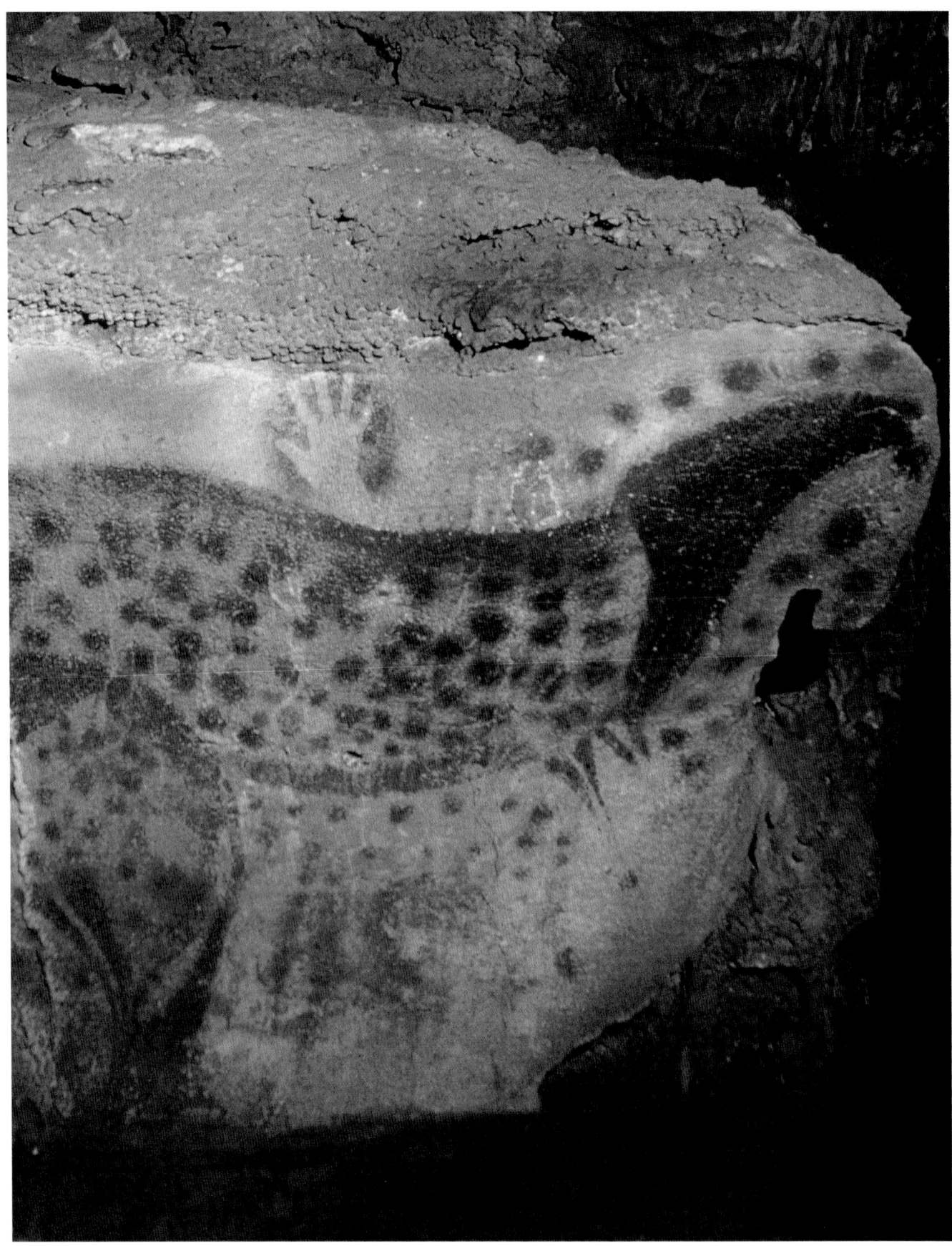

1-1 SPOTTED HORSES AND HUMAN HANDS
Pech-Merle Cave. Dordogne, France. Horses 25,000–24,000 BCE; hands c. 15,000 BCE. Paint on limestone, individual horses over 5′ (1.5 m) in length.

Chapter 1
Prehistoric Art

 ## Learning Objectives

1.a Identify the visual hallmarks of Paleolithic, Neolithic, and Bronze Age art for formal, technical, and expressive qualities.

1.b Interpret the meaning of works of Paleolithic, Neolithic, and Bronze Age art based on their themes, subjects, and symbols.

1.c Relate Paleolithic, Neolithic, and Bronze Age artists and art to their cultural, economic, and political contexts.

1.d Apply the vocabulary and concepts used to discuss Paleolithic, Neolithic, and Bronze Age art, artists, and art history.

1.e Interpret Prehistoric art using appropriate art historical methods, such as observation, comparison, and inductive reasoning.

1.f Select visual and textual evidence in various media to support an argument or an interpretation of Prehistoric art.

This detail shows one of two horses positioned back-to-back on the wall of a chamber within the Pech-Merle Cave, located in the Dordogne region of France (**FIG. 1–1**). The tapering head of this horse follows the natural shape of the rock. Black dots surround portions of its contours and fill most of its body, a striking feature that was believed to be decorative until DNA analysis of the remains of prehistoric horses, published in 2011, proved that one species flourishing at this time actually was spotted. In this instance, at least, prehistoric painters were painting what they saw.

At a later date, a large fish (58 inches long and very difficult to see here) was painted in red on top of the spots. Yet the painters left more than images of horses and fish; they left their own handprints in various places around the animals. These images, and many others hidden in chambers at the ends of long, narrow passages within the cave, connect us to an almost unimaginably ancient world of 25,000 BCE.

Prehistory includes all of human existence before the emergence of writing. When our ancestors were carving objects, painting images, and creating shelters and other structures 30,000 years ago, they were not making "works of art," and there were no "artists" as we use the term today. They were flaking, chipping, and polishing flint into tools—spear points, knives, and scrapers—not sculptures, even if we find these artifacts pleasing to the eye and to the touch

today. Wall paintings must have seemed equally important to their prehistoric makers in terms of everyday survival, not visual delight.

For art historians, archaeologists, and anthropologists, prehistoric "art" provides significant clues—along with fossils, pollen, and other artifacts—to understanding early human life and culture. Specialists continue to discover more about when and how these works were created. In 2012, for instance, an international team of scientists used a refined dating technology known as the uranium-thorium method (see "How Early Art is Dated" on page 12) to prove that some paintings in a Spanish cave known as El Castillo are at least 40,000 years old and probably much older—raising the possibility that they could have been painted by Neanderthals rather than *Homo sapiens*.

We may never know exactly why prehistoric paintings were made. In fact, there may be no single meaning or use for any one image on a cave wall; perhaps it meant different things to different people, depending on their age, their experience, or their specific needs and desires. And the sculpture, paintings, and structures that survive are but a tiny fraction of what must have been created over a very long time span. The conclusions and interpretations we draw from them are only educated guesses, making prehistoric art one of the most speculative, but dynamic and exciting, areas of art history.

The Stone Age

What are the cultural and historical contexts that led to the first artistic impulses of the Stone Age?

How and when modern humans evolved is the subject of ongoing debate, but anthropologists now agree that the species called *Homo sapiens* appeared about 400,000 years ago and that the subspecies to which we belong, *Homo sapiens sapiens* (usually referred to as modern humans), evolved as early as 120,000 years ago. Based on archaeological evidence, it is now clear that modern humans spread from Africa across Asia, into Europe, and finally to Australia and the Americas. This vast movement of people took place between 100,000 and 35,000 years ago.

Scholars began the systematic study of prehistory only about 200 years ago. Nineteenth-century archaeologists, struck by the wealth of stone tools, weapons, and figures found at ancient sites, named the whole period of early human development the Stone Age. Today, researchers divide the Stone Age into two parts: Paleolithic (from the Greek *paleo-*, "old," and *lithos*, "stone") and Neolithic (from the Greek *neo-*, "new"). They divide the Paleolithic period into three phases reflecting the relative position of objects found in layers of excavation: Lower (the oldest), Middle, and Upper (the most recent). In some places archaeologists can identify a transitional, or Mesolithic (from the Greek *meso-*, "middle"), period.

The dates for the transition from Paleolithic to Neolithic vary with geography and with local environmental and social circumstances. For some of the places discussed in this chapter, such as Western Europe, the Neolithic way of living did not emerge until 3000 BCE; in others, such as the Near East, it appeared as early as 8000 BCE. Archaeologists denote time in numbers of years BP ("before present"). However, to ensure consistent style throughout the book, which reflects the usage of art historians, this chapter uses the notations BCE (before the Common Era) and CE (the Common Era) to mark time.

Much is yet to be discovered about prehistoric art. In Australia, some of the world's very oldest images have been dated to between 50,000 and 40,000 years ago, and

1–2 RAINBOW SERPENT ROCK
Western Arnhem Land, Australia.

Appearing in Australia as early as 6000 BCE, images of the Rainbow Serpent play a role in rituals and legends of the creation of human beings, the generation of rains, storms, and floods, and the reproductive power of nature and people.

MAP 1–1 PREHISTORIC EUROPE

As the Ice Age glaciers receded, Paleolithic, Neolithic, Bronze Age, and Iron Age settlements increased from south to north.

the tradition of transient communities who marked the land in complex, yet stunningly beautiful ways continues into historical time. In western Arnhem Land (**FIG. 1-2**), rock art images of the Rainbow Serpent have their origins in prehistory. They were perhaps first created during times of substantial changes in the environment.

Africa, as well, is home to ancient rock art in both its northern and southern regions. And most recently, archaeologists have dated cave paintings on the Indonesian island of Sulawesi to between 35,000 and 40,000 years ago, including stenciled hands very similar to those appearing in Europe at Pech-Merle (SEE FIG. 1-1).

It is the cognitive capability to create and recognize symbols and imagery that sets modern humans apart from all our predecessors and all our contemporary animal relatives. We are defined as a species by our abilities to make and understand art. This chapter focuses primarily on prehistoric European art from the Paleolithic and Neolithic periods and into the Bronze Age (**MAP 1-1**). Later chapters

consider some prehistoric art on other continents and from other cultures, such as China (Chapter 11) and sub-Saharan Africa (Chapter 14).

Tools or Art?

Human beings made tools long before they made what today we call "art." Art, in the sense of image making, is the hallmark of the Upper Paleolithic period and the emergence of our subspecies, *Homo sapiens sapiens*; representational images appear in the archaeological record beginning about 38,000 BCE in Australia, Africa, and Europe. Before that time, during the Lower Paleolithic period in Africa, early humans made tools by flaking and chipping (knapping) flint pebbles into blades and scrapers that had sharp edges. Dating to 2.5 million years ago, the earliest objects made by our human ancestors were simple stone tools used to cut animal skin and meat, smash open bones to reveal the marrow, and cut wood and other plant

1–3 PALEOLITHIC HAND-AXE

From Isimila Korongo, Tanzania. 60,000 years ago. Stone, height 10" (25.4 cm).

Credit: Werner Forman Archive

materials. These first tools have been found at sites such as Olduvai Gorge in Tanzania. Although not art, they document a critical development in our evolution: humans' ability to create specific tools and objects that could be used to complete a task.

By 1.65 million years ago, significant changes in our ancestors' cognitive abilities and manual dexterity can be seen in sophisticated stone tools, such as the teardrop-shaped hand-axes (**FIG. 1–3**) that have been found at sites across Eurasia. These extraordinary objects, symmetrical in form and produced by a complex multistep process, were long thought of as nothing more than tools (or perhaps even as weapons)—but the most recent analysis suggests that they had a social function as well. Some sites (such as Olorgesailie in Kenya) contain hundreds of hand-axes, far more than would have been needed in functional terms, suggesting that they served to announce an individual's skills, status, and standing in his or her community. Although these ancient hand-axes are clearly not art in the representational sense, it is important to see them in terms of performance and process. These concepts, so central to modern Western art, have deep prehistoric roots.

The Paleolithic Period

What do we know about the shelters and representational images from the Paleolithic period?

By 400,000 years ago, during the late Middle Paleolithic period, a *Homo sapiens* subspecies called Neanderthal inhabited Europe. Its members used a wider range of stone tools and may have carefully buried their dead with funerary offerings. Neanderthals survived for thousands of years and overlapped with modern humans, *Homo sapiens sapiens*, which had evolved and spread out of Africa some 300,000 years after the Neanderthals and eventually replaced them, probably between 38,000 and 33,000 BCE.

Critical cognitive abilities set modern humans apart from their predecessors; *Homo sapiens sapiens* outlasted Neanderthals as a species because they had the mental capacity to solve problems of human survival. The new cognitive abilities included improvements in recognizing and benefiting from variations in the natural environment and in managing social networking and alliance making—skills that enabled organized hunting. The most important new ability, however, was the capacity to think symbolically: to create representational analogies between one person, animal, or object, and another and to recognize and remember those analogies. This cognitive development marks the evolutionary origin of what we call art.

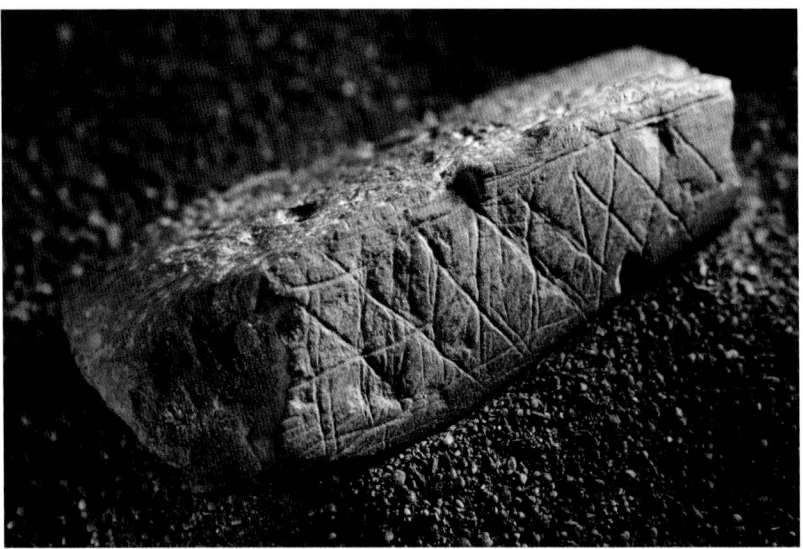

1–4 DECORATED OCHER

From Blombos Cave, southern Cape coast, South Africa. 77,000 years ago.

Credit: Image courtesy of Prof Christopher Henshilwood, University of Bergen, Norway

1–5 RECONSTRUCTION DRAWING OF MAMMOTH-BONE HOUSES
Ukraine. c. 16,000–10,000 BCE

Credit: Jack Unruh/National Geographic Creative

The world's earliest examples of art come from South Africa: two 77,000-year-old, engraved blocks of red ocher (probably used as crayons) found in the Blombos Cave (**FIG. 1–4**). Both blocks are engraved in an identical way with cross-hatched lines on their sides. Archaeologists argue that the similarity of the engraved patterns means these two pieces were intentionally made and decorated following a common pattern. Thousands of fragments of ocher have been discovered at Blombos; there is little doubt that people were using it to draw patterns and images, the remains of which have long since disappeared. It is highly likely that the ocher was used to decorate peoples' bodies, as well as to color objects such as tools or shell ornaments. In an earlier layer on the same site, archaeologists uncovered more than 36 shells, each of which had been perforated so that it could be hung from a string or thong, or attached to clothing or a person's hair; these shells would have been used for personal decoration. An ostrich eggshell bead from the same site would have served the same purpose. The Blombos finds are enormously important. Here our early ancestors, probably modern humans but possibly their predecessors, used the earth's raw materials to decorate themselves with jewelry and body art.

Shelter or Architecture?

"Architecture" usually refers to the enclosure of spaces with some aesthetic intent, and building even a simple shelter requires a degree of imagination and planning deserving of this term. In the Upper Paleolithic period, humans in some regions used great ingenuity to build shelters that were far from simple. In woodlands, evidence of floors indicates that our ancestors built circular or oval huts of light branches and hides that measured

as much as 15 to 20 feet in diameter. (Modern tents to accommodate 6 people vary from 10- by 11-foot ovals to 14- by 7-foot rooms.)

In the treeless grasslands of Upper Paleolithic Russia and Ukraine, builders created settlements of up to ten houses using the bones of the now extinct woolly mammoth, whose long, curving tusks made excellent roof supports and arched door openings (**FIG. 1–5**). This bone framework was probably covered with animal hides and turf. Most activities centered around the inside fire pit, or hearth, where food was prepared and tools were made. Larger houses might have had more than one hearth, and spaces were set aside for specific uses—working stone, making clothing, sleeping, and dumping refuse. Inside the largest dwelling on a site in Mezhirich, Ukraine, archaeologists found 15 small hearths that still contained ashes and charred bones left by the last occupants. Some people colored their floors with powdered ocher in shades that ranged from yellow to red to brown. These Upper Paleolithic structures are important because of their early date: The widespread appearance of durable architecture concentrated in village communities did not occur until the beginning of the Neolithic period in the Near East and southeastern Europe.

Artifacts or Works of Art?

As early as 30,000 BCE small figures, or figurines, of people and animals made of bone, ivory, stone, and clay appeared in Europe and Asia. Today we interpret such self-contained, three-dimensional pieces as examples of **sculpture in the round**. Prehistoric carvers also produced **relief sculpture** in stone, bone, and ivory. In relief sculpture, part of the surrounding material is retained to form a background for the projecting figure.

THE LION-HUMAN An early and puzzling example of a sculpture in the round is a human figure—probably male—with a feline head (**FIG. 1-6**), made about 30,000–26,000 BCE. Archaeologists excavating at Hohlenstein-Stadel, Germany, found broken pieces of ivory (from a mammoth tusk) that they realized were parts of an entire figure. Nearly a foot tall, this remarkable statue surpasses most early figurines in size and complexity.

Instead of copying what he or she saw in nature, the carver created a unique creature, part human and part beast. The figure may have been intended to represent a person wearing a ritual lion mask—or someone who had actually taken on the appearance of an animal. Archaeologists now think that the people who lived at this time held very different ideas than ours about what it meant to be a human and how humans were distinct from animals; it is quite possible that they thought of animals and humans as parts of one common group of beings who shared the world. What is absolutely clear is that the Lion-Human is evidence of the uniquely human ability to conceive and represent a creature never seen in nature.

FEMALE FIGURES While a number of figurines representing men have been found recently, most human figures from the Upper Paleolithic period are female. The most famous of these, the **WOMAN FROM WILLENDORF** (**FIG. 1-7**), Austria, dates from about 24,000 BCE (see "The Power of Naming" opposite). Carved from limestone and originally colored with red ocher, the statuette's swelling,

1-6 LION-HUMAN
From Hohlenstein-Stadel, Germany. c. 40,000–35,000 BCE. Mammoth ivory, 12¼″ × 2⅞″ (31.1 × 7.3 cm). Ulmer Museum, Ulm, Germany.
Credit: Photo: Yvonne Mühleis © Landesamt für Denkmalpflege im RP Stuttgart

1-7 WOMAN FROM WILLENDORF
Austria. c. 24,000 BCE. Limestone, height 4⅜″ (11 cm). Naturhistorisches Museum, Vienna.
Credit: © akg-images/Erich Lessing

Art and its Contexts

THE POWER OF NAMING

Words are only symbols for ideas, and it is no coincidence that the origins of language and of art are often linked in human evolutionary development. But the very words we invent—or our ancestors invented—reveal a certain view of the world and can shape our thinking. Today, we exert the power of naming when we select a name for a baby or call a friend by a nickname. Our ideas about art can also be affected by names. Before the twentieth century, artists usually did not name, or title, their works. Names were eventually supplied by the works' owners or by art historians writing about them, and thus often express the cultural prejudices of the labelers or of the times in which they lived.

An excellent example of such distortion is the naming of the hundreds of small prehistoric statues of women that have been found. Earlier scholars called them by the Roman name Venus. For example, the sculpture in **FIGURE 1–7** was once called the *Venus of Willendorf* after the place where it was found. Using the name of the Roman goddess of love and beauty sent a message that this figure was associated with religious belief, that it represented an ideal of womanhood, and that it was one of a long line of images of "classical" feminine beauty. In a short time, most similar works of sculpture from the Upper Paleolithic period came to be known as Venus figures. The name was repeated so often that even experts began to assume that the statues had to be fertility figures and Mother Goddesses, although there is no proof that this was so.

Our ability to understand and interpret works of art responsibly and creatively is easily compromised by distracting labels. Calling a prehistoric figure a woman instead of Venus encourages us to think about the sculpture in new and different ways.

---

rounded forms make it seem much larger than its actual 4⅜-inch height. The sculptor exaggerated the figure's female attributes by giving it pendulous breasts, a big belly with a deep navel (actually a natural indentation in the stone), wide hips, and dimpled knees and buttocks. By carving a woman with a well-nourished body, the artist may have been expressing health and fertility, which could ensure the ability to produce strong children, thus guaranteeing the survival of the clan.

The most recent analysis of the Paleolithic female sculptures, however, has replaced the traditional emphasis on fertility with more nuanced understandings of how and why the human figure is represented in this way, and who may have had these kinds of objects made. According to archaeologist Clive Gamble, these little sculptures were subtle forms of nonverbal communication among small, isolated groups of Paleolithic people spread out across vast regions. Gamble noted the tremendous (and unusual) similarity in the shapes of figures, even among those found in widely distant parts of Europe. He suggested that when groups of Paleolithic hunter-gatherers did occasionally meet up and interact, the female statues may have been among several signature objects that signaled whether a group was friendly and acceptable for interaction and, probably, for mating. As symbols, these figures would have provided reassurance of shared values about the body, and their size would have demanded engagement at a close personal level. It is not a coincidence, then, that the largest production of these figurines occurred during a period when climatic conditions were at their worst and the need for interaction and alliance building would have been at its greatest.

Another figure, the **WOMAN FROM DOLNÍ VĚSTONICE** (**FIG. 1–8**), takes our understanding of these objects further

1–8 WOMAN FROM DOLNÍ VĚSTONICE

Moravia, Czech Republic. 23,000 BCE. Fired clay, 4¼ × 1⁷⁄₁₀" (11 × 4.3 cm). Moravske Museum, Brno, Czech Republic.

Credit: © akg-images/De Agostini Picture Lib./A. Dagli Orti still. The site of Dolní Věstonice is important because it holds evidence of a very early date (23,000 BCE) for the use of fire to make objects out of mixtures of water and soil. What makes the figures from this site in the Czech Republic and others in the region (Pavlov and Předmosti) unusual is how they were made. But by mixing soil with water according to a very particular recipe and then placing the wet figures in a hot kiln to bake, the makers were not intending to create durable, well-fired statues. On the contrary, the recipe and firing procedure indicate that the intention was to make the figures explode in the kilns before the firing process was complete—before a "successful" figure could be produced. There are very few complete figures, but there are numerous fragments that bear the traces of explosions at high temperatures at these sites. The Dolní Věstonice fragments are records of performance and process art in their rawest and earliest forms.

Another remarkable female image, discovered in the Grotte du Pape in Brassempouy, France, is the tiny ivory head known as the **WOMAN FROM BRASSEMPOUY** (**FIG. 1-9**). Though the finders did not record its archaeological

1-9 WOMAN FROM BRASSEMPOUY
Grotte du Pape, Brassempouy, Landes, France. Probably c. 30,000 BCE. Ivory, height 1¼″ (3.6 cm). Musée des Antiquités Nationales, Saint-Germain-en-Laye, France.

Credit: © akg-images/De Agostini Picture Lib./G. Dagli Orti

context, recent studies prove it to be authentic and date it as early as 30,000 BCE. The carver captured the essence of a head, or what psychologists call the memory image—those generalized elements that reside in our memory of a human head. An egg shape rests on a long neck. A wide nose and strongly defined browline suggest deep-set eyes, and an engraved square patterning may be hair or a headdress. The image is an abstraction (what has come to be known as **abstract** art): the reduction of shapes and appearances to basic yet recognizable forms that are not intended to be exact replications of nature. The result in this case looks uncannily modern to contemporary viewers. Today, when such a piece is isolated in a museum case or as a book illustration we enjoy it as an aesthetic object, but we lose its original cultural context.

Cave Painting

Art in Europe entered a rich and sophisticated phase well before 40,000 years ago, when images began to be painted on the walls of caves in central and southern France and northern Spain. No one knew of the existence of prehistoric cave paintings until one day in 1879, when a young girl, exploring with her father in Altamira in northern Spain, crawled through a small opening in the ground and found herself in a chamber whose ceiling was covered with painted animals (SEE FIG. 1-13). Her father, a lawyer and amateur archaeologist, searched the rest of the cave, told authorities about the remarkable find, and published his discovery the following year. Few people believed that these amazing works could have been made by "primitive" people, and the scientific community declared the paintings a hoax. They were accepted as authentic only in 1902, after many other cave paintings, drawings, and engravings had been discovered at other places in northern Spain and in France.

TECHNIQUE OF PREHISTORIC WALL PAINTING In a dark cave, presumably working by the light of an animal-fat lamp, prehistoric artists chewed a piece of charcoal to dilute it with saliva and water. Then they blew out the mixture on the surface of a wall, using their hands as stencils. This drawing demonstrates how cave archaeologist Michel Lorblanchet and his assistant used this step-by-step process of the original makers of a cave painting at Pech-Merle (SEE FIG. 1-1) in France to create a complex design of spotted horses.

By turning himself into a human spray can, Lorblanchet produced clear lines on the rough stone surface much more easily than he could with a brush. To create the line of a horse's back, for example, with its clean upper edge and blurry lower one, he blew pigment below his hand. To capture its angular rump, he placed his hand vertically against the wall, holding it slightly curved. To produce the sharpest lines, such as those of the upper hind leg and tail,

MICHEL LORBLANCHET SIMULATING THE TECHNIQUE OF PREHISTORIC CAVE PAINTERS

he placed his hands side by side and blew between them. To create the forelegs and the hair on the horses' bellies, he fingerpainted. A hole punched in a piece of leather served as a stencil for the horses' spots. It took Lorblanchet only 32 hours to reproduce the Pech-Merle painting of spotted horses, his speed suggesting that a single artist could have created the original.

Homo sapiens sapiens artists used three painting techniques: the spraying demonstrated by Lorblanchet, drawing with fingers or blocks of ocher, and daubing with a paintbrush made of hair or moss. In some prehistoric caves, three other stages of image creation can be seen: engraved lines using flakes of flint, followed by a color wash of ocher and manganese, and a final engraving to emphasize shapes and details.

THE MEANING OF CAVE PAINTINGS What caused people to paint such dramatic imagery on the walls of caves? The idea that human beings have an inherent desire to decorate themselves and their surroundings—that an aesthetic sense is somehow innate to the human species—found ready acceptance in the nineteenth century. Many believed that people create art for the sheer love of beauty. Scientists now agree that human beings have an aesthetic impulse, but the effort required to accomplish the great cave paintings suggests their creators were motivated by more than simple visual pleasure. Since the discovery at Altamira, anthropologists and art historians have devised several hypotheses to explain the existence of cave art. Like the search for the meaning of prehistoric female figurines, these explanations depend on the cultural views of those who advance them.

In the early twentieth century, scholars believed that art has a social function and that aesthetics are culturally relative. They proposed that cave paintings might be products both of rites to strengthen clan bonds and of ceremonies to enhance the fertility of animals used for food. In 1903, French archaeologist Salomon Reinach suggested that cave paintings were expressions of sympathetic magic: the idea, for instance, that a picture of a reclining bison would ensure that hunters found their prey asleep. Abbé Henri Breuil took these ideas further and concluded that caves were places of worship and settings for initiation rites. During the second half of the twentieth century, scholars rejected these ideas and rooted their interpretations in rigorous scientific methods and then-current social theory. André Leroi-Gourhan and Annette Laming-Emperaire, for example, dismissed the sympathetic magic theory because statistical analysis of debris from human settlements revealed that the animals used most frequently for food were not the ones traditionally portrayed in caves.

Researchers continue to discover new cave images and to correct earlier errors of fact or interpretation. A study of the Altamira Cave in the 1980s led anthropologist Leslie G. Freeman to conclude that the artists had faithfully represented a herd of bison during the mating season. Instead of being dead, asleep, or disabled—as earlier observers had thought—the animals were dust-wallowing, common behavior during the mating season. Similar thinking has led to a more recent interpretation of cave art by archaeologist Steve Mithen. In his detailed study of the motifs of the art and its placement within caves, Mithen argued that hoofprints, patterns of animal feces, and hide colorings were recorded and used as a "text" to teach novice hunters within a group about the seasonal appearance and behavior of the animals they hunted. The fact that so much cave art is hidden deep in almost inaccessible parts of caves—indeed, the fact that it is placed within caves at all—suggested to Mithen that this knowledge was intended for a privileged group and that certain individuals or groups were excluded from acquiring that knowledge.

South African rock-art expert David Lewis-Williams has suggested a different interpretation. Using a deep comparative knowledge of art made by hunter-gatherer communities that are still in existence, Lewis-Williams argued that Upper Paleolithic cave art is best understood in terms of shamanism: the belief that certain people (shamans) can travel outside of their bodies in order to mediate between the worlds of the living and the spirits. Traveling under the ground as a spirit, particularly within caves, or conceptually within the stone walls of the cave, Upper Paleolithic shamans would have participated in ceremonies that involved hallucinations. Images conceived during this trancelike state would likely combine recognizable (the animals) and abstract (the nonrepresentational) symbols. In addition, Lewis-Williams interprets the stenciled human handprints on the cave walls (SEE FIG. 1-1) as traces of the nonshaman participants in the ritual reaching toward and connecting with the shaman spirits traveling within the rock.

Although the hypotheses that seek to explain cave art have changed and evolved over time, there has always been agreement that decorated caves must have had a special meaning because people returned to them time after time over many generations, in some cases over thousands of years. Perhaps Upper Paleolithic cave art was the product of rituals intended to gain the favor of the supernatural. Perhaps because much of the art was made deep inside the caves and nearly inaccessible, its significance may have had less to do with the finished painting than with the very act of creation. Artifacts and footprints suggest that the subterranean galleries, which were far from living quarters, had a religious or magical function. Perhaps the experience of exploring the cave may have been significant to the image-makers. Musical instruments, such as bone flutes, have been found in the caves, implying that even acoustical properties may have had a role to play.

CHAUVET One of the earliest known sites of prehistoric cave paintings is the Chauvet Cave (named after one of the persons who found it) near Vallon-Pont-d'Arc in southeastern France. Discovered in December 1994, it is a trove of hundreds of paintings (**FIG. 1-10**). The most dramatic of the images depict grazing, running, or resting animals, including wild horses, bison, mammoths, bears, panthers, owls, deer, aurochs, woolly rhinoceroses,

and wild goats (or ibex). Also included are occasional humans, both male and female, many handprints, and hundreds of geometric markings such as grids, circles, and dots. Footprints in the Chauvet Cave, left in soft clay by a child, go to a "room" containing bear skulls. The charcoal used to draw the rhinos has been radiocarbon-dated to 32,410 years old, plus or minus 720 years.

LASCAUX The abundant cave paintings found in 1940 at Lascaux, in the Dordogne region of southwest France, have been dated to about 15,000 BCE.

Opened to the public after World War II, the prehistoric "museum" at Lascaux soon became one of the most popular tourist sites in France—too popular, because the visitors brought heat, humidity, exhaled carbon dioxide, and other contaminants. The cave was closed to the public in 1963 so that conservators could battle an aggressive fungus. Eventually they won, but instead of reopening the site, authorities created a facsimile of it. Visitors to what is called Lascaux II may now view copies of the paintings without harming the precious originals.

The scenes they view are remarkable. Lascaux has about 600 paintings and 1,500 engravings. In the **HALL OF BULLS** (**FIG. 1-11**), the Lascaux painters depicted cows, bulls, horses, and deer along the natural ledges of the rock, where the smooth white limestone of the ceiling and upper wall meets a rougher surface below. They also used the curving wall to suggest space. The animals appear singly, in rows, face to face, tail to tail, and even painted on top of

1-10 WALL PAINTING WITH HORSES, RHINOCEROSES, AND AUROCHS
Chauvet Cave. Vallon-Pont-d'Arc, Ardèche Gorge, France. c. 32,000–30,000 BCE. Paint on limestone.

1-11 HALL OF BULLS

Lascaux Cave. Dordogne, France. c. 15,000 BCE. Paint on limestone, length of largest auroch (bull) 18′ (5.50 m).

Credit: © akg-images

one another. Their most characteristic features have been emphasized. Horns, eyes, and hooves are shown as seen from the front, yet heads and bodies are rendered in profile, in a system known as a **composite pose**. The animals are full of life and energy, and the accuracy in the drawing of their silhouettes, or outlines, is impressive.

Painters worked not only in large caverns, but also far back in the smallest chambers and recesses, many of which are almost inaccessible today. Over 100 small stone lamps have been found at Lascaux, indicating that the artists worked in flickering light obtained from burning animal fat. Although 1 pound of fat would burn for 24 hours and produce no soot, the light would not have been as strong as that created by a candle.

One scene at Lascaux was discovered in a remote setting on a wall at the bottom of a 16-foot shaft that contained a stone lamp and spears. The scene is unusual because it is the only painting in the cave complex that seems to tell a story (**FIG. 1-12**), and it is stylistically different from the other paintings at Lascaux. A figure who could be a hunter, greatly simplified in form but recognizably male and with

1-12 BIRD-HEADED MAN WITH BISON

Shaft scene in Lascaux Cave. c. 15,000 BCE. Paint on limestone, length approx. 9′ (2.75 m).

Credit: Photo © Hans Hinz/ARTOTHEK

the head of a bird or wearing a bird's-head mask, appears to be lying on the ground. A great bison looms above him. Below him lie a staff and a spear-thrower, the outer end of which has been carved in the shape of a bird. The long, diagonal line slanting across the bison's hindquarters may be a spear. The bison has been disemboweled and will soon die. To the left of the cleft in the wall a woolly rhinoceros seems to run off. It is unknown why the man was portrayed as a sticklike figure while the bison was rendered with such accurate detail—or whether the painting illustrates a myth, an actual event, or the vision of a shaman.

ALTAMIRA   The cave paintings at Altamira, near Santander in the Cantabrian Mountains in Spain—the first to be discovered and attributed to the Upper Paleolithic period—are now dated to about 12,500 BCE, as discussed below. The Altamira artists created sculptural effects by painting over and around natural irregularities in the cave walls and ceilings. To produce the herd of bison on the ceiling of the main cavern (**FIG. 1-13**), they used red and brown ocher to paint the large areas of the animals' shoulders, backs, and flanks, then sharpened the contours of the rocks and added the details of the legs, tails, heads, and horns in black and brown. They mixed yellow and brown from iron-based ocher to make the red tones, and they derived black from manganese or charcoal.

HOW EARLY ART IS DATED   Since the first discoveries at Altamira, archaeologists have developed increasingly sophisticated ways of dating cave paintings and other excavated objects. Today, they primarily use two approaches to determine an artifact's age. **Relative dating** relies on the relationships among objects in a single excavation or among several sites. If archaeologists have determined, for example, that pottery types A, B, and C follow each other chronologically at one site, they can apply that knowledge to another site. Even if type B is the only pottery present, it can still be assigned a relative date. **Absolute dating**, on the other hand, aims to determine a precise span of calendar years in which an artifact was created.

The most accurate method of absolute dating is **radiometric dating**, which measures the degree to which radioactive materials have disintegrated over time. Used for dating organic (plant or animal) materials—including some pigments used in cave paintings—one radiometric method measures a carbon isotope called radiocarbon, or carbon-14, which is constantly replenished in a living organism. When an organism dies, it starts to lose its store of carbon-14 at a predictable rate. Under the right circumstances, the amount of carbon-14 remaining in organic material can tell us how long ago an organism died.

This method has serious drawbacks for dating works of art. Using carbon-14 dating on a carved antler or wood sculpture shows only when the animal died or when the tree was cut down, not when the artist created the work using those materials. Also, some part of the object must be destroyed in order to conduct this kind of test—something that is never desirable in relation to works of art. For this reason, researchers frequently test organic materials found in the same context as the work of art rather than sacrificing part of the work itself. Radiocarbon dating is most accurate for materials no more than 30,000 to 40,000 years old.

Potassium-argon dating, which measures the decay of a radioactive potassium isotope into a stable isotope of argon, an inert gas, is most reliable with materials over a million years old. **Uranium-thorium dating** measures the decay of uranium into thorium in the deposits of calcium carbonate that cover

1-13 BISON
Ceiling of a cave at Altamira, Spain.
c. 12,500 BCE. Paint on limestone, length approx. 8'3" (2.5 m).

Credit: Sisse Brimberg/National Geographic Creative

1-14 BISON

Le Tuc d'Audoubert, France.
c. 13,000 BCE. Unbaked clay,
length 25″ (63.5 cm) and 24″
(60.9 cm).

Credit: Yvonne Vertut

the surfaces of cave walls, to determine the minimum age of paintings under the crust. **Thermo-luminescence dating** measures the irradiation of the crystal structure of a material subjected to fire, such as pottery, and the soil in which it is found, determined by the luminescence produced when a sample is heated. **Electron spin resonance** techniques use a magnetic field and microwave irradiation to date a material such as tooth enamel and the soil around it.

Recent experiments have helped to date cave paintings with increasing precision. Radiocarbon analysis has determined, for example, that the animal images at Lascaux are 17,000 years old—to be more precise, 17,070 years, plus or minus 130 years.

Cave Sculptures

Caves were sometimes adorned with relief sculpture as well as paintings. At Altamira, an artist simply heightened the resemblance of a natural projecting rock to a similar and familiar animal form. Other reliefs were created by modeling, or shaping, the damp clay of the cave's floor. An excellent example of such work in clay dating to 13,000 BCE is preserved at Le Tuc d'Audoubert, south of the Dordogne region of France. Here the sculptor created two bison leaning against a ridge of rock (**FIG. 1-14**). Although the beasts are modeled in very high relief (they extend well forward from the background), they display the same conventions as earlier painted ones, with emphasis on the broad masses of the meat-bearing flanks and shoulders. To make the animals even more lifelike, their creator engraved short parallel lines below their necks to represent their shaggy coats. Numerous small footprints found in the clay floor of this cave suggest that group rites took place here.

The Neolithic Period

How does the development of prehistoric art and architecture relate to the social and cultural changes of the Neolithic period?

Today, advances in technology, medicine, transportation, and communication change human experience in a generation. Many thousands of years ago, change took place much more slowly. In the tenth millennium BCE the world had already entered the present interglacial period; our modern climate was taking shape. The world was warming up, and this affected the distribution and stability of plant and animal life as well as marine and aquatic resources. However, the Ice Age ended so gradually and unevenly among regions that people could not have known what was happening.

One of the fundamental changes that took place in our prehistoric past was in the relationship people had with their environment. After millennia of established interactions between people and wild plants and animals—ranging from opportunistic foraging to well-scheduled gathering and collecting—people gradually started to exert increasing control over the land and its resources. Seen from the modern perspective, this change in economy (archaeologists use "economy" to refer to the ways people gathered or produced food) seems abrupt and complete. Different communities adopted and adapted new sets of technologies, skills, and plant and animal species that allowed them to produce food. This was the origin of plant and animal domestication. Wheat and barley were cultivated; sheep, goats, cattle, and pigs were bred. This new economy appeared at different rates and to varying degrees of completeness in different parts of the Near East and Europe, and no community relied exclusively on the cultivation of plants or on breeding animals. Instead they balanced hunting, gathering, farming, and animal breeding in order to maintain a steady food supply.

Architecture

At the same time as these new food technologies and species appeared, people began to establish stronger, more lasting connections to particular places in the landscape. The beginnings of architecture in Europe are marked by human social environments made up of simple but durable structures constructed of clay, mud, dung, and straw interwoven among wooden posts. While some of these buildings were simple huts used for no more than a season at a time, others were much more substantial, with foundations made of stone, set into trenches, and supporting walls of large timbers. Some were constructed from simple bricks made of clay, mud, and straw, shaped in rectangular molds and then dried in the sun. Regardless of the technique, the result was the same: People developed a new attachment to the land, and with settlement came a new kind of social life.

At the site of Lepenski Vir, on the Serbian bank of the Danube River, rows of trapezoidal buildings made of wooden posts, branches, mud, and clay—set on stone foundations and with stone-faced hearths—face the river from which the inhabitants took large fish (**FIG. 1–15**). Although this site dates to between 6300 and 5500 BCE, there is little evidence for the domestication of plants and animals that might be expected at this time in association with an architectural settlement. Archaeologists found human burials under the floors of these structures, as well as in the spaces between individual buildings.

1–15 RECONSTRUCTION DRAWING OF LEPENSKI VIR HOUSE/SHRINE
Serbia. 6300–5500 BCE.

Credit: Illustration: John Gordon Swogger

1–16 HUMAN–FISH SCULPTURE
From Lepenski Vir, Serbia. c. 6300–5500 BCE.

Credit: © akg-images/Erich Lessing

In some houses extraordinary art was found, made of carefully shaped river boulders (**FIG. 1–16**). Some of the boulders appear to represent human forms. Others look more like fish. A few seem to consist of mixtures of human and fish features. Here we have a site with a confusing combination of architecture with a nondomesticated economy, very distinctive art, and many burials. Archaeologists interpret such sites as temporary habitations where people carried out special rites and activities linked to death and to the natural and wild worlds.

In some places early architecture was dramatic and long-lasting, with the repeated building—sometimes over 1,000 years or more—of house upon house in successive architectural generations, resulting in the gradual rise of great mounds of villages referred to as tells or mound settlements. A particularly spectacular example is Çatalhöyük (Chatal Huyuk) in the Konya Plain in central Turkey, where the first traces of a village date to 7400 BCE in the early Neolithic period. The oldest part of the site consists of many densely clustered houses separated by areas of rubbish. They were made of rectangular mud bricks held together with mortar; walls, floors, and ceilings were covered with plaster and lime-based paint and were frequently replastered and repainted (see "Closer Look" opposite). The large site was home to as many as 3,000 people at any one time. Beyond the early date of the site and its size and population, the settlement at Çatalhöyük is important to the history of art for two reasons: the picture it provides of the use of early architecture and the sensational art that has been found within its buildings.

A Closer Look

A HOUSE IN ÇATALHÖYÜK

Large wooden beams of juniper or oak supported the roof and the activities that took place above.

The only entrance to the house was through the roof and down a ladder. Natural light was limited to what came through this opening because the house had no windows.

Walls up to 1 foot 4 inches thick and 16 feet high were made of rows of mortared brick. The interior sides of the walls were replastered annually up to 100 times.

Village residents were often buried under house floors.

The walls were used to display special objects. Cattle skulls and horns (bucrania) were attached to the wall as relief art. Conical repositories held special objects.

Domed ovens were placed both on the roof and in the house. The roof was used for cooking and other activities in the summer months.

Side rooms were used for storage, food preparation, and other domestic tasks.

Short walls and ridges created separate areas for different activities or social groups. Within some areas, raised platforms were coated with white plaster and covered with textile mats.

1–17 A HOUSE IN ÇATALHÖYÜK

Reconstruction drawing. Çatalhöyük, Turkey. c. 7400–6200 BCE.

Credit: Illustration: John Gordon Swogger, originally published in Ian Hodder, *The Leopard's Tale: Revealing the Mysteries of Çatalhöyük*. London: Thames & Hudson, 2006, fig. 5.8.

HOUSES AND COMMUNITIES Archaeologists and anthropologists often assume that the decision to create buildings such as the houses at Neolithic sites came from a universal need for shelter from the elements. However, as suggested by the special nature of the activities at Lepenski Vir, recent work at Çatalhöyük also shows clearly that while structures did provide shelter, early houses had much more significant functions. For the Neolithic people of Çatalhöyük, their houses were the key component of their worldview. Most importantly, they became an emblem of the spirit and history of a community. The building of house upon house created a historical continuity that outlasted any human lifetime; some house-rebuilding sequences lasted many hundreds of years. And the seasonal replastering and repainting of walls and floors only enhanced the sense of long-term continuity that made these buildings history-makers. In fact, Ian Hodder, the director of excavations at Çatalhöyük, and his colleagues call some of them "history houses" and have found no evidence to suggest that they were shrines or temples as earlier interpreters had mistakenly concluded.

As at Lepenski Vir, the dead were buried under the floors of many of the buildings at Çatalhöyük, another

way that the site connected the community's past and present. While there were no burials in some houses, a few contained between 30 and 60 bodies (the average is about 6 per house), and one had 62 burials, including people who had lived their lives in other parts of the village. Periodically, perhaps to mark special community events and ceremonies, people dug down into the floors of their houses and removed the heads of the long-deceased, then buried the skulls in new graves under the floors. Skulls were also placed in the foundations of new houses as they were built and rebuilt, and in other special deposits around the settlement. In one extraordinary burial, a deceased woman holds in her arms a man's skull that had been plastered and painted. Perhaps it, too, had been removed from an earlier underfloor grave.

The houses of Çatalhöyük were powerful places not only because of the (literal) depths of their histories, but also because of the art that decorated their interiors. Painted on the walls of some of the houses are violent and wild scenes. In some, humans are represented without heads as if they had been decapitated. Vultures or other birds of prey appear huge next to them, and narratives seem to highlight dangerous interactions between people and animals. In one painting (**FIG. 1-18**) a huge, horned wild animal (probably a deer) is surrounded by small humans who are jumping or running; one of them is pulling on something sticking out of the deer's mouth, perhaps its tongue. There is an emphasis on maleness: some of the human figures are bearded and the deer has an erect penis. Archaeologists have interpreted this scene as a dangerous game or ritual of baiting and taunting a wild animal. In other paintings, people hunt or tease boars or bulls. Conservation of the wall paintings is highly complex, and since many of the most dramatic examples were excavated before modern preservation techniques existed, we must rely on the archaeologist's narrative descriptions or quick field sketches.

Other representations of wild animals, most frequently the heads and horns of bulls, are modeled in relief on the interior walls. In some houses, people placed boar tusks, vulture skulls, and fox and weasel teeth under the floors; in at least one case, they dug into previous house generations to retrieve the plastered and painted heads of bulls.

Sites such as Lepenski Vir and Çatalhöyük have forced archaeologists to think in new ways about the role of architecture and art in prehistoric communities. Critically, the mixture of shelter, architecture, art, spirit, ritual, and ceremony at these and many other Neolithic settlements makes us realize that we cannot easily distinguish between "domestic" and "sacred" architecture. This point re-emerges from the recent work at Stonehenge in England. In addition, the clear and repeated emphasis on death, violence, wild animals, and male body parts at Çatalhöyük has challenged traditional interpretations of the Neolithic worldview that concentrated on representations of the female body, human fertility, and cults of the Mother Goddess.

Most Neolithic architectural sites were not as visually sensational as Çatalhöyük. At the site of Sesklo in northern Greece, dated to 6500 BCE, people built stone-based, long-lasting structures (**FIG. 1-19**) in one part of a village and less substantial mud, clay, and wood buildings in another part. The stone-based buildings may have had a special function within the community—whether ritual, crafts-based, or political is difficult to determine. Since they were rebuilt again and again over a long period of time, the part of the village where they were located "grew" vertically into a mound or tell. Some buildings had parts with easily recognizable functions, such as a place for making ceramic vessels. The distinction between the area of the longer-lasting, often rebuilt buildings and the more temporary structures is clear in the style of architecture as well as in the quality of artifacts found. Finer, decorated pottery is more abundant in the former.

1-18 MEN TAUNTING A DEER (?)

Detail of a wall painting from Çatalhöyük, Turkey. c. 6000 BCE. Museum of Anatolian Civilization, Ankara, Turkey.

1–19 SESKLO STONE-FOUNDATION HOUSE
Sesklo, northern Greece. 6500 BCE.

Credit: From: Stella G. Souvatzi, *A Social Archaeology of Households in Neolithic Greece. An Anthropological Approach.* 2009, fig. 4.8b. Cambridge University Press. After D.R. Theocharis, Neolithiki Hellas, National Bank of Greece, Athens, 1973

In different regions of Europe, people created architecture in different ways. The crowded buildings of Çatalhöyük differed from the structures at Sesklo, and these differed from the trapezoidal huts at Lepenski Vir. To the northwest, in Germany and central Europe, Neolithic villages typically consisted of three or four long timber buildings, each up to 150 feet long, housing 45 to 50 people. The structures were rectangular, with a row of posts down the center supporting a **ridgepole**, a long horizontal beam against which the slanting roof poles were braced. The walls were probably made of **wattle and daub** and roofed with **thatch**, plant material such as reeds or straw tied over a framework of poles. These houses also included large granaries, or storage spaces for the harvest; some buildings contained sections for animals and for people. Around 4000 BCE, Neolithic settlers began to locate their communities at defensible sites—near rivers, on plateaus, or in swamps. For additional protection, they also frequently surrounded their settlements with wooden walls, earth embankments, and ditches.

While much research has focused on the origins and construction technology of the earliest architecture—as at Çatalhöyük, Lepenski Vir, and other sites—some of the most exciting new work has come from studies of how Neolithic houses were destroyed. Excavations of settlements dating to the end of the Neolithic period in eastern and central Europe commonly reveal a level of ash and other evidence for great fires that burned down houses at these sites. The common interpretation had been that

invaders, coming on horseback from Ukraine and Russia, had attacked these villages and burned the settlements.

In one of the most innovative recent studies, Mira Stevanović and Ruth Tringham employed the methods of modern forensic science and meticulously reconstructed the patterns of Neolithic house conflagrations. The results proved that the fires were not part of village-wide destructions, but were individual events, confined to particular houses. Most significantly, they showed that each fire had been deliberately set. In fact, in order to get the fires to consume the houses completely, buildings had been stuffed with combustibles before they were set alight. Repeated tests by experimental archaeologists have supported these conclusions. Each intentional, house-destroying fire was part of a ritual killing of the house and a rupture of the historical and social entity that the house had represented for the community. Critically, even in their destruction, prehistoric buildings played important and complex roles in relation to the ways that individuals and communities created (and destroyed) social identities and continuities.

CEREMONIAL AND TOMB ARCHITECTURE In western and northern Europe, people erected huge stones to build ceremonial structures and tombs. In some cases, they had to transport these great stones over long distances. The monuments thus created are examples of what is known as **megalithic** architecture, the descriptive term derived from the Greek words for "large" (*mega-*) and "stone" (*lithos*).

Archaeologists disagree about the nature of the societies that created these monuments. Some believe they reflect complex, stratified societies in which powerful religious or political leaders dictated the design of these monuments and inspired (and coerced) large numbers of people to contribute their labor to such engineering projects. Skilled "engineers" would have devised the methods for shaping, transporting, and aligning the stones. Other interpreters argue that these massive monuments are clear evidence for collaboration within and between groups on a common project, the successful completion of which fueled social cohesion in the absence of a powerful individual.

Many of these megalithic structures are associated with death. Most recent interpretations stress the role of death and burial as fundamental, public performances in which individual and group identity, cohesion, and disputes were played out. In this reasoning, death and its rituals are viewed as theater, with the deceased as well as grave goods perceived as props, the monument as a stage, the celebrants and mourners as actors, and the entire event proceeding in terms of an (unwritten) script with narrative and plot.

Elaborate megalithic tombs first appeared in the Neolithic period. Some were built for single burials; others had multiple burial chambers. The simplest type was the **dolmen**, formed in **post-and-lintel** construction (construction in which two uprights—the posts—support a horizontal element—the lintel). The tomb chamber was formed of huge upright stones supporting one or more tablelike rocks, or **capstones**. The structure was then mounded over with smaller rocks and dirt to form a **cairn** or artificial hill. A more imposing type of structure was the **passage grave**, in which narrow, stone-lined passageways led into a large room at the center.

At Newgrange, in Ireland, the mound of an elaborate passage grave (**FIG. 1-20**) originally stood 44 feet high and measured about 280 feet in diameter. The mound was built of sod and river pebbles and was set off by a circle of engraved standing stones around its perimeter. Its passageway, 62 feet long and lined with standing stones, leads into a three-part chamber with a **corbeled vault** (an arched structure that spans an interior space) rising to a height of 19 feet.

Some of the stones are engraved with linear designs, mainly rings, spirals, and diamond shapes. These patterns may have been marked out using strings or compasses, then carved by picking at the rock surface with tools made of antlers. Recent detailed analysis of the art engraved on passage graves like Newgrange, but also at Knowth in Ireland, suggest that the images are entoptic (meaning that their significance and function relate to the particularities of perception by the eye), and that we should understand them in terms of the neuropsychological effect they would have had on people visiting the tomb. These effects may

have included hallucinations. Archaeologists argue that key entoptic motifs were positioned at entrances and other important thresholds inside the tomb, and that they played important roles in ritual or political ceremonies that centered around death, burial, and the commemoration and visitation of the deceased by the living.

STONEHENGE   Of all the megalithic monuments in Europe, the one that has stirred the imagination of the public most strongly is **STONEHENGE**, on Salisbury Plain in southern England (**FIGS. 1-21, 1-22**). A **henge** is a circle of stones or posts, often surrounded by a ditch with built-up embankments. Laying out such circles with accuracy would have posed no particular problem. Architects likely relied on the human compass, a simple but effective surveying method that persisted well into modern times. All that is required is a length of cord either cut or knotted to mark the desired radius of the circle. A person holding one end of the cord is stationed in the center; a coworker, holding the other end and keeping the cord taut, steps off the circle's circumference. By the time of Stonehenge's construction, cords and ropes were readily available.

Stonehenge is not the largest such circle from the Neolithic period, but it is one of the most complex, with eight different phases of construction and activity, starting in 3000 BCE during the Neolithic period and stretching over a millennium and a half through the Bronze Age. The site started as a cemetery of cremation burials marked by a circle of bluestones. Through numerous sequences of alterations and rebuildings, it continued to function as a domain of the dead. Between 2900 and 2600 BCE, the bluestones were rearranged into an arc. Around 2500 BCE, a circle of sarsen stones—sarsen is a gray sandstone— gave the site its well-known appearance using post-and-lintel construction. At the same time, the bluestones were rearranged within the sarsens. The center of the site was now dominated by a horseshoe-shaped arrangement of five sandstone, post-and-lintel trilithons— pairs of upright stones topped by **lintels**. The one in the middle stood considerably taller than the rest, rising to a height of 24 feet, and its lintel was more than 15 feet long and 3 feet thick. This group was surrounded by the so-called sarsen circle,

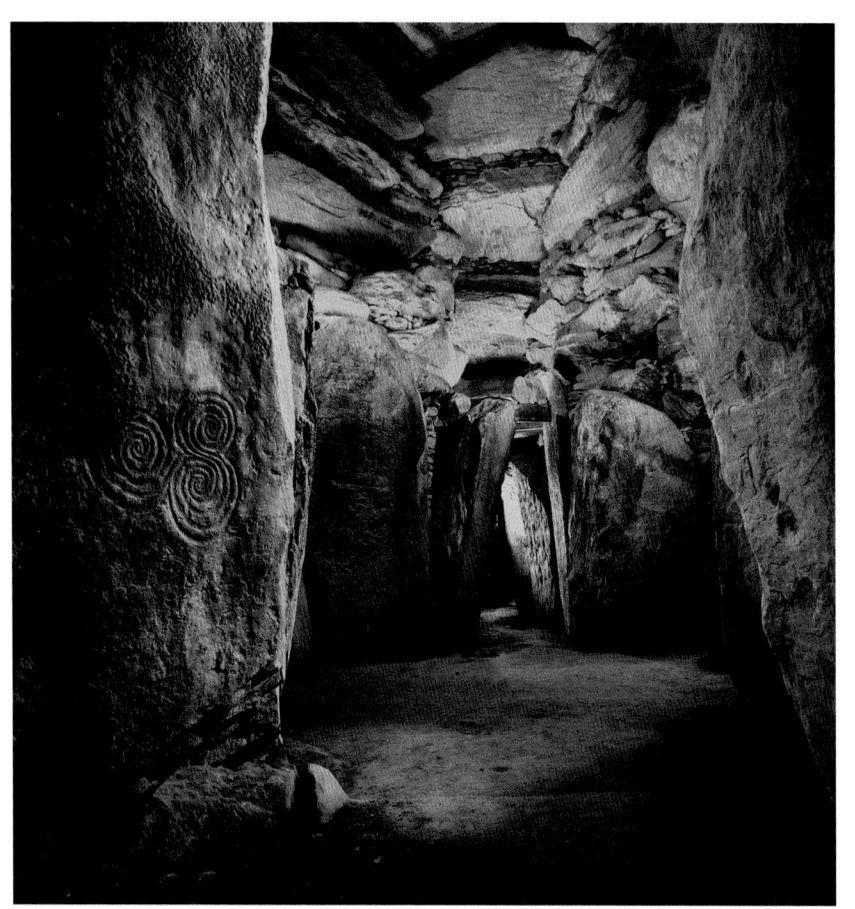

1-20 TOMB INTERIOR WITH CORBELING AND ENGRAVED STONES
Newgrange, Ireland. c. 3000–2500 BCE.

Credit: ©National Monuments Service. Dept of Arts, Heritage and the Gaeltacht

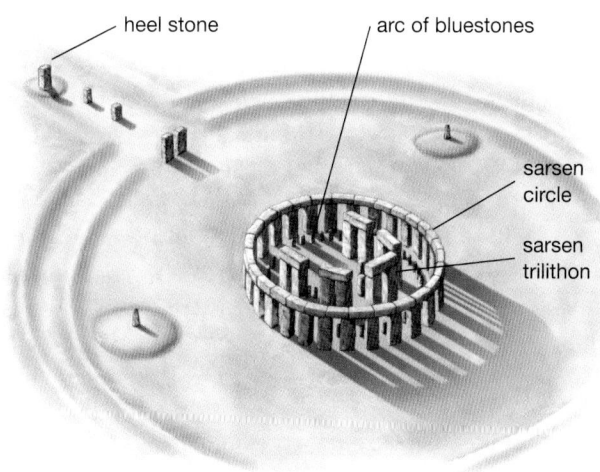

heel stone   arc of bluestones

sarsen circle

sarsen trilithon

1-21 RECONSTRUCTION DRAWING OF STONEHENGE FROM THE AIR
Salisbury Plain, Wiltshire, England. c. 3000–1500 BCE.

a ring of sandstone uprights weighing up to 26 tons each and averaging 13 feet 6 inches tall. This circle, 106 feet in diameter, was capped by a continuous lintel. The uprights taper slightly toward the top, and the gently curved lintel sections were secured by **mortise-and-tenon** joints, that is, joints made by a conical projection at the top of each upright that fits like a peg into a hole in the lintel. Over the next thousand years people continued to alter the arrangement of the bluestones, and cremation burials continued in pits at the site.

The differences in the types of stone used in the different phases of construction are significant. The use of bluestone in the early phases (and maintained and rearranged through the sequence) is particularly important. Unlike the sarsen stone, bluestone was not locally available and would have been transported over 150 miles from the west, where it had been quarried in the mountains of west Wales. The means of transporting the bluestones such distances remains a source of great debate. Some argue that they were floated around the coast on great barges; others hold that they traveled over land on wooden rollers. Regardless, the use of this material tells us that the people who first transformed the Stonehenge landscape into a ceremonial site probably had their ancestral origins in the west. By bringing the bluestones and using them in the early Stonehenge cemetery, these migrants made a powerful connection with their homelands.

Through the ages, many theories have been advanced to explain Stonehenge. In the Middle Ages, people thought that Merlin, the legendary magician of King Arthur, had built it. Later, the site was erroneously associated with the rituals of the Celtic druids (priests). Because it is oriented in relation to the movement of the sun, some people have argued that it may have been an observatory or that it had special importance as a calendar for regulating early agricultural schedules. None of these ideas is supported by the current evidence.

We now believe that Stonehenge was the site of ceremonies linked to death and burial. This theory comes from evidence that looks not only at the stone circles but also at the nearby sites dating from the periods when Stonehenge was in use (FIG. **1-23**). A new generation of archaeologists, led by Mike Parker Pearson, has pioneered this contextual approach.

The settlements built near Stonehenge follow circular layouts, connecting them in plan to the ceremonial site

1-22 STONEHENGE FROM THE GROUND
Credit: © Peter Adams/The Image Bank/Getty Images

1-23 PLAN OF STONEHENGE AND ITS SURROUNDING SETTLEMENTS

Credit: © 1998 Antiquity Publications Ltd. Reprinted with the permission of Cambridge University Press

(FIG. 1-24). Unlike the more famous monument, however, these habitations were built primarily of wood, in particular large posts and tree trunks. A mile from Stonehenge is Durrington Walls, which was a large inhabited settlement (almost 1,500 feet across) surrounded by a ditch. Inside are a number of circles—made not from stone but from wood—and many circular houses constructed with wooden posts. The rubbish left behind at this and similar sites provides archaeologists with insights into the lives of the inhabitants. Chemical analysis of animal bone debris, for example, indicates that the animals consumed came from great distances before they were slaughtered, and therefore that the people who stayed here had come from regions far removed from the site.

Significantly, both Stonehenge and Durrington Walls are connected to the Avon River by banked avenues (SEE FIG. 1-23). These connected the worlds of the living (the wood

settlement) with the domain of the dead (the stone circle). Neolithic people would have moved between these worlds as they walked the avenues, sometimes bringing the deceased to be buried or cremated, other times approaching the stone circle for ceremonies and rituals dedicated to the memories of the deceased and the very ancient ancestors. The meaning of Stonehenge therefore rests within an understanding of the larger landscape that contained not only other ritual sites but also sites of habitation.

Ceramics

In addition to domestic and ceremonial architecture and a food-producing economy, the other critical component of the Neolithic way of life was the ability to make ceramic vessels. This "pot revolution" marked a shift from a complete reliance on skin, textile, and wooden containers to the use of pots made by firing clay. Pottery provided a new medium of extraordinary potential for shaping and decorating durable objects.

The terms pottery and ceramics may be used interchangeably—and often are. Because it covers all baked-clay wares, **ceramics** is technically a more inclusive term than pottery. Pottery includes all baked-clay wares except **porcelain**, which is the most refined product of ceramic technology.

Pottery vessels can be formed in several ways. It is possible, though difficult, to raise up the sides from a ball of raw clay. Another method is to coil long rolls of soft, raw clay, stack them on top of each other to form a container, and then smooth them by hand. A third possibility is simply to press the clay over an existing form, a dried

1-24 RECONSTRUCTION DRAWING OF DURRINGTON WALLS

The settlement at Durrington Walls, near Stonehenge, southern England. 2600 BCE. Private collection.

Credit: © Historic England/Bridgeman Images

gourd for example. By about 4000 BCE, Egyptian potters had developed the potter's wheel, a round, spinning platform on which a lump of clay is placed and then formed with the fingers while rotating, making it relatively simple to produce a uniformly shaped vessel in a very short time. The potter's wheel appeared in the ancient Near East about 3250 BCE and in China about 3000 BCE.

After forming, a pot is allowed to dry completely before it is fired. Special ovens for firing pottery, called **kilns**, have been discovered at prehistoric sites in Europe dating from as early as 26,000 BCE (as at Dolní Věstonice). For effective firing, the temperature must be maintained at a relatively uniform level. Raw clay becomes porous pottery when heated to at least 500° Centigrade. It then holds its shape permanently and will not disintegrate in water. Fired at 800° Centigrade, pottery is technically known as **earthenware**. When subjected to temperatures between 1,200° and 1,400° Centigrade, certain stone elements in the clay vitrify, or become glassy, and the result is a stronger type of ceramic called **stoneware**.

Pottery is relatively fragile, and new vessels were constantly in demand to replace broken ones, so fragments of low-fired ceramics—fired at a hearth, rather than a higher-temperature kiln—are the most common artifacts found in excavations of prehistoric settlements. Pottery fragments, or **potsherds**, serve as a major key in dating sites and reconstructing human living and trading patterns.

Ceramic technology emerged independently, at different times, across the globe. The earliest examples have

1-26 EARLY POTTERY FROM THE FRANCHTHI CAVE, GREECE

6500 BCE.

Credit: Catherine Perlès

been excavated in southern China's Jiangxi Province and date from 20,000 years ago; surviving examples from Japan's Jomon culture date from 12,000 BCE (**FIG. 1-25**). It is extremely difficult to determine with certainty why pottery was first invented or why subsequent cultures adopted it. The idea that pottery would only emerge out of farming settlements has been disproven by recent archaeology. It seems that there was no one set of social, economic, or environmental circumstances that led to the invention of ceramics.

It is likely that the technology for producing ceramics evolved in stages. Archaeologist Karen Vitelli's detailed studies of the early Neolithic site of Franchthi Cave in Greece have shown that pottery making at this site started with an experimental stage during which nonspecialist potters produced a small number of pots. These early pots were used in ceremonies, especially those where medicinal or narcotic plants were consumed (**FIG. 1-26**). Only later did specialist potters share manufacturing recipes to produce enough pots for standard activities such as cooking and eating. A similar pattern may have occurred in other early potting communities.

SCULPTED HUMAN FIGURES   In addition to firing clay to make pots, cups, pitchers, and large storage containers, Neolithic people made thousands of miniature figures of humans. While it was once thought that these figurines refer to fertility cults and matriarchal societies, archaeologists now agree that they had many different functions—for example, as toys, portraits, or votives. More importantly, specialists have shown that there are great degrees of similarity in figurine shape and decoration within distinct cultural regions. Such regional similarities, and the huge numbers of Neolithic figurines that would have been in circulation at any one place and time, have

1-25 EARLY POTTERY FROM JAPAN'S JOMON CULTURE

Approx 7,000 BCE. Excavated at Choshichiyama Shell Midden, Hachinohe, Aomori prefecture.

Art and its Contexts

FIGURES OF A WOMAN AND A MAN

For all we know, the person who created these figurines in around 4500 BCE (**FIG. 1-27**) had nothing particular in mind—people had been modeling clay figures in southeastern Europe for a long time. Perhaps a woman who was making cooking and storage pots out of clay amused herself by fashioning images of the people she saw around her. But because these figures were found in the same grave in Cernavodă, Romania, they suggest to us an otherworldly message.

The woman, wide-hipped and big-bellied, sits directly on the ground, expressive of the mundane world. She exudes stability, and her ample hips and thighs seem to ensure the continuity of her family. But in a lively gesture, she joins her hands on one raised knee, curls up her toes, and tilts her head upward. Her upwardly tilted head could suggest that she is watching the smoke rising from the hearth, worrying about holes in the roof,

gazing adoringly at her partner, or communing with heaven. The man is rather slim, with massive legs and shoulders. He rests his head on his hands, evoking thoughtfulness, weariness, boredom, or sorrow.

We can interpret the Cernavodă woman and man in many ways, but we cannot know what they meant to their makers or owners. Depending on how they are displayed, we make up different stories about them, broadening the potential fields of meaning. When they are set facing each other, or side by side as they are here, we tend to think of them as a couple—a woman and man in a relationship. In fact, we do not know whether the artist conceived of them in this way, or even made them at the same time. For all their visual eloquence, their secrets remain hidden from us, but it is difficult not to speculate.

1-27 FIGURES OF A WOMAN AND A MAN
From Cernavodă, Romania. c. 4500 BCE. Ceramic, height 4½″ (11.5 cm). National History Museum, Bucharest.

Credits: © akg-images/Erich Lessing

convinced experts that the critical significance of these objects is that they mark the emergence of the human body as the core location of human identity. Thus, the central role the body has played in the politics, philosophy, and art, of historical and modern times began over 8,000 years ago with Neolithic figurines.

Neolithic figures of humans were most numerous and diverse in central and eastern Europe, and among the most extraordinary are two figures of a man and woman from around 4500 BCE, excavated in Romania (see "Figures of a Woman and a Man" opposite).

In the Near Eastern site of 'Ain Ghazal in present-day Jordan, archaeologist Gary Rollefson found 32 large **HUMAN FIGURES** (**FIG. 1-28**). Dated to 6500 BCE and constructed by covering bundled-twig cores with layers of plaster, the statues were found in two pits. One contained 12 busts and 13 full figures, and in the other were two full figures, two fragmental busts, and three figures with two heads.

1-28 HUMAN FIGURE

From 'Ain Ghazal, Jordan. 6500 BCE. Fired lime plaster with cowrie shell, bitumen, and paint, height approx. 35″ (90 cm). National Museum, Amman, Jordan.

Credit: © akg-images/Erich Lessing

The stylized faces of these statues are startling for many modern viewers. The eyes—made with cowrie shells outlined with bitumen (a natural asphalt), also used to represent pupils—are wide open, giving them a lifelike appearance. Nostrils are also clearly defined, even exaggerated, but the mouths are discreet and tight-lipped. Clothes and other features were painted on the bodies. The powerful legs and feet are clearly modeled independently with plaster, but the strangely spindly arms and tiny, tapering hands cling closely to the body. The impression is of living, breathing individuals who are unable (or unwilling) to gesture or speak.

Scholars have searched for clues about the function of these figures. The people who lived in 'Ain Ghazal built and rebuilt their houses, replastered walls, buried their dead under house floors, and dug down through the floors to retrieve skulls—just like the inhabitants of Çatalhöyük. They used the same plaster both to coat the walls of their houses and to make the human figures. The site also contains buildings that may have served special, potentially ceremonial functions, and some scholars suggest that the figures are linked to these rites. In addition to the figures' lifelike appearance, the similarity between the burial of bodies under house floors and the burial of the plaster figures in pits is striking. At the same time, however, there are significant differences: The statues are buried in groups while the human bodies are not; the statues are buried in pits, not in houses; and the eyes of the statues are open, as if they are alive and awake. It is difficult to know with certainty how the figures of 'Ain Ghazal were used and what they meant to the people who made them.

Metallurgy

The technology of metallurgy is closely allied to that of ceramics. Although Neolithic culture persisted in northern Europe until about 2000 BCE (and indeed all of its key contributions to human evolution—farming, architecture, and pottery—continue through present times), the age of metals made its appearance in much of Europe about 3000 BCE. In central and southern Europe and in the Aegean region, copper, gold, and tin had been mined, worked, and traded even earlier. Smelted and cast copper beads and ornaments dated to 4000 BCE have been discovered in Poland.

Metals were first used for ornamentation, and gold was one of the first among them; it was used to make jewelry (ear, lip, and nose rings) and to decorate clothing (appliqués sewn onto fabric). Toward the end of the Neolithic period, people shaped simple beads by cold-hammering malachite, a green-colored, copper carbonate mineral that can be found on the surface of the ground in many regions.

Over time, the objects made from gold and copper became more complicated, and technologies of extraction

1–29 GOLD-ADORNED FACE MASK

From Tomb 3, Varna I, Bulgaria. Neolithic, 3800 BCE. Terra cotta and gold. Archaeological Museum, Plovdiv, Bulgaria.

Credit: © akg-images/Erich Lessing

(the mining of copper in Bulgaria) and metalworking (casting copper) improved. Ivan Ivanov discovered some of the most sensational and earliest prehistoric gold and copper objects in the late Neolithic cemetery at Varna on Bulgaria's Black Sea coast. While the cemetery consisted of several hundred graves of men, women, and children, a few special burials contained gold and copper artifacts (**FIGS. 1–29, 1–30**). Objects such as gold-covered scepters, bracelets, beads, arm rings, lip-plugs, and copper axes and chisels distinguish the graves of a small number of adult males. In a very few of those graves, no skeleton was present. Instead, the body was represented by a clay mask richly decorated with gold adornments (SEE FIG. 1–29), and the grave contained extraordinary concentrations of metal and special marine-shell ornaments. As in other prehistoric contexts, death and its attendant ceremonies were the focus for large and visually expressive displays of status and authority.

1–30 GOLD SCEPTERS

From Varna, Bulgaria. 3800 BCE. National Museum of History, Sofia, Bulgaria.

Credit: © akg-images/Erich Lessing

The Bronze Age

How does the Bronze Age transform prehistoric culture and art?

The period that followed the introduction of metalworking is commonly called the Bronze Age. Although copper is relatively abundant in central Europe and in Spain, objects fashioned from it are too soft to be functional and therefore usually have a ceremonial or representational use and value. However, bronze—an **alloy**, or mixture, of tin and copper—is a stronger, harder substance with a wide variety of uses.

The development of bronze, especially for weapons such as daggers and short swords, changed the peoples of Europe in fundamental ways. While copper ore was widely available across Europe, either as surface outcrops or easily mined, the tin that was required to make bronze had a much more limited natural distribution and often required extraction by mining. Power bases shifted within communities as the resources needed to make bronze were not widely available to all. Trade and intergroup contacts across the continent and into the Near East increased, and bronze objects circulated as prized goods.

Rock Carvings

Bronze Age artistry is not limited to metalworking; indeed, some of the most exciting imagery of the period is found in the rock art of northern Europe. For a thousand years starting around 1500 BCE, people created designs by scratching outlines and pecking and grinding the surface of exposed rock faces using stone hammers and sometimes grains of sand as an abrasive. The Swedish region of northern Bohuslän is especially rich in rock carvings dating to this period; archaeologists have recorded over 40,000 individual images from more than 1,500 sites. The range of motifs is wide, including boats, animals (bulls, elk, horses, a few snakes, birds, and fish), people (mostly sexless, some with horned helmets, but also men with erect penises), wheeled

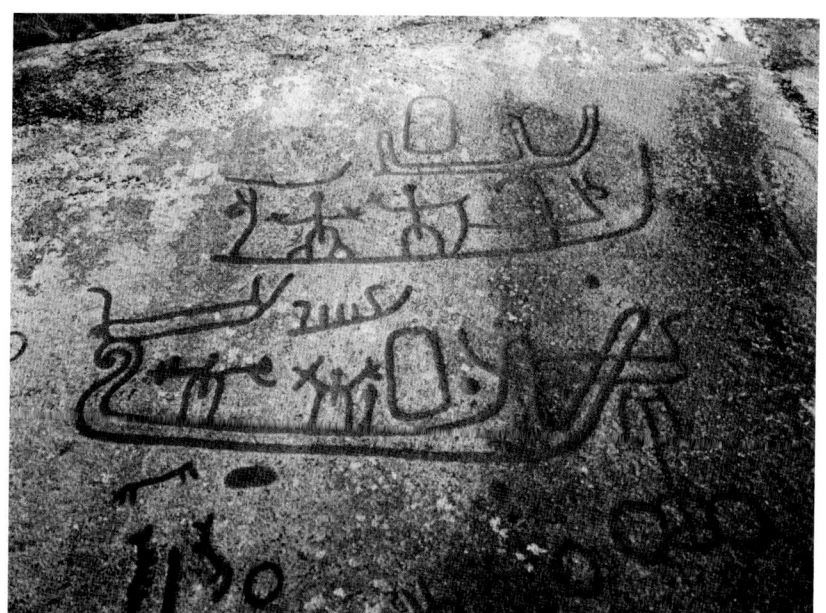

1–31 ROCK ART: BOAT AND SEA BATTLE
Fossum, northern Bohuslän, Sweden. Bronze Age, c. 1500–500 BCE.

Credit: Bridgeman Images

or past shorelines is the critical clue to their meaning. Archaeologist Richard Bradley suggests that rock art connects sky, earth, and sea, perhaps visualizing the community's view of the three-part nature of the universe. Others suggest that the art is intentionally located between water and earth to mark a boundary between the world of the living and the world of spirits. In this view, the permanent character of the rock, grounded deep in the earth, provided a means of communication and connection between distant and distinct worlds.

vehicles and plows (and unassociated disks, circles, and wheels), and weapons (swords, shields, and helmets). Within this range, however, the majority of images are boats (**FIG. 1–31**), not just in Sweden but across northern Europe. Interestingly, the boat images are unlike the boats that archaeologists have excavated. The rock-engraved images do not have masts, nor are they the dugouts or log boats that are known from this period. Instead they represent boats made from wooden planks or with animal skins.

What is the meaning of these boat images? Most agree that the location of the majority of the rock art near current

For people of the prehistoric era, representational and abstract art had critical symbolic importance, justifying the labor required to paint in the deep recesses of caves, move enormous stones great distances, or create elaborately ornamented masks. Prehistoric art and architecture connected the earthly with the spiritual, established social power hierarchies, and perhaps helped people learn and remember information about the natural world that was critical for their survival. This art represents one of the fundamental elements of our development as a human species.

Think About It

1   Prehistoric artists created representations of human figures using a variety of media, styles, and techniques. Compare two examples drawn from different times and places by discussing the relationship between style or technique and expressive character.

2   What are the common motifs found in cave paintings such as those at Lascaux and Altamira? Summarize the current theories about their original meaning and purpose.

3   Many examples of prehistoric art and architecture express relationships between the living and the dead. Discuss how this theme is evoked in one work of architecture and one example of sculpture discussed in this chapter. Why do you think this theme was so important?

4   How did the emergence of ceramics and metallurgy transform art making in the Neolithic era? Select and analyze a work discussed in this chapter that was made in one of these new media and discuss the unique properties of the medium.

Crosscurrents

Although we have limited information about the meanings prehistoric people associated with sacred spaces, art historians and archaeologists have linked these two famous sites with specific social practices and rituals. Discuss and compare current interpretations of Lascaux and Stonehenge, including evidence as well as conclusions.

FIG. 1–11

FIG. 1–22

2–1 STELE OF NARAM-SIN
From Sippar; found at Susa
(present-day Shush, Iran).
Naram-Sin (r. 2254–2218 BCE).
Limestone, height 6′6″ (1.98 m).
Musée du Louvre, Paris.

Chapter 2
Art of the Ancient Near East

 ## Learning Objectives

2.a Identify the visual hallmarks of early Mesopotamian, Assyrian, Neo-Babylonian, and Persian art for formal, technical, and expressive qualities.

2.b Interpret the meaning of works of early Mesopotamian, Assyrian, Neo-Babylonian, and Persian art based on their themes, subjects, and symbols.

2.c Relate early Mesopotamian, Assyrian, Neo-Babylonian, and Persian artists and art to their cultural, economic, and political contexts.

2.d Apply the vocabulary and concepts used to discuss ancient Near Eastern art, artists, and art history.

2.e Interpret ancient Near Eastern art using appropriate art historical methods, such as observation, comparison, and inductive reasoning.

2.f Select visual and textual evidence in various media to support an argument or an interpretation of ancient Near Eastern art.

In public works such as this stone **stele** (upright stone slab), the artists of Mesopotamia developed a sophisticated symbolic visual language—a kind of conceptual art—that both communicated and celebrated the political stratification that gave order to their world. Akkadian ruler Naram-Sin (ruled 2254–2218 BCE) is pictured proudly here (**FIG. 2-1**). His preeminence is signaled by his size: he is by far the largest person in the scene, conforming to an artistic practice we call **hierarchic scale**, where relative size indicates relative importance. Naram-Sin is also elevated well above the other figures and boldly silhouetted against blank ground. Even the shape of the stone slab is an active part of the composition. Its tapering top perfectly accommodates the carved mountain within it, and Naram-Sin is posed to reflect the profile of both, increasing his grandeur. He clasps a full arsenal of weaponry—spear, battleaxe, bow, and arrow—and his helmet sprouts horns, an attribute previously reserved for gods. By wearing such a helmet, he is claiming divinity for himself. Art historian Irene Winter has gone even further, pointing to his eroticized pose and well-formed body. In ancient Mesopotamian culture, male potency and vigor were directly related to mythical heroism and kingship. Thus every aspect of the representation of this ruler supports his authority as leader of the state.

This stele is more than an emblem of Naram-Sin's divine right to rule, however. It also tells the story of one of his important military victories. The ruler stands above a crowded scene of smaller figures. Those to the left, dressed and posed like Naram-Sin, represent his army, marching in diagonal bands up the hillside into battle. The artist has included identifiable native trees to heighten the sense that this portrays an actual event rather than a generic battle scene. In front of and under Naram-Sin are the enemy, in this case the Lullubi people from eastern Mesopotamia (present-day Iran). One has taken a fatal spear to the neck, while others beg for mercy.

Taller than most viewers who might stand in front of it and carved of eye-catching pink stone, this sumptuous work of art communicates with us forcefully and directly even after more than four millennia. Powerful symbolism and dynamic storytelling are not unique to this stele; they are key characteristics of royal art in the ancient Near East.

Early Mesopotamia

How do early Mesopotamian art and architecture develop through the Sumerian and Akkadian empires?

In the sixth or fifth millennium BCE, well before farming communities appeared in Europe, people in Asia Minor and the ancient Near East were already domesticating grains in an area known today as the Fertile Crescent (**MAP 2–1**). These alluvial plains between the Tigris and Euphrates rivers, which the Greeks called *Mesopotamia*, meaning the "land between the rivers," are now in present-day Iraq. Because of problems with periodic flooding as well as drought, there was a need for large-scale systems to control and supply water. Meeting this need may have contributed to the development of the first cities.

Between 4000 and 3000 BCE, a major cultural shift seems to have taken place. Agricultural villages in both northern and southern Mesopotamia evolved into cities simultaneously and independently. These prosperous cities joined with their surrounding territories to create what are known as city-states, each with its own gods and government. As people developed specialized skills beyond those needed for agricultural work, social hierarchies emerged that divided rulers and workers. To grain mills and ovens were added kilns for brick and pottery, and workshops for textiles and metals. With extra goods and increasing wealth came more trade and contact with other cultures.

Organized religion played an important role, and the people who controlled rituals and sacred sites eventually became full-time priests. Numerous gods and goddesses were worshiped. (The names of comparable deities varied over time and place—for example, Inanna, the Sumerian goddess of fertility, love, and war, was equivalent to the Babylonians' Ishtar.) Every city had its special protective deity, and the fate of the city was seen as dependent on the power of that deity. Large complexes of religious, administrative, and service buildings developed in each city as centers of worship and government.

Although the stone-free alluvial plain of southern Mesopotamia was prone to floods and droughts, it was a fertile bed for agriculture, which supported successive,

MAP 2–1 THE ANCIENT NEAR EAST

The green areas represent fertile land that could support early agriculture, notably the area between the Tigris and Euphrates rivers and the strips of land on either side of the Nile in Egypt.

interlinked societies. But Mesopotamia's wealth and agricultural resources, as well as its few natural defenses, made it vulnerable to political upheaval. Over the centuries, the balance of power shifted between north and south and between local powers and outside invaders. First the Sumerians controlled the south, filling their independent city-states with new technology, developed literacy, and impressive art and architecture. But their neighbors to the north, the Akkadians, eventually eclipsed them. When invaders from farther north in turn conquered the Akkadians, the Sumerians regained power locally. During this period the city-states of Ur and Lagash thrived. The Amorites were next to dominate the south. Under them and their king, Hammurabi, a new, unified society arose with its capital in the city of Babylon.

Sumer

The cities and city-states that developed along the rivers of southern Mesopotamia between about 3500 and 2340 BCE are known collectively as Sumer. The Sumerians are credited with important technological and cultural advances. They may have invented the wagon wheel and the plow. But perhaps their greatest contribution was the invention in 3400–3200 BCE of the first form of written script.

WRITING The Sumerians appear to have invented writing as a business accounting system for traded goods. The symbols were pictographs, simple pictures cut into moist clay slabs with a pointed tool called a **stylus**. Eventually the symbols evolved from pictures into a writing system known as **cuneiform** ("wedge-shaped"),

composed of phonograms—representations of syllable sounds—and thus became a writing system comparable to ours.

Thousands of surviving Sumerian tablets have allowed scholars to trace the gradual evolution of writing and arithmetic, another tool of commerce, as well as the Sumerians' organized system of justice. The world's first literary epic is Sumerian in origin, although the fullest surviving version of this tale is written in Akkadian, the language of Sumer's neighbors to the north. The *Epic of Gilgamesh* records the adventures of Gilgamesh, a legendary Sumerian king of Uruk, and his companion Enkidu. When Enkidu dies, the despondent Gilgamesh sets out to find the secret of eternal life from the only man and woman allowed by the gods to survive a great flood. Gilgamesh ultimately accepts his own mortality, abandons his quest, and returns to Uruk, recognizing the majestic city as his lasting accomplishment.

THE ZIGGURAT The Sumerians' most impressive surviving archaeological remains are **ziggurats**, huge, usually stepped structures with a temple or shrine on top. The first ziggurats may have developed from the practice of repeated rebuilding at a sacred site, with rubble from one structure serving as the foundation for the next. Elevating the buildings also protected the shrines from flooding.

Whatever the origin of their design, ziggurats towering above the flat plain proclaimed the wealth, prestige, and stability of a city's rulers and glorified its gods. Ziggurats also functioned symbolically as bridges between the earth and the heavens—a meeting place for humans and their gods. They were given names such as "House of the Mountain" and "Bond between Heaven and Earth."

TEMPLES Two large temple complexes in the 1,000-acre city at Uruk (present-day Warka, Iraq) mark the first independent Sumerian city-state. One was dedicated to Inanna, the goddess of love and war, while the other belonged to the sky god Anu. The temple platform of Anu, built up in stages over the centuries, ultimately became a ziggurat about 40 feet high. Around 3400 BCE, the priests of Uruk erected on top of the platform a whitewashed mud-brick temple that modern archaeologists refer to as the White Temple (**FIG. 2-2**). This now-ruined structure was a simple rectangle with an off-center doorway that led into a large chamber containing an altar; smaller spaces opened to each side.

Statues of gods and donors were placed in Sumerian temples. A striking life-size marble face from Uruk (**FIG. 2-3**) may represent a temple goddess. It could have been attached to a wooden head on a full-size wooden body. Now stripped of its original paint, wig, and the **inlay** set in for brows and eyes, it appears as a

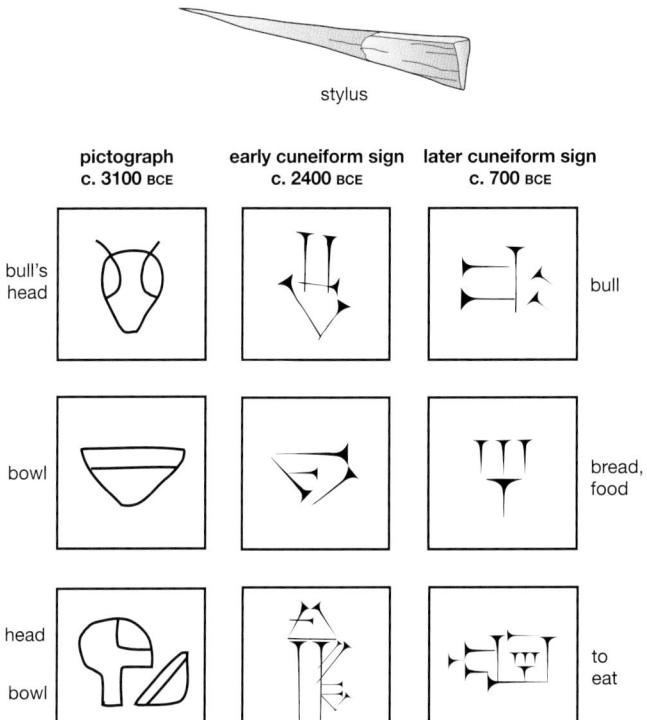

stylus

	pictograph c. 3100 BCE	early cuneiform sign c. 2400 BCE	later cuneiform sign c. 700 BCE	
bull's head				bull
bowl				bread, food
head bowl				to eat

2-2A RUINS OF THE ANU ZIGGURAT AND WHITE TEMPLE
Uruk (present-day Warka, Iraq). c. 3400–3200 BCE.

Many ancient Near Eastern cities still lie undiscovered. In most cases an archaeological site in the region is signaled by a large mound—known locally as a *tell*, *tepe*, or *huyuk*—that represents the accumulated debris of generations of human habitation. When properly excavated, such mounds yield evidence about the people who inhabited the site.

Credit: World Tourism Organization: Iraq

Anu District of Uruk

1. White Temple
2. altar
3. processional stairs
4. NW terrace

2-2B PLAN OF THE ANU ZIGGURAT AND WHITE TEMPLE
Uruk (present-day Warka, Iraq). c. 3400–3200 BCE.

2-3 HEAD OF A WOMAN
From Uruk (present-day Warka, Iraq). c. 3300–3000 BCE. Marble, height approx. 8″ (20.3 cm). Iraq Museum, Baghdad.

Credit: © 2016. Photo Scala, Florence/bpk, Bildagentur für Kunst, Kultur und Geschichte, Berlin

stark white mask. Shells may have formed the whites of the eyes, and lapis lazuli the pupils. The hair may have been gold.

A tall vessel of carved alabaster (a fine-grained, white stone) found in the temple complex of Inanna at Uruk (**FIG. 2-4**) shows how early Mesopotamian sculptors told stories in stone with great clarity and energy. They organized this visual narrative in three **registers**, or horizontal bands, and condensed the story to its essential elements.

The lowest register shows the sources of life in the natural world, beginning with water and plants (variously identified as date palm and barley, wheat and flax) and continuing in a superimposed upper strip, where alternating rams and ewes march single file along a solid ground-line. In the middle register naked men carry baskets of foodstuffs, and in the top register, the goddess Inanna accepts an offering from two standing figures. Inanna stands in front of the gate to her richly filled shrine and storehouse, identified by two reed door poles hung with banners. The two men who face her are probably a naked priest or acolyte presenting an offering-filled basket, followed by a partially preserved, ceremonially dressed figure of the priest-king (not visible in FIG. 2-4). The scene may be a re-enactment of the ritual marriage between the goddess and Dumuzi, her consort—a role taken by the priest-king—that took place during the New Year's festival to ensure the fertility of crops, animals, and people, and thus the continued survival of Uruk.

2-4 CARVED VESSEL

From Uruk (present-day Warka, Iraq). c. 3300–3000 BCE. Alabaster, height 36″ (91 cm). Iraq Museum, Baghdad.

Credits: (left) © 2016. Photo Scala, Florence/bpk, Bildagentur für Kunst, Kultur und Geschichte, Berlin; (right) © 2016. Photo Scala, Florence

VOTIVE FIGURES   Limestone statues dated to about 2900–2600 BCE from the Square Temple in Eshnunna (**FIG. 2-5**), excavated in 1932–1933, reveal another aspect of Sumerian religious art. These **votive figures**—images dedicated to the gods—of men and women are directly related to an ancient Near Eastern devotional practice in which individual worshipers could set up images of themselves in a shrine before a larger, more elaborate image of a god. A simple inscription might identify a votive figure as "one who offers prayers." Longer inscriptions might recount in detail all the things a donor had accomplished in a god's honor. Each sculpture served as a stand-in for the donor, locked in eye contact with the god, perpetually in the act of worship.

The sculptors of these votive statues followed **conventions** (traditional ways of representing forms) that were important in Sumerian art. Figures have stylized faces and bodies and are dressed in clothing that emphasizes pure cylindrical shapes. They stand solemnly, hands clasped, perhaps a posture expected in devotional contexts. The huge, wide-open eyes may relate to contemporary Sumerian texts that advise worshipers to approach their gods with an attentive gaze. As in the face of the woman from Uruk, arched brows were inlaid with dark shell, stone, or bitumen that emphasized the eyes. The male figures, bare-chested and dressed in what appear to be sheepskin skirts, are stocky and muscular, with heavy legs, large feet, big shoulders, and cylindrical bodies. The female figures are as massive as the men. Their long sheepskin skirts reveal sturdy legs and feet.

2-5 TWELVE VOTIVE FIGURES

From the Square Temple, Eshnunna (present-day Tell Asmar, Iraq). c. 2900–2600 BCE. Limestone, alabaster, and gypsum, height of largest figure approx. 30″ (76.3 cm). The Oriental Institute Museum, University of Chicago.

Credit: Courtesy of the Oriental Institute of the University of Chicago

ROYAL TOMBS The British archaeologist Sir Leonard Woolley's excavations at Ur (present-day Muqaiyir, Iraq), south of Uruk during the 1920s initially garnered international attention because of the association of this ancient Mesopotamian city with the biblical patriarch Abraham. It was not long, however, before Woolley's exciting discoveries themselves moved to center stage. Sixteen royal burials yielded spectacular gold objects and lurid evidence of the human sacrifices associated with Sumerian royal burial practices, when retainers were seemingly buried with the rulers they served.

Woolley's work at Ur was a joint venture of the University of Pennsylvania Museum in Philadelphia and the British Museum in London. To conform with Iraq's Antiquities Law of 1922, the uncovered artifacts were divided between

2–6A RECONSTRUCTION OF THE GREAT LYRE WITH BULL'S HEAD

From Royal Tomb (PG 789), Ur (present-day Muqaiyir, Iraq). c. 2600–2500 BCE. Wood with gold, silver, lapis lazuli, bitumen, and shell, reassembled in modern wood support; height of head 14″ (35.6 cm); height of front panel 13″ (33 cm); maximum length of lyre 55½″ (140 cm); height of upright back arm 46½″ (117 cm). University of Pennsylvania Museum of Archaeology and Anthropology, Philadelphia.

Credit: Courtesy of the Penn Museum, image #160104

2–6B FRONT PANEL ON SOUND BOX OF THE GREAT LYRE WITH BULL'S HEAD

Credit: Courtesy of the Penn Museum, image #150888

the sponsoring institutions and Iraq itself. Although Woolley worked with a large team of laborers and assistants during 12 seasons of digging at Ur, he and his wife Katherine reserved for themselves the painstakingly delicate process of uncovering the most important finds. Woolley's own account of work within one tomb outlines the practice: "Most of the workmen were sent away … so that the final work with knives and brushes could be done by my wife and myself in comparative peace. For ten days the two of us spent most of the time from sunrise to sunset lying on our tummies brushing and blowing and threading beads in their order as they lay…. You might suppose that to find three-score women all richly bedecked with jewelry could be a very thrilling experience, and so it is, in retrospect, but I'm afraid that at the moment one is much more conscious of the toil than of the thrill" (quoted in Zettler and Horne, p. 31).

One of the most spectacular discoveries in the royal burials at Ur was an elaborate lyre—a kind of harp—which rested over the body of the woman who had presumably played it during the funeral ceremony for the royal figure buried nearby (**FIG. 2–6A**). Like nine other lyres Woolley found at Ur, the wooden sound box of this one had long since deteriorated and disappeared, but an exquisitely crafted bull's-head finial of gold and lapis lazuli survived, along with a plaque of carved shell inlaid with bitumen, depicting at the top a heroic image of a man interlocked with and in control of two bulls, and below them three scenes of animals mimicking the activities of humans (**FIG. 2–6B**). On one register, a seated donkey plucks the strings of a bull lyre—similar to the instrument on which this set of images originally appeared—stabilized by a standing bear, while a fox accompanies him with a rattle. On the register above, upright animals bring food and drink for a feast. A hyena to the left—assuming the role of a butcher with a knife in his belt—carries a table piled high with meat. A lion follows, toting a large jar and pouring vessel.

The top and bottom registers are particularly intriguing in relation to the *Epic of Gilgamesh*, a 3,000-line poem that is Sumer's great contribution to world literature. Rich in descriptions of heroic feats and fabulous creatures, Gilgamesh's story probes the question of immortality and expresses the heroic aim to understand hostile surroundings and to find meaning in human existence. Gilgamesh encounters scorpion-men like the one pictured in the lowest register, and it is easy to see the hero himself in the commanding but unprotected bearded figure centered in the top register controlling the two human-headed bulls that flank him. Because the poem was first written down 700 years after this lyre was created, this plaque may document a very long oral tradition.

On another level, because we know lyres were used in funeral rites, this imagery might depict a heroic image

of the deceased in the top register and a funeral banquet in the realm of the dead at the bottom. Cuneiform tablets preserve songs of mourning, perhaps chanted by priests accompanied by lyres at funerals. One begins, "Oh, lady, the harp of mourning is placed on the ground," a particularly poignant statement considering that the lyres of Ur may have been buried on top of the sacrificed bodies of the women who originally played them.

Sumerian artists worked in various precious metals and in bronze, often combining them with other materials. Many of these creations were decorated with or shaped like animals or composite animal-human-bird creatures. Archaeologists discovered superb examples of their skill during the excavations of the 16 royal burials from the city of Ur. As we have seen, among the most impressive is the lyre combining wood, gold, lapis lazuli, and shell. Projecting from the base is a wood-sculpted head of a bearded bull overlaid with gold, intensely lifelike despite the blue beard created from the semiprecious gemstone lapis lazuli. Since lapis lazuli had to be imported from Afghanistan, the work documents widespread trade in the region at this time.

The Standard of Ur (**FIG. 2–7**)—a wooden box from the royal tombs at Ur—employs the same techniques and sumptuous materials. Here the theme is Sumerian success in battle on one side and the subsequent banquet celebrating victory on the other. The function of this box is uncertain, but its three registers of scenes are among the best surviving examples of the kind of pictorial narrative that captured the Sumerian imagination and conveyed the culture's most important messages.

The story begins on one of the plaques with a battle scene spread across the bottom register (**SEE FIG. 2–7A**). The action increases in intensity from left to right as the chariot animals (onagers, or wild asses) progress from a calm walk to a run, trampling over the fallen enemy soldiers. In the middle register, rows of Sumerian soldiers move in locked formation toward the removal of armor from the enemy at center, while the defeated shuffle toward the right with conspicuously less order and disjointed postures. The defeated army arrives from the right of the top register, moving toward the Sumerian ruler, easily recognized because hierarchic scale makes him the largest figure in the scene as well as the central figure within the frieze.

On the bottom two registers of the other side of the box (**SEE FIG. 2–7B**), servants carry the provisions necessary for a large celebration banquet. Across the top register, the ruler—this time placed off center, but clearly singled out by hierarchic scale—presides over the banquet, facing his guests, each of whom hoists a drinking cup. At far right, a woman sings to entertain the royal guests, accompanied by the playing of a bull's-head lyre similar to the one in FIGURE 2–6A.

2–7A SCENES OF WAR

The front of a box known as the Standard of Ur. c. 2600–2500 BCE. Shell, lapis lazuli, and red limestone inlaid in bitumen, originally attached to the large sides of a rectangular wooden box, each 8 × 19″ (20.3 × 48.3 cm). British Museum, London.

2–7B SCENES OF THE CELEBRATION OF VICTORY

The back of a box known as the Standard of Ur. c. 2600–2500 BCE. Shell, lapis lazuli, and red limestone inlaid in bitumen, originally attached to the large sides of a rectangular wooden box, each 8 × 19″ (20.3 × 48.3 cm). British Museum, London.

CYLINDER SEALS About the time written records appeared, Sumerians developed stamp seals for identifying documents and establishing property ownership. By 3300–3100 BCE, record keepers redesigned the stamp seal as a cylinder. Sumerian **cylinder seals**, usually less than 2 inches high, were generally made of a hard stone so that their tiny but intricate scenes would not wear away during repeated use. Rolled across documents on clay tablets or over the soft clay applied to a closure that needed sealing—a jar lid, a knot securing a bundle, or a door to a room—the cylinders left a raised mirror image of the design incised (cut) into their surface. Such sealing

proved the authenticity or accuracy of a text or made sure that no unauthorized person could gain access to a room or container. Individuals often acquired seals as signs of status or on appointment to a high administrative position, and the seals were buried with them along with other important possessions. The lapis lazuli **CYLINDER SEAL** (**FIG. 2–8**) is one of over 400 found in excavations of the royal burials at Ur.

This seal comes from the tomb of a powerful royal woman known as Puabi and was found leaning against the right arm of her body. The modern clay impression of its incised design shows two registers of a convivial banquet

2–8 CYLINDER SEAL AND ITS MODERN IMPRESSION

From the tomb of Queen Puabi (PG 800), Ur (present-day Muqaiyir, Iraq). c. 2600–2500 BCE. Lapis lazuli, height 1⁹⁄₁₆″ (4 cm), diameter ²⁵⁄₃₂″ (2 cm). University of Pennsylvania Museum of Archaeology and Anthropology, Philadelphia.

Credit: Courtesy of the Penn Museum, image #10872

at which all the guests appear to be women, with fringed skirts and long hair gathered up in buns. Two seated figures in the upper register raise their glasses, accompanied by standing servants, one of whom, at far left, holds a fan. The single seated figure in the lower register sits in front of a table piled with food, while a figure behind her offers a cup of drink presumably drawn from the jar she carries in her other hand, reminiscent of the container held by the lion on the lyre plaque (SEE FIG. 2–6B). Four women standing to the far right provide background music.

Akkad

A people known as the Akkadians inhabited an area north of Uruk. During the Sumerian period, they adopted Sumerian culture, but unlike the Sumerians, the Akkadians spoke a Semitic language (the family of languages that includes Arabic and Hebrew). Under the powerful military and political figure Sargon I (ruled c. 2332–2279 BCE), they conquered most of Mesopotamia. For more than half a century, Sargon, "King of the Four Quarters of the World," ruled this empire from his capital at Akkad, the actual site of which is yet to be discovered.

DISK OF ENHEDUANNA   A partially preserved circular relief sculpture in alabaster, another of the many objects excavated at Ur by Woolley, is one of the most extraordinary surviving works of ancient Near Eastern art (**FIG. 2–9**). An inscription on the back identifies the central figure on the front—slightly larger than the others and wearing a flounced wool garment and the headgear of a high priestess—as Enheduanna, daughter of Sargon I and high priestess of the moon god Nanna at his temple in Ur. Enheduanna's name also appears in other surviving Akkadian inscriptions, most notably as the author of a series of poems and hymns dedicated to the gods Nanna and Inanna. Hers is the earliest recorded name of an author in human history.

The procession on the front of the disk commemorates the dedication of a dais (raised platform) donated by Enheduanna to the temple of Inanna in Ur. The naked man in front of her pours a ritual libation in front of a ziggurat, while Enheduanna and her two followers—probably female attendants—raise their right hands before their faces in a common gesture of pious greeting (SEE FIG. 2–12). Sargon's appointment of his daughter to this important religious office followed an established tradition, but it may also have been the ruler's attempt to bolster his support and assert dynastic control in the southern part of his domain, largely populated by Sumerians.

2–9 DISK OF ENHEDUANNA

From Ur (present-day Muqaiyir, Iraq). c. 2300–2275 BCE. Alabaster, diameter 10″ (25.6 cm). University of Pennsylvania Museum of Archaeology and Anthropology, Philadelphia.

Credit: Courtesy of the Penn Museum, image #150424

HEAD OF A RULER A life-size bronze head (**FIG. 2-10**) found in the northern city of Nineveh (present-day Ninua, Iraq) and thought to date from the time of Sargon is the earliest known work of hollow-cast sculpture using the **lost-wax casting** process (see "Lost-Wax Casting" in Chapter 14 on page 428). Its artistic and technical sophistication is spectacular.

The facial features and hairstyle may reflect a generalized ideal rather than the unique likeness of a specific individual, although the sculpture was once identified as Sargon himself. The enormous curling beard and elaborately braided hair (circling the head and ending in a knot at the back) indicate both royalty and ideal male appearance. The deliberate damage to the left side of the face and eye suggests that the head was symbolically mutilated at a later date to destroy its power. The ears and the inlaid eyes appear to have been removed to deprive the head of its ability to hear and see.

THE STELE OF NARAM-SIN The concept of imperial authority was literally carved in stone by Sargon's grandson Naram-Sin (**SEE FIG. 2-1**). This stele memorializing one of his military victories is one of the first works of art created to celebrate a specific achievement of an individual ruler. The original inscription- framed in a rectangular box just above Naram-Sin's head—states that the stele commemorates his victory over the Lullubi people of the Zagros Mountains. Watched over by sun gods (symbolized by the rayed suns at the top of the stele) and wearing the horned helmet-crown previously associated only with gods, the hierarchically scaled king stands proudly above his soldiers and his fallen foes, silhouetted against the sky next to the smooth surface of a mountain.

This expression of physical prowess and political power was erected by Naram-Sin in the courtyard of the temple of the sun god Shamash in Sippar, but it did not stay there permanently. During the twelfth century BCE—over a thousand years after the end of Akkadian rule—the Elamite king Shutruk-Nahhunte conquered Sippar and transported the stele of Naram-Sin back to his own capital in Susa, where he rededicated it to an Elamite god. Shutruk-Nahhunte also added a new explanatory inscription in a diagonal band on the mountain in front of Naram-Sin, recounting his own victory and claiming the monument as a statement of his own military and political prowess. The stele remained in Susa until the end of the nineteenth century, when it was excavated by a French archaeologist and taken once more, this time for exhibition in Paris at the Louvre.

Ur and Lagash

The Akkadian Empire fell around 2180 BCE to the Guti, a mountain people from the northeast. For a brief time, the Guti controlled most of the Mesopotamian plain, but ultimately Sumerians under the leadership of King Urnammu of Ur regained control of the region and expelled the Guti in 2112 BCE. Urnammu sponsored magnificent building campaigns, notably a ziggurat dedicated to the moon god Nanna, also called Sin (**FIG. 2-11**). Although located on the site of an earlier temple, this imposing structure—mudbrick faced with kiln-dried brick set with bitumen—was not the accidental result of successive rebuilding. Its base is a rectangle of 205 by 141 feet, with three sets of stairs converging at an imposing entrance gate atop the first of what were three platforms. Each platform's walls slope outward from top to base, probably to prevent rainwater from forming puddles and eroding the mud-brick pavement below. The first two levels of the ziggurat and their retaining walls are recent reconstructions.

2-10 HEAD OF A MAN (KNOWN AS AN AKKADIAN RULER)

From Nineveh (present-day Ninua, Iraq). c. 2300–2200 BCE. Copper alloy, height 14⅜" (36.5 cm). Iraq Museum, Baghdad.

2-11 NANNA ZIGGURAT

Ur (present-day Muqaiyir, Iraq). c. 2100–2050 BCE.

Credit: © Michael S. Yamashita/CORBIS

One large Sumerian city-state remained independent throughout this period: Lagash, whose capital was Girsu (present-day Telloh, Iraq), on the Tigris River. Lagash's ruler, Gudea, built and restored many temples, and within them, following the venerable Mesopotamian tradition, he placed votive statues representing himself as governor and embodiment of just rule (**FIG. 2-12**). The statues are made of diorite, a very hard stone; the difficulty of carving it may have prompted sculptors to use compact, simplified forms for the portraits. Or perhaps it was the desire for powerful, stylized images that inspired the choice of this imported stone. Twenty of the statues survive, making Gudea a familiar figure in the study of ancient Near Eastern art.

Images of Gudea present him as a strong, peaceful, pious ruler worthy of divine favor. Whether sitting or standing, he wears a long garment, which provides plenty of smooth space for long cuneiform inscriptions. In this imposing statue, only 2½ feet tall, his right shoulder is bare, and he wears a cap with a wide brim carved with a pattern to represent fleece. He holds a vessel in front of him from which life-giving water flows in two streams, each filled with leaping fish. The text on his garment states that he dedicated himself, the statue, and its temple to the goddess Geshtinanna, the divine poet and interpreter of dreams. The sculptor has emphasized the power centers of the human body: the eyes, head, and arms. Gudea's face is youthful and serene, and his eyes—oversized and wide open—perpetually meet the gaze of the deity with intense concentration.

2-12 VOTIVE STATUE OF GUDEA

From Girsu (present-day Telloh, Iraq). c. 2090 BCE. Diorite, height 29″ (73.7 cm). Musée du Louvre, Paris.

Credit: Photo © RMN/D. Arnaudet/Louvre, Paris

Babylon

For more than 300 years, political turmoil and stable government alternated in Mesopotamia, until the Amorites (a Semitic-speaking people from the Syrian desert to the west) reunited the region under Hammurabi (ruled 1792–1750 BCE). Hammurabi's capital city was Babylon, and his subjects were called Babylonians. Among Hammurabi's achievements was a written legal code that detailed the laws of his realm and the penalties for breaking them.

THE CODE OF HAMMURABI The Babylonian ruler Hammurabi's systematic codification of his people's rights, duties, and punishments for wrongdoing was engraved on a black basalt slab known as the **STELE OF HAMMURABI** (FIG. 2–13). This imposing artifact, therefore, is both a work of art that depicts a legendary event and a precious historical document.

At the top of the stele, we see Hammurabi standing in an attitude of prayer before Shamash, the sun god and god of justice. Rays rise from Shamash's shoulders as he sits on a backless throne, crowned by a conical horned cap and holding additional symbols of his power—the measuring rod and the rope circle. Shamash gives the law to the king, his intermediary, and the codes of justice flow forth underneath them in horizontal bands of exquisitely engraved cuneiform signs. The idea of god-given laws engraved on

2–13 STELE OF HAMMURABI
Probably from Sippar; found at Susa (present-day Shush, Iran). c. 1792–1750 BCE. Basalt, height of stele approx. 7'4" (2.25 m), height of figural relief 28" (71.1 cm). Musée du Louvre, Paris.

stone tablets will have a long tradition in the ancient Near East. About 500 years later, Moses, the lawgiver of Israel, received two stone tablets containing the Ten Commandments from God on Mount Sinai (Exodus 32:19).

A prologue on the front of the stele lists the temples Hammurabi has restored, and an epilogue on the back glorifies him as a peacemaker, but most of the stele "publishes" the laws themselves, guaranteeing uniform treatment of people throughout his kingdom. Within the inscription, Hammurabi declares that he intends "to cause justice to prevail in the land and to destroy the wicked and the evil, that the strong might not oppress the weak nor the weak the strong." Most of the 300 or so entries that follow deal with commercial and property matters. Only 68 relate to domestic problems, and a mere 20 deal with physical assault.

The wealth, class, and gender of the parties determine the nature of their punishment—the rights of the wealthy are favored over the poor, citizens over slaves, men over women. Most famous are instances when punishments are specifically tailored to fit crimes—an eye for an eye, a tooth for a tooth, a broken bone for a broken bone. Crimes such as stealing from a temple or palace, helping a slave to escape, or being insubordinate in the army merit the death penalty. Trial by water and fire could also be imposed, such as when an adulterous woman and her lover were thrown into the water; if they did not drown, they were considered innocent. Although some of the punishments may seem excessive today, Hammurabi was breaking new ground by regulating laws and punishments rather than leaving them to the whims of rulers or officials.

Assyrians and Neo-Babylonians

How do the design, ornament, and meaning of great palace complexes and urban development projects express the power of Assyrian and Neo-Babylonian rulers?

Around 1400 BCE, a people called the Assyrians rose to dominance in northern Mesopotamia. After about 1000 BCE, they began to conquer neighboring regions. By the end of the ninth century BCE, the Assyrians controlled most of Mesopotamia, and by the early seventh century BCE they had extended their influence as far west as Egypt. Soon afterward they succumbed to internal weakness and external enemies, and by 600 BCE their empire had collapsed.

Assyrian rulers built huge palaces atop high platforms inside a series of fortified cities that served at one time or another as Assyrian capitals. They decorated these palaces with shallow stone reliefs of battle and hunting scenes, Assyrian victories, presentations of tribute to the king, and religious imagery.

Assurnasirpal II

During his reign (883–859 BCE), the Assyrian ruler Assurnasirpal II established his capital at Kalhu (present-day Nimrud, Iraq), on the east bank of the Tigris River, and undertook an ambitious building program. His architects

2–14 ASSURNASIRPAL II KILLING LIONS
From the palace complex of Assurnasirpal II, Kalhu (present-day Nimrud, Iraq). c. 875–860 BCE. Alabaster, height approx. 39″ (99.1 cm). British Museum, London.

fortified the city with mud-brick walls 5 miles long and 42 feet high, and his engineers constructed a canal that irrigated fields and provided water for the expanded population of the city. According to an inscription commemorating the event, Assurnasirpal gave a banquet for 69,574 people to celebrate the dedication of the new capital in 863 BCE.

Most of the buildings in Kalhu were made from mud bricks, but limestone and alabaster slabs—more impressive and durable—covered the walls with architectural decoration. Colossal guardian figures flanked the grand and often decorated major **portals**, and the panels covering the brick walls were carved with scenes in **low relief** (sculpted relief that projects only slightly from a recessed

background) of the king participating in religious rituals, war campaigns, and hunting expeditions.

In a vivid lion-hunting scene (**FIG. 2–14**), Assurnasirpal II stands in a chariot pulled by galloping horses and draws his bow against an attacking lion, advancing from the rear with arrows already protruding from its body. Another expiring beast collapses on the ground under the horses. This was probably a ceremonial hunt, in which the king, protected by men with swords and shields, rode back and forth killing animals as they were released one by one into an enclosed area. The immediacy of this image marks a shift in Mesopotamian art away from a sense of timeless solemnity and toward a more dramatic, even emotional, involvement with the event portrayed.

A Closer Look
ENEMIES CROSSING THE EUPHRATES TO ESCAPE ASSYRIAN ARCHERS

These Assyrian archers are outfitted in typical fashion with protective boots, short "kilts," pointed helmets, and swords, as well as bows and quivers of arrows. Their smaller scale conveys a sense of depth and spatial positioning in this relief, reinforced by the size and placement of the trees.

The detailed landscape setting documents the swirling water of the river, its rocky banks, and the airy environment of the trees, one of which is clearly a palm.

The oblique line of the river bank and the overlapping of the swimmers convey a sense of depth.

If this is the ruler of the enemy citadel, he seems shocked into powerlessness by the Assyrian invasion. Note the contrast between his lowered weapon and those of the archers of the Assyrian vanguard.

The long robes of the three enemy swimmers show their high status. They are not ordinary foot soldiers.

The two lower swimmers were clearly taken by surprise. Already in retreat, they are still blowing through tubes to inflate their flotation devices, made from sewn animal skin.

This beardless swimmer is probably a eunuch, many of whom served as high officials in ancient Near Eastern courts.

Two figures raise their hands in despair, reacting to the fate of their arrow-riddled comrades.

2-15 ENEMIES CROSSING THE EUPHRATES TO ESCAPE ASSYRIAN ARCHERS
Palace complex of Assurnasirpal II, Kalhu (present-day Nimrud, Iraq). c. 875–860 BCE. Alabaster, height approx. 39″ (99.1 cm). British Museum, London.

citadel gate A   Nabu temple   ziggurat   palace   throne room

city wall

palace entrance

citadel gate B

citadel wall

2–16 RECONSTRUCTION DRAWING OF THE CITADEL AND PALACE COMPLEX OF SARGON II

Dur Sharrukin (present-day Khorsabad, Iraq). c. 721–706 BCE. The Oriental Institute Museum, University of Chicago.

Credit: Courtesy of the Oriental Institute of the University of Chicago

In another palace relief, the scene shifts from royal ceremony to the heat of battle, set within a detailed landscape (see "Closer Look" opposite). Three of the Assyrians' enemies—two using flotation devices made of inflated animal skins—swim across a raging river, retreating from a vanguard of Assyrian archers who kneel at its banks to launch their assault. The scene evokes a specific event from 878 BCE described in the annals of Assurnasirpal. As the Assyrian king overtook the army of an enemy leader named Kudurru near the present-day town of Anu, both leader and soldiers escaped into the Euphrates River in an attempt to save their lives.

Sargon II

Sargon II (ruled 721–706 BCE) built a new Assyrian capital at Dur Sharrukin (present-day Khorsabad, Iraq). On the northwest side of the capital a walled citadel, or fortress, straddled the city wall (**FIG. 2-16**). Within the citadel Sargon's **palace complex** (the group of buildings where the ruler governed and resided) stood on a raised, fortified platform about 40 feet high—demonstrating the use of art as political propaganda.

Guarded by two towers, the palace complex could be entered only by a wide ramp leading up from an open

square, around which the homes of important government and religious officials were clustered. Beyond the ramp was the main courtyard with service buildings on the right and temples on the left. The heart of the palace lay past the main courtyard, protected by a reinforced wall with only two small, off-center doors. Within the inner compound was a second courtyard lined with narrative relief panels showing tribute bearers. Visitors would have waited to see the king in this courtyard that functioned as an open-air audience hall; once granted access to the royal throne room, they would have passed through a stone gate flanked, like the other gates of the citadel and palace (**FIG. 2-17**), by awesome guardian figures. These colossal beings, known as **lamassus**, combined the bearded head of a man, the powerful body of a lion or bull, the wings of an eagle, and the horned headdress of a god.

In an open space between the palace complex and temple complex at Dur Sharrukin rose a ziggurat declaring the might of Assyria's kings and symbolizing their claim to empire. It probably had seven levels, each about 18 feet high and painted a different color (SEE FIG. 2-16). The four levels still remaining were once white, black, blue, and red. Instead of separate flights of stairs between the levels, a single, squared-off spiral ramp rose continuously around the exterior from the base.

2-17 GUARDIAN FIGURES AT GATE A OF THE CITADEL OF SARGON II DURING ITS EXCAVATION IN THE 1840S
Dur Sharrukin (present-day Khorsabad, Iraq). c. 721–706 BCE.

Assurbanipal

Assurbanipal (ruled 669–c. 627 BCE), king of the Assyrians three generations after Sargon II, maintained his capital at Nineveh. Like that of Assurnasirpal II two centuries earlier, his palace walls were faced with alabaster panels carved with pictorial narratives in low relief. Most show Assurbanipal and his subjects in battle or hunting.

Occasionally, there are also scenes of palace life. An unusually peaceful example shows the king and queen relaxing in a pleasure garden (**FIG. 2-18**). The king reclines on a couch, the queen sits in a chair at his feet, and a musician plays at far left. Three servants arrive from the left with trays of food, while others wave whisks to protect the royal couple from insects. The king has taken off his rich necklace and hung it on his couch, and he has laid his weapons—a sword, a bow, and a quiver of arrows—on the table behind him. However, this apparently tranquil domestic scene is actually a victory celebration. The severed head of his vanquished enemy hangs from a tree at the far left.

2-18 ASSURBANIPAL AND HIS QUEEN IN THE GARDEN
From the palace at Nineveh (present-day Ninua, Iraq). c. 647 BCE. Alabaster, height approx. 21″ (53.3 cm). British Museum, London.

Neo-Babylonia

At the end of the seventh century BCE, Assyria was invaded by the Medes, a people from western Iran who were allied with the Babylonians and the Scythians, a nomadic people from northern Asia (present-day Russia and Ukraine). In 612 BCE, the Medes' army captured Nineveh. When the dust had settled, Assyria was no more and the Neo-Babylonians—so named because they recaptured the splendor that had marked Babylon 12 centuries earlier under Hammurabi—controlled a region that stretched from present-day Turkey to northern Arabia and from Mesopotamia to the Mediterranean Sea.

The most famous Neo-Babylonian ruler was Nebuchadnezzar II (ruled 605–562 BCE), notorious today for his suppression of the Jews as recorded in the book of Daniel in the Hebrew Bible, in which he may have been confused with the final Neo-Babylonian ruler, Nabonidus. A great patron of architecture, Nebuchadnezzar II built temples dedicated to the Babylonian gods throughout his realm and transformed Babylon—the cultural, political, and economic hub of his empire—into one of the most splendid cities of its day.

Babylon straddled the Euphrates River, its two sections joined by a bridge. The older, eastern sector was traversed by the Processional Way, the route taken by religious processions honoring the city's patron god, Marduk (FIG. 2-19). This street, paved with large stone slabs set in a bed of bitumen, was up to 66 feet

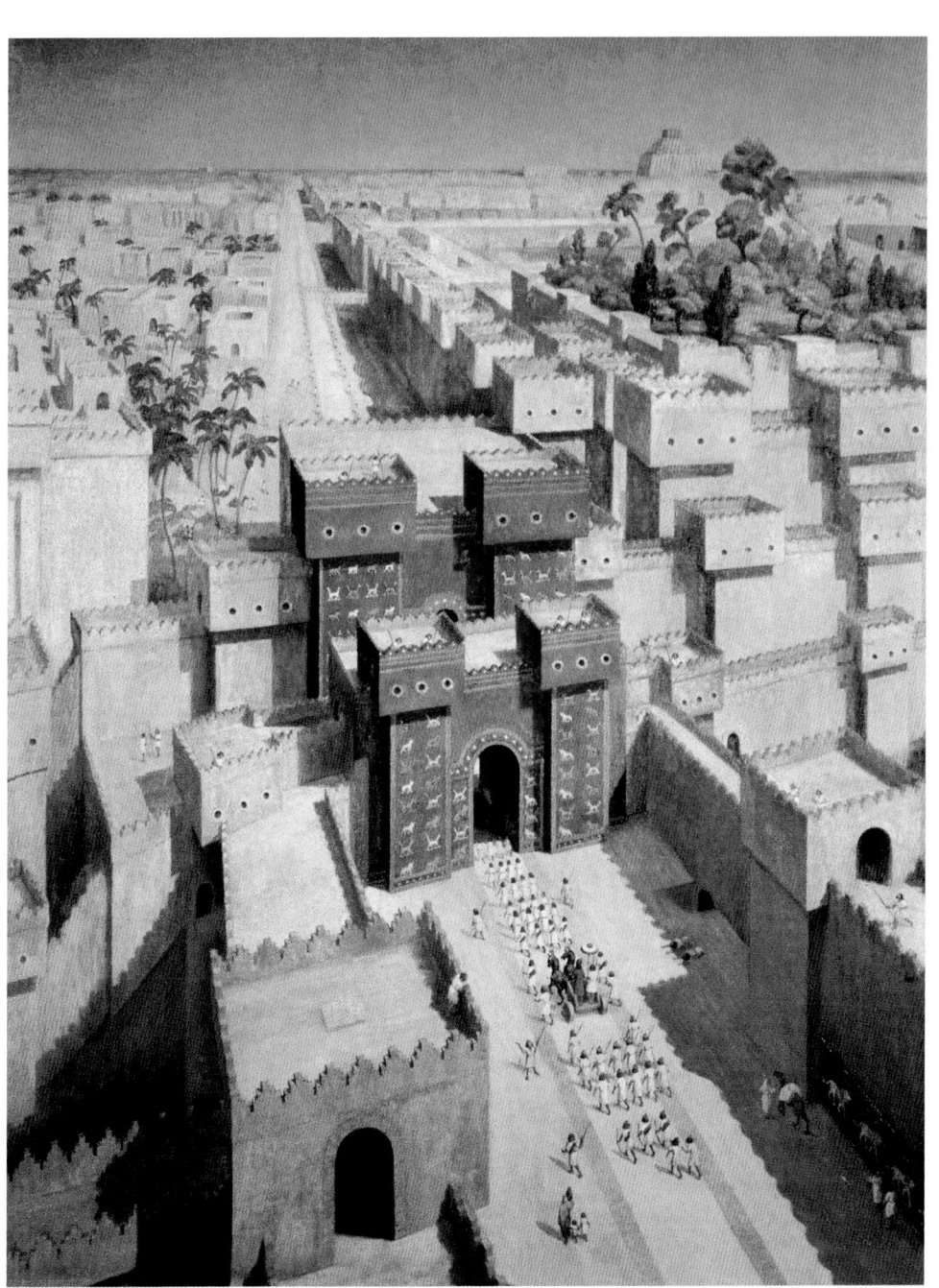

2-19 RECONSTRUCTION DRAWING OF BABYLON IN THE 6TH CENTURY BCE
The Oriental Institute Museum, University of Chicago.

The palace of Nebuchadnezzar II, with its famous Hanging Gardens, can be seen just behind and to the right of the Ishtar Gate, west of the Processional Way. The Marduk Ziggurat looms in the far distance on the east bank of the Euphrates.

Credit: Courtesy of the Oriental Institute of the University of Chicago

wide at some points. It ran from the Euphrates bridge through the temple district and palaces and finally through the Ishtar Gate, the ceremonial entrance to the city.

The Ishtar Gate's four **crenellated** towers (crenellations are notched walls for military defense) symbolized Babylonian power (**FIG. 2-20**). Beyond the Ishtar Gate, dark blue glazed bricks covered the walls on either side of the route. The glaze on the bricks was a film of colored glass adhered to their surface after firing, a process used since about 1600 BCE. Against that blue background, specially molded turquoise-, blue-, and gold-colored bricks formed images of striding lions, mascots of the goddess Ishtar, as well as the dragons that were associated with Marduk.

Persia

What is the impact of the Persian conquest on the history of ancient Near Eastern architecture?

In the sixth century BCE the Persians, a formerly nomadic Indo-European-speaking people, began to seize power in Mesopotamia. From the region of Parsa, or Persis (present-day Fars, Iran), they established a vast empire. The rulers of this new empire traced their ancestry to a semilegendary Persian king named Achaemenes, and consequently they are known as the Achaemenids.

The dramatic expansion of the Achaemenids began in 559 BCE with the ascension of a remarkable leader, Cyrus II (Cyrus the Great, ruled 559–530 BCE). By the

2–21 AERIAL VIEW OF THE CEREMONIAL COMPLEX, PERSEPOLIS
Iran. 518–c. 460 BCE.

Credit: Arazu/Fotolia

time of his death, the Persian Empire included Babylonia, Media (which stretched across present-day northern Iran through Anatolia), and some of the Aegean islands far to the west. Only the Greeks stood fast against them (see Chapter 5). When Darius I (ruled 521–486 BCE) took the throne, he could proclaim, "I am Darius, great King, King of Kings, King of countries, King of this earth."

An able administrator, Darius organized the Persian lands into 20 tribute-paying areas under Persian governors. He often left local rulers in place beneath the governors. This practice, along with a tolerance for diverse native customs and religions, won the Persians the loyalty of large numbers of their subjects. Like many powerful rulers, Darius created palaces and citadels as visible symbols of his authority. He made Susa his first capital and built a 32–acre administrative compound there.

In about 515 BCE, Darius began construction of Parsa, a new capital in the Persian homeland, today known by its Greek name: **PERSEPOLIS**. It is one of the best-preserved and most impressive ancient sites in the Near East (**FIG. 2–21**). Darius imported materials, workers, and artists from all over his empire. He even ordered work to be executed in Egypt and transported to his capital. The result was a new multicultural style of art that combined many different traditions—Persian, Median, Mesopotamian, Egyptian, and Greek.

In Assyrian fashion, the imperial complex at Persepolis was set on a raised platform 40 feet high and measuring 1,500 by 900 feet, accessible only via a single approach made of wide, shallow steps that could be ascended on horseback. Its rectangular grid plan is comparable to Egyptian and Greek cities. Darius lived to see the completion only of the Apadana (audience hall), a treasury, and a very small palace for himself. The **APADANA**, set above the rest of the complex on a second terrace (**FIG. 2–22**), had open porches on three sides and a square hall large enough to hold several thousand people. Darius's son Xerxes I (ruled 485–465 BCE) added a sprawling palace complex for himself, enlarged the treasury building, and began a vast new public reception space, the Hall of 100 Columns.

The central stair of Darius's Apadana displays reliefs of animal combat, tiered ranks of royal guards (the "10,000 Immortals"), and delegations of tribute-bearers. Here, lions attack bulls on either side of the Persian generals. Such animal combats (a theme found throughout the Near East) emphasize the ferocity of the leaders and their men. Ranks of warriors cover the walls with repeated patterns and seem ready to defend the palace. The elegant drawing, balanced composition, and sleek modeling of figures reflect the Persians' knowledge of Greek art and perhaps the use of Greek artists. Other reliefs throughout

2-22 APADANA (AUDIENCE HALL) OF DARIUS AND XERXES

Ceremonial complex, Persepolis, Iran. 518–c. 460 BCE.

Credit: © Melba Photo Agency/Alamy Stock Photo

2-23 DARIUS AND XERXES RECEIVING TRIBUTE

Detail of a relief from the stairway leading to the Apadana, Persepolis, Iran. 491–486 BCE. Limestone, height 8′4″ (2.54 m). The Oriental Institute Museum, University of Chicago.

Credit: Courtesy of the Oriental Institute of the University of Chicago

Persepolis depict displays of allegiance or economic prosperity. In one example, once the centerpiece, Darius holds an audience while his son and heir, Xerxes, listens from behind the throne (**FIG. 2-23**). Such panels would have looked quite different when they were freshly painted in bright colors, with metal objects such as Darius's crown and necklace covered in **gold leaf** (sheets of hammered gold).

At its height, the Persian Empire extended from Africa to India. From Persepolis, Darius in 490 BCE and Xerxes in 480 BCE sent their armies west to conquer Greece, but mainland Greeks successfully resisted the armies of the Achaemenids, preventing them from advancing into Europe. Indeed, it was a Greek who ultimately put an end to their empire. In 334 BCE, Alexander the Great of Macedonia (d. 323 BCE) crossed into Anatolia and swept through Mesopotamia, defeating Darius III and nearly destroying Persepolis in 330 BCE. Although the Achaemenid Empire was at an end, Persia eventually revived. The Persian style in art continued to influence Greek artists (see Chapter 5) and ultimately became one of the foundations of Islamic art (see Chapter 9).

Think About It

1   Describe and characterize the way human figures are represented in the Sumerian votive figures of Eshnunna. What are the potential relationships between style and function?
2   Discuss the development of relief sculpture in the ancient Near East. Choose two specific examples, one from the Sumerian period and one from the Assyrian period, and explain how symbols and stories are combined to express ideas that were important to these two cultures.
3   Select two rulers discussed in this chapter and explain how each preserved his legacy through commissioned works of art and/or architecture.
4   How did the excavations of Sir Leonard Woolley contribute to our understanding of the art of the ancient Near East?

Crosscurrents

Both of these works depict a social gathering involving food and drink, but they are vastly different in scale, materials, and physical context. How do the factors of scale and materials contribute to the visual appearance of the scenes? How does physical context and audience affect the meaning of what is portrayed?

FIG. 2-8

FIG. 2-18

3–1 FUNERARY MASK OF TUTANKHAMUN

From the tomb of Tutankhamun, Valley of the Kings. Eighteenth Dynasty (Tutankhamun ruled c. 1332–1322 BCE), c. 1327 BCE. Gold inlaid with glass and semiprecious stones, height 21¼″ (54.5 cm), weight 24 pounds (11 kg). Egyptian Museum, Cairo. (JE 60672).

Chapter 3
Art of Ancient Egypt

Learning Objectives

3.a Identify the visual hallmarks of Early Dynastic, Old Kingdom, Middle Kingdom, New Kingdom, and Late Egyptian art for formal, technical, and expressive qualities.

3.b Interpret the meaning of works of Early Dynastic, Old Kingdom, Middle Kingdom, New Kingdom, and Late Egyptian art based on their themes, subjects, and symbols.

3.c Relate Early Dynastic, Old Kingdom, Middle Kingdom, New Kingdom, and Late Egyptian artists and art to their cultural, economic, and political contexts.

3.d Apply the vocabulary and concepts used to discuss ancient Egyptian art, artists, and art history.

3.e Interpret ancient Egyptian art using appropriate art historical methods, such as observation, comparison, and inductive reasoning.

3.f Select visual and textual evidence in various media to support an argument or an interpretation of ancient Egyptian art.

On February 16, 1923, *The Times* of London cabled the *New York Times* with dramatic news of a discovery: "This has been, perhaps, the most extraordinary day in the whole history of Egyptian excavation. The entrance today was made into the sealed chamber of [Tutankhamun's] tomb … and yet another door opened beyond that. No eyes have seen the King, but to practical certainty we know that he lies there close at hand in all his original state, undisturbed." And indeed he did. A collar of dried flowers and beads covered the chest, and a linen shroud was draped around the head. A gold **FUNERARY MASK** (**FIG. 3-1**) had been placed over the head and shoulders of his mummified body, which was enclosed in three nested coffins, the innermost made of gold (SEE FIG. 3-32). The coffins were placed in a yellow quartzite **sarcophagus** (stone coffin) that was itself encased within gilt wooden shrines nested inside one another.

The discoverer of this treasure, the English archaeologist Howard Carter, had worked in Egypt for more than 20 years before he undertook a last expedition, sponsored by the wealthy British amateur Egyptologist Lord Carnarvon. Carter was convinced that the tomb of Tutankhamun, one of the last Eighteenth-Dynasty royal burial places still unidentified, lay hidden in the Valley

of the Kings. After 15 years of digging, on November 4, 1922, he unearthed the entrance to Tutankhamun's tomb and found unbelievable treasures in the antechamber: jewelry, textiles, gold-covered furniture, a carved and inlaid throne, and four gold chariots. In February 1923, Carter pierced the wall separating the anteroom from the actual burial chamber and found the greatest treasure of all, Tutankhamun himself.

Since ancient times, tombs have tempted looters; more recently, they also have attracted archaeologists and historians. The first large-scale "archaeological" expedition in history landed in Egypt with the armies of Napoleon in 1798. The French commander must have realized that he would find great wonders there, for he took French scholars with him to study ancient sites. The military adventure ended in failure, but the scholars eventually published richly illustrated volumes of their findings, unleashing a craze for all things Egyptian that has not dimmed since. In 1976, the first blockbuster museum exhibition was born when treasures from the tomb of Tutankhamun began a tour of the United States and attracted over 8 million visitors. Most recently, in 2006, Otto Schaden excavated a tomb containing seven coffins in the Valley of the Kings, the first tomb to be found there since Tutankhamun's in 1922.

The Gift of the Nile

What are the cultural and historical backgrounds for ancient Egyptian art and architecture?

The Greek traveler and historian Herodotus, writing in the fifth century BCE, remarked, "Egypt is the gift of the Nile." This great river, the longest in the world, winds northward from equatorial Africa and flows through Egypt in a relatively straight line to the Mediterranean (MAP 3–1). There it forms a broad delta before emptying into the sea. Before it was dammed in 1970 by the Aswan High Dam, the lower (northern) Nile, swollen with the runoff of heavy seasonal rains in the south, overflowed its banks for several months each year. Every time the floodwaters receded, they left behind a new layer of rich silt, making the valley and delta a continually fertile and attractive habitat.

By about 8000 BCE, the valley's inhabitants had become relatively sedentary, living off the abundant fish, game, and wild plants. Not until about 5000 BCE did they adopt the agricultural village life associated with Neolithic culture (see Chapter 1). At that time, the climate of north Africa grew increasingly dry. To ensure adequate resources for agriculture, the farmers along the Nile began to manage flood waters in a system called basin irrigation.

The Predynastic period, from roughly 5000 to 2950 BCE, was a time of significant social and political transition that preceded the unification of Egypt under a single ruler. (After unification, Egypt was ruled by a series of family dynasties and is therefore characterized as "dynastic.") Rudimentary federations emerged and began conquering and absorbing weaker communities. By about 3500 BCE, there were several larger states, or chiefdoms, in the lower Nile Valley and a centralized form of leadership had emerged. Rulers were expected to protect their subjects, not only from outside aggression, but also from natural catastrophes such as droughts and insect plagues.

The surviving art of the Predynastic period consists chiefly of ceramic figurines, decorated pottery, and reliefs carved on stone plaques and pieces of ivory. A few examples of wall painting—lively scenes filled with small figures of people and animals—were found in a tomb at Hierakonpolis, a Predynastic town of mud-brick houses in Upper Egypt that was once home to as many as 10,000 people.

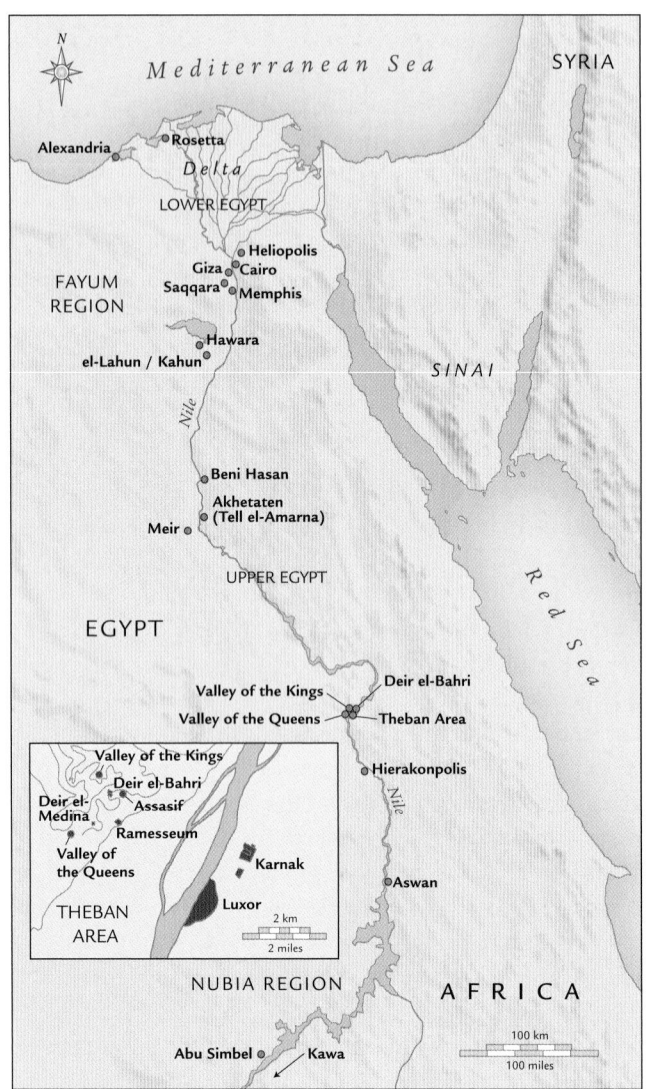

MAP 3–1 ANCIENT EGYPT

Upper Egypt is below Lower Egypt on this map because the designations "upper" and "lower" refer to the directional flow of the Nile, not to our conventions for south and north in drawing maps. The two kingdoms were united c. 3000 BCE, just before the Early Dynastic period.

Early Dynastic Egypt

How are the foundations of ancient Egyptian art established during the Early Dynastic period in the conventions of figural representation and funerary architecture?

Around 3000 BCE, Egypt became a consolidated state. According to legend, the country had previously evolved into two major kingdoms—the Two Lands—Upper Egypt in the south (upstream on the Nile) and Lower Egypt in the north (downstream). But a powerful ruler from Upper Egypt conquered Lower Egypt and unified the two kingdoms. In the art of the subsequent Early Dynastic period we see the development of fundamental and enduring ideas about kingship and the cosmic order. Since the works of art and architecture that survive from ancient Egypt come mainly from tombs and temples—the majority of which were located in secure places and built with the most durable materials—most of what we now know about the ancient art of Egypt is rooted in religious beliefs and practices.

The God-Kings

The Greek historian Herodotus thought the Egyptians were the most religious people he had ever encountered. In their worldview, the movements of heavenly bodies, the workings of gods, and the humblest of human activities were all believed to be part of a balanced and harmonious grand design. Death was to be feared only by those who lived in such a way as to disrupt that harmony. Upright souls could be confident that their spirits would live on eternally.

By the Early Dynastic period, Egypt's kings were revered as gods in human form. A royal jubilee, the *heb sed* or *sed* festival, held in the thirtieth year of the living king's reign, renewed and reaffirmed his divine power, and when kings died, they rejoined their father, the sun god Ra, and rode with him in the solar boat as it made its daily journey across the sky.

In order to please the gods and ensure their continuing goodwill toward the state, kings built splendid temples and provided priests to maintain them. The priests saw to it that statues of the gods, placed deep in the innermost rooms of the temples, were never without fresh food and clothing. Egyptian gods and goddesses were depicted in various forms, some as human beings, others as animals, and still others as humans with animal heads. For example, Osiris, the overseer of the realm of the dead, regularly appears in human form wrapped in linen as a mummy. His son, the sky god Horus, is usually depicted as a falcon or falcon-headed man (see "Egyptian Symbols" below).

Over the course of ancient Egyptian history, Amun (chief god of Thebes, represented as blue and wearing a plumed crown), Ra (of Heliopolis), and Ptah (of Memphis) became the primary national gods. Other gods and their manifestations included Thoth (ibis), god of writing, science, and law; Ma'at (feather), goddess of truth, order, and justice; Anubis (jackal), god of embalming and cemeteries; and Bastet (cat), daughter of Ra.

Artistic Conventions

Egyptian artists followed a set of fairly strict conventions, often based on conceptual principles rather than on the observation of the natural world with an eye to rendering it in lifelike fashion. Eventually a system of mathematical formulas was developed to determine design and proportions (see "Conventions and Technique of Egyptian

---

Art and its Contexts
EGYPTIAN SYMBOLS

Three crowns symbolize kingship in early Egyptian art: the tall, clublike white crown of Upper Egypt (sometimes adorned with two plumes); the flat or scooped red cap with projecting spiral of Lower Egypt; and the double crown representing unified Egypt.

A striped gold and blue linen head cloth, known as the **nemes headdress**, having a cobra and a vulture at the center front, was also commonly used as royal headgear. The upright form of the cobra, known as the *uraeus*, represents the goddess Wadjet of Lower Egypt and is often included in king's crowns as well (SEE FIG. 3–1). The queen's crown included the feathered skin of the vulture goddess Nekhbet of Upper Egypt.

The god Horus, king of the earth and a force for good, is represented as a falcon or falcon-headed man. His eyes symbolize the sun and moon; the solar eye is called the *wedjat*. The looped cross, called the **ankh**, is symbolic of everlasting life. The **scarab** beetle (*khepri*, meaning "he who created himself") was associated with creation, resurrection, and the rising sun.

white crown
of Upper Egypt
(the South)

red crown
of Lower Egypt
(the North)

double crown
of unified Egypt

scepter

ankh

Horus

wedjat
(eye of Horus)

falcon
(the god Horus)

ankh

scarab

Technique

CONVENTIONS AND TECHNIQUE OF EGYPTIAN PICTORIAL RELIEF

Painting usually relies on color and line for its effect, while relief sculpture often depends on the play of light and shadow alone, but in Egypt, relief sculpture was also painted (SEE FIG. 3–17). The walls and closely spaced columns of Egyptian tombs and temples were almost completely covered with colorful scenes and hieroglyphic texts. Until the Eighteenth Dynasty (c. 1539–1292 LM), the only colors used were black, white, red, yellow, blue, and green. Modeling might be indicated by overpainting lines in a contrasting color, although the sense of three-dimensionality was conveyed primarily by the carved forms and incised inscriptions underneath the paint. The crisp outlines created by such carving assured the primacy of line in Egyptian pictorial relief.

With very few exceptions, figures, scenes, and texts were composed in bands, or registers. The scenes were first laid out with inked lines, using a squared grid to guide the designer in proportioning the human figures. The sculptor who executed the carving followed these drawings, and it may have been another person who smoothed the carved surfaces of the relief and eventually covered them with paint.

The lower left corner of the unfinished Twelfth-Dynasty **STELE OF THE SCULPTOR USERWER** shown here still maintains its preliminary underdrawings. In some figures there are also the tentative beginnings of the relief carving. The figures are delineated with black ink, and the grid lines are rendered in red. Every body part had its designated place on the grid. For example, figures are designed 18 squares tall, measuring from the soles of their feet to their hairline; the tops of their knees conform with the sixth square up from the ground-line. Their shoulders align with the top of square 16 and are six squares wide. Slight deviations exist within this structured design format, but this **canon of proportions** represents an ideal system that was standard in pictorial relief throughout the Middle Kingdom.

DETAIL OF THE STELE OF THE SCULPTOR USERWER IN FIG. 3–17

Pictorial Relief" above). The underlying conventions that govern ancient Egyptian art appear early, however, and are maintained, with subtle but significant variations, over almost three millennia of its history.

THE PALETTE OF NARMER This historically and artistically significant work of art (see "Closer Look" opposite) dates from the Early Dynastic period and was found in the temple of Horus at Hierakonpolis. It is commonly interpreted as representing the unification of Egypt and the beginning of the country's growth as a powerful nation-state. It uses many of the representational conventions that would dominate royal Egyptian art from this point on.

On the reverse side of the palette, as in the stele of Naram-Sin (SEE FIG. 2–1), hierarchic scale signals the importance of Narmer by showing him overwhelmingly larger than the other human figures around him. He is also boldly silhouetted against a blank ground, just like Naram-Sin, distancing details of setting and story so they will not distract from his pre-eminence. He wears the white crown of Upper Egypt while striking the enemy who kneels before him with a mace. Above this foe, the god Horus—depicted as a falcon with a human hand—holds a rope tied around

the neck of a man whose head is attached to a block sprouting stylized papyrus, a plant that grew thickly along the Nile and symbolized Lower Egypt. This combination of symbols made the central message clear: Narmer, as ruler of Upper Egypt, is in firm control of Lower Egypt.

A Closer Look
THE PALETTE OF NARMER

This figure, named by hieroglyphic inscription and standing on his own ground-line, holds the king's sandals. Narmer is barefoot because he is standing on sacred ground, performing sacred acts. The same sandal-bearer, likewise labeled, follows Narmer on the other side of the palette.

Phonetic **hieroglyphs** centered at the top of each side of the palette name the king: a horizontal fish (*nar*) above a vertical chisel (*mer*). A depiction of the royal palace—seen simultaneously from above, as a groundplan, and frontally, as a **façade** (front wall of a building)—surrounds Narmer's name to signify that he is king.

Narmer wears the red crown of Lower Egypt and is identified by the hieroglyph label next to his head, as well by as his larger size in relation to the other figures (hierarchic scale).

The royal procession inspects two rows of beheaded enemies with their heads tucked between their feet.

Narmer attacks a figure of comparable size, also identified by a hieroglyphic label, indicating that he is an enemy of real importance, likely the ruler of Lower Egypt.

Next to the heads of these two defeated enemies are, on the left, an aerial depiction of a fortified city, and on the right, a gazelle trap, perhaps to show Narmer's dominion over both city and countryside.

A bull symbolizing the might of the king—he wears a bull's tail on both sides of the palette—tramples another enemy in front of a fortified city.

Palettes were tablets with circular depressions where eye makeup was ground and prepared. Although this example was surely ceremonial rather than functional, a mixing saucer is framed by the elongated, intertwined necks of lions, perhaps signifying the union of Upper and Lower Egypt.

3-2 THE PALETTE OF NARMER
From Hierakonpolis. Early Dynastic Period, c. 2950 BCE. Green schist, height 25″ (64 cm). Egyptian Museum, Cairo. (JE 32169 = CG 14716).
Credit: © akg-images/Erich Lessing

Many of the figures on the palette are shown in composite poses, so that each part of the body is portrayed from its most characteristic viewpoint. Heads are shown in profile, to capture most clearly the nose, forehead, and chin, while eyes are rendered frontally, from their most recognizable and expressive viewpoint. Hips, legs, and feet are drawn in profile, and the figure is usually striding, to reveal both legs. The torso, however, is fully frontal. This conceptualized artistic convention for representing the human figure was to be followed for millennia in Egypt when depicting royalty and other dignitaries. People of lower social rank engaged in active tasks (compare the figure of Narmer with those of his standard-bearers) tend to be represented in ways that seem to us more lifelike.

Funerary Architecture

Ancient Egyptians believed that an essential part of every human personality is its life force, or soul, called the *ka*, which lived on after the death of the body, forever engaged in the activities it had enjoyed in its former existence. But the *ka* needed a body to live in, either the mummified body of the deceased or, as a substitute, a sculpted likeness in the form of a statue. The Egyptians developed elaborate funerary practices to ensure that their deceased moved safely and effectively into the afterlife.

It was especially important to provide a comfortable home for the *ka* of a departed king, so that even in the afterlife he would continue to ensure the well-being of Egypt. Egyptians preserved the bodies of the royal dead with care and placed them in burial chambers filled with sculpted body substitutes and all the supplies and furnishings the *ka* might require throughout eternity (see "Preserving the Dead" below).

MASTABA AND NECROPOLIS In Early Dynastic Egypt, the most common tomb structure—used by the upper level of society, the king's family and relatives—was the **mastaba**, a flat-topped, one-story building with slanted walls erected above an underground burial chamber (see "Mastaba to Pyramid" opposite). Mastabas were at first constructed of mud brick, but toward the end of the Third Dynasty (c. 2650–2575 BCE), many incorporated cut stone, at least as an exterior facing.

In its simplest form, the mastaba contained a **serdab**, a small, sealed room housing the *ka* statue of the deceased, and a chapel designed to receive mourning relatives and offerings. A vertical shaft led from the top of the mastaba down to the actual burial chamber, where the remains of the deceased reposed in a coffin—at times placed within a larger stone sarcophagus—surrounded by appropriate grave goods. This chamber was sealed off after interment. Mastabas sometimes had numerous underground burial chambers to accommodate whole families, and mastaba burial remained the standard for Egyptian elites for centuries.

Mastabas tended to be grouped together in a **necropolis**—literally, a "city of the dead"—at the edge of the desert on the west bank of the Nile, for the land of the dead was believed to be in the direction of the setting sun. Two of the most extensive of these early necropolises are at Saqqara and Giza, just outside present-day Cairo.

DJOSER'S COMPLEX AT SAQQARA For his tomb complex at Saqqara, the Third-Dynasty King Djoser (c. 2650–2631 BCE) commissioned the earliest-known monumental architecture in Egypt (**FIG. 3-3**). The designer of the complex was Imhotep, who served as Djoser's prime minister. Imhotep is the first architect in

---

Technique
PRESERVING THE DEAD

Egyptians developed mummification techniques to ensure that the *ka*, the soul or life force, could live on in the body in the afterlife. No recipes for preserving the dead have been found, but the basic process seems clear enough from images found in tombs, descriptions of later Greek writers such as Herodotus and Plutarch, scientific analysis of mummies, and modern experiments.

By the time of the New Kingdom, the routine was roughly as follows: The body was taken to a mortuary, a special structure used exclusively for embalming. Under the supervision of a priest, workers removed the brains, generally through the nose, and emptied the body cavity—except for the heart—through an incision in the left side. They then covered the body with dry natron, a naturally occurring salt, and placed it on a sloping surface to allow liquids to drain. This preservative caused the skin to blacken, so workers often used paint or powdered makeup to restore some color, using red ocher for a man, yellow ocher for a woman. They then packed the body cavity with clean linen soaked in various herbs and ointments, provided by the family of the deceased. The major organs were wrapped in separate packets and stored in special containers called **canopic jars** to be placed in the tomb chamber.

Workers next wound the trunk and each of the limbs separately with cloth strips before wrapping the whole body in additional layers of cloth to produce the familiar mummy shape. Charms and other smaller objects were often inserted among the wrappings.

Elements of Architecture
MASTABA TO PYRAMID

As the gateway to the afterlife for Egyptian kings and members of the royal court, the Egyptian burial structure began as a low, solid, rectangular mastaba with an external niche that served as the focus of offerings. Later mastabas had either an internal *serdab* (the room where the *ka* statue was placed) and chapel (as in the drawing) or an attached chapel and *serdab* (not

shown). Eventually, mastaba forms of decreasing size were stacked over an underground burial chamber to form the step pyramid. The culmination of this development is the pyramid, in which the actual burial site may be within the pyramid—not below ground—with false chambers, false doors, and confusing passageways to foil potential tomb robbers.

history to be identified; his name is inscribed together with Djoser's on the base of a statue of the king found near the Step Pyramid.

It appears that Imhotep first planned Djoser's tomb as a single-story mastaba, only later deciding to enlarge upon the concept. The final structure is a step pyramid formed by six mastaba-like elements of decreasing size stacked

on top of each other (**FIG. 3-4**). Although the Step Pyramid resembles the ziggurats of Mesopotamia, it differs in both meaning (a stairway to the sun god Ra) and purpose (protecting a tomb). A 92-foot shaft descended from the original mastaba enclosed within the pyramid. A descending corridor at the base of the Step Pyramid provided an entrance from outside to a granite-lined burial vault.

3-3 RECONSTRUCTION DRAWING OF DJOSER'S FUNERARY COMPLEX, SAQQARA

Third Dynasty, c. 2630–2575 BCE.

Situated on a level terrace, this huge commemorative complex—some 1,800′ (544 m) long by 900′ (277 m) wide—was designed as a replica in stone of the wood, brick, and reed buildings used in rituals associated with kingship. Inside the wall, the Step Pyramid dominated the complex.

Credit: © Dorling Kindersley

3-4 THE STEP PYRAMID AND SHAM BUILDINGS, FUNERARY COMPLEX OF DJOSER

Limestone, height of pyramid 204′ (62 m).

Credit: © Jim Henderson/Alamy Stock Photo

The adjacent funerary temple, where priests performed rituals before placing the king's mummified body in its tomb, was used for continuing worship of the dead king. In the form of his *ka* statue, Djoser intended to observe these devotions through two peepholes in the wall between the *serdab* and the funerary chapel. To the east of the pyramid, buildings filled with debris represent actual structures in which the spirit of the dead king could continue to observe the *sed* rituals that had ensured his long reign.

The Old Kingdom

How does the development of ancient Egyptian figural and architectural conventions express political power in the Old Kingdom?

Historians have divided the long royal history of ancient Egypt after the Early Dynastic Period (c. 2950–2575) into three long kingdoms of stability separated by two briefer interludes of instability: the Old Kingdom (c. 2575–2150 BCE), the First Intermediate Period (c. 2125–1975 BCE), the Middle Kingdom (c. 1975–1640 BCE), the Second Intermediate Period (c. 1630–1520 BCE), and the New Kingdom (c. 1539–1075 BCE). This span of close to two millennia —Early Dynastic plus three kingdoms—is further subdivided into 20 family dynasties.

The Old Kingdom was a time of social and political stability, despite increasingly common military excursions to defend the borders. The growing wealth of ruling families of the period is reflected in the enormous and elaborate tomb complexes they commissioned for themselves. Kings were not the only patrons of the arts, however. Upper-level government officials also could afford tombs decorated with elaborate carvings.

The Great Pyramids at Giza

The architectural form most closely identified with Egypt is the true pyramid with a square base and four sloping triangular faces, first erected in the Fourth Dynasty (2575–2450 BCE). The angled sides may have been meant to represent the slanting rays of the sun, for inscriptions on the walls of pyramid tombs built in the Fifth and Sixth Dynasties tell of deceased kings climbing up the rays to join the sun god Ra.

Although not the first pyramids, the most famous are the three great pyramid tombs at Giza (**FIG. 3-5**). These were built by three successive Fourth-Dynasty kings: Khufu (ruled c. 2551– 2528 BCE), Khafre (ruled 2520– 2494 BCE), and Menkaure (ruled c. 2490– 2472 BCE). The oldest and largest pyramid at Giza is that of Khufu, which covers 13 acres at its base. It was originally finished with a thick veneer of polished limestone that lifted its apex to almost 481 feet, some 30 feet above the present summit. The pyramid of Khafre is slightly smaller than Khufu's, and Menkaure's is considerably smaller.

3-5 GREAT PYRAMIDS, GIZA
Fourth Dynasty, c. 2575–2450 BCE. Erected by (from the left) Menkaure, Khafre, and Khufu. Limestone and granite, height of pyramid of Khufu, 450′ (137 m).

The site was carefully planned to follow the sun's east–west path. Next to each of the pyramids was a funerary temple connected by a causeway—an elevated and enclosed pathway or corridor—to a valley temple on the bank of the Nile (**FIG. 3-6**). When a king died, his body was embalmed and ferried west across the Nile from the royal palace to his valley temple, where it was received with elaborate ceremonies. It was then carried up the causeway to his funerary temple and placed in its chapel, where family members presented offerings of food and drink, and priests performed rites in which the deceased's spirit consumed a meal. These rites were to be performed at the chapel in perpetuity. Finally, the body was entombed in a vault deep within the pyramid at the end of a long, narrow, and steeply rising passageway. This tomb chamber was sealed off after the burial with a 50-ton stone block. To further protect the king from intruders, three false passageways obscured the location of the tomb.

CONSTRUCTING THE PYRAMIDS Building a pyramid was a formidable undertaking. A large workers' burial ground discovered at Giza attests to the huge labor force that had to be assembled, housed, and fed. Most of the cut stone blocks—each weighing an average of 2.5 tons—used in building the Giza complex were quarried either on the site or nearby. Teams of workers transported them by sheer muscle power, employing small logs as rollers or pouring water on mud to create a slippery surface over which they could drag the blocks on sleds.

Scholars and engineers have various theories about how the pyramids were raised. Some ideas have been tested in computerized projections and a few models on a small but representative scale have been constructed. The most efficient means of getting the stones into position might have been to build a temporary, gently sloping ramp around the body of the pyramid as it grew higher. The ramp could then be dismantled as the stones were smoothed out or slabs of veneer were laid.

The designers who oversaw the building of such massive structures were capable of the most sophisticated mathematical calculations. They oriented the pyramids to the points of the compass and may have incorporated other symbolic astronomical calculations as well. There was no room for trial and error. The huge foundation layer had to be absolutely level and the angle of each of the slanting sides had to remain constant so that the stones would meet precisely in the center at the top.

KHAFRE'S COMPLEX Khafre's funerary complex is the best preserved. Its pyramid is the only one of the three to have maintained some of its veneer facing at the top. But the complex is most famous for the **GREAT SPHINX** that sits just behind Khafre's valley temple. This colossal portrait of the king—65 feet tall—combines his head with the long body of a crouching lion, seemingly merging notions of human intelligence with animal strength (**FIG. 3-7**).

In the adjacent **VALLEY TEMPLE**, massive blocks of red granite form walls and piers supporting a flat roof

3-6 RECONSTRUCTION DRAWING OF THE GIZA PLATEAU SEEN FROM ABOVE
From left to right: the temples and pyramids of Menkaure, Khafre, and Khufu.

Credit: Russell Barnett © Dorling Kindersley

(**FIG. 3–8**). A **clerestory** (a row of tall, narrow windows in the upper walls, not visible in the figure), lets in light that reflects off the polished Egyptian alabaster floor.

Within the temple were a series of over-life-size statues portraying **KHAFRE** as an enthroned king (**FIG. 3–9**). The falcon god Horus perches on the back of the throne, protecting the king's head with his wings. Lions—symbols of regal authority—form the throne's legs, and the intertwined lotus and papyrus plants beneath the seat symbolize the king's power over Upper (lotus) and Lower (papyrus) Egypt.

Khafre wears the traditional royal costume—a short, pleated kilt, a linen headdress, and a false beard symbolic of royalty. He exudes a strong sense of dignity, calm, and above all permanence. In his right hand, he holds a cylinder, probably a rolled piece of cloth. His arms are pressed tightly within the contours of his body, which is firmly anchored in the stone block from which it was carved. The statue was created from an unusual stone, a type of gneiss (related to diorite) imported from Nubia that produces a rare optical effect: When illuminated by sunlight entering through the temple's clerestory, it glows a deep blue, the celestial color of Horus, filling the space with a blue radiance.

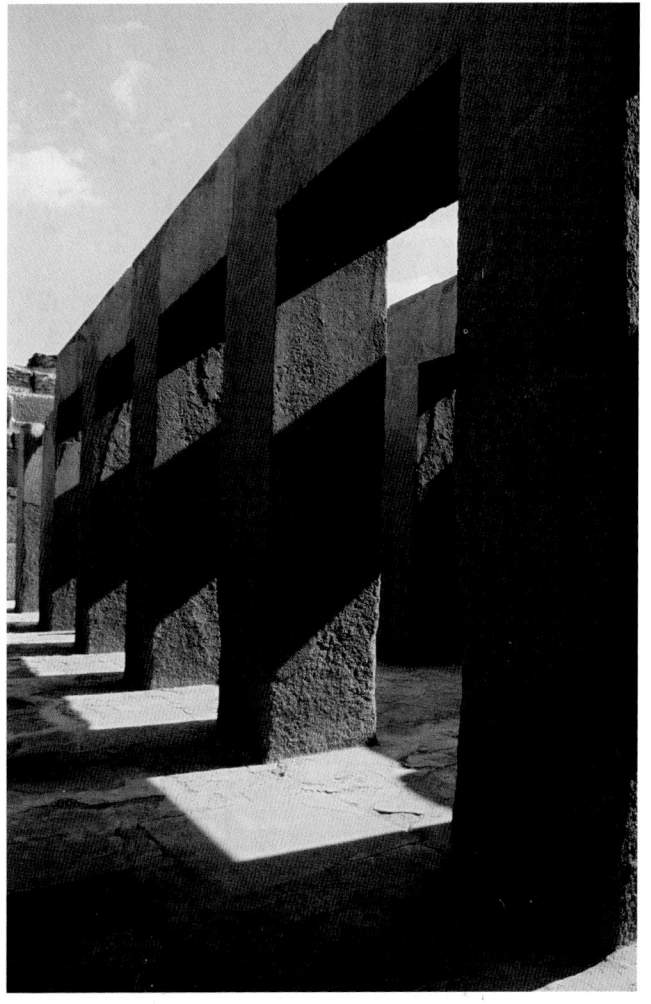

3–8 VALLEY TEMPLE OF KHAFRE
Giza. Old Kingdom, c. 2520–2494 BCE. Limestone and red granite.

3-9 KHAFRE
From Giza, valley temple of Khafre. Fourth Dynasty, c. 2520–2494 BCE. Diorite-gabbro gneiss, height 5'6⅛" (1.68 m). Egyptian Museum, Cairo. (JE 10062 = CG 14).

Credit: Index Ricerca Iconografica/Araldo de Luca

wearing the royal kilt and headcloth—stands in a conventional, balanced pose, striding with the left foot forward, his arms straight at his sides, and his fists clenched over cylindrical objects. His equally youthful queen, taking a smaller step forward, echoes his striding pose. Her sheer, close-fitting garment reveals the curves of her gently swelling body, a foil for the tight muscularity of the king. The time-consuming task of polishing this double statue was never completed, suggesting that the work may have

Sculpture

As the surviving statues of Khafre's valley temple demonstrate, Egyptian sculptors were adept at creating lifelike figures that also express a feeling of strength and permanence consistent with the unusually hard stones from which they were carved.

MENKAURE AND A QUEEN Dignity, calm, and permanence also characterize a sleek double portrait of Khafre's heir King Menkaure and a queen, probably Khamerernebty II, discovered in Menkaure's valley temple (**FIG. 3-10**). The couple's separate figures, close in size, are joined by the stone from which they emerge, forming a single unit. They are further united by the queen's symbolic embrace. Her right hand comes from behind to clasp the king's torso, and her left hand rests over his upper arm.

The king—depicted in accordance with Egyptian ideals as an athletic, youthful figure, nude to the waist and

3-10 MENKAURE AND A QUEEN, PROBABLY KHAMERERNEBTY II
From Giza. Fourth Dynasty, 2490–2472 BCE. Graywacke with traces of red and black paint, height 54½" (142.3 cm). Museum of Fine Arts, Boston. Harvard University—Museum of Fine Arts Expedition. (11.1738).

Credit: Photograph © 2017 Museum of Fine Arts, Boston

3-11 SEATED SCRIBE
Found near the tomb of Kai, Saqqara. Fifth Dynasty,
c. 2450–2325 BCE. Painted limestone with inlaid eyes of rock crystal,
calcite, and magnesite mounted in copper, height 21″ (53 cm).
Musée du Louvre, Paris. (N 2290 = E 3023).

High-ranking scribes could hope to be appointed to one of several
"houses of life," where they would copy, compile, study, and repair
valuable sacred and scientific texts.

Credit: Photo © RMN-Grand Palais (Musée du Louvre)/Franck Raux

been undertaken only a few years before Menkaure's
death in about 2472 BCE. Traces of red paint remain on the
king's face, ears, and neck (male figures were traditionally
painted red), as do traces of black on the queen's hair.

SEATED SCRIBE Old Kingdom sculptors also produced
statues of less prominent people, rendered in a more
relaxed, lifelike fashion. This less formal mode is seen in the
statue of a **SEATED SCRIBE** from early in the Fifth Dynasty
(**FIG. 3-11**)—with round head, alert expression, and close-
cropped hair—that was discovered near the tomb of a government official named Kai. It could be a portrait of Kai
himself. The irregular contours of his engaging face project
a sense of individual likeness and human presence.

The scribe's sedentary vocation has made his sagging
body slightly flabby, proof of a life free from hard physical
labor. As an ancient Egyptian inscription advises, "Become
a scribe so that your limbs remain smooth and your hands
soft and you can wear white and walk like a man of standing whom [even] courtiers will greet" (cited in Strouhal,

p. 216). This scribe sits holding a papyrus scroll partially
unrolled on his lap, his right hand clasping a now-lost
reed brush used in writing. The alert expression on his face
reveals more than a lively intelligence. Because the pupils
are slightly off-center in the irises, the eyes give the illusion of being in motion, and the reflective quality of the
polished crystal inlay reproduces with eerie fidelity the
contrast between the moist surface of eyes and the surrounding soft flesh in a living human face.

STATUETTES OF SERVANTS   Even more lifelike than
the scribe were smaller figures of servants at work that
were made for inclusion in Old Kingdom tombs so that the
deceased could be provided for in the next world. Poses
are rooted directly in the labor these figures were expected
to perform throughout eternity. A painted limestone statuette from the Fifth Dynasty (**FIG. 3-12**) captures a butcher
raised up on the balls of his feet to bend down and lean
forward, poised, knife in hand, over the throat of an ox
that he has just slaughtered. He looks up to acknowledge
us, an action that enhances his sense of lifelike presence.
The emphasis on active poses and engagement with the
viewer may have been an attempt to underscore the ability
of such figures to perform their assigned tasks, or perhaps

3-12 BUTCHER
Perhaps from the tomb of the official Ni-kau-inpu and his wife
Hemet-re, Giza? Fifth Dynasty, c. 2450–2325 BCE. Painted limestone
(knife restored), height 14⅝″ (37 cm). The Oriental Institute Museum,
University of Chicago. (10626).

Although statues such as this have been assumed to represent
the deceased's servants, it has recently been proposed that instead
they depict relatives and friends of the deceased in the role of
servants, allowing these loved ones to accompany the deceased
into the next life.

Credit: © akg-images/Erich Lessing

it was meant to indicate their lower social status by showing them involved in physical labor—or both. The contrast between the detached stylization of upper-class figures and the engaging lifelikeness of laborers can be seen in Old Kingdom pictorial relief works as well.

Pictorial Relief in Tombs

To provide the *ka* with the most pleasant possible living quarters for eternity, wealthy families often had the interior walls and ceilings of their tombs decorated with paintings and reliefs. This decoration carried religious meaning, but it could also show the deceased's everyday life or ceremonial events that proclaimed the deceased's importance. Tombs therefore provide a wealth of information about ancient Egyptian culture.

THE TOMB OF TI On the walls of the large mastaba of a wealthy Fifth-Dynasty government official named Ti, a painted relief shows him watching a hippopotamus hunt—an official duty of royal courtiers (**FIG. 3-13**). It was believed that Seth, the god of chaos, disguised himself as a hippo. Hippos were also destructive, wandering into fields and damaging crops. Tomb depictions of such hunts therefore proclaimed the valor of the deceased and the triumph of good over evil, or at least of order over destruction.

The artists who created this painted limestone relief used a number of established Egyptian representational conventions. The river is shown as if seen from above, a band of parallel wavy lines below the boats. The creatures in this river, however—fish, a crocodile, and hippopotamuses—are shown in profile for easy identification. The shallow boats carrying Ti and his men are shown straight on in relation to the viewer's vantage point, and the papyrus stalks that choke the marshy edges of the river are disciplined into a regular pattern of projecting, linear, parallel, vertical forms that highlight the contrastingly crisp and smooth contour of Ti's body. At the top of the papyrus grove, however, this patterning

3-13 TI WATCHING A HIPPOPOTAMUS HUNT
Tomb of Ti, Saqqara. Fifth Dynasty, c. 2450–2325 BCE. Painted limestone relief, height approx. 45″ (114.3 cm).
Credit: Araldo de Luca

relaxes while animals of prey—perhaps foxes—stalk birds among the leaves and flowers. The hierarchically scaled and sleekly stylized figure of Ti, rendered in the conventional composite pose, looms over all. In a separate boat ahead of him, the actual hunters, being of lesser rank and engaged in more strenuous activities, are rendered in a more lifelike and lively fashion than their master. They are captured at the moment of closing in on their prey, spears at the ready and legs extended for the critical lunge forward.

The Middle Kingdom

How does Middle Kingdom Egyptian art reveal more about individuals and their lives?

The collapse of the Old Kingdom, with its long succession of powerful kings, was followed by roughly 150 years of political turmoil, fragmentation, and warfare traditionally referred to as the First Intermediate period (c. 2125–1975 BCE). About 2010 BCE, a series of kings named Mentuhotep (Eleventh Dynasty, c. 2010–c. 1938 BCE) gained power in Thebes, and the country was reunited under Nebhepetre Mentuhotep, who reasserted royal power and founded the Middle Kingdom.

The Middle Kingdom was another high point in Egyptian history. Arts and writing flourished in the Twelfth Dynasty (1938–1756 BCE), while reflecting a growing awareness of the political upheaval from which the country had just emerged. Using a strengthened military, Middle Kingdom rulers expanded and patrolled the borders, especially in lower Nubia, south of present-day Aswan (SEE MAP 3-1).

By the Thirteenth Dynasty (c. 1755–1630 BCE), however, central control by the government was weakened by a series of short-lived kings and an influx of foreigners, especially in the delta.

Portraits of Senusret III

Some royal portraits from the Middle Kingdom appear to acknowledge the hardship and fragility of human existence. Statues of Senusret III, a king of the Twelfth Dynasty, who ruled from c. 1836 to 1818 BCE, reflect this new sensibility. Old Kingdom rulers such as Khafre (SEE FIG. 3-9) gaze into eternity confident and serene, whereas the portrait **HEAD OF SENUSRET III** seems to capture a monarch preoccupied and emotionally drained (FIG. 3-14). Creases line his cheeks, his eyes are sunken, his eyelids droop, his forehead is flexed, and his jaw is sternly set—a bold image of a resolute ruler, tested but unbowed.

Senusret was a dynamic king and successful general who led four military expeditions into Nubia, overhauled the Egyptian central administration, and regained control

3-14 HEAD OF SENUSRET III
Twelfth Dynasty, c. 1836–1818 LMO. Yellow quartzite, 17¾ × 13½ × 17" (45.1 × 34.3 × 43.2 cm). The Nelson-Atkins Museum of Art, Kansas City, Missouri. Purchase: William Rockhill Nelson Trust (62-11).

over the country's increasingly independent nobles. To modern viewers, his portrait raises questions of interpretation. Are we looking at the face of a man wise in the ways of the world but saddened, and burdened by the weight of his responsibilities? Or are we looking at a reassuring statement: In spite of troubled times that have clearly left their mark on the face of the ruler himself, royal rule endures in Egypt? Given what we know about Egyptian history at this time, it is difficult to be sure.

Rock-Cut Tombs

During the Eleventh and Twelfth Dynasties, high-level officials and members of the nobility commissioned tombs hollowed out of the face of cliffs. A typical rock-cut tomb included an entrance **portico** (projecting porch), a main hall, and a shrine with a burial chamber under the offering chapel. The chambers of these tombs, as well as their ornamental columns, lintels, false doors, and niches, were all carved into the solid rock. An impressive necropolis was created in the cliffs at **BENI HASAN** on the east bank of the Nile (FIG. 3-15).

Painted scenes cover the interior walls of many tombs. Among the best preserved are those in the Twelfth-Dynasty

3-15 ROCK-CUT TOMBS, BENI HASAN

Twelfth Dynasty, 1938–1756 BCE.

At the left is the entrance to the tomb of a provincial governor and the commander-in-chief Amenemhat.

tomb of local noble Khnumhotep, some of which portray vivid vignettes of farm work on his estates. In one painting two men harvest figs, rushing to compete with three baboons who relish the fruit from their perches in the trees (**FIG. 3-16**). One man reaches for a fig to add to the ordered stack in his basket, while his companion arranges the harvest in a larger box for transport. Like the hunters in the much earlier painted relief in the tomb of Ti (SEE FIG. 3-13), the upper torsos of these farm workers take a more lifelike profile posture, deviating from the strict frontality of the royal composite pose.

3-16 PICKING FIGS

Wall painting from the tomb of Khnumhotep, Beni Hasan. Twelfth Dynasty, c. 1890 BCE. Tempera facsimile by Nina de Garis.

Funerary Stelai

Only the wealthiest and noblest of ancient Egyptians could afford elaborately decorated mastabas or rock-cut tombs. Prosperous people, however, could still commission funerary stelai depicting themselves, their family, and offerings of food—meant to preserve the memory of the deceased and inspire the living to make offerings to them. An unfinished stele made for the tomb of the **SCULPTOR USERWER** (**FIG. 3-17**) presents three levels of decoration: one large upper block with five bands of hieroglyphs, beneath which are two registers with figures, each identified by inscription.

The text is addressed to the living, imploring them to make offerings to Userwer: "O living ones who are on the earth who pass by this tomb, as your deities love and favor you, may you say: 'A thousand of bread and beer, a thousand of cattle and birds, a thousand of alabaster [vessels] and clothes, a thousand of offerings and provisions that go forth before Osiris'" (Robins, p. 103).

At left, on the register immediately below this inscription, Userwer sits before a table piled with offerings of food. Behind him is his wife Satdepetnetjer and facing him on the other side of the offering table is Satameni, a standing woman also identified as his wife. (Userwer could have had more than one wife, but one of these women might also be the sculptor's deceased first wife.) At the other side of the stele on this same register but facing the opposite direction sits another couple before another table heaped with food. They are identified as Userwer's parents, and the figure on the other side of their offering table is his son, Sneferuweser. In the lowest register are representations of other family members (probably Userwer's children) and his grandparents.

One of the most striking features of the lowest register of this stele is its unfinished state. The two leftmost figures were left uncarved, but the stone surface still maintains the preparatory ink drawing meant to guide the sculptor, preserving evidence of the system of canonical figure proportions that was established in the Middle Kingdom (see "Conventions and Technique of Egyptian Pictorial Relief" on page 52). The unfinished state of this stele has led to the suggestion that Userwer might have been in the process of carving it for himself when his death left it incomplete.

A more modest stele for a man named **AMENEMHAT** was brought to completion as a vibrantly painted relief (**FIG. 3-18**). Underneath an inscription inviting food offerings for the deceased Amenemhat is a portrait of his family. Amenemhat sits on a lion-legged bench between his wife Iyi and their son Antef, embraced by both. Next to the trio is an offering table heaped with meat, topped with onions, and sheltering two loaves of bread on the floor. On the far right is Amenemhat and Iyi's daughter Hapy,

completing this tableau of family unity. The painter of this relief follows the established Egyptian convention of differentiating gender by skin tonality: dark red-brown for men and lighter yellow-ocher for women.

Town Planning

Although Egyptians used durable materials in the construction of tombs, they built their own dwellings with simple mud bricks, which have either disintegrated over time or been carried away for fertilizer by farmers. Only the foundations of these dwellings now remain.

Archaeologists have unearthed the remains of Kahun, a town built by Senusret II (ruled c. 1842–1837 BCE) for the many officials, priests, and workers who built and maintained his pyramid complex. Parallel streets were laid out on a **grid**, forming rectangular blocks divided into lots for homes and other buildings. The houses of priests, court officials, and their families were large and comfortable, with private living quarters and public rooms grouped around central courtyards. The largest had as many as 70 rooms spread out over half an acre. Workers and their families made do with small, five-room row houses built back-to-back along narrow streets.

A New Kingdom workers' village, discovered at Deir el-Medina on the west bank of the Nile near the Valley of the Kings, has provided us with detailed information about the lives of the people who created the royal tombs. Workers lived together here under the rule of the king's chief minister. During a ten-day week, they worked for eight days and had two days off and also participated in many religious festivals. They lived a good life with their families, were given clothing, sandals, grain, and firewood by the king, and had permission to raise livestock and birds as well as tend a garden. The residents had a council, and the many written records that survive suggest a literate and litigious society that required many scribes. Because the men were away for most of the week working on the tombs, women had a prominent role in the town.

The New Kingdom

How are the conventions of ancient Egyptian art and architecture both refined and transformed during the New Kingdom?

During the Second Intermediate period (1630–1520 BCE)—another turbulent interruption in the succession of dynasties ruling a unified Egypt—an eastern Mediterranean people called the Hyksos invaded Egypt's northernmost regions. The kings of the Eighteenth Dynasty (c. 1539–1292 BCE) eventually regained control of the entire Nile region, extending from Nubia in the south to the Mediterranean Sea in the north, and restored Egypt's political and economic strength. Roughly a century later, one of the same dynasty's most dynamic kings, Thutmose III (ruled 1479–1425 BCE), extended Egypt's influence along the eastern Mediterranean coast as far as present-day Syria. His accomplishment was the result of 15 or more military campaigns and his own skill at diplomacy. The heartland of ancient Egypt was now surrounded by a buffer of empire.

Thutmose III was the first ruler to refer to himself as "pharaoh," a term that literally meant "great house." Egyptians used it in the same way that Americans say "the White House" to mean the current U.S. president and his staff. The successors of Thutmose III continued to call themselves pharaohs, and the term ultimately found its way into the Hebrew Bible—and modern usage—as the title for the kings of Egypt.

The Great Temple Complexes

At the height of the New Kingdom, rulers undertook extensive building programs along the entire length of the Nile. Their palaces, forts, and administrative centers disappeared long ago, but remnants of temples and tombs of this great age have endured. Thebes was Egypt's religious center throughout most of the New Kingdom, and worship of the Theban triad of deities—Amun, his wife Mut, and their son Khons—had spread throughout the country. Temples to these and other gods were a major focus of royal patronage, as were tombs and temples erected to glorify the kings themselves.

THE NEW KINGDOM TEMPLE PLAN   As the home of the god, an Egyptian temple originally took the form of a house—a simple, rectangular, flat-roofed building approached through a courtyard and gateway. The builders of the New Kingdom enlarged and multiplied these elements. The gateway became a massive **pylon** with tapering walls; the semipublic courtyard was surrounded by columns (a **peristyle** court); and the temple itself included an outer **hypostyle hall** (a vast hall filled with columns) and an inner offering hall and sanctuary. The design was symmetrical and axial—that is, all its separate elements were symmetrically arranged along a dominant center line, creating a processional path from the outside straight into the sanctuary. The rooms became smaller, darker, and more exclusive as they neared the sanctuary, where the cult image of the god was housed. Only the pharaoh and the priests entered these inner rooms.

Two temple districts consecrated primarily to the worship of Amun, Mut, and Khons arose within the area of Thebes: a huge complex at Karnak to the north and, joined to it by an avenue of sphinxes, a more compact temple at Luxor to the south.

KARNAK   Karnak was a long-standing sacred site where temples were built and rebuilt for over 1,500 years. During the nearly 500 years of the New Kingdom, successive kings renovated and expanded the complex of the **GREAT TEMPLE OF AMUN** until it covered about 60 acres, an area as large as a dozen football fields (**FIG. 3–19**).

Access to the heart of the temple, a sanctuary containing the statue of Amun, was from the west (on the left side of the reconstruction drawing) through a principal courtyard, a hypostyle hall, and a number of smaller halls and courts. Pylons set off each of these separate elements. Between the reigns of Thutmose I (Eighteenth Dynasty, ruled c. 1493–1482 BCE) and Ramses II (Nineteenth Dynasty, ruled c. 1279–1213 BCE), this area of the complex underwent a great deal of construction and renewal. Most of the pylons leading to the sanctuary and the halls and courts behind them were renovated or newly built and embellished with colorful pictorial wall reliefs. A sacred

3-19 RECONSTRUCTION DRAWING OF THE GREAT TEMPLE OF AMUN AT KARNAK SEEN FROM ABOVE
New Kingdom, c. 1579–1075 BCE.

lake was also added south of the complex, where the king and priests might undergo ritual purification before entering the temple. Thutmose III erected a court and festival temple to his own glory behind the sanctuary of Amun. His great-grandson Amenhotep III (ruled 1390–1353 BCE) placed a large stone statue of the god Khepri—the scarab (beetle) symbolic of the rising sun, rebirth, and everlasting life—next to the sacred lake.

In the sanctuary of Amun, priests washed the god's statue every morning and clothed it in a new garment. Because the god was thought to derive nourishment from the spirit of food, his statue was provided with tempting meals twice a day, which the priests then removed and ate themselves. Ordinary people entered the temple precinct only as far as the forecourts of the hypostyle halls, where they found themselves surrounded by inscriptions and images of kings and the god on columns and walls. During religious festivals, they lined the waterways and submitted petitions to the priests for requests they wished the gods to grant, as statues of the gods circulated along the water in ceremonial boats.

THE GREAT HALL AT KARNAK   One of the most prominent features of the complex at Karnak is the enormous hypostyle hall set between two pylons at the end of the main forecourt. Nineteenth-Dynasty rulers Sety I (ruled c. 1290–1279 BCE) and his son Ramses II (ruled c. 1279–1213 BCE) erected this "Temple of the Spirit of Sety, Beloved of Ptah in the House of Amun," and it may have been used for royal coronation ceremonies. Ramses II referred to it as "the place where the common people extol the name of his majesty." The hall was 340 feet wide and 170 feet long. Its 134 closely spaced columns supported a roof of flat stones, the center section of which rose some 30 feet higher than the broad sides (**FIG. 3-20**).

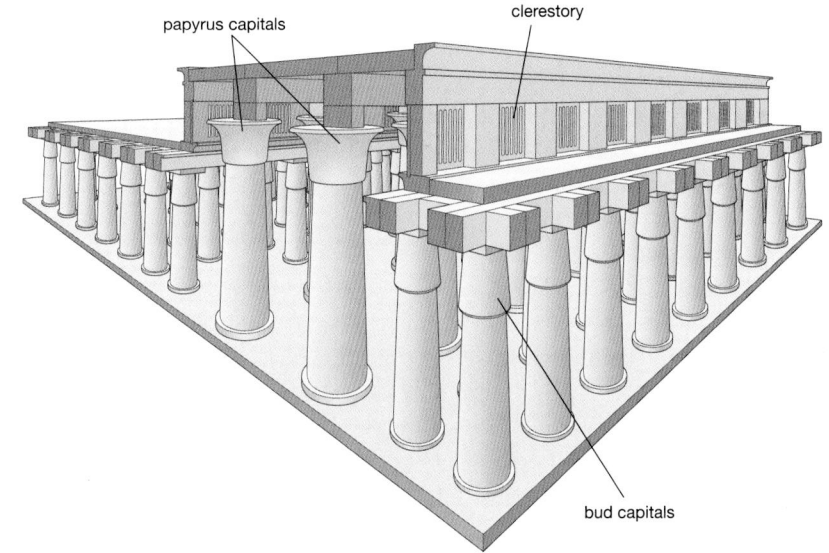

3-20 RECONSTRUCTION DRAWING OF THE HYPOSTYLE HALL, GREAT TEMPLE OF AMUN AT KARNAK
Nineteenth Dynasty, c. 1292–1190 BCE.

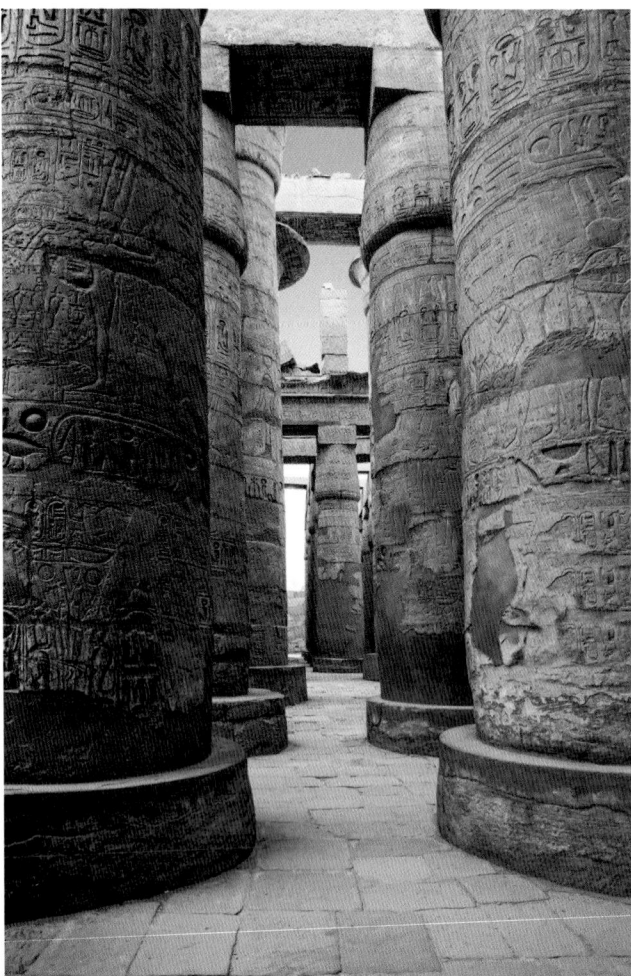

3-21 COLUMNS WITH PAPYRUS AND BUD CAPITALS, HYPOSTYLE HALL, GREAT TEMPLE OF AMUN AT KARNAK

Credit: © pakhnyushchyy/123RF

The columns supporting this higher roof section are 69 feet tall and 12 feet in diameter, ending in huge papyrus **capitals** (**FIG. 3-21**). On each side, smaller columns with bud capitals seem to march off into the darkness. In each of the side walls of the higher center section, a long row of window openings created a clerestory. These openings were filled with stone grillwork, so cannot have provided much light, but they did permit a cooling flow of air through the hall. Despite the dimness of the interior, artists covered nearly every inch of the columns, walls, and crossbeams with painted pictorial reliefs and inscriptions.

Hatshepsut

Across the Nile from Karnak and Luxor lay Deir el-Bahri and the Valleys of the Kings and Queens. These valleys on the west bank of the Nile held the royal necropolis, including the tomb of the pharaoh Hatshepsut. The dynamic Hatshepsut (Eighteenth Dynasty, ruled c. 1473–1458 BCE) is a notable figure in a period otherwise dominated by male warrior-kings. Besides Hatshepsut,

very few women ruled Egypt—they included the little-known Sobekneferu and Tausret, and much later, the well-known Cleopatra VII.

The daughter of Thutmose I, Hatshepsut married her half brother, who then reigned for 14 years as Thutmose II. When he died in c. 1473, she became regent for his underage son—Thutmose III—born to one of his concubines. Within a few years, Hatshepsut had herself declared "king" by the priests of Amun, a maneuver that made her co-ruler with Thutmose III for 20 years.

There was no artistic formula for a female pharaoh in Egyptian art, yet Hatshepsut had to be portrayed in her new role. What happened reveals something fundamentally important about the art of ancient Egypt. She was represented as a male king (**FIG. 3-22**) wearing a kilt and linen headdress, and occasionally even a king's false beard. The formula for portraying kings was not adapted to suit one individual; her appearance was adapted to conform to convention. There could hardly be a more powerful demonstration of the priority given to tradition in Egyptian royal art.

At the height of the New Kingdom, rulers undertook extensive personal building programs, and Hatshepsut was responsible for one of the most spectacular: her **FUNERARY TEMPLE** located at Deir el-Bahri, about a mile away from her actual tomb in the Valley of the Kings (**FIG. 3-23**). This imposing complex was designed for funeral rites and commemorative ceremonies and is much larger and more prominent than the tomb itself,

3-22 HATSHEPSUT KNEELING

From Deir el-Bahri. Eighteenth Dynasty, c. 1473–1458 BCE. Red granite, height 8'6" (2.59 m). Metropolitan Museum of Art, New York.

Credit: © 2016. Image copyright The Metropolitan Museum of Art/Art Resource/ Scala, Florence reversing the scale relationship we saw in the Old Kingdom pyramid complexes.

Magnificently sited and sensitively reflecting the natural three-part layering in the rise of the landscape—from flat desert, through a sloping hillside, to the crescendo of sheer stone cliffs—Hatshepsut's temple was constructed on an axial plan (**FIG. 3-24**). A causeway lined with sphinxes once ran from a valley temple on the Nile to the huge, open space of the first court, where rare myrrh trees were planted in the temple's garden terraces. From there, visitors went up a long, straight ramp to a second court where shrines to Anubis and Hathor occupy the ends of the columned porticos. On the temple's uppermost court, colossal royal statues fronted another **colonnade** (a row of columns supporting a lintel or a series of arches), and behind this lay a large hypostyle hall with chapels

3-23 FUNERARY TEMPLE OF HATSHEPSUT, DEIR EL-BAHRI

Eighteenth Dynasty, c. 1473–1458 BCE.

At the far left, ramp and base of the funerary temple of Mentuhotep III. Eleventh Dynasty, ruled c. 2009–1997 BCE.

Credit: © Brian Lawrence/Getty Images

Temple of Thutmose III

Chapel of Hathor

Temple of Hatshepsut

Temple of Mentuhotep II

3-24 RECONSTRUCTION DRAWING OF THE FUNERARY TEMPLE OF HATSHEPSUT FROM ABOVE

Deir el-Bahri.

Credit: © Dorling Kindersley

Avenue of Sphinxes leading to Karnak

dedicated to Hatshepsut, her father, and the gods Amun and Ra-Horakhty—a powerful form of the sun god Ra combined with Horus. Centered in the hall's back wall was the entrance to the innermost sanctuary, a small chamber cut deep into the cliff.

Tombs of the Elite

The traditional art of pictorial relief, using a representational system that had dominated Egyptian figural art since the time of Narmer, reached a high degree of aesthetic refinement and technical sophistication during the reign of Amenhotep III (Eighteenth Dynasty, ruled c. 1390–1353 BCE), especially in the reliefs carved for the unfinished tomb of Ramose near Thebes (**FIG. 3–25**).

As mayor of Thebes and principal royal advisor to both Amenhotep III and Amenhotep IV (ruled 1353–c. 1336 BCE), Ramose was second only to the pharaoh in power and prestige. Soon after he gained political prominence, he began construction of an elaborate Theban tomb comprised of four rooms, including an imposing hypostyle hall 82 feet wide. Walls were covered with paintings or with shallow pictorial relief carvings celebrating the accomplishments, affiliations, and lineage of Ramose and his wife Merytptah or visualizing the funeral rites that would take place after their death. But the tomb was not used by Ramose. Work on it ceased in the fourth year of Amenhotep IV's reign, when, renamed Akhenaten, he relocated the court from Thebes to the new city of Akhetaten. Presumably Ramose moved with the court to the new capital, but neither his name nor a new tomb has been discovered there.

When the tomb was abandoned, the reliefs had not been painted, and some walls preserve only the preliminary sketches that would have guided sculptors. But the works that were executed are among the most

3-25 RAMOSE'S BROTHER MAY AND HIS WIFE WERENER
From the tomb of Ramose, Thebes. Eighteenth Dynasty, c. 1375–1365 BCE. Limestone relief.

3-26 NEBAMUN HUNTING BIRDS IN THE MARSHES
From the tomb of Nebamun, Thebes. Eighteenth Dynasty, c. 1350 BCE. Wall painting on dry plaster, 31⅝ × 38⅝″ (83 × 98 cm).
British Museum, London.

sophisticated relief carvings in the history of art. On one wall, Ramose and his wife Merytptah appear, hosting a banquet for their family. All are portrayed at the same moment of youthful perfection, even though they represent two successive generations. Carvers lavished their considerable technical virtuosity on the portrayal of these majestic couples, creating clear textural differentiation of skin, hair, clothes, and jewelry. The easy elegance of linear fluidity is not easy to obtain in this medium, and the convincing sense of three-dimensionality in forms and their placement is managed within an extraordinarily shallow depth of relief. In the detail of Ramose's brother May and sister-in-law Werener in FIGURE 3-25, the traditional ancient Egyptian marital embrace (SEE FIGS. 3-10, 3-18) takes on a new tenderness, especially within the eternal stillness of a tomb.

The conceptual conventions of Egyptian royal art are rendered in these carvings with such warmth and refinement that they become almost believable. Our awareness of their artificiality is momentarily eclipsed by their sheer beauty.

But even lesser Eighteenth-Dynasty officials who were less powerful than Ramose created impressive tombs, lined with painted decoration. The walls of the tomb of Nebamun (a common New Kingdom name meaning "my lord is Amun"), who was scribe and grain accountant at the Temple of Amun in Karnak, included scenes of the elite leisure activities of his family during his eternal life after earthly life. In one (**FIG. 3-26**) he strides confidently on a pontoon boat, gliding through the marshes as he hunts for birds. Behind him stands his wife Hatshepsut; his daughter sits under him, grasping his left leg as a gesture of affection or a sign of stability. Just in front of Nebamun, his hunting cat snares three birds, and Nebamun himself holds three egrets. The painters have described the natural environment of Nebamun's hunt with astonishing detail, both on the land and under the water. The composition recalls the hippopotamus hunt of Ti, an Old Kingdom relief (SEE FIG. 3–13) created almost a thousand years before this painting, but employing the same conventions for representing humans and their world—alternately naturalistic and stylized. This New Kingdom version of the scene, however, is more gentle and graceful, freer and energized by spontaneity. To this refined world of convention, however, would come momentous change during the reign of Amenhotep III's successor, Amenhotep IV.

Akhenaten and the Art of the Amarna Period

Amenhotep IV was surely the most unusual ruler in the history of ancient Egypt. During his 17-year reign (c. 1353–1336 BCE), he radically transformed the political, spiritual, and cultural life of the country. He founded a new religion honoring a supreme god, the life-giving sun deity Aten (represented by the sun's disk), and changed his own name in about 1348 BCE to Akhenaten ("One Who Is Effective on Behalf of the Aten"). Abandoning Thebes, the capital of Egypt since the beginning of his dynasty and a city firmly in the grip of the priests of Amun, Akhenaten built a new capital much farther north, calling it Akhetaten ("Horizon of the Aten"). Using the modern name for this site, Tell el-Amarna, historians refer to Akhenaten's reign as the Amarna period.

THE NEW AMARNA STYLE Akhenaten's reign not only saw the creation of a new capital and the rise of a new religious focus, it also led to radical changes in royal artistic conventions. In portraits of the king, artists used startling stylizations, even physical distortions. The new royal figure style can be seen in a colossal statue of Akhenaten, about 16 feet tall, created for a new temple to the Aten that he built near the temple complex of Karnak, openly challenging the state gods (FIG. 3–27). This portrait was placed in one of the porticos of a huge courtyard (c. 426 by 394 feet), oriented to the movement of the sun.

The sculpture's strange, softly swelling forms suggest androgyny to modern viewers. The sagging stomach and inflated thighs contrast with spindly arms, protruding collarbones, and an attenuated neck, on which sits a stylized head. Facial features are exaggerated: Slitlike eyes turn slightly downward, and the bulbous, sensuous lips are flanked by dimples that seem to express emotion. Such stark deviations from convention are disquieting, especially since Akhenaten holds the flail and

shepherd's crook, traditional symbols of the pharoah's super-human sovereignty.

The new Amarna style was used not only in official royal portraits, but also in pictorial relief sculpture portraying the family life of Akhenaten and Queen Nefertiti. In one panel the king and queen sit on cushioned stools playing with their nude daughters (FIG. 3–28), whose elongated, shaved heads conform to the new figural

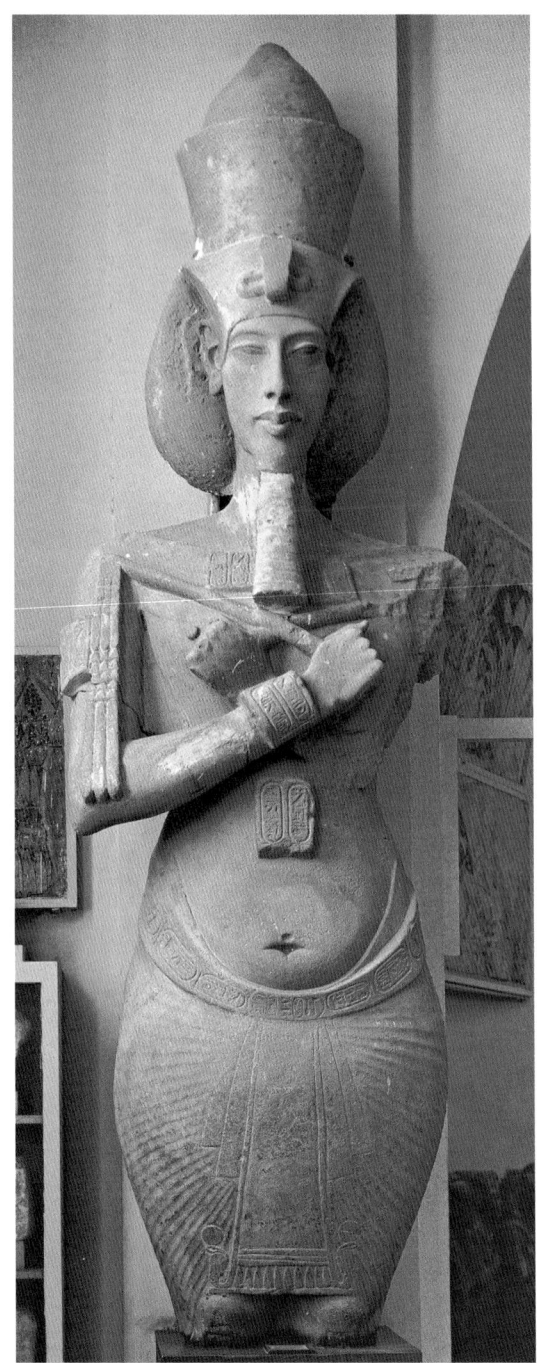

3-27 COLOSSAL FIGURE OF AKHENATEN
From the temple known as the Gempaaten, built early in the reign of Akhenaten (ruled c. 1353–1336 BCE) just southeast of the Temple of Karnak. Sandstone with traces of polychromy, height of remaining portion about 13′ (4 m). Egyptian Museum, Cairo. (JE 49528).

Credit: © akg-images/De Agostini Picture Lib./A. Dagli Orti

3–28 AKHENATEN AND HIS FAMILY

From Akhetaten (present-day Tell el-Amarna). Eighteenth Dynasty, c. 1353–1336 BCE.
Painted limestone relief, 12¼ × 15¼″ (31.1 × 38.7 cm). Staatliche Museen zu Berlin, Preussischer Kulturbesitz, Ägyptisches Museum. (14145).

Egyptian relief sculptors often employed the **sunken relief** technique seen here. In ordinary reliefs, the background is carved back so that the figures project out from the finished surface. In sunken relief, the original flat surface of the stone is reserved as background, and the outlines of the figures are deeply incised, permitting the development of three-dimensional forms within them.

Credit: © 2016. Photo Scala, Florence/bpk, Bildagentur für Kunst, Kultur und Geschichte, Berlin

convention. The royal couple receives the blessings of the Aten, whose rays end in hands that come into the open pavilion to offer ankhs before their nostrils, giving them the "breath of life." The king holds one child and cradles her head while she pulls herself forward to kiss him. The youngest of the three perches on Nefertiti's shoulder, trying to attract her mother's attention by stroking her cheek, while the oldest sits on the queen's lap, tugging at her mother's hand and pointing to her father. In a striking contrast with the serene relief from Ramose's tomb, this artist has conveyed the fidgety behavior of children and the loving involvement of their parents in a manner not even hinted at in earlier royal portraiture.

PORTRAITS OF QUEENS   Akhenaten's goals were actively supported not only by Nefertiti but also by his mother, **QUEEN TIY** (**FIG. 3–29**). She had been the chief wife of the king's father, Amenhotep III, and had played a significant role in affairs of state during his reign. Queen Tiy's personality seems to emerge from a miniature portrait head that highlights the exquisite bone structure of her dark-skinned face with its arched brows, tilted eyes, and full lips. Originally, this portrait included a funerary silver headdress covered with gold cobras and gold jewelry. But after her son came to power and established his new religion, the portrait was altered: A brown cap covered with blue glass beads was placed over the original headdress.

3-29 QUEEN TIY

From Kom Medinet el-Ghurab (near el-Lahun). Eighteenth Dynasty, c. 1352 BCE. Wood (perhaps yew and acacia), ebony, glass, silver, gold, lapis lazuli, cloth, clay, and wax, height 3¾″ (9.4 cm). Staatliche Museen zu Berlin, Preussischer Kulturbesitz, Ägyptisches Museum. (21834).

Credit: © 2016. Photo Scala, Florence/bpk, Bildagentur für Kunst, Kultur und Geschichte, Berlin

The famous head of **NEFERTITI** (**FIG. 3-30**) was discovered in 1912 in the Akhetaten studio of the sculptor Thutmose, along with drawings and other items related to commissions for the royal family. It may have served as a model for full-length sculptures or paintings of the queen. In 2007, analysis using a CT scan revealed the existence of a delicately carved limestone sculpture underneath the modeled **stucco** that forms its outer surface. The two likenesses differ slightly. The sculptor seems to have smoothed out in stucco some of the facial irregularities in the underlying limestone carving—including a bump in Nefertiti's nose and creases around her mouth—and increased the prominence of her cheekbones, probably to bring the queen's face into conformity with contemporary notions of beauty, much in the way we would retouch a photographic image.

The proportions of Nefertiti's refined, regular features, long neck, and heavy-lidded eyes appear almost too ideal to be human, but are eerily consistent with standards of beauty in our own culture. Part of the appeal of this portrait bust, in addition to its stunning beauty, may be the artist's dramatic use of color. The hues of the blue headdress and its striped band are repeated in the rich red, blue, green, and gold of the jeweled necklace. The queen's brows, eyelids, cheeks, and lips are heightened with color, as they no doubt were heightened with cosmetics in real life.

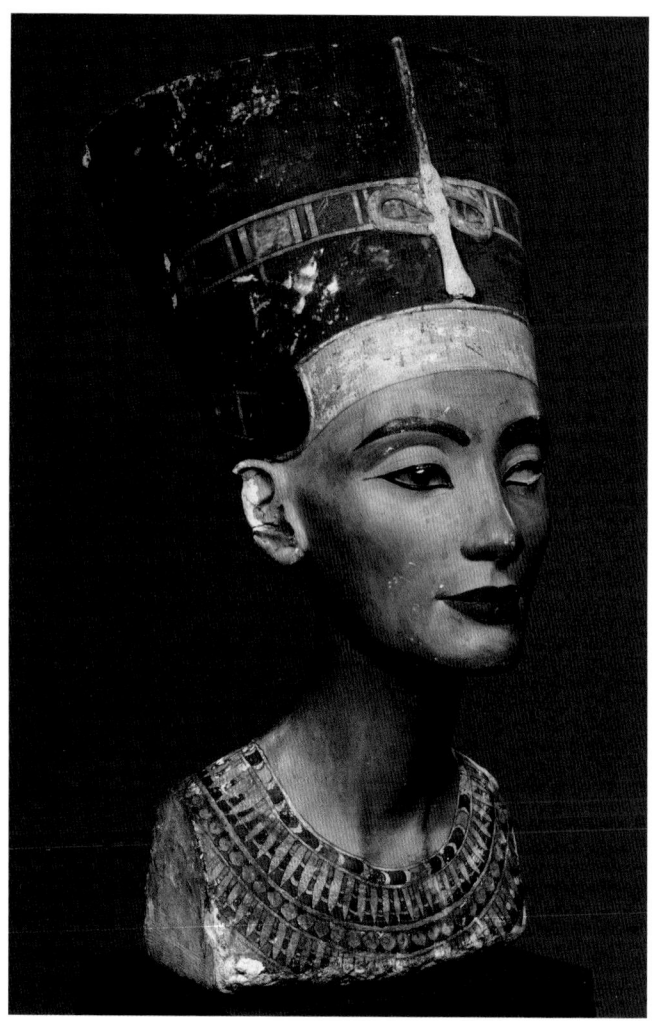

3-30 NEFERTITI

From Akhetaten (present-day Tell el-Amarna). Eighteenth Dynasty, reign of Akhenaten c. 1353–1336 BCE. Painted limestone, height 20″ (51 cm). Staatliche Museen zu Berlin, Preussischer Kulturbesitz, Ägyptisches Museum. (21300).

Credit: © 2016. Photo Scala, Florence/bpk, Bildagentur für Kunst, Kultur und Geschichte, Berlin

GLASS No one knows precisely when or where the technique of glassmaking first developed, but the basics of the process are quite clear. Heating a mixture of sand, lime, and sodium carbonate or sodium sulfate to a very high temperature produces glass. The addition of other minerals can make the glass transparent, translucent, or opaque, as well as create a vast range of colors.

The first objects to be made entirely of glass in Egypt were produced with the technique known as core-formed glass. A lump of sandy clay molded into the desired shape was wrapped in strips of cloth, then skewered on a fireproof rod. It was then briefly dipped into a pot of molten glass. When the resulting coating of glass had cooled, the clay core was removed through the opening left by the skewer. To decorate the vessel, glassmakers frequently heated thin rods of colored glass and fused them on and flattened them against the surface in strips.

3-31 FISH-SHAPED PERFUME BOTTLE

From Akhetaten (present-day Tell el-Amarna). Eighteenth Dynasty, reign of Akhenaten, c. 1353–1336 BCE. Core-formed glass, length 5¾" (14.5 cm). British Museum, London. (EA 55193).

This fish-shaped bottle (**FIG. 3-31**) is an example of core-formed glass from the New Kingdom's Amarna period. The body was created from glass tinted with cobalt, and the surface was then decorated with small rods of white and orange glass. A pointed tool was dragged along the surface to achieve the wavy pattern that resembles fish scales, then two slices of a rod of spiraled black and white glass were fused to the surface to create its eyes.

Glassmaking could only be practiced by artists working for the king, and Akhenaten's new capital had its own glassmaking workshops, where this bottle was made. Meant to hold scented oil, it was fashioned in the shape of a bolti, a species of fish that carries its eggs in its mouth and spits out its offspring when they hatch. The bolti was a common symbol for birth and regeneration, complementing the self-generation that Akhenaten attributed to the sun disk Aten.

The Return to Tradition: Tutankhamun's Tomb

Akhenaten's new religion and revolutionary reconception of pharaonic art outlived him by only a few years. The priesthood of Amun quickly regained its former power, and Akhenaten's young son Tutankhaten (Eighteenth Dynasty, ruled c. 1332–1322 BCE) returned to traditional religious beliefs, changing his name to Tutankhamun— "Living Image of Amun"—and moving the court back to Thebes. He died at age 19 and was buried in the Valley of the Kings, across the Nile from Thebes.

Although some had doubted the royal lineage of the young Tutankhaten, DNA testing of a series of royal mummies from this period has confirmed that he was the son of Akhenaten and one of his sisters. His death at such a young age seems to have been the result of poor health and serious injury. The DNA analysis documented his struggles with malaria, and CT scans revealed a badly broken and seriously infected leg, as well as a series of birth defects that have been ascribed to royal inbreeding.

The sealed inner chamber of Tutankhamun's tomb was never plundered, and when it was found in 1922 its incredible riches were just as they had been left at his interment. His mummified body, crowned with a spectacular mask preserving his likeness (SEE FIG. 3-1), lay inside three nested coffins that identified him with Osiris, the god of the dead. The innermost coffin, in the shape of a mummy, is the richest of the three (**FIG. 3-32**).

Made of over 240 pounds of gold, its surface is decorated with colored glass and semiprecious gemstones,

3-32 INNER COFFIN FROM TUTANKHAMUN'S SARCOPHAGUS

From the tomb of Tutankhamun, Valley of the Kings. Eighteenth Dynasty, c. 1332–1322 BCE. Gold inlaid with glass and semiprecious stones, height 6'7⁄8" (1.85 m), weight nearly 243 pounds (110.4 kg). Egyptian Museum, Cairo. (JE 60671).

Art and its Contexts

THE TEMPLES OF RAMSES II AT ABU SIMBEL

Many art objects are subtle, captivating us through their enduring beauty or complexity. Monuments such as Ramses II's temples at Abu Simbel, however, engage us across the ages with raw power born of sheer scale. This god-king of Egypt, ruler of a vast empire, a virile wonder who fathered nearly a hundred children, is described in an inscription he had carved into an obelisk (now standing in the heart of Paris): "Son of Ra: Ramses-Meryamun ['Beloved of Amun']. As long as the skies exist, your monuments shall exist, your name shall exist, firm as the skies." So far, this is true.

Abu Simbel was an auspicious site for Ramses II's great temples. It is north of the second cataract of the Nile, in Nubia, the ancient land of Kush, which Ramses ruled and which was the source of his gold, ivory, and exotic animal skins. The monuments were carved directly into the rock of the sacred hills. The larger temple is dedicated to Ramses and the Egyptian gods Amun, Ra-Horakhty, and Ptah (**FIG. 3-33**). A row of four colossal seated statues of the king, 65 feet high, dominate the monument, flanked by relatively small statues of family members, including his principal wife Nefertari. Inside the temple, eight 23-foot statues of the god Osiris with the face of Ramses further proclaim Ramses's divinity. The corridor they form leads to seated figures of Ptah, Amun, Ramses II, and Ra.

The corridor was oriented so that twice a year the first rays of the rising sun shot through it to illuminate statues of the king and the three gods placed against the back wall (**FIG. 3-34**).

About 500 feet away, Ramses ordered a smaller temple to be carved into a mountain sacred to Hathor, goddess of fertility, love, joy, and music, and dedicated to Hathor and Nefertari. The two temples were oriented so that their axes crossed in the middle of the Nile, suggesting that they may have been associated with the annual life-giving flood.

Ironically, rising water nearly destroyed them both. Half-buried in the sand over the ages, the temples were only rediscovered early in the nineteenth century. But in the 1960s, construction of the Aswan High Dam flooded the Abu Simbel site. An international team of experts mobilized to find a way to safeguard Ramses II's temples, deciding in 1963 to cut them out of the rock in blocks (**FIG. 3-35**) and re-erect them on higher ground, secure from the rising waters of Lake Nasser. The projected cost of $32 million was financed by UNESCO, with Egypt and the United States each pledging $12 million. Work began in 1964 and was completed in 1968. Thanks to this international cooperation, modern technology, and hard labor, Ramses II's temples were saved to engage future generations.

3-33 TEMPLE OF RAMSES II
Abu Simbel. Nineteenth Dynasty, c. 1279–1213 BCE.

Credit: Bradhenge/Fotolia

**3–34 SCHEMATIC DRAWING
OF THE TEMPLE OF RAMSES II**
Abu Simbel.

Credit: © Dorling Kindersley

inner
sanctuary

vestibule with
scenes of Ramses
and Nefertari
making offerings

statues of Osiris
with the face of
Ramses

storerooms

INTERIOR

a row of baboons
greeting the rising sun

statue of
Ra-Horakhty

colossal statues
of Ramses II

entrance to temple

EXTERIOR

**3–35 REMOVAL OF THE FACE OF ONE OF THE
COLOSSAL SCULPTURES OF RAMSES II AT ABU
SIMBEL IN THE MID-1960S**

Credit: © Terrence Spencer/Time & Life Pictures/Getty Images as well as finely incised linear designs and hieroglyphic inscriptions. The king holds a crook and a flail, symbols that were associated with Osiris and had become a traditional part of the royal regalia. A nemes headdress with projecting cobra and vulture covers his head, and a blue, braided beard is attached to his chin. Nekhbet and Wadjet, vulture and cobra goddesses of Upper and Lower Egypt, spread their wings across his body. The king's features as reproduced on the coffin and masks are those of a very young man, and the unusually full lips, thin-bridged nose, and pierced earlobes suggest the continuing vitality of some Amarna stylizations.

RAMSES II AND NEFERTARI By Egyptian standards Tutankhamun was a rather minor king. Ramses II (Nineteenth Dynasty, ruled c. 1279–1213 BCE), on the other hand, was both powerful and long-lived. He was a bold leader and an effective political strategist and under him, Egypt was a mighty empire. Although he did not win every battle, he was a master of propaganda, able to turn military defeats into glorious victories. He also triumphed diplomatically by making peace with the Hittites, a rival power centered in Anatolia that had tried to expand to the west and south at Egypt's expense. Ramses twice reaffirmed that peace by marrying Hittite princesses.

In the course of a long and prosperous reign, Ramses II initiated building projects on a scale rivaling the Old Kingdom pyramids at Giza. Today, the most awe-inspiring of his many architectural monuments are found at Karnak and Luxor and at Abu Simbel in Egypt's southernmost region (see "The Temples of Ramses II at Abu Simbel" on pages 76–77). At Abu Simbel, Ramses ordered two large temples to be carved into natural rock, one for himself and the other for his principal wife, Nefertari.

The temples at Abu Simbel were not funerary monuments. Ramses's and Nefertari's tombs are in the Valleys

3–36 QUEEN NEFERTARI MAKING AN OFFERING TO HATHOR
Wall painting in the tomb of Nefertari, Valley of the Queens. Nineteenth Dynasty, 1290–1224 BCE.

3–37 JUDGMENT OF HUNEFER BEFORE OSIRIS

Illustration from a Book of the Dead. Nineteenth Dynasty, c. 1285 BCE. Painted papyrus, height 15⅝" (39.8 cm).
British Museum, London. (EA 9901).

Credit:

of the Kings and Queens. The walls of Nefertari's tomb are covered with exquisite paintings. In one mural, Nefertari offers jars of perfumed ointment to the goddess Hathor, known as the "Mistress of the West," who welcomes the dead into their new life (**FIG. 3–36**). The queen wears the vulture-skin headdress and jeweled collar that indicate her royal position and a long, semitransparent white linen gown. Hathor, seated on her throne behind a table heaped with offerings, holds a long scepter in her left hand and the ankh in her right. She wears her signature headdress with horns framing a sun disk. This cow goddess was especially associated with femininity and fertility.

The artists responsible for decorating the tomb diverged very subtly but distinctively from earlier stylistic conventions. The outline drawing and use of pure colors within the lines reflect traditional practices, but quite new is the slight modeling of the body forms by small changes of **hue** to enhance the appearance of three-dimensionality. The skin color of these women is much darker than that conventionally used for females in earlier periods, and lightly brushed-in shading emphasizes their eyes and lips.

The Books of the Dead

Papyrus scrolls visualized New Kingdom beliefs about the final judgment that awaited souls after death. Early collectors of Egyptian artifacts called these scrolls "Books of the Dead." By the time of the New Kingdom, Egyptians had come to believe that only a person free from wrongdoing could enjoy an afterlife. The dead were thought to undergo a last judgment consisting of two tests presided over by Osiris, the god of the underworld, and supervised by Anubis, the jackal-headed god of embalming and cemeteries. After the deceased were questioned about their behavior in life, their hearts—which the Egyptians believed to be the seat of the soul—were weighed on a scale against an ostrich feather, the symbol of Ma'at, goddess of truth, order, and justice.

Family members commissioned scrolls containing magical texts or spells, which embalmers sometimes placed among the wrappings of mummified bodies. A scene in one that was created for a man named Hunefer (Nineteenth Dynasty) shows three successive stages in his induction into the afterlife (**FIG. 3–37**). At the left, Anubis leads Hunefer by the hand to the spot where he will weigh Hunefer's heart against the "feather of Truth." Ma'at appears atop the balancing arm of the scales wearing the feather as a headdress. To the right of the scales, Ammit, the dreaded "Eater of the Dead"—part crocodile, part lion, and part hippopotamus—watches eagerly for a sign from the ibis-headed god Thoth, who prepares to record the result of the weighing.

But Hunefer passes the test, and Horus, on the right, presents him to the enthroned Osiris, who floats on a lake of natron (see "Preserving the Dead" on page 54). Behind the throne, the goddesses Nephthys and Isis support the god's left arm, while in front of him Horus's four sons, each entrusted with the care of one of the deceased's vital organs, stand on a huge lotus blossom rising out of the lake. In the top register, Hunefer, finally accepted into the afterlife, kneels before 14 gods of the underworld.

3-38 KAROMAMA

Third Intermediate period, Twenty-Second Dynasty, c. 945–715 BCE. Bronze inlaid with gold, silver, electrum, glass, and copper; height 23½" (59.5 cm). Musée du Louvre, Paris.

Credit: Photo © RMN-Grand Palais (musée du Louvre)/Hervé Lewandowski

Late Egyptian Art

What traditional and innovative visual and thematic qualities are seen in the later art of ancient Egypt?

After the end of the New Kingdom—during the Third Intermediate Period, c. 1075–715 BCE—Egypt was ruled by a series of new dynasties whose leaders continued the traditional patterns of royal patronage and pushed figural conventions in new and interesting directions. One of the most extraordinary, and certainly one of the largest, surviving examples of ancient Egyptian bronze sculpture (**FIG. 3-38**) dates from this period. An inscription on the base identifies the subject as Karomama, divine consort of Amun and member of a community of virgin priestesses selected from the pharaoh's family or retinue who were dedicated to him. Karomama herself was the granddaughter of King Osorkan I (Twenty-First Dynasty, ruled c. 985–978 BCE). These priestesses amassed great power, held property, and maintained their own court, often passing on their positions to their nieces. The *sistra* (ritual rattles) that Karomama once carried in her hands would have immediately identified her as a priestess rather than a princess.

The main body of this statue was cast in bronze and subsequently covered with a thin sheathing of bronze, which was then exquisitely engraved with patterns inlaid with gold, silver, and electrum (a natural alloy of gold and silver). Much of the inlay has disappeared, but we can still make out the elaborately incised drawing of the bird wings that surround Karomama and accentuate the fullness of her figure, conceived to embody a new female ideal. Her slender limbs, ample hips, and prominent breasts contrast with the uniformly slender female figures of the late New Kingdom (SEE FIG. 3-36).

Foreign Domination

The latest period in the history of ancient Egypt saw the country and its art in the hands and service of foreigners. Nubians, Persians, Macedonians, Greeks, and Romans were all attracted to Egypt's riches and seduced by its art. In the eighth century, Nubians from the powerful kingdom of Kush—ancient Egypt's neighbor to the south—conquered Egypt, establishing capitals at Memphis and Thebes (712–657 BCE) and adopting Egyptian religious, artistic, and architectural practices. The sphinx of the Nubian king Taharqo (ruled c. 690–664 BCE) (**FIG. 3-39**) expresses royal power in a tradition dating back to the Old Kingdom (SEE FIG. 3-7), the two cobras on his forehead perhaps representing Taharqo's two kingdoms—Kush and Egypt. The facial features, however, clearly show him to be African, and an inscription on his chest provides his specific identity.

In 332 BCE, Macedonian Greeks led by Alexander the Great conquered Egypt, and after Alexander's death in 323 BCE, his generals divided up his empire. Ptolemy, a Greek, took Egypt, declaring himself king in 305 BCE. The Ptolemaic dynasty ended with the death of Cleopatra VII (ruled 51–30 BCE), when the Romans succeeded as Egypt's rulers and made it the breadbasket of Rome.

3–39 SPHINX OF TAHARQO

From Temple T, Kawa, Nubia (present-day Sudan). Twenty-Fifth Dynasty, c. 680 BCE. Granite, height 16″ (40.6 cm), length 28¾″ (73 cm). British Museum, London.

Credit: © The Trustees of the British Museum. All rights reserved.

Think About It

1 Explain the pictorial conventions for representing the human figure in ancient Egypt, using the Palette of Narmer (see "Closer Look" on page 53) as an example.

2 Summarize the religious beliefs of ancient Egypt with regard to the afterlife, and explain how their beliefs inspired traditions in art and architecture, citing specific examples both early and late.

3 How do depictions of royalty differ from those of more ordinary people in ancient Egyptian art? Focus your answer on one specific representation of each.

4 Characterize the stylistic transformation that took place during the rule of Akhenaten by comparing **FIGURES 3-25** and **3-28**. Why would there be such a drastic change?

Crosscurrents

What do these two scenes of hunting express about the wealthy and powerful people who commissioned them? How do the artists make their messages clear? How is location related to meaning?

FIG. 2–14

FIG. 3–13

4-1 GIRL GATHERING SAFFRON CROCUS FLOWERS
Detail of wall painting, Room 3 of House Xeste 3, Akrotiri, Thera, Cyclades. Before 1650 BCE. Thera Foundation, Petros M. Nomikos, Greece.

Chapter 4
Art of the Ancient Aegean

 Learning Objectives

4.a Identify the visual hallmarks of Bronze Age Aegean Cycladic, Minoan, and Mycenaean art for formal, technical, and expressive qualities.

4.b Interpret the meaning of works of Bronze Age Aegean Cycladic, Minoan, and Mycenaean art based on their themes, subjects, and symbols.

4.c Relate Bronze Age Aegean Cycladic, Minoan, and Mycenaean artists and art to their cultural, economic, and political contexts.

4.d Apply the vocabulary and concepts used to discuss Bronze Age Aegean art, artists, and art history.

4.e Interpret ancient Aegean art using appropriate art historical methods, such as observation, comparison, and inductive reasoning.

4.f Select visual and textual evidence in various media to support an argument or an interpretation of ancient Aegean art.

This elegantly posed and sharply silhouetted girl, reaching to pluck the crocus flowers blooming on the hillside in front of her (**FIG. 4–1**), offers us a window into life in the ancient Aegean world. The image is from a **fresco** of c. 1650 BCE found in a house in Akrotiri, a town on the Aegean island of Thera that was said to be famous for the saffron harvested from its crocuses. Saffron was valued in the Bronze Age Aegean mainly as a yellow dye in textile production, but it also had medicinal properties and was used to alleviate menstrual cramps. The latter use may be referenced in this image, since the fresco was part of the elaborate painted decoration of a room that some scholars believe housed the coming-of-age ceremonies of young women at the onset of menses. The crocus gatherer's shaved head and looped long ponytail are attributes of childhood, but the light blue color of her scalp indicates that her hair is beginning to grow out, suggesting that she is entering adolescence.

The house that contained this painting disappeared suddenly more than 3,600 years ago when the volcano that formed the island of Thera erupted, spewing pumice that filled and sealed every crevice of Akrotiri—fortunately, after the residents had fled. The rediscovery of the lost town in 1967 was among the most significant archaeological events of the second half of the twentieth century, and excavation of the city is still under way. The opportunity

that Thera affords archaeologists to study works of art and architecture in context has allowed for a deeper understanding of the Bronze Age cultures of the Aegean. As the image of the girl gathering crocuses illustrates, wall paintings may reflect the ritual uses of a room or building, and the meanings of artifacts are better understood by considering where they are found and how they are grouped with one another.

From before 3000 BCE until about 1100 BCE, several Bronze Age cultures flourished simultaneously across the Aegean: on a cluster of small islands (including Thera) called the Cyclades, on Crete and other islands in the eastern Mediterranean, and on mainland Greece (**MAP 4–1**).

To learn about these cultures, archaeologists have studied shipwrecks, homes, and grave sites, as well as the ruins of architectural complexes. Archaeology—uncovering and interpreting material culture to reconstruct its original context—is our principal means of understanding the Bronze Age culture of the Aegean, since only one of its three written languages has been decoded. In recent years, archaeologists and art historians have collaborated with researchers in such areas of study as the history of trade and the history of climate change to provide an ever-clearer picture of ancient Aegean society. But many sites await excavation, or even discovery. The history of the Aegean Bronze Age is still being written.

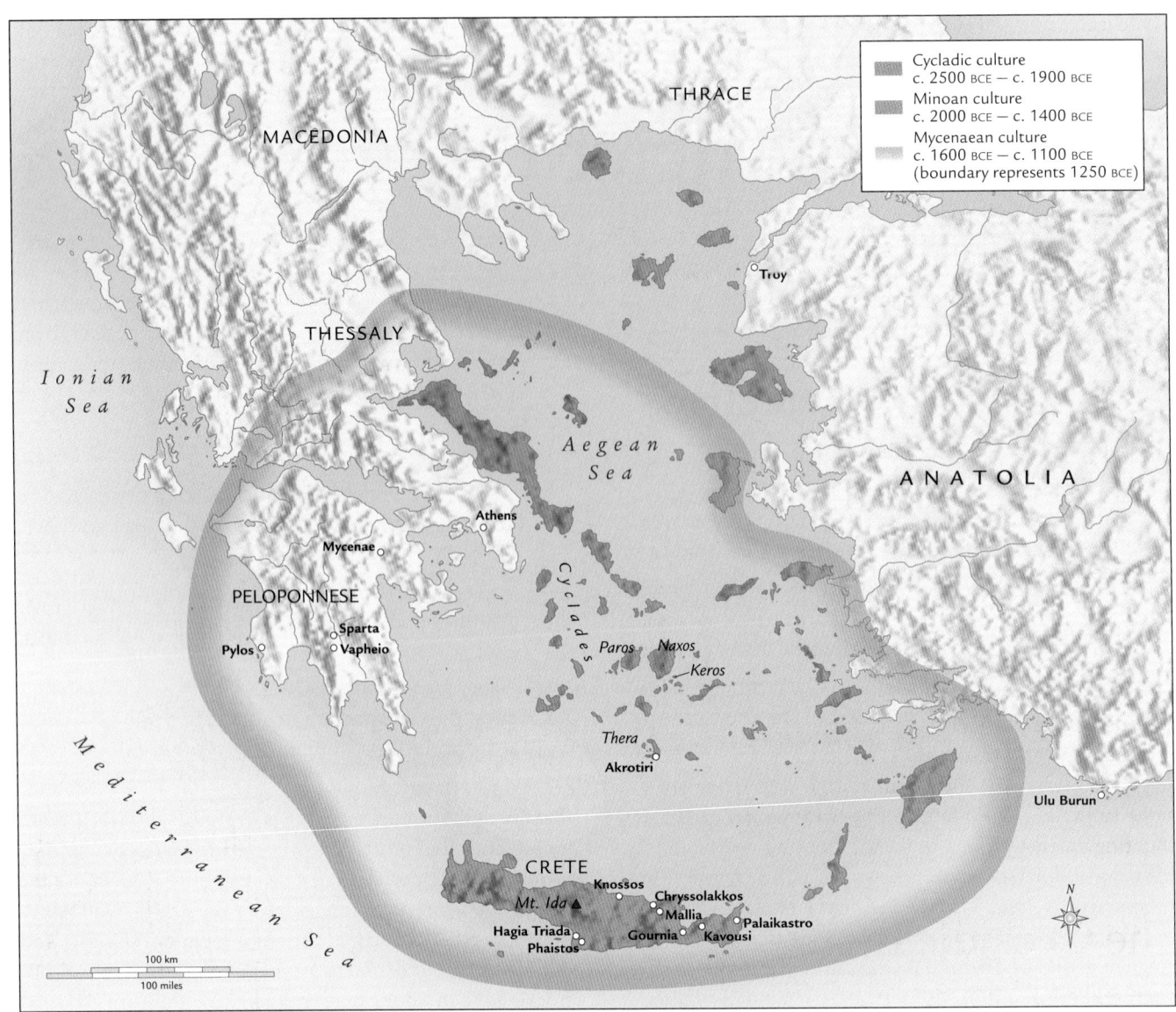

MAP 4–1 THE ANCIENT AEGEAN WORLD

The three main cultures in the ancient Aegean were the Cycladic, in the Cyclades; the Minoan, on Thera and Crete; and the Helladic, including the Mycenaean, on mainland Greece but also encompassing the regions that had been the center of the two earlier cultures.

The Bronze Age in the Aegean

How have scholars learned about the art and culture of the Aegean Bronze Age?

Using metal ores imported from Europe, Arabia, and Anatolia, Aegean peoples created exquisite objects of bronze that were prized for export. This early period when the manufacture of bronze tools and weapons became widespread is known as the Aegean Bronze Age. (See Chapter 1 for the Bronze Age in northern Europe.)

For the ancient Aegean peoples, the sea provided an important link not only between the mainland and the islands, but also to the world beyond. In contrast to the landlocked civilizations of the Near East and to the Egyptians, who used river transportation, the peoples of the Aegean were seafarers, and their ports welcomed ships from other cultures around the Mediterranean. For this reason shipwrecks are a rich source of information about the material culture of these societies. For example, the wreck of a trading vessel (probably from the Levant, the Mediterranean coast of the Near East) thought to have sunk in or soon after 1306 BCE and discovered in the vicinity of Ulu Burun, off the southern coast of present-day Turkey, carried an extremely varied cargo: metal ingots, bronze weapons and tools, aromatic resins, fruits and spices, jewelry and beads, African ebony, ivory tusks, ostrich eggs, disks of blue glass ready to be melted down for reuse, and ceramics from the Near East, mainland Greece, and Cyprus. Among the gold objects was a scarab associated with Nefertiti, wife of the Egyptian pharaoh Akhenaten.

The cargo suggests that this vessel cruised from port to port along the Aegean and eastern Mediterranean seas, loading and unloading goods as it went. It also suggests that the peoples of Egypt and the ancient Near East were trading partners.

Probably the thorniest problem in Aegean archaeology is that of dating the finds. In the case of the Ulu Burun wreck, the dating of a piece of freshly cut firewood on the ship to 1306 BCE—using a technique called dendrochronology that analyzes the spaces between growth rings—allowed unusual precision in pinpointing the moment this ship sank. But archaeologists are not always able to find such easily datable materials. They usually rely on a relative dating system for the Aegean Bronze Age that is based largely on pottery, but assigning specific dates to sites and objects with this system is complicated and controversial. One cataclysmic event has helped: A huge volcanic explosion on the Cycladic island of Thera, as we have seen, devastated Minoan civilization there and on Crete, only 70 miles to the south. Evidence from tree rings from Ireland and California and traces of volcanic ash in ice cores from Greenland put the date of the eruption about 1650–1625 BCE. Sometimes in this book you will find periods cited without attached dates and in other books you may encounter different dates from those given for objects shown here. You should expect dating to change in the future as our knowledge grows and new techniques of dating emerge.

The Cycladic Islands

What stylistic features characterize Bronze Age Cycladic sculpted figures and how do the objects reflect Cycladic culture?

On the Cycladic islands, late Neolithic and early Bronze Age people developed a thriving culture. They engaged in agriculture, herding, crafts, and trade, using local stone to build fortified towns and hillside burial chambers. Because they left no written records, their artifacts are our principal source of information about them. From about 6000 BCE, Cycladic artists used a coarse, poor-quality local clay to make a variety of ceramic objects, including engaging ceramic figurines of humans and animals as well as domestic and ceremonial wares. Some 3,000 years later, they began to produce marble sculptures.

The Cyclades, especially the islands of Naxos and Paros, had ample supplies of a fine and durable white marble. Sculptors used it to create sleek, abstracted representations of human figures ranging from a few inches to almost 5 feet tall. They were shaped—perhaps by women—with scrapers made of obsidian and smoothed using emery polishing stones, both materials easily available on the Cyclades.

These sculptures have been found almost exclusively in graves, and, although there are a few surviving male figures, the overwhelming majority represent nude women and conform to a consistent representational convention (**FIG. 4–2**). They are presented in poses of strict symmetry, with arms folded just under gently protruding breasts, as if they were clutching their abdomens. Necks are long, heads tilted back, and faces featureless except for a prominent, elongated nose. All body parts are pared down to essentials, and some joints are indicated with incised lines. The sculptors carefully designed these figures, laying them out with a compass in conformity to three evenly spaced and equally sized circles—the first delineated by the upper arch of the head and the waist, the second by the sloping shoulders and the line of the knees, and the third beginning with the curving limit of the feet and meeting the bottom of the upper circle at the waist.

For us, these stylizations recall works of modern sculpture, but originally their smooth marble surfaces were enlivened by painted motifs in blue, red, and, more rarely, green paint, emphasizing their surfaces

4–2 FIGURE OF A WOMAN WITH A DRAWING SHOWING EVIDENCE OF ORIGINAL PAINTING AND OUTLINING DESIGN SCHEME
From the Cyclades. c. 2600–2400 BCE. Marble, height 24¾″ (62.8 cm).
Figure: Metropolitan Museum of Art, New York.
Gift of Christos G. Bastis (68.148). Drawing: Elizabeth Hendrix.

rather than their three-dimensional shapes. Today, evidence of such painting is extremely faint, but many patterns have been recovered using controlled lighting and microscopic investigation. Unlike the forms themselves, the painted features are often asymmetrical in organization. In the example illustrated here, wide-open eyes appear on forehead, cheeks, and thigh, as well as on either side of the nose.

Art historians have proposed a variety of explanations for these painted motifs. The angled lines on some figures' bodies could reflect the way Cycladic peoples decorated their own bodies—whether permanently with tattoos or scarification or temporarily with body paint, applied either during their lifetimes or to prepare their bodies for burial. The staring eyes, which seem to demand the viewer's return gaze, may have been a way of connecting these figures to those who owned or used them. And eyes on locations other than faces may aim to draw viewers' attention—perhaps even healing powers—to a particular area of the body. Some have associated eyes on bellies with pregnancy.

4-3 HEAD WITH REMAINS OF PAINTED DECORATION
From the Cyclades. c. 2500–2200 BCE. Marble and red pigment, height 9¹¹⁄₁₆″ (24.6 cm). National Museum, Copenhagen. (4697).

Credit: National Museum, Copenhagen (4697)

Art historian Gail Hoffman has argued that patterns of vertical red lines painted on the faces of some figures (**FIG. 4-3**) were related to Cycladic rituals of mourning their dead. Perhaps these sculptures were used in relation to a succession of key moments throughout their owners' lifetimes—such as puberty, marriage, and death—and were continually repainted with motifs associated with each ritual, before finally following their owners into their graves at death. Since there is no written evidence from Cycladic culture and no information on the archaeological contexts of many works, it is difficult to be certain, but these sculptures were clearly important to Bronze Age Cycladic peoples and seem to have taken on meaning in relationship to their use.

Although some Cycladic islands retained their distinctive artistic traditions, by the Middle and Later Bronze Age, the art and culture of the Cyclades as a whole was overtaken first by Minoan and later by Mycenaean culture.

The Minoan Civilization on Crete

What characterizes the art and architecture of the Minoan Old and New Palace periods, even beyond the island of Crete?

As early as the Neolithic period, there was large-scale migration to and permanent settlement on Crete, the largest of the Aegean islands (155 miles long and 36 miles wide). By the Bronze Age, Crete was economically self-sufficient, producing its own grains, olives and other fruits, cattle, and sheep. With many safe harbors and a convenient location, Crete became a wealthy sea power, trading with mainland Greece, Egypt, the Near East, and Anatolia, thus acquiring the ores necessary for producing bronze.

Between about 1900 BCE and 1375 BCE, a distinctive culture flourished on Crete. The British archaeologist Sir Arthur Evans (see "Pioneers of Aegean Archaeology" opposite) named it Minoan after the legend of Minos, a king who had ruled from the capital, Knossos. According to this legend, a half-man, half-bull monster called the Minotaur—son of the wife of King Minos and a bull belonging to the sea god Poseidon—lived at Knossos in a maze called the Labyrinth. To satisfy the Minotaur's appetite for human flesh, King Minos ordered the mainland kingdom of Athens to send a yearly tribute of 14 young men and women, a practice that ended when the Athenian hero Theseus killed the beast.

Minoan chronology is divided into two main periods, the Old Palace period from about 1900 to 1700 BCE and the New Palace period from around 1700 to 1450 BCE.

RECOVERING THE PAST
PIONEERS OF AEGEAN ARCHAEOLOGY

Heinrich Schliemann (1822–1890) is seen by some as the founder of the modern study of Aegean civilization. Schliemann was the son of an impoverished German minister and a largely self-educated man who spoke several languages. He worked hard, grew rich, and retired in 1863 to pursue his lifelong dream of becoming an archaeologist, inspired by the Greek poet Homer's epic tales, the *Iliad* and the *Odyssey*. In 1869, he began conducting fieldwork in Greece and Turkey. Scholars of that time considered Homer's stories pure fiction, but by studying the descriptions of geography in the *Iliad*, Schliemann located a multilayered site at Hissarlik, in present-day Turkey, whose sixth level up from the bedrock is now generally accepted as the closest chronological approximation of Homer's Troy. After his success in Anatolia, Schliemann pursued his hunch that the grave sites of Homer's Greek royal family would be found inside the citadel at Mycenae. But the graves he found were too early to contain the bodies of Atreus, Agamemnon, and their relatives—a fact only established through recent scholarship, after Schliemann's death.

The uncovering at Knossos of what Schliemann had thought was the palace of the legendary King Minos fell to a British archaeologist, Sir Arthur Evans (1851–1941), who led the excavation between 1900 and 1905. Evans gave the name Minoan—after legendary King Minos—to Bronze Age culture on Crete. He also made a first attempt to establish an absolute chronology for Minoan art, basing his conjectures on datable Egyptian artifacts found in the ruins on Crete and on Minoan artifacts found in Egypt. Later scholars, though, have revised and refined both his dating and his interpretations of what he found at Knossos.

Evans was not the only pioneering archaeologist drawn to excavate on Crete. Boston-born Harriet Boyd Hawes (1871–1945), after graduating from Smith College in 1892 with a major in Classics and a subsequent year of post-graduate study in Athens, traveled to Crete to find a site where she could begin a career in archaeology. She was in Knossos in 1900 to observe Evans's early work and was soon supervising her own excavations, first at Kavousi and then at Gournia, where she directed work from 1901 until 1904. She is famous for the timely and thorough publication of her findings, accomplished while she was not only supervising these Bronze Age digs, but also pursuing her career as a beloved professor of the liberal arts, first at Smith and later at Wellesley College.

The Old Palace Period, c. 1900–1700 BCE

Minoan civilization remained very much a mystery until 1900 CE, when Sir Arthur Evans began uncovering the buried ruins of the architectural complex at Knossos, on Crete's north coast, that had been occupied in the Neolithic period, then built over with a succession of Bronze Age structures.

ARCHITECTURAL COMPLEXES   Like the nineteenth-century excavators before him, Evans called these great architectural complexes "palaces." He believed they had been occupied by a succession of kings. While some scholars continue to believe this, the evidence has suggested to others that Minoan society was not ruled by kings drawn from a royal family, but by a confederation of aristocrats or aristocratic families who established a fluid and evolving power hierarchy. In this light, some scholars interpret these elaborate complexes as sites of periodic religious ritual, perhaps enacted by a community that gathered within the courtyards that are their core architectural feature.

The walls of early Minoan buildings were made of rubble and mud bricks faced with cut and finished local stone, the first evidence of **dressed stone** used as a building material in the Aegean. Columns and other interior elements were made of wood. Both in large complexes and in the surrounding towns, timber appears to have been used for framing and bracing walls. Its strength and flexibility would have minimized damage from the earthquakes common to the area. Nevertheless, an earthquake in c. 1700 BCE severely damaged buildings at several sites, including Knossos and Phaistos.

CERAMICS   During the Old Palace period, Minoans developed elegant new types of ceramics, spurred in part by the introduction of the potter's wheel early in the second millennium BCE. One type is called Kamares ware after the cave on Mount Ida overlooking the architectural complex at Phaistos, in southern Crete, where it was first discovered. The hallmarks of this select ceramic ware—so sought-after that it was exported as far away as Egypt and Syria—were its extreme thinness, its use of color, and its graceful, stylized painted decoration. An example from about 2000–1900 BCE has a globular body and a "beaked" pouring spout (**FIG. 4-4**). Created from brown, red, and creamy white pigments on a black body, the bold, curving forms—derived from plant life—that decorate this jug seem to swell with its bulging contours.

4-4 KAMARES WARE JUG

From Phaistos, Crete. Old Palace period, c. 2000–1900 BCE. Ceramic, height 10⅝" (27 cm). Archaeological Museum, Iraklion, Crete.

Credit: © Craig & Marie Mauzy, Athens

The New Palace Period, c. 1700–1450 BCE

The early architectural complex at Knossos, erected about 1900 BCE, formed the core of an elaborate new one built after a terrible earthquake shook Crete in c. 1700 BCE. This rebuilding, at Knossos and elsewhere, belonged to the New Palace period and is considered by many scholars to be the highest point of Minoan civilization. In its heyday, the Knossos complex covered six acres (FIG. 4-5).

Damaged structures were repaired and enlarged, and the resulting new complexes shared a number of features. Multistoried, flat-roofed, and with many columns, they were designed to maximize light and air, as well as define access and circulation patterns. Daylight and fresh air entered through staggered levels, open stairwells, and strategically placed air shafts and light-wells (FIG. 4-6).

Large, central courtyards—not audience halls or temples—were the most prominent components of these rectangular complexes. Suites of rooms were arranged around them. Corridors and staircases led from the central and subsidiary courtyards through apartments, ritual areas, and storerooms. Walls were coated with plaster, and some were painted with murals. Floors were plaster, or plaster mixed with pebbles, stone, wood, or beaten earth. The residential quarters had many luxuries: sunlit courtyards

4-5 RECONSTRUCTION DRAWING OF THE "PALACE" COMPLEX, KNOSSOS, CRETE

As it would have appeared during the New Palace period. Site occupied since the Neolithic period; the Minoan complex of the Old Palace period (c. 1900–1700 BCE) was rebuilt during the New Palace period (c. 1700–1450 BCE) after earthquakes and fires; final destruction c. 1375 BCE.

Credit: Illustration: Peter Bull

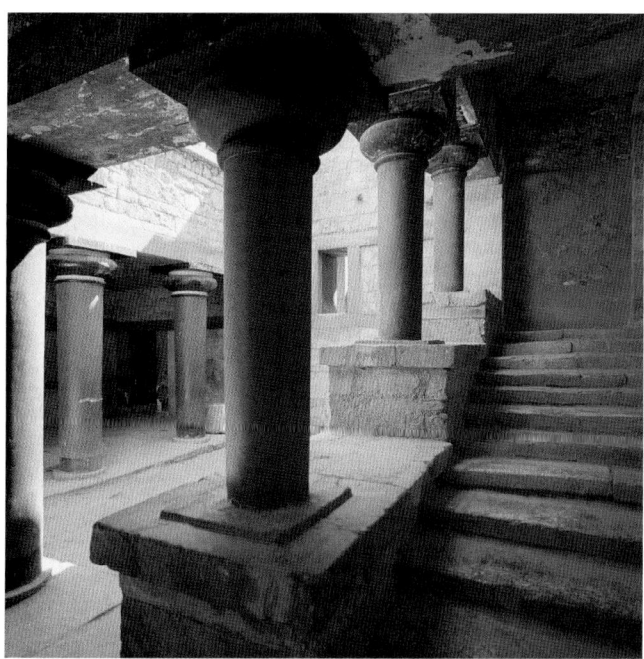

4–6 EAST WING STAIRWELL
"Palace" complex, Knossos, Crete. New Palace period,
c. 1700–1450 BCE.

Credit: © Roger Wood/Corbis

or light-wells, richly colored murals, and sophisticated plumbing systems.

Workshops clustered around the complexes formed commercial centers. Storeroom walls were lined with enormous clay jars for oil and wine, and in their floors stone-lined pits from earlier structures were used for the storage of grain. The huge scale of the centralized food management became apparent when excavators at Knossos found in a single (although more recent) storeroom enough ceramic jars to hold 20,000 gallons of olive oil.

Because double-axe motifs were used in its architectural decoration, the Knossos "palace" was referred to in later Greek legends as the Labyrinth, meaning the "House of the Double Axes" (Greek *labrys*, "double axe"). The organization of the complex seemed so complicated that the word labyrinth eventually came to mean "maze" and became part of the Minotaur legend.

This complicated layout provided the complex with its own internal security system: a baffling array of doors leading to unfamiliar rooms, stairs, yet more corridors, or even dead ends. Admittance could be denied by blocking corridors, and some rooms were accessible only from upper terraces. Close analysis, however, shows that the builders had laid out a square grid following predetermined principles and that the now-confusing layout may partially be the result of later earthquake destruction and rebuilding over the centuries.

In typical Minoan fashion, the rebuilt Knossos complex was organized around a large central courtyard (SEE FIG. 4–5). A few steps led from the courtyard down into

the so-called Throne Room to the west, and a great staircase on the east side descended to the Hall of the Double Axes, an unusually grand example of a Minoan hall. (Evans gave the rooms their misleading but romantic names.) This hall and others were supported by the unique Minoan-type wooden columns that became standard in Aegean palace architecture (SEE FIG. 4–6). The tree trunks from which the columns were made were inverted so that they tapered toward the bottom; they were topped with a broad, flattened capital.

Rooms, following tradition, were arranged around a central space rather than along an axis, as we have seen in Egypt and will see in mainland Greece. During the New Palace period, suites functioned as archives, business centers, and residences. Some must also have had a religious function, though the temples, shrines, and elaborate tombs seen in Egypt are not found in Minoan architecture.

BULL LEAPING AT KNOSSOS Minoan painters worked on a large scale, covering entire walls of rooms with geometric borders, views of nature, and scenes of human activity.

Murals can be painted on a still-wet plaster surface (**buon fresco**) or a dry one (**fresco secco**). The wet technique binds pigments to the wall, but forces the painter to work very quickly. On a dry wall, the painter need not hurry, but the pigments tend to flake off over time. Minoans used both techniques.

Minoan wall painting displays elegant drawing, and Minoan painters, like the Egyptians, filled these linear contours with bright and unshaded fields of pure color. They preferred profile or full-faced views, and they turned natural forms into decorative patterns. One of the most famous paintings of Knossos depicts one of the most prominent subjects in Minoan art: **BULL LEAPING** (FIG. 4–7). The panel—restored from excavated fragments—is one of a group of paintings of bulls from a room in the east wing of the complex. The action—perhaps representing an initiation or fertility ritual—shows three scantily clad youths around a gigantic, dappled bull, which is charging in the **"flying-gallop"** pose. The pale-skinned person at the right—her paleness probably identifying her as a woman—is prepared to catch the dark-skinned man in the midst of his leap, and the pale-skinned woman at the left grasps the bull by its horns, perhaps to help steady it or to begin her own vault. Framing the action are strips of overlapping shapes filled with ornament set within striped bands.

STATUETTE OF A MALE FIGURE FROM PALAIKASTRO Surviving Minoan sculpture consists mainly of small, finely executed work in wood, ivory, precious metals, stone, and ceramic. **Faience** (colorfully glazed fine ceramic) female figurines holding serpents are among the most characteristic images and may have been associated with water, regenerative power, and protection of the

4-7 BULL LEAPING

Wall painting with areas of modern reconstruction, from the "palace" complex, Knossos, Crete. Late Minoan period, c. 1450–1375 BCE. Height approx. 24½" (62.3 cm). Archaeological Museum, Iraklion, Crete.

Careful sifting during excavation preserved many fragments of the paintings that once covered the walls at Knossos. The pieces were painstakingly sorted and cleaned by restorers and reassembled into puzzle pictures; more pieces were missing than found. Areas of color have been used in this reconstruction to fill the gaps, making it obvious which bits are the restored portions, but allowing us to have a sense of the original image.

Credit: © Craig & Marie Mauzy, Athens

home. But among the most impressive works is an unusually large male figure that has been reconstructed from hundreds of fragments excavated in eastern Crete at Palaikastro between 1987 and 1990 (FIG. 4-8). The blackened state of the remains is evidence of a fire that must have destroyed the building where it was kept, since fire damage pervades the archaeological layer in which these fragments were found. The cause or meaning of this fire is a mystery.

The statuette is a multimedia work assembled from a variety of mostly precious materials. The majority of the body was carved in exquisite anatomical detail—including renderings of subcutaneous veins, tendons, and bones—from the ivory of two hippopotamus teeth, with a gap in the lower torso for a wooden insert to which was attached a kilt made of gold foil. Miniature gold sandals slipped onto the small, tapering feet. The head was carved of gray serpentine with inset eyes of rock crystal, just as inlaid wooden nipples

detail the figure's torso. The ivory and gold may have been imported—perhaps from Egypt—but the style is characteristically Minoan (COMPARE FIG. 4-7). We know very little about the context and virtually nothing about the meaning or use of this figure, but the nature of the materials and the large size suggest that it was important. Some have interpreted this as the cult statue of a young god, while others have proposed it was a votive effigy for a religious ceremony, but these remain speculations.

STONE RHYTONS Almost certainly of ritual significance are a series of stone **rhytons**—vessels used for pouring

4-8 STATUETTE OF A MALE FIGURE

From Palaikastro, Crete. c. 1500–1475 BCE. Ivory, gold, serpentine, rock crystal, and wood; height 19½" (50 cm). Archaeological Museum, Siteia, Crete.

Credit: British School at Athens by permission of the Management Committee (courtesy of the Department of Classics, University of Columbia USA. Photo © L.H.Sackett)

4–9 TWO VIEWS OF THE HARVESTER RHYTON
From Hagia Triada, Crete. New Palace period, c. 1650–1450 BCE. Steatite, greatest diameter 4½″ (11.3 cm).
Archaeological Museum, Heraklion, Crete.

Credit: (left) © Craig & Marie Mauzy, Athens; (right) © 2016. Marie Mauzy/Scala, Florence

liquids—that Minoans carved from steatite (a greenish or brown soapstone) and serpentine (usually dull green in color). These have been found in fragments and reconstructed by archaeologists. **THE HARVESTER RHYTON** was a cone-shaped vessel, barely 4½ inches in diameter (**FIG. 4–9**). Only the upper part is preserved.

THE HARVESTER Rhyton may have been covered with gold leaf, a technically demanding process in which artists affix paper-thin sheets of hammered gold to the surface being **gilded** (see "Aegean Metalworking" on page 93).

A rowdy procession of 27 men has been crowded onto its curving surface. The piece is exceptional for relationships among the figures, who overlap and jostle one another instead of marching in patterned single file in the manner of some Near Eastern or Egyptian art. The exuberance of this scene is especially notable in the emotions expressed on the men's faces. They march and chant to a *sistrum*—a rattlelike percussion instrument—lifted by a man whose wide-open mouth seems to signal singing at the top of his lungs. The men have large, bold features and sinewy bodies so trim we can see their ribs. One stands out from the crowd because of his long hair, scale-covered ceremonial cloak, and commanding staff. Archaeologists have proposed a variety of interpretations for the scene—a spring planting or fall harvest festival, a religious procession, a dance, a crowd of warriors, or a gang of forced laborers.

Bulls are a recurrent theme in Minoan art, and rhytons were also made in the form of a bull's head (**FIG. 4–10**). The sculptor carved this one from a block of greenish-black serpentine to create an image that approaches animal portraiture.

4–10 BULL'S-HEAD RHYTON
From Knossos, Crete. New Palace period, c. 1550–1450 BCE. Serpentine with shell, rock crystal, and red jasper; the gilt-wood horns are restorations, height 12″ (30.5 cm). Archaeological Museum, Iraklion, Crete.

Credit: © akg-images/Nimatallah

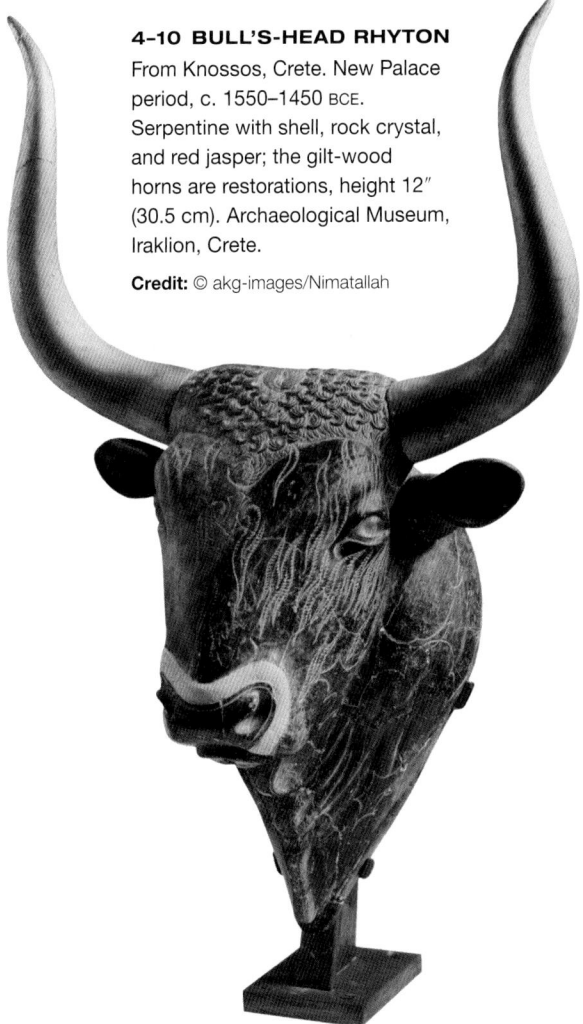

Lightly engraved lines, filled with white powder to make them visible, enliven the animal's coat: short, curly hair on top of the head; longer, shaggy strands on the sides; and circular patterns along the neck suggest its dappled coloring. White bands of shell outline the nostrils, and painted rock crystal and red jasper form the eyes. The horns (here restored) were made of wood covered with gold leaf. This rhyton was filled with liquid through a hole in the bull's neck, and during rituals, fluid was poured out through its mouth.

CERAMICS   The ceramic arts, so splendidly realized early on in Kamares ware, continued throughout the New Palace period. Some of the most striking ceramics are characterized as Marine style because of the depictions of sea life on their surfaces. In a stoppered bottle of this type known as the **OCTOPUS FLASK**, made about 1500–1450 BCE (**FIG. 4–11**), the painter created a dynamic arrangement of marine life, in seeming celebration of Minoan maritime skill. Like microscopic life teeming in a drop of pond water, sea creatures float around an octopus's tangled tentacles. The decoration on the earlier Kamares ware jug (SEE FIG. 4–4) had reinforced the solidity of its surface, but here the pottery surface seems to dissolve. The painter captured the grace and energy of natural forms while presenting them as a stylized design in harmony with the vessel's bulging shape.

4–11 OCTOPUS FLASK
From Palaikastro, Crete. New Palace period, c. 1500–1450 BCE. Marine-style ceramic, height 11″ (28 cm). Archaeological Museum, Heraklion, Crete.

Credit: © Craig & Marie Mauzy, Athens

4–12 PENDANT OF GOLD BEES
From Chryssolakkos, near Malia, Crete. New Palace period, c. 1700–1550 BCE. Gold, height approx. 1¹³⁄₁₆″ (4.6 cm). Archaeological Museum, Heraklion, Crete.

Credit: Studio Kontos Photostock

METALWORK   By about 1700 BCE, Aegean metalworkers were producing objects that rivaled those of Near Eastern and Egyptian jewelers, whose techniques they may have learned and adopted. For a pendant in gold found at Chryssolakkos, the artist arched a pair of easily recognizable but geometrically stylized bees (or perhaps wasps) around a honeycomb of gold granules, providing their sleek bodies with a single pair of outspread wings (**FIG. 4–12**). The pendant hangs from a spiderlike filigree form with what appear to be long legs encircling a tiny gold ball. Small disks dangle from the ends of the wings and the point where the insects' bodies meet.

The Spread of Minoan Culture

About 1450 BCE, a conquering people from mainland Greece known as Mycenaeans arrived in Crete. They occupied the buildings at Knossos and elsewhere until a final catastrophe and the destruction of Knossos about 1375 BCE caused them to abandon the site. But by 1400 BCE, the center of political and cultural power in the Aegean had shifted to mainland Greece.

The skills of Minoan artists, particularly metalsmiths, had made them highly sought after on the mainland. A pair of magnificent gold cups found in a large tomb at Vapheio, on the Greek mainland south of Sparta, were made sometime between 1650 and 1450 BCE either by Minoan artists or by locals trained in Minoan style and techniques. One

Technique

AEGEAN METALWORKING

Aegean artists created exquisite luxury goods from imported gold. Their techniques included lost-wax casting (see "Lost-Wax Casting" in Chapter 14 on page 428), inlay, filigree, granulation, repoussé, niello, and gilding.

The early Minoan pendant with a pair of gold bees (SEE FIG. 4–12) exemplifies early sophistication in **filigree** (delicate decoration with fine wires) and **granulation** (minute granules or balls fused to underlying forms), the latter used to enliven the surfaces and to outline or even create three-dimensional shapes.

The Vapheio Cup (SEE FIG. 4–13) and the funerary mask (SEE FIG. 4–21) are examples of **repoussé**, in which artists gently pushed up relief forms (perhaps by hammering) from the back of

a thin sheet of gold. Experienced goldsmiths may have formed simple designs freehand or used standard wood forms or punches. For more elaborate decorations they would first have sculpted the entire design in wood or clay and then used this form to mold the gold sheet.

The artists who created the Mycenaean dagger blade (SEE FIG. 4–22) not only inlaid one metal into another, but also employed a special technique called **niello**, still a common method of metal decoration. Powdered niellum—a black alloy of lead, silver, and copper with sulfur—was rubbed into very fine engraved lines in a silver or gold surface, then fused to the surrounding metal with heat. The resulting lines appear as black drawings.

side of one cup is shown here (FIG. 4–13). The relief designs were executed in repoussé—the technique of pushing up a sheet of metal from the back. The handles were attached with rivets, and the cup was then lined with sheet gold. In the scenes circling the cups, men are depicted trying to capture bulls in various ways. Here, a scantily clad man has roped a bull's hind leg. The figures dominate the landscape and bulge from the surface with a muscular vitality that belies the cup's small size—it is only 4½ inches tall. The depiction of olive trees could indicate that the scene is set in a sacred grove. The cups may illustrate exploits in some long-lost heroic tale—or just commonplace herding scenes.

WALL PAINTING AT AKROTIRI ON THERA   Minoan cultural influences seem to have spread to the Cyclades as well as mainland Greece. Thera, for example, was so heavily under Crete's influence in the New Palace period that it

4-13 VAPHEIO CUP
One of two cups found near Sparta, Greece. c. 1650–1450 BCE. Gold, height 4½″ (11.3 cm). National Archaeological Museum, Athens.
Credit: © Craig & Marie Mauzy, Athens

was a veritable outpost of Minoan culture. A girl picking crocuses in a fresco in a house at Akrotiri (SEE FIG. 4–1) wears a typically colorful Minoan flounced skirt with a short-sleeved, open-breasted bodice, large earrings, and bracelets. This wall painting demonstrates the sophisticated decorative sense found in Minoan art, both in color selection and in surface detail. The room in which this painting appears seems to have been dedicated to young women's coming-of-age ceremonies, and its frescos provided the visual context for ritual activity, just as the courtyards of architectural complexes in Crete had.

In another Akrotiri house, an artist created an imaginative landscape of hills, rocks, and flowers (FIG. 4–14), the first pure landscape painting we have encountered in ancient art. A viewer standing in the center of the room is surrounded by orange, rose, and blue rocky hillocks sprouting oversized, deep-red lilies. Swallows, sketched by a few deft lines, swoop above and around the flowers. The artist unified the rhythmic flow of the undulating landscape, the stylized patterning of the natural forms, and the decorative use of bright colors alternating with darker, neutral tones, perhaps meant to represent areas of shadow. The colors may seem fanciful to us, but present-day sailors attest to their accuracy, suggesting that these artists recorded the actual colors of Thera's wet rocks in the sunshine—a celebration of the natural world very different from the cool, stable elegance of Egyptian wall painting.

Direct references to the geology of Thera also appear in a long strip of wall painting known as the "Flotilla Fresco" (see "Closer Look" on pages 94–95) running along the tops of the walls in the room of a house in Akrotiri, a domestic context comparable to that of the fresco of the girl gathering crocuses.

This expansive tableau was for years interpreted as a long-distance voyage with a military flavor, but in 2010 art

4-14 LANDSCAPE ("SPRING FRESCO")

Wall painting with areas of modern reconstruction, from Akrotiri, Thera, Cyclades. Before 1630 BCE. National Archaeological Museum, Athens.

Credit: © akg-images/Nimatallah

historian Thomas Strasser argued convincingly that this is a specific seascape viewed from the eastern interior of the island of Thera itself, looking toward the western opening between two peninsular mountainous landmasses, populated by local ships and the dolphins that leap around them. The land and sea of Thera may be the principal subject of this painting.

A Closer Look

THE "FLOTILLA FRESCO" FROM AKROTIRI

The **depiction of lions chasing deer**, perhaps signifying heroism or political power, has a long history in Aegean art.

This block of land seems to represent one of two spits of land in Thera that separate the sea from an enclosed area of water in a volcanic basin at the center of the island. Both the volcanic quality of the painted rocks and their division into horizontal registers as bands of color reproduce the actual geological appearance of this terrain.

The arrangement of ships and leaping dolphins in the center uses vertical perspective (see Starter Kit on page xviii) to indicate spatial recession. In this system, higher placement is given to things that are in the distance, while those placed lower are closer to the viewer.

4-15 "THE FLOTILLA FRESCO"

Detail of the left part of a mural from Room 5 of West House, Akrotiri, Thera. New Palace period, c. 1650 BCE. Height 14⁵⁄₁₆″ (44 cm). National Archaeological Museum, Athens.

Credit: © akg-images/Nimatallah

The Mycenaean (Helladic) Culture

What features distinguish the art and architecture of the Mycenaeans on the Greek mainland from other Aegean Bronze Age cultures?

Archaeologists use the term *Helladic* (from *Hellas*, the Greek name for Greece) to designate the Aegean Bronze Age on mainland Greece. The Helladic period extends from about 3000 to 1000 BCE, contemporary with Cycladic and Minoan cultures. In the early part of the Aegean Bronze Age, Greek-speaking peoples, probably from the northwest, moved into the area. They brought with them advanced techniques for metalworking, ceramics, and architectural design, and they displaced the local Neolithic culture. Later in the Aegean Bronze Age, the people of the mainland city of Mycenae rose to power and extended their influence into the Aegean islands as well.

Helladic Architecture

Mycenaean architecture developed in ways distinct from those of the Minoans. Mycenaeans built fortified strongholds called citadels to protect the palaces of their rulers. These palaces contained a characteristic architectural unit called a **megaron** that was axial in plan, consisting of a large room entered through a porch with columns and sometimes a vestibule. The Mycenaeans also buried their dead in magnificent vaulted tombs, round in floor plan and crafted of cut stone.

MYCENAE Later Greek writers called the walled complex of Mycenae (**FIG. 4-16**) the home of Agamemnon, legendary Greek king and leader of the Greek army that conquered the great city of Troy, as described in Homer's epic poem the *Iliad*. The site was occupied from the Neolithic period to around 1050 BCE. The walls were rebuilt three times—c. 1340 BCE, c. 1250 BCE, and c. 1200 BCE—each

Each of the seven vessels of the fleet (only four can be seen in this partial view) is unique in size, decoration (this one has lions painted on its side), and rigging. This tableau may show a single moment from a nautical festival, perhaps a spring ceremony to kick off a new season of sailing.

Note the difference between the surviving fragments of the original fresco and the modern infill in this restored presentation of a dolphin swimming alongside the ships.

4-16 CITADEL AT MYCENAE
Peloponnese, Greece. Aerial view. Site occupied c. 1600–1200 BCE; walls built c. 1340, 1250, 1200 BCE, creating a progressively larger enclosure.
Credit: © akg-images/Albatross/Duby Tal

time stronger and enclosing more space than the last. The second walls were pierced by the monumental Lion Gate (at bottom left in this view of the archaeological site from above). The final walls were extended to protect the water supply, an underground cistern. These walls were about 25 feet thick and nearly 30 feet high. Their drywall masonry, using largely unworked boulders, is known as **cyclopean**, because at one time it was believed that only the enormous Cyclopes (legendary one-eyed giants) could have moved such massive stones.

Even today, the monumental gateway to the citadel at Mycenae (**FIG. 4-17**) is an impressive reminder of the importance of the city. As in Near Eastern citadels, the Lion Gate was provided with guardian figures, which stand above the door rather than to the sides in the door jambs. The gate is today a simple opening, but its importance is indicated by the material of the flanking walls, a conglomerate stone that can be polished to glistening multicolors. A corbeled relieving **arch** above the lintel forms a triangle filled with a limestone panel bearing a grand heraldic composition—guardian beasts flanking a single Minoan column that swells upward to a large, bulbous capital.

The archival photograph (SEE FIG. 4-17) shows a group posing jauntily outside the gate, including Heinrich

Schliemann standing at the left, and his wife and partner in archaeology, Sophia, sitting at the right. Schliemann had already "discovered" Troy, and when he turned his attention to Mycenae in 1876, he unearthed graves containing rich treasures, including gold masks. The grave circle he excavated lay just inside the Lion Gate.

The Lion Gate has been the subject of much speculation in recent years. What are the animals? What does the architectural feature mean? How is the imagery to be interpreted? The beasts supporting and defending the column are magnificent, supple creatures rearing up on hind legs. Their faces must once have been turned toward the visitor, but today only the attachment holes from their heads remain.

A metaphor for power, the lions rest their feet on Minoan-style altars. Between them stands the mysterious Minoan column, also on the altar base. Clearly the Mycenaeans are borrowing symbolic vocabulary from Crete. But scholars do not agree on what this composition means: It may represent a temple, a palace, the entire city, or the god of the place. The column and capital support a lintel or architrave, which in turn supports the butt ends of logs forming rafters of the horizontal roof, so the most likely theory is that the structure is the symbol of a palace or a temple. But some scholars suggest that by extension it becomes the symbol of a king or a deity. If so, the imagery of the Lion Gate, with its combination of guardian beasts and divine or royal palace, signifies the legitimate power of the ruler of Mycenae.

From the Lion Gate, the Great Ramp led up the hillside past a grave circle to the courtyard for the building occupying the highest point in the center of the city, which may have been the residence of a ruler. From the courtyard one entered a porch, a vestibule, and finally the megaron, which seems to be the intended destination, in contrast to Minoan complexes where the courtyard itself seems to be the destination. The great room of a typical megaron had a central hearth surrounded by four large columns that supported the ceiling. The roof above the hearth was probably raised to admit light and air and permit smoke to escape (SEE FIG. 4-18). Some architectural historians think that the megaron eventually came to be associated with royalty. The later Greeks adapted its form when building temples, which they saw as earthly palaces for their gods.

PYLOS   The rulers of Mycenae fortified their city, but the people of Pylos, in the extreme southwest of the Peloponnese, perhaps felt that their more remote and defensible location made them less vulnerable to attack. This seems not to have been the case, for within a century of its construction in c. 1340 BCE, the palace at Pylos was destroyed by fires, apparently set during the violent upheavals that brought about the collapse of Mycenae itself.

4-17 LION GATE, MYCENAE

c. 1250 BCE. Limestone relief, height of sculpture approx. 9′ 6″ (2.9 m).

In this historic photograph Heinrich Schliemann, director of the excavation beginning in 1876, stands to the left of the gate, and his wife and partner in archaeology, Sophia, sits to the right.

House of Columns

megaron

Great Ramp

postern gate

"Palace" entrance

Warrior Vase House

Grave Circle A

Lion Gate

4-18 RECONSTRUCTION DRAWING OF THE CITADEL AT MYCENAE AT ITS MOST DEVELOPED STATE

Unlike at Knossos and Akrotiri, where we can understand multistory structures because multiple levels survived and have been excavated, at Mycenae we have, for the most part, only foundations. To a certain extent, we can only speculate about the upper portions of these buildings.

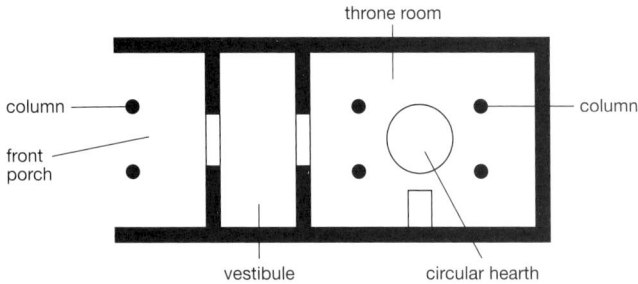

4-19 PLAN OF THE MEGARON OF THE PYLOS PALACE
c. 1300–1200 BCE.

The architectural complex at Pylos was built on a raised site without fortifications, organized around a special area that included an archive, storerooms, workshops, and a megaron (**FIG. 4-19**) with a formal throne room that may also have been used to host feasting rituals involving elite members of the community. Including a porch and vestibule facing the courtyard, the Pylos megaron was a magnificent display of architectural and decorative skill.

The reconstruction shown here (**FIG. 4-20**) shows how it might have looked. Every inch was painted—floors, ceilings, beams, and door frames with brightly colored abstract designs, and walls with paintings of large mythical animals and highly stylized plant and landscape forms. Flanking the throne (on the back wall of the reconstruction) are monumental paintings of lions and griffins. A circular hearth sits in the middle, set into a floor finished with plaster painted with imitations of stone and tile patterns. There was a spot in the megaron where priests and priestesses poured libations to a deity from a ceremonial rhyton, fostering communication between the people of Pylos and their god or gods.

Clay tablets found in the ruins of the palace include an inventory of its elegant furnishings. The listing on one tablet reads: "One ebony chair with golden back decorated with birds; and a footstool decorated with ivory pomegranates. One ebony chair with ivory back carved with a pair of finials and with a man's figure and heifers; one footstool, ebony inlaid with ivory and pomegranates."

Mycenaean Tombs

SHAFT GRAVES   Tombs were given much greater prominence in the Helladic culture of the mainland than they were by the Minoans, and ultimately they became the most architecturally sophisticated monuments of the entire Aegean Bronze Age. The earliest burials were in **shaft graves**, vertical pits 20 to 25 feet deep. In Mycenae, the graves of important people were enclosed in a circle of standing stone slabs. In these graves, the ruling families laid out their dead in opulent dress and jewelry and surrounded them with ceremonial weapons, gold and silver wares, and other articles indicative of their status, wealth, and power.

Among the 30 pounds of gold objects Schliemann found in the shaft graves of Mycenae were five funerary masks, one of which he identified as the face of Agamemnon, commander-in-chief of the Greek forces in Homer's account of the Trojan War (**FIG. 4-21**). We now know the masks have nothing to do with the heroes of the Trojan War, since the Mycenae graves are about 300 years older than Schliemann believed and the burial practices they display were different from those described by Homer.

4-20 RECONSTRUCTION DRAWING OF THE MEGARON (GREAT ROOM) OF THE PYLOS PALACE

c. 1300–1200 BCE. Watercolor by Piet de Jong.

English artist Piet de Jong (1887–1967) began his career as an architect, but his service in the post-World War I reconstruction of Greece inspired him to focus his talents on recording and reconstructing Greek archaeological excavations. In 1922, Arthur Evans called him to work on the reconstructions at Knossos. Piet de Jong spent the rest of his life creating fanciful but archaeologically informed visions of the original appearance of some of the greatest twentieth-century discoveries of ancient Greece and the Aegean during a long association with the British School of Archaeology in Athens.

Credit: © akg-images/De Agostini Picture Lib./G. Dagli Orti

RECOVERING THE PAST

THE "MASK OF AGAMEMNON"

One of Heinrich Schliemann's most famous discoveries in the shaft graves in Mycenae was a solid gold mask that had been placed over the face of a body he claimed was the legendary Agamemnon (SEE FIG. 4–21), uncovered on November 30, 1876. But Schliemann's identification of the mask with this king of Homeric legend has been disproven, and even the authenticity of the mask itself has been called into question over the last 30 years.

Doubts are rooted in a series of stylistic features that separate this mask from the other four excavated by Schliemann in Grave Circle A: the treatment of the eyes and eyebrows, the cut-out separation of the ears from the flap of gold around the face, and, most strikingly, the beard and handlebar mustache that have suspicious parallels with nineteenth-century fashion in facial hair. Suspicions founded on such anomalies are reinforced by Schliemann's own history of deceit and embellishment when characterizing his life and discoveries,

not to mention his freewheeling excavation practices when judged against current archaeological standards.

Some specialists have claimed a middle ground between genuine or fake for the mask, suggesting that the artifact itself may be authentic, but that Schliemann quickly subjected it to an overzealous restoration to make the face of "Agamemnon" seem more heroic and noble—at least to viewers in his own day—than the faces of the four other Mycenaean funerary masks. But another scholar has argued that, in fact, this particular mask is not the one Schliemann associated with Agamemnon, undercutting some of the principal arguments for questioning its authenticity in the first place.

The resolution of these questions awaits a full scientific study to determine the nature of the alloy (gold was regularly mixed with small amounts of other metals to make it stronger) from which this mask was made, as well as a microscopic analysis of its technique and the appearance of its surface.

4–21 "MASK OF AGAMEMNON"
Funerary mask, from Shaft Grave V, Grave Circle A, Mycenae, Greece. c. 1600–1550 BCE. Gold, height approx. 12″ (35 cm). National Archaeological Museum, Athens.

Credit: © Craig & Marie Mauzy, Athens

Also found in these shaft graves were bronze **DAGGER BLADES** (FIG. 4–22) decorated with inlaid scenes, further evidence of the wealth of the Mycenaean ruling elite. To form the decoration of daggers like this, Mycenaean artists cut shapes out of different-colored metals (copper, silver, and gold), inlaid them in the bronze blade, and then added fine details in niello (see "Aegean Metalworking" on page 93). In Homer's *Iliad*, the poet describes similar decoration on Agamemnon's armor and Achilles' shield. The blade shown here depicts four lunging hunters—Minoan in style—attacking a charging lion that has already downed one of their companions, who lies under the lion's front legs. Two other lions retreat in full flight. Like the bull in the Minoan fresco (SEE FIG. 4–7), these fleeing animals stretch out in the "flying-gallop" pose to indicate speed and energy.

4–22 DAGGER BLADE WITH LION HUNT
From Shaft Grave IV, Grave Circle A, Mycenae, Greece. c. 1550–1500 BCE. Bronze inlaid with gold, silver, and niello; length 9⅜″ (23.8 cm). National Archaeological Museum, Athens.

Credit: © akg-images/Nimatallah

4-23 CUTAWAY DRAWING OF THOLOS, THE SO-CALLED TREASURY OF ATREUS

Credit: © Dorling Kindersley

THOLOS TOMBS By about 1600 BCE, members of the elite class on the mainland had begun building large above-ground burial places commonly referred to as **tholos** tombs (popularly known as **beehive tombs** because of their rounded, conical shape). More than 100 such tombs have been found, nine of them in the vicinity of Mycenae. Possibly the most impressive is the so-called **TREASURY OF ATREUS** (FIGS. 4-23, 4-24), which dates from about 1300 to 1200 BCE.

A walled passageway through the earthen mound covering the tomb, about 114 feet long and 20 feet wide and open to the sky, led to the entrance, which was 34 feet high and had a door 16½ feet high faced with bronze plaques. On either side of the entrance were columns created from a green stone found near Sparta and carved with decoration. The section above the lintel had smaller engaged columns on each side, and the relieving triangle was disguised behind a red-and-green engraved marble panel. The main tomb chamber (FIG. 4-25) is a circular room, 47½ feet in diameter and 43 feet high.

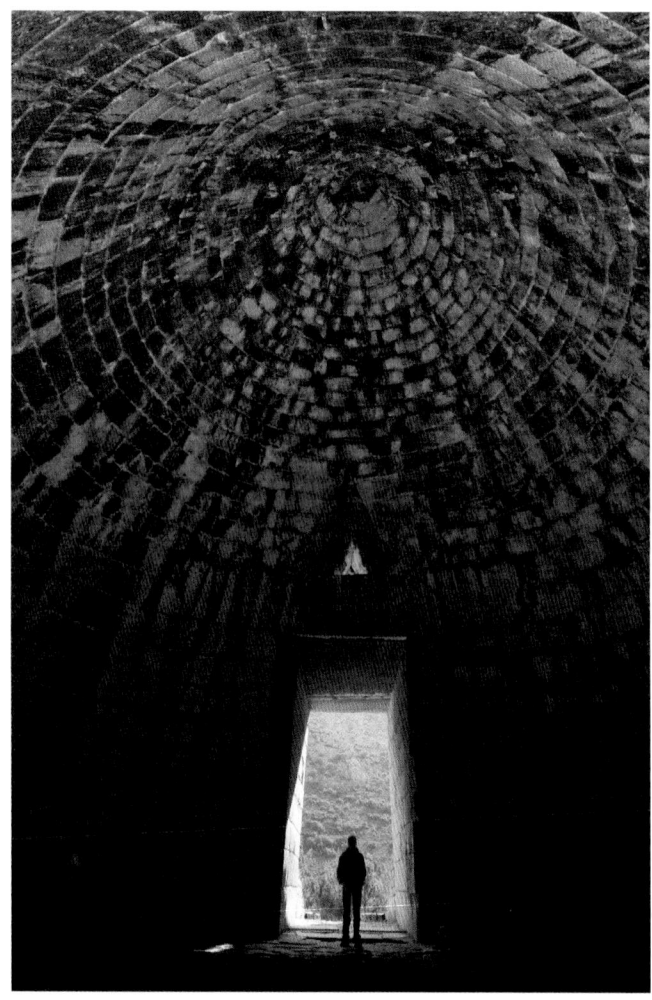

4-25 CORBEL VAULT, INTERIOR OF THOLOS, THE SO-CALLED TREASURY OF ATREUS

Limestone vault, height approx. 43′ (13 m), diameter 47′6″ (14.48 m).

For over a thousand years after it was constructed, this vast vaulted chamber remained the largest unobstructed interior space built in Europe. It was exceeded in size only by the Roman Pantheon (SEE FIG.6–48), built 110–128 CE.

Credit: © Craig & Marie Mauzy, Athens

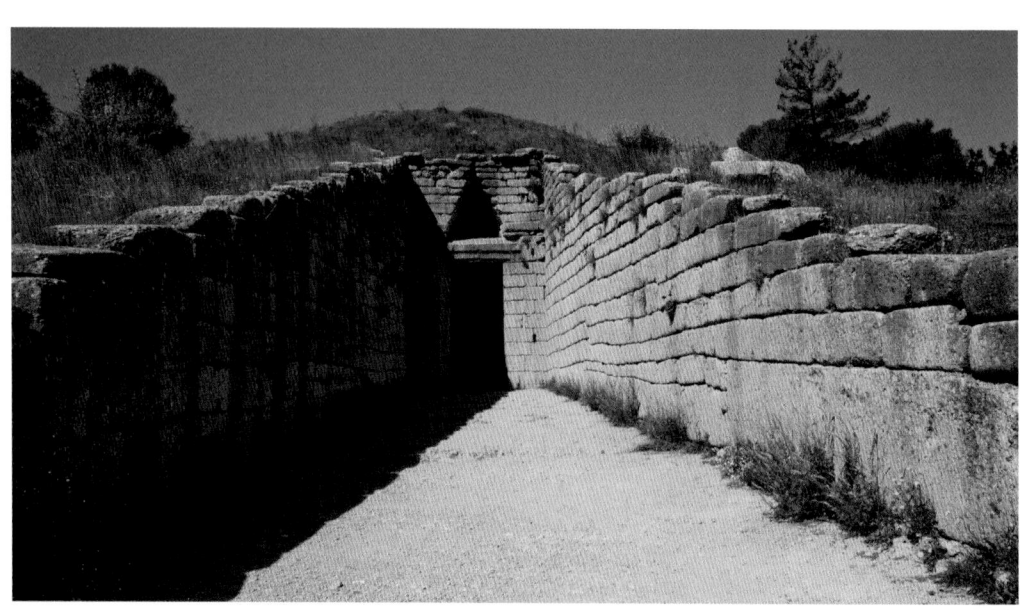

4-24 EXTERIOR VIEW OF THOLOS, THE SO-CALLED TREASURY OF ATREUS

Mycenae, Greece. c. 1300–1200 BCE.

Credit: © Craig & Marie Mauzy, Athens

It is roofed with a **corbeled vault.** The vault is built up in regular **courses**, or layers, of **ashlar**—precisely cut blocks of stone—smoothly leaning inward and carefully calculated to meet in a single capstone (the topmost stone that joins the sides and completes the structure) at the peak. Covered with earth, the tomb became a conical hill. It was a remarkable engineering feat.

Ceramics

In the final phase of the Helladic Bronze Age, Mycenaean potters created highly refined ceramics. A large **krater**—a bowl for mixing water and wine, used both in feasts and as grave markers—is an example of the technically sophisticated wares being produced on the Greek mainland between 1300 and 1100 BCE. Decorations could be highly stylized, like the scene of marching men on the **WARRIOR KRATER** (FIG. 4-26). On the side shown here, a woman at the far left bids farewell to a group of helmeted men with lances and large shields marching off to the right. The vibrant energy of the Harvester Rhyton or the Vapheio Cup has changed to the regular rhythm inspired by the tramping feet of disciplined warriors. The only indication of the woman's emotions is the gesture of an arm raised to her head, a symbol of mourning. The men seem to be interchangeable parts in a rigidly disciplined war machine.

The succeeding centuries, between about 1100 and 900 BCE, were a time of transformation in the Aegean

4-26 WARRIOR KRATER
From Mycenae, Greece. c. 1300–1100 BCE. Ceramic, height 16″ (41 cm). National Archaeological Museum, Athens.

Credit: © Craig & Marie Mauzy, Athens

marked by less political, economic, and artistic complexity and control. A new culture was forming, one that looked back upon the exploits of the Helladic warrior-kings as the glories of a heroic age, while setting the stage for a new Greek civilization.

Think About It

1 Choose a picture or sculpture of a human figure from two of the ancient Aegean cultures examined in this chapter. Characterize how the artist represents the human form and how that representation could be related to the cultural significance of the works in their original contexts.

2 Assess the methods of two archaeologists whose work is discussed in this chapter. How have they recovered, reconstructed, and interpreted the material culture of the Aegean Bronze Age?

3 What explanations have art historians proposed for the use and cultural significance of the figures of women that have been excavated in the Cyclades?

4 Compare the plans of the architectural complexes at Knossos and Mycenae. How have the arrangements of the buildings helped archaeologists to think about how these complexes were related to their cultural contexts and ritual or political uses?

Crosscurrents

Discuss the differences in style between these two works of ancient painting. Consider the different modes of representing human figures as well as the ways those figures are related to their surroundings. Could there be a relationship between the architectural context and the style of presentation?

FIG. 3–36

FIG. 4–1

5-1 Exekias (potter and painter) **AJAX AND ACHILLES PLAYING A GAME**

c. 540–530 BCE. Black-figure painting on a ceramic amphora, height of amphora 24″ (61 cm). Musei Vaticani, Rome.

Credit: Photo © Musei Vaticani/IKONA

Chapter 5
Art of Ancient Greece

 ## Learning Objectives

5.a Identify the visual hallmarks of Greek Geometric, Orientalizing, Archaic, Classical, and Hellenistic period art for formal, technical, and expressive qualities.

5.b Interpret the meaning of works of Greek Geometric, Orientalizing, Archaic, Classical, and Hellenistic period art based on their themes, subjects, and symbols.

5.c Relate artists and works of the distinct periods of Greek Geometric, Orientalizing, Archaic, Classical, and Hellenistic period art to their cultural, economic, and political contexts.

5.d Apply the vocabulary and concepts used to discuss ancient Greek art, artists, and art history.

5.e Interpret ancient Greek art using appropriate art historical methods, such as observation, comparison, and inductive reasoning.

5.f Select visual and textual evidence in various media to support an argument or an interpretation of ancient Greek art.

This elegantly contoured **amphora** was conceived and created to be more than the all-purpose storage jar signaled by its shape, substance, and size (**FIG. 5–1**). A strip around the belly of its bulging form was reserved by Exekias—the mid-sixth-century BCE Athenian artist who signed it proudly as both potter and painter—for a narrative episode from the Trojan War, one of the central stories of the ancient Greeks' mythical conception of their past. Two heroic warriors, Achilles and Ajax, sit across from each other, supporting themselves on their spears as they lean in toward the block between them that serves as a makeshift board for their game of dice. Ajax, to the right, calls out "three"—the spoken word written out on the pot's surface as if coming from his mouth. Achilles counters with "four," the winning number, his victory already suggested by the visual prominence of the boldly silhouetted helmet on his head. (Ajax's headgear has been set aside on his shield, leaning behind him.) Ancient Greek viewers, however, would have understood the tragic irony of Achilles's victory. When these two warriors returned from this playful diversion into the serious contest of battle, Achilles would be killed—and soon afterward, the grieving Ajax would take his own life in despair.

The poignant narrative on this amphora is also a masterful composition. Crisscrossing diagonals and compressed overlapping of spears, bodies, and table describe spatial complexity as well as surface pattern. The varying textures of hair, armor, and clothing are dazzlingly evoked by the alternation between expanses of unarticulated surface and dense patterns of finely incised lines. Careful contours convey a sense of three-dimensional human form. And the arrangement coordinates with the shape of the vessel itself, its curving outline matched by the warriors' bending backs, the line of its handles continued in the tilt of the leaning shields.

There is no hint here of gods or kings. Focus rests on the private diversions of heroic warriors as well as on the identity and personal style of the artist who portrayed them. Supremely self-aware and self-confident, the ancient Greeks developed a concept of human capacity and responsibility that required a new visual expression. Greek art was centered in the material world, but it also conformed to strict ideals of beauty and mathematical concepts of design. This paralleled Greek philosophers' search for the human values of truth, virtue, and harmony, qualities that imbue both subject and style in this celebrated work.

The Emergence of Greek Civilization

What aspects of Greek geography, history, and religion create the background for the emergence of its ancient art and architecture?

Ancient Greece was a mountainous land of spectacular natural beauty. Olive trees and grapevines grew on the steep hillsides, producing oil and wine, but there was little good farmland. In towns, skilled artisans produced metal and ceramic wares to trade abroad for grain and raw materials. Greek merchant ships carried pots, olive oil, and bronzes from Athens, Corinth, and Aegina around the Mediterranean Sea, extending the Greek cultural orbit from mainland Greece south to the Peloponnese, north to Macedonia, and east to the Aegean islands and the coast of Asia Minor (**MAP 5–1**). Greek colonies in Italy, Sicily, and Asia Minor rapidly became powerful, independent commercial and cultural centers, but they remained tied to the homeland by language, heritage, religion, and art.

Within a remarkably brief time, Greek artists developed focused and distinctive ideals of human representation and architectural design that continue to exert a profound influence today. From about 900 BCE until about 100 BCE, they concentrated on a new, rather narrow range of subjects and produced an impressive body of work in a variety of media. Greek artists were restless. They continually sought to change and improve existing artistic trends, resulting in a striking stylistic evolution over the course of a few centuries. This is in stark contrast to the art of ancient Egypt, where a desire for continuity maintained stable artistic conventions for nearly 3,000 years.

Historical Background

In the ninth and eighth centuries BCE, long after Mycenaean dominance in the Aegean had come to an end, the Greeks began to form independently governed city-states. Each city-state was an autonomous region with a city—Athens, Corinth, Sparta—as its political, economic, religious, and cultural center. Each had its own form of government and

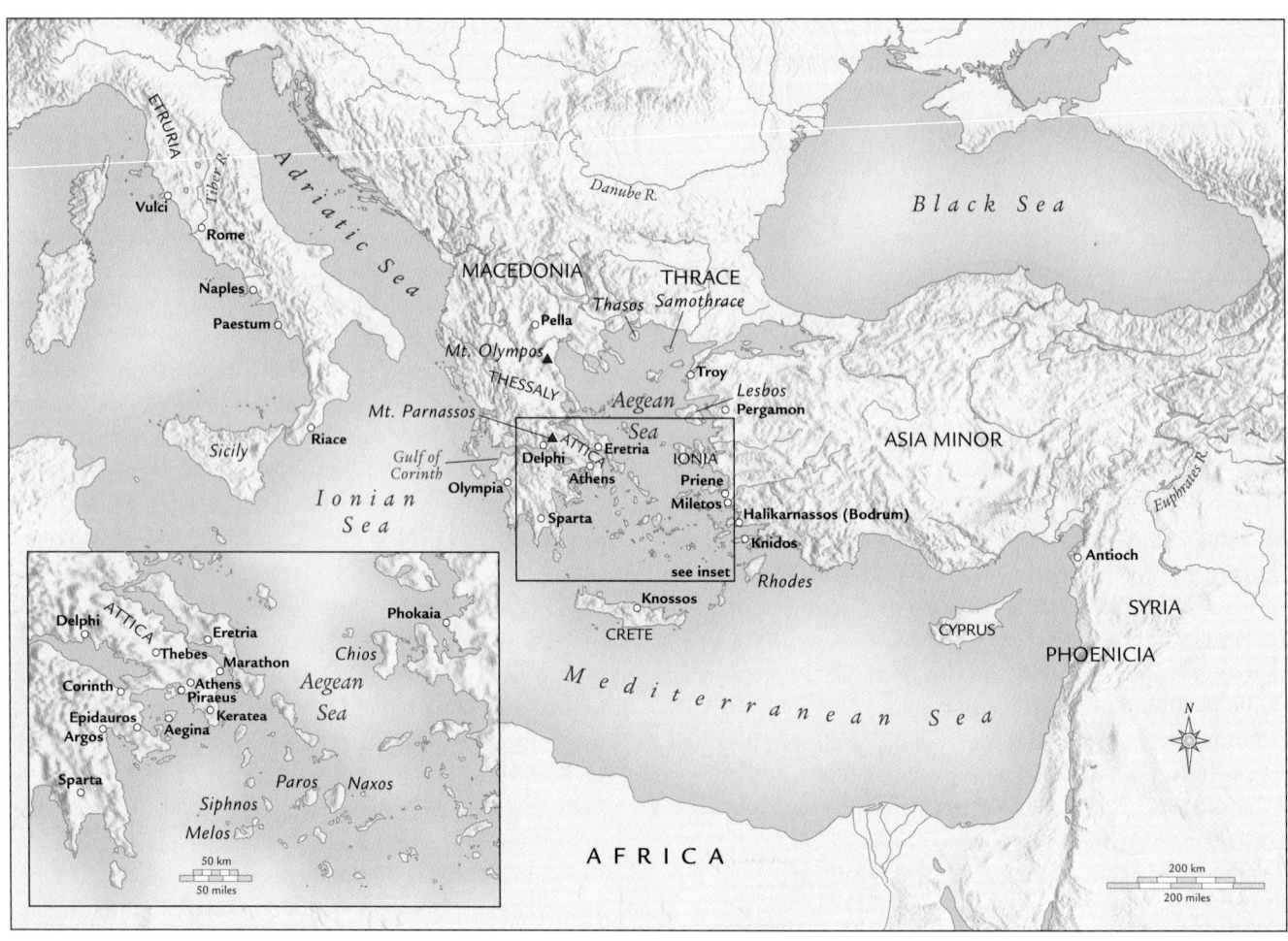

MAP 5–1 ANCIENT GREECE

The cultural heartland of ancient Greece consisted of the Greek mainland, the islands of the Aegean, and the west coast of Asia Minor, but colonies on the Italic peninsula and the island of Sicily extended Greek cultural influence farther west into the Mediterranean.

Art and its Contexts

GREEK AND ROMAN DEITIES

(The Roman form of the name is given after the Greek name.)

The Five Children of Earth and Sky

Zeus (Jupiter), supreme Olympian deity. Mature, bearded man, often holding scepter or lightning bolt; sometimes represented as an eagle.

Hera (Juno), goddess of marriage. Sister/wife of Zeus. Mature woman; cow and peacock are sacred to her.

Hestia (Vesta), goddess of the hearth. Sister of Zeus. Her sacred flame burned in communal hearths.

Poseidon (Neptune), god of the sea. Holds a three-pronged spear (trident).

Hades (Pluto), god of the underworld, the dead, and wealth.

The Seven Sky Gods, Offspring of the First Five

Ares (Mars), god of war. Son of Zeus and Hera.

Hephaistos (Vulcan), god of the forge, fire, and metal handcrafts. Son of Hera (in some myths, also of Zeus); husband of Aphrodite.

Apollo (Phoebus), god of the sun, light, truth, music, archery, and healing. Sometimes identified with Helios (the Sun), who rides a chariot across the daytime sky. Son of Zeus and Leto (a descendant of Earth); brother of Artemis.

Artemis (Diana), goddess of the hunt, wild animals, and the moon. Sometimes identified with Selene (the Moon), who rides a chariot or oxcart across the night sky. Daughter of Zeus and Leto; sister of Apollo. Carries bow and arrows and is accompanied by hunting dogs.

Athena (Minerva), goddess of wisdom, war, victory, and the city. Also goddess of handcrafts and other artistic skills. Daughter of Zeus; sprang fully grown from his head. Wears helmet and carries shield and spear.

Aphrodite (Venus), goddess of love. Daughter of Zeus and the water nymph Dione; alternatively, born of sea foam; wife of Hephaistos.

Hermes (Mercury), messenger of the gods, god of fertility and luck, guide of the dead to the underworld, and god of thieves and commerce. Son of Zeus and Maia, the daughter of Atlas, a Titan who supports the sky on his shoulders. Wears winged sandals and hat; carries caduceus, a wand with two snakes entwined around it.

Other Important Deities

Demeter (Ceres), goddess of grain and agriculture. Daughter of Kronos and Rhea, sister of Zeus and Hera.

Persephone (Proserpina), goddess of fertility and queen of the underworld. Wife of Hades; daughter of Demeter.

Dionysos (Bacchus), god of wine, the grape harvest, and inspiration. His female followers are called **maenads** (Bacchantes).

Eros (Cupid), god of love. In some myths, the son of Aphrodite. Shown as an infant or young boy, sometimes winged, carrying bow and arrows.

Pan (Faunus), protector of shepherds, god of the wilderness and of music. Half-man, half-goat, he carries panpipes.

Nike (Victory), goddess of victory. Often shown winged and flying.

economy, and each managed its own domestic and foreign affairs. The power of these city-states initially depended at least as much on their manufacturing and commercial skills as on their military might.

Among the emerging city-states, Corinth, located on major land and sea trade routes, was one of the oldest and most powerful. By the sixth century BCE, Athens rose to commercial and cultural preeminence. Soon it had also established a representative government in which every community had its own assembly and magistrates. Citizenship was open only to Athenian men, but all citizens participated in the assembly, and all had an equal right to own private property, exercise freedom of speech, vote, hold public office, and serve in the army or navy. The census of 309 BCE in Athens listed 21,000 citizens, 10,000 foreign residents, and 400,000 others—that is, women, children, and slaves.

Religious Beliefs and Sacred Places

According to ancient Greek legend, the creation of the world involved a battle between the earth gods, called Titans, and the sky gods. The victors were the sky gods, whose home was believed to be atop Mount Olympus in the northeast corner of the Greek mainland. The Greeks saw their gods as immortal and endowed with supernatural powers, but they also visualized them in human form and attributed to them human weaknesses and emotions to a greater extent than the Egyptians and peoples of the ancient Near East had done. Among the most important deities were the supreme god and goddess, Zeus and Hera, and their offspring (see "Greek and Roman Deities" above).

Many sites throughout Greece, called **sanctuaries**, were thought to be sacred to one or more gods. The earliest sanctuaries included outdoor altars or shrines and a sacred natural element such as a tree, a rock, or a spring. As more buildings were added, a sanctuary might become a palatial home for the gods, with one or more temples, several treasuries for storing valuable offerings, various monuments and statues, housing for priests and visitors, an outdoor dancefloor or permanent theater for ritual performances and literary competitions, and a stadium for athletic events. The Sanctuary of Zeus near Olympia, in the western Peloponnese, housed an extensive athletic facility with training rooms and arenas for track-and-field events. It was here that athletic competitions, prototypes of today's Olympic Games, were held.

Greek sanctuaries (SEE FIGS. 5-5, 5-6) are quite different from the religious complexes of the ancient Egyptians (see, for example, the Temple of Amun at Karnak, FIG. 3-19). Egyptian builders dramatized the power of gods or god-rulers by organizing their temples along straight, processional ways. The Greeks, in contrast, treated each building and monument as an independent element to be integrated with the natural features of the site in an irregular arrangement that emphasized the exterior of each building as a discrete sculptural form on display.

Greek Art c. 900–c. 600 BCE

What are the distinguishing features of ancient Greek art during its Geometric and Orientalizing periods?

Around the mid eleventh century BCE, a new culture began to form on the Greek mainland. Athens began to develop as a major center of ceramic production, creating both sculpture and vessels decorated with organized abstract designs. In this Geometric period, the Greeks, as we now call them, were beginning to create their own architectural forms and were trading actively with their neighbors to the east. By c. 700 BCE, in a phase called the Orientalizing period, they began to incorporate exotic foreign motifs into their native art.

The Geometric Period

What we call the Geometric period flourished in Greece between 900 and 700 BCE, especially in the decoration of ceramic vessels with linear motifs, such as spirals, diamonds, and cross-hatching. This abstract vocabulary is strikingly different from the stylized plants, birds, and sea creatures that had characterized Minoan pots (SEE FIGS. 4-4, 4-11).

Large funerary vessels like the krater illustrated here (**FIG. 5-2**) were developed at this time for use as grave markers, many of which have been uncovered at the ancient cemetery of Athens just outside the Dipylon Gate, once the main western entrance into the city. This krater seems to provide a detailed pictorial record of funerary rituals associated with the important person whose death is commemorated by it. On the top register, the body of the deceased is shown lying on its side on a funeral bier, perhaps awaiting the relatively new Greek practice of cremation. Male and female figures stand on each side of the body, their arms raised and both hands placed on top of their heads in a gesture of anguish, as if they were literally

tearing their hair out with grief. In the register underneath, horse-drawn chariots and foot soldiers, who look like walking shields with tiny antlike heads and muscular legs, move in solemn procession.

The geometric shapes used to represent human figures on this pot—triangles for torsos; more triangles for the heads in profile; round dots for eyes; long, thin rectangles for arms; tiny waists; and long legs with bulging thigh and calf muscles—are what has given the Geometric style its name. Figures are shown in either full-frontal or full-profile views that emphasize flat patterns and crisp outlines. Any sense of the illusion of three-dimensional forms occupying real space has been avoided. But the artist has captured a deep sense of human loss through the stylized solemnity and strong rhythmic accents of the carefully arranged elements.

Egyptian funerary art reflected the strong belief that the dead in the afterworld could continue to engage in activities they enjoyed while alive. For the Greeks, the deceased entered a place of mystery and obscurity that living humans could not define precisely, and their funerary art, in contrast, focused on the emotional reactions of the survivors. The scene of mourning on this pot contains no

5-2 Attributed to the Hirschfeld Workshop **FUNERARY KRATER**
From the Dipylon Cemetery, Athens. c. 750–735 BCE. Ceramic, height 42⅝″ (108 cm). Metropolitan Museum of Art, New York. Rogers Fund, 1914. (14.130.14).

5-3 MAN AND CENTAUR
Perhaps from Olympia. c. 750 BCE. Bronze, height 4⁵⁄₁₆" (11.1 cm).
Metropolitan Museum of Art, New York. Gift of J. Pierpont Morgan, 1917.
(17.190.2072).

Credit: © 2016. Image copyright The Metropolitan Museum of Art/Art Resource/
Scala, Florence

The Orientalizing Period

By the seventh century BCE, painters in major pottery centers in Greece had moved away from the dense linear decoration of the Geometric style, preferring more open compositions built around large motifs—real and imaginary animals, abstract plant forms, and human figures. The source of these motifs can be traced to the arts of the Near East, Asia Minor, and Egypt. Greek painters did not simply copy the work of Eastern artists, however. Instead, they drew on work in a variety of media—including sculpture, metalwork, and textiles—to invent an entirely new approach to painting vessels.

The Orientalizing style (c. 700–600 BCE) began in Corinth, a port city where luxury wares from the Near East and Egypt inspired artists. The new style is evident in a Corinthian **olpe**, or wide-mouthed pitcher, dating to about 650–625 BCE (**FIG. 5-4**). Silhouetted creatures—lions, panthers, goats, deer, bulls, boars, and swans—stride in

5-4 OLPE (PITCHER)
From Corinth. c. 650–625 BCE. Ceramic with black-figure decoration, height 12⅞" (32.8 cm). J. Paul Getty Museum, Villa Collection, Pacific Palisades, CA (85.AE.89)

supernatural beings, nor any identifiable reference to an afterlife, only poignant evocations of the sentiments and rituals of those left behind on earth.

Greek artists of the Geometric period also produced figurines of wood, ivory, clay, and cast bronze. These small statues of humans and animals are similar in appearance to those painted on pots. A tiny bronze of this type, depicting a **MAN AND CENTAUR**—a mythical creature, part man and part horse (**FIG. 5-3**)—dates to about the same time as the funerary krater. Although there were wise and good centaurs in Greek lore, this work takes up the theme of battling man and centaur, prominent throughout the history of Greek art (SEE FIG. 5-39). The two figures confront each other after the man—perhaps Herakles—has stabbed the centaur; the spearhead is visible on the centaur's left side. Like the painter of the funerary krater from the same period, the sculptor has abstracted the body parts of these figures to basic geometric shapes, arranging them in a composition of solid forms and open, or negative, spaces that makes the piece interesting from multiple viewpoints. Most such sculptures have been found in sanctuaries, suggesting that they may have served as votive offerings to the gods.

horizontal bands against a light background with stylized flower forms called **rosettes** filling the spaces around them. An early example of the **black-figure** technique (see "Black-Figure and Red-Figure" on page 120), dark shapes define the silhouettes of the animals against a background of very pale buff, the natural color of the Corinthian clay. The artist incised fine details inside the silhouetted shapes with a sharp tool and added touches of white and red slip to enliven the design.

The Archaic Period, c. 600–480 BCE

What are the characteristic stylistic features of ancient Greek art and architecture during the Archaic period?

The Archaic period does not deserve its name. "Archaic" means "antiquated" or "old-fashioned," even "primitive," and the term was chosen by art historians who wanted to stress the contrast between what they perceived as the undeveloped art of this time and the subsequent Classical period, once thought to be the most admirable and highly developed phase of Greek art. But the Archaic period was

a time of great new achievement in Greece. In literature, Sappho wrote her inspired poetry on the island of Lesbos, while on another island the legendary storyteller, Aesop, crafted his animal fables. Artists and architects shared in the growing prosperity as city councils and wealthy individuals sponsored the creation of extraordinary sculpture and fine ceramics and commissioned elaborate civic and religious buildings in cities and sanctuaries.

The Sanctuary at Delphi

According to Greek myth, Zeus was said to have released two eagles from opposite ends of the earth, and they met exactly at the rugged mountain site of Apollo's sanctuary (**FIG. 5-5**). From very early times, the sanctuary at Delphi was renowned as an oracle, a place where the god Apollo was believed to communicate with humans by means of cryptic messages delivered through a human intermediary, or medium (the Pythia). The Greeks and their leaders routinely sought advice at oracles and attributed many twists of fate to misinterpretations of the Pythia's statements. Even foreign rulers journeyed to request help at Delphi.

5-5 AERIAL VIEW OF THE SANCTUARY OF APOLLO, DELPHI
Greece, 6th–3rd century BCE.

Credit: © DeAgostini/Superstock

5-6 RECONSTRUCTION DRAWING OF THE SANCTUARY OF APOLLO, DELPHI

Credit: © Dorling Kindersley

theater

Temple of Apollo

Treasury of the Athenians

Meeting Hall of the Knidians

Siphnian Treasury

Sikyonian Treasury

Arkadian monument

Stoa of Attalos

Altar of the Chians

Stoa of the Athenians

Sacred Way

Delphi was the site of the Pythian Games, which, like the Olympian Games, attracted participants from all over Greece. The principal events were athletic, music, dance, and poetry competitions in honor of Apollo. As at Olympia, hundreds of statues dedicated to the victors of the competitions, as well as mythological figures, filled the sanctuary grounds. The sanctuary of Apollo was significantly developed during the Archaic period and included the main temple, performance and athletic areas, treasuries, and other buildings and monuments, which made full use of limited space on the hillside (**FIG. 5–6**).

After visitors had climbed the steep path up the lower slopes of Mount Parnassos, they entered the sanctuary by a ceremonial gate in the southeast corner. From there they zigzagged up the Sacred Way, so named because it was the route of religious processions during festivals. Moving past the numerous treasuries and memorials built by the city-states, they arrived at the long colonnade of the Temple of Apollo, rebuilt in c. 530 BCE on the site of an earlier temple. Below the temple was a **stoa**, a columned pavilion open on three sides, built by the people of Athens. There visitors rested, talked, or watched ceremonial dancing. At the top of the sanctuary hill was a stadium area for athletic contests.

TREASURY OF THE SIPHNIANS Sanctuaries also included treasuries built by the citizens of Greek city-states to house their offerings. The small but luxurious **TREASURY OF THE SIPHNIANS** (**FIG. 5–7**) was built in the sanctuary of Apollo at Delphi by the residents of the island of Siphnos in the Cyclades, between about 530 and 525 BCE.

5-7 RECONSTRUCTION DRAWING OF THE TREASURY OF THE SIPHNIANS

Sanctuary of Apollo, Delphi. c. 530–525 BCE.

This small treasury building at Delphi was originally elegant and richly ornamented. The figure sculpture and decorative moldings were once painted in strong colors, mainly dark blue, bright red, and white, with touches of yellow to resemble gold.

5-8 BATTLE BETWEEN THE GODS AND THE GIANTS
Fragments of the north frieze of the Treasury of the Siphnians, Sanctuary of Apollo, Delphi. c. 530–525 BCE. Marble, height 26″ (66 cm).
Archaeological Museum, Delphi.

Credit: © Craig & Marie Mauzy, Athens

It survives today only in fragments housed in the museum at Delphi. Instead of columns, the builders used two stately **caryatids**—columns carved in the form of women clothed in finely pleated, flowing garments, raised on **pedestals**, and balancing elaborately carved capitals on their heads. The capitals support a tall **entablature** conforming to the **Ionic order**, which features a plain, or three-panel, **architrave** and a continuous carved **frieze** set off by richly carved moldings (see "The Greek Orders" opposite).

Both the continuous frieze and the **pediments** of the Siphnian Treasury were originally filled with relief sculpture. A surviving section of the frieze from the building's north side, which shows a scene from the legendary **BATTLE BETWEEN THE GODS AND THE GIANTS**, is notable for its complex representation of space (**FIG. 5-8**). To give a sense of three-dimensional recession, the sculptors overlapped the figures—sometimes three deep—and varied the depth of the relief to convey different placements in space. Originally such sculptures were painted with bright colors to enhance the lifelike effect.

Temples

For centuries ancient Greeks had worshiped at sanctuaries where an outdoor altar stood within an enclosed sacred area called a **temenos** reserved for worship. Sometimes temples sheltering a statue of a god were incorporated into these sanctuaries, often as later additions to an established sanctuary. A number of standardized temple plans evolved, ranging from simple, one-room structures with columned **porches** (a covered, open space in front of an entrance) to buildings with double porches (located at front and back) surrounded entirely by columns. Builders also experimented with the design of temple

elevations—the arrangement, proportions, and appearance of the columns and the lintels—which now grew into elaborate entablatures. Two specific elevation designs emerged during the Archaic period: the **Doric order** and the Ionic order. The **Corinthian order**, a variant of the Ionic order, would develop later (see "The Greek Orders" opposite).

A particularly well-preserved Archaic Doric temple, built around 550 BCE, still stands at the former Greek colony of Poseidonia (Roman Paestum) about 50 miles south of the present-day city of Naples, Italy (**FIG. 5-9**). Dedicated to Hera, the wife of Zeus, it is known today as Hera I to distinguish it from a second, adjacent temple to Hera built about a century later. A row of columns called the peristyle surrounded the main room, the **cella**. The columns of Hera I are especially robust—only about four times as high as their maximum diameter—and topped with a widely flaring capital and a broad, blocky **abacus**, creating an impression of great stability and permanence. As the column shafts rise, they swell in the middle and contract again toward the top, a refinement known as **entasis**, giving them a sense of energy and lift. Hera I has an uneven number of columns—nine—across the short ends of the peristyle, with a column instead of a space at the center of the two ends. The entrance to the **pronaos** (enclosed vestibule) has three columns in antis (between flanking wall piers), and a row of columns runs down the center of the wide cella to help support the ceiling and roof. The unusual two-aisle, two-door arrangement leading to the small room at the end of the cella suggests that the temple had two presiding deities: Hera and Poseidon (patron of the city), Hera and Zeus, or perhaps Hera in her two manifestations (as warrior and protector of the city and as mother and protector of children).

Elements of Architecture
THE GREEK ORDERS

Each of the three Classical Greek architectural **orders**—Doric, Ionic, and Corinthian—constitutes a system of interdependent parts whose proportions are based on mathematical ratios. No element of an order could be changed without producing a corresponding change in other elements.

The basic components are the **column** and the entablature, which function as post and lintel in the structural system. All three types of columns have a **shaft** and a capital; Ionic and Corinthian also have a base. The shafts are formed of stacked round sections, or **drums**, which are joined inside by metal pegs. In Greek temple architecture, columns stand on the **stylobate**, the "floor" of the temple, which rests on top of a set of steps that form the temple's base, known as the **stereobate**.

In the Doric order, shafts sit directly on the stylobate without a base. They are **fluted**, or channeled, with sharp edges. The height of the substantial columns ranges from five-and-a-half to seven times the diameter of the base. A necking at the top of the shaft provides a transition to the capital itself, composed of the rounded **echinus** and the tabletlike abacus. The entablature includes the architrave, the distinctive frieze of alternating **triglyphs** and **metopes**, and the **cornice**, the topmost, projecting horizontal element. The roofline may have decorative waterspouts and terminal decorative elements called **acroteria**.

The Ionic order has more elongated proportions than the Doric, the height of a column being about nine times the diameter of its base. The flutes on the columns are deeper and are separated by flat surfaces called **fillets**. The capital has a distinctive, spiral-scrolled **volute**; the entablature has a three-panel architrave, continuous sculptured or decorated frieze, and richer decorative moldings.

The Corinthian order, a variant of the Ionic order originally developed by the Greeks for use in interiors, was eventually used on temple exteriors as well. Its elaborate capitals are sheathed with stylized **acanthus** leaves that rise from a convex band called the **astragal**.

Doric order   **Ionic order**   **Corinthian order**

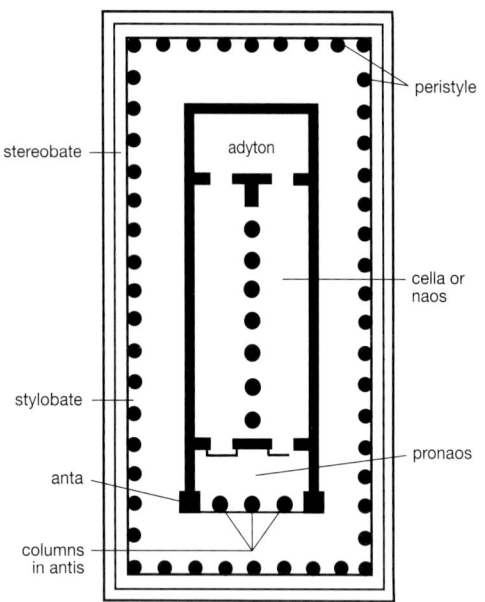

Labels on plan: peristyle, stereobate, adyton, cella or naos, stylobate, anta, pronaos, columns in antis

5-9A PLAN OF THE TEMPLE OF HERA I, POSEIDONIA (ROMAN PAESTUM)

Southern Italy. c. 550–540 BCE.

5-9B EXTERIOR VIEW OF THE TEMPLE OF HERA I, POSEIDONIA (ROMAN PAESTUM)

Southern Italy. c. 550–540 BCE.

Credit: © Fotografica Foglia, Naples

5-10 TEMPLE OF APHAIA, AEGINA

View from the east. c. 500 or c. 475 BCE. Column height about 17′ (5.18 m).

Credit: © Craig & Marie Mauzy, Athens

5-11 RECONSTRUCTION DRAWING OF THE TEMPLE OF APHAIA, AEGINA

c. 500 or c. 475 BCE.

Credit: Courtesy of Laurence King Publishing, John Griffiths Pedley, *Greek Art and Archaeology*, 4th edition ©2007

THE TEMPLE OF APHAIA ON AEGINA A fully developed and somewhat sleeker Doric temple than the one from Poseidonia was built on the island of Aegina during the first quarter of the fifth century BCE in a sanctuary dedicated to a local goddess named Aphaia (**FIG. 5-10**). Spectacularly sited on a hill overlooking the sea, the temple is reasonably well preserved, in spite of the loss of pediments, roof, and sections of its colonnade. Enough evidence remains to form a reliable reconstruction of its original appearance (**FIG. 5-11**).

The plan combines 6 columns on the façades with 12 on the sides, and the cella—whose roof was supported by superimposed colonnades—could be entered from porches on both short sides. The slight swelling of the columns (entasis) seen at Poseidonia is evident here as well, and the outside triglyphs are pushed to the ends of frieze, out of alignment with the column underneath them, to avoid the awkwardness of half a metope (rectangular panel with a relief or painting) at the corner.

Like most Greek temples, this building was neither isolated nor situated in open space, but set in relation to an outside altar where religious ceremonies were focused (**FIG. 5-12**). By enclosing the temple within a walled area, or temenos, the designer could control the viewer's initial experience of the temple. As the viewer entered the sacred space through a gatehouse—the propylon—the temple would be seen at an oblique angle. Unlike ancient Egyptian temples, where long processional approaches led visitors directly to the flat entrance façade of a building (SEE FIGS. 3-19, 3-23), the Greek architect revealed from the outset the full shape of a closed, compact, sculptural mass, inviting viewers not to enter seeking something within, but rather to walk around the exterior, exploring the rich sculptural embellishment on the pediments and frieze. Cult ceremonies, after all, took place at an altar outside Greek temples.

5-12 PLAN OF COMPLEX OF THE TEMPLE OF APHAIA, AEGINA

c. 500 or c. 475 BCE.

ARCHITECTURAL SCULPTURE AT AEGINA Modern viewers will not find exterior sculpture at Aegina. Nothing remains from the metopes, and substantial surviving portions of the two pediments were purchased in the early nineteenth century by the future Ludwig I of Bavaria and are now exhibited in Munich. The triangular pediments in Greek temples created challenging compositional problems for sculptors intent on fitting figures into the tapering spaces at the outside corners, since the scale of figures could not change, only their poses. The west pediment from Aegina (**FIG. 5-13**)—traditionally dated about 500–490 BCE, before its eastern counterpart—represents a creative solution that became a design standard, appearing with variations throughout the fifth century BCE. The subject of the

5–13 WEST PEDIMENT OF THE TEMPLE OF APHAIA, AEGINA
c. 500–490 or 470s BCE. Width about 49′ (15 m). Surviving fragments as assembled in the Staatliche Antikensammlungen und Glyptothek, Munich (early restorations removed).

Credit: Staatliche Antikensammlungen, Munich

pediment, rendered in fully three-dimensional figures, is the participation of local warriors in the military expedition against Troy. Fallen warriors fill the angles at both ends of the pediment base, while others crouch and lunge, rising in height toward an image of Athena as warrior goddess—who can fill the elevated, pointed space at the center peak since she is allowed to be represented larger (hierarchic scale) than the humans who flank her.

Among the best-preserved fragments from the west pediment is the **DYING WARRIOR** from the far right corner (**FIG. 5–14**). This tragic figure struggles to rise up, supported on bent leg and elbow, in order to extract an arrow from his chest even though his death seems certain. The figure originally would have been painted and fitted with authentic bronze accessories, heightening the sense of reality.

A similar figure appeared on the east pediment (**FIG. 5–15**), traditionally seen as postdating the west pediment by a decade or so. The sculptor of this dying warrior also exploited the difficult framework of the pediment corner, only here, instead of an uplifted frontal form in profile, we see a body turning in space. The figure is more precariously balanced on his shield, clearly about to collapse. There is an increased sense of softness in the portrayal of human flesh and a greater sophistication in fitting the bodily posture not only to the tapering shape of the pediment, but also to the expression of the warrior's own agony and vulnerability, which in turn inspires a sense of pathos or empathy in the viewer.

For decades, art historians taught that over the course of a decade, two successive sets of sculptures on Aegina allow us to trace the transition from Archaic toward Early Classical art. Recently, however, Andrew Stewart has reviewed the archaeological evidence on the Athenian Akropolis and Aegina and reached a very different conclusion. He questions the traditional dating of key works from the transition between Archaic and Early Classical

art—notably the Aegina pediment sculpture and the Kritios Boy (SEE FIG. 5–27)—placing them after the Persian invasion of 580–579 BCE and raising the question of whether Greek victory over this outside enemy might have been a factor in the stylistic change. In the case of the Aegina temple, this re-dating becomes especially interesting. Instead of assuming that the difference in style between the western and eastern pediments represents a time gap separating their production, Stewart proposes that the ensembles were both produced during the 470s by two workshops, one conservative and one progressive.

COLOR IN GREEK SCULPTURE For many modern viewers, it comes as a real surprise, even a shock, that the stone sculptures of ancient Greece did not always have stark white marble surfaces, comparable in appearance to—and consistent in taste with—the more recent, but still classicizing sculptures of Michelangelo or Canova (SEE FIGS. 21–14, 2–15; 30–14). But they were originally painted with brilliant colors. A close examination of Greek sculpture and architecture has long revealed evidence of polychromy, even to the unaided eye, but our understanding of the original appearance of these works has been greatly enhanced by the work of German scholar Vinzenz Brinkmann. Since the 1980s, Brinkmann has used visual and scientific analysis to evaluate the traces of painting that remain on ancient Greek sculpture, employing tools such as ultraviolet and x-ray fluorescence, microscopy, and pigment analysis. Based on this research, he and his colleague Ulrike Koch-Brinkmann have made reconstructions to show the exuberant effect these works would have had when they were new. Illustrated here is their painted reconstruction of a kneeling archer (**FIGS. 5–16, 5–17**) from about 500 (or during the 470s) BCE that once formed part of the west pediment of the Temple of Aphaia at Aegina.

5-14 DYING WARRIOR

From the right corner of the west pediment of the Temple of Aphaia, Aegina. c. 500–490 or 470s BCE. Marble, length 5'6" (1.68 m). Staatliche Antikensammlungen und Glyptothek, Munich.

Credit: Staatliche Antikensammlungen, Munich/ Studio Koppermann

5-15 DYING WARRIOR

From the left corner of the east pediment of the Temple of Aphaia, Aegina. c. 490–480 or 470s BCE. Marble, length 6' (1.83 m). Staatliche Antikensammlungen und Glyptothek, Munich.

Credit: Staatliche Antikensammlungen, Munich/ Studio Koppermann

5-16 Vinzenz Brinkmann and Ulrike Koch-Brinkmann **RECONSTRUCTION OF ARCHER**

From the west pediment of the Temple of Aphaia, Aegina. 2004 CE. Staatliche Antikensammlungen und Glyptothek, Munich.

Credit: Staatliche Antikensammlungen, Munich/Studio Koppermann

5-17 ARCHER ("PARIS")

From the west pediment of the Temple of Aphaia, Aegina. c. 500–490 or 470s BCE. Marble. Staatliche Antikensammlungen und Glyptothek, Munich.

Credit: Staatliche Antikensammlungen, Munich/Studio Koppermann

To begin with, they have replaced features of the sculpture that had been lost—ringlet hair extensions, a bow, a quiver, and arrows—probably originally made of bronze or lead and attached to the stone after it was carved, using the holes still evident in the figure's hip and head. The biggest surprise, however, is the restoration of the diamond-shaped patterns originally painted on the archer's leggings and sleeves using pigments derived from malachite, azurite, arsenic, cinnabar, and charcoal. These were not simply colored in. The Greek artists created a sophisticated integration of three-dimensional form, color, and design: The patterning of the figure's leggings actually changes in size and shape in relation to the body beneath it, stretching out on the thighs and constricting on the ankles. Ancient authors indicate that sculpture was painted to make figures more lifelike, and these reconstructions certainly back up their description of the effect.

Free-Standing Sculpture

In addition to statues designed for temple exteriors, sculptors of the Archaic period created a new type of large, free-standing statue made of wood, **terra cotta** (clay fired over low heat), limestone, or white marble from the islands of Paros and Naxos. These figures were brightly painted and sometimes bore inscriptions indicating that individual men or women had commissioned them for a commemorative purpose. They have been found marking graves and in sanctuaries, where they lined the sacred way from the entrance to the main temple.

A female statue of this type is called a **kore** (plural, *korai*), Greek for "young woman," and a male statue is called a **kouros** (plural, *kouroi*), Greek for "young man." Archaic *korai*, always clothed, probably represented deities, priestesses, and nymphs (young female immortals who served as attendants to gods). *Kouroi*, nearly always nude, have been variously identified as gods, warriors, and victorious athletes. Because the Greeks associated young, athletic males with fertility and family continuity, the *kouroi* figures may have symbolized ancestors.

5-18 METROPOLITAN KOUROS

From Attica, Greece. c. 600–590 BCE. Marble, height 6′4⅝″ (1.95 m). Metropolitan Museum of Art, New York. Fletcher Fund, 1932. (32.11.1).

Credit: © 2016. Image copyright The Metropolitan Museum of Art/Art Resource/ Scala, Florence

METROPOLITAN KOUROS A *kouros* dated about 600 BCE (**FIG. 5-18**) recalls the pose and proportions of Egyptian sculpture. As with Egyptian figures such as the statue of Menkaure (SEE FIG. 3-10), this young Greek stands rigidly upright, arms at his sides, fists clenched, and one leg slightly in front of the other. However, the Greek artist has cut away all stone from around the body to make the human form free-standing. Archaic *kouroi* are also much less lifelike than their Egyptian forebears. Anatomy is delineated with linear ridges and grooves that form regular, symmetrical patterns. The head is ovoid and schematized, and the wiglike hair evenly knotted into tufts and tied back with a narrow ribbon. The eyes are relatively large and wide open, and the mouth forms a conventional closed-lip expression known as the **Archaic smile**. In Egyptian sculpture, male figures usually wore clothing associated with their status, such as the headdresses, necklaces, and kilts that identified them as kings. The total nudity of the Greek *kouroi* is unusual in ancient Mediterranean cultures, but it is acceptable—even valued—in the case of young men. Not so with women.

BERLIN KORE   Early Archaic *korai* are as severe and stylized as the male figures. The **BERLIN KORE**, a funerary statue found in a cemetery at Keratea and dated about 570–560 BCE, stands more than 6 feet tall (**FIG. 5-19**). The erect, full-bodied figure takes an immobile pose—accentuated by a bulky crown and thick-soled clogs. The thick robe and tasseled cloak over her shoulders fall in regularly spaced, symmetrically arranged, parallel folds like the fluting on a Greek column. This drapery masks her body but mimics its contours. Traces of red—perhaps the red clay used to attach thin sheets of gold—indicate that the robe was once painted or gilded. The figure holds a pomegranate in her right hand, a symbol of Persephone, who was abducted by Hades, the god of the underworld, and whose annual return brought the springtime.

5-19 BERLIN KORE
From the cemetery at Keratea, near Athens. c. 570–560 BCE. Marble with remnants of red paint, height 6′3″ (1.9 m). Staatliche Museen zu Berlin, Preussischer Kulturbesitz, Antikensammlung.

5-20 ANAVYSOS KOUROS

From the cemetery at Anavysos, near Athens. c. 530 BCE. Marble with remnants of paint, height 6′4″ (1.93 m). National Archaeological Museum, Athens.

Credit: © Craig & Marie Mauzy, Athens

5-21 "PEPLOS" KORE

From the Akropolis, Athens. c. 530 BCE. Marble, height 4′ (1.21 m). Akropolis Museum, Athens.

Credit: © Craig & Marie Mauzy, Athens/Acropolis Museum, Athens, Greece

ANAVYSOS KOUROS   The powerful, rounded, athletic body of a *kouros* from Anavysos, dated about 530 BCE, documents the increasing interest of artists and their patrons in a more lifelike rendering of the human figure (**FIG. 5-20**). The pose, wiglike hair, and Archaic smile echo the earlier style, but the massive torso and limbs have carefully rendered, bulging muscularity, suggesting heroic strength. The statue, a grave monument for a fallen war hero, has been associated with a base inscribed "Stop and grieve at the tomb of the dead Kroisos, slain by wild Ares [god of war] in the front rank of battle." However, there is no evidence that the figure was meant to preserve the likeness of Kroisos or anyone else. It is a symbolic type, not a specific individual.

"PEPLOS" KORE   The kore in **FIG. 5-21** is dated about the same time as the Anavysos Kouros, though she is a votive rather than a funerary statue. Like the *kouros*, she has rounded body forms, but unlike him, she is clothed. She has the same motionless, vertical pose of the Berlin Kore (SEE FIG. 5-19), but her bare arms and head convey a sense of soft flesh covering a real bone structure, and her smile and hair are much less stylized. The original painted colors on both body and clothing must have made her seem even more lifelike, and she also once wore a metal crown and jewelry.

The name we use for this figure is based on an assessment of her clothing as a young girl's peplos—a draped rectangle of cloth pinned at the shoulders and belted to give a bloused effect—but it has recently been argued that this *kore* is actually not wearing a peplos but a sheathlike garment, originally painted with a frieze of animals, identifying her not as a young girl but a goddess, perhaps Athena or Artemis. Her missing left forearm—which was made of a separate piece of marble fitted into the still-visible socket—would have extended forward horizontally, and may have held an attribute that identified her.

Painted Pots

Greek potters created beautiful vessels whose standardized shapes were tailored to specific utilitarian functions (**FIG. 5-22**). Occasionally, these potters actually signed their work, as did the artists who painted scenes on the pots. Greek ceramic painters became highly accomplished at composing their pictures to fit the often awkward fields on utilitarian shapes, and they usually showcased scenes of human interaction evoking a story, rather than isolated figures.

amphora   psykter   hydria   olpe

lip
neck
shoulder
body
foot

volute krater   calyx krater   bell krater

lekythos   oinochoe   kylix   kantharos

5-22 SOME STANDARD SHAPES OF GREEK VESSELS

Technique

BLACK-FIGURE AND RED-FIGURE

The two predominant techniques for painting on Greek ceramic vessels were black-figure (**FIG. 5–23**) and red-figure (**FIG. 5–24**). Both involved applying **slip** (a mixture of clay and water) to the surface of a pot and carefully manipulating the firing process in a kiln (a closed oven) to control the amount of oxygen reaching the ceramics. This firing process involved three stages. In the first stage, oxygen was allowed into the kiln, which "fixed" the whole vessel in one overall shade of red depending on the composition of the clay. Then, in the second (reduction) stage, the oxygen in the kiln was cut back (reduced) to a minimum, turning the vessel black, and the temperature was raised to the point at which the slip partially vitrified (became glasslike). Finally, in the third stage, oxygen was allowed back into the kiln, turning the unslipped areas back to a shade of red. The areas where slip had been applied, however, were sealed against the oxygen and remained black.

In the black-figure technique, artists silhouetted the forms with slip against the unpainted clay of the background. Then, using a sharp tool (a stylus), they cut through the slip to the body of the vessel, **incising** linear details within the silhouetted shape by revealing the unpainted clay underneath. The characteristic color contrast only appeared after firing. Sometimes touches of white and reddish-purple gloss—made of metallic pigments mixed with slip—enhanced the decorative effect.

In the **red-figure** technique, the approach was reversed. Artists painted not the shapes of the forms themselves but the background around forms (negative space), reserving unpainted areas for silhouetted forms. Instead of engraving details, painters drew on the reserved areas with a fine brush dipped in slip. The result was a lustrous black vessel with light-colored figures delineated in fluid black lines.

The contrasting effects obtained by these two techniques are illustrated here in details of two sides of a single amphora of about 525 BCE, both portraying the same figural composition, one painted by an artist using black-figure, and the other painted by an innovative proponent of red-figure technique. The sharp precision and flattened decorative richness of black-figure contrasts strikingly here with the increased fluidity and greater sense of three-dimensionality possible with the red-figure technique.

5–23 Lysippides Painter **HERAKLES DRIVING A BULL TO SACRIFICE**

c. 525–520 BCE. Black-figure decoration on an amphora. Ceramic, height of amphora 20¹⁵⁄₁₆″ (53.2 cm). Museum of Fine Arts, Boston. Henry Lillie Pierce Fund (99.538).

Credit: Photograph © 2017 Museum of Fine Arts, Boston

5–24 Andokides Painter **HERAKLES DRIVING A BULL TO SACRIFICE**

c. 525–520 BCE. Red-figure decoration on an amphora. Ceramic, height of amphora 20¹⁵⁄₁₆″ (53.2 cm). Museum of Fine Arts, Boston. Henry Lillie Pierce Fund (99.538).

Credit: Photograph © 2017 Museum of Fine Arts, Boston

BLACK-FIGURE VESSELS During the Archaic period, Athens became the dominant center for pottery manufacture and trade in Greece, and Athenian painters adopted Corinthian black-figure techniques (SEE FIG. 5-4), which became the principal mode of decoration throughout Greece in the sixth century BCE. At first, Athenian vase painters retained the horizontal banded composition that was characteristic of the Geometric period. Over time, however, they decreased the number of bands and increased the size of figures until a single narrative scene dominated each side of the vessel.

THE AMASIS PAINTER A mid-sixth-century BCE amphora—a large, all-purpose storage jar—with bands of decoration above and below a central figural composition illustrates this development (**FIG. 5-25**). The painting on this amphora has been attributed to an artist we call the Amasis Painter, since this distinctive style was first recognized on vessels such as this one that are signed by a prolific potter named Amasis.

Two maenads (female worshipers of the wine god Dionysos), intertwined with arms around each other's shoulders, skip forward to present their offerings—a long-eared rabbit and a small deer—to the god. (Amasis's signature is just above the rabbit.) The maenad holding the deer wears the skin of a spotted panther or leopard, its head still attached, draped over her shoulders and secured with a belt at her waist. The imposing, richly dressed god clasps a large **kantharos** (wine cup). This encounter between humans and a god appears to be a joyful, celebratory occasion rather than one of reverence or fear. The Amasis Painter favored strong shapes and patterns over conventions for making figures appear to occupy real space. He emphasized fine details, such as the large, delicate petal and spiral designs below each handle, the figures' meticulously arranged hair, and the bold patterns on their clothing.

EXEKIAS Perhaps the most famous of all Athenian black-figure painters, Exekias, signed many of his vessels as both potter and painter. He took his subjects from Greek mythology, which he and his patrons probably considered to be history. On the body of the amphora we saw at the beginning of this chapter, he portrayed Trojan War heroes Ajax and Achilles in a rare moment of relaxation playing dice (SEE FIG. 5-1). This is an episode not included in any literary source, but for Greeks familiar with the story, this anecdotal portrayal of friendly play would have been a poignant reminder that before the end of the war, the heroes would be parted by death. Knowing the story was critical to engaging with such paintings; artists often included identifying labels beside the characters to guide viewers so they could delight in the painters' rich renderings of familiar stories.

5-25 Amasis Painter **DIONYSOS WITH MAENADS**
c. 540 BCE. Black-figure decoration on an amphora. Ceramic, height of amphora 13″ (33.3 cm). Bibliothèque Nationale, Paris.
Credit: Bibliothèque nationale de France

RED-FIGURE VESSELS In the last third of the sixth century BCE, while many painters were still creating handsome black-figure wares, some turned to the new, more fluid technique called red-figure (see "Black-Figure and Red-Figure" opposite). The greater freedom and flexibility that resulted from painting rather than engraving details led ceramic painters to adopt the red-figure technique widely in a relatively short time. It allowed them to create livelier human figures with a more developed sense of bodily form—qualities that were increasingly popular in several media.

EUPHRONIOS One of the best-known red-figure artists was Euphronios. His rendering of the death of Sarpedon, about 515 BCE (see " Closer Look" on page 122), is painted on a krater—called a **calyx krater** because its handles curve up like a flower's calyx. Such a vessel was used as a punchbowl during a **symposium**, a social gathering of rich and powerful men. According to Homer's *Iliad*, Sarpedon, a son of Zeus and a mortal woman, was killed by the Greek warrior Patroclus while fighting for the Trojans. Euphronios captures the scene in which the warrior is being carried off to the underworld, the land of the dead.

Euphronios has created a balanced composition of verticals and horizontals that take the shape of the vessel into account. The bands of decoration above and below the

A Closer Look

THE DEATH OF SARPEDON

Hypnos (Sleep) and Thanatos (Death), identified by inscriptions that seem to emerge from their mouths, face each other on either side of the fallen body of Sarpedon, gently raising the slain warrior.

The god Hermes is identified not only by inscription, but also by his caduceus (staff with coiled snakes) and winged headgear. The attention to contours, distribution of drapery folds, and overlapping of forms give the twisting figure three-dimensionality.

Euphronios makes it appear as if Sarpedon's left leg is projecting into the viewer's space through the technique of foreshortening.

The painting's field is framed by bands of detailed ornament, placed to highlight the contours of the krater.

Sarpedon's body twists up toward the viewer, allowing Euphronios to outline every muscle and ligament of the torso, showing off both his knowledge of anatomy and his virtuosity in the newly developed red-figure technique.

Blood continues illogically to pour from the wounds in Sarpedon's corpse, not out of ignorance on the part of the artist but to heighten the dramatic effect of the scene.

5–26 Euphronios (painter) and Euxitheos (potter) **THE DEATH OF SARPEDON**
c. 515 BCE. Red-figure decoration on a calyx krater. Ceramic, height of krater 18″
(45.7 cm). Museo Nazionale di Villa Giulia, Rome.

Credit: © 2016. Photo Scala, Florence - courtesy of the Ministero Beni e Att. Culturali

scene echo the long horizontal of the dead fighter's body, which seems to levitate in the gentle grasp of its bearers, and the inward-curving lines of the handles mirror the arching backs and extended wings of Hypnos (Sleep) and Thanatos (Death). The upright figures of the lance-bearers on each side and Hermes in the center balance the horizontal and diagonal elements of the composition. While conveying a sense of the mass and energy of human subjects, Euphronios also portrayed the elaborate details of their clothing, musculature, and facial features with the fine tip of a brush. And he created the impression of real space around the figures by gently foreshortening Sarpedon's left leg, which appears to be coming toward the viewer's own space. Such formal features, as well as the scene's sense of pathos, seem to connect Euphronios's work with the dying warriors of the pediments from Aegina (SEE FIGS. 5–14, 5–15).

The Early Classical Period, c. 480–450 BCE

How do increasing naturalism and idealization of the human figure transform sculpture and painting during the Early Classical Period?

Over the brief span of 160 years between c. 480 and 323 BCE, the Greeks established an ideal of beauty that has endured in the Western world to this day. Scholars have associated Greek Classical art with three general concepts: humanism, rationalism, and idealism (see "Classic and Classical" on page 124). The ancient Greeks believed the words of their philosophers and expected to see them embodied in their art: "Man is the measure of all things," that is, seek an ideal based on the human form; "Know thyself," seek the inner significance of forms; and "Nothing in excess," reproduce only essential forms. In their embrace of humanism, the Greeks even imagined their gods as perfect human beings. But the Greeks valued human reason over human emotion. They saw all aspects of life, including the arts, as having meaning and pattern; in their view, nothing happened by accident. It is not surprising that great Greek artists and architects were not only practitioners but also theoreticians. In the fifth century BCE, the sculptor Polykleitos and the architect Iktinos both wrote books on the theory underlying their practices.

Art historians usually divide the Classical into three phases based on the formal qualities of the art: the Early Classical period (c. 480–450 BCE), the High Classical period (c. 450–400 BCE), and the Late Classical period (c. 400–323 BCE). The Early Classical period begins with the defeat of the Persians in 480–479 BCE by an alliance of city-states led by Athens and Sparta. The expanding Persian Empire had posed a formidable threat to the independence of the city-states, and the two sides had been locked in battle for decades until the Greek alliance was able to repulse a Persian invasion and score a decisive victory. Some scholars

have argued that success against the Persians gave the Greeks a self-confidence that accelerated artistic development, inspiring artists to seek new and more effective ways to express their cities' accomplishments. In any case, the period that followed the Persian Wars, extending to about 450 BCE, saw the emergence of a new stylistic direction, away from elegant stylizations and toward a sense of greater faithfulness to the natural appearance of human beings and their world.

Marble Sculpture

In the remarkably short time of only a few generations, Greek sculptors had moved far from the stiff postures and rigid frontality of the Archaic *kouroi* to more relaxed poses in lifelike figures such as the so-called **KRITIOS BOY** of about 480 BCE (**FIG. 5-27**). The softly rounded body forms, broad facial features, and calm expression give the figure an air of self-confident seriousness. His weight rests on his left, or engaged, leg, while his right, or relaxed, leg bends slightly at the knee, and a noticeable curve in his spine counters

5-27 KRITIOS BOY

From the Akropolis, Athens. c. 480 BCE. Marble, height 3′10″ (1.17 m). Akropolis Museum, Athens.

The damaged figure, excavated from the debris on the Athenian Akropolis, was thought by its finders to be by the Greek sculptor Kritios, whose work they knew only from Roman copies.

Art and its Contexts

CLASSIC AND CLASSICAL

The English words "classic" and "classical" both come from the Latin word *classis*, referring to the division of people into classes based on wealth. But they do not mean the same thing today. "Classic" has come to mean "first class" or "the standard of excellence," and in the most general usage, a "classic" is something—a book, a car, a film, even a soft drink—thought to be of lasting quality and universal esteem. However, the meaning of "Classical" is different. In art history, it refers to the work of Greek artists in the fifth century BCE, who sought to create ideal images based on strict mathematical proportions. Since Roman artists were inspired by the Greeks, "Classical" also often refers to the culture of ancient Rome. By extension, the word may also mean "in the style of ancient Greece and Rome," whenever or wherever that style is used. (You will notice that when "Classical" is used in these contexts, it is capitalized.)

the slight shifting of his hips and a subtle drop of one of his shoulders. We see here the beginnings of **contrapposto**, the convention (later developed in full by High Classical sculptors such as Polykleitos) of presenting standing figures with opposing alternations of tension and relaxation around a central axis that will dominate Classical art. The slight turn of the head invites the spectator to move around the figure and admire the small marble statue from every angle.

Bronze Sculpture

Development of the lost-wax process in hollow-cast bronze gave Greek sculptors the potential to create more complex action poses with outstretched arms and legs. These were very difficult to create in marble, since unbalanced figures might topple over and extended limbs might break off due to their weight. Bronze figures were easier to balance, and the metal's greater tensile strength made complicated poses and gestures technically possible.

The painted underside of an Athenian **kylix** (broad, flat drinking cup) portrays work in a late Archaic foundry for casting life-size figures (**FIG. 5–28**), providing clear evidence that the Greeks were creating large bronze statues in active poses as early as the first decades of the fifth century BCE. The walls of the workshop are filled with hanging tools and other foundry paraphernalia including several sketches: a horse, human heads, and human figures in different poses. One worker, wearing what looks like a present-day construction helmet, squats to tend the furnace on the left, perhaps aided by an assistant who peeks from behind. The man in the center, possibly the supervisor, leans on a staff, while a third worker assembles a leaping figure that is braced against a molded support. The unattached head lies between his feet.

THE CHARIOTEER A spectacular and rare life-size bronze, the **CHARIOTEER** (**FIG. 5–29**), cast about 470 BCE, documents the skills of Early Classical bronze-casters. It was found in the sanctuary of Apollo at Delphi together with fragments of a bronze chariot and horses, all buried during an earthquake in 373 BCE that may have saved them from the fate of most ancient bronzes, which were

5–28 Foundry Painter
A BRONZE FOUNDRY
490–480 BCE. Red-figure decoration on a kylix from Vulci, Italy. Ceramic, diameter of kylix 12″ (31 cm). Staatliche Museen zu Berlin, Preussischer Kulturbesitz, Antikensammlung.

The Foundry Painter has masterfully organized this workshop scene within the flaring space that extends upward from the foot of the vessel and along its curving underside to the lip, thereby using a circle as the ground-line for his composition.

Credit: © 2016. Photo Scala, Florence/bpk, Bildagentur für Kunst, Kultur und Geschichte, Berlin. Photo: Ingrid Geske melted down so the material could be recycled into new works. According to its inscription, the sculptural group commemorated a victory in the Pythian Games of 478 or 474 BCE, though it was the team of horses and the owner—not the charioteer—who were being celebrated.

The face of this youth is highly idealized, but there is a lifelike quality to the way his head turns slightly to one side, and the glittering onyx eyes and fine copper eyelashes enhance his intense expression. He stands at attention, sheathed in a long robe with rippling folds that appear to fall naturally under their own weight, varying in width and depth, yet seemingly capable of swaying with the charioteer's movement. The feet, with their closely observed toes, toenails, and swelling veins over the instep, are so realistic that they seem to have been cast from molds made from the feet of a living person.

THE RIACE WARRIORS Shipwreck as well as earthquake has protected ancient bronzes from recycling. As recently as 1972, divers recovered a pair of heavily corroded, larger-than-life-size bronze figures from the seabed off the coast of Italy, dating from about 460–450 BCE.

Initially, a scuba diver in the Ionian Sea near the beach resort of Riace thought he had found a human elbow and upper arm protruding from sand about 25 feet beneath the sea. Taking a closer look, he discovered that the arm was made of metal, not flesh, and was part of a large statue. He uncovered a second statue nearby, and underwater salvagers soon raised the statues: bronze warriors more than 6 feet tall, complete in every respect, except for swords, shields, and one helmet.

5-29 CHARIOTEER

From the Sanctuary of Apollo, Delphi. c. 470 BCE.
Bronze, copper (lips and lashes), silver (hand), onyx (eyes); height 5'11" (1.8 m). Archaeological Museum, Delphi.

The setting of a work of art affects the impression it makes. Today, the *Charioteer* is exhibited on a low base in the peaceful surroundings of a museum, isolated from other works and spotlighted for close examination. Its effect would have been very different in its original outdoor location, standing in a horse-drawn chariot atop a tall monument. Viewers in ancient times, tired from the steep climb to the sanctuary and jostled by crowds of fellow pilgrims, could have absorbed only its overall effect, not the fine details of the face, robe, and body visible to today's viewers.

Credit: © Craig & Marie Mauzy, Athens/Archeological Museum, Delphi

5-30 WARRIOR
Found in the sea off Riace, Italy. c. 460–450 BCE. Bronze with bone and glass eyes, silver teeth, and copper lips and nipples; height 6'9" (2.05 m). National Archeological Museum, Reggio Calabria, Italy.

Credit: © akg-images/Nimatallah

After centuries underwater, however, the bronze *Warriors* were corroded and covered with accretions. The clay cores from the casting process were still inside, adding to the deterioration by absorbing lime and sea salts. Conservators first removed all the exterior corrosion and lime encrustations using surgeon's scalpels, pneumatic drills, and high-technology equipment such as sonar (sound-wave) probes and micro-sanders. Then they painstakingly removed the clay core through existing holes in the heads and feet using hooks, scoops, jets of distilled water, and concentrated solutions of peroxide. Finally, they cleaned the figures thoroughly by soaking them in solvents and sealed them with a fixative specially designed for use on metals before exhibiting them in 1980.

The **WARRIOR** in **FIG. 5-30** reveals a striking balance between the idealized smoothness of "perfected" anatomy conforming to Early Classical standards and the reproduction of details observed from nature, such as the swelling veins in the backs of the hands. Contrapposto is further developed here than in the Kritios Boy, with a more pronounced counterbalance between tension (right leg and left arm) and relaxation (left leg and right arm), seeming to raise the possibility of movement and life. The life-like quality of this bronze is further heightened by inserted eyeballs of bone and colored glass, copper inlays on lips and nipples, silver plating on the teeth that peek between parted lips, and attached eyelashes and eyebrows of separately cast strands of bronze. This accommodation of the intense study of the human figure to an idealism that belies the irregularity of nature will be continued by artists in the High Classical period.

Ceramic Painting

Greek potters and painters continued to work with the red-figure technique throughout the fifth century BCE, refining their ability to create supple, rounded figures posed in ever more complicated and dynamic compositions. One of the most prolific Early Classical artists was Douris, whose signature appears on over 40 surviving pots decorated with scenes from everyday life as well as mythological subjects. His conspicuous skill in composing complex figural scenes that respond to the available pictorial fields of a variety of vessel types is evident in a frieze of frisky satyrs that he painted c. 480 BCE around the perimeter of a **psykter** (**FIG. 5-31**). This strangely shaped pot was a wine cooler, made to float in a krater (see "Closer Look" on page 122) filled with chilled water, its extended bottom serving as a keel to keep it from tipping over.

Like the krater, the psykter was a vessel meant for use in drinking parties know as symposia—lively, elite male gatherings that focused on wine, music, games, and love

5-31 Douris **FROLICKING SATYRS**

c.480 BCE. Red-figure decoration on a psykter. Ceramic, height 11¹⁵⁄₁₆″ (28.7 cm). British Museum, London.

making—and the decoration was chosen with this context in mind. The seeming acrobatic virtuosity of the satyrs' movements is matched by the artist's own virtuosity in composing them as an interlocking set of diagonal gestures that alternately challenge and follow the bulging form around which they are painted. The playful interaction of satyrs with their kylixes must have amused the tipsy revelers, especially when the pot was gently bobbing within a krater, making the satyrs seem to be walking around in circles on top of the wine. One satyr cups his kylix to his buttocks, juxtaposing convex and concave shapes. Another, balanced in a precarious handstand, seems to be observing his own reflection within the wine of his kylix.

But Douris was also capable of more lyrical compositions, as seen in the painting he placed inside a kylix (**FIG. 5-32**) similar in shape to those used as props by the satyrs on the psykter. This **tondo** (circular painting) was an intimate picture. It became visible only to the user of the cup when he tilted up the kylix to drink from it; otherwise, sitting on a table, the painting would have been obscured by the dark wine pool within it. A languidly posed and elegantly draped youth stands behind an altar pouring wine from an **oinochoe** (wine jug) into the kylix of a more dignified, bearded older man. Euphronios's tentative foreshortening of Sarpedon's bent leg on his krater (see "Closer Look" on page 122) blossoms in the work of Douris to become full-scale, formal projection as the graceful youth

on this kylix bends his arm from the background to project his tipping oinochoe over the laterally held kylix of his seated companion.

For the well-educated reveler using this cup at a symposium, there were several possible readings for the scene. This could be the legendary Athenian king Kekrops, who appears, identified by inscription, in the scene Douris painted on the underside of the kylix. Also portrayed there are Zeus and the young Trojan prince Ganymede, whom the supreme god abducted to Olympus to serve as his cupbearer. Or, since the symposia themselves were sites of amorous interactions between older and younger men, the user of this cup might have found his own situation mirrored in what he was observing at the bottom of the cup while he drank.

Wall Painting

Although ancient Greek commentators describe elaborate, monumental wall paintings and discuss the output and careers of illustrious painters from the fifth and fourth centuries BCE, almost nothing of this art has survived. We rely heavily on ceramics to fill gaps in our knowledge of Greek painting, assuming that the decoration of these more modest, utilitarian vessels reflects the glorious painting tradition documented in texts. There are also tantalizing survivals in provincial Greek sites. Principal among

5-32 Douris A YOUTH POURING WINE INTO THE KYLIX OF A COMPANION
c. 480 BCE. Red-figure decoration on a kylix. Ceramic, height 12¾″ (32.4 cm). The Soprintendenza Speciale per i Beni Archeologici di Napoli e Pompei.

Credit: Courtsy Ministero dei Beni e delle Attività Culturali e del Turismo - Museo Archeologico Nazionale di Napoli

5-33 RECONSTRUCTION DRAWING OF THE TOMB OF THE DIVER, POSEIDONIA (ROMAN PAESTUM)

c. 480 BCE.

Credit: Illustration: Peter Bull

On one short side (visible in the reconstruction drawing), a striding nude youth has filled the oinochoe in his right hand with the mixture of wine and water that was served from large kraters (portrayed on the table behind him) as the featured beverage of the symposium. He extends his arm toward a group of revelers reclining along one of the long walls (**FIG. 5-34**), each of whom has a kylix waiting to be filled. The man at the left reclines alone, raising his kylix to salute a couple just arriving—or perhaps toasting their departure—on the other short side. Behind him, the two couples on the long frieze—in each case a bearded, mature man paired with a youthful companion—are already engaged in the party. The young man in the middle pairing is slinging his upraised kylix, presumably to throw the dregs of his wine toward a target, a popular symposium game. His partner turns in the opposite direction to ogle at the amorous pair at the right, who have abandoned their cups on the table in front of them and turned to embrace, gazing into each other's eyes.

The significance of these paintings in relationship to a young man's tomb is not absolutely clear. They may demonstrate the deceased's elevated social status, since only wealthy aristocrats participated in such gatherings. The symposium could also represent funerary feasting or a vision of the pleasures that await the deceased in a world beyond death.

them are the well-preserved Early Classical wall paintings of c. 480–470 BCE in the Tomb of the Diver, discovered in 1968 just south of the Greek colony of Poseidonia (Roman Paestum) in southern Italy.

The paintings cover travertine slabs that formed the four walls and roof of a tomb submerged into the natural rock (**FIG. 5-33**), approximately 7 feet long, 3½ feet wide, and 2½ feet deep. Painted in *buon fresco* (water-based pigments applied to wet plaster) on a white ground in earthy browns, yellows, and blacks with accents of blue, the scenes on the walls surrounded the occupant of this tomb with a group of reclining men assembled for a symposium. Many of the most distinguished of surviving Greek ceramic vessels were made for use in these playfully competitive parties, and they are highlighted in the tomb paintings.

5-34 A SYMPOSIUM SCENE

From the Tomb of the Diver, Poseidonia (Roman Paestum). c. 480 BCE. Fresco on travertine slab, height 31″ (78 cm). Paestum Museum.

Credit: © akg-images/Andrea Baguzzi

5–35 A DIVER

From the Tomb of the Diver, Poseidonia (Roman Paestum). c. 480 BCE. Fresco on travertine slab, height 3′4″ (1.02 m). Paestum Museum.

Credit: © akg-images/Erich Lessing

The transition between this world and the next certainly seems to be the theme of the spare but energetic painting on the roof of the tomb, where a naked boy is caught in mid-dive, poised to plunge into the water portrayed as a blue mound underneath him (**FIG. 5-35**). Whereas the symposium scene follows an ancient Greek pictorial tradition, especially prominent on ceramic vessels made for use by its male participants, this diver finds his closest parallels in Etruscan tomb painting (SEE FIG. 6–5), flourishing at this time farther north in Italy. Since the scene was located directly over the body of the man entombed here, it is likely that it mirrors his own plunge from life into death. And since it combines Greek and Etruscan traditions, perhaps this tomb was made for an Etruscan citizen of Poseidonia, whose tomb was commissioned from a Greek artist working in this flourishing provincial center.

The High Classical Period, c. 450–400 BCE

What qualities constitute the High Classical moment of Greek art and architecture in Athens?

The High Classical period of Greek art lasted only a half-century, 450–400 BCE. The use of the word "high" to qualify the art of this time reflects the value judgments of art historians who have considered this period a pinnacle of artistic refinement, producing works that set a standard of unsurpassed excellence. Some have even referred to this half-century as Greece's "Golden Age," although these decades were also marked by turmoil and destruction. Without a common enemy, Sparta and Athens turned on each other in a series of conflicts known as the Peloponnesian War. Sparta dominated the Peloponnese peninsula and much of the rest of mainland Greece, while Athens controlled the Aegean and became the wealthy and influential center of a maritime empire. Today we remember Athens more for its cultural and intellectual brilliance and its experiments with democratic government, which reached its zenith in the fifth century BCE under the charismatic leader Perikles (c. 495–429 BCE), than for the imperialistic tendencies of its considerable commercial power.

Except for a few brief interludes, Perikles dominated Athenian politics and culture from 462 BCE until his death in 429 BCE. Although comedy writers of the time sometimes mocked him, calling him "Zeus" and "The Olympian" because of his haughty personality, he was a dynamic, charismatic political and military leader. He was also a great patron of the arts, supporting the use of Athenian wealth for the adornment of the city and encouraging artists to promote a public image of peace, prosperity, and power. Perikles said of his city and its accomplishments, "Future generations will marvel at us, as the present age marvels at us now." It was a prophecy he himself helped fulfill.

The Akropolis

Athens originated as a Neolithic **akropolis**, or "city on top of a hill" (*akro* means "high" and *polis* means "city"), that later served as a fortress and sanctuary. As the city grew, the Akropolis became the religious and ceremonial center devoted primarily to the goddess Athena, the city's patron and protector.

After Persian troops destroyed the Akropolis in 480 BCE, the Athenians vowed to keep it in ruins as a memorial, but Perikles convinced them to rebuild it, arguing that this project honored the gods, especially Athena, who had helped the Greeks defeat the Persians. Perikles intended to create a visual expression of Athenian values and civic pride that would bolster the city's status as the capital of the empire. He chose his close friend Pheidias, a renowned sculptor, to supervise the rebuilding and assembled under him the most talented artists in Athens.

The cost and labor involved in this undertaking were staggering. Large quantities of gold, ivory, and exotic woods had to be imported. Some 22,000 tons of marble were transported 10 miles from mountain quarries to city workshops. Perikles was severely criticized by his political opponents for this extravagance, but it never cost

him popular support. In fact, many working-class Athenians—laborers, carpenters, masons, sculptors, and the farmers and merchants who kept them supplied and fed—benefited from his expenditures.

Work on the **AKROPOLIS** continued throughout the fifth century BCE (**FIG. 5–36**). Visitors in 400 BCE would have climbed a steep ramp on the west side of the hill (in the foreground of FIG. 5-36) to the sanctuary entrance, perhaps pausing to admire the small temple dedicated to Athena Nike (Athena as goddess of victory in war) displayed on a projection of rock above the ramp. After passing through an impressive porticoed gatehouse called the Propylaia, they would have seen a huge bronze figure of Athena Promachos (the Defender) designed and executed by Pheidias between about 465 and 455 BCE. Sailors entering the Athenian port of Piraeus, about 10 miles away, could see the sun reflected off her helmet and spear tip. Behind this statue was a walled area that enclosed the Erechtheion, a temple dedicated to several deities, and to its right was the largest building on the Akropolis: the Parthenon, a temple dedicated to Athena Parthenos (the Virgin). Visitors approached the temple from its northwest corner, instantly grasping the imposing width and depth of this building, isolated like a work of sculpture elevated on a pedestal.

5-36 THE AKROPOLIS, ATHENS
Reconstruction drawing as it appeared
c. 447–432 BCE.

5-37A Kallikrates and Iktinos **THE PARTHENON**
Akropolis, Athens. 447–432 BCE. Pentelic marble. Photograph: view from the northwest.

Credit: © Craig & Marie Mauzy, Athens

The Parthenon

Sometime around 490 BCE, Athenians began work on a temple to Athena Parthenos that was still unfinished when the Persians sacked the Akropolis a decade later. In 447 BCE Perikles commissioned the architects Kallikrates and Iktinos to design a larger temple using the existing foundation and stone elements. The finest white marble was used throughout—even on the roof, in place of the more usual terra-cotta tiles (**FIG. 5-37**). The planning and execution of the Parthenon (dedicated in 438 BCE) required extraordinary mathematical, mechanical, and artistic skills from a large number of architects, builders, sculptors, and painters. The result is as much a testament to Pheidias's administrative talent as his artistic vision, since he supervised the entire project.

One key to the Parthenon's sense of harmony and balance is an attention to proportions—especially the ratio of 4:9, expressing the relationship of breadth to length and the relationship of column diameter to space between columns. Also important are subtle refinements of design, deviations from absolute regularity made to create a harmonious effect when the building was actually viewed. For example, since long, straight horizontal lines seem to

5-37B PLAN OF THE PARTHENON
Akropolis, Athens. 447–432 BCE.

opisthodomos

stereobate

stylobate

cella

peristyle colonnade

pronaos

sag when seen from a distance, the Parthenon's base and entablature curve slightly upward to correct this optical distortion. The columns have a gentle swelling (entasis) and tilt inward slightly from bottom to top; the corners are strengthened visually by reducing the space between columns at those points. These refinements give the Parthenon a buoyant, organic appearance and prevent it from looking like a heavy, lifeless stone box. The significance of their achievement was clear to its builders—Iktinos wrote a book on the proportions of this masterpiece.

The sculptural decoration of the Parthenon reflects Pheidias's unifying aesthetic vision, but it also conveys a number of political and ideological themes: the triumph of the democratic Greek city-states over imperial Persia, the preeminence of Athens thanks to the favor of Athena, and the victory of an enlightened Greek civilization over despotism and barbarism.

PEDIMENTS As with most temples, sculpture in the round filled both pediments of the Parthenon, set on the deep shelf of the cornice and secured to the wall with metal pins. Unfortunately, much of the sculpture has been damaged, lost, or removed to museums over the centuries. Using the locations of the pinholes and weathering marks on the cornice, as well as drawings made by French artist Jacques Carrey (1649–1726) on a visit to Athens in 1674, however, scholars have been able to determine the placement of surviving statues and infer the poses of missing ones. We know the subjects from the descriptions of the second-century CE Greek writer Pausanias. The west pediment sculpture, facing the entrance to the Akropolis, presented the contest Athena won over the sea god Poseidon for rule over the Athenians. The east pediment figures, above the entrance to the cella, portrayed the birth of Athena, fully grown and clad in armor, from the brow of her father, Zeus.

The statues from the east pediment are the best preserved of the two groups (**FIG. 5-38**). Flanking the missing central figures—probably Zeus seated on a throne with the newborn adult Athena standing at his side—were groups of goddesses and a single male figure. In the left corner was the sun god Helios in his horse-drawn chariot rising from the sea, while at the right the moon goddess Selene descended in her chariot to the sea, the head of her tired horse hanging over the cornice. The reclining male nude, whose relaxed pose fits so easily into the left pediment, has been identified as either Herakles with his lion's skin or Dionysos (god of wine) lying on a panther skin. The two seated women may be the earth and grain goddesses Demeter and Persephone. The running female figure just to the left of center is Iris, messenger of the gods, spreading the news of Athena's birth.

The three interlocked female figures on the right who seem to be awakening from a deep sleep, two sitting upright and one reclining, are probably Hestia (a sister of Zeus and the goddess of the hearth), Dione (one of Zeus's many consorts), and her daughter, Aphrodite. The sculptor expertly rendered the female forms beneath the draperies, which both cover and reveal the three figures' bodies while uniting them into a single mass.

METOPES The all-marble Parthenon had two sculptured friezes, one above the outer peristyle and another atop the cella wall inside. The Doric frieze on the exterior had 92 metope reliefs depicting legendary battles symbolized by combat between two representative figures: a centaur against a Lapith (a mythical people of pre-Hellenic times); a god against a Titan; a Greek against a Trojan; and a Greek against an Amazon (one of the mythical tribe of female warriors sometimes said to be the daughters of the war god Ares). Each of these struggles represented for the Greeks the triumph of reason over passion.

Among the best-preserved metope reliefs are several depicting the battle between Lapiths and centaurs from

Art and its Contexts

WHO OWNS THE ART? THE ELGIN MARBLES AND THE EUPHRONIOS KRATER

At the beginning of the nineteenth century, Thomas Bruce, the British Earl of Elgin and ambassador to Constantinople, acquired much of the surviving sculpture from the Parthenon, which was at that time being used for military purposes. He shipped it back to London in 1801 to decorate a lavish mansion for himself and his wife, but by the time he returned to England, his wife had left him and the ancient treasures were at the center of a financial dispute and had to be sold. Referred to as the Elgin Marbles, most of the sculpture is now in the British Museum, including all the elements seen in FIGURE 5-38. The Greek government has tried unsuccessfully to have the Elgin Marbles returned.

Another Greek treasure has been in the news more recently. In 1972, a krater painted by Euphronios (see "Closer Look" on page 122) and depicting the death of the warrior Sarpedon during the Trojan War was purchased by the Metropolitan Museum of Art in New York. Museum officials were told that it had come from a private collection, and it became the centerpiece of the museum's galleries of Greek vessels. But in 1995, Italian and Swiss investigators raided a warehouse in Geneva, Switzerland, where they found documents showing that the krater had been stolen from an Etruscan tomb near Rome. The Italian government demanded its return. The controversy was not resolved until 2006. The krater, along with other objects known to have been stolen from Italian sites, was returned, and the Metropolitan Museum is displaying pieces "of equal beauty" under long-term loan agreements with Italy.

5-38 PHOTOGRAPHIC MOCK-UP OF THE EAST PEDIMENT OF THE PARTHENON (USING PHOTOGRAPHS OF THE EXTANT MARBLE SCULPTURE)

c. 447–432 BCE. The gap in the center represents the space that would have been occupied by the missing sculpture. The pediment is over 90 feet (27.45 m) long; the central space of about 40 feet (12.2 m) is missing. British Museum, London.

the south side of the Parthenon. The panel shown here (**FIG. 5–39**) presents a pause within the struggle, a timeless image standing for an extended historical episode. Forms are reduced to their most characteristic essentials, and so dramatic is the X-shaped composition that we easily accept its visual contradictions. The Lapith is caught at an instant of total equilibrium. What could be a grueling tug-of-war between a man and a man-beast has been transformed into an athletic ballet, choreographed to show off the Lapith warrior's flexed muscles and graceful movements against the implausible backdrop of his carefully draped cloak.

PROCESSIONAL FRIEZE Enclosed within the Parthenon's Doric peristyle, a continuous, 525–foot-long Ionic frieze ran along the exterior wall of the cella. Since the eighteenth century, its subject has been seen as a procession celebrating the festival that took place in Athens every four years, when the women of the city wove a new wool peplos and carried it to the Akropolis to clothe an ancient wooden cult statue of Athena. Both the skilled riders in the procession (**FIG. 5–40**) and the graceful but sturdy young walkers (**FIG. 5–41**) are representative types, ideal inhabitants of a successful city-state. The underlying message of the frieze is that Athenians are a healthy, vigorous people united in a democratic civic body favored by the gods. The people are inseparable from and symbolic of the city itself.

5-39 LAPITH FIGHTING A CENTAUR

Metope relief from the Doric frieze on the south side of the Parthenon. c. 447–432 BCE. Marble, height 56″ (1.42 m). British Museum, London.

5-40 HORSEMEN

Detail of the Procession, from the Ionic frieze on the north side of the Parthenon. c. 447–432 BCE. Marble, height 41¾″ (106 cm).
British Museum, London.

5-41 YOUNG WOMEN AND MEN

Detail of the Procession, from the Ionic frieze on the east side of the Parthenon. c. 447–432 BCE. Marble, height 3′6″ (1.08 m).
Musée du Louvre, Paris.

A more recent interpretation by art historian Joan Connelly, however, has challenged the traditional reading of the frieze as an ideal rendering of a contemporary event. She argues that—consistent with what we know of temple decoration elsewhere—what is portrayed is not contemporary but mythological: the legendary Athenian king Erechtheus, who, following the advice of the oracle at Delphi, sacrificed one of his own daughters to save the city of Athens from an external enemy. This theme, also incorporating a procession, would have had obvious resonance with the recent Athenian victory over the Persians.

As with the metope relief of a Lapith fighting a centaur (SEE FIG. 5-39), viewers of the processional frieze easily accept its disproportions, spatial compression, and incongruities, including men and women standing as tall as rearing horses. Carefully planned rhythmic variations contribute to the effectiveness of the frieze. Horses plunge ahead at full gallop; women proceed with a slow, stately step; and men pause to look back at the progress of those behind them.

In executing the frieze, the sculptors took into account the spectators' low viewpoint and the dim lighting inside the peristyle. They carved the top of the frieze band in higher relief than the lower part, thus tilting the figures out to catch the reflected light from the pavement, permitting a clearer reading of the action. The subtleties in the sculpture may not have been as evident to Athenians in the fifth century BCE as they are now: the frieze, seen at the top of a high wall and between columns, was originally completely painted. Figures in red and ocher, accented with glittering gold and real metal details, were set against a contrasting background of dark blue.

STATUE OF ATHENA PARTHENOS After having explored the considerable richness of sculpture on the exterior of the Parthenon, viewers with permission could have climbed the east steps to look into the cella, where they would have seen Pheidias's colossal gold and ivory statue of Athena—outfitted in armor and holding a shield in one hand and a winged Nike (Victory) in the other—which was installed in the temple and dedicated in 438 BCE (**FIG. 5-42**). The original has vanished, but descriptions and later copies allow us a clear sense of its appearance and its imposing size, nearly 40 feet tall.

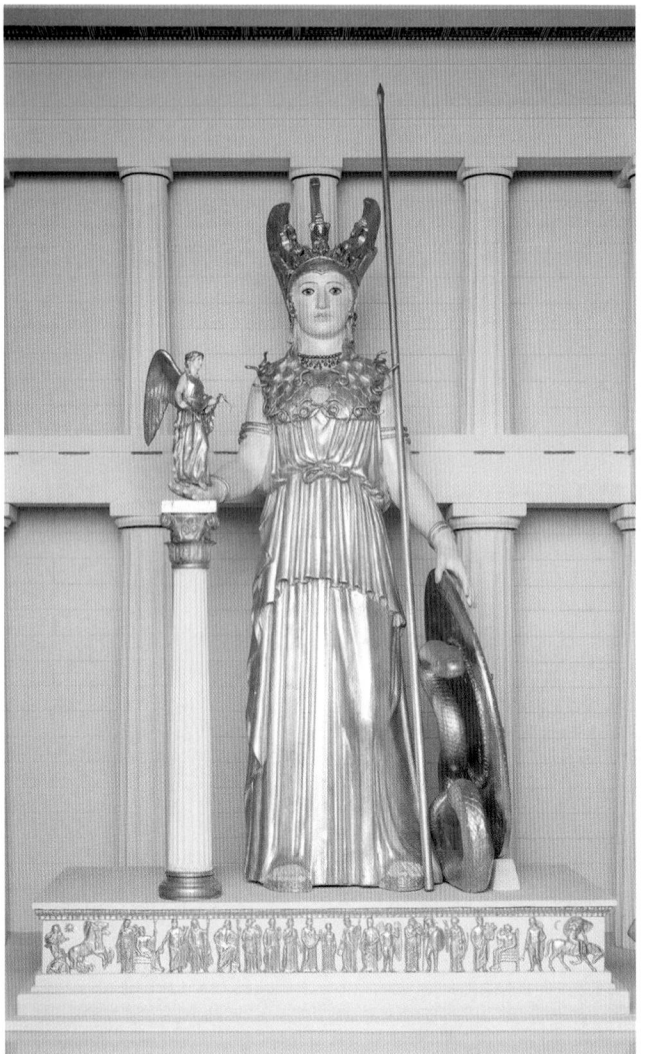

5-42 RE-CREATION OF PHEIDIAS'S HUGE GOLD AND IVORY FIGURE OF ATHENA

Royal Ontario Museum, Toronto.

Credit: With permission of the Royal Ontario Museum © ROM

"The Canon" of Polykleitos

Just as Greek architects defined and followed a set of standards for ideal temple design, Greek sculptors sought an ideal for representing the human body. Studying actual human beings closely and selecting the attributes they considered most desirable—such as regular facial features, smooth skin, and particular body proportions—sculptors combined them into a single ideal of physical perfection.

The best-known theorist of the High Classical period was the sculptor Polykleitos of Argos. About 450 BCE, balancing careful observation with generalizing **idealization**, he developed a set of rules for constructing what he considered the ideal human figure, which he set down in a treatise called the Canon (*kanon* is Greek for "measure," "rule," or "law"). To illustrate his theory, Polykleitos created a bronze statue of a standing man carrying a spear—perhaps the hero Achilles. Neither the treatise nor the original statue has survived, but both were widely discussed in the writings of his contemporaries, and later Roman artists made marble copies of the *Spear Bearer* (*Doryphoros*). By studying these copies, scholars have tried to determine the set of measurements that defined ideal human proportions in Polykleitos's Canon.

The Canon included a system of ratios between a basic unit and the length of various body parts. Some studies suggest that this basic unit may have been the length of the figure's index finger or the width of its hand across the knuckles; others suggest that it was the height of the head from chin to hairline. The Canon also included guidelines for *symmetria* ("commensurability"), by which Polykleitos meant the relationship of body parts to one another. In the *Spear Bearer*, he explored not only proportions, but also the diagonally counterbalanced relationships between weight-bearing and relaxed legs and arms around a central axis, referred to as contrapposto.

The Roman marble copy of the **SPEAR BEARER** (**FIG. 5-43**) shows a male athlete perfectly balanced with the whole weight of the upper body supported over the tense and straight ("engaged") right leg. The relaxed left leg is bent at the knee, with the left foot poised on the ball of the foot, suggesting the weight shift that comes before and after movement. The pattern of tension and relaxation is reversed in the arrangement of the arms, with the right relaxed on the engaged side, and the left bent to support the weight of the (missing) spear. The pronounced tilt of the *Spear Bearer*'s hipline accommodates the raising of the left foot onto its ball, and the head is turned toward the same side as the engaged leg. Hints of this dynamically balanced body pose—characteristic of High Classical standing figure sculpture—had already appeared in the Kritios Boy (SEE FIG. 5–27), and it was developed further in the Riace *Warrior* (SEE FIG. 5–30).

5-43 Polykleitos **SPEAR BEARER (DORYPHOROS)**
Roman copy after the original bronze of c. 450–440 BCE. Marble, height 6'11" (2.12 m); tree trunk and brace strut are Roman additions. National Archaeological Museum, Naples.

Credit: © akg-images/De Agostini Picture Lib./G. Nimatallah

The Propylaia and the Erechtheion

Upon completion of the Parthenon, work began in 437 BCE on the monumental gatehouse, the Propylaia (**FIG. 5-44**), that had been part of the original design of the Akropolis complex. The Propylaia had no sculptural decoration, but its north wing was originally a dining hall that later became the earliest known museum (meaning "home of the Muses"), a gallery built specifically to house a collection of paintings for public view.

Construction of the **ERECHTHEION** (**FIG. 5-45**), the second important temple erected on the Akropolis under Perikles's building program, began in the 430s BCE and ended in 406 BCE, just before the fall of Athens to Sparta. The asymmetrical plan reflects the building's multiple functions in housing several shrines, and also conformed to the sharply sloping terrain on which it is located. The Erechtheion stands on the site of the mythical contest between the sea god Poseidon and Athena for patronage over Athens. During this contest, Poseidon struck a rock with his trident (three-pronged harpoon), bringing forth a spout of water, but Athena gave an olive tree to Athens and won the contest. The Athenians enclosed what they believed to be this sacred rock, bearing the marks of the trident, in the Erechtheion's north porch. The Erechtheion also housed the venerable wooden cult statue of Athena that was the center of the Panathenaic festival.

The north and east porches of the Erechtheion came to epitomize the Ionic order and have served as an important model for European architects since the eighteenth

5-44 THE MONUMENTAL ENTRANCE TO THE AKROPOLIS, ATHENS
The Propylaia (Mnesikles) with the Temple of Athena Nike (Kallikrates) on the bastion at the right. c. 437–423 BCE.

Credit: Studio Kontos Photostock

5-45 ERECHTHEION

Akropolis, Athens. 430s–406 BCE. View from the east. Porch of the Maidens at left; the north porch can be seen through the columns of the east wall.

Credit: © S.Borisov/Shutterstock

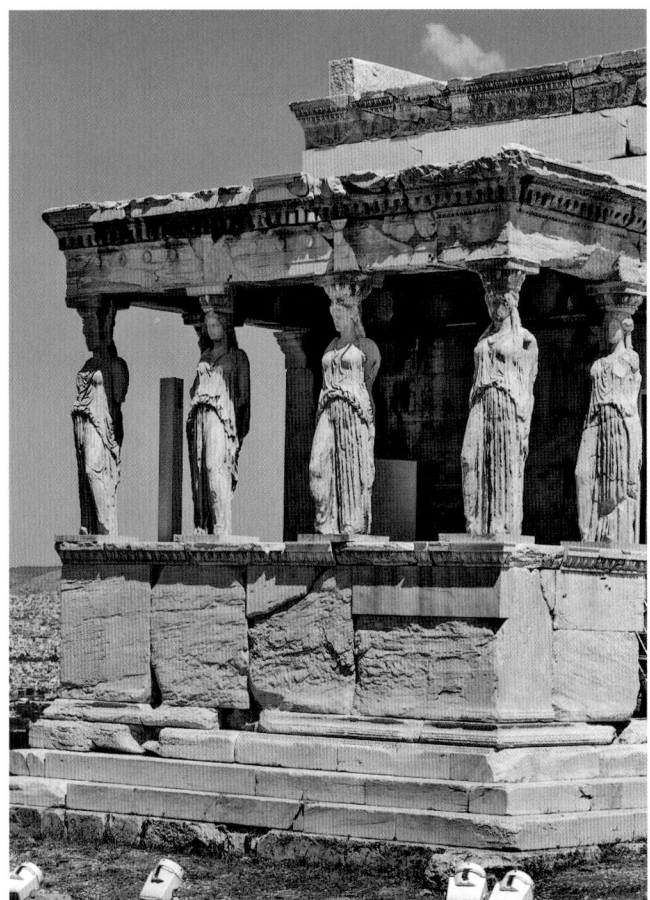

5-46 PORCH OF THE MAIDENS (SOUTH PORCH), ERECHTHEION

Akropolis, Athens. c. 420–410 BCE.

Credit: © Boris17/Shutterstock

century. Taller and more slender in proportion than the Doric, the Ionic order also has richer and more elaborately carved decoration (see "The Greek Orders" on page 111). The columns rise from molded bases and end in volute (spiral) capitals; the frieze is continuous.

The **PORCH OF THE MAIDENS (FIG. 5-46)**, on the south side facing the Parthenon, is even more famous. Raised on a high base, its six stately caryatids support an Ionic entablature made up of bands of carved molding. In a pose characteristic of Classical figures, each caryatid's weight is supported on one engaged leg, while the free leg, bent at the knee, rests on the ball of the foot. The three caryatids on the left have their right legs engaged, and the three on the right have their left legs engaged, creating a sense of closure, symmetry, and rhythm.

THE TEMPLE OF ATHENA NIKE The Ionic Temple of Athena Nike (victory in war), located south of the Propylaia, was designed and built about 425 BCE, probably by Kallikrates (SEE FIG. 5-44). Reduced to rubble during the Turkish occupation of Greece in the seventeenth century CE, the temple has since been rebuilt. Its diminutive size—about 27 by 19 feet—and refined Ionic decoration are in marked contrast to the weightier Doric Propylaia adjacent to it.

Between 410 and 405 BCE, this temple was surrounded by a parapet or low wall faced with sculptured panels depicting Athena presiding over the preparation of a celebration by winged Nikes (victory figures). The parapet no longer exists, but some panels have survived, including

5–47 NIKE (VICTORY) ADJUSTING HER SANDAL

Fragment of relief decoration from the parapet (now destroyed), Temple of Athena Nike, Akropolis, Athens. Last quarter of the 5th century (perhaps 410–405) BCE. Marble, height 3'6" (1.06 m). Akropolis Museum, Athens.

Credit: © Craig & Marie Mauzy, Athens/Akropolis Museum, Athens

the celebrated **NIKE (VICTORY) ADJUST-ING HER SANDAL** (FIG. 5–47). The figure bends forward gracefully, allowing her chiton (tunic) to slip off one shoulder. Her large, overlapping wings effectively balance her unstable pose. Unlike the decorative swirls of heavy fabric covering the Parthenon goddesses and the weighty, pleated robes of the Erechtheion caryatids, the textile covering this Nike appears delicate and light, clinging to her body like wet silk, one of the most discreetly erotic images in ancient art.

The Athenian Agora

In Athens, as in most cities of ancient Greece, commercial, civic, and social life revolved around the marketplace, or **agora**. The Athenian Agora, at the foot of the Akropolis, began as an open space where farmers and artisans displayed their wares. Over time, public and private structures were erected on both sides of the Panathenaic Way, a ceremonial road used during an important festival in honor of Athena (FIG. 5–48). A stone drainage system was installed to prevent flooding, and a large fountain house was built to provide water for surrounding homes, administrative buildings, and shops (see "Women at a Fountain House" on page 142). By 400 BCE, the Agora contained several religious and administrative structures and even a small racetrack. The Agora also had the city mint, its military headquarters, and two buildings devoted to court business.

In design, the stoa, a distinctively Greek structure found nearly everywhere people gathered, ranged from a simple roof held up by columns to a substantial and sometimes architecturally impressive building with two stories and shops along one side. Stoas offered protection from the sun and rain and provided a place for strolling and talking business, politics, or philosophy. While city business could be, and often was, conducted in the stoas, agora districts also came to include buildings with specific administrative functions.

In the Athenian Agora, the 500-member *boule*, or council, met in a building called the *bouleuterion*. This structure, built before 450 BCE but probably after the

5-48 RECONSTRUCTION DRAWING OF THE AGORA (MARKETPLACE), ATHENS
c. 400 BCE.

Persian destruction of Athens in 480 BCE, has a simple, rectangular plan with a vestibule and large meeting room. Near the end of the fifth century BCE, a new *bouleuterion* was constructed west of the old one. This too had a rectangular plan. The interior, however, may have had permanent tiered seating arranged in an ascending semicircle around a ground-level **podium**, or raised platform.

Nearby was a small, round building with six columns supporting a conical roof, a type of structure known as a tholos. Built about 465 BCE, this tholos was the meeting place of the 50-member executive committee of the boule. The committee members dined there at the city's expense, and a few of them always spent the night there in order to be available for any pressing business that might arise.

Private houses surrounded the Agora. Compared with the often grand public buildings, houses of the fifth century BCE in Athens were rarely more than simple rectangular structures of stucco-faced mud brick with wooden posts and lintels supporting roofs of terra-cotta tiles. Rooms were small and included a dayroom in which women could sew, weave, and do other chores, a dining room with couches for reclining around a table, a kitchen,

bedrooms, and occasionally an indoor bathroom. Where space was not limited, houses sometimes opened onto small courtyards or porches.

City Plans

In older Greek cities such as Athens, buildings and streets developed in conformance to the needs of their inhabitants and the requirements of the terrain. As early as the eighth century BCE, however, builders in some western Greek settlements began to use a mathematical concept of urban development based on the **orthogonal** (or grid) plan. New cities or rebuilt sections of old cities were laid out on straight, evenly spaced parallel streets that intersected at right angles to create rectangular blocks. These blocks were then subdivided into identical building plots.

During the Classical period, Hippodamos of Miletos, a major urban planner of the fifth century BCE, held views on the reasoned perfectibility of urban design akin to those of the Athenian philosophers (such as Socrates) and artists (such as Polykleitos). He believed the ideal city should be limited to 10,000 citizens divided into three

Art and its Contexts

WOMEN AT A FOUNTAIN HOUSE

Since most women in ancient Greece were confined to their homes, their daily trip to the communal well or fountain house in the agora was an important event. The Archaic ceramic artist known as the Priam Painter recorded a vignette from this aspect of Greek city life on a black-figure **hydria** (water jug) (**FIG. 5-49**). In the shade of a Doric-columned porch, three women fill hydriae just like the one on which they are painted. A fourth balances her empty jug on her head as she waits, while a fifth woman without a jug seems to be waving a greeting to someone. The building is designed like a stoa, open on one side, but having animal-head spigots on three walls. The Doric columns support a Doric entablature with an architrave above the colonnade and a colorful frieze— here black-and-white blocks replace carved metopes.

5-49 Priam Painter **WOMEN AT A FOUNTAIN HOUSE**

520–510 BCE. Black-figure decoration on a hydria. Ceramic, height 20⅞″ (53 cm). Museum of Fine Arts, Boston. William Francis Warden Fund. (61.195).

Credit: Photograph © 2017 Museum of Fine Arts, Boston

classes—artists, farmers, and soldiers—and three zones— sacred, public, and private. The basic Hippodamian plot was a square 600 feet on each side, divided into quarters. Each quarter was subdivided into six rectangular building plots measuring 100 by 150 feet, a scheme still widely used in American and European cities and suburbs.

Stele Sculpture

Upright stone slabs called stelai (singular, stele) were used in Greek cemeteries as gravestones, carved in low relief with an image (actual or allegorical) of the person or people to be remembered. Instead of the proud warriors or athletes used in the Archaic period, however, Classical stelae place figures in personal or domestic contexts that often feature women and children. A touching mid-fifth-century BCE example found on the island of Paros portrays a young girl seemingly bidding farewell to her pet birds, one of which she kisses on the beak (**FIG. 5-50**). She wears a loose peplos, which is open at the side to reveal parts of her body and clings elsewhere over her form to reveal its three-dimensionality. The extraordinary carving recalls the contemporary reliefs of the Parthenon frieze; like them, this stele would have been painted with color to provide details such as the straps of the girl's sandals or the feathers on her birds.

Another, somewhat later, stele commemorates the relationship between a couple identified by name across an upper frieze resting on two Doric pilasters (**FIG. 5-51**). The husband, Ktesilaos, stands casually with crossed legs and joined hands, gazing at his wife, Theano, who sits before him on a bench, pulling at her gauzy wrap with her right hand in a gesture that is often associated with Greek brides. Presumably this was a tombstone for a joint grave, since both names are inscribed on it, but we do not know which of the two might have died first, leaving behind a mate to mourn and memorialize by commissioning this stele. The air of introspective melancholy here, as well as the softness and delicacy of both flesh and fabric, seem to point forward out of the High Classical period and into the increased sense of narrative and delicacy that was to characterize the fourth century BCE.

5-50 GRAVE STELE OF A LITTLE GIRL
c. 450–440 BCE. Marble, height 31½″ (80 cm). Metropolitan Museum of Art, New York.

Credit: © 2016. Image copyright The Metropolitan Museum of Art/Art Resource/ Scala, Florence

5-51 GRAVE STELE OF KTESILAOS AND THEANO
c. 400 BCE. Marble, height 36⅝″ (93 cm). National Archaeological Museum, Athens.

Credit: © 2016. Photo Scala, Florence

Painting

The Painted Stoa built on the north side of the Athenian Agora (SEE FIG. 5-48) about 460 BCE is known to have been decorated with paintings (hence its name) by the most famous artists of the time, including Polygnotos of Thasos (active c. 475–450 BCE). His contemporaries praised his talent for creating the illusion of spatial recession in landscapes, rendering female figures clothed in transparent draperies, and conveying through facial expressions the full range of human emotions. Ancient writers enthusiastically described his painting, as well as other famous works, but nothing survives for us to see.

White-ground ceramic painting, however, may echo the style of lost contemporary wall and panel painting.

5–52 Style of the Achilles Painter **WOMAN AND MAID**
c. 450–440 BCE. White-ground lekythos. Ceramic, with additional painting in tempera, height 15⅛″ (38.4 cm). Museum of Fine Arts, Boston. Francis Bartlett Donation of 1912. (13.201).

Credit: Photograph © 2017 Museum of Fine Arts, Boston

In this technique, painters applied refined white slip as a ground on which they painted designs with liquid slip. High Classical white-ground painting became a specialty of Athenian potters. Artists enhanced the fired vessel with a full range of colors using paints made by mixing tints with white clay, and also using **tempera**, an opaque, water-based medium mixed with glue or egg white. This fragile decoration deteriorated easily, and for that reason seems to have been favored for funerary, votive, and other non-utilitarian vessels.

Tall, slender, one-handled white-ground **lekythoi** were used to pour libations during religious rituals. Some convey grief and loss, with scenes of departing figures bidding farewell. Others depict grave stelai draped with garlands. Still others envision the deceased returned to the prime of life and engaged in a seemingly everyday activity. A white-ground lekythos dated about 450–440 BCE shows a young servant girl carrying a stool for a small chest of valuables to a well-dressed woman of regal bearing, the dead person whom the vessel memorializes (**FIG. 5–52**). As on the stele of Ktesilaos and Theano (SEE FIG. 5–51), the scene portrayed here contains no overt signs of grief, but a quiet sadness pervades it. The two figures seem to inhabit different worlds, their glances somehow failing to meet.

The Late Classical Period, c. 400–323 BCE

What features separate the style and subjects of Late Classical art from the art of the High Classical period?

After the Spartans defeated Athens in 404 BCE, they set up a pro-Spartan government so oppressive that within a year the Athenians rebelled against it, killed its leader, Kritias, and restored democracy. Athens recovered its independence and its economy revived, but it never regained its dominant political and military status. It did, however, retain its reputation as a center of artistic and intellectual life. In 387 BCE, the great philosopher-teacher Plato founded a school just outside Athens, as his student Aristotle did later. Among Aristotle's students was young Alexander of Macedon, known to history as Alexander the Great.

In 359 BCE, a crafty and energetic warrior, Philip II, had come to the throne of Macedon. In 338, he defeated Athens and rapidly conquered the other Greek cities. When he was assassinated two years later, his kingdom passed to his 20-year-old son, Alexander, who consolidated his power and led a united Greece in a war of revenge and conquest against the Persians. In 334 BCE, he crushed the Persian army and conquered Syria and Phoenicia. By 331, he had occupied Egypt and founded the seaport he named

MAP 5-2 HELLENISTIC GREECE

Alexander the Great created a Greek empire that extended from the Greek mainland and Egypt across Asia Minor and as far east as India.

Alexandria. The Egyptian priests of Amun recognized him as the son of a god, an idea he readily adopted. That same year, he reached the Persian capital of Persepolis and continued east until reaching present-day Pakistan in 326 BCE; his troops then refused to go any farther (**MAP 5-2**). On the way home in 323 BCE, Alexander died of a fever. He was only 33 years old.

Changing political conditions never seriously dampened the Greeks' artistic creativity. Indeed, artists experimented widely with new subjects and styles. Although they maintained a Classical approach to composition and form, they relaxed its conventions, supported by a sophisticated new group of patrons drawn from the courts of Philip and Alexander, wealthy aristocrats in Asia Minor, and foreign aristocrats eager to import Greek works and, sometimes, Greek artists.

Sculpture

Throughout the fifth century BCE, sculptors had accepted and worked within standards for the ideal proportions and forms of the human figure as established by Pheidias

and Polykleitos at mid century. But fourth-century BCE artists began to challenge and modify those standards. On mainland Greece, in particular, a new canon of proportions associated with the sculptor Lysippos emerged for male figures—now eight or more "heads" tall rather than the six-and-a-half or seven-head height of earlier works. The calm, noble detachment characteristic of High Classical figures gave way to more sensitively rendered expressions of wistful introspection, dreaminess, even fleeting anxiety or lightheartedness.

PRAXITELES   According to the Greek traveler Pausanias, writing in the second century CE, the Late Classical sculptor Praxiteles (active in Athens from about 370 to 335 BCE or later) carved a "Hermes of stone who carries the infant Dionysos" for the Temple of Hera at Olympia. In 1875, just such a statue depicting the messenger god Hermes teasing the baby Dionysos with a bunch of grapes was discovered in the ruins of this temple (**FIG. 5-53**). Initially accepted as an original work of Praxiteles because of its high quality, recent studies hold that it is probably an excellent Roman or Hellenistic copy.

5–53 Praxiteles or his followers **HERMES AND THE INFANT DIONYSOS**

Probably a Hellenistic or Roman copy after a Late Classical 4th-century BCE original. Marble, with remnants of red paint on the lips and hair, height 7′1″ (2.15 m). Archaeological Museum, Olympia.

Discovered in the rubble of the ruined Temple of Hera at Olympia in 1875, this statue is now widely accepted as an outstanding Roman or Hellenistic copy. Support for this conclusion comes from certain elements typical of Roman sculpture: Hermes's sandals, which recent studies suggest are not accurate for a fourth-century BCE date; the supporting element of crumpled fabric covering a tree stump; and the use of a reinforcing strut, or brace, between Hermes's hip and the tree stump.

The sculpture highlights the differences between the fourth- and fifth-century BCE Classical styles. Hermes has a smaller head and a more sensual and sinuous body than Polykleitos's *Spear Bearer* (FIG. 5–43). His off-balance, S-curving pose, requires him to lean on a post—a clear contrast with the balanced posture of Polykleitos's work. Praxiteles also created a sensuous play of contrasting textures over the figure's surface, juxtaposing the smooth flesh with crumpled draperies and rough locks of hair. Praxiteles humanizes his subject with a hint of narrative—two gods, one a loving adult and the other a playful child, caught in a moment of absorbed companionship.

Around 350 BCE, Praxiteles created a daring statue of Aphrodite for the city of Knidos in Asia Minor. Although artists of the fifth century BCE had begun to hint boldly at the naked female body beneath tissue-thin drapery—as in the panel showing a Nike adjusting her sandal (SEE FIG. 5–47)—this Aphrodite was apparently the first statue by a well-known Greek sculptor to depict a fully nude woman, and it set a new standard (FIG. 5–54). Although nudity among athletic young men was admired in Greek society, nudity among women was seen as a sign of low character. The acceptance of nudity in statues of Aphrodite may be related to the gradual merging of the Greeks' concept of this goddess with some of the characteristics of the Phoenician goddess Astarte (the Babylonian Ishtar), who was nearly always shown nude in Near Eastern art.

In the version of Praxiteles's statue seen here (actually a composite of two Roman copies), the goddess is preparing to take a bath, with a water jug and her discarded clothing at her side. Her hand is caught in a gesture of modesty that only calls attention to her nudity. Her strong and well-toned body leans forward slightly, with one projecting knee in a seductive pose that emphasizes the swelling forms of her thighs and abdomen. According to an old legend, the sculpture was so realistic that Aphrodite herself journeyed to Knidos to see it and cried out in shock, "Where did Praxiteles see me naked?" The Knidians were so proud of their Aphrodite that they placed it in an open shrine where people could view it from every side. Hellenistic and Roman copies probably numbered in the hundreds, and nearly 50 survive in various collections today.

LYSIPPOS   Compared to Praxiteles, more details of Lysippos's life are known, and, although none of his original works has survived, there are many copies of the sculpture he produced between c. 350 and 310 BCE. Although he claimed to be entirely self-taught and asserted that "nature" was his only model, he must have received some technical training in the vicinity of his home, near Corinth. He expressed great admiration for Polykleitos, but his own figures reflect a different ideal and different proportions. For his famous portrayal of a **MAN SCRAPING HIMSELF (APOXYOMENOS)**, known today only from Roman copies

(**FIG. 5-55**), he chose a typical Classical subject—a nude, male athlete. But instead of a figure actively engaged in his sport, striding, or standing at ease, Lysippos depicted a young man after his workout, methodically removing oil and dirt from his body with a scraping tool called a strigil.

This tall and slender figure with a relatively small head makes a telling comparison with Polykleitos's *Spear Bearer* (SEE FIG. 5-43). Not only does it reflect a different canon of proportions, but the legs are in a wider stance

5-54 Praxiteles **APHRODITE OF KNIDOS**
Composite of two similar Roman copies after the original marble of c. 350 BCE. Marble, height 6'8" (2.04 m). Musei Vaticani, Museo Pio Clementino, Gabinetto delle Maschere, Rome.

The head of this figure is from one Roman copy, the body from another. Seventeenth- and eighteenth-century CE restorers added the nose, the neck, the right forearm and hand, most of the left arm, and the feet and parts of the legs. This kind of restoration would rarely be undertaken today, but it was frequently done and considered quite acceptable in the past, when archaeologists were trying to put together a body of work documenting the appearance of lost Greek statues.

5-55 Lysippos **MAN SCRAPING HIMSELF (APOXYOMENOS)**
Roman copy after the original bronze of c. 350–310 BCE. Marble, height 6'9" (2.06 m). Musei Vaticani, Museo Pio Clementino, Gabinetto dell'Apoxyomenos, Rome.

to counterbalance the outstretched arms, and there is a pronounced curve to the posture. The *Spear Bearer* is contained within fairly simple, compact contours and oriented toward a center-front viewer. In contrast, the arms of the *Man Scraping Himself* break free into the surrounding space, inviting the viewer to move around the statue. Roman authors, who may have been describing the bronze original rather than a marble copy, remarked on the subtle modeling of the statue's elongated body and the spatial extension of its pose.

When Lysippos was summoned to create a portrait of Alexander the Great, he portrayed Alexander as a standing figure with an upraised arm holding a scepter, the same way he posed Zeus. Based on description and later copies, we know Lysippos idealized the ruler as a ruggedly handsome, heavy-featured young man with a large Adam's apple and short, tousled hair. According to the Roman historian Plutarch, Lysippos presented Alexander in a meditative pose, perhaps contemplating grave decisions, waiting to receive divine advice.

Metalwork

The detailed, small-scale work of Greek goldsmiths followed the same stylistic trends and achieved the same high standards of technique and execution characterizing other arts. A specialty of Greek goldsmiths was the design of earrings in the form of tiny works of sculpture. They were often placed on the ears of marble statues of goddesses, but they adorned the ears of living women as well. **EARRINGS** dated about 330–300 BCE depict the abducted youth Ganymede caught in the grasp of an eagle (Zeus) (**FIG. 5-56**),

5-56 EARRINGS

c. 330–300 BCE. Hollow-cast gold, height 2⅜" (6 cm). Metropolitan Museum of Art, New York. Harris Brisbane Dick Fund, 1937. (37.11.9–10).

a technical *tour-de-force*. Slightly more than 2 inches high, they were hollow-cast using the lost-wax process, no doubt to make them light on the ear. Despite their small size, they capture the drama of their subject, evoking swift movement through space.

Painting

Roman observers such as Pliny the Elder praised Greek painters for their skill in capturing the appearance of the real world. Roman patrons also admired Greek murals, and they commissioned copies in fresco or **mosaic** to decorate their homes. (Mosaics—created from **tesserae**, small cubes of colored stone or marble—provide a permanent, waterproof surface that the Romans used for floors in important rooms.) A first-century CE Roman mosaic, **ALEXANDER THE GREAT CONFRONTS DARIUS III AT THE BATTLE OF ISSOS** (**FIG. 5-57**), for example, replicates a Greek painting of about 310 BCE. Pliny the Elder mentions a painting of this subject by Philoxenos of Eretria, but a new theory claims the original as a work of Helen of Egypt.

Such copies document a growing taste for dramatic narrative subjects in late fourth-century BCE Greek painting. The scene here is one of violent action, where diagonal disruption and radical foreshortening draw the viewer in and elicit an emotional response. Astride a rearing horse at the left, his hair blowing free and his neck bare, Alexander challenges the helmeted and armored Persian leader, who stretches out his arm in a gesture of defeat and apprehension as his charioteer whisks him back toward safety within the Persian ranks. The mosaicist has created an illusion of solid figures through modeling, mimicking the play of light on three-dimensional surfaces with highlights and shading.

The interest of fourth-century BCE artists in creating believable illusions of the real world was the subject of anecdotes repeated by later writers. One popular legend involved a floral designer named Glykera—widely praised for her artistry in weaving blossoms and greenery into wreaths, swags, and garlands for religious processions and festivals—and Pausias—the foremost painter of his day. Pausias challenged Glykera to a contest, claiming that he could paint a picture of one of her complex works that would appear as lifelike to the spectator as her real one. According to the legend, he succeeded. It is not surprising, although perhaps unfair, that the opulent floral borders so popular in later Greek painting and mosaics are described as "Pausian" rather than "Glykeran."

A Pausian design frames a mosaic floor from a palace at Pella (Macedonia) dated about 300 BCE (**FIG. 5-58**). The floor features a series of hunting scenes, such as the **STAG HUNT** seen here, prominently signed by an artist named Gnosis. The blossoms, leaves, spiraling tendrils, and twisting, undulating stems that frame this scene echo the linear patterns formed by the hunters, the dog, and

5-57 ALEXANDER THE GREAT CONFRONTS DARIUS III AT THE BATTLE OF ISSOS
Floor mosaic, Pompeii, Italy. 1st-century BCE Roman copy of a Greek wall painting of c. 310 BCE, perhaps by Philoxenos of Eretria or Helen of Egypt. Entire panel 8′10″ × 17′ (2.7 × 5.2 m). Museo Archeologico Nazionale, Naples.

Credit: © Fotografica Foglia, Naples

the struggling stag. The human and animal figures are modeled in light and shade, and the dog's front legs are expertly foreshortened to create the illusion that the animal is turning at a sharp angle into the picture. The work is all the more impressive because it was not made with uniformly cut marble in different colors, but with a carefully selected assortment of natural pebbles.

The Hellenistic Period, 323–31/30 BCE

*What distinguishes the styles and subjects
of Hellenistic art from the Classical art that preceded it?*

When Alexander died unexpectedly at age 33 in 323 BCE, he left a vast empire with no administrative structure and no accepted successor. Almost immediately his generals turned against one another, local leaders fought to

5-58 Gnosis STAG HUNT
Detail of mosaic floor decoration from Pella, Macedonia (in present-day Greece). c. 300 BCE. Pebbles, central panel 10′7½″ × 10′5″ (3.24 × 3.17 m). Signed at top: "Gnosis made it." Archaeological Museum, Pella.

Credit: Studio Kontos Photostock

regain their lost autonomy, and the empire began to break apart. By the early third century BCE, three of Alexander's generals—Antigonus, Ptolemy, and Seleucus—had carved out kingdoms. The Antigonids controlled Macedonia and mainland Greece; the Ptolemies ruled Egypt; and the Seleucids controlled Asia Minor, Mesopotamia, and Persia.

Over the course of the second and first centuries BCE, these kingdoms succumbed to the growing empire centered in Rome. Ptolemaic Egypt endured the longest, and its capital, Alexandria, flourished as a prosperous seaport and great center of learning and the arts. Its library is estimated to have contained 700,000 papyrus and parchment scrolls. The Battle of Actium in 31 BCE and the death in 30 BCE of Egypt's last Ptolemaic ruler, the remarkable Cleopatra, marks the end of the Hellenistic period.

Alexander's lasting legacy was the spread of Greek culture far beyond its original borders, but artists of the Hellenistic period developed visions discernibly distinct from those of their Classical Greek predecessors. Where earlier artists sought to codify a generalized artistic ideal, Hellenistic artists shifted focus to the individual and the specific. They turned increasingly away from the heroic to the everyday, from gods to mortals, from aloof serenity to individual emotion, and from decorous drama to emotional melodrama. Their works appeal to the senses through luscious or lustrous surface treatments and to our hearts as well as our intellects through expressive subjects and poses. Although such tendencies are already evident during the fourth century BCE, they become more pronounced in Hellenistic art.

Architecture

In the architecture of the Hellenistic period, a variant of the Ionic order that had previously been reserved for interiors—called Corinthian by the Romans and featuring elaborate foliate capitals—challenged the dominant Doric and Ionic orders (see "The Greek Orders" on page 111). In Corinthian capitals, curly acanthus leaves and coiled flower spikes surround a basket-shaped core. Above the capitals, the Corinthian entablature, like the Ionic, has a stepped-out architrave and a continuous frieze, but it includes additional bands of carved moldings.

The Corinthian **TEMPLE OF OLYMPIAN ZEUS** (**FIG. 5–59**), located in the lower city of Athens at the foot of the Akropolis, was designed by the Roman architect Cossutius in the second century BCE on the foundations of an earlier Doric temple, but it was not completed until three centuries later, under the patronage of the Roman emperor Hadrian. Viewed through these huge columns—55 feet 5 inches tall—the Parthenon seems modest in comparison. But the new temple followed long-established conventions. It was an enclosed rectangular building surrounded by a screen of columns standing on a three-stepped base. It is simply a Greek temple grown very large.

GREEK THEATERS In ancient Greece, the theater was more than mere entertainment: It was a vehicle for the communal expression of religious beliefs through music, poetry, and dance. In very early times, theater performances took place on the hard-packed dirt or stone-surfaced pavement

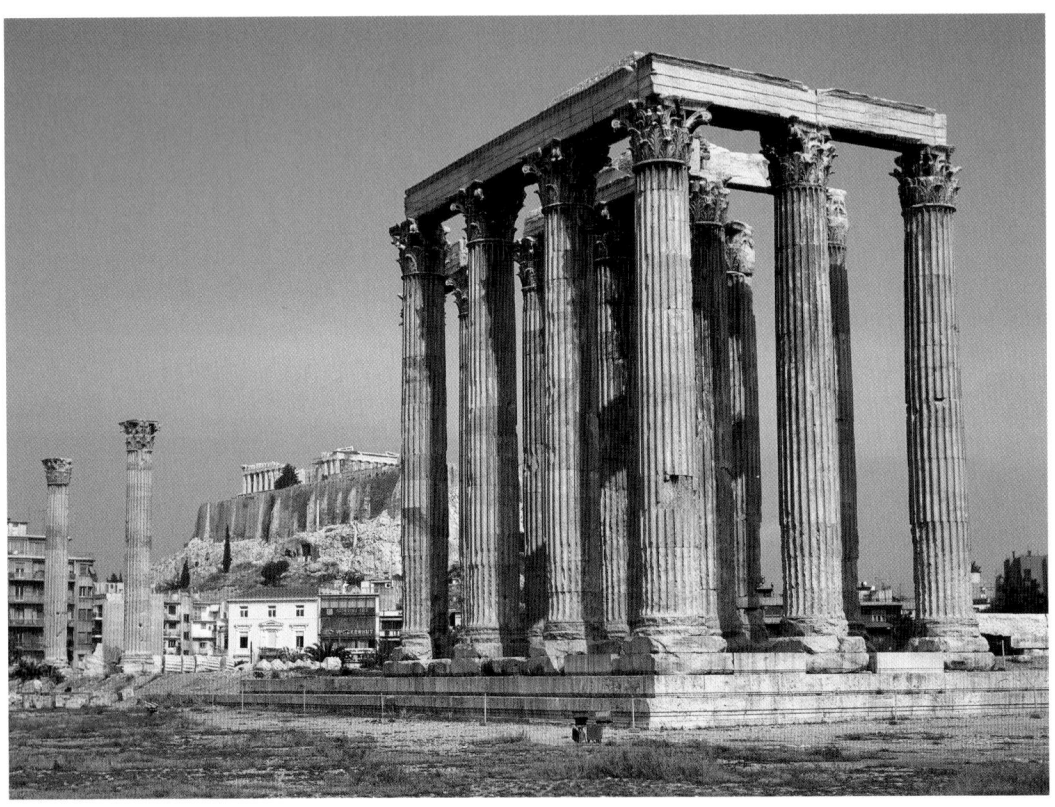

5–59 TEMPLE OF OLYMPIAN ZEUS, ATHENS

View from the southeast with the Akropolis in the distance. Building and rebuilding phases: foundation c. 520–510 BCE, using the Doric order; temple designed by Cossutius begun 175 BCE, left unfinished 164 BCE, completed 132 BCE using Cossutius's design. Height of columns 55'5" (16.89 m).

Credit: © Amanaimages Inc./123RF

of an outdoor threshing floor—the same type of floor later incorporated into religious sanctuaries. Whenever feasible, dramas were also presented facing a steep hill that served as elevated seating for the audience. Eventually such sites were made into permanent open-air auditoriums. At first, tiers of seats were simply cut into the side of the hill. Later, builders improved them with stone.

During the fifth century BCE, the plays were usually tragedies in verse based on popular myths and were performed at festivals dedicated to Dionysos; the three great Greek tragedians—Aeschylus, Sophocles, and Euripides—created works that would define tragedy for centuries. Because they were used continuously and frequently modified over many centuries, early theaters have not survived in their original form.

The theater at Epidauros (**FIG. 5–60**), built in the second half of the fourth century BCE, is characteristic. A semicircle of tiered seats built into the hillside overlooked the circular performance area, called the orchestra, at the center of which was an altar to Dionysos. Rising behind the orchestra was a two-tiered stage structure made up of the vertical *skene* (scene)—an architectural backdrop for performances that also screened the backstage area from view—and the *proskenion* (**proscenium**), a raised platform in front of the *skene* that was increasingly used over time as an extension of the orchestra. Ramps connecting the *proskenion* with lateral passageways provided access for performers. Steps gave the audience access to the 55 rows of seats and divided the seating area into uniform, wedge-shaped sections. The tiers of seats above the wide corridor, or gangway, were added at a much later date. This design provided uninterrupted sight lines and good acoustics and allowed for the efficient entrance and exit of the 12,000 spectators. No better design has ever been created.

5–60 OVERALL VIEW (A) AND RECONSTRUCTION DRAWING (B) OF THE THEATER, EPIDAUROS

Peloponnese, Greece. 4th century BCE and later.

Credit: (above) © Craig & Marie Mauzy, Athens
(right) © Dorling Kindersley

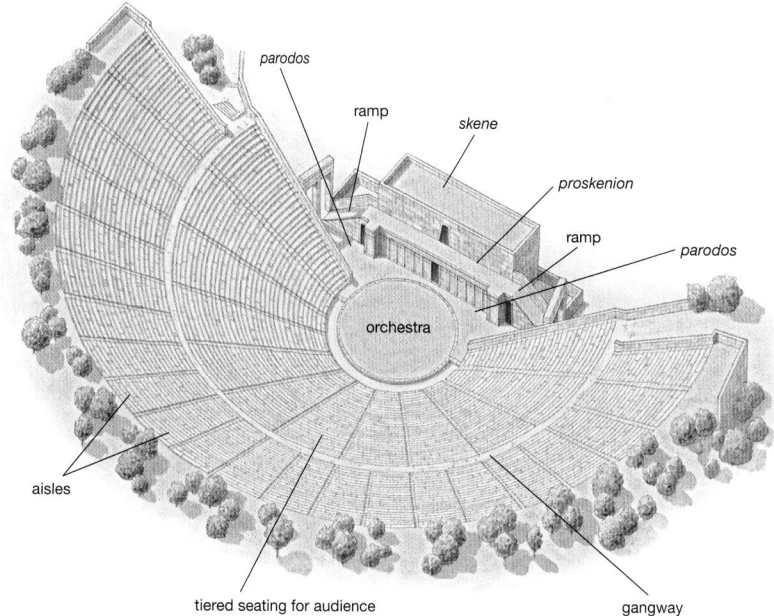

Sculpture in Pergamon

Hellenistic sculptors produced an enormous variety of work in a wide range of materials, techniques, and styles. The period was marked by two broad and conflicting trends. One trend emulated earlier Classical models; sculptors selected aspects of favored works of the fourth century BCE and incorporated them into their own work. The other (sometimes called anti-Classical or Baroque) abandoned Classical strictures and experimented freely with new forms and subjects. This style was especially strong in Pergamon and other eastern centers of Greek culture.

The Anatolian city of Pergamon was the capital of a breakaway state within the Seleucid realm established in the early third century BCE, and it quickly became a leading center of the arts and the hub of an experimental sculptural style that had far-reaching influence throughout the Hellenistic period. This radical style characterizes a monument commemorating the victory in 230 BCE of Attalos I (ruled 241–197 BCE) over the Gauls, a Celtic people (see "The Celts" below). The monument extols the dignity and heroism of the defeated enemies and, by extension, the power and virtue of the Pergamenes.

The bronze figures of Gauls mounted on the pedestal of this monument are known today only from Roman copies in marble. One captures the slow demise of a wounded Celtic soldier-trumpeter (**FIG. 5–62**), whose lime-spiked hair, mustache, and twisted neck ring or **torc** (reputedly the only thing the Gauls wore into battle) identify him as a **barbarian** (a label the ancient Greeks used for all foreigners, whom they considered uncivilized). But the sculpture also depicts his dignity and heroism in defeat, inspiring in viewers both admiration and pity for this fallen warrior. Fatally injured, he struggles to rise, but the slight bowing

Art and its Contexts

THE CELTS

During the first millennium BCE, Celtic peoples inhabited most of central and western Europe. The Celtic Gauls portrayed in the Hellenistic Pergamene victory monument moved into Asia Minor from Thrace during the third century BCE. Pushed out by migrating people, attacked and defeated by challenged kingdoms like that at Pergamon, and then again by the Roman armies of Julius Caesar, the Celts were pushed into the northwesternmost parts of the continent—Ireland, Cornwall, and Brittany. Their wooden sculpture and dwellings and colorful woven textiles have disintegrated, but spectacular funerary goods such as jewelry, weapons, and tableware survive.

This golden **TORC**, dating sometime between the third and first centuries BCE (**FIG. 5–61**), was excavated in 1866 from a Celtic tomb in northern France, but it is strikingly similar to the neck ring worn by the dying trumpeter illustrated in FIGURE 5–62. Torcs were worn by noblemen and were sometimes awarded to warriors for heroic performance in combat. Like all Celtic jewelry, the decorative design of this work consists not of natural forms but of completely abstract ornament, in this case created by the careful twisting and wrapping of strands of pure gold, resolved securely in the definitive bulges of two knobs. In Celtic hands, pattern becomes an integral part of the object itself, not an applied decoration. In stark contrast to the culture of the ancient Greeks, where the human figure was at the heart of all artistic development, here it is abstract, nonrepresentational form and its continual refinement that is the central artistic preoccupation.

5–61 TORC

Found at Soucy, France. Celtic Gaul, 3rd–1st century BCE. Gold, height 5″ (12.7 cm), length 5⅝″ (14.5 cm). Musée Nationale du Moyen-Âge, Paris.

Credit: Photo © RMN/ Jean-Gilles Berizzi

5-62 Epigonos (?) **DYING GALLIC TRUMPETER**

Roman copy (found in Julius Caesar's garden in Rome) after the original bronze of c. 220 BCE. Marble, height 36½" (93 cm). Museo Capitolino, Rome.

Pliny the Elder described a work like the *Dying Gallic Trumpeter*, attributing it to an artist named Epigonos. Recent research indicates that Epigonos probably knew the early fifth-century BCE sculpture of the Temple of Aphaia on Aegina, which included the *Dying Warriors* (SEE FIGS. 5–14, 5–15), and could have had it in mind when he created his own works.

Credit: © Vincenzo Pirozzi, Rome
fotopirozzi@inwind.it

of his supporting right arm and his unseeing, downcast gaze indicate that he is on the point of death. This kind of deliberate attempt to elicit a specific emotional response in the viewer is known as **expressionism**, and it was to become a characteristic of Hellenistic art.

The sculptural style and approach seen in the monument to the defeated Gauls became more pronounced and dramatic in later works, culminating in the sculptured frieze wrapped around the base of a Great Altar on a mountainside at Pergamon (**FIG. 5–63**). Now reconstructed inside a Berlin museum, the original altar was enclosed within a single-story Ionic colonnade raised on a high podium reached by a monumental staircase 68 feet wide and nearly 30 feet deep. The sculptural frieze, over 7 feet in height and probably executed during the reign of Eumenes II (197–159 BCE), depicts the battle between the gods and

the giants, a mythical struggle that the Greeks saw as a metaphor for their conflicts with barbarians. In this case it evokes the Pergamenes' victory over the Gauls.

The Greek gods fight here not only with giants, but also with monsters with snakes for legs that are emerging from the bowels of the earth. In a detail from it (**FIG. 5–64**), the goddess Athena at the left has grabbed the hair of a winged male monster and forced him to his knees. Inscriptions along the base of the sculpture identify him as Alkyoneos, a son of the earth goddess Ge. Ge rises from the ground on the right in fear as she reaches toward Athena, pleading for her son's life. At the far right, a winged Nike rushes to crown Athena with a victor's wreath.

The figures in the Pergamon frieze not only fill the space along the base of the altar, they also break out of their architectural boundaries and invade the spectators'

5-63 RECONSTRUCTED WEST FRONT OF THE ALTAR FROM PERGAMON (IN PRESENT-DAY TURKEY)
c. 175–150 BCE. Marble, height of frieze 7'7" (2.3 m). Staatliche Museen zu Berlin.
Credit: © 2016. Photo Scala, Florence/bpk, Bildagentur für Kunst, Kultur und Geschichte, Berlin

5-64 ATHENA ATTACKING THE GIANTS

Detail of the frieze from the east front of the altar from Pergamon. c. 175–150 BCE. Marble, frieze height 7′7″ (2.3 m). Staatliche Museen zu Berlin.

Credit: © 2016. Photo Scala, Florence/bpk, Bildagentur für Kunst, Kultur und Geschichte, Berlin

5-65 Hagesandros, Polydoros, and Athenodoros of Rhodes LAOCOÖN AND HIS SONS

Original of 1st century BCE or a Roman copy, adaptation, or original of the 1st century BCE. Marble, height 8′ (2.44 m). Musei Vaticani, Museo Pio Clementino, Cortile Ottagono, Rome.

Credit: © 2016. Photo Scala, Florence

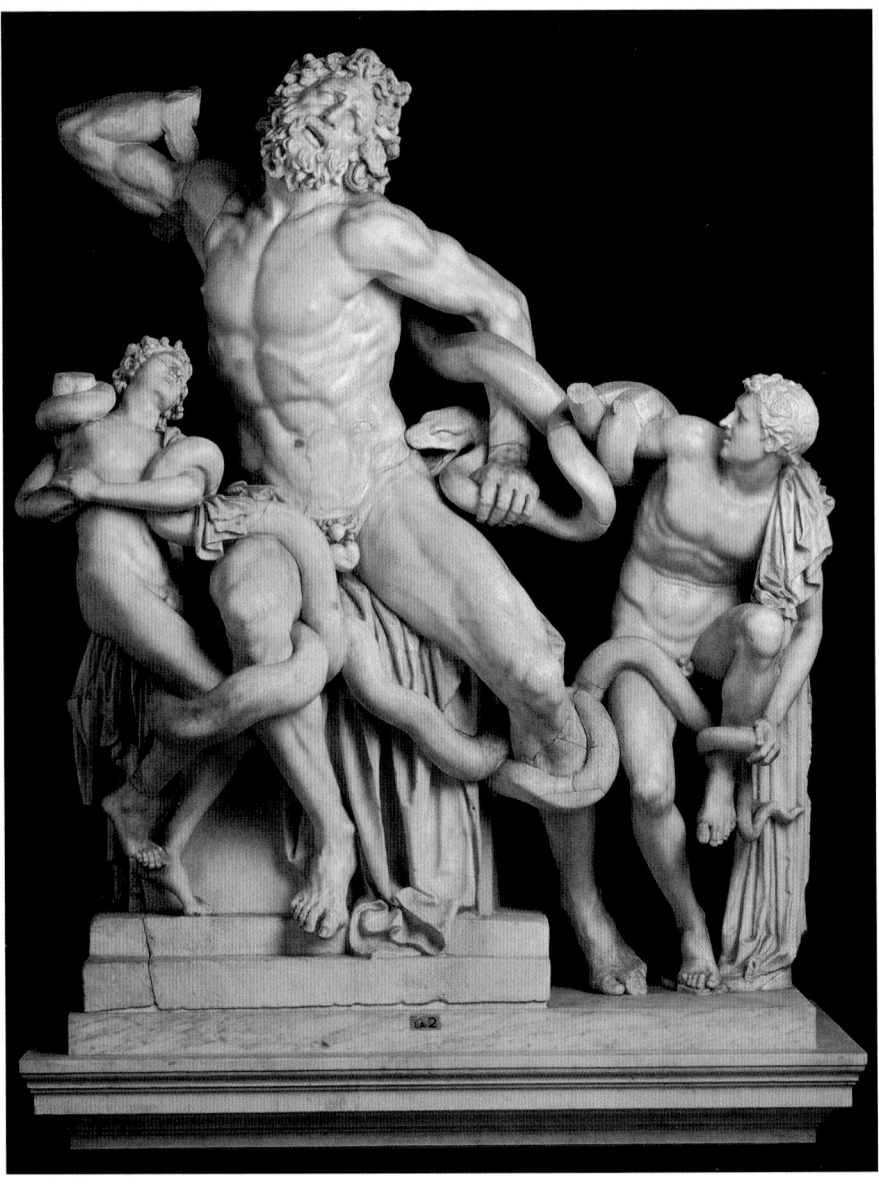

space, crawling out onto the steps that visitors climbed on their way to the altar. Many consider this theatrical and complex interaction of space and form to be a benchmark of the Hellenistic style, just as they consider the balanced restraint of the Parthenon sculpture to be the epitome of the High Classical style. Where fifth-century BCE artists sought horizontal and vertical equilibrium and control, Pergamene artists sought to balance opposing forces in three-dimensional space along dynamic diagonals. Classical preference for smooth, evenly illuminated surfaces has been replaced by dramatic contrasts of light and shade playing over complex forms carved with deeply undercut high relief. The composure and stability admired in the Classical style have given way to extreme expressions of pain, stress, wild anger, fear, and despair. Whereas the Classical artist asked only for an intellectual commitment, the Hellenistic artist demanded that the viewer also empathize.

THE LAOCOÖN Pergamene artists may have inspired the work of Hagesandros, Polydoros, and Athenodoros, three sculptors on the island of Rhodes named by Pliny the Elder as the creators of the famed **LAOCOÖN**

AND HIS SONS (**FIG. 5-65**). This work has been assumed by many art historians to be a Hellenistic original from the first century BCE, although others argue that it is a brilliant copy, a creative adaptation, or a Hellenistic-style invention commissioned by an admiring Roman patron in the first century CE.

The complex sculptural composition illustrates an episode from the Trojan War when the priest Laocoön warned the Trojans not to bring within their walls the giant wooden horse left behind by the Greeks. The gods who supported the Greeks retaliated by sending serpents from the sea to destroy Laocoön and his sons as they walked along the shore. The struggling figures, anguished faces, intricate diagonal movements, and skillful unification of diverse forces in a complex composition all suggest a strong relationship between Rhodian and Pergamene sculptors. Although sculpted in the round, the Laocoön was composed to be seen frontally and from close range, and the three figures resemble the relief sculpture on the altar from Pergamon.

Three Statues of Women

THE NIKE OF SAMOTHRACE This winged figure of Victory (**FIG. 5-66**) is even more theatrical than the Laocoön. In its original setting—in a hillside niche high above the theater in the Sanctuary of the Great Gods at Samothrace, perhaps drenched with spray from a fountain—this huge goddess must have reminded visitors of the god in Greek plays who descends from heaven to determine the outcome of the drama. The forward momentum of the Nike's heavy body is balanced by the powerful backward

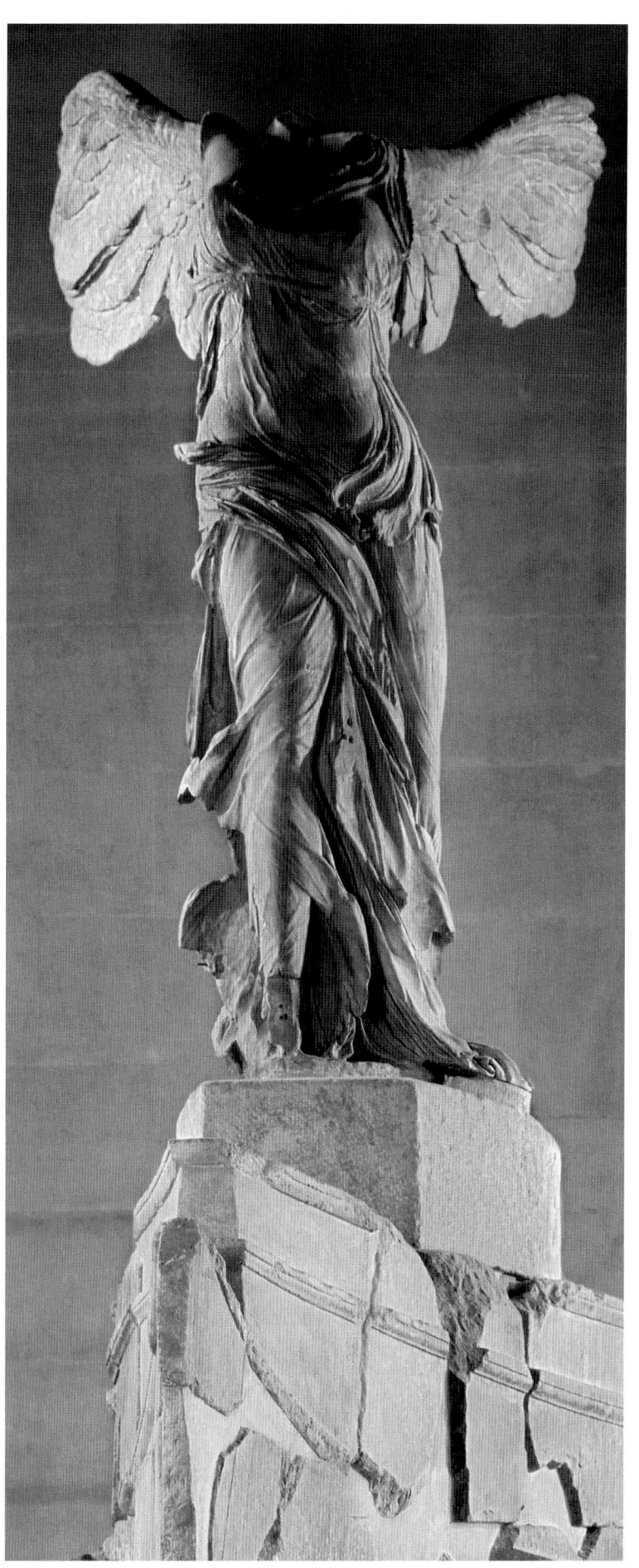

5-66 NIKE (VICTORY) OF SAMOTHRACE
Sanctuary of the Great Gods, Samothrace. c. 180 BCE (?). Marble, height 8′1″ (2.45 m). Musée du Louvre, Paris.

The wind-whipped costume and raised wings of this Nike indicate that she has just alighted on the prow of the stone ship that formed the original base of the statue. The work probably commemorated an important naval victory, perhaps the Rhodian triumph over the Seleucid king Antiochus III in 190 BCE. The Nike (lacking its head and arms) and a fragment of its stone ship base were discovered in the ruins of the Sanctuary of the Great Gods by a French explorer in 1863 (additional fragments were discovered later). Soon after, the sculpture entered the collection of the Louvre Museum in Paris.

5–67 OLD WOMAN

Roman 1st century BCE copy of a Greek work of the 2nd century BCE. Marble, height 49½″ (1.25 m). Metropolitan Museum of Art, New York. Rogers Fund, 1909. (09.39).

Credit: © 2016. Image copyright The Metropolitan Museum of Art/Art Resource/Scala, Florence

5–68 Alexandros from Antioch-on-the-Orontes **APHRODITE OF MELOS (VENUS DE MILO)**

c. 150–100 BCE. Marble, height 6′8″ (2.04 m). Musée du Louvre, Paris.

The original appearance of this famous statue's missing arms has been much debated. When it was dug up in a field on the Cycladean island of Milos in 1820, some broken pieces (now lost) found with it indicated that the figure was holding out an apple in its right hand. Many judged these fragments to be part of a later restoration, not part of the original statue. Another theory is that Aphrodite was admiring herself in the highly polished shield of the war god Ares, an image that was popular in the second century BCE. This theoretical "restoration" would explain the pronounced S-curve of the pose and the otherwise unnatural forward projection of the knee.

Credit: Photo © RMN/Hervé Lewandowski

thrust of her enormous wings. The large, open movements of the figure, the strong contrasts of light and dark on the deeply sculpted forms, and the contrasting textures of feathers, fabric, and skin typify the finest Hellenistic art.

OLD WOMAN The Hellenistic world was varied and multicultural, and some artists turned from generalizing idealism to an attempt to portray the world as they saw it, including representations of people from every level of society, unusual types as well as ordinary individuals. Traditionally, this figure of an aged woman (**FIG. 5-67**) has been seen as a seller on her way to the agora, carrying three chickens and a basket of produce. Despite the bunched and untidy disposition of her dress, however, it is elegant in design and made of fine fabric, and her hair is not in total disarray. These characteristics, along with the woman's sagging lower jaw, unfocused stare, and lack of concern for her exposed breasts, have led to a more recent interpretation that sees her as an aging, dissolute follower of Dionysos on her way to a religious festival, carrying offerings and wearing on her head the ivy wreath associated with the cult of this god of wine. Either way, she is the antithesis of the *Nike of Samothrace*. Yet in formal terms, both sculptures stretch out assertively into the space around them, both demand an emotional response from the viewer, and both display technical virtuosity in the rendering of forms and textures.

APHRODITE OF MELOS Not all Hellenistic artists followed the descriptive and expressionist tendencies of the artists of Pergamon and Rhodes. Some turned to the past, creating an eclectic style by reexamining and borrowing elements from earlier Classical styles and combining them in new ways. Many looked back to Praxiteles and Lysippos for their models. This was the case with Alexandros, son of Menides, the sculptor of an *Aphrodite* (better known as the **VENUS DE MILO**) (**FIG. 5-68**) found on the island of Melos by French excavators in the early nineteenth century. The dreamy gaze recalls Praxiteles's work (SEE FIG. 5-54), and the figure has the heavier proportions of High Classical sculpture, but the twisting stance and the strong projection of the knee are typical of Hellenistic art, as is the rich three-dimensionality of the drapery. The juxtaposition of soft flesh and crisp drapery, seemingly in the process of slipping off the figure, adds a note of erotic tension.

By the end of the first century BCE, the influence of Greek painting, sculpture, and architecture had spread to the artistic communities of the emerging Roman Empire. Roman patrons and artists maintained their enthusiasm for Greek art into Early Christian and Byzantine times. The urge to emulate the work of great Greek artists was so strong that, as we have seen throughout this chapter, much of our knowledge of Greek achievements comes from Roman replicas of Greek artworks and descriptions of Greek art by Roman writers.

Think About It

1 Discuss the development of a characteristically Greek approach to the representation of the male nude by comparing the Anavysos Kouros (**FIG. 5-20**), the Kritios Boy (**FIG. 5-27**), the *Spear Bearer* (**FIG. 5-43**), and *Hermes and the Infant Dionysos* (**FIG. 5-53**). What changes and what remains constant?

2 Choose a work from this chapter that illustrates a scene from a Greek myth or a scene from daily life in ancient Greece. Discuss the nature of the story or event, the particular aspect chosen for illustration by the artist, and the potential meaning of the episode in relation to its cultural context.

3 What ideals are embodied in the term "High Classicism," and what are the value judgments that underlie this art historical category? Select one sculpture and one building discussed in the chapter and explain why these works are regarded as High Classical.

4 Distinguish the attributes of the Doric and Ionic orders, focusing your discussion on a specific building representing each.

Crosscurrents

What is the common theme found in the heroic subjects depicted on these two very different works? What does the specific function and location of each indicate about the importance of that theme in each culture?

FIG. 2-6b

FIG. 5-39

6–1 Novios Plautios **THE FICORONI CISTA**

350–300 BCE. Bronze, height 2′6¼″ (78.6 cm). Museo Nazionale di Villa Giulia, Rome.

Credit: © Vincenzo Pirozzi, Rome fotopirozzi@inwind.it

Chapter 6
Etruscan and Roman Art

 ## Learning Objectives

6.a Identify the visual hallmarks of Etruscan and Roman styles for formal, technical, and expressive qualities.

6.b Interpret the meaning of works of Etruscan and Roman art based on their themes, subjects, and symbols.

6.c Relate Etruscan and Roman artists and art to their cultural, economic, and political contexts.

6.d Apply the vocabulary and concepts relevant to Etruscan and Roman art, artists, and art history.

6.e Interpret a work of Etruscan or Roman art using the art historical methods of observation, comparison, and inductive reasoning.

6.f Select visual and textual evidence in various media to support an argument or an interpretation of a work of Etruscan or Roman art.

Long before the Romans ruled the entire Italic peninsula as the center of an expanding empire, the Etruscans created a thriving culture in northern and central Italy. Etruscan artists were known throughout the Mediterranean world for their special sophistication in casting and engraving on bronze. Some of their most extraordinary works were created for domestic use, including a group of surviving **cistae**—cylindrical containers used by wealthy women as cases for toiletry articles such as mirrors, cosmetics, and perfume.

This exquisitely wrought and richly decorated example—**THE FICORONI CISTA**, named after an eighteenth-century owner—was made in the second half of the fourth century BCE and excavated in Palestrina (**FIG. 6-1**). It was commissioned by an Etruscan woman named Dindia Macolnia as a gift for her daughter, perhaps on the occasion of her marriage. The artist Novios Plautios signed the precisely engraved drawings around the cylinder, accomplished while the hammered bronze sheet from which it was constructed was still flat. First he incised lines within the metal, then filled them with a white substance to make them stand out. The cista's legs and handle—created by the figural group of Dionysus between two satyrs—were cast as separate pieces, attached during the assembly process.

The natural poses and individualization of these figures—both incised and cast—recalls the relaxed but lively naturalism of Etruscan wall paintings, but the Classicizing idealization of bodies and poses seems to come directly from contemporary Greek art. Furthermore, the use of broad foliate and ornamental bands to frame the frieze of figural narrative running around the cylinder matches the practice of famous Greek ceramic painters like Euphronios (see "Closer Look" on page 122). As with Greek pots, the most popular subjects for cistae were Greek myths. Here Novios has engraved sequential scenes drawn from an episode in the story of the Argonauts' quest for the Golden Fleece. The sailors sought water in the land of King Amykos, but the hostile king would give them water from his spring only if they beat him in a boxing match. After the immortal Pollux defeated Amykos, the Argonauts tied the king to a tree, the episode highlighted on the side of the cista seen here.

Novios Plautios probably based this scene on a monumental, mid-fourth-century BCE Greek painting of the Argonauts by Kydias that seems to have been in Rome at this time—perhaps explaining why the artist tells us in his incised signature that he executed this work in Rome. The combination of cultural components coming together in the creation of this cista—Greek stylistic sources in the work of an Etruscan artist living in Rome—will continue as Roman art develops out of the native heritage of Etruria and the emulation of the imported Classical heritage of the Greeks.

The Etruscans

How do the Etruscans develop distinctive types of architecture, tombs, and works in bronze?

At the end of the Bronze Age (about 1000 BCE), a central European people known as the Villanovans occupied the northern and western regions of the boot-shaped Italian peninsula, while the central area was home to people who spoke a closely related group of Italic languages, Latin among them. Beginning in the eighth century BCE, Greeks established colonies on the Italian mainland and in Sicily. From the seventh century BCE, people known as Etruscans, probably related to the Villanovans, gained control of the north and much of today's central Italy, an area known as Etruria. They reached the height of their power in the sixth century BCE, when they expanded into the Po River Valley to the north and the Campania region to the south (**MAP 6–1**).

Etruscan wealth came from fertile soil and an abundance of metal ore. Besides being farmers and metalworkers, the Etruscans were also sailors and merchants, and they exploited their resources in trade with the Greeks and with other people of the eastern Mediterranean. Etruscan artists knew and drew inspiration from Greek and Near Eastern art, assimilating such influences to create a distinctive Etruscan style.

Architecture

In architecture, the Etruscans established patterns of building that would be adopted later by the Romans. Cities were laid out on grid plans, like cities in Egypt and Greece, but more regularly. Two main streets—one usually running north–south and the other east–west—divided the city into quarters, with the town's business district centered at their intersection. We know something about Etruscan domestic architecture within these quarters, because they created house-shaped funerary urns and also decorated the interiors of tombs to resemble houses. Dwellings were designed around a central courtyard (or **atrium**) that was open to the sky, with a pool or cistern fed by rainwater.

MAP 6–1 THE ANCIENT ROMAN WORLD

This map shows the Roman Empire at its greatest extent, which was reached in 106 CE under the emperor Trajan.

TEMPLES The Etruscans incorporated Greek deities and heroes into their pantheon and, like the ancient Mesopotamians, used divination to predict future events. Beyond this and their burial practices (as revealed by the findings in their tombs), we know little about their religious beliefs. Our knowledge of the appearance of Etruscan temples comes from a few excavated foundations, from ceramic votive models, and from the later writings of the Roman architect Vitruvius, who sometime between 33 and 23 BCE compiled descriptions of the nature of Etruscan architecture (see "Roman Writers on Art" on page 168).

Walls with protective gates and towers surrounded Etruscan cities. The third- to second-century BCE city gate of Perugia, called the **PORTA AUGUSTA**, is one of the few surviving examples of Etruscan monumental architecture (**FIG. 6-2**). A tunnel-like passageway between two huge towers, this gate is significant for anticipating the Roman use of the round arch, which is here extended to create a semicircular barrel vault over the passageway. A square frame surmounted by a horizontal decorative element resembling an entablature sets off the entrance arch, which is accentuated by a molding. The decorative section is filled with a row of circular panels, or **roundels**, alternating with rectangular, columnlike upright strips called **pilasters** in an effect reminiscent of the Greek Doric frieze.

Etruscans built their temples with mud-brick walls; columns and entablatures were made of wood or a quarried volcanic rock (tufo) that hardens upon exposure to air. Vitruvius indicates that like the Greeks, Etruscan builders used the post-and-lintel structure and gable roofs, with bases, column shafts, and capitals recalling the Doric or Ionic order and entablatures resembling a Doric frieze (**FIG. 6-3**). Vitruvius used the term "**Tuscan order**" to describe the characteristic Etruscan variation of Doric—an unfluted shaft and simplified base, capital, and entablature (see "Roman Architectural Orders" on page 162).

6-3A MODEL OF AN ETRUSCAN TEMPLE
Based on descriptions by Vitruvius. Università della Sapienza, Rome.

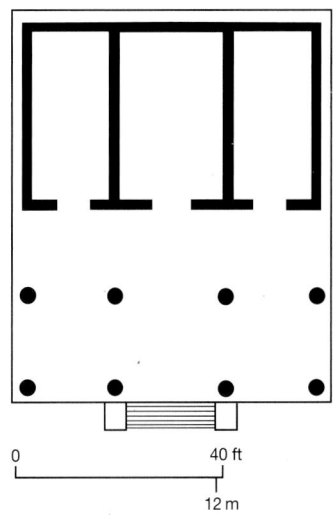

6-3B PLAN OF AN ETRUSCAN TEMPLE
Based on descriptions by Vitruvius.

Elements of Architecture

ROMAN ARCHITECTURAL ORDERS

The Etruscans and Romans adapted Greek architectural orders (see "The Greek Orders" on page 111) to their own tastes, often using them as applied decoration on walls. The Etruscans developed the Tuscan order by modifying the Doric order, adding a base under the shaft, which was often left unfluted. This system was subsequently adopted by the Romans. Later, the Romans created the **Composite order** by combining the volutes of Greek Ionic capitals with the acanthus leaves from the Corinthian order. In this diagram, the two Roman orders are shown on pedestals, which consist of a **plinth**, a **dado**, and a cornice.

Tuscan order   Composite order

Like the Greeks, the Etruscans built rectangular temples on a high platform, but they often imbedded them within urban settings. Rather than surrounding temples uniformly on all sides with a stepped stereobate and peristyle colonnade, as was the practice in Greece (SEE FIGS. 5–10, 5–37), Etruscans built a single flight of stairs leading to a columned porch on one short side. Etruscan siting and orientation also constitutes an important difference from Greek temples, which were built toward the center of an enclosed sacred precinct (SEE FIGS. 5–12, 5–36), rather than the Etruscan practice of siting them on the edge of a courtyard or public square. Also, there was an almost even division in Etruscan temples between porch and interior space, which was often divided into three rooms, presumably for cult statues (SEE FIG. 6–3B).

Although Etruscan temples were simple in form, they were embellished with dazzling displays of painting and terra-cotta sculpture. The temple roof, rather than the pediment, served as a base for large statue groups. Etruscan artists excelled at the imposing technical challenge of making huge terra-cotta figures for placement on temples. A splendid example is a life-size figure of **APULU (APOLLO)** (**FIG. 6–4**). To make such large clay sculptures, artists had to know how to construct figures so that they did not

collapse under their own weight while the raw clay was still wet. They also had to regulate the kiln temperature during the long firing process. The names of some Etruscan terra-cotta artists have come down to us, including that of a sculptor from Veii (near Rome) called Vulca, in whose workshop this figure of Apulu may have been created.

Dating from about 510–500 BCE and originally part of a four-figure scene depicting one of the labors of Hercle (Hercules), this boldly striding Apulu comes from the temple dedicated to Menrva (Minerva) and other gods in the sanctuary of Portonaccio at Veii. Four figures on the temple's ridgepole (horizontal beam at the peak of the roof) depicted Apulu and Hercle fighting for possession of a deer sacred to Aritimi (Diana), while she and Turms (Mercury) looked on.

Apulu's well-developed body and his "Archaic smile" clearly demonstrate that Etruscan sculptors were familiar with the *kouroi* of their Archaic Greek counterparts. But a comparison of the Apulu and a figure such as the Greek Anavysos Kouros (SEE FIG. 5–20) reveals telling differences. Unlike the Greek *kouros*, the body of the Etruscan Apulu is partially concealed by a rippling robe that cascades in knife-edged pleats to his knees. The forward-moving pose of the Etruscan statue also has a dynamic vigor that is avoided in the balanced, rigid stance of the Greek figure. This sense of energy expressed in purposeful movement is a defining characteristic of Etruscan sculpture and painting.

6–4 Master Sculptor Vulca (?) **APULU (APOLLO)**
From the temple of Minerva, Portonaccio, Veii. c. 510–500 BCE. Painted terra cotta, height 5′10″ (1.8 m). Museo Nazionale di Villa Giulia, Rome.

Credit: © Vincenzo Pirozzi, Rome

Tombs

Like the Egyptians, the Etruscans seem to have conceived tombs as homes for the dead. The Etruscan cemetery of La Banditaccia at Cerveteri, in fact, was laid out as a small town, with "streets" running between the grave mounds. The tomb chambers were partially or entirely excavated below the ground, and some were hewn out of bedrock. They were roofed over, sometimes with corbel vaulting, and covered with dirt and stones.

Etruscan painters had a remarkable ability to envision their subjects inhabiting a bright, tangible world just beyond the tomb. Vividly colored scenes of playing, feasting, dancing, hunting, fishing, and other leisure activities decorated the walls. In a late sixth-century BCE tomb from Tarquinia, wall paintings show two boys spending a day in the country, surrounded by the graceful flights of brightly colored birds (**FIG. 6–5**). The boy to the left is climbing a hillside to the promontory of a cliff, soon to put aside his clothes and follow his naked companion, caught by the artist in mid-dive, plunging toward the water below. Such charming scenes of carefree diversions, removed from the routine demands of daily life, seem to promise a pleasurable post-mortem existence to the occupant of this tomb. But this diver could also symbolize the deceased's own plunge from life into death (AS IN FIG. 5–35).

In a painted frieze in the **TOMB OF THE TRICLINIUM**, somewhat later but also from Tarquinia, the diversions are more mature in focus as young men and women frolic to the music of the lyre and double flute within a room whose ceiling is enlivened with colorful geometric decoration (**FIG. 6–6**). These dancers line the side walls, composed within a carefully arranged setting of stylized trees and birds, while at the end of the room couples recline on couches enjoying a banquet as cats prowl underneath the table looking for scraps. The immediacy of this wall painting is striking. Dancers and diners—women as well as men—are engaging in the joyful customs and diversions of human life as we know it.

Some tombs were carved out of the rock to resemble rooms in a house. The **TOMB OF THE RELIEFS**, for example, seems to have a flat ceiling supported by square stone posts (**FIG. 6–7**). Its walls were plastered and painted, and it was fully furnished. Couches were carved from stone, and other fittings were formed of stucco, a slow-drying type of plaster that can be easily molded and carved. Simulated pots, jugs, robes, axes, and other items were molded and carved to look like real objects hanging on hooks—even including what may be a family pet rendered in low relief at the bottom of the post just left of center.

The remains of the deceased were placed in urns or sarcophagi (coffins) made of clay or stone. On the terracotta **SARCOPHAGUS FROM CERVETERI**, dating from

6–5 BOYS CLIMBING ROCKS AND DIVING, TOMB OF HUNTING AND FISHING

Tarquinia, Italy. Late 6th century BCE.

Credit: © 2016. Photo Scala, Florence – courtesy of the Ministero Beni e Att. Culturali

about 520 BCE (**FIG. 6–8**), a husband and wife are shown reclining comfortably on a dining couch. The smooth, lifelike forms of their upper bodies are vertical and square-shouldered, but their hips and extended legs seem to sink into the softness of the couch. Rather than a somber memorial to the dead, we encounter two lively individuals with alert eyes and warm smiles. The man once raised a drinking vessel, addressing the viewer with the lively and engaging gesture of a genial host, perhaps offering an invitation to dine with them for eternity or to join them in the sort of convivial festivities recorded in the paintings on the walls of Etruscan tombs.

6–6 DANCERS AND DINERS, TOMB OF THE TRICLINIUM

Tarquinia, Italy. c. 480–470 BCE.

Credit: © akg-images/ De Agostini Picture Lib./G. Nimatallah

6-7 BURIAL CHAMBER, TOMB OF THE RELIEFS

Cerveteri, Italy. 3rd century BCE.

Credit: © 2016. Photo Scala, Florence - courtesy of the Ministero Beni e Att. Culturali

6-8 RECLINING COUPLE ON A SARCOPHAGUS FROM CERVETERI

c. 520 BCE. Terra cotta, length 6'7" (2.06 m). Museo Nazionale di Villa Giulia, Rome.

Portrait sarcophagi like this one evolved from earlier terra-cotta cinerary urns with sculpted heads of the deceased whose ashes they held.

Credit: © Araldo de Luca/ Corbis

The lid of another Etruscan sarcophagus—slightly later in date and carved of marble rather than molded in clay—also portrays a reclining Etruscan couple, but during a more private moment (**FIG. 6–9**). Dressed only in their jewelry and just partially sheathed by the light covering that clings to the forms of their bodies, this loving pair has been caught for eternity in a tender embrace, absorbed with each other rather than looking out to engage the viewer. The sculptor of this relief was clearly influenced by Greek Classicism in the rendering of human forms, but the human intimacy that is captured here is far removed from the cool, idealized detachment characterizing Greek funerary stelai (SEE FIG. 5–51).

Works in Bronze

The Etruscans were particularly skilled in casting and engraving on bronze. The richly decorated Ficoroni Cista, dated to the second half of the fourth century BCE and found in Palestrina, is inscribed with the words *Dindia Macolnia filea dedit/Novios Plautios med Romai Fecid* ("Novios Plautios made me in Rome/Dindia Macolnia gave [me] to her daughter") (SEE FIG. 6–1).

Since Etruscan bronze artists went to work for Roman patrons after Etruscan lands became part of the Roman Republic, distinguishing between Etruscan and early Roman art is often difficult. A head that was once part of a bronze statue of a man may be an example of an important Roman commission from an Etruscan artist (**FIG. 6-10**). Since it is over life size, this head may have been part of a commemorative work honoring a great man, and the downturned tilt of the head, as well as the flexing of the neck, have led many to propose that it was part of an equestrian figure. Traditionally dated to about 300 BCE, this rendering of a strong, broad face with heavy brows, hawk nose, firmly set lips, and clear-eyed expression is scrupulously detailed. The commanding, deep-set eyes are created with ivory inlay, within which float irises created of glass paste within a ring of bronze. The lifelike effect

6-9 MARRIED COUPLE (LARTH TETNIES AND THANCHVIL TARNAI) EMBRACING

Lid of a sarcophagus. c. 350–300 BCE. Marble, length 7′ (2.13 m). Museum of Fine Arts, Boston. Museum purchase with funds donated by Mrs Gardner Brewer and by contribution and the Benjamin Pierce Cheney Fund (86.145a-b).

Credit: Photograph © 2017 Museum of Fine Arts, Boston

6-10 HEAD OF A MAN (TRADITIONALLY KNOWN AS "BRUTUS")

c. 300 BCE. Bronze, eyes of painted ivory, height 12½″ (31.8 cm). Palazzo dei Conservatori, Rome.

Credit: © Araldo de Luca/Corbis

6–11 CAPITOLINE SHE-WOLF
c. 500 BCE or c. 800 CE? (Boys underneath, 15th century CE). Bronze, height 33½" (85 cm). Museo Capitolino, Rome.

Credit: © 2016 Photo Scala, Florence

is further enhanced by added eyelashes of separately cut pieces of bronze. This work is often associated with a set of male virtues that would continue to be revered by the Romans: stern seriousness, strength of character, the age-worn appearance of a life well lived, and the wisdom and sense of purpose it confers.

A famously ferocious she-wolf has long been considered an—if not the—outstanding example of Etruscan bronze sculpture (**FIG. 6–11**), lauded for its technical sophistication and expressive intensity and traditionally dated to c. 500–470 BCE. The animal confronts us with a vicious snarl, her tense body, thin flanks, and protruding ribs contrasting with her pendulous, milk-filled teats. Since she currently suckles two chubby human boys—Renaissance additions of the fifteenth century—the ensemble now evokes the story of the twins Romulus and Remus, legendary founders of Rome, who were nursed back to health by a she-wolf after having been left to die on the banks of the Tiber.

However, when the bronze she-wolf was restored and cleaned during 1997–2000 under the supervision of

archaeologist Anna Maria Carruba, Carruba mounted a serious challenge to its Etruscan pedigree. She argues that it dates not from antiquity, but from the Middle Ages. Technical as well as stylistic evidence supports her conclusions, specifically the fact that this unusual work, created by the lost-wax process, was formed in the medieval technique of single-pour casting, whereas all surviving Etruscan and Roman bronzes were assembled from separate pieces soldered together. Carruba's proposal of a date of c. 800 CE for the she-wolf has certainly caught the attention of specialists in ancient art, many of whom have revised their assessment of the work. Others are waiting for the full publication of the scientific evidence before removing the she-wolf from the Etruscan canon.

Etruscan art and architectural forms left an indelible stamp on the art and architecture of early Rome that was rivaled only by the influence of Greece. By 88 BCE, when the Etruscans were granted Roman citizenship, their art had already been absorbed into that of Rome.

The Roman Republic, 509–27 BCE

What are the distinctive modes of human representation and architectural design that emerge during the Roman Republic?

At the same time that the Etruscan civilization was flourishing, the Latin-speaking inhabitants of Rome began to develop into a formidable power. For a time, kings of Etruscan lineage ruled them, but in 509 BCE the Romans overthrew them and formed a republic centered in Rome. The Etruscans themselves were absorbed by the Roman Republic at the end of the third century BCE, by which time Rome had steadily expanded its territory in many directions. The Romans unified what is now Italy and, after defeating their rival, the North African city-state of Carthage, they established an empire that encompassed the entire Mediterranean region (SEE MAP 6–1).

At its greatest extent, in the early second century CE, the Roman Empire reached from the Euphrates River in southwest Asia to Scotland. It ringed the Mediterranean Sea—*mare nostrum*, or "our sea," the Romans called it. Those who were conquered by the Romans gradually assimilated Roman legal, administrative, and cultural structures that endured for some five centuries—in the eastern Mediterranean until the fifteenth century CE—and left a lasting mark on the civilizations that emerged in Europe.

The Romans themselves assimilated Greek gods, myths, and religious beliefs and practices into their state religion. During the imperial period, they also deified some of their emperors posthumously. Worship of ancient gods mingled with homage to past rulers, while oaths of allegiance to the living ruler made the official religion a political duty. Religious worship became increasingly ritualized, perfunctory, and distant from the everyday life of most people.

Many Romans adopted the so-called mystery religions of the people they had conquered. Worship of Isis and Osiris from Egypt, Cybele (the Great Mother) from Anatolia, the hero-god Mithras from Persia, and the single, all-powerful God of Judaism and Christianity from Palestine challenged the Roman establishment. These unauthorized religions flourished alongside the state religion with its Olympian deities and deified emperors, despite occasional government efforts to suppress them.

Early Rome was governed by kings and an advisory body of leading citizens called the Senate. The population was divided into two classes: a wealthy and powerful upper class, the patricians, and a lower class, the plebeians. In 509 BCE, Romans overthrew the last Etruscan king and established the Roman Republic as an oligarchy, a government by aristocrats, that would last about 450 years.

As a result of its stable form of government and especially of its encouragement of military conquest, by 275 BCE Rome controlled the entire Italian peninsula. By 146 BCE Rome had defeated its great rival, Carthage, on the north coast of Africa and taken control of the western Mediterranean. By the mid second century BCE Rome had taken Macedonia and Greece, and by 44 BCE it had conquered most of Gaul (present-day France) as well as the eastern Mediterranean (SEE MAP 6–1). Egypt remained independent until Octavian defeated Mark Antony and Cleopatra at the Battle of Actium in 31 BCE.

Art and its Contexts
ROMAN WRITERS ON ART

Only one book devoted specifically to the arts survives from antiquity. (All our other written sources consist of digressions and insertions in works on other subjects.) That one book, the *Ten Books on Architecture* by Vitruvius (c. 80–c. 15 BCE) is invaluable. Written for Augustus in the first century BCE, it is a practical handbook for builders that discusses such things as laying out cities, siting buildings, and using the Greek architectural orders. Vitruvius argued for appropriateness and rationality in architecture, and he also made significant contributions to art theory, including studies on proportion.

Pliny the Elder (c. 23–79 CE) wrote a vast encyclopedia of "facts, histories, and observations" known as *Naturalis Historia* (*Natural History*) that often included discussions of art and architecture. Pliny occasionally used works of art to make his points—for example, citing sculpture within his essays on stone and metals. His scientific turn of mind led to his death, for he was overcome while observing the eruption of Mount Vesuvius that buried Pompeii. His nephew, Pliny the Younger (c. 61–113 CE), a voluminous letter writer, added to our knowledge of Roman domestic architecture with his meticulous descriptions of villas and gardens.

Valuable bits of information can also be found in books by travelers and historians. Pausanias, a second-century CE Greek traveler, wrote descriptions that are basic sources on Greek art and artists. Flavius Josephus (c. 37–100 CE), a historian of the Flavians, wrote in his *Jewish Wars* a description of the triumph of Titus that includes the treasures looted from the Temple in Jerusalem (SEE FIG. 6–36).

During the Republic, Roman art was rooted in its Etruscan heritage, but territorial expansion brought wider exposure to the arts of other cultures. Like the Etruscans, the Romans admired Greek art. As Horace wrote (*Epistulae* ii, 1): "Captive Greece conquered her savage conquerors and brought the arts to rustic Latium." The Romans used Greek designs and Greek orders in their architecture, imported Greek art, and employed Greek artists. In 146 BCE, for example, they stripped the Greek city of Corinth of its art treasures and shipped them back to Rome.

Roman Portraiture

Portrait sculptors of the Republican period created life-like images seemingly based on the careful observation of their subjects. The strong emphasis on portraiture in Roman art may stem from the early practice of creating likenesses—in some cases actual wax death masks—of revered figures and distinguished ancestors for display on public occasions, most notably funerals. Contemporary historians left colorful evocations of this distinctively Roman custom. Polybius, a Greek exiled to Rome in the middle of the second century BCE, wrote home with the following description:

> … after the interment [of the illustrious man] and the performance of the usual ceremonies, they place the image of the departed in the most conspicuous position in the house, enclosed in a wooden shrine. This image is a mask reproducing with remarkable fidelity both the features and the complexion of the deceased. On the occasion of public sacrifices, they display these images, and decorate them with much care, and when any distinguished member of the family dies they take them to the funeral, putting them on men who seem to bear the closest resemblance to the original in stature and carriage…. There could not easily be a more ennobling spectacle for a young man who aspires to fame and virtue. For who would not be inspired by the sight of the images of men renowned for their excellence, all together and as if alive and breathing?… By this means, by the constant renewal of the good report of brave men, the celebrity of those who performed noble deeds is rendered immortal, while at the same time the fame of those who did good services to their country becomes known to the people and a heritage for future generations. (The Histories, 7.53, 54, trans. W.R. Paton, Loeb Library ed.)

Growing out of this heritage, Roman Republican portraiture is frequently associated with the notion of **verism**—an interest in the faithful reproduction of the immediate visual and tactile appearance of subjects. Since

6-12 PORTRAIT HEAD OF AN ELDER FROM SCOPPITO
1st century BCE. Marble, height 11″ (28 cm). Museo Nazionale, Chieti.

Credit: Canali Photobank, Milan, Italy

we find in these portrait busts the same sorts of individualizing physiognomic features that allow us to differentiate among the people we know in our own world, it is easy to assume that they are exact likenesses of their subjects as they appeared during their lifetime. Of course, this is impossible to verify, but our strong desire to believe it must realize the intentions of the artists who made these portraits and the patrons for whom they were made. From this emphasis on verism in the republican period develops a new Roman artistic ideal in human representation, an ideal quite different from the one we encountered in Greek Classicism. Instead of generalizing a human face, smoothed of its imperfections and caught in a moment of detached abstraction, this new Roman idealization emphasized—rather than suppressed—the hallmarks of advanced age and the distinguishing aspects of individual likenesses. This mode is most prominent in portraits of Roman patricians (**FIG. 6-12**), whose time-worn faces embody the wisdom and experience that come with old age. Frequently we take these portraits of wrinkled elders at face value, as highly realistic and faithful descriptions of actual human beings—contrasting Roman realism with Greek idealism—but there is good reason to think that these portraits actually conform to a particularly Roman type of idealization that underscores the effects of aging on the human face.

PORTRAIT SCULPTURE   The life-size bronze portrait of **AULUS METELLUS**—the Roman official's name is inscribed on the hem of his garment in Etruscan letters (**FIG. 6-13**)—dates to about 80 BCE. The statue, known from early times as *The Orator*, depicts a man addressing a gathering, his arm outstretched and slightly raised, a pose expressive of rhetorical persuasiveness. The orator wears sturdy laced leather boots and a folded and draped toga, the characteristic garment of a Roman senator. Perhaps the statue was mounted on an inscribed base in a public space by officials grateful for Aulus's benefactions on behalf of their city.

6-13 AULUS METELLUS (THE ORATOR)
Found near Perugia. c. 80 BCE. Bronze, height 5′11″ (1.8 m). Museo
Credit: © Quattrone, Florence

6-14 DENARIUS WITH PORTRAIT OF JULIUS CAESAR
44 BCE. Silver, diameter approximately ¾″ (2 cm). Ashmolean
Museum, Oxford.

Credit: Bridgeman Images

THE DENARIUS OF JULIUS CAESAR The propaganda value of portraits was not lost on Roman leaders. In 44 BCE, Julius Caesar issued a **DENARIUS** (a widely circulated coin) bearing his portrait (**FIG. 6-14**) conforming to the Roman ideal of advanced age, with notable wrinkles of flesh on the neck and sunken areas on the face. He was the first Roman leader to place his own image on a coin, initiating a practice that would be adopted by his successors, but at the time when this coin was minted it smacked of the sort of megalomaniacal behavior that would ultimately lead to his assassination. Perhaps it is for this reason that Caesar underscores his age, and thus his old-fashioned respectability, in this portrait, which reads as a mark of his traditionalism as a senator. The inscription placed in front of his face—CAESAR IMP—refers to his title of "imperator" or military commander, and the two objects behind him—the spiraling lituus employed by augurs to interpret divine will, and the simpulum or sacrificial jug used for libations—signify his priestly role in religious ceremony.

PATRICIAN CARRYING PORTRAIT BUSTS OF TWO ANCESTORS   A life-size marble statue of a Roman **PATRICIAN** (**FIG. 6-15**) dating from the period of the Emperor Augustus reflects the practices documented much earlier by Polybius and links the man portrayed with a revered tradition and its laudatory associations. The large marble format emulates a Greek notion of sculpture, and its use here signals not only this man's wealth but also his sophisticated artistic tastes, characteristics he shared with the emperor himself. His toga, however, is not Greek but indigenous and signifies his respectability as a Roman

6–15 PATRICIAN CARRYING PORTRAIT BUSTS OF TWO ANCESTORS (KNOWN AS THE BARBERINI TOGATUS)
End of 1st century BCE or beginning of 1st century CE. Marble, height 5′5″ (1.65 m). Palazzo de Conservatori, Rome.

The head of this standing figure, though ancient Roman in origin, is a later replacement and not original to this statue. The separation of head and body in this work is understandable since in many instances the bodies of full-length portraits were produced in advance, waiting in the sculptor's workshop for a patron to commission a head with his or her own likeness that could be attached to it. Presumably the busts carried by this patrician were likewise only blocked out until they could be carved with the faces of the commissioner's ancestors. These faces share a striking family resemblance, and the stylistic difference reproduced in the two distinct bust formats reveals that these men lived in successive generations. They could be the father and grandfather of the man who carries them.

Credit: © Araldo de Luca/Corbis

citizen of some standing. The busts of ancestors that he holds in his hands document his distinguished lineage in the privileged upper class (laws regulated which members of society could own such collections), and the statue as a whole proclaims his adherence to the family tradition by having his own portrait created.

The Roman Arch

The round arch was not an Etruscan or Roman invention, but the Etruscans and Romans were the first to make widespread use of it (SEE FIG. 6-2)—both as an effective structural idea and an elegant design motif.

Round arches displace most of their weight, or downward **thrust** (see arrows on diagram), along their curving sides, transmitting that weight to adjacent supporting uprights (door or window jambs, columns, or piers). From there, the thrust goes to, and is supported by, the ground. To create an arch, brick or cut stones are formed into a curve by fitting together wedge-shaped pieces, called **voussoirs**, until they meet and are locked together at the top center by the final piece called the **keystone**. These voussoirs exert an outward as well as a downward thrust, so arches may require added support, called **buttressing**, from adjacent masonry elements.

Until the keystone is in place and the mortar between the bricks or stones dries, an arch is held in place by wooden scaffolding called **centering**. The points from which the curves of the arch rise are called **springings**, and their support is often reinforced by **impost blocks**. The wall areas adjacent to the curves of the arch are **spandrels**. In a succession of arches, called an **arcade**, the space encompassed by each arch and its supports is called a **bay**.

keystone
spandrel   spandrel   extrados
voussoirs   intrados
impost   springing   centering
jamb   pier   pier
bay
round arch

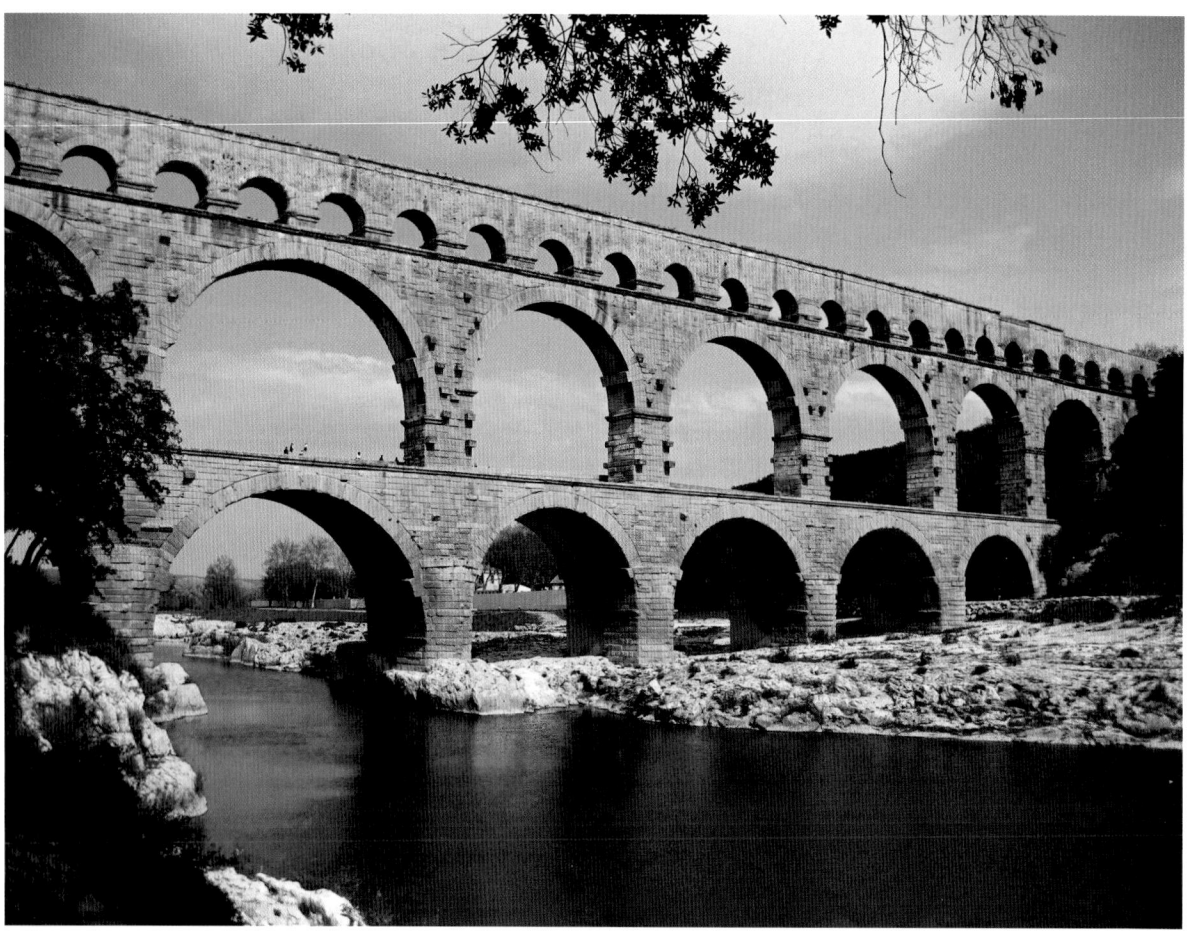

6–16 PONT DU GARD

Nîmes, France. Late 1st century BCE. Height above river 160′ (49 m), width of road bed on lower arcade 20′ (6 m).

Credit: © Filipa Fuxa/Shutterstock

A stunning example of the early Roman use of the round arch is a bridge known as the **PONT DU GARD** (**FIG. 6–16**), part of an aqueduct built in the late first century BCE near Nîmes, in southern France. An ample water supply was essential for a city, and the Roman invention to supply this water was the aqueduct, built with arcades—a linear series of arches. This aqueduct brought water from springs 30 miles to the north using a simple gravity flow, and it provided 100 gallons a day for every person in Nîmes. Each arch buttresses its neighbors and the huge arcade ends solidly in the hillsides. The structure conveys the balance, proportions, and rhythmic harmony of a great work of art, and although it harmonizes with its natural setting, it also makes a powerful statement about Rome's ability to control nature in order to provide for its cities. Both structure and function are marks of Roman civilization.

Temples

Architecture during the Roman Republic reflected both Etruscan and Greek practices. Like the Etruscans, the Romans built urban temples in commercial centers as well as in special sanctuaries. An early example is a small rectangular temple standing on a raised platform, or podium, beside the Tiber River in Rome (**FIG. 6–17**), probably from the second century BCE and perhaps dedicated to Portunus, the god of harbors and ports. This temple uses the Etruscan system of a rectangular cella and a front porch at one end reached by a broad, inviting flight of steps, but the Roman architects have adopted the Greek Ionic order, with full columns on the porch and half-columns **engaged** (set into the wall) around the exterior walls of the cella (SEE FIG. 6–17B) and a continuous frieze in the entablature. The overall effect resembles a Greek temple, but there are two major differences. First, Roman architects liberated the form of the column from its post-and-lintel structural roots and engaged it onto the surface of the wall as a decorative feature. Second, while a Greek temple encourages viewers to walk around the building and explore its uniformly articulated sculptural mass, Roman temples are defined in relation to interior spaces, which visitors are invited to enter through one opening along the longitudinal axis of a symmetrical plan.

By the first century BCE nearly a million people lived in Rome, which had evolved into the capital of a formidable commercial and political power with a growing overseas empire. As long as Republican Rome was essentially a large city-state, its form of government—an oligarchy under the control of a Senate—remained feasible. But as the empire around it grew larger and larger, a government of competing senators and military commanders could not enforce taxation and maintain order in what was becoming a vast and complicated territorial expanse. As governance of the Republic began to fail, power became concentrated in fewer and fewer leaders, until it was ruled by one man, an emperor, rather than by the Senate.

The Early Empire, 27 BCE–96 CE

What changes and innovations in art and architecture take place when Rome becomes an empire?

The first Roman emperor was born Octavian in 63 BCE. When he was only 18 years old, his brilliant great-uncle, Julius Caesar, adopted him as son and heir, recognizing in him qualities that would make him a worthy successor. Shortly after Julius Caesar refused the Senate's offer of the imperial crown early in 44 BCE, a group of conspirators murdered him, and the 19-year-old Octavian stepped up to take his place. Over the next 17 years, acting as a

general, politician, and public-relations genius, Octavian vanquished warring internal factions and brought peace to fractious provinces. By 27 BCE the Senate had conferred on him the title of Augustus (meaning "exalted," or "sacred"). Assisted by his astute and pragmatic second wife, Livia, Augustus led the state and the empire for 45 years. He established efficient rule and laid the foundation for an extended period of stability, domestic peace, and economic prosperity known as the *Pax Romana* ("Roman Peace"), which lasted more than 200 years (27 BCE to 180 CE). In 12 BCE he became Pontifex Maximus ("High Priest"), the empire's highest religious official, as well as its political leader.

Conquering and maintaining a vast empire required not only the inspired leadership and tactics of Augustus, but also careful planning and great administrative skill, backed by massive logistical support. These qualities are reflected in some of Rome's most enduring contributions to Western civilization: its system of law, its governmental and administrative structures, and its sophisticated civil engineering and architecture.

To facilitate the development and administration of the empire, as well as to make city life comfortable and attractive to its citizens, the Roman state undertook building programs of unprecedented scale and complexity, mandating the construction of central administrative and legal centers (forums and basilicas), recreational facilities

6-17A EXTERIOR VIEW OF A TEMPLE, PERHAPS DEDICATED TO PORTUNUS
Forum Boarium (Cattle Market), Rome. Late 2nd century BCE.

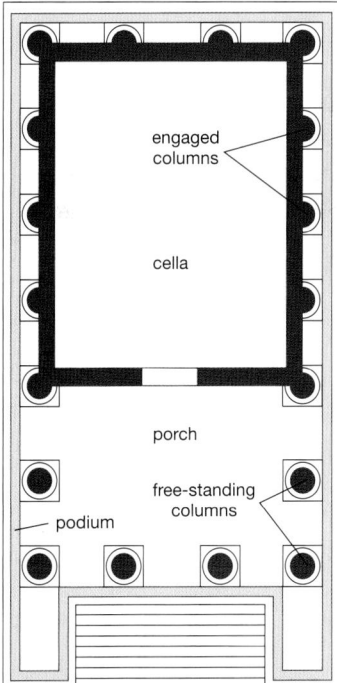

engaged columns

cella

porch

free-standing columns

podium

6-17B PLAN OF A TEMPLE, PERHAPS DEDICATED TO PORTUNUS
Forum Boarium (Cattle Market), Rome. Late 2nd century BCE.

6–18 AUGUSTUS OF PRIMAPORTA

Early 1st century CE. Perhaps a copy of a bronze statue of c. 20 BCE. Marble, originally painted with color, height 6′8″ (2.03 m). Musei Vaticani, Braccio Nuovo, Rome.

Credit: © Araldo de Luca/Corbis

(racetracks, stadiums), temples, markets, theaters, public baths, aqueducts, middle-class housing, and even entire new towns. To accomplish these tasks without sacrificing beauty, efficiency, and human well-being, Roman builders and architects developed rational plans using easily worked but durable materials and highly sophisticated engineering methods.

To move their armies about efficiently, to speed communications between Rome and the farthest reaches of the empire, and to promote commerce, the Romans built a vast and complex network of roads and bridges. Many modern European streets and highways still follow the lines laid down by Roman engineers; some Roman bridges are even still in use.

Art in the Age of Augustus

Roman artists of the Augustan age created a new style—a new Roman form of idealism that, though still grounded in the appearance of the everyday world, revived Greek Classical ideals. They enriched the art of portraiture in both official images and representations of private individuals, they recorded contemporary historical events on public monuments, and they contributed unabashedly to Roman imperial propaganda.

AUGUSTUS OF PRIMAPORTA In the sculpture known as **AUGUSTUS OF PRIMAPORTA** (**FIG. 6–18**)—because it was discovered in Livia's villa at Primaporta, near Rome (SEE FIG. 6–31)—we see the emperor as he wanted to be seen and remembered. This work demonstrates the creative combination of earlier sculptural traditions that is a hallmark of Augustan art. In its idealization of a specific ruler and his prowess, the sculpture also illustrates the way Roman emperors would continue to use portraiture for propaganda that not only expressed their authority directly, but rooted it in powerfully traditional stories and styles.

The sculptor of this larger-than-life marble statue adapted the standard pose of a Roman orator (SEE FIG. 6–13) by melding it with the contrapposto and canonical proportions developed by the Greek High Classical sculptor Polykleitos, as exemplified by his *Spear Bearer* (SEE FIG. 5–43). Like the heroic Greek figure, Augustus's portrait captures him in the physical prime of youth, far removed from the image of advanced age idealized in the coin portrait of Julius Caesar (SEE FIG. 6–14). Although Augustus lived almost to age 76, in his portraits he is always a vigorous ruler, eternally young. But like Caesar, and unlike the *Spear Bearer*, Augustus's face is rendered with the kind of details that make this portrait an easily recognizable likeness.

To this combination of Greek and Roman traditions, the sculptor of the *Augustus of Primaporta* added mythological and historical imagery that exalts Augustus's family and celebrates his accomplishments. Cupid, son of the

goddess Venus, rides a dolphin next to the emperor's right leg, a reference to the claim of the emperor's family, the Julians, to descent from the goddess Venus through her human son Aeneas. Augustus's anatomically conceived cuirass (torso armor) is also covered with figural imagery. Mid-torso is a scene representing Augustus's 20 BCE diplomatic victory over the Parthians; a Parthian (on the right) returns a Roman military standard to a figure variously identified as a Roman soldier or the goddess Roma. Looming above this scene at the top of the cuirass is a celestial deity who holds an arched canopy, implying that the peace signified by the scene below has cosmic implications. The personification of the earth at the bottom of the cuirass holds an overflowing cornucopia, representing the prosperity brought by Augustan peace.

THE ARA PACIS AUGUSTAE One of the most extraordinary surviving Roman monuments from the time of Augustus is the **ARA PACIS AUGUSTAE**, or Altar of Augustan Peace (**FIG. 6–19**), begun in 13 BCE and dedicated in 9 BCE on the occasion of Augustus's triumphal return to the capital after three years spent establishing Roman rule in Gaul and Hispania. In its original location in the Campus Martius (Plain of Mars), the Ara Pacis was aligned with a giant sundial, marked out on the pavement with lines and bronze inscriptions and using as its pointer an Egyptian obelisk that Augustus had earlier brought from Heliopolis to signify Roman dominion over this ancient land.

The Ara Pacis itself consists of a walled rectangular enclosure surrounding an open-air altar, emulating Greek custom (**FIG. 6–20**). Made entirely of marble panels carved with elaborate sculpture, the monument presented powerful propaganda, uniting portraiture and allegory, religion and politics, the private and the public. On the inner walls, a series of foliate garlands hang in swags from ox skulls. The skulls symbolize sacrificial offerings at the altar during annual commemorations, and the garlands—including fruits and flowers from every season—signify the continuing peace and prosperity that Augustus brought to the Roman world.

On the exterior, this theme of natural prosperity continues in lower reliefs of lavish, scrolling acanthus leaves populated by animals. Above them, decorative allegory gives way to figural tableaux. On the front and back are framed allegorical scenes evoking the mythical history of Rome and the divine ancestry of Augustus. The longer sides portray two continuous processions, seemingly representing actual historical events rather than myth or allegory. Perhaps they document Augustus's triumphal return, or they could memorialize the dedication and first sacrifice performed by Augustus on the completed altar itself. In any event, the arrangement of the participants is emblematic of the fundamental dualism characterizing Roman rule under Augustus. On one side march members

6–19 ARA PACIS AUGUSTAE (ALTAR OF AUGUSTAN PEACE)
Rome. 13–9 BCE. View of west side. Marble, approx. 34′5″ × 38′ (10.5 × 11.6 m).

This monument was begun when Augustus was 50 (in 13 BCE) and was dedicated on Livia's 50th birthday (9 BCE).

Credit: © akg-images/Andrea Jemolo

of the Senate, a stately line of male elders. But on the other is Augustus's imperial family (**FIG. 6-21**)—men, women, and, notably, children, who stand in the foreground as Augustus's hopes for dynastic succession. Whereas most

6-20 RECONSTRUCTION DRAWING OF THE ARA PACIS AUGUSTAE

Credit: © Dorling Kindersley

of the adults maintain their focus on the ceremonial event, the imperial children are allowed to fidget, look at their cousins, or reach up to find comfort in holding the hands or tugging at the garments of the adults around them, one of whom puts her finger to her mouth in a shushing gesture, perhaps seeking to mitigate their distracting behavior. The lifelike aura brought by such anecdotal details underlines the earthborn reality of the ideology embodied here. Rome is now subject to the imperial rule of the family of Augustus, and this stable system will bring continuing peace and prosperity since his successors have already been born.

The processional friezes on the exterior sides of the enclosure wall clearly reflect Classical Greek works like the Ionic frieze of the Parthenon (SEE FIG. 5-40), with their three-dimensional figures wrapped in revealing draperies that also create rhythmic patterns of rippling folds. But unlike the Greek sculptors of the Parthenon, the Roman sculptors of the Ara Pacis depicted actual individuals participating in a specific event at a known time. The Classical style may evoke the general notion of a Golden Age, but the historical references and identifiable figures in the Ara Pacis procession associate that Golden Age specifically with Augustus and his dynasty.

6–21 IMPERIAL PROCESSION
Detail of a relief on the south side of the Ara Pacis. Height 5′2″ (1.6 m).

The figures in this frieze represent members of Augustus's extended family, and scholars have proposed some specific, if tentative, identifications. The middle-aged man with the shrouded head at the far left is generally accepted to be a posthumous portrait of Marcus Agrippa, who would have been Augustus's successor had he not predeceased him in 12 BCE. The bored but well-behaved youngster pulling at Agrippa's robe—and being restrained gently by the hand of the man behind him—is probably Agrippa's son Gaius Caesar. The heavily swathed woman next to Agrippa on the right may be Augustus's wife, Livia, followed perhaps by Tiberius, who would become the next emperor. Behind Tiberius could be Antonia, the niece of Augustus, looking back at her husband, Drusus, Livia's younger son. She may grasp the hand of Germanicus, one of her younger children. The depiction of children and real women in an official relief was new to the Augustan period and reflects Augustus's desire to promote private family life as well as to emphasize his potential heirs and thus the continuity of his dynasty.

Credit: © akg-images/Andrea Jemolo

The Ara Pacis did not survive from antiquity in the form we see today. The monument eventually fell into disuse, ultimately into ruin. Remains were first discovered in 1568, but complete excavation took place only in 1937–1938 under the supervision of archaeologist Giuseppe Moretti, sponsored by the Italian dictator Benito Mussolini, who was fueled by his own ideological objectives. Once the monument had been unearthed, Mussolini had it reconstructed and commissioned a special building to house it, close to the **Mausoleum** (monumental tomb) of Augustus, all in preparation for celebrating the 2,000th anniversary of Augustus's birth, and associating the Roman imperial past with Mussolini's fascist state. The dictator even planned his own burial within Augustus's mausoleum.

More recently, the City of Rome commissioned American architect Richard Meier to design a new setting for the Ara Pacis, this time within a sleek, white box with huge walls of glass that allow natural light to flood the exhibition space (SEEN IN FIG. 6-19). Many Italian critics decried the Modernist design of Meier's building—completed in 2006—but this urban renewal project focused on the Ara Pacis has certainly revived interest in one of the most precious remains of Augustan Rome.

The Gemma Augustea

After Augustus's death in 14 CE, the Roman Senate deified him by decree, and his stepson Tiberius became emperor (ruled 14–37 CE). In acknowledgment of the lineage of both—Augustus from Julius Caesar and Tiberius from his father, Tiberius Claudius Nero, Livia's first husband—the dynasty is known as the Julio-Claudian (14–68 CE). It ended with the death of Nero in 68 CE.

An exquisite large onyx **cameo** (a gemstone carved in low relief) known as the **GEMMA AUGUSTEA** glorifies Augustus as triumphant over barbarians (a label for foreigners that the Romans adopted from the Greeks) and as the deified emperor (**FIG. 6-22**). The emperor, crowned with a victor's wreath, sits at the center right of the upper register. He has assumed the pose and identity of Jupiter, the king of the gods; an eagle, sacred to Jupiter, stands at his feet. Sitting next to him is a personification of Rome that seems to have Livia's features. The sea goat in the roundel between them may represent Capricorn, the emperor's zodiac sign.

Tiberius, as the adopted son of Augustus, steps out of a chariot at far left, returning victorious from the German

6-22 GEMMA AUGUSTEA

Early 1st century CE.
Onyx, 7½ × 9" (19 × 23 cm).
Kunsthistorisches Museum,
Vienna.

Credit: © KHM-
Museumsverband

front prepared to assume the throne as Augustus's chosen heir. Below this realm of godlike rulers, Roman soldiers are raising a post or standard on which armor captured from the defeated enemy is displayed as a trophy. The cowering, shackled barbarians on the bottom right wait to be tied to it. The artist of the Gemma Augustea brilliantly combines idealized, heroic figures based on Classical Greek art with recognizable Roman portraits, bringing together the dramatic action of Hellenistic art with Roman attention to descriptive detail and historical specificity.

Roman Cities

In good times and bad, individual Romans—like people everywhere at any time—tried to live a decent or even comfortable life with adequate shelter, food, and clothing. Romans loved to have contact with the natural world. The middle classes enjoyed their gardens, wealthy city dwellers maintained rural estates, and Roman emperors had country villas that were both functioning farms and places of recreation. Wealthy Romans even brought nature indoors by commissioning artists to paint landscapes on the interior walls of their homes. Through the efforts of the modern archaeologists who have excavated them, Roman cities and towns, houses, apartments, and country villas still evoke for us the ancient Roman way of life with amazing clarity.

Roman architects who designed new cities or expanded and rebuilt existing ones based their urban plans on the layout of Roman army camps. Like Etruscan towns, they were designed as a grid with two bisecting main streets crossing at right angles to divide the layout into quarters. The **forum** and other public buildings were generally located at this intersection, the site of the commander's headquarters in a military camp.

Much of the housing in a Roman city consisted of brick apartment blocks called *insulae*. These apartment buildings had internal courtyards, multiple floors joined by narrow staircases, and occasionally overhanging balconies. City dwellers—then as now—were social creatures who spent much of their lives in public markets, squares, theaters, baths, and neighborhood bars. The city dweller returned to the *insulae* to sleep, perhaps to eat. Even women enjoyed a public life outside the home—a marked contrast to the circumscribed lives of Greek women.

The affluent southern Italian city of Pompeii, a thriving center of between 10,000 and 20,000 inhabitants, gives a vivid picture of Roman city life. In 79 CE Mount Vesuvius erupted, burying the city under more than 20 feet of volcanic ash and preserving it until its rediscovery and excavation beginning in the eighteenth century (**FIGS. 6-23, 6-24**). Temples and government buildings surrounded a main square, or forum; shops and houses lined mostly straight, paved streets; and a protective wall enclosed the

**6-23 AERIAL VIEW
OF THE RUINS OF
POMPEII**

Destroyed 79 CE.

Credit: © David Hiser/National
Geographic Creative/Corbis

**6-24 DRAWING OF CENTRAL POMPEII
IN ITS CURRENT STATE**

Credit: © Dorling Kindersley

House of
the Vettii

Stabian baths

theater

forum baths

market

forum

temple of Apollo

forum basilica

sea gate

heart of the city. The forum was the center of civic life in Roman cities, as the agora was in Greek cities. Business was conducted in its basilicas and porticos, religious duties performed in its temples, and speeches delivered in its open square. For recreation, people went to the nearby baths or to events in the theater or amphitheater.

Roman Houses

Wealthy city dwellers lived in private houses with enclosed gardens; these houses were often fronted by shops facing the street. The Romans emphasized the interior rather than the exterior in such gracious domestic architecture.

A Roman house usually consisted of small rooms laid out around one or two open courts, the atrium and the peristyle (**FIG. 6-25**). People entered the house from the street through a vestibule and stepped into the atrium, a large space with an **impluvium** (pool for catching rainwater). The peristyle was a planted courtyard, farther into the house and enclosed by columns. Off the peristyle was the formal reception room or office called the tablinum; here the head of the household conferred with clients. Portrait busts of the family's ancestors might be displayed in the tablinum or in the atrium. Private areas—such as the family dining room, sitting rooms, and bedrooms (*cubicula*)—and service areas—such as the kitchen and servants' quarters—could be arranged around the peristyle or the atrium.

6-25 PLAN AND RECONSTRUCTION DRAWING OF THE HOUSE OF THE SILVER WEDDING
Pompeii. 1st century CE.

Credit: Reprinted with the permission of Cambridge University Press

In Pompeii, where the mild southern climate permitted gardens to flourish year-round, the peristyle was often turned into an outdoor living room with painted walls, fountains, and sculpture, as in the mid-first-century CE remodeling of the second-century BCE **HOUSE OF THE VETTII** (**FIG. 6-26**). Since Roman houses were designed in

6-26 PERISTYLE GARDEN, HOUSE OF THE VETTII
Pompeii. Rebuilt 62–79 CE.

Credit: © Mimmo Jodice/Corbis

relation to a long axis that runs from the entrance straight through the atrium and into the peristyle, visitors were greeted at the door of the house with a deep vista, showcasing the lavish residence of their host and its beautifully designed and planted gardens extending into the distance.

Little was known about these gardens until archaeologist Wilhelmina Jashemski (1910–2007) excavated the peristyle in the House of G. Polybius in Pompeii, beginning in 1973. Earlier archaeologists had usually ignored, or unwittingly destroyed, evidence of gardens, but Jashemski developed a new way to find and analyze their layouts and the plants cultivated in them. Workers first removed layers of debris and volcanic material to expose the level of the soil as it was before the eruption in 79 CE. They then collected samples of pollen, seeds, and other organic material and carefully injected plaster into underground root cavities. When the surrounding earth was removed, the roots, now in plaster, enabled botanists to identify the types of plants and trees cultivated in the garden and to estimate their size.

The garden in the house of Polybius was surrounded on three sides by a portico, which protected a large cistern on one side that supplied the house and garden with water. Young lemon trees in pots lined the fourth side of the garden, and nail holes in the wall above the pots indicated that the trees had been espaliered—pruned and trained to grow flat against a support—a practice still in use today. Fig, cherry, and pear trees filled the garden space, and traces of a fruit-picking ladder, wide at the bottom and narrow at the top to fit among the branches, was found on the site.

An aqueduct built during the reign of Augustus eliminated Pompeii's dependence on wells and rainwater basins and allowed residents to add to their gardens pools, fountains, and flowering plants that needed heavy watering. In contrast to earlier, unordered plantings, formal gardens with low, clipped borders and plantings of ivy, boxwood, laurel, myrtle, acanthus, and rosemary—all mentioned by writers of the time—became fashionable. There is also evidence of topiary work (the clipping of shrubs and hedges into fanciful shapes), sculpture, and fountains. The peristyle garden of the House of the Vettii, for example, had more than a dozen fountain statues jetting water into marble basins (SEE FIG. 6-26). In the most elegant peristyles, mosaic decorations covered the floors, walls, and fountains.

Wall Painting

The interior walls of Roman houses were plain, smooth plaster surfaces with few architectural moldings or projections. On these invitingly blank fields artists created pictures at the House of the Vettii. Some used mosaic, but most painted with pigment suspended in a water-based solution of lime and soap, sometimes with a little wax. After such paintings were finished, they were polished with a special metal, glass, or stone burnisher and then buffed with a cloth. Many fine wall paintings in a series of developing styles have come to light through excavations, first in Pompeii and other communities surrounding Mount Vesuvius, near Naples, and more recently in and around Rome.

In the 1870s, German art historian August Mau (1840–1909) analyzed Pompeian wall painting and proposed a schematic organizing system that is still used by many today to categorize its stylistic development. In the earliest wall paintings from Pompeii, artists covered the walls with illusionistic paintings of thin slabs of colored marble and projecting architectural moldings. Mau referred to this as First-Style wall painting (c. 300–100 BCE). Later, painters began to extend the space of a room visually with scenes of figures on a shallow platform or with landscapes or cityscapes (SEE FIGS. 6-29, 6-30)—Mau's Second Style (c. 100–20 BCE). During the late first century BCE, Third-Style wall painting replaced vistas with solid planes of color decorated with fine, lively architectural and floral details and small, delicate vignettes (c. 20 BCE–c. 50 CE). The final phase of Pompeian wall painting, the Fourth Style (c. 50–79 CE), united all three earlier styles into compositions of enormous complexity (SEE FIG. 6-28), where some wall surfaces seem to recede or even disappear behind a maze of floating architectural forms, while other flat areas of color become the support for simulated paintings of narrative scenes or still lifes (compositions of inanimate objects).

HOUSE OF THE VETTII   Some of the finest surviving Roman wall paintings are found in the Pompeian House of the Vettii, whose peristyle garden we have already explored (SEE FIG. 6-26). The house was built to the axial house plan—with its entrance leading through an atrium to a peristyle garden (**FIG. 6-27**)—by two brothers, wealthy freed slaves A. Vettius Conviva and A. Vettius Restitutus. Between its damage during an earthquake in 62 CE and the eruption of Vesuvius in 79 CE, the walls of the house were repainted, and this spectacular Fourth-Style decoration was uncovered in a splendid state of preservation during excavations at the end of the nineteenth century.

A complex combination of painted fantasies fills the walls of a reception room off the peristyle garden (**FIG. 6-28**). At the base of the walls is a lavish frieze of simulated colored-marble revetment, imitating the actual stone veneers that are found in some Roman residences. Above this "marble" dado are broad areas of pure red or white, onto which are painted pictures resembling framed panel paintings, swags of floral garlands, or unframed figural vignettes. The framed picture here illustrates a Greek mythological scene from the story of Ixion, who was bound by Zeus to a spinning wheel in punishment for attempting

**6-27 PLAN OF THE
HOUSE OF THE VETTII**
Pompeii. Rebuilt 62–79 CE.

6-27 PLAN OF THE HOUSE OF THE VETTII
Pompeii. Rebuilt 62–79 CE.

to seduce Hera. Between these pictorial fields, and along a long strip above them that runs around the entire room, are fantastic architectural vistas with multicolored columns and undulating entablatures that recede into fictive space through the use of fanciful linear perspective. The fact that this fictive architecture is occupied here and there by volumetric figures only enhances the sense of three-dimensional spatial definition.

VILLAS Villas were the country houses of wealthy Romans, and their plans, though resembling town houses, were often more expansive and irregular. The eruption of Vesuvius in 79 CE preserved not only the houses along the city streets within Pompeii, but also the so-called **VILLA OF THE MYSTERIES** just outside the city walls. Here a series of elaborate figural murals from the mid first century BCE (**FIG. 6-29**) seem to portray the initiation rites of a mystery religion, probably the cult of Bacchus, which were often performed in private homes as well as in special buildings or temples. Perhaps this room was a shrine or meeting place for such a cult to this god of vegetation, fertility, and

wine. Bacchus (or Dionysus) was one of the most important deities in Pompeii.

The entirely painted architectural setting consists of a simulated marble dado (similar to that in the House of the Vettii) and, around the top of the wall, an elegant frieze supported by painted pilaster strips. The figural scenes take place on a shallow "stage" along the top of the dado, with a background of a brilliant, deep red—now known as Pompeian red—that, as we have already seen, was very popular with Roman painters. The tableau unfolds around the entire room.

The walls of a room from another villa, this one at Boscoreale, farther removed from Pompeii and dating slightly later, open onto a fantastic urban panorama (**FIG. 6-30**). Surfaces seem to dissolve; a painted series of columns and lintels frames the view of a maze of complicated architectural forms, like the painted scenic backdrops of a stage. Indeed, the theater may have inspired this kind of decoration, as the theatrical masks hanging from the lintels seem to suggest. By using a kind of **intuitive perspective**, the artists have created the impression of real space

**6-28 WALL PAINTING
IN THE "IXION ROOM,"
HOUSE OF THE VETTII**
Pompeii. Rebuilt 62–79 CE.

Credit: © Fotografica Foglia, Naples

**6-29 INITIATION RITES
OF THE CULT OF BACCHUS (?),
VILLA OF THE MYSTERIES**
Pompeii. Wall painting. c. 60–50 BCE.
Photo taken after 2015 restoration.

Credit: © Fotografica Foglia, Naples - courtesy of
the Ministero Beni e Att. Culturali e del Turismo -
Suprintendenza Pompei

6–30 CITYSCAPE, HOUSE OF PUBLIUS FANNIUS SYNISTOR

Boscoreale. Detail of a wall painting from a bedroom. c. 50–30 BCE. Metropolitan Museum of Art, New York. Rogers Fund, 1903. (03.14.13).

Credit: © 2016. Image copyright The Metropolitan Museum of Art/Art Resource/Scala, Florence

beyond the wall. In intuitive perspective, architectural details follow diagonal lines that the eye interprets as parallel lines receding into the distance, and objects meant to be perceived as far away from the surface plane of the wall are shown gradually smaller and smaller than those intended to appear in the foreground.

Close to Rome, the late first-century BCE paintings on the dining-room walls of Livia's villa at Primaporta exemplify yet another approach to creating a sense of expanded space with murals (FIG. 6-31). Instead of rendering a stage set or opening onto an expansive architectural vista, the artists here created the illusion of being on a porch or pavilion looking out over a low wall into an orchard of flowering shrubs and heavily laden fruit trees populated by a variety of wonderfully observed birds—an idealized view of the natural world. Here the painters used **atmospheric perspective**, where the world becomes progressively less distinct as it recedes into the distance.

A PAINTER AT WORK This fresco—portraying a painter absorbed in her art—once decorated the walls of a house in Pompeii (FIG. 6-32). Like women in Egypt and

Crete, Roman women were far freer and more worldly than their Greek counterparts. Many received a formal education and became physicians, writers, shopkeepers, or even overseers in such male-dominated businesses as shipbuilding. But we have little information about the role women played in the visual arts, making the testimony of this picture precious.

The painter sits within a room that opens behind her to the outdoors, holding her **palette**, a sign of her profession. She wears a long robe covered by an ample mantle, and a gold headband holds back her hair; but lighting and composition highlight two other aspects of her body: her centralized face, which focuses intently on the subject of her painting—a sculptured rendering of the bearded fertility god Priapus appearing in the shadows of the right background—and her right arm, which extends downward so she can dip her brush into a paintbox that rests precariously on a column drum next to her folding stool. A small child steadies the panel on which she paints, and two elegantly posed and richly dressed women—perhaps her patrons—stand next to a pier behind her. The art she is practicing reflects well on her social position. Pliny

6–31 GARDEN VISTA, VILLA OF LIVIA AT PRIMAPORTA
Near Rome. Late 1st century BCE. Museo Nazionale Romano, Rome.

Like the garlands and curling vine scrolls on the Ara Pacis Augustae (SEE FIG. 6–19), the lush fertility of nature seems to celebrate the vitality and prosperity of Rome under Augustan peace.

Credit: © Vincenzo Pirozzi, Rome

the Elder claimed that "Among artists, glory is given only to those who paint panel paintings" (*Natural History*, 35.118). Wall paintings, he claimed, are of lesser value because they cannot be removed in case of fire. For this fresco, however, fixed positioning facilitated survival. When Mount Vesuvius erupted, it was wall paintings like this one that were preserved.

6–32 A PAINTER AT WORK
From the House of the Surgeon, Pompeii. 1st century BCE –1st century CE. Fresco, 17⅞″ × 17⅜″ (45.5 × 45.3 cm). Museo Archeologico Nazionale, Naples.

This painting of a female artist at work was conceived as a simulated panel painting, positioned on the yellow wall of a small room (compare the red wall in FIG. 6–29). It was revered so highly by the archaeologists who discovered it in 1771 that it was cut out of the wall to be exhibited as a framed picture in a museum, a practice that would be anathema today but was far from unusual in the eighteenth century.

Credit: © 2016. Photo Scala, Florence/Fotografica Foglia – courtesy of the Minstero Beni e Att. Culturali

STILL LIFES AND PORTRAITS In addition to cityscapes, landscapes, and figural tableaux, other subjects that appeared in Roman art included exquisitely rendered genre scenes (SEE FIG. 6–32), still lifes, and portraits. A still-life panel from Herculaneum, a community in the vicinity of Mount Vesuvius near Pompeii, depicts everyday domestic objects—still-green peaches and a glass jar half-filled with water (FIG. 6–33). The items have been carefully arranged on two stepped shelves to give the composition clarity and balance. Strong light floods the picture from left to right, casting shadows, picking up highlights, and enhancing the illusion of solid objects in real space.

Few Pompeian paintings are more arresting than a double portrait of a young husband and wife (FIG. 6–34) who look out from their simulated spatial world beyond the wall into the viewer's space within the room. The swarthy, wispy-bearded man addresses us with a direct stare and holds a scroll, a conventional sign of educational achievement seen frequently in Roman portraits. Though his wife overlaps him to stake her claim to the foreground, she gazes out at us less directly. She also holds fashionable attributes of literacy—a stylus she elevates in front of her chin and a folding writing tablet on which she would have

6-33 STILL LIFE, HOUSE OF THE STAGS (CERVI)
Herculaneum. Detail of a wall painting. Before 79 CE. Approx. 1′2″ × 1′1½″ (35.5 × 31.7 cm). Museo Archeologico Nazionale, Naples.
Credit: © akg-images/Erich Lessing

6-34 PORTRAIT OF A MARRIED COUPLE
Wall painting from Pompeii. Mid 1st century CE. Height 25½″ (64.8 cm). Museo Archeologico Nazionale, Naples.

Credit: © Fotografica Foglia, Naples - courtesy of the Ministero Beni e Att. Culturali used the stylus to inscribe words into a wax infill. This picture is comparable to modern studio portrait photography with its careful lighting and retouching, conventional poses and accoutrements. Its attention to physiognomic detail—note the differences in the spacing of the two figures' eyes and the shapes of their noses, ears, and lips—makes it clear that we are in the presence of actual human likenesses.

The Flavians

The Julio-Claudian dynasty ended with the suicide of Nero in 68 CE, which led to a brief period of civil war. Eventually an astute general, Vespasian, seized control of the government in 69 CE, founding a new dynasty known as the Flavian. Led by practical military men who inspired confidence and ruled for the rest of the first century, the Flavian dynasty restored the imperial finances and stabilized the frontiers. The Julio-Claudian fashion for classicizing imperial portraiture was replaced by a return to the ideal of time-worn faces with the effects of old age enhanced to project a sense of wisdom and accomplishment.

THE ARCH OF TITUS   When Domitian assumed the throne in 81 CE, he immediately commissioned a triumphal arch to honor the capture of Jerusalem in 70 CE by his brother and deified predecessor, Titus. Part architecture, part sculpture, and distinctly Roman, free-standing triumphal arches commemorate a triumph, or formal victory celebration, during which a victorious general or emperor paraded through Rome with his troops, captives, and booty. Constructed of concrete and faced with marble, **THE ARCH OF TITUS** (FIG. 6–35) is essentially a free-standing gateway whose passage is covered by a barrel vault. It served as a giant base, 50 feet tall, for a now-lost bronze statue of the emperor in a four-horse chariot, a typical triumphal symbol. Applied to the faces of the arch are columns in the Composite order supporting an entablature. The inscription on the uppermost story declares that the Senate and the Roman people erected the monument to honor Titus.

Titus's capture of Jerusalem ended a fierce campaign to crush a revolt of the Jews in Palestine.

6–35 THE ARCH OF TITUS
Rome. c. 81 CE (restored 1822–1824).
Concrete and white marble,
height 50' (15 m).

The dedication inscribed across the tall attic story above the arch opening reads: "The Senate and the Roman people to the Deified Titus Vespasian Augustus, son of the Deified Vespasian." The perfectly sized and spaced Roman capital letters, meant to be read from a distance and cut with sharp terminals (serifs) to catch the light, established a standard that calligraphers and font designers still follow today.

6-36 SPOILS FROM THE TEMPLE IN JERUSALEM
Relief in the passageway of the Arch of Titus. Marble, height 6'8″ (2.03 m).

Credit: © 2016. Photo Scala, Florence

The Romans sacked and destroyed the Temple in Jerusalem, carried off its sacred treasures, and displayed them in a triumphal procession in Rome (**FIG. 6-36**). A relief on the inside walls of the arch captures the drama of the occasion, depicting Titus's soldiers flaunting this booty as they carry it through the streets of Rome. The soldiers head toward the right through an arch, turned obliquely to project into the viewer's own space, thus allowing living spectators a sense of the press of a boisterous, disorderly crowd.

The mood of the procession depicted in this relief contrasts with the relaxed but formal solemnity of the procession portrayed on the Ara Pacis (SEE FIG. 6-21), but like the sculptors of the Ara Pacis, the sculptors of the Arch of Titus showed the spatial relationships among figures by rendering nearer elements in higher relief than those more distant. A **menorah** (seven-branched lampholder) from the Temple in Jerusalem dominates the scene with its relatively high relief.

THE COLOSSEUM Romans were huge sports fans, and the Flavian emperors catered to their tastes by building splendid facilities. Construction of Rome's greatest arena, the **FLAVIAN AMPHITHEATER** (**FIGS. 6-37, 6-38**), began under Vespasian in 70 CE and was completed under Titus, who dedicated it in 80 CE. The Flavian Amphitheater came to be known as the "Colosseum," because a gigantic statue of Nero called the *Colossus* stood next to it. "Colosseum" is a most appropriate description of this enormous entertainment center. Its outer wall stands 159 feet high. It is an oval,

measuring 615 by 510 feet, with a floor 280 by 175 feet. This floor was laid over a foundation of service rooms and tunnels that provided an area for the athletes, performers, animals, and equipment. The floor was covered by sand, *arena* in Latin, hence the English term "arena" for a building of this type.

Roman audiences watched a variety of athletic events, blood sports, and spectacles, including animal hunts, fights to the death between gladiators or between gladiators and wild animals, performances of trained animals and acrobats, and even mock sea battles, for which the arena would be flooded. The opening performances in 80 CE lasted 100 days, during which time it was claimed that 9,000 wild animals and 2,000 gladiators died for the amusement of the spectators.

The amphitheater is so remarkably efficient—with easy access, perfect sight lines, and effective crowd control—that stadiums today still use its plan. Some 50,000 spectators could move easily through the 76 entrance doors to the 3 levels of seats—laid over barrel-vaulted access corridors and entrance tunnels—and the standing area at the top. Each spectator had an uninterrupted view of the events below, and the walls on the top level supported a huge awning that could shade the seats. Sailors, who had experience in handling ropes, pulleys, and large expanses of canvas, worked the apparatus that extended the awning.

The curving, outer wall of the Colosseum consists of three levels of arcades (linear series of arches) surmounted by a wall-like attic (top) story. Each arch is framed by engaged columns. Entablature-like friezes mark the divisions between levels. Each level also uses a different architectural order, increasing in complexity from bottom to top: the plain Tuscan order on the ground level, Ionic on the second level, Corinthian on the third, and Corinthian pilasters on the fourth. The attic story is broken by small, square windows, which originally alternated with gilded-bronze shield-shaped ornaments called **cartouches**, supported on brackets that are still in place.

All these elements are purely decorative. As we saw in the Etruscan Porta Augusta (SEE FIG. 6-2), the addition of post-and-lintel decoration to arched structures was an Etruscan innovation. The systematic use of the orders in a logical succession from sturdy Tuscan to lighter Ionic to decorative Corinthian follows a tradition inherited from Hellenistic architecture. This orderly, dignified, and visually satisfying way of organizing the façades

6-37 RECONSTRUCTION DRAWING OF THE FLAVIAN AMPHITHEATER (COLOSSEUM)
Rome. 70–80 CE.

Credit: © Dorling Kindersley

6-38 OUTER WALL OF THE FLAVIAN AMPHITHEATER (COLOSSEUM)
Rome. 70–80 CE.

Credit: © 123RF.com

Elements of Architecture

ROMAN VAULTING

The Romans became experts in devising methods of covering large, open architectural spaces with concrete and masonry, using barrel vaults, groin vaults, or domes.

A **barrel vault** is constructed in the same manner as the round arch. In a sense, it is a series of connected arches extended in sequence along a line. The outward pressure exerted by the curving sides of the barrel vault requires buttressing within or outside the supporting walls.

When two barrel-vaulted spaces intersect each other at the same level, the result is a **groin vault**. Both the weight and

outward thrust of the groin vault are concentrated on four corner piers; only the piers require buttressing, so the walls on all four sides can be opened. The Romans used the groin vault to construct some of their grandest interior spaces.

A third type of vault brought to technical perfection by the Romans is the **dome**. The rim of the dome is supported on a circular wall, as in the Pantheon (SEE FIGS. 6–48, 6–49, 6–51). This wall is called a drum when it is raised on top of a main structure. Sometimes a circular opening, called an **oculus**, is left at the top.

barrel vault

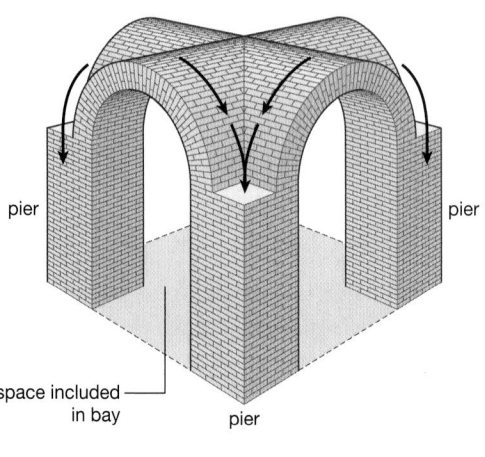

groin vault

of large buildings is still popular. Unfortunately, much of the Colosseum was dismantled in the Middle Ages as a source of marble, metal fittings, and materials for buildings such as churches.

PORTRAIT SCULPTURE Roman patrons continued to expect recognizable likenesses in their portraits, but this did not preclude idealization. A portrait sculpture of a **YOUNG FLAVIAN WOMAN** (FIG. 6–39) is idealized in a manner similar to the *Augustus of Primaporta* (SEE FIG. 6–18). Her features—a strong nose and jaw, heavy brows, deep-set eyes, and a long neck—are well observed and her hair is piled high in an extraordinary mass of ringlets following the latest court fashion. Executing the head required skillful chiseling and **drillwork**, a technique for rapidly cutting deep grooves with straight sides, used here to render the holes in the center of the curls. The overall effect is quite lifelike, as the play of light over the subtly sculpted marble surfaces simulates the textures of real skin and hair.

A contemporary bust of an older woman (FIG. 6–40) presents a strikingly different image of its subject. Although she also wears her hair in the latest fashion, it

is less elaborate than that of her younger counterpart. The work emphasizes not the fresh sheen of an unblemished face, but a visage clearly marked by the passage of time. We may regard this portrait as less idealized and more naturalistic, but for a Roman viewer, it conformed to an ideal of accomplishment by showcasing signs of aging, cherished since the Republican period as reflections of virtue and venerability.

The High Imperial Art of Trajan and Hadrian

What are the salient features of Roman art and architecture at the height of imperial power and expanse?

Domitian, the last Flavian emperor, was assassinated in 96 CE and succeeded by a senator, Nerva (ruled 96–98 CE), who designated as his successor Trajan, a general born in Spain who had commanded Roman troops in Germany. For nearly a century, the empire was under the control of brilliant administrators. Instead of depending on the vagaries

6-39 YOUNG FLAVIAN WOMAN
c. 90 CE. Marble, height 25″ (65.5 cm). Museo Capitolino, Rome.
Credit: © Araldo de Luca/Corbis

6-40 MIDDLE-AGED FLAVIAN WOMAN
Late 1st century CE. Marble, height 9½″ (24.1 cm). Musei Vaticani,
Museo Gregoriano Profano, ex-Lateranese, Rome.

of fate (or genetics) to produce intelligent heirs, the emperors Nerva (ruled 96–98 CE), Trajan (ruled 98–117 CE), Hadrian (ruled 117–138 CE), and Antoninus Pius (ruled 138–161 CE) each selected an able administrator to follow himself, thus "adopting" his successor. Italy and the provinces flourished, and official and private patronage of the arts increased.

Under Trajan, the empire reached its greatest territorial expanse. By 106 CE, he had conquered Dacia, roughly present-day Romania (SEE MAP 6-1). His successor, Hadrian, consolidated the empire's borders and imposed far-reaching social, governmental, and military reforms. Hadrian was well educated and widely traveled, and his admiration for Greek culture spurred new building programs and classicizing works of art throughout the empire. Unfortunately, his successor, Marcus Aurelius (ruled 161–180 CE), broke the tradition of adoption and let his son, Commodus, inherit the throne. Within 12 years, Commodus (ruled 180–192 CE) had destroyed the stable government his predecessors had so carefully built.

Imperial Architecture

The Romans believed their rule extended to the ends of the Western world, but the city of Rome remained the nerve center of the empire. During his long and peaceful reign, Augustus had paved the city's old Republican Forum, restored its temples and basilicas, and followed Julius Caesar's example by building an Imperial Forum. These projects marked the beginning of a continuing effort to transform the capital into a magnificent monument to imperial rule. Such grand structures as the Imperial Forums, the Colosseum, the Circus Maximus (a track for chariot races), the Pantheon, and aqueducts stood amid the temples, baths, warehouses, and homes in the city center as expressions of successive emperors' beneficence and their desire to leave their mark on, and preserve their memory in, the capital. A model of Rome's city center makes apparent the dense building plan (**FIG. 6–41**).

THE FORUM OF TRAJAN In about 110–113 CE, Trajan began the last and largest Imperial Forum on a large piece of property next to the earlier forums of Augustus and

6–41 MODEL OF IMPERIAL ROME

c. 324 CE.

Colosseum

Temple of Venus and Rome

Arch of Titus

Basilica of Maxentius and Constantine

Forum of Vespasian (Peace)

Forum of Augustus

Forum of Julius Caesar

Rostrum

Forum of Trajan

Markets of Trajan

Basilica Ulpia

Column of Trajan

Pantheon

Credit: Index/Vasari

Julius Caesar; Hadrian finished the project about 117 CE (**FIG. 6–42**). For this major undertaking, Trajan chose Apollodorus of Damascus, a Greek architect and experienced military engineer. A straight, central axis leads from the Forum of Augustus through a triple-arched gate surmounted by a bronze chariot group into a large, colonnaded square with a statue of Trajan on horseback at its center.

The **BASILICA ULPIA** (**FIG. 6–43**) closed off the courtyard at the north end. Dedicated in c. 112 CE, the building was named for the family to which Trajan belonged. A **basilica** was a large, rectangular building with an extensive interior space, adaptable for a variety of administrative governmental functions. The Basilica Ulpia was a court of law, but other basilicas served as imperial audience chambers, army drill halls, and schools. The Basilica Ulpia was a particularly grand interior space, 385 feet long (not including the apses) and 182 feet wide. A large central area (the **nave**) was flanked by double colonnaded aisles surmounted by open galleries or by a clerestory, an upper nave wall with windows. The timber truss roof had a span

of about 80 feet. The two **apses**, rounded extensions at each end of the building, provided imposing settings for judges when the court was in session.

During the site preparation for Trajan's forum, part of a commercial district had to be razed and excavated. To make up for the loss, Trajan ordered the construction of a handsome public market (**FIGS. 6–44, 6–45**). The market, comparable in size to a large modern shopping mall, had more than 150 individual shops on several levels and included a large, groin-vaulted main hall. In compliance with a building code that was put into effect after a disastrous fire in 64 CE, the market, like most Roman buildings of the time, was constructed of concrete (see "Concrete" on page 196) and faced with brick, with only occasional detailing in stone and wood.

Behind the Basilica Ulpia stood twin libraries built to house the emperor's collections of Latin and Greek manuscripts. These buildings flanked an open court, the location of the great spiral column commemorating Trajan's victory over the Dacians that was erected either c. 113 CE, at about

6–42 PLAN OF TRAJAN'S FORUM AND MARKET

c. 110–113 CE.

N

Temple to the Divine Trajan

Column of Trajan

Greek and Latin libraries

market hall

Markets of Trajan

Via Biberatica

Basilica Ulpia

Temple of Venus Genetrix in the Forum of Julius Caesar

equestrian statue of Trajan

0   50 m

0   100 ft

6–43 Gilbert Gorski RESTORED PERSPECTIVE VIEW OF THE CENTRAL HALL, BASILICA ULPIA

Rome. As it was c. 112 CE.

Trajan's architect was Apollodorus of Damascus. The building may have had clerestory windows instead of the gallery shown in this drawing. The Column of Trajan can be seen through the upper colonnade at right.

Credit: Dr. James E. Packer

6-44 RECONSTRUCTION DRAWING OF TRAJAN'S MARKET

Rome. As it was 100–112 CE.

Credit: Kevin Jones and Associates © Dorling Kindersley

the same time as the Basilica Ulpia, or by Hadrian after Trajan's death in 117 CE. The column became Trajan's tomb when Hadrian placed a golden urn containing his predecessor's ashes in its base.

THE COLUMN OF TRAJAN The relief decoration on the **COLUMN OF TRAJAN** spirals upward in a band that would stretch almost 625 feet if laid out straight. Like a giant, unfurled version of the scrolls housed in the libraries next to it, the column presents a continuous pictorial narrative of the Dacian campaigns of 102–103 and 105–106 CE (**FIG. 6-46**). The remarkable sculpture includes more than 2,500 individual figures linked by landscape and architecture and punctuated by the recurring figure of Trajan. The narrative band slowly expands from about 3 feet in height at the bottom of the column to 4 feet at the top, where it is farther from view. The natural and architectural elements in the scenes have been kept small so that the important figures can occupy as much space as possible.

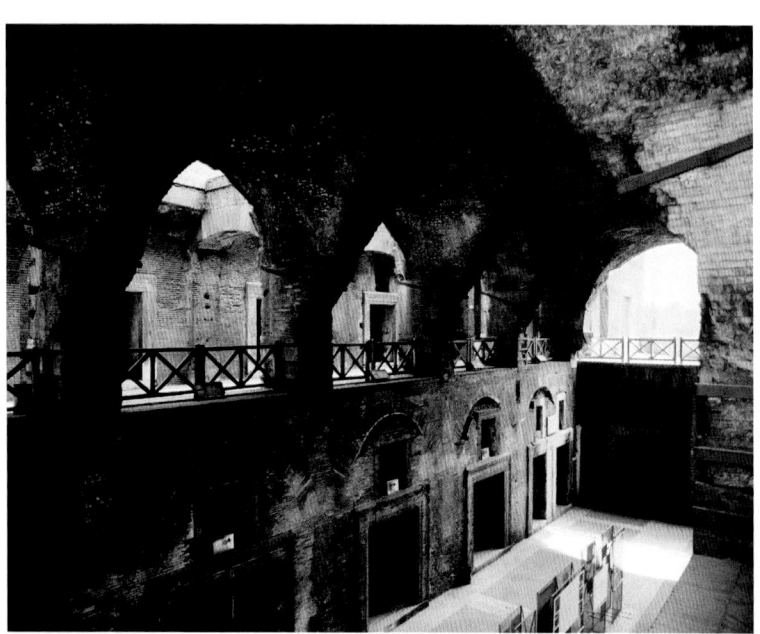

6-45 MAIN HALL, TRAJAN'S MARKET
Rome. 100–112 CE.

Credit: © 2016. Photo Scala, Florence - courtesy of the Ministero Beni e Att. Culturali

6-46 COLUMN OF TRAJAN

Rome. 113–116 CE, or after 117 CE. Marble, overall height with base 125′ (38 m); column alone 97′8″ (29.77 m); length of relief 625′ (190.5 m).

The height of the column may have recorded the depth of the excavation required to build the Forum of Trajan. The gilded bronze statue of Trajan that once stood on the top was replaced in 1588 CE with the statue of St. Peter seen today.

Credit: © Vincenzo Pirozzi, Rome

The scene at the beginning of the spiral, at the bottom of the column, shows Trajan's army crossing the Danube River on a pontoon bridge to launch the first Dacian campaign of 101 CE (FIG. 0-47). Soldiers construct battlefield headquarters in Dacia from which the men on the frontiers will receive orders, food, and weapons. In this spectacular piece of imperial ideology or propaganda, Trajan is portrayed as a strong, stable, and efficient commander of a well-run army, and his barbarian enemies are shown as worthy opponents of Rome.

6-47 ROMANS CROSSING THE DANUBE AND BUILDING A FORT

Detail of the lowest part of the Column of Trajan. 113–116 CE, or after 117 CE. Marble, height of the spiral band approx. 36″ (91 cm).

Credit: © 2016. Photo Scala, Florence - courtesy of the Ministero Beni e Att. Culturali

Elements of Architecture

CONCRETE

The Romans were pragmatic builders, and their practicality extended from recognizing and exploiting undeveloped potential in construction methods and physical materials to organizing large-scale building works. Their exploitation of the arch and the vault is typical of their adapt-and-improve approach. But their innovative use of concrete, beginning in the first century BCE, was a technological breakthrough of the greatest importance in the history of architecture.

In contrast to stone—which was expensive and difficult to quarry and move—the components of concrete were cheap, relatively light, and easily transported. Building stone structures required highly skilled masons, but a large, semiskilled workforce directed by a few experienced supervisors could construct brick-faced concrete buildings.

Roman concrete consisted of powdered lime, a volcanic sand called *pozzolana*, and various types of rubble, such as small rocks and broken pottery. Mixing these materials in water caused a chemical reaction that blended them, and they hardened into a strong, solid mass as they dried. At first, concrete was used mainly for poured foundations, but with technical advances it became indispensable for the construction of walls, arches, and vaults for ever-larger buildings such as

the Flavian Amphitheater (SEE FIG. 6–38) and the Market of Trajan (SEE FIG. 6–45). In the earliest concrete wall construction, workers filled a framework of rough stones with concrete. Soon they developed a technique known as *opus reticulatum*, in which the framework is a diagonal web of smallish bricks set in a cross pattern. Concrete-based construction freed the Romans from the limits of right-angle forms and comparatively short spans. With this new freedom, Roman builders pushed the established limits of architecture, creating some very large and highly original spaces by pouring concrete over wooden frameworks to mold it into complex curving shapes.

Concrete's one weakness was that it absorbed moisture and would eventually deteriorate if unprotected, so builders covered exposed concrete with a veneer, or facing, of finer materials—such as marble, stone, stucco, or painted plaster—to protect it. An essential difference between Greek and Roman architecture is that Greek builders reveal the building material itself and accept the design limitations of post-and-lintel construction, whereas Roman buildings expose only an externally applied surface covering. The sophisticated structural underpinnings are hidden from view.

6–48 PANTHEON
Rome. c. 110–128 CE.

Today a huge fountain dominates the square in front of the Pantheon. Built in 1578 by Giacomo della Porta, it now supports an Egyptian obelisk placed there in 1711 by Pope Clement XI.

Credit: © Vincenzo Pirozzi, Rome

6-49 RECONSTRUCTION DRAWING OF THE PANTHEON

Credit: © Dorling Kindersley

THE PANTHEON Perhaps the most remarkable ancient building surviving in Rome—and one of the marvels of world architecture in any age—is a temple to Mars, Venus, and the divine Julius Caesar known as the **PANTHEON** (**FIG. 6-48**). Although this monument was designed and constructed during the reigns of emperors Trajan and Hadrian, the long inscription on the architrave states that it was built by "Marcus Agrippa, son of Lucius, who was consul three times." Agrippa, the son-in-law and valued advisor of Augustus, sponsored a building on this site in 27–25 BCE. After a fire in 80 CE, Domitian either restored the Pantheon or built a new temple, which burned again after being struck by lightning in 110 CE. Although for some time scholars have believed that it was Hadrian who reconstructed the building in its current state in 118–128 CE, a recent study of the brick stamps has argued convincingly that the Pantheon was begun soon after 110 under Trajan, but completed during the reign of his successor, Hadrian. The Pantheon's spectacular and influential design may represent another work of Apollodorus of Damascus.

6-50 PLAN OF THE PANTHEON

Credit: After William L. MacDonald, The Architecture of the Roman Empire I: An Introductory Study. New Haven and London: Yale University Press, 1965, fig 9

The current setting of the temple gives little suggestion of its original appearance. Centuries of dirt and street construction hide its podium and stairs. Attachment holes in the pediment indicate the placement of bronze sculpture, perhaps an eagle within a wreath representing the imperial Jupiter. Today we can see the sides of the rotunda flanking the entrance porch, but when the Pantheon was constructed, the façade of this porch—resembling the façades of typical, rectangular temples—was literally all viewers could see of the building. Since their approach was controlled by an enclosed courtyard (SEE FIG. 6-41), the actual circular shape of the Pantheon was concealed.

Viewers were therefore surprised to pass through the rectilinear and restricted aisles of the portico and the huge main door to encounter the gaping space of the giant **rotunda** (circular room) topped with a vast, bowl-shaped dome, 143 feet in diameter and 143 feet from the floor at its summit (**FIGS. 6-49, 6-50**). Even without the controlled courtyard approach, encountering this space today is still an overwhelming experience—for many of

6-51 INTERIOR OF THE PANTHEON LOOKING UP INTO THE DOME

With light from the oculus on its coffered ceiling. c. 110–128 CE. Brick, concrete, marble veneer, diameter of dome 143′ (43.5 m).

Credit: © Insadco Photography/Alamy Stock Photo

us, one that is repeated on successive visits to the rotunda.

Standing at the center of this hemispherical temple (**FIG. 6-51**), the visitor feels isolated from the outside world and intensely aware of the shape and tangibility of the luminous space itself. Our eyes are drawn upward over the patterns made by the sunken panels, or **coffers**, in the dome's ceiling to the light entering the 29-foot-wide oculus, or round central opening. This disk of light illuminates a brilliant circle against the surface of the dome and moves around this microcosm throughout the day like a sun. Clouds travel across the opening as well; when rain falls in, it drains off through conduits on the floor planned by the original engineer. Occasionally a bird flies in.

The simple shape of the Pantheon's dome belies its sophisticated design and engineering. Marble veneer and richly colored architectural detail conceal the internal brick arches and concrete structure of the rotunda's 20-foot-thick walls. More than half of the original decoration— two tiers of columns, pilasters, and entablatures—survives. The simple repetition of square against circle, established on a large scale by juxtaposing the rectilinear portico against the circular rotunda, dominates the building's ornamentation. Seven **exedrae** (niches)—rectangular alternating with semicircular—punctuate the wall. Originally they

held statues of gods. The boxlike coffers inside the dome, which help lighten the weight of the masonry, may once have contained gilded bronze rosettes or stars suggesting the heavens. In 609 CE, Pope Boniface IV rededicated the Pantheon as the Christian church of St. Mary of the Martyrs, thus ensuring its survival through the Middle Ages and down to our day.

HADRIAN'S VILLA AT TIVOLI To imagine imperial Roman life at its most luxurious, one must go to Tivoli, a little more than 20 miles from Rome. **HADRIAN'S VILLA**, or country residence, was not a single building but an architectural complex of many buildings, lakes, and gardens spread over half a square mile (**FIG. 6-52**). Each section had its own inner logic and took advantage of natural

6-52 PLAN OF HADRIAN'S VILLA
Tivoli. c. 125–135 CE.

private suite (libraries)

maritime theater

Poikile

triclinium

stadium

Piazza d'Oro

small baths

vestibule

Piazza d'Oro

great baths

Canal

N

0 ____ 25 m
0 ____ 50 ft

0 ____ 250 m
0 ____ 500 ft

academy

land formations and attractive views. Hadrian instructed his architects to re-create his favorite places throughout the empire so he could pretend to enjoy the Athenian Grove of Academe, the Painted Stoa from the Athenian Agora, and buildings of the Ptolemaic capital of Alexandria in Egypt.

Landscapes with pools, fountains, and gardens turned the villa into a place of delight. An area with a long reflecting pool, called **THE CANAL**, was framed by a colonnade with alternating semicircular and straight entablatures (**FIG. 6-53**). Copies of famous Greek

6-53 THE CANAL (REFLECTING POOL), HADRIAN'S VILLA
Tivoli. c. 125–135 CE.

Credit: © Vincenzo Pirozzi, Rome

statues—sometimes even originals—filled the spaces between columns. So great was Hadrian's love of Greek sculpture that he had the caryatids of the Erechtheion (SEE FIG. 5–46) replicated for his pleasure palace.

The individual buildings were not large, but they were extremely complex and imaginatively designed, exploiting fully the flexibility offered by concrete vaulted construction. Walls and floors had veneers of marble and travertine or of exquisite mosaics and paintings. A panel from one of the floor mosaics (FIG. 6–54) demonstrates the artistry of Hadrian's mosaicists. In a rocky landscape with only a few bits of greenery, a desperate male centaur raises a large boulder over his head to crush a tiger that has severely wounded a female centaur. Two other felines apparently took part in the attack—the white leopard on the rocks to the left and the dead lion at the feet of the male centaur. The artist rendered the figures with three-dimensional shading, foreshortening, and a great sensitivity to a range of figure types, including human torsos and animals in a variety of poses.

Roman Mosaics

Mosaics were used widely in Hellenistic times and became enormously popular for decorating homes in the Roman period. Mosaics were created with pebbles (SEE FIG. 5–58) or with small, regularly shaped pieces of colored stone and marble called tesserae. The stones were pressed into a kind of soft cement called grout. When the stones were firmly set, the spaces between them were also filled with grout. After the surface dried, it was cleaned and polished. Since the natural stones produced only a narrow range of colors, glass tesserae were also used to extend the palette as early as the third century BCE.

Some skilled mosaicists even copied well-known paintings, often by famous Greek artists. Employing a technique in which very small tesserae in a wide range of colors were laid down in irregular, curving lines, they effectively imitated painted brushstrokes. One example is **THE UNSWEPT FLOOR** (FIG. 6–55). Herakleitos, a second-century CE Greek mosaicist living in Rome, made this copy

6–54 BATTLE OF CENTAURS AND WILD BEASTS
From Hadrian's Villa, Tivoli. c. 125 CE. Mosaic, 23 × 36″ (58.4 × 91.4 cm). Staatliche Museen zu Berlin, Preussischer Kulturbesitz, Antikensammlung.

This floor mosaic may be a copy of a much-admired scene of a fight between centaurs and wild animals painted by the late fifth-century BCE Greek artist Zeuxis.

6–55 Herakleitos **THE UNSWEPT FLOOR**
Mosaic variant of a 2nd-century BCE painting by Sosos of Pergamon. 2nd century CE. Musei Vaticani, Museo Gregoriano Profano, Rome.

Credit: © akg-images/Pirozzi

of an original work by the renowned second-century BCE artist Sosos. Pliny the Elder, in his *Natural History*, mentions a mosaic of an unswept floor and another of doves that Sosos made in Pergamon.

A dining room would be a logical location for a floor mosaic of this theme with table scraps recreated in meticulous detail, even to the shadows they cast, and a mouse foraging among them. Guests reclining on their banquet couches would certainly have been amused by the pictures on the floor, and they could also have shown off their knowledge of the Greek precedent for the mosaic beneath their feet.

Imperial Portraits

Imperial portraits were objects of propaganda, proclaiming the accomplishments and pretensions of emperors. Marcus Aurelius, like Hadrian, was a successful military commander who was equally proud of his intellectual attainments. In a lucky error—or twist of fortune—a

gilded-bronze equestrian statue of the emperor dressed as a military commander in a tunic and short, heavy cloak (**FIG. 6–56**) came mistakenly to be revered during the Middle Ages as a statue of Constantine, the first Christian emperor, and consequently escaped being melted down to recycle the bronze. The raised foreleg of the horse once trampled a crouching barbarian.

Marcus Aurelius's head, with its thick, curly hair and full beard (a fashion initiated by Hadrian), resembles traditional "philosopher" portraits from the Greek world. The emperor wears no armor and carries no weapons; like Egyptian kings, he conquers effortlessly by divine will. And like his illustrious predecessor Augustus, he reaches out to those around him in a rhetorical gesture of address. It is difficult to create an equestrian portrait in which the rider stands out as the dominant figure without making the horse look too small. The sculptor of this statue found a balance acceptable to viewers of the time and, in doing so, created a model for later artists.

6-56 EQUESTRIAN STATUE OF MARCUS AURELIUS

c. 176 CE. Bronze, originally gilded, height 11'6″ (3.5 m). Museo Capitolino, Rome.

Between 1187 and 1538, this statue stood in the piazza fronting the palace and church of St. John Lateran in Rome. In January 1538, Pope Paul III had it moved to the Capitoline Hill, and Michelangelo made it the centerpiece of his newly redesigned Capitoline Piazza. After being removed from its base for cleaning and restoration during the 1980s, it was taken inside the Capitoline Museum to protect it from air pollution, and a copy has replaced it in the piazza.

Credit: © akg-images/Pirozzi

Marcus Aurelius's son Commodus succeeded him as emperor. Commodus was a man without political skill, administrative competence, or intellectual distinction. During his unfortunate reign (180–192 CE), he devoted himself to luxury and frivolous pursuits, claiming at various times to be the reincarnation of Hercules and the incarnation of the god Jupiter. When he proposed to assume the consulship dressed and armed as a gladiator, his associates, including his mistress, arranged to have him strangled in his bath by a wrestling partner. In a spectacular marble bust, the emperor poses as **HERCULES** (**FIG. 6-57**), adorned with references to the hero's legendary labors: Hercules's club, the skin and head of the Nemean lion, and the golden apples from the Garden of the Hesperides. Commodus's likeness emphasizes his family resemblance to his more illustrious and powerful father (SEE FIG. 6-56), but the bust also captures his vanity through the grand pretensions of the costume and the Classical associations of the body type. The sculptor's sensitive modeling and expert drillwork exploit the play of light on the figure to bring out the textures of the hair, beard, facial features, and drapery and create an illusion of movement.

Funerary Sculpture

During the second and third centuries, a shift from cremation to inhumation created a growing demand for sarcophagi in which to bury the bodies of the deceased. Wealthy Romans commissioned thousands of massive and elaborate marble sarcophagi encrusted with sculptural relief, created in large production workshops throughout the Roman Empire.

In 1885, nine particularly impressive sarcophagi were discovered in private underground burial chambers built for use by a powerful, aristocratic Roman family—the Calpurnii Pisones. One of these sarcophagi, from c. 190 CE, portrays the **INDIAN TRIUMPH OF DIONYSUS** (see "Closer Look" on page 204). This is a popular theme in late second-century CE sarcophagi, but here the carved

relief is of especially high quality—complex but highly legible at the same time. The mythological composition owes a debt to imperial ceremony: Dionysus, at far left in a chariot, receives from a personification of Victory standing behind him a laurel crown, identical to the headdress worn by Roman emperors during triumphal processions. Also derived from state ceremony is the display of booty and captives carried by the elephants at the center of the composition. But religion, rather than statecraft, is the real theme here. The set of sarcophagi to which this belongs proclaims the family's adherence to a mystery cult of Dionysus that focused on themes of decay and renewal, death and rebirth. The triumph of the deceased over death is the central message here, not one particular episode in the life of Dionysus himself.

A Closer Look

SARCOPHAGUS WITH THE INDIAN TRIUMPH OF DIONYSUS

Semele, mortal mother of the god Dionysus, gives birth prematurely and then dies. Once grown, Dionysus would travel to the underworld and bring his mother to paradise. Semele's death therefore suggests the promise of eternal life through her son.

These hooked sticks are identical to the *ankusha* still used by *mahouts* (elephant drivers) in India today.

As part of their worship, followers of Dionysiac mystery religions re-created the triumphant return of the god from India by parading in the streets after dark. A dancing maenad beats her tambourine here, suggesting the sounds and movements that would accompany such re-enactments.

The presence of exotic animals such as elephants, a lion, a giraffe, and panthers identifies this scene as Dionysus's triumphant return from India.

Snakes were not only used in the rites of Dionysiac mystery religions, they were also powerful symbols of rebirth and phallic fertility, making them especially appropriate in the context of a sarcophagus. Three snakes appear along the ground-line of the sculptural frieze.

The aged god Silenus leans on a *thyrsos* staff, a giant fennel stalk wound with ivy and topped with a pinecone, symbolizing fertility. Dionysus, with whom such staffs were associated, also carries one here as his triumphal scepter.

6-58 SARCOPHAGUS WITH THE INDIAN TRIUMPH OF DIONYSUS
c. 190 CE. Marble, 47½ × 92½ × 35¹³⁄₁₆″ (120.7 × 234.9 × 90.96 cm). The Walters Art Museum, Baltimore (23.31)

Credit: Photo © The Walters Art Museum, Baltimore

The Late Empire, Third and Fourth Centuries CE

What continues and what changes in the art and architecture of the Late Roman Empire?

The comfortable life suggested by the wall paintings in Roman houses and villas was to be challenged by hard times within a century. The reign of Commodus marked the beginning of a period of political and economic decline. Barbarian groups had already begun moving into the empire in the time of Marcus Aurelius. Now they pressed on Rome's frontiers. Many crossed the borders and settled within them, disrupting provincial governments. As perceived threats spread throughout the empire, imperial rule became increasingly authoritarian. Eventually the army controlled the government, and the Imperial Guards set up and deposed rulers almost at will, often selecting candidates from among poorly educated, power-hungry provincial leaders in their own ranks.

The Severan Dynasty

Despite the pressures brought by political and economic change, the arts continued to flourish under the Severan emperors (193–235 CE) who succeeded Commodus. Septimius Severus (ruled 193–211 CE), who was born in Africa, and his Syrian wife, Julia Domna, restored public buildings, commissioned official portraits, and revitalized the old cattle market in Rome into a well-planned center of bustling commerce. Their sons, Geta and Caracalla, succeeded Septimius Severus as co-emperors in 211 CE, but Caracalla murdered Geta in 212 CE and then ruled alone until he in turn was murdered in 217 CE.

PORTRAITS OF CARACALLA   The Emperor Caracalla appears in his portraits as a fierce and courageous ruler, capable of confronting Rome's enemies and safeguarding the security of the Roman Empire. In the example shown here (**FIG. 6-59**), the sculptor has enhanced the intensity of the emperor's expression by producing strong contrasts of light and dark with chiseling and drillwork. Even the eyes have been drilled and engraved to catch the light in a way that makes them dominate Caracalla's expression. The contrast between this style and that of the portraits of Augustus is a telling reflection of the changing character of imperial rule. Augustus envisioned himself as the suave initiator of a Golden Age of peace and prosperity; Caracalla presents himself as a no-nonsense ruler of iron-fisted determination with a militaristic, close-cropped haircut and a glare of fierce intensity.

THE BATHS OF CARACALLA   The year before his death in 211 CE, Septimius Severus had begun a popular public-works project: the construction of magnificent new public baths on the southeast side of Rome as a new recreational and educational center. Caracalla completed and inaugurated the baths today known by his name in 216–217 CE. The impressive brick-and-concrete structure was hidden under a sheath of colorful marble and mosaic. The builders used soaring groin and barrel vaults, which allow the maximum space with the fewest possible supports. The groin vaults also made possible large windows in every bay (the space encompassed by each arch and its supports). Windows were important, since the baths depended on natural light and could only be open during daylight hours.

The **BATHS OF CARACALLA** (**FIG. 6-60**) were laid out on a strictly symmetrical plan. The bathing facilities were grouped in the center of the main building to make efficient use of the

6-59 CARACALLA

Early 3rd century CE. Marble, height 14½″ (36.2 cm). Metropolitan Museum of Art, New York. Samuel D. Lee Fund, 1940. (40.11.1A).

Credit: © 2016. Image copyright The Metropolitan Museum of Art/Art Resource/ Scala, Florence. Photo: Schechter Lee

6-60A AERIAL VIEW OF THE BATHS OF CARACALLA
Rome. c. 211–217 CE.

gymnasium   gymnasium

natatio
(swimming pool)

caldarium
(hot bath)

frigidarium (cold bath)

tepidarium (warm bath)

0   150 ft

40 m

6-60B PLAN OF THE BATHS OF CARACALLA
Rome. c. 211–217.

below-ground furnaces that heated them and to allow bathers to move comfortably from hot to cold pools and then finish with a swim. Many other facilities—exercise rooms, shops, latrines, and dressing rooms—were housed on each side of the bathing block. The bath buildings alone covered 5 acres. The entire complex, which included gardens, a stadium, libraries, a painting gallery, auditoriums, and huge water reservoirs, covered an area of 50 acres.

6-61 PORTRAIT OF A TETRARCH (GALERIUS?)
Early 4th century CE. Porphyry, 2′5½″ (65 cm). Egyptian Museum, Cairo.

The Tetrarchy

Following the assassination of the last Severan emperor by one of his military commanders in 235 CE, Rome was plunged into a period of anarchy that lasted for 50 years. A series of soldier emperors attempted to rule the empire, but real order was only restored by Diocletian (ruled 284–305 CE), also a military commander. This brilliant politician and general reversed the empire's declining fortunes, but he also initiated an increasingly autocratic form of rule, and the social structure of the empire became increasingly rigid.

To divide up the task of defending and administering the Roman world and assure an orderly succession, in 286 CE Diocletian divided the empire in two. According to his plan, he would rule in the East with the title of "Augustus," while another Augustus, Maximian, would rule in the West. Then in 293 CE he devised a form of government called a tetrarchy, or "rule of four," in which each Augustus designated a subordinate and heir who held the title of "Caesar." Four individuals would rule the Roman Empire, which was now divided into four quadrants.

PORTRAITURE   The introduction of a radically new, hard style of geometricized abstraction, especially notable in portraits of the tetrarchs themselves, parallels Diocletian's political restructuring. A powerful bust of a tetrarch, startlingly alert with searing eyes (FIG. 6–61) embodies this strong stylistic shift away from the suave Classicism seen in the portrait of Commodus as Hercules (SEE FIG. 6–57). There is no clear sense of likeness. Who this individual is seems to be less significant than the powerful position he holds. Some art historians have interpreted this change in style as

a conscious embodiment of Diocletian's new concept of government, while others have pointed to parallels with the provincial art of Diocletian's Dalmatian homeland or with the Neoplatonic aesthetics of idealized abstraction promoted by Plotinus, a third-century CE philosopher who was widely read in the late Roman world. In any event, these riveting works represent not a degeneration of the Classical tradition but its conscious replacement by a different aesthetic viewpoint—militaristic, severe, and abstract rather than suave, slick, and classicizing.

This new mode is famously represented by a sculptural group of **THE TETRARCHS** (FIG. **6–62**). The four

6-62 THE TETRARCHS
c. 300 CE. Porphyry, height of figures 51" (129 cm). Installed at the corner of the façade of the Cathedral of St. Mark, Venice.

This particular sculpture may have been made in Egypt and moved to Constantinople after 330 CE. Christian crusaders who looted Constantinople in 1204 CE took the statue to Venice and installed it at the Cathedral of St. Mark, where it remains today.

Credit: © Cameraphoto Arte, Venice

6-63 EXTERIOR OF THE AUDIENCE HALL OF CONSTANTIUS CHLORUS (NOW KNOWN AS THE BASILICA)
Trier, Germany.
Early 4th century CE.

Credit: © Achim Bednorz, Cologne

figures are nearly identical, except that the senior Augusti have beards while their juniors, the Caesars, are clean-shaven. Dressed in military garb and clasping swords at their sides, they embrace each other in a show of impe-rial unity, proclaiming an alliance rooted in strength and vigilance. The sculpture is made of porphyry, an extremely hard, purple stone from Egypt that was reserved for impe-rial use (SEE FIG. 6–61).

ARCHITECTURE   The tetrarchs ruled the empire from administrative headquarters in Milan (Italy), Trier (Ger-many), Thessaloniki (Greece), and Nicomedia (Turkey). Imposing architecture was created to house the govern-ment in these new capital cities. In Trier, for example, Con-stantius Chlorus (Caesar, 293–305; Augustus, 305–306 CE) and his son Constantine fortified the city with walls and a monumental gate that still stand. They built public ameni-ties, such as baths, and a palace with a huge **AUDIENCE HALL**, later used as a Christian church (FIG. **6-63**). This early fourth-century basilica's large size and simple plan and structure exemplify the architecture of the tetrarchs: no-nonsense, imposing buildings that would impress their subjects. The audience hall is a large rectangular building, 190 by 95 feet, with a strong directional focus given by a single apse opposite the door. Two rows of arched win-dows pierce the brick walls, originally stuccoed on the out-side and covered with marble veneer inside.

A flat roof nearly 100 feet above the floor covers both the nave and the apse (FIG. **6-64**). In a concession to the northern climate, the building was centrally heated with hot air flowing under the floor, a technique also used in

Roman baths. The windows of the apse create an interest-ing optical effect. Slightly smaller than the windows in straight side walls, they create the illusion of greater dis-tance, so that the tetrarch enthroned in the apse would appear larger than life and the hall would seem longer than it actually is.

Constantine the Great

In 305 CE, Diocletian abdicated and forced his fellow Augustus, Maximian, to do so as well. The orderly suc-cession he had planned, however, failed to occur, and a struggle for position and advantage followed almost immediately. Two main contenders appeared in the West-ern Empire: Maximian's son Maxentius and Constantine, son of Tetrarch Constantius Chlorus. Constantine emerged victorious in 312, defeating Maxentius at the Battle of the Milvian Bridge at the entrance to Rome.

According to Christian tradition, Constantine had a vision the night before the battle in which he saw a flaming cross in the sky and heard these words: "In this sign you shall conquer." The next morning he ordered that his army's shields and standards be inscribed with the monogram XP (the Greek letters *chi* and *rho*, standing for *Christos*). The vic-torious Constantine then showed his gratitude by ending the persecution of Christians and recognizing Christianity as a lawful religion. It is possible that his mother, Helena—a devout Christian, later canonized—influenced his decision. Whatever his motivation, Constantine and Licinius, who ruled the Eastern Empire, issued the Edict of Milan, an early model of religious toleration, in 313 CE.

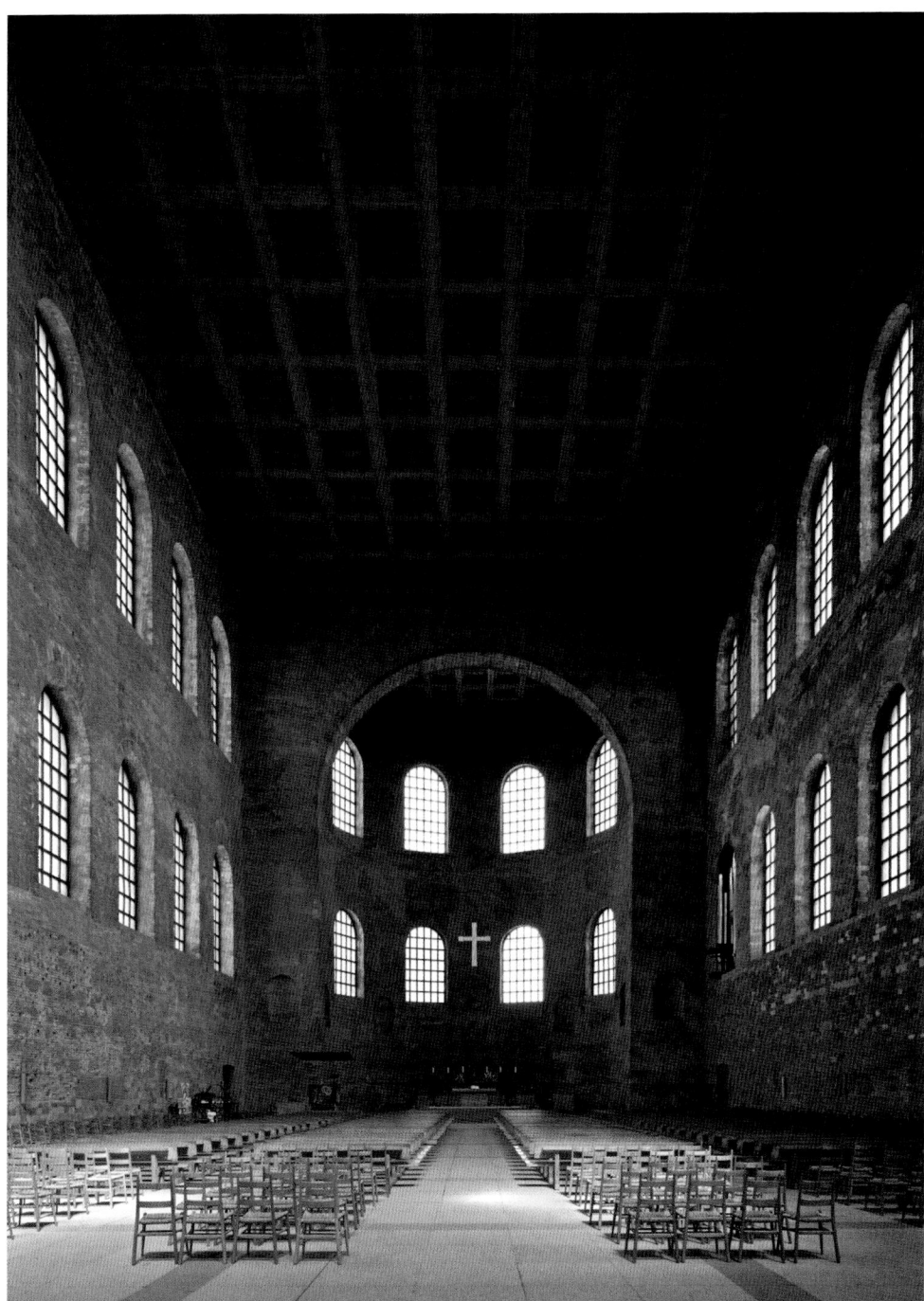

6-64 INTERIOR OF THE AUDIENCE HALL OF CONSTANTIUS CHLORUS (NOW KNOWN AS THE BASILICA)

Trier, Germany. Early 4th century CE. Height of room 100′ (30.5 m).

Only the left wall and apse survive from the original Roman building. The hall became part of the bishop's palace during the medieval period.

Credit: © Achim Bednorz, Cologne

The Edict granted freedom to all religious groups, not just Christians. Constantine, however, remained the Pontifex Maximus of Rome's state religion. He also reaffirmed his devotion to the military's favorite god, Mithras, and to the Invincible Sun, Sol Invictus, a manifestation of Helios Apollo, the sun god. In 324 CE, Constantine defeated Licinius, his last rival, and ruled as sole emperor until his death in 337. After his last visit to Rome in 325, he made the port city of Byzantium the new capital of the Roman Empire and renamed it after himself: Constantinople (present-day Istanbul, in Turkey). Rome, which had already ceased to be the seat of government in the West, further declined in importance.

THE ARCH OF CONSTANTINE In Rome, next to the Colosseum, the Senate erected a triumphal arch to commemorate Constantine's victory over Maxentius (**FIG. 6-65**), a huge, triple arch that dwarfs the nearby Arch of Titus (SEE FIG. 6-35). Its three barrel-vaulted passageways are flanked by columns on high pedestals and topped with a large attic story with elaborate sculptural decoration and a laudatory inscription: "To the Emperor Constantine from the Senate and the Roman People. Since through divine inspiration and great wisdom he has delivered the state from the tyrant and his party by his army and noble arms, [we] dedicate this arch, decorated with triumphal insignia." The "triumphal insignia" were in part appropriated from earlier monuments made for Constantine's illustrious predecessors—Trajan, Hadrian, and Marcus Aurelius. The reused items visually transferred the old Roman virtues of strength, courage, and piety associated with these earlier exemplary emperors to Constantine himself. New reliefs were made for the arch to recount the story of Constantine's victory and to symbolize his own power and generosity. They run in strips underneath the reused Hadrianic tondi (plural for tondo, a circular composition) (**FIG. 6–66**).

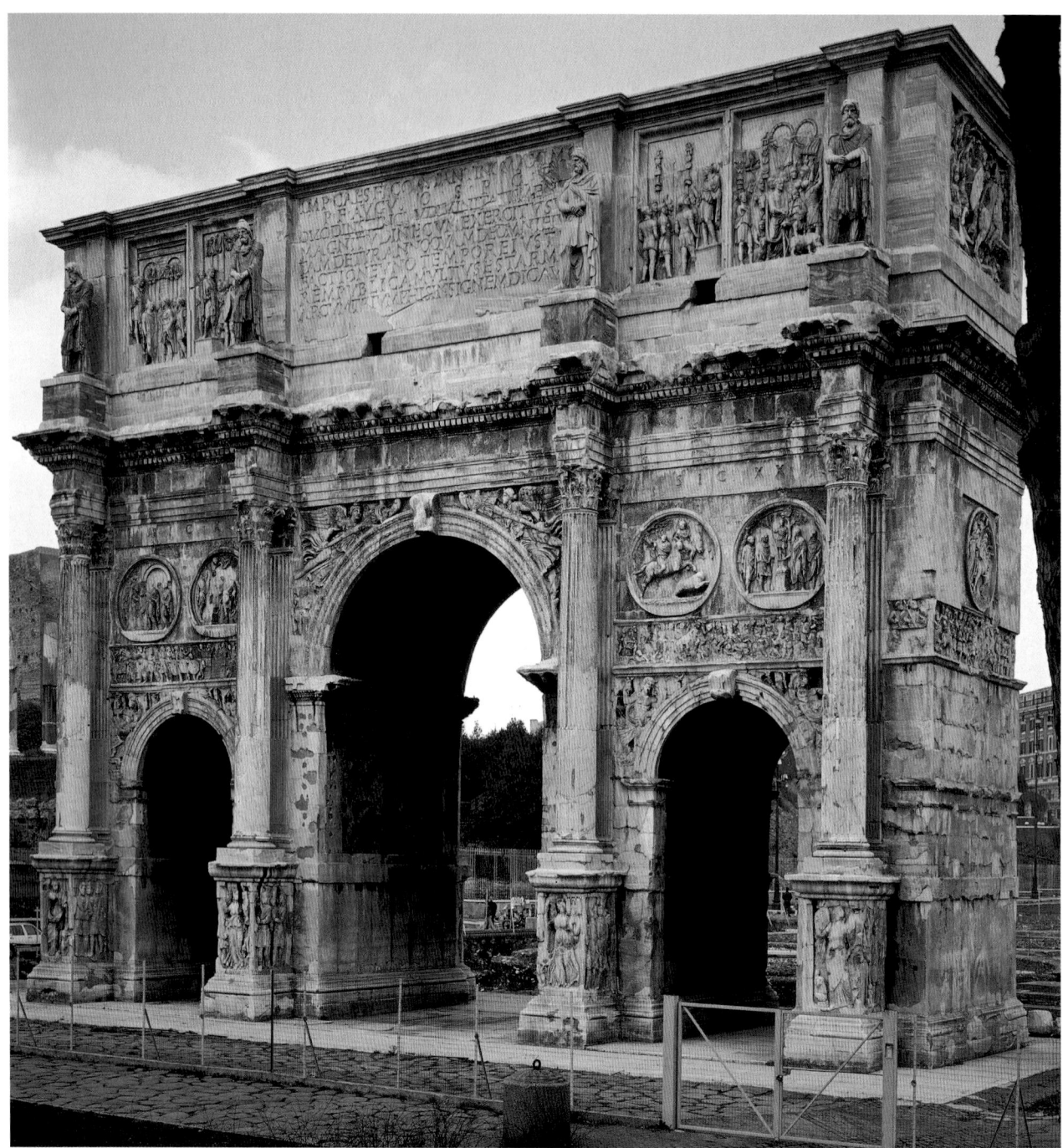

6–65 ARCH OF CONSTANTINE
Rome. 312–315 CE (dedicated July 25, 315). 69 × 85′ (21 × 26 m).

This massive, triple-arched monument to Emperor Constantine's victory over Maxentius in 312 CE is a wonder of recycled sculpture. On the attic story, flanking the inscription over the central arch, are relief panels taken from a monument celebrating the victory of Marcus Aurelius over the Germans in 174 CE. On the attached piers framing these panels are large statues of prisoners made to celebrate Trajan's victory over the Dacians in the second century CE. On the inner walls of the central arch and on the attic of the short sides (neither seen here) are reliefs also commemorating Trajan's conquest of Dacia. Over each of the side arches is a pair of large tondi (circular compositions) taken from a monument to Hadrian (SEE FIG. 6–66). The rest of the decoration is early fourth century CE, contemporary with the arch.

6–66 HADRIAN/CONSTANTINE HUNTING BOAR AND SACRIFICING TO APOLLO; CONSTANTINE ADDRESSING THE ROMAN PEOPLE IN THE ROMAN FORUM

Tondi made for a monument to Hadrian and reused on the Arch of Constantine. c. 130–138 CE. Marble, diameter 6′6″ (2 m). Frieze by Constantinian sculptors 312–315 CE. Marble, height 3′4″ (1 m).

The two tondi were originally part of a lost monument erected by the emperor Hadrian (ruled 117–138 CE). The boar hunt demonstrates his courage and physical prowess, and his sacrificial offering to Apollo shows his piety and gratitude to the gods for their support. The classicizing heads, form-enhancing drapery, and graceful poses of the figures betray a debt to the style of Late Classical Greek art. In the fourth century CE, Constantine appropriated these tondi, had Hadrian's head recarved with his own or his father's features, and incorporated them into his own triumphal arch (SEE FIG. 6–65) so that the power and piety of this predecessor could reflect on him and his reign. In a strip of relief underneath the tondi, sculptors from his own time portrayed a ceremony performed by Constantine during his celebration of the victory over his rival, Maxentius, at the Battle of the Milvian Bridge (312 CE). Rather than the Hellenizing mode popular during Hadrian's reign, the Constantinian sculptors employ the blocky and abstract stylizations that became fashionable during the Tetrarchy.

Although the new Constantinian reliefs reflect the long-standing Roman predilection for depicting important events with recognizable detail, they nevertheless represent a significant change in style, approach, and subject matter (see lower figural frieze in FIG. 6–66). In this scene of Constantine addressing the Roman people in the Roman Forum, the Constantinian reliefs are easily distinguished from the reused Hadrianic tondi mounted just above them because of the faithfulness of the new reliefs to the avant-garde tetrarchic style we have already encountered in portraiture. The forceful, blocky, mostly frontal figures are compressed into the foreground plane. The participants to the sides, below the enthroned Constantine (his head is missing), almost congeal into a uniformly patterned mass that isolates the new emperor and connects him visually with the statues of his illustrious predecessors flanking him on the dais. This two-dimensional, hierarchical approach, with its emphasis on authority and power rather than on individualized outward form, is far removed from the classicizing illusionism of earlier imperial reliefs. It is one of the Roman styles that will be adopted by the emerging Christian Church.

THE BASILICA NOVA Constantine's rival Maxentius, who controlled Rome throughout his short reign (ruled 306–312), ordered the repair of older buildings there and had new ones built. His most impressive undertaking was a huge new basilica, just southeast of the Imperial Forums,

6-67 VIEW OF THE REMAINS OF THE BASILICA OF MAXENTIUS AND CONSTANTINE (BASILICA NOVA)
Rome. 306–313 CE.

Credit: © JIPEN/Shutterstock

6-68A RECONSTRUCTION DRAWING OF THE BASILICA OF MAXENTIUS AND CONSTANTINE (BASILICA NOVA)
Rome. 306–313 CE.

6-68B PLAN OF THE BASILICA OF MAXENTIUS AND CONSTANTINE (BASILICA NOVA)
Rome. 306–313 CE.

apse added later

barrel-vaulted bay

original apse

groin-vaulted nave

original entrance

groin-vaulted porch

barrel-vaulted bay

entrance added later

called the **BASILICA NOVA,** or New Basilica (**FIG. 6–67**). Now known as the Basilica of Maxentius and Constantine, this was the last important imperial government building erected in Rome. Like all basilicas, it functioned as an administrative center and provided a magnificent setting for the emperor when he appeared as supreme judge.

Earlier basilicas, such as Trajan's Basilica Ulpia (SEE FIG. 6–43), had been columnar halls, but Maxentius ordered his engineers to create the kind of large, unbroken, vaulted space found in public baths. Groin vaults covered the central hall, while the lower barrel vaults of the side aisles acted as buttresses, or projecting supports, for the central vault and allowed generous window openings in the clerestory areas over the side walls.

Three of these brick-and-concrete barrel vaults still loom over the streets of present-day Rome (SEE FIG. 6–67). The basilica originally measured 300 by 215 feet and the vaults of the central nave rose to a height of 114 feet. A groin-vaulted porch extended across the short side and sheltered a triple entrance to the central hall. At the opposite end of the long axis of the hall was an apse of the same width, which acted as a focal point for the building (**FIG. 6–68**). Christians would adopt this directional focus along a central axis from entrance to apse when designing basilican churches.

Constantine, seeking to impress the people of Rome with visible symbols of his authority, put his own stamp on projects Maxentius had started, including this one. He may have changed the orientation of the Basilica Nova by adding an imposing new entrance in the center of the long side facing the Via Sacra and a giant apse facing it across the three aisles. He also commissioned a colossal, 30-foot statue of himself for placement within an apse (**FIG. 6–69**). Sculptors used white marble for the head, chest, arms, and legs, and sheets of bronze for the drapery, all supported on a wooden frame. This statue became a permanent stand-in for the emperor, representing him whenever the conduct of business legally required his presence. The head combines features of traditional Roman portraiture with some of the abstract qualities evident in images of the tetrarchs (SEE FIG. 6–62). The defining characteristics of Constantine's face—his heavy jaw, hooked nose, and jutting chin—have been incorporated into a stylized, symmetrical pattern in which other features, such as his eyes, eyebrows, and hair, have been simplified into repeated geometric arcs. The result is a work that projects imperial power and dignity with no hint of human frailty or imperfection.

Roman Art after Constantine

Although Constantine was baptized only on his deathbed in 337, Christianity had become the official religion of the empire by the end of the fourth century, and non-Christians had become targets of persecution.

6–69 CONSTANTINE THE GREAT

From the Basilica of Maxentius and Constantine, Rome. 325–326 CE. Marble, height of head 8′6″ (2.6 m). Palazzo dei Conservatori, Rome.

Credit: © Vincenzo Pirozzi, Rome

This religious shift, however, did not diminish Roman interest in the artistic traditions of their pagan Classical past. A large silver **PLATTER** dating from the mid fourth century CE (**FIG. 6–70**) proves that artists working for Christian patrons continued to use pagan themes, allowing them the opportunity to create elaborate figural compositions displaying the nude or lightly draped human body in complex, dynamic poses.

The Bacchic revelers on this platter whirl, leap, and sway in a dance to the piping of satyrs around a circular central medallion. In the centerpiece, nude females frolicking in the waves with fantastic sea creatures surround the head of the sea god Oceanus. In the figural composition that rings the outer circle, the figure of Bacchus is the one stable element. With a bunch of grapes in his right hand, a krater at his feet, and one foot on the haunches of his panther, he focuses his attention on a male follower begging for another drink. Only a few figures away, the drunken hero Hercules has lost his lion-skin mantle and collapsed in a stupor into the arms of two satyrs. The detail, clarity, and liveliness of this platter reflect the work of a virtuoso artist. Deeply engraved lines emphasize the contours of the subtly modeled bodies, echoing the technique of **undercutting** used to add depth to figures in stone and marble reliefs and suggesting a connection between silver-working and relief sculpture.

A farmer accidentally discovered this extraordinary platter—one of the greatest archaeological finds of the twentieth century—while plowing a field in 1942 outside the town of Mildenhall in Suffolk, England, located near the site of an ancient Roman villa. In total he unearthed 34 pieces of Roman silver tableware dating from the fourth century CE, including spoons engraved with Christian symbols. The find was not made public until four years later, since the farmer and his associates claimed they were unaware of how valuable it was, both materially and historically. When word of the discovery leaked out, however, the government confiscated the silver to determine if it was a "Treasure Trove"—gold or silver objects that have been intentionally hidden (rather than, for example, included in a burial) and that by law belong not to the finder, but to the Crown. The silver found at Mildenhall was deemed a "Treasure Trove" and is now one of the great glories of the British Museum in London.

The original owner of the hoard was thought to be a wealthy Roman Christian living in the provinces. Such opulent items were often hidden or buried to protect them from theft and looting, a sign of the breakdown of the Roman peace, especially in provincial areas. But there are those who do not believe the official story of the discovery. None of the silver in the hoard showed any sign of having been dented by a plow, and some believe that the quality and style of the objects are inconsistent with a provincial Roman context, especially so far in the hinterlands in England. Could the treasure have been looted from Italy during World War II, brought back to England (Mildenhall is not far from an American airfield), and buried to set up a staged discovery? The farmer who discovered the hoard and his associates, some argue, changed their story several times over the course of its history. Most scholars do believe the official story—that the silver was buried quickly for safekeeping by wealthy provincial Romans in Britain who felt threatened by a possible invasion or attack, and was forgotten (perhaps its owners were killed in the expected turmoil) until its accidental discovery in 1942. But when the history of art is founded on undocumented archaeological finds, there is usually some room for doubt.

Unlike the original owners of the Mildenhall platter, however, not all fourth-century Romans converted to Christianity. Among the champions of paganism were the Roman patricians Quintus Aurelius Symmachus and Virius Nicomachus Flavianus. A famous ivory diptych (**FIG. 6–71**) attests to the close relationship between their families, perhaps through marriage, as well as to their firmly held beliefs. A diptych was a pair of panels attached with hinges, not unlike the modest object held by the woman in FIGURE 6–34, but in this case made of a very precious material and

6–70 PLATTER
From Mildenhall, England. Mid 4th century CE. Silver, diameter approx. 24" (61 cm). British Museum, London.

6-71 PRIESTESS OF BACCHUS (?)
Right panel of the diptych of Symmachus and Nicomachus. c. 390–401 CE.
Ivory, 11¾ × 4¾" (29.9 × 12 cm). Victoria & Albert Museum, London.

Credit: V&A Images/Victoria and Albert Museum

carved with reliefs on the exterior sides. On the interior of a diptych there were shallow, traylike recessions filled with wax, into which messages could be written with a stylus and sent with a servant as a letter to a friend or acquaintance, who could then smooth out the wax surface, incise a reply with his or her own stylus, and send the diptych back to its owner with the servant. Here, one family's name is inscribed at the top of each panel. On the panel inscribed "Symmachorum" (illustrated here), a stately, elegantly attired priestess burns incense at a beautifully decorated altar. On her head is a wreath of ivy, sacred to Bacchus. She is assisted by a small child, and the event takes place out of doors under an oak tree, sacred to Jupiter. Like the silversmiths, Roman ivory carvers of the fourth century CE were highly skillful, and their work was widely admired. They imitated the Augustan style effortlessly for conservative patrons like the Nicomachus and Symmachus families. The exquisite rendering of the drapery and foliage recalls the reliefs of the Ara Pacis (SEE FIG. 6–21).

Classical subject matter remained attractive to artists and patrons throughout the late Roman period. Even such great Christian thinkers as the fourth-century CE bishop Gregory of Nazianzus spoke out in support of the right of the people to appreciate and enjoy their Classical heritage, as long as it did not seduce them to return to pagan practices. As a result, stories of the ancient gods and heroes entered the secular realm as lively, visually delightful, even erotic decorative elements. As Roman authority gave way to local rule by powerful "barbarian" tribes in much of the West, many people continued to appreciate Classical learning and to treasure Greek and Roman art. In the East, patrons and artists cultivated Classical traditions, and they became an enduring element of Byzantine art.

Think About It

1   Characterize the salient stylistic features of the murals that survive from Roman houses in Pompeii, discussing specific examples from this chapter.

2   Explain how the Roman interest in portraits grew out of early funeral rituals and developed into a powerful aspect of imperial self-fashioning.

3   Describe and evaluate the subjects used in Etruscan tomb paintings and sarcophagi. How do Etruscan practices relate to what we have discovered about tombs in other ancient cultures?

4   Identify two key structural advances made by Roman builders and discuss their use in one large civic building. Why do you think the ancient Romans built on such a large scale?

Crosscurrents

Greek and Roman temples have features in common, but they are fundamentally different in important respects. Evaluate the significant similarities and dissimilarities by comparing these two buildings.

FIG. 5–37A

FIG. 6–17A

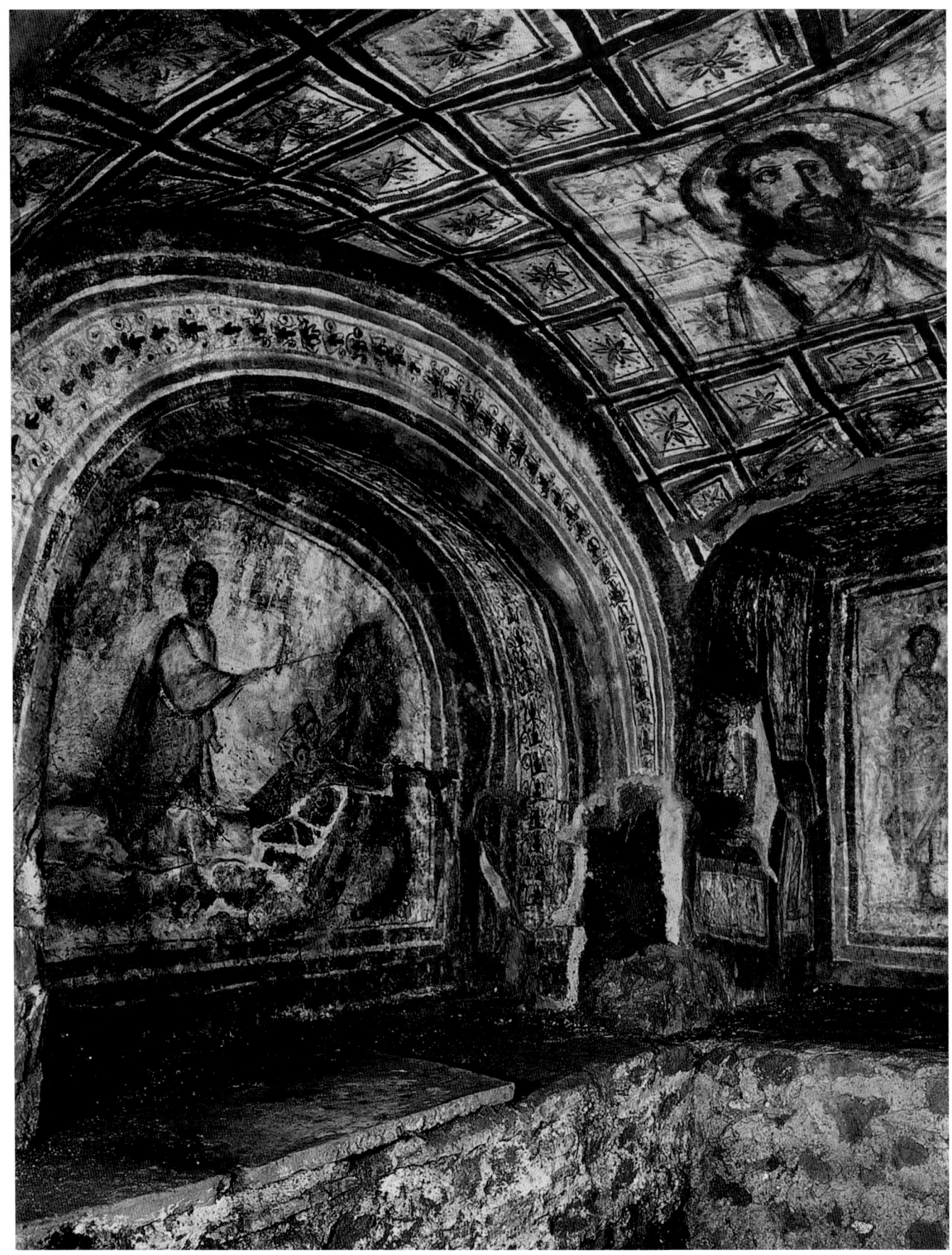

7-1 CUBICULUM OF LEONIS, CATACOMB OF COMMODILLA
Near Rome. Late 4th century.

Credit: Index Ricerca Iconografica

Chapter 7
Jewish and Early Christian Art

 ## Learning Objectives

7.a Identify the visual hallmarks of Jewish and Early Christian art for formal, technical, and expressive qualities.

7.b Interpret the meaning of works of Jewish and Early Christian art based on their themes, subjects, and symbols.

7.c Relate Jewish and Early Christian artists and art to their cultural, economic, and political contexts.

7.d Apply the vocabulary and concepts relevant to Jewish and Early Christian art, artists, and art history.

7.e Interpret a work of Jewish and Early Christian art using the art historical methods of observation, comparison, and inductive reasoning.

7.f Select visual and textual evidence in various media to support an argument or an interpretation of a work of Jewish and Early Christian art.

In this painting in a Roman **catacomb** (underground cemetery) (**FIG. 7–1**), St. Peter, like Moses before him, strikes a rock and water flows from it (scene at left). Imprisoned in Rome at the end of his missionary journeys, Peter was said to have converted his fellow prisoners and jailers to Christianity, but he needed water with which to baptize them. Miraculously, a spring gushed forth at the touch of his staff. In spite of his all too human frailty, Peter became the rock (Greek *petros*) on which Jesus founded the Church. He was considered the first bishop of Rome, predecessor of today's pope. By including this episode from the life of Peter in the chamber's decoration, the early Christians who dug this catacomb as a place to bury their dead may have sought to emphasize the importance of their own city in Christian history.

In the star-studded heavens painted on the vault of this chamber floats the face of Christ, flanked by the first and last letters of the Greek alphabet, alpha and omega. Here Christ takes on the guise not of the youthful teacher or miracle worker seen so often in Early Christian art, but of a more mature Greek philosopher with long beard and hair. The **halo** (circle) of light around his head indicates his importance and his divinity, a symbol appropriated from the conventions of late Roman imperial art, where haloes often appeared around the heads of emperors.

These two catacomb paintings represent two major directions of Early Christian art—the narrative and the iconic—that will continue to be important as this visual tradition develops. The **narrative image** recounts an event drawn from St. Peter's life—striking the rock for water—which in turn evokes the establishment of the Church as well as the essential Christian rite of baptism. The **iconic image**—Christ's face flanked by alpha and omega—offers a tangible expression of an intangible concept. The letters signify the beginning and end of time, and, combined with the image of Christ, symbolically represent not a story, but an idea—the everlasting dominion of the heavenly Christ.

Throughout the long and continuing history of Christian art these two tendencies will be apparent—the narrative urge to tell a good story, in which moral or theological implications often have instructional value, and the desire to create iconic images that symbolize the core concepts and values of the developing religious tradition. In both cases, the works of art take on meaning only in relation to viewers' stored knowledge of Christian stories and beliefs. This art was made not to teach non-readers new stories or concepts, as is so often claimed, but rather to remind faithful viewers of stories they had already heard—perhaps to draw specific lessons in their retelling—or to highlight ideas that were central to religious belief and would guide the religious devotional practice it inspired.

Judaism and Christianity in the Late Roman World

What features of late antique Jewish and Christian art and architecture derive from Roman conventions?

Three religions that arose in the Near East still dominate the spiritual life of the Western world today: Judaism, Christianity, and Islam. All three are monotheistic—believing that the same God of Abraham created and rules the universe and hears the prayers of the faithful. Jews believe that God made a covenant, or pact, with their ancestors, the Hebrews, and that they are God's chosen people. They await the coming of a savior, the Messiah, "the anointed one." Christians believe that Jesus of Nazareth was that Messiah (the name Christ is derived from the Greek term meaning "Messiah"). They believe that in Jesus, God took human form, preached among men and women, suffered execution, rose from the dead, and ascended to heaven after establishing the Christian Church under the leadership of the apostles (his closest disciples). Muslims, while accepting the Hebrew prophets and Jesus as divinely inspired, believe Muhammad to be the last and greatest prophet of God (Allah), the Messenger of God through whom Islam was revealed some six centuries after Jesus's lifetime.

All three are "religions of the book," that is, they have written records of God's will and words: the Hebrew Bible; the Christian Bible, which includes the Hebrew Bible as its Old Testament as well as the Christian New Testament; and the Muslim Qur'an, believed to be the Word of God as revealed in Arabic directly to Muhammad through the archangel Gabriel.

Both Judaism and Christianity existed within the Roman Empire, along with various other religions devoted to the worship of many gods. The variety of religious buildings excavated in present-day Syria at the abandoned Roman outpost of Dura-Europos represents the cosmopolitan religious character of Roman society in the second and third centuries. The settlement—destroyed in 256 CE—included a Jewish house-synagogue, a Christian house-church, shrines to the Persian cults of Mithras and Zoroaster, and temples to Greek and Roman gods, including Zeus and Artemis.

Early Jewish Art

Although we concentrate here on the art and architecture of the late Roman world, Jewish art has a much longer history. The Jewish people trace their origin to a Semitic people called the Hebrews, who lived in the land of Canaan. Canaan, known since the second century CE by the Roman name Palestine, was located along the eastern edge of the Mediterranean Sea (MAP 7-1). According to the Torah—the first five books of the Hebrew Bible—God promised the

MAP 7–1 THE LATE ROMAN AND BYZANTINE WORLD

During the period that saw the early spread of Christianity and ultimately its legalization by Constantine, the Roman Empire still extended completely around the shores of the Mediterranean Sea.

7-2 ARK OF THE COVENANT AND MENORAHS

Wall painting in a Jewish catacomb, Villa Torlonia, Rome. 3rd century. 3′11″ × 5′9″ (1.19 × 1.8 m).

The menorah form probably derives from the ancient Near Eastern Tree of Life, symbolizing for the Jewish people both the end of exile and the paradise to come.

Credit: Soprintendenza Archeologica di Roma / IKONA

patriarch Abraham that Canaan would be a homeland for the Jewish people (Genesis 17:8), a belief that remains important for some Jews to this day.

Jewish settlement of Canaan probably began sometime in the second millennium BCE. According to Exodus, the second book of the Torah, the prophet Moses led the Hebrews out of slavery in Egypt to the promised land of Canaan. At one crucial point during the journey Moses climbed alone to the top of Mount Sinai, where God gave him the Ten Commandments, the cornerstone of Jewish law. The commandments, inscribed on tablets, were kept in a gold-covered wooden box known as the Ark of the Covenant.

Jewish law forbade the worship of idols, a prohibition that often made the representational arts—especially sculpture in the round—suspect. Nevertheless, artists working for Jewish patrons depicted both symbolic and narrative Jewish subjects, and they drew from the traditions of both Near Eastern and Classical Greek and Roman art.

THE FIRST TEMPLE IN JERUSALEM   In the tenth century BCE, the Jewish king Solomon built a temple in Jerusalem to house the Ark of the Covenant. According to the Hebrew Bible (2 Chronicles 2–7), he sent to nearby Phoenicia for cedar, cypress, and sandalwood and for a superb construction supervisor. The building later known as the First Temple was the spiritual center of Jewish life. Biblical texts describe courtyards, two bronze pillars (large, freestanding architectural forms), an entrance hall, a main hall, and the Holy of Holies, the innermost chamber that housed the Ark and its guardian cherubim, or attendant angels.

In 586 BCE, the Babylonians under King Nebuchadnezzar II conquered Jerusalem. They destroyed the Temple, exiled the Jews, and carried off the Ark of the Covenant. When Cyrus the Great of Persia conquered Babylonia in 539 BCE, he permitted the Jews to return to their homeland (Ezra 1:1–4) and rebuild the Temple, which became known as the Second Temple. When Canaan became part of the Roman Empire, Herod the Great (king of Judaea, 37–34 BCE) restored the Second Temple. In 70 CE, Roman forces led by the general and future emperor Titus destroyed and looted the Second Temple and all of Jerusalem, a campaign the Romans commemorated on the Arch of Titus (SEE FIG. 6-36). The site of the Second Temple, the Temple Mount, is also an Islamic holy site, the Haram al-Sharif, and is now occupied by the shrine called the Dome of the Rock (SEE FIGS. 9-3, 9-4).

JEWISH CATACOMB ART IN ROME   Most of the earliest surviving examples of Jewish art date from the Hellenistic and Roman periods. Six Jewish catacombs, discovered on the outskirts of Rome and in use from the first to fourth centuries CE, display wall paintings with Jewish themes. In one example from the third century CE, two menorahs flank the long-lost **ARK OF THE COVENANT (FIG. 7-2)**. The continuing representation of the menorah, one of the precious objects looted from the Second Temple, kept the memory of the lost Jewish treasures alive.

SYNAGOGUES   Judaism has long emphasized religious learning. Jews gather in synagogues for study of the Torah—considered a form of worship. A synagogue can be any large room where the Torah scrolls are kept and read; it was also the site of communal social gatherings. Some synagogues were located in private homes or in buildings originally constructed like homes. The first synagogue in

7-3 WALL WITH TORAH NICHE

From a house-synagogue, Dura-Europos, Syria. 244–245 CE. Tempera on plaster, section approx. 40′ (12.19 m) long. Reconstructed in the National Museum, Damascus, Syria.

Credit: Princeton University Press/Art Resource, NY

Dura-Europos, Syria, consisted of an assembly hall, a separate alcove for women, and a courtyard. After a remodeling of the building completed in 244–245 CE, men and women shared the hall, and residential rooms were added. Two architectural features distinguished the assembly hall: a bench along its walls and a niche for the Torah scrolls (**FIG. 7-3**).

Scenes from Jewish history and the story of Moses, as recorded in Exodus, unfold in a continuous visual narrative around the room, employing the Roman tradition of epic historical presentation (SEE FIG. 6-47). In the scene of

THE CROSSING OF THE RED SEA (**FIG. 7-4**), Moses appears twice to signal sequential moments in the dramatic narrative. To the left he leans toward the army of Pharaoh, which is marching along the path that had been created for the Hebrews by God's miraculous parting of the waters, but at the right, wielding his authoritative staff, he returns the waters over the Egyptian soldiers to prevent their pursuit. Over each scene hovers a large hand, representing God's presence in both miracles—the parting and the unparting—using a symbol that will also be frequent in Christian art. Hierarchic scale makes it clear who is the

7-4 THE CROSSING OF THE RED SEA

Detail of a wall painting from a house-synagogue, Dura-Europos, Syria. 244–245 CE. National Museum, Damascus, Syria.

Credit: Image courtesy Yale University Art Gallery, Dura-Europos Collection

A Closer Look

THE MOSAIC FLOOR OF THE BETH ALPHA SYNAGOGUE

The shrine that holds the Torah is flanked by menorahs and growling lions, the latter perhaps as a security system to protect such sacred objects.

The figures in the four corners are winged personifications of the seasons; this figure holding a shepherd's crook and accompanied by a bird is Spring.

At the center of the zodiac wheel is a representation of the sun in a chariot set against a night sky studded with stars and a crescent moon.

The 12 signs of the zodiac appear in chronological order following a clockwise arrangement around the wheel of a year, implying perpetual continuity since the series has no set beginning and no end. This is Scorpio.

The peaceful coexistence of the lion and the ox (predator and prey) may represent a golden age or peaceable kingdom (Isaiah 11:6–9; 65:25).

Torah shrine and ritual objects.
•
The Metaphysical Realm

The sun, seasons, and signs of the zodiac.
•
The Celestial Realm

The Sacrifice of Isaac (Genesis 22:1–19).
•
The Terrestrial Realm

This ram (identified by inscription) will ultimately take Isaac's place as sacrificial offering. Throughout the mosaic, animals are shown consistently in profile, human beings frontally.

These two texts—one in Aramaic and one in Greek—identify the artists of the mosaic as Marianos and his son Hanina, and date their work to the reign of either Emperor Justin I (518–527) or Justin II (565–578).

Abraham, preparing to sacrifice Isaac, is interrupted by the hand of God rather than by the angel specified in the Bible. Both Abraham and Isaac are identified by inscription, but Abraham's advanced age is signaled pictorially by the streaks of gray in his beard.

7-5 Marianos and Hanina **RITUAL OBJECTS, CELESTIAL DIAGRAM, AND SACRIFICE OF ISAAC**
Mosaic floor of the Beth Alpha Synagogue, Galilee, Israel. 6th century CE.

Credit: © akg-images/Bible Land Pictures/Jerusalem Photo: Zev Radovan hero in this two-part narrative, but the clue to his identity is provided only by the context of the story, which observers would have already known.

In addition to house-synagogues, Jews built meeting places designed on the model of the ancient Roman basilica. A typical basilica synagogue had a central nave; an aisle on both sides, separated from the nave by a line of columns; a semicircular apse with Torah shrine in the wall facing Jerusalem; and perhaps an atrium and porch, or **narthex** (vestibule). The small fifth-century CE synagogue at Beth Alpha—discovered between the Gilboa mountains and the River Jordan by farmers in 1928—fits well into this pattern with a three-nave interior, vestibule, and courtyard. Like some other very grand synagogues, it also has a mosaic floor, in this case a later addition from the sixth century. Most of the floor decoration is geometric in design, but in the central nave there are three complex panels full of figural compositions and symbols (see "Closer Look" on page 221) created using 21 separate colors of stone and glass tesserae. The images of ritual objects, a celestial diagram of the zodiac, and a scene of Abraham's near-sacrifice of Isaac, bordered by strips of foliate and geometric ornament, draw on both Classical and Near Eastern pictorial traditions.

Early Christian Art

At age 30, a Palestinian Jew named Jesus gathered a group of followers, male and female. Accounts of his life written by his followers credit him with performing miracles of healing and preaching on the value of loving God and neighbor, on the sanctity of social justice, on the forgiveness of sins, and on the promise of life after death. Christian belief holds that after his ministry on Earth Jesus was executed by crucifixion, and after three days rose from the dead.

The Christian scriptures include what Christians call the Old Testament (from the Hebrew Bible) and the New Testament (written well after Jesus's lifetime). The story of Jesus's life and collections of his teachings were recorded between about 70 and 100 CE in four Gospels at the beginning of the New Testament, attributed to four evangelists (from the Greek *evangelion*, meaning "good news"): Matthew, Mark, Luke, and John.

The New Testament also includes the Acts of the Apostles and the Epistles, 21 letters of advice and encouragement written to Christian communities in Greece, Asia Minor, and other parts of the Roman Empire. The final book is Revelation (or Apocalypse), a series of enigmatic visions and prophecies concerning the eventual triumph of God at the end of the world, written about 95 CE.

THE EARLY CHURCH Jesus limited his ministry primarily to Jews; it was his apostles, as well as later followers such as Paul, who took his teachings to gentiles (non-Jews). Despite sporadic persecutions, Christianity persisted and spread throughout the Roman Empire. The imperial government formally recognized the religion in 313, and Christianity grew rapidly during the fourth century. As well-educated, upper-class Romans joined the Christian Church, they established increasingly elaborate organizational structures, rituals, doctrines, and works of art and architecture.

Christian communities became organized by geographic units, or dioceses, along the lines of Roman provincial governments. Senior church officials called bishops served as governors of dioceses made up of smaller units known as parishes and headed by priests. A bishop's church is a **cathedral**, a word derived from the Latin *cathedra*, which means "chair" but took on the meaning of "bishop's throne."

Communal Christian worship focused on the ritual consumption of bread and wine, identified as the Body and Blood of Christ, which Jesus had inaugurated at the Last Supper, a Passover Seder meal with his disciples just before his crucifixion. Around these acts developed a complicated religious ceremony, or liturgy, called the **Eucharist** (also known as Holy Communion or the Mass).

The earliest Christians gathered to worship in private apartments or houses or in buildings constructed after domestic models such as the third-century house-church excavated at Dura-Europos, Syria (see FIG. 7-6). As their worship became more ritualized and complex, however, they developed special buildings—churches and baptisteries—as well as specialized ritual equipment. They also began to use art to visualize their most important stories and ideas (SEE FIG. 7-1). The earliest surviving Christian art dates to the early third century and derives its styles and its imagery from Jewish and Roman visual traditions. In this process, known as **syncretism**, artists assimilate images from other traditions—either unconsciously or deliberately—and give them new meanings. For example, **orant** figures—worshipers with arms outstretched in prayer—can be pagan, Jewish, or Christian, depending on the context in which they occur. Perhaps the best-known syncretic image is the Good Shepherd. In pagan art, he was Apollo, or Hermes the shepherd, or Orpheus among the animals, or a personification of philanthropy. For Early Christians, he became the Good Shepherd of the Psalms (Psalm 23) and the Gospels (Matthew 18:12–14, John 10:11–16). Such images, therefore, do not have a stable meaning, but are associated with the meaning or meanings that a particular group of viewers brings to them. They remind rather than instruct.

DURA-EUROPOS Our understanding of buildings used for worship by third-century Jews and Christians was greatly enhanced—even revolutionized—by the spectacular discoveries made in the 1930s while excavating the Roman military garrison and border town of Dura-Europos

7–6 RECONSTRUCTION OF BAPTISTERY, WITH FRAGMENTS OF ORIGINAL FRESCO

From Christian house-church, Dura-Europos, Syria. Before 256. Yale University Art Gallery, New Haven, Connecticut.

Credit: Image courtesy Yale University Art Gallery

(in present-day Syria). In 256, threatened by the Parthians attacking from the east, residents of Dura built a huge earth-work mound around their town in an attempt to protect themselves from the invading armies. In the process—since they were located on the city's margins right against its defensive stone wall—the houses used by Jews and Christians as places of worship were buried under the earthwork perimeter. In spite of this enhanced fortification, the Parthians conquered Dura-Europos. But since the victors never unearthed the submerged margins of the city, an intact Jewish house-synagogue and Christian house-church remained underground awaiting the explorations of modern archaeologists.

We have already seen the extensive strip narratives flanking the Torah shrine in the house-synagogue (SEE FIG. 7–3). The discovery of this expansive pictorial decoration contradicted a long-held scholarly belief that Jews of this period avoided figural decoration of any sort, in conformity with Mosaic law (Exodus 20:4). A few blocks down the street that ran along the city wall, a typical Roman house built around a central courtyard held another surprise. Only a discreet red cross above the door distinguished it from the other houses on its block, but the arrangement of the interior clearly documents its use as a Christian place of worship. A large assembly hall that could seat 60–70 people lies on one side of the courtyard, and across from it is a smaller but extensively decorated room with a water tank set aside for baptism, the central rite of Christian initiation (**FIG. 7–6**).

Along the walls of this room were scenes from Christ's miracles and a monumental portrayal of women visiting his tomb about to discover his resurrection. Even this early in Christian art, sacred spaces were decorated with pictures proclaiming the theological meaning of the rituals they housed. Above the baptismal basin is a **lunette** (semicircular wall section) with a painting (**FIG. 7–7**) in which Adam and Eve's fall from grace is juxtaposed with a larger image of the Good Shepherd (representing Jesus) who came to Earth to care for and guide his sheep (Christian believers) toward redemption and eternal life—a message that was especially appropriate juxtaposed with the rite of Christian baptism, which signaled the converts' passage from sin to salvation.

7–7 THE GOOD SHEPHERD WITH ADAM AND EVE AFTER THE FALL

Detail of lunette fresco in FIG. 7–6.

Credit: Image courtesy Yale University Art Gallery, Dura-Europos Collection

7–8 THE GOOD SHEPHERD, ORANTS, AND THE STORY OF JONAH

Painted ceiling of the Catacomb of SS. Peter and Marcellinus, Rome. Late 3rd–early 4th century.

Credit: Canali Photobank, Milan, Italy

CATACOMB PAINTING AND SCULPTURE Christians, like Jews, used catacombs for burials and funeral ceremonies. They were not sites of communal worship. In the Christian Catacomb of Commodilla, dating from the fourth century, long rectangular niches in the walls called *loculi* each held two or three bodies. Affluent families created small rooms, or **cubicula** (singular, *cubiculum*), off the main passages to house sarcophagi (SEE FIG. 7-1). The *cubicula* were hewn out of tufo, a soft volcanic rock, then plastered and painted with imagery related to their owners' religious beliefs. The finest Early Christian catacomb paintings resemble murals in houses such as those preserved at Rome and Pompeii.

One fourth-century Roman catacomb contained remains, or relics, of SS. Peter and Marcellinus, two third-century Christians martyred for their faith. Here, the ceiling of a *cubiculum* is partitioned by a central **medallion**, or round compartment, and four semicircular lunettes, framed by arches (**FIG. 7-8**). At the center is a Good Shepherd, whose pose has roots in Classical sculpture. In its new context, the image was a reminder of Jesus's promise "I am the good shepherd. A good shepherd lays down his life for the sheep" (John 10:11).

The semicircular compartments surrounding the Good Shepherd tell the story of Jonah and the sea monster from the Hebrew Bible (Jonah 1–2), in which God caused Jonah to be thrown overboard, swallowed by the monster,

7–9 THE GOOD SHEPHERD

Eastern Mediterranean, probably Anatolia (present-day Turkey). Second half of the 3rd century. Marble, 19½ × 10 × 6″ (49.5 × 26 × 16.2 cm). Cleveland Museum of Art. John L. Severance Fund (1965.241).

Credit: Bridgeman Images

and released, repentant and unscathed, three days later. Christians reinterpreted this story as a parable of Christ's death and resurrection—and hence of the everlasting life awaiting true believers—and it was a popular subject in Christian catacombs. On the left, Jonah is thrown from the boat; on the right, the monster spits him up; and below, between these two scenes, Jonah reclines in the shade of a vine, a symbol of paradise. Orant figures stand between the lunettes, presumably images of the faithful Christians who were buried here.

SCULPTURE Early Christian sculpture before the fourth century is rarer than painting. What survives are mainly sarcophagi and small statues and reliefs. A remarkable set of small marble figures, discovered in the 1960s and probably made in third-century Asia Minor, features a gracious **GOOD SHEPHERD** (**FIG. 7-9**). Because it was found with sculptures depicting Jonah—as we have already seen, a popular Early Christian theme—it is probably from a Christian context.

Imperial Christian Architecture and Art in Rome

How is Christian art and architecture transformed in Rome after its acceptance by Constantine?

When Constantine issued the Edict of Milan in 313 granting all people in the Roman Empire freedom to worship whatever god they wished, Christianity and Christian art and architecture entered a new phase. Sophisticated philosophical and ethical systems developed, incorporating many ideas from Greek and Roman pagan thought. Church scholars edited and commented on the Bible, and the papal secretary who would become St. Jerome (c. 347–420) undertook a new Bible translation from Hebrew and Greek versions into Latin, the language of the Western Church. The so-called Vulgate (from the same root as the word "vulgar," the Latin *vulgaris*, meaning "common" or "popular") became the official version of the Bible.

The developing Roman Christian community had special architectural needs. Greek temples had served as the house and treasury of the gods, forming a backdrop for ceremonies that took place at altars in the open air, but with Christianity, an entire community needed to gather inside a building to worship. Christians also needed locations for special activities such as the initiation of new members, private devotion, and burials. Beginning with the age of Constantine, **longitudinal-plan** pagan basilicas provided the model for congregational churches, and **central-plan** tombs provided a model for baptisteries and martyrs' shrines.

Old St. Peter's

Constantine ordered the construction of a large new basilican church to mark the place where Christians believed St. Peter was buried (**FIG. 7-10**). Our knowledge of what is now called Old St. Peter's (it was destroyed and replaced by a new building in the sixteenth century) is based on written descriptions, drawings made before and while it was being dismantled, the study of other churches inspired by it, and modern archaeological excavations at the site.

7-10 PLAN (A) AND RECONSTRUCTION DRAWING (B) OF OLD ST. PETER'S
c. 320–327; atrium added in later 4th century. Approx. 394′ (120 m) long and 210′ (64 m) wide.

Old St. Peter's included architectural elements in a longitudinal-plan arrangement that has characterized Christian basilican churches ever since. An atrium, or courtyard, in front of the basilica and a narthex across its width at the entrance end provided a place for people who had not yet been baptized. Five doorways—a large, central portal into the nave and two portals on each side—gave access to the church. Columns supporting an entablature lined the tall nave, forming what is called a nave colonnade, and above the entablature windows within the upper walls brought light directly into the nave space. Running parallel to the nave colonnade on each side was another row of columns that created shorter double side aisles; these columns supported round arches rather than an entablature (**FIG. 7-11**). The roofs of both nave and aisles were supported by wooden rafters. Sarcophagi and tombs lined the side aisles and graves were dug under the floor. At the apse end of the nave, Constantine's architects added an innovative **transept**—a perpendicular hall crossing in front of the apse, giving the plan of the building a T-shape. This area provided additional space for the large number of clergy serving the church, and it also accommodated pilgrims visiting the tomb of St. Peter. Old St. Peter's could hold at least 14,000 worshipers, and it remained the largest church in Christendom until the eleventh century.

Art and its Contexts

NAMING CHRISTIAN CHURCHES: DESIGNATION + DEDICATION + LOCATION

Christian churches are identified by a three-part descriptive title combining (1) designation (or type), (2) dedication (often to a saint), and (3) geographic location, in that order.

Designation: There are various types of churches fulfilling a variety of liturgical and administrative objectives, and the identification of a specific church often begins with an indication of its function within the system. For example, an **abbey church** or monastery church is the place of worship within a monastery or convent; a **pilgrimage church** is a site that attracts visitors wishing to venerate **relics** (material remains or objects associated with a saint) as well as attend services. A cathedral is a bishop's primary church (the word derives from the Latin *cathedra*, meaning "chair," since the chair or throne of a bishop is contained within his cathedral). A bishop's domain is called a diocese, and there can be only one church in the diocese designated as its bishop's cathedral, but a diocese has numerous parish churches where local residents attend regular services.

Dedication: Christian churches are always dedicated to Christ, the Virgin Mary, a saint, or a sacred concept or event, for example St. Peter's Basilica or the church of Hagia Sophia (Christ as the embodiment of Holy Wisdom). In short-hand identification, when we omit the church designation at the beginning, we always add an apostrophe and an *s* to a saint's name, as when using "St. Peter's" to refer to the Vatican Basilica of St. Peter in Rome.

Location: The final piece of information that clearly pinpoints the specific church indicated in a title is its geographic location, as in the church of San Vitale in Ravenna or the Cathedral of Notre-Dame (French for "Our Lady," referring to the Virgin Mary) in Paris. "Notre-Dame" alone usually refers to this Parisian cathedral, in spite of the fact that many contemporary cathedrals elsewhere (e.g. at Chartres and Reims) were also dedicated to "Notre-Dame." Similarly, "St. Peter's" usually means the Vatican church of the pope in Rome.

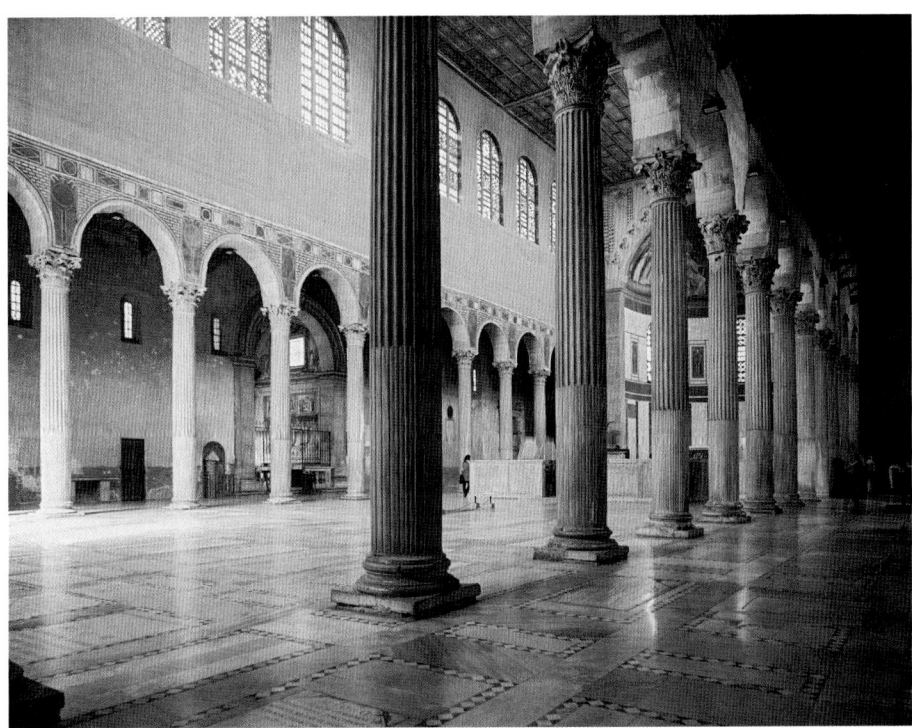

7–12 INTERIOR, CHURCH OF SANTA SABINA, ROME
View from the south aisle near the sanctuary toward the entrance. c. 422–432.

Credit: © akg-images/Andrea Jemolo

Santa Sabina

Old St. Peter's is gone, but the church of Santa Sabina in Rome, constructed by Bishop Peter of Illyria (a region in the Balkan peninsula) a century later between about 422 and 432, appears much as it did in the fifth century (**FIGS. 7-12, 7-13**). The basic elements of the Early Christian basilica are clearly visible here, inside and out: a nave lit by clerestory windows, flanked by single side aisles, and ending in a rounded apse.

Santa Sabina's exterior is simple brickwork. In contrast, the church's interior displays a wealth of marble veneer and 24 fluted marble columns with Corinthian capitals reused from a second-century pagan building. (Material reused from earlier buildings is known as **spolia**, Latin for "spoils.") The columns support round arches, creating a nave arcade, in contrast to the straight nave colonnade on an architrave in Old St. Peter's. The spandrels between the arches are faced with marble veneer that portrays chalices (wine cups) and paten (bread plates), essential equipment for the Eucharistic rite that took place at the altar. In such basilicas, the expanse of wall between the arcade and the clerestory typically had paintings or mosaics with biblical scenes, but here the decoration of the upper walls has been lost.

7–13 CHURCH OF SANTA SABINA, ROME
Exterior view from the southeast. c. 422–432.

Credit: © Vincenzo Pirozzi, Rome

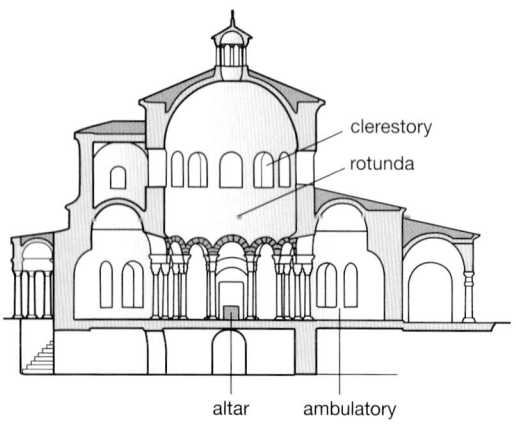

**7-14 PLAN (A) AND SECTION (B)
OF THE CHURCH OF SANTA COSTANZA, ROME**

c. 350.

Santa Costanza

Central-plan Roman buildings with vertical (rather than longitudinal) axes served as models for Christian tombs, churches dedicated to or built over the tombs of martyrs, and baptisteries (where Christians "died"—giving up their old life—and were reborn as believers). One of the earliest surviving central-plan Christian buildings is the mausoleum of Constantina, daughter of Constantine. Her tomb was built outside the walls of Rome just before 350 (**FIG. 7-14**), and it was consecrated as a church in 1256, dedicated to Santa Costanza (the Italian form of Constantina, who was sanctified after her death).

The building is a tall rotunda with an encircling barrel-vaulted passageway called an **ambulatory**. Paired columns with Composite capitals and richly molded entablature blocks support the arcade and dome (**FIG. 7-15**). Unlike basilicas, where the longitudinal axis draws worshipers forward along a line from the entrance toward the apse, central-plan buildings such as this have a vertical axis from the center up through the dome, which may have functioned as a symbolic "vault of heaven."

Originally, the interior was entirely sheathed in mosaics and veneers of fine marble; mosaics still surviving in the ambulatory vault recall the syncretic images in the catacombs. In one section, for example, a bust portrait of Constantina at the crest of the vault is surrounded by a tangle of grapevines filled with **putti**—naked cherubs, derived from pagan art—who vie with the birds to harvest the grapes (**FIG. 7-16**). Along the bottom edges on each side, other *putti* drive wagonloads of grapes toward pavilions housing large vats in which more *putti* trample the grapes into juice for the making of wine. The technique and style are Roman; the subject is traditional, associated with Bacchus and his cult; but the meaning here is new. In a Christian context, the wine refers to the Eucharist and the trampling of grapes for the making of wine becomes an image of death and resurrection. Constantina's pagan

7-15 CHURCH OF SANTA COSTANZA, ROME

c. 350. View from ambulatory into rotunda.

7–16 HARVESTING OF GRAPES
Ambulatory vault, church of Santa Costanza, Rome. c. 350. Mosaic.

Credit: © 2016 Photo Scala, Florence

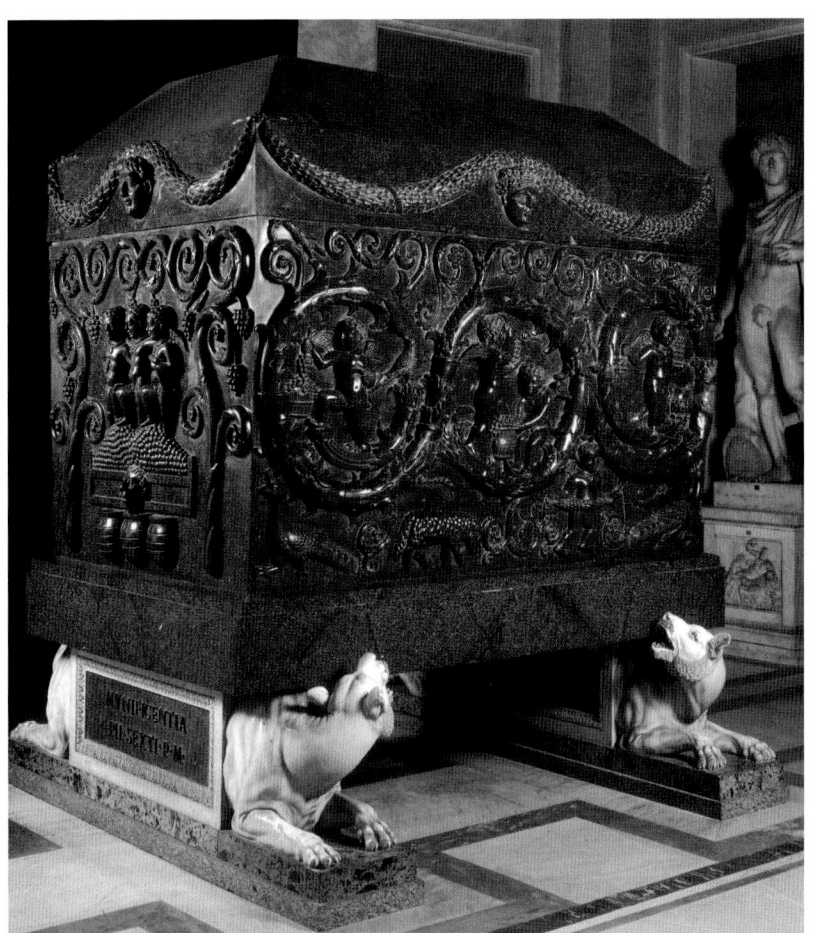

husband, however, may have appreciated the parallel, pagan reference.

Within her mausoleum, Constantina (d. 354) was buried within a spectacularly huge porphyry sarcophagus (**FIG. 7-17**) that was installed across from the entrance on the other side of the ambulatory in a rectangular niche (visible on the plan in FIG. 7–14; an in-place replica peeks over the altar in **FIG. 7-15**). The motifs are already familiar—the *putti* making wine that were in the mosaics of the ambulatory vaults. Here the scenes are framed by a huge, undulating grapevine whose subsidiary shoots curl above and below to fill the flat sides of the box. Striding along its base, peacocks symbolize eternal life in paradise, while a lone sheep could represent a member of Jesus's flock, presumably Constantina herself.

7–17 SARCOPHAGUS OF CONSTANTINA
c. 350. Porphyry, height 7′5″ (2.26 m).
Musei Vaticani, Rome.

Credit: © akg-images/Nimatallah

Sarcophagus of Junius Bassus

Carved about the same time as the Sarcophagus of Constantina but made of marble, the **SARCOPHAGUS OF JUNIUS BASSUS** (FIG. 7–18) is packed with figural scenes like the second-century CE Dionysiac sarcophagus (see "Closer Look" in Chapter 6 on page 204), only here they are separated into two registers, where columns, entablatures, and gables divide the space into fields for individual scenes. Junius Bassus was a Roman official who, as the inscription here tells us, was "newly baptized" and died on August 25, 359, at age 42.

In the center of both registers is a triumphant Christ. Above, he appears as a Roman emperor, distributing legal authority in the form of scrolls to flanking figures of SS. Peter and Paul and resting his feet on the head of Coelus, the pagan god of the heavens, here identifying Christ as ruler of the cosmos. In the bottom register, the earthly Jesus makes his triumphal entry into Jerusalem like a Roman emperor entering a conquered city.

Jesus, however, rides on a humble ass rather than a powerful horse.

Even in the earliest Christian art, such as that in catacomb paintings and here on the sarcophagus of Junius Bassus, artists employed episodes from the Hebrew Bible allegorically since Christians saw them as prefigurations of important events in the New Testament. At the top left, Abraham passes the test of faith and need not sacrifice his son Isaac. Christians saw in this story an allegory that foreshadowed God's sacrifice of his own son, Jesus, which culminates not in Jesus's death, but in his resurrection. Under the triangular gable, second from the end at bottom right, the Hebrew Bible story of Daniel saved by God from the lions prefigures Christ's emergence alive from his tomb. At bottom far left, God tests the faith of Job, who provides a model for the sufferings of Christian martyrs. Next to Job, Adam and Eve have sinned to set in motion the entire Christian redemption story. Lured by the serpent, they have eaten the forbidden fruit and, conscious of their nakedness, are trying to hide their genitals with leaves.

Art and its Contexts
THE LIFE OF JESUS

Episodes from the life of Jesus as recounted in the Gospels form the principal subject matter of Christian visual art. What follows is a list of main events in his and his mother's life with parenthetical references when there are textual sources in the Gospel texts.

Maternity of Mary and Childhood of Jesus

Annunciation: The archangel Gabriel informs the Virgin Mary that God has chosen her to bear his Son. A dove often represents the Incarnation, her miraculous conception of Jesus through the Holy Spirit. (Lk 1:26–28)

Visitation: The pregnant Mary visits her older cousin Elizabeth, pregnant with the future St. John the Baptist. (Lk 1:29–45)

Nativity: Jesus is born in Bethlehem. The Holy Family—Jesus, Mary, and her husband, Joseph—is usually portrayed in a stable or, in Byzantine art, a cave. (Lk 2:4–7)

Annunciation to and Adoration of the Shepherds: Angels announce Jesus's birth to shepherds, who hurry to Bethlehem to honor him. (Lk 2:8–20)

Adoration of the Magi: Wise men from the east follow a bright star to Bethlehem to honor Jesus as king of the Jews, presenting him with precious gifts. Eventually these Magi became identified as three kings, often differentiated through facial type as young, middle-aged, and old. (Mat 2:1–12)

Presentation in the Temple: Mary and Joseph bring the infant Jesus to the Temple in Jerusalem, where he is presented to the high priest. (Lk 2:25–35)

Massacre of the Innocents and Flight into Egypt: An angel warns Joseph that King Herod plans to murder all male babies in Bethlehem to eliminate the threat of a newborn rival king. The Holy Family flees to Egypt. (Mat 2:13–16)

Jesus's Ministry

Baptism: At age 30, Jesus is baptized by John the Baptist in the River Jordan. The Holy Spirit appears in the form of a dove, and a heavenly voice proclaims Jesus as God's Son. (Mat 3:13–17, Mk 1:9–11, Lk 3:21–22)

Marriage at Cana: At his mother's request Jesus turns water into wine at a wedding feast, his first public miracle. (Jn 2:1–10)

Miracles of Healing: Throughout the Gospels, Jesus performs miracles of healing the blind, possessed (mentally ill), paralytic, and lepers; he also resurrects the dead.

Calling of Levi/Matthew: Jesus calls to Levi, a tax collector, "Follow me." Levi complies, becoming the disciple Matthew. (Mat 9:9, Mk 2:14)

Raising of Lazarus: Jesus brings his friend Lazarus back to life four days after his death. (Jn 11:1–44)

Transfiguration: Jesus reveals his divinity in a dazzling vision on Mount Tabor as his closest disciples—Peter, James, and John—look on. (Mat 17:1–5, Mk 9:2–6, Lk 9:28–35)

Tribute Money: Challenged to pay the temple tax, Jesus sends Peter to catch a fish, which turns out to have the required coin in its mouth. (Mat 17:24–27, Lk 20:20–25)

Jesus's Passion, Death, and Resurrection

Entry into Jerusalem: Jesus, riding an ass and accompanied by his disciples, enters Jerusalem, while crowds honor him,

7-18 SARCOPHAGUS OF JUNIUS BASSUS
Grottoes of St. Peter, Vatican, Rome. c. 359. Marble, 4 × 8′ (1.2 × 2.4 m).

Credit: © 2016. Photo Scala, Florence

spreading clothes and palm fronds in his path. (Mat 21:1–11, Mk 11:1–11, Lk 19:30–44, Jn 12:12–15)

Last Supper: During the Jewish Passover Seder, Jesus reveals his impending death to his disciples. Instructing them to drink wine (his blood) and eat bread (his body) in remembrance of him, he lays the foundation for the Christian Eucharist (Mass). (Mat 26:26–30, Mk 14:22–25, Lk 22:14–20)

Washing the Disciples' Feet: At the Last Supper, Jesus humbly washes the disciples' feet. (Jn 13: 4–12)

Agony in the Garden: In the Garden of Gethsemane on the Mount of Olives, Jesus struggles between his human fear of pain and death and his divine strength to overcome them. The apostles sleep nearby, oblivious. (Lk 22:40–45)

Betrayal/Arrest: Judas Iscariot (a disciple) has accepted a bribe to point out Jesus to an armed band of his enemies by kissing him. (Mat 26:46–49, Mk 14:43–46, Lk 22:47–48, Jn 18:3–5)

Jesus before Pilate: Jesus is taken to Pontius Pilate, Roman governor of Judaea, and charged with treason for calling himself king of the Jews. Pilate proposes freeing Jesus but is shouted down by the mob, which demands Jesus be crucified. (Mat 27:11–25, Mk 15:4–14, Lk 23:1–24, Jn 18:28–40)

Crucifixion: Jesus is executed on a cross, often shown between two crucified criminals and accompanied by the Virgin Mary, John the Evangelist, Mary Magdalen, and other followers standing at the foot of the cross. Roman soldiers sometimes torment Jesus, extending a sponge on a pole with vinegar instead of water for him to drink and stabbing him in the side with a spear. (Mat 27:35–50, Mk 15:23–37, Lk 23:38–49, Jn 19:18–30)

Descent from the Cross (Deposition): Jesus's followers take his body down from the cross. (Mat 27:55–59, Mk 15:40–46, Lk 23:50–56, Jn 19:38–40)

Lamentation/Pietà and Entombment: Jesus's sorrowful followers gather around his body to mourn and then place his body in a tomb. An image of the grieving Virgin alone with Jesus across her lap is known as a **pietà** (from Latin *pietas*, "pity"). (Mat 27:60–61, Jn 19:41–42)

Resurrection/Holy Women at the Tomb: Three days after his entombment, Christ rises from the dead, and his female followers—usually including Mary Magdalen—discover his empty tomb. An angel announces Christ's resurrection. (Mat 28, Mk 16, Lk 24:1–35, Jn 20)

Descent into Limbo/Harrowing of Hell (Anastasis): The resurrected Jesus descends into limbo, or hell, to free deserving predecessors, among them Adam, Eve, David, and Moses. (Apocryphal Gospel of Nicodemus, not in the New Testament)

Noli Me Tangere ("Do Not Touch Me"): Christ appears to Mary Magdalen as she weeps at his tomb. When she reaches out to him, he warns her not to touch him. (Lk 24:34–53, Jn 20:11–31)

Ascension: Christ ascends to heaven from the Mount of Olives, disappearing in a cloud, while his mother and apostles watch. (Acts 1)

Mary's Death

Dormition of the Virgin: Literally Mary's "falling asleep." She dies surrounded by the apostles, while her soul, in the form of a baby or child, appears above her in the arms of the risen Christ. (Not in the Gospels)

Assumption of the Virgin: Mary's body ascends to heaven. (Not in the Gospels)

On the upper right side, spread over two compartments, Jesus appears before Pontius Pilate, who is about to wash his hands, symbolizing his denial of responsibility for Jesus's death. Jesus's position here, held captive between two soldiers, recalls (and perhaps could also be read as) his arrest in Gethsemane, especially since the composition of this panel is reflected in the arrests of the apostles Peter (top, second frame from the left) and Paul (bottom, far right).

Ravenna and Thessaloniki

How do the art and architecture in the provincial capitals of Ravenna and Thessaloniki continue Imperial Roman conventions?

As the city of Rome's political importance dwindled, that of other imperial cities grew. In 395, Emperor Theodosius I split the Roman Empire into Eastern and Western divisions, each ruled by one of his sons. Heading the West, Honorius (ruled 395–423) first established his capital at Milan, but in 402, to escape the siege by Germanic settlers, he moved his government to Ravenna, on the east coast of Italy. Its naval base, Classis (present-day Classe), had been important since the early days of the empire. In addition to military security, Ravenna offered direct access by sea to Constantinople. When Italy fell in 476 to the Ostrogoths, Ravenna became one of their headquarters, but the beauty and richness of Early Christian buildings can still be experienced there in a remarkable group of especially well-preserved fifth- and sixth-century churches, baptisteries, and oratories, encrusted with mosaics.

The history of Thessaloniki (in present-day Greece) as an imperial capital dates back even earlier to the reorganization of Roman imperial government under Diocletian (see Chapter 6). Galerius—at first Diocletian's Caesar after the creation of the Tetrarchy in 293 and then emperor of the East from Diocletian's retirement in 305 to his own

7–19 ORATORY OF GALLA PLACIDIA, RAVENNA
c. 425–426.

7–20 ORATORY OF GALLA PLACIDIA
View from entrance, barrel-vaulted arms housing sarchophagi, lunette mosaic of the martyrdom of St. Lawrence. c. 425–426.

Credit: Canali Photobank, Milan, Italy

death in 311—made Thessaloniki his capital, initiating an ambitious building program that included a hippodrome, a palace, and a triumphal arch. After Constantine eliminated his rivals and became sole emperor of the Roman world in 324, Thessaloniki decreased in importance, though it remained a provincial capital and the seat of a powerful bishop. The local Christian community dates to the first century CE. St. Paul's letters written to the church in Thessaloniki during the 50s became part of the New Testament.

The Oratory of Galla Placidia in Ravenna

One of the earliest surviving Christian structures in Ravenna is a magnificent **oratory** (small chapel) that was attached c. 425–426 to the narthex of the palace church of Santa Croce (**FIG. 7-19**). This building was dedicated to St. Lawrence, but today it bears the name of the remarkable Galla Placidia—daughter of Roman emperor Theodosius I, wife of a Gothic king, sister of emperors Honorius and Arcadius, and mother of Emperor Valentinian III. As regent for her son after 425, she ruled the Western Empire

until 437/438. The oratory came to be called the Mausoleum of Galla Placidia because she and her family were once believed to be buried there. This small building is **cruciform**, or cross-shape.

A barrel vault covers each arm of the oratory, and a pendentive dome—a dome continuous with its pendentives—covers the square space at the center (see "Pendentives and Squinches" in Chapter 8 on page 241). The interior of the chapel contrasts markedly with the unadorned exterior, a transition seemingly designed to simulate the passage from the real world into the supernatural realm (**FIG. 7-20**). The worshiper looking from the western entrance across to the eastern bay of the chapel sees brilliant mosaics in the vaults and panels of veined marble sheathing the walls below. Bands of luxuriant floral designs and geometric patterns cover the arches and barrel vaults, and figures of standing apostles, gesturing like orators, fill the upper walls of the central space. Doves flanking a small fountain between the apostles symbolize eternal life in heaven.

In the lunette at the end of the barrel vault opposite the entrance (seen here), a mosaic depicts the third-century St. Lawrence, to whom the building was dedicated. The triumphant martyr carries a cross over his shoulder like a

7–21 THE GOOD SHEPHERD

Lunette over the entrance, Oratory of Galla Placidia. c. 425–426. Mosaic.

Credit: © Cameraphoto Arte, Venice

trophy and gestures toward the fire-engulfed metal grill on which he was literally roasted at his martyrdom. At the left stands a tall cabinet containing the Gospels, signifying the faith for which he gave his life.

Opposite St. Lawrence, in a lunette over the entrance portal, is a mosaic of **THE GOOD SHEPHERD** (FIG. **7–21**). A comparison with third- and fourth-century renderings of the same subject reveals significant changes in content and design.

The Rotunda Church of St. George in Thessaloniki

Galerius constructed within his palace complex in Thessaloniki a grand rotunda that may have been intended for his tomb. During the fifth century, this imperial building was converted into a church through the addition of an apse on the east side, an entrance on the west, and an ambulatory encircling the entire rotunda. The interior surface of

the huge dome—almost 100 feet in diameter—was covered with lavish golden mosaics, perhaps created by artists who were called here from Constantinople, which was developing into one of the great artistic centers of the Christian Roman world (FIG. **7–22**).

Forming a circle around and above worshipers within the building, 16 standing figures of saints dressed in liturgical vestments make orant gestures of prayer, as if celebrating the liturgy in paradise concurrent with the services held here on earth. Behind them is a backdrop of elaborate architectural fantasies composed of Classical forms, decorated with gems, and inhabited by peacocks. The figures are equally Classical with their careful modeling, lavish drapery, and most notably their air of grace, eloquence, and composure. Classicizing features such as these will continue to develop as the Early Christian art of the Eastern Roman Empire blossoms into Byzantine art, which will flourish until the fifteenth century, centered in Constantinople.

7–22 SS. ONESIPHOROS AND PORPHYRIOS STANDING BEFORE AN ARCHITECTURAL BACKDROP
Mosaics on the interior of the dome of the church of St. George (formerly the mausoleum of Galerius). Thessaloniki, northern Greece. Rotunda 4th century; mosaics 5th century

Credit: Hirmer Fotoarchiv

Think About It

1   Discuss the Roman foundations of Early Christian sculpture, focusing your answer on the sarcophagus of Junius Bassus (**FIG. 7–18**). Look back to Chapter 6 to help form your ideas.

2   Distinguish the "iconic" from the "narrative" in two works of late antique Jewish or Christian art discussed in this chapter. How were these two traditions used by the communities that created these works?

3   How did the location of the Jewish and Christian buildings in Dura-Europos on the outskirts of the Roman Empire affect their design and decoration?

4   Identify the distinctive features of basilicas and central-plan churches, and discuss how the forms of these early churches were geared toward specific types of Christian worship and devotional practice.

Crosscurrents

Both Etruscans and Early Christians often painted the interior walls of their tombs. Discuss the themes chosen for the murals in these two examples. Are the images related to life, to death, or to life after death? How are the styles and subjects related to these two cultures?

FIG. 6–6

FIG. 7–1

8-1 DAVID BATTLING GOLIATH

One of the "David Plates," made in Constantinople. 629–630 CE. Silver, diameter 19⅞″ (49.4 cm). Metropolitan Museum of Art, New York.

Chapter 8
Byzantine Art

 ## Learning Objectives

8.a Identify the visual hallmarks of Byzantine art for formal, technical, and expressive qualities.

8.b Interpret the meaning of works of Byzantine art based on their themes, subjects, and symbols.

8.c Relate Byzantine artists and art to their cultural, economic, and political contexts.

8.d Apply the vocabulary and concepts relevant to Byzantine art, artists, and art history.

8.e Interpret a work of Byzantine art using the art historical methods of observation, comparison, and inductive reasoning.

8.f Select visual and textual evidence in various media to support an argument or an interpretation of a work of Byzantine art.

The robust figures on this huge silver plate (**FIG. 8-1**) enact three signature episodes in the youthful hero David's combat with the Philistine giant Goliath (1 Samuel 17:41–51). In the upper register, David—easily identified by his youth and as the "good guy" by his prominent halo—and Goliath challenge each other on either side of a seated Classical personification of the stream that will be the source of David's stones for the ensuing battle. The confrontation itself appears in the middle of the plate, in a broad figural frieze whose size signals its primary importance. Goliath is most notable here for his superior armaments—helmet, spear, sword, and an enormous shield. At the bottom, David, stones and slingshot flung behind him, seals his victory by severing the head of his foe, whose imposing weapons and armor are scattered uselessly behind him.

Some may be surprised to see a Judeo-Christian subject portrayed in a style that was developed for the exploits of Classical heroes, but this mixture of traditions is typical of the eclecticism that characterized the visual arts as the Christianized Roman world became the Byzantine Empire. Patrons saw no conflict between the artistic principles of the pagan past and the Christian teaching undergirding their imperial present. To them, this Jewish subject created for a Christian patron in a pagan style would

have attracted notice only because of its sumptuousness and its artistic virtuosity.

This was one of nine "David Plates" unearthed in Cyprus in 1902. Control stamps—guaranteeing the purity of the material much like the stamps of "sterling" on silver today—date them to the reign of the Byzantine emperor Heraclius (ruled 613–641 CE). Displayed in the home of their owners, they were visual proclamations of wealth, education, and refined taste, just like collections of art and antiques in homes now. A constellation of iconographic and historical factors, however, allows us to uncover a subtler message. For the original owners, the single combat of David and Goliath might have recalled a situation involving their own emperor and enemies.

The reign of Heraclius was marked by war with the Sasanian Persians. A decisive moment in the final campaign of 628–629 CE occurred when Heraclius himself stepped forward for single combat with the Persian general Razatis, and the emperor prevailed, presaging Byzantine victory. Some contemporaries referred to Heraclius as a new David. Is it possible that the set of David Plates was produced for the emperor to offer as a diplomatic gift to one of his aristocratic allies, who subsequently took them to Cyprus? Perhaps the owners later buried them for safekeeping—like the early silver platter from Mildenhall (SEE FIG. 6–70).

Early Byzantine Art

How does early Byzantine art develop in the Eastern Roman Empire?

Art historians apply the term "Byzantine" broadly to the art and architecture of Constantinople—whose ancient name, before Constantine renamed the revitalized city after himself, was Byzantium—and of the regions under its influence. Constantine had chosen well in selecting the site of his new capital city—his "New Rome." Constantinople lay at the crossroads of the overland trade routes between Asia and Europe and the sea route connecting the Black Sea and the Mediterranean. Even as the territories controlled by Byzantine rulers diminished in size and significance up to the fall of Constantinople in 1453, Byzantine emperors continued to conceive themselves as successors to the rulers of ancient Rome, their domain as an extension of the Roman Empire, and their capital city as an enduring manifestation of the glory that was ancient Rome.

In this chapter, we will focus on what have been considered the three "golden ages" of Byzantine art. The Early Byzantine period, most closely associated with the reign of Emperor Justinian I (ruled 527–565), began in the fifth century and ended in 726 at the onset of the iconoclast controversy that led to the destruction of religious images. The Middle Byzantine period began in 843, when Empress Theodora (wife of Emperor Theophilus, 830–842, and regent of their son Emperor Michael III, 842–855) reinstated the veneration of icons, and continued until 1204, when Christian crusaders from western Europe occupied Constantinople. The Late Byzantine period began with the restoration of Byzantine rule in 1261 and ended with the empire's fall to the Ottoman Turks in 1453, at which point Russia succeeded Constantinople as the "Third Rome" and the center of the Eastern Orthodox Church. Late Byzantine art continued to flourish into the eighteenth century in Ukraine, Russia, and much of southeastern Europe.

MAP 8–1 THE LATE ROMAN AND BYZANTINE WORLD

The eastern shores of the Mediterranean, birthplace of Judaism and Christianity, were the focal point of the Byzantine Empire. The empire expanded farther west under Emperor Justinian, though by 1025 CE it had contracted again to the east.

The Golden Age of Justinian

The Eastern Roman Empire prospered during the fifth and sixth centuries, while invasions and religious controversy racked the Italian peninsula. In fact, during the sixth century under Emperor Justinian I and his wife, Empress Theodora (d. 548), Byzantine political power, wealth, and culture were at their peak. Imperial forces held northern Africa, Sicily, much of Italy, and part of Spain. Ravenna became the Eastern Empire's administrative capital in the west, and Rome remained under nominal Byzantine control until the eighth century.

HAGIA SOPHIA IN CONSTANTINOPLE In Constantinople, Justinian and Theodora embarked on a spectacular campaign of building and renovation, but little now remains of their architectural projects or of the old imperial capital itself. The church of Hagia Sophia, meaning "Holy Wisdom" (referring to the dedication of this church to Christ as the embodiment of divine wisdom) is a spectacular exception (**FIG. 8-2**). It replaced a fourth-century church destroyed when crowds, spurred on by Justinian's foes during the devastating urban Nika Revolt in 532, set the old church on fire and cornered the emperor within his palace. Theodora, a brilliant and politically shrewd woman, is said to have shamed Justinian, who was plotting to escape, into not fleeing the city, saying "Purple makes a fine shroud"—a reference to purple as the imperial color. Theodora meant that she would

rather remain and die an empress than flee and preserve her life. Taking up her words as a battle cry, Justinian led the imperial forces in crushing the rebels and restoring order, reputedly slaughtering 30,000 of his subjects in the process.

To design a new church that embodied imperial power and Christian glory, Justinian chose two scholar-theoreticians, Anthemius of Tralles and Isidorus of Miletus. Anthemius was a specialist in geometry and optics, and Isidorus a specialist in physics who had also studied vaulting. They developed an audacious and awe-inspiring design that was executed by builders who had refined their masonry techniques by building the towers and domed rooms that were part of the city's defenses.

The new Hagia Sophia was not constructed by the miraculous intervention of angels, as was rumored, but by mortal builders in only five years (532–537). Procopius of Caesarea, who chronicled Justinian's reign, claimed poetically that Hagia Sophia's gigantic dome seemed to hang suspended on a "golden chain from heaven." Legend has it that Justinian himself, aware that architecture can be a potent symbol of earthly power, compared his accomplishment with that of the legendary builder of the First Temple in Jerusalem, saying "Solomon, I have outdone you."

Hagia Sophia is an innovative hybrid of longitudinal and central architectural planning. The building is clearly dominated by the hovering form of its gigantic dome (**FIG. 8-3**). But flanking **conches**—halfdomes—extend the

8-2 Anthemius of Tralles and Isidorus of Miletus **CHURCH OF HAGIA SOPHIA, CONSTANTINOPLE**
Present-day Istanbul. 532–537. View from the southwest.

The body of the original church is now surrounded by later additions, including the minarets built after 1453 by the Ottoman Turks. Today the building is a museum.

8-3 INTERIOR OF THE CHURCH OF HAGIA SOPHIA

Credit: Photo © Ayhan Altun

**8-4 PLAN (A) AND ISOMETRIC DRAWING (B)
OF THE CHURCH OF HAGIA SOPHIA**

central space into a longitudinal nave that expands outward from the central dome to connect with the narthex on one end and the halfdome of the sanctuary apse on the other. This processional core, called the **naos** in Byzantine architecture, is flanked by side aisles with **galleries** above them (**FIG. 8–4**).

Since its idiosyncratic mixture of basilica and rotunda precludes a ring of masonry underneath the dome to provide support around its circumference (as in the Pantheon,

SEE FIGS. 6–48, 6–49), the main dome of Hagia Sophia rests instead on four **pendentives** (triangular curving vault sections) that connect the base of the dome with the huge supporting piers at the four corners of the square area beneath it (see "Pendentives and Squinches" below). And since these piers are essentially submerged back into the darkness of the aisles, rather than expressed within the main space itself (SEE FIG. 8-4), the dome seems to float over a void.

Elements of Architecture
PENDENTIVES AND SQUINCHES

Pendentives and squinches are two methods of supporting a round dome or its drum over a square space. Pendentives are concave, triangular forms between the arches under a dome. They rise upward and inward to form a circular base of support on which the dome rests. **Squinches** are diagonal lintels placed across the upper corner of the wall and supported by an arch or a series of corbeled arches that give it a nichelike shape. Because squinches create an octagon, which is close in shape to a circle, they provide a solid base around the perimeter of a dome, usually elevated on a drum (a circular wall), whereas pendentives project the dome slightly inside the square space it covers, making it seem

to float. Byzantine builders preferred pendentives (as at Hagia Sophia, SEE FIG. 8-4), but elaborate, squinch-supported domes became a hallmark of Islamic architecture.

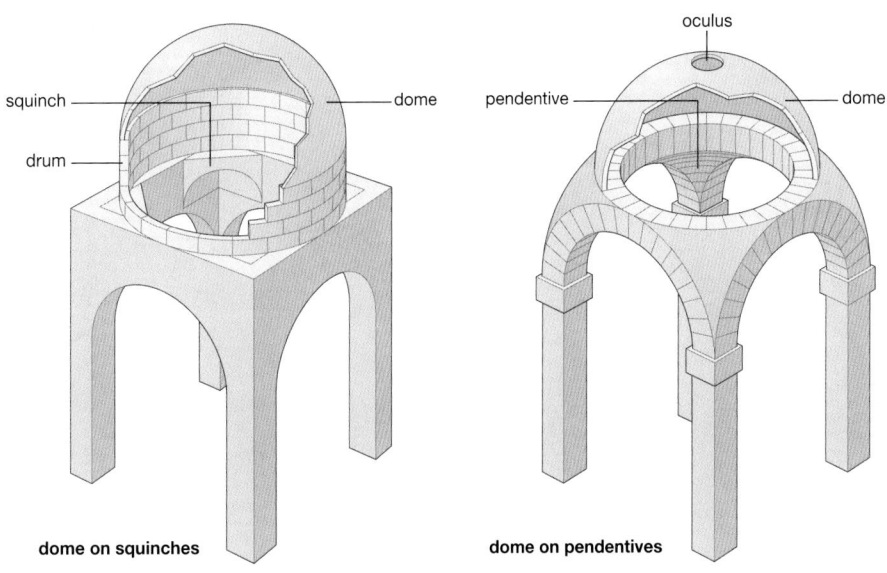

dome on squinches   dome on pendentives

The weightless effect was reinforced by the light-reflecting gold mosaic that covered the surfaces of dome and pendentives alike, as well as by the band of 40 windows that perforate the base of the dome right where it meets its support (SEE FIG. 8-3). This daring move challenges architectural logic by seeming to weaken the integrity of the masonry at the very place where it needs to be strong, but the windows created the circle of light that helps the dome appear to hover, and a reinforcement of buttressing on the exterior made the solution strong as well as shimmering. The origin of the dome on pendentives is obscure, but its large-scale use at Hagia Sophia was unprecedented and represents one of the boldest experiments in the history of architecture. It was to become the preferred method of supporting domes in Byzantine architecture.

The architects and builders of Hagia Sophia clearly stretched building materials to their physical limits, denying the physicality of the building in order to emphasize its spirituality. In fact, when the first dome fell in 558, it did so because a pier and pendentive shifted and because the dome was too shallow and exerted too much outward force at its base, not because the windows weakened the support. Confident of their revised technical methods, the architects designed a steeper dome that raised the summit 20 feet higher. They also added exterior buttressing. Although repairs had to be made in 869, 989, and 1346, the church has since withstood numerous earthquakes.

The liturgy used in Hagia Sophia in the sixth century has been lost, but it presumably resembled the rites described in detail for the church in the Middle Byzantine period. The celebration of the Eucharist took place behind a screen that separated the sanctuary from the nave. The emperor was the only layperson permitted to enter the sanctuary. Other men and women stood in the aisles or in the galleries, where they witnessed the processions of clergy moving in a circular path from the sanctuary into the nave and back five or six times during the ritual.

Hagia Sophia was thus a gigantic theater for public, imperial worship of God, created by a culture within which Church and state were inextricably intertwined. Justinian had the sanctuary embellished with 40,000 pounds of silver that he donated himself. This precious material was crafted into sumptuous decorations on the altar, ciborium (canopy sheltering the altar), ambo (pulpit), and screen. Since there was no figural decoration on the walls of the building in Justinian's time to focus the attention of viewers in any one place, worshipers standing on the church floor must have surveyed the whole expanse of the interior, shifting their attention from one shimmering vista to the next.

SAN VITALE IN RAVENNA   In 540, Byzantine forces captured Ravenna from the Arian Christian Ostrogoths who had themselves taken it from the Romans in 476. Much of our knowledge of the art of this turbulent period comes from the well-preserved monuments in Ravenna. In 526, Ecclesius, bishop of Ravenna, commissioned two new churches, one for the city and one for its port, Classis. In the 520s, construction began on a central-plan church, a **martyrium** (church built over the grave of a martyr) dedicated to the fourth-century Roman martyr St. Vitalis (Vitale in Italian), but it was not finished until after Justinian had conquered Ravenna and established it as the administrative capital of Byzantine Italy (**FIG. 8-5**).

8–5 PLAN (A) AND CUTAWAY DRAWING (B) OF THE CHURCH OF SAN VITALE, RAVENNA
Under construction from c. 520; consecrated 547.

8-6 CHURCH OF SAN VITALE

View into the sanctuary toward the northeast. c. 547.

Credit: © 2016, Photo Scala, Florence

wall shows an altar table set for the meal that Abraham offers to three disguised angels (Genesis 18:1–15), and next to it is a portrayal of his near-sacrifice of Isaac. In the spandrels and other framed wall spaces appear prophets and evangelists.

The framed wall spaces are bristling with symbolic references to Jesus, but the focus of the sanctuary program is the courtly tableau in the halfdome of the apse. A youthful, classicizing Christ appears on axis (**FIG. 8-7**), dressed in imperial purple and enthroned on a cosmic orb in paradise, the setting indicated by the four rivers that flow from the ground underneath him. Two winged angels flank him like imperial bodyguards or attendants. In his left hand Christ holds a scroll with seven seals that he will open at his Second Coming at the end of time, proclaiming his authority not only over this age, but over the age to come. He extends his right hand to offer a crown of martyrdom to St. Vitalis, the saint to whom this church is dedicated. On the other side is the only figure in the tableau without a halo. Labeled as Bishop Ecclesius, he is the founder of San Vitale, who offers a model of the church itself to Christ. The artist has imagined a scene of courtly protocol in paradise, where Christ, as emperor, gives a gift to and receives a gift from members of the celestial entourage.

In separate, flanking rectangular compositions along the curving wall of the apse underneath the scene in the halfdome appear Justinian and Theodora and their retinues (Justinian can be seen in FIG. 8-6). The royal couple did not attend the dedication ceremonies for the church of San Vitale, conducted by Archbishop Maximianus in 547, and there is no evidence that they actually set foot in Ravenna, but these two large mosaic panels that face each other across its sanctuary picture their presence here in perpetuity. Justinian (**FIG. 8-8**), on the north wall, carries a large golden paten that will be used to hold the Eucharistic bread and stands next to Maximianus, who holds a golden, jewel-encrusted cross. The priestly celebrants at the right carry the Gospels encased in a golden, jeweled book cover, symbolizing the coming of Christ

San Vitale was designed as a central-domed octagon surrounded by eight radiating exedrae (wall niches), surrounded in turn by an ambulatory and gallery, all covered by vaults. A rectangular sanctuary and semicircular apse project from one of the sides of the octagon, and circular rooms flank the apse. A separate oval narthex, set off-axis, joined church and palace and also led to cylindrical stair towers that gave access to the second-floor gallery.

The floor plan of San Vitale only hints at the effect of the complex, interpenetrating interior spaces of the church, an effect that was enhanced by the offset narthex with its double sets of doors leading into the church. People entering from the right saw only arched openings, whereas those entering from the left approached on an axis with the sanctuary visible straight ahead of them. The dome rests on eight large piers that frame the exedrae and the sanctuary. The undulating, two-story exedrae open through superimposed arcades into the outer aisles on the ground floor and into galleries on the second floor. They push out the circular central space and create an airy, floating sensation, reinforced by the liberal use of veined marble veneer and colored glass and gold mosaics in the surface decoration. As in Hagia Sophia, structure seems to dissolve into shimmering light and color.

Here, however, an elaborate program of figural mosaics focuses the worshiper's attention within the sanctuary (**FIG. 8-6**).

In the halfdome of the sanctuary apse St. Vitalis and Bishop Ecclesius flank an image of Christ enthroned. The other sanctuary images relate to its use for the celebration of the Eucharist. The lunette on the north as the Word, and a censer containing burning incense to purify the altar prior to the Eucharist.

On the south wall, Theodora, standing beneath a fluted shell canopy and singled out by a golden halo and elaborate crown, carries a huge golden chalice studded with jewels (**FIG. 8-9**). The rulers present these gifts as precious offerings to Christ—emulating most immediately Bishop Ecclesius, who offers a model of the church to Christ in the halfdome of the apse, but also the three Magi who brought valuable gifts to the infant Jesus, depicted in "embroidery" at the bottom of Theodora's purple cloak. In fact, the paten and chalice offered by the royal couple will be used by this church to offer Eucharistic bread and wine to the local Christian community during the liturgy. In this way the entire program of mosaic decoration revolves around themes of offering, extended into the theme of the Eucharist itself.

Theodora's group stands beside a fountain, presumably in a courtyard leading to the entrance to the church. The open doorway and curtain are Classical space-creating devices, but here the mosaicists have deliberately avoided allowing their illusionistic power to overwhelm the mosaic's flat surface patterns. Notice, too, that the figures cast no shadows, and, though modeled, their outlines as

8-8 EMPEROR JUSTINIAN AND HIS ATTENDANTS, NORTH WALL OF THE APSE
Church of San Vitale, Ravenna. c. 547. Mosaic, 8'8″ × 12' (2.64 × 3.65 m).

As head of state, the haloed Justinian wears a huge jeweled crown and a purple cloak; he carries a large golden paten that he is donating to San Vitale for the celebration of the Eucharist. Bishop Maximianus at his left holds a jeweled cross and another churchman holds a jewel-covered book. Government officials stand at Justinian's right, followed by barbarian mercenary soldiers, one of whom wears a neck torc, another a Classical cameo cloak clasp.

Credit: © Cameraphoto Arte, Venice

8-9 EMPRESS THEODORA AND HER ATTENDANTS, SOUTH WALL OF THE APSE
Church of San Vitale, Ravenna. c. 547. Mosaic, 8'8″ × 12' (2.64 × 3.65 m).

Like Justinian, Theodora has a halo, wears imperial purple, and carries in her hands a liturgical vessel—the chalice that held the Eucharistic wine—that she will donate to the church. Her elaborate jewelry includes a wide collar of embroidered and jeweled cloth. A crown, hung with long strands of pearls (thought to protect the wearer from disease), frames her face. Her attendants also wear the rich textiles and jewelry of the Byzantine court.

Credit: © Cameraphoto Arte, Venice

silhouetted shapes are more prominent than their sense of three-dimensionality. Still, especially in Justinian's panel, a complex and carefully controlled system of overlapping allows us to see these figures clearly and logically situated within a shallow space, moving in a stately procession from left to right toward the entrance to the church and the beginning of the liturgy. So the scenes portrayed in these mosaic paintings are both flattened and three-dimensional, abstract and representational, patterned and individualized. Like Justinian and Theodora, their images are both there and not there at the same time.

THE MONASTERY OF ST. CATHERINE ON MOUNT SINAI   Justinian's imperial architectural projects extended across the breadth of the Byzantine Empire, emulating the example of the great emperors of ancient Rome. Soon after the dedication of San Vitale, he sponsored the reconstruction of the monastery of St. Catherine at Mount Sinai in Egypt (FIG. 8–10). This pilgrimage destination and spiritual retreat had been founded much earlier, during the fourth century, at the place where Moses had encountered God in the burning bush (Exodus 4 and 5) and in the shadow of the peak on which he had met God to receive the Ten Commandments (Exodus 19 and 20). Justinian's reconstruction focused on two aspects of the complex. In conjunction with the installation of a frontier garrison to protect both monks and pilgrims from Bedouin attacks on this remote border outpost, Justinian had the walls of the monastery fortified. He also commissioned a new church dedicated to the Virgin Mary and—according to inscriptions carved into the wooden beams that support its roof—built in memory of Theodora, who died in 548.

Procopius's description of this project focuses on the lives of the monks who lived there:

> On this Mount Sinai dwell monks whose life is a kind of careful rehearsal of death, and they enjoy without fear the solitude which is very precious to them. Since these monks have nothing to desire, for they are superior to all human wishes and they have no interest in owning anything or in caring for their bodies, nor do they seek pleasure in any other thing whatever, therefore the emperor Justinian built them a church which he dedicated to the Mother of God, so that they might be enabled to pass their lives within it, praying and holding services. (*Buildings*, V, viii, translated by H.B. Dewing, Loeb Library ed.)

The origins of monasticism in the eastern Christian world can be traced back to the third century, when some devout Christians began to retire into the desert to become hermits, living a secluded life of physical austerity and devoted to continual meditation and prayer. By the fourth century, groups of men and women began assembling around these hermits, ultimately forming independent secluded communities devoted to prayer and work. These monks and nuns practiced celibacy, poverty, and obedience to a spiritual leader, and they aspired to self-sufficiency so as to minimize contact with the outside world. The monastic movement grew rapidly; by 536 there were about 70 monasteries in Constantinople alone. Although they continued to function as retreats from the secular world—places where pious men and women could devote themselves almost exclusively to the contemplative life and safe havens for orphans, the poor, and the elderly—the monasteries, being tax-exempt, also amassed enormous wealth from the donations and bequests of the rich.

A local architect designed the new basilica church that

8–10 THE MONASTERY OF ST. CATHERINE, SINAI
Mount Sinai, Egypt. Fortifications and church constructed under the patronage of Emperor Justinian, c. 548–566.

Founded in the fourth century, this monastery was initially associated with the burning bush, since it was built on the site where Moses was believed to have encountered this startling theophany, but in the tenth or eleventh century it was rededicated to St. Catherine of Alexandria after acquiring her relics.

Credit: © age fotostock/Corbis RF/José Fuste Raga

8–11 THE TRANSFIGURATION OF CHRIST
Apse mosaic in the church of the Virgin, monastery of St. Catherine, Mount Sinai, Egypt. c. 565.

Framing the scene of the Transfiguration are medallion portraits of the 12 apostles, 2 monastic saints, and the 17 major and minor prophets. Sixth-century viewers would probably have associated David—in the medallion directly under Jesus and dressed in the robes and crown of a Byzantine emperor—with the patron, Emperor Justinian, and an inscription running above the lower row of medallions to the right identifies the monastic leaders at the time the mosaic was made and dates them to 565/6, near the time of Justinian's death.

Justinian commissioned for the monks and pilgrims of Mount Sinai. The building was constructed of local materials, but the sumptuous decoration of the sanctuary derives from more cosmopolitan artistic centers. The marble revetment that faces the lower walls of the apse was imported from an island quarry near Constantinople, and the artists who covered the halfdome of the apse and the end wall of the nave above it with powerful scenes in sumptuous mosaics were probably called in from Jerusalem, or even Constantinople. As at San Vitale, mosaic decoration is concentrated in the sanctuary, where the apse would have glistened with vivid color and divine light—a spotlighted destination at the end of the longitudinal axis of the processional nave (**FIG. 8–11**).

The mosaics integrate a series of stories and themes into a coherent program around the notion of theophany—the appearance of God to human beings. Two rectangular scenes on the end wall of the nave above the apse (only partially visible in FIG. 8-11) picture two local theophanies—Moses before the burning bush and Moses receiving the law. The halfdome of the apse highlights the Transfiguration, an episode from the life of Jesus during which he was transformed "on a high mountain" from human to divine and set between apparitions of Moses and Elijah before the eyes of Peter, James, and John, three of his disciples (Matthew 17:1–6, NRSV). The central figure of Jesus fits the description in the Gospel text—"his face shone like the sun, and his clothes became dazzling white." The artists have flattened Jesus's form and set him against a contrasting deep blue **mandorla** (body halo), through which pass rays of light emanating from him and touching the figures around him. Unlike Jesus, the three apostles below him—who "fell to the ground and were overcome by fear"—are active rather than static, aggressively three-dimensional rather than brilliantly flattened, in a visual contrast between celestial apparition and earthly form. The entire tableau takes place against a background of golden light, with no indication of a landscape setting other than the banded lines of color at the bottom of the scene.

Luxury Objects

The court workshops of Constantinople excelled in the production of luxurious small-scale works in gold, ivory, and textiles. The Byzantine elite also sponsored vital **scriptoria** (writing centers for scribes—professional document writers) for the production of **manuscripts** (handwritten books), often located within monasteries.

IVORY DIPTYCHS Commemorative ivory diptychs—two carved panels hinged together—originated with ancient Roman politicians elected to the post of consul. New consuls would send notices of their election to friends and colleagues by inscribing them in wax that filled a recessed rectangular area on the inner sides of a pair of ivory panels carved with elaborate decoration on the outside. Christians adapted the practice for religious use, inscribing a diptych with the names of people to be remembered with prayers during the liturgy.

This large panel portraying the **ARCHANGEL MICHAEL**—the largest surviving Byzantine ivory—was half of such a diptych (**FIG. 8-12**). In his classicizing serenity, imposing physical presence, and elegant architectural setting, the archangel is comparable to the (supposed) priestess of Bacchus in the fourth-century pagan Symmachus diptych panel (SEE FIG. 6-71) and reminiscent of the standing saints in the dome mosaics of St. George in Thessaloniki (SEE FIG. 7-22). His relationship to the architectural

8-12 ARCHANGEL MICHAEL
Panel of a diptych, probably from the court workshop at Constantinople. Early 6th century. Ivory, 17 × 5½" (43.3 × 14 cm). British Museum, London.

space and the frame around him, however, is more complex. His heels rest on the top step of a stair that clearly lies behind the columns and pedestals, but the rest of his body overlaps the architectural setting and thus seems to project in front of them—creating a striking tension between the celestial figure and his terrestrial backdrop.

The angel is outfitted as a divine messenger, holding a staff of authority in his left hand and a sphere symbolizing worldly power in his right. Within the arch is a similar cross-topped orb, set against the background of a scallop shell and framed by a wreath bound by a ribbon with long, rippling extensions. The lost half of this diptych would have completed the Greek inscription across the top, which reads: "Receive these gifts, and having learned the cause…." Perhaps the other panel contained a portrait of the emperor—many think he would be Justinian—or of another high official who presented the panels as a gift to an important colleague, acquaintance, or family member. Nonetheless, the emphasis here is on the powerfully classicized celestial messenger, who does not need to obey the laws of earthly scale or human perspective.

ILLUMINATED MANUSCRIPTS   Since people began to write, they have kept records on a variety of materials, including clay or wax tablets, pieces of broken pottery, papyrus, animal skins, and paper. Books have taken two forms: scroll and codex.

Scribes made scrolls from sheets of papyrus glued end to end or from thin sheets of cleaned, scraped, and trimmed sheepskin or calfskin, a material known as **parchment** or, when softer and lighter, **vellum** (an especially fine writing surface made from calfskin). Each end of the scroll was attached to a rod; readers slowly unfurled the scroll from one rod to the other as they read. Scrolls could be written to be read either horizontally or vertically.

At the end of the first century CE, the more practical and manageable **codex** (plural, codices)—sheets bound together like the modern book—replaced the scroll as the primary form of recording texts. The basic unit of the codex was the eight-leaf quire, made by folding a large sheet of parchment twice, cutting the edges free, then sewing the sheets together up the center. Heavy covers kept the sheets of a codex flat. The thickness and weight of parchment and vellum made it impractical to produce a very large manuscript, such as an entire Bible, in a single volume. As a result, individual sections were made into separate books.

Until the invention of printing in the fifteenth century, all books were manuscripts—that is, they were written by hand. Manuscripts often included illustrations, called **miniatures** (from *minium*, the Latin word for a reddish lead pigment). Manuscripts decorated with gold and colors were said to be **illuminated**.

Byzantine manuscripts were often made with very costly materials. For example, sheets of purple-dyed

vellum and gold and silver inks were used to produce a codex now known as the Vienna Genesis. It was probably made in Syria or Palestine, and the purple vellum indicates that it may have been created for an imperial patron, since costly purple dye, made from the secretions of murex mollusks, was usually restricted to imperial use. The Vienna Genesis is written in Greek and illustrated with pictures that appear below the text at the bottom of the pages.

A painter who worked on the Vienna Genesis visualized the story of **REBECCA AT THE WELL** (**FIG. 8-13**) (Genesis 24) as a single composition. But—clinging to the **continuous narrative** tradition that had characterized the illustration of scrolls—this scene combines events that take place at different times in the story within a single narrative space. Rebecca, the heroine, appears at the left walking away from the walled city of Nahor with a large jug on her shoulder, going to fetch water. A colonnaded road leads toward a spring, personified by a reclining pagan water nymph who holds a flowing jar. In the foreground, Rebecca appears again, clearly identifiable by continuity of costume. Her jug now full, she encounters a thirsty camel driver and offers him water to drink. Since he is

8-13 REBECCA AT THE WELL
Page from a codex featuring the book of Genesis (known as the Vienna Genesis). Made in Syria or Palestine. Early 6th century. Tempera, gold, and silver paint on purple-dyed vellum, 13½ × 9⅞″ (33.7 × 25 cm). Österreichische Nationalbibliothek, Vienna.

Abraham's servant, Eliezer, in search of a bride for Abraham's son Isaac, Rebecca's generosity results in her marriage to Isaac. The lifelike poses and rounded, full-bodied figures of this narrative scene conform to the conventions of traditional Roman painting. The sumptuous purple of the background and the glittering metallic letters of the text situate the book within the world of the privileged and powerful in Byzantine society.

SILVER The imperial court at Constantinople had a monopoly on the production of some luxury goods, especially those made of precious metals. A seventh-century court workshop seems to have been the origin of a spectacular set of nine silver plates portraying events in the early life of the biblical King David, including the plate that we examined at the beginning of the chapter (SEE FIG. 8–1).

The plates would have been made by hammering a large silver ingot (the plate in FIG. 8–1 weighs 12 pounds 10 ounces) into a round shape and raising on it the rough semblance of the human figures and their environment. With finer chisels, silversmiths then refined these shapes, and at the end of their work, they punched ornamental motifs and incised fine details. The careful modeling, lifelike postures, and intricate engraving document the highly refined artistry and technical virtuosity of these cosmopolitan artists at the imperial court, who still practiced a classicizing art that had characterized some works of Christian art for centuries (SEE FIGS. 7–9, 7–18, 7–21, 8–12).

Icons

Christians in the Byzantine world prayed to Christ, Mary, and the saints while gazing at images of them on independent panels known as **icons**. Church doctrine toward the veneration of icons was ambivalent.

Christianity inherited from Judaism an uneasiness with the power of religious images, rooted in the Mosaic prohibition of "graven images" (Exodus 20:4). The lingering effects of the early persecution of Christians because of their refusal to venerate images of Roman emperors only intensified this anxiety. But key figures of the Eastern Church, such as Basil the Great of Cappadocia (c. 329–379) and John of Damascus (c. 675–749), distinguished between idolatry—the worship of images—and the veneration of an idea or holy person depicted in a work of art. Icons were thus accepted as aids to meditation and prayer, intermediaries between worshipers and the holy personages they depicted. Honor showed to the image was believed to transfer directly to its spiritual prototype.

Surviving early icons are rare. A few precious examples exist at the monastery of St. Catherine on Mount

8–14 VIRGIN AND CHILD WITH SAINTS AND ANGELS

Icon. Second half of the 6th century. Encaustic on wood, 27 × 18⅞" (69 × 48 cm). Monastery of St. Catherine, Mount Sinai, Egypt.

Sinai, among them **VIRGIN AND CHILD WITH SAINTS AND ANGELS** (**FIG. 8–14**). As Theotokos (Greek for "bearer of God"), Jesus's earthly mother was viewed as a powerful, ever-forgiving intercessor, who could be counted on to appeal to her divine son for mercy on behalf of devout and repentant worshipers. The Virgin and Child are flanked here by Christian warrior-saints Theodore (left) and George (right)—both legendary figures said to have slain dragons, representing the triumph of the Church over the "evil serpent" of paganism. Angels behind them twist their heads to look heavenward. The artist has painted the Christ Child, the Virgin, and especially the angels, with an illusionism that renders them lifelike and three-dimensional in appearance. But the warrior-saints—who look out to meet directly the worshipful gaze of viewers—are more stylized. Here the artist barely hints at bodily form beneath the richly patterned textiles of their cloaks, and their faces are frozen in frontal stares of gripping intensity, addressing viewers directly.

Iconoclasm

During the eighth century, mounting discomfort with the place of icons in Christian devotion grew into a major controversy in the Byzantine world, and between 726 and 730, Emperor Leo III (ruled 717–741) imposed **iconoclasm** ("image breaking"), initiating the systematic destruction of images of saints and sacred stories on icons and in churches, as well as the persecution of those who made them and defended their use. Only a few early icons survived in isolated places like Mount Sinai, which was no longer a part of the Byzantine Empire at this time (FOR EXAMPLE, FIG. 8–14). Leo III's successor, Constantine V (ruled 741–775), enforced these policies and practices with even greater fervor, but at the end of the reign of Leo IV (ruled 775–780), his widow, Empress Irene, who ruled as regent for their son Constantine IV (ruled 780–797), put an end to iconoclasm in 787 through a church council held in Nicea. Leo V (ruled 813–820) instituted a second phase of iconoclasm in 813, and it remained imperial policy until March 11, 843, when the widowed Empress Theodora reversed her husband Theophilus's policy and reinstated the central place of images in Byzantine devotional practice.

A number of explanations have been proposed for these two interludes of Byzantine iconoclasm. Some Church leaders feared that the use of images in worship could lead to idolatry or at least distract worshipers from their spiritual exercises. Specifically, there were questions surrounding the relationship between images and the Eucharist, the latter considered by iconoclasts as sufficient representation of the presence of Christ in the church. But there was also anxiety in Byzantium about the weakening state of the empire, especially in relation to the advances of Arab armies into Byzantine territory. It was easy to pin

8-15 CRUCIFIXION AND ICONOCLASTS
From the Chludov Psalter. Mid 9th century. Tempera on vellum, 7¾ × 6" (19.5 × 15 cm). State Historical Museum, Moscow. MS. D. 29, fol. 67v.

This page and its illustration of Psalm 69:21—made soon after the end of the iconoclastic controversy in 843—record the iconophiles' harsh judgment of the iconoclasts. Painted in the margin at the right, a scene of the Crucifixion shows a soldier tormenting Christ with a vinegar-soaked sponge. In a striking visual parallel, two named iconoclasts—identified by inscription—in the adjacent picture along the bottom margin employ a whitewash-soaked sponge to obliterate an icon portrait of Christ, thus linking them by their actions with those who had crucified him.

these hard times on God's displeasure with the idolatrous use of images. Coincidentally, Leo III's success fighting the Arabs could be interpreted as divine sanction of his iconoclastic position, and its adoption might appease the iconoclastic Islamic enemy itself as well. Finally, since the production and promotion of icons was centered in monasteries—at that time rivaling the state in strength and wealth—attacking the use of images might check their growing power. Perhaps all these factors played a part, but with the triumph of the **iconophiles** (literally "lovers of images") in 843, the place of images in worship was again secure: Icons proclaimed Christ as God incarnate and facilitated Christian worship by acting as intermediaries between humans and saints. Those who had suppressed icons were considered heretics (**FIG. 8–15**).

Middle Byzantine Art

What traditions of Byzantine art and architecture are established during its middle period?

With the turmoil and destruction of iconoclasm behind them, Byzantine patrons and artists turned during the second half of the ninth century to ambitious projects of restoration and renewal, redecorating church interiors with figural images and producing new icons in a variety of media for the devotional practices of the faithful. This period also saw a renewal and expansion of the power and presence of monasteries in the Byzantine world. A new Macedonian dynasty of rulers—founded in 866 by Emperor Basil I (ruled 866–886) and continuing until 1056—increased Byzantine military might, leading to an expansion of imperial territory, only checked in the mid eleventh century by the growing power of the Turks, who dealt the Byzantine army a series of military setbacks that would continue to erode the empire until the fifteenth century. But after the empire stabilized under the Komnenian dynasty (1081–1185), it was not the Turks who instigated the end of the Middle Byzantine period. It ended abruptly when Christian crusaders from the west, who had set out on a holy war against Islam, diverted their efforts to conquering the wealthy Christian Byzantine Empire, taking Constantinople in 1204. The crusaders looted the capital and set up a Latin dynasty of rulers to replace the Byzantine emperors, who fled into exile.

The patronage of the Macedonian dynasty stimulated a new golden age of Byzantine art, often referred to as the "Macedonian Renaissance," since it was marked by an intensified interest in the styles and themes of Classical art, as well as by a general revitalization of intellectual life. As the Middle Byzantine period developed, the geography of Byzantine art changed significantly. As we have seen, early Byzantine civilization had been centered in lands along the rim of the Mediterranean Sea that had been within the Roman Empire. During the Middle Byzantine period, Constantinople's scope was reduced to present-day Turkey and other areas by the Black Sea, as well as the Balkan peninsula, including Greece, and southern Italy. The influence of Byzantine culture also extended into Russia and Ukraine, and to Venice, Constantinople's trading partner in northeastern Italy, at the head of the Adriatic Sea.

Architecture and Wall Painting in Mosaic and Fresco

Although the restitution of images led to the creation of new mosaics in the major churches of the capital, comparatively few Middle Byzantine churches in Constantinople have survived intact. Better-preserved examples of the central-plan domed churches that were popular in the

Byzantine world survive in Greece to the southwest and Ukraine to the northeast, and within the western medieval world are reflected in Venice. These structures document the Byzantine taste for a multiplicity of geometric forms, for verticality, and for rich decorative effects both inside and out.

APSE MOSAIC OF HAGIA SOPHIA   The upper parts of Justinian's church of Hagia Sophia were originally encrusted with broad expanses of gold mosaic framed by strips of vegetal and geometric ornament, but figural mosaics highlighting sacred individuals or sacred stories seem not to have been part of the original design. With the end of iconoclasm, however, there was an urgency to assert the significance of images within Byzantine churches, and the great imperial church of the capital was an important location to proclaim the orthodoxy of icons. By 867, mosaicists had inserted an iconic rendering of the Incarnation in the form of an image of the Virgin Mary holding the child Jesus in her lap (**FIG. 8-16**), flanked by angels and accompanied by an inscription claiming that "the images which the imposters [the iconoclast emperors] had cast down here, pious emperors have set up again."

8-16 VIRGIN AND CHILD IN THE APSE OF HAGIA SOPHIA

Constantinople (present-day Istanbul). Dedicated in 867. Mosaic.

Credit: Photo © Ayhan Altun

8-17 MONASTERY CHURCHES AT HOSIOS LOUKAS, STIRIS
Central Greece. Katholikon (left), early 11th century, and church of the Theotokos, late 10th century. View from the east.

Credit: © Ioannis Mantas/Alamy Stock Photo

The design of Hagia Sophia—especially the disposition of the sanctuary apse perforated from top to bottom with bands of windows—provided no obvious areas to highlight a figural mosaic, and working at the extreme height of the halfdome—where the mosaic is located—required the erection of immense wooden scaffolding to accommodate the artists at work (SEE FIG. 8-3, where the Virgin and Child appear at the top of the central lower apse, floating above the middle of the five windows at the bottom of the halfdome). Adding this mosaic was an expensive project.

Floating on an expansive sweep of gold mosaic with neither natural nor architectural setting—like a monumental icon presented for the perpetual veneration of the faithful—the Virgin and Child in Hagia Sophia recalls the pre-iconoclastic rendering on a surviving icon from Mount Sinai (SEE FIG. 8-14), but their gracefully modeled faces, their elegantly attenuated bodily proportions, and the jewel-studded bench that serves as their throne all proclaim the singular importance of their placement in Constantinople's principal imperial church. Co-emperors Michael III and Basil I were present in Hagia Sophia on March 29, 867, when the patriarch Photios preached the sermon at the dedication of the apse mosaics, laying claim to the historic moment this represented and challenging the rulers to maintain the orthodoxy it represented.

MONASTERY OF HOSIOS LOUKAS Although an outpost, Greece was part of the Byzantine Empire, and the eleventh-century Katholikon (main church) of the monastery of Hosios Loukas, built a few miles from the village of Stiris in central Greece, is an excellent example of Middle Byzantine architecture (FIG. 8-17). It stands next to the earlier church of the Theotokos (Virgin Mary) within the courtyard of the walled enclosure that contained the life of the monks (FIG. 8-18). They slept in individual rooms—called "cells"—incorporated into the walls around the periphery of the complex, and they ate their meals together in a long rectangular hall parallel to the main church.

The Katholikon has a compact central plan with a dome supported on squinches rising over an octagonal core (see "Pendentives and Squinches" on page 241). Outside, the rising forms of apses, walls, and roofs disguise the vaulting roofs of the interior. The Greek builders created a polychromed decorative effect on the exterior, alternating stones with bricks set both vertically and horizontally and using diagonally set bricks to form saw-toothed moldings. Inside the churches, the high central space carries the eyes of worshipers upward into the main dome, which soars above a ring of tall arched openings.

Unlike Hagia Sophia, with its clear, sweeping geometric forms, the Katholikon has a complex variety of architectural

warm rooms
for winter

old entrance

monks' cells

courtyard

gardens

gardens

older church
of the Virgin
(Theotokos)

Katholikon
(main church
of Hosios Loukas)

refectory

underground
cistern

current entrance

chapel and
clock tower

monks' cells

0   20m

shapes and spaces, including domes, groin vaults, barrel vaults, pendentives, and squinches, all built on a relatively small scale (**FIG. 8–19**). The barrel vaults and tall sanctuary apse with flanking rooms further complicate the spatial composition. Single, double, and triple windows create intricate and unusual patterns of light that illuminated a mosaic of Christ Pantokrator (now lost) looming at the center of the main dome. A mosaic of the Lamb of God surrounded by the Twelve Apostles at Pentecost fills the secondary,

sanctuary dome, and the apse halfdome presents a rendering of the Virgin and Child Enthroned reminiscent of the ninth-century mosaic in the apse halfdome of Hagia Sophia (SEE FIG. 8–16). Scenes of Christ's life on earth (the Nativity appears on the squinch visible in FIG. 8–19) and figures of saints fill the upper surfaces of the interior with brilliant color and dramatic images. As at Hagia Sophia, the lower walls are faced with a multicolored stone veneer. A screen with icons separates the congregation from the sanctuary.

8-19 CENTRAL DOMED SPACE AND APSE (THE NAOS), KATHOLIKON
Monastery at Hosios Loukas. Early 11th century and later.

The subjects of the mosaics in Middle Byzantine churches such as the Katholikon at Hosios Loukas were organized into three levels according to meaning. Heavenly subjects like Christ Pantokrator, the Virgin Mary, Pentecost (Acts 2:1–3), or angels, appear on the tops of domes or in apse halfdomes. Below them, in a middle register are scenes from Christ's life on earth—here the Nativity in a squinch. Below, at the lowest level of mosaics are iconic representations of saints, closer to the viewer and thus more available for individual prayerful veneration.

CATHEDRAL OF SANTA SOPHIA IN KIEV During the ninth century, the rulers of Kievan Rus—Ukraine, Belarus, and Russia—adopted Orthodox Christianity and Byzantine culture. These lands had been settled by eastern Slavs in the fifth and sixth centuries, but later were ruled by Scandinavian Vikings who had sailed down the rivers from the Baltic to the Black Sea. In Constantinople, the Byzantine emperor hired the Vikings as his personal bodyguards, and Viking traders established a headquarters in the upper Volga region and in the city of Kiev, which became the capital of the area under their control.

The first Christian member of the Kievan ruling family was Princess Olga (c. 890–969), who was baptized in Constantinople by the patriarch himself with the Byzantine emperor as her godfather. Her grandson Grand Prince Vladimir (ruled 980–1015) established Orthodox Christianity as the state religion in 988 and cemented his relations with the Byzantines by accepting baptism and marrying Anna, the sister of the powerful Emperor Basil II (ruled 976–1025).

Vladimir's son Grand Prince Yaroslav (ruled 1036–1054) founded the **CATHEDRAL OF SANTA SOPHIA** in Kiev (**FIG. 8-20**). The church—originally designed as a typical Byzantine multiple-domed cross—was expanded with double side aisles leading to five apses and incorporating a large central dome surrounded by 12 smaller domes, all of which creates a complicated and compartmentalized interior. The central domed space of the crossing, however,

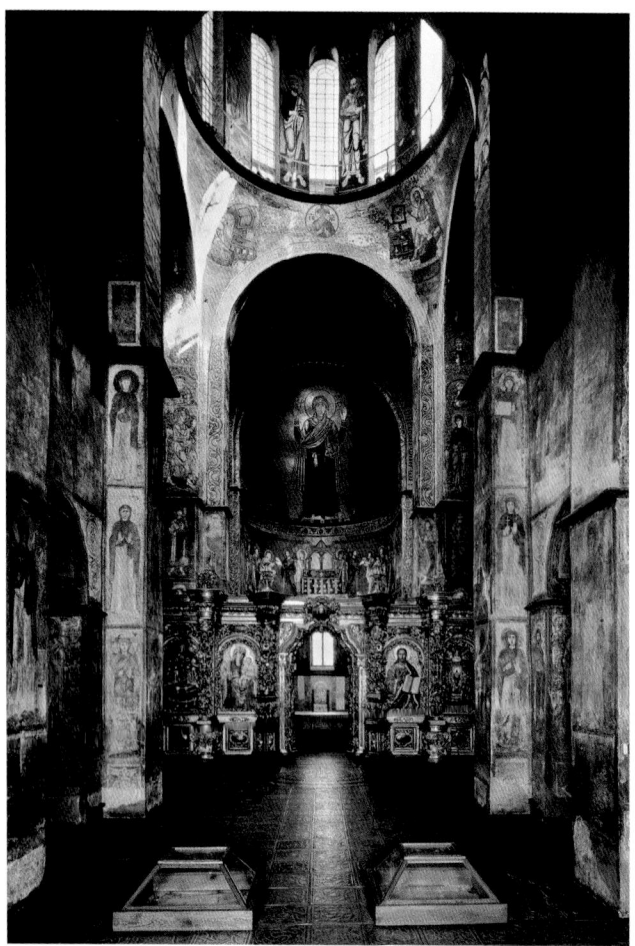

8-20 INTERIOR, CATHEDRAL OF SANTA SOPHIA, KIEV
1037–1046. Apse mosaics: Orant Virgin and Communion of the
Apostles.

focuses attention on the nave and the main apse, where the
walls glow with lavish decoration, including the mosaics
of the central dome, the apse, and the arches of the crossing. The remaining surfaces are frescoed with scenes from
the lives of Christ, the Virgin, the apostles Peter and Paul,
and the archangels.

The Kievan mosaics established a standard iconographic system used in Russian Orthodox churches. A
Christ Pantokrator fills the curving surface at the crest of the
main dome (not visible above the window-pierced drum in
FIG. 8-20). At a lower level, the apostles stand between the
windows of the drum, with the four evangelists occupying
the pendentives. An orant figure of the Virgin Mary seems
to float in a golden heaven on the halfdome and upper wall
of the apse, and on the wall below her is the Communion
of the Apostles. Christ appears not once, but twice, in this
scene, offering the Eucharistic bread and wine to the apostles, six on each side of the altar. With such extravagant use
of costly mosaic, Prince Yaroslav made a powerful political declaration of his own power and wealth—and that of
the Kievan Church as well.

**MONASTERY CHURCH OF THE DORMITION AT
DAPHNI**   The refined mosaicists who worked c. 1100 at
the monastery church of the Dormition at Daphni, near
Athens, seem to have conceived their compositions in relation to an intellectual ideal. They eliminated all "unnecessary" detail to focus on the essential elements of a narrative
scene, conveying its mood and message in a moving but
elegant style. The main dome of this church has retained
its riveting image of the Pantokrator, centered at the crest
of the dome like a seal of divine sanction and surveillance
(FIG. 8-21). This imposing figure manages to be elegant
and awesome at the same time. Christ blesses or addresses
the assembled congregation with one hand, while the slender, attenuated fingers of the other spread to clutch a massive book securely. In the squinches of the corner piers are
four signal episodes from his life: Annunciation, Nativity,
Baptism, and Transfiguration.

A mosaic of the **CRUCIFIXION** from the lower part of
the church (FIG. 8-22) exemplifies the focus on emotional
appeal to individuals that appears in late eleventh-century
Byzantine art. The figures inhabit an otherworldly space, a
golden universe anchored to the material world by a few
flowers, which suggest the promise of new life. A nearly
nude Jesus is shown with bowed head and gently sagging
body, his eyes closed in death. The witnesses have been
reduced to two isolated mourning figures, Mary and the

**8-21 CHRIST PANTOKRATOR WITH SCENES FROM THE
LIFE OF CHRIST**

Central dome and squinches, church of the Dormition, Daphni,
Greece. c. 1100. Mosaic.

This depiction of the Crucifixion has symbolic as well as emotional power. The mound of rocks and the skull at the bottom of the cross represent Golgotha, the "place of the skull," the hill outside ancient Jerusalem where Adam was thought to be buried and where the Crucifixion was said to have taken place. Christians saw Jesus Christ as the new Adam, whose sacrifice on the cross saved humanity from the sins brought into the world by Adam and Eve. The arc of blood and water springing from Jesus's side refers to Eucharistic and baptismal rites. As Paul wrote in his First Letter to the Corinthians: "For just as in Adam all die, so too in Christ shall all be brought to life" (1 Corinthians 15:22). The timelessness and simplicity of this image were meant to aid the Christian worshiper seeking to achieve a mystical union with the divine through prayer and meditation, both intellectually and emotionally.

MONASTERY CHURCH OF ST. PANTELEIMON AT NEREZI Dedicated in 1164, the church of St. Panteleimon—the Katholikon of the small monastery at Nerezi in Macedonia—was built under the patronage of Alexios Komnenos, nephew of Emperor John II (ruled 1118–1143). Here the wall paintings were created in fresco rather than mosaic, with a stylistic delicacy and **painterly** spontaneity characteristic of Byzantine art under the Komnenians. It represents well the growing emphasis on capturing the emotionalism of sacred narrative, already noted at Daphni. In the upper part of one wall, the scene of the **LAMENTATION** over the dead body of Christ (**FIG. 8-23**)—a non-biblical episode that seems to have been developed during the twelfth century—forges a direct link with viewers'

8-22 CRUCIFIXION

Church of the Dormition, Daphni, Greece. c. 1100. Mosaic.

Credit: Studio Kontos Photostock

young apostle John, to whom Jesus had just entrusted the care of his mother. The elegant cut of the contours and the eloquent restraint of the gestures only intensify the emotional power of the image. The nobility and suffering of these figures was meant to move monks and visiting worshipers toward a deeper involvement with their own meditations.

8-23 LAMENTATION

North wall of the church of the monastery of St. Panteleimon, Nerezi (near Skopje), Macedonia. 1164. Fresco.

Credit: © akg-images/Erich Lessing

emotions. The narrative emphasis is on the Virgin's anguish as she cradles the lifeless body of her son in the broad extension of her lap, pulling his head toward her, cheek to cheek, in a final embrace. Behind her, St. John bends to lift Jesus's hand to his cheek, conforming to a progressively descending diagonal arrangement of mourners that tumbles from the mountainous backdrop toward resolution in the limp torso of the savior. Such emotional expressions of human grief in human terms will be taken up again in Italy by Giotto over a century later (SEE FIG. 18–8).

THE CATHEDRAL OF ST. MARK IN VENICE The northeastern Italian city of Venice, set on the Adriatic at the crossroads of Europe and Asia Minor, was in certain ways an outpost of Byzantine art in Italy. Venice had been subject to Byzantine rule in the sixth and seventh centuries, and up to the tenth century, the city's ruler, the doge ("duke" in Venetian dialect), had to be ratified by the Byzantine

emperor. At the end of the tenth century, Constantinople granted Venice a special trade status that allowed its merchants to control much of the commerce between east and west, and the city grew enormously wealthy.

Venetian architects looked to Byzantine domed churches for inspiration in 1063, when the doge commissioned a church to replace the palace chapel that had housed the relics of St. Mark the apostle since they had been brought to Venice from Alexandria in 828/29 (**FIG. 8–24**). The **CATHEDRAL OF ST. MARK** is designed as a Greek cross, with arms of equal length. A dome covers each square unit—five great domes in all, separated by barrel vaults and supported by pendentives. Unlike Hagia Sophia in Constantinople, where the space seems to flow from the narthex up into the dome and through the nave to the apse, St. Mark's domed compartments produce a complex space in which each dome maintains its own separate vertical axis. As we have seen elsewhere, marble veneer covers the lower walls, and golden mosaics glimmer above on the vaults, pendentives, and domes.

8-24A INTERIOR OF THE CATHEDRAL OF ST. MARK

Venice. Begun 1063. View looking toward apse.

This church is the third one built on the site. It was both the palace chapel of the doge and the burial place for the bones of the patron of Venice, St. Mark. The church was consecrated as a cathedral in 1807. The mosaics have been reworked continually to the present day.

Credit: © Cameraphoto Arte, Venice

8-24B PLAN OF THE CATHEDRAL OF ST. MARK

Venice. Begun 1063.

Precious Objects of Commemoration, Veneration, and Devotion

As in the Early Byzantine period, tenth-, eleventh-, and twelfth-century artists produced small, often portable, luxury items for wealthy members of the imperial court as well as for Church dignitaries. These patrons often commissioned such precious objects as official gifts for one another. They had to be portable, sturdy, and refined, representing the latest trends in style and subject. These works frequently combined exceptional beauty and technical virtuosity with religious meaning; many were icons or devotional objects. Ivory carving, gold and **enamel** work, fine books, and intricate panel paintings were especially prized.

IVORIES Standing slightly over 9 inches tall, the small ivory ensemble known as the **HARBAVILLE TRIPTYCH** (named after a nineteenth-century owner) was made as a portable devotional object with two hinged wings that could be folded shut for travel. Its privileged owner used this work as the focus for private prayer; its luxuriousness also signaled high status and wealth. When opened (**FIG. 8-25A**), the triptych features across the top of the central panel a tableau with an enthroned Christ flanked by Mary and St. John the Baptist. This is a composition known as the "Deësis" (meaning "entreaty" in Greek), which shows Mary and John interceding with Christ, presumably pleading for forgiveness and salvation for the owner of this work. St. Peter stands directly under Christ, gesturing upward toward him and flanked by four other apostles—SS. James, John, Paul, and Andrew, all identified by inscriptions. The figures in the outer panels (both back and front) are military saints, bishop saints, and martyrs.

These holy figures stand in spatial settings given definition only by the small bases under their feet, effectively removing their gently modeled forms from the physical world. As a whole, they represent a celestial court of saints attending the enthroned Christ in paradise, categorized into thematic groups in an organization that recalls the ordered distribution of subjects in a Middle Byzantine church (SEE FIGS. 8–19, 8–20). On the back of the central panel (**FIG. 8-25B**) is a symbolic

evocation of paradise itself in the form of a large, stable cross surrounded by luxurious vegetation inhabited by animals, presumably an evocation of the longed-for destination of the original owner, a reminder to focus attention

8-25A FRONT OF THE HARBAVILLE TRIPTYCH
From Constantinople. Mid 10th century. Ivory, closed 9½ × 5⅝" (24.2 × 14.3 cm); open 9½ × 11" (24.2 × 28 cm). Musée du Louvre, Paris.

Credit: Photo © RMN-Grand Palais (Musée du Louvre)/Daniel Arnaudet

8-25B BACK OF THE HARBAVILLE TRIPTYCH
From Constantinople. Mid 10th century. Ivory, closed 9½ × 5⅝" (24.2 × 14.3 cm); open 9½ × 11" (24.2 × 28 cm). Musée du Louvre, Paris.

Credit: Photo © RMN-Grand Palais (Musée du Louvre)/Daniel Arnaudet

8-26 CHRIST CROWNING EMPEROR ROMANOS II AND EMPRESS EUDOKIA

From Constantinople. 945–949. Ivory, 7⅜ × 3¾″ (18.6 × 9.5 cm). Cabinet des Médailles, Bibliothèque Nationale, Paris.

Credit: Bibliothèque nationale de France

child—of the fusion of imperial authority with the religious faith that sanctioned and supported it. The carefully modeled figure of Christ, whose drapery is arranged to give three-dimensionality to his bodily form, offers a striking contrast to the stiff and flattened figures of the imperial couple, all but consumed by the elaborate decoration of their royal robes.

MANUSCRIPTS Painted books were some of the most impressive products of the Middle Byzantine period, and of the Macedonian Renaissance in particular. The luxurious Paris **Psalter** (named after its current library location) is a noteworthy example. This personal devotional book—meant to guide the prayer life of its aristocratic owner—includes the complete text of the Psalms and a series of odes or canticles drawn from the Bible that were a standard part of Byzantine psalters. The annotation of the biblical texts with passages from interpretive commentaries gives this book a scholarly dimension consistent with a revival of learning that took place under the Macedonian emperors. Indeed, it seems to have been commissioned in Constantinople by the intellectual Emperor Constantine

8-27 DAVID COMPOSING THE PSALMS

Page from the Paris Psalter. Constantinople. c. 950. Paint and gold on vellum, sheet size 14½ × 10½″ (37 × 26.5 cm). Bibliothèque Nationale, Paris.

Credit: Bibliothèque nationale de France

on devotional practice and enlist the aid of the congregation of saints to assure the attainment of salvation. An abbreviated inscription above the cross—IC XC NIKA—backs up the pictorial reminder with words—"Jesus Christ is victorious."

Related to the Harbaville Triptych in both figure style and compositional format is an independent ivory panel portraying an emperor and empress standing on either side of and gesturing toward an elevated figure of Christ, who reaches out to touch their crowns (**FIG. 8-26**). The imperial figures are identified by inscription as Romanos and Eudokia—most likely Emperor Romanos II, son and co-emperor of Constantine VII Porphyrogenitos (ruled 945–959), and his first wife, Eudokia, the daughter of Hugo of Provence, King of Rome, whom Romanos married in 944 when she was only 4 years old and who died in 949. This is not a scene of coronation but an emblem—Eudokia, for instance, is represented as an adult rather than as a

VII Porphyrogenitos as a gift for his son Romanos II, whom we have already encountered (SEE FIG. 8–26).

This book is best known, however, neither for its learned texts nor for its imperial patron or owner, but for its set of 14 full-page miniatures. The fresh spontaneity of these paintings and the complicated abstraction underlying their compositional structure—salient stylistic features of the Macedonian Renaissance—make this book one of the true glories of Byzantine art. Eight of the framed miniatures portray episodes from the life of Israel's King David, who as a boy had saved the people of God by killing the giant Goliath (SEE FIG. 8–1) and who was traditionally considered the author of the Psalms. The first of these depicts David seated outdoors against a background of lush foliage while he composes the Psalms to the accompaniment of his harp (FIG. 8–27). Groups of animals surround him in the foreground, while his native city of Bethlehem looms through the atmospheric mist in the background.

The Macedonian Renaissance emphasis on a Classical revival is evident here in the personification of abstract ideas and landscape features: Melody, a languorous female figure, leans casually on David's shoulder to inspire his compositions, while another woman, perhaps Echo, peeks from behind a column in the right background. The swarthy reclining youth in the lower foreground is a personification of Mount Bethlehem, as we learn from his inscription. The motif of the dog watching over the sheep and goats while his master strums the harp invokes the Classical subject of Orpheus charming wild animals with music. The strongly modeled three-dimensionality of the forms, the integration of the figures into a three-dimensional space, and the use of atmospheric perspective all enhance the Classical flavor of the painting, in yet another example of the enduring vitality of pagan artistic traditions at the Christian court in Constantinople.

ICONS In the centuries after the end of iconoclasm, one of the major preoccupations of Byzantine artists was the creation of independent devotional images in a variety of media. The revered twelfth-century icon of Mary and Jesus known as the **VIRGIN OF VLADIMIR** (FIG. 8–28) was probably painted in Constantinople but brought to Kiev. This distinctively humanized image is another example of the growing desire for a more immediate and personal religion that we have already seen in the Crucifixion mosaic at Daphni, dating slightly earlier. Here the artist used an established iconographic type known as the "Virgin of Compassion," showing Mary and the Christ Child pressing their cheeks together and gazing at each other with tender affection. This type of image is found as early as the tenth century and was believed to have been first painted by St. Luke, reproducing what he had seen in a vision. The *Virgin of Vladimir* was thought to protect the people of the city where it resided. It arrived in Kiev sometime in the

8–28 VIRGIN OF VLADIMIR
Probably from Constantinople. Faces, 12th century; the figures have been retouched. Tempera on panel, height approx. 31″ (78 cm). Tretyakov State Gallery, Moscow.

Credit: © 2016. Photo Scala, Florence

1130s, was subsequently taken to the city of Suzdal, and finally came to Vladimir in 1155. In 1480, it was moved to the Cathedral of the Dormition in the Moscow Kremlin.

Also from the twelfth century, but made from more precious materials and presenting a saintly image more hieratic than intimate, is a representation of the archangel Michael in silver-gilt and enamel (see "Closer Look" on page 262), whose technical virtuosity and sumptuous media suggest it may have been an imperial commission for use within the palace complex itself. St. Michael is dressed here as a confrontational military commander in the heavenly forces, a real contrast with the calmly classicizing angelic form he takes in the large ivory panel we examined from the Early Byzantine period (SEE FIG. 8–12).

This icon did not remain in Constantinople. It is now in the treasury of the Cathedral of St. Mark in Venice, one of many precious objects looted by Latin crusaders in 1204 at the fall of Constantinople during the ill-conceived Fourth Crusade. This devastating event brought an abrupt end to the Middle Byzantine period.

A Closer Look

ICON OF ST. MICHAEL THE ARCHANGEL

This bust portrait of Christ, created with **cloisonné** enamel, appears directly over the head of St. Michael, sanctioning his power with a gesture of blessing or recognition. The medallions on the upper corners portray SS. Peter and Menas, but the enamels once filling comparable medallions on the lower strip of the frame have been lost.

Heavily abbreviated inscriptions identify each saint by name.

In 1834, restorers replaced the wings of St. Michael, which are now probably disproportionately large in relation to the originals. In the same restoration, the precious gemstones once set into the frame were replaced with colored glass.

Four pairs of military saints in oval compartments flank St. Michael on the lateral strips of the frame. This entourage emphasizes the military character of St. Michael, who is dressed and equipped for battle as the leader of a heavenly army.

Luminous enamel (glass heated to the melting point at which it bonds to the underlying or surrounding metal) completely covers the face of St. Michael to give it the appearance of human flesh.

Lavish and intricate patterns created from enamel fill the background around St. Michael. Byzantine artists were virtuosos in the cloisonné technique, in which gold strips or wires are soldered to the underlying metal surface to separate the different colors of enamel from each other, forming a network of delicate gold lines that delineate the decorative forms and enliven the surface with reflected light.

A series of separately fabricated forms—haloed head, torso, legs, arms, wings, sword, and fully three-dimensional orb and sword—have been assembled to create the projecting figure of St. Michael.

8-29 ICON OF ST. MICHAEL THE ARCHANGEL
Made in Constantinople. 12th century. Silver-gilt on wood, cloisonné enamels, gemstones; 18⅛ × 13¾″ (46 × 35 cm). Treasury of the Cathedral of St. Mark, Venice.

Credit: © Cameraphoto Arte, Venice

Late Byzantine Art

How is Byzantine art transformed during its late period?

A third great age of Byzantine art began in 1261 after the Byzantines expelled the Christian crusaders who had occupied Constantinople for nearly 60 years. Although the empire had been weakened and its domain decreased to small areas of the Balkans and Greece, the arts underwent a resurgence known as the Palaeologue Renaissance after the new dynasty of emperors who regained Constantinople.

The patronage of emperors, wealthy courtiers, and the Church stimulated renewed church building as well as the production of icons, books, and precious objects.

Constantinople: The Chora Church

In Constantinople, many existing churches were renovated, redecorated, and expanded during the Palaeologue Renaissance. Among these is the church of the monastery of Christ in Chora (meaning "in the country"), part of an influential monastery on the outskirts of Constantinople.

8-30 PLAN OF THE MONASTERY CHURCH OF CHRIST IN CHORA KARIYE MÜZESI, CONSTANTINOPLE
Present-day Istanbul. Original construction 1077–1081; expanded and refurbished c. 1315–1321.

Metochites became a powerful intellectual figure in Constantinople. As a poet, philosopher, and astronomer who wrote scores of complicated commentaries in an intentionally cultivated, arcane, and mannered literary style, he ridiculed a rival for his prose style of "excess clarity." In 1290, Emperor Andronicus II Palaeologus (ruled 1282–1328) called Metochites to court service, where the prolific young scholar became an influential senior statesman, ascending to the highest levels of the government and amassing power and wealth second only to that of the emperor himself. Metochites's political and financial status plummeted when the emperor was overthrown by his grandson in 1328. Stripped of his wealth and sent into exile, Metochites was allowed to return to the capital two years later, retiring to house arrest at the Chora monastery, where he died and was buried in 1332.

It is his association with this monastery that has become Theodore Metochites's greatest claim to enduring fame. He was at the peak of his power and wealth when he funded the expansion and restoration of the monastery's church, and the **FUNERARY CHAPEL** (or parekklesion) that was built adjacent to the main church (**FIG. 8–31**), was designed with the intention of creating a location for his own funeral and tomb.

The expansion of this church (known today as the Kariye Müzesi) was one of several projects that Theodore Metochites (1270–1332), a humanist poet and scientist and the administrator of the imperial treasury at Constantinople, sponsored between c. 1315 and 1321. He added a two-story annex on the north side, two narthexes on the west, and a parekklesion (side chapel) used as a funerary chapel on the south (**FIG. 8–30**). These structures contain the most impressive interior decorations remaining in Constantinople from the Late Byzantine period, rivaling in splendor and technical sophistication the works of the age of Justinian, but on a more intimate scale. The walls and vaults of the parekklesion are covered with frescos, and the narthex vaults are encrusted with mosaics.

Theodore Metochites was one of the most fascinating personalities of the Late Byzantine world. Son of an intellectual cleric who had been condemned and exiled for championing the union of the Roman and Byzantine Churches,

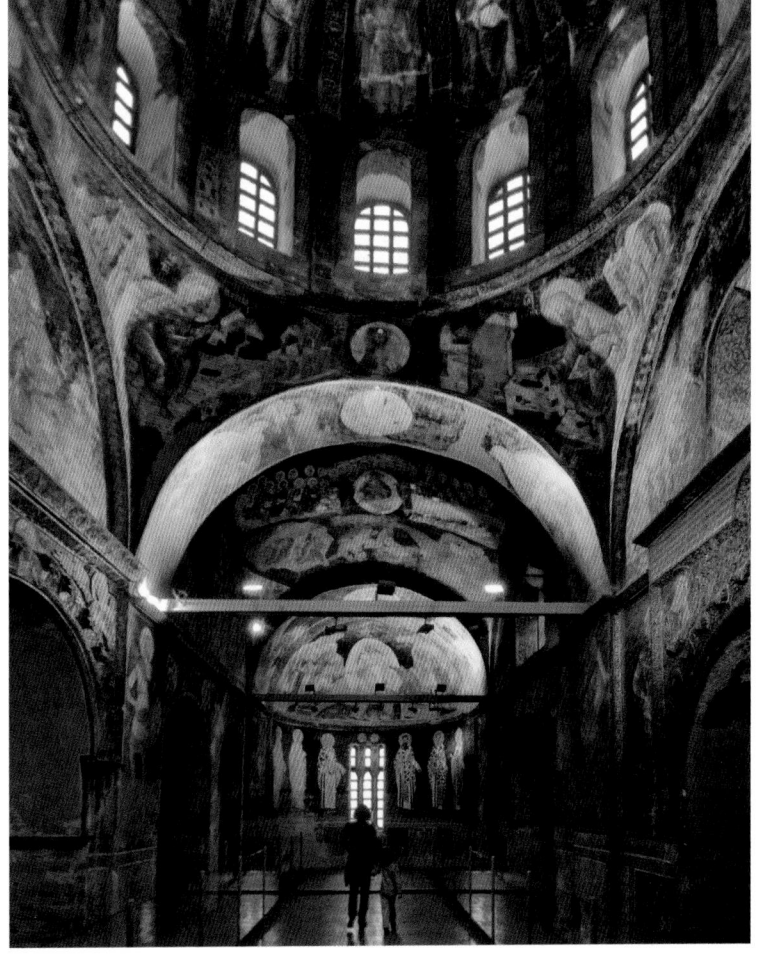

8-31 FUNERARY CHAPEL (PAREKKLESION)
Church of the monastery of Christ in Chora, present-day Istanbul. c. 1315–1321.

Credit: Photo © Ayhan Altun

8–32 ANASTASIS
Apse of the funerary chapel, church of the monastery of Christ in Chora, present-day Istanbul. c. 1321. Fresco.

Credit: Photo © Ayhan Altun

The extensive and highly integrated program of frescos covering every inch of the walls and vaults of this jewel box space focuses on funerary themes and expectations of salvation and its rewards. Above a dado of imitation marble stands a frieze of 34 military saints ready to fulfill their roles as protectors of those buried in the chapel. Above them on the side walls of the main space are stories from the Hebrew Bible interpreted in Byzantine Christianity as prefigurations of the Virgin Mary's intercessory powers. A portrayal of Jacob's ladder (Genesis 28:11–19), for example, evokes her position between heaven and earth as a bridge from death to life. On the pendentives of the dome over the main space (two of which are seen in the foreground), famous Byzantine hymn writers sit at their desks surrounded by quotations from their work. These carefully chosen passages highlight texts associated with funerals, including one that refers to the story of Jacob's ladder.

The climax of the decorative program, however, is the powerful rendering of the **ANASTASIS** that occupies the halfdome of the apse (**FIG. 8-32**). In this popular Byzantine representation of the Resurrection—drawn not from the Bible but from the apocryphal Gospel of Nicodemus—Jesus demonstrates his powers of salvation by descending into limbo after his death on the cross to save his righteous Hebrew forebears from Satan's grasp. Here a boldly striding Christ—brilliantly outfitted in a pure white that makes him shine to prominence within the fresco program—lunges to rescue Adam and Eve from their tombs, pulling them upward with such force that they seem to float under the spell of his power. Satan lies tied into a helpless bundle at his feet, and patriarchs, kings, and prophets look on in admiration, perhaps waiting for their own turn to be rescued. During a funeral in this chapel, the head of the deceased would have been directed toward this engrossing

tableau, closed eyes facing upward toward a painting of the Last Judgment strategically positioned on the vault over the bier. In 1332, this was the location of Metochites's own dead body since this parekklesion was the site of his funeral. He may have been buried in one of the niche tombs cut into the walls of the chapel or within a tomb under the floor of the sanctuary itself, directly under the painted image of the archangel Michael, guardian of souls.

The mosaic decoration Metochites commissioned for the church's expansive narthexes, however, may be the most sumptuous product of his beneficence. Above an expanse of traditional marble revetment on the lower walls, mosaics cover every surface—the domical groin vaults, the wall lunettes, even the undersides of arches—with narrative scenes and their ornamental framework (**FIG. 8-33**). The small-scale figures of these mosaics seem to dance with enthusiasm through the narrative episodes they enact from the lives of Christ and his mother. Unlike the stripped-down narrative scenes of Daphni (SEE FIG. 8-22), here the artists have lavished special attention on the settings, composing their stories against backdrops of architectural fantasies and stylized plants. The architecture of the background is presented in an innovative system of perspective, charting its three-dimensionality not in relation to a point of convergence in the background—as will be the case in the linear, **one-point perspective** of fifteenth-century Florentine art—but projecting forward in relationship to a point in the foreground, thereby drawing attention to the figural scenes themselves.

The Chora mosaics build on the growing Byzantine interest in the expression of emotions within religious narrative, presenting a level of human tenderness that surpasses anything we have seen in Byzantine art thus far. The artists invite viewers to see the participants in these venerable, sacred stories as human beings just like themselves, only wealthier and holier. For example, the entire narrative field in one vault is devoted to a scene where the infant Mary is cuddled between her adoring parents, Joachim and Anna (**FIG. 8-34**; part of the scene is visible in FIG. 8-33). Servants on either side of the family look on with gestures and expressions of admiration and approval, perhaps modeling the response that is expected from viewers within the narthex itself. The human interaction extends to details such as the nuzzling of Mary's head into the beard

of her father as she leans back to look into his eyes, and her tentative reach toward her mother's face at the same time. In another scene, the young Jesus rides on the shoulders of Joseph in a pose still familiar to fathers and children today. The informality and believability that these anecdotal details bring to sacred narrative recalls developments as far away as Italy, where at this same time Giotto and Duccio were using similar devices to bring their stories to life (see Chapter 18).

8-33 MOSAICS IN THE VAULTING OF THE INNER NARTHEX

Church of the monastery of Christ in Chora, present-day Istanbul. c. 1315–1321.

Credit: Photo © Ayhan Altun

Icons

Late Byzantine artists of Constantinople created icons as well as painting murals and making mosaics on walls. Among the most dynamic and engaging is a representation of the Annunciation on one side of an early fourteenth-century double-sided icon (**FIG. 8-35**)—the other side has an image of the Virgin and Child—roughly contemporary with the redecoration of the Chora church. This icon was made in the capital, perhaps under imperial patronage, and sent from there to the archbishop of Ohrid. Over 3 feet tall, it was probably mounted on a pole and carried in processions, where both sides would be visible. Characteristic of Constantinopolitan art under the Palaeologues are the small heads, inflated bodies, and light shot-silk clothing of the figures; the forward-projecting perspective of the architecture of background and throne, similar in concept to that of the Chora mosaics (SEE FIG. 8-34); and the fanciful caryatids perched on the tops of the columns.

The practice of venerating icons intensified in Russia during the late Byzantine period; regional schools of icon painting flourished, fostering the work of remarkable artists. One of these was the renowned artist-monk Andrey Rublyov, who created a magnificent icon of **THE HOSPITALITY OF ABRAHAM** sometime between about 1410 and 1425 (**FIG. 8-36**). It was commissioned in honor of Abbot Sergius of the Trinity-Sergius Monastery, near Moscow. The theme is the Trinity, represented here by three identical angels. Rublyov's source for this idea was a story in the Hebrew Bible of the patriarch Abraham and his wife Sarah, who entertained three strangers who were in fact God represented by three divine beings in human form

(Genesis 18). Tiny images of Abraham and Sarah's home and the oak of Mamre can be seen above the angels. The food the couple offered to the strangers becomes a chalice on an altarlike table.

Rublyov's icon clearly illustrates how Late Byzantine artists—like the artists of ancient Greece—relied on mathematical conventions to create ideal figures, giving their works remarkable consistency. But unlike the Greeks, who based their formulas on close observation of nature, Byzantine artists invented an ideal geometry to evoke a spiritual realm and conformed their representations of human forms and features to it. Here the circle forms the basic underlying structure for the composition. Despite this formulaic approach, talented artists like Rublyov worked within it to create a personal, expressive style. Rublyov relied on typical Late Byzantine conventions—salient contours, small heads and long bodies, and a focus on a limited number of figures—to capture the sense of the spiritual in his work, yet he distinguished his art by imbuing it with a sweet, poetic ambience.

The Byzantine tradition continued for centuries in the art of the Eastern Orthodox Church and is carried on to this day in Greek and Russian icon painting. But in Constantinople, Byzantine art—like the empire itself—came to an end in 1453. When the forces of the Ottoman sultan Mehmed II overran the capital, the Eastern Empire became part of the Islamic world. The Turkish conquerors were so impressed with the splendor of the Byzantine art and architecture in the capital, however, that they adopted its traditions and melded them with their own rich aesthetic heritage into a new, and now Islamic, artistic efflorescence.

8–35 ANNUNCIATION TO THE VIRGIN
Sent from Constantinople to the church of the Virgin Peribleptos, Ohrid, Macedonia. Early 14th century. Tempera on panel, 36⅝ × 26¾″ (93 × 68 cm). Icon Gallery, Ohrid, Macedonia.

Credit: © 2016. Photo Scala, Florence

8–36 Andrey Rublyov **THE HOSPITALITY OF ABRAHAM**
c. 1410–1425. Tempera on panel, 55½ × 44½″ (141 × 113 cm). Tretyakov State Gallery, Moscow.

Credit: © 2016. Photo Scala, Florence

Think About It

1 Characterize the role of the Classical tradition, already notable in the Early Christian period, in the developing history of Byzantine art. When was it used? In what sorts of contexts? Develop your discussion in relation to two specific examples from two different periods of Byzantine art.

2 Compare the portrayals of the Byzantine rulers in the mosaics of San Vitale in Ravenna (**SEE FIGS. 8-8, 8-9**) and those on a tenth-century ivory plaque

(**SEE FIG. 8-26**). Discuss the subjects of the scenes themselves as well as the way the emperor and empress are incorporated within them.

3 How were images used in Byzantine worship? Why were images suppressed during iconoclasm?

4 How do the mosaics of the Chora Church in Constantinople emphasize the human dimensions of sacred stories? Consider in particular how the figures are represented, what kinds of stories are told, and in what way.

Crosscurrents

Both of these grand churches were built under the patronage of powerful rulers and were meant to glorify them as well as serve the Christian community. What features do they share? In what ways are they fundamentally different? What functions did they serve for both Church and state?

FIG. 7–10A

FIG. 8–4A

9-1 Yahya Ibn al-Wasiti **THE MAQAMAT OF AL-HARIRI**

From Baghdad, Iraq. 1237. Ink, pigments, and gold on paper, 13¾ × 10¼″ (35 × 25 cm). Bibliothèque Nationale, Paris. Arabic MS. 5847, fol. 18v.

Chapter 9
Islamic Art

 ## Learning Objectives

9.a Identify the visual hallmarks of Islamic art for formal, technical, and expressive qualities.

9.b Interpret the meaning of works of Islamic art based on their themes, subjects, and symbols.

9.c Relate Islamic artists and art to their cultural, economic, and political contexts.

9.d Apply the vocabulary and concepts relevant to Islamic art, artists, and art history.

9.e Interpret a work of Islamic art using the art historical methods of observation, comparison, and inductive reasoning.

9.f Select visual and textual evidence in various media to support an argument or an interpretation of a work of Islamic art.

THE MAQAMAT (*"Assemblies"*) by al-Hariri (1054–1122) belongs to a popular Islamic literary genre of cautionary tales. Al-Hariri's stories revolve around a silver-tongued scoundrel named Abu Zayd, whose cunning inevitably triumphs over other people's naivety. His exploits take place in a world of colorful settings—including desert camps, ships, pilgrim caravans, apothecary shops, mosques, gardens, libraries, cemeteries, and courts of law. Comic stories of trickery in such settings would seem perfectly suited for illustration, and that is the case in this engaging manuscript, made in Baghdad during the thirteenth century. Human activity permeates the compositions. And the vivid visualizations provide us with rare windows into ordinary Muslim life: here, prayer in the congregational **mosque** (FIG. 9-1), a religious and social institution at the center of Islamic culture.

The congregation has gathered to hear a sermon preached by the deceitful Abu Zayd, who plans to make off with the alms collection. The men sit directly on the ground, as is customary not only in mosques, but in traditional dwellings. The listener in the front row tilts his chin upward to focus his gaze directly upon the speaker. He is framed and centered by the arch of the **mihrab** (the niche indicating the direction of Mecca) on the rear wall; his white turban contrasts noticeably with the darker gold background. Perhaps he stands in for the manuscript's readers who pause while perusing these illustrations to project themselves into the scene.

The columns of the mosque's arcades have ornamental capitals from which spring half-round arches. Glass mosque lamps hang from the center of each arch. Figures wear turbans and flowing, loose-sleeved robes with epigraphic borders (*tiraz*) embroidered in gold. Abu Zayd delivers his sermon from the steps of a **minbar** (pulpit) with an arched gateway opening at the lowest level. This *minbar* and the arcades that form the backdrop of the scene are reduced in scale so the painter can describe the entire setting and still make the figures the main focus of the composition. Likewise, although in an actual mosque the *minbar* would share the same wall as the *mihrab*, here they have been separated, perhaps to keep the *minbar* from hiding the *mihrab*, and to rivet our attention on what is most important—the rapt attention Abu Zayd commands from his captive audience, a group we ourselves join as we relish the anecdotal and pictorial delights of this splendid example of Islamic visual narrative.

Islam and Early Islamic Society

How do early Islamic society and culture foster the development of new forms of art and architecture?

Islam arose in seventh-century Arabia, a land of desert oases that was sparsely inhabited by tribal nomads and had no cities of great size. Yet under the leadership of its founder, the Prophet Muhammad (c. 570–632 CE), and his successors, Islam spread rapidly throughout northern

Africa, southern and eastern Europe, and into Asia, gaining territory and converts with astonishing speed. Because Islam encompassed geographical areas with a variety of long-established cultural traditions, and because it admitted diverse peoples among its converts, it absorbed and combined many different techniques and ideas about art and architecture. The result was a highly sophisticated artistic eclecticism.

Muslims ("those who have submitted to God") believe that in the desert outside of Mecca in 610 Muhammad received revelations that led him to found the religion called Islam ("submission to God's will"). Many powerful Meccans were hostile to the message preached by the young visionary, and in 622 he and his companions fled to Medina. There Muhammad built a house that became a gathering place for the converted and thus the first mosque. Muslims date their history as beginning with this *hijira* ("emigration").

In 630, Muhammad returned to Mecca with an army of 10,000, routed his enemies, and established the city as the spiritual capital of Islam. After his triumph, he went to the **KAABA** (**FIG. 9–2**), a cubelike, textile-draped shrine said to have been built for God by Ibrahim (Abraham) and Isma'il (Ishmael) and long the focus of pilgrimage and polytheistic worship. He emptied the shrine, repudiating its accumulated pagan idols, while preserving the enigmatic structure itself and dedicating it to God.

The Kaaba is the symbolic center of the Islamic world, the place to which all Muslim prayer is directed, and the ultimate destination of Islam's obligatory pilgrimage, the *hajj*. Each year, huge numbers of Muslims from all over the world travel to Mecca to circumambulate the Kaaba during the month of pilgrimage. The exchange of ideas that occurs during the intermingling of these diverse groups of pilgrims has contributed to Islam's cultural eclecticism.

Muhammad's act of emptying the Kaaba of its pagan idols instituted the fundamental practice of avoiding figural imagery in Islamic religious architecture. This did not, however, lead to a ban on art. Figural imagery is frequent in palaces and illustrated manuscripts, and Islamic artists also elaborated a rich vocabulary of nonfigural ornament, including complex geometric designs and scrolling foliate vines (that Europeans labeled **arabesques**), which were appropriate in all contexts. Islamic art revels in surface

9–2 THE KAABA, MECCA
The Kaaba represents the center of the Islamic world. Its cubelike form is draped with a black textile that is embroidered with a few Qur'anic verses in gold.

Credit: Ayazad/Fotolia

MAP 9-1 THE ISLAMIC WORLD

Within 200 years after 622 CE, the Islamic world expanded from Mecca to India in the east, and to Morocco and Spain in the west.

decoration and in manipulating line, color, and especially pattern, often highlighting the interplay of pure abstraction, organic form, and script.

According to tradition, the Qur'an assumed its final form during the time of the third caliph (successor to the Prophet), Uthman (ruled 644–656). As the language of the Qur'an, Arabic and its script have been a powerful unifying force within Islam. From the eighth through the eleventh centuries, Arabic was the universal language among scholars in the Islamic world and in some Christian lands as well. Inscriptions frequently ornament works of art, sometimes written clearly to provide a readable message, but in other cases written as complex patterns to also delight the eye.

The Prophet was succeeded by a series of caliphs. The accession of Ali as the fourth caliph (ruled 656–661) provoked a power struggle that led to his assassination and resulted in enduring divisions within Islam. Followers of Ali, known as Shi'ites (referring to the party or *shi'a* of Ali), regard him alone as the Prophet's rightful successor. Sunni Muslims, in contrast, recognize all of the first four caliphs as "rightly guided." Ali was succeeded by his rival Muawiya (ruled 661–680), a close relative of Uthman and the founder of the first Muslim dynasty, the Umayyad (661–750).

Islam expanded dramatically. Within two decades, seemingly unstoppable Muslim armies conquered the Sasanian Persian Empire, Egypt, and the Byzantine provinces of Syria and Palestine. By the early eighth century, the Umayyads had reached India, conquered northern Africa and Spain, and penetrated France before being turned back (**MAP 9-1**). In these newly conquered lands, the treatment of Christians and Jews who did not convert to Islam was not consistent, but in general, as "People of the Book"—followers of a monotheistic religion based on a revealed scripture—they enjoyed a protected status, though they were subject to a special tax and restrictions on dress and employment.

Muslims participate in congregational worship at a mosque (*masjid*, "place of prostration"). The Prophet Muhammad himself lived simply and instructed his followers in prayer at his house, now known as the Mosque of the Prophet, where he resided in Medina. This was a square enclosure that framed a large courtyard with rooms along the east wall where he and his family lived. Along the south wall, a thatched portico supported by palm-tree trunks sheltered both the faithful as they prayed and Muhammad as he spoke from a low platform. This simple arrangement inspired the design of later mosques. Without the architectural focus provided by chancels, altars, naves, or domes, the space of this prototypical hypostyle (multi-columned) mosque reflected the founding spirit of Islam in which the faithful pray as equals directly to God, led by an imam, but without the intermediary of a priesthood.

The Five Pillars of Islam

Islam emphasizes a direct personal relationship with God. The Pillars of Islam, sometimes symbolized by an open hand with the five fingers extended, enumerate the duties required of Muslims by their faith.

- The first pillar (*shahadah*) is to proclaim that there is only one God and that Muhammad is his messenger. While monotheism is common to Judaism, Christianity, and Islam, and Muslims worship the God of Abraham while also acknowledging Hebrew and Christian prophets such as Musa (Moses) and Isa (Jesus), Muslims deem the Christian Trinity polytheistic and assert that God was not born and did not give birth.

- The second pillar requires prayer (*salat*) to be performed by turning to face the Kaaba in Mecca five times daily: at dawn, noon, late afternoon, sunset, and nightfall. Prayer can occur almost anywhere, although the prayer on Fridays takes place in the congregational mosque. Because ritual ablutions are required for purity, mosque courtyards usually have fountains.

- The third pillar is the voluntary payment of annual tax or alms (*zakah*), equivalent to one-fortieth of one's assets. *Zakah* is used for charities such as feeding the poor, housing travelers, and paying the dowries of orphan girls. Among Shi'ites, an additional tithe is required to support the Shi'ite community specifically.

- The fourth pillar is the dawn-to-dusk fast (*sawm*) during Ramadan, the month when Muslims believe Muhammad received the revelations set down in the Qur'an. The fast of Ramadan is a communally shared sacrifice that imparts purification, self-control, and fellowship with others. The end of Ramadan is celebrated with the feast day 'Id al-Fitr (Festival of the Breaking of the Fast).

- For those physically and financially able to do so, the fifth pillar is the pilgrimage to Mecca (*hajj*), which ideally is undertaken at least once in the life of each Muslim. Among the extensive pilgrimage rites are donning simple garments to remove distinctions of class and culture; collective circumambulations of the Kaaba; kissing the Black Stone inside the Kaaba (probably a meteorite that fell in pre-Islamic times); and the sacrificing of an animal, usually a sheep, in memory of Abraham's readiness to sacrifice his son at God's command. The end of the *hajj* is celebrated by the festival 'Id al-Adha (Festival of Sacrifice).

The directness and simplicity of Islam have made the Muslim religion readily adaptable to numerous varied cultural contexts throughout history. The Five Pillars instill not only faith and a sense of belonging, but also a commitment to Islam in the form of actual practice.

Early Islamic Art and Architecture

What characterizes the early formation of Islamic art and architecture?

Under the caliphs of the Umayyad dynasty (661–750), while Mecca and Medina remained the holiest Muslim cities, the political center shifted to the Syrian city of Damascus, which became the Umayyad capital in 656. Throughout the Islamic empire the Umayyads built mosques and palaces that projected the authority of the new rulers and reflected the growing acceptance of Islam. In the eastern Mediterranean, they built shrines, mosques, and palaces under the influence of Roman and Byzantine architecture.

In 750 the Abbasid clan replaced the Umayyads in a coup d'état, ruling as caliphs until 1258 from Baghdad, in Iraq. Their long and cosmopolitan reign saw achievements in medicine, mathematics, the natural sciences, philosophy, literature, music, and art. They were generally tolerant of the ethnically diverse populations in the territories they subjugated, and they admired the past achievements of Roman civilization as well as the living traditions of Byzantium, Persia, India, and China, freely borrowing artistic techniques and styles from all of them.

In the tenth century, the Islamic world split into separate kingdoms ruled by independent caliphs. In addition to the Abbasids of Iraq, there was a Fatimid Shi'ite caliph ruling Tunisia and Egypt and a descendant of the Umayyads ruling Spain and Portugal (together then known as al-Andalus). The Islamic world did not reunite under the myriad dynasties who thereafter ruled from northern Africa to Asia, but loss in unity was gain to artistic diversity.

The Dome of the Rock

In the center of Jerusalem rises the Haram al-Sharif ("Noble Sanctuary"), a rocky outcrop from which Muslims believe Muhammad ascended to the presence of God on the "Night Journey" described in the Qur'an, as well as the site of the First and Second Jewish Temples. Jews and Christians variously associate this place with Solomon, the site of the creation of Adam, and the place where the patriarch Abraham prepared to sacrifice his son Isaac at the command of God. In 691–692, a domed shrine was built over the rock (**FIG. 9–3**), employing artists trained in the

9–3A EXTERIOR VIEW OF THE DOME OF THE ROCK, JERUSALEM
Israel. Begun 691.

Credit: © Zoonar GmbH/Alamy Stock Photo

Byzantine tradition to create the first great monument of Islamic art. By assertively appropriating a site holy to Jews and Christians, the Dome of the Rock manifested Islam's view of itself as completing and superseding the prophecies of those faiths.

Structurally, the Dome of the Rock imitates the centrally planned form of Early Christian and Byzantine

9–3B CUTAWAY DRAWING OF THE DOME OF THE ROCK, JERUSALEM
Israel. Begun 691.

Credit: © Dorling Kindersley

martyria (SEE FIGS. 7–14, 8–5). However, unlike the plain exteriors of its models, it is crowned by a golden dome that dominates the skyline. The ceramic tiles on the lower portion of the exterior were added later, but the opulent marble veneer and mosaics of the interior are original. The dome, surmounting a circular drum pierced with windows and supported by arcades of alternating **piers** and columns, covers the central space containing the rock (**FIG. 9–4**), and concentric aisles (ambulatories) permit devout visitors to circumambulate it.

Inscriptions from the Qur'an are interspersed with passages from other texts, including information about the building itself, to form a frieze around the inner and outer arcades. As pilgrims walk around the central space to read the inscriptions in brilliant gold mosaic on turquoise green ground, the building communicates both as a text and as a dazzling visual display. These inscriptions are especially notable because they are the oldest surviving written verses from the Qur'an and the first use of Qur'anic inscriptions in architecture. Below them, the walls are faced with marble—the veining of which creates abstract symmetrical patterns—and the rotunda is surrounded by columns of gray marble with gilded capitals. Above the calligraphic frieze is another mosaic frieze depicting symmetrical vine scrolls and trees in turquoise, blue, and green embellished with imitation jewels over a gold ground. The mosaics are variously thought to represent the gardens of Paradise and trophies of Muslim victories offered to God. Though the decorative program is extraordinarily rich, the focus of the building is neither art nor architecture but the plain rock it shelters.

9-4 INTERIOR, DOME OF THE ROCK
Israel. Begun 691.

The arches of the inner and outer face of the central arcade are encrusted with golden mosaics, a Byzantine technique adapted for Islamic use to create ornament and inscriptions. The pilgrim must walk around the central space first clockwise and then counterclockwise to read the inscriptions. The carpets and ceilings are modern but probably reflect the original intent.

Credit: © akg-images/Jean-Louis Nou

The Great Mosque of Damascus

Muslim congregations gather on Fridays for regular worship in a mosque. The earliest mosque type followed the model of the Prophet's own house. The **GREAT MOSQUE** of Damascus (**FIG. 9-5**), built in 706 through the patronage of the Umayyad caliph al-Walid I (ruled 705–715), is a large rectangular space divided into a courtyard surrounded by arcaded porticos on three sides and a broad hypostyle prayer hall oriented toward Mecca. One of the hallmarks of the early hypostyle plan is its system of repeated bays and aisles that can easily be extended as the congregation grows in size. Another characteristic feature is the incorporation of large **minarets** (tall towers from which the faithful are called to prayer) that stand as powerful signs of Islam's presence in the city.

The **qibla** wall—the wall of the prayer hall that is closest to Mecca—included a *mihrab* niche, indicating the direction toward which prayer should be oriented. In the Great Mosque of Damascus, the *qibla* wall is given heightened importance by a perpendicular nave crowned by a dome and intersecting the three long aisles of the prayer hall to mark the axis that extends from the courtyard entrance to the *mihrab*. The *mihrab* (for a fourteenth-century example, SEE FIG. 9-22) belongs to the historical tradition of niches that signify a holy place—the Torah shrine in a synagogue, the frame for sculptures of gods or ancestors in Roman architecture, and the apse in a Christian church.

The design of the Damascus mosque and the architectural forms that compose it recall Roman and Byzantine architecture. An ancient Roman sanctuary platform was

9-5 VIEW FROM ABOVE OF THE GREAT MOSQUE, DAMASCUS
Syria. 706.

Credit: © akg-images/Gerard Degeorge

actually reused for its foundation, and Roman columns and carved stonework were incorporated into the building fabric during its construction. But the lavish glass mosaics encrusting the interior courtyard arcades (FIG. 9-6)—portraying lush landscapes and elaborate cityscapes—date from the period of Umayyad construction and were probably created by Byzantine artists from Constantinople.

9-6 MOSAICS ON THE COURTYARD ARCADE OF THE GREAT MOSQUE, DAMASCUS
Syria. 706–715.

Credit: © age fotostock/Mondadori Portfolio/Luca Mozzati

The Great Mosque of Cordoba

When the Umayyads were toppled in 750, a survivor of the dynasty, Abd al-Rahman I (ruled 756–788), fled across north Africa into southern Spain (al-Andalus) where with the support of Muslim settlers he established himself as the provincial ruler, or emir. This newly transplanted Umayyad dynasty ruled in Spain from its capital in Cordoba (756–1031). The Hispano-Umayyads were noted patrons of the arts, and one of the finest surviving examples of Umayyad architecture is the Great Mosque of Cordoba (**FIGS. 9-7, 9-8**).

In 785, the Umayyad conquerors began building the Cordoba mosque on the site of a Christian church built by the Visigoths, the pre-Islamic rulers of Spain. The choice of site was both practical—the Muslims had already been renting space within the church—and symbolic, an appropriation of place (similar to the Dome of the Rock) that affirmed their presence. Later rulers expanded the

building three times, and today the walls enclose an area of about 620 by 460 feet, about a third of which is the courtyard. This patio was planted with fruit trees beginning in the early ninth century; today orange trees seasonally fill the space with color and sweet scent. Inside, the proliferation of pattern in the repeated columns and double flying arches is both colorful and dramatic. The marble columns and capitals in the hypostyle prayer hall were recycled from the Christian church that had formerly occupied the site, as well as from classical buildings in the region, which had been a wealthy Roman province. The mosque's interior incorporates *spolia* (reused) columns of slightly varying heights. There are two tiers of arches, one over the other, above these columns, the upper tier springing from rectangular piers that rise from the columns. This double-tiered design dramatically increases the height of the interior space, inspiring a sense of awe. The distinctively shaped **horseshoe arches**—a form known from Roman times and favored by the Visigoths—came to be

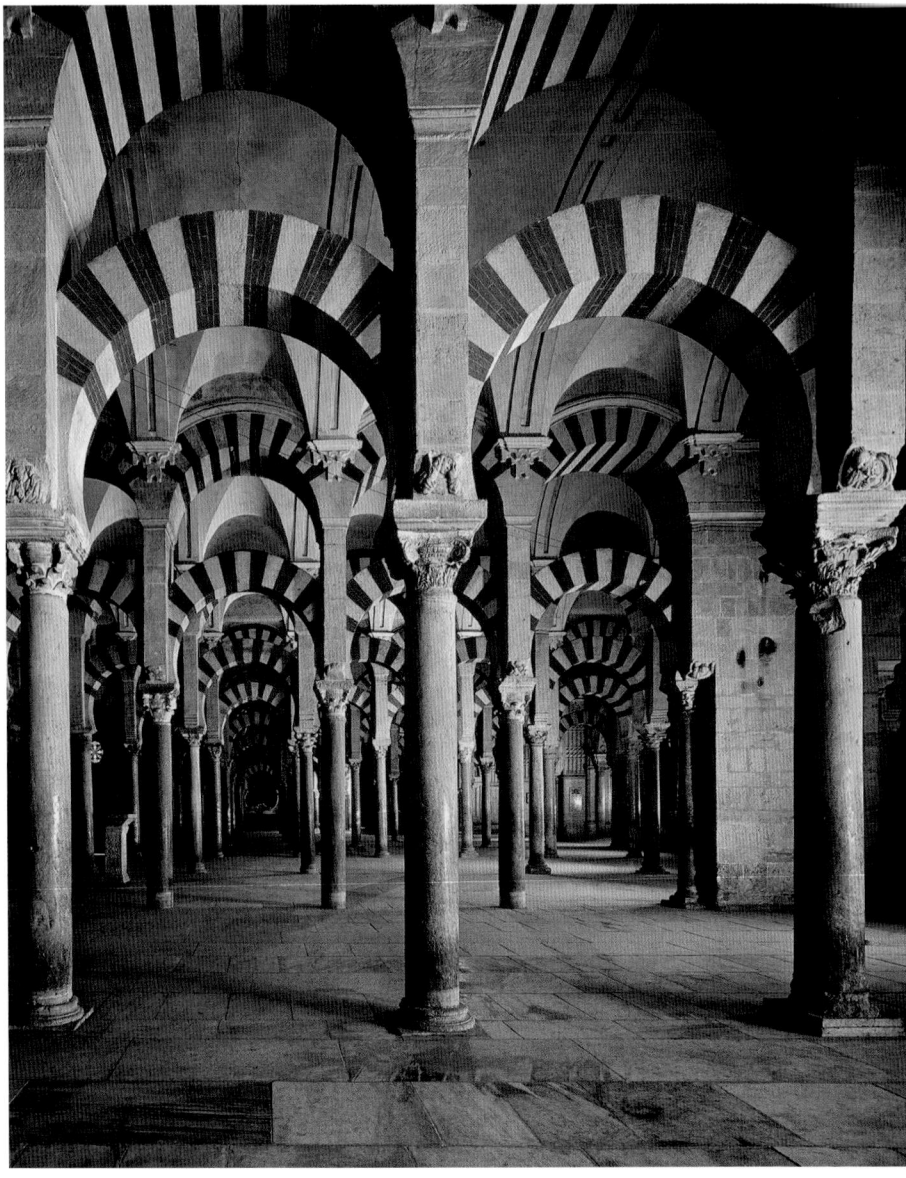

9-7 PRAYER HALL, GREAT MOSQUE, CORDOBA

Spain. Begun 785/786.

Credit: © Raffaello Bencini/Archivi Alinari, Firenze

Elements of Architecture
ARCHES

The simple **semicircular arch**, inherited from the Romans and Byzantines, has a single center point that is level with the points from which the arch springs.

Credit: Kathy Mrozek

The **horseshoe arch** pre-dates Islam but became the prevalent arch form in the West (SEE FIG. 9–7). The center point is above the level of the arch's springing point, so that it pinches inward above the capital.

The **pointed arch**, introduced after the beginning of Islam, has two (sometimes four) center points, the points generating different circles that overlap (SEE FIG. 9–16).

A **keel arch** has flat sides, and slopes where other arches are curved. It culminates at a pointed apex (SEE FIG. 9–22).

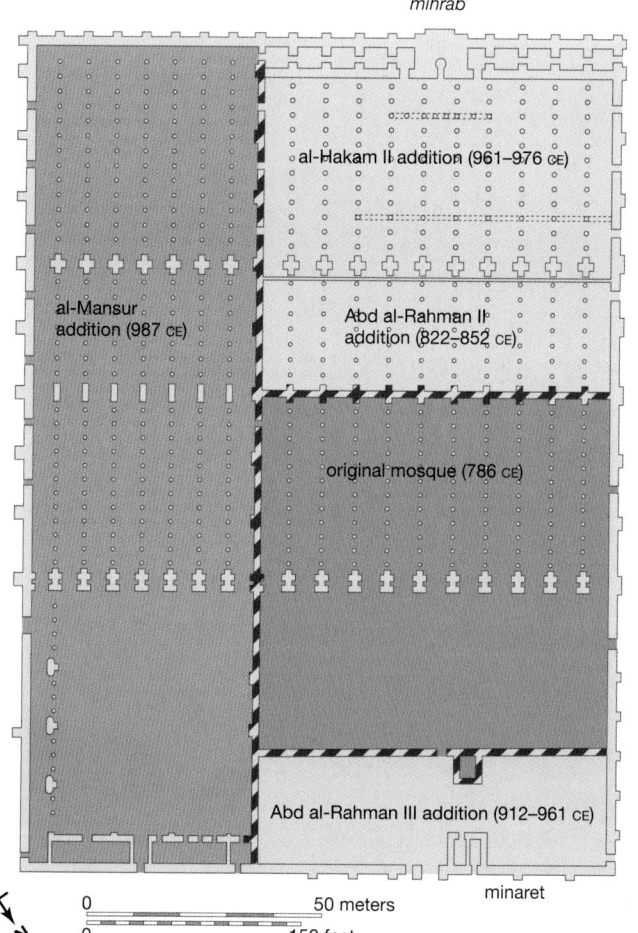

mihrab

al-Hakam II addition (961–976 CE)

al-Mansur addition (987 CE)

Abd al-Rahman II addition (822–852 CE)

original mosque (786 CE)

Abd al-Rahman III addition (912–961 CE)

0   50 meters
0   150 feet

minaret

9-8 PLAN OF THE GREAT MOSQUE, CORDOBA
Begun 785/786.

closely associated with Islamic architecture in the West (see "Arches" above). Another distinctive feature of these arches, adopted from Roman and Byzantine precedents, is the alternation of white stone and red-brick voussoirs forming the curved arch. This mixture of materials may have helped the building withstand earthquakes.

In the final century of Umayyad rule, Cordoba emerged as a major commercial and intellectual hub and a flourishing center for the arts, surpassing Christian European cities in science, literature, and philosophy. As a sign of this new wealth, prestige, and power, Abd al-Rahman III (ruled 912–961) boldly reclaimed the title of caliph in 929. He and his son al-Hakam II (ruled 961–976) made the Great Mosque a focus of patronage, commissioning costly and luxurious renovations such as a new *mihrab* with three bays in front of it (FIG. 9-9). These capped the **maqsura**, an enclosure in front of the *mihrab* reserved for the ruler and other dignitaries, which became a feature of congregational mosques after an assassination attempt on one of the Umayyad rulers. A *minbar* formerly stood by the *mihrab* as the place for the prayer leader and as a symbol of

9-9 DOME IN FRONT OF THE MIHRAB, GREAT MOSQUE, CORDOBA

965.

Credit: © Raffaello Bencini/Archivi Alinari, Firenze

Minbar from the Kutubiya Mosque in Marrakesh

In the Kutubiya Mosque, the principal mosque of Marrakesh, Morocco, survives an exceptionally exquisite twelfth-century wooden **minbar** made originally for the Booksellers' Mosque in Marrakesh (**FIG. 9-10**). It consists of a staircase from which the weekly sermon was delivered to the congregation (SEE FIG. 9-1), and it is completely covered with intricate ornament. The sides are paneled in wooden marquetry with strapwork in a geometric pattern of eight-pointed stars and elongated hexagons inlaid with ivory (see "Ornament" on page 279). Wood carved in swirling vines fills the areas between the strapwork. Reflecting the arcades of its original architectural context, the risers of the stairs represent horseshoe arches (see "Arches" on page 277) resting on columns with ivory capitals and bases. This *minbar* is much like others across the Islamic world, but those at the Kutubiya Mosque and the Great Mosque of Cordoba were the finest, according to Ibn Marzuq (1311–1379), a distinguished preacher who had given sermons from 48 *minbars*.

9-10 MINBAR

From the Kutubiya Mosque, Marrakesh, Morocco. 1125–1130. Wood and ivory, 12′8″ × 11′4″ × 2′10″ (3.86 × 3.46 × 0.87 m). Badi Palace Museum, Marrakesh.

Credit: © akg-images/Erich Lessing

authority. The melon-shaped, ribbed dome over the central bay may be a metaphor for the celestial canopy. It seems to float upon a web of crisscrossing arches, the complexity of the design reflecting the Islamic interest in mathematics and geometry, not purely as abstract concepts but as sources for artistic inspiration. Lushly patterned mosaics with inscriptions, geometric motifs, and stylized vegetation clothe both this dome and the *mihrab* below in brilliant color and gold. These were installed by a Byzantine master sent by the emperor in Constantinople, who brought with him boxes of small glazed ceramic and glass pieces (tesserae). Such artistic exchange is emblematic of the interconnectedness of the medieval Mediterranean—through trade, diplomacy, and competition.

Art and its Contexts
ORNAMENT

Islamic art delights in complex ornament that sheathes surfaces, distracting the eye from the underlying structure or physical form.

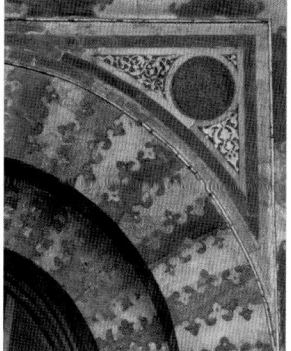

Credit: © akg-images/François Guénet

ablaq masonry (Madrasa-Mausoleum-Mosque of Sultan Hasan, Cairo; SEE FIG. 9–16) juxtaposes stone of contrasting colors. The ornamental effect is enhanced here by the interlocking jigsaw shape of the blocks, called **joggled voussoirs**.

Credit: © Alen Laguta/123RF

cut tile (Shah-i Zinda, Samarkand; SEE FIG. 9–23), made up of dozens of individually cut ceramic tile pieces fitted precisely together, emphasizes the clarity of the colored shapes.

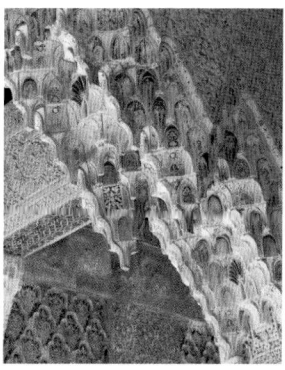

Credit: © VLADJ55/Shutterstock

muqarnas (Palace of the Lions, Alhambra, Granada; SEE FIG. 9–21) consist of small nichelike components, usually stacked in multiples as successive, non-load-bearing units in arches, cornices, and domes, hiding the transition from the vertical to the horizontal plane.

Credit: © akg Images/Erich Lessing

wooden strapwork (Kutubiya *minbar*, Marrakesh; SEE FIG. 9–10) assembles finely cut wooden pieces to create the appearance of geometrically interlacing ribbons, often framing smaller panels of carved wood and inlaid ivory or mother-of-pearl (shell).

Credit: © B.O'Kane/Alamy Stock Photo

mosaic (Dome of the Rock, Jerusalem; SEE FIG. 9–4) is comprised of thousands of small glass or glazed ceramic tesserae set on a plaster ground. Here the luminous white circular shapes are mother-of-pearl.

Credit: Loisclare/Fotolia

water (Court of the Myrtles, Alhambra, Granada) as a fluid architectural element reflects surrounding architecture, adds visual dynamism and sound, and, running in channels between areas, unites disparate spaces.

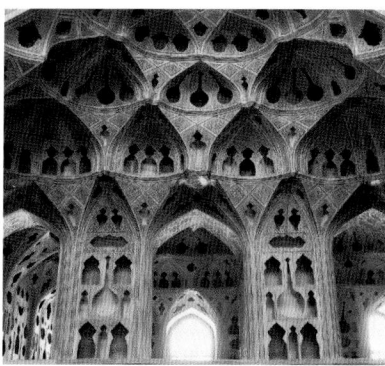

Credit: Credit: K.M. Westermann

chini khana (Ali Qapu Pavilion, Isfahan)—literally "china cabinet"—is a panel of niches, sometimes providing actual shelving, but used here for its contrast of material and void which reverses the typical figure–ground relationship.

Calligraphy

From the beginning, Arabic script was held in high esteem in Islamic society. Reverence for the Qur'an as the word of God extended—and continues to extend—by association to the act of writing itself, and **calligraphy** (the art of the finely written word) became one of the glories of Islamic art. Writing was not limited to books and documents but—as we have seen—was displayed on the walls of buildings and will appear on works in many media throughout the history of Islamic art. The written word played two roles: It could convey information about a building or object, describing its beauty or naming its patron, and it could delight the eye as a manifestation of beauty.

Arabic script is written from right to left, and a letter's form varies depending on its position in a word. With its rhythmic interplay between verticals and horizontals, Arabic lends itself to many variations. Calligraphers enjoyed the highest status of all artists in Islamic society. Apprentice scribes had to learn secret formulas for inks and paints and become skilled in the proper ways to sit, breathe, and manipulate their tools. They also had to absorb the complex literary traditions and number symbolism that had developed in Islamic culture. Their training was long and arduous, but unlike other artists, who were generally anonymous in the early centuries of Islam, outstanding calligraphers received public recognition.

Formal **Kufic** script (after Kufa, a city in Iraq) is blocky and angular, with strong upright strokes and long horizontals. It may have developed first for carved or woven inscriptions where clarity and practicality of execution were important. Most early Qur'ans were horizontal in orientation and had large Kufic letters creating only three to five lines per page. Visual clarity was essential because one book was often shared simultaneously by multiple readers. A page from a ninth-century Syrian Qur'an exemplifies the style common from the eighth to the tenth century (**FIG. 9-11**). Red diacritical marks (pronunciation guides) accent the dark brown ink; the surah ("chapter") title is embedded in the burnished ornament at the bottom of the sheet. Instead of page numbers, the brilliant gold of the framed words and the knoblike projection in the left-hand margin mark chapter breaks.

By the tenth century, more than 20 cursive scripts had come into use. They were standardized by Ibn Muqla (d. 940), an Abbasid official who fixed the proportions of the letters in each script and devised a method for teaching calligraphy that is still in use today. The Qur'an was usually written on parchment (treated sheep- or calfskin) and vellum (a fine parchment made of calfskin). Paper was first manufactured in Central Asia during the mid eighth century, having been introduced earlier by Buddhist monks. Muslims learned how to make high-quality, rag-based paper and eventually established their own paper mills. By about 1000, paper had largely replaced the more costly parchment for everything but Qur'an manuscripts, which adopted the new medium much later. It was a change as momentous as that brought about by movable type or the Internet, affecting not only the appearance of books but also their content. The inexpensive new medium sparked a surge in book production and a proliferation of increasingly elaborate and decorative cursive scripts, which had generally superseded Kufic by the thirteenth century.

Kufic script remained popular, however, in other media. It was the sole decoration on a type of white pottery made from the tenth century onward in and around the region of Nishapur (in Khurasan, in present-day Iran) and Samarkand (in present-day Uzbekistan) known as epigraphic ware. These elegant earthenware bowls and plates employ a clear lead glaze over a painted black inscription on a white slip ground (**FIG. 9-12**). Here the script's horizontals and verticals have been elongated to

9-11 PAGE FROM THE QUR'AN
Surah 2:286 and title of surah 3 in Kufic script. Syria. 9th century. Black ink, pigments, and gold on vellum; 8⅜ × 11⅛″ (21.8 × 29.2 cm). Metropolitan Museum of Art, New York. Rogers Fund, 1937. (37.99.2).

9-12 PLATE WITH KUFIC BORDER
From Khurasan. 10th–12th century. Earthenware with white
and black slip, and lead glaze; diameter 14½" (33.8 cm).
Musée du Louvre, Paris.

Credit: Photo © RMN/Thierry Ollivier

fill the plate's rim, stressing the letters' verticality in such a way that they seem to radiate from the bold spot at the center of the circle. The fine quality of the lettering indicates that a calligrapher furnished the model. The inscription translates as "Knowledge [or magnanimity]: the beginning of it is bitter to taste, but the end is sweeter than honey," an apt choice for tableware made to appeal to an educated patron. Inscriptions on Islamic ceramics provide a storehouse of such popular aphorisms.

Developments in Ceramics

In the ninth century, Islamic potters developed a means of producing a lustrous metallic surface on their ceramics. They may have learned the technique from Islamic glassmakers in Syria and Egypt, who had produced luster-painted vessels a century earlier. First the potters applied a paint laced with silver, copper, or gold oxides to the surface of already fired and glazed tiles or vessels. In a second firing with relatively low heat and less oxygen, these oxides burned away to produce a reflective, metallic sheen. The finished **lusterware** resembled precious metal. Lusterware tiles dated 862/863 decorated the *mihrab* of the Great Mosque at Kairouan. At first a carefully guarded secret of Abbasid potters in Iraq, lusterware soon spread throughout the Islamic world to North Africa, Egypt, Iran, Syria, and Spain.

Early potters covered the entire surface with luster, but soon they began to use luster to paint patterns using geometric designs, foliate motifs, animals, and human figures in brown, red, purple, and/or green. Most common was monochrome lusterware in shades of brown, as in this tenth-century jar from Iraq (**FIG. 9-13**). The form of the vessel is emphasized by the distribution of decorative motifs—the lip and neck are outlined with a framed horizontal band of scalloped motifs, the shoulder singled out with dots within circles (known as the "peacock's eye"

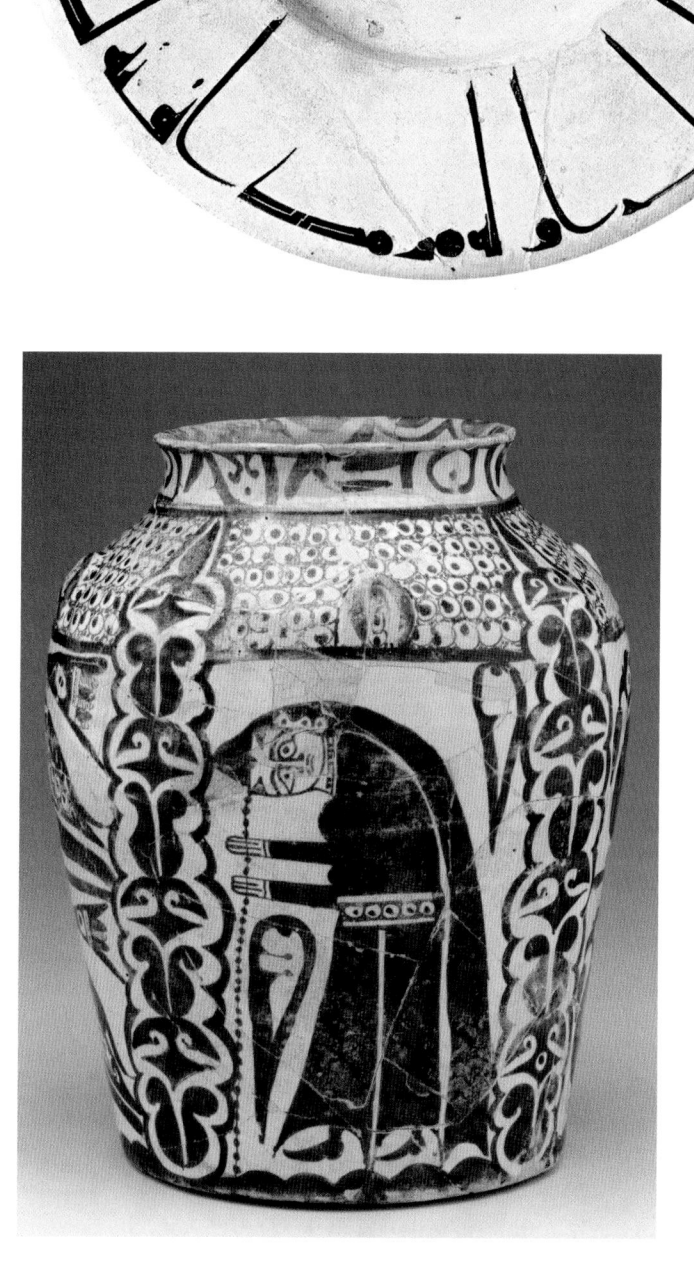

9-13 LUSTERWARE JAR
Iraq. 10th century. Glazed earthenware with luster, 11⅛ × 9⅛"
(28.2 × 23.2 cm). Freer Gallery of Art, Smithsonian Institution,
Washington, DC.

Credit: Bridgeman Images

9–14 MINA'I BOWL WITH BAHRAM GUR AND AZADA
Iran. 12th–13th century. *Mina'i* ware (stoneware with polychrome in-glaze and overglaze), diameter 8½″ (21.6 cm). Metropolitan Museum of Art, New York.

Credit: © 2016 Image copyright The Metropolitan Museum of Art/Art Resource/ Scala, Florence

foolishly belittled his skills as a hunter. To prove his peerless marksmanship, the king pins with his arrow the hoof and ear of a gazelle that had lifted its hind leg to scratch an itch. In this continuous narrative (representing multiple scenes from the same story within a single composition), the subsequent action is also portrayed: Azada trampled to death under the camel after Bahram Gur had pushed her from her mount as punishment for mocking him.

motif), and the height emphasized by boldly ornamented vertical strips with undulating outlines moving up toward pointed tops and dividing the surface of the jar into quadrants. Emphasis, however, is placed on representations of enigmatic human figures dressed in dark, hooded garments. They stand in bended postures and hold beaded strands while looking directly out toward viewers, engaged in an activity whose meaning and significance remains a mystery to us.

MINA'I WARE   From the beginning, Islamic civilization in Iran was characterized by the production of exceptionally sophisticated and strikingly beautiful luxury ceramic ware. During the twelfth century, Persian potters developed a technique of multicolor ceramic overglaze painting known as *mina'i* ware, the Persian word for "enamel" (**FIG. 9-14**). *Mina'i* bowl, plate, and beaker decoration often references stories and subjects popular with potential owners. The circular scene at the bottom of this bowl is drawn from the royal life of Bahram Gur (Sasanian king Bahram V, ruled 420–438), legendary in the Islamic world for his prowess in love and hunting; this episode combines both. Bahram Gur rides proudly atop a large camel next to his favorite, the ill-fated lute player Azada, who has

Regional Dynasties

How do Islamic art and architecture develop in Egypt, Spain, Iran, Uzbekistan, and Afghanistan?

The Abbasid caliphate began a slow disintegration in the ninth century, and power in the Islamic world became distributed among more or less independent regional rulers. During the eleventh century, the Saljuqs, a Turkic people, swept from north of the Caspian Sea into Khurasan and took Baghdad in 1055, becoming the virtual rulers of the Abbasid lands. The Saljuqs united most of Iran and Iraq, establishing a dynasty that endured from 1037/38 to 1194. A branch of the dynasty, the Saljuqs of Rum, ruled much of Anatolia (Turkey) from the late eleventh to the beginning of the fourteenth century. The central and eastern Islamic world suffered a dramatic rift in the early thirteenth century when the nomadic Mongols—non-Muslims led by Genghiz Khan (ruled 1206–1227) and his successors—attacked northern China, Central Asia, and ultimately Iran. The Mongols captured Baghdad in 1258 and encountered weak resistance until they reached Egypt, where they were firmly defeated by the new ruler of the Mamluk dynasty (1250–1517). In Spain, the borders of Islamic territory were gradually pushed southward by Christian forces until the rule of the last Muslim dynasty there, the Nasrids (1230–1492), was ended. Morocco was ruled by the Berber Marinids from the mid thirteenth century until 1465.

Although the religion of Islam remained a dominant and unifying force throughout these developments, the history of later Islamic society and culture reflects largely regional phenomena. Only a few works have been selected here and in Chapter 24 to characterize Islamic art, and they by no means provide a comprehensive history.

The new dynasties built on a grand scale, expanding their patronage from mosques and palaces to include new functional buildings such as tombs, **madrasas** (colleges for religious and legal studies), public fountains, and urban hostels. To encourage long-distance trade, remote caravanserais (inns) were constructed for traveling merchants. A distinguishing characteristic of architecture in the later period is its complexity. Multiple building types were now combined in large and diverse complexes supported by perpetual endowments (called *waqf*) that funded not only the building, but its administration and maintenance. Increasingly, these complexes included the patron's own tomb, thus giving visual prominence to the act of individual patronage and expressing personal identity through commemoration. A new plan emerged, organized around a central courtyard framed by four large **iwans** (large vaulted halls with rectangular plans and monumental arched openings); this four-*iwan* plan was used for schools, palaces, and especially mosques.

The Mamluks in Egypt

Beginning in the eleventh century, Muslim rulers and wealthy individuals endowed hundreds of charitable complexes that displayed piety as well as personal wealth and status. The combined *madrasa*-mausoleum-mosque complex established in mid-fourteenth-century Cairo by the Mamluk Sultan Hasan (**FIG. 9-15**) is a splendid example. A deflected entrance—askew from the building's orientation—leads from the street, through a dark corridor, into a central, well-lit courtyard of majestic proportions. The complex has a classic four-*iwan* plan, each *iwan* serving as a classroom for students following a different branch of study who are housed in a surrounding, multi-storied cluster of tiny rooms.

The sumptuous *qibla iwan* served as the prayer hall for the complex (**FIG. 9-16**). Its walls are ornamented with typically Mamluk panels of sharply contrasting marbles (*ablaq* masonry, see "Ornament" on page 279) that culminate in a doubly recessed *mihrab* framed by slightly pointed arches on columns. The marble blocks of the arches are ingeniously joined in interlocking pieces called joggled voussoirs. The paneling is surmounted by a wide band of

9-15 PLAN (A) AND DRAWING OF EXTERIOR (B) OF THE SULTAN HASAN MADRASA-MAUSOLEUM-MOSQUE COMPLEX, CAIRO

1356–1363.

Credit: Robert Hillenbrand, *Islamic Architecture: Form, Function and Meaning*, 1994, Edinburgh University Press, p.195

Kufic script in stucco set against a background of scrolling vines, both the text and the abundant foliage referring to the paradise that is promised to the faithful. Next to the *mihrab*, an elaborate *minbar* stands behind a platform for reading the Qur'an. Just beyond the *qibla iwan* is the patron's monumental domed tomb, ostentatiously asserting his identity with the architectural complex. The Sultan Hasan complex is vast in scale and opulent in decoration, but money was not a problem: The project was financed by the estates of victims of the bubonic plague that had raged in Cairo from 1348 to 1350.

GLASS, METALWORK, AND BOOK ARTS Partly because the mosque in the Sultan Hasan complex—and many smaller establishments—required hundreds of lamps, glassmaking was a booming industry in Egypt and Syria. Made of ordinary sand and ash, glass is the most ethereal of materials. The ancient Egyptians were producing glassware by the second millennium BCE (see Chapter 3), and the tools and techniques for making it have changed little since then. Islamic artists also used glass for beakers and bottles, but lamps, lit from within by oil and wick, glowed with special brilliance inside expansive architectural interiors (see "Closer Look" opposite).

Islamic metalsmiths enlivened the surface of vessels with scrolls, interlacing designs, human and animal figures, and calligraphic inscriptions. A shortage of silver in the mid twelfth century prompted the development of inlaid brasswork that used the more precious metal

sparingly, as in this basin (**FIG. 9-17**), among the finest works of metal produced by a Muslim artist. The dynamic surface is crowded with overlapping figures in vigorous poses that nevertheless remain distinct by means of hatching, modeling, and framing. The outside is divided into three bands. The upper and lower depict running animals, and the center shows scenes of horsemen flanked by attendants, soldiers, and falcons—scenes of the princely arts of horsemanship and hunting. In later metalwork, such pictorial cycles were replaced by elegant large-scale inscriptions.

The art of book production had flourished from the first century of Islam because an emphasis on the study of the Qur'an promoted a high level of literacy among both men and women. With the availability of paper, books on a wide range of religious as well as secular subjects became available, although since they were hand-copied, they always remained fairly costly. (Muslims did not adopt the printing press until the eighteenth and nineteenth centuries.) Libraries, often associated with *madrasas*, were endowed by members of the educated elite. Books made for royal patrons had luxurious bindings and highly embellished pages, the result of workshop collaboration between noted calligraphers and illustrators.

Mamluk manuscript illustrators executed intricate nonfigural designs filled with sumptuous botanical ornamentation for Qur'ans. As in architectural decoration, the exuberant ornament adheres to a strict geometric organization. On an impressive frontispiece, the design radiates on each page from a 16-pointed starburst, filling the central

9-16 QIBLA WALL WITH MIHRAB AND MINBAR
Sultan Hasan Madrasa-Mausoleum-Mosque Complex, Cairo. 1356–1363.

9-17 Muhammad Ibn al-Zain
BAPTISTERY OF ST. LOUIS

Syria or Egypt. c. 1300. Brass inlaid with silver and gold, 8¾ × 19¾″ (22.2 × 50.2 cm). Musée du Louvre, Paris.

Judging by its emblems and coats of arms, this beautifully crafted basin, with its princely themes of hunting and horsemanship, was made for an unidentified, aristocratic Mamluk patron. However, it became known as the Baptistery of St. Louis because it was acquired by the French sometime before the end of the fourteenth century (long after the era of St. Louis [king Louis IX, ruled 1226–1270]) and used for royal baptisms.

Credit: Photo © RMN-Grand Palais (Musée du Louvre)/Franck Raux

A Closer Look

A MAMLUK GLASS OIL LAMP

The inscription on the lamp's flared neck is a quotation from the Qur'an (surah 24:35): "God is the light of the heavens and the earth. His light might be compared to a niche that enshrines a lamp, the lamp within a crystal of star-like brilliance."

During the thirteenth and fourteenth centuries, Mamluk glassmakers in Egypt and Syria imparted an elegant thinness to their vessels through refined glass-blowing and molding techniques. The blue, red, and gold enamel used to decorate the lamp was affixed to the glass surface by reheating the painted vessel.

This emblem of a cup in a medallion is called a blazon. It identifies the commissioner of the lamp as a cup-bearer to the sultan. The use of blazons traveled to western Europe during the crusades, where it evolved into the system we know as heraldry.

This inscription around the body of the lamp identifies the patron, Sayf al-Din Qawsun (d. 1342), emir and cup-bearer of the Mamluk sultan al-Nasir Muhammad (ruled 1293–1341). It was probably intended for one of the patron's architectural commissions in Cairo.

The artist, 'Ali ibn Muhammad al-Barmaki, signed this work discreetly on the upper band of the foot, asking for God's protection.

9-18 'Ali ibn Muhammad al-Barmaki **GLASS OIL LAMP**

Cairo, Egypt. c. 1329–1335. Blown glass, polychrome enamel, and gold; diameter 9⅜″ (23.89 cm), height 14″ (35.56 cm). Metropolitan Museum of Art, New York.

Credit: © 2016. Image copyright The Metropolitan Museum of Art/Art Resource/Scala, Florence

9-19 QUR'AN FRONTISPIECE
Cairo. c. 1368. Ink, pigments, and gold on paper, 24 × 18″
(61 × 45.7 cm). National Library, Cairo. MS. 7.

The Qur'an to which this page belonged was donated in 1369 by
Sultan Shaban to the *madrasa* established by his mother. A close
collaboration between illuminator and scribe can be seen here and
throughout the manuscript.

Credit: From: *Qur'ans of the Mamluks* by David James, fig. 132, p. 132.
Courtesy of Alexandria Press

square (**FIG. 9-19**). The surrounding frames contain interlacing foliage and stylized flowers that embellish the holy
scripture. The page's resemblance to court carpets was not
coincidental. Designers often worked in more than one
medium, leaving the execution of their efforts to specialized artisans. In addition to religious works, scribes copied and recopied famous secular texts—scientific treatises,
manuals of all kinds, stories, and especially poetry. Painters supplied illustrations for these books and also created
individual small-scale paintings—miniatures—that were
collected by the wealthy and placed in albums.

The Nasrids in Spain

Muslim patrons also spent lavishly on luxurious palaces
set in gardens. The Alhambra in Granada, in southeastern
Spain, is an outstanding and sumptuous example. Built
on the hilltop site of an early Islamic fortress, this palace
complex was the seat of the Nasrids (1232–1492), the last
Spanish Muslim dynasty, by which time Islamic territory

had shrunk from covering most of the Iberian peninsula
to covering only the region around Granada. To the conquering Christians at the end of the fifteenth century, the
Alhambra represented the epitome of luxury. Thereafter,
they preserved the complex as much to commemorate the
defeat of Islam as for its beauty. Essentially a small town
extending for about half a mile along the crest of a high hill
overlooking Granada, it included government buildings,
royal residences, gates, mosques, baths, servants' quarters,
barracks, stables, a mint, workshops, and gardens. Much
of what one sees at the site today was built in the fourteenth century or by Christian patrons in later centuries.

The Alhambra offered dramatic views of the settled valley and snowcapped mountains around it, while enclosing
gardens within its courtyards. One of these is the **COURT
OF THE LIONS**, which stood at the heart of the so-called Palace of the Lions, the private retreat of Sultan Muhammad V
(ruled 1354–1359 and 1362–1391). The Court of the Lions is
divided into quadrants by cross-axial walkways—a garden
form called a *chahar bagh*. The walkways carry channels that
meet at a central marble fountain held aloft on the backs
of 12 stone lions (**FIG. 9-20**). Water animates the fountain,
filling the courtyard with the sound of its abundance. In
an adjacent courtyard, the Court of the Myrtles, a basin's
round shape responds to the naturally concentric ripples of
the water that spouts from a central jet (see "Ornament" on
page 279). Water has a practical role in the irrigation of gardens, but here it is raised to the level of an art form.

The Court of the Lions is encircled by an arcade of
stucco arches embellished with **muqarnas** (nichelike components stacked in tiers, see "Ornament" on page 279) and
supported on single columns or clusters of two and three.
Second-floor **miradors**—windows that frame intentional
views—look over the courtyard, which was originally
either gardened or more likely paved, with aromatic citrus
confined to corner plantings. Protected from view by the
latticework screens in these windows, the women of the
court, who did not appear in public, would watch the activities of the men below. At one end of the Palace of the Lions,
a particularly magnificent *mirador* looks out onto a large,
lower garden and the plain below. From here, the sultan literally oversaw the fertile valley that was his kingdom.

Pavilions used for dining and musical performances
open off the Court of the Lions. One of these, the so-called
Hall of the Abencerrajes, in addition to having excellent
acoustics, is covered by a ceiling of dazzling geometrical
complexity and exquisitely carved stucco (**FIG. 9-21**). The
star-shaped vault is formed by a honeycomb of clustered
muqarnas arches that alternate with corner squinches themselves filled with more *muqarnas*. The square room thus
rises to an eight-pointed star, pierced by 16 windows, that
culminates in a burst of *muqarnas* floating high overhead—
a dematerialized architectural form, perceivable and yet
ultimately unknowable, like the heavens themselves.

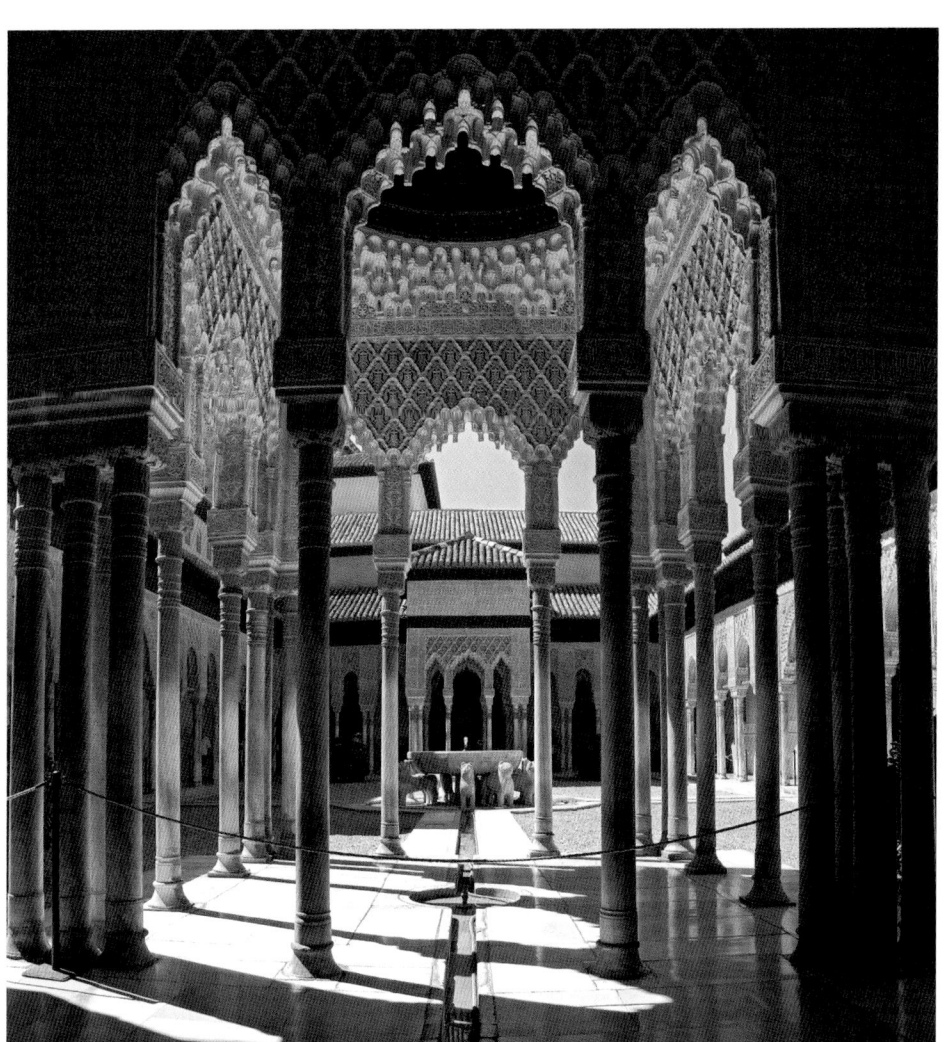

9-20 COURT OF THE LIONS, ALHAMBRA

Granada, Spain. 1354–1391.

Credit: Rafael Ramirez/Fotolia

9-21 MUQARNAS DOME, HALL OF THE ABENCERRAJES, PALACE OF THE LIONS, ALHAMBRA

Granada, Spain. 1354–1391.

The stucco *muqarnas* (stalactite) ornament does not support the dome but is actually suspended from it, composed of some 5,000 individual plaster pieces. Of mesmerizing complexity, the vault's effect can be perceived, but its structure cannot be fully comprehended.

Credit: © Roberto Tetsuo Okamura/ Shutterstock

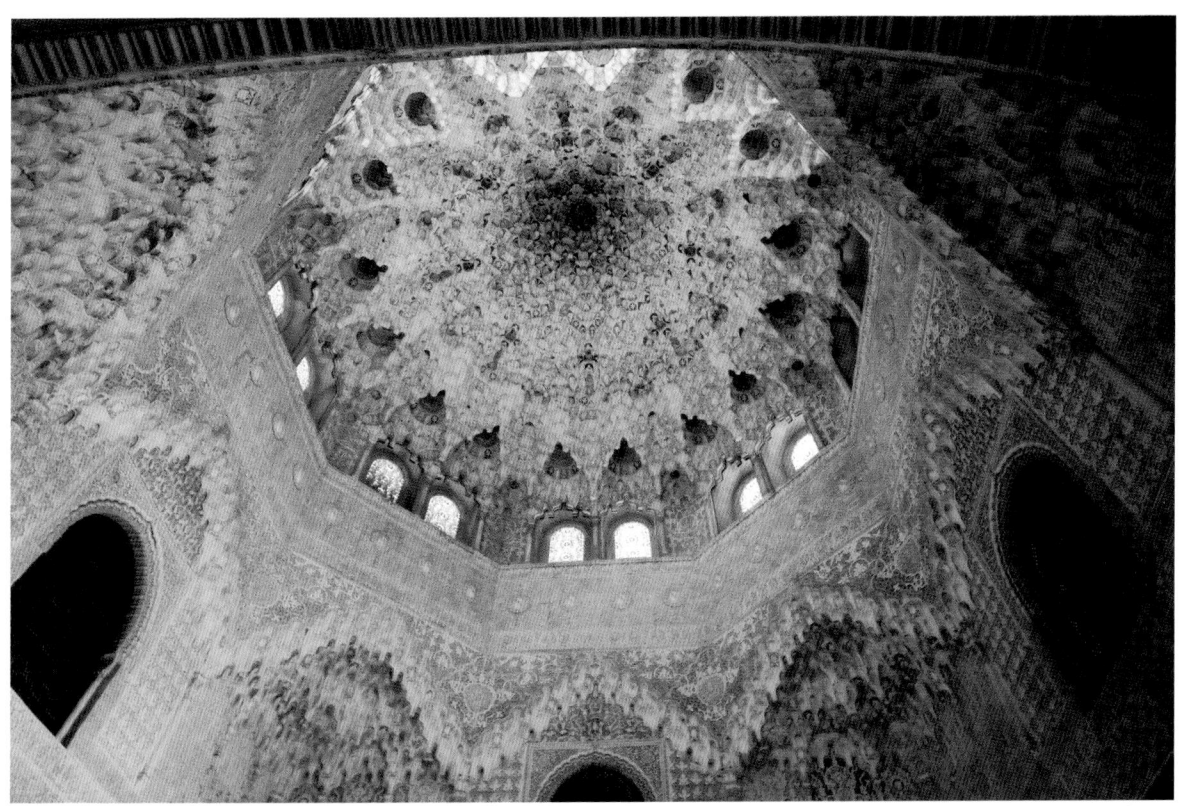

The Timurids in Iran, Uzbekistan, and Afghanistan

The Mongol invasions brought devastation and political instability, but also renewal and artistic exchange that provided the foundation for successor dynasties with a decidedly Eastern identity. One of the empires to emerge after the Mongols was the vast Timurid Empire (1370–1506), which conquered Iran, Central Asia, and the northern part of South Asia. Its founder, Timur (known in the West as Tamerlane), was a Mongol descendant, his lineage strengthened through marriage to a descendant of Genghiz Khan. Timur made his capital at Samarkand (in present-day Uzbekistan), which he embellished

9-22 TILE MOSAIC MIHRAB

From the Madrasa Imami, Isfahan, Iran. Founded 1354. Glazed and cut tiles, 11′3″ × 9′5¹¹⁄₁₆″ (3.43 × 2.89 m). Metropolitan Museum of Art, New York. Harris Brisbane Dick Fund. (39.20).

This *mihrab* has three inscriptions: the outer inscription, in cursive, contains Qur'anic verses (surah 9) that describe the duties of believers and the Five Pillars of Islam. Framing the niche's pointed arch, a Kufic inscription contains sayings of the Prophet. In the center, a panel with a line in Kufic and another in cursive states: "The mosque is the house of every pious person."

by means of the forcible relocation of expert artists from the areas he conquered. Because the empire's compass was vast, Timurid art could integrate Chinese, Persian, Turkic, and Mediterranean artistic ideas into a Mongol base. Its architecture is characterized by axial symmetry, tall double-shelled domes (an inner dome capped by an outer shell of much larger proportions), modular planning with rhythmically repeated elements, and brilliant cobalt blue, turquoise, and white glazed ceramics. Although the empire itself lasted only 100 years after the death of Timur, its legacy endured in the art of the later Safavid dynasty in Iran and the Mughals of South Asia.

Made during a period of uncertainty as Iran shifted from Mongol to Timurid rule, this *mihrab* (1354), originally from a *madrasa* in Isfahan, is one of the finest examples of architectural ceramic decoration from this era (**FIG. 9-22**). More than 11 feet tall, it was made by painstakingly cutting each individual piece of tile, including the pieces making up the letters on the curving surface of the keel-profiled niche. The color scheme—white against turquoise and cobalt blue with accents of dark yellow and green—was typical of this type of decoration, as were the harmonious, dense, contrasting patterns of organic and geometric forms. The cursive inscription of the outer frame is rendered in elegant white lettering on a blue ground, while the Kufic inscription bordering the pointed arch reverses these colors for a striking contrast.

Near Samarkand, the preexisting Shah-i Zinda ("Living King") **FUNERARY COMPLEX** was adopted for the tombs of Timurid family members, especially princesses, in the late fourteenth and fifteenth centuries (**FIG. 9-23**). The mausolea are arrayed along a central avenue that descends from the tomb of Qutham b. Abbas (a cousin of the Prophet and a saint). The women sought burial in the vicinity of the holy man in order to gain *baraka* (blessing) from his presence. Like all Timurid architecture, the tombs reflect modular planning—noticeable in the repeated dome-on-square unit—and a preference for blue glazed tiles. The domes of the individual structures were double-shelled and, for exaggerated effect, stood on high drums inscribed with Qur'anic verses in interwoven Kufic calligraphy. The ornament on the exterior façades consists of an unusually exuberant array of patterns and techniques, from geometry to chinoiserie, and both painted and cut tiles (see "Ornament" on page 279). The tombs reflect a range of individual taste and artistic experimentation that was possible precisely because they were private commissions that served the patrons themselves, rather than the city or state (as in a congregational mosque).

BOOK ARTS One of the great royal centers of Islamic miniature painting was at Herat in western Afghanistan, where a Persian **school of painting** and calligraphy was

9-23 SHAH-I ZINDA FUNERARY COMPLEX
Samarkand, Uzbekistan. Late 14th–15th century.

Timurid princesses were buried here and built many of the tombs. The lively experimentation in varied artistic motifs indicates that women were well versed in the arts and empowered to exercise personal taste.

Credit: © Evgeniy Agarkov/Shutterstock

founded by the Timurids in the early fifteenth century. One of the most famous painters of the Herat School was Kamal al-Din Bihzad (c. 1450–1536/37), who worked under the patronage of Sultan Husayn Bayqara (ruled 1470–1506). When the Safavids supplanted the Timurids in 1506/07 and established their capital at Tabriz in northwestern Iran, Bihzad moved to Tabriz, where he headed the Safavid royal workshop.

Bihzad's key paintings, including his only signed works, appear in a manuscript of the thirteenth-century Persian poet Sa'di's *Bustan* ("Orchard") made for the royal library in 1488. Sa'di's narrative anthology in verse includes the story of Yusuf, the biblical Joseph, whose virtue was proven by resisting seduction by his master Potiphar's wife, named Zulayhka in the Islamic tradition (Genesis 39:6–12; Qur'an 12:23–25). Bihzad's vizualization of this event (**FIG. 9-24**) is one of the masterpieces of Persian narrative painting. The dazzling and elaborate

9-24 Kamal al-Din Bihzad YUSUF FLEEING ZULAYHKA
From a copy of the *Bustan* of Sa'di. Herat, Afghanistan. 1488.
Ink and pigments on paper, approx. 12 × 8½″ (30.5 × 21.5 cm).
National Library, Cairo. (MS Adab Farsi 908, f. 52v).

Credit: © Roland and Sabrina Michaud/akg-images

architectural setting is inspired not by Sa'di's account, but by the Timurid poet Jami's more mystical version of the story (quoted in an architectural frame around the central *iwan* under the two figures), written only five years before Bihzad's painting. Jami sets his story in a seduction palace that Zulayhka had built specifically for this encounter, and into which she leads Yusuf ever inward from room to room, with entrance doors locked as they pass from one room to the next. As the scarlet-garbed Zulayhka lunges to possess him, the fire-haloed Yusuf flees her advances as the doors miraculously open in front of him.

The brilliant, jewel-like color of Bihzad's architectural forms and the exquisite detail with which each is rendered are salient characteristics of his style, as is the dramatic lunge of Zulayhka and Yusuf's balletic escape. The asymmetrical composition depends on a delicately balanced placement of flat screens of colorful ornament and two emphatically three-dimensional architectural features—a projecting balcony to the right and a zigzagging staircase to the left. Bihzad signed this work in a calligraphic panel over a window at upper left.

Art and Architecture of later Empires

What features characterize Islamic art and architecture under the Ottoman and Safavid dynasties?

In the pre-modern era, the introduction of gunpowder for use in cannons and guns caused a shift in military strategy. Isolated lords in lone castles could not withstand gunpowder sieges; power lay not in thick walls but in strong centralized governments that could invest in firepower and train armies in its use. Three great powers emerged in the Islamic world. To the west was the Ottoman Empire (1342–1918), which grew from a small principality in Asia Minor. In spite of setbacks inflicted by the Mongols, the Ottomans ultimately controlled Anatolia, western Iran, Iraq, Syria, Palestine, western Arabia (including Mecca and Medina), northern Africa (excepting Morocco), and part of eastern Europe. In 1453, their stunning capture of Constantinople (ultimately renamed Istanbul) brought the Byzantine Empire to an end. To the east of the Ottomans, Iran was ruled by the Safavid dynasty (1501–1732), distinguished for their Shi'ite branch of Islam. Their patronage of art and architecture brought a new refinement to artistic ideas and techniques drawn from the Timurid period. The other heirs to the Timurids were the Mughals of South Asia (1526–1858). The first Mughal emperor, Babur, invaded Hindustan (India and Pakistan) from Afghanistan, bringing with him a taste for Timurid gardens, architectural symmetry, and modular planning. Here we will focus on the Ottomans and the Safavids.

The Ottomans

Imperial Ottoman mosques were strongly influenced by Byzantine church plans. Prayer-hall interiors are dominated by ever-larger domed spaces uninterrupted by structural supports. Worship is directed, as in other mosques, toward a *qibla* wall and *mihrab* opposite the entrance.

Upon conquering Constantinople, Ottoman rulers converted the great Byzantine church of Hagia Sophia into a mosque, framing it with two graceful Turkish-style minarets in the fifteenth century and two more in the sixteenth century (SEE FIG. 8–2). In conformance with Islamic practice, the church's figural mosaics were destroyed or whitewashed. Huge calligraphic disks with the names of God (Allah), Muhammad, and the early caliphs were added to the interior in the mid nineteenth century (SEE FIG. 8–3). At present, Hagia Sophia is neither a church nor a mosque but a state museum.

SINAN Ottoman architects had already developed the domed, centrally planned mosque, but the vast open interior and structural clarity of Hagia Sophia inspired them to strive for a more ambitious scale. For the architect Sinan (c. 1489–1588), the development of a monumental, centrally planned mosque was a personal quest. Sinan began his career in the army, serving as engineer in the Ottoman campaigns at Belgrade, Vienna, and Baghdad. He rose through the ranks to become, in 1528, chief architect for Suleyman "the Magnificent," the tenth Ottoman sultan (ruled 1520–1566). Suleyman's reign marked the height of Ottoman power, and the sultan sponsored an ambitious building program on a scale not seen since the days of the Roman Empire. Serving Suleyman and his successor, Sinan is credited with more than 300 imperial commissions, including palaces, *madrasas* and Qur'an schools, tombs, public kitchens, hospitals, caravanserais, treasure houses, baths, bridges, viaducts, and 124 large and small mosques.

Sinan's crowning accomplishment, completed in about 1579 when he was over 80, was a mosque he designed in the provincial capital of Edirne for Suleyman's son, Selim II (ruled 1566–1574) (**FIG. 9–25**). The gigantic hemispheric dome that tops the Selimiye Mosque is more than 102 feet in diameter—larger than the dome of Hagia Sophia, as Sinan proudly pointed out. It crowns a building of extraordinary architectural coherence. The transition from square base to the central dome is accomplished by corner halfdomes that enhance the spatial plasticity and openness of the prayer hall's airy interior (**FIG. 9–26**). The eight massive piers that bear the dome's weight are visible both within and without; on the exterior they resolve in pointed towers that encircle the main dome, revealing the structural logic of the building and clarifying its form. In the arches that support the dome and span from one pier to the next—indeed at every level—light mosque courtyard — minaret — minaret — quibla wall — minaret — minaret

9-25A PLAN OF THE MOSQUE OF SULTAN SELIM, EDIRNE

Western Turkey. 1568–1575.

Credit: Necipoglu Gülru, *The Age of Sinan: Architectural Culture in the Ottoman Empire*, 2005, London: Reaktion Books, p.239

9-25B EXTERIOR VIEW OF THE MOSQUE OF SULTAN SELIM, EDIRNE

Western Turkey. 1568–1575.

The minarets that pierce the sky around the prayer hall of this mosque, their sleek, fluted walls and needle-nosed spires soaring to more than 295 feet, are only 12½ feet in diameter at the base, an impressive feat of engineering. Only royal Ottoman mosques were permitted multiple minarets, and having more than two was unusual.

Credit: © Mehmet Cetin/Shutterstock

9-26 INTERIOR, MOSQUE OF SULTAN SELIM

Credit: Photo © Ayhan Altun

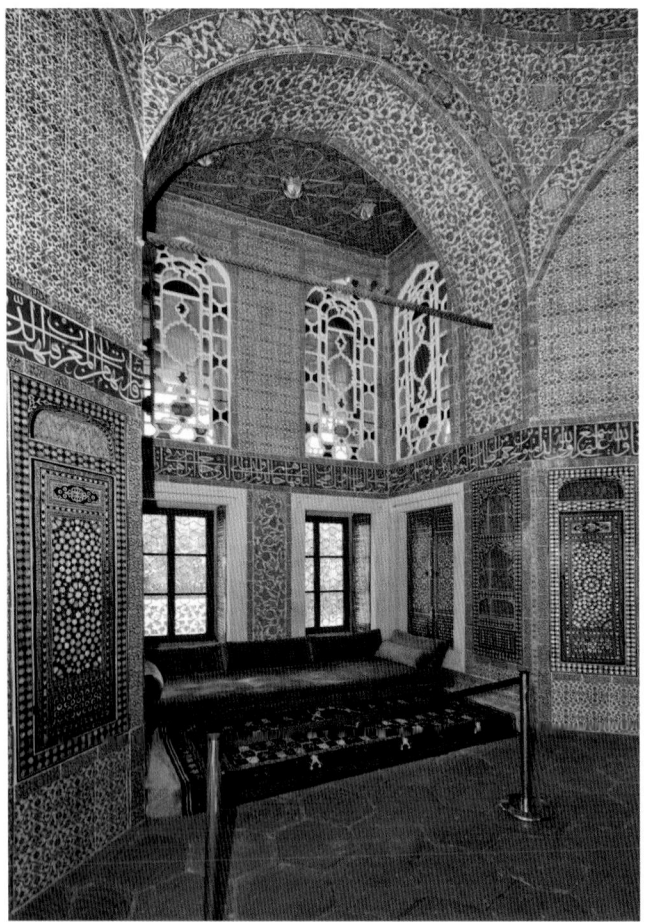

9-27 BAGHDAD KIOSK ALCOVE
Topkapi Palace, Istanbul. 1638.

Credit: Photo © Ayhan Altun

pours through windows into the interior, a space at once soaring and serene.

The interior was clearly influenced by Hagia Sophia—an open expanse under a vast dome floating on a ring of light—but it rejects Hagia Sophia's longitudinal pull from entrance to sanctuary. The Selimiye Mosque is truly a centrally planned structure. In addition to the mosque, the complex housed a *madrasa* and other educational buildings, a cemetery, a hospital, and charity kitchens, as well as the income-producing covered market and baths. Framed by the vertical lines of four minarets and raised on a platform at the city's edge, the Selimiye Mosque dominates the skyline.

TOPKAPI PALACE The Topkapi, the Ottomans' enormous palace in Istanbul, was a city unto itself. Built and inhabited from 1473 to 1853, it consisted of enclosures within walled enclosures, mirroring the immense political bureaucracy of the state. Inside, the sultan was removed from virtually all contact with the public. At the end of the inner palace, a free-standing pavilion, the Baghdad Kiosk (1638), provided him with a sumptuous retreat (**FIG. 9-27**). The kiosk consists of a low dome set above a cruciform hall with four alcoves. Each recess contains a low sofa (a Turkish word) laid with cushions and flanked by cabinets of wood inlaid with ivory and shell. Alternating with the cabinets are niches with ornate profiles; when stacked in profusion such niches—called *chini khana*—form decorative panels. On the walls, the blue-and-turquoise glazed tiles contain an inscription of the Throne

9-28 ILLUMINATED TUGRA OF SULTAN SULEYMAN

From Istanbul, Turkey. c. 1555–1560. Ink, paint, and gold on paper, removed from a *firman* and trimmed to 20½ × 25⅜" (52 × 64.5 cm). Metropolitan Museum of Art, New York. Rogers Fund, 1938. (38.149.1).

The *tugra* shown here is from a document endowing an institution in Jerusalem that had been established by Suleyman's powerful wife, Hurrem.

Credit: © 2016. Image copyright The Metropolitan Museum of Art/Art Resource/Scala, Florence

9-29 PAINTED CERAMIC DISH WITH BIRDS AND FLOWERS

From Iznik, Turkey. c. 1575–1590. Stonepaste and polychrome painting under transparent glaze, diameter 11⅛″ (28.4 cm). Metropolitan Museum of Art, New York. Gift of James J. Rorimer in appreciation of Maurice Dimand's curatorship, 1933–1959. (59.69.1).

Credit: © 2016. Image copyright The Metropolitan Museum of Art/Art Resource/Scala, Florence

in the body of the *tugra* may have been inspired by Chinese blue-and-white porcelain; similar designs appear on Ottoman ceramics and textiles.

The most important center for ceramic production under the Ottomans was Iznik (the Byzantine city of Nicea) in northwestern Turkey. Iznik potters specialized in polychrome underglaze painting, used on tiles made for architectural revetment as well as on plates and vessels intended for display. The three-color palette used on this dish (**FIG. 9-29**) is characteristic of their work. The sprawling floral spray that fills the interior—a rose, a tulip, and sprigs of honeysuckle and hyacinth—is a common motif in Iznik decoration, as is the energetic border of circles, spirals, and leaves, inspired by Chinese ceramics. The birds are more unusual. Perhaps they are the nightingales, which—with roses—are popular allegorical imagery in Ottoman love poetry.

Verse (Qur'an 2:255) which proclaims God's dominion "over the heavens and the earth," a reference to divine power that appears in many throne rooms and places associated with Muslim sovereigns. Sparkling light glows in the **stained glass** above.

CALLIGRAPHY AND CERAMICS Following a practice begun by the Saljuqs and Mamluks, the Ottomans put calligraphy to political use, developing the design of imperial ciphers—**tugras**—into a specialized art form. Ottoman *tugras* combined the ruler's name and title with the motto "Eternally Victorious" into a monogram denoting the authority of the sultan and of those select officials who were also granted an emblem. *Tugras* appeared on seals, coins, and buildings, as well as on official documents called *firmans*, imperial edicts supplementing Muslim law. Suleyman issued hundreds of edicts, and a high court official supervised specialist calligraphers and illuminators who produced the documents with fancy *tugras* (**FIG. 9-28**).

Tugras were drawn in black or blue with three long, vertical strokes to the right of two concentric horizontal teardrops. Decorative foliage patterns fill the area within the script. By the 1550s, this fill decoration became more naturalistic, and in later centuries it spilled outside the emblems' boundary lines. This rare, oversized *tugra* has a sweeping, fluid but controlled line, drawn to set proportions. The color scheme of delicate floral interlace enclosed

The Safavid Dynasty

When Shah Isma'il (ruled 1501–1524) solidified Safavid rule over the land of the Timurids in the early years of the sixteenth century, he called Bihzad, the most distinguished member of the Herat School, to the capital city of Tabriz to supervise the Safavid royal workshop, which established a new golden age of book production by blending the Herat style with that of other regional Persian traditions. But it was Isma'il's son and successor, Shah Tahmasp (ruled 1524–1576), who emerged as the most important early patron.

SULTAN MUHAMMAD As a child, Tahmasp was trained in the art of calligraphy and drawing in Herat, where Shah Isma'il had dispatched him to serve as titular governor. Shortly after succeeding his father, the youthful Tahmasp commissioned from the royal workshop in Tabriz a spectacular manuscript copy of the *Shahnama* ("Book of Kings"), Firdawsi's poetic history of Persian rulers written in the late tenth and early eleventh centuries.

9-30 Sultan Muhammad **THE "COURT OF GAYUMARS"**
From the *Shahnama* of Shah Tahmasp (fol. 20v). Tabriz, Iran.
c. 1525–1535. Ink, pigments, and gold on paper, page size
18½ × 12½" (47 × 31.8 cm). Aga Khan Museum, Toronto. (AKM165).

Tahmasp's monumental volume—with pages 18½ inches tall, larger than any book produced during the Timurid period—consists of 742 folios whose margins are embellished with pure gold; 258 full-page pictures highlight the important kings and heroes of Persian royal history. The paintings were produced by a series of artists over an extended period during the 1520s and into the 1530s. This was the most important royal artistic project of the early Safavid period.

Among the most impressive paintings—indeed, a work that many consider the greatest of all Persian manuscript paintings—is a rendering of **THE "COURT OF GAYUMARS"** (**FIG. 9-30**) painted by Sultan Muhammad, the most renowned artist in the royal workshop. This assessment is not only modern. In 1544, Dust Muhammad—painter, chronicler, and **connoisseur**—cited this painting in particular when singling out Sultan Muhammad as the premier painter participating in the project, claiming that "although it has a thousand eyes, the celestial sphere

has not seen his like" (Blair and Bloom, page 168). Sultan Muhammad portrayed the idyllic reign of the legendary first Shah, Gayumars, who ruled from a mountaintop over a people who were the first to make clothing from leopard skins and develop the skill of cooking. The elevated and central figure of the king is surrounded by the members of his family and court, each rendered with individual facial features and varying body proportions to add a sense of naturalism to the unleashed fantasy characterizing the

9-31 ARDABIL CARPET
Produced in the Safavid royal workshops, probably for the shrine of Shaykh Safi al-Din in Ardabil, Iran. 1539–1540. Dyed wool pile, undyed silk warp and weft, 34'6" × 17'6" (10.51 × 5.34 m). Victoria and Albert Museum, London.

Technique

CARPET MAKING

Because textiles are made of organic materials that are destroyed through use, very few carpets from before the sixteenth century have survived. Carpets fall into two basic types: flat-weave carpets and pile, or knotted, carpets. Both can be made on either vertical or horizontal looms.

The best-known flat-weaves today are kilims, which are typically woven in wool with bold, geometric patterns and sometimes with brocaded details. Kilim weaving is done with a **tapestry** technique called slit tapestry (see A).

Knotted carpets are an ancient invention. The oldest known example, excavated in Siberia and dating to the fourth or fifth century LM, has designs evocative of Achaemenid art, suggesting that the technique may have originated in Central Asia. In knotted carpets, the pile—the plush, thickly tufted surface—is made by tying colored strands of yarn, usually wool but occasionally silk for deluxe carpets, onto the vertical elements (the **warp**) of a yarn grid (see B and C). These knotted

loops are later trimmed and sheared to form the plush pile surface of the carpet. The **weft** strands (crosswise threads) are shot horizontally, usually twice, after each row of knots is tied, to hold the knots in place and to form the horizontal element common to all woven structures. The weft is usually an undyed yarn and is hidden by the colored knots of the warp. Two common knotting techniques are the asymmetrical knot (formerly called the Sehna knot), used in many carpets from Iran, Egypt, and Central Asia, and the symmetrical knot (formerly called the Gördes knot), more commonly used in Anatolian Turkish carpet weaving. The greater the number of knots, the shorter the pile. The finest carpets can have as many as 2,400 knots per square inch, each one tied separately by hand.

Although royal workshops produced luxurious carpets (SEE FIG. 9–31), most knotted rugs have traditionally been made in tents and homes by, depending on local custom, either women or men.

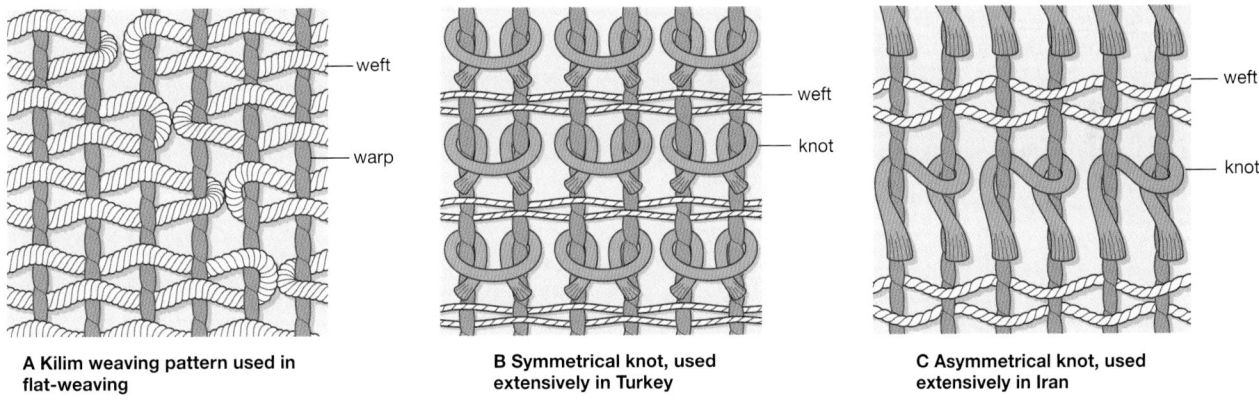

A Kilim weaving pattern used in flat-weaving

B Symmetrical knot, used extensively in Turkey

C Asymmetrical knot, used extensively in Iran

surrounding world. The landscape sparkles with brilliant color, encompassing the detailed delineation of lavish plant life as well as melting renderings of pastel rock formations, into which are tucked the faces of the spirits and demons animating this primitive paradise. Packed with surprises, this is a painting meant to be savored slowly by an elite audience within the Safavid court.

CARPETS Shah Thamasp also sponsored royal workshops for the production of finely woven carpets that were often signed, an indication of the growing prestige associated with this medium. Maqsud of Kashan's name—presumably he was the designer—and the production date of 1539–40 (year 946 in the Islamic calendar) is woven into the design of one of the most spectacular surviving carpets of Thamasp's court, one of a pair that seem to have originally come from the funerary mosque of Shayke Safi al-Din in Ardabil (**FIG. 9–31**). This is a huge rug, measuring almost 35 by 18 feet, and densely woven with 340 knots in each

square inch (25 million knots in total). The central medallion—orbited by 16 radiating, pointed ovals in alternating colors—is flanked along the rug's long axis by two stylized representations of mosque lamps, one smaller than the other. Some have suggested that the difference in size may have been calculated to make the rug seem even longer when viewed from the end of the long rectangle when entering the room where it was displayed.

Rugs have long been used for Muslim prayer, which involves repeatedly kneeling and touching the forehead to the floor before God. While individuals often had their own small prayer rugs with representations of *mihrab* niches to orient them in prayer, many mosques were furnished with wool-pile rugs received as pious donations, such as this one from Ardabil. Rugs from Iran, Turkey, and elsewhere were historically highly valued by Westerners, who often displayed them on tables rather than floors. They remain one of the predominant forms of Islamic art known in the West.

ARCHITECTURE Whereas the Ottomans took their inspiration from works of the Byzantine Empire, the Safavids looked to Timurid architecture with its tall, double-shell domes sheathed in blue tiles. In the later Safavid capital of Isfahan, the typically Timurid taste for modular construction re-emerged on a grand scale that extended well beyond buildings to include avenues, bridges, public plazas, and gardens. To the preexisting city of Isfahan, Safavid Shah Abbas I (1588–1629) added an entirely new extension, planned around an immense central plaza (*maydan*) and a broad avenue called the Chahar Bagh that ran through a zone of imperial palace pavilions and gardens down to the river. The city's prosperity and beauty so amazed visitors who flocked from around the world to conduct trade and diplomacy that it led to the popular saying, "Isfahan is half the world."

With Isfahan's **MASJID-I SHAH**, or Royal Mosque (1611–1638), the four-*iwan* mosque plan reached its apogee (**FIG. 9–32**). Stately and huge, it anchors the south end of the city's *maydan*. Its 90-foot portal and the passageway through it aligns with the *maydan*, which is oriented astrologically, but the entrance corridor soon turns to conform to the prayer hall's orientation to Mecca. The portal's great *iwan* is framed by a *pishtaq* (a rectangular panel framing an *iwan*) that rises above the surrounding walls and is enhanced by the soaring verticality of its minarets.

9–32A PLAN OF THE MASJID-I SHAH, ISFAHAN
Iran. 1611–1638.

Credit: Drawing by Keith Turner after Henri Stierlin, courtesy of the Aga Khan Documentation Center at MIT.

The *iwan*'s profile is reflected in the repeated, double-tiered *iwans* that parade across the façade of the mosque courtyard and around the *maydan* as a whole. Achieving unity through the regular replication of a single element—here

9–32B EXTERIOR VIEW OF THE MASJID-I SHAH, ISFAHAN
Iran. 1611–1638.

The tall, bulbous dome behind the *qibla iwan* and the large *pishtaqs* with minarets are pronounced vertical elements that made royal patronage visible not only from the far end of the *maydan* but throughout the city and beyond.

Credit: Klange76/Fotolia

the arch—is a hallmark of Safavid architecture inherited from Timurid aesthetics, but achieved on an unprecedented scale and integrated within a well-planned urban setting.

Into the Modern Era

Islamic art is not restricted to the distant past. But with the dissolution of the great Islamic empires and the formation of smaller nation-states during the twentieth century, questions of identity and its expression in art changed significantly. Muslim artists and architects began to participate in international movements that swept away many of the visible signs that formerly expressed their cultural character and difference. More recently, Islamic architects have sought to reconcile modernity with an Islamic cultural identity distinct from the West. In this spirit Iraqi architect Sami Mousawi and the Italian firm of Portoghesi-Gigliotti designed the **ISLAMIC CULTURAL CENTER** in Rome (completed 1992) with clean, modern lines, exposing the structure while at the same time taking full advantage of opportunities for ornament (**FIG. 9-33**). The structural logic appears in the prayer hall's concrete columns, which rise to meet abstract capitals in the form of plain rings, then spring upward to make a geometrically dazzling eight-pointed star supporting a dome of concentric circles. There are references here to the interlacing ribs of the *mihrab* dome in the Great Mosque of Cordoba (SEE FIG. 9-9), to the great domed spans of Sinan's prayer halls (SEE FIG. 9-26), and to the simple palm-tree trunks that supported the roof of the Mosque of the Prophet in Medina.

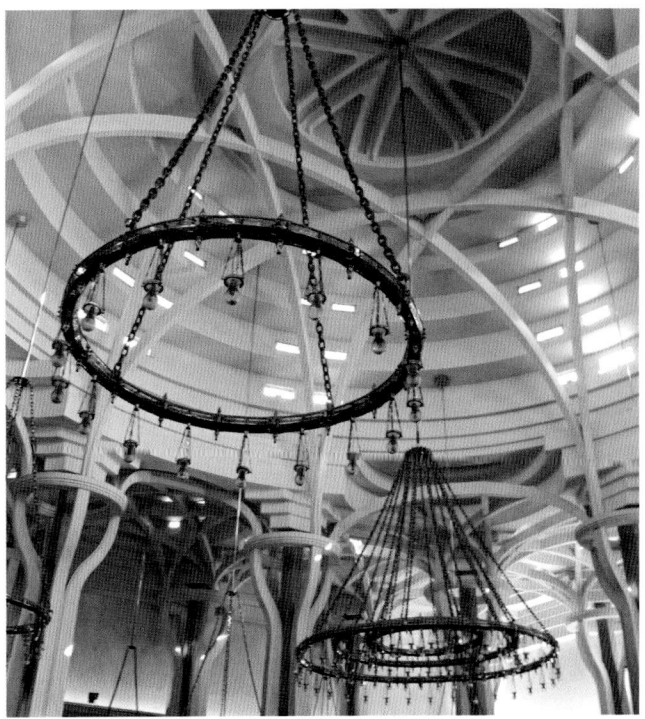

9-33 Paolo Portoghesi, Vittorio Gigliotti, and Sami Mousawi **ISLAMIC MOSQUE AND CULTURAL CENTER, ROME**
1984–1992.

The prayer hall, 197 × 131' (60 × 40 m), which has an ablution area on the floor below, can accommodate a congregation of 2,500 on its main floor and balconies. The large central dome, 65½' (20 m) in diameter, is surrounded by 16 smaller domes, all similarly articulated with concrete ribs.

Credit: © Gari Wyn Williams/Alamy Stock Photo

Think About It

1   Explain how the design of the mosque varies across the Islamic world with reference to three examples. Despite the differences, what features do mosques typically have in common?

2   Images of people are not allowed in Islamic religious contexts, but mosques and other religious buildings are lavishly decorated. What artistic motifs and techniques are used and why?

3   Compare the painted pages from sumptuous manuscripts in **FIGURES 9-24 and 9-30**. How does the comparison reveal the distinctive aspirations of religious and secular art in Islamic society? How are they different, and what features do they share?

4   Select an Islamic structure that is influenced by Roman or Byzantine architecture. Which forms are borrowed? Why and how, in their new Islamic context, are they transformed?

Crosscurrents

These buildings were constructed for worship during the formative years of Christianity and Islam. Explain why they appear similar and discuss the ways in which their designs are consistent with the religious and cultural contexts.

FIG. 7-10B

FIG. 9-5

10-1 ASHOKAN PILLAR

Kutagarasala Vihara near Vaishali, Bihar, India. Maurya period, c. 279–232 BCE.

Chapter 10
Art of South and Southeast Asia before 1200

Learning Objectives

10.a Identify the visual hallmarks of South and Southeast Asian art for formal, technical, and expressive qualities.

10.b Interpret the meaning of works of South and Southeast Asian art based on their themes, subjects, and symbols.

10.c Relate South and Southeast Asian artists and art to their cultural, economic, and political contexts.

10.d Apply the vocabulary and concepts relevant to South and Southeast Asian art, artists, and art history.

10.e Interpret a work of South or Southeast Asian art using the art historical methods of observation, comparison, and inductive reasoning.

10.f Select visual and textual evidence in various media to support an argument or an interpretation of a work of South or Southeast Asian art.

The heroic qualities of the great ruler Ashoka Maurya are well recorded in the Indian cultural tradition. His accomplishments served as inspiration for later kings, like those of the Gupta dynasty, and Buddhist literary sources credit him with a wide range of miraculous deeds. But in spite of this fame, early historians had great difficulty distinguishing the historical man from the legend. In 1837, when examining inscriptions on a series of massive monolithic pillars (**FIG. 10-1**) in northern India, scholars realized that the designation "Beloved of the Gods" was one of King Ashoka's personal epithets. This realization made clear that the pillars dated to the time of King Ashoka (c. 273–232 BCE) and lifted some of the mystery surrounding this renowned figure. Once properly identified, his name appeared in numerous Maurya-dynasty inscriptions. What they reveal about the humanity of this man is in many ways more captivating than the larger-than-life figure encountered in the legends.

Notably, in his Thirteenth Rock Edict, Ashoka presents himself as a man weary of battle and intensely remorseful for the death and suffering generated by his political ambitions. In it, he recalls a horrific battle in the region of Kalinga that took place eight years into his reign. By his estimation 100,000 died and many thousands more were dispossessed or left in despair from the conflict. In surveying this carnage, Ashoka admits to being deeply pained and resolves henceforth to seek conquest through moral teachings (*dharma*) rather than by the sword. His profound

change of heart also proved to be a sound policy for establishing legal consistency over his vast empire. This stability stimulated a rich period of artistic production.

As part of this conversion, Ashoka supported religious institutions and gave special attention to the nascent Buddhist community. He also widely distributed royal inscriptions by having them carved directly onto boulders and mountainsides. These rock edicts were far more plentiful than the inscribed columns, commonly called Ashokan pillars, which are few in number and appear to have been concentrated in the heart of the Maurya empire. The remains of about 19 such pillars exist, but not all bear inscriptions that can be attributed with certainty to Ashoka. Most were placed at the sites of Buddhist monasteries along a route leading from Punjab in the northwest to Ashoka's capital, Pataliputra, in the northeast.

Pillars and pillared halls had been used as emblems of kingship in the Persian Achaemenid Empire (Chapter 2, pages 44–47), and it is possible that Ashoka was familiar with these precedents when he decided to display his words on columns detached from an architectural setting. Most of these edicts are inscribed in Prakrit, a language closely related to classical Sanskrit, but others were written in the languages spoken locally, like Greek and Aramaic. These observations are indicative of the size and reach of Ashoka's empire, which set the model for South Asian kingship over the centuries to come.

The Origins of Civilization in South Asia

What are the geographical and cultural contexts of the earliest art in South Asia?

It is difficult to make inclusive claims about South and Southeast Asia because the two areas were and are home to a broad range of ethnic communities, political units, language groups, and cultural traditions. One of the few things both regions share is the historical importance to trade networks and, consequently, an exposure to similar ideological and religious ideas, most notably Hinduism, Buddhism, and Islam. And the same proximity to the sea that played a role in trade also ensured exposure to the monsoon rains, which pull moisture from the oceans each summer and have traditionally enabled vigorous agricultural production. Due to their wealth and accessibility, both regions have historically been subject to periods of invasion, immigration, and colonization.

This sporadic influx of new peoples has, at times, been a source of great hardship, but each wave added to the rich diversity of these regions and contributed new layers to their remarkable artistic heritage.

The South Asian subcontinent, or Indian subcontinent, as it is commonly called, is a peninsular region that includes the present-day countries of India, Afghanistan, Pakistan, Nepal, Bhutan, Bangladesh, and Sri Lanka (**MAP 10-1**). This land mass is slowly pressing northward into the rest of Asia, and the collision has given rise to the Himalayas, the world's highest mountains, which capture the snows and feed the subcontinent's major rivers throughout the year. It is along these vast river systems that we can find the first evidence of organized settlements in the region.

The earliest civilization of South Asia was nurtured in the lower reaches of the Indus River, in present-day Pakistan and northwestern India. Known as the Indus or Harappan civilization (after Harappa, the first-discovered site), it flourished from approximately 2600 to 1900 BCE, or during roughly the same time as the Old Kingdom period

MAP 10–1 SOUTH AND SOUTHEAST ASIA

As the deserts in western China heat during the summer months, the hot air rises and pulls cool air north off the oceans. As this water-laden air hits the Himalayas and the Tibetan plateau, it drops the torrential monsoon rains over much of South and Southeast Asia.

10-2 SEAL IMPRESSIONS

A, D: horned animal; B: Bull; C: sacrificial rite to a goddess (?);
E: yogi; F: three-headed animal. Indus Valley civilization, c. 2500–
1500 BCE. Steatite, each seal approx. 1¼ × 1¼" (3.2 × 3.2 cm).
National Museum of Karachi, Pakistan.

The more than 2,000 small seals and impressions that have been
found offer an intriguing window on the Indus Valley civilization.
Usually carved from steatite stone, the seals were coated with alkali
and then fired to produce a lustrous, white surface. A perforated
knob on the back of each may have been for suspending them. The
most popular subjects are animals, most commonly a one-horned
bovine standing before an altarlike object (A, D). The function of the
seals may relate to trade but this remains uncertain since the script
that is so prominent in the impressions has yet to be deciphered.

Credit: A-F, National Museum of Karachi, Karachi, Pakistan/Bridgeman Images

of Egypt, the Minoan civilization of the Aegean, and the
dynasties of Ur and Babylon in Mesopotamia. In fact, there
is evidence of trade contact between the Harappan civilization and Mesopotamia.

The presence of city mounds and the occasional discovery of small **SEALS** (such as those whose impressions
are shown in **FIG. 10-2**) preserved the memory that an
ancient civilization had existed in the Indus River Valley. Systematic excavations did not begin, however, until
the 1920s, and they have continued to the present. These
efforts have uncovered a number of major urban areas at
points along the lower Indus River, including Harappa,
Mohenjo-Daro, and Chanhu-Daro.

The Indus Civilization

MOHENJO-DARO   The ancient cities of the Indus Valley
resemble each other in design and construction, suggesting
a coherent culture. At Mohenjo-Daro, the best preserved
of the sites, archaeologists discovered an elevated citadel
area about 50 feet high, surrounded by a wall. Among
the citadel's buildings is a remarkable **WATER TANK**, a
large watertight pool that may have been a public bath
but could also have had a ritual use (**FIG. 10-3**). Stretching out below the elevated area was the city, arranged in
a gridlike plan with wide avenues and narrow side streets.
Its houses, often two stories high, were generally built
around a central courtyard. Like other Indus Valley cities,
Mohenjo-Daro was constructed of fired brick, in contrast
to the less durable sun-dried brick used in other cultures of
the time. The city included a network of covered drainage
systems that channeled away waste and rainwater. Clearly
the technical and engineering skills of this civilization
were highly advanced. At its peak, about 2500 to 2000 BCE,

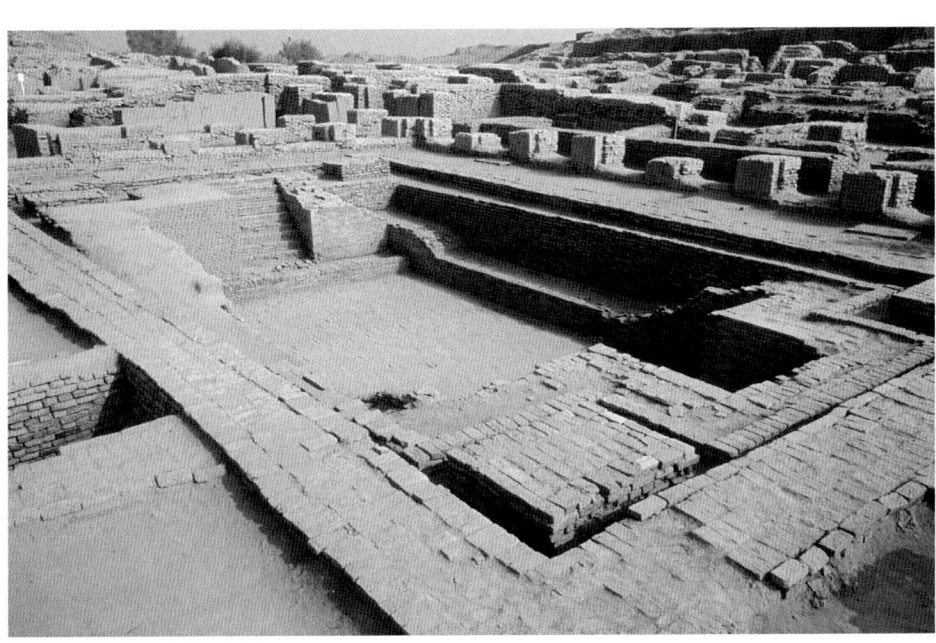

**10-3 LARGE WATER TANK,
MOHENJO-DARO**

Indus Valley (Harappan) civilization,
c. 2600–1900 BCE.

This was possibly a public or ritual
bathing area.

Credit: © akg-images/Gerard Degeorge

Mohenjo-Daro was approximately 6–7 square miles in size and had a population of about 20,000–50,000. The uniformity of its architecture and plans suggests some form of central political control, but in the absence of any clear political or religious structures we can say very little about how the cities were governed.

INDUS VALLEY SEALS Although our knowledge of the Indus civilization is limited by the fact that we cannot read its writing, motifs on seals as well as the few discovered artworks strongly suggest continuities with later South Asian cultures. The seal in FIGURE 10-2E, for example, depicts a man in a meditative posture that resembles later forms of yoga, traditional physical and mental exercises usually undertaken for spiritual purposes. In FIGURE 10-2C, people with elaborate headgear stand in a row or procession observing a figure standing in a tree—possibly a goddess—and a kneeling worshiper. This scene may offer some insight into the religious or ritual customs of Indus people, whose deities may have been ancient prototypes of later Indian gods and goddesses.

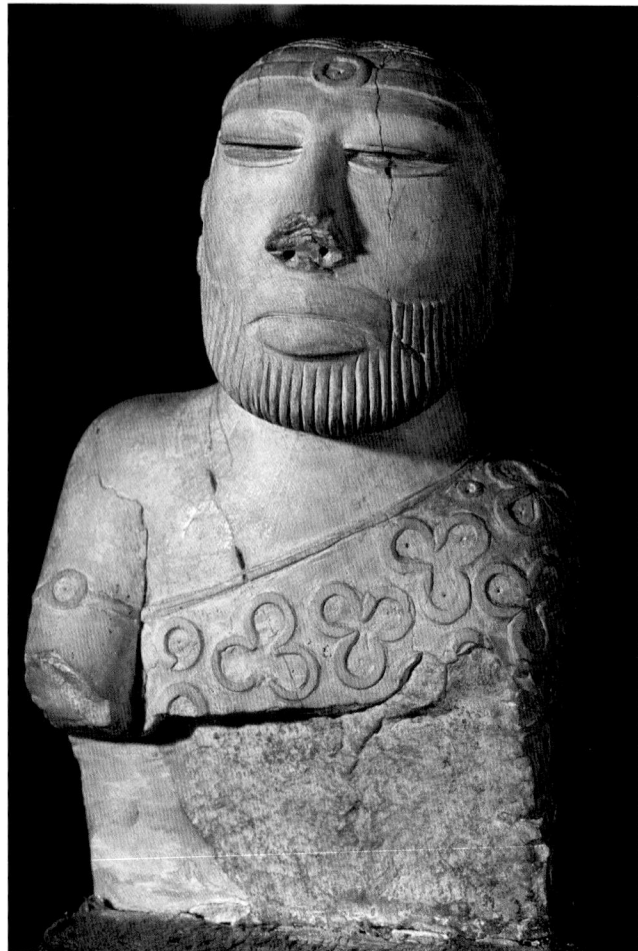

10-4 TORSO OF A "PRIEST-KING"
From Mohenjo-Daro. Indus Valley civilization, c. 2600–1900 BCE. Steatite, height 6⅞″ (17.5 cm). National Museum of Pakistan, Karachi.

Credit: © akg-images/Jean-Louis Nou

Numerous terra-cotta figurines and a few stone and bronze statuettes have been found at Indus sites. They reveal a confident maturity of artistic conception and technique. Both the terra-cotta and the stone figures foreshadow the later Indian artistic tradition in their sensuous naturalism.

"PRIEST-KING" FROM MOHENJO-DARO The male torso sometimes called the "priest-king" (**FIG. 10-4**) suggests by this name a structure of society where priests functioned as kings—for which we have no evidence at all. Several features of this figure, including a low forehead, a broad nose, thick lips, and long slit eyes, are seen on other works from Mohenjo-Daro. The man's garment is patterned with a **trefoil** (three-lobed) motif. The depressions of the trefoil pattern were originally filled with red pigment, and the eyes were inlaid with colored shell or stone. Narrow bands with circular ornaments adorn the upper arm and the head. The headband falls in back into two long strands, which may be an indication of rank. Certainly, with its formal pose and simplified, geometric form, the statue conveys a commanding human presence.

NUDE TORSO FROM HARAPPA Although its date is disputed, a nude **MALE TORSO** (**FIG. 10-5**) found at Harappa is an example of a contrasting naturalistic style of ancient Indus origin. Less than 4 inches tall, it is one of the most extraordinary portrayals of the human form to survive from any early civilization. Its lifelike rendering emphasizes the soft texture of the human body and the subtle nuances of muscular form. With these characteristics the Harappa torso forecasts the essential aesthetic attributes of later Indian sculpture.

The reasons for the demise of this flourishing civilization are not yet understood. Recent research has suggested that between 2000 and 1750 BCE there was a gradual breakdown of the architectural regularity characteristic of earlier periods. Many now think this was due to climate change and a dramatic shift in the course of local rivers. These changes made it impossible to practice the agriculture and river trade on which these cities depended. The cities of the Indus civilization declined, and predominantly rural and nomadic societies emerged.

The Vedic Period

About 2000 BCE nomadic herdsmen, the Aryans, entered India from Central Asia and the Russian steppes. Gradually they blended with the indigenous populations and introduced the horse and chariot, the Sanskrit language, a hierarchical social order, and religious practices that centered on the propitiation of gods through fire sacrifice. The earliest of their sacred writings, known as the Vedas, contain hymns to various gods including the divine king Indra. The importance of the fire sacrifice,

10-5 MALE TORSO

From Harappa. Indus Valley civilization, c. 2600–1900 BCE. Red sandstone, height 3¾″ (9.5 cm). National Museum, New Delhi.

Credit: © akg-images/Jean-Louis Nou

the *Ramayana*, the most popular and enduring religious epic in India and Southeast Asia, were taking shape. These texts relate histories of gods and humans, bringing profound philosophical ideas to a more accessible and popular level. In this way, the religious tradition continued to evolve, emerging later as Hinduism, a loose term that encompasses the many religious forms that resulted from the mingling of Vedic culture with indigenous beliefs.

In this stimulating religious, philosophical, and literary climate, numerous religious communities arose, some of which did not accept the primacy of the Brahmins. Among these heterodox groups the Jains and the Buddhists were the most successful. The last of the 24 Jain spiritual pathfinders (*tirthankara*), Mahavira, is believed to have taught in the sixth century BCE. His were the earliest teachings ever to recognize nonviolence as a central moral principle. The Buddha Shakyamuni is thought to have lived shortly thereafter in the fifth century BCE. Both traditions espoused some basic Upanishadic tenets, such as the cyclical nature of existence and the need for liberation from the material world. However, they rejected the authority of the Vedas, and with it the legitimacy of the fire sacrifice and the hereditary class structure of Vedic society, including its powerful, exclusive priesthood. In further contrast with the Brahmins, who often held important positions in society, both Jainism and Buddhism were renunciant (*shramana*) traditions, centered on communities of monks and nuns who chose to separate themselves from worldly concerns. Over time, these communities did begin to play important social roles. But asceticism held, and continues to hold, an important place within most South Asian religious traditions.

overseen by a powerful priesthood—the Brahmins—and religiously sanctioned social classes, persisted through the Vedic period. At some point, the class structure became hereditary and immutable, with lasting consequences for Indian society.

During the latter part of this period, from about 800 BCE, the Upanishads were composed. These texts, written primarily by Brahmins, attempted to reform the Vedic ritual by emphasizing the unity between the individual and the divine. Some authors asserted that the material world is illusory and that only the universal divine (Brahman) is real and eternal. Others held that our existence is cyclical and that beings are caught in *samsara*, a relentless cycle of birth, life, death, and rebirth. Believers aspire to attain liberation from *samsara* and to unite the individual soul with the eternal, universal Brahman.

The latter portion of the Vedic period also saw the flowering of India's epic literature, written in the melodious and complex Sanskrit language. By around 400 BCE, the *Mahabharata*, the longest epic in world literature, and

The Flourishing of Buddhism and Hinduism

How does South Asian art develop with the flourishing of Buddhism and Hinduism across a series of regional dynasties through the twelfth century CE?

Buddhism

Many of the renunciant traditions developed from the efforts of gifted and insightful teachers. For the Buddhists, this man was Shakyamuni Buddha, who lived during the fifth century BCE in the present-day regions of southern Nepal and northern India. At his birth, it is believed, seers foretold that the infant prince, named Siddhartha Gautama, would become either a *chakravartin* (world-conquering ruler) or a *buddha* (literally an "awakened one" or a fully enlightened being). Hoping for a ruler like himself, Siddhartha's father tried to surround his son with pleasure and shield him from pain. Yet the prince was eventually exposed to the sufferings of old age, sickness, and death—the inevitable fate of all mortal beings. Deeply troubled by the human condition, Siddhartha at age 29 left the palace, his family, and his inheritance to live as an ascetic in the wilderness. After six years of meditation, he attained complete enlightenment at a site in India now called Bodh Gaya.

Following his enlightenment, the Buddha gave his first teaching in the Deer Park at Sarnath. Here he expounded the Four Noble Truths that are the foundation of Buddhism: (1) life is suffering; (2) this suffering has a cause, which is ignorance and desire; (3) this ignorance and desire can be overcome and extinguished; (4) the way to overcome them is by following the eightfold path of right view, right resolve, right speech, right action, right livelihood, right effort, right mindfulness, and right concentration. After the Buddha's death at age 80, his many disciples developed his teachings and established the world's oldest monastic institutions.

A buddha is not a god, but rather one who sees the ultimate nature of the world and is therefore no longer subject to *samsara*, the cycle of birth, death, and rebirth that otherwise holds all in its grip, whether they are gods, humans, animals, demons, tortured spirits, or hellish beings.

The early form of Buddhism, known as Theravada or Nikaya, stresses self-cultivation for the purpose of attaining *nirvana*, which is the extinction of *samsara* for oneself. Theravada Buddhism has continued mainly in Sri Lanka and Southeast Asia. Almost equally old is another form of Buddhism known as Mahayana, which became popular mainly in northern India; it eventually flourished in China, Korea, Japan, and in Tibet (as Vajrayana). Compassion for all beings is the foundation of Mahayana Buddhism, whose goal is not only *nirvana* for oneself but buddhahood (enlightenment) for every being throughout the universe. Many schools of Buddhism recognize buddhas other than Shakyamuni from the past, present, and future. One such is Maitreya, the next buddha destined to appear on earth. Several Buddhist schools also accept the existence of **bodhisattvas** ("those whose essence is wisdom"), saintly beings who are on the brink of achieving buddhahood but have vowed to help others achieve buddhahood before crossing over themselves. In art, bodhisattvas and buddhas are most clearly distinguished by their clothing and adornments: bodhisattvas wear the princely garb of India, while buddhas wear monks' robes.

The Maurya Period

In about 700 BCE, hundreds of years after their decline along the Indus, cities began to reappear on the subcontinent, particularly in the north, where numerous kingdoms arose. For most of its subsequent history, India was a shifting mosaic of regional kingdoms. From time to

10-6 LION CAPITAL
From Ashokan pillar at Sarnath, Uttar Pradesh, India. Maurya period, c. 250 BCE. Polished sandstone, height 7' (2.13 m). Archaeological Museum, Sarnath.

Credit: Borromeo/Art Resource, NY

time, however, a particularly powerful dynasty formed an empire. The first of these was the Maurya dynasty (c. 322–185 BCE), which claimed to rule over all but the southernmost portion of the subcontinent.

During the reign of the third Maurya king, Ashoka (ruled c. 273–232 BCE), Buddhism expanded from a religion largely localized in the Maurya heartland, a region known as Magadha, to one extending across the entire empire. Among the monuments Ashoka erected were monolithic pillars set up primarily at the sites of Buddhist monasteries. The fully developed Ashokan pillar—a slightly tapered sandstone shaft that usually rested on a stone foundation slab sunk more than 10 feet into the ground—rose to a height of around 50 feet (SEE FIG. 10-1). On it were often carved inscriptions relating to rules of *dharma*, the divinely ordained moral law believed to keep the universe from falling into chaos. Ideal kings were enjoined to uphold this law, and many later Buddhists interpreted the rules as also referring to Buddhist teachings. At the top were placed elaborate animal-shaped capitals carved from separate blocks of sandstone. Both shaft and capital were given the high polish characteristic of Maurya stonework. Scholars believe that the pillars, which served as royal standards, symbolized the **axis mundi** ("axis of the world"), joining earth with the cosmos and representing the vital link between the human and celestial realms.

LION CAPITAL FROM SARNATH This capital (**FIG. 10–6**) originally crowned the pillar erected at Sarnath, the site of the Buddha's first sermon. It represents four addorsed, or back to back, Asiatic lions with open mouths standing atop a circular platform depicting a bull, horse, lion, and elephant separated by large chariot wheels. The base is an inverted lotus blossom whose bell shape formed a transition to the column. The deeply cut carving promotes an active play of light and shadow, resulting in details that must have been readily visible even when this image was placed high atop its pillar.

Some poetic references allude to the Buddha's sermon as the "Lion's Roar," whereas others refer to it as the turning of the "Wheel of the Law" (*dharmachakra*). This designation likens the Buddha's teachings to a chariot wheel and the sermon to the first push that set the wheel rolling across the world. The four lions and spoked wheels on the capital face the cardinal directions, thus referencing these descriptive titles.

However, the imagery works on two levels; it also holds important political associations. The lion may have served as a metaphor for the Buddha's preaching, but prior to that it was a symbol of kingship, and the elephant, horse, and bull were similarly potent as emblems of worldly and military power. When considered in conjunction with the wheel motifs, this imagery almost certainly also references the king as a *chakravartin*. This term refers to a universal king of such power that the wheels of his chariot pass everywhere unimpeded. The designation held great significance in South Asia, and Ashoka is here associating the worldly might of his empire with the moral authority of Buddhism. This relationship would have been further reinforced by the large wheel, now lost, that is believed to have rested atop the lions.

FEMALE FIGURE FROM DIDARGANJ Alongside the formal religious institutions of the Brahmins, Buddhists, and Jains, there existed a host of popular religious practices centered on local gods of villages and fields who were believed to oversee worldly matters such as health, wealth, and fertility. A spectacular **FEMALE FIGURE HOLDING A FLY-WHISK**, or *chauri* (**FIG. 10–7**), found at Didarganj, near the Maurya capital of Pataliputra, may represent one such deity. Possibly representing a **yakshi**, a spirit associated with the productive and reproductive forces of nature,

10–7 FEMALE FIGURE HOLDING A FLY-WHISK
From Didarganj, Patna, Bihar, India. Probably Maurya period, c. 250 BCE. Polished sandstone, height 5′4¼″ (1.63 m). Patna Museum, Patna.

Often identified as a *yakshi*, this sculpture has become one of the most famous works of Indian art. Holding a fly-whisk in her raised right hand, the figure wears only a long shawl and a skirtlike cloth. The nubbled tubes about her ankles probably represent anklets made of beaten gold. Her hair is bound behind in a large bun, and a small bun sits on her forehead. This hairstyle appears again in Indian sculpture of the later Kushan period (c. second century CE).

the figure embodies female associations with procreative abundance, bounty, and auspiciousness.

The statue's date is still debated by scholars, but many place it in the Maurya period. Sculpted from fine-grained sandstone, the statue conveys the *yakshi*'s authority through the frontal rigor of her pose, the massive volumes of her form, and the strong, linear patterning of her ornaments and dress. Alleviating and counterbalancing this hierarchical formality are her soft, youthful face, the precise definition of prominent features such as the stomach muscles, and the polished sheen of her exposed flesh. As noted above, this lustrous polish is a special feature of Maurya sculpture.

The Period of the Shunga and Early Satavahana

With the demise of the Maurya empire, India returned to rule by regional dynasties. Between the second century BCE and the early centuries CE, two of the most important of these dynasties were the Shunga dynasty (185–72 BCE) in central India and the Satavahana dynasty (third century BCE–third century CE), which initially ruled in central India and after the first century in the south. During this period, some of the most magnificent early Buddhist structures were created.

Elements of Architecture

STUPAS AND TEMPLES

Buddhist architecture in South Asia consists mainly of stupas and temples, often at monastic complexes containing *viharas* (monks' cells and common areas). These monuments may be either structural (built up from the ground) or rock-cut (hewn out of a mountainside). **Stupas** derive from burial mounds and contain relics beneath a solid, dome-shaped core. A major stupa is surrounded by a railing that creates a sacred path for ritual circumambulation at ground level. This railing is punctuated by gateways, called **toranas** in Sanskrit, aligned with the cardinal points of the compass. The stupa sits on a round or square terrace; stairs may lead to an upper circumambulatory path around the platform's edge. On top of the stupa a railing defines a square, from the center of which rises a mast supporting tiers of disk-shaped "umbrellas."

Hindu architecture in South Asia consists mainly of temples, either structural or rock-cut, executed in a number of styles and dedicated to diverse deities. The two general Hindu temple types are the northern and southern styles, prevalent in northern India and southern India respectively. Within these broad categories is great stylistic diversity, though all are raised on plinths and dominated by their superstructures. In north India, the term **shikhara** is used to refer to the entire towerlike superstructure, which often curves inward, sloping more steeply near its peak. By contrast, the southern superstructure is comprised of angular, steplike terraces, and the term *shikhara* refers only to its **finial**, that is, the uppermost member of the superstructure. North Indian *shikharas* are crowned by **amalakas**. Inside, a series of **mandapas** (halls) leads to an inner sanctuary, the **garbhagriha**, which contains a sacred image. An axis mundi is imagined to run vertically up from the Cosmic Waters below the earth, through the *garbhagriha*'s image, and out through the top of the tower.

Jain architecture consists mainly of structural and rock-cut monasteries and temples that have much in common with their Buddhist and Hindu counterparts.

stupa

northern-style temple

southern-style temple

Religious monuments called stupas, solid mounds enclosing a relic, are fundamental to Buddhism (see "Stupas and Temples" opposite). The exact nature of the relic varies, but in ideal cases they are connected directly to the Buddha himself or to one of his important disciples. The form, size, and decoration of stupas differ from region to region, but their symbolic meaning remains virtually the same, and their plan is a carefully calculated **mandala**, or diagram of the cosmos as envisioned in Buddhism. Stupas are open to all for private worship.

The first stupas were constructed to house the Buddha's remains after his cremation. According to tradition, these relics were divided into eight portions and given to important kings, who then further divided and encased the remains in burial mounds. Since the early stupas held actual remains of the Buddha, they were venerated as his body and, by extension, his enlightenment and attainment of *nirvana* (liberation from rebirth). The method of veneration was, and still is, to circumambulate, or walk around, the stupa in a clockwise direction.

THE GREAT STUPA AT SANCHI   Probably no early Buddhist structure is more famous than the **GREAT STUPA** at Sanchi in central India (**FIG. 10–8**). Most likely dating to the time of Ashoka, the Great Stupa originally formed part of a large monastery complex crowning a hill. During the mid second century BCE, it was enlarged to its present size, and the surrounding stone railing was constructed. About 100 years later, elaborately carved stone gateways were added to the railing.

Representative of the early central Indian stupa type, the solid, hemispherical mound of the Great Stupa at Sanchi was built up from rubble and dirt, faced with dressed stone, and covered with a shining white plaster made from lime and powdered seashells. A 10-foot-tall stone railing demarcates a circumambulatory path at ground level. Another walkway, approached by a staircase on the south side, creates a second raised level for circumambulation. On top of the mound a square enclosure designated by another railing contains the top of a mast bearing three stone disks, or "umbrellas," of decreasing size. Interpreted in various ways, these disks are probably an architectural form derived from the parasols used to shade kings and indicate people of importance. They may also correspond to the "Three Jewels of Buddhism"—the Buddha, the Law, and the Monastic Order.

The railing provides a protective boundary and demarcates a ritual path around the central structure. Carved with octagonal uprights and lens-shaped crossbars, it probably simulates the wooden railings of the time. Four stone gateways, or *toranas,* aligned with the four cardinal directions punctuate the railing. An inscription on the south gateway indicates that it was provided by ivory carvers from the nearby town of Vidisha, while another inscription on the same *torana* specifies a gift during the reign of King Satakarni of the Satavahana dynasty, providing the first-century BCE date for the gateways. The vast majority of the inscriptions at Sanchi, however, record modest donations by individual devotees from all walks of life. This collaborative patronage points to Buddhism's expanding popularity.

10–8 STUPA 1 (THE GREAT STUPA) AT SANCHI
Madhya Pradesh, India. Founded 3rd century BCE; enlarged c. 150–50 BCE.

Credit: © veice/Shutterstock

Rising to a height of 35 feet, the gateways are the only elements of the Great Stupa at Sanchi to be ornamented with sculpture.

The four gates support a three-tiered array of architraves in which posts and crossbars are elaborately carved with symbols and scenes drawn mostly from the Buddha's life and the **Jataka tales**, stories of the Buddha's past lives. These relief sculptures employ two distinctive features of early South Asian visual narrative. The first is that the Buddha himself is not shown in human form prior to the late first century BCE. Instead, he is represented by symbols such as his footprints, an empty "enlightenment" seat, or a plank. The reasons for this absence are still widely debated but, since Vedic gods and Jinas are very rarely depicted in this period, it seems likely that this was the result of a wider cultural practice rather than a uniquely Buddhist prohibition. The second is that South Asian sculpture frequently employs continuous narrative. This means that several moments in time are represented in the same visual frame. This visual narrative technique is used in the portrayal of the Great Departure covering the outer surface of a curving architrave of the eastern *torana*.

The *toranas* are further decorated with free-standing sculptures depicting such subjects as *yakshis* and their male counterparts, *yakshas*, riders on real and mythical animals, and the Buddhist wheel. Forming a bracket between each capital and the lowest crossbar on the east gate is a sculpture of a **YAKSHI** (**FIG. 10–10**). These *yakshis* are some of the finest female figures in Indian art, and they make an instructive comparison with the Didarganj image of the Maurya period (SEE FIG. 10–7). The earlier figure was distinguished by a formal, somewhat rigid pose, an emphasis

A Closer Look

THE GREAT DEPARTURE

Before he became the Buddha, Prince Siddhartha resolved to give up his royal comforts in order to pursue the life of an ascetic. Confiding only in his charioteer Channa, the prince slipped out of his palace in the dead of night, and, mounting his horse, headed for the gates. The local gods, *yakshas*, were eager for the prince to succeed on his spiritual quest and cupped their hands under the horse's hooves so that no one would awaken from the noise. Indeed, in some versions, they carry the horse and its rider right over the palace walls. This story is depicted, using some distinctive forms of visual narrative, on the middle architrave of the east gate of the Great Stupa at Sanchi.

The presence of the prince is indicated by the riderless horses shaded by a royal parasol and fly-whisk. This is the same horse shown at various moments in the story.

All the action is organized geographically in the scene as it plays out between the palace and the forest. This tree indicates the transition into the forest setting.

The *yakshas* accompany the creature only when ridden by the prince. In the lower right, the horse and charioteer turn back on their own, unaccompanied by the local gods and leaving Shakyamuni to begin his life as an ascetic.

The footprints on the far right of the relief indicate the place Prince Siddhartha dismounted.

10–9 THE GREAT DEPARTURE
East *torana* (exterior middle architrave) of Stupa 1 (the Great Stupa) at Sanchi. 1st century BCE. Sandstone.

Credit: Dinodia/Bridgeman Images

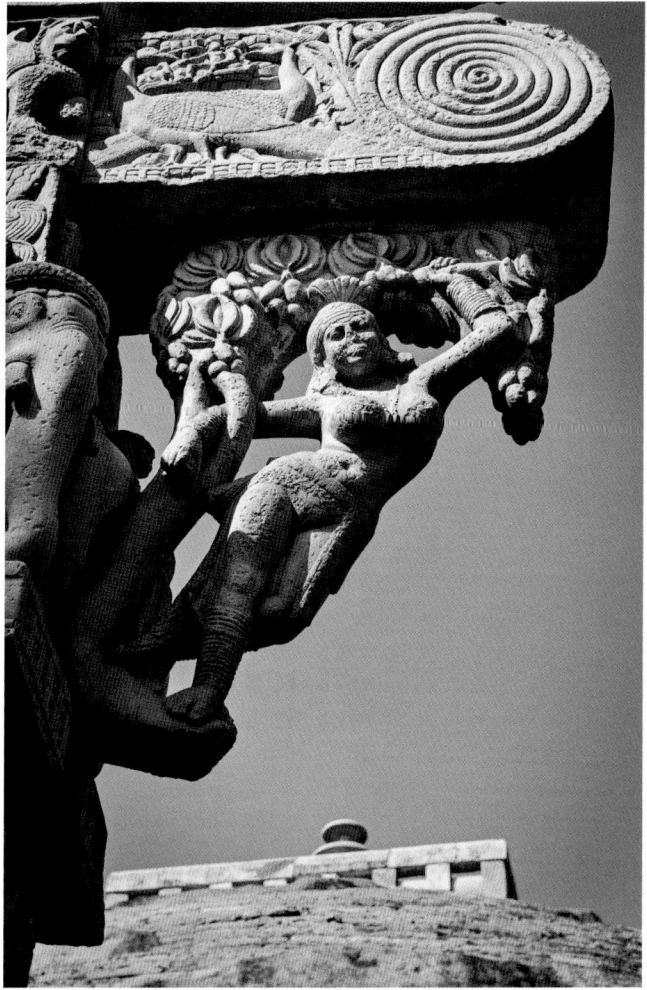

10–10 YAKSHI BRACKET FIGURE

East *torana* of the Great Stupa at Sanchi. 1st century BCE. Sandstone, height approx. 60″ (152.4 cm).

Credit: © veice/Shutterstock

on realistic details, and a clear distinction between clothed and nude parts of the body. In contrast, the Sanchi *yakshi* leans daringly into space with casual abandon, supported by one leg as the other charmingly crosses behind. Her diaphanous garment is noticeable only by its hems, and so she appears almost nude, which emphasizes her form. The mango tree on which she hangs is heavy with fruit, reasserting the fecundity and bounty associated with these mercurial deities. This semidivine figure's presence on a Buddhist gateway implies her role as a guardian or devotee, which, in turn, speaks to Buddhism's inclusiveness. Even deities were understood to benefit from the Buddha's teachings.

THE CHAITYA HALL AT KARLE   From ancient times, caves have been considered hallowed places in India, because they were frequently the abodes of holy men and ascetics. Around the second century BCE, cavelike sanctuaries were hewn out of the stone plateaus in the region of south-central India known as the Deccan. Made for the use of Jain and Buddhist monks, these sanctuaries were

carved from top to bottom like great pieces of sculpture, with all details completely finished in stone. The cool, dark interior and the echo that magnifies the smallest sound combine to promote a state of heightened awareness in these remarkable halls.

The monastic community used two types of rock-cut halls. The **vihara** functioned as the monks' living quarters, and the **chaitya** ("sanctuary") usually enshrined a stupa. A **CHAITYA HALL** at Karle (**FIG. 10–11**), dating from the first century BCE to the first century CE, is one of the largest and most fully developed examples of these early Buddhist works. At the entrance, columns once supported a wooden façade, in front of which stands a pillar, inspired by Ashokan precedents. The walls of the vestibule are carved in relief with rows of small balcony railings and arched windows, simulating the appearance of a great multi-storied palace. At the base of the side walls, enormous statues of elephants seem to support the entire structure on their backs. Dominating the upper portion of the main façade is a large, horseshoe-shaped opening that provides the hall's main source of light.

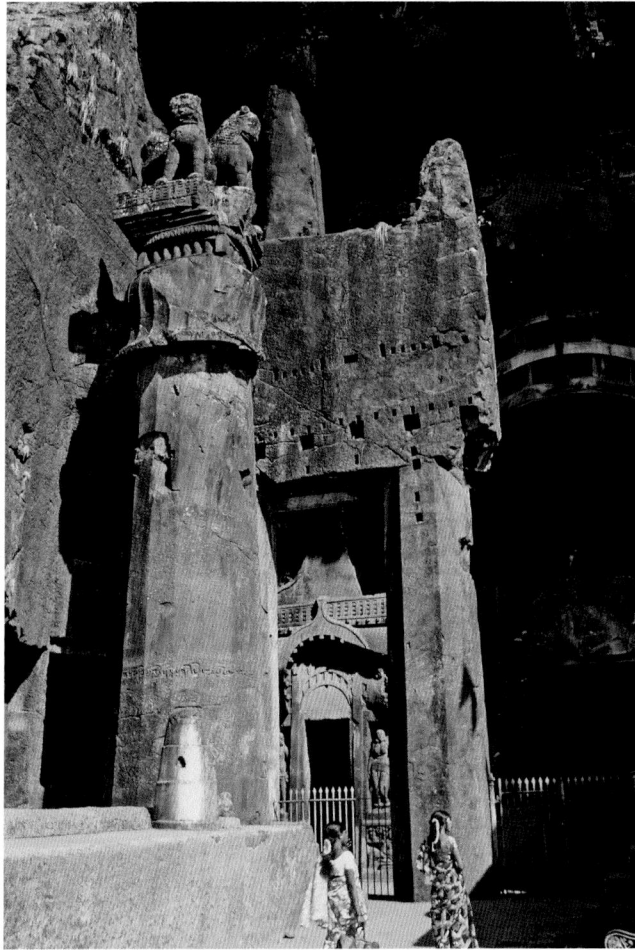

10–11 EXTERIOR OF CHAITYA HALL, KARLE

Maharashtra, India. 1st century BCE–1st century CE.

Credit: Image: Regents of the University of Michigan, History of Art Department, Visual Resources Collections

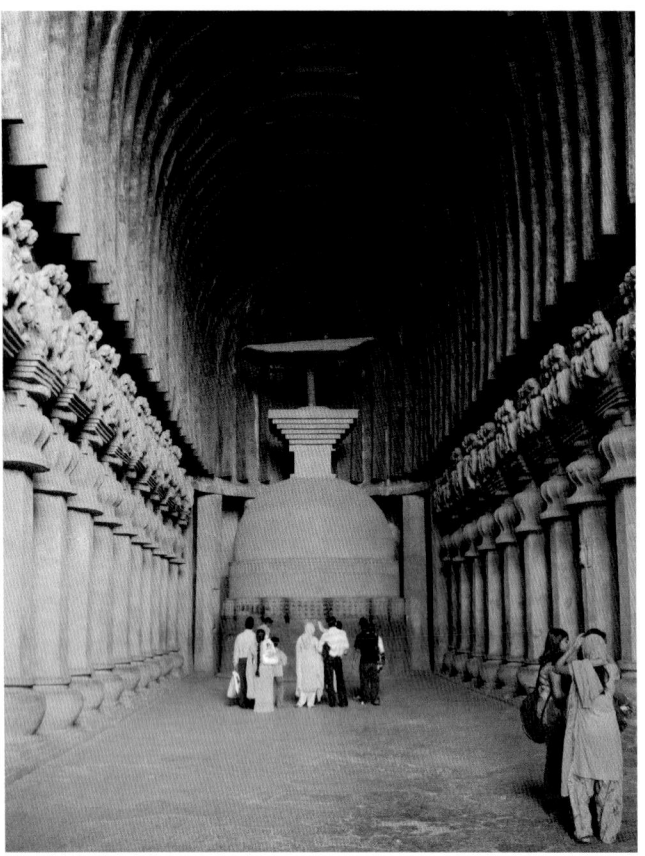

10-12 INTERIOR OF CHAITYA HALL, KARLE

Maharashtra, India. 1st century BCE–1st century CE.

Credit: © Ivan Vdovin/JAI/Corbis

The opening was originally fitted with a carved wooden screen, some of which remains, that filtered the light streaming inside.

Three entrances allow access to the interior. Flanking the doorways are sculpted panels of **mithuna** couples, amorous male and female figures that evoke the auspicious qualities of harmony and fertility in life. The **INTERIOR HALL** (**FIG. 10-12**), 123 feet long, has a 46-foot-high ceiling carved in the form of a barrel vault ornamented with arching wooden ribs. Both the interior and exterior of the hall were once brightly painted. Pillars demarcate a pathway for circumambulation around the stupa in the apse at the far end.

The side aisles are separated from the main aisle by closely spaced columns whose bases resemble a large pot set on a stepped pyramid of planks. The statues that comprise the upper capitals of these columns depict pairs of kneeling elephants, each bearing a *mithuna* couple. These figures, the only sculpture within this austere hall, may represent the nobility coming to pay homage. The pillars around the apse are plain, and the stupa is simple. A railing motif ornaments its base. The stupa was once topped with wooden umbrellas, only one of which remains. As with nearly everything in the cave, the stupa is carved from the rock of the cliff.

The Kushan Period

Around the first century CE, the regions of present-day Afghanistan, Pakistan, and north India came under the control of the Kushans, originally a nomadic people forced out of northwest China by the Han. Exact dates are uncertain, but they ruled from the first to the third century CE.

These heavily bearded warrior-kings made widespread use of royal portraiture on coins and in sculptural form. An image of **KING KANISHKA** (**FIG. 10-13**), whose reign is thought to have begun in 127 CE, represents one of the Kushans' most illustrious rulers. This boldly frontal work stands over 5 feet tall even with the head missing. The fact that his hands rest on his sword and massive club makes his martial authority clear even before reading the inscription, which identifies him as "The great king, king of kings." Attired in a coat and heavy felt riding boots, he is ill-suited for the warm South Asian climate; his garments reflect his Central Asian heritage. The hundreds of pearls that line the hem of his outfit are indicative of his great wealth and were particularly rare in the inland territories from which the Kushan migrated.

10-13 KING KANISHKA

Uttar Pradesh, India. c. 2nd–3rd century CE. Sandstone, height 5'3" (1.6 m). Government Museum, Mathura.

Credit: © T Paramjit/Ancient Art & Architecture Collection Ltd

These rulers were remarkably eclectic in their religious views and, judging from their coins, supported a wide range of religious institutions. In this tolerant climate, and perhaps spurred on by Kushan royal images, innovative figural art began to blossom in the Jain, Brahmanic, and Buddhist traditions.

Among these innovations are the first depictions of the Buddha himself in art. (Previously, as in the Great Stupa at Sanchi, the Buddha had been indicated solely by symbols.) Distinctive styles arose in the Gandhara region in the northwest (present-day Pakistan and Afghanistan) and in the important religious center of Mathura in central India. While the images from these Kushan-controlled regions are stylistically quite distinct, they shared a basic visual language, or iconography, in which the Buddha is readily recognized by specific characteristics. For instance, he wears a monk's robe, a long length of cloth draped over the left shoulder and around the body. The Buddha also is said to have had 32 major distinguishing marks, called **lakshanas**, some of which are reflected in the iconography (see "Buddhist Symbols" in Chapter 12 on page 370). These marks of a perfected being include a golden-colored body, long arms that reached to his knees, the impression of a wheel (*chakra*) on the palms of his hands and the soles of his feet, and the **urna**—a mark between his eyebrows. A prince in his youth, he had worn the customary heavy earrings, and so his earlobes are usually shown elongated. The top of his head is said to have had a protuberance called an **ushnisha**, which in images often resembles a bun or topknot and symbolizes his enlightenment.

THE GANDHARA STYLE   Combining elements of Hellenistic, Persian, and Indian styles, Gandhara sculptors typically portrayed the Buddha as an athletic figure, more powerful and heroic than an ordinary human. Carved from gray schist, a fine-grained stone, this **STANDING BUDDHA** (**FIG. 10–14**) dates to the fully developed stage of the Gandhara style, during the second or early third century CE. The Buddha's body, whose contours are revealed through the folds of his garment, is broad and massive, with heavy shoulders and limbs and powerful legs. His left knee bends gently, suggesting a slightly relaxed posture.

The treatment of the robe is especially characteristic of the Gandhara manner. Naturalistic folds alternate with clinging cloth, setting up a clear, rhythmic pattern of heavy creases and shallow depressions. On the upper part of the figure, the folds break irregularly along the Buddha's left arm; below his waist they drape in a symmetric U shape. The strong tension of the complex fold pattern brings life and power to the figure. It resembles the treatment of togas on certain Roman statues (SEE FIG. 6–21) that exerted a strong influence on portrayals of the Buddha in Central and East Asia. The Gandhara region's relations with the Hellenistic world may have brought this strong

10–14 STANDING BUDDHA
From Gandhara, Pakistan. Kushan period, c. 2nd–3rd century CE. Gray schist, height 47½" (1.2 m). Los Angeles County Museum of Art. Gift of Mr. and Mrs. Eric Lidow in honour of the museum's twenty-fifth anniversary (M.91.90)

Mediterranean feeling to its art. Pockets of Hellenistic culture had thrived in neighboring Bactria (present-day northern Afghanistan and southern Uzbekistan) since the fourth century BCE, when the Greeks under Alexander the Great had reached the borders of India. Also, Gandhara's position near the east–west trade routes stimulated contact with Roman culture in the Near East during the early centuries of the first millennium CE.

THE MATHURA STYLE The second major style of Buddhist art in the Kushan period—that found at Mathura—was not allied with the Hellenistic-Roman tradition. Instead, the Mathura style evolved from representations of *yakshas*, the indigenous male nature deities. Early images of the Buddha produced at Mathura draw on this sculptural tradition, often portraying him in a frontal stance with broad shoulders and wide eyes.

The stele shown here (**FIG. 10-15**) is one of the finest of the early Mathura images. The sculptors worked in a distinctive red sandstone flecked with cream-colored spots. Carved in **high relief** (forms projecting strongly from the background), it depicts a seated Buddha with two

10-15 BUDDHA AND ATTENDANTS
From Katra Keshavdev, Mathura, Madhya Pradesh, India. Kushan period, c. late 1st–early 2nd century CE. Red sandstone, height 27¼" (69.2 cm). Government Museum, Mathura.

Credit: Photo: Frederick M. Asher

attendants. His right hand is raised in a symbolic gesture meaning "have no fear." Images of the Buddha rely on a repertoire of such gestures, called **mudras**, to communicate certain ideas, such as teaching, meditation, or the attaining of enlightenment (see "Mudras" opposite). The Buddha's *urna*, his *ushnisha*, and the impressions of wheels on his palms and soles are all clearly visible in this figure. Behind his head is a large, circular halo; the scallop points of its border represent radiating light. Behind the halo are branches of the pipal tree, the tree under which the Buddha was seated when he achieved enlightenment. Two celestial beings hover above.

As in Gandhara sculptures, the Mathura work gives a powerful impression of the Buddha. The diaphanous quality of his robe is suited to the warm climate of Mathura, just as the thick robe of the Gandhara example is appropriate in the cooler weather of the northwest. The robe is pulled tightly over the body, allowing the fleshy form to be seen as almost nude. Where the pleats of the robe appear, such as over the left arm and fanning out between the legs, they are depicted abstractly through compact parallel formations of ridges with an incised line in the center of each ridge. This characteristic Mathura tendency to abstraction also appears in the face, whose features take on geometric shapes, as in the rounded forms of the widely opened eyes. Nevertheless, the torso with its subtle and soft modeling is strongly naturalistic. This Buddha's riveting outward gaze and alert posture impart an intense, concentrated energy that draws on imagery associated with nature deities and reveals a spiritual power contained in physical form.

Hinduism

Alongside the development of Buddhism, the older Vedic traditions underwent a long process of reform. These reforms were largely undertaken by members of the Brahmin community who had grown unsatisfied with the older systems of rituals. What emerged from these reforms was a series of practices and beliefs that we now collectively refer to as Hinduism. Hinduism is not one religion but many related beliefs and innumerable sects. It results from the mingling of Vedic beliefs with indigenous, local beliefs and practices. All three major Hindu sects draw upon the texts of the Vedas, which are believed to be sacred revelations set down about 1200–800 BCE. The gods lie outside the finite world, but they can appear in visible form to believers. Each Hindu sect takes its particular deity as supreme. By worshiping gods with rituals, meditation, and intense love, individuals may be reborn into increasingly higher positions until they escape the cycle of life, death, and rebirth, which is called *samsara*. The most popular deities are Vishnu, Shiva, and the Great Goddess, Devi. Deities are revealed and depicted in multiple aspects.

Art and its Contexts

MUDRAS

Mudras (Sanskrit for "signs") are ancient symbolic hand gestures that first appeared in a manual on dance, but came to be regarded as physical expressions of a particular action or state of being. In Buddhist art, they function iconographically. *Mudras* are also used during meditation to invoke specific states of mind. The following are the most common *mudras* in Asian art.

Dharmachakra mudra

Appears as if the subject is counting on his fingers. The gesture of teaching, setting the *chakra* (wheel) of the *dharma* (law or doctrine) in motion. Hands are at chest level.

Dhyana mudra

A gesture of meditation and balance, symbolizing the path toward enlightenment. Hands are in the lap, the lower representing *maya*, the physical world of illusion, the upper representing *nirvana*, enlightenment and release from the world.

Vitarka mudra

This variant of *dharmachakra mudra* stands for intellectual debate. The right and/or left hand is held at shoulder level with thumb and forefinger touching. The gesture resembles counting on the fingers with one hand.

Abhaya mudra

The gesture of reassurance, blessing, and protection, this *mudra* means "have no fear." The right hand is at shoulder level, with the palm outward.

Bhumisparsha mudra

This gesture calls upon the earth to witness Shakyamuni Buddha's enlightenment at Bodh Gaya. A seated figure's right hand reaches toward the ground, palm inward.

Varada mudra

The gesture of charity, symbolizing the fulfillment of all wishes. Alone, this *mudra* is made with the right hand; but when combined with *abhaya mudra* in standing Buddha figures (as is most common), the left hand is occasionally shown in *varada mudra*.

mudras

VISHNU: Vishnu is a regal god who works for the order and well-being of the world. He is often represented lying in a trance or asleep on the Cosmic Waters, where he dreams the world into existence. His attributes include the discus, conch shell, mace, and lotus. He usually has four arms and wears a crown and lavish jewelry. He rides a man-bird, Garuda. Vishnu appears in ten different incarnations (*avatara*), including Rama and Krishna, who have their own sects. Rama embodies virtue, and, assisted by the monkey king, he fights the demon Ravana. As Krishna, Vishnu is a supremely beautiful, blue-skinned youth who lives with the cowherds, loves the maiden Radha, and battles the demon Kansa.

SHIVA: Shiva is both creative and destructive, light and dark, male and female, ascetic and family man. His symbol is the *linga*, originally an upright phallus, which is typically represented as a low pillar set in a low base, or *yoni*, which represents the feminine. As an expression of his power and creative energy, he is often depicted as Lord of the Dance, dancing the Cosmic Dance, the endless cycle of death and rebirth, destruction and creation (SEE FIG. 10–33). He dances within a ring of fire, his four hands holding fire, carrying a drum, and gesturing to the worshipers. Shiva's animal vehicle is the bull. His consort is Parvati; their sons are the elephant-headed Ganesha, the remover of obstacles, and Karttikeya, often associated with war.

DEVI: Devi, the Great Goddess, controls material riches and fertility. She has forms indicative of beauty, wealth, and auspiciousness, but also forms of wrath, pestilence, and power. As the embodiment of cosmic energy, she provides the vital force to all the male gods. When armed and riding a lion (as the goddess Durga), she personifies righteous fury. As the goddess Lakshmi, she is the goddess of wealth and the auspicious.

There are countless other deities, but central to Hindu practice are *puja* (forms of worship) and *darshan* (beholding a deity), generally performed to obtain a deity's favor in the hope that this favor will lead to liberation from *samsara*. Because desire for the fruits of our actions traps us, the ideal is to consider all earthly endeavors as sacrificial offerings to a god. Pleased with our devotion, he or she may grant us an eternal state of pure being, pure consciousness, and pure bliss.

The Gupta Period and its Successors

The Guptas, who founded a dynasty in the eastern region of central India, expanded their territories during the fourth century CE to form an empire that encompassed northern and much of central India. Although Gupta rule was not long-lasting (ending in 550) or the most expansive, the influence of Gupta culture was tremendous and its impact was felt long after its decline. Renowned for their flourishing artistic, mathematical, and literary culture, the Guptas and their contemporaries brought forth some of India's most widely admired works of art. While Buddhism continued to be a major religion, the earliest surviving Hindu temples also date from this time.

By the fourth century the Vedic sacrifice, in which burnt offerings were ritually sent up to the gods, had given way to temple-based practices that invoked the divine presence into a sanctified architectural setting. These practices, collectively termed Hinduism by later observers, were still presided over by Brahmin priests but often brought new deities into prominence.

TEMPLE OF VISHNU AT DEOGARH One of the earliest northern-style temples, dedicated to the Hindu god Vishnu, is at Deogarh in north-central India and dates to 530 CE (**FIG. 10-16**). The entire temple site is patterned on a *mandala*, or sacred diagram. Much of the central tower, or *shikhara*, has crumbled away, so we cannot determine its original shape with precision. Clearly a massive, solid structure built of large cut stones, it would have given the impression of a mountain, one of several metaphoric meanings of a Hindu temple. The temple has only one chamber, the *garbhagriha*, literally the womb chamber, which corresponds to the center of a *mandala*. As the deity's residence, the *garbhagriha* is likened to a sacred cavern within the "cosmic mountain" of the temple.

Large panels sculpted in relief with images of Vishnu appear as "windows" on the temple's exterior. These elaborately framed panels do not function literally to let light

10-16 VISHNU TEMPLE, DEOGARH
Uttar Pradesh, India.
Gupta dynasty, c. 530 CE.

Credit: Borromeo/Art Resource, NY

10-17 VISHNU LYING ON THE COSMIC WATERS
Relief panel in the Vishnu Temple, Deogarh. c. 530 CE. Sandstone, height approx. 5' (1.5 m).

Credit: © akg-images/Jean-Louis Nou

richly ornamented. The ideal of the Gupta style is evident in the smooth, perfected shape of the body and in the lavishly detailed jewelry, including Vishnu's characteristic cylindrical crown. The four figures on the right in the frieze below Vishnu personify his four attributes. They stand ready to fight the appearance of evil, represented at the left of the frieze by two demons who threaten to kill Brahma and jeopardize all creation.

The birth of the universe and the appearance of evil are thus portrayed here in three clearly organized registers. Typical of Indian religious and artistic expression, these momentous events are set before our eyes not in terms of abstract symbols, but as a drama acted out by gods in superhuman form.

SEATED BUDDHA FROM SARNATH Buddhism continued to thrive during the Gupta period. Although the Gandhara style

into the temple; they function symbolically to let the light of the deity *out* of the temple to be seen by those outside.

One panel depicts **VISHNU LYING ON THE COSMIC WATERS** at the beginning of creation (**FIG. 10-17**). He sleeps on the serpent of infinity, Ananta, whose body coils endlessly into space. Stirred by his female aspect (*shakti*, or female energy), personified here by the goddess Lakshmi, seen holding his foot, Vishnu dreams the universe into existence. From his navel springs a lotus (shown in this relief behind Vishnu), from which emerges the god Brahma (not to be confused with Brahman), who appears here as the central, four-headed figure in the row of gods portrayed above the reclining Vishnu. Brahma subsequently turns himself into the universe of space and time by thinking, "May I become many."

The sculptor has depicted Vishnu as a large, resplendent figure with four arms. His size and his multiple arms denote his omnipotence. He is lightly garbed but

eventually declined in influence, the Mathura style gave rise to the Buddhist visual forms found over much of north India, including at sites like Sarnath.

A seated Buddha (**FIG. 10-18**) embodies the fully developed Sarnath Gupta style. Carved from fine-grained sandstone, the figure sits in a yogic posture making the teaching gesture indicative of the First Sermon. This event is further indicated by the devotees/listeners represented on the pedestal along with a wheel whose tread faces toward the viewer. The devotees, who may also represent the donors of this image, are joined in their devotion by two divine beings flying in from above. The Buddha's plain robe, portrayed with none of the creases and folds so prominent in the Kushan-period images, is typical of the Sarnath style. The body, clearly visible through the clinging robe, is graceful and slight, with broad shoulders and a well-proportioned torso. Only a few lines of the garment at the neck, waist, and hems interrupt the purity of its subtly

10-18 BUDDHA PREACHING HIS FIRST SERMON
From Sarnath, Uttar Pradesh, India. Gupta period, c. 465–485 CE.
Sandstone, height 5'3" (1.6 m). Archaeological Museum, Sarnath.

Credit: Luca Tettoni/Robert Harding

shaped surfaces; the face, smooth and ovoid, has the same refined elegance. The downcast eyes suggest otherworldly introspection, yet the gentle, open posture maintains a human quality. Behind the head is a large, circular halo. Carved in concentric circles of pearls and foliage, the ornate halo contrasts dramatically with the plain surfaces of the figure.

THE AJANTA CAVES Prior to the late fifth century, the Vakataka dynasty had been subject to Gupta rule. Shortly after winning regional control, people affiliated with their court began to sponsor a new phase of construction at the rock-cut monastery of Ajanta. Each of these large caves, over 20 in all, appears to have had its own major patron. Whether inspired by devotion or competition, these caves are among the finest rock-cut architecture found anywhere. Adding to their importance is the fact that they preserve examples of wall painting, giving us a rare glimpse of a refined art form that has almost entirely been lost to time. Of these examples, Cave I, a large *vihara* hall with monks' chambers around the sides and a Buddha shrine chamber in the back, houses some of the finest. Murals painted in

mineral pigments on a prepared plaster surface cover the walls of the central court. Some depict episodes from the Buddha's past lives, while two large bodhisattvas, one of which is seen here (**FIG. 10-19**), flank the entrance to the shrine chamber.

Bodhisattvas are enlightened beings who postpone *nirvana* and buddhahood to help others achieve enlightenment. They are distinguished from buddhas in art by their princely garments. This bodhisattva is lavishly adorned with delicate ornaments: a bejeweled crown, large earrings, a pearl necklace, armbands, and bracelets. A striped cloth covers his lower body. The graceful bending posture and serene gaze impart a sympathetic attitude. The lotus flower in his right hand indicates his possible identity as the compassionate bodhisattva Avalokiteshvara.

The naturalistic style balances outline and softly graded color tones. Outline drawing, always a major ingredient of Indian painting, clearly defines shapes; tonal gradations impart the illusion of three-dimensional form, with lighter tones used for protruding parts such as the

10-19 BODHISATTVA
Detail of a wall painting in Cave I, Ajanta, Maharashtra, India.
Vakataka dynasty, c. 475 CE.

Credit: © age fotostock/Dinodia

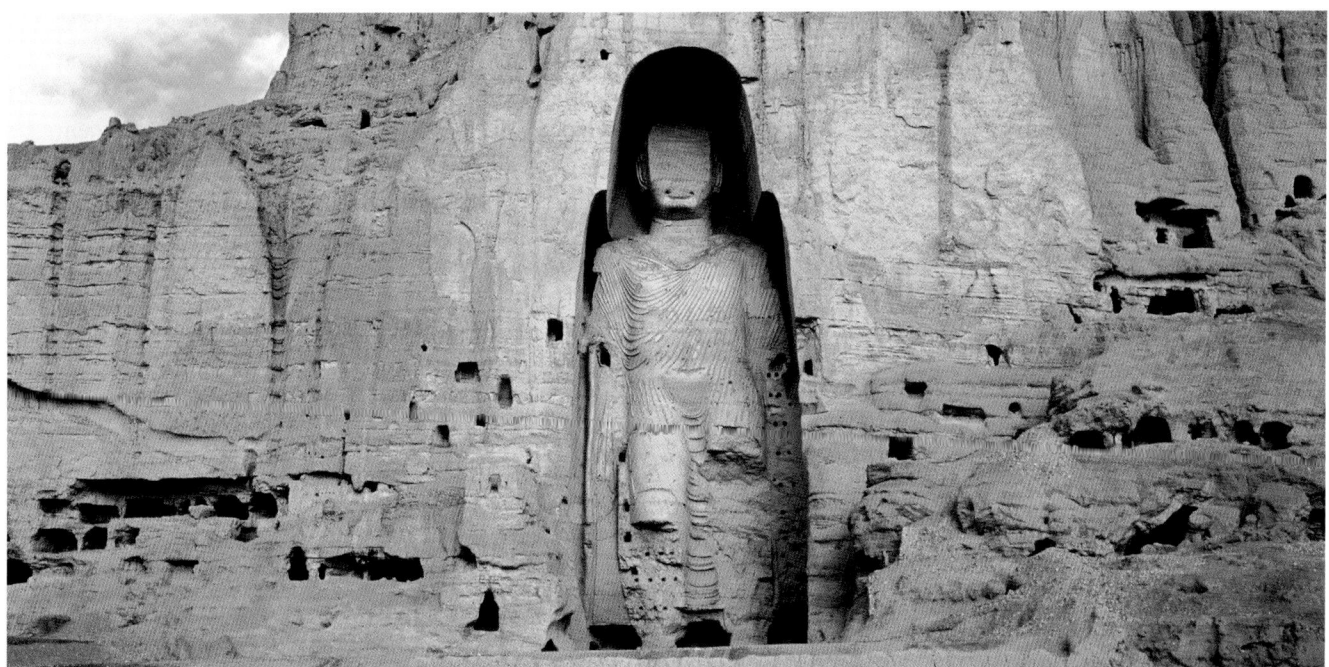

10–20 STANDING BUDDHA

Bamiyan, Afghanistan. c. 5th century CE. Sandstone coated in stucco, 165′ (50 m).

This photograph pre-dates the destruction of the Buddhas in 2001. Their recesses now stand empty.

Credit: Borromeo/Art Resource, NY

nose, brows, shoulders, and chest muscles. Together with the details of the jewels, these highlighted areas resonate against the subdued tonality of the figure. Sophisticated, realistic detail is balanced by the languorous human form. This particular synthesis is evident also in the Sarnath statue (SEE FIG. 10–18), which has much in common as well with the sculpture of Ajanta.

Other Developments, Fifth to the Seventh Centuries

After the fall of Gupta, north Indian empires struggled to match the splendor and stability of their predecessor, and by the late sixth century power shifted to the south where new and expansive empires emerged. These empires grew wealthy on trade and solidified their positions as transregional powers. As trade networks expanded, South Asian ideas and religions spread with them. This was good news for Buddhism, because as competition with Hinduism increased, the Buddhists found more receptive communities abroad.

THE BAMIYAN BUDDHAS   The Gupta and their feudatories were by no means the only kingdoms to flourish in fifth- to seventh-century South Asia. Bamiyan, about 155 miles northwest of Kabul, Afghanistan, was one example. Located just west of one of the most treacherous portions of the Silk Road, it was both a haven and crossroad on the lucrative trade routes that reached from China to the West. There, two enormous Buddhas were carved from

the rock of a cliff, one some 115 feet in height, the other about 165 feet tall (**FIG. 10–20**). Recorded by a Chinese pilgrim who came to Bamiyan in the seventh century, these Buddhas must date from before his visit. Buddhist travelers may have offered gifts of thanks or prayers for safety, depending on their destinations. On the right side of the smaller figure, pilgrims could walk within the cliff up a staircase that ended at the Buddha's shoulder. There they could look into the vault of the niche and see a painted image of the sun god, suggesting a metaphoric pilgrimage to the heavens. They could then circumambulate the figure at the level of the head and return to ground level by a staircase on the figure's left side. These huge figures likely served as the model for those at rock-cut sanctuaries in China, for example, at Yungang. Despite the historical and religious importance of these figures, and ignoring the pleas of world leaders, the Taliban demolished the Bamiyan Buddhas in 2001.

SIGIRIYA, SRI LANKA   Far away from Afghanistan, in the south, the palace site of **SIGIRIYA** was built on a dramatic plateau that rises abruptly above the forest canopy in north-central Sri Lanka (**FIG. 10–21**). According to the royal chronicles, this structure was built by King Kassapa in the late 400s CE after he usurped the throne from his father and drove off his brother. Visitors to the palace first passed through a broad moat and elaborate terraced gardens before beginning their ascent. At its base, the staircase passed through the chest of a massive sculptural lion, of which only the naturalistically rendered feet still exist.

10–21 SIGIRIYA
Matale District, Central Province, Sri Lanka. 5th century CE. Aerial view.

Credit: © Tuul and Bruno Morandi/Getty Images

As visitors climbed higher they were greeted by painted murals depicting elegant **HEAVENLY MAIDENS** moving among clouds (**FIG. 10-22**) before emerging at the top of the plateau. Only the foundations of the palace buildings, cisterns, and a few sculptures remain, but they are sufficient to convey a sense of the site's imposing splendor and spectacular elevation. Kassapa did not have long to enjoy his luxurious and well-fortified home, however, because within approximately 11 years the rightful heir, his brother Moggallana, returned with an army and took back the kingdom. After his victory, Moggallana gave Sigiriya to the Buddhists as a monastery.

TEMPLE OF SHIVA AT ELEPHANTA The Hindu god Shiva exhibits a wide range of aspects or forms, both gentle and wild: He is the Great Yogi who dwells for vast periods of time in meditation in the Himalayas; he is also the husband par excellence who makes love to the goddess Parvati for eons at a time; he is the Slayer of Demons; and he is the Cosmic Dancer who dances the destruction and re-creation of the world. Many of these forms of Shiva appear in the monumental relief panels adorning a cave-temple carved in the mid sixth century on the island of Elephanta off the coast of Mumbai in western India. The cave-temple is complex in layout and conception and is

10-22 HEAVENLY MAIDENS
Detail of wall painting, Sigiriya. 5th century CE.

Credit: Fuchsphotography/Fotolia

**10-23 CAVE-TEMPLE
OF SHIVA, ELEPHANTA**
Maharashtra, India. Post-Gupta
period, mid 6th century CE.
View along the east–west axis to
the *linga* shrine.

Credit: © age fotostock/Dinodia

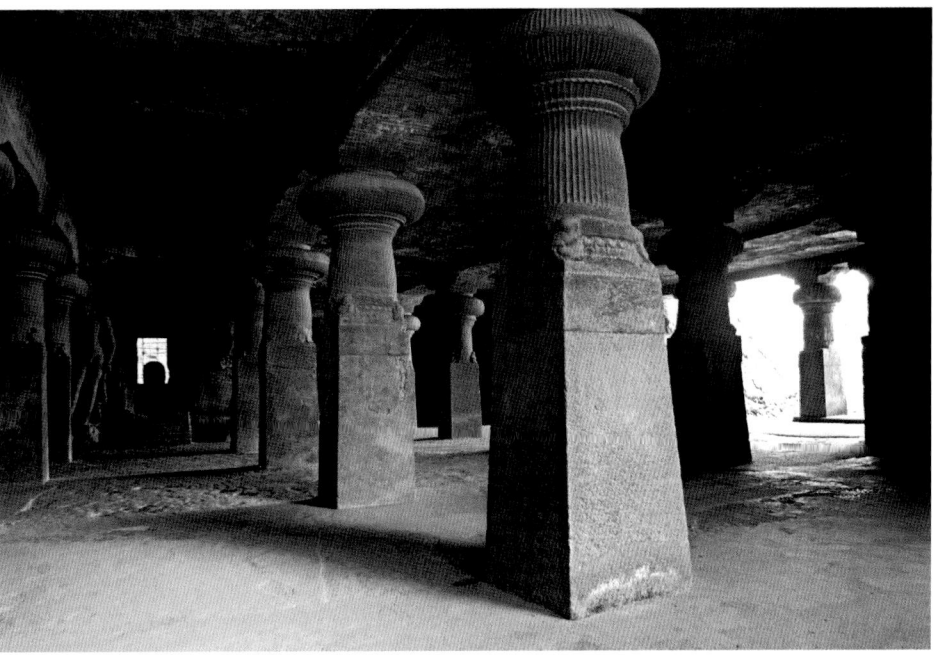

a fine example of Hindu rock-cut architecture. While most temples have one entrance, this temple offers three—one facing north, one east, and one west. The interior, impressive in its size and grandeur, is designed along two main axes, one running north–south, the other east–west. The three entrances provide the only source of light, and the resulting cross- and back-lighting effects add to the sense of the cave as a place of mysterious, almost confusing complexity.

Along the east–west axis, large pillars cut from the rock appear to support the low ceiling and its beams, although, as with all architectural elements in a cave-temple, they are not structural (**FIG. 10-23**). The pillars form orderly rows, but the rows are hard to discern within the framework of the cave shape, which is neither square nor longitudinal, but formed of overlapping *mandalas* that create a symmetric yet irregular space. The pillars each have an unadorned, square base rising to nearly half the pillar's total height. Above is a circular column, which has a curved contour and a billowing "cushion" capital. Both

column and capital are delicately fluted, adding a surprising refinement to these otherwise sturdy forms. The focus of the east–west axis is a square **linga shrine** (SEE FIG. 10–23, center left). A pair of colossal standing guardian figures flank each of its four entrances. In the center of the shrine is the *linga*, the abstracted symbol of Shiva that represents his presence as the unmanifest Formless One, or Brahman. Synonymous with Shiva, the *linga* is seen in nearly every Shiva temple and shrine.

The focus of the north–south axis, in contrast, is a relief on the south wall with a huge bust of Shiva representing his Sadashiva, or **ETERNAL SHIVA**, aspect (**FIG. 10-24**). Three heads rest upon the broad shoulders of the upper body, but five heads are implied: the fourth behind and the fifth, never depicted, on top. The head in the front depicts Shiva deep in introspection. The massiveness of the broad head, the large, barely delineated eyes, and the mouth with its heavy lower lip all suggest the

10-24 ETERNAL SHIVA
Rock-cut relief in the cave-temple of Shiva, Elephanta.
Mid 6th century CE.
Height approx. 11′ (3.4 m).

Credit: © ephotocorp/Alamy Stock Photo

god's serious depths. Lordly and majestic, he easily supports his huge crown, intricately carved with designs and jewels, and the matted, piled-up hair of a yogi. On his left shoulder, his creative nature is depicted as female, with curled hair and a pearl-festooned crown. On his right shoulder, his wrathful, destroyer nature wears a fierce expression, and snakes adorn his ear and hand.

The Pallava Period

Rising to power in the late sixth century, the Pallava dynasty spread from its heartland in southeastern India, drawing wealth from overseas trade. The kingdom grew to its peak during the reigns of King Mahendravarman I (c. 600–630 CE) and his successor Narasimhavarman I (c. 630–668 CE), who was also referred to by his nickname "Mamalla" (which alludes to his skill at wrestling). Both men sponsored rock-cut shrines and sculpture at the coastal city of Mamallapuram, near Chennai. Often religious in subject matter, the carving is at times infused with a whimsical humor. This good-natured irreverence emerges most clearly in the Pallava literary tradition. One well-known farcical drama attributed to Mahendravarman himself pokes fun at Tantric ascetics, Buddhist monks, and Brahmin priests.

At Mamallapuram there are many large boulders and cliffs along the shore from which the Pallava-period stonecutters carved entire temples as well as reliefs. Among the most interesting of these rock-cut temples is a group known as the Five Rathas, which preserve diverse early architectural styles that probably reflect contemporary wood or brick structures.

DHARMARAJA RATHA AT MAMALLAPURAM One of this group, today called the **DHARMARAJA RATHA** (**FIG. 10-25**), epitomizes the early southern-style temple. Each story of the superstructure is articulated by a cornice and carries a row of miniature shrines. Both shrines and cornices are decorated with a window motif from which faces peer. The shrines not only demarcate each story, but also provide loftiness for this palace intended to enshrine a god. The temple, square in plan, remains unfinished, and what would have been a pillared hall on the first floor was never hollowed out, suggesting that, like cave-temples, Dharmaraja Ratha was executed from the top downward. On the lower portion, only the columns and niches have been carved. The presence of a single deity in each niche forecasts the main trend in temple sculpture in the centuries ahead: The tradition of narrative reliefs declined, and the stories they told became concentrated in statues of individual deities, which conjure up entire mythological episodes through characteristic poses and a few symbolic objects. On the south side of this ratha, among the images of deities, is an unusual two-armed image identified as a representation of King Mamalla, who appears to be visually associating himself with Shiva. This practice of depicting royalty in the likeness of divinity became more common over time and was widely practiced in parts of Southeast Asia.

THE GREAT RELIEF AT MAMALLAPURAM There are many possible ways to interpret an enormous relief at Mamallapuram (**FIG. 10-26**), and this ambiguity was almost certainly intended by its creators. In Sanskrit poetry, the use of overlapping meaning is called *slesha*, and it was appreciated for its sophistication. The most prominent interpretation of this scene is that it depicts the penance of a king, Bhagiratha, who sought to purify the bones of his deceased relatives by subjecting himself to terrible austerities. In response to his penance, the god Shiva sent the sacred Ganges River, represented by the natural cleft in the rock, to earth, thereby allowing the holy man to ensure his relatives some peace in their next lives. Bhagiratha is shown

10-25 DHARMARAJA RATHA, MAMALLAPURAM
Tamil Nadu, India. Pallava period, c. mid 7th century CE.

Credit: Arvind Balaraman/Fotolia

10-26 DESCENT OF THE GANGES

Rock-cut relief, Mamallapuram, Tamil Nadu, India. Mid 7th century CE. Granite, approx. 20′ (6 m).

Credit: Snowwhiteimages/Fotolia

staring directly at the sun through his parted fingers, standing for interminable periods on one foot, and in deep prayer before a temple. In the upper left part of the relief, Shiva, shown four-armed, appears before Bhagiratha to grant his wish. Elsewhere in the relief animal families are depicted, generally in mutually protective roles. But in a characteristically Pallava twist, this pious scene is mimicked by a cat who does his best to imitate Bhagiratha's pose (**FIG. 10-27**). The reference is to the story of an aging cat who pretends to be an ascetic who has renounced meat, so as to lure the local mice into complacency, much to their misfortune. This cautionary tale about false ascetics serves as an apt and humorous foil to the upper scene of consummate penance and faith. Both tales are set on the banks of the Ganges.

This richly carved relief was executed under the Pallava dynasty, which continued to flourish in southeastern India until the ninth century CE. The relief must have been visible to anyone heading inland from the sea and likely served as an allegory for benevolent kingship. It was possibly even an attempt to invoke the presence of the sacred Ganges River right at the heart of the Pallavas' southern empire.

10-27 CAT IN YOGIC POSTURE

Detail from rock-cut relief, Mamallapuram, Tamil Nadu, India. Mid 7th century CE.

Credit: Nstanev/Fotolia

The Eighth through Twelfth Centuries

During the eighth through twelfth centuries, regional styles developed in ruling kingdoms that were generally smaller than those that had preceded them. Hindu gods Vishnu, Shiva, and the Great Goddess (mainly Durga) grew increasingly popular. Monarchs rivaled each other in the building of temples to their favored deity, and complicated and subtle variations of the Hindu temple emerged with astounding rapidity in different regions. By around 1000 the Hindu temple reached unparalleled heights of grandeur and engineering.

KAILASHA TEMPLE, ELLORA Occupied and expanded from the fifth to the tenth century, the rock-cut site of Ellora has 34 caves in all, variously dedicated to Buddhism, Jainism, and Hinduism. Among the most spectacular of these is "Cave" 16, the **KAILASHA TEMPLE** (FIG. 10–28), which

was most likely started in the reign of the Rashtrakuta king Krishna I (ruled 757–83 CE) and completed under his successors. In many ways, this structure marks the apex of the South Asian rock-cut tradition, as the skilled architects and artists successfully sculpted an entire two-story, highly ornamented Shiva temple out of a single mass of stone. The structure is set back in the mountainside, which required cutting straight down 107 feet so that the rock would be high enough to accommodate the stepped, southern-style tower.

Passing the outer gateway, devotees can circumambulate at ground level and admire the narrative sculptural scenes and large elephants that adorn the lower plinth. Alternately, visitors can climb an internal staircase to a second level where a relatively small shrine dedicated to Shiva's bull-mount, Nandi, faces the main temple across a bridge. The interior of the main temple hall (*mandapa*) was originally painted with additional narrative imagery. The *garbhagriha* can be circumambulated from the second story by coming out onto a balcony from which a

10-28 KAILASHA TEMPLE, CAVE 16, ELLORA
Aurangabad District, Maharashtra, India. Mid 8th century CE.

Credit: Michalknitl/Fotolia

10-29 KANDARIYA MAHADEVA TEMPLE, KHAJURAHO
Madhya Pradesh, India. Chandella dynasty, c. 1000 CE.

Credit: © Westend61 GmbH/Alamy Stock Photo

number of subsidiary shrines radiate. The narrative sculpture throughout the site depicts a wide range of deities and events from Hindu literature, many of which feature Shiva.

This site takes the metaphorical association between temples and mountains to an extreme as it is constructed, quite literally, from a mountain. Even the temple itself is named for Shiva's abode on Mount Kailasha in the Himalayas. Despite this association, remote mountainside locations better suited the needs of Buddhist and Jain monastic communities. Such locations proved to fit poorly with the public nature and ritual requirements of Hindu temples. The Kailasha Temple stands as the last of the great rock-cut Hindu temples. From this point on, architects and donors favored built structures placed in or near major urban centers.

KANDARIYA MAHADEVA TEMPLE, KHAJURAHO In 950 CE, the Chandella court moved against the weakened Pratihara dynasty, to whom they were vassals. This rebellion proved successful, and the Chandella marked their new status by undertaking an ambitious project of temple building. The earliest of these structures housed an image of Vishnu taken directly from their previous overlords, but this temple was only the first among many. Khajuraho remained the capital and main temple site for the Chandellas, who constructed more than 80 temples there, about 25 of which are well preserved.

The **KANDARIYA MAHADEVA** (**FIG. 10-29**), a temple dedicated to Shiva at Khajuraho, was probably built by a ruler of the Chandella dynasty in the late tenth or early

eleventh century. In the northern style, a curvilinear *shikhara* rises over the *garbhagriha* of the temple. Extensively ornamented with additional halls on the front and porches to the sides and back, the temple rests on a stone terrace that sets off a sacred space from the mundane world. A steep flight of stairs at the front (to the right in the illustration) leads to a series of three *mandapas* (distinguished on the outside by pyramidal roofs), preceding the *garbhagriha*. The *mandapas* serve as spaces for ritual, such as dances performed for the deity, and for the presentation of offerings. The temple is built of stone blocks using only post-and-lintel construction. Despite this architectural challenge, the *shikhara* rises more than 100 feet over the *garbhagriha* and is crowned by a small *amalaka*, or bulbous ornament. The *shikhara* is bolstered by the many smaller subsidiary towers bundled around it. This decorative scheme adds a complex richness to the surface, but it also obscures the shape of the main *shikhara*, which is slender, with a swift and impetuous upward movement. The roofs of the *mandapas* contribute to the impression of rapid ascent by growing progressively taller as they near the *shikhara*.

Despite its apparent complexity, the temple has a clear structure and unified composition. Strong horizontal **moldings** (shaped or sculpted strips) and open spaces over the *mandapas* and porches separate the towers of the superstructure from the lower portion. Three rows of sculpture—some 600 figures—are integrated into the exterior walls. Approximately 3 feet tall and carved in high relief, the sculptures depict gods and goddesses, as well as figures in erotic postures.

ideal relationship between humans and deities. Rather than focusing on ritual and the performance of *dharma* according to the Vedas, *bhakti* stresses an intimate, personal, and loving relation with the god, and complete devotion and surrender to the deity. Tantrism, by contrast, is pursued under the guidance of a teacher and employs various techniques designed to help the devotee self-identify with the deity. Ultimately this leads to a profound understanding that there is no separation between oneself and the divine. Although not typical, both traditions have, at times, employed erotic or romantic imagery as a visual means of expressing ideas of devotion and unity.

GAL VIHARA, SRI LANKA   During the twelfth century, when Buddhism had all but disappeared from India, it was still thriving in Sri Lanka. This island kingdom played a large role in exporting Buddhist ideas to parts of Southeast Asia, with which it had maintained close economic and cultural ties. Sri Lanka was central to strengthening and maintaining the conservative Theravada Buddhist traditions, especially by preserving scriptures and relics. Sri Lankan sculptors further refined Indian styles and iconography in colossal Buddhist sculptures but rarely initiated further elaboration on traditional Buddhist forms. Because the Buddha's image was believed to have been based on a portrait made during his lifetime, intentional variation was considered unnecessary and inaccurate.

The construction of the Gal Vihara is linked to an ambitious series of construction projects undertaken by King Parakramabahu in the mid twelfth century. The rock-cut **PARINIRVANA OF THE BUDDHA** at this monastic complex (**FIG. 10–31**) is one of three colossal Buddhas at the site. This serene and dignified image restates one of the early themes of Buddhist art, that of the Buddha's final death and transcendence, with a sophistication of modeling and proportion that updates and localizes the classical Buddhist tradition. Postholes in the rock face reveal that this sculpture was originally housed in a wooden superstructure that has since decayed. Fortunately granite is

The Khajuraho temples are especially well known for their **EROTIC SCULPTURES** (**FIG. 10–30**). These carvings are not placed haphazardly, but rather in a single vertical line at the juncture of the walls enclosing the *garbhagriha* and the last *mandapa*. Their significance is uncertain; perhaps they derive from the amorous couples (*mithuna*) found at the entrances of many temples and *chaityas*. It is also possible that they relate to two growing traditions within Hinduism: *tantra* and *bhakti*.

These terms are associated with two major religious movements that were developing throughout this period and affected Hindu practice and art: the tantric, or esoteric, and the *bhakti*, or devotional. Although both movements evolved throughout India, the influence of tantric sects appeared during this period primarily in the art of the north, while the *bhakti* movements found artistic expression across South Asia. *Bhakti* revolves around the

10-31 PARINIRVANA OF THE BUDDHA

Gal Vihara, near Polonnaruwa, Sri Lanka. 11th–12th century CE. Granite.

Credit: © ziggymars/123RF

more durable, and this fine example of Sri Lankan colossal sculpture has been preserved. This monastery, located north of the capital in Polonnaruwa, was occupied until the capital fell in the late 1200s.

The Chola Period

The Cholas, who succeeded the Pallavas in the mid ninth century, founded a dynasty that governed most of the far south of India well into the late thirteenth century. Their extensive trade networks and powerful navy also made them a potent cultural force in many parts of Southeast Asia over these centuries. The Chola dynasty reached its peak during the reign of Rajaraja I (ruled 985–1014). As an expression of gratitude for his many victories in battle, Rajaraja built the Rajarajeshvara Temple to Shiva in his capital, Thanjavur (formerly known as Tanjore). The name Rajarajeshvara means the temple of "Rajaraja's Lord," that is, Shiva, which also has the effect of linking the name of the king with that of Shiva. His patronage of the temple was in part a reflection of the fervent Shiva *bhakti* movement which had reached its peak by that time. Now commonly called the Brihadeshvara Temple (Temple of the Great Lord), this temple is a remarkable achievement of the southern style of Hindu architecture (**FIG. 10-32**). It stands within a huge walled compound near the banks of the Kaveri River. Although smaller shrines dot the compound, the Rajarajeshvara dominates the area.

10-32 RAJARAJESHVARA TEMPLE OF SHIVA, THANJAVUR

Tamil Nadu, India. Chola dynasty, 1003–1010 CE.

Credit: © 123RF.com

Rising to an astonishing height of 216 feet, this temple was probably the tallest structure in India in its time. Each story is decorated with miniature shrines, window motifs, and robust dwarf figures who seem to be holding up the next story. Like the contemporaneous Kandariya Mahadeva Temple at Khajuraho (SEE FIG. 10–29), the Rajarajeshvara has a longitudinal axis and greatly expanded dimensions, especially with regard to its superstructure, a four-sided, hollow pyramid. Typical of the southern style, the *mandapa* at the front of the Rajarajeshvara has a flat roof, as opposed to the pyramidal roofs of the northern style. The walls of the sanctum rise for two stories, with each story emphatically articulated by a large cornice. The interior was originally painted, and portions of this decoration have recently been uncovered as sections of the overpainting were removed. The exterior walls are ornamented with niches, each of which holds a single statue, usually depicting a form of Shiva. Because the Rajarajeshvara's superstructure is not obscured by its decorative motifs, it forcefully ascends skyward and is topped by an octagonal dome-shaped capstone. This huge capstone is exactly the same size as the *garbhagriha* housed 13 stories directly below. It thus evokes the shrine a final time before the eye ascends to the point separating the worldly from the cosmic sphere above.

Perhaps no sculpture is more representative of Hinduism than the statues of Shiva Nataraja, or Shiva as the Lord of Dance, a form perfected by sculptors under the royal patronage of the south Indian Chola dynasty during the late tenth to eleventh centuries (**FIG. 10–33**). The particularly striking Chola version of the Dancing Shiva was introduced and promoted primarily through the efforts of one woman, Queen Sembiyan Mahadevi. Donation records spanning over 60 years reveal that she was a major patron both of temple building and bronze casting, and many of her projects involved increasing the prominence of Shiva Nataraja. It was not unusual for Hindu royal families to associate themselves with a particular aspect of a deity, and her efforts were instrumental in forging such a bond between Shiva Nataraja and the Chola state.

By the thirteenth or fourteenth century, the dance of Shiva came to represent a dance of cosmic proportions, signifying the universe's cycle of death and rebirth; it is also a dance for each individual, signifying the liberation of the believer through Shiva's compassion. In the iconography of the Nataraja, this sculpture shows Shiva with four arms dancing on the prostrate body of Apasmara, a dwarf figure who symbolizes "becoming" and whom Shiva controls. Shiva's extended left hand holds a ball of fire; a circle of fire rings the god. The fire is emblematic of the destruction

10–33 SHIVA NATARAJA (SHIVA AS LORD OF THE DANCE)

South India. Chola dynasty, 11th century CE. Bronze, 43⅞ × 40″ (111.5 × 101.65 cm). Cleveland Museum of Art. Purchase from the J.H. Wade Fund (1930.331).

Credit: Bridgeman Images

of *samsara* and the physical universe as well as the destruction of *maya* (illusion) and our ego-centered perceptions. Shiva's back right hand holds a drum; its beat represents the irrevocable rhythms of creation and destruction, birth and death. His front right arm shows the *abhaya* "have no fear" *mudra* (see "Mudras" on page 313). The front left arm, gracefully stretched across his body with the hand pointing to his raised foot, signifies the promise of liberation.

The artist has rendered the complex pose with great clarity. The central axis, which aligns the nose, navel, and insole of the weight-bearing foot, maintains the figure's equilibrium while the remaining limbs extend asymmetrically far to each side. Shiva wears a short loincloth, a ribbon tied above his waist, and delicately tooled ornaments. The scant clothing reveals his perfected form with its broad shoulders tapering to a supple waist. The jewelry is restrained, and the detail does not detract from the beauty of the body. This work was made using the lost-wax method and is a testament to the extraordinary skill routinely exhibited by Chola artists.

Early Art and Architecture of Southeast Asia

How do Southeast Asian art and architecture develop through a series of early cultures and dynasties?

Geographically, Southeast Asia is part of the Asian continental plate and can be divided into two broad regions. The first part is its peninsular or mainland portion, which emerges from the southern edge of Asia and includes Myanmar, Cambodia, Laos, Malaysia, Singapore, Thailand, and Vietnam. The second region is comprised of a vast archipelago of islands that spreads out into the Pacific and Indian oceans. This maritime region includes the states of Brunei, East Timor, Indonesia, and the Philippines.

With its high mountainous interior and dense vegetation, Southeast Asia's earliest human settlements naturally formed along the rivers and coastlines, facilitating both food production and trade. Additionally, the presence of rich mineral deposits allowed for the development of metallurgy. Bronze casting developed early in the region, and the oldest bronze finds, located on the mainland, have been, with some disagreement, dated to 1500 BCE.

Early Southeast Asia

Archaeological work at sites such as Ban Chiang in northeastern Thailand has uncovered a wide range of bronze tools and jewelry as well as finely decorated ceramics. Because its distinctive bronzework has been found as far afield as Java, the archaeological site of Dongson in

northern Vietnam reveals evidence of short-range ocean trade having developed shortly after 600 BCE. By the first century CE, these trade networks had expanded, and evidence for a kingdom or collection of states called Funan in the southern reaches of the Southeast Asian peninsula is provided by third-century CE Chinese sources. As long-distance trade increased, the Southeast Asians found themselves in a strategic and lucrative location for controlling and mediating exchanges between East Asia and points west. Having no shortage of locally produced and highly prized commodities like hardwoods and spices, regional merchants were also active participants in this trade network. It was perhaps inevitable that over these centuries of trade, new ideas also arrived. By the sixth century CE there is ample evidence that Buddhism and Hinduism had taken firm root in the Mon kingdom of Dvaravati (present-day Thailand and southern Myanmar), as well as in the pre-Angkorian art of the Khmer (in today's Cambodia).

Sixth to the Ninth Century

As trade networks strengthened and expanded, Southeast Asian communities gained increased access to foreign goods and foreign ideas. The South Asian religions of Hinduism and Buddhism were of particular influence and gained popularity just as some of the earliest large-scale kingdoms were emerging. These religions supported and inspired emerging dynasties and became closely intertwined with early Southeast Asian concepts of kingship.

DVARAVATI-STYLE BUDDHA, THAILAND   The Mon ethnic group was among the first in Southeast Asia to adopt Buddhism. Starting in the sixth century CE they organized into a kingdom whose name, Dvaravati, is preserved thanks to a cache of ritual coins unearthed from a stupa in Nakhon Pathom, Thailand. The archaeological remains from this kingdom are quite varied in form, media, and subject, which is not surprising given that the Mon controlled this region until the Khmer gained influence in the tenth century.

Characteristic of the sculpture associated with early Mon sites are the standing Buddha images in bronze, as seen in an eighth-century example (**FIG. 10–34**). Stylistically, this image exhibits the arched brows, outlined facial features, and curled hair reminiscent of the Mathura style; however, the double robe is flattened in a distinctive manner against the body with a capelike angularity at its base. The iconography is consistent with that seen in South Asia, but Dvaravati Buddhas almost invariably display the same *mudra* in both hands, in this case the *vitarka*. The reasons for this insistence on symmetry are not known, but it suggests a local preference. The typically small size of these images may indicate that they were inspired by portable icons carried along the trade routes.

10–34 STANDING DVARAVATI BUDDHA
Mon Dvaravati style, from Thailand. 8th century CE. Bronze, 52″
(1.3 m). The Nelson-Atkins Museum of Art, Kansas City, Missouri.
Purchase: William Rockhill Nelson Trust (51-23).

HARIHARA, CAMBODIA Local preferences are exhibited clearly in a late seventh-century CE sculpture from
Phnom Da, Cambodia. This pre-Angkorian Khmer work
depicts a merged form of the Hindu gods Shiva and
Vishnu known as **HARIHARA** (FIG. 10–35). Such images
are only rarely encountered in South Asia, but in Southeast Asia, in the absence of a long history of sectarian differences between devotees of the two gods, this unified
expression of Hindu divinity became extremely popular.
Iconographically, the right side of the image depicts Shiva
with his trident, matted hair, third eye, and animal skins.
The left half, correspondingly, represents Vishnu, whose
cylindrical crown, *chakra* (throwing disk), and fine garments indicate his identity. The artist has rendered this

complex subject with great skill, but in this early period
the Khmer still did not fully trust the strength of the stone,
so the sculptor cautiously linked the hands to the head
with a supporting arch of stone.

BOROBUDUR, INDONESIA The mainland was not
alone in transforming new ideas from abroad. The islands
of Southeast Asia, Java in particular, produced some of the
earliest and grandest responses to imported Buddhist ideas.
The remarkable structure of **BOROBUDUR** (FIG. 10–36) was
built in its central Java location by the Shailendra dynasty
about the year 800. It appears to have been the endpoint of
a processional road that linked this site with the Buddhist
sacred structures at Mendut and Pawon. Borobudur has
characteristics typical of a stupa as well as those suggestive
of a three-dimensional *mandala*, or cosmic diagram, but many
aspects of the structure's use are still poorly understood.

The monument itself rises more than 100 feet from
ground level. This stepped pyramid of volcanic-stone
blocks has five lower quadrilateral terraces that support
three roughly circular terraces topped with a large, bell-
shaped stupa, itself ringed by 72 smaller openwork stupas. Each of the squared terraces is enclosed by a high
wall bearing extensive relief sculpture and adorned with
Buddha images in niches and small, bell-shaped projections. The decoration on the lowest level was hidden for
centuries because shortly after the monument was built, it
was bolstered by a heavy architectural foot in order to stop
the structure from spreading as the dirt in its core settled
under the weight of the stone. During the restoration of
the monument that began in 1975, these **bas-reliefs** were

10–35 HARIHARA
From Phnom Da, Angkor Barei, Cambodia. Pre-Angkorian Khmer,
7th century CE. Sandstone, 68″ (76 cm). Musée Guimet, Paris.

Credit: Photo © RMN-Grand Palais (musée Guimet, Paris)/Thierry Ollivier

10-36 BOROBUDUR
Central Java, Magelang District, Indonesia.
c. 800 CE. Aerial view.

Credit: © Luca Tettoni/ Corbis

exposed and carefully photographed. As with all sculpture at the site, the figures are elegant, with full, rounded bodies whose smooth forms are sporadically accentuated by delicately carved adornments.

The decorative program of these relief carvings displays a carefully calculated arrangement that moves from pragmatic moral lessons at the base up to more abstract religious ideas at the summit. The lowest gallery, which had been covered by the foot, depicts instructive scenes of karmic reward and punishment (**FIG. 10-37**). As one circumambulates to the next set of terraces, scenes of the Buddha's past lives and other moral tales share space with

10-37 SCENE OF DRUNKENNESS AND MODERATION
Borobudur, east side. Central Java, Indonesia. c. 800 CE.

This scene depicts a lesson from the Karmavibhanga on the rewards for moderation in food and drink. The figures on the upper right turn away from the scene of debauchery played out in front of them. In reward for this good judgment they are reborn as individuals with few diseases, indicated by the hearty couple surrounded by supplicants on the right side of the panel. The tree divides the cause from the effect.

10–38 LORO JONGGRANG

Prambanan, Central Java, Indonesia. 9th century CE.

Credit: NJ/Fotolia

the life story of Shakyamuni Buddha. Moving upward, terraces four and five visually recount the story of Sudhana, an ordinary man who seeks personal enlightenment, eventually achieving it with the guidance of a bodhisattva. At this point visitors exit to the upper three circular terraces, whose rows of stupas and wide vista may be a metaphor for the enlightened state. Each of these perforated stupas holds a seated Buddha except for the large, central stupa, whose surface is solid. The placement of Buddha images on the monument and their differing *mudras* corresponds to the arrangement found in some Buddhist *mandalas* and points to another layer of meaning in this exceptionally complex architectural plan.

LORO JONGGRANG, INDONESIA   Slightly later than Borobudur, but clearly influenced by its example, is the extensive site of **LORO JONGGRANG** in Prambanan, Java (**FIG. 10–38**). Although not a stepped pyramid, this Hindu monument employs a concentric plan and shares

Borobudur's repetition of bell-shaped forms. This temple complex was begun in the mid ninth century by the Sanjaya dynasty, regional rivals to the Shailendra, under the reign of Rakai Pikatan. It was then further expanded by later kings.

The buildings in the complex are arranged around the central temple dedicated to Shiva. The central sacred area, housing the biggest temples, is enclosed in an outer wall, beyond which the remains of 224 shrines are arrayed in four concentric squares. Most of these shrines are now badly damaged and their function is not clear, but some have speculated that their locations may reflect the social status of their donors. The towering central structure stands almost 155 feet high and is flanked by two somewhat smaller structures dedicated to Vishnu and Brahma, each just over 108 feet in height. The primary image of Shiva is an anthropomorphic representation rather than a *linga*. Its east-facing chamber is surrounded by subsidiary shrines aligned to the other

10–39 ABDUCTION OF SITA

Illustration of the *Ramayana*, relief 13, scene 2, Chandi Shiva, Prambanan, central Java, Indonesia. 9th century CE.

Credit: ©1983 Visual Resources Collections, Department of History of Art, Regents of the University of Michigan cardinal directions and housing images of deities associated with Shiva. The flanking temples have only one chamber each, which contain beautifully carved images of Vishnu and Brahma respectively. A row of three smaller chambers is located just across from the entrances to the main temples. It is believed that these buildings were dedicated to the mounts (*vahana*) of the three gods, but only the image of Shiva's mount, the bull Nandi, has survived. All the temples are raised on high plinths decorated with narrative scenes in relief.

A portion of these reliefs depicts scenes from the *Ramayana*. This Hindu epic was known in Indonesia from an early date, and aspects of the story were adjusted to better suit the needs and expectations of its Southeast Asian audience. Some of this local influence can be seen in a relief (**FIG. 10-39**) portraying the moment the wicked demon king Ravana (Rawana) abducts Sita, the wife of the hero Rama. Ravana, disguised as a Brahmin, seizes Sita in the midst of a Javanese village and in the process overturns a number of objects as the witnesses to the event react in horror and surprise. The wildlife in this panel exploit the distraction—a dog in the foreground grabs at food fallen from an overturned pot, a rat can be seen sneaking into the storehouse, and a monkey reaches for food held by a seated man. The addition of these details not mentioned in the text reinforces the shamefully animalistic nature of Ravana's actions, which ultimately lead to his own destruction. Typical for the art of Java in this period, the panel is full of activity; each event is accompanied by a host of attendants, onlookers, and references to the natural world.

Tenth to the Twelfth Century

By the tenth through twelfth centuries the powerful kingdoms in Angkor and Bagan were reaching their peaks. Their great wealth and success found expression in innovative forms of architectural construction whose ambitious design and grand scale took earlier forms of Southeast Asian construction to new heights.

ANANDA TEMPLE, MYANMAR King Anawrahta came to power in 1044, uniting the disparate regional rulers in northern Myanmar under his rule and the local gods (*nats*) under Buddhism. Lavish temple-building projects were not just a means for the king to demonstrate his legitimacy and accrual of good *karma* (the concept that one's deeds, good or bad, eventually produce correspondingly positive or negative consequences); they were also seen as ensuring the welfare of state interests and public well-being. The focus of this fervent generosity was the Buddhist monastic order based near the capital in Bagan (also called Pagan). Over the course of generations of public and royal patronage this semiarid valley came to house several thousand spectacular Buddhist structures, large and small, in various states of repair.

Among these, one of the grandest is the **ANANDA TEMPLE** (**FIG. 10-40**), built in 1105 by King Kyanzittha, Anawrahta's adopted son and eventual successor. According to the legends, the head monk at Bagan, Shin Arahan, introduced the king to eight monks from India who were seeking support abroad. The ensuing discussions inspired the king to undertake a major act of patronage, which culminated in the construction of the Ananda Temple. The unique architectural plan of this temple is rather complex, but it can be envisioned as four temples placed up against the sides of a massive square-based stupa, which rises to almost 175 feet. The temples each face a cardinal direction and house large Buddha images covered in gold leaf, most of which have been renovated or replaced over the centuries. The walls of these temples have openings that make way for two covered circumambulation pathways. While most of the sculpture in niches along these pathways

10-40 ANANDA TEMPLE
Bagan, Mandalay Division, Myanmar. 12th century CE. Height approx. 35' (10.5 m).

Credit: Noelbynature/ Fotolia

10–41 PORTRAIT OF KING KYANZITTHA
West shrine, Ananda Temple, Bagan. 11th century CE.
Gilded lacquer, height 30″ (76 cm).

Credit: Photo: John Listopad

remains, almost none of the painting does. The exterior is embellished with rising spires and flamelike decoration over the windows and doors. The central roof rises to the main tower in five tiers. These are decorated with horizontal bands of inset glazed ceramic plaques, many of which display scenes from the Buddha's past lives.

Of particular note are two gilded lacquer images of figures in postures of reverence flanking the Buddha image in the west-facing shrine. These images are believed to depict **KING KYANZITTHA** (FIG. 10–41), shown in elaborate attire, and his chief monk Shin Arahan, bald and in simple robes. The details of these figures have been somewhat obscured by accumulated layers of gold leaf, but this accretion may also have protected the lacquer from decay.

The Ananda is just one grand temple among many in Bagan. Unfortunately, misguided attempts by the government in Myanmar to restore these structures have resulted in conjectural and inaccurate renovations that have hidden or destroyed much of the early material.

ANGKOR WAT, CAMBODIA   In 802, the Khmer king Jayavarman II, newly returned from Java, climbed Mount Kulen in what is now northwestern Cambodia. He was accompanied on this trip by a Brahmin who performed a ritual on the mountaintop that marked a special relationship between Jayavarman II and the Hindu god Shiva.

Thereafter, Jayavarman II and subsequent rulers in his lineage claimed the title of "god-king" (*devaraja*). The special religious status indicated by this designation was further solidified through architectural projects that invoked divine symbolism on behalf of the ruler. While Jayavarman II had ascended an actual mountain, his descendants opted to construct elaborate temple mountains near the major urban centers of Roluos and Angkor. These immense structures recalled the sacred mountains on which the gods dwell and marked the political and religious center of the Khmer empire.

Among the grandest and most unusual of these structures is Suryavarman II's temple mountain, known today as **ANGKOR WAT** (FIG. 10–42). Having come to power after a period of turmoil, Suryavarman II (ruled 1113–1150),

10–42 ANGKOR WAT
Angkor, Cambodia.
12th century CE.

Credit: © Olga Lipatova/Shutterstock

10-43 VISHNU CHURNING THE OCEAN OF MILK
Detail of relief sculpture, Angkor Wat. 12th century CE.
Credit: © Kevin R. Morris/Corbis

many of which depict scenes from the great Hindu epics or glorified depictions of the king.

One relief on the east side of the outer gallery portrays a Hindu story known as the "Churning of the Ocean of Milk" (**FIG. 10-43**). In this tale, set in a time before the world was fully formed, Vishnu orchestrates the production of the elixir of immortality. He achieves this by wrapping the cosmic serpent around a great mountain emerging from the sea. Then by pulling on the serpent, the gods, working with their enemies, the *asura*, manage to churn up the elixir of immortality from the ocean's depths. This relief may hold a clue to understanding the monument as a whole. With its mountainlike towers, broad moat, and serpent balustrades, the entire complex at Angkor Wat parallels the setting of the legend and may speak to Suryavarman II's hopes for gaining a sort of immortality through his own special union with Vishnu.

unlike most of his predecessors, chose to devote himself to the god Vishnu rather than to Shiva. He further broke with tradition by having his temple face west to the setting sun, a direction which had funerary associations.

The temple is a massive structure, comprised of three concentric galleries that frame a stepped pyramid crowned by five delicately tapered towers. This entire structure is surrounded by lakelike moats over 820 feet wide and crossed by walkways adorned with balustrades shaped like multi-headed serpents. The inner walls of the three outer galleries contain elaborate bas-relief sculptures,

Think About It

1   Consider the use of rock-cut architecture. What were the benefits and drawbacks to this architectural technique? How did it influence, and how was it influenced by, built architecture? Give examples.

2   Select one architectural work and one work of sculpture from this chapter. Explain how either Buddhist or Hindu ideas are expressed through their decoration, form, or iconography.

3   Describe the typical form of Indian temples, northern and southern. Directly contrast the stupa and the temple, paying attention to specific building features and how they are used.

4   How do sites like Mamallapuram, the Ananda Temple, and Angkor Wat help legitimize the authority of the ruler?

Crosscurrents

Water symbolism occurs frequently in the art of South and Southeast Asia. Consider how practical concerns over climate and commerce may have shaped the way this imagery was understood. Why would such symbolism be appropriate for royally sponsored sculpture, and what was its significance?

FIG. 10–26

FIG. 10–43

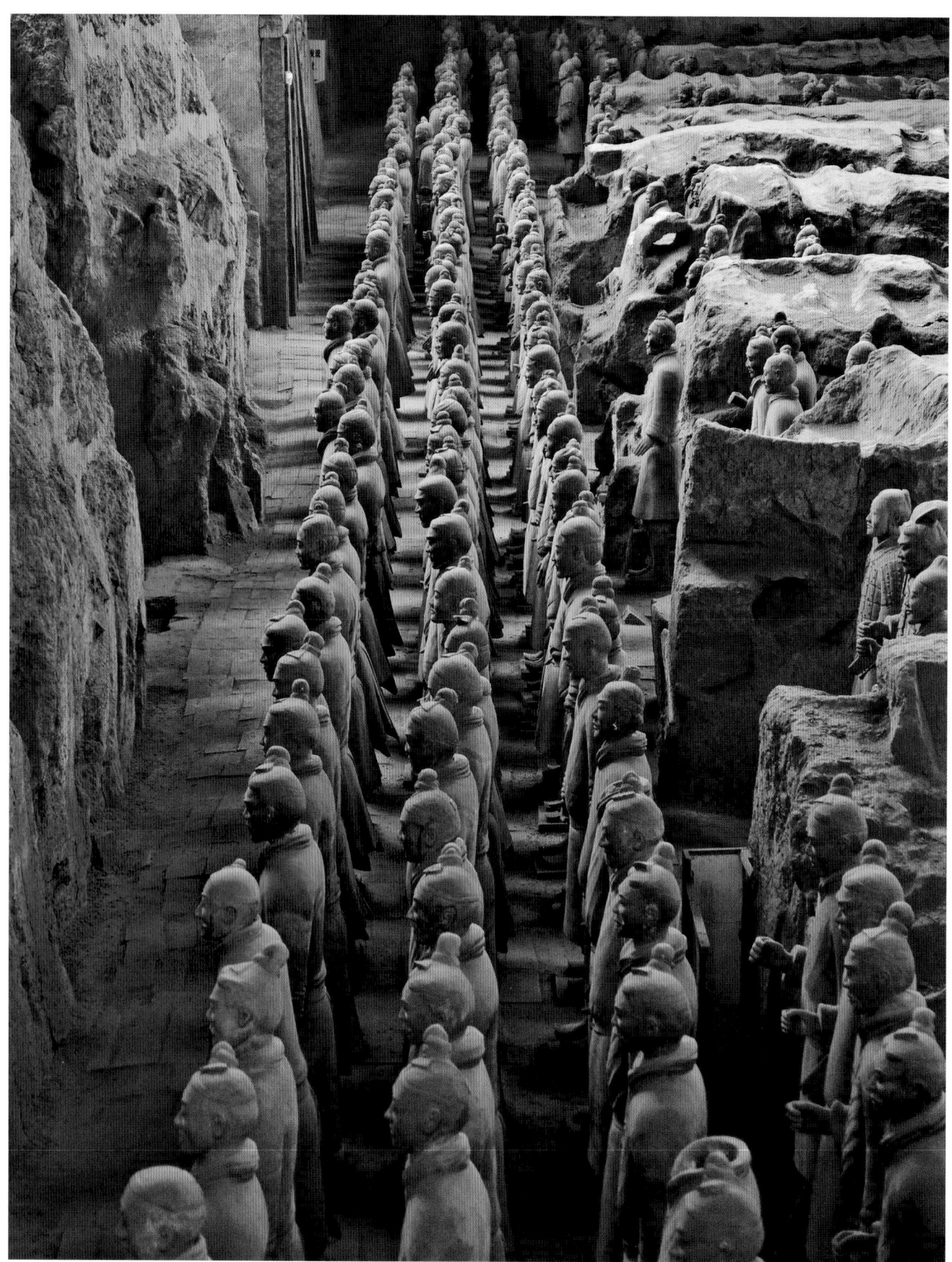

11-1 TERRA-COTTA SOLDIERS

From the mausoleum of Emperor Shihuangdi, Lintong, Shaanxi. Qin dynasty, c. 210 BCE. Earthenware, life-size.

Chapter 11
Chinese and Korean Art before 1279

 Learning Objectives

11.a Identify the visual hallmarks of early Chinese and Korean art for formal, technical, and expressive qualities.

11.b Interpret the meaning of works of early Chinese and Korean art based on their themes, subjects, and symbols.

11.c Relate early Chinese and Korean artists and art to their cultural, economic, and political contexts.

11.d Apply the vocabulary and concepts relevant to early Chinese and Korean art, artists, and art history.

11.e Interpret a work of early Chinese or Korean art using the art historical methods of observation, comparison, and inductive reasoning.

11.f Select visual and textual evidence in various media to support an argument or an interpretation of a work of early Chinese or Korean art.

As long as anyone could remember, the huge mound in Shaanxi Province in northern China had been just part of the landscape. But one day in 1974, peasants digging a well accidentally brought to light the first hint of riches. When archaeologists began to excavate, they were stunned by what they found: a vast underground army of some 8,000 life-size terra-cotta soldiers with 100 life-size ceramic horses standing in military formation and ready for battle (**FIG. 11–1**). For more than 2,000 years, while the tumultuous history of China unfolded overhead, they had guarded the tomb of Emperor Shihuangdi, the ruthless ruler who first united the states of China into an empire, the Qin. In ongoing excavations, additional bronze carriages and horses were found, further evidence of the technology and naturalism achieved during Qin Shihuangdi's reign.

China has had a long-standing fascination with antiquity, but archaeology is a relatively young discipline there. Only since the 1920s have scholars methodically dug into the layers of history, yet so much has been unearthed that ancient Chinese history has been rewritten many times. The archaeological record shows that Chinese civilization arose several millennia ago and was distinctive for its early advances in ceramics and metalwork, as well as for the elaborate working of jade. Early use of the potter's wheel, mastery of reduction firing, and invention of high-fired stoneware and porcelain distinguish the technological advancement of Chinese ceramics. Highly imaginative bronze casting and proficient techniques of mold making characterize early Chinese metalworking. Early attainments in jade reflect a technological competence with rotary tools and abrasion, as well as an aesthetic passion for the subtleties of shape, proportion, and surface texture.

Archaeology has supplemented our understanding of historically appreciated Chinese art forms, which explored human relationships and exemplified Confucian values, teaching the standards of conduct that underlie social order. Later, China also came to embrace the Buddhist tradition from India. In princely representations of Buddhist divinities and in sublime and powerful, but often meditative, figures of the Buddha, China's artists presented the divine potential of the human condition. Perhaps the most distinguished Chinese tradition is the presentation of philosophical ideals through the theme of landscape. Paintings of mountains and water in simple black ink became the ultimate artistic medium for expressing the vastness, abundance, and endurance of nature.

Chinese civilization radiated its influence throughout East Asia, repeatedly stimulating the growth of culture in Korea, which in turn transmitted influence to Japan.

The Middle Kingdom

How do the geography and early history of China lead to distinctive forms of art?

Among the cultures of the world, China is distinguished by its long, uninterrupted development, now traced back some 8,000 years. From Qin (pronounced "chin") comes our name for the country that the Chinese call the Middle Kingdom, the country in the center of the world. Present-day China occupies a large landmass in the center of East Asia, covering an area slightly larger than the continental United States. Within its borders lives one fifth of the human race.

The historical and cultural heart of China is the land watered by its three great rivers, the Yellow (Huang Ho), the Yangzi, and the Xi (MAP 11-1). The Qinling Mountains divide Inner China into north and south, regions with strikingly different climates, cultures, and historical fates. In the south, the Yangzi River flows through lush green hills to the fertile plains of the delta. Along the southern coastline, rich with natural harbors, arose China's port cities, the focus of a vast maritime trading network. The Yellow River, nicknamed "China's Sorrow" because of its disastrous floods, winds through the north—a dry land of steppe and desert, hot in the summer and lashed by cold winds in the winter. Over its vast and vulnerable frontier have come the nomadic invaders that are a recurring theme in Chinese history, but emissaries from Central Asia, India, Persia, and Europe also crossed this border.

Neolithic Cultures

Early archaeological evidence led scholars to believe that agriculture, the cornerstone technology of the Neolithic period, made its way to China from the ancient Near East. More recent findings, however, suggest that agriculture based on rice and millet arose independently in East Asia before 5000 BCE and that knowledge of Near Eastern grains followed some 2,000 years later. One of the clearest archaeological signs of Neolithic culture in China is evidence of the vigorous emergence of towns and cities. At Jiangzhai, near present-day Xi'an, for example, the foundations of more than 100 dwellings have been discovered surrounding the remains of a communal center, a cemetery, and a kiln. Dated to about 4000 BCE, the ruins point to the existence of a highly developed early society. Elsewhere, the foundations of the earliest-known Chinese palace have been uncovered and dated to about 2000 BCE.

PAINTED POTTERY CULTURES In China, as in other places, distinctive forms of Neolithic pottery identify different cultures. One of the most interesting objects recovered is a shallow red **BOWL** with a turned-out rim (FIG. 11-2). Found in the village of Banpo near Xi'an and the Yellow

11-2 BOWL
From Banpo, near Xi'an, Shaanxi. Neolithic period, Yangshao culture, 5000–4000 BCE. Painted pottery, height 7″ (17.8 cm). Banpo Museum.

Credit: Cultural Relics Publishing House

River, it was crafted sometime between 5000 and 4000 BCE. The bowl is an artifact of the Yangshao culture, one of the most important of the so-called Painted Pottery cultures of Neolithic China. Although not made on a potter's wheel, the bowl is perfectly round, and its surfaces are highly polished, bearing witness to a distinctly advanced technology. In addition, markings on shards from this location may be evidence of the beginnings of writing in China, which was fully developed by the second millennium BCE, in the later Bronze Age.

Inside the bowl, a pair of stylized fish suggests that fishing was an important activity for the villagers. The images between the two fish represent human faces flanked by fish, one on each side. Although there is no certain interpretation of the images, they may depict an ancestral figure who could assure an abundant catch, since the worship of ancestors and nature spirits was fundamental to later Chinese beliefs.

LIANGZHU CULTURE Banpo lies near the great bend in the Yellow River, in the area traditionally regarded as the cradle of Chinese civilization, but archaeological finds have revealed that Neolithic cultures spread over a far broader geography. Recent excavations in sites more than 800 miles away, near Hangzhou Bay in the southeastern coastal region, have uncovered human and animal images—often masks or faces—more than 5,000 years old from the Liangzhu culture (FIG. 11-3). Large, round eyes, a flat nose, and a rectangular mouth protrude slightly from the background pattern of wirelike lines. Above the

MAP 11–1 CHINA AND KOREA

The map shows the borders of contemporary China and Korea. Bright-colored areas indicate the extent of China's Han dynasty (206 BCE–220 CE).

11-3 DRAWING OF THE MASK DECORATION ON A JADE CONG

Neolithic period, Liangzhu culture, 3200–2200 BCE.

Credit: Line drawing © Michael Sullivan, *The Arts of China, 5th Edition, Revised and Expanded*. Published by the University of California Press, 2009, p. 12, fig. 1-14.

forehead a second, smaller face grimaces from under a huge headdress. The upper face may be human, perhaps riding the animal figure below. The drawing reproduces one of eight masks that were carved in low relief on the outside of a large jade *cong*, an object resembling a cylindrical tube encased in a rectangular block.

Another **CONG** (**FIG. 11–4**), also from Liangzhu, bears a lustrous, smooth finish and similar—if more stylized—mask motifs. Both *congs* were found near the remains of persons buried with what appear to be sets of numerous jade objects. The intricacy of these carvings documents the technical sophistication of the jade-working Liangzhu culture, which seems to have emerged around 3300 BCE. Jade, a stone cherished by the Chinese throughout their history, is extremely hard and is difficult to carve. Liangzhu artists must have used sand as an abrasive to slowly grind the stone down; modern artisans marvel at the refinement and virtuosity of the work they produced.

The meaning of the masklike image in FIGURE 11–3 is open to interpretation. Its combination of human and animal features seems to show how the ancient Chinese imagined supernatural beings, either deities or dead ancestors. Similar masks later formed the primary decorative motif of Bronze Age ritual objects. Still later, Chinese historians began referring to the ancient mask motif as the **taotie**, but the motif's original meaning had already been lost. The jade carving here seems to be a forerunner of this most central and mysterious image.

11–4 CONG
Neolithic period, Liangzhu culture, 3200–2200 BCE. Jade, 1⁷⁄₈ × 2⁵⁄₈" (5 × 6.6 cm). Shanghai Museum.

The *cong* is one of the most prevalent and mysterious of early Chinese jade shapes. Originating in the Neolithic period, it continued to play a prominent role in burials through the Shang and Zhou dynasties. Many experts believe the *cong* was connected with the practice of contacting the spirit world.

Bronze Age China

How are the advanced metalworking traditions of Bronze Age China used within the cultures of the Shang and Zhou dynasties?

China entered its Bronze Age in the second millennium BCE. As with agriculture, scholars at first theorized that the technology had been imported from the Near East. Archaeological evidence now makes clear, however, that bronze casting using the **piece-mold casting** technique arose independently in China, where it eventually attained an extraordinary level of sophistication (see "Piece-Mold Casting" opposite).

Shang Dynasty

Traditional Chinese histories tell of three Bronze Age dynasties: the Xia, the Shang, and the Zhou. Experts at one time tended to dismiss the Xia and Shang as legendary, but twentieth-century archaeological discoveries fully established the historical existence of the Shang (c. 1700–1100 BCE) and point strongly to the historical existence of the Xia as well.

Shang kings ruled from a succession of capitals in the Yellow River Valley, where archaeologists have found walled cities, palaces, and vast royal tombs. The Shang were surrounded by many other states—some rivals, others clients—and their culture spread widely. Society seems to have been highly stratified, with a ruling group that had the bronze technology needed to make weapons and ritual vessels. They maintained their authority in part by claiming power as intermediaries between the supernatural and human realms. The chief Shang deity, Shangdi, may have been a sort of "Great Ancestor." It is thought that nature and fertility spirits were also honored, and that regular sacrifices were carried out to keep the spirits of dead ancestors vital so that they might help the living.

Shang priests communicated with the supernatural world through oracle bones. An animal bone or piece of tortoiseshell was inscribed with a question and heated until it cracked; the crack was then interpreted as an answer. Many oracle bones have been recovered and deciphered. They contain the earliest known form of Chinese writing, a script fully recognizable as the ancestor of the system still in use today (see "Chinese Characters" on page 340).

RITUAL BRONZES Shang tombs reveal a warrior culture of great splendor and violence. Many humans and animals were sacrificed to accompany the deceased into death. In one tomb, for example, chariots were found with the skeletons of their horses and drivers; in another, dozens of human skeletons lined the approaches to the central burial chamber. The tombs contain hundreds of jade,

Technique
PIECE-MOLD CASTING

The early piece-mold technique for bronze casting is different from the lost-wax process developed in the ancient Mediterranean and Near East. Although we do not know the exact steps ancient Chinese artists followed, we can deduce the general procedure for casting a vessel.

First, a model of the bronze-to-be was made of clay and dried. Then, to create a mold, damp clay was pressed onto the model; after the clay mold dried, it was cut away in pieces, which were keyed for later reassembly and then fired. The original model was shaved down to serve as the core for the mold. After this, the pieces of the mold were reassembled around the core and held in place by bronze spacers, which locked the core in position and ensured an even casting space around the core. The mold was then covered with another layer of clay, and a sprue, or pouring duct, was cut into the clay to receive the molten metal. A riser duct may also have been cut to allow the hot gases to escape. Molten bronze was then poured into the mold. When the metal cooled, the mold was broken apart to reveal a bronze copy of the original clay model. Finely cast relief decoration could be worked into the model or carved into the sectional molds, or both. Finally, the vessel could be burnished—a long process that involved scouring the surface with increasingly fine abrasives.

The vessel shown here is a **fang ding** recovered from the royal tombs near Yin, the last of the Shang capitals (present-day Anyang). A *ding* is a ceremonial rectangular cooking vessel standing on four legs that was used in Shang rituals and buried in Shang tombs. Weighing nearly 2,000 pounds, this *ding* is the largest Shang *ding* ever recovered.

Sectional clay molds for casting bronze vessels. This sketch is based on a vessel in the Zhengzhou Institute of Cultural Relics and Archaeology.

ivory, and lacquer objects, gold and silver ornaments, and bronze vessels. The enormous scale of Shang burials illustrates the great wealth of the civilization and the power of a ruling class able to consign such great quantities of treasure to the earth. It also documents this culture's reverence for the dead.

Bronze vessels are the most admired and studied of Shang artifacts. Like oracle bones and jade objects, they were connected with ritual practices, serving as containers for offerings of food and wine. A basic repertoire of about 30 shapes evolved. Some derive from earlier pottery forms, while others seem to reproduce wooden containers.

Still others are highly sculptural and take the form of fantastic composite animals. A ritual pouring vessel, known as a **GUANG** (**FIG. 11–5**), shows a highly sculptural rendition of animal forms. The pouring spout and cover take the form of the head and body of a tiger, while the rear portion of the vessel and cover are conceived as an owl. Overall geometric decoration combines with suggestive zoomorphic forms. Such images seem to be related to the hunting life of the Shang, but their deeper significance is unknown. Shang creatures seem always to have a sense of mystery, evoking the Shang attitude toward the supernatural world.

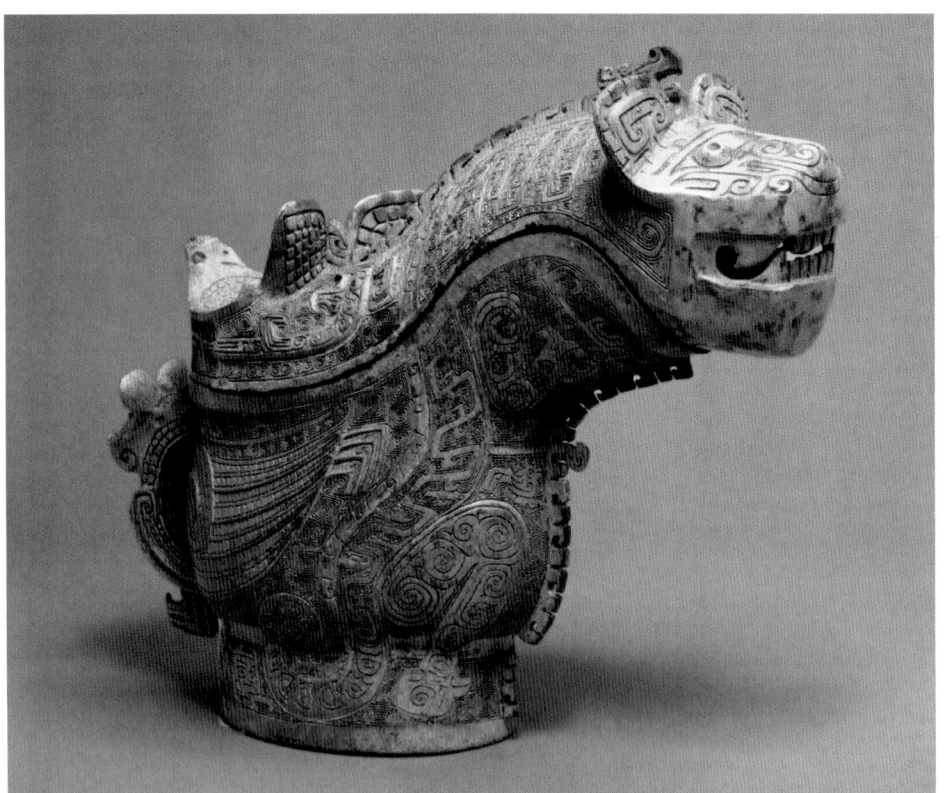

11–5 COVERED RITUAL WINE-POURING VESSEL (GUANG) WITH TIGER AND OWL DÉCOR

Shang dynasty, 13th century BCE. Cast bronze, height with cover 9¾″ (25 cm), width including handle 12⅜″ (31.5 cm). Arthur M. Sackler Museum, Harvard University Art Museums, Cambridge, Massachusetts. Bequest of Grenville L. Winthrop (1943.52.103).

Credit: Bridgeman Images

Art and its Contexts

CHINESE CHARACTERS

Each word in Chinese is represented by its own unique symbol, called a character. Some characters originated as **pictographs**, images that mean what they depict. Writing reforms over the centuries have often disguised the resemblance, but if we place modern characters next to their ancestors, the pictures come back into focus:

	water	horse	moon	child	tree	mountain
Ancient	巛	馬	月	𢀛	朱	山
Modern	水	馬	月	子	木	山

Other characters are ideographs, pictures that represent abstract concepts or ideas:

sun	+	moon	=	bright
日		月		明
woman	+	child	=	good
女		子		好

Most characters were formed by combining a radical, which gives the field of meaning, with a phonetic, which originally hinted at pronunciation. For example, words that have to do with water have the character for "water" 木 abbreviated to three strokes 氵 as their radical. Thus "to bathe," 沐 pronounced *mu*, consists of the water radical and the phonetic 木, which by itself means "tree" and is also pronounced *mu*. Here are other "water" characters. Notice that the connection to water is not always literal.

river	sea	weep	pure, clear	extinguish, destroy
河	海	泣	清	滅

These phonetic borrowings took place centuries ago. Many words have shifted in pronunciation, and for this and other reasons there is no way to tell how a character is pronounced or what it means just by looking at it. While at first this may seem like a disadvantage, in the case of Chinese it is advantageous. Spoken Chinese has many dialects. Some are so far apart in sound as to be virtually different languages. But while speakers of different dialects cannot understand each other, they can still communicate through writing, for no matter how they say a word, they write it with the same character. Writing has thus played an important role in maintaining the unity of Chinese civilization through the centuries.

Zhou Dynasty

Around 1100 BCE, the Shang were conquered by the Zhou from western China. During the Zhou dynasty (1100–221 BCE) a feudal society developed, with nobles related to the king ruling over numerous small states. (Zhou nobility are customarily ranked in English by such titles as duke and marquis.) The supreme deity became known as Tian, or Heaven, and the king ruled as the Son of Heaven. Later Chinese ruling dynasties continued to follow the belief that imperial rule emanated from a mandate from Heaven.

The first 300 years of this longest-lasting Chinese dynasty were generally stable and peaceful. In 771 BCE, however, the Zhou suffered defeat in the west at the hands of a nomadic tribe. Although they quickly established a new capital to the east, their authority had been crippled, and the later Eastern Zhou period was a troubled one. States grew increasingly independent, giving only nominal allegiance to the Zhou kings. Smaller states were swallowed up by their larger neighbors. During the time historians call the Spring and Autumn period (722–481 BCE), 10 or 12 states, later reduced to 7, emerged as powers. The ensuing Warring States period (481–221 BCE) saw intrigue, treachery, and increasingly ruthless warfare.

Against this background of social turmoil, China's great philosophers arose—such thinkers as Confucius (551–479 BCE), Laozi (flourished in sixth century BCE), Mozi (c. 470–391 BCE), and Zhuangzi (369–286 BCE). Traditional histories speak of China's "one hundred schools" of philosophy, indicating a shift of focus from the supernatural to the human world. Nevertheless, elaborate burials on an even larger scale than before reflected the continuation of traditional beliefs.

BRONZE BELLS   Ritual bronze objects continued to play an important role during the Zhou dynasty, and new forms developed. One of the most spectacular recent discoveries is a carillon of 65 bronze components, mostly bells arranged in a formation 25 feet long (**FIG. 11-6**), found in the tomb of Marquis Yi of the state of Zeng. Each bell is precisely calibrated to sound two tones—one when struck at the center, another when struck at a corner. They are arranged in scale patterns in a variety of registers. Several musicians would have moved around the carillon, striking the bells in an appointed order.

Music may well have played a part in rituals for communicating with the supernatural, for the *taotie* typically appears on the front and back of each bell. The image is now much more intricate and stylized, a complexity made possible in part by the more refined lost-wax casting process (see "Lost-Wax Casting" in Chapter 14 on page 428), which had replaced the older piece-mold technique. The marquis, who died in 433 BCE, must have considered music important, for among the more than 15,000 objects recovered from his tomb were many musical instruments. Zeng was one of the smallest and shortest-lived states of the Eastern Zhou, but the contents of this tomb attest in quantity and quality to its high cultural level.

11-6 SET OF BELLS
From the tomb of Marquis Yi of Zeng, Suixian, Hubei. Zhou dynasty, 433 BCE. Bronze, with bronze and timber frame, frame height 9' (2.74 m), length 25' (7.62 m). Hubei Provincial Museum, Wuhan.

Credit: © Asian Art & Archaeology, Inc./Corbis

Early Chinese Empires

How do Chinese art and architecture develop during the Qin, Han, and Six dynasties periods?

Toward the middle of the third century BCE, the state of Qin launched military campaigns that led to its triumph over the other states by 221 BCE. For the first time in its history, China was united under a single ruler. This first emperor of Qin, Shihuangdi, a man of exceptional ability, power, and ruthlessness, was fearful of both assassination and rebellion. Throughout his life, he sought ways to attain immortality. Even before uniting China, he began his own mausoleum at Lintong, in Shaanxi Province. This project continued throughout his life and after his death, until rebellion abruptly ended the dynasty in 206 BCE. Since that time, the mound over the mausoleum has always been visible, but not until an accidental discovery in 1974 was its army of terra-cotta soldiers and horses revealed (SEE FIG. 11–1). Modeled from clay with individualized faces and meticulously rendered uniforms and armor and then fired, the figures claim a prominent place in the great tradition of Chinese ceramic art. The tomb itself has not yet been opened, but literary sources suggest that it reproduces the world as it was known to the Qin, with stars overhead and rivers and mountains below. Thus did the tomb's architects try literally to ensure that the underworld—the world of souls and spirits—would match the human world.

Qin rule was harsh and repressive. Laws were based on a totalitarian philosophy called legalism, and all other philosophies were banned, their scholars executed, and their books burned. Yet the Qin also established the mechanisms of centralized bureaucracy that molded China both politically and culturally into a single entity. Under the Qin, the country was divided into provinces and prefectures, the writing system and coinage were standardized, roads were built to link different parts of the country with the capital, and battlements on the northern frontier were connected to form the Great Wall. To the present day, China's rulers have followed the administrative framework first laid down by the Qin.

Han Dynasty

The commander who overthrew the Qin became the next emperor and founded the Han dynasty (206 BCE–220 CE). During this period China enjoyed peace, prosperity, and stability. Borders were extended and secured, and Chinese control over strategic stretches of Central Asia led to the opening of the Silk Road, a land route that linked China by trade all the way to Rome. In addition to spices, one of the precious goods traded was silk, which had been cultivated and woven in China since at least the third millennium BCE and treasured in Greece and Rome since the third century BCE (see "The Silk Road during the Tang Period" on page 353).

PAINTED BANNER FROM CHANGSHA The early Han dynasty marks the twilight of China's so-called mythocentric age, when people believed in a close relationship between the human and supernatural worlds. The most

11–7 PAINTED BANNER

From the tomb of the Marquess of Dai, Mawangdui, Changsha, Hunan. Han dynasty, c. 160 BCE. Colors on silk, height 6'8½" (2.05 m). Hunan Provincial Museum, Changsha.

Credit: © Asian Art & Archaeology, Inc./Corbis

Art and its Contexts

DAOISM

Daoism is an outlook on life that brings together many ancient ideas regarding humankind and the universe. Its primary text, a slim volume called the *Daodejing* (*The Way and Its Power*), is ascribed to the Chinese philosopher Laozi, who is said to have been a contemporary of Confucius (551–479 ʙᴄᴇ). Later, a philosopher named Zhuangzi (369–286 ʙᴄᴇ) explored many of the same ideas in a book that is known simply by his name: *Zhuangzi*. Together the two texts formed a body of ideas that crystallized into a school of thought during the Han period.

A *dao* is a way or path. The Dao is the Ultimate Way, the Way of the universe. The Way cannot be named or described, but it can be hinted at. It is like water. Nothing is more flexible and yielding, yet water can wear down the hardest stone. Water flows downward, seeking the lowest ground. Similarly, a Daoist sage seeks a quiet life, humble and hidden, unconcerned with worldly success. The Way is great precisely because it is small. The Way may be nothing, yet nothing turns out to be essential.

To recover the Way, we must unlearn. We must return to a state of nature. To follow the Way, we must practice *wu wei* (nondoing). "Strive for nonstriving," advises the *Daodejing*.

All our attempts at asserting ourselves, at making things happen, are like swimming against a current and are thus ultimately futile, even harmful. If we let the current carry us, however, we will travel far. Similarly, a life that follows the Way will be a life of pure effectiveness, accomplishing much with little effort.

It is often said that the Chinese are Confucians in public and Daoists in private, and the two approaches do seem to balance each other. Confucianism is a rational political philosophy that emphasizes propriety, deference, duty, and self-discipline. Daoism is an intuitive philosophy that emphasizes individualism, nonconformity, and a return to nature. If a Confucian education molded scholars outwardly into responsible, ethical officials, Daoism provided some breathing room for the artist and poet inside.

---

elaborate and best-preserved painting from this time is a T-shaped silk **BANNER** that summarizes this early worldview (**FIG. 11–7**). Found in the tomb of a noblewoman on the outskirts of present-day Changsha in Hunan Province, the banner dates from the second century BCE and is painted with scenes representing three levels of the universe—heaven, earth, and underworld—as well as a portrait of the deceased.

The heavenly realm appears at the top, in the crossbar of the T. In the upper-right corner is the sun, inhabited by a mythical crow; in the upper left, a mythical toad stands on a crescent moon. Between them is an image of the Torch Dragon, a primordial deity shown as a man with a long serpent's tail. Dragons and other celestial creatures swarm underneath him.

A gate guarded by two seated figures stands where the horizontal of heaven meets the banner's long, vertical stem. Two intertwined dragons loop through a circular jade piece known as a *bi*, itself usually a symbol of heaven, dividing this vertical segment into two areas. The portion above the *bi* represents the first stage of the heavenly realm. Here, the deceased woman and three attendants stand on a platform while two kneeling attendants welcome her. The portion beneath the *bi* represents the earthly world and the underworld. Silk draperies and a stone chime hanging from the *bi* form a canopy for the platform below. Like the bronze bells we saw earlier, stone chimes were ceremonial instruments dating from Zhou times. On the platform, ritual bronze vessels contain food and wine for the deceased, just as they did in Shang tombs. The squat, muscular man holding up the platform stands on a pair of fish whose

bodies form another *bi*. The fish and the other strange creatures in this section are inhabitants of the underworld.

Philosophy and Art

The Han dynasty marked the beginning of a new age, when the philosophical ideals of Daoism and Confucianism, formulated during the troubled times of the Eastern Zhou, became central to Chinese thought. Since this period, their influence has been continuous and fundamental.

DAOISM AND NATURE   Daoism emphasizes the close relationship between humans and nature. It is concerned with bringing the individual life into harmony with the Dao, or the Way, of the universe (see "Daoism" above). For some a secular, philosophical path, Daoism on a popular level developed into an organized religion, absorbing many traditional folk practices as well as the search for immortality.

Immortality was as intriguing to Han rulers as it had been to the first emperor of Qin. Daoist adepts experimented with diet, physical exercise, and other techniques in the belief that immortal life could be achieved on earth. A popular Daoist legend of the Land of Immortals in the Eastern Sea takes form in a bronze **INCENSE BURNER** from the tomb of Prince Liu Sheng, who died in 113 BCE (**FIG. 11–8**). Around the bowl, gold inlay outlines the stylized waves of the sea. Above them rises the mountainous island, crowded with birds, animals, and the immortals themselves, all cast in bronze with highlights of inlaid gold. This visionary world would have been shrouded in the shifting mist of incense when the burner was in use.

11–8 INCENSE BURNER

From the tomb of Prince Liu Sheng, Mancheng, Hebei. Han dynasty, 113 BCE. Bronze with gold inlay, height 10½″ (26 cm). Hebei Provincial Museum, Shijiazhuang.

Technically, this exquisite work represents the ultimate development of the long and distinguished tradition of bronze casting in China.

Credit: © Asian Art & Archaeology, Inc./Corbis

CONFUCIANISM AND THE STATE In contrast to the metaphysical focus of Daoism, Confucianism is concerned with the human world; its goal is the attainment of social harmony. To this end, it proposes a system of ethics based on reverence for ancestors and correct relationships among people. Beginning with self-discipline in the individual, Confucianism teaches how to rectify relationships within the family, and then, in ever-widening circles, with friends and others, all the way up to the level of the emperor and the state (see "Confucius and Confucianism" below).

Emphasis on social order and respect for authority made Confucianism especially attractive to Han rulers, who were eager to distance themselves from the disastrous legalism of the Qin. The Han emperor Wudi (ruled 141–87 BCE) made Confucianism the official imperial

---

Art and its Contexts
CONFUCIUS AND CONFUCIANISM

Confucius was born in 551 BCE into a declining aristocratic family in the state of Lu, roughly present-day Shandong Province. While still in his teens he set his heart on becoming a scholar; by his early twenties he had begun to teach.

By this time, wars for supremacy had begun among the various states of China, and the traditional social fabric seemed to be breaking down. Looking back to the early Zhou dynasty as a sort of golden age, Confucius thought about how a just and harmonious society could again emerge. For many years he sought a ruler who would put his ideas into effect, but to no avail. Frustrated, he spent his final years teaching. After his death in 479 BCE, his conversations with his students were collected by his disciples and their followers into a book known in English as the *Analects*, which is the only record of his teaching.

At the heart of Confucian thought is the concept of *ren* (human-heartedness). *Ren* emphasizes morality and empathy as the basic standards for all human interaction. The virtue of *ren* is most fully realized in the Confucian ideal of the *junzi* (gentleman). Originally indicating noble birth, the term was redefined to mean one who through education and self-cultivation had become a superior person, right-thinking and right-acting in all situations. A *junzi* is the opposite of a petty or small-minded person. His characteristics include moderation, integrity, self-control, loyalty, reciprocity, and altruism. His primary concern is justice.

Together with human-heartedness and justice, Confucius emphasized *li* (etiquette). *Li* includes everyday manners as well as ritual, ceremony, and protocol—the formalities of all social conduct and interaction. Such forms, Confucius felt, choreographed life so that an entire society moved in harmony. *Ren* and *li* operate in the realm of the Five Constant Relationships that define Confucian society: parent and child, husband and wife, elder sibling and younger sibling, elder friend and younger friend, ruler and subject. Deference to age is clearly built into this view, as is the deference to authority that made Confucianism attractive to emperors. Yet responsibilities flow the other way as well: The duty of a ruler is to earn the loyalty of subjects, of a husband to earn the respect of his wife, of age to guide youth wisely.

During the early years of the People's Republic of China, and especially during the Great Proletarian Cultural Revolution (1966–1976), Confucius and Confucian thought were denigrated. Recently, however, Confucian temples in Beijing and elsewhere have been restored. Notably, the Chinese government has used the philosopher's name officially in establishing hundreds of Confucius Institutes in more than 80 countries to promote the learning of the Chinese language abroad.

A Closer Look

A RECEPTION IN THE PALACE

Birds and small figures, possibly alluding to mythical creatures or immortals.

Women—and an empress?—receiving visitors on the upper floor.

The legendary archer Yi saves the world by shooting the extra sun-crows that were threatening it.

The procession of visitors in horse-drawn chariots on their way to the palace.

Men—and the emperor?—receiving visitors on the lower floor.

11–9 A RECEPTION IN THE PALACE

Detail from a rubbing of a stone relief in the Wu family shrine (Wuliangci). Jiaxiang, Shandong. Han dynasty, 151 CE. 27½ × 66½″ (70 × 169 cm). Princeton University Art Museum. Far Eastern Seminar Collection. (2002-307.24)

Credit: © 2016. Princeton University Art Museum/Art Resource NY/Scala, Florence. Photo: Bruce M. White

philosophy, and it remained the state ideology of China for more than 2,000 years, until the end of imperial rule in the twentieth century. Once institutionalized, Confucianism took on so many rituals that it eventually assumed the form and force of a religion. Han philosophers contributed to this process by infusing Confucianism with traditional Chinese cosmology. They emphasized the Zhou idea, taken up by Confucius, that the emperor ruled by the mandate of Heaven. Heaven itself was reconceived more abstractly as the moral force underlying the universe. Thus the moral system of Confucian society became a reflection of universal order.

Confucian subjects turn up frequently in Han art. Among the most famous examples are the reliefs from the Wu family shrines built in 151 CE in Jiaxiang. Carved and engraved in low relief on stone slabs, the scenes were meant to teach Confucian themes such as respect for the emperor, filial piety, and wifely devotion. Daoist motifs also appear, as do figures from traditional myths

and legends in a synchronism characteristic of Han art (see "Closer Look" above).

When compared with the Han-dynasty banner (SEE FIG. 11-7), this late Han relief clearly shows the change that took place in the Chinese worldview in the span of 300 years. The banner places equal emphasis on heaven, earth, and the underworld; human beings are dwarfed by a great swarm of supernatural creatures and divine beings. In the relief, the focus is clearly on the human realm and human behavior.

ARCHITECTURE   Contemporary literary sources are eloquent on the wonders of the Han capital. Unfortunately, our only information about Han architecture is in the form of ceramic models of buildings found in tombs, where they were intended to house or support the dead in the afterlife. This model represents a typical Han dwelling (**FIG. 11–10**). Its four stories are crowned with a watchtower and face a small walled courtyard. Pigs and oxen probably occupied

11–10 TOMB MODEL OF A HOUSE AND TOWER
Eastern Han dynasty, 1st-mid 2nd century CE. Painted earthenware,
52 × 33½ × 27" (132.1 × 85.1 × 68.6 cm). The Nelson-Atkins Museum
of Art, Kansas City, Missouri.

The main house in this ceramic model is assembled from a stack of
13 individual components. Hand-written inscriptions on several of
them indicate their specific placement in the assembly process.

the ground floor, while the family lived in the upper stories, where larger windows provided light and air.

Aside from the multi-level construction, the most
interesting feature of the house is the **bracketing** system
(architectural elements projecting from the wall) that supports the rather broad eaves of its tiled roofs. Bracketing
became a standard element of East Asian architecture, not
only in private homes but more typically in palaces and
temples (SEE FIG. 11-16). Another interesting aspect of the
model is the elaborate painting on the exterior walls, much
of it decorative but some of it illustrating structural features such as posts and lintels while other images evoke
the world outdoors such as the trees flanking the gateway.
Literary sources describe the walls of Han palaces as decorated with paint and lacquer, as well as inlaid with precious metals and stones.

Six Dynasties

With the fall of the Han in 220 CE, China splintered into
three warring kingdoms. In 280 CE, the empire was briefly
reunited, but invasions by nomadic peoples from central
Asia, a source of disruption throughout Chinese history,
soon forced the court to flee south. For the next three centuries, northern and southern China developed separately.
In the north, 16 kingdoms carved out by invaders rose and
fell before giving way to a succession of largely foreign
dynasties. Warfare was commonplace. Tens of thousands
of Chinese fled south, where six short-lived dynasties succeeded each other in an age of almost constant turmoil
broadly known as the Six Dynasties period or the period of
the Southern and Northern dynasties (265–589 CE).

In this chaotic context, the Confucian system lost
influence. In the south, especially, many intellectuals—the
creators and custodians of China's high culture—turned
instead to Daoism, which contained a strong escapist element. Educated to serve the government, they increasingly
withdrew from public life. They wandered the landscape,
drank, wrote poems, practiced calligraphy, and expressed
their disdain for the social world through willfully eccentric behavior.

The rarefied intellectual escape route of Daoism was
available only to the educated elite. Most people sought
answers in the magic and superstitions of Daoism in its
religious form. Though weak and disorganized, the southern courts remained centers of traditional Chinese culture,
and Confucianism survived as official doctrine. Yet ultimately it was a newly arrived religion—Buddhism—that
flourished in the troubled China of the Six Dynasties.

PAINTING   Although few paintings survive from the
Six Dynasties, abundant literary sources describe the
period as an important one for painting. Landscape, later
a major theme of Chinese art, first appeared as an independent subject. Daoists wandered through China's countryside seeking spiritual refreshment, and both painters and
scholars of the Six Dynasties found that wandering in the
mind's eye through a painted landscape could serve the
same purpose. This new emphasis on the spiritual value
of painting contrasted with the Confucian view, which had
emphasized its moral and didactic usefulness.

Reflections on painting traditions also inspired the
first works on theory and aesthetics. Some of the earliest
and most succinct formulations of the ideals of Chinese
painting are the six principles set out by the scholar Xie He
(active c. 500–535 CE). The first two principles in particular offer valuable insight into the context in which China's
painters worked.

The first principle announces that "spirit consonance"
imbues a painting with "life's movement." This "spirit"
is the Daoist *qi*, the breath that animates all creation, the
energy that flows through all things. When a painting has

11–11 Attributed to Gu Kaizhi **DETAIL OF ADMONITIONS OF THE IMPERIAL INSTRUCTRESS TO COURT LADIES**
Six Dynasties period or later, 5th–8th century CE. Handscroll, ink and colors on silk, 9¾″ × 11′6″ (24.8 × 348.2 cm). British Museum, London.

qi, it will be alive with inner essence, not merely outward resemblance. Artists must cultivate their own spirit so that this universal energy flows through them and infuses their work. The second principle recognizes that brushstrokes are the "bones" of a picture, its primary structural element. Traditionally, a Chinese painting is judged above all by the quality of its brushwork. Each brushstroke is a vehicle of expression; it is through the vitality of a painter's brushwork that "spirit consonance" makes itself felt.

We can sense this attitude already in the rapid, confident brushstrokes that outline the figures of the Han banner (SEE FIG. 11-7) and again in the more controlled, rhythmical lines of one of the most important works associated with the Six Dynasties period, a painted scroll known as **ADMONITIONS OF THE IMPERIAL INSTRUCTRESS TO COURT LADIES**. Attributed to the painter Gu Kaizhi (344–407 CE), it alternates illustrations and text to relate seven Confucian stories of wifely virtue from Chinese history, based on a text written as a reprimand of the empress. The first illustration depicts the courage of Lady Feng (**FIG. 11-11**). An escaped circus bear rushes toward her startled husband, a Han emperor. Behind his throne, two female servants have turned to run away. Before him, two male attendants try to fend off the bear with spears. Only Lady Feng is calm as she rushes forward to place herself between the beast and the emperor.

The figures are drawn with a brush in a thin, even-width line, and a few outlined areas are filled with color. Facial features, especially those of the men, are carefully delineated. Movement and emotion are shown through conventions—the scarves flowing from Lady Feng's dress, indicating that she is rushing forward, and the upturned strings on both sides of the emperor's head, suggesting his fear. There is no hint of a setting; the artist's careful placement of figures creates a sense of depth.

The painting is on silk, which was typically woven in bands about 12 inches wide and up to 20 or 30 feet long. Early Chinese painters thus developed the format used here, the **handscroll**—a long, narrow, horizontal composition compact enough to be held in the hand when rolled up. Handscrolls are intimate works, meant to be viewed by only two or three people at a time. They were not displayed completely unrolled as we commonly see them today in museums. Rather, viewers would open a scroll and savor it slowly from right to left, displaying only an arm's length at a time.

CALLIGRAPHY The emphasis on the expressive quality and structural importance of brushstrokes finds its purest embodiment in calligraphy. The same brushes are used for both painting and calligraphy, and a relationship between them was recognized as early as Han times. In his teachings, Confucius had extolled the importance of the pursuit of knowledge and the arts. Among the visual arts, painting was felt to reflect moral concerns, while calligraphy was believed to reveal the character of the writer.

Calligraphy is regarded as one of the highest forms of artistic expression in China. For more than 2,000 years, China's literati—Confucian scholars and literary men who also served the government as officials—have been connoisseurs and practitioners of this art. During the fourth century CE, calligraphy came to full maturity. The most important practitioner of the day was Wang Xizhi (c. 307–365), whose works have served as models of excellence for subsequent generations. The example here comes from a letter, now somewhat damaged and mounted as part of an album, known as **FENG JU** (**FIG. 11-12**).

Feng Ju is an example of "running" or semicursive style, neither too formal nor too free but with a relaxed, easygoing manner. Brushstrokes vary in width and length,

11–12 Wang Xizhi **PORTION OF A LETTER FROM THE FENG JU ALBUM**

Six Dynasties period, mid 4th century CE. Ink on paper, 9¾ × 18½" (24.7 × 46.8 cm). National Palace Museum, Taibei, Taiwan, Republic of China.

The stamped characters that appear on Chinese artworks are seals—personal emblems. The use of seals dates from the Zhou dynasty, and to this day such seals traditionally employ the archaic characters, known appropriately as "seal script," of the Zhou or Qin. Cut in stone, a seal may state a formal, given name, or it may state any of the numerous personal names that China's painters and writers adopted throughout their lives. A treasured work of art often bears not only the seal of its maker, but also those of collectors and admirers through the centuries. In the Chinese view, these do not disfigure the work but add another layer of interest. This sample of Wang Xizhi's calligraphy, for example, bears the seals of two Song-dynasty emperors, a Song official, a famous collector of the sixteenth century, and two Qing-dynasty emperors of the eighteenth and nineteenth centuries.

Credit: © National Palace Museum, Taipei, Taïwan, Dist. RMN-Grand Palais/ image NPM

creating rhythmic vitality. Individual characters remain distinct, yet within each character the strokes are connected and simplified as the brush moves from one to the other without lifting off the page. The effect is fluid and graceful, yet strong and dynamic. Wang Xizhi's running style came to be officially accepted and learned along with other script styles by those who practiced this art.

BUDDHIST ART AND ARCHITECTURE Buddhism originated in India during the fifth century BCE (see Chapter 10), then gradually spread north into central Asia. With the opening of the Silk Road during the Han dynasty, its influence reached China. To the Chinese of the Six Dynasties, beset by constant warfare and social devastation, Buddhism offered consolation in life and the promise

11–13 SEATED BUDDHA, CAVE 20, YUNGANG

Datong, Shanxi. Northern Wei dynasty, c. 460. Stone, height 45′ (13.7 m).

Credit: Takashi Images/Fotolia

of salvation after death. The faith spread throughout the country across all social levels, first in the north, where many of the invaders promoted it as the official religion, then slightly later in the south, where it found its first great patron in the emperor Liang Wu Di (ruled 502–549 CE). Thousands of temples and monasteries were built, and many people became monks and nuns.

Almost nothing remains in China of the Buddhist architecture of the Six Dynasties, but we can see what it must have looked like in the Japanese Horyuji Temple (SEE FIG. 12-4), which was based on Chinese models of this period.

ROCK-CUT CAVES OF THE SILK ROAD   The most impressive works of Buddhist art surviving from the Six Dynasties are the hundreds of northern rock-cut caves along the trade routes between Xinjiang in Central Asia and the Yellow River Valley. Both the caves and the sculptures that fill them were carved from the solid rock of the cliffs. Small caves high above the ground were retreats for monks and pilgrims, while larger caves at the base of the cliffs were wayside shrines and temples.

The caves at Yungang, near Datong in Shanxi Province in central China, contain many examples of the earliest phase of Buddhist sculpture in China, including the monumental **SEATED BUDDHA** in Cave 20 (**FIG. 11-13**). The figure was carved in the latter part of the fifth century by the imperial decree of a ruler of the Northern Wei dynasty (386–534 CE), the longest-lived and most stable of the northern kingdoms. Most Wei rulers were avid patrons of Buddhism, and under their rule the religion made its greatest advances in the north.

The front part of the cave has crumbled away, and the 45-foot statue, now exposed to the open air, is clearly visible from a distance. The elongated ears, protuberance on the head (*ushnisha*), and monk's robe are traditional attributes of the Buddha. The masklike face, full torso, massive shoulders, and shallow, stylized drapery indicate strong Central Asian influence. The overall effect of this colossus is remote and austere, less human than the more sensuous expression of the early Buddhist traditions in India.

Sui and Tang Dynasties

What significant contributions are made to the history of Chinese art under the Sui and Tang dynasties?

In 581 CE, a general from the last of the northern dynasties replaced a child emperor and established a dynasty of his own, the Sui. Defeating all opposition, he molded China into a centralized empire as it had been in Han times. The short-lived Sui dynasty fell in 618, but in reunifying the empire paved the way for one of the greatest dynasties in Chinese history: the Tang (618–907). Even today many Chinese living abroad still call themselves "Tang people." To them, Tang implies that part of the Chinese character

that is strong and vigorous (especially in military power), noble and idealistic, but also realistic and pragmatic.

Buddhist Art and Architecture

The new Sui emperor was a devout Buddhist, and his reunification of China coincided with a fusion of the several styles of Buddhist sculpture that had developed. This new style is seen in a bronze **ALTAR TO AMITABHA BUDDHA** (**FIG. 11-14**), one of the many Buddhas of Mahayana Buddhism. Amitabha dwelled in the Western Pure Land, a paradise into which his faithful followers were promised rebirth. With its comparatively simple message of salvation, the Pure Land sect eventually became the most popular form of Buddhism in China and one of the most popular in Japan (see Chapter 12).

11–14 ALTAR TO AMITABHA BUDDHA
Sui dynasty, 593. Bronze, height 30⅛" (76.5 cm). Museum of Fine Arts, Boston. Gift of Mrs. W. Scott Fitz (22.407) and Gift of Edward Holmes Jackson in memory of his mother, Mrs. W. Scott Fitz (47.1407–1412).

Credit: Photograph © 2017 Museum of Fine Arts, Boston

The altar depicts Amitabha in his paradise, seated on a lotus throne beneath a canopy of trees. Each leaf cluster is set with jewels. Seven celestial figures sit on the topmost clusters, and ropes of "pearls" hang from the tree trunks. Behind Amitabha's head is a halo of flames. To his left, the bodhisattva Guanyin holds a pomegranate; to his right, another bodhisattva clasps his hands in prayer. Behind are four disciples who first preached the teachings of the Buddha. On the lower level, an incense burner is flanked by seated lions and two smaller bodhisattvas. Focusing on Amitabha's benign expression and filled with objects symbolizing his power, the altar combines the sensuality of Indian styles, the schematic abstraction of central Asian art, and the Chinese emphasis on linear grace and rhythm into a harmonious new style.

Buddhism reached its greatest development in China during the subsequent Tang dynasty, which for nearly three centuries ruled China and controlled much of Central Asia. Virtually the entire country adopted the Buddhist faith. A Tang vision of the popular Pure Land sect was expressed in a wall painting from a cave in Dunhuang (**FIG. 11–15**). A major stop along the Silk Road, Dunhuang has nearly 500 caves carved into its sandy cliffs, all filled with painted clay sculpture and decorated with wall paintings from floor to ceiling. The site was worked on continuously from the fourth to the fourteenth century, a period of almost 1,000 years. In the detail shown here, a seated Amitabha Buddha appears at center, flanked by four bodhisattvas, his messengers to the world. Two other groups of bodhisattvas are clustered at right and left. Great halls and towers rise in the background, representing the Western Paradise in terms of the grandeur of Tang palaces. Indeed, the aura of opulence could just as easily be that of the imperial court. This worldly vision of paradise provides our best indication of the splendor of Tang civilization at a time when Chang'an (present-day Xi'an) was probably the greatest city in the world.

The early Tang emperors proclaimed a policy of religious tolerance, but during the ninth century a conservative reaction developed. Confucianism was reasserted and Buddhism was briefly suppressed as a "foreign" religion. Thousands of temples, shrines, and monasteries were destroyed and innumerable bronze statues melted down. Fortunately, several Buddhist structures do survive from the Tang dynasty. One of them, the Nanchan Temple, is the earliest important surviving example of Chinese architecture.

11–15 THE WESTERN PARADISE OF AMITABHA BUDDHA
Detail of a wall painting in Cave 217, Dunhuang, Gansu. Tang dynasty, c. 750. 10'2" × 16' (3.1 × 4.86 m).

Credit: © dbimages/Alamy Stock Photo

11-16 NANCHAN TEMPLE, WUTAISHAN
Shanxi. Tang dynasty, 782.

Credit: ©
ChinaFotoPress/Getty Images

NANCHAN TEMPLE The Nanchan Temple shows characteristics of both temples and palaces of the Tang dynasty (**FIG. 11–16**). Located on Mount Wutai (Wutaishan) in the eastern part of Shanxi Province, this small hall was constructed in 782. The tiled roof, seen earlier in the Han tomb model (SEE FIG. 11–10), has taken on a curved silhouette. Quite subtle here, this curve became increasingly pronounced in later centuries. The very broad overhanging eaves are supported by a correspondingly elaborate bracketing system.

Also typical is the bay system of construction, in which a cubic unit of space, a bay, is formed by four posts and their lintels. The bay functioned in Chinese architecture as a **module**, a basic unit of construction. To create larger structures, an architect multiplied the number of bays. Thus, though modest in scope with only three bays, the Nanchan Temple still gives an idea of the vast, multistoried palaces of the Tang depicted in such paintings as FIGURE 11–15.

GREAT WILD GOOSE PAGODA The Great Wild Goose Pagoda of the Ci'en Temple in the Tang capital of Chang'an (present-day Xi'an) also survives (**FIG. 11–17**). The temple, constructed in 645 for the famous monk Xuanzang (600–664) on his return from a 16-year pilgrimage to India, was where he taught and translated the Sanskrit Buddhist scriptures he had brought back with him.

Built entirely in brick, the Great Wild Goose Pagoda nevertheless imitates the wooden architecture of the time. The walls are decorated in low relief to resemble bays, and bracket systems are reproduced under the projecting roofs of each story. Although modified and repaired in later times (its seven stories were originally five, and a

new finial has been added), the pagoda still preserves the essence of Tang architecture in its simplicity, symmetry, proportions, and grace.

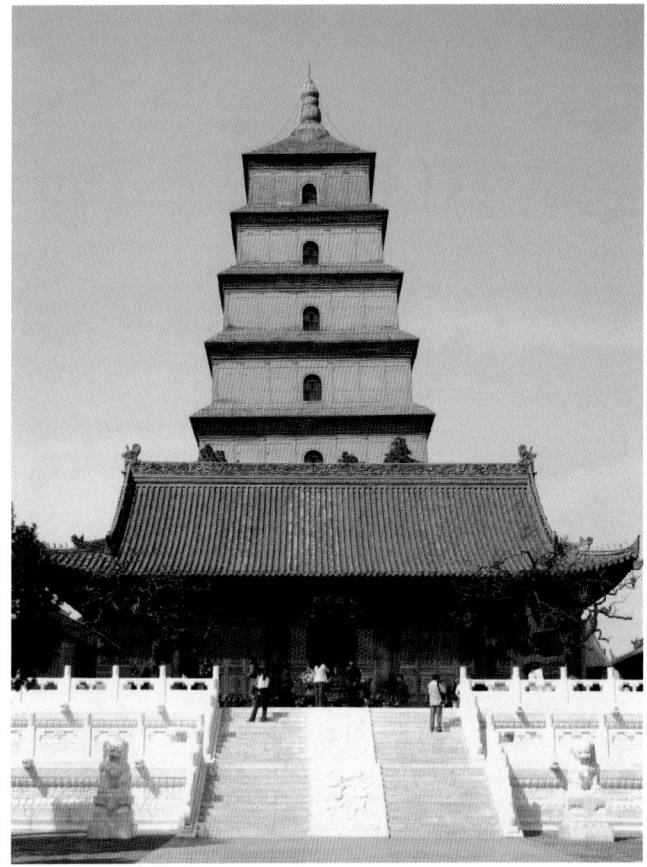

11-17 GREAT WILD GOOSE PAGODA AT CI'EN TEMPLE, CHANG'AN
Shanxi. Tang dynasty, first erected 645; rebuilt mid 8th century CE.
Credit: © Amy Harris/123RF.com

Elements of Architecture

PAGODAS

Pagodas developed from Indian stupas as Buddhism spread northeast along the Silk Road. Stupas merged with the watchtowers of Han-dynasty China in multi-storied stone or wood structures with projecting tiled roofs. This transformation culminated in wooden pagodas with upward-curving roofs supported by elaborate bracketing in China, Korea, and Japan. Buddhist pagodas retain the axis mundi masts of stupas. Like their South Asian prototypes, early East Asian pagodas were symbolic rather than enclosing structures. Later examples often provided access to the ground floor and sometimes to upper levels.

early stupa
India, 2nd century BCE

later stupa
Central Asia,
5th–6th century CE

watchtower
China, Han dynasty,
c. 206 BCE–220 CE

stone pagoda
northwestern China,
c. 5th century CE

wooden pagoda
Japan, 7th century CE

Tang Figure Painting and Ceramics

Later artists looking back on their heritage recognized the Tang dynasty as China's great age of figure painting. Unfortunately, very few Tang **scroll paintings** still exist. However, the wall paintings of Dunhuang (SEE FIG. 11–15) give us some idea of the character of Tang figure painting, and we can look at copies of lost Tang paintings made by later Song-dynasty artists. **LADIES PREPARING NEWLY WOVEN SILK** is an outstanding example of such copies, this one attributed to Huizong (ruled 1101–1126 CE),

11–18 Attributed to Emperor Huizong **DETAIL OF LADIES PREPARING NEWLY WOVEN SILK**
Copy after a lost Tang-dynasty painting by Zhang Xuan. Northern Song dynasty, early 12th century CE. Handscroll with ink and colors on silk, 14^{9}/$_{16}$ × 57^{3}/$_{16}$″ (37 × 145.3 cm). Museum of Fine Arts, Boston. Special Chinese and Japanese Fund (12.886).

Confucius said of himself, "I merely transmit, I do not create; I love and revere the ancients." In this spirit, Chinese painters regularly copied paintings of earlier masters. Painters made copies both to absorb the lessons of their great predecessors and to perpetuate the achievements of the past. In later centuries, they took up the practice of regularly executing a work "in the manner of" some particularly revered ancient master. This was at once an act of homage, a declaration of artistic allegiance, and a way of reinforcing a personal connection with the past.

Credit: Photograph © 2017 Museum of Fine Arts, Boston

the last emperor of the Northern Song dynasty (**FIG. 11–18**). An inscription on the scroll identifies the Tang original as a famous work by Zhang Xuan, an eighth-century painter known for his depictions of women at the Tang court.

Since the original no longer exists, we cannot know how faithful the copy is, but its refined lines and bright colors seem to share the grace and dignity of Tang sculpture and architecture.

Art and its Contexts
THE SILK ROAD DURING THE TANG PERIOD

Under a series of ambitious and forceful Tang emperors, Chinese control once again extended over Central Asia. Goods, ideas, and influence flowed along the Silk Road. In the South China Sea, Arab and Persian ships carried on a lively trade with coastal cities. Chinese cultural influence in East Asia was so important that Japan and Korea sent thousands of students to study Chinese civilization.

Cosmopolitan and tolerant, Tang China was confident and curious about the world. Many foreigners came to the splendid new capital Chang'an (present-day Xi'an), and they are often depicted in the art of the period. A ceramic statue of a camel carrying a troupe of musicians (**FIG. 11–19**) reflects the Tang fascination with the "exotic" Turkic cultures of Central Asia. The three bearded musicians (one with his back to us) are Central Asian, while the two smooth-shaven ones are Han Chinese. Bactrian, or two-humped, camels, themselves exotic Central Asian "visitors," were beasts of burden in the caravans that traversed the Silk Road. The stringed lute (which the Chinese called the *pipa*) came from Central Asia to become a lasting part of Chinese music.

Stylistically, the statue reveals a new interest in naturalism, an important trend in both painting and sculpture. Compared with the rigid, staring ceramic soldiers of the first emperor of Qin (SEE FIG. 11-1), this Tang band is alive with gesture and expression. The camel throws its head back; the musicians are captured in mid-performance. Ceramic figurines such as this, produced by the thousands for tombs, offer glimpses into the gorgeous variety of Tang life. The statue's three-color glaze technique was a specialty of Tang ceramicists. The glazes— usually chosen from a restricted palette of amber-yellow, green, and blue—were splashed freely and allowed to run over the surface during firing to convey a feeling of spontaneity. The technique is emblematic of Tang culture itself in its colorful and cosmopolitan expressiveness.

The Silk Road had first flourished in the second century CE. A 5,000-mile network of caravan routes from the Han capital (near present-day Luoyang, Henan, on the Yellow River) to Rome, it brought Chinese luxury goods to Western markets.

The journey began at the Jade Gate (Yumen) at the westernmost end of the Great Wall, where Chinese merchants turned their goods over to Central Asian traders. Goods would change hands many more times before reaching the Mediterranean. Caravans headed first for the nearby desert oasis of Dunhuang. Here northern and southern routes diverged to skirt the vast Taklamakan Desert. At Khotan, in western China, farther west than the area shown in MAP 11–1, travelers on

the southern route could turn off toward a mountain pass into Kashmir, in northern India. Or they could continue on, meeting up with the northern route at Kashgar, on the western border of the Taklamakan, before proceeding over the Pamir Mountains into present-day Afghanistan. From there, travelers could head toward present-day Pakistan and India, or travel west through present-day Uzbekistan, Iran, and Iraq, arriving finally at Antioch, in Syria, on the coast of the Mediterranean. After that, land and sea routes led to Rome.

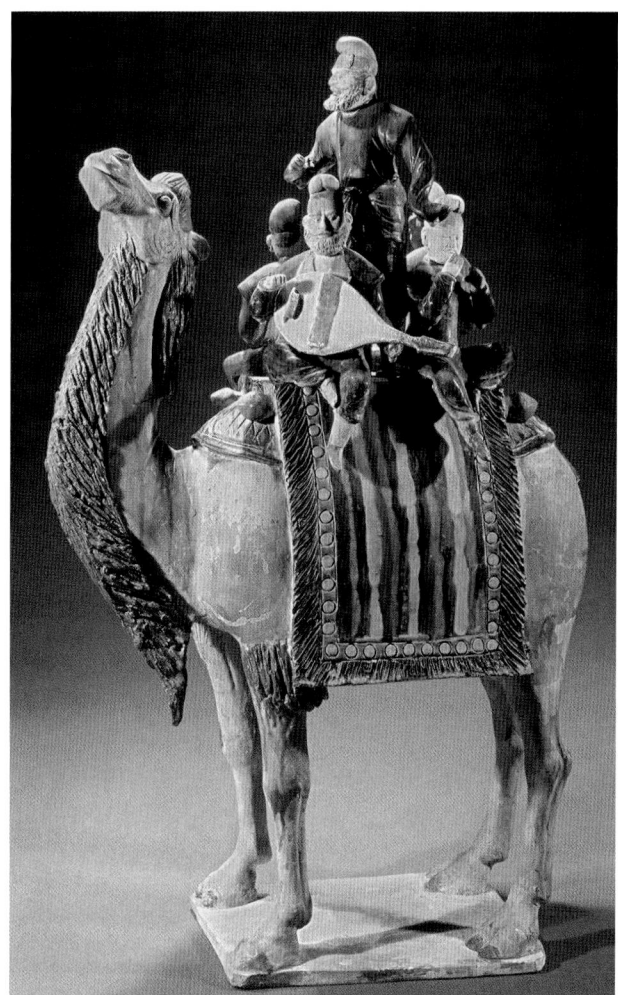

11–19 CAMEL CARRYING A GROUP OF MUSICIANS
From a tomb near Xi'an, Shanxi. Tang dynasty, c. mid 8th century CE. Earthenware with three-color glazes, height 26⅛″ (66.5 cm). National Museum, Beijing.

Credit: Cultural Relics Publishing House

11–20 TWO EQUESTRIAN FIGURES
Tang dynasty, first half of 8th century CE.
Molded, reddish-buff earthenware with cold-
painted pigments over white ground, height
(male figure) 14½″ (37 cm). Arthur M. Sackler
Museum, Harvard Art Museums, Cambridge,
Massachusetts. Gift of Anthony M. Solomon
(2003.207.1-2).

This pair documents the participation of women
as well as men in sport and riding. Both have
pointed boots and are mounted on standing,
saddled, and bridled horses; their hands are
positioned to hold the reins. The male figure
wears a tall, elaborately embellished hat,
and the female figure has her hair arranged in
a topknot.

Credit: Bridgeman Images

Two earthenware **EQUESTRIAN FIGURES** (FIG. 11–20), a man and a woman made for use as tomb furnishings, reveal more directly the robust naturalism and exuberance of figural representation during the Tang period. Accurate in proportion and lively in demeanor, the statuettes are not glazed (as is the tomb figure in FIG. 11-19), but are "cold-painted" with pigments after firing to render details of costume and facial features.

Song Dynasty

What are the important developments in Chinese art during the Song dynasty?

A brief period of disintegration followed the fall of the Tang, but eventually China was again united, this time under the Song dynasty (960–1279). A new capital was founded at Bianjing (present-day Kaifeng), near the Yellow River. In contrast to the outgoing confidence of the Tang, the mood during the Song was more introspective, a reflection of China's weakened military situation. In 1126, the Jurchen tribes of Manchuria invaded China, sacked the capital, and took possession of much of the northern part of the country. Song forces withdrew south and established a new capital at Hangzhou. From this point on, the dynasty is known as the Southern Song (1127–1279), with the first portion called in retrospect the Northern Song (960–1126).

Although China's territory had diminished, its wealth had increased because of advances in agriculture, commerce, and technology begun under the Tang. Patronage was plentiful, and the arts flourished. Song culture is noted for its refined taste and intellectual grandeur. Where the Tang had reveled in exoticism, eagerly absorbing

influences from Persia, India, and Central Asia, Song culture was more self-consciously Chinese. Philosophy experienced its most creative era since the "one hundred schools" of the Zhou. Song scholarship was brilliant, especially in history, and its poetry is noted for its depth. Perhaps the finest expressions of the Song, however, are in art, especially painting and ceramics.

No hint of political disruption or religious questioning intrudes on the sublime grace and beauty of this **SEATED GUANYIN BODHISATTVA** (FIG. 11–21), carved from wood in the eleventh or twelfth century in a territory on the northern border of Song China, a region ruled by the Liao dynasty (907–1125). Bodhisattvas are represented as young princes wearing royal garments and jewelry, their finery indicative of their worldly but virtuous lives. Guanyin is the Bodhisattva of Infinite Compassion, who appears in many guises, in this case as the Water and Moon Guanyin. He sits on rocks by the sea, in the position known as royal ease. His right arm rests on his raised and bent right knee and his left arm and foot hang down, the foot touching a lotus blossom.

Philosophy: Neo-Confucianism

Song philosophers continued the process, begun during the Tang, of restoring Confucianism to dominance. In strengthening Confucian thought, they drew on Daoist and especially Buddhist ideas, even as they openly rejected Buddhism itself as foreign. These innovations provided Confucianism with a new metaphysical aspect, allowing it to propose a richer, all-embracing explanation of the universe. This new synthesis of China's three main paths of thought is called Neo-Confucianism.

11–21 SEATED GUANYIN BODHISATTVA
Liao dynasty, 11th–12th century CE (the painting and gilding were restored in the 16th century). Wood with paint and gold, 95 × 65″ (241.3 × 165.1 cm). The Nelson-Atkins Museum of Art, Kansas City, Missouri. Purchase: William Rockhill Nelson Trust (34–10).

Neo-Confucianism teaches that the universe consists of two interacting forces known as *li* (principle or idea) and *qi* (matter). All pine trees, for example, consist of an underlying *li* we might call "Pine Tree Idea" brought into the material world through *qi*. All the *li* of the universe, including humans, are but aspects of an eternal first principle known as the Great Ultimate (*taiji*), which is completely present in every object. Our task as human beings is to rid our *qi* of impurities through education and self-cultivation so that our *li* may realize its oneness with the Great Ultimate. This life-long process resembles the striving to attain buddhahood, and, if we persist in our attempts, one day we will be enlightened—the term itself coming directly from Buddhism.

Northern Song Painting

Neo-Confucian ideas found visual expression in art, especially in landscape, which became the most highly esteemed subject for painting. Northern Song artists studied nature closely to master its many appearances: the way each species of tree grows; the distinctive character of each rock formation; the changes of the seasons; the myriad birds, blossoms, and insects. This passion for descriptive detail was the artist's form of self-cultivation. Mastering outward forms showed an understanding of the principles behind them.

Yet despite the convincing accumulation of detail, Song landscape paintings do not record a specific site. The artist's goal was to paint the eternal essence of "mountain-ness," for example, not to reproduce the appearance of a particular mountain. Painting landscapes required artists to orchestrate their cumulative understanding of *li* in all its aspects—mountains and rocks, streams and waterfalls, trees and grasses, clouds and mist. A landscape painting thus expressed the desire for the spiritual communion with nature that was the key to enlightenment. As the tradition progressed, landscape also became a vehicle for conveying human emotions, even for speaking indirectly of one's own deepest feelings.

In the earliest times, art had reflected the mythocentric worldview of the ancient Chinese. Later, as religion came to dominate people's lives, the focus of art shifted, and religious images and human actions became important subjects. Subsequently, during the Song dynasty, artists developed landscape as the chief means of expression, preferring to avoid direct depiction of the human condition and to instead convey ideals in a symbolic manner. Chinese artistic expression thus moved from the mythical, through the religious and ethical, and finally to the philosophical and aesthetic.

FAN KUAN   One of the first great masters of Song landscape was the eleventh-century painter Fan Kuan (active c. 990–1030 CE), whose surviving major work, **TRAVELERS AMONG MOUNTAINS AND STREAMS**, is regarded as one of the great monuments of Chinese art (**FIG. 11-22**). The work is physically large—almost 7 feet high—but the sense of monumentality also radiates from the composition itself.

The composition unfolds in three stages comparable to three acts of a drama. At the bottom a large, low-lying group of rocks establishes the extreme foreground. In anticipating the shape and substance of the mountains to come, the rocks introduce the main theme of the work, much as the first act of a drama introduces the principal characters. In the middle ground, travelers and their mules are coming from the right. Their size confirms our human scale—how small we are against the vastness of nature. This middle ground takes up twice as much picture surface as the foreground, and, like the second act of a play, shows variation and development. Instead of a solid mass, the rocks here are separated into two groups by a waterfall that is spanned by a bridge. In the hills to the right, the rooftops of a temple stand out above the trees.

11–22 Fan Kuan **TRAVELERS AMONG MOUNTAINS AND STREAMS**
Northern Song dynasty, early 11th century CE. Hanging scroll with ink and colors on silk, height 6′9½″ (2.06 m). National Palace Museum, Taibei, Taiwan, Republic of China.

Credit: © Corbis

Mist veils the transition to the background, with the result that the mountain looms suddenly. This background area, almost twice as large as the foreground and middle ground combined, is the climactic third act of the drama. The mountain's ponderous weight increases as it extends upward, finally bursting into the sprays of energetic brushstrokes that describe the scrubby growth on top. To the right, a slender waterfall plummets, enhancing the mountain's upward thrust by contrast. The whole painting conveys the feeling of climbing a high mountain, leaving the human world behind to come face to face with the Great Ultimate in a spiritual communion.

All the elements are depicted with precise detail and in proper scale. Jagged brushstrokes describe the contours of rocks and trees and express their rugged character. Layers of short, staccato strokes (translated as "raindrop texture" from the Chinese) accurately mimic the texture of the rock surface. Spatial recession from foreground through middle ground to background is convincingly handled.

Although it contains realistic details, the landscape represents no specific place. In its forms, the artist expresses the ideal forms behind appearances; in the rational, ordered composition, he expresses the intelligence of the universe. The arrangement of the mountains, with the central peak flanked by lesser peaks on each side, seems to reflect both the ancient Confucian notion of social hierarchy, with the emperor flanked by his ministers, and the Buddhist motif of the Buddha with bodhisattvas at his side. The landscape, a view of nature uncorrupted by human habitation, expresses a kind of Daoist ideal. Thus we find the three strains of Chinese thought united, much as they are in Neo-Confucianism itself.

The ability of Chinese landscape painters to take us out of ourselves and to let us wander freely through their sites is closely linked to the avoidance of perspective as it is understood in the West. Fifteenth-century European painters, searching for fidelity to appearances, developed a scientific system for recording exactly the view that could be seen from a single, stable vantage point. In contrast, the goal of Chinese painting is to show a totality beyond what we are normally given to see. If the ideal for centuries of Western painters was to render what can be seen from a fixed viewpoint, that of Chinese artists was to reveal nature through a distant, all-seeing, and mobile viewpoint.

XU DAONING This sense of shifting perspective is clearest in the handscroll, where our vantage point changes constantly as we move through the painting. One of the finest handscrolls to survive from the Northern Song is **FISHING IN A MOUNTAIN STREAM** (**FIG. 11–23**), executed in the middle of the eleventh century by Xu Daoning (c. 970–c. 1052). Starting from a thatched hut in the right foreground, we follow a path that leads to a broad, open view of a deep vista dissolving into distant mists and mountain peaks. (Remember that viewers observed only a small section of the scroll at a time, moving from right to left. To mimic this effect, use two pieces of paper to frame a small viewing area, then move them slowly leftward.) Crossing over a small footbridge, we are brought back to the foreground with the beginning of a central group of high mountains that show extraordinary shapes. Again our path winds back along the bank, and we have a view of the highest peaks from another small footbridge. At the far side of the bridge, we find ourselves looking up into a deep valley, where a stream lures our eyes far into the distance. We can imagine ourselves resting in the small pavilion halfway up

11–23 Xu Daoning **SECTION OF FISHING IN A MOUNTAIN STREAM**
Northern Song dynasty, mid 11th century CE. Handscroll with ink on silk, 19″ × 6′10″ (48.9 cm × 2.09 m). The Nelson-Atkins Museum of Art,
Kansas City, Missouri. Purchase, William Rockhill Nelson Trust (33–1559).

the valley on the right or perhaps fishing from the boats visible as the valley gives way to a second, smaller group of mountains, serving both as an echo of the central group and as a transition to the painting's finale, a broad, open vista. Gazing out into the distance and reflecting on our journey, we again feel that communion with nature that is the goal of Chinese artistic expression.

Such handscrolls have no counterpart in the Western visual arts and are often compared instead to the tradition of Western music, especially symphonic compositions. Both are generated from opening motifs that are developed and varied, both are revealed over time, and in both our sense of the overall structure relies on memory, for we do not see the scroll or hear the composition all at once.

ZHANG ZEDUAN   The Northern Song fascination with precision extended to details within landscape. The emperor Huizong, whose copy of *Ladies Preparing Newly Woven Silk* was seen in FIGURE 11–18, gathered around himself a group of court painters who shared his passion for quiet, exquisitely detailed, delicately colored paintings of birds and flowers. Other painters specialized in domestic

and wild animals, still others in palaces and buildings. One of the most spectacular products of this passion for observation is **PEACE REIGNS ALONG THE RIVER**, a long handscroll painted in the late eleventh or early twelfth century by Zhang Zeduan, an artist connected to the court (**FIG. 11–24**). Beyond its considerable visual delights, the painting is also a valuable record of daily life in the Song capital.

On the long expanse of the painted scroll an idealized view of city life unfolds. The scene reproduced here takes place at the Rainbow Bridge (its name derived from its shape), crowded with merchants and shoppers. The large boat approaching the bridge from the right is probably bringing goods from the southern part of China up the Grand Canal that ran through the city at that time. The sailors are preparing to pass beneath the bridge by lowering the sail and taking down the mast. Figures on ship and shore gesture wildly, shouting orders and advice, while a crowd gathers at the bridge railing to watch. Stalls on the bridge are selling food and other merchandise; wine shops and eating places line the banks of the canal. Some people are busy carrying goods, some are shopping, some are

11–24 Zhang Zeduan **SECTION OF PEACE REIGNS ALONG THE RIVER**
Northern Song dynasty, late 11th–early 12th century CE. Handscroll with ink and colors on silk, 9½″ × 7′4″ (24.8 cm × 2.28 m). The Palace Museum, Beijing.

Credit: Werner Forman Archive/ Palace Museum, Beijing

simply enjoying themselves. The bustling activity is meant to signify the economic prosperity that results from successful governance by the Northern Song emperor.

Little is known about the painter Zhang Zeduan other than that he was a member of the scholar-official class, the highly educated elite of imperial China. His painting demonstrates skill in the fine-line architectural drawing called *jiehua* ("ruled-line") painting. Interestingly, some of Zhang Zeduan's peers were already beginning to cultivate quite a different attitude toward painting as a form of artistic expression, one that placed overt display of technical skill at the lowest end of the scale of values. This emerging scholarly aesthetic, developed by China's literati, later came to dominate Chinese thinking about art.

Southern Song Painting and Ceramics

Landscape painting took a very different course after the fall of the north to the Jurchen in 1127 and the removal of the court to its new southern capital in Hangzhou.

XIA GUI A new sensibility is reflected in the surviving portion of **TWELVE VIEWS OF LANDSCAPE** (**FIG. 11–25**) by Xia Gui (active c. 1195–1235), a member of the newly established Academy of Painters. In general, academy members continued to favor such subjects as birds and flowers in the highly refined, elegantly colored court style patronized earlier by Huizong (SEE FIG. 11–18). Xia Gui, however, was interested in landscape and cultivated his own style. Only the last four of the 12 views that originally made up this long handscroll have survived, but they are enough to illustrate the unique quality of his approach.

In contrast to the majestic, austere landscapes of the Northern Song painters, Xia Gui presents an intimate and lyrical view of nature. Subtly modulated, carefully controlled ink washes evoke a landscape veiled in mist, while a few deft brushstrokes indicate the details

showing through the mist—the grasses growing by the bank, the fishers at their work, the trees laden with moisture, the two bent-backed figures carrying their loads along the path that skirts the hill. Simplified forms, stark contrasts of light and dark, asymmetrical composition, and great expanses of blank space suggest a fleeting world that can be captured only in glimpses. The intangible has more presence than the tangible. By limiting himself to a few essential details, the painter evokes a deep feeling for what lies beyond.

This development in Song painting from the rational and intellectual to the emotional and intuitive had a parallel in philosophy. During the late twelfth century, a new school of Neo-Confucianism called School of the Mind insisted that self-cultivation could be achieved through contemplation, which might lead to sudden enlightenment. The idea of sudden enlightenment may have come from Chan Buddhism, better known in the West by its Japanese name, Zen. Chan Buddhists rejected formal paths to enlightenment such as scripture, knowledge, and ritual, in favor of meditation and techniques designed to "short-circuit" the rational mind. Xia Gui's painting seems to suggest this intuitive approach.

The subtle and sophisticated paintings of the Song were created for a highly cultivated audience who were equally discerning in other arts such as ceramics. Building on the considerable accomplishments of the Tang, Song potters achieved a technical and aesthetic perfection that has made their wares models of excellence throughout the world. Like their painter contemporaries, Song potters turned away from the exuberance of Tang styles to create more quietly beautiful pieces.

GUAN WARE Among the most prized of the many types of Song ceramics is Guan ware, made mainly for imperial use (**FIG. 11–26**). The rounded body, high neck, and extended lip of this simple vessel show a strong sense of harmony. Enhanced by a lustrous grayish-blue glaze, the

11–25 Xia Gui **SECTION OF TWELVE VIEWS OF LANDSCAPE**
Southern Song dynasty, early 13th century CE. Handscroll with ink on silk, height 11″ (28 cm); length of extant portion 7′7½″ (2.31 m). The Nelson-Atkins Museum of Art, Kansas City, Missouri. Purchase: William Rockhill Nelson Trust (32–159/2).

11-26 GUAN WARE VESSEL

Southern Song dynasty, 13th century CE. Gray stoneware with crackled grayish-blue glaze, height 6⅝" (16.8 cm). Percival David Foundation of Chinese Art, British Museum, London.

form flows without break from base to lip, evoking an introspective quality as eloquent as the blank spaces in Xia Gui's painting. The aesthetic of the Song is most evident in the crackle pattern on the glazed surface. The crackle technique was probably discovered accidentally, but it came

to be used deliberately in some of the most refined Song wares. In the play of irregular, spontaneous crackles over a perfectly regular, perfectly planned form we can sense the same spirit that hovers behind the self-effacing virtuosity and freely intuitive insights of Xia Gui's landscape.

In 1279 the Southern Song dynasty fell to the conquering forces of the Mongol leader Kublai Khan (1215–1294). China was subsumed into the vast Mongol empire. Mongol rulers founded the Yuan dynasty (1279–1368), setting up their capital in the northeast in what is now Beijing. Yet the cultural center of China remained in the south, in the cities that rose to prominence during the Song, especially Hangzhou. This separation of political and cultural centers, coupled with a lasting resentment toward "barbarian" rule, created the climate for later developments in Chinese art.

The Arts of Korea

What features characterize the early art of Korea from the Three Kingdoms period through the Goryeo dynasty?

Set between China and Japan, Korea occupies a peninsula in northeast Asia. Inhabited for millennia, the peninsula gave rise to a distinctively Korean culture during the Three Kingdoms period.

The Three Kingdoms Period

Traditionally dated 57 BCE–668 CE, the Three Kingdoms period saw the establishment of three independent nation-states: Silla in the southeast, Baekje in the southwest, and Goguryeo in the north. Large tomb mounds built during the fifth and sixth centuries CE are enduring monuments of this period.

A GOLD HEADDRESS   The most spectacular items recovered from these tombs are trappings of royal authority (**FIG. 11-27**). Made expressly for burial, this elaborate crown was assembled from cut pieces of thin gold sheet held together by gold wire. Spangles of gold embellish the crown, as do comma-shaped ornaments of green and white jadeite—a form of jade mineralogically distinct from the nephrite prized by the early Chinese. The tall, branching

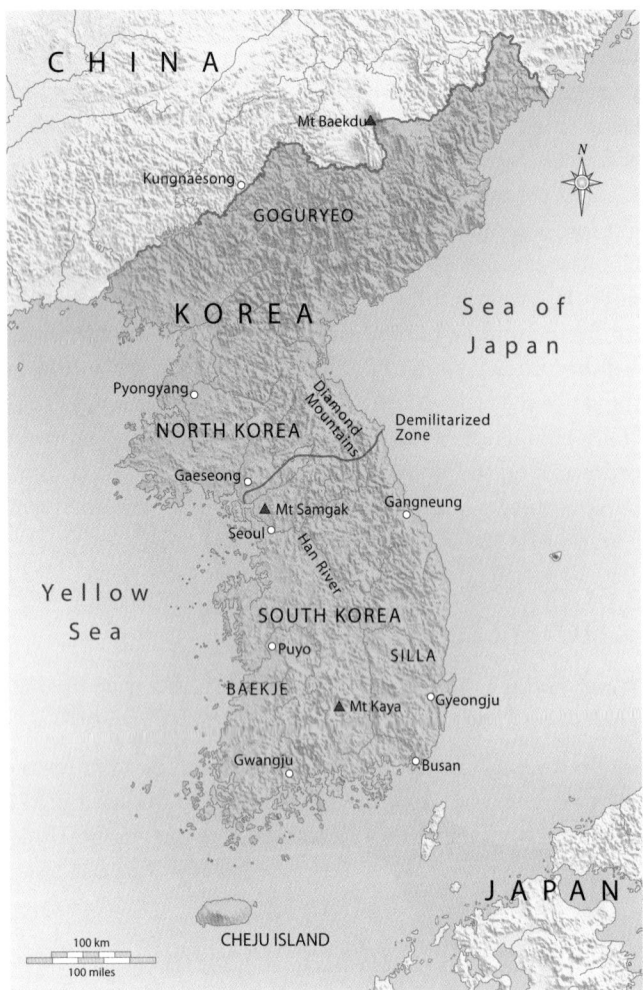

MAP 11–2 KOREA

The map shows Korea, with its division into North and South, and
indicates major sites mentioned in this chapter.

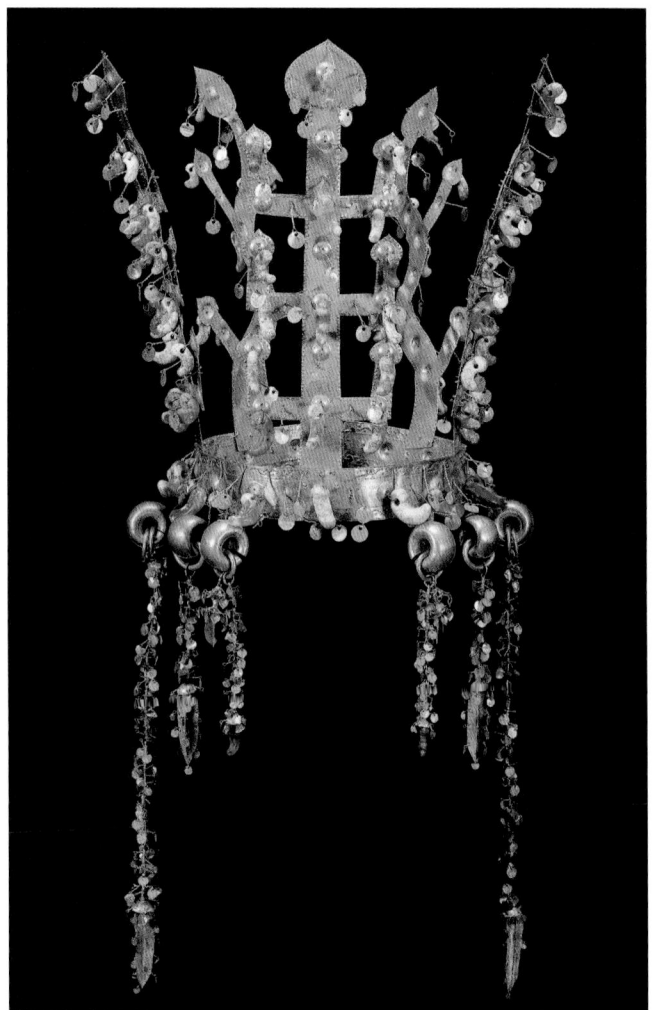

11–27 CROWN

From the Gold Crown Tomb, Gyeongju, North Gyeongsang
Province, Korea. Three Kingdoms period, Silla kingdom, probably
6th century CE. Gold with jadeite ornaments, height 17½″ (44.5 cm).
National Museum of Korea, Seoul, Republic of Korea.

Credit: National Museum of Korea, Seoul, Republic of Korea

forms rising from the crown's periphery resemble trees
and antlers. Within the crown is a conical cap woven of
narrow strips of sheet gold and ornamented with append-
ages that suggest wings or feathers.

HIGH-FIRED CERAMICS The tombs have also yielded
ceramics in abundance. Most are containers for offerings
of food placed in the tomb to nourish the spirit of the
deceased. These items generally are of unglazed stoneware, a high-fired ceramic that is impervious to liquids,
even without glaze.

The most imposing ceramic shapes are tall **STANDS**
(**FIG. 11-28**), typically designed as a long, cylindrical shaft
set on a bulbous base and used to support round-bottomed
jars. Openwork apertures cut into the moist clay before firing lighten what otherwise would be rather ponderous
forms. Few examples of Three Kingdoms ceramics exhibit
surface ornamentation, other than an occasional combed
wave pattern or an incised configuration of circles and
chevrons (V shapes), but in this piece snakes inch their
way up the shaft of the stand.

A BODHISATTVA SEATED IN MEDITATION Buddhism was introduced into the Goguryeo kingdom from
China in 372 CE and into Baekje by 384. Although it probably reached Silla in the second half of the fifth century, it
gained recognition as the official religion of the Silla state
only in 527.

At first, Buddhist art in Korea imitated Chinese examples. By the late sixth century, however, Korean sculptors
had created a distinctive style, exemplified by a magnificent gilt-bronze image of a bodhisattva (probably the bodhisattva Maitreya) seated in meditation that likely dates to
the early seventh century (**FIG. 11-29**). Although the pose
derives from late sixth-century Chinese sculpture, the slender body, elliptical face, elegant drapery folds, and trilobed
crown are distinctly Korean.

Buddhism was introduced to Japan from Korea—from
the Baekje kingdom, according to literary accounts. Historical sources indicate that numerous Korean sculptors

11–28 CEREMONIAL STAND WITH SNAKE, ABSTRACT, AND OPENWORK DECORATION
Reportedly recovered in Andong, North Gyeongsang Province, Korea. Three Kingdoms period, Silla kingdom, 5th–6th century CE. Gray stoneware with combed, stamped, applied, and openwork decoration and with traces of natural ash glaze, height 23⅛″ (58.7 cm). Arthur M. Sackler Museum, Harvard Art Museums, Cambridge, Massachusetts. Partial gift of Maria C. Henderson and partial purchase through the Ernest B. and Helen Pratt Dane Fund for the Acquisition of Oriental Art (1991.501).

Credit: Bridgeman Images

11–29 BODHISATTVA SEATED IN MEDITATION
Korea. Three Kingdoms period, probably Silla kingdom, early 7th century CE. Gilt bronze, height 35⅞″ (91 cm). National Museum of Korea, Seoul, Republic of Korea (formerly in the collection of the Toksu Palace Museum of Fine Arts, Seoul).

Credit: Pictures from History/National Museum of Korea/Bridgeman Images

were active in Japan in the sixth and seventh centuries; several early masterpieces of Buddhist art in Japan show pronounced Korean influence (SEE FIG. 12–6).

The Unified Silla Period

In 660, the Silla kingdom conquered Baekje, and, in 668, through an alliance with Tang-dynasty China, it vanquished Goguryeo, uniting the peninsula under the rule of the Unified Silla dynasty, which lasted until 935. Buddhism prospered under Unified Silla, and many large, important temples were erected in and around Gyeongju, the Silla capital.

SEOKGURAM The greatest monument of the Unified Silla period is Seokguram, an artificial cave-temple constructed under royal patronage atop Mount Toham, near

Gyeongju. The temple is modeled after Chinese cave-temples of the fifth, sixth, and seventh centuries, which were in turn inspired by the Buddhist cave-temples of India.

Built in the mid eighth century of cut blocks of granite, Seokguram consists of a small rectangular antechamber joined by a narrow vestibule to a circular main hall with a domed ceiling. More than 11 feet in height, a huge seated Buddha dominates the main hall (**FIG. 11–30**). Seated on a lotus pedestal, the image represents the historical Buddha Shakyamuni at the moment of his enlightenment, as indicated by his earth-touching gesture, or *bhumisparsha mudra.*

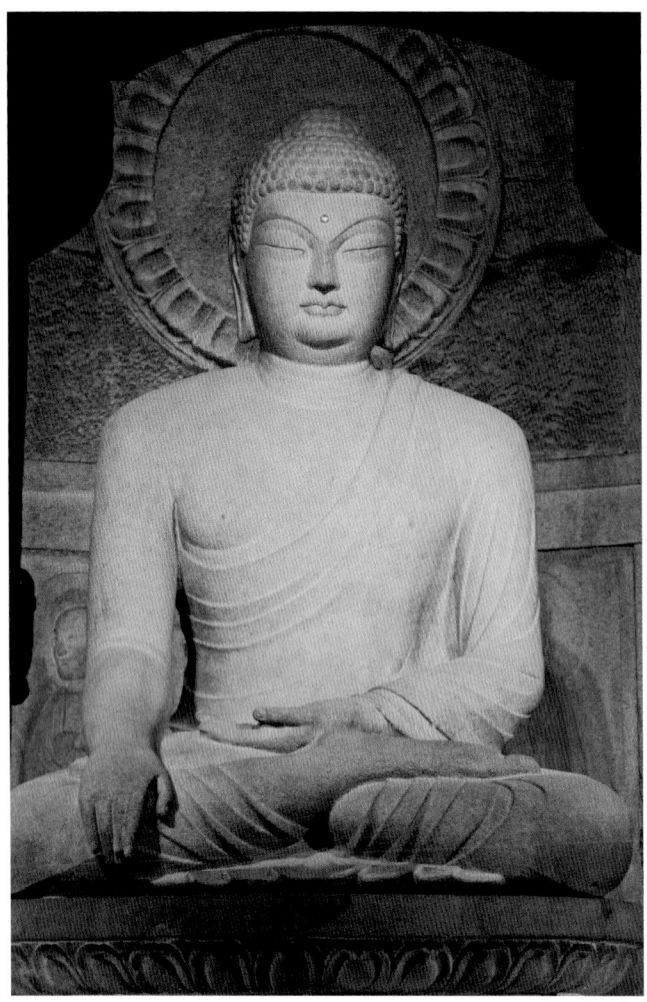

11–30 SEATED SHAKYAMUNI BUDDHA

Seokguram Grotto, near Gyeongju, North Gyeongsang Province, Korea. Unified Silla period, c. 751 CE. Granite, height of Buddha 11′2½″ (3.42 m).

The Buddha's hands are in the *bhumisparsha mudra*, the earth-touching gesture symbolizing his enlightenment.

Credit: © Prisma Bildagentur AG/Alamy Stock Photo

The full, taut forms, diaphanous drapery, and anatomical details of his chest relate this image to eighth-century Chinese sculptures. Exquisitely carved low-relief images of bodhisattvas and lesser deities grace the walls of the antechamber, vestibule, and main hall.

The Goryeo Dynasty

Established in 918, the Goryeo dynasty eliminated the last vestiges of Unified Silla rule in 935; it would continue until 1392, ruling from its capital at Gaeseong—to the northwest of present-day Seoul and now in North Korea. A period of courtly refinement, the Goryeo dynasty is best known for its celadon-glazed ceramics.

CELADON-GLAZED CERAMICS The term **celadon** refers to a high-fired, transparent glaze of pale bluish-green hue, typically applied over a pale gray stoneware body. Chinese potters invented celadon glazes and had initiated the continuous production of celadon-glazed wares as early as the first century CE. Korean potters began to experiment with such glazes in the eighth and ninth centuries, and soon the finest Goryeo celadons rivaled the best Chinese court ceramics. Although these wares were used by people of various socioeconomic classes during the Goryeo dynasty, the finest examples went to the palace, to nobles, or to powerful Buddhist clergy.

Prized for their classic simplicity, eleventh-century Korean celadons often have little decoration, but during the twelfth century potters added incised, carved, or molded embellishments, either imitating those of contemporary Chinese ceramics or exploring new styles and techniques of ornamentation. Most notable among their

11–31 MAEBYEONG BOTTLE WITH DECORATION OF BAMBOO AND BLOSSOMING PLUM TREE

Korea. Goryeo dynasty, late 12th–early 13th century CE. Inlaid celadon ware: light gray stoneware with decoration inlaid with black and white slips under celadon glaze, height 13¼″ (33.7 cm). Tokyo National Museum, Tokyo, Japan. (TG-2171).

Credit: TNM Image Archives

11–32 SEATED WILLOW-BRANCH GWANSE'EUM BOSAL (THE BODHISATTVA AVALOKITESHVARA)
Korea. Goryeo dynasty, late 14th century CE. Hanging scroll with ink, colors, and gold pigment on silk, height 62½″ (159.6 cm). Arthur M. Sackler Museum, Harvard Art Museums, Cambridge, Massachusetts. Bequest of Grenville L. Winthrop (1943.57.12).

Credit: Bridgeman Images

inventions was inlaid decoration, in which black and white slips, or finely ground clays, were inlaid into the intaglio lines of decorative elements incised or stamped in the clay body, creating underglaze designs in contrasting colors, as seen in a bottle (**FIG. 11–31**) displaying three different pictorial scenes inlaid in black and white slips. The scene shown here depicts a clump of bamboo growing at the edge of a lake, the stalks intertwined with the branches of a blossoming plum tree (which flowers in late winter before sprouting leaves). Geese swim in the lake and butterflies flutter above, linking the several scenes around the bottle. Known as a *maebyeong* ("plum bottle"), such broad-shouldered vessels were used as storage jars for wine, vinegar, and other liquids. A small, bell-shaped cover originally capped the bottle, protecting its contents and complementing its curves.

BUDDHIST PAINTING   Buddhism, the state religion of Goryeo, enjoyed royal patronage, allowing many temples to commission the very finest architects, sculptors, and painters. The most sumptuous Buddhist works produced during the Goryeo period were paintings. Created with ink and colors on silk, a fourteenth-century hanging scroll (**FIG. 11–32**) depicts Gwanse'eum Bosal (whom the Chinese called Guanyin), the bodhisattva of compassion. The rich colors and gold pigment reflect the luxurious taste of the period. Numerous paintings of this type were exported to Japan, where they influenced the course of Buddhist painting.

Think About It

1   To what extent is naturalism—the artistic goal of reproducing the visual appearance of the natural world—a motivating force in early Chinese and Korean art?

2   Compare and contrast the Chinese seated Guanyin bodhisattva (**FIG. 11–21**) and the Korean bodhisattva seated in meditation (**FIG. 11–29**). Define "bodhisattva," and examine how the artists gave visual expression to each deity's attributes.

3   Summarize the main principles of Confucianism. Then select a work from this chapter that gives visual form to Confucian philosophy and explain how it does so.

4   Select one of the Song-era Chinese landscape paintings included in this chapter. Describe it carefully and explain how it may embody philosophical or religious ideals.

Crosscurrents

These two imposing complexes from Egypt and China are royal tombs. Explain how they represent the political stature of the entombed and the beliefs of their cultures.

FIG. 3–4

FIG. 11–1

12–1 KASUGA SHRINE MANDALA

Kamakura period, early 14th century CE. Hanging scroll with ink, color, and gold on silk, 39½ × 15⅝″ (100.3 × 39.8 cm). Mary Griggs Burke Collection. Gift of the Mary and Jackson Burke Foundation, 2015.

Chapter 12
Japanese Art before 1333

Learning Objectives

12.a Identify the visual hallmarks of early Japanese art for formal, technical, and expressive qualities.

12.b Interpret the meaning of works of early Japanese art based on their themes, subjects, and symbols.

12.c Relate early Japanese artists and art to their cultural, economic, and political contexts.

12.d Apply the vocabulary and concepts relevant to early Japanese art, artists, and art history.

12.e Interpret a work of early Japanese art using the art historical methods of observation, comparison, and inductive reasoning.

12.f Select visual and textual evidence in various media to support an argument or an interpretation of a work of early Japanese art.

A group of Buddhist deities hovers at the top of this painting (**FIG. 12–1**), poised above a vast expanse of verdant hills and meadows filled with blossoming cherry and plum trees and a diagrammatic, bird's-eye view of a religious compound. The sacred site depicted in idealized but recognizable form is the Kasuga Shrine in Nara, dedicated to deities, known as *kami*, of Japan's native Shinto religion. It served as the family shrine for the most powerful aristocratic clan in ancient Japan, the Fujiwara, who chose the site for its proximity to their home, as well as for its natural beauty.

Life in Japan revolved around seasonal rhythms and the conceptions of *kami*, who give and protect life and embody the renewable, life-sustaining forces of nature. The *kami* were believed to have descended from the heavens at supremely beautiful places such as majestic mountains, towering waterfalls, old and gnarled trees, or unusual rock formations, thus rendering such locations holy—places where one might seek communion with *kami*. The deer prominently silhouetted at the very bottom of the painting are considered sacred messengers of *kami*. They roam freely in this area even today.

That foreign deities associated with Buddhism preside over a native Shinto shrine presented no anomaly. By the Heian period (794–1185 CE), the interaction of Buddhist and Shinto doctrines in Japan resulted from the belief that Buddhist deities were their original forms of *kami*. When Buddhism first entered Japan in the sixth century, the effort to integrate it with the indigenous Japanese religious belief system centered around *kami*, which only later came to be called Shinto. Until the latter part of the nineteenth century, when the government forcibly separated the two religions and elevated Shinto to bolster worship of the emperor, Buddhism and Shinto were intimately intertwined, evolving together as complementary systems. Shinto explains the origins of the Japanese people and its deities protect them, while Buddhism offers salvation after death.

This painting encapsulates various aspects of ancient and early medieval Japanese art and culture. Like all religious art from early Japan, it was created to embody religious teachings and beliefs and was not considered a work of art. It represents how reverence for the natural world informed religious practice and visual vocabulary, and shows how the foreign religion of Buddhism was integrated with indigenous belief systems without sacrificing either. We will discover other creative syntheses of disparate traditions as we survey the art of early Japan.

The Origins of Art in Japan

What characterizes the earliest art produced by the prehistoric cultures of Japan?

Human habitation in Japan dates to around 30,000 years ago (**MAP 12–1**). Sometime after 15,000 years ago Paleolithic peoples gave way to Neolithic hunter-gatherers, who gradually developed the ability to make and use ceramics. Recent scientific dating methods have shown that some works of Japanese pottery date to earlier than 10,000 BCE.

MAP 12–1 JAPAN

Melting glaciers at the end of the Ice Age in Japan 15,000 years ago raised the sea level and formed the four main islands of Japan: Hokkaido, Honshu, Shikoku, and Kyushu.

Jomon Period

The early potters lived during the Jomon ("cord markings") period (c. 12,000–400 BCE), named for the patterns on much of the pottery they produced. They made functional earthenware vessels, probably originally imitating reed baskets, by building them up with coils of clay, then firing them in bonfires at relatively low temperatures (SEE FIG. 1-25). They also created small humanoid figures known as **dogu**, which were probably effigies that manifested a kind of sympathetic magic. Around 5000 BCE agriculture emerged with the planting and harvesting of beans and gourds.

Yayoi Period

During the succeeding Yayoi era (c. 400 BCE–300 CE), the introduction of rice cultivation by immigrants from Korea helped transform Japan into an agricultural nation. As it did elsewhere in the world, this shift to agriculture brought larger permanent settlements, class structure with the division of labor into agricultural and nonagricultural tasks, and more hierarchical forms of social organization. Korean settlers also brought metal technology. Bronze was used to create weapons as well as ceremonial objects such as bells. Iron metallurgy developed later in this period, eventually replacing stone tools in everyday life.

Kofun Period

Centralized government developed during the ensuing Kofun ("old tombs") period (c. 300–552 CE), named for its large royal tombs. With the emergence of a more complex social order, the veneration of leaders grew into the beginnings of an imperial system. Still in existence today in Japan, this system eventually explained that the emperor (or, very rarely, empress) descended directly from Shinto deities. When an emperor died, chamber tombs were constructed following Korean examples. Various grave goods were placed inside the tomb chambers, including large amounts of pottery, presumably to pacify the spirits of the dead and to serve the emperor in his next life. As part of a general cultural transfer from China through Korea, fifth-century potters in Japan gained knowledge of finishing techniques and improved kilns and began to produce high-fired ceramic ware.

The Japanese government has never allowed the major sacred tombs to be excavated, but much is known about the mortuary practices of Kofun-era Japan. Some huge tombs of the fifth and sixth centuries were constructed in a shape resembling a large keyhole and surrounded by moats dug to protect the sacred precincts. Tomb sites might extend over more than 400 acres, with artificial hills built over the tombs themselves. On the top of the hills were placed ceramic sculptures called **haniwa**.

HANIWA The first *haniwa* were simple cylinders that may have held jars with ceremonial offerings. By the fifth century, these cylinders came to be made in the shapes of ceremonial objects, houses, and boats. Gradually, animals were added to the repertoire of *haniwa* subjects, including birds, deer, dogs, monkeys, cows, and horses. By the sixth century, **HANIWA** in human shapes were crafted, including males and females of various types, professions, and classes (FIG. **12-2**).

Haniwa embody aesthetic characteristics that we will encounter again in Japanese art. Their clay bodies were left

12-2 HANIWA
From Kyoto. Kofun period, 6th century CE. Earthenware, height 27″
(68.5 cm). Collection of the Tokyo National Museum. Important
Cultural Property.

There have been many theories on the function of *haniwa*. The
figures seem to have served as some kind of link between the world
of the dead, over which they were placed, and the world of the living,
from which they could be viewed. This figure has been identified
as a seated female shaman, wearing a robe, belt, and necklace
and carrying a mirror at her waist. In early Japan, shamans acted
as agents between the natural and the supernatural worlds, just as
haniwa figures were links between the living and the dead.

Credit: TNM Image Archives

unglazed and do not show a preoccupation with technical
virtuosity. Instead, their makers explored the expressive
potentials of simple and bold forms. *Haniwa* are never perfectly symmetrical; their slightly off-center eye-slits, irregular cylindrical bodies, and unequal arms seem to impart
the idiosyncrasy of life and individuality.

Shinto

As described at the beginning of this chapter, Shinto is
Japan's indigenous religious belief system. It encompasses
a variety of ritual practices that center around family, village, and devotion to *kami*. The term Shinto was not coined
until after the arrival of Buddhism in the sixth century CE;
as *kami* worship was influenced by and incorporated into
Buddhism it became more systematized, with shrines, a
hierarchy of deities, and more strictly regulated ceremonies.

THE ISE SHRINE   One of the great Shinto monuments
is the Grand Shrine of Ise, on the coast southwest of Tokyo
(**FIG. 12–3**), where the main deity worshiped is the sun
goddess Amaterasu-o-mi-kami, the legendary progenitor
of Japan's imperial family. Japan's earliest written historical texts, recorded by the imperial court in the eighth century, claim that the Ise Shrine dates to the first century CE.
Although we do not know for certain if this is true, we do
know that it has been ritually rebuilt, alternately on two
adjoining sites, at 20-year intervals with few breaks since
the year 690, when the imperial family was solidifying its
hegemony. Its most recent rebuilding was in 2013 by carpenters who trained for the task from childhood. After the
kami is ceremonially escorted to the freshly copied shrine,
the old shrine is dismantled. Thus—like Japanese culture
itself—this exquisite shrine is both ancient and constantly
renewed. In this sense it embodies one of the most important characteristics of Shinto faith—ritual purification—
derived from respect for the cycle of the seasons in which
pure new life emerges in springtime and gives way to
death in winter, yet is reborn again in the following year.

Although Ise is visited by millions of pilgrims each
year, only members of the imperial family and a few Shinto
priests are allowed within the enclosure that surrounds its
inner shrine. Detailed documents on its appearance date
back to the tenth century, but shrine authorities denied
photographers access to its inner compound until 1953,
when the iconic photograph of it reproduced in FIGURE 12–3
was taken by a photographer officially engaged by a quasi-
governmental cultural relations agency. The reluctance of
shrine officials to permit photography even then may stem
from beliefs that such intimate pictures would violate the
privacy of the shrine's most sacred spaces.

Many aspects of the Ise Shrine are typical of Shinto
architecture, including the wooden piles that elevate the
building above the ground, a thatched roof held in place
by horizontal logs, the use of unpainted cypress wood,
and the overall feeling of natural simplicity rather than
overwhelming size or elaborate decoration. The building's
shape seems indebted to early raised granaries known
from drawings on bronze artifacts of the Yayoi period. The
sensitive use of unornamented natural materials suggests
an early origin for an aspect of Japanese taste that persists
to the present day.

Writing, Language, and Culture

Chinese culture enjoyed great prestige in East Asia. Written Chinese served as an international language of scholarship and cultivation, much as Latin did in medieval Europe. Educated Koreans, for example, wrote almost exclusively in Chinese until the fifteenth century. In Japan, Chinese continued to be used for certain kinds of writing, such as Buddhist *sutras*, philosophical and legal texts, and Chinese poetry (by Japanese writers), into the nineteenth century.

When it came to writing their own language, the Japanese initially borrowed Chinese characters, or *kanji*. Differences between the Chinese and Japanese languages made this system extremely unwieldy, so during the ninth century they developed two syllabaries, or *kana*, from simplified Chinese characters. (A syllabary is a system of lettering in which each symbol stands for a syllable.)

Katakana, consisting of angular symbols, was developed to aid pronunciation of Chinese Buddhist texts and now is generally used for foreign words. *Hiragana*, comprised of graceful, cursive symbols, was the written language the Japanese first used to write native poetry and prose. Eventually it came to be used to represent only the grammatical portions of the written Japanese language in conjunction with Chinese characters that convey meaning. Japanese written in *hiragana* was once called "women's hand" because its rounded forms looked feminine. During the Heian period *hiragana* was used to create a large body of literature, written either by women or sometimes for women by men.

A charming poem originated in Heian times to teach the new writing system. In two stanzas of four lines each, it uses almost all of the syllable sounds of spoken Japanese and thus almost every *kana* symbol.

12-3 MAIN HALL, INNER SHRINE, ISE
Mie Prefecture. Last rebuilt 2013. Photograph by Watanabe Yoshio (1907–2000), 1953. National Treasure.

Credit: Watanabe Yoshio/PPS

It was memorized as we would recite our ABC's. The first stanza translates as:

> Although flowers glow with color
> They are quickly fallen,
> And who in this world of ours
> Is free from change?
> (Translation by Earl Miner)

Like Chinese, Japanese is written in columns from top to bottom and across the page from right to left. (Following this logic, Chinese and Japanese handscrolls also read from right to left.) Below is the stanza written three ways. At the right, it appears in *katakana* glossed with the original phonetic value of each symbol. In the center, the stanza appears in flowing *hiragana*. To the left is the mixture of *kanji* and *hiragana* that eventually became standard.

kanji and *hiragana* mixed	*hiragana*	*katakana*

常ならむ 我世誰ぞ 散りぬるを 色は匂へど つねならむ わかよたれそ ちりぬるを いろはにほへと

ツネナラム (Tsu-ne-na-ra-mu) ワカヨタレソ (Wa-ka-yo-ta-re-so) チリヌルヲ (Chi-ri-nu-ru-wo) イロハニホヘト (I-ro-ha-ni-he-to)

Asuka and Nara Periods

How do the introduction and flourishing of Buddhism during the Asuka and Nara periods change Japanese art and architecture?

During the single century of the Asuka period (552–645 CE), new forms of philosophy, medicine, music, food, clothing, agriculture, city planning, religion, visual art, and architecture entered Japan from Korea and China at an astonishing pace. Most significant among these were Buddhism, a centralized governmental structure, and a system of writing. Each was adopted and gradually modified to suit local Japanese conditions, and each has had an enduring legacy.

Buddhism reached Japan in Mahayana form, with its many buddhas and bodhisattvas (see Chapter 10). After being accepted by the imperial family, it was soon adopted as a state religion. Buddhism represented not only different gods from Shinto but an entirely new concept of religion. Worship of Buddhist deities took place in temples situated close to imperial cities. The Chinese-influenced temples looked nothing like previous Japanese buildings. They housed anthropomorphic and elaborately symbolic Buddhist icons at a time when *kami* were not portrayed in human form (see "Buddhist Symbols" on page 370).

Yet Buddhism attracted followers because it offered a rich cosmology with profound teachings of meditation and enlightenment. The protective powers of its deities enabled the ruling elites to justify their own power, and they called upon Buddhist deities to nurture and protect the populace over whom they ruled. Many highly developed aspects of continental Asian art traveled to Japan with the new religion, including new methods of painting and sculpture.

Art and its Contexts

BUDDHIST SYMBOLS

A few of the most important Buddhist symbols, which have myriad variations, are described here in their most generalized forms.

Lotus flower: Usually shown as a white waterlily, the lotus (Sanskrit, *padma*) symbolizes spiritual purity, the wholeness of creation, and cosmic harmony. The flower's stem is an *axis mundi* ("axis of the world").

Lotus throne: Buddhas are frequently shown seated on an open lotus, either single or double, a representation of *nirvana* (SEE FIG. 12–10).

Chakra: An ancient sun symbol, the *chakra* (wheel) symbolizes both the various states of existence (the Wheel of Life) and the Buddhist doctrine (the Wheel of the Law). A *chakra*'s exact meaning depends on how many spokes it has.

Marks of a buddha: A buddha is distinguished by 32 physical attributes (*lakshanas*). Among them are a bulge on top of the head (*ushnisha*), a tuft of hair between the eyebrows (*urna*), and 1,000-spoked *chakras* on the soles of the feet.

Mandala: *Mandalas* are diagrams of cosmic realms, representing order and meaning within the spiritual universe. They may be simple or complex, three- or two-dimensional, and in a wide array of forms—such as an Indian stupa (SEE FIG. 10–8) or a Womb World *mandala* (SEE FIG. 12–8), an early Japanese type.

lotus flower

double lotus flower

chakra

Credit:
Kathy Mrozek

marks of a buddha

Horyuji

The most significant surviving early Japanese temple is Horyuji, located on Japan's central plains not far from Nara. The temple was founded in 607 by Prince Shotoku (574–622), who ruled Japan as a regent and became the most influential early proponent of Buddhism. Rebuilt after a fire in 670, Horyuji is the oldest wooden temple in the world.

The main compound of Horyuji consists of a rectangular courtyard surrounded by covered corridors, one of which contains a gateway. Within the compound are two buildings: the **kondo** (main hall) and a five-story pagoda. In a simple asymmetrical layout, the large golden *kondo*

12–4 AERIAL VIEW OF THE HORYUJI COMPOUND
Pagoda to the west (left), golden hall (*kondo*) to the east (right). Nara Prefecture. Asuka period, 7th century CE. UNESCO World Heritage Site, National Treasure.

Credit: © Shashinkoubou

balances the tall, slender pagoda (**FIG. 12–4**). The *kondo*, filled with Buddhist images, is used for worship and ceremonies, while the pagoda serves as a **reliquary** and is not entered. Other monastery buildings lie outside the main compound, including an outer gate, a lecture hall, a repository for sacred texts, a belfry, and dormitories for monks.

Among the many treasures still preserved in Horyuji is a portable shrine decorated with paintings in lacquer. It is known as the Tamamushi Shrine after the *tamamushi* beetle, whose iridescent wings were originally affixed to the shrine to make it glitter, much like mother-of-pearl. Its architectural form replicates an ancient palace-form building type that pre-dates Horyuji itself.

HUNGRY TIGRESS JATAKA Paintings on the sides of the Tamamushi Shrine are among the few two-dimensional works of art to survive from the Asuka period. Most celebrated among them are two that illustrate Jataka tales, stories about former lives of the Buddha. One depicts the future Buddha nobly sacrificing his life in order to feed his body to a starving tigress and her cubs (**FIG. 12–5**).

12–5 HUNGRY TIGRESS JATAKA
Panel of the Tamamushi Shrine, Horyuji. Asuka period, c. 650 CE. Lacquer on wood, height of shrine 7′7½″ (2.33 m). Horyuji Treasure House, Nara. National Treasure.

Credit: © Iberfoto/Alinari Archives

12–6 Attributed to Tori Busshi **BUDDHA SHAKA AND ATTENDANT BODHISATTVAS IN THE HORYUJI KONDO**

Asuka period, c. 623 CE. Gilt bronze, height of seated figure 34½″ (87.5 cm). Horyuji, Nara Prefecture. National Treasure.

Credit: © Iberfoto/Alinari Archives

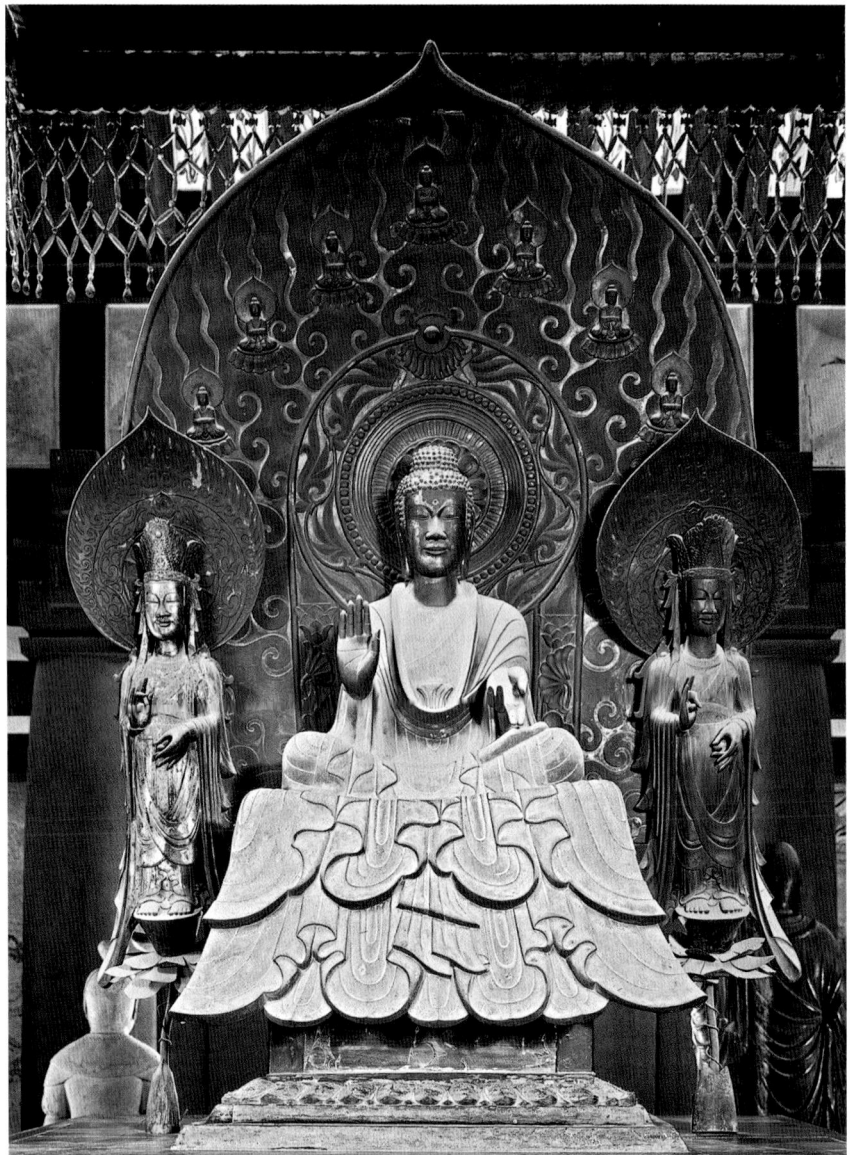

Since the tigers are at first too weak to eat him, he jumps off a cliff to break open his flesh. The painter has created a full narrative within a single frame. The graceful form of the Buddha appears three times in three sequential stages of the story, harmonized by the curves of the rocky cliff and tall wands of bamboo. First, he hangs his shirt on a tree, then he dives downward onto the rocks, and finally the starving animals devour his body. The elegantly slender renditions of the figure and the stylized treatment of the cliff, trees, and bamboo represent an international Buddhist style that was transmitted to Japan via China and Korea. Such illustrations of Jataka tales helped popularize Buddhism in Japan.

SHAKA TRIAD   Another example of the international style of early Buddhist art at Horyuji is the sculpture called the Shaka Triad, traditionally attributed to sculptor Tori Busshi (**FIG. 12–6**). (Shaka is the Japanese name for Shakyamuni, the historical Buddha.) Tori Busshi (Busshi means Buddhist image-maker) may have been a descendant of Korean craftspeople who emigrated to Japan as part of an influx of Buddhists and artisans from Korea. The Shaka Triad reflects the strong influence of Chinese art of the Northern Wei dynasty (SEE FIG. 11–13). The frontal pose, the outsized face and hands, and the linear treatment of the drapery all suggest that the maker of this statue was well aware of earlier continental models, while the fine bronze casting of the figures shows his advanced technical skill.

Nara Period

The Nara period (645–794) is named for Japan's first permanent imperial capital, founded in 710. Previously, an emperor's death was thought to taint his entire capital city, so for reasons of purification (and perhaps also of politics), his successor usually selected a new site. As the

government adopted ever more complex aspects of the Chinese political system, necessitating construction of huge administrative complexes, it abandoned this custom in the eighth century when Nara was founded. During this period, divisions of the imperial bureaucracy grew exponentially and hastened the swelling of the city's population to perhaps 200,000 people.

One result of the strong central authority was the construction in Nara of magnificent Buddhist temples and Shinto shrines that dwarfed those built previously. The expansive park in the center of Nara today is the site of the largest and most important of these, including the Shinto Kasuga Shrine depicted in FIGURE 12–1. The grandest of the Buddhist temples in Nara Park is Todaiji, which the deeply religious Emperor Shomu (ruled 724–749) conceived as the headquarters of a vast network of branch temples throughout the nation. Todaiji served as both a state-supported central monastic training center and as the setting for public religious ceremonies. The most spectacular of these took place in 752 and celebrated the consecration of the main Buddhist statue of the temple in a traditional "eye-opening" ceremony. The statue, a giant gilt-bronze image of the Buddha Birushana (Vairochana in Sanskrit), was inspired by the Chinese tradition of erecting monumental stone Buddhist statues in cave-temples (SEE FIG. 11–13).

The ceremony, which took place in the vast courtyard in front of the newly constructed Great Buddha Hall, was presided over by an illustrious Indian monk and included *sutra* chanting by over 10,000 Japanese Buddhist monks and sacred performances by 4,000 court musicians and dancers. Vast numbers of Japanese courtiers and emissaries from the Asian continent were the audience. Numerous ritual objects used in the ceremony came from exotic Asian and Near Eastern lands. The resulting cosmopolitan atmosphere reflected the position Nara then held as the eastern terminus of the Central Asian Silk Road.

Many of these treasures have been preserved in the Shosoin Imperial Repository at Todaiji, which today contains some 9,000 objects. The Shosoin came into being in the year 756 when Emperor Shomu died and his widow, the devout Buddhist empress Komyo, donated some 600 of his possessions to the temple, including a number of objects used during the Great Buddha's consecration ceremony. Many years later, objects used in Buddhist rituals and previously stored elsewhere at Todaiji were incorporated into the collection. The objects formerly owned by Emperor Shomu consisted mainly of his personal possessions, such as documents, furniture, musical instruments, games, clothing, medicine, weapons, some Buddhist ritual objects, and food and beverage vessels of metal, glass, and lacquer. Some of these had been made in Japan, while others came from as far away as China, India, Iran, Greece,

Rome, and Egypt. They reflect the vast international trade network that existed at this early date.

One of the items Empress Komyo donated in 756 is a magnificently crafted five-stringed lute (*biwa*) made of lacquered red sandalwood and chestnut and inlaid with mother-of-pearl, amber, and tortoiseshell. Its plectrum guard portrays a central Asian musician (his ethnicity apparent from his clothing and physical features) sitting on a camel and playing a lute (**FIG. 12–7**). This is the only existing example of an ancient five-stringed lute, an instrument invented in India and transmitted to China and Japan via the Silk Road. The Shosoin piece is generally identified as Chinese, but, as with many of the objects preserved in the Shosoin, the location of its manufacture is not certain. While it was most likely crafted in China and imported to Japan for use in the consecration ceremony (researchers have recently conclusively determined that it was indeed played), it is also plausible that Chinese (or Japanese) craftspeople made it in Japan using imported materials. Its meticulous workmanship is characteristic of the high level of craft production achieved by artists of this era.

Influenced by Emperor Shomu, the Buddhist faith permeated all aspects of Nara court society. Indeed, in 749 Shomu abdicated the throne to spend the remainder of his life as a monk. His daughter, also a devout Buddhist, succeeded him as empress but wanted to cede her throne to a Buddhist monk. This so dismayed her advisors that they moved the capital city away from Nara, where they felt Buddhist influence had become overpowering, and established a new one in Kyoto, within whose bounds only a few Buddhist temples would be allowed at first. The move of the capital to Kyoto marked the end of the Nara period.

12–7 FIVE-STRINGED LUTE (BIWA) WITH DESIGN OF A CENTRAL ASIAN MAN PLAYING A BIWA ATOP A CAMEL
Chinese. Tang dynasty, 8th century CE. Red sandalwood and chestnut inlaid with mother-of-pearl, amber, and tortoiseshell; length 42½" (108.1 cm), width 12" (30.9 cm), depth 3½" (9 cm). Shosoin Repository, Todaiji.

Credit: Shosoin, Todaiji, Nara

Heian Period

How are Japanese art and architecture transformed during the Heian period?

During the Heian period (794–1185) the Japanese fully absorbed and transformed their cultural borrowings from China and Korea. Generally peaceful conditions contributed to a new air of self-reliance, and the imperial government severed ties to China in the ninth century, a time when the power of related aristocratic families increased. An efficient method of writing the Japanese language was developed, and the rise of vernacular literature generated such prose masterpieces as Lady Murasaki's *The Tale of Genji*. During these four centuries of splendor and refinement, two major streams of Buddhism emerged—esoteric sects and, later, those espousing salvation in the Pure Land Western Paradise of the Buddha Amida.

Esoteric Buddhist Art

With the capital's move to Kyoto, the older Nara temples lost their influence. Soon two new esoteric sects of Buddhism, Tendai and Shingon, grew to dominate Japanese religious life. Strongly influenced by polytheistic religions such as Hinduism, Esoteric Buddhism (known as Tantric Buddhism in Nepal and Tibet) included a daunting number of deities, each with magical powers. The historical Buddha was no longer very important. Instead, most revered was the universal Buddha, called Dainichi ("Great Sun" in Japanese), who was believed to preside over the universe. He was accompanied by buddhas and bodhisattvas, as well as guardian deities who formed fierce counterparts to the more benign gods.

Esoteric Buddhism is hierarchical, and its deities have complex relationships to one another. Learning all the different gods and their interrelationships was assisted greatly by paintings, especially *mandalas*, cosmic diagrams

12–8 WOMB WORLD MANDALA

Heian period, late 9th century CE. Hanging scroll with colors on silk, 6′ × 5′1½″ (1.83 × 1.54 m). Toji, Kyoto. National Treasure.

Mandalas are used not only in teaching, but also as vehicles for practice. A monk, initiated into secret teachings, may meditate upon and assume the gestures of each deity depicted in the *mandala*, gradually working out from the center, so that he absorbs some of each deity's powers. The monk may also recite magical phrases, called mantras, as an aid to meditation. The goal is to achieve enlightenment through the powers of the different forms of the Buddha. *Mandalas* are created in sculptural and architectural forms as well as in paintings (SEE FIG. 10–36). Their integration of the two most basic shapes, the circle and the square, is an expression of the principles of ancient geomancy (divining by means of lines and figures) as well as Buddhist cosmology.

of the universe that portray the deities in schematic order. The **WOMB WORLD MANDALA** from Toji, for example, is entirely filled with depictions of gods (**FIG. 12–8**). Dainichi is at the center, surrounded by buddhas of the four directions. Other deities, including some with multiple heads and limbs, branch out in diagrammatical order, each with a specific symbol of power and targeted to various levels of potential worshipers, some of whom needed to be frightened to awaken to Buddhist teaching. To believers, the *mandala* represents an ultimate reality beyond the visible world.

Perhaps the most striking attribute of many Esoteric Buddhist images is their sense of spiritual force and potency, especially in depictions of the wrathful deities, which are often surrounded by flames like those visible in the Womb World *mandala* just below the main circle of buddhas. With its intricate theology and complex doctrines, Esoteric Buddhism was a religion for the educated aristocracy, not for the masses. Its elaborate network of deities, hierarchy, and ritual found parallels in the elaborate social divisions of the Heian court.

Pure Land Buddhist Art

Rising militarism, political turbulence, and excesses of the imperial court marked the beginning of the eleventh century in Japan. To many, the unsettled times seemed to confirm the coming of *Mappo*, the Buddhist concept of a long-prophesied dark age of spiritual degeneration. Japanese of all classes reacted by increasingly turning to the promise of salvation after death through their faith in a Buddhist realm known as the Western Paradise of the Pure Land, a resplendent place filled with divine flowers and music. Amida (Amitabha in Sanskrit) and his attendant bodhisattvas preside there as divine protectors who compassionately accept all who submit wholeheartedly to their benevolent powers. Pure Land beliefs had spread to Japan from China by way of Korea, where they also enjoyed great popularity. They offered an easier and more immediate way to achieve salvation than the elaborate rituals of the esoteric sects. Pure Land Buddhism held that merely by chanting *Namu Amida Butsu* ("Hail to Amida Buddha"), the faithful would be reborn into the Western Paradise.

BYODOIN   One of the most beautiful temples of Pure Land Buddhism is the Byodoin, located in the Uji Mountains not far from central Kyoto (**FIG. 12–9**). The temple itself was originally a secular villa whose form was intended to suggest the appearance of the palatial residence of Amida in his Western Paradise (SEE FIG. 11–15). It was built for a member of the powerful Fujiwara family who served as the leading counselor to the emperor. After the counselor's death in the year 1052, his descendants converted the palace into a memorial temple to honor his

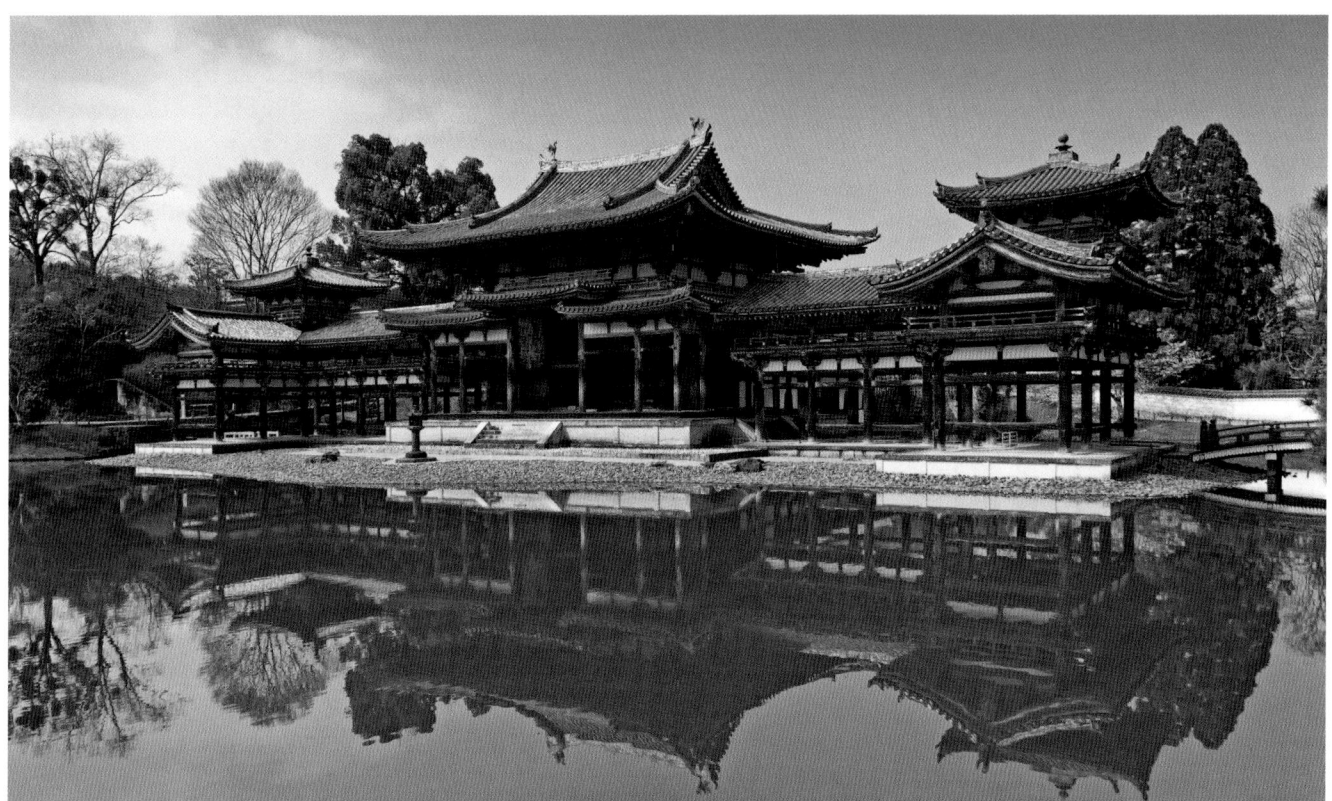

12–9 BYODOIN (PHOENIX HALL), UJI
Kyoto Prefecture. Heian period, c. 1053 CE. UNESCO World Heritage Site, National Treasure.

spirit. The Byodoin is often called the Phoenix Hall, not only for the pair of phoenix images on its roof, but also because the shape of the building itself suggests the mythical bird. Its thin columns give the Byodoin a sense of airiness, as though the temple could rise up through the sky to Amida's Western Paradise. The hall rests gently in front of an artificial pond created in the shape of the Sanskrit letter A, the sacred symbol for Amida.

The Byodoin's central image of Amida, carved by the master sculptor Jocho (died 1057), exemplifies the serenity and compassion of this Buddha (**FIG. 12–10**). When reflected in the water of the pond before it, the Amida image seems to shimmer in its private mountain retreat. Surrounding the Amida on the walls of the Byodoin are smaller wooden figures of bodhisattvas and angels, some playing musical instruments. Everything about the Byodoin was designed to simulate the appearance of the paradise that awaits the believer after death. Its remarkable state of preservation after more than 900 years allows visitors to experience the late Heian religious ideal at its most splendid.

Jocho's figure was not carved from a single block of wood like earlier sculpture, but from several blocks in his new **joined-block** method of construction (see "Joined-Block Wood Sculpture" opposite).

Secular Painting and Calligraphy

Parallel with the permeation of Buddhism during the Heian era (794–1185) was a refined secular culture that developed at court. Gradually over the course of these four centuries, the pervasive influence of Chinese culture in aristocratic society gave rise to new, uniquely Japanese developments. Above all, Heian court culture greatly valued refinement; pity any man or woman at court who was not accomplished in several forms of art. A woman would be admired for the way she arranged the 12 layers of her robes by color, or a man for knowing which kind of incense was being burned. Concurrently, court life became preoccupied by the poetical expression of human love. In this climate, women became a vital force in Heian society.

Although the status of women was to decline in later periods, they contributed greatly to art at the Heian court and became famous for their prose and poetry.

Although male courtiers continued to be required to read and write Chinese, both men and women of court society wrote prose and poetry in their native Japanese language using the newly devised *kana* script. They also used *kana* on text portions of new types of small-scale secular paintings: handscrolls or folding albums designed to be appreciated in private settings.

At the beginning of the eleventh century, the lady-in-waiting Lady Murasaki transposed the lifestyle of Heian aristocrats into fiction for the amusement of her fellow court ladies in *The Tale of Genji*, which some consider the world's first novel. Japanese today still admire this tale of 54 chapters as a pinnacle of Japanese literary achievement. (In 2009, the official 1,000-year anniversary of its completion, numerous exhibitions and celebrations took place throughout Japan.) Underlying the story of the love affairs of Prince Genji and his companions is the Heian conception of fleeting pleasures and ultimate sadness in life, an echo of the Buddhist view of the vanity of earthly pleasures.

12–10 Jocho **AMIDA BUDDHA**
Byodoin (Phoenix Hall). Heian period, c. 1053 CE.
Gold leaf and lacquer on wood, height 9′8″ (2.95 m).
National Treasure.

Credit: © Prisma Bildagentur AG/Alamy Stock Photo

Technique

JOINED-BLOCK WOOD SCULPTURE

Wood is a temperamental material because fluctuations in moisture content cause it to swell and shrink. Cut from a living, sap-filled tree, it takes many years to dry to a state of stability. While the outside of a piece of wood dries fairly rapidly, the inside yields its moisture only gradually, causing a difference in the rates of shrinkage between the inside and the outside, which induces the wood to crack. Consequently, a large statue carved from a single log must inevitably crack as it ages. Natural irregularities in wood, such as knots, further accentuate this problem. Thus, wood with a thinner cross section and fewer irregularities is less susceptible to cracking because it can dry more evenly. (This is the logic behind sawing logs into boards before drying.)

   Japanese sculptors developed an ingenious and unique method, the joined-block technique, to reduce cracking in heavy wooden statues. This allowed them to create larger statues in wood than ever before, enabled standardization of body proportions, and encouraged division of labor among teams of carvers, some of whom became specialists in certain parts, such as hands or crossed legs or lotus thrones. To create large statues seated in the lotus pose, sculptors first put four blocks together vertically two by two in front and back, to form the main body, then added several blocks horizontally at what would become the front of the statue for the lap and knees. After carving each part, they assembled the figure and hollowed out the interior. This cooperative approach also had the added benefit of enabling workshops to produce large statues more quickly to meet a growing demand. Jocho is credited as the master sculptor who perfected this technique. The diagram shows how he assembled the Amida Buddha at the Byodoin (SEE FIG. 12–10).

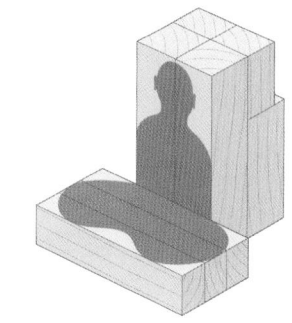

Diagram of the joined-block wood sculpture technique used on the Amida statue by Jocho.

Credit:
Kathy Mrozek

YAMATO-E HANDSCROLLS—THE TALE OF GENJI   A new secular painting style arose called **yamato-e**, or native Japanese-style pictures; Yamato is the old Japanese word for Japan. One of the earliest surviving examples is an illustrated handscroll from the twelfth century depicting a series of scenes from *The Tale of Genji*. The handscroll alternates sections of text with illustrations of scenes from the story and features delicate lines, strong (but sometimes muted) mineral colors, and asymmetrical compositions. The paintings have a refined, subtle emotional impact. They generally show court figures in architectural settings, with the frequent addition of natural elements and gardens that help to convey the mood of the scene. Thus a blossoming cherry tree appears in a scene of happiness, while unkempt weeds appear in a depiction of loneliness. Such correspondences between nature and human emotion are an enduring theme of Japanese poetry and art. The figures in *The Tale of Genji* paintings do not show their emotions directly on their faces, which are rendered with a few simple lines. Instead, their feelings are conveyed by colors, poses, fluttering of curtains, and the overall composition of the scenes.

   One scene portrays Prince Genji viewed from behind while visiting his favorite consort, Murasaki (not the same person as the author of the novel), who faces him across a narrow interior space (see "Closer Look" on page 378). Although Genji was especially fond of her, Murasaki could not become his principal wife because she was not from an aristocratic family. Here he comes to see her shortly before her death. One might expect the visualization of such a poignant moment to focus on the people involved. Instead the figures are relatively small and all but consumed by their clothing. The screens of the domestic interior dominate the scene, effectively squeezing Genji and Murasaki into a confined corridor. The composition, not the facial expressions or bodily postures, conveys the melancholy of the moment. The airy openness of the outdoor garden to the left—and the sketchy delicacy of the plants within it—heighten the sense of confinement and impending loss.

A Closer Look

THE TALE OF GENJI

Only 19 illustrated scenes survive from this earliest known example of an illustrated handscroll of *The Tale of Genji*, created about 100 years after the novel was written. Scholars assume that it originally contained illustrations from the entire novel of 54 chapters, approximately 100 pictures in all. Each scroll seems to have been produced by a team of artists. One was the calligrapher, most likely a member of the nobility.

Another was the master painter, who outlined two or three illustrations per chapter in fine brushstrokes and indicated the color scheme. Next, colorists went to work, applying layer after layer of color to build up patterns and textures. After they had finished, the master painter returned to reinforce outlines and apply the finishing touches, among them the details of the faces.

Thickly applied mineral colors are now cracking and flaking.

Following courtly convention, Murasaki's body is concealed beneath voluminous robes; she holds a fan to shield her face, and her loosened hair cascades around her face and over her clothes.

The roof has been removed so we can see what is happening.

Wooden verandas surrounded Japanese houses, merging interior and exterior to provide vantage points for admiring the gardens.

The non-individualized faces of the prince and his consort betray none of the emotional content of the scene.

Murasaki's daughter is discretely tucked between a "privacy" curtain and the wall.

12-11 SCENE FROM THE TALE OF GENJI
Heian period, 12th century CE. Handscroll with ink and colors on paper, 8⅝ × 18⅞" (21.9 × 47.9 cm). Gotoh Museum, Tokyo.

CALLIGRAPHY IN JAPANESE The text portions of the *The Tale of Genji* handscroll were written in *kana* script, which was also used to write poetry in Japanese. In the Heian period, the most significant form of native poetry was a 31-syllable format known as *waka*, which had first been composed earlier than the eighth century. During the Heian era, the finest *waka* by various writers were collected together and hand-copied in albums, the most popular of which featured writers collectively known as the Thirty-Six Immortal Poets, an anthology still appreciated

by educated Japanese today. The earliest of many surviving examples of this iconic collection originally contained 39 volumes of poems. Two volumes were taken apart and sold in 1929, and now survive in single-page sections (**FIG. 12-12**). Collectively these separated volumes are known as the *Ishiyamagire* (Ishiyama fragments, named after Ishiyamadera, the temple that originally owned the volumes).

With its simple, flowing letters, characters, or syllables, interspersed occasionally with more complex Chinese characters, this style of writing gave a distinctive asymmetrical balance to the appearance of the written words. In these pages, the poems seem to float elegantly on fine dyed papers decorated with painting, block printing, scattered sheets, and particles of gold and silver, and sometimes paper collage. Often, as in FIGURE 12–12, the irregular pattern of torn paper edges adds a serendipitous element. The page shown here reproduces two verses by the eighth-century courtier Ki no Tsurayuki that express melancholy emotions. One reads:

> Until yesterday
> I could meet her,
> But today she is gone—
> Like clouds over the mountain
> She has been wafted away.

The spiky, flowing calligraphy, the patterning of the papers, the rich use of gold, and the suggestions of natural imagery all match the elegance of the poetry, epitomizing courtly Japanese taste.

YAMATO-E HANDSCROLLS—FROLICKING ANIMALS In its sedate and sophisticated portrayal of courtly life, *The Tale of Genji* scroll represents one side of *yamato-e*. But another style of native painting emerged contemporaneously. Characterized by bold, confident strokes of the brush and little if any use of color, it depicted subjects outside the court engaged in playful and irreverent activities. One of the early masterpieces of this style is a set of handscrolls known as *Frolicking Animals* (*Choju Giga*) that satirizes human behavior through animal antics. Freely executed entirely in black ink, the humorous parodies are attributed to Toba Sojo (1053–1140), abbot of a Buddhist monastery.

In one particularly amusing scene, a monkey—robed as a monk preoccupied with the passionate

12–13 Attributed to Toba Sojo **SCENE FROM FROLICKING ANIMALS**
Heian period, 12th century CE. Handscroll with ink on paper, height 12″ (30.5 cm). Kozanji, Kyoto. National Treasure.

Credit: TNM Image Archives

incantations that emerge from his gaping mouth like wisps of smoke—offers a peach branch on an altar, behind which a frog is posed as a buddha enthroned on a lotus leaf (**FIG. 12–13**). Around this monkey-monk is an assembly of animals—rabbits, monkey, foxes, and frog—representing monastic and secular worshipers, some bored and distracted, others focusing on their prayers, which are either read from texts or guided by the Buddhist prayer beads clutched in their hands. Although unlike the *Genji* scroll there is no accompanying text to *Frolicking Animals*, making it difficult to know exactly what was being satirized, the universality of the humorous antics remains.

Kamakura Period

How do the priorities of secular and religious patrons shape Japanese art of the Kamakura period?

The courtiers of the Heian era seem to have become so engrossed in their own refinement that they neglected their responsibilities for governing the country. Clans of warriors—samurai—from outside the capital grew increasingly strong. Two of these, the Taira and Minamoto, were especially powerful. They took opposing sides in the factional conflicts of the imperial court in order to control the weakened emperor and take charge of the government.

The Kamakura era (1185–1333) began when the head of the Minamoto clan, Yoritomo (1147–1199), defeated the Taira family and ordered the emperor to appoint him as

shogun (general-in-chief). To resist what he perceived as the softening effects of courtly life in Kyoto, he established his military capital in Kamakura, while the emperor continued to reside in Kyoto. Although Yoritomo's newly invented title of shogun nominally respected the authority of the emperor, it also assured him of supreme military and political power. The shogunate initiated by Yoritomo endured in various forms until 1868.

A Battle Handscroll

The battles for domination between the Minamoto and the Taira became famous not only in medieval Japanese history but also as subjects in literature and art. One of the great painted handscrolls depicting these battles is **NIGHT ATTACK ON THE SANJO PALACE** (**FIG. 12–14**). Though it was painted perhaps a century after the actual event, the artist conveyed the sense of eyewitness reporting even though imagining the scene from verbal—at best semifactual—descriptions. The style of the painting includes some of the brisk and lively linework of *Frolicking Animals* and also aspects of the more refined brushwork, use of color, and bird's-eye viewpoint of *The Tale of Genji* scroll. The relentless focus, however, is on the dynamic depiction of the savagery of warfare across expansive lateral compositions (see "Arms and Armor" opposite). Unlike the *Genji* scroll, *Night Attack* is full of action. The sense of energy and violence is pervasive, conveyed with sweeping power. There is no trace here of courtly poetic refinement and melancholy; the new world of the samurai is dominating the secular arts.

12–14 SECTION OF NIGHT ATTACK ON THE SANJO PALACE

Kamakura period, late 13th century CE. Handscroll with ink and colors on paper, 16¼″ × 22′ 9¹¹⁄₁₆″ (41.3 cm × 700.3 cm). Museum of Fine Arts, Boston. Fenollosa-Weld Collection (11.4000).

The battles between the Minamoto and Taira clans were fought primarily by mounted and armored warriors, who used swords as well as bows and arrows. In the year 1160, some 500 Minamoto rebels opposed to the retired emperor Go-Shirakawa carried out a daring raid on the Sanjo Palace. In a surprise attack in the middle of the night, they abducted the emperor. The scene was one of great carnage, much of it caused by the burning of the wooden palace. Despite the drama of the scene, this was not the decisive moment in the war. The Minamoto rebels would lose more-important battles to their Taira enemies, yet the Minamoto heirs to those who carried out this raid would eventually prove victorious, destroying the Taira clan in 1185.

Art and its Contexts

ARMS AND ARMOR

Battles such as the one depicted in *Night Attack on the Sanjo Palace* (SEE FIG. **12–14**) were fought largely by archers on horseback. Samurai archers charged the enemy at full gallop and loosed their arrows just before they wheeled away. The scroll clearly shows their distinctive bow with its asymmetrically placed handgrip. The lower portion of the bow is shorter than the upper so it can clear the horse's neck. The samurai wear long, curved swords at their waists.

By the tenth century, Japanese swordsmiths had perfected techniques for crafting their legendarily sharp swords. Sword-makers face a fundamental difficulty: Steel hard enough to hold a razor-sharp edge is brittle and breaks easily, but steel resilient enough to withstand rough use is too soft to hold a keen edge. The Japanese ingeniously forged a blade which laminated a hard cutting edge within less brittle support layers.

The earliest form of samurai armor, illustrated here, known as *yoroi*, was intended for use by warriors on horseback, as seen in FIGURE **12–14**. It was made of overlapping iron and lacquered leather scales, punched with holes and laced together with leather thongs and brightly colored silk braids. The principal piece wrapped around the chest, left side, and back. Padded shoulder straps hooked it together back to front. A separate piece of armor was tied to the body to protect the right side. The upper legs were protected by a four-sided skirt that attached to the body armor, while two large rectangular panels tied on with cords guarded the arms. The helmet was made of iron plates riveted together. From it hung a neck guard flared sharply outward to protect the face from arrows shot at close range.

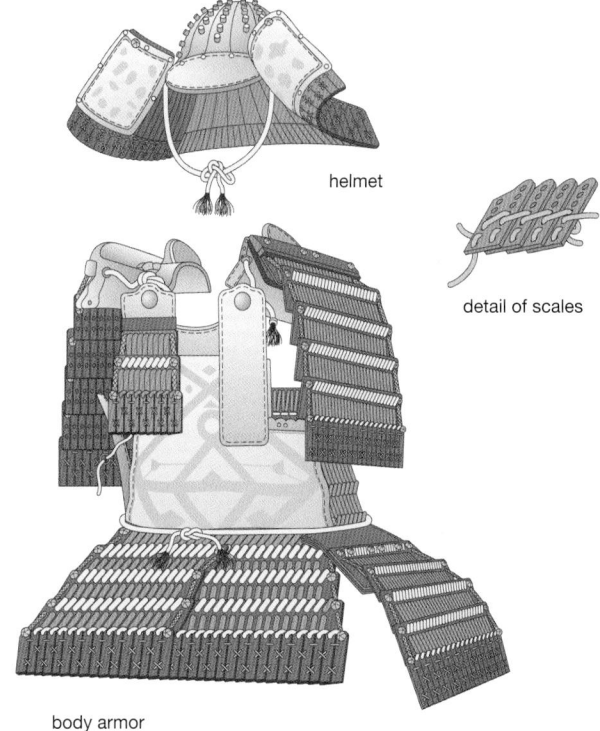

helmet

detail of scales

body armor

Pure Land Buddhist Art

By the beginning of the Kamakura period, Pure Land Buddhist beliefs had swept throughout Japan, and several charismatic priests founded new sects to promote this ideology. They traveled throughout the country, spreading the new gospel in ways that appealed to people of all levels of education and sophistication. They were so successful that Pure Land Buddhist sects have remained the most popular form of Buddhism in Japan ever since.

RAIGO PAINTINGS Pure Land Buddhism taught that even one sincere invocation of the sacred chant could lead the most wicked sinner to the Western Paradise. Popular paintings called **raigo** ("welcoming approach") depicted the Amida Buddha, accompanied by bodhisattvas, coming down to earth to welcome the soul of the dying believer. Golden cords were often attached to these paintings, which were taken to the homes of the dying. A person near death held onto these cords, hoping that Amida would escort the soul directly to paradise.

Raigo paintings differ significantly in style from the complex *mandalas* and fierce guardian deities of Esoteric Buddhism. The earliest-known example of this subject is found on the walls and doors of the Byodoin, surrounding Jocho's sculpture of Amida (SEE FIG. 12-10). Like that statue, they radiate warmth and compassion. In the Kamakura

12-15 DESCENT OF AMIDA AND THE TWENTY-FIVE BODHISATTVAS
Kamakura period, 13th century CE. Hanging scroll with colors and gold on silk, 57¼ × 61½″ (145 × 155.5 cm). Chion-in, Kyoto. National Treasure.

Credit: Photo Courtesy of Kyoto National Museum. Property of Chion-in period, *raigo* paintings were made in great numbers, reflecting the popularity of Pure Land Buddhism at that time. One magnificent example portrays Amida Buddha and 25 bodhisattvas descending over mountains (**FIG. 12-15**). The artist used gold paint and thin slivers of gold leaf cut in elaborate patterns to suggest the divine radiance of the deities. This painstaking cut–gold leaf technique, known as *kirikane*, is one of the great achievements of early Japanese Buddhist artists. It originated in China, but Japanese artists refined and perfected it. In this painting, the darkened silk behind the figures heightens the sparkle of their golden aura. In the flickering light of oil lamps and torches, *raigo* paintings would have appeared magical, whether in a temple or in a dying person's home.

One of the most remarkable aspects of this painting is its sensitive rendering of the landscape, full of rugged peaks and flowering trees. Perhaps this emphasis on the natural setting derives from a traditional Japanese appreciation for the beautiful land in which they dwelled, an appreciation that may stem from Shinto beliefs. In fact, Shinto pictures portraying the landscape of Japan as divine first appeared in the Kamakura period, just as Pure Land Buddhism was growing in popularity. One of these is the Kasuga Shrine *mandala* of FIGURE 12-1, demonstrating how Kamakura artists represented the merging of the two faiths of Buddhism and Shinto. The artist of this work made the shrine buildings resemble those of the palatial abode of Amida in his Western Paradise and rendered the landscape details with the radiant charm of Amida's heaven.

Zen Buddhist Art

Zen Buddhism was introduced to Japan from China, where it was already highly developed and known as Chan. Relations between the two countries had been interrupted during the Heian period. But during the Kamakura era, both emigrant Chinese and Japanese monks—who went to China to study Buddhism and returned home enthused about the new teachings they learned there—brought Zen to Japan. They secluded themselves in monasteries, leading an austere life of simplicity and self-responsibility.

Chan (Zen) monks modeled their behavior on that of the founder of their lineage, the mythical Indian Buddhist sage Daruma (Bodhidharma in Sanskrit), who emigrated to China in the sixth century CE and famously transmitted his teachings to a Chinese disciple who became the second Chan patriarch. This portrait of **DARUMA** (**FIG. 12-16**) is one of the earliest surviving examples of Japanese Zen painting. Using fine ink outlines and a touch of color for the robe and the figure's sandals, the artist portrays the Chan master seated meditating atop a rock with an unwavering gaze that is intended to convey his inner strength and serenity. At the top of the scroll is an inscription in Chinese by Yishan Yining (1247–1317), one of several influential

early Chinese Chan masters to emigrate to Japan. He had planned only to visit Japan as head of an official diplomatic delegation from China in 1299, but he stayed for the remainder of his life. Although the Japanese were wary of him at first, his sincere intentions to teach Chan and his erudite abilities quickly attracted influential supporters. Soon after arrival, Yishan was appointed as the tenth head abbot of the large Zen temple of Kenchoji in Kamakura, a post he held briefly before moving on to head several other Zen temples.

12-16 DARUMA
Inscription by Chinese Chan master Yishan Yining (1247–1317). Kamakura period, early 14th century CE. Hanging scroll with ink and colors on silk, 39⅝ × 20″ (100.8 × 50.8 cm). Tokyo National Museum. Important Cultural Property.

Credit: TNM Image Archives

Kenchoji had been founded in 1253 by another emigrant Chan master, Lanxi Daolong (1213–1278). Lanxi was the first Chan master to travel to Japan. There, he was warmly received by the fifth Minamoto shogun, who

12-17 PORTRAIT OF THE CHINESE CHAN MASTER LANXI DAOLONG

Inscription by Lanxi Daolong. Kamakura period, 1271 CE. Hanging scroll with colors on silk, 41⅓ × 18″ (105 × 46.1 cm). Kenchoji, Kamakura. National Treasure.

Credit: Kenchoji, Kamakura

helped him plan construction of Kenchoji where, for the first time, authentic Chinese Chan Buddhism was to be taught in Japan. Kenchoji remains one of the most important Zen monasteries in Japan. The temple owns many formal portraits of its founder, including this one (**FIG. 12-17**), considered by many to be the best because it seems to capture Daolong's inner spirit as well as his outer form. This type of painting is peculiar to Chan and Zen sects and is known as *chinso*. These paintings were often gifts given by a master to disciples when they completed their formal training and departed to officiate at their own temples. The paintings served as personal reminders of the master's teachings and tangible evidence (like a diploma) of the disciples' right to transmit Zen teachings to their own pupils. Lanxi Daolong dedicated the inscription of this painting to an important regent (samurai official), a confidant of the shogun, and not an ordained Zen monk. This shows that Zen, from its early days in Japan, also strove to attract followers from among those in power who could not abandon their secular life for the rigorous, cloistered existence of Zen monks who lived in temples.

In some ways, Zen resembles the original teachings of the historical Buddha: it emphasizes individual enlightenment through meditation, without the help of deities or magical chants. It especially appealed to the self-disciplined spirit of samurai warriors, who were not satisfied with the older forms of Buddhism connected with the Japanese court. Zen was the last major form of Buddhism to reach Japan from the Asian mainland, and it had a profound and lasting impact on Japanese arts and culture.

Just as the *Night Attack* (SEE FIG. 12-14) reveals a propensity for recording the consequences of political turbulence by representing gruesome and detailed battle scenes in vivid colors, Kamakura-era Buddhist sculpture and painting also emphasized realism. Various factors account for this new taste. Society was dominated by samurai warriors, who possessed a more pragmatic outlook on the world than the Heian-period courtiers, who had lived a dreamlike, insular existence at court. In addition, renewed contacts with China introduced new styles for Buddhist art that emphasized lifelike portrayal. Finally, forging personal connections with heroic exploits and individuals—both past and present, political and religious—greatly concerned the people of the Kamakura period. Representing these figures in arresting pictorial and sculpted images helped reinforce legends and perpetuate their influence.

As the Kamakura era ended, the seeds of the future were planted both politically and culturally. The coming age witnessed the nation's continued dominance by the warrior class and the establishment of Zen as the religion of choice among those warriors who wielded power at the highest levels. As before, the later history of Japanese art continued to be marked by an intriguing interplay between native traditions and imported foreign tendencies.

Think About It

1   Discuss the influence of Chinese art on the early Japanese Buddhist complex at Horyuji, referring to Chapter 11 as necessary.

2   Compare the Heian-period Womb World *mandala* (**FIG. 12-8**) with the Kamakura-period *Descent of Amida and the Twenty-Five Bodhisattvas* (**FIG. 12-15**). How do these pictures embody the specific type of Buddhism from which each emerged? How would they have been used by believers?

3   Discuss a work of art in this chapter that combines aspects of the foreign traditions of Buddhism with native Shinto traditions. How do the artists blend the disparate traditions? How would the blending affect the way the work functioned within a religious context?

4   Characterize and compare one representative secular work of art from Heian courtly culture with one from the warrior culture that replaced it during the Kamakura period. How do these works relate to the political climates of these two distinct eras in early Japanese history?

Crosscurrents

These two works of art proclaim political power by documenting military conquest, but their artists chose vastly different media and contexts to achieve this goal. How do the differences between these battle narratives relate to the cultural context that gave rise to each? Be sure to consider the perspective of the viewer when forming your answer.

6–47

12–14

13-1 OFFERING 4, LA VENTA

Mexico. Olmec culture, c. 750–550 BCE. Jade, greenstone, granite, and sandstone; height of figures 6¼–7″ (16–18 cm). Museo Nacional de Antropología, Mexico City.

Credit: © akg-images/De Agostini Picture Lib./G. Dagli Orti

Chapter 13
Art of the Americas before 1300

 ## Learning Objectives

13.a Identify the visual hallmarks of the art of early cultures in the Americas for formal, technical, and expressive qualities.

13.b Interpret the meaning of works of art of early cultures in the Americas based on their themes, subjects, and symbols.

13.c Relate artists and the art of early cultures in the Americas to their distinct cultural, economic, and political contexts.

13.d Apply the vocabulary and concepts relevant to the art, artists, and art history of early cultures in the Americas.

13.e Interpret a work of art of the early Americas using the art historical methods of observation, comparison, and inductive reasoning.

13.f Select visual and textual evidence in various media to support an argument or an interpretation of a work of art of the early Americas.

To modern viewers, this group of 16 stone figurines (**FIG. 13–1**) hints at a story or resembles a ritual in progress. Since they were "standing" in this manner when they were excavated in 1955 at the Olmec site of La Venta, in Mexico, we know these small statues were deposited as a group along with the six stela-like shafts of jade, called **celts**, lined up behind them. Their "standing" poses are identical and specific; they flex their knees so they can tuck in their tailbones, straighten their spines, and lift their heads while keeping their arms relaxed at their sides. Today this pose is used in practices such as tai chi to strengthen the body and maintain mental focus. Also, each figure appears to have cranial deformation, which would have been created intentionally shortly after birth, probably by bandaging the head for several months. With similar postures and heads, the figurines seem strikingly uniform.

If we look closely, however, we see that despite these obvious similarities, each figure is carved from a distinctive stone, with varying degrees of care. Each is slightly different in size and proportions. Recent scholarship proposes that these statuettes were made by different sculptors and used for other purposes before their burial in this cache. Their gender identity is also perplexing. While 14 wear male clothing and 2 have small breasts and a female pubic area, several of the "male" figures were originally ungendered or female. These figurines were seemingly brought to La Venta and may have been modified before their deposition around 750–550 BCE. At that time, La Venta was an important ritual center, the site of many buried offerings, or caches. These 16 figurines—known as Offering 4—were placed in a walled courtyard above a massive offering and adjacent to a long mound containing caches of royal regalia and numerous ceramic bowls. Perhaps the figurines were brought here to provide permanent representation of a village's spiritual practitioner in this important pilgrimage center.

About 100 years after the figurines were initially buried, someone checked to make sure they were still there. A hole was dug directly over the offering, but nothing was removed and the figurines were reburied. The precision of this later excavation shows that people remembered the exact location of the cache. This extraordinary find is an example of the importance of scientific archaeological excavations for understanding ancient art. Had these objects been torn out of the ground by looters and sold piecemeal on the black market, we might never have known that Olmec sculptures such as these were used to create meaningful installations, nor could we have imagined that once buried, art such as this could be remembered for so long.

The Rise of Civilizations in the Americas

What are the early geographic and cultural backgrounds for the development of art in the Western Hemisphere?

In recent years the question of the original settlement of the Americas has become an area of debate. The traditional view has been that human beings arrived in North and South America from Asia during the last Ice Age, when glaciers trapped enough of the world's water to lower the level of the oceans and expose a land bridge across the Bering Strait. Although most of present-day Alaska and Canada was covered by glaciers at that time, an ice-free corridor along the Pacific coast would have provided access from Asia to the south and east. Thus, this theory holds that sometime before 12,000 years ago, perhaps as early as 20,000 to 30,000 years ago, Paleolithic

hunter-gatherers emerged from this corridor and began to spread out into two vast, uninhabited continents. This view is now challenged by the early dates of some new archaeological finds and by evidence suggesting the possibility of early connections with Europe as well, perhaps along the Arctic coast of the North Atlantic. Recently, some have theorized that Pacific Islanders could have sailed to the coast of Chile and spread out from there. In any event, by 10,000 to 12,000 years ago bands of hunters roamed throughout the Americas, and after the ice had retreated, the peoples of the Western Hemisphere were essentially cut off from the rest of the world until they were overrun by European invaders, beginning at the end of the fifteenth century CE.

In this isolation, the peoples of the Americas experienced cultural transformations similar to those seen elsewhere after the Paleolithic era. In most regions they developed an agricultural way of life. A trio of native

MAP 13–1 THE AMERICAS BEFORE 1300

Human beings moved across North America, then southward through Central America until they eventually reached the Tierra del Fuego region of South America.

plants—corn, beans, and squash—was especially important, but people cultivated potatoes, tobacco, cacao, tomatoes, and avocados as well. New World peoples also domesticated many animals: dogs, turkeys, guinea pigs, llamas, and their camelid cousins—alpacas, guanacos, and vicuñas.

As elsewhere, the shift to agriculture in the Americas was accompanied by population growth and, in some places, the rise of hierarchical societies, the appearance of ceremonial centers and towns with monumental architecture, and the development of sculpture, ceramics, and other arts. The people of Mesoamerica—the region that extends from central Mexico well into Central America—developed writing, astronomy, a complex and accurate calendar, and a sophisticated system of mathematics. Central and South American peoples had advanced metallurgy and produced exquisite gold, silver, and copper objects. The metalworkers of the Andes, the mountain range along the western coast of South America, began to produce metal jewelry, weapons, and agricultural implements in the first millennium CE, and people elsewhere in the Americas made tools, weapons, and art from other materials such as bone, ivory, stone, wood, and, where it was available, obsidian, a volcanic glass capable of a cutting edge 500 times finer than surgical steel. Basketry and weaving became major art forms. The inhabitants of the American Southwest built multi-storied, apartmentlike village and cliff dwellings, as well as elaborate irrigation systems with canals. Evidence of weaving in the American Southwest dates to about 7400 BCE.

The extraordinary early arts of the Americas served as an essential mode of communicating beliefs and displaying status. This chapter explores the accomplishments of selected cultures in five of those areas: Mesoamerica, Central America, the central Andes of South America, the Southeastern Woodlands and great river valleys of North America, and the North American Southwest.

Mesoamerica and Central America

What distinguishes the art and architecture of the Olmec, Teotihuacan, Maya, and Diquis cultures in Mesoamerica and Central America?

Ancient Mesoamerica encompasses the area from north of the Valley of Mexico (the location of Mexico City) to present-day Belize, Honduras, and western Nicaragua in Central America (MAP 13–1). The region is one of great contrasts, ranging from tropical rainforest to semiarid mountains. The civilizations that arose in Mesoamerica varied, but they were linked by cultural similarities and trade. Among their shared features were a ballgame with

religious and political significance (see "The Cosmic Ballgame" on page 390), monumental building construction, and a complex system of multiple calendars including a 260-day divinatory cycle and a 365-day ritual and agricultural cycle. Many Mesoamerican societies were sharply divided into elite and commoner classes.

The transition to farming began in Mesoamerica between 7000 and 6000 BCE, and by 3000 to 2000 BCE settled villages were widespread. The region's subsequent history is usually divided into three broad periods: Formative or Preclassic (1500 BCE–250 CE), Classic (250–900 CE), and Postclassic (900–1521 CE). This chronology derives primarily from the archaeology of the Maya—the people of Guatemala, southern Mexico, and the Yucatan Peninsula—with the Classic period bracketing the era during which the Maya erected dated stone monuments. As with the study of ancient Greek art, the term "Classic" reflects the view of early scholars that this period was a kind of golden age. Although this view is no longer current—and the periods are only roughly applicable to other cultures of Mesoamerica—the terminology has endured.

The Olmec

Mesoamericans used skillfully crafted objects to communicate with the powerful forces of nature. From the Gulf of Mexico to the Pacific, Formative Period peoples were developing technologies for marking time, maintaining health, and visualizing cherished ideas. Around 1700 BCE, the earliest major site along the Gulf Coast was not a village but a depository for precious objects. Within a spring at the base of Cerro Manatí, for over six centuries pilgrims deposited perfectly balanced and polished celts of imported jade and balls fashioned from local rubber, along with ceramics and seeds, before burying them under a thick layer of silt. Around 1300 BCE, the offerings were more frequently human busts carved of wood and wrapped in fiber bundles along with seeds, which were deposited in the spring along with more celts, wooden staffs, and a few infant bones.

At the same time, 11 miles away, a town—now called San Lorenzo—was developed on a leveled plateau surrounded by several watercourses and constructed low mounds. This first urban center in Mesoamerica flourished between 1300 and 900 BCE, and its inhabitants, in an astonishing explosion of creativity, created over 100 basalt sculptures of subjects for which there are no known precedents. After transporting basalt boulders from a volcano 30 miles away, they carved **COLOSSAL HEADS** (FIG. 13–4) weighing up to 25 tons, thrones depicting caves in rock walls with overhanging ledges, some remarkably naturalistic seated human figures, and a variety of animal forms.

Ten colossal heads have been excavated at San Lorenzo, and there is considerable speculation about what

Art and its Contexts

THE COSMIC BALLGAME

The ritual ballgame was one of the defining characteristics of Mesoamerican society. It was generally played on a long, rectangular court with a large, solid, heavy rubber ball. Using their elbows, knees, or hips—but not their hands—heavily padded players directed the ball toward a goal or marker. The rules, size, and shape of the court, the number of players on a team; and the nature of the goal varied. The largest surviving ballcourt, at Chichen Itza, is bigger than a modern football field. Large stone rings set in the walls of this court about 25 feet above the field served as goals. The **BALLCOURT** in **FIGURE 13–2** was constructed at the heart of the ceremonial center in the southernmost Maya city of Copan.

The game was a common subject in Mesoamerican art. This scene, painted on a **CYLINDRICAL VESSEL** (**FIG. 13–3**), shows four lords playing the ballgame, the architectural space of the ballcourt suggested by a few horizontal lines. The men wear elaborate headdresses and padded gear to protect them from the heavy rubber ball. The painter has chosen a moment of arrested movement: One player kneels to hit the ball—or has just hit it—while the others gesture and lean toward him.

The ballgame may have had religious and political significance: It is part of creation stories and was sometimes associated with warfare. Captive warriors might have been forced to play the game, and when the stakes were high the game may have culminated in human sacrifice.

13–2 BALLCOURT
Copan, Honduras. Maya culture, c. 711–736 CE.

Credit: © Keren Su/Getty Images

13–3 CYLINDRICAL VESSEL WITH BALLGAME SCENE

Maya culture, 600–800 CE. Painted ceramic, diameter 6⅜″ (15.9 cm), height 8⅛″ (20.5 cm). Dallas Museum of Art. Gift of Mr. and Mrs. Raymond Nasher 1983.148.

This roll-out photograph shows the entire scene painted around the cylinder; a person holding the vessel would have to turn it to see what was happening. The text around the rim is a standard dedicatory inscription naming the vessel as one to be used for drinking chocolate, and tests of residues inside similar vessels have confirmed this use. Without sugar or milk, Maya chocolate was very different from ours; it was a frothy and bitter beverage consumed on courtly and ritual occasions.

Credit: Rollout photograph © Justin Kerr, K2803

13–4 COLOSSAL HEAD, SAN LORENZO
Mexico. Olmec culture, c. 1200–900 BCE. Basalt, height 7′5″ (2.26 m).
Anthropology Museum, Veracruz University, Jalapa.

Credit: Werner Forman Archive

they represent. All have broad features and flat noses, and all wear helmets. The overall shape is reminiscent of the rubber balls offered at El Manatí. As later civilizations would describe the ballgame, it had mythological cosmic and generative significance, and the decapitated heads of the heroic ballplayers were often used as a ball. These bodiless heads could represent balls or heroic ballplayers. However, some scholars think their monumentality and lack of uniformity suggests that they are more likely portraits of rulers. San Lorenzo was the most important town in the region. Despite evidence of social stratification and recognition that the elite must have amassed wealth, no deposits like those of El Manatí have been found in over 40 years of archaeology in the region.

However, the practice of buried offerings was revived at La Venta, which thrived from 1000 to 400 BCE. To initiate the second of four construction phases in an enclosed ritual courtyard, people carried 200 tons of serpentine (a dark green semiprecious mineral) from a source 180 miles away to create two massive offerings. These were 20-feet-deep pits, measuring 19 by 20 feet. Layers of pink, green, gold, and rose clay created settings for the serpentine blocks. The massive offerings served as effigies of lakes or springs, while on the uppermost layer, serpentine blocks formed a mosaic design that signified the sacred female earth surface, covered by an array of celts. Additional massive offerings initiated later phases of construction at La Venta. The number of small caches of stone figurines, celts, and jade ornaments in the form of earflares, hands, frogs, clamshells, canoes, and animal teeth increased, showing the growing importance of this center as a sacred site (SEE FIG. 13–1).

Meanwhile, like their counterparts at San Lorenzo, the La Venta Olmec built earthen mounds and set over 100 monumental sculptures in their plazas (**FIG. 13–5**). Unlike San Lorenzo, the mounds and enclosed

13–5 GREAT PYRAMID AND PLAZA, LA VENTA
Mexico. Olmec culture, c. 900–400 BCE. Pyramid height approx. 100′ (30 m).

Credit: © 2016. Image copyright The Metropolitan Museum of Art/Art Resource/Scala, Florence

courtyard at La Venta were designed to symmetrically flank the site's central axis, which pointed south toward the nearest mountain on the horizon, presumably a sacred location. The sculptures included colossal heads, cave-niche thrones, basalt columns, and other enormous carvings. A 100-foot-high earthen mound in the center of the site was the largest in Mesoamerica at the time. These earthen forms and stone sculptures formed a processional narrative array along the central axis that portrayed the Olmec creation story. The climax of the story was portrayed in a series of gigantic stelai in the form of stylized human embryos from which maize sprouted; the fetuses, like the colossal heads, wore helmets.

The Olmec traded across Mesoamerica, obtaining jade from the Motagua River Valley in Honduras and malachite pigments from northwestern Mexico. As Formative Period people interacted, the ideas that Olmec art expressed so powerfully—about the parallels between maize plants and human life, reciprocal relations with natural forces, the preciousness of jade as a symbol of vital energy, and the cosmic ramifications of the ballgame—were adopted and transformed by groups throughout Mesoamerica. As Olmec civilization waned around 300 BCE, people in the Maya area and Teotihuacan in the Valley of Mexico forged new civilizations from these foundational ideas.

Teotihuacan

Located some 30 miles northeast of present-day Mexico City, the city of Teotihuacan experienced a period of rapid growth early in the first millennium CE. By 200 CE, it had emerged as Mesoamerica's first truly urban settlement,

13-7 PLAN OF THE CEREMONIAL CENTER OF TEOTIHUACAN

13-6 CEREMONIAL CENTER OF THE CITY OF TEOTIHUACAN
Mexico. Teotihuacan culture, c. 100–650 CE.

Credit: V Korostyshevskiy/Fotolia

13-8 PYRAMID OF THE FEATHERED SERPENT

The Ciudadela, Teotihuacan, Mexico. Teotihuacan culture, c. 200 CE.

Credit: NoraDoa/Fotolia

a significant center of commerce and manufacturing. At its height, between 300 and 650, Teotihuacan covered nearly 9 square miles and had a population of at least 125,000, making it the largest city in the Americas and one of the largest in the world at that time (**FIG. 13-6**). Its residents lived in walled "apartment compounds," and the entire city was organized on a grid (**FIG. 13-7**), its orientation chosen both for its calendrical significance and to respond to the surrounding landscape.

Although Teotihuacan declined after 650, it was never forgotten. Centuries later, it remained a legendary pilgrimage center. Aztec people (c. 1300–1525) revered the site, believing it to be the place where the gods created the sun and the moon, and they gave the city its name— "Teotihuacan," meaning place of divinity in the Nahuatl language of the Aztec. The names we use for its principal monuments are also Nahuatl. Despite a century of modern research, the ethnicity of the principal inhabitants of Teotihuacan remains unknown, because while they used a bit of pictographic writing, they did not name themselves or their city in their glyphs.

We do know about how the city developed. By 100 CE, planners established an orthogonal grid plan. The Avenue of the Dead (a series of plazas at different levels about 150 feet wide and over a mile long) runs 15 degrees east of north, or almost north–south, and creates a central axis like the one at earlier La Venta. All north–south streets and walls parallel this axis. The grid is further enforced by the Teotihuacan Measurement Unit (TMU) of 83 cm. All buildings and their components are even multiples of this measurement. Three pyramid complexes dominate the center of the city. At the north end of the central axis stands the Pyramid of the Moon, facing a large plaza flanked by

smaller, symmetrically placed platforms. It seems to echo the shape of the mountain behind it, and as one walks toward the pyramid, it looms above, eclipsing the mountain completely. The Pyramid of the Moon was enlarged several times, as were many Mesoamerican pyramids; each enlargement completely enclosed the previous structure and was accompanied by rich sacrificial offerings and caches including stone standing and seated figurines.

The largest of Teotihuacan's architectural monuments, the Pyramid of the Sun (SEE FIG. 13-6), located just to the east of the Avenue of the Dead, is slightly over 200 feet high and measures about 720 feet on each side at its base— similar in size to, but not as tall as, the largest Egyptian pyramid at Giza (see Chapter 3). The pyramid rises in a series of sloping steps to a flat platform where a small temple once stood. A monumental stone stairway led from level to level up the front of the pyramid to the temple platform. The exterior was faced with stone, which was then stuccoed and painted.

The Pyramid of the Sun was built over a tunnel that may have been an enlargement of a natural cave. Excavations from 2008 to 2011 within the tunnel revealed several burials and offering caches containing stone masks, anthropomorphic figurines, and shells. A similar tunnel has recently been discovered in the Ciudadela complex at the southern end of the ceremonial center. This complex consists of a series of temple platforms surrounding a plaza for religious and political gatherings of more than 60,000 people. The tunnel descends below the plaza floor, running eastward to terminate under the **PYRAMID OF THE FEATHERED SERPENT** (**FIG. 13-8**), and like the tunnel under the Pyramid of the Sun, this one also contained offerings. The pyramid uses the *talud-tablero* (slope-and-panel) system of construction that is a hallmark of the Teotihuacan architectural style. The *talud* (sloping base) of each platform supports a *tablero* (entablature) that rises vertically and is surrounded by a frame.

Archaeological excavations of the temple's early phase have revealed reliefs portraying undulating, feathered serpents floating in a watery space punctuated by aquatic shells. Their flat, angular, abstract style, typical of Teotihuacan art, is in marked contrast to the curvilinear, organic forms of Olmec art. While the bodies of the feathered serpents are rendered in low relief, in the vertical *tablero* sections three-dimensional sculptures of fanged serpent heads emerge from rings of stylized feathers. Each serpent carries on its body a squarish headdress with a protruding upper jaw; huge, round eyes originally inlaid with obsidian; and a pair of round goggles on its forehead between the eyes. These mosaic headdresses seem to represent an aspect of the Teotihuacan Storm God associated with warfare—other works of art at Teotihuacan and elsewhere in Mesoamerica show armed warriors wearing the same headdress. Inside the pyramid, this militaristic message was reinforced by the burials of dozens of sacrificial victims, some of them wearing necklaces made of human jawbones (or shell imitations thereof), their arms tied behind their backs.

The residential sections of Teotihuacan surrounded the city's center. The spacious palaces of the elite, with as many as 45 rooms and 7 patios, stood nearest the ceremonial center. Artisans, foreign traders, and peasants lived farther away, in more crowded compounds, all aligned with the Teotihuacan grid. Palaces and more humble homes alike were rectangular, one-story structures with high walls—plastered and covered with paintings—and suites of rooms arranged around open courtyards.

Teotihuacan's artists created wall paintings in a fresco technique, applying pigments directly on damp lime plaster. Once the paint was applied, the walls were polished to give them a smooth, shiny, and durable surface. The style, like that of the sculpture, was flat, angular, and abstract, often featuring processions of similarly dressed figures, rows of mythological animals, or other sequences of repeated images. Teotihuacan painters worked in several different color schemes, including a bright polychrome and a more restricted palette emphasizing tones of red. One detached fragment of a wall painting from the Techinantitla complex, which was 500 meters east of the Pyramid of the Moon, depicts a feathered serpent pouring liquids and flowers around trees (**FIG. 13-9**). In typical Central Mexican fashion, the trees (in the lower strip) appear in elevation view, with their roots showing below ground. Above each of the grey root systems sits a place glyph that forms a base for the trunk of the tree. This place name and tree configuration forms a toponym (place-name) in the Teotihuacan system of writing, and the visible roots of the trees implies attachment to each particular place. For example, the left-most place glyph is called "mask-step," followed by "yellow platform" and "hand-shell-yellow petals." Six more trees and glyphs (three more than are shown here) followed these first three around the room, then the nine place-trees series was repeated seven more times within the room. Such toponyms were integral to all Mesoamerican writing systems, both pictorial and phonetic.

Sometime in the early seventh century disaster struck Teotihuacan. The ceremonial center was sacked and

13-9 FEATHERED SERPENT AND FLOWERING TREES
Fragment of a fresco from Techinantitla building, Teotihuacan, Mexico. Teotihuacan culture, c. 500–650 CE. Earthen aggregate, lime plaster, and mineral pigments. 23¼ × 159½ × 2¼" (59.1 × 405.1 × 5.7 cm). The Fine Arts Museums of San Francisco. Bequest of Harald Wagner (1985.104.1).

These fragments are among a group of numerous mural fragments that collector Harald Wagner unexpectedly bequeathed to the Fine Arts Museums of San Francisco in 1976. Because accessioning parts of ancient architectural complexes had been prohibited by the 1970 United Nations Educational, Scientific, and Cultural Organization Convention on cultural property, the museum was diligent in establishing the entry date of the pieces into the United States and initiated a cooperative effort among Mexican museums and conservation experts to jointly conserve the murals and return some of them to Mexico.

burned, and the city went into a permanent decline. Nevertheless, its influence continued as other centers throughout Mesoamerica, as far south as the Maya region, borrowed and transformed its imagery, as can be seen in the rectangular headdress and Storm God headdress ornament that Lady Xok wears on Yaxchilan Lintel 24 (SEE FIG. 13–14).

The Maya

More than any other ancient American civilization, the Maya developed their cities as works of art. Each of the hundreds of kingdoms that arose in the tropical rainforests of southeastern Mesoamerica created a unique visual identity by elaborating and individualizing the basic building forms—the plaza, pyramid, palace, and ballcourt—and by creating unusual modifications of the basic sculptural forms—the stela, lintel, altar, and throne. City founders chose to build near distinctive topographic features, and each city devised a strategy for the alignment of architecture to an astronomical phenomenon. Stucco reliefs transformed the flat walls of buildings into undulating forms that were brightly painted. Both images and hieroglyphs enlivened the surfaces, documenting the deeds of the rulers, their ancestors, and the city's patron deities. Decorated textiles, polychrome painted ceramics, and bark paper books added further visual complexity to the spectacle of the Maya court.

An increasingly detailed picture of the Maya has been emerging from recent archaeological research and from advances in deciphering their writing. That picture shows a society divided into competing city-states in a near-constant state of war with each other. A hereditary ruler and an elite class of nobles and priests governed each city-state, supported by a large group of farmer-commoners. Rulers established their legitimacy, maintained links with their divine ancestors, commemorated important calendrical dates, and sustained the gods through elaborate rituals, including ballgames, bloodletting ceremonies, and human sacrifice. Rulers commemorated such events and their military exploits on carved stelae.

Maya civilization emerged during the Late Preclassic period (400 BCE–250 CE), reached its peak in the southern lowlands of Mexico and Guatemala during the Classic period (250–900 CE), and shifted to the northern Yucatan Peninsula during the Postclassic period (900–1521 CE). Throughout this time, the Maya maintained strong ties with other regions of Mesoamerica: They inherited many ideas and technologies from the Olmec, had trade and military interactions with Teotihuacan, and, centuries later, were in contact with the Aztec Empire.

Art and its Contexts
MAYA WRITING

Maya writing is logosyllabic—it consists of ideographs or logographs that represent entire words as well as a set of symbols that stand for the sound of each syllable in the Maya language. Thus, a word like *balam* (jaguar) could be written in many different ways: with the logograph "BALAM," a picture of the head of a jaguar (top right); with three syllables, "ba-la-ma," for the sounds of the word *balam* (bottom right); or a combination of the two systems—the logograph "BALAM" complemented with one or more phonetic syllables, to make it clear which logograph was represented (and avoid the possibility of confusing this logograph with the symbol for *hix*, another kind of feline, for example) (middle right). The combination of these two systems allowed Maya scribes extraordinary flexibility, and some calligraphers seem to have delighted in finding as many different ways as possible to write the same word. Many Maya logographs remained very pictorial, like the glyph for jaguar illustrated here, which meant that Maya writing was never too distant from other kinds of image making. In fact, the same word, *ts'ib*, signified both writing and painting in the Classic Maya language.

With major advances in the decipherment of Maya hieroglyphic writing—beginning in the 1950s and continuing to this day—it has become clear that the inscriptions on Maya architecture and stelae are almost entirely devoted to a ceremonial recording of historical events. They document the dates of royal marriages, births of heirs, alliances between cities, and great military victories, and they tie these events to astronomical events and propitious dates in the Maya calendar. We know that the Maya also wrote books, but only four of these fragile manuscripts—called codices—have survived, all of them from the Postclassic period.

BALAM

ba-BALAM

BALAM-ma

ba-BALAM-ma

Credit: Kathy Mrozek

ba-la-ma

TIKAL   The monumental buildings of Maya cities were masterly examples of the use of architecture for public display and as the backdrop for social and sacred ritual. Tikal (in present-day Guatemala) was one of the largest Maya cities, with a population of up to 70,000 at its height. Unlike Teotihuacan, with its grid plan, Maya cities, including Tikal, conformed to the uneven terrain of the rainforest. Plazas, pyramid-temples, ballcourts, and other structures stood on high ground connected by wide elevated roads, or causeways.

Tikal was settled in the Late Preclassic period, in the fourth century BCE, and continued to flourish through the Early Classic period. The kings of Tikal were buried in funerary pyramids like the one visible on the right in **FIGURE 13–10**, which was separated by a wide plaza from the royal palace to the south. Tikal suffered a major upheaval in 378 CE, recorded in texts from the city and surrounding centers, when some scholars believe the arrival of strangers from Teotihuacan precipitated the death of Tikal's king and the installation of a new ruler with ties to Central Mexico. Art from this period shows strong Teotihuacan influence in ceramic and architectural forms, though both were soon adapted to suit local Maya aesthetics. The city enjoyed a period of wealth and regional dominance until a military defeat led to a century of decline.

In the eighth century, Tikal finally succeeded in defeating the military alliance that dominated them when King Jasaw Chan K'awiil (ruled 682–734) captured Ich'aak K'ak, the king of mighty Calakmul. He initiated an extensive construction program, including ritual complexes for celebrating the K'atun, or 20-year period, which held the stela and altar that embodied both the K'atun and the ruler. His building program culminated in the construction of Temple I (SEE FIG. 13–10), a tall pyramid that faces a companion pyramid, Temple II, across a large central plaza. Containing Jasaw Chan K'awiil's tomb in the limestone bedrock below, Temple I rises above the forest canopy to a height of more than 140 feet. Its base has nine layers, probably reflecting the belief that the underworld had nine levels. Priests climbed the steep stone staircase on the exterior to the temple on top, which consists of two narrow, parallel rooms covered with a steep roof supported by corbel vaults. The crest that rises over the roof of the temple, known as a **roof comb**, was originally covered with brightly painted sculpture. Ritual performances on the narrow platform at the top of the pyramid would have been visible throughout the plaza. Inspired by Jasaw Chan K'awiil's building program, later kings of Tikal also built tall funerary pyramids that still tower above the rainforest canopy.

13–10 BASE OF NORTH ACROPOLIS (LEFT) AND TEMPLE I (RIGHT), TIKAL
Guatemala. Maya culture. North Acropolis, 4th century BCE–5th century CE; Temple I (Tomb of Jasaw Chan K'awiil), c. 734 CE.
Credit: © Daniel Loncarevic/Shutterstock

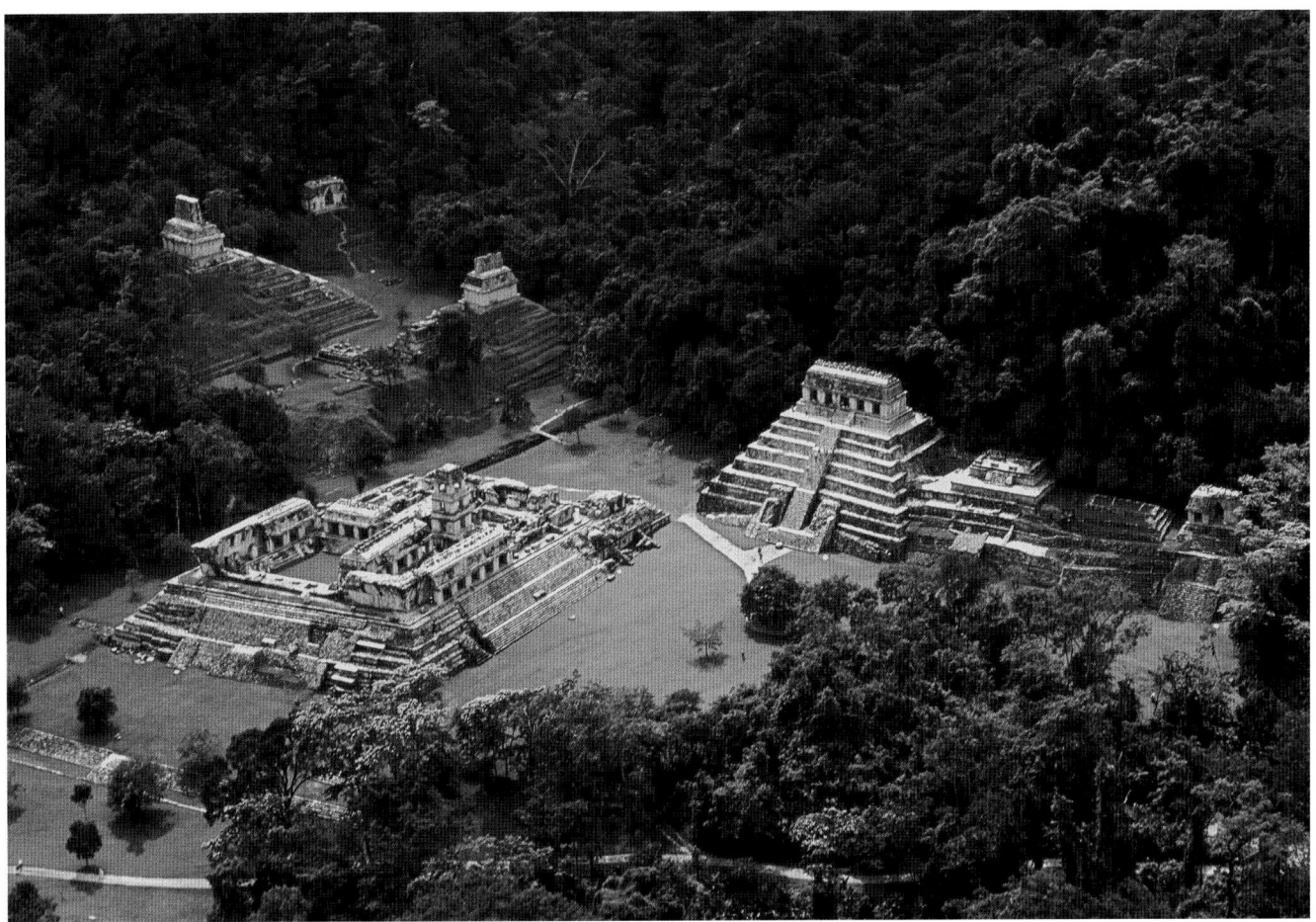

13–11 PALACE (FOREGROUND) AND TEMPLE OF THE INSCRIPTIONS, PALENQUE

Mexico. Maya culture. Palace, 5th–8th century CE; Temple of the Inscriptions (Tomb of Pakal the Great), c. 683 CE.

Credit: © Danny Lehman/Corbis

PALENQUE The small city-state of Palenque (in the present-day Mexican state of Chiapas) rose to prominence later than Tikal, during the Classic period. Hieroglyphic inscriptions record the beginning of its royal dynasty in 431 CE, but the city had only limited regional importance until the ascension of a powerful ruler, K'inich Janahb Pakal (*pakal* is Maya for "shield"), who ruled from 615 to 683. Known as Pakal the Great, he and his sons, who succeeded him, commissioned most of the structures visible at Palenque today. As at Tikal, urban planning responds to the landscape. Perched on a ridge over 300 feet above the swampy lowland plains, the buildings of Palenque are terraced into the mountains with a series of aqueducts channeling rivers through the urban core. The center of the city houses the palace, the Temple of the Inscriptions, and various temples (**FIG. 13–11**). Other temples, elite palaces, and a ballcourt surround this central group.

The palace was an administrative center as well as a royal residence. At its core was the throne room of Pakal the Great, a spacious structure whose stone roof imitated the thatched roofs of more humble dwellings. Over time, the palace grew into a complex series of buildings organized around four courtyards, where the private business

of the court was transacted. From the outside, the palace presented an inviting façade of wide staircases and open colonnades decorated with stucco sculptures, but access to the interior spaces was tightly limited.

Next to the palace stands the Temple of the Inscriptions, Pakal the Great's funerary pyramid. Rising 75 feet above the plaza, it has nine levels like Temple I at Tikal (SEE FIG. 13–10). The shrine on the summit consists of a portico with five entrances and a vaulted inner chamber originally surmounted by a tall roof comb. Its façade still retains much of its stucco sculpture. The inscriptions that give the building its name consist of three large panels of text that line the back wall of the outer chamber at the top of the temple, linking Pakal's accomplishments to the mythical history of the city.

A corbel-vaulted stairway beneath the floor of the shrine at the top of Pakal's funerary pyramid zigzags down 80 feet to a small subterranean chamber that contained his tomb, discovered in 1952. A huge slab of carved limestone nearly filled the chamber. It covered a monolithic limestone sarcophagus with reliefs of ancestors merged with fruiting trees, both emerging from crevices in the earth to witness his death and rebirth, the subject of the elaborate relief sculpture on the lid (**FIG. 13–12**). Scholars have linked Pakal's unusual pose to birthing iconography. The Maya conventionalized symbol for a tree emerges from his midsection. In this case, logographs for "divinity" mark the tree, which is adorned with jade-beaded, square-nosed serpents on its branches, while a jade-bodied, double-headed serpent—a device held by rulers— wraps around it. The principal bird deity, which sits atop the tree, appears in Maya art during events of great creative and transformative power, and the jade beads and symbols of divinity that float around the tree provide the context for Pakal's rebirth. That this event occurs in the celestial realm is signaled by the solar, lunar, and planetary symbols in the "skybands" on the side borders.

Underneath the lid, archaeologists found the bones of Pakal in a uterus-shaped cavity within the sarcophagus.

13–13 BURIAL MASK OF PAKAL THE GREAT

From Pakal's tomb, Temple of the Inscriptions, Palenque, Mexico. Maya culture, c. 683 CE. Jade, shell, and pearl; life-size mask. Museo Nacional de Antropología, Mexico City.

Credit: © akg-images/Album/J.Enrique Molina

13–12 REPRODUCTION OF LID OF THE SARCOPHAGUS OF PAKAL THE GREAT

From Pakal's tomb, Temple of the Inscriptions, Palenque, Mexico. Maya culture, c. 683 CE. Limestone, 12'1½" × 7'1½" (3.72 × 2.17 m).

Credit: © Fine Art Images/Alinari Archives, Firenze

Rich burial offerings covered him, including a jade mask, jewelry, and figurines. The mask (**FIG. 13–13**) shows the aesthetic modifications of Pakal's body during his lifetime. The shape of his head had been elongated during his infancy and an artificial bridge enhanced his long, curved nose. His compact chin and protruding lower lip conform to Maya ideals of beauty, and since the overall shape of his face is consistent with his portrayal in other portraits, this mask seems to have blended individual likeness with idealized conventions.

YAXCHILAN Yaxchilan differed from most Maya cities in its use of lintels as a major location for relief sculpture and in the prominence of women in its art. More than 60 lintels have been recovered. While some contain only hieroglyphic texts, most portray the rulers, royal women, and other nobles in elaborate costumes performing a variety of rituals. On Lintel 24, one of a series dedicated in 726 by Lady Xok (Shoke), she appears kneeling on the ground, drawing a thick, thorny cord through her tongue (see "Closer Look" opposite). Her husband, Shield Jaguar, stands next to her, holding a flaming torch, with which he may set fire to the strips of paper dotted with blood in the basket between them. The reason for the bloodletting may be linked to the fact that the date was an anniversary of Shield Jaguar's accession to the throne. This is one of the most explicit portrayals of bloodletting in Maya art as well as a rare depiction of a female perforating her tongue.

This lintel is unusual for another reason. Artist's signatures appear on some lintels, but the finished products appear to have been the result of the collaborative work of several hands. At least two sculptors seem to have created this scene, and one did something radical for Maya art. While the faces of both figures appear in strict profile view and Shield Jaguar's body takes the same orientation, Lady Xok's torso is frontal, and her right hand—highlighted against the ground at the center of the composition—twists

elegantly in a three-quarter view. This "3/4 artist" likely drew the composition, with its swirling flames and the foreshortening of Lady Xok's lower limbs and may also have written the text, with its irregular outlines and coarse detailing. A second artist, nicknamed "Elegant Knot," took charge of the delicate detailing of the complex textile patterns and knots, using carefully controlled parallel lines and regular edges.

POSTCLASSIC PERIOD After warfare and environmental crisis led to the abandonment of the lowland Maya city-states around 800, the focus of Maya civilization shifted north to the Yucatan Peninsula. One of the principal cities of the Postclassic period was Chichen Itza, which means "at the mouth of the well of the Itza," and may refer to the deep *cenote* (sinkhole) at the site that was sacred to the

A Closer Look

SHIELD JAGUAR AND LADY XOK

Shield Jaguar's elaborate headgear includes the shrunken head of a sacrificial victim, proclaiming his past piety in another ritual pleasing to the gods.

The two inscriptions—almost acting as an internal frame for the standing figure—record the date and the nature of the ritual portrayed: bloodletting on October 28, 709. They also identify the standing king as Shield Jaguar and the kneeling woman as Lady Xok.

The sharply outlined subjects, as well as the way they project forward from a deeply recessed, blank background, focus viewers' attention on the bodies of Shield Jaguar and his kneeling wife, Lady Xok.

Shield Jaguar holds a huge torch, indicating that this ritual took place within a dark room or during the night.

Tasseled headdresses are associated with bloodletting rituals.

Lady Xok pulls a rope of thorns through her perforated tongue, while spiraling dotted lines show the blood she is sacrificing to the gods. The spiny rope falls to a basket with blood-spotted paper and a stingray spine (also sometimes used for bloodletting). This ritual of self-mutilation was required of royalty since it was believed to maintain royal rule and continuation of human life within the kingdom by gaining favor with the gods.

Lady Xok is lavishly dressed in a garment made of patterned fabric edged with a fringe. The mosaics on her cuffs and collar could be made of jade or shell.

13–14 SHIELD JAGUAR AND LADY XOK (LINTEL 24)
Yaxchilan, Mexico. Maya culture, 726 CE. Limestone, 43½ × 31¾"
(110.5 × 80.6 cm). British Museum, London.

Credit: Photograph © Justin Kerr, K2887

13-15 PYRAMID ("EL CASTILLO") WITH CHACMOOL IN FOREGROUND

Chichen Itza, Yucatan, Mexico. Maya culture, 9th–12th century CE.

From the top of the Temple of the Warriors, where a reclining *chacmool* sculpture graces the platform, there is a clear view of the radial pyramid nicknamed "El Castillo."

Credit: © akg-Images/ Hedda Eid

Maya. The city flourished from the ninth to the thirteenth century, and at its height covered about 6 square miles.

One of Chichen Itza's most conspicuous structures is a massive nine-level pyramid in the center of a large plaza, nicknamed **"EL CASTILLO"** ("the castle" in Spanish) **(FIG. 13–15)**. A stairway on each side of the radial pyramid leads to a square temple on the summit. At the spring and fall equinoxes, the setting sun casts undulating shadows on the stairway, forming bodies for the serpent heads carved at the base of the north balustrades, pointing toward the Sacred Cenote. Many prominent features of Chichen Itza are markedly different from earlier Maya sites and recall complexes in central Mexico, including long, colonnaded halls and inventive columns in the form of descending serpents. Brilliantly colored relief sculpture and painting covered the buildings of Chichen Itza. Many of the surviving works show narrative scenes that emphasize military conquests. Sculpture at Chichen Itza, including the serpent columns and balustrades and the half-reclining figures known as **chacmools**, has the sturdy forms, proportions, and angularity of architecture, rather than the curving complexity and subtle modeling of Classic Maya sculpture. The *chacmools* may represent fallen warriors and were used to receive sacrificial offerings.

After Chichen Itza's decline, Mayapan, in the middle of the Yucatan Peninsula, became the principal Maya center. But by the time the Spanish arrived in the early sixteenth century, Mayapan, too, had declined (destroyed in the mid fifteenth century), and smaller cities like Tulum, located on the Caribbean coast, were all that remained. The Maya people and much of their culture would survive the devastation of the conquest, adapting to the imposition of Hispanic customs and beliefs. However, many Maya continue to speak their own languages, venerate traditional sacred places, and follow traditional ways.

Central America

Unlike their neighbors in Mesoamerica, who lived in complex hierarchical societies, the people of Central America lived in extended family groups in towns led by chiefs. A notable example of these small chiefdoms was the Diquis culture (located in present-day Costa Rica), which lasted from about 700 to 1500 CE. The Diquis occupied fortified villages and seem to have engaged in constant warfare with one another. Although they did not produce monumental architecture or the large-scale sculpture found in other parts of Costa Rica, they created fine featherwork, ceramics, textiles, and objects of gold and jade.

Metallurgy and the use of gold and copper–gold alloys were widespread in Central America. The technique of lost-wax casting probably first appeared in present-day Colombia between 500 and 300 BCE. From there it spread north to the Diquis. A small, exquisite pendant **(FIG. 13–16)** illustrates the style and technique of Diquis goldwork. The pendant depicts a male figure wearing bracelets, anklets, and a belt with a snake-headed penis sheath. He plays a drum while holding the tail of a snake in his teeth and its head in his left hand. The wavy forms with serpent heads emerging from his scalp suggest an elaborate headdress, and the creatures emerging from his legs suggest some kind of reptile costume. The inverted triangles on the headdress probably represent birds' tails.

In Diquis mythology, serpents and crocodiles inhabited a lower world, humans and birds a higher one. Diquis art depicts animals and insects as fierce and dangerous. The man in the pendant is clearly a performer, and some have interpreted him as a shaman transforming himself into a composite serpent-bird or enacting a ritual snake dance surrounded by serpents or crocodiles. The scrolls on the sides of his head may represent a shaman's power

13–16 SUPERNATURAL FIGURE WITH DRUM AND SNAKE

Costa Rica. Diquis culture, c. 13th–16th century CE. Gold, 4¼ × 3¼″ (10.8 × 8.2 cm). Museos del Banco Central de Costa Rica, San José, Costa Rica.

Credit: Photo: John Bigelow Taylor

to hear and understand the speech of animals. Whatever its specific meaning, the pendant evokes a ritual of mediation between earthly and cosmic powers involving music, dance, and costume.

Whether gold figures of this kind were protective amulets or signs of high status, they were certainly more than personal adornment. Shamans and warriors wore gold to inspire fear, perhaps because gold was thought to capture the energy and power of the sun. This energy was also thought to allow shamans to leave their bodies and travel into cosmic realms.

South America: The Central Andes

What distinguishes the art and architecture of the early cultures in the central Andes?

Like Mesoamerica, the central Andes of South America—primarily present-day Peru and Bolivia—saw the development of complex hierarchical societies with rich and varied artistic traditions. The area is one of dramatic contrasts.

The narrow coastal plain, bordered by the Pacific Ocean on the west and the abruptly soaring Andes Mountains on the east, is one of the driest deserts in the world. Life here depends on the rich marine resources of the Pacific Ocean and the rivers that descend from the Andes, forming a series of valley oases. The Andes themselves are a region of lofty snowcapped peaks, high grasslands, steep slopes, and deep, fertile river valleys. The high grasslands are home to the Andean camelids that have served for thousands of years as beasts of burden and a source of wool and meat. The lush eastern slopes of the Andes descend to the tropical rainforest of the Amazon basin.

In contrast to developments in other parts of the world, Andean peoples developed monumental architecture and textiles long before ceramics and intensive agriculture, usually the two hallmarks of early civilization. Thus the earliest period of monumental architecture, beginning around 3000 BCE, is called the Preceramic period. On the coast, sites with ceremonial mounds and plazas were located near the sea, while in the highlands early centers consisted of multi-roomed, stone-walled structures with sunken central fire pits for burning ritual offerings. In the second millennium BCE (the Initial Period), as agriculture became more important both in the highlands and on the coast, the scale and pace of construction increased dramatically. Communities in the coastal valleys built massive, U-shaped ceremonial complexes, while highland religious centers focused on sunken, circular courtyards. By adding to these constructions bit by bit over generations and using older constructions as the nucleus of new buildings, relatively small communities could generate mountain-size pyramids.

Chavin de Huantar

Located on a trade route between the coast and the Amazon basin, the highland site of Chavin de Huantar was an important religious center between 900 and 200 BCE, home to a style of art that spread through much of the Andes. In Andean chronology, this era is known as the Early Horizon, the first of three so-called Horizon periods. The period was one of artistic and technical innovation in ceramics, metallurgy, and textiles.

The architecture of Chavin synthesizes coastal and highland traditions, combining the U-shaped pyramid typical of the coast with a sunken circular plaza lined with carved reliefs, a form common in the highlands. The often fantastical animals that adorn Chavin sculpture have features of jaguars, hawks, caimans, and other tropical Amazonian beasts.

Within the U-shaped Old Temple at Chavin is a maze-like system of narrow galleries, at the very center of which lies a sculpture called the **LANZÓN** (FIG. **13–17**). Wrapped around a 15-foot-tall blade-shaped stone with a narrow projection at the top—a form that may echo the shape of traditional Andean planting sticks—this complex carving depicts a powerful creature with a humanoid body, clawed hands and feet, and enormous fangs. Its eyebrows and strands of hair terminate in snakes—a kind of composite and transformational imagery shared by many Chavin images. The creature is bilaterally symmetrical, except that it has one hand raised and the other lowered. Compact frontality, flat relief, curvilinear design, and the combination of human, animal, bird, and reptile parts characterize this early art.

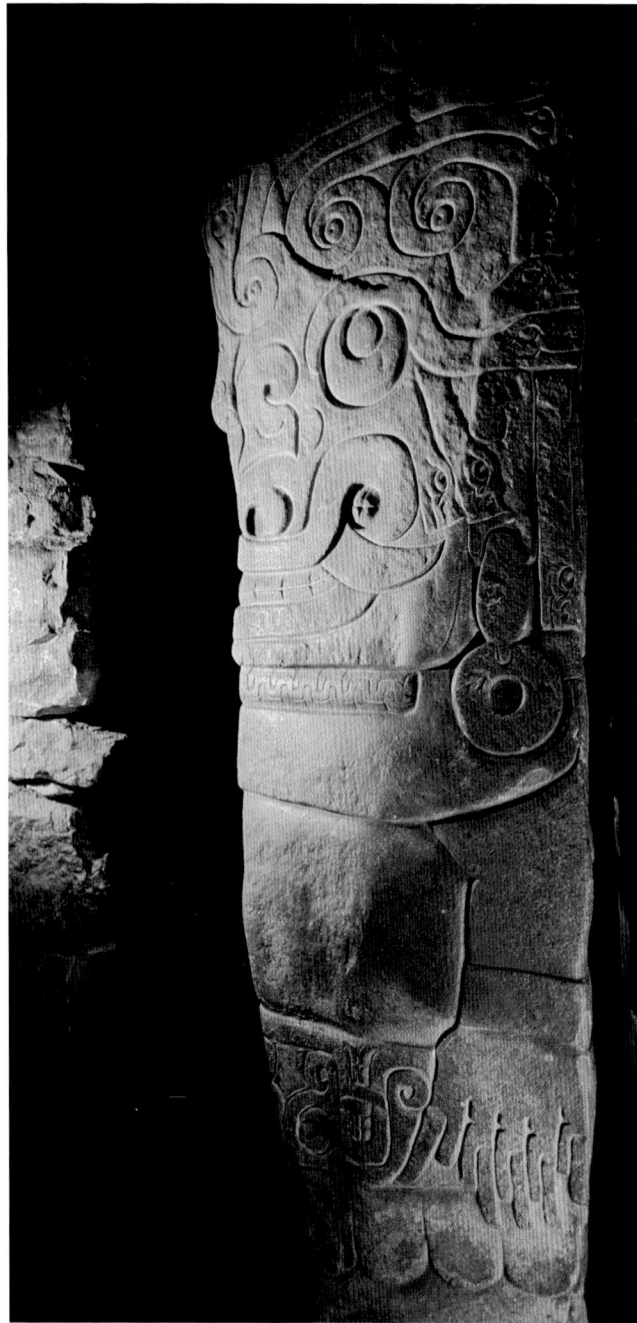

13-17 LANZÓN, CHAVIN DE HUANTAR
Peru. Chavin culture, c. 900 BCE. Granite, height 15′ (4.5 m).

It has been suggested that the Lanzón was an oracle (a chamber directly above the statue allowed priests' disembodied voices to filter into the room below), which would explain why people from all over the Andes made pilgrimages to Chavin, bringing exotic goods to the highland site and spreading the style of its art throughout the Andean region as they returned home.

The Paracas and Nazca Cultures

While Chavin de Huantar was flourishing as a highland center whose art was enormously influential, different valleys on the Pacific coast developed distinctive art styles and cultures.

PARACAS   The Paracas culture of the Peruvian south coast flourished from about 600 BCE to 200 CE, overlapping the Chavin period. It is best known for its stunning textiles, which were found in cemeteries as wrappings, in many layers, around the bodies of the dead. Some bodies were wrapped in as many as 200 pieces of cloth.

Weaving is of great antiquity in the central Andes and continues to be among the most prized arts in the region (see "Andean Textiles" opposite). Fine textiles were a source of prestige and wealth.

The designs on Paracas textiles include repeated embroidered figures of warriors, dancers, composite creatures, and animals (FIG. 13-18). Tiny overlapping stitches on this example create a colorful, curvilinear pattern of paired fish—probably sharks, based on the placement of the gills—striking against the dark blue field and red border. Paracas embroiderers sometimes used as many as 22 different colors within a single figure, but only one simple stitch.

NAZCA   The Nazca culture, which dominated portions of the south coast of Peru during the first seven centuries CE, overlapped the Paracas culture to the north. Nazca artisans wove fine fabrics and also produced multicolored pottery with painted and modeled images reminiscent of those on Paracas textiles.

The Nazca are best known for their colossal **earthworks**, or **geoglyphs**, which dwarf even the most ambitious twentieth-century environmental sculpture. On great stretches of desert they literally drew in the earth. By removing dark, oxidized stones, they exposed the light underlying stones. In this way they created gigantic images—including a **HUMMINGBIRD** with a beak 120 feet long (FIG. 13-19), a killer whale, a monkey, a spider, a duck, and other birds—similar to those with which they decorated their pottery. They also made abstract patterns and groups of straight, parallel lines that extend for up to 12 miles. The purpose and meaning of the glyphs remain a mystery, but the "lines" of stone are wide enough to have been ceremonial pathways.

Technique

ANDEAN TEXTILES

Textiles were one of the most important forms of art and technology in Andean society. Specialized fabrics were developed for everything from ritual burial shrouds and ceremonial costumes to rope bridges and knotted cords for record keeping. Clothing indicated ethnic group and social status and was customized for certain functions, the most rarefied being royal ceremonial garments made for specific occasions and worn only once. Andean textiles are among the most technically complex cloths ever made, and their creation consumed a major portion of societal resources.

Andean textile artists used two principal materials: cotton and camelid fiber. (Camelid fiber—llama, alpaca, guanaco, or vicuña hair—is the Andean equivalent of wool.) Cotton grows on the coast, while camelids—such as llamas and alpacas—thrive in the highlands. The presence of cotton fibers in the highlands and camelid fibers on the coast documents trade between the two regions from very early times and suggests that the production of textiles was an important factor in the domestication of both plants (cotton) and animals (camelids).

The earliest Peruvian textiles were made by twining, knotting, wrapping, braiding, and looping fibers. Those techniques continued to be used even after the invention of weaving looms in the early second millennium BCE. Most Andean textiles were woven on a simple, portable backstrap loom in which the undyed warp (the lengthwise threads) was looped and stretched between two bars. One bar was tied to a stationary object and the other strapped to the waist of the weaver. The weaver controlled the tension of the warp threads by leaning back and forth while threading a shuttle from side to side to insert the weft (crosswise threads). Changing the arrangement of the warp threads between each passage of the weft created a stable interlace of warp and weft: a textile.

Andean artists used a variety of different techniques to decorate their textiles, creating special effects that were prized for their labor intensiveness and difficulty of manufacture as well as their beauty. In tapestry weaving, a technique especially suited to representational textiles, the weft does not run the full width of the fabric; each colored section is woven as an independent unit. **Embroidery** with needle and thread on an already woven textile allows even greater freedom from the rigid warp-and-weft structure of the loom, allowing the artist to create curvilinear forms with thousands of tiny stitches (SEE FIG. 13–18). As even more complex techniques developed, the production of a single textile might involve a dozen processes requiring highly skilled workers. Dyeing technology, too, was an advanced art form in the ancient Andes, with some textiles containing dozens of colors.

Because of their complexity, deciphering how these textiles were made can be a challenge, and investigators rely on contemporary Andean weavers—inheritors of this tradition—for guidance. Now, as then, fiber and textile arts are primarily in the hands of women.

13–18 MANTLE WITH DOUBLE FISH PATTERN
Paracas Necropolis, Peru. Paracas culture, 1st century CE. Cotton and camelid fiber, plain weave with stem-stitch embroidery, 118⅛ × 63¾″ (3 × 1.62 m). Brooklyn Museum, New York. Alfred W. Jenkins Fund (34.1560).

13–19 EARTH DRAWING (GEOGLYPH) OF A HUMMINGBIRD, NAZCA PLAIN
Southwest Peru. Nazca culture, c. 1–700 CE. Length approx. 450′ (137 m); wingspan approx. 220′ (60.9 m).

Credit: © Stéphane Compoint

The Moche Culture

The Moche culture dominated the north coast of Peru from the Piura Valley to the Huarmey Valley—a distance of some 370 miles—between about 100 and 700 CE. Moche lords ruled each valley in this region from a ceremonial-administrative center. The largest of these, in the Moche Valley (from which the culture takes its name), contained the so-called Huaca del Sol (Pyramid of the Sun) and Huaca de la Luna (Pyramid of the Moon), both built of **adobe** brick (sun-baked blocks of clay mixed with straw). The Huaca del Sol, one of the largest ancient structures in South America, was originally 1,100 feet long by 500 feet wide, rising in a series of terraces to a height of 59 feet. Much of this pyramid was destroyed in the seventeenth century, when a Spanish mining company diverted a river through it to wash out the gold contained in its many burials. Recent excavations at the Huaca de la Luna have revealed brightly painted reliefs of deities, captives, and warriors, remade during successive renovations of the pyramid. This site had been thought to be the capital of the entire Moche realm, but the accumulating evidence indicates that the Moche maintained a decentralized social network.

The Moche were exceptional potters and metalsmiths. Vessels were made in the shapes of naturalistically modeled human beings, animals, and architectural structures, at times combined in complex figural scenes. They developed ceramic molds, which allowed them to mass-produce some forms. They also created **PORTRAIT VESSELS** that seem to preserve individual likenesses (**FIG. 13-20**) and recorded mythological narratives and ritual scenes in intricate fine-line painting. Similar scenes were painted on the walls of temples and administrative buildings. Moche metalsmiths, the most sophisticated in the central Andes, developed several innovative metal alloys.

THE TOMB OF THE WARRIOR PRIEST A central theme in Moche iconography is a ceremony in which prisoners captured in battle are sacrificed and several elaborately dressed figures then drink their blood. Archaeologists have labeled the principal figure in this sacrifice ceremony as the Warrior Priest and other important figures as the Bird Priest and the Priestess. The recent discovery of a number of spectacularly rich Moche tombs indicates that the sacrifice ceremony was an actual Moche ritual and that Moche lords and ladies assumed the roles of the principal figures. The occupant of a tomb at Sipán, in the Lambayeque Valley on the northwest coast, was buried with the regalia of the Warrior Priest. In tombs at the site of

San José de Moro, just south of Sipán, several women were buried with the regalia of the Priestess.

Among the riches accompanying the Warrior Priest at Sipán was a pair of exquisite gold-and-turquoise **EARSPOOLS**, each of which depicts three Moche warriors (**FIG. 13–21**). The central figure bursts into three dimensions, while his companions are shown in profile, in a flat inlay technique. All three are adorned with tiny gold-and-turquoise earspools, simpler versions of the object they themselves adorn. They wear gold-and-turquoise headdresses topped with delicate sheets of gold that resemble the crescent-shaped knives used in sacrifices. The central figure has a crescent-shaped nose ornament and carries a removable gold club and shield. A necklace of owl's-head beads strung with gold thread hangs around his shoulders; similar objects have been found in other tombs at Sipán. These earspools illustrate two of the most notable features of Moche art: its capacity for naturalism and its close attention to detail.

13–21 EARSPOOL

From Sipán, Peru. Moche culture, c. 300 CE. Gold, turquoise, quartz, and shell; diameter approx. 3″ (9.4 cm). Bruning Archaeological Museum, Lambayeque, Peru.

Credit: Photo: Susan Einstein

North America

How do the art and architecture of early cultures differ across North America?

Compared to the densely inhabited agricultural regions of Mesoamerica and South America, most of North America remained sparsely populated. Early people lived primarily by hunting, fishing, and gathering edible plants. Agriculture was developed on a limited scale with the cultivation of squash, sunflowers, and other plants to supplement a diet comprised largely of game, fish, and berries.

The East

We are only beginning to understand the early culture of eastern North America. Archaeologists have discovered that people lived in communities that included both burial and ceremonial earthworks—mounds of earth-formed platforms that probably supported a chief's house and served as the shrines of ancestors and places for a sacred fire, tended by special guardians. Poverty Point, Louisiana, is one of the largest of the earthwork ceremonial centers (though not the earliest—this distinction goes to Watson

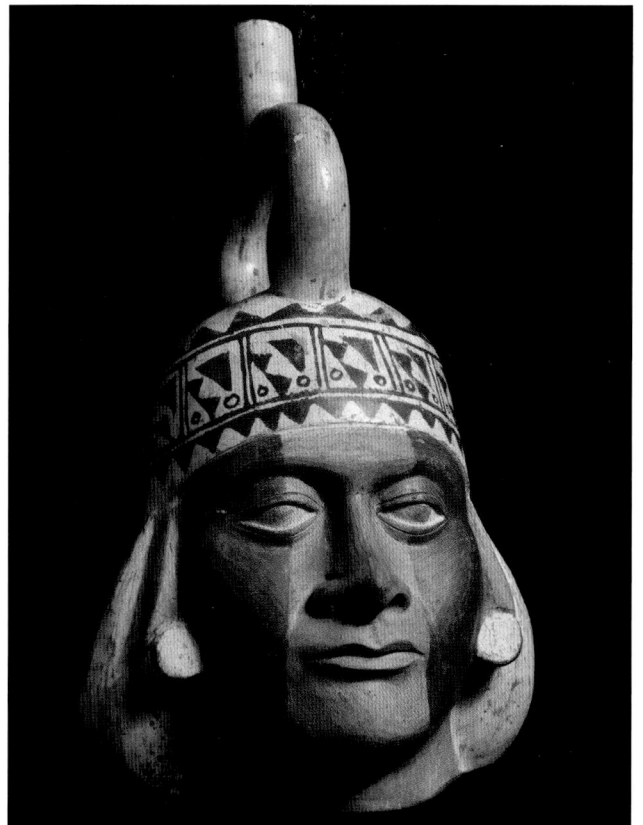

13–20 MOCHE PORTRAIT VESSEL

Peru. Moche culture, c. 100–700 CE. Clay, height 11″ (28 cm). Staatliche Museen zu Berlin, Ethnologisches Museum.

This is one of several portrait vessels made from the same mold that seems to portray a particular individual.

Brake, Louisiana, dating to 3400–3000 BCE). Dated between 1800 and 500 BCE—essentially contemporary with Stonehenge in England (SEE FIG. 1-22) and with Olmec constructions in Mexico (SEE FIG. 13-5)—Poverty Point consisted of huge, concentric earthen arcs three quarters of a mile wide.

The Woodland Period

The Woodland period (300 BCE–1000 CE) saw the creation of impressive earthworks along the great river valleys of the Ohio and Mississippi, where people built monumental mounds and buried individuals with valuable grave goods. Objects discovered in these burials indicate that the people of the Mississippi, Illinois, and Ohio river valleys traded widely with other regions of North and Central America. For example, the burial sites of the Adena (c. 1100 BCE–200 CE) and the Hopewell (c. 100 BCE–550 CE) cultures contained objects made with copper from present-day Michigan's Upper Peninsula, as well as cut sheets of mica from the Appalachian Mountains, turtle shells and sharks' teeth from Florida, and obsidian from Wyoming and Idaho. The pipes that the Hopewell people created from fine-grained pipestone for the ritual smoking of tobacco have been found from Lake Superior to the Gulf of Mexico.

The Hopewell carved their pipes with representations of forest animals and birds, sometimes with inlaid eyes and teeth of fresh-water pearls and bone. Combining realism and elegant simplification, a beaver crouching on a platform forms the bowl of a pipe found in present-day Illinois (FIG. 13-22). As in a modern pipe, the bowl—a hole in the beaver's back—could be filled with tobacco or other dried leaves, the leaves lighted, and smoke drawn through the hole in the stem. Using the pipe in this way, the smoker would be face to face with the beaver, whose shining pearl eyes may suggest an association with the spirit world.

The Mississippian Period

The Mississippian period (c. 700–1550 CE) is characterized by the widespread distribution of complex chiefdoms, both large and small, that proliferated throughout the region. The people of the Mississippian culture continued the mound-building tradition begun by the Adena, Hopewell, and others. From 1539 to 1543 Hernando de Soto encountered Mississippian societies while exploring the region, and this contact between native North American people and Europeans resulted in catastrophe. The Europeans introduced diseases, especially smallpox, to which native populations had had no previous exposure and hence no immunity. In short order, 80 percent of the native population perished, an extraordinary disruption of society, far worse than the Black Death in fourteenth-century Europe. By the time other Europeans reached the area, the great earthworks of the Mississippian culture had long been abandoned.

One of the most impressive Mississippian-period earthworks is the **GREAT SERPENT MOUND** in present-day Adams County, Ohio (FIG. 13-23). Researchers using carbon-14 dating have recently proposed dating the mound to about 1070 CE. There have been many interpretations of the twisting snake form, especially the "head" at the highest point, a Y shape and an oval enclosure that some see as the serpent opening its jaws to swallow a huge egg. Perhaps the people who built it were responding to the spectacular astronomical display of Halley's Comet in 1066.

Mississippian peoples built a major urban center known as Cahokia near the juncture of the Illinois, Missouri, and Mississippi rivers (now East St. Louis, Illinois). Although the site may have been inhabited as early as about 3000 BCE, most monumental construction at Cahokia took place between about 1000 and 1300 CE. At its height the city had a population of up to 15,000 people, with another 10,000 in the surrounding countryside (FIG. 13-24).

The most prominent feature of Cahokia—a feature also found at other Mississippian sites—is an enormous earth mound called Monk's Mound, covering 15 acres and originally 100 feet high. A small, rounded platform on its summit initially supported a wooden fence and a rectangular building. The mound is aligned with the sun at the equinox and may have had a special use during planting or harvest festivals. Smaller rectangular and rounded mounds in front of the principal

13-22 BEAVER EFFIGY PLATFORM PIPE

From Bedford Mound, Pike County, Illinois. Hopewell culture, c. 100–400 CE. Pipestone, river pearls, and bone, 4⁹⁄₁₆ × 1⁷⁄₈ × 2" (11.6 × 4.8 × 5.1 cm). Gilcrease Museum, Tulsa, Oklahoma.

Credit: Photo: John Bigelow Taylor

13-23 GREAT SERPENT MOUND

Adams County, Ohio. Mississippian culture, c. 1070 CE. Length approx. 1,254′ (328.2 m).

Credit: © Tony Linck/ SuperStock

mound surrounded a large, roughly rectangular plaza. The city's entire ceremonial center was protected by a stockade, or fence, of upright wooden posts. In all, the walled enclosure contained more than 100 mounds, platforms, wooden enclosures, and houses. The various earthworks functioned as tombs and bases for palaces and temples, and also served to make astronomical observations.

Postholes indicate that woodhenges (circles of wooden columns) were a significant feature of Cahokia. The largest (seen to the extreme left in FIG. 13-24) had 48 posts forming a circle with a diameter of about 420 feet. Sight lines

between a 49th post set east of the center of the enclosure and points on the perimeter enabled early astronomers to determine solstices and equinoxes.

FLORIDA GLADES CULTURE   In 1895, excavators working in submerged mud and shell mounds off Key Marco on the west coast of Florida made a remarkable discovery: posts carved with birds and animals that had been preserved in the swamps. The large mound called Fort Center, in Glades County, Florida, gives the Florida Glades culture its name.

13-24 RECONSTRUCTION OF CENTRAL CAHOKIA

As it would have appeared about 1150 CE. Collinsville, Illinois. Mississippian culture, c. 1000–1300 CE. East–west length approx. 3 miles (4.82 km), north–south length approx. 2¼ miles (3.6 km); base of great mound 1,037 × 790′ (316 × 241 m), height approx. 100′ (30 m). Monk's Mound is the large platform in the center of the image.

Credit: Painting by William Iseminger, Reconstruction of Central Cahokia Mounds. c. 1150 CE. Courtesy of Cahokia Mounds State Historic Site

13-25 PELICAN FIGUREHEAD
Key Marco, Florida. Florida Glades culture, c. 1000 CE. Wood and
paint, 4⅜ × 2⅜ × 3⅛" (11.2 × 6 × 8 cm). University of Pennsylvania
Museum of Archaeology and Anthropology, Philadelphia.

Credit: Courtesy of the Penn Museum, image #160303

At Key Marco, painted wooden animal and bird
heads, a human mask, and the figure of a kneeling cat-
human were found in circumstances that suggested a
ruined shrine. Recently, carbon-14 dating of these items
has confirmed a date of about 1000 CE. Although the heads
are spare in details, the artists show a remarkable power of
observation in reproducing the creatures they saw around
them, such as the **PELICAN** in **FIGURE 13-25**. The surviving
head, neck, and breast of the pelican are made of carved
wood painted black, white, and gray (other images also
had traces of pink and blue paint). The bird's outstretched
wings were found nearby, but the wood shrank and disintegrated as it dried. Carved wooden wolf and deer heads
were also found. Archaeologists think the heads might
have been attached to ceremonial furniture or posts. Some
see evidence here of a bird and animal cult or perhaps the
use of birds and animals as clan symbols.

The Southwest

Farming cultures were slower to arise in the arid American Southwest, which became home to three major early
cultures. The Hohokam culture, centered in the central and
southern parts of present-day Arizona, emerged around
200 BCE and endured until sometime around 1300 CE. The
Hohokam built large-scale irrigation systems, multi-story
residences, and ballcourts that demonstrate ties with Mesoamerica. The Mimbres/Mogollon culture, located in the
mountains of west-central New Mexico and east-central

Arizona, flourished from about 200 to about 1150 CE. Potters made deep bowls painted with lively, imaginative, and
sometimes complex scenes of humans and animals (**FIG.
13-26**). Much of our knowledge of this ceramic tradition
is based on examples excavated in burials under the floors
of Mimbres dwellings, where food bowls—most of them
intentionally punctured before burial—were inverted and
placed over the head of the deceased. Some experts believe
these perforated bowls could have represented the dome
of the sky and embodied ideas about the transport of the
dead from the earth into the spirit world.

The third southwestern culture, the Ancestral
Puebloans (formerly called Anasazi), emerged around
500 CE in the Four Corners region, where present-day Colorado, Utah, Arizona, and New Mexico meet. The Puebloans
adopted the irrigation technology of the Hohokam and
began building elaborate, multi-storied, apartmentlike
"great houses" with many rooms for specialized purposes,
including communal food storage and ritual.

As in Mimbres culture, Ancestral Puebloan people
found aesthetic expression in their pottery. Women were
the potters in ancient Pueblo society. They developed a
functional, aesthetically pleasing, coil-built earthenware,
or low-fired ceramic, initiating a tradition of ceramic production that continues to be important today among the
Pueblo peoples of the Southwest. One type of vessel, a
wide-mouthed **SEED JAR** with a globular body and holes

13-26 BOWL WITH SCORPIONS
Swarts Ruin, Southwest New Mexico. Mimbres culture, c. 1000–
1150 CE. Earthenware with white slip and black paint, height 4¾"
(12 cm), diameter 11⅝" (29.5 cm). Peabody Museum of Archaeology
and Ethnology, Harvard University.

Credit: © President and Fellows of Harvard College, Peabody Museum of
Archaeology and Ethnology, Harvard University, PM# 24-15-10/94585

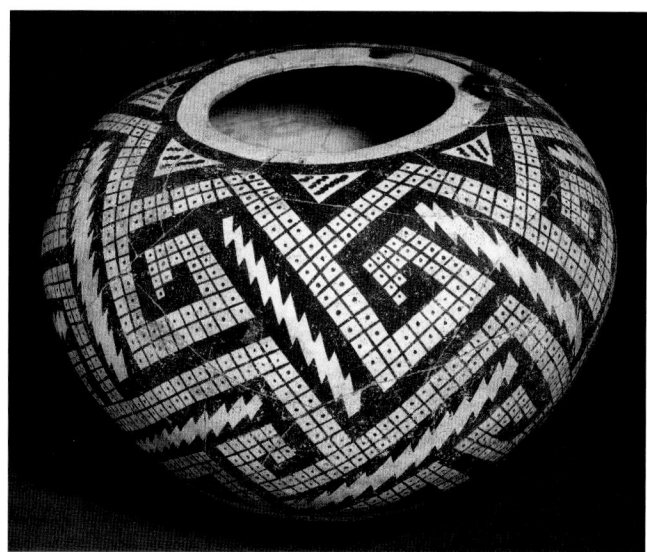

13-27 SEED JAR

Ancestral Puebloan culture, c. 1150 CE. Earthenware with black-and-white pigment, diameter 14½″ (36.9 cm). Saint Louis Art Museum.
Funds given by the Children's Art Festival (175:1981).

near the rim (**FIG. 13-27**), would have been suspended from roof poles by thongs attached to the jar's holes, out of reach of voracious rodents. The example shown here is decorated with black-and-white dotted squares and zig-zag patterns. The patterns conform to the body of the jar, enhancing its curved shape by focusing the energy of the design around its bulging expansion.

CHACO CANYON   Chaco Canyon, covering about 30 square miles in present-day New Mexico with nine great houses, or pueblos, was an important center of Ancestral Puebloan civilization. The largest-known "great house" is a ruin known as **"PUEBLO BONITO"** (**FIG. 13-28**), which was built in stages between the ninth and mid twelfth centuries. Eventually it included over 800 rooms in four or five stories, arranged in a D shape. Within the crescent part of the D, 32 **kivas** recall the round, semi-submerged pit houses of earlier Southwestern cultures. Here men performed religious rituals and instructed youths in their responsibilities. Interlocking pine logs formed a shallow, domelike roof with a hole in the center through which the men entered by climbing down a ladder. Based on what we know of later Pueblo beliefs, a small indentation in the floor of the kiva directly under the entrance and behind the fire pit may have symbolized the "navel of the earth"—the place where ancestors of the Ancestral Pueblo had emerged to settle on the earth in mythic "first times." The top of the kivas formed the floor of the communal plaza.

Pueblo Bonito stood at the hub of a network of wide, straight roads—almost invisible today, but discovered through aerial photography—that radiated out to some 70 other communities. They make no detour to avoid topographic obstacles; when they encounter cliffs, they become stairs. Their undeviating course suggests that they were more than practical thoroughfares: They may have served as processional ways. Given its place at the intersection

13-28 "PUEBLO BONITO"

Chaco Canyon, New Mexico. Ancestral Puebloan culture, 830–1150 CE.

Credit: © Richard A. Cooke/Corbis

13–29 "CLIFF PALACE"
Mesa Verde National Park, Colorado. Ancestral Puebloan culture, c. 1150–1300 CE.

Credit: © MarclSchauer/Shutterstock

of this road system and the prominence of kivas in the design of great houses such as Pueblo Bonito, some have suggested that Chaco Canyon may have been a gathering place or pilgrimage site for people from the entire region at specific times of year.

Though no one knows for certain why Chaco Canyon was abandoned, the Ancestral Puebloan population declined during a severe drought in the mid twelfth century, and building at Pueblo Bonito ceased around 1150. Ancestral Puebloans may have moved to the Rio Grande and Mogollon river valleys, where they built new apartmentlike dwellings on ledges under sheltering cliffs (**FIG. 13–29**). One of the most impressive surviving cliff

dwellings from this period is the "Cliff Palace" in Mesa Verde, Colorado, comprised of 150 rooms and 23 kivas, with an estimated population of about 100. Difficult as it must have been to live high on canyon walls and commute to farm the valley below, the cliff communities had the advantage of being relatively secure. The cliffs also acted as insulation, protecting the dwellings from the extremes of heat and cold that characterize this part of the world. The many rooms housed an entire community comfortably, and close proximity built communal solidarity.

ROCK ART   The rock art of the American Southwest consists of pictographs, which are painted, and petroglyphs,

13–30 ANTHROPOMORPHS
The Great Gallery, Horseshoe (Barrier) Canyon, Utah. c. 1–1000 CE. Largest figure about 8′ (2.44 m) tall.

These may represent holy or priestly figures and are often associated with snakes, dogs, and other small, energetic creatures. Big-eyed anthropomorphs may be rain gods. Painters used their fingers and yucca-fiber brushes to apply the reddish pigment made from hematite (iron oxide).

Credit: © Whit Richardson/Aurora Open/ SuperStock

which are pecked or engraved. While occurring in numerous distinctive styles, rock art images include humans, animals, and geometric figures represented singly and in multi-figured compositions.

In the Great Gallery of Horseshoe Canyon, Utah, the painted human figures have long, decorated rectangular bodies and knoblike heads (**FIG. 13-30**). One large, wide-eyed figure popularly known as the "Holy Ghost" is nearly 8 feet tall. Archaeologists have dated these paintings to about 1,000 to 2,000 years ago; rock art is very difficult to date with any precision.

Petroglyphs are often found in places where the dark brown bacterial growths and staining known as **"desert varnish"** streak down canyon walls. To create an image, the artist scrapes through the layer of varnish, exposing the lighter sandstone beneath. In the petroglyphs of Nine Mile Canyon in central Utah—attributed to the Fremont people (800–1300 CE), who were agriculturists as well as hunters—a large human hunter draws his bow and arrow on a flock of bighorn sheep (**FIG. 13-31**). Other hunters and a large, rectangular, armless figure wearing a horned headdress mingle with the animals. The scene gives rise to the same questions and arguments we have noted with regard to the prehistoric art discussed in Chapter 1: Is this a record of a successful hunt, a ritual activity, or a mythic story?

Throughout the Americas for the next several hundred years artistic traditions would continue to emerge, develop, and be transformed as the indigenous peoples of various regions interacted. But more than anything else, the sudden incursions of Europeans beginning in the late fifteenth century would have a dramatic and lasting impact on these civilizations and their art.

13-31 HUNTER'S MURAL

Nine Mile Canyon, Utah. Fremont people, 800–1300 CE.

Credit: © Ed Warner/Alamy Stock Photo

Think About It

1   Characterize and compare the differing figure styles of paintings from Teotihuacan and Maya culture as seen in **FIGURES 13-9** and **13-3**.

2   Discuss the significance of bloodletting as a recurring theme in early Mesoamerican art, focusing your answer on one specific work of art in this chapter.

3   Evaluate what we can learn about the broad cultural values of Olmec civilization from the figural group (**FIG. 13-1**) that was the subject of the opening discussion in this chapter.

4   Compare the architectural complexes of Teotihuacan and Chaco Canyon. Evaluate the arguments for understanding both of these early monuments of American art as ceremonial sites. What do we know of the rituals that would have been performed in each location?

Crosscurrents

Both of these works, representing activities and relationships critical to royal power, were created in pictorial relief sculpture. Compare the two very different techniques of carving and figural styles. How are style and technique related to the cultural traditions of the time when and place where they were made?

FIG. 3–28

FIG. 13–14

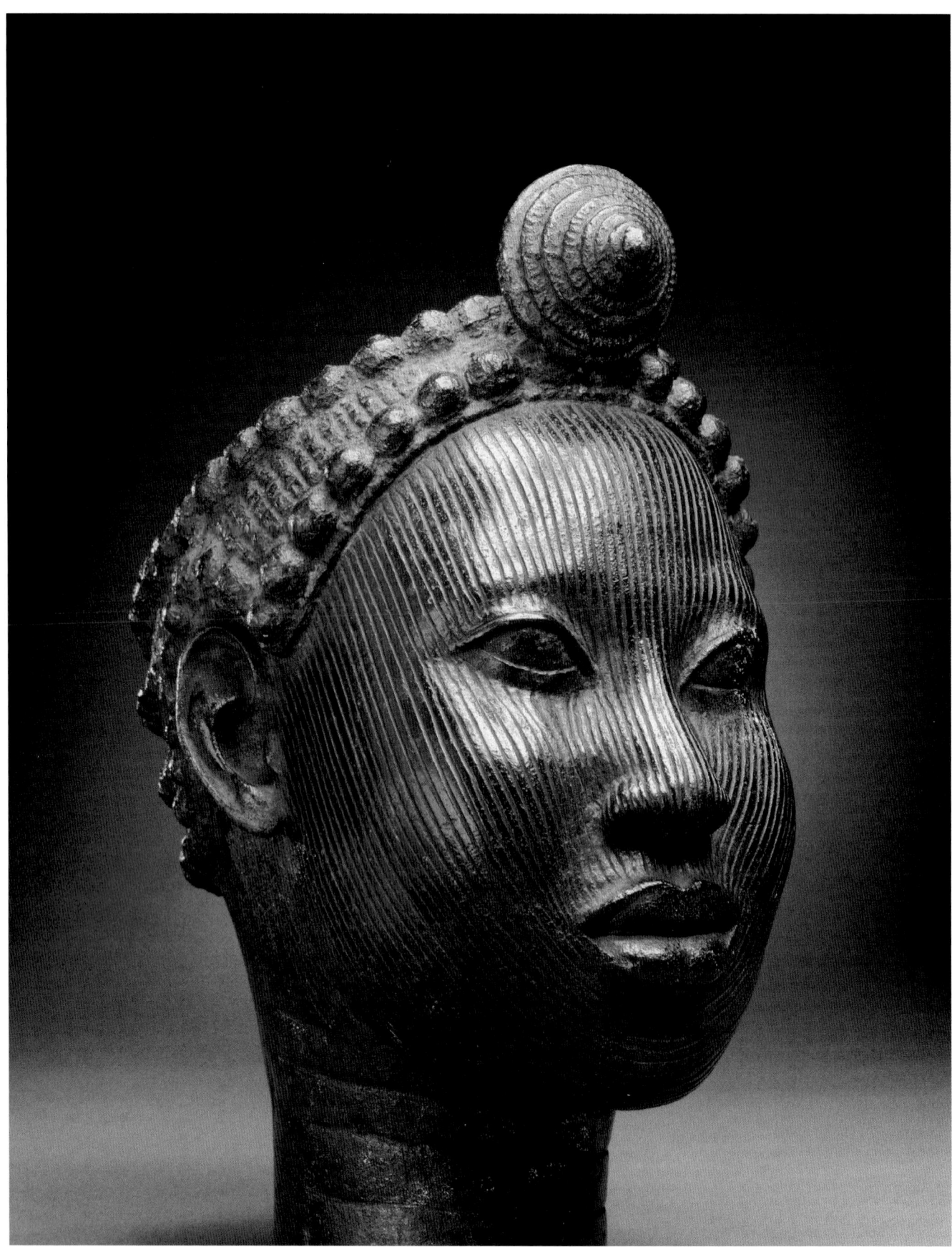

14–1 CROWNED HEAD OF A YORUBA RULER FROM IFE

Nigeria. Yoruba, 12th–15th century CE. Zinc brass, height 9⁷⁄₁₆″ (24 cm). National Commission for Museums and Monuments, Nigeria, Museum of Ife Antiquities.

Chapter 14
Arts of Africa to the Sixteenth Century

 ## Learning Objectives

14.a Identify the visual hallmarks of the art of pre-1600 cultures in Africa for formal, technical, and expressive qualities.

14.b Interpret the meaning of works of pre-1600 cultures in Africa based on their themes, subjects, and symbols.

14.c Relate the art and artists in pre-1600 Africa to their distinct cultural, economic, and political contexts.

14.d Apply the vocabulary and concepts relevant to pre-1600 African art, artists, and art history.

14.e Interpret a work of pre-1600 African art using the art historical methods of observation, comparison, and inductive reasoning.

14.f Select visual and textual evidence in various media to support an argument or an interpretation of a work of pre-1600 African art.

The brass head seen here demonstrates the extraordinary talents of the artist who produced it using the lost-wax casting technique (**FIG. 14–1**). The modeling of the flesh—covered with thin, parallel **scarification** patterns (decorations made by scarring)—is remarkably sensitive, especially the subtle transitions around the nose and mouth.

This head portrays a Yoruba *oni* (king) and could represent either a male or female ruler. The full, delicate lips and expressive eyes bulge organically, stressing the artist's desire to connect human anatomy with the spiritual nature of the *oni*. The *oni* in fact was seen as an intermediary between Yoruba people and the spiritual realms of their gods, ancestors, and demons. The *oni* was understood to live in a human body, but be mostly spirit (or godlike) in nature.

Cast metal heads of kings and queens like the one seen here are part of a sculptural tradition that began in the city of Ife (also known as Ile-Ife) in about 1050 CE in what is today Nigeria. The Yoruba religion regards Ife as the "navel of the world," the site of creation where Ife's first ruler—Oni Oduduwa—came down from heaven to create Earth. By the eleventh century CE, Ife was a lively metropolis. It was, and remains, a sacred city for Yoruba people.

The Yoruba kings at Ife were but a small part of a tremendous series of ancient empires that stretched from West Africa to the central Saharan region (**MAP 14–1**). The Ghana and Akan empires south of the Sahara traded gold with those possessing salt in the north. Mobile populations such as the Fulani in the Sahara region and the Khoekhoe and San in the Kalahari region built wealth in herding domesticated animals across the savanna biomes of the continent. They displayed this wealth on their bodies in the form of elaborately made jewelry and clothing, as well as painstakingly elaborate hairstyles, body art, and patterned skin scarification. Nubian kings along the upper Nile influenced and were influenced by the Egyptian pharaohs farther downriver. Their temples and commemorative statues attest to their political power and artistic might.

By following the trade routes that linked African empires such as the Yoruba to each other and to the lands beyond their continent, we can gain insight into social, cultural, religious, and artistic desires of each region. Undoubtedly more research will lead to new interpretations and better understanding of the myriad of objects produced by Africans from prehistory to today. This is what makes the study of African art so exciting and dynamic, as well as vital to our understanding of art history around the world.

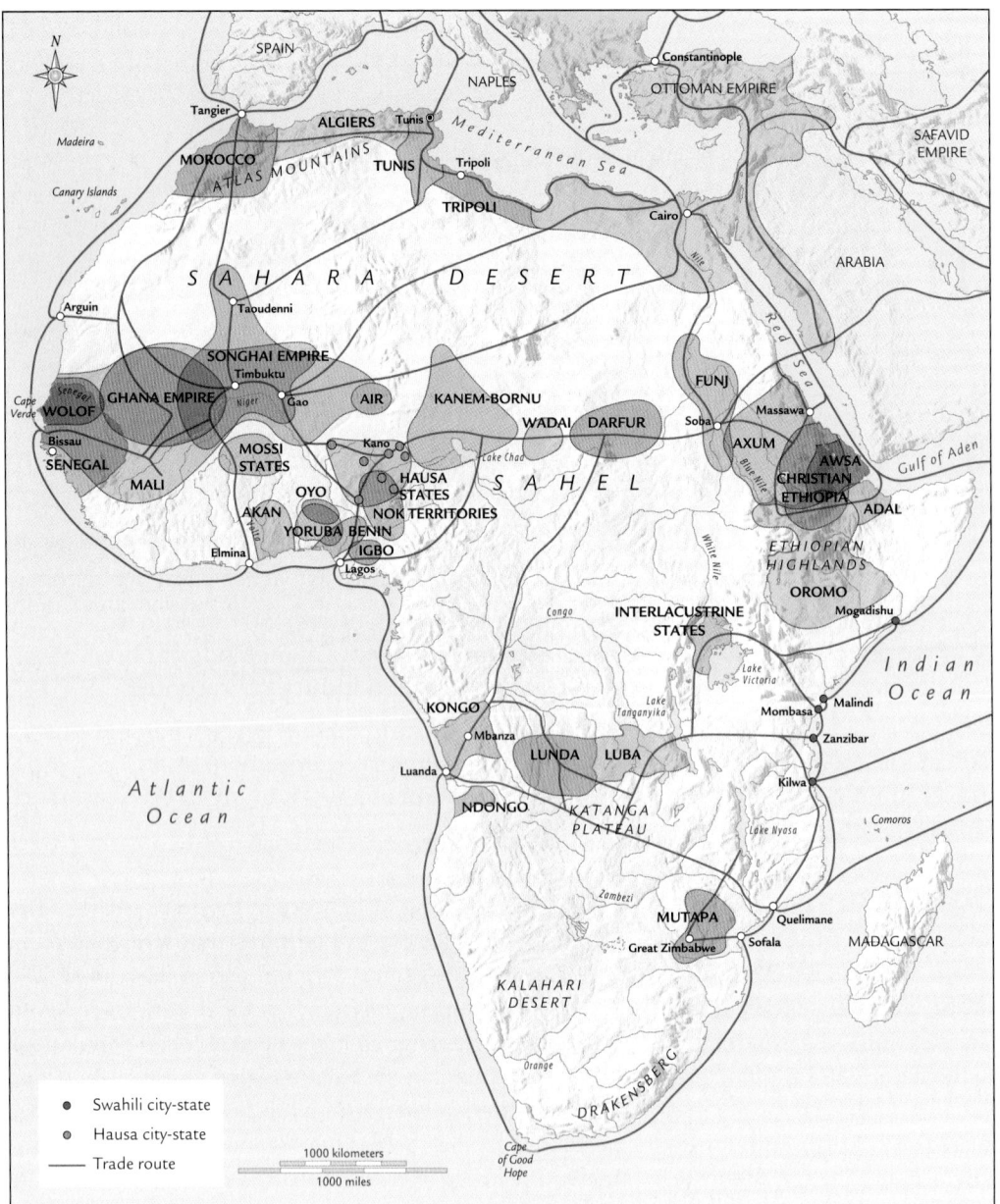

MAP 14-1 INDIGENOUS KINGDOMS IN 11TH–16TH CENTURY AFRICA

The Origins of Art in Africa

How do the prehistoric arts of Africa communicate spirituality, power, and identity?

Africa is a continent with over 54 countries and a twenty-first-century population estimated at 1.2 billion people, who speak more than 2,000 languages and live on a landmass large enough to encompass the entire United States three times over.

With such a sheer volume of cultures, arts, and languages, as well as a chronology going back 80,000 years, this field of study is constantly being updated and expanded, and it improves with each generation of scholarship. This chapter, therefore, can merely introduce some of the early artistic moments and monuments from across the continent of Africa, as we understand them at the beginning of the twenty-first century.

Concepts

Three concepts of great importance are present in the works of art covered in this chapter.

SPIRITUALITY Whether prehistoric or from the 1500s, many works of art are created to honor, harness, or communicate with spiritual forces. Ancient African religions seem to have focused on the spiritual forces of animals and the shamanistic capacities of gifted human individuals to communicate with spirits beyond the visible world.

POWER Massive architectural monuments for religious and political use clearly demonstrate the wealth, engineering expertise, and skill of the populations that built them. Trade networks that date back to prehistoric times created wealth and control for civilizations that were able to dominate the flow of goods from one area to the next.

Individual rulers commissioned works of art and architecture made from local and imported materials to display their control over their own people and their cosmopolitan connections to far-flung regions.

IDENTITY   During these formative centuries, group identity and unity were more important than individual distinction. When rulers commissioned works of art representing people, even themselves, these images more accurately represented the role of their office than the likeness or personality of the individual. Thus "portraits," or personal likenesses of an individual, are not as important as the role of king, shaman, ancestor, historian, dancer, mother, or initiate. Societies were built on the organization of individuals into occupations that served the good of all. Works of art, like the *Crowned Head of a Yoruba Ruler* from Nigeria, represent the ideals of a good king or queen, without copying the particular king or queen's features.

Prehistoric Arts

Images painted on rocks are found throughout the African continent in places where the environment has been conducive to preservation. These rock paintings and engravings date back in some cases to 25,000 BCE. They range from highly abstract geometric designs to naturalistic representations of human and animal forms often arranged to tell stories. These include dramatic hunting scenes, views of domestic family life, and costumed dancing figures.

NAMIBIA AND SOUTH AFRICA   Namibia is a sparsely populated country that is perhaps best known as a haven for safari vacationers and nature enthusiasts. Much of the country is on an elevated plateau that sits between the coastal Namib Desert in the west and the Kalahari Desert to the east. The dry climate has allowed for the preservation of countless works of rock art spread across the plateau, as well as in caves and rocky outcrops. The most famous rock art sites in Namibia are Twyfelfontein in the northwest, which is home to many scenes of herd animals, hunters, and groups of humans both painted and engraved on the rocky and hilly terrain, and the so-called "Apollo 11" cave in the southern part of the country.

The "Apollo 11" cave is the site of the earliest known figurative artworks on the African continent. They are animal figures dating to about 25,000 BCE, painted in red and black pigment on flat stones (**FIG. 14–2**). The stones were found in the late 1960s by archaeologist W.E. Wendt. He named the cave in honor of NASA's Apollo 11 mission, which had just successfully landed astronauts on the moon. While the name he gave to the cave has nothing to do with the ancient plaques he discovered there, it has stuck, and the site still goes by this appellation today.

The small slab seen here, despite being broken in half, contains the readily discernable image of an animal marked on the stone in a charcoal-based pigment. The animal is abstracted, with a large head and elongated thick neck, making it difficult to determine if the painter was attempting to render a specific species. More likely, the artist was attempting to capture the essence or spirit of the animal; in that case, naturalistic depiction would have been unnecessary, and perhaps even undesirable.

In parts of South Africa, the landscape is very similar to that in Namibia, making it home to an equally exciting number of carved and painted images on living rock. The majority of central and western South Africa is desert and semiarid desert, while a rocky escarpment, the

14–2 QUARTZITE SLABS DEPICTING ANIMALS

"Apollo 11" Cave. Namibia. c. 25,000 BCE. State Museum of Namibia, Windhoek.

Credit: Photo: W.E. Wendt. © State Museum of Namibia

14-3 "GAME PASS" SHELTER
Drakensberg, South Africa. San.

Credit: © Ariadne Van Zandbergen/Alamy Stock Photo

Drakensberg Mountain range, runs the length of its eastern region.

Numerous examples of rock painting are found in the Drakensberg Mountains. Almost 600 sites have been located in rock shelters and caves, with approximately 35,000 individual images catalogued. Around 2,400 years ago, ancestors of the San peoples began painting the walls of the Drakensberg cliffs. Ethnographic research among contemporary San people suggests possible interpretations for some of the paintings. For example, scholars have been studying contemporary San rituals performed to heal individuals or to cleanse communities. These ceremonies look very similar to images painted on the rock walls of the Drakensberg range. The San people have also continued their ancestral tradition of rock painting into today, making theirs one of the longest continually practiced art forms in the world.

In the **"GAME PASS" SHELTER** site seen here, the primary subject is a group of eland (a species of large-bodied antelope) with much smaller running and leaping humans positioned above them (**FIG. 14-3**). At its most literal, it is a scene of hunting, with men chasing the herd of eland. However, the artistic treatment of the eland certainly prioritizes them as the subject of this enormous wall painting.

The animals are painted in multiple hues of red, white, brown, and ocher. They overlap each other as well as appearing as solo depictions. The human figures, in contrast, are quite small and painted in only one color.

Game Pass is so named for the paintings along the wall but also for the vantage point it commands over the valley below. From here, hunters could watch undetected the movements of eland herds across the open plains. Most likely the paintings document this strategic viewing point and mark the site as a ritual location for hunters preparing physically and spiritually for the rigors of the hunt.

One small group of figures painted on the walls of Game Pass give proof to this theory. An eland is painted in profile with its rear legs stylized into a cross-legged pose that living animals do not make. A male figure stands behind the animal holding its tail and displaying the same awkward crossed-leg position. To the right of them, three human figures appear in contorted poses, and all the humans are painted with antelope hooves. Scholars interpret these gestures as those of a dying eland with a successful hunter who holds the animal directly while it dies in order to absorb its spiritual power. The three other human figures are interpreted as shamans in the middle of a trance who are also absorbing the spiritual energy of the eland before it dies. The transfer of energy between humans and animals via trance was and remains a vital component of San ritual hunting. Trance is still a respected and feared practice among the San today, who describe it as a ritual "death" that allows humans access to forces beyond their capacities.

ALGERIA To the far north of the African continent, the mountains of the central Sahara Desert—principally the Tassili-n-Ajjer range in the south of present-day Algeria and the Acacus Mountains in present-day Libya—contain painted images that span the years between 8000 and 2000 BCE. They record not only the artistic and cultural development of the peoples who lived in the region, but also the transformation of the Sahara from fertile grassland to the vast desert we know today.

A variety of scenes found on rock walls in southern Algeria and Libya depict men and women dancing or performing various ceremonial activities (**FIG. 14–4**). The artists who created these works paid close attention to details of clothing, body decoration, and headdresses; in some examples the figures are depicted wearing masks that cover their faces. While scholars are still unsure of

their exact meaning, some have suggested the figures are engaged in rituals intended to ensure adequate rainfall or success in hunting, or to honor their dead.

By 4000 BCE the savanna-like climate of the Sahara had become increasingly arid, and hippopotamuses, elephants, giraffes, and antelopes were disappearing from the region (and also as subjects in the rock art paintings of this time). Eventually, hunting gave way to herding as the primary life-sustaining activity of the Sahara's inhabitants. Paintings from Tassili-n-Ajjer dating to this period illustrate men and women gathered in front of round, thatched houses. As the men tend cattle, women prepare meals and care for children.

The continued drying of the Sahara into desert coincided with the rise of Egyptian civilization to the east. Similarities between Egyptian art and Saharan rock art include images of rams with disks between their horns. These were originally interpreted as evidence of Egyptian influence on the Saharan regions. Yet in light of the great age of Saharan rock art, it seems just as plausible that the influence flowed the other way, carried by people who migrated into the Nile Valley when the grasslands of the Sahara disappeared.

14–4 DANCERS IN CEREMONIAL ATTIRE
Section of rock wall painting, Tassili-n-Ajjer, Algeria. c. 5000–2000 BCE.

North and East Africa

What features define the arts and architecture of the distinct cultures of North and East Africa, and what does this tell us about the political power of each culture?

The word "Africa" comes from the name given to a large territory encompassing what is today Tunisia, northern Algeria, and coastal Libya. Named by the Romans in the second century BCE when they annexed the city of Carthage in present-day Tunisia, "Africa Proconsularis" was one part of the much larger Roman Empire that at its height encompassed the entire Mediterranean Sea. Over time the name given to this colony eventually came to represent the entire continent.

Well before Rome folded northern Africa into its empire, the local populations had built sophisticated and long-standing empires and kingdoms. Dynastic and religious rulers in North and East Africa were natural trading partners, making use of trade route connections along the North African coast to Egypt and up the Nile to Nubia (now Sudan), as well as to the Axumite kingdom, which spread from present-day Ethiopia to Yemen and south to Sudan. Mercantile trade, exchange of objects of religious and royal value, and shared architectural technologies created the massive political and religious structures built across the region, many of which can still be seen today.

Ancient Nubia (Sudan)

Inhabited as of 5000 BCE, the lands of Nubia stretched from Khartoum, at the juncture of the Blue and White Nile rivers in what is now Sudan, north to the city of Aswan in present-day Egypt. At Aswan, the Nile is non-navigable due to a series of rapids known as the First Cataract, which served as the historical boundary between Egypt and Nubia. The Egyptians called the kingdom to their south "Kush." Powerful dynastic kings ruled over these lands from 2000 BCE up until the fourth century CE. When the Romans encountered the Kushites, they called them Nubians. Nubia has since been adopted to refer to the region and its inhabitants from 5000 BCE through the sixth century CE.

"I descended [the Nile] with three hundred [donkeys] laden with incense, ebony, grain, panthers, ivory, and every good product." Thus the Egyptian envoy Harkhuf described his return from Nubia in 2300 BCE. The riches of Nubia attracted merchants and envoys in ancient times, and trade brought the region into contact with not only Egyptians, but also Phoenicians, Greeks, and Romans.

THE KINGDOM OF KUSH The Kushite kings and queens established themselves first at the city of Kerma (2000–1650 BCE) and subsequently at the cities of Napata and Meroë. During the Napatan period (800–270 BCE), Nubian kings also assumed control over Egypt, entering the dynastic line of pharaohs around 750 BCE and remaining kings of the combined Nubian and Egyptian kingdoms until around 661 BCE. As a result, the later sculpture and architecture of the Kushite kingdom reflect both Nubian and Egyptian influences.

A **COLOSSAL STATUE OF KING ASPELTA** dating to the Napatan period is one example (**FIG. 14–5**). Aspelta became the King of Kush after the sudden death of his older brother, Anlamani. In the statue, measuring over 10 feet in height, Aspelta assumes a posture seen in Egyptian sculptures of kings (SEE FIG. 3–10): arms held rigidly at the sides and the left leg forward in a striding position.

14–5 COLOSSAL STATUE OF KING ASPELTA
From Jebel Barkal, Sudan. Nubian, Napatan period, 593–568 BCE. Height 130¾" (332.1 cm). Museum of Fine Arts, Boston (23.730), Harvard University/Boston Museum of Fine Arts Expedition 1916.

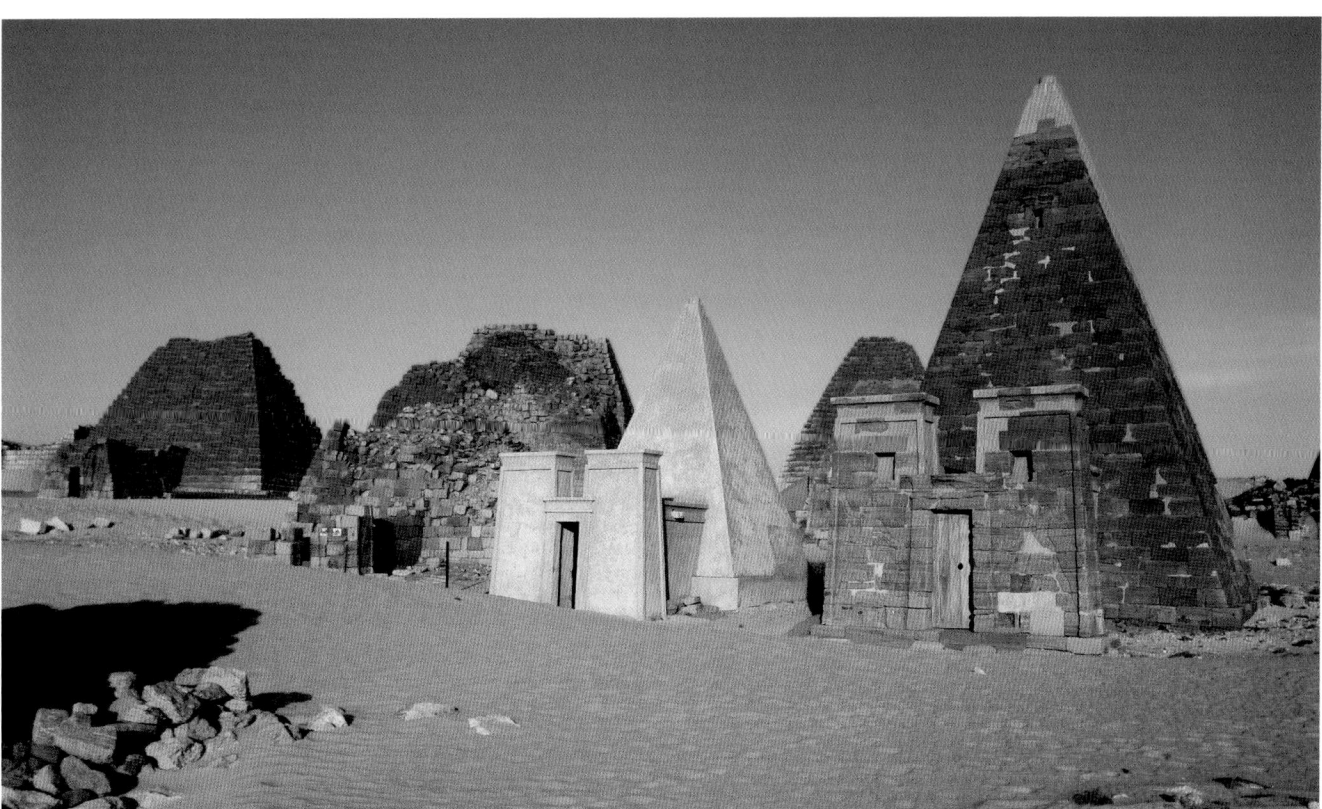

14–6 PYRAMIDS AT MEROË

Sudan. Nubian, 337 BCE–339 CE.

The damage seen to the pyramids in the background of this photograph was caused by looters and European explorers in the nineteenth century who dynamited the structures looking for the burial chambers and the troves of gold and valuable objects buried with each king and queen. Note that the two smaller pyramids at the front have been restored in modern times with lighter colored stone to distinguish the rebuilt sections from the original structures.

Credit: Robnaw/Fotolia

The sculptural treatment of the eyes also resembles Egyptian imagery with thick raised lines outlining the pupil. However, the designations that show him to be the king of Napata are Nubian. He wears a close-fitting cap on his head, and carved in low relief around his neck is a loop of cord that drapes over the front of each shoulder. These regalia are different than those used for Egyptian kings. Aspelta appears to have been the last Nubian king elected at the city of Napata. After his reign the Nubian kings moved farther south to establish their reign at the city of Meroë.

The Nubian **PYRAMIDS AT MEROË** were constructed between 337 BCE and 339 CE (**FIG. 14-6**) They are burial temples for Nubian rulers, both kings and queens. A clearly Nubian feature is the H-shaped entrance gateway known as a *bekhenet* in front of each burial pyramid. These sit in front of each major temple structure and symbolize the passage between the human realm and the world of the gods. The coffin containing the deceased king or queen would be moved through the doorway of the *bekhenet* into a small, rectangular tunnel that connected to the funerary chamber deep inside the pyramid behind it. While the use of a pyramid as a burial chamber is of ancient Egyptian influence, these are modified by Kushite architects to

distinguish them from those to the north. The pyramids at Meroë are not nearly as large as those in Giza, Egypt, for example, and they are narrower, shaped like isosceles triangles. In addition, each course of brickwork is slightly inset from the row beneath, creating horizontal ridges, unlike the smooth façades preferred by Egyptian pharaohs.

Ethiopia

Ethiopia's role in the history of humanity from prehistoric times to the present is unparalleled. This region is where our species, *homo sapiens*, first emerged; some of the oldest languages and alphabetic scripts in the world came from here; and it was home to some of the earliest incarnations of Christianity and Islam.

Ethiopia was a major contributor to the civilizations of the ancient world, including Greece, Egypt, Rome, Byzantium, and Arabia. In the second century BCE the kings in the Ethiopian highlands increased their importance through their control of trade routes from the African interior to the Red Sea port of Adulis. The city of Axum generated wealth for its kings by exporting ivory, gold, enslaved peoples, frankincense, myrrh, and salt. These ancient connections to vast swaths of human civilization have left a rich legacy in Ethiopia. Its people speak over 80 languages, and their written languages include the ancient Ge'ez (also Gə'əz) and Amharic scripts, both still in use today. Ethiopia was the sole territory on the African continent able to avoid territorial annexation by European nations during the colonial conquest. As a result, the colors of its flag—red, yellow, and green—were used by other African nations when they achieved independence from Europe in the mid twentieth century.

EARLY CHRISTIANITY In the mid fourth century CE the Axumite king Ezana converted to Christianity. His conversion made Axum only the second politically Christian region in the world after Armenia, whose king Tiridates had converted his court in 301 CE.

The power and influence of the kings of Axum were only diminished by the displacement of the Red Sea trade routes after the Persian conquest of south Arabia, which among other things disrupted pilgrimage routes between Ethiopia and Jerusalem (the holy city revered by Christians, Jews, and Muslims). Subsequently, the Zagwe from Ethiopia's western highlands conquered Axum around 960 CE.

LIVING ROCK CHURCHES In the mid twelfth century, Gebre (king) Mesqel Lalibela, a dynastic Zagwe ruler, wished to create a "new" Jerusalem in Ethiopia. He founded a holy site, which he named Lalibela after himself, in the highlands south of Axum. The numerous rock-hewn sanctuaries that were created in the hills above the city of Lalibela date from about 1181 to 1221. Rather than being built from the ground up, the churches and secondary structures were carved down from the ground level into living volcanic rock called tuff. In total, 11 churches were carved in close proximity to each other, creating a remarkable destination for Christian pilgrimages. UNESCO has declared all 11 churches at Lalibela a World Heritage Site.

BIETE GHIORGIS (CHURCH OF ST. GEORGE) possesses the most unique floor plan of the group, being in the shape of a square orthodox cross (**FIG. 14-7**). In order to construct it, a wide trench was first cut around what would become the 12 sides of the cross-shaped church. Stonemasons then carved out the windows on the uppermost level of the sanctuary and used these openings as a means by which to excavate the stone material from the inside ceiling of the church. Work progressed in this way

14-7 BIETE GHIORGIS (CHURCH OF ST. GEORGE)
Lalibela, Ethiopia. 13th century CE. Volcanic rock.
Credit: Milosk50/Fotolia

from roof to interior ceiling down through the levels of the structure until the desired "height" was reached. Finally the doors and windows of the ground-floor entry level could be carved. Then the exterior courtyard was widened and access tunnels dug to allow pilgrims and priests to enter the church. This top-down construction meant that each aspect of the structure had to be planned with precision before work could begin. The interior of the church is topped with a hemispherical domed ceiling in the style of the Byzantine churches that Ethiopian priests would have been familiar with from their pilgrimages to Jerusalem. This dome contains a large square cross carved in low relief, which mirrors a cross carved directly above it on the roof of the church. The exterior cross, while decorative, also serves in a drainage capacity: The channels formed by its sides carry water to the four downspouts at each side of the roof.

MANUSCRIPT ARTS Due to their long-standing connections with the ancient Christian world in the Middle East and then Byzantium and Rome, Ethiopian monks and monastic scribes most likely began using illuminated manuscripts from the moment the Axumite dynasty converted to Christianity in the fourth century. While their earliest texts do not survive, the scribes' practice of copying older manuscripts when they fell into disrepair means that many of the thirteenth- to twentieth-century manuscripts hearken back centuries in their texts and designs. We know that manuscripts from Byzantium and Rome were housed in Ethiopian repositories, while Ethiopian illuminated books also traveled to major Christian centers in Europe. Some Ethiopian Christian texts, such as **EUSEBIUS'S LETTER TO CARPIANUS**, illuminated by Mätre Krestos, were modeled on Byzantine predecessors (**FIG. 14–8**). However, these were always translated from the Greek or Latin into the local language of Ge'ez. Ge'ez remains the liturgical language of the Ethiopian Orthodox Church and is still the primary language used for religious documents.

Eusebius of Caesarea (c. 260–339 CE) was a Roman theologian and scholar who became Bishop of Caesarea (a coastal Roman city in the contemporary country of Israel). Among his most famous contributions to Christianity was his system of dividing the four Christian Gospels into canon tables, in order to identify where the four authors converged or diverged on their narrations of the life of Christ. In an important letter to a fellow Christian by the name of Carpianus, Eusebius explained how to use his table system.

From the time of its writing until about the fifteenth century, Eusebius's letter was often copied in Latin, Greek, or, in this case, Ge'ez at the beginning of illuminated manuscripts of Gospel books. After the letter, the canon tables would be presented, followed by pictures of the evangelists and scenes from the life of Christ.

14–8 Mätre Krestos **EUSEBIUS'S LETTER TO CARPIANUS**
Gospel book. Tegray, northern Ethiopia. Early 14th century CE. Ink and pigment on parchment. The Walters Art Museum, Baltimore. Museum purchase with funds provided by the W. Alton Jones Foundation Acquisition Fund, 1996.

Mätre Krestos was a fourteenth-century monastic scribe in Tegray, in northern Ethiopia. His illuminations of Eusebius's letter and canon tables occupy 10 pages in his 248-page manuscript. Krestos had access to centuries-old Byzantine manuscripts, and some scholars believe his gospel is based on a sixth-century text that he may have used for reference. Like the earlier Byzantine models, Krestos uses a rounded arch to frame both the letter seen here and the canon tables that follow it. Surrounding the arch and its columns are birds of varying sizes. Birds were a favorite image in Ethiopian manuscripts, referring to the idea that the Holy Spirit took the form of a dove. Birds also appear in Early Christian versions of the Eusebian canon tables, a clear example of the convergence of local Ethiopian artistic preferences with those of early Christianity.

Tunisia

Present-day Tunisia is home to an extraordinarily long history of cultures. Berbers have been the area's inhabitants since prehistory. In the first millennium BCE, they were joined by Phoenicians, who established the ancient city of Carthage in 814 BCE. The Romans followed in the second century BCE, only to fall to the Byzantine Empire in 534 CE. Their leadership gave way to the Islamic conquest, which created the territory of Ifriqiya in the seventh century CE. Ifriqiya fell to the Ottoman Empire in the sixteenth century, the Ottomans fell to the French in 1881, and the French were forced out in 1956. Tunisia today bears both scars and glories from this history, and the Berbers are still a dynamic and powerful population in the area, as they were during and between all of the above political regimes. In 2010, the Tunisian revolution launched the Arab Spring, resulting in the Tunisian people taking the lead role in the movement toward democratic governance across North Africa.

ROMAN RUINS   Rome established its first colony in Tunisia in 146 BCE. Roman colonization of what is today Morocco, Algeria, Tunisia, Libya, and Egypt expanded until 117 CE and lasted intact until the end of the third century CE.

Around 238 CE, the aging Gordian I and his son, Gordian II, assumed dual control over the Roman colony of Africa Proconsularis and ordered the construction of a large **AMPHITHEATER AT EL JEM** (called Thysdrus by the Romans) to replace a smaller structure deemed insufficient (**FIG. 14–9**). The new amphitheater was to hold 35,000 spectators (although it arguably could have held almost double that) and was modeled on the Flavian Amphitheater (the Colosseum) in Rome (SEE FIGS. 6–37, 6–38). It is oval in form, four stories high, and measures 453 feet long by 374 feet wide. While smaller than the Colosseum, it was the largest amphitheater built by Rome on the African continent, and had it been completed, it would have rivaled the Colosseum in grandeur and capabilities.

The amphitheater at El Jem was never completed, however, because Gordian I suffered a military defeat at

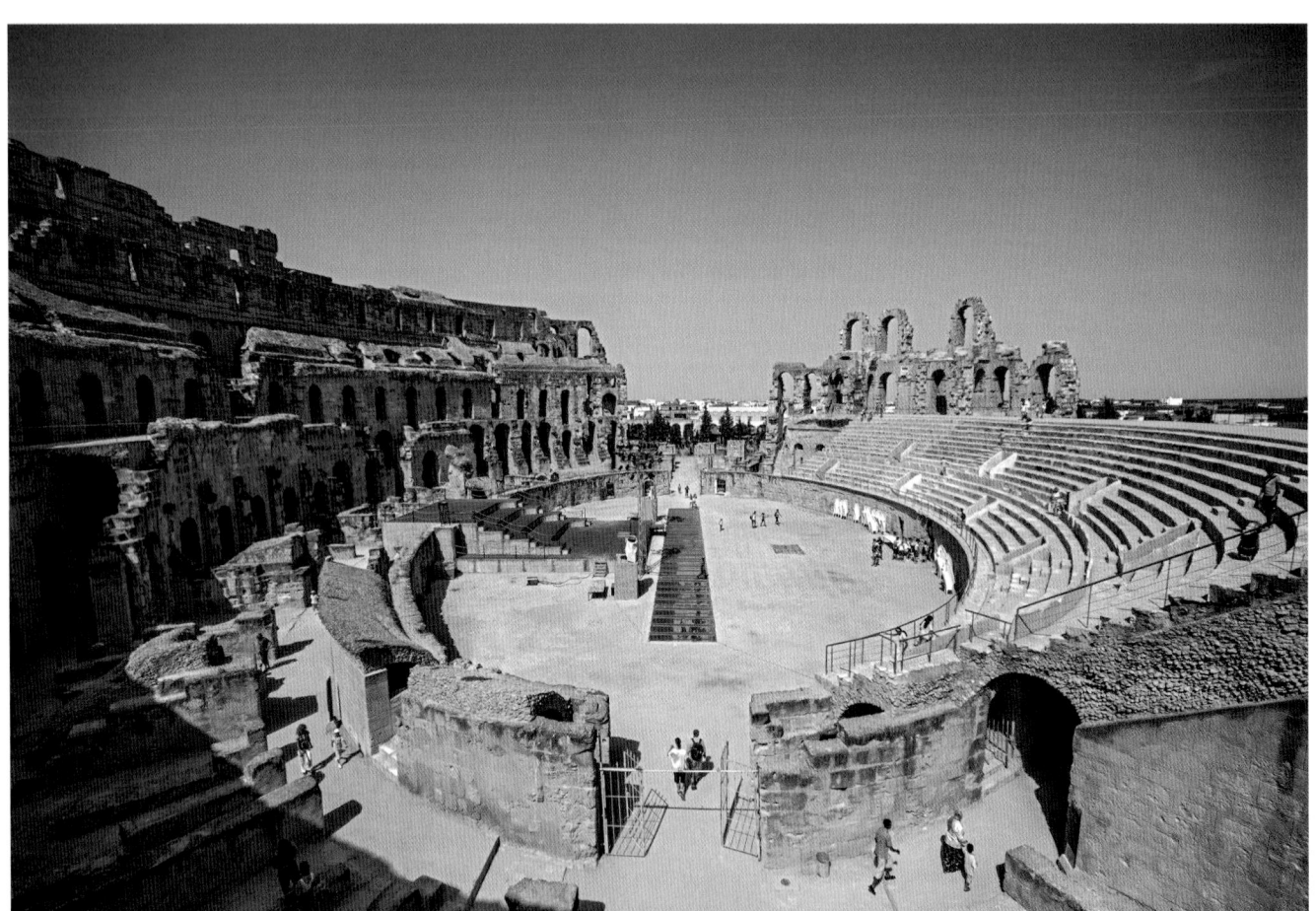

14–9 ROMAN AMPHITHEATER AT EL JEM
Tunisia. c. 238 CE (never completed).

After the fall of the Roman Empire in North Africa, the El Jem amphitheater was used as a fortress and citadel by various clashing groups up through the seventeenth century. Damage to the amphitheater from cannon fire is still visible as a result. What remains of the amphitheater is well preserved, and UNESCO named it a World Heritage Site in 2010.

14–10 Ziadet-Allah I **GREAT MOSQUE OF KAIROUAN**
Tunisia. 836–875 CE.

Credit: Palmenpe/Fotolia

Carthage (the capital of the African colony) one month after assuming office and committed suicide. A rapid succession of Roman leaders came and went for the African colony. The North African chaos was surpassed only by greater chaos elsewhere in the Roman Empire, resulting in the eventual division of the empire into two parts.

ISLAMIC ARCHITECTURE The arrival of Islam in North Africa came as a result of long-standing trade routes along the Silk Road from China to southern Europe and sub-Saharan Africa. As the Middle East converted to follow the teachings of the prophet Muhammad in the seventh century, Arab traders in the region, who largely controlled the Silk Road trade through the Middle East, North Africa, and the western Mediterranean, brought their faith with them into North Africa. As the populations of northern Africa converted to the new religion, the need arose for both small neighborhood mosques (*masjid*) for prayers and large congregational or Friday mosques (*jama masjid*) for communal prayer and celebration.

There are no specific dictates in the Qur'an as to what a mosque must look like, only what it must achieve: a respectful, non-distracting space for prayer and purification. As a result, much religious architecture, whether in Tunisia or elsewhere, follows local architectural styles and material preferences.

The **GREAT MOSQUE OF KAIROUAN** (**FIG. 14–10**) sits in the center of the religious city of Kairouan, which was founded in 670 CE by Uqba Ibn Nafi, an Arab general for the Umayyad Caliphate. The mosque was largely constructed between 836 and 875 CE, although it replaced a series of smaller mosques on the site going back to the original built by Uqba Ibn Nafi himself in 670. As it was conceived in 836 by Ziadet-Allah I, then emir of the ruling Aghlabid dynasty in Ifriqiya, the mosque has a hypostyle plan that follows an irregular rectangular format. It is built from local stone quarried and cut to look like bricks. Large arcades form bays and galleries surrounding a central open courtyard; this is derived from what the house of Prophet Muhammad is believed to have looked like in plan.

One of the most unusual features of this mosque is its reuse of marble and porphyry columns from antiquity. Columns in the prayer hall and courtyard are of Roman manufacture and were taken from Carthage and other sites. The columns are topped by capitals that do not always match the columns themselves; they came from various Roman and Byzantine temples that were dismantled during the seventh century. The columns are placed in pairs throughout, supporting the massive round arches of the arcades. Upon first glance, the arches also appear to be Roman in design, but they are actually modified in two substantial ways. Some are slightly pointed at the top, which allowed for the architect to span greater distances at a greater height, and all curve slightly inward at their bases where they meet the capitals of their columns. Each arch therefore looks like the letter C turned on its side: These are known as horseshoe arches. The mosque at Kairouan made the horseshoe arch synonymous with Islamic architecture as it was copied for centuries afterward and around the world. A dome sits on squinches at the *mihrab* wall of the mosque; this feature is both Byzantine and Islamic in origin.

The Great Mosque of Kairouan is the oldest surviving mosque on the African continent, and it bears remarkable witness to ninth-century changes in northern Tunisia. Kairouan was the founding capital city of Ifriqiya and the seat of the Aghlabid dynasty for the entirety of the ninth century. The mosque documents the Islamic victory over Roman and Byzantine empires, because it literally was built from their remains. Yet, at the same time, respect for the architectural traditions of earlier inhabitants of the area is obvious, as great care was taken to preserve the ancient columns and to use the local stone to tie the building to the indigenous history of this sacred site.

West and Central Africa

What are the features of West and Central African arts that reflect the societies and religions that produced them?

Historically, the Western and Central coastal cultures of the African continent have been the most well known to art historians. This is because of their long-standing contact with European nations, beginning during the fifteenth century, at the height of the European Renaissance. Art history and anthropology did not emerge as academic disciplines until the eighteenth century in Europe, as part of the Age of Enlightenment. By then, Europe's connections to West and Central Africa were 300 years old, and the arts of these areas formed the largest part of European art historical and anthropological research inquiries. Prior to the 1960s, in fact, a visit to any European or American art museum would reveal "African art" collections that were primarily the arts of Nigeria, the Ivory Coast, Sierra Leone, the Congo/Angola region, and Gabon. Greater surveys of the larger continent and the arts of northern, eastern, and southern Africa would not come until the end of the twentieth century and are still areas of growth for museum collection and display to this day.

That being said, the arts of West and Central Africa date back to well before the Common Era, and they are as diverse in nature as the cultures that produced them. Aesthetic objects in West and Central Africa served many societal needs: Some were for religious use; some were to honor ancestors and kings; some honored group identity, recorded history or promoted community; and some were for personal adornment and ornamentation. West and Central Africa hosted several of the major early kingdoms and empires on the African continent, including some of the wealthiest in the world during their time.

Mali

One of the first empires established in the territory now known as the Republic of Mali was the Ghana Empire that emerged in the fourth century CE; it ruled a large swath of what is now southern Mali, eastern Senegal, and southern Mauritania (SEE MAP 14–1). In the thirteenth century the Ghana Empire fell to the strengthening Mali Empire, from which the current country claims its name. Yet a third major empire arose here: The Songhai Empire dominated the area in the fifteenth through sixteenth centuries. Together these three empires were among the richest and most powerful the continent has ever known.

Islam had arrived very early in the ninth century due to the trade routes connecting the area to the northern Sahara empires. Rulers of the tenth-century Ghana Empire, as well as those of the subsequent Mali and Songhai empires, embraced the tradition. The cities of Timbuktu, Djenne, Gao, and Kano were early centers of Islamic learning and research in West Africa, roles they still occupy today.

GREAT MOSQUE OF DJENNÉ Archaeologists have determined that the city of Djenné was established by the third century CE, and that by the middle of the ninth century it had become a major urban center. Koi Konboro, the 26th king of Djenné, converted to Islam in the thirteenth century and transformed his palace into a huge mosque built from adobe brick (a sun-dried mixture of clay, mud, and dry fill). With its great surrounding wall and tall towers, locals claimed it was more beautiful and more lavishly decorated than the Kaaba, the central shrine of Islam, at Mecca.

Konboro's mosque eventually attracted the attention of austere Muslim rulers who objected to its sumptuous furnishings. Among these was the early nineteenth-century ruler Sekou Amadou, who destroyed the mosque by plugging the drains built to direct rain away from the fragile adobe surface. A few rainy seasons were all it took to melt the mosque into the ground. In the meantime, Amadou erected a new mosque nearby. But he and his followers were soon forced out of Mali by French colonial leaders, and the local community returned to Konboro's vision of a grand mosque at its original site. The current mosque, constructed between 1906 and 1907, sits on the ancient site and is of adobe construction in the style of the original (**FIG. 14–11**). Architect Ismaila Traoré, the head of

14–11 Ismaila Traoré (lead architect) and the Djenné Mason's Guild **GREAT MOSQUE AT DJENNÉ**
Eastern and northern façades. Mali. 1906–1907 CE.

The plan of the mosque is not quite rectangular. Inside, nine rows of heavy adobe columns, each 33′ (10 m) tall and linked by pointed arches, support a flat ceiling of palm logs, which is covered by adobe slip with raised conical air vents on the roof. A great double wall encloses an open courtyard on the west side (seen at the back right of the image). The main entrances to the men's prayer hall are in the north wall (to the right of the photograph).

Credit: Africanway/Fotolia

the Djenné **guild** (an artisans' organization) of masons, supervised the reconstruction.

The mosque's finials, or crowning ornaments, at the top of each tower are taken from Malian pre-Islamic shrine architecture and are symbols of fertility and purity. The façade and sides of the mosque are distinguished by tall, narrow engaged buttresses, which support the heavy arcades of the interior prayer hall. A significant feature of this mosque, and one incorporated into West African adobe architecture in general, is the **toron**: a wooden beam that projects from the exterior walls. Torons provide permanent supports for the wooden scaffolding erected each year so that the exterior of the mosque can be replastered. In addition they provide aesthetic interest, for they not only produce shadows that striate the surface of the mosque over the course of the day, but also break up the flat austerity of the windowless adobe walls.

CERAMICS   At a site near Djenné known as Djenné-Djenno or Old Jenné, excavations by both archaeologists and looters have uncovered hundreds of terra-cotta figures dating from the thirteenth to the sixteenth century. The figures were polished, covered with a red clay slip, and fired at a low temperature.

A **HORSEMAN** sculpture armed with a quiver, arrows, and a dagger is a good example of the technique (**FIG. 14-12**). The rider and his horse were formed from coils of rolled clay, which were then smoothed together. The details of the face, clothing, and harness were subsequently carved, engraved, and painted on the figure prior to firing. The rider has a long, oval head and jutting chin; pointed oval eyes set in multiple framing lids; and a long, straight nose. He wears short pants and a helmet with a chinstrap, and his horse has an ornate bridle. Such elaborate trappings suggest that the horseman could be a guardian figure, hero, or even a deified ancestor.

To reduce the illegal looting and trading of these ceramics on the international art market, archaeologists have worked with the Malian government to put strict rules into place preventing them from being exported under any circumstances. Public museums and private collectors are now wrestling with the problem of

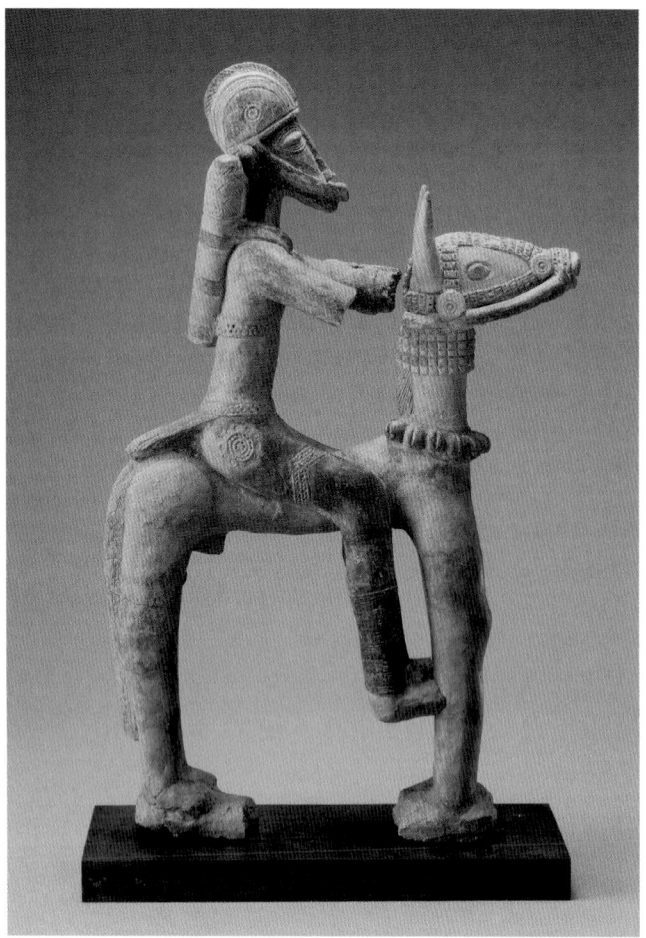

14–12 HORSEMAN

From Djenné-Djenno (Old Djenné), Mali. 13th–15th century CE. Terra cotta, height 27¾" (70.5 cm). National Museum of African Art, Smithsonian Institution, Washington, DC. Museum Purchase (86.12.2).

Credit: Photo: Franko Khoury

determining if their Djenné-Djenno ceramics were looted, bought, or sold illegally, in which case they would need to be returned to Mali.

Nigeria

Nigeria today is the most populous nation on the continent, with over 181 million people. Perhaps startlingly, considering its small size relative to other global nations, it is also the eighth most populous nation in the world. More than 250 ethnic groups are documented within its borders, and Nigerians cumulatively speak over 500 indigenous languages, with Hausa, Yoruba, Igbo (Ibo), and Fulani being the most widespread.

Historically, the Yoruba (pronounced YOR-u-ba) claim earliest settlement of the area; it is believed that the Yoruba language in fact goes back to the first millennium BCE. Small, archaeologically well-known cities such as Nok and Igbo-Ukwu were also present in the first millennium, but the Yoruba were the first to organize into a kingdom with far-reaching power and religious influence. Their capital,

Ife, was founded in the eighth century CE. It was a religious, linguistic, and artistic center from its inception, and the arts it produced influenced every subsequent society in the area—in particular, the Edo kingdom (thirteenth through nineteenth centuries) based at Benin City to the south of Ife.

ANCIENT NOK Nok is a small town in the geographic center of Nigeria. Masterful clay sculptures of humans have been—and continue to be—found here, as well as in neighboring regions. Many of the objects were not archaeologically excavated, however, and thus our knowledge of their creation and function remains very limited. During the 1950s, local miners digging for tin uncovered hundreds of broken pieces from ceramic figures of humans and animals. Two types of dating, carbon-14 and thermoluminescence, subsequently fixed the ages of the Nok ceramics to between 800 BCE and 600 CE, with most dating to a briefer window from about 500 BCE to the very beginning of the Common Era. These dates make the Nok ceramics some of the oldest artworks from West Africa

Nok ceramics range from miniatures to over-life-size figures, and this head is the latter (**FIG. 14-13**). Most remains are broken; scholars believe that heads like this

14–13 HEAD

From Nok, Nigeria. 500 BCE–200 CE. Terra cotta, height 14³⁄₁₆" (36 cm). National Museum Lagos, Nigeria.

Credit: Werner Forman Archive/National Museum, Lagos, Nigeria. Location: 02.

were originally attached to complete bodies either in wood or ceramic. The triangular or D-shaped eyes are characteristic of Nok style and also appear on sculptures of animals. Holes in the pupils, nostrils, and mouth allowed air to pass freely when the figure was fired.

IGBO-UKWU Located in southern Nigeria, the cultural heartland of the Igbo people, Igbo-Ukwu is one of the oldest archaeological sites in West Africa. To date, only three sites at Igbo-Ukwu have been archaeologically excavated: a burial for an important ruler, a storehouse of valued objects, and a midden (trash pit). These excavations revealed that bronze casting was a developed, specialized, and highly important method of art production in the region from as early as the ninth century. All objects recovered from these excavations are now in important museum collections around the world, foremost among them the National Museum in Lagos, Nigeria.

Like a number of other objects excavated at Igbo-Ukwu, the **ROPED POT ON A STAND** (**FIG. 14–14**) is a **skeuomorph**, an object created in a different material from an original but made to resemble it in form, shape, or texture. Scholars assume that the original item upon which this skeuomorph is based was a water vessel, made in ceramic, tied to a basketry or wooden base. Here, the object is made entirely of leaded bronze. The "rope" is nonfunctional, as the vessel is welded to its base, but its presence is required in order to refer to the original that this object replicates.

The vessel was made during the ninth or tenth century using the lost-wax method, although latex was most likely used instead of wax in this case. When it was found in the 1960s, scholars and artists debated for years whether it had been made from a single mold or cast in parts and soldered together. Microscopic analysis finally revealed that the flaring neck of the vessel (just below the rim) and the lower half of the pot stand were cast separately. Molten metal was then applied to the edges of the separate castings to join them. The knotted rope element was also cast separately and then slid over the vessel before the rim and lower half of the stand were attached to the pot.

Techniques for hammering and plating were known to the artists at Igbo-Ukwu, but they did not use them. Clearly, what was important to the culture at Igbo-Ukwu in the ninth and tenth centuries was to possess a unique, virtuoso style of cast-bronze metalwork that mimicked natural forms.

EDO KINGDOM AT BENIN CITY Benin City is a long-standing royal city in Nigeria. It is not to be confused with the present-day country of Benin (formerly Dahomey), which lies to the west of Nigeria. The population that has inhabited Benin City since at least the tenth century CE speaks Edo. They organized a sophisticated kingdom under the *oba* (king) Ogiso around 900, and a second

14–14 ROPED POT ON A STAND
From Igbo-Ukwu, Nigeria. 9th–10th century CE. Leaded bronze, height 12¹¹⁄₁₆″ (32.3 cm). National Museum Lagos, Nigeria.

Credit: Photo © Dirk Bakker/Bridgeman Images

powerful dynasty arose under the warrior-king Eweka I in the thirteenth century. Eweka I is credited with bringing Benin City to the height of its power. From the twelfth through nineteenth centuries, in fact, Benin City was an internationally renowned sacred city, as well as the political capital of the Edo Empire. In the fifteenth and sixteenth centuries, three important *oba*, Ewuare, Ozolua, and Esigie, ignited an artistic revival in their capital. Thousands of art objects in cast brass, ivory, wood, and red ocean coral were created during their reigns. Many of the objects remaining to us from Benin City date to these centuries.

New research suggests that Oba Esigie (ruled 1517–1550s) and his son, Oba Orhogbua (ruled 1550s–1570s), commissioned the major group of decorative brass plaques that once adorned columns in the court chamber used by the *oba* and their retinues in the royal palace. The chamber was rectangular, with solid outer walls and a covered arcade supported by rectangular columns. The center of

Technique

LOST-WAX CASTING

In the lost-wax casting process a metal copy is produced from an original image made of wax. The usual metals for this casting process are bronze, an alloy of copper and tin, and brass, an alloy of copper and zinc. First, the sculptor models a wax original. Then the wax is dipped into clay slip and packed with hard clay to make a heat-resistant mold. Next, the wax is melted, leaving an empty cavity into which molten metal is poured. After the metal cools and solidifies, the mold is broken away and the metal copy is chased (trimmed of excess metal) and polished.

The progression of drawings here shows the steps used by the Benin sculptors of Africa. A heat-resistant "core" of clay (A) approximating the shape of the sculpture-to-be (and eventually becoming the hollow inside the sculpture) was covered by a

layer of wax that had the thickness of the final sculpture. The sculptor carved or modeled (B) the details in the wax. Rods and a pouring cup made of wax (C) were attached to the model. A thin layer of fine, damp sand was pressed very firmly into the surface of the wax model, and then model, rods, and cup were encased in thick layers of clay (D). When the clay was completely dry, the mold was heated (E) to melt out the wax. The mold was then placed upside down in the ground to receive the molten metal (F). When the metal was completely cool, the outside clay cast and the inside core were broken up and removed (G), leaving the cast-brass sculpture. Details were polished to finish the piece, which could not be duplicated because the mold had been destroyed.

clay core
A

wax
tool
B

layer of clay
layer of fine sand
wax rods (drains) and wax cup
C

D

E
draining wax

molten metal
F

G
finished cast

the room was open to the sky. More than 850 brass plaques in two sizes were produced for this chamber using the lost-wax casting method. Wide plaques were hung on the sides of the columns that faced the *oba* as he sat at the end of his audience hall on a dais, as well as on the

opposite sides of the columns, where they faced visitors as they entered. A second set of narrow plaques hung on the sides of the columns that faced the side walls of the *oba*'s court, visible to those gathered along the walls to witness the audiences held by the *oba*. In this manner, each

14–15 PALACE PLAQUE OF A WAR CHIEF, WARRIORS, AND ATTENDANTS
Benin City Kingdom, Nigeria. Edo, 17th century CE. Brass, height 14¾ × 15½″ (37.5 × 39.4 cm). The Nelson-Atkins Museum of Art, Kansas City, Missouri. Purchase: William Rockhill Nelson Trust (58.3).

of the columns was covered on all four sides, floor to ceiling, with plaques presenting a visual narrative of Esigie and Orhogbua, their courtiers, and the organization of Benin City royal society.

In the plaque seen here a warrior and his attendants are shown in service to the *oba*. The central figures on the plaque are in such high relief that they approach sculpture-in-the-round (**FIG. 14–15**). They are prominently raised from a textured background of foliate patterns representing four-petaled water flowers, the symbol of the water god Olokun, the patron deity of the *oba*.

The plaque uses hierarchical scale, which should not be confused with perspectival distance (in which objects

that are far away are represented as smaller than those that are close to the viewer). The warrior chief is larger in size and in the center of the composition, as he is more important than the figures that accompany him. He holds a spear in one hand and in the other an *eben* sword, a distinctive leaf-shaped sword only used by high-ranked court officials. Two lesser-ranked military officers carrying shields accompany him. Completing the group are a musician who plays a sideblown ivory oliphant (horn) that announces the warrior chief's presence, and an attendant who carries a ceremonial box for conveying gifts to the *oba*.

Another example of the virtuosity of artists in service to the *oba* at Benin City is the ivory **HIP PENDANT OF THE**

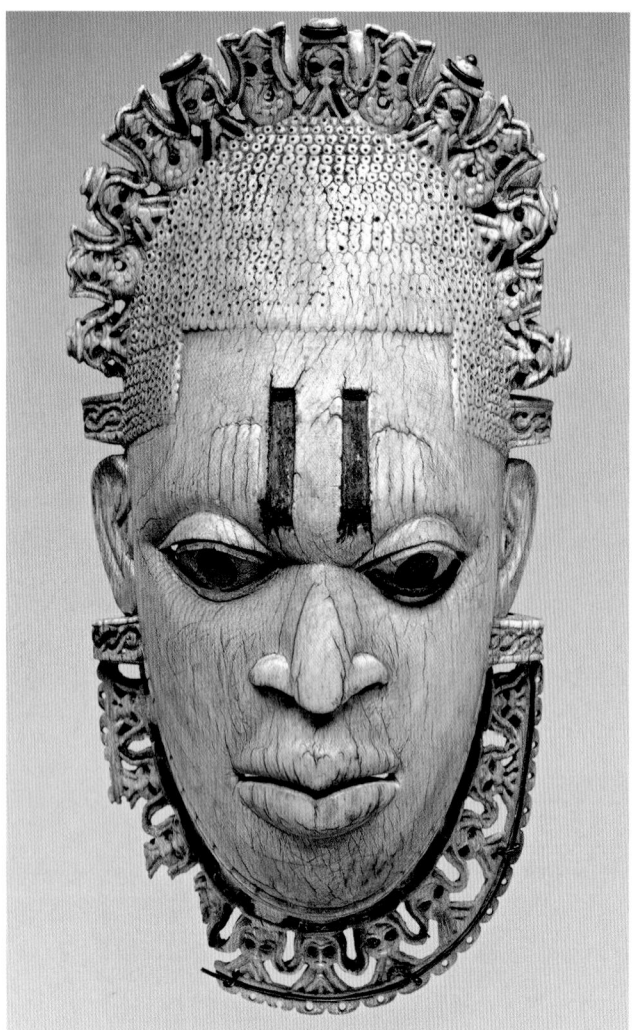

**14–16 HIP PENDANT OF THE IYOBA
(QUEEN MOTHER) IDIA**

Benin City Kingdom, Nigeria. 16th century CE. Ivory, iron, and copper, height 9⅜″ (23.8 cm). The Metropolitan Museum of Art, New York. The Michael C. Rockefeller Memorial Collection, Gift of Nelson A. Rockefeller (1978.412.323).

Credit: © 2016. Image copyright The Metropolitan Museum of Art/Art Resource/ Scala, Florence

IYOBA (QUEEN MOTHER) IDIA seen here (**FIG. 14–16**). It is one of two nearly matched ivory hip ornaments made at the same time for the famous Oba Esigie. One is in the Metropolitan Museum of Art in New York, and the other is held by the British Museum in London. Both represent the same woman, Idia, who held the title of *iyoba* (queen mother) while her son, Esigie, was *oba*.

Idia helped to negotiate the end of the war with the neighboring Igala in the early years of Esigie's reign, thus stabilizing the Edo Empire. For her efforts, Esigie created the title of *iyoba* for his mother. Most likely the two ivory pendants were made to commemorate her new status based on her political achievements.

The minutely detailed headdress and neck ruff of the pendant depict Portuguese men, identifiable through their round, European-style hats and long hair and beards. In

Idia's headdress, each Portuguese face alternates with a mudfish, a local species of catfish recognizable by its broad flat body, whiskers, and eyes on the top of its head.

The Portuguese were an important symbol in Benin City art. They supplied coral, satin, hats, and other items of value to the *oba*, who in turn provided them with red pepper, metal, animal skins, and eventually ivory and captives to be sold as slaves. The Portuguese therefore became associated with the wealth and power of the *oba*; co-opting their image into the royal arts presented them as subjects to the king and queen mother, clearly under their economic and political control.

The mudfish seen in the ivory sculpture of Idia also signify the power of the *oba*. Mudfish have an extraordinary ability to dig into the mud of riverbanks and go into a state of hibernation during the dry season, waiting to re-emerge until the rains come. Some mudfish also carry an electrical charge. This ability to "defeat" death and electrocute enemies inspired their use as animal symbols for the *oba*.

Hip pendants were generally made of brass or bronze and worn where a man's rectangular cloth wrapper was knotted closed at his waist. In other sixteenth-century artworks from Benin City, we see warrior chiefs and kings wearing face pendants on their hips. Most of these depict kings, leopards, or the queen mother. Only a few ivory hip pendants have been found, making this piece and its partner at the British Museum almost unique in Edo art.

Cameroon

Cameroon is a relatively small country on the continent, roughly the size of Colorado and Utah combined. Yet over 240 languages are spoken there by a population of just under 22 million people. The earliest people in the area were the Bantu, who were skilled agriculturalists. About 2000 BCE, the Bantu migrated south for unknown reasons. They went on, however, to become the most dominant population in Central and Southern Africa.

MOUSGOUM ARCHITECTURE   The Mousgoum people have lived in northern Cameroon on the river border between Cameroon and Chad, just south of Lake Chad, since at least the sixteenth or seventeenth century. They are primarily fishermen and farmers and are also very well respected for their architecture. The Mousgoum invented a style of adobe construction in which bricks are stacked in circular arrangements that decrease in diameter with each laid course. This produces a conical dome, or beehive, structure called a teleuk (**FIG. 14–17**).

As the Mousgoum add each subsequent ring of adobe brick to the dome, they cover the exterior of the teleuk in thick clay. The exterior clay is molded into a series of stacked, pointed ridges known as "feet." The tops of the

14-17 MOUSGOUM FAMILY ENCLOSURE WITH TELEUK HOUSES
Northern Cameroon. Adobe. Photo: Ernst M. Heims, 1911, from Adolf Friedrich, *From the Congo to the Niger and the Nile*, 1913.

This building type, as well as the circular arrangement of rooms in the family household, dates back to at least the sixteenth and seventeenth centuries. By the mid twentieth century, many Mousgoum had abandoned teleuk architecture and converted to construction in pre-fabricated cement block. However, in the late 1990s a revival of the style in the region began, with towns building teleukakay (teleuk plural) to serve as public community buildings and tourist centers, and individual families once again began incorporating the teleuk into their homesteads.

Credit: From: *Adolf Friedrich Duke of Mecklenburg, From the Congo to the Niger and the Nile: An account of the German Central African Expedition of 1910-1911*, Volume 1. London: Duckworth & Co, 1913, p.130.

ridges serve as places where the masons can stand as they stack the upper layers of the building. The feet also serve to guide rainwater off the structure during the rainy season, and they cast shadows on the walls' surfaces, reducing the amount of heat the structure absorbs from the sun. Lastly, the feet add aesthetic interest to the teleuk. When French colonial officials and missionaries began documenting Mousgoum buildings in the early twentieth century, they were so taken by the teleuk designs that they copied the style to build the French West African colonial pavilion that was exhibited at the 1931 International Colonial Exposition in Paris.

Teleuk architecture tells us much about Mousgoum society and culture. For example, family homes are constructed out of a circular ring of independent rooms. The two largest rooms house the father of the family and the grain produced by each family's farming activities. The mother of the family and any additional adult female relatives each have their own room, and small children and girls sleep with their mothers. Young men who have not yet established their own families share a room. Mousgoum society is organized around adults mentoring children of their own gender; this is reflected in the organization of family housing.

Republic of the Congo, Democratic Republic of the Congo, and Angola

Some of the biggest kingdoms on the continent were spread across what are now the Republic of the Congo, the Democratic Republic of the Congo, and Angola. The kingdoms of Loango, Kongo, Angola, and Benguela stretched across the coastal region, while inland, the kingdoms of the Luba, Kuba, Lunda, Matamba, and hundreds more existed for centuries. This region is home to some of the most valuable natural resources on earth. Huge copper and tin belts stretch through the region; diamonds, gold, copper, coltan (used in cell phones), lead, zinc, uranium, and more are also mined here.

The Republic of the Congo is the smallest of the three nations, separated from its much larger neighbor, the Democratic Republic of the Congo, by the enormous Congo River. All three of these entities are named for the Kingdom of Kongo, which controlled the region from the fourteenth through nineteenth centuries. The Democratic Republic of the Congo is large enough, in fact, to encompass all of Europe inside its borders, while Angola is about twice the size of Texas. The Bantu from Cameroon migrated to all three countries sometime during the first millennium BCE.

14–18 "THE BANSA, OR RESIDENCE OF THE KING OF KONGO, CALLED SÃO SALVADOR"
View of M'banza Kongo, capital city of the Kongo Kingdom, Angola. Engraving after Olfert Dapper, 17th century CE.

Credit: Thomas Astley, A new general collection of voyages and travels : consisting of the most esteemed relations, which have been hitherto published in any language; comprehending everything remarkable in its kind, in Europe, Asia, Africa, and America. London, 1745-47 [1968]. Volume 3/4, folding plate p.245. Picture Collection, The New York Public Library. Astor, Lenox and Tilden Foundations

Bantu languages are still widely spoken in the region and include Shona, Swahili, Luba, and Kongo. In Bantu languages, noun modifiers are attached to the beginnings of words, not at the end as in English. The prefix "ba-" means people and "ki-" means language. Therefore, it is most correct to state that the Bakongo speak Kikongo, the Bakuba speak Kikuba, and so on. In English usage, however, the prefixes are often dropped in order to avoid confusion.

THE KONGO KINGDOM   The Kingdom of Kongo encompassed over 100,000 square miles of present-day northwestern Angola and the western part of the Democratic Republic of the Congo. In the fifteenth century, the capital city M'banza Kongo was the center of major trade networks, all of which were controlled by the Kongo king (**FIG. 14–18**).

Along with items made for trade, artists working for the kings of Kongo excelled at making luxury items for royal use. Textile squares, carved wooden cups, and

14–19 WOVEN AND CUT-PILE TEXTILE
Democratic Republic of the Congo. Kongo, before 1400 CE. Raffia, 18½ × 9½″ (47 × 24 cm). Pitt Rivers Museum, University of Oxford, England. (1886.1.254.1).

This textile was dated by the Pitt Rivers Museum using carbon-14 analysis. When the textile first came into the museum's collection in 1886, its earliest documentation was a brief mention in a 1656 catalogue that may or may not have referred to this specific textile. Until carbon-14 dating was used in the twentieth century, this textile could only be dated as a "seventeenth-century" object. Carbon-14 dating proved that the textile was much older and had in fact been made before 1400.

woven hats and garments formed the bulk of this industry. The textile seen here is a rare early example of one such royal item, and would have been highly prized by royal and elite individuals alike (**FIG. 14–19**).

A 1508 account of Kongo textiles by Portuguese sea captain Duarte Pacheco Pereira indicates how much these items were appreciated in Europe: "In the kingdom of the Congo they produce cloths from palm fibers with velvet-like pile of such beauty that better ones are not made in Italy."

Woven of raffia fiber with both raised and plushed bands and embroidered decorations, this small square was most likely made to serve two purposes: a valuable form of currency and a small section of a larger wearable garment.

In the textile's lightest bands, called "streets," the design was achieved by embroidering raffia fibers in a simple whipstitch pattern. The diamond or lozenge shapes, or "blocks," created between the lighter "streets" were embroidered in raffia dyed a darker color. The darkest color on the textile, used to form a border around the "streets," is done in a plush pile technique. Raffia fibers dyed a dark brown are pushed through from the back of the textile and then cut close to the surface to form a velvet-like pile. This gives the textile depth as well as visual contrast.

The primary symbol of the Kongo religion is a cosmogram, a cross shape within a diamond, usually with four circles drawn at each point of the diamond. This cosmogram is visible in the patterns of "streets" on this textile. The cosmogram represents the "Four Moments of the Sun"; the points on the diamond represent sunrise, midday, sunset, and night. These points also represent the four cardinal directions (north, south, east, and west) and four life stages (birth, adulthood, death, and ancestry/rebirth). Royal textiles such as this used cosmogram imagery to stress the kingdom's spirituality and the divine right of its kings to rule.

CHRISTIANITY IN THE KONGO KINGDOM   The Kingdom of Kongo's religion surprised fifteenth- and sixteenth-century Portuguese and Dutch traders for its parallels with Christianity, including the cosmogram symbol, which to the Portuguese looked like their orthodox Christian cross. In fact, the Kongo readily assimilated European Christianity into their own religious practice.

In 1491, King Nzinga aNkuwa converted to Christianity, as did his son and successor Afonso I, who established Christianity as the official religion of the Kongo Kingdom. The conversions helped to solidify trade relations with the Portuguese, who had first arrived at M'banza Kongo in 1482. The ensuing trade in copper, salt, ivory, cloth, and, later, enslaved peoples brought increased prosperity to the kingdom.

Due to its shared geometry with the Kongo cosmogram, the crucifix became especially popular as a potent symbol of both Christian conversion and

adherence to traditional political and religious authorities. Cast in solid brass, this example somewhat mirrors a European prototype, but the imagery is restated in Kongolese terms (**FIG. 14–20**).

The features of the crucified Christ, as well as his hands and feet and those of the supporting figures, are stylized according to Kongo tradition. In the biblical telling, two thieves were crucified on either side of Jesus, while his mother Mary and many apostles watched his death. In the Kongo narration seen here, this well-known story is modified so that four of these individuals appear on the same cross as Jesus. The two thieves are depicted as small figures sitting on either side of Jesus's outstretched arms, while Mary kneels at his feet. The topmost figure may be John the Baptist, a saint or apostle, or even God the father. The Kongo artist has made the cross large enough to hold them all—in dramatic distinction from Portuguese depictions of the same subject, which would have been well known to this artist. The four supporting figures all kneel in prayer, which doubles in Kongo symbolism as clapping, a central African gesture of respect for another person.

14–20 CRUCIFIX
From the Democratic Republic of the Congo, Republic of the Congo, or Angola. Kongo, 16th–17th century CE. Solid cast brass, height 10¾" (27.3 cm). Metropolitan Museum of Art, New York. Gift of Ernst Anspach (1999.295.7).

14–21 SITE OF GREAT ZIMBABWE

Credit: © akg-images/Interfoto

Southern Africa

How do the arts of early societies in Zimbabwe and South Africa transmit information about their societies and community structures?

Southern Africa is the traditional home of the San and Khoekhoe peoples and their ancestors. These groups were mobile and pastoral, herding their livestock across the vast savannas of the region. Encroached upon by the Bantu migrations from the north, the San and Khoekhoe were joined (and largely displaced) by the Zulu, Shona, Xhosa, and others. As we have seen, the region is famous for its rock art. It is also home to sites of architectural and artistic importance.

Zimbabwe

Known best for its national parks and safari excursions, Zimbabwe is the homeland of the Shona peoples. The country takes its name from the archaeological site of Great Zimbabwe, an early Shona kingdom that rose to prominence based on its trade networks with Arab merchants traversing the Indian Ocean.

GREAT ZIMBABWE At its height in the fourteenth century, **GREAT ZIMBABWE** is believed to have been a city of over 10,000 people, with the Great Enclosure serving as its religious and/or administrative hub (**FIG. 14-21**). The city was an important commercial center for the East African gold trade as well as commerce with Swahili traders along the coast. When Great Zimbabwe and its surrounding area were excavated in the early twentieth century, a large cache of goods including Portuguese medallions, Persian pottery from Iran, and even Chinese porcelain were found, testifying to the former extent of its trade.

The current ruins at Great Zimbabwe were originally three related sites. The oldest, known as Hill Ruin, was built on the top of a hill around 1250 CE. It sits atop a natural cave that has the unique feature of amplifying sound made from within it directly out and down to the valley below. About a century later, a second construction known as the Great Enclosure (c. 1350–1450 CE) was begun in the valley. The Great Enclosure consists of a 32-foot exterior wall with smaller concentric walls and solid stone tower structures inside. The third section of Great Zimbabwe, the Valley Ruins, is where the trade objects were found.

The exterior walls at the Great Enclosure were made from even, smoothly finished courses (rows) of locally quarried granite. The stones are carved to fit together so precisely that no mortar was needed to hold the walls together. The walls are still remarkably stable and have eroded very little over time. Near the top of the exterior wall, two rows of granite stones were carved in a double row of chevrons (diamond patterns), part of which is still visible at the ruins today.

Inside the Great Enclosure are two solid **CONICAL TOWERS**, the larger of which still stands over 30 feet tall (FIG. 14–22). Their exact original heights are unknown, but they were taller than the external walls. The larger conical tower is a massive stone construction made of very finely hewn granite. The stones fit together so tightly that

nothing can be slipped in between them; as a result, the tower looks as if it is made out of a solid stone block.

South Africa

When the government of South Africa officially ended the racially motivated segregationist practice of **apartheid** in 1994, the country took to euphemistically calling itself the "Rainbow Nation" based on its existing cultural diversity and its desire to recognize all the peoples that had been disenfranchised under the apartheid political system. While the contemporary dream for equality and freedom in South Africa is still a work in progress, culturally speaking, South Africa has always been a region of incredible artistic diversity.

MAPUNGUBWE HILL   The Limpopo River forms South Africa's northeastern border with Zimbabwe and Botswana. The three countries converge where the Shashe River, which separates Zimbabwe and Botswana, joins the Limpopo. At this juncture lies the historical site of the Kingdom of Mapungubwe, which arose around 1220 CE as a regional kingdom. It remained viable only until about 1300, when its power was eclipsed by Great Zimbabwe to its north. It is believed that the inhabitants of the kingdom were Khoe or San peoples who located there due to the abundance of wildlife, including elephants, as well as for the agricultural fertility of the region. We know that trade for ivory was increasing during the period Mapungubwe was inhabited, and given its strategic location at the convergence of two rivers, we can safely understand that part, if not all, of the kingdom's wealth was procured through this trade.

Archaeological excavations determined that elite men and women lived separately from each other, while the general population lived apart from both elite genders. Those with elite status lived higher up on the hillside, while the lower classes were confined to the low-lying areas of the city. Several important burials were discovered in 1932; they have provided us with all the knowledge we have of Mapungubwe, as no other records survive.

In one tomb, archaeologists found a male skeleton assumed to be that of the king, or else an elite ruler. They found many gold objects buried with him, including a small rhinoceros made of gold known as the **MAPUNGUBWE GOLD RHINO** (FIG. 14–23). The rhinoceros was not solid gold, but rather gold sheeting that was pounded flat and then molded over a wooden sculpture. A bowl and a short scepter produced in the same technique of gold over wood were also in this grave. The man was buried in a seated position, knees drawn up to his chest, and holding the golden scepter in his hand. So far, more than 20 skeletons have been found at Mapungubwe Hill, three of them being elite burials.

The significance of this short-lived kingdom lies in the fact that it is one of the earliest examples of a kingdom

14–22 CONICAL TOWER IN THE GREAT ENCLOSURE
Great Zimbabwe, Zimbabwe. c. 1350–1450 CE. Stone, height 30′ (9.1 m).

Credit: © Lynn Y/Shutterstock

14-23 MAPUNGUBWE GOLD RHINO
From Mapungubwe Hill excavations, South Africa. 1220–1300 CE. 6 × 1⅝ × 2³⁄₁₆″ (152 × 42 × 55mm). The University of Pretoria, Department of UP Arts: Mapungubwe Collection.

In 2009, the South African post office issued a series of stamps featuring the Gold Rhino and a golden bowl and scepter from the Mapungubwe Hill World Heritage Site to commemorate this early civilization and its history.

with a stratified societal structure on the continent. It is also one of the first areas where goldsmithing developed in southern Africa. For these reasons, the site was designated as a UNESCO World Heritage Site in 2003.

International Art Trade

Who are the primary trade partners with early African regions and what are the important items of exchange?

Long-distance trade developed in African regions, as it did elsewhere in the world, to take advantage of products and raw materials that were produced in one place and desired in another. Along with agricultural and mercantile goods, items we now consider art moved along trade routes. Regular trade caravans are believed to have been crossing the Sahara Desert since the establishment of dynastic Egypt, and most likely much earlier than that.

North and East Africa

In the medieval period, Arab traders navigated the routes between Europe and sub-Saharan Africa bringing gold, salt, and spices from the kingdoms of Mali, Ghana, and the Songhai to trade partners as far north as the Netherlands. Islamic scholars chronicled these great West African empires, most famously that of Emperor Musa Keita I (known as Mansa Moussa) of Timbuktu, who in 1324 journeyed from Timbuktu in present-day Mali to Alexandria (Egypt) and then to Mecca (Saudi Arabia). He brought an entourage of tens of thousands of people with him and such a fortune in gold that he crashed the gold markets throughout the regions he visited, damage from which they took decades to recover. He traded gold for souvenirs

and art objects and purchased the services of architects who returned home with him to build extravagant mosques and Islamic schools in Timbuktu. He was undoubtedly not the first king to make such an extensive voyage, however; the documentation of his trip indicates the strength of trade connections across northern Africa that were in place before his time.

East Africa, meanwhile, had been drawn since at least the beginning of the Common Era into the maritime trade that ringed the Indian Ocean and extended east to Indonesia and the South China Sea. Arab, Indian, and Persian ships plied the coastline. A new language, Swahili, evolved from centuries of contact between Arabic-speaking merchants and Bantu-speaking East Africans, and great port cities such as Kilwa, Mombasa, Dar es-Salaam, and Mogadishu arose.

West and Central Africa

Trade in fine objects between regions in West and Central Africa and European partners began in earnest during the late fifteenth and early sixteenth centuries as a result of Portuguese advances in maritime navigation, which allowed them to navigate down the western coast of Africa, around the Cape of Good Hope, and over to East African port cities on their way to India. Encountering the continent firsthand, they were often astonished by what they found. "Dear King My Brother," wrote a fifteenth-century Portuguese king to his new trading partner, the *oba* (king) of Benin City in West Africa. The Portuguese king's respect was well founded—the Edo Empire at Benin City was vastly wealthier and more powerful than the small European country that had just stumbled upon it.

Benin City was not the only place where Europeans found artistic objects that fascinated them. The kingdoms of West and Central Africa supplied Europeans with the majority of their African art collections from the fifteenth through the nineteenth centuries. Over 800 African art objects brought to Europe between 1400 and 1800 still exist in collections today. Of these, over half originated in West Africa, and 113 came from Central Africa.

A Portuguese sea captain, Valentim Fernandez, commented that artists from Sierra Leone were "very talented in making ivory artifacts such as saltcellars and spoons; whatever sort of object is designed for them, they can carve it in ivory." Two objects of the sort described by Fernandez can be seen here. One is a Sapi-Portuguese **OLIPHANT (HUNTING HORN)**; virtually all its decorative motifs are European-inspired (**FIG. 14–24**). The mouthpiece is at the narrow end rather than on the side, as is typical for African horns. The carvings, including the coat of arms of Portugal and Spain, the motto of Spain's Ferdinand V, heraldic emblems, and hunting scenes, were derived from illustrations found in European prayer books and other publications given to the Sapi artist as source material.

However, not all of the designs found on some export ivories are derived from European sources. For example, the lidded **SALTCELLAR** seen here was also commissioned by a Portuguese individual, who described what he wanted to an artist working in coastal Sierra Leone (**FIG. 14–25**). Ivory saltcellars were popular items on aristocratic dining tables in the fifteenth and sixteenth

14–24 END-BLOWN OLIPHANT (HUNTING HORN)
From Sierra Leone. Bullom or Temne (Sapi) and Portuguese collaboration, late 15th century CE. Ivory and metal, length 25¼" (64.2 cm). National Museum of African Art, Smithsonian Institution, Washington, DC. Gift of Walt Disney World Co., a subsidiary of the Walt Disney Company (2005.6.9).

Credit: Photo: Frank Khoury

14–25 LIDDED SALTCELLAR
From Sierra Leone. Bullom or Temne (Sapi) and Portuguese collaboration, 15th–16th century CE. Ivory, height 11¾" (29.8 cm). Metropolitan Museum of Art, New York. Gift of Paul and Ruth W. Tishman (1991.435a,b).

Credit: © 2016. Image copyright The Metropolitan Museum of Art/Art Resource/ Scala, Florence centuries across Italy, Germany, and France. The round globe at the top is divided into two semispheres; the top one lifts off and table salt is kept in the bowl formed by the lower half. The floral and dot motifs on the top of the cellar display the artist's virtuosity with his chisel. The object is less than a foot tall, so this detail work is very delicate and difficult to achieve at such small scale. The lower half of the vessel is even more impressive. Alternating male and female figures with Sapi facial features and Sapi garments are separated from each other by crouching dogs, which are poised to leap up into the mouths of serpents that descend from a coil at the base of the globe. The serpents even have their tongues sticking out, a detail from nature that would have been sure to impress wealthy European patrons.

Europeans did not come empty-handed to West and Central Africa. They brought items of European manufacture such as French fabrics, Dutch tableware, tools, and most significantly for the course of history, guns. They also transported items from the Far East to African trade partners. Indonesian batik fabrics and Chinese porcelain proved very popular with African buyers.

Foremost among all of the European goods exchanged in African markets, however, were the glass beads made in Venice, Bohemia, and the Netherlands. Glassmaking technology was widespread in Europe and rare in African nations, making the beads a highly desirable commodity. The bead trade was so extensive that by the mid nineteenth century, manufacturers in Europe were making cards with bead samples and prices on them so that wealthy prospective buyers (primarily kings and chiefs) in Africa could order their beads in advance, ensuring that they would have the newest and most fashionable styles from Europe (**FIG. 14–26**).

14–26 TRADE BEAD CARD

London, c. 1860s CE. Labeled "Beads employed in the African trade for ivory"; used in Ghana for trade with Asante. Group of 133 glass beads mounted on cardboard in 37 strings and 2 singles. British Museum, London. Gift of M. L. Levin (Af1863,0717.1).

Southern Africa

Coastal South Africans primarily traded with Dutch partners early in the Atlantic trade system, as the Dutch had quickly supplanted the Portuguese in this area. Key goods were food and water needed to restock Dutch ships on their journey home from Indonesia. The Dutch offered metal, alcoholic beverages, and beads in exchange. Trade beads from Europe were also extremely popular elsewhere in southern Africa, and they were widely distributed north from the coast into regions now encompassed by Botswana, Zimbabwe, and Zambia.

As the European trade market grew in scope, Dutch and British populations began to settle in southern Africa, with the result that trade in this area moved away from foodstuffs for ships and toward raw materials (such as diamonds and minerals) that could be sent to Europe in exchange for goods of European manufacture supplied by the British.

By the seventeenth century, labor needs were increasing around the world to support large, European-run plantations producing sugar, cotton, tobacco, and agricultural items for international markets. Horrifically, from the seventeenth through nineteenth centuries, the most valuable and popular commodity traded in European and African exchanges was African people themselves. What had begun in the fifteenth century as a system for exchange of goods to the mutual benefit of Europe and Africa would become a brutal source of incalculable suffering, the repercussions of which are still felt today.

Think About It

1   Animals are often portrayed in a spiritual, rather than naturalistic, manner in prehistoric rock art. Discuss some of the techniques artists used to convey the spiritual qualities of the animals they painted.

2   Even when art objects and monuments were religious in nature, political power was often the means by which they could be produced. Select a religious object or monument from North or East Africa and discuss the role specific political forces played in its creation and history.

3   Give an example of an art object from West or Central Africa that conveys the cultural ideals of its society. What techniques did the artist employ to depict these social and cultural values in the object?

4   How did the architecture at Great Zimbabwe convey the city's political power to its neighbors and rivals?

5   How does studying the international trade of art objects across regions of Africa give us insight into the social, cultural, religious, and artistic desires of each region?

Crosscurrents

When the Kongolese people adopted Christianity in the late fifteenth century, they were interested in European depictions of Christ on the cross, but they did not adopt this imagery wholesale for their own Christian images. Discuss how this Kongolese image of the Crucifixion scene differs from that of the European example. What was important for the Kongolese artist to convey? Which elements does this Crucifixion share with European imagery, and which are new Kongolese innovations?

FIG. 8–22

FIG. 14–20

15–1 CHI RHO IOTA PAGE FROM THE BOOK OF KELLS

Probably made at Iona, Scotland. Late 8th or early 9th century. Oxgall inks and pigments on vellum, 12¾ × 9½″ (32.5 × 24 cm).

The Board of Trinity College, Dublin. MS. 58, fol. 34r.

Chapter 15
Early Medieval Art in Europe

 ## Learning Objectives

15.a Identify the visual hallmarks of Early Medieval art for formal, technical, and expressive qualities.

15.b Interpret the meaning of works of Early Medieval art based on their themes, subjects, and symbols.

15.c Relate Early Medieval art and artists to their cultural, economic, and political contexts.

15.d Apply the vocabulary and concepts relevant to Early Medieval art, artists, and art history.

15.e Interpret a work of Early Medieval art using the art historical methods of observation, comparison, and inductive reasoning.

15.f Select visual and textual evidence in various media to support an argument or an interpretation of a work of Early Medieval art.

The explosion of ornament surrounding—almost suffocating—the words on this page from an early medieval manuscript clearly indicates the importance of what is being expressed (**FIG. 15-1**). The large Greek letters *chi rho iota* (*XPI*) abbreviate the word *Christi*, which starts the Latin phrase *Christi autem generatio*. The last word is written out fully and legibly at bottom right, clear of the decorative expanse. These words begin Matthew 1:18 (NRSV): "Now the birth of Jesus the Messiah took place in this way." So what is signaled here—not with a picture of the event, but with an ornamental celebration of its initial mention in the text—is Christ's first appearance within this Gospel book.

Known as the Book of Kells and produced in Ireland or Scotland sometime around the year 800, the lavish book not only contains the four biblical accounts of Christ's life; it would also have evoked Christ's presence on the altar of the monastery church where it was once housed. It is precisely the sort of ceremonial book carried in the hands of a deacon in Justinian's procession into San Vitale in Ravenna to begin the liturgy (SEE FIG. 8–8).

There is nothing explicitly Christian about the ornamental motifs on this page celebrating the first mention of the birth of Christ in the Gospels. The swirling spirals and interlaced tangles of stylized animal forms have their roots

in jewelry created by the migrating, so-called barbarian tribes that formed the "other" of the Greco-Roman world. But by this time, this ornamental repertory had been subsumed into the flourishing art of Irish monasteries. Irish monks became as famous for writing and copying books as for their intense spirituality and missionary fervor.

Wealthy, isolated, and undefended, Irish monasteries were easy victims to Viking attacks. In 806, monks fleeing Viking raids on the island of Iona (off the coast of present-day Scotland) established a refuge at Kells on the Irish mainland. They probably brought the Book of Kells with them. It was precious, and its production had entailed lavish expenditure: Four scribes and three major painters worked on it (modern scribes take about a month to complete such a page), 185 calves were slaughtered to make the vellum, and colors for some of its paintings came from as far away as Afghanistan.

Throughout the Middle Ages and across Europe, monasteries were principal centers of art and learning. While prayer and acts of mercy represented their primary vocation, some talented monks and nuns also worked as painters, jewelers, carvers, weavers, and embroiderers. Few, however, could claim a work of art as spectacular as this one.

The Early Middle Ages

*What are the geographical and historical backgrounds
for the early art and architecture of the European
Middle Ages?*

As Roman authority crumbled at the dissolution of the
Western Empire in the fifth century, it was replaced by rule
of people from outside the Romans' cultural orbit whom
the Romans—like the Greeks before them—called "barbarians," since they could only "barble" the Greek or Latin
languages (MAP 15-1). Thus far we have seen these "barbarians" as adversaries viewed through Greek and Roman
eyes—the defeated Gauls at Pergamon (SEE FIG. 5-62), the
captives on the Gemma Augustea (SEE FIG. 6-22), or the
enemy beyond the Danube River on Trajan's Column (SEE
FIG. 6-47). But by the fourth century many Germanic tribes
were allies of Rome. In fact, most of Constantine's troops
in the decisive battle with Maxentius at the Milvian Bridge
were Germanic "barbarians."

A century later the situation was entirely different. The
adventures of the Roman princess Galla Placidia, whom
we have already met as a patron of the arts (SEE FIG. 7-20),
bring the situation to life. She had the misfortune to be in
Rome when Alaric and the Visigoths sacked the city in 410
(the emperor and pope were living safely in Ravenna).
Carried off as a prize of war by the Goths, Galla Placidia
had to join their migrations through France and Spain and
eventually married the Gothic king, who was soon murdered. Back in Italy, married and widowed yet again, Galla
Placidia ruled the Western Empire as regent for her son
from 425 to 437/438. She died in 450, thus escaping yet
another sack of Rome, this time by the Vandals, in 455. The
fall of Rome shocked the Christian world, although the
wounds were more psychological than physical. Bishop
Augustine of Hippo (St. Augustine, d. 430) was inspired
to write *The City of God*, a cornerstone of Christian philosophy, as an answer to people who claimed that the Goths
represented the vengeance of the pagan gods on people
who had abandoned them for Christianity.

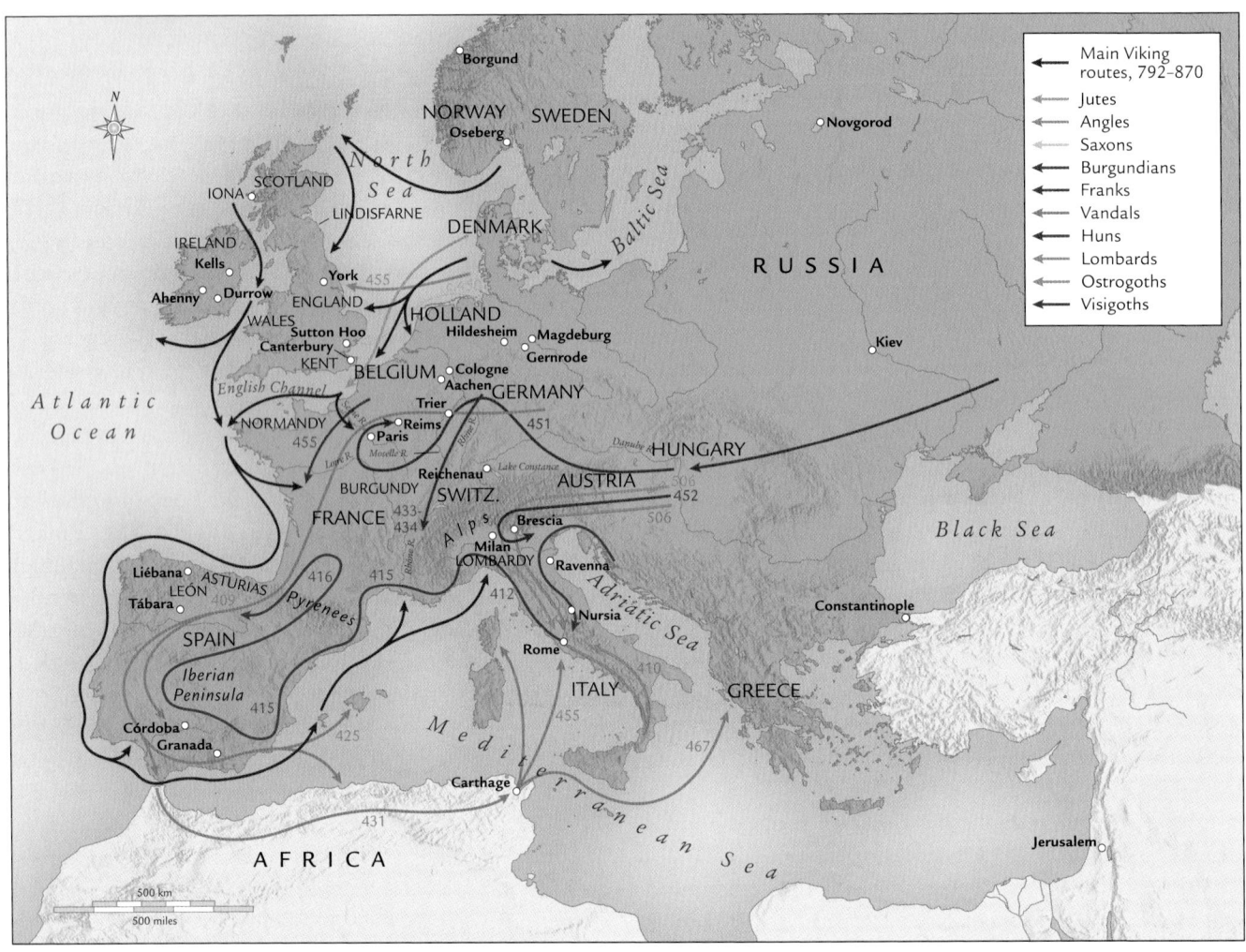

MAP 15-1 EUROPE OF THE EARLY MIDDLE AGES

This map shows the routes taken by the groups of people who migrated into and through the Western Roman world at the dawn of the Middle
Ages. Modern country names have been used here for convenience, but at this time, these countries as we know them did not yet exist.

Art and its Contexts

DEFINING THE MIDDLE AGES

The roughly 1,000 years of European history between the dissolution of the Western Roman Empire during the fifth century and the Florentine Renaissance in the fifteenth century are generally referred to as the Middle Ages, or the medieval period. These terms reflect the view of Renaissance humanists who regarded the period that preceded theirs as a "dark age" of ignorance, decline, and barbarism separating their own "golden age" from the golden ages of ancient Greece and Rome. Although scholars now acknowledge the ridiculousness of this self-serving formulation and recognize the millennium of the "Middle Ages" as a period of great richness, complexity, creativity, and innovation, the term has endured.

Art historians commonly divide the Middle Ages into three periods: early medieval (ending c. 1000), Romanesque (eleventh and twelfth centuries), and Gothic (beginning in the mid twelfth and extending into the fifteenth century). In this chapter we can look at only a few of the many cultures that flourished during the early medieval period. For convenience, we will use modern geographic names as familiar points of reference (SEE MAP 15–1), but, in fact, European nations as we know them today did not yet exist.

Who were these people living outside of the Mediterranean orbit? Their wooden architecture has been lost to fire and decay, but their metalwork and its animal and geometric ornament have survived. They were hunters and fishermen, shepherds and farmers, living in villages with a social organization based on extended families and tribal loyalties. They engaged in pottery, weaving, and woodwork, and they fashioned metals into weapons, tools, and jewelry.

The Celts controlled most of western Europe (see "The Celts" in Chapter 5 on page 152), and the Germanic people—Goths and others—lived around the Baltic Sea. Increasing population evidently forced the Goths to begin to move south into better lands and climate around the Mediterranean and Black Sea, but the Romans had extended the borders of their empire across the Rhine and Danube rivers. Seeking the relative security and higher standard of living they saw in the Roman Empire, the Germanic people crossed the borders and settled within the Roman world.

The tempo of migration speeded up in the fifth century when the Huns from Central Asia swept down on western Europe; the Ostrogoths (Eastern Goths) moved into Italy and deposed the last Western Roman emperor in 476; the Visigoths (Western Goths) ended their wanderings in Spain; the Burgundians settled in Switzerland and eastern France; the Franks in Germany, France, and Belgium; and the Vandals crossed over into Africa, making Carthage their headquarters before circling back to Italy, sacking Rome in 455.

As these "barbarian" groups gradually converted to Christianity, the Church served to unify Europe's heterogeneous population. As early as 345, the Goths adopted Arian Christianity, beliefs considered heretical by the Church in Rome. (Arian Christians did not believe that Christ was divine or co-equal with God the Father.) Not until 589 did they accept Roman Christianity. But the Franks under Clovis (ruled 481–511), influenced by his Burgundian wife Clotilda, converted to Roman Christianity in 496, beginning a fruitful alliance between French rulers and the popes. Kings and nobles defended the claims of the Roman Church, and the pope, in turn, validated their authority. As its wealth and influence increased throughout Europe, the Church emerged as the principal patron of the arts, commissioning buildings and liturgical equipment including altars, altar vessels, crosses, candlesticks, containers for the remains of saints (reliquaries), vestments (ritual garments), images of Christian symbols and stories, and copies of sacred texts.

"Barbarians" in Europe

What characterizes the metalworking traditions of migrating people from the east who settled in the former territory of the Western Roman Empire?

Weaving a rich fabric of themes and styles originating from inside and out of the empire, from pagan and Christian beliefs, and from urban and rural settlements, new artistic styles were born across Europe as people migrated from the east to settle within the former Western Roman Empire. Many of the "barbarian" groups were superb metalworkers and created magnificent, colorful jewelry with precious metals and inlays of gems. Most of the motifs were geometric or highly abstracted natural forms.

The Merovingians

Among the "barbarian" people who moved into the Western Roman world during the fifth century were the Franks, migrating westward from what is now Belgium and settling in the northern part of Roman Gaul (present-day France). There they were soon ruled by a succession of leaders from a dynasty named "Merovingian" after its legendary founder, Merovech. The Merovingians established a powerful kingdom during the reigns of Childeric I (ruled c. 457–481) and his son Clovis I, whose conversion to Christianity in 496 connected the Franks to the larger European world through an ecclesiastical network of communication and affiliation.

Some early illuminated books (books that include not only text but also pictures and decoration in color and gold) have been associated with the dynasty, but our knowledge of Merovingian art is based primarily on the jewelry that has been uncovered in the graves of kings, queens, and aristocrats, indicating that both men and women expressed their wealth in death as presumably in life by wearing earrings, necklaces, finger rings, bracelets, and weighty leather belts from which they suspended even more metalwork. One of the most spectacular royal tombs was that of Queen Arnegunde, unearthed during

excavations in 1959 at the Abbey of Saint-Denis, near Paris, which was a significant center of Merovingian patronage.

Arnegunde was discovered within a stone sarcophagus that had been undisturbed since her burial in c. 580–590. From her bodily remains, archaeologists determined that she was slight and blond, 5 feet tall, and about 70 years old at the time of her death. The inscription of her name on a gold ring on her left thumb provided the first clue to her identity, and her royal pedigree was confirmed by the sumptuousness of her clothing. She wore a short, purple silk tunic cinched at the waist by a substantial leather belt from which hung ornamental metalwork. Her stockings were supported by leather garters with silver strap tongues and dangling ornaments. Over this ensemble was a dark red gown embroidered in gold thread. This overgarment was open at the front, but clasped at neck and waist by round brooches and a massive buckle (**FIG. 15–2**).

15–2 JEWELRY OF QUEEN ARNEGUNDE
Discovered in her tomb, excavated at the Abbey of Saint-Denis, Paris. Burial c. 580–590. Gold, silver, garnets, and glass beads; length of pin 10⅜″ (26.4 cm). Musée des Antiquités Nationales, Saint-Germain-en-Laye, France.

Credit: Photo © RMN/Jean-Gilles Berizzi

These impressive objects were made by casting their general shape in two-piece molds, refining and **chasing** them with tools, and inlaying cut garnets to provide color and sparkle. Not long after Arnegunde's interment, Merovingian royalty ceased the practice of burying such precious items with the dead—encouraged by the Church to donate them instead to religious institutions in honor of the saints—but we are fortunate to have a few early examples that presumably document the way these royal figures presented themselves on state occasions.

The Norse

In Scandinavia (present-day Denmark, Norway, and Sweden), which was never part of the Roman Empire, people spoke variants of the Norse language and shared a mythology with other Germanic peoples. Scandinavian artists had exhibited a fondness for abstract patterning since early prehistoric times. During the first millennium BCE, trade, warfare, and migration had brought a variety of jewelry, coins, textiles, and other portable items into northern Europe, where artists incorporated the solar disks and stylized animals on these objects into their already rich artistic vocabulary.

By the fifth century CE, the so-called **animal style** dominated the arts, resulting in an impressive array of serpents, four-legged beasts, and squat human figures. The **GUMMERSMARK BROOCH** (**FIG. 15–3**), for example, is a large silver-gilt pin from Denmark, dating from the sixth century. Its elegant ornament consists of a large, rectangular panel connected by an arched bow to a medallion-like plate covering the pin's catch. The surface of the pin seethes with human, animal, and geometric forms. An eye-and-beak motif frames the rectangular panel, a man is compressed between dragons just below the bow, and a pair of monster heads and crouching dogs with spiraling tongues frame the covering of the catch.

Certain underlying principles govern animal-style design: The compositions are generally symmetrical, and artists depict animals in their entirety either in profile or from above. Ribs and spinal columns are exposed as if they had been x-rayed; hip and shoulder joints are pear-shape; tongues and jaws extend and curl; and legs end in large claws.

The northern jewelers carefully crafted their molds to produce a glittering surface on the cast metal, turning a process intended to speed production into an art form of great refinement.

Celts and Anglo-Saxons in Britain

After the Romans departed Britain at the beginning of the fifth century, Angles and Saxons from Germany and the Low Countries (present-day Belgium and Holland)

15–3 GUMMERSMARK BROOCH

Denmark. 6th century. Silver gilt, height 5¾″ (14.6 cm). National Museum, Copenhagen.

Credit: Photo: Kit Weiss

and Jutes from Denmark crossed the sea to southeastern Britain. Gradually they extended their control northwest across the island. Over the next 200 years, the arts experienced a spectacular efflorescence. A fusion of Celtic, Roman, Germanic, and Norse cultures generated a new style of art, sometimes known as Hiberno-Saxon (from Hibernia, the Roman name for Ireland). Anglo-Saxon literature is filled with references to sumptuous jewelry and weapons made of or decorated with gold and silver. Some of these objects—Celtic and Scandinavian, as well as Anglo-Saxon—have survived.

The Anglo-Saxon epic *Beowulf*, composed as early as the seventh century, describes its hero's burial with a hoard of treasure in a grave mound near the sea. Such a burial site was discovered near the North Sea coast in Suffolk at a site called Sutton Hoo (*hoo* means "hill"). The grave's occupant had been buried in a ship—90 feet long and designed for rowing, not sailing—whose traces in the earth were recovered by careful excavators. The wood and the hero's body had disintegrated, and no inscriptions record his name. He has sometimes been identified with the ruler Raedwald, who died about 625. Whoever he was, the treasures buried with him prove that he was a wealthy and powerful man. They include weapons, armor, other equipment to provide for the ruler's afterlife, and many luxury items. The

objects from Sutton Hoo represent the broad multicultural heritage characterizing the British Isles at this time: Celtic, Scandinavian, and classical Roman, as well as Anglo-Saxon. There was even a Byzantine silver bowl.

One of the most exquisite finds was a gold clasp that once secured the leather body armor of its owner over his shoulder (**FIG. 15-4**). The two sides of the clasp—almost identical in design—would have been connected when a long gold pin, attached to one half by a delicate

RECOVERING THE PAST
SUTTON HOO

The story of the excavation of Sutton Hoo—unquestionably one of the most important archaeological discoveries in Britain—begins with Edith May Pretty, who decided late in her life to explore the burial mounds that were located on her estate in southeast Suffolk, securing the services of a local amateur archaeologist, Basil Brown. Excavations began in 1938 as a collaborative effort between the two of them, and in the following year they encountered the famous ship burial. As rumors spread of the importance of the find, its excavation was gradually taken over by renowned experts and archaeologists who moved from the remains of the ship to the treasures of the burial chamber for which Sutton Hoo is most famous. Police officers were posted to guard the site, and the treasures were sent for safekeeping to the British Museum in London, although, since Sutton Hoo was determined not to be "Treasure Trove" (buried objects meant to be retrieved by their original owners and now considered property of the Crown—see Chapter 6), it was Pretty's legal property. She, however, decided to donate the entire contents of the burial mound to the British Museum.

Excavation of Sutton Hoo was interrupted by World War II, but in 1945 Rupert Bruce-Mitford of the British Museum began

a scholarly study of its treasures that would become his life's work. He not only subjected each piece to detailed scrutiny, but also proposed reconstructions of objects that were only partially preserved, such as the harp, helmet, and drinking horns. Using evidence that had been gathered in a famous murder case, he proposed that Sutton Hoo was actually a burial despite no human remains having ever been found, since they could have disappeared completely in the notably acidic soil of the mound. Other scholars used radiocarbon dating of timber fragments and close analysis of coins to focus the dating of the burial to c. 625, which happened to coincide with the death date of King Raedwald of East Anglia, the most popular candidate for the identity of the person buried at Sutton Hoo.

After heated discussions and considerable controversy, new excavations were carried out in the area around Sutton Hoo during the 1980s and 1990s. These revealed a series of other discoveries in what emerged as an important early medieval burial ground and proved that the area had been inhabited since the Neolithic period—but they uncovered nothing to rival the collection of treasures at Sutton Hoo.

but strong gold chain, was inserted through a series of aligned channels on the back side of the inner edge of each. The superb decoration of this work was created with thin pieces of garnet and blue-checkered glass (known as **millefiori**, from the Italian for "a thousand flowers") cut into precisely stepped geometric shapes and sinuous animal forms. The cut shapes were then inserted into channels and supplemented by granulation (the use of minute granules of gold fused to the surface; see also "Aegean Metalworking," page 93). Under the geometric pieces that form a rectangular patterned field on each side, jewelers placed gold foil stamped with incised motifs that reflect light back up through the transparent garnet to spectacular effect. Around these carpetlike rectangles are borders of interlacing snakes, and in the curving compartments to the outside stand pairs of semitransparent, overlapping boars stylized in ways that reflect the traditions of Scandinavian jewelry. Their curly tails overlap their rumps at the outer edges on each side of the clasp and connect through visible vertebrae along the arched backs to heads with floppy ears and extended tusks. Boars represented strength and bravery, important virtues in warlike Anglo-Saxon society.

The Early Christian Art of the British Isles

How do stylistic aspects of "barbarian" metalworking traditions continue in the Early Christian art of the British Isles?

Although the Anglo-Saxons who settled in Britain had their own gods and myths, Christianity survived. Monasteries flourished in the Celtic north and west, and

Christians from Ireland founded influential missions in Scotland and northern England. Cut off from Rome, these Celtic Christians developed their own liturgical practices, calendar, and distinctive artistic traditions. Then, in 597, Pope Gregory the Great (pontificate 590–604) dispatched missionaries from Rome to the Anglo-Saxon king Ethelbert of Kent, whose Christian wife, Bertha, was sympathetic to their cause. The head of this successful mission, the monk Augustine (St. Augustine of Canterbury, d. 604), became the first archbishop of Canterbury in 601. The Roman Christian authorities and the Irish monasteries, although allied in the effort to Christianize Britain, came into conflict over their divergent practices. The Roman Church eventually triumphed, but local traditions continued to influence British Christian art.

Illustrated Books

Among the richest surviving artworks of the period are lavishly decorated Gospel books, essential not only for spiritual and liturgical life within established monasteries, but also for the missionary activities of the Church, since a Gospel book was required in each new foundation. Often bound in gold and jeweled covers, they were placed on church altars, carried in processions, and even thought to protect parishioners from enemies, predators, diseases, and other misfortunes. The sumptuous books were produced by monks in local monastic workshops called scriptoria (see "The Medieval Scriptorium" below).

THE BOOK OF DURROW One of the earliest surviving decorated Gospels of the period is the **BOOK OF DURROW**, dating to the second half of the seventh century (**FIG. 15–5**). The book's format reflects Roman Christian models, but its

Art and its Contexts
THE MEDIEVAL SCRIPTORIUM

Today books are made with computer software that can lay out pages, set type, and insert and prepare illustrations—and modern presses can produce hundreds of thousands of identical copies in full color. In medieval Europe, however, before the invention of printing from movable type in the mid-1400s, books were made by hand, one at a time. Each one was a time-consuming and expensive undertaking, and no two were exactly the same.

At first, medieval books were usually made by monks and nuns in a workshop called a scriptorium (plural, scriptoria) within the monastery. As the demand for books increased, rulers set up palace workshops employing both religious and lay scribes and artists, supervised by scholars. Books were written on carefully prepared animal skin—either vellum, which was fine

and soft, or parchment, which was heavier and shinier. Ink and water-based paints required time and experience to prepare, and many pigments—particularly blues and greens—were derived from costly semiprecious stones. In very rich books, artists also used gold leaf or gold paint.

Work on a book was often divided between scribes, who copied the text, and artists, who painted or drew illustrations, large initial letters, and other decorations. Occasionally, scribes and artists signed and dated their work on the last page, in what was called the **colophon**. One scribe even took the opportunity to warn: "O reader, turn the leaves gently, and keep your fingers away from the letters, for, as the hailstorm ruins the harvest of the land, so does the injurious reader destroy the book and the writing" (cited in Dodwell, p. 247).

15-5 SYMBOL OF THE EVANGELIST MATTHEW, GOSPEL BOOK OF DURROW

Page from the Gospel of Matthew. Probably made at Iona, Scotland, or in northern England. Second half of 7th century. Ink and tempera on parchment, 9⅝ × 6⅛″ (24.4 × 15.5 cm). Trinity College, Dublin. MS. 57, fol. 21v.

Credit: © The Board of Trinity College, Dublin, Ireland/Bridgeman Images

paintings are an encyclopedia of Hiberno-Saxon design. Each of the four Gospels is introduced by a three-part decorative sequence: a page with the symbol of its evangelist author, followed by a page of pure ornament, and finally elaborate decoration highlighting the initial words of the text (the *incipit*).

The Gospel of Matthew is preceded by his symbol, the man, which demonstrates a great difference from the way humans were represented in the Greco-Roman tradition. The armless body is formed of a colorful checkered pattern recalling the rectangular panels of the Sutton Hoo clasp (SEE FIG. 15–4). Set on the body's rounded shoulders, a schematic, symmetrical, frontal face stares directly out at the viewer, and the tiny feet that emerge at its other end are seen from a contrasting profile view, as if to deny any hint of lifelike form or earth-based spatial placement. Equally prominent is the bold band of complicated but coherent interlacing ornament that borders the figure's field.

THE LINDISFARNE GOSPEL BOOK The **LINDISFARNE GOSPEL BOOK** (FIG. 15-6) is one of the most extraordinary manuscripts ever created, admired for the astonishing beauty of its words and pictures, but also notable for the wealth of information we have about its history. Two and a half centuries after it was made, a priest named Aldred added a colophon to the book, outlining with rare precision its history, as he knew it—that it had been written by Eadfrith, bishop of the island of Lindisfarne (698–721), and bound by Ethelwald, his successor. Producing this stupendous work of art was an expensive and laborious proposition—requiring 300 calfskins to make the vellum and pigments imported from as far away as the Himalayas for the decoration. Preliminary outlines were made for each of the pictures using compasses, dividers, straight edges, and sharp points of silver or lead—forerunner to our pencils.

The full pages of ornament set within cross-shape frameworks are breathtakingly complex visual puzzles that require patient and extended viewing. Hybrid animal

15-6 CARPET PAGE, LINDISFARNE GOSPEL BOOK

Lindisfarne, England. c. 715–720. Ink and tempera on vellum, 13⅜ × 9⁷⁄₁₆″ (34 × 24 cm). The British Library, London. Cotton MS.

Credit: © The British Library Board (Cotton Nero D. IV, f.26v)

15–7 PAGE WITH THE BEGINNING OF THE TEXT OF MATTHEW'S GOSPEL, LINDISFARNE GOSPEL BOOK

Lindisfarne. c. 715–720. Ink and tempera on vellum, 13⅜ × 9⁷⁄₁₆″ (34 × 24 cm). The British Library, London.

The words written in the right margin, just beside the frame, are an Old English gloss translating the Latin text, added here in the middle of the tenth century by the same Aldred who added the colophon. They represent the earliest surviving English text of the Gospels.

Credit: © The British Library Board (Cotton Nero D. IV, f.27)

forms tangle in acrobatic interlacing, disciplined by strict symmetry and sharp framing. Some have speculated that members of the religious community at Lindisfarne might have deciphered the patterns as a spiritual exercise.

This book was carried in processions and displayed on the altar, not shelved in a library to be consulted as a part of intellectual life. The text is heavily ornamented and abbreviated, making it difficult to read. The words that begin the Gospel of Matthew (**FIG. 15–7**)—*Liber generationis ihu xpi filii david filii abraham* ("The book of the generation of Jesus Christ, son of David, son of Abraham")—are jammed together, even stacked on top of each other. They are also surrounded by a proliferation of decorative forms deriving from barbarian visual traditions, which we have already seen moving from jewelry into books in the Book of Durrow (SEE FIG. 15–5) and the Book of Kells (SEE FIG. 15–1).

But the paintings in the Lindisfarne Gospels document more than the developing sophistication of an abstract artistic tradition. Instead of beginning each Gospel with a symbol of its author, the designer of this book introduced portraits of the evangelists writing their texts, drawing on a Roman tradition (**FIG. 15–8**). The monastic library at Wearmouth-Jarrow, near Lindisfarne, had a collection of Roman books, and an author portrait in one of them seems to have provided the model for an artist there to portray **EZRA RESTORING THE SACRED SCRIPTURES** within a huge Bible (**FIG. 15–9**). This painter worked to emulate Greco-Roman illusionistic traditions. Ezra is a modeled, three-dimensional form, sitting on a foreshortened bench and stool drawn in perspective to make them appear to recede into the distance. In the background, the obliquely placed books on the shelves of a cabinet seem to occupy the depth of its interior space.

Judging from the number of details these two portraits share, especially the figures' poses, the artist of the Matthew portrait in the Lindisfarne Gospels worked with the same Roman prototype. But instead of striving to capture the lifelike features of his Roman model, the Lindisfarne artist sought to undermine them. Matthew appears against a blank background. All indications of modeling have been stripped from his clothing to emphasize the decorative pattern and contrasting color created by the drapery folds. By carefully arranging the ornament on the legs of Matthew's bench, the three-dimensional shading and perspective seen in the portrait of Ezra have been suppressed. The footstool has been liberated from its support to float freely on the surface, while still resting under the evangelist's silhouetted feet. Playing freely with an acknowledged and well-understood alien tradition, the painter situates an enigmatic figure in the "background" at upper right behind a gathered drape—suspended from a curtain rod hanging from a screw eye sunk into the upper frame—that is not long enough to conceal the entire figure. Clearly there were important cultural reasons for such divergent reactions to a Mediterranean model—Wearmouth-Jarrow seeking to emphasize its Roman connections and Lindisfarne its indigenous roots. We are extremely fortunate to have two surviving works of art that embody the contrast so clearly.

THE BOOK OF KELLS This chapter began with a close look at the most celebrated page in the Book of Kells—the page introducing Matthew's account of Jesus's birth (SEE FIG. 15–1). It is a dense thicket of patterns derived from metalworking traditions that embellish—in fact practically overwhelm—the Chi Rho monogram of Christ. The illuminators outlined each letter in the Chi Rho monogram, and then they subdivided the letters into panels filled with interlaced animals and snakes, as well as extraordinary spiral and knot motifs. The spaces

15–8 MATTHEW WRITING HIS GOSPEL, LINDISFARNE GOSPEL BOOK

Lindisfarne. c. 715–720. Ink and tempera on vellum, 13⅜ × 9⁷⁄₁₆″ (34 × 24 cm). The British Library, London.

The identity of the haloed figure peeking from behind the curtain is still a topic of debate. Some see him as Christ confronting us directly around the veil that separated the holy of holies from worshipers in the Jewish Temple; others think he is Moses, holding the closed book of the law that was meant to be seen in contrast to the open book into which Matthew writes his Gospel. Also curious here is the Greek form of "saint" in Matthew's title (*O Agios* or "the holy"), written, however, with letters from the Latin alphabet.

between the letters form a whirling ornamental field dominated by spirals.

In the midst of these abstractions, the painters inserted numerous pictorial and symbolic references to Christ—a fish (the Greek word for "fish," *ichthus*, comprises in its spelling the first letters of Jesus Christ, Son of God, Savior), moths (symbols of rebirth), the cross-inscribed wafer of the Eucharist, and numerous chalices and goblets. In a particularly intriguing image at bottom left, two cats pounce on a pair of mice nibbling the Eucharistic wafer, and two more mice torment the vigilant cats. This may be a metaphor for the struggle between good (cats) and evil (mice) or an acknowledgment of the perennial problem of keeping the sacred Host safe from rodents—or both.

15–9 EZRA RESTORING THE SACRED SCRIPTURES, IN THE BIBLE KNOWN AS THE CODEX AMIATINUS

Wearmouth-Jarrow, England. c. 700–715. Ink and tempera on vellum, 20 × 13½″ (50.5 × 34.3 cm). Biblioteca Medicea Laurenziana, Florence.

This huge manuscript (at over 2,000 pages, it weighs more than 75 pounds) is the earliest surviving complete text of the Bible in the Latin Vulgate translation of St. Jerome.

Irish High Crosses

Metalworking traditions influenced not only manuscript decoration, but also the monumental stone crosses erected in Ireland during the eighth century, called high crosses because of their size. The **SOUTH CROSS** of Ahenny, in County Tipperary, is an especially well-preserved example (**FIG. 15-10**). It seems to have been modeled on metal ceremonial or reliquary crosses, that is, cross-shape containers for holy relics. It is outlined with ropelike, convex moldings and covered with spirals and interlace. The large **bosses** (broochlike projections), which form a cross within this cross, resemble the jewels that were similarly placed on metal crosses. The circle enclosing the arms of high crosses has been interpreted as both a ring of heavenly light and a purely practical means of supporting the projecting arms.

15-10 SOUTH CROSS, AHENNY
County Tipperary, Ireland. 8th century. Sandstone.

Credit: Courtesy of Marilyn Stokstad

The Viking Era

What are the distinctive ornamental styles and enduring timber architectural traditions of the Vikings?

During the eighth century, seafaring bands of Norsemen known as Vikings (*viken*, "people from the coves") descended on the rest of Europe. Setting off in flotillas of as many as 350 ships, they explored, plundered, traded with, and colonized a vast area during the ninth and tenth centuries. The earliest recorded Viking incursions were two devastating attacks on wealthy isolated Christian monasteries: one in 793, on the religious community on Lindisfarne, off the northeast coast of England; and another in 795, at Iona, off Scotland's west coast.

Norwegian and Danish Vikings subsequently raided a vast territory stretching from Iceland and Greenland—where they settled in 870 and 985, respectively—to Ireland,

England, Scotland, and France. The Viking Leif Eriksson reached North America in 1000. In good weather a Viking ship could sail 200 miles in a day. In the early tenth century, the rulers of France bought off Scandinavian raiders (the Normans, or "northmen") with a large grant of land that became the duchy of Normandy. Swedish Vikings turned eastward and traveled down the Russian rivers to the Black Sea and Constantinople, where the Byzantine emperor recruited them to form an elite personal guard. Others, known as Rus, established settlements around Novgorod, one of the earliest cities in what would become Russia. They settled in Kiev in the tenth century and by 988 had become Orthodox Christians (see Chapter 8).

Carving in Wood and Stone

Since prehistoric times northerners had represented their ships as sleek sea serpents, and, as we saw at Sutton Hoo, they used them for burials as well as sea journeys. The ship of a dead warrior symbolized his passage to Valhalla (a legendary great hall that welcomed fallen warriors), and Viking chiefs were sometimes cremated in a ship in the belief that this hastened their journey. Women as well as men were honored by ship burials. A 75-foot-long ship, discovered in Oseberg, Norway, and dated c. 815–820, served as the vessel for two women on their journey to eternity in 834, a queen and her companion or servant. Although the burial chamber was long ago looted of jewelry and precious objects, the ship itself and its equipment attest to the wealth and prominence of its owner. A cart and four sleds, all made of wood with beautifully carved decorations, were stored on board. At least 12 horses, several dogs, and an ox had been sacrificed to accompany the women on their last journey.

The Oseberg ship itself was designed to be propelled by both sail and oars for travel in the relatively calm waters of fjords (narrow coastal inlets), not for voyages in the open sea. The rising prow spirals into a serpent's head, and bands of interlaced animals are carved in low relief along the edges (**FIG. 15-11**). Viking beasts are grotesque, broad-bodied creatures with bulging eyes, short muzzles, snarling mouths, and large teeth and claws. They adorned all sorts of Viking belongings—jewelry, houses, tent poles, beds, wagons, and sleds. Traces of color indicate that the carved wood of this ship was originally painted black, white, red, brown, and yellow.

All women, including the most elite, worked in the fiber arts. The Oseberg queen took her spindles (a frame for braiding), tablets for tablet-weaving, and two upright looms with her to the grave. Her cabin walls had been hung with tapestries, fragments of which survive. Women not only produced woven and embroidered garments and wall hangings, but also wove the huge sails of

15–11 GRIPPING BEASTS, DETAIL OF OSEBERG SHIP

c. 815–820. Wood. Vikingskiphuset, Universitets Oldsaksamling, Oslo, Norway.

Credit: © IAM/akg-images

waterproof unwashed wool that gave Viking ships their long-distance capability. The entire community—men and women—worked to create these ships, which represent the Vikings' most important surviving contribution to world architecture.

PICTURE STONES AT JELLING Both at home and abroad, the Vikings erected large memorial stones. Those covered mostly with inscriptions are called **rune stones** (runes are twiglike letters of an early Germanic alphabet). Those with figural decoration are called picture stones. Traces of pigments suggest that the memorial stones were originally painted in bright colors.

About 980, the Danish king Harald Bluetooth (c. 940–987) ordered a picture stone to be placed near an old, smaller rune stone and the family burial mounds at Jelling (**FIG. 15–12**). Carved in runes on a boulder 8 feet high is the inscription "King Harald had this memorial made for Gorm his father and Thyra his mother: that Harald who won for himself all Denmark and Norway and made the Danes Christians." Harald and the Danes had accepted Christianity in c. 960, but Norway did not become Christian until 1015.

During the tenth century, a new style emerged in Scandinavia and the British Isles, one that combined interlacing foliage and ribbons with animals that are more recognizable than the gripping beasts of the Oseberg ship. On one face of the larger Jelling stone the sculptor carved the image of Christ robed in the Byzantine manner, with arms outstretched as if crucified. He is entangled in a

15–12 ROYAL RUNE STONES, RIGHT-HAND STONE ORDERED BY KING HARALD BLUETOOTH

Jelling, Denmark. 983–985. Granite, 3-sided, height about 8′ (2.44 m).

Credit: © Carmen Redondo/Corbis

double-ribbon interlace instead of nailed to a cross. A second side holds runic inscriptions, and a third, a striding creature resembling a lion fighting a snake. The loosely twisting double-ribbon interlace covering the surface of the stone could have been inspired by Hiberno-Saxon art.

Timber Architecture

The vast forests of Scandinavia provided the materials for timber buildings of many kinds. Two forms of timber construction evolved: one that stacked horizontal logs, notched at the ends, to form a rectangular building (the still-popular log cabin); and another that stood the wood on end to form a palisade or vertical plank wall, with timbers set directly in the ground or into a sill (a horizontal beam). More modest buildings consisted of wooden frames filled with wattle-and-daub. Typical buildings

had a turf or thatched roof supported on interior posts. The same basic structure was used for almost all building types—feasting and assembly halls, family homes (which were usually shared with domestic animals), workshops, barns, and sheds. The great hall had a central open hearth (smoke escaped through a louver in the roof) and an off-center door designed to reduce drafts. People secured their residences and trading centers by building massive circular earthworks topped with wooden palisades.

THE BORGUND STAVE CHURCH   Subject to decay and fire, early timber buildings have largely disappeared, leaving only postholes and other traces in the soil. In rural Norway, however, a few later **stave churches** survive—named for the four huge timbers (staves) that form their structural core. Borgund church (**FIG. 15–13**) has four corner staves supporting the central roof, with additional interior posts

15–13A EXTERIOR OF STAVE CHURCH, BORGUND, NORWAY
c. 1125–1150.

Credit: PHB.cz/Fotolia

15–13B CUTAWAY DRAWING OF STAVE CHURCH, BORGUND, NORWAY
c. 1125–1150.

Credit: Kathy Mrozek

that create the effect of a nave and side aisles, narthex, and **choir** (for the clergy). A rounded apse covered with a timber tower is attached to the choir. Steeply pitched roofs covered with wooden shingles protect the walls—planks slotted into the sills—from the rain and snow. Openwork timber stages set on the roof ridge create a tower and give the church a steep pyramidal shape. On all the gables either crosses or dragon heads protect the church and its congregation from trolls and demons.

The Vikings were not always victorious. Their colonies in Iceland and the Faeroe Islands survived, but in North America their trading posts eventually had to be abandoned. In Europe, south of the Baltic Sea, a new German dynasty challenged and then defeated the Vikings. By the end of the eleventh century the Viking era had come to an end.

Mozarabic Art in Spain

What style emerges from the synthesis of early Christian and Islamic traditions in the Mozarabic manuscripts of early medieval Spain?

In 711, Islamic invaders conquered Spain, ending Visigothic rule. Bypassing the small Christian kingdom of Asturias on the north coast, they crossed the Pyrenees Mountains into France, but in 732 Charles Martel and the Frankish army stopped them before they reached Paris. Islamic rulers remained in the Iberian peninsula (Spain and Portugal) for nearly 800 years, until the fall of Granada to the Christians in 1492.

With some exceptions, Christians and Jews who acknowledged the authority of the Islamic rulers and paid

15–14 Maius **WOMAN CLOTHED WITH THE SUN, THE MORGAN BEATUS**
Monastery of San Salvador at Tábara, León, Spain. 940–945. Tempera on vellum, 15⅛ × 22⅛″ (38.5 × 56 cm). The Morgan Library and Museum, New York. MS. M644, fols. 152v–153r.

When the modern abstract French painter Fernand Léger (1881–1955; SEE FIG. 32–21) was visiting the great art historian Meyer Schapiro (1904–1996) in New York during World War II, the artist asked the scholar to suggest the single work of art that was most important for him to see while there. Schapiro took him to the Morgan Library to leaf through this manuscript. The strong impact it had on Léger can be clearly seen in the boldness of his later paintings.

higher taxes because they were non-Muslims were left free to follow their own religious practices. The Iberian peninsula became a melting pot of cultures in which Muslims, Christians, and Jews lived and worked together, even as they were officially and firmly separated. Christians in the Muslim territories were called Mozarabs (from the Arabic *mustarib*, meaning "would-be Arab"). In an exchange of artistic influences, Christian artists incorporated some features of Islamic art into a colorful new style known as **Mozarabic**. When the Mozarabic communities migrated to northern Spain, which returned to Christian rule not long after the initial Islamic invasion, they took this Mozarabic style with them.

Beatus Manuscripts

One of the most influential books of the early Middle Ages was a Commentary on the Apocalypse compiled during the eighth century by Beatus, abbot of the monastery of San Martín at Liébana in the northern kingdom of Asturias. Beatus described the end of the world and the Last Judgment of the Apocalypse, rooted in the Revelation to John at the end of the New Testament, which vividly describes Christ's final, fiery triumph.

A lavishly illustrated copy of Beatus's Commentary, called the Morgan Beatus, was produced c. 940–945, probably at the monastery of San Salvador at Tábara, by an artist named Maius (d. 968), who both wrote the text and painted the illustrations. His gripping portrayal of the **WOMAN CLOTHED WITH THE SUN**, based on the biblical text of Apocalypse (Revelation) 12:1–18, extends over two pages to cover an entire opening of the book (**FIG. 15-14**). Maius has stayed close to the text in composing his tableau, which is dominated by the long, seven-headed, red dragon that slithers across practically the entire width of the picture to threaten at top left the "woman clothed with the sun, with the moon under her feet, and on her head a crown of twelve stars" (12:1). With his tail, at upper right, he sweeps a third of heaven's stars toward Earth while the woman's male child appears before the throne of God. Maius presents this complex allegory of the triumph of the Church over its enemies with a forceful, abstract, ornamental style that accentuates the nightmarish qualities of the events outlined in the text. The background has been distilled into horizontal strips of color; the figures become striped bundles of drapery capped with faces dominated by staring eyes and silhouetted, framing haloes. Apocalyptic events have been transformed by Maius into exotic abstractions that still maintain their power to captivate.

Another copy of Beatus's Commentary was produced about 30 years later for Abbot Dominicus of San Salvador at Tábara. A colophon identifies Senior as the scribe for this project. Emeterius and a woman named Ende

(or simply En), who signed herself "painter and servant of God," shared the task of illustration. For the first time in the West, a woman artist is identified by name with a specific surviving work of art. In an allegory of the triumph of Christ over Satan (**FIG. 15-15**), the painters show a peacock grasping a red-and-orange snake in its beak. The text explains that a bird with a powerful beak and beautiful plumage (Christ) covers itself with mud to trick the snake (Satan). Just when the snake decides the bird is harmless, the bird swiftly attacks and kills it. "So Christ in his Incarnation clothed himself in the impurity of our [human] flesh that through a pious trick he might fool the evil deceiver.... [W]ith the word of his mouth [he] slew the venomous killer, the devil" (cited in Williams, page 95).

15-15 Emeterius and Ende, with the scribe Senior **BATTLE OF THE BIRD AND THE SERPENT, COMMENTARY ON THE APOCALYPSE BY BEATUS AND COMMENTARY ON DANIEL BY JEROME**
Made for Abbot Dominicus, probably at the monastery of San Salvador at Tábara, León, Spain. Completed July 6, 975. Tempera on parchment, 15¾ × 10¼" (40 × 26 cm). Cathedral Library, Gerona, Spain. MS. 7[11], fol. 18v.

Credit: Archivo Fotográfico Oronoz, Madrid

The Carolingian Empire

How do Roman traditions influence the development of art and architecture during the Carolingian Empire?

During the second half of the eighth century, a new force emerged on the Continent. Charlemagne (the French form of Carolus Magnus, Latin for "Charles the Great") established a dynasty and an empire known today as the Carolingian. He descended from a family that had followed the Merovingians in the late seventh century as rulers of the Franks in northern Gaul (parts of present-day France and Germany). Under Charlemagne (ruled 768–814), the Carolingian realm reached its greatest extent, encompassing western Germany, France, the Lombard kingdom in Italy,

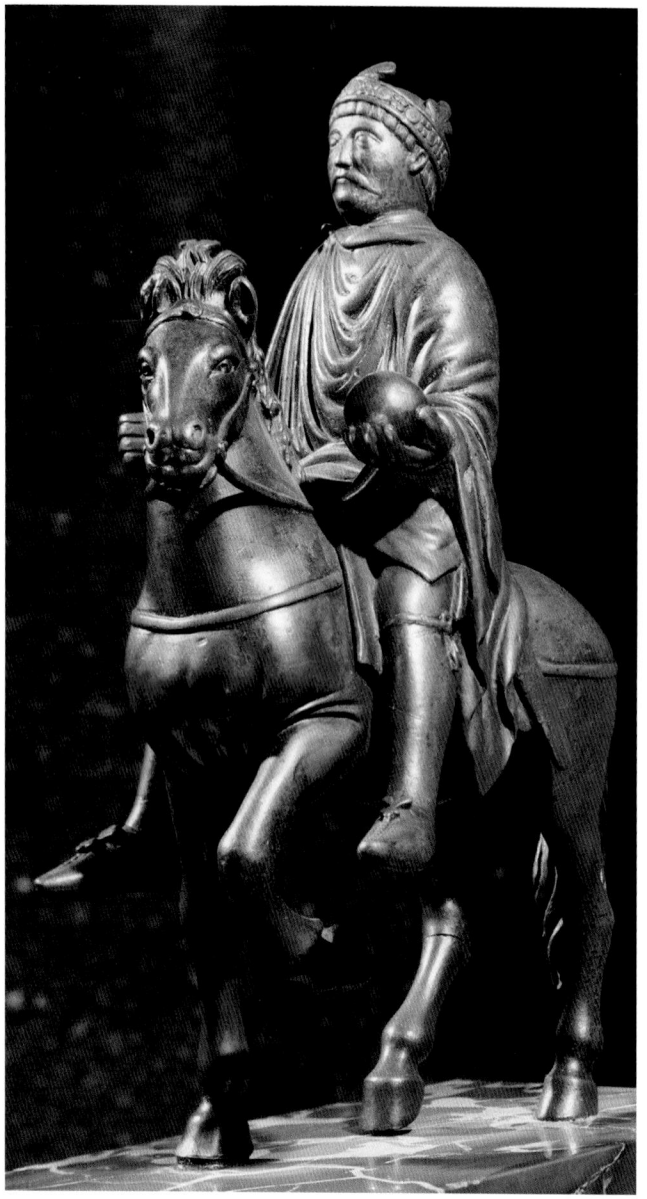

15–16 EQUESTRIAN PORTRAIT OF CHARLES THE BALD (?)

9th century. Bronze, height 9½" (24.4 cm). Musée du Louvre, Paris.

Credit: © akg-images /Erich Lessing

and the Low Countries. Charlemagne imposed Christianity throughout this territory, and in 800, Pope Leo III (pontificate 795–816) crowned him emperor in a ceremony in St. Peter's Basilica in Rome, declaring him the rightful successor to Constantine, the first Christian emperor. This endorsement reinforced Charlemagne's authority and strengthened the bonds between the papacy and secular government in the West.

The Carolingian rulers' ascent to the Roman *imperium*, and the political pretensions it implied, are clearly signaled in a small bronze equestrian statue—once thought to be a portrait of Charlemagne himself but now usually identified with his grandson **CHARLES THE BALD** (FIG. 15–16). The idea of representing an emperor as a proud equestrian figure recalls the much larger image of Marcus Aurelius (SEE FIG. 6–56) that was believed during the Middle Ages to portray Constantine, the first Christian emperor. But unlike the bearded Roman, this Carolingian king sports a mustache, a Frankish sign of nobility that had also been common among the Celts (SEE FIG. 5–62). Works of art such as this are not a slavish mimicking of Roman prototypes, but a creative appropriation of Roman imperial typology to glorify rulers who are clearly Carolingian.

Charlemagne sought to restore the Western Empire as a Christian state and to revive the arts and learning: as inscribed on his official seal, "the Renewal of the Roman Empire." To lead this revival, he turned to Benedictine monks and nuns. By the early Middle Ages, monastic communities had spread across Europe. In the early sixth century, Benedict of Nursia (c. 480–547) wrote his *Rule for Monasteries*, and this set of guidelines for a secluded life of monastic work and prayer became the model for Benedictine monasticism, soon the dominant form throughout Europe. The Benedictines became Charlemagne's "cultural army," and the imperial court at Aachen, Germany, one of the leading intellectual centers of western Europe.

Architecture

To proclaim the glory of the new empire in monumental form, Charlemagne's architects turned for inspiration to two former Western imperial capitals, Rome and Ravenna. Charlemagne's biographer Einhard reported that the ruler "beyond all sacred and venerable places... loved the church of the holy apostle Peter in Rome." Not surprisingly, Constantine's basilica of St. Peter, with its long nave and side aisles ending in a transept and projecting apse (SEE FIG. 7–10A), served as a model for many important churches in Charlemagne's empire. The basilican plan, which had fallen out of favor since the Early Christian period, emerged again as the preferred arrangement of large congregational churches and would remain so throughout the Middle Ages and beyond.

CHARLEMAGNE'S PALACE AT AACHEN Charlemagne's palace complex provides an example of the Carolingian synthesis of Roman, Early Christian, and northern styles. Charlemagne, who enjoyed hunting and swimming, built a headquarters and palace complex amid the forests and natural hot springs of Aachen, in the northern part of his empire, and installed his court there in about 794. The palace complex included a large masonry audience hall and chapel facing each other across a large square (reminiscent of a Roman forum), and a monumental gateway supporting a hall of judgment. Other administrative buildings, a palace school, homes for his advisors and his large family, and workshops supplying all the needs of Church and state were mostly constructed using the wooden building traditions indigenous to this part of Europe.

The **PALACE CHAPEL** (FIG. **15–17**) functioned as Charlemagne's private place of worship, the church of his imperial court, a place for precious relics, and, after the emperor's death, the imperial mausoleum. The central, octagonal plan recalls the church of San Vitale in Ravenna (SEE FIG. 8–5), but the Carolingian architects added a monumental western entrance block. Known as a **westwork**, this structure combined a ground-floor narthex (vestibule) and an upper-story throne room which opened onto the chapel interior, allowing the emperor an unobstructed view of the liturgy at the high altar while assuring his privacy and safety. The room also opened outside into a large walled forecourt where the emperor could make public appearances and speak to assembled crowds.

The soaring core of the chapel is an octagon, surrounded at the ground level by an ambulatory (curving aisle passageway) and on the second floor by a gallery (upper-story passageway overlooking the main space) and rising to a clerestory above the gallery level and

15–17A INTERIOR VIEW, PALACE CHAPEL OF CHARLEMAGNE
Aachen (Aix-la-Chapelle), Germany. 792–805.

Extensive renovations took place here in the nineteenth century, when the chapel was reconsecrated as the cathedral of Aachen, and in the twentieth century, after it was damaged in World War II.

Credit: © Achim Bednorz, Cologne

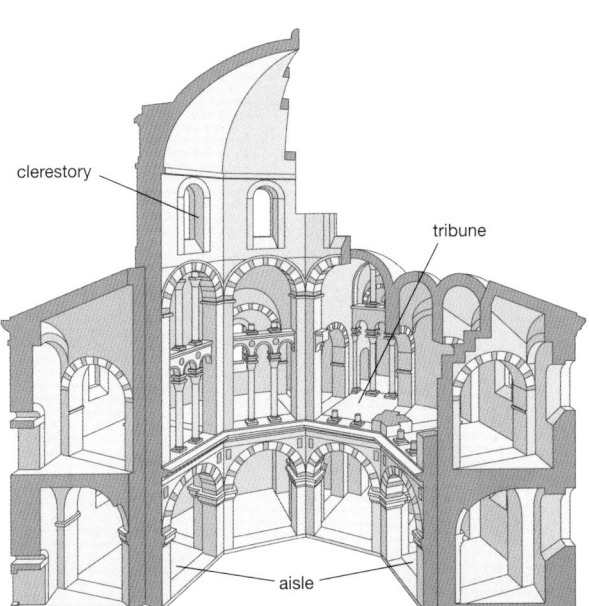

15–17B SECTION DRAWING, PALACE CHAPEL OF CHARLEMAGNE
Aachen (Aix-la-Chapelle), Germany. 792–805.

Credit: Kathy Mrozek

under the octagonal dome. At the gallery level, two tiers of paired Corinthian columns and railings form a screen that re-emphasizes the flat, pierced walls of the octagon and enhances the clear, planar geometry of its design. The effect is quite different from the dynamic spatial play and undulating exedrae of San Vitale, but the veneer of richly patterned and multicolored stone—some imported from Italy—on the walls and the mosaics covering the dome at Aachen were clearly inspired by Byzantine architecture.

THE WESTWORK AT CORVEY   Originally designed to answer practical requirements of protection and display in buildings such as Charlemagne's palace chapel, the soaring, multi-towered westwork came to function as the very visible sign of an important building; it is one of the hallmarks of Carolingian architecture. A particularly well-preserved example is the late ninth-century westwork at the

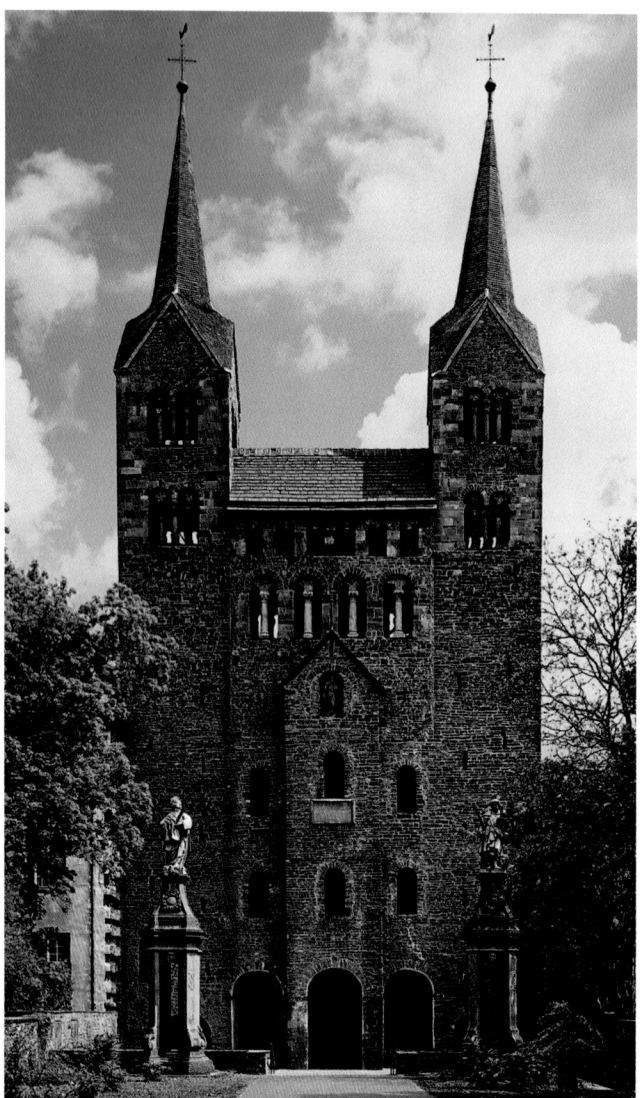

15–18 WESTWORK, ABBEY CHURCH OF CORVEY
Westphalia, Germany. Late 9th century (upper stories mid 12th century).

Credit: © Achim Bednorz, Cologne

ABBEY CHURCH OF CORVEY (FIG. 15–18). Even discounting the pierced upper story and towers that were added in the middle of the twelfth century, this is a broad and imposing block of masonry construction. The strong, austere exterior is a symmetrical arrangement of towers flanking a central core punched with a regular pattern of windows and doors, free of elaborate carving or decoration. In addition to providing private spaces for local or visiting dignitaries, the interiors of westworks may have been used for choirs—medieval musical graffiti were discovered inside this one—and they were the starting point for important liturgical processions.

THE SAINT GALL PLAN   Monastic life centered on prayer and work, and since it also demanded seclusion, it required a special type of architectural planning. While contemplating how best to house a monastic community, Abbot Haito of Reichenau developed, at the request of his colleague Abbot Gozbert of Saint Gall, a conceptual plan for the layout of monasteries. This extraordinary ninth-century drawing survives in the library of the Abbey of Saint Gall in modern Switzerland and is known as the **SAINT GALL PLAN** (FIG. 15–19). This is not a blueprint in the modern sense, intended to guide the construction of an actual monastery, but a record of Carolingian thinking about the nature of monastic life. It does, however, reflect the basic layout of medieval monasteries, an efficient and functional arrangement that continues to be used by Benedictine monasteries today.

At the center of the Saint Gall plan is the **cloister**, an enclosed courtyard onto which open all the buildings that are central to the lives of monks. Most prominent is a large basilican church north of the cloister, with towers and multiple altars in nave and aisles as well as in the sanctuary at the east end, where monks would gather for communal prayer throughout the day and night. On the north side of the church were public buildings such as the abbot's house, the school, and the guesthouse. The monks' living quarters lie off the southern and eastern sides of the cloister, with a dormitory, a refectory (dining room), and work rooms. For night services the monks could enter the church directly from their dormitory. The kitchen, brewery, and bakery were attached to the refectory, and a huge cellar (indicated on the plan by giant barrels) was on the west side. Along the east edge of the plan are a cemetery, a hospital, and an educational center for novices (monks in training).

The Saint Gall plan indicates beds for 77 monks in the dormitory. Practical considerations for group living include latrines attached to every unit—dormitory, guesthouse, and abbot's house. Six beds and places in the refectory were reserved for visiting monks. In the surrounding buildings were special spaces for scribes and painters, who spent much of their day in the scriptorium studying and

15–19 SAINT GALL PLAN (ORIGINAL AND REDRAWN WITH CAPTIONS)
c. 817. Original in red ink on parchment, 28 × 44⅛″ (71.1 × 112.1 cm). Stiftsbibliothek, Saint Gall, Switzerland. Cod. Sang. 1092.

Credit: (left) Stiftsbibliothek, St. Gallen; (right) Kathy Mrozek

copying books, and for teachers who staffed the monastery's schools and library. St. Benedict had directed that monks extend hospitality to all visitors, and the plan includes a hospice for the poor. South and west of the central core were workshops, farm buildings, and housing for the lay support staff.

Illustrated Books

Books played a central role in the efforts of Carolingian rulers to promote learning, propagate Christianity, and standardize church law and practice. Imperial workshops produced authoritative copies of key religious texts, weeding out the errors that had inevitably crept into books over centuries of copying them by hand. The scrupulously edited versions of ancient and biblical texts that emerged are among the lasting achievements of the Carolingian period. For example, the Anglo-Saxon scholar Alcuin of York, whom Charlemagne called to his court, spent the last eight years of his life producing a corrected copy of the Latin Vulgate Bible. His revision served as the standard

text of the Bible for the remainder of the medieval period and is still in use.

Carolingian scribes also worked on standardizing script. Capitals (majuscules) based on ancient Roman inscriptions continued to be used for very formal writing, titles and headings, and luxury manuscripts. But they also developed a new, clear script called Carolingian minuscule, based on Roman forms but with a uniform lowercase alphabet that increased legibility and streamlined production. So, like those who transformed other revived Roman types—such as basilicas, central-plan churches, and equestrian Roman portraits—into creative new works, scribes and illuminators revitalized established traditions of book production. Notably, they returned the representation of lifelike human figures to a central position. For example, portraits of the evangelists (the authors of the Gospels) began to look like pictures of Roman authors.

As can be seen in a comparison of the author portraits in two Carolingian Gospel books, however, a common source in the Roman tradition did not preclude considerable variation in both style and expressive content.

15–20 PAGE WITH ST. MATTHEW THE EVANGELIST, CORONATION GOSPELS

Gospel of Matthew. Early 9th century. 12¾ × 9¹³⁄₁₆″ (32.4 × 24.9 cm). Kunsthistorisches Museum, Vienna. Inv.Nr. SK XIII 18, folio 15r

Tradition holds that this Gospel book was buried with Charlemagne in 814, and that in the year 1000 Emperor Otto III removed it from his tomb. Its title derives from its use in the coronation ceremonies of later German emperors.

Credit: © KHM-Museumsverband

THE CORONATION GOSPELS The portrait of Matthew (**FIG. 15–20**) in the early ninth-century **CORONATION GOSPELS** of Charlemagne conforms to the idealized, lifelike representation of the Greco-Roman Classical tradition. The full-bodied, white-robed figure is modeled in brilliant white and subtle shading and seated on the cushion of a folding chair set within a freely painted landscape. The way his foot lifts up to rest on the solid base of his writing desk emphasizes his three-dimensional placement within an outdoor setting, and the frame enhances the Classical effect of a view seen through a window. Conventions for creating the illusion of solid figures in space may have been learned from Byzantine manuscripts in a monastic library or from artists fleeing Byzantium as a result of the iconoclastic controversy (see Chapter 8).

15–21 PAGE WITH ST. MATTHEW THE EVANGELIST, EBBO GOSPELS

Gospel of Matthew. Second quarter of 9th century. Ink, gold, and colors on vellum, each page 10¼ × 8¾″ (26 × 22.2 cm). Médiathèque d'Épernay, France. MS. 1, fol. 18v.

THE EBBO GOSPELS   One of the most innovative and engaging Carolingian variations on Greco-Roman tradition is a Gospel book made for Archbishop Ebbo of Reims (archbishop 816–835, 840–841) at the nearby Abbey of Hautvillers (**FIG. 15-21**). The calm, carefully painted grandeur characterizing Matthew's portrait in the Coronation Gospels (SEE FIG. 15-20) has given way to spontaneous, calligraphic painting suffused with energetic abandon. The passion is apparent in the intensity of Matthew's gaze, but the whole composition is charged with energy, from the evangelist's wiry hairdo and rippling drapery to the rapidly sketched landscape and the windblown acanthus leaves of the frame. These forms are related to content, evoking the evangelist's spiritual excitement as he hastens to transcribe the Word of God delivered by the angel (also serving as Matthew's symbol), who is almost lost in the

upper right corner. As if swept up in the saint's turbulent emotions, the footstool tilts precariously and the top of the desk seems about to detach itself from the pedestal.

THE UTRECHT PSALTER   One of the most famous Carolingian manuscripts, the Utrecht Psalter (**FIG. 15-22**), is illustrated with ink drawings that match the linear vitality encountered in Ebbo's Gospel book. Psalms do not tell straightforward stories but use metaphor and allegory in poems of prayer; they are exceptionally difficult to illustrate. Some psalters bypass this situation by illustrating scenes from the life of the presumed author (SEE FIG. 8-27). The artists of the Utrecht Psalter, however, decided to interpret the words and images of individual psalms literally (see "Closer Look" on page 529). Sometimes the words are acted out, as in a game of charades.

A Closer Look

PSALM 23 IN THE UTRECHT PSALTER

The basilica curtains are drawn back to reveal an altar and hanging votive crown: "I will dwell in the house of the Lord forever" (verse 6).

The artist has situated the psalmist in a pasture filled with sheep, goats, and cattle "beside the still water" (verse 2) of a gently flowing stream.

The text of Psalm 23 (22 in the Latin Vulgate) begins here with the words *Dominus regit me* ("The Lord ruleth me"). This is the Latin translator's rewording of the Hebrew text of the opening, which is more familiar to Christians today as: "The Lord is my shepherd."

An angel supports the psalmist with a "rod and staff" while anointing his head with oil (verses 4 and 5).

"Thou preparest a table before me in the presence of mine enemies" (verse 5).

Enemies gather and shoot arrows, but the psalmist ignores them to focus on the table and the house of the Lord, holding a conspicuous cup in his hand, presumably overflowing (verses 5 and 6).

15-22 PSALM 23, THE UTRECHT PSALTER
c. 816–835. Ink on parchment, 13 × 9⅞" (33 × 25 cm). Utrecht University Library.
MS. 32, fol. 13r.

15–23 CRUCIFIXION WITH ANGELS AND MOURNING FIGURES, LINDAU GOSPELS

Outer cover. c. 870–880. Gold, pearls, sapphires, garnets, and emeralds, 13¾ × 10⅞″ (36.9 × 27.5 cm). The Morgan Library and Museum, New York. MS. 1.

Metalwork

The sumptuously illustrated manuscripts of the medieval period represented an enormous investment of time, talent, and materials, so it is not surprising that they were often protected with equally sumptuous covers. But because these covers were made of valuable materials—ivory, enamelwork, precious metals, and jewels—they were frequently recycled or stolen. The elaborate book cover of gold and jewels now on the Carolingian manuscript known as the **LINDAU GOSPELS** (**FIG. 15–23**) was probably made between 870 and 880 at one of the monastic workshops of Charlemagne's grandson, Charles the Bald (ruled 840–877), but not for this book. Sometime before the sixteenth century it was reused on a late ninth-century manuscript from the monastery of Saint Gall.

The cross and the Crucifixion were common themes for medieval book covers. This one is crafted in pure gold with figures in repoussé (low relief produced by pushing or hammering up from the back of a panel of metal to produce raised forms on the front) surrounded by heavily jeweled frames. The jewels are raised on miniature arcades to allow reflected light to pass through them from beneath, imparting a lustrous glow, and also to allow light traveling in the other direction to reflect from the shiny surface of the gold.

Grieving angels hover above the arms of the cross, and earthbound mourners twist in agony below. Over Jesus's head personifications of the sun and the moon hide their faces in anguish. The gracefully animated poses of these figures, who seem to float around the jeweled bosses in the compartments framed by the arms of the cross, extend the expressive style of the Utrecht Psalter illustrations into another medium and a later moment. Jesus, on the other hand, has been modeled in a more rounded and calmer Classical style. He seems almost to be standing in front of the cross—straight, wide-eyed, with outstretched arms, as if to prefigure his ultimate triumph over death. The flourishes of blood that emerge from his wounds are almost decorative. There is little, if any, sense of his suffering.

Ottonian Europe

How do architecture, sculpture, and painting develop in Ottonian Europe?

In 843, the Carolingian Empire was divided into three parts ruled by three grandsons of Charlemagne. One of them was Charles the Bald, whom we have already encountered (SEE FIG. 15–16). Another, Louis the German, took the eastern portion, and when his family died out at the beginning of the tenth century, a new Saxon dynasty came to power in lands corresponding roughly to present-day Germany and Austria. We call this dynasty Ottonian

after its three principal rulers—Otto I (ruled 936–973), Otto II (ruled 973–983), and Otto III (ruled 983–1002; queens Adelaide and Theophanu ruled as regents for him, 983–994). After the Ottonian armies defeated the Vikings in the north and the Magyars (Hungarians) on the eastern frontiers, the resulting peace permitted increased trade and the growth of towns, making the tenth century a period of economic recovery. In 951, Otto I added northern Italy to his domain by marrying the widowed Lombard queen, Adelaide. He also re-established Charlemagne's Christian Roman Empire when he was crowned emperor by the pope in 962. The Ottonians and their successors so dominated the papacy and appointments to other high offices of the Church that in the twelfth century this union of Germany and Italy under a German ruler came to be known as the Holy Roman Empire. The empire survived in modified form as the Habsburg Empire into the early twentieth century.

The Ottonian ideology, rooted in unity of Church and state, takes visual form on an ivory plaque, one of several that may once have been part of the decoration of an altar or pulpit presented to Magdeburg Cathedral at the time of its dedication in 968 (**FIG. 15–24**). Otto I presents a model of the cathedral to Christ and St. Peter. Following hierarchic

15–24 OTTO I PRESENTING MAGDEBURG CATHEDRAL TO CHRIST

One of a series of 17 ivory plaques known as the Magdeburg Ivories, possibly carved in Milan. c. 962–968. Ivory, 5 × 4½" (12.7 × 11.4 cm). Metropolitan Museum of Art, New York. *Gift of George Blumenthal, 1941 (41.100.157).*

Credit: © 2016. Image copyright The Metropolitan Museum of Art/Art Resource/Scala, Florence

scale, the mighty emperor is the smallest figure and the saints and angels, in turn, are taller than Otto but smaller than Christ. Otto is embraced by the patron saint of this church, St. Maurice, a third-century military commander who was martyred for refusing to worship pagan gods. The cathedral Otto holds is a basilica with prominent clerestory windows and a rounded apse. Like the Carolingian basilicas before it, it was intended to recall the Early Christian churches of Rome.

Architecture

As we have seen, Ottonian rulers sought to replicate the splendors of both the Christian architecture of Rome and the Christian empire of their Carolingian predecessors. German officials knew Roman basilicas well, since the German court in Rome was located near the Early Christian church of Santa Sabina (SEE FIGS. 7–12, 7–13). The buildings of Byzantium were another important influence, especially after Otto II married a Byzantine princess, cementing a tie with the East. But large timber-roofed basilicas were terribly vulnerable to fire. Magdeburg Cathedral burned down in 1008, only 40 years after its dedication; it was rebuilt in 1049, burned down again in 1207, and rebuilt yet again. In 1009, the Cathedral of Mainz burned down on the day of its consecration. The church of St. Michael at Hildesheim was destroyed in World War II. Luckily the convent church of St. Cyriakus at Gernrode, Germany, still survives.

THE CONVENT CHURCH OF ST. CYRIAKUS IN GERNRODE During the Ottonian Empire, aristocratic women often held positions of authority, especially as leaders of religious communities. When the provincial military governor Gero founded the convent and **CHURCH OF ST. CYRIAKUS** in 961, he installed his widowed daughter-in-law as the convent's first abbess. The church was designed as a basilica with a westwork flanked by circular towers (FIG. 15–25). At the eastern end, a transept with chapels leads to a choir with an apse built over a crypt.

Like an Early Christian or Carolingian basilica, the interior of St. Cyriakus (SEE FIG. 15–25B) has a nave flanked by side aisles. But the design of the three-level wall elevation—nave arcade, gallery, and clerestory—creates a rhythmic effect distinct from the uniformity that characterized earlier basilicas. Rectangular piers alternate with round columns in the two levels of arcades, and at gallery level pairs of openings are framed by larger arches and then grouped in threes. The central rectangular piers, aligned on the two levels, bisect the walls vertically into two units, each composed of two broad arches of the nave arcade topped by three pairs of arches at the gallery level. This seemingly simple system with its rhythmic alternation of heavy and light supports, its balance of rectangular and rounded forms, and its combination of horizontal and vertical movements seems to prefigure the aesthetic exploration of wall design that will characterize the Romanesque architecture of the next two centuries.

Sculpture

Ottonian sculptors worked in ivory, bronze, wood, and other materials rather than stone. Like their Early Christian and Byzantine predecessors, they and their patrons focused on church furnishings and portable art rather than architectural sculpture. Drawing on Roman, Early Christian, Byzantine, and Carolingian models, they created large works in wood and bronze that would have a significant influence on later medieval art.

15–25A PLAN OF CHURCH OF ST. CYRIAKUS, GERNRODE
Harz, Saxony-Anhalt, Germany.
Begun 961; consecrated 973.

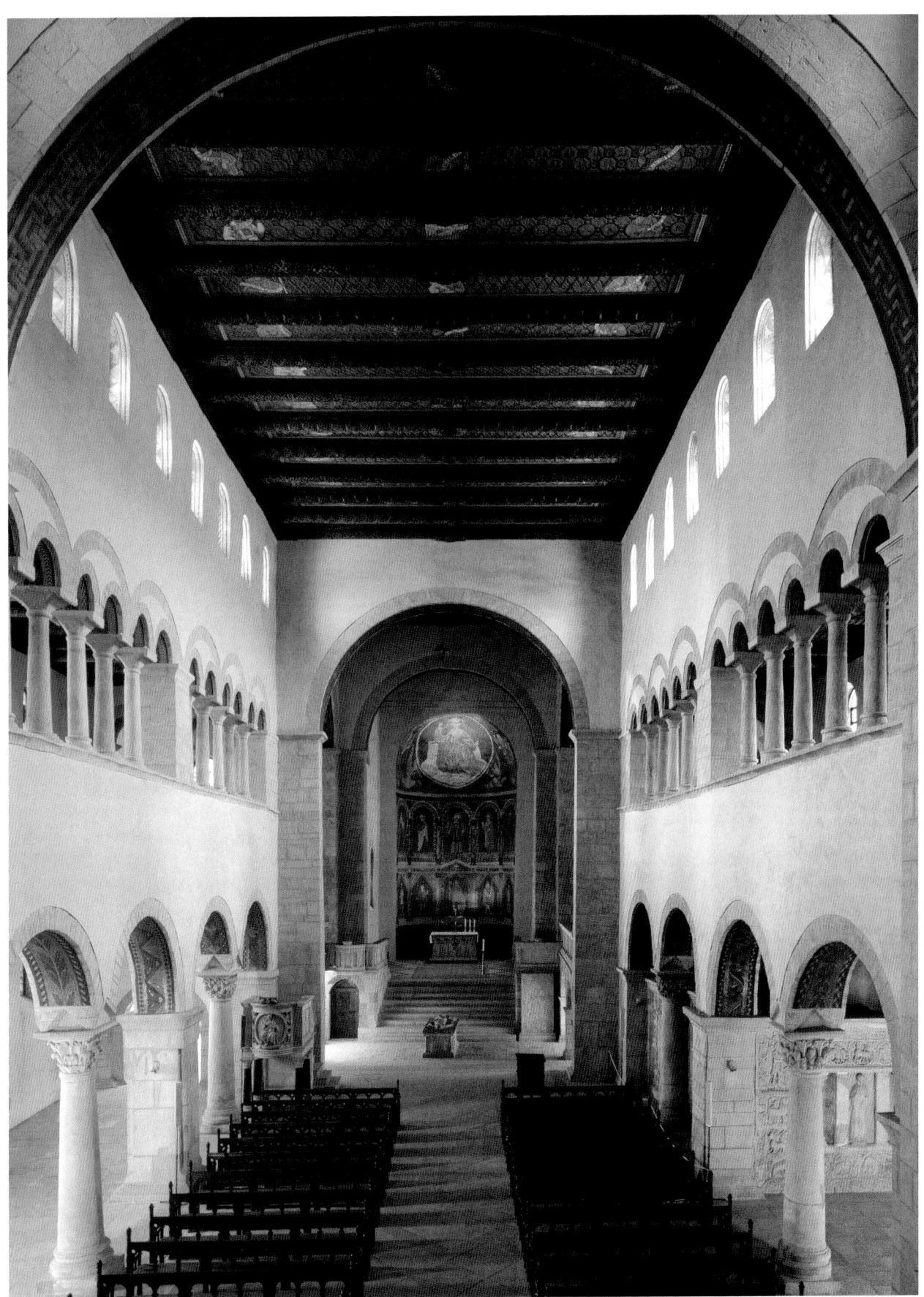

15–25B INTERIOR OF CHURCH OF ST. CYRIAKUS, GERNRODE

Harz, Saxony-Anhalt, Germany. Begun 961; consecrated 973.

Credit: © Achim Bednorz, Koln

15–26 GERO CRUCIFIX

Cologne Cathedral, Germany. c. 970. Painted and gilded wood, height of figure 6′2″ (1.88 m).

This life-size sculpture is both a crucifix to be suspended over an altar and a special kind of reliquary. A cavity in the back of the head was made to hold a piece of the Host, or Communion bread, already consecrated by the priest. Consequently, the figure not only represents the body of the dying Jesus but also contains a "relic" of the Eucharistic body of Christ. In fact, the Ottonian chronicle of Thietmar of Meresburg (written 1012–1018) claims that Gero himself placed a consecrated Host, as well as a fragment of the true cross, in a crack that formed within the head of this crucifix and prayed that it be closed, which it was.

Credit: Rheinisches Bildarchiv, Museen der Stadt Köln

THE GERO CRUCIFIX One of the few large works of carved wood to survive from the early Middle Ages is the **GERO CRUCIFIX** (**FIG. 15–26**). Archbishop Gero of Cologne (archbishop 969–976) commissioned the sculpture for his cathedral in about 970. The life-size figure of Christ is made of painted and gilded oak. The focus here is on Jesus's human suffering. He is shown as a tortured martyr, not as the triumphant hero of the Lindau Gospels cover (SEE FIG. 15–23). His broken body sags on the cross, and his head falls forward, eyes closed. The straight, linear fall of his golden drapery heightens the impact of his drawn face, emaciated arms and legs, sagging torso, and limp, bloodied hands. This is a poignant image of distilled anguish, meant to inspire pity and awe in its viewers.

THE HILDESHEIM DOORS Under the last of the Ottonian rulers, Henry II and Queen Kunigunde (ruled 1002–1024), Bishop Bernward of Hildesheim emerged as an important patron. His biographer, the monk Thangmar, described Bernward as a skillful goldsmith who closely supervised the artists working for him. Bronze doors made under his direction for the abbey church of St. Michael in Hildesheim—and installed by him in 1015, according to the inscription on them—represented the most ambitious bronze-casting project undertaken since antiquity (**FIG. 15–27**). Each door, including the impressive lion heads holding the ring handles, was cast as a single piece using the lost-wax process (see "Lost-Wax Casting" in Chapter 14 on page 428) and later detailed and reworked with chisels and fine tools. Rounded, animated figures populate spacious backgrounds. Architectural elements and features of the landscape are depicted in lower relief so that the figures stand out prominently, with their heads fully modeled in three dimensions. The result is lively, visually stimulating, and remarkably spontaneous in feeling for so monumental an undertaking.

The doors, standing more than 16 feet tall, portray events from the Hebrew Bible on the left (reading downward from the creation of Eve at the top to Cain's murder of Abel at the bottom) and from the New Testament on the right (reading upward from the Annunciation at the bottom to the *Noli me tangere* at the top). In each pair of scenes placed across from each other, the Hebrew Bible event is meant to prefigure or complement the New Testament event. For instance, the third panel down on the left shows Adam and Eve picking the forbidden fruit in the Garden of Eden, believed by Christians to be the source of human sin, suffering, and death. The paired scene on the right shows the Crucifixion of Jesus, whose sacrifice was believed to have atoned for Adam and Eve's original sin, bringing the promise of eternal life. At the center of the doors, six panels down—between the door pulls—Eve (left) and Mary (right) are paired, holding their sons. Cain (who murdered his brother) and Jesus (who was unjustly executed) signify the opposition of evil and good, damnation and salvation. Other telling combinations are the murder of Abel (the first sin) paired with the Annunciation (the advent of salvation) at the bottom, and the passing of blame from Adam and

Life in Paradise

Formation of Eve

Eve presented to Adam

The Fall

Temptation and Fall of Adam and Eve

Accusation and Judgment of Adam and Eve

Life in the World

Expulsion of Adam and Eve from Paradise

Adam and Eve Laboring

Eve's Children

Offerings by Cain (grain) and Abel (lamb)

Cain murders Abel

Promise of Return to Paradise

Noli me tangere

Three Marys at the Tomb

The Passion

Crucifixion

Judgment of Jesus by Pilate

Infancy of Jesus

Presentation of Jesus in the Temple

Adoration of the Magi

Mary's Child

Nativity

Annunciation

15–27 DOORS OF BISHOP BERNWARD

Cathedral of the Assumption of Mary, Hildesheim, Germany. 1015. Bronze, height 16′6″ (approx. 5 m).

Credit: Dommuseum Hildesheim. Photo: Florian Monheim

Eve to the serpent paired with Pilate washing his hands of any responsibility in the execution of Jesus, fourth from the top.

Illustrated Books

Like their Carolingian predecessors, Ottonian monks and nuns created richly illuminated manuscripts, which were often funded by secular rulers. Styles varied from place to place, depending on the traditions of the particular scriptorium, the models available in its library, and the creativity of its artists.

THE HITDA GOSPELS The presentation page of a Gospel book made in the early eleventh century for Abbess Hitda (d. 1041) of Meschede, near Cologne (**FIG. 15–28**) represents one of the most distinctive local styles. The

abbess herself appears here offering the book to St. Walpurga, her convent's patron saint. The artist has angled the buildings of the sprawling convent in the background to frame the figures and draw attention to their interaction. The size of the architectural complex underscores the abbess's position of authority. The foreground—a rocky, undulating strip of landscape—is meant to be understood as holy ground, separated from the rest of the world by golden trees and the huge arch-shape aura that silhouettes St. Walpurga. The energetic spontaneity of the painting's style suffuses the scene with a sense of religious fervor appropriate to the visionary encounter.

THE GOSPELS OF OTTO III This Gospel book, made in a German monastery near Reichenau about 1000, shows another Ottonian painting style, in this case inspired by Byzantine art in its use of sharply outlined drawing and

15–28 PRESENTATION PAGE WITH ABBESS HITDA AND ST. WALPURGA, HITDA GOSPELS

Early 11th century. Ink and colors on vellum, 11⅜ × 5⅝″ (29 × 14.2 cm). Universitäts- und Landesbibliothek, Darmstadt.

lavish fields of gold (**FIG. 15-29**). Backed by a more controlled and balanced architectural canopy than the one that sheltering Hitda and St. Walpurga, these tall, slender men gesture dramatically with long, thin fingers. The scene captures the moment when Jesus washes the feet of his disciples during their final meal together (John 13:1–17). At left is Peter, who had tried to stop his Savior from performing this ancient ritual of hospitality, with one leg reluctantly poised over the basin, while a centrally silhouetted and hierarchically scaled Jesus gestures emphatically to underscore the necessity and significance of the act. Another disciple at far right enthusiastically raises his leg to untie his sandals so he can be next in line. With selective stylization, the artist has transformed the Classical tradition into a style of stunning expressiveness and narrative power, features that will also characterize the figural styles associated with Romanesque art.

15-29 PAGE WITH CHRIST WASHING THE FEET OF HIS DISCIPLES, GOSPELS OF OTTO III

c. 1000. Ink, gold, and colors on vellum, approx. 13⅛ × 9½" (33.4 × 24.2 cm). Bayerische Staatsbibliothek, Munich. Clm 4453, fol. 237r.

Think About It

1   Characterize the styles of painting that developed in Spain for the illustration of commentaries on the Apocalypse and in the Ottonian world for visualizing sacred narratives. Focus your answer on specific examples discussed in this chapter.

2   Discuss the themes and subjects used for paintings in early medieval Gospel books by comparing two specific examples from different parts of Europe.

3   Explain the references to early Christian Roman traditions in Carolingian architecture. How did Carolingian builders transform their models?

4   Compare the renderings of the crucified Christ on the cover of the Lindau Gospels (**FIG. 15-23**) and on the Gero Crucifix (**FIG. 15-26**). Consider the differences in media and expressive effect, as well as in style and scale.

Crosscurrents

The equestrian portrait on the right consciously emulates the Roman tradition represented by the work on the left. For the early Middle Ages, this sort of creative appropriation was common artistic practice. Discuss what it tells us about the Carolingians, grounding your answer in a discussion of these two works.

FIG. 6–56

FIG. 15–16

16–1 CHRIST AND DISCIPLES ON THE ROAD TO EMMAUS
Cloister of the abbey of Santo Domingo, Silos, Castilla y Leon, Spain. c. 1100. Pier relief, figures nearly life-size.

Chapter 16
Romanesque Art

16.a Identify the visual hallmarks of Romanesque art for formal, technical, and expressive qualities.

16.b Interpret the meaning of works of Romanesque art based on their themes, subjects, and symbols.

16.c Relate Romanesque art and artists to their cultural, economic, and political contexts.

16.d Apply the vocabulary and concepts relevant to Romanesque art, artists, and art history.

16.e Interpret a work of Romanesque art using the art historical methods of observation, comparison, and inductive reasoning.

16.f Select visual and textual evidence in various media to support an argument or an interpretation of a work of Romanesque art.

Three men seem to glide forward on tiptoe as their leader turns back (**FIG. 16–1**). Their bodies are smooth and elongated, their legs cross in gentle angles, and their shoulders, elbows, and fingers form soft curves. Draperies delicately delineate shallow contours, and the bearded faces stare out with large, wide eyes from under strong brows. The figures interrelate and interlock, pushing against the limits of their architectural frame.

Medieval viewers would have quickly identified the leader as Christ, not only by his commanding size, but specifically by his cruciform halo. The sanctity of his companions is signified by their own haloes. The scene reminds faithful Christians of the resurrected Christ and two of his disciples on the road from Jerusalem to Emmaus (Luke 24:13–35). Christ has the distinctive attributes of a medieval pilgrim—a hat, a satchel, and a walking stick. The scallop shell on his satchel is the badge worn by pilgrims to a specific site: the shrine of St. James at Santiago de Compostela. Early pilgrims who reached this destination in the far northwestern corner of the Iberian peninsula continued to the coast to pick up a shell as evidence of their journey. Soon shells were gathered (or fabricated from metal as brooches) and sold to the pilgrims—a lucrative business for both the sellers and the church. On the return journey home, the shell became the pilgrims' passport, a badge attesting to their piety and accomplishment.

Other distinctive badges were adopted at other pilgrimage sites, too.

This relief was carved on a corner pier in the cloister of the monastery of Santo Domingo in Silos, a major eleventh- and twelfth-century center of religious and artistic life south of the pilgrimage road across Spain (see "The Pilgrim's Journey to Santiago" on page 476). It engaged an audience of monks—who were well versed in the meaning of Christian images—through a sculptural style that we call Romanesque. Not since the art of ancient Rome half a millennium earlier had sculptors carved monumental figures in stone within an architectural fabric. During the early Middle Ages, sculpture was small-scale, independent, and created from precious materials—a highlighted object within a sacred space, rather than a part of the space's architectural envelope. But during the Romanesque period, narrative and iconic figural imagery in deeply carved ornamental frameworks was placed especially heavily around the entrances to churches, focusing attention on their compelling portal complexes. These public displays of Christian doctrine and moral teaching would have been part of the cultural landscape experienced by pilgrims journeying along the road to Santiago. Traveling as a pilgrim opened the mind to a world beyond the familiar towns and agricultural villages of home, signaling a new era in the social, economic, and artistic life of Europe.

MAP 16-1 EUROPE IN THE ROMANESQUE PERIOD

Although a few large political entities began to emerge in places like England and Normandy, Burgundy, and León/Castile, Europe remained a land of small economic entities. Pilgrimages, monasticism, and crusades acted as unifying international forces.

Romanesque Europe

What are the geographical and historical backgrounds for Romanesque art and architecture?

At the beginning of the eleventh century, Europe was still divided into many small political and economic units ruled by powerful families, such as the Ottonians in Germany (**MAP 16-1**). The nations we know today did not exist, although for convenience we shall use present-day names of countries. The king of France ruled only a small area around Paris known as the Île-de-France. The southern part of today's France had close linguistic and cultural ties to northern Spain; in the north the duke of Normandy (heir of the Vikings) and in the east the duke of Burgundy paid the French king only token homage.

When in 1066 Duke William II of Normandy (ruled 1035–1087) invaded England and, as William the Conqueror, became that country's new king, Norman nobles replaced the Anglo-Saxon nobility there, and England became politically and culturally allied with Normandy. As astute and skillful administrators, the Normans formed a close alliance with the Church, supporting it with grants of land and gaining in return the allegiance of abbots and bishops. Normandy became one of Europe's most powerful domains. During this period, the Holy Roman Empire, re-established by the Ottonians, encompassed much of Germany and northern Italy, while the Iberian peninsula remained divided between Muslim rulers in the south and Christian rulers in the north. By 1085, Alfonso VI of Castile and León (ruled 1065–1109) had conquered the Muslim stronghold of Toledo, a center of Islamic and Jewish culture in the kingdom of Castile. Catalunya (Catalonia) emerged as a power along the Mediterranean coast.

By the end of the twelfth century, however, a few exceptionally intelligent and aggressive rulers had begun to create national states. The Capetians in France and the Plantagenets in England were especially successful. In Germany and northern Italy, the power of local rulers and towns prevailed, and Germany and Italy remained politically fragmented until the nineteenth century.

Political, Economic, and Social Life

Although towns and cities with artisans and merchants grew in importance, Europe remained an agricultural society, and developing agricultural practices in this period led to expanded food supplies and population growth.

Land was the primary source of wealth and power for a hereditary aristocracy. Allegiances, obligations, and social relations among members of the upper echelons of society, as well as between them and the peasants who lived and worked on their land, were not static, but were subject to long- and short-term changes in power and wealth. Patterns of political and social dependencies, expectations, and obligations varied extensively from place to place and from community to community. Life was often difficult, and people from all levels of society were vulnerable to the violence of warfare—both local and general—as well as recurrent famine and disease.

The Church

In the early Middle Ages, Church and state had forged some fruitful alliances. Christian rulers helped ensure the spread of Christianity throughout Europe and supported monastic communities with grants of land. Bishops and abbots were often royal relatives, younger brothers and cousins, who supplied the rulers with crucial social and spiritual support and a cadre of educated administrators. As a result, secular and religious authority became tightly intertwined; this continued through the Romanesque period. Monasteries remained at the center of European culture, but there were two new cultural forces fostered by the Church: pilgrimages and crusades.

MONASTICISM   Although the first universities were established in the eleventh and twelfth centuries in the growing cities of Bologna, Paris, Oxford, and Cambridge, monastic communities continued to play a major role in intellectual life and—as in the early Middle Ages—provide valuable social services, including caring for the sick and destitute, housing travelers, and educating the elite. Because monasteries were major landholders, abbots and priors were part of the political power structure. The children of aristocratic families continued to join religious orders, strengthening links between monastic communities and the ruling elite.

As life in Benedictine communities grew increasingly comfortable and intertwined with the secular world, reform movements sought a return to earlier monastic austerity and spirituality. The first important group of reformers for the arts was the Burgundian congregation of Cluny, established in the tenth century. Later came the Cistercians, who sought reform of what they saw as Cluniac decadence and corruption of monastic values.

PILGRIMAGES   Pilgrimages to three of the holiest places of Christendom—Jerusalem, Rome, and Santiago de Compostela—increased (see "The Pilgrim's Journey to Santiago" on page 476), although the majority of pilgrimages were probably more local. Rewards awaited courageous travelers along the routes, whether long or short. Pilgrims

on long journeys could venerate the relics of local saints along the route, and artists and architects were commissioned to create spectacular and enticing new buildings and works of art to capture their attention.

CRUSADES   In the eleventh and twelfth centuries, Christian Europe, previously on the defensive against the expanding forces of Islam, became the aggressor. In Spain, Christian armies of the north waged increasingly successful invasions against Islamic kingdoms in the south. At the same time, the Byzantine emperor asked the pope for help in his war with the Muslims surrounding his domain. The Western Church responded in 1095 by launching a series of holy wars, military offensives against Islamic powers known collectively as the crusades (from the Latin *crux*, referring to the cross crusaders wore).

This First Crusade was preached by Pope Urban II (pontificate 1088–1099) and fought by the lesser nobility of France, who had economic and political as well as spiritual objectives. The crusaders captured Jerusalem in 1099 and established a short-lived kingdom. The Second Crusade in 1147, preached by St. Bernard and led by France and Germany, accomplished nothing. In 1187, the Muslim leader Saladin united the Muslim forces and captured Jerusalem, inspiring the Third Crusade, led by German, French, and English kings. The Europeans recaptured some territory, but not Jerusalem, and in 1192 they concluded a truce with the Muslims, permitting the Christians access to the shrines in Jerusalem. Although the crusades were brutal military failures, the movement had far-reaching cultural and economic consequences, providing western Europeans with direct encounters with the more sophisticated material culture of the Islamic world and the Byzantine Empire. This in turn helped stimulate trade, and with trade came the development of an increasingly urban society during the eleventh and twelfth centuries.

Romanesque Architecture

How is architecture transformed across Europe during the Romanesque period?

The word "Romanesque," meaning "in the Roman manner," was coined in the early nineteenth century to describe early medieval European church architecture, which often displayed the solid masonry walls and rounded arches and vaults characteristic of imperial Roman buildings. Soon the term was applied to all the arts of the period from roughly the mid eleventh century to the second half of the twelfth century, even though that art derives from a variety of sources and reflects a multitude of influences, not just Roman.

This was a period of great construction activity in Europe. New castles, manor houses, churches, and monasteries arose everywhere. One eleventh-century monk claimed that the Christian faithful were so relieved to have passed through the apocalyptic anxiety that had gripped their world at the millennial change around the year 1000, that, in gratitude, "Each people of Christendom rivaled with the other, to see which should worship in the finest buildings. The world shook herself, clothed everywhere in a white garment of churches" (Radulphus Glaber, cited in Holt, vol. I, p. 18). The desire to glorify the house of the Lord and his saints (whose earthly remains in the form of relics kept their presence alive in the minds of the people) increased throughout Christendom.

Romanesque architecture and art was a trans-European phenomenon, but it was inflected regionally, and the style varied in character from place to place. Although timber remained common in construction, Romanesque builders used stone masonry extensively. Masonry vaults were stronger and more durable, and they enhanced the acoustical effect of Gregorian chant (plainsong, named after Pope Gregory the Great, pontificate 590–604). Stone towers sometimes marked the church as the most important building in the community. Portals were often encrusted with sculptures that broadcast the moral and theological messages of the Church to a wide public.

16–2 SAINT-MARTIN-DU-CANIGOU

French Pyrenees. 1001–1026.

Credit: © akg-images/Stefan Drechsel

"First Romanesque"

Soon after the year 1000, patrons and builders in Catalunya (northeast Spain), southern France, and northern Italy were already constructing all-masonry churches, employing the methods of late Roman builders. The picturesque Benedictine monastery of **SAINT-MARTIN-DU-CANIGOU**, nestled into the Pyrenees on a building platform stabilized by strongly buttressed retaining walls, is a typical example (**FIG. 16–2**). Patronized by the local Count Guifred, who took refuge in the monastery and died here in 1049, the complex is capped by a massive stone tower next to the sanctuary of the two-story church. Art historians call such early stone-vaulted buildings "First Romanesque," employing the term that Catalan architect and theorist Josep Puig I Cadafalch first associated with them in 1928.

THE CHURCH OF SANT VINCENÇ, CARDONA
Another fine example of "First Romanesque" is the **CHURCH OF SANT VINCENÇ** (St. Vincent) in the Catalan castle of Cardona (**FIG. 16–3**). Begun in the 1020s, it was consecrated in 1040. Castle residents entered the church through a two-story narthex into a nave with low narrow side aisles that permitted clerestory windows in the nave wall. The sanctuary was raised dramatically over an aisled crypt. The Catalan masons used local materials—small split stones, bricks, river pebbles, and very strong mortar—to raise plain walls and round barrel or groin vaults. Today we can admire their skillful stonework both inside and out, but the builders originally covered their masonry with stucco.

To strengthen the exterior walls and enrich their sculptural presence, the masons added vertical bands of projecting masonry (called strip buttresses) joined by arches and additional courses of masonry to counter the weight and outward thrust of the vault. On the interior these masonry strips project from the piers and continue up and over the vault, creating a series of **transverse arches**. Additional projecting bands line the underside of the arches of the nave arcade. The result is a compound, sculptural pier that works in concert with the transverse arches to divide the nave into a series of bays. This system of bay division became standard in Romanesque architecture. It is a marked contrast to the flat-wall continuity and undivided space within a pre-Romanesque church like the one in Gernrode (SEE FIG. 15–25).

Pilgrimage Churches

The growth of a cult of relics and the desire to visit holy shrines such as St. Peter's in Rome or St. James's in Spain, as well as the shrines of local saints, increasingly inspired Christians in western Europe to travel on pilgrimages (see "The Pilgrim's Journey to Santiago" on page 476). To accommodate the faithful and proclaim Church doctrine,

many monasteries—including those on the major pilgrimage routes—built large new churches, filled them with sumptuous altars and reliquaries, and encrusted them with elaborate stone sculpture on the exterior, especially around entrances.

16-3 INTERIOR, CHURCH OF SANT VINCENÇ, CARDONA
Spain. 1020s–1030s.

Credit: Archivo Fotográphico Oronoz, Madrid

Art and its Contexts

THE PILGRIM'S JOURNEY TO SANTIAGO

Western Europe in the eleventh and twelfth centuries saw the growing popularity of religious pilgrimage—much of it local, but some of it international. The rough roads that led to the holiest destinations—the tomb of St. Peter and other martyrs in Rome, the church of the Holy Sepulcher in Jerusalem, and the cathedral of St. James in Santiago de Compostela in the northwest corner of Spain—were often crowded with pilgrims. Journeys could last a year or more; church officials going to Compostela were given 16 weeks' leave of absence. Along the way the pilgrims had to contend with bad food and poisoned water, as well as bandits and dishonest innkeepers and merchants.

In the twelfth century, the priest Aymery Picaud wrote a guidebook for pilgrims on their way to Santiago through what is now France. Like travel guides today, Picaud's book provided advice on local customs, comments on food and the safety of drinking water, and a list of useful words in the Basque language. In Picaud's time, four main pilgrimage routes to Santiago crossed France, merging into a single road in Spain at Puente la Reina and leading on from there through Burgos and León to Compostela (MAP 16–2). Conveniently spaced monasteries and churches offered food and lodging, as well as relics to venerate. Roads and bridges were maintained by a guild of bridge builders and guarded by the Knights of Santiago.

Picaud described the best-traveled routes and most important shrines to visit along the way. Chartres, for example, housed the tunic that the Virgin was said to have worn when she gave birth to Jesus. The monks of Vézelay had the bones of St. Mary Magdalen, and at Conques, the skull of Sainte Foy was to be found. Churches associated with miraculous cures—Autun, for example, which claimed to house the relics of Lazarus, raised by Jesus from the dead—were filled with the sick and injured praying to be healed.

MAP 16–2 THE PILGRIMAGE ROUTES TO SANTIAGO DE COMPOSTELA

THE CATHEDRAL OF ST. JAMES IN SANTIAGO DE COMPOSTELA One major goal of pilgrimage was the **CATHEDRAL OF ST. JAMES** in Santiago de Compostela (**FIG. 16–4**), which held the body of St. James, the apostle to the Iberian peninsula. Builders of this and several other major churches along the roads leading through France to the shrine developed a distinctive plan designed to accommodate the crowds of pilgrims and allow them to move easily from chapel to chapel to venerate relics. This "pilgrimage plan" is a model of functional planning and traffic control. To the aisled nave the builders added aisled transepts with eastern chapels leading to an ambulatory (curving walkway) with additional radiating chapels around the apse. This expansion of the basilican plan allowed worshipers to circulate freely around the church's perimeter, visiting chapels and venerating relics without disrupting services within the main space.

At Santiago, pilgrims entered the church through large double doors at the ends of the transepts rather than through the western portal, which served ceremonial processions. Pilgrims from France entered the north transept portal; the approach from the town was through the south portal. All found themselves in a transept in which the design exactly mirrored the nave in height and structure (**FIG. 16–5**). Both nave and transept have two stories—an arcade and a gallery. Compound piers with attached half-columns on all four sides support the immense barrel vault and are projected over it vertically through a rhythmic series of transverse arches. They give sculptural form to the interior walls and also mark off individual vaulted bays in which the sequence is as clear and regular as the ambulatory chapels of the choir. Three different kinds of vaults are used here: barrel vaults with transverse arches cover the nave, groin vaults span the side aisles, and half-barrel or quadrant vaults cover the galleries and strengthen the building by countering the outward thrust of the high nave vaults and transferring it to the outer walls and buttresses. Without a clerestory, light enters the nave and transept only indirectly, through windows in the outer walls of the aisles and upper-level galleries. Light from the choir clerestory and the large windows of an octagonal **lantern** tower (a structure built above the height of the main

**16-4 PLAN (A) AND
RECONSTRUCTION DRAWING (B)
OF THE CATHEDRAL OF ST. JAMES,
SANTIAGO DE COMPOSTELA**

Galicia, Spain. 1078–1122; western portions
later. View from the east.

Credit: Kathy Mrozek

ceiling with windows that illuminate the space below) over the crossing would therefore spotlight the glittering gold and jeweled shrine of the principal relic at the high altar.

In its own time, Santiago was admired for the excellence of its construction—"not a single crack is to be found," said the twelfth-century pilgrims' guide, "admirable and beautiful in execution… large, spacious, well-lighted, of fitting size, harmonious in width, length, and height…." Pilgrims arrived at Santiago de Compostela weary after weeks or months of difficult travel through dense woods and mountains. Grateful to St. James for his protection along the way, they entered a church that welcomed them with open portals covered with the dynamic, moralizing sculpture that characterized Romanesque churches. The cathedral had no doors to close—it was open day and night.

**16-5 NAVE, CATHEDRAL
OF ST. JAMES, SANTIAGO DE COMPOSTELA**

1078–1122. View toward the choir.

Credit: © akg-images/Andrea Jemolo

Relics and Reliquaries

Christians turned to the heroes of the Church, especially martyrs who had died for their faith, to answer their prayers and to intercede with Christ on their behalf; prayers offered to saints while in close proximity to their relics were considered especially effective. Bodies, parts of bodies, and things associated with the Holy Family or the saints were kept in richly decorated containers called reliquaries. Reliquaries could be simple boxes, but they might also be created in more elaborate shapes, sometimes in the form of body parts such as arms, ribs, or heads. By the eleventh century, many different arrangements of crypts, chapels, and passageways gave people access to the relics

16–6 RELIQUARY STATUE OF SAINTE FOY (ST. FAITH)

Abbey church, Conques, France. Late 9th or 10th century with later additions. Silver gilt over a wood core, with gems and cameos of various dates. Height 33″ (85 cm). Church Treasury, Conques.

Credit: © akg-images/Erich Lessing

kept in churches. When the Church decided that every altar required a relic, the saints' bodies and possessions were subdivided. In this way relics were multiplied; for example, hundreds of churches held relics of the true cross.

Owning and displaying these relics so enhanced the prestige and wealth of a community that people went to great lengths to acquire them, not only by purchase but also by theft. In the ninth century, for example, the monks of Conques stole the relics of the child martyr Sainte Foy (St. Faith) from her shrine at Agen. Such a theft was called "holy robbery," for the new owners insisted that it had been sanctioned by the saint, who had communicated to them her desire to move. In the late ninth or tenth century, the monks of Conques encased their new relic—the skull of Sainte Foy—in a gold and jeweled statue whose unusually large head was made from a reused late Roman work. During the eleventh century, they added the crown and more jeweled banding, and, over subsequent centuries, jewels, cameos, and other gifts added by pilgrims continued to enhance the statue's splendor (FIG. 16–6).

This type of reliquary—taking the form of a statue of the saint—was quite popular in the region around Conques, but not everyone was comfortable with the way these works functioned as cult images. Early in the eleventh century, Bernard of Angers prefaces his tendentious account of miracles associated with the cult of Sainte Foy by confessing his initial misgivings about such reliquaries, specifically the way simple folks adored them. Bernard thought it smacked of idolatry: "To learned people this may seem to be full of superstition, if not unlawful, for it seems as if the rites of the gods of ancient cultures, or that the rites of demons, are being observed" (*The Book of Sainte Foy*, p. 77). But when he witnessed firsthand the interaction of the reliquary statue with the faithful, he altered his position: "For the holy image is consulted not as an idol that requires sacrifices, but because it commemorates a martyr. Since reverence to her honors God on high, it was despicable of me to compare her statue to statues of Venus or Diana. Afterwards I was very sorry that I had acted so foolishly toward God's saint." (ibid., p. 78)

Cluny

In 909, the duke of Burgundy gave land for a monastery to Benedictine monks intent on strict adherence to the original rules of St. Benedict. They established the reformed congregation of Cluny. From its foundation, Cluny had an independent status; its abbot answered directly to the pope in Rome rather than to the local bishop or lord. This freedom, safeguarded by a series of long-lived and astute abbots, enabled Cluny to keep the profits from extensive gifts of both land and treasure. Independent, wealthy, and a center of culture and learning, Cluny and its affiliates became important patrons of architecture and art.

stables and guest house

abbot's residence

main gate

second church

monks' cloister

kitchen

third church

monks' refectory

novices' dormitory

novices' cloister

monks' dormitory

cemetery and chapel

infirmaries

latrines

16–7 RECONSTRUCTION DRAWING OF THE ABBEY OF CLUNY
Burgundy, France. 1088–1130. View from the east.

Credit: Stephen Conlin © Dorling Kindersley

The monastery of Cluny was a city unto itself. By the second half of the eleventh century, there were some 200 monks in residence, supplemented by many laymen on whom they depended for material support. Just as in the Saint Gall plan of the Carolingian period (SEE FIG. 15–19), the cloister lay at the center of this monastic community, joining the church with domestic buildings and workshops (FIG. 16–7). In wealthy monasteries such as Cluny, the arcaded galleries of the cloister had elaborate carved capitals as well as relief sculpture on piers (SEE FIG. 16–1). The capitals may have served as memory devices or visualized theology to direct and inspire the monks' thoughts and prayers.

Cluniac monks observed the traditional eight Benedictine Hours of the Divine Office (including prayers, scripture readings, psalms, and hymns) spread over the course of each day and night. Mass was celebrated after the third hour (terce), and the Cluniac liturgy was especially elaborate. During the height of this liturgy's use, plainsong, or Gregorian chant, filled the church with music 24 hours a day. And the design of the church at Cluny—like that of many of the churches of its numerous dependent

monasteries—was conceived largely as an elegant and extravagant setting for the performance of this liturgy. Cluniac churches were notable for their fine stone masonry with rich sculptured and painted decoration. In Burgundy the churches were distinguished by their use of classicizing elements drawn from Roman art, such as fluted pilasters and Corinthian capitals. Cluniac monasteries elsewhere, however, were free—perhaps even encouraged—to follow regional traditions and styles.

THE THIRD CHURCH AT CLUNY   The original church at Cluny, a small, barnlike building, was soon replaced by a basilica with two towers and narthex on the west side and a choir with tower and chapels on the east. Hugh de Semur, abbot of Cluny for 60 years (1049–1109), began rebuilding the abbey church for the third time in 1088 (FIG. 16–8), financed by money paid in tribute by Muslims to victorious Christians in Spain. When King Alfonso VI of Castile and León captured Toledo in 1085, he sent 10,000 pieces of gold to Cluny; German rulers were also generous donors. Cluny III (as this third church is often referred to by art historians) was the largest church in Europe when it was completed in 1130: 550 feet long, with five aisles like Old St. Peter's in Rome. Built with superbly cut masonry and richly carved, painted, and furnished, it was a worthy home for the relics of St. Peter and St. Paul, which the monks had acquired from the church of St. Paul's Outside the Walls in Rome. It was also a fitting headquarters for a monastic order that eventually became so powerful within Europe that popes were chosen from its ranks.

In simple terms, the church was a basilica with five aisles, double transepts with chapels, and a high altar within the main choir space surrounded by an ambulatory and radiating chapels. The large number of chapels was necessary so that each monk-priest had an altar at which to perform daily Mass. Octagonal towers over the two crossings and additional towers over the transept arms created a dramatic pyramidal design at the east end. The nave had a three-part elevation. A nave arcade with tall compound piers, faced by pilasters to the inside and engaged columns at the sides, supported pointed arches lined by Classical ornament. At the next level a blind arcade and pilasters created a continuous sculptural strip that could have been modeled on an imperial Roman triumphal monument. Finally, triple clerestory windows in each bay let sunlight directly into the church around its perimeter. The pointed barrel vault with transverse arches rose to a daring height of 98 feet with a span of about 40 feet, made possible by giving the vaults a steep profile, rather than the weaker rounded profile used at Santiago de Compostela.

Cluny III was consecrated in 1130, but it no longer exists. The monastery was suppressed during the French Revolution, and this grandest of French Romanesque churches was sold stone by stone

for building materials. Today the site is an archaeological park, with only one transept arm from the original church still standing.

The Cistercians

New religious orders devoted to an austere spirituality arose in the late eleventh and early twelfth centuries. Among these were the Cistercians, who spurned Cluny's elaborate liturgical practices and aspects of their arts, especially figural sculpture in cloisters (see "St. Bernard and Theophilus: The Monastic Controversy over the Visual Arts" opposite). The Cistercian reform began in 1098 with the founding of the abbey of Cîteaux (Cistercium in Latin, hence the order's name). Led in the twelfth

16–8 RECONSTRUCTION DRAWING OF THE INTERIOR LOOKING TOWARD THE CHOIR, THIRD ABBEY CHURCH AT CLUNY
1088–1130. From Kenneth Conant, Carolingian and Romanesque Architecture, 800 to1200, Yale University Press, fig. 103.

Credit: Reproduced courtesy of Yale University Press, London.

Art and its Contexts

ST. BERNARD AND THEOPHILUS: THE MONASTIC CONTROVERSY OVER THE VISUAL ARTS

The twelfth century saw a heated controversy over the place and appropriateness of lavish art in monasteries. In a letter to William of Saint-Thierry, Bernard of Clairvaux wrote:

> ...in the cloisters, before the eyes of the brothers while they read—what is that ridiculous monstrosity doing, an amazing kind of deformed beauty and yet a beautiful deformity? What are the filthy apes doing there? The fierce lions? The monstrous centaurs? The creatures part man and part beast? The striped tigers? The fighting soldiers? The hunters blowing horns? You may see many bodies under one head, and conversely many heads on one body. On one side the tail of a serpent is seen on a quadruped, on the other side the head of a quadruped is on the body of a fish. Over there an animal has a horse for the front half and a goat for the back; here a creature which is horned in front is equine behind. In short, everywhere so plentiful and astonishing a variety of contradictory forms is seen that one would rather read in the marble than in books, and spend the whole day wondering at every single one of them than in meditating on the law of God. Good God! If one is not ashamed of the absurdity, why is one not at least troubled at the expense?
>
> (Rudolph, *Things of Greater Importance*, pp. 11–12)

"Theophilus" is the pseudonym used by a monk who wrote a book during the first half of the twelfth century on the practice of artistic craft, voiced as a defense of the place of the visual arts within the monastic traditions of work and prayer. The book gives detailed instructions for panel painting, stained glass (colored glass assembled into ornamental or pictorial windows), and goldsmithing. In contrast to the stern warnings of Bernard, perhaps even in response to them, "Theophilus" assured artists that "God delights in embellishments" and that artists worked "under the direction and authority of the Holy Spirit."

He wrote:

> Therefore, most beloved son, you should not doubt but should believe in full faith that the Spirit of God has filled your heart when you have embellished His house with such great beauty and variety of workmanship...
>
> ...do not hide away the talent given to you by God, but, working and teaching openly and with humility, you faithfully reveal it to those who desire to learn.
>
> ...if a faithful soul should see a representation of the Lord's crucifixion expressed in the strokes of an artist, it is itself pierced; if it sees how great are the tortures that the saints have endured in their bodies and how great the rewards of eternal life that they have received, it grasps at the observance of a better life; if it contemplates how great are the joys in heaven and how great are the torments in the flames of hell, it is inspired with hope because of its good deeds and shaken with fear on considering its sins.
>
> (Theophilus, *On Divers Arts*, pp. 78–79)

As we will see in the next chapter, Abbot Suger of Saint-Denis shared the position of Theophilus, rather than that of Bernard, and from this standpoint would sponsor a reconstruction of his abbey church that gave birth to the Gothic style.

century by the commanding figure of Abbot (later St.) Bernard of Clairvaux, the Cistercians advocated strict mental and physical discipline and a life devoted to prayer and intellectual pursuits combined with shared manual labor. Like the Cluniacs, however, Cistercians depended on the work of laypeople. To seclude themselves as much as possible from the outside world, they settled in reclaimed swamps and wild forests, where they then farmed and raised sheep. In time, their monasteries extended from Russia to Ireland.

FONTENAY Cistercian architecture embodies the ideals of the order—simplicity, austerity, and purity. Always practical, the Cistercians made a significant change to the already very efficient monastery plan. They placed key buildings such as the refectory at right angles to the cloister walk so they could easily be extended should the community grow. The cloister fountain was relocated from the center to the side, conveniently in front of the refectory, where the monks could wash when coming from their work in the fields for communal meals. For easy access to the sanctuary during their prayers at night, monks entered the church directly from the cloister into the south transept or from the dormitory by way of the "night stairs."

The **ABBEY OF NOTRE-DAME** in Fontenay, is among the best-preserved early Cistercian monasteries (**FIG. 16–9**). The abbey church, begun in 1139, has a regular geometric plan with a long bay-divided nave, rectangular chapels off the square-ended transept arms, and a shallow choir with a straight east wall. One of its characteristic features is the use of pointed barrel vaults over the nave and pointed arches in the nave arcade and side-aisle bays. Although pointed arches are usually associated with Gothic architecture, they are actually common in the Romanesque buildings of some regions, including Burgundy—we have already seen them at Cluny. Pointed arches are structurally more stable than round ones, directing more weight down into the floor instead of outward against the walls. Consequently, they can span greater distances at greater heights without collapsing.

night stairs
to dormitory

chapter house

great hall
(dormitory above)

entrance from
church

warming
room

cloister

fountain

refectory

kitchen

abbey church

16–9A PLAN OF THE ABBEY OF NOTRE-DAME, FONTENAY

Burgundy, France. 1139–1147.

Although Fontenay and other early Cistercian monasteries fully reflect the architectural developments of their time in masonry construction, vaulting, and planning, the Cistercians concentrated on harmonious proportions, superbly refined stonework, and elegantly carved foliate and ornamental decoration to achieve beauty in their architecture. The figural scenes and monstrous animals found on many Romanesque churches are avoided here. The large windows in the end wall, rather than a clerestory, provided light, concentrated here as at Santiago, on the sanctuary. The sets of triple windows may have reminded the monks of the Trinity. Some scholars have suggested that the numerical and proportional systems guiding the design of such seemingly simple buildings are saturated with the sacred numerical systems outlined by such eminent early theologians as St. Augustine of Hippo.

16–9B CHURCH INTERIOR OF THE ABBEY OF NOTRE-DAME, FONTENAY

Burgundy, France. 1139–1147.
View toward the choir.

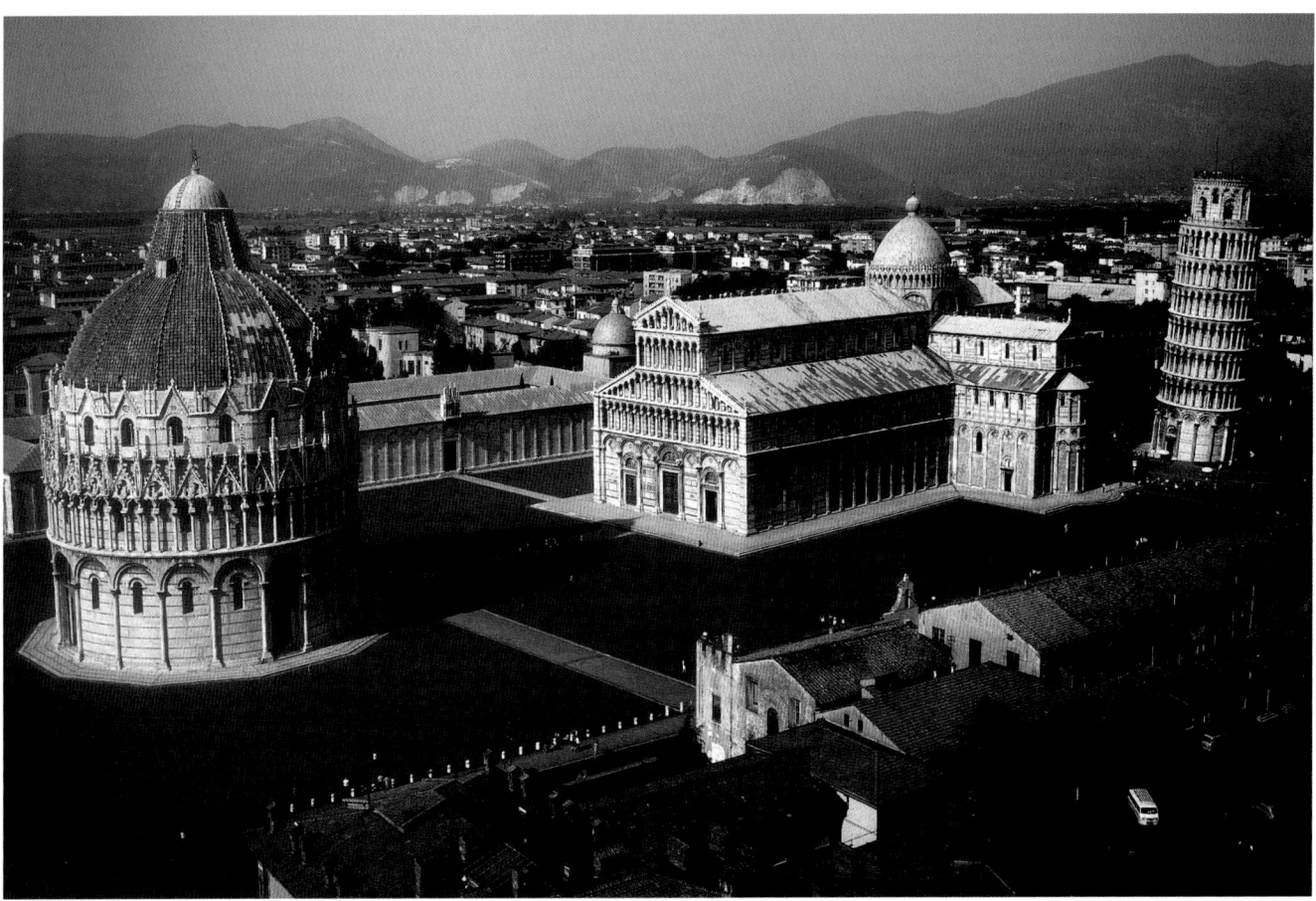

16–10 CATHEDRAL COMPLEX, PISA
Tuscany, Italy. Cathedral, begun 1063; baptistery, begun 1153; campanile, begun 1174; Campo Santo, 13th century.

When finished in 1350, the Leaning Tower of Pisa stood 179 feet high. The campanile had begun to tilt while still under construction, and today it leans about 13 feet off the perpendicular. In the latest effort to keep it from toppling, engineers filled the base with tons of lead.

Credit: Folco Quilici © Fratelli Alinari

The streamlined but sophisticated architecture favored by the Cistercians spread from their homeland in Burgundy to become an international style. From Scotland and Poland to Spain and Italy, Cistercian designs and building techniques varied only slightly in relation to local building traditions. Cistercian experiments with masonry vaulting and harmonious proportions influenced the development of the French Gothic style in the middle of the twelfth century.

Regional Styles in Romanesque Architecture

The cathedral of Santiago de Compostela and the abbey church at Cluny reflect the cultural exchanges and international connections fostered by powerful monastic orders, and to a certain extent by travel along the pilgrimage roads, but Europe remained a land divided by competing kingdoms, regions, and factions. Romanesque architecture reflects this regionalism in the wide variety of its styles, traditions, and building techniques. Only a few examples can be examined here.

THE CATHEDRAL OF ST. MARY OF THE ASSUMPTION IN PISA Throughout Italy artists looked to the still-standing remains of imperial Rome and early Christianity. The influence remained especially strong in Pisa, on the west coast of Tuscany. Pisa became a maritime power, competing with Barcelona and Genoa as well as the Muslims for control of trade in the western Mediterranean. In 1063, after a decisive victory over the Muslims, the jubilant Pisans began an imposing new cathedral dedicated to the Virgin Mary (**FIG. 16–10**). The cathedral was designed as a cruciform basilica by the master builder Busketos. A long nave with double side aisles (usually an homage to Old St. Peter's) is crossed by projecting transepts, designed like basilicas with their own aisles and apses. The builders added galleries above the side aisles, and a dome covers the crossing. Unlike Early Christian basilicas, the exteriors of Tuscan churches were richly decorated with marble—either panels of green and white marble or arcades. At Pisa, pilasters, applied arcades, and narrow galleries in white marble adorn the five-story façade.

In addition to the cathedral itself, the complex eventually included a baptistery, a campanile, and the later Gothic Campo Santo, a walled burial ground. The baptistery, begun in 1153, has arcading and galleries on the lower levels of its exterior that match those on the cathedral; the baptistery's present exterior dome and ornate upper levels were built later. The campanile (a free-standing bell tower now known for obvious reasons as "the Leaning Tower of Pisa") was begun in 1174 by master builder Bonanno Pisano. Built on inadequate foundations, it began to lean almost immediately. The cylindrical tower is encased in tier upon tier of marble columns. This creative reuse of the Classical theme of the colonnade, turning it into a decorative arcade, is characteristic of Tuscan Romanesque art.

THE BENEDICTINE CHURCH OF SAN CLEMENTE IN ROME The Benedictine **CHURCH OF SAN CLEMENTE** in Rome was rebuilt beginning in the eleventh century (it was consecrated in 1128) on top of the previous church, which had itself been built over a Roman sanctuary of Mithras. The architecture and decoration reflect a conscious effort to reclaim the artistic and spiritual legacy of the early church (**FIG. 16–11**). As with the columns of Santa Sabina (SEE FIG. 7–12), the columns in San Clemente are *spolia*: that is, they were reused from ancient Roman buildings. The church originally had a timber roof, now disguised by an ornate eighteenth-century ceiling. Even given the Romanesque emphasis on stone vaulting, the construction of timber-roofed buildings continued throughout the Middle Ages.

16–11 INTERIOR, CHURCH OF SAN CLEMENTE, ROME
Consecrated 1128.

San Clemente contains one of the finest surviving collections of early church furniture: choir stalls, pulpit, lectern, candlestick, and also the twelfth-century inlaid pavement. Ninth-century choir-screen panels were reused from the earlier church on the site. The upper nave wall and ceiling decoration date from the eighteenth century.

Credit: © akg-images/Erich Lessing

16–12 STAGS DRINKING FROM STREAMS FLOWING UNDER THE CRUCIFIED CHRIST
Detail of mosaics in the apse of the church of San Clemente, Rome. Consecrated 1128.

Credit: © Dagli Orti G./De Agostini Picture Library, licenced via Alinari

At San Clemente, the nave ends in a semicircular apse opening directly off the rectangular hall without a sanctuary extension or transept crossing. To accommodate the increased number of participants in the twelfth-century liturgy, the liturgical choir for the monks was extended into the nave itself, defined by a low barrier made up of ninth-century relief panels reused from the earlier church. In Early Christian basilicas, the area in front of the altar had been similarly enclosed by a low stone parapet (SEE FIG. 7-12), and the Romanesque builders may have wanted to revive what they considered a glorious Early Christian tradition. A **baldacchino** (a canopy suspended over a sacred space, also called a ciborium) symbolizing the Holy Sepulcher covers the main altar in the apse.

The apse of San Clemente is richly decorated with marble revetment on the curving walls and mosaic in the semidome, in a system familiar from the Early Christian and Byzantine worlds (SEE FIGS. 7-20, 8-6). The mosaics recapture this past glory, portraying the trees and rivers of paradise in a lavish vine scroll inhabited by figures, in the midst of which emerges the crucified Christ flanked by Mary and St. John. Twelve doves on the cross and the 12 sheep that march in single file below represent the apostles. Stags drink from streams flowing from the base of the cross, an evocation of the tree of life in paradise (**FIG. 16-12**). An inscription running along the base of the apse explains, "We liken the Church of Christ to this vine that the law causes to wither and the Cross causes to bloom," a statement that recalls Jesus's reference to himself as the

true vine and his followers as the branches (John 15:1–11). The learned monks of San Clemente would have been prepared to derive these and other meanings from the evocative symbols within this elaborate, glowing composition.

Although the subject of the mosaic recalls Early Christian art, the style and technique are clearly Romanesque. The artists have suppressed the sense of lifelike illusionism that characterized earlier mosaics in favor of ornamental patterns and schemas typical of the twelfth century. The doves silhouetted on the dark blue cross, the symmetrical repetition of circular vine scrolls, even the animals, birds, and humans among their leaves conform to an overriding formal design. With an irregular setting of mosaic tesserae in visibly rough plaster, the artists heighten color and increase the glitter of the pervasive gold field, allowing the mosaic to sparkle.

THE ABBEY CHURCH OF SAINT-SAVIN-SUR-GARTEMPE At the Benedictine **ABBEY CHURCH OF SAINT-SAVIN-SUR-GARTEMPE** in western France, a tunnel-like barrel vault runs the length of the nave and choir (**FIG. 16-13**). Without galleries or clerestory windows, the nave at Saint-Savin approaches the form of a "hall church," where the nave and aisles rise to an equal height. And unlike other churches we have seen (for example, FIG. 16-5), at Saint-Savin the barrel vault is unbroken by projecting transverse arches, making it ideally suited for paintings.

The paintings on the high vaults of Saint-Savin survive almost intact, presenting scenes from the Hebrew

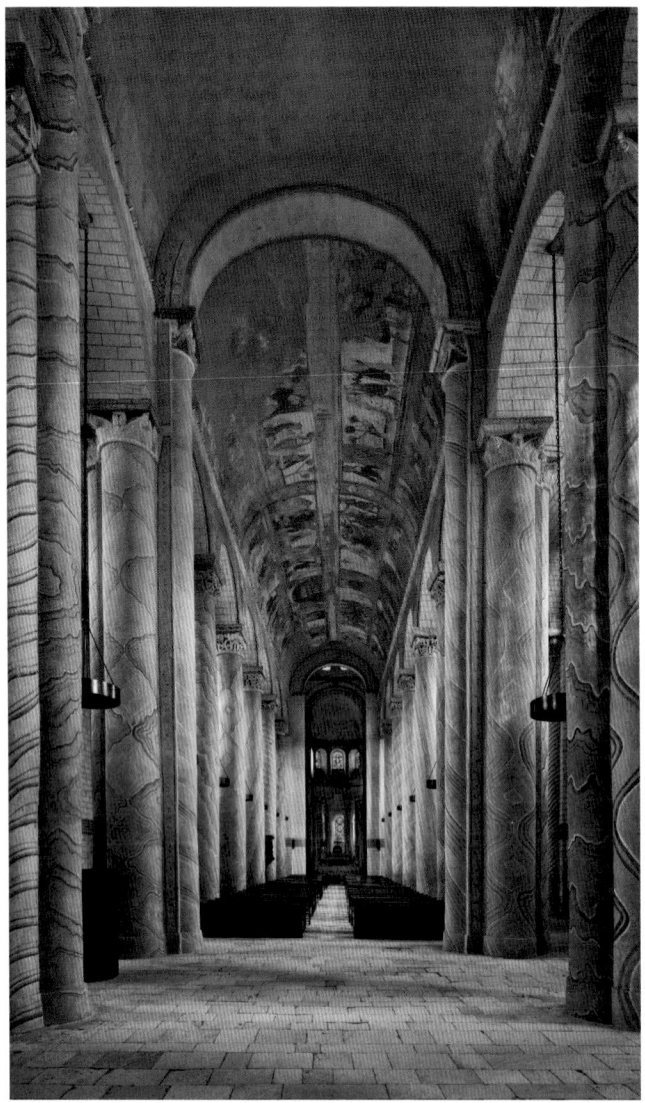

16–13 ABBEY CHURCH OF SAINT-SAVIN-SUR-GARTEMPE
Poitou, France. Choir c. 1060–1075; nave c. 1095–1115.

Credit: © Achim Bednorz, Cologne

Bible and New Testament. The nave was built c. 1095–1115, and the painters seem to have followed the masons immediately, probably using the same scaffolding. Perhaps their intimate involvement with the building process accounts for the vividness with which they portrayed the biblical story of the **TOWER OF BABEL** (FIG. 16–14).

According to the account in Genesis (11:1–9), God (represented here by a striding figure of Christ on the left) punished the prideful people who had tried to reach heaven by means of their own architectural ingenuity by scattering them and making their languages mutually unintelligible. The tower in the painting is Romanesque in style, reflecting the medieval practice of visualizing all stories in contemporary settings to stress their relevance for the contemporary audience. Workers haul heavy stone blocks toward the tower, presumably intending to lift them to masons on the top with the same hoist that has been used to haul up a bucket of mortar. The giant Nimrod, on the far right, simply hands over the blocks. These paintings embody the energy and narrative vigor that characterizes Romanesque art. A dynamic figure of God confronts the wayward people, stepping away from them even as he turns back, presumably to scold them. The dramatic movement, monumental figures, bold outlines, broad areas of color, and patterned drapery all promote the legibility of these pictures to viewers looking up in the dim light from far below. The team of painters working here did not use the *buon fresco* technique favored in Italy for its durability, but they did moisten the walls before painting, which allowed some absorption of pigments into the plaster and made them more permanent than paint applied to a dry surface.

SAN CLIMENT IN TAULL As we have seen at San Clemente in Rome and at Saint-Savin-sur-Gartempe (SEE FIGS.

16–14 TOWER OF BABEL
Detail of painting in nave vault, abbey church of Saint-Savin-sur-Gartempe, Poitou, France. c. 1115.

Credit: © akg-images/De Agostini Picture Lib.

16-15 CHRIST IN MAJESTY

Detail of apse fresco, church of San Climent, Taull, Catalunya, Spain. Consecrated 1123. MNAC - Museu Nacional d'Art de Catalunya, Barcelona.

Credit: © akg-images/Album/Oronoz

16–11, 16–13), Romanesque church interiors were not bare expanses of stone, but were often covered with images that glowed in flickering candlelight amid clouds of incense. Outside Rome during the Romanesque period, murals largely replaced mosaics on the walls of churches. Wall painting was subject to the same influences as the other visual arts: that is, the mural painters could be inspired by illuminated manuscripts, or ivories, or enamels in their treasuries or libraries. Some artists must have seen examples of Byzantine art; others had Carolingian or even Early Christian models.

Artists in Catalunya brilliantly combined the Byzantine style with their own Mozarabic and Classical heritage in the apse paintings of the church of San Climent in the mountain village of Taull (Tahull), consecrated in 1123 just a few years before the church of San Clemente in Rome. The curve of the semidome of the apse contains a magnificently expressive **CHRIST IN MAJESTY** (FIG. 16–15) holding

an open book inscribed *Ego sum lux mundi* ("I am the light of the world," John 8:12)—recalling in his commanding presence the imposing Byzantine depictions of Christ Pantokrator, ruler and judge of the world, in Middle Byzantine churches (SEE FIG. 8–21).

The San Climent artist was one of the finest painters of the Romanesque period, but where he came from and where he learned his art is unknown. His use of elongated oval faces, large staring eyes, and long noses, as well as the placement of figures against flat bands of color and his use of heavy outlines, reflect the Mozarabic past (SEE FIG. 15–14). At the same time, the influence of Byzantine art is revealed in his painting technique of modeling from light to dark through repeated colored lines of varying width in three shades—dark, medium, and light. Instead of blending the colors, he delights in the striped effect, as well as in the potential for pattern in details of faces, hair, hands, and muscles.

SPEYER AND DURHAM The imperial cathedral at Speyer in the Rhine River Valley was a colossal structure. An Ottonian, wooden-roofed church built between 1030 and 1060 was given a masonry vault c. 1080–1106 (**FIG. 16-16**). Massive compound piers mark each nave bay and support the transverse ribs of a groin vault that rises to a height of over 100 feet. The compound piers alternate with smaller piers supporting the vaults of the aisle bays. This rhythmic, alternating pattern of heavy and light elements, first suggested in Ottonian wooden-roofed architecture (SEE FIG. 15-25B), became an important design element in Speyer. Since groin vaults concentrate the weight and thrust of the vault on the four corners of the bay, they relieve the stress on the side walls of the building—so large windows can be safely inserted in each bay to flood the building with light.

The exterior of Speyer Cathedral emphasizes its Ottonian and Carolingian background. Soaring towers and wide transepts mark both ends of the building, although a narthex, not an apse, stands to the west. A large apse housing the high altar abuts the flat wall of the choir; transept

16–17 EXTERIOR, SPEYER CATHEDRAL
c. 1080–1106 and second half of the 12th century.

Credit: © akg-images/Erich Lessing

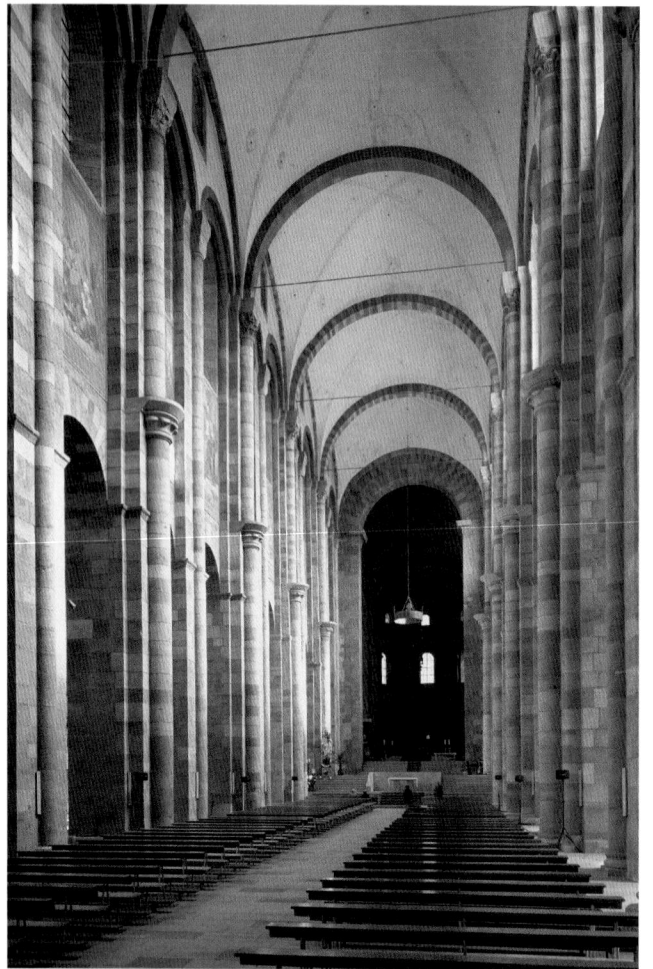

16–16 INTERIOR, SPEYER CATHEDRAL
Rhineland-Palatinate, Germany. As remodeled c. 1080–1106.

Credit: © akg-images/Bildarchiv Monheim

arms project at each side; a large octagonal tower rises over the crossing; and a pair of tall, slender towers flanks the choir (**FIG. 16-17**). A horizontal arcade forms an exterior gallery at the top of the apse and transept wall, recalling the Italian practice at Pisa (SEE FIG. 16-10).

In Durham, an English military outpost near the Scottish border, a prince-bishop held both secular and religious authority. For his headquarters he chose a defensive site where the bend in the River Wear formed a natural moat. Durham grew into a powerful fortified complex including a castle, a monastery, and a cathedral. The great tower of the castle defended against attack from the land, and an open space between buildings served as the courtyard of the castle and the cathedral green.

DURHAM CATHEDRAL, begun in 1087 and vaulted starting in 1093, is an impressive example of Norman Romanesque, but like most buildings that have been in continuous use, it has been altered several times (**FIG. 16-18**). The nave retains its Norman character, but the huge circular window lighting the choir is a later Gothic addition.

The cathedral's size and décor are ambitious. Enormous compound piers and robust columnar piers form the nave arcade and establish a rhythmic alternation. The columnar piers are carved with chevrons, spiral fluting, and diamond patterns, and some have scalloped, cushion-shape capitals. The richly carved arches that sit on them have multiple round moldings and chevron ornaments. All this carved ornamentation was originally painted.

Above the cathedral's massive piers and walls rises a new system of ribbed groin vaults. Romanesque masons in Santiago de Compostela, Cluny, Fontenay, Speyer, and Durham were all experimenting with stone vaulting—and adopted different solutions. The Durham builders divided each bay with two pairs of diagonal crisscrossing rounded ribs and so kept the crowns of the vaults close in height to the keystones of the pointed transverse arches. Although this allows the eye to run smoothly down the length of the vault, and from vault to vault down the expanse of the nave, the richly carved zigzagging moldings on the ribs themselves invite us to linger over each bay, acknowledging traditional Romanesque bay division. This new system of ribbed groin vaulting will become a hallmark of Gothic architecture, though there it will create a very different aesthetic effect.

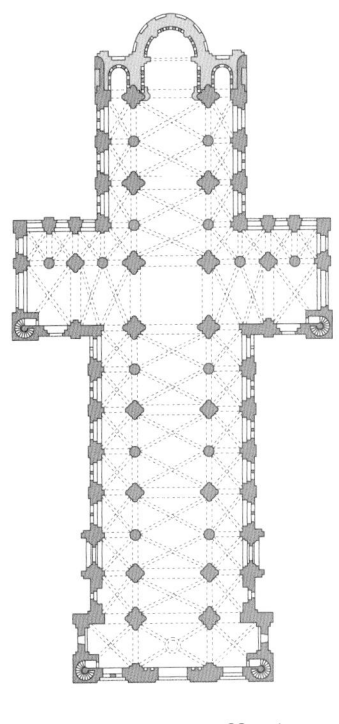

0   30 meters
0   100 feet

16–18A PLAN OF DURHAM CATHEDRAL
Northern England. 1087–1133.
Original east end replaced by
a Gothic choir, 1242–c. 1280.

16–18B INTERIOR OF DURHAM CATHEDRAL
Northern England. 1087–1133.
Original east end replaced by
a Gothic choir, 1242–c. 1280.
Vault height about 73′ (22.2 m).

Credit: © akg-images/A.F.Kersting

Secular Architecture

The need to provide for personal security in a time of periodic local warfare and political upheaval, as well as the desire to glorify the house of Christ and his saints, meant that communities used much of their resources to build castles and churches. Fully garrisoned, castles were sometimes as large as cities. In the twelfth century, **DOVER CASTLE** was a bold manifestation of military power that safeguarded the southeastern coast of England from invasion (**FIG. 16–19**). It illustrates the way in which a key defensive position developed over the centuries.

The Romans had built a lighthouse on the point where the English Channel separating England and France narrows. The Anglo-Saxons added a church (both lighthouse and church can be seen in FIG. 16-19 behind the tower,

surrounded by the remains of earthen walls). In the early Middle Ages, earthworks topped by wooden walls provided a measure of security, and a wooden tower signified an important administrative building and residence. The advantage of fire-resistant walls was obvious, and in the twelfth and thirteenth centuries, military engineers replaced the timber tower and palisades with stone walls. They added the massive stone towers we see today.

The Great Tower, as it was called in the Middle Ages (later known as a **keep** in England and donjon in France), stood in a courtyard called the bailey, surrounded by additional walls. Ditches outside the walls added to their height. In some castles, ditches were filled with water to form moats. A gatehouse—perhaps with a drawbridge—controlled the entrance. In all castles, the bailey was filled with buildings, the most important of which was the lord's

16–19 DOVER CASTLE
Southern England.

Aerial view. Center: Norman Great Tower, surrounding earthworks and wall, twelfth century. Outer walls, thirteenth century. Modern buildings have red tiled roofs. The castle was used in World War II and is now a museum.

Elements of Architecture

THE ROMANESQUE CHURCH PORTAL

The most important imagery on a Romanesque portal appears on the semicircular **tympanum** directly over the door—often a hierarchically scaled image of abstract grandeur such as Christ in Majesty or Christ presiding over the Last Judgment—as well as on the lintel beneath it. **Archivolts**—curved moldings composed of the wedge-shaped stone voussoirs of the arch—frame the tympanum. On both sides of the doors, the **jambs** (vertical elements) and occasionally a central pier called the **trumeau** support the lintel and archivolts, providing further fields for figures, columns, or narrative friezes. The jambs can extend forward to form a porch.

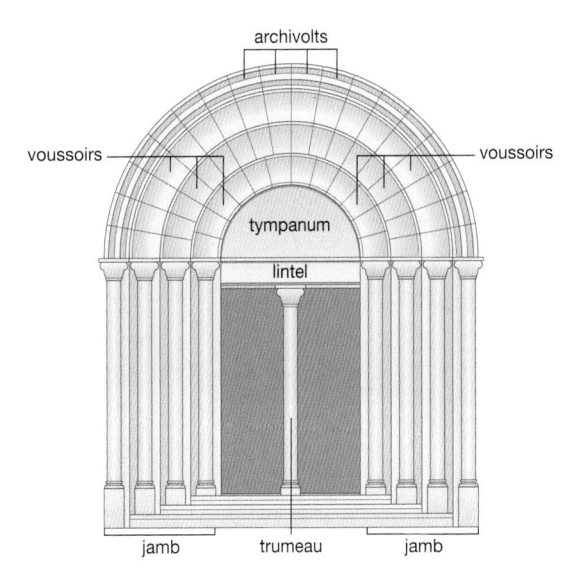

hall; it was used to hold court and for feasts and ceremonial occasions. Timber buildings housed troops, servants, and animals. Barns, workshops, ovens, and wells were also needed—the castle had to be self-sufficient.

If enemies broke through the outer walls, the castle's defenders retreated to the Great Tower. In the thirteenth century, the builders at Dover doubled the walls and strengthened them with towers, even though the castle's position on cliffs overlooking the sea made scaling the walls nearly impossible. It could be forced to surrender only by starving its occupants.

During Dover Castle's heyday, improvements in farming and growing prosperity provided the resources for increased building activity across Europe. The secular and religious buildings that still stand—despite the ravages of weather, vandalism, neglect, and war—testify to the technical skills and creative ingenuity of the builders and the power, local pride, and faith of the patrons.

Romanesque Sculpture

Why is monumental architectural stone sculpture revived in the Romanesque period and how is the style extended into works in wood and bronze?

Architecture dominated the arts in the Romanesque period—not only because it required the material and human resources of entire communities, but because it provided the physical context for a revival of the art of monumental stone sculpture, which had been almost dormant in Europe for 500 years. The "mute" façades used in early medieval buildings (SEE FIG. 15–18) were transformed by Romanesque sculptors into "speaking" façades with richly carved portals that projected bold symbolic and

didactic programs to the outside world (SEE FIG. 16–21). Christ Enthroned in Majesty might be carved over the entrance, and increasing importance was accorded to the Virgin Mary. The prophets, kings, and queens of the Hebrew Bible were seen by medieval Christians as precursors of people and events in the New Testament, so they were depicted; we can also find representations of contemporary bishops, abbots, other noble patrons, and even ordinary folk. A profusion of monsters, animals, plants, geometric ornament, allegorical figures such as Lust and Greed, and depictions of real and imagined buildings surround the sculpture within its architectural setting. The elect rejoice in heaven with the angels; the damned suffer in hell, tormented by demons; biblical and historical tales come alive in a contemporary medieval setting, juxtaposed with scenes drawn from the viewer's everyday life.

These innovative portals are among the greatest artistic achievements of Romanesque art, taking the central messages of the Christian Church out of the sanctuary (SEE FIGS. 8–6, 8–11) and into the public spaces of medieval towns. And figural sculpture did not appear only at entrances—it was also on the capitals of interior and exterior piers and columns, as well as in friezes, on corbels, even peeking around cornices or from behind moldings. There was plenty of work for stone sculptors on Romanesque building sites.

Wiligelmo at the Cathedral of Modena

The spirit of ancient Rome pervades the sculpture of Romanesque Italy, and the sculptor Wiligelmo may have been inspired by Roman sarcophagi still visible in cemeteries when he carved horizontal reliefs across the west façade of Modena Cathedral, c. 1099. Wiligelmo took his

16–20 Wiligelmo **CREATION AND FALL OF ADAM AND EVE, WEST FAÇADE, MODENA CATHEDRAL**
Emilia, Italy. Building begun 1099; sculpture c. 1099. Height approx. 3′ (92 cm).

Credit: © 2016. Photo Scala, Florence

subjects here from Genesis, focusing on events from the **CREATION AND FALL OF ADAM AND EVE** (FIG. 16–20). On the far left, God, in a mandorla (body halo) supported by angels, appears as both Creator and Christ, identified by a cruciform halo. Following this iconic image, the narrative of creation unfolds in three scenes from left to right: God brings Adam to life, then brings forth Eve from Adam's side, and finally Adam and Eve cover their genitals in shame as they eat fruit from the forbidden tree, around which the wily serpent twists.

Wiligelmo's deft carving gives these figures a strong three-dimensionality. The framing arcade establishes a stagelike setting, with the rocks on which Adam lies and the tempting tree of paradise serving as stage props. Wiligelmo's figures exude life and personality; they convey an emotional connection with the narrative they enact. Bright paint, now almost all lost, must have increased their lifelike impact still further. An inscription at Modena proclaims, "Among sculptors, your work shines forth, Wiligelmo." This self-confidence turned out to be justified. Wiligelmo's influence can be traced throughout Italy and as far away as Lincoln Cathedral in England.

The Priory Church of Saint-Pierre at Moissac

The Cluniac priory of Saint-Pierre at Moissac was a major stop on the pilgrimage route to Santiago de Compostela. The shrine at the site dates back to the Carolingian period, and after affiliating with Cluny in 1047, the monastery prospered from the donations of pilgrims and

local nobility, as well as from its control of shipping on the nearby Garonne River. During the twelfth century, Moissac's monks launched an ambitious building campaign, and much of the sculpture from the cloister (c. 1100, under Abbot Ansquetil) and the church portal and porch (1100–1130, under Abbot Roger) has survived. The quantity and quality of the carving here are outstanding.

A flattened figure of **CHRIST IN MAJESTY** dominates the huge tympanum (FIG. 16–21), visualizing a description of the Second Coming in Chapters 4 and 5 of Revelation. This gigantic Christ is an imposing, iconic image of enduring grandeur. He is enclosed by a mandorla; a cruciform halo rings his head. Although Christ is stable, even static, in this apocalyptic appearance, the four winged creatures symbolizing the evangelists—Matthew the man (upper left), Mark the lion (lower left), Luke the ox (lower right), and John the eagle (upper right)—who frame him on either side move with dynamic force, as if activated by his dramatic appearance. Rippling bands extend across the tympanum at Christ's sides and under him—perhaps representing waves in the "sea of glass like crystal" (Revelation 4:6). They delineate three registers in which 24 elders with "gold crowns on their heads" and either a harp or a gold bowl of incense (Revelation 4:4 and 5:8) twist to catch a glimpse of Christ's majestic arrival. Each of them takes an individually conceived pose and gesture, as if the sculptors were demonstrating their ability to represent three-dimensional human figures turning in space in a variety of postures, some quite challengingly contorted. Foliate and geometric ornament covers every surface surrounding this tableau. Monstrous heads in the lower corners of

16–21 SOUTH PORTAL, TYMPANUM SHOWING CHRIST IN MAJESTY, PRIORY CHURCH OF SAINT-PIERRE, MOISSAC

Tarn-et-Garonne, France. c. 1115.

the tympanum spew ribbon scrolls, and other creatures appear at each end of the lintel, their tongues growing into ropes encircling acanthus rosettes.

Two side jambs and a trumeau (central portal pier) support the weight of the lintel and tympanum. These elements have scalloped profiles that playfully undermine the ability of the colonettes on the door jambs to perform their architectural function. They give a sense of instability to the lower part of the portal, as if to underline the ability of the stable figure of Christ in Majesty to provide his own means of support. St. Peter and the prophet Isaiah flank the doorway on the jambs. Peter, a tall, thin saint, steps away from the door but twists back to look through it.

16-22 TRUMEAU, SOUTH PORTAL, PRIORY CHURCH OF SAINT-PIERRE, MOISSAC

c. 1115.

Credit: © Achim Bednorz, Cologne

The **TRUMEAU** (**FIG. 16-22**) is faced by a crisscrossing pair of lions. On the side visible here, a prophet, usually identified as Jeremiah, twists toward the viewer, with legs crossed in a pose that would challenge his ability to stand, much less move. The sculptors placed him in skillful conformity with the constraints of the scalloped trumeau; his head, pelvis, knees, and feet moving into the pointed cusps. This decorative scalloping, as well as the trumeau lions and lintel rosettes, may reveal the influence of Islamic art. Moissac was under construction shortly after the First Crusade, when many Europeans first encountered the Islamic art and architecture of the Holy Land. People from the region around Moissac participated in the crusade; perhaps they brought Islamic objects and ideas home with them.

A porch covering the area in front of the portal at Moissac provided a sheltered space for pilgrims to congregate and view the sculpture. The side walls of this porch are filled with yet more figural sculptures (**FIG. 16-23**), but the style of presentation changes here with the nature of the subject matter and the response that was sought from the audience. Instead of the stylized and agitated figures on the tympanum and its supports, here sculptors have substituted more lifelike and approachable human beings. Rather than embodying unchanging theological notions or awe-inspiring apocalyptic appearances, these figures convey human frailties and torments in order to persuade viewers to follow the Church's moral teachings.

Behind the double arcade framework of the lower part of the wall are hair-raising portrayals of the torments of those who fall prey to the two sins that particularly preoccupied twelfth-century moralists: avarice (greed and the hoarding of money) and lust (sexual misconduct). At bottom left, a greedy man is attacked by demons while the money bags around his neck weigh him down, strangling him. On the other side of the column, his counterpart, the female personification of lust (*luxuria*), is confronted by a pot-bellied devil while snakes bite at her breasts and another predator attacks her pubic area. In the scene that extends behind the column and across the wall above them, *luxuria* reappears, kneeling beside the deathbed of the miser, as devils make off with his money. These scenes are made as graphic as possible so that medieval viewers could identify with the situations, perhaps even feel the pain in their own bodies as a warning to avoid behaviors that lead to such gruesome consequences.

In the strip of relief running across the top of the wall, the mood is calmer, but the moral message remains clear, at least for those who know the story. The sculpture tells the tale of Lazarus and Dives (Luke 16:19–31), the most popular parable of Jesus in Romanesque art. The broad scene to the right shows the rich and greedy Dives, relishing the feast that is being laid before him by his servants and refusing to give even his table scraps to the leprous

16–23 RELIEFS ON THE LEFT (WEST) WALL OF THE SOUTH PORCH, PRIORY CHURCH OF SAINT-PIERRE, MOISSAC

c. 1115.

The parable of Lazarus and Dives that runs across the top of this wall has retained its moral power to our own day. This was the text of Martin Luther King's last Sunday sermon, preached only a few days before his assassination in Memphis, where he was supporting a strike by sanitation workers. Perhaps he saw the parable's image of the table scraps of the rich and greedy as particularly appropriate to his context. Just as in this portal, in Dr. King's sermon the story was juxtaposed with other stories and ideas to craft its interpretive message in a way that was both clear and compelling for the audience addressed.

Credit: © Achim Bednorz, Cologne

beggar Lazarus, spread out at lower left. Under the table, dogs—unsatisfied by leftovers from Dives's feast—turn to lick the pus from Lazarus's sores as he draws his last breath. The angel above Lazarus, however, transfers his soul (once represented as a naked baby, now missing) to the lap of Abraham (a common image of paradise), where he is cuddled by the patriarch, the eternal reward for a pious life. The fate of Dives is not portrayed here, but it is

certainly evoked on the lower section of the wall in the torments of the miser, whom we can now identify with Dives himself. Clearly some knowledge is necessary to recognize the story of this sculpture, and a guide may have been present to aid those viewers who did not readily understand. Nonetheless, the moral of sin and its consequences can be read easily from the narrative presentation. This is not scripture for an illiterate population. It is a sermon sculpted in stone.

The Church of Saint-Lazare at Autun

A different sculptural style and another subject appear at Autun on the portal of the church of Saint-Lazare (see "Closer Look" on page 496), which was built in the first half of the twelfth century as part of a cathedral complex to house the relics of St. Lazarus, becoming the cathedral of Autun itself only in 1195. The tympanum portrays the Last Judgment, in which Christ—enclosed in a mandorla held by two svelte angels—has returned at the end of time to judge the cowering, naked humans whose bodies rise from their sarcophagi along the lintel at his feet. The damned writhe in torment at Christ's left (our right), while on the opposite side the saved savor serene bliss. The inscribed message on the side of the damned reads: "Here let fear strike those whom earthly error binds, for their fate is shown by the horror of these figures," and under the blessed: "Thus shall rise again everyone who does not lead an impious life, and endless light of day shall shine for him" (translations from Grivot and Zarnecki).

Another text, right under the feet of Christ, ascribes the Autun tympanum to a man named Gislebertus—*Gislebertus hoc fecit* ("Gislebertus made this"). Traditionally, art historians have interpreted this inscription as a rare instance of a twelfth-century artist's signature, assigning this façade and related sculpture to an individual named Gislebertus, who was at the head of a large workshop of sculptors. Recently, however, art historian Linda Seidel has challenged this reading, arguing that Gislebertus was actually a late Carolingian count who had made significant donations to local churches. Like the names inscribed on many academic buildings of American universities, this legendary donor's name would have been evoked here as a reminder of the long and rich history of secular financial support in Autun, and perhaps also as a challenge to those currently in power to respect and continue that venerable tradition of patronage themselves.

Thinner and taller than their counterparts at Moissac, stretched out and bent at sharp angles, the stylized figures at Autun are powerfully expressive and hauntingly beautiful. As at Moissac, a huge, **hieratic** (highly stylized) figure of Christ dominates the composition at the center of the tympanum, but the surrounding figures are not arranged here in regular compartmentalized tiers. Their posture

A Closer Look

THE LAST JUDGMENT TYMPANUM AT AUTUN

In one of the most endearing vignettes, an angel pushes one of the saved up through an open archway and into the glorious architectural vision of heaven. Another figure at the angel's side reaches up, impatient for his turn to be hoisted up into paradise.

Christ's mother, Mary, is enthroned as queen of heaven. Below, St. Peter—identified by the large keys slung over his shoulder—performs his duties as heavenly gatekeeper, clasping the hands of someone waiting to gain entrance.

This inscription proclaims "I alone dispose of all things and crown the just. Those who follow crime I judge and punish." Clearly, some of the viewers could read Latin.

The cross (a badge of Jerusalem) and scallop shell (a badge of Santiago de Compostela) identify these two figures as former pilgrims. The clear message is that participation in pilgrimage will be a factor in their favor at the Last Judgment.

The incised ornament on these sarcophagi is quite similar to that on ancient Roman sarcophagi, one of many indications that the Autun sculptors and masons knew the ancient art created when Autun was a Roman city.

Interestingly, hell is represented here as a basilica, with a devil emerging from the toothy maw that serves as a side entrance, capturing sinners for eternal torment. The devil uses a sharp hook to grab *luxuria*, the female personification of lust.

16–24 Gislebertus (?) **THE LAST JUDGMENT**

West portal tympanum, Cathedral of Saint-Lazare, Autun, Burgundy, France. c. 1120–1130 or 1130–1145.

Credit: © Achim Bednorz, Cologne

and placement conform to their involvement in the story they enact. Since that story is filled with human interest and anecdotal narrative detail, viewers can easily project themselves into what is going on. On the lintel, angels physically assist the resurrected bodies rising from their tombs, guiding them to line up and await their turn at being judged. Ominously, a pair of giant, pincerlike hands descends to snatch one of the damned on the right side of the lintel (as we look at it). Above these hands, the archangel Michael competes with devils over the fate of someone

whose judgment is being weighed on the scales of good and evil. The man himself perches on the top of the scale, hands cupped to his mouth to project his pleas for help toward the Savior. Another man hides nervously in the folds of Michael's robe, perhaps hoping to escape judgment or cowering from the prospect of eternal damnation.

By far the most riveting players in this drama are the grotesque, screaming demons who grab and torment the damned and even try to cheat by yanking the scales to favor damnation. The fear they inspire, as well as the poignant portrayal of the psychological state of those whom they torment, would have been reminders to medieval viewers to examine the way they were leading their own lives, or perhaps to seek the benefits of entering the doors in front of them to participate in the community of the Church.

16–25 THE MAGI ASLEEP (A) AND THE FLIGHT INTO EGYPT (B)
Capitals from the choir pier pilasters, Cathedral of Saint-Lazare, Autun, Burgundy, France. c. 1125.

Credit: Bridgeman Images

The creation of lively narrative scenes within the geometric confines of capitals (called **historiated capitals**) was an important Romanesque innovation in architectural sculpture. The same sculptors who worked on the Autun tympanum carved historiated capitals for pier pilasters inside the church. Two capitals (**FIG. 16–25**) depict scenes from the childhood of Jesus drawn from Matthew 2:1–18. In one capital, the Magi—who have previously adored and offered gifts to the child Jesus—are interrupted in their sleep by an angel who warns them not to inform King Herod of the location of the newborn king of the Jews. In an ingenious compositional device, the sculptor has shown the reclining Magi and the head of their bed as if viewed from above, whereas the angel and the foot of the bed are viewed from the side. This allows us to see clearly the angel—who is appearing to them in a dream—as he touches the hand of the upper Magus, whose eyes have popped open. As on the façade, the sculptor has conceived this scene in ways that emphasize the human qualities of its story, not its deep theological significance. With its charming, doll-like figures, the other capital shows an event that occurred just after the Magi's dream: Joseph, Mary, and Jesus are journeying toward Egypt to escape King Herod's order to murder all young boys so as to eliminate the newborn royal rival the Magi had journeyed to venerate.

Sculpture in Wood and Bronze

Painted wood was commonly used when abbey and parish churches of limited means commissioned statues. Wood was not only cheap, it was lightweight, a significant consideration since these devotional images were frequently carried in processions. But whereas wood seems to have been a sculptural medium that spread across Europe, three geographic areas—the Rhineland, the Meuse River Valley, and German Saxony—were the principal metalworking centers. Bronze sculpture was produced only for wealthy aristocratic and ecclesiastical patrons. It drew on a variety of stylistic sources, including the work of contemporary Byzantine and Italian artists, as well as Classical precedents as reinterpreted by the sculptors' Carolingian and Ottonian forebears.

CHRIST ON THE CROSS (MAJESTAT BATLLÓ) This mid-twelfth-century painted wooden crucifix from Catalunya, known as the **MAJESTAT BATLLÓ** (**FIG. 16–26**), presents a clothed, triumphant Christ, rather than the seminude figure we have seen at Byzantine Daphni (SEE FIG. 8–22) or on the Ottonian Gero Crucifix (SEE FIG. 15–26). This Christ's royal robes emphasize his kingship, although his bowed head, downturned mouth, and heavy-lidded eyes seem to convey sadness or introspection. The hem of his long, medallion-patterned tunic has pseudo-kufic

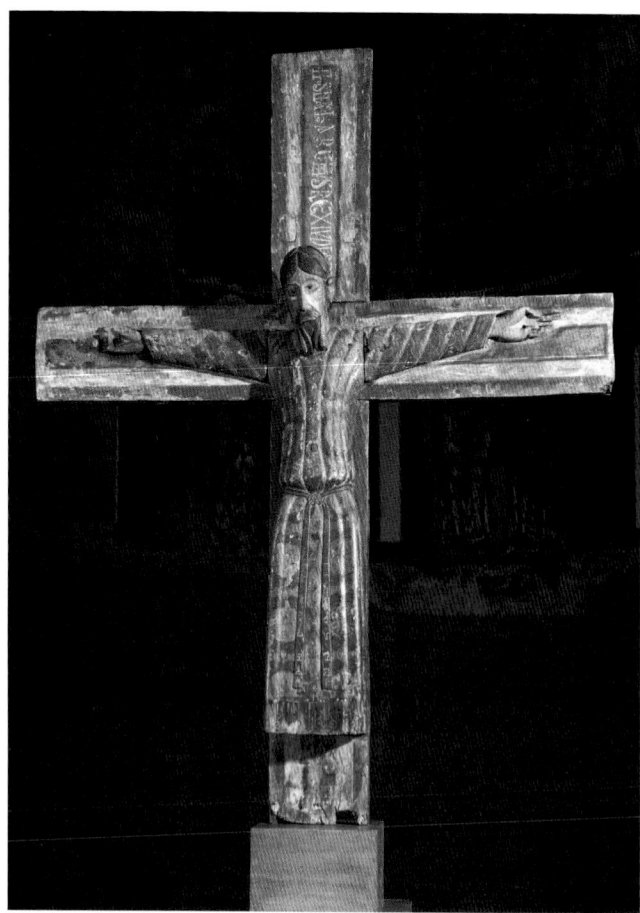

16–26 CRUCIFIX (MAJESTAT BATLLÓ)
Catalunya, Spain. Mid 12th century. Polychromed wood, height
approx. 37¾″ (96 cm). MNAC - Museu Nacional d'Art de Catalunya,
Barcelona.

Credit: © 2016. Photo Scala, Florence

inscriptions—designs meant to resemble Arabic script—a
reminder that silks from Islamic Spain were highly prized
in Europe at this time.

MARY AS THE THRONE OF WISDOM   Any Romanesque image of Mary seated on a throne and holding the
Christ Child on her lap is known as "The Throne of Wisdom." In a well-preserved example in painted wood dating from the second half of the twelfth century (**FIG. 16–27**),
Mother and Child are frontal and regal. Mary's thronelike
bench symbolized the lion-throne of Solomon, the Hebrew
Bible king who represented earthly wisdom in the Middle Ages. Mary, as Mother and "God-bearer" (the Byzantine *Theotokos*), gave Jesus his human nature. She forms a
throne on which he sits in majesty, but she also represents
the Church. Although the Child's hands are missing, we
can assume that the young Jesus held a book—the Word of
God—in his left hand and raised his right hand in blessing.

Such statues of the Virgin and Child served as cult
objects on the altars of many churches during the twelfth
century. They also sometimes took part in the liturgical dramas becoming popular in church services at this

time. At the feast of the Epiphany, celebrating the arrival
of the Magi to pay homage to the young Jesus, townspeople representing the Magi acted out their journey by
searching through the church for the newborn king. The
roles of Mary and Jesus were "acted" by such sculptures,
which the "Magi" discovered on the altar. The Flight into
Egypt capital from Autun in FIGURE 16–25 may record the
theatrical use of a wooden statue, strapped to the back of
a wooden donkey, that would have been rolled into the
church on wheels, possibly referenced by the round forms
at the base of the capital.

TOMB OF RUDOLF OF SWABIA   The oldest-known
bronze tomb effigy (recumbent portrait of the deceased) is
that of **KING RUDOLF OF SWABIA** (**FIG. 16–28**), who died

16–27 VIRGIN AND CHILD
Auvergne region, France. Late 12th century. Oak with polychromy,
height 31″ (78.7 cm). Metropolitan Museum of Art, New York. Gift of
J. Pierpont Morgan, 1916 (16.32.194).

Credit: © 2016. Image copyright The Metropolitan Museum of Art/Art Resource/
Scala, Florence

16–28 TOMB COVER WITH EFFIGY OF KING RUDOLF OF SWABIA

Saxony, Germany. c. 1080. Bronze with niello, approx. 6′5½″ × 2′2½″ (1.97 × 0.68 m). Cathedral of Merseburg, Germany.

16–29 Renier of Huy **BAPTISMAL FONT, NOTRE-DAME-AUX-FONTS**

Liège, Belgium. 1107–1118. Bronze, height 23⅝″ (60 cm), diameter 31¼″ (79 cm). Now in the church of Saint-Barthélemy, Liège.

in battle in 1080. The spurs on his oversized feet identify him as a heroic warrior, and he holds a scepter and cross-surmounted orb, emblems of Christian kingship. Although the tomb is in the cathedral of Merseburg, in Saxony, the effigy has been attributed to an artist originally from the Rhine Valley. Nearly life-size, it was cast in one piece and gilded, though few traces of the gilding survive. The inscription around the frame was incised after casting, and glass paste or semiprecious stones may have originally been set into the eyes and crown. We know that during the battle that ultimately led to Rudolph's death he lost a hand—which was mummified separately and kept in a leather case—but the sculptor of his effigy presents him idealized and whole.

RENIER OF HUY Bronze sculptor Renier of Huy (Huy is near Liège in present-day Belgium) worked in the Mosan region under the profound influence of classicizing early medieval works of art, as well as the humanistic learning of Church scholars. Hellinus of Notre-Dame-aux-Fonts in Liège (abbot 1107–1118) commissioned a bronze **BAPTISMAL FONT** from Renier (**FIG. 16–29**) that was inspired by the basin carried by 12 oxen in Solomon's Temple in Jerusalem (I Kings 7:23–24).

Christian commentators identified the 12 oxen as the 12 apostles and the basin as the baptismal font, and this interpretation is given visual form in Renier's work. On the sides of the font are images of St. John the Baptist preaching and baptizing Christ, St. Peter baptizing the Roman soldier Cornelius, and St. John the Evangelist baptizing the philosopher Crato. Renier models sturdy but idealized bodies—nude or with clinging drapery—that move and gesture with lifelike conviction, infused with dignity, simplicity, and harmony. His understanding of human anatomy and movement must have derived from close observation of the people around him. He placed these figures within defined landscape settings, standing on an undulating ground-line, and separated into scenes by miniature trees. Water rises in a mound of rippling waves (in Byzantine fashion) to cover nude figures discreetly.

Textiles and Books

What are the characteristic features of the Romanesque style in textiles and manuscript painting?

Among the most admired arts during the Middle Ages were those that later critics patronized as the "minor" or "decorative" arts. Although small in scale, these works were often produced with technical virtuosity from very precious materials, and they were vital to the Christian mission and devotion of the institutions that housed them.

Artists in the eleventh and twelfth centuries were still often monks and nuns. They labored within monasteries as calligraphers and painters in scriptoria to produce books and as metalworkers to craft the enamel- and jewel-encrusted works used in liturgical services. They also embroidered the vestments, altar coverings, and wall hangings that clothed both celebrants and settings in the Mass. Increasingly, however, secular urban workshops supplied the aristocratic and royal courts with textiles, tableware, books, and weapons for their own use or as donations to religious institutions.

Chronicling History

Romanesque artists were commissioned not only to illustrate engaging stories and embody important theological ideas within the context of sacred buildings and sacred books. They also created visual accounts of secular history, where moralizing was one of the principal objectives of pictorial narrative.

THE WORCESTER CHRONICLE   The earliest-known illustrated history book, written in the twelfth century by a monk named John, is the **WORCESTER CHRONICLE** (FIG. 16–30). The pages shown here concern Henry I (ruled 1100–1135), the second of William the Conqueror's sons to sit on the English throne. The text relates a series of nightmares the king had in 1130, in which his subjects demanded tax relief. The artist depicts the dreams with energetic directness. On the first night, farmers confront the sleeping king; on the second, armed knights surround his bed; and on the third, monks, abbots, and bishops present their case. In the fourth illustration, the king travels in a storm-tossed ship and saves himself by promising God that he will rescind the tax increase for seven years. The author of the Worcester Chronicle assured his readers that this story came from a reliable source, the royal physician Grimbald, who appears in the margins next to three of the scenes. The farmers capture our attention today because we seldom see working men with their equipment and simple clothing depicted in painting from this time.

THE BAYEUX EMBROIDERY   Rarely has art spoken more vividly than in the eleventh-century **BAYEUX EMBROIDERY**, a strip of embroidered linen that recounts the history of the Norman Conquest of England. Its designer was a skillful storyteller who used a staggering number of images to tell the tale. In the 50 surviving scenes there are more than 600 human figures; 700 horses, dogs, and other creatures; and 2,000 inch-high letters. This work represents the kind of secular art that

16–30 John of Worcester **THOSE WHO WORK; THOSE WHO FIGHT; THOSE WHO PRAY—THE DREAM OF HENRY I, WORCESTER CHRONICLE**

Worcester, England. c. 1140. Ink and tempera on vellum, each page 12¾ × 9⅜" (32.5 × 23.7 cm). Corpus Christi College, Oxford.

Credit: By Permission of the President and Fellows of Corpus Christi College, Oxford (CCC Ms 157)

16–31 MESSENGERS SIGNAL THE APPEARANCE OF HALLEY'S COMET, THE BAYEUX EMBROIDERY
Norman–Anglo-Saxon, perhaps from Canterbury, Kent, England. c. 1066–1082. Linen with wool embroidery, height 20″ (50.8 cm). Centre Guillaume le Conquérant, Bayeux, France.

Credit: Musée de la Tapisserie, Bayeux, France/With special authorisation of the city of Bayeux/Bridgeman Images

must once have been part of most royal courts. It could have been rolled up and transported from residence to residence as the noble Norman owner traveled throughout his domain, and some have speculated that it may have been the backdrop at banquets for stories sung by professional performers who could have received their cues from the identifying inscriptions that accompany most scenes. Eventually the embroidery was given to Bayeux Cathedral, perhaps by Bishop Odo, William's half brother; we know it was displayed around the walls of the cathedral on the feast of the relics.

Flanked by narrower bands of ornament, the broad, central narrative strip of the Bayeux Embroidery chronicles the events that led to Duke William of Normandy's conquest of England on October 14, 1066, when, after a long day of fighting, he became William the Conqueror, king of England. It may have been drawn by a Norman designer since there is a clear Norman bias in the telling of the story; it justifies William's conquest with the intensity of an eyewitness account. The style of the embroidery, however, suggests that Anglo-Saxons did the actual needlework.

Early in the story, the Anglo-Saxon nobleman Harold swears his allegiance to William, but later he betrays this vow, accepting the crown of England for himself. Harold begins as a heroic figure, but then events overtake him. After his coronation, cheering crowds celebrate—until Halley's Comet crosses the sky (**FIG. 16–31**). The Anglo-Saxons, seeing the comet as a portent of disaster, cringe and point at this brilliant ball of fire with a flaming tail, and a man rushes to inform the new king. Harold slumps on his throne in the Palace of Westminster. He foresees what is to come: Below his feet is his vision of a ghostly fleet of Norman ships already riding the waves. Duke William has assembled the last great Viking flotilla on the Normandy coast. Unworthy to be king, Harold dies in the ensuing battle at the hands of William and the Normans.

In another extended tableau, Duke William and his brother Odo, Bishop of Bayeux, are feasting before the battle (**FIG. 16–32**). Attendants bring in roasted birds on skewers, placing them on a makeshift table made of the knights' shields set on trestles. The diners, summoned by the blowing of a horn, gather at a curved table laden with food and drink. Bishop Odo—seated at the center, head and shoulders above William to his right—blesses the meal while others eat. The kneeling servant in the middle proffers a basin and towel so that the diners may wash their hands. The man on Odo's left points to the next event, a council

16–32 BISHOP ODO BLESSING THE FEAST, THE BAYEUX EMBROIDERY
Norman–Anglo-Saxon, perhaps from Canterbury, Kent, England. c. 1066–1082. Linen with wool embroidery, height 20″ (50.8 cm). Centre Guillaume le Conquérant, Bayeux, France.

Credit: Musée de la Tapisserie, Bayeux, France/With special authorisation of the city of Bayeux/Bridgeman Images

stem
stitching

crosswise
stitches

laid
threads

couching
stitches

16–33 DETAIL OF FIG. 16–32 HIGHLIGHTING THE EMBROIDERY STICHING

Credit: Musée de la Tapisserie, Bayeux, France/With special authorisation of the city of Bayeux/Bridgeman Images

Although traditionally referred to as the "Bayeux Tapestry," this work is really an embroidery. In tapestry, the colored threads that create images or patterns are woven together during the process of production, completely covering the canvas ground that serves as their support; in embroidery, stitches are applied on top of a tightly woven fabric that serves as their support, as well as the ground behind the patterns they create (**FIG. 16–33**).

The embroiderers—probably Anglo-Saxon women based on the style—worked in tightly twisted wool that was dyed in eight colors and sewed onto fine linen cloth. They used only two stitches: the quick, overlapping stem stitch that produced a slightly jagged line or outline, and the time-consuming laid-and-couched work used to form blocks of color.

For the latter, the embroiderer first "laid" a series of long, parallel covering threads; then anchored them with a second layer of regularly spaced crosswise stitches; and finally tacked all the strands down with tiny "couching" stitches. Some of the laid-and-couched work was done in contrasting colors to achieve particular effects. The creative coloring is often fanciful: for example, some horses have legs in four different colors. Skin and other light-toned areas are represented by the bare linen cloth that formed the ground of the work.

of war between William (now the central and tallest figure), Odo, and a third man labeled "Rotbert," probably Robert of Mortain, another of William's half brothers. The text reads: "and here the servants (*ministra*) perform their duty. / Here they prepare the meal (*prandium*) / and here the bishop blesses the food and drink (*cibu et potu*). Bishop Odo. William. Robert."

The tragedy of this drama has spoken movingly to audiences over the centuries. It is the story of a good man—Harold—who, like Shakespeare's Macbeth, is overcome by his lust for power and so betrays his lord—Duke William. The images of this Norman invasion also spoke to people during the darkest days of World War II. When the Allies invaded Nazi-occupied Europe in June 1944, they took the same route in reverse from England to beaches on the coast of Normandy. The Bayeux Embroidery still speaks to us of the folly of human greed and ambition and of two battles that changed the course of history.

Sacred Books

Monastic scriptoria continued to be the centers of illustrated book production, which increased dramatically during the twelfth century. But the scriptoria sometimes employed lay scribes and artists who traveled from place to place. In addition to the books needed for church services, scribes produced copies of sacred texts, scholarly commentaries, visionary devotional works, lives of saints, and collections of letters and sermons.

THE CODEX COLBERTINUS The portrait of **ST. MATTHEW** from the Codex Colbertinus (**FIG. 16–34**) is an entirely Romanesque conception, quite different from Hiberno-Saxon and Carolingian author portraits. Like the sculptured pier figures of Silos (SEE FIG. 16–1), the evangelist stands within an architectural frame that completely surrounds him. Instead of writing in his book, he blesses and holds it within the compact silhouette of his body. His dangling feet bear no weight, and his body has little sense of three-dimensionality, with solid blocks of color filling its strong outlines.

The text of Matthew's Gospel begins with a complementary block of ornament to the left of Matthew's portrait. The "L" of *Liber generationis* ("The book of the generation") is a framed picture formed of plants and animals—what art historians call a historiated initial. Dogs or catlike creatures and long-necked birds twist, claw, and bite each other and themselves while, in the center, two humans—one dressed and one nude—clamber up the letter. This manuscript was made in the region of Moissac at about the same time that sculptors were working on the abbey church, and the stacking of intertwined animals here recalls the outer face of the Moissac trumeau (SEE FIGS. 16–21, 16–22).

16–35 The Nun Guda **BOOK OF HOMILIES**
Westphalia, Germany. Early 12th century. Ink on parchment. Universitätsbibliothek Johann Christian Senckenberg, Frankfurt am Main, Germany. MS. Barth. 42, fol. 110v.

16–34 ST. MATTHEW FROM THE CODEX COLBERTINUS
c. 1100. Tempera on vellum, 7½ × 4" (19 × 10.16 cm). Bibliothèque Nationale, Paris. MS lat. 254, fol. 10r.

THE GERMAN NUN GUDA In another historiated initial, this one from Westphalia in Germany, the nun Guda has a more modest presentation. In a **BOOK OF HOMILIES** (sermons), she inserted her self-portrait into the letter *D* and signed it as scribe and painter, "Guda, the sinful woman, wrote and illuminated this book" (**FIG. 16–35**). This is a simple colored drawing with darker blocks of color in the background, but Guda and her monastic sisters played an important role in the production of books in the twelfth century, and not all of them remain anonymous. Guda's image is the earliest signed self-portrait by a woman in western Europe. Throughout the Middle Ages, women were involved in the production of books as authors, scribes, painters, and patrons.

A CISTERCIAN TREE OF JESSE The Cistercians were particularly devoted to the Virgin Mary and are also credited with popularizing themes such as the Tree of Jesse as a device for showing her position as the last link in the genealogy connecting Jesus to King David. (Jesse, the father of King David, was an ancestor of Mary and, through her, of Jesus.) A manuscript of St. Jerome's Commentary on Isaiah, made in the scriptorium of the Cistercian mother house of Cîteaux in Burgundy about 1125, contains an image of an abbreviated **TREE OF JESSE** (FIG. 16–36).

A monumental Mary, with the Christ Child sitting on her veiled arm, stands over the forking branches of the tree, dwarfing the sleeping patriarch, Jesse, from whose body a small tree trunk grows. The long, vertical folds of Mary's voluminous drapery—especially the flourish at lower right, where a piece of her garment billows up, as if caught in an updraft—recall the treatment of drapery in the portal at Autun (SEE FIG. 16-24), also in Burgundy. The artist has drawn, rather than painted, with soft colors, using subtle tints that seem somehow in keeping with Cistercian restraint. Christ embraces his mother's neck, pressing his cheek against hers in a display of affection that recalls Byzantine icons of the period, like the *Virgin of Vladimir* (SEE FIG. 8-28). The foliate form Mary holds in her hands could be a flowering sprig from the Jesse Tree, or it could be a lily symbolizing her purity.

The building held by the angel on the left equates Mary with the Church, and the crown held by the angel on the right is hers as queen of heaven. The dove above her halo represents the Holy Spirit; Jesse Trees often have doves sitting in the uppermost branches. In the early decades of the twelfth century, Church doctrine came increasingly to stress the role of the Virgin Mary and the saints as intercessors who could plead for mercy on behalf of repentant sinners, and devotional images of Mary became increasingly popular during the later Romanesque period. As we will see, this popularity would continue into the Gothic period, not only in books but on the sculpted portals and within the stained-glass windows of cathedrals.

16–36 PAGE WITH THE TREE OF JESSE, EXPLANATIO IN ISAIAM (ST. JEROME'S COMMENTARY ON ISAIAH)

Abbey of Cîteaux, Burgundy, France. c. 1125. Ink and tempera on vellum, 15 × 4¾" (38 × 12 cm). Bibliothèque Municipale, Dijon, France. MS. 129, fol. 4v.

Credit: © 2016. Photo Scala, Florence

HILDEGARD OF BINGEN We might expect women to have had subordinate positions in the hierarchical and militaristic society of the twelfth century. On the contrary, aristocratic women took responsibility for managing estates during their male relatives' frequent absences in wars or while serving at court. And some women also achieved positions of authority and influence as the heads of religious communities. Notable among them was Hildegard of Bingen (1098–1179).

Born into an aristocratic German family, Hildegard transcended the barriers that limited most medieval women. She began serving as leader of her convent in 1136, and about 1147 she founded a new convent near Bingen.

Hildegard also wrote important treatises on medicine and natural science, invented an alternate alphabet, and was one of the most gifted and innovative composers of her age, writing not only motets and liturgical settings, but also a musical drama that is considered by many to be the first opera. Clearly a major, multitalented figure in the intellectual and artistic life of her time—comparison with the later Leonardo da Vinci comes to mind—she also corresponded with emperors, popes, and the powerful abbots Bernard of Clairvaux and Suger of Saint-Denis.

Following a command she claimed to have received from God in 1141, and with the assistance of her nuns and the monk Volmar, Hildegard began to record the mystical visions she had been experiencing since she was just 5 years old. The resulting book, called the *Scivias* (from the Latin *scite vias lucis*, "know the ways of the light"), is filled not only with words but with striking images of the strange and wonderful visions themselves (**FIG. 16–37**).

The opening page (**FIG. 16-38**) shows Hildegard receiving a flash of divine insight, represented by the tongues of flame encircling her head—she said "a fiery light, flashing intensely, came from the open vault of heaven and poured through my whole brain"—while her scribe Volmar writes to her dictation. But was she also responsible for the arresting pictures that accompany the text in this book? Art historian Madeline Caviness thinks so, both because of their unconventional nature and because they conform in several ways to the "visionary" effects experienced by many people during migraines, which plagued Hildegard throughout her life but especially during her forties while she was composing the *Scivias*. She said of her visions, "My outward eyes are open. So I have never fallen prey to ecstasy in the visions, but I see them wide awake, day and night. And I am constantly fettered by sickness, and often in the grip of pain so intense that it threatens to kill me." (Translated in Newman, p. 16.)

Perhaps in this miniature Hildegard is using the large stylus to sketch on the wax tablets in her lap the pictures of her visions that were meant to accompany the verbal descriptions she dictates to Volmar, who sits at the right with a book in his hand, ready to write them down.

16–37 Hildegard of Bingen **THE UNIVERSE**
1927–1933 facsimile of Part I, Vision 3 of the *Liber Scivias* of
Hildegard of Bingen. Original, 1150–1175.

Hildegard begins her description of this vision with these words:
"After this I saw a vast instrument, round and shadowed, in the
shape of an egg, small at the top, large in the middle, and narrowed
at the bottom; outside it, surrounding its circumference, there was
a bright fire with, as it were, a shadowy zone under it. And in that
fire there was a globe of sparkling flame so great that the whole
instrument was illuminated by it."

Credit: © akg-images/Erich Lessing

16–38 HILDEGARD AND VOLMAR
1927–1933 facsimile of the frontispiece of the *Liber Scivias* of
Hildegard of Bingen. Original, 1150–1175.

This author portrait was once part of a manuscript of Hildegard's
Scivias that many believe was made in her own lifetime, but it was
lost in World War II. Today we can study its images only from prewar
black-and-white photographs or from a full-color facsimile that was
lovingly hand-painted by the nuns of the abbey of St. Hildegard in
Eibingen under the direction of Joesepha Krips between 1927 and
1933, the source of both pictures reproduced here.

Credit: © akg-images/Erich Lessing

Think About It

1   Discuss what the term "Romanesque" means
and distinguish some of the key stylistic features
associated with architecture in this style.

2   Discuss the sculpture that was integrated into
the exteriors of Romanesque churches. Why was
it there? Whom did it address? What were the
prominent messages? Refer to at least one church
discussed in this chapter.

3   What is a pilgrimage site? How did pilgrimage sites
function for medieval Christians? Ground your
answer in a discussion of Santiago de Compostela,
focusing on specific features that were geared
toward pilgrims.

4   Analyze one example of a Romanesque work of art
in this chapter that tells a story of human frailty.
Who was the intended audience? How does its style
relate to the intended moral message?

Crosscurrents

These pages served as the beginning of
the Gospel of Matthew in two medieval
manuscripts, one Hiberno-Saxon and the
other Romanesque. Compare the designs
of these two pages and the relationship
that is established between words and
images. How does the work of these two
artists relate to work in other media during
the period in which each was made?

FIG. 15–7

FIG. 16–34

17–1 SCENES FROM GENESIS

Detail of the Good Samaritan Window, south aisle of nave, Cathedral of Notre-Dame, Chartres, France. c. 1200–1210.
Stained and painted glass.

Chapter 17

Gothic Art of the Twelfth and Thirteenth Centuries

 ## Learning Objectives

17.a Identify the visual hallmarks of Gothic art and its regional variations for formal, technical, and expressive qualities.

17.b Interpret the meaning of works of Gothic art based on their themes, subjects, and symbols.

17.c Relate Gothic art and artists to their cultural, economic, and political contexts.

17.d Apply the vocabulary and concepts relevant to Gothic art, artists, and art history.

17.e Interpret a work of Gothic art using the art historical methods of observation, comparison, and inductive reasoning.

17.f Select visual and textual evidence in various media to support an argument or an interpretation of a work of Gothic art.

The Gothic style—originating in the powerful monasteries of the Paris region—dominated European art and architecture for 400 years. By the mid twelfth century, advances in building technology, increasing financial resources, and new intellectual and spiritual aspirations led to the development of a new art and architecture that expressed the religious and political values of monastic communities. Just as residents of twentieth-century American cities raced to erect higher and higher skyscrapers, the patrons of western Europe competed to build cathedrals and churches with ever-taller naves and towers, increasingly diaphanous walls of glowing glass, and breathtakingly airy interiors that seemed to open in all directions.

The light captured in stained-glass windows created luminous pictures and interior atmospheres that must have captivated worshipers whose everyday existence included little color. Gothic churches became the glorious jeweled houses of God: evocations of the heavenly Jerusalem and invitations to faithful living. And stained glass became the major medium of monumental painting.

This detail from the Good Samaritan Window at Chartres Cathedral (**FIG. 17-1**), created in the early years of the thirteenth century, well into the development of French Gothic architecture, includes scenes from Genesis, the first book of the Bible. The window portrays God's creation of Adam and Eve and continues with their subsequent temptation, fall into sin, and expulsion from the paradise of the Garden of Eden to lead a life of work and woe. Adam and Eve's story is used here to interpret the meaning of

the parable of the Good Samaritan for medieval viewers, reminding them that Christ saves them from the original sin of Adam and Eve just as the Good Samaritan saves the injured and abused traveler (SEE FIG. 17-10). The stained-glass windows of Gothic cathedrals were radiant sermons, preached with pictures rather than with words. They were directed at a diverse audience of worshipers, drawn from a broad spectrum of medieval society, who derived multiple meanings from gloriously complicated works of art.

Gothic Europe

What are the cultural and historical backgrounds for Gothic art and architecture?

In the middle of the twelfth century, a distinctive new architecture known today as Gothic emerged in the Île-de-France, the French royal domain around Paris (**MAP 17-1**). The appearance there of a new style and technique of building coincided with the emergence of the monarchy as a powerful centralizing force. Within 100 years, an estimated 2,700 Gothic churches were built in the Île-de-France region alone.

Advances in building technology allowed progressively larger windows and ever loftier vaults, supported by exterior buttressing that was more and more streamlined and skeletal. The Gothic style spread throughout western Europe, gradually displacing Romanesque forms while taking on regional characteristics inspired by them.

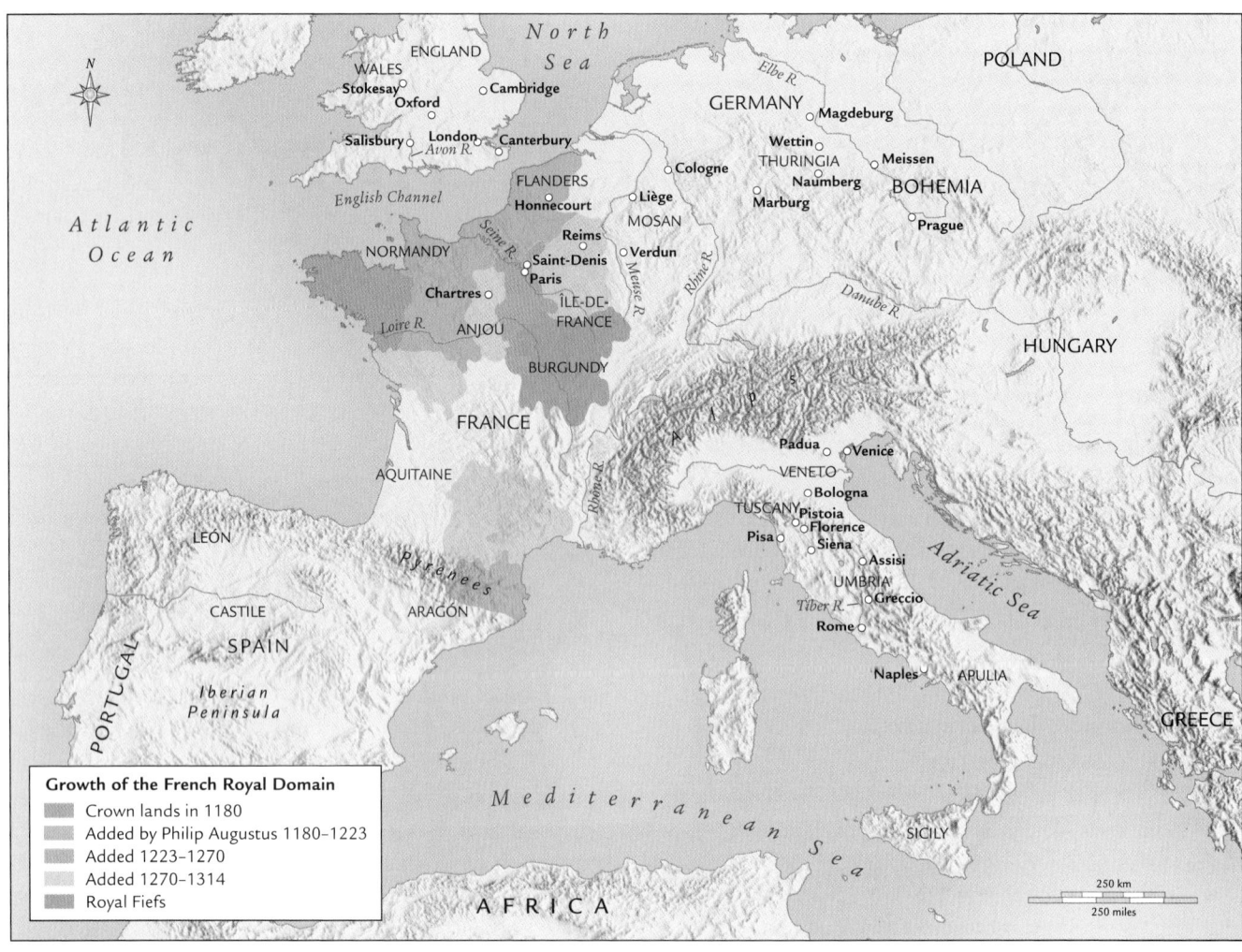

MAP 17–1 EUROPE IN THE GOTHIC ERA

The color changes on this map chart the gradual expansion of territory ruled by the king of France during the period when Gothic was developing as a modern French style.

Gothic prevailed until about 1400, and even longer in some regions. It was adapted to all types of structures, including town halls and residences, as well as Christian churches and synagogues.

The term "Gothic" was popularized by the sixteenth-century Italian artist and historian Giorgio Vasari, who disparagingly attributed the by-then-old-fashioned style to the Goths, Germanic invaders who had "destroyed" the Classical civilization of the Roman Empire that Vasari preferred. In its own day the Gothic style was simply called "modern art" or the "French style."

The Rise of Urban and Intellectual Life

The Gothic period was an era of communal achievement and social change. Although Europe remained rural, towns became important centers of artistic patronage, fostering strong communal identity by public projects and ceremonies. Intellectual life was also stimulated by the interaction of so many people living side by side. Universities in Bologna, Padua, Paris, Cambridge, and Oxford supplanted monastic and cathedral schools as centers of learning. Brilliant teachers like Peter Abelard (1079–1142) drew crowds of students, and in the thirteenth century an Italian theologian, Thomas Aquinas (1225–1274), made Paris the intellectual center of Europe.

A system of reasoned analysis known as Scholasticism emerged from these universities, intent on reconciling Christian theology with Classical philosophy. Scholastic thinkers used a question-and-answer method of argument and arranged their ideas into logical outlines. Thomas Aquinas, the foremost Scholastic, applied Aristotelian logic to comprehend religion's supernatural aspects, setting up the foundation on which Catholic thought rests to this day. Some have seen a relationship between the development of these new ways of thinking and the geometrical order that permeates the design of Gothic cathedrals, as well as with the new interest in describing the appearance of the natural world in sculpture and painting.

The Age of Cathedrals

Urban cathedrals, the seats of the ruling bishops, superseded rural monasteries as centers of religious culture and patronage. So many cathedrals were rebuilt between 1150 and 1400—often to replace earlier churches destroyed in the fires that were a byproduct of population growth and housing density within cities—that some have dubbed the period the "Age of Cathedrals." Cathedral precincts functioned almost as towns within towns—containing a palace for the bishop, housing for the clergy, and workshops for the multitude of artists and laborers necessary to support building campaigns. These gigantic churches certainly dominated their urban surroundings. But even if their grandeur inspired admiration, their enormous expense and some bishops' intrusive displays of power inspired resentment, even rioting.

France and the Origins of the Gothic Style

How does the Gothic style originate at the monastery of Saint-Denis in the 1140s and develop in France over the next century?

The development and initial flowering of the Gothic style in France took place against the backdrop of the growing power of the Capetian monarchy. Louis VII (ruled 1137–1180) and Philip Augustus (ruled 1180–1223) consolidated royal authority in the Île-de-France and began to exert more control over powerful nobles in other regions. Louis VII's queen, Eleanor of Aquitaine, brought southwestern France into the royal domain, but when their marriage was annulled, Eleanor reclaimed her lands and married Henry Plantagenet—count of Anjou, duke of Normandy—who became King Henry II of England. The resulting tangle of conflicting claims kept France and England at odds for centuries.

As French kings continued to consolidate royal authority and increase their domains and privileges, the growing centralization of their government sparked a building boom in Paris, which developed from a small provincial town into a thriving urban center beginning in the middle of the twelfth century. Concentrated architectural activity in the capital provided the impetus—or perhaps simply the opportunity—for the developments in architectural technology and the new ways of planning and thinking about buildings that ultimately led to the birth of a new style.

The Birth of Gothic at the Abbey Church of Saint-Denis

Many consider the church of the Benedictine abbey of Saint-Denis, just north of Paris, to be the first Gothic building. This monastery had been founded in the fifth century over the tomb of St. Denis, the Early Christian martyr who had been sent from Rome to convert the local pagan population, becoming the first bishop of Paris. Early on, the abbey developed special royal significance. It housed tombs of the kings of France, the regalia of the French crown, and the relics of St. Denis, patron saint of France.

Construction began in the 1130s of a new church to replace the early medieval church at the abbey, under the supervision of Abbot Suger (abbot 1122–1151). Suger discusses the building of the church in a written account of his administration of the abbey, a rare firsthand chronicle and justification of a medieval building program. Suger prized magnificence, precious materials, and especially fine workmanship (see "Abbot Suger on the Value of Art in Monasteries" on page 512). He invited an international team of masons, sculptors, metalworkers, and glass painters, making this building site a major center of artistic exchange. Such a massive undertaking was extraordinarily expensive. The abbey received substantial annual revenues from the town's inhabitants, and Suger was not above forging documents to increase the abbey's landholdings, which constituted its principal source of income.

Suger began building c. 1135, with a conservative new west façade and narthex attached to the old church, but it was in the new choir—completed in three years and three months between July 14, 1140 and its consecration on June 11, 1144—where the fully formed Gothic architectural style may first have appeared. In his account of the reconstruction, Suger argues that the older building was inadequate to accommodate the crowds of pilgrims who arrived on feast days to venerate the body of St. Denis, and too modest to express the importance of the saint himself. In working with builders to conceive a radically new church design, he turned for inspiration to texts that were attributed erroneously to a follower of St. Paul named Dionysius (the Greek form of Denis), who considered radiant light a physical manifestation of God. Through the centuries, this Pseudo-Dionysius had become identified with the martyred Denis, so Suger was adapting what he believed was the patron saint's concept of divine luminosity in designing the new abbey church with walls composed essentially of stained-glass windows. In inscriptions he composed for the bronze doors (now lost), he was specific about the motivations for the church's innovative style: "being nobly bright, the work should lighten the minds, so that they may travel, through the true lights, to the True Light where Christ is the true door" (Panofsky, p. 49).

The **PLAN OF THE CHOIR** (FIG. 17-2A) retains key features of the Romanesque pilgrimage plan (SEE FIG. 16-4A), with a semicircular apse surrounded by an ambulatory, around which radiate seven chapels of uniform size. And the structural elements of the choir had already appeared in Romanesque buildings, including pointed arches, ribbed groin vaults, and external buttressing to relieve stress on the walls. The dramatic achievement of Suger's builders was the coordinated use of these features to create an architectural whole that emphasized open, flowing space enclosed by non-load-bearing walls of glowing stained glass (FIG. 17-2B). In Suger's words, the church becomes "a circular string of chapels by virtue of which the whole would shine with the wonderful and uninterrupted light of most luminous windows, pervading the interior beauty" (Panofsky, p. 101). And since Suger saw

the contemplation of light as a means of illuminating the soul and uniting it with God, he was providing his monks with an environment especially conducive to their primary vocation of prayer and meditation.

The revolutionary stained-glass windows of Suger's Saint-Denis were almost lost in the wake of the French Revolution, when this royal abbey represented everything the new leaders were intent on suppressing. Thanks to an enterprising antiquarian named Alexandre Lenoir, however, the twelfth-century windows, though removed from their architectural setting, were saved from destruction. During the nineteenth century, some stained glass returned to the abbey, but many panels are now in museums. One of the best-preserved—from a window that narrated Jesus's childhood—portrays **THE FLIGHT INTO EGYPT** (FIG. 17-3). The crisp elegance of the delineation of faces, foliage, and

17-2A PLAN OF THE CHOIR OF THE ABBEY CHURCH OF SAINT-DENIS
France. 1140–1144.

17-2B VIEW OF AMBULATORY AND APSE CHAPELS OF THE ABBEY CHURCH OF SAINT-DENIS
France. 1140–1144.

Envisioning the completion of the abbey church with a transept, and presumably also a nave, Abbot Suger had the following inscription placed in the church to commemorate the 1144 dedication of the choir: "Once the new rear part is joined to the part in front, the church shines with its middle part brightened. For bright is that which is brightly coupled with the bright, and bright is the noble edifice which is pervaded by the new light." (Panofsky, p. 51).

Credit: © akg-images/Bildarchiv Monheim

Elements of Architecture

RIB VAULTING

An important innovation of Romanesque and Gothic builders was **rib vaulting**. Rib vaults are a form of groin vault (see "Roman Vaulting" in Chapter 6 on page 190), in which the diagonal ridges (groins) rest on and are covered by curved moldings called ribs. After the walls and piers of the building reached the desired height, timber scaffolding to support these masonry ribs was constructed. When the mortar of the ribs was set, the web of the vault was then laid on forms built on the ribs themselves. After all the temporary forms were removed, the ribs may have provided strength at the intersections of the webbing to channel the vaults' thrust outward and downward to the foundations; they certainly add decorative interest. In short, ribs formed the "skeleton" of the vault; the webbing, a lighter masonry "skin." In Late Gothic buildings, additional decorative ribs give such vaults a lacelike appearance.

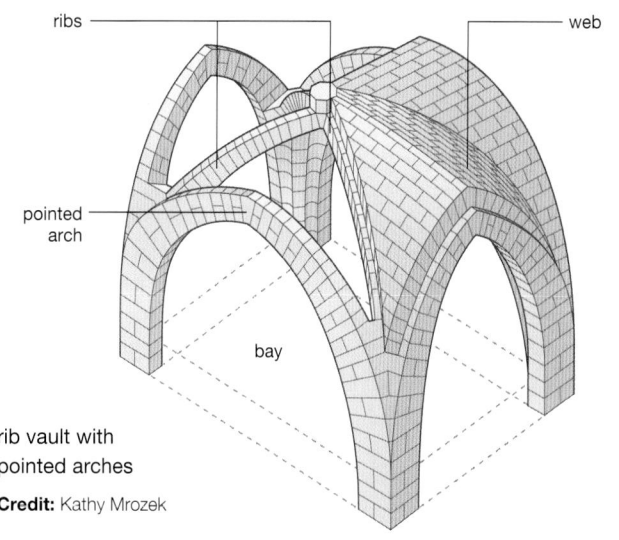

ribs   web

pointed arch

bay

rib vault with pointed arches

Credit: Kathy Mrozek

drapery—painted with vitreous enamel on the vibrantly colored pieces of glass that make up the panel (see "Stained Glass Windows" on page 512)—is almost as clear today as it was when the windows were new. One unusual detail—the Virgin reaching to pick a date from a palm tree that has bent down at the infant Jesus's command to accommodate her—is based on an apocryphal Gospel that was not included in the canonical Christian scriptures but remained a popular source for twelfth-century artists.

Louis VII and Eleanor of Aquitaine attended the consecration of the new choir in June 1144, along with a constellation of secular and sacred dignitaries. Since the bishops and archbishops of France were assembled at the consecration—celebrating Mass simultaneously at altars throughout the choir and crypt—they had the opportunity to experience firsthand this new Gothic style of building. The history of French architecture over the next few centuries indicates that they were quite impressed.

17-3 THE FLIGHT INTO EGYPT
Detail of the Incarnation (Infancy of Christ) Window, axial choir chapel, abbey church of Saint-Denis. c. 1140–1144. Glencairn Museum, Bryn Athyn, Pennsylvania.

Credit: © Glencairn Museum, Bryn Athyn, Pennsylvania.

Technique

STAINED-GLASS WINDOWS

The "wonderful and uninterrupted light" that Suger sought in the reconstruction of the choir of Saint-Denis in the 1140s was provided by stained-glass artists that—as he tells us—he called in from many nations to create glowing walls for the radiating chapels and perhaps the clerestory as well. As a result of their exquisite work, this influential building program not only constituted a new architectural style; it catapulted what had been a minor curiosity among pictorial techniques into the major medium of monumental European painting. For several centuries, stained glass would be integral to architectural design, not decoration added to an already completed building. Windows were produced at the same time that masons were building walls and carving capitals and moldings.

Our knowledge about the medieval art of stained glass is based on a precious twelfth-century text—*De Diversis Artibus* (*On Divers Arts*)—written by a German monk who called himself Theophilus Presbyter (see "St. Bernard and Theophilus" in Chapter 16 on page 481). In fact, the basic procedures of producing a stained-glass window have changed little since the Middle Ages. It is not a lost art, but it is a complex and costly process. The glass itself was made by bringing sand and ash to a molten state under intense heat and "staining" it with color through the addition of metallic oxides. This molten material was then blown and flattened into sheets. Guided by a **cartoon** (full-scale drawing) painted on a whitewashed board, the glass painter would cut from these sheets the individual shapes that would make up a figural scene or ornamental passage. A hot iron was used to crack the glass into a rough approximation that could later be refined by chipping away at the edges with an iron tool—a process called **grozing**—to achieve the precise shape needed in the composition.

The artists used a vitreous paint (made, Theophilus tells us, of iron filings and ground glass suspended in wine or urine) at full strength to block light and delineate features such as facial expressions or drapery folds. It could also be diluted to create modeling washes. Once painted, the pieces of glass would be fired in a kiln to fuse the painting with the glass surface. Only then did the artists assemble these shapes of color—like pieces of a complex compositional puzzle—with strips of lead (called **cames**), and subsequently mount a series of the resulting panels on an iron framework within the architectural opening to form an ensemble we call a stained-glass window. Lead was used in the assembly process because it was strong enough to hold the glass pieces together, but flexible enough to bend around their complex shapes and—perhaps more critically—absorb the impact from gusts of wind and prevent the glass itself from cracking.

Art and its Contexts

ABBOT SUGER ON THE VALUE OF ART IN MONASTERIES

Suger, who masterminded the reconstruction of the abbey church at Saint-Denis while he was its abbot (1122–1151), weighed in on the twelfth-century monastic debate concerning the appropriateness of elaborate art in monasteries (see "St. Bernard and Theophilus" in Chapter 16 on page 481), both through the magnificence of the new church he built and by the way he described and discussed the project in the account he wrote of his administration of the abbey.

These are his comments on the bronze doors, which were destroyed in 1794:

> Bronze casters having been summoned and sculptors chosen, we set up the main doors on which are represented the Passion of the Saviour and His Resurrection, or rather Ascension, with great cost and much expenditure for their gilding as was fitting for the noble porch…

The verses on the door are these:

> Whoever thou art, if thou seekest to extol the glory of these doors,
> Marvel not at the gold and the expense but at the craftsmanship of the work,
> Bright is the noble work; but being nobly bright, the work
> Should lighten the minds, so that they may travel, through the true lights,
> To the True Light where Christ is the true door,
> In what manner it be inherent in this world the golden door defines:
> The dull mind rises to truth through that which is material
> And, in seeing this light, is resurrected from its former subversion.

On the lintel, just under the large figure of Christ at the Last Judgment on the tympanum, Suger had inscribed:

> Receive, O stern Judge, the prayers of Thy Suger; grant that I be mercifully numbered among Thy own sheep.
>
> (Translations from Panofsky, pp. 47, 49)

The Cathedral of Notre-Dame at Chartres

The abbey church of Saint-Denis became the prototype for a new architecture of space and light based on a highly adaptable skeletal framework that supported rib vaulting on the points of slender piers—rather than along massive Romanesque walls—reinforced by external buttress systems. It initiated a period of competitive experimentation in France that resulted in ever-larger churches—principally cathedrals—enclosing increasingly taller interior spaces, walled with ever-greater expanses of stained glass.

The new Gothic conceptions of space and wall and the structural techniques that made them possible were developed further at the Cathedral of Notre-Dame at Chartres. The great cathedral dominates this town southwest of Paris and, for many people, is a near-perfect embodiment of the Gothic style. Constructed in several stages beginning in the mid twelfth century and extending into the mid thirteenth, with additions such as the north spire as late as the sixteenth century, Chartres Cathedral reflects the transition from an experimental twelfth-century architecture to a mature thirteenth-century style.

Chartres was the site of a pre-Christian virgin-goddess cult, and later, dedicated to the Virgin Mary, it became one of the oldest and most important Christian shrines in France. Its main treasure was a piece of linen believed to have been worn by the Virgin Mary when she gave birth to Jesus. This relic was a gift from the Byzantine empress Irene to Charlemagne, whose grandson Charles the Bald donated it to Chartres in 876. It was kept below the high altar in a huge basement crypt. The healing powers attributed to the cloth made Chartres a major pilgrimage destination, especially as the cult of the Virgin grew in popularity in the twelfth and thirteenth centuries. Its association with important market fairs—especially cloth markets—held at Chartres on the feast days of the Virgin put the textile relic at the intersection of local prestige and the local economy, increasing the income of the cathedral not only through pilgrimage but also through tax revenue it received from the markets.

The **WEST FAÇADE** of Chartres (**FIG. 17-4**) preserves an early sculptural program created within a decade of the reconstruction of Saint-Denis. Surrounding these three doors—the so-called Royal Portal, used only for important ceremonial entrances of the bishop and his retinue—sculpted figures calmly and comfortably fill their architectural settings.

On the central tympanum, Christ is enthroned in majesty, returning at the end of time surrounded by the four evangelists (**FIG. 17-5**). Although imposing, he seems more serene and human than in the hieratic and stylized portrayal of the same subject at the priory church at Moissac (SEE FIG. 16-21). The apostles, organized into four groups of

three, fill the lintel, and the 24 elders of the Apocalypse line the archivolts.

The right portal is dedicated to the Incarnation (God's first earthly appearance), highlighting the role of Mary in the early life of Christ, from the Annunciation to the Presentation in the Temple. On the left portal is the Ascension (the Incarnate God's return from earth to heaven). Jesus floats heavenward in a cloud supported by angels. Running across all three portals on the top of the jambs just underneath the level of the lintels, historiated capitals depict Jesus's life on earth in a series of small, lively narrative scenes.

17-4 WEST FAÇADE, CHARTRES CATHEDRAL (CATHEDRAL OF NOTRE-DAME)

France. West façade begun c. 1134; cathedral rebuilt after a fire in 1194; building continued to 1260; north spire 1507–1513.

Credit: © akg-images/Schütze/Rodemann

17-5 ROYAL PORTAL, WEST FAÇADE, CHARTRES CATHEDRAL

c. 1145–1155.

Credit: © Achim Bednorz, Cologne

Flanking all three openings on the jambs are column statues (**FIG. 17-6**) of kings, queens, and prophets from the Hebrew Bible, evocations of Christ's royal and spiritual ancestry as well as a reminder of the close ties between the Church and the French royal house. The prominence of kings and queens here is what has given the Royal Portal its name. The elegantly elongated proportions and linear, but lifelike, drapery of these column statues echo the cylindrical shafts behind them. Their meticulously carved, idealized heads radiate a sense of beatified calm. In fact, tranquility and order prevail in the overall design as well as in the individual components of this portal, a striking contrast to the dynamic configurations and energized figures on the portals of Romanesque churches.

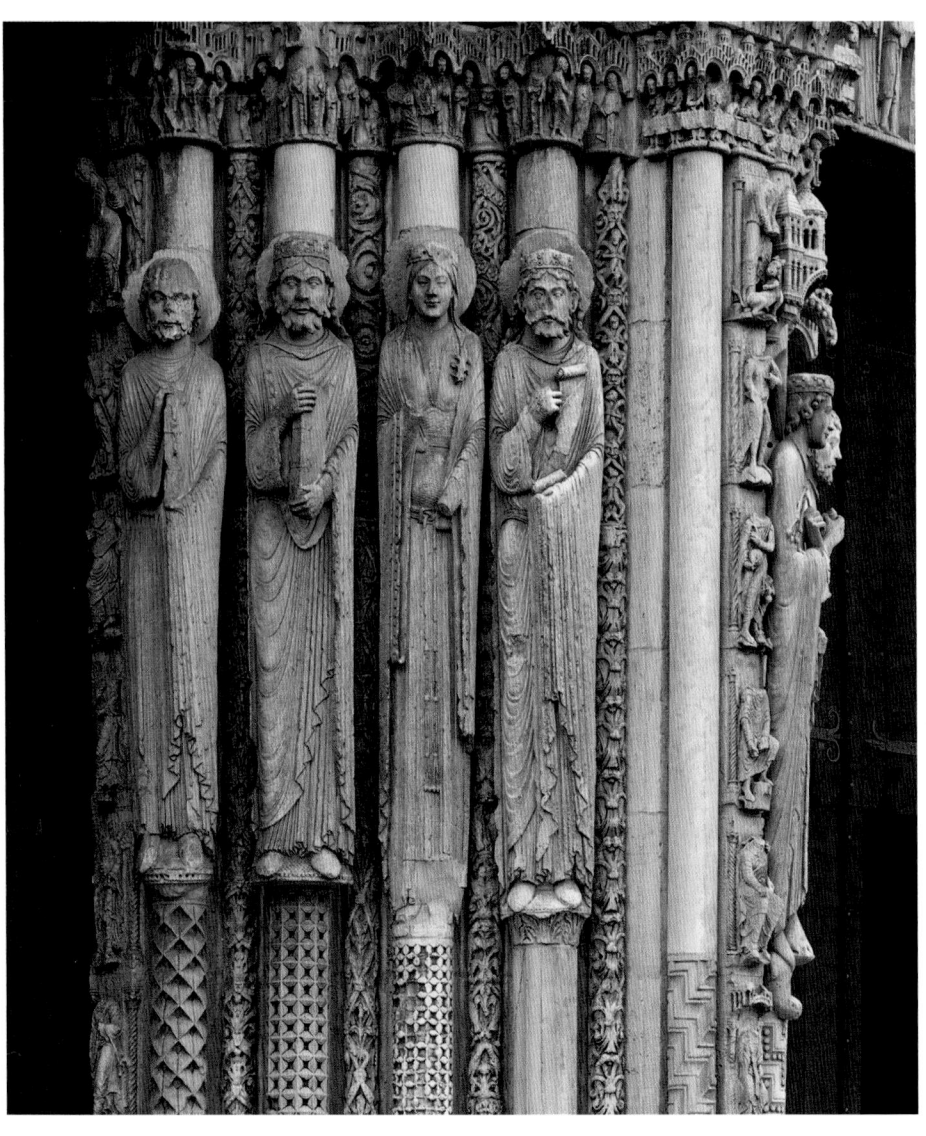

17-6 ROYAL PORTAL, WEST FAÇADE, CHARTRES CATHEDRAL

Detail of prophets and ancestors of Christ (kings and queens of Judea), right side, central portal. c. 1145–1155.

Credit: © Achim Bednorz, Cologne

17-7 MASONS AT WORK

Detail of a miniature from a Picture Bible made in Paris. 1240s. The Morgan Library and Museum, New York. MS. M638, fol. 3r.

Credit: © 2016. Photo Pierpont Morgan Library/Art Resource/ Scala, Florence

ARCHITECTURE   The bulk of Chartres Cathedral was constructed after a fire in 1194 destroyed an earlier Romanesque church but spared the Royal Portal, the windows above it, and the crypt with its precious relics. A papal representative convinced reluctant local church officials to rebuild. He argued that the Virgin had permitted the fire because she wanted a new and more beautiful church to be built in her honor. Between 1194 and about 1260 that new cathedral was built (see "The Gothic Church" on page 517).

Such a project required vast resources— money, raw materials, and skilled labor (see "Master Masons" below). A contemporary painting shows a building site with the **MASONS AT WORK** (FIG. **17-7**). Carpenters have built scaffolds, platforms, and a lifting machine. Master stonecutters measure and cut the stones; workers carry and hoist the blocks by hand or with a lifting wheel. Thousands of stones had to be cut and placed accurately. Here a laborer carries mortar up a ladder to

Art and its Contexts

MASTER MASONS

Master masons oversaw all aspects of church construction in the Middle Ages, from design and structural engineering to construction and decoration. The master mason at Chartres coordinated the work of roughly 400 people, scattered with their equipment and supplies, across many locations, from distant stone quarries to high scaffolding. It has been estimated that this workforce set in place some 200 blocks of stone each day.

Funding shortages and technical delays, such as the need to let mortar harden for three to six months, made construction sporadic, so master masons and their crews moved constantly from job to job; often, several masters and many teams of masons contributed to the construction of a single building. Fewer than 100 master builders are estimated to have been responsible for all the major architectural projects around Paris during the century-long building boom there, some of them working on parts of as many as 40 churches. This was dangerous work. Masons were always at risk of injury, which could cut short a career in its prime. King Louis IX of

France actually provided sick pay to a mason injured in the construction of Royaumont Abbey in 1234, but not all workers were this lucky. Master mason William of Sens, who supervised construction at Canterbury Cathedral, fell from a scaffold. His injuries forced him to return to France in 1178 because of his inability to work. Some medieval contracts had pension arrangements or provisions that took potential injury or illness into account, but some did not.

Today, the names of more than 3,000 master masons are known to us, and the close study of differences in construction techniques often discloses the participation of specific masters. Master masons gained in prestige during the thirteenth century as they increasingly differentiated themselves from the laborers they supervised. In some cases their names were prominently inscribed in the labyrinths on cathedral floors. From the thirteenth century on, in what was then an exceptional honor, masters were buried along with patrons and bishops in the cathedrals they built.

men working on the top of the wall, where the lifting wheel delivers cut stones. To fund this work, bishops and cathedral officials usually pledged all or part of their incomes for up to ten years. Royal and aristocratic patrons joined in the effort. In a scheme that seems very modern, the churchmen at Chartres solicited contributions by sending the cathedral relics, including the Virgin's tunic, on tour as far away as England.

As the new structure rose higher during the 1220s, the work grew more costly and funds dwindled. But when the bishop and the cathedral clergy tried to make up the deficit by raising taxes, the townspeople drove them into exile for four years. This action in Chartres was not unique; people often opposed the building of cathedrals because of the burden of new taxes.

Building on the principles pioneered at Saint-Denis—a glass-filled masonry skeleton enclosing a large, open space—the masons at Chartres erected a church over 45 feet wide with vaults that soar approximately 120 feet above the floor. As at Saint-Denis, the plan is rooted in the Romanesque pilgrimage plan, but with a significantly enlarged sanctuary occupying a full third of the building (**FIG. 17–8A**).The Chartres builders codified what were to become the typical Gothic structural devices: pointed arches and ribbed groin vaults rising from compound piers over rectangular bays. The vaults were supported externally by the recently developed **flying buttress** system (**SEE FIG. 17–9**) in which arched exterior supports countered the lateral thrust of the nave vault and transferred its weight outward, over the side aisles, where it was resolved into and supported by a buttressing pier, rising from the ground. Flying buttresses permitted larger clerestory windows, nearly equal in height to the nave arcade (**FIG. 17–8B**). Paired **lancets** (tall openings with pointed tops) surmounted by small circular **rose windows** are created in a technique known as **plate tracery**—holes are cut into the stone wall and nearly half the wall surface is filled with stained glass. The band between the clerestory and nave arcade was now occupied by a **triforium** (arcaded wall passageway) rather than a tall gallery,

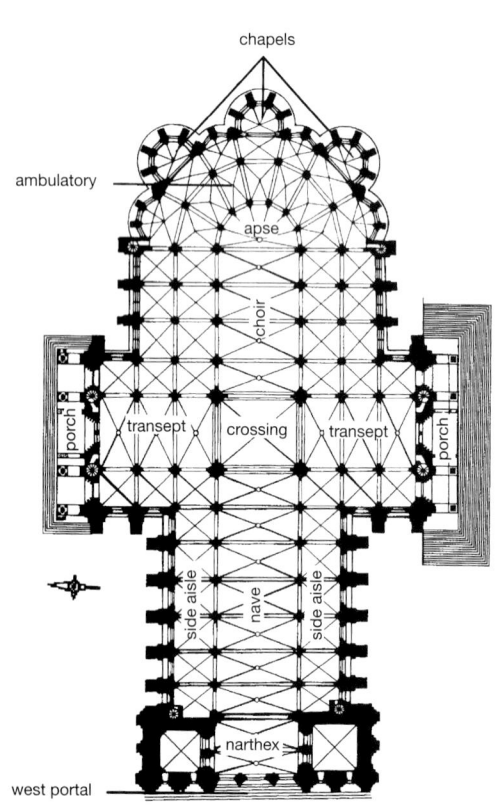

17–8A PLAN, CHARTRES CATHEDRAL
1194–c. 1220.

17–8B INTERIOR LOOKING EAST, CHARTRES CATHEDRAL
1194–c. 1220.

Credit: © Achim Bednorz, Cologne

Elements of Architecture

THE GOTHIC CHURCH

Most large Gothic churches in western Europe were built on the Latin cross plan, with a projecting transept marking the transition from nave to choir, an arrangement that derives ultimately from the fourth-century Constantinian basilica of Old St. Peter's (SEE FIG. 7–10A). The main entrance portal was generally on the west, with the choir and its apse on the east. A western narthex could precede the entrance to the nave and side aisles. An ambulatory with radiating chapels circled the apse and facilitated the movement of worshipers through the church. Many Gothic churches have a three-story elevation, with a triforium sandwiched between the nave arcade and a clerestory full of stained glass. Rib vaulting usually covered all spaces. Flying buttresses helped support the soaring nave vaults by transferring their outward thrust over the aisles to

massive, free-standing, upright external buttresses. Church walls were decorated inside and out with arcades of round or pointed arches, engaged columns and colonnettes, an applied filigree of **tracery**, and horizontal moldings called **stringcourses**. The pitched roofs above the vaults—necessary to shed rainwater from the building—were supported by wooden frameworks. A spire or crossing tower above the junction of the transept and nave was usually planned, though often never finished. Portal façades were also customarily marked by high, flanking towers or gabled porches ornamented with **pinnacles** and finials. Architectural sculpture proliferated on each portal's tympanum, archivolts, and jambs (SEE FIGS. 17–5, 17–6), and in France a magnificent rose window typically formed the centerpiece of the flat portal façades (**FIG. 17–9**).

17–9 SCHEMATIC DRAWING OF CHARTRES CATHEDRAL

STAINED GLASS　Chartres is distinctive among French Gothic buildings in that most of its stained-glass windows have survived. Stained glass is an enormously expensive and complicated medium of painting, but its effect on the senses and emotions made the effort worthwhile for medieval patrons and builders (see "Stained Glass Windows" on page 512). By 1260, glass painters had installed about 22,000 square feet of stained glass in 176 windows. Most of the glass dates from between about 1200 and 1250, but a few earlier windows from the 1150s—comparable in style to the windows of Suger's Saint-Denis—survived the fire of 1194 and remain in the west wall above the Royal Portal.

In the aisles and chapels, where the windows were low enough to be easily seen, there were elaborate multi-scene narratives, with small figures composed into individual episodes within the irregularly shaped compartments of windows, designed as stacked medallions set against dense, multicolored fields of ornament. Art historians refer to these as cluster medallion windows. The **GOOD SAMARITAN WINDOW** of c. 1200–1210 in the south aisle of the nave is a typical example of the design (**FIG. 17-10**). Its learned allegory on sin and salvation also typifies the complexity of Gothic narrative art.

The principal subject is a parable Jesus told his followers to teach a moral truth (Luke 10:25–37). The protagonist is a traveling Samaritan who cares for a stranger who has been beaten, robbed, and left for dead by thieves. Jesus's parable is an allegory for his imminent redemption of humanity's sins, and within this window a story from Genesis unfolds above the parable to make that association clear (SEE FIG. 17-1). Adam and Eve's fall introduced sin into the world, but Christ (the Good Samaritan) rescues humanity (the traveler) from sin (the thieves) and ministers to them within the Church, just as the Good Samaritan takes the wounded traveler for refuge and healing to an inn (bottom scene, FIG. 17-1). Stylistically, these willowy, expressive figures avoid the classicizing stockiness in Wiligelmo's folksy Romanesque rendering of the Genesis narrative at Modena (SEE FIG. 16-20). Instead they take the dancelike postures that will come to characterize Gothic figures as the style spreads.

In the clerestory windows, the Chartres glass painters mainly used not multi-scene narratives, but large-scale single figures that could be seen at a distance because of their size, bold drawing, and strong colors. Iconic ensembles were easier to "read" in lofty openings more removed from viewers, such as the huge north transept **ROSE WINDOW** (**FIG. 17-11**), which is over 42 feet in diameter. Surmounting five lancets, the ensemble proclaims the royal and

17-10 GOOD SAMARITAN WINDOW
South aisle of nave, Chartres Cathedral. c. 1200–1210.
Stained and painted glass.

Credit: Sonia Halliday Photographs

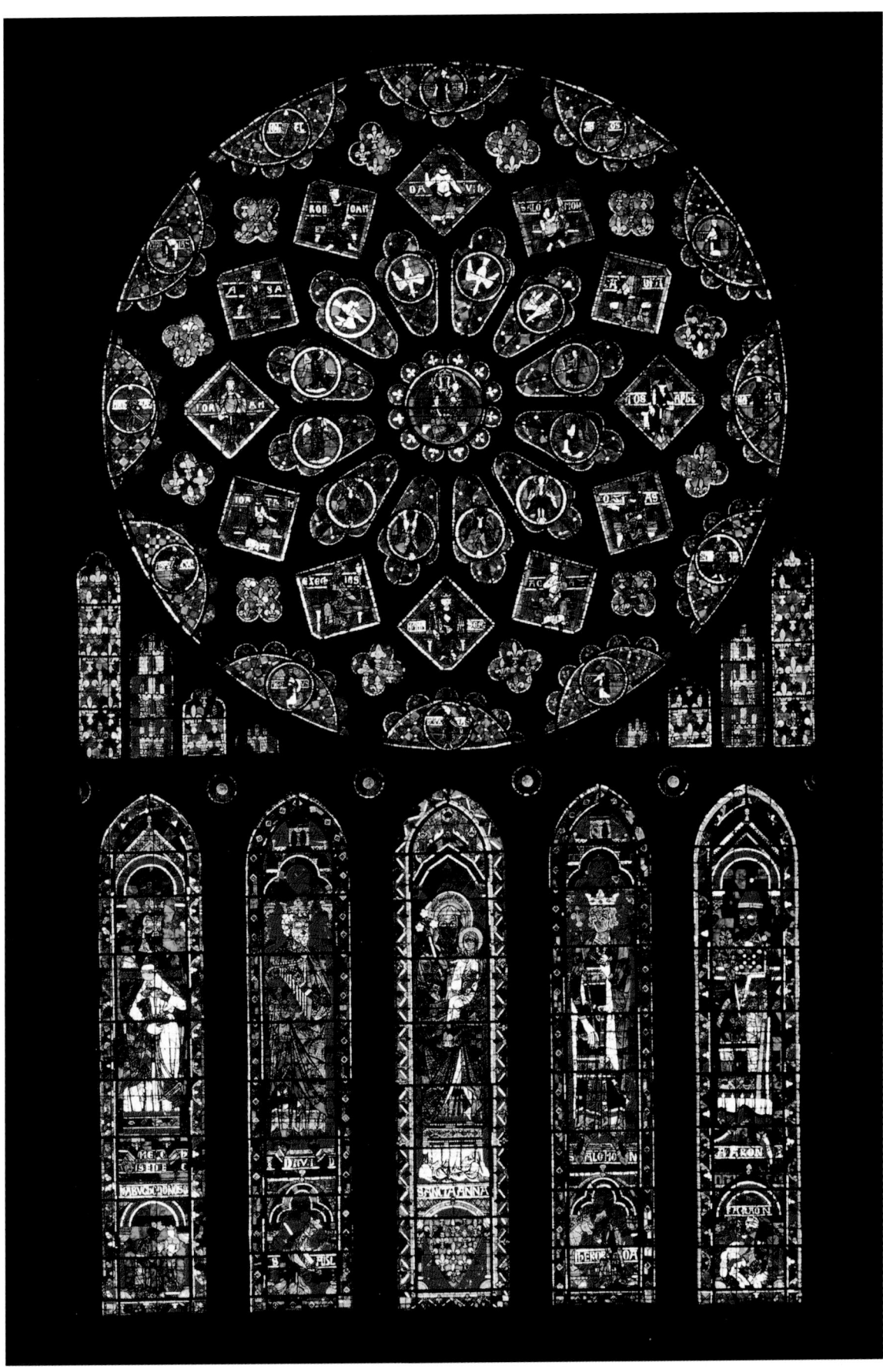

17–11 ROSE WINDOW AND LANCETS, NORTH TRANSEPT, CHARTRES CATHEDRAL

c. 1230–1235. Stained and painted glass.

Credit: © Angelo Hornak/Corbis

priestly heritage of Mary and Jesus and, through them, of the Church itself. In the central lancet, St. Anne holds her infant daughter Mary, flanked left to right by statuesque figures of Hebrew Bible leaders Melchizedek, David, Solomon, and Aaron. Above, in the very center of the rose window itself, Mary and Jesus are enthroned, surrounded by a radiating array of doves, angels, and Hebrew Bible kings and prophets.

This vast wall of glass was a gift from the young King Louis IX (ruled 1226–1270), perhaps arranged by his powerful mother, Queen Blanche of Castile (1188–1252), who ruled as regent (1226–1234) during Louis's minority. Royal heraldic emblems proclaim the window's association with

the king. The arms of France—golden *fleurs-de-lis* on a blue ground—fill a prominent shield under St. Anne at the bottom of the central lancet. *Fleurs-de-lis* also appear in the graduated lancets bracketing the base of the rose window, and in a series of **quatrefoils** (four-lobed designs) within the rose itself. But also prominent is the Castilian device of golden castles on a red ground, a reference to the royal lineage of Louis's powerful mother. Light radiating from the deep blues and reds creates a hazy purple atmosphere in the soft light of the north side of the building. On a sunny day the masonry may seem to dissolve in color, but the bold theological and political messages of the rose window remain clear.

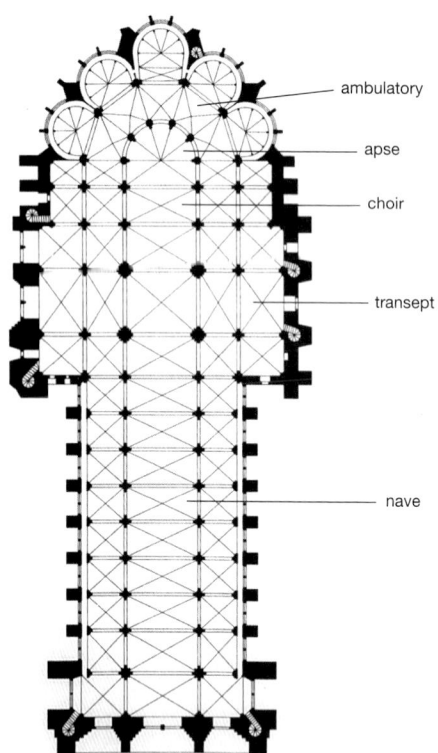

17–12 PLAN OF CATHEDRAL OF NOTRE-DAME, REIMS

France. Begun in 1211.

17–13 WEST FAÇADE, CATHEDRAL OF NOTRE-DAME, REIMS

Rebuilding begun 1211; façade begun c. 1225; to the height of rose window by 1260; finished for the coronation of Philip the Fair in 1286; towers left unfinished 1311; additional work 1406–1428.

Credit: © zechal/123RF

The Cathedral of Notre-Dame at Reims

Reims Cathedral, northeast of Paris in the region of Champagne, was the coronation church of the kings of France and, like Saint-Denis, had been a cultural and educational center since Carolingian times. When fire destroyed this historic building in 1210, the community at Reims began to erect a new Gothic structure, planned as a large basilica (**FIG. 17-12**). It is similar to the model set earlier at Chartres (SEE FIG. 17-8A), but at Reims priority is given to an extended nave rather than an expanded choir, perhaps a reference to the processional emphasis of the coronation ceremony. The cornerstone of the cathedral was laid in 1211, and work continued throughout the century. The expense of the project sparked such local opposition that twice in the 1230s revolts drove the archbishop and canons into exile. At Reims, five master masons directed the work on the cathedral over the course of a century—Jean d'Orbais, Jean le Loup, Gaucher de Reims, Bernard de Soissons, and Robert de Coucy.

The west front of the Cathedral of Reims is a magnificent ensemble in which almost every square inch of stone surface seems encrusted with sculptural decoration (**FIG.** 17-13). Its tall, gabled portals form a broad, horizontal base and project forward to display an expanse of sculpture, while the tympana they enclose are filled with stained-glass windows rather than stone carvings. Their soaring peaks—the middle one reaching to the center of the dominating rose window—unify the façade vertically. In a departure from tradition, Mary rather than Christ is featured in the central portal, a reflection of the growing popularity of her cult. Christ crowns her as queen of heaven in the central gable. The towers were later additions, as was the row of carved figures that runs from the base of one tower to the other above the rose window. This "gallery of kings" is the only strictly horizontal element of the façade.

The sheer quantity of sculpture envisioned for this elaborate cathedral front required the skills of many sculptors, working in an impressive variety of styles over several decades. Four figures from the right jamb of the **CENTRAL PORTAL** illustrate this rich stylistic diversity (**FIG. 17-14**). The pair on the right portrays the Visitation, in which Mary (left), pregnant with Jesus, visits her older cousin, Elizabeth (right), pregnant with St. John the Baptist. The sculptor of these figures, active in Reims about 1230–1235, drew heavily on ancient sources. Reims had been a major Roman city, and there were remaining Roman works at

17-14 CENTRAL PORTAL, RIGHT SIDE, WEST FAÇADE, REIMS CATHEDRAL

Annunciation (left pair: Mary [right] c. 1240, angel [left] c. 1250) and Visitation (right pair: Mary [left] and Elizabeth [right] c. 1230).

Credit: © Angelo Hornak/Corbis

the disposal of medieval sculptors. The bulky bodies show the same solidity seen in Roman sculpture (SEE FIG. 6-15), and the women's full faces, wavy hair, and heavy mantles recall imperial portrait statuary, including the two imperial facial ideals of unblemished youth (Mary) and aged accomplishment (Elizabeth) (SEE FIGS. 6-39, 6-40). The figures shift their weight to one leg in contrapposto as they turn toward each other in conversation.

The pair to the left of the Visitation enacts the Annunciation, in which the archangel Gabriel announces to Mary that she will bear Jesus. This Mary's slight body, broad planes of simple drapery, restrained gesture, inward focus, and delicate features contrast markedly with the bold tangibility of the Mary in the Visitation next to her. She is clearly the work of a second sculptor. The archangel Gabriel (at the far left) represents a third artist, active at the middle of the century. This sculptor created tall, gracefully swaying figures with small, fine-featured heads, whose expressions, hairdos, and mannered poses of aristocratic refinement grew to characterize the figural arts in later Gothic sculpture and painting. These characteristics became the basis for what is called the International Gothic Style, fashionable across Europe well into the fifteenth century.

Inside the church (FIG. 17-15), the wall is designed, as at Chartres, as a three-story elevation with nave arcade and clerestory of equal height, divided by the continuous arcade of a narrow triforium passageway. The designer at Reims gives a subtle emphasis to the center of each bay in the wall elevation, coordinating the central division of the clerestory into two lancets with a slightly enlarged colonnette at the middle of the triforium. This design feature was certainly noticed by one contemporary viewer, since it is (over)emphasized in the drawings Villard de Honnecourt made during a visit to Reims Cathedral c. 1230 (SEE FIG. 17-16). Villard also highlighted one of the principal innovations at Reims: the development of **bar tracery**, in which thin stone bars called **mullions** are inserted into an expansive opening in the wall to form a lacy framework for the stained glass (see the rose window in FIG. 17-15). Bar tracery replaced the older plate tracery— still used at Chartres (SEE FIG. 17-11)—and made possible even larger areas of stained glass in relation to wall surface.

A remarkable ensemble of sculpture and stained glass fills the interior west wall at Reims. A great rose window fills the clerestory level; a row of lancets illuminates the triforium; and a smaller rose window replaces the stone of the portal tympanum. The lower level is anchored visually

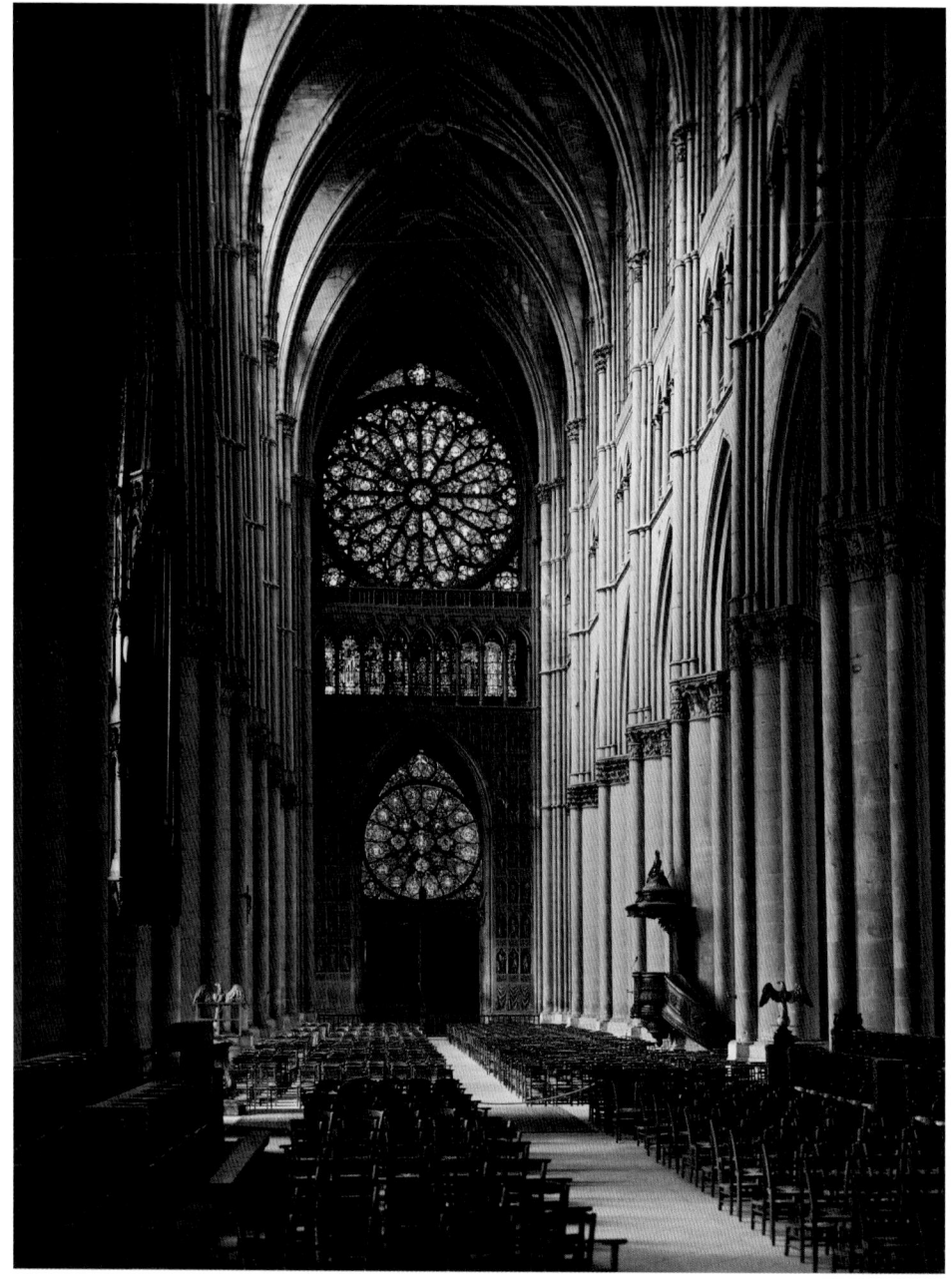

17-15 INTERIOR LOOKING WEST, REIMS CATHEDRAL
Begun 1211; nave c. 1220.

by an expanse of sculpture covering the inner wall of the façade. Here ranks of carved prophets and royal ancestors represented moral guides for the newly crowned monarchs who faced them while proceeding down the nave and out of the cathedral following the coronation ceremony as they began the job of ruling France.

Villard de Honnecourt

One of the most fascinating and enigmatic works surviving from Gothic France is a set of 33 sheets of parchment covered with about 250 drawings in leadpoint and ink, signed

17–17 Villard de Honnecourt **SHEET OF DRAWINGS WITH GEOMETRIC FIGURES**

c. 1230. Ink on vellum, 9¼ × 6″ (23.5 × 15.2 cm). Bibliothèque Nationale, Paris. MS. fr. 19093.

This page, labeled "help in drawing figures according to the lessons taught by the art of geometry," demonstrates how geometric configurations underlie the shapes of natural forms and the designs of architectural features. They seem to give insight into the design process of Gothic artists, but it is also possible that they represent the doodlings of a passionate amateur.

Credit: Bibliotheque nationale de France

17–16 Villard de Honnecourt **DRAWINGS OF THE INTERIOR AND EXTERIOR ELEVATION OF THE NAVE OF REIMS CATHEDRAL**

c. 1230. Ink on vellum, 9¼ × 6″ (23.5 × 15.2 cm). Bibliothèque Nationale, Paris. MS. fr. 19093.

Scholars still debate whether Villard's drawings of Reims Cathedral—the church he documented most extensively, with five leaves showing views and two containing details—were made from observing the building itself, during construction, or copied from construction drawings that had been prepared to guide the work of the masons. But in either case, what Villard documents here are those aspects of Reims that distinguish it from other works of Gothic architecture, such as the use of bar tracery, the enlarged central colonnettes of the triforium, the broad bands of foliate carving on the pier capitals, and the statues of angels that perch on exterior buttresses. He seems to have grasped what it was that separated this building from the other cathedrals rising across France at the same time.

Credit: Bibliotheque nationale de France

by a man named Villard from the Picardy town of Honnecourt and now bound into a book housed in the French National Library. Judging from the identifiable buildings that he recorded, Villard made these drawings in the 1220s and 1230s during extensive travels, mainly in France but also in Switzerland and Poland. Included are plans or individual details of the cathedrals of Cambrai, Chartres, Laon, and especially Reims (**FIG. 17–16**).

Villard seems simply to have drawn those things that interested him—animals, insects, human beings, church furnishings, buildings, and construction devices (**FIG. 17–17**). Although the majority of his drawings have nothing to do with architecture, his renderings of aspects of Gothic buildings have received the most attention since the book was rediscovered in the mid nineteenth century and have led to a widespread belief that he was an architect or master mason. There is no evidence for this. In fact, the evidence we have argues against it, since the architectural drawings appear to be the work of someone without a great deal of knowledge of the structural systems and design priorities of Gothic builders. This in no way diminishes the value of this amazing document, which allows us rare access into the mind of a curious, well-traveled thirteenth-century amateur who drew the things that caught his fancy in the extraordinary world around him.

Art in the Age of St. Louis

During the time of Louis IX (ruled 1226–1270; canonized as St. Louis in 1297), Paris became the artistic center of Europe. Artists from all over France were lured to the capital, responding to the growing local demand for new and remodeled buildings, as well as to the international demand for the extraordinary works of art that were the specialty of Parisian commercial workshops. Especially valued were richly illuminated manuscripts and small-scale objects in precious materials. The Parisian style of this period is often called the "Court Style," since its association with the court of St. Louis was one reason it spread beyond the capital to the courts of other European rulers. Parisian works became trans-European benchmarks of artistic quality and sophistication.

THE SAINTE-CHAPELLE IN PARIS The masterpiece of mid-thirteenth-century Parisian style is the Sainte-Chapelle (Holy Chapel) of the royal palace, commissioned by Louis IX to house his collection of relics of Christ's Passion, especially the Crown of Thorns. In many ways this huge chapel can be seen as the culmination of the Gothic style that emerged from Suger's pioneering choir at Saint-Denis. The interior walls have been reduced to a series of slender piers and mullions that act as skeletal support for a vast skin of stained glass (**FIG. 17-18**). The structure itself is stabilized by external buttressing that projects from the piers around the exterior of the building. Interlocking iron bars between the piers and concealed within the windows run around the entire building, adding further stabilization. The viewer inside is unaware of these systems of support, being focused instead on the kaleidoscopic nature of this jewelbox reliquary and the themes of sacred kingship that dominate the program of stained-glass windows.

The building project has a rich history. In 1237, Baldwin II, Latin ruler of Constantinople—a descendant of the crusaders who had snatched the Byzantine capital from Emperor Alexius III Angelus in 1204—was in Paris, offering to sell the relic of Christ's Crown of Thorns to his cousin, King Louis IX of France. The relic was at that time hocked in Venice, securing a loan to the

17-18 UPPER CHAPEL INTERIOR, THE SAINTE-CHAPELLE
Paris. 1239–1248.

Credit: © F1 ONLINE/SuperStock

cash-poor Baldwin, who had decided, rather than redeem-ing it, to sell it to the highest bidder. Louis purchased the relic in 1239, and on August 18, when the newly acquired treasure arrived at the edge of Paris, the humble king, barefoot, carried it through the streets of his capital to the royal palace. Soon after its arrival, plans were underway to construct a glorious new palace building to house it—the Sainte-Chapelle, completed for its ceremonial conse-cration on April 26, 1248. In the 1244 charter establishing services in the Sainte-Chapelle, Pope Innocent IV claimed that Christ had crowned Louis with his own crown, strong

confirmation for Louis's own sense of the sacred under-pinnings of his kingship.

The Sainte-Chapelle is an extraordinary manifestation of the Gothic style. The two-story building (**FIG. 17–19**)—there are both lower and upper liturgical spaces—is large for a chapel, and though it is now swallowed up by modern Paris, when it was built it was one of the tallest and most elaborately decorated buildings in the capital. The upper chapel is a completely open interior space surrounded by walls composed almost entirely of stained glass (SEE FIG. 17–18), presenting viewers with a glittering, multicolored expanse. Not only the king and his court experienced this chapel; members of the public came to venerate and celebrate the relic, as well as to receive the indulgences offered to pious visitors. The Sainte-Chapelle resembles a reliquary made of painted stone and glass instead of gold and gems, turned inside out so that we experience it from within. But this arresting visual impression is only part of the story.

The stained-glass windows present extensive narra-tive cycles related to the special function of this chapel. Since they are painted in a bold, energetic style, the stories are easily legible, in spite of their breadth and complexity. Around the sanctuary's **hemicycle** (apse or semicircular interior space) are standard themes relating to the cele-bration of the Mass. But along the straight side walls are broader, four-lancet windows whose narrative expanse is dominated by the exploits of the sacred kings and queens of the Hebrew Bible, heroes Louis claimed as his royal ancestors. Above the recessed niche where Louis sat at Mass was a window filled with biblical kings, whereas in the corresponding niche on the other side of the chapel, his mother, Queen Blanche of Castile, and his wife, Queen Marguerite of Provence, sat under windows devoted to the lives of Judith and Esther, alternatively appropriate role models for medieval queens. Everywhere we look we see kings being crowned, leading soldiers into holy warfare, or performing royal duties, all framed with heral-dic references to Louis and the French royal house. There is even a window that includes scenes from the life of Louis IX himself.

17–19 SCHEMATIC DRAWING OF THE SAINTE-CHAPELLE
Paris. 1239–1248.

Credit: © Dorling Kindersley

17–20 HOLOFERNES'S ARMY CROSSING THE EUPHRATES RIVER

Detail of the Judith Window, from the Sainte-Chapelle, Paris. c. 1245. Stained, painted, and leaded glass, diameter 23⅝″ (59.2 cm). Philadelphia Museum of Art.

Credit: © 2016. Photo The Philadelphia Museum of Art/Art Resource/Scala, Florence

the progressive climate of the mid-thirteenth-century Parisian art world.

ILLUMINATED MANUSCRIPTS Paris gained renown in the thirteenth century not only for its new architecture and sculpture but also for the production of books. Manuscript painters flocked to Paris from other regions to join workshops supervised by university officials who controlled the production and distribution of books. These works ranged from small Bibles used as textbooks by university students to extravagant devotional and theological works filled with exquisite miniatures for wealthy patrons.

After the French Revolution, the Sainte-Chapelle was transformed into an archive, and some stained glass was removed to allow more light into the building. Deleted panels made their way onto the art market, and in 1803 the wealthy Philadelphia merchant William Powell bought three medallions from the Judith Window during a European tour; his collection was the first in America to concentrate on medieval art. One medallion portrays the armies of Holofernes crossing the Euphrates River (**FIG. 17-20**). A compact crowd of equestrian warriors to the right conforms to a traditional system of representing crowds as a measured, overlapping mass of essentially identical figures, but the warrior at the rear of the battalion breaks the pattern, turning to acknowledge a knight behind him. The foreshortened rump of this soldier's horse projects out into our space, as if he were marching from our real world into the fictive world of the window—an avant-garde touch from a major artist working in

17–21 QUEEN BLANCHE OF CASTILE AND KING LOUIS IX

From a Moralized Bible made in Paris. 1226–1234. Ink, tempera, and gold leaf on vellum, each page 15 × 10½″ (38 × 26.6 cm). The Morgan Library and Museum, New York. MS. M. 240, fol. 8r.

Credit: © 2016. Photo Pierpont Morgan Library/Art Resource, NY/Scala, Florence

A particularly sumptuous Parisian book from the time of Louis IX is a three-volume Moralized Bible from c. 1230, in which selected scriptural passages are paired with allegorical or moralized interpretations, using pictures as well as words to convey the message. The dedication page (**FIG. 17-21**) shows the teenage King Louis IX and his mother, Queen Blanche of Castile. The royal pair—emphasized by their elaborate thrones and slightly oversized heads—appear against a solid gold background under a multicolored architectural framework. Below them, a clerical scholar (left) dictates to a scribe, who seems to be working on a page from this very manuscript, with a column of roundels already outlined for paintings.

The design of stacked medallions—forming the layout for most of this monumental manuscript (**FIG. 17-22**)—clearly derives from stained-glass lancets with their columns of superimposed images (SEE FIG. 17-10). In the book, however, the schema combines pictures with words. Each page has two vertical strips of painted scenes set against a mosaiclike field and filled out by half-quatrefoils in the interstices—the standard format of mid-thirteenth-century windows. Adjacent to each medallion is an excerpt of text, either a summary of a scriptural passage or a terse contemporary interpretation or allegory. Both painted miniatures and texts alternate between scriptural summaries and their moralizing explications, outlined in words and visualized with pictures. This adds up to a very learned and complicated compilation, perhaps devised by clerical scholars at the University of Paris, but certainly painted by some of the most important professional artists in the cosmopolitan French capital.

England

How does the new French Gothic style combine with distinctive local materials and traditions in England?

Plantagenet kings ruled England from the time of Henry II and Eleanor of Aquitaine until 1485. Many were great patrons of the arts. During this period, London grew into a large city, but most people continued to live in rural villages and bustling market towns. Textile production dominated manufacture and trade, and fine embroidery continued to be an English specialty. The French Gothic style influenced English architecture and manuscript illumination, but these influences were tempered by local materials, methods, traditions, and tastes.

Manuscript Illumination

The universities of Oxford and Cambridge dominated intellectual life, but monasteries continued to house active scriptoria, in contrast to France, where book production became centralized in the professional workshops of Paris. By the end of the thirteenth century, secular workshops became increasingly active in England, meeting demand for books from students as well as from royal and noble patrons.

17-22 MORALIZATIONS FROM THE APOCALYPSE

From a Moralized Bible made in Paris. 1226–1234. Ink, tempera, and gold leaf on vellum, each page 15 × 10½" (38 × 26.6 cm). The Morgan Library and Museum, New York. MS. M. 240, fol. 6r.

MATTHEW PARIS The monastic tradition of history writing that we saw in the Romanesque Worcester Chronicle (SEE FIG. 16–30) flourished into the Gothic period at the Benedictine monastery of St. Albans, where monk Matthew Paris (d. 1259) compiled a series of historical works. Paris wrote the texts of his chronicles, and he also added hundreds of marginal pictures that were integral to his history writing. The tinted drawings have a freshness that reveals the artist as someone working outside the rigid strictures of compositional conventions—or at least pushing against them. In one of his books, Paris included an almost full-page, framed image of the Virgin and Child in a tender embrace (**FIG. 17–23**). Under this picture, outside the sacred space of Mary and Jesus, Paris drew a picture of himself—identified not by likeness but by a label with his name, strung out in alternating red and blue capital letters behind him. He looks not at the holy couple, but at the words in front of him. These offer his commentary on the image, pointing to the affection shown in the playful Christ Child's movement toward his earthly mother, but emphasizing the authority he has as the divine incarnation of his father. Matthew Paris seems almost to hold his words in his hands, pushing them upward toward the object of his devotion.

THE WINDMILL PSALTER The dazzling artistry and delight in ambiguity and contradiction that had marked early medieval manuscripts in the British Isles (SEE FIG. 15–1) also survived into the Gothic period in the Windmill Psalter of c. 1270–1280 (see "Closer Look" opposite).

The letter *B*—the first letter of Psalm 1, which begins with the words *Beatus vir qui non abit in consilio impiorum* ("Happy are those who do not follow the advice of the wicked", NRSV)—fills an entire left-hand page and outlines a densely interlaced thicket of tendrils and figures. This is a Tree of Jesse, a genealogical diagram of Jesus's royal and spiritual ancestors in the Hebrew Bible based on a prophesy in Isaiah 11:1–3. An oversized, semi-reclining figure of Jesse, father of King David, appears sheathed in a red mantle with the blue trunk of a vinelike tree emerging from his side. Above him is his majestically enthroned royal son, who, as an ancestor of Mary (shown just above him), is also an ancestor of Jesus, who appears at the top of the sequence. In the circling foliage flanking this sacred royal family tree is a series of prophets representing Jesus's spiritual heritage.

E, the second letter of the psalm's first word, appears at the top of the right-hand page and is formed from large tendrils emerging from delicate background vegetation to support characters in the story of the Judgment of Solomon portrayed within it (I Kings 3:16–27). Two women (one above the other at the right) claiming the same baby appear before King Solomon (enthroned on the crossbar) to settle their dispute. The king orders a guard to slice the baby in half

17–23 Matthew Paris **SELF-PORTRAIT KNEELING BEFORE THE VIRGIN AND CHILD**

From the *Historia Anglorum*, made in St. Albans, England. 1250–1259. Ink and color on parchment, 14 × 9¾" (35.8 × 25 cm). The British Library, London.

Credit: © The British Library Board (Royal 14 C VII, fol.6r)

A Closer Look

PSALM 1 IN THE WINDMILL PSALTER

Although this page initially seems to have been trimmed at left, the flattened outside edge of the roundels marks the original end of the page. What might have started as an independent Jesse Tree may later have been expanded into the initial B, widening the pictorial composition farther than originally planned.

The four evangelists appear in the corner roundels as personified symbols writing at desks.

The windmill that has given this psalter its name seems to be a religious symbol based on the fourth verse of this psalm: "Not so the wicked, not so: but like the dust, which the wind driveth from the face of the earth."

Tucked within the surrounds of the letter B are scenes from God's creation of the world, culminating in the forming of Adam and Eve. Medieval viewers would meditate on how the new Adam (Christ) and Eve (Mary)—featured in the Jesse Tree—had redeemed humankind from the sin of the first man and woman. Similarly, Solomon's choice of the true mother would recall Christ's choice of the true Church. Medieval manuscripts are full of cross-references and multiple meanings, intended to stimulate extended reflection and meditation, not embody a single truth or tell a single story.

Participants in this scene of the Judgment of Solomon have been creatively distributed within the unusual narrative setting of the letter *E*. Solomon sits on the crossbar; the two mothers are stacked one above the other; and the knight balancing the baby has to hook his toe under the curling extension of the crossbar to maintain his balance.

17–24 THE OPENING OF PSALM 1

From the Windmill Psalter, made in England, probably London. Late 13th century. Ink, color, and gold on vellum, each page 12¾ × 8¾" (32.3 × 22.2 cm). The Morgan Library and Museum, New York. MS. M102, fols. 1v-2r.

Credit: © 2016. Photo Pierpont Morgan Library/Art Resource/Scala, Florence

with his sword and give each woman her share. This trick exposed the real mother, who hastened to give up her claim in order to save the baby's life. It has been suggested that the positioning of this story within the letter *E* may have made a subtle association between Solomon and the reigning King Edward I. The rest of the psalm's five opening words appear on a banner carried by an angel who swoops down at the bottom of the *E*.

Architecture

The Gothic style in architecture appeared early in England, introduced by Cistercian and Norman builders and by traveling master masons. But in England there was less emphasis on height than in France. English churches have long, broad naves and screenlike façades.

SALISBURY CATHEDRAL   The thirteenth-century cathedral in Salisbury is an excellent example of English Gothic. It has unusual origins. The first cathedral in this diocese had been built within the castle complex of the local lord. In 1217, Bishop Richard Poore petitioned the pope to relocate the church, claiming the wind on the hilltop howled so loudly that the clergy could not hear themselves sing the Mass. A more pressing concern was probably his desire to escape the lord's control. As soon as he moved, the bishop established a new town called Salisbury. Material from the old church was carted down the hill and used in the new cathedral, along with dark, fossil-filled Purbeck stone from quarries in southern England and limestone imported from Caen. Building began in 1220, and most of the cathedral was finished by 1258, an unusually short period for such an undertaking (**FIG. 17-25**).

The west façade, however, was not completed until 1265. The small flanking towers project beyond the side walls and buttresses, giving the façade an increased width; the slightly later cloister and chapter house provided for the cathedral's clergy. The huge crossing tower (the French preferred a slender spire) and its 400-foot spire are a fourteenth-century addition, as are the flying buttresses, which were added to stabilize the tower. The crossing tower became the focal point of the building.

17-25 SALISBURY CATHEDRAL

England. Church building 1220–1258; west façade finished 1265; spire c. 1320–1330; cloister and chapter house 1263–1284.

Credit: © Skyscan/Corbis

17-26 PLAN OF SALISBURY CATHEDRAL

17-27 INTERIOR LOOKING EAST, SALISBURY CATHEDRAL

In the eighteenth century, the English architect James Wyatt subjected the building to radical renovations, during which the remaining stained glass and figure sculpture were removed or rearranged. Similar campaigns to refurbish medieval churches were common at the time. The motives of the restorers were complex and their results were far from our own notions of historical authenticity.

Credit: © Robert Preston Photography/Alamy Stock Photo

Salisbury has a distinctive plan (FIG. 17-26) with wide projecting double transepts, a square east end with a single chapel, and a spacious sanctuary—more like a monastic church. The nave interior reflects the Norman building tradition of heavy walls and a tall nave arcade topped with a gallery and a clerestory with simple lancet windows (FIG. 17-27). The walls alone are substantial enough to support the four-part ribbed vault. The emphasis on the horizontal movement of the arcades, unbroken by continuous vertical colonnettes extending from the compound piers, directs worshipers' attention forward toward the altar behind the choir screen. The use of color in the stonework is reminiscent of the decorative effects in Romanesque interiors. The shafts supporting the four-part rib vaults are made of dark Purbeck stone that contrasts with the lighter limestone of the rest of the interior. The original painting and gilding of the stonework would have enhanced the effect.

MILITARY AND DOMESTIC ARCHITECTURE Cathedrals were not the only Gothic buildings. Western European knights who traveled east during the crusades were impressed by the architectural forms they saw in Muslim castles and Byzantine fortifications. When they returned home, they had their own versions of these fortifications built. Castle gateways became more complex, nearly independent fortifications, often guarded by twin towers rather than just one. New rounded towers eliminated the corners that had made earlier square towers vulnerable to battering rams, and crenellations (notches) were added to tower tops to provide stone shields for more effective defense. The outer, enclosing walls were likewise strengthened. The open, interior space was enlarged and filled with more comfortable living quarters for the lord and wooden buildings to house the garrison and the support staff. Barns and stables for animals, including the extremely valuable war horses, were also erected within the enclosure.

17–28 EXTERIOR OF THE GREAT HALL, STOKESAY CASTLE
England. Late 13th century.

Credit: Fotomicar/Fotolia

STOKESAY CASTLE Military structures were not the only secular buildings outfitted for defense. In uncertain times, the manor (a landed estate), which continued to be an important economic unit in the thirteenth century, also had to fortify its buildings. And country houses equipped with a tower and crenellated rooflines became a status symbol as well as a necessity. **STOKESAY CASTLE**, a remarkable fortified manor house, survives in England near the Welsh border. In 1291, a wool merchant, Lawrence of Ludlow, acquired the property of Stokesay and secured permission from King Edward I to fortify his dwelling— officially known as a "license to crenellate" (**FIG. 17–28**). Two towers—including a massive crenellated south tower—and a great hall still survive.

Life in the Middle Ages revolved around the hall. Windows on each side of Stokesay's hall open both toward the courtyard and out across a moat toward the countryside. By the thirteenth century, people began to expect some privacy as well as security; therefore at both ends of the hall are two-story additions that provided retiring rooms for the family and workrooms where women could spin and weave. Rooms at the north end could be reached from the hall, but the upper chamber at the south was accessible only by means of an exterior stairway. A tiny window— a peephole—let women and members of the household observe the often rowdy activities in the hall below. In layout, there was essentially no difference between this manor, far from the London court, and the mansions built by the nobility in the city. Palaces followed the same pattern of hall and retiring rooms; they were simply larger.

Germany and the Holy Roman Empire

How do the Gothic architecture and sculpture of Germany and the Holy Roman Empire compare with the foundational monuments in France?

The Holy Roman Empire, weakened by internal strife and a prolonged struggle with the papacy, ceased to be a significant power in the thirteenth century. England and France were becoming strong nation-states, and the empire's hold on southern Italy and Sicily ended at mid century with the death of Emperor Frederick II. Subsequent emperors—who were elected—had only nominal authority over a loose conglomeration of independent principalities, bishoprics, and free cities. As in England, the French Gothic style, avidly embraced in the western Germanic territories, shows regional adaptations and innovations.

Architecture

In the thirteenth century, the increasing importance of the sermon in church services led architects in Germany to develop the **hall church**, a type of open, light-filled interior space that had appeared in Europe in the early Middle Ages. Characterized by a nave and side aisles of equal height, these spacious and well-lit hall churches accommodated the large crowds drawn by charismatic preachers.

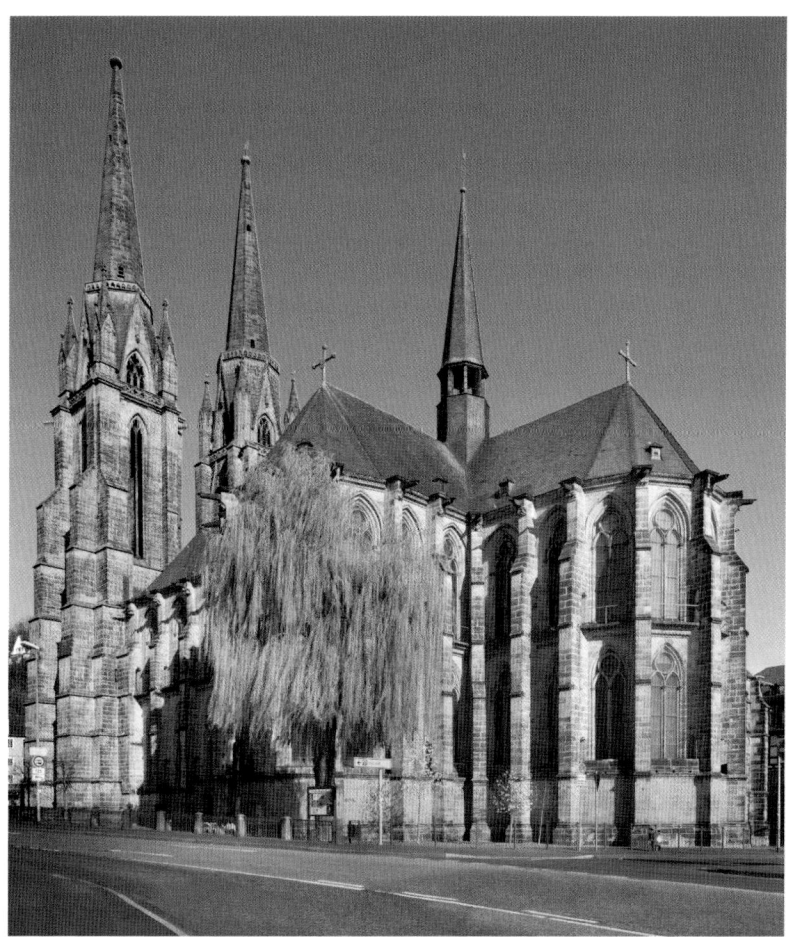

17–29 EXTERIOR, CHURCH OF ST. ELIZABETH OF HUNGARY

Marburg, Germany. 1235–1283.

Credit: © Achim Bednorz, Cologne

which is not the case. Inside, the closely spaced piers of the nave support the ribbed vault and, as with the buttresses, give the building a vertical, linear quality (**FIG. 17–30**). Light from the two stories of windows fills the interior, unimpeded by walls or galleries. The hall-church design was adopted widely for civic and residential buildings in Germanic lands and also for Jewish architecture.

THE OLD-NEW SYNAGOGUE Built in the third quarter of the thirteenth century using the hall-church design, Prague's **OLD-NEW SYNAGOGUE** (Altneuschul) is the oldest functioning synagogue in Europe and one of two principal synagogues serving the Jews of Prague (**FIG. 17–31**). Like a hall church, the vaults of the synagogue are all the same height. Unlike a basilican church, however, with its division into nave and side aisles, the Old-New Synagogue has only two aisles, each with three bays supported by the walls and

CHURCH OF ST. ELIZABETH OF HUNGARY IN MARBURG Perhaps the first true Gothic hall church, and one of the earliest Gothic buildings in Germany, was the **CHURCH OF ST. ELIZABETH OF HUNGARY** in Marburg (**FIG. 17–29**). The Hungarian princess Elizabeth (1207–1231) had been sent to Germany at age 4 to marry the ruler of Thuringia. He soon died of the plague, and she devoted herself to caring for people with incurable diseases. It was said that she died at age 24 from exhaustion, and she was canonized in 1235. Between 1235 and 1283, the knights of the Teutonic Order (who had moved to Germany from Jerusalem) built a church to serve as her mausoleum and pilgrimage center.

The plan of the church is an early German form with choir and transepts of equal size, each ending in apses. The elevation of the building, however, is new, with nave and aisles of equal height. On the exterior, tall buttresses emphasize its verticality, and the two rows of windows suggest a two-story building,

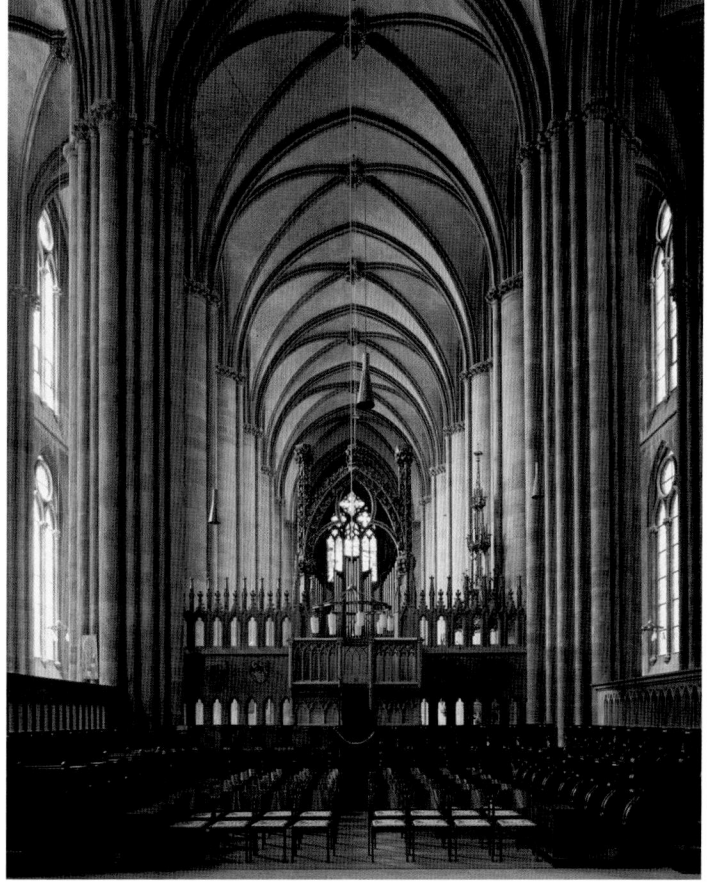

17–30 INTERIOR, CHURCH OF ST. ELIZABETH OF HUNGARY

Marburg, Germany. 1235–1283.

Credit: © Achim Bednorz, Cologne

17–31 INTERIOR, OLD-NEW SYNAGOGUE (ALTNEUSCHUL)

Prague, Bohemia (Czech Republic). c. late 13th century; *bimah* after 1483.

two octagonal piers. Each bay has Gothic four-part ribbed vaulting to which a nonfunctional fifth rib has been added. Some say that this fifth rib was added to undermine the cross form made by the intersecting diagonal ribs.

Medieval synagogues were both places of prayer and communal centers of learning and inspiration where men gathered to read and discuss the Torah. The synagogue had two focal points: a shrine for the Torah scrolls (the *aron*) and a raised platform for reading from them (the *bimah*). The congregation faced the Torah shrine, which was located on the east wall, in the direction of Jerusalem, while the reading platform stood in the center of the hall straddling the two center bays. In Prague it was surrounded by an ironwork open screen. The single entrance was placed off-center in a corner bay at the west end. Men worshiped and studied in the main space; women had to worship in annexes on the north and west sides.

Sculpture

Since the eleventh century, among the most creative centers of European sculpture were the Rhine River Valley and the region known as the Mosan (named after the Meuse River, in present-day Belgium), with centers in Liège and Verdun. Ancient Romans had built camps and cities in this area, and Classical influence lingered through the Middle Ages, when Nicholas of Verdun and his fellow goldsmiths initiated a new classicizing style in the arts.

SHRINE OF THE THREE KINGS For the archbishop of Cologne, Nicholas created the magnificent **SHRINE OF THE THREE KINGS** (c. 1190–c. 1205/1210), a reliquary for what were believed to be relics of the three Magi (**FIG. 17-32**). Shaped in the form of a basilican church, it is made of gilded bronze and silver set with gemstones and dark blue enamel plaques that accentuate its architectural details. Like his fellow Mosan artists, Nicholas was inspired by ancient Roman art still found in the region, as well as by classicizing Byzantine works. The figures are lifelike, fully modeled, and swathed in voluminous but revealing drapery. The three Magi and the Virgin fill the front gable end, and prophets and apostles sit in the niches in the two levels of arcading on the sides. The work combines robust, expressively mobile sculptural forms with a jeweler's exquisitely ornamental detailing to create an opulent, monumental setting for its precious contents.

17-32 Nicholas of Verdun and workshop **SHRINE OF THE THREE KINGS**

Cologne Cathedral, Germany. c. 1190–c. 1205/1210. Silver and gilded bronze with enamel and gemstones, 5′8″ × 6′ × 3′8″ (1.73 × 1.83 × 1.12 m).

Credit: © akg-images/Erich Lessing

17–33 ST. MAURICE
Magdeburg Cathedral, Germany. c. 1240–1250. Dark sandstone with traces of polychromy.

Credit: © akg-images/Hilbich

17–34 EKKEHARD AND UTA
West chapel, Naumburg Cathedral, Germany. c. 1245–1260. Stone with polychromy, height approx. 6'2" (1.88 m).

Credit: © akg-images/Erich Lessing

ST. MAURICE   A powerful current of realism runs through German Gothic sculpture. Some works seem to be carved after a living model. Among them is an arresting mid-thirteenth-century statue of **ST. MAURICE** in Magdeburg Cathedral (**FIG. 17-33**), the location of his relics since 968. The Egyptian Maurice, a commander in the Roman army, was martyred in 286 together with his Christian battalion while they were stationed in Germany. As patron saint of Magdeburg, he was revered by Ottonian emperors, who were anointed in St. Peter's in Rome at the altar of St. Maurice. He remained a favorite saint of military aristocrats. This is the first surviving representation of Maurice as a black African, an acknowledgment of his Egyptian origins and an aspect of the growing German interest in realism, which extends here to the detailed rendering of his costume of chain mail and riveted leather.

EKKEHARD AND UTA   Equally portraitlike is the depiction of this couple, commissioned about 1245 by Dietrich II, bishop of Wettin, for the family funeral chapel, built at the west end of Naumburg Cathedral. Bishop Dietrich ordered life-size statues of 12 of his ancestors, who had been patrons of the church, to be placed on pedestals mounted at window level around the chapel.

In the representations of Margrave Ekkehard of Meissen (a margrave—count of the march or border—was a territorial governor who defended the frontier) and his Polish-born wife, Uta (**FIG. 17-34**), the sculptor created highly individualized figures and faces. Since these are eleventh-century people sculpted in the thirteenth century, we are not looking at their portrait likenesses, but it is still possible that live models were used to heighten the sense of a living presence in their portraits. But more than their faces contribute to this liveliness. The margrave nervously fingers the strap of the shield that is looped over his arm, and the coolly elegant Uta pulls her cloak around her neck as if to protect herself from the cold, while the extraordinary spread of her left hand is necessary to control the cloak's voluminous, thick cloth. The survival of original **polychromy** (multicolored painting on the surface of sculpture or architecture) indicates that color added to the impact of the figures. The impetus toward descriptive realism and psychological presence, initiated in the thirteenth century, will expand in the art of northern Europe into the fifteenth century and beyond.

Italy

What are the important developments in Italian sculpture and painting during the late Middle Ages?

The thirteenth century was a period of political division and economic expansion for the Italian peninsula. Part of southern Italy and Sicily was controlled by Frederick II von Hohenstaufen (1194–1250), Holy Roman Emperor from 1220. Frederick was a politically unsettling force. He fought with a league of north Italian cities and briefly controlled the Papal States. On his death, however, Germany and the Holy Roman Empire ceased to be an important factor in Italian politics and culture.

In northern Italy, in particular, organizations of successful merchants created communal governments in their prosperous and independent city-states and struggled against powerful families for political control. Artists began to emerge as independent agents, working directly with wealthy clients and with civic and religious institutions.

It was during this time that new religious orders known as the mendicants (begging monks) arose to meet the needs of the growing urban population. They espoused an ideal of poverty, charity, and love, and they dedicated themselves to teaching and preaching while living among the urban poor. Most notable in the beginning were the Franciscans, founded by St. Francis of Assisi (1182–1226; canonized in 1228). This son of a wealthy merchant gave away his possessions and devoted his life to God and the poor. As others began to join him, he wrote a simple rule for his followers, who were called brothers, or friars (from the Latin *frater*, meaning "brother"), and the pope approved the new order in 1209–1210.

Sculpture of the Pisano Family

During the first half of the thirteenth century, the culturally enlightened Frederick II fostered a Classical revival at his southern Italian court. In the Romanesque period, artists in southern Italy had already turned to ancient sculpture for inspiration, and Frederick, mindful of his imperial status as Holy Roman Emperor, encouraged this tendency to help communicate a message of power. He also encouraged artists to emulate the world around them. Nicola Pisano (active in Tuscany c. 1258–1278), who moved from the southern region of Apulia to Tuscany at mid century, became the leading exponent of this classicizing and naturalistic style.

NICOLA PISANO'S PULPIT AT PISA In an inscription on a free-standing marble **PULPIT** in the Pisa Baptistery (**FIG. 17-35**), Nicola identifies himself as a supremely self-confident sculptor: "In the year 1260 Nicola Pisano carved this noble work. May so gifted a hand be praised as it deserves." Columns topped with leafy Corinthian capitals

17-35 Nicola Pisano **PULPIT**
Baptistery, Pisa, Italy. 1260. Marble, height approx. 15′ (4.6 m).
Credit: © Studio Fotografico Quattrone, Florence

17–36 Nicola Pisano
ANNUNCIATION, NATIVITY, AND ADORATION OF THE SHEPHERDS

Detail of pulpit, Baptistery, Pisa, Italy. 1260. Marble, 33½ × 44½″ (85 × 113 cm).

Credit: © Studio Fotografico Quattrone, Florence

support standing figures and Gothic trefoil arches, which in turn provide a platform for the six-sided pulpit. The columns rest on high bases carved with crouching figures, domestic animals, and shaggy-maned lions. Panels forming the pulpit enclosure illustrate New Testament subjects, each framed as an independent composition.

Each panel illustrates several scenes in a continuous narrative; **FIGURE 17-36** depicts the **ANNUNCIATION, NATIVITY, AND ADORATION OF THE SHEPHERDS**.

The Virgin reclines in the middle of the composition after having given birth to Jesus, who below receives his first bath from midwives. The upper left corner holds the Annunciation—the moment of Christ's conception, as announced by the archangel Gabriel. The scene in the upper right combines the Annunciation to the Shepherds with their Adoration of the Child. The viewer's attention moves from group to group within the shallow space, always returning to the regally detached Mother of God.

17–37 Giovanni Pisano **ANNUNCIATION, NATIVITY, AND ADORATION OF THE SHEPHERDS**

Detail of pulpit, Sant'Andrea, Pistoia, Italy. 1298–1301. Marble, 33 × 40⅛″ (83 × 102 cm).

Credit: © 2016. Photo Scala, Florence - courtesy Diocesi di Pistoia, Ufficio Beni Culturali

The format, style, and technique of Roman sarcophagus reliefs—readily accessible in the burial ground near the baptistery—may have provided Nicola's models for this carving. The sculptural treatment of the deeply cut, full-bodied forms is certainly Classical in inspiration, as are the heavy, placid faces.

GIOVANNI PISANO'S PULPIT AT PISTOIA   Nicola's son Giovanni (active c. 1265–1314) assisted his father while learning from him, and he may also have worked or studied in France. By the end of the thirteenth century, he had emerged as a versatile artist in his own right. Between 1298 and 1301, he and his workshop carved a pulpit for Sant'Andrea in Pistoia that is similar to his father's in conception but significantly different in style and execution. In his more dramatic rendering of the **ANNUNCIATION, NATIVITY, AND ADORATION OF THE SHEPHERDS**, Giovanni places graceful but energetic figures in an uptilted, deeply carved setting (**FIG. 17-37**). He replaces Nicola's imperious, stately Roman matron with a lithe, younger Mary, who recoils from Gabriel's advance at left, and at center, exhausted from giving birth, pulls at her bed-sheets for support while reaching toward her newborn baby. Sheep, shepherds, and angels spiral up through the trees at the right. Giovanni's sculpture is as dynamic as Nicola's is static.

Painting

The capture of Constantinople by crusaders in 1204 brought an influx of Byzantine art and artists to Italy. The imported style of painting, the *maniera greca* ("the Greek manner"), influenced thirteenth- and fourteenth-century Italian painting in style and technique and introduced a new emphasis on pathos and emotion.

PAINTED CRUCIFIXES   One example, a large wooden **CRUCIFIX** attributed to the thirteenth-century Florentine painter Coppo di Marcovaldo (**FIG. 17-38**), represents an image of a suffering Christ on the cross, a Byzantine type with closed eyes and bleeding, sagging body that encourages viewers to respond emotionally and empathetically to the image (SEE FIGS. 8-22, 15-26). This is a "historiated crucifix," meaning that narrative scenes flank Christ's body, in this case episodes from the story of his Passion. Such monumental crosses—this one is almost 10 feet high—were mounted on the choir screens that separated the clergy in the sanctuary from the laypeople in the nave, especially in the churches of the Italian mendicants. One such cross can be seen from behind with its wooden bracing in FIGURE 17-40, tilted out to lean toward the worshiper's line of vision and increase the emotional impact.

17–38 Coppo di Marcovaldo **CRUCIFIX**
From the Franciscan convent of Santa Chiara, San Gimignano, Italy. c. 1250–1270.
Tempera and gold on wood panel, 9'7⅜" × 8'1¼" (2.93 × 2.47 m). Pinacoteca, San Gimignano, Italy.

THE CHURCH OF ST. FRANCIS AT ASSISI Two years after St. Francis's death in 1226, the church in his birthplace, Assisi, was begun. It was nearly finished in 1239 but was not dedicated until 1253. This building was unusually elaborate in its design, with upper and lower churches on two stories and a crypt at the choir end underneath both (**FIG. 17–39**). Both upper and lower churches have a single nave of four square vaulted bays, and both end in a transept and a single apse. The lower church has massive walls and a narrow nave flanked by side chapels. The upper church is a spacious, well-lit hall with excellent visibility and acoustics, designed to accommodate the crowds of pilgrims who came to see and hear the friars preach as well as to participate in church rituals and venerate the tomb of the saint. The church walls presented expanses of uninterrupted wall surface where sacred stories could unfold in murals. In the wall paintings of the upper church, the focus was on the story of Francis himself, presented as a model Christian life to which pilgrims, as well as resident friars, might aspire.

Scholars differ over whether the murals of the upper church were painted as early as 1290, but they agree on their striking narrative effectiveness. Like most Franciscan paintings, these scenes were designed to engage with viewers by appealing to their memories of their own life experiences, evoked by the inclusion of recognizable anecdotal details and emotionally expressive figures.

A good example is **THE MIRACLE OF THE CRIB AT GRECCIO** (**FIG. 17–40**), portraying St. Francis making the first Christmas manger scene in the church at Greccio.

The scene—like all Gothic visual narratives, set in the present, even though the event portrayed took place in the past—unfolds within a Gothic church that would have looked very familiar to late thirteenth-century viewers. A large wooden crucifix similar to the one by Coppo di Marcovaldo (SEE FIG. 17–38) has been suspended from a stand on top of a screen separating the sanctuary from the nave. The cross has been reinforced on the back and tilted forward to hover over people in the nave, whom we see crowding behind an open door in the choir screen. A pulpit, with stairs leading up to its entrance and candlesticks at its corners, rises above the screen at the left. An elaborate carved *baldacchino* (canopy) shelters the altar at the right, and an adjustable wooden lectern stands in front of the altar. Other small but telling touches include a seasonal liturgical calendar posted on the lectern, foliage swags decorating the *baldacchino*, and an embroidered altar cloth. Sound as well as sight is referenced in the figures of the friars who throw their heads back, mouths wide open, to provide the liturgical soundtrack to this cinematic tableau.

The focus on the sacred narrative is confined to a small area at lower right, where St. Francis reverently holds the Holy Infant above a plain, boxlike crib next to miniature representations of various animals that might have been

17–39 SCHEMATIC DRAWING OF THE CHURCH OF ST. FRANCIS, ASSISI
Umbria, Italy. 1228–1253.

Credit: Maltings Partnership © Dorling Kindersley

present at the Nativity, capturing the miraculous moment when the Christ Child appeared in the manger. But even if the story is about a miracle, it takes place in a setting full of worldly references that allowed contemporary viewers to imagine themselves as part of the scene, either as worshipers kneeling in front of the altar or as spectators pushing toward the doorway to get a better view. This narrative goal of engaging with viewers through references to their own lives, initiated during the Middle Ages, will continue into the Renaissance.

17-40 THE MIRACLE OF THE CRIB AT GRECCIO

From a cycle of the Life of St. Francis, church of St. Francis, Assisi. Late 13th or early 14th century. Fresco.

Credit: © 2016. Photo Scala, Florence

Think About It

1   Characterize the most important of the technological innovations and sociocultural formations that made the "Age of Cathedrals" possible.

2   Explain how manuscript illumination was used to convey complex theological ideas during the Gothic period. Analyze the iconography of one manuscript discussed in this chapter.

3   How was St. Francis's message of empathy conveyed in the frescos of the church of St. Francis in Assisi?

4   Analyze Salisbury Cathedral in England and the German church of St. Elizabeth of Hungary in Marburg. How does each reflect characteristics of French Gothic style, and how does each depart from that style and express architectural features characteristic of its own region?

Crosscurrents

These two works of art, one Romanesque and one Gothic, portray events from the same Bible story in a public context where they would have been seen by a diverse cross section of viewers. Compare the style of presentation. What features do these visual narratives have in common? How are they different? Is there a relationship between style, meaning, and medium?

FIG. 16–20

FIG. 17–1

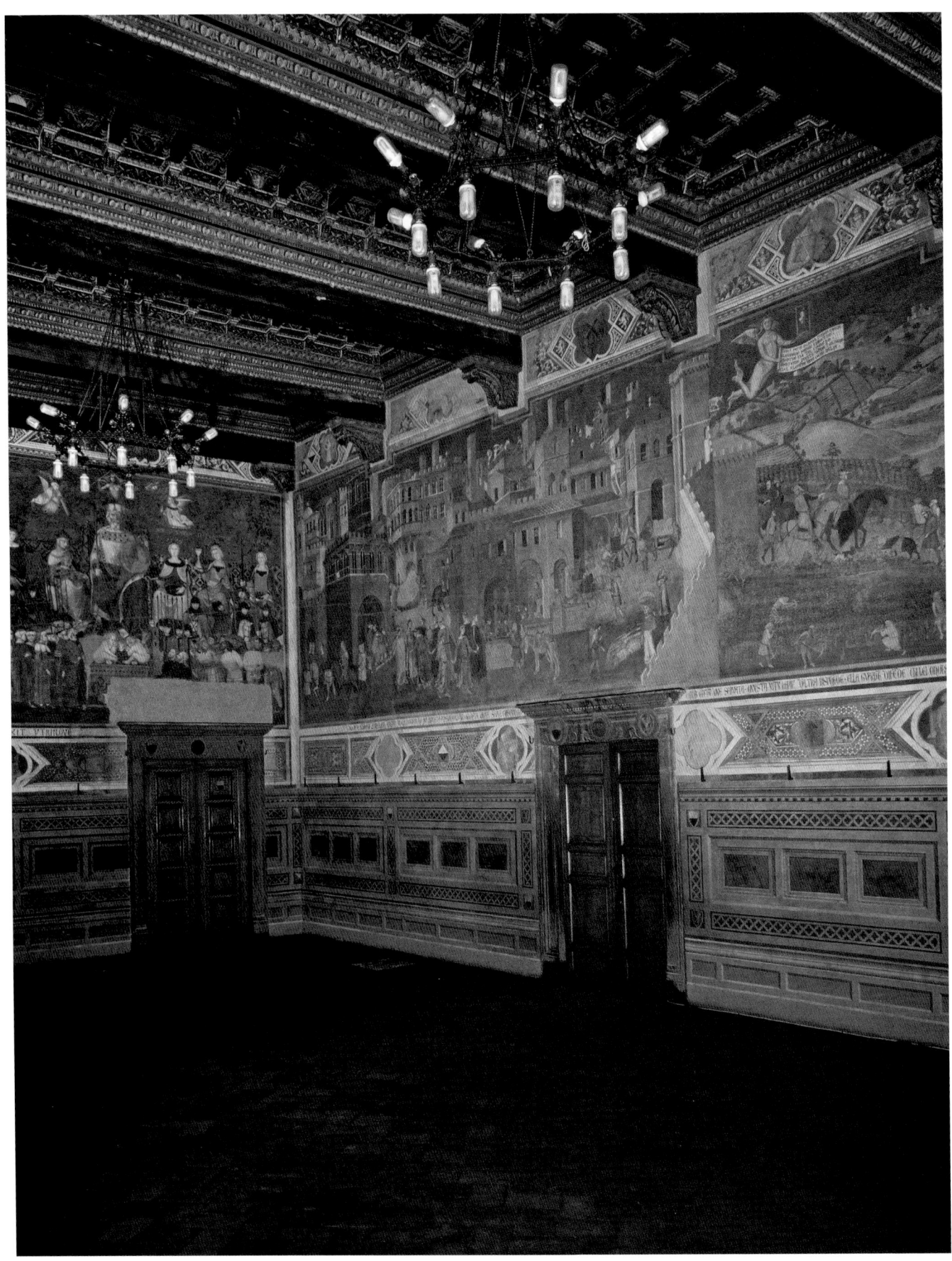

18–1 Ambrogio Lorenzetti **FRESCOS OF THE SALA DEI NOVE (OR SALA DELLA PACE)**

Palazzo Pubblico, Siena, Italy. 1338–1339. Length of long wall approx. 46′ (14 m).

Credit: © Studio Fotografico Quattrone, Florence

Chapter 18
Fourteenth-Century Art in Europe

 ## Learning Objectives

18.a Identify the visual hallmarks of fourteenth-century European art for formal, technical, and expressive qualities.

18.b Interpret the meaning of works of fourteenth-century European art based on its themes, subjects, and symbols.

18.c Relate fourteenth-century European art and artists to their cultural, economic, and political contexts.

18.d Apply the vocabulary and concepts relevant to fourteenth-century European art, artists, and art history.

18.e Interpret a work of fourteenth-century European art using the art historical methods of observation, comparison, and inductive reasoning.

18.f Select visual and textual evidence in various media to support an argument or an interpretation of a work of fourteenth-century European art.

In 1338, the Nine—a council of merchants and bankers that governed Siena as an oligarchy—commissioned frescos from the renowned Sienese painter Ambrogio Lorenzetti (c. 1295–c. 1348) for three walls in the chamber of the Palazzo Pubblico where they met to conduct city business. This commission came at the moment of Siena's greatest prosperity and security since the establishment of their government in 1287.

Lorenzetti's frescos combine allegory with panoramic landscapes and cityscapes to visualize and justify the beneficial effects of the Sienese form of government. The moral foundation of the rule of the Nine is outlined in a complicated allegory in which seated personifications (far left in **FIG. 18–1**) of Concord, Justice, Peace, Strength, Prudence, Temperance, and Magnanimity, not only diagram good governance but actually reference the Last Judgment in a bold assertion of the relationship between secular rule and divine authority. This tableau contrasts with a similar presentation of bad government, where Tyranny is flanked by the personified forces that keep tyrants in power—Cruelty, Treason, Fraud, Fury, Division, and War. A group of scholars would have devised this complex program of symbols and meanings; it is unlikely that Lorenzetti would have known the philosophical works that underlie them. Lorenzetti's fame, however, and the wall paintings' secure

position among the most remarkable surviving mural programs of the period, rests on the other part of this ensemble—the effects of good and bad government in city and country life (SEE FIG. 18–16).

Unlike the tableau showing the perils of life under tyrannical rule, the panoramic view of life under good government—which in this work of propaganda means life under the rule of the Nine—is well preserved. A vista of fourteenth-century Siena—identifiable by the cathedral dome and tower peeking over the rooftops in the background—showcases carefree life within shops, schools, taverns, and worksites, as the city streets bustle with human activity. Outside, an expansive landscape highlights agricultural productivity.

Unfortunately, within a decade of the frescos' completion, life in Siena was no longer so stable and carefree. The devastating bubonic plague came in 1348—Ambrogio Lorenzetti himself was probably one of the victims—and the rule of the Nine collapsed in 1355. But this glorious vision of joyful prosperity preserves the dreams and aspirations of a stable government using some of the most progressive and creative ideas in fourteenth-century Italian art, ideas we will see developed at the very beginning of the century, and whose history we will trace over the next two centuries through the Renaissance.

Fourteenth-Century Europe

What are the cultural and historical backgrounds for the transformation of European art during the fourteenth century?

Literary luminaries Dante, Petrarch, Boccaccio, Chaucer, and Christine de Pizan (see "A New Spirit in Fourteenth-Century Literature" below) and the visionary painters Giotto, Duccio, Jean Pucelle, and Master Theodoric participated in a cultural explosion that swept through fourteenth-century Europe, and especially Italy. The poet Petrarch (1304–1374) was a towering figure in this change, writing his love lyrics in Italian, the language of everyday life, rather than Latin, the language of ceremony and high art. Similarly, the deeply moving murals of Florentine painter Giotto di Bondone (c. 1277–1337) were rooted in his observation of the people around him, giving the characters in sacred narratives both great dignity and a striking new humanity. Even in Paris—still the artistic center of Europe as far as refined taste and technical sophistication were concerned—the painter Jean Pucelle began to show an interest in experimenting with established conventions.

Changes in the way that society was organized were also underway, and an expanding class of wealthy merchants supported the arts as patrons. Artisan guilds—organized by occupation—exerted quality control among members and supervised education through an apprenticeship system. Admission to a guild came after examination and the creation of a "masterpiece"—literally, a piece fine enough to achieve master status. The major guilds included cloth finishers, wool merchants, and silk manufacturers, as well as pharmacists and doctors. Painters belonged to the pharmacy guild, perhaps because they used mortars and pestles to grind their colors. Their patron saint, Luke, who was believed to have painted the first image of the Virgin Mary, was also a physician—or so they thought. Sculptors who worked in wood and stone had their own guild, while those who worked in metals belonged to another. Guilds provided social services for their members, including care of the sick and funerals for the deceased. Each guild had its patron saint, maintained a chapel, and participated in religious and civic festivals.

Despite the cultural flourishing and economic growth of the early decades, by the middle of the fourteenth century much of Europe was in crisis. Prosperity had fostered population growth, which began to exceed food production. A series of bad harvests compounded this problem with famine. To make matters worse, a prolonged conflict known as the Hundred Years' War (1337–1453) erupted between France and England. Then, in mid century, a lethal plague known as the Black Death swept across Europe (MAP 18–1), wiping out as much as 40 percent of the population. In spite of these catastrophic events, however, the strong current of cultural change still managed to persist through to the end of the century and beyond.

Art and its Contexts

A NEW SPIRIT IN FOURTEENTH-CENTURY LITERATURE

For Petrarch and his contemporaries, the essential qualifications for a writer were an appreciation of Greek and Roman authors and an ability to observe the people living around themselves. Although fluent in Latin, each chose to write in the language of their own time and place—whether Italian, English, or French. Leading the way was Dante Alighieri (1265–1321), who wrote *The Divine Comedy*, his great summation of human virtue and vice, in Italian, establishing his daily language as worthy to express great literary themes.

Francesco Petrarca, called simply Petrarch (1304–1374), raised the status of secular literature with his sonnets to his unattainable beloved, Laura, his histories and biographies, and his writings on the joys of country life in the Roman manner. Petrarch's imaginative updating of Classical themes in a work called *The Triumphs*—which examines the themes of Chastity triumphant over Love, Death over Chastity, Fame over Death, Time over Fame, and Eternity over Time—provided later Renaissance poets and painters with a wealth of allegorical subject matter.

The earthier Giovanni Boccaccio (1313–1375) perfected the art of the short story in *The Decameron*, a collection of amusing and moralizing tales told by a group of young Florentines who move to the countryside to escape the Black Death. With wit and sympathy, Boccaccio presents the full spectrum of daily life in Italy. Such secular literature, written in Italian as it was then spoken in Tuscany, provided a foundation for fifteenth-century Renaissance writers.

In England, Geoffrey Chaucer (c. 1342–1400) was inspired by Boccaccio to write his own series of stories, *The Canterbury Tales*, as if told by pilgrims traveling to the shrine of St. Thomas à Becket (1118?–1170) in Canterbury. Observant and witty, Chaucer depicted the pretensions and foibles, as well as the virtues, of humanity.

Christine de Pizan (1364–c. 1431), born in Venice but living and writing at the French court, became an author out of necessity when she was left a widow with three young children and an aged mother to support. Among her many works are a poem in praise of Joan of Arc and a history of famous women—including artists—from antiquity to her own time. In *The Book of the City of Ladies*, she defended women's abilities and argued for women's rights and status.

These writers, as surely as the visual artists Giotto, Duccio, Peter Parler, and Master Theodoric, led the way into a new era.

MAP 18–1 EUROPE IN THE FOURTEENTH CENTURY

Following its outbreak in the Mediterranean in 1347, the Black Death swept across the European mainland over the next four years.

Italy

How do political, religious, and cultural changes transform the artistic traditions of Florence and Siena during the first half of the fourteenth century?

As great wealth promoted patronage of art in fourteenth-century Italy, artists began to emerge as individuals in the modern sense, both in their own eyes and in the eyes of patrons. Although their methods and working conditions remained largely unchanged from the Middle Ages, artists in Italy contracted freely with wealthy townspeople and nobles as well as with civic and religious bodies. Perhaps it was their economic and social freedom that encouraged their self-confidence, individuality, and innovation.

Florentine Architecture and Metalwork

The typical medieval Italian city was a walled citadel on a hilltop. Houses clustered around a church and an open city square. Powerful families added towers to their houses, both for defense and as expressions of family pride. In Florence, by contrast, the ancient Roman city—with its axial rectangular plan and open city squares—formed the basis for the civic layout. The cathedral stood northeast of the ancient forum, and a street following the Roman plan connected it with the Piazza della Signoria, the seat of the government.

THE PALAZZO DELLA SIGNORIA

The Signoria (ruling body, from *signore*, meaning "Lord") that governed Florence met in the **PALAZZO DELLA SIGNORIA**, a massive, fortified building with a bell tower 300 feet tall (**FIG. 18-2**). The building faces a large square, or piazza, which became the true center of Florence. The town houses around the piazza often had benches along their walls to provide convenient public seating. Between 1376 and 1382, master builders Benci di Cione and Simone Talenti constructed a huge **loggia**, or covered open-air corridor, at one side—now known as the Loggia dei Lanzi (Loggia of the Lancers)—to provide a sheltered place for ceremonies and speeches.

THE BAPTISTERY DOORS

In 1330, Andrea Pisano (c. 1290–1348) was awarded the prestigious commission for a pair of gilded bronze doors for Florence's Baptistery of San Giovanni, situated directly in front of the cathedral. (Andrea's last name means "from Pisa," and he was not related to Nicola and Giovanni Pisano.) The doors were completed within six years and display 20 scenes from the **LIFE OF ST. JOHN THE BAPTIST** (the San Giovanni to whom the baptistery is dedicated), set above eight personifications of the Virtues (**FIG. 18-3**). The overall effect is two-dimensional and decorative: a grid of 28 rectangles with repeated quatrefoils filled with the graceful, patterned poses of delicate human figures. Within the quatrefoil frames, however, the figural compositions create the illusion of three-dimensional forms moving within natural and architectural spaces.

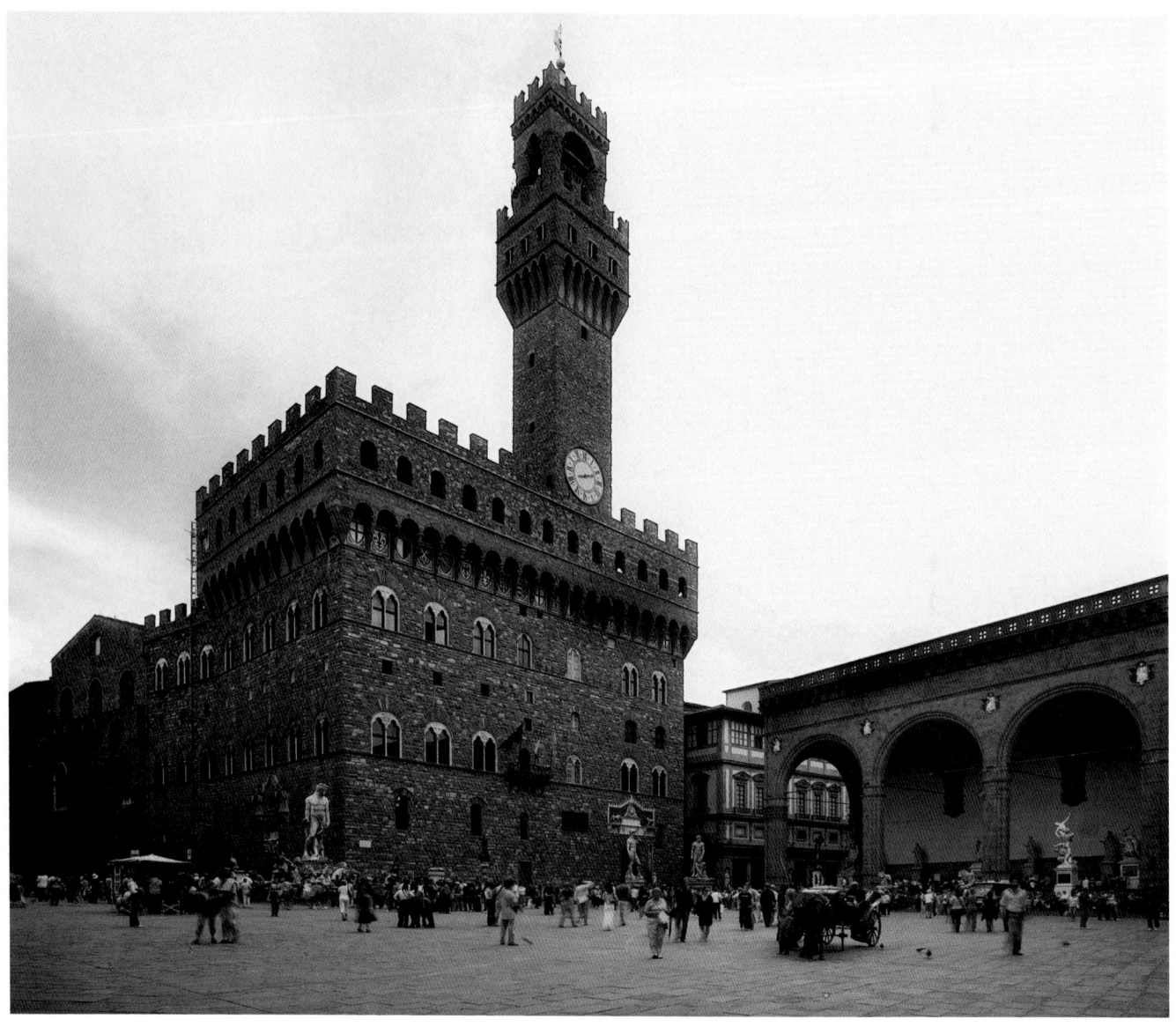

18-2 PIAZZA DELLA SIGNORIA WITH PALAZZO DELLA SIGNORIA (TOWN HALL) AND LOGGIA DEI LANZI (LOGGIA OF THE LANCERS)

Florence. Palazzo della Signoria, 1299–1310; Loggia dei Lanzi, 1376–1382.

Credit: © Achim Bednorz, Cologne

18-3 Andrea Pisano **LIFE OF ST. JOHN THE BAPTIST**
South doors, Baptistery of San Giovanni, Florence. 1330–1336. Gilded bronze, each panel 19¼ × 17″ (48 × 43 cm). Frame, Ghiberti workshop, mid 15th century.

The bronze vine scrolls filled with flowers, fruits, and birds on the lintel and jambs framing the door were added in the mid fifteenth century.

18-4 Andrea Pisano **THE BAPTISM OF THE MULTITUDE**
Detail of the south doors, Baptistery of San Giovanni, Florence. 1330–1336. Gilded bronze, 19¼ × 17″ (48 × 43 cm).

Credit: Photo: David G. Wilkins

The scene of John baptizing a multitude (**FIG. 18-4**) takes place on a shelflike stage created by a forward extension of the rocky natural setting, which also expands back behind the figures into a corner of the quatrefoil frame. Composed as a rectangular group, the gilded figures present an independent mass of modeled forms. The illusion of three-dimensionality is enhanced by the way the curving folds of their clothing wrap around their bodies. At the same time, their graceful gestures and the elegant fall of their drapery reflect the soft curves and courtly postures of French Gothic art.

Florentine Painting

Florence and Siena, rivals in so many ways, each supported a flourishing school of painting in the fourteenth century. Both grew out of local thirteenth-century painting traditions and engendered individual artists who became famous in their own time. The Byzantine influence—the *maniera greca* ("Greek style")—continued to provide models of dramatic

pathos and narrative iconography, as well as stylized features including the use of gold for drapery folds and striking contrasts of highlights and shadows in the modeling of individual forms. By the end of the fourteenth century, the painter and commentator Cennino Cennini (see "Cennino Cennini on Panel Painting" on page 556) would be struck by the accessibility and modernity of Giotto's art, which, though it retained traces of the *maniera greca*, was moving toward the depiction of a lifelike, contemporary world anchored in solid, three-dimensional forms.

CIMABUE In Florence, this stylistic transformation began a little earlier than in Siena. About 1280, a painter named Cenni di Pepi (active c. 1272–1302), better known by his nickname "Cimabue," painted a panel portraying the **VIRGIN AND CHILD ENTHRONED** (**FIG. 18-5**), perhaps for the main altar of the church of Santa Trinità in Florence. At over 12 feet tall, this enormous egg-tempera panel painting set a new precedent for monumental altarpieces. Cimabue surrounds the Virgin and Child with angels and places a row of Hebrew Bible prophets beneath them. The hierarchically scaled figure of Mary holds the infant Jesus in her lap. Looking out at the viewer while gesturing toward her son as the path to salvation, she adopts a formula popular in Byzantine iconography since at least the sixth century (SEE FIG. 8–14).

Mary's huge throne, painted to resemble gilded bronze with inset enamels and gems, provides an architectural framework for the figures. Cimabue creates highlights on the drapery of Mary, Jesus, and the angels with thin lines of gold, as if to capture their divine radiance. The viewer seems suspended in space in front of the image, simultaneously looking down on the projecting elements of the throne and Mary's lap and looking straight ahead at the prophets at the base of the throne and the angels at each side. These spatial ambiguities, the subtle asymmetries within the centralized composition, the Virgin's engaging gaze, and the individually conceived faces of the old men give the picture a sense of life and the figures a sense of presence. Cimabue's ambitious attention to spatial volumes, his use of delicate light-to-dark modeling to simulate three-dimensional form, and his efforts to give naturalistic warmth to human figures had an impact on future Florentine painting.

18–5 Cimabue
VIRGIN AND CHILD ENTHRONED
Most likely painted for the high altar of the church of Santa Trinità, Florence. c. 1280. Tempera and gold on wood panel, 12′7″ × 7′4″ (3.53 × 2.2 m). Galleria degli Uffizi, Florence.

Credit: © Studio Fotografico Quattrone, Florence

GIOTTO DI BONDONE According to the sixteenth-century chronicler Giorgio Vasari, Cimabue discovered a talented shepherd boy, Giotto di Bondone (active c. 1300–1337) and taught him to paint; "not only did the young boy equal the style of his master, but he became such an excellent imitator of nature that he completely banished that crude Greek [Byzantine] style and revived the modern and excellent art of painting, introducing good drawing from live natural models, something which had not been done for more than two hundred years" (Vasari, translated by Bondanella and Bondanella, p. 16). After his training, Giotto may have collaborated on murals at the prestigious church of St. Francis in Assisi. We know he worked for the Franciscans in Florence and absorbed facets of their teaching. St. Francis's message of humility, simple devotion, direct experience of God, and love for all creatures was gaining followers throughout western Europe, and it had a powerful impact on thirteenth- and fourteenth-century Italian literature and art.

Compared to Cimabue's *Virgin and Child Enthroned*, Giotto's altarpiece of the same subject (**FIG. 18–6**), painted about 30 years later for the church of the Ognissanti (All Saints) in Florence, exhibits greater spatial consistency and sculptural solidity while retaining some of Cimabue's

18–6 Giotto di Bondone **VIRGIN AND CHILD ENTHRONED**

Most likely painted for the high altar of the church of the Ognissanti (All Saints), Florence. 1305–1310. Tempera and gold on wood panel, 10′8″ × 6′8¼″ (3.53 × 2.05 m). Galleria degli Uffizi, Florence.

Technique
BUON FRESCO

The two techniques used in mural painting are *buon* ("true") *fresco* ("fresh"), in which water-based paint is applied on wet plaster, and *fresco secco* ("dry"), in which paint is applied to a dry plastered wall. Both methods can be used on the same wall painting.

The advantage of *buon fresco* is its durability. A chemical reaction occurs as the painted plaster dries, which bonds the pigments into the wall surface. In *fresco secco*, by contrast, the color does not become part of the wall and tends to flake off over time. The chief disadvantage of *buon fresco* is that it must be done quickly without mistakes. The painter plasters and paints only as much as can be completed in a day, which explains the Italian term for each of these sections: **giornata**, or a day's work. The size of a *giornata* varies according to the complexity of the painting within it. A face, for instance, might take an entire day, whereas large areas of sky can be painted quite rapidly. In Giotto's Scrovegni Chapel, scholars have identified 852 separate *giornate*, some worked on concurrently within a single day by assistants in Giotto's workshop.

In medieval and Renaissance Italy, a wall to be frescoed was first prepared with a rough, thick undercoat of plaster known as the *arriccio*. When this was dry, assistants copied the master painter's composition onto it with reddish-brown pigment or charcoal. The artist made any necessary adjustments. These underdrawings, known as **sinopia**, have an immediacy and freshness that are lost in the finished painting. Work proceeded in irregularly shaped *giornate* conforming to the contours of

major figures and objects. Assistants covered one section at a time with a fresh, thin coat of very fine plaster—the *intonaco*—over the *sinopia*, and when this was "set" but not dry, the artist worked with pigments mixed with water, painting from the top down so that drips fell on unfinished portions. Gilding and pigments such as ultramarine blue (which was unstable in *buon fresco*) would be added after the wall was dry using the *fresco secco* technique.

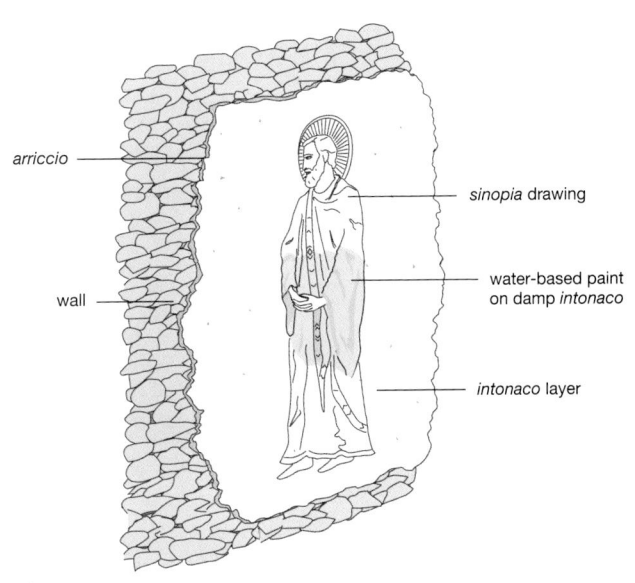

conventions. The position of the figures within a symmetrical composition reflects Cimabue's influence. Gone, however, are Mary's modestly inclined head and the delicate gold folds in her drapery. Instead, light and shadow play gently across her stocky form, and her action—holding her child's leg instead of pointing him out to us—seems less contrived. This colossal Mary overwhelms her slender Gothic tabernacle of a throne, where figures peer through openings and haloes overlap faces. In spite of the hierarchic scale, the formal, enthroned image, and the flat, gold background, Giotto has created the sense that these are fully three-dimensional beings, whose plainly draped, bulky bodies inhabit real space. The Virgin's torso is revealed by her thin tunic, and the angels are substantial solids whose foreshortened postures project from the foreground toward us, unlike those of Cimabue, who stay on the surface along lateral strips composed of overlapping screens of color.

Although Giotto was trained in the Florentine tradition, many of his principal works were produced elsewhere. After a sojourn in Rome during the last years of the thirteenth century, he was called to Padua in northern

Italy soon after 1300 to paint frescos (see *"Buon Fresco"* above) for a new chapel being constructed at the site of an ancient Roman arena—explaining why it is often referred to as the Arena Chapel. The chapel was commissioned by Enrico Scrovegni, whose family fortune was made through the practice of usury, or charging interest when loaning money, a sin considered so grave at the time that it resulted in exclusion from the Christian sacraments. Enrico's father, Regibaldo, was an egregious case (he appears in Dante's *Inferno* as the prototypical usurer), but evidence suggests that Enrico followed in his father's footsteps, and the building of the Arena Chapel next to his new palatial residence seems to have been conceived at least in part as an attempt to atone not only for his father's sins, but also for his own. He was pardoned by Pope Benedict XI (pontificate 1303–1304).

That Scrovegni called two of the most famous artists of the time—Giotto and Giovanni Pisano (SEE FIG. 17-37)—to decorate his chapel indicates that his goals were to express his power, sophistication, and prestige, as well as to atone for his sins. The building itself has little architectural distinction. It is a simple, barrel-vaulted room with broad walls to showcase Giotto's paintings (**FIG. 18–7**). Giotto covered the entrance wall with the *Last Judgment* (not visible here) and the sanctuary wall with three highlighted scenes from the life of Christ. The Annunciation spreads over the two painted architectural frameworks on either side of the tall, arched opening into the sanctuary itself. Below this are, to the left, the scene of Judas receiving payment for betraying Jesus and, to the right, the scene of the Visitation, where the Virgin, pregnant with God incarnate, embraces her cousin Elizabeth, pregnant with St. John the Baptist. The compositions and color arrangement of these two scenes create a symmetrical pairing that encourages viewers to relate them, comparing the ill-gotten financial gains of Judas (a rather clear reference to Scrovegni usury) to the miraculous pregnancy that brought the promise of salvation.

Giotto subdivided the side walls of the chapel into framed pictures. A dado of faux-marble and allegorical **grisaille** paintings (monochrome paintings in shades of gray) of the Virtues and Vices support vertical bands painted to resemble marble inlay into which are inserted painted imitations of carved medallions. The central band of medallions spans the vault, crossing a brilliant, lapis-blue, star-spangled sky in which large portrait disks float like glowing moons. Set into this framework are three horizontal bands of rectangular narrative scenes from the life of the Virgin and her parents at the top and Jesus along the middle and lower registers, which make up the primary religious program of the chapel.

Both the individual scenes and the overall program display Giotto's genius for distilling complex stories into a series of compelling moments. He concentrates on the human dimensions of the unfolding drama—from touches of anecdotal humor to expressions of profound anguish—rather than on its symbolic or theological weight. His prodigious narrative skills are apparent in a set of scenes from Christ's life on the north wall (**FIG. 18–8**). At top left Jesus performs his first miracle, changing water into wine at the wedding feast at Cana. The wine steward—looking very much like the jars of new wine himself—sips the results.

18–7 Giotto di Bondone **SCROVEGNI (ARENA) CHAPEL, VIEW TOWARD EAST WALL**

Padua. 1305–1306. Frescos.

Credit: © Studio Fotografico Quattrone, Florence

18–8 Giotto di Bondone **MARRIAGE AT CANA, RAISING OF LAZARUS, LAMENTATION, AND RESURRECTION/ NOLI ME TANGERE**

North wall of Scrovegni (Arena) Chapel, Padua. 1305–1306. Fresco, each scene approx. 6′5″ × 6′ (2 × 1.85 m).

Credit: © Studio Fotografico Quattrone, Florence

To the right is the Raising of Lazarus, where boldly modeled and individualized figures twist in space. Through their postures and gestures they react to the human drama by pleading for Jesus's help or by expressing either astonishment at the miracle or revulsion at the smell of death. Jesus is separated from the crowd. His transforming gesture is highlighted against the dark blue of the background, his profile face locked in communication with the similarly isolated Lazarus, whose eyes—still fixed in death—let us know that the miracle has not yet happened.

On the lower register, where Jesus's followers lament over his dead body, Giotto portrays palpable human suffering, drawing viewers into a circle of personal grief. The stricken Virgin pulls her dead son close, while John the Evangelist flings his arms back in convulsive despair and others hunch over the corpse. Much as Giotto linked the scene of Judas's pact and the Visitation across the

sanctuary arch, he links this scene to the mourning of Lazarus on the register above using the continuous diagonal implied by the sharply angled hillside behind both scenes, and the rhyming repetition of mourners in each scene— facing in opposite directions—who throw back their arms to express their emotional state. Viewers would know that the mourning in both scenes is resolved by resurrection, portrayed in the last picture in this set.

Following traditional medieval practice, the fresco program is full of scenes and symbols that are intended to be seen as coordinated or contrasting juxtapositions. What is new here is the way Giotto draws us into the experience of these events. This direct emotional appeal not only allows viewers to imagine the scenes in relation to their own life experiences, it also embodies the new Franciscan emphasis on personal devotion rooted in empathetic responses to sacred stories.

18–9 Giotto di Bondone
KISS OF JUDAS
South wall of Scrovegni
(Arena) Chapel, Padua.
1305–1306. Fresco,
6'6¾" × 6'⅞" (2 × 1.85 m).

Credit: © Studio Fotografico
Quattrone, Florence

One of the most gripping paintings in the chapel is Giotto's portrayal of the **KISS OF JUDAS**, the moment of betrayal that represents the first step on Jesus's road to the Crucifixion (**FIG. 18-9**). Savior and traitor are slightly off-center in the near foreground. The expansive sweep of Judas's strident yellow cloak—the same outfit he wore at the scene of his payment for the betrayal on the strip of wall to the left of the sanctuary arch—almost completely swallows Christ's body. Surrounding them, faces glare from all directions. A bristling array of weapons radiating from the confrontation draws attention to the encounter between Christ and Judas and documents the militarism of the arresting soldiers. Jesus stands solid, a model of calm resolve that recalls his visual characterization in the *Raising of Lazarus*, and forms a striking foil to the noisy and chaotic aggression that engulfs him. Judas, in simian profile, purses his lips for the kiss that will betray Jesus to his captors, setting up a mythic confrontation of good and evil. In a subplot to the left, Peter lunges forward to sever the ear of the high priest's assistant. They are behind another broad sweep of fabric, this one extended by a figure completely concealed except for the hand that pulls at Peter's cloak. Indeed, a broad expanse of cloth and lateral gestures creates a barrier along the picture plane—as if to protect viewers from the compressed chaos of the scene itself. Rarely has this poignant event been visualized with such riveting power.

Sienese Painting

Like their Florentine rivals, Sienese painters were rooted in thirteenth-century pictorial traditions, especially those of Byzantine art. Sienese painting emphasized the decorative potential of narrative painting with brilliant, jewel-like colors and elegantly posed figures. For this reason, some art historians consider Sienese art more conservative than Florentine art, but we will see that it has its own charm and its own narrative strategies.

DUCCIO DI BUONINSEGNA Siena's foremost painter was Duccio di Buoninsegna (active 1278–1318), whose creative synthesis of Byzantine and French Gothic sources transformed the tradition in which he worked. Between 1308 and 1311, Duccio and his workshop painted a huge altarpiece commissioned for Siena Cathedral and known as the **MAESTÀ** ("Majesty") (**FIG. 18-10**). Creating this altarpiece—assembled from many wood panels bonded together before painting—was an arduous undertaking. The work was not only large—the central panel alone was 7 by 13 feet—but it had to be painted on both sides since it could be seen from all directions when installed on the main altar at the center of the sanctuary.

Because the *Maestà* was dismantled in 1771, its power and beauty can only be imagined from scattered parts, some still in Siena but others elsewhere. FIGURE 18-10A is a

18–10 Duccio di Buoninsegna
CONJECTURAL RECONSTRUCTION OF THE FRONT (A) AND BACK (B) OF THE MAESTÀ ALTARPIECE

Made for Siena Cathedral. 1308–1311. Tempera and gold on wood, main front panel 7 × 13′ (2.13 × 4.12 m).

Credit: © Lew Minter

Technique

CENNINO CENNINI ON PANEL PAINTING

Il Libro dell' Arte (*The Book of Art*) of Cennino Cennini (c. 1370–1440) is a compendium of Florentine painting techniques from about 1400 that includes step-by-step instructions for making panel paintings, a process also used in Sienese paintings of the same period.

The wood for the panels, he explains, should be fine-grained, free of blemishes, and thoroughly seasoned by slow drying. The first step in preparing such a panel for painting was to cover its surface with clean white linen strips soaked in a **gesso** (primer) made from gypsum, a task, he tells us, best done on a dry, windy day. Gesso provided a ground, or surface, on which to paint, and Cennini specified that at least nine layers should be applied. The gessoed surface should then be burnished until it resembles ivory. Only then could the artist sketch the composition of the work with charcoal made from burned willow twigs. At this point, advised Cennini, "When you have finished drawing your figure, especially if it is in a very valuable [altarpiece], so that you are counting on profit and reputation from it, leave it alone for a few days, going back to it now and then to look it over and improve it wherever it still needs something. When it seems to you about right (and bear in mind that you may copy and examine things done by other good masters; that it is no shame to you), when the figure is satisfactory, take the feather and rub it over the drawing very lightly, until the drawing is practically effaced" (Cennini, trans. Thompson, p. 75). At this point, the final design would be inked in with a fine squirrel-hair brush. Gold leaf, he advises, should be affixed on a humid day, the tissue-thin sheets carefully glued down with a mixture of fine powdered clay and egg white on the reddish clay ground called bole. Then the gold is burnished with a gemstone or the tooth of a carnivorous animal. Punched and incised patterning should be added to the gold leaf later.

Fourteenth- and fifteenth-century Italian painters worked principally in tempera paint: powdered pigments mixed with egg yolk, a little water, and an occasional touch of glue. Apprentices were kept busy grinding pigments and mixing paints, setting them out for more senior painters in wooden bowls or shell dishes.

Cennini outlined a detailed and highly formulaic painting process. Faces, for example, were always to be done last, with flesh tones applied over two coats of a light greenish pigment and highlighted with touches of red and white. The finished painting was to be given a layer of varnish to protect it and intensify its colors.

18–11 Duccio di Buoninsegna **RAISING OF LAZARUS**

From the predella of the back of the *Maestà* altarpiece (lower right corner of FIG. 18–10B), made for Siena Cathedral. 1308–1311. Tempera and gold on wood, 17⅛ × 18¼″ (43.5 × 46.4 cm). Kimbell Art Museum, Fort Worth, Texas.

18–12 Duccio di Buoninsegna **BETRAYAL OF JESUS**
From the back of the *Maestà* altarpiece (lower center of FIG. 18–10B), made for Siena Cathedral. 1308–1311.
Tempera and gold on wood, 22½ × 40″ (57.2 × 101.6 cm). Museo dell'Opera del Duomo, Siena.

Credit: © 2016. Photo Opera Metropolitana Siena/Scala, Florence

reconstruction of how the front of the original altarpiece might have looked. It is dominated by a large representation of the Virgin and Child in Majesty (thus its title of *Maestà*), flanked by 20 angels and 10 saints, including the 4 patron saints of Siena kneeling in the foreground. Above and below this lateral tableau were small narrative scenes from the last days of the life of the Virgin (above) and the infancy of Christ (spread across the **predella**, the lower zone of the altarpiece). An inscription running around the base of Mary's majestic throne places the artist's signature within an optimistic framework: "Holy Mother of God, be thou the cause of peace for Siena and life to Duccio because he painted thee thus." This was not Duccio's first work for the cathedral. In 1288, he had designed a stunning stained-glass window portraying the Death, Assumption, and Coronation of the Virgin for the huge circular opening in the east wall of the sanctuary. It would have hovered over the installed *Maestà* when it was placed on the altar in 1311.

The enthusiasm with which citizens greeted a great painting or altarpiece like the *Maestà* demonstrates the power of images as well as the association of such magnificent works with the glory of a city itself. According to a contemporary account, on December 20, 1311, the day that Duccio's altarpiece was carried from his workshop to the cathedral, all the shops were shut, and everyone in the city participated in the procession, with "bells ringing joyously, out of reverence for so noble a picture as is this" (Holt, p. 69).

On the back of the *Maestà* (SEE FIG. 18–10B) were episodes from the life of Christ focusing on his Passion. Sacred narrative unfolds in elegant episodes enacted by graceful figures who seem to dance their way through these stories while still conveying emotional content. Characteristic of Duccio's narrative style is the scene of the **RAISING OF LAZARUS** (FIG. 18–11). Lyrical figures enact the event with graceful decorum, but their highly charged glances and expressive gestures—especially the bold reach of Christ—convey a strong sense of dramatic urgency that contrasts with the tense stillness that we saw in Giotto's rendering of this same moment of confrontation (SEE FIG. 18–8). Duccio's shading of drapery, like his modeling of faces, faithfully describes the figures' three-dimensionality, but the crisp outlines of the jewel-colored shapes created by their clothing, as well as the sinuous continuity of folds and gestures, generate rhythmic patterns crisscrossing the surface. Duccio's experimentation with the portrayal of space extends from the receding rocks of the mountainous landscape to the carefully studied interiors, including the tomb of Lazarus, the door of which was removed by a bystander to reveal Jesus's resurrected friend.

Duccio's rendering of the **BETRAYAL OF JESUS** (FIG. 18–12) is more expansive, both pictorially and temporally, occupying one of the broadest panels in the altarpiece (SEE FIG. 18–10B, lower center) and encompassing within one composition several moments in the sequential narrative of its subject matter. The tableau is centered and stabilized by the frontal figure of Jesus, whose dark mantle with its sinuous gold trim stands out from the densely packed, colorful crowd of figures surrounding him. Judas approaches from the left to identify Jesus. Although the heads of betrayer and betrayed touch in this moment, Duccio avoids the psychological power of Giotto's face-to-face confrontation in the Scrovegni Chapel (SEE FIG. 18-9). Flanking Duccio's stable, packed central scene of betrayal are two subsequent moments in the story, each pulling our attention to the sides. To the left, the apostle Peter lunges with a dynamic gesture to sever the ear of a member of the arresting party, while on the other side of the composition a group of apostles rushes to escape the central scene, abandoning Jesus to his fate. Through the postures and facial expressions of the many figures in this broad, continuous narrative, Duccio expresses the emotional charge of these pivotal moments

in the narrative of Christ's Passion. At the same time, he creates a dazzling picture, as rich in color and linear elegance as it is faithful to the human dimensions of the situations it portrays.

SIMONE MARTINI   The generation of painters who followed Duccio continued to paint in the elegant style he established, combining the evocation of three-dimensional form with a graceful continuity of linear pattern. One of Duccio's most successful and innovative followers was Simone Martini (c. 1284–1344), whose paintings were in high demand throughout Italy, including in Assisi where he covered the walls of the St. Martin Chapel with frescos between 1312 and 1319. His most famous work, however, was commissioned in 1333 for the cathedral of his native Siena, an altarpiece of the **ANNUNCIATION** flanked by two saints (**FIG. 18-13**) that he painted in collaboration with his brother-in-law, Lippo Memmi.

18–13 Simone Martini and Lippo Memmi **ANNUNCIATION**
Made for Siena Cathedral. 1333. Tempera and gold on wood, 10′ × 8′9″ (3 × 2.67 m). Galleria degli Uffizi, Florence.

Art and its Contexts

THE BLACK DEATH

A deadly outbreak of the bubonic plague, known as the Black Death after the dark sores that developed on the bodies of its victims, spread to Europe from Asia by both land and sea in the middle of the fourteenth century. At least half the urban population of Florence and Siena—some estimate 80 percent—died during the summer of 1348, probably including the artists Andrea Pisano and Ambrogio Lorenzetti. Death was so quick and widespread that basic social structures crumbled in the resulting chaos; people did not know where the disease came from, what caused it, or how long the pandemic would last.

Mid-twentieth-century art historian Millard Meiss proposed that the Black Death had a significant impact on the development of Italian art in the middle of the fourteenth century. Pointing to what he saw as a reactionary return to hieratic linearity in religious art, Meiss theorized that artists had retreated from the rounded forms that had characterized the work of Giotto to old-fashioned styles, and that this artistic change reflected a growing reliance on traditional religious values in the wake of a disaster that some interpreted as God's punishment of a world in moral decline.

An altarpiece painted in 1354–1357 by Andrea di Cione, nicknamed "Orcagna" ("Archangel"), under the patronage of Tommaso Strozzi—the so-called **STROZZI ALTARPIECE** (**FIG. 18–14**)—is the sort of painting that led Meiss to his interpretation. It is dominated by a central figure of Christ,

presumably enthroned, but without any hint of an actual seat, evoking the image of the judge at the Last Judgment, outside time and space. The silhouetted outlines of the standing and kneeling saints emphasize surface over depth; the gold floor beneath them does not offer any reassuring sense of spatial recession to contain them and their activity. Throughout, line and color are more prominent than form.

Recent art historians have stepped back from Meiss's contextual explanation of stylistic change. Some have pointed out logical relationships between style and subject in the works Meiss cites; others have seen in them a mannered outgrowth of current style rather than a reversion to an earlier style; still others have discounted the underlying notion that stylistic change is connected with social situations. But there is a clear relationship of works such as the Strozzi Altarpiece with death and judgment, sanctity, and the promise of salvation—themes also suggested in the narrative scenes on the predella: Thomas Aquinas's ecstasy during Mass, Christ's miraculous walk on water to rescue Peter, and the salvation of Emperor Henry II because of a pious donation. While these are not uncommon scenes in sacred art, it is easy to see a relationship between their choice as subject matter here and the specter cast by the Black Death over a world that had recently imagined its prosperity in art firmly rooted in references to everyday life (SEE FIG. 18–16).

18–14 Andrea di Cione (nicknamed "Orcagna") **ENTHRONED CHRIST WITH SAINTS, FROM THE STROZZI ALTARPIECE**
Strozzi Chapel, Santa Maria Novella, Florence. 1354–1357. Tempera and gold on wood, 9′ × 9′8″ (2.74 × 2.95 m).

Credit: © Studio Fotografico Quattrone, Florence

The smartly dressed figure of Gabriel—the extended flourish of his drapery behind him suggesting he has just arrived, and with some speed—raises his hand to address the Virgin. The words of his message are actually incised into the gold-leafed gesso of the background, running from his opened mouth toward the Virgin's ear: *Ave gratia plena dominus tecum* (Luke 1:28: "Hail, full of grace, the Lord is with thee"). Seemingly frightened—at the very least

18–15 AERIAL VIEW OF THE CAMPO IN SIENA WITH THE PALAZZO PUBBLICO (CITY HALL INCLUDING ITS TOWER) FACING ITS STRAIGHT SIDE

Siena. Palazzo Pubblico 1297–c. 1315; tower 1320s–1340s.

Credit: © Archivi Alinari, Firenze

startled—by this unexpected celestial messenger, Mary recoils into her lavish throne, her thumb inserted into the book she had been reading to safeguard her place, while her other hand pulls at her clothing in an elegant gesture of nobility that relates back to the courtly art of thirteenth-century Paris (see Solomon, second lancet from the right in FIG. 17–11).

AMBROGIO LORENZETTI   The most important civic structure in Siena was the **PALAZZO PUBBLICO** (FIG. 18–15), the town hall which served as the seat of government, just as the Palazzo della Signoria did in rival Florence (SEE FIG. 18-2). There are similarities between these two buildings. Both are designed as strong, fortified structures sitting on the edge of a public piazza, and both have a tall tower, making them visible signs of the city from a considerable distance. The Palazzo Pubblico was constructed from 1297 to c. 1315, but the tower was not completed until 1348, when the bronze bell used to signal meetings of the ruling council was installed.

The interior of the Palazzo Pubblico was the site of important commissions by some of Siena's most famous artists. In c. 1315, Simone Martini painted a large mural of the Virgin in Majesty surrounded by saints—clearly based on Duccio's recently installed *Maestà*. Then, in 1338, the Siena city council commissioned Ambrogio Lorenzetti to paint frescos for the council room of the Palazzo known as the Sala dei Nove (Chamber of the Nine), or Sala della Pace (Chamber of Peace), on the theme of the contrast between good and bad government (SEE FIG. 18–1).

Lorenzetti painted the results of both good and bad government on the two long walls. For the expansive scene of **THE EFFECTS OF GOOD GOVERNMENT IN THE CITY AND IN THE COUNTRY**, and in tribute to his patrons, he created an idealized but recognizable portrait of the city of Siena and its immediate environs (FIG. 18–16). The cathedral dome and the distinctive striped campanile are visible in the upper left-hand corner; the streets are filled with the bustling activity of productive citizens who also have time for leisurely diversions. Lorenzetti shows the city from shifting viewpoints so we can see as much as possible, and renders its inhabitants larger in scale than the buildings around them to highlight their activity. Featured in the foreground is a circle of dancers—probably a professional troupe of male entertainers masquerading as women as part of a spring festival—and above them, at the top of the painting, a band of masons on exterior scaffolding is constructing the wall of a new building.

The Porta Romana, Siena's gateway leading to Rome, divides the thriving city from its surrounding countryside. In this panoramic landscape painting, Lorenzetti describes a natural world marked by agricultural productivity, showing activities of all seasons simultaneously—sowing, hoeing, and harvesting. Hovering above the gate that separates city life and country life is a woman clad in a wisp of transparent drapery, a scroll in one hand and a miniature gallows complete with a hanged man in the other. She represents Security, and her scroll bids those coming to the city to enter without fear because she has taken away the power of the guilty who would harm them.

18–16 Ambrogio Lorenzetti **THE EFFECTS OF GOOD GOVERNMENT IN THE CITY AND IN THE COUNTRY**
Sala dei Nove (also known as Sala della Pace), Palazzo Pubblico, Siena, Italy. 1338–1339. Fresco, total length approx. 46' (14 m).
Credit: © Studio Fotografico Quattrone, Florence

The world of the Italian city-states—which had seemed so full of promise in Ambrogio Lorenzetti's *Good Government* fresco—was transformed into uncertainty and desolation by a series of natural and societal disasters as the middle of the century approached. In 1333, a flood devastated Florence, followed by banking failures in the 1340s, famine in 1346–1347, and epidemics of the bubonic plague, especially virulent in the summer of 1348. Some art historians have traced the influence of these calamities on the visual arts at the middle of the fourteenth century (see "The Black Death" on page 559). Yet as dark as those days must have seemed to the men and women living through them, the cultural and artistic changes initiated earlier in the century would persist. In a relatively short span of time, the European Middle Ages gave way in Florence to a new movement that would blossom in the Italian Renaissance.

France

What features characterize the small-scale works of art produced in Parisian workshops during the fourteenth century?

At the beginning of the fourteenth century, the royal court in Paris was still the arbiter of taste in western Europe, as it had been in the days of King Louis IX (St. Louis). During the Hundred Years' War, however, the French countryside was ravaged by armed struggles and civil strife. The power of the nobility, weakened significantly by warfare, was challenged by townsmen, who took advantage of new economic opportunities that opened up in the wake of the conflict. As centers of art and architecture, the duchy of Burgundy, England, and, for a brief moment, the court of Prague began to rival Paris.

French sculptors found lucrative new outlets for their work—not only in stone, but in wood, ivory, and precious metals, often decorated with enamel and gemstones—in the growing demand among wealthy patrons for religious art intended for homes as well as churches. Manuscript painters likewise created lavishly illustrated books for the personal devotions of the wealthy and powerful. And architectural commissions focused on exquisitely detailed chapels or small churches, often under private patronage, rather than on the building of grand cathedrals funded by Church institutions.

Manuscript Illumination

By the late thirteenth century, private prayer books became popular among wealthy patrons. Because they contained special prayers to be recited at the eight canonical devotional "hours" between morning and night, an individual copy of one of these books came to be called a **Book of Hours**.

Such a book included everything the layperson needed for pious practice—psalms, prayers and offices of the Virgin and other saints (such as the owner's patron or the patron of their home church), a calendar of feast days, and sometimes prayers for the dead. During the fourteenth century, a richly decorated Book of Hours was worn or carried like jewelry, counting among a noble person's most important portable possessions.

THE BOOK OF HOURS OF JEANNE D'ÉVREUX King Charles IV gave his 14-year-old queen, Jeanne d'Évreux, a tiny Book of Hours illuminated by the Parisian painter Jean Pucelle, perhaps on the occasion of their marriage in 1324. When opened, it fits easily within one hand (see "Closer Look" opposite). This book was so precious to the queen that she mentioned it and its illuminator specifically in her will, leaving this royal treasure to King Charles V. Pucelle painted the book's pictures in *grisaille*. His style clearly derives from the courtly mode established in Paris at the time of Louis IX—softly modeled, voluminous draperies gathered loosely and falling in projecting diagonal folds around tall, elegantly posed figures with carefully coiffed, curly hair, broad foreheads, and delicate features. But his conception of space, with figures placed within coherent, discrete architectural settings, suggests a firsthand knowledge of contemporary Sienese art.

Jeanne appears in the initial *D* below the Annunciation, kneeling in prayer before a lectern, perhaps using this Book of Hours to guide her meditations, beginning with the words written on this page: *Domine labia mea aperies* (Psalm 51:15: "O Lord, open thou my lips"). The juxtaposition of the praying Jeanne with a scene from the life of the Virgin Mary suggests that the sacred scene is actually a vision inspired by Jeanne's meditations. The young queen might have identified with and sought to feel within herself Mary's joy at Gabriel's message. Given what we know of Jeanne's life and her royal husband's predicament, it might also have directed the queen's prayers toward the fulfillment of his wish for a male heir.

In the Annunciation, Mary is shown receiving the archangel Gabriel in a Gothic building that seems to project outward from the page toward the viewer, while rejoicing angels look on from windows under the eaves. The group of children at the bottom of the page at first glance seems to echo the angelic jubilation. Folklorists have suggested, however, that the children are playing "froggy in the middle" or "hot cockles," games in which one child was tagged by the others. To the medieval viewer, if the game symbolized the mocking of Christ or the betrayal of Judas, who "tags" his friend, it would have evoked a darker mood—referring to the picture on the other page of this opening and foreshadowing Jesus's imminent death even as his life is beginning.

A Closer Look

THE HOURS OF JEANNE D'ÉVREUX

In this opening Pucelle juxtaposes complementary scenes drawn from the Infancy and Passion of Christ, placed on opposing pages in a scheme known as the Joys and Sorrows of the Virgin. The "joy" of the Annunciation on the right is paired with the "sorrow" of the betrayal and arrest of Christ on the left.

Christ sways back as Judas betrays him with a kiss. The S-curve of his body mirrors the Virgin's pose on the opposite page, as both accept their fate with courtly decorum.

The prominent lamp held aloft by a member of the arresting battalion informs the viewer that this scene takes place at night, in the dark.

The angel who holds up the boxlike enclosure where the Annunciation takes place is an allusion to the legend of the miraculous transportation of this building from Nazareth to Loreto in 1294.

Christ reaches casually down to heal Malchus, the assistant of the high priest, whose ear Peter had just cut off in angry retaliation for his participation in the arrest of Jesus.

Visual puns, off-color jokes, and scenes of secular amusements from everyday life appear at the bottom of many pages of this book. Sometimes they relate to the themes of the sacred scenes above them. These comic knights riding goats may be a commentary on the lack of valor shown by the soldiers assaulting Jesus, especially if this wine barrel conjured up for Jeanne an association with the Eucharist.

The candle held by the cleric who guards the "door" to Jeanne's devotional retreat, as well as the rabbit emerging from its burrow in the marginal scene, are sexually charged symbols of fertility that seem directly related to the prayers of a child bride required to produce a male heir.

18–17 Jean Pucelle **THE KISS OF JUDAS AND THE ANNUNCIATION**

Two-page opening from the Hours of Jeanne d'Évreux. Paris. c. 1324–1328. *Grisaille* and color on vellum, each page 3⅝ × 2⁷⁄₁₆″ (9.2 × 6.2 cm). Metropolitan Museum of Art, New York. The Cloisters Collection (54.1.2), fols. 15v–16r.

Metalwork and Ivory

Fourteenth-century French sculpture is intimate in character. Religious subjects became more emotionally expressive; objects became smaller and demanded closer scrutiny from the viewer. In the secular realm, tales of love and valor were carved on luxury items to delight the rich. Precious materials—gold, silver, and ivory—were preferred.

18–18 VIRGIN AND CHILD

c. 1324–1339. Silver gilt and enamel, height 27⅛" (69 cm). Musée du Louvre, Paris.

Credit: © Jacqueline Guillot/akg-images

A VIRGIN AND CHILD FROM SAINT-DENIS A silver-gilt image of a standing **VIRGIN AND CHILD** (FIG. 18–18) is a rare survivor that verifies the acclaim that was accorded fourteenth-century Parisian goldsmiths. An inscription on the base documents the statue's donation to the abbey church of Saint-Denis in 1339 and the donor's name, the same Queen Jeanne d'Évreux whose Book of Hours we have just examined. In a style that recalls the work of artist Jean Pucelle in that Book of Hours, the Virgin holds Jesus in her left arm with her weight on her left leg, standing in a graceful, characteristically Gothic S-curve pose. Mary originally wore a crown, and she still holds a large enameled and jeweled *fleur-de-lis*—the heraldic symbol of royal France—which served as a reliquary container for strands of Mary's hair. The Christ Child, reaching out tenderly to caress his mother's face, is babylike in both form and posture. On the base, minuscule statues of prophets stand on projecting piers to separate 14 enameled scenes from Christ's Infancy and Passion, reminding us of the suffering to come. The apple in the baby's hand carries the theme further with its reference to Christ's role as the new Adam, whose sacrifice on the cross redeemed humanity from the first couple's fall into sin when Eve bit into the forbidden fruit.

AN IVORY CHEST WITH SCENES OF ROMANCE Fourteenth-century Paris was renowned for more than its goldsmiths (SEE FIG. 18–18). Among the most sumptuous and sought-after Parisian luxury products were small chests assembled from carved ivory plaques that were used by wealthy women to store jewelry or other personal treasures. The entirely secular subject matter of these chests explored romantic love. Indeed, they seem to have been courtship gifts from smitten men to desired women or wedding presents offered by grooms to their brides.

A chest from around 1330 to 1350, now in the Walters Museum (FIG. 18–19), is one of seven that have survived intact; there are fragments of a dozen more. It is a delightful and typical example. Figural relief covers five exterior sides of the box: around the perimeter and on the hinged top. The assembled panels were joined by hardware originally wrought in silver. Although some chests tell a single romantic story in sequential episodes, most, like this one, anthologize scenes drawn from a group of stories, combining courtly romance, secular allegory, and ancient fables.

On the lid of the Walters casket (FIG. 18–20), jousting is the theme. Spread over the central two panels, a single scene catches two charging knights in the heat of a tournament, while trumpeting heralds call the attention of spectators, lined up above in a gallery to observe this public display of virility. The panel at right mocks the very ritual showcased in the middle panels by pitting a woman against a knight, battling not with lances but with

18-19 SMALL IVORY CHEST WITH SCENES FROM COURTLY ROMANCES

Made in Paris. c. 1330–1350. Elephant ivory with modern iron mounts, height 4½ × 9¹¹⁄₁₆ × 4⅞″ (11.5 × 24.6 × 12.4 cm). The Walters Art Museum, Baltimore. 71.264

Credit: Photo © The Walters Art Museum, Baltimore

18-20 ATTACK ON THE CASTLE OF LOVE
Top of the chest in FIG. 18-19.

Credit: Photo © The Walters Art Museum, Baltimore

18-21 TRISTAN AND ISEULT AT THE FOUNTAIN; CAPTURE OF THE UNICORN
Left short side of the chest in FIG. 18-19.

Credit: Photo © The Walters Art Museum, Baltimore

a long-stemmed rose (symbolizing sexual surrender) and an oak bough (symbolizing fertility). Instead of observing these goings-on, however, the spectators tucked into the upper architecture pursue their own flirtations. Finally, in the scene on the left, knights use crossbows and a catapult to hurl roses at the Castle of Love, while Cupid returns fire.

On the front of the chest (SEE FIG. 18-19), generalized romantic allegory gives way to vignettes from a specific story. At left, the long-bearded Aristotle teaches the young Alexander the Great, using exaggerated gestures and an authoritative text to emphasize his point. Today's lesson is a warning not to allow women to distract the young prince from his studies. The subsequent scene, however, pokes fun at the eminent teacher, who has become so smitten by a young beauty named Phyllis that he lets her ride

him around like a horse while his student observes from the castle in the background. The two scenes at right relate to an Eastern legend of the fountain of youth, popular in medieval Europe. A line of bearded elders approaches the fountain from the left, steadied by their canes; on the right, two newly rejuvenated couples, now nude, bathe and flirt within the fountain's basin. The man first in line for treatment looks suspiciously like the figure of Aristotle, forming a link between the two stories on the casket front.

Two other well-known medieval themes are juxtaposed on the left short side of the ivory chest (**FIG. 18-21**). At left, Tristan and Iseult have met secretly for an illicit romantic tryst, while Iseult's husband, King Mark, tipped off by an informant, observes them from a tree. But when they see his reflection in a fountain between them, they alter their behavior accordingly, and the king believes them innocent of the adultery he had (rightly) suspected. The medieval bestiary ("book of beasts") claimed that only a virgin could capture the mythical unicorn, which at right lays his head, with its aggressively phallic horn, into the lap of just such a pure maiden so that the hunter can take advantage of her alluring powers over the animal to kill it with his phallic counterpart of its horn, a large spear.

Unlike royal marriages of the time, which were essentially business contracts based on political or financial exigencies, the romantic love of the aristocratic wealthy involved passionate devotion. Images of gallant knights and their coy paramours captured the popular Gothic imagination and formed the principal subject matter on personal luxury objects—not only chests like this, but mirror backs, combs, writing tablets, even ceremonial saddles. These stories evoke themes that still captivate us: desire and betrayal, cruel rejection and blissful folly. In this way they allow us some access to the lives of the people who owned these precious objects, even if we ourselves are unable to afford them.

England

What is distinctive about English textiles and architecture during the fourteenth century?

Fourteenth-century England prospered in spite of the ravages of the Black Death and the Hundred Years' War with France. English life at this time is described in the brilliant social commentary of Geoffrey Chaucer in the *Canterbury Tales* (see "A New Spirit in Fourteenth-Century Literature" on page 544). The royal family—especially Edward I (ruled 1272–1307), the castle builder—and many nobles and bishops were generous patrons of the arts.

Embroidery: *Opus Anglicanum*

Since the thirteenth century, the English had been renowned for pictorial needlework, using colored silk and gold threads to create images as detailed as contemporary painters produced in manuscripts. Popular throughout Europe, the art came to be called *opus anglicanum* ("English work"). The popes had more than 100 pieces in the Vatican treasury. The names of several prominent embroiderers are known, but in the thirteenth century no one surpassed Mabel of Bury St. Edmunds, who created both religious and secular articles for King Henry III (ruled 1216–1272).

THE CHICHESTER-CONSTABLE CHASUBLE   This *opus anglicanum* liturgical vestment, worn by a priest during Mass (**FIG. 18-22**), was embroidered c. 1330–1350 with

18–22 LIFE OF THE VIRGIN, BACK OF THE CHICHESTER-CONSTABLE CHASUBLE

From a set of vestments embroidered in *opus anglicanum* from southern England. c. 1330–1350. Red velvet with silk and metallic thread and seed pearls; length 4′3″ (129.5 cm), width 30″ (76 cm). Metropolitan Museum of Art, New York. Fletcher Fund, 1927 (27 162.1).

images formed by subtle gradations of colored silk. Where gold threads were laid and couched (tacked down with colored silk), the effect resembles the burnished gold-leaf backgrounds of manuscript illuminations. The Annunciation, the Adoration of the Magi, and the Coronation of the Virgin are set in cusped, crocketed ogee (S-shape) arches, supported on animal-head corbels and twisting branches of oak leaves with seed-pearl acorns. Because the star and crescent moon in the Coronation of the Virgin scene are heraldic emblems of Edward III (ruled 1327–1377), perhaps he or a family member commissioned this luxurious vestment.

During the celebration of the Mass, especially as the priest moved, *opus anglicanum* would have glinted in the candlelight. Court dress was just as rich and colorful as the treasures on the altar, and at court such embroidered garments proclaimed the rank and status of the wearer. Such gold and bejeweled garments became so heavy that their wearers often needed help to move.

Architecture

In the later years of the thirteenth century and early years of the fourteenth, a distinctive and influential Gothic architectural style popularly known as the "Decorated style" developed in England. This change in taste has been credited to Henry III's ambition to surpass Louis IX, who was his brother-in-law, as a royal patron of the arts.

THE DECORATED STYLE AT EXETER   One of the most complete Decorated-style buildings is **EXETER CATHEDRAL**. Thomas

of Witney began construction in 1313 and remained master mason from 1316 to 1342, supervising construction of the nave and redesigning upper parts of the choir. He left the towers of the original Norman cathedral, but turned the interior into a dazzling stone forest of colonnettes, moldings, and vault ribs (**FIG. 18-23**). From piers formed by a cluster of colonnettes rise multiple moldings that make the arcade seem to ripple. Bundled colonnettes spring from sculptured foliate corbels (brackets that project from a wall) between the arches and rise up the wall to support conical clusters of 13 ribs that meet at the summit of the vault, a modest 69 feet above the floor. The basic structure

18-23 INTERIOR, EXETER CATHEDRAL

Devon, England. Thomas of Witney, choir, 14th century and bishop's throne, 1313–1317; Robert Lesyngham, east window, 1389–1390.

Credit: © akg/Bildarchiv Monheim

here is the four-part vault with intersecting cross-ribs, but the designer added additional ribs, called tiercerons, to create a richer linear pattern. Elaborately carved bosses (decorative knoblike elements) signal the point where ribs meet along the ridge of the vault. Large bar-tracery clerestory windows illuminate the 300-foot-long nave. Unpolished gray marble shafts, yellow sandstone arches, and a white French stone, shipped from Caen, add subtle gradations of color to the upper wall.

Detailed records survive for the building of Exeter Cathedral, documenting work over the period from 1279 to 1514, with only two short breaks. They record where masons and carpenters were housed (in a hostel near the cathedral) and how they were paid (some by the day with extra for drinks, some by the week, some for each finished piece); how materials were acquired and transported (including horseshoes and fodder for the horses); and, of course, payments for the building materials (not only stone and wood, but rope for measuring and parchment on which to draw forms for the masons). The bishops contributed generously to the building funds. This was not a labor only of love.

Thomas of Witney also designed the intricate, 57-foot-high bishop's throne (at right in FIG. 18–23), constructed by Richard de Galmeton and Walter of Memburg, who led a team of a dozen carpenters. The canopy resembles embroidery translated into wood, with its maze of pinnacles bursting with leafy crockets and tiny carved animals and heads. To finish the throne in splendor, Master Nicolas painted and gilded the wood. When the bishop was seated on his throne wearing embroidered vestments like the Chichester-Constable Chasuble (SEE FIG. 18–22), he must have resembled a golden image in a shrine—more a symbol of the power and authority of the Church than a specific human being.

THE PERPENDICULAR STYLE AT EXETER During the years following the Black Death, work at Exeter Cathedral came to a standstill. The nave had been roofed but not vaulted, and the windows had no glass. When work could be resumed, tastes had changed. The exuberance of the Decorated style gave way to an austere style in which rectilinear patterns and sharp, angular shapes replaced intricate curves, and luxuriant foliage gave way to simple, stripped-down patterns. This phase is known as the Perpendicular style.

In 1389–1390, well-paid master mason Robert Lesyngham rebuilt the great east window (SEE FIG. 18–23, far wall), designing its tracery in the new Perpendicular style. The window fills the east wall of the choir like a luminous altarpiece. A single figure in each light stands under a tall, painted canopy that flows into and blends with the stone tracery. The Virgin with the Christ Child stands in the center over the high altar with four female saints at the left

and four male saints on the right, including St. Peter, to whom the church is dedicated. At a distance, the colorful figures silhouetted against the silver *grisaille* glass become a band of color, reinforcing the rectangular pattern of the mullions and transoms. The combination of *grisaille*, silver-oxide stain (staining clear glass with shades of yellow or gold), and colored glass produces a glowing wall and casts a cool, silvery light over the nearby stonework.

Perpendicular architecture heralds the Renaissance style in its regularity, its balanced horizontal and vertical lines, and its plain wall or window surfaces. When Tudor monarchs introduced Renaissance art into the British Isles, builders were not forced to rethink the form and structure of their buildings; they simply changed the ornament from the pointed cusps and crocketed arches of the Gothic style to the round arches and columns and capitals of Roman Classicism. The Perpendicular style itself became an English architectural vernacular. It has even been popular in the United States, especially for churches and college buildings.

The Holy Roman Empire

How do the expressive qualities of the figural arts and the architectural supremacy of Prague lead to a distinctive form of Gothic in the Holy Roman Empire?

By the fourteenth century, the Holy Roman Empire existed more as idealized fiction than fact. The Italian territories had established their independence, and in contrast to England and France, Germany had become further divided into multiple states with powerful regional associations and princes. The Holy Roman emperors, now elected by Germans, concentrated on securing the fortunes of their families. They continued to be patrons of the arts, promoting local styles.

Mysticism and Suffering

The by-now-familiar ordeals of the fourteenth century—famines, wars, and plagues—helped inspire a mystical religiosity in Germany that emphasized both ecstatic joy and extreme suffering. Devotional images, known as *Andachtsbilder* in German, inspired worshipers to contemplate Jesus's first and last hours, especially during evening prayers, or vespers, giving rise to the term *Vesperbild* for the image of Mary mourning her son. Through such religious exercises, worshipers hoped to achieve understanding of the divine and union with God.

VESPERBILD In this well-known example (FIG. 18–24), blood gushes from the hideous rosettes that form the wounds of an emaciated and lifeless Jesus who teeters improbably on the lap of his hunched-over mother.

The Virgin's face conveys the intensity of her ordeal. Such images took on greater poignancy since they would have been compared, in the worshiper's mind, to the familiar, almost ubiquitous images of the young Virgin mother holding her innocent and loving baby Jesus.

THE HEDWIG CODEX   The extreme physicality and emotionalism of the *Vesperbild* finds parallels in the actual lives of some medieval saints in northern Europe. St. Hedwig (1174–1243), married at age 12 to Duke Henry I of Silesia and mother of his seven children, entered the Cistercian convent of Trebniz (in present-day Poland) on her husband's death in 1238. She devoted the rest of her life to caring for the poor and seeking to emulate the suffering of Christ by walking barefoot in the snow. As described in her *vita* (biography), she had a particular affection for a small ivory statue of the Virgin and Child, which she carried with her at all times; "she often took it up in her hands to envelop it in love, so that out of passion she could see it more often and through the seeing could prove herself more devout, inciting her to even greater love of the glorious Virgin. When she once blessed the sick with this image they were cured immediately" (translation from Schleif, p. 22). Hedwig was buried clutching the statue, and when her tomb was opened after her canonization in 1267, it was said that although most of her body had deteriorated, the fingers that still gripped the beloved object had miraculously not decayed.

18–24 VESPERBILD (PIETÀ)

From the Middle Rhine region, Germany. c. 1330. Wood and polychromy, height 34½″ (88.4 cm). Landesmuseum, Bonn.

Credit: © akg-images/Erich Lessing

18-25 ST. HEDWIG OF SILESIA WITH DUKE LUDWIG I OF LIEGNITZ-BRIEG AND DUCHESS AGNES

Dedication page of the Hedwig Codex. 1353. Ink and paint on parchment, 13⁷/₁₆ × 9¾″ (34 × 25 cm). The J. Paul Getty Museum, Los Angeles. MS. Ludwig XI 7, fol. 12v.

A picture of Hedwig serves as the frontispiece (**FIG. 18-25**) of a manuscript of her *vita* known as the Hedwig Codex, commissioned in 1353 by one her descendants, Ludwig I of Liegnitz-Brieg. Duke Ludwig and his wife, Agnes, are shown here kneeling on either side of St. Hedwig, dwarfed by the saint's architectural throne and her own imposing scale. With her prominent, spidery hands, she clutches the famous ivory statue, as well as a rosary and a prayer book, inserting her fingers within it to maintain her place as if our arrival had interrupted her devotions. She has draped her leather boots over her right wrist in a reference to her practice of removing them to walk in the snow. Hedwig's highly volumetric figure stands in a swaying pose of courtly elegance derived from French Gothic, but the intensity of her gaze and posture are far removed from the mannered graciousness of the smiling angel of Reims (see statue at far left in FIG. 17-14), whose similar gesture and extended finger are employed simply to grasp his drapery and assure its elegant display.

The Supremacy of Prague

Charles IV of Bohemia (ruled 1346–1378) was raised in France, and his admiration for the French king Charles IV was such that he changed his own name from Wenceslas to Charles. He was officially crowned King of Bohemia in 1347 and Holy Roman Emperor in 1355. He established his capital in Prague, which, in the view of his contemporaries, replaced Constantinople as the "New Rome." Prague had a great university, a castle, and a cathedral overlooking a town that spread on both sides of a river joined by a stone bridge, a remarkable structure itself.

When Pope Clement VI made Prague an archbishopric in 1344, construction began on a new cathedral in the Gothic style to be named for St. Vitus. It would also serve as the coronation church and royal pantheon. But the choir was not finished for Charles's first coronation, so he brought Peter Parler from Swabia to complete it.

THE PARLER FAMILY In 1317, Heinrich Parler, a former master of works on Cologne Cathedral, designed and began building the church of the Holy Cross in Schwäbisch Gmünd, in southwest Germany. In 1351, his son Peter

(c. 1330–1399), the most brilliant architect of this talented family, joined the workshop. Peter designed the choir (**FIG. 18-26**) in the manner of a hall church whose triple-aisled form was enlarged by a ring of deep chapels between the buttresses. The contrast between Heinrich's nave and Peter's choir (seen clearly in **FIG. 18-26B**) illustrates the increasing complexity of rib patterns covering the vaults, which emphasizes the unity of interior space rather than its division into bays.

Called by Charles IV to Prague in 1353, Peter turned the unfinished St. Vitus Cathedral into a "glass house," adding a vast clerestory and glazed triforium supported by double flying buttresses, all covered by net vaults that

18-26A Heinrich and Peter Parler **PLAN OF THE CHURCH OF THE HOLY CROSS, SCHWÄBISCH GMÜND**

Germany. Begun in 1317 by Heinrich Parler; choir by Peter Parler begun in 1351; vaulting completed 16th century.

Credit: © Achim Bednorz, Cologne

18-26B Heinrich and Peter Parler **INTERIOR OF THE CHURCH OF THE HOLY CROSS, SCHWÄBISCH GMÜND**

Germany. Begun in 1317 by Heinrich Parler; choir by Peter Parler begun in 1351; vaulting completed 16th century.

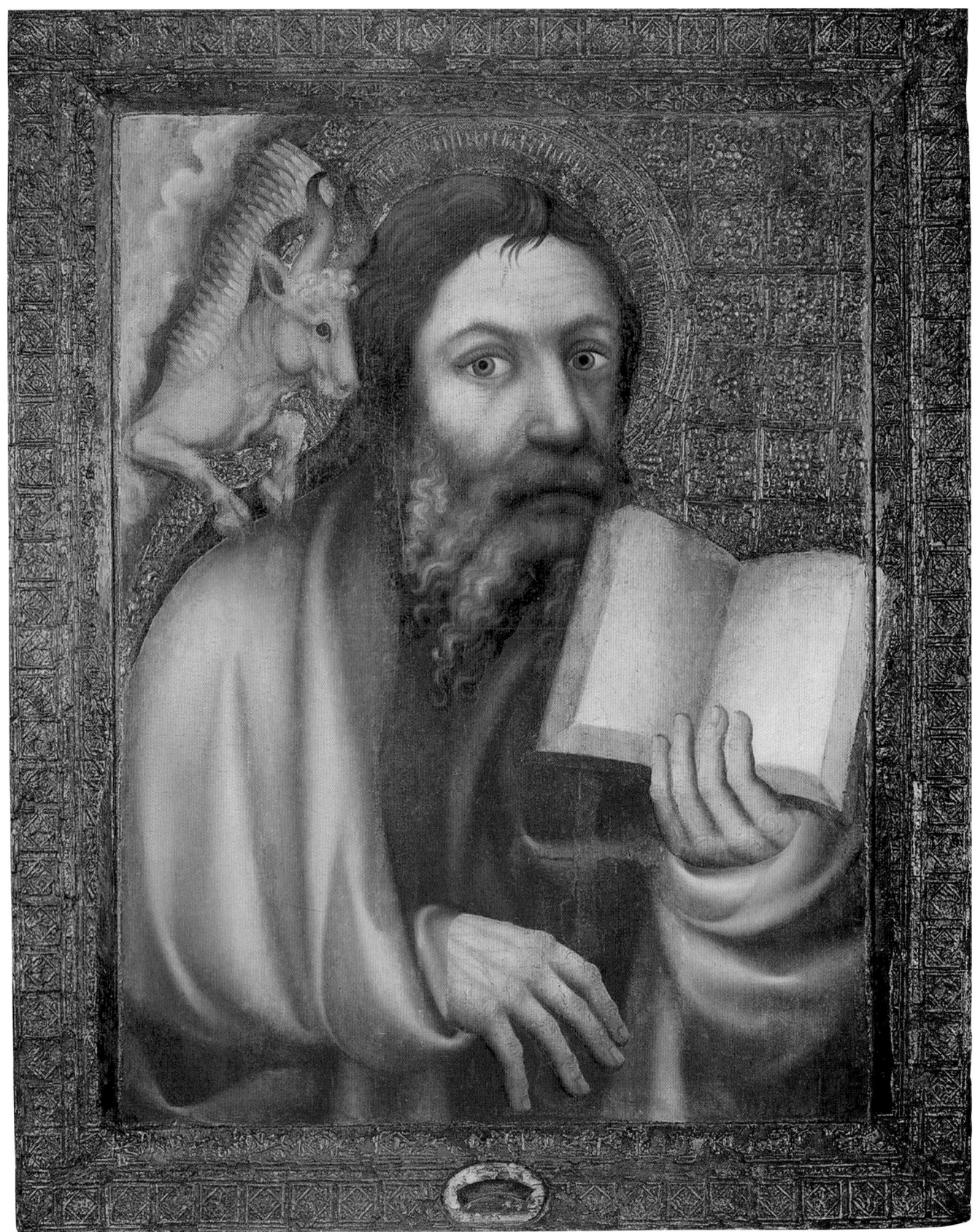

18–27 Master Theodoric **ST. LUKE**

Holy Cross Chapel, Karlstejn Castle, near Prague. 1360–1364. Paint and gold on panel, 45¼ × 37″ (115 × 94 cm).

Credit: Photo: Radovan Boček

created a continuous canopy over the space. Because of the success of projects such as this, Peter and his family became the most successful architects in the Holy Roman Empire. Their concept of space, luxurious decoration, and intricate vaulting dominated central European architecture for three generations.

MASTER THEODORIC   At Karlstejn Castle, a day's ride from Prague, Charles IV built another chapel, covering the walls with gold and precious stones as well as with paintings. There were 130 paintings of the saints serving as reliquaries, with relics inserted into their frames. Master Theodoric, the court painter, provided drawings on the wood panels, and he painted about 30 images himself. Figures are crowded into—even extend over—their frames, emphasizing their size and power. Master Theodoric was head of the Brotherhood of St. Luke, and the way that his painting of **ST. LUKE** (**FIG. 18–27**), patron saint of painters, looks out at the viewer has suggested

to scholars that this may be a self-portrait. His personal style combined a preference for substantial bodies, oversized heads and hands, dour and haunted faces, and soft, deeply modeled drapery, with a touch of grace derived from the French Gothic style. The chapel, consecrated in 1365, so pleased the emperor that in 1367 he gave the artist a farm.

Prague and the Holy Roman Empire under Charles IV had become a multicultural empire where people of different religions (Christians and Jews) and ethnic heritages (German and Slav) lived side by side. But Charles died in 1378, and without his strong central government, political and religious dissent overtook the empire. Jan Hus, dean of the philosophy faculty at Prague University and a powerful reforming preacher, denounced the immorality he saw in the Church. He was burned at the stake, becoming a martyr and Czech national hero. The Hussite Revolution in the fifteenth century ended Prague's—and Bohemia's—leadership in the arts.

Think About It

1   Compare and contrast Giotto's and Duccio's renderings of the biblical story of Christ's Raising of Lazarus (**FIGS. 18–8**, **18–11**).

2   Discuss Ambrogio Lorenzetti's engagement with secular subject matter in his frescos for Siena's Palazzo Pubblico (**FIG. 18–16**). How did these paintings relate to their sociopolitical context?

3   Discuss the circumstances surrounding the construction and decoration of the Scrovegni (Arena) Chapel, paying special attention to its relationship to the life and aspirations of its patron.

4   Choose one small work of art in this chapter that was crafted from precious materials with exceptional technical skill. Explain how it was made and how it was used. How does the work of art relate to its cultural and social contexts?

Crosscurrents

Depictions of the Virgin Mary holding the infant Jesus represent a theme that developed early in the history of European Christian art and continues to this day. Describe the relationship between the mother and child in these two examples. Characterize the difference in artistic style. How does the choice of medium contribute to the differences between them? How were they used?

FIG. 16–27

FIG. 18–18

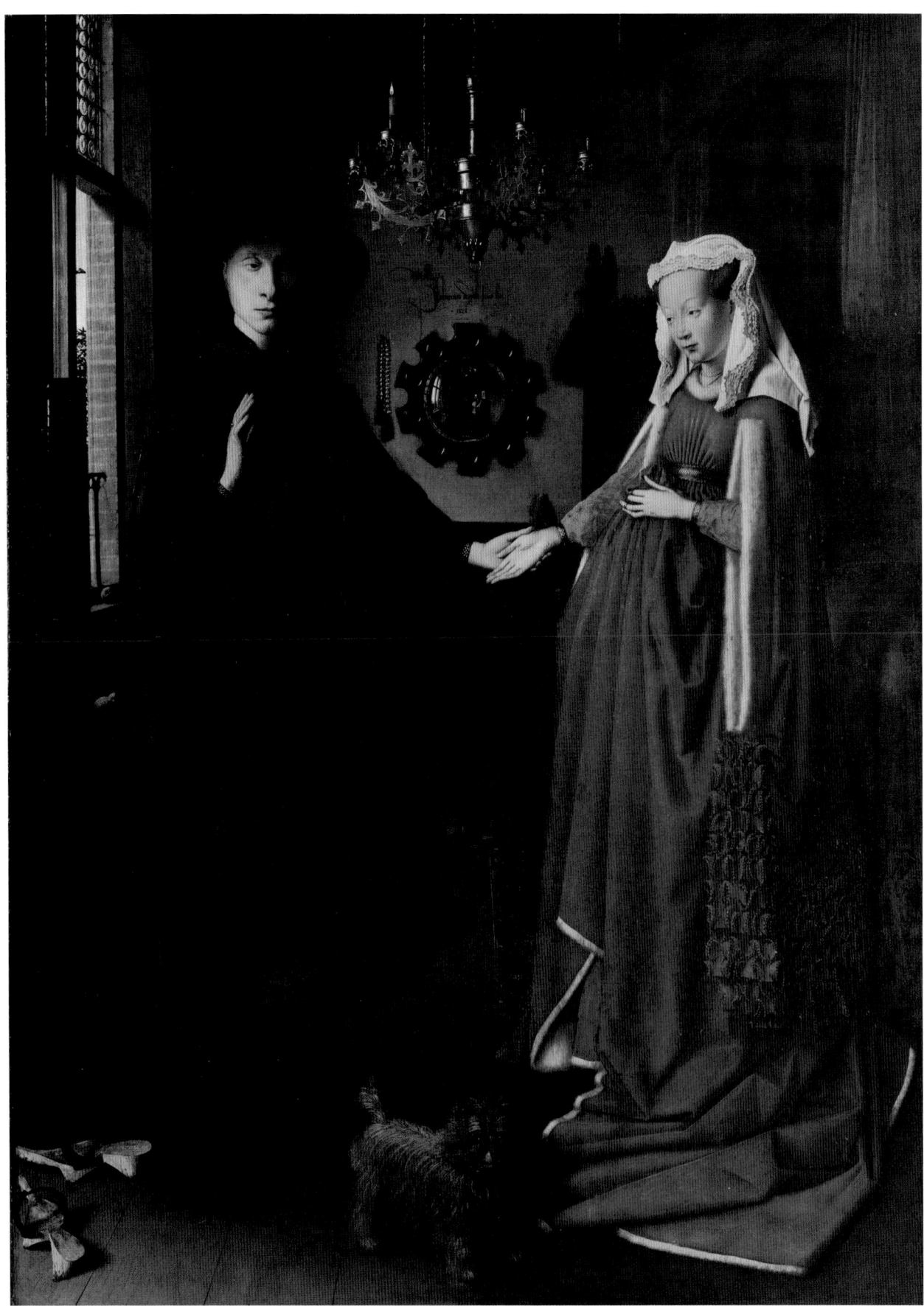

19-1 Jan van Eyck **DOUBLE PORTRAIT OF GIOVANNI ARNOLFINI AND HIS WIFE**

1434. Oil on wood panel, 33 × 22½″ (83.8 × 57.2 cm). National Gallery, London.

Chapter 19
Fifteenth-Century Art in Northern Europe

⌄ Learning Objectives

19.a Identify the visual hallmarks of fifteenth-century Northern European art for formal, technical, and expressive qualities.

19.b Interpret the meaning of works of fifteenth-century Northern European art based on their themes, subjects, and symbols.

19.c Relate fifteenth-century Northern European art and artists to their cultural, economic, and political contexts.

19.d Apply the vocabulary and concepts relevant to fifteenth-century Northern European art, artists, and art history.

19.e Interpret a work of fifteenth-century Northern European art using the art historical methods of observation, comparison, and inductive reasoning.

19.f Select visual and textual evidence in various media to support an argument or an interpretation of a work of fifteenth-century Northern European art.

Fifteenth-century Europe saw the emergence of wealthy merchants whose rise to power was fueled by individual accomplishment, rather than hereditary succession within noble families. Certainly Giovanni Arnolfini—the pasty gentleman with the extravagant hat in this double portrait (**FIG. 19-1**)—earned, rather than inherited, the right to have himself and his wife recorded by renowned artist Jan van Eyck. It was the wealth and connections he made as an Italian cloth merchant providing luxury fabrics to the Burgundian court that put him in the position to commission such a precious picture, in which both patron and painter are identified with conspicuous clarity. Giovanni's face looks more like a personal likeness than anything we have seen since ancient Rome, and not only did Jan van Eyck inscribe his name above the convex mirror ("Jan van Eyck was here 1434"), but his personal painting style also carries the stamp of authorship. The doll-like face of the woman standing next to Giovanni is less individualized. She may be lifting her skirt over her belly so she can follow Giovanni, who has taken her by the hand—or, as most modern observers assume, she may be pregnant. This painting is full of mysteries.

The identity of the couple is still open to scholarly debate, as is the nature of the subject. Is it a wedding, a betrothal, security for a shady financial deal, or a memorial to a beloved wife lost to death, perhaps in childbirth? Only the wealth of the couple is beyond dispute. They are surrounded by luxury objects: lavish bed hangings, a sumptuous chandelier, precious oriental carpet, and rare oranges, not to mention their extravagant clothing. The man wears a fur-lined, silk velvet *heuque* (sleeveless overgarment). The woman's gown not only employs more costly wool fabric than necessary to cover her slight body; the elaborate cutwork decoration and white fur lining of her sleeves is an ostentatious indicator of cost. In fact, the painting itself—probably hung in the couple's home—was an object of considerable value.

Even within its secular setting, however, the picture resonated with sacred meaning. The Church still provided spiritual grounding for men and women of the Renaissance. The crystal prayer beads hanging next to the convex mirror imply the couple's piety, and the mirror itself—a symbol of the all-seeing eye of God—is framed with a circular cycle of scenes from Christ's Passion. A figure of St. Margaret—protector of women in childbirth—is carved at the top of a post in the high-backed chair beside the bed, and the perky *affenpinscher* in the foreground may be more than a pet. In art, dogs served as symbols of fidelity and also had funerary associations, but choosing a rare, ornamental breed for inclusion here may have been yet another opportunity to express wealth.

The Northern Renaissance

What are the cultural and historical backgrounds for the Northern Renaissance?

Revitalized civic life and economic growth in the late fourteenth century gave rise to a prosperous middle class that supported scholarship, literature, and the arts. Their patronage resulted in the explosion of learning and creativity that we refer to as the Renaissance (French for "rebirth")—a term that was assigned to this period by later historians.

A major trait of the Renaissance in northern Europe was a growing, newly intense interest in the natural world. Artists observed birds, plants, and animals closely and depicted their appearance with breathtaking accuracy. They applied the same scrutiny to people and objects, modeling forms with light and shadow to give them

MAP 19–1 FIFTEENTH-CENTURY NORTHERN EUROPE

The dukes of Burgundy—whose territory included much of present-day Belgium and Luxembourg, the Netherlands, and eastern France—became the cultural and political leaders of western Europe. Their major cities of Bruges (Belgium) and Dijon (France) were centers of art and industry as well as politics.

the semblance of three-dimensionality. These carefully described subjects were situated in spatial settings, applying an intuitive perspective system by diminishing their scale as they receded into the distance. In the portrayal of landscapes—which became a northern specialty—artists used atmospheric perspective in which distant elements appear increasingly indistinct and less colorful as they approach the background. The sky, for instance, becomes paler near the horizon, and the distant landscape turns bluish-gray.

One aspect of the desire for accurate visual depictions of the natural world was a new interest in individual personalities. Fifteenth-century portraits have an astonishingly lifelike quality, combining careful—sometimes seemingly unflattering—surface description with an uncanny sense of vitality. Indeed, the individual becomes important in every sphere. More names of artists survive from the fifteenth century, for example, than in the entire span from the beginning of the Common Era to the year 1400, and some artists begin regularly to sign their work.

The new power of cities in Flanders and the greater Netherlands (present-day Belgium, Luxembourg, and the Netherlands) (**MAP 19–1**) provided a critical tension and balance with the traditional powers of royalty and the Church. Increasingly, the urban lay public sought to express personal and civic pride by sponsoring secular architecture, monuments, or paintings directed toward the community. The commonsense values of merchants formed a solid underpinning for the Northern Renaissance, but their influence remained intertwined with the continuing power of the Church and the royal and noble courts. Giovanni Arnolfini's success at commerce and negotiation provided the funding for his extraordinary double portrait (SEE FIG. 19–1), but he was able to secure the services of Jan van Eyck only with the cooperation of the duke of Burgundy.

Art for the French Ducal Courts

What characterizes the works of art in diverse media created for the ducal courts of Burgundy and France during the fifteenth century?

The dukes of Burgundy (controlling present-day east-central France, Belgium, Luxembourg, and the Netherlands) were the most powerful rulers in northern Europe for most of the fifteenth century. Their domain encompassed not only Burgundy itself but also the Flemish and Netherlandish centers of finance and trade, including the thriving cities of Ghent, Bruges, Tournai, and Brussels. The major seaport, Bruges, was the commercial center of northern Europe, rivaling the Italian city-states of Florence, Milan,

and Venice as an economic hub. In the late fourteenth century, Burgundian duke Philip the Bold (ruled 1363–1404) had acquired territory in the Netherlands—including the politically desirable region of Flanders—by marrying the daughter of the Flemish count. But although he and the dukes Jean of Berry and Louis of Anjou were brothers of King Charles V of France, their interests rarely coincided. Even the threat of a common enemy, England, during the Hundred Years' War was not a strong unifying factor, since Burgundy and England were often allied because of common financial interests in Flanders.

While the French king held court in Paris, the dukes held even more splendid courts in their own cities. The dukes of Burgundy and Berry (central France), not the king in Paris, were the real arbiters of taste. Especially influential was Jean, duke of Berry, who commissioned many works from Flemish and Netherlandish painters in the fashionable International Gothic style.

This new, composite style emerged in the late fourteenth century from the multicultural papal court in Avignon in southern France, where artists from Italy, France, and Flanders worked side by side. The International Gothic style became the prevailing manner of late fourteenth-century Europe. It is characterized by slender, gracefully posed figures whose delicate features are framed by masses of curling hair and extraordinarily complex headdresses. Noble men and women wear rich brocaded and embroidered fabrics and elaborate jewelry. Landscape and architectural settings are miniaturized; however, details of nature—leaves, flowers, insects, birds—are rendered in breathtaking detail. Spatial recession is represented by rising tiled floors in rooms that are like stage sets; fanciful mountains and meadows with high horizon lines; progressive diminution in the size of receding objects; and atmospheric perspective. Artists and patrons preferred light, bright colors and a liberal use of gold in manuscript and panel paintings, tapestries, and polychromed sculpture. International Gothic was so appealing that it endured well into the fifteenth century.

Painting and Sculpture for the Chartreuse de Champmol

One of Philip the Bold's most lavish projects was the Carthusian monastery, or *chartreuse* ("charterhouse"), at Champmol, outside Dijon, his Burgundian capital city. Land was acquired in 1377 and 1383, and construction began in 1385. The monastic church was intended to house the family's tombs, and the monks were expected to pray continuously for the souls of Philip and his family. Carthusian monasteries were particularly expensive to maintain because Carthusian monks did not provide for themselves by farming or other physical work, but instead were dedicated exclusively to prayer and solitary meditation.

MELCHIOR BROEDERLAM The duke ordered a magnificent carved and painted altarpiece (see "Altars and Altarpieces" opposite) for the Chartreuse de Champmol. The interior of the altarpiece, carved and gilded by Jacques de Baerze, depicts scenes of the Crucifixion flanked by the Adoration of the Magi and the Entombment. The exteriors of the protective shutters of this triptych were covered not by carvings but by two paintings by Melchior Broederlam (active 1381–1410) showing scenes from the life of the Virgin and the infancy of Christ (**FIG. 19-2**). Broederlam situates his closely observed, International-Style figures within fanciful, miniature architectural and landscape settings. His lavish use of brilliantly seductive colors demonstrates one of the features that made International Gothic so popular.

The archangel Gabriel greets Mary while she is at prayer. She sits in a Gothic room with a back door leading into the dark interior of a Romanesque rotunda that symbolizes the Temple of Jerusalem as a repository of the Old Law. According to legend, Mary was an attendant in the temple prior to her marriage to Joseph. The tiny enclosed garden and conspicuous pot of lilies are symbols of Mary's virginity. In International Gothic fashion, both the interior and exterior of the building are shown, and the floors are tilted up at the back to give clear views of the action. Next, in the Visitation, just outside the temple walls, the now-pregnant Mary greets her older cousin Elizabeth, who will soon give birth to John the Baptist.

On the right shutter is the Presentation in the Temple. Mary and Joseph have brought the newborn Jesus to the temple for his redemption as a first-born son and for Mary's purification, where Simeon takes the baby in his arms to bless him (Luke 2:25–32). At the far right, the Holy Family flees to Egypt to escape King Herod's order that all Jewish male infants be killed. The family travels along treacherous terrain similar to that in the Visitation scene, where a path leads viewers' eyes into the distance along a rising ground plane. Broederlam has created a sense of light and air around solid figures. Details drawn from the real world are scattered throughout the pictures—a hawk flies through the golden sky, the presented baby looks anxiously back at his mother, and Joseph drinks from a flask and carries the family belongings in a satchel over his shoulder on the journey to Egypt. The statue of a pagan god, visible at the upper right, breaks and tumbles from its pedestal as the Christ Child approaches. A new era dawns and a new religion replaces the old, among both Jews and gentiles.

19-2 Melchior Broederlam **ANNUNCIATION, VISITATION, PRESENTATION IN THE TEMPLE, AND FLIGHT INTO EGYPT**
Exterior of the wings of the altarpiece of the Chartreuse de Champmol. 1393–1399. Oil on wood panel, 5'5¾" × 4'1¼" (1.67 × 1.25 m). Musée des Beaux-Arts, Dijon.

Art and its Contexts

ALTARS AND ALTARPIECES

The altar in a Christian church symbolizes both the table of Jesus's Last Supper and the tombs of Christ and the saints. As a table, the altar is the site where priests celebrate Mass. And as a tomb, before the Reformation it traditionally contained a relic—placed in a reliquary on the altar, beneath the floor on which the altar rests, or even enclosed within the altar itself.

Altarpieces are painted or carved constructions placed at the back of or behind the altar so that altar and altarpiece appear visually to be joined. By the fifteenth century, important altarpieces had evolved into large and elaborate architectural structures filled with images and protected by movable wings that function like shutters. An altarpiece can sit on a base, called a predella. A winged altarpiece can be a **diptych**, in which two panels are hinged together; a **triptych**, in which two wings fold over a center section, forming a diptych when closed; or a **polyptych**, consisting of more than three panels.

altar and polyptych altarpiece

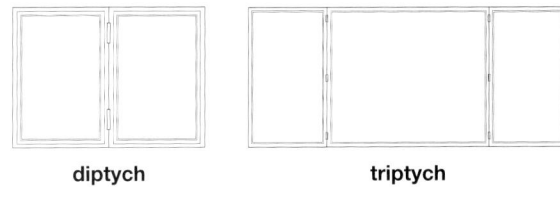

diptych   triptych

CLAUS SLUTER   Flemish sculptor Jean de Marville (active 1366–1389) initially directed the decoration of the Chartreuse, and when he died in 1389, he was succeeded by his talented assistant Claus Sluter (c. 1360–1406), from Haarlem, in Holland. Sluter's distinctive work survives in a monumental **WELL OF MOSES** carved for the main cloister (**FIG. 19-3**), begun in 1395 and left unfinished at Sluter's death.

The design of this work was complex. A pier rose from the water to support a large free-standing figure of Christ on the cross, mourned by the Virgin Mary, Mary Magdalen, and John the Evangelist. Forming a pedestal for this Crucifixion group at the viewer's eye level are life-size stone figures from the Hebrew Bible who Christians believe foretold the coming of

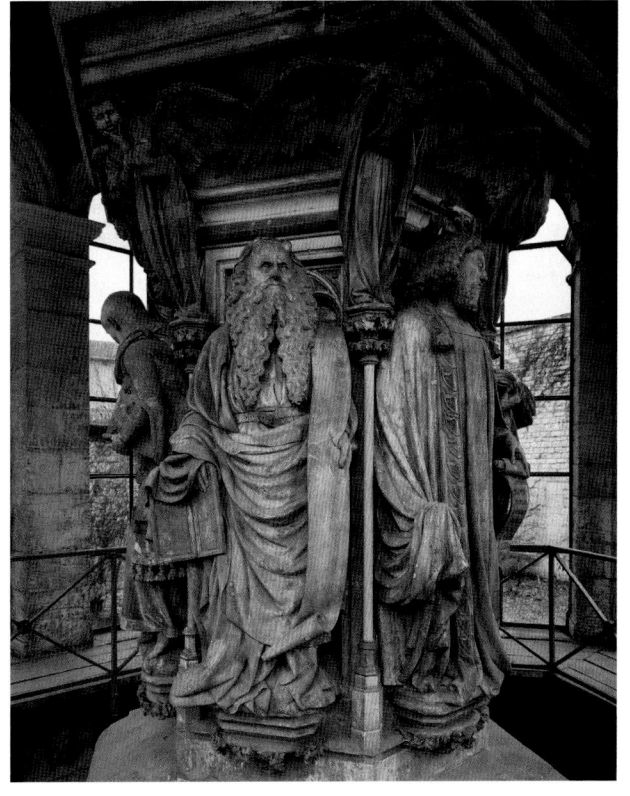

19-3 Claus Sluter **WELL OF MOSES, DETAIL OF MOSES AND DAVID**

The Chartreuse de Champmol, Dijon, France. 1395–1406. Limestone with traces of paint, height of figures about 5′8″ (1.69 m).

The sculpture's original details included metal used for buckles and even eyeglasses. It was also painted: Moses wore a gold mantle with a blue lining over a red tunic; David's gold mantle had a painted lining of ermine, and his blue tunic was covered with gold stars and wide bands of ornament.

Christ: Moses, David, and the prophets Jeremiah, Zachariah, Daniel, and Isaiah. This concept may have been inspired by contemporary mystery plays, in which prophets foretell and explain events of Christ's Passion. Sluter's patriarchs and prophets are distinct individuals, physically and psychologically. Moses's eyes blaze out from a memorable face entirely covered with a fine web of wrinkles. Even his horns are wrinkled. (These horns are traditional attributes based on a mistranslation of Exodus 34:29–35 in the Latin Vulgate Bible, where the rays of light radiating from Moses's face become horns.) A mane of curling hair and beard cascades over his heavy shoulders and chest, and an enormous cloak envelops his body. Beside him stands David in the voluminous robes of a medieval king, the personification of nobility.

Sluter looked at the human figure in a new way—as a weighty mass defined by voluminous drapery that lies in deep folds, falls in horizontal arcs and cascading lines, and both conceals and reveals the body, creating strong highlights and shadows. With the vigorous, imposing, and highly individualized figures of the *Well of Moses*, Sluter abandoned the idealized faces, elongated figures,

and vertical drapery of International Gothic. He retained, however, the detailed naturalism and rich colors (almost lost, but revealed in recent cleaning) and surfaces still preferred by his patrons.

Manuscript Illumination

Besides religious texts, wealthy patrons treasured richly illuminated secular writings such as herbals (encyclopedias of plants), health manuals, and works of history and literature. A typical manuscript page (**FIG. 19–4**) might have leafy tendrils framing the text, decorated opening initials, and perhaps a small inset picture. Only the most lavish books would have full-page miniature paintings set off with frames. The pictures in these books are conceived as windows looking into rooms or out onto landscapes with distant horizons.

THE LIMBOURG BROTHERS Among the finest Netherlandish painters at the beginning of the century were three brothers—Paul, Herman, and Jean Limbourg—their "last" name referring to their home region. At this time people generally did not have family names in the modern sense, but were known instead by their first names, often followed by a reference to their place of origin, parentage, or occupation.

About 1404, the Limbourg brothers entered the service of avid book-lover Duke Jean of Berry (1340–1416), for whom they produced their most impressive surviving work, the so-called **TRÈS RICHES HEURES** ("Very Sumptuous Book of Hours"), between 1411 and 1416. A Book of Hours, in addition to containing prayers and readings used in daily devotion, also included a calendar of holy days. The Limbourgs created full-page illustrations for the calendar in the *Très Riches Heures*. For each month, subjects including both peasant labors and aristocratic pleasures appeared in a framed lower field, while elaborate calendar devices, with the chariot of the sun and the zodiac symbols, filled a

19–4 PAGE WITH A MINIATURE PAINTING OF THAMYRIS

From Giovanni Boccaccio's *De Claris Mulieribus* (*Concerning Famous Women*). 1402. Ink and tempera on vellum, 14 × 9½″ (35.5 × 24 cm). Bibliothèque Nationale, Paris.

This page from a French edition of a work by the Italian author Boccaccio entitled *Concerning Famous Women* includes a picture of Thamyris, an artist of antiquity, at work in her studio. She appears in fifteenth-century dress, painting an image of the Virgin and Child. At the right, an assistant grinds and mixes her colors. In the foreground, her brushes and paints are laid out neatly and conveniently on a table.

Credit: Bibliothèque nationale de France

semicircular area on the upper part of the page. Like most European artists of the time, the Limbourgs showed the working class in a light acceptable to aristocrats—that is, either happily working for the nobles' benefit or displaying an uncouth lifestyle for aristocratic amusement. At times, however, the peasants seem to be enjoying the pleasures of their leisure moments.

In the February page (FIG. 19-5), farm folks relax before a fire. Although many country people at this time lived in hovels, this farm looks comfortable and well maintained, with timber-framed buildings, a row of beehives, a sheepfold, and tidy woven-wattle fences. In the distance are a village and church. Within this scene, although all are much lower in social standing than the duke, there is still a hierarchy of class. Largest in scale and most elegantly dressed is the woman closest to us, perhaps the owner of the farm, who carefully lifts her overgarment with both hands as she warms herself. She shares her fire with a couple, smaller because they are farther away, who wear more modest clothing and are considerably less well behaved, especially the man, who exposes himself as he lifts his clothing to take advantage of the fire's warmth.

One of the most remarkable aspects of this painting is the way it conveys the feeling of cold winter weather: the heavy sky and bare trees, the soft snow and huddled sheep, the steamy breath of the worker blowing on his hands, and the comforting smoke curling from the farmhouse chimney. The artists employ several International Gothic conventions: the high placement of the **horizon line**, the small size of trees and buildings in relation to people, and the cutaway view of the house showing both interior and exterior. The muted palette is sparked with touches of yellowish-orange, blue, and bright red, including the man's turban at the lower left. Scale relationships seem consistent with our experience in the natural world since as the landscape recedes, the size of figures and buildings diminishes progressively from foreground to background.

In contrast, the illustration for the other winter month—January—depicts an aristocratic household (FIG. 19-6). The duke of Berry himself sits behind a table laden with food and expensive tableware, presiding over his New Year's feast and surrounded by servants and allies. His chamberlain invites smartly dressed courtiers to greet the duke (the words written overhead say "approach"),

19-5 Paul, Herman, and Jean Limbourg **FEBRUARY: LIFE IN THE COUNTRY, TRÈS RICHES HEURES**
1411–1416. Colors and ink on parchment, 11⅜ × 8¼″ (29 × 21 cm). Musée Condé, Chantilly, France.

Credit: Photo © RMN-Grand Palais (domaine de Chantilly)/René-Gabriel Ojéda

19-6 Paul, Herman, and Jean Limbourg **JANUARY: THE DUKE OF BERRY AT TABLE, TRÈS RICHES HEURES**
1411–1416. Colors and ink on parchment, 11⅜ × 8¼″ (29 × 21 cm). Musée Condé, Chantilly, France.

Credit: Photo © RMN-Grand Palais (domaine de Chantilly)/René-Gabriel Ojéda who is singled out visually by the red cloth of honor with his heraldic arms—swans and the lilies of France—hanging over him and by a large fire screen that circles his head like a secular halo. Tapestries with battle scenes cover the walls. Such luxury objects attest to the wealth of this great patron of the arts, a striking contrast to the farm life depicted in February, encountered when turning to the next page of the book.

THE MARY OF BURGUNDY PAINTER   One of the finest painters of Books of Hours later in the century was an artist known as the Mary of Burgundy Painter—so called because he painted a Book of Hours for Mary of Burgundy (1457–1482), the only child of Charles the Bold. Within a full-page miniature in a book only 7½ by 5¼ inches, earthly reality and a religious vision have been rendered equally tangible (**FIG. 19–7**). The painter conjures up a complex pictorial space. We look not only through the "window" of the illustration's frame, but also through an actual window in the wall of the room depicted in the foreground of the painting. The artist shows considerable virtuosity in representing these worlds. Spatial recession leads the

19–7 Mary of Burgundy Painter **MARY AT HER DEVOTIONS, HOURS OF MARY OF BURGUNDY**
Before 1482. Colors and ink on parchment, size of image 7½ × 5¼" (19.1 × 13.3 cm). Österreichische Nationalbibliothek, Vienna.

Credit: © 2016. DeAgostini Picture Libary/Scala, Florence

viewer into the far reaches of the church interior, past the Virgin and the gilded altarpiece in the sanctuary to two people conversing in the far distance. The filmy veil covering Mary of Burgundy's steeple headdress is exquisitely described, as is the transparency of the glass vase, and the distinctive bull's-eye glass (circular panes whose center "lump" was formed by the glassblower's pontil) filling the foreshortened, open window.

Mary of Burgundy appears twice. She is seated in the foreground by a window reading from, or contemplating a picture within, her Book of Hours, held carefully and protected by a lush green cloth, perhaps from the small dog cuddled into her lap. She appears again in the background, within the representation of the personal vision inspired by her private meditations. A glorious Gothic church may form the setting for her vision, but it does not result from attendance at Mass or the direction of a priest. She experiences it in private, a reward for her personal faith. Christians were encouraged in this period to imagine themselves participating in biblical stories and sacred events so they could personally feel the experiences of the protagonists. Secluded in her private space and surrounded by devotional aids on the window ledge—book, rosary, and symbolic flowers (carnations symbolized the nails of the Crucifixion, the irises Mary's sorrow)—it seems that Mary of Burgundy is doing just that. In her vision, she kneels with attendants and angels in front of a gracefully human Virgin and Child.

Textiles

In the fifteenth and sixteenth centuries, the best European tapestries came from Flanders. Major weaving centers at Brussels, Tournai, and Arras produced intricately woven wall hangings for royal and aristocratic patrons across Europe, important church officials including the pope, and even town councils. Among the most common subjects were foliage and flower patterns, scenes from the lives of the saints, and themes from Classical mythology and history, such as the Battle of Troy seen hanging on the walls of Duke Jean of Berry's reception room (SEE FIG. 19-6). Tapestries provided both insulation and decoration for the stone walls of castle halls, churches, and municipal buildings, and because they were much more expensive than wall or panel paintings, they also showed off the owners' wealth. They were also portable, a valuable quality as courts moved from residence to residence.

The price of a tapestry depended on the artists involved, the work required, and the materials used. Rarely was a fine, commissioned series woven only with wool; instead, tapestry producers enhanced the weaving with silk, and with silver and gold threads that must have glittered on the walls, especially at night, illuminated by flickering lamps or candles. Because silver and gold threads were made of silk wrapped with real silver and gold, people later burned many tapestries to retrieve the precious materials. As a result, few royal tapestries in France survived the French Revolution. If a greater percentage had survived, these luxurious and monumental textile wall paintings would surely figure more prominently in the history of art.

THE UNICORN TAPESTRY   Tapestries were often produced in series. One of the best known is the 1495–1505 "Hunt of the Unicorn" series. Four of the seven surviving hangings present scenes of people and animals set against a dense field of trees and flowers, with a distant view of a castle, as in the **UNICORN IS FOUND AT THE FOUNTAIN** (**FIG. 19–8**). The unusually fine condition of the tapestry allows us to appreciate its rich colors, the subtlety in

modeling the faces, the tonal variations in the animals' fur, and even the depiction of reflections in the water. The technical skill of its weavers is astonishing.

In tapestry, designs are woven directly into the fabric. The Unicorn tapestries seem to have been woven on huge, horizontal looms, where weavers interwove fine weft yarn of wool and silk—dyed a multitude of colors from the creative combination of three vegetal dyes—onto the parallel strands of the coarser wool warp. Weavers worked from behind what would be the front surface of the finished tapestry, following the design on a full-scale cartoon laid on the floor under the loom. They could only see the actual effect of their work by checking the front with mirrors. Making a tapestry panel this large was a collaborative effort that required the organizational skills of a talented production manager and five or six weavers working side

19–8 UNICORN IS FOUND AT THE FOUNTAIN
From the "Hunt of the Unicorn" tapestry series. c. 1495–1505. Wool, silk, and silver- and gilt-wrapped thread (13–21 warp threads per inch), 12'1" × 12'5" (3.68 × 3.78 m). Metropolitan Museum of Art, New York. Gift of John D. Rockefeller Jr., The Cloisters Collection, 1937 (37.80.2).

19–9 COPE OF THE ORDER OF THE GOLDEN FLEECE
Flemish. Mid 15th century. Cloth with gold and colored silk embroidery, 5′4⁹⁄₁₆″ × 10′9⁵⁄₁₆″ (1.64 × 3.3 m). Imperial Treasury, Vienna.

Credit: © KHM-Museumsverband

by side on a single loom. What is so extraordinary about their work is the skillful way they created curving lines— since the tapestry process is based on a rectilinear network of threads, curves have to be simulated—and the lighting effects of shading and reflections, which require using yarn in the same hue with a multitude of values.

The subject of this series is the unicorn, a mythical, horselike animal with a single long, twisted horn and supernatural speed; it could only be captured by a virgin, to whom it came willingly. Thus, the unicorn became both a symbol of the Incarnation (Christ is the unicorn captured by the Virgin Mary) and also a metaphor for romantic love (SEE FIG. 18–21). The capture and killing of the unicorn was also equated with Christ's death on the cross to save humanity.

The natural world represented so splendidly in this tapestry also has potential symbolic meaning. For instance, lions represented faith, courage, mercy, and even—because they were thought to breathe life into their cubs—the Resurrection of Christ. The stag is another Resurrection symbol (it sheds and grows its antlers) and a protector against poisonous serpents and evil in general. Even today we see rabbits as symbols of fertility, and dogs of fidelity. Many of the easily identifiable flowers and trees also carry both religious and secular meanings. There is a strong theme of marriage: the strawberry is a common symbol of sexual love; the pansy means remembrance; and the periwinkle, a cure for spiteful feelings and jealousy. The trees include oak for fidelity, beech for nobility, holly for protection against evil, hawthorn for the power of love, and pomegranate and orange for fertility.

COPE OF THE ORDER OF THE GOLDEN FLEECE Surviving vestments of the Order of the Golden Fleece are remarkable examples of Flemish textiles. The Order of the Golden Fleece was an honorary fraternity founded by Duke Philip the Good of Burgundy in 1430 with 23 knights chosen for their moral character and bravery. Religious services were an integral part of the order's meetings, and opulent liturgical and clerical objects were created for the purpose.

The surface of the sumptuous cope (cloak) in **FIGURE 19–9** is divided into compartments filled with the standing figures of saints. At the top of the neck edge, as if presiding over the company, is an enthroned figure of Christ, flanked along the front edge by scholar-saints in their studies. The embroiderers worked with great precision to match the illusionistic effects of contemporary Flemish painting; gold threads are sewn to the surface using unevenly spaced colored silk threads, creating images and an iridescent effect.

Painting in Flanders

What innovative features characterize the Northern Renaissance oil painting tradition established by the Master of Flémalle, Jan van Eyck, Rogier van der Weyden, and their followers?

A strong economy based on the textile industry and international trade provided stability and money for a rapid Flemish flowering in the arts. Civic groups, town councils, and wealthy merchants were important patrons in the Netherlands, where cities were self-governing and largely independent of landed nobility. Guilds oversaw nearly every aspect of their members' lives, and high-ranking guild members served on town councils and helped run city governments. Even experienced artists who moved from one city to another usually had to work as assistants in a local workshop until they met the requirements for guild membership.

Throughout most of the fifteenth century, Flemish art and artists were greatly admired across Europe. Artists from abroad studied Flemish works, and their influence spread even to Italy. Only at the end of the fifteenth century did the broad preference for Netherlandish painting give way to a taste for the new styles of art and architecture developing in Italy.

Flemish panel painters preferred using an oil medium rather than the tempera paint that was standard in the works of Italian artists. Since it was slow to dry, **oil paint** provided flexibility, and it had a luminous quality. Like manuscript illuminations, Flemish panel paintings provided a window onto a scene rendered with keen attention to describing individual features—people, objects, or aspects of the natural world—with consummate skill.

The Master of Flémalle

Some of the earliest and most outstanding artists using the new Flemish style were painters in the workshop of an artist known as the Master of Flémalle, identified by some art historians as Robert Campin (active 1406–1444). From about 1425 to 1430, these artists painted the triptych now called the **MÉRODE ALTARPIECE**, after its later owners (**FIG. 19–10**). Its relatively small size—slightly over 2 feet tall and about 4 feet wide with the wings open—suggests that it was probably made for a small private chapel.

The Annunciation of the central panel is set in a Flemish home and incorporates common household objects, many invested with symbolic religious meaning. The lilies in the **majolica** (glazed earthenware) pitcher on the table, for example, often appear in Annunciations to symbolize Mary's virginity. The hanging water pot in the background niche refers to Mary's purity and her role as the vessel for the Incarnation of God (God assuming human form). What seems at first to be a towel hung over the prominent, hinged rack next to the niche may be a tallis (Jewish prayer shawl). Some art historians have referred to these as "hidden" or "disguised" symbols because they are treated as a normal part of the setting, but their routine religious meanings would have been obvious to the intended audience.

Some have interpreted the narrative in the central panel as the moment immediately following Mary's acceptance of her destiny. A rush of wind riffles the pages of the book and snuffs the candle (the flame, symbolic of God's divinity, extinguished at the moment he takes human form) as a tiny figure of Christ carrying a cross descends on a ray of light. Having accepted the miracle of the Incarnation, Mary reads her Bible while sitting humbly on the footrest of the long bench. Her position becomes a symbol of her submission to God's will. Other art historians have proposed that the scene represents the moment just prior to the Annunciation. In this view, Mary is not yet aware of Gabriel's presence, and the rushing wind is the result of the angel's rapid entry into the room, where he appears before her, half kneeling and raising his hand in salutation.

In the left wing of the triptych, the donors—presumably a married couple—kneel in an enclosed garden, another symbol of Mary's virginity, before the open door of

Technique
OIL PAINTING

Whereas Italian artists favored tempera, using it almost exclusively for panel painting until the end of the fifteenth century, Flemish artists preferred oil paints, in which powdered pigments are suspended in linseed—and occasionally walnut—oil. They exploited the potential of this medium during the fifteenth century with a virtuosity that has never been surpassed.

Tempera has to be applied in a very precise manner because it dries almost as quickly as it is applied. Shading is restricted to careful, overlapping strokes in graded tones ranging from white and gray to dark brown and black. Because tempera is opaque—light striking its surface does not penetrate to lower layers of color and reflect back—the resulting surface is **matte**, or dull, taking on a sheen only if burnished or overlaid with varnish.

On the other hand, oil paint is a viscous medium which takes hours or even days to dry, and while it is still wet changes can be made easily. Once applied, the paint has time to smooth out as it dries, erasing traces of individual brushstrokes on the surface of the finished panel. Perhaps even more importantly, oil paint is translucent when applied in very thin layers, called glazes. Light striking a surface built up of glazes penetrates to the lower layers and is reflected back, creating the appearance of an interior glow. These luminous effects enabled artists to capture jewel-like colors and the varying effects of light on changing textures, enhancing the illusion that viewers are looking at real objects rather than their painted imitation.

So brilliant was Jan van Eyck's use of oil paint that he was credited by Giorgio Vasari with inventing the medium. Actually, it had been in use since at least the twelfth century, when it was described in Theophilus Presbyter's *De Diversis Artibus* (see "Stained-Glass Windows" in Chapter 17 on page 512).

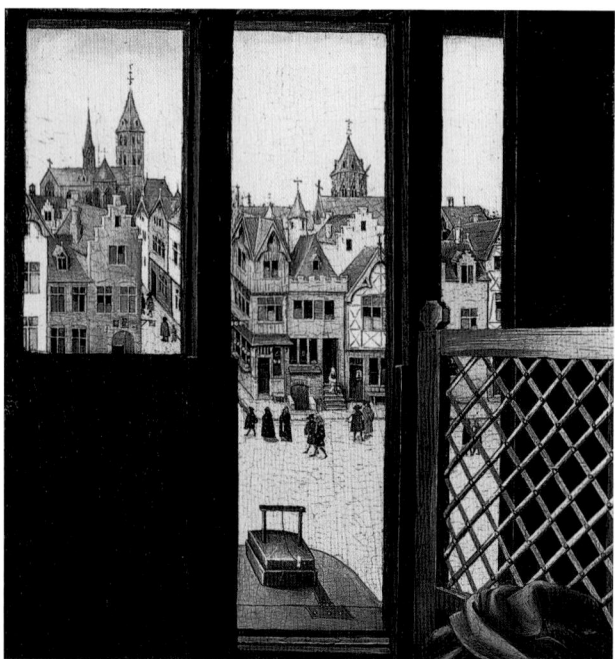

19–11 Workshop of the Master of Flémalle **A FLEMISH CITY**
Detail of the right wing of the Mérode Altarpiece (FIG. 19–10).

the house where the Annunciation is taking place, implying that the scene is a vision engendered by their faithful meditations, comparable to the vision in the Hours of
Mary of Burgundy (SEE FIG. 19–7). Such presentations, very
popular with Flemish patrons, allowed those who commissioned a religious work to appear in the same space
and time, and often on the same scale, as religious figures.
The donors' eyes, which seem unfocused, are directed not
outward but inward, intent on the spiritual exercise of
imagining their own presence within this sacred narrative.

On the right wing, Joseph is working in his carpentry workshop. A prosperous Flemish city is exquisitely
detailed in the view through the shop window, with people going about their daily business (FIG. 19–11). Even here
there is religious symbolism. On the windowsill of Joseph's
shop and on the workbench beside him are mousetraps,
which fifteenth-century viewers would understand as references to Christ as the bait in a trap set by God to catch
Satan. Joseph is drilling holes in a small board used as a
drainboard for making wine, calling to mind the Eucharist
and Christ's Passion.

The complex and consistent treatment of light in the
altarpiece represents a major preoccupation of Flemish

19–10 Workshop of the Master of Flémalle **MÉRODE ALTARPIECE (OPEN), (TRIPTYCH OF THE ANNUNCIATION)**

c. 1425–1430s. Oil on wood panel, center 25¼ × 24⅞″ (64.1 × 63.2 cm); each wing approx. 25⅜ × 10¾″ (64.5 × 27.6 cm). Metropolitan Museum of Art, New York. The Cloisters Collection, 1956 (56.70).

In the late nineteenth century, this triptych was associated with a group of stylistically related works and assigned to an artist called the Master of Flémalle, who was subsequently identified by some art historians as a documented artist named Robert Campin. Recently, however, experts have questioned this association and proposed that the triptych we now see was the work of several artists working within the workshop that created the stylistic cluster. Current opinion holds that the *Annunciation* was initially created as an independent panel, and shortly afterward expanded into a triptych with the addition of the side panels under the patronage of the donor in the foreground at left. Finally, sometime later in the 1430s, the figure of his wife was added behind him, presumably on the occasion of his marriage.

painters. The strongest light comes from an unseen source at upper left in front of the **picture plane** (the picture's front surface), as if sunlight were entering through the open front of the room. More light comes from the rear windows, and painted, linear rays come from the round window at left, a symbolic vehicle for Jesus's descent. Jesus seems to slide down the rays of light linking God with Mary, carrying the cross of human salvation over his shoulder. The light falling on the Virgin's lap emphasizes this connection, and the transmission of the symbolic light through a transparent panel of glass (which remains intact) recalls the virginal nature of Jesus's conception.

Jan van Eyck

In 1425, Jan van Eyck (active 1420s–1441) became court painter to Duke Philip the Good of Burgundy (ruled 1419–1467), who was the uncle of the king of France and one of the most sophisticated men in Europe. Philip made Jan one of his confidential employees and even sent him on a diplomatic mission to Portugal, charged with painting a portrait of a prospective bride for the duke. Philip alluded to Jan's remarkable technical skills in a letter of 1434–1435, saying that he could find no other painter equal to his taste and abilities in art and science. So brilliant was Jan's use of oil glazes that he was mistakenly credited with the invention of oil painting (see "Oil Painting" on page 585).

Jan's 1433 portrait of a **MAN IN A RED TURBAN** (**FIG. 19–12**) projects a particularly strong sense of personality, and the signed and dated frame also bears Jan's personal

motto—"As I can, [but not as I would]"—in Greek letters at the top. Since these letters also form an anagram of his own name, most scholars see this painting as a self-portrait in which physical appearance seems recorded in a magnifying mirror. We see the stubble of a day's growth of beard on his chin and cheeks, and every carefully described wrinkle around the artist's eyes, reddened from the strain of his work and reflecting light that seems to emanate from our own space. That same light source gives the inscriptions the **trompe l'oeil** ("trick of the eye") sense of having been

19–12 Jan van Eyck **MAN IN A RED TURBAN**

1433. Oil on wood panel, 13⅛ × 10¼″ (33.3 × 25.8 cm). National Gallery, London.

engraved into the frame, heightening the illusionistic wizardry of Jan's painting.

THE GHENT ALTARPIECE In Jan van Eyck's lifetime, one of his most famous works was a huge polyptych with a very complicated and learned theological program that he painted (perhaps in collaboration with his brother Hubert) for a chapel in what is now the Cathedral of St. Bavo in Ghent; the piece is now known as the **GHENT ALTARPIECE** (**FIG. 19-13**). Jan's artistic wizardry is magnificently demonstrated in the three-dimensional mass of the figures, the volume and remarkable surface realism of the draperies, and the scrupulous attention to luminous details of textures as variable as jewels and human flesh. He has carefully controlled the lighting within this multi-panel ensemble to make it appear that the objects represented are illuminated by sunlight coming through the window of the chapel where it was meant to be installed. Jan's painting is firmly grounded in the terrestrial world, even when he is rendering a visionary subject.

An inscription on the frame of the Ghent Altarpiece seems to identify both Jan and Hubert van Eyck as its artists: "The painter Hubert van Eyck, greater than whom no one was found, began [this work]; and Jan, his brother, second in art, having carried through the task at the expense of Jodocus Vyd, invites you by this verse, on the sixth of May [1432], to look at what has been done."

Many art historians believe Hubert began this altarpiece, and after Hubert's death in 1426 Jan completed it, when free of ducal responsibilities in 1430–1432. Others believe the entire painting was produced by Jan and his workshop, Hubert perhaps being responsible for the frame. At least the commission and situation are clear. Jodocus Vijd, who appears with his wife Isabella Borluut on the outside of the polyptych's two shutters (**FIG. 19-14**), commanded the work. One of a wealthy family of financiers, Jodocus was a city official in Ghent comparable to mayor in 1433–1434; the altarpiece was part of a renovation he funded for the family chapel at the parish church of St. John (now the Cathedral of St. Bavo). He also endowed

19-13 Jan and Hubert (?) van Eyck **GHENT ALTARPIECE (OPEN), ADORATION OF THE MYSTIC LAMB**
Completed 1432. Oil on panel, 11′5¾″ × 15′1½″ (3.5 × 4.6 m). Cathedral of St. Bavo, Ghent.

Credit: © akg-images/Erich Lessing

daily Masses in the chapel for the salvation of himself, his wife, and their ancestors.

When the altarpiece was closed (SEE FIG. 19–14), the exterior of the shutters displayed the striking likenesses of the donor couple kneeling to face painted statues of John the Baptist (patron of Ghent) and John the Evangelist (patron of this church) that recall those on Sluter's *Well of Moses* (SEE FIG. 19–3). Above this row is an expansive rendering of the Annunciation—whose somber color scheme coordinates with the *grisaille* statues below—situated in an upstairs room that looks out over a panoramic cityscape. As in Simone Martini's *Annunciation* altarpiece (SEE FIG. 10 10), the words that issue from Gabriel's mouth ("Hail, full of grace, the Lord is with thee") appear on the painting's surface, and here there is Mary's response as well ("Behold the handmaid of the Lord"), only it is painted upside down since it is directed to God, who hovers above her head as the dove of the Holy Spirit. Prophets and sibyls perch in the irregular compartments at the top, unfurling scrolls recording their predictions of Christ's coming.

19–14 Jan and Hubert (?) van Eyck **GHENT ALTARPIECE (CLOSED), ANNUNCIATION WITH DONORS**
Completed 1432. Oil on panel, height 11′5″ (3.48 m). Cathedral of St. Bavo, Ghent.

Credit: © akg-images/Erich Lessing

When the shutters were opened (SEE FIG. 19–13) on Sundays and feast days, the mood changed. The effect is no longer muted, but rich in both color and implied sound. Dominating the altarpiece by size, central location, and brilliant color is the enthroned, red-robed figure of God, wearing the triple papal crown, with an earthly crown at his feet, and flanked by the Virgin Mary and John the Baptist holding open books. To either side are first angel musicians and then Adam and Eve, represented as lifelike nudes. Adam seems to have been painted from a model, from whom Jan reproduced even the "farmer's tan" of his hands and face. Eve displays clear features of the female anatomy; the pigmented line running downward from her navel appears frequently during pregnancy. Each of the three themes of the upper register—God with Mary and John, musical angels, and Adam and Eve—is set in a distinct space: the holy trio in a golden shrine, angels against a blue sky, Adam and Eve in shallow stone niches.

The five lower panels present a unified field. A vast landscape with meadows, woods, and distant cities is set against a continuous horizon. A diverse array of saints—apostles, martyrs, confessors, virgins, hermits, pilgrims, warriors, judges—assembles to adore the Lamb of God as described in the book of Revelation. The Lamb stands on an altar, blood flowing into a chalice, ultimately leading to the fountain of life.

The Ghent Altarpiece became a famous work of art almost as soon as it was completed. To celebrate Duke Philip the Good's visit to the city in 1458, citizens of Ghent welcomed him with *tableaux vivants* (living pictures) of its scenes. German artist Albrecht Dürer traveled to Ghent to see the altarpiece in 1521. During the French occupation of Flanders in 1794 it was transferred to Paris (returned in 1815), and during World War II it was confiscated by the Nazis. It is now displayed within a secure glass case in the baptismal chapel of the church for which it was made.

THE ARNOLFINI DOUBLE PORTRAIT The Ghent altarpiece may have been Jan's most famous painting during his lifetime, but his best-known painting today is the distinctive double portrait of Giovanni Arnolfini and his wife encountered earlier (SEE FIG. 19–1). Early interpreters saw this fascinating work as depicting a wedding or betrothal. Above the mirror on the back wall, the artist inscribed the words *Johannes de eyck fuit hic 1434* ("Jan van Eyck was here 1434"). More normal as a signature would have been, "Jan van Eyck made this," so the words "was here" might suggest that Jan served as a witness to a matrimonial episode portrayed in the painting. Jan is not the only witness recorded in the painting. The convex mirror between the figures reflects not only the back of the couple but a front view of two visitors standing in the doorway, entering the room. Perhaps one of them is the artist himself.

New research has complicated the developing interpretation of this painting by revealing that the Giovanni Arnolfini traditionally identified as the man in this painting married his wife Giovanna Cenami only in 1447, long after the date on the wall and Jan van Eyck's own death. One scholar has proposed that the picture is actually a prospective portrait of Giovanni and Giovanna's marriage in the future, painted in 1434 to secure the early transfer of the dowry from her father to her future husband. Others have more recently suggested that the man portrayed here is a different Giovanni Arnolfini, accompanied either by his first wife, Costanza Trenta, who died the year before this picture was painted—which would make the painting a memorial portrait—or by a hypothetical second wife whose name is unknown. The true meaning of this masterpiece may remain a mystery, but it is doubtful that scholars will stop trying to solve it.

Rogier van der Weyden

Little as we know about Jan van Eyck, we know even less about the life of Rogier van der Weyden (c. 1400–1464). Not a single existing work of art bears his name. He may have studied under the Master of Flémalle, but the relationship is not completely clear. Rogier established himself in 1432 as an independent master in Tournai; at the peak of his career he maintained a large workshop in Brussels, where he was the official city painter, attracting apprentices and shop assistants from as far away as Italy. To establish the stylistic characteristics of Rogier's art, scholars have turned to a painting of the **DEPOSITION** (**FIG. 19–15**), an altarpiece commissioned by the Louvain crossbowmen's guild (crossbows can be seen in the tracery painted in the upper corners) sometime before 1443, the date of the earliest known copy of it by another artist.

19–15 Rogier van der Weyden **DEPOSITION**
From an altarpiece commissioned by the crossbowmen's guild, Louvain, Belgium. Before 1443, possibly c. 1435–1438. Oil on wood panel, 7'2⅝" × 8'7⅛" (2.2 × 2.62 m). Museo del Prado, Madrid.

19–16 Rogier van der Weyden
**ST. LUKE DRAWING THE VIRGIN
AND CHILD**
c. 1435–1440. Oil and tempera on wood
panel, 54¼ × 43⅝″ (137.7 × 110.8 cm).
Museum of Fine Arts, Boston.

Credit: Photograph © 2017 Museum of Fine Arts,
Boston

The Deposition was a popular theme in the fifteenth century
because of its potential for dramatic,
personally engaging portrayal.
Rogier sets the act of removing
Jesus's body from the cross on the
shallow stage of a gilt wooden box,
just like the case of a carved and
painted altarpiece. The ten solid,
three-dimensional figures, however,
are not simulations of polychromed
wood carving, but near-life-size renderings of human figures who seem
to press forward into the viewer's
space, allowing no escape from the
forceful expressions of grief. Jesus's
friends seem real, with their portraitlike faces and scrupulously
described contemporary dress, as
they remove his body from the cross
for burial. Jesus's corpse dominates the center of the composition,
drooping in a languid curve framed
by jarringly thin, angular arms.
His pose is echoed by the rhyming
form of the swooning Virgin. It is as
if mother and son share in the redemptive passion of his
death on the cross, encouraging viewers to identify with
them or to join their assembled companions. Although
united by sorrow, the mourning figures react in different
ways, from the intensity of Mary Magdalen at far right,
wringing her hands, to John the Evangelist's blank stare
at left as he reaches to support the collapsing Virgin, to the
anguish of the woman behind him, mopping her eyes with
the edge of her veil.

Rogier's choice of color and pattern balances and
enhances his composition. The complexity of the gold brocade worn by Joseph of Arimathea, who offered his new
tomb for the burial, and the contorted pose and vivid dress
of Mary Magdalen increase the visual impact of the right
side of the panel to counter the pictorial weight of the
larger number of figures at the left. The palette contrasts
subtle, slightly muted colors with brilliant expanses of
blue and red, while white accents focus the viewer's attention on the main subjects. The whites of the winding cloth
and the tunic of the youth on the ladder set off Jesus's pale

body, as the white turban and shawl emphasize the ashen
face of Mary.

Another work by Rogier, painted at about the same
time as the *Deposition*, is both quieter and more personal.
It represents the evangelist St. Luke executing a preparatory drawing for a painting of the Virgin and Child, who
seem to have materialized to pose for him (**FIG. 19–16**). The
painting is based on a legend with origins in sixth-century
Byzantium of a miraculous appearance of the Virgin and
Child to Luke so he could record their appearance and
pass on his authentic witness to his Christian followers.
Rogier's version takes place in a carefully defined interior
space that opens onto a garden, and from there into a distant vista of urban life, before dissolving into the countryside through which a winding river guides our exploration
all the way to the horizon. The Virgin is preoccupied with
nursing her baby, who has pulled away from her breast,
smiling and flexing his hand—familiar gestures of actual
nursing babies. Luke, half-kneeling, captures the scene in
a **silverpoint** sketch, a common preliminary step used by

A Closer Look

A GOLDSMITH IN HIS SHOP

The coat of arms of the dukes of Guelders hangs from a chain around this man's neck, leading some to speculate that the woman, who is the more active of the pair, is Mary of Guelders, niece of Duke Philip the Good, who married King James II of the Scots the same year this picture was painted.

Goldsmiths were expected to perform all their transactions, including the weighing of gold, in public view to safeguard against dishonesty. Here the scales tip toward the couple, perhaps an allusion to the scales of the Last Judgment, which always tip to the side of the righteous.

Three types of coin rest on the shop counter: "florins" from Mainz, "angels" from English king Henry VI's French territories, and "riders" minted under Philip the Good. Such diversity of currency could show the goldsmith's cosmopolitanism, or they could indicate his participation in money changing, since members of that profession belonged to the same guild as goldsmiths.

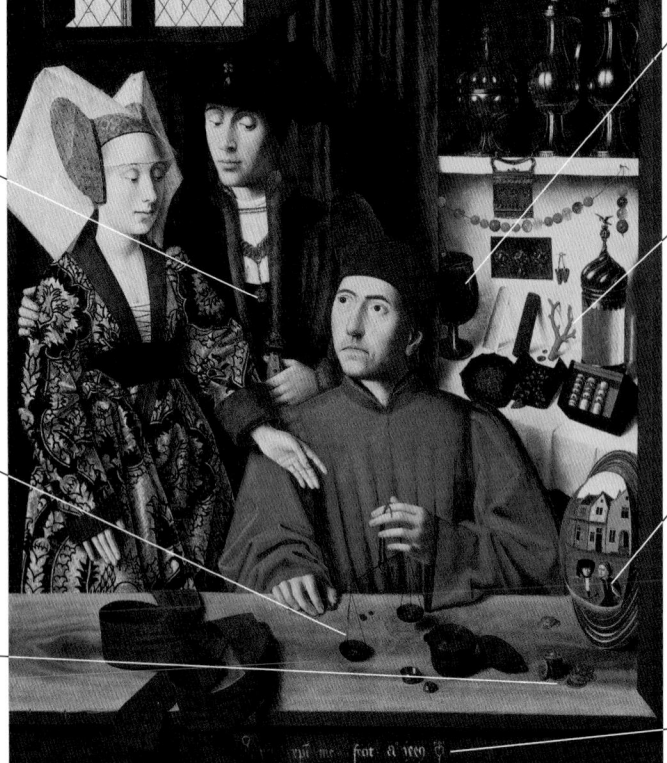

This coconut cup was supposed to neutralize poison. The slabs of porphyry and rock crystal were "touchstones," used to test gold and precious stones.

The red coral and serpents' tongues (actually fossilized sharks' teeth) were intended to ward off the evil eye.

Two men, one with a falcon on his arm, are reflected in the obliquely placed mirror as they stand in front of the shop. The edges of the reflection catch the red sleeve of the goldsmith and the door frame, uniting the interior and exterior spaces and drawing the viewer into the painting.

The artist signed and dated his work in a bold inscription that appears just under the tabletop at the bottom of the painting: "Master Petrus Christus made me in the year 1449."

19–17 Petrus Christus **A GOLDSMITH IN HIS SHOP**
1449. Oil on oak panel, 38⅝ × 33½″ (98 × 85 cm). Metropolitan Museum of Art, New York. Robert Lehman Collection, 1975. 1975.1.110.

Credit: © 2016. Image copyright The Metropolitan Museum of Art/Art Resource/ Scala, Florence

---

fifteenth-century Flemish painters in the planning of their paintings, especially portraits. The portraitlike quality of Luke's face here has led scholars to propose that this image of the saint is a self-portrait of the artist himself.

Art historians have traditionally interpreted this painting in two ways. Some see it—especially if Luke is a self-portrait—as a document of Rogier's sense of his own profession. They see him distancing himself and his fifteenth-century Flemish colleagues from identification with the laboring artisans of the Middle Ages and staking a claim for his special role as an inspired creator who recorded sacred visions in valuable, individualistic works of art. The notion of Rogier's own identification with Luke in this painting is supported by the fact that later artists emulated his composition in creating their own self-portraits as the century progressed. But other art historians, proposing that this painting was created for the chapel

of the guildhall of the painters in Brussels (the evidence is suggestive but unclear), have interpreted it as a claim for the importance of the painters' profession because it is rooted in saintly legend. Perhaps this extraordinary picture was both self-fashioning and professional propaganda. But it was also a devotional image. Luke's tenuous, half-kneeling posture, and his dreamy, introspective gaze certainly remind us that one of the tasks of painters in this period was to create inspiring pictures of religious visions that are made to feel real by meticulous references to the earthly world.

For another painting by Rogier van der Weyden that seems to have had a close connection with his life story and is characterized by a similar blending of the real and the visionary, see the discussion of one of his last—and perhaps one of his greatest—works in the "Introduction" and FIG. Intro–6.

Painting at Mid Century: The Second Generation

The extraordinary accomplishments of the Master of Flémalle, Jan van Eyck, and Rogier van der Weyden attracted many followers in Flanders. The work of this second generation of Flemish painters may be simpler, more direct, and often easier to understand than that of their predecessors, but they still produced extraordinary works of great emotional power. They were in large part responsible for the rapid spread of the Flemish style throughout Europe.

PETRUS CHRISTUS   Among the most interesting of these painters was Petrus Christus (active 1444–c. 1475/1476), who became a citizen of Bruges in 1444 and signed and dated six paintings in a career that extended over three decades.

In 1449, Christus painted a portrait of a goldsmith serving two well-dressed customers in his shop (see "Closer Look" opposite). A halo around the head of the seated figure—not originally a part of the painting—was removed by restorers in 1993. This coincided with a reevaluation of the subject matter of the work, now seen as a vocational portrait of an actual goldsmith, rather than an image of St. Eloi, patron saint of goldsmiths, set in the present. Finished products and raw materials of the jeweler's trade sit on the shelves behind the goldsmith: containers, rings, brooches, a belt buckle, a string of beads, pearls, gemstones, coral, and crystal cylinders. A betrothal belt curls across the counter. Such a combination of objects suggests that the painting expresses a hope for health and well-being for the couple, who may be in the process of procuring rings for their upcoming marriage.

As in Jan van Eyck's double portrait, a convex mirror extends the viewer's field of vision, in this instance to the street outside, where two men appear. One is stylishly dressed in red and black, and the other holds a falcon, another indication of high status. Whether or not the reflected image has symbolic meaning, the mirror would have had practical value in a goldsmith's shop, allowing him to observe the approach of potential customers to the counter outside his window.

DIERIC BOUTS   Dieric Bouts (active c. 1444–1475) is best known among Flemish painters as a storyteller, and he exercised those skills in a series of large altarpieces with narrative scenes drawn from the life of Christ and the lives of the saints. But he also created more intimate pictures, such as this tender rendering of the **VIRGIN AND CHILD**, just 8½ inches tall (**FIG. 19–18**). Even it evokes a story. Mary holds her baby securely, using both of her plain, strong hands to surround completely the lower part of his body. The baby reaches across his mother's chest and around her neck, pulling himself closer to press his face next to hers,

19–18 Dieric Bouts **VIRGIN AND CHILD**
c. 1455–1460. Oil on wood panel, 8½ × 6½″ (21.6 × 16.5 cm).
Metropolitan Museum of Art, New York.

Credit: © 2016. Image copyright The Metropolitan Museum of Art/Art Resource/
Scala, Florence

cheek to cheek, nose to nose, mouth to mouth, eyes locked together, forming a symmetrical system that links them in pattern and almost melds them into a single mirrored form. It is as if a fifteenth-century St. Luke had captured a private moment between the Virgin and Child—a dimpled mother and baby looking very much like the actual people in the artist's world—during their miraculous appearance to sit as his models (compare FIG. 19–16). The concept is actually not so far-fetched. Bouts's painting is modeled after a fourteenth-century Italian image in the cathedral of Cambrai that in the fifteenth century was believed to have been painted by St. Luke himself.

Hugo van der Goes and Hans Memling

Hugo van der Goes (c. 1440–1482), dean of the painters' guild in Ghent (1468–1475), united the intellectual prowess of Jan van Eyck with the emotional sensitivity of Rogier van der Weyden to create an entirely new personal style. Hugo's major work was an exceptionally large altarpiece, more than 8 feet tall, of the Nativity (**FIG. 19–19**), commissioned by Tommaso Portinari, head of the Medici bank in Bruges. Probably painted between 1474 and 1476, the triptych was sent to Florence and installed in 1483 in the Portinari family chapel, where it had a noticeable impact on Florentine painters.

Tommaso, his wife Maria Baroncelli, and their three oldest children are portrayed kneeling in prayer on the side panels of the wing interiors. On the left wing, looming larger than life behind Tommaso and his son Antonio, are their name saints—SS. Thomas and Anthony of Egypt. Since the younger son, Pigello, born in 1474, was apparently added after the original composition was set, his saintly counterpart is lacking. On the right wing, Maria and her daughter Margherita are presented by SS. Mary Magdalen and Margaret.

The theme of the altarpiece is the Nativity as told by Luke (2:10–19). The central panel represents the Adoration of the newborn Christ Child by Mary and Joseph, a host of angels, and the shepherds who have rushed in from the fields. In the middle ground of the wings are additional scenes. Winding their way through the winter landscape are two groups headed for Bethlehem. On the left wing, Mary and Joseph travel there to take part in a census. Near the end of her pregnancy, Mary has dismounted from her donkey and staggers, supported by Joseph. On the right wing, a servant of the three Magi, who are coming to honor the awaited Savior, asks directions from a peasant.

Hugo paints meadows and woods meticulously, and he uses atmospheric perspective to approximate distance in the landscape. He shifts figure size hierarchically for emphasis: The huge figures of Joseph, Mary, and the shepherds are the same size as the patron saints on the wings, in contrast to the much smaller Portinari family and still smaller angels. Hugo also uses light, as well as the gestures and gazes of the figures, to focus our eyes on the center panel where the mystery of the Incarnation takes place. Instead of lying swaddled in a manger or in his mother's arms, Jesus rests naked and vulnerable on the barren ground. Rays of light emanate from his body. This image was based on the visionary writing of the medieval Swedish mystic St. Bridget (who composed her work c. 1360–1370), which describes Mary kneeling to adore the Christ Child immediately after giving birth.

As in the work of Jan van Eyck, aspects of the setting of this painting are infused with symbolic meaning. In the foreground, the wheatsheaf refers both to the location of the event at Bethlehem, which in Hebrew means "house of bread," and to the Eucharistic Host, which represents the body of Christ. The majolica vessel is decorated with vines and grapes, alluding to the Eucharistic wine, which represents the blood of Christ. It holds a red lily for Christ's blood and three irises—white for purity and purple for Christ's royal ancestry. The seven blue columbines in the glass vessel remind the viewer of the Virgin's future sorrows, and scattered on the ground are violets, symbolizing humility. But Hugo's artistic vision transcends such formal religious symbolism. For example, the shepherds, who stand in awe before the miraculous event, are among the most sympathetically rendered images of common people to be found in the art of any period, and the portraits of the

19–20 Hans Memling **DIPTYCH OF MAARTEN VAN NIEUWENHOVE**

1487. Oil on wood panel, each panel (including frames) 20½ × 16¼″ (52 × 41.5 cm). Hans Memling Museum, Musea Brugge, Sint-Jans Hospital, Bruges.

Credit: © akg-images/ Erich Lessing

Portinari children are unusually sensitive renderings of the delicate features of youthful faces.

HANS MEMLING   The artist who seems to summarize and epitomize painting in Flanders during the second half of the fifteenth century is German-born Hans Memling (c. 1435–1494). Memling combines the intellectual depth and virtuoso rendering of his predecessors with a delicacy of feeling and exquisite grace, a "prettiness" that made his work exceptionally popular. He may have worked in

19–19 Hugo van der Goes **PORTINARI ALTARPIECE (OPEN)**

c. 1474–1476. Tempera and oil on wood panel; center 8′3½″ × 10′ (2.53 × 3.01 m), wings each 8′3½″ × 4′7½″ (2.53 × 1.41 m). Galleria degli Uffizi, Florence.

Credit: © Studio Fotografico Quattrone, Florence

Rogier van der Weyden's Brussels workshop in the 1460s, but soon after Rogier's death in 1464, Memling moved to Bruges, where he developed an international clientele that supported a thriving workshop. He also worked for local patrons.

In 1487, the 24-year-old Maarten van Nieuwenhove (1463–1500), member of a powerful political family in Bruges (he became mayor of Bruges in 1497), commissioned from Memling a diptych that combined a meticulously detailed portrait of Maarten with a visionary apparition of the Virgin and Child, presented as a powerful fiction of their physical encounter in Maarten's own home (**FIG. 19–20**). This type of devotional diptych was a specialty of Rogier van der Weyden, but Memling transforms the type into something more intimate by placing it in a domestic setting. An expensively outfitted figure of Maarten appears in the right wing of the diptych, seen from an oblique angle, hands folded in prayer. He seems caught in a moment of introspection inspired by personal devotions—his Book of Hours lies still open on the table in front of him. The window just over his shoulder holds a stained-glass rendering of his name saint, Martin, in the top pane, while a recognizable landmark in Bruges can be seen through the opening below. The Virgin and Child on the adjacent panel are presented frontally, and the strong sense of specific likeness characterizing Maarten's portrait has given way to an idealized delicacy and grace in the visage of the Virgin that complements the extravagance of her clothing. Although she does not seem to be focusing on her baby, a completely nude Jesus stretches out on the pillow in front of her; she stabilizes him with one hand and offers him an apple with the other. This seems a clear reference to their roles as the new Adam and Eve, ready to redeem the sin brought into the world by the first couple. The stained glass behind them is filled with heraldry, devices, and a motto associated with Maarten's family.

Memling's construction of a coherent interior space for these figures is both impressive and meaningful. We are looking through two windows into a rectangular room containing this devotional group. The pillow under the Christ Child casts a shadow, painted on the lower frame of the left panel, to intensify the illusion, and the Virgin's scarlet mantle extends under the division between the two wings of the diptych to reappear on Maarten's side of the painting underneath his Book of Hours. This mantle not only connects the two sides of the painting spatially but also relates Maarten's devotional exercise to the apparition of the Virgin and Child. This relationship is also documented with a device already familiar to us in paintings by Jan van Eyck (SEE FIG. 19-1) and Petrus Christus (SEE FIG. 19-17). On the shadowy back wall, over the Virgin's right shoulder and set against the closed shutters of a window, is a convex mirror that reflects the backs of both Maarten and Mary, bearing visual witness to their presence together within his domestic space and undoing the division between them that is endemic to the diptych format. Maarten's introspective gaze signals that for him the encounter is internal and spiritual, but Memling transforms Maarten's private devotion into a concrete public statement that promotes an image of his piety and freezes him in perpetual prayer. We bear witness to his vision as an actual event.

France

How are painting and architecture transformed in fifteenth-century France?

Flemish art—with its complex symbolism, visionary subjects, atmospheric space, luminous colors, and sensuous surface textures—delighted wealthy patrons and well-educated courtiers both inside and outside Flanders. At first, Flemish artists worked in foreign courts, or their works were commissioned and exported abroad. Flemish manuscripts, tapestries, altarpieces, and portraits appeared in palaces and chapels throughout Europe. But soon regional artists traveled to Flanders to learn oil-painting techniques and practice the Flemish style. By the end of the fifteenth century, distinctive regional variations of Flemish art could be found throughout Europe, from the Atlantic Ocean to the Danube.

The centuries-long struggle for power and territory between France and England continued well into the fifteenth century. When King Charles VI of France died in 1422, England claimed the throne for the king's 9-month-old grandson, Henry VI of England. The plight of Charles VII, the late French king's son, inspired Joan of Arc to raise an army to return him to the throne. Thanks to Joan's efforts, Charles was crowned at Reims in 1429. Although Joan was burned at the stake in 1431, the revitalized French forces drove the English from French lands. In 1461, Louis XI succeeded his father, Charles VII, as king of

19–21 Jean Fouquet **ÉTIENNE CHEVALIER AND ST. STEPHEN, VIRGIN AND CHILD**
The Melun Diptych. c. 1452–1455. Oil on oak panel. Left wing: 36½ × 33½″ (92.7 × 85.5 cm), Staatliche Museen zu Berlin, Preussischer Kulturbesitz, Gemäldegalerie; right wing: 37¼ × 33½″ (94.5 × 85.5 cm), Koninklijk Museum voor Schone Kunsten, Antwerp, Belgium.

France. Under his rule the French royal court again became a major source of patronage for the arts.

Jean Fouquet and Jean Hey

The leading court artist of fifteenth-century France, Jean Fouquet (c. 1425–1481), was born in Tours and may have trained in Paris as an illuminator and in Bourges in the workshop of Jacob de Littemont, Flemish court painter to Charles VII. He was part of a French delegation to Rome in 1446–1448, but by mid century he had established a workshop in Tours and was a renowned painter. Fouquet drew from contemporary Italian Classicism, especially in rendering architecture, and he was also strongly influenced by Flemish illusionism. He painted pictures of Charles VII, the royal family, and courtiers; he also illustrated manuscripts and designed tombs.

Among the court officials who commissioned paintings from Fouquet was Étienne Chevalier, treasurer of France under Charles VII. Fouquet painted a diptych for him that was installed over the tomb of Chevalier's wife Catherine Budé (d. 1452) in the church of Notre-Dame in Melun (**FIG. 19–21**). Chevalier appears in the left panel, kneeling in prayer with clasped hands and a meditative gaze within an Italianate palace, accompanied by his name saint Stephen (Étienne in French). Fouquet describes the courtier's ruddy features with a mirrorlike precision that is reminiscent of Flemish art. He is expensively dressed in a heavy red wool garment lined with fur, and his "bowl cut" hairstyle represents the latest Parisian fashion. St. Stephen's features convey a comparable sense of likeness and sophistication. A deacon in the Early Christian church in Jerusalem, Stephen was the first Christian martyr, stoned to death for defending his beliefs. Here he wears the fifteenth-century liturgical vestments of a deacon and carries a large stone on a closed Gospel book as evidence of his martyrdom. A trickle of blood can be seen on his tonsured head (male members of religious orders shaved the tops of their heads as a sign of humility). Placing his arm around Étienne Chevalier's back, the saint seems to be introducing the treasurer to the Virgin and Child in the adjacent panel.

The Virgin and Child, however, exist in another world. A supernatural vision unfolds as the queen of heaven is enthroned surrounded by red and blue seraphim and cherubim, who form a tapestrylike background. The Virgin seems a celestial being, conceived by Fouquet as a hybrid of careful description and powerful abstraction. Her fashionable, tightly waisted bodice has been unlaced so she can present her spherical breast to a substantial, seated baby who points across the juncture between the two wings of the diptych to acknowledge Chevalier. According to tradition, Fouquet gave this image of the Virgin the features of the king's much loved and respected mistress, Agnès Sorel, who died in 1450. The original frame that united these

19–22 Jean Hey (The Master of Moulins) **PORTRAIT OF MARGARET OF AUSTRIA**

c. 1490. Oil on wood panel, 12⅞ × 9⅛" (32.7 × 23 cm). Metropolitan Museum of Art, New York. Robert Lehman Collection.

Credit: © 2016. Image copyright The Metropolitan Museum of Art/Art Resource/ Scala, Florence

two panels into a diptych—now divided between two museums—is lost, but among the fragments that remain is a stunning medallion self-portrait that served as the artist's signature.

JEAN HEY, THE MASTER OF MOULINS Perhaps the greatest French follower of Jean Fouquet is an artist who for many years was known as the Master of Moulins after a large triptych he painted at the end of the fifteenth century under the patronage of Duke Jean II of Bourbon, for the Burgundian cathedral of Moulins. This triptych combines Flemish attention to color and surface texture with a characteristically French air of reserved detachment. Recently the work of this artist has been associated with the name Jean Hey, a painter of Flemish origin who seems to have been trained in the workshop of Hugo van der Goes, but who pursued his career at the French court.

This charming portrait (**FIG. 19–22**)—which may have been one half of a devotional diptych comparable to that painted by Memling for Maarten van Nieuwenhove (SEE FIG. 19-20)—portrays Margaret of Austria (1480–1530), daughter of Emperor Maximilian I, who had been betrothed to the future French king Charles VIII (ruled 1483–1498) at age 2 or 3 and was being brought up at the French court. She would return home to her father in 1493 after Charles decided to pursue another, more politically expedient marriage (after two political marriages of her own, the widowed Margaret would eventually become governor of the Habsburg Netherlands), but Hey captures her at a tender moment a few years before those troubled times. She kneels in front of a strip of wall between two windows that open onto a lush country landscape, fingering the pearl beads of her rosary. Details of her lavish velvet and ermine outfit not only proclaim her wealth but provide the clues to her identity—the Cs and Ms embroidered on her collar signal her betrothal to Charles and the ostentatious *fleur-de-lis* pendant set with large rubies and pearls proclaims her affiliation with the French court. But it is the delicacy and sweet vulnerability of this 10-year-old girl that are most arresting. They recall Hugo van der Goes's sensitivity to the childlike qualities of the young members of donor families (SEE FIG. 19-19) and provide strong evidence for ascribing Hey's training to the workshop of this Flemish master.

Flamboyant Architecture

The great age of cathedral building that had begun in the second half of the twelfth century was essentially over by the end of the fourteenth century—but growing urban populations needed houses, city halls, guildhalls, and more parish churches. It was in buildings such as these that late Gothic architecture took form in a style we call "Flamboyant" because of its repeated, twisted, flamelike tracery patterns. Late Gothic masons covered their buildings with increasingly elaborate and at times playful architectural decoration. Like painters, sculptors also turned to describing the specific nature of the world around them, and they covered capitals and moldings with ivy, hawthorn leaves, and other vegetation, not just the conventional acanthus motifs inherited from the Classical world.

The **CHURCH OF SAINT-MACLOU** in Rouen, which was begun after a fund-raising campaign in 1432 and dedicated in 1521, is an outstanding and well-preserved example of Flamboyant Gothic (**FIG. 19-23**) probably designed by the Paris architect Pierre Robin. A projecting porch bends to enfold the façade of the church in a screen of tracery. Sunlight on the flame-shape openings casts ever-changing shadows across the intentionally complex surface. **Crockets**—small, knobby, leaflike ornaments that line the steep gables and slender buttresses—break every defining line. In the Flamboyant style, decoration sometimes disguises structural elements with an overlay of tracery and ornament in geometric and natural shapes, all to dizzying effect.

The house of Jacques Coeur, a wealthy merchant in Bourges, reflects the popularity of the Flamboyant style for secular architecture (**FIG. 19-24**). Built at great expense between 1443 and 1451, it survives almost intact, although it has been stripped of its rich furnishings. The rambling, palatial house is built around an irregular open courtyard, with spiral stairs in octagonal towers giving access to the upper-floor rooms. Tympana over doors indicate the function of the rooms within; for example, over the door to the kitchen a cook stirs the contents of a large bowl. Among the carved decorations are puns on the patron's surname, Coeur (meaning "heart" in French). The house was also Jacques Coeur's place of business, so it had large storerooms for goods and a strongroom for treasure.

19-23 Pierre Robin (?) **CHURCH OF SAINT-MACLOU, ROUEN**

Normandy, France. West façade, 1432–1521; façade c. 1500–1514.

Credit: © Achim Bednorz, Cologne

19-24A PLAN OF JACQUES COEUR HOUSE
Bourges, France. 1443–1451.

The Germanic Lands

How is the Northern Renaissance style expressed in painting and the graphic arts in Germany and Switzerland?

Present-day Germany and Switzerland were situated within the Holy Roman Empire, a loose confederation of primarily German-speaking states. Artisan guilds grew powerful and trade flourished under the auspices of the Hanseatic League, an association of cities and trading outposts, stimulating a strengthening of the merchant class. The Fugger family, for example, began their spectacular rise from simple textile workers and linen merchants to bankers for the Habsburgs and the popes.

Painting and Sculpture

Germanic fifteenth-century painters worked in two very different styles. Some, clustered around Cologne, continued the International Gothic style with increased prettiness, softness, and sweetness of expression. Other artists began an intense investigation and detailed description of

19-24B INTERIOR COURTYARD OF JACQUES COEUR HOUSE
Bourges, France. 1443–1451.

Credit: © Hervé Champollion/akg-images

the physical world. The major exponent of the latter style was Konrad Witz (active 1434–1446). A native of Swabia in southern Germany, Witz moved to Basel (in present-day Switzerland), where he found a rich source of patronage in the Church.

Witz's last large commission before his early death in 1446 was an altarpiece dedicated to St. Peter for the cathedral of Geneva, signed and dated to 1444. In one of its scenes—the **MIRACULOUS DRAFT OF FISHES (FIG. 19-25)**—Jesus appears posthumously to his disciples as they fish on the Sea of Galilee, and Peter leaps from the boat to greet him. But Witz sets the scene on the Lake of Geneva, with the distinctive dark mountain (the Mole) rising on the north shore and the snow-covered Alps shining in the distance. Witz records every nuance of light and water—the rippling surface, the reflections of boats, figures, and

buildings, and even the lake bottom. Peter's body and legs, visible through the water, are distorted by the refraction. It is one of the earliest times in European art that an artist captures both the appearance and the spirit of nature.

Some patrons in Germanic lands preferred altarpieces that featured polychromed wood carvings rather than the ensembles of panel paintings that we saw in Flanders—for example, the Ghent Altarpiece (SEE FIGS. 18-13, 18-14). One of the greatest artists working in this tradition was painter and sculptor Michael Pacher (1435–1498), based in Bruneck, now in the Italian Alps. In 1471, Benedict Eck, abbot of Mondsee, commissioned from Pacher for the pilgrimage church of St. Wolfgang a grand high altarpiece that is still installed in its original church setting (FIG. 19-26). The surviving contract specifies materials and subject matter and even documents the cost—1,200 Hungarian florins—but

19-25 Konrad Witz MIRACULOUS DRAFT OF FISHES
From an altarpiece for the Cathedral of St. Peter, Geneva, Switzerland. 1444. Oil on wood panel, 4′3″ × 5′1″ (1.29 × 1.55 m). Musée d'Art et d'Histoire, Geneva.

Credit: © Musée d'art et d'histoire, Ville de Genève. Photo: Flora Bevilacqua

19–26 Michael Pacher **ST. WOLFGANG ALTARPIECE**
Church of St. Wolfgang, Austria. 1471–1481. Carved, painted, and gilt wood; wings are oil on wood panel.

sets no time limit for its completion. Pacher and his shop worked on it for ten years.

When it is open (as in FIG. 19-26), a dizzyingly complicated sculptural ensemble aligns up the middle, flanked by four large panel paintings portraying scenes from the life of the Virgin on the opened shutters. Both the design and execution were supervised by Pacher, but many other artists collaborated with him on the actual carving and painting. In the main scene, the wood carvings create a vision of Paradise where Christ crowns his mother as the queen of heaven, flanked by imposing images of local saints. The use of soft wood facilitated deep undercutting and amazing detail in the rendering of these figures, and the elaborate polychromy and gold leaf give them a finish that glitters in the changing patterns of natural light or the flickering glow of candles.

The Graphic Arts

Printmaking emerged in Europe at the end of the fourteenth century with the development of printing presses and the increased local manufacture and wider availability of paper. The techniques used by printmakers during the fifteenth century were woodcut and engraving on metal (see "Woodcuts and Engravings on Metal" below). **Woodblocks** cut in relief had long been used to print designs on cloth, but only in the fifteenth century did the printing of images and texts on paper and the production of books in multiple copies of a single edition, or version, begin to replace the copying of each book by hand. Both hand-written and printed books were often illustrated, and printed images were sometimes hand-colored.

Large quantities of single-sheet prints were also made using woodcut and engraving techniques in the early

Technique
WOODCUTS AND ENGRAVINGS ON METAL

Woodcuts are made by drawing on the surface of a block of fine-grained wood, then cutting away all the areas around the lines with a sharp tool called a gouge, leaving the lines in high relief. When the block's surface is inked and a piece of paper pressed down hard on it, the ink on the relief areas transfers to the paper to create a reverse image. The effects can be varied by making thicker and thinner lines, and shading can be achieved by placing the lines closer or farther apart. Sometimes color was painted onto the resulting black-and-white images by hand.

Engraving on metal requires a technique called **intaglio**, in which the lines are cut into the plate with tools called gravers or **burins**. The engraver then carefully polishes the plate to ensure a clean, sharp image. Ink is applied over the whole plate and forced down into the lines, then the plate's surface is carefully wiped clean of the excess ink. When paper and plate are held tightly together by a press, the ink in the recessed lines transfers to the paper.

Woodblocks and metal plates could be used repeatedly to make nearly identical images. If the lines of the block or plate wore down, the artists could repair them. Printing large numbers of identical prints of a single version, called an edition, was usually a team effort in a busy workshop. One artist would make the drawing. Sometimes it was drawn directly on the block or plate with ink, in reverse of its printed direction, sometimes on paper to be transferred in reverse onto the plate or block by another person, who then cut the lines. Others would ink and print the images.

In the illustration of books, the plates or blocks would be reused to print later editions and even adapted for use in other books. A set of blocks or plates for illustrations was a valuable commodity and might be sold by one workshop to another. Early in publishing, there were no copyright laws, and many entrepreneurs simply had their workers copy book illustrations onto woodblocks and cut them for their own publications.

relief printing

intaglio printing

19-27 THE BUXHEIM ST. CHRISTOPHER
Mid 15th century. Hand-colored woodcut, 11⅜ × 8⅛″ (28.85 × 20.7 cm). Private collection.

The Latin text reads, "Whenever you look at the face of St. Christopher, you will not die a terrible death that day."

Credit: © Fine Art Images/Archivi Alinari, Firenze

decades of the fifteenth century. Often artists drew the images and then professional woodworkers would cut them from the block.

THE BUXHEIM ST. CHRISTOPHER Devotional images were sold as souvenirs to pilgrims at holy sites. **THE BUX-HEIM ST. CHRISTOPHER** was found in the Carthusian monastery of Buxheim, in southern Germany, glued to the inside of the back cover of a manuscript (**FIG. 19-27**). St.Christopher, patron saint of travelers and protector from the plague, carries the Christ Child across the river. His efforts are witnessed by a monk holding out a light to guide him to the monastery door, but ignored by the hardworking millers on the opposite bank. Both the cutting of the block and the quality of the printing are very high. Lines vary in width to strengthen major forms. Delicate lines are used for inner modeling (facial features) and short, parallel lines indicate shadows (the inner side of draperies). The date 1423, which is cut into the block, was once thought to

identify this print as among the earliest to survive. Recent studies have determined that the date refers to some event, and the print is now dated at mid century.

MARTIN SCHONGAUER Engraving may have originated with goldsmiths and armorers, who recorded their work by rubbing lampblack into the engraved lines of their products and pressing paper over the metal. German artist Martin Schongauer (c. 1435–1491), who learned engraving from his goldsmith father, was an immensely skillful printmaker who excelled both in drawing and in the difficult technique of shading from deep blacks to faintest grays using only line. In **THE TEMPTATIONS OF ST. ANTHONY**, probably engraved during the 1470s (**FIG. 19-28**), Schongauer illustrated the original biblical meaning of temptation as a physical assault rather than a subtle inducement. Wildly acrobatic, slithery, spiky demons lift Anthony up off the ground to torment him in midair. The engraver intensified the horror of the moment by condensing the action into a swirling vortex of

19-28 Martin Schongauer **THE TEMPTATIONS OF ST. ANTHONY**
c. 1470–1480. Engraving, 12¼ × 9″ (31.1 × 22.9 cm). Metropolitan Museum of Art, New York. Rogers Fund, 1920 (20.5.2).

Credit: © 2016. Image copyright The Metropolitan Museum of Art/Art Resource/Scala, Florence figures beating, scratching, poking, tugging, and no doubt shrieking at the stoical saint, who remains impervious to all, perhaps because of his power to focus inwardly on his private meditations.

Printed Books

The explosion of learning in Europe in the fifteenth century encouraged experiments in faster and cheaper ways of producing books than by hand-copying them. The earliest printed books were block books, for which each page of text, with or without illustrations, was cut in relief on a single block of wood. Movable-type printing, in which individual letters could be arranged and locked together, inked, and then printed onto paper, was first achieved in Europe in the workshop of Johann Gutenberg in Mainz, Germany. More than 40 copies of Gutenberg's Bible, printed around 1455, still exist. As early as 1465, two German printers were working in Italy, and by the 1470s there

were presses in France, Flanders, Holland, and Spain. With the invention of this fast way to make a number of identical books, the intellectual and spiritual life of Europe—and with it the arts—changed forever.

THE NUREMBERG CHRONICLE The publication of the *Nuremberg Chronicle* by prosperous Nuremberg printer Anton Koburger was the culmination of his complicated collaboration with scholars, artists, and investors in an early capitalist enterprise that is a landmark in the history of printed books. The text of this history of the world was compiled by physician and scholar Hartmann Schedel, drawing from the work of colleagues and the extensive holdings of his private library. When Koburger set out to publish Schedel's compilation, he sought financial support from Sebald Schregel and his brother-in-law Sebastian Kammermaister, who had a proven record of patronage in book publishing. He also contracted in the 1480s with artists Michael Wolgemut and

19–29 Michael Wolgemut, Wilhelm Pleydenwurff, and workshop **THE CITY OF NUREMBERG**
Nuremberg Chronicle, published by Anton Koburger in 1493. Woodcut within a printed book, hand-colored after printing, each page 18½ × 12¾″ (47 × 32.4 cm). Staatliche Museen zu Berlin.

Wilhelm Pleydenwurff to produce the woodcut illustrations and in 1491 to work on the layout.

The *Nuremberg Chronicle* was published in 1493 in an edition of 2,500. Woodcut illustrations—1,809 in total—were dispersed throughout the book, spreading across the width of whole pages or tucked into the text along either margin. Those interested in purchasing the book could obtain it in Latin or German, on parchment or on paper, bound or unbound, as it came from the press or tinted with color. It seems fitting that the only instance of a double-page picture—filling the entire expanse of an opening with text restricted to headings and labels—is a panoramic view of the city of Nuremberg where this collaborative enterprise was centered (**FIG. 19–29**). Illustrated here is a view of this expansive cityscape in a copy of the book that was originally owned by a bibliophile who could afford to have the woodcuts hand-painted with color to enhance the appearance of this proud Renaissance city's portrait. As we will see, Nuremberg was the site of significant artistic developments in the sixteenth century as well.

Think About It

1   Explain how oil-painting technique allowed fifteenth-century Flemish painters to achieve unprecedented descriptive effects in their work. Support your answer by discussing one specific work in this chapter.

2   Discuss the symbolic meanings that fifteenth-century viewers would have comprehended in the objects in the domestic environment of either the Mérode Altarpiece (**FIG. 19–10**) or the Arnolfini double portrait (**FIG. 19–1**).

3   How have fifteenth-century northern paintings been characterized as devotional visions of the patrons who are portrayed in them? Use a specific work discussed in this chapter as the focus of your answer.

4   Why did printmaking become a major pictorial medium in northern Europe during the fifteenth century? Choose a work discussed in this chapter and explain how it supports your answer.

Crosscurrents

These two paintings portray one of the most popular subjects in Christian art: the Annunciation. They were painted by artists working in different places and trained in different traditions, and they are very different in medium and size. Characterize the differences in style and narrative presentation. How are these features related to the cultural context of each?

FIG. 18–13

FIG. 19–10

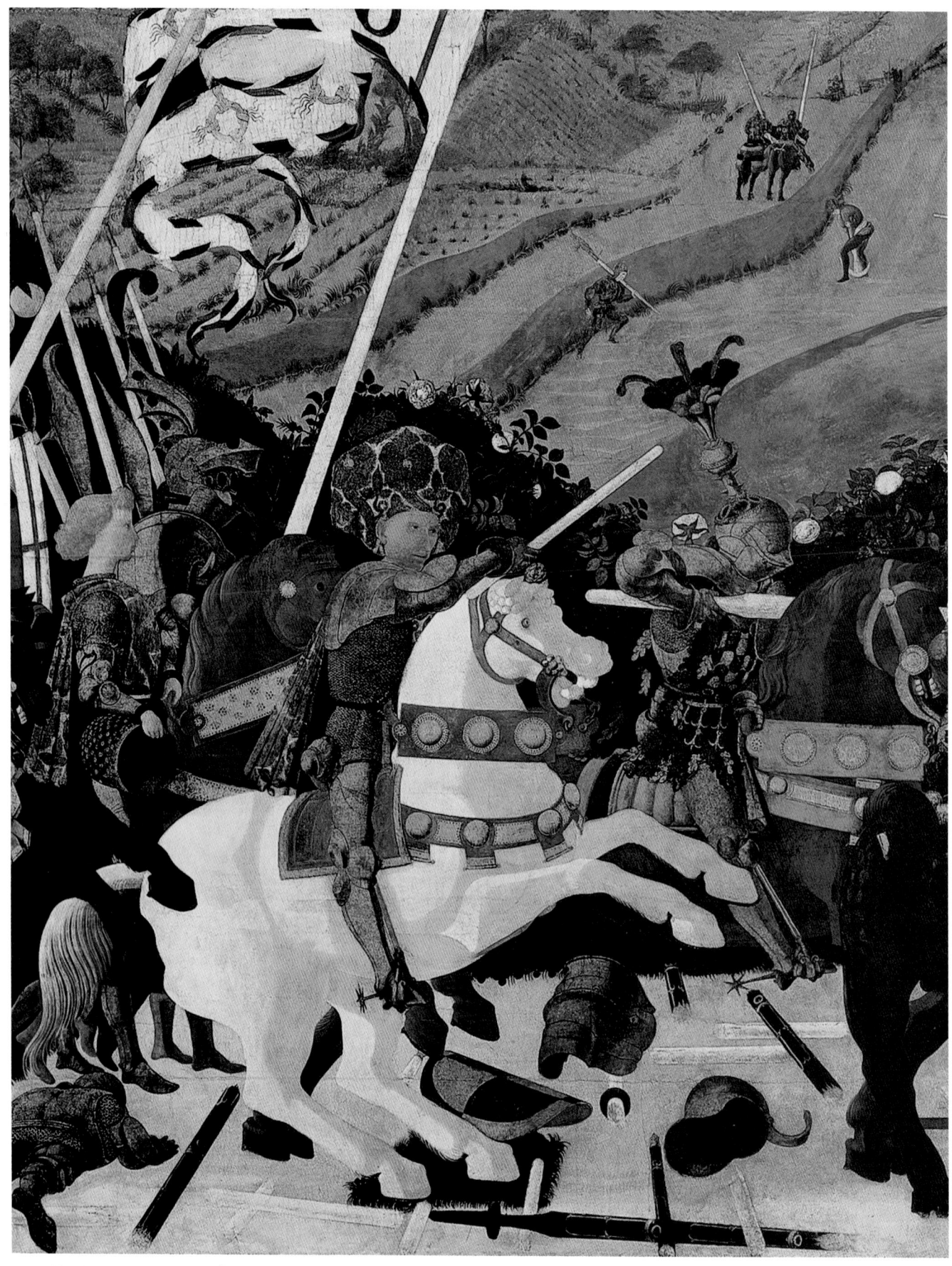

20–1 Paolo Uccello **NICCOLÒ DA TOLENTINO LEADING THE CHARGE**

Detail from *The Battle of San Romano* (FIG. 20–24), 1438–1440. Tempera on wood panel. National Gallery, London.

Chapter 20
Renaissance Art in Fifteenth-Century Italy

Learning Objectives

20.a Identify the visual hallmarks of fifteenth-century Italian art for formal, technical, and expressive qualities.

20.b Interpret the meaning of works of fifteenth-century Italian art based on their themes, subjects, and symbols.

20.c Relate fifteenth-century Italian art and artists to their cultural, economic, and political contexts.

20.d Apply the vocabulary and concepts relevant to fifteenth-century Italian art, artists, and art history.

20.e Interpret a work of fifteenth-century Italian art using the art historical methods of observation, comparison, and inductive reasoning.

20.f Select visual and textual evidence in various media to support an argument or an interpretation of a work of fifteenth-century Italian art.

This ferocious but bloodless battle seems to take place in a dream, but it depicts a historical event (**FIG. 20–1**). Under an elegantly fluttering banner, the Florentine general Niccolò da Tolentino leads his men against the Sienese at the Battle of San Romano, which took place on June 1, 1432. The battle rages across a shallow stage defined by the debris of warfare arranged in a neat pattern on a pink ground and backed by blooming hedges. In the center foreground, Niccolò holds up a baton of command, the sign of his authority. His bold gesture—together with his white horse and crimson-and-gold damask hat—ensures that he dominates the scene. His knights charge into the fray, and when they fall, like the soldier at the lower left, they join the many broken lances on the ground—all in conformity with the new mathematical depiction of receding space called **linear perspective**, posed to align with implied lines that converge at a single point on the horizon.

An eccentric Florentine painter nicknamed Paolo Uccello ("Paul Bird") created the panel painting (SEE FIG. 20–24) from which the detail in FIGURE 20–1 is taken. It is one of three related panels—now separated, hanging in major museums in Florence, London, and Paris—commissioned by Lionardo Bartolini Salimbeni (1404–1479), who led the Florentine governing Council of Ten during the war against Lucca and Siena. Uccello's remarkable accuracy when depicting armor from the 1430s, heraldic banners, and even fashionable fabrics and crests surely would have appealed

to Lionardo's civic pride. The hedges of oranges, roses, and pomegranates—all ancient fertility symbols—suggest that Lionardo might have commissioned the paintings at the time of his wedding in 1438. Lionardo and his wife, Maddalena, had six sons, two of whom inherited the paintings.

According to a later complaint brought by Damiano, one of the heirs, Lorenzo de' Medici, the powerful *de facto* ruler of Florence, "forcibly removed" the paintings from Damiano's house. They were never returned, and Uccello's masterpieces are recorded in a 1492 inventory as hanging in the Medici palace. Perhaps Lorenzo, who was called "the Magnificent," saw Uccello's heroic pageant as a trophy more worthy of a Medici merchant prince. Princely patronage was certainly a major factor in the genesis of the Italian Renaissance as it developed in Florence during the early years of the fifteenth century.

Humanism and the Italian Renaissance

What are the cultural and historical backgrounds of Italian Renaissance art and architecture?

By the end of the Middle Ages, the most important Italian cultural centers lay north of Rome in the cities of Florence, Milan, and Venice, and in the smaller court cities of

MAP 20–1 FIFTEENTH-CENTURY ITALY

Powerful families divided the Italian peninsula into city-states: the Medici in Florence, the Visconti and Sforza in Milan, the Montefeltro in Urbino, the Gonzaga in Mantua, and the Este in Ferrara. After 1420, the popes ruled Rome, while in the south Naples and Sicily were French and then Spanish (Aragonese) territories. Venice maintained its independence as a republic.

Mantua, Ferrara, and Urbino. Political power and artistic patronage were both dominated by wealthy families: the Medici in Florence, the Montefeltro in Urbino, the Gonzaga in Mantua, the Visconti and Sforza in Milan, and the Este in Ferrara (MAP 20-1). Cities grew in wealth and independence as people migrated from the countryside in unprecedented numbers. Like in northern Europe, commerce became increasingly important. Money conferred status, and a shrewd business or political leader could become very powerful. The period saw the rise of mercenary armies led by entrepreneurial (and sometimes brilliant) military commanders called *condottieri*, who owed allegiance only to those who paid them well; their employer might be a city-state, a lord, or even the pope. Some *condottieri*, like Niccolò da Tolentino (SEE FIG. 20-1), became rich and famous. Others, like Federico da Montefeltro (SEE FIG. 20-39), were lords or dukes themselves, with territories of their own in need of protection. Patronage of the arts was an important public activity with political overtones. As one Florentine merchant, Giovanni Rucellai, succinctly noted, he supported the arts "because they serve the glory of God, the honour of the city, and the commemoration of myself" (cited in Baxandall, p. 2).

The term Renaissance (French for "rebirth") was only applied to this period by later historians. However, its origins lie in the thought of Petrarch and other fourteenth-century Italian writers, who emphasized the power and potential of human beings for great individual accomplishment. These Italian humanists also looked back at the thousand years extending from the disintegration of the Western Roman Empire to their own day and determined that the achievements of the Classical world were followed by what they perceived as a period of decline—a "middle" or "dark" age. They proudly saw their own era as a third age characterized by a revival or rebirth ("renaissance"), when humanity began to emerge from what they erroneously saw as intellectual and cultural stagnation to appreciate once more the achievement of the ancients and the value of rational, scientific investigation. They looked to the accomplishments of the Classical past for inspiration and instruction, and in Italy this centered on the heritage of ancient Rome. They sought the physical and literary records of the ancient world—assembling libraries, collecting sculpture and fragments of architecture, and beginning archaeological investigations. Their aim was to live a rich, noble, and productive life—usually within the framework of Christianity, but always adhering to a school of philosophy as a moral basis.

Artists, like the humanists, turned to Classical antiquity for inspiration, emulating ancient Roman sculpture and architecture even as they continued to fulfill commissions for predominantly Christian subjects and buildings. But a number of home furnishings from the secular world, such as birth trays and marriage chests, have survived, richly painted with allegorical and mythological themes. Patrons began to collect art for their personal enjoyment.

Like Flemish artists, Italian painters and sculptors increasingly focused their attention on rendering the illusion of physical reality. They did so in a more analytical way than the northerners. Rather than seeking to describe the visual appearance of nature through luminosity and detailed textural differentiation, Italian artists aimed at achieving lifelike but idealized weighty figures set in a space organized through strict adherence to linear perspective, a mathematical system that gave the illusion of a measured and continuously receding space (see "Renaissance Perspective" on page 623).

The Early Renaissance in Florence

What characterizes the early development of Italian Renaissance architecture, sculpture, and painting in Florence?

In taking Uccello's battle painting (SEE FIG. 20-1), Lorenzo de' Medici was asserting the role his family had come to expect to play in Florence. The fifteenth century witnessed the rise of the Medici from among the most successful of a

newly rich middle class (primarily merchants and bankers) to the city's virtual rulers. Unlike the hereditary aristocracy, the Medici emerged from obscure roots to make their fortune in banking; from their money came their power.

The competitive Florentine atmosphere that had fostered mercantile success and civic pride also cultivated competition in the arts and encouraged an interest in ancient literary texts. This has led many to consider Florence the cradle of the Italian Renaissance. Under Cosimo the Elder (1389–1464), the Medici became leaders in intellectual and artistic patronage. They sponsored philosophers and other scholars who wanted to study the Classics, especially the works of Plato and his followers, the Neoplatonists. Neoplatonism distinguished between the spiritual (the ideal or Idea) and the physical (Matter) and encouraged artists to represent ideal figures. But it was writers, philosophers, and musicians—and not artists—who dominated the Medici Neoplatonic circle. Architects, sculptors, and painters learned their craft in apprenticeships and were therefore considered manual laborers. Nevertheless, interest in the ancient world rapidly spread from the Medici circle to visual artists, who gradually began to see themselves as more than laborers. Florentine society soon recognized their best works as achievements of a very high order.

Although the Medici were the *de facto* rulers, Florence was considered a republic. The Council of Ten (headed for a time by Salimbeni, who commissioned Uccello's *Battle of San Romano*) was a kind of constitutional oligarchy where wealthy men formed the government. At the same time, the various guilds wielded tremendous power; guild membership was a prerequisite for holding government office. Consequently, artists could look to the Church and the state—the state including both the city government and the guilds—as well as private individuals for patronage. All these patrons expected the artists to reaffirm and glorify their achievements with works that were not only beautiful but intellectually powerful.

The Competition Reliefs

In 1401, the building supervisors of the baptistery of Florence Cathedral decided to commission a new pair of bronze doors, funded by the powerful wool merchants' guild. Instead of choosing a well-established sculptor with a strong reputation, a competition was announced for the commission. This prestigious project would be awarded to the artist who demonstrated the greatest talent in executing a trial piece: a bronze relief representing Abraham's sacrifice of Isaac (Genesis 22:1–13) composed within the same Gothic quatrefoil framework used in Andrea Pisano's first set of bronze doors for the baptistery, made in the 1330s (SEE FIG. 18-3).

Two competition panels have survived, those submitted by the presumed finalists—Filippo Brunelleschi and

20-2 Filippo Brunelleschi **SACRIFICE OF ISAAC**
1401–1402. Bronze with gilding, 21 × 17½″ (53 × 44 cm) inside molding. Museo Nazionale del Bargello, Florence.

Credit: © Studio Fotografico Quattrone, Florence

20-3 Lorenzo Ghiberti **SACRIFICE OF ISAAC**
1401–1402. Bronze with gilding, 21 × 17½″ (53 × 44 cm) inside molding. Museo Nazionale del Bargello, Florence.

Credit: © Studio Fotografico Quattrone, Florence

Lorenzo Ghiberti, both young artists in their early twenties (**FIGS. 20-2, 20-3**). Brunelleschi's composition is rugged and explosive, marked by raw dramatic intensity. At the right, Abraham lunges forward, grabbing his son by the neck, while the angel swoops to stop him just as the knife is about to strike. Isaac's awkward pose embodies his fear and struggle. Ghiberti's version is quite different, suave and graceful rather than powerful and dramatic. Poses are controlled and choreographed; the harmonious pairing of son and father contrasts sharply with the wrenching struggle in Brunelleschi's rendering. And Ghiberti's Isaac is not a stretched, scrawny youth, but a fully idealized Classical figure exuding calm composure.

Brunelleschi's biographer, Antonio di Tuccio Manetti, claimed that the competition ended in a tie, and that when the committee decided to split the commission between the two young artists, Brunelleschi withdrew. It is possible, however, that the cloth merchants actually chose Ghiberti to make the doors. They might have preferred the elegance of his figural composition. Perhaps they liked the prominence of gracefully arranged swags of cloth, reminders of the source of their patronage and prosperity. But they also could have been swayed by the technical superiority of Ghiberti's relief. Unlike Brunelleschi, Ghiberti cast background and figures mostly as a single piece, making his bronze stronger, lighter, and less expensive to produce. The finished doors—installed in the baptistery in 1424—were

so successful that Ghiberti was commissioned to create another set (SEE FIG. 20-16), his most famous work, hailed by Michelangelo as the "Gates of Paradise." Brunelleschi would refocus his career on buildings rather than bronzes, becoming one of the most important architects of the Italian Renaissance (SEE FIGS. 20-4, 20-6).

Filippo Brunelleschi, Architect

The defining civic project of the early years of the fifteenth century was the completion of Florence Cathedral with a magnificent dome over the high altar. The construction of the cathedral had begun in the late thirteenth century and had continued intermittently during the fourteenth. As early as 1367, builders had envisioned a very tall dome to span the huge interior space of the crossing, but they lacked the engineering know-how to construct it. When interest in completing the cathedral revived around 1407, the technical solution was proposed by the young sculptor-turned-architect Filippo Brunelleschi.

FLORENCE CATHEDRAL Filippo Brunelleschi (1377–1446) achieved what many had considered impossible: He solved the problem of the dome of Florence Cathedral. Brunelleschi had originally trained as a goldsmith. To further his education, he traveled to Rome to study ancient Roman sculpture and architecture, and it was on his return to Florence that he tackled the dome. After the completion

20-4 Filippo Brunelleschi **DOME OF FLORENCE CATHEDRAL (SANTA MARIA DEL FIORE)**
1420–1436; lantern completed 1471.

Credit: © Javier Martin/123RF

of a tall octagonal drum in 1412, Brunelleschi designed the
dome itself in 1417, and it was built between 1420 and 1436
(**FIGS. 20-4, 20-5**). A revolutionary feat of engineering,
the dome is a double shell of masonry 138 feet across. The
octagonal outer shell is supported on 8 large and 16 lighter
ribs. Instead of using a costly and even dangerous scaffold and centering, Brunelleschi devised a system in which
temporary wooden supports were cantilevered out from
the drum. He moved these supports up as building progressed. As the dome was built up course by course, each
portion of the structure reinforced the next one. Vertical

**20-5 SCHEMATIC
DRAWING OF FLORENCE
CATHEDRAL**

The separate, central-plan
building in front of the façade is
the baptistery. Adjacent to the
façade is a tall tower designed
by Giotto in 1334.

Credit: © Dorling Kindersley

marble ribs interlocked with horizontal sandstone rings, connected and reinforced with iron rods and oak beams. The inner and outer shells were linked internally by a system of arches. When completed, this self-buttressed unit required no external support to keep it standing.

An oculus (round opening) in the center of the dome was topped with a lantern designed in 1436. After Brunelleschi's death, this crowning structure, made up of Roman architectural forms, was completed by another Florentine architect, Michelozzo di Bartolomeo (1396–1472). The final touch—a gilt-bronze ball by Andrea del Verrocchio—was added in 1468–1471 (but replaced in 1602 with a smaller one).

Other commissions came quickly after the cathedral dome project established Brunelleschi's fame. From about 1418 until his death in 1446, Brunelleschi was involved in a series of influential projects. Between 1419 and 1423, he built the elegant Capponi Chapel in the church of Santa Felicità (SEE FIG. 21-37). In 1419, he also designed a foundling hospital for the city.

THE FOUNDLING HOSPITAL In 1419, the guild of silk manufacturers and goldsmiths (Arte della Seta) in Florence undertook a significant public service: It established a large public orphanage and commissioned Filippo Brunelleschi to build it near the church of the Santissima Annunziata (Most Holy Annunciation), which housed a miracle-working painting of the Annunciation, making it a popular pilgrimage site. Completed in 1444, the Foundling Hospital—**OSPEDALE DEGLI INNOCENTI**—was unprecedented in terms of scale and design (FIG. 20-6).

Brunelleschi created a building that paid homage to traditional forms while introducing features that we associate with the Italian Renaissance style. Traditionally, a charitable foundation's building had a portico open to the street to provide shelter, and Brunelleschi built an arcade of striking lightness and elegance, using smooth round columns and richly carved capitals—his own interpretation of the Classical Corinthian order. Although we might initially assume that the sources for this arcade lay in the Roman architecture of Classical antiquity, columns were not actually used in antiquity to support free-standing arcades, only to support straight architraves. In fact, it was local Romanesque architecture that was the source for Brunelleschi's design. It is the details of capitals and moldings that bring an air of the antique to this influential building.

The underlying mathematical basis for Brunelleschi's design—traced to the same Pythagorean proportional systems that were believed to create musical harmony—creates a distinct sense of harmony in this graceful arcade. Each bay encloses a cube of space defined by the 10-*braccia* (20–foot) height of the columns and the diameter of the arches. Domical vaults, half as high again as the columns, cover the cubes. The bays at the end of the arcade are slightly larger than the rest, creating a subtle frame for the composition. Brunelleschi defined the perfect squares

20–6 Filippo Brunelleschi **OSPEDALE DEGLI INNOCENTI (FOUNDLING HOSPITAL), FLORENCE**
Designed 1419; begun under Brunelleschi's direct supervision 1421–1427; construction continued into the 1440s.

20–7 Andrea della Robbia **INFANT IN SWADDLING CLOTHES (ONE OF THE HOLY INNOCENTS MASSACRED BY HEROD)**
Ospedale degli Innocenti (Foundling Hospital), Florence. c. 1487. Glazed terra cotta.

Credit: pio3/Fotolia

and semicircles of his building with **pietra serena**, a gray Tuscan sandstone, against plain white walls. His training as a goldsmith and sculptor served him well as he led his artisans to carve crisp, elegantly detailed capitals and moldings for the covered gallery.

A later addition to the building seems especially suitable: About 1487, Andrea della Robbia, who had inherited the family ceramics firm and its secret **glazing** formulas from his uncle Luca, created for the spandrels between the arches glazed terra-cotta medallions (**FIG. 20-7**) that signified the building's function. Molds were used in the ceramic workshop to facilitate the production of the series of similar babies in swaddling clothes, one of which was placed at the center of each medallion. The terra-cotta forms were covered with a tin glaze to make the sculptures both weatherproof and decorative, and the baby-blue ceramic backgrounds—a signature color for the della Robbia family workshop—makes the babies seem to float as celestial apparitions. This is not altogether inappropriate. Although they clearly refer to the foundlings (*innocenti*) cared for in the hospital, they are also meant to evoke the innocent baby boys martyred by King Herod in his attempt to rid his realm of the potential rival the Magi had journeyed to venerate (Matthew 2:16).

Andrea della Robbia's ceramic babies—which remain among the most beloved images of the city of Florence—seem to lay claim to the human side of Renaissance humanism, reminding viewers that the city's wealthiest

guild cared for the most helpless members of society. Perhaps the Foundling Hospital spoke to fifteenth-century Florentines' increased sense of social responsibility. Or perhaps, by so publicly demonstrating social concerns, the wealthy guild that sponsored the hospital solicited the support of the lower classes in the cut-throat power politics of the day.

SAN LORENZO   For the Medicis' parish church of San Lorenzo, Brunelleschi designed and built a centrally planned sacristy (a room where ritual attire and vessels are kept) from 1421 to 1428 and also conceived plans for a new church. The church has a basilican plan with a long nave flanked by side aisles that open into shallow lateral chapels (**FIG. 20-8**). A short transept and square crossing lead to a square sanctuary flanked by additional chapels opening off the transept. Brunelleschi based his mathematically regular plan on a square module—a basic unit of measure that could be multiplied or divided and applied to every element of the design, creating a series of clear, harmonious spaces. Architectural details, all in a Classical style, were carved in the dark gray *pietra serena*, that became synonymous with Brunelleschi's interiors. Below the plain clerestory with its unobtrusive openings, the arches of the nave arcade are carried on tall, slender Corinthian columns made even taller by the insertion of an impost block between the column capital and the springing of the round arches—one of Brunelleschi's

20–8A Filippo Brunelleschi (continued by Michelozzo di Bartolomeo) **INTERIOR OF CHURCH OF SAN LORENZO, FLORENCE**

c. 1421–1428; nave (designed 1434?) 1442–1470.

Credit: © Studio Fotografico Quattrone, Florence

20–8B Filippo Brunelleschi (continued by Michelozzo di Bartolomeo) **PLAN OF CHURCH OF SAN LORENZO, FLORENCE**

c. 1421–1428; nave (designed 1434?) 1442–1470.

favorite details. Flattened architectural moldings in *pietra serena* repeat the arcade in the outer walls of the side aisles, and each bay is covered by its own shallow domical vault. Brunelleschi's rational approach, clear sense of order, and innovative incorporation of Classical motifs inspired later Renaissance architects, many of whom learned from his work firsthand by completing his unfinished projects.

THE MEDICI PALACE Brunelleschi may have been involved in designing the nearby Medici Palace (now known as the **PALAZZO MEDICI-RICCARDI**) in 1446. According to Giorgio Vasari, the sixteenth-century artist and theorist who wrote the first modern history of art, Cosimo de' Medici the Elder rejected Brunelleschi's model for the **palazzo** as too grand (any large house was called a *palazzo*—"palace"). Many now attribute the design of the building to Michelozzo. The austere exterior (**FIG. 20-9**) was in keeping with the Florentine political climate and religious attitudes, both imbued with the Franciscan ideals of poverty and charity. Like many other European cities, Florence had sumptuary laws that forbade ostentatious displays of wealth—but they were often ignored. For example, private homes were supposed to be limited to a dozen rooms, but Cosimo acquired and demolished 20 small houses to provide the site for his new residence. His house was more than a dwelling place; it was his place of business, his company headquarters. The palazzo symbolized the family and established its place in the Florentine social hierarchy.

Huge in scale—each story is more than 20 feet high—the building is marked by harmonious proportions and elegant, Classically inspired details. On one side, the ground floor originally opened through large, round arches onto the street, creating in effect a loggia that provided space for the family business. These arches were walled up in the sixteenth century and given windows designed by Michelangelo. The large, **rusticated** stone blocks—that is, blocks with their outer faces left rough—facing the lower story clearly set it off from the upper two levels. In fact, all three stories are distinguished by stone surfaces that vary from sculptural at the ground level to almost smooth dressed stone on the third floor.

The builders followed the time-honored tradition of placing rooms around a central courtyard. Unlike the plan of the house of Jacques Coeur (SEE FIG. 19–24A), however, the Palazzo Medici-Riccardi courtyard is square in plan with rooms arranged symmetrically (**FIG. 20–10**). Round arches on slender columns form a continuous arcade under an enclosed second story. Disks bearing the Medici arms top each arch in a frieze decorated with swags in **sgraffito** work (decoration produced by scratching through a darker layer of plaster or glaze). Such classicizing elements, inspired by the study of Roman ruins, gave the great house an aura of dignity and stability that enhanced the status of its owners. The Medici Palace inaugurated a new fashion for monumentality and regularity in residential Florentine architecture.

Sculpture

The new architectural language inspired by ancient Classical forms was accompanied by a similar impulse in sculpture. By 1400, Florence had enjoyed internal stability and economic prosperity for over two decades. However, until 1428, the city and its independence were challenged by two great anti-republican powers: the duchy of Milan and the kingdom of Naples. In an atmosphere of wealth and civic patriotism, Florentines turned to commissions that would express their self-esteem and magnify the importance of their city. A new attitude toward realism, space, and the Classical past set the stage for more than a century of creativity. Sculptors led the way.

20–9 Attributed to Michelozzo di Bartolomeo **FAÇADE, PALAZZO MEDICI-RICCARDI, FLORENCE**
Begun 1446 (the view shown here includes a two-bay extension constructed during the 18th century).

For the palace site, Cosimo de' Medici the Elder chose the Via de' Gori at the corner of the Via Larga, the widest city street at that time. Despite his practical reasons for constructing a large residence and the fact that he chose simplicity and austerity over grandeur in the exterior design, his detractors commented and gossiped. As one exaggerated, "[Cosimo] has begun a palace which throws even the Colosseum at Rome into the shade."

Credit: © Achim Bednorz, Cologne

20–10 COURTYARD WITH SGRAFFITO DECORATION, PALAZZO MEDICI-RICCARDI, FLORENCE
Begun 1446.

Credit: © Studio Fotografico Quattrone, Florence

20-11 EXTERIOR VIEW OF ORSANMICHELE SHOWING SCULPTURE IN NICHES
Florence. Begun 1337.

At street level, Orsanmichele was constructed originally as an open loggia (similar to the Loggia dei Lanzi in FIG. 18–2); in 1380 the spaces under the arches were filled in. In this view of the southeast corner, appearing on the receding wall to the left is first (in the foreground on the corner pier) Donatello's *St. George*, then, Nanni di Banco's *Four Crowned Martyrs*. However, the sculptures seen in this photograph are modern replicas; the originals have been removed to museums for safekeeping.

Credit: © Studio Fotografico Quattrone, Florence

ORSANMICHELE In 1339, 14 of Florence's most powerful guilds had been commissioned to fill the ground-floor niches that decorated the exterior of **ORSANMICHELE**—a newly completed loggia that served as a grain market—with sculpted images of their patron saints (**FIG. 20–11**). By 1400, only three had fulfilled this assignment. In the new climate of republicanism and civic pride, the government pressured the guilds to fill their niches. This directive resulted in a dazzling display of sculpture produced by the most impressive local practitioners, including Nanni di Banco, Lorenzo Ghiberti, and Donatello, each of whom took responsibility for filling three niches.

In about 1409, Nanni di Banco (c. 1385–1421), son of a sculptor in the Florence Cathedral workshop, was commissioned by the stonecarver and woodworkers' guild (to which he himself belonged) to produce **THE FOUR CROWNED MARTYRS** (**FIG. 20–12**). According to tradition, these third- or fourth-century Christian martyrs were sculptors executed for refusing to make an image of a pagan Roman god for Emperor Diocletian. Although the architectural setting is Gothic in style, Nanni's

figures—with their solid bodies, heavy yet form-revealing togas, noble hair and beards, and portraitlike features—reveal his interest in ancient Roman sculpture, particularly portraiture (SEE FIG. 6–15). They testify to this sculptor's role in the Florentine revival of interest in antiquity.

The saints convey a new spatial relationship to the building and to the viewer. They stand in a semicircle, with feet and drapery protruding beyond the floor of the niche and into the viewer's space. The saints appear to be four individuals interacting within their own world, but a world that opens to engage with passing pedestrians (SEE FIG. 20–11). The relief panel below the niche shows the four sculptors at work, embodied with a similar solid vigor. Nanni deeply undercut both figures and objects to cast shadows that enhance the illusion of three-dimensionality.

DONATELLO Donatello (Donato di Niccolò di Betto Bardi, c. 1386/1387–1466) also received three commissions for the niches at Orsanmichele during the first quarter of the century. Like Nanni a member of the guild of stonecarvers and woodworkers, he worked in both media, as well as in bronze. During a long and productive career, he developed into one of the most influential and distinguished figures in the history of Italian sculpture, approaching each commission as if it were the opportunity for a new experiment. One of Florence's lesser guilds—the armorers and sword-makers—called on Donatello to carve a majestic and self-assured **ST. GEORGE** for their niche (**FIG. 20-13**). As originally conceived, the saint would have been a standing advertisement for their trade, carrying a metal sword in his right hand and probably wearing a metal

20-12 Nanni di Banco **THE FOUR CROWNED MARTYRS**

c. 1409–1417. Marble, height of figures 6′ (1.83 m). Photographed *in situ* before removal of the figures to the Museo di Orsanmichele, Florence.

Credit: © Studio Fotografico Quattrone, Florence

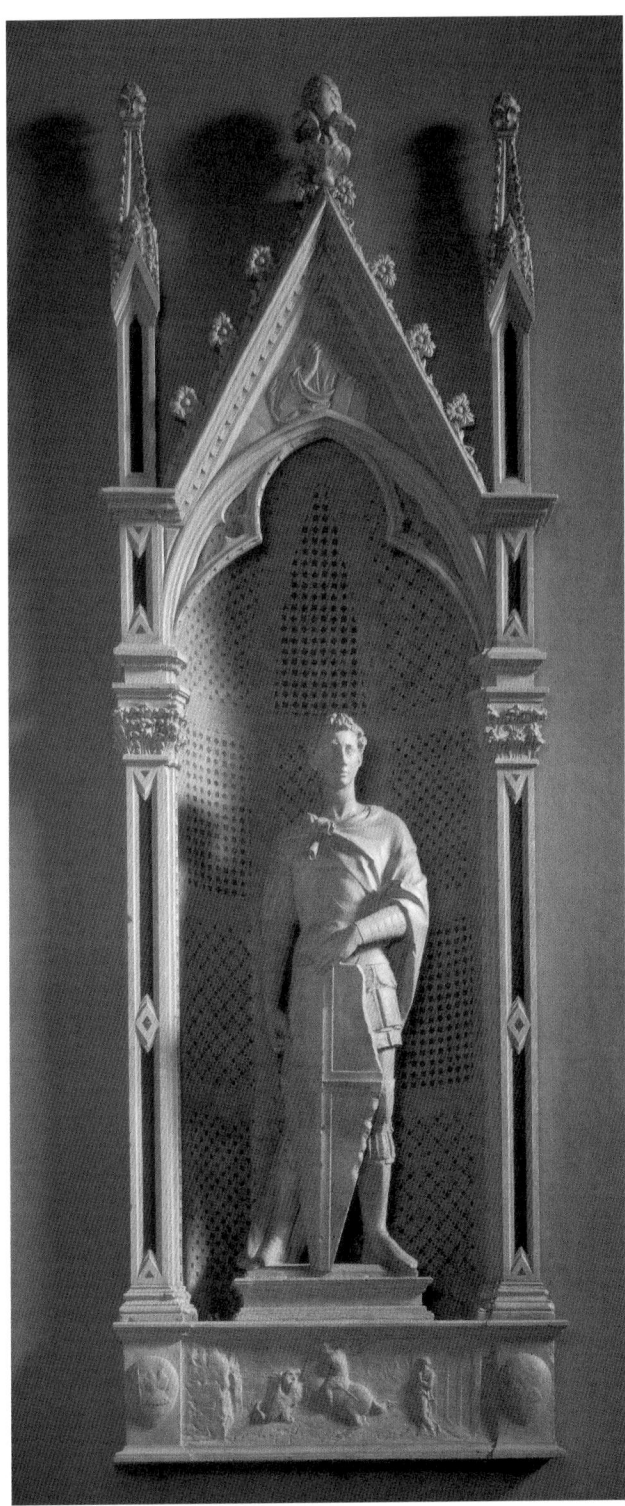

20–13 Donatello **ST. GEORGE**

Formerly in Orsanmichele, Florence. 1417–1420. Marble, height 6′5″ (1.95 m). Museo Nazionale del Bargello, Florence.

Credit: © Studio Fotografico Quattrone, Florence

20-14 Donatello **DAVID**

c. 1446–1460 (?). Bronze, height 5'2¼" (1.58 m). Museo Nazionale del Bargello, Florence.

This sculpture is first recorded as being in the courtyard of the Medici Palace in 1469, where it stood on a base inscribed with these lines:

> The victor is whoever defends the fatherland.
> All-powerful God crushes the angry enemy.
> Behold, a boy overcomes the great tyrant.
> Conquer, O citizens!

helmet and sporting a scabbard, all now lost. The figure has remarkable presence, even without his accessories. St. George stands in solid defiance, legs braced to support his armor-heavy torso. He seems to stare out into our world, perhaps sizing up his most famous adversary—a dragon that was holding a princess captive—lurking in the space behind us. With his wrinkled brow and determined expression, he is alert and focused, if perhaps also slightly worried. This complex psychological characterization of the warrior-saint particularly impressed Donatello's contemporaries, not least among them his potential patrons.

For the base of the niche, Donatello carved a remarkable shallow relief showing St. George slaying the dragon and saving the princess, a well-known part of his story. The contours of the foreground figures are slightly undercut to emphasize their mass, while the landscape and architecture are in progressively lower relief until they are barely incised rather than carved, an ingenious emulation of the painter's technique of atmospheric perspective. This is also a pioneering example of linear perspective (see "Renaissance Perspective" on page 623), in which the orthogonals converge on the figure of the saint himself. Donatello used this timely representational system not only to simulate spatial recession, but also to provide narrative focus.

Donatello's long career as a sculptor in a broad variety of media established him as one of the most successful and admired sculptors of the Italian Renaissance. He excelled in part because of his attentive exploration of human emotions and expression, as well as his ability to solve the technical problems posed by various media—from lost-wax casting in bronze and carved marble to polychromed wood.

Donatello's bronze **DAVID** was the first life-size, free-standing nude since antiquity (**FIG. 20-14**). Since nothing is known about the circumstances of its creation, this statue has been the subject of continuing inquiry and speculation. Although the representation of David clearly draws on the Classical tradition of heroic nudity, the meaning of this sensuous, pre-pubescent boy in a jaunty, laurel-trimmed shepherd's hat and boots has long piqued interest. Some art historians have stressed an overt homoeroticism, especially in the openly effeminate conception of David and the way a wing from the helmet on Goliath's severed head brushes the young hero's inner thigh. Others have seen in David's angular pose and boyish torso a sense that he is poised between childish interests and adult responsibility, an image of improbable heroism. David was a potent political image in Florence, a symbol of the citizens' resolve to oppose tyrants regardless of their superior power, since virtue brings divine support and preternatural strength, and we will see other Florentine Renaissance renderings of this biblical hero. Indeed, an inscription engraved into the base where the sculpture once stood suggests that it could have celebrated the Florentine triumph over the Milanese in 1425, a victory that brought resolution to a quarter-century struggle with despots and helped give Florence a vision of itself as a strong, virtuous republic.

Probably in 1443, Donatello traveled to Padua to execute one of the first life-size bronze equestrian portraits of the Renaissance—an **EQUESTRIAN STATUE** (**FIG. 20-15**) commemorating the Paduan general of the Venetian army, Erasmo da Narni, nicknamed "Gattamelata" (meaning "Honeyed Cat"—a reference to his mother, Melania Gattelli). If any image could be said to characterize the self-made men of the Italian Renaissance, surely it would be those of the *condottieri*—the brilliant generals such as Gattamelata and Niccolò da Tolentino (SEE FIG. 20-1) who organized the armies and fought for any city-state willing to pay for their services. As guardians for hire, they were tough, opportunistic mercenaries. But they also subscribed to an ideal of military and civic virtue. Horsemanship was more than a necessary skill for the *condottieri*. The horse, a beast of enormous strength, symbolized animal passions, and skilled horsemanship demonstrated physical and intellectual control—self-control, as well as control of the animal—the triumph of "mind over matter."

Donatello's sources for this statue were surviving Roman bronze equestrian portraits, notably the famous image of Marcus Aurelius (SEE FIG. 6-56), which the sculptor certainly knew from his stay in Rome, and the famous set of Roman bronze horses installed on the façade of St. Mark's Cathedral in Venice. Viewed from a distance, Donatello's man–animal juggernaut, installed on a high marble base in front of the church of Sant'Antonio in Padua, seems capable of thrusting forward at the first threat. Seen up close, however, the man's sunken cheeks, sagging jaw, ropy neck, and stern but sad expression suggest a warrior grown old and tired from the constant need for military vigilance and rapid response.

20-16 Lorenzo Ghiberti **"GATES OF PARADISE"** (EAST BAPTISTERY DOORS)

Formerly on the Baptistery of San Giovanni, Florence. 1425–1452. Gilt bronze, height 15′ (4.57 m). Museo dell'Opera del Duomo, Florence.

The door panels, commissioned by the wool manufacturers' guild, depict ten scenes from the Hebrew Bible beginning with the Creation in the upper left panel. The murder of Abel by his brother, Cain, follows in the upper right panel, succeeded in the same left–right paired order by the Flood and the drunkenness of Noah, Abraham sacrificing Isaac; the story of Jacob and Esau, Joseph sold into slavery by his brothers; Moses receiving the Tablets of the Law, Joshua and the fall of Jericho; and finally David and Goliath, Solomon and the queen of Sheba. Ghiberti placed his own portrait as a signature in the frame at the lower right corner of the Jacob and Esau panel. He wrote in his *Commentaries* (c. 1450–1455): "I strove to imitate nature as clearly as I could, and with all the perspective I could produce, to have excellent compositions with many figures."

GHIBERTI'S GATES OF PARADISE   The bronze doors that Lorenzo Ghiberti (1381?–1455) produced for the Florentine Baptistery after winning his famous competition with Brunelleschi in 1401 were such a success that in 1425 he was awarded the commission for yet another set of bronze doors for the east side of the baptistery, facing the doors of the cathedral; his first set of doors was moved to the north side. The new door panels, funded by the wool manufacturers' guild, were a significant conceptual leap from the older schemes of 28 small scenes employed for Ghiberti's earlier doors and those of Andrea Pisano in the fourteenth century (SEE FIG. 18–3). Ghiberti departed entirely from the old arrangement, producing a set of ten scenes from the Hebrew Bible—from the Creation to the reign of Solomon—composed in rectangular fields, like a set of framed paintings. Michelangelo reportedly said that the results, installed in 1452, were worthy of the **"GATES OF PARADISE"**—the name by which they are now commonly known (FIG. 20–16).

Ghiberti organized the space in the ten square reliefs either by a system of linear perspective with obvious orthogonal lines (see "Renaissance Perspective" on page 623) or more intuitively by a series of arches, rocks, or trees charting a path into the distance. Foreground figures are grouped in the

20-17 Lorenzo Ghiberti **JACOB AND ESAU, PANEL OF THE "GATES OF PARADISE"** (EAST BAPTISTERY DOORS)

Formerly on the Baptistery of San Giovanni, Florence. c. 1435. Gilded bronze, 31¼″ (79 cm) square. Museo dell'Opera del Duomo, Florence.

lower third of each panel, while the other figures decrease gradually in size to map their positioning in deep space. The use of a system of perspective, with clearly differentiated background and foreground, also helped Ghiberti combine a series of related events, separated by narrative time, within a single pictorial frame.

The story of **JACOB AND ESAU** (Genesis 25 and 27) fills the center panel of the left door. Ghiberti creates a coherent and measurable space peopled by graceful, idealized figures (FIG. 20–17). He pays careful attention to one-point perspective in laying out the architectural setting. Squares in the pavement establish the receding lines of the orthogonals that converge on a vanishing point under the loggia, while towering arches overlap and gradually diminish in size from foreground to background to define the receding space above the figures. The story unfolds in a series of individual episodes beginning in the background. On the rooftop (upper right) Rebecca stands, listening as God warns of her unborn sons' future conflict; under the left-hand arch she gives birth to the twins. The adult Esau sells his rights as oldest son to his brother Jacob, and when he goes hunting (center right), Rebecca and Jacob plot against him. Finally, in the right foreground, Jacob receives Isaac's blessing, while in the center, Esau faces his father. Ghiberti's portrayal of the scene relates more closely to developments in painting than to contemporary sculpture. Ghiberti not only signed his work, but also included his self-portrait in the medallion beside the lower right corner of this panel.

Masaccio

Even though his career lasted less than a decade, Tommaso di Ser Giovanni di Mone Cassai (1401–1428/1429?), nicknamed "Masaccio" (meaning "Big Tom"), established a new direction in Florentine painting much as Giotto had a century earlier. He did this by integrating monumental and consistently scaled figures into rational architectural and natural settings using linear perspective. The chronology of Massaccio's works is uncertain, but his fresco of the **TRINITY** in the church of Santa Maria Novella in Florence must have been painted around 1426, the date on the Lenzi family tombstone that once stood in front of it (**FIGS. 20–18, 20–19**).

Masaccio's fresco was meant to give the illusion of a stone funerary monument and altar table set below a deep **aedicula** (framed niche) in the wall. The effect of looking up into a barrel-vaulted niche was made plausible through precisely rendered linear perspective. The eye level of an adult male viewer standing within the church determined the horizon line on which the vanishing point was centered, just below the kneeling figures above the altar. And the painting demonstrates not only Masaccio's intimate

20–18 Masaccio **TRINITY WITH THE VIRGIN, ST. JOHN THE EVANGELIST, AND DONORS**
Church of Santa Maria Novella, Florence. c. 1425–1427/1428. Fresco, 21′ × 10′5″ (6.4 × 3.2 m).

Credit: © Studio Fotografico Quattrone, Florence

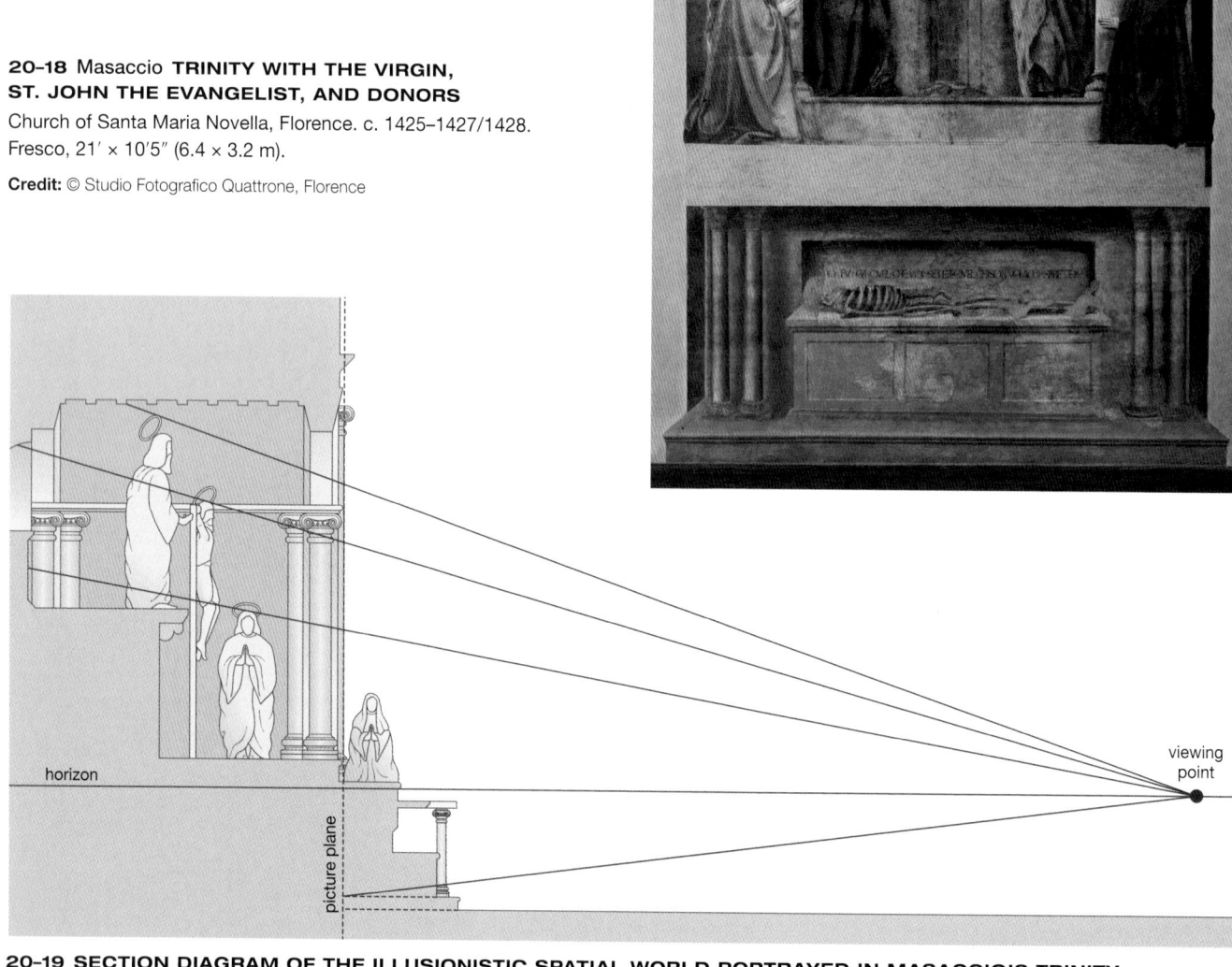

20–19 SECTION DIAGRAM OF THE ILLUSIONISTIC SPATIAL WORLD PORTRAYED IN MASACCIO'S TRINITY

Technique

RENAISSANCE PERSPECTIVE

Fifteenth-century Italian artists developed a system known as linear, or mathematical, perspective that enabled them to represent three dimensions on a two-dimensional surface, simulating the recession of space in the visible world pictorially in a way they found convincing. The sculptor and architect Filippo Brunelleschi first demonstrated the system about 1420, and the theorist and architect Leon Battista Alberti codified it in 1436 in his treatise *Della Pittura (On Painting)*.

For Alberti, in one-point linear perspective a picture's surface was conceived as a flat plane that intersected the viewer's field of vision at right angles. This highly artificial concept presumed a viewer standing dead center at a prescribed distance from a work of art. From this single fixed vantage point, everything would appear to recede into the distance at the same rate, following imaginary lines called orthogonals that met at a single **vanishing point** on the horizon. By using orthogonals in concert with controlled diminution of scale as forms move back toward the vanishing point, artists could replicate the optical illusion that things appear to grow smaller, rise higher, and come closer together as they get farther away from us. Linear perspective makes pictorial spaces seem almost like extensions of the viewer's real space, creating a compelling, even exaggerated sense of depth (**FIG. 20-20**).

Linear perspective is not the only way to simulate spatial recession in two dimensions (see "Pictorial Devices for Depicting Recession in Space" in the Starter Kit on page xviii). In atmospheric perspective, for example, variations in color and clarity convey the feeling of distance: objects and landscape are portrayed less clearly, and colors become grayer, in the background, imitating the natural effects of a loss of clarity and color when viewing things in the distance through an atmospheric haze.

20-20A Perugino **CHRIST GIVING THE KEYS TO ST. PETER**

Fresco on the right wall of the Sistine Chapel (SEE FIG. 20-41), Vatican, Rome. c. 1480–1482. 11′5½″ × 18′8½″ (3.48 × 5.70 m).

Perugino's painting is, among other things, a representation of Alberti's ideal city, described in *De Re Aedificatoria* as having a "temple" (that is, a church) at the very center of a great open space, raised on a dais and separate from any other buildings that might obstruct it.

Credit: Canali Photobank, Milan, Italy

20-20B SCHEMATIC DRAWING SHOWING THE ORTHOGONALS AND VANISHING POINT OF CHRIST GIVING THE KEYS TO ST. PETER

Christ Giving the Keys to St. Peter is a remarkable study in linear perspective. The clear demarcation of the paving stones of the piazza provides a network of orthogonal and horizontal lines for the measured placement of the figures. People and buildings become systematically smaller as the space recedes. Horizontally, the composition is divided between the foreground frieze of figures and the widely spaced background buildings; it is vertically divided by the open space at the center between Christ and Peter and by the symmetrical architectural forms on either side of this central axis.

20–21 Masaccio **THE EXPULSION OF ADAM AND EVE FROM PARADISE**

Brancacci Chapel, church of Santa Maria del Carmine, Florence. c. 1427. Fresco, 7′ × 2′11″ (214 × 90 cm).

Cleaning and restoration of the Brancacci Chapel paintings revealed the remarkable speed and skill with which Masaccio worked. He painted Adam and Eve in four *giornate* (each *giornata* of fresh plaster representing a day's work). Working from the top down and left to right, he painted the angel on the first day, the portal on the second day, Adam on the third day, and Eve on the fourth.

Credit: © Studio Fotografico Quattrone, Florence

knowledge of Brunelleschi's perspective experiments (see "Renaissance Perspective" on page 623), but also his architectural style (SEE FIG. 20–8). The painted architecture is an unusual combination of Classical orders. On the wall surface, Corinthian pilasters support a plain architrave below a cornice, while inside the niche Renaissance variations on Ionic columns support framing arches at the front and rear of the barrel vault. The "source" of the consistent illumination of the architecture lies in front of the picture, casting reflections on the coffers, or sunken panels, of the ceiling.

The figures are organized in a measured progression through space. At the near end of the recessed, barrel-vaulted space is the Trinity—Jesus on the cross, the dove of the Holy Spirit poised in downward flight above his tilted halo, and God the Father, who stands behind to support the cross from his perch on a high platform. As in many scenes of the Crucifixion, Jesus is flanked by the Virgin Mary and John the Evangelist, who contemplate the scene on either side of the cross. Mary gazes calmly out at us, her raised hand drawing our attention to the Trinity. Members of the Lenzi family kneel in front of the pilasters—thus closer to us than the Crucifixion; the red robes of the male donor signify that he was a member of the governing council of Florence. Below these donors, in an open sarcophagus, is a skeleton, a grim reminder of the Christian belief that since death awaits us all, our only hope is redemption and the promise of life in the hereafter, rooted in Christ's sacrifice on the cross. The inscription above the skeleton reads: "I was once that which you are, and what I am you also will be."

THE BRANCACCI CHAPEL Masaccio's brief career culminated in the frescos he painted on the walls of the Brancacci Chapel in the church of Santa Maria del Carmine in Florence. Two of the best-known scenes are **THE EXPULSION OF ADAM AND EVE FROM PARADISE** (FIG. 20–21) and **THE TRIBUTE MONEY** (FIG. 20–22). In *The Expulsion*, Masaccio presented Adam and Eve as monumental nude figures, combining his studies of the human figure with an intimate knowledge of ancient Roman sculpture. In contrast to Flemish painters, who sought to record every detail of a figure's surface (compare Adam and Eve from FIG. 19–13), Masaccio focused on the mass of the bodies formed by the underlying bone and muscle structure; a single light source emphasizes their physicality with modeled forms and cast shadows. Departing from earlier interpretations of the event, which emphasized wrong-doing and the fall from grace, Masaccio concerns himself with the psychological impact of shame on these first humans, who have been cast out of paradise and thrown naked into the world.

In *The Tribute Money* (SEE FIG. 20–22), Masaccio portrays an incident from the life of Jesus that highlights St. Peter (Matthew 17:24–27), to whom this chapel was dedicated.

20–22 Masaccio **THE TRIBUTE MONEY**
Brancacci Chapel, church of Santa Maria del Carmine, Florence. c. 1427. Fresco, 8′1″ × 19′7″ (2.46 × 6 m).

Credit: © Studio Fotografico Quattrone, Florence

In the central scene a tax collector (dressed in a short red tunic and seen from behind) asks Peter (in the left foreground with the short gray beard) if Jesus pays the Jewish temple tax (the "tribute money" of the title). Set against the stable backdrop of a semicircular block of apostolic observers, a masterful series of dynamic diagonals in the postures and gestures of the three main figures interlocks them in a compositional system that gives their interaction a sense of tension calling out for resolution. Jesus instructs Peter to "go to the sea, drop in a hook, and take the first fish that comes up," which Peter does at the far left. In the fish's mouth is a coin, which Peter gives to the tax collector at the far right. The tribute story was especially significant for Florentines because in 1427, to raise money for defense against military aggression, the city enacted a graduated tax, based on the value of people's personal property.

The Tribute Money is particularly remarkable for its early use of both linear and atmospheric perspective to integrate figures, architecture, and landscape into a consistent whole. Jesus and the apostles surrounding him form a clear central focus, from which the landscape seems to recede naturally into the far distance. To create this illusion, Masaccio used linear perspective in the depiction of the house, and then reinforced it by diminishing the sizes of the distant trees and the crouching Peter at far left. The central vanishing point established by the orthogonals of the house corresponds with the head of Jesus.

The cleaning of the painting in the 1980s revealed that it was painted in 32 *giornate* (a *giornata* is a section of fresh

plaster that could be prepared and painted in a single day; see "*Buon Fresco*" in Chapter 18 on page 551). The cleaning also uncovered Masaccio's subtle use of color to create atmospheric perspective in the distant landscape: Mountains fade from grayish-green to grayish-white, and the houses and trees on their slopes are loosely sketched to simulate the lack of clear definition when viewing things in the distance through a haze. Green leaves were painted on the branches *al secco* (meaning "on the dry plastered wall").

As in *The Expulsion*, Masaccio modeled the foreground figures here with bold highlights and long shadows on the ground toward the left, giving a strong sense of volumetric solidity and implying a light source at the far right, as if the scene were lit by the actual window in the rear wall of the Brancacci Chapel. Not only does the lighting give the forms sculptural definition, but the colors also vary in tone according to the strength of the illumination. Masaccio used a wide range of hues—pale pink, mauve, gold, blue-green, seafoam green, apple green, peach— and a sophisticated shading technique using contrasting colors, as in Andrew's green robe, which is shaded with red instead of darker green. The figures of Jesus and the apostles originally had gold-leaf haloes, several of which have flaked off. Rather than silhouette the heads against consistently flat gold circles (for example, see FIG. 18–6), however, Masaccio conceived of haloes as gold disks hovering in space above each head that moved with the heads as they moved, and he foreshortened them depending on the angle from which each head is seen.

Some stylistic innovations take time to be fully accepted, and Masaccio's innovative depictions of volumetric solidity, consistent lighting, and spatial integration—though they clearly had an impact on his immediate successors—were perhaps best appreciated by a later generation of painters. Many important sixteenth-century Italian artists, including Michelangelo, studied and sketched Masaccio's Brancacci Chapel frescos, as they did Giotto's work in the Scrovegni Chapel. In the meantime, painting in Florence after Masaccio's death developed along somewhat different lines.

Painting in Florence After Masaccio

The tradition of covering walls with frescos continued uninterrupted through the fifteenth century. Between 1438 and 1445, Fra Angelico's decoration of the Dominican monastery of San Marco in Florence was one of the most extensive projects.

FRA ANGELICO Guido di Piero da Mugello (c. 1395/1400–1455) earned his nickname "Fra Angelico" ("Angelic Brother") through his piety as well as his painting: In 1982, he was beatified, the first step toward sainthood. Fra Angelico is first documented painting in Florence in 1417–1418, and he remained an active painter after taking vows as a Dominican monk in nearby Fiesole between 1418 and 1421.

Between 1438 and 1445, in the monastery of San Marco, Fra Angelico and his assistants—probably working under the patronage of Cosimo de' Medici—created paintings to inspire meditation in each monk's cell (44 in all; see FIGS. Intro-8, Intro-9), in the chapter house (meeting room), and even in the hallways. At the top of the stairs in the north corridor, where the monks passed frequently on their way to their individual cells, Fra Angelico painted a serene picture of the **ANNUNCIATION** (FIG. 20-23). To describe the quiet, measured space where the demure archangel greets the unassuming, youthful Mary, Fra Angelico used linear perspective with striking sensitivity, extending the monks' stairway and corridor outward into an imagined portico and garden beside the Virgin's home. The slender, graceful figures wear quietly flowing draperies and assume modest poses. Natural light falling from the left models their forms gently, casting an almost supernatural radiance over their faces and hands. This is a sacred vision rendered in a contemporary setting, welcoming the monks to the most intimate areas of the monastery and preparing them for their private meditations. The line of Latin text running along the bottom of the picture directs the monks, "As you revere this figure of the intact Virgin while passing before it, beware lest you omit to say a Hail Mary."

20-23 Fra Angelico **ANNUNCIATION**
North dormitory corridor, monastery of San Marco, Florence. c. 1438–1445. Fresco, 7'1" × 10'6" (2.2 × 3.2 m).

The shadowed vault of the portico is supported by a wall on one side and by slender Ionic and Corinthian columns on the other, a new building technique used by Brunelleschi (SEE FIG. 20-6).

Credit: © Studio Fotografico Quattrone, Florence

20-24 Paolo Uccello **THE BATTLE OF SAN ROMANO**
1438–1440. Tempera on wood panel, approx. 6′ × 10′6″ (1.82 × 3.2 m). National Gallery, London.

Credit: © 2016. Copyright The National Gallery, London/Scala, Florence

UCCELLO At mid century, when Fra Angelico was still painting his radiant visions of Mary and Jesus in the monastery of San Marco, other artists explored different directions. Thoroughly familiar with the theories of Brunelleschi and Alberti, they had mastered the techniques of depicting figures in a constructed architectural space. Paolo Uccello devoted himself with special fervor to the study of linear perspective (**FIG. 20-24**; see also FIG. 20-1). In his biographies of Italian artists, Vasari described Uccello as a man so obsessed with the science of perspective that he neglected his painting, his family, and even his pet birds (his *uccelli*). According to Vasari, Uccello's wife complained that he sat up drawing all night, and when she called to him to come to bed he would say, "Oh, what a sweet thing this perspective is!" (Vasari, trans. Bondanella and Bondanella, p. 83).

CASTAGNO Andrea del Castagno (c. 1417/1419–1457) is best known for a fresco of **THE LAST SUPPER** painted for a convent of Benedictine nuns in 1447 (**FIG. 20-25**). The subject was often painted in monastic refectories (dining halls) to remind the monks or nuns of Christ's Last Supper with his first followers and encourage them to see their daily gatherings for meals almost as a sacramental act rooted in this biblical tradition. Here Castagno has not portrayed the

20-25 Andrea del Castagno **THE LAST SUPPER**
Refectory, convent of Sant'Apollonia, Florence. 1447. Fresco, width approx. 16 × 32′ (4.6 × 9.8 m).

Castagno worked quickly, completing this huge mural in at most 32 days.

scene in the biblical setting of an "upper room." Rather, the humble house of the original account has become a great palace with sumptuous marble revetment. The most brilliantly colored and wildly patterned marble panel frames the off-center heads of Christ and Judas to focus viewers on the most important part of the picture. Judas takes his traditional position on the viewer's side of the table, separated from the other apostles. Equally conventional is the seemingly sleeping figure of St. John, head collapsed onto the tabletop (John 13:23). The lines of floor tiles, ceiling rafters, and paneled walls draw viewers into the scene; the

nuns would have seen the painting as an extension of their own dining hall. At first, the lines of the orthogonals seem perfectly logical, but close examination reveals that only the lines of the ceiling converge to a single point. Two windows light the painting's room from the direction of the actual refectory windows, further unifying the two spaces.

FRA FILIPPO LIPPI During the middle of the fifteenth century, portraiture came into its own as a major artistic form in Italy, and among the most extraordinary—if enigmatic—examples is this **PORTRAIT OF A WOMAN AND MAN (FIG. 20-26)**, an early work of Fra Filippo Lippi (c. 1406–1469). This painting is also the earliest surviving double portrait of the Italian Renaissance. Lippi grew up as an orphan in the Carmelite church where Masaccio had painted frescos in the Brancacci Chapel, and art historians have stressed the impact this work had on Lippi's development as an artist. But although he may have absorbed Masaccio's predilection for softly rounded forms situated in carefully mapped spaces, in Lippi's hands these artistic tools became the basis for pictures that often ask more questions than they answer, by stressing outline at the same time as form and creating complex and often confusing spatial systems.

The emphasis in this double portrait is squarely on the woman. She is spotlighted in the foreground, sharply profiled against a window that serves as an unsettling internal frame, not big enough to contain her. This window opens onto a vista, clearly a fragment of a larger world, but one that highlights an orthogonal to emphasize a spatial recession only partially revealed. The woman blocks most of this vista with her shining visage and sumptuous costume—notably its embroidered velvet, fur lining, and luminous pearls. There is no engagement with the viewer and little sense of likeness. And it is not at all clear what she is looking at, especially since the gaze of the man in the background does not meet hers. He is even more of a mystery. We see only a masklike sliver of his profile, capped by the red *berretta* that signals his high status—although the substantiality of his face is reinforced by the strong shadow it casts against the window casement through which he looks. Unlike the woman, who clasps her inert hands in front of her as if to highlight her rings, this man fidgets with his fingers, perhaps to draw our attention to the heraldic device below him that may identify him as a member of the Scolari family. This could be a double portrait of Lorenzo di Ranieri Scolari and Angiola di Bernardo Sapiti, who married in 1436 and welcomed a son in 1444. But what does the painting say about them? Does it commemorate their marriage, celebrate the birth of their child, or memorialize one of their deaths? All have been proposed by art historians as an explanation for this innovative double portrait, but it remains a puzzle to be pondered. Could that pondering be the point of the picture?

20–26 Fra Filippo Lippi **PORTRAIT OF A WOMAN AND MAN (ANGIOLA DI BERNARDO SAPITI AND LORENZO DI RANIERI SCOLARI?)**
c. 1435–1445. Tempera on wood panel, 25¼ × 16½"
(64.1 × 41.9 cm). Metropolitan Museum of Art, New York.

Some art historians have seen in the sumptuousness of this woman's costume an indication that she is a newlywed, outfitted in the extravagant clothing and jewelry presented to her by her husband at the time of their marriage, especially since the pearls sewn with gold threads into the embroidery on her sleeve spell out the word *lealtà*, meaning "loyalty." Florentine law prevented a woman from wearing such ostentatious expressions of wealth—particularly the jewelry—more than three years after her marriage.

Florentine Art in the Second Half of the Fifteenth Century

How do Renaissance sculpture and painting continue to develop in Florence during the second half of the fifteenth century?

Florence remained a thriving artistic center throughout the fifteenth century. Sculptors continued to explore Classical themes and experiment with the representation of the human form. Florentine painting pursued a love of material opulence, an interest in describing the natural world, and a poetic, mystical spirit, motivated by the patronage of citizens who sought to advertise their wealth and social standing, as well as by the religious fervor that arose at the very end of the century.

20–27 Andrea del Verrocchio **DAVID**
Commissioned by Lorenzo de' Medici for the Medici Palace.
c. 1470–1475. Bronze with gilded details, height 49⅝" (1.26 m).
Museo Nazionale del Bargello, Florence.

Credit: © Studio Fotografico Quattrone, Florence

Verrocchio

One of the most prestigious and active workshops in Florence was that of Andrea di Michele Cioni (1435–1488), nicknamed "Verrocchio" ("true eye"). Trained as a goldsmith, but best known for his works as a painter and bronze sculptor, Verrocchio was also a gifted teacher, counting among his pupils Perugino and Leonardo da Vinci. Around 1470, Lorenzo de' Medici commissioned a bronze statue of David from Verrocchio for the Palazzo Medici, the location where Donatello's sculpture of the same subject (SEE FIG. 20-14) was then displayed. Verrocchio's work (**FIG. 20-27**) seems to have been conceived as a response to the demure, sleek, but awkwardly boyish nude of his famous predecessor. Verrocchio's triumphant biblical hero is a poised and proud adolescent, modestly clothed and confidently looking out to meet the gaze of the viewer. Although slight, he is equipped with the developing musculature required for the daunting task—whose accomplishment is signaled by the severed head of his foe, displayed like a trophy between his feet. The careful attention to the textural details of hair and clothing reveal Verrocchio's training as a goldsmith.

Pollaiuolo

Florentine sculptors created not only large-scale figures, but also small works. The ambitious and multi-talented Antonio del Pollaiuolo (c. 1431–1498)—a goldsmith, embroidery designer, printmaker, sculptor, and painter who came to work for the Medici family in Florence about 1460—created mostly small bronze sculptures. His **HERCULES AND ANTAEUS** of about 1475 is one of the largest (**FIG. 20-28**). This study of complex, interlocking figures has an explosive energy that can best be appreciated by viewing it from every angle.

Statuettes of religious subjects were still popular, but humanist patrons were beginning to collect bronzes of Classical subjects. Many sculptors, especially those trained as goldsmiths, started to cast small copies of well-known ancient works. Some artists also executed original designs *all'antica* ("in the antique style") to appeal to a cultivated humanist taste. Hercules was always a popular figure; as a patron of Florence, he was on the city seal. Among the many courageous acts by which Hercules gained immortality was the slaying of the evil Antaeus in a wrestling match by lifting him off the Earth, the source of the giant's great physical power.

An engraving by Pollaiuolo, **THE BATTLE OF THE NUDES** (**FIG. 20-29**), reflects two interests of Renaissance scholars—anatomical research and the study of Classical sculpture. Although this is Pollaiuolo's only known print, it was still highly influential. He may have intended it as a compositional study of the human figure in action.

The naked men fighting each other ferociously against a tapestrylike background of foliage seem to represent the same individual in a variety of poses, many of which were taken from Classical sources. Like the artist's *Hercules and Antaeus,* much of the engraving's fascination lies in its depiction of the muscles of the male body reacting under tension. This depiction is more impressive than realistic; anatomical accuracy was clearly not the point.

The Morelli-Nerli Wedding Chests

The palazzos of wealthy Florentine families were outfitted with massive pieces of elaborate furniture. Constructed of richly carved wood that was gilded and often covered with paintings, these household objects were a central feature of the fifteenth-century Florentine art world. Some of the most impressive surviving examples of Renaissance furniture are great chests—called **cassoni**—that were used to store clothing and other precious personal objects in a couple's bedroom. They were frequently commissioned in pairs on the occasion of a wedding.

Marriages between members of wealthy Florentine families were not the result of romantic connections between two young people. They were political alliances and economic transactions that involved the transfer of capital and gifts as displays of wealth. In preparation for such marriages, husbands refurbished their living quarters in the family palazzo, where they would bring a bride into the household. We have a detailed accounting of the extent of work required, as well as the expenditure, when 30-year-old Lorenzo di Matteo Morelli prepared his apartments for the arrival of his young bride, Vaggia di Tanai

20–30 Jacopo del Sellaio, Biagio d'Antonio (painters), and Zanobi di Domenico (woodworker) **CASSONE MADE FOR THE MARRIAGE OF LORENZO DI MATTEO MORELLI AND VAGGIA DI TANAI NERLI (ONE OF A SET OF TWO)**

1472. Tempera and gold on wood, chest 83½ × 75 × 30″ (212 × 193 × 76.2 cm). The Samuel Courtauld Trust, the Courtauld Gallery, London. (F.1947.LF.4).

Credit: © Samuel Courtauld Trust, The Courtauld Gallery, London, UK/Bridgeman Images

Nerli, after their marriage in 1472. His commissioning of a pair of *cassoni*—one for him and one for Vaggia—represented almost two-thirds of the entire cost of redecoration. Fortunately, the two chests still survive (**FIG. 20–30**). They are among the most important and best-preserved Renaissance *cassoni* that have come down to us, especially since they still maintain the original backboard—called a *spalliera*—that was produced concurrent with and hung on the wall directly behind the chests when they were placed in Lorenzo's bedroom. The lion's feet on which the chests now stand are modern additions, and the *spalliera* was originally hung as one continuous painting above both *cassoni*, not two separate panels mounted behind each lid as in the current configuration. Otherwise these chests give a strong sense of their original appearance.

Like most Renaissance *cassoni*, Lorenzo's chest is painted with pictures drawn from stories that extol moral virtues and reflect some of their values and glories on Lorenzo himself. The long painted scene on the front tells the story of ancient Roman hero Marcus Furius Camillus

defeating the Gauls as he chases them out of Rome. On the *spalliera*, *trompe l'oeil* ("fool-the-eye") curtains part to reveal the scene of another Roman hero defending a bridge against insurmountable odds. Presumably Lorenzo wanted to be seen as the heroic descendant of such illustrious Romans—strong, brave, and triumphant. The scenes portrayed on Vaggia's chest (like Lorenzo's, identified by her coat of arms) challenge her to care for the children she is expected to produce and to practice the virtues of temperance, prudence, and patience that were valued in Florentine patrician brides.

The Morelli–Nerli *cassoni* passed from Lorenzo to his son, and they remained in the Morelli family at least until 1680, maybe into the nineteenth century, when they first appeared together on the art market. Elaborate Renaissance furniture became coveted items in the homes of wealthy art collectors in late nineteenth-century Europe and America, where the new owners doubtless saw themselves as worthy successors to the rich and powerful merchants who had originally commissioned them.

Ghirlandaio

The most prolific later fifteenth-century Florentine paint-ing workshop was that of Domenico di Tommaso Bigordi (1449–1494), known as "Ghirlandaio" ("Garland-Maker"), a nickname first adopted by his father, who was a gold-smith noted for his floral wreaths. A skilled storyteller, the younger Ghirlandaio reinterpreted the art of ear-lier fifteenth-century painters into a visual language of descriptive immediacy and structural clarity. Among Ghir-landaio's most impressive narrative programs was the fresco cycle of the **LIFE OF ST. FRANCIS**, commissioned by the wealthy manager of the Medici bank, Francesco Sas-setti, and painted between 1483 and 1486 on the walls of the Sassetti family burial chapel in the Florentine church of Santa Trinità (**FIG. 20–31**).

In the uppermost tier of the paintings (**FIG. 20–32**), Pope Honorius gives a confirmation of the Franciscan

order to the kneeling figure of St. Francis, with the Log-gia dei Lanzi and the Palazzo della Signoria (SEE FIG. 18–2) in the background. The foreground figures—arranged in a composition that parallels the sacred scene behind them—are portrait likenesses of well-known Florentines. At far right are (from left to right) poet Antonio Pucci, Lorenzo de' Medici, the patron Francesco Sassetti, and Sassetti's son Federigo, all of whom seem to be receiving the approaching retinue coming up the stairs at the lower center of the fresco—humanist poet Poliziano leading his pupils, the sons of Lorenzo de' Medici. Just below this scene, in the middle register (SEE FIG. 20–31), a small boy who has fallen from an upper window is resurrected by St. Francis. This miracle is likewise witnessed by contem-porary Florentines, including other members of the Sas-setti family and Ghirlandaio himself, and the scene takes place in the piazza outside the actual church of Santa Trinità. Ghirlandaio has thus transferred both events from thirteenth-century Rome to contemporary Flor-ence, painting recognizable views of the city and portraits of living Florentines, and delighting in local color and anecdotal detail. Perhaps Renais-sance painters, like Gothic painters, represented sacred narratives in contemporary settings to emphasize their current relevance, or perhaps they and their patrons simply enjoyed seeing themselves dressed in their finery, witnessing these dramas within the cities of which they were justifiably proud.

The altarpiece Ghirlandaio painted for the Sassetti Chapel portrays the **NATIVITY AND ADO-RATION OF THE SHEPHERDS** (**FIG. 20–33**). It is still in its original frame in the place for which it was painted (SEE FIG. 20–31). The influence of Hugo van der Goes's Portinari Altarpiece (SEE FIG. 19–19), which had been placed on the high altar of the church of Sant'Egidio in 1483, two years ear-lier, is strong. Ghirlandaio's Christ Child also lies on the ground, adored by the Virgin while rug-ged shepherds kneel at the right. Ghirlandaio even copies some of Hugo's flowers—although here the iris, a symbol of the Passion, springs not from a vase, but from the earth in the lower right corner. But Ghirlandaio highlights references to Classical Rome. First to catch the eye are two

20–31 Domenico Ghirlandaio **SCENES FROM THE LIFE OF ST. FRANCIS; ALTARPIECE WITH NATIVITY AND ADORATION OF THE SHEPHERDS**

Sassetti Chapel, church of Santa Trinità, Florence. 1483–1486. Fresco, chapel 12′2″ deep × 17′2″ wide (3.7 × 5.25 m).

Credit: © Archivi Alinari, Firenze

20–32 Domenico Ghirlandaio **CONFIRMATION OF THE FRANCISCAN RULE BY POPE HONORIUS III**
Sassetti Chapel, church of Santa Trinità, Florence. 1483–1486. Fresco, width at base 17′2″ (5.25 m).

Credit: © Studio Fotografico Quattrone, Florence

Classical pilasters with Corinthian capitals, one of which is dated by inscription to 1485. The manger is an ancient sarcophagus with an inscription that promises resurrection (as in the fresco directly above the altarpiece where St. Francis is reviving a child), and in the distance a Classical arch inscribed with a reference to the Roman general Pompey the Great frames the road along which the Magi travel. Weighty, restrained actors replace the psychologically intense figures of Hugo's painting. Ghirlandaio joins a clear foreground, middle ground, and background in part with the road and in part with **aerial perspective**, which creates a seamless transition of color from the sharp details and primary hues of the Adoration to the soft gray mountains in the distance.

20–33 Domenico Ghirlandaio **NATIVITY AND ADORATION OF THE SHEPHERDS**
Altarpiece in the Sassetti Chapel, church of Santa Trinità, Florence. 1485. Panel, 65¾″ (1.67 m) square.

Credit: © Studio Fotografico Quattrone, Florence

A Closer Look

PRIMAVERA

Mercury, the sign for the month of May, disperses the winter clouds with his caduceus. This staff, wound about with serpents, became a symbol for the medical profession. The name Medici means "doctors."

Venus, clothed in contemporary costume and crowned with a marriage wreath, appears in her role as the goddess of wedded love. The presence of both Venus and Mercury may be an astrological reference; prominent Neoplatonist Marsilio Ficino told Lorenzo di Pierfrancesco de' Medici that these planets were aligned in his horoscope.

The setting of the painting is a grove of orange trees. These hold a double meaning—suggestive of Venus's Garden of the Hesperides, with its golden fruit, and also perhaps an allusion to the Medici, whose coat of arms featured golden orbs.

This three-figure grouping tells a story. Zephyrus, the west wind, is accosting the virgin nymph Chloris, identifiable from the roses pouring out of her mouth. Once Zephyrus makes her his bride, Chloris is transformed into the goddess Flora, the elaborately dressed personification of spring at the front of the group.

The gold flames decorating Mercury's garment are also an attribute of St. Lawrence, the namesake of Lorenzo di Pierfrancesco de' Medici, for whom this painting was made. The laurel tree (*laurus* in Latin) behind Zephyrus also alludes to Lorenzo's name.

The Three Graces symbolize ideal female virtues—Chastity, Beauty, Love. Venus's son Cupid—the embodiment of romantic desire—playfully aims his arrow at them.

So accurate is the representation of the flowering plants in the painting that 138 of the 190 total have been identified. Almost all grow in the neighborhood of Florence between the months of March and April, and most carry symbolic associations with love and marriage.

Flora scatters flowers held in a fold of her dress at the level of her womb, equating female procreative fertility with the fecundity brought about by changing seasons.

20–34 Sandro Botticelli **PRIMAVERA**
c. 1482. Tempera on wood panel, 6′8″ × 10′4″ (2.03 × 3.15 m). Galleria degli Uffizi, Florence.

Credit: © Studio Fotografico Quattrone, Florence

Botticelli

Like most artists in the second half of the fifteenth century, Alessandro di Mariano di Vanni Filipepi (1445–1510), called "Botticelli" ("the little barrel," a nickname borrowed from his older brother), painted sculptural figures that were modeled by light from a consistent source and placed in a setting rendered illusionistic by linear perspective. An outstanding portraitist, he, like Ghirlandaio, often included recognizable contemporary figures among the saints and angels in religious paintings. He worked in Florence, frequently for the Medici, before being called to Rome in 1481 by Pope Sixtus IV to help decorate the new Sistine Chapel along with Ghirlandaio, Perugino, and other artists.

Botticelli returned to Florence that same year and entered a new phase of his career. Like other artists working for patrons steeped in Classical scholarship and humanistic thought, he was exposed to philosophical speculations on beauty—as well as to the examples of ancient art in his employers' collections. For the Medici, Botticelli produced secular paintings of mythological subjects inspired by ancient works and by contemporary Neoplatonic thought. Art historian Michael Baxandall has shown that these works were also patterned on the slow movements of fifteenth-century Florentine dance, in which the dancers acted out their relationships to one another in public performances that would have influenced the thinking and viewing habits of both painters and their audience.

The overall appearance of Botticelli's **PRIMAVERA**, or *Spring* (see "Closer Look" opposite), recalls Flemish tapestries (SEE FIG. 19–8), which were very popular in Italy at the time. And its subject—like the subjects of many tapestries—is a highly complex **allegory** (a symbolic illustration of a concept or principle) interweaving Neoplatonic ideas with esoteric references to Classical sources. In simple terms, Neoplatonic philosophers and poets conceived Venus, the goddess of love, as having two natures. The first ruled over earthly, human love and the second over universal, divine love. In this way the philosophers could argue that Venus was a Classical equivalent of the Virgin Mary. *Primavera* was painted at the time of the wedding of Lorenzo di Pierfrancesco de' Medici and Semiramide d'Appiano in 1482. The theme suggests love and fertility in marriage, and the painting can be read as a lyrical wish for a similar fecundity in the union of Lorenzo and Semiramide—a sort of highly refined fertility dance.

Several years later, some of the same mythological figures reappeared in Botticelli's **BIRTH OF VENUS** (FIG. **20-35**), in which the central image represents the Neoplatonic idea of divine love in the form of a nude Venus based on an antique statue type known as the "modest Venus" ultimately deriving from Praxiteles's *Aphrodite of Knidos* (SEE FIG. 5-54). Botticelli's Classical goddess of love and beauty, born of sea foam, averts her eyes from our gaze as she floats ashore on a scallop shell, carefully arranging her hands and hair to hide—but actually drawing attention

20–35 Sandro Botticelli **BIRTH OF VENUS**
c. 1484–1486. Tempera and gold on canvas, 5'8⅞" × 9'1⅞" (1.8 × 2.8 m). Galleria degli Uffizi, Florence.

Credit: © Studio Fotografico Quattrone, Florence

to—her sexuality. Indeed, she is an arrestingly alluring figure, set within a graceful composition organized by Botticelli's characteristically decorative use of line. Blown by the wind, Zephyrus (with his love, the nymph Chloris), Venus arrives at her earthly home. She is welcomed by a devotee who offers her a garment embroidered with flowers. The circumstances of this commission are uncertain. It is painted on canvas, which suggests that it may have been a banner or a painted, tapestrylike wall hanging.

Botticelli's later career was apparently affected by a profound spiritual crisis. While the artist was creating his mythologies for the Medici, a Dominican monk, Fra Girolamo Savonarola (active in Florence 1490–1498), was preaching impassioned sermons denouncing the worldliness of Florence. Many Florentines reacted with orgies of self-recrimination, and processions of weeping penitents wound through the streets. Botticelli, too, may have fallen into a state of religious fervor. In a gesture of repentance, he burned many of his earlier paintings and began to produce highly emotional pictures dominated by an intense religiosity.

Urbino, Mantua, Rome, and Venice

How does the Renaissance style spread from Florence to other Italian cities?

In the second half of the fifteenth century, the ideas and ideals of artists like Brunelleschi, Donatello, and Masaccio began to spread from Florence to the rest of Italy, as artists who had trained or worked in Florence traveled to other cities to work. Northern Italy embraced the new Classical ideas swiftly, especially in the court cities of Urbino and Mantua. Venice and Rome also emerged as innovative art centers in the last quarter of the century.

Urbino

Under Federico da Montefeltro, Urbino developed into a thriving artistic center. A new palace was under construction, and prominent architects and artists were brought into the court to make the new princely residence a showcase of ducal splendor.

THE PALACE AT URBINO   Construction of the palace had been underway for about 20 years in 1468 when Federico hired Luciano Laurana (c. 1420/1425–1479) to direct the work. Among Laurana's major contributions to the palace were closing the courtyard with a fourth wing and redesigning the courtyard façades (**FIG. 20-36**). The result is a superbly rational solution to the problems created in courtyard design by the awkward juncture of the arcades at the four corners. The ground-level portico on each side has arches supported by columns, but piers embellished with pilasters bridge the corner angles. This arrangement avoided the awkward visual effect of two arches springing from a single column (SEE FIG. 20-10) and gave the corner a greater sense of stability. A variation of the composite capital (a Corinthian capital with added Ionic volutes) was used, perhaps for the first time, on the ground level. Corinthian pilasters flank the windows in the story above, forming divisions that repeat the bays of the portico. (The two low upper stories were added later.) The plain architrave was engraved with inscriptions praising Federico, added when the count became duke of Urbino in 1476.

The interior of the Urbino palace likewise reflected its patron's embrace of new Renaissance ideas and interest in Classical antiquity, seen in carved marble fireplaces and window and door surrounds. In creating luxurious home furnishings and interior decorations for sophisticated clients such as Federico, Italian artists found freedom to experiment with new subjects, treatments, and techniques. Among these was the creation of remarkable *trompe l'oeil* effects using exacting linear perspective and foreshortening in **intarsia** (wood inlay) decoration. An extraordinary example is on the walls of Federico da Montefeltro's **STUDIOLO**, or study, a room for private conversation and the owner's collection of fine books and art objects (**FIG. 20-37**). The work,

20-36 Luciano Laurana **COURTYARD, DUCAL PALACE, URBINO**
Courtyard c. 1468–1472; palace begun c. 1450.

Credit: © akg-images/De Agostini Picture Lib./L. Romano

20–37 Giuliano da Maiano (?) **STUDIOLO OF FEDERICO DA MONTEFELTRO**
Ducal palace, Urbino. 1476. Intarsia, height 7′3″ (2.21 m).

Credit: © 2016. Photo Scala, Florence – courtesy of the Ministero Beni e Att. Culturali

probably done by the architect and woodworker Giuliano da Maiano (1432–1490), carries the date 1476.

The elaborate scenes in the small room are created entirely of wood inlaid on flat surfaces. Each detail is rendered with convincing illusionism: pilasters, carved cupboards with latticed doors, niches with statues, paintings, and built-in tables. Prominent in the decorative scheme is the prudent and industrious squirrel, a Renaissance symbol of the ideal ruler—in other words, of Federico da Montefeltro. A large "window" looks out onto an elegant marble loggia with a distant view of the countryside through its arches, and the shelves, cupboards, and tables are filled with all manner of fascinating things: scientific instruments, books, even the duke's armor hanging like a suit in a closet.

PIERO DELLA FRANCESCA Federico also brought the artist Piero della Francesca (c. 1415–1492) to Urbino. Piero had worked in Florence in the 1430s before settling in his native Borgo San Sepolcro, a Tuscan hill town under papal control. He knew current art theory and art practice—including Brunelleschi's system of spatial illusion and linear perspective, Masaccio's powerful modeling of forms and atmospheric perspective, and Alberti's theoretical treatises. Piero was one of the few practicing artists who also wrote his own books of theory. Not surprisingly, in his treatise on perspective he emphasized the geometry and the volumetric construction of forms and spaces that were so apparent in his own work.

These characteristic features are clearly apparent in a serene image of the **BAPTISM OF CHRIST** that has become one of Piero's signature works (**FIG. 20–38**). It was commissioned by the Graziani family, probably

20–38 Piero della Francesca **BAPTISM OF CHRIST**
c. 1450. Tempera on wood panel, 66 × 45¾″ (1.67 × 1.16 m). National Gallery, London.

The three angels standing in a cluster at left, partially overlapped by the foreground tree, have been interpreted as an emblem of concord—representing the rapprochement reached between the Roman and Byzantine Christian churches in 1439 at the Council of Florence. Another reference to this council has been seen in the exotic costumes of the figures in the far background. Since the accord reached at the council was very short-lived, this interpretation would move the date of the painting into the early 1440s rather than the 1450s.

Credit: © 2016. Copyright The National Gallery, London/Scala, Florence

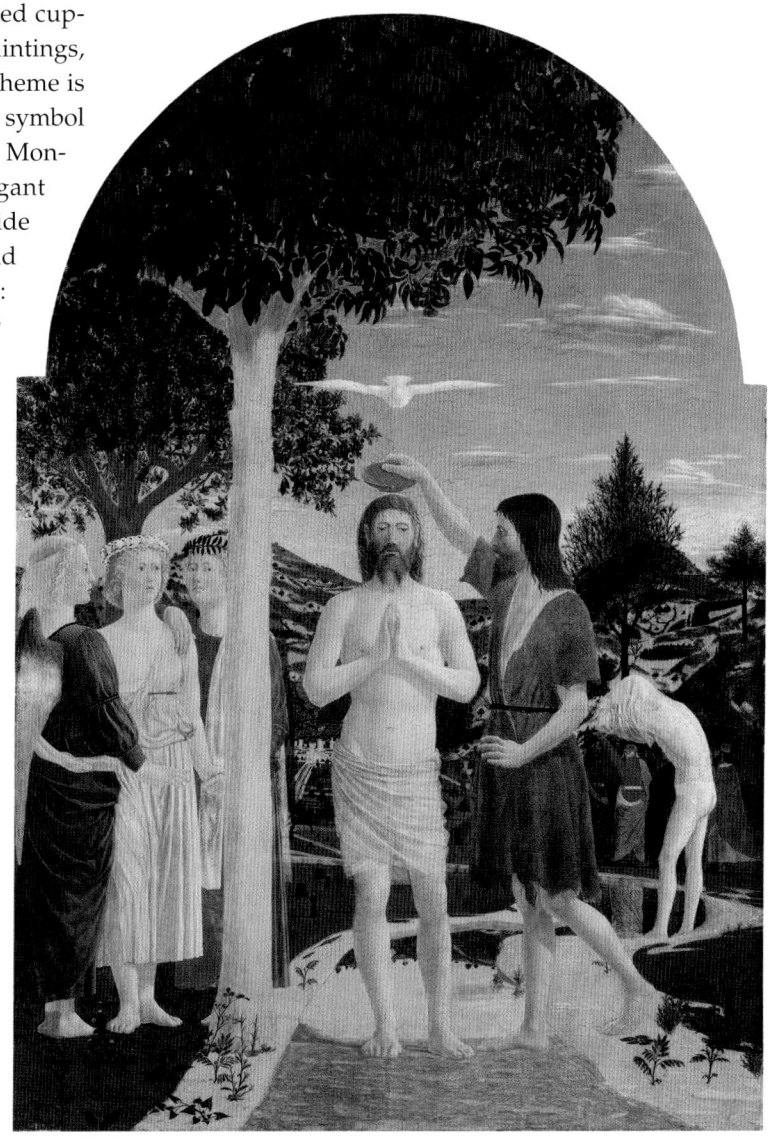

during the 1450s, for the priory of San Giovanni Battista in Borgo San Sepolchro. The central figure of Christ dominates the painting, standing in a shallow stream of glassy water under a tree of manicured regularity. Christ's legs and the sleek tree trunk set up a series of emphatically upright forms, one of many formal relationships that reverberate both across the picture's surface and into its carefully measured space. Feet and ankles rotate across the lower quarter of the painting, providing a clear and well-distributed sense of grounding for the figural composition, while the radically foreshortened dove (Holy Spirit), John's baptismal dish, and the clouds create a rhythmic line of horizontals that adds stability above and creates a staccato rhythm that merges foreground and background on the painting's surface. The mirrored profiles and gestures of the outside angel and the baptizing John provide an internal frame for the central action. Such carefully crafted formal correspondences infuse this picture with an air of quiet calm and peaceful stasis—a stillness suggesting that nothing will ever change, no one will ever move in this frozen moment within a story that, for Christian believers, actually changed everything.

Piero traveled widely—to Rome, to the Este court in Ferrara, and especially to Urbino. In about 1474, he painted the portraits of **FEDERICO DA MONTEFELTRO** and his recently deceased wife, **BATTISTA SFORZA** (**FIG. 20-39**). The small panels resemble Flemish painting in their detail and luminosity, their record of surfaces and textures, and their vast landscapes. But in traditional Italian fashion, figures are portrayed in strict profile, disengaged psychologically from the viewer. The profile format also allowed for an accurate recording of Federico's likeness without emphasizing two disfiguring scars—the loss of his right eye from a lance blow and his broken nose. His good left eye is shown, and the angular profile of his nose might easily be merely a distinctive family trait. Typically, Piero emphasized the underlying geometry of the forms. Dressed in the most elegant fashion (Federico wears his red ducal robe and Battista's jewels are meticulously recorded), they are silhouetted against a panoramic landscape. These are the hills around Urbino, seemingly dissolving into infinity through an atmospheric perspective as subtle and luminous as in any Flemish panel painting. Piero used another Northern European device: In the harbor view just in front of Federico,

20–39 Piero della Francesca **BATTISTA SFORZA AND FEDERICO DA MONTEFELTRO**
c. 1474. Oil on wood panel, each 18½ × 13″ (47 × 33 cm). Galleria degli Uffizi, Florence.

Battista Sforza died in 1472 at age 26, shortly after the birth of her ninth child, a son who would one day be duke. We are told that Federico was disconsolate. Some arranged aristocratic marriage alliances blossomed into loving partnerships, and it seems that one of them was memorialized in this double portrait.

20–40 Andrea Mantegna **TWO VIEWS OF THE CAMERA PICTA, DUCAL PALACE, MANTUA**

1465–1474. Fresco, diameter of false oculus 8′9″ (2.7 m); room 26′6″ (8 m) square.

Credit: (left) © 2016. Photo Scala, Florence - courtesy of the Ministero Beni e Att. Culturali., (below) © Studio Fotografico Quattrone, Florence

the water narrows into a river that leads us into the distant landscape (SEE FIG. 19-16). He would have had contact in Urbino with the Flemish artists who were also working there.

Mantua

Ludovico Gonzaga, the marquis of Mantua, ruled a territory that lies on the north Italian plain between Venice and Milan. Like Federico, he made his fortune as a *condottiere*. Ludovico was schooled by humanist teachers and created a court where humanist ideas flourished in art as well as in literature.

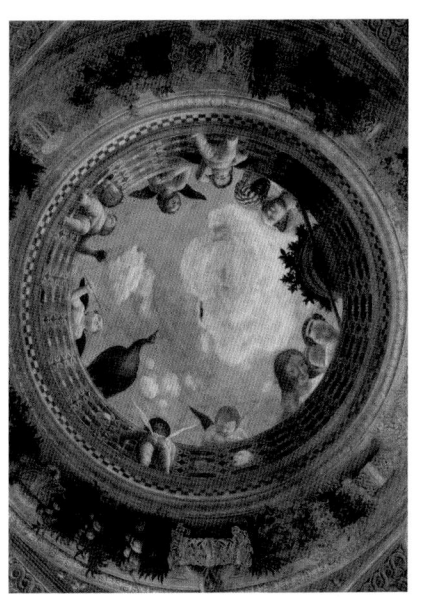

MANTEGNA Working at Ludovico's court was Andrea Mantegna (1431–1506), a painter trained in Padua and profoundly influenced by the sculptor Donatello, who arrived in Padua in 1443 and worked there for a decade. Mantegna learned the Florentine system of linear perspective and pushed it to its limits with radically foreshortened forms and dramatic spatial recessions. He went to work for Ludovico Gonzaga in 1460 and continued to work for the Gonzaga family for the rest of his life.

Perhaps his finest works are the frescos of the **CAMERA PICTA** ("Painted Room"), a tower chamber in Ludovico's palace, which Mantegna decorated between 1465 and 1474 (**FIG. 20-40**). Around the walls the family—each member seemingly identified by a portrait likeness—learns of the return of and ultimately welcomes Ludovico's son, Cardinal Francesco Gonzaga. On the domed ceiling, the artist painted a *tour-de-force* of radical perspective in a technique called *di sotto in sù* ("from below upwards"). The room appears to be open to a cloud-filled sky through a large oculus in a simulated marble- and mosaic-covered vault. On each side of a precariously balanced planter, four young women—one an African, outfitted in an exotic turban—peer over a marble balustrade into the room below, while a fourth looks dreamily upward. Joined by a large peacock, several *putti* play around the balustrade, seemingly oblivious to the danger of their perch. Three stand on the interior ledge of a cornice unprotected by the balustrade, toes projecting into space. This ceiling began a long tradition of illusionistic ceiling painting that culminated in the extravagant and explosive ceilings of Baroque churches (see Chapter 23).

20–41 VIEW OF THE SISTINE CHAPEL SHOWING PAINTINGS COMMISSIONED FOR THE SIDE WALLS BY POPE SIXTUS IV
Vatican, Rome. At lower right, Perugino's *Christ Giving the Keys to St. Peter*, c. 1480–1482. 11′5½″ × 18′8½″ (3.48 × 5.7 m).

Credit: Photo © Musei Vaticani/IKONA

his contributions, *Christ Giving the Keys to St. Peter* (foreground painting at lower right in FIG. 20–41; also FIG. 20–20A), portrayed the event that provided biblical support for the supremacy of papal authority (Matthew 16:19). In a light-filled piazza in which banded paving stones provide a geometric grid for perspectival recession, the figures stand like chess pieces on the squares, scaled to size according to their distance from the picture plane and modeled by a consistent light source from the upper left. Triumphal arches inspired by ancient Rome frame the church and focus attention on the center of the composition, where the vital key is being transferred. The carefully calibrated scene is softened by the subdued colors, the distant idealized landscape and cloudy skies, and the variety of the figures' positions.

Rome

Rome's development into a Renaissance center of the arts was greatly enhanced in the early 1480s when Pope Sixtus IV called to the city a group of young Florentine and Umbrian artists to decorate the walls of his newly built chapel (1479–1481), now named the **SISTINE CHAPEL** after him (FIG. 20–41). Botticelli and Ghirlandaio were among the most famous artists summoned to the chapel to paint, but many art historians believe that Perugino was the supervising artist in charge of the project.

PERUGINO Pietro Vannucci, called "Perugino" (c. 1445–1523), was originally from near the town of Perugia in Umbria (thus the nickname), and he worked for a while in Florence, but by 1479 he was in Rome. Two years later, he was working on the Sistine murals. One of

Venice

In the last quarter of the fifteenth century, Venice emerged as a major Renaissance art center. Ruled as an oligarchy (government by a select few) with an elected duke (*doge* in the Venetian dialect), the city government was founded at the end of the Roman Empire and survived until the Napoleonic era. In building their city, the Venetians had turned marshes into a commercial seaport, and they saw the sea as a resource, not a threat. They depended on naval power and on the natural defense of their lagoons rather than city walls. Venice turned toward the east, especially after the crusaders' conquest of Constantinople in 1204, designing the church of St. Mark as a great Byzantine building sheathed in mosaics (SEE FIG. 8–24A). In addition to its long history of painting and sculpture, Venice excelled in the arts of textiles and jewelry, gold and enamel, glass and mosaic, fine printing and bookbinding.

VENETIAN PALACES   Venice was a city of waterways with few large public spaces. Even palaces had only small interior courtyards and tiny gardens and were separated by narrow alleys. Their façades overlooked the canals, permitting owners to display on these major thoroughfares the large portals, windows, and loggias that proclaimed their importance through the lavishness of their residences—a sharp contrast to the fortresslike character of most Florentine town houses (SEE FIG. 20-9). Similar to the Florentine great houses, however, Venetian structures combined a place of business with a dwelling.

The **CA D'ORO** (House of Gold), home of the wealthy nobleman Marino Contarini, has a splendid front with three superimposed loggias facing the Grand Canal (**FIG. 20-42**). The house was constructed between 1421 and 1437, and its asymmetrical elevation is based on a traditional Byzantine plan. A wide central hall ran from front to back all the way through the building to a small inner courtyard with a well and garden. The entrance on the canal permitted goods to be delivered directly into the warehouse that constituted the ground floor. An outside stair led to the main floor on the second level, which had a salon and reception room opening on the richly decorated loggia. It was filled with light from large windows, and more light reflected off the polished terrazzo floor. Private family rooms filled the upper stories. Contarini specified that the façade was to be painted with white enamel and ultramarine blue and that the red stones in the patterned wall should be oiled to make them even brighter. Details of carving, such as coats of arms and balls on the crest at the roofline, were to be gilded. Beautiful as the palace is today, in the fifteenth and sixteenth centuries it must have been truly spectacular.

THE BELLINI BROTHERS   The domes of the church of St. Mark dominated the city center, and the rich colors of its glowing mosaics captured painters' imaginations. Perhaps it was their love of color that encouraged the Venetian painters to embrace the oil medium for both panel and canvas painting.

The most important Venetian artists of this period were two brothers: Gentile (c. 1429–1507) and Giovanni (c. 1430–1516) Bellini, whose father, Jacopo (c. 1400–1470), had also been a central figure in Venetian art. Andrea Mantegna became part of this circle when he married Jacopo's daughter in 1453.

Gentile Bellini celebrated the daily life of the city in large, lively narratives, such as the **PROCESSION OF THE RELIC OF THE TRUE CROSS BEFORE THE CHURCH OF ST. MARK** (**FIG. 20-43**). Every year on the feast of St. Mark (April 25), the Confraternity of St. John the Evangelist carried the miracle-working relic of the True Cross in a procession through the square in front of the church. Bellini's painting of 1496 depicts an event that had occurred in 1444: the miraculous recovery of a sick child whose father (the man in red kneeling to the right of the relic) prayed for help as the relic passed by. Gentile has rendered the cityscape with great attention to detail. The mosaic-encrusted Byzantine Cathedral of St. Mark (SEE FIG. 8-24A) forms a backdrop for the procession, and the doge's palace and base of the bell tower can be seen at the right. The gold reliquary is carried under a canopy, surrounded by marchers with giant candles led by a choir and followed at the far right by the doge and other officials. Gentile's procession serves as a reminder that fifteenth-century piazzas and buildings were sites of ceremony, and it was in moments such as this that they were brought to life.

Gentile's brother Giovanni amazed and attracted patrons with his artistic virtuosity for almost 60 years. The **VIRGIN AND CHILD ENTHRONED WITH SS. FRANCIS, JOHN THE BAPTIST, JOB, DOMINIC, SEBASTIAN, AND LOUIS OF TOULOUSE** (**FIG. 20-44**), painted in about 1478 for the chapel of the Hospital of San Giobbe (St. Job), exhibits a dramatic perspective view

20-42 CA D'ORO (CONTARINI PALACE), VENICE
1421–1437.

Credit: © Cameraphoto Arte, Venice

20–43
Gentile Bellini
PROCESSION OF THE RELIC OF THE TRUE CROSS BEFORE THE CHURCH OF ST. MARK

1496. Oil on canvas, 12′ × 24′5″ (3.67 × 7.45 m). Galleria dell'Accademia, Venice.

Credit: © Cameraphoto Arte, Venice

up into a tunnel vault that leads to an apse. Giovanni may have known his brother-in-law Mantegna's early experiments in radical foreshortening and the use of a low vanishing point. Here Giovanni positions the vanishing point for the rapidly converging lines of the architecture at bottom center, just above the floor. His figures stand in a Classical architectural interior with a coffered barrel vault reminiscent of Masaccio's *Trinity* (SEE FIG. 20–18). The gold mosaic, with its identifying inscription and stylized seraphim (angels of the highest rank), recalls Byzantine art and the long tradition of Byzantine-inspired painting and mosaics in Venice.

Giovanni Bellini's painting of **ST. FRANCIS IN ECSTASY (FIG. 20–45)**, also from the 1470s, recalls Flemish painting in the fine detail with which the natural world is rendered. The saint stands bathed in early morning sunlight, his outspread hands displaying his stigmata. Francis had moved to a cave in the barren wilderness in his search for communion with God, but in the world Giovanni creates for him, the fields blossom and flocks of animals graze. The grape arbor over his desk adds to the atmosphere of sylvan delight. Like

20–44 Giovanni Bellini **VIRGIN AND CHILD ENTHRONED WITH SS. FRANCIS, JOHN THE BAPTIST, JOB, DOMINIC, SEBASTIAN, AND LOUIS OF TOULOUSE**
Originally commissioned for the chapel of the Hospital of San Giobbe, Venice. c. 1478. Oil on wood panel, 15′4″ × 8′4″ (4.67 × 2.54 m). Galleria dell'Accademia, Venice.

Art historians have given the name **sacra conversazione** ("holy conversation") to this type of composition that shows saints, angels, and sometimes even the painting's donors in the same pictorial space with the enthroned Virgin and Child. Despite the name, no "conversation" or spoken interaction takes place in a literal sense. Instead, the individuals portrayed are joined in a mystical and eternal communion that occurs outside human time and space.

Credit: © Cameraphoto Arte, Venice

most of the fifteenth-century religious art we have seen, however, Giovanni presents viewers with a natural world saturated in symbolism. Here a relationship between St. Francis and Moses is outlined. The tree symbolizes the burning bush; the stream, the miraculous spring brought forth by Moses. The crane and donkey represent the monastic virtue of patience. The detailed description, luminous palette, and symbolic surroundings suggest Flemish art, but the golden light suffusing the painting is unmistakably Venetian.

20–45 Giovanni Bellini
ST. FRANCIS IN ECSTASY
c. 1470s. Oil on wood panel,
49¹⁄₁₆ × 55⅞″ (124.6 × 142 cm).
The Frick Collection, New York.

Think About It

1　Explain how one of the Florentine sculptors discussed in this chapter helped establish the increasing naturalism and emulation of Classical models that would be central to the early Italian Renaissance.

2　Discuss Masaccio's use of linear perspective in either *The Tribute Money* or *Trinity with the Virgin, St. John the Evangelist, and Donors*. How does he use this technique? Illustrate your points with a comparative reference to a work discussed earlier in this chapter or in a previous chapter.

3　Choose a wealthy merchant or *condottiere* and discuss how his patronage fostered the emergence of the Renaissance in fifteenth-century Italy. Make reference to specific works in forming your answer.

4　Discuss the 1401 competition to choose an artist to create the bronze doors of the Florence Baptistery. How did the competition affect the careers of the two finalists, Ghiberti and Brunelleschi?

Crosscurrents

Compare the representation of the human nude in these two examples of Renaissance art, one from Flanders and one from Florence. How do these works relate to the character of art in these two parts of Europe in the early fifteenth century? How do they embody the cultural expectations of their time and place?

FIG. 19–13

FIG. 20–21

21–1 Leonardo da Vinci **MONA LISA**

c. 1503–1506. Oil on wood panel, 30¼ × 21″ (77 × 53 cm). Musée du Louvre, Paris. (INV. 779).

Chapter 21
Sixteenth-Century Art in Italy

Learning Objectives

21.a Identify the visual hallmarks of sixteenth-century Italian Renaissance art and architecture for formal, technical, and expressive qualities.

21.b Interpret the meaning of sixteenth-century Italian Renaissance works of art based on their themes, subjects, and symbols.

21.c Relate sixteenth-century Italian Renaissance artists and art to their cultural, economic, and political contexts.

21.d Apply the vocabulary and concepts relevant to sixteenth-century Italian Renaissance art, artists, and art history.

21.e Interpret a work of sixteenth-century Italian Renaissance art using the art historical methods of observation, comparison, and inductive reasoning.

21.f Select visual and textual evidence in various media to support an argument or an interpretation of a work of sixteenth-century Italian Renaissance art.

Is it Mona Lisa's "smile" that grabs us? Or the sense of mystery created by the smoky haze that envelops both her and the weird landscape behind her—or the way she turns to confront us directly with such self-confidence? Compelling to centuries of art lovers, this may be the world's most famous European painting.

Actually the **MONA LISA** (**FIG. 21-1**) is not especially mysterious. No secret code needs to be cracked. Leonardo da Vinci, one of the most famous painters and most fertile minds of the Italian Renaissance, painted this portrait between 1503 and 1506, while he was living in Florence. Although there is lingering uncertainty, most art historians agree with the sixteenth-century Italian biographer Giorgio Vasari, who claimed that the *Mona Lisa* portrays Lisa di Antonio Maria Gherardini, the wife of Florentine merchant Francesco del Giocondo. ("Mona" is a term of respect, a contraction of "Madonna," meaning "my lady"). Lisa married Francesco in 1495, when she was 16, so Leonardo painted her during her mid-twenties. But he never delivered the painting. He kept it with him for the rest of his life, continuing to tinker with it, probably working on it while he was in Rome after 1513 and taking it with him in 1516 when he moved to France at the invitation of Francis I. After Leonardo's death in 1519, the king purchased the *Mona Lisa* for Fontainebleau. Louis XIV moved it to Versailles, and Napoleon hung it in his bedroom in the Tuileries Palace. It now hangs at the Louvre. It is one of the most popular destinations for tourists visiting Paris.

This was an unusual portrait for its time. Leonardo abandoned the long-standing Italian tradition of painting wealthy wives in profile view, wearing the sumptuous clothing and jewelry that signified their status and their husbands' wealth (SEE FIGS. 20–26, 20–39). Mona Lisa seems to be the likeness of a specific woman who turns with calm assurance to engage viewers, hands relaxed in her lap. Her expression has been called enigmatic. It hides rather than reveals her thoughts and personality, and it lacks the warmth one expects to see in her eyes, which have shifted to the side to look straight out at us. The psychological complexity Leonardo has given to this face may explain the spell it has cast over viewers.

One thing is clear. This portrait embodies many of the hallmarks of the High Renaissance style that will solidify in Rome during the first two decades of the sixteenth century—the blend of naturalistic description and classicizing idealism, and the clarity and balanced structure of the pyramidal composition that gives utter stability to the monumentally sculptural human form.

Europe in the Sixteenth Century

What are the cultural and historical backgrounds for the development of Italian Renaissance art and architecture during the sixteenth century?

The sixteenth century was an age of social, intellectual, and religious ferment that transformed European culture. It was marked by continual armed conflict triggered by the expansionist ambitions of warring rulers. The humanism of the fourteenth and fifteenth centuries, with its medieval roots and its often uncritical acceptance of the authority of Classical texts, slowly developed into a critical exploration of new ideas, the natural world, and distant lands. Cartographers began to acknowledge the Earth's curvature and the degrees of distance, giving Europeans a more accurate understanding of their place within the world. The printing press sparked an explosion in book production, spreading new ideas through the translation and publication of ancient and contemporary texts, broadening the horizons of educated Europeans, and encouraging the development of literacy. Since travel was growing more common, artists and their work became mobile, and the world of art was transformed into a more international community.

At the start of the sixteenth century, England, France, and Portugal were nation-states under strong monarchs. German-speaking central Europe was divided into dozens of principalities, counties, free cities, and small territories. But even states as powerful as Saxony and Bavaria acknowledged the supremacy of the Habsburg Holy Roman Empire—in theory the greatest power in Europe. Charles V, elected emperor in 1519, also inherited Spain, the Netherlands, and vast territories in the Americas. Italy, which was divided into numerous small states, was a diplomatic and military battlefield where for much of the century the Italian city-states, Habsburg Spain, France, and the papacy fought each other in shifting alliances. Popes behaved like secular princes, using diplomacy and military force to regain control over central Italy and in some cases to establish family members as hereditary rulers.

The popes' incessant demands for money, to finance the rebuilding of St. Peter's as well as their self-aggrandizing art projects and luxurious lifestyles, aggravated the religious dissent that had long been developing, especially north of the Alps. Early in the century, religious reformers within the established Church challenged its beliefs and practices, especially Julius II's sale of indulgences promising forgiveness of sins and assurance of salvation in exchange for a financial contribution to the Church. Because they protested, these northern European reformers came to be called Protestants; their demand for reform gave rise to a movement called the Reformation.

The political maneuvering of Pope Clement VII (pontificate 1523–1534) led to a direct clash with Holy Roman Emperor Charles V. In May 1527, Charles's troops attacked Rome, beginning a six-month orgy of killing, looting, and burning. The Sack of Rome, as it is called, shook the sense of stability and humanistic confidence that until then had characterized the Renaissance, and it sent many artists fleeing from the ruined city. Nevertheless, Charles saw himself as the leader of the Catholic forces—and he was the sole Catholic ally Clement had at the time. In 1530, Clement VII crowned Charles emperor in Bologna.

Sixteenth-century patrons valued artists highly and rewarded them well, not only with generous commissions but sometimes even with high social status. Charles V, for example, knighted the painter Titian. Some painters and sculptors became entrepreneurs and celebrities, selling prints of their works on the side and creating international reputations for themselves. Many artists recorded their activities—professional and private—in diaries, notebooks, and letters that have come down to us. In addition, contemporary writers began to report on the lives of artists, documenting their physical appearance and assessing their individual reputations. In 1550, Giorgio Vasari wrote the first survey of Italian art history (revised and expanded in 1568)—*Lives of the Most Excellent Architects, Painters, and Sculptors*. It was organized as a series of critical biographies, but at its core was a work of critical judgment. Vasari also commented on the role of patrons and argued that art had become more realistic and more beautiful over time, reaching its apex of perfection in his own age. From his characterization developed our notion of this period as the High Renaissance—that is, as a high point in art after the early experiments of Cimabue and Giotto, marked by a balanced synthesis of Classical ideals and a lifelike rendering of the natural world.

During this period, the fifteenth-century humanists' notion of painting, sculpture, and architecture not as manual arts but as liberal (intellectual) arts, requiring education in the Classics and mathematics as well as in the techniques of the craft, became a topic of intense interest. And from these discussions arose the Renaissance formulation—still with us today—of artists as divinely inspired creative geniuses, a step above most of us in their gifts of hand and mind. This idea weaves its way through Vasari's work like an organizing principle. And this newly elevated status favored men. Although few artists of either sex had access to the humanist education required by the often esoteric subject matter used in paintings (usually devised by someone other than the artist), women were also denied the studio practice necessary to study and draw from nude models. Furthermore, it was almost impossible for an artist to achieve international status without traveling extensively and frequently relocating to follow commissions—something most women could not do. Still, some European women managed to establish careers as artists during this period despite these obstacles.

The Roman High Renaissance

What characterizes the art of the High Renaissance in Rome as embodied by the works of Leonardo, Raphael, Michelangelo, and Bramante?

Italian art between the mid-1480s and the 1520s has been called the High Renaissance. As we have already seen with the High Classical period in ancient Athens, the term "High Renaissance" encapsulates an art historical judgment, claiming that what happened in Italy at this time represents a pinnacle of achievement within a longer artistic movement, and that it set standards for the future (**MAP 21–1**). High Renaissance art is characterized by a sense of gravity and decorum, a complex but ordered relationship of individual parts to the whole, and an emulation of the principles artists saw in ancient Classical art. Art historian Sydney Freedberg has stressed the way High Renaissance art fuses the real and the ideal, characterizing Leonardo's *Mona Lisa*, for example, as "a rare perfection between art and reality; an image in which a breathing instant and a composure for all time are held in suspension" (Freedberg, p. 28).

Two important practical developments at the turn of the sixteenth century affected the arts in Italy. Technically, the use of tempera had almost completely given way to the more flexible oil painting medium; and economically, with increasing commissions from private sources, artists no longer depended so heavily on the patronage of the Church, the court, or civic associations.

Florence's renowned artistic tradition had attracted a stream of young artists to that city throughout the fifteenth century. They traveled there to study its many

MAP 21–1 RENAISSANCE AND EARLIER MONUMENTS IN ROME

In addition to situating the principal works of the Roman Renaissance that emerged from Julius II's campaign to revitalize the papal city, this map also locates the surviving works of Roman antiquity that would have been available to the Renaissance artists and architects who masterminded the Classical revival.

artistic treasures, not least of which were Masaccio's solid, monumental figures in the Brancacci Chapel paintings (SEE FIGS. 20–21, 20–22), with their eloquent facial features, poses, and gestures. The young Michelangelo's sketches of the chapel frescos document the importance of Masaccio to his developing style. In fact, Leonardo, Michelangelo, and Raphael—the three leading artists of the High Renaissance—all worked in Florence early in their careers, although they soon moved to other centers of patronage and their influence spread well beyond that city, even beyond Italy.

Leonardo da Vinci

Leonardo da Vinci (1452–1519) was 12 or 13 when his family moved to Florence from the Tuscan village of Vinci. After an apprenticeship in the shop of the Florentine painter and sculptor Andrea del Verrocchio and a few years on his own, Leonardo traveled to Milan in 1481 or 1482 to work for the ruling Sforza family.

Leonardo spent much of his time in Milan on military and civil engineering projects, including both urban-renewal and fortification plans for the city, but he also created a few key monuments of Renaissance painting. In April 1483, Leonardo contracted with the Confraternity of the Immaculate Conception to paint an altarpiece for their chapel in the church of San Francesco Grande in Milan, a painting now known as **THE VIRGIN OF THE ROCKS** (FIG. 21-2). The contract stipulated a painting of the Virgin and Child with angels, but Leonardo added a figure of the young John the Baptist, who balances the composition at the left, pulled into dialogue with his younger cousin Jesus by the long, protective arm of the Virgin. She draws attention to her child by extending her other hand over his head, while the enigmatic figure of the angel—who looks out without actually making eye contact with the viewer—points to the center of interaction. The stable, balanced, pyramidal figural group—a compositional formula that will become a standard feature of High Renaissance Classicism—is set against an exquisitely detailed landscape that dissolves mysteriously into the misty distance.

To assure their dominance in the picture, Leonardo picks out the four figures with spotlights, creating a

21-2 Leonardo da Vinci **THE VIRGIN OF THE ROCKS**

c. 1485. Oil on wood panel (now transferred to canvas), 6′6″ × 4′ (1.9 × 1.2 m). Musée du Louvre, Paris.

Credit: Photo © Réunion des Musées Nationaux/Musée du Louvre, Paris

Art and its Contexts

THE VITRUVIAN MAN

Artists throughout history have turned to geometric shapes and mathematical proportions to seek the ideal representation of the human form. Leonardo, following the first-century ᴸᴹ Roman architect and engineer Vitruvius, equated the ideal man with both circle and square. Ancient Egyptian artists had laid out square grids as aids to design (see "Conventions and Technique of Egyptian Pictorial Relief" in Chapter 3 on page 52). Medieval artists adapted a variety of figures, from triangles to pentagrams (SEE FIG. 17–17).

Vitruvius, in his ten-volume *De architectura* (*On Architecture*), wrote: "For if a man be placed flat on his back, with his hands and feet extended, and a pair of compasses centered at his navel, the fingers and toes of his two hands and feet will touch the circumference of a circle described therefrom. And just as the human body yields a circular outline, so too a square figure may be found from it. For if we measure the distance from the soles of the feet to the top of the head, and then apply that measure to the outstretched arms, the breadth will be found to be the same as the height" (Book III, Chapter 1, Section 3). Vitruvius determined that the ideal body should be eight heads high. Leonardo added his own observations in the reversed writing he always used in his notebooks when he created his well-known diagram for the ideal male figure, called the **VITRUVIAN MAN** (**FIG. 21–3**).

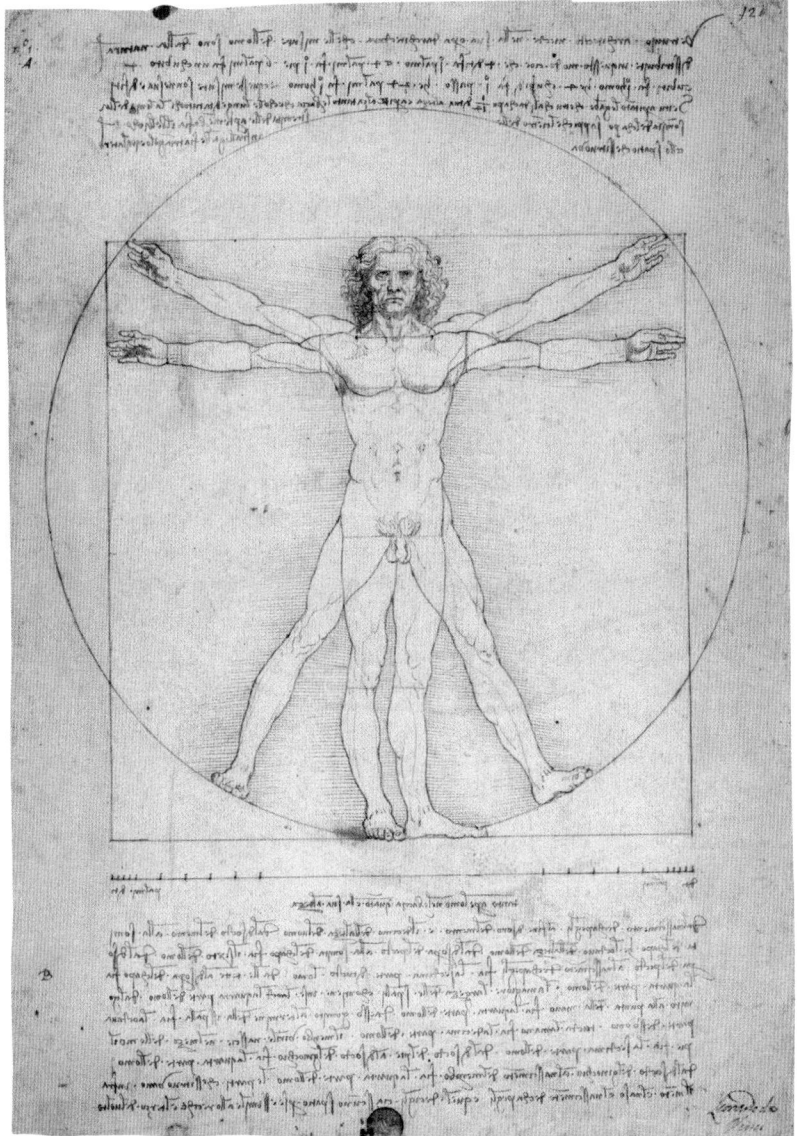

21–3 Leonardo da Vinci **VITRUVIAN MAN**
c. 1490. Ink, 13½ × 9⅝" (34.3 × 24.5 cm). Galleria dell'Accademia, Venice.

Credit: © Cameraphoto Arte, Venice

strong **chiaroscuro** (from the Italian words *chiaro*, meaning "light," and *oscuro*, meaning "dark") that enhances their modeling as three-dimensional forms. This painting is an excellent early example of a specific variant of this technique, called **sfumato** ("smoky"), in which there are subtle, almost imperceptible, transitions between light and dark in shading. *Sfumato* became a hallmark of Leonardo's style, although the effect is artificially enhanced in this painting by the yellowing of its thick varnish, which masks the original vibrancy of its color.

At Duke Ludovico Sforza's request, Leonardo painted **THE LAST SUPPER (FIGS. 21-4, 21-5)** in the refectory, or dining hall, of the monastery of Santa Maria delle Grazie in Milan between 1495 and 1498. In fictive space defined by a coffered ceiling and four pairs of tapestries that seem to extend the refectory into another room, Jesus and his disciples are seated at a long table placed parallel to the picture plane and to the monastic diners who would have been seated in the hall below. In a sense, Jesus's meal with his disciples prefigures the daily gathering of this local monastic community at mealtimes. The stagelike space recedes from the table to three windows on the back wall, where the vanishing point of the one-point linear perspective lies behind Jesus's head. A stable, pyramidal Jesus at the center is flanked by his 12 disciples, grouped in four interlocking sets of three.

On one level, Leonardo has painted a scene from a story—one that captures the individual reactions of the apostles to Jesus's announcement that one of them will betray him. Leonardo was an acute observer of human behavior, and his art captures human emotions with compelling immediacy. On another level, *The Last Supper* is a symbolic evocation of Jesus's coming sacrifice for the salvation of humankind, the foundation of the institution of the Mass. Breaking with traditional representations of the subject (SEE FIG. 20-25) to create compositional clarity, balance, and cohesion, Leonardo placed the traitor Judas—clutching his money bags in the shadows—within the first triad to Jesus's right, along with the young John the Evangelist and the elderly Peter, rather than isolating Judas on the opposite side of the table. Judas, Peter, and John were each to play an essential role in Jesus's mission: Judas set in motion the events leading to Jesus's sacrifice; Peter led the Church after Jesus's death; and John, the visionary, foretold the Second Coming and the Last Judgment in the book of Revelation.

The painting's careful geometry, the convergence of its perspective lines, the stability of its pyramidal forms, and Jesus's calm demeanor at the mathematical center of all the commotion, work together to reinforce the sense of gravity, balance, and order. The clarity and stability of this painting epitomize High Renaissance style.

The French, who had invaded Italy in 1494, next claimed Milan by defeating Leonardo's Milanese patron,

Ludovico Sforza, and Leonardo returned to Florence in 1500. Perhaps the most famous of his Florentine works is the portrait he painted between about 1503 and 1506 known as the **MONA LISA** (SEE FIG. 21-1). In a departure from tradition, the young woman is portrayed without jewelry, not even a ring. The solid pyramidal form of her halflength figure—another departure from traditional portraiture, which was limited to the upper torso—is silhouetted against distant hazy mountains, giving the painting a sense of mystery reminiscent of *The Virgin of the Rocks* (SEE FIG. 21-2). The expressive complexity of Mona Lisa's smile and the sense of psychological presence it gives the human face—especially in the context of the masklike detachment that was more characteristic of Renaissance portraiture (compare FIG. 20-39 or even FIG. 21-8)—is what makes this innovative painting so arresting and haunting, even today.

A fiercely debated topic in Renaissance Italy was the relative merits of painting and sculpture. Leonardo insisted on the supremacy of painting as the best and most complete means of creating an illusion of the natural world, while Michelangelo argued for sculpture. Yet in creating a painted illusion, Leonardo considered color to be secondary to the depiction of sculptural volume, which he achieved through his virtuosity in *sfumato*. He also unified his compositions by covering them with a thin, lightly tinted varnish, which enhanced the overall smoky haze. Because early evening light tends to produce a similar effect naturally, Leonardo considered dusk the finest time of day and recommended that painters set up their studios in a courtyard with black walls and a linen sheet stretched overhead to reproduce twilight.

Leonardo's fame as an artist is based on only a few works, for many other interests took him away from painting. Unlike his humanist contemporaries, he was not particularly interested in Classical literature or archaeology. Instead, his passions were mathematics, engineering, and the natural world. He compiled volumes of detailed drawings and notes on anatomy, botany, geology, meteorology, architectural design, and mechanics. In his drawings of human figures, he sought not only the precise details of anatomy but also the geometric basis of perfect proportions (see "The Vitruvian Man" on page 649). Leonardo's searching mind is evident in his drawings not only of natural objects and human beings, but also of machines, so clearly and completely worked out that modern engineers have used them to construct working models. He designed flying machines, a kind of automobile, a parachute, and all sorts of military equipment, including a mobile fortress. His imagination outran his means to bring his creations into being. For one thing, he lacked a source of power other than men and horses. For another, he may have lacked focus and follow-through. His contemporaries complained that he never finished anything and that his inventions distracted him from his painting.

21–4 Leonardo da Vinci **THE LAST SUPPER**

Refectory of the monastery of Santa Maria delle Grazie, Milan. 1495–1498. Tempera and oil on plaster, 15′2″ × 28′10″ (4.6 × 8.8 m).

Credit: © Studio Fotografico Quattrone, Florence

21–5 REFECTORY OF THE MONASTERY OF SANTA MARIA DELLE GRAZIE, SHOWING LEONARDO'S LAST SUPPER

Milan.

Instead of painting in fresco, Leonardo devised an experimental technique for this mural. Hoping to achieve the freedom and flexibility of painting on wood panel, he worked directly on dry *intonaco*—a thin layer of smooth plaster—with an oil-and-tempera paint for which the formula is unknown. The result was disastrous. Within a short time, the painting began to deteriorate, and by the middle of the sixteenth century its figures could be seen only with difficulty. In the seventeenth century, the monks saw no harm in cutting a doorway through the lower center of the composition. The work has barely survived the intervening period, despite many attempts to halt its deterioration and restore its original appearance. It narrowly escaped complete destruction in World War II, when the refectory was bombed to rubble. The coats of arms at the top are those of patron Ludovico Sforza, duke of Milan (ruled 1494–1499), and his wife, Beatrice.

Credit: © Studio Fotografico Quattrone, Florence

Leonardo returned to Milan in 1508 and lived there until 1513. He also lived for a time in the Vatican at the invitation of Pope Leo X, but there is no evidence that he produced any works of art during his stay. In 1516, he accepted the French king Francis I's invitation to relocate to France as an advisor on architecture, taking the *Mona Lisa*, as well as other important works, with him. He remained at Francis's court until his death in 1519.

Raphael

In about 1505—while Leonardo was working on the *Mona Lisa*—Raphael (Raffaello Santi or Sanzio, 1483–1520) arrived in Florence from his native Urbino after studying in Perugia with the city's leading artist, Perugino (SEE FIG. 20–20A). Raphael quickly became successful in Florence, especially with small, polished paintings of the Virgin and

21-6 Raphael **THE SMALL COWPER MADONNA**
c. 1505. Oil on wood panel, 23⅜ × 17⅜″ (59.5 × 44.1 cm). National Gallery of Art, Washington, DC. Widener Collection (1942.9.57).

In the distance on a hilltop, Raphael has painted a scene he knew well from his childhood, the domed church of San Bernardino, 2 miles outside Urbino. The church contains the tombs of dukes of Urbino, Federico and Guidobaldo da Montefeltro, along with their wives (SEE FIG. 20–39). Donato Bramante, whose architecture was key in establishing the High Renaissance style, may have designed the church.

Child, such as **THE SMALL COWPER MADONNA** (named for a modern owner) of about 1505 (**FIG. 21-6**). Already a superb painter technically, the youthful Raphael shows his indebtedness to his teacher in the delicate tilt of the figures' heads, the brilliant tonalities, and the pervasive sense of serenity. But Leonardo's impact is also evident here in the simple grandeur of the monumental shapes, the pyramidal composition activated by the spiraling movement of the child, and the draperies that cling to the Virgin's substantial form. In other Madonnas from this period, Raphael included the young John the Baptist (**FIG. 21-7**) and experimented with the multiple-figure interactions pioneered by Leonardo in *The Virgin of the Rocks* (SEE FIG. 21-2).

At the same time as he was producing engaging images of elegant Madonnas, Raphael was also painting flawlessly executed portraits of prosperous Florentine patrons like the 30-year-old cloth merchant Agnelo Doni, who commissioned **pendant** portraits (**FIG. 21-8**) to commemorate his marriage in 1504 to Maddalena Strozzi, the 15-year-old daughter of a powerful banking family. As Piero della Francesca had done in his portraits of Battista Sforza and Federico da Montefeltro (SEE FIG. 20–39), Raphael silhouettes Maddalena and Agnelo against a meticulously described panoramic landscape. But unlike his predecessors, Raphael turned his subjects to address the viewer. Agnelo is commanding but casual, leaning his arm on a balustrade to add three-dimensionality to his posture. Maddalena's pose imitates Leonardo's innovative presentation of his subject in the *Mona Lisa* (SEE FIG. 21-1), which Raphael had obviously seen in progress. But with Maddalena there is no sense of mystery, indeed little psychological presence, and Raphael follows tradition in emphasizing the sumptuousness of her clothing and making ostentatious display of her jewelry. The wisps of hair that escape from her sculpted coiffure are the only hint of human vulnerability.

Raphael left Florence about 1508 for Rome, where Pope Julius II put him to work almost immediately decorating rooms (*stanze*, singular *stanza*) in the papal apartments. In the Stanza della Segnatura (**FIG. 21-9**)—the pope's private library and study—Raphael painted the four branches of knowledge as conceived in the sixteenth century: Religion (the *Disputà*, depicting discussions concerning the true presence of Christ in the Eucharistic Host), Philosophy (*The School of Athens*, to the right in FIG. 21-9), Poetry (*Parnassus*, home of the Muses, to the left in FIG. 21-9), and Law (the *Cardinal Virtues* under a figure of *Justice*).

Raphael's most influential achievement in the papal rooms was *The School of Athens*, painted about 1510–1511 (see "Closer Look" on page 655). Here, the painter summarizes the ideals of the Renaissance papacy in a grand conception of harmoniously arranged forms in a rational space, as well as in the calm dignity of the figures that

21–7 Raphael **MADONNA OF THE GOLDFINCH (MADONNA DEL CARDELLINO)**
1506. Oil on panel, 42 × 29½″ (106.7 × 74.9 cm).
Galleria degli Uffizi, Florence.

The vibrant colors of this important work were revealed in the course of a careful, ten-year restoration completed in 2008.

Credit: © Studio Fotografico Quattrone, Florence

occupy it. If the learned Julius II did not actually devise the subjects, he certainly must have approved them. Greek philosophers Plato and Aristotle take center stage—placed to the right and left of the vanishing point—silhouetted against the sky and framed under three successive barrel vaults. Surrounding Plato and Aristotle are mathematicians, naturalists, astronomers, geographers, and other philosophers debating and demonstrating their theories with and to onlookers and each other. The scene takes place in an immense interior flooded with a clear, even light from a single source, seemingly inspired by the new design for St. Peter's, under construction at the time. The grandeur of the building is matched by the monumental dignity of the philosophers themselves, each of whom has a distinct physical and intellectual presence. The sweeping arcs of the composition are activated by the variety and energy of their poses and gestures, creating a dynamic unity that is a prime characteristic of High Renaissance art.

21–8 Raphael **AGNELO DONI AND MADDALENA STROZZI**
c. 1506. Oil on wood panel, each 24½ × 17¼″ (63 × 45 cm). Palazzo Pitti, Florence.

These portraits were not the only paintings commissioned by Agnelo Doni to commemorate his upwardly mobile marriage alliance with Maddalena Strozzi. He ordered a tondo portraying the Holy Family from rival artist Michelangelo (see "Closer Look" in the Introduction on page xxviii). Vasari reports that although the original price for that painting was set at 70 ducats, Doni only sent Michelangelo 40. In order to obtain his painting, the patron eventually had to pay the artist double the original price— 140 ducats.

Credit: © Studio Fotografico Quattrone, Florence

21-9 Raphael **STANZA DELLA SEGNATURA**
Vatican, Rome. Fresco in the left lunette, *Parnassus*; in the right lunette, *The School of Athens*. 1510–1511.

Credit: Photo © Musei Vaticani/IKONA

A Closer Look

THE SCHOOL OF ATHENS

Looking down from niches in the walls are sculptures of Apollo (the god of sunlight, rationality, poetry, music, and the fine arts) and Minerva (the goddess of wisdom and the mechanical arts).

Plato points upward to the realm of ideas and pure forms that were at the center of his philosophy. His pupil Aristotle gestures toward his surroundings, signifying the empirical world that for him served as the basis for understanding.

The figure bent over a slate with a compass is Euclid, the father of geometry. Vasari claimed that Raphael gave this mathematician the portrait likeness of Bramante, the architect whose redesigned St. Peter's was under construction not far from this room and who was also a distant relative of Raphael.

Raphael placed his own portrait in a group that includes the geographer Ptolemy, who holds a terrestrial globe, and the astronomer Zoroaster, who holds a celestial globe.

The brooding figure of Heraclitus, a late addition to the composition, is a portrait of Michelangelo, who was working next door on the ceiling of the Sistine Chapel and whose monumental figural style is here taken (or mimicked) by Raphael. The stonecutter's boots on his feet refer to Michelangelo's self-identification—or Raphael's insistence that he be seen—as a sculptor rather than a painter.

Vasari's account of the painting identifies this figure as Diogenes the Cynic. It is more likely that he is Socrates, however. The cup next to him could refer to his deadly draught of hemlock, and his reclining position recalls his teaching from his prison bed.

The group of figures gathered around Euclid illustrate the various stages of understanding: literal learning, dawning comprehension, anticipation of the outcome, and assisting the teacher. Raphael was praised for his ability to communicate so clearly through the poses and expressions of his figures.

21–10 Raphael **THE SCHOOL OF ATHENS**
Fresco in the Stanza della Segnatura, Vatican, Rome. c. 1510–1511. 19 × 27′ (5.79 × 8.24 m).

TAPESTRIES FOR THE SISTINE CHAPEL In 1515, Raphael was commissioned by Pope Leo X (pontificate 1513–1521) to provide designs on themes from the Acts of the Apostles to be woven into a lavish set of tapestries for the strip of blank wall below the fifteenth-century wall paintings of the Sistine Chapel (this surface is now decorated with painted simulations of hanging drapery: see FIG. 21-16). Raphael produced full-scale cartoons for the weavers in Brussels to match. Pictorial weaving was the most prestigious and costly kind of wall decoration. With murals by the leading painters of the fifteenth century above his work and Michelangelo's work circling over all, Raphael must have felt both honored and challenged: The pope had chosen him for the chapel's most valuable works of art. They cost Leo X more than five times what Julius II had paid Michelangelo to paint the ceiling. Raphael only received a sixteenth of the total cost of the tapestries, however, for designing the program and producing the cartoons; the expense here involved production more than design.

The cartoons were created in Raphael's workshop between 1515 and 1516. Raphael was clearly the intellect behind the compositions, and he participated in the actual preparation and execution. This was a prestigious commission that would reflect directly on the reputation of the master. But he could not have accomplished this imposing task in a little over a year without the collaboration of numerous assistants. The cartoons were first drawn with charcoal on paper (160–170 separate sheets were glued together to form the expanse of a single tapestry), then overpainted with color, and finally sent to Brussels, where they were woven into tapestries in the workshop of Pieter van Aelst. The first was complete in 1517, seven were hanging in the chapel for Christmas 1519, and the entire cycle was installed by Leo X's death in 1521.

The process of creation, from design through production, can be charted by examining the tapestry portraying **CHRIST'S CHARGE TO PETER** (John 21:15–17; Matthew 16:17–19) at three stages in its development. We have Raphael's preliminary drawing (FIG. 21-11), where models—it is tempting to see these as Raphael's assistants, stripped to their underwear to help the master work out his composition—are posed to enact the moment when Jesus addresses his apostles. This is a preliminary idea for the pose of Christ. In the final cartoon (FIG. 21-12), Raphael changes Christ's gesture so that he addresses the kneeling Peter specifically rather than the whole apostolic group; for the patron, this would be an important detail since papal power rested in the belief that Christ had transferred authority to Peter, who was considered the first pope, with subsequent popes inheriting this authority in unbroken succession. Comparison of drawing and cartoon also reveals an important aspect of the design process. The cartoon reverses the figural arrangement of the drawing because in the production process the tapestry would be woven from the back—so the weavers would need to follow a reversed version of the original drawing in order to come out with the intended orientation for the resulting tapestry (FIG. 21-13). Comparison of cartoon and tapestry also indicates that the weavers were not required to follow their models slavishly. They embellished the costume of Christ, perhaps in an attempt to ensure that the viewer's attention would be immediately drawn to this most important figure in the scene.

After they had been used to create the tapestries hung in the Sistine Chapel, Raphael's cartoons remained in Brussels, where several additional sets of tapestries were made from them—one for Henry VIII of England, another for Francis I of France—before seven surviving cartoons were acquired in 1623 by the future Charles I of England. They remain in the British Royal Collection. The tapestries themselves, although still in the Vatican, are displayed in the museum rather than on the walls of the chapel for which they were originally conceived, as one of the most prestigious artistic projects from the peak of the Roman High Renaissance.

21-11 Raphael STUDY FOR CHRIST'S CHARGE TO PETER
c. 1515. Red chalk. Royal Library, Windsor Castle, England.

Credit: Royal Collection Trust © Her Majesty Queen Elizabeth II, 2016/Bridgeman Images

21–12 Raphael and assistants **CARTOON FOR TAPESTRY PORTRAYING CHRIST'S CHARGE TO PETER**
c. 1515–1516. Distemper on paper (now transferred to canvas), 11'1″ × 17'4″ (3.4 × 5.3 m). Lent by Her Majesty the Queen
to the Victoria & Albert Museum, London.

Credit: V&A Images/Victoria and Albert Museum

21–13 Shop of Pieter van Aelst, Brussels, after cartoons by Raphael and assistants **CHRIST'S CHARGE TO PETER**
Woven 1517, installed 1519 in the Sistine Chapel. Wool and silk with silver-gilt-wrapped threads. Musei Vaticani, Pinacoteca,
Rome.

Credit: Photo © Musei Vaticani/IKONA

Michelangelo

Michelangelo Buonarroti (1475–1564) was born in the Tuscan town of Caprese into an impoverished Florentine family that laid a claim to nobility—a claim the artist carefully advanced throughout his life. He grew up in Florence, where at age 13 he was apprenticed to Ghirlandaio (SEE FIG. 20–31), in whose workshop he learned the technique of fresco painting and studied drawings of Classical monuments. Soon the talented youth joined the household of Lorenzo the Magnificent, head of the ruling Medici family, where he came into contact with Neoplatonic philosophy and the family's distinguished sculpture collection. After Lorenzo died in 1492, Michelangelo traveled to Venice and Bologna, then returned to Florence.

Michelangelo's major early work at the turn of the century was a marble sculpture of the **PIETÀ** commissioned by a French cardinal and installed as a tomb monument in Old St. Peter's (**FIG. 21-14**). The theme of the *pietà* (in which the Virgin supports and mourns the dead Jesus in her lap), long popular in northern Europe (SEE FIG. 18–24), was an unusual theme in Italy at the time. Michelangelo traveled to the marble quarries at Carrara in central Italy to select the block from which to make this large work, a practice he was to continue for nearly all his sculpture. The choice of stone was important to him because he envisioned his sculpture as already existing within the marble, needing only his tools to set it free. Michelangelo was a poet as well as an artist and later wrote in his Sonnet 15: "The greatest artist has no conception which a single block of marble

21-14 Michelangelo
PIETÀ
c. 1500. Marble, height 5′8½″ (1.74 m). St. Peter's, Vatican, Rome.

Credit: Canali Photobank, Milan, Italy

21–15 Michelangelo **DAVID**

1501–1504. Marble, height 17′ (5.18 m) without pedestal. Galleria dell'Accademia, Florence.

Michelangelo's most famous sculpture was cut from an 18-foot-tall marble block. The sculptor began with a small model in wax, then sketched the contours of the figure as they would appear from the front on one face of the marble. According to his friend and biographer Vasari, Michelangelo then chiseled in from the drawn-on surface, as if making a figure in very high relief. The completed statue took four days to move on tree-trunk rollers down the narrow streets of Florence from the cathedral workshop to its location outside the Palazzo della Signoria (SEE FIG. 18–2). In 1504, the Florentines gilded the tree stump and added a gilded wreath to the head and a belt of 28 gilt-bronze leaves, since removed. In 1873, the statue was replaced by a copy, and the original was moved into the museum of the Florence Academy.

Credit: © Studio Fotografico Quattrone, Florence

does not potentially contain within its mass, but only a hand obedient to the mind can penetrate to this image."

Michelangelo's Virgin is a young woman of heroic stature holding the unnaturally smaller, lifeless body of her grown son. Inconsistencies of scale and age are forgotten, however, when contemplating the sweetness of expression, technical virtuosity of the carving, and smooth interplay of the forms. Michelangelo's compelling vision of beauty was meant to be seen up close so that the viewer can look directly into Jesus's face. The 25-year-old artist is said to have slipped into the church at night to sign the statue on a strap across the Virgin's breast after it was finished, answering directly questions that had come up about the identity of its creator.

In 1501, Michelangelo accepted a Florentine commission for a statue of the biblical hero **DAVID** (**FIG. 21–15**) to be placed high atop a buttress of the cathedral. But when it was finished in 1504, the *David* was so admired that the city council instead placed it in the principal city square, next to the Palazzo della Signoria (SEE FIG. 18–2), the seat of Florence's government. There it stood as a reminder of Florence's republican status, which was briefly reinstated after the expulsion of the powerful Medici oligarchy in 1494. Although in its muscular nudity Michelangelo's *David* embodies the antique ideal of the athletic male nude, the emotional power of its expression and its concentrated gaze are entirely new. Unlike Donatello's bronze *David* (SEE FIG. 20–14), this is not a triumphant hero with the trophy head of the giant Goliath already under his feet. Slingshot over his shoulder and a rock in his right hand, Michelangelo's *David* knits his brow and stares into space, seemingly preparing himself psychologically for the danger ahead, a mere youth confronting a gigantic experienced warrior. This *David* stands for the supremacy of right over might— a perfect emblem for the Florentines, who had recently fought the forces of Milan, Siena, and Pisa and still faced political and military pressure.

THE CEILING OF THE SISTINE CHAPEL Despite Michelangelo's contractual commitment to Florence Cathedral for additional statues, Pope Julius II, who saw Michelangelo as an ideal collaborator in the artistic aggrandizement of the papacy, arranged in 1505 for him to come to Rome to work on the spectacular tomb Julius planned for himself. Michelangelo began the tomb project, but two years later the pope ordered him to begin painting the ceiling of the **SISTINE CHAPEL** instead (**FIG. 21–16**).

Michelangelo considered himself a sculptor, but the strong-minded pope wanted paintings; work began in 1508. Michelangelo complained bitterly in a sonnet to a friend: "This miserable job has given me a goiter…. The force of it has jammed my belly up beneath my chin. Beard to the sky….Brush splatterings make a pavement of my face…. I'm not a painter." Despite his physical misery as he stood on a scaffold, painting the ceiling just above him, the results were extraordinary, and Michelangelo

21–16 INTERIOR, SISTINE CHAPEL
Vatican, Rome. Built 1475–1481; ceiling painted 1508–1512; end wall, 1536–1541. The ceiling measures 45 × 128′ (13.75 × 39 m).

Credit: Musei Vaticani/Zigrossi, Brachetti/IKONA

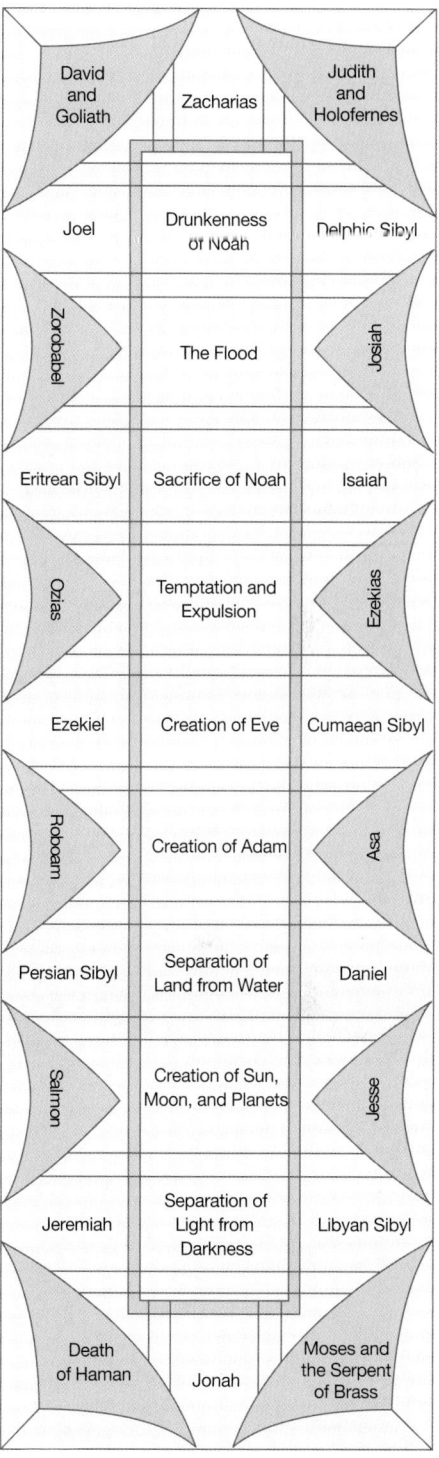

CHAPEL ENTRANCE

David and Goliath	Zacharias	Judith and Holofernes
Joel	Drunkenness of Noah	Delphic Sibyl
Zorobabel	The Flood	Josiah
Eritrean Sibyl	Sacrifice of Noah	Isaiah
Ozias	Temptation and Expulsion	Ezekias
Ezekiel	Creation of Eve	Cumaean Sibyl
Roboam	Creation of Adam	Asa
Persian Sibyl	Separation of Land from Water	Daniel
Salmon	Creation of Sun, Moon, and Planets	Jesse
Jeremiah	Separation of Light from Darkness	Libyan Sibyl
Death of Haman	Jonah	Moses and the Serpent of Brass

ALTAR

21–17 Michelangelo SISTINE CHAPEL CEILING WITH DIAGRAM IDENTIFYING SCENES
1508–1512. Fresco.

Credit: Photo © Musei Vaticani/IKONA

established a new and remarkably powerful style in Renaissance painting.

Julius's initial order for the ceiling was simple: *trompe l'oeil* coffers to replace the original star-spangled blue decoration. Later he wanted the 12 apostles seated on thrones on the triangular spandrels between the lunettes framing the windows. According to Michelangelo, when he objected to the limitations of Julius's plan, the pope told him to paint whatever he liked. This Michelangelo presumably did, although he was certainly guided by a theological advisor and his plan no doubt required the pope's approval.

In Michelangelo's design, an illusionistic marble architecture establishes a framework for the figures and narrative scenes on the vault of the chapel (FIG. 21-17). Running completely around the ceiling is a painted cornice with projections supported by pilasters decorated with "sculptured" *putti*. Between the pilasters are figures of prophets and sibyls (female seers from the Classical world) who were believed to have foretold Jesus's birth. Seated on the fictive cornice are heroic figures of nude young men called *ignudi* (singular, *ignudo*), holding sashes attached to large gold medallions. Rising behind the *ignudi*, shallow bands of fictive stone span the center of the ceiling and divide it into nine compartments containing successive scenes from Genesis—recounting the Creation, the Fall, and the Flood—beginning over the altar and ending near the chapel entrance. God's earliest acts of creation are therefore closest to the altar, the Creation of Eve at the center of the ceiling, followed by the imperfect actions of humanity: Temptation, Fall, Expulsion from Paradise, and God's eventual destruction of all people except Noah and his family by the Flood. The eight triangular spandrels over the windows, as well as the lunettes crowning them, contain paintings of the ancestors of Jesus.

Perhaps the most familiar scene on the ceiling is the **CREATION OF ADAM** (FIG. 21-18), where Michelangelo captures the moment when God charges the languorous Adam—in a pose adapted from the Roman river-god type—with the spark of life. As if to echo the biblical text, Adam's heroic body, outstretched arm, and profile almost mirror those of God, in whose image he has been created. Emerging under God's other arm and looking across him in the direction of her future mate is the robust and energetic figure of Eve before her creation.

21-18 Michelangelo **CREATION OF ADAM, SISTINE CHAPEL CEILING**
1511–1512. Fresco, 9'2" × 18'8" (2.8 × 5.7 m).

Credit: Photo © Musei Vaticani/IKONA

SAN LORENZO After the Medici regained power in Florence in 1512 and Leo X (Giovanni de' Medici) succeeded Julius in 1513, Michelangelo became chief architect for Medici family projects at the church of San Lorenzo in Florence—including a new chapel for the tombs of Lorenzo the Magnificent, his brother Giuliano, and two younger dukes, also named Lorenzo and Giuliano, ordered in 1519 for the so-called New Sacristy (SEE FIG. 20–8B). The older men's tombs were never built to Michelangelo's designs, but the unfinished tombs for the younger relatives were placed on opposite side walls (FIG. 21–19).

Each of the two monuments consists of an idealized portrait of the deceased, who turns to face the family's unfinished ancestral tomb. The men are dressed in a sixteenth-century interpretation of Classical armor and seated in wall niches above pseudo-Classical sarcophagi. Balanced precariously atop the sarcophagi are male and female figures representing the times of day. Their positions would not seem so unsettling had reclining figures of river gods been installed below them, as originally planned, but even so there is a conspicuous tension here between the substantiality of the figures and the limitations imposed on them by their architectural surrounds. In the tomb illustrated here, Michelangelo represents Giuliano as the Active Life, and his sarcophagus figures are allegories of Night and Day. Night at left is accompanied by her symbols: a star and crescent moon on her tiara; poppies, which induce sleep; and an owl under the arch of her leg. The huge mask at her back may allude to Death, since Sleep and Death were said to be the children of Night. Some have seen in this mask that glares out at viewers in the chapel a self-portrait of the artist, serving both as signature and as a way of proclaiming his right to be here because of his long relationship with the family. On the other tomb, Lorenzo, representing the Contemplative Life, is supported by Dawn and Evening.

Concurrent with work on the Medici tombs was the construction of a new library at San Lorenzo. The idea for the library belongs to Cardinal Giulio de' Medici and dates to 1519, but it was only after he was elected Pope Clement VII in 1523 that the money became available to realize it. Michelangelo was commissioned to design and also supervise construction of the new

21–19 Michelangelo **TOMB OF GIULIANO DE' MEDICI WITH ALLEGORICAL FIGURES OF NIGHT AND DAY**
New Sacristy (Medici Chapel), church of San Lorenzo, Florence. 1519–1534. Marble, height of seated figure approx. 5'10" (1.8 m).

Credit: © Studio Fotografico Quattrone, Florence

VESTIBULE (FIG. **21-20**) and reading room and to spare no expense in making them both grand and ambitious. The pope paid keen attention to the library's progress—not, he said, to verify the quality of the design, but because the project had a special interest for him.

Michelangelo coordinated his work within a decorative tradition established at San Lorenzo when Brunelleschi designed the church itself a century earlier (SEE FIG. 20-8A), using stylized architectural elements carved in dark gray *pietra serena*, set against and within a contrasting white wall. However, Michelangelo plays with the Classical architectural etiquette that Brunelleschi had used to create such clarity, harmony, and balance in the nave. In Michelangelo's vestibule, chunky columns are recessed into rectangular wall niches that can barely contain them. They are crowded and overlapped by the aggressive lateral extension of the pediment over the door. The door itself is broken into parts, sides jutting forward as fluted pilasters that are then partially obscured by the frame around the opening. The three flights of stairs leading up to the reading room almost fill the vestibule, and the central stairs cascade forward forcefully toward visitors, who are hardly encouraged to go against the flow and step up. Through their playfulness, these creative combinations of architectural forms draw attention to themselves and their design rather than the function of the building itself or the comfortable accommodation of its users, prime characteristics of the Mannerist architecture then coming into fashion.

Fearing for his life when ongoing political struggles flared up in Florence, Michelango returned to Rome in 1534 and settled permanently. He had left both the Medici Chapel and the library unfinished. In 1557, he sent a plaster model of the library staircase to Florence to ensure that its completion conformed to his design. In 1545, his students had assembled the tomb sculptures, including unfinished figures of the times of day, into the composition we see today.

The figures of the dukes are finely finished, but the times of day are notable for their contrasting areas of rough unfinished and polished marble. These are the only unfinished sculptures Michelangelo apparently permitted to be put in place, and we do not know what his reasons were. Specialists in Renaissance art history characterize these works with the word *nonfinito* ("unfinished"), proposing that Michelangelo had begun to view his artistic creations as symbols of human imperfection. Indeed, Michelangelo's poetry often expressed his belief that humans could achieve perfection only in death.

21–20 Michelangelo
VESTIBULE OF THE LAURENTIAN LIBRARY
Church of San Lorenzo, Florence. Begun 1524; stairway designed 1550s.

Credit: © Studio Fotografico Quattrone, Florence

Architecture in Rome and the Vatican

The election of Julius II as pope in 1503 crystallized a resurgence of papal power, but France, Spain, and the Holy Roman Empire all had designs on Italy. During his ten-year papacy, Julius fought wars and formed alliances to consolidate his power. He also enlisted Bramante, Raphael, and Michelangelo to carry out his vision of a revitalized Rome as the center of a new Christian architecture, inspired by the achievements of their fifteenth-century predecessors as well as the monuments of antiquity. Although most commissions were for churches, opportunities also arose to create urban palaces and country villas.

BRAMANTE Donato Bramante (1444–1514) was born near Urbino and trained as a painter, but turned to architectural design early in his career. About 1481, he became attached to the Sforza court in Milan, where he would have known Leonardo da Vinci. In 1499, Bramante settled in Rome, but work came slowly. The architect was nearing 60 when Julius II asked him to redesign St. Peter's (see "St. Peter's Basilica" on page 687) and the Spanish rulers Queen Isabella and King Ferdinand commissioned a small shrine over the spot in Rome where the apostle Peter was believed to have been crucified (**FIG. 21–21**). In this tiny building, known as Il Tempietto ("Little Temple"), Bramante combined his interpretation of the principles of Vitruvius and Alberti, from the stepped base to the Tuscan columns and Doric frieze (Vitruvius had advised that the Doric order be used for temples to gods of particularly forceful character) to the elegant balustrade. The centralized plan and the tall drum supporting a hemispheric dome recall Early Christian shrines built over martyrs' relics, as well as ancient Roman circular temples. Especially notable is the sculptural effect of the building's exterior, with its deep wall niches and sharp contrasts of light and shadow. Bramante's design called for a circular cloister around the church, but the cloister was never built.

21-21 Donato Bramante **IL TEMPIETTO, CHURCH OF SAN PIETRO IN MONTORIO**

Rome. 1502–1510; dome and lantern were restored in the 17th century.

Credit: © Vincenzo Pirozzi, Rome

Northern Italy

How are the sixteenth-century Renaissance buildings, paintings, and sculptures in northern Italy distinctive from what was created at the same time in Rome?

While Rome was Italy's preeminent arts center at the beginning of the sixteenth century, wealthy and powerful families elsewhere also patronized the arts and letters, just as the Montefeltros and Gonzagas had in Urbino and Mantua during the fifteenth century. The architects and painters working for these sixteenth-century patrons created fanciful structures and developed a new colorful, illusionistic painting style. The result was witty, elegant, and finely executed art designed to appeal to the jaded taste of the intellectual elite in cities such as Mantua, Parma, Bologna, and Venice.

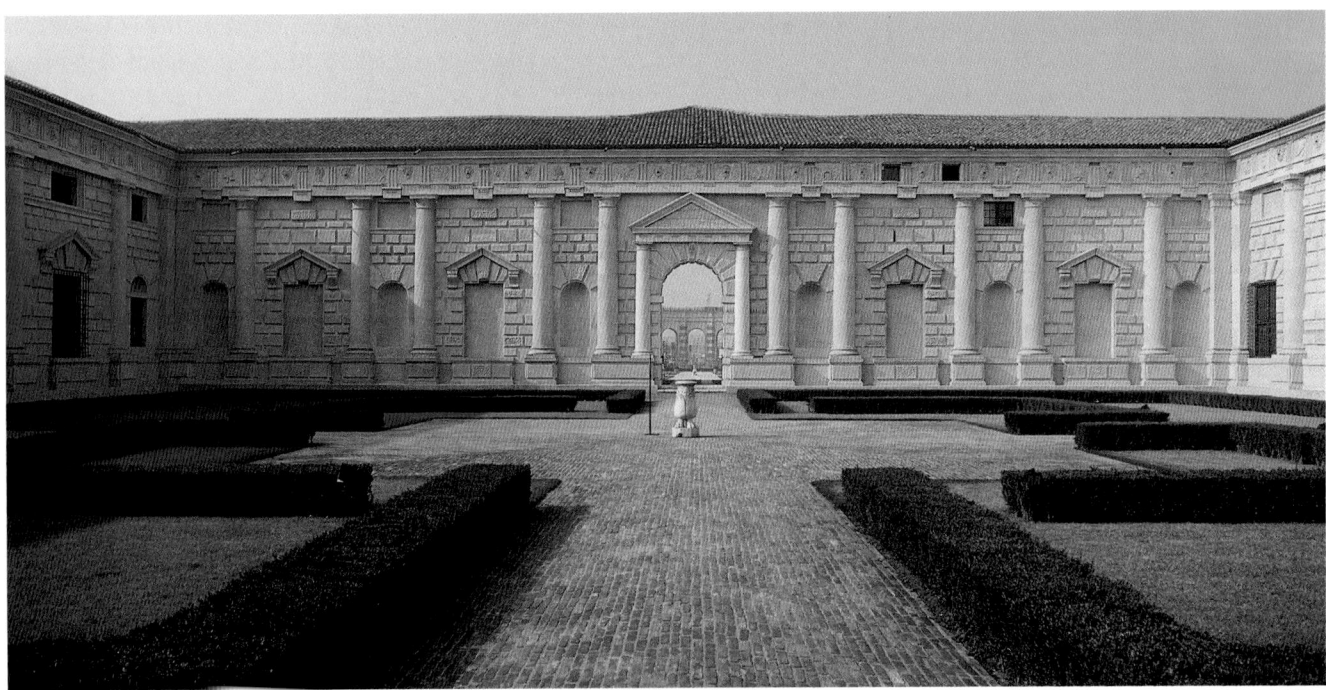

21-22 Giulio Romano **COURTYARD FAÇADE, PALAZZO DEL TE, MANTUA**
1527–1534.

Credit: © SuperStock

GIULIO ROMANO In Mantua, Federigo II Gonzaga (ruled 1519–1540) continued the family tradition of patronage when, in 1524, he lured a Roman follower of Raphael, Giulio Romano (c. 1499–1546), to build him a pleasure palace. Indeed, the **PALAZZO DEL TE** (**FIG. 21-22**) devoted more space to gardens, pools, and stables than to rooms for residential living. Since Federigo and his well-educated friends would have known Classical orders and proportions, they could appreciate the playfulness with which they are used here. The building is full of visual jokes, such as lintels masquerading as arches and triglyphs that slip sloppily out of place. Like the similar, if more sober, subversions of Classical architectural decorum in Michelangelo's contemporary Laurentian Library (SEE FIG. 21-20), the Palazzo del Te's sophisticated humor and exquisite craft have been seen as a precursor to Mannerism or as a manifestation of Mannerism itself.

Giulio Romano continued his witty play in the decoration of the two principal rooms. One, dedicated to the loves of the

21-23 Giulio Romano **FALL OF THE GIANTS**
Sala dei Giganti, Palazzo del Te. 1530–1532. Fresco.

Credit: © 2016. Photo Scala, Florence

gods, depicted the marriage of Cupid and Psyche. The other room is a remarkable feat of *trompe l'oeil* painting in which the entire building seems to be collapsing around the viewer as the gods defeat the giants (**FIG. 21-23**). Here, Giulio Romano accepted the challenge Andrea Mantegna had laid down in the Camera Picta of the Gonzaga Palace (SEE FIG. 20-40), painted for Federigo's grandfather: to dissolve architectural barriers and fantasize a world of playful delight beyond the walls and ceilings. But the Palazzo del Te was not just fun and games. The unifying themes were love and politics, the former focused on the separate apartments built to house Federigo's mistress, Isabella Boschetti. The palace was constructed in part as a place where they could meet beyond the watchful gaze of her husband, but the decoration also seems to reflect Federigo's dicey alliance

with Charles V, who stayed in the palace in 1530 and again in 1532, when the scaffolding was removed from the Sala dei Giganti so the emperor could see the paintings in progress. He must have been impressed with his host's lavish new residence, and doubtless he saw a connection between these reeling paintings and his own military successes.

CORREGGIO At about the same time that Giulio Romano was building and decorating the Palazzo del Te, in nearby Parma an equally skillful master, Correggio (Antonio Allegri da Correggio, c. 1489–1534), was creating similarly theatrical effects with dramatic foreshortening in Parma Cathedral. Correggio's great work, the **ASSUMPTION OF THE VIRGIN** (**FIG. 21-24**), a fresco painted between about 1526 and 1530 in the cathedral's

21-24 Correggio ASSUMPTION OF THE VIRGIN
Main dome, interior, Parma Cathedral, Italy. c. 1526–1530. Fresco, diameter of base of dome approx. 36′ (11 m).
Credit: © 2016. Photo Scala, Florence

21-25 Properzia de' Rossi **JOSEPH AND POTIPHAR'S WIFE**

Cathedral of San Petronio, Bologna. 1525–1526. Marble, 1′9″ × 1′11″ (54 × 58 cm). Museo de San Petronio, Bologna.

Credit: Berardi/IKONA

in the 1550 edition of *Lives of the Artists*; he wrote that a rival male sculptor prevented her from being paid fairly for this piece and from securing additional commissions.

Venice and the Veneto

In the sixteenth century the Venetians did not see themselves as rivals of Florence and Rome, but rather as their superiors. Their city was the greatest commercial sea power in the Mediterranean, they had challenged Byzantium, and now they confronted the Muslim Turks. Favored by their unique geographical situation—protected by water and controlling sea routes in the Adriatic Sea and the eastern Mediterranean—the Venetians became wealthy and secure patrons of the arts.

Their Byzantine heritage, preserved by their conservative tendencies, encouraged an art of rich patterned surfaces emphasizing light and color.

The idealized style and oil-painting technique initiated by the Bellini family in the late fifteenth century (see Chapter 20) were developed further by sixteenth-century Venetian painters. Venetians were the first in Italy to use oils for painting on both wood panel and canvas. Possibly because they were a seafaring people accustomed to working with large sheets of canvas, and possibly because humidity made their walls crack and mildew, the Venetians were also the first to cover walls with large canvas paintings instead of frescos. Because oils dried slowly, errors could be corrected and changes made easily during the work. The flexibility of the canvas support, coupled with the radiance and depth of oil-suspended pigments, eventually made oil on canvas the preferred medium, especially since it was particularly well suited to the rich color and lighting effects favored by Giorgione and Titian, two of the city's major painters of the sixteenth century.

GIORGIONE The career of Giorgione (Giorgio da Castelfranco, c. 1475–1510) was brief—he died from the plague, and most scholars accept fewer than ten paintings as entirely by his hand. But his importance to Venetian painting is critical. He introduced new, enigmatic pastoral themes, known as **poesie** (or "painted poems"), that were inspired by the contemporary literary revival of ancient pastoral verse but defy specific narrative or symbolic interpretation. He is significant above all for his appreciation of

dome, distantly recalls the illusionism of Mantegna's ceiling in the Gonzaga Palace, but Correggio has also assimilated Leonardo da Vinci's use of *sfumato* and Raphael's idealism into his own style. Correggio's *Assumption* is a dazzling illusion—the architecture of the dome seems to dissolve and the forms seem to explode through the building, drawing viewers into the swirling vortex of saints and angels who rush upward amid billowing clouds to accompany the Virgin as she soars into heaven. Correggio's sensual rendering of the figures' flesh and clinging draperies contrasts with the spirituality of the theme (the miraculous transporting of the Virgin to heaven at the moment of her death). The viewer's strongest impression is of a powerful, upward-spiraling motion of alternating cool clouds and warm, alluring figures.

PROPERZIA DE' ROSSI Very few women had the opportunity to become sculptors. Properzia de' Rossi (c. 1490–1529/1530), who lived in Bologna, was an exception. She mastered many arts, including engraving, and was famous for her miniature sculptures, including an entire *Last Supper* carved on a peach pit. She carved several pieces in marble—two sibyls, two angels, and this relief of **JOSEPH AND POTIPHAR'S WIFE**—for the Cathedral of San Petronio in Bologna (**FIG. 21-25**). According to Vasari, it was inspired by Properzia's own love for a young man, which she got over by carving this panel. Joseph escapes, running, as the partially clad seductress snatches at his cloak. Properzia is the only woman Vasari included nature in landscape painting. His early life and training are undocumented, but his work suggests that he studied with Giovanni Bellini. Perhaps Leonardo da Vinci's subtle lighting system and mysterious, intensely observed landscapes also inspired him.

One of Giorgione's most compelling works, called today **THE TEMPEST** (FIG. 21-26), was painted shortly before his death, potentially in response to personal, private impulses—as with many modern artists—rather than to fulfill an external commission. Simply trying to understand what is happening in this enigmatic picture piques our interest. At the right, a woman is seated on the ground, nude except for the end of a long white cloth thrown over her shoulders. Her nudity seems maternal, her sensuality generative rather than erotic, as she nurses the baby protectively and lovingly embraced at her side. Across the dark, rocky edge of her elevated perch stands a mysterious man, variously interpreted as a German mercenary soldier and as an urban dandy wandering in the country. His shadowed head turns in the direction of the

21-26 Giorgione **THE TEMPEST**
c. 1506. Oil on canvas, 32 × 28¾″ (82 × 73 cm). Galleria dell'Accademia, Venice.

Credit: © Cameraphoto Arte, Venice

woman, but he only appears to have paused for a moment before turning back toward the viewer or resuming his journey along the path. X-rays of the painting show that Giorgione altered the composition while he was still working on the painting—the man replaced a second nude woman who was bathing. Between the figures, a spring gushes to feed a lake surrounded by substantial houses, and in the far distance a bolt of lightning splits the darkening sky. Indeed, the artist's attention seems focused as much on the landscape and the unruly elements of nature as on the figures posed within it. Some interpreters have seen references to the Classical elements of water, earth, air, and fire in the lake, the verdant ground, the billowing clouds, and the lightning bolt.

For a few years before Giorgione's untimely death in 1510, he was associated with Tiziano Vecellio, a painter better known today as Titian (c. 1488–1576). The painting known as **THE PASTORAL CONCERT** (FIG. **21-27**) has been attributed to both of them, although scholarly opinion

today favors Titian. As in Giorgione's *The Tempest*, the idyllic landscape, here bathed in golden, hazy, late-afternoon sunlight, seems to be one of the main subjects of the painting. In this mythic world, two men—an aristocratic musician in rich red silks and a barefoot, singing peasant in homespun cloth—turn toward each other, seemingly unaware of the two naked women in front of them. One woman plays a pipe and the other pours water into a well; the white drapery sliding to the ground enhances rather than hides their nudity. Perhaps they are the musicians' muses. Behind the figures, the sunlight illuminates another shepherd and his animals near lush woodland. The painting evokes a golden age of love and innocence recalled in ancient Roman and Italian Renaissance pastoral poetry. In fact, the painting is now interpreted as an allegory on the invention of poetry. Both artists were renowned for painting sensuous female nudes whose bodies seem to glow with an incandescent light, inspired by flesh and blood as much as any source from poetry or art.

21-27 Giorgione or Titian **THE PASTORAL CONCERT OR ALLEGORY ON THE INVENTION OF PASTORAL POETRY**
c. 1510. Oil on canvas, 41¼ × 54¾" (105 × 136.5 cm). Musée du Louvre, Paris.

TITIAN Titian's early life is obscure. He supposedly began an apprenticeship as a mosaicist, then studied painting under Gentile and Giovanni Bellini, perhaps working later with Giorgione. He certainly absorbed Giorgione's style and completed at least one of Giorgione's unfinished paintings.

In 1519, Jacopo Pesaro, commander of the papal fleet that had defeated the Turks in 1502, commissioned Titian to commemorate the victory in a votive altarpiece for a side-aisle chapel in the Franciscan church of Santa Maria Gloriosa dei Frari in Venice. Titian worked on the painting for seven years and changed the concept three times before he finally came up with a revolutionary composition—one that complemented the viewer's approach from the left.

He created an asymmetrical setting of huge columns on high bases soaring right out of the frame (**FIG. 21–28**). Into this architectural setting, he placed the Virgin and Child on a high throne at one side and arranged saints and the Pesaro family below on a diagonal axis, crossing at the central figure of St. Peter (a reminder of Jacopo's role as head of the papal forces in 1502). The red of Francesco Pesaro's brocade garment and of the banner diagonally across sets up a contrast of primary colors against St. Peter's blue tunic and yellow mantle and the red and blue draperies of the Virgin. St. Maurice (behind the kneeling Jacopo at the left) holds the banner with the papal arms, and a cowering Turkish captive reminds the viewer of the Christian

victory. A youth turning to meet our gaze at lower right guarantees our engagement, and light floods in from above, illuminating not only this and other faces, but also the great columns, where *putti* in the clouds carry a cross. Titian was famous for his mastery of light and color, but this altarpiece demonstrates that he also could draw and model as solidly as any Florentine. The perfectly balanced composition, built on color and diagonals instead of a vertical and horizontal grid, looks forward to the art of the seventeenth century.

In 1529, Titian, who was well known outside Venice, began a long professional relationship with Emperor Charles V, who vowed to let no one else paint his portrait and ennobled Titian in 1533. The next year Titian was commissioned to paint a portrait of

21–28 Titian **PESARO MADONNA**
1519–1526. Oil on canvas, 16′ × 8′10″ (4.9 × 2.7 m). Side-aisle altarpiece, Santa Maria Gloriosa dei Frari, Venice.

Credit: © Cameraphoto Arte, Venice

21–29 Titian **ISABELLA D'ESTE**
1534–1536. Oil on canvas, 40⅛ × 25³⁄₁₆″ (102 × 64.1 cm).
Kunsthistorisches Museum, Vienna.

Credit: © KHM-Museumsverband

the marchesa of Mantua, Isabella d'Este (1474–1539; **FIG. 21-29**), a patron of painters, musicians, composers, writers, and literary scholars. Married to Francesco II Gonzaga at age 15, she had great wealth and a brilliant mind that made her a successful diplomat and administrator. A true Renaissance woman, she was an avid collector of manuscripts and books and sponsored the publication of an edition of Virgil while still in her twenties. She also collected ancient art and objects, as well as works by contemporary Italian artists such as Mantegna, Leonardo, Perugino, Correggio, and Titian. Her study in her Mantuan palace was a veritable museum. The walls above the storage and display cabinets were painted with frescos by Mantegna, and the carved wood ceiling was covered with mottoes and visual references to Isabella's literary interests.

Isabella was past 60 when Titian portrayed her in 1534–1536, but she asked to appear as she had in her

21–30 Titian **"VENUS" OF URBINO**
c. 1538. Oil on canvas, 3′11″ × 5′5″ (1.19 × 1.65 m). Galleria degli Uffizi, Florence.

Credit: © Studio Fotografico Quattrone, Florence

21–31 Veronese **FEAST IN THE HOUSE OF LEVI**
From the refectory of the monastery of SS. Giovanni e Paolo, Venice. 1573. Oil on canvas, 18′3″ × 42′ (5.56 × 12.8 m).
Galleria dell'Accademia, Venice.

Credit: © Cameraphoto Arte, Venice

twenties. Titian was able to satisfy her wish by referring to an early portrait by another artist, but he also conveyed the mature Isabella's strength, self-confidence, and energy.

No photograph can convey the vibrancy of Titian's paint surfaces, which he built up in layers of pure colors, chiefly red, white, yellow, and black, on his canvases. A recent scientific study of Titian's paintings revealed that he ground his pigments much finer than had earlier, wood-panel painters. The complicated process by which he produced many of his works began with a charcoal drawing on the prime coat of lead white that was used to seal the pores and smooth the surface of the rather coarse Venetian canvas. The artist then built up the forms with fine glazes of different colors, sometimes in as many as 15 layers. Titian had the advantage of working in Venice, the first place to have professional retail "color sellers." These merchants produced a wide range of specially prepared pigments, even mixing their oil paints with ground glass to increase their glowing transparency. Not until the second half of the sixteenth century did color sellers open their shops in other cities.

Paintings of nude, reclining women became especially popular in court circles, where men could appreciate the "Venuses" under the cloak of respectable Classical mythology. Seemingly typical of such paintings is the **"VENUS"** Titian delivered to Guidobaldo della Rovere, duke of Urbino, in spring 1538 (**FIG. 21–30**). Here, we seem to see a beautiful Venetian courtesan with deliberately provocative gestures, stretching languidly on her couch in a spacious palace, her glowing flesh and golden hair set off by white sheets and pillows. But for its original audience, art

historian Rona Goffen has argued, the painting was more about marriage than mythology or seductiveness. The multiple matrimonial references in this work include the pair of *cassoni* (SEE FIG. 20–30) where servants are removing or storing the woman's clothing in the background, the bridal symbolism of the myrtle and roses she holds in her hand, and even the spaniel snoozing at her feet—a traditional symbol of fidelity and domesticity, especially when sleeping so peacefully. Titian's picture might be associated with Duke Guidobaldo's marriage in 1534 to the 10-year-old Giulia Verano. Four years later, when this painting arrived, she would have been considered an adult rather than a child bride. It seems to represent neither a Roman goddess nor a Venetian courtesan, but a bride welcoming her husband into their lavish bedroom.

VERONESE AND TINTORETTO Later sixteenth-century Venetian oil painters expanded upon the color, light, and expressively loose brushwork initiated by Giorgione and Titian. Paolo Caliari (1528–1588) took his nickname, "Veronese," from his hometown, Verona, but he worked mainly in Venice. His paintings are nearly synonymous today with the popular image of Venice as a splendid city of pleasure and pageantry sustained by a nominally republican government and great mercantile wealth. Veronese's elaborate architectural settings and costumes, still lifes, anecdotal vignettes, and other everyday details—often unconnected with the main subject—proved immensely appealing to Venetian patrons.

One of Veronese's most famous works is a *Last Supper* that he renamed **FEAST IN THE HOUSE OF LEVI** (**FIG. 21–31**),

21–32 Tintoretto **THE LAST SUPPER**
Church of San Giorgio Maggiore, Venice. 1592–1594. Oil on canvas, 12′ × 18′8″ (3.7 × 5.7 m).

Tintoretto, who had a large workshop, often developed a composition by creating a small-scale model like a miniature stage set, which he populated with wax figures. He then adjusted the positions of the figures and the lighting until he was satisfied with the entire scene. Using a grid of horizontal and vertical threads placed in front of this model, he could easily sketch the composition onto squared paper for his assistants to copy onto a large canvas. His assistants also primed the canvas, blocking in the areas of dark and light, before the artist himself, free to concentrate on the most difficult passages, finished the painting. This efficient working method allowed Tintoretto to produce a large number of paintings in all sizes.

Credit: © Cameraphoto Arte, Venice

painted in 1573 for the Dominican monastery of SS. Giovanni e Paolo. At first glance, the subject of the painting seems to be primarily its architectural setting and only secondarily Christ seated at the table. Symmetrically disposed, balustraded stairways lead to an enormous loggia framed by colossal arches, beyond which sits an imaginary city of white marble. Within this grand setting, lifelike figures in lavish costumes strike theatrical poses, surrounded by the sort of anecdotal details loved by the Venetians—such as parrots, monkeys, a man picking his teeth, and foreign soldiers—but the painting's monastic patrons were shocked. They saw these as profane distractions, especially in a representation of the Last Supper.

As a result of the furor, Veronese was called before the Inquisition, a papal office that prosecuted heretics, to explain his painting. There he justified himself first by asserting that the picture actually depicted not the Last Supper, but rather the feast in the house of Simon, a small dinner held shortly before Jesus's final entry into

Jerusalem. He also noted that artists customarily invent details in their pictures and that he had received a commission to paint the piece in his own way. His argument fell on unsympathetic ears, and he was ordered to change the painting. Later he sidestepped the issue by changing its title to that of another banquet, one given by the tax collector Levi, whom Jesus had called to follow him (Luke 5:27–32). Perhaps with this change of subject, Veronese took a modest revenge on the Inquisitors: When Jesus himself was criticized for associating with such unsavory people at this meal, he replied, "I have not come to call the righteous to repentance but sinners" (Luke 5:32).

Jacopo Robusti (1518–1594), called Tintoretto ("Little Dyer," because his father was a dyer), carried Venetian painting in another direction. Tintoretto's goal, declared on a sign in his studio, was to combine Titian's coloring with the drawing of Michelangelo. His large painting of **THE LAST SUPPER** (FIG. 21–32) for the choir of Palladio's church of San Giorgio Maggiore (SEE FIG. 21–33) is quite different from Leonardo da Vinci's painting of the same subject almost a century earlier (SEE FIG. 21-4). Instead of Leonardo's frontal view of a closed and logical space with massive figures reacting in individual ways to Jesus's statement, Tintoretto views the scene from a corner, with the vanishing point on a high horizon line at far right. The table, coffered ceiling, and inlaid floor all seem to plunge dramatically into the distance. The figures, although still large bodies modeled by flowing draperies, turn and move in a continuous serpentine line that unites apostles, servants, and angels. Tintoretto used two internal light sources: one real, the other supernatural. Over the near end of the table, light streams from the oil lamp flaring exuberantly, with angels swirling out from the flame and smoke. A second light emanates from Jesus himself and is repeated in the glow of the apostles' haloes. The intensely spiritual, otherworldly mood is enhanced by deep colors flashed with dazzling highlights on elongated figures, consistent with Mannerist tendencies. Homey details like the still lifes on the tables and the cat in the foreground connect with viewers' own experiences. And the narrative emphasis has shifted from Leonardo's more worldly study of personal betrayal to Tintoretto's reference to the institution of the Eucharist. Jesus offers bread and wine to a disciple in the same way that a priest would administer the sacrament at the altar next to the painting.

Although the brilliance and immediacy of Tintoretto's work are much admired today—twentieth-century gestural painters particularly appreciated his slashing brushwork—the speed with which he drew and painted was cited as evidence of carelessness in his own time. Rapid production may have been a byproduct of his working methods. Tintoretto

had a large workshop of assistants, and he usually provided only the original conception, the early drawings, and the final brilliant touches on the finished paintings. His workshop also included members of his family: Four of his eight children became artists. His oldest daughter, Marietta Robusti, worked with him as a portrait painter, and two or three of his sons also joined the shop. So skillfully did Marietta capture her father's style and technique that today art historians cannot separate their work.

The Architecture of Palladio

Just as Veronese and Tintoretto built on the rich Venetian tradition of oil painting initiated by Giorgione and Titian, Andrea Palladio dominated architecture during the second half of the century by expanding upon the principles of Alberti and the ancient Romans. His buildings—whether villas, palaces, or churches—were characterized by harmonious symmetry and controlled ornamentation. Born

21-33 Palladio **CHURCH OF SAN GIORGIO MAGGIORE, VENICE**

Plan 1565; construction 1565–1580; façade 1597–1610; campanile 1791. Finished by Vincenzo Scamozzi following Palladio's design.

Credit: © Cameraphoto Arte, Venice

21-34 NAVE, CHURCH OF SAN GIORGIO MAGGIORE, VENICE
Begun 1566. Tintoretto's *Last Supper* (not visible) hangs to the left of the altar.

Credit: © Cameraphoto Arte, Venice

Andrea di Pietro della Gondola (1508–1580), probably in Padua, Palladio began his career as a stonecutter. After moving to Vicenza, he was hired by Giangiorgio Trissino, a nobleman, humanist scholar, and amateur architect who gave him the nickname "Palladio" for the Greek goddess of wisdom, Pallas Athena, and the fourth-century Roman writer Palladius. Palladio learned Latin at Trissino's small academy and accompanied his benefactor on three trips to Rome, where he made drawings of Roman monuments.

Over the years, Palladio became involved in several publishing ventures, including a guide to Roman antiquities and an illustrated edition of Vitruvius. He also published his own books on architecture—including ideal plans for country estates using proportions derived from ancient Roman buildings—that would be valued for centuries as resources for architectural design. Despite their theoretical bent, his writings were often more practical than earlier treatises. Perhaps his early experience as a stonemason enabled him to discuss technical problems

with the same clarity as theories of ideal proportion and uses of the Classical orders. By the eighteenth century, Palladio's *Four Books of Architecture* were in the libraries of most educated people. Thomas Jefferson had one of the first copies in America.

SAN GIORGIO MAGGIORE By 1559, when he settled in Venice, Palladio was one of the foremost architects in Italy. In 1565, he undertook a major architectural commission: the monastery **CHURCH OF SAN GIORGIO MAGGIORE** (FIG. 21-33). His variation on the traditional Renaissance façade for a basilica—a wide lower level fronting the nave and side aisles, surmounted by a narrower front for the nave clerestory—creates the illusion of two temple fronts of different heights and widths, one set inside the other. At the center, colossal columns on high pedestals support an entablature and pediment; these columns correspond to the width of the nave within. Behind the taller temple front, a second front consists of pilasters supporting another entablature and pediment; this wider front spans the entire width of the church, aisles as well as nave. Although the façade was not built until after the architect's death, his original design was followed.

The interior of San Giorgio (**FIG. 21–34**) is a fine example of Palladio's harmoniously balanced geometry, expressed here in strong verticals and powerfully opened arches. The tall engaged columns and shorter pilasters of the nave arcade piers echo the two levels of orders on the façade, helping to unify the building's exterior and interior.

THE VILLA ROTONDA Palladio's versatility was already apparent in numerous villas built early in his career. In the 1560s, he started his most famous and influential villa just outside Vicenza (**FIGS. 21–35, 21–36**). Although villas were working farms, Palladio designed this one in part as a retreat—literally a party house. To maximize vistas of the countryside, he placed a porch elevated at the top of a wide staircase on each face of the building. The main living quarters are on this second level, and the lower level is reserved for the kitchen, storage, and other utility rooms. Upon its completion in 1569, the building was dubbed the **VILLA ROTONDA** because it had been inspired by another round building, the Roman Pantheon. The plan shows the geometric clarity of Palladio's

conception: a circle inscribed in a small square inside a larger square, with symmetrical rectangular compartments and identical rectangular projections from each of its faces. The use of a central dome on a domestic building was a daring innovation that effectively secularized the dome and initiated what was to become a long tradition of domed country houses, particularly in England and the United States.

21-35 Palladio **PLAN OF VILLA ROTONDA, VICENZA**
Italy. Begun 1560s.

21-36 Palladio **EXTERIOR VIEW OF VILLA ROTONDA, VICENZA**

After its purchase in 1591 by the Capra family, the Villa Rotonda became known as the Villa Capra.

Mannerism

How do art historians define Mannerism, the new style that appears in Florentine painting and sculpture during the 1520s?

A new style developed in Florence and Rome in the 1520s that some art historians have associated with the death of Raphael and labeled "Mannerism," a word deriving from the Italian *maniera* (meaning "style"). Mannerism developed into an anti-Classical movement in which artificiality, grace, and elegance took priority over the ordered balance and lifelike references that were hallmarks of High Renaissance art. Patrons favored esoteric subjects, displays of extraordinary technical virtuosity, and the pursuit of beauty for its own sake. Painters and sculptors quoted from ancient and modern works of art in the same self-conscious manner that contemporary poets and authors were quoting from ancient and modern literary classics.

Architects working in the Mannerist style designed buildings that defied uniformity and balance and used Classical orders in unconventional, even playful, ways.

Painters working in the Mannerist style fearlessly manipulated and distorted accepted formal conventions, creating contrived compositions and irrational spatial environments. Figures take on elongated proportions, enigmatic gestures, dreamy expressions, and complicated, artificial poses. The pictures are full of quoted references to the works of illustrious predecessors.

Pontormo, Parmigianino, and Bronzino

The frescos and altarpiece painted between 1525 and 1528 by Jacopo Carucci da Pontormo (1494–1557) for the 100-year-old **CAPPONI CHAPEL** in the church of Santa Felicità in Florence (**FIG. 21–37**) bear the hallmarks of early Mannerist painting. Open on two sides, Brunelleschi's chapel forms an interior loggia in which frescos on the right-hand wall depict the Annunciation, and tondi (circular paintings) on the pendentives under the cupola represent the four evangelists. In the *Annunciation* the Virgin accepts the angel's message but also seems moved by the adjacent vision of her future sorrow, as she turns to see her son's body lowered from the cross in the altarpiece on the adjoining wall.

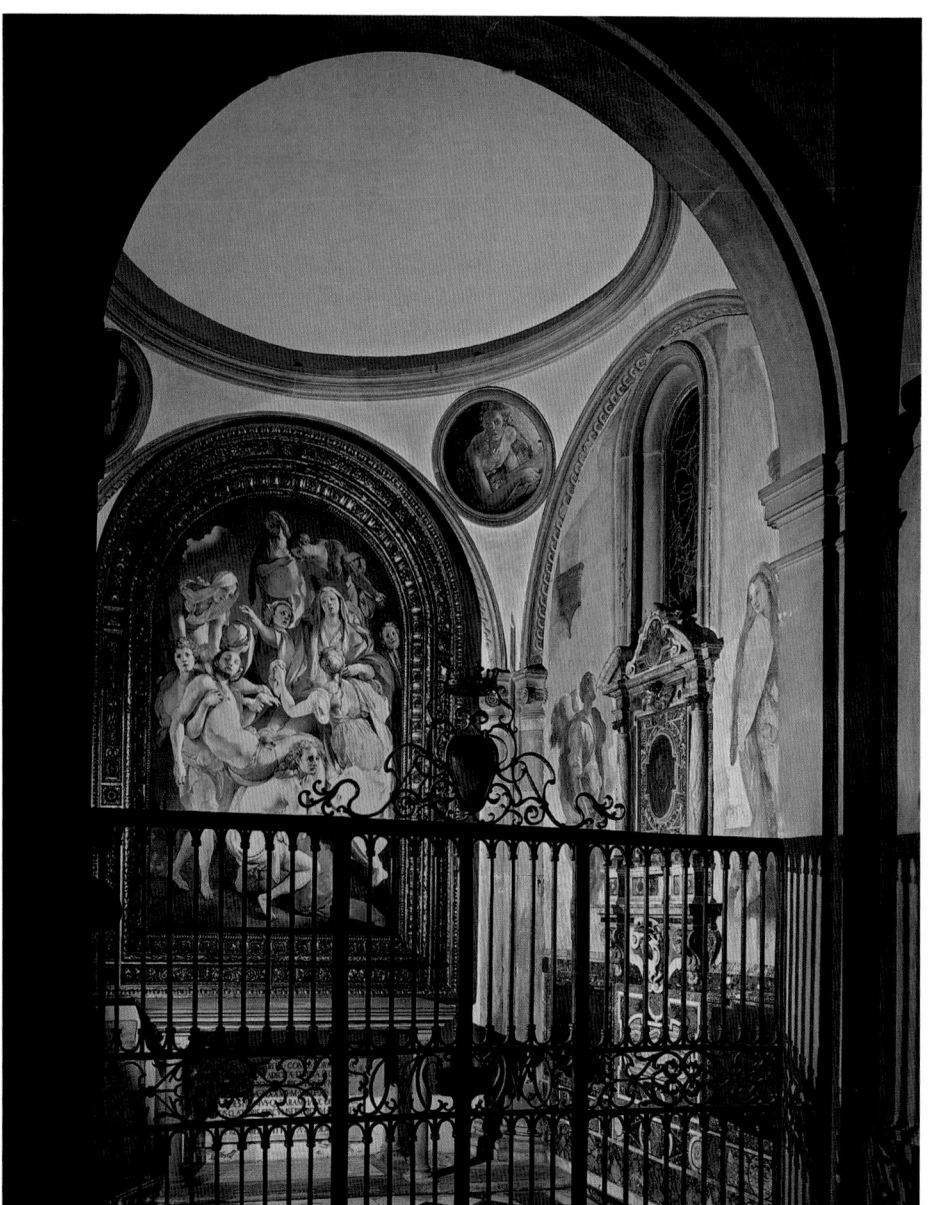

21–37 CAPPONI CHAPEL, CHURCH OF SANTA FELICITÀ, FLORENCE

Chapel by Filippo Brunelleschi for the Barbadori family, 1419–1423; acquired by the Capponi family, who ordered paintings by Pontormo, 1525–1528.

Credit: Index Ricerca Iconografica

Pontormo's ambiguous composition in the **DEPOSI-TION** (**FIG. 21–38**) enhances the visionary quality of the altarpiece. The shadowy ground and cloudy sky give no sense of a specific location and little sense of grounding for the figures. Some press forward into the viewer's space, while others seem to levitate or stand precariously on tip-toe. Pontormo chose a moment just after Jesus's removal from the cross, when the youths who have lowered him pause to regain their hold on the corpse, which recalls Michelangelo's Vatican *Pietà* (SEE FIG. 21–14). Odd poses and drastic shifts in scale charge the scene emotionally, but per-haps most striking is the use of strange colors in unusual combinations—baby blue and pink with accents of olive green, yellow, and scarlet. The overall tone of the picture

21–38 Pontormo
DEPOSITION
Altarpiece in the Capponi Chapel, church of Santa Felicità, Florence. 1525–1528. Oil and tempera on wood panel, 10′3″ × 6′4″ (3.1 × 1.9 m).

The dreamy-eyed male figure in the background shadows at upper right is a self-portrait by the artist.

Credit: © Studio Fotografico Quattrone, Florence

21–39 Parmigianino **MADONNA OF THE LONG NECK**
1534–1540. Oil on wood panel, 7'1" × 4'4" (2.16 × 1.32 m). Galleria degli Uffizi, Florence.

Art historian Elizabeth Cropper has noted the visual relationship between the shape of the swelling, tapering-necked, ovoid vessel held by the figure at far left and the form of the figure of the Virgin herself, and has proposed that this visual analogy references a sixteenth-century literary conceit that related ideal beauty in women to the slender necks and swelling shapes of antique vessels.

Credit: © Studio Fotografico Quattrone, Florence

is set by the unstable youth crouching in the foreground, whose skintight bright pink shirt is shaded in iridescent, pale gray-blue, and whose anxious expression projects out of the painting, directly at the viewer.

When Parmigianino (Francesco Mazzola, 1503–1540) left his native Parma in 1524 for Rome, the strongest influence on his work was Correggio (SEE FIG. 21–24). In Rome, however, Parmigianino met Giulio Romano; he also studied the work of Raphael and Michelangelo. What he assimilated developed into a distinctive Mannerist style, calm but strangely unsettling. After the Sack of Rome in 1527, he moved to Bologna and then back to Parma.

Left unfinished at the time of his early death is a disconcerting painting known as the **MADONNA OF THE LONG NECK** (FIG. 21–39). The unnaturally proportioned figure of Mary, whose massive legs and lower torso contrast with her narrow shoulders and long neck and fingers, is presumably seated on a throne, but there is no seat in sight. The languid expanse of the sleeping child recalls the pose of the ashen Christ in a *pietà*; indeed, there is more than a passing resemblance here to Michelangelo's famous sculpture in the Vatican, even to the inclusion of a diagonal band across the Virgin's chest (SEE FIG. 21–14). The plunge into a deep background to the right reveals a startlingly small St. Jerome, who unrolls a scroll in front of huge, white columns from what was to be a temple in the unfinished background, whereas at the left a crowded mass of blushing boys blocks any view into the background. Like Pontormo, Parmigianino presents a well-known image in a challenging manner calculated to intrigue viewers.

About 1522, Agnolo di Cosimo di Mariano Tori (1503–1572), whose nickname of "Bronzino" means "copper-colored" (just as we might call someone "Red"), became Pontormo's pupil and assistant, probably helping with the tondi on the pendentives of the Capponi Chapel (SEE FIG. 21–37). In 1530, he established his own workshop, though he continued to work with Pontormo on occasional large

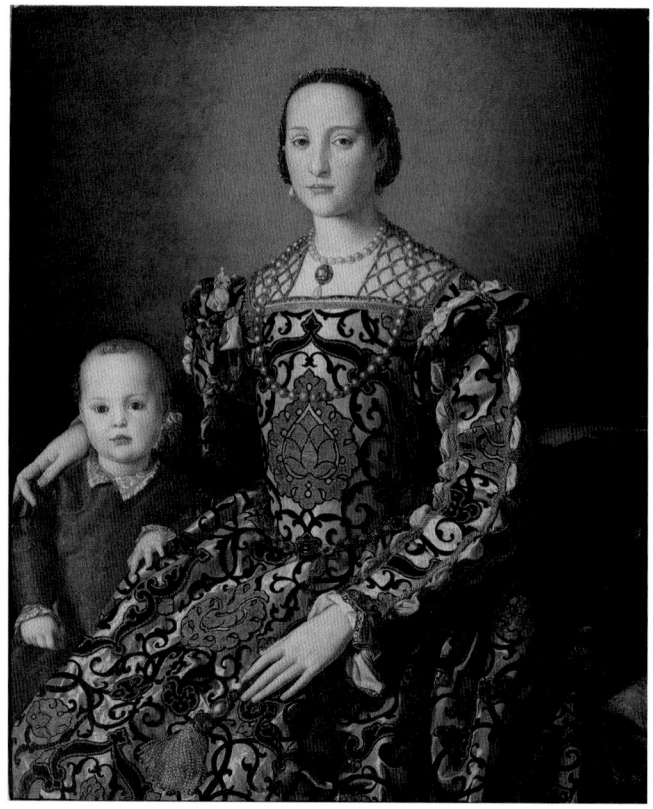

21–40 Bronzino **PORTRAIT OF ELEONORA OF TOLEDO AND HER SON GIOVANNI DE' MEDICI**
1545. Oil on wood panel, 45¼ × 37¾" (115 × 96 cm). Galleria degli Uffizi, Florence.

Credit: © Studio Fotografico Quattrone, Florence

21–41 Bronzino **ALLEGORY WITH VENUS AND CUPID**

Mid-1540s. Oil on panel, 57½ × 46″ (1.46 × 1.16 m). National Gallery, London.

Credit: © 2016. Copyright The National Gallery, London/Scala, Florence

Church. Already archbishop of Pisa as a teenager, he became a cardinal in 1560 at age 17, only two years before both he and his mother died of malaria.

Bronzino's **ALLEGORY WITH VENUS AND CUPID** is one of the strangest paintings of the sixteenth century (**FIG. 21–41**). It contains all the formal, iconographical, and psychological characteristics of Mannerist art and could almost stand alone as a summary of the movement. Seven figures, three masks, and a dove interweave in an intricate, formal composition pressed claustrophobically into the foreground plane. Taken as individual images, the figures display the exaggerated poses, graceful forms, polished surfaces, and delicate colors that characterize Mannerist art. But a closer look into this composition uncovers disturbing erotic attachments and bizarre irregularities. The painting's complex allegory and relentless ambiguity probably delighted mid-sixteenth-century courtiers who enjoyed equally sophisti-

projects. By 1540, he was court painter to the Medici. Although he produced altarpieces, fresco decorations, and tapestry designs over his long career, he is best known today for his elegant portraits, the focus of his work for Duke Cosimo I de' Medici (ruled 1537–1574). Bronzino's virtuosity in rendering costumes and settings, combined with the self-contained, masklike quality given to the faces, results in cold and formal portraits that admirably convey the haughtiness of his subjects and the absolutism of Cosimo's rule.

Typical is an elegantly restrained state portrait of 1545 portraying Cosimo's wife, **ELEONORA OF TOLEDO** (1522–1562), and their second son, Giovanni de' Medici (**FIG. 21–40**). Bronzino characteristically portrays this mother and son as aloof and self-assured, their class connection much more prominent than any sense of individual likeness or personality. This double portrait is an iconic embodiment of dynastic power and an assurance of Medici succession. Giovanni, however, did not succeed his father as duke—that path was taken by his elder brother Francesco. Instead he pursued a fast-tracked career in the

cated wordplay and esoteric Classical references, but for us it defies easy explanation. Nothing is quite what it seems.

Venus and her son Cupid engage in an unsettlingly lascivious dalliance, encouraged by a *putto* striding in from the right—representing Folly, Jest, or Playfulness—who is about to throw pink roses at them while stepping on a thorny branch that draws blood from his foot. Cupid gently kisses his mother and pinches her erect nipple while she snatches an arrow from his quiver, leading some scholars to suggest that the painting's title should be *Venus Disarming Cupid*. Venus holds the golden apple of discord given to her by Paris; her dove conforms to the shape of Cupid's foot without actually touching it, while a pair of masks lying at her feet reiterates the theme of duplicity. An old man, Time or Chronos, assisted by an outraged Truth or Night, pulls back a curtain to expose the couple. Lurking just behind Venus, a monstrous serpent—which has the upper body and head of a beautiful young girl and the legs and claws of a lion—crosses her hands to hold a honeycomb and the stinger at the end of her tail. This strange hybrid has been interpreted both as Fraud and Pleasure.

In the shadows to the left, a pale and screaming man tearing at his hair has recently been identified as a victim of syphilis, which raged as an epidemic during this period. The painting could, therefore, be a warning of the dangers of this disease, believed in the sixteenth century to be spread principally by coitus, kissing, and breast feeding, all of which are alluded to in the intertwined Cupid and Venus. But the complexity of the painting makes room for multiple meanings, and deciphering them would be typical of the sorts of games enjoyed by sixteenth-century intellectuals. Perhaps the allegory tells of the impossibility of constant love and the folly of lovers, which becomes apparent across time. Or perhaps it is a warning of the dangers of illicit sexual liaisons, including the pain, hair loss, and disfiguration of venereal disease. It could be both, and even more. Duke Cosimo commissioned the painting and presented it as a diplomatic gift to the French king Francis I, who would doubtless have relished its overt eroticism and flawless execution.

Anguissola and Fontana

Northern Italy, more than any other part of the peninsula, produced a number of gifted women artists. In the latter half of the sixteenth century, Bologna, for example, boasted some two dozen women painters and sculptors, as well as a number of learned women who lectured at the university. Sofonisba Anguissola (c. 1532–1625), born into a noble family in Cremona (between Bologna and Milan), was unusual in that she was not the daughter of an artist. Her father gave all his children a humanistic education and encouraged them to pursue careers in literature, music, and especially painting. He consulted Michelangelo about his daughter's artistic talents in 1557, asking for a drawing that she might copy and return to be critiqued. Michelangelo evidently obliged, because her father wrote an enthusiastic letter of thanks.

Anguissola was a gifted portrait painter who also created miniatures, an important aspect of portraiture in the sixteenth century, when people had few means of recording the features of a lover, friend, or family member. Anguissola painted a miniature **SELF-PORTRAIT** holding a medallion, the border of which spells out her name and hometown, Cremona (**FIG. 21–42**). The interlaced letters at the center of the medallion pose a riddle; they seem to form a monogram with the first letters of her sisters' names: Minerva, Europa, Elena. Such names are further evidence of the Anguissola family's enthusiasm for the Classics.

In 1560, Anguissola accepted the invitation of the queen of Spain to become a lady-in-waiting and court painter, a post she held for 20 years. Unfortunately, most of her Spanish works were lost in a seventeenth-century palace fire, but a 1582 Spanish inventory described her as the best portrait painter of the age—extraordinary praise

in a court that patronized Titian. After her years at court, she retired to Spanish-controlled Sicily, where she died in her nineties. Anthony van Dyck met her in Palermo in 1624, where he sketched her and claimed that she was then 96 years old. He wrote that she advised him on positioning the light for her portrait, asking that it not be placed too high because the strong shadows would bring out her wrinkles.

Bolognese artist Lavinia Fontana (1552–1614) learned to paint from her father. By the 1570s her success was so well rewarded that her husband, the painter Gian Paolo Zappi, gave up his own painting career to care for their large family and help his wife with the technical aspects of her work, such as framing. In 1603, Fontana moved to Rome as an official painter to the papal court. She also soon came to the attention of the Habsburgs, who became major patrons.

While still in her twenties, Fontana painted a **NOLI ME TANGERE** (**FIG. 21–43**), where Christ reveals himself for the first time to Mary Magdalen following his Resurrection, warning her not to touch him (John 20:17). Christ's broad-brimmed hat and spade refer to the passage in John's Gospel claiming that Mary Magdalen at first thought Christ

21–42 Sofonisba Anguissola **SELF-PORTRAIT**
c. 1556. Varnished watercolor on parchment, 3¼ × 2½" (8.3 × 6.4 cm). Museum of Fine Arts, Boston. Emma F. Munroe Fund 60.155.

Credit: Photograph © 2017 Museum of Fine Arts, Boston

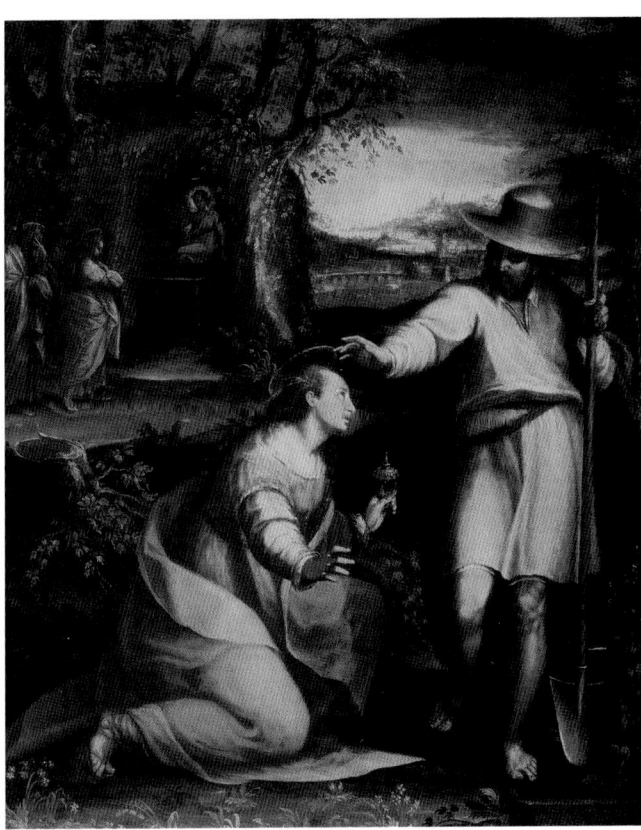

21–43 Lavinia Fontana **NOLI ME TANGERE**

1581. Oil on canvas, 47⅜ × 36⅝″ (120.3 × 93 cm). Galleria degli Uffizi, Florence.

Credit: Canali Photobank, Milan, Italy

was the gardener. In the middle distance Fontana portrays a second version of the Resurrection, where women followers of Christ discover an angel in his empty tomb. This secondary scene's dizzying diagonal plunge into depth is a typical feature of late Mannerist painting in Italy, as are the affected pose of the foreground Christ and the elongated proportions of Mary Magdalen.

Sculpture

Mannerist sculpture—often small in size and made from precious metals—stylizes body forms and emphasizes technical skill in ways that are reminiscent of Mannerist painting.

CELLINI   The Florentine goldsmith and sculptor Benvenuto Cellini (1500–1571), who wrote a dramatic—and scandalous—autobiography and a practical handbook for artists, worked in the French court at Fontainebleau. There he made the famous **SALTCELLAR OF KING FRANCIS I** (**FIG. 21-44**), a table accessory transformed into an elegant sculptural ornament by fanciful imagery and superb execution. In gold and enamel, the Roman sea god Neptune, representing the source of salt, sits next to a tiny, boat-shaped container for the seasoning, while a personification of Earth guards the plant-derived pepper contained in the triumphal arch to her right. Representations of the seasons and the times of day on the base refer to both daily meal schedules and festive seasonal celebrations. The two main figures lean away from each other at impossible angles yet are connected and visually balanced by glance, gestures, and coordinated poses—mirroring each other with one bent and one straight leg. Their supple, elongated bodies and small heads reflect the Mannerist conventions of artists like Parmigianino (SEE FIG. 21-39). Cellini wrote, "I represented the Sea and the Land, both seated, with their legs intertwined just as some branches of the sea run into the land and the land juts into the sea…" (Cellini, *Autobiography*, translated by G. Bull, p. 291).

GIAMBOLOGNA   In the second half of the sixteenth century, the most influential sculptor in Italy was probably Jean Boulogne, better known by his Italian names, Giovanni Bologna or Giambologna (1529–1608). Born in Flanders, he settled during the 1550s in Florence, where he worked at the court of Duke Cosimo I de' Medici.

21–44 Benvenuto Cellini **SALTCELLAR OF KING FRANCIS I OF FRANCE**

1540–1543. Gold and enamel, 10½ × 13⅛″ (26.67 × 33.34 cm). Kunsthistorisches Museum, Vienna.

Credit: © KHM-Museumsverband

He not only influenced and trained a later generation of Italian sculptors, he also spread the Mannerist style to the north through artists who came to study his work.

Although Giambologna's prodigious artistic output included elaborate fountains and many works in bronze—both imposing public monuments and exquisitely rendered statuettes—his most famous sculpture is a monumental marble carving now known as **THE CAPTURE OF A SABINE WOMAN** (FIG. 21–45), a title given to it by a member of the Florentine Academy of Design after it was finished. Giambologna himself conceived of this composition of three nude figures—rising in an energetic, tightly wound column—not in relation to any particular subject or story, but as a formal exercise in figural representation and technical virtuosity. In spite of the deep undercutting and dramatically projecting gestures, the entire sculpture was carved from a single block of marble. Because of the spiraling composition, viewers must walk around the sculpture to explore it; it cannot be fully grasped from any single viewpoint. Grand Duke Francesco I de' Medici installed Giambologna's masterpiece in a place of honor at the front of the Loggia dei Lanzi, where it remains today (SEE FIG. 18–2).

21–45 Giambologna **THE CAPTURE OF A SABINE WOMAN**
1581–1582. Marble, height 13'6" (4.1 m). Loggia dei Lanzi, Florence.

Art and the Counter-Reformation

What is the impact of the Counter Reformation on Roman painting and architecture?

Pope Clement VII, whose miscalculations had spurred Emperor Charles V to attack and destroy Rome in 1527, also misjudged the threat to the Church and to papal authority posed by the Protestant Reformation. His failure to address the issues raised by the reformers enabled the movement to spread. His successor, Paul III (pontificate 1534–1549), the rich and worldly Roman noble Alessandro Farnese, was the first pope to pursue Church reform in response to the rise of Protestantism. In 1536, he appointed a commission to investigate charges of Church corruption and later convened the Council of Trent (1545–1563) to define Catholic dogma, initiate disciplinary reforms, and regulate the training of clerics.

Pope Paul III also addressed Protestantism through repression and censorship. In 1542, he instituted the Inquisition, a papal office that sought out heretics for interrogation, trial, and sentencing. The enforcement of religious unity extended to the arts. Guidelines issued by the Council of Trent limited what could be represented in Christian art and led to the destruction of some works. Traditional images of Christ and the saints were approved, but art was examined closely for traces of heresy and profanity. At the same time, art became a powerful weapon of propaganda, especially in the hands of members of the Society of Jesus, a new religious order founded by the Spanish nobleman Ignatius of Loyola (1491–1556) and confirmed by Paul III in 1540. Dedicated to piety, education, and missionary work, the Jesuits, as they are known, spread worldwide and became important leaders of the Counter-Reformation movement and the revival of the Catholic Church.

Rome and the Vatican

To restore the heart of the city of Rome, Paul III began rebuilding the Capitoline Hill as well as continuing work on St. Peter's. His commissions include some of the finest art and architecture of the late Italian Renaissance. His first major commission brought Michelangelo, after a quarter of a century, back to the Sistine Chapel.

MICHELANGELO'S LATE WORK In his early sixties, Michelangelo complained bitterly of feeling old, but he nonetheless undertook the important and demanding task of painting the **LAST JUDGMENT** on the 48-foot-high end wall above the Sistine Chapel altar between 1536 and 1541 (FIG. 21–46).

Abandoning the clearly organized medieval conception of the Last Judgment, in which the saved are neatly separated from the damned, Michelangelo painted a writhing swarm of resurrected humanity. At left, the dead are dragged from their graves and pushed up into a vortex of figures around Christ, who wields his arm like a sword of justice. The shrinking Virgin under Christ's raised right arm represents a change from Gothic tradition, where she had sat enthroned beside, and equal in size to, her son. To the right of Christ's feet is St. Bartholomew, who was

21–46 Michelangelo **LAST JUDGMENT, SISTINE CHAPEL**
1536–1541. Fresco, 48 × 44′ (14.6 × 13.4 m).

Dark, rectangular patches intentionally left by recent restorers (visible, for example, in the upper left and right corners) contrast with the vibrant colors of the chapel's frescos. These dark areas show just how dirty the walls had become over the centuries before their cleaning.

Credit: Photo: Vatican Museums/IKONA

martyred by being skinned alive. He holds his flayed skin, and Michelangelo seems to have painted his own distorted features on the skin's face. Despite the efforts of several saints to save them, the damned are plunged toward hell on the right, leaving the elect and still-unjudged in a dazed state. On the lowest level of the mural, right above the altar, is the gaping, fiery entrance to hell, toward which Charon, the ferryman of the dead to the underworld, propels his craft. The painting was long interpreted as a grim and constant reminder to celebrants of the Mass—the pope and his cardinals—that ultimately they too would face stern judgment at the end of time. Conservative clergy criticized it for its nudity, and after Michelangelo's death they ordered bits of drapery to be added by artist Daniele da Volterra to conceal the offending areas, earning Daniele the unfortunate nickname "Il Braghettone" ("breeches painter").

Another of Paul III's ambitions was to complete the new St. Peter's, a project that had been underway for 40 years (see "St. Peter's Basilica" opposite). Michelangelo was well aware of the work done by his predecessors—from Bramante to Raphael to Antonio da Sangallo the Younger. When he began his own work on the project, the 71-year-old sculptor, confident of his architectural expertise, demanded the right to deal directly with the pope, rather than through a committee of construction deputies. Michelangelo further shocked the deputies—but not the pope—by undoing parts of Sangallo's design, then simplifying and strengthening Bramante's central plan, long associated with shrines of Christian martyrs.

Although seventeenth-century additions and renovations dramatically changed the original plan of the church and the appearance of its interior, Michelangelo's **ST. PETER'S** (**FIG. 21-47**) still can be seen in the contrasting forms of the flat and angled exterior walls and the three surviving hemicycles (semicircular structures). Colossal pilasters, blind windows (frames without openings), and niches surround the sanctuary of the church. The current dome, erected by Giacomo della Porta in 1588–1590, retains Michelangelo's basic design: segmented with regularly spaced ribs, seated on a high drum with pedimented windows between paired columns, and topped with a tall lantern.

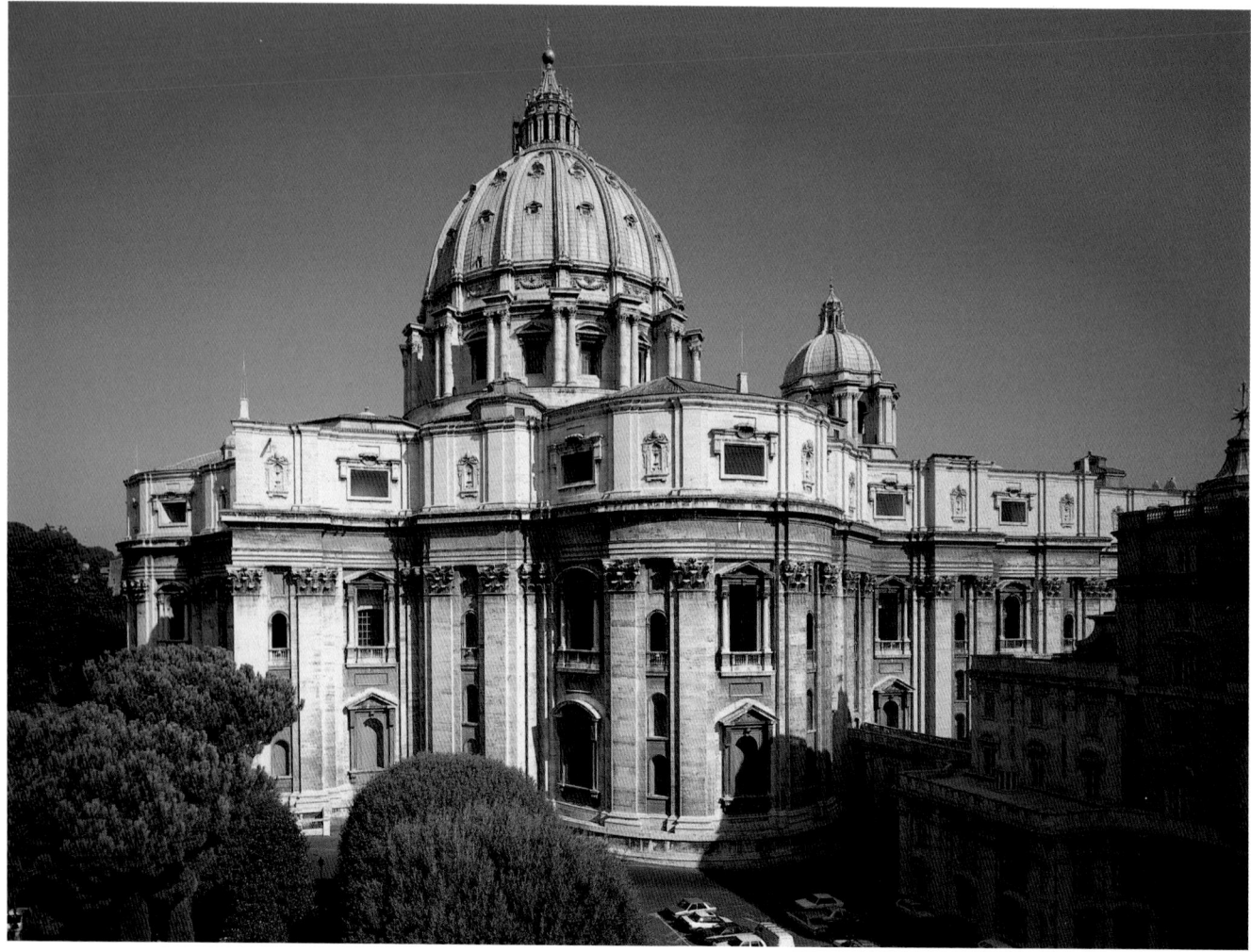

21-47 Michelangelo **ST. PETER'S BASILICA, VATICAN**
c. 1546–1564; dome completed 1590 by Giacomo della Porta; lantern 1590–1593. View from the west.

Credit: Canali Photobank, Milan, Italy. © James Morris, Ceredigion

Art and its Contexts

ST. PETER'S BASILICA

The history of St. Peter's in Rome is a case study of the effects of individual and institutional demands on the design, construction, and remodeling of a major religious building. The original church—now called Old St. Peter's—was built in the fourth century by Constantine, the first Christian Roman emperor, to mark the grave of the apostle Peter, the first bishop of Rome and therefore considered the first pope. Because the site was so holy, Constantine's architect had to build a structure large enough to hold the crowds of pilgrims who came to visit St. Peter's tomb. To provide a platform for the church, a huge terrace was cut into the side of the Vatican Hill across the Tiber River from the city. Here Constantine's architect erected a basilica with a new feature, a transept, to allow large numbers of visitors to approach the shrine at the front of the apse. The rest of the church was, in effect, a covered cemetery, carpeted with the tombs of believers who wanted to be buried near the apostle's grave. When it was built, Constantine's basilica, as befitted an imperial commission, was one of the largest buildings in the Roman world (interior length 368 feet, width 190 feet). For more than a thousand years it was the most important pilgrimage site in Europe.

In 1506, Pope Julius II made the astonishing decision to demolish the Constantinian basilica, which had fallen into disrepair, and replace it with a new building. That anyone, even a pope, should have had the nerve to pull down such a venerated building is an indication of the extraordinary self-assurance of the Renaissance—and of Julius himself. To design and build the new church, the pope appointed Donato Bramante, who envisioned the new St. Peter's as a central-plan building, in the shape of a cross with four arms of equal length, crowned by an enormous dome. This design was intended to emulate the Early Christian tradition of constructing domed and round buildings over the tombs of martyrs, itself derived from the Roman practice of building centrally planned tombs. In Renaissance thinking, the central plan and dome symbolized the perfection of God.

The deaths of pope and architect in 1513 and 1514 put a temporary halt to the project. Successive plans by Raphael, Antonio da Sangallo, and others extended one arm of the cross to provide the church with an extended nave. However, when Michelangelo was appointed architect in 1546, he returned to the centralized plan and simplified Bramante's design to create a single, unified space covered with a hemispherical dome. The dome was finally completed some years after Michelangelo's death by Giacomo della Porta, who retained Michelangelo's basic design but gave the dome a taller profile (SEE FIG. 21–47).

During the Counter-Reformation, the Catholic Church emphasized congregational worship; as a result, more space was needed to house the congregation and allow for processions. To expand the church—and to make it more closely resemble Old St. Peter's—Pope Paul V in 1606 commissioned the architect Carlo Maderno to change Michelangelo's central plan back once again into a longitudinal plan. Maderno extended the nave to its final length of slightly more than 636 feet and added a new façade, thus completing St. Peter's as we see it today. Later in the seventeenth century, the sculptor and architect Gianlorenzo Bernini created an elaborate approach to the basilica by surrounding the space in front of it with a great colonnade, like a huge set of arms extended to embrace the faithful as they approach the principal church of Western Christendom.

Old St. Peter's
4th century

Bramante, plan for
New St. Peter's
1506

Michelangelo, plan
for New St. Peter's
1546–1564

Maderno, plan of
St. Peter's Basilica
1607–1615

The aging Michelangelo, often described by his contemporaries as difficult and even arrogant, alternated between periods of depression and frenzied activity. Yet he was devoted to his friends and helpful to young artists. He believed that his art was divinely inspired and became increasingly devoted to religious works—many left unfinished—that subverted Renaissance ideals of human perfectibility and denied the idealism of youth. In the process he pioneered new stylistic directions that would inspire succeeding generations of artists.

VIGNOLA A young artist who worked to meet the need for new Roman churches was Giacomo Barozzi (1507–1573), known as Vignola after his native town. He worked in Rome during the late 1530s, surveying ancient Roman monuments and providing illustrations for an edition of Vitruvius. From 1541 to 1543, he was in France with

apse

crossing

nave

chapels

21–48B Vignola and Giacomo della Porta
PLAN OF THE CHURCH OF IL GESÙ, ROME
c. 1568–1584.

Francesco Primaticcio at the château of Fontainebleau. After returning to Rome, he secured the patronage of the Farnese family and profited from the Counter-Reformation church-building initiatives.

Catholicism's new emphasis on individual, emotional participation brought a focus on sermons and music, requiring churches with wide naves and unobstructed views of the altar, instead of the complex interiors of medieval and earlier Renaissance churches. Ignatius of Loyola was determined to build **IL GESÙ**, the Jesuit headquarters church in Rome, according to these precepts, although he did not live to see it finished (**FIG. 21-18**). The cornerstone was laid in 1540, but construction did not begin until 1568, after a period of fund-raising. Cardinal Alessandro Farnese (Paul III's namesake and grandson) donated to the project in 1561 and selected Vignola as architect. After Vignola died in 1573, Giacomo della Porta finished the dome and façade to his own designs.

Il Gesù was admirably suited for congregational worship. Vignola designed a wide, barrel-vaulted nave with shallow, connected side chapels. There are no aisles and only truncated transepts contained within the line of the outer walls—enabling all worshipers to gather in the central space. A single, huge apse and dome over the crossing directed attention to the altar. The design also allows the building to fit compactly into a city block—a requirement that now often overrode the desire to orient a church along an east–west axis. The symmetrical façade, in Vignola's original design as well as della Porta's variation on it, emphasized the central portal with Classical pilasters, engaged columns and pediments, and volutes scrolling out laterally to hide the buttresses of the central vault and link the tall central section with the lower sides.

As finally built by Giacomo della Porta, the façade design had significant influence well into the next century. The early Renaissance grid of Classical pilasters and entablatures was abandoned for a two-story design that coordinates paired columns or pilasters, aligned vertically to tie together the two stories of the central block, which corresponds with the nave elevation. The main entrance, with its central portal aligned with a tall upper-story window, became the focus of the composition. Centrally aligned pediments break into the level above, leading the eye upward to the cartouches with coats of arms—here of both Cardinal Farnese, the patron, and the Jesuits (whose arms display the initials IHS, the monogram of Christ).

Think About It

1 Some art historians have claimed that Rome and Florence were oriented toward drawing, but Venice was oriented toward color. Evaluate this claim, discussing specific works from each tradition in your answer.

2 Analyze either the Palazzo del Te (**FIG. 21-22**) or the Villa Rotonda (**FIG. 21-36**). Explain how the design of the building differs from the design of grand churches during this same period, even though architects clearly used Classical motifs in both sacred and secular contexts.

3 Discuss Julius II's efforts to aggrandize the city of Rome and create a new golden age of papal art. Focus your answer on at least two specific works that he commissioned—one in painting and the other architectural.

4 Select either Pontormo's *Deposition* (**FIG. 21-38**) or Parmigianino's *Madonna of the Long Neck* (**FIG. 21-39**) and explain why it characterizes Mannerist style. How does your chosen work depart from the Classical norms of the High Renaissance? How would you characterize its relationship to Michelangelo's *Last Judgment* (**FIG. 21-46**)?

Crosscurrents

These two paintings, each commissioned by a powerful political figure, combine Classical and allegorical themes in unusual ways. Each addresses a select audience. Compare the nature of the message each painting presents and evaluate how the style of presentation relates to the traditions and objectives of Florentine art during the period in which it was painted.

FIG. 20-34

FIG. 21-41

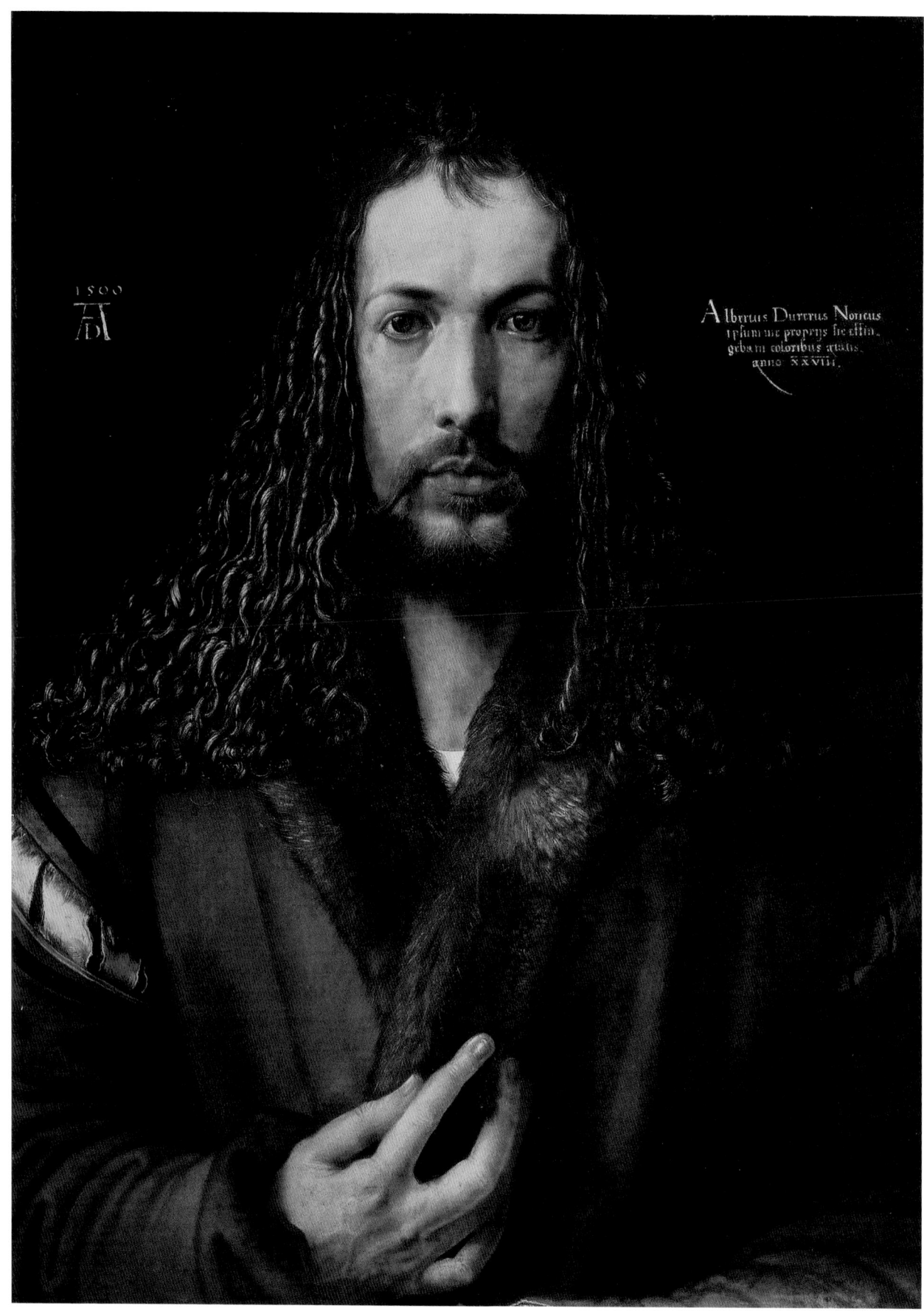

22–1 Albrecht Dürer **SELF-PORTRAIT**

1500. Signed "Albrecht Dürer of Nuremberg … age 28." Oil on wood panel, 26¼ × 19¼″ (66.3 × 49 cm). Alte Pinakothek, Munich.

Chapter 22

Sixteenth-Century Art in Northern Europe and the Iberian Peninsula

Learning Objectives

22.a Identify the visual hallmarks of sixteenth-century Northern European and Iberian Peninsular art and architecture for formal, technical, and expressive qualities.

22.b Interpret the meaning of works of sixteenth-century Northern European and Iberian Peninsular art based on their themes, subjects, and symbols.

22.c Relate sixteenth-century Northern European and Iberian Peninsular artists and art to their cultural, economic, and political contexts.

22.d Apply the vocabulary and concepts relevant to sixteenth-century Northern European and Iberian Peninsular art, artists, and art history.

22.e Interpret a work of sixteenth-century Northern European or Iberian Peninsular art using the art historical methods of observation, comparison, and inductive reasoning.

22.f Select visual and textual evidence in various media to support an argument or an interpretation of a work of sixteenth-century Northern European or Iberian Peninsular art.

This striking image (**FIG. 22-1**), dated 1500, seems to depict a blessing Christ, meant to rivet our attention and focus our devotion. But an inscription to the right of the face identifies this as a **SELF-PORTRAIT** by Albrecht Dürer, painted when he was 28 years old. We are already familiar with the practice of artists painting their own image. Self-portraits appear with some frequency during the Middle Ages (SEE FIGS. 16–35, 17–23); they truly blossom during the Renaissance (SEE FIGS. 19–12, 21–42). But this image still seems peculiar, marked by an artistic hubris that may embarrass us. The picture becomes less puzzling, however, seen in context.

Dürer strikes an odd pose for a self-portrait—frontal and hieratic, intentionally recalling iconic images of Christ as *Salvator Mundi* (Savior of the World) that were very popular in northern Europe. Dürer even alters the natural color of his own hair to align the image more closely with contemporary notions of Christ's physical appearance. But there is no reason to see this as blasphemous. Since a principal component of Christian devotion in Dürer's time was the attempt to imitate Christ in the believer's own life, Dürer could be visualizing a popular spiritual practice. He could also be depicting literally the biblical statement that humans are created in the image

of God. But he is also claiming that artists are learned and creative geniuses—perhaps Godlike—not laboring craftspeople. He wrote, "The more we know, the more we resemble the likeness of Christ who truly knows all things" (Snyder, p. 314).

Dürer had traveled to Italy in 1494–1495, where he encountered a new conception of artists as noble intellectuals: participants in humanistic discourse and purveyors of ideas as well as pictures. In 1498, back in Nuremberg, he published a woodcut series on the Apocalypse (SEE FIG. 22-7) that brought him a kind of international notice that was new to the German art world. He certainly had reason to feel pride. This stable, triangular composition—so consistent with High Renaissance norms of harmony and balance—could reflect Dürer's Italian adventure. But at its core, this picture fits into a long-standing Northern European interest in the meticulous description of surface texture—the soft sheen of human flesh, the reflective wetness of eyes, the matte softness of cloth, and the tactile quality of hair, emphasized here by the way Dürer's hand fingers his fur collar, encouraging viewers to feel it as they see it. Ultimately what is showcased here are Dürer's awesome artistic gifts of hand as much as his intellectual gifts of mind, two aspects perhaps emblemized by the brightly illuminated body parts that align on a vertical axis to dominate this arresting self-portrait.

The Reformation and the Arts

How does the Protestant Reformation affect sixteenth-century Northern European art and artists?

In spite of the dissident movements and heresies that had challenged the Roman Catholic Church through the centuries, its authority and that of the pope always prevailed—until the sixteenth century (**MAP 22-1**). Then, against a backdrop of broad dissatisfaction with financial abuses and decadent lifestyles among the clergy, religious reformers from within the Church itself challenged first its practices and then its beliefs.

Two of the most important reformers in the early sixteenth century were themselves Catholic priests and trained theologians: Desiderius Erasmus (1466?–1536) of Rotterdam in Holland, who worked to reform the Roman Catholic Church from within, and Martin Luther (1483–1546) in Germany, who eventually broke with it. Indeed, many locate the beginning of the Reformation in 1517, when Luther issued his "95 Theses" calling for Church reform. Among Luther's concerns were the practice of selling indulgences (guarantees of relief from the punishment required after death for forgiven sins) and the excessive veneration of saints and their relics, which he considered superstitious. Luther and others emphasized individual faith and regarded the Bible as the ultimate religious authority. As they challenged the pope's supremacy, it became clear that the Protestants had to break away from Rome. The Roman Catholic Church condemned Luther in 1521.

MAP 22-1 WESTERN EUROPE DURING THE REFORMATION, C. 1560

Sixteenth-century Europe remained largely Roman Catholic, except in Switzerland and the far north, where the impact of the Protestant Reformation was strongest.

Increased literacy and the widespread use of the printing press aided the reformers and allowed scholars throughout Europe to enter the religious debate. In Germany, the wide circulation of Luther's writings—especially his German translation of the Bible and his works maintaining that salvation comes through faith alone—eventually led to the establishment of the Protestant (Lutheran) Church there. In Switzerland, John Calvin (1509–1564) led an even more austere Protestant revolt; and in England, King Henry VIII (ruled 1509–1547) broke with Rome in 1534 for reasons of his own. By the end of the sixteenth century, Protestantism in some form prevailed throughout northern Europe.

Leading the Catholic cause was Holy Roman Emperor Charles V. Europe was racked by religious war from 1546 to 1555 as Charles battled Protestant forces in Germany, until a meeting of the provincial legislature of Augsburg in 1555 determined that the emperor must accommodate the Protestant Reformation in his lands. By the terms of

the peace, local rulers could select the religion of their subjects—Catholic or Protestant. Tired of the strain of government and prematurely aged, Charles abdicated in 1556 and retired to a monastery in Spain, where he died in 1558. His son Philip II inherited Habsburg Spain and the Spanish colonies, while his brother Ferdinand led the Austrian branch of the dynasty.

The years of political and religious strife had a grave impact on artists and art. Some artists found their careers at an end because of their reformist religious sympathies. Then, as Protestantism gained ascendancy, it was Catholic artists who had to leave their homes to seek patronage abroad. There was also widespread destruction of religious art. In some places, Protestant zealots smashed sculpture and stained-glass windows and destroyed or whitewashed religious paintings to rid churches of what they considered idols—though Luther himself never directly supported iconoclasm (the destruction of religious images). With the sudden loss of patronage for religious art in the newly

Art and its Contexts

GERMAN METALWORK: A COLLABORATIVE VENTURE

In Nuremberg, a city known for its master metalworkers, Hans Krug (d. 1519) and his sons Hans the Younger and Ludwig were among the finest. They created marvelous display pieces for the wealthy, such as this silver-gilt **APPLE CUP** (**FIG. 22-2**). Made in about 1510, a gleaming apple, in which the stem forms the handle of the lid, balances on a leafy branch that serves as its base.

The Krug family was responsible for the highly refined casting and finishing of the final product, but several artists worked together to produce such pieces—one drawing designs, another making the models, and others creating the final piece in metal. A drawing by Dürer may have been the basis for the apple cup. Though we know of no piece of goldwork by the artist himself, Dürer was a major catalyst in the growth of Nuremberg as a key center of German goldsmithing. He accomplished this by producing designs for metalwork throughout his career. Designers played an essential role in the metalwork process. With design in hand, the modelmaker created a wooden form for the goldsmith to follow. The result of this artistic collaboration was a technical *tour-de-force* and an exquisitely clever object.

22-2 Workshop of Hans Krug (?) **APPLE CUP**
c. 1510–1515. Gilt silver, height 8½″ (21.5 cm). Germanisches Nationalmuseum, Nuremberg.
Credit: © 2016. Photo Scala, Florence

Protestant lands, many artists turned to portraiture and other secular subjects, including moralizing depictions of human folly and weaknesses, still lifes, and landscapes. The popularity of these themes stimulated the burgeoning of a free art market centered in Antwerp.

Germany

What are the diverse trends in sixteenth-century German sculpture and painting?

In German-speaking regions, the arts flourished until religious upheavals and iconoclastic purges took their toll at mid century. German cities had strong business and trade interests, and their merchants and bankers accumulated self-made, rather than inherited, wealth. They ordered portraits of themselves and fine furnishings for their large, comfortable houses. Entrepreneurial artists like Albrecht Dürer became major commercial successes. And, as in the Middle Ages, the production of small luxury objects crafted with high finish out of precious materials was an important aspect of artistic production.

Sculpture

Although, like the Italians, German Renaissance sculptors worked in stone and bronze, they produced their most original work in wood, especially fine-grained limewood. Most of these wooden images were gilded and painted, continuing an interest in heightening naturalism, until Tilman Riemenschneider began to favor natural wood finishes.

TILMAN RIEMENSCHNEIDER Tilman Riemenschneider (c. 1460–1531) became a master in 1485 and soon had the largest workshop in Würzburg, including specialists in both wood and stone sculpture. Riemenschneider attracted patrons from other cities, and in 1501 he signed a contract with the church of St. James in Rothenburg, where a relic said to be a drop of Jesus's blood was preserved. The **ALTARPIECE OF THE HOLY BLOOD** (**FIG. 22-3**) is a spectacular limewood construction standing nearly 30 feet high. Erhart Harschner, a specialist in architectural shrines, had begun work on the elaborate Gothic frame in 1499, and was paid 50 florins for his work. Riemenschneider was commissioned to provide the figures and scenes to be placed within this frame. He was paid 60 florins for the sculpture, giving us a sense of the relative value patrons placed on their contributions.

The main panel of the altarpiece portrays the moment at the Last Supper when Christ revealed that one of his followers would betray him. Unlike Leonardo da Vinci, who chose the same moment (SEE FIG. 21-4), Riemenschneider puts Judas at center stage and Jesus off-center at the left. The disciples sit around the table. As the event is described

in the Gospel of John (13:21–30), Jesus extends a morsel of food to Judas, signifying that he will be the traitor who sets in motion the events leading to the Crucifixion. One apostle points down, a strange gesture until we realize that he is pointing to the crucifix in the predella, to the relic of Christ's blood, and to the altar table, the symbolic representation of the table of the Last Supper and the tomb of Christ.

22-3 Tilman Riemenschneider **ALTARPIECE OF THE HOLY BLOOD (OPEN)**

Sankt Jakobskirche (church of St. James), Rothenburg ob der Tauber, Germany. Center, *Last Supper*. c. 1499–1505. Limewood, glass, height of tallest figure 39″ (99.1 cm), height of altar 29′6″ (9 m).

Credit: © akg-images/Erich Lessing

Rather than creating individual portraits of the apostles, Riemenschneider repeated an established set of facial types. His figures have large heads, prominent features, sharp cheekbones, sagging jowls, baggy eyes, and elaborate hair with thick wavy locks and deeply drilled curls. The muscles, tendons, and raised veins of hands and feet are also especially lifelike. His assistants and apprentices copied these features either from drawings or from three-dimensional models made by the master. In the altarpiece, deeply hollowed folds create active patterns in the voluminous draperies whose strong highlights and dark shadows harmonize the figural composition with the intricate carving of the framework. The Last Supper is set in a real space containing actual benches for the figures. Windows in the back wall are glazed with bull's-eye glass so that natural light shines in from two directions to illuminate the scene, producing changing effects depending on the time of day and the weather. Although earlier sculpture had been painted and gilded, Riemenschneider introduced the use of a natural wood finish toned with varnish. This meant that details of both figures and environment had to be carved into the wood itself, not added later with paint. Since this required more skillful carvers and more time for them to carve, this new look was a matter of aesthetics, not cost-saving.

In addition to producing an enormous number of religious images for churches, Riemenschneider was politically active in Würzburg, serving as mayor in 1520. His career ended during the Peasants' War (1524–1526), an early manifestation of the Protestant movement. His support for the peasants led to a fine and imprisonment in 1525, and although he survived, Riemenschneider produced no more sculpture and died in 1531.

NIKOLAUS HAGENAUER Prayer was the principal source of solace and relief to the ill before the advent of modern medicine. About 1505, the Strasbourg sculptor Nikolaus Hagenauer (active 1493–1530s) carved an altarpiece for the abbey of St. Anthony in Isenheim near Colmar (**FIG. 22-4**), where a hospital specialized in the care of patients with skin diseases, including the plague, leprosy, and St. Anthony's Fire (caused by eating rye and other grains infected with the ergot fungus). The shrine includes images of SS. Anthony, Jerome, and Augustine. Three tiny men—their size befitting their subordinate status—kneel at the feet of the saints: the donor, Jean d'Orliac, and two men offering a rooster and a piglet.

In the predella, Jesus and the apostles bless the altar, Host, and assembled patients in the hospital. The flesh of the sculpted figures was painted in lifelike colors, but most of the altarpiece was gilded to enhance its resemblance to a metalwork reliquary. A decade later, Matthias Grünewald painted wooden shutters to cover the shrine (SEE FIGS. 22-5, 22-6).

Painting

The work of two very different German artists has come down to us from the first decades of the sixteenth century. Matthias Grünewald continued currents of medieval mysticism and emotional spirituality to create extraordinarily moving paintings. Albrecht Dürer, on the other hand, used intense observation of the world to render lifelike representations of nature, mathematical perspective to create convincing illusions of space, and a reasoned canon of proportions to standardize depictions of the human figure.

MATTHIAS GRÜNEWALD As a court artist to the archbishop of Mainz, Matthias Grünewald (Matthias Gothart Neithart, c. 1470/1475–1528) was a man of many talents who worked as an architect and hydraulic engineer as well as a painter. He is best known today for paintings on the shutters or wings attached to Nikolaus Hagenauer's carved Isenheim Altarpiece (SEE FIG. 22-4). The completed altarpiece is impressive in its size and complexity. Grünewald painted one set of fixed wings and two sets of movable ones, plus one set of panels to cover the predella. The altarpiece could be exhibited in different configurations depending upon the church calendar. The wings and carved wooden shrine complemented one another, the inner sculpture seeming to bring the surrounding paintings to life, and the painted wings in turn protecting the precious carvings.

On weekdays, when the altarpiece was closed, viewers saw a grisly image of the Crucifixion in a darkened landscape, a *Lamentation* below it on the predella, and life-size figures of SS. Sebastian and Anthony Abbot—both associated with the plague—standing on *trompe l'oeil* pedestals on the fixed wings (**FIG. 22-5**). The intensity of feeling here has suggested that Grünewald may have been inspired by the visions of St. Bridget of Sweden, a fourteenth-century mystic whose works—including morbidly detailed descriptions of the Crucifixion—were published in Germany beginning in 1492. Grünewald has scrupulously described the horrific character of the tortured body of Jesus, covered with gashes from his beating and pierced by the thorns used to form a crown for his head. His ashen body, clotted blood, open mouth, and blue lips signal his death. In fact, he appears already to be decaying, an effect enhanced by the palette of putrescent green, yellow, and purplish-red—all described by St. Bridget. She wrote, "The color of death spread through his flesh…." An immaculately garbed Virgin Mary has collapsed in the arms of a ghostlike John the Evangelist, and Mary Magdalen has fallen in anguish to her knees; her clasped hands with outstretched fingers seem to echo Jesus's fingers, cramped in rigor mortis. At the right, John the Baptist points to Jesus and repeats his prophecy, "He shall increase." The Baptist and the lamb, holding a cross and bleeding from its breast into a golden chalice, allude to baptism, the Eucharist, and

22–4 Nikolaus Hagenauer (central panels and predella) and Matthias Grünewald (wings) **ISENHEIM ALTARPIECE (OPEN)**
From the Community of St. Anthony, Isenheim, Alsace, France. Center panels and predella: *St. Anthony Enthroned between SS. Augustine and Jerome; Christ and the Apostles*, c. 1500. Painted and gilt limewood, center panel 9′9½″ × 10′9″ (2.97 × 3.28 m), predella 2′5½″ × 11′2″ (0.75 × 3.4 m). Wings: *SS. Anthony and Paul the Hermit* (left); *The Temptation of St. Anthony* (right). 1510–1515. Oil on wood panel, 8′2½″ × 3′½″ (2.49 × 0.93 m). Musée d'Unterlinden, Colmar, France.

Credit: Bridgeman Images

to Christ as the sacrificial Lamb of God. In the predella, Jesus's bereaved mother and friends prepare his racked body for burial—an activity that must have been a common sight in the abbey's hospital.

In contrast to these grim scenes, the first opening displays events of great joy—the Annunciation, the Nativity, and the Resurrection—appropriate for Sundays and feast days (**FIG. 22-6**). Praying in front of these pictures, the patients must have hoped for miraculous recovery and taken comfort in these visions of divine rapture and orgiastic color. Unlike the darkness of the Crucifixion, the inner scenes are brilliantly illuminated, in part by phosphorescent auras and haloes; stars glitter in the night sky of the Resurrection. The technical virtuosity of Grünewald's painting is enough to inspire euphoria.

The central panels show the heavenly and earthly realms joined in one space. In a variation on the Northern European visionary tradition, the new mother adores her miraculous Christ Child while envisioning her own future as queen of heaven amid angels and cherubim. Grünewald portrayed three distinct types of angels in the foreground—young, mature, and a feathered hybrid

with a birdlike crest on its human head. The range of ethnic types in the heavenly realm may have emphasized the global dominion of the Church, whose missionary efforts were expanding as a result of European exploration. St. Bridget describes the jubilation of the angels as "the glowing flame of love."

The second opening of the altarpiece (SEE FIG. 22-4) reveals Hagenauer's sculpture and was reserved for the special festivals of St. Anthony. The wings in this second opening show to the left the meeting of St. Anthony with the hermit St. Paul, and to the right St. Anthony attacked by horrible demons, perhaps inspired by the horrors of the diseased patients, but also modeled in part on Schongauer's well-known print of the same subject (SEE FIG. 19-28). The meeting of the two hermits in the desert glorifies the monastic life, and in the wilderness Grünewald depicts medicinal plants used in the hospital's therapy. Grünewald painted the face of St. Paul with his own self-portrait, while St. Anthony is a portrait of the donor and administrator of the hospital, the Italian Guido Guersi, whose coat of arms Grünewald painted on the rock next to him.

22–5 Matthias Grünewald **ISENHEIM ALTARPIECE (CLOSED)**

From the Community of St. Anthony, Isenheim, Alsace, France. Center panels: *Crucifixion*; predella: *Lamentation*; side panels: *SS. Sebastian* (left) and *Anthony Abbot* (right). c. 1510–1515. Date 1515 on ointment jar. Oil on wood panel, center panels 9′9½″ × 10′9″ (2.97 × 3.28 m) overall, each wing 8′2½″ × 3′1½″ (2.49 × 0.93 m), predella 2′5½″ × 11′2″ (0.75 × 3.4 m). Musée d'Unterlinden, Colmar, France.

Credit: Bridgeman Images

22–6 Matthias Grünewald **ISENHEIM ALTARPIECE (FIRST OPENING)**

Left to right: *Annunciation, Virgin and Child with Angels, Resurrection*. c. 1510–1515. Oil on wood panel, center panels 9′9½″ × 10′9″ (2.97 × 3.28 m) overall, each wing 8′10″ × 4′8″ (2.69 × 1.42 m). Musée d'Unterlinden, Colmar, France.

Credit: Bridgeman Images

22–7 Albrecht Dürer **THE FOUR HORSEMEN OF THE APOCALYPSE**
From *The Apocalypse*. 1497–1498.
1511 edition. Woodcut, 15½ × 11¹⁄₁₆"
(39.4 × 28.1 cm). Yale University Art Gallery,
New Haven, Connecticut. Library transfer, Gift
of Paul Mellon, B.A. 1929 (1956.16.3e).

Credit: Image courtesy Yale University Art Gallery

Venture" on page 693). Dürer did complete an apprenticeship in gold working, as well as in stained-glass design, painting, and the making of woodcuts—which he learned from Michael Wolgemut, illustrator of the *Nuremberg Chronicle* (SEE FIG. 19–29). It was as a painter and graphic artist, however, that he built his artistic fame.

In 1490, Dürer began traveling to extend his education. He went to Basel, Switzerland, hoping to meet Martin Schongauer, but arrived after the master's death. By 1494, Dürer had moved from Basel to Strasbourg. His first trip to Italy (1494–1495) introduced him to Italian Renaissance ideas and attitudes and, as we considered at the beginning of this chapter, to the concept of the artist as an independent creative genius. In his self-portrait of 1500 (SEE FIG. 22–1), Dürer represents himself as an idealized, Christlike figure in a severely frontal pose, staring self-confidently at the viewer.

As with Riemenschneider, Grünewald's involvement with the Peasants' War may have damaged his artistic career. He left Mainz and spent his last years in Halle, whose ruler was the chief protector of Martin Luther and a long-time patron of Grünewald's contemporary Albrecht Dürer.

ALBRECHT DÜRER Studious, analytical, observant, and meticulous—and as self-confident as Michelangelo—Albrecht Dürer (1471–1528) was the foremost artist of the German Renaissance. He made his home in Nuremberg, where he became a prominent citizen. Nuremberg was a center of culture as well as of business, with an active group of humanists and internationally renowned artists. It was also a leading publishing center. Dürer's father was a goldsmith and must have expected his son to follow in his trade (see "German Metalwork: A Collaborative

On his return to Nuremberg, Dürer began to publish his own prints to bolster his income, and ultimately it was prints, not paintings, that made his fortune. His first major publication, *The Apocalypse*, appeared simultaneously in German and Latin editions in 1497–1498. It consisted of a woodcut title page and 14 full-page illustrations with the text printed on the back of each. Perhaps best known is **THE FOUR HORSEMEN OF THE APOCALYPSE (FIG. 22–7)**, based on figures described in Revelation 6:1–8: a crowned rider, armed with a bow, on a white horse (Conquest); a rider with a sword, on a red horse (War); a rider with a set of scales, on a black horse (Plague and Famine); and a rider on a sickly pale horse (Death). Earlier artists had simply lined up the horsemen in the landscape, but Dürer created a compact, overlapping group of wild riders charging across the world and trampling its cowering inhabitants.

Dürer probably did not cut his own woodblocks but employed a skilled carver who followed his drawings faithfully. The dynamic figures show affinities with Schongauer's *Temptations of St. Anthony* (SEE FIG. 19–28). Dürer adapted Schongauer's metal-engraving technique to the woodcut medium, using a complex pattern of lines to model the forms. His early training as a goldsmith is evident in his meticulous attention to detail and in his decorative cloud and drapery patterns. Following the tradition established by his late fifteenth-century predecessors, he fills the foreground with large, active figures.

Perhaps as early as the summer of 1494, Dürer began to experiment with engravings, cutting the metal plates himself with an artistry rivaling Schongauer's. His growing interest in Italian art and his theoretical investigations are reflected in his 1504 engraving **ADAM AND EVE** (**FIG. 22-8**), which represents his first documented use of ideal human proportions based on Roman copies of ancient Greek sculpture. He may have seen figures of Apollo and Venus in Italy, and he would have known ancient sculpture from contemporary prints and drawings. But around these idealized human figures he represents plants and animals with typically Northern attention to descriptive detail.

Dürer filled the landscape with symbolic content reflecting the medieval theory that after Adam and Eve disobeyed God, they and their descendants became vulnerable to imbalances in the body fluids that controlled human temperament. An excess of black bile from the liver would produce melancholy, despair, and greed; yellow bile caused anger, pride, and impatience; phlegm in the lungs resulted in lethargy and apathy; and an excess of blood made a person unusually optimistic but also compulsively interested in the pleasures of the flesh. These four human temperaments, or personalities, are symbolized here by the melancholy elk, the choleric cat, the phlegmatic ox, and the sanguine (or sensual) rabbit. The mouse

22-8 Albrecht Dürer **ADAM AND EVE**

1504. Engraving, 9⅝ × 7⅝″ (24.4 × 19.3 cm). Yale University Art Gallery, New Haven, Connecticut. Fritz Achelis Memorial Collection, Gift of Frederic George Achelis, B.A. 1907; reacquired in 1972 with the Henry J. Heinz II, B.A. 1931, Fund; Everett V. Meeks, B.A. 1901, Fund; and Stephen Carlton Clark, B.A. 1903, Fund (1925.29).

Credit: Image courtesy Yale University Art Gallery

is a symbol of Satan (see the mousetrap in FIG. 19–11), whose earthly power, already manifest in the Garden of Eden, was capable of bringing human beings to a life of woe through their own bad choices. Adam seems to be releasing the mouse into the world of his paradise as he thinks about eating the forbidden fruit that Eve receives from the snake. Dürer placed his signature prominently on a placard hung on a tree branch in Adam's grasp on which perches a parrot—possibly symbolizing false wisdom, since it can only repeat mindlessly what it hears.

Dürer's familiarity with Italian art was greatly enhanced by a second, leisurely trip over the Alps in 1505–1506. Thereafter, he seems to have resolved to reform the art of his own country by publishing theoretical writings and manuals that discussed Italian Renaissance problems of perspective, ideal human proportions, and the techniques of painting.

Dürer admired Martin Luther, but they never met. In 1526, the artist openly professed his Lutheranism in a pair of inscribed panels, the **FOUR APOSTLES** (FIG. **22-9**).

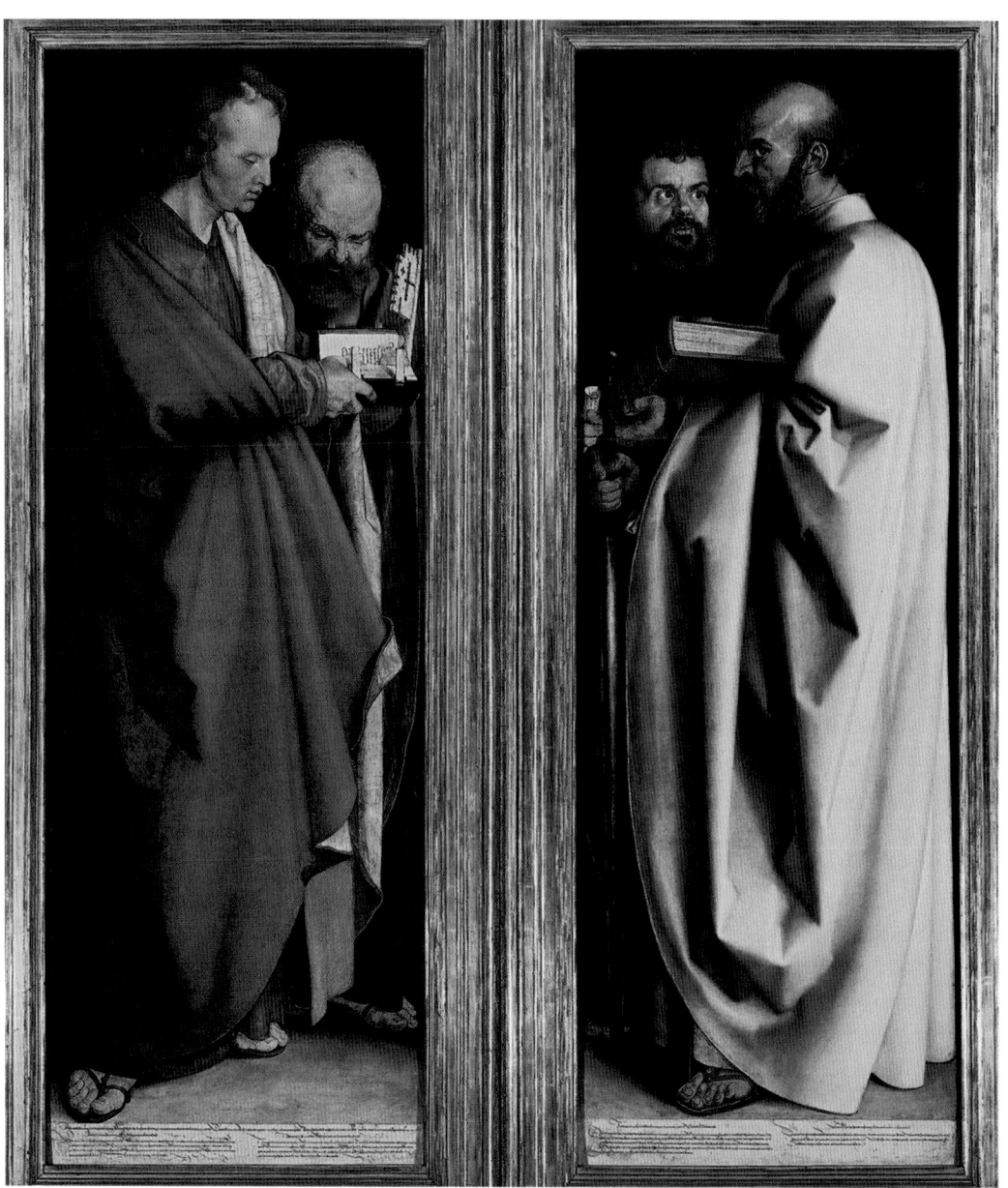

22-9 Albrecht Dürer **FOUR APOSTLES**

1526. Oil on wood panel, each panel 7′½″ × 2′6″ (2.15 × 0.76 m). Alte Pinakothek, Munich.

Dürer presented these panels to the city of Nuremberg, which had already adopted Lutheranism as its official religion. Dürer wrote, "For a Christian would no more be led to superstition by a picture or effigy than an honest man to commit murder because he carries a weapon by his side. He must indeed be an unthinking man who would worship picture, wood, or stone. A picture therefore brings more good than harm, when it is honourably, artistically, and well made" (Snyder, p. 333).

Credit: Photo © Bayer@Mitko/ARTOTHEK

On the left panel, the elderly Peter, who normally has a central position as the first pope, has been displaced with his keys to the background by Luther's favorite evangelist, John, who holds an open Gospel that reads "In the beginning was the Word," reinforcing the Protestant emphasis on the Bible. On the right panel, Mark stands behind Paul, whose epistles were particularly admired by the Protestants. A long inscription on the frame warns the viewer not to be led astray by "false prophets" but to heed the words of the New Testament as recorded by these "four excellent men." Below each figure are excerpts from their letters and from the Gospel of Mark—drawn from Luther's German translation of the New Testament—warning against those who do not understand the true Word of God. These paintings were surely meant to chart the possibility of a Protestant visual art.

CRANACH, BALDUNG, AND ALTDORFER Martin Luther's favorite painter, Lucas Cranach the Elder (1472–1553), moved his workshop to Wittenberg in 1504 after a number of years in Vienna. In addition to the humanist milieu of its university and library, Wittenberg offered the patronage of the Saxon court. Appointed court painter to Elector Frederick the Wise, Cranach created woodcuts, altarpieces, and many portraits.

Just how far German artists' style and conception of the figure could differ from Italian Renaissance idealism is easily seen in Cranach's **NYMPH OF THE SPRING** (**FIG. 22-10**), especially when compared with Titian's *"Venus" of Urbino* (SEE FIG. 21-30). The sleeping nymph was a Renaissance theme, not an ancient one. Cranach was inspired by a fifteenth-century inscription on a fountain beside the Danube, cited in the upper left corner of the painting: "I am the nymph of the sacred font. Do not interrupt my sleep for I am at peace." Cranach records the Danube landscape with characteristic Northern attention to detail and turns his nymph into a rather provocative young woman, who glances slyly out at the viewer through half-closed eyes. She has cast aside a fashionable red velvet gown, but still wears her jewelry, which together with her transparent veil enhances rather than conceals her nudity—especially those coral beads that fall between her breasts, mapping their contours. Unlike other artists working for Protestant patrons, many of whom looked on earthly beauty as a sinful vanity, Cranach seems delighted by earthly things—the lush foliage that provides the nymph's couch, the pair of partridges (symbols of Venus and married love), and Cupid's bow and quiver of arrows hanging on the tree. This nymph is certainly not an embodiment of an idealized, Classical Venus; perhaps she was a living beauty from the Wittenberg court.

Cranach's slightly younger contemporary, Hans Baldung Grien (1484/1485–1545)—his nickname tag "Grien" ("green," apparently a favorite color) dates from his apprenticeship days and was used to distinguish him from the numerous other apprentices named Hans—is known for very different visualizations of women. Born into an affluent and well-educated family, Baldung was working in Strasbourg by 1500, before moving to Nuremberg in 1503 and eventually joining Dürer's workshop in 1505–1507. Over the course of his long career, he also worked in Halle and Freiburg, but his principal artistic home was Strasbourg, where he lived out a prosperous professional life as a painter, printmaker, and stained-glass designer.

During the first half of his career, Baldung created a series of paintings on the theme of **DEATH AND THE MATRON** that juxtapose sensuality with mortality, voluptuousness with decay, attraction with repulsion. The example in **FIG. 22-11** (painted in about 1520–1525 for a private collector in Basel) uses brilliant illumination and open poses to draw our attention first to the nude, who is fleshier and considerably more sensual than Cranach's nymph (SEE FIG. 22-10) or Dürer's Eve (SEE FIG. 22-8). But this focus is soon overtaken by a sense of surprise that mirrors her own, as she turns her head to discover that the figure stroking her hair and clutching at her breast is not her lover but Death himself. The putrid decay of his yellowing flesh contrasts sharply with her soft contours, and his bony, molting head is the antithesis of her full, pink cheeks, flowing tresses, and soft traces of body hair. That the encounter takes place in a cemetery, on top of a tombstone, serves to underline the warning against the transitory pleasures of the flesh, but Baldung also seems to depend on the viewer's own erotic engagement to make the message not only moral but personal.

Landscape, with or without figures, became a popular theme in the sixteenth century. In the fifteenth century, Northern artists had examined and recorded nature with the care and enthusiasm of biologists, but painted landscapes were reserved for the backgrounds of figural compositions, usually sacred subjects. In the 1520s, however, religious art found little favor among Protestants. Landscape painting, on the other hand, had no overt religious content, although it could be seen as a reflection or even glorification of God's works on Earth. The most accomplished German landscape painter of the period was Albrecht Altdorfer (c. 1480–1538).

Altdorfer probably received his early training in Bavaria from his father, but he became a citizen of Regensburg in 1505 and remained there painting the Danube River Valley for the rest of his life. **DANUBE LANDSCAPE** of about 1525 (**FIG. 22-12**) is an early example of pure landscape painting, without a narrative subject, human figures, or overt religious significance. A small work on vellum laid down on a wood panel, it shows a landscape that seems to be a minutely detailed reproduction of the natural terrain, but the forest seems far more poetic and

22–10 Lucas Cranach the Elder **NYMPH OF THE SPRING**

c. 1537. Oil on panel, 19 × 28½″ (48.5 × 72.9 cm).
National Gallery of Art, Washington, DC. (1925.29)

Credit: Image courtesy the National Gallery of Art, Washington

mysterious than Dürer's or Cranach's carefully observed views of nature. The low mountains, gigantic lacy pines, neatly contoured shrubberies, and fairyland castle with red-roofed towers at the end of a winding path announce a new sensibility. The eerily glowing yellow–white horizon below moving gray and blue clouds in a sky that takes up more than half the composition prefigures the Romanticism of German landscape painting in later centuries.

22–11 Hans Baldung Grien **DEATH AND THE MATRON**

c. 1520–1525. Oil on wood panel, 12⅜ × 7⅜″
(31.3 × 18.7 cm). Öffentliche Kunstsammlung, Basel.

Although more erotically charged and certainly more dramatic than Dürer's Eve in FIG. 22–8, Baldung's woman is based in certain ways on that famous image, which was engraved while he was assisting in Dürer's workshop. In many respects, the similarities in pose (especially the feet) and form (wide hips with narrowing waist and torso) only point up the differences in expressive content.

Credit: Photo © Hans Hinz/ARTOTHEK

22–12 Albrecht Altdorfer
DANUBE LANDSCAPE
c. 1525. Oil on vellum on wood
panel, 12 × 8½″ (30.5 × 22.2 cm).
Alte Pinakothek, Munich.

Credit: © 2016. Photo Scala,
Florence/bpk, Bildagentur für Kunst,
Kultur und Geschichte, Berlin

France

How does King Francis I's enthusiasm for Italian art transform Renaissance art and architecture in France?

Renaissance France followed a different path from that taken in Germany. In 1519, Pope Leo X came to an agreement with the French king Francis I (ruled 1515–1547) that spared the country the turmoil suffered in Germany. Furthermore, whereas Martin Luther had devoted followers in France, French reformer John Calvin (1509–1564) fled to Switzerland in 1534, where he led a theocratic state in Geneva.

During the second half of the century, however, warring political factions favoring either Catholics or Huguenots (Protestants) competed to exert power over the French crown, with devastating consequences. In 1560, the devoutly Catholic Catherine de' Medici, widow of Henry II (ruled 1547–1559), became regent for her young son, Charles IX, and tried, but failed, to find a balance between the two sides. Her machinations ended in religious polarization and a bloody conflict that began in 1562. When her third son, Henry III (ruled 1574–1589), was murdered by a fanatical Dominican friar, a Protestant cousin, Henry, king of Navarre, inherited the throne

22–13 Jean Clouet **FRANCIS I**
1525–1530. Oil and tempera on wood panel,
37¾ × 29⅛" (95.9 × 74 cm). Musée du Louvre, Paris.

Credit: © 2016. Photo Scala, Florence

created a flattering image of Francis by softening the king's distinctive features with shading and highlighting the nervous activity of his fingers. At the same time he conceived an image of pure power. Elaborate, puffy sleeves broaden the king's shoulders to fill the entire width of the panel, much as Renaissance parade armor turned scrawny men into giants. The detailed rendering of the delicately worked costume of silk, satin, velvet, jewels, and gold embroidery could be painted separately from the portrait itself. Royal clothing was often loaned to the artist or modeled by a servant to spare the "sitter" (the subject of the portrait) the boredom of posing. In creating such official portraits, the artist sketched the subject, then painted a prototype that, upon approval, became the model for numerous replicas made for diplomatic and family purposes.

Royal Residences

With the enthusiasm of Francis for things Italian and the widening distribution of Italian books on architecture, the Italian Renaissance style soon infiltrated French architecture. Builders of elegant rural palaces, called **châteaux**, were quick to introduce Italianate decoration to otherwise Gothic buildings, but French architects soon adapted Classical principles of building design as well.

One of the most beautiful châteaux was not built as a royal residence, although it soon became one. In 1512, Thomas Bohier, a royal tax collector, bought the castle of Chenonceau on the River Cher, a tributary of the Loire (**FIG. 22-14**) (see "The Castle of the Ladies" opposite). He demolished the old castle, leaving only a tower. Using the piers of a water mill on the river bank as part of the foundation, he and his wife erected a new Renaissance home. The plan reflects the Classical principles of geometric regularity and symmetry—a rectangular building with rooms arranged on each side of a wide central hall. Only the library and chapel, which are corbelled out over the water, break the line of the walls. In the upper story, the builders used traditional features of medieval castles—battlements, corner turrets, steep roofs, and dormer windows. The owners died soon after the château was finished in 1521, and their son gave it to Francis I, who turned it into a hunting lodge.

and became the first Bourbon king. Henry converted to Catholicism and ruled as Henry IV. Backed by a country sick of bloodshed, he quickly settled the religious question by proclaiming tolerance of Protestants in the Edict of Nantes in 1598.

A French Renaissance Under Francis I

Immediately after his ascent to the throne, Francis I sought to "modernize" the French court by acquiring the versatile talents of Leonardo da Vinci, who moved to France in 1516. Officially, Leonardo was there to advise the king on royal architectural projects and, the king said, for the pleasure of his conversation. Francis supported an Italian-inspired Renaissance in French art and architecture throughout his long reign.

JEAN CLOUET Not all the artists working at the court of Francis I, however, were Italian. Flemish artist Jean Clouet (c. 1485–c. 1540) found great favor at the royal court, especially as a portrait painter. About the same time that he became principal court painter in 1527, he produced an official portrait of the king (**FIG. 22-13**). Clouet

22-14 CHÂTEAU OF CHENONCEAU
Touraine, France. Original building (at right) 1513–1521; gallery on bridge at left by Philibert de l'Orme, finished c. 1581.

Chenonceau continued to play a role in the twentieth century. During World War I, it was used as a hospital. During the German occupation in World War II (1940–1942), when the River Cher formed the border with Vichy "Free" France, the gallery bridge at Chenonceau became an escape route.

Credit: Wildman/Fotolia

Art and its Contexts

THE CASTLE OF THE LADIES

Women played an important role in the patronage of the arts during the Renaissance. Nowhere is their influence stronger than in the châteaux of the Loire River Valley. At Chenonceau (SEE FIG. 22-14), women built, saved, and restored the château, which now is often referred to as "The Castle of the Ladies." Catherine Briconnet and her husband, Thomas Bohier, originally acquired the property, including a fortified mill, on which they built their country residence. Catherine supervised the construction, which included such modern conveniences as a straight staircase (an Italian and Spanish feature) instead of traditional medieval spiral stairs, and a kitchen inside the château instead of in a distant outbuilding. After Thomas died in 1524 and Catherine in 1526, their son gave Chenonceau to King Francis I.

King Henry II, Francis's son, gave Chenonceau to his mistress Diane de Poitiers in 1547. She managed the estate astutely, increased its revenue, developed the vineyards, added intricately planted gardens in the Italian style, and built a bridge across the Cher. When Henry died in a tournament, his queen, Catherine de' Medici (1519–1589), appropriated the château for herself.

Catherine, like so many in her family a great patron of the arts, added the two-story gallery to the bridge at Chenonceau, as well as outbuildings and additional formal gardens. Her parties were famous: mock naval battles on the river, fireworks, banquets, dances, and on one occasion two choruses of young women dressed as mermaids in the moat and nymphs in the shrubbery—who were then chased about by young men costumed as satyrs.

When Catherine's third son became king as Henry III in 1574, she gave the château to his wife, Louise of Lorraine, who lived in mourning at Chenonceau after Henry III was assassinated in 1589. She wore only white and covered the walls, windows, and furniture in her room with black velvet and damask. She left Chenonceau to her niece when she died.

In the eighteenth and nineteenth centuries, women continued to determine the fate of Chenonceau. During the French Revolution (1789–1793), the owner, Louise Dupin, was so beloved by the villagers that they protected her and saved her home. Then, in 1864, Marguerite Pelouze bought Chenonceau and restored it by removing Catherine de' Medici's Italian "improvements."

Later, Roman-trained French Renaissance architect Philibert de l'Orme (d. 1570) designed for Catherine de' Medici a gallery for an existing bridge across the river. Completed about 1581, it incorporates contemporary Italianate window treatments, wall molding, and cornices that harmonized almost perfectly with the forms of the original turreted building.

FONTAINEBLEAU Having chosen as his primary residence the medieval hunting lodge at Fontainebleau, Francis I began transforming it into a grand country palace. In 1530, he imported a Florentine artist, the Mannerist painter Rosso Fiorentino (1495–1540), to direct the project. After Rosso died, he was succeeded by his Italian colleague Francesco Primaticcio (1504–1570), who had joined Rosso in 1532 after working with Giulio Romano in Mantua (SEE FIG. 21-23). Primaticcio would spend the rest of his career working on the decoration of Fontainebleau. During that time, he also commissioned and imported a large number of copies and casts of original Roman sculpture, from the newly discovered Laocoön (SEE FIG. 5-65) to the relief decoration on the Column of Trajan (SEE FIG. 6-47). These works provided an invaluable visual resource of figures and techniques for the Northern European artists employed on the Fontainebleau project.

Among Primaticcio's first projects at Fontainebleau was the redecoration in the 1540s of the rooms of the king's official mistress, Anne, duchess of Étampes (**FIG. 22-15**). Woodwork, stucco relief, and fresco painting are combined in a complex interior design. The stucco nymphs, with their elongated bodies and small heads,

recall Parmigianino's paintings (SEE FIG. 21-39). Their spiraling postures and bits of clinging drapery are playfully erotic. Garlands, mythological figures, and Roman architectural ornament almost overwhelm the walls with visual enrichment, yet the whole remains graceful, orderly, and lighthearted. The first School of Fontainebleau, as this Italian phase of the palace decoration is called, established an Italianate tradition of Mannerism in painting and interior design that spread to other centers in France and into the Netherlands.

THE LOUVRE Before Francis I's defeat at Pavia by Holy Roman Emperor Charles V and subsequent imprisonment in Spain in 1525, the French court had been a mobile unit, and the locus of French art resided outside Paris in the Loire Valley. After his release in 1526, Francis made Paris his bureaucratic seat, and the Île-de-France—Paris and its region—took the artistic lead. The move to the capital gave birth to a style of French Classicism when Francis I and Henry II decided to modernize the medieval castle of the Louvre. Work began in 1546 with the replacement of the west wing of the square court, or **COUR CARRÉE** (**FIG. 22-16**), by architect Pierre Lescot (c. 1510–1578) working with sculptor Jean Goujon (1510–1568). They designed a building that incorporated Renaissance ideals of balance and regularity with Classical architectural details and rich sculptural decoration. The irregular rooflines seen in a château such as the one at Chenonceau (SEE FIG. 22-14, right part of the building) gave way to discreetly rounded arches and horizontal balustrades. Classical pilasters and entablatures replaced Gothic buttresses and stringcourses.

22–15 Primaticcio **STUCCO AND WALL PAINTING, CHAMBER OF THE DUCHESS OF ÉTAMPES, CHÂTEAU OF FONTAINEBLEAU**
France. 1540s.

22–16 Pierre Lescot and Jean Goujon **WEST WING OF THE COUR CARRÉE, PALAIS DU LOUVRE, PARIS**
Begun 1546.

Credit: © akg-images/Erich Lessing

A round-arched arcade on the ground floor suggests an Italian loggia. On the other hand, the sumptuousness of the decoration recalls the French Flamboyant style (see Chapter 19), only with Classical pilasters and acanthus replacing Gothic colonnettes and cusps.

Spain and Portugal

How do the Escorial, the Convent of Christ in Tomar, and the paintings of El Greco embody the religion and politics of Renaissance Spain and Portugal?

The sixteenth century saw the peak of Spanish political power. The country had been united in the fifteenth century by the marriage of Isabella of Castile and Ferdinand of Aragon. Only Navarre (in the Pyrenees) and Portugal remained outside the union. When Isabella and Ferdinand's grandson Charles V abdicated in 1556, his son Philip II (ruled 1556–1598) became the king of Spain, the Netherlands, and the Americas, as well as ruler of Milan, Burgundy, and Naples, but Spain was Philip's permanent residence. For more than half a century, he supported artists in Spain, Italy, and the Netherlands. His navy, the famous Spanish Armada, halted the advance of Islam in the Mediterranean and secured control of most of the Americas. Despite enormous effort, however, Philip could not suppress the revolt of the northern provinces of the Netherlands, nor could he prevail in his war against the English, who destroyed his

navy in 1588. He was able to gain control of the entire Iberian peninsula, however, by claiming Portugal in 1580, and it remained part of Spain until 1640.

Architecture

Philip built **THE ESCORIAL** (**FIG. 22–17**), the great monastery-palace complex outside Madrid, partly to comply with his father's direction to construct a "pantheon" in which all Spanish kings might be buried, and partly to house his court and government. In 1559, Philip summoned from Italy Juan Bautista de Toledo (d. 1567), who had been Michelangelo's supervisor of work at St. Peter's from 1546 to 1548. Juan Bautista's design for the monastery-palace reflected his indoctrination in Bramante's Classical principles in Rome, but the king himself dictated the severity and size of the structure. The Escorial's grandeur comes from its overwhelming size, fine proportions, and excellent masonry. The complex includes not only the royal residence but also the Royal Monastery of San Lorenzo, a school, a library, and a church, its crypt serving as the royal burial chamber. The plan was said to resemble a gridiron, the instrument of martyrdom of its patron saint, Lawrence, who was roasted alive.

In 1572, Juan Bautista's assistant, Juan de Herrera, was appointed architect, and he immediately changed the design, adding second stories on all wings and breaking the horizontality of the main façade with a central frontispiece

22–17 Juan Bautista de Toledo and Juan de Herrera **THE ESCORIAL**
Madrid. 1563–1584. Detail from an anonymous 17th-century painting. Oil on canvas, 30¼ × 35⅞ (77 × 91cm). Monasterio-Pintura, San Lorenzo Del Escorial, Madrid.

Credit: © akg-images/Album/Oronoz

that resembled the superimposed temple fronts that were fashionable on Italian churches at this time (SEE FIGS. 21-33, 21-48A). Before beginning the church in the center of the complex, Philip solicited the advice of Italian architects including Vignola and Palladio. The final design combined ideas that Philip approved and Herrera carried out, and it embodies Italian Classicism in its geometric clarity, symmetry, and superimposed temple-front façade. In its austerity, it embodies the deep religiosity of Philip II.

Sculpture

One of the most beautiful, if also one of the strangest, sixteenth-century sculptures in Portugal seems to float over the cloisters of the convent of Christ in Tomar. In the heart of the castle-monastery complex, one comes unexpectedly face to face with the Old Man of the Sea. He supports on his powerful shoulders an extraordinary growth—part roots and trunk of a gnarled tree and part tangled mass of seaweed, algae, ropes, and anchor chains. Barnacle- and coral-encrusted piers lead the eye upward, revealing a large, lattice-covered window, the great **WEST WINDOW** of the church of the Knights of Christ (**FIG. 22-18**).

When Pope Clement V disbanded the Templars (a monastic order of knights founded in Jerusalem after the First Crusade) in 1314, King Dinis of Portugal offered them

a renewed existence as the Knights of Christ. As a result, in 1356, they made the former Templar castle and monastery in Tomar their headquarters. When Prince Henry the Navigator (1394–1460) became the grand master of the order, he invested their funds in the exploration of the African coast and the Atlantic Ocean. The Templar insignia, the squared cross, became the emblem used on the sails of Portuguese ships.

King Manuel I of Portugal (ruled 1495–1521) commissioned the present church, with its amazing sculpture by Diogo de Arruda, in 1510. So distinctive is the style developed under King Manuel by artists like the Arruda brothers, Diogo (active 1508–1531) and Francisco (active 1510–1547), that Renaissance art in Portugal is called "Manueline." In the window at Tomar, every surface is carved with architectural and natural detail associated with the sea. Twisted ropes form the corners of the window; the coral pillars support great swathes of seaweed. Chains and cables drop to the place where the head of a man—perhaps a self-portrait of Diogo de Arruda—emerges from the roots of a tree. Above the window, more ropes, cables, and seaweed support the emblems of the patron—armillary spheres at the upper outside corners (topped by pinnacles) and at dead center, the coat of arms of Manuel I with its Portuguese castles framing the five wounds of Christ. Topping the composition is the square

22-18 Diogo de Arruda **WEST WINDOW, CHURCH IN THE CONVENT OF CHRIST, TOMAR**

Portugal. c. 1510. Commissioned by King Manuel I of Portugal.

Credit: Lemtal/Fotolia

Painting

The most famous painter working in Spain during the last quarter of the sixteenth century was Domenikos Theotokopoulos (1541–1614), who arrived in Spain in 1577 after working for ten years in Italy. El Greco ("The Greek"), as he is called, was trained as an icon painter in the Byzantine manner in his native Crete, then under Venetian rule. In about 1566, he entered Titian's studio in Venice, where he also studied the paintings of Tintoretto and Veronese. From about 1570 to 1577, he worked in Rome, living for a time in the Farnese Palace. Probably encouraged by Spanish church officials whom he met in Rome, El Greco eventually settled in Toledo, seat of the Spanish archbishop. He had hoped for a court appointment, but Philip II—a great patron of the Venetian painter Titian and a collector of Netherlandish artists such as Bosch—disliked the painting he had commissioned from El Greco for the Escorial and never again gave him work.

In Toledo, El Greco joined the circle of humanist scholars. He wrote that the artist's goal should be to copy nature, that Raphael relied too heavily on the ancients, and that the Italians' use of mathematics to achieve ideal proportions hindered their painting of nature. At this same time an intense religious revival was underway in Spain, expressed in the impassioned preaching of Ignatius of Loyola, as well as in the poetry of two great Spanish mystics: St. Teresa of Ávila (1515–1582) and her follower, St. John of the Cross (1542–1591). El Greco's style—rooted in Byzantine icon painting and strongly reflecting the rich colors and loose brushwork of Venetian painting—was well equipped to express the intense spirituality of these mystics.

cross of the Order of Christ, clearly delineated against the wall of the chapel.

The armillary sphere became a symbol of the era. This complex form of a celestial globe, with the sun at the center surrounded by rings marking the paths of the planets, was a teaching device for the new scientific theory that the Sun, not the Earth, was the center of the solar system. (Copernicus published his theories about this in 1531 and 1543.) King Manuel's use of the armillary sphere as his emblem signals his determination to make Portugal the leader in the exploration of the sea. Indeed, in Manuel's reign the Portuguese reached India and Brazil.

In 1586, Andrés Nuñez, parish priest of the church of Santo Tomé, commissioned a painted altarpiece from El Greco to honor Count Orgaz, a great benefactor of the Church. At Count Orgaz's funeral in 1323, SS. Augustine and Stephen were said to have appeared to lower the body into his tomb as his soul was seen ascending to heaven. El Greco's painting the **BURIAL OF COUNT ORGAZ** (**FIG. 22-19**) captures these miracles in a Mannerist composition that recalls Pontormo (SEE FIG. 21-38), packing the pictorial field with figures and eliminating specific reference to the spatial setting. An angel lifts Orgaz's soul along the central axis of the painting toward the enthroned Christ at the apex of the canvas. The otherworldly light emanating from

Christ in this heavenly vision is quite unlike the natural light below, where El Greco surrounded the burial scene with portraits of the local aristocracy and religious notables. He placed his own 8-year-old son at the lower left next to St. Stephen and signed the painting on the boy's white kerchief. El Greco may also have put his own features on the man just above the saint's head, the only other figure who, like the child, looks straight out at the viewer.

22-19 El Greco **BURIAL OF COUNT ORGAZ**
Church of Santo Tomé, Toledo, Spain. 1586. Oil on canvas, 16′ × 11′10″ (4.88 × 3.61 m).

Credit: Courtesy of Marilyn Stokstad

The Netherlands

How do the diverse interests of wealthy bourgeois and noble patrons affect painting in the Netherlands during the sixteenth century?

In the Netherlands, the sixteenth century was an age of bitter religious and political conflict. Despite the opposition of the Spanish Habsburg rulers, the Protestant Reformation took hold in the northern provinces. Seeds of unrest were sown still deeper over the course of the century by continued religious persecution, economic hardship, and inept governors. Widespread iconoclasm characterized 1566–1567, and a long battle for independence began with a revolt in 1568 that lasted until Spain relinquished all claims to the region 80 years later. As early as 1579, when the seven northern Protestant provinces declared themselves the United Provinces, the discord split the Netherlands, eventually dividing it along religious lines into the United Provinces (the present-day Netherlands) and Catholic Flanders (present-day Belgium).

Despite such turmoil, Antwerp and other cities developed into thriving art centers. The Reformation led artists to seek patrons outside the Church. While courtiers and burghers alike continued to commission portraits, the demand arose for small paintings with interesting secular subjects appropriate for homes. For example, some artists became specialists known for their landscapes or satires. In addition to painting, textiles, ceramics, printmaking, and sculpture in wood and metal flourished in the Netherlands. Flemish tapestries were sought after and highly prized across Europe, as they had been in the fifteenth century, and leading Italian artists made cartoons to be woven into tapestries in Flemish workshops (see Chapter 21). The **graphic arts** emerged as an important medium, providing many artists with another source of income. Pieter Bruegel the Elder, for instance, began his career drawing amusing moralizing images to be printed and published by At the Four Winds, an Antwerp publishing house.

Like Vasari in Italy, Carel van Mander (1548–1606) recorded the lives of his Netherlandish contemporaries in engaging biographies that mix fact and gossip. He, too, intended his 1604 book *Het Schilder-boeck* (*The Painter's Book*) to be a survey of the history of art, and he included material from the ancient Roman writers Pliny and Vitruvius as well as from Vasari's revised and expanded *Lives*, published in 1568.

Painting for Aristocratic and Noble Patrons

Artistic taste among the wealthy bourgeoisie and noble classes in the early sixteenth-century Netherlands was characterized by a striking diversity, encompassing the imaginative and difficult visions of Hieronymus Bosch as well as the more Italianate compositions of Jan Gossaert. In the later years of his life, Bosch's membership in a local but prestigious confraternity called the Brotherhood of Our Lady seems to have opened doors to noble patrons such as Count Hendrick III of Nassau and Duke Philip the Fair. His younger contemporary Gossaert left the city of Antwerp as a young man to spend the majority of his active years as the court painter for the natural son of Duke Philip the Good. His art also attracted members of the Habsburg family, including Charles V, who were seduced by Gossaert's combination of Northern European and Italian styles.

HIERONYMUS BOSCH   Among the most fascinating Netherlandish painters to modern viewers is Hieronymus Bosch (1450–1516), who depicted the sort of imaginative fantasies more often associated with medieval than Renaissance art. A superb colorist and virtuoso technician, Bosch spent his career in the town whose name he adopted, 's-Hertogenbosch. Bosch's religious devotion is certain, and his range of subjects shows that he was well educated. Challenging and unsettling paintings such as his **GARDEN OF EARTHLY DELIGHTS (FIG. 22-20)** have led modern scholars to label Bosch both a mystic and a social critic. The subject of the triptych seems to be founded on Christian belief in the natural state of human sinfulness, but it was not painted for a church.

In the left wing, God introduces doll-like figures of Adam and Eve under the watchful eye of the owl of perverted wisdom. The owl symbolizes both wisdom and folly. Folly had become an important concept to the Northern European humanists, who believed in the power of education. They believed that people would choose to follow the right way once they knew it. Here the owl peers out from an opening in the spherical base of a fantastic pink fountain in a lake from which vicious creatures creep out into the world.

In the central panel, the Earth teems with such monsters, but also with vivacious human revelers and huge fruits, symbolic of fertility and sexual abandon. In hell, at the right, sensual pleasures—eating, drinking, music, and dancing—become instruments of torture in a dark world of fire and ice. The emphasis in the right wing on the torments of hell, with no hint of the rewards of heaven, seems to caution that damnation is the natural outcome of a life lived in ignorant folly and that humans ensure their damnation through their self-centered pursuit of pleasures of the flesh—the sins of gluttony, lust, greed, and sloth—outlined with such fantastic and graphic abandon in the central panel.

One scholar has proposed that the central panel is a parable on human salvation in which the practice of alchemy—the process that sought to turn common metals

22–20 Hieronymus Bosch **GARDEN OF EARTHLY DELIGHTS (OPEN)**
c. 1505–1515. Oil on wood panel; center panel 7′2½″ × 6′4¾″ (2.20 × 1.95 m), each wing 7′2½″ × 3′2″ (2.20 × 0.97 m).
Museo del Prado, Madrid.

Despite—or perhaps because of—its bizarre subject matter, this triptych was woven in 1566 into tapestries, and at least one painted copy
was made as well. Bosch's original triptych was sold at the onset of the Netherlands Revolt and sent in 1568 to Spain, where it entered the
collection of Philip II.

into gold—parallels Christ's power to convert human dross
into spiritual gold. In this theory, the bizarre fountain at
the center of the lake in the middle distance can be seen
as an alchemical "marrying chamber," complete with the
glass vessels for collecting the vapors of distillation. Others see the theme as the power of women over men. In this
interpretation, the central pool is the setting for a display
of seductive women and sex-obsessed men. Women frolic
alluringly in the pool while men dance and ride in a mad
circle trying to attract them. In this strange garden, men
are slaves to their own lust. An early seventeenth-century
critic focused on the fruit, writing that the triptych was
known as *The Strawberry Plant* because it represented the
"vanity and glory and the passing taste of strawberries or
the strawberry plant and its pleasant odor that is hardly

remembered once it has passed." Luscious fruits of obvious sexual symbolism—strawberries, cherries, grapes, and
pomegranates—appear everywhere in the garden, serving
as food, as shelter, and even as a boat. The message may be
that human life is as fleeting and insubstantial as the taste
of a strawberry. But yet another modern reading sees the
central tableau as depicting the course of life in paradise
if Adam and Even had not consigned humanity to sin by
eating the forbidden fruit.

Conforming to a long tradition of triptych altarpieces
made for churches, Bosch painted a more sober *grisaille*
picture on the reverse of the side wings. When the triptych
is closed, a less enigmatic, but equally fascinating, scene is
displayed (**FIG. 22–21**). A transparent, illusionistic rendering of a receding sphere floating within a void encloses the

22-21 Hieronymus Bosch **GARDEN OF EARTHLY DELIGHTS (CLOSED)**

Credit: © 2916. Photo Scala, Florence

flat circular shelf of Earth on its third day of creation. Fragments of the fantastic fruit that will appear fully formed in the interior pictures float here in the primordial sea, while dark clouds promise the rain that will nurture them into their full ripeness. A tiny, crowned figure of God the Creator hovers in a bubble within clouds at the upper left, displaying a book, perhaps a Bible opened to the words from Psalm 33:9 that are inscribed across the top: "For he spoke, and it came to be; he commanded, and it stood firm."

The *Garden of Earthly Delights* was commissioned by an aristocrat (probably Count Hendrick III of Nassau) for his Brussels town house, and the artist's choice of a triptych format, which suggests an altarpiece, may have been an understated irony. In a private home the painting surely inspired lively discussion, even

ribald commentary, much as it does today in the Prado Museum. Perhaps that, rather than a single meaning, is the true intention behind this dazzling display of artistic imagination.

JAN GOSSAERT   In contrast to the private visions of Bosch, Jan Gossaert (c. 1478–c. 1533) maintained traditional subject matter and embraced the new Classical art of Italy. Gossaert (who later called himself Mabuse after his native city Maubeuge) entered the service of Philip, the illegitimate son of the duke of Burgundy, accompanying him to Italy in 1508 and remaining in his service after Philip became archbishop of Utrecht in 1517.

Gossaert's "Romanizing" style—inspired by Italian Mannerist paintings and decorative details drawn from

22-22 Jan Gossaert **ST. LUKE DRAWING THE VIRGIN MARY**
1520. Oil on panel, 43⅜ × 32¼″ (110.2 × 81.9 cm). Kunsthistorisches Museum, Vienna.

Credit: © akg-images/Erich Lessing

ancient Roman art—is evident in his painting of **ST. LUKE DRAWING THE VIRGIN MARY** (FIG. **22-22**), a traditional subject we already know from a painting by Rogier van der Weyden (SEE FIG. 19-16). In Gossaert's version, the artist's studio is an extraordinary structure of Classical piers and arches, carved with a dense ornament of foliage and medallions. Mary and the Christ Child appear in a blaze of golden light and clouds in front of the saint, who kneels at a desk, his hand guided by an angel as he records the vision in a drawing. Luke's crumpled red robe replicates fifteenth-century drapery conventions in a seeming reference to Rogier's famous picture. Seated above and behind Luke on a columnar structure, Moses holds the Tablets of the Law, referencing his own visions of God on Mount Sinai. Just as Moses had removed his shoes in God's presence, so has Luke in the presence of his vision. Gossaert, like Dürer before him, seems to be staking a claim for the divine inspiration of the artist.

Antwerp

During the sixteenth century, Antwerp was the commercial and artistic center of the southern Netherlands. Its deep port made it an international center of trade (it was one of the European centers for trade in spices), and it was the financial center of Europe. Painting, printmaking, and book production flourished in this environment, attracting artists and craftspeople from all over Europe. The demand for luxury goods fostered the birth of the art market, in which art was transformed into a commodity for both local and international consumption. In response to this market, many artists became specialists in one area, such as portraiture or landscape, and worked with art dealers, who emerged as middlemen, further shaping the commodification of art, its production, and its producers.

QUENTIN MASSYS Early accounts of the prosperous Antwerp artist Quentin Massys (1466–1530) claim that he began working in his native Louvain as a blacksmith (his father's profession) but changed to painting to compete with a rival for the affections of a young woman; Carel van Mander claims he was a self-trained artist. We know he entered the Antwerp painters' guild in 1491, and at his death in 1530 he was among its most prosperous and renowned members, supervising a large workshop to meet the market in this burgeoning art center.

One of his most fascinating paintings—**MONEY CHANGER AND HIS WIFE** (FIG. 22-23)—recalls, like Gossaert's *St. Luke*, a famous fifteenth-century work, in this case the picture of a goldsmith painted for the Antwerp goldsmiths' guild by Petrus Christus (see "Closer Look" in Chapter 19 on page 592). Here, however, a couple is in charge of the business, and they present us with two different profiles of engagement. The soberly dressed proprietor

22-23 Quentin Massys **MONEY CHANGER AND HIS WIFE**
1514. Oil on panel, 27¾ × 26⅜″ (70.5 × 67 cm). Musée du Louvre, Paris.

Credit: Photo © RMN-Grand Palais (Musée du Louvre)/Tony Querrec focuses intently on weighing coins. His brightly outfitted wife—dressed in an archaic fifteenth-century costume that harks back to a golden age of Flemish painting—looks to the side, her husband's activity distracting her from the meticulously described Book of Hours spread out on the table in front of her. It would be easy to jump to the conclusion that this is a moral fable, warning of the danger of losing sight (literally) of religious obligations because of a preoccupation with affairs of business. But the painting is not that simple. An inscription that ran around the original frame quoted Leviticus 19:36—"You shall have honest balances and honest weights"—claiming just business practices as a form of righteous living. Perhaps the painting's moral juxtaposes not worldliness and spirituality, but attentive and distracted devotional practice. The wife seems to have been idly flipping through her prayer book before turning to observe her husband, whereas a man reflected in the convex mirror next to her Book of Hours is caught in rapt attention to the book in front of him, and the nature of his reading is suggested by the church steeple through the window behind him. The sermon here concerns the challenge of godly living in a worldly society, but wealth itself is not necessarily the root of the problem.

CATERINA VAN HEMESSEN Antwerp painter Caterina van Hemessen (1528–1587) developed an illustrious reputation as a portraitist. She had learned to paint from her father, the Flemish Mannerist Jan Sanders van Hemessen, who was dean of the Antwerp painters' guild in 1548, but the quiet realism and skilled rendering of her subjects is distinctively her own. To direct viewers' focus to her foreground subjects, Van Hemessen painted them against even, dark-colored backgrounds, on which she identified the sitter by name and age, signing and dating each work. The inscription in her **SELF-PORTRAIT** (**FIG. 22-24**) reads: "I Caterina van Hemessen painted myself in 1548. Her age 20." In delineating her own features, Van Hemessen presented a serious young person who looks up to acknowledge us, interrupting her work on a portrait of a woman client. Between the date of this self-portrait and 1552, she painted ten signed and dated portraits of women, which seems to have been a specialty. She became a favored court artist to Mary of Hungary, sister of Emperor Charles V and regent of the Netherlands, for whom she painted not only portraits but also religious works, and whom she followed back to Spain when Mary ceased to be regent in 1556.

PIETER BRUEGEL THE ELDER The works of Hieronymus Bosch remained so popular that nearly half a century after Bosch's death, Pieter Bruegel (c. 1525–1569) began his career by imitating them. Like Bosch, he often painted large narrative works crowded with figures, and he chose moralizing or satirical subject matters. He traveled throughout Italy,

22-24 Caterina van Hemessen
SELF-PORTRAIT
1548. Oil on wood panel, 12¼ × 9¼" (31.1 × 23.5 cm). Öffentliche Kunstsammlung, Basel.

Credit: Kunstmuseum Basel. Photo: Martin Buhler/ Kunstmuseum Basel

22–25 Pieter Bruegel the Elder **RETURN OF THE HUNTERS**
1565. Oil on wood panel, 3′10½″ × 5′3¾″ (1.18 × 1.61 m). Kunsthistorisches Museum, Vienna.

Credit: © akg-images/Erich Lessing

but, unlike many Renaissance artists, he did not record the ruins of ancient Rome or the wonders of Italian cities. Instead, he was fascinated by the landscape, particularly the formidable, jagged rocks and sweeping panoramic views of Alpine valleys, which he recorded in detailed drawings. Back home in his studio, he made an impressive leap of the imagination as he painted the flat and rolling lands of Flanders as broad panoramas, even adding imaginary mountains on the horizon. He also visited country fairs to sketch the farmers and townspeople who became the focus of his paintings. Bruegel presented humans not as unique individuals, but as well-observed types whose universality makes them familiar even today.

Cycles, or series, of paintings unified by a developing theme or allegorical subject—for instance, the Times of the Day, the Four Seasons, or the Five Senses—became popular wall decorations in prosperous Flemish homes during the sixteenth century. In 1565, Bruegel was commissioned to paint a series of six large paintings, each over 5 feet wide, surveying the months of the year, two months to a picture. They were made to be hung together in a room—probably

the dining room, since food figures prominently in them—in the suburban villa of wealthy merchant Nicolaes Jonghelinck just outside Antwerp.

RETURN OF THE HUNTERS (FIG. **22–25**), representing December and January, captures the bleak atmosphere of early winter nightfall with a freshness that recalls the much earlier paintings of his compatriots the Limbourgs (SEE FIG. 19-5). Hunters are returning home at dusk with meager results: a fox slung over the largest man's shoulder. But the landscape, rather than the figures, seems to be the principal subject. On the left, a receding row of trees, consistently diminishing in scale, draws our attention into the space of the painting along the same orthogonal descent as the hillside of houses. Like the calendar illustrations of medieval Books of Hours, the landscape is filled with behavior emblematic of the time of year: the singeing of the pig outside the farmhouse at left, the rhythmic movement of ice skaters across frozen fields. We see it all from an elevated viewpoint, like one of the birds that perch in the trees or glide across the snow-covered fantasy of an alpine background.

The mood is very different in the painting representing the late summer days of August and September, another slice of everyday life faithfully reproduced within a carefully calculated composition (**FIG. 22-26**). Here the light is warmer, the landscape lush, and the human activity rooted in agricultural labor or a momentary respite from it. Birds still perch and glide, and a silhouetted tree still dominates the foreground—as if Bruegel wanted to set up obvious relationships between the scenes so that viewers would assess them comparatively—but the setting here is more rural. Architecture keeps its distance or is screened by foliage. Farm workers harvest grain and gather stalks into tidy sheaves. The figural focus, however, is in the foreground, on a shift of workers on their lunch break—serving themselves from baskets, gnawing on pieces of bread, spooning milk from bowls, or gulping from an uplifted jug. One man takes the opportunity for a quick nap. Some have seen in this figure an emblem of sloth or a display of uncouth behavior, reminiscent of the embarrassing exposure of the peasant couple before the fire in the February page of Duke

Jean de Berry's *Très Riches Heures* (SEE FIG. 19-5), painted by the Netherlandish Limbourg brothers a century and a half earlier.

Indeed, Bruegel's series invites comparison with this venerable tradition—dating to the early Middle Ages—of showing peasant activity within the calendar cycles of prayer books made for wealthy patrons. Perhaps the rich were amused by peasant behavior, enjoyed representations of the productivity of their land, or even longed for a simpler life, idealized here as a harmony between the natural world and the people who live from it. But the peasants in this sunny scene are only on a lunch break. Another shift is already at work in the fields, and the wealth of the patrons who supported the growth of an art market was dependent on the labor of countless others like them.

As a depiction of Netherlandish life, these landscape-focused peasant scenes represent a relative calm before the storm. Three years after they were painted, the anguished struggle of the northern provinces for independence from Spain began.

22-26 Pieter Bruegel the Elder **THE HARVESTERS**
1565. Oil on wood panel, 46⅞ × 63¾" (1.17 × 1.6 m). Metropolitan Museum of Art, New York. Rogers Fund, 1919. (19.164).

A Closer Look

THE FRENCH AMBASSADORS

Embossing on the sheath of the dagger tells us that de Dinteville is 29, while an inscription on the edge of the book (Bible?) under de Selve's arm records that he is 25.

This globe perched on the shelf above the table has Polisy, the de Dinteville family estate, marked at the center. It was here that this painting was hung when the ambassador returned to France at the end of 1533.

These objects on the top shelf were used to observe natural heavenly phenomena and chart the passage of time. The items displayed on the lower shelf relate more to terrestrial concerns.

Music is a common symbol of harmony in this period, and the broken string on this lute has been understood as an allusion to the discord created by the sweep of Protestant reform across Europe.

This bizarre, but prominently placed skull—as well as the skull badge that appears on de Dinteville's cap—reminded viewers of their own mortality. The foreground skull is distorted by anamorphosis, in which images are stretched horizontally with the use of a trapezoidal grid so that they must be viewed from the side to appear correctly proportioned.

This pavement—known as "Cosmati work" after the thirteenth-century Italian family that specialized in it—is copied from the floor in Westminster Abbey and may proclaim the ambassadors' involvement in a holy enterprise of reconciliation. The artist signed the painting on the left edge of the floor: "Johannes Holbein pingebat, 1533."

This is a Lutheran hymnal published in 1527, open at one of Luther's best-known compositions: "Come, Holy Ghost, our souls inspire." Neither man was a Protestant, but some of de Selve's contemporaries saw him as sympathetic to the cause of the reformers.

22–27 Hans Holbein the Younger **THE FRENCH AMBASSADORS**
1533. Oil on wood panel, 81⅛ × 82⅝″ (2.07 × 2.1 m). National Gallery, London.

Credit: © 2016. Copyright The National Gallery, London/Scala, Florence

England

How do painting and architecture reflect the interests of the English Tudor court?

Tudor England, in spite of the disruption caused by the Reformation, was economically and politically stable enough to provide sustained support for the arts, as Henry VIII strived to compete with the wealthy, sophisticated court of Francis I. Music, literature, and architecture flourished, but painting was principally left to foreigners.

As a young man, Henry VIII (ruled 1509–1547) was loyal to the Church, defending it against Luther's attacks. He was rewarded by the pope in 1521 by being granted the title "Defender of the Faith." But when the pope refused to annul his marriage to Catherine of Aragon, Henry broke with Rome. By action of Parliament in 1534 he became the "Supreme Head on Earth of the Church and Clergy of England." He mandated an English translation of the Bible in every church, and in 1536 and 1539 he dissolved the monasteries, confiscating their great wealth and rewarding his followers with monastic lands and buildings. Shrines and altars were stripped of their jewels and precious metals to bolster the royal purse, and in 1548, during the reign of Henry's son, Edward VI, religious images were officially prohibited.

During the brief reign of Mary (ruled 1553–1558), England officially returned to Catholicism, but the accession of Elizabeth in 1558 confirmed England as a Protestant country. So effective was Elizabeth, who ruled until 1603, that the last decades of the sixteenth century in England are called the Elizabethan Age.

Painting at the Tudor Court

A remarkable record of the appearance of Tudor notables survives in portraiture. Since the Tudors had long favored Netherlandish and German artists, it is hardly surprising that it was a German-born painter, Hans Holbein the Younger (c. 1497–1543), who shaped the taste of the English court and upper classes.

HANS HOLBEIN Holbein first visited London from 1526 to 1528 and was introduced by the Dutch scholar Erasmus to the humanist circle around the English statesman Thomas More. He returned to England in 1532 and was appointed court painter to Henry VIII about four years later. During the 1530s, he created a spectacular series of portraits of nobles and diplomats associated with the Tudor court. The court's climate of international interaction is captured in a double portrait that Holbein painted in 1533 (see "Closer Look" on page 719)—a German painter's rendering in England of two French diplomats,

one of them representing the court of Francis I in the Vatican. *The French Ambassadors* foregrounds Holbein's virtuosity as a painter and constructs a rich characterization of Jean de Dinteville, French ambassador to England, and his friend Georges de Selve, bishop of Lavaur and ambassador to the Holy See. With detail that recalls the work of Jan van Eyck, the artist describes the textures and luminosity of the many objects placed in the painting to reflect the intellectual gifts and evoke the political accomplishments of these two men. References in these objects to the conflicts between European states and within the Catholic Church itself imply that these confident young ambassadors will apply their diplomatic skills to finding a resolution.

PORTRAITS OF ELIZABETH Queen Elizabeth I carefully controlled the way artists represented her in official portraits and was known to have imprisoned artists whose unofficial images did not meet with her approval. A stark and hieratic regal image by Flemish artist Marcus Gheeraerts typifies the look she was after (**FIG. 22-28**). Called the *Ditchley Portrait* because it seems to have been commissioned for Ditchley, the estate of her courtier Sir Henry Lee, to commemorate the queen's visit in 1592, the full-length figure of Elizabeth—more costume than body—stands supreme on a map of her realm with her feet in Oxfordshire, near Ditchley. The stark whiteness of her elaborate dress and the pale abstraction of her severe face assert the virginal purity that she cultivated as a part of her image. A storm passes out of the picture on the right while the sun breaks through on the left. It is as if the queen is in control not only of England but of nature itself.

NICHOLAS HILLIARD In 1570, Nicholas Hilliard (1547–1619) arrived in London from southwest England to pursue a career as a jeweler, goldsmith, and painter of miniatures. Hilliard never received a court appointment, but he created miniature portraits of the queen and court notables, including **GEORGE CLIFFORD** (1558–1605), third Earl of Cumberland (**FIG. 22-29**). Cumberland was a regular participant in the annual tilts and festivals celebrating the anniversary of Elizabeth's ascent to the throne. In Hilliard's miniature, Cumberland, a man of about 30, wears a richly engraved and gold-inlaid suit of armor forged for his first appearance in 1583 (see "Armor for Royal Games" on page 722). Hilliard gives him a marked air of courtly jauntiness, with a stylish beard, mustache, and curled hair, but Cumberland is also humanized by his direct gaze and receding hairline. His motto—"I bear lightning and water"—is inscribed on a stormy sky with a lightning bolt in the form of a caduceus, one of his emblems. After all, he was that remarkable Elizabethan type—a naval commander and gentleman pirate.

22–28 Marcus Gheeraerts the Younger **QUEEN ELIZABETH I (THE DITCHLEY PORTRAIT)**

c. 1592. Oil on canvas, 95 × 60″ (2.4 × 1.5 m). National Portrait Gallery, London.

Credit: Photo © Stefano Baldini/Bridgeman Images

22–29 Nicholas Hilliard **GEORGE CLIFFORD, THIRD EARL OF CUMBERLAND**

c. 1595. Watercolor on vellum on card, oval 2¾ × 2³⁄₁₆″ (7.1 × 5.8 cm). The Nelson-Atkins Museum of Art, Kansas City, Missouri. Gift of Mr. and Mrs. John W. Starr through the Starr Foundation. F58-60/188.

Architecture

To increase support for the Tudor dynasty, Henry and his successors granted titles to rich landowners. To display their wealth and status, many of these newly created aristocrats embarked on extensive building projects, constructing lavish country residences that sometimes surpassed the French châteaux in size and grandeur. Rooted in the Perpendicular Gothic style (SEE FIG. 18–23, far wall), Elizabethan architecture's severe walls and broad expanses of glass were modernized by replacing medieval ornament with Classical motifs copied from architectural handbooks and pattern books. The first architectural manual in English, published in 1563, was written by John Shute, one of the few builders who had spent time in Italy. Most influential were the

treatises on architectural design by the Italian architect Sebastiano Serlio.

HARDWICK HALL   One of the grandest of all the Elizabethan houses was Hardwick Hall, the home of Elizabeth, countess of Shrewsbury, known as "Bess of Hardwick" (**FIG. 22–30**). When she was in her seventies, the countess—who inherited riches from all four of her deceased husbands—employed Robert Smythson (c. 1535–1614), England's first Renaissance architect, to build Hardwick Hall (1591–1597).

The medieval great hall was transformed into a two-story entrance hall with rooms arranged symmetrically around it—a nod to Classical balance. A sequence of rooms leads to a grand stair up to the long gallery and **HIGH**

22–30 Robert Smythson
HARDWICK HALL
Derbyshire, England. 1591–1597.

Credit: © Phil MacD Photography/Shutterstock

GREAT CHAMBER on the second floor that featured an ornately carved fireplace (**FIG. 22–32**). It was here the countess received guests, entertained, and sometimes dined. Illuminated by enormous windows, the room seems designed to showcase a precious set of six Brussels tapestries featuring the story of Ulysses. They serve as yet another reminder of the international character of the lavish decoration of residences created for wealthy Renaissance patrons throughout Europe during the sixteenth century.

Art and its Contexts

ARMOR FOR ROYAL GAMES

The medieval tradition of holding tilting, or jousting, competitions at English festivals and public celebrations continued during Renaissance times. Perhaps most famous were the Accession Day Tilts, held annually to celebrate the anniversary of Elizabeth I's coming to the throne. The gentlemen of the court, dressed in armor made especially for the occasion, held mock battles in the queen's honor. They rode their horses from opposite directions, trying to strike each other with long lances during six passes as judges rated their performances.

The elegant armor worn by George Clifford, third Earl of Cumberland, at the Accession Day Tilts has been preserved in the collection of the Metropolitan Museum of Art in New York (**FIG. 22–31**). Tudor roses and back-to-back capital *E*s in honor of the queen decorate the armor's surface. As the queen's champion, beginning in 1590, Clifford also wore her jeweled glove attached to his helmet as he met all comers in the tiltyard of Whitehall Palace in London.

Made by Jacob Halder in the royal armories at Greenwich, the 60-pound suit of armor is recorded in the sixteenth-century Almain Armourers' Album along with its "exchange pieces." These allowed the owner to vary his appearance by changing mitts, side pieces, or leg protectors, and also provided backup pieces if one were damaged.

22–31 Jacob Halder **ARMOR OF GEORGE CLIFFORD, THIRD EARL OF CUMBERLAND**

Made in the royal workshop at Greenwich, England. c. 1580–1583. Steel and gold, height 5′9½″ (1.77 m). Metropolitan Museum of Art, New York. Munsey Fund, 1932 (32.130.6).

Credit: © 2016. Image copyright The Metropolitan Museum of Art/Art Resource/ Scala, Florence

22–32 Robert Smythson **HIGH GREAT CHAMBER, HARDWICK HALL**
Derbyshire, England. 1591–1597. Brussels tapestries 1550s; painted plaster sculpture by Abraham Smith.

Credit: National Trust Photographic Library/Andreas von Einsiedel/Bridgeman Images

Think About It

1   Explore the influence of Italian art and ideas on the work and persona of German artist Albrecht Dürer. Choose one of his works from this chapter and discuss its Italianate features and the ways in which it departs from and draws on earlier Northern European traditions.

2   Discuss the impact of the Protestant Reformation on the visual arts in northern Europe, focusing your discussion on types of subject matter that patrons sought.

3   Choose one European court that employed artists working in a "foreign" tradition from another part of Europe and assess how this internationalism fostered the breaking down of regional and national boundaries in European art. Ground your discussion in the work of specific artists.

4   Choose a work of art from this chapter that displays extraordinary technical skill in more than one medium. How was its virtuosity achieved, and how is that virtuosity highlighted as an important factor in the work's significance?

Crosscurrents

Gossaert's painting of St. Luke drawing the Virgin Mary suggests that he knew Rogier van der Weyden's famous earlier painting of the same subject. Compare these two works, separated in date by almost a century, discussing Gossaert's references to Rogier's painting but also describing the way each of these two artists embodied the style that characterized their particular moment in the history of art. What did these paintings mean for their original audiences?

FIG. 19–16

FIG. 22–22

23-1 Gianlorenzo Bernini **ST. TERESA OF ÁVILA IN ECSTASY**

Cornaro Chapel, church of Santa Maria della Vittoria, Rome. 1645–1652. Marble, height of the group 11′6″ (3.5 m).

Chapter 23

Seventeenth-Century Art in Europe

 ## Learning Objectives

23.a Identify the visual hallmarks of seventeenth-century European art for formal, technical, and expressive qualities.

23.b Interpret the meaning of works of seventeenth-century European art based on their themes, subjects, and symbols.

23.c Relate seventeenth-century European art and artists to their cultural, economic, and political contexts.

23.d Apply the vocabulary and concepts relevant to seventeenth-century European art, artists, and art history.

23.e Interpret a work of seventeenth-century European art using the art historical methods of observation, comparison, and inductive reasoning.

23.f Select visual and textual evidence in various media to support an argument or an interpretation of a work of seventeenth-century European art.

In the church of Santa Maria della Vittoria in Rome, the sixteenth-century Spanish mystic **ST. TERESA OF ÁVILA** (1515–1582, canonized 1622) swoons in ecstasy on a bank of billowing marble clouds (**FIG. 23-1**). A smiling angel tugs at her clothing while balancing an arrow pointed in her direction. Gilded bronze rays of supernatural light descend, even as actual light illuminates the figures from a hidden window above. This dramatic scene, created by Gianlorenzo Bernini (1598–1680) between 1645 and 1652, represents a famous vision described with startling clarity by Teresa, in which an angel pierced her body repeatedly with an arrow, transporting her to a state of ecstatic oneness with God.

The sculpture is an exquisite example of the emotional, theatrical style perfected by Bernini in response to the religious and political climate in Rome during the period of spiritual renewal known as the Counter-Reformation. Many had seen the Protestant Reformation of the previous century as an outgrowth of Renaissance humanism with its emphasis on rationality and independent thinking. In response, the Catholic Church took a reactionary, authoritarian position, supported by the new Society of Jesus founded by Ignatius of Loyola (d. 1556, canonized 1622). In the "spiritual exercises" (1522–1523) initiated by

St. Ignatius, Christians were enjoined to use all their senses to transport themselves emotionally as they imagined the events on which they were meditating. They were to feel the burning fires of hell or the bliss of heaven, the lashing of the whips and the flesh-piercing crown of thorns. Art became an instrument of propaganda and also a means of leading the spectator to a reinvigorated Christian practice and belief.

Of course, the arts had long been used to convince or inspire, but the Catholic Church in the seventeenth century pushed this practice to a new height of effectiveness. To serve the educational and evangelical mission of the revitalized and conservative Church, paintings and sculpture had to depict events and people accurately and clearly, following guidelines established by religious leaders. Throughout Catholic Europe, painters such as Rubens and Caravaggio created brilliant religious art under official Church sponsorship. And although today some viewers find this sculpture of St. Teresa uncomfortably charged with sexuality, the Church approved of the depictions of such sensational and supernatural mystical visions. They helped worshipers achieve the emotional state of religious ecstasy that was a goal of the Counter-Reformation.

"Baroque"

*What are the cultural and historical backgrounds
for the development of European art during the
seventeenth century?*

The intellectual and political forces set in motion by the Renaissance and Reformation of the fifteenth and sixteenth centuries intensified during the seventeenth century. Religious wars continued, although gradually the Protestant forces gained control in the north, where Spain recognized the independence of the Dutch Republic in 1648. Catholicism maintained its primacy in southern Europe, the Holy Roman Empire, and France through the efforts of an energized papacy aided by the new Society of Jesus, also known as the Jesuit Order (**MAP 23-1**). At the same time, scientific advances compelled people to question their

worldview. Of great importance was the growing understanding that the Earth was not the center of the universe, but a planet revolving around the Sun. As rulers' economic strength began to slip away, artists found patrons in the Church and the secular state, as well as in the newly confident and prosperous urban middle classes. What evolved was a style that art historians have called "Baroque." The label may be related to the Italian word *barocco*, a jeweler's term for an irregularly shaped pearl—something beautiful, fascinating, and strange.

Baroque art deliberately evokes intense emotional responses from viewers. Dramatically lit, theatrical compositions often combine several media within a single work as artists highlight their technical virtuosity. But the seventeenth century also saw its own version of Classicism, a more moving and dramatic variant of Renaissance principles featuring idealization based on observation of

MAP 23-1 SEVENTEENTH-CENTURY EUROPE

Protestantism still dominated northern Europe, while in the south Roman Catholicism remained strong after the Counter-Reformation.
The Habsburg Empire was now divided into two parts, under separate rulers.

the material world; balanced (though often asymmetrical) compositions; diagonal movement in space; rich, harmonious colors; and visual references to ancient Greece and Rome. Many seventeenth-century artists sought lifelike depiction of their world in portraiture, **genre paintings** (scenes from everyday life), still life, and religious scenes enacted by ordinary people in ordinary settings. Intense emotional involvement, lifelike renderings, and Classical references may all exist in the same work.

The role of viewers also changed. Italian Renaissance painters and patrons had been fascinated with the visual possibilities of perspective; they treasured an idealism of form and subject that kept viewers at a distance, reflecting intellectually on what they were seeing. Seventeenth-century artists, on the other hand, sought to engage viewers as participants in the work of art and often reached out to incorporate or activate the surrounding environment into the meaning of the work itself. In Catholic countries, representations of horrifying scenes of martyrdom or the passionate spiritual life of mystics sought to inspire viewers to a reinvigorated faith by making them feel what was going on, not simply contemplate it. In Protestant countries, images of communal parades and city views sought to inspire pride in civic accomplishments. Viewers participated in works of art like audiences in a theater—vicariously but completely—as the work of art drew them visually and emotionally into its orbit. The seventeenth-century French critic Roger de Piles (1635–1709) described this exchange when he wrote: "True painting … calls to us; and has so powerful an effect, that we cannot help coming near it, as if it had something to tell us" (Puttfarken, p. 55).

Italy

How is the Baroque style established and developed in Rome?

Seventeenth-century Italy remained a divided land in spite of a common history, language, and geography. The Kingdom of Naples and Sicily was Spanish; the Papal States crossed the center; Venice maintained its independence as a republic; and the north remained divided among small principalities. Churchmen and their families remained powerful patrons of the arts, especially as they sought to use art in revitalizing the Roman Catholic Church. The Council of Trent (concluded 1563) had set guidelines for church art that went against the arcane, worldly, and often lascivious trends exploited by Mannerism. The clergy's call for clarity, simplicity, chaste subject matter, and the ability to rouse a very Catholic piety in the face of Protestant revolt found a response in the fresh approaches to subject matter and style offered by a new generation of artists.

A major goal of the Counter-Reformation was the proper embellishment of churches and their settings. Pope Sixtus V (pontificate 1585–1590) had begun the renewal in Rome by cutting long, straight avenues through the city to link the major pilgrimage churches with one another and with the main gates of Rome. Sixtus also ordered open spaces—piazzas—to be cleared in front of major churches, marking each site with an Egyptian obelisk. In a practical vein, he also reopened one of the ancient aqueducts to stabilize the city's water supply. Unchallengeable power and vast financial resources were required to carry out such an extensive plan of urban renewal and to refashion Rome—parts of which had been neglected since the Middle Ages—once more into the center of spiritual and worldly power.

The Counter-Reformation popes had great wealth, although they eventually nearly bankrupted the Church with their building programs. Sixtus began to renovate the Vatican and its library; he completed the dome of St. Peter's and built splendid palaces. The Renaissance ideal of the central-plan church continued to be used for the shrines of saints, but Counter-Reformation thinking called for churches with long, wide naves to accommodate large congregations assembled to hear inspiring sermons as well as to participate in the Mass. In the sixteenth century, the decoration of new churches had been relatively austere, but seventeenth- and eighteenth-century Catholic taste favored opulent and spectacular visual effects to heighten the emotional involvement of worshipers.

Maderno and Bernini at St. Peter's

Half a century after Michelangelo had returned St. Peter's Basilica to Bramante's original vision of a central-plan building, Pope Paul V Borghese (pontificate 1605–21) commissioned Carlo Maderno (1556–1629) to provide the church with a longitudinal nave and a new façade (**FIG. 23–2**). Construction began in 1607, and everything but the façade bell towers was completed by 1615 (see "St. Peter's Basilica" in Chapter 21 on page 687). Rooted in the design of Il Gesù's façade (SEE FIG. 21–48A), Maderno's façade for St. Peter's steps forward in three progressively projecting planes: from the corners to the doorways flanking the central entrance area, then the entrance area, then the central doorway itself. Similarly, the colossal orders connecting the first and second stories are flat pilasters at the corners but fully round columns where they flank the doorways. These columns support a continuous entablature that also steps out—following the columns—as it moves toward the central door.

When Maderno died in 1629, Gianlorenzo Bernini (1598–1680), his collaborator of five years, succeeded him as Vatican architect. Bernini was taught by his father, and part of his training involved sketching the Vatican collection of ancient sculpture, such as *Laocoön and His Sons* (SEE FIG. 5–65), as well as the many examples of Renaissance painting in the papal palace. Throughout his life, Bernini

23-2 Carlo Maderno and Gianlorenzo Bernini **ST. PETER'S BASILICA AND PIAZZA, VATICAN, ROME**
Maderno, façade, 1607–1626; Bernini, piazza design, c. 1656–1657.

Perhaps only a Baroque artist of Bernini's talents could have unified the many artistic periods and styles that come together in St. Peter's Basilica (starting with Bramante's original design for the building in the sixteenth century). The basilica in no way suggests a piecing together of parts made by different builders at different times but rather presents itself as a triumphal unity of all the parts in one coherent whole.

admired antique art and, like other artists of this period, considered himself a Classicist. Today, we not only appreciate his strong debt to the Renaissance tradition but also acknowledge the way he broke through that tradition to develop a new, Baroque style.

When Urban VIII was elected pope in 1623, he unhesitatingly gave the young Bernini the daunting task of designing an enormous bronze *baldacchino*, or canopy, over the high altar of St. Peter's. The church was so large that a dramatic focus on the altar was essential. The resulting **BALDACCHINO (FIG. 23-3)**, completed in 1633, stands almost 100 feet high and exemplifies the Baroque objective to create multimedia works—combining architecture, sculpture, and sometimes painting as well—that defy simple categorization. The gigantic corner columns symbolize the union of Christianity and its Jewish tradition; the vine of the Eucharist climbs the twisted columns associated with the Temple of Solomon. They support an entablature

with a crowning element topped with an orb (a sphere representing the universe) and a cross (symbolizing the reign of Christ). Figures of angels and *putti* decorate the entablature, which is hung with tasseled panels in imitation of a cloth canopy. This imposing work not only marks the site of the tomb of St. Peter, but also serves as a tribute to Urban VIII and his family, the Barberini, whose emblems are prominently displayed—honeybees and suns on the tasseled panels and laurel leaves on the climbing vines.

Between 1627 and 1641, Bernini and several other sculptors, again in multimedia extravaganzas, rebuilt Bramante's crossing piers as giant reliquaries. Statues of SS. Helena, Veronica, Andrew, and Longinus stand in niches below alcoves containing their relics to the left and right of the *baldacchino*. Visible through the *baldacchino*'s columns in the apse of the church is another reliquary: the Chair of Peter, a gilded-stone, bronze, and stucco shrine made by Bernini between 1657 and 1666 for the ancient

23-3 Gianlorenzo Bernini **BALDACCHINO**

St. Peter's Basilica, Vatican, Rome. 1624–1633. Gilt bronze, height approx. 100′ (30.48 m). Chair of Peter shrine, 1657–1666; gilt bronze, marble, stucco, and glass. Pier decorations, 1627–1641; gilt bronze and marble.

Credit: © akg-images/Bildarchiv Monheim

wooden throne thought to have belonged to St. Peter as the first bishop of Rome. It symbolized the direct descent of Christian authority from Peter to the current pope, a belief rejected by Protestants and therefore deliberately emphasized in Counter-Reformation Catholicism. Above the shrine, a brilliant stained-glass window portrays the Holy Spirit as a dove surrounded by an oval of golden rays. Gilded angels and gilt-bronze rays fan out around the window and seem to extend the penetration of the natural light—and the Holy Spirit—into the apse of the church. The gilding also reflects the light back to the window itself, creating a dazzling, ethereal effect that the seventeenth century, with its interest in mystics and visions, would see as the activation of divinity.

At approximately the same time that he was at work on the Chair of Peter, Bernini designed and supervised the building of a colonnade to form a huge double piazza in front of the entrance to St. Peter's (SEE FIG. 23-2). The open space that he had to work with was irregular, and an Egyptian obelisk and a fountain previously installed by Sixtus V had to be incorporated into the overall plan. Bernini's remarkable design frames the oval piazza with two enormous curved porticos, or covered walkways, supported by Tuscan columns. These curved porticos are connected to two straight porticos, which lead up a slight incline to the two ends of the church façade. Bernini characterized his design as the "maternal arms of the church" reaching out to the world. He had intended to build a third section of the colonnade closing the side of the piazza facing the church, so that only after pilgrims had crossed the Tiber River bridge and made their way through narrow streets would they encounter

the enormous open space before the imposing church. This element of surprise would have made the basilica and its setting an even more awe-inspiring vision. The approach today—along the grand avenue of the Via della Conciliazione running from the Tiber to the Basilica—was conceived by Mussolini in 1936 as part of his master plan to transform Rome into a grand fascist capital.

Bernini as Sculptor

Even after Bernini's appointment as Vatican architect in 1629, he was still able to accept outside commissions thanks to his large workshop. In fact, he first became famous as a sculptor, and he continued to create sculpture throughout his career for both the papacy and private clients. He was also a painter and even a playwright—an interest that dovetailed with his genius for dramatic presentation.

Bernini's **DAVID** (**FIG. 23-4**), made for a nephew of Pope Paul V in 1623, introduced a new type of three-dimensional composition that intrudes forcefully into the viewer's space. The young hero bends at the waist and twists far to one side, ready to launch the lethal rock at Goliath. Unlike Donatello's sassy boy (SEE FIG. 20-14) and Verrocchio's poised and proud adolescent (SEE FIG. 20-27)—both already victorious—or Michelangelo's pensive young man contemplating the task ahead (SEE FIG. 21-15), Bernini's more mature David, with his sinewy body, lightly clenched mouth, and straining muscles, is all tension, action, and determination. By creating a twisting figure caught in movement, Bernini incorporates the surrounding space within his composition, implying the presence of an unseen adversary somewhere behind the viewer. Thus, the viewer becomes part of the action, rather than its displaced and dispassionate observer.

23-5 Gianlorenzo Bernini **CORNARO CHAPEL, CHURCH OF SANTA MARIA DELLA VITTORIA, ROME**
1642–1652.

Credit: © Vincenzo Pirozzi, Rome

23-4 Gianlorenzo Bernini **DAVID**
1623. Marble, height 5'7" (1.7 m). Galleria Borghese, Rome.

Credit: © Per concessione del Ministero per i Beni e le Attività Culturali/Archivi Alinari, Firenze

From 1642 until 1652, Bernini worked on the decoration of the funerary chapel of the Venetian cardinal Federigo Cornaro (**FIG. 23-5**) in the Roman church of Santa Maria della Vittoria, designed by Carlo Maderno earlier in the century. The Cornaro family chapel was dedicated to the Spanish saint Teresa of Ávila, canonized only 20 years earlier. Bernini designed it as a rich and theatrical setting for the portrayal of a central event in Teresa's life. He covered the walls with multicolored marble panels and crowned them with a projecting cornice supported by marble pilasters.

In the center of the chapel, framed by columns in the huge oval niche above the altar, is Bernini's marble group *St. Teresa of Ávila in Ecstasy* (SEE FIG. 23-1), which represents an eroticized vision described by the Spanish mystic in which an angel pierced her body repeatedly with an arrow, transporting her to a state of indescribable pain, religious ecstasy, and a sense of oneness with God. St. Teresa and the angel, who seem to float upward, are cut from a heavy mass of solid marble supported on a seemingly drifting pedestal that was fastened by hidden metal bars to the chapel wall. Bernini's skill at capturing the movements and emotions of these figures is matched by his virtuosity in simulating different textures and colors in the pure white marble; the angel's gauzy, clinging draperies seem silken in contrast with Teresa's heavy woolen monastic robe. Bernini effectively used the configuration of the garment's folds to convey the saint's swooning, sensuous body beneath, even though only Teresa's face, hands, and bare feet are actually visible.

Kneeling against what appear to be balconies on both sides of the chapel are marble portrait sculptures of Federigo, his deceased father (a Venetian doge), and six cardinals of the Cornaro family. The figures are informally posed and naturalistically portrayed. Two read from their prayer books, others exclaim at the miracle taking place in the light-infused realm above the altar, and one leans out from his seat, apparently to look at someone entering the chapel—perhaps the viewer, whose space these figures share. Bernini's intent was not to produce a spectacle for its own sake, but to capture a critical, dramatic moment at its emotional and sensual height, and by doing so guide viewers to identify totally with the event—and perhaps be transformed in the process.

Borromini

The intersection of two of the wide, straight avenues created by Pope Sixtus V inspired city planners to add a special emphasis, with fountains marking each of the four corners of the crossing. In 1634, Trinitarian monks decided to build a new church at the site and awarded the commission for San Carlo alle Quattro Fontane (St. Charles at the Four Fountains) to Francesco Borromini (1599–1667). Borromini, a nephew of architect Carlo Maderno, had arrived in Rome in 1619 from northern Italy to enter his uncle's workshop. Later, he worked under Bernini's supervision on the decoration of St. Peter's. Some details of the *baldacchino*, as well as its structural engineering, are now attributed to him, but San Carlo was his first independent commission. Unfinished at Borromini's death, the church was nevertheless completed according to his design.

SAN CARLO ALLE QUATTRO FONTANE stands on a narrow piece of land with one corner cut off to accommodate one of the fountains that give the church its name (**FIG. 23-6**). To fit the irregular site, Borromini created an elongated central-plan interior space with undulating walls. Robust pairs of columns support a massive entablature, over which an oval dome, supported on pendentives,

23-6A Francesco Borromini **FAÇADE OF THE CHURCH OF SAN CARLO ALLE QUATTRO FONTANE**
Rome. 1638–1667.

23-6B Francesco Borromini **PLAN OF THE CHURCH OF SAN CARLO ALLE QUATTRO FONTANE**
Rome. 1638–1667.

23–7 Francesco Borromini **VIEW INTO THE DOME OF THE CHURCH OF SAN CARLO ALLE QUATTRO FONTANE**
Rome. 1638–1667.

Credit: © View Pictures Ltd/Alamy Stock Photo

seems to hover (**FIG. 23–7**). The coffers (inset panels in geometric shapes) filling the interior of the oval dome form an eccentric honeycomb of crosses, elongated hexagons, and octagons. These coffers decrease sharply in size as they approach the apex, or highest point, where the dove of the Holy Spirit hovers in a climax that brings together the geometry used in the chapel: oval, octagon, circle, and—very important—a triangle, symbol of the Trinity as well as of the church's patrons. The dome appears to be shimmering and inflating—almost floating up and away—thanks to light sources placed in the lower coffers and the lantern.

It is difficult today to appreciate how audacious Borromini's design for this small church was. He abandoned the modular, additive system of planning taken for granted by every architect since Brunelleschi. He worked instead from an overriding geometrical scheme, as a Gothic architect

might, subdividing modular units to obtain more complex, rational shapes. For example, the elongated, octagonal plan of San Carlo is composed of two triangles set base to base along the short axis of the plan (**SEE FIG. 23–6B**). This diamond shape is then subdivided into secondary triangular units made by calculating the distances between what will become the concave centers of the four major and five minor niches. Yet Borromini's conception of the whole is not medieval. The chapel is dominated horizontally by a Classical entablature that breaks any surge upward toward the dome. Borromini's treatment of the architectural elements as if they were malleable was also unprecedented. His contemporaries understood immediately what an extraordinary innovation the church represented; the Trinitarian monks who had commissioned it received requests for plans from visitors from all over Europe. Although Borromini's innovative work had little impact on the architecture of Classically minded Rome, it was widely imitated in northern Italy and beyond the Alps.

Borromini's design for San Carlo's façade (**SEE FIG. 23–6A**), executed more than two decades later, was as innovative as his planning of the interior. He turned the building's front into an undulating, sculpture-filled screen punctuated with large columns and deep concave and convex niches that create dramatic effects of light and shadow. He also gave his façade a strong vertical thrust in the center by placing over the tall doorway a statue-filled niche, then a windowed niche covered with a canopy, then a giant, forward-leaning cartouche held up by angels carved in such high relief that they appear to hover in front of the wall. The entire composition is crowned with a balustrade broken by the sharply pointed frame of the cartouche. As with the design of the building itself, Borromini's façade was enthusiastically imitated in northern Italy and especially in northern and eastern Europe.

Painting

Painting in seventeenth-century Italy followed one of two principal paths: the ordered Classicism of the Carracci family or the dramatic naturalism of Caravaggio. Although the leading exponents of these paths were northern Italians—the Carracci were from Bologna, and Caravaggio was born in or near Milan—they were all eventually drawn to Rome, the center of power and patronage. All, too, were schooled in northern Italian Renaissance traditions, with its emphasis on *chiaroscuro*, as well as in Venetian color and *sfumato*. However, the Carracci quite consciously rejected the artifice of the Mannerist style and fused their northern roots with the central Italian High Renaissance insistence on line (*disegno*), compositional structure, and figural solidity. They looked to Raphael, Michelangelo, and antique Classical sculpture for their ideal figural types and their expressive but decorous compositions. Caravaggio, on the other hand, satisfied the Baroque demand for drama and clarity by developing realism in a powerful new direction. He painted people he saw in the world around him—even the lowlife of Rome—and worked directly from models without elaborate drawings and compositional notes. Unlike the Carracci, he claimed to ignore the influence of the great masters so as to focus steadfastly on a sense of immediacy and invention.

THE CARRACCI The brothers Agostino (1557–1602) and Annibale (1560–1609) Carracci and their cousin Ludovico (1555–1619) shared a studio in Bologna. As their re-evaluation of the High Renaissance masters attracted interest among their peers, they opened their doors to friends and students and then, in 1582, founded an art academy, where students drew from live models and studied art theory, Renaissance painting, and antique Classical sculpture. The Carracci placed a high value on accurate drawing, complex figure compositions, complicated narratives, and technical expertise in both oil and fresco painting. During its short life, the academy had an impact on the development of the arts and art education through its insistence on both life drawing (to achieve naturalism) and aesthetic theory (to achieve artistic harmony).

In 1595, Annibale was hired by Cardinal Odoardo Farnese to decorate the principal rooms of his family's immense Roman palace. In the long *galleria* (gallery), the artist was requested to paint scenes of love based on Ovid's *Metamorphoses* (**FIG. 23-8**) to celebrate the wedding of Duke Ranuccio Farnese of Parma to the niece of the pope. Undoubtedly, Annibale and Agostino, who assisted him, felt both inspiration and competition from the important collection of antique sculpture exhibited throughout the palace.

The primary image, set in the center of the vault, is *The Triumph of Bacchus and Ariadne*, a joyous procession celebrating the wine god Bacchus's love for Ariadne, whom he rescued after her lover, Theseus, abandoned her on the island of Naxos. Annibale combines the great northern Italian

23-8 Annibale Carracci **CEILING OF GALLERY, PALAZZO FARNESE**

Rome. 1597–1601. Fresco, approx. 68 × 21′ (20.7 × 6.4 m).

Credit: Canali Photobank, Milan, Italy

tradition of ceiling painting—seen in the work of Mantegna and Correggio (SEE FIGS. 20–40, 21–24)—with his study of central Italian Renaissance painters and the Classical heritage of Rome. He organized his complex theme by using illusionistic devices to create multiple levels of reality. Painted imitations of gold-framed easel paintings called *quadri riportati* ("transported paintings") appear to rest on the actual cornice of the vault and overlap painted bronze medallions that are flanked, in turn, by realistically colored *ignudi*, dramatically lit from below. The viewer is invited to compare the warm flesh tones of these youths and their lifelike poses with the more idealized painted bodies in the framed scenes next to them. Above, paintings of stucco-colored sculptures of herms (plain shafts topped by human torsos) twist and turn as they support the painted framework of the vault, exposing a variety of feelings with their expressions and seemingly communicating with one another. Many of Annibale's ideas are inspired by motifs in Michelangelo's Sistine Chapel ceiling (SEE FIG. 21–17). The figure types, true to their source, are heroic, muscular, and drawn with precise anatomical accuracy. But instead of Michelangelo's cool illumination and intellectual detachment, the Carracci ceiling glows with a warm light that recalls the work of the Venetian painters Titian and Veronese and seems buoyant with optimism and lively engagement.

The ceiling was highly admired, famous from the moment it was finished. The proud Farnese family generously allowed young artists to sketch the figures there, so that Carracci's masterpiece influenced Italian art well into the following century.

CARAVAGGIO Michelangelo Merisi (1571–1610), known as "Caravaggio" after his family's home town in Lombardy, introduced a powerfully frank realism and dramatic, theatrical lighting and gesture to Italian Baroque art.

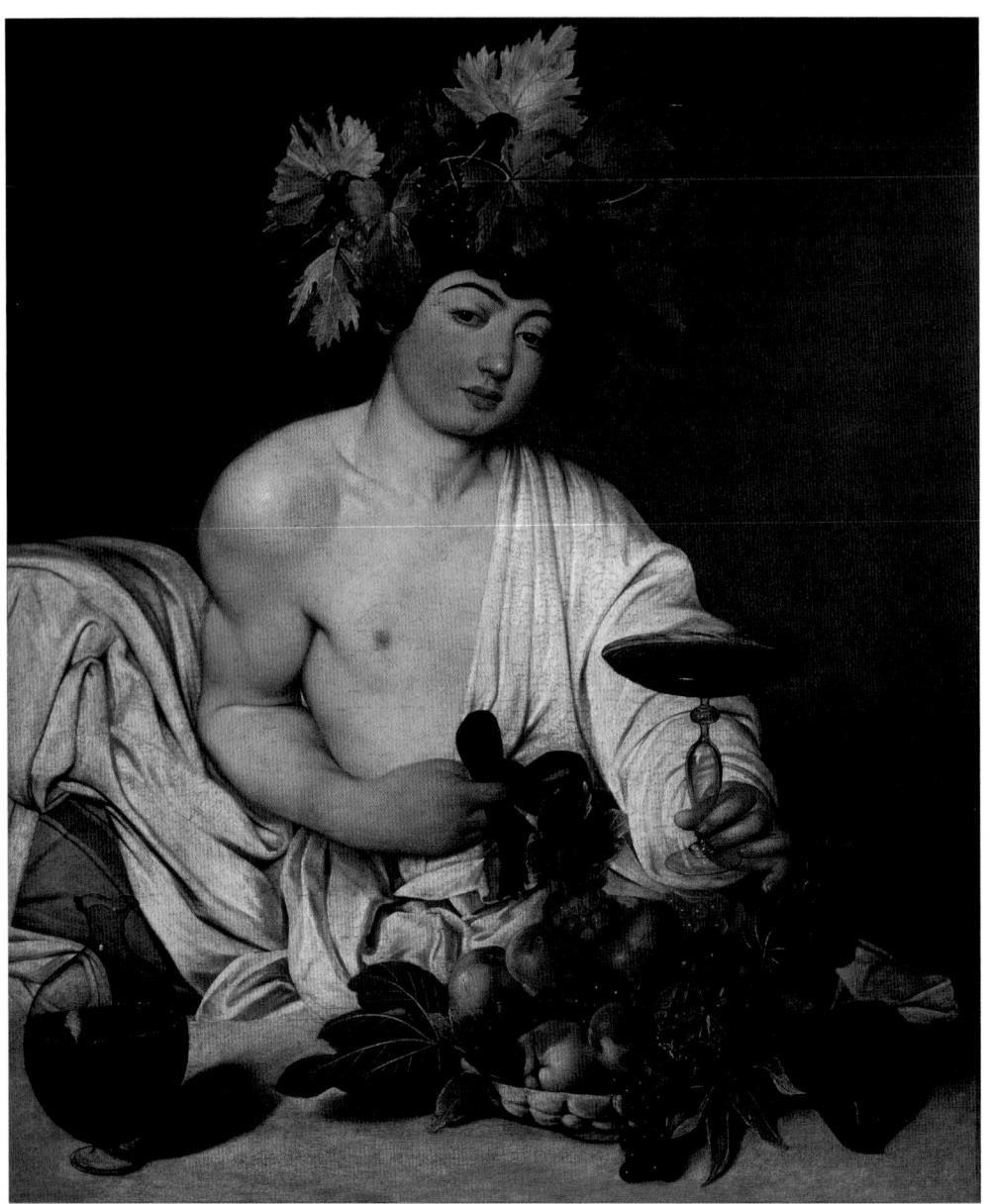

23-9 Caravaggio
BACCHUS
1595–1596. Oil on canvas,
37 × 33½" (94 × 85.1 cm).
Galleria degli Uffizi, Florence.

A restoration of this painting in 2009 revealed in the reflection on the surface of the glass carafe at lower left, a self-portrait of the artist, brush in hand, caught in the process of painting this picture.

Credit: © Quattrone, Florence

The young painter brought an interest, perhaps a specialization, in still-life painting with him when he arrived in Rome from Milan late in 1592 and found studio work as a specialist painter of fruit and vegetables. When he began to work on his own, he continued to paint still lifes, but began to include half-length figures with them. By this time, his reputation had grown to the extent that an agent offered to market his pictures.

Caravaggio painted for a small, sophisticated circle associated with the household of art patron Cardinal del Monte, where the artist was invited to live. His subjects from the 1590s include not only still lifes but also genre scenes featuring fortune-tellers, cardsharps, and glamorous young men dressed as musicians or mythological figures. The **BACCHUS** of 1595–1596 (**FIG. 23-9**) is among the most polished of these early works. Caravaggio seems to have painted exactly what he saw, reproducing the "farmer's tan" of those parts of this partially dressed youth's skin—hand and face—that have been exposed to the sun, as well as the dirt under his fingernails. The figure himself is strikingly androgynous. Made up with painted lips and smoothly arching eyebrows, he seems to offer the viewer the gorgeous goblet of wine held delicately in his left hand, while fingering the black bow that holds his loose clothing together at the waist. This may be a provocative invitation to an erotic encounter or a young actor outfitted for the role of Bacchus, god of wine—and the juxtaposition of the youth's invitation with a still life of rotting fruit may add a message about the transitory nature of sensual pleasure, either admonishing viewers to avoid sins of the flesh or encouraging them to enjoy life's pleasures while they can. The ambiguity makes the painting even more provocative.

One of Caravaggio's first religious commissions, obtained through the efforts of Cardinal del Monte, was oil paintings to be installed in the Contarelli Chapel in the French community's church of St. Louis (San Luigi dei Francesi) (**FIG. 23-10**).

San Luigi dei Francesi served the French community in Rome, and the building itself was constructed between 1518 and 1589, its completion made possible by the patronage of Catherine de' Medici, queen of France. The chapel Caravaggio decorated was founded in 1565 by Mathieu Cointrel—Matteo Contarelli—a French noble at the papal court who would serve as a financial administrator under Gregory XIII (pontificate 1572–1585). Although earlier artists had been called on to provide paintings for the chapel, it was only after Contarelli's death in 1585 that the executors of his will brought the decoration to completion, hiring Giuseppe Cesare in 1591 to paint the ceiling frescos and Caravaggio in 1599 to provide paintings of scenes from the life of the patron's patron saint: **THE CALLING OF ST. MATTHEW** on the left wall (**FIG. 23-11**) and *The Martyrdom of St. Matthew* on the right (not visible in **FIG. 23-10**), both installed in July 1600.

The subject is conversion, a common Counter-Reformation theme. Jesus calls Levi, the tax collector, to join his apostles (Matthew 9:9; Mark 2:14). Levi—who will become St. Matthew—sits at a table, counting or collecting money, surrounded by elegant young men in plumed hats, velvet doublets, and satin shirts. Nearly hidden behind the back of a beckoning apostle—probably St. Peter—at the right, the gaunt-faced Jesus points dramatically at Levi. An intense raking light enters the painting from upper right, as if it were coming from the chapel's actual window above the altar to spotlight the important features of this darkened scene. Viewers encountering the painting obliquely across the empty space of the chapel interior seem to be witnessing the scene as it is occurring, elevated on a recessed stage opening through the wall before them.

The commissioning document was explicit, requiring the artist to show in *The Calling of St. Matthew* the saint rising from his seat to follow Christ in ministry. But Caravaggio was never very good at following rules. Among the group of smartly dressed Romans who form Matthew's circle of friends seated around the table at the left, no one rises to leave. Art historians have not even been able to agree on which figure is Matthew. Many identify him with the bearded man in the center, interpreting his pointing gesture as a self-referential, questioning response to Jesus's call, as if to say, "Who, me?". But some see Matthew in the figure hunched over the scattered coins at far left, seemingly unmoved by Jesus's presence. In this case, the bearded figure's pointing would question whether this bent-over colleague was the one Jesus sought. The painting is marked by mystery, not by the clarity sought by Counter-Reformation guidelines.

In February 1602, Caravaggio received a second commission for the Contarelli Chapel, this time for a painting over the altar showing St. Matthew accompanied by his angelic symbol and writing his Gospel. It was to be completed within three months, but Caravaggio did not receive payment for the picture until September of that year, and the painting he delivered was rejected. The clergy considered Caravaggio's rendering of the saint unacceptably crude and common, his cross-legged pose uncouth and unnecessarily revealing. The fleshiness of the angel, who sidled cozily up to Matthew, was judged inappropriately risqué. In short, the painting was inconsistent with guidelines for saintly decorum set for artists by the Council of Trent. Caravaggio had to paint a second, more decorous altarpiece for the chapel (seen in **FIG. 23-10**), with a nobler Matthew and a more distant angel. The rejected version was snapped up by Roman collector Vincenzo Giustiniani, who actually paid for the replacement in order to acquire the more sensational original. Unfortunately, this first painting was destroyed in the 1945 bombing of Berlin during World War II.

23–10 CONTARELLI CHAPEL, SAN LUIGI DEI FRANCESI
Rome. Paintings by Caravaggio 1599–1600.

Credit: © 2016. Photo Scala, Florence

a heavenly apparition, only Paul's response to it. There is no clear physical setting, only mysterious darkness. And Paul's experience is personal. Whereas he has been flung from his horse and threatens to tumble into the viewer's own space— arms outstretched and legs akimbo, bathed in a strong spotlight—the horse and groom behind him seem oblivious to Paul's experience. The horse takes up more space in the painting than the saint, and the unsettling position of its lifted foreleg, precariously poised over Paul's sprawled body, adds further tension to an already charged presentation.

Most of Caravaggio's commissions after 1600 were religious, and reactions to them were

The emotional power of Caravaggio's theatrical approach to sacred narrative is nowhere more evident than in his **CONVERSION OF ST. PAUL** for the Cerasi Chapel in Santa Maria del Popolo (**FIG. 23-12**). This is one of two paintings commissioned for this chapel in 1600; the other portrayed the Crucifixion of St. Peter. As with Caravaggio's *St. Matthew* for the Contarelli Chapel, the first pair was rejected when Caravaggio delivered them and later acquired by a private collector. This second version of Paul's conversion is direct and simple. Caravaggio focuses on Paul's internal involvement with a pivotal moment, not its external cause. There is no indication of

mixed. Sometimes patrons rejected his powerful, sometimes brutal, naturalism as unsuitable to the subject's dignity. Critics differed as well. An early critic, the Spaniard Vincente Carducho, wrote in his *Dialogue on Painting* (Madrid, 1633) that Caravaggio was an "omen of the ruin and demise of painting" because he painted "with nothing but nature before him, which he simply copied in his amazing way" (Enggass and Brown, pp. 173–174). Others recognized him as a great innovator who reintroduced realism into art and developed new, dramatic lighting effects. Seventeenth-century art historian Giovanni Bellori described Caravaggio's painting as

... reinforced throughout with bold shadows and a great deal of black to give relief to the forms. He went so far in this manner of working that he never brought his figures out into the daylight, but placed them in the dark brown atmosphere of a closed room, using a high light that descended vertically over the principal parts of the bodies while leaving the remainder in shadow in order to give force through a strong contrast of light and dark.... (Bellori, *Lives of the Painters*, Rome, 1672, in Enggass and Brown, p. 79)

Caravaggio's approach has been compared to the preaching of Filippo Neri (1515–1595), the Counter-Reformation priest and mystic who founded a Roman religious group called the Congregation of the Oratory. Neri, called the Apostle of Rome and later canonized, focused his missionary efforts on ordinary people for whom he strove to make Christian history and doctrine understandable and meaningful. Caravaggio, too, interpreted his religious subjects directly and dramatically, combining intensely observed figures, poses, and expressions with strongly contrasting effects of light and color. His knowledge of

23–11 Caravaggio THE CALLING OF ST. MATTHEW
Contarelli Chapel, church of San Luigi dei Francesi, Rome. 1599–1600. Oil on canvas, 10′7½″ × 11′2″ (3.24 × 3.4 m).
Credit: © Quattrone, Florence

23-12 Caravaggio **THE CONVERSION OF ST. PAUL**

Cerasi Chapel, Santa Maria del Popolo, Rome. c. 1601. Oil on canvas, 7′6″ × 5′8″ (2.3 × 1.75 m).

Credit: © Vincenzo Pirozzi, Rome

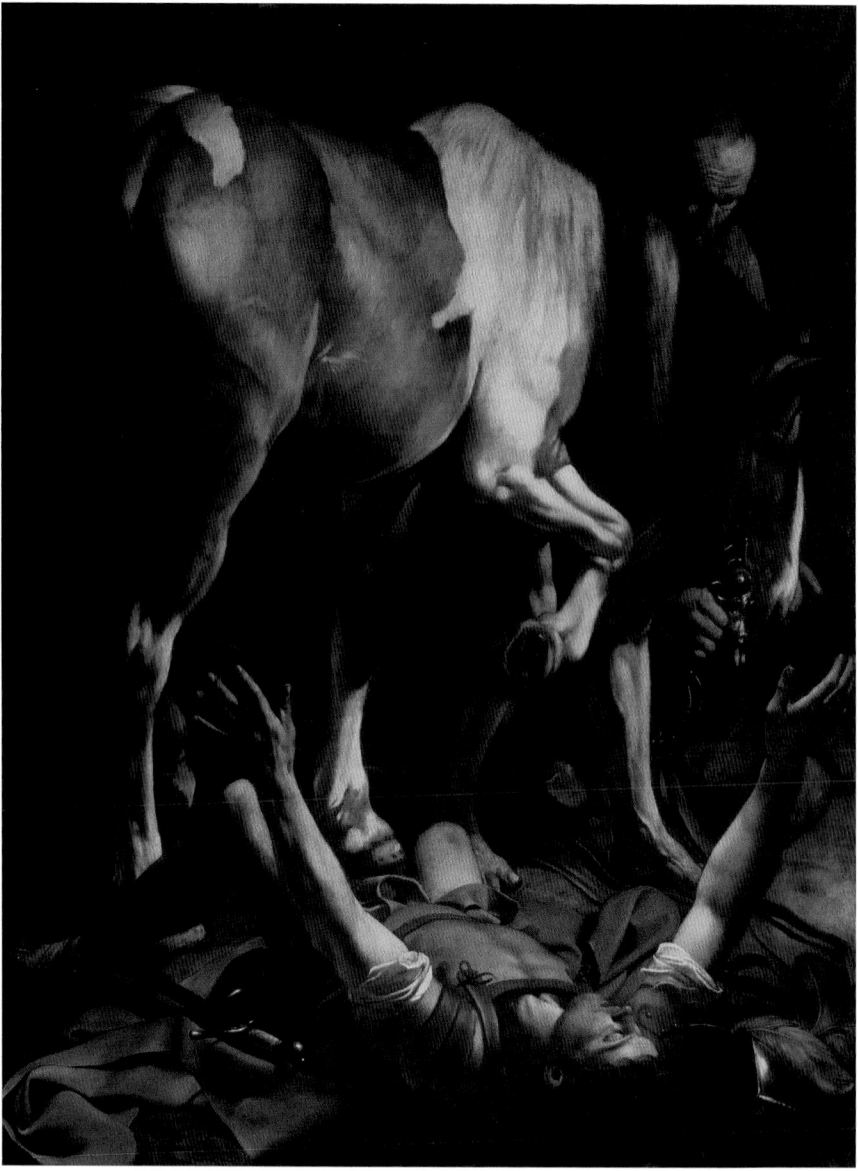

Lombard painting, where the influence of Leonardo was strong, must have facilitated his development of the technique now known as **tenebrism**, in which forms emerge from a dark background into a strong light that often falls from a single source outside the painting. The effect is that of a theatrical spotlight.

Despite the great esteem in which Caravaggio was held by some, especially the younger generation of artists, his violent temper repeatedly got him into trouble. During the last decade of his life, he was frequently arrested, initially for minor offenses such as carrying arms illegally or street brawling. But in May of 1606 he killed a man in a duel fought over a disputed tennis match and had to flee Rome as a fugitive under a death sentence. He supported himself while on the run by painting in Naples, Malta, and Sicily. The Knights of Malta awarded him the cross of their religious and military order in July 1608, but in October he was imprisoned for insulting one of them, and again he escaped and fled. Caravaggio died on July 18, 1610, just short of his 39th birthday, of a fever contracted during a journey back to Rome, where he had expected to be pardoned of his capital offense. Caravaggio's realism and tenebrism influenced nearly every important European artist of the seventeenth century.

ARTEMISIA GENTILESCHI One of Caravaggio's most brilliant Italian followers was Artemisia Gentileschi (1593– c. 1652/1653), whose international reputation helped spread the Caravaggesque style beyond Rome. Gentileschi first studied and worked under her father, Orazio, one of the earliest followers of Caravaggio. In 1616 she moved from Rome to Florence, where she worked for Grand Duke Cosimo II de' Medici and was elected, at the age of 23, to the Florentine Academy of Design.

One of her most famous paintings, a clear example of her debt to Caravaggio's tenebrism and naturalism, is

JUDITH BEHEADING HOLOFERNES (**FIG. 23-13**), which she gave to Cosimo II shortly before she left Florence to return to Rome in 1620. The subject is drawn from the biblical book of Judith, which recounts the story of the destructive invasion of Judah by the Assyrian general Holofernes, when the brave Jewish widow Judith risked her life to save her people. Using her charm to gain Holofernes's trust, Judith enters his tent with her maidservant while he is drunk and beheads him with his own sword. Gentileschi emphasizes the grisly facts of this heroic act, as the women struggle to subdue Holofernes while blood spurts from the severing of his jugular. Dramatic spotlighting and a convergence of compositional diagonals rivet our attention on the most sensational aspects of the scene, which have been pushed toward us in the foreground. Throughout her life, Gentileschi painted many such images of heroic biblical women, which art historians have interpreted in relation to her own struggle to claim her rightful place in an art world dominated by men.

CORTONA AND GAULLI: BAROQUE CEILINGS Theatricality, intricacy, and the opening of space reached an apogee in Baroque ceiling decoration—complex constructions combining architecture, painting, and stucco sculpture. These grand, illusionistic projects were carried out in the domes and vaults of churches, civic buildings, palaces, and villas, and went far beyond even Michelangelo's Sistine Chapel ceiling (SEE FIG. 21–17) or Correggio's dome at Parma (SEE FIG. 21–24). Baroque ceiling painters sought the drama of an immeasurable heaven that extended into vertiginous zones far beyond the limits of High Renaissance taste. To achieve this, they employed the system of *quadratura* (literally, "squaring" or "gridwork"): an architectural setting painted in meticulous perspective and usually requiring viewing from a specific spot to achieve the desired effect of soaring space. The resulting viewpoint is called *di sotto in sù* ("from below upwards"), which we first saw, in a limited fashion, in Mantegna's ceiling in Mantua (SEE FIG. 20–40). Because it required such careful calculation, figure painters usually had specialists in *quadratura* paint the architectural frame for them.

Pietro Berrettini (1596–1669), called "Pietro da Cortona" after his hometown, carried the development of the Baroque ceiling away from Classicism into a more strongly unified and illusionistic direction. Trained in Florence and inspired by Veronese's ceiling in the Doge's Palace, which he saw on a trip to Venice in 1637, the artist was commissioned in the early 1630s by the Barberini family of Pope Urban VIII to decorate the ceiling of the audience hall of their Roman palace.

Pietro da Cortona's great fresco **THE GLORIFICATION OF THE PAPACY OF URBAN VIII** became a model for a

23–13 Artemisia Gentileschi **JUDITH BEHEADING HOLOFERNES**

c. 1619–20. Oil on canvas, 6′6⅜″ × 5′4″ (1.99 × 1.63 m). Galleria degli Uffizi, Florence.

with deep shadows, fuses the ceiling into a dense but unified whole.

The subject is an elaborate allegory of the virtues of the pope. Just below the center of the vault, seated at the top of a pyramid of clouds and figures personifying Time and the Fates, Divine Providence (in gold against an open sky) gestures toward three giant bees surrounded by a huge laurel wreath (both Barberini emblems) carried by Faith, Hope, and Charity. Immortality offers a crown of stars, while other figures present the crossed keys and the triple-tiered crown of the papacy. Around these figures are scenes of Roman gods and goddesses, who demonstrate the pope's wisdom and virtue by triumphing over the vices. So complex was the imagery that a guide gave visitors an explanation, and one member of the household published a pamphlet explaining the painting that is still in use today.

The most spectacular of all illusionistic Baroque ceilings is Giovanni Battista Gaulli's **THE TRIUMPH OF THE NAME OF JESUS AND FALL OF THE DAMNED** (**FIG. 23–15**), which fills the vault of the Jesuit church Il Gesù (SEE FIG. 21–48A). In the 1560s, Giacomo da Vignola had designed an austere interior for Il Gesù, but when the Jesuits renovated their church a century later, they commissioned a religious allegory to cover the nave's plain ceiling. Gaulli (1639–1709) designed and executed the spectacular illusion between 1672 and 1685, fusing sculpture and painting to eliminate any appearance of architectural division. It is difficult to sort carved three-dimensional figures from the painted imitations, and some paintings are on real panels that extend over the actual architectural frame. Gaulli, who arrived in Rome from Genoa in 1657, had worked in his youth for Bernini, from whom he absorbed a taste for drama and multimedia effects. The elderly Bernini, who worshiped daily at Il Gesù, may well have offered his personal advice to his former assistant, and Gaulli was certainly familiar with other

succession of Baroque illusionistic palace ceilings throughout Europe (**FIG. 23–14**). He structured his mythological scenes around a vaultlike skeleton of architecture painted in *quadratura* that appears to be attached to the actual cornice of the room. But in contrast to Annibale Carracci's neat separations and careful *quadro riportato* framing (SEE FIG. 23–8), Pietro's figures weave in and out of their setting in active and complex profusion; some rest on the actual cornice, while others float weightlessly against the sky. Instead of Annibale's warm, nearly even light, Pietro's dramatic illumination, with its bursts of brilliance alternating illusionistic paintings in Rome as well, including Pietro da Cortona's Barberini ceiling (SEE FIG. 23–14).

Gaulli's astonishing creation went beyond anything that had preceded it in unifying architecture, sculpture, and painting. Every element is dedicated to creating the illusion that clouds and angels have descended through an opening in the top of the church into the upper reaches of the nave. The extremely foreshortened figures are projected as if seen from below, and the whole composition is focused off-center on the golden aura around the letters IHS, the monogram of Jesus and the insignia of the Jesuits. The subject is the Last Judgment, with the elect rising toward the name of God and the damned plummeting through the ceiling toward the nave floor. The sweeping extension of the work into the nave space, the powerful appeal to the viewer's emotions, and the near-total unity of the multimedia visual effect—all hallmarks of Italian Baroque—were never surpassed.

23–15 Giovanni Battista Gaulli **THE TRIUMPH OF THE NAME OF JESUS AND FALL OF THE DAMNED**

Vault of the church of Il Gesù, Rome. 1672–1685. Fresco with stucco figures.

Credit: © Vincenzo Pirozzi, Rome

Spain

What constitutes the "Golden Age" of painting in Spain?

When the Holy Roman Emperor Charles V abdicated in 1556, he left the Holy Roman Empire (Germany and Austria) to his brother Ferdinand, while Spain and its American colonies, as well as the Netherlands, Burgundy, Milan, and the Kingdom of Naples and Sicily, went to his son Philip II. Ferdinand and the Habsburg emperors who succeeded him ruled their territories from Vienna in Austria, but much of German-speaking Europe remained divided into small units in which local rulers decided on the religion of their territory. Catholicism prevailed in southern and western Germany and in Austria, while the north was Lutheran.

The Spanish Habsburg kings Philip III (ruled 1598–1621), Philip IV (ruled 1621–1665), and Charles II (ruled 1665–1700) reigned over a weakening empire. After repeated local rebellions, Portugal re-established its independence in 1640. The Kingdom of Naples remained in a constant state of unrest. After 80 years of war, the Protestant northern Netherlands—which had formed the United Provinces—gained independence in 1648. Amsterdam grew into one of the wealthiest cities in Europe, and the Dutch Republic became an increasingly serious threat to Spanish trade and colonial possessions. The Catholic southern Netherlands (Flanders) remained under Spanish and then Austrian Habsburg rule.

What had seemed an endless flow of gold and silver from the Americas to Spain diminished, as precious-metal production in Bolivia and Mexico lessened. Agriculture, industry, and trade at home also suffered. As the Spanish kings tried to defend the Roman Catholic Church and their empire on all fronts, they squandered their resources and finally went bankrupt in 1692. Nevertheless, despite the decline of the Habsburgs' Spanish empire, seventeenth-century writers and artists produced some of the greatest Spanish literature and art, and the century is often called the Spanish Golden Age.

Painting in Spain's Golden Age

The primary influence on Spanish painting in the fifteenth century had been the art of Flanders; in the sixteenth, it had been the art of Florence and Rome. Seventeenth-century Spanish painting, profoundly influenced by Caravaggio, was characterized by an ecstatic religiosity, as well as realistic surface detail that emerges from the deep shadows of tenebrism.

JUAN SÁNCHEZ COTÁN   Late in the sixteenth century, Spanish artists developed a significant interest in paintings of artfully arranged objects rendered with intense attention to detail. Juan Sánchez Cotán (1561–1627) was one of the earliest painters of these pure still lifes in Spain. In **STILL LIFE WITH QUINCE, CABBAGE, MELON, AND CUCUMBER** (**FIG. 23-16**), of about 1602, he contrasts the irregular, curved shapes of the fruits and vegetables with the angular geometry of their setting. His precisely ordered subjects—two of which are suspended from strings—form a long, sagging arc from the upper left to the lower right. The fruits and vegetables appear within a *cantarero* (primitive pantry), but it is unclear why they have been arranged in this way. Set in a strong light against impenetrable darkness, this highly artificial arrangement of strikingly lifelike forms suggests not only a fascination with spatial ambiguity, but also a contemplative sensibility and interest in the qualities of objects that look forward to the work of Zurbarán and Velázquez.

JUSEPE DE RIBERA   Jusepe (or José) de Ribera (c. 1591–1652) was born in Seville but studied in Rome and settled in Spanish-ruled Naples; in Italy, he was known as "Lo Spagnoletto" ("the Little Spaniard"). He combined the Classical and Caravaggesque styles he had learned in Rome to create a new Neapolitan—and eventually

23-16 Juan Sánchez Cotán **STILL LIFE WITH QUINCE, CABBAGE, MELON, AND CUCUMBER**

c. 1602. Oil on canvas, 27⅛ × 33¼" (68.8 × 84.4 cm). San Diego Museum of Art.
Gift of Anne R. and Amy Putnam.

Credit: © akg-images/De Agostini Picture Lib.

23–17 Jusepe de Ribera **MARTYRDOM OF ST. BARTHOLOMEW**

1634. Oil on canvas, 41¼ × 44⅞″ (1.05 × 1.14 m). National Gallery of Art, Washington, DC. Rosenwald Collection (1950.14.744).

Credit: Image courtesy the National Gallery of Art, Washington

realistic faces with the dramatic light of tenebrism and describes the aging, wrinkled flesh in great detail. The compression of the figures into the foreground space heightens our sense of being witness to this scene (SEE FIG. 23–12).

FRANCISCO DE ZURBARÁN Francisco de Zurbarán (1598–1664) represents another martyrdom, in this case already accomplished, in his 1628 painting of **ST. SERAPION** (FIG. 23–18). Little is known of Zurbarán's early years before 1625, but he came under the influence of the Caravaggesque taste prevalent in Seville, the

Spanish—style. Ribera became the link extending from Caravaggio in Italy to the Spanish masters Zurbarán and Velázquez.

During this period, the Church—aiming to draw people back to Catholicism—commissioned portrayals of heroic martyrs who had endured shocking torments as witness to their faith. Ribera's painting of the **MARTYRDOM OF ST. BARTHOLOMEW** (the apostle who was martyred by being skinned alive) captures the horror of the violence to come while emphasizing the saint's spirituality and acceptance (FIG. 23–17). The bound Bartholomew looks heavenward as his executioner tests the sharpness of the knife that he will soon use on his victim. Ribera has learned the lessons of Caravaggio well, as he highlights the intensely

23–18 Francisco de Zurbarán **ST. SERAPION**

1628. Oil on canvas, 47½ × 40¾″ (120.7 × 103.5 cm). Wadsworth Atheneum, Hartford, Connecticut. Ella Gallup Sumner and Mary Catlin Sumner Collection Fund.

Credit: Wadsworth Atheneum, Photo: Allen Phillips

major city in southwestern Spain, while his interest in abstract design has been traced to the heritage of Islamic art in Spain.

Zurbarán primarily worked for the monastic orders. In this painting, he portrays the martyrdom of Serapion, a member of the thirteenth-century Mercedarians, a Spanish order founded to rescue the Christian prisoners of the Moors. Following the vows of his order, Serapion sacrificed himself in exchange for Christian captives. The dead man's pallor, his rough hands, and the coarse ropes contrast with the off-white of his creased habit, its folds arranged in a pattern of highlights and varying depths of shadow. The only colors are the red and gold of the insignia. This timelessly immobile composition is like a tragic still life, a study of fabric and flesh become inanimate.

VELÁZQUEZ AND MURILLO   Diego Rodríguez de Silva y Velázquez (1599–1660), the greatest painter to emerge from the Caravaggesque school of Seville, shared Zurbarán's fascination with objects. He entered Seville's painters' guild in 1617. Like Ribera, he began his career as a tenebrist and naturalist. During his early years, he painted scenes set in taverns, markets, and kitchens, and emphasized still lifes of various foods and kitchen utensils. His early **WATER CARRIER OF SEVILLE** (FIG. 23-19) is a study of the surfaces and textures of the splendid ceramic pots that have characterized folk art through the centuries. Velázquez was devoted to studying and sketching from life: The man in the painting was a well-known Sevillian waterseller. Like Sánchez Cotán, Velázquez arranged the elements of his paintings with almost mathematical rigor. The objects and figures allow the artist to exhibit his virtuosity in rendering volumes and contrasting textures in dramatic natural light. Light reflects in different ways off the glazed waterpot at the left and the coarser clay jug in the foreground; it is absorbed by the rough wool and dense velvet of the costumes; it is refracted as it passes through the clear glass held by the man and the waterdrops on the jug's surface.

In 1623, Velázquez moved to Madrid, where he became court painter to the young King Philip IV, a prestigious position that he held until his death in 1660. The opportunity to study paintings in the royal collection, as well as to travel, enabled the development of his distinctive personal style. The Flemish painter Peter Paul Rubens, during a 1628–1629 diplomatic visit to the Spanish court, convinced the king that Velázquez should visit Italy. Velázquez made two trips, the first in 1629–1631 and the second in 1649–1651. He was profoundly influenced by contemporary Italian painting, and on the first trip seems to have taken a special interest in narrative paintings with complex figure compositions.

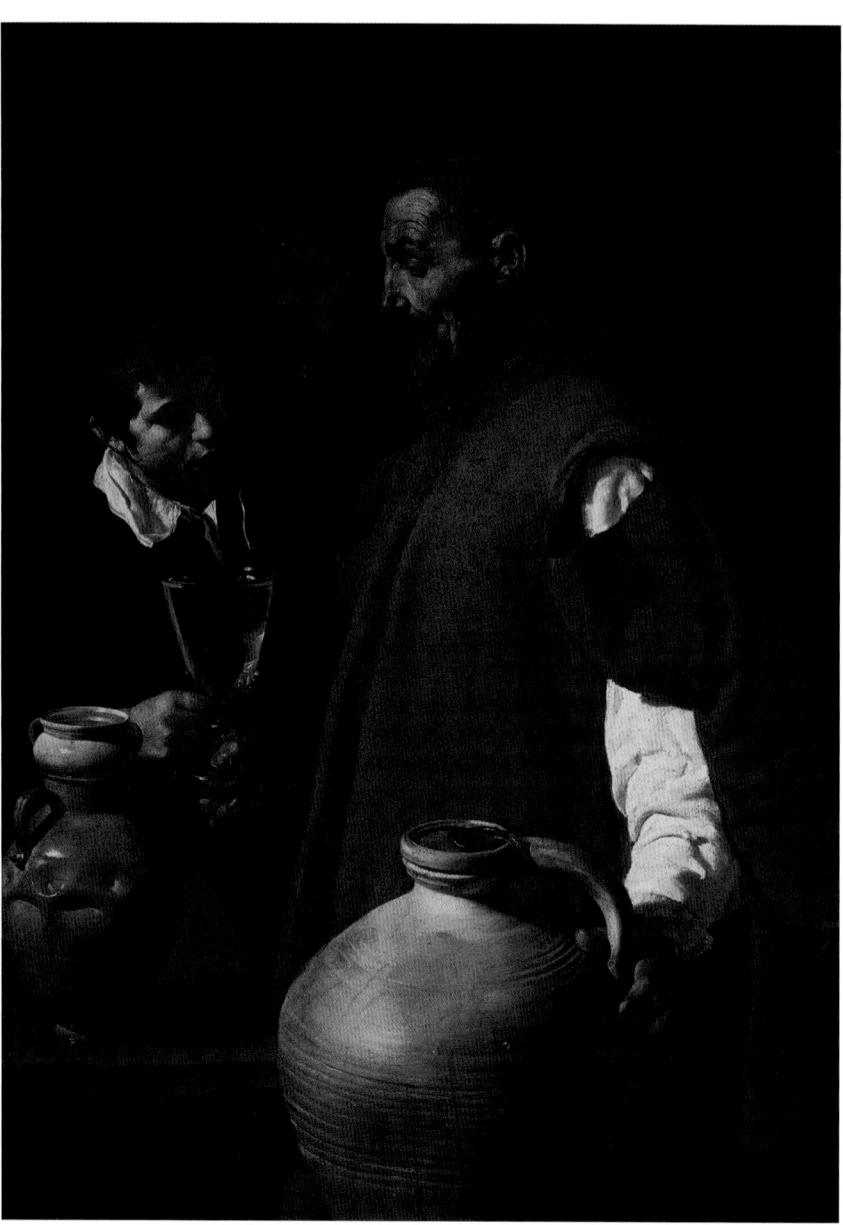

23-19 Diego Velázquez **WATER CARRIER OF SEVILLE**

c. 1619. Oil on canvas, 41½ × 31½″ (105.3 × 80 cm). Victoria & Albert Museum, London.

Credit: V&A Images/Victoria and Albert Museum

23-20 Diego Velázquez **THE SURRENDER AT BREDA (THE LANCES)**
1634–1635. Oil on canvas, 10'⁷⁄₈" × 12'½" (3.07 × 3.67 m). Museo del Prado, Madrid.

Credit: © 2016. Image Copyright Museo Nacional del Prado. © Photo MNP/Scala, Florence

Velázquez's Italian studies and his growing skill in composition are apparent in both figure and landscape paintings. In **THE SURRENDER AT BREDA** (**FIG. 23-20**), painted in 1634–1635, Velázquez treats the theme of triumph and conquest in an entirely new way—far removed from traditional gloating military propaganda. Years earlier, in 1625, Ambrosio Spinola, the duke of Alba and the Spanish governor, had defeated the Dutch at Breda. As Velázquez imagined the scene of surrender, the opposing armies stand on a hilltop overlooking a vast valley where the city of Breda burns and soldiers are still deployed. The Dutch commander, Justin of Nassau, hands over the keys of Breda to the victorious Spanish commander. The entire exchange seems extraordinarily gracious, an emblem of a courtly ideal of gentlemanly conduct. The victors stand at attention, holding their densely packed lances upright in a vertical pattern—giving the painting its popular name, *The Lances*—while the defeated Dutch, a motley group, stand out of order, with pikes and banners drooping.

In fact, according to reports, no keys were involved and the Dutch were more presentable in appearance than the Spaniards. Velázquez has taken liberties with historical fact to create for his Spanish patron a work of art that focuses on the meaning of the surrender, rather than its actual appearance.

Velázquez displays here his compositional virtuosity and his extraordinary gifts as a visual storyteller. A strong diagonal, starting in the sword of the Dutch soldier in the lower left foreground and ending in the checked banner on the upper right, unites the composition and moves the viewer from the defeated to the victorious soldiers in the direction of the surrender itself. Portraitlike faces, meaningful gestures, and controlled color and texture convince us of the reality of the scene. Across the upper half of the huge canvas, the landscape background is startling. Velázquez painted an entirely imaginary Netherlands in greens and blues worked with flowing, liquid brushstrokes. Luminosity is achieved by laying

23–21 Diego Velázquez **LAS MENINAS (THE MAIDS OF HONOR)**
1656. Oil on canvas, 10′5″ × 9′1½″ (3.18 × 2.76 m). Museo del Prado, Madrid.

The cleaning of *Las Meninas* in 1984 revealed much about Velázquez's methods. He used a minimum of underdrawing, building up his forms with layers of loosely applied paint and finishing off the surfaces with dashing highlights in white, lemon yellow, and pale orange. Rather than using light to model volumes in the time-honored manner, Velázquez tried to depict the optical properties of light reflecting from surfaces. On close inspection his forms dissolve into a maze of individual strokes of paint.

Credit: © 2016. Photo Scala, Florence

down a thick layer of lead white and then flowing the layers of color over it. The silvery light forms a background for dramatically silhouetted figures and weapons. Velázquez revealed a breadth and intensity unsurpassed in his century, and became an inspiration to modern artists such as Manet and Picasso.

Velázquez's most enigmatic, and perhaps most striking, work is the enormous multiple portrait known as **LAS MENINAS (THE MAIDS OF HONOR)** (FIG. 23-21), painted in 1656, near the end of his life. Nearly 10½ feet tall and over 9 feet wide, this painting continues to challenge viewers and stimulate debate among art historians. Velázquez draws viewers directly into the scene. In one interpretation, the viewer stands in the very space occupied by King Philip and his queen, whose reflections can be seen in the large mirror on the back wall, perhaps a clever reference to Jan van Eyck's *Double Portrait of Giovanni Arnolfini and his Wife* (SEE FIG. 19-1), which was a part of the Spanish royal collection at this time. Echoing pictorially the claim made in Jan's signature, Velázquez himself is also present, brushes in hand, beside a huge canvas. The central focus, however, is neither the artist nor the royal couple but their brilliantly illuminated 5-year-old daughter, the Infanta (princess) Margarita, who is surrounded by her attendants, most of whom are identifiable portraits.

No consensus exists today on the meaning of this monumental painting. It is a royal portrait; it is also a self-portrait of Velázquez standing at his easel. But fundamentally, *Las Meninas* is a personal statement. Throughout his life, Velázquez had sought respect and acclaim for himself and for the art of painting. Here, dressed as a courtier, the Order of Santiago on his chest (added later) and the keys of the palace tucked into his sash, Velázquez proclaims the dignity and importance of painting itself.

The Madrid of Velázquez was the center of Spanish art. Seville declined after an outbreak of plague in 1649, but it remained a center for trade with the Spanish colonies, where the work of Bartolomé Esteban Murillo (1617–1682) had a profound influence on art and religious iconography. Many patrons wanted images of the Virgin Mary and especially of the Immaculate Conception, the controversial

idea that Mary was born free from original sin. Although the Immaculate Conception became Catholic dogma only in 1854, the concept, as well as devotion to Mary, grew during the seventeenth and eighteenth centuries.

Counter-Reformation authorities had provided specific instructions for artists painting the Virgin of the Immaculate Conception: Mary was to be dressed in blue and white, her hands folded in prayer as she is carried upward by angels, sometimes in large flocks. She may be surrounded by an unearthly light ("clothed in the sun") and may stand on a crescent moon in reference to the woman of the Apocalypse (SEE FIG. 15-14). Angels often carry palms and symbols of the Virgin, such as a mirror, a fountain, roses, and lilies, and they may vanquish the serpent, Satan. The Church exported to the New World many paintings faithful to these orthodox guidelines by Murillo, Zurbarán, and others. When the indigenous population began to visualize the Christian story (SEE FIG. 30-47), paintings such as Murillo's **THE IMMACULATE CONCEPTION** (FIG. 23-22) provided prompts for their imaginings.

23-22 Bartolomé Esteban Murillo
THE IMMACULATE CONCEPTION
c. 1660–1665. Oil on canvas, 81⅛ × 56⅝″ (2.06 × 1.44 m). Museo del Prado, Madrid.

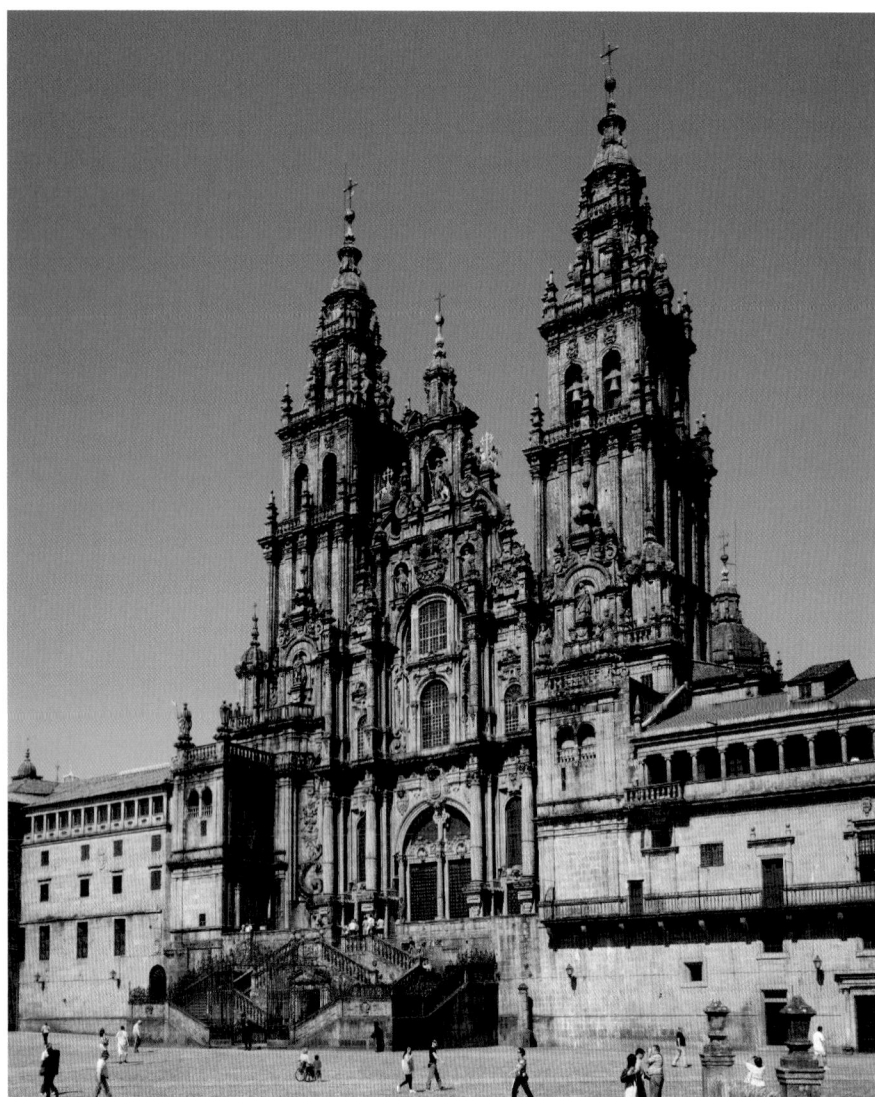

23-23 WEST FAÇADE, CATHEDRAL OF ST. JAMES, SANTIAGO DE COMPOSTELA, SPAIN

South tower 1667–1680; north tower and central block finished mid 18th century by Fernando de Casas y Nóvoas.

Credit: © Bartosz Turek/Shutterstock

Architecture

Turning away from the severity displayed in the sixteenth-century El Escorial monastery-palace (SEE FIG. 22-17), seventeenth-century Spanish architects again embraced the lavish decoration that had characterized their art since the fourteenth century. Profusions of ornament swept back into fashion, first in huge *retablos* (altarpieces), then in portals (main doors often embellished with sculpture), and finally in entire buildings.

THE CATHEDRAL OF SANTIAGO DE COMPOSTELA

In the seventeenth century, the role of St. James as patron saint of Spain was challenged by the supporters of St. Teresa of Ávila and then by supporters of St. Michael, St. Joseph, and other popular saints. It became important to the archbishop and other leaders in Santiago de Compostela, where the Cathedral of St. James was located, to re-establish their primacy. They reinforced their efforts to revitalize the regular flow of pilgrims to the city, undertaken by Spaniards since the ninth century, and used architecture as part of their campaign.

Renewed interest in pilgrimages to the shrines of saints in the seventeenth century brought an influx of pilgrims, and consequently financial security, to the city and the Church. The cathedral chapter ordered an elaborate façade to be added to the twelfth-century pilgrimage church (FIG. 23-23). A south tower was built in 1667–1680 and then later copied as the north tower.

The last man to serve as architect and director of works at the cathedral, Fernando de Casas y Nóvoas (active 1711–1749), tied the disparate elements—towers, portal, stairs—together at the west end in a grand design focused on a veritable wall of glass, popularly called "The Mirror." His design culminates in a free-standing gable soaring above the roof, visually linking the towers and framing a statue of St. James. The extreme simplicity of the cloister walls and the archbishop's palace at each side of the portal heightens the dazzling effect of this enormous expanse of windows, glittering, jewel-like, in their intricately carved granite frame.

Flanders

What new developments in Flemish painting are evident in the workshop of Peter Paul Rubens?

Led by the nobleman Prince William of Orange, the Netherlands' Protestant northern provinces (present-day Holland) began to rebel against Spain in 1568. The seven provinces joined together as the United Provinces in 1579 and began a long struggle for independence, achieved only in the seventeenth century. The king of Spain considered the Dutch heretical rebels, but finally the Dutch prevailed. In 1648, the United Provinces joined emissaries from Spain, the Vatican, the Holy Roman Empire, and France on equal footing in peace negotiations. The resulting Peace of Westphalia officially recognized the independence of the northern Netherlands.

Flanders, the southern—and predominantly Catholic—part of the Netherlands, enjoyed a period of relative autonomy under Habsburg regents starting in 1598, but returned to direct Spanish rule in 1621. Catholic churches were restored and important commissions focused on sacred art. As Antwerp, Flanders' capital city and major arts center, gradually recovered from the turmoil of the religious wars, artists of great talent flourished there. Painters like Peter Paul Rubens and Anthony van Dyck established international reputations that brought them important commissions from foreign as well as local patrons.

Rubens

Peter Paul Rubens (1577–1640), whose painting has become synonymous with Flemish Baroque art, was born in Germany, where his father, a Protestant, had fled from his native Antwerp to escape religious persecution. Rubens's mother returned with her children to Antwerp and

to Catholicism in 1587, after her husband's death. Rubens decided in his late teens to become an artist and at age 21 was accepted into the Antwerp painters' guild, a testament to his energy, intelligence, and skill. Shortly thereafter, in 1600, he left for Italy. In Venice, his work came to the attention of the duke of Mantua, who offered him a court post. Rubens's activities on behalf of the duke over the next eight years did much to prepare him for the rest of his long and successful career. The duke had him copy famous paintings in collections all over Italy to add to the ducal collection.

Rubens visited every major Italian city, went to Madrid as the duke's emissary, and spent two extended periods in Rome, where he studied the great works of Roman antiquity and the Italian Renaissance. While in Italy, Rubens studied the paintings of two contemporaries, Caravaggio and Annibale Carracci. By 1607 Rubens had persuaded the duke of Mantua to buy the former's *Death of the Virgin*

23–24 Peter Paul Rubens
SELF-PORTRAIT WITH ISABELLA BRANDT
1609–1610. Oil on canvas, 5′9″ × 4′5″ (1.78 × 1.36 m). Alte Pinakothek, Munich.

Credit: Photo © Blauel Gnamm/ARTOTHEK

23–25 Peter Paul Rubens **RUBENS'S HOUSE**
Italianate addition built 1610–1615. Looking toward the garden: house at left, studio at right; house restored and opened as a museum in 1946. From an engraving of 1684. Rijksmuseum, Amsterdam.

(c. 1601–1602), which had been rejected by Caravaggio's patrons because of its shocking realism.

In 1608, Rubens returned to Antwerp, where in 1609 he accepted a position as court painter to the Habsburg

regents of Flanders, Archduke Albert and Princess Isabella Clara Eugenia, the daughter of Philip II. Ten days after that appointment, he married the 18-year-old Isabella Brandt (1596–1626), an alliance that was financially beneficial to the artist, then almost twice the age of his bride. He commemorated the marriage with a spectacular double portrait of himself and his bride seated together in front of a honeysuckle bower that evokes a state of marital bliss (**FIG. 23–24**). The self-confident couple looks out to engage viewers directly, and the rich detail of their lavish costumes is described with precision, demonstrating both the artist's virtuosity and the couple's wealth and sophistication. They join right hands in a traditional gesture of marriage,

23–26 Peter Paul Rubens **THE RAISING OF THE CROSS**
Made for the church of St. Walpurga, Antwerp, Belgium. 1610–1611. Oil on panel, center panel 15′1⅞″ × 11′1½″ (4.62 × 3.39 m), each wing 15′1⅞″ × 4′11″ (4.62 × 1.52 m). Now in the Cathedral of Our Lady, Antwerp.

Credit: Onze Lieve Vrouwkerk, Antwerp Cathedral, Belgium/Bridgeman Images

23–27 Peter Paul Rubens **HENRY IV RECEIVING THE PORTRAIT OF MARIE DE' MEDICI**

1621–1625. Oil on canvas, 12′11⅛″ × 9′8⅛″ (3.94 × 2.95 m). Musée du Louvre, Paris.

Credit: Photo © RMN-Grand Palais (Musée du Louvre)/René-Gabriel Ojéda/Thierry Le Mage

Rubens's first major commission in Antwerp was a large canvas triptych for the main altar of the church of St. Walpurga, **THE RAISING OF THE CROSS** (**FIG. 23–26**), painted in 1610–1611. He extended the central action and the landscape through all three panels. At the center, Herculean figures strain to haul upright the wooden cross with Jesus already stretched upon it. At the left, the followers of Jesus join in mourning, and at the right, soldiers supervise the execution. The drama and intense emotion of Caravaggio is merged here with the virtuoso technique of Annibale Carracci, but transformed and reinterpreted according to Rubens's own unique ideal of thematic and formal unity. The heroic nude figures, dramatic lighting effects, dynamic diagonal composition, and intense emotions show his debt to Italian art, but the rich colors and careful description of surface textures reflect his native Flemish tradition.

Rubens's expressive visual language was considered just as appropriate for representing secular rulers as it was for religious subjects. Moreover, his intelligence, courtly manners, and personal charm made him a valuable and trusted courtier to his royal patrons, who included Philip IV of Spain, Queen Marie de' Medici of France, and Charles I of England. In 1621, Marie de' Medici, who had been regent for her son Louis XIII, asked Rubens to paint the story of her life, to glorify her role in ruling France and commemorate the founding of the new Bourbon royal dynasty. In 24 paintings, Rubens portrayed Marie's life and career as one continuous triumph overseen by the ancient gods of Greece and Rome.

In the painting depicting the royal engagement (**FIG. 23–27**), Henry IV immediately falls in love with Marie as he gazes at her portrait, shown to him—at the exact center of the composition—by Cupid and Hymen, the god of marriage. The supreme Roman god Jupiter and his wife Juno look down approvingly from the clouds. A personification of France encourages Henry, outfitted with steel

and the artist slips his foot into the folds of Isabella's flowing red skirt, suggesting a more intimate connection between them. They would have three children before Isabella's untimely death in 1626.

In 1611, Rubens purchased a residence in Antwerp. The original house was large and typically Flemish, but Rubens added a studio in the Italian manner across a courtyard, joining the two buildings by a second-floor gallery over the entrance portal (**FIG. 23–25**). Beyond the courtyard lay the large formal garden, laid out in symmetrical beds. The living room permitted access to a gallery overlooking Rubens's huge studio, a room designed to accommodate large paintings and to house what became virtually a painting factory. The tall, arched windows provided ample light for the single, two-story room, and a large door permitted the assistants to move finished paintings out to their designated owners. Through the gates at one side of the courtyard, one can see the architectural features of the garden.

breastplate and silhouetted against a landscape in which the smoke of a battle lingers in the distance, to abandon war for love, as *putti* play below with the rest of his armor. The ripe colors, lavish textures, and dramatic diagonals give sustained visual excitement to these enormous canvases, making them not only important works of art but also political propaganda of the highest order.

To satisfy his clients all over Europe, Rubens employed dozens of assistants, many of whom were, or became, important painters in their own right. Using workshop assistants was standard practice for a major artist, but Rubens was particularly methodical, training or hiring specialists in costumes, still lifes, landscapes, portraiture, and animal painting who together could complete works from his detailed sketches. Some of his most spectacular paintings were collaborations. Frans Snyders (1579–1657), a specialist in painting animals and flowers, was brought in by Rubens to paint the enormous eagle who devours the liver of the mythical hero in **PROMETHEUS BOUND** (see

"Closer Look" below), begun in 1611–1612 and perhaps worked on as late as 1618. The dramatic lighting, dynamic composition, and loose, energetic brushwork of this painting—which the artist kept for a while in his own personal collection—was clearly Rubens's own, while Snyders's tight and detailed technique sets up within the painting a telling representational contrast between the massive predator and its writhing victim. Among Rubens's other collaborators were his friend and neighbor Jan Brueghel the Elder (1568–1625, son of Pieter Bruegel the Elder, see Chapter 22) and Anthony van Dyck.

Van Dyck and Peeters: Portraits and Still Lifes

Anthony van Dyck (1599–1641) had an illustrious independent career as a portraitist in addition to collaborating with Rubens. Son of an Antwerp silk merchant, he was listed as a pupil of the dean of Antwerp's Guild of St. Luke at age

A Closer Look
PROMETHEUS BOUND

The eagle in this picture was painted by Frans Snyders, a specialist in painting animals and flowers whom Rubens brought in to render the detailed feathers and powerful posture of this bird of prey.

During the seventeenth century, the struggle between Prometheus and the eagle was interpreted allegorically sometimes as the struggle involved in artistic creativity, other times as the heroism involved in enduring suffering of body or soul. Some saw in Prometheus a prototype of the Christ of the Crucifixion, an association furthered here by the placement of the gash on Prometheus's side.

After the main composition was complete, Rubens added this 17½-inch strip of canvas to the left side of the painting to provide more space for the dramatic action, allowing the inclusion at lower left of the fire that got Prometheus into trouble and, on the horizon, the bright light that some have interpreted as a touch of optimism to counteract the punishment in the foreground.

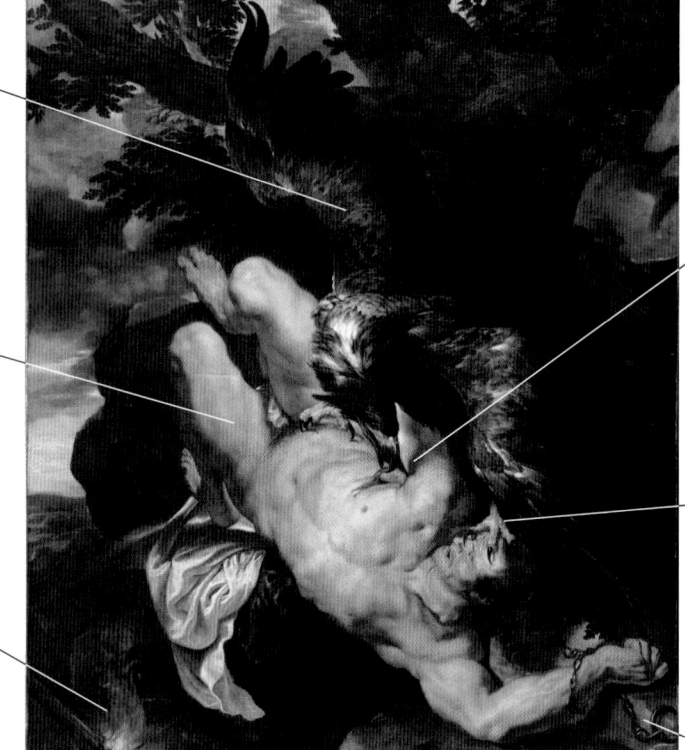

The eagle has pierced Prometheus's side to devour his liver, an action that identifies the subject here. This hero of Greek myth was chained to Mount Caucasus and sentenced to this sensational punishment because, in direct defiance of Zeus's command, he stole fire from Mount Olympus and brought it to earth so humankind would no longer be confined to cold and darkness. Since Prometheus's liver regrew each night, his fate was to have it plucked out again and again, day after day.

The talons of the eagle are poised to dig into the groin and face of the struggling hero to underline for viewers the excruciating nature of his pain.

These small chains that confine Prometheus to the rock seem hardly adequate to confine the powerfully muscular hero, leading some to speculate that the artist wanted his incarceration to seem more psychological than physical.

23-28 Peter Paul Rubens and Frans Snyders **PROMETHEUS BOUND**
c. 1611–1618. Oil on canvas, 95½ × 82½" (2.43 × 2.1 m). Philadelphia Museum of Art.
Credit: © 2016. Photo The Philadelphia Museum of Art/Art Resource/Scala, Florence

23–29 Anthony van Dyck **CHARLES I AT THE HUNT**

1635. Oil on canvas, 8'11" × 6'11" (2.75 × 2.14 m). Musée du Louvre, Paris.

Credit: Photo © Photo RMN (Musee du Louvre, Paris)

to enhance the stature of Henry IV; see FIG. 23-27), Charles, who was in fact very short, appears here taller than his pages and even than his horse, since its head is down and its heavy body is partly off the canvas. The viewer's gaze is diverted from the king's delicate frame to his pleasant features, framed by his jauntily cocked cavalier's hat and the graceful cascade of his hair. As if in polite homage, the tree branches bow gracefully toward him, echoing the curving lines of the hat.

Our use of the term "still life" for paintings of objects on a table comes from the Dutch *stilleven*, a word coined about 1650. The Antwerp artist Clara Peeters (1594– c. 1657) specialized in still lifes (see "Closer Look" in the Introduction on page xxxi). She was a precocious young woman whose career seems to have begun before she was 14. Of some 50 paintings now attributed to her (of which more than 30 are signed), many are of the type called "breakfast pieces," showing a table set for a meal of bread and fruit. Peeters was one of the first artists to combine flowers and food in a single painting, as in her **STILL LIFE WITH FLOWERS, GOBLET, DRIED FRUIT, AND PRETZELS** (**FIG. 23-30**) of 1611. Peeters arranged rich tableware and food against neutral, almost black backgrounds, the better to emphasize the fall of light over the contrasting surface textures. In a display of precious objects that must have appealed to her clients, the luxurious goblet and bowl contrast with simple stoneware and pewter, as do the delicate flowers with the homey pretzels. The pretzels are a particularly interesting Baroque element, with their complex multiple curves.

10. He had his own studio and roster of pupils at age 16 but was not made a member of the guild until 1618, the year after he began his association with Rubens as a specialist in painting heads. The need to blend his work seamlessly with that of Rubens enhanced Van Dyck's technical skill. After a trip to the English court of James I (ruled 1603– 1625) in 1620, Van Dyck traveled to Italy and worked as a portrait painter for seven years before returning to Antwerp. In 1632, he returned to England as the court painter to Charles I (ruled 1625–1649), by whom he was knighted and given a studio, a summer home, and a large salary.

Van Dyck's many portraits of the royal family provide a sympathetic record of their features and demeanor. In **CHARLES I AT THE HUNT** (**FIG. 23-29**), of 1635, Van Dyck was able, by clever manipulation of the setting, to portray the king truthfully and still present him as an imposing figure. Dressed casually for the hunt and standing on a bluff overlooking a distant view (a device used by Rubens

23–30 Clara Peeters **STILL LIFE WITH FLOWERS, GOBLET, DRIED FRUIT, AND PRETZELS**

1611. Oil on panel, 20½ × 28¾" (52 × 73 cm). Museo del Prado, Madrid.

Like many "breakfast pieces," this painting features a pile of pretzels among the elegant tableware. The salty, twisted bread was called *pretzel* (from the Latin *pretiola*, meaning "small reward") because it was invented by German monks to reward children who had learned their prayers. The twisted shapes represented the crossed arms of a child praying.

Credit: © 2016. Image Copyright Museo Nacional del Prado. © Photo MNP/Scala, Florence

The Dutch Republic

What are the distinctive styles and subjects preferred in paintings from the Protestant Netherlands?

The House of Orange was not notable for its patronage of the arts, but patronage improved significantly under Prince Frederick Henry (ruled 1625–1647), and Dutch artists found many other eager patrons among the prosperous middle class in Amsterdam, Leiden, Haarlem, Delft, and Utrecht. The Hague was the capital city and the preferred residence of the House of Orange, but Amsterdam was the true center of power, because of its sea trade and the enterprise of its merchants, who made the city an international commercial center. The Dutch delighted in depictions of themselves and their country—the landscape, cities, and domestic life—not to mention beautiful and interesting objects in still-life paintings and interior scenes.

A well-educated people, the Dutch were also fascinated by history, mythology, the Bible, new scientific discoveries, commercial expansion abroad, and colonial exploration.

Visitors to the Netherlands in the seventeenth century noted the popularity of art among merchants and working people. This taste for art stimulated a free market for paintings that functioned like other commodity markets. Artists had to compete to capture the interest of the public by painting on speculation—completing paintings before offering them for sale, in contrast to commissions, which were created only after a purchase agreement was made. Specialists in particularly popular types of images were most likely to be financially successful, and what most Dutch patrons wanted were paintings of themselves, their country, their homes, their possessions, and the life around them—characterized by active trade, bustling mercantilism, Protestant religiosity, and jarring class distinctions. The demand for art also gave rise to an active market for the graphic arts, both for original compositions and for copies of paintings, since one copperplate could produce hundreds of impressions, and worn-out plates could be reworked and used again.

Painting

Hendrick ter Brugghen (1588–1629) spent time in Rome, perhaps between 1608 and 1614, where he must have seen Caravaggio's works and became an enthusiastic follower. On his return home, in 1616, Ter Brugghen entered the Utrecht painters' guild, introducing Caravaggio's style into the Netherlands in paintings such as **ST. SEBAS-TIAN TENDED BY ST. IRENE** (**FIG. 23-31**), and becoming the best known of the Utrecht "Caravaggisti." The sickly gray-green flesh of the nearly dead St. Sebastian, painted in an almost monochromatic palette, contrasts with the brilliant red-and-gold brocade of what seems to be his

crumpled garment. (Actually this is the cope of the bishop of Utrecht, which had survived destruction by Protestants and become a symbol of Catholicism in Utrecht.) The saint is cast as a heroic figure, his strong, youthful body still bound to the tree. But St. Irene (the patron saint of nurses) delicately removes one of the arrows that pierce him, and her maid reaches to untie his wrists. In a typically Baroque manner, the powerful diagonal created by St. Sebastian's left arm dislodges him from the triangular stability of the group. The immediacy and emotional engagement of the work are enhanced by crowding all the figures into the foreground plane, an effect strengthened by the low horizon line, another aspect of this painting that recalls the work of Caravaggio. The tenebrism and dramatic lighting effects are likewise Caravaggesque, as is the frank realism of the women's faces, with reddened noses and rosy cheeks. Rembrandt, Vermeer, and Rubens all admired Ter Brugghen's painting.

HALS AND LEYSTER Frans Hals (c. 1581/1585–1666), the leading painter of Haarlem, developed a style grounded in the Netherlandish love of description and inspired by the Caravaggesque style introduced by artists such as Ter Brugghen. Like Velázquez, he tried to recreate the optical effects of light on the shapes and textures of objects. He painted boldly, with slashing strokes and angular patches of paint. Only when seen at a distance do the colors merge into solid forms over which a flickering light seems to move. In Hals's hands, this loose and seemingly effortless technique suggests the spontaneity of an infectious joy in life. He was known primarily as a portraitist.

23-31 Hendrick ter Brugghen
ST. SEBASTIAN TENDED BY ST. IRENE
1625. Oil on canvas, 58¹⁵⁄₁₆ × 47½" (149.6 × 120 cm). Allen Memorial Art Museum, Oberlin College, Ohio. R.T. Miller Jr. Fund (1953.256).
Credit: Bridgeman Images

23–32 Frans Hals
OFFICERS OF THE HAARLEM MILITIA COMPANY OF ST. ADRIAN

c. 1627. Oil on canvas, 6′ × 8′8″ (1.83 × 2.67 m). Frans Hals Museum, Haarlem.

Credit: Frans Hals Museum, Haarlem. Photo: © Margareta Svensson

Seventeenth-century Dutch portraiture took many forms, ranging from single figures in sparsely furnished settings to allegorical depictions of groups in elaborate costumes surrounded by symbols and attributes. Although the faithful description of facial features and costumes was the most important gauge of a portrait's success, some painters, like Hals, went beyond likeness to convey a sense of mood or emotion in the sitter. Fundamentally, portraits functioned as social statements of the sitters' status coupled with a clear sense of identity rooted in recognizable faces.

Group portraiture documenting the membership of corporate organizations was a Dutch specialty, and Hals painted some of the greatest examples. These large canvases, filled with many individuals who shared the cost of the commission, challenged painters to present a coherent, interesting composition that nevertheless gave equal attention to each individual portrait. Most artists arranged their sitters in neat rows to depict every face clearly, but in **OFFICERS OF THE HAARLEM MILITIA COMPANY OF ST. ADRIAN** (FIG. **23-32**) of about 1627, Hals transforms the group portrait into a lively social event. The company, made up of several guard units, was charged with the military protection of Haarlem. Officers came from the upper middle class and held their commissions for three years, whereas the ordinary guards were tradespeople and crafts-people. Each company was organized like a guild, traditionally under the patronage of a saint, and functioned mainly as a fraternal order, holding archery competitions and taking part in city processions. Hals's composition is based on a strong underlying geometry of diagonal lines—gestures, banners, and sashes—balanced by the stabilizing

perpendiculars of table, window, and tall glass. The black suits and hats make the white ruffs and sashes of rose, white, and baby blue even more brilliant.

Although Hals focused his career on portraits of wealthy members of Haarlem's merchant class, he also painted images of eccentric local figures that, although they follow the format of portraiture, functioned as genre paintings by commenting on the nature of modern life. Among the most striking of these is a painting of the 1630s, portraying a laughing—presumably drunk—older woman with a large beer tankard in her right hand and a shadowy owl perched on her shoulder, known as **MALLE BABBE** (FIG. **23-33**). The figure is based on a well-known Haarlem barmaid who was eventually confined to a charitable mental institution; the word "Malle" means loony or mad, and the owl was a popular symbol of folly. Hals's painting technique in this character study is looser and more energetic than in most of his formal portraits, where he often restrained his stylistic exuberance to conform to the expectations of his wealthy sitters. Here he felt freer in a painting that may have had personal significance. The historical Malle Babbe was confined to the same workhouse for the mentally impaired as Hals's own son Pieter, raising the question of whether this lively vignette of pub life was meant as a bracing social commentary.

A painting that was long praised as one of Hals's finest works is actually by Judith Leyster (c. 1609–1660), Hals's contemporary. A cleaning uncovered her distinctive signature, the monogram "JL" with a star, which refers to her surname, meaning "pole star." Leyster's work clearly shows her exposure to the Utrecht painters who had enthusiastically adopted the principal features

23–33 Frans Hals **MALLE BABBE**
c. 1630–1633. Oil on canvas, 30⅞ × 26″ (78.5 × 66.2 cm). Staatliche Museen zu Berlin.

Credit: © 2016. Photo Scala, Florence/bpk, Bildagentur für Kunst, Kultur und Geschichte, Berlin

whose popularity was based on the very type of painting in progress on her easel. One critic has suggested that her subject—a man playing a violin—may be a visual pun on the painter with palette and brush. Leyster's understanding of light and texture is remarkable. The brushwork she used to depict her own flesh and delicate ruff is more controlled than Hals's loose technique and forms an interesting contrast to the broad strokes of thick paint she used to create her full, stiff skirt. She further emphasized the difference between her portrait and her painting by executing the image on her easel in lighter tones and softer, looser brushwork. The narrow range of colors sensitively dispersed in the composition and the warm spotlighting are typical of Leyster's mature style.

REMBRANDT VAN RIJN The most important painter working in Amsterdam in the seventeenth century was Rembrandt van Rijn (1606–1669). One of nine children born in Leiden to a miller and his wife, Rembrandt studied under Pieter Lastman (1583–1633), the principal painter in Amsterdam at the time. From Lastman, a history painter who had worked in Rome, Rembrandt absorbed an interest in the naturalism, drama, and tenebrism championed by Caravaggio. By the 1630s, Rembrandt was established in Amsterdam primarily as a portrait painter, although he also painted a wide range of narrative themes and landscapes.

of Caravaggio's style. Since Leyster signed in 1631 as a witness at the baptism of one of Hals's children, it is assumed they were close; she may also have worked in his shop. She entered Haarlem's Guild of St. Luke in 1633, which allowed her to take pupils into her studio, and her competitive relationship with Frans Hals around that time is made clear by the complaint she lodged against him in 1635 for luring away one of her apprentices.

Leyster is known primarily for informal scenes of daily life, which often carry an underlying moralistic theme. In her lively **SELF-PORTRAIT** of 1635 (**FIG. 23–34**), the artist has interrupted her work to lean back and look at viewers, as if they had just entered the room. Her elegant dress and the fine chair in which she sits are symbols of her success as an artist

23–34 Judith Leyster **SELF-PORTRAIT**
1635. Oil on canvas, 29⅜ × 25⅝″ (74.6 × 65.1 cm). National Gallery of Art, Washington, DC. Gift of Mr. and Mrs. Robert Woods Bliss (1949.6.4).

Credit: Image courtesy the National Gallery of Art, Washington

23–35 Rembrandt van Rijn **THE ANATOMY LESSON OF DR. NICOLAES TULP**
1632. Oil on canvas, 5′3¾″ × 7′1¼″ (1.6 × 2.1 m). Mauritshuis, The Hague.

Credit: © 2016. Photo Scala, Florence

In his first group portrait, **THE ANATOMY LESSON OF DR. NICOLAES TULP** (**FIG. 23–35**) of 1632, Rembrandt combined his scientific and humanistic interests. Frans Hals had activated the group portrait rather than conceiving it as a simple reproduction of posed figures and faces; Rembrandt transformed it into a charged moment from a life story. Dr. Tulp, head of the surgeons' guild from 1628 to 1653, sits right of center, while a group of fellow physicians gathers around to observe the cadaver and learn from the famed anatomist. Rembrandt built his composition on a sharp diagonal that pierces space from right to left, uniting the cadaver on the table, the calculated arrangement of speaker and listeners, and the open book into a dramatic narrative event. Rembrandt makes effective use of Caravaggio's tenebrist technique, as the figures emerge from a dark and undefined ambience, their attentive faces framed by brilliant white ruffs. Light streams down to spotlight the ghostly flesh of the cadaver, drawing our attention to the extended arms of Dr. Tulp, who flexes his own left hand to demonstrate the action of the cadaver's arm

muscles that he lifts up with silver forceps. Unseen by the viewers are the illustrations of the huge book, presumably an edition of Andreas Vesalius's study of human anatomy, published in Basel in 1543, which was the first attempt at accurate anatomical illustrations in print. Rembrandt's painting has been seen as an homage to Vesalius and to science, as well as a portrait of the members of the Amsterdam surgeons' guild.

Prolific and popular with his Amsterdam clientele, Rembrandt ran a busy studio producing works that sold for high prices. The prodigious output of his large workshop and of the many followers who imitated his manner has made it difficult for scholars to define his body of work, and many paintings formerly attributed to Rembrandt have recently been assigned to other artists. Rembrandt's mature work reflected his cosmopolitan city environment, his study of science and nature, and the broadening of his artistic vocabulary by the study of Italian Renaissance art, chiefly from engravings and paintings imported by the busy Amsterdam art market.

In 1642, Rembrandt was one of several artists commissioned by a wealthy civic-guard company to create large group portraits of its members for its new meeting hall. The result, **THE COMPANY OF CAPTAIN FRANS BANNING COCQ** (FIG. 23–36), carries the idea of a group portrait as a dramatic event even further. Because a dense layer of grime had darkened and obscured its colors, this painting was once thought to be a nocturnal scene and was therefore called *The Night Watch*. After cleaning and restoration in 1975–1976, it now exhibits a natural golden light that sets afire the palette of rich colors—browns, blues, olive-green, orange, and red—around a central core of lemon yellow in the costume of a lieutenant. To the dramatic group composition, showing a company forming for a parade in an Amsterdam street, Rembrandt added several colorful but seemingly unnecessary figures. While the officers stride purposefully forward, the rest of the men and several

mischievous children mill about. The radiant young girl in the left middle ground, carrying a chicken with prominent claws (*klauw* in Dutch), may be a pun on the kind of guns (*klower*) that gave the name (the *Kloveniers*) to the company. Chicken legs with claws also are part of its coat of arms. The complex interactions of the figures and the vivid, individualized likenesses of the militiamen make this one of the greatest group portraits in the Dutch tradition.

In his enthusiasm for printmaking as an important art form with its own aesthetic qualities, Rembrandt was remarkably like Albrecht Dürer (SEE FIGS. 22-7, 22-8). Beginning in 1627, he focused on **etching**, which uses acid to inscribe a design on metal plates. About a decade later, he began to experiment with making additions to his compositions in the **drypoint** technique, in which the artist uses a sharp needle to scratch shallow lines in a plate. Because etching and drypoint allow the artist to work directly

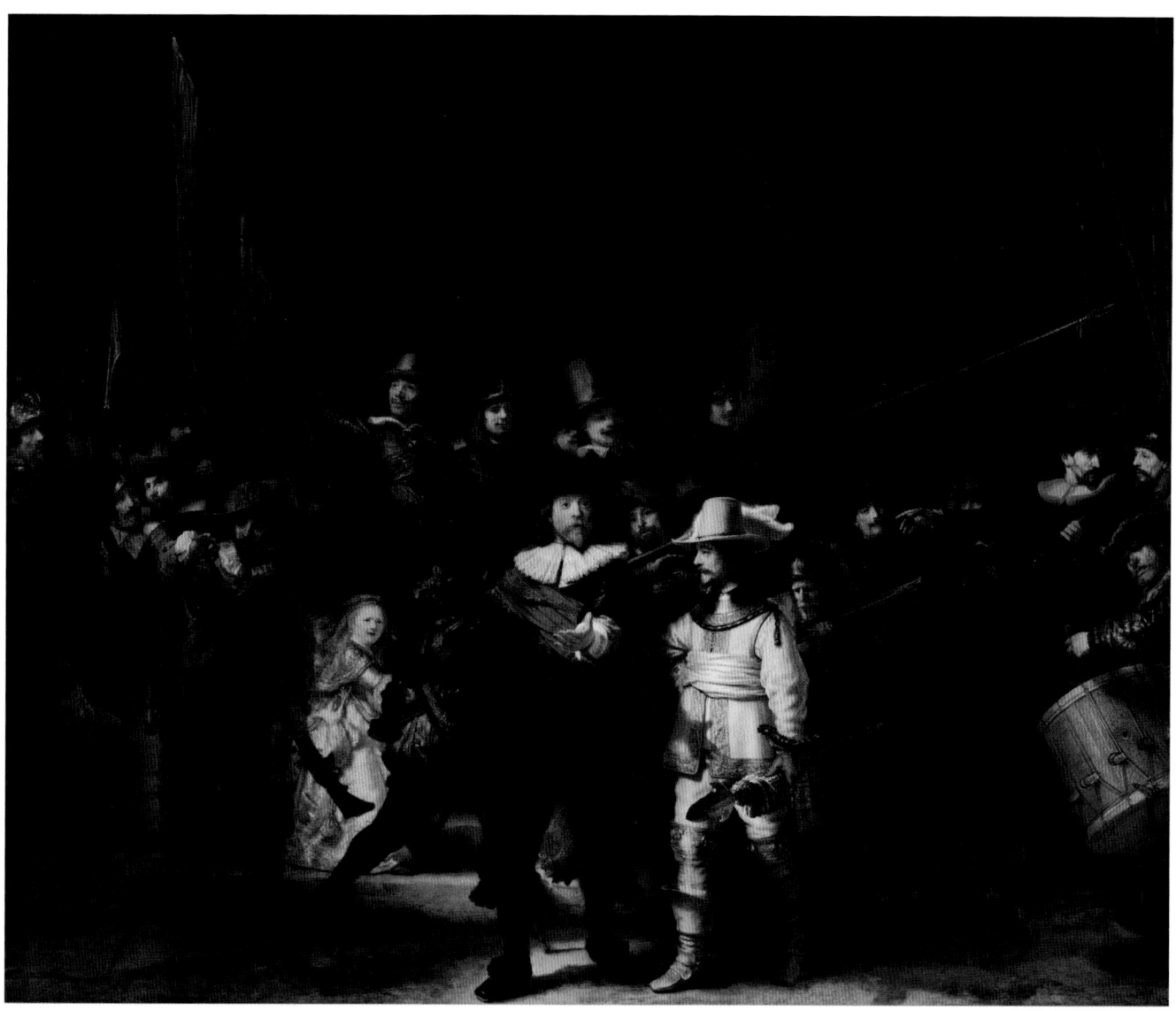

23–36 Rembrandt van Rijn **THE COMPANY OF CAPTAIN FRANS BANNING COCQ (THE NIGHT WATCH)**
1642. Oil on canvas, 11′11″ × 14′4″ (3.63 × 4.37 m) (cut down from the original size). Rijksmuseum, Amsterdam.

Technique

ETCHING AND DRYPOINT

Rembrandt was the first artist to popularize etching as a major form of artistic expression. Etching is an intaglio technique, meaning that the design is carved out of the surface of the printing plate. First the metal plate is coated on both sides with an acid-resistant resin that dries hard without being brittle. Then, instead of laboriously cutting the lines of the desired image directly into the plate as in an engraving (see "Woodcuts and Engravings on Metal" in Chapter 19 on page 603) the artist scratches delicately through the resin with a sharp needle to expose the metal. The plate is then immersed in acid, which eats into the metal exposed by the drawn lines. By controlling the time the acid stays on different parts of the plate, the artist can make shallow, fine lines or deep, heavy ones. After the resin coating is removed from the surface of the plate, an impression is taken. If changes need to be made, lines can be "erased" with

a sharp metal scraper. Not surprisingly, a complex image with a wide range of tones requires many steps.

Another intaglio technique for registering images with incised lines on a metal plate is called drypoint, in which a sharp needle is used to scratch lines directly into the metal. In drypoint, however, the burr (metal pushed up by the drypoint needle) is left in place. Unlike engraving, in which the burr is scraped off, here both the burr and the groove hold the ink. This creates a printed line with a rich black appearance that is impossible to achieve with engraving or etching alone. Unfortunately, drypoint burr is fragile, and no more than a dozen prints can be made before it flattens and loses its character. Rembrandt's earliest prints were entirely etched, but later he added drypoint to develop tonal richness.

on the plate, the style of the finished print can have the relatively free and spontaneous character of a drawing (see "Etching and Drypoint" above). In these works Rembrandt alone took charge of the creative process, from the preparation of the plate to its inking and printing, and he constantly experimented with the technique, with methods of inking, and with papers for printing. Rembrandt's prints were widely collected and attracted high prices even in his lifetime.

Rembrandt's deep speculations on the meaning of the life of Christ evolve in a series of prints of the **THREE**

CROSSES that comes down to us in five states, or stages, of the creative and printing process, in this case created entirely with the drypoint technique. (Only the first and fourth states are reproduced here.) Rembrandt sought to capture the moment described in the Gospels when, during the Crucifixion, darkness covered the Earth and Jesus cried out, "Father, into thy hands I commend my spirit." In the first state (**FIG. 23–37**), the centurion kneels in front of the cross while other people run. The Virgin Mary and St. John share the light flooding down from heaven. By the fourth state (**FIG. 23–38**), Rembrandt has completely

23–37 Rembrandt van Rijn **THREE CROSSES (FIRST STATE)**
1653. Drypoint, 15⅛ × 17¾" (38.5 × 45 cm). Rijksmuseum, Amsterdam.

23–38 Rembrandt van Rijn **THREE CROSSES (FOURTH STATE)**
1653. Drypoint, 15⅛ × 17¾" (38.5 × 45 cm). Rijksmuseum, Amsterdam.

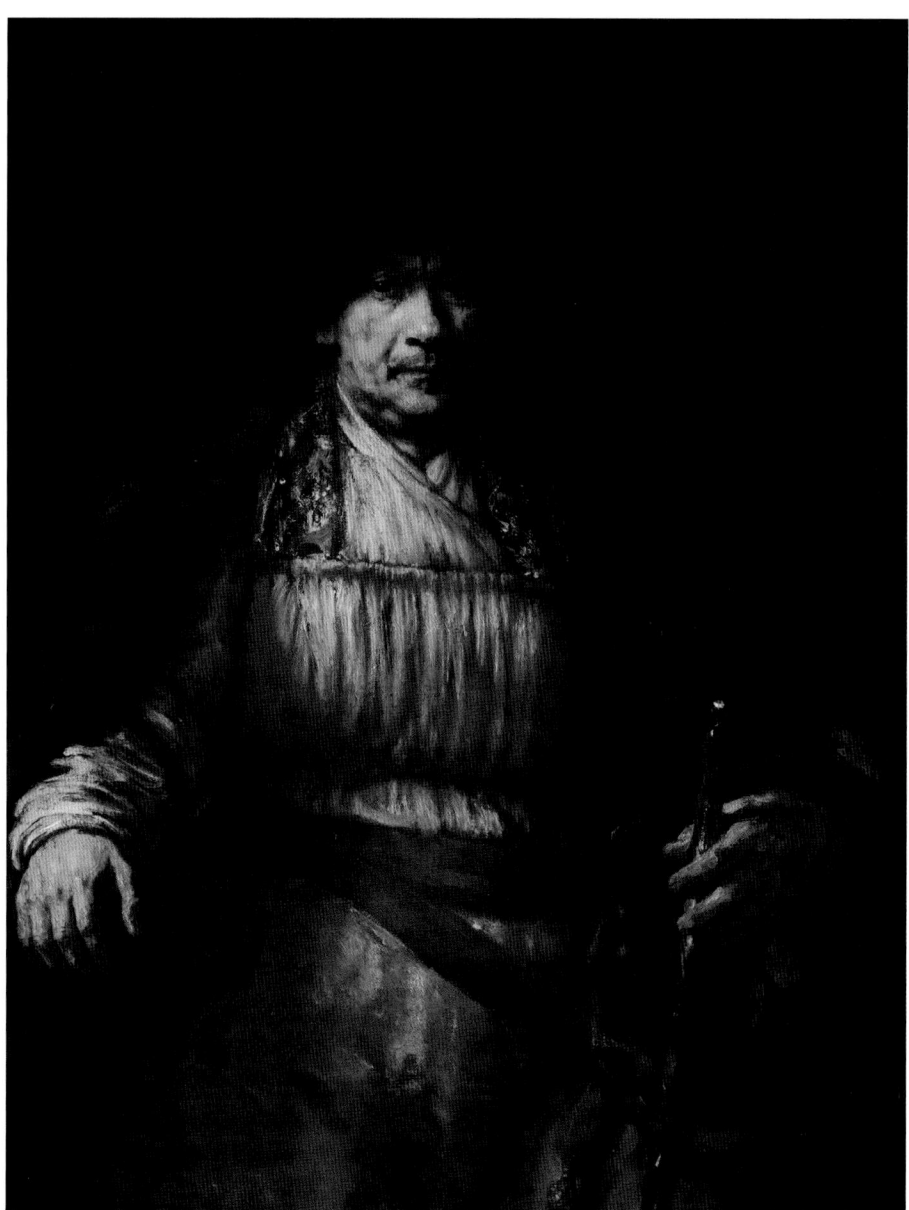

23–39 Rembrandt van Rijn
SELF-PORTRAIT
1658. Oil on canvas, 52⅝ × 40⅞″
(133.6 × 103.8 cm). The Frick Collection,
New York. Henry Clay Frick Bequest.
(1906.1.97)

Credit: Photo: Michael Bodycomb

reworked and reinterpreted the theme. As in the first state, the shattered hill of Golgotha dominates the foreground, but now the scene is considerably darker, and some of the people in the first state, including even Mary and Jesus's friends, have almost disappeared. The horseman holding the lance now faces Jesus. The composition has become more compact, the individual elements are simplified, and the emotions are intensified. An oval of light below the base of the cross draws viewers' attention to the figure of Jesus, and the people around him are trapped in mute confrontation. The first state is a rendering of a narrative moment, bustling with detail; the fourth state reduces the event to its mysterious essence.

As he aged, Rembrandt painted ever more brilliantly, varying textures and paint from the thinnest glazes to thick **impasto** (heavily applied paint), creating a rich, luminous *chiaroscuro* ranging from deepest shadow to brilliant highlights in a dazzling display of gold, red, and chestnut-brown. His sensitivity to the human condition is perhaps nowhere more powerfully expressed than in his late self-portraits, which became more searching as he aged. Distilling a lifetime of study and contemplation, he expressed an internalized spirituality new in the history of art. In his **SELF-PORTRAIT** of 1658 (**FIG. 23–39**), the artist assumes a regal pose, at ease, with arms and legs spread, holding a staff as if it were a baton of command. Yet we know that fortune no longer smiled on him; he had declared bankruptcy in 1656, and over the two-year period between that moment and this self-portrait he had sold his private art collection and even his house to cover his debts. It is possible to relate the stress of this situation to the way he represents himself here. A few well-placed brushstrokes suggest physical tension in the fingers and weariness in the deep-set eyes. Mercilessly analytical, the portrait depicts the furrowed brow, sagging flesh, and aging face of one who has suffered pitfalls but managed to survive, retaining his dignity.

JOHANNES VERMEER One of the most intriguing Dutch artists of this period is Johannes Vermeer (1632–1675), who was also an innkeeper and art dealer. He entered the Delft artists' guild in 1653 and painted only for local patrons. Meticulous in his technique, with a unique and highly structured compositional approach and soft, liquid painting style, Vermeer produced fewer than 40 canvases that can be securely attributed to him. The more these paintings are studied, the more questions arise about the artist's life and his methods. Vermeer's **VIEW OF DELFT** (**FIG. 23–40**), for example, is no simple cityscape. Although the artist convinces the viewer of its authenticity, he does not paint a photographic reproduction of the scene; he moves buildings around to create an ideal composition. Vermeer endows the city with a timeless stability through a stress on horizontal lines, the careful placement of buildings, the quiet atmosphere, and the clear, even light that seems to emerge from beneath low-lying clouds. Vermeer may also have experimented with the mechanical device known as the **camera obscura** (a cameralike box used to record images from the real world; see Chapter 31). This would not have been used by Vermeer as a method of reproducing the image but as another tool in the visual analysis of the composition. The camera obscura would have enhanced optical distortions that led to the "beading" of highlights (seen here on the harbored ships and dark

gray architecture), which creates the illusion of brilliant light but does not dissolve the underlying form.

Most of Vermeer's paintings portray enigmatic scenes of women in their homes, alone or with a servant, occupied with a refined activity such as writing, reading letters, or playing a musical instrument. These are quiet and still interior scenes, gentle in color, asymmetrical but strongly geometric in organization. By creating a contained and consistent architectonic world in which each object adds to the clarity and balance of the composition, Vermeer transports everyday scenes to a level of unearthly perfection. An even, pearly light from a window often gives solidity to the figures and objects in a room. All emotion is subdued, evoking a mood of quiet meditation. Vermeer's brushwork is so controlled that it becomes invisible, except when he paints his characteristic pools of reflected light as tiny, pearl-like droplets of color.

In **WOMAN HOLDING A BALANCE** (**FIG. 23–41**), studied equilibrium creates a monumental composition and a moment of supreme stillness. The woman contemplates the balance in her right hand, drawing our attention to the act of weighing and judging. Her hand and the scale are central, but directly behind her head is a painting of the Last Judgment, highlighting the figure of Christ the Judge in a gold oval above her head. The juxtaposition seems to turn Vermeer's genre scene into a metaphor for eternal

23–40 Johannes Vermeer **VIEW OF DELFT**

c. 1662. Oil on canvas, 38½ × 46¼" (97.8 × 117.5 cm). Royal Picture Gallery, Mauritshuis, The Hague.

23–41 Johannes Vermeer **WOMAN HOLDING A BALANCE**
c. 1664. Oil on canvas, 15⅝ × 14″ (39.7 × 35.5 cm). National Gallery of Art, Washington, DC. Widener Collection (1942.9.97).

Credit: Image courtesy the National Gallery of Art, Washington

judgment, a sobering religious reference that may reflect the artist's own position as a Catholic living in a Protestant country. The woman's moment of quiet introspection in front of the gold and pearls displayed on the table before her, shimmering with reflected light from the window, also evokes the *vanitas* theme of the transience of earthly life.

GENRE SCENES Continuing a long Netherlandish tradition, seventeenth-century genre paintings—generally made for private patrons and depicting scenes of contemporary daily life—were often laden with symbolic references, although their meaning is not always clear to us

now. A clean house might indicate a virtuous housewife and mother, while a messy household suggested laziness and the sin of sloth. Ladies dressing in front of mirrors certainly could be succumbing to vanity, and drinking parties led to overindulgence and lust.

Gerard ter Borch (1617–1681) was one of the most refined of the genre painters. In his painting traditionally known as **THE SUITOR'S VISIT** (**FIG. 23-42**), from about 1658, a well-dressed man bows gracefully to an elegant woman in white satin, who stands in a sumptuously furnished room in which another woman plays a lute. Another man, in front of a fireplace, turns to observe

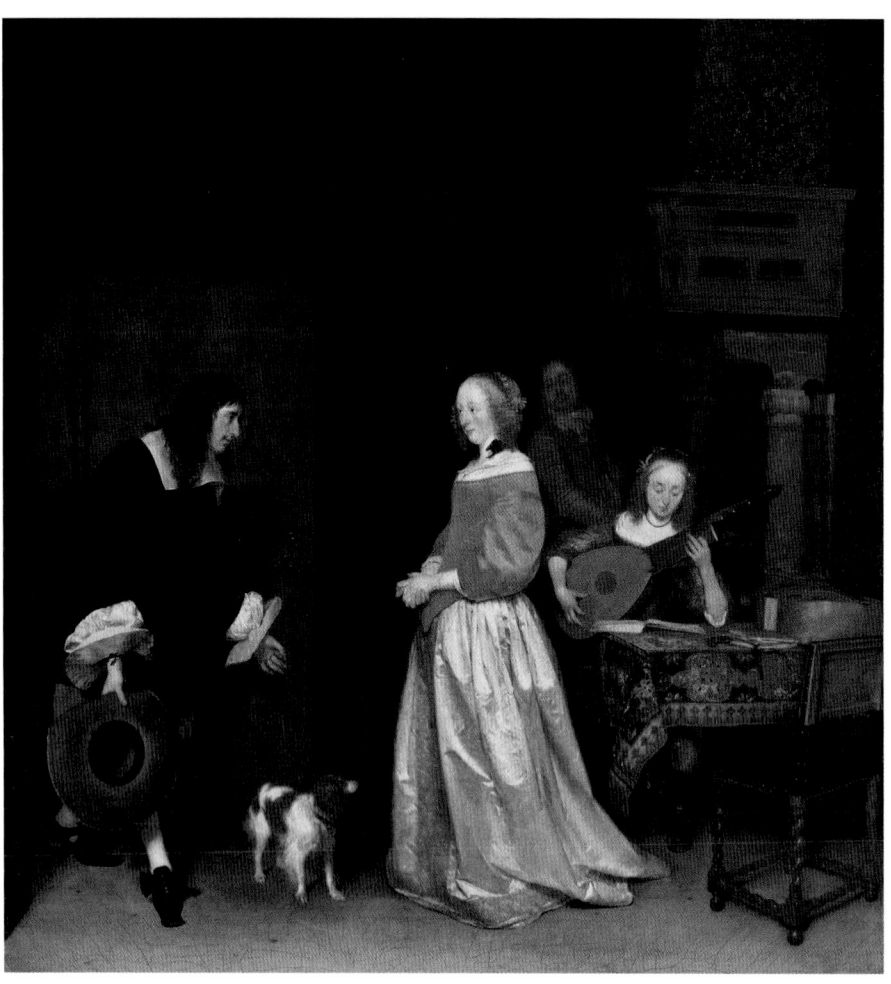

23–42 Gerard ter Borch **THE SUITOR'S VISIT**

c. 1658. Oil on canvas, 32½ × 29⅝" (82.6 × 75.3 cm). National Gallery of Art, Washington, DC. Andrew W. Mellon Collection.

Credit: Image courtesy the National Gallery of Art, Washington

success. Most of his scenes used everyday life to portray moral tales, illustrate proverbs and folk sayings, or make puns to amuse the spectator. Since Steen traveled throughout the Netherlands all his life and was a tavern owner in Leiden during the 1670s, he had many sources of inspiration for the lively human dramas in his paintings.

Steen's paintings of children are especially remarkable, for he captured not only their childish physiques but also their fleeting moods and expressions with rapid, fluid brushstrokes. A characteristic example is **THE FEAST OF ST. NICHOLAS** (**FIG. 23–43**), from the 1660s. Steen's household setting holds neither the intimate order and stillness favored

the newcomer. The painting appears to represent a prosperous gentleman paying a call on a lady of equal social status, possibly a courtship scene. The spaniel and the musician seem to be simply part of the scene, but we are already familiar with the dog as a symbol of fidelity, and stringed instruments were said to symbolize, through their tuning, the harmony of souls and thus, possibly, a loving relationship. On the other hand, music making was also associated with sensory pleasure evoked by touch. Ter Borch's exquisite rendering highlights the lace, velvet, and especially the satin of these opulent outfits, potentially symbols of personal excess. If there is a moral lesson, it is presented discreetly and ambiguously.

Another important genre painter is Jan Steen (1626–1679), whose larger brushstrokes contrast with the meticulous treatment of Ter Borch and reveal an artistic affinity with Frans Hals. Steen painted over 800 works but never achieved financial

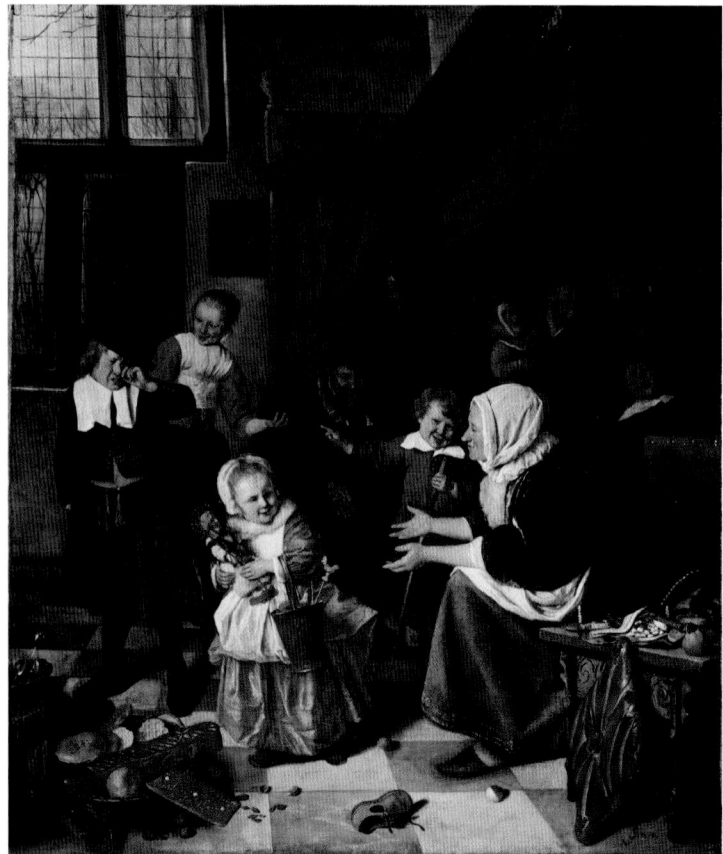

23–43 Jan Steen **THE FEAST OF ST. NICHOLAS**
c. 1660–1665. Oil on canvas, 32¼ × 27¾" (82 × 70.5 cm). Rijksmuseum, Amsterdam.

23–44 Emanuel de Witte
**PORTUGUESE SYNAGOGUE,
AMSTERDAM**
1680. Oil on canvas, 43½ × 39″
(110.5 × 99.1 cm). Rijksmuseum,
Amsterdam.

Architects Daniel Stalpaert and
Elias Bouman built the synagogue in
1671–1675.

by Vermeer, nor the elegant decorum and guarded interaction portrayed by Ter Borch. This is a scene of noisy commotion within a joyous family get-together, where children react in various ways—disappointment, delight, possessiveness—to the pre-Christmas gifts St. Nicholas has left for them in their shoes. Steen renders the objects scattered in the disordered foreground with meticulous attention to the details of surface texture, but the focus here is the festive atmosphere of a boisterous holiday morning and the folksy figures who delight in the celebration.

Emanuel de Witte (1617–1692) of Rotterdam specialized in architectural interiors, first in Delft in the 1640s and then in Amsterdam after settling there permanently in 1652. Although many of his interiors were composites of features from several locations combined in one idealized architectural view, De Witte also painted faithful "portraits" of actual buildings. One of these is his **PORTUGUESE SYNAGOGUE, AMSTERDAM** (**FIG. 23–44**) of 1680. The synagogue shown here, which still stands in Amsterdam, is a rectangular hall divided into one wide central aisle with narrow side aisles, each covered with a wooden barrel vault resting on lintels supported by columns. De Witte's shift of the viewpoint slightly to one side has created an

intriguing spatial composition, and strong contrasts of light and shade add dramatic movement to the simple interior. The elegant couple and the dogs in the foreground provide both a sense of scale for the architecture and some human interest for viewers.

Today, this painting is interesting not only as a work of art, but also as a record of seventeenth-century synagogue architecture, documenting Dutch religious tolerance in an age when European Jews were often persecuted. Expelled from Spain and Portugal from the late fifteenth century on, many Jews had settled in Amsterdam, and their community numbered about 2,300 people, most of whom were well-to-do merchants. Fund-raising for a new synagogue began in 1670, and in 1671 Elias Bouman and Daniel Stalpaert began work on the building. With its classical architecture, Brazilian jacaranda-wood furniture, and 26 brass chandeliers, this synagogue was considered one of the most impressive buildings in Amsterdam.

LANDSCAPE AND STILL LIFE   The Dutch loved the landscapes and vast skies of their own country, but landscape painters worked in their studios rather than in nature, and they were never afraid to rearrange, add to, or subtract from a scene in order to give their compositions formal organization or a desired mood. Starting in the 1620s, landscape painters generally followed a convention in which little color was used beyond browns, grays, and beiges. After 1650, they used more individualistic styles, but nearly all brought a broader range of colors into play. One continuing motif was the emphasis on cloud-filled expanses of sky dominating a relatively narrow horizontal band of earth below.

The Haarlem landscape specialist Jacob van Ruisdael (1628/1629–1682), whose popularity drew many pupils to his workshop, was especially adept at both the invention of dramatic compositions and the projection of moods. His **VIEW OF HAARLEM FROM THE DUNES AT OVERVEEN** (FIG. 23–45), painted about 1670, celebrates the flatlands outside Haarlem that had been reclaimed from the sea as part of a massive landfill project that the Dutch compared with God's restoration of the Earth after Noah's Flood. Such a religious interpretation may be referenced here in the prominent Gothic church of St. Bavo looming on the horizon. There may be other messages as well. While almost three-quarters of this painting is devoted to a rendering of the powerfully cloudy sky, tiny humans can be seen laboring below, caught in the process of spreading white linen across the broad fields to bleach in the sun. This glorification of the industriousness of citizens engaged in one of Haarlem's principal industries must have made the painting particularly appealing to the patriotic local market.

23–45 Jacob van Ruisdael **VIEW OF HAARLEM FROM THE DUNES AT OVERVEEN**
c. 1670. Oil on canvas, 22 × 24¼" (55.8 × 62.8 cm). Royal Picture Gallery, Mauritshuis, The Hague.

23–46 Pieter Claesz **STILL LIFE WITH TAZZA**

1636. Oil on panel, 17⅜ × 24″ (44 × 61 cm). Royal Cabinet of Paintings, Mauritshuis, The Hague.

The heavy round glass is a Roemer, a relatively inexpensive, everyday item, as are the pewter plates. The silver cup (*tazza*) was a typical ornamental piece. Painters owned and shared such valuable props, and this and other showpieces appear in many paintings.

The Dutch were so proud of their still-life painting tradition that they presented a flower painting by Rachel Ruysch to the French queen Marie de' Medici during her state visit to Amsterdam. Like genre paintings, a still-life painting might carry moralizing connotations and commonly had a *vanitas* theme, reminding viewers of the transience of life and material possessions, even art. Yet it could also document and showcase the wealth of its owner.

One of the first Dutch still-life painters was Pieter Claesz (1596/1597–1660) of Haarlem, who, like Antwerp artist Clara Peeters (SEE FIG. 23–30), painted "breakfast pieces," that is, meals of bread, fruits, and nuts. In subtle, nearly monochromatic paintings such as **STILL LIFE WITH TAZZA** (FIG. 23–46), Claesz seems to give life to inanimate objects. He organizes dishes in diagonal positions to give a strong sense of space—here reinforced by the spiraling strip of lemon peel, foreshortened with the plate into the foreground and reaching toward the viewer's own space—and

he renders the maximum contrast of textures within a subtle palette of yellows, browns, greens, and silvery whites. The tilted silver *tazza* contrasts with the half-filled glass, which becomes a monumental presence and permits Claesz to display his skill with transparencies and reflections. Such paintings suggest the prosperity of Claesz's patrons. The food might be simple, but a silver ornamental cup like this would have graced the tables of only the wealthy. The meticulously painted timepiece could suggest deeper meanings—it alludes to human technological achievement, but also to the inexorable passage of time and the fleeting nature of human life, thoughts also prompted by the interrupted breakfast, casually placed knife, and toppled tableware.

Still-life paintings in which cut-flower arrangements predominate were referred to simply as "flower pieces." Significant advances were made in botany during the seventeenth century through the application of orderly scientific methods and objective observation (see "Science and the Changing Worldview" opposite). Then, as now, the Dutch were major growers and exporters of flowers, especially the tulips that appear in nearly every flower piece in dozens of exquisite variations. The Dutch tradition of flower painting peaked in the long career of Rachel Ruysch (1664–1750) of Amsterdam. Her flower pieces were highly prized for their sensitive, free-form arrangements and their unusual and beautiful color harmonies. During her 70-year career, she became one of the most sought-after and highest-paid still-life painters in Europe—her paintings brought in twice what Rembrandt's did.

In her **FLOWER STILL LIFE** (**FIG. 23–47**) painted shortly after the end of the century, Ruysch placed the container at the center of the canvas's width, then created an asymmetrical floral arrangement of pale oranges, pinks, and yellows rising from lower left to top right of the picture, offset by the strong diagonal of the tabletop. To further balance the painting, she placed highlighted blossoms and leaves on the dark left half of the canvas and silhouetted them against the light wall area on the right. Ruysch often emphasized the beauty of curving flower stems and enlivened her compositions with interesting additions, such as casually placed pieces of fruit or insects, in this case a large gray moth (lower left) and two snail shells.

Flower painting was almost never a straightforward depiction of actual fresh flowers. Instead, artists made color sketches of fresh examples of each type of flower and studied scientifically accurate color illustrations in botanical publications. In the studio, using their sketches and notebooks, they would compose bouquets of perfect specimens of a variety of flowers that could never be found blooming at the same time. The short life of flowers was a poignant reminder of the fleeting nature of beauty and of human life.

23–47 Rachel Ruysch **FLOWER STILL LIFE**
After 1700. Oil on canvas, 30 × 24″ (76.2 × 61 cm). The Toledo Museum of Art, Ohio. Purchased with funds from the Libbey Endowment. Gift of Edward Drummond Libbey (1956.57).

Credit: The Toledo Museum of Art, Toledo, Ohio (1956.57)

Art and its Contexts

SCIENCE AND THE CHANGING WORLDVIEW

From the mid sixteenth through the seventeenth centuries, new discoveries about the natural world brought a sense of both the grand scale and the microscopic detail of the universe. To publish their theories and research, early scientists learned to draw or depended on artists to draw what they discovered in the world around them. This practice would continue until the invention of photography in the nineteenth century.

Artist and scientist were seldom the same person, but Anna Maria Sibylla Merian (1647–1717) contributed to botany and entomology both as a researcher and as an artist. German by birth and Dutch by training, Merian was once described by a Dutch contemporary as a painter of unclean and undesirable subjects such as worms, flies, mosquitoes, and spiders. In 1699, the city of Amsterdam subsidized Merian's research on plants and insects in the Dutch colony of Surinam in South America, where she spent two years exploring the jungle and recording insects. On her return to the Dutch Republic, she published the results of her research as **THE METAMORPHOSIS OF THE INSECTS OF SURINAM**, illustrated with 72 large prints created as copies of her watercolors (**FIG. 23–48**). For all her meticulous scientific accuracy, Merian arranged her depictions of exotic insects and elegant fruits and flowers into skillful and harmonious compositions.

But interest in scientific exploration was not limited to the Netherlands. The writings of philosophers Francis Bacon (1561–1626) in England and René Descartes (1596–1650) in France helped establish a new scientific method of studying the world by insisting on scrupulous objectivity and logical reasoning. Bacon argued that the facts be established from observation and tested by controlled experiments. Descartes, who was also a mathematician, argued for the deductive method of reasoning, in which conclusions were arrived at logically from basic premises.

In 1543, the Polish scholar Nicolaus Copernicus (1473–1543) published *On the Revolutions of the Heavenly Spheres*, which contradicted the long-held view that the Earth was the center of the universe (the Ptolemaic theory) by arguing instead that it and the other planets revolved around the Sun. The Church put Copernicus's work on its *Index of Prohibited Books* in 1616, but Johannes Kepler (1571–1630) continued demonstrating that the planets revolve around the Sun in elliptical orbits. Galileo Galilei (1564–1642), an astronomer, mathematician, and physicist, developed the telescope as a tool for observing the heavens and provided further confirmation of Copernican theory, but since

23–48 Anna Maria Sibylla Merian **PLATE 9 FROM THE METAMORPHOSIS OF THE INSECTS OF SURINAM**
1719. Hand-colored engraving, 18⅞ × 13″ (47.9 × 33 cm). Getty Research Institute, Los Angeles (89-B10750).

the Church prohibited its teaching, Galileo was tried for heresy by the Inquisition and forced to deny his views.

The new seventeenth-century science turned to the study of the very small as well as to the vast reaches of space. This included the development of the microscope by the Dutch lens-maker and amateur scientist Anton van Leeuwenhoek (1632–1723). Leeuwenhoek perfected grinding techniques and increased the power of his lenses far beyond what was required for a simple magnifying glass. Ultimately, he was able to study the inner workings of plants and animals and even see micro-organisms.

France

How does the art of France differ from art and architecture produced elsewhere in Europe?

Early seventeenth-century France was marked by almost continuous foreign and civil wars. The assassination of King Henry IV in 1610 left France in the hands of the queen, Marie de' Medici (regency 1610–1617; SEE FIG. 23–27), as regent for her 9-year-old son, Louis XIII (ruled 1610–1643). When Louis came of age, the brilliant and unscrupulous Cardinal Richelieu became chief minister and set about increasing the power of the crown at the expense of the French nobility. The death of Louis XIII again left France with another child king, the 5-year-old Louis XIV (ruled 1643–1715). His mother, Anne of Austria, became regent, with the assistance of another powerful minister, Cardinal Mazarin. At Mazarin's death in 1661, Louis XIV began his long personal reign, assisted by yet another able minister, Jean-Baptiste Colbert.

An absolute monarch whose reign was the longest in European history, Louis XIV made the French court the envy of every ruler in Europe. He became known as "le Roi Soleil" ("the Sun King") and was sometimes glorified in art through identification with the Classical sun god, Apollo. In a 1701 portrait by court painter Hyacinthe Rigaud (1659–1743), the richly costumed **LOUIS XIV** is framed by a lavish, billowing curtain (**FIG. 23-49**). Proudly showing off his elegant legs, the 63-year-old monarch poses in a blue robe of state, trimmed with gold *fleurs-de-lis* and lined with white ermine. He wears the high-heeled shoes he devised to compensate for his shortness. Despite his pompous pose and magnificent surroundings, the

23-49 Hyacinthe Rigaud **LOUIS XIV**

1701. Oil on canvas, 9′2″ × 7′10¾″ (2.19 × 2.4 m). Musée du Louvre, Paris.

Louis XIV had ordered this portrait as a gift for his grandson, the future Philip V of Spain (ruled 1700–1746), but when Rigaud finished the painting, Louis liked it too much to give it away and only three years later ordered a copy from Rigaud to give to his grandson. The request for copies of royal portraits was not unusual since the aristocratic families of Europe were linked through marriage. Paintings made appropriate gifts and at the same time memorialized important political alliances by recording them in visual form.

Credit: Photo © Centre Pompidou, MNAM-CCI, Dist. RMN-Grand Palais/ Philippe Migeat

Art and its Contexts

GRADING THE OLD MASTERS

The members of the French Royal Academy of Painting and Sculpture considered ancient Classical art to be the standard by which contemporary art should be judged. By the 1680s, however, younger artists of the academy began to argue that modern art might equal, or might even surpass, the art of the ancients—a radical thought that sparked controversy.

A debate arose over the relative merits of drawing and color in painting. The conservatives argued that drawing was superior to color because drawing appealed to the mind while color appealed to the senses. They saw Nicolas Poussin as embodying perfectly the Classical principles of subject and design. But the young artists who admired the vivid colors of Titian, Veronese, and Rubens claimed that painting should deceive the eye, and since color achieves this deception more convincingly than drawing, application of color should be valued over drawing. Adherents of the two positions were called *poussinistes* (in honor of Poussin) and *rubénistes* (for Rubens).

The portrait painter and critic Roger de Piles (1635–1709) took up the cause of the *rubénistes* in a series of pamphlets. In *The Principles of Painting*, de Piles evaluated the most important painters on a scale of 0 to 20 in four categories. He gave no score higher than 72 (18 in each category), since no mortal artist could achieve perfection. Caravaggio received a 0 in expression and a 6 in drawing, while Michelangelo and Leonardo both got a 4 in color and Rembrandt a 6 in drawing.

Most of the painters examined here do not do very well. Raphael and Rubens get 65 points (A on our grading scale), Van Dyck comes close with 55 (C+). Poussin and Titian earn 53 and 51 (solid Cs), while Rembrandt slips by with 50 (C–). Leonardo da Vinci gets 49 (D), and Michelangelo and Dürer with 37 and Caravaggio with 28 are resounding failures in de Piles's view. Tastes change. Someday our own ideas may seem just as misguided as those of the academicians.

---

directness of the king's gaze and the frankness of his aging face make him appear surprisingly human.

The arts, like everything else, came under royal control. In 1635, Cardinal Richelieu had founded the French Royal Academy, directing the members to compile a definitive dictionary and grammar of the French language. In 1648, the Royal Academy of Painting and Sculpture was founded, which, as reorganized by Colbert in 1663, maintained strict control over the arts (see "Grading the Old Masters" above). Although it was not the first European arts academy, none before it had exerted such dictatorial authority—an authority that would last in France until the late nineteenth century. Membership of the academy assured an artist of royal and civic commissions and financial success, but many talented artists did well outside it.

Versailles

French architecture developed along Classical lines in the second half of the seventeenth century under the influence of François Mansart (1598–1666) and Louis Le Vau (1612–1670). When the Royal Academy of Architecture was founded in 1671, its members developed guidelines for architectural design based on the belief that mathematics was the true basis of beauty. Their chief sources for ideal models were the books of Vitruvius and Palladio.

In 1668, Louis XIV began to enlarge the small château built by Louis XIII at Versailles, not far from Paris. Louis moved to the palace in 1682 and eventually required his court to live in Versailles; 5,000 aristocrats lived in the palace itself, together with 14,000 servants and military staff

members. The town had another 30,000 residents, most of whom were royal employees. The designers of the palace and park complex at Versailles were Le Vau, Charles Le Brun (1619–1690), who oversaw the interior decoration, and André Le Nôtre (1613–1700), who planned the gardens (see "Garden Design" on page 772). For both political and sentimental reasons, the old château was left standing, and the new building went up around it. This project consisted of two phases: the first additions by Le Vau, begun in 1668; and an enlargement completed after Le Vau's death by his successor, Jules Hardouin-Mansart (1646–1708), from 1670 to 1685.

Hardouin-Mansart was responsible for the addition of the long lateral wings and the renovation of Le Vau's central block on the garden side to match these wings (**FIG. 23-50**). The three-story façade has a lightly rusticated ground floor, a main floor lined with enormous arched windows separated by Ionic columns or pilasters, an attic level whose rectangular windows are also flanked by pilasters, and a flat, terraced roof. The overall design is a sensitive balance of horizontals and verticals relieved by a restrained overlay of regularly spaced projecting blocks with open, colonnaded porches.

In his renovation of Le Vau's center-block façade, Hardouin-Mansart enclosed the previously open gallery on the main level, creating the famed **HALL OF MIRRORS** (**FIG. 23-51**), which is about 240 feet long and 47 feet high. He achieved architectural symmetry and a sense of both splendor and expansiveness by lining the interior wall with glass mirrors, matching in size and shape the arched windows in the opposing wall. Mirrors were small

Elements of Architecture

GARDEN DESIGN

Wealthy and aristocratic French landowners commissioned garden designers to transform their large properties into gardens extending over many acres. The challenge for garden designers was to unify diverse elements—buildings, pools, monuments, plantings, and natural land formations—into a coherent whole. At Versailles, André Le Nôtre imposed order upon the vast expanses of palace gardens and park by using broad, straight avenues radiating from a series of round focal points. He succeeded so thoroughly that his plan inspired generations of urban designers as well as landscape architects.

In Le Nôtre's hands, the palace terrain became an extraordinary work of art and a visual delight for its inhabitants. Neatly contained expanses of lawn and broad, straight vistas seemed to stretch to the horizon, while the formal gardens became an exercise in precise geometry. The gardens at Versailles are classically harmonious in their symmetrical, geometric design but Baroque in their vast size and extension into the surrounding countryside, where the gardens thickened into woods cut by straight avenues.

The most formal gardens lay nearest the palace, and plantings became progressively less elaborate and larger in scale as their distance from the palace increased. Broad, intersecting paths separated reflecting pools and planting beds, which are called embroidered **parterres** for their colorful patterns of flowers outlined with trimmed hedges. After the formal zone of parterres came lawns, large fountains on terraces, and trees planted in thickets to conceal features such as an open-air ballroom and a colonnade. Statues carved by at least 70 sculptors also adorned the park. A mile-long canal, crossed by a second canal nearly as large, marked the main axis of the garden. Fourteen waterwheels brought the water from the river to supply the canals and the park's 1,400 fountains. Only the fountains near the palace played all day; the others were turned on only when the king approached.

At the north end of the secondary canal, a smaller pavilion-palace, the Trianon, was built in 1669. To satisfy the king's love of flowers year-round, the gardens of the Trianon were bedded out with blooming plants from the south shipped in by the French navy. Even in midwinter, the king and his guests could stroll through a summer garden. The head gardener is said to have had nearly 2 million flowerpots at his disposal. In the eighteenth century, Louis XV added greenhouses and a botanical garden. The facilities of the fruit and vegetable garden that supplied the palace in 1677–1683 today house the National School of Horticulture.

Grand Canal

orangerie

parterre

château

parterre

reflecting pools

Grand Trianon

Petit Trianon

PLAN OF THE GARDENS OF THE PALACE OF VERSAILLES (LOUIS LE VAU AND ANDRÉ LE NÔTRE, c. 1661-1785)

Credit: John Woodcock © Dorling Kindersley

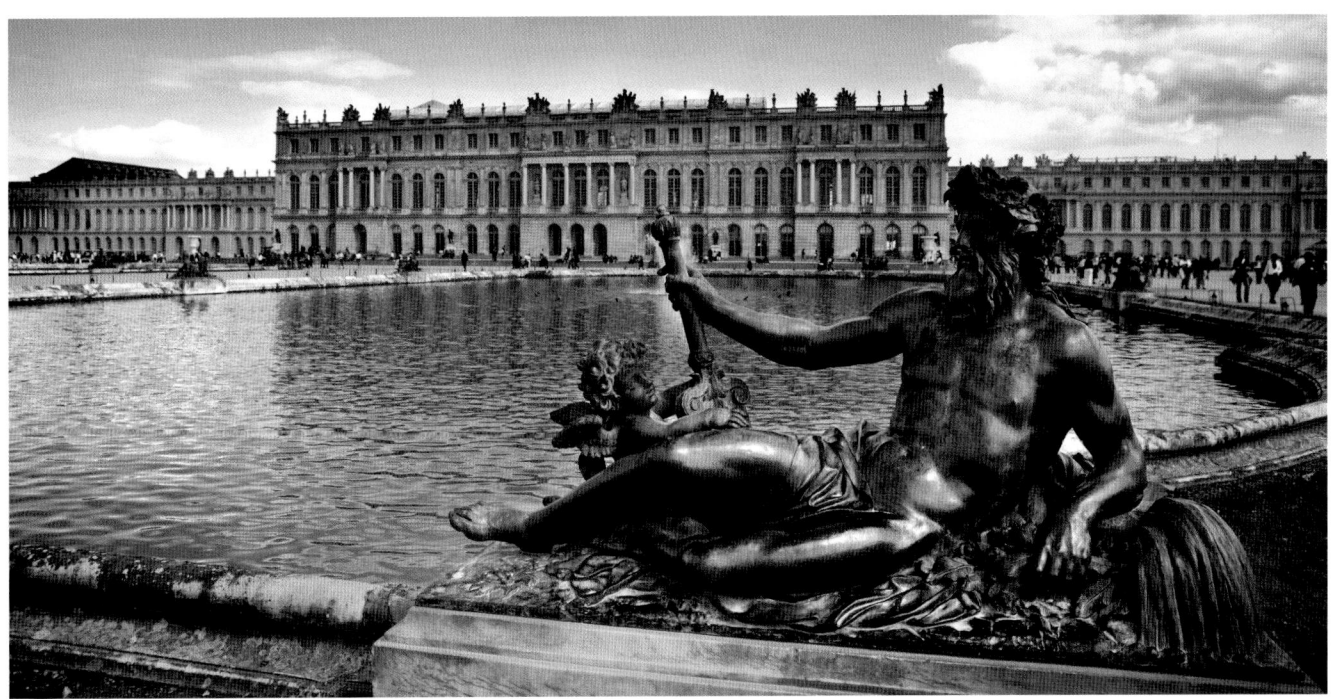

23–50 Louis Le Vau and Jules Hardouin-Mansart **GARDEN FAÇADE OF THE PALACE OF VERSAILLES**
1678–1685. Foreground: Jean-Baptiste Tuby's *Neptune*.

Credit: © Onairda/Shutterstock

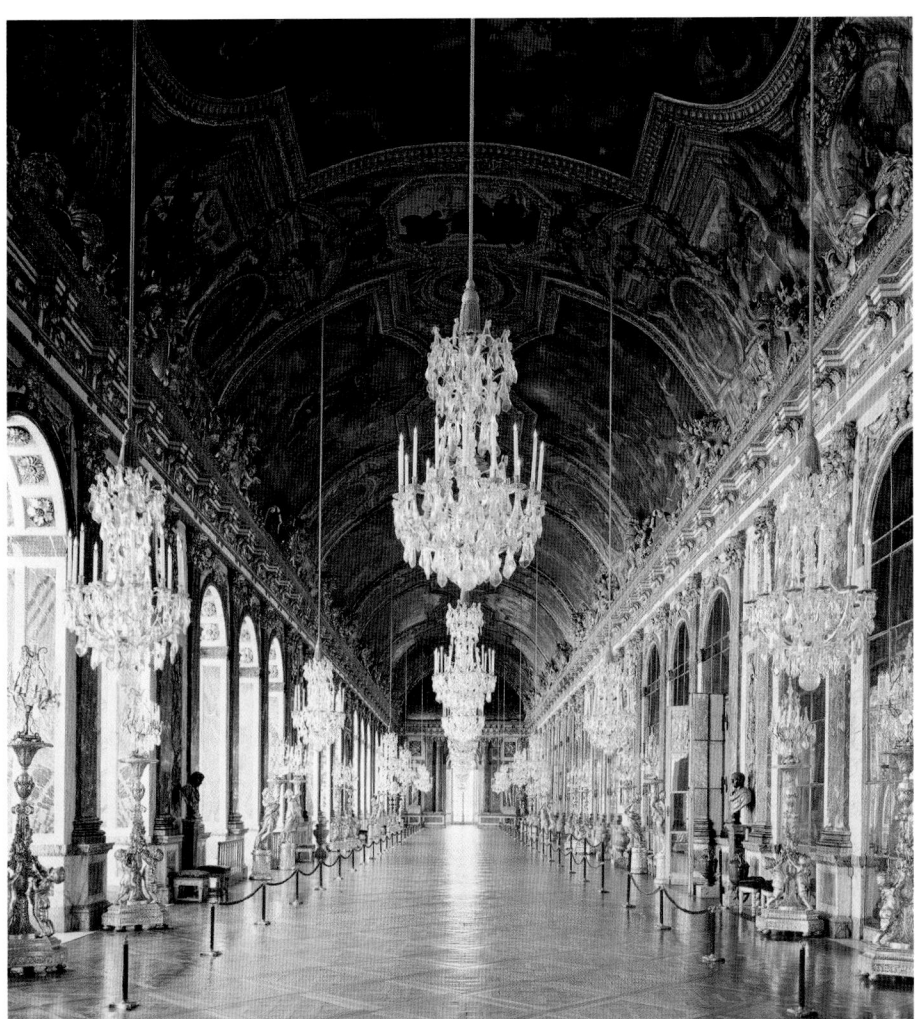

23–51 Jules Hardouin-Mansart and Charles Le Brun **HALL OF MIRRORS, PALACE OF VERSAILLES**
Begun 1678. Length approx. 240′ (73 m).

In the seventeenth century, mirrors and clear window glass were enormously expensive. To furnish the Hall of Mirrors, hundreds of glass panels of manageable size had to be assembled into the proper shape and attached to one another with glazing bars, which became part of the decorative pattern of the vast room.

Credit: © Massimo Listri/Corbis

and extremely expensive in the seventeenth century, and these huge walls of reflective glass were created by fitting 18-inch panels together. They reflect the natural light from the windows and give the impression of an even larger space; at night, the reflections of flickering candles must have turned the mirrored gallery into a shimmering tableau in which the king and courtiers saw themselves as they promenaded.

Inspired by Carracci's Farnese ceiling (SEE FIG. 23-8), Le Brun decorated the vaulted ceiling with paintings on canvas (more stable in the damp northern climate) glorifying the reign and military triumphs of Louis XIV, accompanied by Classical gods. In 1642, Le Brun had studied in Italy, where he came under the influence of the Classical style of his compatriot Nicolas Poussin. As "first painter to the king" and director of the Royal Academy of Painting and Sculpture, Le Brun controlled art education and patronage from 1661/1663 until his death in 1690. He tempered the warmly exuberant Baroque ceilings he had seen in Rome with Poussin's cool Classicism. The underlying theme for his design and decoration of Versailles was the glorification of the king as Apollo the sun god, with whom Louis

identified. Louis XIV thought of the duties of kingship, including its pageantry, as a solemn performance, so it is most appropriate that Rigaud's portrait presents him on a raised, stagelike platform, with a theatrical curtain (SEE FIG. 23-49). Versailles became the splendid stage on which the king played the principal role in the grandiose drama of state.

Painting

Sixteenth-century French Mannerism began to give way in the 1620s to Classicism and the impact of Caravaggio, especially his tenebrism and compression of large-scale figures into the foreground. As the century progressed, the control of the Royal Academy and its encouragement of studies of the Classics and the surviving antiquities in Rome guided French painting toward the Classicism promoted by Le Brun.

CARAVAGGIO'S INFLUENCE: GEORGES DE LA TOUR AND THE LE NAIN BROTHERS   One of Caravaggio's most important followers in France, Georges de La Tour (1593–1652) received major royal and ducal commissions and became court painter to Louis XIII in 1639. La Tour may have traveled to Italy in 1614–1616, and in the 1620s he almost certainly visited the Netherlands, where Caravaggio's style was having an impact (SEE FIG. 23-31). Like Caravaggio, La Tour filled the foreground of his compositions with imposing figures, but in place of Caravaggio's focus on descriptive detail, La Tour's work revels in the dramatic effects of lighting, usually from sources within the paintings themselves. Often, it seems, light is his real subject (see "Closer Look" in the Introduction on page xxvi).

23-52 Georges de La Tour **MARY MAGDALEN WITH THE SMOKING FLAME** c. 1640. Oil on canvas, 46¼ × 36⅛" (117 × 91.8 cm). Los Angeles County Museum of Art. Gift of the Ahmanson Foundation (M. 77.73).

23-53 Louis or Antoine Le Nain **A PEASANT FAMILY IN AN INTERIOR**
c. 1640. Oil on canvas, 44½ × 62½" (1.13 × 1.59 m). Musée du Louvre, Paris.

Credit: © akg-images/Erich Lessing

La Tour painted many images of Mary Magdalen. In **MARY MAGDALEN WITH THE SMOKING FLAME** (**FIG. 23-52**), as in many of his other paintings, the light emanates from a source shown in the painting, in this case the flame from an oil lamp. Its warm glow gently brushes over hand and skull—symbol of mortality—to establish the foreground. The compression of the figure into the front of the pictorial space conveys a sense of intimacy between the saint and viewers, although she is completely unaware of our presence. Light not only unifies the painting, its controlled character also creates its somber mood. Mary Magdalen has put aside her rich clothing and jewels to meditate on the frailty and vanity of human life. Even the flickering light that rivets our attention on her meditative face and gesture is of limited duration.

The same feeling of timelessness and a comparable interest in effects of light characterize the paintings of the Le Nain brothers, Antoine (c. 1588–1648), Louis (c. 1593–1648), and Mathieu (1607–1677). Although all three were working in Paris by about 1630 and were founding members of the Royal Academy of Painting and Sculpture in

1648, little else is known about their lives and careers. Because they collaborated closely with each other, art historians have only recently begun to sort out their individual styles. They are best known for their painting of genre scenes in which French peasants pause from labor for quiet family diversions. **A PEASANT FAMILY IN AN INTERIOR** (**FIG. 23-53**) of about 1640, probably by Louis Le Nain, is the largest and one of the most lyrical of these noble scenes of peasant life. Three generations of this family are gathered around a table. The adults acknowledge our presence—a spotlighted woman at left even seems to offer us some wine—whereas the children remain lost in dreams or focused on play. The casualness of costume and behavior is underlined by the foreground clutter of pets and kitchen equipment. It is only after we survey the frieze of figures illuminated around the table that the painting reveals one of its most extraordinary passages—a boy in the left background, warming himself in front of a fireplace and represented only as a dark silhouette from behind, edged by the soft golden firelight. Why the brothers chose to paint these peasant families, and who bought their paintings, are questions still unresolved.

23–54
Nicolas Poussin
**LANDSCAPE
WITH ST.
MATTHEW AND
THE ANGEL**
1639–1640. Oil on
canvas, 39 × 53⅛"
(99 × 135 cm).
Staatliche Museen
zu Berlin.

Credit: © 2016.
Photo Scala, Florence/
bpk, Bildagentur für
Kunst, Kultur und
Geschichte, Berlin.
Photo: Joerg P. Anders

**THE CLASSICAL LANDSCAPE: POUSSIN AND
CLAUDE LORRAIN**   French painters Nicolas Poussin
(1594–1665) and Claude Gellée (called "Claude Lorrain" or
simply "Claude," 1600–1682) pursued their careers in Italy
although they usually worked for French patrons. They
perfected the French ideal of the "Classical" landscape and
profoundly influenced painters for the next two centuries.
We refer to Poussin and Claude as Classicists because they
organized natural elements and figures into gently illuminated, idealized compositions. Both were influenced by
Annibale Carracci and to some extent by Venetian painting, yet each evolved an unmistakably personal style that
conveyed an entirely different mood from that of their
sources and from each other.

Nicolas Poussin was born in Normandy but settled in
Paris, where his initial career as a painter was unremark-
able. He arrived in Rome, and the Barberini family became
his foremost patrons. Bernini considered Poussin one of
the greatest painters in Rome, and others clearly agreed.
In 1639, Giovanni Maria Roscioli, secretary to Pope Urban
VIII, commissioned from Poussin two large paintings
showing the evangelists John and Matthew composing
their texts within expansive landscapes dotted with Classical buildings and antique ruins (**FIGS. 23–54, 23–55**).
The paintings were completed by October 1640, just before
Poussin left for two years in Paris to work for Louis XIII.
Perhaps they were the first installment of a set of four

evangelists within landscapes, but only these two had
been painted when the patron died in 1644.

These paintings epitomize and are among the earliest
examples of a new style of rigorously ordered and highly
idealized Classical landscapes with figures—an artistic
theme and format created by Poussin that would have a
long future in European painting. Although each is individually composed to create an ordered whole on its own, the
paintings were designed as a pair. The large clumps of trees
at the outside edges form "bookends" that bring lateral
closure to the broad panorama that stretches across both
canvases. Their unity is emphasized by the evangelists'
postures, turned inward toward each other, and solidified
at the lower inside corners where huge blocks of Classical masonry converge from both pictures as coordinated
remains of the same ruined monument. A consistent perspective progression in both pictures moves from the picture plane back into the distance through a clearly defined
foreground, middle ground, and background, illuminated
by an even light with gentle shadows and highlights. In the
middle distance, behind St. John, are a ruined temple and
an obelisk; the round building in the distant city is Hadrian's Tomb, which Poussin knew from Rome. Precisely
placed trees, hills, mountains, water, and even clouds take
on a solidity of form that seems almost as structural as this
architecture. The subject of Poussin's paintings is not the
writing evangelists but the balance and order of nature.

23–55
Nicolas Poussin
**LANDSCAPE
WITH ST. JOHN
ON PATMOS**
1640. Oil on canvas,
39½ × 53⅝″
(100.3 × 136.4 cm).
The Art Institute of
Chicago. A.A. Munger
Collection (1930.500).

Credit: Photo © The Art
Institute of Chicago

When Claude Lorrain went to Rome in 1613, he first studied with Agostino Tassi, an assistant of Guercino and a specialist in architectural painting. Claude, however, preferred landscape. He sketched outdoors for days at a time, then returned to his studio to compose paintings. Claude was fascinated with light, and his works are often studies of the effect of the rising or setting sun on colors and the atmosphere. A favorite and much-imitated device was to place one or two large objects in the foreground—a tree, building, a figural group, or hill—past which the viewer's

23–56 Claude Lorrain **A
PASTORAL LANDSCAPE**
c. 1648. Oil on copper, 15½ × 21″
(39.3 × 53.3 cm). Yale University Art
Gallery, New Haven, Connecticut.
Leonard C. Hanna, Jr., B.A. 1913,
Fund (1959.47).

Credit: Image courtesy Yale University
Art Gallery

eye enters the scene and proceeds, often by diagonal paths, into the distance.

Claude used this compositional device to great effect in paintings such as **A PASTORAL LANDSCAPE** of the late 1640s (**FIG. 23–56**). Instead of balancing symmetrically placed elements in a statement of stable order, Claude leads viewers actively into the painting in a continuing, zigzagging fashion. A conversing couple frames the composition at the right. Their gestures and the ambling of the cows they are tending lead our attention toward the left on a slightly rising diagonal, where a bridge and the traveler moving across it establish a middle ground. Across the bridge into the distance is a city, setting up a contrast between the warm, soft contours of the pastoral right foreground and the misty angularity of the fortified walls and blocks of the distant fortress. More distant still are the hazy outlines of hills that seem to take this space into infinity. The picture evokes a city dweller's nostalgia for the simpler and more sensuous life of the country, and it is easy to imagine the foreground shepherd boasting to his companion the superior virtues of their life in contrast to that in the city, toward which he gestures.

England

What features characterize the Classicism of English architecture?

England and Scotland were joined in 1603 with the ascent to the English throne of James VI of Scotland, who reigned over Great Britain as James I (ruled 1603–1625). James increased royal patronage of British artists, especially in literature and architecture. William Shakespeare wrote *Macbeth*, featuring the king's legendary ancestor Banquo, in tribute to the new royal family, and the play was performed at court in December 1606.

Although James's son Charles I was an important collector and patron of painting, religious and political tensions that erupted into civil war cost Charles his throne and his life in 1649. A succession of republican and monarchical rulers who alternately supported Protestantism or Catholicism followed, until the Catholic king James II was deposed in the Glorious Revolution of 1689 by his Protestant son-in-law and daughter, William and Mary. After Mary's death in 1694, William (the Dutch great-

23–57 Inigo Jones **BANQUETING HOUSE, WHITEHALL PALACE**
London. 1619–1622.

Credit: © akg-images /A.F.Kersting

grandson of William of Orange, who had led the Netherlands' independence movement) ruled on his own until his death in 1702. He was succeeded by Mary's sister, Anne (ruled 1702–1714).

Architecture

In sculpture and painting, the English court favored foreign artists. The field of architecture, however, was dominated in the seventeenth century by the Englishmen Inigo Jones, Christopher Wren, and Nicholas Hawksmoor. They replaced the country's long-lived Gothic style with Classicism.

INIGO JONES In the early seventeenth century, Inigo Jones (1573–1652) introduced to England his version of Renaissance Classicism, based on the style of Italian architect Andrea Palladio. Jones had studied Palladio's work in Venice, and he filled his copy of Palladio's *Four Books of Architecture*—still preserved—with notes. Appointed surveyor-general in 1615, Jones was commissioned to design the Queen's House in Greenwich and the Banqueting House for the royal palace of Whitehall.

The **BANQUETING HOUSE** (**FIG. 23-57**), built in 1619–1622 to replace an earlier hall destroyed by fire, was used for court ceremonies and entertainments such as the popular masques—stylized dramas combining theater, music, and dance in spectacles performed by professional actors, courtiers, and even members of the royal family itself. The west front, shown here, consisting of what appears to be two upper stories

with superimposed Ionic and Composite orders raised over a plain basement level, exemplifies the understated elegance of Jones's interpretation of Palladian design. Pilasters flank the end bays, and engaged columns subtly emphasize the three bays at the center, a disposition repeated in the balustrade along the roofline. A rhythmic effect results from varying window treatments—triangular and segmental (semicircular) pediments on the first level, cornices with volute (scroll-form) brackets on the second. The sculpted garlands just below the roofline add an unexpected decorative touch.

Although the exterior suggests two stories, the interior of the Banqueting House (**FIG. 23-58**) is actually one large hall divided by a balcony, with antechambers at each end. Ionic columns and pilasters suggest a colonnade but do

23-58 INTERIOR, BANQUETING HOUSE, WHITEHALL PALACE

Ceiling paintings of the apotheosis of King James and the glorification of the Stuart monarchy by Peter Paul Rubens. 1630–1635.

Credit: Historic Royal Palaces Enterprises Ltd

23–59 SCHEMATIC DRAWING OF ST. PAUL'S CATHEDRAL, LONDON

Credit: © Dorling Kindersley

not impinge on the ideal, double-cube space, which measures 55 feet in width by 110 feet in length by 55 feet in height. In 1630, Charles I commissioned Peter Paul Rubens—who was in England on a peace mission—to decorate the ceiling. Jones had divided the flat ceiling into nine compartments, for which Rubens painted canvases glorifying the reign of James I. Installed in 1635, the central oval shows the triumph of the Stuart dynasty with the king carried to heaven on clouds of glory. The large rectangular panel beyond it depicts the birth of the new nation, flanked by allegorical paintings of heroic strength and virtue overcoming vice. In the long paintings alongside the oval, *putti* holding the fruits of the earth symbolize the peace and prosperity of England and Scotland under Stuart rule. So proud was Charles of the result that, rather than allow the smoke of candles and torches to harm the ceiling decoration, he moved evening entertainments to an adjacent pavilion.

23–60 Christopher Wren **FAÇADE OF ST. PAUL'S CATHEDRAL, LONDON**

Designed 1673, built 1675–1710.

Credit: © Angelo Hornak/Getty Images

CHRISTOPHER WREN After Jones's death, English architecture was dominated by Christopher Wren (1632–1723) who began his professional career in 1659 as a professor of astronomy. For Wren, architecture was a sideline until 1665, when he traveled to France to further his education. While there, he met with French architects and with Bernini, who was in Paris to consult on designs for the Louvre. Wren returned to England with architecture books, engravings, and a greatly increased admiration for French Classical Baroque design. In 1669, he was made surveyor-general, the position once held by Jones, and in 1673, he was knighted.

After the Great Fire of 1666 destroyed large parts of central London, Wren was continuously involved in rebuilding the city, including more than 50 churches. His major project from 1675 to 1710 was the rebuilding of **ST. PAUL'S CATHEDRAL** (**FIG. 23-59**). Attempts to salvage the burned-out Gothic church on the site failed, and a new cathedral was needed. Wren's famous second design for St. Paul's (which survives in the so-called "Great Model" of 1672–1673) was for a centrally planned building with a great dome in the manner of Bramante's original plan for St. Peter's. This was rejected, but Wren ultimately succeeded in reconciling Reformation tastes for a basilica with the unity inherent in the use of a dome. St.

Paul's has a long nave and equally long sanctuary articulated by small, domed bays. Semicircular, colonnaded porticos open into short transepts that compress themselves against the crossing, where the dome rises 366 feet from ground level. Wren's dome has an interior masonry vault with an oculus and an exterior sheathing of lead-covered wood, but also has a brick cone rising from the inner oculus to support a tall lantern. The ingenuity of the design and engineering remind us that Wren had been a mathematician and professor of astronomy at Oxford. The columns surrounding the drum on the exterior recall Bramante's Tempietto in Rome (SEE FIG. 21-21), although Wren never went to Italy and knew Italian architecture only from books.

On the façade of St. Paul's (**FIG. 23-60**), two levels of paired Corinthian columns support a carved pediment. The deep-set porticos and columned pavilions atop the towers create dramatic areas of light and shadow. The huge size of the cathedral combines with its triumphant verticality, complexity of form, and *chiaroscuro* effects to make it a major monument of English architecture. Wren recognized the importance of the building. On the simple marble slab that forms his tomb in the crypt of the cathedral, he had engraved: "If you want to see his memorial, look around you."

Think About It

1   Discuss how Bernini and Caravaggio established the Baroque style in sculpture and painting, respectively. Locate the defining traits of the style in at least one work from this chapter by each artist.
2   Discuss the development of portraiture, still life, and genre painting in the Dutch Republic during the seventeenth century. What accounts for the increased importance of these subjects at this time?
3   Choose two paintings of monarchs in this chapter and explain how the artists who painted them embodied the ruler's prestige and power. Are the strategies of these painters different from those employed by painters of powerful people in the sixteenth century?
4   Determine how Poussin's landscapes depart from other stylistic currents at the time. What is meant by the term "Classicism" in relation to Poussin's style? Comment on its importance for the future of French art.

Crosscurrents

These two works visualize the same religious theme—the Last Judgment. But they are placed in different locations within their buildings, engaging different audiences in distinct ways. How do they represent the cultural goals and stylistic systems of their time and place? Do they have anything other than their subject in common?

FIG. 16–24

FIG. 23–15

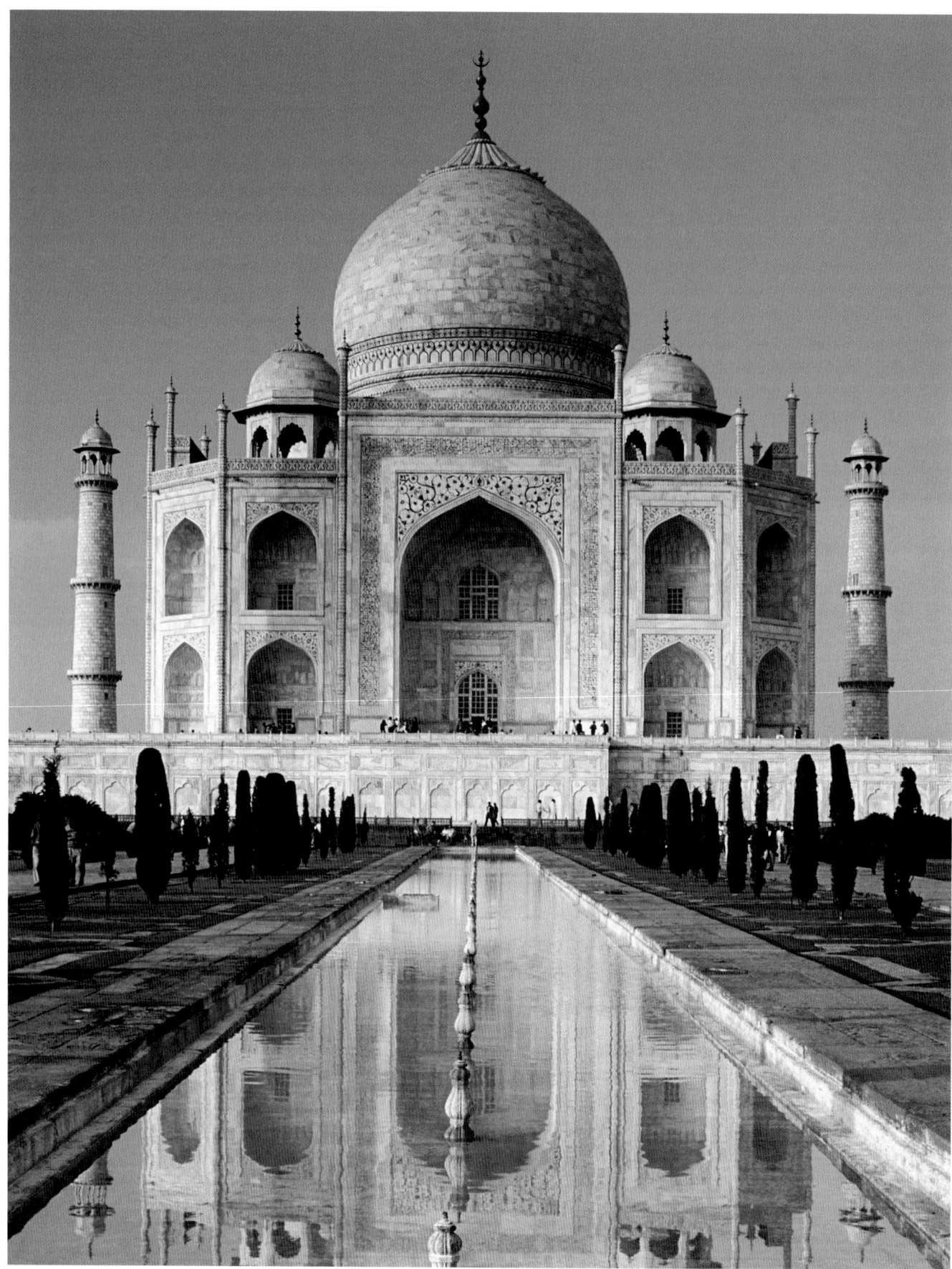

24–1 TAJ MAHAL

Agra, India. Mughal period, reign of Shah Jahan, c. 1631–1648.

Credit: © Peter Adams/Corbis

Chapter 24
Art of South and Southeast Asia after 1200

 ## Learning Objectives

24.a Identify the visual hallmarks of South and Southeast Asian art after 1200 for formal, technical, and expressive qualities.

24.b Interpret the meaning of works of South and Southeast Asian art after 1200 based on their themes, subjects, and symbols.

24.c Relate artists and art of South and Southeast Asia after 1200 to their cultural, economic, and political contexts.

24.d Apply the vocabulary and concepts relevant to the art, artists, and art history of South and Southeast Asia after 1200.

24.e Interpret a work of South or Southeast Asian art after 1200 using the art historical methods of observation, comparison, and inductive reasoning.

24.f Select visual and textual evidence in various media to support an argument or an interpretation of a work of South or Southeast Asian art after 1200.

Upon entering the gateway that today serves as the entrance to the great Taj Mahal complex, the visitor beholds the majestic white marble structure that is one of the world's best-known monuments. Its reflection shimmers in the pools of the garden meant to evoke a vision of paradise as described in the Qur'an. The building's façades are delicately inlaid with inscriptions designed by India's foremost calligrapher of the time, Amanat Khan, and floral arabesques in semiprecious stones: carnelian, agate, coral, turquoise, garnet, lapis, and jasper. Above, its luminous white marble dome reflects each shift in light, flushing rose at dawn, dissolving in its own brilliance in the noonday sun. This extraordinary building—originally and appropriately called the Illuminated Tomb and only since the nineteenth century known as the **TAJ MAHAL** (FIG. 24–1)—was built between 1631 and 1648 by the Mughal ruler Shah Jahan as a mausoleum for his favorite wife, Mumtaz Mahal, who died in childbirth, and likely as a tomb for himself.

Inside, the Taj Mahal invokes the *hasht behisht* ("eight paradises") with the eight small chambers that ring the interior—one at each corner and one behind each *iwan*, a vaulted opening with an arched portal that is a typical feature of eastern Islamic architecture. In two stories (for a total of 16 chambers), the rooms ring the octagonal

central area, which rises the full two stories to a domed ceiling that is lower than the outer dome. In this central chamber, surrounded by a finely carved octagonal openwork marble screen, are the exquisite inlaid **cenotaphs** (funerary monuments to someone whose remains lie elsewhere) of Shah Jahan and his wife, whose actual tombs lie in the crypt below.

The Taj Mahal complex includes much more than the white marble tomb. On one side is a mosque, while opposite and very similar in appearance is a building that may have served as a rest house. The enormous garden, both in front of the building and in its continuation on the opposite side of the Jamuna River, lends a lush setting consistent with Islamic notions of paradise. The side buildings and the two parts of the garden provide a sense of perfect symmetry to the entire complex.

A dynasty of Central Asian origin, the Mughals were the most successful of the many Islamic groups that established themselves in India beginning in the twelfth century. Under their patronage, Persian and Central Asian influences continued, but the Mughals intentionally cultivated connections with older traditions of the South Asian subcontinent, adding yet another dimension to the already ancient and complex artistic heritage of India.

Foundations of Indian Culture

What aspects of the early history, culture, and art of South Asia form a critical background for the development of art and architecture after 1200?

The earliest civilization on the Indian subcontinent flourished toward the end of the third millennium BCE along the Indus River in present day Pakistan. Remains of its expertly engineered brick cities have been uncovered, together with works of art that intriguingly suggest spiritual practices and reveal artistic traits known in later Indian culture.

The decline of the Indus civilization during the mid second millennium BCE coincides with the arrival from the northwest of a seminomadic people who spoke an Indo-European language and referred to themselves as Aryans. Over the next millennium they were influential in formulating the new civilization that gradually emerged. The most important Aryan contributions to this new civilization included the Sanskrit language and the sacred texts called the Vedas. The evolution of Vedic thought under the influence of indigenous Indian beliefs culminated in the mystical philosophical texts called the Upanishads, which took shape sometime after 800 BCE.

The Upanishads teach that the material world is illusory; only Brahman, the universal soul, is real and eternal. We—that is, our individual souls—are trapped in this illusion in a relentless cycle of birth, death, and rebirth. The ultimate goal of religious life is to liberate ourselves from this cycle and to unite our individual soul with Brahman.

Buddhism and Jainism are two of the many religions that developed in the wake of Upanishadic thought. Buddhism is based on the teachings of Shakyamuni Buddha, who lived in central India about 500 BCE. Jainism was shaped slightly earlier by the followers of the spiritual leader Mahavira. Both religions acknowledged the cyclical nature of existence and taught a means of liberation from it, but they rejected the authority, rituals, and social strictures of Vedic religion. The Vedic religion was in the hands of a hereditary priestly class, but Buddhist and Jain communities welcomed all members of society, which gave them great appeal. The Vedic tradition eventually evolved into the many sects now collectively known as Hinduism.

Through most of its history India was a mosaic of regional dynastic kingdoms, but from time to time empires emerged that unified large parts of the subcontinent. The first was that of the Maurya dynasty (c. 322–185 BCE), whose great king Ashoka patronized Buddhism. From this time Buddhist doctrines spread widely and its artistic traditions were established.

In the first century CE the Kushans, a Central Asian people, created an empire extending from present-day Afghanistan down into central India. Buddhism prospered under Kanishka, the most powerful Kushan king, and spread into Central Asia and East Asia. Under the new Kushan cultural and political climate, the image of the Buddha first appeared.

Later, under the Gupta dynasty (c. 320–550 CE) in northern India, Buddhist art and culture reached a high point. However, Gupta monarchs also patronized Hindu art, and from this time Hinduism grew to become the dominant Indian religious tradition, with its emphasis on the great gods Vishnu, Shiva, and the Goddess—all with multiple forms.

After the tenth century, numerous regional dynasties prevailed, some quite powerful and long-lasting. Hindu temples, in particular, developed monumental and complex forms that were rich in symbolism and ritual function, with each region of India producing its own variation.

South Asia 1200–1800

What are the characteristic features of the Buddhist, Jain, Islamic, and Hindu art and architecture of India from 1200 to 1800?

By 1200, India was already among the world's oldest civilizations. The art that survives from its earlier periods is often inspired by the three principal religions: Buddhism, Hinduism, and Jainism. These three religions remained a primary focus for Indian art, even as dynasties arriving from the northwest began to expand the influential religious culture of Islam.

Changes in Religion and Art

After many centuries of prominence, Buddhism began to decline as a cultural force in India after the eighth century, many of its sacred centers and much of its imagery having been absorbed into Hinduism. As patronage diminished, many Indian Buddhist monks sought out more supportive communities in Southeast Asia, where Buddhism remained an important religion. At the start of the twelfth century, Kyanzittha, the Burmese king of Bagan, who was known to have hosted Indian monks, actually sent crews to Buddhist centers in South Asia to repair the neglected monuments. By 1200, the remaining Buddhist enclaves in South Asia were concentrated in the northeast, in the region that had been ruled by the Pala dynasty (c. 750–1199). There, in great monastic universities that attracted monks from as far away as China, Korea, and Japan, a form of Buddhism known as Tantrism or Vajrayana was cultivated.

Over these same centuries, Hinduism quickly rose to new prominence, inspiring grand temples, sculpture, and poetry across the subcontinent. Jainism continued to prosper as its relatively small community of adherents grew in regional influence. And the new religion of Islam entered from the northwest, eventually to have a profound influence on South Asian culture.

MAP 24-1 SOUTH AND SOUTHEAST ASIA

Throughout its history, the kingdoms comprising the Indian subcontinent engaged—sometimes peacefully, sometimes militarily—with neighboring and more distant people, contributing significantly to the development of its art.

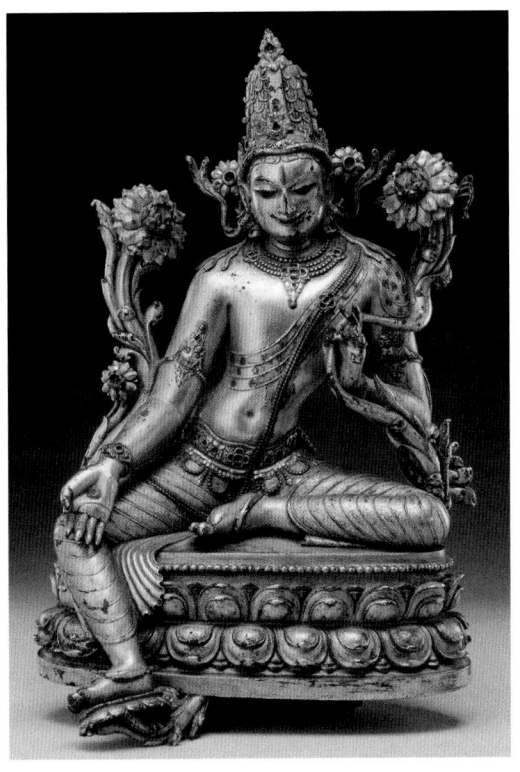

THE BODHISATTVA AVALOKITESHVARA   The practices of Tantric Buddhism, which include techniques for visualizing deities, encouraged the development of images with precise iconographic details, such as the twelfth-century gilt-bronze sculpture of **THE BODHISATTVA AVALOKITESHVARA (FIG. 24-2)** from the site of Kurkihar in eastern India. Bodhisattvas are compassionate beings who are well advanced on the path to buddhahood (enlightenment) and who have vowed to help others achieve enlightenment. Avalokiteshvara, the bodhisattva of greatest compassion who vowed to forgo buddhahood until all others become buddhas, became the most popular of these saintly beings in India and in East Asia.

Characteristic of bodhisattvas, Avalokiteshvara is distinguished in art by his princely garments, unlike a buddha, who wears monk's robes. Avalokiteshvara is specifically recognized by the lotus flower he holds and by the presence in his crown of his "parent" Buddha, in this case Amitabha, the Buddha of the Western Pure Land (a Buddhist paradise). Other marks of Avalokiteshvara's extraordinary status are

24-2 THE BODHISATTVA AVALOKITESHVARA
From Kurkihar, Bihar. Pala dynasty, 12th century. Gilt-bronze, height 10" (25.5 cm). Patna Museum, Patna.

Credit: Photo © Dirk Bakker/Bridgeman Images

the third eye (symbolizing his omniscience) and the wheel on his palm (an emblem of the Buddhist *dharma*). Avalokiteshvara is shown here in the relaxed pose known as the posture of "royal ease." One leg angles down; the other is drawn up onto the lotus seat.

With the fall of the Pala dynasty in the late twelfth century, the last centers of Buddhism in northern India collapsed, and most of the monks dispersed, mainly into Nepal and Tibet (**MAP 24–1**)—which have remained the principal stronghold of Tantric Buddhist practice and its arts since that time. The artistic style perfected under the Palas, however, came to influence international style throughout East and Southeast Asia.

LUNA VASAHI, MOUNT ABU The history of Jainism makes an interesting counterpoint to that of Buddhism. Although both are monastic traditions, the Jains never gained the widespread popularity of Buddhism—but neither did they suffer a precipitous decline. The Jain religion traces its roots to a spiritual leader called Mahavira (c. 599–527 BCE), whom it regards as the last in a series of 24 saviors known as pathfinders (*tirthankaras*). Devotees seek through purification and moral action to become worthy of escaping the cycle of rebirth. Jain monks live a life of austerity, and even laypeople avoid killing any living creature. The Jain commitment to nonviolence means that there are relatively few Jain kings in South Asian history, but this same commitment led many Jains to gravitate toward lucrative professions in banking and trade. It is from these ranks of merchants and ministers that some of the most important donors of Jain art come, as in the case of the Dilwara Temples erected on Mount Abu in Rajasthan, India. The modest exterior enclosure walls and relatively small size of the five Dilwara Temples do little to prepare the visitor for the lacelike splendor of the interior. Every inch of these spaces is filled with deeply cut relief carvings in white marble whose complicated details had to be produced through abrasion and rubbing rather than with a chisel. One of the most impressive of these temples, the Luna Vasahi, was dedicated to the 22nd Jain *tirthankara*, Neminatha, and was built in 1230 by two brothers, Tejpala and Vastupala, who served as ministers to the local ruler. They are known to have sponsored temples in at least two other locations. The structure has had to be repaired in places, the damage most likely caused by raids, but most of the delicate sculpture is still intact.

The main sanctuary is set in a courtyard surrounded by two columned arcades. These open to reveal the temple's most impressive architectural feature, the ornate dome that crowns the *mandapa* hall. This corbeled dome is made of concentric bands of sculpted stone capped with a meticulously carved pendant which hangs down from the apex. Surrounding this decorative element are images of 16 goddesses of wisdom, attached individually to the

24–3 LUNA VASAHI, MANDAPA CEILING
Mount Abu, India. 1230.

Credit: © Eye Ubiquitous/Alamy Stock Photo

surface of the dome. This, in turn, is held aloft by eight pillars linked by undulating architraves (**FIG. 24–3**). Every surface is adorned with narrative scenes, animals, protective deities, and plant motifs. These riotous forms highlight the calm, unadorned image of the *tirthankara*, which looks out from the quietude of the sanctuary. The dramatic contrast speaks to the difference between the active world of constant rebirth and the steady peace of enlightenment.

QUTB MINAR Traders and merchants were the first to bring Islam to South Asia, but the backing of political rulers, which helped to establish it across the region, did not occur until the eighth century when Arab communities established a small territory near the Indus River. Later, beginning around 1000, Turkic factions from Central Asia, relatively recent converts to Islam, began military campaigns into north India—at first purely for plunder, then seeking territorial control. From the thirteenth century various Turkic and Afghan dynasties ruled portions of the subcontinent from the northern city of Delhi. These sultanates, as they are known, constructed forts, mausoleums, monuments, and mosques.

The first Delhi Sultanate was founded in 1206 by Qutb-ud-din Aibak of the Slave dynasty, so named because Aibak had begun his life as a soldier-slave (*mamluk*) under the Ghorids. Although he did not reign long, he began construction of a large mosque adorned with a truly massive minaret. The mosque complex, called Quwwat ul-Islam ("strength of Islam"), was built over the citadel of Delhi's previous rulers, and portions of the Jain and Hindu religious structures from this location were reused in the construction of the mosque. By far the most visible element of this complex is the tower known as the **QUTB MINAR** (**FIG. 24-4**). This minaret was begun by Aibak and completed under his successor, Iltutmish. It stands over 237 feet high and was among the tallest structures in South Asia at the time. It was constructed of sandstone in five segments, each of which is marked by the presence of a balcony that encircles the tower. The stories get smaller farther up the tower, and the final balcony rests on the top. Minarets are traditionally used to call Muslims to prayer, but this tower is too tall to serve that purpose easily and serves more clearly as an expression of power and political authority than as a functioning religious structure.

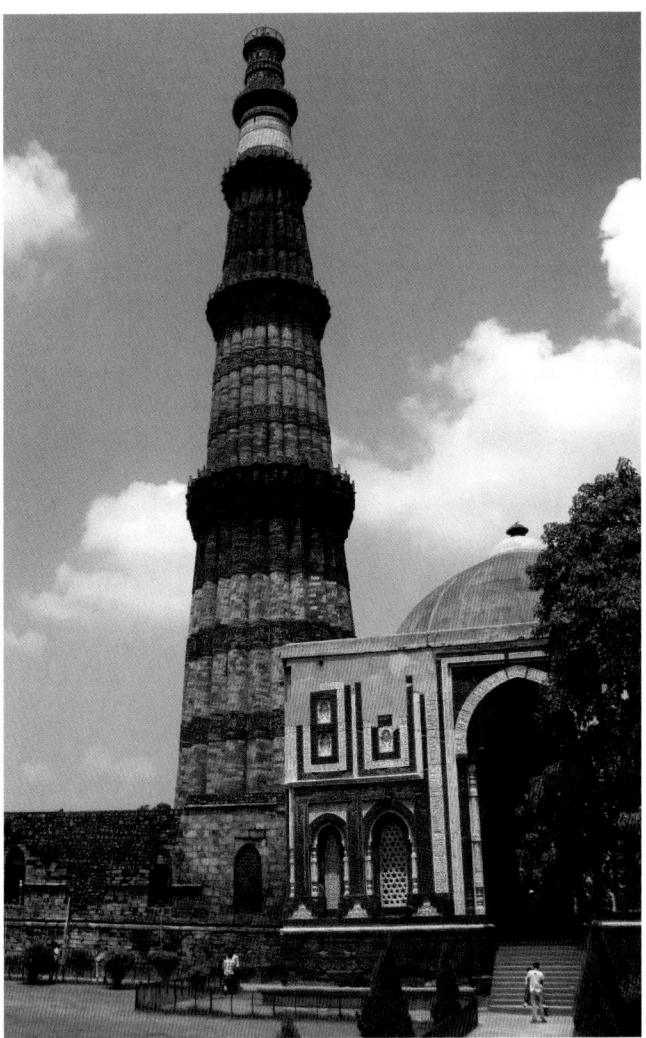

24-4 QUTB MINAR
Quwwat ul-Islam Mosque, Mehrauli Archaeological Park, Delhi. 1211–1236.

Credit: Icon72/Fotolia

Hindu Architectural Developments

With the increasing popularity of Hindu sects came the rapid development of Hindu temples. Spurred by the ambitious building programs of wealthy donors, well-formulated regional styles had evolved by about 900. The most spectacular structures of the era were monumental, with a complexity and grandeur of proportion rarely equaled even in later Indian art.

Emphasis on monumental temples gave way to the building of vast temple complexes and more moderately scaled, yet more richly ornamented, individual temples. These developments took place largely in the south of India, although some of the largest temples are in the north—for example, the Sun Temple at Konarak, built in the thirteenth century, and the Govind Deva Temple in Brindavan, built in the sixteenth century under the patronage of the Mughal emperor Akbar. The mightiest of the southern Indian kingdoms was Vijayanagara (c. 1336–1565), whose rulers successfully countered the potential incursions of neighboring dynasties, both Hindu and Muslim, for more than 200 years. Under the patronage of the Vijayanagara kings and their successors, the Nayaks, some of India's most spectacular Hindu architecture was created.

VIJAYANAGARA ("the City of Victory") was the capital of an empire that flourished in South India between the fourteenth and sixteenth centuries. Scholars estimate that at its peak the city was the second most populous in the world and had fortifications encompassing an area of 250 square miles. As a center of trade, Vijayanagara housed small, itinerant communities from across Asia, Europe, and the Middle East, and within the settled population were devotees of Hinduism, Islam, Jainism, and Christianity. Among the visitors drawn by this city's wealth and fame were those who left travel accounts praising its lush gardens, expansive waterways, abundant markets, grand temples, and stone arcades. At the heart of this sprawling urban center stood the **VIRUPAKSHA TEMPLE** (**FIG. 24-5**); its founding pre-dates the birth of the city, but it was expanded in size and splendor along with the empire's capital.

The brothers Bukka and Harihara first enlarged this temple to Shiva in the mid fourteenth century as they prayed for the protection and success of their new empire. Most of the temple as it now stands, however, was built by later donors in the fifteenth and sixteenth centuries. The temple is notable for its grand eastward-facing **gopura** (entrance gateway), whose nine-tiered tower reaches over 160 feet in height. This gateway connects the outer temple courtyard to a long, colonnaded road that was used for ceremonial processions and may also have contained stalls for vendors. A smaller *gopura*, which along with the central pillared hall was donated by the great king Krishnadevaraya in the early 1500s, provides access to the inner courtyard. Krishnadevaraya, like all kings of Vijayanagara,

24-5 VIRUPAKSHA TEMPLE, VIJAYANAGARA

Hampi, India. Founded before the 9th century but expanded in the 14th–16th centuries.

Credit: © Eugil Chandran/Alamy Stock Photo

continued to recognize the Virupaksha form of Shiva as the special defender of the empire and the royal line.

While the temples in Vijayanagara tend to follow conservative South Indian architectural forms, the civic architecture exhibits hybrid forms that reflect the religious and ethnic diversity of the city's population. This appropriation of diverse architectural techniques is apparent in the royal **ELEPHANT STABLES** (FIG. 24–6). The structure utilizes both traditional South Indian architectural forms and elements associated with Islamic (or sultanate) architecture, namely the arch and dome, to span the large spaces needed to comfortably house such massive animals. The court stabled its elephants in grand fashion because these powerful animals had both ceremonial and military functions. They were living emblems of the state's pageantry and power. The structure contains ten chambers divided by a central structure capped with a rooftop pavilion. This pavilion most likely held musicians and served as a viewing platform from which important individuals could observe military maneuvers conducted in the parade grounds that stretch out in front of the stables. The individual chambers are placed in a row and alternate between two types, one

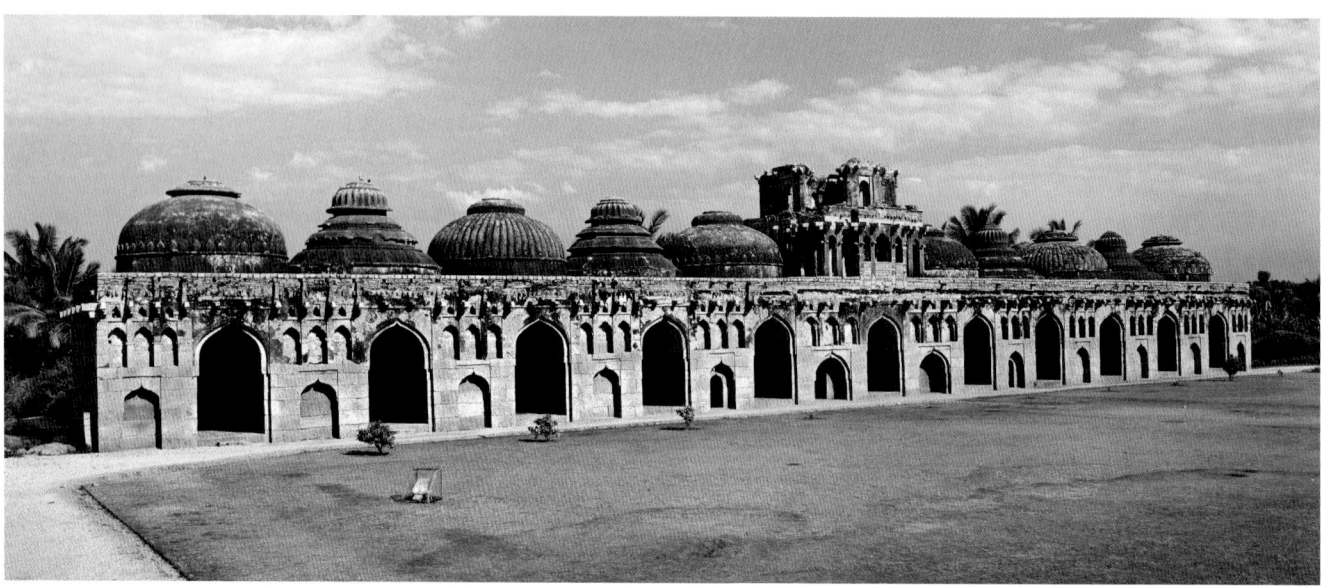

24-6 ELEPHANT STABLES, VIJAYANAGARA

Hampi, India. 15th century.

Credit: © age fotostock/Alamy Stock Photo

crowned by a semicircular dome and the other by a conical vault. As with many structures in Vijayanagara this building is unique, and its style reflects the court's comfort with foreign ideas.

TEMPLE AT MADURAI   The enormous temple complex at Madurai, one of the capitals of the Nayaks, is a fervent expression of Hindu faith. Founded around the fourteenth century and greatly expanded in the seventeenth, it is dedicated to the goddess Minakshi (the local name for Parvati, the consort of the god Shiva) and to Sundareshvara (the local name for Shiva himself). The temple complex stands in the center of the city and is the focus of Madurai life. At its heart are the two oldest shrines, one to Minakshi and the other to Sundareshvara. Successive additions over the centuries gradually expanded the complex around these small shrines and came to dominate the visual landscape. The most dramatic features of this and similar southern "temple cities" were the thousand-pillar halls, large

ritual-bathing pools, and especially the entrance gateways (*gopuras*) that tower above the temple site and the surrounding city like modern skyscrapers (**FIG. 24–7**).

As a temple city grew, it needed bigger enclosing walls, and thus new gateways. Successive rulers and powerful merchants of the Chettiyar community, often seeking to outdo their predecessors, donated taller and taller *gopuras*. As a result, the tallest structures in temple cities are often at the periphery, rather than at the central temples, which are sometimes totally overwhelmed by the height of the surrounding structures. The temple complex at Madurai has 11 *gopuras*, the largest over 160 feet tall.

Formally, the *gopura* has its roots in the pyramidal tower characteristic of the seventh-century southern temple style. As the *gopura* evolved, it took on the graceful concave silhouette shown here. The exterior is embellished with thousands of sculpted figures, evoking a teeming world of gods and goddesses. Inside, stairs lead to the top for an extraordinary view.

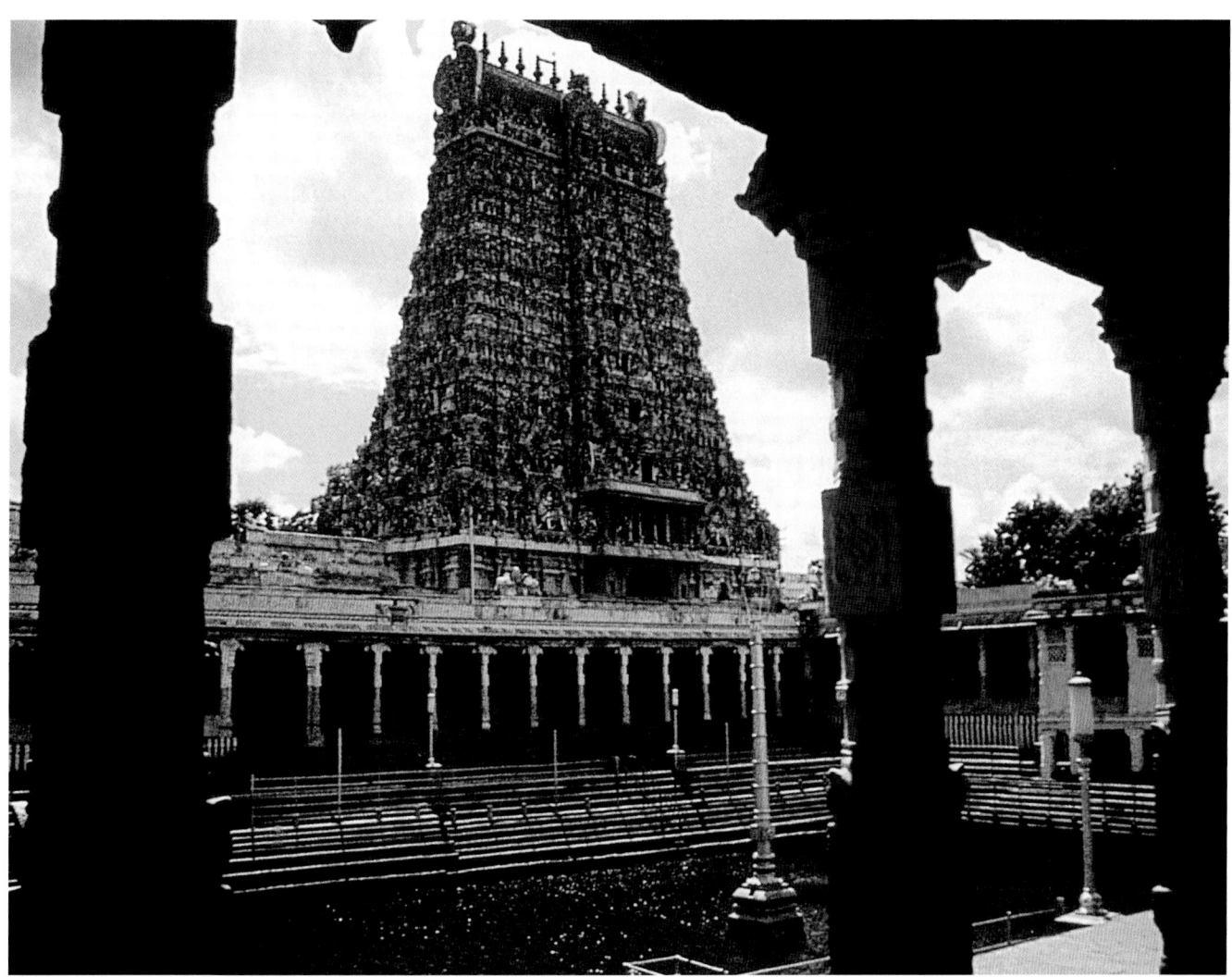

24–7 OUTER GOPURA OF THE MINAKSHI-SUNDARESHVARA TEMPLE
Madurai, Tamil Nadu, India. Nayak dynasty, mostly 13th to mid 17th century, with modern renovations.

Credit: Courtesy of Marilyn Stokstad

Mughal Period

The Mughals, like many of the Delhi sultans, came from Central Asia. Muhammad Zahir-ud-Din, known as Babur ("Lion" or "Panther"), was the first Mughal emperor of India (ruled 1526–1530). He emphasized his Turkic heritage, though he had equally impressive Mongol ancestry. After some initial conquests in Central Asia, he amassed an empire stretching from Afghanistan to Delhi, which he conquered in 1526. Akbar (ruled 1556–1605), the third ruler, extended Mughal control over most of north India, and under his two successors, Jahangir and Shah Jahan, northern India was generally unified by 1658. The Mughal Empire lasted until 1858, when the last Mughal emperor was deposed and exiled to Burma (today's Myanmar) by the British.

Mughal architects were heir to a 300-year-old tradition of Islamic building in India. The Delhi sultans who preceded them had great forts housing government and court buildings. Their architects had introduced two fundamental Islamic structures, the mosque and the tomb, along with construction based on the arch and the dome. (Earlier Indian architecture had been based primarily on post-and-lintel construction.) They had also drawn freely on Indian architecture, borrowing both decorative and structural elements to create a variety of hybrid styles, and had especially benefited from the centuries-old Indian virtuosity in stonecarving and masonry. The Mughals followed in this tradition, synthesizing Indian, Persian, and Central Asian elements for their forts, palaces, mosques, tombs, and cenotaphs.

The third emperor, Akbar, presided over a period of openness and expansion. His inclusive policies and tolerance toward religious difference did much to help solidify and stabilize his massive empire. A dynamic, humane, and just leader, Akbar enjoyed religious discourse and loved the arts, especially painting. He created an imperial **atelier** (workshop) of painters, which he placed under the direction of two artists from the Persian court. Learning from these two masters, the Indian painters of the atelier soon transformed Persian styles into the more vigorous, naturalistic styles that mark Mughal painting (see "Indian Painting on Paper" below).

FATEHPUR SIKRI Despite all this success Akbar was concerned about who would follow him on the throne. In desperation, he sought the advice of the Sufi mystic Shaikh Salim Chishti. This Muslim holy man foretold the birth of a prince, and when his prediction proved accurate, Akbar built a new capital near Chishti's home to commemorate and celebrate the event. Built primarily during Akbar's residence at the site from about 1572 to 1585, there are two major components to Fatehpur Sikri: one section including the Jami Mosque, which houses the tomb of Salim Chishti, and another containing the administrative and residential section. Among the most extraordinary buildings in the administrative and residential section is the private audience hall or **DIWAN-I-KHAS** (FIG. 24-8). In the center of the hall is a tall pillar supporting a circular platform reached by four walkways. On this perch Akbar could have sat majestically as he received his nobles and dispensed

---

Technique

INDIAN PAINTING ON PAPER

Before the fourteenth century most painting in India had been on walls or palm leaves. With the introduction of paper, about the same time in India as in Europe, Indian artists adopted painting techniques from Persia and over the ensuing centuries produced jewel-toned works on paper.

Painters usually began their training early. As young apprentices, they learned to make brushes and grind pigments. Brushes were made from the curved hairs of a squirrel's tail, arranged to taper from a thick base to a single hair at the tip. Paint came from pigments of vegetables and minerals—lapis lazuli to make blue, malachite for pale green—that were ground to a paste with water, then bound with a solution of gum from the acacia plant. Paper was made by crushing fibers of cotton and jute to a pulp, pouring the mixture onto a woven mat, drying it, and then burnishing with a smooth piece of agate, often achieving a glossy finish.

First, the painter applied a thin wash of a chalk-based white, which sealed the surface of the paper while allowing any underlying sketches to show through. Next, outlines were filled with thick washes of brilliant, opaque, unmodulated color. When the colors were dry, the painting was laid face down on a smooth marble surface and burnished with a rounded agate stone, rubbing first up and down, then side to side. The indirect pressure against the marble polished the pigments to a high luster. Then outlines, details, and modeling—depending on the style—were added with a fine brush.

Sometimes certain details were purposely left until last, such as the eyes, which were said to bring the painting to life. Gold and raised details were applied when the painting was nearly finished. Gold paint, made from pulverized, 24-carat gold leaf bound with acacia gum, was applied with a brush and burnished to a high shine. Raised details such as the pearls of a necklace were made with thick, white, chalk-based paint, with each pearl a single droplet hardened into a tiny raised mound.

My liking for painting and my practice in judging it have arrived at such a point that when any work is brought before me, either of deceased artists or of those of the present day, without their names being told me I say on the spur of the moment that it is the work of such and such a man, and if there be a picture containing many portraits, and each face be the work of a different master, I can discover which face is the work of each of them. And if any other person has put in the eye and eyebrow of a face, I can perceive whose work the original face is and who has painted the eye and eyebrows.

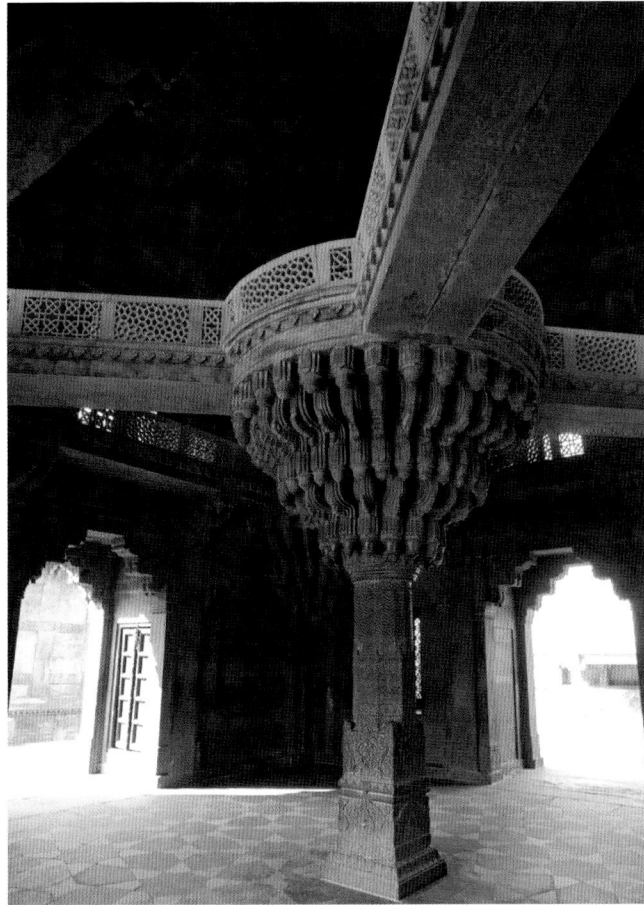

24-8 DIWAN-I-KHAS (PRIVATE AUDIENCE HALL)
Fatehpur Sikri, India. 1570.

Credit: MrPeak/Fotolia

24-9 AKBAR INSPECTING THE CONSTRUCTION OF FATEHPUR SIKRI
From the *Akbarnama*. c. 1590. Opaque watercolor on paper, 14¾ × 10″ (37.5 × 25 cm). Victoria & Albert Museum, London. (I.S.2-1896 91/117).

Many of the painters in the Mughal imperial workshops are recorded in texts of the period. Based on those records and on signatures that occur on some paintings, the design of this work has been attributed to Tulsi Kalan (Tulsi the Elder), the painting to Bandi, and the portraits to Madhu Kalan (Madhu the Elder) or Madhu Khurd (Madhu the Younger).

Credit: V&A Images/Victoria and Albert Museum

justice. The structure recalls, perhaps consciously, the pillars erected by Ashoka to publicize his law.

Unlike most Mughal emperors, Akbar did not write his own biography; instead he entrusted its creation to his vizier Abul Fazl. This text, the *Akbarnama* (**FIG. 24-9**), details the actions and accomplishments of the emperor, including the events leading to the construction of Fatehpur Sikri.

Paintings commissioned to illustrate this event round out our understanding of Mughal building techniques and reveal Akbar's personal interest in the progress. Among the most fascinating illustrations in this manuscript are those that record Akbar's supervision of the construction of Fatehpur Sikri. One painting (SEE FIG. 24-9) documents his inspection of the stonemasons and other craftspeople. Akbar's love of painting set a royal precedent that his successors enthusiastically continued.

PAINTING IN THE COURT OF JAHANGIR   Jahangir (ruled 1605–1627), Akbar's son and successor, was a connoisseur of painting; he had his own workshop, which he established even before he became emperor. His focus on detail was much greater than that of his father. In his memoirs, he claimed:

24–10 Nadir al-Zaman (Abu'l Hasan)
JAHANGIR AND SHAH ABBAS
From the St. Petersburg Album. Mughal period,
c. 1618. Opaque watercolor, gold, and ink on
paper; 9⅜ × 6″ (23.8 × 15.4 cm). Freer Gallery
of Art, Smithsonian Institution, Washington, DC.
Purchase, F1945.9.

Credit: Bridgeman Images

together, an ancient symbol of harmony, also appears to bolster this interpretation. Indeed, the fact that the men are framed by the sun and moon while standing on a map of the world might imply that these bonds of trust and peace extend even to their respective states. Yet nothing could be further from the truth.

This painting was created in a moment of high tension between Shah Abbas and the Mughal throne. The trouble centered on Kandahar in Afghanistan. The prosperous city had been given to Shah Abbas's ancestor by the Mughal emperor Humayun, but later, in the time of Akbar, the Mughals took back control of the city. Shah Abbas then waited for a chance to reclaim it, believing it was his right to do so. When the Mughals were distracted by civil conflict in South Asia, he seized the opportunity and recaptured Kandahar in a swift assault. He immediately made conciliatory gestures to Jahangir, who was furious but unable to spare the military force needed to retake the city.

Another look at the painting reveals new details. Jahangir is depicted much larger than Shah Abbas, who appears to bow deferentially to the Mughal emperor. Jahangir's head is centered in the halo and he stands on the predatory lion, whose body spans a vast territory, including Shah Abbas's own holdings in Afghanistan and Iran. These details invert the initial impression conveyed by the subject, revealing a new meaning. The painting, cloaked in the diplomatic language of cordiality and reconciliation, is a strong reminder of Mughal superiority and a potent warning against further expansion

Despite the proliferation of portrait painting, depictions of court women occur rarely in Mughal art, due in part to the restricted access male painters had to the women's quarters. An important exception to this was Jahangir's favorite wife, Empress Nur Jahan, of whom a few images exist. As Jahangir grew older he succumbed to addiction and illness. During this period, in which he was largely incapacitated, Nur Jahan ran the empire on his behalf, carrying his seal

Portraits became a major art under Jahangir. We can only speculate on the target audience for the portrait Jahangir commissioned of himself with the Safavid-dynasty Persian ruler, Shah Abbas. The painting of **JAHANGIR AND SHAH ABBAS** (FIG. 24–10) is of such small size it could not be publicly displayed and was, therefore, certainly not intended for Jahangir's subjects. But because we know that paintings were commonly conveyed by embassies from one kingdom to another, it may have been intended to be taken, or even just seen, by one of Shah Abbas's representatives at court.

At first glance this painting of two rulers embracing seems to tell of a close bond of friendship between the men. The presence of a lion and lamb laying peacefully and issuing decrees in his name. Although she ruled in Jahangir's name, the images of her at court and the imperial coins that bore her name suggest her role was no secret.

The idyllic scene depicted in **FIGURE 24-11** portrays Nur Jahan serving food and drink to Jahangir and his son by another wife, Prince Khurram. Seated on ornate carpets the royal family members sit near a fountain as court women bring food and wave fans. This deceptively harmonious tableau is qualified by the verses in Persian surrounding the painting. These refer to Jahangir's displeasure over Khurram's attempts to take the throne, an outcome that Nur Jahan also wished to prevent. After Jahangir died, however, and Nur Jahan was confined to her palace, Khurram managed to seize the throne, taking the royal name Shah Jahan.

THE TAJ MAHAL Shah Jahan (ruled 1628–58) achieved a number of military and political victories, but he is best known as the patron of what is perhaps the most famous of all Indian Islamic structures, the Taj Mahal. Built between

24-11 JAHANGIR AND PRINCE KHURRAM FEASTED BY NUR JAHAN

Mughal period, 1617. Paint and gold on paper, 9¹⁵⁄₁₆ × 5⅝″ (25.2 × 14.3 cm). Freer Gallery of Art, Smithsonian Institution, Washington, DC. Gift of Charles Lang Freer (F1907.258).

Credit: Bridgeman Images

1631 and 1648 on the banks of the Jamuna River, it was commissioned as a mausoleum for Mumtaz Mahal, the wife of Shah Jahan, who is believed to have taken a major part in overseeing its design and construction. Shah Jahan's personal motivations add a poignancy to this structure, but it must also be recalled that this was the first major architectural undertaking of Shah Jahan's reign. That the Taj Mahal effectively evokes both personal loss and imperial authority is perhaps its most remarkable strength.

As visitors enter through a monumental, hall-like gate, the tomb rises before them across a spacious garden set with long reflecting pools (SEE FIG. 24-1). Measuring some 1,000 by 1,900 feet, the enclosure is unobtrusively divided into quadrants planted with trees and flowers, and framed by broad walkways and stone inlaid in geometric patterns. In Shah Jahan's time, fruit trees and cypresses—symbolic of life and death, respectively—lined the walkways, and fountains played in the shallow pools. Collectively these features evoked paradise on earth.

Recent archaeology has revealed that the garden continued on the far bank of the Jamuna River. A garden filled with night-blooming plants and a large octagonal fountain provided a vantage point for viewing the Taj Mahal from across the river. Thus while the structure appears to visitors to be set at the end of a garden, it is in fact in the center of a four-part garden, a traditional Mughal tomb setting used for earlier tombs. The tomb is flanked by two smaller structures not visible in FIGURE 24-1, one a mosque and the other a hall designed to mirror it. Like the entrance hall, they are made mostly of red sandstone, rendering even more startling the full glory of the tomb's white marble, a material previously reserved for the tombs of saints and here implying an elevated religious stature for Shah Jahan and Mumtaz Mahal. The tomb is raised higher than these structures on its own marble platform, emphasizing its importance. This aggrandizement of the tomb is further achieved by having the minarets flank the tomb rather than the mosque. The minarets' three levels correspond to those of the tomb, creating a bond between them. Crowning each minaret is a **chattri** (pavilion). Traditional embellishments of Indian palaces, *chattris* quickly passed into the vocabulary of Indian Islamic architecture, where they appear prominently. A lucid geometric symmetry pervades the tomb. It is basically square, but its **chamfered** (sliced-off)

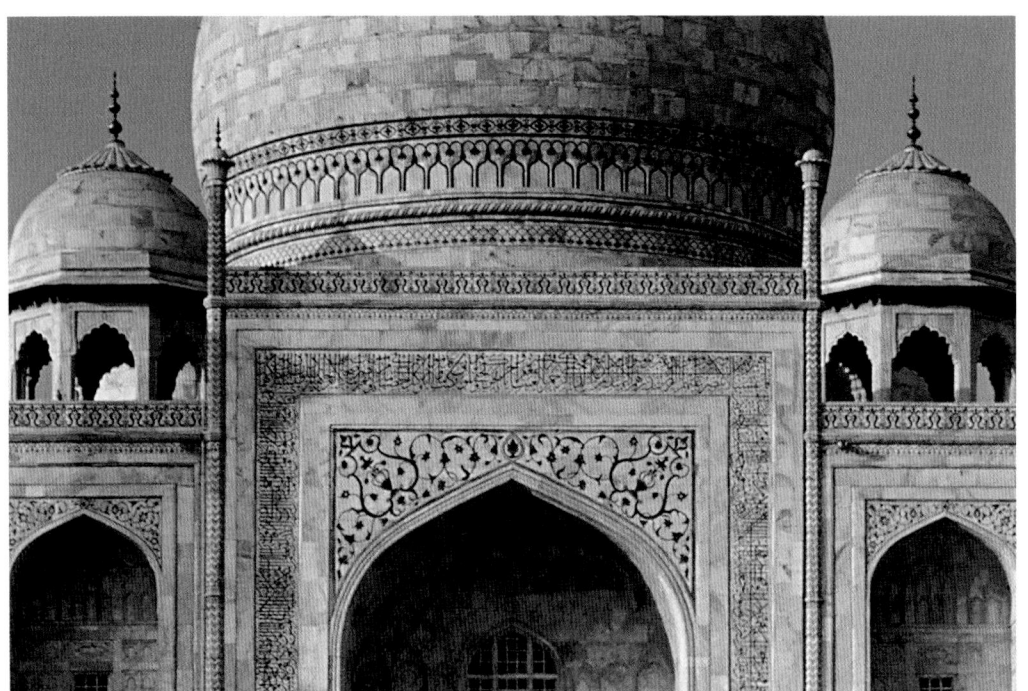

Rajput painting, more abstract than the Mughal style, included subjects like those treated by Mughal painters: royal portraits and court scenes, as well as indigenous subjects such as Hindu myths, love poetry, and Ragamala illustrations (illustrations of musical modes).

corners create a subtle octagon. Measured to the base of the finial (the spire at the top), the tomb is almost exactly as tall as it is wide. Each façade is identical, with a central *iwan* flanked by two stories of smaller *iwans*. By creating voids in the façades, these *iwans* contribute to the building's sense of weightlessness. On the roof, four octagonal *chattris*, one at each corner, create a visual transition to the lofty, bulbous dome. Framed but not obscured by the *chattris*, the dome rises gracefully and is lifted higher by its drum than in earlier Mughal tombs, allowing the swelling curves and elegant lines of its surprisingly large form to emerge with perfect clarity.

The pristine surfaces of the Taj Mahal are embellished with utmost subtlety (**FIG. 24-12**). Even the sides of the platform on which the Taj Mahal stands are carved in relief with a **blind arcade** (decorative arches set into a wall) motif and carved relief panels of flowers. The portals are framed with verses from the Qur'an and inlaid in black marble, while the spandrels are decorated with floral arabesques inlaid in colored semiprecious stones, a technique known by its Italian name, *pietra dura*. Not strong enough to detract from the overall purity of the white marble, the embellishments enliven the surfaces of this impressive yet delicate masterpiece.

RAJPUT PAINTING   Outside the Mughal strongholds at Delhi and Agra, much of northern India was governed regionally by local princes, often descendants of the so-called Hindu Rajput warrior clans, who were allowed to keep their lands in return for allegiance to the Mughals. Like the Mughals, Rajput princes frequently supported painters at their courts, and in these settings a variety of strong, indigenous Indian painting styles were perpetuated.

The Hindu devotional movement known as *bhakti*, which had done much to spread the faith in the south from around the seventh century, now experienced a revival in the north. As it had earlier in the south, *bhakti* inspired an outpouring of poetic literature, this time devoted especially to Krishna, the popular human incarnation of the god Vishnu. Most renowned is the *Gita Govinda*, a cycle of rhapsodic poems about the love between God and humans expressed metaphorically through the love between the young Krishna and the cowherd Radha.

The illustration here (**FIG. 24-13**) is from a manuscript of the *Gita Govinda* probably produced about 1525–1550 in what is present-day Rajasthan. The blue god Krishna sits in dalliance with a group of cowherd women. Standing with her maid and consumed with love for Krishna, Radha peers through the trees, overcome by jealousy. Her feelings are indicated by the cool blue color behind her, while the crimson red behind the Krishna grouping suggests passion. The bold patterns of curving stalks and flowering vines express both the exuberance of springtime, when the story unfolds, and the heightened emotional tensions of the scene. Birds, trees, and flowers are as brilliant against the black, hilly landscape edged in an undulating white line. All the figures are of a single type, with plump faces in profile and oversized eyes. Yet the resilient line of the drawing gives them life, and the variety of textile patterns provides some individuality. The intensity of the color and resolute flatness of the scene engage the viewer in the drama.

Quite a different mood dominates **HOUR OF COW-DUST**, a work from the Kangra School in the Punjab Hills, foothills of the Himalayas north of Delhi (**FIG. 24-14**). Painted around 1790, some 250 years later than the *Gita Govinda* illustration, it shows the influence of Mughal

24–13 KRISHNA AND THE GOPIS

From the *Gita Govinda*, Rajasthan, India. Mughal period, c. 1525–1550. Gouache on paper, 4⅞ × 7½" (12.3 × 19 cm). Prince of Wales Museum, Mumbai.

The lyrical poem *Gita Govinda*, by the poet-saint Jayadeva, was probably written in eastern India during the latter half of the twelfth century. The poem traces the progress of Krishna and Radha's love through separation, reconciliation, and fulfillment.

naturalism on the later schools of Indian painting. The theme is again Krishna. Wearing his peacock crown, garland of flowers, and yellow garment—all traditional iconography of Krishna-Vishnu—he returns to the village with his fellow cowherds and their cattle. All eyes are upon him as he plays his flute, said to enchant all who hear it. Women with water jugs on their heads turn to look; others lean from windows to watch and call out to him. We are drawn into this village scene by the diagonal movements of the cows as they surge through the gate and into the courtyard beyond. Pastel houses and walls create a sense of space, and in the distance we glimpse other villagers going about their work or peacefully sitting in their houses. A rim of dark trees softens the horizon, and an atmospheric sky completes the aura of enchanted naturalism. Again, all the figures are similar in type, this time with refined proportions and a gentle, lyrical movement that complement the idealism of the setting.

24–14 HOUR OF COWDUST

From the Punjab Hills, India. Mughal period, Kangra School, c. 1790. Gouache on paper, 14¹⁵⁄₁₆ × 12⁹⁄₁₆" (38 × 31.9 cm). Museum of Fine Arts, Boston. Denman W. Ross Collection (22.683).

24-15 CITY PALACE, UDAIPUR

India, 1559 onward.

Credit: © Ozphotoguy/Getty Images

RAJPUT ARCHITECTURE Just as each Rajput court had a distinctive style of painting, so too was each royal household situated within its own majestic architectural setting. Due to both tradition and political reality, these massive structures often combined regal splendor with imposing fortifications. Royal families typically placed these palaces at strategic hilltop locations and gradually expanded them over the course of generations. As a result, the plans of such structures are often asymmetrical and exceedingly complex, with multiple terraces and courtyards opening into complicated arrangements of chambers and hallways, some of which were intended for public use and others reserved solely for members of the royal family.

Many spectacular examples of Rajput palaces and forts remain; a fine example is the **CITY PALACE** in Udaipur (**FIG. 24-15**). Construction on the palace began in 1559 when Maharana Udai Singh II relocated the capital of the Mewar Kingdom from Chittor after the town had been sacked by Mughal forces under Akbar. The new location proved to be more defensible, and the Mewar rulers expanded both the city and their royal residences almost continuously over the next 300 years. Located on a ridge above a lake, this extensive architectural complex is better understood as a linked series of palaces rather than as a single building.

The structure is built primarily of granite and marble, but architects ornamented the dull stone with bright flourishes of paint, inlaid stone, silverwork, and inset pieces of mirror and colored glass. Despite its vast size, artists lavished attention on the finest points of decoration. This attention to detail reminds us that the palace was far more than just a military center; it functioned equally well as a backdrop for political events and displays of state

24-16 MOR CHOWK OF THE CITY PALACE, UDAIPUR

India. 17th century with 19th-century additions.

Credit: Donyanedomam/Fotolia

power. One such lavishly ornamented space in the Udaipur City Palace complex is the **MOR CHOWK** (**FIG. 24-16**) or "Peacock Courtyard." Built in the seventeenth century by Maharana Sajjan Singh, it housed ceremonial gatherings. The public nature of this space and its function as an extension of royal authority are reflected in the decoration. The court gets its name from the three molded, high-relief images of peacocks inset with colored glass that adorn the courtyard's lower level, but the decoration becomes even more elaborate on the upper story. Here images of courtiers and carved stone screens depicting trees flank a projecting balcony with Mewari cusped arches. The entire surface is ornamented with delicately inset foliage patterns of colored tile and stained glass. Although the courtyard was first constructed in the 1600s, much of the current decoration represents the work of later centuries. This longevity attests to the continued importance of display as a component of court politics.

Art and its Contexts
SOUTHEAST ASIAN CERAMICS

Before the fourteenth century, China dominated the international trade in ceramics, but with the rise of the Ming dynasty, China began to look inward, limiting and regulating most forms of international trade. The resulting scarcity of Chinese trade ceramics, sometimes called the "Ming gap," was an opportunity for the merchants and artists of Southeast Asia. Both the Burmese and Thai kingdoms produced ceramics, often inspired by stonewares and porcelains from China. Sukhothai potters, for example, made green-glazed and brown-glazed wares at the renowned kilns of Sawankhalok. But it was the potters of Vietnam who were most successful in meeting the international demand for porcelains. So many ceramics were exported from Vietnam that most of what remained to be found by archaeologists were the broken or discarded leftovers.

This changed with the excavation of a sunken ship laden with ceramics for export, found 22 miles off the coast of Hoi An. This wreck brought to light over 250,000 ceramic works made by Vietnamese potters dating back to the late fifteenth to early sixteenth century (**FIG. 24-17**). Painted in underglaze cobalt blue and further embellished with overglaze enamels, these wares were shipped throughout Southeast Asia and beyond, as far east as Japan and as far west as England and the Netherlands.

24-17 GROUP OF VIETNAMESE CERAMICS FROM THE HOI AN HOARD
Late 15th to early 16th century. Porcelain with underglaze blue decoration; barbed-rim dishes: (left) diameter 14″ (35.1 cm); (right) diameter 13¼″ (34.7 cm). Phoenix Art Museum, Arizona. (2000.105–109).
Credit: Photo: Craig Smith.

Southeast Asia 1200–1800

What characterizes the Buddhist art and architecture of Southeast Asia from 1200 to 1800?

India's Buddhist and Hindu traditions found acceptance in Southeast Asia and were instrumental in validating newly rising kingdoms. Buddhism, in particular, was quickly and widely adopted. Starting in the twelfth century, Islam, carried by Arab and Chinese traders, began to gain influence in the region as well. Religious ideas, however, were not the only foreign influence at work in Southeast Asia. Throughout this time trade expanded and, as demand for Southeast Asian goods rose abroad, colonial powers saw the region as an attractive target (see "Southeast Asian Ceramics" on page 797). European, East Asian, and American economic and military interests had profound consequences on regional history, culture, and society.

Buddhist Art and Kingship

As Buddhism declined in the land of its origin, it continued to thrive in Southeast Asia, where it was shaped and developed in new ways. As it gained adherents among the population, rulers at times found it vital to align themselves with Buddhist ideas. Yet the individual incentives for espousing Buddhist ideas were as varied as the artistic forms they employed.

SEATED BUDDHA When Khmer king Jayavarman VII took the throne of Angkor in 1181, it marked the end of a long struggle against internal rebellions and foreign invaders. During his reign, he raised up the kingdom of Angkor in a final flowering, building more than any of his royal predecessors. In an unusual move, he elected to associate himself with the Buddha, rather than with a Hindu deity, and in so doing adapted Buddhist ideas to the Khmer concept of the god-king or, in his case, the buddha-king (*buddharaja*). Before starting construction of his massive temple-mountain complex at Angkor Thom, he sought legitimacy for his claims of Buddhist authority by dedicating large temples to each of his parents in the guise of bodhisattvas. This process reached its logical conclusion when he associated himself directly with the Buddha (as well as with the bodhisattva Lokeshvara).

Although Jayavarman VII's artists and architects produced a staggering number of spectacular sculptures and grand temples, few are as sublime as a simple sandstone Buddha image in the collection of the National Museum of Cambodia in Phnom Penh (**FIG. 24-18**). A few similar images exist, and in each example the seated Buddha displays nearly identical facial features. This consistency has led scholars to believe that these works are in fact portraits of Jayavarman VII seated serenely in the guise of the Buddha. Just as his ancestors had linked themselves

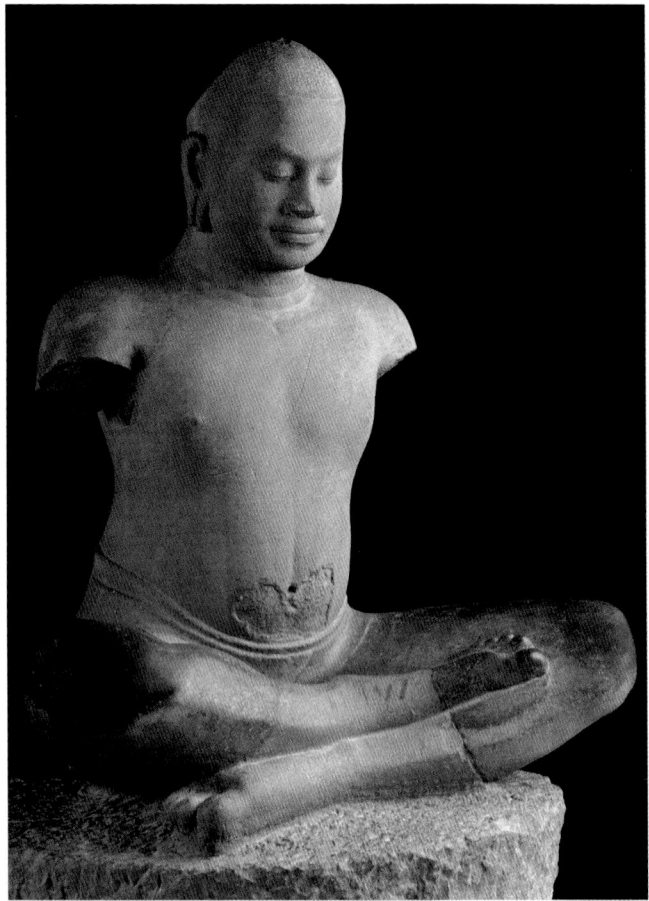

24-18 SEATED BUDDHA
From Angkor Thom. Reign of Jayavarman VII, late 12th–early 13th century. Sandstone, 4′6″ (1.4 m). National Museum of Cambodia, Phnom Penh.

Credit: © Luca Tettonni/Getty Images

with Hindu deities, Jayavarman VII represented himself as a Buddha: with downturned, meditative eyes, distended earlobes, hair pulled back into a topknot, and a simple garment. The authority of the king and Buddha are here expressed in a single understated, almost humble, image.

SHWEDAGON STUPA, MYANMAR In northern Burma from the eleventh to the thirteenth century, rulers raised thousands of religious monuments—temples, monasteries, and stupas—in the Bagan Plain, following the scriptures of Theravada Buddhism. To the south arose the port city now called Yangon (founded as Dagon and also formerly known as Rangoon). Established by Mon rulers before the eleventh century, Yangon is the site of the **SHWEDAGON STUPA** (**FIG. 24-19**), which enshrines relics of the four past Buddhas, including hair from Shakyamuni. The modern structures of Shwedagon ("Golden Dagon") rise from an ancient Mon core that was rebuilt and enlarged in the fourteenth century. In subsequent decades it underwent continual restoration and enhancement by pious Burmese kings and queens. The site continues to be a focus for lavish devotion and generosity. The bell-shaped spire is capped by an umbrella-like ornament (*hti*) adorned with a large diamond, and the sides of the terraces are covered in gold plate. While most of this wealth was donated by royalty, over the centuries people from all walks of life have offered gold for its construction and maintenance. Images of the Buddha, and sometimes his footprints alone, provide focal points for devotion.

TEMPLE OF THE EMERALD BUDDHA, THAILAND

The Dvaravati culture remained regionally dominant until Khmer invasions in the tenth century. During this turmoil a new ethnic group, the Thai, entered the scene from the north, gradually gaining control and adopting Buddhism, as well as some aspects of Hinduism, from the Mon. The first Thai kingdom, Sukhothai, was established in 1238 and flourished under the guidance of kings like the renowned Ram Khamhaeng before falling to rival Thai states.

The Sukhothai period was a formative time of innovation in Thai art. Among the creations of Sukhothai artists was an elegant new style of Buddha image. Featuring draping, almost boneless, limbs and attenuated heads adorned with spire-like flames, the Buddha images of this period are immediately recognizable. Art historians have explored diverse explanations for the distinctive, otherworldly features of Sukhothai Buddhas. One strong possibility is that they are literally poetry given tangible form (see "Closer Look" on page 800). The artists may have been working from descriptions found in the Indian Buddhist texts, which use evocative similes to describe the Buddha's beautiful appearance.

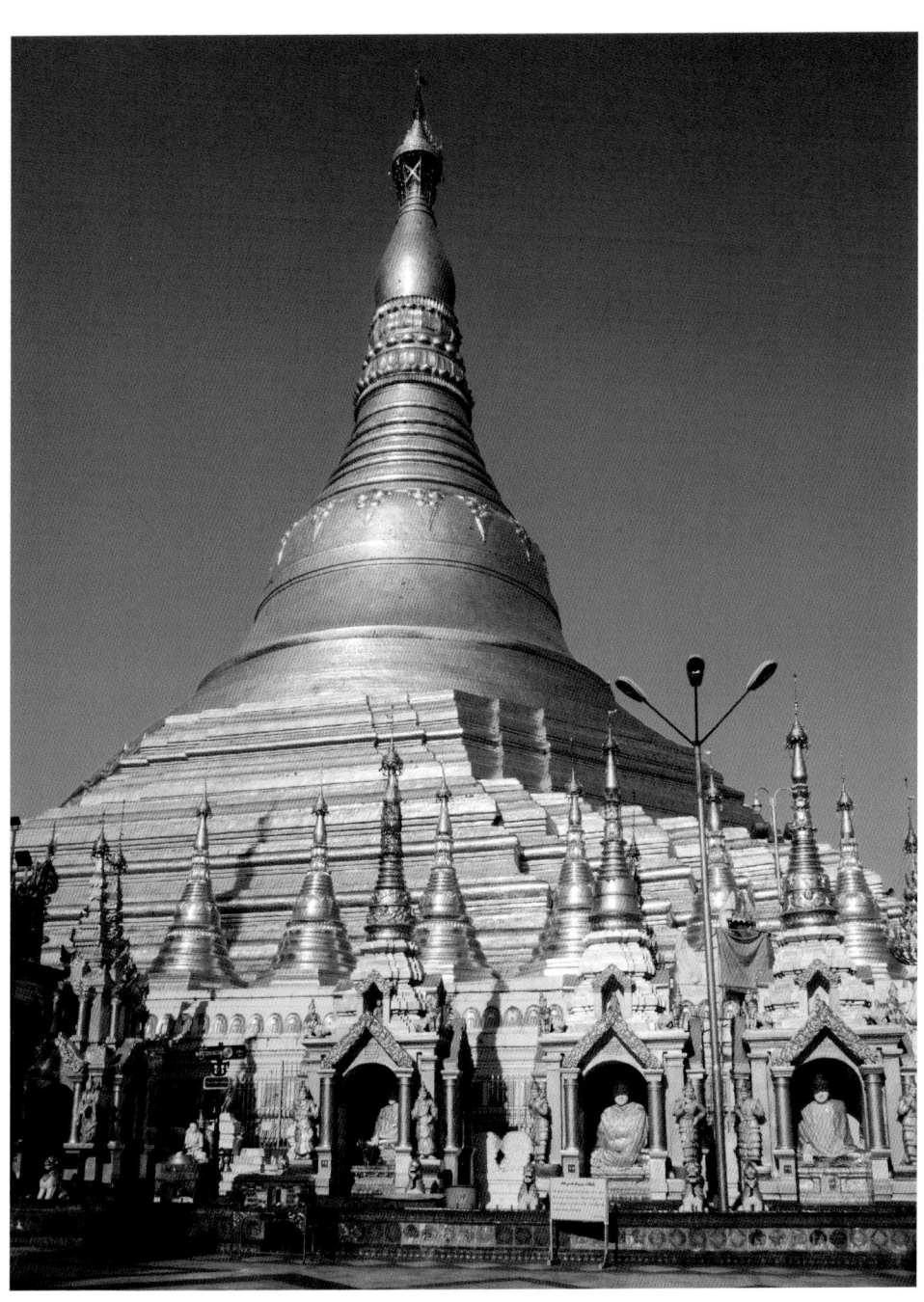

24–19 SHWEDAGON STUPA (PAGODA)

Yangon, Myanmar. 15th century; construction at the site dates from at least the 14th century, with continuous replastering and redecoration to the present.

Credit: Thor Jorgen Udvang/Fotolia

A Closer Look

THE SUKHOTHAI BUDDHA

The graceful Buddhas of the Sukhothai period were at times further enhanced by a second Sukhothai innovation: the walking Buddha pose. Sukhothai Buddhas reveal not just the surface of the Buddha's form, but also aspects of his character and life. Smooth skin is indicative of royal upbringing; long arms and broad shoulders mark someone born into a lineage of warriors; and lack of genitals alludes to his celibacy as an ascetic. Consider the following descriptions taken from Buddhist texts in relation to this example,

"Eyebrows like arched bows"

"Chin like a mango pit"

"Broad shoulders like an elephant's head"

"Arms tapering like an elephant's trunk"

"Thighs like banana-tree stalks"

"Fingertips like lotus petals"

24-20 SUKHOTHAI BUDDHA
From Wat Mahathat, now in Wat Benchamabophit, Bangkok, Thailand. Bronze, 7′22″ (2.2 m). Sukhothai period, 14th–15th century.

Credit: © Luca Tettoni/Corbis

Despite its cultural importance, the kingdom of Sukhothai did not last long, giving way to a succession of dynasties. The capital was eventually moved south to Bangkok, and under the rule of the Chakri king Rama I, construction began there on a grand new temple to house the Thais' most sacred Buddha image.

The Emerald Buddha ("emerald" refers to its color; it is actually made of jadeite) is featured in legends that place its creation in India under the direction of major Buddhist figures and trace its travels through great Buddhist nations

of the past. These stories, although not grounded in historical evidence, suggest that the image has a special link to the world's foremost Buddhist kings, among whose lineage the Thai king is the most recent. The king himself ritually changes the image's golden garments three times a year. In one of these costumes the Emerald Buddha is dressed as a king, further strengthening the association between the Buddha and the state.

The temple complex that houses this sacred image is suitably spectacular (**FIG. 24-21**). The enclosure covers

24–21 TEMPLE OF THE EMERALD BUDDHA (WAT PHRA KAEW)
Grand Palace Complex, Bangkok, Thailand. 1782, and greatly expanded in later centuries.

Credit: psstockfoto/Fotolia

over 200 acres and contains hundreds of buildings, most of which are crowned by high, pointed roofs tiled in vibrant orange and green. These colorful rooftops shade the walls and pillars, whose surfaces are inset with intricate patterns of glass, gold leaf, and tile that shimmer in the intense sunlight. Although the core of this complex dates to 1782, it has been greatly expanded since then and remains an important Thai religious and political center.

Islamic Art in Southeast Asia

Muslim merchants played a major role in overseas trade, and they frequently spent months at port waiting for the trade winds to change. Over time their faith, Islam, was accepted by local populations living in Malaysia and the island of Sumatra (Indonesia) around the Straits of Malacca. From there it spread across island Southeast Asia. Indonesia is today the world's most populous Muslim country.

KUDUS MOSQUE, INDONESIA   Islamic monuments in Indonesia, like the earlier Hindu and Buddhist ones, draw from a rich and diverse repertoire of styles and motifs. One of the earliest examples of Islamic architecture in Java is the Kudus mosque, dedicated to one of Java's nine great saints. Although the mosque itself has been renovated, most of the tower-like **MINARET** still survives from the earliest phase of construction in 1549 (**FIG. 24–22**). Its brickwork and decorative niches are reminiscent of earlier Hindu shrine towers, but this structure served to call Muslims to worship five times daily. In a traditional Javanese fashion, this was done with a large drum (*bedug*) along

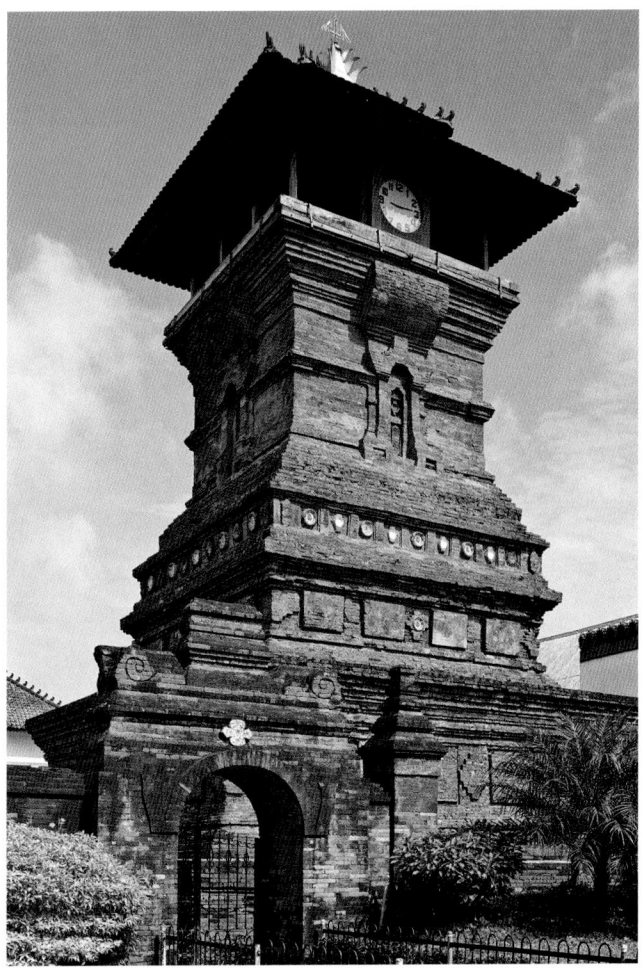

24–22 MINARET, KUDUS MOSQUE
1549. Kudus, Java, Indonesia.

Credit: © B.O'Kane/Alamy Stock Photo

with the sung prayers typical in other parts of the world. The lower bands of the tower are decorated with inset porcelain plates imported from China, which add color to the exterior. The various indigenous and international influences that helped shape this tower speak to the remarkably cosmopolitan nature of sixteenth-century Java.

The Colonial Period and the Modern Era

How are South and Southeast Asian art and architecture transformed during colonialism and the modern era?

By the late eighteenth century, India's regional rulers, both Hindu and Muslim, had reasserted themselves, and the vast Mughal Empire had shrunk to a small area around Delhi. At the same time, however, a new power, Britain, was making itself felt, inaugurating a markedly different period in Indian history.

British Imperialism in South Asia

First under the commercial interests of the British East India Company in the seventeenth and eighteenth centuries, and then under the direct control of the British government as a part of the British Empire in the nineteenth century, India was brought forcefully into contact with the West and its culture. The political concerns of the British Empire extended even to the arts. Over the course of the nineteenth century, the small settlements of Calcutta (present-day Kolkata), Madras (Chennai), and Bombay (Mumbai) were transformed into cities to serve trade with the British Empire. In the process, they took on a European aspect as British architects built in the revivalist styles favored in England.

VICTORIA TERMINUS, MUMBAI The British insistence on European styles of architecture was at its most strident in the early years of colonial rule. Even after South Asia transitioned to direct control by the British Crown in 1858, a period known as the Raj, British architects strove to emphasize difference. Nowhere is this more visible than at the **VICTORIA TERMINUS** (now Chhatrapati Shivaji Terminus) in Mumbai (**FIG. 24-23**). This massive train station built in a Gothic Revival style was designed by architect Frederick William Stevens and opened in 1887, the year of Queen Victoria's Golden Jubilee. The building makes a few concessions to its South Asian setting, as with the inclusion of turret-like domes, but it is overwhelmingly a self-conscious statement of British imperial power. This pairing of cathedral architecture and train station celebrates ideas of British technology and authority. In place of the saints that might normally decorate a cathedral, personifications of Progress, Commerce, Agriculture, and Science adorn the exterior. Originally, this structure was crowned by an image of Queen Victoria, which was later removed.

24-23 Frederick Stevens **VICTORIA TERMINUS**
Mumbai, India. 1887.

24–24 George Wittet
GATEWAY OF INDIA
Mumbai, India. 1924.

Credit: © Pete Burana/Shutterstock

24–25 Abanindranath
Tagore **BHARAT MATA
(MOTHER INDIA)**
1905. Watercolor on paper,
10½ × 6″ (26.7 × 15.3 cm).
Rabindra Bharati Society,
Kolkata.

Credit: Courtesy of Marilyn Stokstad

GATEWAY OF INDIA, MUMBAI Over time, the British reduced their insistence on promoting difference through their choice of architectural forms and began to appreciate aspects of indigenous style. Completed in 1924, the **GATEWAY OF INDIA** was built to welcome King George V on his visit to India (**FIG. 24-24**). The British constructed the monument in the form of a European triumphal arch, while embellishing it with South Asian architectural features. Stone screens, ornate brackets, pointed arches, and floral decorations were taken directly from earlier Hindu and Muslim architectural practices in the subcontinent. This hybrid style, known as the Indo-Saracenic style, became the preferred architectural style for British governmental buildings and elite private estates in India by the late nineteenth century; a few examples were built in England and in other parts of the empire as well. India won its independence in 1947, and the last British troops in South Asia departed through this gate a year later in 1948.

MOTHER INDIA Well before Britain's consolidation of imperial power in New Delhi, a new spirit of Indian independence and pan-Asiatic solidarity was awakening. For example, working near Calcutta (Kolkata), the painter Abanindranath Tagore (1871–1951)—nephew of the poet Rabindranath Tagore (1861–1941), who won the Nobel Prize for Literature in 1913—deliberately rejected the medium of oil painting and the academic realism of Western art. Like the Nihonga artists of Japan (SEE FIG. 26-18) with whom he was in contact, Tagore strove to create a style that reflected his ethnic origins. In **BHARAT MATA (MOTHER INDIA)** he invents a nationalistic icon by using Hindu symbols while also drawing upon the format and techniques of Mughal and Rajput painting (**FIG. 24-25**).

24–26 Maqbool Fida Husain **VEDIC**
From the "Theorama" series, 1994. Limited-edition color print, 23½ × 36″ (60 × 92 cm).

Credit: Photo: Philip de Bay

The Modern Period

Marked by both inspirational expressions of peaceful resistance and bloody warfare, the modern history of South and Southeast Asia has been a study in extremes. But as the turmoil of earlier decades fades across most of the region, many states have emerged as leaders in international commerce, technology, and finance. In an international age, they are capitalizing on the region's centuries-old tradition of bridging cultures and adapting new ideas. These qualities are seen clearly in the South and Southeast Asian art of the modern period, which blends the traditional with the new.

MODERN SOUTH ASIA In the wake of World War II, the imperial powers of Europe began to shed their colonial domains. The attainment of self-rule had been five long decades in the making, when finally—pressured by the nonviolent example of Mahatma Gandhi (1869–1948)—the British Empire gave up its "Jewel in the Crown," which was partitioned to form the modern nations of India, Pakistan, and (in 1972) Bangladesh. After independence in 1947, the exuberant young nations welcomed a modern, internationalist approach to art and architecture.

One of India's most influential and prolific modern artists was Maqbool Fida Husain (1915–2011). Beginning his career in the 1940s, he embraced Modernism and used its techniques to express South Asian

24–27 César Pelli and Deejay Cerico **PETRONAS TOWERS**
Kuala Lumpur, Malaysia. 1998.

Credit: © Travelpix Ltd/Getty Images

themes. He drew his subjects from diverse sources such as Hindu literature, historical events, and the natural world, as well as from the traditions of his Muslim upbringing. He was highly productive, and his range of subject matter at times drew objections from religious groups, who opposed his use of religious imagery. These complaints led him reluctantly to spend the final years of his life in Qatar, but he consistently returned to South Asian themes for his inspiration.

His simplified and schematic style can be seen in the "Theorama" series, which addresses nine of the world's major religions. Pictured here is **VEDIC** (**FIG. 24–26**), Husain's tribute to Hinduism. Despite its abstraction, the figure of Krishna can be seen dancing on the serpent deity Kaliya, whose body merges with the story of the Churning of the Ocean of Milk (SEE FIG. 10–43). The event pivots on a triangular form with three faces reminiscent of the Shiva from Elephanta (SEE FIG. 10-24), and a goddess on elephant-back dispenses abundance in the form of coins or seeds from her outstretched hand. The composition is framed on the right by a seated ascetic whose head is a spoked wheel. This wheel may reference the spinning wheels whose use Gandhi advocated to break dependence on British textiles, but it also reaches back further into the South Asian past and evokes the wheel of *dharma*.

MODERN SOUTHEAST ASIA   The transition from colonial control varied greatly across Southeast Asia, due largely to the range of colonial powers in the region and their varying attitudes toward relinquishing power. Some nations, like Thailand, managed to avoid imperial domination entirely, whereas others fought long wars to establish their independence. In some cases, the power vacuum was filled by local regimes that brought new hardship, like the horrors perpetrated by the Khmer Rouge in Cambodia. The region has gradually achieved stability and growing prosperity, as exemplified by its internationally recognized artwork and contemporary architecture.

Dominating the skyline of Kuala Lumpur, Malaysia, are the **PETRONAS TOWERS** (**FIG. 24–27**), which from 1998 to 2004 were the tallest structures in the world. These paired skyscrapers, linked by a sky bridge at the 41st and 42nd floors, are built primarily of reinforced concrete surrounded by a casing of steel and glass. They were designed collaboratively by Argentine architect César Pelli and Filipino-Malaysian engineer Deejay Cerico, who drew inspiration for their designs from traditional Malaysian Islamic forms. The towers stand 1,242 feet tall and took seven years to build. Today they house many business offices, a shopping mall, and the Malaysian Philharmonic Orchestra. They are characteristic of the growth and development across the region.

Think About It

1   Consider the Qutb Minar (**FIG. 24–4**) and Fatehpur Sikri (**FIG. 24–8**). Do these structures reveal differences in the way each kingdom viewed itself in relation to wider Indian culture? If so, explain how. Can similar differences be seen when comparing the Victoria Terminus and the Gateway of India? Explain.

2   Great wealth is often required to build grand structures, and typically this wealth rests in the hands of rulers. Who were the patrons of the Luna Vasahi (**FIG. 24–3**) and the *gopuras* at the temple in Madurai (**FIG. 24–7**)? What does this tell us about the importance of trade and increased access to public displays of piety?

3   The Emerald Buddha and the Seated Buddha from the reign of Jayavarman VII are both closely associated with royal power. Explain how each Buddhist image lends authority to the king; emphasize both similarities and differences between the two examples.

4   Consider the paintings *Jahangir and Shah Abbas* (**FIG. 24–10**) and *Mother India* (**FIG. 24–25**). What are their political messages and to whom were these messages directed? Who would have seen these works?

Crosscurrents

Consider some of the ways that Islamic art and culture impacted South and Southeast Asia. Explain how the Taj Mahal and the Kudus mosque minaret are similar. In what ways do they differ from one another? What historical and cultural influences help account for those differences?

FIG. 24–1   FIG. 24–22

25-1 Wang Hui **A THOUSAND PEAKS AND MYRIAD RAVINES**

Qing dynasty, 1693. Hanging scroll with ink on paper, 8′2½″ × 3′4½″ (2.54 × 1.03 m). National Palace Museum, Taibei, Taiwan, Republic of China.

Chapter 25
Chinese and Korean Art after 1279

 ## Learning Objectives

25.a Identify the visual hallmarks of Chinese and Korean art after 1279 for formal, technical, and expressive qualities.

25.b Interpret the meaning of works of Chinese and Korean art after 1279 based on their themes, subjects, and symbols.

25.c Relate artists and art of China and Korea after 1279 to their cultural, economic, and political contexts.

25.d Apply the vocabulary and concepts relevant to the art, artists, and art history of China and Korea after 1279.

25.e Interpret a work of Chinese or Korean art after 1279 using the art historical methods of observation, comparison, and inductive reasoning.

25.f Select visual and textual evidence in various media to support an argument or an interpretation of a work of Chinese or Korean art after 1279.

Mountains, rivers, waterfalls, trees, rocks, temples, pavilions, houses, bridges, boats, wandering scholars, fishers—all are included in **A THOUSAND PEAKS AND MYRIAD RAVINES** (**FIG. 25-1**), painted by Wang Hui (1632–1717). These are common motifs and subjects in the landscape tradition of Chinese ink painting, already many centuries old when this large work was painted in 1693. At the top of the hanging scroll, the artist himself has written:

> Moss and weeds cover the rocks and mist hovers over the water.
> The sound of dripping water is heard in front of the temple gate.
> Through a thousand peaks and myriad ravines the spring flows,
> And brings the flying flowers into the sacred caves.
> In the fourth month of the year 1693, in an inn in the capital, I painted this based on a Tang-dynasty poem in the manner of [the painters] Dong [Yuan] and Ju[ran].
> (Translation by Chu-tsing Li)

The inscription refers to the artist's inspiration—for the subject, found in the lines of a Tang-dynasty poem, and for the style, found in the work of tenth-century painters Dong Yuan and Juran. Wang Hui's art embodies the ideals of the scholar in imperial China.

China's scholar class was unique, the product of an examination system designed to recruit the finest minds in the country for government service. Instituted during the Tang dynasty (618–907) and based on even earlier traditions, the civil service examinations were excruciatingly difficult, but for the tiny percentage who passed at the highest level, the rewards were great—prestige, position, power, and wealth. Steeped in philosophy, literature, and history, China's scholars—often called *wenren* (literati)—shared an outlook. Following Confucianism, they became officials to fulfill their obligation to the world, but pulled by Daoism, they retreated from society in order to come to terms with nature and the universe—to create a garden, to write poetry, or to paint.

During the Song dynasty (960–1279) the examinations were expanded and regularized. More than half of all government positions came to be filled by scholars. In the subsequent Yuan and Ming periods, the tradition of **literati painting** (a style that reflected the taste of the educated class) developed further. When the Yuan period of foreign rule came to an end, the new Ming ruling house revived the court traditions of the Song. The Ming also became the model for the rulers of Korea's Joseon dynasty, under whose patronage these styles achieved a distinctive and austere beauty.

In the Qing era, China was again ruled by an outside group, this time the Manchus. While maintaining their traditional connections to Tibet and inner Asia through patronage of Tibetan Buddhism, the Manchu rulers also embraced Chinese ideals, especially those of the literati. Practicing painting and calligraphy, composing poetry in Chinese, and collecting esteemed Chinese works of art, these rulers amassed the great palace collections that can now be seen in Beijing and Taibei.

Foundations of Chinese Culture

What aspects of the early history, culture, and art of China form a critical background for the development of art and architecture after 1279?

Chinese culture is distinguished by a long and continuous development that traces to the prehistoric period. Between 6000 and 2000 BCE a variety of Neolithic cultures flourished across China. Through long interaction these cultures became increasingly similar, and they eventually gave rise to the three Bronze Age dynastic states with which Chinese history traditionally begins: the Xia, the Shang (c. 1700–1100 BCE), and the Zhou (1100–221 BCE).

The Shang developed traditions of casting ritual vessels in bronze, working jade in ceremonial shapes, and writing consistently in scripts that directly evolved into the modern Chinese written language. Society was stratified, and the ruling group maintained its authority in part by claiming power as intermediaries between the human and spirit worlds. Under the Zhou a feudal society developed, with nobles related to the king ruling over numerous small states.

During the latter part of the Zhou dynasty, states began to vie with each other for supremacy through intrigue and increasingly ruthless warfare. The collapse of social order profoundly influenced China's first philosophers, who largely concerned themselves with the pragmatic question of how to bring about a stable society.

In 221 BCE, rulers of the state of Qin triumphed over the remaining states, unifying China as an empire for the first time. The Qin created the mechanisms of China's centralized bureaucracy, but their rule was harsh and the dynasty was quickly overthrown. The ensuing Han dynasty (206 BCE–220 CE) brought peace and prosperity to China as Confucianism became the official state ideology, and in the process assumed the form and force of a religion. Developed from the thought of Confucius (551–479 BCE), one of the many philosophers of the Zhou, Confucianism is an ethical system for the management of society based on establishing correct relationships among people. Providing a counterweight was Daoism, which also came into its own during the Han dynasty. Based on the thought of Laozi, a possibly

legendary contemporary of Confucius, and the philosopher Zhuangzi (369–286 BCE), Daoism is a view of life that seeks to harmonize the individual with the Dao, or Way, the process of the universe. Confucianism and Daoism remained central to Chinese thought—one addressing the public realm of duty and conformity, and the other the private world of individualism and creativity.

Following the collapse of the Han dynasty, China experienced a centuries-long period of disunity (220–589 CE). Invaders from the north and west established numerous kingdoms and dynasties, while a series of six precarious Chinese dynasties held sway in the south. Buddhism, which had spread from India into China over trade routes during the Han era, began to flourish.

China was reunited under the Sui dynasty (581–618 CE), which quickly fell to the Tang (618–907), one of the most successful dynasties in Chinese history. Strong and confident, Tang China fascinated and, in turn, was fascinated by the cultures around it. Caravans streamed across central Asia to the capital, Chang'an (present-day Xi'an), then the largest city in the world. Japan and Korea sent thousands of students to study Chinese culture, and Buddhism reached the height of its influence before a period of persecution signaled the start of its decline.

The mood of the Song dynasty (960–1279) was quite different. The martial vigor of the Tang gave way to a culture of increasing refinement and sophistication, and Tang openness to foreign influences was replaced by a conscious cultivation of China's own traditions. In art, landscape painting emerged as the most esteemed genre, capable of expressing both philosophical and personal concerns. With the fall of the north to invaders in 1126, the Song court set up a new capital in the south, which became the cultural and economic center of the country.

The Mongol Invasions and the Yuan Dynasty

How is Chinese art transformed after the Mongol invasions during the Yuan dynasty?

At the beginning of the thirteenth century the Mongols, a nomadic people from the steppes north of China, began to amass an empire. Led first by Genghiz Khan (c. 1162–1227), then by his sons and grandsons, they swept westward into central Europe and overran Islamic lands from Central Asia through present-day Iraq. To the east, they quickly captured northern China, and in 1279, led by Kublai Khan, they conquered southern China as well. Grandson of the mighty Genghiz, Kublai proclaimed himself emperor of China and founded the Yuan dynasty (1279–1368).

The Mongol invasions were traumatic; their effect on China was long-lasting. During the Song dynasty, China had grown increasingly introspective. Rejecting foreign ideas and influences, intellectuals had focused on defining the qualities that constituted true "Chinese-ness." They drew a clear distinction between their own people, whom they characterized as gentle, erudite, and sophisticated, and the "barbarians" outside China's borders, whom they regarded as wild and uncivilized. Now, faced with the reality of foreign occupation, China's inward gaze intensified in spiritual resistance. For centuries to come, long after the Mongols had gone, leading scholars continued to seek intellectually more challenging, philosophically more profound, and artistically more subtle expressions of all that could be identified as authentically Chinese.

The Mongols established their capital in the northern city now known as Beijing (**MAP 25-1**). The cultural centers of China, however, remained the great cities of the south, where the Song court had been located for the previous 150 years. Combined with the tensions of Yuan rule, this

separation of China's political and cultural centers created a new dynamic in the arts.

Throughout most of Chinese history, the imperial court had set the tone for artistic taste: Artisans attached to the court produced architecture, paintings, gardens, and objects of jade, lacquer, ceramics, and silk especially for imperial use. Over the centuries, painters and calligraphers gradually moved higher up the social scale, for these "arts of the brush" were often practiced by scholars and even emperors, whose high status reflected positively on whatever interested them. With the establishment of an imperial painting academy during the Song dynasty, painters finally achieved a status equal to that of court officials. For the literati, painting came to be grouped with calligraphy and poetry as the trio of accomplishments suited to members of the cultural elite.

But while the literati elevated the status of painting by virtue of practicing it, they also began to develop their own

MAP 25-1 CHINA AND KOREA

The map shows the borders of both contemporary China and Korea. The colored areas indicate the historical extent of the Qing-dynasty empire (1644–1911), including its tributary states.

ideas of what painting should be. Not needing to earn an income from their art, they cultivated an amateur ideal in which personal expression counted for more than professional skill. They created for themselves a status as artists totally separate from and superior to professional painters, whose art they felt was inherently compromised, since it was done to please others and tainted by money.

The conditions of Yuan rule now encouraged a clear distinction between court taste, ministered to by professional artists and artisans, and literati taste. The Yuan dynasty continued to see patronage of the arts as an imperial responsibility, commissioning buildings, murals, gardens, paintings, and decorative arts. Western visitors, such as the Italian Marco Polo (c. 1254–1324), who spent 17 years in the service of Kublai Khan, were mightily impressed by the magnificence of the Yuan court. But scholars, profoundly alienated from the new government, took little notice of these accomplishments. Nor did Yuan rulers have much use for scholars, especially those from the south. The civil service examinations were abolished, and the highest government positions were bestowed, instead, on Mongols and their foreign allies. Scholars now tended to turn inward to search for solutions of their own and try to express themselves in personal and symbolic terms.

Painting

Zhao Mengfu (1254–1322) was a descendant of the imperial line of Song. Unlike many scholars of his time, he eventually chose to serve the Yuan government and was made a high official. A distinguished painter, calligrapher, and poet, Zhao was especially known for his carefully rendered paintings of horses, but he also practiced traditional landscape painting. One of his best-known works is a sensitively composed and beautifully balanced painting of two farm animals, **SHEEP AND GOAT** (FIG. 25-2), which he claimed to have drawn from life. This may be too simplistic an assessment, because the two animals are portrayed in clearly different styles. The goat, on the right, is carefully described and lifelike in appearance, but the sheep, on the left, is more abstracted, almost flattened. The markings on its body create a sense of pattern rather than the appearance of natural irregularities. Some have seen pride in the sheep's posture and submission in the pose of the goat—although with head down, the goat could also be prepared to attack. Some have proposed that Zhao was expressing either acceptance of or resistance to the rule of the foreign Yuan dynasty, or since the same Chinese word is used for these two animals, perhaps he implies that the Mongols and the Chinese are not as different as they seem.

Zhao Mengfu became a prime practitioner of literati painting with his unassuming brushwork, sparing use of color (many literati paintings, like FIG. 25-2, give up color altogether), and use of traditional painting to convey personal meaning. The literati did not paint for public display but for each other, and Zhao's *Sheep and Goat* was actually created at the request of a friend of the artist. The literati favored small formats such as handscrolls, **hanging scrolls**, or **album** leaves (book pages), which could easily be shown to friends or shared at small gatherings (see "Formats of Chinese Painting" opposite).

25-2 Zhao Mengfu **SHEEP AND GOAT**
Yuan dynasty, c. 1300. Handscroll with ink on paper, 9⅞ × 19″ (25.2 × 48.4 cm). Freer Gallery of Art, Smithsonian Institution, Washington, DC.
Credit: Bridgeman Images

Technique
FORMATS OF CHINESE PAINTING

With the exception of large wall paintings that typically decorated palaces, temples, and tombs, most Chinese paintings were created from ink and water-based colors on silk or paper. Finished works were generally mounted as handscrolls, hanging scrolls, or leaves in an album.

An album is made up of a set of paintings of identical size mounted in a book. (A single painting from an album is called an album leaf.) The paintings in an album are usually related in subject, such as various views of a famous site or a series of scenes glimpsed on one trip.

Album-size paintings might also be mounted as a handscroll, generally a horizontal format about 12 inches high and anywhere from a few feet to dozens of feet long. More typically, however, a handscroll would be a single, continuous painting. Handscrolls were not meant to be displayed all at once, the way they are commonly presented today in museums. Rather, they were unrolled only occasionally, to be savored in much the same spirit as we might view a favorite film. Placing the scroll on a flat surface such as a table, a viewer would unroll it a foot or two at a time, moving gradually through the entire scroll from right to left, lingering over favorite details. The scroll was then rolled up and returned to its box until the next viewing.

Like handscrolls, hanging scrolls were not displayed permanently but were taken out for a limited time: a day, a week, or a season. Unlike a handscroll, however, the painting on a hanging scroll was viewed as a whole—unrolled and hung on a wall, with the roller at the lower end acting as a weight to help the scroll hang flat. Although some hanging scrolls are quite large, they are still fundamentally intimate works, not intended for display in a public place.

Creating a scroll was a time-consuming and exacting process accomplished by a professional mounter. The painting was first backed with paper to strengthen it. Next, strips of paper-backed silk were pasted to the top, bottom, and sides, framing the painting on all four sides. Additional silk pieces were added to extend the scroll horizontally or vertically, depending on the format. The assembled scroll was then backed again with paper and fitted with a half-round dowel, or wooden rod, at the top of a hanging scroll or on the right end of a handscroll, with ribbons for hanging and tying, and with a wooden roller at the other end. Hanging scrolls were often fashioned from several patterns of silk, and a variety of piecing formats were developed and codified. On a handscroll, a painting was generally preceded by a panel giving the work's title and often followed by a long panel bearing colophons—inscriptions related to the work, such as poems in its praise or comments by its owners over the centuries. A scroll would be remounted periodically to better preserve it, and colophons and inscriptions would be preserved in each remounting. Seals added another layer of interest. A treasured scroll often bears not only the seal of its maker but also those of collectors and admirers through the centuries.

colophon panel   frontispiece   label

秋華鵲色

handscroll rolled for storage
handscroll

handscroll

front   back
hanging scroll

NI ZAN   Of the considerable number of Yuan painters who took up Zhao's ideas, several became models for later generations. One was Ni Zan (1301–1374), whose most famous surviving painting is **THE RONGXI STUDIO** (**FIG. 25–3**). Done entirely in ink, the painting depicts the lake region in Ni's home district. Mountains, rocks, trees, and a pavilion are sketched with a minimum of detail using a dry brush technique—a technique in which the

25-3 Ni Zan **THE RONGXI STUDIO**
Yuan dynasty, 1372. Hanging scroll with ink on paper, height 29⅜″
(74.6 cm). National Palace Museum, Taibei, Taiwan, Republic of China.

The idea that a painting is not an attempt to capture the visual
appearance of nature or to satisfy others but is executed freely for
the artist's own amusement is at the heart of the literati aesthetic.
Ni Zan once wrote this comment on a painting: "What I call painting
does not exceed the joy of careless sketching with a brush. I do
not seek formal likeness but do it simply for my own amusement.
Recently I was rambling about and came to a town. The people
asked for my pictures, but wanted them exactly according to their
own desires and to represent a specific occasion. [When I could
not satisfy them,] they went away insulting, scolding, and cursing in
every possible way. What a shame! But how can one scold a eunuch
for not growing a beard?" (translated in Bush and Shih, p. 266).

Credit: Photo © National Palace Museum, Taipei, Taïwan, Dist. RMN-Grand
Palais/image NPM

brush is not fully loaded with ink but rather is about to
run out, so that white paper "breathes" through the ragged
strokes. The result is a painting with a light touch and a
sense of simplicity and purity. Literati styles were believed
to reflect an individual painter's personality, and Ni's
spare, dry style became associated with a noble spirit.
Many later painters adopted or paid homage to it.

Ni Zan's eccentric behavior became legendary in the
history of Chinese art. In his early years he was one of the
richest men in the region, the owner of a large estate. His
pride and his aloofness from daily affairs often got him
into trouble with the authorities. His cleanliness was notorious. In addition to washing himself several times daily,
he ordered his servants to wash the trees in his garden and
to clean the furniture after his guests had left. He was said
to be so unworldly that late in life he gave away most of
his possessions and lived as a hermit in a boat, wandering
on rivers and lakes.

Whether these stories are true or not, they were important elements of Ni's legacy to later painters, for Ni's life
as well as his art served as a model. Literati painting was
associated with a viewpoint concerning what constituted
an appropriate life. The ideal, as embodied by Ni Zan and
others, was a brilliantly gifted scholar whose spirit was
too refined for the dusty world of government service and
who thus preferred to live as a recluse or had retired after
having become frustrated by a brief stint as an official.

The Ming Dynasty

*What characterizes Chinese painting and architecture
during the Ming Dynasty?*

The founder of the next dynasty, the Ming (1368–1644),
came from a family of poor, uneducated peasants. As Zhu
Yuanzhang rose through the ranks in the army, he enlisted
the help of scholars to gain power and solidify his following. Once he had driven the Mongols from Beijing and
firmly established himself as emperor, however, he grew
to distrust intellectuals. His rule was despotic, even ruthless. Throughout the nearly 300 years of Ming rule, most
emperors shared his attitude, so although the civil service
examinations were reinstated, scholars remained alienated
from the government they were trained to serve.

MING BLUE-AND-WHITE WARES   Ming China
became famous the world over for its exquisite ceramics,
especially porcelain. The imperial kilns in Jingdezhen, in
Jiangxi Province, became the most renowned center for
porcelain not only in China, but in all the world. During the
reigns of the Yongle (1403–1424) and Xuande (1426–1435)
emperors, major trade and diplomatic missions traveled
to the Middle East, and Ming porcelain made its way to
Turkey and Iran, where its refined decoration and flawless
glazing was admired. The shapes of two porcelain flasks

used for decanting wine in the Chinese imperial household (**FIG. 25-4**) were probably inspired by Islamic glass vessels brought back to China with traders returning from these missions. The underglaze cobalt blue decoration shows the variety of ornamental motifs and representational systems that were used by the painters of Ming porcelain: The body of one dragon is rendered with fine descriptive detail against a background of delicate plant motifs, whereas the other dragon is a bold white silhouette reserved from the densely painted waves of its ocean habitat.

25-4 TWO FLASKS

Ming dynasty, 1403–1424 (reign of Yongle emperor). Porcelain with decoration painted in underglaze cobalt blue. Percival David Foundation Collection, British Museum, London.

Dragons have featured prominently in Chinese folklore from earliest times—Neolithic examples have been found painted on pottery and carved in jade. In Bronze Age China, dragons came to be associated with powerful and sudden manifestations of nature, such as wind, thunder, and lightning. At the same time, they became associated with superior beings such as virtuous rulers and sages. With the emergence of China's first firmly established empire during the Han dynasty, the dragon was appropriated as an imperial symbol, and it remained so throughout Chinese history. Dragon sightings were duly recorded and considered auspicious. Yet even the Son of Heaven could not monopolize the dragon. During the Tang and Song dynasties the practice arose of painting pictures of dragons to pray for rain, and for Chan (Zen) Buddhists, the dragon was a symbol of sudden enlightenment.

Technique
THE SECRET OF PORCELAIN

Marco Polo, it is said, was the one who named a new type of ceramic he found in China. Its translucent purity reminded him of the smooth whiteness of the cowrie shell, *porcellana* in Italian. Porcelain is made from kaolin, an extremely refined white clay, and petuntse, a variety of the mineral feldspar. When properly combined and fired at a high-enough temperature (generally in the range of 1300° to 1400°C), the two materials fuse into a glasslike, translucent ceramic that is far stronger than it looks.

Porcelaneous stoneware, fired at lower temperatures, was known in China by the seventh century, but true porcelain was perfected during the Song dynasty. To create blue-and-white porcelain such as the flasks in FIGURE 25-4, blue pigment was made from cobalt oxide, finely ground and mixed with water. The decoration was painted directly onto the unfired porcelain vessel, then a layer of clear glaze was applied over it. (In this technique, known as **underglaze** painting, the pattern is painted beneath the glaze.) After firing, the piece emerged from the kiln with a clear blue design set sharply against a snowy white background.

Entranced with the exquisite properties of porcelain, European potters tried for centuries to duplicate it. The technique was finally "discovered" in 1709 by Johann Friedrich Böttger in Dresden, Germany, who tried—but failed—to keep it a secret.

Court and Professional Painting

The contrast between the luxurious world of the court and the austere ideals of the literati continued through the Ming dynasty.

A typical example of Ming court taste is **HUNDREDS OF BIRDS ADMIRING THE PEACOCKS (FIG. 25-5)**, a large painting on silk by Yin Hong, an artist active during the late fifteenth and early sixteenth centuries. A pupil of well-known courtiers, Yin probably served in the court at Beijing. This painting is an example of the birds-and-flowers genre, which had been popular with artists of the Song academy. Here the subject takes on symbolic meaning, with the homage of the birds to the peacocks representing the homage of court officials to the imperial state. Although the style is faithful to Song academic models, the large format and intense attention to detail are traits of the Ming.

A related, yet bolder and less constrained, landscape style was also popular during this period. It is sometimes called the Zhe style since its roots were in Hangzhou, Zhejiang Province, where the Southern Song court had been located. An example is **RETURNING HOME LATE FROM**

A SPRING OUTING (FIG. 25-6), unsigned but attributed to Dai Jin (1388–1462). Zhe-style works such as this will become sources for Korean and Japanese artists such as An Gyeon (SEE FIG. 25-19) and Sesshu (SEE FIG. 26-3).

QIU YING A preeminent professional painter in the Ming period was Qiu Ying (1494–1552), who lived in Suzhou, a prosperous southern city. He inspired generations of imitators with exceptional works such as a long handscroll known as **SPRING DAWN IN THE HAN PALACE**

25-5 Yin Hong **HUNDREDS OF BIRDS ADMIRING THE PEACOCKS**

Ming dynasty, late 15th–early 16th century. Hanging scroll with ink and color on silk, 7′10½″ × 6′5″ (2.4 × 1.96 m). The Cleveland Museum of Art. Purchase from the J.H. Wade Fund (1974.31).

Credit: Bridgeman Images

25-6 Attributed to Dai Jin **RETURNING HOME LATE FROM A SPRING OUTING**

Ming dynasty. Hanging scroll with ink on silk, 5′6″ × 2′8¾″ (1.68 × 0.83 m). National Palace Museum, Taibei, Taiwan, Republic of China.

Credit: © Corbis

25–7A Qiu Ying **SECTION OF SPRING DAWN IN THE HAN PALACE**

Ming dynasty, 1500–1550. Handscroll with ink and color on silk, 1′ × 18′¹³⁄₁₆″ (0.3 × 5.7 m). National Palace Museum, Taibei, Taiwan, Republic of China.

Credit: Photo © National Palace Museum, Taipei, Taïwan, Dist. RMN-Grand Palais/image NPM

(**FIG. 25–7**). The painting is based on Tang-dynasty depictions of women in the court of the Han dynasty (206 BCE–220 CE). While in the service of a well-known collector, Qiu Ying had the opportunity to study many Tang paintings, whose artists usually concentrated on figures set on blank backgrounds. Qiu's graceful and elegant figures—although modeled after those in Tang works—are situated within a carefully described setting of palace buildings. They engage in courtly pastimes, such as chess, music, calligraphy, and painting. With its antique subject matter, refined technique, brilliant color, and controlled composition, *Spring Dawn in the Han Palace* brought professional painting to another level (see a detail from this scroll in "Closer Look" below).

A Closer Look

SPRING DAWN IN THE HAN PALACE

Two ladies of the court unwrap a *qin*, the zither or lute that was the most respected musical instrument at the time.

A seated woman plays the *pipa*, an instrument introduced from Central Asia during the Tang dynasty.

Antique vessels of bronze, lacquer, and porcelain adorn the room and suggest the women's refined taste.

A tray landscape featuring an eroded rock provides a sculptural counterpart to landscape (mountain-and-water) painting and suggests a place where immortals might dwell.

Two women dance together, letting their sleeves and sashes swirl.

25–7B DETAIL OF FIG. 25–7A

Credit: Photo © National Palace Museum, Taipei, Taïwan, Dist. RMN-Grand Palais/image NPM

Architecture and City Planning

Centuries of warfare and destruction have left very few early Chinese architectural monuments intact. The most important remaining example of traditional architecture is **THE FORBIDDEN CITY**, the imperial palace compound in Beijing, whose principal buildings were constructed during the Ming dynasty (**FIG. 25-8**).

THE FORBIDDEN CITY   The basic plan of Beijing was the work of the Mongols, who laid out their capital city according to traditional Chinese principles. City planning had begun early in China—in the seventh century, in the case of Chang'an (present-day Xi'an), the capital of the Sui and Tang emperors. The walled city of Chang'an was organized on a rectangular grid with evenly spaced streets that ran north–south and east–west. At the northern end stood a walled imperial complex.

Beijing, too, was developed as a walled, rectangular city with streets laid out in a grid. The palace enclosure occupied the center of the northern part of the city, which was reserved for the Mongols. Chinese lived in the southern third of the city. Later, Ming and Qing emperors preserved this division, with officials living in the northern or Inner City and commoners living in the southern or Outer City. The third Ming emperor, Yongle (ruled 1403–1424), rebuilt the Forbidden City as we see it today.

The approach was impressive. Visitors entered through the Meridian Gate, a monumental complex with perpendicular side wings (in the center of FIG. 25-8). Next they encountered a broad courtyard crossed by a bow-shaped waterway spanned by five arched marble bridges. At the opposite end of this courtyard is the Gate of Supreme Harmony, opening onto an even larger courtyard that houses three ceremonial halls raised on a broad platform. First is the Hall of Supreme Harmony, where on the most important state occasions the emperor sat on his throne, facing south. Beyond is the smaller Hall of Central Harmony, then the Hall of Protecting Harmony. Behind these vast ceremonial spaces, still on the central axis, is the inner court, again with a progression of three buildings, this time more intimate in scale. In its balance and symmetry the plan of the Forbidden City reflects ancient Chinese beliefs about the harmony of the universe, and it emphasizes the emperor's role as the Son of Heaven, maintaining the cosmic order from his throne in the middle of the world.

The Literati Aesthetic

In the south, particularly in the district of Suzhou, literati painting, associated with the educated men who served the court as government officials, remained the dominant artistic trend. One of the major literati painters from the Ming period is Shen Zhou (1427–1509), who had no desire to enter government service and spent most of his life in Suzhou. He studied the Yuan painters avidly and tried to recapture their spirit in such works as *Poet on a Mountaintop* (see "*Poet on a Mountaintop*" opposite). Although the style of the painting recalls the freedom and simplicity of Ni Zan (SEE FIG. 25-3), the motif of a poet surveying the landscape from a mountain plateau is Shen's creation.

25-8 THE FORBIDDEN CITY
Now the Palace Museum, Beijing. Mostly Ming dynasty. View from the southwest.

Credit: © View Stock/Getty

Art and its Contexts

POET ON A MOUNTAINTOP

In earlier landscape paintings, human figures were typically shown dwarfed by the grandeur of nature. Travelers might be seen scuttling along a narrow path by a stream, while overhead towered mountains whose peaks were in the clouds and whose heights were inaccessible. But in **FIGURE 25–9** the poet has climbed the mountain and dominates the landscape. Even the clouds are beneath him. Before his gaze, a poem hangs in the air, as though he were projecting his thoughts.

The poem, composed by Shen Zhou himself, and written in his distinctive hand, reads:

White clouds like a scarf enfold the
　　mountain's waist;
Stone steps hang in space—a long,
　　narrow path.
Alone, leaning on my cane, I gaze
　　intently at the scene,
And feel like answering the murmuring
　　brook with the music of my flute.
　　(Translation by Jonathan Chaves,
　　The Chinese Painter as Poet, p. 46.)

Shen Zhou composed the poem and wrote the inscription at the time he painted the album. The style of the calligraphy, like the style of the painting, is informal, relaxed, and straightforward—qualities that were believed to reflect the artist's character and personality.

The painting visualizes Ming philosophy, which held that the mind, not the physical world, was the basis for reality. With its tight synthesis of poetry, calligraphy, and painting and its harmony of mind and landscape, *Poet on a Mountaintop* represents the essence of Ming literati painting.

25–9 Shen Zhou **POET ON A MOUNTAINTOP**
Leaf from an album of landscapes; painting mounted as part of a handscroll. Ming dynasty, c. 1500. Ink and color on paper, 15¼ × 23¾″ (40 × 60.2 cm). The Nelson-Atkins Museum of Art, Kansas City, Missouri. Purchase: William Rockhill Nelson Trust (46-51/2).

**LITERATI INFLUENCE ON FURNITURE, ARCHITEC-
TURE, AND GARDEN DESIGN**   The taste of the literati
also influenced the design of furniture, architecture, and
especially gardens. Characteristic of Chinese furniture
during the Ming period, the **ARMCHAIR** in **FIGURE 25-10** is
constructed without the use of glue or nails. Instead, pieces
fit together based on the principle of the mortise-and-
tenon joint, in which a projecting element (tenon) on one
piece fits snugly into a cavity (mortise) on another. Each
piece of the chair is carved—not bent or twisted—and the
joints are crafted with great precision. The patterns of the
wood grain provide subtle interest, unconcealed by painting or other embellishment. The style, like that of Chinese
architecture, is simple, clear, symmetrical, and balanced.
The effect is formal and dignified but natural and simple—
virtues central to the traditional Chinese view of proper
human conduct as well.

The art of landscape gardening also flourished during the Ming dynasty, as many literati surrounded their
homes with gardens. The most famous gardens were created in the southern cities of the Yangzi Delta, especially
in Suzhou, including the largest surviving garden of the
era—the **GARDEN OF THE CESSATION OF OFFICIAL LIFE**

25-10 ARMCHAIR
Ming dynasty, 16th–17th century. Huanghuali wood (hardwood),
39⅜ × 27¼ × 20″ (100 × 69.2 × 50.8 cm). The Nelson-Atkins Museum
of Art, Kansas City, Missouri. Purchase: William Rockhill Nelson Trust
(46–78/1).

(**FIG. 25-11**). Although modified and reconstructed many
times since the sixteenth century, it still reflects many of the
basic ideas of the original Ming owner. About one third of
the garden is devoted to water through artificially created
brooks and ponds. The landscape is dotted with pavilions,
kiosks, libraries, studios, and corridors—many with poetic
names, such as Rain Listening Pavilion and Bridge of the
Small Flying Rainbow.

DONG QICHANG, LITERATI THEORIST   The ideas
underlying literati painting found their most influential
expression in the writings of Dong Qichang (1555–1636).
This high official in the late Ming period embodied the literati tradition as poet, calligrapher, and painter. He developed a view of Chinese art history that divided painters
into two opposing schools, northern and southern. The
categorization is unrelated to the actual geographic homes
of the painters—a painter from the south might well be
classed as northern—but reflects parallels Dong perceived
with the northern and southern schools of Chan (Zen)
Buddhism in China. The southern school of Chan, founded
by the eccentric monk Huineng (638–713), was unorthodox, radical, and innovative; the northern Chan school
was traditional and conservative. Similarly, Dong's two
schools of painters represented progressive and conservative traditions. In Dong's view, the conservative northern
school was dominated by professional painters whose academic, often decorative, style emphasized technical skill.
In contrast, the progressive southern school preferred ink
to color and free brushwork to meticulous detail. Its painters aimed for poetry and personal expression. In promoting this theory, Dong privileged literati painting, which he
positioned as the culmination of the southern school, and
this viewpoint fundamentally influenced the way the Chinese viewed their own tradition.

Dong Qichang summarized his views on the proper
training for literati painters in the famous statement "Read
ten thousand books and walk ten thousand miles." By
this he meant that one must first study the works of the
great masters, then follow "heaven and earth," the world
of nature. Such study would prepare the way for greater
self-expression through brush and ink, the goal of literati painting. Dong's views rested on an awareness that
a painting of scenery and the actual scenery are two very
different things. The excellence of a painting does not lie
in its degree of resemblance to the natural world—that
gap can never be bridged—but in its expressive power. In
this view, the expressive language of painting is inherently
abstract, rooted in the construction of its brushstrokes.
For example, in a painting of a rock, the rock itself is not
expressive; rather, the brushstrokes that suggest the rock
are expressive.

With such thinking Dong brought painting close to the
realm of calligraphy, which had long been considered the

25-11 GARDEN OF THE CESSATION OF OFFICIAL LIFE (ALSO KNOWN AS THE HUMBLE ADMINISTRATOR'S GARDEN)

Suzhou, Jiangsu. Ming dynasty, early 16th century.

Early in the sixteenth century, an official in Beijing, frustrated after serving in the capital for many years without promotion, returned home. Taking an ancient poem, "The Song of Leisurely Living," for his model, he began to build a garden. He called his retreat the Garden of the Cessation of Official Life to indicate that he had exchanged his career as a bureaucrat for a life of leisure. By leisure, he meant that he could now dedicate himself to calligraphy, poetry, and painting, the three arts most valued by scholars in China.

Credit: © Meiqianbao/Shutterstock

highest form of artistic expression in China. More than a thousand years before Dong's time, a body of critical terms and theories had evolved to discuss calligraphy in relation to the formal and expressive properties of brushwork and composition. Dong incorporated some of these terms—categories such as opening and closing, rising and falling, and void and solid—into the criticism of painting.

Dong's theories take visual form in his painting of **THE QINGBIAN MOUNTAINS** (FIG. 25-12). As documented in his own inscription, he based this painting on a work by the tenth-century artist Dong Yuan. Dong Qichang's style, however, is quite different from the styles of the masters he admired. Although there is some indication of foreground, middle ground, and distant mountains, the space is ambiguous, as if all the elements were compressed to the surface of the picture. With this flattening of space, the trees, rocks, and mountains become more readily legible as semiabstract forms made of brushstrokes.

Six trees arranged diagonally at the lower right define the extreme foreground and announce themes that the rest of the painting repeats, varies, and develops. The left-most of these foreground trees, with its outstretched branches and full foliage, is echoed first in the shape of another tree just across the river and again in a tree farther up and to the left. The tallest tree of the foreground grouping anticipates the high peak that towers in the distance almost directly above it, while the forms of the smaller foreground trees, especially the one with the darkest leaves, are repeated in many variations across the painting. At the same time, the ordinary-looking boulder in the foreground is transformed in the conglomeration of rocks, ridges, hills, and mountains above. This double reading—both abstract and representational, on the surface and into space—parallels the work's dual nature as a painting of a landscape and an interpretation of a traditional landscape painting.

25–12 Dong Qichang **THE QINGBIAN MOUNTAINS**
Ming dynasty, 1617. Hanging scroll with ink on paper, 21′8″ × 7′4⅜″
(6.72 × 2.25 m). Cleveland Museum of Art. Leonard C. Hanna, Jr., Fund.

Credit: Bridgeman Images

The influence of Dong Qichang on the development of Chinese painting of later periods cannot be overstated. Indeed, nearly all Chinese painters since the early seventeenth century have engaged with his ideas in one way or another.

From the Qing Dynasty to the Modern Era

What traditions and styles endure and what are the new developments in Chinese art from the Qing Dynasty into the modern era?

In 1644, when the armies of the Manchu people northeast of China marched into Beijing, many Chinese reacted as though their civilization had come to an end. Yet the Manchus had already adopted many Chinese customs and institutions. After gaining control of all of China, a process that took decades, they showed great respect for Chinese tradition. All the major artistic trends of the late Ming dynasty eventually continued into the Manchu, or Qing, dynasty (1644–1911).

Orthodox and Individualist Painting

Literati painting had been established as the dominant tradition; it now became orthodox. Scholars followed Dong Qichang's recommendation, basing their approach on the study of past masters—especially Song and Yuan artists—and imitating antique styles as a way of expressing their own learning, technique, and taste.

The Qing emperors of the late seventeenth and eighteenth centuries were painters themselves. They collected literati painting, and their taste was shaped mainly by artists such as Wang Hui (SEE FIG. 25–1). Thus literati painting, long associated with reclusive scholars, ultimately became an academic style practiced at court. Imbued with values associated with scholarship and virtue, these paintings constituted the highest art form of the Qing court. The emperors also valued a style of bird-and-flower painting developed by Yun Shouping (1633–1690) that, like the orthodox style of landscape painting, was embraced by literati painters, many of them court officials themselves. Most often seen in albums or fans, the style recalled aspects of Song- and Yuan-dynasty bird-and-flower painting, and artists cited their ancient models as a way to enrich both the meaning and the beauty of these small-format works. In a leaf from an album of flowers, bamboo,

25-13 Yun Shouping **AMARANTH**
Leaf from an album of flowers, bamboo, fruits, and vegetables. Qing dynasty, 1633–1690. Album of 10 leaves; ink and color on paper; each leaf 10 × 13″ (25.3 × 33.5 cm). Collection of Phoenix Art Museum, Arizona. Gift of Marilyn and Roy Papp. (2006.164)

The leaf is inscribed by the artist: "Autumn garden abounds in beauty, playfully painted by Ouxiangguan (Yun Shouping)."
(Translation by Momoko Soma Welch)

fruits, and vegetables that employs a variety of brush techniques (**FIG. 25-13**), Yun Shouping painted flowers representing the autumn season.

INDIVIDUALIST PAINTING The first few decades of Qing rule had been both traumatic and dangerous for those who were loyal—or worse, related—to the Ming. Some committed suicide, while others sought refuge in monasteries or wandered the countryside. Among them were several painters—now known as the individualists—who expressed their anger, defiance, frustration, and melancholy in their art. They took Dong Qichang's idea of painting as an expression of the artist's personal feelings very seriously and cultivated highly original styles. Among the most accomplished was Zhu Da, whose painting of quince we have already encountered in the Introduction (**FIG. 25-14**; see the Introduction on pages xxx–xxxiii).

SHITAO Another individualist was Shitao (1642–1707), Zhu Da's distant imperial cousin, who was descended from the first Ming emperor and, like Zhu Da, took refuge in Buddhist temples when the dynasty fell. In his later life he brought his painting to the brink of abstraction in such works as **REMINISCENCES OF QINHUAI RIVER**, the final leaf of a landscape album (**FIG. 25-15**). In this painting, a monk stands in a boat, looking up at the mountains that seem to be reaching downward toward him, lined by inverted trees. The inscription filling the negative space above the mountains explains that the painting was made for one of Shitao's friends who had sent him paper for a requested painting. In these nostalgic paintings the artist refers to a happier time in the 1680s when the two friends had searched for plum blossoms along the Qinhuai River. Throughout his life Shitao identified himself with the fallen Ming, filled with longing for the secure world that had turned to chaos with the Manchu conquest.

25–14 Zhu Da (Bada Shanren) **QUINCE (MUGUA)**
Qing dynasty, 1690. Album leaf mounted as a hanging scroll; ink and colors on paper, 7⅞ × 5¾″ (20 × 14.6 cm). Princeton University Art Museum.

Credit: © 2016. Princeton University Art Museum/Art Resource, NY/Scala, Florence

25–15 Shitao **REMINISCENCES OF QINHUAI RIVER**
One of eight leaves from an album. Qing dynasty, c. 1695–1700. Ink and color on paper, 10 × 8″ (25.5 × 20.2 cm). Cleveland Museum of Art.

Credit: Bridgeman Images

The Modern Period

In the mid and late nineteenth century, China was shaken from centuries of complacency by a series of humiliating military defeats at the hands of Western powers and Japan. Only then did the government finally realize that these new rivals were not like the Mongols of the thirteenth century. China was no longer at the center of the world, a civilized country surrounded by "barbarians." Spiritual resistance was no longer sufficient to solve the problems brought on by change. New ideas from Japan and the West began to filter in, and the demand arose for political and cultural reforms. In 1911, the Qing dynasty was overthrown, ending 2,000 years of imperial rule, and China was reconceived as a republic.

During the first decades of the twentieth century Chinese artists traveled to Japan and Europe to study Western art. Returning to China, many sought to introduce the ideas and techniques they had learned, and they explored ways to synthesize Chinese and Western traditions. After the establishment of the present-day Communist government in 1949, individual artistic freedom was curtailed as

the arts were pressed into the service of the state and its vision of a new social order. After 1979, however, cultural attitudes began to relax, and Chinese painters again pursued their own paths.

WU GUANZHONG   One artist who emerged during the 1980s as a leader in Chinese painting was Wu Guanzhong (1919–2010). Combining his French artistic training with his Chinese background, Wu Guanzhong developed a semiabstract style to depict scenes from the Chinese landscape. He made preliminary sketches on site. Then, back in his studio, he developed these sketches into free interpretations based on his feeling and vision. An example of his work, **PINE SPIRIT**, depicts a scene in the Huang (Yellow) Mountains (**FIG. 25–16**). The technique, with its sweeping gestures of paint, is clearly linked to Abstract Expressionism, an influential Western movement of the post–World War II years (Chapter 32); yet the painting also claims a place in the long tradition of Chinese landscape as exemplified by such masters as Shitao.

25–16 Wu Guanzhong **PINE SPIRIT**

1984. Ink and color on paper, 2′5⅝″ × 5′3½″ (0.70 × 1.61 m). Spencer Museum of Art, University of Kansas, Lawrence. Gift of the E. Rhodes and Leonard B. Carpenter Foundation (1991.0003).

Credit: © Wu Guanzhong

Like all aspects of Chinese society, Chinese art has felt the strong impact of Western influence, and the question remains whether Chinese artists will absorb Western ideas without losing their traditional identity. Interestingly, landscape remains an important subject, as it has been for more than a thousand years, and calligraphy continues to play a vital role. Using the techniques and methods of the West, some of China's artists have joined an international avant-garde (see, for example, Wenda Gu in Chapter 33, FIG. 33–54), while other painters still seek communion with nature through their ink brushstrokes as a means to come to terms with human life and the world.

Arts of Korea from the Joseon Dynasty to the Modern Era

How do Korean ceramics and painting develop from the fifteenth to the twentieth century?

In 1392, General Yi Seonggye (1335–1408) overthrew the Goryeo dynasty (918–1392), establishing the Joseon dynasty (1392–1910), sometimes called the Yi dynasty. He first maintained his capital at Gaeseong, the old Goryeo capital, but moved it to Seoul in 1394, where it remained through the end of the dynasty. The Joseon regime rejected Buddhism, espousing Neo-Confucianism as the state philosophy. Taking Ming-dynasty China as its model, the new government patterned its bureaucracy on that of the Ming emperors, even adopting as its own such outward symbols of Ming imperial authority as blue-and-white porcelain. The early Joseon era was a period of cultural refinement and scientific achievement during which Koreans invented Han'geul (the Korean alphabet) and movable type, not to mention the rain gauge, astrolabe, celestial globe, sundial, and water clock.

Joseon Ceramics

Like their Silla and Goryeo forebears, Joseon potters excelled in the manufacture of ceramics, taking their cue from contemporaneous Chinese wares but seldom copying them directly.

BUNCHEONG CERAMICS Descended from Goryeo celadons, Joseon-dynasty stonewares, known as *buncheong* wares, enjoyed widespread usage throughout the peninsula. Their decorative effect relies on the use of white slip that makes the humble stoneware resemble more expensive white porcelain. In fifteenth-century examples, the slip is often seen inlaid into repeating design elements stamped into the clay body.

Sixteenth-century *buncheong* wares are characteristically embellished with wonderfully fluid, calligraphic brushwork painted in iron-brown slip on a white slip ground. Most painted *buncheong* wares have stylized floral

25–17 HORIZONTAL WINE BOTTLE WITH DECORATION OF A BIRD CARRYING A NEWLY CAUGHT FISH
Korea. Joseon dynasty, 16th century.
Buncheong ware: light gray stoneware with decoration painted in iron-brown slip on a white slip ground; 6¹/₁₀ × 9½″ (15.5 × 24.1 cm). Museum of Oriental Ceramics, Osaka, Japan.
Gift of the Sumitomo Group (20773).

décor, but rare pieces, such as a charming **WINE BOTTLE** (**FIG. 25–17**), feature pictorial decoration. In fresh, lively brushstrokes, a bird with outstretched wings grasps a fish that it has just caught in its talons; waves roll below, while two giant lotus blossoms frame the scene.

Japanese armies repeatedly invaded the Korean peninsula between 1592 and 1597, destroying many of the *buncheong* kilns and essentially bringing ceramic production to a halt. Tradition holds that the Japanese took many *buncheong* potters home with them to produce *buncheong*-style wares, which were greatly admired by connoisseurs of the tea ceremony. In fact, the spontaneity

25–18 BROAD-SHOULDERED JAR WITH DECORATION OF A FRUITING GRAPEVINE
Korea. Joseon dynasty, 17th century. Porcelain with decoration painted in underglaze iron-brown slip, height 22⅛″ (53.8 cm). Ewha Women's University Museum, Seoul, Republic of Korea.
Credit: Courtesy of Ewha Woman's University Museum, Seoul

of Korean *buncheong* pottery has inspired Japanese ceramics to this day.

PAINTED PORCELAIN Korean potters produced porcelains with designs painted in underglaze cobalt blue as early as the fifteenth century, inspired by Chinese porcelains of the early Ming period (SEE FIG. 25–4). The Korean court dispatched artists from the royal painting academy to the porcelain kilns—located some 30 miles southeast of Seoul—to train porcelain painters. As a result, from the fifteenth century onward, the painting on the best Korean porcelains closely approximated that on paper and silk, unlike in China, where ceramic decoration followed a path of its own with little reference to painting traditions.

In another unique development, Korean porcelains from the sixteenth and seventeenth centuries often feature designs painted in underglaze iron-brown rather than the cobalt blue customary in Ming porcelain. Also uniquely Korean are porcelain jars with bulging shoulders, slender bases, and short, vertical necks, which appeared by the seventeenth century and came to be the most characteristic ceramic shapes in the later Joseon period. One example, a seventeenth-century jar painted in underglaze iron-brown (**FIG. 25–18**), depicts a fruiting grape branch around its shoulder. In typical Korean fashion, the painting spreads over a surface unconstrained by borders, resulting in a balanced but asymmetrical design that incorporates the Korean taste for unornamented spaces.

Joseon Painting

Korean secular painting came into its own during the Joseon dynasty. Continuing Goryeo traditions, early Joseon examples employ Chinese styles and formats, their range of subjects expanding from botanical motifs to include landscapes, figures, and a variety of animals.

Painted in 1447 by An Gyeon (b. 1418), **DREAM JOURNEY TO THE PEACH BLOSSOM LAND** (**FIG. 25–19**) is the

25–19 An Gyeon **DREAM JOURNEY TO THE PEACH BLOSSOM LAND**
Korea. Joseon dynasty, 1447. Handscroll with ink and light colors on silk, 15¼ × 41¾″ (38.7 × 106.1 cm). Central Library, Tenri University, Tenri (near Nara), Japan.

Credit: Photo courtesy of Central Library, Tenri University, Tenri, Japan

earliest extant and dated Joseon secular painting. It illustrates a fanciful tale by China's revered nature poet Tao Qian (365–427) about chancing upon a utopia secluded from the world for centuries while meandering among the peach blossoms of spring.

As with their Goryeo forebears, the monumental mountains and vast, panoramic vistas of such fifteenth-century Korean paintings echo Northern Song painting styles. Chinese paintings of the Southern Song (1127–1279) and Ming (1368–1644) periods also influenced Korean painting of the fifteenth, sixteenth, and seventeenth centuries, though these styles never completely supplanted the imprint of the Northern Song masters.

THE SILHAK MOVEMENT   In the eighteenth century, a truly Korean style emerged, inspired by the *silhak* ("practical learning") movement, which emphasized the study of things Korean in addition to the Chinese classics. The impact of the movement is exemplified by the painter Jeong Seon (1676–1759), who chose well-known Korean vistas as the subjects of his paintings, rather than the Chinese themes favored by earlier artists. Among Jeong Seon's paintings are numerous representations of the Diamond Mountains (Geumgang-san), a celebrated range of craggy peaks along Korea's east coast. One hanging scroll painted in 1734 (**FIG. 25–20**) aptly captures the Diamond Mountains' needle-like peaks. The subject is Korean, and so is the energetic spirit and the intensely personal style,

25–20 Jeong Seon **PANORAMIC VIEW OF THE DIAMOND MOUNTAINS (GEUMGANG-SAN)**
Korea. Joseon dynasty, 1734. Hanging scroll with ink and colors on paper, 40⅝ × 37″ (130.1 × 94 cm). Lee'um, Samsung Museum, Seoul, Republic of Korea.

Credit: National Treasure # 217

25–21 Kim Hongdo **ROOF TILING**

From *Album of Genre Paintings*. Korea. Joseon dynasty,18th century. Ink and light colors on paper, 10⅝ × 8⅞" (27 × 22.7 cm). National Museum of Korea, Seoul, Republic of Korea. Treasure No. 527.

Credit: National Museum of Korea, Seoul, Republic of Korea.

with its crystalline mountains, distant clouds of delicate ink wash, and individualistic brushwork.

Other artists expanded the growing interest in Korean themes to different sorts of subject matter. Kim Hongdo (1745–1806) painted genre scenes that showcased the everyday lives and occupations not of the nobility, but of commoners. His painting of **ROOF TILING** (**FIG. 25–21**)—one of a series of 25 album leaves portraying genre scenes—shows a team of six laborers engaged in various aspects of their roofing job. At lower right a carpenter smooths a propped-up board with his plane, while two colleagues perch on the roof itself, one about to hoist up a bundle of materials and the other catching a tile that has been heaved to him from below. The seventh man, leaning on his staff at upper right to survey the work, is presumably the roofers' supervisor. The circular figural composition animates the compressed foreground tableau and organizes the viewer's examination of the carefully detailed workers, whose depiction is energized by active poses and expressive faces. Kim creates a strong sense of narrative; we seem to have come unexpectedly into the middle of an unfolding story.

Modernist Painting

Long known as "the Hermit Kingdom," the Joseon dynasty pursued a policy of isolationism, closing its borders to most of the world except China, until 1876. Japan's annexation of Korea in 1910 brought the Joseon dynasty to a close, but effectively prolonged the country's seclusion from the outside world. The legacy of self-imposed isolation was compounded by colonial occupation (1910–1945)—not to mention the harsh circumstances imposed by World War II (1939–1945) and the even worse conditions of the Korean War (1950–1953)—and impeded Korea's artistic and cultural development during the first half of the twentieth century.

Despite these privations, some modern influences did reach Korea indirectly via China and Japan, and beginning in the 1920s and 1930s a few Korean artists experimented with contemporary Western styles, typically painting in the manner of Cézanne or Gauguin, but sometimes trying abstract, nonrepresentational styles. Among these, Whanki Kim (1913–1974) was influenced by Constructivism and geometric abstraction and would become one of twentieth-century Korea's influential painters. Like many Korean artists after the Korean War, Kim wanted to examine Western Modernism at its source. He visited Paris in 1956 and then, from 1964 to 1974, lived and worked in New York, where he produced his best-known works. His painting **UNIVERSE 5-IV-71 #200** presents a large pair of circular, radiating patterns composed of small dots and squares in tones of blue, black, and gray (**FIG. 25–22**). While appearing wholly Western in style, medium, concept, and even the adoption of the date of the work's creation as part of its title, this work also seems related to East Asia's venerable tradition of monochrome **ink painting**, while suggesting a transcendence that seems Daoist or Buddhist in feeling. Given that the artist was Korean, that he learned the Chinese classics in his youth, that he studied art in Paris, and that he then worked in New York, it is possible that his painting embodies all of the above. It illustrates the dilemma faced by many modern artists seeking to find a distinctive, personal style: whether to paint in an updated version of a traditional style, in a wholly international style, in an international style with a distinctive local twist, or in an eclectic, hybrid style that incorporates both native and naturalized elements from diverse artistic traditions.

By addressing these questions, Whanki Kim blazed a trail for subsequent Korean-born artists, such as the renowned video artist Nam June Paik (1932–2006), whose work will be discussed in Chapter 33.

25–22 Whanki Kim **UNIVERSE 5-IV-71 #200**
Korea. 1971. Oil on cotton, 8'4" × 8'4" (254 × 254 cm). Whanki Museum, Seoul, Republic of Korea.

Credit: © Whanki Foundation - Whanki Museum

Think About It

1   Discuss the place of Dong Qichang's *The Qingbian Mountains* (**FIG. 25-12**) within the history of Chinese landscape painting, drawing specific comparisons with works that came before and after it.

2   Examine a work commissioned by the court at Beijing and distinguish which of its features are typical of court art.

3   Characterize the culture of the literati, including their values and their art patronage.

4   Theorize reasons for the emergence of individualist painting in China, using specific works to support your argument.

Crosscurrents

Both of these expansive paintings use landscape, figures, and text in compositions that embody important ideas, values, and themes characteristic of two very different cultures. Discuss the meanings in these two works. How do they represent the aspirations of the artists who created them and the viewers who originally encountered them?

FIG. 18–15

FIG. 25–9

26–1 Suzuki Harunobu **THE FLOWERS OF BEAUTY IN THE FLOATING WORLD: MOTOURA AND YAEZAKURA OF THE MINAMI YAMASAKIYA**

Edo period, 1769. Polychrome woodblock print on paper, 11⅜ × 8½″ (28.9 × 21.8 cm). Honolulu Museum of Art, Gift of James A. Michener, 1957 (14044)

Chapter 26
Japanese Art after 1333

 ## Learning Objectives

26.a Identify the visual hallmarks of Japanese art after 1333 for formal, technical, and expressive qualities.

26.b Interpret the meaning of works of Japanese art after 1333 based on their themes, subjects, and symbols.

26.c Relate artists and art of Japan after 1333 to their cultural, economic, and political contexts.

26.d Apply the vocabulary and concepts relevant to post-1333 Japanese art, artists, and art history.

26.e Interpret a work of Japanese art after 1333 using the art historical methods of observation, comparison, and inductive reasoning.

26.f Select visual and textual evidence in various media to support an argument or an interpretation of a work of Japanese art after 1333.

Perched on a window seat, a young woman pauses from smoking her pipe while the girl at her side peers intently through a telescope at boats in the bay below (**FIG. 26–1**). The scene takes place in the city of Edo (now Tokyo) in the 1760s, during an era of peace and prosperity that had started some 150 years earlier when the Tokugawa shoguns unified the nation. Edo was then the largest city in the world, with over 1 million inhabitants: samurai-bureaucrats and working-class townspeople. The commoners possessed a vibrant culture centered in urban entertainment districts, where geisha and courtesans, such as the lady and her young trainee portrayed in this woodblock print, worked.

In the 1630s, the Tokugawa shogunate banned Japanese citizens from traveling abroad and restricted foreign access to the country. Nagasaki became Japan's sole international port, which only Koreans, Chinese, and Dutch could enter—and they could not travel freely in the country once there. The government did this to deter Christian missionaries and to assert authority over foreign powers. Not until 1853, when Commodore Matthew Perry of the United States forced Japan to open additional ports, did these policies change. But even prior to 1853, foreign influences and products could not be prevented, as the tobacco pipe and telescope in this print testify.

The Japanese had first encountered Westerners—Portuguese traders—in the mid sixteenth century. The Dutch reached Japan by 1600 and brought tobacco and, soon after that, the telescope and other exotic optical devices—including spectacles and microscopes—as well as other objects, including books, many illustrated. The Japanese eagerly welcomed these foreign goods and imitated foreign customs, which conferred an air of sophistication on the user. Looking through telescopes like the one in this print was a popular amusement of courtesans and their customers. It conveyed the sort of sexual overtones—because of the telescope's phallic shape—that characterized the ribald humor then in vogue. Western optical devices, all readily available by the mid eighteenth century, offered a new way of seeing that affected the appearance of Japanese pictorial art. As in the early history of Japanese art, however, Chinese influence remained strong and now spread throughout the population as never before, due to new efforts to educate the broader populace in Chinese studies. In varying degrees, the intermingling of diverse native and foreign artistic traditions continued to shape the arts of Japan.

Foundations of Japanese Culture

What aspects of the early history, culture, and art of Japan form a critical background for the development of art and architecture after 1333?

With the end of the last Ice Age roughly 15,000 years ago, rising sea levels submerged the lowlands connecting Japan to the Asian landmass, creating the chain of islands we

MAP 26-1 JAPAN

Japan's wholehearted emulation of many aspects of Chinese culture began in the fifth century. It was challenged by new influences from the West only in the mid nineteenth century after Western powers forced Japan to open its treaty ports to international trade.

know today as Japan (**MAP 26-1**). Not long afterward, early Paleolithic cultures gave way to a Neolithic culture known as Jomon (c. 11,000–400 BCE) after its characteristic cord-marked pottery. During the Jomon period, a sophisticated hunter-gatherer culture developed. Agriculture supplemented hunting and gathering by around 5000 BCE, and rice cultivation began some 4,000 years later.

A fully settled agricultural society emerged during the Yayoi period (c. 400 BCE–300 CE), accompanied by hierarchical social organization. As people learned to manufacture bronze and iron, use of those metals became widespread. Yayoi architecture, with its unpainted wood and thatched roofs, already showed the Japanese affinity for natural materials and clean lines; the style of Yayoi granaries in particular persisted in the design of shrines in later centuries. The trend toward social organization continued during the Kofun period (c. 300–552 CE), an era characterized by the construction of large royal tombs following the Korean practice. Veneration of leaders grew into the beginnings of the imperial system that has lasted to the present day.

The Asuka era (552–645 CE) began with a period of profound change as elements of Chinese civilization flooded into Japan, initially through the intermediary of Korea. The three most significant Chinese contributions to the developing Japanese culture were Buddhism (with its attendant art and architecture), a system of writing, and the structures of a centralized bureaucracy. The earliest extant Buddhist temple compound in Japan, Horyuji, which contains the oldest currently existing wooden buildings in the world, dates from this period (SEE FIG. 12–4).

The arrival of Buddhism also prompted some formalization of Shinto, the loose collection of indigenous Japanese beliefs and practices. Shinto is a religion that connects people to nature. Its rites are shamanistic and emphasize ceremonial purification. These include the invocation and appeasement of spirits, including those of the recently dead. Many Shinto deities are thought to inhabit various aspects of nature, such as particularly magnificent trees, rocks, and waterfalls, and living creatures such as deer. Shinto and Buddhism have in common an intense awareness of the transience of life, and as their goals are complementary—purification in the case of Shinto, enlightenment in the case of Buddhism—they have generally existed comfortably alongside each other.

The Nara period (645–794 CE) takes its name from the location of Japan's first permanently established imperial capital. During this time the founding works of Japanese literature were compiled, and Buddhism became the most important force in Japanese culture. Its influence at court grew so great that in 794 the emperor moved the capital from Nara to Heian-kyo (present-day Kyoto), far from powerful monasteries.

During the Heian period (794–1185 CE) an extremely refined court culture thrived, embodied today in an exquisite legacy of poetry, calligraphy, and painting. An efficient method for writing the Japanese language was developed, and with it a woman at the court wrote Japan's most celebrated fictional story, which some describe as the world's first novel: *The Tale of Genji*. Esoteric Buddhism, as hierarchical and intricate as the aristocratic world of the court, became popular.

The end of the Heian period was marked by civil warfare as regional warrior (samurai) clans were drawn into the factional conflicts at court. Pure Land Buddhism, with its simple message of salvation, offered consolation to many in troubled times. In 1185, the Minamoto clan defeated their arch rivals, the Taira, and their leader, Minamoto Yoritomo, assumed the position of shogun (general-in-chief). While paying respect to the emperor, Minamoto Yoritomo took actual military and political power for himself, setting up his own capital in Kamakura. The Kamakura era (1185–1333 CE) began a tradition of rule by shogun that lasted in various forms until 1868. It was also the time in which renewed contacts with China created the opportunity for Zen Buddhism, which was then flourishing in China (and was known there as Chan), to be introduced to Japan. By the end of the Kamakura period, numerous Zen monasteries had been founded in Kyoto and Kamakura, and Chinese and Japanese Chan/Zen monks were regularly visiting each other's countries.

Muromachi Period

What is the impact of Zen aesthetics on ink painting and garden design during the Muromachi period?

By the year 1333, the history of Japanese art was already long and rich. Very early, a particularly Japanese sensitivity to artistic production had emerged, including a love of natural materials, a fondness for representing elements of the natural world, and a cultivation of fine craft. Aesthetically, Japanese art manifested a taste for asymmetry, abstraction, boldness of expression, and humor—characteristics that will continue to distinguish Japanese art in its evolving history.

Late in the twelfth century, the authority of the emperor had been superseded by powerful and ambitious warriors (samurai) under the leadership of the shogun, the general-in-chief. But in 1333, Emperor Go-Daigo attempted to retake power. He failed and was forced into hiding in the mountains south of Kyoto where he set up a "southern court." Meanwhile, the shogunal family then in power, the Minamoto, was overthrown by warriors of the Ashikaga clan, who placed a rival to the upstart emperor on the throne in Kyoto, in a "northern court," and had him declare their clan head as shogun. They ruled the country from the Muromachi district in Kyoto and finally vanquished the southern court emperors in 1392. The Muromachi period, also known as the Ashikaga era (1392–1573), formally began with this event.

The Muromachi period is marked by the ascendance of Zen Buddhism, introduced into Japan in the late twelfth century, whose austere ideals particularly appealed to the highly disciplined samurai. While Pure Land Buddhism, which had spread widely during the latter part of the Heian period (794–1185), remained popular, Zen (which means meditation) became the dominant cultural force in Japan among the ruling elite.

Zen Ink Painting

During the Muromachi period, the creation of brightly colored narrative handscrolls in traditional Japanese style continued, but monochrome painting in black ink and its diluted grays—which had just been introduced to Japan from the continent at the end of the Kamakura period (1185–1333)—reigned supreme. Muromachi ink painting was heavily influenced by the aesthetics of Zen, but unlike

earlier Zen paintings that had concentrated on portrayals of important individuals associated with the Zen monastic tradition, Chinese-style landscapes in ink also began to be produced. Traditionally, the monk-artist Shubun (active c. 1418–1463) is regarded as Japan's first great master of ink landscape painting. Unfortunately, no undisputed work of his survives. Two landscapes by Shubun's pupil Bunsei (active c. 1450–1460), however, do survive. The one reproduced in **FIGURE 26-2** is closely modeled on Korean

26-2 Bunsei LANDSCAPE
Muromachi period, mid 15th century. Hanging scroll with ink and light colors on paper, 28¾ × 13″ (73.2 × 33 cm). Museum of Fine Arts, Boston. Special Chinese and Japanese Fund (05.203).

Credit: Photograph © 2017 Museum of Fine Arts, Boston

ink landscape paintings, which were themselves copied from Ming-period Chinese models (such as FIG. 25-6). The foreground consists of a spit of rocky land with an overlapping series of motifs—a spiky pine tree, a craggy rock, a poet seated in a hermitage, and a brushwood fence surrounding a small garden of trees and bamboo. In the middle ground is open space—emptiness, the void. We are expected to "read" the unpainted expanse as water. Beyond the blank space, subtle tones of gray ink delineate a distant shore where fishing boats, a small hut, and two people stand. The two parts of the painting seem to echo each other across a deep expanse. The painting illustrates well the pure, lonely, and ultimately serene spirit of the Zen poetic landscape tradition.

SESSHU Another of Shubun's pupils, Sesshu (1420–1506), has come to be regarded as one of the greatest Japanese painters of all time. Although Shubun and his followers completed training to become Zen monks at the monastery, they specialized in art rather than in religious ritual or teaching. This distinguished them from earlier Zen monk-painters, for whom painting was but one facet of their lives. By Shubun's day, temples had formed their own professional painting ateliers in order to meet the large demand from warrior patrons for paintings. Sesshu trained as a Zen monk at Shokokuji, where Shubun had his studio. He worked in the painting atelier under Shubun for 20 years before leaving Kyoto to head a small provincial Zen temple in western Japan, where he could concentrate on painting unencumbered by monastic duties and entanglements with the political elite. His new temple was under the patronage of a wealthy warrior clan that engaged in trade with China. Funded by them, he had the opportunity to visit China in 1467 on a diplomatic mission. He traveled extensively there for three years, viewing the scenery, stopping at Chan (Zen) monasteries, and studying Chinese paintings by professional artists rather than those by contemporary literati masters.

When Sesshu returned from China, he remained in the provinces to avoid the turmoil in Kyoto, at that time devastated by civil warfare that would last for the next hundred years. Only a few paintings created prior to his sojourn in China have come to light. They are in a style closer to Shubun, and Sesshu signed them with another name. In contrast, the paintings he produced after his return demonstrate a conscious break artistically with the refined landscape style of his teacher. These masterful later paintings exhibit a bold, new spirit, evident in his **WINTER LANDSCAPE** (FIG. 26-3). A cliff descending from the mist seems to cut the composition in two parts. Jagged brushstrokes delineate a series of rocky hills, where a lone figure makes his way to a Zen monastery. Instead of a gradual recession into space, flat, overlapping planes fracture the composition into crystalline facets. The white of the paper is left to indicate snow, while the sky is suggested by tones of gray. A few trees cling to the rocky land. The harsh chill of winter is almost palpable.

Zen Dry Gardens

Zen monks led austere lives in their quest for the attainment of enlightenment. In addition to daily meditation, they engaged in manual labor to provide for themselves and maintain their temple properties. Many Zen temples constructed dry landscape courtyard gardens, not for strolling in but for the purpose of contemplative viewing. Cleaning and maintaining these gardens—pulling weeds, tweaking unruly shoots, and raking the gravel—was a kind of active meditation that helped to keep the monks' minds grounded.

The dry landscape gardens of Japan, *karesansui* ("dried-up mountains and water"), exist in perfect

26-3 Sesshu **WINTER LANDSCAPE**
Muromachi period, c. 1470s. Hanging scroll with ink on paper, 18¼ × 11½" (46.3 × 29.3 cm). Collection of the Tokyo National Museum. National Treasure.

26–4 ROCK GARDEN, RYOANJI, KYOTO

Muromachi period, c. 1480. Photographed spring 1993. UNESCO World Heritage Site, National Treasure.

The American composer John Cage, who composed a piece entitled "Ryoanji" in 1983, loved this garden, believing that every stone was in just the right place but also claiming that if they were rearranged, they would still be in the right place. His remark is thoroughly Zen in spirit. There are many ways to experience Ryoanji. For example, we can imagine the rocks as having different visual "pulls" that relate them to one another. Yet there is also enough space between them to give each a sense of self-sufficiency and permanence.

Credit: © Michael S. Yamashita/Corbis

harmony with Zen Buddhism. The dry garden in front of the abbot's quarters in the Zen temple at Ryoanji is one of the most renowned Zen creations in Japan (**FIG. 26–4**). A flat rectangle of raked gravel, about 29 by 70 feet, surrounds 15 stones of different sizes in islands of moss. The stones are set in asymmetrical groups of two, three, and five. Low, plaster-covered walls establish the garden's boundaries, but beyond the perimeter wall maple, pine, and cherry trees add color and texture to the scene. Called "borrowed scenery," these elements are a considered part of the design even though they grow outside the garden. This garden is celebrated for its severity and its emptiness.

Dry gardens began to be built in the fifteenth and sixteenth centuries in Japan. By the sixteenth century, Chinese landscape painting influenced the gardens' composition, and miniature clipped plants and beautiful stones were arranged to resemble famous paintings. Especially fine and unusual stones were coveted and even carried off as war booty, such was the cultural value of these seemingly mundane objects.

The Ryoanji garden's design, as we see it today, probably dates from the mid seventeenth century, at which point such stone and gravel gardens had become highly intellectualized, abstract reflections of nature. This garden has been interpreted as representing islands in the sea or mountain peaks rising above the clouds, perhaps even a swimming tigress with her cubs, or constellations of stars and planets. All or none of these interpretations may be equally satisfying—or irrelevant—to a monk seeking clarity of mind through contemplation.

Momoyama Period

What are the major contributions of the Momoyama period in architectural design and art?

The civil wars that were sweeping Japan laid bare the basic flaw in the Ashikaga system—samurai were primarily loyal to their own feudal lord (*daimyo*), rather than to the central government. Battles between feudal clans grew more frequent, and it became clear that only a warrior powerful and bold enough to unite the entire country could control Japan. As the Muromachi period drew to a close, three leaders emerged who would change the course of Japanese history.

The first of these leaders was Oda Nobunaga (1534–1582), who marched his army into Kyoto in 1568 and overthrew the reigning Ashikaga shogun in 1573, initiating a new age of Japanese politics. A ruthless warrior, Nobunaga went so far as to destroy a Buddhist monastery because the monks refused to join his forces. Yet he was also a patron of the most rarefied and refined arts.

After he took his own life to avoid succumbing to his enemies in the midst of a military campaign, he was succeeded by one of his generals, Toyotomi Hideyoshi (1537–1598), who soon gained complete power in Japan. He, too, was a patron of the arts when not leading his army, since he considered culture a vital adjunct to his rule. Hideyoshi, however, was overly ambitious. He believed he could conquer both Korea and China, and he wasted much of his resources on two ill-fated invasions. A stable and long-lasting military regime finally emerged soon after 1600 with the triumph of a third leader, Tokugawa Ieyasu (1543–1616), a former ally of Nobunaga who served as a senior retainer to Hideyoshi and only asserted his power after Hideyoshi's death. But despite its turbulence, the era of Nobunaga and Hideyoshi, known as the Momoyama period (1573–1615), was one of the most creative eras in Japanese history.

Today the very word Momoyama conjures up images of bold warriors, luxurious palaces, screens shimmering with gold leaf, and, in contrast, rustic tea-ceremony ceramics. Europeans first made an impact in Japan at this time. After the arrival of a few wayward Portuguese explorers in 1543, traders and missionaries soon followed. It was only with the rise of Nobunaga, however, that Westerners were able to extend their activities beyond the ports of Kyushu, Japan's southernmost island. Nobunaga welcomed foreign traders, who brought him various products, the most influential of which were firearms.

Architecture

European muskets and cannons quickly changed the nature of Japanese warfare and Japanese castle architecture. In the late sixteenth century, castles became heavily fortified garrisons to defend against these new weapons. Some were eventually lost to warfare or torn down by victorious enemies, and others have been extensively altered over the years. One of the most beautiful of the few that have survived intact is **HIMEJI**, not far from the city of Osaka (**FIG. 26-5**). Rising high on a hill above the plains, Himeji has been given the name White Heron. To reach the upper fortress, visitors must follow angular paths beneath steep walls, climbing from one area to the next past stone ramparts and through narrow, fortified gates, all the while feeling lost in a maze with no sense of direction or progress. At the main building, a further climb up a series of narrow ladders leads to the uppermost chamber. There, the footsore visitor is rewarded with a stunning 360-degree view of the surrounding countryside.

Shoin Rooms

Castles such as Himeji were sumptuously decorated, offering artists unprecedented opportunities to work on a grand scale. Interiors were divided into *shoin*-style rooms by paper-covered sliding doors (**fusuma**). Alcoves were created for specialized placement of art and activities.

26-5 HIMEJI CASTLE, HYOGO, NEAR OSAKA
Momoyama period, 1601–1609. UNESCO World Heritage Site, National Treasure.

Credit: © Louis W/Shutterstock

The use of *fusuma* provided expansive surfaces for large-scale murals. Free-standing folding screens (*byobu*) were also popular. Some of these paintings had gold-leaf backgrounds, whose glistening surfaces reflected light back into rooms and demonstrated the wealth of the warrior leaders who commissioned them. They were used in castles, as well as in grand reception rooms in temples where the monks met with visitors, notably the patrons themselves (see "*Shoin* Design" below). Artists working in the famous Kano School were often called on to meet the growing need for paintings to decorate *shoin*-style rooms.

A sumptuous set of *fusuma* in full color on a gold background was commissioned from Kano School artists for the reception room in a subtemple of Ryonji; the patron was a member of the ruling elite from the

Elements of Architecture
SHOIN DESIGN

The Japanese tea ceremony and *shoin*-style interior used in residential architecture were undoubtedly the most significant and enduring expressions of Japanese taste established during the Momoyama period. **Shoin** combine a number of interior features in more or less standard ways, though no two rooms are ever the same. These features include wide verandas, walls divided by wooden posts, floors covered with woven straw **tatami** mats, recessed panels in ceilings, sometimes painted and sometimes covered with reed matting, several shallow alcoves for prescribed purposes, *fusuma* (paper-covered sliding doors), and **shoji** screens—wood frames covered with translucent rice paper. The *shoin* illustrated here was built in 1601 as a guest hall, called Kojoin, at the Buddhist temple of Onjoji near Kyoto.

The *shoin* is a formal room for receiving important upper-class guests. With some variations due to differences in status, these rooms were designed for buildings used by samurai, aristocrats, and even well-to-do commoners. They are found in various types of buildings: private residences; living quarters, guesthouses, and reception rooms at religious complexes (both Shinto shrines and Buddhist temples); and the finest houses of entertainment (such as seen in FIG. 26–1) where geisha and courtesans entertained important guests. The owner of the building or the most important guest would be seated in front of the main alcove (*tokonoma*), which would contain a hanging scroll, an arrangement of flowers, or a large painted screen. Alongside that alcove was another that featured staggered shelves, often for displaying precious objects. The veranda side of the room also contained a writing space fitted with a low writing desk.

The architectural harmony of a *shoin* is derived from standardization of its basic units, or modules. In Japanese carpentry, the common module of design and construction is the bay, reckoned as the distance from the center of one post to the center of another, which is governed in turn by the standard size of *tatami* floor mats. Although varying slightly from region to region, the size of a single *tatami* is about 3 by 6 feet. Room area in Japan is still expressed in terms of the number of *tatami* mats; for example, a room may be described as an eight-mat room.

shoji — veranda — writing alcove — *tokonoma* — *tatami* — staggered shelves — *fusuma*

ARTIST'S RENDERING OF THE KOJOIN GUEST HOUSE AT ONJOJI
Otsu, Shiga prefecture. Momoyama period, 1601. National Treasure.

26-6 Kano School APPRECIATION OF PAINTING
Fusuma (sliding screens) from the patron's reception room of the abbot's quarters, Ryoanji, Kyoto. Momoyama period, c. 1606. Ink, color, and gold leaf on paper; 72″ × 24′ (1.83 × 7.32 m). Metropolitan Museum of Art, New York.

Credit: © 2016. Image copyright The Metropolitan Museum of Art/Art Resource/Scala, Florence

Hosokawa family, either Hosokawa Yusai (1534–1610) or his son Sansai (1564–1645), powerful samurai warriors who were also intellectual and political figures in Momoyama Japan. Portraying secular Chinese themes, the *fusuma* were once installed within the *hojo* (or abbot's quarters) overlooking the famous rock garden at Ryoanji (SEE FIG. 26-4). **FIGURE 26-6** shows one of a set of screens from this room that portrayed the Confucian scholarly arts of music, painting, calligraphy, and chess. To the right a gathering of sages admires an unrolled hanging scroll, while the celebrated Tang poet Li Bo approaches from the left. In his inebriated state, the poet needs the assistance of two boys, one to each side. The drunken Li Bo was a popular Momoyama subject, representing the ideal of an unencumbered life.

The Tea Ceremony

Japanese art is never one-sided. Along with castles and their opulent interior decoration, there was an equal interest during the Momoyama period in the quiet, the restrained, and the natural. This was expressed primarily through the tea ceremony.

The term "tea ceremony," a phrase now in common use, does not convey the full meaning of *chanoyu*, the Japanese ritual drinking of tea. There is no counterpart in Western culture. Tea had been introduced to Japan in the ninth century, when it was molded into cakes and boiled. However, the advent of Zen brought to Japan a different way of preparing tea, with the leaves ground into powder and then whisked in bowls with hot water. Zen monks used such tea as a mild stimulant to aid meditation. Others found it had medicinal properties.

SEN NO RIKYU The most famous tea master in Japanese history was Sen no Rikyu (1522–1591). He conceived of the tea ceremony as an intimate gathering in which a few people, often drawn from a variety of backgrounds—warriors, courtiers, wealthy merchants—would enter a small rustic room, drink tea carefully prepared in front of them by their host, and quietly discuss the tea utensils or a Zen scroll hanging on the wall. He largely established the aesthetic of modesty, refinement, and rusticity that permitted the tearoom to serve as a respite from the busy and sometimes violent world outside. A traditional tearoom combines simple elegance and rusticity. It is made of natural materials such as bamboo and wood, with mud walls, paper windows, and a floor covered with *tatami*. One tearoom that preserves Rikyu's design is named **TAIAN** (**FIG. 26-7**). Built in 1582, it has a tiny door (guests must crawl to enter) and miniature *tokonoma* (alcove) for displaying a Zen scroll or a simple flower arrangement. At first glance, the room seems symmetrical. But a longer look reveals the disposition of the *tatami* does not match the

26-7 Sen no Rikyu **TAIAN TEAROOM**
Myokian Temple, Kyoto. Momoyama period, 1582. National Treasure.

Credit: Myoki-an/PPS

spacing of the *tokonoma*, providing a subtle undercurrent of irregularity. The walls seem scratched and worn with age, but the *tatami* are replaced frequently to keep them clean and fresh. The mood is quiet; the light is muted and diffused through three small paper windows. Above all, there is a sense of spatial clarity. Since nonessentials have been eliminated, there is nothing to distract from focused attention. This tearoom aesthetic became an important element in Japanese culture.

THE TEA BOWL Every utensil connected with tea, including the water jar, the kettle, the tea scoop, the whisk, the tea caddy, and, above all, the tea bowl, came to be appreciated for its aesthetic quality, and many works of art were created for use in *chanoyu*.

The age-old Japanese admiration for the natural and the asymmetrical found full expression in tea ceramics. Korean-style rice bowls made for peasants were suddenly considered the epitome of refined taste, and tea masters urged potters to mimic their imperfect shapes. But not every misshapen bowl would be admired. A rarified appreciation of beauty developed that took into consideration such factors as how well a tea bowl fitted into the hands, how subtly the shape and texture of the bowl appealed to the eye, and who had previously used and admired it. For this purpose, the inscribed storage box became almost as important as the ceramic that it held, and if a bowl had been given a name by a leading tea master, it was especially treasured by later generations.

intellectual force by a form of Neo-Confucianism, a philosophy formulated in Song-dynasty China that emphasized loyalty to the state, although the popularity of Buddhism among the commoner population surged at this time.

The shogunate officially divided Edo society into four classes. Samurai officials constituted the highest class, followed by farmers, artisans, and finally merchants. As time went on, however, merchants began to control the money supply, and in Japan's increasingly mercantile economy, their accumulation of wealth soon exceeded that of the samurai, which helped, unofficially, to elevate their status. Reading and writing became widespread at all levels of society, and with literacy came intellectual curiosity and interest in the arts. All segments of the population—including samurai, merchants, townspeople, and rural peasants—were able to acquire art. A rich cultural atmosphere developed unlike anything Japan had experienced before, in which artists worked in a wide variety of styles to appeal to these different groups of consumers.

Rinpa School Painting

During the Edo period, Edo was the shogun's city while life in Kyoto took its cues from the resident emperor and his court. Kyoto was also home to wealthy merchants, artists, and craftspeople who served the needs of the courtiers and shared their interest in refined pursuits, such as the tea ceremony, and also their appreciation of art styles that recalled those perfected by aristocratic artists in the Heian period. The most famous and original Kyoto painter who worked for this group of patrons was Tawaraya Sotatsu (active c. 1600–1640). Sotatsu is considered the first great painter of the Rinpa school, the modern name given to a group of artists whose art reinterpreted ancient courtly styles. These artists are grouped together because of their shared artistic interests; they did not constitute a formal school, such as the Kano. Rinpa masters were not just painters, however: They sometimes collaborated with craftspeople.

One of Sotatsu's most famous pairs of screens probably depicts the islands of Matsushima near the northern city of Sendai (**FIG. 26-9**). On the right screen (shown here on top), mountainous islands echo the swing and sweep of the waves, with stylized gold clouds emerging from the gold ground at upper left. On the left screen (here below) the gold clouds continue until they become a sand spit from which twisted pines grow. One branch to the left seems to stretch down toward a strange island in the lower left, composed of an organic, amoebalike form in gold surrounded by mottled ink. This mottled effect was a specialty of Rinpa-school painters.

As one of the "three famous beautiful views of Japan," Matsushima was often depicted in art. Most painters chose a viewpoint above the pine-covered islands that make the area famous. Sotatsu's genius was to portray the islands in

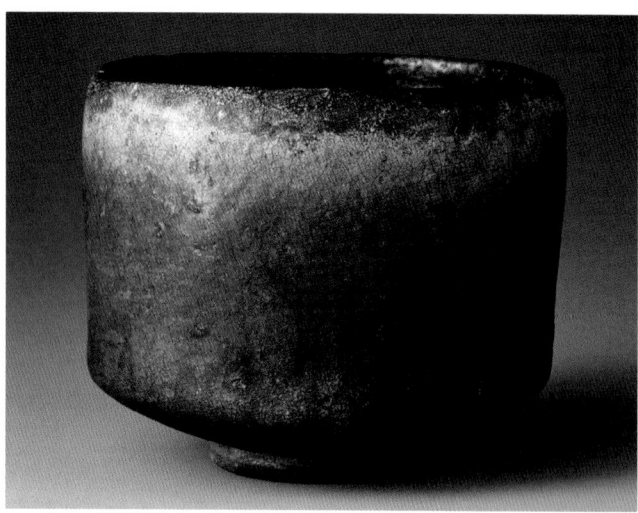

26-8 Chojiro **TEA BOWL, CALLED YUGURE ("TWILIGHT")**
Momoyama period, late 16th century. *Raku* ware, height 3½" (9 cm). Gotoh Museum, Tokyo.

Connoisseurs developed a subtle vocabulary to discuss the aesthetics of tea. A favorite term was *sabi* ("loneliness"), which refers to the tranquility found when feeling alone. Other virtues were *wabi* ("poverty"), which suggests the artlessness of humble simplicity, and *shibui* ("bitter" or "astringent"), meaning elegant restraint. Tea bowls embody these aesthetics.

Credit: Photo courtesy the Gotoh Museum, Tokyo

One of the finest surviving early **TEA BOWLS** (**FIG. 26-8**) is attributed to Chojiro (1516–1592), the founder of the Raku family of potters. Named *Yugure* ("Twilight") by tea master Sen no Sotan (1578–1658), a grandson of Rikyu, this bowl is an excellent example of red **raku** ware—a hand-built, low-fired ceramic of gritty red clay, developed especially for use in the tea ceremony. The glaze-shaded red hue and lively surface texture evoke a gentle landscape, illuminated by the setting sun. With its small foot, straight sides, irregular shape, and crackled texture, this bowl exemplifies tea taste at the beginning of its development.

Edo Period

What diverse forms, subjects, and media characterize art from the Edo period?

When Tokugawa Ieyasu gained control of Japan, he forced the emperor to proclaim him shogun, a title neither Nobunaga nor Hideyoshi had held. His reign initiated the Edo period (1615–1868), named after the city that he founded (present-day Tokyo) as his capital. This period is alternatively known as the Tokugawa era. Under the rule of the Tokugawa family, peace and prosperity came at the price of a rigid and repressive bureaucracy. The problem of a potentially rebellious *daimyo* was solved by ordering all feudal lords to spend either half of each year, or every other year, in Edo, where their families were required to live. Zen Buddhism was supplanted as the prevailing

26-9 Tawaraya Sotatsu **WAVES AT MATSUSHIMA**

Edo period, 17th century. Pair of six-panel folding screens with ink, mineral colors, and gold leaf on paper; each screen 4'9⅞" × 11'8½" (1.52 × 3.56 m). Freer Gallery of Art, Smithsonian Institution, Washington, DC. Gift of Charles Lang Freer (F1906.231 & 232).

The six-panel screen format was a triumph of scale and practicality. Each panel consisted of a light wood frame surrounding a latticework interior covered with several layers of paper. Over this foundation was pasted a high-quality paper, silk, or gold-leaf ground, ready to be painted by the finest artists. Held together with ingenious paper hinges, a screen could be folded for storage or transportation, resulting in a mural-size painting, light enough to be carried by a single person and ready to be displayed as needed.

an abbreviated manner and from a fresh vantage point, as though the viewer were passing them in a boat on the roiling waters. The artist's asymmetrical composition and his use of thick mineral colors in combination with soft, playful brushwork and sparkling gold leaf create the boldly decorative effect that is the hallmark of the Rinpa tradition.

LACQUER BOX Rinpa-school painters also participated in the collaborative production of luxury objects. The painter Ogata Korin (1658–1716) designed the **LACQUER BOX** shown here (**FIG. 26-10**) and oversaw its execution, although he left the actual work to highly trained craftspeople. He also frequently collaborated with his brother Kenzan, a celebrated potter.

The upper tray of the box housed writing implements, and the larger bottom section stored paper (see "Inside a Writing Box" on page 840). Korin's design sets a motif of irises and a plank bridge in a dramatic asymmetrical

26-10 Ogata Korin **EXTERIOR (A) AND VIEWS OF INTERIOR AND LID (B) OF A LACQUER BOX FOR WRITING IMPLEMENTS**

Edo period, late 17th–early 18th century. Lacquer, lead, silver, and mother-of-pearl, 5⅝ × 10¾ × 7¾" (14.2 × 27.4 × 19.7 cm). Tokyo National Museum, Tokyo. National Treasure.

composition created from mother-of-pearl, silver, lead, and gold lacquer. The subject was one he frequently represented in painting because it was immensely popular with the educated Japanese of his day, who would have recognized the imagery as an allusion to a famous passage from the tenth-century Japanese literary classic *Tales of Ise*. A nobleman poet, having left his wife in the capital, pauses at a place called Eight Bridges, where a river branches into eight streams, each covered with a plank bridge. Irises are in full bloom, and his traveling companions urge the poet to write a *waka*—a 5-line, 31-syllable poem—beginning each line with a syllable from the word for "iris": *Kakitsubata* (*ka-ki-tsu-ba-ta; ba* is the voiced form of *ha*, which here begins the penultimate line). The poet responds:

> *Karagoromo*
> *kitsutsu narenishi*
> *tsuma shi areba*
> *harubaru kinuru*
> *tabi o shi zo omou.*
> When I remember
> my wife, fond and familiar
> as my courtly robe,
> I feel how far and distant
> my travels have taken me.
> (Translated by Stephen Addiss)

The poem in association with the scene became so famous that any image of a group of irises, with or without a plank bridge, immediately called the episode to mind.

Lacquer is derived in Asia from the sap of the lacquer tree, *Rhus verniciflua*, indigenous to China but also grown commercially throughout East Asia very early in history. It is gathered by tapping into a tree and letting the sap flow into a container, and it can be colored with vegetable or mineral dyes. Applied in thin coats to a surface of wood or leather, lacquer hardens into a glasslike protective coating that is waterproof, heat- and acid-resistant, and airtight. Its practical qualities made it ideal for storage containers and vessels for food and drink. The creation of a piece of lacquer can take several years. First, the item is fashioned of wood and sanded smooth. Next, up to 30 layers of lacquer are thinly applied, each dried and polished before the next is brushed on.

Japanese craftspeople exploited the decorative potential of lacquer to create expensive luxury items such as this box, which was created when lacquer arts had been perfected. It features inlays of mother-of-pearl and precious metals in a style known as *makie* ("sprinkled design"), in which flaked or powdered gold or silver was embedded in a still-damp coat of lacquer.

Naturalistic and Literati Painting

NAGASAWA ROSETSU By the middle of the eighteenth century, the taste of wealthy Kyoto merchants had shifted, influencing the styles of artists who competed for their patronage. The public was enthralled with novel imagery captured in magnifying glasses, telescopes, and an optical device that enhanced the three-dimensional effects of

---

Art and Its Contexts

INSIDE A WRITING BOX

Writing boxes hold tools basic for both writing and painting: ink stick, ink stone, brushes, and paper—all beautiful objects in their own right.

Ink sticks are basically soot from burning wood or oil that is bound into a paste with resin and pressed into small, stick-shaped or cake-shaped molds to harden.

Fresh ink is made for each writing or painting session by grinding the hard, dry ink stick in water against a fine-grained stone. A typical ink stone has a shallow well at one end sloping up to a grinding surface at the other. The artist fills the well with water from a waterpot. The ink stick, held vertically, is dipped into the well to pick up a small amount of water, then is rubbed in a circular motion firmly on the grinding surface. Grinding ink is viewed as a meditative task, time for collecting one's thoughts and concentrating on the painting or calligraphy ahead.

Brushes are made from animal hair set in simple bamboo or hollow-reed handles. Brushes taper to a fine point that responds sensitively to any shift in pressure. Although great painters and

calligraphers do eventually develop their own styles of holding and using the brush, all begin by learning the basic position for writing. The brush is held vertically, grasped firmly between the thumb and first two fingers, with the fourth and fifth fingers often resting against the handle for more subtle control.

writing implements

26–11 Nagasawa Rosetsu
BULL AND PUPPY
Edo period, late 18th century.
Left of a pair of six-panel
screens with ink and gold
wash on paper, 5'7¼" × 12'3"
(1.70 × 3.75 m). Los Angeles
County Museum of Art. Joe and
Etsuko Price Collection (L.83.45.3a).

Credit: © 2016. Digital Image
Museum Associates/LACMA/Art
Resource NY/Scala, Florence

Western-style perspective pictures. Schools of independent artists emerged in Kyoto to satisfy demands for naturalistic-style paintings that reflected this fascination. The most influential was founded by Maruyama Okyo, who had perfected methods to incorporate Western shading and perspective into a more native Japanese decorative style, creating a sense of volume new to East Asian painting, while still retaining a sense of familiarity.

Okyo's most famous pupil was Nagasawa Rosetsu (1754–1799), a painter of great natural talent who added his own boldness and humor to his master's tradition. Rosetsu delighted in surprising his viewers with odd juxtapositions and unusual compositions. One of his finest works is a pair of screens, the left one depicting a **BULL AND PUPPY** (FIG. **26-11**). The bull is so immense that his mammoth body exceeds the borders of the screen, an effect undoubtedly influenced by new optical devices. The tiny puppy, white against the dark gray of the bull, helps to emphasize the bull's huge size through its contrasting smallness. The puppy's relaxed and informal pose, looking happily straight out at the viewer, gives this powerful painting a humorous touch that increases its charm. In the hands of a master such as Rosetsu, simple and common subject matter became simultaneously delightful and monumental.

LITERATI PAINTING   Because the city of Kyoto was far from the watchful eyes of the government in Edo, and the emperor resided there with his court, it enjoyed a degree of privilege and independence not found in any other Japanese city. These conditions allowed for the creation of art in the new Rinpa and naturalistic styles. They also encouraged the emergence of new schools of philosophy based on interpretations of Chinese Confucianism that disagreed with those taught at schools sponsored by Tokugawa shoguns. These new interpretations incorporated ideas from Chinese Daoism, which promoted the cultivation of a person's uniqueness, thus encouraging artistic creativity. Kyoto's intellectuals, who admired Chinese culture, even created a new, more informal tea ceremony of their own,

featuring steeped tea called *sencha* because this was the tea drunk by Ming-dynasty Chinese literati. They did this as a political protest—by then *chanoyu* had become encumbered by rules and was closely associated with the repressive shogunate.

Influenced by such new ideas, a Chinese manner of painting arose in the mid eighteenth century in emulation of literati painting. Artists who embraced this style—both professionals who painted for paying clients and amateurs who painted for their own enjoyment—quickly grew to number in the hundreds as its popularity spread throughout Japan, along with increased interest in drinking *sencha* and other aspects of Chinese culture. These artists learned about Chinese literati painting not only from the paintings themselves, but also from woodblock-printed painting manuals imported from China, and Chinese emigrant monks and merchants who lived in Japan.

The best and most successful of these artists took Chinese literati painting models as starting points for their own original interpretations of literati themes. One of them was Ike Taiga (1723–1776), admired as much for his magnetic personality as for his art. He was born into a poor farming family near Kyoto and showed innate talent for painting at a young age. Moving to Kyoto in his teens, he became friends with Chinese scholars there, including those who promoted drinking *sencha*. Taiga became a leader in this group, attracting admirers who were enamored of both his quasi-amateurish painting style and his quest for spiritual self-cultivation. His character and personal style are seen in the scintillating, rhythmic layering of strokes used to define the mountains in his **VIEW OF KOJIMA BAY** (FIG. **26-12**), which blends Chinese models, Japanese aesthetics, and personal brushwork. The gentle rounded forms of the mountains intentionally recall the work of famous Chinese literati painters, and Taiga utilizes a stock landscape composition that separates foreground and background mountains with a watery expanse (COMPARE FIG. **26-2**). However, he did not paint an imaginary Chinese landscape but a personal vision of an actual Japanese place that he had visited—Kojima Bay—as a document accompanying the

26-12 Ike Taiga **VIEW OF KOJIMA BAY**
Edo period, third quarter of 18th century. Hanging scroll with ink and color on silk, 39¼ × 14⅝" (99.7 × 37.6 cm). Hosomi Museum, Kyoto.

painting explains. Still, in deference to his admiration for Chinese literati, Taiga places two figures clad in Chinese robes on the right, midway up the mountain.

Ukiyo-e: Pictures of the Floating World

Edo served as the shogun's capital as well as the center of a flourishing popular culture associated with tradespeople.

Deeply Buddhist, commoners were acutely aware of the transience of life, symbolized, for example, by the cherry tree which blossoms so briefly. Putting a positive spin on this harsh realization, they sought to live by the mantra: Let's enjoy life to the fullest as long as it lasts. This they did to excess in the restaurants, theaters, bathhouses, and brothels of the city's pleasure quarters, named after the Buddhist phrase *ukiyo* ("floating world"). Every major city in Japan had these quarters, and most were licensed by the government. But those of Edo were the largest and most famous. The heroes of the floating world were not famous samurai or aristocratic poets. Instead, swashbuckling kabuki actors and beautiful courtesans were admired. These paragons of pleasure soon became immortalized in paintings and—because paintings were too expensive for common people—in woodblock prints known as **ukiyo-e** ("pictures of the floating world;" see "Japanese Woodblock Prints" opposite). Most prints were inexpensively produced by the hundreds and not considered serious fine art. Yet when first imported to Europe and America, they were immediately acclaimed and strongly influenced late nineteenth- and early twentieth-century Western art (see Chapter 31).

HARUNOBU The first woodblock prints had no color, only black outlines. Soon artists were adding colors by hand, but to produce colored prints more rapidly they gradually devised a system to print them using multiple blocks. The first artist to design prints that took advantage of this new technique, known as *nishiki-e* ("brocade pictures"), was Suzuki Harunobu (1724–1770), famous for his images of courtesans (SEE FIG. 26-1).

SHARAKU Toshusai Sharaku is one of the most mysterious, if today among the most admired, masters of *ukiyo-e*. He seems to have been active less than a year in 1794–1795, during which he produced 146 prints, of which all but ten are pictures of famous actors in a popular form of theater known as kabuki. He was renowned for half-length portraits that captured the dramatic intensity of noted performers outfitted in the costumes and makeup of the characters they played on stage. Much as people today buy posters of their favorite sports, music, or movie stars, in the Edo period people clamored for images of their kabuki idols. The crossed eyes, craning neck, and stylized gestures of Sharaku's portrayal of actor **OTANI ONIJI** (**FIG. 26-13**) capture a frozen, tension-filled moment in an action-packed drama, precisely the sort of stylized intensity that was valued in kabuki performance.

HOKUSAI During the first half of the nineteenth century, pictures of famous sights of Japan grew immensely popular. The two most famous *ukiyo-e* printmakers,

Technique

JAPANESE WOODBLOCK PRINTS

The production of woodblock prints combined the expertise of three individual specialists: the artist, the carver, and the printer. Coordinating and funding this collaborative endeavor was a publisher, who commissioned the project and distributed the prints to stores or traveling vendors, who would sell them.

The artist designed and supplied the master drawing for the print, executing its outlines with brush and ink on tissue paper. Colors might be indicated, but more often they were understood or determined later. The drawing was passed on to the carver, who pasted it face down on a hardwood block—preferably cherrywood—so that the outlines were visible through the tissue paper in reverse. A light coating of oil might be brushed on to make the paper more transparent, allowing the drawing to stand out even more clearly. The carver then cut around the lines of the drawing with a sharp knife, always working in the same direction as the original brushstrokes. The rest of the block was then chiseled away, leaving only the outlines in relief. This block, which reproduced the master drawing, was called the **key block**. If the print was to be polychrome, involving multiple colors, prints made from the key block were in turn pasted face down as carving guides on blocks that would become the color blocks. Each color generally required a separate block, although both sides of a block might be used for economy.

Once the blocks were completed, the printer took over. Paper for printing was covered lightly with animal glue (gelatin), and before printing, the coated paper was lightly moistened so that it would take ink and color well. Water-based ink or color was brushed over the blocks, and the paper was placed on top and rubbed with a smooth, padded device called a *baren* until the design was completely transferred. The key block was printed first, then the colors, one by one. Each block was carved with two small marks called **registration marks**, in exactly the same place in the margins, outside of the image area—an L in one corner, and a straight line in another. By aligning the paper with these marks before letting it fall over the block, the printer ensured that the colors would be placed correctly within the outlines. One of the most characteristic effects of later Japanese prints is a grading of color from dark to pale. This was achieved

by wiping some of the color from the block before printing or by moistening the block and then applying the color gradually with an unevenly loaded brush—a brush loaded on one side with full-strength color and on the other with diluted color.

26-13 Toshusai Sharaku **OTANI ONIJI IN THE ROLE OF YAKKO EDOBE**

Edo period, 1794. Polychrome woodblock print with ink, colors, and white mica on paper, 15 × 9⅞″ (38.1 × 25.1 cm). Metropolitan Museum of Art, New York. Henry L. Phillips Collection, Bequest of Henry L. Phillips, 1939 (JP2822).

Credit: © 2016. Image copyright The Metropolitan Museum of Art/Art Resource/Scala, Florence

Utagawa Hiroshige (1797–1858) and Katsushika Hokusai (1760–1849) (see Chapter 31), specialized in this genre. Hiroshige's *Fifty-Three Stations of the Tokaido* and Hokusai's *Thirty-Six Views of Mount Fuji* became the most successful sets of graphic art the world has known. The woodblocks were printed, and printed again, until they wore out. They were then recarved, and still more copies were printed. This process continued for decades, and thousands of prints from the two series still survive.

THE GREAT WAVE (**FIG. 26-14**) is the most famous of the scenes from *Thirty-Six Views of Mount Fuji*. The great wave rears up like a dragon with claws of foam,

ready to crash down on the figures huddled in the boats below. Exactly at the point of imminent disaster, but far in the distance, rises Japan's most sacred peak, Mount Fuji, whose slopes swing up like waves and whose snowy crown is like foam—comparisons the artist makes clear in the wave nearest us. In the late nineteenth century when Japonisme, a style of French and American nineteenth-century art that was highly influenced by Japanese art, became the vogue in the West, Hokusai's art was greatly appreciated, even more so than it had been in Japan: The first book on the artist was published in France.

26–14 Katsushika Hokusai **THE GREAT WAVE**

From *Thirty-Six Views of Mount Fuji*. Edo period, c. 1831. Polychrome woodblock print on paper, 9⅞ × 14⅝″ (25 × 37.1 cm). Honolulu Academy of Art. Gift of James A. Michener 1995 (HAA 13, 695).

Credit: Image courtesy Yale University Art Gallery

Zen Painting: Buddhist Art for Rural Commoners

Outside Japan's urban centers, art for commoners also flourished, much of it tied to their devotion to Buddhism. Deprived of the support of the samurai officials who now favored Confucianism, Buddhism nevertheless thrived during the Edo period through patronage from private individuals, many of them rural peasants. In the early eighteenth century, one of the great monks who preached in the countryside was the Zen master Hakuin Ekaku (1685–1769), born in a small village near Mount Fuji. After hearing a fire-and-brimstone sermon in his youth he resolved to become a monk, and for years he traveled around Japan seeking out the strictest Zen teachers. He became the most important Zen master in 500 years and composed many *koan* (questions posed to novices by Zen masters to guide their progression toward enlightenment during meditation), including the famous "What is the sound of one hand clapping?" In his later years he taught himself painting and calligraphy and freely gave away his scrolls to admirers—who included not only farmers but also artisans, merchants, and even samurai—as a way of spreading his religious message.

Hakuin's art differed from that of Muromachi period monk-painters like Bunsei and Sesshu (SEE FIGS. 26–2, 26–3). It featured everyday Japanese subjects or Zen themes that conveyed his ideas in ways his humble followers could easily understand. He often painted Daruma (Bodhidharma in Sanskrit) (FIG. 26–15), the semilegendary Indian monk who founded Zen. Hundreds of Zen monks of the Edo period and later created simply brushed Zen ink paintings, largely within the standards that Hakuin had set.

Cloth and Ceramics

The ingenuity and technical proficiency that contributed to the development of *ukiyo-e* came about because of Japan's long and distinguished history of what the Western tradition considers fine crafts. Japanese artists had excelled in the design and production of textiles, ceramics, lacquer, woodwork, and metalwork for centuries, and in premodern Japan, unlike the West, no separate words distinguished fine arts (painting and sculpture) from "crafts." (The Japanese word for fine art and corresponding modern Japanese language words for various types of craft were not coined until 1872.) This was largely because professional Japanese artistic studios basically followed the same hereditary, hierarchical structure, regardless of medium. A master artist directed all activity in a workshop of trainees, who gradually gained seniority through innate talent and years of apprenticeship. Sometimes, such as when a pupil was not chosen to succeed the master, he would leave to establish his own studio. Teamwork under masterful supervision was the approach to artistic production.

KOSODE In the West, the robe most often known as a kimono has become as emblematic of Japanese culture as the "tea ceremony." These loose, unstructured garments, wrapping around the body and cinched with a sash, were the principal outer article of clothing for both men and women by the end of the fifteenth century. Robes with short sleeves were known as *kosode* ("small sleeves"). Because they wore out from being worn, few *kosode* prior to the Edo period have survived, but the early examples that remain reveal the opulent tastes of affluent women at this time (see "Closer Look" on page 846). In this early

26–15 Hakuin Ekaku **GIANT DARUMA**

Edo period, mid 18th century. Hanging scroll with ink on paper, 4'3½" × 1'9¾" (130.8 × 55.2 cm). Los Angeles County Museum of Art. Gift of Murray Smith (M.91.220)

As a self-taught amateur painter, Hakuin's painting style is the very antithesis of that of professionals, such as painters of the Kano or Rinpa schools. The appeal of his art lies in its artless charm, humor, and astonishing force. Here Hakuin has portrayed the wide-eyed Daruma during his nine years of meditation in front of a temple wall in China. Intensity, concentration, and spiritual depth are conveyed by a minimal number of broad, forceful brushstrokes. The inscription is the ultimate Zen message, attributed to Daruma himself: "Pointing directly to the human heart, see your own nature and become Buddha."

eighteenth-century *kosode*, the curving branches of a citrus tree (the *tachibana*, native to Japan) emerge above a bamboo fence along the bottom of the robe to grow up its height and across its sleeves, creating an asymmetrical composition with an area of undecorated fabric concentrated at the center toward the left. The textile artists employed many techniques to create the rich interplay of textures and pictures. The extensive use of stencil dyeing and embroidery associate this *kosode* with the tastes of wives of warriors during the early eighteenth century. The individual design elements and the principles of composition resemble those found in paintings and on ceramics during the Edo period, when the pattern books created for garment-makers disseminated motifs among artists working in a variety of media.

JAPANESE PORCELAIN   While the history of ceramic production dates to the earliest days of Japanese civilization, production of glazed, high-fired stoneware ceramics proliferated in Japan only from the sixteenth century. The industry thrived in southern Japan, where, in the years following 1600, influxes of more highly skilled Korean potters helped native artisans learn new continental technologies that allowed them to manufacture porcelain for the first time. One town, Arita, became the center for the production of porcelain, created not only for domestic use but for export to the West. While tea ceremony aesthetics still favored rustic wares

such as Chojiro's tea bowl (SEE FIG. 26–8), porcelain was widely adopted for everyday use in response to a growing fashion for Chinese arts. Porcelains made in Arita are known by various names according to their dating and decorative schemes. The plate in **FIGURE 26–17** is an example of Nabeshima ware, produced in kilns that had been established in Arita by the Nabeshima samurai clan as early as 1628. Initially, ceramics from these kilns were reserved for family use or as gifts to the Tokugawa shogunate, but eventually Nabeshima ware was also acquired by other powerful noble families. The multicolor decorative motifs often combine an organically irregular natural form (here a branch of flowering wisteria) and a more abstracted, stabilizing design drawn from the built environment (here a trellis on which the wisteria can grow). Contemporary textile designs—well known through the publication of pattern books that documented the latest fashion—frequently served as source material for the decoration of Nabeshima ware.

The Modern Period

How is Japanese art transformed during the period between the forced opening of the country to the West and the aftermath of World War II?

The tensions that resulted from Commodore Matthew Perry's forced opening of trade ports in Japan in 1853 precipitated the downfall of the Tokugawa shogunate. In 1868, the emperor was formally restored to power, an event known as the Meiji Restoration. The court soon moved from Kyoto to Edo, which was renamed Tokyo ("Eastern Capital"). After two decades of intense industrialization, influential private individuals and government officials, sometimes working cooperatively, created new arts institutions including juried exhibitions, artists' associations, arts universities, and cultural heritage laws. These rekindled appreciation for the art of the past, encouraged perpetuation of artistic techniques threatened by adoption of Western ways, and stimulated new artistic production. Many of these arts institutions still exist today.

A Closer Look

WOMAN'S *KOSODE*

Embroidery with vermilion threads gives a vibrant tonality to this citrus fruit and other motifs throughout the design.

The white silk damask fabric of this robe is woven with a key-fret pattern, most visible with reflected light as the wearer moves.

Some of the leaves and citrus fruits are embroidered with radiant gold threads. Some of these threads have become loose, revealing the written inscriptions that told the embroiderer which kind of thread to use.

The decoration flows up the back of the robe in the form of an inverted *C*, leaving an area of unornamented silk at middle left. This design demonstrates an early 18th-century taste for asymmetry.

There is extensive use of the *kata-kanoko* technique, in which stencils were used to create dotted patterns with the application of resist paste and dipping and/or painting with dye. This imitated the elaborate tie-dying that had been popular in earlier robes but was now too time-consuming to meet a growing demand for garments.

26–16 WOMAN'S *KOSODE* WITH DESIGN OF BAMBOO FENCE AND CITRUS TREE (TACHIBANA)
Edo period, early 18th century. White figured satin (*rinzu*), with embroidery (gold and silk thread) and stencil dyeing. Length 62½" (158.8 cm). Philadelphia Museum of Art. Gift of Mr. and Mrs. Rodolphe Meyer de Schauensee, 1951.

Credit: © 2016. Photo The Philadelphia Museum of Art/Art Resource/Scala, Florence

Meiji-Period Nationalist Painting

The Meiji period (1868–1912) marked a major change for Japan. Japanese society adopted various aspects of Western education, governmental systems, clothing, medicine, industrialization, and technology in efforts to modernize the nation. Teachers of sculpture and oil painting came from Italy, while adventurous Japanese artists traveled to Europe and America to study.

A MEIJI PAINTER Ernest Fenollosa (1853–1908), an American who had recently graduated from Harvard, traveled to Japan in 1878 to teach philosophy and political economy at Tokyo University. Within a few years, he and a former student, Okakura Kakuzo (1862–1913), began urging artists to study traditional Japanese arts rather than focusing exclusively on Western art styles and media, but to infuse these traditional practices with a modern sensibility. Yokoyama Taikan (1868–1958) subsequently developed his personal style within the Nihonga (modern Japanese painting) genre promoted by Okakura. Encouraged by Okakura, who had gone there before him, Taikan visited India in 1903. He embraced Okakura's ideals of pan-Asian cultural nationalism, expressed in the first line of Okakura's book *Ideals of the East* (1903) with the words "Asia is one."

26–17 PLATE WITH WISTERIA AND TRELLIS PATTERN
Edo period, 18th century. Nabeshima ware. Porcelain with underglaze blue decoration and overglaze enamels, diameter 12³⁄₁₆″ (31 cm). Kyushu National Museum, Japan. Important Cultural Property.

Credit: Photographer: FUJIMORI Takeshi

This outlook later contributed to fueling Japan's imperialist ambitions. Taikan's **FLOATING LIGHTS** (**FIG. 26–18**) was inspired by a visit to Calcutta (Kolkata), where he observed women engaged in divination on the banks of the Ganges. The naturalism of their semitransparent robes and the gently rippling water reveal his indebtedness to Western art. In contrast, the lightly applied colors and gracefully composed branches with delicate, mottled brushwork defining the leaves recall techniques of Rinpa-school artists.

Japan after World War II

In the aftermath of World War II (1941–1945), Japan was a shambles, her great cities ruined. Nevertheless, under the U.S.-led Allied Occupation (1946–1952), the Japanese people immediately began rebuilding, unified by a sense of national purpose. Within ten years, Japan established nascent automobile, electronics, and consumer goods industries. Rail travel, begun in 1872, expanded and improved significantly after the war, and by the time of the Tokyo Olympics in 1964, the capital had an extensive commuter rail system. Japan became the world leader in city-to-city high-speed rail transit with its new Shinkansen (bullet train). As the rest of the world came to know Japan, foreign interest in its arts focused especially on the country's still thriving "crafts" traditions. Not only were these a source of national pride and identity, the skills and attitudes they fostered also served as the basis for Japan's national revival.

TANGE KENZO The **HIROSHIMA PEACE MEMORIAL MUSEUM** and Park (**FIG. 25–19**) was one of the first

monuments constructed after World War II. A memorial to those who perished on August 6, 1945, and an expression of prayers for world peace, it attests the spirit of the Japanese people at this difficult juncture in history. Tange Kenzo (1913–2005), who would eventually become one of the masters of Modernist architecture, designed the complex after winning an open competition as a young, up-and-coming architect.

The building's design befits the solemnity of its context. Concrete piers raise its compact concrete form 20 feet off the ground. The wood formwork of the concrete recalls

26–18 Yokoyama Taikan **FLOATING LIGHTS**
Meiji period, 1909. Hanging scroll with ink, colors, and gold on silk, 56½ × 20½″ (143 × 52 cm). Museum of Modern Art, Ibaraki.

Credit: Photographer: Kodaira Tadao

26–19 Tange Kenzo **HIROSHIMA PEACE MEMORIAL MUSEUM**
Showa period, 1955. Main building (center) repaired in Heisei period, 1991. East building (right), the former Peace Memorial Hall, which first opened in 1955, was rebuilt in June 1994 and attached to the main building. Designated UNESCO World Heritage Site in 1996.

Credit: Courtesy Tange Kenzo and Hiroshima Peace Memorial Museum

the wooden forms of traditional Japanese architecture, but the use of concrete as a building material was inspired by Le Corbusier's 1920s Modernist villas (see Chapter 32). Evenly spaced vertical concrete fins lining the façade provide light shade. They suggest both the regular spacing of elements present in modular *shoin* architecture (see "Shoin Design" on page 835) and the values of Modernist architects, who demanded a strict correlation between structure and form. In this commission Tange infused Modernist tendencies and materials with a Japanese sense of interval and refinement, characteristics still seen in the work of younger contemporary Japanese architects.

FUKAMI SUEHARU Perhaps because the arts of tea ceremony and flower arrangement both require ceramic vessels, the Japanese have long had a particular affection for pottery. While some ceramicists continue to create *raku* tea bowls and other traditional wares, others experiment with new styles and techniques.

Fukami Sueharu (b. 1947) is among the most innovative clay artists in Japan today. Yet his art has roots in the past—in his case, in Chinese porcelains with pale bluish-green glazes (*seihakuji*). Even so, his forms and fabrication methods, as in his **SKY II**, are ultramodern (**FIG. 26–20**). He created the piece using a slip casting technique in which he injected liquid clay into a mold using a high-pressure compressor. Although Fukami sometimes makes functional pieces, mainly cylinders that could hold flower arrangements, he shows his mastery of pure form in *Sky II*. The title suggests sources of this abstract sculptural shape: a wing or a blade of an aircraft slicing through the sky. The pale sky-blue glaze only enhances this reference. The fusion of traditions, media, techniques, and forms looks back to a distinguished artistic heritage, but the suave mastery of abstraction and subtle evocation of thematic meaning point forward to a global art world, where Japanese artists are clearly taking their place.

CRAFTSPEOPLE AS LIVING NATIONAL TREA-SURES Throughout the history of Japanese art, there has been a salient sensitivity toward the surface quality of things, for polish, for line, for exquisite facture and stylish articulation. This is certainly the case with an exquisite wooden box (**FIG. 26–21**) by Eri Sayoko (1945–2007). In 2002, the government designated her a Living National Treasure for her accomplishment in the art of cut-gold leaf (*kirikane*), traditionally used to decorate Buddhist sculpture and paintings. The National Treasure designation originated in Japanese laws of 1897 that were intended to safeguard the nation's artistic heritage at a time when art was

26–20 Fukami Sueharu **SKY II**
Heisei period, c. 1990. Celadon-glazed porcelain with wood base, 3 × 44⅛ × 9½" (7.7 × 112.1 × 24.2 cm). Spencer Museum of Art, University of Kansas, Lawrence. Museum purchase: R. Charles and Mary Margaret Clevenger Fund (1992.0072).

Credit: © Fukami Sueharu. Courtesy Erik Thomsen Gallery, New York being bought by Western collectors but suffering neglect at home. In 1955, the government added provisions to honor living individuals who excel in traditional craft techniques with the title Living National Treasure. This historic preservation system is the most complex of its type in the world.

In its encouragement of traditional arts, the Living National Treasure system has greatly assisted women in gaining much-deserved recognition. In pre-modern Japan (up to the start of the Meiji period in 1868), women mostly operated in the private sphere of the home where they created crafts for their own enjoyment or for devotional purposes. By the eighteenth century, this situation had begun to change, so that women could be poets, calligraphers, and painters; the wives or daughters of famous male artists gained the most recognition. Among the most famous was Gyokuran, wife of the literati painter Ike Taiga (SEE FIG. 26–12). However, the conservative nature of traditional Japanese craft workshops meant women could not hold leadership positions in them, and until the post–World War II period they were seldom recognized for their achievements. Eri Sayoko flourished in the new climate as one of the first women to work in the medium of cut-gold, which she took up via an unorthodox route.

Eri specialized in Japanese painting in high school and in design-dyeing in junior college. After marriage to a traditional Buddhist sculptor she started producing Buddhist paintings and began an apprenticeship with a master *kirikane* craftsman. She was so talented that after only three years she was able to exhibit her work professionally.

Her art is informed by her deep study of the history of the technique, and her special sensitivity for color betrays her training in dyeing. Eri's elegant, functional objects are infused with modern sensibilities, proving that a traditional technique can still result in artistic originality.

26–21 Eri Sayoko ORNAMENTAL BOX: DANCING IN THE COSMOS
Heisei period, 2006. Wood with polychrome and cut gold, 33⅞ × 6½ × 6½″ (86 cm × 16.5 cm × 16.5 cm). Collection of Eri Kokei.

Credit: Courtesy Koukei Eri

Think About It

1 Discuss how the Japanese tea ceremony works and observe the role that art plays within it. Include the unique aesthetics of the tearoom and the artistic practices associated with the ceremony, making reference to at least one work from this chapter.

2 Chose one woodblock print discussed in this chapter and explain how its subject matter represents the culture of the "floating world" in Edo.

3 Reflect on the differences between the styles of artists from Kyoto and artists from Edo. How do they relate to the variations in the social status and cultural and intellectual interests of residents of these two cities? How would you fit the lacquer box by a Rinpa-school artist from Kyoto (**FIG. 26–10**) and the *kosode* robe made in Edo ("Closer Look" on page 846) into your discussion?

4 Chose one of the three Japanese works in this chapter from the period after World War II and evaluate how it draws from both traditional Japanese and foreign artistic practices. Is the larger debt to tradition or to innovation?

Crosscurrents

Garden design weaves its way throughout the history of art. These two examples were produced for two very different architectural complexes to serve very different populations. Assess how the gardens were used and discuss how their form is related to their function. How are they representative of their cultural contexts?

PAGE 772

FIG. 26–4

27-1 Julia Jumbo **TWO GREY HILLS TAPESTRY WEAVING**
Navajo, 2003. Handspun wool, 36 × 24½″ (91.2 × 62.1 cm).

Credit: Photo: Addison Doty

Chapter 27
Art of the Americas after 1300

Learning Objectives

27.a Identify the visual hallmarks of post-1300 art of the Americas in its distinct cultures for formal, technical, and expressive qualities.

27.b Interpret the meaning of post-1300 works of art of the Americas in its distinct cultures based on their themes, subjects, and symbols.

27.c Relate the art of the Americas after 1300 to its distinct cultural, economic, and political contexts.

27.d Apply the vocabulary and concepts relevant to the art of the Americas after 1300.

27.e Interpret a work of art of the Americas after 1300 using the art historical methods of observation, comparison, and inductive reasoning.

27.f Select visual and textual evidence in various media to support an argument or an interpretation of a work of art of the Americas after 1300.

According to Navajo mythology, the universe itself is a weaving, its fibers spun by Spider Woman out of sacred cosmic materials. Spider Woman taught the art of weaving to Changing Woman (an aspect of Mother Earth), and she in turn taught it to Navajo women, who continue to keep this art vital, seeing its continuation as a sacred responsibility. Early Navajo blankets were composed of simple horizontal stripes, but over time weavers have introduced more intricate patterns, and today Navajo rugs are woven in numerous distinctive styles.

The tapestry weaving in **FIGURE 27-1** is designed in the Two Grey Hills style that developed during the early twentieth century around a trading post of that name in northwest New Mexico. Weavers who work in this style use the natural colors of undyed sheep's wool (only the black wool is sometimes dyed) to create dazzling geometric patterns. Julia Jumbo (1928–2007), who learned to weave as a child, used her weavings to support her family. She raised her own sheep and carded and spun her wool by hand before incorporating it into painstakingly made textiles. Jumbo is renowned for the clarity of her designs and the technical perfection of her fine weave.

When the first Europeans arrived, the Western Hemisphere had been inhabited for 10,000 years by peoples with long histories and rich cultural traditions (**MAP 27-1**).

After 1492, when Christopher Columbus and his companions first sailed to the Western Hemisphere, the arrival of Europeans completely altered the destiny of the Americas. In Mesoamerica and South America the break with the past was sudden and violent: Two great empires—the Aztec in Mexico and the Inca in South America—that had risen to prominence in the fifteenth century were rapidly destroyed. In North America the change took place more gradually, but the outcome was much the same. In both North and South America, indigenous peoples contracted European diseases to which they had no immunity, especially smallpox, leading to massive population loss and social disruption. Over the next 400 years, many Native Americans were displaced from their ancestral homelands, and many present-day Native American ethnic groupings were formed by combinations of various survivor groups.

Despite all the disruption, during the past century the indigenous arts of the Americas have undergone a re-evaluation and revitalization. Native American artists like Julia Jumbo continue to revive and reimagine indigenous traditions, revisit traditional outlooks, and restate their ancient customs and ideas in new ways, while at the same time contemporary painters like Jaune Quick-to-See Smith (SEE FIG. 27-25) engage with European traditions to challenge European assessments.

The Aztec Empire

What characterizes the art and architecture produced during the Aztec Empire in Mesoamerica?

In November 1519, the army of the Spanish soldier Hernán Cortés saw for the first time the great Aztec capital of Tenochtitlan. The shimmering city, which seemed to be floating on the water, was built on an island in the middle of Lake Texcoco in the Valley of Mexico and linked by broad causeways to the mainland. One of Cortés's companions later recalled the wonder the Spanish felt at that moment: "When we saw so many cities and villages built on the water and other great towns on dry land and that straight and level causeway going towards [Tenochtitlan], we were amazed … on account of the great towers and temples and buildings rising from the water, and all built of masonry. And some of our soldiers even asked whether the things that we saw were not a dream." (Bernal Díaz del Castillo, cited in Coe and Koontz, p. 190.)

The Mexica people who lived in the remarkable city that Cortés found were then rulers of much of the land that later took their name, Mexico. Their rise to power had been recent and swift. Only 400 years earlier, according to their own legends, they had been a nomadic people living far north of the Valley of Mexico in a distant place called Aztlan. The term Aztec derives from the word Aztlan and refers to all those living in Central Mexico who came from this mythical homeland, not just to the Mexica of Tenochtitlan.

The Mexica arrived in the Valley of Mexico in the thirteenth century and settled—according to their mythologized account—on an island in Lake Texcoco where they had seen an eagle perching on a prickly pear cactus (*nochtli*) growing out of a stone (*tetl*), a sign that their god Huitzilopochtli told them would mark the end of their wandering. They called the place Tenochtitlan. The city on the island was gradually expanded by reclaiming land from the lake and serviced by a grid of artificial canals.

MAP 27-1 THE AMERICAS AFTER 1300

Diverse cultures inhabited the Americas, each shaping a distinct artistic tradition.

A Closer Look

CALENDAR STONE

According to Mexica belief, the gods created the world four times before the present era. These cartouches name the days on which the four previous suns were destroyed: 4 Jaguar, 4 Wind, 4 Rain, and 4 Water.

Together, these four calendrical glyphs and the face and claws of the central god combine to form the glyph for 4 Motion, the day on which the fifth Sun will be destroyed by a giant earthquake.

This central face combines elements of the sun god as the night sun in the underworld, with the clawed hands and flint tongue of earth gods, symbolizing the night sun and the hungry earth.

This band forms the Aztec symbol for the sun, a round disk with triangular projections denoting the sun's rays.

Two fire serpents encircle the outer part of the disk. Stylized flames rise off their backs. Their heads meet at the bottom, and human faces emerge from the mouths of the serpents.

This band contains the 20 day signs of the 260-day ritual calendar.

27-2 CALENDAR STONE

Mexico. Aztec, c. 1500. Diameter 11′6¾″ (3.6 m). Museo Nacional de Antropología, Mexico City.

Credit: © Jejim/Shutterstock

In the fifteenth century, the Mexica joined allies in a triple alliance and began an aggressive campaign of expansion. The tribute they exacted from all over the Aztec Empire transformed Tenochtitlan into a glittering capital.

Aztec religion was based on a complex pantheon that combined Aztec deities with more ancient ones that had long been worshiped in Central Mexico. According to Aztec belief, the gods had created the current era, or sun, at the ancient city of Teotihuacan in the Valley of Mexico. The continued existence of the world depended on human actions, including rituals of bloodletting and human sacrifice, because blood was the life force that was owed the gods to help keep the cosmos going and time running. Many Mesoamerican peoples believed that the world had been created multiple times before the present era. But while most Mesoamericans believed that they were living in the fourth era, or Sun, the Mexica asserted that they lived in the fifth Sun, a new era that coincided with

the Aztec Empire. The Calendar Stone (see "Closer Look" above) boldly makes this claim, using the dates of the destructions of the four previous eras to form the glyph that names the fifth sun, 4 Motion.

Tenochtitlan

The first Spanish viceroy of New Spain from 1535 to 1550, Antonio Mendoza, is believed to have commissioned a book with drawings by indigenous artists for presentation to Holy Roman Emperor Charles V (who was also king of Spain) so that the emperor could learn about his new subjects. The frontispiece of the Codex Mendoza shows a schematized version of Tenochtitlan and its founding, Mexica war victories, and the Spanish invasions (**FIG. 27–3**). An eagle perched on a prickly pear cactus growing out of a stone—the symbol of the city—fills the center of the page. Waterways divide the city into four quarters and indicate

27-3 THE FOUNDING OF TENOCHTITLAN
Page from Codex Mendoza. Mexico. Aztec, 1545. Ink and color on paper, 12⅜ × 8⁷⁄₁₆″ (31.5 × 21.5 cm). Bodleian Library, University of Oxford, England. MS. Arch Selden. A.1, fol. 2r.

Credit: The Bodleian Libraries, The University of Oxford

the lake surrounding the city. Early leaders of Tenochtitlan are shown sitting in the four quadrants. The victorious warriors at the bottom of the page represent Aztec conquests, and a count of years surrounds the entire scene. This image combines historical narration with idealized cartography, showing the city in the middle of the lake at the moment of its founding.

At the center of Tenochtitlan was the sacred precinct, a walled enclosure that contained dozens of temples and other buildings. This area has been the site of intensive archaeological excavations in Mexico City since 1978, work that has greatly increased our understanding of this aspect of the Aztec city. The focal point of the sacred precinct was the Great Pyramid (or Templo Mayor), with paired temples on top: The one on the north was dedicated to Tlaloc, an ancient rain god with a history extending back to Teotihuacan, and the one on the south to Huitzilopochtli, the solar god of the newly arrived Mexica tribe (**FIG. 27-4**). During the winter rainy season the sun rose behind the temple of Tlaloc, and

during the dry season it rose behind the temple of Huitzilopochtli. The double temple thus united two natural forces, sun and rain, or fire and water. During the spring and autumn equinoxes, the sun rose between the two temples.

Two steep staircases led up the west face of the pyramid from the plaza in front. Sacrificial victims climbed these stairs to the temple of Huitzilopochtli, where priests threw them over a stone, quickly cut open their chests, and pulled out their still-throbbing hearts, a sacrifice that ensured the survival of the sun, the gods, and the Aztecs. The bodies were then rolled down the stairs and dismembered. Thousands of severed heads were said to have been kept on a skull rack in the plaza, represented in FIGURE 27-3 by the rack with a single skull to the right of the eagle. In addition to major works of Aztec sculpture, current excavations have uncovered a series of deep shafts containing multiple levels of offerings—precious objects as well as animals—and some believe that eventually human burials will be discovered, perhaps those of Aztec kings.

27-4 RECONSTRUCTION OF THE GREAT PYRAMID (TEMPLO MAYOR) OF TENOCHTITLAN, c. 1500

Credit: Hernan Canellas/National Geographic Creative

Sculpture

Aztec sculpture was monumental, powerful, and often unsettling. A particularly striking example is an imposing statue of **COATLICUE**, mother of the Mexica god Huitzilopochtli (**FIG. 27-5**). Coatlicue means "she of the serpent skirt," and this broad-shouldered figure with clawed feet has a skirt of twisted snakes. The sculpture may allude to the moment of Huitzilopochtli's birth: When Coatlicue conceived Huitzilopochtli from a ball of down, her other children—the stars and the moon—jealously conspired to kill her. As they attacked, Huitzilopochtli emerged from his mother's body fully grown and armed, drove off his half-brothers, and destroyed his half-sister, the moon goddess Coyolxauhqui. Coatlicue, however, did not survive the encounter. In this sculpture, she has been decapitated and a pair of serpents, symbols of gushing blood, rise from her neck to form her head. Their eyes are her eyes; their fangs, her teeth. Around her stump of a neck hangs a necklace of human hands, hearts, and a dangling skull. Despite the surface intricacy, the statue's massive form creates an impression of solidity, and the entire sculpture leans forward, looming over the viewer. The colors with which it was originally painted—red, white, ocher, black, and blue—would have heightened its dramatic impact.

27-5 THE GODDESS COATLICUE
Mexico. Aztec, c. 1500. Basalt, height 8′6″ (2.65 m).
Museo Nacional de Antropología, Mexico City.

Credit: Werner Forman Archive

Featherwork and Manuscripts

Other Aztec art was colorful as well. An idea of its splendor is captured in the **FEATHER HEADDRESS** (FIG. 27–6) said to have been given by the Aztec emperor Moctezuma to Cortés, and thought to be the one listed in the inventory of treasures Cortés shipped to Charles V, the Habsburg emperor in Spain, in 1519. Featherwork was one of the glories of Mesoamerican art, but very few of these extremely fragile artworks survive. The tropical feathers in this headdress exemplify the exotic tribute paid to the Aztecs; the long, iridescent green feathers that make up most of the headdress are the exceedingly rare tail feathers of the quetzal bird—each male quetzal has only two such plumes. The feathers were gathered in small bunches, reinforced with reed tubes, and then sewn to the frame in overlapping layers, the joins concealed by small gold plaques. Featherworkers were esteemed artists. After the Spanish invasion, they turned their exacting skills to "feather paintings" of Christian subjects.

MANUSCRIPTS   Aztec scribes also created brilliantly colored books: histories, maps, and divinatory almanacs. Instead of being bound on one side like European books, Mesoamerican books were accordion-pleated so that each page was connected only to the two adjacent pages. This format allowed great flexibility: A book could be opened to show two pages, or unfolded to show six or eight pages simultaneously; different sections of the book could also be opened next to one another at the same time. A rare manuscript that survived the Spanish conquest provides a concise summary of Mesoamerican cosmology (FIG. 27–7). Mesoamerican peoples recognized five key directions: north, south, east, west, and center. At the center of the image is Xiuhtecuhtli, god of fire, time, and the calendar. Radiating from him are the four cardinal directions—each associated with a specific color, a deity, and a tree with a bird in its branches. The 260 dots that trace the eight-lobed path around the central figure refer to the 260-day Mesoamerican divinatory calendar; the 20 day signs of this calendar are also distributed throughout the image. By linking the 260-day calendar to the four directions, this image speaks eloquently of the unity of space and time in the Mesoamerican worldview.

The Inca Empire

What characterizes the architecture, textiles, and metalwork produced during the Inca Empire in the Andes region of South America?

At the beginning of the sixteenth century the Inca Empire was one of the largest states in the world. It extended more than 2,600 miles along western South America, encompassing most of present-day Peru, Ecuador, Bolivia, and northern Chile and reaching into Argentina. Like the Aztec Empire, its rise was rapid and its destruction abrupt.

The Incas called their empire the "Land of the Four Quarters." At its center was their capital, Cusco, "the navel of the world," located high in the Andes Mountains. The Inca state began as one of many small competing

27–6 FEATHER HEADDRESS OF MOCTEZUMA
Mexico. Aztec, before 1519. Quetzal, blue cotinga, and other feathers and gold on a fiber frame; 45⅝ × 68⅞" (116 × 175 cm). Weltmuseum, Vienna.

This extraordinary and fragile work from the late Aztec Empire has been in Europe since the sixteenth century, presumably sent or taken back across the Atlantic by someone connected with the invading Spanish army in 1519. During 2010–2012, the headdress was the subject of a thorough collaborative conservation study sponsored by the Kunsthistorisches Museum of Vienna and the Instituto Nacional de Antropología e Historia of Mexico City.

Credit: Bridgeman Images

kingdoms that emerged in the highlands. In the fifteenth century the Incas began to expand, suddenly and quickly, and had subdued most of their vast domain through conquest, alliance, and intimidation by 1500.

To hold this linguistically and ethnically diverse empire together, the Inca ("Inca" refers to both the ruler and the people) relied on religion, an efficient bureaucracy, and various forms of labor taxation, in which the payment was a set amount of time spent performing tasks for the state. In return the state provided gifts through local leaders and sponsored lavish ritual entertainments. Men might cultivate state lands, serve in the army, or work periodically on public works projects—building roads and terracing hillsides, for example—while women wove cloth as tribute. Inca writing took the form of complex knotted and color-coded cords known as *khipus*; according to the Spanish, these devices recorded and communicated tribute, census, history, poetry, and astronomy.

To move their armies and speed transport and communication within the empire, the Incas built more than 23,000 miles of roads. These varied from 50-foot-wide thoroughfares to 3-foot-wide paths. Two main north–south roads, one along the coast and the other through the highlands, were linked by east–west roads. Travelers journeyed on foot, using llamas as pack animals. Stairways helped them negotiate steep mountain slopes, and rope suspension bridges allowed river gorge crossings. All along the roads, storehouses and lodgings—more than a thousand have been found—were spaced a day's journey apart. A relay system of runners could carry messages between Cusco and the farthest reaches of the empire in about a week.

Cusco

Cusco, a capital of great splendor, was home to the Inca, ruler of the empire. Its urban plan was said to have been designed by the Inca Pachacuti (ruled 1438–1471) in the shape of a puma, its head the fortress of Sacsayhuaman, and its belly the giant plaza at the center of town. The city was divided into upper and lower parts, reflecting the dual organization of Inca society. Cusco was the symbolic as well as the political center of the Inca Empire: Everyone had to carry a burden when entering the city, and gold, silver, or textiles brought into the city could not afterward be removed from it.

Cusco was a showcase of the finest Inca masonry, some of which can still be seen in the city today (see "Inca Masonry" on page 858). Architecture was a major

27–8 INCA MASONRY, DETAIL OF A WALL AT MACHU PICCHU

Peru. Inca, 1450–1530.

Credit: © Galyna Andrushko/Shutterstock

expressive form for the Inca—the very shape of individually worked stones conveyed a sense of power, and the way they come together to make up walls without needing mortar expressed Inca social order (**FIG. 27–8**). In contrast to the massive walls, Inca buildings had gabled, thatched roofs.

Doors, windows, and niches were trapezoids, narrower at the top than the bottom.

Machu Picchu

MACHU PICCHU was originally a vibrant city and is now one of the most spectacular archaeological sites in the world (**FIG. 27–9**). At almost 8,000 feet above sea level, it straddles a ridge between two high peaks in the eastern slopes of the Andes and looks down on the Urubamba River. Stone buildings, today lacking only their thatched roofs, occupy terraces around central plazas, and narrow agricultural terraces descend into the valley. The site, near the eastern limits of the empire, was the royal estate of the Inca ruler Pachacuti. The court might have retired to this warmer, lower-altitude palace when the Cusco winter became too harsh. Important diplomatic negotiations and ceremonial feasts may also have taken place at this country retreat. It provides an excellent example of Inca architectural planning: The entire complex is designed with great sensitivity to its surroundings. Walls and plazas frame stupendous vistas of the surrounding landscape, and carefully selected stones echo the shapes of the mountains beyond.

Elements of Architecture

INCA MASONRY

Working with the simplest of tools—mainly heavy stone hammers—and using no mortar, Inca builders created stonework of great refinement and durability: roads and bridges that linked the entire empire, terraces for growing crops, and structures both simple and elaborate. Great effort was expended on stone construction. Fine Inca masonry used in elite contexts consisted of either rectangular blocks or irregular polygonal blocks (SEE FIG. 27–8). In both types, adjoining blocks were painstakingly shaped to fit tightly together without mortar. Their stone faces might be slightly beveled along their edges so that each block presented a "pillowed" shape with recessed joins, or walls might be smoothed into a continuous, flowing surface in which the individual blocks formed a seamless whole. At a few Inca sites, the stones used in construction were boulder-size: up to 27 feet tall. In Cusco, and elsewhere in the Inca Empire, Inca masonry has survived earthquakes that destroyed later structures.

At Machu Picchu (SEE FIGS. 27–8, 27–9), all buildings and terraces within its 3-square-mile extent were made of granite, the hard stone occurring at the site. Commoners' houses and some walls were constructed of irregular stones that were carefully fitted together, while fine polygonal or smoothed masonry distinguished palaces and temples.

polygonal-stone wall

smooth-surfaced wall

27-9 MACHU PICCHU
Peru. Inca, 1450–1530.

Credit: © Ocphoto/ Shutterstock

Textiles and Metalwork

The production of fine textiles was already an important art in the Andes by the third millennium BCE. Among the Incas, textiles of cotton and camelid fibers (from llama, vicuña, and alpaca) were an indication of wealth. One form of labor taxation required the manufacture of fibers and cloth, and textiles as well as agricultural products filled Inca storehouses. Cloth was deemed a fitting gift for the gods, so fine garments were draped around statues and even burned as sacrificial offerings.

The patterns and designs on garments were not simply decorative; they carried symbolic messages, including indications of a person's ethnic identity and social rank. In the elaborate **TUNIC** in **FIGURE 27-10**, some squares represent miniature tunics. For example, tunics with checkerboard patterns were worn as military uniforms.

27-10 TUNIC
Peru. Inca, c. 1500. Camelid fiber and cotton, 35⅞ × 30″ (91 × 76.5 cm). Dumbarton Oaks Research Library and Collections, Pre-Columbian Collection, Washington, DC.

Credit: Justin Kerr/Dumbarton Oaks, Byzantine Photograph and Fieldwork Archives, Washington, DC

Perhaps an exquisite tunic such as this, containing patterns associated with multiple ranks and statuses, was woven as a royal garment.

METALWORK When they arrived in Peru in 1532, the Spanish were far less interested in Inca cloth than in their vast quantities of gold and silver. The Inca valued objects made of gold and silver not for their precious metal, but because they saw in them symbols of the sun and the moon. They are said to have called gold the "sweat of the sun" and silver the "tears of the moon." On the other hand, the Spanish exploration of the New World was propelled by feverish tales of native treasure. Whatever gold and silver objects the Spanish could obtain were melted down to enrich their royal coffers. Only a few small figures buried as offerings, like the little **LLAMA** shown in **FIGURE 27-11**, escaped destruction. The llama was thought to have a special connection with the sun, with rain, and with fertility, and a white llama was sacrificed to the sun every morning in Cusco. In this small silver figurine, the essential character of a llama is rendered with only a few well-chosen details, but in keeping with the value that Andeans placed on textiles the blanket on its back is thoroughly described.

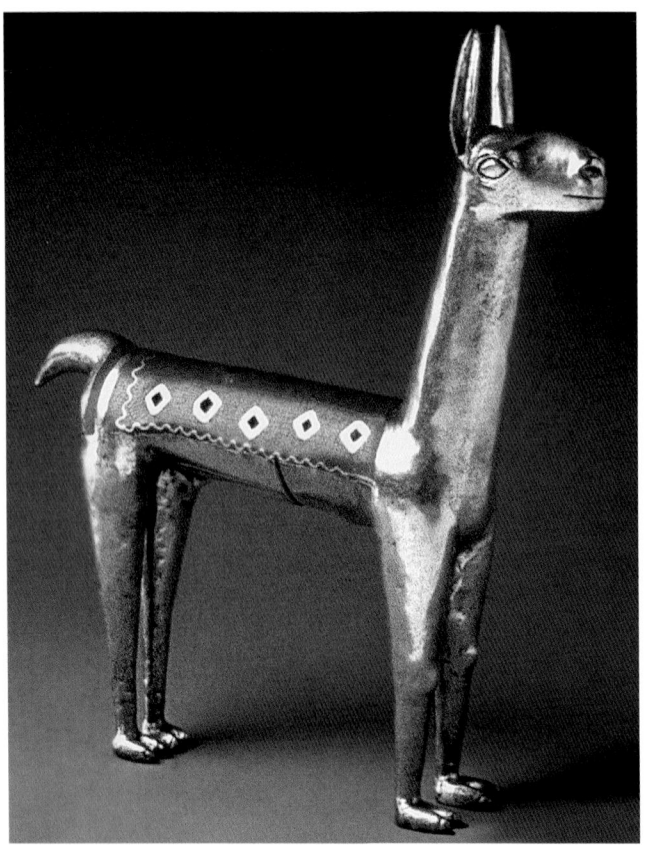

27-11 LLAMA

From Bolivia or Peru, found near Lake Titicaca. Inca, 15th century. Cast silver with gold and cinnabar, 9 × 8½ × 1¾" (22.9 × 21.6 × 4.4 cm). American Museum of Natural History, New York.

Credit: Courtesy Dept. of Library Services, American Museum of Natural History. Photo: John Bigelow Taylor, NY

The Aftermath of the Spanish Conquest

Native American populations declined sharply after the Spanish invasions of the Aztec and Inca empires because of the exploitative policies of the conquerors and the ravages of smallpox and other European diseases. This demographic collapse meant that the population of the Americas declined by as much as 90 percent in the century after contact with Europe. European missionaries suppressed local beliefs and practices and worked to spread Christianity throughout the Americas. Although increasing numbers of Europeans began to settle and dominate the land, the production of art did not end with the Spanish conquest. Traditional media, including fine weaving, continue to flourish to this day, transforming and remaining vital as indigenous peoples adjust to a changing world.

North America

How do the style and functions of art and architecture differ among cultures across North America?

In America north of Mexico, from the upper reaches of Canada and Alaska to the southern tip of Florida, many different peoples with widely varying cultures coexisted. Here, the Europeans came less as military men seeking riches to plunder than as families seeking land to farm. Unlike the Spaniards, they found no large cities with urban populations to resist them. However, although they imagined that the lands they settled were an untended wilderness, in fact nearly all of North America was occupied by indigenous peoples. Over the next 400 years, by means of violence, bribery, and treaties, the English colonies and, in turn, the United States displaced nearly all Native Americans from their ancestral homelands. For example, beginning in the 1830s and continuing through the nineteenth century, thousands of Native Americans (46,000 by 1938) were relocated from their ancestral homelands to newly assigned territory in present-day Oklahoma, a forced migration that became known as the Trail of Tears.

Euro-Americans did not recognize indigenous aesthetic objects as anything more than ethnographic curiosities. Native American works that were small, portable, and usually fragile, were often collected—sometimes forcibly—as souvenirs or anthropological artifacts. Today, Native peoples have begun to reclaim sacred objects and human remains that were forcibly taken from them, and museums are beginning to work with Native communities to present their art in respectful and culturally sensitive ways. Here, we will be able to look at art from only four North American cultural areas: the Eastern Woodlands, the Great Plains, the Northwest Coast, and the Southwest (**MAP 27-2**).

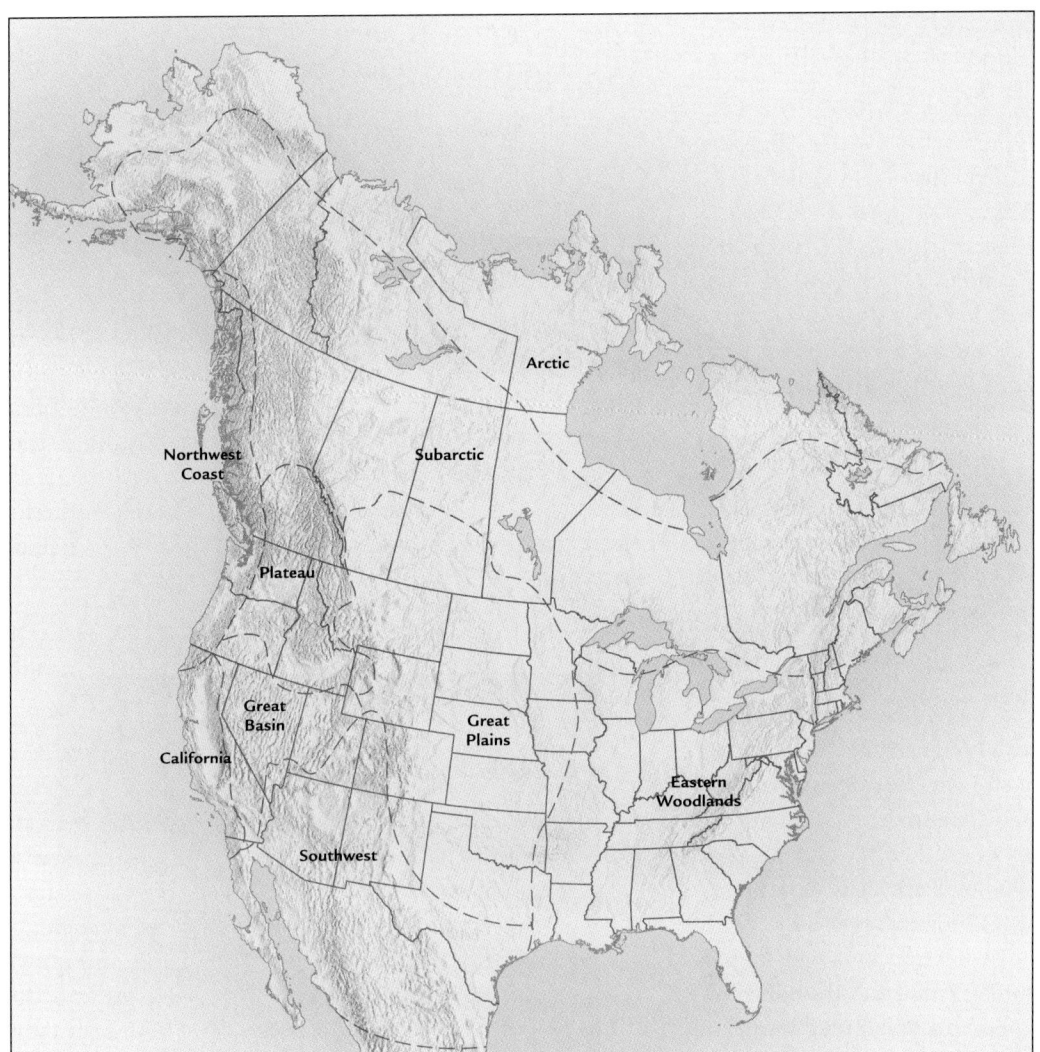

MAP 27-2 NORTH AMERICAN CULTURAL AREAS
The varied geographic regions of North America supported diverse cultures adapted to their distinct environments.

The Eastern Woodlands

In the Eastern Woodlands, after the decline of the great Mississippian centers, most tribes lived in stable villages, and they combined hunting, gathering, and agriculture for their livelihood. In the sixteenth century, the Iroquois formed a powerful confederation of five northeastern Native American nations, which played a prominent military and political role until after the American Revolution. The Huron and Illinois also formed sizable confederacies.

In the seventeenth century, the arrival on the Atlantic coast of a few boatloads of Europeans seeking religious freedom, farmland, and a new life for themselves brought major changes. Trade with these settlers gave the Woodlands peoples access to things they valued, while the colonists learned Native forms of agriculture, hunting, and fishing—skills they needed in order to survive. Native Americans traded furs for such useful items as metal tools, cookware, needles, and cloth, and they especially prized European glass beads and silver. These trade items largely replaced older materials, such as crystal, copper, and shell.

WAMPUM   Woodlands peoples made belts and strings of cylindrical purple and white beads—made from whelk and clam shells—called wampum. The Iroquois and Delaware peoples used wampum to keep records (the purple and white patterns served as memory aids) and exchanged belts of wampum to seal treaties (**FIG. 27-12**). Few actual wampum treaty belts have survived, so this one, said to commemorate an unwritten treaty when the land that is now the state of Pennsylvania was ceded by the Delawares in 1682, is especially prized. The belt, with two figures of equal size holding hands, suggests the mutual respect enjoyed by the Delaware and Penn's Society of Friends (Quakers), a respect that later collapsed into land fraud and violence. In general, wampum strings and belts had the authority of legal agreement and also symbolized a moral and political order.

QUILLWORK   Woodlands art focused on personal adornment—tattoos, body paint, and elaborate dress—and fragile arts such as **quillwork**. Quillwork involved dyeing porcupine and bird quills with a variety of natural dyes, soaking the quills to soften them, and then working them

27-12 WAMPUM BELT, TRADITIONALLY CALLED WILLIAM PENN'S TREATY WITH THE DELAWARE
1680s. Shell beads, 17⅜ × 6⅛" (44 × 15.5 cm). Royal Ontario Museum, Canada.

Credit: With permission of the Royal Ontario Museum © ROM

into rectilinear, ornamental surface patterns on deerskin clothing and on birch-bark items like baskets and boxes. A Sioux legend recounts how a mythical ancestor, Double-woman ("double" because she was both beautiful and ugly, benign and dangerous), appeared to a woman in a dream and taught her the art of quillwork. As the legend suggests, quillwork was a woman's art form, as was basketry. The Sioux **BABY CARRIER** in **FIGURE 27-13** is richly decorated with symbols of protection and well-being, including bands of antelopes in profile and thunderbirds flying with their heads turned and tails outspread. The thunderbird was an especially helpful symbol, thought to be capable of protecting against both human and super-natural adversaries.

BEADWORK AND BASKETRY Shell beads were used in wampum, but decorative beadwork did not become commonplace until Native American artists began to acquire European colored-glass beads in the late eighteenth century; in the nineteenth century they favored the tiny seed beads from Venice and Bohemia. Early bead-work mimicked the patterns and colors of quillwork. In the nineteenth century it largely replaced quillwork and incorporated European designs. Among other sources of inspiration were Canadian nuns, who introduced the young women in their schools to embroidered European floral motifs, European needlework techniques, and pat-terns from European garments, all of which Native embroi-derers began to adapt into their own work. Functional aspects of garments might be transformed into purely decorative motifs; for example, a pocket would be replaced by an area of beadwork shaped like a pocket. A **BANDO-LIER BAG** from Kansas, made by a Delaware woman (**FIG. 27-14**), is covered with curvilinear plant motifs in contrast to the rectilinear patterns of traditional quillwork. White

27-13 BABY CARRIER
Upper Missouri River area. Eastern Sioux, 19th century. Wooden board, buckskin, porcupine quill length 31" (78.8 cm). Department of Anthropology, Smithsonian Institution Libraries, Washington, DC. Catalog No. 7311.

Credit: Catalogue No. 73311, Department of Anthropoogy, Smithsonian Institution

27-14 BANDOLIER BAG
Kansas. Delaware people, c. 1860. Wool fabric, cotton fabric and thread, silk ribbon, and glass beads, 22 × 17" (56 × 43 cm); bag without strap, 8⅝ × 7¾" (22 × 19.7 cm). The Detroit Institute of Arts. Founders Society Purchase (81.216).

Credit: Bridgeman Images

lines outline brilliant pink and blue leaf-shaped forms on both bag and shoulder straps, heightening the intensity of the colors, which alternate within repeated patterns, exemplifying the evolution of beadwork design and its adaptation to a changing world. The shape of bandolier bags is adapted from ammunition pouches carried by European soldiers and trappers.

Basketry is the weaving of reeds, grasses, and other plant materials to form containers. In North America the earliest evidence of basketwork, found in Danger Cave, Utah, dates to as early as 8400 BCE. Over the subsequent centuries, Native American women across North America developed basketry into an art form that combined utility with great beauty. There are three principal basket-making techniques: coiling, twining, and plaiting. **Coiling** involves sewing together a spiraling foundation of rods with some other material. **Twining** twists

Art and Its Contexts

CRAFT OR ART?

In many cultures, the distinction between "fine art" and "craft" does not exist. The traditional Western academic hierarchy of materials (in which marble, bronze, oil paint, and fresco are valued more than ceramic, glass, and watercolor) and the equally artificial hierarchy of subjects (in which history painting, including religious history, stands supreme) are irrelevant to non-Western art and to much art produced in the West before the modern era.

Indigenous peoples of the Americas did not produce objects as works of art to be displayed in museums. In their eyes all pieces were utilitarian objects, adorned in ways necessary for their intended purposes. A work was valued for its effectiveness and for the role it played in society. Some, like a Sioux baby carrier (SEE FIG. 27-13), enrich mundane life with their aesthetic qualities. Others, such as Pomo baskets, commemorate important events. The function of an Inca tunic may have been to identify or confer status on its owner or user through its material value or symbolic associations. And as with art in all cultures, many pieces had great spiritual power. Such works of art cannot be fully comprehended or appreciated when they are seen only on pedestals or encased in glass boxes in museums

or galleries. They must be imagined, or better yet seen, as acting in their societies: Kwakwaka'wakw masks (SEE FIG. 27-20), for example, functioning in religious drama, changing not only the outward appearance, but also the very essence of the individuals wearing them.

At the beginning of the twentieth century, European and American artists broke away from the academic bias that promoted the Classical heritage of Greece and Rome. They found new inspiration in the art—or craft, if you will—of many different non-European cultures. Artists explored a new freedom to use absolutely any material or technique that challenged outmoded assumptions and opened the way for a free and unfettered delight in, and an interest in understanding, Native American art as well as the art of other non-Western cultures. The more recent twentieth- and twenty-first-century conception of art as a multimedia adventure has helped validate works of art once seen only in ethnographic collections. Today, objects once called "primitive" are recognized as works of art and acknowledged to be an essential dimension of a twenty-first-century worldview. The line between "art" and "craft" seems more artificial and less relevant than ever before.

27-15 FEATHERED BASKET

California. Pomo culture, c. 1877. Willow, bulrush, fern, feather, shells, glass beads; height 5½″ (14 cm), diameter 12″ (36.5 cm). Philbrook Museum of Art, Inc., Tulsa, Oklahoma.

Gift of Clark Field (1948.39.37).

multiple elements around a vertical warp of rods. Plaiting weaves strips over and under each other.

The coiled basket shown here was made by a Pomo woman in California (**FIG. 27-15**). According to Pomo legend, the Earth was dark until their ancestral hero stole the sun and brought it to Earth in a basket. He hung the basket first just over the horizon, but, dissatisfied with the light it gave, he kept suspending it in different places across the dome of the sky. He repeats this process every day, which is why the sun moves across the sky from east to west.

In the Pomo basket, the structure of coiled willow and bracken fern root produces a spiral surface into which the artist worked sparkling pieces of clam shell, trade beads, and soft tufts of woodpecker and quail feathers. The underlying patterns in the basket, the glittering shells,

and the softly waving feathers create layers and textural contrasts characteristic of works of art. This blending of aesthetics and functionality is found throughout Native North American art.

The Great Plains

Between the Eastern Woodlands region and the Rocky Mountains to the west lay an area of prairie grasslands called the Great Plains. On the Great Plains, two differing ways of life developed, one a relatively recent and short-lived (1700–1870) nomadic lifestyle—dependent on the region's great migrating herds of buffalo for food, clothing, and shelter—and the other a much older sedentary and agricultural lifestyle. Horses, taken from wild herds that had descended from feral horses brought to America by Spanish explorers in the sixteenth and seventeenth centuries, made travel, and thus a nomadic way of life, easier for the dispossessed eastern groups that moved to the plains.

On the eastern seaboard, both Native Americans and European backcountry settlers were living in loosely village-based, farming societies and thus were competing for the same resources. Increasingly, European settlers pressured the Eastern Woodlands peoples, seizing their farmlands and forcing them westward. The resulting interaction of Eastern Woodlands artists with one another and with Plains artists led in some cases to the emergence of new hybrid styles, while other artists consciously fought to maintain their own traditional cultures.

PORTABLE ARCHITECTURE The nomadic Plains peoples hunted buffalo for food and hides from which they created clothing and a light, portable dwelling known as a tipi (formerly spelled teepee) (**FIG. 27-16**). The tipi was well adapted to withstand the strong and constant wind, the dust, and the violent storms of the prairies. The framework of a tipi consisted of a stable pyramidal frame of three or four long poles, filled out with about 20 additional poles, in a roughly oval plan. The framework was covered with hides specially prepared to make them flexible and waterproof—later, canvas was used—to form a conical structure. Between 20 and 40 hides were needed for a tipi, depending on its size. An opening at the top served as the smoke hole for a central hearth. The tipi leaned slightly into

27-16 BLACKFOOT WOMEN RAISING A TIPI

Photographed c. 1900. Montana Historical Society Research Center.

the prevailing west wind while the flap-covered door and smoke hole faced east, away from the wind. An inner lining covered the lower part of the walls and the perimeter of the floor to protect the occupants from drafts.

Tipis were the property and responsibility of women, who set them up at new encampments and lowered them when the group moved on. Blackfoot women could set up their huge tipis in less than an hour. Women quilled, beaded, and embroidered tipi linings, as well as backrests, clothing, and equipment. The patterns with which tipis were decorated, like the tipis' proportions and colors, varied from nation to nation, family to family, and individual to individual. In general, the bottom was covered with traditional motifs and the center section held personal images. When disassembled and packed to be dragged by a horse to another location, the tipi served as a platform for transporting other possessions. The Sioux arranged

their tipis in two half-circles—one for the sky people and one for the earth people—divided along an east–west axis. When the Blackfeet people gathered in the summer for their ceremonial Sun Dance, their encampment contained hundreds of tipis in a circle a mile in circumference.

PLAINS INDIAN PAINTING Plains men recorded their exploits in paintings on tipis and on buffalo-hide robes. The earliest documented painted buffalo-hide robe, presented to Lewis and Clark during their transcontinental expedition, illustrates a battle fought in 1797 by the Mandan (of what is now North Dakota) and their allies against the Sioux (**FIG. 27-17**). The painter, trying to capture the full

27-17 BATTLE SCENE, HIDE PAINTING
North Dakota. Mandan, 1797–1800. Tanned buffalo hide, dyed porcupine quills, and black, red, green, yellow, and brown pigment, 7′10″ × 8′6″ (2.44 × 2.65 m). Peabody Museum of Archaeology and Ethnology, Harvard University.

This robe, "collected" in 1804 by Meriwether Lewis and William Clark on their expedition into western lands acquired by the United States in the Louisiana Purchase, is the earliest documented example of Plains painting. It was one of a number of Native American artworks that Lewis and Clark sent to President Thomas Jefferson, who displayed the robe in the entrance hall of his home at Monticello, Virginia.

extent of a conflict in which five nations took part, shows a party of warriors in 22 separate episodes. The party is led by a man with a pipe and an elaborate eagle-feather headdress, and the warriors are armed with bows and arrows, lances, clubs, and flintlock rifles. Details of equipment and emblems of rank—headdresses, sashes, shields, feathered lances, powder horns for the rifles—are depicted carefully. Horses are shown in profile with stick legs, C-shaped hooves, and either clipped or flowing manes.

The figures stand out clearly against the light-colored background of the buffalo hide. The painter pressed lines into the hide, then filled in the forms with black, red, green, yellow, and brown pigments. A strip of colored porcupine quills runs down the spine of the buffalo hide. The robe would have been worn draped over the shoulders of the powerful warrior whose deeds it commemorates. As the wearer moved, the painted horses and warriors would seem to come alive, transforming him into a living representation of his exploits.

Life on the Great Plains changed abruptly in 1869, when the transcontinental railway linking the east and west coasts of the United States was completed, providing easy access to Native American lands. Between 1871 and 1890, Euro-American hunters killed off most of the buffalo, and soon ranchers and then farmers moved into the Great Plains. The U.S. government forcibly moved the outnumbered and outgunned Native Americans to reservations, land considered worthless until the later discovery of oil and, in the case of the Black Hills, gold.

The Northwest Coast

From southern Alaska to northern California, the Pacific coast of North America is a region of unusually abundant resources. Its many rivers fill each year with salmon returning to spawn. Harvested and dried, the fish could sustain large populations throughout the year. The peoples of the Northwest Coast—among them the Tlingit, the Haida, and the Kwakwaka'wakw (formerly spelled Kwakiutl)—exploited this abundance to develop a complex and distinctive way of life in which the arts played a central role.

ANIMAL IMAGERY   Animals feature prominently in Northwest Coast art because each extended family group (clan) claimed descent from a mythic animal or animal-human ancestor, from whom the family took its name and the right to use certain animals and spirits as totemic emblems, or crests. These emblems appear frequently in Northwest Coast art, notably in carved cedar house poles and the tall, free-standing mortuary poles erected to memorialize dead chiefs. Chiefs, who were males in the most direct line of descent from the mythic ancestor, validated their status and garnered prestige for themselves and their families by holding ritual feasts known

as potlatches, during which they gave valuable gifts to the invited guests. Shamans, who were sometimes also chiefs, mediated between the human and spirit worlds. Some shamans were female, giving them unique access to certain aspects of the spiritual world.

Northwest Coast peoples lived in large, elaborately decorated communal houses made of massive timbers and thick planks. Carved and painted partition screens separated the chief's quarters from the rest of the house. The Tlingit screen illustrated in **FIGURE 27–18** came from the house of Chief Shakes of Wrangell (d. 1916), whose family crest was the grizzly bear. The image of a rearing grizzly painted on the screen is itself made up of smaller bears and bear heads that appear in its ears, eyes, nostrils, joints, paws, and body. The oval door opening is a symbolic vagina; passing through it re-enacts the birth of the family from its ancestral spirit.

27–18 GRIZZLY BEAR HOUSE-PARTITION SCREEN
From the house of Chief Shakes of Wrangell, Canada. Tlingit people, c. 1840. Cedar, paint, and human hair, 15 × 8' (4.57 × 2.74 m). Denver Art Museum. Native Arts acquisition funds (1951.315).

27–19 CHILKAT BLANKET
Southeast Alaska. Tlingit people, c. 1850. Mountain-goat wool, yellow cedar bark, linen thread, approx. 55 × 72″ (130 × 183 cm). Thaw Collection, Fenimore Art Museum, Cooperstown, New York.

Credit: Photo: John Bigelow Taylor

TEXTILES Blankets and other textiles produced collaboratively by the men and women of the Chilkat Tlingit had great prestige among Northwest Coast peoples (**FIG. 27-19**). Men drew the patterns on boards, and women wove them into the blankets, using shredded cedar bark and mountain-goat wool. The weavers did not use looms; instead, they hung cedar warp threads from a rod and twined colored goat wool back and forth through them to make the pattern, which in this technique can be defined by curving lines. The ends of the warp form the fringe at the bottom of the blanket.

The popular design used here is known as the diving whale—the central panel shows the downward-facing whale(s), while the panels to the sides have been interpreted as this animal's body or seated ravens seen in profile. Characteristic of Northwest painting and weaving, the images are composed of two basic elements: the ovoid (a slightly bent rectangle with rounded corners) and the formline (a continuous, shape-defining line). Here, subtly swelling black formlines define gently curving ovoids and C shapes. When the blanket was worn, its two-dimensional shapes would have become three-dimensional, with the dramatic central figure curving over the wearer's back and the intricate side panels crossing over his shoulders and chest.

MASKS To call upon guardian spirits, many Native American cultures staged ritual dance ceremonies in which dancers wore complex costumes and striking carved and painted wooden masks. Isolated in museums as "art," the masks doubtless lose some of the shocking vivacity they have in performance; nevertheless their bold forms and color schemes retain power and meaning that can be activated by the viewer's imagination.

Some of the most elaborate masks are those used by the Kwakwaka'wakw in the Winter Ceremony that initiates members into the shamanistic Hamatsa society. The dance re-enacts the taming of Hamatsa, a cannibal spirit, and his three attendant bird spirits. Magnificent carved and painted masks transform the dancers into Hamatsa and the attendants, who search for victims to eat. Strings allow the dancers to manipulate the masks so that the beaks open and snap shut with spectacular effect. With snapping beaks and cries of "Hap! Hap! Hap!" ("Eat! Eat! Eat!"), Hamatsa and his three assistants threaten and even attack the Kwakwaka'wakw people who gather for the Winter Ceremony.

In the Winter Ceremony, youths are captured, taught the Hamatsa lore and rituals, and then in a spectacular theater–dance performance are "tamed" and brought back into civilized life. All the members of the community, including singers, gather in the main room of the great house, which is divided by a painted screen (SEE FIG. 27-18). The audience members fully participate in the performance; in early times, they brought containers of blood so that when the bird-dancers attacked them, they could appear to bleed and have flesh torn away.

27–20 Attributed to Willie Seaweed **KWAKWAKA'WAKW BIRD MASK**

Alert Bay, Vancouver Island, Canada. Prior to 1951. Cedar wood, cedar bark, feathers, and fiber, 10 × 72 × 15″ (25.4 × 183 × 38.1 cm). Collection of the Museum of Anthropology, Vancouver, Canada. (A6120).

The name "Seaweed" is an anglicization of the Kwakwaka'wakw name *Siwid*, meaning "Paddling Canoe," "Recipient of Paddling," or "Paddled To"—referring to a great chief to whose potlatches guests paddled from afar. Willie Seaweed was not only the chief of his clan, but a great orator, singer, and tribal historian who kept the tradition of the potlatch alive during years of government repression.

Credit: Courtesy of the UBC Museum of Anthropology, Vancouver, Canada

Whistles from behind the screen announce the arrival of the Hamatsa (danced by an initiate), who enters through the central hole in the screen in a flesh-craving frenzy. Wearing hemlock, a symbol of the spirit world, he crouches and dances wildly with outstretched arms as attendants try to control him. He disappears but returns again, now wearing red cedar and dancing upright. Finally tamed, a full member of society, he even dances with the women.

Then the masked bird-dancers appear—first Raven-of-the-North-End-of-the-World, then Crooked-Beak-of-the-End-of-the-World, and finally the untranslatable Huxshukw, who cracks open skulls with his beak and eats the brains of his victims. Snapping their beaks, these masters of illusion enter the room backward, their masks pointed up as though the birds are looking skyward. They move slowly counterclockwise around the floor. At each change in the music they crouch, snap their beaks, and let out their wild cries of "Hap! Hap! Hap!" Essential to the ritual dances are the huge wooden masks. Among the finest are those by Willie Seaweed (1873–1967), a Kwakwaka'wakw chief, whose brilliant colors and exuberantly decorative carving style determined the direction of twentieth-century Kwakwaka'wakw sculpture (**FIG. 27–20**).

The Canadian government, abetted by missionaries, outlawed the Winter Ceremony and potlatches in 1885, claiming the event was injurious to health, encouraged prostitution, endangered children's education, damaged the economy, and was cannibalistic. But the Kwakwaka'wakw refused to give up their "oldest and best" festival—one that spoke powerfully to them in many ways, establishing social rank and playing an important role in arranging marriages. By 1936, the government and the missionaries, who called the Kwakwaka'wakw

"incorrigible," gave up. But not until 1951 could the Kwakwaka'wakw people gather openly for winter ceremonies, including the initiation rites of the Hamatsa society.

The Southwest

The Native American peoples of the southwestern United States include, among others, the modern Puebloans (sedentary village-dwelling groups) and the Navajo. The Puebloans (living, for example, in Hopi, Acoma, Zuni, and a series of pueblos along the Rio Grande in New Mexico) are heirs of the Ancestral Puebloans (former Anasazi), Hohokam, and Mogollan cultures (see Chapter 13). The Ancestral Puebloans built apartmentlike villages and cliff dwellings whose ruins are found throughout the Four Corners region of New Mexico, Colorado, Arizona, and Utah. The Navajo, who arrived in the region sometime between 1100 and 1500 CE, developed a semisedentary way of life based on agriculture and (after the introduction of sheep by the Spaniards) shepherding. Being among the very few Native American tribal groups whose reservations are located on their actual ancestral homelands, both groups have succeeded in maintaining the continuity of their traditions despite Euro-American pressure. Today, their arts reflect the adaptation of traditional forms to new technologies, new media, and the dominant American culture that surrounds them.

THE PUEBLOS Some Pueblos, like those of their ancient ancestors, consist of multi-storied dwellings made of adobe. One of these, **TAOS PUEBLO** (**FIG. 27–21**), is located in north-central New Mexico. Continually occupied and modified for over 500 years, the up-to-five-story house blocks of Taos Pueblo provide flexible, communal

27-21 TAOS PUEBLO

Taos, New Mexico. Acetate negative, 1947. © 1979 Amon Carter Museum of American Art, Fort Worth, Texas. Bequest of the artist (P1979.208.698).

Laura Gilpin (1891–1979), an American photographer of the landscape, architecture, and people of the American Southwest, began her series on the Pueblos and Navajos in the 1930s. She published her work in four volumes of photographs between 1941 and 1968.

Credit: © 1979 Amon Carter Museum of American Art, Fort Worth, Texas. P1979.208.698.

dwellings. Ladders provide access to the upper stories and to insulated inner rooms entered through holes in the ceiling. Two large house blocks are arrayed around a central plaza that opens toward the neighboring mountains, rising in a stepped fashion to provide a series of roof terraces that can serve as viewing platforms. The plazas and roof terraces are centers of communal life and ceremony, as can be seen in Pablita Velarde's painting of the winter solstice celebrations (SEE FIG. 27-23).

CERAMICS   Traditionally, pottery was women's art among Pueblo peoples. Wares were made by coiling and other hand-building techniques and then fired at low temperature in wood fires. The best-known twentieth-century Pueblo potter was Maria Montoya Martinez (1887–1980) of San Ildefonso Pueblo in New Mexico. Inspired by prehistoric pottery that was unearthed at nearby archaeological excavations and by the then-fashionable Art Deco style, she and her husband, Julian Martinez (1885–1943), developed a distinctive **blackware** ceramic style notable for its elegant forms and subtle textures (**FIG. 27-22**). Maria Martinez made pots covered with a slip that was then burnished. Using additional slip, Julian Martinez painted the pots with designs that interpreted traditional Pueblo and Ancestral Puebloan imagery. After firing, the burnished ground became a lustrous black and the slip painting retained a matte surface. By the 1930s, production of blackware in San Ildefonso had become a communal enterprise. Family members and friends all worked making pots, and Maria Martinez signed all the pieces so that, in typical Pueblo communal solidarity, everyone profited from her fame within the art market.

THE SANTA FE INDIAN SCHOOL   In the 1930s, Anglo-American art teachers and dealers worked with Native Americans of the Southwest to create a distinctive, stereotypical "Indian" style in several media—including jewelry, pottery, weaving, and painting—to appeal to tourists and collectors. A leader in this effort was Dorothy Dunn (1903–1991), who opened an art studio known as the Studio School within the Santa Fe Indian School, an off-reservation government boarding school in New Mexico, from 1932 to 1937. Dunn inspired her students to create a painting style that combined the outline drawing and flat colors of folk art, the decorative qualities of Art Deco, and exotic "Indian" subject matter. Restrictive as the Studio School was, Dunn's success made painting a viable occupation for some young Native American artists.

Pablita Velarde (1918–2006), from Santa Clara Pueblo in New Mexico and a 1936 graduate of Dorothy Dunn's Studio School, was only a teenager when one of her paintings was selected for exhibition at the Chicago World's Fair in 1933. Thereafter, Velarde documented Pueblo ways of

27-22 Maria Montoya Martinez and Julian Martinez **BLACK-ON-BLACK STORAGE JAR**

New Mexico. c. 1942. Ceramic, height 18¾″ (47.6 cm), diameter 22½″ (57.1 cm). Museum of Indian Arts and Culture/Laboratory of Anthropology, Museum of New Mexico, Santa Fe. Gift of Henry Dendahl.

Credit: Museum of Indian Arts and Culture/Laboratory of Anthropology, Santa Fe.

27-23 Pablita Velarde **KOSHARES OF TAOS**
New Mexico. 1940s. Watercolor on paper, 13⅞ × 22⅜″ (35.3 × 56.9 cm). Philbrook Museum of Art, Tulsa, Oklahoma. Museum purchase (1947.37).

Credit: © Helen Tindel. Photograph © 2017. The Philbrook Museum of Art, Inc., Tulsa, Oklahoma

life in a large series of murals for the Bandelier National Monument (a small Ancestral Puebloan site near Los Alamos, New Mexico), launching a long and successful career. In smaller works on paper, such as the one illustrated here, she continued this focus on Pueblo life. **KOSHARES OF TAOS (FIG. 27-23)** illustrates a moment during a ceremony celebrating the winter solstice when *koshares*, or clowns, take over the plaza from the Katsinas. Katsinas—the supernatural counterparts of animals, natural phenomena like clouds, and geological features like mountains—are central to traditional Pueblo religion. They manifest themselves in the human dancers who impersonate them during ceremonies throughout the year, as well as in the small figures known as Katsina dolls that are given to children to help them learn to identify the masks. Velarde's painting combines bold, flat colors and a simplified decorative line with European perspective. Her paintings, with their Art Deco abstraction, helped establish the popular idea of the "Indian" style in art.

THE NAVAJOS While some Navajo arts, like sand painting, have deep traditional roots, others have developed over the centuries of European contact. Navajo weaving (SEE FIG. 27-1) depends on the wool of sheep introduced by the Spaniards, and the designs and colors of Navajo blankets continue to evolve today in response to tourism and

changing aesthetics. Similarly, jewelry made of turquoise and silver did not become an important Navajo art form until the mid nineteenth century. Traditionally, Navajo arts had strict gender divisions: women wove cloth, and men worked metal.

Sand painting, a traditional Navajo art, is the exclusive province of men. Sand paintings are made to the accompaniment of chants by shaman-singers in the course of healing and blessing ceremonies, and they have great sacred significance. The Night Chant, sung toward the end of the ceremony, signals the restoration of inner harmony and balance:

> In beauty (happily) I walk.
> With beauty before me I walk.
> With beauty behind me I walk.
> With beauty below me I walk.
> With beauty all around me I walk.
> It is finished (again) in beauty.
> It is finished in beauty.

Navajo sand paintings depict mythic heroes and events; and as ritual art, they follow prescribed rules and patterns that ensure their power. To make them, the singer dribbles pulverized colored stones, pollen, flowers, and other natural colors over a hide or sand ground. The rituals are intended to cure by restoring harmony to the world. The paintings are not meant to be seen by the public and certainly not to be displayed in museums. They are meant to be destroyed by nightfall of the day on which they are made.

In 1919, a respected shaman-singer named Hosteen Klah (1867–1937) began to incorporate sand-painting images into weaving, breaking with the traditional prohibitions. Many Navajos took offense at Klah both for recording the sacred images and for doing so in what was traditionally a woman's art form. But the Navajo traditionally recognize at least three genders; Hosteen Klah was a *nadle*, or Navajo third-gender, and he had learned to weave from his mother and sister. Hence, he could learn both female and male arts; that is, he was trained both to weave and to heal. Hosteen Klah was not breaking artistic barriers in a conventional sense, but rather exemplifying the complexities of the traditional Navajo gender system. Klah's work was ultimately accepted because of his great skill and prestige.

The **WHIRLING LOG CEREMONY** sand painting, woven into tapestry (**FIG. 27-24**), depicts part of the Navajo creation myth. The Holy People create the earth's surface and divide it into four parts. They create humans, and bring forth corn, beans, squash, and tobacco—the four sacred plants. A male–female pair of humans and one of the sacred plants stand in each of the four quarters, defined by the central cross. The four Holy People (the elongated figures) surround the image, and the guardian figure of Rainbow Maiden frames the scene on three sides. Like all

Navajo artists, Hosteen Klah hoped that the excellence of the work would make it pleasing to the spirits. Recently, shaman-singers have made permanent sand paintings on boards for sale, but they usually introduce slight errors in them to render the paintings ceremonially harmless.

A New Beginning

How are Native American artists and arts institutions responding to the contemporary global art world?

While Native American art has long been displayed in anthropology and natural history museums, today the art of indigenous peoples is finally achieving full recognition by the art establishment (see "Craft or Art?" on page 863). The Institute of American Indian Arts (IAIA), founded in 1962 in Santa Fe and attended by Native American students from all over North America, supports Native American aspirations in the arts today just as Dorothy Dunn's Studio School did in the 1930s. Staffed by Native American artists, the school encourages the incorporation of indigenous ideals in the arts without creating an official "style." As alumni have achieved distinction and the IAIA museum in Santa Fe has established a reputation for excellence, the institute has led Native American art into the mainstream of contemporary art (see Chapter 33).

Contemporary Native American artist Jaune Quick-to-See Smith (b. 1940) borrowed a well-known image by Leonardo da Vinci for **THE RED MEAN** (**FIG. 27-25**), a work she describes as a self-portrait. Indeed, the center of the work has a bumper sticker that reads "Made in the U.S.A." above an identification number. The central figure quotes Leonardo's *Vitruvian Man* (see "The Vitruvian Man" in Chapter 21 on page 649), but the message here is autobiographical. Leonardo inscribed the human form within perfect geometric shapes to emphasize the perfection of the human body, while Smith put her silhouette inside the red X that signifies nuclear radiation. This image alludes both to the uranium mines found on some Indian reservations and to the fact that many have become temporary repositories for nuclear waste. The image's background is a collage of Native American tribal newspapers. Her self-portrait thus includes her ethnic identity and life on the reservation as well as allusions to the history of Western art.

Other artists, such as Canadian Haida artist Bill Reid (1920–1998), have sought to sustain and revitalize traditional art in their work. Trained as a woodcarver, painter, and jeweler, Reid revived the art of carving totem poles and dugout canoes in the Haida homeland of Haida Gwaii—"Islands of the People"—known on maps today as the Queen Charlotte Islands. Late in life he began to create large-scale sculptures in bronze. With their black patina, these works recall traditional Haida carvings in shiny black argillite.

27-24 Hosteen Klah WHIRLING LOG CEREMONY
Sand painting; tapestry by Mrs. Sam Manuelito. Navajo, c. 1925. Wool, 5′5″ × 5′10″ (1.69 × 1.82 m). Heard Museum, Phoenix, Arizona.

Reid's imposing **THE SPIRIT OF HAIDA GWAII** now stands outside the Canadian Embassy in Washington, DC (**FIG. 27-26**). This sculpture, which Reid viewed as a metaphor for modern Canada's multicultural society, depicts a boatload of figures from the natural and mythic worlds struggling to paddle forward. The dominant figure is a shaman in a spruce-root basket hat and Chilkat blanket holding a speaker's pole. On the prow, the place reserved for the chief in a war canoe, sits the Bear. He faces backward rather than forward, and is bitten by an Eagle, with formline-patterned wings. The Eagle, in turn, is bitten by the Seawolf. The Eagle and the Seawolf, together with the man behind them, nevertheless continue paddling. At the stern, steering the canoe, is the Raven, the trickster in Haida mythology. The Raven is assisted by Mousewoman, the traditional guide and escort of humans in the spirit realms. According to Reid, the work represents a "mythological and environmental lifeboat," where "the entire family of living things … whatever their differences, … are paddling together in one boat, headed in one direction" (Bringhurst 1991).

27-26 Bill Reid **THE SPIRIT OF HAIDA GWAII**
Haida, 1991. Bronze, approx. 13 × 20′ (4 × 6 m). Canadian Embassy, Washington, DC.

THE NATIONAL MUSEUM OF THE AMERICAN INDIAN In September 2004, the National Museum of the American Indian finally opened on the Mall in Washington, DC, directly below Capitol Hill and across from the National Gallery of Art. Inspired by the colors, textures, and forms of the American Southwest, the museum building established a new presence for Native Americans on the Mall (**FIG. 27-27**). Symbolizing the Native relationship to the environment, the museum is surrounded by boulders ("Grandfather Rocks"), water, and plantings that recall the varied landscapes of North America, including wetlands, meadows, forest, and traditional cropland with corn, squash, and tomatoes. The entrance to the museum on the east side faces the morning sun and recalls the orientation of prairie tipis. Inside the building a Sun Marker of stained glass in the south wall throws its dagger of light across the vast atrium as the day progresses. The Native peoples of North America have at last taken their rightful place alongside other American ethnicities and many artistic traditions from around the globe.

27-27 NATIONAL MUSEUM OF THE AMERICAN INDIAN

The Smithsonian Institution, Washington, DC. Opened September 2004. Architectural design: GBQC in association with Douglas Cardinal (Blackfoot). Architectural consultants: Johnpaul Jones (Cherokee-Choctaw) and Ramona Sakiestewa (Hopi). Landscape consultant: Donna House (Navajo-Oneida), ethno-botanist.

Credit: J. Scott Applewhite/AP Photos

Think About It

1   Distinguish characteristic styles and techniques developed by two Native American cultures—one in the north, and one in the south—and discuss how they are demonstrated in one specific work from each culture.

2   Explain how symbols and themes are used in **FIGURE 27-7** to articulate the Aztec worldview.

3   Choose a work of art in this chapter that is best understood in connection with its use in religious or political ritual. Discuss its meaning in relation to its ceremonial context. How could such works be displayed in museums in such a way that viewers would be able to understand this critical aspect of their meaning?

4   Evaluate the ways in which two Native North American works from this chapter show influences from European culture.

Crosscurrents

As is frequently the case in the history of art, artist Jaune Quick-to-See Smith has drawn, in *The Red Mean: Self-Portrait*, on a famous work of art from the past—in this case Leonardo da Vinci's *Vitruvian Man*. Discuss how grasping the meaning of Smith's work depends on the viewer's understanding of Leonardo's drawing. Does thinking about the comparison change the way you understand the earlier work?

FIG. 21-3

FIG. 27-25

The following text appears within the artwork (collage of printed text on paper):

THE BARUNGA STATEMENT

We the indigenous owners and occupiers of Australia call on the Australian Government and people to recognise our rights

to self determination and self management including the freedom to pursue our own economic, social religious and cultural development;

to permanent control and enjoyment of our ancestral lands;

to compensation for the loss of use of lands, there having been no extinction of original title;

to protection and control of access to our sacred sites, sacred objects, artifacts, designs, knowledge and works of art;

to the return of the remains of our ancestors for burial in accordance with our traditions;

to respect for and promotion of our Aboriginal identity, including the cultural, linguistic, religious and historical aspects, including the right to be educated in our own languages, and in our own culture and history;

in accordance with the Universal Declaration of Human Rights, the International Covenant on Economic, Social and Cultural Rights, the International Covenant on Civil and Political Rights, and the International Convention on the Elimination of All Forms of Racial Discrimination, including rights to life, liberty, security of person, food, clothing, housing, medical care, education and employment opportunities, necessary social services and other basic human rights.

We call on the Commonwealth Parliament to pass laws providing:

a national elected Aboriginal and Islander organisation to oversee Aboriginal and Islander affairs;

a national system of land rights;

a police and justice system which recognises our customary laws and frees us from discrimination and any activity which may threaten our identity or security, interfere with our freedom of expression or association, or otherwise prevent our full enjoyment and exercise of universally recognised human rights and fundamental freedoms.

We call on the Australian Government to support Aborigines in the development of an International Declaration of Principles for Indigenous Rights, leading to an International Covenant.

And we call on the Commonwealth Parliament to negotiate with us a Treaty or Compact recognising our prior ownership, continued occupation and sovereignty and affirming our human rights and freedoms.

28–1 Galarrwuy Yunupingu Wenten Rubuntja, Lindsay Turner Jampikina, Dennis Williams Japanangka, Bakulangay Marawili, Djambawa Marawili, Marrirra Marawili, Djewiny Ngurruwithun **THE BARUNGA STATEMENT**

1988. Ochers on composition board with collage of printed text on paper, 48 x 47¼" (122 x 120 cm). Parliament House Art Collection, Parliament House, Canberra.

Chapter 28
Art of Pacific Cultures

Learning Objectives

28.a Identify the visual hallmarks of the art of Pacific cultures for formal, technical, and expressive qualities.

28.b Interpret the meaning of works of art of Pacific cultures based on their themes, subjects, and symbols.

28.c Relate artists and art of Pacific cultures to their cultural, economic, and political contexts.

28.d Apply the vocabulary and concepts relevant to the art, artists, and art history of Pacific cultures.

28.e Interpret the art of Pacific cultures using the art historical methods of observation, comparison, and inductive reasoning.

28.f Select visual and textual evidence in various media to support an argument or an interpretation of the art of Pacific cultures.

In 1788, when Captain James Cook arrived in Australia, it was home to at least 300,000 Indigenous Australians, whose ancestors had arrived 50,000 years earlier and who spoke over 250 languages. For 40,000 years Indigenous Australians had been creating rock art; they were the oldest continuous culture in the world. Nevertheless, Cook claimed Australia for Britain as a *terra nullius*, a land that belonged to no one. Within a few decades, European diseases had killed 50 percent of Indigenous Australians. Colonization and the arrival of missionaries changed their lives forever.

Two hundred years later, Indigenous Australians presented what is now known as **THE BARUNGA STATEMENT** (**FIG. 28–1**) to the then prime minister Bob Hawke. It was inspired by the Yirrkala Bark Petitions, which 25 years earlier had gained national attention when indigenous land rights claims were presented to the government on traditional bark paintings from Arnhem Land in the Northern Territory. The Barunga Statement placed its call for broader Aboriginal rights in text on paper collaged onto composition board decorated with two different styles of indigenous painting: one from Arnhem Land (on the left; see also FIG. 28–3) and the other from the Central Desert area (on the right; see also "Closer Look" on page 892). Painted in natural ochers, the cross hatching (*rarrk*) and zigzag patterns from the north contrast with the more fluid curved lines and dots that fill the central desert painting. In both, the artists used a dazzling array of symbols to retell stories about the adventures of ancestral beings.

In 1992, the Australian High Court rejected Cook's *terra nullius* argument and granted land rights to Indigenous Australians. When no treaty between the national government and Indigenous Australians followed, Galarrwuy Yunupingu, an indigenous leader, asked for the Barunga Statement back so that he could bury it. Today, however, it still hangs in Parliament and the struggle for full rights for Indigenous Australians continues.

Throughout the Pacific, contact with the West has had a significant impact on indigenous cultures, though to different degrees. In New Zealand, for example, the Treaty of Waitangi (1840) recognized Maori ownership of land and gave Maori the rights of British subjects, establishing early on a different political dynamic. Nonetheless, although numerous issues remain there, as well as in other parts of the region, Pacific islanders continue to use the arts to express and preserve their own rich and distinctive cultural identities.

The Peopling of the Pacific

What are the geographic and cultural backgrounds for the art of the Pacific islands?

On a map with the Pacific Ocean as its center, only the peripheries of the great landmasses of Asia and the Americas appear. Nearly one third of the earth's surface is taken up by this vast watery expanse. Europeans arriving in

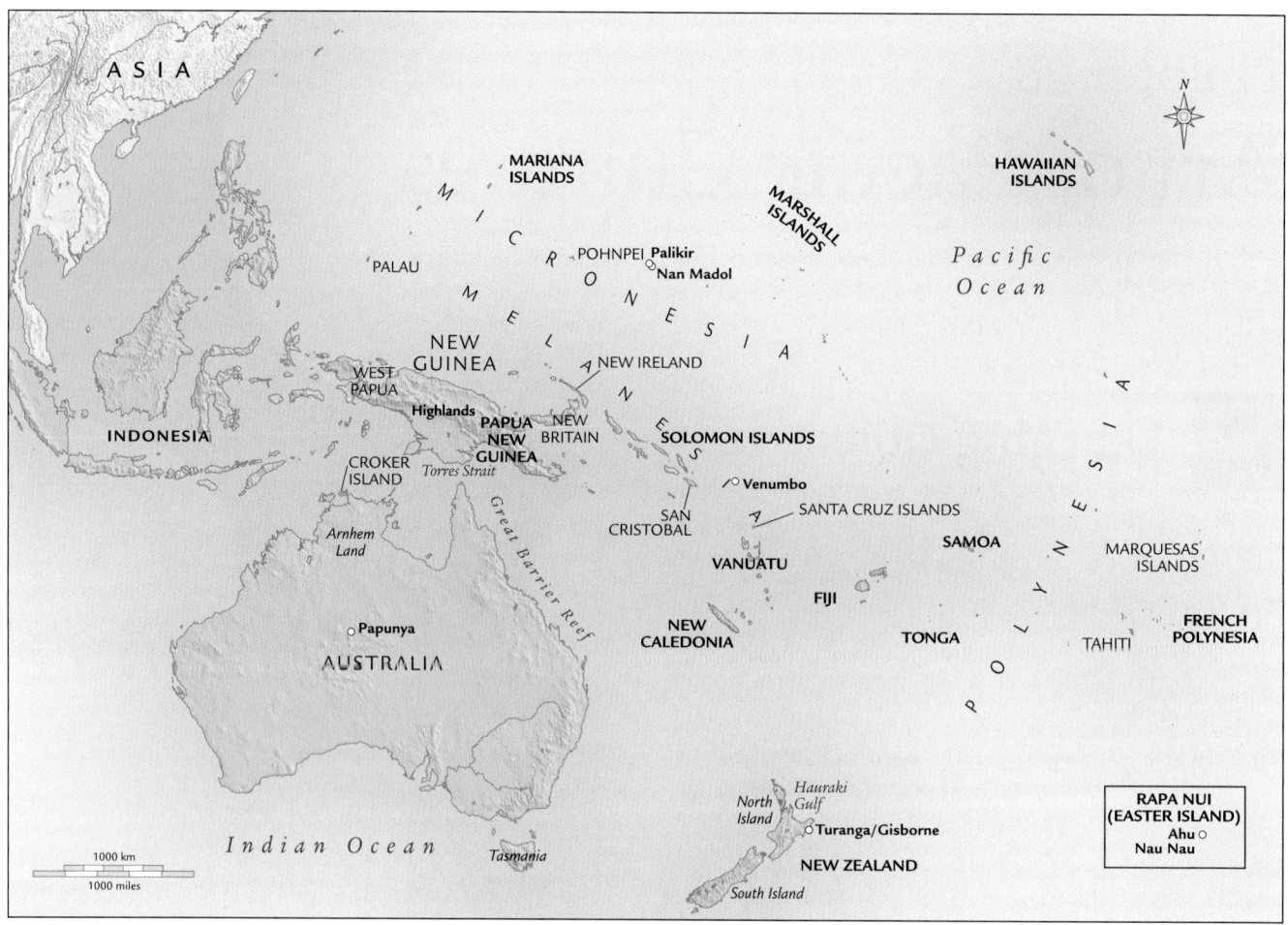

MAP 28–1 PACIFIC CULTURAL-GEOGRAPHIC REGIONS

The Pacific cultures are spread over four vast areas: Australia, Melanesia, Micronesia, and Polynesia.

Oceania in the late eighteenth and early nineteenth centuries noted four distinct but connected cultural-geographic areas: Australia, Melanesia, Micronesia, and Polynesia (**MAP 28–1**). Australia includes the continent, as well as the island of Tasmania to the southeast. Melanesia ("black islands," a reference to the dark skin color of its inhabitants) includes New Guinea and the string of islands that extends eastward from it as far as Fiji and New Caledonia. Micronesia ("small islands"), to the north of Melanesia, is a region of small islands and coral atolls. Polynesia ("many islands") is scattered over a huge, triangular region defined by New Zealand in the south, Rapa Nui (Easter Island) in the east, and the Hawaiian islands to the north. The last region on earth to be inhabited by humans, Polynesia covers some 7.7 million square miles, of which fewer than 130,000 square miles are dry land—and most of that is New Zealand. With the exception of temperate New Zealand, with its marked seasons and snowcapped mountains, Oceania is in the tropics, that is, between the tropic of Cancer in the north and the tropic of Capricorn to the south.

Australia, Tasmania, and New Guinea formed a single continent during the last Ice Age, which began some 2.5 million years ago. About 50,000 years ago, when the sea level was about 330 feet lower than it is today, people moved to this continent from Southeast Asia, making at least part of the journey over open water. Around 27,000 years ago, humans were settled on the large islands north and east of New Guinea as far south as San Cristobal, but they ventured no farther for another 25,000 years. By about 4000 BCE—possibly as early as 7000 BCE—the people of Melanesia were raising pigs and cultivating taro, a plant with edible rootstocks. As the glaciers melted, the sea level rose, flooding low-lying coastal land. By around 4000 BCE a 70-mile-wide waterway, now called the Torres Strait, separated New Guinea from Australia, whose indigenous people continued their hunting and gathering way of life into the twentieth century.

The settling of the rest of the islands of Melanesia and the westernmost islands of Polynesia—Samoa and Tonga—coincided with the spread of the Lapita culture, named for a site in New Caledonia. The Lapita people were Austronesian speakers who probably migrated from Taiwan to Melanesia about 6,000 years ago and spread throughout the islands of Melanesia beginning around

1500 BCE. They were farmers and fisherfolk who cultivated taro and yams and brought dogs, pigs, and chickens with them for food. They also brought the distinctive ceramics whose remnants today enable us to trace the extent of their travels. Lapita potters produced dishes, platters, bowls, and jars. Sometimes they covered their wares with a red slip, and they often decorated them with bands of incised and stamped patterns—dots, lines, and hatching—that may also have been used on bark cloth and in tattoos. Most of the decoration was geometric, but some was figurative. The human face that appears in the example in **FIGURE 28-2** is among the earliest representations of a human being, one of the most important subjects in Oceanic art. The Lapita people were skilled shipbuilders and navigators and engaged in inter-island trade. Over time the Lapita culture lost its widespread cohesion and evolved into various local forms. Its end is generally dated to the early centuries of the Common Era.

Polynesian culture emerged in the eastern Lapita region on the islands forming Tonga and Samoa. Just before the beginning of the first millennium CE, daring Polynesian seafarers, probably in double-hulled sailing canoes, began settling the scattered islands of Far Oceania and eastern Micronesia. Voyaging over open water, sometimes for thousands of miles, they reached Hawaii and Rapa Nui after about 500 CE and settled New Zealand around 800/900–1200 CE.

While this history of migrations across Melanesia to Polynesia and Micronesia allowed for cross-cultural borrowings, there are distinctions between these areas and within the regions as well. The islands that make up Micronesia, Melanesia, and Polynesia include both low-lying coral atolls and the tall tops of volcanic mountains that rise from the ocean floor. Raw materials available to residents of these islands vary greatly, and islander art and architecture use these materials in different ways. The soil of volcanic islands can be very rich, supporting densely populated settlements with a local diversity of plants and animals. On the other hand, the poorer soil of coral atolls cannot support large populations. Similarly, whereas volcanic islands provide good stone for tools and building (as at Nan Madol, see FIG. 28-10), coral is sharp but not particularly hard, and the strongest tools on a coral atoll are often those made from giant clam shells. Generally, the diversity of both plants and animals decreases from west to east among the Pacific islands.

The arts of this vast and diverse region display an enormous variety that is closely linked to each community's ritual and religious life. In this context, the visual arts were often just one strand in a rich weave that also included music, dance, and oral literature.

Australia

How is the concept of the "dreaming" fundamental in Indigenous Australian art?

Until European settlers disrupted their way of life, the hunter-gatherers of Australia were closely attuned to the environments in which they lived. Their only modification of the landscape was regular controlled burning of the underbrush, which encouraged new plant life and attracted animals. Their intimate knowledge of plants, animals, and water sources enabled them to survive and thrive in a wide range of challenging environments.

Indigenous Australian life is intimately connected with the concept of the Dreamtime, or the Dreaming. Not to be confused with our notions of sleep and dreams, the Dreaming refers to the period before humans existed. (The term, a translation from Arrente, one of the more than 250 languages spoken in Australia when Europeans arrived, was first used in the late nineteenth century in an attempt to understand the indigenous worldview.) According to this complex belief system, the world began as a flat, featureless place. Ancestral Spirit Beings emerged from the earth or arrived from the sea, taking many different forms. The Spirit Beings had numerous adventures, and in crossing the continent, they created all of its physical features: mountains, sand hills, creeks, and water holes. They also brought about the existence of animals, plants, and humans and created the ceremonies and sacred objects needed to ensure that they themselves were remembered, a system sometimes referred to as Aboriginal Laws. The Spirit Beings eventually returned to the earth or became

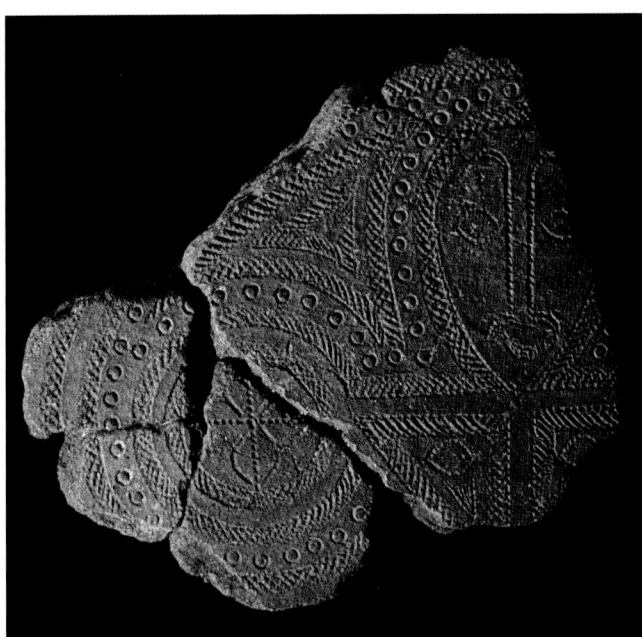

28-2 FRAGMENTS OF A LARGE LAPITA JAR
From Venumbo Reef, Santa Cruz Island, Solomon Islands. c. 1200–1100 BCE. Clay, height of human face motif approx. 1½" (4 cm).

Credit: Courtesy of the Anthropology Photographic Archive, Department of Anthropology, The University of Auckland

28-3 Jimmy Midjaw Midjaw **THREE DANCERS AND TWO MUSICIANS: CORROBOREE OF MIMI, SPIRITS OF THE ROCKS**

Minjilang (Croker Island), West Arnhem Land, Australia. Mid 20th century. Natural pigments on eucalyptus bark, 23 × 35″ (59 × 89 cm). Musée du Quai Branly, Paris, France. (MNAO 64.9.103).

Credit: Photo © RMN-Grand Palais (musée du quai branly)/Jean-Gilles Berizzi

literally one of its features. Thus, they are identified with specific places, which are honored as sacred sites. Indigenous Australians who practice this traditional religion believe that they are descended from the Spirit Beings and associate themselves with particular places related to the ancestors' stories and transformations.

Knowledge of the Dreaming stories and of the objects related to them is sacred and secret. Multiple levels of meaning are learned over a lifetime and restricted to those properly trained and initiated to know each level. As a result, an outsider's understanding of the stories and related art (objects and motifs) is strictly limited to what is allowed to be public. Some stories are shared by many tribes across great distances, while others are specific to one area. Men and women have their own stories, women's often associated with food and food gathering.

Since the Dreaming has never ceased, the power of the ancestral Spirit Beings still exists. Indigenous Australians have developed a rich artistic life to relive the stories of the ancestors and transmit knowledge about them to subsequent generations. Ceremonial art forms include paintings on rock and bark, sand drawings, and ground sculptures. Sacred objects, songs, and dances are used to renew the supernatural powers of the ancestors in ceremonial meetings called corroborees. In **FIGURE 28-3**, Western Arnhem Land artist Jimmy Midjaw Midjaw depicts such a meeting held by a group of Mimi, spirits who live

in the narrow spaces between rocks by day and come out at night. Specific to this area, they taught humans how to hunt and cook animals, as well as to dance, sing, and play instruments in ceremonies. Tall, thin, humanlike figures, often in motion, they were painted in ancient rock shelters, and since at least the late nineteenth century, on eucalyptus bark.

Bark paintings are found throughout northern Australia, where numerous regional styles exist. In Western Arnhem Land, the background is usually a monochromatic red ocher wash, with figures in white, black, and red pigments. In the 1950s and 1960s, Midjaw Midjaw was part of a prolific group of artists on Minjilang (Croker Island) that became well known through the anthropologists and collectors working in the area.

Melanesia and Micronesia

What are the diverse forms of art and architecture found on the islands that make up Melanesia and Micronesia?

Since the inhabitants of Melanesia usually rely at least partially on agriculture for survival, they live in permanent settlements, many of which feature spaces set aside for ritual use. Social position and status are not inherited or determined by birth, but are achieved by the accumulation of wealth (often in the form of pigs), by the demonstration of leadership, and, often, by participation in men's societies. Much ceremony is related to rituals associated with these societies, including initiation into different levels or grades. Other important rituals facilitate relationships with the deceased and with supernatural forces.

Melanesian art is frequently bold, and masking and body decoration—often as part of ceremonial performances—are important, though they can be ephemeral. Men are prominent in the sculptural and masking traditions; women play significant roles as audience and also make bark cloth, woven baskets, pottery, and other aesthetically pleasing objects.

New Guinea

New Guinea, at 1,500 miles long and 1,000 miles wide, is the largest island in the Pacific and the second-largest in the world. It is today divided between two countries. Its eastern half is part of the modern nation of Papua New Guinea; the western half is West Papua, a province of present-day Indonesia. Located near the equator and with mountains that rise to 16,000 feet, the island has a variety of environments, from coastal mangrove marshes to grasslands, dense rainforests to swampy river valleys. The population is equally diverse, with coastal fishermen, riverine hunters, slash-and-burn agriculturalists, and more-stable farmers in the highlands. Among New Guinea and its smaller neighboring islands, more than 700 languages have been identified.

THE KORAMBO (CEREMONIAL HOUSE) OF THE ABELAM OF PAPUA NEW GUINEA   The Abelam, who live in the foothills of the mountains on the north side of the Sepik River in Papua New Guinea, raise pigs and cultivate yams, taro, bananas, and sago palms. In traditional Abelam society, people live in extended families or clans in hamlets. Wealth among the Abelam is measured in pigs, but men gain status from participation in a yam cult that has a central place in Abelam society. The yams that are the focus of this cult—some of which reach an extraordinary 12 feet in length—are associated with clan ancestors and the potency of their growers. Village leaders renew their relationship with the forces of nature as represented by yams during the Long Yam Festival, which is held at harvest time and involves processions, masked figures, singing, and the ritual exchange of the finest yams.

An Abelam hamlet includes sleeping houses, cooking houses, storehouses for yams, a central space for rituals, and a ceremonial or spirit house, the **korambo** (*haus tambaran* in Pidgin). In this ceremonial structure reserved for the men of the village, the objects associated with the yam cult and with clan identity are kept hidden from women and uninitiated boys. Men of the clan gather in

the *korambo* to organize rituals, especially initiation rites, and to conduct community business. The prestige of a hamlet is linked to the quality of its *korambo* and the size of its yams. Constructed on a frame of poles and rafters and roofed with split cane and thatch, *korambo* are built with a triangular floor plan, the side walls meeting at the back of the building. The elaborately decorated façade consists of three parts, beginning at the bottom: a woven mat, a painted and carved wooden lintel, and painted sago bark panels (**FIG. 28–4**). In this example, built about 1961, red, white, and black faces of spirits (*nggwal*) appear on the façade's bark panels, and the figure at the top is said to represent a female flying witch. This last figure is associated with the feminine power of the house itself. The projecting pole at the top of the *korambo* is the only male element of the architecture, and is said to be the penis of the house. The small door at the lower right is a female element, a womb; entering and exiting the house is the symbolic equivalent to death and rebirth. The Abelam believe the paint itself has magical qualities. Regular, ritual repainting revitalizes the images and ensures their continued potency.

28–4 EXTERIOR OF KORAMBO (HAUS TAMBARAN)
Kinbangwa village, Sepik River, Papua New Guinea. Abelam, 20th century.

Credit: Mandeville Special Collections Library Geisel Library University of California, San Diego. Photo: Anthony Forge, 1962

Every stage in the construction of a *korambo* is accompanied by ceremonies, which are held in the early morning while women and boys are still asleep. The completion of the façade of a house is celebrated with a ceremony called *mindja*, which includes all-night dancing, and which may continue for six months, until the roof is completely thatched. Women participate in these inaugural ceremonies and are allowed to enter the new house, which afterward is ritually cleansed and closed to them.

BILUM—CONTEMPORARY NET BAGS OF HIGHLAND NEW GUINEA Women's arts in Papua New Guinea tend to be less spectacular than men's, but nonetheless significant. Both functionally and symbolically, they contribute to a balance between male and female roles in society. **Bilum**, for example, are netted bags made mainly by women throughout the central highlands of New Guinea (**FIG. 28-5**). Looped from a single long thread spun on the thigh, *bilum* are very strong and, as loosely woven work bags, are used to carry items from vegetables to beer. The bones of a deceased man may be stored in a special *bilum* in a village's men's house (which is similar

in function to the Abelam *korambo* in FIG. 28-4), while his widow wears his personal bag as a sign of mourning. Women wear decorative *bilum*, into which marsupial fur is often incorporated, as adornment, exchange them as gifts, and use them to carry babies.

Bilum are rich metaphorical symbols. Among the women of the Wahgi tribe, who live in the Wahgi Valley of the central highlands, seen in FIGURE 28-5, the term *bilum* may be used as a synonym for womb and bride, and they are also associated with ideas of female attractiveness. Depending on how they are worn, they can indicate whether a girl is eligible for marriage.

In the past, *bilum* were made from natural fibers, most commonly the inner bark of a ficus plant. Today, while the technique for making them remains unchanged, a wide array of colorful contemporary fibers, including nylon and acrylic yarn, are used, and new designs incorporating complicated patterns and words are constantly appearing. *Bilum* are now made by women throughout Papua New Guinea, not just in the highlands. They are sold commercially in markets and towns and have become one of the country's national symbols.

28-5 WOMEN WEARING NET BAGS (BILUM)
Wahgi Valley, Western Highlands Province, Papua New Guinea. 1990.
Credit: Michael O'Hanlon

28-6 ASMAT ANCESTRAL SPIRIT POLES (BISJ)
Buepis village, Fajit River, West Papua Province, Indonesia. c. 1960.
Wood, paint, palm leaves, and fiber, height approx. 18' (5.48 m).

Credit: © 2016. Image copyright The Metropolitan Museum of Art/
Art Resource, NY

SPIRIT POLES OF THE ASMAT OF WEST PAPUA The
Asmat, who live along rivers in the coastal swamp forests
of the southwest coast, were known in the past as warriors
and headhunters. In Asmat culture, trees are identified
with human beings, their fruit with human heads. Fruit-
eating birds were thus the equivalent of headhunters, and
were often represented in war and mortuary arts, along
with the praying mantis, whose female bites off the head
of the male during mating. In the past, the Asmat believed
that death was always caused by an enemy, either by direct
killing or through magic, and that it required revenge, usually in the form of taking an enemy's head, to appease the
spirit of the person who had died and thus maintain balance between hostile groups.

Believing that the spirit of the dead person remained in
the village, the Asmat erected elaborately sculpted memorial poles (**FIG. 28-6**) known as *bisj* (pronounced bish),
which embodied the spirits of the ancestors and paid tribute to them. Placed in front of special houses belonging to

the village's men's society, *bisj* poles are generally carved
from mangrove trees, although some have been identified
as wild nutmeg wood. The felling of a tree is a ritual act
in which a group of men attack the tree as if it were an
enemy. The figures on the poles represent the dead individuals who are to be avenged; small figures represent
dead children. The bent pose of the figures associates them
with the praying mantis. The large, lacy phalluses emerging from the figures at the top of the poles are carved from
the projecting roots of the tree and symbolize male fertility, while the surface decoration suggests body ornamentation. The poles faced the river to ensure that the spirits of
the dead would travel to the realm of the ancestors (*safan*),
which lay beyond the sea. The *bisj* pole also served symbolically as the dugout canoe that would take the spirit of
the deceased down the river to *safan*.

By carving *bisj* poles (usually for several deceased at
the same time) and organizing a *bisj* feast, relatives publicly indicated their responsibility to avenge their dead in a
headhunting raid. As part of the ceremonies, mock battles
were held, the men boasting of their bravery, the women
cheering them on. After the ceremonies, the poles were left
in the swamp to deteriorate and transfer their supernatural
power back to nature. Today, Asmat continue to carve *bisj*
poles and use them in funerary ceremonies, although they
stopped headhunting in the 1970s. Poles are also made to
sell to outsiders.

New Ireland and New Britain

MALAGAN DISPLAY OF NEW IRELAND New Ireland is one of the large eastern islands of the nation of
Papua New Guinea. The northern people on the island
still practice a complex set of death and commemorative rites known as *malagan* (pronounced malang-gan),
which can take place as much as two years after a person's death. In the past, clan leaders rose to prominence
primarily through *malagan* ceremonies that honored their
wives' recently deceased family members. The greater
the *malagan* ceremony, the greater prominence the clan
leader had achieved.

Malagan also include rites to initiate young men and
women into adulthood. After several months' training in seclusion in a ritual enclosure, they are presented
to the public and given carved and painted figures. The
combined funerary and initiation ceremonies include
feasts, masked dances, and the creation of a special
house to display elaborately carved and painted sculptures (**FIG. 28-7**) that honor the dead. The display house
illustrated, which dates to the early 1930s, is more
than 11 feet wide and honors 12 deceased individuals. The carvings are large (the first on the left is nearly
6 feet in height) and take the form of horizontal friezes,
standing figures, and poles containing several figures.

28–7 MALAGAN DISPLAY

Medina village, New Ireland, Papua New Guinea. c. 1930. 6′10⅝″ × 11′5¾″ (2.1 m × 3.5 m). Museum für Völkerkunde, Basel, Switzerland.

They are visually complex, with tensions created between solids and voids and between the two-dimensional painted patterns on three-dimensional sculptural forms. Such displays are kept secret until their unveiling at the climax of festivities. After the ceremonies they are no longer considered ritually "active" and are destroyed or, since the late nineteenth century, sold to outsiders. *Malagan* figures are still being carved in association with continuing ceremonies.

TUBUAN MASK OF NEW BRITAIN In the Papua New Guinea province of New Britain—including the Duke of York Islands—Tubuan masks represent the Tolai male secret society, which has different levels of increasing knowledge and power and wields both spiritual and social control, especially during the three months of ceremonies known as the "Time of the Tubuan." Though initiation to the society is the main purpose of the ceremonies, the men of the village, who have achieved power through the accumulation of wealth (in the past through bravery in war), use this period to call up the spirits represented by the masks, who have the authority to settle disputes, stop fights, punish lawbreakers, and force the payment of debts. Political power and authority are underscored and enhanced by their appearance. In the past they had the power of life and death.

The masks represent both female and male spirits, though all the masks are danced by men. Local stories say women originally owned the masks and that men

28–8 TUBUAN MASK BEING DANCED

Tolai people, Duke of York Islands, New Britain, Papua New Guinea. c. 1990. Cloth, paint, fiber, and feathers.

stole them. The **TUBUAN MASK** (**FIG. 28-8**) represents the Mother, who gives birth to her children, the Duk Duk masks, representing the new initiates into the society. With the appearance first of the Mother masks, then of the Duk Duk masks, the initiates return to the village from the bush, where they have undergone intensive preparation to enter the society. The Tubuan mask has a distinctive, tall conical shape and prominent eyes formed by concentric white circles. The green leaf skirt is a very sacred part of the mask, which is itself made from painted bark cloth, various fibers, and feathers. Black feathers on top indicate a more powerful spirit than white feathers.

MICRONESIA   The majority of Micronesia's islands are small, low-lying coral atolls, but in the western region several are volcanic in origin. The eastern islands are more closely related culturally to Polynesia, while those in the west show connections to Melanesia, especially in the men's houses found on Palau and Yap. The atolls—circular coral reefs surrounding lagoons where islands once stood—have a limited range of materials for creating objects of any kind. Micronesians are known especially for their navigational skills and their fine canoes. They also create textiles from banana and coconut fibers, bowls from turtle shells, and abstract human figures from wood, which is scarce. As in other parts of the Pacific, tattooing and performative arts remain central to life.

WAPEPE NAVIGATION CHART   Sailors from the Marshall Islands relied on celestial navigation—using the sun and moon and stars—as well as a detailed understanding of the ocean currents and trade winds to travel from one island to another. To teach navigation to younger generations, elders traditionally used stick charts (*wapepe* or *mattang*)—maps that showed land, but also the path from one island to the next over the water (**FIG. 28-9**).

In common use until the 1950s, stick charts were schematic diagrams of the prevailing ocean currents and the characteristic wave patterns encountered between islands. Currents are represented by sticks held together by coconut fibers; attached shells mark islands along the route. The arrangement of sticks around a shell indicates a zone of distinctive waves shaped by an island deflecting the prevailing wind. Such refracted waves enable a navigator to sense the proximity of land without being able to see it and to discern the least difficult course for making landfall. Although *wapepe* are primarily functional, their combination of clarity, simplicity, and abstraction has an aesthetic impact.

NAN MADOL   The basalt cliffs of the island of Pohnpei provided the building material for one of the largest and most remarkable stone architectural complexes in Oceania. Nan Madol, on Pohnpei's southeast coast,

28-9 WAPEPE NAVIGATION CHART
Marshall Islands. 19th century. Sticks, coconut fiber, and shells, 29½ × 29½" (75 × 75 cm). Peabody Essex Museum, Salem.

Credit: Courtesy Peabody Essex Museum. Photo: Jeffrey Dykes.

consists of 92 artificial islands set within a network of canals covering about 170 acres (**MAP 28-2**). Seawalls and breakwaters 15 feet high and 35 feet thick protect the area from the ocean. When it was populated, openings in the breakwaters gave canoes access to the ocean and allowed seawater to flow in and out with the tides, flushing clean the canals. While other similar complexes have been identified in Micronesia, Nan Madol is the largest and most impressive, reflecting the importance of the kings who ruled from the site. The artificial islands and the buildings atop them were constructed between the early thirteenth century and the dynasty's political decline in the seventeenth. The site had already been abandoned by the time Europeans discovered it in the nineteenth century Nan Madol was an administrative and ceremonial center for powerful kings, who commanded a local labor force to construct this monumental city of as many as 1,000 people.

Both the buildings and the underlying islands are built of massive masonry set in alternating layers of log-shaped stones and boulders of prismatic basalt. The largest of the artificial islets is more than 100 yards long, and one basalt cornerstone alone is estimated to weigh about 50 tons. The stone logs were split from the cliffs by alternately heating the stone and dousing it with water. Most of the islands are oriented northeast–southwest, receiving the benefit of the cooling prevailing winds.

MAP 28-2 THE
COMPLEX OF
NAN MADOL

Pohnpei, Federated
States of Micronesia.
c. 1200/1300–
c. 1500/1600.

The walls of the **ROYAL MORTUARY COMPOUND**, which once dominated the northeast side of Nan Madol (**FIG. 28-10**), rise in subtle upward and outward curves to a height of 25 feet. To achieve the sweeping, rising lines, the builders increased the number of stones in the header courses (those with the ends of the stones laid facing out along the wall) relative to the stretcher courses (those with the lengths of the stones laid parallel to the wall) as they came to the corners and entryways. The plan of the structure consists of progressively higher rectangles within rectangles—the outer walls leading by steps up to interior walls that lead up to a central courtyard with a small, cubical tomb.

Polynesia

How are the art and architecture of Polynesia distinct from that of Melanesia and Micronesia?

The settlers of the far-flung islands of Polynesia developed distinctive cultural traditions but also retained linguistic and cultural affinities that reflect their common origin. Traditional Polynesian society was generally far more stratified than Melanesian society: A person's genealogy, tracing his or her descent from an ancestral god, determined his or her place in society. First-born children of the hereditary elite were considered the most sacred because they inherited more spiritual power (*mana*) at their birth. *Mana* could be gained through leadership, courage, or skill, but it could be lost because

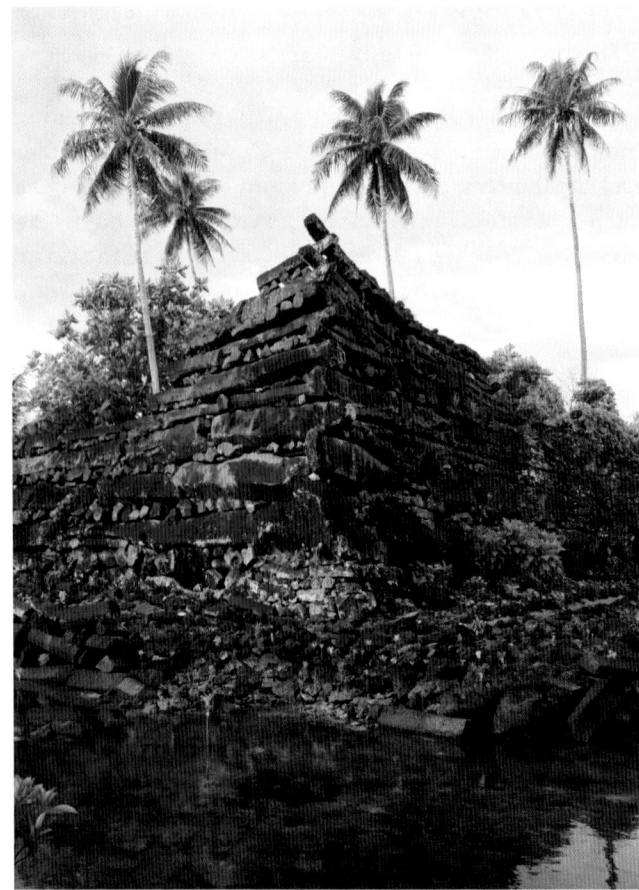

28-10 ROYAL MORTUARY COMPOUND, NAN MADOL
Pohnpei, Federated States of Micronesia. Basalt blocks, wall height up to 25′ (7.62 m).

Credit: © Stephen Alvarez/ National Geographic/Getty Images of failure in warfare. It was protected by strict laws of conduct called *tapu,* a word that came into the English language as "taboo."

All of the arts in Polynesia were sacred, and their creation was a sacred act. Master artists were also ritual specialists. Objects were crafted from a variety of materials, some of which, like jadeite in New Zealand, were considered spiritually powerful. Some objects were practical, such as canoes, fishhooks, and weapons; others indicated the status and rank of the society's elite. Objects had their own *mana,* which could increase or decrease depending on how successful they were in performing their functions. Quality and beauty were important. Objects were made to endure, and many were handed down as heirlooms from generation to generation. In addition, the human body itself was the canvas for the art of tattoo (*tatau* in several Polynesian languages).

Polynesian religions included many levels of gods, from creator gods and semidivine hero-gods (such as Maui, who appears in the stories of many of the Polynesian cultures) to natural forces, but the most important were ancestors, who became gods at their death. Since they remained influential in daily life, they had to be honored and placated, and their help was sought for important projects and in times of trouble. Throughout much of Polynesia, figures in human form—often generically called *tiki*—were carved in stone, wood, and in some places, including the Marquesas Islands, human bone. These statues represented the ancestors and were often placed on sacred ritual sites attended by ritual specialists (SEE FIG. 28-12) or, as in New Zealand, incorporated into meeting houses.

Te-Hau-Ki Turanga

New Zealand was settled sometime after 800 CE by intrepid seafaring Polynesians now known as the Maori. As part of the process of adapting their Polynesian culture to the temperate New Zealand environment, they began to build wooden-frame homes, the largest of which, the chief's house, evolved after Western contact into the meeting house (*whare nui*). The meeting house stands on an open plaza (*marae*), a sacred place where a Maori tribe (*iwi*) or subtribe (*hapu*) still today greets visitors, discusses important issues, and mourns the dead. In it, tribal history and genealogy are recorded and preserved. Created by the master carver Raharuhi Rukupo and his 18 named assistants in the early 1840s, **TE-HAU-KI-TURANGA** is the oldest existing, fully decorated meeting house in New Zealand (**FIG. 28-11**). Built by Rukupo as a memorial to his elder brother, its name refers to the region of New Zealand where it was made—Turanga, today Gisborne and its region, on the northeast coast of the North Island. It has been translated as "The Breezes of Turanga" or "The Spirit of Turanga."

In this area of New Zealand, the meeting house symbolizes the tribe's founding ancestor, for whom it is often named. The ridgepole is the backbone, the rafters are the ribs, and the slanting bargeboards—the boards attached to the projecting end of the gable—are the outstretched enfolding arms. The face appears in the gable mask. Relief figures of ancestors cover the support poles, wall planks, and the lower ends of the rafters. The ancestors, in effect, support the house. They were thought to take an active interest in community affairs and to participate in the discussions held in the meeting house. Rukupo, who was an

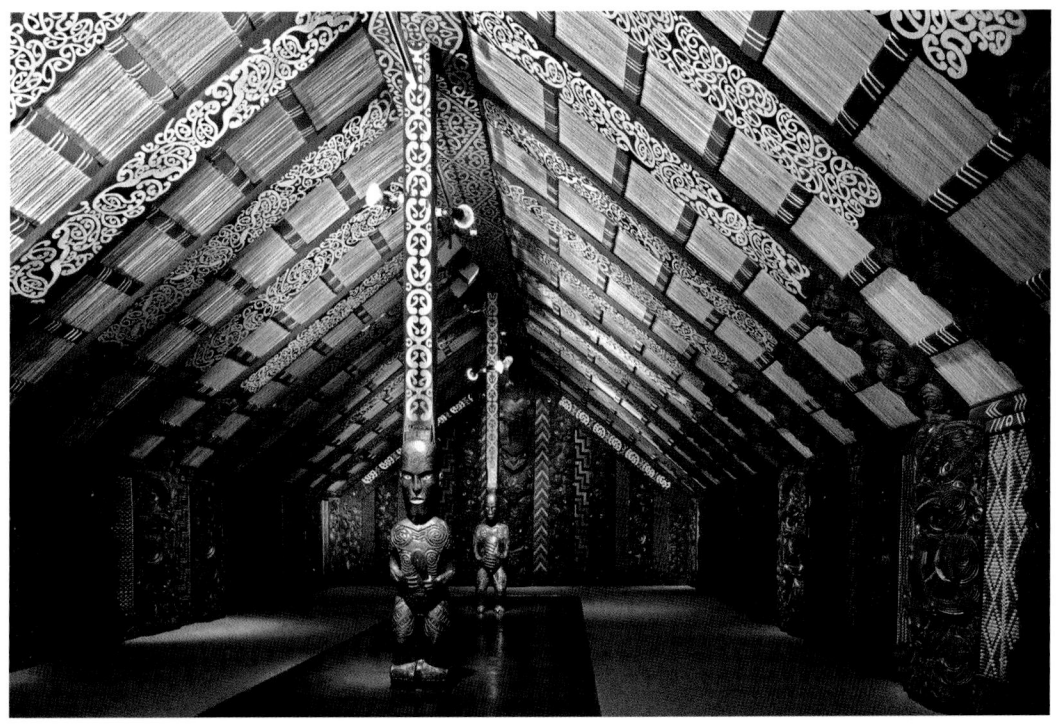

28–11 Raharuhi Rukupo, master carver **TE-HAU-KI-TURANGA (MAORI MEETING HOUSE)**
Gisborne/Turanga, New Zealand; built and owned by the Rongowhakaata people of Turanga. 1842–1843, restored in 1935. Wood, shell, grass, flax, and pigments. Museum of New Zealand/Te Papa Tongarewa, Wellington. (Neg. B18358).

Credit: Museum of New Zealand Te Papa Tongarewa

front

parts of the meeting house

interior side wall

interior rear wall

important political and religious leader as well as a master carver, included an unusual naturalistic portrait of himself among them.

Painted curvilinear patterns (**kowhaiwhai**) decorate the rafters in white on a red-and-black background. The **koru** pattern, a curling stalk with a bulb at the end that resembles the young tree fern, dominates the design system. Lattice panels (**tukutuku**) made by women fill the spaces between the wall planks. Because ritual prohibitions, or taboos, prevented women from entering the meeting house, they worked from the outside and wove the panels from the back. They created the black, white, and orange patterns from grass, flax, and flat slats. Each pattern has a symbolic meaning: chevrons representing the teeth of the sea monster Taniwha, steps the stairs of heaven climbed by the hero-god Tawhaki, and diamonds the flounder.

When Captain Cook arrived in New Zealand in the second half of the eighteenth century, each tribe and geographical region had its own style. A storehouse doorway from the Ngäti Päoa tribe (**FIG. 28–12**), which lived in the Hauraki Gulf area to the west of Turanga, dates to this period of time (or earlier) and shows the soft, shallow surface carving resulting from the use of stone tools. In comparison, a house panel (**poupou**) from Te-Hau-ki-Turanga (**FIG. 28–13**), carved with steel tools, shows the deeply cut, very precisely detailed surface carving characteristic of that time.

As is typical throughout Polynesia (SEE FIG. 28–17), the figures face frontally and have large heads with open eyes. The Hauraki Gulf figure has both hands placed on its stomach and represents a male ancestor, while the Te-Hau-ki-Turanga figure is a female ancestor nursing a child. In both, a small figure, representing their descendants, stands between their legs.

Considered a national treasure by the Maori, this meeting house was restored in 1935 by Maori artists who knew the old, traditional methods; it is now preserved at the Museum of New Zealand / Te Papa Tongarewa in Wellington and considered *taonga* (cultural treasure).

28–12 CARVED FIGURE FROM STOREHOUSE DOORWAY

Ngäti Päoa, Hauraki Gulf, New Zealand. 1500–1800. Wood, height 33⅞" (86 cm). Museum of New Zealand/Te Papa Tongarewa, Wellington.

Credit: Museum of New Zealand Te Papa Tongarewa/ Michael Hall

28–13 POUPOU (PANEL)

From Te-Hau-ki-Turanga. Wood and red pigment, height 4'7" (140 cm). Museum of New Zealand/Te Papa Tongarewa, Wellington.

Credit: Museum of New Zealand Te Papa Tongarewa

Marquesas Islands

TATTOO IN THE MARQUESAS ISLANDS   The art of tattoo was widespread and ancient in Oceania. Tattoo chisels made of bone have been found in Lapita sites. They are quite similar to the tools used to decorate Lapita pottery, suggesting some symbolic connection between the marking of pottery and human skin. The Polynesians, descendants of the Lapita people, brought tattooing with them as they migrated throughout the Pacific, and as they became isolated from each other over time, distinctive styles evolved. Spirals became a hallmark of the Maori facial tattoo (*moko*), and rows of triangles became prominent in Hawaiian designs.

The people of the Marquesas Islands—an archipelago about 900 miles northeast of Tahiti—were the most extensively tattooed of all Polynesians. The process of tattooing involves shedding blood, the most *tapu* (sacred) substance in Polynesia. In the Marquesas, the process for a young man of high social rank began around age 18; by age 30 he would be fully tattooed (**FIG. 28–14**). Because of the sacredness and prestige of the process, some men continued to be tattooed until their skin was completely covered and the designs

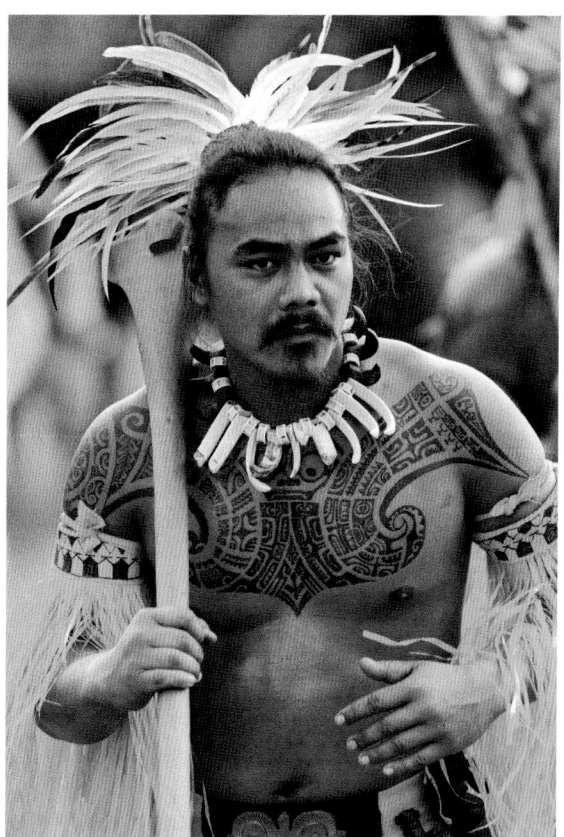

28–15 DANCER FROM THE MARQUESAS ART AND CULTURE FESTIVAL

2015. Ua Huka, Marquesas. Photo: Lionel Gouverneur.

Credit: Photographer Lionel Gouverneur

28–14 TATTOOED NATIVE OF NUKAHIVA

Plate 10 in A. J. von Krusenstern's *Voyage Round the World in the Years 1803, 1804, 1805, 1806, ...* 1813. Richard Belgrave Hoppner (trans.). London: J. Murray.

Credit: © The British Library Board (981.i.8 frontispiece)

disappeared. Marquesan women were also tattooed, usually on the hands, ankles, lips, and behind the ears.

Tattooing was painful and expensive. Though women could be tattooed with little ceremony in their own homes, in the case of both men and women of high rank, special houses were built for the occasion. The master tattooer and his assistants had to be fed and paid, and at the end of the session a special feast was held to display the new tattoos. Each design had a name and a meaning. Tattooing marked passages in people's lives and their social positions; it commemorated special events or accomplishments. Some tattoos denoted particular men's societies or eating groups. Especially for men, tattoos demonstrated courage and were essential to their sexual attractiveness.

Tattooing was forbidden in the nineteenth century by French colonial administrators and Catholic missionaries, and it died out in the Marquesas. Beginning in the 1970s, however, there was a resurgence of the art throughout the Pacific, and in 1980 Teve Tupuhia became the first Marquesan in modern times to be fully tattooed. Marquesans quickly reclaimed their tattoo heritage as a mark of identity and pride in their culture (**FIG. 28–15**). Because of the beauty and complexity of contemporary Marquesan-style tattoo designs, they are seen today throughout French Polynesia.

Hawaii, Rapa Nui, Samoa

FEATHER CLOAK FROM HAWAII   The Hawaiian islanders had one of the most highly stratified of all Polynesian societies, with valleys and whole islands ruled by high chiefs. Soon after contact with the West, the entire archipelago was unified for the first time under the rule of Kamehameha I (ruled 1810–1819), who assumed the title of king in the European manner.

Among the members of the Hawaiian elite, feathered capes and cloaks were emblems of high social status. A full-length cloak made with thousands of red and yellow feathers (**FIG. 28-16**) was reserved for the highest ranks of the elite men and called an *'ahu 'ula* ("red cloak")—the color red is associated with high status and rank throughout Polynesia. Often given as gifts to important visitors to Hawaii, this particular cloak was presented in 1843 to Commodore Lawrence Kearny, commander of the USS *Constellation*, by King Kamehameha III (ruled 1825–1854).

Draped over the wearer's shoulders, such a cloak creates a sensuously textured and colored abstract design, which in this example joins to create matching patterns of paired crescents on front and back. The cloak's foundation consisted of coconut fiber netting onto which were tied bundles of feathers. The red, and especially the yellow, feathers were highly prized and came from several species of birds including the *i'iwi, apapane, 'o'o,* and *mamo* (which is now extinct). In some cases, each bird yielded only seven or eight feathers, making the collecting of feathers very labor-intensive and increasing the value of the cloaks.

Cloaks were so closely associated with the spiritual power (*mana*) of the elite person that they could be made only by specialists trained in both the complicated technique of manufacture and the rituals attending their fabrication. Surrounded by protective objects, they created the cloak while reciting the chief's genealogy to imbue it with the power of his ancestors. As a result, the cloaks were seen as protective of the wearer, while also proclaiming his elite status and political and economic power.

Feathers were also used for decorating helmets, capes, blankets, and garlands (*leis*), all of which conferred status and prestige. The annual tribute paid to the king by his subjects included feathers, and tall feather pompons (*kahili*) mounted on long slender sticks were symbols of royalty. Even the effigies of gods that Hawaiian warriors carried into battle were made of light, basketlike structures covered with feathers.

MONUMENTAL MOAI ON RAPA NUI   Rapa Nui (Easter Island) is the most isolated inhabited locale in Oceania, located 2,300 miles west of the coast of South America and 1,200 miles from Pitcairn Island, the nearest Polynesian outpost. Three volcanoes, one at each corner, make up the small triangular island. Originally known to its native inhabitants as Te Pito o te Henúa ("Navel of the World") and now known as Rapa Nui, it was named Easter Island by Captain Jacob Roggeveen, the Dutch explorer who first landed there on Easter Sunday in 1722. Rapa Nui became part of Chile in 1888.

Rapa Nui is the site of Polynesia's most impressive stone sculpture. Though many imaginative theories have been posited regarding the origins of its statues—from space aliens to Native Americans—they are definitely part of an established Polynesian tradition. Sacred religious sites (*marae*) with stone altar platforms (*ahu*) are common throughout Polynesia. On Rapa Nui the Polynesians who arrived at the island in canoes between 800 and 1200 CE built most of the *ahu* near the coast, parallel

28-16 FEATHER CLOAK (KNOWN AS THE KEARNY CLOAK)
Hawaii. c. 1843. Red, yellow, and black feathers, olona cordage, and netting; length 55¾" (143 cm). Bishop Museum, Honolulu.

King Kamehameha III (ruled 1825–1854) presented this cloak to Commodore Lawrence Kearny, commander of the frigate USS *Constellation*.

28-17 MOAI ANCESTOR FIGURES

Ahu Nau Nau, Rapa Nui (Easter Island). c. 1000?–1500 CE, restored 1978. Volcanic stone (tufa), average height approx. 36′ (11 m).

Credit: © Shin/ Shutterstock

to the shore, and began to erect stone figures on them, perhaps as memorials to deceased chiefs or ancestors. Nearly 1,000 of these figures, called **moai**, have been found on the island, including some 400 unfinished ones in the quarry at Rano Raraku where they were being carved. The statues themselves are made from yellowish-brown volcanic tuff. On their heads, *pukao* (topknots of hair) were rendered in red scoria, another volcanic stone. When the statues were in place, the insertion of white coral and stone "opened" the eyes. In 1978, several figures on Ahu Nau Nau (**FIG. 28-17**) were restored to their original condition. These are about 36 feet tall, but *moai* range in size from much smaller to a 65-foot statue that is still in the quarry. A recent theory proposes that the completed *moai* were "walked" up to 11 miles from the quarry to the sites of the *anu* as handlers rocked them from side to side using attached ropes. The fragmentary remains of statues, which line the road away from the quarry, indicate that not all *moai* completed the journey.

Like other Polynesian statues, the *moai* face frontally. Their large heads have deep-set eyes under a prominent brow ridge; a long, concave, pointed nose; a small mouth with pursed lips; and an angular chin. The extremely elongated earlobes have parallel engraved lines that suggest ear ornaments. The figures have schematically indicated breastbones and pectorals, and small arms with hands pressed close to the sides. Since their bodies emerge from the ground at just below waist level, they have no legs.

The island's indigenous population, which has been estimated at 3,000 people when the Dutch arrived in 1722, was nearly eradicated in 1877 when Peruvian slave traders set off an epidemic of smallpox and tuberculosis that left only 110 inhabitants alive. Today, a vibrant population of some 5,000 people is known especially for its energetic and athletic dance performances and thrives primarily on tourism.

TAPA (SIAPO) IN SAMOA   As they migrated across the Pacific, Polynesians brought with them the production of bark cloth. Known by various names throughout the Pacific, most commonly as **tapa**, in Samoa bark cloth is called **siapo**. It is usually made by women, although sometimes men help obtain the bark or decorate the completed cloth. In Samoa, *siapo* is made by stripping the inner bark from branches of the paper mulberry tree (banyan and breadfruit are sometimes used in other archipelagos). The bark is beaten with a wooden mallet, then folded over and beaten again, to various degrees of softness. Larger pieces can be made by building up the cloth in a process of felting or by using natural pastes as glue. The heavy wooden mallets used for beating the cloth are often incised with complex patterns, which leave impressions like watermarks in the cloth, viewable when held up to the light.

28–18 TAPA (SIAPO VALA)
Samoa, 20th century. 58⅝ × 57" (149 × 145 cm). Auckland Museum, New Zealand. (AM 46892).

Credit: Photo: Krzysztof Pfeiffer, Auckland Museum

Plain and decorated *tapa* of various thicknesses and qualities was used throughout Polynesia for clothing, sails, mats, and ceremonial purposes, including wrapping the dead. *Tapa* was also used to cover wooden or wicker frames to make human effigies in the Marquesas and Rapa Nui, serving a purpose we still do not completely understand. In western Polynesia (Samoa and Tonga), very large pieces, 7–10 feet across and hundreds of feet long, were traditionally given in ceremonial exchanges of valuables and as gifts. Along with fine mats, *siapo* is still sometimes given on important ceremonial occasions. And *tapa* was widely used for clothing. Samoan men and women wore large pieces of *siapo* as wraparound skirts (*lavalava*) (SEE FIG. 28-19). Special chiefs, called talking chiefs, who spoke on behalf of the highest-ranking chief in the village council, wore special *tapa* skirts called *siapo vala* (FIG. 28-18).

Distinctive design styles for *tapa* evolved across the Pacific, even when the cloth used was essentially the same from one island to the next. It could be dyed bright yellow with turmeric or brown with dyes made from nuts. It could also be exposed to smoke to turn it black or darker brown. Today, contemporary fabric paint is often used. Decorative designs were made through a variety of means from freehand painting to printing with tiny bamboo stamps or using stencils, as is done in Fiji. This Samoan *siapo vala* has designs that were produced by first placing the cloth over a wooden design tablet, an **upeti**, and then rubbing pigment over the cloth to pick up the carved pattern. Subsequently, this lighter rubbed pattern was overpainted by hand. The result is a boldly patterned, symmetrical design.

Recent Art in Oceania

What are some recent developments in the art of Oceania?

In the late 1960s and early 1970s, a cultural resurgence swept across the Pacific. Growing independence and autonomy throughout the region, the model of civil rights and other movements in the United States, and dramatic increases in tourism, among other factors, brought a new awareness of the importance of indigenous cultures. Many of them had been fundamentally changed, if not nearly destroyed, by colonial rule and missionary efforts to eradicate local customs and beliefs.

Festival of Pacific Arts

In the early 1970s, the South Pacific Commission conceived the idea of an arts festival that would promote traditional song and dance. The first Festival of Pacific Arts was held in 1972 in Fiji; subsequent festivals, held every four years, have been hosted by New Zealand, Papua New Guinea, Tahiti, Australia, the Cook Islands, Samoa, New Caledonia, Palau, and American Samoa.

Musicians from the highlands of Papua New Guinea (FIG. 28-19) were among the more than 2,000 participants from 27 countries at the tenth festival at Pago Pago, American Samoa, in 2008. Carrying traditional drums, they wore elaborate headdresses topped with bird of paradise feathers and neck ornaments made from kina shells, a once valuable medium of exchange in New Guinea.

In the decades since their founding, the festivals have had an enormous impact on the arts. Many Pacific cultures now have their own festivals; in the Marquesas Islands one is held every four years. In an age of globalization and the Internet, festivals are one of the main ways in which young people become involved in and learn about their culture and heritage. However, the festivals are not without controversy: Some people are critical of an increasing level of professionalism and commercialism.

Central Desert Painting

In Australia, indigenous artists have adopted canvas and acrylic paint for rendering imagery traditionally associated with more ephemeral media like body and sand drawing. Sand drawing is an ancient ritual art form that involves creating large colored designs on bare earth. Made with red and yellow ochers, seeds, and feathers arranged on the ground in symbolic patterns, they are used to convey tribal knowledge to initiates. In 1971, several indigenous Pintubi men living in government-controlled Papunya Tula in the Central Desert of Australia who were trained and initiated in sacred knowledge were encouraged by a non-indigenous art teacher to transform their ephemeral art into a

28–19 MUSICIANS FROM PAPUA NEW GUINEA AT THE FESTIVAL OF PACIFIC ARTS

Pago Pago, American Samoa, 2008.

Credit: Photo: Caroline Yacoe

painted mural on the school wall. The success of the public mural encouraged community elders to allow others to try their hand at painting. In Utopia, a neighboring community, it was the women who began painting in 1988 after success in tie-dyeing with fabrics. Starting in Alice Springs, art galleries spread the art form, and "dot paintings" were a worldwide phenomenon by the late 1980s. Paintings became an economic mainstay for many Indigenous Australian groups in the central and western Australia desert. Although the artists are creating work for sale, they can paint only stories to which they have earned rights and must be careful to depict only what a non-initiated person is allowed to know.

Clifford Possum Tjapaltjarri (c. 1932–2002), a founder of the Papunya Tula Artists Cooperative in 1972, gained an international reputation after a 1988 exhibition of his paintings. He worked with his canvases on the floor, as in traditional sand painting, using ancient patterns and colors, principally red and yellow, as well as touches of blue. The superimposed layers of concentric circles and undulating lines and dots in a painting like *Man's Love Story* (see "Closer Look" on page 892) create an effect of shifting colors and lights that was highly valued in the global art world.

The painting seems entirely abstract, but it actually conveys a narrative involving two mythical ancestors. One of these ancestors—represented by the white U shape on the left, seated in front of a water hole with an ants' nest indicated by concentric circles—came to Papunya in search of honey ants. His digging stick lies to his right, and white sugary leaves to his left. The straight white "journey line" represents his trek from the west. The second ancestor—represented by the brown-and-white U-shaped

form—came from the east, leaving footprints, and sat down by another water hole nearby. He began to spin a hair string on a spindle (the form leaning toward the upper right of the painting), but was distracted by thoughts of the woman he loved, who belonged to a kinship group into which he could not marry. When she approached, he let his hair string blow away (represented by the brown flecks below him) and lost all his work. Four women (the dotted U shapes) came at night and surrounded the camp to guard the lovers. Symbolism also fills other areas of the painting: the white footprints are those of another ancestral figure following a woman, and the wavy line at the top is the path of yet another ancestor. The black, dotted oval area indicates the site where young men were taught this story. The long horizontal bars are mirages, while the wiggly shapes represent caterpillars, a source of food. Possum Tjapaltjarri painted numerous variations of this Dreaming story.

The painting is effectively a map showing the ancestors' journeys. To begin the work Possum Tjapaltjarri first painted the landscape features and the impressions left on the earth by the figures—their tracks, direction lines, and the U-shaped marks they left when sitting. Then, working carefully, dot by dot, he captured the vast expanse and shimmering light of the arid landscape. The painting's resemblance to modern Western painting styles such as Abstract Expressionism, gestural painting, Pointillism, or color field painting (see Chapters 31 and 32) is coincidental. Possum Tjapaltjarri's work is rooted in the mythic narratives of the Dreaming. It serves as a model for other contemporary indigenous artists, who use both age-old and new media to express the deepest meanings of their culture.

A Closer Look

MAN'S LOVE STORY

Designs may have multiple meanings. A circle can represent a water hole or ant hole, as here, but also a hole where the ancestral Spirit Beings exited and entered the earth, a person viewed from above, or a campfire.

Honey ants are a sweet delicacy. A digging stick is used to open up the nest, exposing the ant colony so that the ants can be removed and eaten.

Hair is spun into string using a spindle that is rotated across the thigh. The string is surprisingly strong and was used for utilitarian and ceremonial purposes, depending on the region.

Acrylic paint replaces the earth-toned ochers used in the sand paintings that provide the model for paintings such as this.

Women are important figures in the Dreaming stories and are represented in several places in this painting. Indigenous women artists paint their own stories, too, which usually center on food and food gathering.

The dots are made using a stick with a round, flat end that is dipped into the paint. Several people can work at the same time to fill in dotted areas.

28–20 Clifford Possum Tjapaltjarri **MAN'S LOVE STORY**
1978. Synthetic polymer paint on canvas, 6′11¾″ × 8′4¼″ (2.15 × 2.57 m). Art Gallery of South Australia, Adelaide. Visual Arts Board of the Australia Council Contemporary Art Purchase Grant, 1980.

Credit: © Estate of the artist 2016, licensed by Aboriginal Artists Agency Ltd

Shigeyuki Kihara

Many contemporary Pacific artists live in urban settings, were trained at colleges and universities, and create artworks in modern media that deal with a range of political issues, including the colonial legacy, discrimination, misappropriation, cultural identity, and land rights.

Shigeyuki Kihara is a multimedia and performance artist of Samoan and Japanese descent who lives in New Zealand. In **ULUGALI'I SAMOA: SAMOAN COUPLE** (**FIG. 28–21**), she explores culture, stereotypes, authenticity, and gender roles through a reappropriation of nineteenth- and early twentieth-century colonial photographs. Made in studio settings, colonial photographs were often turned into postcards depicting Pacific island men and women, both alone and in couples, the women as bare-breasted and sexualized "dusky maidens" and the men as emasculated "noble savages." Kihara confronts these stereotyped images in carefully staged, sepia-toned photographs that, through ironic twists, also challenge the viewer's understanding of gender and gender roles.

In this photograph of a male and female couple both figures are clothed as they might have been in the nineteenth century, wearing large pieces of Samoan bark cloth (SEE FIG. 28-18), and holding traditional Samoan status objects—a plaited fan and a fly-whisk. Kihara herself poses as the native woman, but has also superimposed her own face, with wig and mustache, onto the body of the male figure. *Ulugali'i Samoa: Samoan Couple* is part of a series of photographs called "Fa'a fafine: In a Manner of a Woman." *Fa'a fafine* is the Samoan term for a biological male who lives as a woman, the "third gender" socially accepted historically throughout much of Polynesia (as in the Americas, see FIG. 27-24). Kihara is herself *fa'a fafine*, a transgender woman who lives and identifies in that gender role. In this photograph and the others in the series, she blurs stereotyped notions of who or what is male or female, original or copy, reality or perception. This work was part of the exhibition "Shigeyuki Kihara: Living Photographs," the first solo exhibition by a Samoan in the Metropolitan Museum of Art in New York. Her work and that of other urban artists draws on the richness of Pacific cultures while addressing global issues of the twenty-first century.

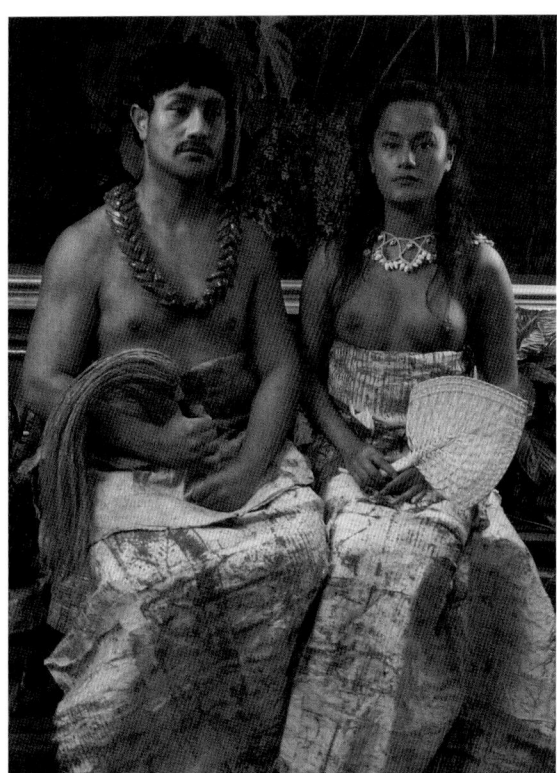

28-21 Shigeyuki Kihara **ULUGALI'I SAMOA: SAMOAN COUPLE**

2004–2005. C-type photograph, edition of 5, 31½ × 23⅗" (80 × 60 cm). Metropolitan Museum of Art, New York.

Gift of Shigeyuki Kihara, 2009.

Credit: © 2016. Image copyright The Metropolitan Museum of Art/Art Resource/Scala, Florence

---

Think About It

1   Explain how differences in environment, including available resources, affect the nature of the visual arts in the Pacific. Include architectural forms and body adornment in your answer.

2   How is the human body adorned and/or depicted in art across the Pacific? How do these adornments and depictions define or enhance status, authority, and gender roles?

3   Assess the importance of ancestors and the different ways in which they are engaged, honored, or invoked through various Pacific art forms. Focus your answer on two works from two different cultural and geographic settings.

4   Discuss the impact of contact with Western society on the arts and cultures of the peoples of the Pacific. How are contemporary indigenous artists throughout the Pacific addressing the issues of their own time and place?

Crosscurrents

The production of fabric was an important aspect of the cultures of both Peru and Samoa. Although there are strong similarities in the designs of these two cloths, their style, media, and context of production are distinct in significant ways. Discuss these differences and how they relate to the cultural values and distinctive environments of the artists who made them and the societies that valued them.

FIG. 27-10

FIG. 28-18

29–1 Amir Nour **GRAZING AT SHENDI**

1969. Steel, 202 pieces. Collection of the artist.

Credit: © Amir Nour

Chapter 29
Arts of Africa from the Sixteenth Century to the Present

 ## Learning Objectives

29.a Identify the visual hallmarks of post-1500 African art in its distinct cultures for formal, technical, and expressive qualities.

29.b Interpret the meaning of works of post-1500 African art in their distinct cultures based on their themes, subjects, and symbols.

29.c Relate African artists and art after 1500 to their distinct cultural, economic, and political contexts.

29.d Apply the vocabulary and concepts relevant to post-1500 African art, artists, and art history.

29.e Interpret a work of African art after 1500 using the art historical methods of observation, comparison, and inductive reasoning.

29.f Select visual and textual evidence in various media to support an argument or an interpretation of a work of African art after 1500.

Sudanese sculptor Amir Nour (b. 1939) works with metal and stone materials that are frequently industrially made to his specifications. His objects sit directly on the ground, often in **site-specific** locations, and as a result, they engage directly with both their setting and the audience—no pedestal, barrier, or other staging device separates them from the viewer. **GRAZING AT SHENDI** (1969), his best-known work (**FIG. 29–1**), is composed of 202 bent stainless steel tubes of varying sizes. When arranged on the ground in a group, they form an abstract image of herd animals grazing in the fields. Shendi, a farming town and trade center in Sudan, is located not far from the famous pyramids at Meroë (see Chapter 14). Nour grew up in Shendi, and this sculpture speaks to both his observations of animals grazing in the town of his birth and to a greater global perspective. Trained as an artist and art historian in London, the United States, and Scotland, Nour's education allows him to see his own work as participating in more than just African art history and art making. In *Grazing at Shendi*, he displays his virtuosity with techniques used by artists of the Minimalist movement in the United States in the 1960s and 70s (see Chapter 33) as well as the international projects of conceptualism and Postmodernism. Nour epitomizes the artistic choices of many artists of African descent working today. Globally educated and historically motivated, they see their work as interrogating the complex histories of the continent and countries of their birth.

Arguably, since the sixteenth century these histories of Africa and the art they produced have dramatically impacted world art history: One cannot tell the story of art without them.

The Sixteenth through Twentieth Centuries: Royal Arts and Architecture

What are the key concepts of African art after 1500, and how do art objects participate in royal activities in early modern African architecture and sculpture?

The continent of Africa is the second largest in the world (**MAP 29–1**). More than 2,000 African languages have been identified, and an even greater number of distinct cultural groups call the continent home. With this kind of linguistic and cultural diversity, it is impossible to easily summarize four centuries of African culture and creativity, as well as their connectivity to one another and to the global world.

This chapter traces some important moments in African art history, from royal arts of the sixteenth century through the colonial period, which dramatically reshaped art making across the continent. Also considered are examples of postcolonial and contemporary art, which frequently involve techniques, technologies, and materials that are both African and global in reach.

MAP 29-1 POLITICAL MAP OF AFRICA IN 2015

The vast continent of Africa is home to 54 internationally recognized countries, each of which is home to multiple cultural and ethnic groups with their own linguistic and religious practices.

Key Concepts

This chapter focuses on four key concepts that permeate African art from the sixteenth century to the present day.

PARTICIPATION   More so than in European art, African art objects are intended to be part of human activities. Seldom is one meant to simply look at or contemplate them from a distance. They are meant to physically participate in human aesthetic events. They are frequently portable and can be changed or altered depending on the circumstances of their use.

CONTEMPORANEITY   Art objects not made for museum or gallery display are often made for temporary use, either to be part of a particular ceremony or masquerade or to serve a single town or individual. When the

ceremony is over or the user no longer needs the object, it can be discarded or reworked. Old and worn-out objects are far less desirable than newly made ones. In this way, art objects are always "contemporary" or new. They keep up with the times, and innovation is always prized in the creation of a new variation on a favorite object.

ABSTRACTION   From the Renaissance through the nineteenth century, European artists strove to emulate nature or to idealize the world around them in their arts. Artists in Africa during this time took a very different trajectory. Their objects were not made to describe or imitate anything (or anyone) in the real world. Rather, African artists were aiming to convey intangible or non-visual ideas with their objects, such as modesty, justice, or the abuse of political power. Artists were often expected to depict individuals as part human and part supernatural (as ancestors, deities, or spirits). This chapter explains how African artists have taken these conceptual ideas and given them physical form. Often the resulting work is far removed from what can be observed in the natural world.

CULTURAL FLUENCY African artists who work in African countries or who live and work elsewhere value their ability to function in multiple cultures at once. Given that African countries are some of the most linguistically and culturally diverse in the world, it is no wonder that the most skilled artists are those who can communicate with people from a variety of cultural backgrounds. Along with defining the cultural ideals of a particular group, art objects must also incorporate those ideals into relationships with others.

Art made for royal use in the sixteenth through twentieth centuries exhibits all of these traits. Wealthy kings and queens who ruled the Asante, Bamum, Edo, Kuba, and Yoruba kingdoms, to name but a few, commissioned dynamic works of art ranging from textiles, sculptures, decorated architectural palaces, and houses to personal items. Many of these items survive today because their unique combinations of abstraction and naturalism appealed not only to African rulers, but also to European collectors. They were often exchanged as gifts between African kings and their European counterparts, or else admired and collected by museum curators for the quality and diversity they brought to their art collections and the evolving understanding of global art history. In fact, the royal art objects produced during the eighteenth and nineteenth centuries are some of the best represented in the world's museums.

Ghana

The Republic of Ghana took its name from the ancient Ghana Empire that flourished during the fourth to thirteenth centuries in what is present-day Mali, far to the north of the country of Ghana. One of the shared traits between the ancient empire and the modern country is that both are situated over massive deposits of gold. This gold was used strategically in trade and certainly solidified the power of the Akan Empire, which divided the region into kingdoms during the thirteenth century. The most powerful of these was the Asante (formerly spelled Ashanti), who initially occupied the southern and coastal regions of the area and controlled a majority of the gold trade.

THE ASANTE EMPIRE By the eighteenth century, the Asante Empire stretched nearly the entirety of the contemporary country of Ghana. When the Portuguese first arrived along the coast of present-day Ghana in the 1470s, they were so impressed by the abundance of Asante gold mines they called the territory El Mina ("the Mine"). The contemporary city of Elmina on the coast of Ghana draws its name from the fifteenth-century Portuguese trading castle that was built there.

Until the kings of the Asante (called *Asantehene*) were forced into power sharing with the British beginning in the mid-1800s, they ruled from their capital city of Kumasi. After independence, the nation of Ghana recognized the Asante Empire as a traditional subnation state. Today the lineage of *Asantehene* continues, and the king still presides at the royal palace in Kumasi.

Asante royal households were famous during the eighteenth century for their prized **KENTE CLOTH** (**FIG. 29-2**)

29-2 KENTE CLOTH
Asante, c. 1980. Rayon, 10'3½" × 7'1½" (3.14 × 2.17 m). Fowler Museum of Cultural History, University of California in Los Angeles.

Credit: © Photo courtesy of the Fowler Museum at UCLA

and their wealth of sculptural objects, adornments, and ritual paraphernalia, all covered with or made entirely of gold. Not many early examples of **kente** fabric have survived over the centuries, for new ones were commissioned to replace older worn fabrics or to update the patterns to the newest styles.

Kente is a term derived from the Asante word for "basket," acknowledging the woven nature of the fabric. Asante weavers—traditionally men—work on double-heddle looms, allowing them to produce long, narrow strips of cloth with vertical stripes that alternate with horizontal bands and geometric patterns. The strips are then sewn together to form large rectangles of finished *kente* cloth. The strips are joined in such a way that their patterns do not exactly line up with each other. This is intentional, in order to make the finished fabric more dazzling and less predictable.

Kente was originally produced under royal control. Weaving guilds at Kumasi produced cloth exclusively for royal patrons. *Kente* cloth is still worn by the royal family and the *Asantehene* in Kumasi, although Ghanaians of all descent can now also wear it. It is very expensive and worn only on special occasions.

29-3 Attributed to Kojo Bonsu **FINIAL OF AN OKYEAME POMA (SPEAKER'S STAFF)**
Ghana. Asante, 1960s–70s. Wood and gold, height 11¼" (28.57 cm). Barbier-Muller Collection, Gold of Africa Museum, Cape Town, South Africa.

Along with royal *kente* cloth, the Asante used sculptural objects to identify those who held power and to validate their right to their authority. Expensive gold jewelry, royal staffs, and a ritual throne known as the Golden Stool represented the importance of the *Asantehene* to his community and communicated his authority to members of society. The Asante also greatly admire fine language and poetic speech. Consequently their governing system includes the special post of *okyeame*, or spokesman, for the *Asantehene*.

Whenever the *okyeame* for an Asante king was conferring with that ruler or announcing the ruler's words to an audience, he held a staff called an **OKYEAME POMA** to symbolize his authority to speak on behalf of the *Asantehene* (**FIG. 29-3**). This twentieth-century staff was made following traditions established at the inception of the Asante Empire. It is composed of a long, wooden pole with a sculpture covered in gold leaf on top. The sculpture, of a seated man holding an egg, enters into direct conversation with the *Asantehene* and his *okyeame* and participates in their shared rituals of rulership and speech. "Political power is like an egg," says an Asante proverb. "Grasp it too tightly and it will shatter in your hand; hold it too loosely and it will slip from your fingers." The sculptural imagery reminds the *Asantehene* and his *okyeame* to always speak carefully and refrain from abusing their political and social power.

Cameroon

In Cameroon, hundreds of city-states and small kingdoms existed during the sixteenth to twentieth centuries. The most dominant of these included the Bamileke, the Tikar, and the Bamum. Cameroon is also the ancestral home of the Bantu-speaking peoples who migrated southward and went on to become the dominant cultural group across the entirety of Africa south of the equator.

BAMUM KINGDOM The Bamum kingdom is based at the walled city of Fumban in the elevated grasslands region of what is now Northwestern Cameroon. It was founded by King Nchare in 1394 and, except for the period 1924–1933, has lasted uninterrupted until the present. In 1918, *Fon* (chief) Ibrahim Njoya came to power and led the Bamum in a period of wealth accumulation, advanced learning, and calculated interactions with German, then British, then French colonial powers. Njoya established a written script for the Bamum language in order to prove to colonial powers that his culture was not lacking in literature, history, and the written arts. He alternately practiced Christianity and Islam when it served him in his negotiations with the Germans, French, and North Africans, and was well known for variously adopting European colonial, Islamic, and traditional Bamum clothing as the political occasion warranted (**FIG. 29-4**). When his ancestral wooden palace burned in a fire, he and his son designed a new palace built in stone at Fumban. Njoya was an avid

29–4 KING NJOYA OF BAMUM IN THE UNIFORM OF AN OFFICER WITH HIS FATHER'S THRONE IN FRONT OF THE OLD PALACE AT FUMBAN

1906 photo from Basel Mission Archives, E-30.29.042. Beaded throne of King Nsangu, father of King Njoya. Bamum, Cameroon. Late 1880s.

The king stands next to his father's throne, which he gifted to Kaiser Wilhelm II in 1908.

supporter of all arts, and Bamum sculptures and beadwork became world famous under his rule. He went on to declare himself Sultan, in lieu of the historical title of *Fon*, and his heirs have continued this tradition. Njoya was deposed by the French in 1924 and exiled in 1931 under the pretense that he was a threat to French authority. He passed away in 1933, and today, his grandson Sultan Ibrahim Mbombo Njoya rules the Bamum kingdom from Fumban.

In this 1906 photograph, King Njoya stands next to his father's beaded throne wearing what is clearly a German officer's outfit. The photograph documents a truly significant event in Bamum and German history, one that also exemplifies the impressive level of cultural fluency achieved by Bamum artists. Captain Hans Ramsey, an administrator for a German trading company, had traveled to Fumban for the first time in 1902 in the hopes of expanding German trade farther inland. In all his written records,

we can see he was captivated by Njoya and impressed with the beauty of the palace's architecture and the organization and power of the kingdom. After several trade negotiations were worked out, Ramsey asked Njoya if he would consider giving a gift to the Kaiser of Germany, from one king to another. Ramsey wanted Njoya's beaded throne, a monumental, multipart work that Njoya had inherited from his father, King Nsangu, who had commissioned it in the late 1880s. In this photograph, Njoya shows off the handsome throne, carved in wood and entirely covered in brightly colored seed beads acquired from European trade. On the back of the throne is a standing ancestral couple. When Nsangu (and later Njoya) was seated on this throne, this gave the effect of the ancestors looking over his shoulders as he ruled and passed judgments. The footrest depicts two attendants carrying guns; the king would rest his feet upon the barrels of the guns, showing that military might literally rested under his feet.

Njoya consented to give the royal ancestral throne to the Kaiser, but only after Ramsey offered to pay for a new throne to be carved and beaded for Njoya and gave him a German officer's uniform, complete with pith helmet and saber—which Njoya is wearing in this official photograph. Njoya's new throne, finished in 1912, is still at the palace of Fumban, while Nsangu's throne, along with many other smaller beaded stools and thrones that Njoya gave as gifts to the German Kaiser, eventually made its way to the Ethnographic Museum (now the Staatliche Museen) in Berlin. Njoya remained a key ally for the Germans until their defeat in World War I, when the German colony of Kamerun was ceded to the French and renamed Cameroon.

After the French sent Njoya into exile for challenging their authority in the region, his son Seidou Njimouluh Njoya was able to ascend the throne at Fumban. He continued much of his father's work in support of the arts, literature, and culture. The Bamum kingdom today is recognized as a semi-autonomous political entity within the nation of Cameroon.

Democratic Republic of the Congo

The earliest of the powerful kingdoms along the Congo River and its tributaries (today encompassed by the Republic of the Congo, the Democratic Republic of the Congo [DRC] and Angola) was the Kongo kingdom founded at the turn of the fourteenth century. A century later the powerful Luba and Lunda kingdoms emerged in the DRC, followed by the Kuba kingdom in the early 1600s. All were founded by Bantu speakers from the north and spoke variations of Bantu languages. They shared similar religious and political structures, although they often clashed over control of significant river trade routes.

KUBA KINGDOM The Kuba people—more properly called Bakuba, given the nature of their Bantu language

29-5 SLEEPING HOUSE OF THE NYIM
Royal Compound at Nsheng, Democratic Republic of the Congo. 1980.
Credit: Photo: Angelo Turconi

structure—live near the geographic center of the Democratic Republic of the Congo. In the seventeenth and eighteenth centuries, their kingdom was an artistic powerhouse in the region. Kuba sculptures, textiles, and luxury domestic goods were reserved for royal use locally, but could be sold or traded outside of the kingdom with those willing to pay the very high price required for their manufacture.

The Kuba king, or *nyim*, ruled from his royal compound, which was composed of multiple highly ornamented buildings to house all the functions required of an elite political and religious government system. Of these buildings, the *nyim's* sleeping house was one of the most spectacularly decorated (**FIG. 29-5**). The structure itself is not elaborate: a rectangular building made of wood and palm canes with a thatched gable roof. The exterior, however, is decorated in its entirety. Palm fronds attach reeds to the façade, creating geometric interlocking patterns of diamonds created by right-angled "streets." A border of contrasting natural and dyed palm fronds creates honeycomb patterns along the ridgeline, corners, and tops and sides of the walls. The patterns are similar to the woven diamonds and "streets" seen on the Kongo textile in Chapter 14 (SEE FIG. 14-19) because the two neighboring kingdoms shared many religious and aesthetic values.

The interlocking diamond patterns on the *nyim's* sleeping house are also found on the base of this wooden commemorative portrait (**FIG. 29-6**), called an **ndop**—a Kuba word meaning "portrait statue." The patterns are associated with royalty, so it is very appropriate that they appear on all the *nyim's* possessions. Kuba *nyim* often had their portraits sculpted, not to commemorate how they looked in real life, but rather to show how they conducted themselves in the role of king. This particular portrait depicts the *nyim* Mishe miShyaang maMbul, who reigned during the mid-eighteenth century. The facial features are remarkably similar to those of many other *ndop* produced of Kuba *nyim*, stressing the importance of the office as ongoing, even though its power would pass from man to man. The forehead is high and rounded and the facial expression still, with the body carved smoothly and to a smaller scale than the head. All *ndop* show the king seated cross-legged

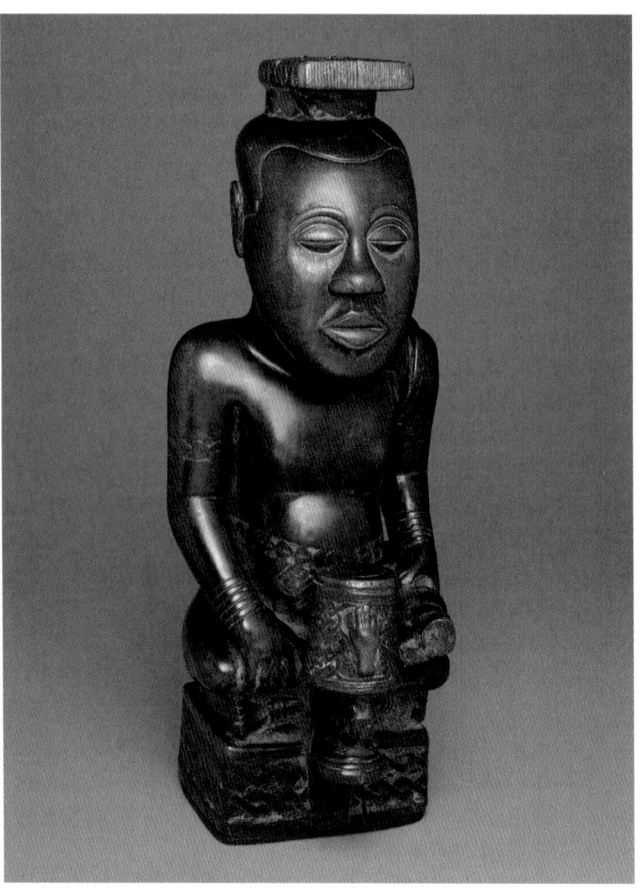

29-6 NDOP PORTRAIT OF KING MISHE MISHYAANG MAMBUL
Kuba. c. 1760–80. Wood, camwood powder, 19½ × 7⅝ × 8⅝″ (49.5 × 19.4 × 21.9 cm). Lulua Province (Democratic Republic of the Congo). Brooklyn Museum, New York.

and holding the regalia of his office (a staff, belt, armbands and bracelets). In fact the only way to identify this sculpture as the *ndop* of Mishe miShyaang maMbul is the symbol of an open hand placed on the side of the drum in front of him. This was his personal attribute, and anyone in his kingdom would have recognized it as his symbol. *Ndop* were used to commemorate kings while they lived, and they participated in his rule, for the sculptures were frequently placed near the king to absorb his power. Upon the king's death, the sculpture, now invested with the life force of its owner, was passed to the next king. Subsequent *nyim* spent time with the *ndop*, including keeping it in their sleeping house, in order to absorb the wisdom and spirit of the deceased king.

Nigeria

Along with the powerful Edo kingdom that ruled from its palace in Benin City, many Yoruba kingdoms are well known to history. Important palaces were constructed at the city-states of Ise, Ikere and Osi-Ilorin, to name but a few. The Yoruba people have been known throughout history as prolific carvers. Monumental sculptures, masquerade headpieces, and architectural sculptures such as columns and doors were masterfully worked in wood. Even today, Yoruba artists keep these traditional arts alive for wealthy kings, political leaders, and private patrons.

YORUBA Among the most important Yoruba artists of the early twentieth century was Olowe of Ise (c. 1873–1938), who carved doors and veranda posts for the rulers of the Ekiti-Yoruba kingdoms in southwestern Nigeria. His unique style of carving means that sculptural programs for several royal palaces can be attributed to him.

Olowe was a royal court carver for the kings of Ise and Ikere, both located to the east of the holy city of Ife and north of Benin City. His competitor was a sculptor named Arowogun, who worked around the same time for the kings at Osi-Ilorin to the north. These two artists are among a huge class of specialized artists who worked for the Yoruba kings in Nigeria in pre-colonial and colonial times. Olowe and Arowogun were more than just artists. Along with their fellow royal carvers, they depicted histories, lineages, important events, and rituals, all in the most unique, up-to-date styles possible so as to demonstrate the kings' prosperity and capacity for innovation.

Olowe worked on a large scale, doing entire design sequences for palaces at Ise and Ikere. One of his most well-known compositions is the figural column sequence for the veranda of the king's palace at Ikere. Olowe carved three massive columns, each from a single tree trunk, to support the roof of the veranda (**FIG. 29-7**). The left column as one faces the porch from the courtyard depicts a royal wife standing with her hands on top of her twin daughters' heads. The threesome faces sideways, in order to look at the central column, which shows the seated

Yoruba *arinjale* (king) of the city of Ikere with his senior wife standing behind him. The column on the right portrays an equestrian soldier who also faces the royal couple.

The columns were fully painted, but that paint is now largely faded. The queen was painted mostly in blue, a color the Yoruba associate with women and their female ancestors, while the king was done in red. Notice that the scale of the two figures on this central column is not proportional: The queen is much larger than her smaller, seated husband. Olowe uses this hierarchy of scale to show that even though the king is the ruler, he rules only with the help and guidance of others, particularly his female ancestors and his senior wife.

Olowe has also balanced this important column of the king and queen geometrically; the angle of the queen's jaw is picked up in the angle of her breasts, and then in the king's own jawline. These diagonals counterbalance the rigid horizontal lines of the seat of the king's throne and his bent legs. Vertical lines of the throne are repeated in

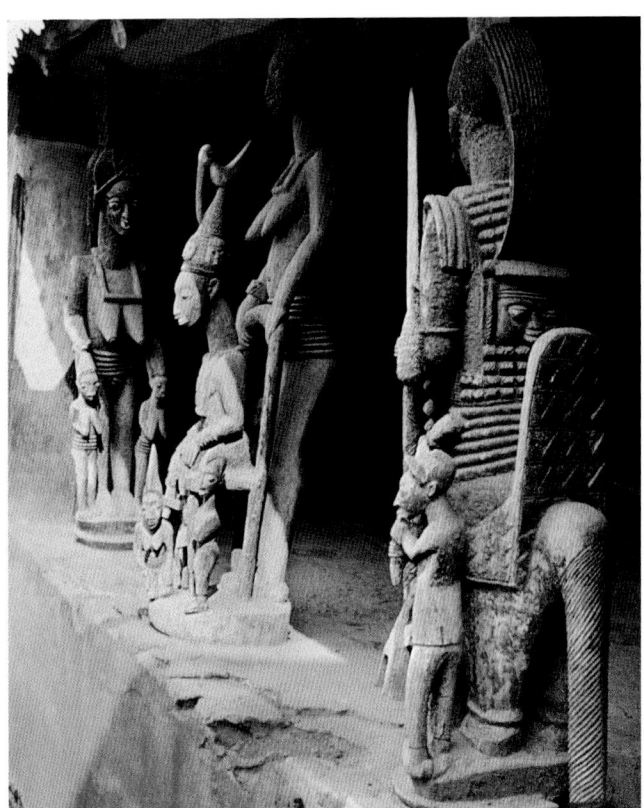

29-7 Olowe of Ise **VERANDA POSTS (LEFT TO RIGHT): ROYAL WIFE WITH TWIN DAUGHTERS, ENTHRONED KING AND SENIOR WIFE (OPO OGOGA), AND ROYAL WARRIOR ON HORSEBACK**

From the palace of the king of Ikere, Ekiti region, Nigeria. Yoruba, 1910/1914. Wood and pigment, 60 × 12½ × 16" (152.5 × 31.75 × 40.6 cm) each. Photograph 1964. Memorial Art Gallery, Rochester, New York, Marion Stratton Gould Fund (71.13) (royal wife); Art Institute of Chicago, Major Acquisitions Centennial Fund, 1984.550 (king and wife); and New Orleans Museum of Art museum purchase, Ella West Freeman Foundation Matching Fund (70.20) (royal warrior).

Credit: Photo: John Picton

the strict columnar forms of the queen's legs. The geometries give a sense of order, balance, strength, and calm—all desired attributes of a king. Furthermore, the king and queen, along with the soldier and royal wife at their sides, literally hold up the palace roof, symbolic of the way a king supports his community.

At the nearby palace at Ise, Olowe was commissioned to make a set of doors commemorating the *arinjale*'s reception of Major W. R. Reeve-Tucker, the first British traveling commissioner for the province, and his entourage (**FIG. 29-8**). This door panel depicts the Yoruba court as they welcome the British to the palace of Ise; a second door panel (not shown) presents the European entourage. The door is carved very deeply on a massive single plank of wood. Tall figures with bodies in profile turn their heads outward to confront the viewer. Their long necks and elaborate hairstyles make them appear even taller, unlike typical Yoruba sculpture, which until Olowe's time favored shorter figures. The relief is so high that the figures' upper portions are actually carved in the round. The figure of the *arinjale* on horseback, for example, has a body carved in the round, while his legs and the horse upon which he sits are done in relief. Olowe intended his viewers to understand that the more fully carved the figure, the more important he or she was in Yoruba royal society. Combining relief and sculpture-in-the-round in the same figure had not been done before; it is one of the attributes of Olowe's innovative style.

In the second register of this panel, the *arinjale* appears on horseback wearing a conical crown and accompanied by court messengers. Other registers contain other members of the court—royal wives lifting their breasts (a gesture of generosity and affection performed by older women), men carrying kegs of gunpowder, royal guards, and priests. The bottom register portrays a deceased person, perhaps a criminal, with birds (standing in for the ancestors, who mete out justice) pecking at the corpse. The two rows of heads on the left side of the panel may represent either ancestors of the king or enemies taken in battle. The entire surface of the doors was originally painted, but only traces of the original colors remain.

Olowe's sculptures for the *arinjale* of Ise and Ikere, among others, were emulated throughout the Yoruba kingdom. His style marked the art of his generation and he was renowned for his contemporary, cosmopolitan compositions and his ability to capture the abstract workings of political rule (interdependence on others, respect for tradition, and willingness to engage in new relations) in visual form. All of Olowe's surviving carved monuments are now in museum collections and are highly prized sculptural masterpieces.

29-8 Olowe of Ise **ONE OF TWO DOORS FROM THE KING'S PALACE AT ISE**
Nigeria. Yoruba, c. 1904–1910.
Wood and pigment, 81½ × 34⅝ × 6¼"
(207 × 88 × 15.9 cm). National Museum of African Art, Smithsonian Institution, Washington, DC. Gift of Dr. and Mrs Robert Kuhn (88-13-1).

Credit: Photo: Frank Khoury

The Nineteenth Century: Colonialism and Modernity

How do art and artists respond to the new conditions created by European colonialism?

Modernism and modernity in art history have usually been understood as European and North American, while colonialism was applied to Africa, and yet both concepts ought to be applied equally to both regions. Modernity on the African continent is defined through increasing urbanization, trade, travel, and war, which occurred in tandem with the continent's deepening entanglements with European nations. The synthesis of these dynamic changes created the burgeoning artistic production in African nations during the nineteenth century. Artists gained European patrons who desired "traditional" African objects for their collections, while local patrons needed new types of objects to negotiate the new political and social realities of their lives

under colonial rule. The arts of nineteenth-century Africa give visual form to Africans' merging and modern ties with Europe as a result of their colonial power struggles.

The Colonial Conquest

Early in the nineteenth century the trade in human slaves was becoming less profitable to European traders and was also under increasing moral attack from abolitionists in Great Britain. In an attempt to redirect their business to more profitable and less reprehensible activities, European explorers began to investigate the African interior, looking for ways to expand their control over natural and trade resources. They were joined by missionaries and eager anthropologists and adventurers, whose reports created even wider European interest in the continent.

THE BERLIN CONFERENCE OF 1884–1885 Drawn by the potential wealth of Africa's natural resources, European governments began to seek territorial concessions from African rulers. Diplomacy eventually gave way to force, and by the end of the nineteenth century, competition among rival European powers fueled the so-called Scramble for Africa, during which England, France, Germany, Belgium, Italy, Spain, and Portugal raced to lay claim to whatever part of the continent they could. This resulted in a conference called by German Chancellor Otto von Bismarck in 1884 where the European nations effectively divided up African territories among themselves (**MAP 29-2**). In many cases, the boundaries drawn up at this conference are still the active borders between countries today.

MAP 29-2 THE COLONIAL CONQUEST OF AFRICA

The political boundaries shown are those of 1914, resulting from the divisions created at the Berlin Conference of 1884–1885.

The borders between territories they devised had everything to do with the European desire to control resources and trade routes and nothing to do with cultural or political boundaries as they had been established by Africans themselves. As a result, unified ethnic groups often found themselves split into two or more partitions, unable to rule themselves with any autonomy and often unable to visit each other across the new colonial borders. The treaties signed at the Berlin Conference of 1884–1885 meant that by 1914 virtually all of Africa (except for Ethiopia and Liberia) had fallen under European colonial rule.

THE BRITISH PUNITIVE EXPEDITION OF 1897 As territory was taken under European control, vast quantities of art objects flowed into European city, state, national, and private collections due to expanding interest in cultural trade items. Objects also entered Western collections through conflict. The most infamous of these occurred in 1897 when a British delegation headed by the newly appointed Acting Council-General James Phillips

embarked on a mission to gain more favorable trade agreements with the *oba* (king) of the Edo people in Benin City, then located in the British protectorate of Nigeria. Outside the city walls, Philips was told he could not enter the city or meet with the king without permission granted in advance. Phillips refused to leave, and the *oba*'s warrior chiefs defended their king by attacking the British delegation, killing all but two of them.

To retaliate for the Benin City attack, the British organized an expedition that destroyed much of Benin City; the *oba* was imprisoned and the royal palace stripped of all valuables and then burned to the ground (**FIG. 29–9**). The British Punitive Expedition of 1897 resulted in the seizure of over 2,000 objects, including Edo antiquities, royal shrine sculptures, carved ivory tusks, brass palace plaques, and vast quantities of jewelry and royal body adornment—nearly the entire store of artifacts from the royal palace. The objects taken by the British were brought to England. After the customary third was given to Queen Victoria, the rest were auctioned. These objects are now

29–9 MEMBERS OF THE BRITISH PUNITIVE EXPEDITION TO BENIN CITY

Seen in the Royal Palace with objects from the *oba's* treasury. 1897 photograph.

All of these items were subsequently taken to England. The jugs at the soldiers' feet are filled with palm oil, the subject of the trade agreement desired by the British when they were refused entry to the city by the *oba's* royal guards. The three brass standing figures and the brass leopard in the foreground (along with the ivory leopard sculpture at the left, cut off by the frame of the photo) can now be seen at the British Museum.

29-10 BENIN CITY PALACE ANCESTRAL ALTAR DEDICATED TO OBA OVONRAMWEN

Benin City, Nigeria c.1959. Image no. EEPA EECL 7584. Eliot Elisofon Photographic Archives, National Museum of African Art, Smithsonian Institution, Washington, DC.

Credit: Photograph by Eliot Elisofon 1959

dispersed in museums and private collections throughout the world. Visible in the foreground of this photograph are three standing figures cast in brass, along with the *oba*'s bronze stool decorated with frogs, a brass leopard, and the back of an ivory leopard with copper disks forming the spots. These sculptures, along with several of the carved ivory tusks, are now in the British Museum in London.

As part of the 1897 Punitive Expedition, the British exiled the city's *oba*, Ovonramwen, to the city of Calabar, and the Edo had no formal state recognition until the restoration of the Benin monarchy in 1914. The newly instated *oba* Enweka II commissioned new ancestral altar shrines, as the previous ones had been dismantled and taken by the British (**FIG. 29-10**). This altar, complete with copies of the traditional brass, ivory, and coral objects that would have been on the original, is dedicated to Enweka II's father, Ovonramwen, who died in exile.

Both the Edo kingdom at Benin City and the nation of Nigeria have pressured the British government to return items taken from Benin City during the 1897 Punitive Expedition, but no decision has been reached as to whether the brass plaques will be returned to the palace walls in Benin City. In the meantime, the kingdom has continued to rebuild and resurrect the art objects that were taken or destroyed by the British.

Modern Objects

The colonial experience spurred the creation of modern objects that responded to the new conditions of life and society on the African continent. In the best of circumstances, artists gained new appreciative patrons in the European residents of their continent, and wealth gained

from doing business with Europeans increased for the few willing to cooperate with European law and political control. The Europeans also introduced the idea of the art object as an object simply for aesthetic appreciation, not for actual use. Once artists understood that their European buyers had no interest in using an object in any purposeful ritual or sacred manner, they modified objects for these buyers to be larger and more decorative than the ones they made for local use. This in turn inspired local African buyers to buy these new variations themselves to show off their financial means and their cosmopolitan awareness of the international value of their culture's art objects. One sculpture that may have been created and purchased in this manner is a **LIDDED VESSEL** from South Africa (**FIG. 29-11**).

The vessel is almost 25 inches tall, much larger than earlier wooden containers with lids, and is carved with deep, parallel grooves over the entire surface. Unlike other carved patterns we have seen that have royal or religious meaning, these grooves appear to have been done purely for the visual effect, as well as for the tactile pleasure they would have given to those who handled the vessel. The entire object was carved from a single piece of wood, making the four handles and the ring that joins them particularly remarkable and difficult to produce. Analysis of the inside of the vessel revealed that it had never been used to hold anything (no traces of foods or liquids were found), and therefore was most likely to have been carved as a display item. We do not know if the patron who purchased the sculpture was European or African, but the fact that it was used for visual appreciation certainly demonstrates the European influence on how art objects were understood in the nineteenth century.

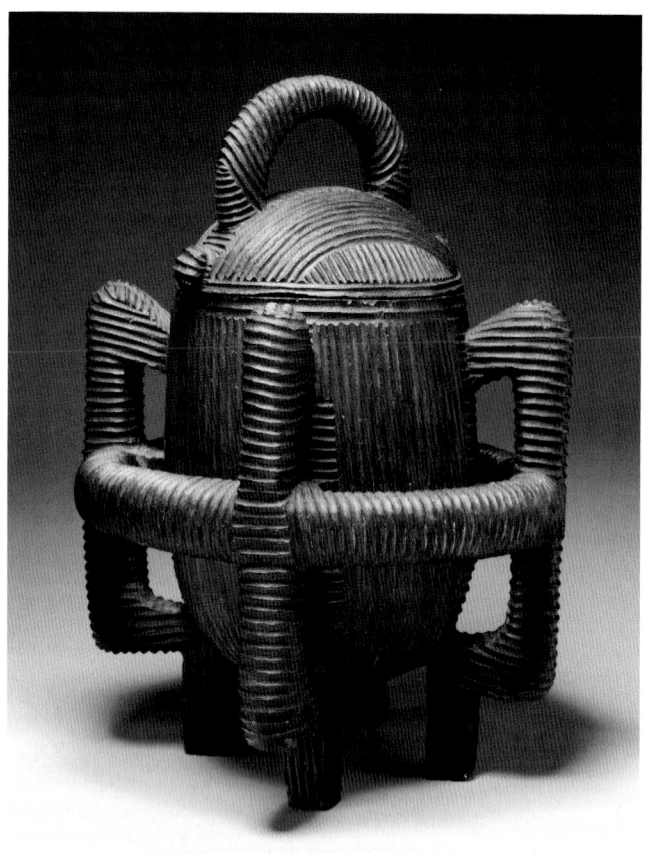

29-11 LIDDED VESSEL
South Africa or kingdom of Swaziland, southern Africa. North Nguni, 19th century. Wood, height 24¹³⁄₁₆″ (63 cm). Metropolitan Museum of Art. Purchase, Anonymous Gift, Richard, Ann, John, and James Solomon Families Foundation, Adam Lindemann and Amalia Dayan, and Herbert and Lenore Schorr Gifts, Rogers Fund, and funds from various donors, (2013.165a, b).

Credit: © 2016. Image copyright The Metropolitan Museum of Art/Art Resource/ Scala, Florence

NEW OBJECTS: THE NKISI NKONDI In less positive circumstances, artists had to create new forms of objects due to European interference in their daily lives. One example of this is found with the *nkisi nkondi* class of objects made by the Kongo peoples. The *nkisi nkondi* (also *n'kondi*) was a hunter object used by chiefs, elders, and diviners to help administer justice in their local communities (FIG. 29–12).

In the territories now contained by the Democratic Republic of the Congo, Belgian colonial authorities removed local systems of justice and handled all arbitration through their own colonial courts based on Belgian law, which was foreign and inapplicable to the traditions of most local populations. The emerging consensus among scholars is that *minkisi* (plural of *nkisi*) *nkondi* were invented to solve the lack of access to local, recognizable systems of justice.

When a dispute arose between members of the community that they alone could not resolve, they would take their case to the chief, who served as caretaker for the *nkisi*

nkondi. The chief would bring out the sculpture to hear the case, and then, if the clients still could not reach an agreement, even when faced with the threatening figure of the *nkondi,* they would drive a nail, blade, or other pointed object into the figure to capture the *nkisi nkondi*'s attention and prick it into action. The object could then recognize, hunt down, and punish whichever party was in the wrong.

The *nkisi nkondi* seen here was carved from a single block of wood. It is a rare example in that it retains its original bundled raffia skirt, packed earthen neck ruff,

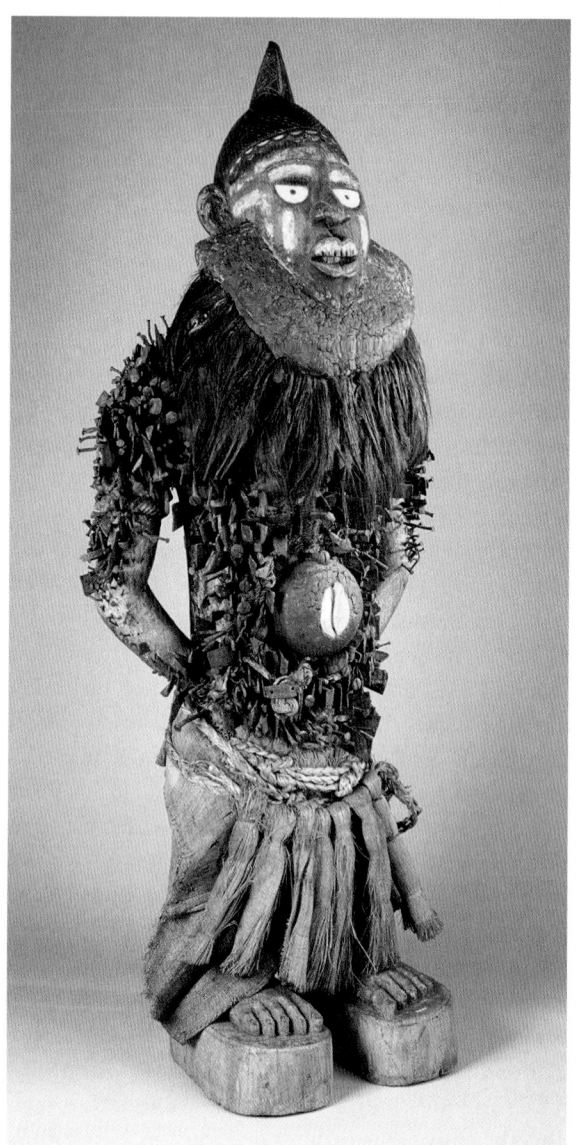

29-12 NKISI NKONDI
Democratic Republic of the Congo. Kongo, 19th century. Wood, nails, raffia, organic materials, and pigment, height 44″ (111.7 cm). The Field Museum, Chicago.

Near the end of the colonial period in the mid-twentieth century, *minkisi nkondi* stopped being made for judicial use; most likely they were no longer needed after independence from Europe and judicial systems returned to African control. The objects are still made now, but for tourist and collector markets.

Credit: © The Field Museum, Image No. A109979_Ac, Cat. No. 91300. Photo: Diane Alexander White and fur collar. These types of items were frequently lost or removed from *minkisi nkondi* as they disintegrated or become damaged over time. The large number of objects driven into this *nkondi* suggests that its powers were both formidable and efficacious.

The *nkisi nkondi* stands with its hands on its hips, its knees bent, and its mouth and eyes wide open in a pose called *pakalala*, a stance of alertness like a wrestler challenging an opponent. Other *minkisi nkondi* hold a knife or spear in an upraised right hand, ready to attack. This posture was used to convey to petitioners the power that was contained within the body of the *nkisi nkondi*, ready to be unleashed at the first sign of wrongdoing on the part of either party.

Kongo culture is based in oral, not written history. One's word was one's honor, and the spoken word of chiefs or elders was the word of law. Here, the *nkisi nkondi*'s mouth is open, indicating that it is breathing or speaking, therefore capable of speaking justice. Additionally, it has filed teeth. This is not to make it look frightening; rather, it followed the local custom of important members of society filing their teeth. This painful process was a marker of important status and also drew attention to the speaker's mouth, focusing listeners on the power of the words being spoken.

PRIVATE OBJECTS: THE SPIRIT SPOUSE   While the *minkisi nkondi* were public objects, used in the service of entire communities, it was not uncommon for objects to be made for very private use. One example comes from the Baule peoples who live in the present-day country of the Ivory Coast (Côte d'Ivoire).

The Baule make a particular type of object known as the spirit spouse (*blolo bla* if female and *blolo bian* if male) **(FIG. 29-13)**. It is sculpted to represent an idealized individual. The objects do not, however, imitate actual living people—they are a synthesis of physical, moral, and spiritual ideals of beauty in a carved wooden form.

If an individual is suffering in his or her romantic or married life, Baule spirituality explains it as an otherworldly lover who is making trouble for the living person who is the object of their affection. To remedy the situation, the person imagines what this spirit spouse looks like and commissions an artist to produce a sculpture that will flatter the spirit. By pleasing the spirit with a beautiful object, it is hoped that the spirit will assist his or her earthly lover to have a more productive and healthy life, marriage, and family. The objects therefore, transfer the burden of romantic failure away from the individual and onto an intangible spirit. Psychologically, this has the effect of freeing the person from his or her own guilt or inhibition. The spirit spouse allows the person to realize that he or she *is* loved already, despite the temporary lack of a love relationship on earth.

This spirit wife, or *blolo bla*, stands upright with a slight bend at the knees. The spine and neck are rigid and create a strong vertical line from the head to the feet. The vertical axis is softened by the curving forms of the face, belly, buttocks, and calves, which create a gentle zigzag movement from the front to the back of the figure. This figure holds her hands on her swelling belly, symbolizing maternity and a woman's ability to bear and nurture children. The bent knees indicate preparedness, a readiness to

29-13 BLOLO BLA (FEMALE SPIRIT SPOUSE)
Ivory Coast. Baule, early–mid 20th century. Wood and glass beads, height 19¼" (48.9 cm). National Museum of African Art, Smithsonian Institution, Washington DC. Museum purchase (85.15.2).

The cheeks, torso, and back of this figure are decorated with raised bumps called cicatrizations. On this sculpture the scarifications created a tactile sensation when the figure was touched or rubbed with oil. The scarifications also contribute to creating subtle patterns of light and shadow, adding visual interest to the object.

Credit: Photo: Frank Khoury

move, contrasting with the stillness of the overall figure. This symbolizes not only a woman's physical strength, but also patience and the ability to think or wait before acting.

The eyes occupy the majority of her face. They are proportionally much larger than human eyes and appear to be closed or downcast. The figure's eyes and small mouth signify characteristics of restraint: She is not a gossip and will not pry into the affairs of others. Her breasts are small and constrained, symbolizing female physical beauty without overt eroticism. The full calves indicate health and beauty, and the shiny, well-oiled surface of the sculpture resembles healthy skin.

The head of this figure is proportionally oversized compared to the rest of the body. Also, the torso and neck are elongated. These deviations from human proportion indicate the supernatural aspect of the object. It prevents anyone from understanding the sculpture as a portrait of a living woman and encourages viewers to see the abstractions as markers of what the Baule considered intangible aspects of character and moral beauty.

Ironically, these private objects that were once kept in bedrooms are now some of the most widely displayed in public museums. Certainly the fine workmanship of the sculptures makes them visually stunning to display, but the bright lights and glass vitrines around them make it difficult to remember that these were once very intimate objects, certainly not meant to be seen by strangers.

ALTERED OBJECTS: THE BIERI FIGURE Along with new objects that emerged during the colonial period, existing objects were frequently modified due to changing circumstances. In these cases, the uses of the original objects were still necessary, but often their use had to be concealed to prevent European colonizers' awareness of the objects and their functions, which were often seen as threatening to European social control.

The Fang (pronounced "fong"), who live in Gabon, traditionally preserved the skulls, bones, and relics of their family ancestors in a cylindrical bark container. On top of this container, they placed a carved wooden guardian figure, or **BIERI** (also spelled *byeri*) (**FIG. 29-14**). These sculptures were attached to their boxes with a post that descended from their buttocks and inserted into a hole in the top of the bark container. The sculptures functioned as points of contact for ancestral support and as guardians to protect the relics from malevolent spirit forces.

Bieri were carved in a number of different forms and styles. Some are large heads with long necks that were inserted into the lid of the container, which represents the ancestral body. Other *bieri*, such as this one, were created as full figures with carefully arranged hairstyles, fully rounded torsos, and heavily muscled legs and arms. Here, the figure's firmly set jaw and powerful, muscular body exudes a sense of authority and confidence.

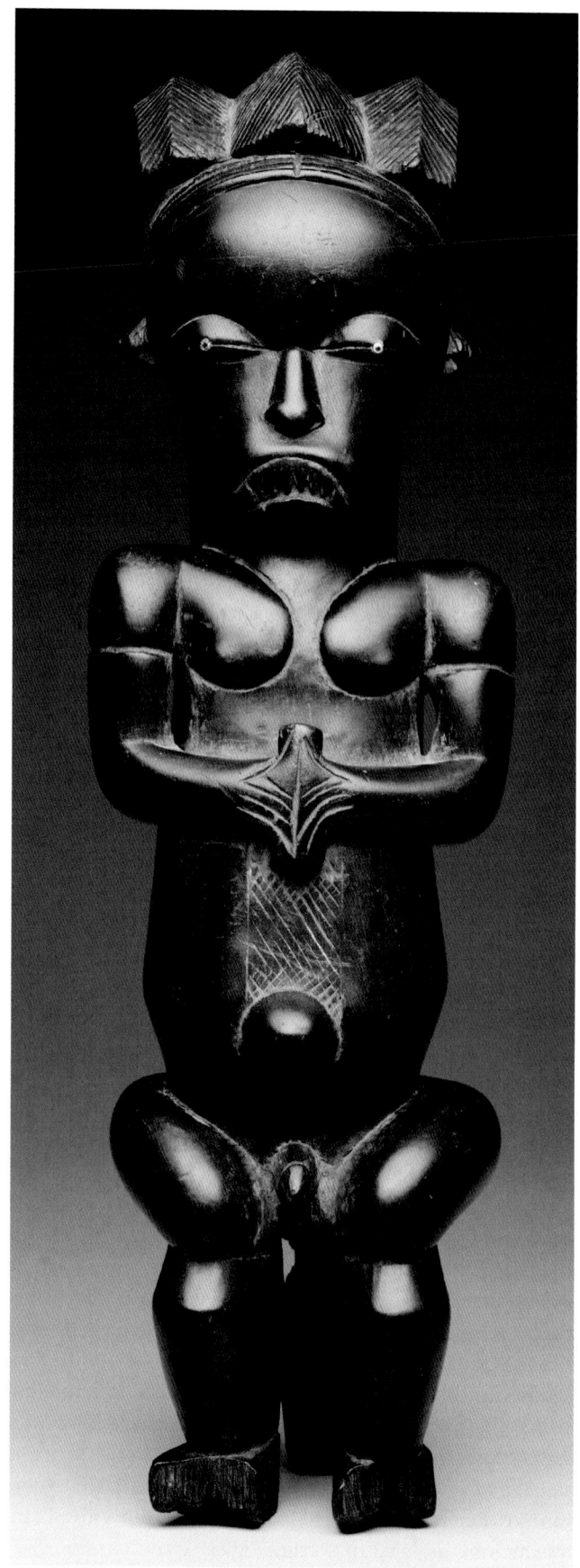

29-14 EYEMA-O-BYERI (RELIQUARY FIGURE)
Gabon. Fang, mid–late 19th century. Wood, metal, and shell; height 21¼" (53.97 cm). Dallas Museum of Art. The Eugene and Margaret McDermott Art Fund, Inc. (2000.3.MCD).

These sculptures were often enhanced by feathers, beads, clothing, and the frequent application of cleansing and purifying palm oil. The entire object served as a reliquary, not unlike the medieval practice in Europe of preserving the bones or clothing of saints in ornamented reliquary altars in cathedrals.

Due to the similarity of Fang reliquary objects to their own Christian relics, the French, who colonized the area in 1885, viewed the Fang *bieri* objects as idols and a threat to the Christian religion. Colonial officials banned many Fang ritual practices and often confiscated and destroyed the *bieri* sculptures. In order to preserve the bones of their ancestors, which were the most important part of the *bieri* reliquary, the Fang willingly turned over their sculptures for destruction or sale to the French. As the bark boxes themselves were not figurative in nature like the sculptures, they were less threatening to the French. During the early colonial period, therefore, the Fang ceased almost entirely to sculpt guardian figures for their *bieri* boxes.

Those *bieri* that were not burned by missionaries or otherwise destroyed ended up in Europe as curiosities. To make them more appealing to collectors, European dealers frequently modified them to look more like "sculpture" and less like functional objects. The posts used to secure them to their boxes were cut off, feathers and beads were removed, and some were even polished black to render them uniform in color. Like the private Baule spirit spouses, Fang *bieri* are most often seen today under glass in museums. They are all missing their bark boxes with the ancestral remains they guarded; many are also missing their support posts, beads, feathers, and other decorations. Fang *bieri* as we see them today in museums are among the objects most heavily altered from their original appearance.

DECONTEXTUALIZED OBJECTS: MOVING INTO MUSEUMS   The earliest collections of African art were, for the most part, acquired by European museums of natural history or ethnography, which exhibited the works as curious artifacts of the "less civilized" cultures that had come under European control during the colonial expansion. By the latter half of the twentieth century, however, African objects were better understood and were steadily moved into art museums, where their aesthetic qualities were studied. As with any object in a museum that was originally made for a different venue or use, the original context of the object is missing in museum displays and has to be reconstructed through wall labels, videos, maps, and written essays to help viewers understand how these objects were used in their original societies.

For example, this sculpture from Madagascar of a male and female couple was once the topmost portion of a *hazomanga*, a ritual post placed outside a family's home to honor their ancestors (**FIG. 29–15**). The *hazomanga* serve as

markers of lineage, like a family tree. They are therefore the focal points of ceremonies where families come together at marriages or enlarge through births or are reduced in number by death. The post in its entirety would have been almost 6 feet tall. This couple—at some point in history cut off from the bottom of their column—stands only 39 inches tall. In the Sakalava language, *hazo* means tree or wood, while *manga* means blue and beauty simultaneously. The "blue tree" or "beautiful wood" was in some ways a symbolic phallus, representing fertility and continuation of the family line.

29–15 STANDING COUPLE, PINNACLE COMPONENT OF HAZOMANGA POLE
Madagascar. Sakalava/Menabe, 17th–late 18th century. Wood and pigment, height 39″ (99.06 cm). Metropolitan Museum of Art, New York. Purchase, Lila Acheson Wallace, Daniel and Marian Malcolm, and James J. Ross Gifts, 2001 (2001.408).

Given this context, the image of the male and female in this sculpture makes perfect sense; they are the original matriarch and patriarch of the family, the pinnacle of the family that grows underneath them. In a museum, however, this aspect is more difficult to imagine.

RECONTEXTUALIZED OBJECTS: THE BRITISH MUSEUM SOWEI MASK

In 2013, the British Museum in London organized an exhibition called "*Sowei* Mask: The Spirit of Sierra Leone" to display their large collection of polished black masks called *sowei*, made for the Sande women's society in Sierra Leone. Most of the museum's *sowei* masks had been collected during the 1880s by Thomas Joshua Alldridge, who was asked to form a collection of Sierra Leone objects to display at the "Colonial and Indian Exhibition" held in 1886 in London. Now the museum was looking for a more contemporary and accurate way to display these objects and to

break away from their colonial history, which had presented the masks as primitive, exotic, and the opposite of civilized European society. To do this, they invited members of the Sierra Leone diaspora community living in London to assist with the development of the exhibition and its programming. The women of the Sande society in London found one mask in particular to have an especially troubled past, so they worked with the British Museum to create a series of programs to adjudicate its colonial history (**FIG. 29–16**).

With its glossy black surface, high forehead, and refined facial features, the **SOWEI MASK** seen here, as with all *sowei* masks, represents ideal female beauty for the Mende, Temne, Vai, and Kpelle peoples who live in what is today Liberia and Sierra Leone. When in use, the mask would have been worn by a senior member of the Sande women's society at the initiation ceremony of young girls into the society. The Sande society is unique: While men are the musicians at the initiation ceremony and carve the *sowei* masks worn by the dancers, Sande women dance the masquerade. The performance honors the female ancestors of the past and welcomes the newest generation of young women into the society.

The meanings of the mask are complex. Its rounded conical form refers to the chrysalis of a butterfly. Thus, the young woman entering adulthood is like a butterfly emerging from its cocoon. The small eyes and lips indicate modesty, and that the voice will only be used when it is important, never in gossip or slander. The high forehead symbolizes wisdom and generosity of thoughts and actions. This mask also wears a European style top hat. In Europe in the 1880s, the top hat was a symbol of male sophistication, wealth, and elite status in society. By coopting this symbol into their mask, Sande women used it to articulate the power of Sande to create women of sophistication, wealth, and power, who would of course go on to attract husbands of similar rank and wealth.

By 2013, the mask had lost the raffia fringe around its collar due to decay, and the Sande society women in London asked that a new fringe be made for it. They were also concerned that the mask had lost its name. When Alldridge acquired it, he did not realize that all *sowei* masks are individually named, so did not record that information. Therefore, the Sande women held a naming ceremony (**FIG. 29–17**) during which they sang songs to the mask and asked it to accept a name by suggesting historical ancestors and throwing cowrie shells to see if the mask agreed. Finally, the name Gbavo (meaning "to attract the attention of crowds") emerged, a highly appropriate choice for a mask in a world museum. The Sande women then formally presented the newly named mask with its new fringe collar to the museum, righting the past wrongs of its colonial collection and incomplete display.

29–16 SOWEI MASK FROM THE SHERBRO DISTRICT
Mende, 1880–1886. Wood, pigment, and raffia fiber; height 16.9" (43 cm) (mask), 17.3" (44 cm) (fringe). British Sixteum, London. Purchase from Thomas Joshua Alldridge (Af1886,1126.1).

The Twentieth Century: Independence-Era Art

What are the predominant conceptual concerns of African artists working in the 1960s to 1980s, and how do they differ from those of colonial-period artists?

In the years following World War I, nationalistic movements resisting European domination arose across Africa. Their leaders were inspired by the Pan-African movement, the Harlem Renaissance, and later the American civil rights movement, as well as Marxism and communism. African political and religious leaders demanded the transformation of colonial divisions into modern nation-states governed by Africans. By the mid-1950s all of North Africa had broken away from European colonial rule, and Ghana was the first sub-Saharan nation to declare independence (from Britain) in 1957. It would take until the late 1970s, however, for all African nations to be free of colonial rule. Portugal finally gave up its claim on Angola in 1975 and Britain and France subsequently let go of the Seychelles (1976) and Djibouti (1977), respectively.

Ghana

Great pride exists among Ghanaians for their status as the first sub-Saharan nation to gain independence from Europe. Indeed, Ghana inspired many other African regions to push for their own independence. Kwame Nkrumah, the first president of independent Ghana, was inspired by the power wielded by the ancient Ghana Empire and their resources of gold. Therefore, he elected to use its name for his new country, which had been dubbed the "Gold Coast" by the British.

Since independence, Ghana has celebrated its long cultural history by maintaining the Asante kingdom at its traditional capital city Kumasi and encouraging the development and sustenance of African history, language learning, and the arts. Ghana is one of many African nations to use the arts as an important component of nation building in the independence era by preserving historical and traditional forms of local art and architecture and celebrating innovative new work by contemporary artists such as El Anatsui, who is discussed later in this section.

One example of keeping traditional arts alive comes from the Nankani people, a community of farmers that lives in an arid region on the northern border of Ghana. This region lies just south of the Sahara desert and is part of the wide swath of agriculturally important land called the Sahel. The rainy season lasts three months; otherwise the area is hot and dry.

Nankani farming communities create distinctive painted adobe homes (**FIG. 29-18**). Adobe is a material used worldwide in arid climates. Sand and clay are mixed with water and fill material (such as straw, grasses, animal bones, or compost). The mixture is then molded into bricks and allowed to bake in the sun. When the bricks are hard, they are stacked with layers of adobe mortar between the courses. These buildings have no windows, which keeps them cool by preventing the hot sun from entering during the day. No windows also mean that blowing dust and sand do not enter the house during the dry season. Once the bricks and mortar are dry, a thick adobe slip is applied by hand over the entire surface of the building (inside and out) and allowed to harden. This seals the structure, making it temporarily waterproof, and during the hardening process, the slip can be sculpted and painted with decorative designs.

29-18 HOUSE COMPOUND IN SIRIGU

Ghana. Nankani, 1972.

Among the Nankani people, creating living areas is a cooperative but gender-specific project. Men build the structures; women decorate the surfaces. The structures are also gendered. The round dwellings shown here are women's houses, located in an interior courtyard; men occupy rectangular flat-roofed houses.

Credit: © Margaret Courtney-Clarke/Corbis

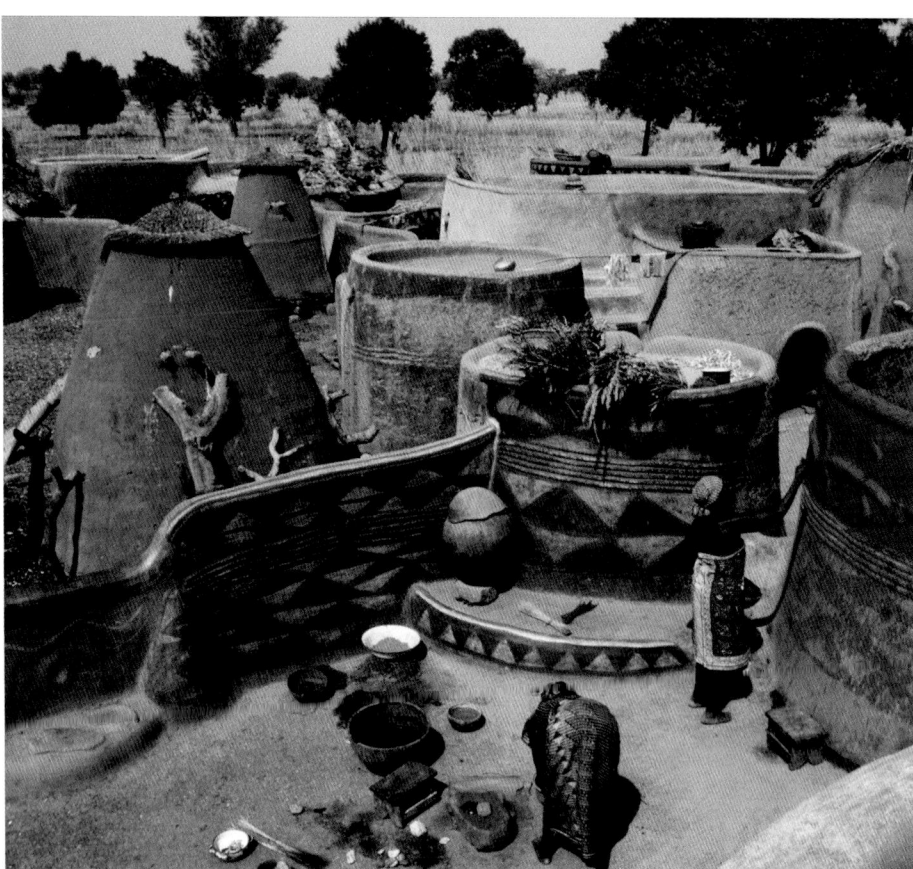

The homes seen in this 1972 photograph were most likely built during the first half of the twentieth century. Women are shown repainting their homes where the exterior decorations have faded. They have decorated one set of the walls with horizontal molded ridges called *yidoor* ("rows in a cultivated field") and then surrounded them with blue diamond-shaped "long life" symbols to express good wishes and agricultural success for the family. The triangular patterns contrast elegantly with the curvature of the walls.

The Nankani use these same geometric motifs on pottery and baskets and for scarification of the skin. The fact that the Nankani were continuing to use historic, and most likely ancient, symbols in the 1970s to enhance their homes, their possessions, and even their bodies sheds light on how important those symbols were in connecting the Nankani to their own past, and not that of British colonial occupation. Certainly the Nankani, like many Ghanaians, were looking for ways to celebrate their own history and traditions after so many centuries of having the traditions, languages, and cultures of others imposed on them.

Burkina Faso

The Bwa people in Burkina Faso are another cultural group that has elected to maintain much of their historic religion and traditions despite French colonialism and the presence of both Islam and Christianity in the region. The Bwa continue to initiate young men and women into adulthood following the onset of puberty. Initiation provides young people with instruction on the social, familial, and religious obligations they need to follow as adults. At the end of their initiation period, the initiates display their new knowledge in a public masquerade ceremony (**FIG.**

29-19). Each young man performs one of the masks, while the young women sing the accompanying songs. At the end of the ceremony all the initiates rejoin their families as adults, ready to marry, start farms, and begin families of their own.

The masks seen in this 1984 masquerade are made of painted wood and represent animal messengers of the important spiritual figure, Do, who mediates between the Bwa people and their creator god. Do's realm is wild, untamed nature and the life force that it generates. Along with initiations, masquerades honoring Do are performed at funerals, as well as at planting and harvest ceremonies. Dancing a masquerade for a funeral, for example, assists the deceased family member in making the journey from the world of the living to the world of the spirits and ancestors.

The masks are commissioned and maintained by family groups who compete with each other to make and dance the most spectacular masks. The imagery consists of human and animal forms combined with painted abstract symbols using only three colors: red, black, and white. The dance costume, traditionally made of leaves, is now frequently made with fibers dyed a brilliant red or black to match the bold colors of the masks.

Bwa masks draw from the natural world to depict people, animals, and insects in a highly abstract manner. The red beaks seen on three of these masks imitate those of the hornbill, a water bird, while the horned figure (second from left) represents a buffalo, and the incredibly long, slender mask at center represents a serpent. The mask at the far right features three small figures on top of the central plank. This type of mask stresses the commissioning family's own connection to the spirit world.

While the theatrical masquerade performance can only be appreciated by participating in the event, the masks and costumes are often all that is viewed by outsiders, as the Bwa have traded or sold these objects in the past and still produce them on commission for sale to collectors. Collecting and displaying Bwa masks for others to view, however, poses significant problems for museums. Few institutions can exhibit such large objects, and museums often only have the wooden headpieces. The feather, leaf, and fiber costumes have typically either been lost or removed due to damage or deterioration. In museum cases, it is difficult for viewers to imagine how a Do mask would have looked when worn and performed. Only by participating in an actual masquerade do the size and grandeur of the masks, and the incredible talent of the dancers, become fully evident.

Postcolonial/Postmodern: Photography, *Récupération*, Painting

Along with retaining pre-colonial artistic traditions, artists working in the 1950s to 1980s engaged with new materials and theories to give aesthetic voice to the changes occurring with continental independence from Europe. The technology of photography, imported from Europe in the nineteenth century, became a tool by which Africans could reclaim their own image from the colonial gaze and display their bodies on their own terms for the camera. Painting proved equally popular with independence-era artists. Painting, after all, was the backbone of European

art up through the colonial period, and a measure by which artists around the world were being judged. African artists took to disrupting this narrative; they interfered with painting's precious status by using organic materials (such as earth, milk, and clay) as pigments or by painting on canvas taken from flour or potato sacks. They painted with brushes, with palette knives, or with their feet. They also adopted oil on canvas to great success, showing European artists that they could master the art of painting as well as anybody.

Along with co-opting photography and painting, two of Europe's prized contemporary art forms, African artists, particularly in French-speaking countries, began to develop their own contemporary theoretical explorations, this time focusing on the found object. The influence of the European **readymade** (an object from popular or material culture presented without further manipulation as an artwork by the artist; see Chapter 32) was certainly part of this impulse, but African modes of art making that use found objects as their primary materials go back centuries. The French term **récupération** (to re-find, reuse, or re-make) defines the African practices of converting preexisting objects from the man-made and natural world into political, aesthetic, and three-dimensional objects; it became one of the most widely used and influential art practices mastered by African artists during the second half of the twentieth century.

PHOTOGRAPHY One of the best-known photographers of the late colonial and early independence era was Seydou Keïta (c. 1921–2001). Born in the capital city of Bamako, Mali (then French West Africa), Keïta's interest in photography was sparked by his uncle's gift to him of a Kodak Brownie Flash camera in 1935. He acquired a large-format camera in 1948 and opened his own studio in

29-19 THREE PLANK MASKS, BUFFALO MASK, AND SERPENT MASK PERFORMING IN THE TOWN OF DOSSI

Burkina Faso. Bwa, 1984. Wood, pigments, and raffia fiber. Plank masks height 7' (2.13 m); serpent mask height over 14' (4.3 m).

Bigger masks symbolize greater means and influence on the part of the family that commissioned the mask, as well as greater talent on the part of the sculptor. Some Bwa masks, especially serpent masks, reach over 25 feet in height, while most plank masks average between 5 and 7 feet tall. Others, such as those representing birds or butterflies, may only be a couple feet high but possess wingspans of over 6 feet.

Credit: © Charles & Josette Lenars/Corbis

Bamako where he became renowned as a portraitist, taking engaging black-and-white photographs of the cosmopolitan residents of the city. He photographed his sitters as prosperous and urban, often providing props such as jewelry, watches, radios, televisions, and glasses, which his sitters readily adopted to enhance their portraits. Along with depicting people as they were in reality, he captured how they wished to be seen and who they aspired to be. His approach fought back against a century of colonial photography where Malians (and all Africans) were photographed by Europeans as ethnographic subjects, exotic others, or naked "savages," so as to belittle African civilizations as inferior to those of Europe.

Keïta's aesthetic approach was unique in that he used a very shallow depth of field, which had the effect of making his sitters pop out against the patterned fabrics he used as backdrops. He shot most of his "studio" portraits outside to make the most of the sharp black-and-white contrasts afforded by natural light. In the family portrait shown here, the sitters occupy a visually luxurious space (**FIG. 29-20**). The heavy, strong patterns of the wife's clothing contrast with the stark white worn by her husband and child. Keïta's elegant composition monumentalizes individuals whose power and pride are communicated through their commanding poses, impeccable dress, and relaxed gestures. While Keïta made his photographs for domestic consumption (his studio archive comprised over 10,000 negatives), his work found its way to France in the 1990s, and his photographs have been frequently exhibited in Europe and the United States ever since.

RÉCUPÉRATION The complex, multimedia work of El Anatsui (b. 1944) affirms African artists' extensive history of using unexpected materials, and he is one of many in his generation to work with the powerful technique of *récupération*. Born in Ghana, Anatsui studied art in Kumasi, where he took coursework he describes as predominantly Western in orientation, while Ghana's own rich artistic legacy was ignored. Following his own inclinations, he began to study Ghanaian surface design traditions as produced by Ewe and Asante textile artists. In 1975, Anatsui took a position in the Fine Arts Department of the University of Nigeria at Nsukka. There he found a like-minded spirit in Uche Okeke, who was intensely interested in revitalizing *uli*, an important Igbo surface design system. Anatsui began to create what would become a large body of work inspired by *uli* and other graphic systems using tools such as chainsaws and blowtorches.

Later, while still concerned with the survival and transmission of inherited traditions, Anatsui began to use found objects, including soda- and beer-bottle caps, aluminum can lids from canned goods, and the tops and neck labels from liquor bottles, to create revelatory art forms in a variety of media. These include immense wall sculptures that fold and undulate like textiles but are made from metal bottle caps "sewn" together with copper wire (**FIG. 29-21**).

Anatsui's wall hangings have proven immensely popular around the world, and he gives several reasons for this global appeal. First, they are glittering, massive objects; they look like tapestries made of gold and silver, so they speak to the love of big objects that look expensive. Second, they carry historical meaning; Anatsui creates them in the spirit of *kente* cloth, where small segments are made and then "stitched" together. He names his works, just as *kente* patterns have their own names, and thus brings a long-standing tradition to the awareness of a new generation of African and international audiences alike. Third, they speak to environmental concerns, where humans worldwide are consuming and throwing away more than we need and more than the earth can handle. Anatsui's bottle-cap sculptures and tin-can-lid objects keep thousands of pounds of material out of the trash stream. Finally, his works carry the weight of political critique. In **FLAG FOR A NEW WORLD POWER**, we are all asked to examine how the world's political systems operate, including the importance we attach to nationalism and to flags that announce the nation-state to the world. Anatsui's work asks us to consider if a unified

29-20 Seydou Keïta **UNTITLED (FAMILY PORTRAIT)**
Bamako, Mali. Gelatin silver print, 1952–1955.

Credit: *Courtesy The Contemporary African Art Collection, Geneva*

29–21 El Anatsui FLAG FOR A NEW WORLD POWER

2004. Aluminum (bottle caps) and copper wire, 16'4" × 14'9" (5 × 4.5 m). Private collection.

Credit: © El Anatsui. Courtesy October Gallery, London.

shops, movie theaters, and event venues. In 1973, he began working with an eastern European anthropologist who encouraged him to paint scenes of life in Zaire. Tshibumba found great pleasure in this topic and subsequently embarked on a project to document the entirety of the history of the Congo in a painted series of over 100 acrylic paintings on floursack canvases. Using vivid colors and willfully violating the traditional rules of European linear perspective in favor of the more African hierarchical perspective, Tshibumba painted early kings and queens, the violence of the regime of King Leopold II and the Belgian colonial powers, the excitement at independence, and the violence that tore his country apart in the post-independence years. In **TOMBEAU SANS CERCUEIL** ("Tomb without a Coffin"), Tshibumba paints one of the hero figures of Congolese independence, Patrice Lumumba, who also served briefly as the first democratically elected leader of the independent country of Congo (**FIG. 29–22**). Lumumba was assassinated under suspicious circumstances less than four months after taking office, a victim of the international power struggle for control over the Congo and its natural resources.

world will be made from our ruins, our trash, or our commitment to overcome humanity's own destructive impulses.

PAINTING   Politics in fact, are one of the most common subjects explored by independence-era artists. Logically, artists were leaders in giving visual presence to the rapidly changing and complex political and social realities for Africans in the 1960s and 70s. One artist whose work is particularly poignant today is Tshibumba Kanda Matulu, born in 1947 in the city of Lubumbashi (then the Belgian Congo, renamed Zaire in 1971, now the Democratic Republic of the Congo). Tshibumba never trained as a painter, but found local success painting signboards for barber

29–22 Tshibumba Kanda Matulu TOMBEAU SANS CERCUEIL (TOMB WITHOUT A COFFIN)

ca. 1974. Canvas (recycled flour sack), paint, wood, and staples, 39.2 × 60.2" (99.5 × 152.9 cm). Fowler Museum at UCLA. Anonymous Gift (2002.30.2).

Credit: © Photo courtesy of the Fowler Museum at UCLA

Tshibumba paints Lumumba as a Christlike figure. Despite his bound arms, ripped T-shirt, and signs of being tortured, he is peaceful, seemingly resigned to his fate. As Lumumba's death by firing squad was not announced to the Congolese until a month after the fact, rumors circulated that he had escaped and survived or that, like Jesus, he had risen from the dead and would come again to liberate his people.

Tragically, Tshibumba disappeared under similar circumstances in the early 1980s. It is not known whether he lived or died during the civil war that raged near his hometown in the late 1970s. His paintings, however, bear substantial witness to the political turmoil witnessed by generations of Congolese during the twentieth century, and they remain invaluable historical and visual documents of the violent end of the colonial era.

Late Twentieth and Early Twenty-First Century: New Directions

How do today's artists make use of past cultural styles even as they push in new artistic and global directions?

In addition to continuing traditional art making, adopting new materials and technologies, and confronting the politics of their time, African artists today have broadened their study of art. Along with training with local masters, many study abroad at renowned art schools worldwide and live between two or more countries. The diversity of influences on contemporary artists of African descent makes it impossible to render a single view of what makes up African art in the twenty-first century.

However, one significant attribute of many contemporary artists, as mentioned at the beginning of this chapter, is their cultural fluency. Each artwork by the four artists discussed below translates meanings across cultures, and often across time and space, in order to present specific issues and cultural concerns to a broad audience. Asking a global audience to consider the lasting colonial burden on the Congo, for example, requires Aimé Mpane not only to know the colonial history of his country, but also to realize that many others around the world do not know it. Incorporating aesthetics, history, awareness, and insight into art objects is what these four artists, and many of their contemporaries not discussed here, do so brilliantly.

Mpane: The Burden of History

In a manner related to El Anatsui's *recuperation* use of bottle caps and tin can lids, Aimé Mpane cut the sulfurous heads off of thousands of wooden matches and glued the sticks together into the life-size hollow framework of a man to produce a signature work: **CONGO: SHADOW OF A SHADOW** (**FIG. 29-23**). Mpane lives between Kinshasa in the Democratic Republic of the Congo, where he was born in 1968, and Brussels, Belgium. He is a painter, sculptor, and installation artist and *Congo: Shadow of a Shadow* brought him instant international recognition. It is a *tour-de-force* in wood, not sculpted from a single block as a traditional carver would do (and as Mpane himself has done in other works), but rather painstakingly assembled from small sticks of wood. The matchstick sculpture of the man stands at the foot of a grave, meant to be his own, where the tombstone is a cross marked with the words "Congo … 1885." A

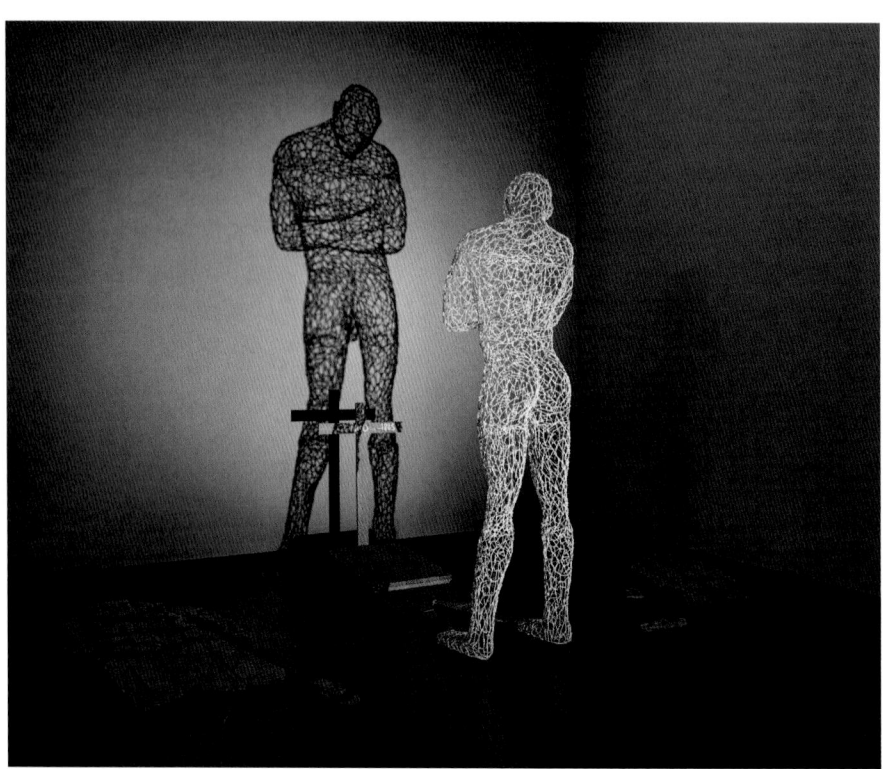

29-23 Aimé Mpane **CONGO: SHADOW OF A SHADOW**
2005. Installed in the exhibition "Shaping Power: Luba Masterworks from the Royal Museum for Central Africa," July 7, 2013–May 4, 2014), Los Angeles County Museum of Art (LACMA). Mixed media (matchsticks, wood, shoes, beads, and metal), dimensions variable. National Museum of African Art, Smithsonian Institution, Washington, D.C. Museum purchase (2009.10.1).

Credit: © 2016. Digital Image Museum Associates/LACMA/Art Resource NY/ Scala, Florence bright light is positioned out of view behind the man, casting the shadow of his transparent body onto the wall in front of him. He can literally be seen as a shadow of his former self. Around the man lie silhouettes made from assembled planks of wood, shaped to resemble a man, woman, and child. Actual shoes are placed at the feet of each silhouette, and the impression is one of white lines drawn around fallen bodies on the ground to mark the places they died.

By personifying the Congo as a man, Mpane humanizes the brutality that was visited upon the Congolese people during the colonial era and in the civil wars that have wracked the country ever since. By giving a "death date" of 1885, Mpane clearly indicates that the Berlin Conference killed his home country. At that conference, in fact, the territory now comprising the Democratic Republic of the Congo was granted to King Leopold II of Belgium as his personal property. It would eventually pass into the hands of the Belgian government until independence was achieved in 1960. Throughout the period of King Leopold's and Belgian control, Congolese men were forced to work in deplorable conditions on rubber plantations and in diamond and mineral mines. Those who resisted were sent to brutal work camps. Women and children were forced into slavery-like conditions for Belgian investors and residents in the region. The history of the Congo under colonialism is one of the most tragic and brutal accounts of human suffering. Mpane's sculpture mourns the countless dead and the loss of his indigenous country to the greed of the European powers around the conference table in Berlin.

Wangechi Mutu: The International Artist Experience

Wangechi Mutu was born in Nairobi, Kenya, in 1972 and currently works in New York. She trained as both an anthropologist and artist and originally thought to pursue a career in film. She instead discovered a powerful medium in **collage** (pasting separate elements together on a surface) and a way to make it describe the experiences of women across international borders. Mutu cuts out images of women's bodies from fashion magazines, historical books on fashion, medical and botanical textbooks, and gynecological drawings of the female body. She reassembles these images together with her own painted imagery onto diverse grounds of paper, reflective Mylar, and original pages cut from manuscripts. Mutu points out that women carry the marks of culture more than men do, for better or for worse. In making women the subject of her work, she can cross cultural boundaries more explicitly and focus on the demands that various cultures place on women and their bodies.

In **LE NOBLE SAUVAGE**, Mutu spins off of the colonial-period stereotype of non-European women as being somehow exotic or savage due to their skin color, their clothing, and their body shape (**FIG. 29-24**). The collage contains cut-outs of animals stereotypically associated with Africa: parrots, lions, cheetahs, water buffalo, and snakes, while shredded papers create grass, palm fronds, and the woman's skirt. Part woman, part tree, the figure seems wild and untamed, and the lions depicted are all in the act of eating their freshly killed prey, making the image rather gruesome. The woman's skin color is ambiguous; mottled spots and geometric shapes of light and dark skin tones indicate she is a universal female figure, rather than one who can be associated with any particular race. The snakes emerge from her head, reminiscent of Medusa in ancient Greek mythology. By exposing stereotypes associated not only with wild African animals, but also the dangerous Greek goddess, Mutu points out that many

29-24 Wangechi Mutu **LE NOBLE SAUVAGE**
2006. Ink and collage on Mylar, 7'7¾" × 4'6" (233 × 137.2 cm).
Collection of Martin and Rebecca Eisenberg, Scarsdale, New York.

Credit: © Wangechi Mutu. Image courtesy the artist.

societies negatively view the bodies of women of color as dangerous, uncivilized, and animalistic. Ironically, this is the exact opposite of how women's bodies appear in the fashion magazines where Mutu gets her images. Her work points out that beauty is always contrived and that women around the world are held to unnatural standards in regard to their looks, behavior, and cultural backgrounds.

Yinka Shonibare MBE: The Global Flows of History

Yinka Shonibare MBE (Member of the British Empire) has made the interconnected histories of Europe and Africa his primary artistic subject. He was born in England to Nigerian parents, and in his artistic career he focuses on the nineteenth century, when colonialism was at its height. His works expose the uneven power exchanges between Europeans and Africans and the damages they created over time. And yet, he does this in a disarmingly beautiful manner. He has made **wax-print fabric** his signature material, largely for the way it conveys the flow of history between Europe and Africa (**FIG. 29–25**).

Cotton wax-print fabrics came to African coastal cities in the nineteenth century. In their journeys to Indonesia for trade, the Dutch had bought expensive, hand-made Indonesian batik (wax-printed) fabrics, thinking to trade them back home in Europe, but discovered that African traders loved them. In order to capitalize on this trade on both the inbound and outbound legs of their travels, the Dutch began industrially manufacturing less expensive, brightly colored wax-print fabrics in the Netherlands in order to sell them to African traders on their way to Indonesia. The fabrics were hugely popular, so much so that in order to meet demand, African people began printing them locally. These fabrics, now ubiquitously associated with "African" fashion, are in fact, Dutch in origin.

In **SCRAMBLE FOR AFRICA** (2003), Shonibare imagines the cast of European heads of state during the Berlin Conference of 1884–1885 assembled around a table arguing over which pieces of the African "pie" they want to claim for themselves. He dresses his mannequins in the traditional style of European nineteenth-century men's dress: straight trousers worn with a tuxedo shirt, vest, and bow-tie paired with a long or short waistcoat. He has replaced the traditional plain wool and silk fabrics with the wax print. Initially it looks like he has dressed European men in African fabric, and the effect is rather funny. However, upon recognizing that the "African" fabric is actually European, viewers realize that what is perceived to be authentically European or authentically African cannot be so easily separated after all. Rather, cultures influence each other throughout history, largely inspired by the global flows of trade and art. Shonibare points out that the results can be beautiful and ugly at the same time.

Muholi: Changing the Political and Cultural Discourse

Zanele Muholi was born in Durban, South Africa, in 1972. She lived under the brutal racially based political system known as **apartheid** until it was abolished in 1994. Identifying as a black lesbian, Muholi found herself not only constantly subjected to discrimination against black women under apartheid, but also targeted for her same-sex relationships. Her work in photography, installation, and film has always been part of her political activism, geared toward raising awareness of gender and sexual equality and fighting for equal civil rights.

29–25 Yinka Shonibare **SCRAMBLE FOR AFRICA** 2003. 14 life-size fiberglass mannequins, 14 chairs, table, and Dutch wax-printed cotton. The Pinnell Collection, Dallas.

Credit: Courtesy James Cohan Gallery, NY

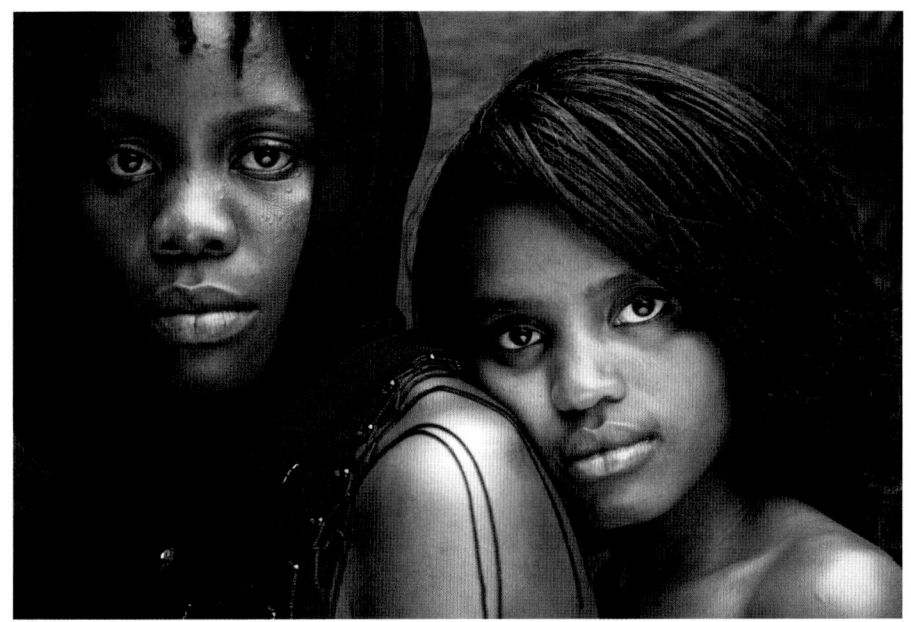

29-26 Zanele Muholi **THOBE AND PHILA I**

2012. Silver gelatin print, 19⅞ × 30⅛" (50.5 × 76.5 cm). Edition of 5 + 2 AP.

Credit: © Zanele Muholi. Courtesy of Stevenson, Cape Town/Johannesburg and Yancey Richardson, New York.

One of Muholi's longest-standing art projects is the "Faces and Phases" series begun in 2006, in which the artist takes half-length portrait photographs in black and white of individual people who identify as lesbian, gay, bisexual, transgender, or queer. Her goal with this project is to document people on their own terms, giving visual and aesthetic strength to one of South Africa's most targeted minority communities. In another series, "Being," which she began in 2007, Muholi presents photographs of individuals and couples, honoring their relationships and normalizing them as just "being" people, existing side by side with the rest of their communities (**FIG. 29-26**). In **THOBE AND PHILA I**, Muholi photographs the couple standing one behind the other. Phila gently leans her cheek on her partner's shoulder in a gesture of comfort and ease. Both women gaze directly at the camera, Phila's soft expression balanced by Thobe's stronger, more aggressive stare. The close-up confrontation between the couple and the viewer is not a violent or challenging one; rather, the women demand to be looked at as equals: as South African, as lovers, as people.

As Muholi explains, "Every individual in my photographs has her own or his own story to tell. But sadly we come from spaces in which most black people never had that opportunity. I'm not [here] to speak for the people, but to share and change the portrayal of black bodies.... It's about time that we bring positive imagery of us in space where we are there, but hardly seen."

Think About It

1   How do the royal arts of the sixteenth to twentieth centuries display the attributes of participating in society, cultural fluency of artists, contemporary nature, and abstract subjects?

2   How did African objects made during the colonial period respond to the new contemporary situations of colonial society?

3   How did the arts of the independence period participate in redefining African art in the 1950s to 1980s?

4   Cultural fluency arguably means something different for artists working for royal patrons than it does for artists working for a global art market. How are late twentieth- and early twenty-first-century artists interpreting cultural and global fluency?

Crosscurrents

Njoya's father's throne and Yinka Shonibare's sculpture both present the sustained and complex relationship between Europe and Africa during the colonial period. How does each object display its "Europeanness" and its "Africanness"? How does the combination of elements from both African and European cultures contribute to the power and meaning of each work of art?

FIG. 29–4

FIG. 29–25

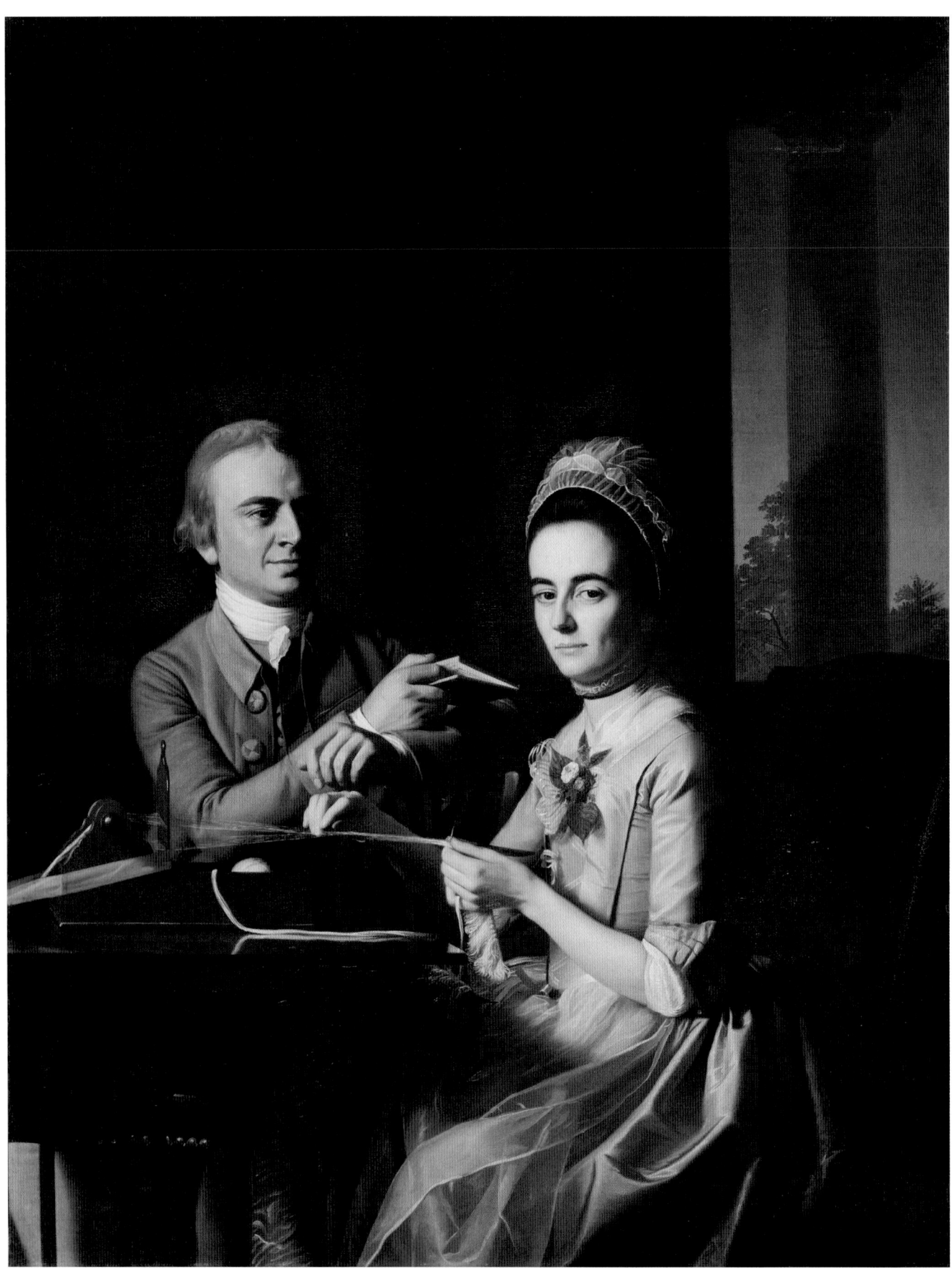

30–1 John Singleton Copley **THOMAS MIFFLIN AND SARAH MORRIS (MR. AND MRS. MIFFLIN)**
1773. Oil on canvas, 61⅝ × 48″ (156.5 × 121.9 cm). Philadelphia Museum of Art.

Chapter 30
European and American Art, 1715–1840

Learning Objectives

30.a Identify the visual hallmarks of eighteenth- and early nineteenth-century European and American art for formal, technical, and expressive qualities.

30.b Interpret the meaning of eighteenth- and early nineteenth-century European and American works of art based on their themes, subjects, and symbols.

30.c Relate eighteenth- and early nineteenth-century European and American art and artists to their cultural, economic, and political contexts.

30.d Apply the vocabulary and concepts relevant to eighteenth- and early nineteenth-century European and American art, artists, and art history.

30.e Interpret a work of eighteenth- or early nineteenth-century European and American art using the art historical methods of observation, comparison, and inductive reasoning.

30.f Select visual and textual evidence in various media to support an argument or an interpretation of a work of eighteenth- or early nineteenth-century European and American art.

John Singleton Copley (1738–1815) painted this double portrait of Thomas Mifflin and his wife, Sarah Morris (**FIG. 30-1**), in 1773 when the Philadelphia couple was visiting Boston for a family funeral. This was the same year when American colonists protested against the British tax on tea by staging the Boston Tea Party—seizing British tea and tossing it into Boston harbor. The painting must have hung in the couple's Philadelphia home when Thomas Mifflin, a prominent merchant and politician, and other leading representatives of the colonies negotiated a strategy for the impending break with Britain at the First Continental Congress. The painting proclaims the couple's identity as American patriots, committed to the cause of independence.

Sarah—not her famous husband—is the center of attention. She sits in the foreground, wearing a stylish silk dress decorated with expensive laces, a finely wrought lace cap atop her smoothly coiffed head. She is certainly rich and elegant, but she wears no jewelry except for a modest choker. In fact, rather uncharacteristically for a woman of her social status, she is shown with her sleeves rolled up, working silk threads on the large wooden frame that sits on her polished table. Her work is domestic and pragmatic, not the kind of activity we expect to see highlighted in a large and expensive formal portrait, but it was included here for important political reasons. Sarah is weaving a

type of decorative silk fringe that in the past would have been imported from England. By portraying her involved in this work, Copley demonstrates her commitment both to her home as a good and industrious wife and to the revolutionary cause as a woman without pretension who can manage well without British imported goods. Meeting the viewer's gaze with confidence and intelligence, she is clearly a full partner with her husband in the important work of resisting British colonial power. He is content to sit in the background of this picture, interrupting his reading to look admiringly at his beloved Sarah.

By 1773, John Singleton Copley was Boston's preeminent portrait painter and a wealthy man. His reputation stood on his remarkable ability to represent the upper level of society in a clear, precise painting style that seemed to reveal not only every detail of a sitter's physical appearance and personality, but also the gorgeous satins, silks, and laces of the women's dresses and the expensive polished furniture that signified his patrons' wealth and status. Although his father-in-law was the Boston representative of the East India Company (whose tea was dumped into the harbor), Copley was sympathetic to the revolutionary cause and, in fact, tried unsuccessfully to mediate the crisis in Boston. This portrait of Sarah Morris and Thomas Mifflin was painted when Copley himself was ambivalent about the political future of the colonies—he would flee the unsettled climate of the colonies the following year to begin a second career in London—but his sitters reveal only their own sober commitment to the cause.

Industrial, Intellectual, and Political Revolutions

What are the political and social backgrounds for eighteenth- and early nineteenth-century European and American art and architecture?

The American War of Independence was just one of many revolutions to shake the established order during the eighteenth and early nineteenth centuries. This was an age of radical change in society, thought, and politics, and while these transformations were felt especially in England, France, and the United States, they had consequences throughout the West and, eventually, the world.

The transformations of this period were informed by a new way of thinking that had its roots in the scientific revolution of the previous century (see "Science and the Changing Worldview" in Chapter 23 on page 769). In England, John Locke (1632–1704) argued that reasonable and rational thought should supplant superstition, and Isaac Newton (1643–1727) insisted upon empirical observation, rational evaluation, and logical consideration in mathematics and science. In 1702, Bernard de Fontenelle (1657–1757), a French popularizer of scientific innovation, wrote that he anticipated "a century which will become more enlightened day by day, so that all previous centuries will be lost in darkness by comparison." Over the course of the eighteenth century, this emphasis on thought "enlightened" by reason was applied to political and moral philosophy as well as science. Enlightenment thinking is marked by a conviction that humans are not superstitious beings ruled by God or the aristocracy, and that all men (some thinkers also included women) should have equal rights and opportunities for "life, liberty, and the pursuit of happiness." Most Enlightenment philosophers believed that, when freed of past religious and political shackles, men and women could and would act rationally and morally. The role of the state was to protect and facilitate these rights, and when the state failed, the moral solution was to change it. Both the American Revolution of 1776 and the French Revolution of 1789 were justified on this basis.

The eighteenth century was also a period of economic and social transformation set in motion by the Industrial Revolution. In the Europe of 1700, wealth and power belonged to the aristocracy, who owned the land and controlled the lives of poor tenant farmers. The Industrial Revolution eventually replaced the land-based power of the aristocracy with the financial power of capitalists, who were able to use new sources of energy to mechanize manufacturing and greatly increase the quantity and profitability of saleable goods. Factory work lured the poor away from the countryside to the cities with the promise of wages and greater independence. The conditions that urban workers endured, however, were dreadful, both at their grueling factory jobs and in their overcrowded and unsanitary neighborhoods. These conditions would sow the seeds of dissent and revolution in several European countries in the mid nineteenth century. Industrialization also produced a large middle class that both bought and sold the new goods made in factories.

By the early nineteenth century, the aristocracy was weak and ineffectual in many nations and virtually eliminated in France. Upper-middle-class industrialists and merchants dominated European commerce, industry, and politics, and their beliefs and customs defined social norms. At the same time, the idealism of the Enlightenment had eroded, particularly in France in the wake of the Revolution, when the new republican form of government "by the people" brought chaos and bloodshed rather than order and stability. A new intellectual trend, known as Romanticism, started as a literary movement in the 1790s and served as a counterpoint to Enlightenment rationalism. It critiqued the idea that the world was knowable and ruled by reason alone. The central premise of Romanticism was that an exploration of emotions, the imagination, and intuition—areas of the mind not addressed by Enlightenment philosophy—could lead to a more nuanced understanding of the world. Rather than one replacing the other, Romanticism and Enlightenment thought coexisted as different parts of a complex cultural whole.

Rococo

How does the ornate style of Rococo art and architecture originate in salon life among the aristocracy and develop more broadly?

In the modern age, the shift from art produced for individual or institutional patrons—the monarchy, aristocracy, Church, and wealthy merchants—to art produced as a commodity to be sold to the industrial rich and the emerging middle classes had its roots in the Rococo, when the court culture of Versailles was replaced by the salon culture of Paris. The term Rococo combines the Italian word *barocco* (an irregularly shaped pearl, possibly the source of the word "baroque") and the French *rocaille* (a popular form of garden or interior ornamentation using shells and pebbles) to describe the refined and fanciful style that became fashionable in parts of Europe during the eighteenth century. The Rococo developed in France around 1715, when the duc d'Orléans, regent for the boy-king Louis XV (ruled 1715–1774), moved his home and the French court from Versailles to Paris. The movement spread quickly across Europe (MAP 30–1).

MAP showing Europe and North America with British lands, French lands, and Spanish lands indicated. Labels include: CANADA, NORTH AMERICA, UNITED STATES, MEXICO, QUEBEC, Quebec City, Boston, New York, Philadelphia, Charlottesville, Washington D.C., Richmond, Tucson, Havana, CUBA, HAITI, Mexico City, Gulf of Mexico, Caribbean Sea, Pacific Ocean, Atlantic Ocean, GREAT BRITAIN, SCOTLAND, IRELAND, WALES, London, Paris, EUROPE, GERMANY, Berlin, Dresden, Würzburg, POLAND, HABSBURG AUST. EMPIRE, SWITZ., Venice, Bologna, Rome, DENMARK, RUSSIA, St. Petersburg, PORTUGAL, SPAIN, Madrid, Marseille, OTTOMAN EMPIRE, Chios, PALESTINE, Jaffa, MOROCCO, ALGERIA, AFRICA, SENEGAL, Mississippi R., Severn R., Rhine R., Danube R., Tiber R.

Inset map (HOLLAND/FRANCE): Burslem, Derby, Coalbrookdale, Birmingham, Bath, London, Stourhead, Chiswick, Twickenham, Valenciennes, English Channel, Sèvres, Paris, Versailles, Fontainebleau, Loire R., FRANCE, 200 km / 200 miles.

Inset map (ITALY): Florence, Rome, Naples, Herculaneum, Pompeii, Mt. Vesuvius, Adriatic Sea, Tiber R., ITALY, 100 km / 100 miles. 1000 km / 1000 miles.

MAP 30-1 EUROPE AND NORTH AMERICA IN THE EIGHTEENTH CENTURY

During the eighteenth century, three major artistic styles—Rococo, Neoclassicism, and Romanticism—flourished in Europe and North America.

Rococo Salons

The French court was happy to escape its confinement in the rural palace of Versailles and relocate to Paris. There courtiers built elegant town houses (in French, *hôtels*), whose social rooms may have been smaller than at Versailles, but were no less lavishly decorated. These became the center of social life for aristocrats who cultivated witty exchanges, elegant manners, and a playfully luxurious life specifically dedicated to pleasure, leisure, and sensuality that frequently masked social insecurity and ambivalence. **Salons**, as the rooms and the events held in them were known, were intimate, fashionable, and intellectual gatherings, often including splendid entertainments that mimicked in miniature the rituals of the Versailles court. The salons were hosted on a weekly basis by accomplished, educated women of the upper class including Mesdames de Staël, de La Fayette, de Sévigné, and du Châtelet.

30-2 Germain Boffrand **SALON DE LA PRINCESSE, HÔTEL DE SOUBISE**

Paris. Begun 1732.

Credit: © Hervé Champollion/akg-images

The Rococo style cannot be fully appreciated through single objects, but is evident everywhere in the salons, with their profusely decorated walls and ceilings bursting with exquisite three-dimensional embellishments in gold, silver, and brilliant white paint; their intimate, sensual paintings hung among the rich ornament; and their elaborate crystal chandeliers, mirrored walls, and delicate decorated furniture and tabletop sculptures. When these Parisian salons were lit by candles, they must have glittered with light reflected and refracted by the gorgeous surfaces. The rooms were no doubt also enlivened by the energy of aristocrats, fancifully dressed in a profusion of pastel blues, yellows, greens, and pinks to complement the light, bright details of the Rococo architecture, paintings, and sculptures around them.

The **SALON DE LA PRINCESSE** in the Hôtel de Soubise (**FIG. 30-2**), designed by Germain Boffrand (1667–1754), was the setting for such intimate gatherings of the Parisian aristocracy in the years prior to the French Revolution. Its delicacy and lightness are typical of French Rococo salon design of the 1730s, with architectural elements rendered in sculpted stucco including arabesques (characterized by flowing lines and swirling shapes), S shapes, C shapes, reverse C shapes, volutes, and naturalistic plant forms. Intricate polished surfaces included carved wood panels called boiseries and inlaid wood designs on furniture and floors. The glitter of silver and gold against white and pastel shades and the visual confusion of mirror reflections all enhanced this Rococo interior.

Painting

The paintings and sculpture that decorated Rococo salons and other elegant spaces were instrumental in creating their atmosphere of sensuality and luxury. Pictorial themes were often taken from Classical love stories, and both pictures and sculpted ornament were typically filled with playful *putti*, lush foliage, and fluffy clouds. The paintings of Jean-Antoine Watteau, François Boucher, and Jean-Honoré Fragonard and the tabletop sculpture of Claude Michel, known as Clodion, were highly coveted in salon culture.

WATTEAU   Jean-Antoine Watteau (1684–1721) has been seen as the originator, and for some the greatest practitioner, of the French Rococo style in painting. Born in the

30–3 Jean-Antoine Watteau **THE SIGNBOARD OF GERSAINT**

c. 1721. Oil on canvas, 5'4" × 10'1" (1.62 × 3.06 m). Stiftung Preussische Schlössen und Gärten Berlin-Brandenburg, Schloss Charlottenburg.

Watteau painted this signboard for the Paris art gallery of Edmé-François Gersaint, a dealer who introduced to France the English idea of selling paintings by catalog. The systematic listing of works for sale gave the name of the artist and the title, the medium, and the dimensions of each work of art. The shop depicted on the signboard, however, is not Gersaint's but a gallery created from Watteau's imagination and visited by typically elegant and cultivated patrons. The sign was so admired that Gersaint sold it only 15 days after it was installed. Later it was cut down the middle, and each half was framed separately, which resulted in the loss of some canvas along the sides of each section. The painting was restored and its two halves reunited only in the twentieth century.

30-4 Jean-Antoine Watteau **PILGRIMAGE TO THE ISLAND OF CYTHERA**
1717. Oil on canvas, 4′3″ × 6′4½″ (1.3 × 1.9 m). Musée du Louvre, Paris.

Credit: Photo © RMN-Grand Palais (musée du Louvre)/Stéphane Maréchalle

provincial town of Valenciennes, Watteau came to Paris around 1702, where he studied Rubens's paintings for Marie de' Medici (SEE FIG. 23-27), then displayed in the Luxembourg Palace, and the paintings and drawings of sixteenth-century Venetians such as Giorgione and Titian (SEE FIGS. 21-26, 21-27), which he saw in a Parisian private collection. Incorporating the fluent brushwork and rich colors of such works from the past, Watteau perfected a graceful personal style that embodied the spirit of his own time.

Watteau painted for the new urban aristocrats who frequently purchased paintings for their homes through art dealers in the city. The signboard he painted for the art dealer Edmé-François Gersaint (FIG. 30-3) shows the interior of one of these shops—an art gallery filled with paintings from the Venetian and Netherlandish schools that Watteau admired. Indeed, the glowing satins and silks of the women's gowns pay homage to artists such as Gerard ter Borch (SEE FIG. 23-42). The visitors to the gallery are elegant ladies and gentlemen, at ease in these surroundings and apparently knowledgeable about painting; they create an atmosphere of aristocratic sophistication. At the left, a woman in shimmering pink satin steps across the threshold, ignoring her companion's outstretched hand, to watch the two porters packing. While one porter holds a mirror, the other carefully lowers into the wooden case a portrait of Louis XIV, which may be a reference to the name of Gersaint's shop,

Au Grand Monarque ("At [the Sign of] the Great Monarch"). It also suggests the passage of time, for Louis had died six years earlier.

Other elements in the work also suggest transience. On the left, the clock directly above the king's portrait, topped with an allegorical figure of Fame and sheltering a pair of lovers, is a **memento mori**, a reminder of mortality, suggesting that both love and fame are subject to the ravages of time. Well-established *vanitas* emblems are the easily destroyed straw (in the foreground) and the young woman gazing into the mirror (set next to a vanity case on the counter)—mirrors and images of young women looking at their reflections had been familiar symbols of the fragility of human life since the Baroque period. Notably, the two gentlemen at the end of the counter also appear to gaze at the mirror, and are thus also implicated in the *vanitas* theme. Watteau, who died from tuberculosis before he was 40, produced this painting during his last illness. Gersaint later wrote that Watteau had completed the painting in eight days, working only in the mornings because of his failing health. When the *Signboard* was installed, it was greeted with almost universal admiration; Gersaint sold it in less than a month.

In **PILGRIMAGE TO THE ISLAND OF CYTHERA** (FIG. **30-4**), painted four years earlier, Watteau portrayed an imagined vision of the idyllic and sensual life of Rococo

30–5 François Boucher
**GIRL RECLINING:
LOUISE O'MURPHY**
1751. Oil on canvas,
23¼ × 28¾″ (59 × 73 cm).
Wallraf-Richartz Museum,
Cologne.

Credit: Rheinisches Bildarchiv,
Museen der Stadt Köln

aristocrats, but with the same undertone of melancholy that hints at the fleeting quality of human happiness. This is a dream world in which beautifully dressed and elegantly posed couples, accompanied by *putti*, conclude the romantic trysts of their day on Cythera, the island sacred to Venus, the goddess of love, whose garlanded statue appears at the extreme right. The lovers, dressed in exquisite satins, silks, and velvets, gather in the verdant landscape. Such idyllic and wistfully melancholic visions of aristocratic leisure charmed both early eighteenth-century Paris and most of Europe. Watteau painted *Pilgrimage to the Island of Cythera* in 1717 as his official examination canvas for admission to membership of the French Royal Academy of Painting and Sculpture. Although there was no academic category to cover the painting, the academicians were so impressed by the canvas that they created a new category, the **fête galante**, or elegant outdoor entertainment, to describe this genre.

BOUCHER The artist most closely associated with Parisian Rococo painting after Watteau's death is François Boucher (1703–1770). The son of a minor painter, Boucher in 1723 entered the workshop of an engraver where he was hired to reproduce Watteau's paintings for a collector, laying the groundwork for the future direction of his career.

After studying in Rome from 1727 to 1731 at the academy founded there by the French Royal Academy of Painting and Sculpture, Boucher settled in Paris and became an academician. Soon his life and career were intimately bound up with two women. The first was his artistically talented wife, Marie-Jeanne Buseau, who was her husband's frequent model as well as his studio assistant. The other was Louis XV's mistress, Madame de Pompadour, who became his major patron and supporter. Pompadour was an amateur artist herself and took lessons in printmaking from Boucher. After he received his first royal commission in 1735, Boucher worked almost continuously on the decorations for the royal residences at Versailles and Fontainebleau. In 1755, he was made chief inspector at the Gobelins tapestry manufactory; he provided designs for it as well as for the Sèvres porcelain and Beauvais tapestry manufactories. Boucher operated in a much more commercial market than artists in the previous century had done—all these workshops produced both furnishings for the royal household and wares for sale on the open market by merchants such as Edmé-François Gersaint.

In 1765, Boucher became First Painter to the King. In this role he painted portraits of Louis XV, scenes of daily life, mythological pictures, and a series of erotic works for private enjoyment, often depicting the adventures of Venus. The subject of one such painting—**GIRL RECLINING: LOUISE O'MURPHY (FIG. 30-5)**—however, is hardly mythological. The teenage Louise O'Murphy, who would soon be one of the mistresses of Louis XV, appears provocatively pink and completely naked, sprawled across a day bed on her stomach, looking out of the painting and completely unaware of our presence. Her satiny clothing is crushed beneath her, and her spread legs sink into a pillow; braids and a blue ribbon decorate her hair, while a fallen pink rose is highlighted on the floor. Louise's plump buttocks are displayed at the very center of the painting, leaving little doubt about the painting's subject. In contrast to Watteau's *fête galante*, in which imaginary aristocrats and *putti* frolic decorously in idyllic settings, the overtly sensual woman shown here is clearly human, a known contemporary personality, and presented to us in a very real Rococo room.

FRAGONARD Another master of French Rococo painting, Jean-Honoré Fragonard (1732–1806), studied with Boucher, who encouraged him to enter the competition for the Prix de Rome, a three- to five-year scholarship awarded to the top students graduating from the art school of the French Royal Academy of Painting and Sculpture. Fragonard won the prize in 1752 and spent the years 1756 to 1761 in Italy, but it was not until 1765 that he was finally accepted as a member of the Academy. He catered to the tastes of an aristocratic clientele, and, as a decorator of interiors, began to fill the vacuum left by Boucher's death in 1770.

Fragonard's **THE SWING** (**FIG. 30–6**) of 1767 was originally commissioned from another painter, Gabriel-François Doyen, although the identity of the patron is unknown. Doyen described the subject he was asked to paint as sensually explicit, and he refused the commission, giving it to Fragonard, who created a small jewel of a painting. A pretty young woman is suspended on a swing, her movement created by an elderly guardian obscured by the shadow of the bushes on the right who pulls her with a rope. On the left, the girl's blushing lover hides in the bushes, swooning with anticipation. As the swing approaches, he is rewarded with an unobstructed view up her skirt, lifted on his behalf by an

30–6 Jean-Honoré Fragonard **THE SWING**

1767. Oil on canvas, 31⅞ × 25¼″ (81 × 64.2 cm). The Wallace Collection, London.

Credit: © Wallace Collection, London, UK/ Bridgeman Images extended leg. The young man reaches out toward her with his hat as if to make a mockingly useless attempt to conceal the view, while she glances down, seductively slinging one of her shoes toward him. The playful abandon of the lovers, the complicity of the sculpture of Cupid on the left, his shushing gesture assuring that he will not tell, the *putti* and dolphin beneath the swing who seem to urge the young woman on, and the poor, duped guardian to the right all work together to create an image that bursts with anticipation and desire, but also maintains a robust sense of humor.

Sculpture and Architecture

CLODION In the last quarter of the eighteenth century, Rococo largely fell out of favor in France, its style and subject matter attacked for being frivolous at best and immoral at worst. One sculptor who clung to the style almost until the French Revolution, however, was Claude Michel, known as Clodion (1738–1814). Most of his work consisted of playful, erotic tabletop sculpture, mainly in unpainted terra cotta. Typical of his Rococo designs is the terra-cotta model he submitted to win a 1784 royal commission for a large monument to **THE INVENTION OF THE BALLOON** (**FIG. 30-7**). In the eighteenth century, hot-air balloons were elaborately decorated with painted Rococo scenes, gold braid, and tassels. Clodion's balloon, circled with bands of ornament, rises from a columnar launching pad belching billowing clouds of smoke, assisted at the left by a puffing wind god with butterfly wings and heralded at the right by a trumpeting Victory. Some *putti* stoke the fire basket, providing the hot air that allows the balloon to ascend, while others gather reeds for fuel and carry them up to feed the fire.

CHURCH DESIGN AND DECORATION The beginning of the Rococo coincided with the waning importance of the Church as a major patron of art in northern Europe. Although churches continued to be built and decorated, the dominance of both the Church and the hereditary aristocracy as patrons diminished significantly. The Rococo proved, however, to be a powerful vehicle for spiritual experience. Several important churches were built in the style, showing how visual appearance can be tailored to a variety of social meanings. One of the most opulent Rococo churches is dedicated to the Vierzehnheiligen (the "Fourteen Auxiliary Saints" or "Holy Helpers"); it was designed by Johann Balthasar Neumann (1687–1753) and constructed in Bavaria between 1743 and 1772. The plan (**FIG. 30-8**), based on six interpenetrating oval spaces of varying sizes around a vaulted ovoid center, recalls that of Borromini's Baroque church of San Carlo alle Quattro Fontane in Rome (SEE FIG. 23-6B). But the effect here is airy lightness. In the nave (**FIG. 30-9**), the Rococo love of undulating surfaces with overlays of decoration creates a

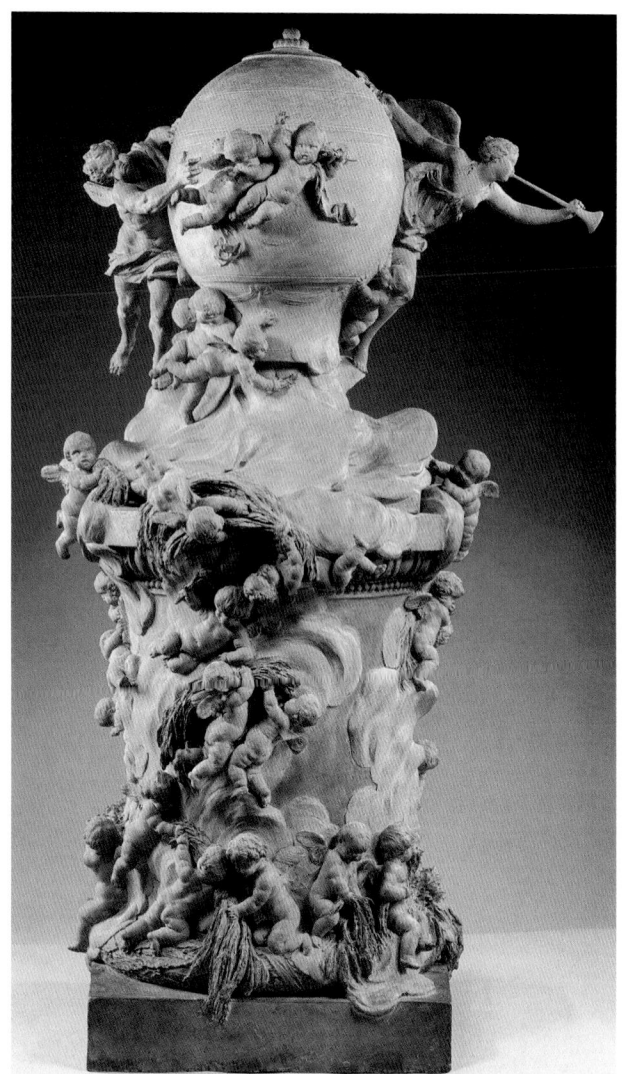

30-7 Clodion **THE INVENTION OF THE BALLOON**
1784. Terra-cotta model for a monument, height 43½" (110.5 cm). Metropolitan Museum of Art, New York. Rogers Fund and Frederick R. Harris Gift, 1944 (44.21a b).

Clodion had a long career as a sculptor in the exuberant Rococo manner seen in this work commemorating the 1783 invention of the hot-air balloon. During the austere revolutionary period of the First Republic (1792–1804), he became one of the few Rococo artists to adopt successfully the more acceptable Neoclassical manner. In 1806, he was commissioned by Napoleon to provide the relief sculpture for two Paris monuments, the Vendôme Column and the Carrousel Arch near the Louvre.

visionary world where surfaces scarcely exist. Instead, the viewer is surrounded by clusters of pilasters and engaged columns interspersed with two levels of arched openings to the side aisles, and large clerestory windows illuminating the gold and white of the interior. The foliage of the fanciful capitals is repeated in arabesques, wreaths, and the ornamented frames of irregular panels lining the vault. An ebullient sense of spiritual uplift is achieved by the complete integration of architecture and decoration.

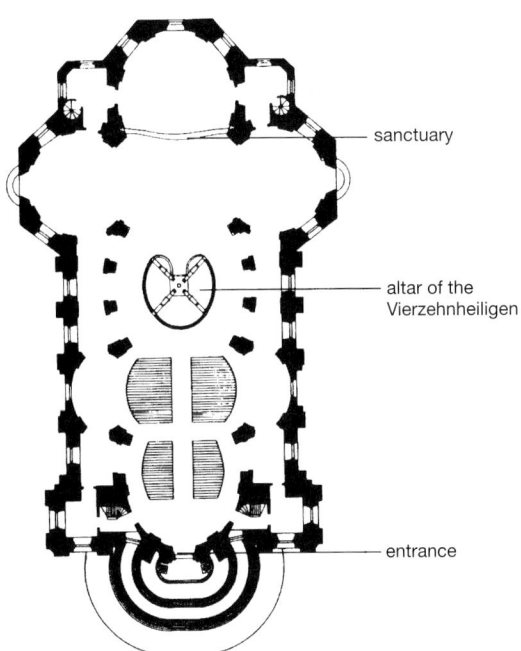

30-8 Johann Balthasar Neumann **PLAN OF THE CHURCH OF THE VIERZEHNHEILIGEN**

Near Bamberg, Bavaria, Germany. c. 1743.

30-9 Johann Balthasar Neumann **INTERIOR, CHURCH OF THE VIERZEHNHEILIGEN**

Near Bamberg, Bavaria, Germany. 1743–1772.

Credit: © Achim Bednorz, Cologne

The Grand Tour and Neoclassicism in Italy

What is the relationship between the Grand Tour and the development of Neoclassicism in Italy?

From the late 1600s until well into the nineteenth century, the education of a wealthy young northern European or American gentleman—few women were considered worthy of such education—was completed on the **Grand Tour**, an extended visit to the major cultural sites of southern Europe. Accompanied by a tutor and an entourage of servants, the Grand Tourist began in Paris, moved on to southern France to visit a number of well-preserved Roman buildings and monuments there, then headed to Venice, Florence, Naples, and Rome. As the repository of the Classical and Renaissance pasts, Italy was the focus of the Grand Tour.

Italy— Rome in particular—was also the primary destination for artists and scholars interested in the Classical past. In addition to the ancient architecture and sculpture throughout Rome, the nearby sites of Pompeii and Herculaneum offered sensational new material for study and speculation. In the mid eighteenth century, archaeologists began the systematic excavation of these two prosperous Roman towns buried by a sudden volcanic eruption in 79 CE.

The artists and intellectuals who found inspiration in the Classical past were instrumental in the development of Neoclassicism, which was both a way of viewing the world and an influential movement in the visual arts. Neoclassicism (*neo* means "new") sought to present Classical ideals and subject matter in a style derived from Classical Greek and Roman sources. Neoclassical paintings reflect the clear forms, tight compositions, and shallow space of ancient relief sculpture. Because the ancient world was considered the source of British and European democracy, secular government, and civilized thought and action, its art was viewed as the embodiment of timeless civic and moral lessons. Neoclassical paintings and sculptures were frequently painted for and displayed in public places in order to inspire patriotism, nationalism, and courage. Neoclassicism was especially popular in Britain, America, and France as a visual expression of the state and political stability.

Grand Tour Portraits and Views

Artists in Italy benefited not only from their access to authentic works of antiquity, but also from the steady stream of wealthy art collectors on the Grand Tour. Tourists visited the studios of important Italian artists in order to view and purchase works that could be brought home and displayed as evidence of their cultural travels.

CARRIERA Wealthy European visitors to Italy frequently sat for portraits by Italian artists. Rosalba Carriera (1675–1757), the leading portraitist in Venice in the first half of the eighteenth century, worked mainly in pastel, a medium better suited than slow-drying oil to accommodate sitters whose time in the city was limited. **Pastel** is fast and versatile: Pastel crayons, made of pulverized pigment bound to a chalk base by weak gum water, can be used to sketch quickly and spontaneously, or they can be rubbed and blended on the surface of paper to produce a shiny and highly finished surface.

Carriera began her career designing lace patterns and painting miniature portraits on the ivory lids of snuffboxes before she graduated to pastel portraits. Her portraits were so widely admired that she was awarded honorary membership of Rome's Academy of St. Luke in 1705 and was later admitted to the academies in Bologna and Florence. In 1720, she traveled to Paris, where she made a pastel portrait of the young Louis XV and was elected to

30–10 Rosalba Carriera **GUSTAVUS HAMILTON, 2ND VISCOUNT BOYNE**

1730–1731. Pastel on blue paper, 22¼ × 16⅞″ (56.5 × 42.9 cm). Metropolitan Museum, New York.

Credit: © 2016. Image copyright The Metropolitan Museum of Art/Art Resource/Scala, Florence

30–11 Canaletto **THE DOGE'S PALACE AND THE RIVA DEGLI SCHIAVONI**

Late 1730s. Oil on canvas, 24⅛ × 39¼″ (61.3 × 99.8 cm). National Gallery, London. Wynn Ellis Bequest 1876 (NG 940).

Credit: © 2016. Copyright The National Gallery, London/Scala, Florence

30-12 Giovanni Battista Piranesi **VIEW OF THE PANTHEON, ROME**

From the *Views of Rome* series, first printed in 1756. Etching, 18⁹⁄₁₆ × 27⅛" (47.2 × 69.7 cm). Yale University Art Gallery, The Arthur Ross Collection (2012.159.11.60.)

Credit: Image courtesy Yale University Art Gallery

the French Royal Academy of Painting and Sculpture, despite the 1706 rule forbidding the further admission of women. Returning to Italy in 1721, she established herself in Venice as a portraitist of handsome young men such as the Irish aristocrat **GUSTAVUS HAMILTON, 2ND VISCOUNT BOYNE (FIG. 30-10)**. He visited Venice in both 1730 and 1731, and Carriera portrays him dressed for carnival with a half mask and lace veil under his stylish tricorne hat.

CANALETTO A painted city view was by far the most prized souvenir of a stay in Venice. Two kinds of views were produced in Venice: the **capriccio** ("caprice," plural *capricci*), an imaginary landscape or cityscape in which the artist mixed actual structures, such as famous ruins, with imaginary ones to create attractive compositions; and the **veduta** ("view," plural *vedute*), a more naturalistic rendering of famous views and buildings, well-known tourist attractions, and local color in the form of tiny figures of Venetian people and visiting tourists. *Vedute* often encompassed panoramic views of famous landmarks, as in **THE DOGE'S PALACE AND THE RIVA DEGLI SCHIAVONI (FIG. 30-11)** by the Venetian artist Giovanni Antonio Canal, called Canaletto (1697–1768). It was thought that Canaletto used a camera obscura (see Chapter 31) to render his *vedute* with exact topographical accuracy, but his drawings show that he seems to have worked freehand. In fact, his views are rarely topographically accurate; more often than not, they are composite images, so skillfully composed that we can easily believe that Canaletto's *vedute* are "real." He painted and sold so many to British visitors that his dealer sent him to London from 1746 to 1755 to paint views of the English capital city for his British clients, who included several important aristocrats as well as King George III.

PIRANESI The city of Rome was also captured in *vedute* for tourists and armchair travelers, notably by Giovanni Battista Piranesi (1720–1778). Trained in Venice as an architect, he moved to Rome in 1740 and studied etching, eventually establishing a publishing house and becoming one of the century's most successful printmakers. Piranesi produced a large series of *vedute* of ancient Roman monuments, whose ruined, deteriorating condition made them even more interesting for his customers. His **VIEW OF THE PANTHEON (FIG. 30-12)** demonstrates his careful study of this great work of ancient Roman architecture, which seems even more monumental in relation to the dramatic clouds that frame it and the small figures who surround it on the ground, admiring its grandeur from all directions.

Neoclassicism in Rome

The intellectuals and artists who came to study and work in Rome often formed communities with a shared interest in Neoclassical ideals. One such British group included Angelica Kauffmann (SEE FIG. 30-28), Benjamin West (SEE FIG. 30-29), and Gavin Hamilton (1723–1798), all of whom contributed to early Neoclassicism, and there were similar gatherings of artists from France and Germany. One of the most influential communities was formed at the Villa Albani on the outskirts of Rome, under the sponsorship of Cardinal Alessandro Albani (1692–1779).

Cardinal Albani built his villa in 1760–1761 specifically to house and display his vast collection of antique sculpture, sarcophagi, intaglios (objects with designs carved into the surface), cameos, and ceramics, and it became one of the most important stops on the Grand Tour. The villa was more than a museum: It was also a place to buy art and artifacts. Albani sold items to artists and tourists alike to help satisfy the growing craze for antiquities; unfortunately, many had been faked or heavily restored by artisans in the cardinal's employ.

In 1758, Albani hired Johann Joachim Winckelmann (1717–1768), the leading theoretician of Neoclassicism, as his secretary and librarian. The Prussian-born Winckelmann had become an expert on Classical art while working in Dresden, where the French Rococo style that he deplored was still fashionable. In 1755, he had published a pamphlet, *Thoughts on the Imitation of Greek Works in Painting and Sculpture*, in which he attacked the Rococo as decadent, arguing that modern artists could only claim their status as legitimate artists by imitating Greek art. After relocating to Rome to work for Albani, Winckelmann published a second influential treatise, *The History of Ancient Art* (1764), often considered the beginning of modern art-historical study. In it Winckelmann was the first to analyze the history of art as a succession of period styles, an approach which later became the norm for art history books (including this one).

MENGS Winckelmann's closest friend and colleague in Rome was a fellow German, the painter Anton Raphael Mengs (1728–1779). In 1761, Cardinal Albani commissioned Mengs to paint the ceiling of the great gallery in his new villa. To our eyes Mengs's **PARNASSUS** ceiling (**FIG. 30-13**) may seem stilted, but it is nevertheless significant as the first full expression of Neoclassicism in painting. The scene is taken from Classical mythology. Mount Parnassus in central Greece was where the ancients believed Apollo (god of poetry, music, and the arts) and

the nine Muses (female personifications of artistic inspiration) resided. Mengs depicted Apollo—practically nude and holding a lyre and olive branch to represent artistic accomplishment—standing at the compositional center, his pose copied from the famous *Apollo Belvedere* in the Vatican collection, one of Winckelmann's favorite Greek statues. Around Apollo are the Muses and their mother, Mnemosyne (Memory, leaning on a Doric column). Mengs arranged his figures in a roughly symmetrical, pyramidal composition parallel to the picture plane, like the relief sculpture he had studied at Herculaneum. Winckelmann praised this work, claiming that it captured the "noble simplicity and calm grandeur" of ancient Greek sculpture. Shortly after its completion, Mengs left for Spain, where he served as court painter until 1777, bringing Neoclassical ideas with him. Other artists from Rome carried the style elsewhere in Europe.

CANOVA The theories of the Albani–Winckelmann circle were applied most vigorously by sculptors in Rome, who remained committed to Neoclassicism for almost 100 years. The leading Neoclassical sculptor of the late eighteenth and early nineteenth centuries was Antonio Canova (1757–1822). Born near Venice into a family of stonemasons, he settled in Rome in 1781, where he adopted the Neoclassical style under the guidance of the Scottish painter Gavin Hamilton and quickly became the most sought-after European sculptor of the period.

30-13 Anton Raphael Mengs **PARNASSUS**
Ceiling fresco in the Villa Albani, Rome. 1761.

Credit: © akg-images/Mondadori Portfolio/Sergio Anelli

30-14 Antonio Canova **CUPID AND PSYCHE**

1787–1793. Marble, 61 × 68″ (1.55 × 1.73 m). Musée du Louvre, Paris.

Credit: Photo © Musée du Louvre, Dist. RMN-Grand Palais/Raphaël Chipault

One of Canova's most admired works depicts the erotically charged mythological subject **CUPID AND PSYCHE** (**FIG. 30-14**) in a way that recalls the ancient Classical sculpture that attracted artists and scholars to Rome. Condemned to a death-like sleep by a jealous Venus, Psyche revives at Cupid's kiss. His projecting wings offset the rounded forms of the two linked bodies and balance the downward diagonal extensions of the figures' legs. The lustrous finish of their marble skin shines against the contrasting textures of drapery and rocks. Although carved fully in the round, the work is meant to be experienced frontally, as a symmetrically stable composition of interlocking triangles and ovals. The effect is ordered, decorous, and calming, if still titillating.

Neoclassicism and Early Romanticism in Britain

What distinguishes Neoclassicism and Romanticism in the eighteenth-century art and architecture of England?

British tourists and artists in Italy became leading supporters of early Neoclassicism, partly because of the early burgeoning taste for revival styles at home, but the Classical revival in Britain had a slightly different focus from what we saw in Rome. It is in British art and literature that we find the beginnings of Romanticism.

While Roman Neoclassicism looked to the past in order to revive a sense of moral and civic virtue, many later eighteenth-century British artists harnessed the concept of civic virtue to patriotism to create more Romantic works of art dedicated specifically to the British nation.

Like Neoclassicism, Romanticism describes not only a style but also an attitude: It celebrates the individual and the subjective, while Neoclassicism celebrates the universal and the rational. Romanticism takes its name and many of its themes from the "romances"—novellas, stories, and poems written in Romance (Latin-derived) languages. The term "Romantic" suggests something fantastic or novelistic, perhaps set in a remote time or place, infused by a poetic melancholy, occasionally inciting terror or horror. One of the best examples of early Romanticism in literature is *The Sorrows of Young Werther* (1774) by Johann Wolfgang von Goethe (1749–1832), in which a sensitive, outcast young man fails at love and kills himself. This is a story about a troubled individual who loses his way; it does not recall ancient virtues or civic responsibility.

Neoclassicism and Romanticism existed side by side in the later eighteenth and early nineteenth centuries—two ways of looking at the world, serving distinct purposes in society. Neoclassicism tended to be a more public art form, and Romanticism more individual and private. Sometimes Neoclassicism even functioned within Romanticism. Distinctions were not always clear.

30–15A Richard Boyle (Lord Burlington) **EXTERIOR VIEW OF CHISWICK HOUSE**
West London, England. 1724–1729. Interior decoration (1726–1729) and new gardens (1730–1740) by William Kent.

Credit: © Achim Bednorz, Cologne

The Classical Revival in Architecture and Design

Ancient Greece and Rome provided a morally elevated inspiration for eighteenth-century British buildings, utensils, poetry, and even clothing. Women started wearing white muslin gowns and men curled their hair forward in imitation of Classical statues. In the 1720s, a group of professional architects and wealthy amateurs in Britain, led by a Scot, Colen Campbell (1676–1729), stood against what they viewed as the immoral extravagance of the Italian Baroque. They advocated a return to the austerity and simplicity of the Classically inspired architecture of Andrea Palladio, and his country houses in particular.

CHISWICK HOUSE   Designed in 1724 by its owner, Richard Boyle, the third Earl of Burlington (1695–1753), **CHISWICK HOUSE (FIG. 30-15)** is a fine example of British Neo-Palladianism. In visiting Palladio's country houses in Italy, Burlington was particularly struck by the Villa Rotonda (SEE FIGS. 21-35, 21-36), which inspired his design for Chiswick House. The plan shares the bilateral symmetry of Palladio's villa, although its central core is octagonal rather than round and there are only two entrances. The main entrance, flanked here by matching staircases, is a Roman temple front, an imposing entrance for the earl. Chiswick's elevation is characteristically Palladian, with

30–15B Richard Boyle (Lord Burlington) **PLAN OF CHISWICK HOUSE**
West London, England. 1724.

a main floor resting on a basement, and tall, rectangular windows with triangular pediments. The few, crisp details seem perfectly suited to the refined proportions of the whole. The result is a lucid evocation of Palladio's design.

When in Rome, Burlington persuaded the English expatriate William Kent (1685–1748) to return to London as his collaborator. Kent designed Chiswick's surprisingly ornate interior as well as its grounds, the latter in a style that became known throughout Europe as the English landscape garden. Kent's garden abandoned the regularity and rigid formality of Baroque gardens (see "Garden Design" in Chapter 23 on page 772). It featured winding paths, a lake with a cascade, irregular plantings of shrubs, and other effects that imitated the appearance of a natural, rural landscape. In fact, it was carefully designed and manicured.

STOURHEAD Following Kent's lead at Chiswick, landscape architecture flourished in England in the hands of such designers as Lancelot ("Capability") Brown (1716–1783) and Henry Flitcroft (1697–1769). In the 1740s, the banker Henry Hoare began redesigning the grounds of his estate at Stourhead in Wiltshire (**FIG. 30-16**) with the assistance of Flitcroft, a protégé of Burlington. The resulting gardens at Stourhead carried Kent's ideas for the English garden much further. Stourhead is a perfect example of the English **picturesque** garden: Its conception and views intentionally mimic the compositional devices of "pictures" by French landscape painter Claude Lorrain (SEE FIG. 23-56), whose paintings were popular in England. The picturesque view illustrated here shows a garden designed with "counterfeit neglect," intentionally

contrived to look natural and unkempt. The small lake is crossed by a rustic bridge, while in the background we see a "folly," a miniature version of the Pantheon in Rome. The park is punctuated by other Classically inspired temples, copies of antique statues, artificial grottoes, a rural cottage, a Chinese bridge, a Gothic spire, and even a Turkish tent. The result is a delightful mixture of styles and cultures that combines aspects of both the Neoclassical and the Romantic. Inside the house, Hoare commissioned Mengs to paint *The Meeting of Antony and Cleopatra*, a blended work that chooses from Classical history a Romanticized subject.

DECORATIVE ARTS The interiors of country houses like Chiswick and Stourhead were designed partly as settings for the art collections of British aristocrats, which included antiquities as well as a range of Neoclassical paintings, sculpture, and decorative wares (see "Closer Look" on page 936).

The most successful producer of Neoclassical decorative art was Josiah Wedgwood (1730–1795). In 1769, near his native village of Burslem, he opened a pottery factory called Etruria after the ancient Etruscan civilization in central Italy known for its pottery. His production-line shop had several divisions, each with its own kilns and workers trained in diverse specialties. A talented chemist, in the mid-1770s Wedgwood perfected a fine-grained, unglazed, colored pottery which he called **jasperware**. His most popular jasperware featured white figures against a

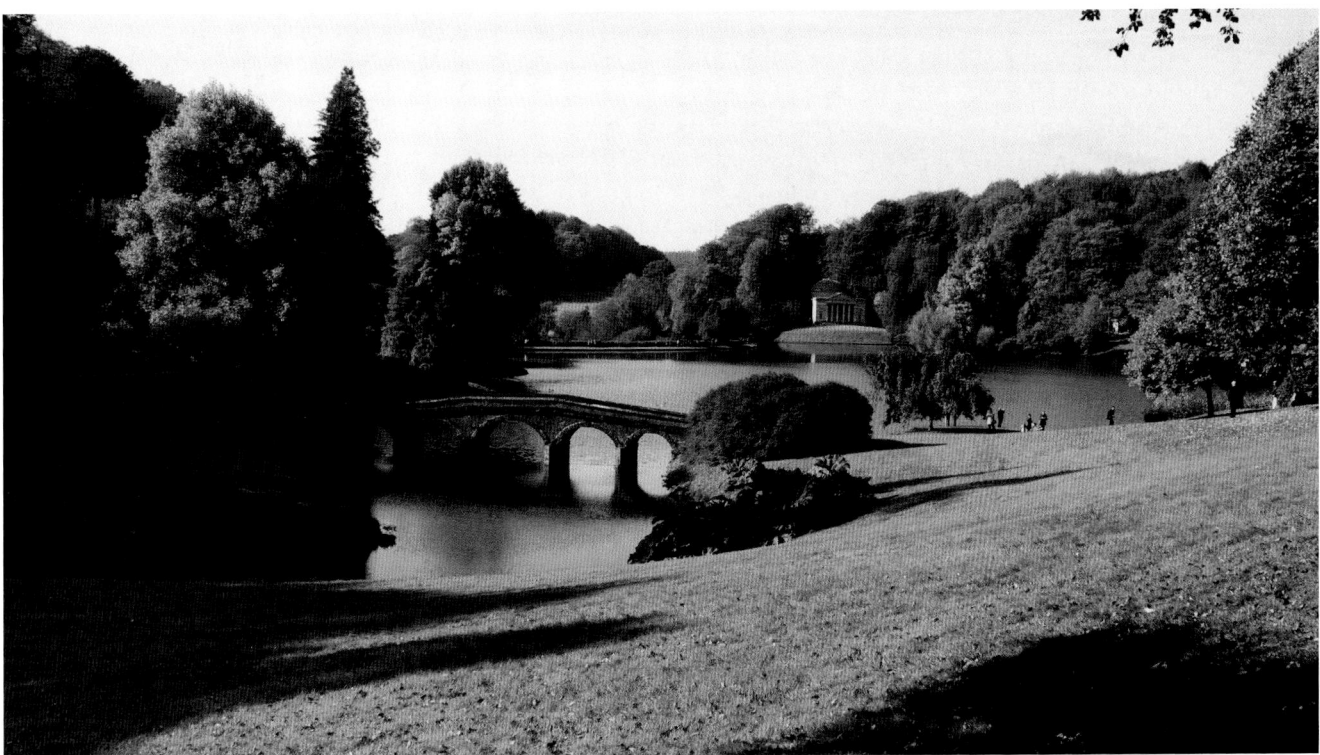

30-16 Henry Flitcroft and Henry Hoare **THE PARK AT STOURHEAD**
Wiltshire, England. Laid out 1743, executed 1744–1765, with continuing additions.

Credit: Gail Johnson/Fotolia

A Closer Look

GEORGIAN SILVER

All of the objects shown here bear the marks of silver shops run either wholly or partly by women, who played a significant role in the production of silver during the Georgian period—the years from 1714 to 1830, when Great Britain was ruled by four successive kings named George.

This goblet was used for drinking punch, a potent alcoholic beverage enjoyed by British high society. The gilded interior protected the silver from the acid in punch.

The filled goblets would have been served from a tray called a salver.

This snuffbox was made to hold snuff, a pulverized tobacco inhaled by both men and women of the upper class. It has curved sides for easy insertion into the pocket of a gentleman's tight-fitting trousers.

These "double beaker" cups were also for drinking punch. The smaller size made them convenient for use when traveling.

This ladle was used to pour punch from a bowl into a goblet. Its twisted whalebone handle floats, making it easy to retrieve from the bowl.

30–17 GEORGIAN SILVER

Elizabeth Morley: George III toddy ladle, 1802; Alice and George Burrows: George III snuffbox, 1802; Elizabeth Cooke: George III salver, 1767; Ann and Peter Bateman: George III goblet, 1797; Hester Bateman: George III double beaker, 1790.

National Museum of Women in the Arts, Washington, DC. Silver collection assembled by Nancy Valentine. Purchased with funds donated by Mr. and Mrs. Oliver Grace and family.

blue ground, as in **THE APOTHEOSIS OF HOMER** jar (**FIG. 30–18**). The low-relief decoration was designed by the sculptor John Flaxman Jr. (1755–1826), who worked for Wedgwood from 1775 to 1787. Flaxman based this scene on a book illustration portraying a particular Greek vessel in the collection of William Hamilton (1730–1803), a leading collector of antiquities and one of Wedgwood's major patrons. Flaxman simplified the original design to accommodate the popular, idealized notion of ancient Greek art and the demands of mass production.

The socially conscious Wedgwood, informed by Enlightenment thinking, established a village for his employees and showed concern for their well-being. He was also active in the international effort to halt the

African slave trade and abolish slavery. To publicize the abolitionist cause, he commissioned the sculptor William Hackwood (c. 1757–1839) to design an emblem for the British Committee to Abolish the Slave Trade, formed in 1787. Hackwood created a small medallion of black-and-white jasperware with a cameo likeness of an African man kneeling in chains and the legend **"AM I NOT A MAN AND A BROTHER?"** (**FIG. 30–19**). Wedgwood sent copies of the medallion to Benjamin Franklin, the president of the Philadelphia Abolition Society, and to others in the abolitionist movement. The image was so compelling that the women's suffrage movement in the United States later modified it to represent a woman in chains with the motto "Am I Not a Woman and a Sister?"

30–18 Josiah Wedgwood **THE APOTHEOSIS OF HOMER**
Made at the Wedgwood Etruria factory, Staffordshire, England. 1790–1795. White jasperware body with a mid-blue dip and white relief, height 18″ (45.7 cm). *Relief of the Apotheosis of Homer* adapted from a plaque by John Flaxman, Jr., 1778. Trustees of the Wedgwood Museum, Barlaston, Staffordshire, England.

Credit: Photo © Wedgwood Museum/WWRD

30–19 William Hackwood for Josiah Wedgwood **"AM I NOT A MAN AND A BROTHER?"**
1787. Black-and-white jasperware, 1⅜ × 1⅜″ (3.5 × 3.5 cm).
Trustees of the Wedgwood Museum, Barlaston, Staffordshire, England.

Credit: Photo © Wedgwood Museum/WWRD

The Gothic Revival in Architecture and Design

The Gothic Revival emerged alongside Neoclassicism in Britain in the mid eighteenth century and spread to several other nations after 1800. An early advocate of the Gothic Revival was the conservative politician and author Horace Walpole (1717–1797), who in 1764 published *The Castle of Otranto*, widely regarded as the first Gothic novel. This tale of mysterious and supernatural happenings set in the Middle Ages almost single-handedly launched a fashion for the Gothic. In 1749, Walpole began to remodel his country house, **STRAWBERRY HILL**, transforming it into the kind of Gothic castle that he described in his fiction (**FIG. 30–20**).

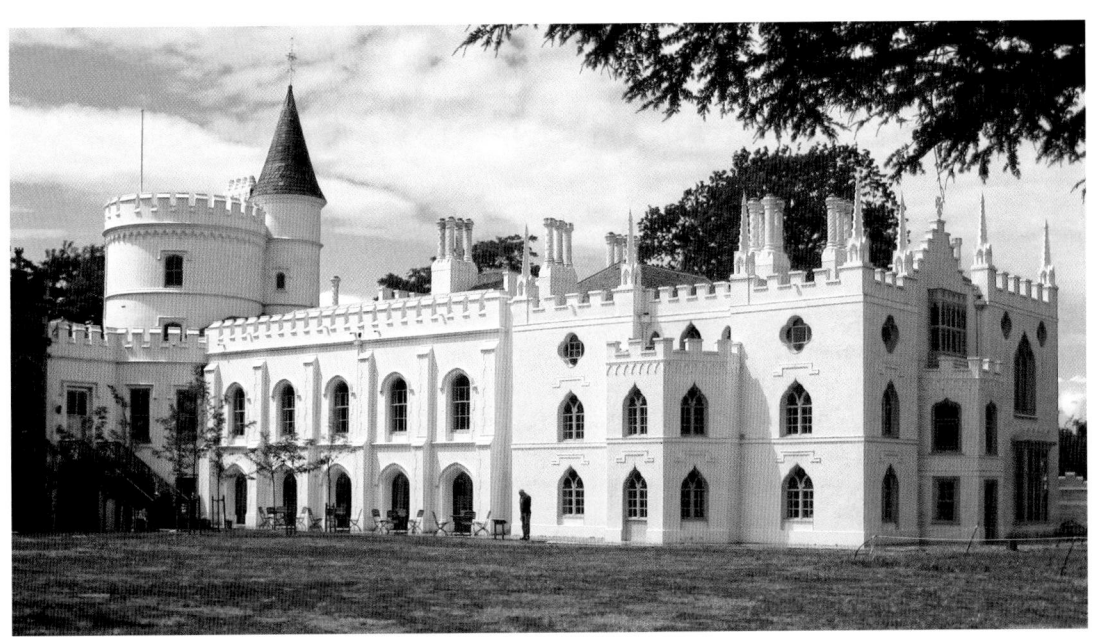

30–20 Horace Walpole and others **STRAWBERRY HILL**
Twickenham, England. 1749–1776.

Credit: Photo: Robert Neuman

Working with several friends and architects, over the next 30 years he added decorative crenellations (higher and lower sections alternating along the top of a wall), tracery windows, and turrets. The interior, too, was redesigned according to Walpole's fanciful Gothic interpretation of the British historical past. His **PICTURE GALLERY** (**FIG. 30-21**) drew on engravings of medieval architecture from antiquarian books in his library. The gallery ceiling is modeled on that of the Chapel of Henry VII at Westminster, but transformed to suit Walpole's taste. For example, the strawberry design on the fan vaults would not have appeared in medieval architecture.

Iron as a Building Material

In 1779, Abraham Darby III built a bridge over the Severn River (**FIG. 30-22**) at Coalbrookdale in Shropshire, England, a town typical of industrial England, with factories and workers' housing filling the valley. Built primarily for function, the bridge demonstrated a need for newer, better transportation routes for moving industrial goods. Its importance lies in the fact that it is probably the first large-scale example of the use of structural metal in bridge building: Iron struts replace the heavy, hand-cut stone voussoirs of earlier bridges.

Five pairs of cast-iron, semicircular arches form a strong, economical 100-foot span. In functional architecture such as this, the form is determined in large part by the available technology, the properties of the material, and the requirements of engineering, often producing an unintended new aesthetic. Here, the use of metal made possible the light, open, skeletal structure sought by builders since the twelfth century. Cast iron was quickly adopted for the construction of engineering wonders like the soaring train stations of the nineteenth century, leading ultimately to such marvels as the Eiffel Tower (SEE FIG. 31–1).

30–22 Abraham Darby III **SEVERN RIVER BRIDGE**
Coalbrookdale, England. 1779.

Credit: © Dorling Kindersley

Trends in British Painting

In the mid eighteenth century, portraits remained popular in British painting among those with the means to commission them. But a taste was also developing for other subjects, such as moralizing satire and caricature, ancient and modern history, scenes from British literature, and the actual British landscape and its people. Whatever their subject matter, many of the paintings and prints created in Britain reflected Romantic sensibilities and Enlightenment values, including an interest in social change, the embracing of natural beauty, and an enthusiasm for science and technology.

THE SATIRIC SPIRIT   The industrialization of Britain created a large and affluent middle class with enough disposable income to purchase smaller and less formal paintings such as landscapes and genre scenes, as well as prints. Relatively inexpensive printed versions of paintings could also be sold to large numbers of people. William Hogarth (1697–1764) capitalized on this new market for art and was largely responsible for reviving the British print industry in the eighteenth century.

Trained as a portrait painter, Hogarth believed art should contribute to the improvement of society. As part of a flourishing culture of satire in Britain directed at a variety of political and social targets, he illustrated works by John Gay, a writer whose 1728 play *The Beggar's Opera* portrayed all classes as corrupt, but caricatured aristocrats in particular as feckless. In about 1730, Hogarth began illustrating moralizing tales of his own invention in sequences of four to six paintings, which he then produced in sets of mass-produced prints, enabling him to both maximize his profits and reach as many people as possible.

Between 1743 and 1745, Hogarth produced his *Marriage à la Mode* suite, inspired by Joseph Addison's 1712 essay in the *Spectator* promoting the concept of marriage based on love rather than on aristocratic machinations. In his series of paintings and later prints, Hogarth portrays the sordid story and sad end of an arranged marriage between the children of an impoverished aristocrat and a social-climbing member of the newly wealthy merchant class. In the opening scene of the series, **THE MARRIAGE CONTRACT** (**FIG. 30-23**), the cast of characters is assembled to legalize the union. At the right of the painting sits Lord Squanderfield, raising his gout-ridden right foot on

30-23 William Hogarth **THE MARRIAGE CONTRACT**
From *Marriage à la Mode*, 1743–1745. Oil on canvas, 27½ × 35¾" (69.9 × 90.8 cm). National Gallery, London.

a footstool as he points to his lengthy family tree (with a few wilted branches), which goes all the way back to medieval knights, as if to say that the pile of money in front of him on the table is not payment enough for the marriage contract he is being asked to sign. Young Squanderfield, a fop and a simpleton, sits on the far left, admiring himself in the mirror and ignoring his future wife as he takes a pinch of snuff. His neck is already showing signs of syphilis. The unhappy bride-to-be is extravagantly dressed but rather plain, and her wedding ring is threaded through a handkerchief to wipe away her tears. In the center, her father, the uncultured but wealthy merchant in the brash red coat, leans forward to study Lord Squanderfield's pedigree, an empty sack of money at his feet. The other men are lawyers, including the slippery Silvertongue, who is sharpening the quill that will seal the young couple's fate. The next five scenes of the tale describe the progressively disastrous results of such a union, culminating in murder and suicide.

Hogarth hoped to create a distinctively British style of art, free of obscure mythological references and encouraging the self-improvement in viewers that would lead to social progress. His contempt for the decadent tastes of the aristocracy can be seen in the comic detail of the paintings hanging on Lord Squanderfield's walls. Hogarth wanted to entertain and amuse his audiences, but at the same time his acerbic wit lays open the tensions of class and wealth so prevalent in the Britain of his day. Hogarth's work became so popular that in 1745 he was able to give up portraiture, which he considered a deplorable form of vanity.

PORTRAITURE Sir Joshua Reynolds (1723–1792) was a generation younger than Hogarth, and represented the mainstream of British art at the end of the century. After studying Renaissance art in Italy, Reynolds settled in London in 1753, where he worked vigorously to educate artists and patrons to appreciate Classically inspired history painting. In 1768, he was appointed the first president of the Royal Academy. His *Fifteen Discourses to the Royal Academy* (1769–1790) set out his theories on art in great detail. He argued that artists should follow rules derived from studying the great masters of the past, especially those who worked in the Classical tradition; he claimed that the ideal image communicated universal truths, and that artists should avoid representations based solely on observation, as these paintings merely communicated base reality.

Reynolds was able to combine his own taste for history painting with his patrons' desire for images of themselves by developing a type of historical or mythological portraiture called the **Grand Manner**. **LADY SARAH BUNBURY SACRIFICING TO THE GRACES** (FIG. 30–24) is a good example. The large scale of the canvas suggests that it is a history painting, and its details evoke a Classical setting. Framed by a monumental Classical pier and arch and dressed in a classicizing costume, Lady Sarah plays the part of a Roman priestess making a sacrifice to the Three Graces, personifications of female beauty. Portraits such as this were intended for the public rooms, halls, and stairways of aristocratic residences. Reynolds's Grand Manner portraits were widely celebrated, and his London studio was abuzz with sitters, patrons, and assistants. But Reynolds experimented with his paints, so many of his canvases have faded badly.

A counterpoint to Reynolds's style of portraiture is found in the art of Thomas Gainsborough (1727–1788), who catered to his rich and fashionable clients' tastes for the informal poses and natural landscapes introduced to England by Van Dyck in the 1620s (SEE FIG. 23–29).

30–24 Joshua Reynolds **LADY SARAH BUNBURY SACRIFICING TO THE GRACES**

1765. Oil on canvas, 7'10" × 5' (2.42 × 1.53 m). The Art Institute of Chicago. Mr. and Mrs. W. W. Kimball Collection, 1922.4468.

Lady Sarah Bunbury was one of the great beauties of her era. A few years before this portrait was painted, she turned down a proposal of marriage from George III.

30-25 Thomas Gainsborough **ROBERT ANDREWS AND FRANCES CARTER (MR. AND MRS. ANDREWS)**
c. 1748–1750. Oil on canvas, 27½ × 47″ (69.7 × 119.3 cm). National Gallery, London.

Gainsborough was engaged to paint this couple's portrait shortly after the 20-year-old Robert Andrews married 16-year-old Frances Carter in November 1748. An area of painting in Frances's lap has been left unfinished, perhaps anticipating the later addition of a child for her to hold.

Credit: © 2016. Copyright The National Gallery, London/Scala, Florence

Gainsborough's early, unfinished **ROBERT ANDREWS AND FRANCES CARTER** (**FIG. 30–25**), painted soon after their wedding in 1748, shows the wealthy young rural landowner and his wife posed on the grounds of their estate, with the Sudbury River and the hills of Suffolk in the background. The youthful Frances Carter sits stiffly on a decorative seat, the shimmering satin of her fine dress arranged around her, while her husband appears more relaxed, his hunting rifle tucked casually under his arm and his favorite dog at his side. The couple's good care of the land is revealed as well: The neat rows of grain stocks and stubble in the foreground show the use of the seed drill and plant husbandry. Sheep and horses graze in separate fields. The significance of this painting lies in the informal pose of the couple; the depictions of their land, the pride they take in it, and the wealth and power it provides; and the artist's emphasis on nature as the source of bounty and beauty.

THE ROMANCE OF SCIENCE   In the English Midlands, artist Joseph Wright of Derby (1734–1797) shows an Enlightenment fascination with the drama and romance of science in his depiction of **AN EXPERIMENT ON A BIRD IN THE AIR-PUMP** (**FIG. 30–26**). Wright set up his studio during the first wave of the Industrial Revolution, and many of his patrons were self-made, wealthy industrial entrepreneurs.

He belonged to the Lunar Society, a group of industrialists (including Wedgwood), merchants, traders, and progressive aristocrats who met monthly in or near Birmingham to exchange ideas about science and technology. As part of the society's attempts to popularize science, Wright painted a series of "entertaining" scenes of scientific experiments.

The second half of the eighteenth century was an age of rapid technological change, and the development of the air-pump was among the many scientific innovations of the time. Although primarily used to study the properties of gas, it was also widely used in dramatic public demonstrations of scientific principles. In the experiment shown here, air was pumped out of the large glass vessel above the scientist's head until the bird inside collapsed from lack of oxygen. Before the animal died, air was reintroduced by a simple mechanism at the top. Wright depicts the exciting moment before air is reintroduced. Dramatically lit from below by a single light source on the table, the scientist peers out of the picture and gestures like a magician about to perform a trick. By delaying the reintroduction of air, the scientist has created considerable suspense. The three men on the left watch the experiment with great interest, while the young girls on the right have a more emotional response to the proceedings. Near the window at upper right—through which a full moon shines

30–26 Joseph Wright of Derby
**AN EXPERIMENT ON A BIRD
IN THE AIR-PUMP**

1768. Oil on canvas, 6 × 8′
(1.82 × 2.43 m). National Gallery,
London.

Credit: © 2016. Copyright The National
Gallery, London/Scala, Florence

(an allusion to the "Lunar"
Society)—a boy stands ready
to lower a cage when the bird
revives. Science, the painting
suggests, holds the potential
for wonder, excitement, and
discovery about matters of life
and death.

ACADEMIES AND ACADEMY EXHIBITIONS During
the seventeenth century, the French government founded
a number of **academies** for the support and instruction
of students in literature, painting and sculpture, music
and dance, and architecture. In 1664, the French Royal
Academy of Painting and Sculpture in Paris began to
mount occasional exhibitions of members' recent work.
This exhibition came to be known as the Salon because it
was held in the Salon Carré in the Palace of the Louvre. As
of 1737, the Salon was held every other year, with a jury of
members selecting the works to be shown.

History paintings (based on historical, mythological, or biblical narratives and generally conveying a high
moral or intellectual idea) were accorded highest place in
the Academy's hierarchy of genres, followed by historical portraiture, landscape painting, various other forms
of portraiture, genre painting, and still life. The Salon
shows were the only public art exhibitions of importance
in Paris, so they were highly influential in establishing
officially approved styles and in molding public taste;
they also consolidated the Academy's control over the
production of art.

In recognition of Rome's importance as a training ground for aspiring history painters, the French
Royal Academy of Painting and Sculpture opened
a French Academy in Rome in 1666. A competitive
"Prix de Rome," or Rome Prize, enabled the win-
ners to study in Rome for three to five years. A similar
prize was established by the French Royal Academy of
Architecture in 1720. Many Western cultural capitals
emulated the French academic model: Academies were
established in Berlin in 1696, Dresden in 1705, London

in 1768 (**FIG. 30–27**), Boston in 1780, Mexico City in 1785,
and New York in 1802.

Although there were several women members of the
European academies of art before the eighteenth century,
their inclusion amounted to little more than an honorary

30–27 Johann Zoffany **ACADEMICIANS OF
THE ROYAL ACADEMY**

1771–1772. Oil on canvas, 47½ × 59½″ (120.6 × 151.2 cm).
The Royal Collection, Windsor Castle, England.

Zoffany's group portrait of members of the London Royal Academy
reveals how mainstream artists were taught in the 1770s. The
painting shows artists, all men, setting up a life-drawing class and
engaging in lively conversation. The studio is decorated with the
academy's study collection of Classical statues and plaster copies.
Propriety prohibited the presence of women in life-drawing studios,
so Zoffany includes Royal Academicians Mary Moser and Angelica
Kauffmann in portraits on the wall on the right.

Credit: Royal Collection Trust © Her Majesty Queen Elizabeth II, 2016/
Bridgeman Images.

recognition of their achievements. In France, Louis XIV proclaimed in his founding address to the French Royal Academy that its purpose was to reward all worthy artists "without regard to the difference of sex," but this resolve was not put into practice. Only seven women gained the title of "Academician" between 1648 and 1706, after which the Academy was closed to women. Despite this, four more women were admitted by 1770; however, the men, worried that women would become "too numerous," limited the total number of female members to four. Young women were neither admitted to the French Academy School nor allowed to compete for Academy prizes, both of which were required for professional success. They fared even worse at London's Royal Academy. The Swiss painters Mary Moser and Angelica Kauffmann were both founding members in 1768, but no other women were elected until 1922, and then only as associates.

HISTORY PAINTING By the time it was adapted to Neoclassicism, history painting had long been considered the highest form of art. The Swiss history painter Angelica Kauffmann (1741–1807) trained in Italy and was one of the greatest exponents of early Neoclassicism. Already accepting portrait commissions at age 15, Kauffmann painted

Winckelmann's portrait in Rome, became an ardent practitioner of Neoclassicism, and was elected to the Roman Academy of St. Luke. Most eighteenth-century women artists specialized in the "lower" painting genres of portraiture or still life, but Kauffmann boldly embarked on an independent career as a history painter. She arrived in London in 1766 to great acclaim and lived there until 1781, inspiring British artists to paint Classical history paintings and British patrons to buy them. She was welcomed immediately into Joshua Reynolds's inner circle and, as mentioned, was one of only two women named among the founding members of the Royal Academy.

After her return to Italy, Kauffmann painted **CORNELIA POINTING TO HER CHILDREN AS HER TREASURES** (**FIG. 30–28**) for an English patron. The scene in the painting took place in the second century BCE during the republican era of Rome. A woman visitor shows Cornelia her jewels and then asks to see those of her hostess. In response, Cornelia shows off her daughter and two sons, saying: "These are my most precious jewels." Cornelia exemplifies the "good mother," a popular theme among some later eighteenth-century patrons who preferred Classical subjects that taught metaphorical lessons of civic and moral virtue. The value of Cornelia's maternal dedication

30–28 Angelica Kauffmann **CORNELIA POINTING TO HER CHILDREN AS HER TREASURES**
c. 1785. Oil on canvas, 40 × 50" (101.6 × 127 cm). Virginia Museum of Fine Arts, Richmond, Virginia. The Adolph D. and Wilkins C. Williams Fund.

Credit: Virginia Museum of Fine Arts, Richmond. Photo: Katherine Wetzel

30-29 Benjamin West **THE DEATH OF GENERAL WOLFE**
1770. Oil on canvas, 4'11½" × 7' (1.51 × 2.14 m). National Gallery of Canada, Ottawa. Transfer from the Canadian War Memorials, 1921. Gift of the 2nd Duke of Westminster, Eaton Hall, Cheshire, 1918.

The famous actor David Garrick was so moved by this painting that he enacted an impromptu interpretation of the dying Wolfe in front of the work when it was exhibited at the Royal Academy.

is emphasized by the fact that her sons, Tiberius and Gaius Gracchus, grew up to be political reformers. Kauffmann's composition is severe and Classical, but she softens the image with warm, subdued lighting and the tranquil grace of her figures.

During her early years in Rome, Kauffmann had been friends with the American-born Benjamin West (1738–1820), who studied in Philadelphia before he left for Rome in 1759, where he met Winckelmann and became a student of Mengs. In 1763, he moved permanently to London, where he specialized in Neoclassical history painting. In 1768, along with Kauffmann and Reynolds, he became a founding member of the Royal Academy.

Two years later, West shocked Reynolds and his other academic friends with his painting **THE DEATH OF GENERAL WOLFE** (**FIG. 30-29**), which seemed to break completely with Neoclassicism and academic history painting. West argued that history painting was not dependent on dressing figures in Classical costume; in fact, it could represent a contemporary subject as long as the grand themes and elevated message remained intact. Thus, West's painting, and the genre it spawned, came to be known as "modern history" painting. At first, King George III and Joshua

Reynolds were appalled, but modern history pieces had a very strong attraction for both British collectors and the British public, and the king eventually commissioned one of the four replicas of the painting.

West's painting glorifies the British general James Wolfe, who died in 1759 in a British victory over the French for the control of Quebec during the Seven Years' War (1756–1763). West depicted Wolfe in his red uniform expiring in the arms of his comrades under a cloud-swept sky. Wolfe actually died at the base of a tree accompanied by two or three attendants, but the laws of history painting demanded a nobler scene. Thus, though West's painting seems naturalistic, it is not an objective document, nor was it intended to be. West employs the Grand Manner that Reynolds proposed in his *Discourses*, celebrating the valor of the fallen hero, the loyalty of the British soldiers, and the justice of their cause. To indicate the North American setting, West also included at the left a Native American warrior who contemplates the fallen Wolfe— another fiction, since the Native Americans in this battle fought on the side of the French. The dramatic lighting increases the emotional intensity of the scene, as do the poses of Wolfe's attendants, arranged to suggest a Lamentation over the dead Christ. Extending the analogy, the British flag above Wolfe replaces the Christian cross. Just as Christ died for humanity, Wolfe sacrificed himself for the good of the nation. The brilliant color, emotional intensity, and moralizing message made this image extremely popular with the British public. It was translated into a print and received the widest circulation of any image in Britain up to that time.

ROMANTIC PAINTING The emotional drama of West's painting helped launch Romanticism in Britain. Among its early practitioners was John Henry Fuseli (1741–1825), who arrived in London from his native Switzerland in 1764. Trained in theology, philosophy, and the Neoclassical aesthetics of Winckelmann (whose writings he translated into English), Fuseli quickly became a member of London's intellectual elite. Joshua Reynolds encouraged Fuseli to become an artist, and in 1770 he left England to study in Rome, where he spent most of the next eight years. His encounter with the sometimes tortured and expressive aspects of both Roman sculpture and Michelangelo's painting led him not to Neoclassicism, but to his own powerfully expressive style.

Back in London, Fuseli established himself as a history painter, but he specialized in dramatic subjects drawn from Homer, Dante, Shakespeare, and Milton. His interest in the dark recesses of the human mind led him to paint supernatural and irrational subjects. In **THE NIGHTMARE** (FIG. 30-30), he depicts a sleeping woman sprawled across a divan with her head thrown back, oppressed by a gruesome incubus (or *mara*, an evil spirit) crouching on her pelvis in an erotic dream. According to legend, the incubus

30–30 John Henry Fuseli THE NIGHTMARE
1781. Oil on canvas, 39¾ × 49½″ (101 × 127 cm). The Detroit Institute of Arts. Founders Society purchase with Mr. and Mrs. Bert L. Smokler and Mr. and Mrs. Lawrence A. Fleischmann funds.

Fuseli was not popular with the English critics. One writer said that his 1780 entry in the London Royal Academy exhibition "ought to be destroyed," and Horace Walpole called another painting in 1785 "shockingly mad, mad, mad, madder than ever." Even after achieving the highest official acknowledgment of his talents, Fuseli was called "the Wild Swiss" and "Painter to the Devil." But the public appreciated his work, and *The Nightmare*, exhibited at the Royal Academy in 1782, was repeated in at least three more versions and its imagery was disseminated through prints published by commercial engravers. One of these prints would later hang in the office of the Austrian psychoanalyst Sigmund Freud, who believed that dreams were manifestations of the dreamer's repressed desires.

was believed to feed by stealing women and having sex with them. In the background a horse with wild, phosphorescent eyes thrusts its head into the room through a curtain. The image communicates fear of the unknown and unknowable, and sexuality without restraint. The painting was exhibited at the Royal Academy in 1782, and although not well received by Fuseli's peers, it struck a chord with the public. He painted at least four versions of this subject, and prints of it had a wide circulation.

Fuseli's friend William Blake (1757–1827), a highly original poet, painter, and printmaker, was also inspired by the dramatic aspect of Michelangelo's art. Trained as an engraver, he enrolled briefly at the Royal Academy, where he quickly rejected the teachings of Reynolds, believing that rules limit rather than aid creativity. He became a lifelong advocate of probing the unfettered imagination. For Blake, imagination provided access to the higher realm of the spirit while reason was confined to the lower world of matter.

Blake was interested in exploring the nature of good and evil and developed an idiosyncratic form of Christian belief that drew on elements from the Bible, Greek mythology, and British legend. His "prophetic books,"

designed and printed in the mid-1790s, brought together painting and poetry to explore themes of spiritual crisis and redemption. Thematically related to the prophetic books is an independent series of 12 large color prints that he executed mostly in 1795. These include a large print of Isaac Newton (**FIG. 30-31**), the epitome of eighteenth-century rationalism, heroically naked in a cave, obsessed with reducing the universe to a mathematical drawing with his compasses—an image that recalls medieval representations of God the Creator designing the world.

John Singleton Copley, whose portrait of Sarah Morris and Thomas Mifflin opened this chapter (SEE FIG. 30-1), moved from Boston to London just before the Revolutionary War, never to return to his native land. In London, he established himself as a portraitist and painter of modern history in the vein of fellow American expatriate Benjamin West. Copley's most distinctive modern history painting was **WATSON AND THE SHARK** (**FIG. 30-32**), commissioned by Brook Watson, a wealthy London merchant and Tory politician, in 1778. Copley's painting dramatizes an episode of 1749 in which the 14-year-old Watson was attacked by a shark while swimming in Havana Harbor

30-31 William Blake **NEWTON**

1795–c. 1805. Color print finished in ink and watercolor, 18⅛ × 23⅝" (46 × 60 cm). Tate, London.

Credit: Photo © Peter Willi/ARTOTHEK

30–32 John Singleton Copley **WATSON AND THE SHARK**
1778. Oil on canvas, 5′10¾ × 7′6½″ (1.82 × 2.29 m). National Gallery of Art, Washington, DC. Ferdinand Lammot Belin Fund.

Credit: Image courtesy the National Gallery of Art, Washington

and lost part of his right leg before being rescued by his comrades. Copley's pyramidal composition is made up of figures in a boat and Watson in the water with a highly imaginary shark set against the backdrop of the harbor. Several of the figures were inspired by Classical sources, but the scene portrayed is anything but Classical. In the foreground, the ferocious shark lunges toward the helpless, naked Watson, while at the prow of the rescue boat a man raises his harpoon to attack the predator. At the left, two of Watson's shipmates strain to reach him while others look on in alarm. An African man standing at the apex of the painting holds a rope that curls over Watson's extended right arm, connecting him to the boat.

Some scholars have read the African figure as a servant waiting to hand the rope to his white master, but his inclusion has also been interpreted in more overtly political terms. The shark attack had occurred while Watson was working as a crew member in the transatlantic shipping trade, which included the shipment of slaves from Africa to the West Indies. At the time when Watson commissioned this painting, debate was raging in the British Parliament over the interconnected issues of the Americans' recent Declaration of Independence and the slave trade. Several Tories, including Watson, opposed American independence, highlighting the hypocrisy of American calls for freedom from the British crown while the colonists continued to deny freedom to African slaves. Indeed, during the Revolutionary War the British offered freedom to every runaway American slave who joined the British army or navy.

Copley's painting, its subject doubtless dictated by Watson, may therefore indicate Watson's sympathy for American slaves—or the figure may be included simply to indicate that the event took place in Havana, much as the inclusion of a Native American in West's painting of the death of Wolfe (SEE FIG. 30–29) sites that picture. Copley was one of the first artists in London to exhibit his large modern history paintings in public places around the capital, making money by charging admission fees and advertising his paintings for sale. His extraordinary images and exhibitions took advantage of the spectacular displays of early nineteenth-century London's Phantasmagoria (a sensational magic lantern display with smoke, mirrors, lights, and gauze "ghosts"), panoramas, dioramas, and the Eidophusikon (a miniature theater with special effects).

Later Eighteenth-Century Art in France

How do Neoclassical architecture, history painting, and portraiture, as well as moralizing genre painting, replace Rococo in France?

In late eighteenth-century France, the Rococo was replaced by Enlightenment ideas and growing signs of revolution. French art moved increasingly toward Neoclassicism as French architects held closer to Roman proportions and sensibility, while painters and sculptors increasingly embraced didactic presentations in a sober, Classical style.

Architecture

French architects of the late eighteenth century generally considered Classicism not one of many possible artistic styles, but the single, true style. Winckelmann's argument that "imitation of the ancients" was the key to good taste was taken to heart in France. The leading French Neoclassical architect was Jacques-Germain Soufflot (1713–1780), whose church of Sainte-Geneviève, known today as the **PANTHÉON** (FIG. 30–33), is the most typical Neoclassical building in Paris. In it, Soufflot attempted to integrate three traditions: Roman architecture he had seen on two trips to Italy; French and English Baroque Classicism; and the

30–33 Jacques-Germain Soufflot **PANTHÉON (CHURCH OF SAINTE-GENEVIÈVE), PARIS**
1755–1792.

This building has an interesting history. Before it was completed, the revolutionary government in control of Paris confiscated all religious properties to raise desperately needed public funds. Instead of selling Sainte-Geneviève, however, they voted in 1791 to make it the Temple of Fame for the burial of Heroes of Liberty. Under Napoleon I (ruled 1799–1814), the building was resanctified as a Catholic church and was again used as such under King Louis-Philippe (ruled 1830–1848) and Napoleon III (ruled 1852–1870). Then it was permanently designated a nondenominational lay temple. In 1851, the building was used as a physics laboratory. Here the French physicist Jean-Bernard Foucault suspended his now-famous pendulum in the interior of the high crossing dome, and by measuring the path of the pendulum's swing proved his theory that the Earth rotated on its axis in a counterclockwise motion. In 1995, the ashes of Marie Curie, who had won the Nobel Prize for Chemistry in 1911, were moved into this "memorial to the great men of France," making her the first woman to be enshrined there.

Palladian style being revived at the time in England. The façade of the Panthéon with its huge portico is modeled on the proportions of ancient Roman temples. The dome, on the other hand, was inspired by seventeenth-century architecture, including Sir Christopher Wren's St. Paul's Cathedral in London (SEE FIGS. 23–59, 23–60), and the radical geometry of the central-plan layout (FIG. 30–34) owes as much to Burlington's Neo-Palladian Chiswick House (SEE FIG. 30–15B) as it does to Christian tradition. The Panthéon, however, is not simply the sum of its parts. Its rational, ordered plan is constructed with rectangles, squares, and circles, while its relatively plain surfaces communicate severity and powerful simplicity.

Painting

French painters such as Boucher, Fragonard, and their followers continued to work in the Rococo style in the later decades of the eighteenth century, but a strong reaction against the Rococo had set in by the 1760s. A leading detractor of the Rococo was Denis Diderot (1713–1784), whose 32-volume compendium of knowledge and skill, the *Encyclopédie* (produced in collaboration with Jean le Rond d'Alembert, 1717–1783) served as an archive of Enlightenment thought in France. In 1759, Diderot began

to write reviews of the official Salon for a periodic newsletter for wealthy subscribers; he is generally considered to be the founder of modern art criticism. Diderot believed that art should be moralizing, that it should promote virtuous behavior and inspire refined manners—a function that the Rococo was not designed to fulfill.

CHARDIN   Diderot greatly admired Jean-Siméon Chardin (1699–1779), an artist who as early as the 1730s began to create moralizing pictures of refined intimacy in the tradition of seventeenth-century Dutch genre painting by focusing on touching scenes of everyday middle-class life, with an emphasis on the moral goodness of everyday familial routines. **SAYING GRACE** (FIG. 30–35), for instance, shows a mother leaning to set the family table for a meal. Across from her sit two children: an older daughter partially concealed by the table and her younger brother in the foreground who has hung his toy drum on the back of his chair so he can join his hands to say grace. His mother pauses from her domestic chore to admire her son's simple piety. We might initially assume the praying child to be a girl, but young boys wore skirts in France until the twentieth century (see FIG. Intro-5 in the "Introduction"), and the toy drum would have identified this youngster as a boy for an eighteenth-century audience.

GREUZE Diderot reserved his highest praise for Jean-Baptiste Greuze (1725–1805), and his own plays of the late 1750s served as a source of inspiration for Greuze's painting. Diderot expanded the traditional range of theatrical works in Paris from mostly tragedy and comedy to include the *drame bourgeois* ("middle-class drama") and "middle tragedy" (later called the "melodrama"), both of which communicated moral and civic lessons through simple stories of ordinary life. Greuze's domestic genre paintings, such as **THE VILLAGE BRIDE** (FIG. 30-36), were visual counterparts to Diderot's preferred theatrical subjects. In this painting, Greuze presents the action as a carefully constructed composition on a shallow, stagelike space under a dramatic spotlight. As an elderly father hands the dowry for his daughter to his new son-in-law, he conveys what contemporary critics saw as a moral lesson on financial management; a notary at far right records the event with cool concentration, in marked contrast to the clearly emotional reaction of the father. The mother and sister who embrace the bashful bride seem reluctant to let her go. A

strong contrast to the deception and self-serving objectives highlighted in Hogarth's *Marriage Contract* (SEE FIG. 30-23), Greuze's painting visualizes the utopian notion that moral virtue and relative prosperity can coexist in village life. This kind of highly emotional, theatrical, and moralizing genre scene was widely praised in Greuze's time, offering a counterpoint to early Neoclassical history painting in France.

VIGÉE-LEBRUN While Greuze painted scenes of the poor and middle class, Marie-Louise-Élisabeth Vigée-Lebrun (1755–1842) became famous as Queen Marie Antoinette's favorite portrait painter. Vigée-Lebrun was also notable for her election into the French Royal Academy of Painting and Sculpture, which then made only four places available to women. In 1787, she painted **MARIE ANTOINETTE WITH HER CHILDREN** (FIG. 30-37). Drawing on the "good mother" theme seen earlier in Angelica Kauffmann's Neoclassical painting of Cornelia (SEE FIG. 30-28), Vigée-Lebrun portrays the queen as a kind, stabilizing mother—a work of royal propaganda

30–36 Jean-Baptiste Greuze **THE VILLAGE BRIDE, OR THE MARRIAGE, THE MOMENT WHEN A FATHER GIVES HIS SON-IN-LAW A DOWRY**

1761. Oil on canvas, 36 × 46½″ (91.4 × 118.1 cm). Musée du Louvre, Paris.

Credit: Photo © RMN-Grand Palais (musée du Louvre)/ Franck Raux

aimed at counteracting public perceptions of Marie Antoinette as selfish, extravagant, and immoral. The queen maintains an appropriately regal pose, but her children are depicted more sympathetically. The princess leans affectionately against her mother's arm and the little dauphin—heir to a throne he would never inherit—poignantly points to the empty cradle of a recently deceased sibling. The image alludes to the allegory of Abundance and thus is also intended to signify peace and prosperity for France under the reign of Marie Antoinette's husband, Louis XVI, who came to the throne in 1774 but would be executed along with the queen in 1793.

30–37 Marie-Louise-Élisabeth Vigée-Lebrun **PORTRAIT OF MARIE ANTOINETTE WITH HER CHILDREN**

1787. Oil on canvas, 9′1½″ × 7′5⅝″ (2.75 × 2.15 m). Musée National du Château de Versailles.

As the favorite painter to the queen, Vigée-Lebrun escaped from Paris with her daughter on the eve of the Revolution of 1789 and fled to Rome. After a very successful self-exile working in Italy, Austria, Russia, and England, the artist finally resettled in Paris in 1805 and again became popular with Parisian art patrons. Over her long career, she painted about 800 portraits in a vibrant style that changed very little over the decades.

Credit: © Jean Feuillie/Centre des monuments nationaux

DAVID The most important French Neoclassical painter of the era was Jacques-Louis David (1748–1825), who dominated French art for over 20 years during the French Revolution and the subsequent reign of Napoleon. In 1774, he won the Prix de Rome and spent six years in that city, studying antique sculpture and learning the principles of Neoclassicism. After his return to Paris, he produced a series of severely plain Neoclassical paintings celebrating the antique virtues of stoicism, masculinity, and patriotism.

Perhaps the most significant of these works was the **OATH OF THE HORATII** (FIG. 30-38) of 1784–1785. A royal commission that David returned to Rome to paint, the work reflects the taste and values of Louis XVI, who, along with his minister of the arts, Count d'Angiviller, was sympathetic to the Enlightenment. Like Diderot, d'Angiviller and the king believed that art should improve public morals. Accordingly, one of d'Angiviller's first official acts was

to ban indecent nudity from the Salon of 1775 and commission a series of didactic history paintings. The commission for David's *Oath of the Horatii* in 1784 was part of that general program.

The subject of the painting was inspired by the drama *Horace*, written by the great French playwright Pierre Corneille (1606–1684), which had in turn been based on ancient Roman historical texts. The patriotic oath-taking incident David depicted, however, is not taken directly from these sources and was apparently the artist's own invention. The story is set in the seventh century BCE at a time when Rome and its rival, Alba, a neighboring city-state, agreed to settle a border dispute and avert a war by holding a battle to the death between the three sons of Horace (the Horatii), representing Rome, and the three Curatii, representing Alba. In David's painting, the Horatii stand with arms outstretched toward their father, who reaches toward them with the swords on which they pledge to fight and die for

30-38 Jacques-Louis David **OATH OF THE HORATII**
1784–1785. Oil on canvas, 10'8¼" × 14' (3.26 × 4.27 m). Musée du Louvre, Paris.

Credit: Photo © RMN-Grand Palais (musée du Louvre)/Gérard Blot/Christian Jean

30–39 Jacques-Louis David
DEATH OF MARAT
1793. Oil on canvas, 5'5" × 4'2½"
(1.65 × 1.28 m). © Royal Museums of Fine
Arts of Belgium, Brussels.

Credit: © Royal Museums of Fine Arts of
Belgium, Brussels/Photo: J. Geleyns - Roscan

Rome. The powerful gesture of the young men's outstretched hands almost pushes their father back. In contrast to the upright, tensed, muscular angularity of the men, the group of swooning women and frightened children are limp. They weep for the lives of both the Horatii and the Curatii. Sabina (in the center) is a sister of the Curatii and also married to one of the Horatii; Camilla (at the far right) is sister to the Horatii and engaged to one of the Curatii. David's composition, which separates the men from the women and children spatially by the use of framing background arches, dramatically contrasts the young men's stoic and willing self-sacrifice with the women's emotional collapse.

The emotional intensity of this history painting pushed French academic rules on decorum to their limit. Originally a royal commission, it quickly and ironically became an emblem of the 1789 French Revolution, since its message of patriotism and sacrifice for the greater good effectively captured the mood of the leaders of the new French Republic established in 1792. As the revolutionaries abolished the monarchy and titles of nobility, took education out of the hands of the Church, and wrote a declaration of human rights, David joined the leftist Jacobin party.

In 1793, David painted the death of the Jacobin supporter, Jean-Paul Marat (**FIG. 30–39**). A radical journalist, Marat lived simply among the packing cases that he used as furniture, writing pamphlets urging the abolition of aristocratic privilege. Because he suffered from a painful skin ailment, he would often write while sitting in a medicinal bath. Charlotte Corday, a supporter of an opposition party, held Marat partly responsible for the 1792 riots in which hundreds of political prisoners judged sympathetic to the king were killed, and in retribution she stabbed Marat as he sat in his bath. David avoids the potential for sensationalism in the subject by portraying not the violent event but its tragic aftermath—the dead Marat slumped in his bathtub, his right hand still holding a quill pen, while his left hand grasps the letter that Corday used to gain access to his home. The simple wooden block beside the bath, which Marat used as a desk, bears a dedicatory inscription with the names of both Marat and the painter—"to Marat, David." It almost serves as the martyr's tombstone.

David's painting is tightly composed and powerfully stark. The background is blank, adding to the quiet mood and timeless feeling of the picture, just as the very different background of the *Oath of the Horatii* added to its drama. The color of Marat's pale body coordinates with the blood-stained sheets on which he lies, creating a compact shape that is framed by the dark background and green blanket draped over the bathtub. David transforms a brutal event into an elegiac statement of somber eloquence. Marat's pose, which echoes Michelangelo's Vatican *Pietà* (SEE FIG. 21-14), implies that, like Christ, Marat was a martyr for the people.

The French Revolution degenerated into mob rule in 1793–1794 as Jacobin leaders orchestrated the ruthless execution of thousands of their opponents in what became known as the Reign of Terror. David, as a Jacobin, was elected a deputy to the National Convention and served a two-week term as president, during which time he signed several arrest warrants. When the Jacobins lost power in 1794, he was twice imprisoned, albeit under lenient conditions that allowed him to continue to paint. He later emerged as a supporter of Napoleon and re-established his career at the height of Napoleon's ascendancy.

GIRODET-TRIOSON AND LABILLE-GUIARD David was a charismatic and influential teacher who trained most of the major French painters of the 1790s and early 1800s, including Anne-Louis Girodet-Trioson (1767–1824). Girodet-Trioson's **PORTRAIT OF JEAN-BAPTISTE BELLEY** (**FIG. 30–40**) combines the restrained color and tight composition of David with a relaxed elegance that makes the subject more lifelike and self-possessed, accessible and inaccessible at the same time. And like many of David's works, this portrait was political. The Senegalese-born Belley (1747?–1805) was a former slave who was sent to Paris as a representative to the French Convention by the colony of Saint-Domingue (now Haiti). The Haitian Revolution of 1791, in which African slaves overturned the French colonial power, resulted in the first republic to be ruled by freed African slaves. In 1794, Belley led a successful legislative campaign to abolish slavery in the colonies and grant full citizenship to people of African descent. In the portrait, Belley leans casually on the pedestal of a bust of the abbot Guillaume Raynal (1711–1796), a French philosopher whose 1770 book condemned slavery and paved the way for such legislation—making the portrait a tribute to both Belley and Raynal. Napoleon re-established slavery in the Caribbean islands in 1801, but the revolt continued until 1804, when Haiti finally achieved full independence.

Also reflecting the revolutionary spirit of the age, the painter Adélaïde Labille-Guiard (1749–1803) championed the rights of women artists. Elected to the French Royal Academy of Painting and Sculpture in the same year as Vigée-Lebrun, Labille-Guiard asserted her worthiness for this honor in a **SELF-PORTRAIT WITH TWO PUPILS** that she submitted to the Salon of 1785 (**FIG. 30–41**). The painting was a response to sexist rumors that her work and that of Vigée-Lebrun had actually been painted by men. In a witty role reversal, the only male in this monumental painting of the artist at her easel is her father, shown in a bust behind her canvas, as her muse, a role usually played by women. While the self-portrait flatters Labille-Guiard, it also portrays her as a force to be reckoned with, a woman who engages our gaze uncompromisingly and whose students are serious and intent on their study. In the year following the French Revolution, Labille-Guiard successfully petitioned the French Academy of Painting and Sculpture to end the restriction that limited its membership to four women. The reform was later reversed by the revolutionary government as it became more authoritarian.

30–40 Anne-Louis Girodet-Trioson **PORTRAIT OF JEAN-BAPTISTE BELLEY**

1797. Oil on canvas, 5′2½″ × 3′8½″ (1.59 × 1.13 m). Musée National du Château de Versailles.

Credit: Photo © RMN-Grand Palais (Château de Versailles)/ Gérard Blot

30–41 Adélaïde Labille-Guiard
SELF-PORTRAIT WITH TWO PUPILS

1785. Oil on canvas, 6'11" × 4'11½"
(2.11 × 1.51 m). Metropolitan
Museum of Art, New York. Gift of
Julia A. Berwind, 1953 (53.225.5).

Credit: © 2016. Image copyright The
Metropolitan Museum of Art/Art Resource/
Scala, Florence

Sculpture

The French Neoclassical sculptor Jean-Antoine Houdon (1741–1828), who studied in Italy between 1764 and 1768 after winning the Prix de Rome, imbued the Classical style with a new sense of realism. He carved busts and full-length statues of a number of the important figures of his time, including Diderot, Voltaire, Jean-Jacques Rousseau, Catherine the Great, Thomas Jefferson, Benjamin Franklin, Lafayette (a Revolutionary hero), and Napoleon, and his studio produced a steady supply of replicas, much in demand because of the cult of great men promoted by Enlightenment thinkers to provide models of virtue and patriotism. On the basis of his bust of

Benjamin Franklin, Houdon was commissioned by the Virginia State Legislature to make a portrait of its native son **GEORGE WASHINGTON** to be installed in the Neoclassical Virginia state capitol building designed by Jefferson. In 1785, Houdon traveled to the United States to make a cast of Washington's features and create a bust in plaster, returning to Paris to execute the life-size marble figure (**FIG. 30–42**). The sculpture represents Washington in the Classical manner but dressed in contemporary clothes, much as Benjamin West had represented General Wolfe (SEE FIG. 30–29). Houdon imbued the portrait with Classical ideals of dignity, honor, and civic responsibility. Washington wears the uniform of a general, the rank he held in the Revolutionary War, but he also rests his left hand on a Roman *fasces*, a bundle of 13 rods (representing the 13 colonies) and an axe face, that served as a Roman symbol of authority. Attached to the *fasces* are both a sword of war and a plowshare of peace. Significantly, Houdon's Washington does not touch the sword.

30–42 Jean-Antoine Houdon **GEORGE WASHINGTON**
1788–1792. Marble, height 6'2" (1.9 m). State Capitol, Richmond, Virginia.

The plow share behind Washington alludes to Cincinnatus, a Roman soldier of the fifth century ʟʙᴄ who was appointed dictator and dispatched to defeat the Aequi, who had besieged a Roman army. After the victory, Cincinnatus resigned the dictatorship and returned to his farm. Washington's contemporaries compared him with Cincinnatus because, after leading the Americans to victory over the British, he resigned his commission and went back to farming rather than seeking political power. Just below Washington's waistcoat hangs the badge of the Society of the Cincinnati, founded in 1783 by the officers of the disbanding Continental Army who were returning to their peacetime occupations. Washington lived in retirement at his Mount Vernon, Virginia, plantation for five years before his 1789 election as the first president of the United States.

Spain and Spanish America

What characterizes the art and architecture of Spain and its American colonies during the late eighteenth and early nineteenth centuries?

In the first half of the eighteenth century, Philip V (ruled 1700–1746) marginalized the Spanish art world by awarding most royal commissions to foreign artists. The German painter Mengs introduced Neoclassicism into Spain with his work for Charles III (ruled 1759–1788), but Spanish artists did not embrace Neoclassicism the way they had Baroque during the previous century. At the end of the eighteenth century, however, the Spanish court appointed one of the greatest Spanish artists of the period as court painter: Francisco Goya y Lucientes (1746–1828).

Since the sixteenth century, the Spanish had commissioned art in the distant lands of their American colonies as well as in the homeland. During the eighteenth century this colonial art and architecture remained rooted in the traditions of the Spanish Baroque, intermingled with the artistic traditions of native peoples, joining the symbolism and the artistic vocabulary of two distinct cultures into a new art in Mexico and the American Southwest.

Goya

Goya was introduced to the Spanish royal workshop in 1774, when he produced tapestry cartoons under the direction of Mengs. He painted for Charles III and served as court painter to Charles IV (ruled 1788–1808), but he also belonged to an intellectual circle that embraced the ideals of the French Revolution, and his work began subtly to criticize the court in which he served.

Soon after the French Revolution, Charles IV, threatened by the possibility of similar social upheaval in Spain, reinstituted the Inquisition, halted reform, and even prohibited the entry of French books into Spain. Goya responded to this new situation by creating a series of prints aimed at the ordinary people, with whom he identified. The theme of *Los Caprichos* (*The Caprices*, a folio of 80 etchings produced between 1796 and 1798) is that reason ignored is a sleeping monster. In the print entitled **THE SLEEP OF REASON PRODUCES MONSTERS** (**FIG. 30-43**), the slumbering personification of Reason is haunted by a menagerie of demonic-looking owls, bats, and a cat that are let loose when Reason sleeps. Other *Caprichos* enumerate the follies of Spanish society that Goya and his circle considered equally monstrous. His goal with this series was to incite action, to alert the Spanish people to the errors of their foolish ways, and to reawaken them to reason. He tried to market his etchings as Hogarth had done in England, but it aroused controversy and was brought to the attention of his royal patrons. To deflect additional trouble, Goya presented the metal plates of the series to

30-43 Francisco Goya **THE SLEEP OF REASON PRODUCES MONSTERS**

No. 43 from *Los Caprichos* (*The Caprices*). 1796–1798; published 1799. Etching and aquatint, 8½ × 6″ (21.6 × 15.2 cm). Yale University Art Gallery. Bequest of Ralph Kirkpatrick, Hon. M.A. 1965 (1984.54.92.43)

After printing about 300 sets of this series, Goya offered them for sale in 1799. He withdrew them two days later without explanation. Historians believe that he was probably warned by the Church that if he did not do so he might have to appear before the Inquisition because of the unflattering portrayal of the Church in some of the etchings. In 1803, Goya donated the plates to the Royal Printing Office.

Credit: Image courtesy Yale University Art Gallery

the king, suggesting that the images were not intentionally critical of the monarchy. He was torn between his position as a court painter who owed allegiance to the king and his passionate desire for a more open Spain.

A large portrait of the **FAMILY OF CHARLES IV** (FIG. **30-44**) reveals some of Goya's ambivalence. He clearly wanted his patron to connect this portrait to an earlier Spanish royal portrait, *Las Meninas* by Velázquez (SEE FIG. 23-21), thereby raising his own status as well as that of the king. Like Velázquez, Goya includes himself in the painting, to the left behind the easel. The king and queen appear at the center of this large family portrait, surrounded by their immediate family. The figures are formal and stiff. Much has been written about how Goya seems to show his patrons as faintly ridiculous here. Some seem bored; the somewhat dazed king,

30-44 Francisco Goya **FAMILY OF CHARLES IV**

1800. Oil on canvas, 9'2″ × 11' (2.79 × 3.36 m). Museo del Prado, Madrid.

Credit: © 2016. Image copyright Museo Nacional del Prado. © Photo MNP/Photo Scala, Florence chest full of medals, stands before a relative who looks distractedly out of the painting (perhaps the face was added at the last minute); the double-chinned queen gazes obliquely toward the viewer (at that time she was having an open affair with the prime minister); their eldest daughter, to the left, stares into space; and another, older relative behind seems almost surprised to be there. One French art critic even described the painting as resembling "the corner baker and his family after they have won the lottery." Yet the royal family was apparently satisfied with Goya's depiction. At a time when the authority of the Spanish aristocracy was crumbling, this complex representation of conflicted emotions, aspirations, and responsibilities may have struck a chord with them. Some viewers who first saw it may have thought its candid representations were refreshingly modern.

In 1808, Napoleon launched a campaign to conquer Spain; he would eventually place his brother, Joseph Bonaparte (1768–1844), on the Spanish throne. At first many Spanish citizens, Goya included, welcomed the French, who brought political reform, including a new, more liberal constitution. But on May 2, 1808, a rumor spread through Madrid that the French planned to kill the royal family. The populace rose up against the French, and a day of bloody street fighting ensued, followed by mass arrests. Hundreds were herded into a convent and then executed by a French firing squad before dawn on May 3. In Goya's impassioned memorial to that slaughter (**FIG. 30–45**), the violent gestures of the defenseless rebels and the mechanical efficiency of the tight row of executioners in the firing squad create a nightmarish tableau. A spotlighted victim in a brilliant white shirt confronts his faceless killers with outstretched arms recalling the crucified Christ, an image of searing pathos. This painting is not a cool, didactic representation of civic sacrifice like David's Neoclassical *Oath of the Horatii* (SEE FIG. 30–38). It is an image of blind terror and desperate fear, the essence of Romanticism—the sensational current event, the loose brushwork, the lifelike poses, the unbalanced composition, and the dramatic lighting. There is no moral here, only hopeless rage. When asked why he painted such a brutal scene, Goya responded: "To warn men never to do it again."

30–45 Francisco Goya **THIRD OF MAY, 1808**
1814–1815. Oil on canvas, 8'9″ × 13'4″ (2.67 × 4.06 m). Museo del Prado, Madrid.

Soon after, the Spanish monarchy was restored. Ferdinand VII (ruled 1808, 1814–1833) once again reinstated the Inquisition and abolished the new constitution. In 1815, Goya was called before the Inquisition and charged with obscenity for an earlier painting of a female nude. He was acquitted and retired to his home outside Madrid, where he vented his anger at the world in a series of nightmarish "black paintings" rendered directly on the walls, and then spent the last four years of his life in France.

The Art of the Americas under Spain

The sixteenth-century Spanish conquest of Central and South America led to the suppression of indigenous religions. Temples were demolished and replaced with Roman Catholic churches, while Franciscan, Dominican, and Augustinian friars worked to convert the indigenous populations. Some missionaries were so appalled by the conquerors' brutal treatment of the native peoples that they petitioned the Spanish king to help improve conditions.

In the course of the Mesoamericans' forced conversion to Roman Catholicism, Christian symbolism became inextricably blended with the symbolism of indigenous religious beliefs. An example can be seen in colonial **atrial crosses**, carved early on by indigenous sculptors. Missionaries placed these crosses in church atriums, where converts gathered for education in Christianity. The sixteenth-century **ATRIAL CROSS** now in the basilica of Guadalupe near Mexico City (**FIG. 30-46**) is richly carved in the low relief of native sculptural traditions and interweaves images from Christian and native religions into a dense symbolic whole. The Christian images were probably copied from the illustrated books and Bibles of the missionaries. Visible here are the Arms of Christ (the "weapons" that Christ used to defeat the devil); the holy face, placed where his head would appear on a crucifix; the crown of thorns, draped around the cross bar; and the holy shroud, wrapped around the cross's arms. Winged angel heads and pomegranates surround the inscription at the top as symbols of regeneration. While the cross represents the redemption of humanity in Christianity, it symbolizes the tree of life in Mesoamerican religions. The blood that sprays out where the nails pierce the hands and feet of Christ are a reference to his sacrifice; such representations of sacrificial blood were also common in indigenous religious art.

Images of the Virgin Mary also took on a Mesoamerican inflection after she was believed to have appeared in Mexico. In one such case, in 1531, a Mexican peasant named Juan Diego claimed that the Virgin Mary visited him to tell him in his native Nahuatl language to build a church on a hill where an Aztec goddess had once been worshiped, subsequently causing flowers to bloom so that Juan Diego could show them to the archbishop as proof of his vision. When Juan Diego opened his bundle

30-46 ATRIAL CROSS
Before 1556. Stone, height 11′3″ (3.45 m). Chapel of the Indians, basilica of Guadalupe, Mexico City.

Credit: © Jamie Lara

of flowers, the cloak he had used to wrap them is said to have borne the image of a Mexican Mary in a composition used in Europe to portray the Virgin of the Immaculate Conception, popular in Spain (SEE FIG. 23-22). The site of Juan Diego's vision was renamed Guadalupe after Our Lady of Guadalupe in Spain, and it became a venerated pilgrimage center. In 1754, Pope Benedict XIV declared the **VIRGIN OF GUADALUPE**, as depicted here in a 1779 work by Sebastian Salcedo, the patron saint of the Americas (**FIG. 30-47**).

Spanish colonial builders sought to replicate the architecture of their native country in the Americas. One of the finest examples is the **MISSION SAN XAVIER DEL BAC**, in the American Southwest near Tucson, Arizona (**FIG. 30-48**). In 1700, the Jesuit priest Eusebio Kino (1644–1711) began laying the foundations for San Xavier del Bac using stone quarried locally by people of the Pima nation. The Pima had already laid out the desert site with irrigation ditches so there would be running water in every room

30–47 Sebastian Salcedo **VIRGIN OF GUADALUPE**

1779. Oil on panel and copper, 25 × 19″ (63.5 × 48.3 cm). Denver Art Museum. Funds contributed by Mr. and Mrs. George G. Anderman and an anonymous donor (1976.56).

At the bottom right is the female personification of New Spain (Mexico) and at the left is Pope Benedict XIV (pontificate 1740–1758), who in 1754 declared the Virgin of Guadalupe to be the patroness of the Americas. Between the figures, the sanctuary of Guadalupe in Mexico can be seen in the distance. The four small scenes circling the Virgin represent the story of Juan Diego, and at the top three scenes depict Mary's miracles. The six figures above the Virgin represent Hebrew Bible prophets and patriarchs and New Testament apostles and saints.

30–48 MISSION SAN XAVIER DEL BAC

Near Tucson, Arizona. 1784–1797.

Credit: Paul Moore/Fotolia

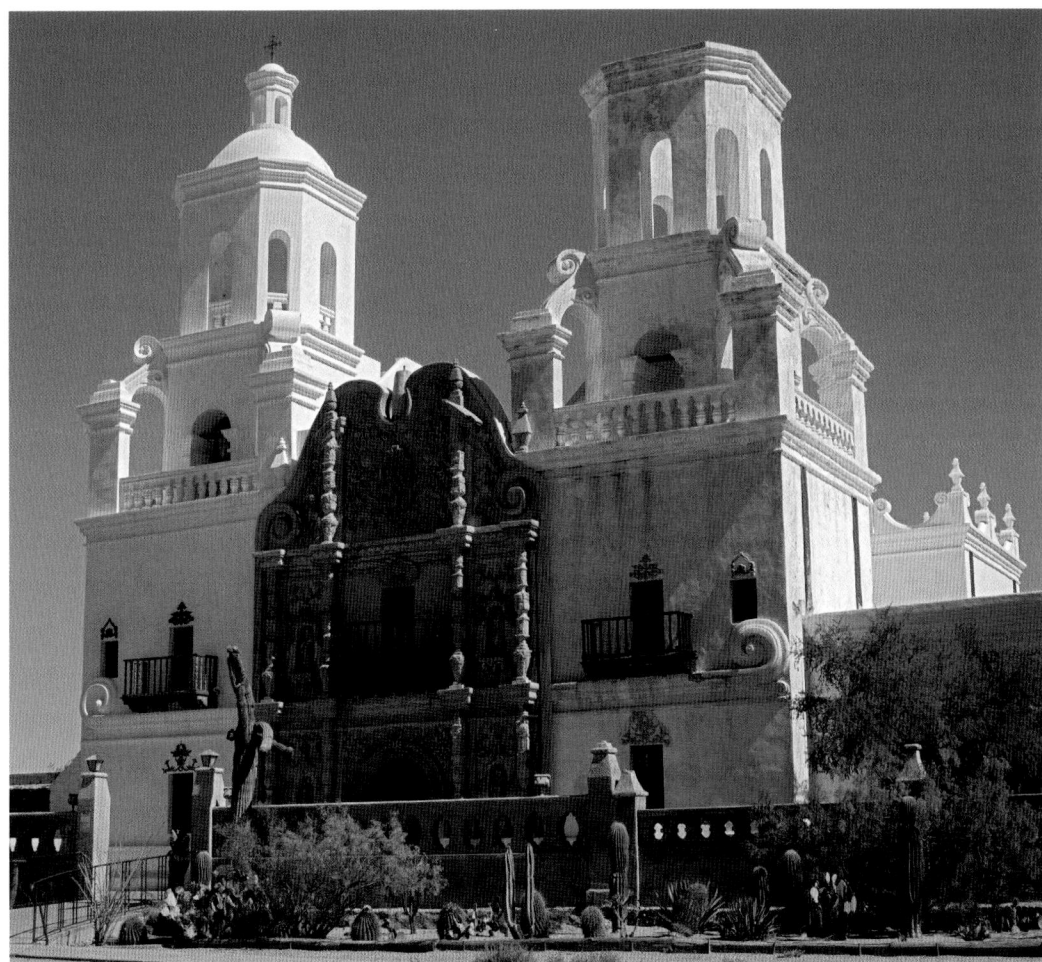

and workshop of the new mission. In 1768, before construction began, the site was turned over to the Franciscans as part of a larger change in Spanish policy toward the Jesuits. Father Kino's vision was eventually realized by the Spanish Franciscan Juan Bautista Velderrain, who arrived at the mission site in 1776.

This huge church, 99 feet long with a domed crossing and flanking bell towers, is unusual for the area because it was built of bricks and mortar rather than adobe, which is made from earth and straw. The basic structure was finished by the time of Velderrain's death in 1790, and the exterior decoration was completed by his successor in 1797. The façade of San Xavier is not a copy of Spanish architecture, although the focus of visual attention on the central entrance to the church and the style of the decoration are consistent with Spanish Baroque. Since the mission was dedicated to Francis Xavier, his statue once stood at the top of the portal decoration, and there are still four female saints, tentatively identified as Lucy, Cecilia, Barbara, and Catherine of Siena, in the niches. Hidden in the sculpted mass is one humorous element: a cat confronting a mouse, which inspired a local Pima saying: "When the cat catches the mouse, the end of the world will come" (cited in Chinn and McCarty, p. 12).

The Development of Neoclassicism and Romanticism into the Nineteenth Century

How do Neoclassicism and Romanticism develop in the early nineteenth-century art of France, England, Germany, and the United States?

Neoclassicism and Romanticism existed side by side well into the nineteenth century in European and American art. In fact, Neoclassicism survived in both architecture and sculpture beyond the middle of the century, as patrons and artists continued to use it to promote the virtues of democracy and republicanism. The longevity of Neoclassicism was also due in part to its embrace by art academies, where training was grounded in the study of antique sculpture and the work of Classical artists such as Raphael. The Neoclassical vision of art as the embodiment of universal standards of taste and beauty complemented the academy's idea of itself as a repository of venerable tradition in fast-changing times.

Romanticism, whose roots in eighteenth-century Britain we have already seen, took a variety of forms in the early nineteenth century. The common connecting thread continued to be an emphasis on emotional expressiveness and the unique experiences and tastes of the individual. Romantic paintings continued to explore dramatic subject matter taken from literature, current events, the natural world, or the artist's own imagination, with the goal of stimulating the viewer's emotions.

Developments in France

Paris increasingly established itself as a major artistic center during the nineteenth century. Between 1800 and 1830, the French academy system was the arbiter of artistic success in Paris. The École des Beaux-Arts attracted students from all over Europe and the Americas, as did the ateliers (studios) of Parisian academic artists who offered private instruction. Artists competed fiercely for a spot in the Paris Salon, the annual exhibition that gradually opened to those who were not academy members. At the beginning of the nineteenth century there was a deep division between the *poussinistes* and *rubénistes* (see "Grading the Old Masters" in Chapter 23 on page 771). The *poussinistes*

argued that line, as used in the work of Poussin (SEE FIGS. 23-54, 23-55), created fundamental artistic structure and should be the basis of all painting. The *rubénistes* argued that essential structure could be achieved more eloquently through a sophisticated use of rich, warm color, as exemplified by the paintings of Rubens (SEE FIG. 23-27). Similarly, the relative value of the **esquisse**, a preliminary sketch for a much larger work, was hotly debated. Some claimed that it was simply a tool for the larger, finished work, while others began to argue that the fast, impulsive expression of imagination captured in the *esquisse* made the finished painting seem dull and flat by comparison. This emphasis on expressiveness blossoms in Romanticism between 1815 and 1830.

THE GRAND MANNER PAINTINGS OF DAVID AND GROS With the rise of Napoleon Bonaparte, Jacques-Louis David re-established his dominant position in French painting. David saw in Napoleon the best hope for realizing France's Enlightenment-oriented political goals, and Napoleon saw in David a tested propagandist for revolutionary values. As Napoleon gained power and extended his rule across Europe, reforming law codes and abolishing aristocratic privilege, he commissioned David and his students to document his deeds.

In 1800, four years before Napoleon became emperor, David had already begun to glorify him in **NAPOLEON CROSSING THE SAINT-BERNARD** (or *Bonaparte Crossing the Alps*) **(FIG. 30–49)**. Napoleon is represented in the Grand Manner, and David used artistic license to imagine how he might have appeared as he led his troops over the Alps into Italy. Framed by a broad shock of red drapery, he exhorts his troops to follow as he charges uphill on his powerful, rearing horse. The horse's flying mane and wild eyes, combined with the swirl of the cape, convey energy, impulsiveness, and power, backed up by the heavy guns and troops in the background. When Napoleon fell from power in 1814, David went into exile in Brussels, where he died in 1825.

30–49 Jacques-Louis David **NAPOLEON CROSSING THE SAINT-BERNARD**
1800–1801. Oil on canvas, 8'11" × 7'7" (2.7 × 2.3 m). Versailles, Châteaux de Versailles et de Trianon.

Credit: Photo © RMN-Grand Palais (Château de Versailles)/ Franck Raux

30-50 Antoine-Jean Gros **NAPOLEON IN THE PLAGUE HOUSE AT JAFFA**
1804. Oil on canvas, 17′5″ × 23′7″ (5.32 × 7.2 m). Musée du Louvre, Paris.

The huddled figures to the left were based on those around the mouth of hell in Michelangelo's *Last Judgment* (SEE FIG. 21–46).

Credit: Photo © RMN-Grand Palais (musée du Louvre)/Thierry Le Mage

Antoine-Jean Gros (1771–1835) began working in David's studio as a teenager and eventually competed with his master for commissions from Napoleon, traveling with Napoleon in Italy in 1797 and later becoming an official chronicler of his military campaigns. His painting **NAPOLEON IN THE PLAGUE HOUSE AT JAFFA** (**FIG. 30-50**), like David's portrait, represents an actual event in the Grand Manner. During Napoleon's campaign against the Ottoman Turks in 1799, bubonic plague broke out among his troops. To quiet fears and forestall panic among his soldiers, Napoleon decided to visit the sick and dying, who were housed in a converted mosque in the town of Jaffa (now in Israel but then part of the Ottoman Empire). The format of Gros's painting—a shallow stage with a series of pointed arches framing the main protagonists—recalls David's *Oath of the Horatii* (SEE FIG. 30-38). But Gros's painting is quite different from that of his teacher. His color is more vibrant and his brushwork more spontaneous. The overall effect is Romantic, not simply because of the dramatic lighting and the wealth of details, both exotic and

horrific, but also because the main action is meant to incite veneration of Napoleon the man more than republican sentiments in general. Near the center of the painting, surrounded by a small group of soldiers and a doctor who keep a cautious distance from the contagious patients or hold handkerchiefs to their noses to block their stench, a heroic and fearless Napoleon reaches his bare hand toward the sores of one of the victims in a pose that was meant to evoke Christ healing the sick with his touch.

GÉRICAULT The life of Théodore Géricault (1791–1824), a major proponent of French Romanticism, was cut short by his untimely death at age 32, but his brief career had a large impact on the early nineteenth-century Parisian art world. After a short stay in Rome in 1816–1817, where he discovered the art of Michelangelo, Géricault returned to Paris determined to paint a great modern history painting. He chose for his subject the scandalous and sensational shipwreck of the *Medusa* (**FIG. 30-51**). In 1816, this French ship bound for Senegal ran aground close to its destination.

30–51 Théodore Géricault **THE RAFT OF THE MEDUSA**
1818–1819. Oil on canvas, 16′1″ × 23′6″ (4.9 × 7.16 m). Musée du Louvre, Paris.

Credit: © akg-images/Erich Lessing

Its captain, an incompetent aristocrat commissioned by the newly restored monarchy of Louis XVIII, reserved all six lifeboats for himself, his officers, and several government representatives. The remaining 152 passengers were set adrift on a makeshift raft. When those on the raft were rescued 13 days later, just 15 had survived, some only by eating human flesh. Since the captain had been a political appointee, the press used the horrific story to indict the monarchy for this and other atrocities in French-ruled Senegal. The moment in the story that Géricault chose to depict is one fraught with emotion, as the survivors on the raft experience both the fear that the distant ship might pass them by and the hope that they will be rescued.

Géricault's monumental *The Raft of the Medusa* fits the definition of a history painting in that it is a large (16 by 23 feet), multi-figured composition that represents an event in history. It may not qualify, however, on the basis of its function—to expose incompetence and a willful disregard for human life rather than to ennoble, educate, or remind viewers of their civic responsibility. The hero of this painting is also an unusual choice for a history painting; he is not an emperor or a king, nor even an

intellectual, but Jean Charles, a black man from French Senegal who showed endurance and emotional fortitude in the face of extreme danger.

Géricault's painting is arranged in a pyramid of bodies. The diagonal axis that begins in the lower left extends upward to the waving figure of Jean Charles; a complementary diagonal beginning with the dead man in the lower right extends through the mast and billowing sail, directing our attention to a huge wave. The figures are emotionally suspended between hope of salvation and fear of imminent death. Significantly, the "hopeful" diagonal in Géricault's painting terminates in the vigorous figure of Jean Charles. By placing him at the top of the pyramid of survivors and giving him the power to save his comrades by signaling to the rescue ship, Géricault suggests metaphorically that freedom is often dependent on the most oppressed members of society.

Géricault prepared his painting carefully, using each of the prescribed steps for history painting in the French academic system. The work was the culmination of extensive study and experimentation. An early pen drawing (*The Sighting of the Argus*, **FIG. 30–52**) depicts the survivors' hopeful response to the appearance of the rescue

30–52 Théodore Géricault **THE SIGHTING OF THE ARGUS**
1818. Pen and ink on paper, 13¾ × 16⅛" (34.9 × 41 cm).
Musée des Beaux-Arts, Lille.

Credit: Photo © RMN-Grand Palais/Philipp Bernard

30–53 Théodore Géricault **THE SIGHTING OF
THE ARGUS**
1818. Pen and ink, sepia wash on paper, 8⅛ × 11¼" (20.6 × 28.6 cm).
Musée des Beaux-Arts, Rouen.

Credit: Photo © RMN-Grand Palais/Philipp Bernard

ship on the horizon at the extreme left. Their excitement is in contrast to the mournful scene of a man grieving over a dead youth on the right side of the raft. The drawing is quick, spontaneous, and bursting with energy.

A later pen-and-wash drawing (FIG. 30–53) reverses the composition, creates greater unity among the figures, and establishes the modeling of their bodies. This is primarily a study of light and shade. Other studies would have focused on further analyses of the composition, arrangement of figures, and overall color scheme. The drawings look ahead to the final composition of *The Raft of the Medusa*, but both still lack the figure of Jean Charles at the apex of the painting, and the dead and dying figures at the extreme left and lower right, which fill out the composition's base.

Géricault also made separate studies of many of the figures, as well as of actual corpses, severed heads, and dissected limbs (FIG. 30–54) supplied to him by friends who worked at a nearby hospital. For several months, according to Géricault's biographer, "his studio was a kind of morgue. He kept cadavers there until they were half-decomposed, and insisted on working in this charnel-house atmosphere...." However, he did not use cadavers for any specific figures in *The Raft of the Medusa*. Rather, he traced the outline of his final composition onto its large canvas, and then painted each body directly from a living model, gradually building up his composition figure by figure. He drew from corpses and body parts in his studio to make sure that he understood the nature of death and its impact on the human form.

Indeed, Géricault did not describe the actual physical condition of the survivors on the raft: exhausted, emaciated, sunburned, and close to death. Instead, following the Grand Manner, he gave his men athletic bodies and vigorous poses, evoking the work of Michelangelo and Rubens (see Chapters 21 and 23). He did this to generalize and ennoble his subject, elevating it above the particulars of a specific shipwreck in the hope that it would speak to more fundamental human conflicts: humanity against nature, hope against despair, and life against death.

Géricault exhibited *The Raft of the Medusa* (entitled *A Shipwreck* since identifying its actual subject overtly would have been too politically inflammatory) at the 1819 Salon, where it caused considerable controversy. Most contemporary French critics and royalists interpreted the painting as a political jibe at the king, on whose favor many academicians depended, while independent liberals praised Géricault's attempt to expose corruption. The debate raised

30–54 Théodore Géricault **STUDY OF HANDS AND FEET**
1818–1819. Oil on canvas, 20½ × 25³⁄₁₈" (52 × 64 cm).
Musée Fabre, Montpellier.

Credit: Musée Fabre de Montpellier Agglomération. Photo: Frédéric Jaulmes the question of the point at which a painting crosses the line between art and political advocacy. Although it was intended to shock rather than to edify, the painting conforms to academy rules in every other way. The king refused to buy it, so Géricault exhibited *The Raft of the Medusa* commercially on a two-year tour of Ireland and England; the London exhibition alone attracted more than 50,000 paying visitors.

DELACROIX AND RUDE The French novelist Stendhal characterized the Romantic spirit when he wrote, "Romanticism in all the arts is what represents the men of today and not the men of those remote, heroic times which probably never existed anyway." Eugène Delacroix (1798–1863), the most important Romantic painter in Paris after Géricault's death, depicted contemporary heroes and victims engaged in the violent struggles of the times. In 1830, he created what has become his masterpiece, **LIBERTY**

LEADING THE PEOPLE: JULY 28, 1830 (FIG. 30–55), a painting that encapsulated the history of France after the fall of Napoleon. When Napoleon was defeated in 1815, the victorious neighboring nations reimposed the French monarchy under Louis XVIII (ruled 1815–1824), brother of Louis XVI. The king's power was limited by a constitution and a parliament, but the government became more conservative as years passed, undoing many revolutionary reforms. Louis's younger brother and successor, Charles X (ruled 1824–1830), reinstated press censorship, returned education to the control of the Catholic Church, and limited voting rights. These actions triggered a large-scale uprising in the streets of Paris. Over the course of three days in July 1830, the Bourbon monarchical line was overthrown and Louis-Philippe d'Orléans (ruled 1830–1848) replaced his cousin Charles X, promising to abide by a new constitution. This period in French history is now referred to as the "July Monarchy."

30–55 Eugène Delacroix **LIBERTY LEADING THE PEOPLE: JULY 28, 1830**
1830. Oil on canvas, 8'6½" × 10'8" (2.6 × 3.25 m). Musée du Louvre, Paris.

30-56 François Rude **DEPARTURE OF THE VOLUNTEERS OF 1792 (THE MARSEILLAISE)**

Arc de Triomphe, Place de l'Étoile, Paris. 1833–1836. Limestone, height approx. 42′ (12.8 m).

Credit: © Kiev.Victor/Shutterstock

In his large modern history painting Delacroix memorialized the July 1830 revolution just a few months after it took place. Although it records aspects of the actual event, it also departs from the facts in ways that further the intended message. Delacroix's revolutionaries are a motley crew of students, artisans, day laborers, and even children and top-hatted intellectuals. They stumble forward through the smoke of battle, crossing a barricade of refuse and dead bodies. The towers of Notre-Dame loom through the smoke and haze of the background. This much of the work is plausibly accurate. Their leader, however, is an energetic, allegorical figure of Liberty, personified by a gigantic, muscular, half-naked woman charging across the barricade with the revolutionary flag in one hand and a bayoneted rifle in the other. Delacroix has placed a Classical allegorical figure within the battle itself, outfitted with a contemporary weapon and Phrygian cap—the ancient symbol for a freed slave that was worn by the insurgents. He presents the event as an emotionally charged moment just before the ultimate sacrifice, as the revolutionaries charge the barricades to near-certain death. This dramatic example of Romantic painting is full of passion, turmoil, and danger—part real and part dream.

Artists working for the July Monarchy increasingly used the more dramatic subjects and styles of Romanticism to represent the 1830 revolution, just as Neoclassical principles had been used to represent the previous one. Early in the regime, the minister of the interior decided, as an act of national reconciliation, to complete the triumphal arch on the Champs-Élysées in Paris begun by Napoleon in 1806. François Rude (1784–1855) received the commission for a sculpture to decorate the main arcade with a scene that commemorated the volunteer army that had halted a Prussian invasion in 1792–1793. Beneath the urgent exhortations of the winged figure of Liberty, the volunteers surge forward, some nude, others in Classical armor (**FIG. 30-56**). Despite these Classical details, the overall impact is Romantic. The crowded, excited group stirred patriotism in Paris, and the sculpture quickly became known simply as the *Marseillaise*, the name of the French national anthem written in 1792, the same year as the action depicted.

INGRES Jean-Auguste-Dominique Ingres (1780–1867), perhaps David's most famous student, served as director of the French Academy in Rome between 1835 and 1841. As a teacher and theorist, Ingres became one of the most influential artists of his time. His paintings offer another variant on the Romantic and Neoclassical, combining the precise drawing, formal idealization, Classical composition, and graceful lyricism of Raphael (SEE FIG. 21–7) with an interest in creating sensual and erotically charged images that appeal to viewers' emotions.

Although Ingres fervently desired to be accepted as a history painter, he was made famous by his paintings of male fantasies of female slaves and his portraits of aristocratic women. He painted numerous versions of the **odalisque**, an exoticized version of a female slave or harem concubine. In his **LARGE ODALISQUE** (FIG. 30–57), the woman's calm gaze is leveled directly at her master, while she twists her reclined, naked body in a snakelike, concealing pose of calculated eroticism. The saturated, cool blues of the couch and the curtain at the right set off the effect of her cool, pale skin and blue eyes, while the tight angularity of the crumpled sheets accentuates the sensual contours of her body. The exotic details of her headdress and the brush

of the peacock fan against her thigh only intensify her sensuality. Ingres's commitment to academic line and formal structure was grounded in his Neoclassical training, but his fluid, attenuated female nudes speak more strongly of the Romantic tradition.

Although Ingres complained that making portraits was a "considerable waste of time," his skill in rendering physical likeness with scintillating clarity and in mimicking in paint the material qualities of clothing, hairstyles, and jewelry was unparalleled. He painted many life-size and highly polished portraits, but he also produced— usually in just a day—exquisite, small portrait drawings that are extraordinarily fresh and lively. The charming **PORTRAIT OF MADAME DÉSIRÉ RAOUL-ROCHETTE** (FIG. 30–58) is a flattering yet credible representation of the relaxed and elegant sitter. Her gloved right hand draws attention to her social status; fine kid gloves were worn only by members of the upper class, who did not work with their hands. And her ungloved left hand reveals her marital status with a wedding band. Ingres renders her shiny taffeta dress, with its fashionably high waist and puffed sleeves, with great economy and spontaneity, using subdued marks that suggest rather than describe the

30–57 Jean-Auguste-Dominique Ingres **LARGE ODALISQUE**
1814. Oil on canvas, approx. 35 × 64″ (88.9 × 162.5 cm). Musée du Louvre, Paris.

During Napoleon's campaigns against the British in North Africa, the French discovered the exotic Near East. Upper-middle-class European men were particularly attracted to the institution of the harem, partly as a reaction against the egalitarian demands of women of their own class that had been unleashed by the French Revolution.

30–58 Jean-Auguste-Dominique Ingres **PORTRAIT OF MADAME DÉSIRÉ RAOUL-ROCHETTE**

1830. Graphite on paper, 12⅝ × 9½″ (32.2 × 24.1 cm). Cleveland Museum of Art. Purchase from the J. H. Wade Fund (1927.437).

Madame Raoul-Rochette (1790–1878), née Antoinette-Claude Houdon, was the youngest daughter of the famous Neoclassical sculptor Jean-Antoine Houdon (SEE FIG. 30–42). In 1810, at age 20, she married Désiré Raoul-Rochette, a noted archaeologist, who later became the secretary of the Académie des Beaux-Arts (Academy of Fine Arts, founded in 1816 to replace the French Royal Academy of Painting and Sculpture) and a close friend of Ingres. Ingres's drawing of Madame Raoul-Rochette is inscribed to her husband ("Ingres to his friend and colleague, Mr. Raoul-Rochette"), whose portrait Ingres also drew around the same time.

fabric. As a result, emphasis rests on the sitter's face and elaborate coiffure, which Ingres has drawn precisely and modeled with subtle evocations of light and shade.

DAUMIER Honoré Daumier (1808–1879) came to Paris from Marseille in 1816. He studied drawing at the Académie Suisse, but he learned the technique of **lithography** (see "Lithography" on page 970) as assistant to the printmaker Bélaird. Daumier published his first lithograph in 1829 at age 21 in the weekly satirical magazine *La Silhouette*.

In the wake of the 1830 revolution in Paris, Daumier began supplying pictures to *La Caricature*, an anti-monarchist, pro-republican magazine, and the equally partisan *Le Charivari*, the first daily newspaper illustrated with lithographs. His 1834 lithograph calling attention to the atrocities on **RUE TRANSNONAIN** (FIG. 30-60) was part

of a series of large prints sold by subscription to raise money for *Le Charivari*'s legal defense fund and thus further freedom of the press. A government guard had been shot and killed on the rue Transnonain—only a few blocks from Daumier's home—during a demonstration by workers, and in response, the riot squad killed everyone in the building where they believed the marksman was hiding. Daumier shows the bloody aftermath of the event: an innocent family disturbed from their sleep and then murdered. The wife lies in the shadows to the left, her husband in the center of the room, and an elderly man to the right. It takes a few minutes for viewers to realize that under the central figure's back there are also the bloody head and arms of a murdered child. Daumier was known for his biting caricatures and social commentary, but this image is one of his most powerful.

Technique
LITHOGRAPHY

Lithography, invented in the mid-1790s, is based on the natural antagonism between oil and water. The artist draws on a flat surface—traditionally, fine-grained stone (*lithos* is Greek for "stone")—with a greasy substance. After the drawing is completed, the stone's surface is wiped first with water and then with an oil-based ink. The ink adheres to the greasy areas but not to the damp ones. After a series of such steps, a sheet of paper is laid face down on the inked stone, pressed against it with a scraper, and then rolled through a flatbed press. This transfers ink from stone to paper, thus making lithography (like relief and intaglio) a direct method of creating a printed image. Unlike earlier processes, however, grease-based lithography enables the artist to capture the subtleties of drawing with crayon and a liquid mixture called *tusche*. Francisco Goya, Théodore Géricault, Eugène Delacroix, Honoré Daumier, and Henri de Toulouse-Lautrec used the medium to great effect.

Daumier was probably the greatest exponent of lithography in the nineteenth century. The technique was widely used in France for fine-art prints and to illustrate popular magazines and even newspapers. By the 1830s, the print trade in France had exploded. Artists could use lithography to produce their own prints without the cumbersome, expensive, and time-consuming intermediary of the engraver. Daumier's picture of **THE PRINT LOVERS** (**FIG. 30–59**) shows three men who have fixed their attention on the folio of prints in front of them, despite being surrounded by works of art packed tightly on the wall behind them. By the end of the nineteenth century, inexpensive prints were in every house and owned by people at every level of society.

30–59 Honoré Daumier **THE PRINT LOVERS**
c. 1863–1865. Watercolor, black pencil, black ink, gray wash, 10⅛ × 12⅛″ (25.8 × 30.7 cm). Musée du Louvre, Paris.

Credit: Photo © RMN-Grand Palais (musée du Louvre)

scraper   paper   inked stone   moving base

diagram of the lithographic process

30–60 Honoré Daumier **RUE TRANSNONAIN, LE 15 AVRIL 1834**
1834. Lithograph, 11 × 17⅜″ (28 × 44 cm). Yale Univesity Art Gallery. Everett V. Meeks, B.A. 1901, Fund (1982.120.4)

Credit: Image courtesy Yale University Art Gallery

Romantic Landscape Painting

The Romantics saw nature as ever-changing, unpredictable, and uncontrollable, and they saw in it an analogy to equally changeable human emotions. They found nature awesome, fascinating, powerful, domestic, and delightful, and landscape painting became an important visual theme in Romantic art.

CONSTABLE   John Constable (1776–1837), the son of a successful miller, claimed that the quiet domestic landscape of his youth in southern England had made him a painter before he ever picked up a paintbrush. Although he was trained at the Royal Academy, he was equally influenced by the seventeenth-century Dutch landscape-painting tradition (SEE FIG. 23–45). After moving to London in 1816, he dedicated himself to painting monumental views of the agricultural landscape (known as "six-footers"), which he considered as important as history painting. Constable's commitment to contemporary English subjects was so strong that he opposed the establishment of the English National Gallery of Art in 1832 on the grounds that it might distract painters by enticing them to paint foreign or ancient themes in unnatural styles.

THE HAY WAIN (FIG. **30-61**) of 1821 shows a quiet, slow-moving scene with the fresh color and sense of visual exactitude that persuade viewers that it must have been painted directly from observation. But although Constable made numerous drawings and small-scale color studies for his paintings, the final works were carefully constructed images produced in the studio. (His paintings are very large, even for landscape themes of historic importance, never mind views derived from the local countryside.) *The Hay Wain* represents England as Constable imagined it had been for centuries—comfortable, rural, and idyllic. Even the carefully rendered and meteorologically correct details of the sky seem natural. The painting is, however, deeply nostalgic, harking back to an agrarian past that was fast disappearing in industrializing England.

TURNER   Joseph Mallord William Turner (1775–1851) is often paired with Constable. The two were English landscape painters of roughly the same period, but Turner's career followed a different path. He entered the Royal Academy in 1789, was elected a full academician at the unusually young age of 27, and later became a professor at the Royal Academy Schools. By the late 1790s, he was

30–61 John Constable **THE HAY WAIN**
1821. Oil on canvas, 51¼ × 73″ (130.2 × 185.4 cm). National Gallery, London. Gift of Henry Vaughan, 1886.

30–62 Joseph Mallord William Turner **SNOWSTORM: HANNIBAL AND HIS ARMY CROSSING THE ALPS**
1812. Oil on canvas, 4′9″ × 7′9″ (1.46 × 2.39 m). Tate, London.

Credit: © akg-images/De Agostini Picture Library

30–63 Joseph Mallord William Turner **THE BURNING OF THE HOUSES OF LORDS AND COMMONS, 16TH OCTOBER 1834**

Oil on canvas, 36¼ × 48½″ (92.1 × 123.2 cm). Philadelphia Museum of Art.

The John Howard McFadden Collection, 1928.

Credit: © 2016. Photo The Philadelphia Museum of Art/Art Resource/Scala, Florence exhibiting large-scale oil paintings of grand natural scenes and historical subjects, in which he sought to capture the **sublime**, a concept defined by philosopher Edmund Burke (1729–1797). According to Burke, when we witness something that instills fascination mixed with fear, or when we stand in the presence of something far larger than ourselves, our feelings transcend those we encounter in normal life. Such savage grandeur strikes awe and terror into the heart of the viewer, but there is no real danger. Because the sublime is experienced vicariously, it is thrilling and exciting rather than threatening, and it often evokes the transcendent power of God. Turner translated this concept of the sublime into powerful paintings of turbulence in the natural world and the urban environment.

His **SNOWSTORM: HANNIBAL AND HIS ARMY CROSSING THE ALPS** (FIG. **30-62**) of 1812 epitomizes Romanticism's view of the awesomeness of nature. An enormous vortex of wind, mist, and snow masks the sun and threatens to annihilate the soldiers marching below it. Barely discernible in the distance is the figure of Hannibal, mounted on an elephant to lead his troops through the Alps toward their encounter with the Roman army in 218 BCE. Turner probably meant his painting as an allegory of the Napoleonic Wars. Napoleon himself had crossed the Alps, an event celebrated by David in his laudatory portrait (SEE FIG. 30-49). But while David's painting, which Turner saw in Paris in 1802, presented Napoleon as a powerful figure, commanding not only his troops but nature itself, Turner reduced Hannibal to a speck on the horizon, threatened with his troops by natural disaster, as if foretelling their eventual defeat.

Closer to home, Turner based another dramatic and thrilling work on the tragic fire that severely damaged London's historic Parliament building. Blazing color and light dominate **THE BURNING OF THE HOUSES OF LORDS AND COMMONS, 16TH OCTOBER 1834** (FIG. **30-63**), and the foreground of the painting shows the south bank of the Thames packed with spectators. This fire was a national tragedy; these buildings had witnessed some of the most important events in English history. Turner himself was witness to the scene and hurriedly made watercolor sketches on site; within a few months he had the large painting ready for exhibition. The painting's true theme is the brilliant light and color that spirals across the canvas in the explosive energy of loose brushwork, explaining why Turner was called "the painter of light."

COLE AND FRIEDRICH Thomas Cole (1801–1848) was one of the first great professional landscape painters in the United States. Cole emigrated from England at age 17 and by 1820 was working as an itinerant portrait painter. With the help of a patron, he traveled in Europe between 1829 and 1832, and upon his return to the United States he settled in New York and became a successful landscape painter. He frequently worked from observation when making sketches for his paintings. In fact, his self-portrait is tucked into the foreground of **THE OXBOW** (FIG. **30-64**), where he turns back to look at us while pausing from his work. He is executing an oil sketch on a portable easel, but like most landscape painters of his generation, he produced his large finished works in the studio during the winter months.

30-64 Thomas Cole **THE OXBOW** 1836. Oil on canvas, 51½ × 76" (1.31 × 1.94 m). Metropolitan Museum of Art, New York. Gift of Mrs. Russell Sage, 1908 (08.228).

Credit: © 2016. Image copyright The Metropolitan Museum of Art/Art Resource/Scala, Florence

30-65 Caspar David Friedrich **ABBEY IN AN OAK FOREST**
1809–1810. Oil on canvas, 44 × 68½" (111.8 × 174 cm). Nationalgalerie, Berlin.

Credit: © Photo Scala, Florence/bpk, Bildagentur für Kunst, Kultur und Geschichte, Berlin. Photo. Joerg P. Anders

Cole painted this work in the mid-1830s for exhibition at the National Academy of Design in New York. He considered it one of his "view" paintings because it represents a specific place and time. Although most of his other view paintings were small, this one is monumentally large, probably because it was created for exhibition at the National Academy. Its scale allows for a sweeping view of a spectacular oxbow bend in the Connecticut River from the top of Mount Holyoke in western Massachusetts. Cole wrote that the American landscape lacked the historic monuments that made European landscape interesting; there were no castles on the Hudson River of the kind found on the Rhine, and there were no ancient monuments in America of the kind found in Rome. On the other hand, he argued, America's natural wonders, such as this oxbow, should be viewed as America's natural antiquities. The painting's title tells us that Cole depicts an actual spot, but, like other landscape painters who wished to impart a larger message about the course of history in their work, he composed the scene to stress the landscape's grandeur and significance, exaggerating the steepness of the mountain and setting the scene below a dramatic sky. Along a sweeping arc produced by the dark clouds and the edge of the mountain, he contrasts the two sides of the American landscape: its dense, stormy wilderness and its congenial, pastoral valleys with settlements. The fading storm seems to suggest that the land is bountiful and ready to yield its fruits to civilization.

In Germany, the Romantic landscape painter Caspar David Friedrich (1774–1840) saw landscape as a vehicle through which to achieve spiritual revelation. As a young man, he had been influenced by the writings and teachings of Gotthard Kosegarten, a local Lutheran pastor and poet who taught that the divine was visible through a deep personal connection with nature. Kosegarten argued that just as God's book was the Bible, the landscape was God's "Book of Nature." Friedrich studied at the Copenhagen Academy before settling in Dresden, where the poet Johann Wolfgang von Goethe encouraged him to make landscape the principal subject of his art. He sketched from nature but painted in the studio, synthesizing his sketches with his memories of and feelings about nature. In **ABBEY IN AN OAK FOREST** (**FIG. 30-65**), a funeral procession of monks in the lower foreground is barely visible through the gloom that seems to be settling heavily on the snow-covered world of human habitation. Most prominent are the boldly silhouetted trunks and bare branches of a grove of oak trees, and nestled among them the ruin of a Gothic wall, a formal juxtaposition that creates a natural cathedral from this cold and mysterious landscape.

British and American Architecture

A mixture of Neoclassicism and Romanticism motivated architects in the early nineteenth century, many of whom worked in either mode, depending on the task at hand. Neoclassicism in architecture often imbued secular public buildings with a sense of grandeur and timelessness, while Romanticism evoked, for instance, the Gothic past with its associations of spirituality and community.

GOTHIC ARCHITECTURE The British claimed the Gothic as part of their patrimony and erected many Gothic Revival buildings during the nineteenth century, prominent among them the new **HOUSES OF PARLIAMENT** (**FIG. 30-66**). After Westminster Palace burned in 1834 in

30–66 Charles Barry and Augustus Welby Northmore Pugin **HOUSES OF PARLIAMENT, LONDON**
1836–1860. Royal Commission on the Historical Monuments of England, London.

Pugin published two influential books in 1836 and 1841, in which he argued that the Gothic style of Westminster Abbey was the embodiment of true English genius. In his view, the Greek and Roman Classical orders were stone replications of earlier wooden forms and therefore fell short of the true principles of stone construction.

Credit: © S.Borisov/Shutterstock

the fire so memorably painted by Turner (SEE FIG. 30–63), the British government announced a competition for a new building to be designed in the English Perpendicular Gothic style, harmonizing with the neighboring thirteenth-century church of Westminster Abbey where English monarchs are crowned.

Charles Barry (1795–1860) and Augustus Welby Northmore Pugin (1812–1852) won the commission. Barry devised the essentially Classical plan of the new building, whose symmetry suggests the balance of powers within the British parliamentary system, while Pugin designed the intricate Gothic decoration. The leading advocate of Gothic architecture at this time, Pugin published *Contrasts* in 1836, in which he compared the troubled modern era of materialism and mechanization unfavorably with the Middle Ages, which he represented as an idyllic time of deep spirituality and satisfying handcraft. For Pugin, Gothic was not a style but a principle, like Classicism. The Gothic, he insisted, embodied two "great rules" of architecture: "first, that there should be no features about a building which are not necessary for convenience, construction or propriety; second, that all ornament should consist of enrichment of the essential structure of the building."

Most Gothic Revival buildings of this period, however, were churches, usually either Roman Catholic or Anglican (Episcopalian in the United States). The British-born American architect Richard Upjohn (1802–1878) designed many of the most important American examples, including **TRINITY CHURCH** in New York (**FIG. 30–67**). With its tall spire, long nave, and squared-off chancel, Trinity

30–67 Richard Upjohn **TRINITY CHURCH, NEW YORK CITY**
1839–1846.

Credit: Leo Sorel Photography

Church quotes the early fourteenth-century British Gothic style particularly admired by Anglicans and Episcopalians. Every detail is rendered with historical accuracy, but the vaults are plaster, not masonry. The stained-glass windows above the altar were among the earliest of their kind in the United States.

NEOCLASSICAL ARCHITECTURE In several European capitals in the early nineteenth century, the Neoclassical designs of national museums positioned these buildings as both temples of culture and expressions of nationalism. Perhaps the most significant was the **ALTES MUSEUM** (Old Museum) in Berlin, designed in 1822 by Karl Friedrich Schinkel (1781–1841) and built between 1824 and 1830 (**FIG. 30–68**). Commissioned to display the royal art collection, the building was built directly across from the Baroque royal palace on an island in the Spree River in the heart of the city. The museum's imposing façade consists of a screen of 18 Ionic columns raised on a platform with a central staircase. Attentive to the problem of lighting artworks on both the ground and the upper floors, Schinkel created interior courtyards on either side of a central rotunda. Tall windows on the museum's outer walls provide natural illumination, and partition walls perpendicular to the windows eliminate glare on the varnished surfaces of the paintings on display.

Neoclassical style was also popular for large public buildings in the United States, perhaps most significantly and symbolically in the U.S. Capitol, in Washington, DC, initially designed in 1792 by William Thornton (1759–1828), an amateur architect. His monumental plan featured a large dome over a temple front flanked by two wings to accommodate the House of Representatives and the Senate. In 1803, President Thomas Jefferson (1743–1826), also an amateur architect, hired a British-trained professional, Benjamin Henry Latrobe (1764–1820), to oversee the actual construction of the Capitol. Latrobe modified Thornton's design by adding a grand staircase and Corinthian colonnade on the east front (**FIG. 30–69**). After the British gutted the building in the war of 1812, Latrobe repaired the wings and designed a higher dome. Seeking new symbolic forms for the nation within the traditional Classical vocabulary, he also created a variation on the Corinthian order for the interior by substituting indigenous crops such as corn and tobacco for the Corinthian order's acanthus leaves. In 1817, Latrobe resigned his post. The reconstruction was completed under Charles

30–69 Benjamin Henry Latrobe **U.S. CAPITOL, WASHINGTON, DC**

c. 1808. Engraving by T. Sutherland, 1825. Library of Congress, Prints and Photographs division, Washington D.C.

Credit: Courtesy the Library of Congress

Bulfinch (1763–1844), and another major renovation, resulting in a much larger dome, began in 1850.

Thomas Jefferson's graceful designs for the mountaintop home he called **MONTICELLO** (Italian for "little mountain"), near Charlottesville, Virginia, employ Neoclassical architecture in a private setting (**FIG. 30-70**). Jefferson began the first phase of construction (1769–1782) when Virginia was still a British colony, using the English Palladian style (see Chiswick House, FIG. 30-15). By 1796, however, he had become disenchanted with both the English and their architecture and had come to admire French architecture while serving as the American minister in Paris. He then embarked upon a second building campaign at Monticello (1796–1809), enlarging the house and redesigning its brick and wood exterior so that its two stories appeared from the outside as one large story in the manner then fashionable in Paris. The modern worlds of England, France, and America, as well as the ancient worlds of Greece and Rome, come together in this residence. In the second half of the nineteenth century, cultural borrowings would take on an even broader global scope.

30-70 Thomas Jefferson **MONTICELLO**
Charlottesville, Virginia.
1769–1782, 1796–1809.

Credit: © Ffooter/Shutterstock

Think About It

1   Summarize some of the key stylistic traits of French Rococo art and architecture and explain how these traits relate to the social context of salon life. Then analyze one Rococo work from this chapter and explain how it is typical of the period style.

2   Explain why artists as visually diverse as Delacroix and Friedrich can be classified under the category of Romanticism. How useful is "Romanticism" as a classifying term?

3   How did the political climate during Francisco Goya's life affect his art? Focus your answer on a discussion of *Third of May, 1808* (**FIG. 30-45**).

4   Discuss the relationship of the Enlightenment interest in archaeology with the new movement of Neoclassicism in the eighteenth century.

Crosscurrents

Double portraits of couples are common in the history of European and American art. Assess the ways in which these two examples portray the nature of the marital relationship of these men and women. How do the portrayals represent the social structures and concerns of the cultural situations in which the couples lived?

FIG. 19-1

FIG. 30-1

31-1 Gustave Eiffel **EIFFEL TOWER, PARIS**
1889 (also the date of this photograph). Height 984′ (300 m).

Credit: Courtesy the Library of Congress

Chapter 31

Mid- to Late Nineteenth-Century Art in Europe and the United States

 ## Learning Objectives

31.a Identify the visual hallmarks of mid- to late nineteenth-century European and American art and architecture for formal, technical, and expressive qualities.

31.b Interpret the meaning of works of mid- to late nineteenth-century European and American art based on their themes, subjects, and symbols.

31.c Relate mid- to late nineteenth-century European and American art and artists to their cultural, economic, and political contexts.

31.d Apply the vocabulary and concepts relevant to mid- to late nineteenth-century European and American art, artists, and art history.

31.e Interpret a work of mid- to late nineteenth-century European or American art using the art historical methods of observation, comparison, and inductive reasoning.

31.f Select visual and textual evidence in various media to support an argument or an interpretation of a work of mid- to late nineteenth-century European or American art or architecture.

The world-famous **EIFFEL TOWER** (**FIG. 31-1**) is a proud reminder of the nineteenth-century French belief in the progress and ultimate perfectibility of civilization through science and technology. Structural engineer Gustave Eiffel (1832–1923) designed and constructed the tower to serve as a monumental approach to the 1889 Universal Exposition in Paris. When completed, it stood 984 feet high and was the tallest structure in the world, taller than the Egyptian pyramids or Gothic cathedrals. The Eiffel Tower was the main attraction of the Universal Exposition, one of more than 20 such international fairs staged throughout Europe and the United States in the second half of the nineteenth century. These events showcased and compared international industry, science, and the applied, decorative, and fine arts. An object of pride for the French nation, the Eiffel Tower was intended to demonstrate France's superior engineering, technological, and industrial knowledge and power. Although originally conceived as a temporary structure, it still stands today.

The initial response to the Eiffel Tower was mixed. In 1887, a group of 47 writers, musicians, and artists wrote to *Le Temps* protesting "the erection … of the useless and monstrous Eiffel Tower," which they described as "a black and gigantic factory chimney." Gustave Eiffel, however, said, "I believe the tower will have its own beauty," and that it "will show that [the French] are not simply an amusing people, but also the country of engineers." Indeed, the Eiffel Tower quickly became an international symbol of advanced thought and modernity among artists and was admired by the public as a wondrous spectacle. Today it is the symbol of Paris itself.

The tower was one of the city's most photographed structures in 1889, its immensity dwarfing the seemingly tiny buildings below. Thousands of tourists to the Exposition bought souvenir photographs taken by professional and commercial photographers. This one shows the imposing structure rising above the exhibition buildings around and behind it along the Champ de Mars.

Europe and the United States in the Mid to Late Nineteenth Century

What are the political and social backgrounds for mid- to late nineteenth-century European and American art and architecture?

The technological, economic, and social transformations initiated by the Industrial Revolution intensified during the nineteenth century. Increasing demands for coal and iron prompted improvements in mining, metallurgy, and transportation. Likewise, the development of the locomotive and steamship facilitated the shipment of raw materials and merchandise, made passenger travel easier, and encouraged the growth of cities (**MAP 31-1**). These changes also set in motion a vast population migration, as the rural poor moved to cities to find work in factories, mines, and mechanical manufacturing. Industrialists and entrepreneurs enjoyed new levels of wealth and prosperity in this system, but conditions for workers—many of them women and children—were often terrible. Although new

government regulations led to some improvements, socialist movements condemned the exploitation of workers by capitalist factory owners and argued for communal or state ownership of the means of production and distribution.

In 1848, workers' revolts broke out in several European capitals, and Karl Marx and Friedrich Engels published the *Communist Manifesto*, which predicted the violent overthrow of the bourgeoisie (middle class) by the proletariat (working class); the abolition of private property; and the creation of a classless society. At the same time, the Americans Lucretia Mott and Elizabeth Cady Stanton organized the country's first women's rights convention, in Seneca Falls, New York. They called for the legal equality of women and men, property rights for married women, acceptance of women into institutions of higher education, admission of women to all trades and professions, equal pay for equal work, and women's right to vote.

The nineteenth century also saw the rise of imperialism. In order to create new markets for their products and to secure access to cheap raw materials and cheap labor, European nations established numerous new colonies by dividing up most of Africa and nearly a third of Asia. Colonial rule often suppressed indigenous cultures while

MAP 31-1 EUROPE AND THE UNITED STATES IN THE NINETEENTH CENTURY

In the nineteenth century, Europe and the United States became increasingly industrialized, and many European nations established colonial possessions around the world. Paris was firmly established as the center of the Western art world.

exploiting the colonies for the economic development of the European colonial powers.

Scientific discoveries led to the invention of the telegraph, telephone, and radio. By the end of the nineteenth century, electricity powered lighting, motors, trams, and railroads in most European and American cities. Developments in chemistry created many new products, such as aspirin, disinfectants, photographic chemicals, and more-effective explosives. Steel, a new alloy of iron and carbon, was lighter, harder, and more malleable than iron and replaced it in heavy construction and transportation. In medicine and public health, Louis Pasteur's purification of beverages through heat (pasteurization) and the development of vaccines, sterilization, and antiseptics led to a dramatic decline in mortality rates all over the Western world.

Some scientific discoveries challenged traditional religious beliefs and changed social philosophy. Geologists concluded that the Earth was far older than the estimated 6,000 years sometimes claimed by biblical literalists. In 1859, Charles Darwin proposed that life evolved gradually through natural selection. Religious conservatives attacked Darwin's account, which seemed to deny divine creation and even the existence of God. Some of Darwin's more extreme supporters, however, suggested that the "survival of the fittest" had advanced the human race, with certain types of people—particularly the Anglo-Saxon upper classes—achieving the pinnacle of social evolution. "Social Darwinism" provided a rationalization for the poor conditions of the working class and the colonization of the "underdeveloped" parts of the world.

Industrialists, merchants, professionals, the middle classes, some governments, and national academies of art became sources of patronage in the arts. Large annual exhibitions in European and American cultural centers took on increasing importance as a means for artists to show their work, win prizes, attract buyers, and gain commissions. Cheap illustrated newspapers and magazines published art criticism that influenced the reception and production of art, both making and breaking artistic careers, and commercial art dealers emerged as important brokers of taste.

The second half of the nineteenth century saw vast changes in how art was conceptualized and created. Some artists became committed political or social activists as industrialization and social unrest continued, while others retreated into their own imagination. Some responded to the ways in which photography transformed vision and perception, either setting themselves up as photographers or emulating the new medium's clarity in their own work. Many investigated the difference between photography's detailed but superficial description of visual reality and a deeper, more human reality as a source of inspiration—as well as the artistic potential of photography's sometimes visually unbalanced compositions, its tendency to compress the illusion of depth, its sharp framing and abrupt cropping, its lack of an even focus across the picture plane (or sometimes the reverse), and the inability of early photography to "see" red and green equally, causing undifferentiated areas of white and black in a photograph. By the end of the century, while many artists were still exploring the reliability of observed reality, others were venturing ever further into the realm of abstraction.

French Academic Architecture and Art

What are the hallmarks of academic taste in French art and architecture?

The Académie des Beaux-Arts (founded in 1816 to replace the disbanded Royal Academy of Painting and Sculpture) and its official art school, the École des Beaux-Arts, continued to exert a powerful influence over the visual arts in France during the nineteenth century. Academic artists controlled the Salon juries, and major public commissions routinely went to academic architects, painters, and sculptors. It was to Paris that artists and architects from Europe and the United States came to study the conventions of academic art.

Academic art and architecture frequently used motifs drawn from historic models—a practice called **historicism**. Elaborating on earlier Neoclassical and Romantic revivals, historicist art and architecture encompassed the sweep of history. Historicists often referred to several different historical periods in a single work. Some academic artists catered to the public taste for exotic sights with Orientalist paintings (see "Orientalism" on page 982). These works also combined disparate elements, borrowing from Egyptian, Turkish, and Indian cultures to create an imaginary Middle Eastern world.

Architecture

In 1848, after rioting over living conditions erupted in French cities, Napoleon III (ruled as emperor 1852–1870) launched sweeping new reforms. The riots had devastated Paris's central neighborhoods, and Georges-Eugène Haussmann (1809–1891) was engaged to redraw the street grid and rebuild the city. Haussmann imposed a new, rational plan of broad avenues, parks, and open public places upon the medieval heart of Paris. He demolished entire neighborhoods, erasing networks of narrow, winding, medieval streets and evicting the poor from their slums rapidly and without exceptions. Then he replaced what he had destroyed with grand new buildings erected along wide, straight, tree-lined avenues that were more suitable for horse-drawn carriages and strolling pedestrians.

Art and Its Contexts

ORIENTALISM

In **THE SNAKE CHARMER** (**FIG. 31-2**), French academic painter Jean-León Gérôme (1824–1904) creates a nineteenth-century fantasy of the Middle East—a characteristic example of **Orientalism**, the European fascination with Middle Eastern cultures. A young boy, entirely naked, handles a python, while an older man behind him plays a fipple flute, and an audience huddles within the background shadows in a blue-tiled room decorated with calligraphic patterns. Gérôme paints the scene with photographic clarity and scrupulous attention to detail, leading us to think that it is an accurate representation of a specific event and locale. He traveled to the Middle East several times and was praised by critics of the 1855 Salon for his ethnographic accuracy, but his *Snake Charmer* is a complete fiction, mixing Egyptian, Turkish, and Indian cultures together in a fantasized pastiche.

Orientalism dates to Napoleon's 1798 invasion of Egypt and his rampant looting of Egyptian objects for the Louvre Museum, which he opened in 1804, and the 24-volume *Description de l'Egypte* (1809–1822), recording Egyptian people, lands, and culture, that followed. In the 1840s and 1850s, British, French, and Italian photographers established studios at major tourist sites in the Middle East in order to provide photographs for both visitors and armchair tourists, thus fueling a popular interest in the region.

Characterizing both academic and avant-garde art in the nineteenth century, the scholar Edward Said described Orientalism as the colonial gaze upon the colonized Orient (the Middle East rather than Asia), seen as something to possess by the colonizer and as a "primitive" or "exotic" playground by the "civilized" European visitor. "Native" men become savage and despotic, and "native" women—and in this painting, boys—are sensuously described and sexually available

31-2 Jean-Léon Gérôme **THE SNAKE CHARMER** c. 1870. Oil on canvas, 33 × 48⅛″ (83.8 × 122.1 cm). Clark Art Institute, Williamstown, Massachusetts. Acquired by Sterling and Francine Clark, 1942. (1955.51).

Credit: Bridgeman Images

The **OPÉRA** (**FIG. 31-3**), a city opera house designed by Charles Garnier (1825–1898) that is still a major Parisian landmark, was built at an intersection newly created by Haussmann's grand avenues. Accessible from many directions, the Opéra was designed with transportation and vehicular traffic in mind and had a modern cast-iron internal frame; yet in other respects it is a masterpiece of historicism derived mostly from the Baroque style, revived to recall an earlier period of greatness in France. The massive façade, featuring a row of paired columns over an arcade, refers to the seventeenth-century wing of the Louvre, an association meant to assert the continuity of the French nation and to flatter Napoleon III by comparing him favorably with Louis XIV. The building's primary function—as a place of entertainment for the emperor, his entourage, and the high echelons of French society—accounts for its luxurious exterior detail. The interior, described as a "temple of pleasure," was even more opulent, with neo-Baroque sculptural groupings, heavy gilded decoration, and a lavish mix of expensive, polychromed materials. More spectacular than any performance on stage was the one on the grand, sweeping Baroque staircase (**FIG. 31-4**), where members of the Paris elite displayed themselves. As Garnier said, the purpose of the Opéra was to fulfill the human desire to hear, to see, and to be seen.

31–3 Charles Garnier **OPÉRA, PARIS**

1861–1874.

Credit: © akg-images

31–4 GRAND STAIRCASE, OPÉRA

Credit: © John Kellerman/Alamy Stock Photo

Painting and Sculpture

The taste that dominated painting and sculpture in the Académie des Beaux-Arts by the mid nineteenth century is well represented by **THE BIRTH OF VENUS** by Alexandre Cabanel (1823–1889), one of the leading academic artists of the time (**FIG. 31-5**). After studying with an academic master, Cabanel won the Prix de Rome in 1845 and garnered top honors at the Salon three times in the 1860s and 1870s. In his version of this popular mythological subject (compare FIG. 20-35), Venus floats above the waves as flying *putti* playfully herald her arrival with conch shells. Cabanel's technical mastery of anatomy, flesh tones, and the rippling sea derives from his academic training. But the image also carries a strong erotic charge in the languid

limbs, arched back, and diverted eyes of Venus. The combination of mythological pedigree and sexual allure proved irresistible to Napoleon III, who bought *The Birth of Venus* for his private collection.

Although academic and avant-garde art are often seen as polar opposites, the relationship was more complex. Some academic artists experimented while maintaining academic conventions, while avant-garde artists held many academic practices in high esteem and sought academic approval. The academic artist Jean-Baptiste Carpeaux (1827–1875) illustrates the kind of experimentation that took place even within the academy. Carpeaux, who had studied at the École des Beaux-Arts under the Romantic sculptor François Rude (SEE FIG. 30-56), was commissioned to carve a large sculptural group for the façade of

31-5 Alexandre Cabanel **THE BIRTH OF VENUS**

1863. Oil on canvas, 52 × 90″ (1.35 × 2.29 m). Musée d'Orsay, Paris.

Credit: Photo © RMN-Grand Palais (musée d'Orsay)/ Hervé Lewandowski

Art and Its Contexts

THE MASS DISSEMINATION OF ART

Just as contemporary artists can distribute photographic reproductions of their work, artists in the nineteenth century used engraving or etching to reproduce their work for distribution to a larger audience.

Works of art that won prizes or created controversy were often engraved for reproduction by specialists in printmaking; the prints were sold at bookstores or magazine stands. J. M. W. Turner hired a team of engravers to capture the delicate tonal shadings of his works. An engraved copper plate could be printed upward of 100 times before the repeated pressing wore down the plate and affected image quality. In the later nineteenth century, artists increasingly used steel

engraving, wood engraving, and lithography for printing. These more durable surfaces could print up to 10,000 copies of an image without much loss of quality, though only a few artists experienced such demand.

One of the canniest self-marketers of the century was Alexandre Cabanel. After Napoleon III bought *The Birth of Venus* (SEE FIG. 31-5), the artist sold the reproduction rights to the art dealer Adolphe Goupil, who in turn hired other painters to create at least two smaller-scale copies of the work. After the original artist had approved the copies and signed them, the dealer used them as models for engravers who cut steel plates so prints could be made. The dealer then sold the painted copies.

Garnier's Opéra. His work, **THE DANCE** (**FIG. 31-6**), shows a winged male personification of Dance leaping up joyfully in the midst of a compact group of mostly nude female dancers, an image of uninhibited Dionysian revelry. Like Cabanel's *Birth of Venus*, the work imbues a mythological subject with an erotic charge.

Unlike Cabanel's figures, Carpeaux's were not smooth and generalized in a Neoclassical manner, and this drew criticism from some academicians. The arrangement of his sculptural group also seemed too spontaneous, the facial expressions of the figures too vivid, their musculature too exact, and their bone structure and proportions too much of this world, rather than reflections of an ideal one. Carpeaux's work signaled a new direction in academic art, responding to the values of a new generation of patrons from the industrial and merchant classes. These practical new collectors were less interested in art that idealized than in art that brought the ideal down to earth.

31-6 Jean-Baptiste Carpeaux THE DANCE
1867–1868. Plaster, height approx. 15′ (4.6 m).
Musée d'Orsay, Paris.

Credit: © akg-images/Erich Lessing

Early Photography in Europe and the United States

How does photography establish itself as a new art form?

The nineteenth-century desire to record the faces of the new mercantile elite, their achievements and possessions, and even the imperial possessions of nations, found expression in photography. Since the late Renaissance, artists and others had sought a mechanical method for drawing from nature. One early device was the camera obscura (Latin, meaning "dark chamber"), which consists of a darkened room or box with a lens through which light passes, projecting an upside-down image of the scene onto the opposite wall (or box side), which an artist can then trace. By the nineteenth century, a small, portable camera obscura or even lighter *camera lucida* had become standard equipment for artists. Photography developed as a way to fix—that is, to make permanent—the images produced by a camera obscura (later called simply a "camera") on light-sensitive material.

Photography had no single inventor. Several individuals worked on the technique simultaneously, each contributing some part to a process that emerged over many years. Around 1830, a handful of experimenters had found ways to "record" the image, but the last step, "stopping" or "fixing" that image so that further exposure to light would not further darken the image, was more challenging.

In France, while experimenting with ways to duplicate his paintings, Louis-Jacques-Mandé Daguerre (1787–1851) discovered that a plate coated with light-sensitive chemicals and exposed to light for 20 to 30 minutes would reveal a "latent image" when later exposed to mercury vapors. By 1837, he had developed a method of fixing his image by bathing the plate in a solution of salt, and he vastly improved the process by using the chemical hyposulfate of soda (known as "hypo") as suggested by Sir John Frederick Herschel (1792–1871). The final image was negative, but when viewed upon a highly polished silver plate it appeared positive. The resulting picture could not be duplicated easily and was very fragile,

Technique

THE PHOTOGRAPHIC PROCESS

A camera is essentially a lightproof box with a hole, called an aperture, which is usually adjustable in size and controls how much light reaches the film. The aperture is covered with a lens, to focus the image on the film, and a shutter, a hinged flap that opens for a controlled amount of time to expose the film to light—usually a small fraction of a second. Small, modern cameras with viewfinders are usually used at eye level; looking through them, the photographer sees almost the same image that will be captured on film.

In black-and-white chemical photography, silver halide crystals (silver combined with iodine, chlorine, or other halogens) are suspended in a gelatin base to make an emulsion that coats the film; in early photography, before the invention of plastic, a glass plate was coated with a variety of emulsions. When the shutter is open, light reflected off objects enters the camera and strikes the film, exposing it. Pale objects reflect more light than dark ones. The silver in the emulsion collects most densely where it is exposed to the most light, producing a "negative" image on the film. Later, when the film is placed in a chemical bath (developed), the silver deposits turn black, as if tarnishing. The more light the film receives in the camera, the denser the black tone created by the chemicals. The final image is created in the darkroom, where the film (now called a negative) is placed over a sheet of paper that, like the film, has been treated to

make it light-sensitive. Light is directed through the negative onto the paper to create a positive image. Multiple positive prints can be generated from a single negative.

Today the chemical process has been largely replaced by digital photography, which records images as digital information files that can be manipulated on computers rather than in darkrooms. Exploiting the artistic potential of this new photographic medium is a major preoccupation of contemporary artists.

but its quality was remarkably precise. In Daguerre's photograph of his studio tabletop (**FIG. 31-7**) the details are exquisite (though impossible to see in reproduction, even using today's technology), and the composition mimics the conventions of still-life painting. Daguerre, after he patented and announced his new technology, produced an early type of photograph called a **daguerreotype** in August 1839.

Even before Daguerre announced his photographic technique in France, the American artist Samuel Finley Breese Morse (1791–1872) traveled to Paris to exchange information about his own invention, the telegraph, for information about Daguerre's photography. Morse introduced the daguerreotype process to America within weeks of Daguerre's announcement and by 1841 had reduced exposure times enough to take portrait photographs (**FIG. 31-8**).

31-7 Louis-Jacques-Mandé Daguerre
THE ARTIST'S STUDIO
1837. Daguerreotype, 6½ × 8½" (16.5 × 21.6 cm). Société Française de Photographie, Paris.

Credit: © akg-images

At the same time in England, Henry Fox Talbot (1800–1877), a wealthy amateur, made negative copies of engravings, lace, and plants by placing them on paper soaked in silver chloride and exposing them to light. He also discovered that the negative image on paper could be exposed again on top of another piece of paper to create a positive image: the negative–positive process that became the basis of photographic printing. Talbot's negative could be used more than once, so he could produce a number of positive images inexpensively. But the **calotype**, as he later called it, produced a soft, fuzzy image. When he heard of Daguerre's announcement, Talbot rushed to make his own announcement and patent his process. The term for these processes—photography, derived from the Greek for "drawing with light"—was coined by Herschel.

Photography was quickly put to use in making visual records of the world. From the beginning, however, photographers also experimented with the expressive possibilities of the new medium and worked to create striking compositions. Between 1844 and 1846, Talbot published a book in six parts entitled *The Pencil of Nature*, illustrated entirely with salt-paper prints made from calotype negatives. Most of the photographs were of idyllic rural scenery or carefully arranged still lifes; they were presented as works of art rather than documents of reality. Talbot realized that the imprecision of his process could not compete with the commercial potential of the daguerreotype, and so rather than trying to do so, he chose to view photography in visual and artistic terms. In **THE OPEN DOOR** (**FIG. 31–9**), for example, shadows create a repeating pattern of diagonal lines that contrast with the rectilinear lines of the architecture. And it conveys meaning, expressing

31–8 DAGUERREOTYPE OF SAMUEL FINLEY BREESE MORSE

c. 1845. Sixth-plate daguerreotype, 2¾ × 3¼″ (7 × 8.3 cm). The Daguerreotype Collection of the Library of Congress, Washington, DC.

Credit: Courtesy the Library of Congress

nostalgia for a rural way of life that was fast disappearing in industrial England.

In 1851, Frederick Scott Archer, a British sculptor and photographer, took a major step in the development of early photography. Archer found that silver nitrate would adhere to glass if it was mixed with collodion, a combination of guncotton, ether, and alcohol used in medicinal bandages. When wet, this collodion–silver nitrate mixture needed only a few seconds' exposure to light to create an image. The result was a glass negative, from which countless positive proofs with great tonal subtleties could be made.

31–9 Henry Fox Talbot
THE OPEN DOOR

1843. Salt-paper print from a calotype negative, 5⅝ × 7¹¹⁄₁₆″ (14.3 × 19.5 cm). Science Museum, London. Fox Talbot Collection.

Credit: © National Media Museum/Science & Society Picture Library

31-10 Alexander Gardner **THE HOME OF THE REBEL SHARPSHOOTER: BATTLEFIELD AT GETTYSBURG**

1863. Albumen print, 7 × 9″ (18 × 23 cm). Library of Congress, Washington, DC.

Credit: Courtesy the Library of Congress

Alexander Gardner and Julia Margaret Cameron

American photographers used this newly refined process to document the momentous events of the Civil War (1861–1865) in artfully composed pictures. Alexander Gardner (1821–1882) was a "camera operator" for Mathew Brady (1822–1896) at the beginning of the conflict and working with an assistant, Timothy O'Sullivan (c. 1840–1882), made war photographs that were widely distributed. **THE HOME OF THE REBEL SHARPSHOOTER** (FIG. 31-10) was taken after the Battle of Gettysburg in July 1863. The technical difficulties were considerable. The glass plate used to make the negative had to be coated with a sticky substance holding the light-sensitive chemicals. If the plate dried, the photograph could not be taken, and if dust contaminated the plate, the image would be ruined. Since long exposure times made action photographs impossible, early war photographs were taken in camp or in the aftermath of battle. Gardner's image seems to show a sharpshooter who has been killed in his look-out. But this rock formation was in the middle of the battlefield and had neither the height nor the view needed for a sharpshooter. In fact, the photographers dragged the dead body to the site and posed it; the rifle propped against the wall was theirs. The staging of this photograph raises questions about visual fact and fiction. Like a painting, a photograph is composed to create a picture, but photography promises a kind of factuality that we do not expect from painting. Interestingly, the manipulation of this photograph

31-11 Julia Margaret Cameron **PORTRAIT OF THOMAS CARLYLE**

1867. Silver print, 10 × 8″ (25.4 × 20.3 cm). The Royal Photographic Society, Collection at the National Museum of Photography, Film, and Television, England.

Credit: © National Media Museum/Science & Society Picture Library did not concern nineteenth-century viewers, who understood clearly that photography could not record the visual world without bias.

One of the most creative early photographers was Julia Margaret Cameron (1815–1879), who received her first camera as a gift from her daughters when she was 49. Her principal subjects were the great men and women of British arts, letters, and sciences, many of whom had long been family friends. Cameron's approach was experimental and radical. Like many of her portraits, that of the famous British historian **THOMAS CARLYLE** is deliberately slightly out of focus (**FIG. 31-11**): Cameron consciously rejected the sharp focus of commercial portrait photography, which she felt accentuated the merely physical attributes and neglected the inner character of the subject. By blurring the details, she sought to call attention to the light that suffused her subjects and to their thoughtful expressions. In her autobiography, Cameron said, "When I have had such men before my camera my whole soul has endeavoured to do its duty towards them in recording faithfully the greatness of the inner as well as the features of the outer man."

Realism and the Avant-Garde

How do Realism and the avant-garde in art represent the rejection of academic taste and practice, fueled by social and political concerns?

In reaction to the rigidity of academic training, some French artists began to consider themselves members of an **avant-garde**, meaning "advance guard" or "vanguard." The term was coined by the French military during the Napoleonic era to designate the forward units of an advancing army that scouted territory that the main force would soon occupy. Avant-garde artists saw themselves as working in advance of an increasingly bourgeois society. The term was first mentioned in connection with art around 1825 in the political programs of French utopian socialists. Henri de Saint-Simon (1760–1825) suggested that in order to transform modern industrialized society into an ideal state, it would be necessary to gather together an avant-garde of intellectuals, scientists, and artists to lead France into the future.

In 1831, the architect Eugène Viollet-le-Duc applied the term to the artists of Paris in the aftermath of the revolution of 1830. Viollet-le-Duc vehemently opposed the French academic system of architectural training. His concept of the avant-garde called for a small elite of independent radical thinkers, artists, and architects to break away from the Académie des Beaux-Arts and the norms of society in order to forge new thoughts, ideas, and ways

of looking at the world and art. He foresaw that this life would require the sacrifice of artists' reputations and reduce sales of their work. Most avant-garde artists were neither as radical nor as extreme as Viollet-le-Duc, and, as we have seen, the relationship between the Académie des Beaux-Arts and the avant-garde was complex. Nonetheless, the idea was embraced by a number of artists who have come to characterize the period.

Realism and Revolution

In the modern world of Paris at mid-century—a world plagued by violence, social unrest, overcrowding, and poverty—the grand, abstract themes of academic art seemed irrelevant to the thinkers who would come to represent the avant-garde. Rising food prices, high unemployment, political disenfranchisement, and government inaction ignited in a popular rebellion known as the Revolution of 1848, led by a coalition of socialists, anarchists, and workers. It brought an end to the July Monarchy and established the Second Republic (1848–1852). Conflicts among the reformers, however, led to another uprising, in which more than 10,000 of the working poor were killed or injured in their struggle against the new government's forces. Against this social and political backdrop a new intellectual movement known as Realism originated in the novels of Émile Zola, Charles Dickens, Honoré de Balzac, and others who wrote about the real lives of the urban lower classes. What art historians have labeled Realism is less of a style than a commitment to paint the modern world honestly, without turning away from the brutal truths of life for all people, poor as well as privileged.

COURBET   Gustave Courbet (1819–1877) was one of the first artists to call himself avant-garde or a Realist. A big, blustery man, he was, in his own words, "not only a Socialist but a democrat and a Republican: in a word, a supporter of the whole Revolution." Born and raised near the Swiss border in the French town of Ornans, he moved to Paris in 1839. The street fighting in Paris in 1848 radicalized him and became a catalyst for two large canvases that have come to be regarded as the defining works of the Realist Movement.

Painted in 1849, the first of these, **THE STONE BREAKERS** (**FIG. 31-12**), depicts a young boy and an old man crushing rock to produce the gravel used for roadbeds. Stone breakers represent the disenfranchised peasants on whose backs modern life was being built. The younger figure strains to lift a large basket of rocks to the side of the road, dressed in tattered shirt and trousers but wearing modern work boots. His older companion, seemingly broken by the lowly work, pounds the rocks as he kneels, wearing the more traditional clothing of a peasant, including wooden clogs. The boy thus seems to represent a grim future,

31–12 Gustave Courbet
THE STONE BREAKERS
1849. Oil on canvas, 5'3" × 8'6"
(1.6 × 2.59 m). Formerly
Gemäldegalerie, Dresden;
destroyed in World War II.

Credit: © Staatliche Kunstsammlungen
Dresden/Bridgeman Images

while the man signifies an increasingly obsolete rural past. Both are conspicuously faceless.

Courbet recorded his inspiration for this painting:

> [N]ear Maisières [in the vicinity of Ornans], I stopped to consider two men breaking stones on the highway. It's rare to meet the most complete expression of poverty, so an idea for a picture came to me on the spot. I made an appointment with them at my studio for the next day.... On the one side is an old man, seventy.... On the other side is a young fellow … in his filthy tattered shirt.... Alas, in labor such as this, one's life begins that way, and it ends the same way.

Two things are clear from this description: Courbet set out to make a political statement, and he invited the men back to his studio so that he could study them more carefully, following academic practice.

By depicting labor at the size of a history painting—the canvas is over 5 by 8 feet—Courbet intended to provoke. In academic art, monumental canvases were reserved for heroic subjects, so Courbet was asserting that peasant laborers should be venerated as heroes. Bypassing the highly finished style and inspiring message of history painting, he signifies the brutality of modern life in his rough use of paint and choice of dull, dark colors, awkward poses, and a stilted composition. The scene feels realistically gloomy

31–13 Gustave Courbet **A BURIAL AT ORNANS**
1849. Oil on canvas, 10'3½" × 21'9" (3.1 × 6.6 m). Musée d'Orsay, Paris.

Credit: Photo © RMN-Grand Palais (musée d'Orsay)/Gérard Blot/Hervé Lewandowski and degrading. In 1865 his friend the anarchist philosopher Pierre-Joseph Proudhon (1809–1865) described *The Stone Breakers* as the first socialist picture ever painted, "an irony of our industrial civilization, which continually invents wonderful machines to perform all kinds of labor … yet is unable to liberate man from the most backbreaking toil." Courbet himself described the work as a portrayal of "injustice."

Courbet began to paint **A BURIAL AT ORNANS (FIG. 31-13)** immediately after *The Stone Breakers* and exhibited the two paintings together at the 1850–1851 Salon. *A Burial at Ornans* was inspired by the 1848 funeral of Courbet's maternal grandfather, Jean-Antoine Oudot, a veteran of the French Revolution of 1789. It is not meant as a record of that particular funeral, however, since Oudot is shown alive in profile at the extreme left of the canvas, his image adapted by Courbet from an earlier portrait. The two men to the right of the open grave, dressed not in contemporary but in late eighteenth-century clothing, are also revolutionaries of Oudot's generation. Their proximity to the grave suggests that one of their peers is being buried. Perhaps Courbet's picture links the revolutions of 1789 and 1848, both of which sought to advance the cause of democracy in France.

This is a vast painting, measuring roughly 10 by 21 feet, and depicts a rural burial life-size. A crush of people forms irregular rows across the width of the picture. The grave-digger kneels over the gaping hole in the ground, placed front and center and flanked by a bored altar boy and a distracted dog; to the left, clergy dressed in red seem indifferent while to the right, the huddle of rural mourners—Courbet's heroes of modern life—weeps. Although painted

on a scale befitting the funeral of a hero, Courbet's depiction has none of the idealization of traditional history painting; instead, it captures the awkward, blundering numbness of a real funeral and emphasizes its brutal, physical reality. When shown at the Salon, the painting was attacked by critics who objected to the elevation of a provincial funeral to this heroic scale, to Courbet's disrespect for the rules of academic composition, and even to the painting's lack of any suggestion of the afterlife. But Courbet had submitted his work to the Salon knowing that it would be denounced; he wanted to challenge the prescribed subjects, style, and finish of academic painting, to establish his position in the avant-garde, and to create controversy. After the rejection of some of his works by the International Exposition of 1855, Courbet constructed a temporary building on rented land near the fair's Pavilion of Art and installed a show of his own works that he called the "Pavilion of Realism," boldly asserting his independence from the Salon. Many artists after him would follow in his footsteps.

MILLET Similar accusations of political radicalism were leveled against Jean-François Millet (1814–1875). This artist grew up on a farm and despite living and working in Paris between 1837 and 1848, he never felt comfortable with urban life. A state commission (with stipend) awarded for his part in the 1848 revolution allowed him to move to the village of Barbizon, just south of Paris, where he painted the hardships and pleasures of the rural poor.

Among his best-known works is **THE GLEANERS (FIG. 31-14)**, which shows three women gathering stray grain

31–14 Jean-François Millet **THE GLEANERS**
1857. Oil on canvas, 33 × 44" (83.8 × 111.8 cm). Musée d'Orsay, Paris.

Credit: Photo © RMN-Grand Palais (musée d'Orsay)/Jean Schormans from the ground after harvest. Despite its soothing, warm colors, the scene is one of extreme poverty. Gleaning was a form of relief offered to the rural poor by landowners, but it required hours of backbreaking work to collect enough wheat to make a single loaf of bread. Two women bend over to reach the tiny stalks of grain remaining on the ground, while a third straightens to ease her back. When Millet exhibited the painting in 1857, critics noted its implicit social criticism and described the work as "Realist." Millet denied the accusations, but his paintings contradict him.

COROT The landscape paintings of Jean-Baptiste-Camille Corot (1796–1875) take a more romantic and less political approach to depicting rural life. After painting historical landscapes early in his career, Corot steadily moved toward more naturalistic and intimate scenes of rural France. **FIRST LEAVES, NEAR MANTES** (FIG. 31–15) depicts a scene infused with the soft mist of early spring in the woods. Corot's feathery brushwork representing soft, new foliage contrasts with the stark, vertical tree trunks and branches and together with the fresh green of the new undergrowth evokes a lyrical mood. A man and woman pause to talk on the road winding from left to right through the painting, while a woman labors in the woods

at the lower right. These images of peaceful country life held great appeal for Parisians who had experienced the chaos of the 1848 revolution and who lived in an increasingly crowded, noisy, and fast-paced metropolis.

BONHEUR Rosa Bonheur (1822–1899) was one of the most popular French painters of farm life. Her success in a male domain owed much to the socialist convictions of her parents, who belonged to a radical utopian sect founded by the Comte de Saint-Simon that believed not only in the equality of women but also in a future female Messiah. Bonheur's father, a drawing teacher, provided most of her artistic training.

Bonheur dedicated herself to accurate depictions of modern draft animals, which were becoming increasingly obsolete as technology and industrialization transformed farming. She studied her subjects by reading zoology books and making detailed studies in stockyards and slaughterhouses; to gain access to these all-male preserves, she had to obtain police permission to dress in men's clothing. Her professional breakthrough came at the Salon of 1848, where she showed eight paintings and won a first-class medal. **THE HORSE FAIR** (FIG. 31–16), painted in 1853, was based on a horse market near Salpêtrière, but

31–15 Jean-Baptiste-Camille Corot **FIRST LEAVES, NEAR MANTES**
c. 1855. Oil on canvas, 13⅜ × 18⅛″ (34 × 46 cm). Carnegie Museum of Art, Pittsburgh, Pennsylvania.

Credit: Photograph © 2016 Carnegie Museum of Art, Pittsburgh. Photo: Richard Stoner

31–16 Rosa Bonheur **THE HORSE FAIR**
1853–1855. Oil on canvas, 8'¼" × 16'7½" (2.45 × 5.07 m). Metropolitan Museum of Art, New York.

Credit: © 2016. Image copyright The Metropolitan Museum of Art/Art Resource, NY/ Scala, Florence

was also partly inspired by the Parthenon marbles in London and by the art of Géricault. The scene shows grooms displaying splendid Percheron horses, some walking obediently in their circle, others rearing up. Some have interpreted the painting as a commentary on the lack of rights for women in the 1850s, but it was not read that way at the time. Although unusually monumental for a painting of farm animals, it was highly praised at the 1853 Salon. When the painting later toured throughout Britain and the United States, members of the public paid to see it, and it was widely disseminated in print form on both sides of the Atlantic. In 1887, Cornelius Vanderbilt purchased it for the new Metropolitan Museum of Art in New York. Bonheur became so famous working within the Salon system that in 1865 she received France's highest award, membership in the Legion of Honor, becoming the first woman to be awarded its Grand Cross.

Manet: "The Painter of Modern Life"

Along with the concept of the avant-garde, the idea of "modernity" also shaped art in France at this time. The experience of modern life—of constant change and renewal—was linked to the dynamic nature of the city. Themes of the modern city and of political engagement with modern life in an industrialized world are key to understanding the development of painting and literature in France in the second half of the nineteenth century.

In his 1863 essay "The Painter of Modern Life," poet Charles Baudelaire argued that in order to speak for their time and place, artists' work had to be infused with

modernity. He called for artists to be painters of contemporary manners and "of the passing moment and of all the suggestions of eternity that it contains," using both modern urban subjects and new approaches to seeing and representing the visual world. This break with the past was critical in order to comprehend and comment on the present. Especially after the invention of photography, art was expected to offer new ways of representing reality. One artist who rose to Baudelaire's challenge was the French painter Édouard Manet (1832–1883).

LUNCHEON ON THE GRASS At mid-century, the Académie des Beaux-Arts increasingly opened Salon exhibitions to non-academic artists, resulting in a surge in the number of works submitted, and inevitably rejected by, the Salon jury. In 1863, the jury turned down nearly 3,000 works. A storm of protest erupted, prompting Emperor Napoleon III to order an exhibition of the rejected work called the "Salon des Refusés" ("Salon of the Rejected Ones"). Featured in it was Manet's painting **LUNCHEON ON THE GRASS (LE DÉJEUNER SUR L'HERBE) (FIG. 31–17)**. A well-born Parisian who had studied in the early 1850s with the independent artist Thomas Couture (1815–1879), Manet had by the early 1860s developed a strong commitment to Realism and modernity, largely as a result of his friendship with Baudelaire. *Luncheon on the Grass* scandalized contemporary viewers all the way up to Napoleon III himself, provoking a critical avalanche that mixed shock with bewilderment. Ironically, the resulting *succès de scandale* ("success from scandal") helped establish Manet's career as a radical, avant-garde, modern artist.

The most scandalous aspect of the painting was the "immorality" of Manet's theme: a suburban picnic featuring two fully dressed bourgeois gentlemen seated alongside a completely naked woman with another scantily dressed woman in the background. Manet's audience assumed that these women were prostitutes, and the men their customers. Equally shocking were the painting's references to important works of art of the past, which Académie des Beaux-Arts artists were expected to make, combined with its crude, unvarnished modernity. In contrast, one of the paintings that gathered most renown at the official Salon in that year was Alexandre Cabanel's *Birth of Venus* (SEE FIG. 31-5), which, because it presented nudity in a conventionally acceptable, Classical environment and mythological context, was favorably reviewed and quickly entered the collection of Napoleon III.

Manet apparently conceived of *Luncheon on the Grass* as a modern version of a Venetian Renaissance painting in the Louvre, *The Pastoral Concert*, then believed to be by Giorgione but now attributed to both Titian and Giorgione or to Titian exclusively (SEE FIG. 21-27). Manet's composition also refers to a Marcantonio Raimondi engraving of Raphael's *The Judgment of Paris*, itself based on Classical reliefs of river gods and nymphs. Presenting the seamier side of city life in the guise of Classical art was intentionally provocative. And the stark lighting and sharp outlining of his nude, the cool colors, and the flat quality of his figures, who seem as if they are silhouetted cut-outs set against a painted backdrop, were unsettling to viewers accustomed to traditional, controlled gradations of shadows modeling smoothly rounded forms in perspectively mapped spaces.

OLYMPIA Shortly after completing *Luncheon on the Grass*, Manet painted **OLYMPIA** (FIG. 31-18), its title alluding to a socially ambitious prostitute of the same name in a novel and play by Alexandre Dumas the Younger. Like *Luncheon on the Grass*, Manet's *Olympia* was based on a Venetian Renaissance source, Titian's *"Venus" of Urbino* (SEE FIG. 21-30), which Manet had earlier copied in Florence.

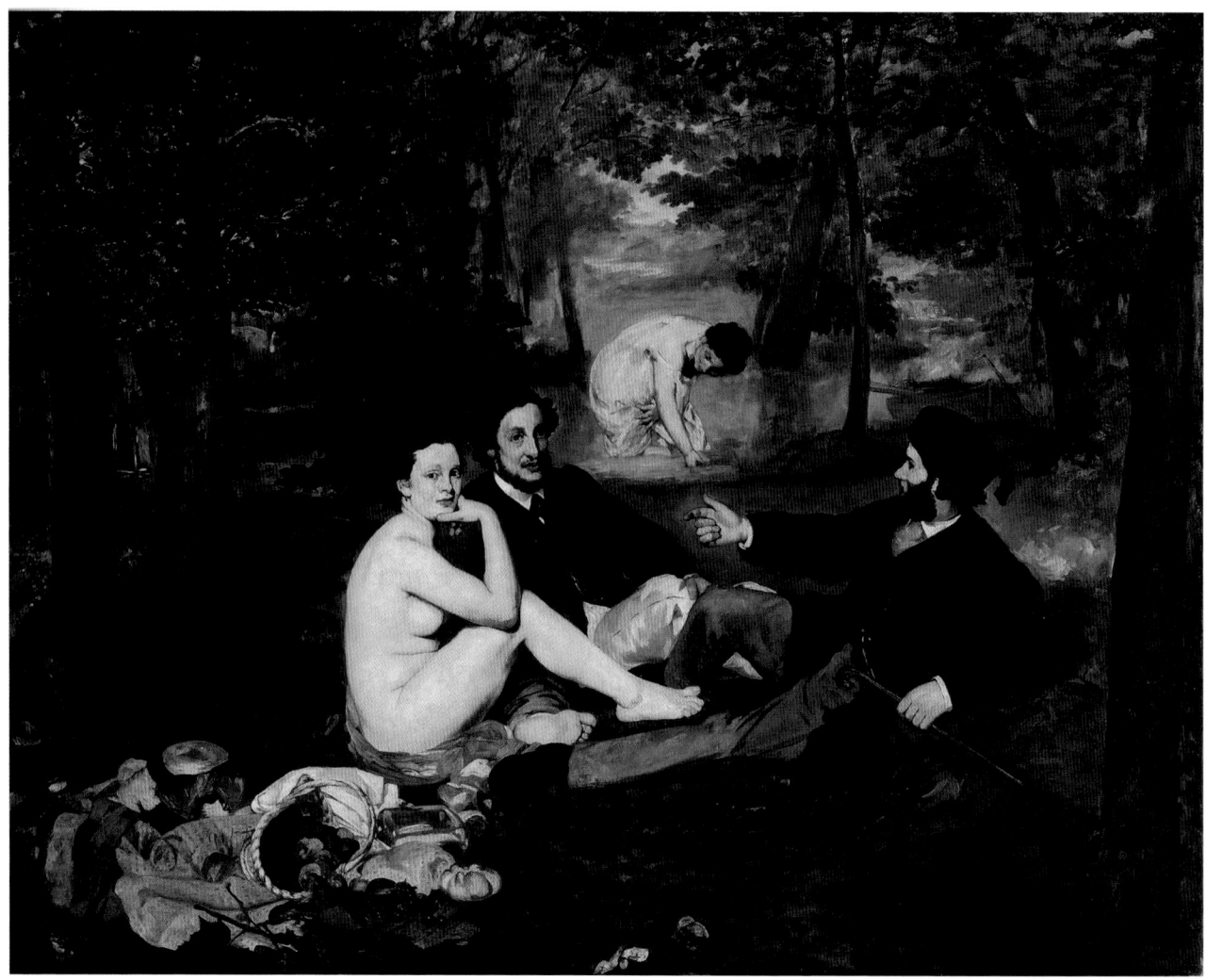

31-17 Édouard Manet **LUNCHEON ON THE GRASS (LE DÉJEUNER SUR L'HERBE)**
1863. Oil on canvas, 7′ × 8′8″ (2.13 × 2.64 m). Musée d'Orsay, Paris.

31–18 Édouard Manet **OLYMPIA**
1863. Oil on canvas, 4'3" × 6'2¼" (1.31 × 1.91 m). Musée d'Orsay, Paris.

Credit: Photo © RMN-Grand Palais (musée d'Orsay)

At first, his painting appears to pay homage to Titian's in its subject matter (at that time believed to be a Venetian courtesan) and composition, but Manet made his reclining nude the very antithesis of Titian's. Titian's female is curvaceous and softly rounded; Manet's is angular and flattened. Titian's colors are warm and rich; Manet's are cold and harsh. Titian's "Venus" looks coyly at the male spectator; Manet's Olympia appears indifferent. And instead of looking up at us, Olympia gazes down at us, indicating that she is in the position of power and that we are subordinate, like the black servant at the foot of the bed who brings her a bouquet of flowers. Olympia's relationship with us is underscored by her cat, which—unlike the sleeping dog in the Titian—arches its back at the viewer. Manet overturns the entire tradition of the accommodating female nude. Not surprisingly, conservative critics vilified *Olympia* when it was exhibited at the Salon of 1865.

Manet generally submitted his work to every Salon, but when several were rejected in 1867, he did as Courbet had done in 1855: He asserted his independence by renting a hall nearby and staging his own show. This made Manet the unofficial leader of a group of forward-thinking artists and writers who gathered at the Café Guerbois in the Montmartre district of Paris. Among the artists who frequented the café were Edgar Degas, Claude Monet, Camille Pissarro, and Pierre-Auguste Renoir, all of whom would soon exhibit together as the Impressionists and follow Manet's lead in challenging academic conventions.

LATER WORKS   Manet worked closely with all of these artists and frequently painted themes similar to those favored by the Impressionists, but he always retained his dedication to the portrayal of modern urban life. In his last major painting, **A BAR AT THE FOLIES-BERGÈRE (FIG. 31-19)**, he maintains his focus on the complex theme of gender and class relations. A young woman serves drinks at a bar in the famous nightclub that offered circuses, musicals, and vaudeville acts (note the legs of a trapeze artist in the upper left corner of the painting). She has an unfashionably ruddy face, and her hands look raw. In the glittering light created by the electric bulbs and mirrors of the music hall she seems stiff and distant, certainly self-absorbed, and perhaps even depressed, refusing to meet the gaze of the customer in front of her. The barmaid is at once detached from the scene and part of it, one of the many items among the still life of liquor bottles, tangerines, and flowers on display for purchase. This image is about sexualized looking, and the barmaid's uneasy reflection in the mirror seems to acknowledge that both her class and gender expose her to visual and even sexual consumption.

31–19 Édouard Manet
**A BAR AT THE
FOLIES-BERGÈRE**

1881–1882. Oil on canvas.
37¾ × 51¼" (95.9 × 130 cm).
The Samuel Courtauld
Trust, the Courtauld Gallery,
London. (P.1934.SC.234).

Credit: © Samuel Courtauld Trust,
The Courtauld Gallery, London,
UK/Bridgeman Images

Responses to Realism beyond France

Artists of other nations embraced their own forms of realism in the period after 1850 as the social effects of urbanization and industrialization began to be felt in their countries. While these artists did not label themselves as Realists like their contemporaries in France, they did share an interest in presenting unflinching looks at reality that exposed the difficult lives of the working poor and the complexities of urban life.

REALISM IN RUSSIA: THE WANDERERS   In Russia, a variant on French Realism developed in relation to a new concern for the peasantry. In 1861, the tsar abolished serfdom, emancipating Russia's peasants from the virtual slavery they had endured on the large estates of the aristocracy. Two years later, a group of painters inspired by the emancipation declared allegiance both to the peasant cause and to freedom from the St. Petersburg Academy of Art, which had controlled Russian art since 1754. Reacting against what they considered the escapist aesthetics of the academy, the members of the group dedicated themselves to a socially useful realism. Committed to bringing art to the people in traveling exhibitions, they called themselves "the Wanderers." By the late 1870s, members of the group, like their counterparts in music and literature, had also joined a nationalist movement to reassert what they considered to be an authentic Russian culture rooted in the traditions of the peasantry, rejecting the Western European customs that had long predominated among the Russian aristocracy.

Ilya Repin (1844–1930), who attended the St. Petersburg Academy and won a scholarship to study in Paris, joined the Wanderers in 1878 after his return to Russia. He painted a series of works illustrating the social injustices then prevailing in his homeland, including **BARGEHAULERS ON THE VOLGA** (FIG. 31–20), which features a group of peasants condemned to the brutal work of pulling ships up the Volga River. To heighten our sympathy for these workers, Repin placed in the center of the group a young man who will soon be as worn out as his companions unless something is done to rescue him. This painting was a call to action.

REALISM IN THE UNITED STATES: A CONTINUING TRADITION   Although it was not a term used in the United States, realism—often with a political edge—was an unbroken tradition stretching back to colonial portrait painters (SEE FIG. 30–1) and continuing in the pioneering work of photographers during the Civil War (SEE FIG. 31–10). There were several kinds of realism in later nineteenth-century American art. Thomas Eakins (1844–1916), for instance, made a series of uncompromising paintings that were criticized for their controversial subject matter. Born in Philadelphia, Eakins trained at the Pennsylvania Academy of the Fine Arts, but since he thought the training in anatomy lacked rigor, he supplemented his studies at the Jefferson Medical College nearby. He later enrolled at the École des Beaux-Arts in Paris and then spent six months in Spain, where he encountered the profound realism of Baroque artists such as Jusepe de Ribera and Diego Velázquez (SEE FIGS. 23–17, 23–19). After he returned to

31-20 Ilya Repin **BARGEHAULERS ON THE VOLGA**
1870–1873. Oil on canvas, 4′3¾″ × 9′3″ (1.3 × 2.81 m). State Russian Museum, St. Petersburg.

Credit: © akg-images

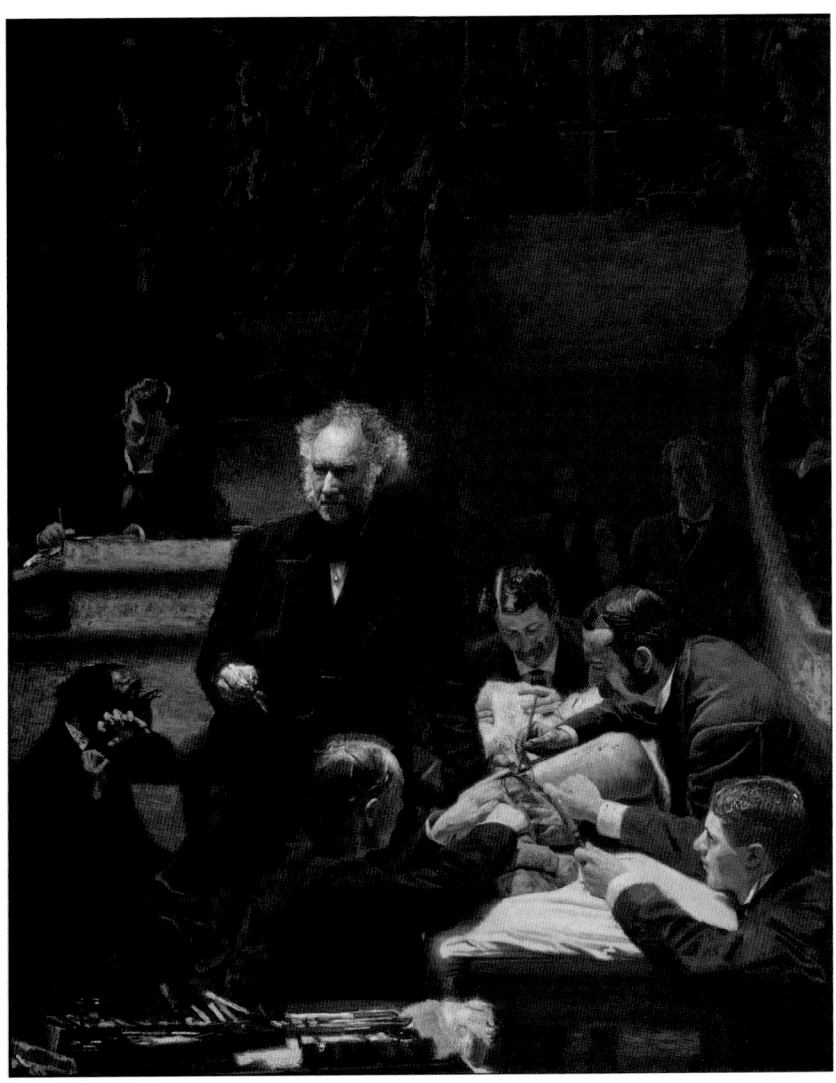

Philadelphia in 1870, Eakins specialized in frank portraits and scenes of everyday life whose lack of conventional charm generated little popular interest. But he was a charismatic teacher and was soon appointed director of instruction at the Pennsylvania Academy.

THE GROSS CLINIC (FIG. 31-21) was one of Eakins's most controversial paintings. Although created specifically for the 1876 Philadelphia Centennial Exhibition, it was rejected for the fine-art exhibition—the jury did not consider surgery a fit subject for art—and relegated to the

31-21 Thomas Eakins **THE GROSS CLINIC**
1875. Oil on canvas, 8′ × 6′5″ (2.44 × 1.98 m). Philadelphia Museum of Art. Gift of the Alumni Association to Jefferson Medical College in 1878 and purchased by the Pennsylvania Academy of the Fine Arts and the Philadelphia Museum of Art in 2007.

Eakins, who taught anatomy and figure drawing at the Pennsylvania Academy of the Fine Arts, disapproved of the academic technique of drawing from plaster casts. In 1879, he said, "At best, they are only imitations, and an imitation of an imitation cannot have so much life as an imitation of nature itself." He added, "The Greeks did not study the antique … the draped figures in the Parthenon pediment were modeled from life, undoubtedly."

Credit: © 2016. Photo The Philadelphia Museum of Art/ Art Resource/Scala, Florence

31–22 Winslow Homer
THE LIFE LINE
1884. Oil on canvas,
28¾ × 44⅝" (73 ×
113.3 cm). Philadelphia
Museum of Art.
The George W. Elkins
Collection, 1924.

In the early sketches for
this work, the man's face
was visible. The decision
to cover it focuses
attention on the victim,
and also on the true
hero, the mechanical
apparatus known as the
"breeches buoy."

Credit: © 2016. Photo The
Philadelphia Museum of Art/
Art Resource/Scala, Florence

scientific and medical display. The monumental painting shows Dr. Samuel David Gross performing an operation that he pioneered in the surgical amphitheater of Jefferson Medical College. Dr. Gross pauses to lecture to medical students taking notes in the background, as well as to Eakins himself, whose self-portrait appears along the painting's right edge. A woman at left, presumably a relative of the patient, cringes in horror at the bloody spectacle. At this time, surgeons were regarded with fear—especially teaching surgeons, who frequently thought of the poor as objects on which to practice. But Eakins portrays Gross as a heroic figure, spotlighted by beams of light on his forehead and bloodied right hand with glinting scalpel. Principal illumination, however, is reserved for the patient, presented here not as an entire body but as a dehumanized jumble of thigh, buttock, socked feet, and bunches of cloth. In conceiving this portrait, Eakins must have had Rembrandt's famous Baroque painting of Dr. Tulp in mind (SEE FIG. 23–35), and the American painter's use of light seems to point to a similar homage to scientific achievement: Amid the darkness of ignorance and fear, modern science is the light of knowledge and the source of progress. The procedure showcased here, in fact, was a surgical innovation that allowed Dr. Gross to save a patient's leg that previously would have routinely been amputated.

Winslow Homer (1836–1910) also developed into a realist painter. Born in Boston, he began his career as a 21-year-old freelance illustrator for popular periodicals such as *Harper's Weekly*, which sent him to cover the Civil War in 1862. In 1867, after a ten-month sojourn in France, Homer returned to paint nostalgic visions of the rural scenes that had figured in his magazine illustrations. But following a sojourn during 1881–1882 in a tiny English

fishing village on the rugged North Sea coast, Homer developed a commitment to depicting the working poor. Moved by the hard lives and strength of character of the people he encountered in England, he set aside idyllic subjects for themes of heroic struggle against natural adversity. In England, he had been particularly impressed by the "breeches buoy," a mechanical apparatus used for rescues at sea. During the summer of 1883, he made sketches of one imported by the lifesaving crew in Atlantic City, New Jersey. The following year he painted **THE LIFE LINE** (FIG. **31–22**), which depicts a coastguard saving a shipwrecked woman with the use of a breeches buoy—a testament not simply to valor but also to human ingenuity.

The sculptor Edmonia Lewis (1845–c. 1911) was born in New York State to a Chippewa mother and an African-American father, orphaned at the age of 4, and raised by her mother's family. As a teenager, with the help of abolitionists, she attended Oberlin College, the first college in the United States to grant degrees to women, and then moved to Boston. Her highly successful busts and medallions of abolitionist leaders and Civil War heroes financed her move to Rome in 1867, where she was welcomed into the sculptural circle of American expatriate artist Harriet Hosmer (1830–1908) and used Neoclassical style to address modern, realist concerns. Galvanized by the struggle of recently freed slaves for equality, Lewis created **FOREVER FREE** (FIG. **31–23**) in 1867 as a memorial to the Emancipation Proclamation (1862–1863). A diminutive woman kneels in gratitude beside the looming figure of her male companion, who boosts himself up on the ball that once bound his ankle and raises his broken shackles in a gesture of liberation. This sculpture not only celebrates the freeing of American slaves, but also reflects white attitudes toward women and people of color. Lewis's female figure is less racialized and more submissive than her male counterpart to align her with the contemporary ideal of womanhood and make her more appealing to white audiences. Lewis had to borrow money to pay for the marble for this work. She shipped it from Rome back to Boston hoping that a subscription drive among abolitionists would pay back her loan. The effort was only partially successful, but the steady income from the sale of commemorative medallions eventually paid off Lewis's debt.

Other women and African Americans, groups often excluded from art schools, were among Eakins's students at the Pennsylvania Academy of the Fine Arts. One of the star pupils was Henry Ossawa Tanner (1859–1937), who became the most successful African-American painter of the late nineteenth and early twentieth centuries. The son of a bishop in the African Methodist Episcopal Church,

31-24 Henry Ossawa Tanner **THE BANJO LESSON**
1893. Oil on canvas, 49 × 35½" (124.4 × 90 cm). Hampton University Museum, Virginia.

Credit: Hampton University's Archival and Museum Collection Hampton University

31-23 Edmonia Lewis **FOREVER FREE**
1867. Marble, 41¼ × 22 × 17" (104.8 × 55 × 43.2 cm). Howard University Gallery of Art, Washington, DC.

Tanner grew up in Philadelphia and after studying at the academy, he worked as a photographer and drawing teacher in Atlanta. In 1891, to further his academic training, he moved to Paris, where his painting received favorable critical attention. In the early 1890s, he painted scenes from African-American and rural French life that combined Eakins's realism with the delicate brushwork he encountered in France. With strongly felt, humanizing images like **THE BANJO LESSON** (**FIG. 31-24**), he sought to counter caricatures of African-American life created by other artists. An elderly man is giving a young boy a music lesson: two figures connected by their seriousness and concentration. The use of the banjo here is especially significant since it had become identified with images of minstrels—just the sort of derogatory caricatures that Tanner sought to replace with his sympathetic genre scenes focused on the intimate interactions that brought dignity and pride to family life. After a trip to Palestine in 1897, Tanner turned to religious subjects, believing that Bible stories could illustrate the struggles and hopes of contemporary African Americans.

DEVELOPMENTS IN BRITAIN Britain also encountered social and political upheaval at the middle of the nineteenth century. The depression of the "hungry forties," the Irish Potato Famine, and the Chartist Riots threatened social stability in England. Mid-century British artists painted scenes of religious, medieval, or moral exemplars using a tight, realistic style that was quite different from both French and American realism.

In 1848, seven young London artists formed the Pre-Raphaelite Brotherhood in response to what they considered the misguided practices of contemporary British art. Instead of the "Raphaelesque" conventions taught at the Royal Academy, the Pre-Raphaelites looked back to the Middle Ages and early Renaissance (before Raphael) for a beauty and spirituality that they found lacking in their own time. They believed this earlier art was more moralistic and "real."

Dante Gabriel Rossetti (1828–1882) was a leading member of the Pre-Raphaelite Brotherhood. His painting **LA PIA DE' TOLOMEI** (FIG. 31-25) illustrates a scene from Dante's *Purgatory* in which La Pia (the Pious One), wrongly accused of infidelity and imprisoned by her husband in a castle, is dying. The rosary and prayer book at her side refer to her piety, while the sundial and ravens suggest the passage of time and her impending death. La Pia's continuing love for her husband is represented by his letters, which lie under her prayer book. The luxuriant fig leaves that surround her are traditionally associated with shame, and they seem to suck her into themselves. They have no source in Dante, but had personal relevance for Rossetti: Jane Burden, his model for this and many other paintings, was the wife of his friend William Morris, but she had also become Rossetti's lover. By fingering her wedding ring,

31-25 Dante Gabriel Rossetti **LA PIA DE' TOLOMEI**
1868–1869. Oil on canvas, 41½ × 47½" (105.4 × 119.4 cm). Spencer Museum of Art, University of Kansas, Lawrence. (1956.0031).

The massive, gilded frame Rossetti designed for *La Pia de' Tolomei* features simple moldings on either side of broad, sloping boards, embellished with a few large roundels. The title of the painting is inscribed above the paired roundels at the lower center. On either side of them appear four lines from Dante's *Purgatory*, spoken by the spirit of La Pia, in Italian at the left and in Rossetti's English translation at the right: "Remember me who am La Pia,—me/From Siena sprung and by Maremma dead./This in his inmost heart well knoweth he/With whose fair jewel I was ringed and wed."

31-26 Philip Webb and William Morris "SUSSEX" CHAIR AND "PEACOCK AND DRAGON" CURTAIN

Chair (by Webb): in production from c. 1865. Ebonized wood with rush seat, 33 × 16½ × 14″ (83.8 × 42 × 35.6 cm). Curtain (by Morris): 1878. Handloomed jacquard-woven woolen twill, 12′10½″ × 11′5⅝″ (3.96 × 3.53 m). Chair and curtain manufactured by Morris & Company. The William Morris Gallery, London Borough of Waltham Forest.

Morris and his principal furniture designer, Philip Webb (1831–1915), adapted the company's Sussex line of chairs from traditional rush-seated chairs of the Sussex region. The handwoven curtain in the background is typical of Morris's fabric designs in its use of flat patterning that affirms the two-dimensional character of the textile medium. The pattern's prolific organic motifs and soothing blue and green hues—the decorative counterpart to those of naturalistic landscape painting—were meant to provide relief from the stresses of modern urban existence.

Credit: The William Morris Gallery, London, E17, England

La Pia/Jane suggests that she is a captive not of her husband but of her marriage, evoking Rossetti's own situation.

Other British artists drew inspiration from the medieval past as a panacea for modern life in London. William Morris (1834–1896) worked briefly as a painter under the influence of the Pre-Raphaelites before turning his attention to interior design and decoration. Morris's interest in crafts developed in the context of a widespread reaction against the shoddy design of industrially produced goods. Unable to find satisfactory furnishings for his new home after his marriage in 1859, Morris designed and constructed them himself with the help of friends, later founding a decorating firm to produce a full range of medieval-inspired objects. Although many of the furnishings offered by Morris & Company were expensive,

one-of-a-kind items, others, such as the rush-seated chair illustrated here (**FIG. 31-26**), were inexpensive and simple, intended as a handcrafted alternative to machine-made furniture. Concerned with creating a "total" environment, Morris and his colleagues designed not only furniture but also stained glass, tiles, wallpaper, and fabrics, such as the "Peacock and Dragon" curtain seen in FIGURE 31-26.

Morris inspired what became known as the Arts and Crafts Movement. He rebelled against the idea that art was a highly specialized product made for a small elite, and he hoped to usher in a new era of art for the people. He said in lectures: "I do not want art for a few, any more than education for a few, or freedom for a few." A socialist, Morris opposed mass production and the deadening impact of factory life on the industrial worker. He argued that when laborers made handcrafted objects, they derived satisfaction from being involved in the entire process of creation and thus produced honest and beautiful things.

The American expatriate James Abbott McNeill Whistler (1834–1903) also focused his attention on the rooms and walls where art was hung, but he did so to satisfy elitist tastes for beauty as its own reward. He also became embroiled in several artistic controversies that laid the groundwork for abstraction in the next century. After flunking out of West Point in the early 1850s, Whistler studied art in Paris, where he was briefly influenced by Courbet's Realism; the two artists painted several seascapes together. Whistler settled in London in 1859, after which his art began to take on a more decorative quality that he called "aesthetic" and that increasingly diverged from observed reality. He believed that the arrangement of a room (or a painting) could be aesthetically pleasing in itself, without reference to the outside world. He occasionally designed exhibition rooms for his own art, with the aim of creating a total harmony of objects and space.

Whistler's ideas about art were revolutionary. He was among the first artists to conceive of his paintings as abstractions from rather than representations of observed reality, and he was among the first patrons to collect Japanese art, fascinated by what he perceived as decorative line, color, and shape, although he understood little about its meaning or intent. By the middle of the 1860s, Whistler began to call his works "symphonies" and "arrangements," suggesting that their themes resided in their compositions rather than their subject matter, and he painted several landscapes with another musically derived title, *Nocturne*. (Whistler took the term "nocturne" from the titles of piano compositions by Frédéric Chopin.) When he exhibited some of these in 1877, he drew the scorn of England's leading art critic, John Ruskin (1819–1900), a supporter of the Pre-Raphaelites and their moralistic intentions. Decrying Whistler's work as carelessly lacking in finish and purpose, Ruskin's review asked how an artist could "demand 200 guineas for flinging a pot of paint in the public's face."

31–27 James Abbott McNeill Whistler **NOCTURNE IN BLACK AND GOLD, THE FALLING ROCKET** 1875. Oil on panel, 23¾ × 18⅜″ (60.2 × 46.7 cm). The Detroit Institute of Arts. Gift of Dexter M. Ferry Jr. (46.309).

Credit: Bridgeman Images

The most controversial painting in Whistler's 1877 exhibition was **NOCTURNE IN BLACK AND GOLD, THE FALLING ROCKET** (**FIG. 31–27**), and Ruskin's objections to it set off one of the most notorious court dramas in art history. Painted in restricted tonalities, at first glance the work appears completely abstract. In fact, the painting is a night scene depicting a fireworks show over a lake at Cremorne Gardens in London, with viewers vaguely discernible along the lake's edge in the foreground. After reading Ruskin's review, Whistler sued the critic for libel (see "Art on Trial in 1877" below). He deliberately turned the courtroom into a public forum, both to defend and to advertise his art. On the witness stand, he maintained that art has no higher purpose than creating visual delight and denied the need for paintings to have "subject matter." While Whistler never made a completely abstract painting, his theories were integral to the development of abstract art in the next century.

Art and Its Contexts

ART ON TRIAL IN 1877

This is a partial transcript of James Abbott McNeill Whistler's testimony at the libel trial that he initiated against the art critic John Ruskin. Whistler's responses often provoked laughter, and the judge at one point threatened to clear the courtroom.

Q: What is your definition of a Nocturne?

A: I have, perhaps, meant rather to indicate an artistic interest alone in the work, divesting the picture from any outside sort of interest which might have been otherwise attached to it. It is an arrangement of line, form, and color first … The *Nocturne in Black and Gold* [SEE FIG. 31–27] is a night piece, and represents the fireworks at Cremorne.

Q: Not a view of Cremorne?

A: If it were called a view of Cremorne, it would certainly bring about nothing but disappointment on the part of beholders. It is an artistic arrangement. It was marked 200 guineas …

Q: I suppose you are willing to admit that your pictures exhibit some eccentricities; you have been told that over and over again?

A: Yes, very often.

Q: You send them to the gallery to invite the admiration of the public?

A: That would be such a vast absurdity on my part that I don't think I could.

Q: Did it take you much time to paint the *Nocturne in Black and Gold*? How soon did you knock it off?

A: I knocked it off in possibly a couple of days; one day to do the work, and another to finish it.

Q: And that was the labor for which you asked 200 guineas?

A: No, it was for the knowledge gained through a lifetime.

The judge ruled in Whistler's favor; Ruskin had indeed libeled him. But he awarded Whistler damages of only one farthing. Since in those days the person who brought the suit had to pay all the court costs, the case ended up bankrupting the artist.

Impressionism

What are the origins, objectives, and subjects of Impressionist painting?

The generation of French painters maturing around 1870 continued to paint modern urban subjects, but their perspective differed from that of Manet and the Realists. Instead of challenging social commentary, these younger artists painted pretty pictures of the upper middle class at leisure in the countryside and in the city, and although several members of this group painted rural scenes, their point of view tended to be that of a city person on holiday. They also began to paint not in the studio, but **en plein air** (French for "in the open air," or outdoors), in an effort to record directly the fleeting effects of light and atmosphere by applying many small touches of pure color directly onto the canvas. *Plein air* painting was greatly facilitated by the invention in 1841 of collapsible metal tubes for oil paint, which artists could conveniently pack and take out of the studio. Setting aside the boredom of the academic program for painting, with its elaborate preparatory drawings and underpainting followed by laborious work in the studio, the Impressionists sought instead to capture the play of light quickly, before it changed.

In April 1874, a group of these artists—including Paul Cézanne, Edgar Degas, Claude Monet, Berthe Morisot, Camille Pissarro, and Pierre-Auguste Renoir—exhibited together in Paris under the title of the Société Anonyme des Artistes Peintres, Sculpteurs, Graveurs, etc. (Anonymous Corporation of Artist-Painters, Sculptors, Engravers, etc.). Pissarro organized the group along the lines advocated by anarchists such as Pierre-Joseph Proudhon, who urged citizens to band together into self-supporting grassroots organizations, rather than relying on state-sanctioned institutions. Pissarro envisioned the Société as a mutual aid group for artists who opposed the state-funded Salons. While the Impressionists are the most famous of its members today, at the time the group included artists working in several styles. All 30 participants agreed not to submit anything that year to the Salon, which had in the past often rejected their work. This was a declaration of independence from the Académie and a bid to gain the public's attention directly.

While their exhibition received some positive reviews, one critic, Louis Leroy, writing in the satirical journal *Le Charivari*, seized upon the title of Claude Monet's painting *Impression: Sunrise* (SEE FIG. 31–28) and dubbed the entire exhibition "impressionist." Leroy was ridiculing the fast, open brushstrokes and unfinished look of some of the paintings, but Monet and his colleagues embraced the term because it aptly described their aim of rendering the instantaneous impression and fleeting moment in paint. Seven more Impressionist exhibitions were held between 1876 and 1886, with the membership of the group varying slightly on each occasion; only Pissarro participated in all eight shows. The relative success of these exhibitions prompted other artists to organize their own alternatives to the Salon, and by 1900 an independent exhibition and gallery system had all but eradicated the French academic Salon system. The Academy's centuries-old stranglehold on determining and controlling artistic standards was effectively ended.

Landscape and Leisure

Claude Monet (1840–1926) was a leading exponent of Impressionism. Born in Paris but raised in the port city of Le Havre, he trained briefly with an academic teacher but soon established his own studio. His friend Charles-François Daubigny urged him to trust his personal impressions and suggested that he paint *en plein air*. Like other Impressionists, Monet's focus was the creation of a modern painting style, not the production of biting social commentary. Initially, the Impressionists celebrated the semirural pleasures of outings to the suburbs, which the Paris train system had made possible for the middle class. Few early works depict locations far from Paris; most feature Parisians at leisure—walking, boating, and visiting fashionable new parks within the city or just outside of town.

In the summer of 1870 the Franco-Prussian War broke out, and Monet fled to London, where he spent time with Pissarro and Paul Durand-Ruel, who would later be Monet's art dealer. The disastrous loss of the major industrial regions of Alsace and Lorraine to Prussia at the end of the war devastated the French economy. In Paris, for two months between March and May 1871 workers rose up and established the Commune, a working-class city government, the suppression of which led to an estimated 20,000 dead and 7,500 imprisoned. The horror rocked Paris. Courbet was imprisoned for a short time and in artists' circles, the fear of being branded as an enemy of the state sent a chill through everyone. After 1871, overt political commentary in French art diminished even more, and the challenge of the avant-garde was expressed increasingly as an insular stylistic rebellion.

In 1873, just after returning to Paris, Monet painted **IMPRESSION: SUNRISE** (FIG. 31–28), a view of the sun rising in the morning fog over the harbor in his hometown of Le Havre. The painting is rendered almost entirely of strokes of color (Leroy sneeringly called them "tongue-lickings"). The foreground is ambiguous, and the horizon line disappears among the shimmering shapes of steamships and docks in the background, clouded by a thick atmosphere of mist. Monet registers the intensity and shifting forms of a first sketch and presents it as the final work of art. He records the ephemeral play of reflected light and color and its effect on the eye, rather than describing the physical substance of forms and the spatial volumes

31–28 Claude Monet
IMPRESSION: SUNRISE

1872. Oil on canvas,
19 × 24⅜" (48 × 63 cm).
Musée Marmottan, Paris.

Credit: Bridgeman Images

they occupy. The American painter Lilla Cabot Perry, who befriended Monet in his later years, recalled him telling her:

> When you go out to paint, try to forget what objects you have before you—a tree, a house, a field, or whatever. Merely think, Here is a little square of blue, here an oblong of pink, here a streak of yellow, and paint it just as it looks to you, the exact color and shape, until it gives your own naïve impression of the scene before you.

Monet continued to explore personal impressions of light and color during a long career that extended well into the twentieth century. Beginning in the 1880s and 1890s he focused his vision even more intently, exploring a limited number of outdoor subjects through several series of paintings: haystacks, poplar trees silhouetted against the sky, and the façade of Rouen Cathedral (**FIG. 31–29**). He painted the cathedral not as an expression of personal religious conviction, but because of his fascination with the way light played across its undulating stone surface, changing its appearance constantly as the lighting changed throughout the day. He painted more than 30 canvases of the Rouen

31–29 Claude Monet **ROUEN CATHEDRAL, WEST FAÇADE, SUNLIGHT**

1894. Oil on canvas, 39⅜ × 25⅞" (100.1 × 65.8 cm).
National Gallery of Art, Washington, DC., Chester Dale Collection (1963.10.179)

Credit: Image courtesy the National Gallery of Art, Washington

façade, begun from direct observation of the cathedral from a second-story window across the street and finished later in his studio at nearby Giverny. In these paintings, Monet continued his Impressionist pursuit of capturing the fleeting effects of light and atmosphere, but his extensive reworking of the paintings in his studio produced pictures that were more carefully orchestrated and laboriously executed than his earlier, more spontaneous, *plein air* works.

Monet's friend and fellow artist Camille Pissarro (1830–1903) offered a new Impressionist image of the landscape, painting scenes where the urban meets the rural. At times he portrayed the rural landscape on its own, but he often shows urban visitors to the countryside and small towns or factories embedded in the land as the city encroaches upon them. Born in the Dutch West Indies to French parents and raised near Paris, Pissarro studied art in Paris during the 1850s and early 1860s. In 1870, while he and Monet lived in London, Pissarro had already taken up the principles that would later blossom in Impressionism. The two artists worked together in England, trying to capture what Pissarro described as "*plein air* light and fugitive effects" by lightening color intensity and hue and loosening brushstrokes.

Following his return to France, Pissarro settled in Pontoise, a small, hilly village northwest of Paris where he worked for most of the 1870s in an Impressionist style, using high-keyed color and short brushstrokes to capture fleeting qualities of light and atmosphere. In the late 1870s, his work became more visually complex, with darkened colors. In his **WOODED LANDSCAPE AT L'HERMITAGE, PONTOISE** (**FIG. 31-30**), for instance, a foreground composition of trees screens the view of a rural path and village behind, flattening space and partly masking the figure at the lower right. Pissarro applies his paint thickly here, with a multitude of short, multidirectional brushstrokes.

In contrast, Impressionist painter Pierre-Auguste Renoir (1841–1919) focused most of his attention not on landscapes but on figures, producing mostly images of the middle class at leisure. When he met Monet at the École des Beaux-Arts in 1862, he was already working as a figure painter. Monet encouraged him to lighten his palette and to paint outdoors, and by the mid-1870s Renoir was combining a spontaneous handling of natural light with animated figural compositions. In **MOULIN DE LA GALETTE** (**FIG. 31-31**), for example, Renoir depicts a convivial crowd relaxing on a Sunday afternoon at an old-fashioned dance hall—the Moulin de la Galette (the "Pancake Mill") in the Montmartre area of Paris, which opened its outdoor courtyard during good weather. Renoir glamorizes the working-class clientele by placing his attractive bourgeois artist friends and their models among them, striking poses of relaxed congeniality, smiling, dancing, and chatting. He underscores the innocence of their flirtations by including children in the painting in the lower

31-30 Camille Pissarro **WOODED LANDSCAPE AT L'HERMITAGE, PONTOISE**
1878. Oil on canvas, 18⁵⁄₁₆ × 22¹⁄₁₆" (46.5 × 56 cm). The Nelson-Atkins Museum of Art, Kansas City, Missouri. Gift of Dr. and Mrs. Nicholas S. Pickard.

31–31 Pierre-Auguste Renoir **MOULIN DE LA GALETTE**

1876. Oil on canvas, 4′3½″ × 5′9″ (1.31 × 1.75 m). Musée d'Orsay, Paris.

Credit: Photo © RMN-Grand Palais (musée d'Orsay)/Hervé Lewandowski

31–32 Berthe Morisot **SUMMER'S DAY**

1879. Oil on canvas, 17¹³⁄₁₆ × 29⁵⁄₁₆″ (45.7 × 75.2 cm). National Gallery, London. Lane Bequest, 1917.

Credit: © 2016. Copyright The National Gallery, London/Scala, Florence

left, while emphasizing the ease of social relations through the relaxed informality of the scene. The overall mood is knit together by the dappled sunlight falling through the trees and Renoir's soft brushwork weaving blues and purples through the crowd and around the canvas. This naïve image of a carefree life of innocent leisure—a kind of bourgeois paradise removed from the real world—encapsulates Renoir's idea of the essence of art: "For me a picture should be a pleasant thing, joyful and pretty—yes pretty! There are quite enough unpleasant things in life without the need for us to manufacture more."

Impressionist artist Berthe Morisot (1841–1895) defied societal conventions to become a professional painter. Morisot and her sister, Edma, copied paintings in the Louvre and studied with several teachers, including Corot, in the late 1850s and early 1860s. The sisters exhibited their art in the five Salons between 1864 and 1868, the year they met Manet. In 1869, Edma married and gave up painting to devote herself to domestic duties, but Berthe continued painting even after her 1874 marriage to Manet's brother, Eugène, and the birth of their daughter in 1879. Morisot sent nine paintings to the first exhibition of the Impressionists in 1874 and showed her work in all but one of their subsequent shows.

As a respectable bourgeois lady, Berthe Morisot was not free to prowl the city looking for modern subjects, so she concentrated on depictions of women's lives, a subject she knew well. In the 1870s, she painted in an increasingly fluid and painterly style, flattening her picture plane and making her brushwork more prominent. In **SUMMER'S** **DAY** (**FIG. 31-32**), Morisot shows two elegant young ladies enjoying an outing on the lake of the fashionable Bois de Boulogne. First shown in the fifth Impressionist exhibition in 1880, the painting exemplifies the emphasis on formal features in Impressionist painting—the brushstrokes and the colors are as much its subject as the figures themselves.

Modern Life

Subjects from urban life also attracted Edgar Degas (1834–1917), although his paintings are closer to Realism in their intensely frank portrayals that often suggest social commentary. Instead of painting outdoors, Degas composed his pictures in the studio from working drawings and photographs. His rigorous academic training at the École des Beaux-Arts in the mid-1850s and his three years in Italy studying the Old Masters blossomed in paintings characterized by complex compositional structure and striking representational clarity. In many respects his themes and style were closer to Manet's than to the Impressionists.

After a period of painting psychologically probing portraits of friends and relatives, during the 1870s, Degas began painting the modern life of Paris, especially its venues of entertainment and spectacle—the racetrack, the music hall, and the opera, usually focusing on the entertainers rather than on the bourgeois audience. He was especially drawn to the ballet in the 1870s and 1880s, at a time when it was in decline. Occasionally Degas drew or painted actual dancers in rehearsal, but he also hired dancers, often very young "ballet rats" (as he called them), to come to his studio to pose for him. **THE REHEARSAL ON STAGE** (**FIG. 31-33**), for example, is a contrived scene based on such studio studies, calculated to delight the eye but also to refocus the

31-33 Edgar Degas **THE REHEARSAL ON STAGE**

c. 1874. Pastel over brush-and-ink drawing on thin, cream-colored wove paper, laid on bristol board, mounted on canvas, 21⅜ × 28¾" (54.3 × 73 cm). Metropolitan Museum of Art, New York. Bequest of Mrs. H. O. Havemeyer Collection, Gift of Horace Havemeyer, 1929 (29.160.26).

31–34 Edgar Degas **THE TUB**
1886. Pastel on cardboard,
23⅝ × 32⅝" (60 × 83 cm).
Musée d'Orsay, Paris.

Credit: Photo © RMN-Grand Palais (musée d'Orsay)/Hervé Lewandowski

mind on the stern realities of modern life. Several of the dancers look bored or exhausted; others stretch, perhaps to mitigate the toll this physical work took on their bodies. Because ballerinas generally came from lower-class families and showed their scantily clad bodies in public—something that "respectable" bourgeois women did not do—they were widely assumed to be sexually available, and they often attracted the attentions of wealthy men willing to support them in exchange for sexual favors. In the right background of this painting slouch two well-dressed, middle-aged men, each probably a wealthy "protector" of one of the dancers.

The composition is set in a space that seems to tilt upward, as if viewed from a box close to the stage. The abrupt foreshortening is emphasized by the dark scrolls of the double basses that jut up from the lower left. The angular viewpoint from above may derive from Japanese prints, which Degas collected, while the seemingly arbitrary cropping of figures on the left suggests photography, which he also practiced.

Whereas Degas's ballet paintings highlight informal moments associated with public performance, his later images of bathing women are furtive glimpses of intimate moments drawn from private life, usually rendered in the medium of pastel, which only heightens their sense of immediacy. **THE TUB** of 1886 (**FIG. 31–34**) represents a crouching woman perched within a small tub, washing her neck with a sponge. Initially, this may seem to be two separate pictures: at the left the compactly posed woman, balanced precariously on the steep floor of a receding interior space, and on the right a tipped-up table with a still life of objects associated with bathing. But when coordinated, they establish the viewer's elevated, domineering vantage point. The dramatic, flattened juxtaposition, as well as the

compression and cropping of the close frame, are further examples of the impact of Japanese prints and photography on Degas's art.

Another artist who exhibited with the Impressionists but whose art soon diverged from them in both style and technique—conditioned in part by her contact with Degas—was American expatriate Mary Cassatt (1844–1926). Born near Pittsburgh to a well-to-do family and raised in the cosmopolitan world of Philadelphia, she studied at the Pennsylvania Academy of the Fine Arts between 1861 and 1865, then moved to Paris for further academic training and lived there for most of the rest of her life. The realism of the figure paintings she exhibited at the Salons of the early and mid-1870s attracted the attention of Degas, who invited her to participate in the fourth Impressionist exhibition in 1879. Although she, like Degas, remained a studio painter and printmaker, her distaste for what she called the "tyranny" of the Salon jury system made her one of the group's staunchest supporters.

Like Morisot, Cassatt focused her paintings on the world she knew best: the domestic and social life of bourgeois women. She is known for extraordinarily sensitive representations of women with children, which, like the genre paintings of fellow expatriate Henry Ossawa Tanner (SEE FIG. 31–24), sought to counteract the clichéd stereotypes of her age. In **MOTHER AND CHILD** from about 1890 (**FIG. 31–35**), she contrasts the loosely painted, Impressionist treatment of clothing and setting and the solidly modeled forms of faces and hands to rivet our attention on the tender connection between mother and child at bedtime, right after a bath. The drowsy face, flushed cheeks, and weighty limbs of the child have a natural quality, even though the space occupied by the figures seems flattened. Because the composition and subject recall much earlier portrayals of the Virgin and Child, Cassatt elevates this modest scene of private life into a homage to motherhood and a dialogue with the history of art.

Gustave Caillebotte (1848–1894), another friend of Degas, was instrumental in organizing several Impressionist exhibitions and used his wealth to purchase the work

31–35 Mary Cassatt **MOTHER AND CHILD**
c. 1890. Oil on canvas, 35½ × 25⅜″ (90.2 × 64.5 cm).
Wichita Art Museum, Kansas.

of his friends, amassing a large collection of paintings. He studied with an academic teacher privately and qualified for the École des Beaux-Arts, but never attended. Caillebotte was fascinated by the regularized, radiating streets of Haussmann's Paris (SEE FIG. 31–3), and his subjects and compositions often represent life along the boulevards. **PARIS STREET, RAINY DAY** (FIG. **31–36**) has an unconventional, almost telescopic, asymmetrical composition with a tipped perspective. The broad, wet streets create the subject of this painting, with anonymous, huddled Parisians mostly pushed to the periphery, their shiny umbrellas as prominent as their silhouetted bodies. Only the connected couple strolling toward us is fully realized and personalized. Squeezed between the lamppost and the saturated red and green of a shopfront, they stand within an internally framed rectangular composition capped by the strong horizontal of the two umbrellas.

31–36 Gustave Caillebotte **PARIS STREET, RAINY DAY**
1877. Oil on canvas, 83½ × 108¾″ (212.2 × 276.2 cm). The Art Institute of Chicago.
Charles H. and Mary F.S. Worcester Collection (1964.336).

Credit: Photo © The Art Institute of Chicago

Japonisme

Japan was forcibly opened by the U. S. Navy to Western trade and diplomacy in 1853. Two years later, when France, England, Russia, and the United States signed trade agreements that permitted regular exchange of goods, Japanese art became available to European and American artists. One of the first works that engaged the attention of modern painters was a sketchbook called *Manga* by Katsushika Hokusai (1760–1849), which several Parisian artists eagerly passed around.

The Paris International Exposition of 1867 hosted the first exhibition of Japanese prints in Europe, and soon, Japanese lacquers, fans, bronzes, hanging scrolls, kimonos, ceramics, illustrated books, and *ukiyo-e* (prints of the "floating world," the realm of geishas and popular entertainment) began to appear for sale in specialty shops, art galleries, and even some department stores. Soon it became fashionable for those in the art world to collect Japanese objects for their homes. The French obsession with Japan and its arts reached such proportions by 1872 that the art critic Philippe Burty gave it a name: **Japonisme**.

Japanese art had a profound impact on Western painting and printmaking, and eventually also on architecture, but the influence was extraordinarily diverse. How individual artists responded depended on their own interests.

Whistler found encouragement for his purely aesthetic conception of art, liberated from Renaissance rules of representation and perspective. Degas discovered both realistic subjects and complex, diagonal compositional arrangements and elevated viewpoints. Those interested in the reform of late nineteenth-century industrial design found in Japanese objects both the fine craft and honest elegance they thought lacking in the West.

Cassatt directly emulated the compositions, designs, and colors of *ukiyo-e* after multiple visits to an influential 1890 exhibition of 725 woodblock prints mounted at the École des Beaux-Arts in Paris. This art appealed to Cassatt because its concentration on the private lives of women (**FIG. 31-37**) coordinated well with her own preferred subject matter (SEE FIG. 31-35), but she also felt a connection to the stylistic character of these prints—their cropped, diagonally structured, and often asymmetrical compositions; their use of broad, flat, unmodulated areas of color or tone; their emphasis on outline and pattern over form and space; and their oblique vantage points. This exhibition inspired Cassatt to create her own portfolio of ten prints (**FIG. 31-38**) using the contemporary medium of aquatint and drypoint. The exhibition of these prints in 1891 was her first solo show, and her work was acclaimed by her fellow artists. Cassatt's friend and mentor Degas was dumbfounded—"I do not admit that a woman can draw like that."

31-37 Suzuki Harunobu **YOUNG WOMAN LOOKING AT A POT OF PINKS**

c. 1767. Woodblock print, 10⅝ × 7½" (27 × 19.2 cm). The Cleveland Museum of Art.

Credit: Bridgeman Images

31-38 Mary Cassatt **WOMAN BATHING**

1890–1891. Color drypoint and aquatint, 16⅝ × 12" (42.3 × 30.5 cm). National Gallery of Art, Washington, DC., Dale Collection (1963.10.253)

Credit: Image courtesy the National Gallery of Art, Washington

The Late Nineteenth Century

What are the diverse stylistic innovations of the generation of artists who came after the Impressionists?

The Realists and Impressionists continued to create art until the end of the century, but by the mid-1880s they had relinquished their dominance to a younger generation of innovative artists. This period seems less unified, less directed, and less restricted geographically. Artists increasingly defined the avant-garde in terms of visual experimentation, developing new visual languages more appropriate to newly formulated messages.

These artists included French Post-Impressionists, who expressed an interior world of the imagination or imposed a new scientific rigor on representations of the world around them; late nineteenth-century French sculptors, who studied the passionate physicality of the human form; Symbolists, who retreated into fantastical and sometimes horrifying worlds of the imagination; Art Nouveau artists, who rejected the rational order of the industrial world to create images and designs ruled by the writhing, asymmetrical shapes of growing plants; and even landscape architects, who recast the urban cityscape into a rambling, natural landscape.

Post-Impressionism

The English critic Roger Fry coined the term "Post-Impressionism" in 1910 in order to describe a diverse group of painters whose work he had collected for an exhibition. He acknowledged that these artists did not share a unified approach to art, but they all used Impressionism as a springboard for developing their individual styles.

SEURAT Georges Seurat (1859–1891), who was born in Paris and trained at the École des Beaux-Arts, sought to "correct" Impressionism, which he found too intellectually shallow and improvisational. He preferred the clarity of structure he saw in Classical relief sculpture and the seemingly systematic but actually quite emotive use of color suggested by optics and color theory. He was particularly interested in the "law of the simultaneous contrast of colors" formulated by Michel-Eugène Chevreul in the 1820s. Chevreul observed that adjacent objects not only cast reflections of their own color onto their neighbors, but also create the effect of their **complementary color**. Thus, when a blue object is set next to a yellow one, the eye will detect in the blue object a trace of purple, the complement of yellow, and in the yellow object a trace of orange, the complement of blue.

Seurat's goal was to find ways to create such retinal vibrations to enliven the painted surface, using distinctively short, multidirectional strokes of almost pure color in what came to be known as "Divisionism" or "Pointillism." In theory, these juxtaposed strokes of color would merge in the viewer's eye to produce the impression of other colors. When perceived from a certain distance they would appear more luminous and intense than the same colors seen separately, while on close inspection the strokes and colors would remain distinct and separate.

Seurat's monumental painting **A SUNDAY AFTERNOON ON THE ISLAND OF LA GRANDE JATTE** (FIG. 31-39) was first exhibited at the eighth and final Impressionist exhibition in 1886. The theme of weekend leisure is typically Impressionist, but the rigorous technique, the stiff formality of the figures, and the highly calculated geometry of the composition produce a solemn effect quite at odds with the casual naturalism of Impressionism. Seurat painted the entire canvas using only 11 colors in three values. When viewed from a distance of about 9 feet, the painting reads as figures in a park rendered in many colors and tones; but when viewed from a distance of 3 feet, the individual marks of color become more apparent, while the forms dissolve into abstraction.

From its first appearance, the painting has been the subject of a number of conflicting interpretations. Contemporary accounts of the island indicate that on Sundays (the newly designated official day off for French working families) it was noisy, littered, and chaotic. Seurat may have intended to represent an ideal image of harmonious, blended working-class and middle-class life and leisure. But some art historians see Seurat satirizing the sterile habits, rigid attitudes, and domineering presence of the growing Parisian middle class—or simply engaging in an intellectual exercise on the nature of form and color.

VAN GOGH AND GAUGUIN Among the most famous Post-Impressionist artists is the Dutch painter Vincent van Gogh (1853–1890), who transformed his artistic sources into a highly expressive personal style. The oldest son of a Protestant minister, Van Gogh worked as an art dealer, a teacher, and an evangelist before deciding in 1880 to become an artist. After brief periods of study in Brussels, The Hague, and Antwerp, in 1886 he moved to Paris, where he encountered the Parisian avant-garde. Van Gogh adapted Seurat's Pointillism by applying brilliantly colored paint in multidirectional strokes of impasto (thick applications of paint) to give his pictures a turbulent emotional energy and a palpable surface texture.

Van Gogh was a socialist who believed that modern life, with its constant social change and focus on progress and success, alienated people from one other and from themselves. His paintings are efforts to communicate his emotional state by establishing a direct connection

31–39 Georges Seurat **A SUNDAY AFTERNOON ON THE ISLAND OF LA GRANDE JATTE**
1884–1886. Oil on canvas, 6'9½" × 10'1¼" (207 × 308 cm). The Art Institute of Chicago.
Helen Birch Bartlett Memorial Collection (1926.22).

There was a social hierarchy in Parisian parks in the late nineteenth century; the Bois de Boulogne (SEE FIG. 31–32) was an upper-middle-class park in an area of grand avenues, whereas the Grande Jatte faced a lower-class industrial area across the river and was easily accessible by train. The figures represent a range of "types" that would have been easily recognizable to the nineteenth-century viewer, such as the middle-class strolling man and his companion to the right—usually identified as a *boulevardier* (or citified dandy) and a *cocotte* (a single woman assumed to be a prostitute)—or the working-class *canotier* (oarsman) to the left.

Credit: Photo © The Art Institute of Chicago

between artist and viewer, thereby overcoming the emotional barrenness of modern society. In a prolific output over only ten years, he produced paintings that contributed significantly to the later emergence of Expressionism, in which the intensity of an artist's emotional state would override any desire for fidelity to the actual appearance of things. Van Gogh described his working method in a letter to his brother:

I should like to paint the portrait of an artist friend who dreams great dreams, who works as the nightingale sings, because it is his nature. This man will be fair-haired. I should like to put my appreciation, the love I have for him, into the picture. So I will paint him as he is, as faithfully as I can—to begin with. But that is not the end of the picture. To finish it, I shall be an obstinate colorist. I shall exaggerate the fairness of the hair, arrive at tones of orange, chrome, pale yellow. Behind the head—instead of painting the ordinary wall of the shabby apartment, I shall paint

infinity, I shall do a simple background of the richest, most intense blue that I can contrive, and by this simple combination, the shining fair head against this rich blue background, I shall obtain a mysterious effect, like a star in the deep blue sky.

One of the most famous examples of Van Gogh's approach is **THE STARRY NIGHT** (FIG. 31–40), painted near the asylum of Saint-Rémy. Above the quiet town, the sky pulsates with celestial rhythms and exploding stars. Contemplating life and death in a letter, Van Gogh wrote: "Just as we take the train to get to Tarascon or Rouen, we take death to reach a star." This idea is made visible here by the cypress tree, a traditional symbol of both death and eternal life, which rises to link the terrestrial and celestial realms. The brightest star in the sky is actually a planet, Venus, which is associated with love: It is possible that the picture's extraordinary energy also expresses Van Gogh's euphoric hope of gaining in death the love that had eluded him in life. The painting is a riot of brushstrokes of intense color that writhe across the surface. This is clearly more a record of what Van Gogh felt than what he saw. During the last year and a half of his life, before he made this painting, he had experienced repeated psychological crises that lasted for days or weeks. While they were raging, he wanted to hurt himself, heard loud noises in his head, and could not paint. The stress of these attacks led him to the asylum where he painted *The Starry Night*, and eventually to suicide in July 1890.

In painting from imagination more than from nature in *The Starry Night*, Van Gogh may have been following the advice of his close friend Paul Gauguin (1848–1903), who once counseled another artist, "Don't paint from nature too much. Art is an abstraction. Derive this abstraction from nature while dreaming before it, and think more of the creation that will result." Born in Paris to a Peruvian mother and a radical French journalist father, Gauguin lived in Peru until age 7. During the 1870s and early 1880s, he enjoyed a comfortable bourgeois life as a stockbroker, painting in his spare time as a student of Pissarro. Between 1880 and 1886, he exhibited in the final four Impressionist exhibitions. In 1883, he lost his job during a stock market crash, and three years later he abandoned his wife and five children to pursue a full-time painting career. Gauguin knew firsthand the business culture of his time and came to despise it. Believing that escape to a more "primitive" place would bring with it the simpler pleasures of preindustrial life, Gauguin lived for extended periods in the French province of Brittany between 1886 and 1891, traveled to Panama and Martinique in 1887, spent two months in Arles with Van Gogh in 1888, and in 1891 sailed for Tahiti, a French colony in the South Pacific. After a final sojourn in France in 1893–1895, Gauguin returned to French Polynesia, where he died in 1903.

Gauguin's art was inspired by sources as varied as medieval stained glass, folk art, and Japanese prints; he sought to paint in a "primitive" way, employing the so-called decorative qualities of folk art, such as brilliantly colored flat shapes, anti-naturalist color, and bold, black outlines. Gauguin called his style "synthetism," because he believed it synthesized observation and the artist's feelings in an abstracted application of line, shape, space, and color.

31–40 Vincent van Gogh **THE STARRY NIGHT**
1889. Oil on canvas, 28¾ × 36¼" (73 × 93 cm). Museum of Modern Art, New York. Acquired through the Lillie P. Bliss Bequest (472.1941).

MAHANA NO ATUA (*Day of the God*) (see "Closer Look" below) is very much a product of such synthesis. Despite its Tahitian subject, it was painted in France during Gauguin's brief return after two years in the South Pacific. He had gone to Tahiti hoping to find an unspoiled, preindustrial paradise, imagining the Tahitians to be childlike and close to nature. What he discovered was a thoroughly colonized country whose native culture was rapidly disappearing under the pressures of Westernization. In paintings such as this, however, Gauguin chose to ignore this reality and depict instead the Edenic ideal of his own imagination.

A Closer Look
MAHANA NO ATUA (DAY OF THE GOD)

Gauguin divided the painting into three horizontal zones, increasingly abstract from top to bottom. The upper zone, painted in the most lifelike manner, centers on the statue of a god set in a beach landscape populated by Tahitians.

The central female bather dips her feet in the water and looks coyly out at viewers, while, on either side of her, two androgynous figures recline in fetuslike postures. The three poses perhaps symbolize—left to right—birth, life, and death.

As was his practice in many of his Tahitian paintings, Gauguin did not base this sculpted idol on a statue he saw in Tahiti, but rather on pictures he owned of the Buddhist temple complex at Borobudur (SEE FIG. 10–36).

Filling the bottom third of the painting is a striking pool of water, abstracted into a dazzling array of bright colors and arranged in a puzzlelike pattern of flat, curvilinear shapes. The left half of this pool seems rooted in natural description, evoking spatial recession. But on the right it becomes flatter and more stylized.

This middle zone contains three figures posed on an unnaturalistically pink beach. The green, arched form behind the central woman links her visually to the idol immediately above her.

By reflecting a strange and unexpected reality exactly where we expect to see a mirror image of the familiar world, this magic pool seems the perfect symbol of Gauguin's desire to evoke "the mysterious centers of thought." His aim was symbolic rather than descriptive works of art.

31–41 Paul Gauguin **MAHANA NO ATUA (DAY OF THE GOD)**
1894. Oil on canvas, 27⅜ × 35⅝″ (69.5 × 90.5 cm). The Art Institute of Chicago. Helen Birch Bartlett Memorial Collection (1926.198).

Credit: Photo © The Art Institute of Chicago

Symbolism

Symbolism was an international movement in art and literature championed by a loose affiliation of artists interested in the irrational aspects of the human mind. A fascination with the dark recesses of the psyche emerged over the last decades of the nineteenth century, encompassing photographic and scientific examinations of the nature of insanity as well as a popular interest in the spirit world of mediums. Some Symbolist artists sought escape from modern life in irrational worlds of unrestrained emotion as described by authors such as Edgar Allan Poe (1809–1849), whose terrifying stories of the supernatural were popular across Europe. It is hardly coincidental that Sigmund Freud (1856–1939), who compared artistic creation to the process of dreaming, wrote his pioneering *The Interpretation of Dreams* (1900) during this period.

The Symbolists rejected the value placed on rationalism and material progress in modern Western culture, choosing instead to explore the realms of emotion, imagination, and spirituality. They sought a deeper and more mysterious reality beyond everyday life, which they conveyed through strange, ambiguous subject matter and stylized forms that suggest hidden and elusive meanings. They often compared their works to dreams.

Symbolism in painting closely paralleled a similar movement among poets and writers. For example, Joris-Karl Huysmans's novel *À Rebours* (*Against the Grain*), published in 1884, has a single character, an aristocrat named Des Esseintes, who locks himself away from the world because "Imagination could easily be substituted for the vulgar realities of things." Claiming that nature was irrelevant, Des Esseintes muses that "Nature has had her day" and "wearied aesthetes" should take refuge in artworks "steeped in ancient dreams or antique corruptions, far removed from the manner of our present day."

MOREAU   A visionlike atmosphere pervades the later work of Gustave Moreau (1826–1898), an academic artist whom the Symbolists regarded as a precursor. They particularly admired Moreau's renditions of the biblical Salomé, the young Judaean princess who at the instigation of her mother, Herodias,

performed an erotic dance before her stepfather, Herod, and demanded as reward the head of John the Baptist (Mark 6:21–28). In **THE APPARITION** (**FIG. 31–42**), exhibited at the Salon of 1876, the seductive Salomé confronts a vision of the saint's severed head, which hovers open-eyed in midair, dripping blood and radiating holy light. Moreau depicted this sensual and macabre scene and its exotic setting in meticulous detail with touches of jewel-like color, creating an atmosphere of voluptuous decadence that amplifies Salomé's role as *femme fatale*.

The Symbolists, like many smaller groups of artists in the late nineteenth century, staged independent art exhibitions, but unlike the Impressionists, who hired halls, printed programs, and charged a small admission fee for their exhibitions, the Symbolists mounted modest shows with little expectation of public interest. During the 1889 Universal Exposition, for example, they hung a few works in a café close to the fairgrounds, with the result that the exhibition went almost unnoticed by the press.

31–42 Gustave Moreau **THE APPARITION**
1874–1876. Watercolor on paper, 41⁵⁄₁₆ × 28³⁄₁₆″
(106 × 72.2 cm). Musée du Louvre, Paris.

Credit: Photo © RMN-Grand Palais (musée d'Orsay)/
Jean-Gilles Berizzi

MUNCH Symbolism originated in France but had a profound impact on the avant-garde in other countries, where it frequently took on Expressionist tendencies. In Norway, Edvard Munch (1863–1944) produced a body of work that shows the terrifying workings of an anguished mind. **THE SCREAM** (FIG. 31–43) is the stuff of nightmares and horror movies; its harsh, swirling colors and lines direct us wildly around the painting, but bring us right back to the human head at the center and the echoes of its haunting scream, sensed visually. Munch described how the painting began: "One evening I was walking along a path; the city was on one side, and the fjord below. I was tired and ill…. I sensed a shriek passing through nature…. I painted this picture, painted the clouds as actual blood."

31–43 Edvard Munch **THE SCREAM**
1893. Tempera and oil on unprimed canvas, 33 × 26″ (83.5 × 66 cm). Munch Museum, Oslo.

Credit: © 2016 Artists Rights Society (ARS), New York. Nasjonalgalleriet, Oslo, Norway/ Bridgeman Images.

31–44 James Ensor **THE INTRIGUE**
1890. Oil on canvas, 35½ × 59″ (90.3 × 150 cm). Koninklijk Museum voor Schone Kunsten, Antwerp.

Credit: © Lukas - Art in Flanders VZW/Photo: Hugo Maertens/Bridgeman Images

ENSOR   The Belgian painter and printmaker James Ensor (1860–1949) studied for four years at the Brussels Academy, but spent the rest of his life in the nearby coastal resort town of Ostend, where like Munch he produced terrifying paintings combining Symbolist and Expressionist tendencies. **THE INTRIGUE** (**FIG. 31–44**) shows a tightly packed group of agitated people pushed toward the viewer into the foreground. Masks—modeled on the grotesque papier-mâché masks Ensor's family sold for the pre-Lenten carnival—conceal their faces, giving them a disturbing, mindless, menacing quality. Ensor's acidic colors and energetic paint handling only increase the viewer's anxiety.

French Sculpture

A defiance of conventional expectations and an interest in emotional expressiveness also characterize the work of late nineteenth-century Europe's most successful and influential sculptor, Auguste Rodin (1840–1917). Born in Paris, Rodin failed three times to gain entrance to the École des Beaux-Arts and consequently spent the first 20 years of his career as an assistant to other sculptors and decorators. After an 1875 trip to Italy, where he saw the sculpture of Donatello and Michelangelo, Rodin developed a style of vigorously modeled figures in unconventional, even awkward poses, which was simultaneously scorned by academic critics and admired by the general public.

Rodin's status as a major sculptor was confirmed in 1884 when he won a competition to create **THE BURGHERS OF CALAIS** (**FIG. 31–45**) for the city of Calais, commemorating a local event from the Hundred Years' War. In 1347, Edward III of England had offered to spare the besieged city if six leading citizens (burghers) surrendered themselves to him for execution. Edward's wife, Queen Philippa of Hainault, convinced her husband to pardon the men

31–45 Auguste Rodin **THE BURGHERS OF CALAIS**
1884–1889. Bronze, 6′10½″ × 7′11″ × 6′6″ (2.1 × 2.4 × 2 m). Hirshhorn Museum and Sculpture Garden, Smithsonian Institution, Washington, DC. Gift of Joseph H. Hirshhorn, 1966.

Rodin's relocation of public sculpture from a high pedestal to a low base would lead to the twentieth-century elimination of the pedestal itself, thus presenting sculpture in the "real" space of the viewer.

31–46 Camille Claudel **THE WALTZ**
1892–1905. Bronze, height 9⅞" (25 cm). Neue Pinakothek, Munich.

Credit: Photo © Blauel/Gnamm/ARTOTHEK

She soon became his mistress, and their relationship lasted 15 years. Claudel enjoyed independent professional success but suffered a breakdown that sent her to a mental hospital for the last 30 years of her life.

One of Claudel's most celebrated works is **THE WALTZ** (**FIG. 31–46**), produced in several versions and sizes between 1892 and 1905. The subject of the waltz alone was controversial at this time because of the close body contact demanded of dancers. The sculpture depicts a dancing couple, both nude, although the woman's lower body is covered with long, flowing drapery, a concession she made after an inspector from the Ministry of Fine Arts declared their sensuality unacceptable, recommending against a state commission for a marble version of the work. Claudel added enough drapery to regain the commission, but she never finished it. She did, however, cast the modified version in bronze as this tabletop sculpture, in which the spiral flow of the cloth creates the illusion of rapturous movement as the embracing dancers twirl through space.

Art Nouveau

The swirling mass of drapery in Claudel's *The Waltz* has a stylistic affinity with Art Nouveau (French for "new art"), a movement launched in the early 1890s that permeated all aspects of European design for more than a decade. Art Nouveau embraced the use of modern industrial materials but rejected the functional aesthetic of works such as the Eiffel Tower (**SEE FIG. 31–1**) that showcased exposed structure as architectural design. Art Nouveau artists and architects drew particular inspiration from nature, especially from vines, snakes, flowers, and winged insects, whose delicate and sinuous forms were consistent with the graceful and attenuated aesthetic principles of the movement. The goal was to harmonize all aspects of design into an integrated whole, as found in nature itself.

because she feared their execution would be a bad omen for their unborn child, but Rodin's sculpture captures a moment before this pardon was known.

The Calais commissioners were pleased neither with Rodin's conception of the event nor with his plan to display the figures on a low base, almost at street level, to suggest to viewers that ordinary people like themselves were capable of noble acts. Instead of calm, idealized heroes, Rodin presented ordinary-looking men in various attitudes of resignation and despair, dressed only in sackcloth with rope halters and carrying the keys to the city. He exaggerated their facial expressions, lengthened their arms, greatly enlarged their hands and feet, and swathed them in heavy fabric, showing not only how they may have looked but also how they must have felt as they forced themselves to take one difficult step after another. Rodin's willingness to stylize the human body for expressive purposes opened the way for subsequent sculptural abstractions.

Camille Claudel (1864–1943), who was Rodin's assistant while he worked on *The Burghers of Calais*, had already studied sculpture formally before joining Rodin's studio.

HORTA The artist most responsible for developing the Art Nouveau style in architecture was the Belgian Victor Horta (1861–1947). After academic training in Ghent and Brussels, Horta worked in the office of a Neoclassical architect in Brussels for six years before opening his own practice in 1890. In 1892, he received his first important commission, a private residence in Brussels for a Professor Emile Tassel. The result, especially the house's entry hall and staircase (**FIG. 31–47**), was strikingly original. The ironwork, wall decoration, and floor tiles were all designed in an intricate series of long, graceful curves. Although Horta's sources are still debated, he was apparently impressed by the stylized linear designs of the English Arts and Crafts Movement of the 1880s. His concern for integrating the various arts into a more unified whole, like his reliance on sinuous decorative line, derived in part from English reformers such as William Morris.

31–47 Victor Horta
STAIRWAY, TASSEL HOUSE, BRUSSELS
1892–1893.

Credit: © 2016 – Victor Horta, Bastin & Evrard/ARS NY/SOFAM, Brussels

GAUDÍ The application of graceful linearity to all aspects of design spread across Europe. In Spain, where the style was called *Modernismo*, the major practitioner was the Catalan architect Antoni Gaudí i Cornet (1852–1926). Gaudí integrated natural forms into the design of buildings and parks that are still revolutionary in their dynamic freedom of line.

In 1904, the wealthy industrialist Josep Batlló commissioned Gaudí to design a private residence to surpass the lavish houses of other prominent families in Barcelona. Gaudí convinced his patron to retain the underlying structure of an existing building, but transform its façade and interior spaces. Gaudí's façade (**FIG. 31–48**) is a dreamlike fantasy of undulating sandstone sculptures and multicolored glass and tile surfaces, imaginatively mixing the Islamic, Gothic, and Baroque visual traditions of Barcelona. The gaping lower-story windows are the source of the building's nickname, the "house of yawns,"

31-48 Antoni Gaudí **CASA BATLLÒ, BARCELONA**

43 Passeig de Gràcia. 1900–1907.

Credit: Vincent Abbey Photography

while the use of what look like giant human shinbones for upright supports led others to call it the "house of bones." The roof resembles a recumbent dragon with overlapping tiles as scales. A fanciful turret at its edge recalls the sword of St. George—patron saint of Catalunya—plunged into the back of the dragon, his legendary foe. Gaudí's highly personal alternative to academic historicism and modern industrialization reflects his affinity with Iberian traditions as well as his concern to provide imaginative surroundings to enrich the lives of city dwellers.

GUIMARD The leading French practitioner of Art Nouveau was Hector Guimard (1867–1942), who embraced the movement after meeting Horta in 1895. Guimard is most famous for his designs of entrances to the Paris Métro (subway) at the turn of the century, but he devoted much of his career to interior design and furnishings, such as this **DESK** that he made for himself (**FIG. 31–49**). Instead of a static and stable object, Guimard handcrafted an asymmetrical, organic entity that seems to undulate and grow around the person who sits at it.

31–49 Hector Guimard **DESK**
c. 1899 (remodeled after 1909).
Olive wood with ash panels,
28¾ × 47¾″ (73 × 121 cm).
Museum of Modern Art, New York.
Gift of Madame Hector Guimard.

Credit: © 2016. Digital Image, The Museum of Modern Art/Scala, Florence/Art Resource, NY

TOULOUSE-LAUTREC Henri de Toulouse-Lautrec (1864–1901) suffered from a genetic disorder that stunted his growth and left him physically disabled. Born into an aristocratic family in southern France, he moved to Paris in 1882, where his private academic training was transformed when he discovered the work of Degas. He also discovered Montmartre, the entertainment district of Paris that housed the most bohemian of the avant-garde artists. From the late 1880s, Toulouse-Lautrec dedicated himself to depicting the nightlife of Montmartre—the cafés, theaters, dance halls, and brothels that he himself frequented.

Between 1891 and 1901, Toulouse-Lautrec designed roughly 30 lithographic posters for Montmartre's more famous nightspots, advertising their most popular entertainers. One features the notoriously limber dancer **JANE AVRIL** performing the infamous can-can (**FIG. 31–50**). Toulouse-Lautrec places Avril on a stage that zooms into the background. The hand and face of a double-bass player, part of his instrument, and pages of music frame the poster in the extreme foreground at lower right—a bold foreshortening that recalls the compositions of Degas (SEE FIG. 31–33). But Toulouse-Lautrec's image emphasizes Avril's sexuality in order to draw in the crowds, while Degas's pictures

coax visual beauty from frank Realism. Toulouse-Lautrec outlines forms, flattens space, and suppresses modeling to accommodate the cheap colored lithographic printing technique he used, but the resulting bold silhouettes and curving lines are distinctively Art Nouveau.

31–50 Henri de Toulouse-Lautrec **JANE AVRIL**
1893. Four-color lithograph, 51⅛ × 37⅜″ (129.85 × 94.93 cm). Los Angeles County Museum of Art. Gift of Mr and Mrs Billy Wilder (59.80.15).

The Beginnings of Modernism

In what way do the innovative use of new technology in architectural design and the highly structured painting style of Paul Cézanne point toward twentieth-century Modernism?

The history of late nineteenth-century architecture reflects a dilemma faced by the industrial city, caught between the classicizing tradition of the Beaux-Arts academic style and the materials, construction methods, and new aesthetic of industry. The École des Beaux-Arts, although marginalized by the end of the century by new trends in painting, came into its own after 1880 as the training ground for European and American architects, while industrialization in places like Chicago simultaneously demanded new ways of thinking about tall and large buildings.

At the same time, Paul Cézanne, late in his life, altered the course of avant-garde painting by returning to an intense visual scrutiny of the world around him. In 1906, the year Cézanne died, a retrospective exhibition of his life's work in Paris revealed his methods to the next generation of artists, who would be the creators of Modernism.

European Architecture: Technology and Structure

The pace of life speeded up considerably over the course of the nineteenth century. Industrialization allowed people to manufacture more, consume more, travel more, and do more, in greater numbers than before. Industrialization caused urbanization, which in turn demanded more industrialization. A belief in the perfectibility of society spawned more than 20 international fairs celebrating innovations in industry and technology. One of the first of these took place in London in 1851. The Great Exhibition of the Industry of All Nations was mounted by the British to display their industrial might, assert their right to empire, and subdue lingering public unrest after the 1848 revolutions elsewhere in Europe. The centerpiece of the Great Exhibition, the Crystal Palace, introduced new building techniques and aesthetics.

THE CRYSTAL PALACE   The revolutionary construction of **THE CRYSTAL PALACE** (**FIG. 31-51**), created by Joseph Paxton (1803–1865), featured a structural skeleton of cast iron that held iron-framed glass panes measuring 49 by 30 inches, the largest size that could be mass-produced at the time. Prefabricated wooden ribs and bars supported the panes. The triple-tiered edifice was the largest space that had ever been enclosed—1,851 feet long, covering more than 18 acres, and providing almost a million square feet of exhibition space. The central vaulted transept—based on the design for new cast-iron train stations—rose 108 feet to accommodate a row of the elm trees dear to Prince Albert, the husband of Queen Victoria (ruled 1837–1901). By the end of the exhibition, 6 million people had visited it, most agreeing that the Crystal Palace was a technological marvel. Even so, most architects and critics, still wedded to Neoclassicism and Romanticism, considered it a work of engineering rather than legitimate architecture because the novelty of its iron-and-glass frame overshadowed its Gothic Revival style.

31–51 Joseph Paxton
THE CRYSTAL PALACE
London. 1850–1851. Iron, glass, and wood. (Print of the Great Exhibition of 1851; printed and published by Dickinson Brothers, London, 1854. Illustration by Joseph Nash and Robert Haghe. British Library, London.)

BIBLIOTHÈQUE NATIONALE Henri Labrouste (1801–1875)—trained as an architect at the École des Beaux-Arts, where he also taught—had a radical desire to combine the Academy's historicizing approach to architecture with the technical innovations of industrial engineering. Although reluctant to push his ideas at the École, he pursued them in his architecture. The **READING ROOM** of the Bibliothèque Nationale (**FIG. 31-52**) is an example of this fusion. A series of domes form the ceiling—faced with bright white ceramic tiles, crowned with glass-covered oculi that light the reading room, and supported on thin iron arches and columns that open the space visually. The mixture of historical allusions in the Classical detailing, combined with the vast open space made possible by industrial materials, is thoroughly modern.

The Chicago School

In the United States up until this time, as in Europe, major architectural projects were expected to embody Beaux-Arts historicism. But the modern city required new building types for industry, transportation, commerce, storage, and habitation—types that would accommodate more people and more activities in urban areas where land prices were skyrocketing. Chicago was a case in point.

As the transportation hub for grain, livestock, and other produce headed from the rural Midwest to the cities of the east and west coasts, Chicago had become a populous, wealthy city by the 1890s. As new department stores, commercial facilities, and office buildings were designed, primarily with practical needs in mind, Chicago also became the cradle for a novel way of thinking about urban design and construction in which function gave birth to architectural form.

WORLD'S COLUMBIAN EXPOSITION Richard Morris Hunt (1827–1895) was the first American to study architecture at the École des Beaux-Arts in Paris. Extraordinarily skilled in Beaux-Arts historicism and determined to raise the standards of American architecture, he built in every accepted style, including Gothic, French Classicist, and Italian Renaissance. After the Civil War, Hunt built many lavish mansions for a growing class of wealthy eastern industrialists and financiers, emulating aristocratic European models.

Late in his career, Hunt supervised the design of the 1893 World's Columbian Exposition in Chicago, commemorating the 400th anniversary of Christopher Columbus's arrival in the Americas. Rather than focus on engineering wonders as in previous fairs, the Chicago planning board decided to build "permanent buildings—a dream city." To create a sense of unity among these buildings (which were, in fact temporary, constructed from a mixture of plaster and fibrous materials rather than masonry), a single style for the fair was settled upon—the Classical style, alluding to ancient Greece and republican Rome to reflect America's pride in its own democratic institutions as well as its emergence as a world power. A photograph of the **COURT OF HONOR** (FIG. 31-53) shows the Beaux-Arts style of the so-called "White City."

The World's Columbian Exposition was intended to be a model of the ideal American city—clean, spacious, carefully planned, and Classically styled—in contrast to the soot and overcrowding of most unplanned American cities. Frederick Law Olmsted, the designer of New York City's Central Park, was responsible for the exhibition's landscape design. He converted the marshy lakefront into a series of lagoons, canals, ponds, and islands, some laid out formally, as in the White City, and others informally, as in the Midway, which contained the busy conglomerate of pavilions representing "less civilized" nations. Between these two parts stood the world's first Ferris wheel, which provided a spectacular view of the fair and the city. After the fair, most of its buildings were demolished, but Olmsted's landscaping has remained.

RICHARDSON The second American architect to study at the École des Beaux-Arts was Henry Hobson Richardson (1838–1886). Born in Louisiana and educated at Harvard and Tulane, Richardson returned from Paris in 1865 to settle in New York. He designed architecture in a variety of revival styles but is most famous for a robust, rusticated style known as Richardsonian Romanesque. In 1885, he designed the **MARSHALL FIELD WHOLESALE STORE** in Chicago (FIG. 31-54), drawing on the design and scale of Italian Renaissance palaces such as the Palazzo Medici-Riccardi in Florence (SEE FIG. 20-9). Although the rough, blocklike stone facing, the arched windows, and the decorated cornice all evoke historical architecture, Richardson's mixture of diverse features resulted in a readily identifiable personal style.

Plain and sturdy, Richardson's building was a revelation to the young architects of Chicago, then engaged in rebuilding the city after the disastrous fire of 1871. About the same time, new technology for producing steel—a strong, cheap alloy of iron—created new structural opportunities for architects. The rapidly rising cost of urban land made tall buildings desirable; structural steel and the electric elevator (developed during the 1880s) made them possible. William Le Baron Jenney (1832–1907) built the first steel-skeleton building in Chicago; his lead was quickly

31-53 COURT OF HONOR, WORLD'S COLUMBIAN EXPOSITION, CHICAGO
1893. View from the east.

Surrounding the Court of Honor were, from left to right, the Agriculture Building by McKim, Mead, and White; the Administration Building by Richard Morris Hunt; and the Manufactures and Liberal Arts Building by George B. Post. The architectural ensemble was collectively called the White City, a nickname by which the exposition was also popularly known. The statue in the foreground is *The Republic* by Daniel Chester French.

Credit: © Corbis

31–54 Henry Hobson Richardson **MARSHALL FIELD WHOLESALE STORE, CHICAGO**

1885–1887. Demolished c. 1935.

Credit: Courtesy the Library of Congress

utilities. A richly decorated foliate frieze in terra-cotta relief crowns the building, punctuated by bull's-eye windows and capped by a thick cornice slab.

The Wainwright Building's outward appearance clearly articulates three different levels of function: shops at the bottom, offices in the middle, and mechanical utilities at the top. It illustrates Sullivan's stated architectural philosophy: "Form ever follows function." This idea was adopted as a credo by Modernist architects, who used it to justify removal of all surface decoration from buildings. However, although Sullivan designed the Wainwright Building for function, he also created an expressive building. The thick corner piers, for example, are not structurally necessary—an internal steel-frame skeleton supports the building—but they emphasize its vertical thrust. The thinner piers between the office windows, which rise uninterrupted from the third story to the attic, echo and reinforce its spring and verticality. As Sullivan put it, a tall office building "must be every inch a proud and soaring thing, rising in sheer exultation."

followed by younger architects in what was known as the Chicago School.

SULLIVAN The Chicago School architects produced not only a new style of architecture but a new kind of building—the skyscraper. An early example is Louis Sullivan's **WAINWRIGHT BUILDING** in St. Louis, Missouri (**FIG. 31-55**). The Boston-born Sullivan (1856–1924) studied for a year at the Massachusetts Institute of Technology (MIT), home of the United States' first formal architecture program, and for an equally brief period at the École des Beaux-Arts in Paris, where he developed a distaste for historicism. He settled in Chicago in 1875, partly because of the building boom there that had followed the fire of 1871. In 1883 he entered into a partnership with the Danish-born engineer Dankmar Adler (1844–1900).

Sullivan's first major skyscraper, the Wainwright Building has a U-shaped plan that provides an interior light-well for the illumination of inside offices. The ground floor, designed to house shops, has wide plate-glass windows for the display of merchandise. The second story, or mezzanine, also features large windows for the illumination of the shop offices. Above the mezzanine rise seven identical floors of offices lit by rectangular windows, and an attic story houses the building's mechanical plant and

In the Wainwright Building that exultation culminates in the rich vegetative ornament that swirls around the crown of the building like the foliated capital of a Corinthian column. The tripartite structure of the building itself suggests the Classical column with its base, shaft, and capital, reflecting the lingering influence of Classical design principles. Only in the twentieth century would Modernist architects reject tradition entirely to create an architectural aesthetic stripped of applied decoration.

31–55 Louis Sullivan **WAINWRIGHT BUILDING, ST. LOUIS** Missouri. 1890–1891.

Credit: © Art on File/Corbis

The City Park

Parks originated during the second millennium BCE in China as enclosed hunting reserves for kings and the nobility. In Europe from the Middle Ages to the eighteenth century, they remained private recreation grounds for the privileged. The first urban park intended for the public was in Munich, Germany. Laid out by Friedrich Ludwig von Sckell in 1789–1795 in the picturesque style of an English landscape garden (SEE FIG. 30–16), it contained irregular lakes, gently sloping hills, broad meadows, and paths meandering through wooded areas.

The crowding and pollution of cities during the Industrial Revolution prompted the creation of large public parks whose green open spaces helped purify the air and provided city dwellers of all classes with a place for recreation. Numerous municipal parks were built in Britain during the 1830s and 1840s and in Paris during the 1850s and 1860s, when Georges-Eugène Haussmann redesigned the former royal hunting forests of the Bois de Boulogne and the Bois de Vincennes in the English style favored by Emperor Napoleon III.

In American cities before 1857, the only public outdoor spaces were small squares found between certain intersections, and larger gardens, such as the Boston Public Garden, neither of which filled the growing need for varied recreational facilities in the city. For a time, landscaped suburban cemeteries in the picturesque style were popular sites for strolling, picnicking, and even horse racing—an incongruous set of uses that strikingly demonstrated the need for more urban parks.

The rapid growth of Manhattan in the nineteenth century spurred civic leaders to set aside parkland while open space still existed. The city purchased an 843-acre tract in the center of the island and in 1857 announced a competition for its design as Central Park. The competition required that designs include a parade ground, playgrounds, a site for an exhibition or concert hall, sites for a

31–56 Frederick Law Olmsted and Calvert Vaux **PLAN OF CENTRAL PARK, NEW YORK CITY**
Revised and extended park layout as shown on a map of 1873.

Credit: Frederick Law Olmsted & Calvert Vaux/City of New York, Department of Parks fountain and for a viewing tower, a flower garden, a pond for ice skating, and four east–west cross-streets so that the park would not interfere with the city's vehicular traffic. The latter condition was pivotal to the winning design, drawn up by architect Calvert Vaux (1824–1895) and park superintendent Frederick Law Olmsted (1822–1903), which sank the crosstown roads in trenches hidden below the surface of the park and designed separate routes for carriages, horseback riders, and pedestrians (**FIG. 31–56**).

Believing that the "park of any great city [should be] an antithesis to its bustling, paved, rectangular, walled-in streets," Olmsted and Vaux designed picturesque landscaping in the English tradition, with the irregularities of topography and planting used as positive design elements. Except for a few formal elements, such as the tree-lined mall that leads to the Classically designed Bethesda Terrace and Fountain, the park is remarkably informal and naturalistic. Where the land was low, Olmstead and Vaux further depressed it, installing drainage tiles and carving out ponds and meadows. They planted clumps of trees to contrast with open spaces, and exposed natural outcroppings of schist to provide dramatic, rocky scenery. They arranged walking trails, bridle paths, and carriage drives through the park with a series of changing vistas. Intentionally appealing were the views from the apartment houses of the wealthy on the streets surrounding the park. An existing reservoir divided the park into two sections. Olmsted and Vaux developed the southern half more completely and located most of the sporting facilities and amenities there, while leaving the northern half more like a nature reserve. Largely complete by the end of the Civil War, Central Park

was widely considered a triumph, launching a movement to build similar parks in cities across the United States.

Cézanne

No artist had a greater impact on the next generation of Modernist painters than Paul Cézanne (1839–1906). The son of a prosperous banker in the southern French city of Aix-en-Provence, Cézanne studied art first in Aix and then in Paris, where he participated in the circle of Realist artists around Manet. His early pictures, somber in color and coarsely painted, often depicted Romantic themes of drama and violence and were consistently rejected by the Salon.

In the early 1870s under the influence of Pissarro, Cézanne changed his style. He adopted a bright palette and broken brushwork and began painting landscapes. Like the Impressionists, with whom he exhibited in 1874 and 1877, Cézanne dedicated himself to the study of what he called the "sensations" of nature. Unlike the Impressionists, however, he did not seek to capture transitory effects of light and atmosphere; instead, he created highly structured paintings through a methodical application of color that merged drawing and modeling into a single process. His professed aim was to "make of Impressionism something solid and durable, like the art of the museums."

Cézanne's dedicated pursuit of this goal is evident in his repeated paintings of **MONT SAINTE-VICTOIRE**, a mountain close to his home in Aix, which he depicted in hundreds of drawings and about 30 oil paintings between the 1880s and his death in 1906. The painting in **FIGURE 31–57** presents the mountain rising above the Arc Valley, which is dotted with buildings and trees and crossed at the far right by a railroad viaduct. Framing the scene to the left is an evergreen tree, which echoes the contours of the mountains, creating visual harmony between the two principal elements of the composition. The even

31–57 Paul Cézanne **MONT SAINTE-VICTOIRE**

c. 1885–1887. Oil on canvas, 25½ × 32″ (64.8 × 92.3 cm). The Samuel Courtauld Trust, the Courtauld Gallery, London. (P.1934.SC.55).

Credit: © Samuel Courtauld Trust, The Courtauld Gallery, London, UK/ Bridgeman Images light, stable atmosphere, and absence of human activity create the sensation of timeless stillness.

Cézanne's handling of paint is deliberate and controlled. His brushstrokes, which vary from short, parallel hatchings to light lines to broader swaths of flat color, weave together the elements of the painting into a unified but flattened visual space. The surface design vies with the pictorial effect of receding space, generating tension between the illusion of three dimensions within the picture and the physical reality of its two-dimensional surface. Recession into depth is suggested by the tree in the foreground—a *repoussoir* (French for "something that pushes back") that helps draw the eye into the valley—and by the transition from the saturated hues in the foreground to the lighter values in the background, creating an effect of atmospheric perspective. But recession into depth is challenged by other more intense colors in both the foreground and background and by the tree branches in the sky, which follow the contours of the mountain, avoiding overlapping and subtly suggesting that the two are on the same plane. Photographs of this scene show that Cézanne created a composition in accordance with a harmony that he felt the scene demanded, rather than reproducing in detail the appearance of the lansdscape. His commitment to the painting as a work of art, which he called "something other than reality"—not a representation of nature but "a construction after nature"—was a crucial step toward the modern art of the next century.

Spatial ambiguities of a different sort appear in Cézanne's later still lifes, in which many of the objects may seem at first glance to be incorrectly drawn. In **STILL LIFE WITH BASKET OF APPLES** (FIG. 31–58), for example, the right side of the table is higher than the left, the wine bottle has two distinct silhouettes, and the pastries on the table next to it tilt upward toward the viewer, while we seem to see the apples head-on. Such shifting viewpoints are not evidence of incompetence; they come from Cézanne's rejection of the rules of traditional perspective. Although linear perspective requires that the eye of the artist (and thus the viewer) occupy a fixed point relative to the scene (see "Renaissance Perspective" in Chapter 20 on page 623), Cézanne presents the objects in his still lifes from a variety of different positions just as we might move around or turn our heads to take everything in. The composition as a whole, assembled from multiple sightings, is consequently complex and dynamic. Instead of faithfully reproducing static objects from a stable vantage point, Cézanne recreated, or reconstructed, our viewing experiences through time and space.

Cézanne enjoyed little professional success until the last years of his life, when his paintings became more complex internally and more detached from observed reality. **THE LARGE BATHERS** (FIG. 31–59), probably begun in the last year of his life and left unfinished, was the largest canvas he ever painted. It returns in several ways to the academic conventions of history painting as a monumental, multi-figured composition of nude figures in a landscape setting that suggests a mythological theme. The bodies cluster in two pyramidal groups at left and right, beneath a canopy of trees that opens in the middle onto a triangular

31–58 Paul Cézanne **STILL LIFE WITH BASKET OF APPLES**

1880–1894. Oil on canvas, 24⅜ × 31″ (62.5 × 79.5 cm). The Art Institute of Chicago. Helen Birch Bartlett Memorial Collection (1926.252).

Credit: Photo © The Art Institute of Chicago

expanse of water, landscape, and sky. The figures assume statuesque, often Classical poses and seem to exist outside recognizable time and space. Using a restricted palette of blues, greens, ochers, and roses laid down over a white ground, Cézanne suffused the picture with a cool light that emphasizes the scene's remoteness from everyday life.

Despite its unfinished state, *The Large Bathers* brings nineteenth-century painting full circle by reviving the Arcadian landscape, a much earlier category of academic painting, while opening a new window on some radical rethinking about the fundamental practice and purpose of art.

31–59 Paul Cézanne **THE LARGE BATHERS**
1906. Oil on canvas, 6′10″ × 8′2″ (2.08 × 2.49 m). Philadelphia Museum of Art. The W.P. Wilstach Collection.

Credit: © 2016. Philadelphia Museum of Art/Art Resource, NY/Scala, Florence

Think About It

1   Discuss the interests and goals of French academic painters and sculptors and explain how their work differed from other art of the same time and place, such as that of the Realists and Impressionists.

2   Discuss the innovative content of Impressionist paintings and explain how it differs from that of traditional European paintings by focusing on one specific work from the chapter.

3   Discuss Gustave Courbet's Realism in works such as *The Stone Breakers* (**FIG. 31-12**) and *A Burial at Ornans* (**FIG. 31-13**) in relation to the social and political issues of mid-century France.

4   Explain how the photographic process works and evaluate the roles played by Louis-Jacques-Mandé Daguerre and Henry Fox Talbot in the emergence of this medium.

Crosscurrents

European artists often include reflections of art from the past in works that address concerns of the present. This is certainly the case here, where Manet's *Olympia* recalls aspects of the composition and subject of this famous painting by Titian. The messages of the two paintings are very different, however. Analyze the meanings of these paintings. Do they express the concerns of artist, patron, or society, or some mixture of the three?

FIG. 21–30

FIG. 31–18

32–1 Pablo Picasso **MA JOLIE**

1911–1912. Oil on canvas, 39⅜ × 25¾″ (100 × 65.4 cm). Museum of Modern Art, New York.

Acquired through the Lillie P. Bliss Bequest (176.1945).

Chapter 32
Modern Art in Europe and the Americas, 1900–1950

Learning Objectives

32.a Identify the visual hallmarks of modern European and American art and architecture from 1900–1950 for formal, technical, and expressive qualities.

32.b Interpret the meaning of works of modern European and American art from 1900–1950 based on their themes, subjects, and symbols.

32.c Relate modern European and American art and artists from 1900–1950 to their cultural, economic, and political contexts.

32.d Apply the vocabulary and concepts relevant to modern European and American art, architecture, artists, and art history from 1900–1950.

32.e Interpret a work of modern European or American art from 1900–1950 using the art historical methods of observation, comparison, and inductive reasoning.

32.f Select visual and textual evidence in various media to support an argument or an interpretation of a work of modern European or American art from 1900–1950.

Pablo Picasso was a towering presence at the center of the Parisian art world throughout much of the twentieth century, continually transforming the style, forms, meanings, and conceptual frameworks of his art in relation to the many factors at play in the world around him. Early in the century in his great Cubist work **MA JOLIE** (**FIG. 32-1**) of 1911–1912, Picasso challenged his viewers to think about the very nature of communication through painting. Remnants of the subjects Picasso worked from are evident throughout, but any attempt to reconstruct the "subject"—a woman with a stringed instrument—poses difficulties for the viewer. *Ma Jolie* ("My Pretty One," the nickname Picasso used for his lover of the time, Marcelle Humbert) is in some sense a portrait, though Picasso makes us work to see and to understand the figure. We can discover several things about Ma Jolie from the painting; we can see parts of her head, her shoulders, the curve of her body, and a hand. But in Paris in 1911, "Ma Jolie" was also the title of a popular song, so the inclusion of writing and a musical staff and treble clef in the painting suggests other meanings. Our first impulse might be to wonder what exactly is pictured. Picasso provided the sarcastic answer, "My Pretty One."

On the other hand, it might be argued that the human subject provided only the raw material for a formal, abstract arrangement. A subtle tension between order and disorder is maintained throughout this painting. For example, the shifting effect of the surface—a delicately patterned texture of grays and browns—is unified through the use of short, horizontal brushstrokes. Similarly, with the linear elements, horizontals and verticals at first seem to dominate, but strong diagonals and occasional curves challenge the grid-like regularity. The combination of horizontal brushwork and right angles firmly establishes a grid that effectively counteracts the surface flux. Moreover, the repetition of certain diagonals and the relative lack of details in the upper left and upper right create a pyramidal shape reminiscent of Classical systems of compositional stability (SEE FIG. 21-1). Thus, what at first may seem a chaotic composition of lines and muted colors turns out to be a carefully organized design. For many, the aesthetic satisfaction of such a work depends on the way chaos seems to resolve itself into order.

In 1923, Picasso said, "Cubism is no different from any other school of painting. The same principles and the same elements are common to all. The fact that for a long time Cubism has not been understood … means nothing. I do not read English, [but] this does not mean that the English language does not exist, and why should I blame anyone … but myself if I cannot understand [it]?"

Europe and America in the Early Twentieth Century

What are the political and social backgrounds for early twentieth-century European and American art and architecture?

At the beginning of the twentieth century, the fragile idea that "civilization" would inexorably continue to progress began to crack and finally fell apart in an orgy of violence during World War I. Beginning in August 1914, the war initially pitted the Allies (Britain, France, and Russia) against the Central Powers (Germany and the Austro-Hungarian Empire) and the Ottoman Empire. The United States eventually entered the war on the side of Britain and France in 1917, helping to guarantee victory for the Allies the following year.

World War I transformed almost every aspect of Western society, including politics, economics, and culture (MAP 32-1). The war was fought with twentieth-century technology but nineteenth-century strategies. Trench warfare and the Maxim gun (an early machine gun) caused the deaths of millions of soldiers and the horrible maiming of millions more. Europe lost an entire generation of young men; whole societies were shattered. Europeans began to question the nineteenth-century imperial social and political order that had brought about this carnage and foreshadowed a change in the character of

warfare itself. Future wars would be fought over ideology as well as territory.

In the first half of the twentieth century, three very different political ideologies struggled for world supremacy: communism (as in China and the Union of Soviet Socialist Republics, or U.S.S.R.), fascism (as in Italy and Germany), and liberal–democratic capitalism (as in North America, Britain, and Western Europe). The October 1917 Russian Revolution led to the Russian Civil War and the eventual triumph of the Bolshevik ("Majority") Communist Party led by Vladimir Lenin (1870–1924), as well as to the founding of the U.S.S.R. in 1922. After Lenin's death and an internal power struggle, Joseph Stalin (1878–1953) emerged as leader of the U.S.S.R. Under Stalin, the U.S.S.R. took over several neighboring states, suffered through the Great Purge of the 1930s, and lost tens of millions during the war against Nazi Germany.

Fascism first took firm root in Italy in October 1922 when Benito Mussolini (1883–1945) came to power. In Germany, meanwhile, the postwar democratic Weimar Republic collapsed under a combination of rampant hyperinflation and the enmity between communists, socialists, centrists, Christian Democrats, and fascists. By the time of the 1932 parliamentary election, Germany's political and economic deterioration had paved the way for a Nazi Party victory and the chancellorship of its leader, Adolf Hitler (1889–1945). Fascism was not limited to Germany and Italy—it was widespread throughout Central and

MAP 32-1 EUROPE, THE AMERICAS, AND NORTH AFRICA, 1900–1950

Eastern Europe and on the Iberian peninsula, where General Francisco Franco (1892–1975) emerged victorious from the Spanish Civil War.

The economic impact of World War I was global. Although the United States emerged from it as the leading economic power in the world, hyperinflation in Germany during the 1920s, the repudiation of German war debt under the Versailles Treaty, and the United States stock market crash of 1929 plunged the Western world into a widespread economic depression that exacerbated political hostility between the major European countries, served as an incubator for fascism and communism in Europe, and tore apart the social and political fabric of Britain and America. In the United States, President Franklin D. Roosevelt (1882–1945, president 1933–1945) created the New Deal programs in 1933 to stimulate the economy with government spending, and France and Britain took their first steps toward the modern welfare state. But ultimately only the military build-up of World War II would end the United States's Great Depression. This war lasted from 1939 to 1945, and the human carnage it caused to both soldiers and civilians, particularly in German concentration camps, raised difficult questions about the very nature of our humanity.

Changes in scientific knowledge were also dramatic. Albert Einstein's publication of his Special Theory of Relativity in 1905 had shaken the foundations of Newtonian physics; they collapsed with the subsequent development of quantum theory by Niels Bohr, Werner Heisenberg, and Max Planck. These developments in physics also unlocked the Pandora's box of nuclear energy; first opened when the British split the atom in 1919, it was fully unleashed on the world when America dropped nuclear bombs on Japan in 1945.

The early twentieth century also witnessed a multitude of innovations in technology and manufacturing: the first powered flight (1903); the mass manufacture of automobiles (1909); the first public radio broadcast (1920); the electrification of most of Western Europe and North America (1920s); and the development of both television (1926) and the jet engine (1937), to mention only a few. Technology led both to better medicines for prolonging life and to more efficient warfare, which shortened it. Information about the outside world became ever more accessible with the advent of radio, television, and film. The visual popular culture of the nineteenth century had been based on paper, but that of the early twentieth century was centered in photographs and films.

Just as quantum physics fundamentally altered our understanding of the physical world, developments in psychology transformed our conception of the workings of the mind and consequently how we viewed ourselves. In 1900, Austrian psychiatrist Sigmund Freud published *The Interpretation of Dreams*, which argues that our behavior

is often motivated not only by reason, but also by powerful forces that work below our level of awareness. The human unconscious, as he described it, includes strong urges for love and power that must be managed if society is to remain peaceful and whole. For Freud, we are always attempting to strike a balance between our rational and irrational sides, often erring on one side or the other. Also in 1900, Russian scientist Ivan Pavlov began feeding dogs only after ringing a bell. Soon the dogs salivated not at the sight of food, but at the sound of the bell. The later discovery that these "conditioned responses" also exist in humans showed that if we manage external stimuli we can control people's appetites. Political leaders of all stripes soon exploited this realization.

Thus the first half of the twentieth century was a time of exciting new theories and technologies, as well as increased access of ordinary people to consumer items, but it was also a time of cataclysmic social, economic, and political change when millions died in wars and concentration camps. These changes, whether for the better or for the worse, shaped the art of the early twentieth century.

Early Modern Art and Architecture in Europe

How is Modernism established and spread in Europe?

Modern artists explored many new ways of seeing their world. Few read academic physics or psychology texts, but their day-to-day life was being transformed by such fields, as well as by many technological advances. Modernist art was frequently subversive and intellectually demanding, and it was often visually, socially, and politically radical. It seems as if every movement in early twentieth-century art chose or acquired a distinctive label and wrote a manifesto or statement of intent, leading this to be described later as the age of "isms."

Most Modern art was still bound to the idea that works of art, regardless of how they challenged vision and thought, were still precious objects—primarily pictures or sculptures. But a few artistic movements—notably Dada and some elements of Surrealism, both prompted by the horrors of World War I—challenged this idea. Their preoccupations built the foundation for much art after 1950.

The Fauves: Wild Beasts of Color

In 1903, a group of discontented artists organized and founded the Salon d'Automne (Autumn Salon), so named to distinguish it from the official Salon that took place every spring. The Autumn Salon provided a showcase for progressive artists, and many major Modernist movements of the twentieth century made their debut in this Salon's

32–2 André Derain **MOUNTAINS AT COLLIOURE**

1905. Oil on canvas, 32 × 39½″ (81.5 × 100 cm). National Gallery of Art, Washington, DC.

John Hay Whitney Collection.

Credit: © 2016 Artists Rights Society (ARS), New York/ADAGP, Paris. Image courtesy the National Gallery of Art, Washington

disorderly halls. The paintings exhibited in 1905 by André Derain (1880–1954), Henri Matisse (1869–1954), and Maurice de Vlaminck (1876–1958) were filled with such brilliant colors and blunt brushwork that the critic Louis Vauxcelles described the young painters as *fauves* ("wild beasts"), the French term by which they soon became known. These artists took the French tradition of color and strong brushwork to new heights of intensity and expressive power and entirely rethought the painting's surface.

Among the first major Fauve works were paintings that Derain and Matisse made in 1905 in the French Mediterranean port town of Collioure. In **MOUNTAINS AT COLLIOURE** (**FIG. 32–2**), Derain used short, broad strokes of pure color, placing next to each other the complementary colors of blue and orange (as in the mountain range) or red and green (as in the trees) to intensify the hue of each. He chose a range of semi-naturalistic colors—the grass and the trees are green, the trunks are close to brown. This is recognizable as a landscape, but it is also a self-conscious exercise in

32–3 Henri Matisse **THE WOMAN WITH THE HAT**

1905. Oil on canvas, 31¾ × 23½″ (80.6 × 59.7 cm). San Francisco Museum of Modern Art. Bequest of Elise S. Haas.

Credit: © 2016 Succession H. Matisse/Artists Rights Society (ARS), New York painting. The uniform brightness of the colors undermines any effect of atmospheric perspective. As a consequence, viewers remain aware that they are looking at a flat canvas covered with paint, not an illusionistic rendering of the natural world. This tension between image and painting, along with the explosive effect of the color, generates a visual energy that positively pulses from the painting. Derain described his colors as "sticks of dynamite" and his stark juxtapositions of complementary hues as "deliberate disharmonies."

Matisse was equally interested in "deliberate disharmonies." His **WOMAN WITH THE HAT** (FIG. 32–3) was particularly controversial at the 1905 Autumn Salon because of its thick swatches of crude, seemingly arbitrary, non-naturalistic color and its broad and blunt brushwork. For instance, the face of the subject—Matisse's wife Amélie, who was a milliner and probably sold elaborate hats like the one she wears here—includes bold green stripes across her brow and down her nose, as well as a blue rectangle between her lips and her chin. The uproar, however, did not stop siblings Gertrude and Leo Stein, among the most important American patrons of avant-garde art at this time, from purchasing the work in 1905.

The same year, Matisse also began painting **THE JOY OF LIFE (LE BONHEUR DE VIVRE)** (FIG. 32–4), a large pastoral landscape depicting a golden age—a reclining nude in the foreground plays pan pipes, another piper herds goats in the right mid-ground, lovers embrace in the foreground, and others dance in the background. Like Cézanne's *The Large Bathers* painted in the same year (SEE FIG. 31–59), *The Joy of Life* is academic in scale and theme, but avant-garde in most other respects—notably in the way the figures appear "flattened" and in the distortion of the spatial relations between them. Matisse emphasized expressive color, drawing on folk-art traditions in his use of unmodeled forms and bold outlines. In the past, artists might have expressed feeling through the figures' poses or facial expressions, but now, he wrote, "The whole arrangement of my picture is expressive. The place occupied by figures or objects, the empty spaces around them, the proportions, everything plays a part…. The chief aim of color should be to serve expression as well as possible."

32–4 Henri Matisse **THE JOY OF LIFE (LE BONHEUR DE VIVRE)**
1905–1906. Oil on canvas, 5′8½″ × 7′9¾″ (1.74 × 2.38 m). The Barnes Foundation, Merion, Pennsylvania. (BF 719).

Credit: The Bridgeman Art Library © 2016 Succession H. Matisse/Artists Rights Society (ARS), New York/Bridgeman Images

Picasso, "Primitivism," and the Coming of Cubism

Of all Modern art "isms" created before World War I, Cubism was probably the most influential. The joint invention of Pablo Picasso (1881–1973) and Georges Braque (1882–1963)—who worked side by side in Paris, the undisputed capital of the art world before 1950—Cubism proved a fruitful launching pad for both artists, allowing them to comment on modern life and investigate the ways in which artists perceive and represent the world around them.

PICASSO'S EARLY ART Born in Málaga, Spain, Picasso was an artistic child prodigy. During his teenage years at the National Academy in Madrid, he painted highly polished works that presaged a conservative artistic career, but his restless temperament led him to Barcelona in 1899, where he involved himself in avant-garde circles. In 1900, he first traveled to Paris, and in 1904 he moved there and would live in France for the rest of his life. During this early period Picasso painted urban outcasts in weary poses using a coldly expressive blue palette that led art historians to label this his Blue Period. These paintings seem motivated by Picasso's political sensitivity to those he considered victims of modern capitalist society, which eventually led him to join the Communist Party.

In 1904–1905, Picasso joined a larger group of Paris-based avant-garde artists and became fascinated with the subject of *saltimbanques* ("traveling acrobats"). He rarely painted these entertainers performing, however, focusing instead on the hardships of their existence on the margins of society. In **FAMILY OF SALTIMBANQUES** (**FIG. 32–5**), a painting from his Rose Period (so called because of the introduction of that color into his palette), five *saltimbanques* stand in weary silence to the left, while a sixth, a woman, sits in curious isolation on the right. All seem psychologically withdrawn, as uncommunicative as the empty landscape they occupy. The harlequin figure to the far left is commonly identified as a self-portrait of the artist, suggesting his identification with the circus performers as marginalized and melancholy illusionists. By 1905, Picasso had begun to sell these works to a number of important collectors.

Soon Picasso became one of the first artists in Paris to use images from African art in his paintings. In 1906, the Louvre installed a newly acquired collection of sculpture

32–5 Pablo Picasso **FAMILY OF SALTIMBANQUES** 1905. Oil on canvas, 6'11¾ × 7'6⅜" (2.1 × 2.3 m). National Gallery of Art, Washington, DC. Chester Dale Collection (1963.10.190).

Credit: © 2016 Estate of Pablo Picasso/Artists Rights Society (ARS), New York. Image courtesy the National Gallery of Art, Washington

32-6 Pablo Picasso
LES DEMOISELLES D'AVIGNON (THE YOUNG LADIES OF AVIGNON)

1907. Oil on canvas, 8′ × 7′8″ (2.43 × 2.33 m). Museum of Modern Art, New York. Acquired through the Lillie P. Bliss Bequest (333.1939).

Credit: © 2016 Estate of Pablo Picasso/Artists Rights Society (ARS), New York. © 2016. Digital image, The Museum of Modern Art, New York/Scala, Florence

from the Iberian peninsula (present-day Spain and Portugal) dating from the sixth and fifth centuries BCE. Picasso certainly saw those works, but it was an exhibition of African masks that he saw around the same time that really changed the way he thought about art. The exact date of this encounter is not known, but it might have occurred at the Musée d'Éthnographie du Trocadéro, which had opened to the public in 1878. Picasso greatly admired the expressive power and formal strangeness of African masks, and since African art was relatively inexpensive, he also bought several pieces from Parisian shops and kept them in his studio.

The term **primitivism** refers to the widespread tendency among Modern artists to scour the art of other cultures beyond the Western tradition for inspiration. It is not benignly descriptive; it carries modern European perceptions that Western culture is more civilized, more developed, and more complex than other cultures, which are less civilized, less developed, and simpler. It could be argued that just as colonizing nations exploited "primitive" lands in the nineteenth century for raw materials and labor to increase their own wealth and power, so did

Western artists exploit the visual cultures of "primitive" nations to amplify ideas about themselves. Many early Modern artists thus represented other cultures and used aspects of their art without understanding—or really caring to understand—how those cultures actually functioned or how their art was used. This was the case with Picasso.

His contact with African art had a huge impact on **LES DEMOISELLES D'AVIGNON (THE YOUNG LADIES OF AVIGNON)** (**FIG. 32-6**), one of the most radical and complex paintings of the twentieth century. "*Demoiselle*" was a common euphemism for prostitute at this time, and Avignon was the name of a street in the red-light district in Barcelona. The work's boldness, however, resides not only in its subject matter, but also in its size: nearly 8 feet square. Picasso may have undertaken such a large painting in 1907 to compete with both Matisse—who had exhibited *The Joy of Life* (SEE FIG. 32-4) in the Salon des Indépendants of 1906—and Cézanne—whose *Large Bathers* (SEE FIG. 31-59) was shown the same year. Like Matisse and Cézanne, Picasso revived and changed the ideas of large-scale academic history painting, using the traditional subject of nude women shown in an interior space. There are other echoes of the

Western tradition in the handling of the figures. The two women in the center display themselves to the viewer like Venus rising from the sea (SEE FIGS. 20–35, 31–5), while the one to the left takes a rigid pose with a striding stance, recalling a Greek *kouros* (SEE FIG. 5–18), and the one seated on the right might suggest the pose of Manet's *Luncheon on the Grass* (SEE FIG. 31–17). But not all visual references point to the Western tradition. Iberian sources stand behind the faces of the three leftmost figures, with their flattened features and wide, almond-shaped eyes. The masklike faces of the two figures at right imitate African art.

Picasso has created an unsettling picture from these sources. The women are shielded by masks, flattened and fractured into sharp, angular shapes. The space they inhabit is incoherent and convulsive. The central pair raise their arms in a conventional gesture of accessibility but contradict it with their hard, piercing gazes and tight mouths that create what art historian Leo Steinberg called "a tidal wave of female aggression." Even the fruit displayed in the foreground, symbols of female sexuality, seems brittle and dangerous. These women, Picasso suggests, are not the gentle and passive creatures that men would like them to be. This viewpoint contradicts an enduring tradition, prevalent at least since the Renaissance, of portraying sexual availability in the female nude, just as strongly as Picasso's treatment of space shatters the reliance on orderly perspective, also standard since the Renaissance.

Most of Picasso's friends were shocked by his new work. Matisse, for example, accused Picasso of making a joke of Modern art and threatened to break off their friendship. But one artist, Georges Braque, enthusiastically embraced Picasso's radical ideas—he saw in *Les Demoiselles d'Avignon* a potential for new visual experiments. In 1907–1908, Picasso and Braque began a close working relationship that lasted until the latter went to war in 1914. Together, they developed Picasso's formal innovations by flattening pictorial space, incorporating multiple perspectives within a single picture, and fracturing form, all features that they had admired in Cézanne's late paintings. According to Braque, "We were like two mountain climbers roped together."

ANALYTIC CUBISM Braque, a year younger than Picasso, was born near Le Havre, France, where he trained as a decorator. In 1900, he moved to Paris and began painting brightly colored Fauvist landscapes, but it was the 1906 Cézanne retrospective and Picasso's *Demoiselles* in 1907 that established his future course by sharpening his interest in altered form and compressed space. In his landscapes after 1908, he reduced nature's complexity to its essential colors and elemental geometric shapes, but the Autumn Salon rejected his work. Fellow artists dismissively referred to Braque's "little cubes," and the critic Louis Vauxcelles picked up the phrase, claiming that

Braque "reduced everything to cubes," thereby giving birth to the art historical label of Cubism.

Braque's 1909–1910 **VIOLIN AND PALETTE** (FIG. 32-7) shows the kind of relatively small still-life paintings that the two artists created during their initial collaborative

32-7 Georges Braque **VIOLIN AND PALETTE**
1909–1910. Oil on canvas, 36⅛ × 16⅞″ (91.8 × 42.9 cm). Solomon R. Guggenheim Museum, New York. (54.1412).

experimentation in the gradual abstraction of recognizable subject matter and space. The still-life items here are not arranged in a measured progression from foreground to background, but push close to the picture plane, confined to a shallow space. Braque knits the various elements—a violin, an artist's palette, and some sheet music—together into a single shifting surface of forms and colors. In some areas of the painting, these formal elements have lost not only their natural spatial relations but their coherent shapes as well. Where representational motifs remain—the violin, for example—they have been fragmented by Braque to facilitate their integration into the compositional whole.

Picasso's 1910 Cubist **PORTRAIT OF DANIEL-HENRY KAHNWEILER** (**FIG. 32–8**) depicts the artist's first and most important art dealer in Paris, who saved many artists from destitution by buying their early works. Kahnweiler (1884–1979) was an early champion of Picasso's art and one of the first to recognize the significance of *Les Demoiselles d'Avignon*. His impressive stable of artists included Picasso, Braque, Derain, Fernand Léger, and Juan Gris. Since he was German, Kahnweiler fled France for Switzerland during World War I; the French government confiscated all his possessions, including his stock of paintings, which was sold by the state at auction after the war. Being Jewish, he was forced into hiding during World War II.

Braque's and Picasso's paintings of 1909 and 1910 initiated what is known as Analytic Cubism because of the way the artists broke objects into parts as if to analyze them. In works of 1911 and early 1912, such as Picasso's *Ma Jolie* (**SEE FIG. 32–1**), they begin to take a somewhat different approach to the breaking up of forms, in which they did not simply fracture objects visually, but also rearranged their components. Thus, Analytic Cubism begins to resemble the actual process of perception, during which we examine objects from various points of view and reassemble our glances into a whole object in our brain. Except Picasso and Braque reassembled their shattered subjects not according to the process of perception, but conforming to principles of artistic composition, to communicate meaning rather than to represent observed reality. For example, remnants of the subject are evident throughout Picasso's *Ma Jolie*, but any attempt to reconstruct them into the image of a woman with a stringed instrument would be misguided since the subject provided only the raw material for a formal composition. *Ma Jolie* is not a representation of a woman, a place, or an event; it is simply a painting.

SYNTHETIC CUBISM Works such as *Ma Jolie* brought Picasso and Braque to the brink of complete abstraction, but in the spring of 1912 they pulled back and began to create works that suggested more clearly discernible subjects. Neither artist wanted to break the link to reality; Picasso said that there was no such thing as completely abstract art, because "You have to start somewhere." This second

32–8 Pablo Picasso **PORTRAIT OF DANIEL-HENRY KAHNWEILER**
1910. Oil on canvas, 39½ × 28⅝" (100.6 × 72.8 cm).
The Art Institute of Chicago. Gift of Mrs. Gilbert W. Chapman in memory of Charles B. Goodspeed.

Credit: © 2016 Estate of Pablo Picasso/Artists Rights Society (ARS), New York. Photo © The Art Institute of Chicago

major phase of Cubism is known as Synthetic Cubism because of the way the artists created complex compositions by combining and transforming individual elements, as in a chemical synthesis. Picasso's **BOTTLE OF SUZE (LA BOUTEILLE DE SUZE)** (**FIG. 32–9**), like many of the works he and Braque created from 1912 to 1914, is a collage (from the French *coller*, meaning "to glue"), a work composed of separate elements pasted together. At the center, assembled newsprint and construction paper suggest a tray or round table supporting a glass and a bottle of liquor with an actual label. Around this arrangement Picasso pasted larger pieces of newspaper and wallpaper.

As in earlier Cubism, Picasso offers multiple perspectives. We see the top of the blue table, tilted to face us, and simultaneously the side of the glass. The bottle stands on the table, its label facing us, while we can also see the round profile of its opening, as well as the top of the cork that plugs it. The elements together evoke not only a place—a bar—but also an activity—the viewer alone with a newspaper, enjoying a quiet drink.

The newspaper clippings glued to this picture, however, disrupt the quiet mood. They address the First Balkan War of 1912–1913, which contributed to the outbreak of World War I. Picasso may have wanted to underline the disorder in his art by comparing it with the disorder building in the world around him, or to warn viewers not to sit blindly and sip Suze while political events threatened to shatter the peaceful pleasures this work evokes—or this may simply be a collage.

Picasso employed collage three-dimensionally to produce Synthetic Cubist sculpture, such as **MANDOLIN AND CLARINET** (**FIG. 32-10**). Composed of wood scraps, the sculpture suggests the Cubist subject of two musical instruments, here shown at right angles to each other. Sculpture had traditionally been carved, modeled, or cast. Picasso's sculptural collage was a new idea and introduced **assemblage**, giving sculptors the option not only of carving or modeling masses to sit within space, but also of constructing three-dimensional works from combinations of found objects and unconventional materials, assembled in such a way that each part maintains its own identity while at the same time contributing to a new, combined form.

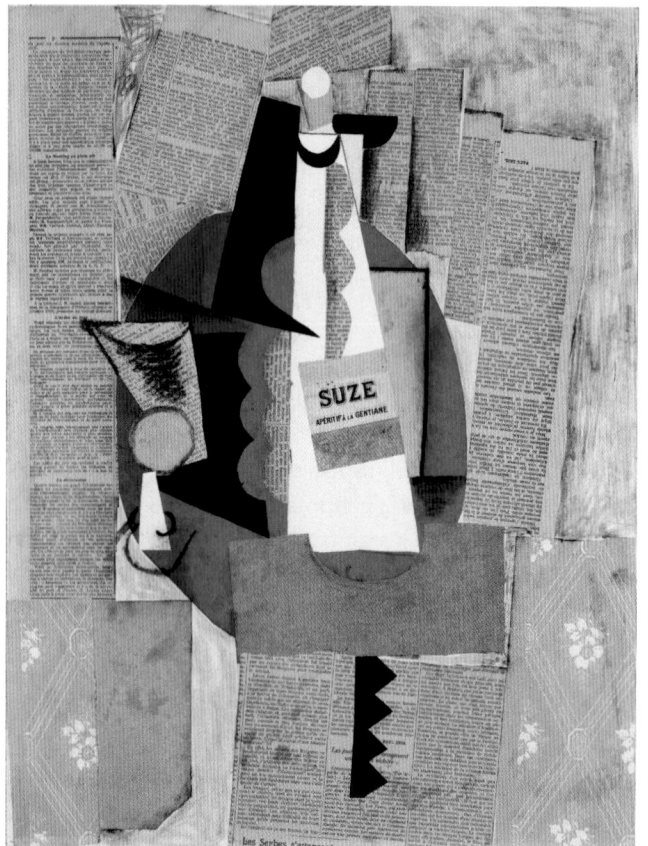

32-9 Pablo Picasso **BOTTLE OF SUZE (LA BOUTEILLE DE SUZE)**
1912. Pasted paper, gouache, and charcoal, 25¾ × 19¾″ (65.4 × 50.2 cm). Mildred Lane Kemper Art Museum, Washington University in St. Louis. University purchase, Kende Sale Fund, 1946.

Credit: © 2016 Estate of Pablo Picasso/Artists Rights Society (ARS), New York. Photo © Hans Hinz/ARTOTHEK.

32-10 Pablo Picasso **MANDOLIN AND CLARINET**
1913. Construction of painted wood with pencil marks, 25⅝ × 14⅛ × 9″ (58 × 36 × 23 cm). Musée Picasso, Paris.

Credit: © 2016 Estate of Pablo Picasso / Artists Rights Society (ARS), New York. Photo © RMN-Grand Palais (musée Picasso de Paris)/Béatrice Hatala.

Die Brücke and Primitivism

At the same time that Picasso and Braque were transforming painting in Paris, a group of radical German artists came together in Dresden as Die Brücke (The Bridge), taking their name from a passage in Friedrich Nietzsche's *Thus Spake Zarathustra* (1883) that describes contemporary humanity's potential as a bridge to a more perfect humanity in the future. Formed in 1905, Die Brücke included architecture students Fritz Bleyl (1880–1966), Erich Heckel (1883–1970), Ernst Ludwig Kirchner (1880–1938), and Karl Schmidt-Rottluff (1884–1976). Other German and northern European artists later joined the group, which continued until 1913. These artists hoped Die Brücke would be a gathering place for "all revolutionary and surging elements" who opposed Germany's "pale, over-bred, and decadent" society.

Drawing on the work of northern visual predecessors such as Van Gogh and Munch and adopting traditional northern media such as woodcuts, these artists created intense, brutal, expressionistic images of alienation and anxiety in response to Germany's rapid and intensive

32–11 Erich Heckel **STANDING CHILD**
1910. Color woodcut, 14¾ × 10¾″ (37.5 × 27.5 cm).
Los Angeles County Museum of Art.

urbanization. Not surprisingly, among their favorite motifs were the natural world and the nude body—nudism was also a growing cultural trend in Germany in those years, as city dwellers forsook the city to reconnect with nature. Erich Heckel's three-color woodcut print **STANDING CHILD** (**FIG. 32–11**) of 1910 presents a strikingly stylized but powerfully expressive image of a naked girl—whose flesh is the reserved color of the paper itself—isolated against a spare landscape created from broad areas of pure black, green, and red. The girl stares straight out at the viewer with a confident sexuality that becomes more unsettling when we learn that this girl was the 12-year old Fränzi Fehrmann, a favorite of Die Brücke artists who, with her siblings, modeled to provide financial support for her widowed mother.

Although not part of the original Die Brücke group, Emil Nolde (1867–1956) joined in 1906 and quickly became its most committed member. Originally trained in industrial design, Nolde studied academic painting privately in Paris for a few months in 1900, but he never painted as he was taught. Nolde regularly visited Parisian ethnographic museums to study the art of Africa and Oceania, which impressed him with the radical and forceful visual presence of the human figure, especially in masks. His painting **MASKS** (**FIG. 32–12**) of 1911 seems to come both from what he saw in Paris and from the masquerades familiar to him from European carnivals (**SEE FIG. 31–44**). By merging these traditions, Nolde transforms his African and Oceanic sources into a European nightmare full of horror and implicit violence. The gaping mouths and hollow eyes of the hideously colored and roughly drawn masks taunt viewers, appearing to advance from the picture plane into their space. Nolde also uses the juxtaposition of complementaries to intensify his colors and the painting's emotionality. Nolde stopped frequenting Die Brücke's studio in 1907 but remained friendly with the group's members. On the eve of World War I, Nolde accompanied a German scientific expedition to New Guinea, explaining that what attracted him to the "native art" of Pacific cultures was their "primitivism," their "absolute originality, the intense and often grotesque expression of power and life in very simple forms."

32–12 Emil Nolde **MASKS**
1911. Oil on canvas, 28¾ × 30½″
(73.03 × 77.47 cm). The Nelson-Atkins
Museum of Art, Kansas City, Missouri.
Gift of the Friends of Art (54-90).

32-13 Ernst Ludwig Kirchner STREET, BERLIN
1913. Oil on canvas, 47½ × 35⅞" (120.6 × 91 cm). Museum of
Modern Art, New York. Purchase (274.39).

and fur-trimmed coats—strut past a group of well-dressed bourgeois men whom they view as potential clients. The figures are dehumanized, with masklike faces and stiff gestures. Their bodies crowd together, but they are psychologically distant, ambiguously related to one another. The biting colors, tilted perspective, and forceful brushstrokes make this a disturbing Expressionistic image of urban degeneracy and alienation.

Independent Expressionists

Beyond the members of Die Brücke, many other artists in Germany and Austria worked Expressionistically before World War I. For example, Käthe Kollwitz (1867–1945) used her art to further working-class causes and pursue social change. She preferred printmaking because its affordability gave it the potential to reach a wide audience. Between 1902 and 1908, she produced a series of seven etchings showing the sixteenth-century German Peasants' War. **THE OUTBREAK (FIG. 32-14)**, a lesson in the power of group action, portrays the ugly fury of the peasants as they charge forward, armed only with their farm tools, bent on revenge against their oppressors. The faces of the two figures at the front of the charge are particularly grotesque, while the leader, Black Anna—whom Kollwitz modeled on herself—signals the attack with a fierce gesture, her arms silhouetted against the sky. Behind her, the crowded and chaotic mass of workers forms a passionate picture of political revolt.

Like Kollwitz, Paula Modersohn-Becker (1876–1907) studied at the Berlin School of Art for Women. In 1898, she moved to Worpswede, an artists' retreat in rural northern

Each summer, members of Die Brücke returned to nature, visiting remote areas of northern Germany, but in 1911 they moved to Berlin instead—perhaps preferring to imagine rather than actually live the natural life. Their images of cities, especially Berlin, are powerfully critical of urban existence. In Ernst Ludwig Kirchner's **STREET, BERLIN (FIG. 32-13)**, two prostitutes—their profession advertised by their large, feathered hats

32-14 Käthe Kollwitz THE OUTBREAK
From the "Peasants' War" series. 1903. Etching, 20 × 23⅓" (50.7 × 59.2 cm). Kupferstichkabinett, Staatliche Museen zu Berlin.

Germany. Dissatisfied with the Worpswede artists' naturalistic approach to rural life, she made four trips to Paris after 1900 to view recent developments in Post-Impressionist painting and was especially attracted to the "primitivizing" tendencies of Gauguin's Tahitian paintings (SEE FIG. 31–41). Many of her most powerful works were painted during 1906, her last year in Paris. **RECLINING MOTHER AND CHILD** (FIG. **32–15**) highlights a monumental mother who encloses her young (perhaps nursing) child within a protective embrace. Coordinated curves and rhyming poses knit the two frankly naked figures together into a composition of interconnected flesh with no hint of glamour or allure. This iconic portrayal of motherhood becomes even more poignant with the knowledge that the artist herself was to die the year following soon after giving birth to her first child.

In contrast, the 1911 **SELF-PORTRAIT NUDE** (FIG. **32–16**) of Austrian artist Egon Schiele (1890–1918) challenges viewers with his physical and psychological torment. The impact of Schiele's father's death from untreated syphilis when the artist was just 14 led him to conflate suffering with sexuality throughout his life. In many drawings and watercolors, Schiele portrays women in tormented poses that emphasize their raw sexuality and the artist's sense of its dangerous allure. In this self-portrait, Schiele turns the same harsh gaze on himself, expressing deep ambivalence toward his own sexuality and body. He stares at us with anguish, his emaciated body stretched and displayed in a halo of harsh light, lacking both hands and genitals. Some have interpreted this representational mutilation in Freudian fashion as the artist's symbolic self-punishment for indulgence in masturbation, then commonly believed to lead to insanity.

32–16 Egon Schiele **SELF-PORTRAIT NUDE**

1911. Gouache and pencil on paper, 20¼ × 13¾″ (51.4 × 35 cm). Metropolitan Museum of Art, New York. Bequest of Scofield Thayer, 1982 (1984.433.298).

32–17 Franz Marc **THE LARGE BLUE HORSES**

1911. Oil on canvas, 3′5⅜″ × 5′11¼″ (1.05 × 1.81 m). Walker Art Center, Minneapolis. Gift of T.B. Walker Collection, Gilbert M. Walter Fund, 1942.

32–18 Vassily Kandinsky **IMPROVISATION 28 (SECOND VERSION)**

1912. Oil on canvas, 43⅞ × 63⅞″ (111.4 × 162.2 cm). Solomon R. Guggenheim Museum, New York. Solomon R. Guggenheim Founding Collection (37.239).

Credit: © 2016 Artists Rights Society (ARS), New York. The Solomon R. Guggenheim Foundation/Art Resource, NY.

Spiritualism of Der Blaue Reiter

Formed in Munich by the Russian artist Vassily Kandinsky (1866–1944) and the German artist Franz Marc (1880–1916), Der Blaue Reiter ("The Blue Rider") was named for a popular image of St. George, who wears a blue cloak on the city emblem of Moscow. Just as St. George had been a spiritual leader in society, so Der Blaue Reiter aspired to offer spiritual leadership in the arts. Its first exhibition was held in December 1911 and included the work of 14 artists working in a wide range of styles from realism to radical abstraction.

By 1911, Marc was mostly painting animals rather than humans, rendering them in big, bold forms and highly saturated colors. He felt animals were more "primitive" and thus purer than humans, enjoying a more spiritual relationship with nature. In **THE LARGE BLUE HORSES** (**FIG. 32-17**), the animals—painted in blue, a color that the artist considered spiritual—merge into a homogeneous whole. Their sweeping contours reflect the harmony of their collective existence and echo the curved lines of the hills behind them, suggesting that they live in harmony with their surroundings.

Born into a wealthy Moscow family, Kandinsky initially trained as a lawyer, but after visiting exhibitions of Modernist art in Germany and taking private art lessons, he abandoned his legal career, moved to Munich, and established himself as an artist. Kandinsky was one of the first artists to investigate the theoretical possibility of purely abstract painting. Like Whistler (SEE FIG. 31-27)—an artist he both studied and admired—Kandinsky gave many of his works musical titles such as *Composition* and *Improvisation* and aspired to make paintings that responded to his own inner state and would be entirely autonomous, making no reference to the visible world.

Between 1911 and 1914, Kandinsky painted a series of works, including **IMPROVISATION 28** (**FIG. 32-18**), that, although they make clear references to landscape, architecture, and figures, initiate a progressive movement toward abstraction. In them, brilliant colors and veiled images leap and dance to express a variety of emotions and spiritualities. For Kandinsky, painting was a utopian force. He saw art's traditional focus on accurate rendering of the physical world as a misguided, materialistic quest; he hoped that his paintings would lead humanity toward a deeper awareness of spirituality and the inner world. He asks us to look at the painting as if we were hearing a symphony, responding instinctively and spontaneously to this or that passage and then to the total experience. Kandinsky further explained the musical analogy in his book *Concerning the Spiritual in Art* (1912): "Color directly influences the soul. Color is the keyboard, the eyes are the hammers, the soul is the piano with many strings. The artist is the hand that plays, touching one key or another purposively, to cause vibrations in the soul."

Extending Cubism and Questioning Art Itself

What additional transformations in European and American art and architecture emerge from Modernism?

As Cubist paintings emerged from the studios of Braque and Picasso, they altered the artistic discourse irrevocably. Cubism's way of viewing the world resonated with artists all over Europe, in Russia, and even in the United States—significantly broadening and extending its visual message beyond the ideas and objects of Picasso and Braque.

FRANCE   Robert Delaunay (1885–1941) and his wife, the Ukrainian-born Sonia Delaunay (1885–1979), took the relatively monochromatic and static forms of Cubism in a new direction. Fauvist color had inflected Delaunay's early work; his deep interest in communicating spirituality through color led him to participate in Der Blaue Reiter exhibitions. In 1910, he began to fuse his interest in color with Cubism to create paintings celebrating the modern city and modern technology. In **HOMAGE TO BLÉRIOT** (**FIG. 32-19**), Delaunay pays tribute to Louis Blériot—the French pilot who in 1909 became the first person to fly across the English Channel—by portraying his airplane

32-19 Robert Delaunay **HOMAGE TO BLÉRIOT**
1914. Watercolor on paper, 31 × 26" (78 × 67 cm). Musée d'Art Moderne de la Ville de Paris. Donation of Henry-Thomas, 1976.

Credit: © 2016 White Images/Scala, Florence

flying over the Eiffel Tower, the Parisian symbol of modernity. The brightly colored circular forms that fill the rest of the painting suggest the movement of the airplane's propeller, a blazing sun in the sky, and the great rose window of the Cathedral of Notre-Dame, representing Delaunay's ideas of progressive science and spirituality. This painting's fractured colors also suggest the fast-moving parts of modern machinery.

The critic Guillaume Apollinaire labeled the art of both Robert and Sonia Delaunay "Orphism" after Orpheus, the legendary Greek poet whose lute playing charmed wild beasts, thus implying that their art had similar power. They preferred the term "simultaneity," a concept based on Michel-Eugène Chevreul's law of the simultaneous contrast of colors that proposed collapsing spatial distance and the sequence of time into a simultaneous "here and now"—creating a harmonic unity out of the disharmonious world. The Delaunays envisioned a simultaneity

32–20 Sonia Delaunay **CLOTHES AND CUSTOMIZED CITROËN B-12 (EXPO 1925 MANNEQUINS AVEC AUTO)**

From *Maison de la Mode*. 1925.

32–21 Fernand Léger **THREE WOMEN**

1921. Oil on canvas, 6'½" × 8'3" (1.84 × 2.52 m). Museum of Modern Art, New York. Mrs. Simon Guggenheim Fund.

that combined the modern world of airplanes, telephones, and automobiles with spirituality.

Sonia Delaunay produced Orphist paintings with Robert, but she also designed fabric and clothing on her own. She created new fabric patterns and dress designs similar to her paintings and exhibited a line of inexpensive ready-to-wear garments that she called Simultaneous Dresses at the important 1925 International Exposition of Modern Decorative and Industrial Arts. Delaunay also decorated a Citroën sports car to match one of her ensembles for the exhibition (**FIG. 32–20**). She saw the small three-seater as an expression of a new age because, like her clothing, it was produced inexpensively for a mass market and was designed specifically to appeal to the newly independent woman of the time. Sadly, there are only black-and-white photographs of these designs.

Technology also fascinated Fernand Léger (1881–1955), who painted a more static but brilliantly colored version of Cubism based on machine forms. **THREE WOMEN** (**FIG. 32–21**) is a Purist, machine-age version of the French academic subject of the reclining nude. Purism was developed in Paris by Le Corbusier (b. Charles-Édouard Jeanneret, 1887–1965) and Amédée Ozenfant in a 1925 book, *The Foundation of Modern Art*, that argued for a return to clear, ordered forms and ideas to express the efficient clarity of the machine age—a desire commonly understood as a reaction to the chaotic horrors of World War I. In Léger's painting, the women's bodies are constructed from large, machinelike shapes arranged in an asymmetrical geometric grid that evokes both cool Classicism and an arrangement of interchangeable plumbing parts. The women are dehumanized, with identical, bland, round faces; the exuberant colors and patterns that surround them suggest an orderly industrial society in which everything has its place.

ITALY In Italy, Cubism developed into Futurism, with an emphasis on portraying technology and a sense of speed. In 1908, Italy was a state in crisis. Huge disparities of wealth separated the north from the south; four-fifths of the country was illiterate; poverty and near-starvation were rampant; and as many as 50,000 people had recently died in one of the nation's worst earthquakes. On February 20, 1909, Milanese poet and editor Filippo Tommaso Marinetti (1876–1944) published "Foundation and Manifesto of Futurism" on the front page of the Parisian

newspaper *Le Figaro*. He attacked everything old, dull, and "feminine" and proposed to shake Italy free of its past by embracing an exhilarating, "masculine," "futuristic," and even dangerous world based on the thrill, speed, energy, and power of modern urban life.

In April 1911, a group of Milanese artists followed Marinetti's manifesto with the "Technical Manifesto of Futurist Painting," in which they demanded that "all subjects previously used must be swept aside in order to express our whirling life of steel, of pride, of fever, and of speed." Some of these artists traveled to Paris for a Futurist exhibition in 1912, after which they used the visual forms of Cubism to express in art their love of machines, speed, and war.

Gino Severini (1883–1966) signed the "Technical Manifesto" while living in Paris, where he served as an intermediary between the Italian-based Futurists and the French avant-garde. Perhaps more than other Futurists, Severini embraced the concept of war as a social cleansing agent. In **ARMORED TRAIN IN ACTION** (**FIG. 32–22**) of 1915—probably based on a photograph of a Belgian armored car on a train going over a bridge—Severini uses the jagged forms and splintered, overlapping surfaces of Cubism to describe a tumultuous scene of smoke, violence, and cannon blasts issuing from the speeding train seen from a disorienting viewpoint.

32–22 Gino Severini **ARMORED TRAIN IN ACTION**
1915. Oil on canvas, 45⅝ × 34⅞" (115.8 × 88.5 cm). Museum of Modern Art, New York. Gift of Richard S. Zeisler (287.86).

32-23 Umberto Boccioni
**UNIQUE FORMS OF
CONTINUITY IN SPACE**

1913. Bronze, 43⅞ × 34⅞ × 15¾″
(111 × 89 × 40 cm). Museum of
Modern Art, New York. Acquired
through the Lillie P. Bliss Bequest
(231.1948).

Credit: © 2016. Digital image, The
Museum of Modern Art, New York/Scala,
Florence

Russian Futurist artists—also known as Cubo-Futurists—claiming to have emerged independently of Italian Futurism began to move increasingly toward abstraction.

ELECTRIC LIGHT (**FIG. 32-24**), painted in 1913 by Natalia Goncharova (1881–1962), shows the brightly artificial light from a new electric lamp fracturing and dissolving its surrounding forms like an analytical Cubist force. Goncharova turned to mixtures of Russian folk art and Modernist abstraction in costumes and sets she designed for Sergei Diaghilev's Ballets Russes stagings, including *Le Coq d'Or* (1914), *Night on Bald Mountain* (1923), and the revival of Igor Stravinsky's *Firebird* (1926).

After 1915, Kazimir Malevich (1878–1935) emerged as the leader of the Moscow avant-garde. He later remembered, "In the year 1913, in my desperate attempt to free art from the burden of the object, I took refuge in the square form and exhibited a picture which consisted of nothing more than a black square on a white field." *The Black Square* was one of the backdrops for Mikhail Matiushin's Russian Futurist

In 1912, Umberto Boccioni (1882–1916) argued for a Futurist "sculpture of environment" in which form should explode in a violent burst of motion from the closed and solid mass into the surrounding space. In **UNIQUE FORMS OF CONTINUITY IN SPACE** (**FIG. 32-23**), Boccioni portrays a figure striding powerfully through space with muscular forms like wings flying out energetically behind it. Many of Boccioni's sculptures made use of unconventional materials; this sculpture was actually made of plaster and only cast in bronze after the artist's death. In keeping with his Futurist ideals, Boccioni celebrated Italy's entry into World War I by enlisting. He was killed in combat.

RUSSIA By 1900, Russian artists and art collectors in the cosmopolitan cities of St. Petersburg and later Moscow had begun to embrace avant-garde art, making trips to Paris to see it. Russian artists also drew on Futurist tendencies to celebrate technology and the aesthetic of speed. In 1912,

32-24 Natalia Goncharova **ELECTRIC LIGHT**

1913. Oil on canvas, 41½ × 32″ (105.5 × 81.3 cm).
Musée National d'Art Moderne, Centre National d'Art et de Culture
Georges-Pompidou.

Credit: © 2016 Artists Rights Society (ARS), New York/ADAGP, Paris.
Photo © Centre Pompidou, MNAM-CCI, Dist. RMN-Grand Palais/Droits réservés

32–25 Kazimir Malevich
SUPREMATIST PAINTING (EIGHT RED RECTANGLES)
1915. Oil on canvas, 22½ × 18⅞″ (57 × 48 cm). Stedelijk Museum, Amsterdam.

Credit: Collection Stedelijk Museum Amsterdam

opera, *Victory Over the Sun*. At the "Last Futurist Exhibition of Paintings: 0.10" held in St. Petersburg in the winter of 1915–1916, Malevich exhibited 39 works of art consisting of flat, assembled, geometric shapes in a style he termed Suprematism, defined as "the supremacy of pure feeling in creative art." One of these works, **SUPREMATIST PAINTING (EIGHT RED RECTANGLES)** (**FIG. 32-25**), arranges eight red rectangles diagonally on a white ground—a pure abstraction.

Toward Abstraction in Sculpture

Sculpture underwent a revolution as profound as that of painting in the years prior to World War I. Perhaps Picasso's creation of three-dimensional works from diverse materials assembled and hung on a wall rather than placed on pedestals (SEE FIG. 32-10) was the most radical innovation, but not all change involved new

materials and display contexts. The Romanian artist Constantin Brancusi (1876–1957), who settled in Paris in 1904, became immediately captivated by the "primitive" art on display in the city. He admired the semiabstracted forms of much art beyond the Western tradition, believing that the artists who made such art succeeded in capturing the "essence" of their subject. Brancusi, like Picasso, rejected superficial realism. He wrote, "What is real is not the external form but the essence of things. Starting from this truth it is impossible for anyone to express anything essentially real by imitating its exterior surface."

For Brancusi, the egg symbolized the potential for birth, growth, and development—the essence of life contained in a perfect, organic, abstract ovoid. In **THE NEWBORN** (**FIG. 32-26**) of 1915, he conflates its shape with the head of a human infant to suggest the essence of humanity at the moment of birth.

32-26 Constantin Brancusi **THE NEWBORN**
1915. Marble, 5¾ × 8¼ × 5⅞" (14.6 × 21 × 14.8 cm).
Philadelphia Museum of Art. Louise and Walter Arensberg Collection.
(195.134.10).

Credit: © 2016 Artists Rights Society (ARS), New York/ADAGP, Paris. © 2016.
Photo The Philadelphia Museum of Art/Art Resource/Scala, Florence

In his 1924 **TORSO OF A YOUNG MAN** (**FIG. 32-27**), Brancusi distills the figure's torso and upper legs into three highly polished metal cylinders, a machinelike regularity that might relate to the works of Léger or the Futurists. This bold abstraction carries a Classical gravity and stillness, especially when perched atop the elemental earthiness of the impressive pedestal Brancusi created for it in wood and stone. On the other hand, although the sleek torso lacks a penis, the phallic nature of the displayed form itself transforms the ensemble into a sexually charged symbol of essential masculinity.

Dada: Questioning Art Itself

When World War I broke out in August 1914, most European leaders thought it would be over by Christmas. Both sides reassured their citizens that the efficiency of their armies and bravery of their soldiers would ensure a speedy resolution and that the political status quo would resume. These hopes proved illusory. World War I was the most brutal and costly in human history up to that time. On the Western Front in 1916 alone, Germany lost 850,000 soldiers, France 700,000, and Great Britain 400,000. The conflict settled into a vicious stalemate on all fronts as each side deployed new killing technologies, such as improved machine guns, flame throwers, fighter aircraft, and poison gas. On the home fronts, governments exerted control over industry and labor to manage the war effort, and ordinary people were forced to endure food rationing, propaganda attacks, and war profiteering.

Horror at the enormity of the carnage arose on many fronts. One of the first artistic movements to address the

32-27 Constantin Brancusi **TORSO OF A YOUNG MAN**
1924. Bronze on stone and wood bases; combined figure and bases
40⅜ × 20 × 18¼" (102.4 × 50.5 × 46.1 cm). Hirshhorn Museum and
Sculpture Garden, Smithsonian Institution, Washington, DC. Gift of
Joseph H. Hirshhorn 1966 (HMSG 66.61)

Credit: © 2016 Artists Rights Society (ARS), New York/ADAGP, Paris slaughter and moral questions of the war was Dada—a transnational movement with distinct local manifestations that arose during the war in Zürich and New York, then spread to Berlin, Paris, Cologne, and Hannover. If Modern art until that time questioned the traditions of art, Dada went further to question the concept of art itself. Witnessing how thoughtlessly life was discarded in the trenches, Dada mocked the senselessness of rational thought and even the foundations of modern society. It embraced a "mocking iconoclasm" even in its name, which has no real or fixed meaning. *Dada* is baby talk in German; in French it means "hobbyhorse"; in Romanian and Russian, "yes, yes"; in the Kru African dialect, "the tail of a sacred cow." Dada artists annihilated the conventional understanding of art as something precious, replacing it with a strange and irrational art focused on ideas and actions rather than objects.

HUGO BALL AND THE CABARET VOLTAIRE One of Dada's first great moments was the first performance of poet Hugo Ball's poem "Karawane" at the Cabaret Voltaire on June 23, 1916. Ball (1886–1927) and his companion, Emmy Hennings (1885–1949), a nightclub singer, moved from Germany to neutral Switzerland when World War I broke out and opened the Cabaret Voltaire in Zürich in February of 1916. Cabaret Voltaire was based loosely on the bohemian artists' cafés of prewar Berlin and Munich, and its mad, irrational world became a meeting place for exiled avant-garde writers and artists of various nationalities who shared Ball and Hennings's disgust for the war.

It was here that Ball solemnly recited one of his sound poems, **"KARAWANE"** (FIG. 32–28) with his legs and body encased in blue cardboard tubes and a white-and-blue "witch doctor's hat," as he called it, on his head. He also wore a huge, gold-painted cardboard cape that flapped when he moved his arms, and lobsterlike cardboard hands or claws. The text of Ball's poem—included in the photograph documenting the event—consists of a string of nonsensical sounds, renouncing "the language devastated and made impossible by journalism," and mocking traditional poetry. He self-consciously abandoned the rationality of adulthood and created a new and wholly incomprehensible private language of random sounds that seemed to mimic baby talk.

MARCEL DUCHAMP Although not formally a member of the Dada movement, Marcel Duchamp (1887–1968) created some of its most complex and challenging works. He also took Dada to New York when he crossed the Atlantic in 1915 to escape the war in Europe. In Paris in 1912, Duchamp had experimented with Cubism, painting *Nude Descending a Staircase No. 2*, which would be one of the most controversial works included in the notorious Armory Show in New York in 1913 (discussed later in this chapter). But by the time Duchamp himself arrived in the United States, he had discarded painting, which he claimed had become for him a mindless activity, and had devised the Dada genre that he termed the readymade, in which he transformed ordinary, often manufactured objects into works of art.

Duchamp was warmly welcomed into the American art world. The American Society of Independent Artists invited him to become a founding member, and he chaired the hanging committee for its annual exhibition in 1917. The show advertised itself as unjuried—any work of art submitted with the entry fee of $6 would be hung. His anonymous submission was a common porcelain urinal that he purchased in a plumber's shop and turned on its side so that it was no longer functional, signing it "R. Mutt" in a play on the name of the urinal's manufacturer, J.L. Mott Iron Works. It was rejected.

FOUNTAIN (FIG. 32–29) remains one of the most controversial works of art of the twentieth century. It incites laughter, anger, embarrassment, and disgust by openly referring to private bathroom activities and to human carnality and vulnerability. But more significantly, in it Duchamp questions the essence of what constitutes a work of art. How much can be stripped away before an object's status as art disappears? Since Whistler's famous court case (see "Art on Trial in 1877" in Chapter 31 on page 1002), most avant-garde artists had agreed that a work of art did not have to be descriptive or well crafted, but before 1917, none would have argued, as Duchamp does in this piece, that art was primarily conceptual. For centuries, perhaps millennia, artists had regularly employed studio assistants to make parts, if not all, of the art objects that they designed. On one level, Duchamp updates that practice into modern terms by arguing that art objects can actually

32–29 Marcel Duchamp FOUNTAIN

1917. Porcelain plumbing fixture and enamel paint. Photograph by Alfred Stieglitz. Philadelphia Museum of Art. Louise and Walter Arensberg Collection (1998-74-1).

Stieglitz's photograph is the only known image of Duchamp's original *Fountain*, which mysteriously disappeared after it was rejected by the jury of the American Society of Independent Artists exhibition. In 1964, Duchamp supervised the production of a small edition of replicas of the original *Fountain* based on the Stieglitz photograph. One of these replicas sold at auction in 1999 for $1.76 million, setting a record for a work by Duchamp.

32–30 Marcel Duchamp L.H.O.O.Q.

1919. Pencil on reproduction of Leonardo da Vinci's *Mona Lisa*, 7¾ × 4¾" (19.7 × 12.1 cm). Philadelphia Museum of Art. Louise and Walter Arensberg Collection.

be mass-produced for the artist by industry. Duchamp creates a commentary simultaneously about consumption and about the irrationality of the modern age by claiming that the "readymade" simply bypasses the craft tradition, qualifying as a work of art because of its human conceptualization rather than its human making.

When *Fountain* was rejected, as Duchamp anticipated it would be, the artist resigned from the Society of Independent Artists in mock horror. An unsigned editorial in a Dada journal (which could have been written by the artist himself) detailed what it described as the scandal of the R. Mutt case. It claimed, "The only works of art America has given are her plumbing and bridges," and added, "Whether Mr. Mutt with his own hands made the fountain or not has no importance. He CHOSE it. He took an ordinary article of life, placed it so that its useful significance disappeared under the new title and point of view—created a new thought for that object."

After Duchamp returned to Paris, he challenged the French art world with a work that he entitled **L.H.O.O.Q.** (**FIG. 32-30**) and described as a "modified readymade." In 1911, a Louvre employee had stolen Leonardo's famous *Mona Lisa* (SEE FIG. 21-1), believing it should be returned to Italy. It took two years to recover it. While missing, however, the *Mona Lisa* became even more famous and was widely and badly reproduced in postcards, posters, and advertising. Duchamp chose to comment on the nature of fame and on the degraded image of the *Mona Lisa* by purchasing a cheap postcard reproduction and drawing a mustache and beard on its subject's famously enigmatic face. In doing so he turned a revered cultural artifact into an object of ridicule. The letters that he scrawled across the bottom of the card, "L.H.O.O.Q.," when read aloud sound phonetically similar to the French slang phrase *elle a chaud au cul*, politely translated as "she's hot for it," thus adding a crude sexual innuendo to the already cheapened image. Like *Fountain*, this work challenges traditional notions about what constitutes art and makes ridicule and bodily functions its central artistic content. As one of Dada's founders said, "Dada was born of disgust."

Duchamp made only a few readymades. In fact, he created very little art at all after about 1922, when he devoted himself almost entirely to chess. When asked about his occupation, he described himself as a "retired artist," but his radical ideas about art continued to exert influence, especially in the period after 1960.

BERLIN DADA   Early in 1917, Hugo Ball and the Romanian-born poet Tristan Tzara (1896–1963) organized the Galerie Dada in Zürich. Tzara also edited the magazine *Dada*, which quickly attracted the attention of like-minded artists and writers in several European capitals and the United States. The movement spread farther when expatriate members of Ball's circle in Switzerland returned to their homelands after the war. Richard Huelsenbeck (1892–1974), for instance, took Dada to Germany, where he helped found the Club Dada in Berlin in April 1918.

Dada pursued a slightly different agenda and took on different forms in each of its major centers. One distinctive feature of Berlin Dada was its use of provocative propaganda. Compared to the more literary forms of Dada elsewhere, Berlin Dada also produced an unusually large amount of visual art—especially collage and **photomontage** (photographic collage).

One example of this is the work of Kurt Schwitters (1887–1948), who worked in Hannover and met Huelsenbeck and other Dadaists in 1919. Schwitters used discarded rail tickets, postage stamps, ration coupons, beer labels, and other street trash to create visual poetry. He called the resulting two- and three-dimensional works of art *Merzbilder* (German for "refuse pictures"). In these works Schwitters combined fragments of newspaper and other

32–31 Kurt Schwitters **MERZBILD 5B (PICTURE-RED-HEART-CHURCH)**

April 26, 1919. Collage, tempera, and crayon on cardboard, 32⅞ × 23¾" (83.4 × 60.3 cm). Solomon R. Guggenheim Museum, New York. (52.1325).

printed material with drawn or painted images, incorporating them into an overall visual structure that recalled Cubism. He wrote that garbage demanded equal rights with painting. In **MERZBILD 5B** (**FIG. 32-31**), Schwitters's collage includes printed fragments from the street with newspaper scraps to comment on the postwar disorder of defeated Germany. One fragment describes the brutal overthrow of the short-lived socialist republic in Bremen.

Hannah Höch (1889–1978) produced even more pointed political photomontages. Between 1916 and 1926, she worked for Ullstein Verlag, Berlin's largest publishing house, designing decorative patterns and writing articles on crafts for a women's magazine. Höch considered herself part of the women's movement in the 1920s and disapproved of contemporary mass-media representations of women. She had to fight for her place as the sole woman in the Berlin Dada group, one of whose male members described her contribution disparagingly as merely conjuring up beer and sandwiches. In **CUT WITH THE KITCHEN KNIFE DADA THROUGH THE LAST WEIMAR BEER-BELLY**

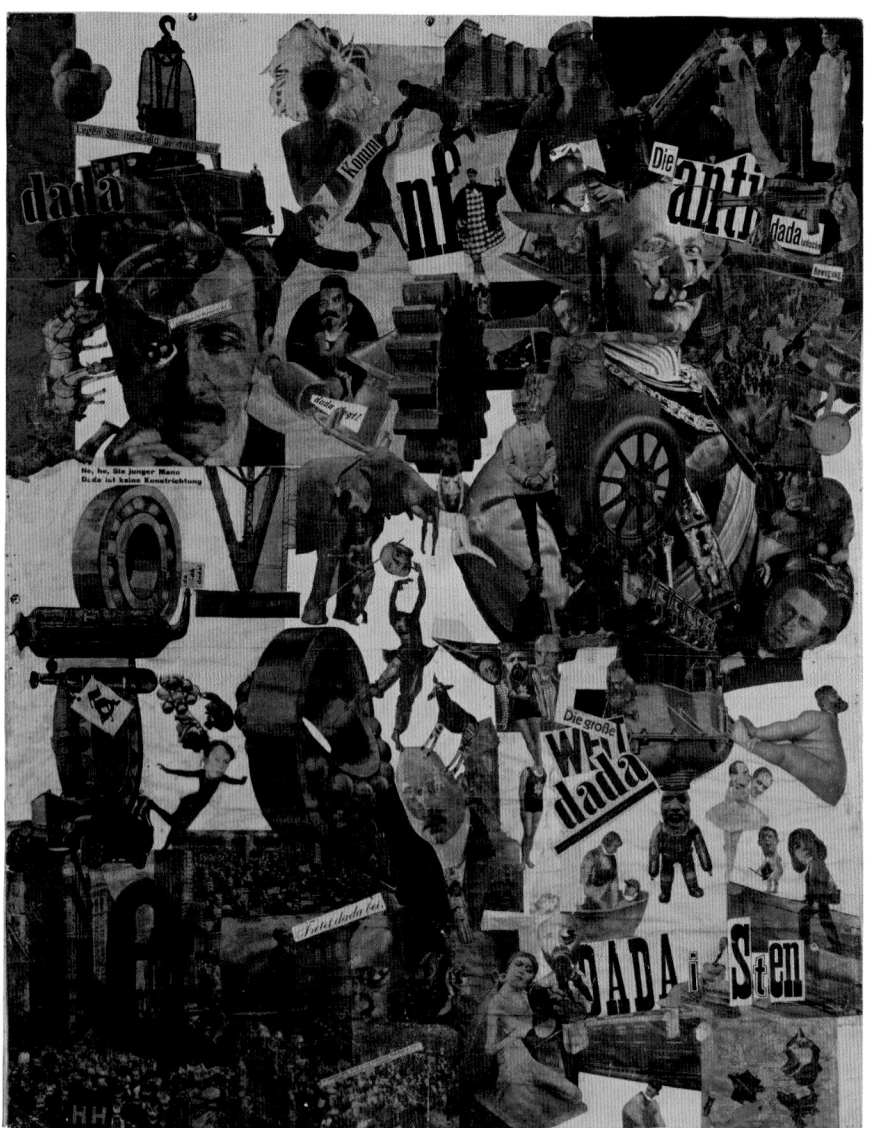

32–32 Hannah Höch **CUT WITH THE KITCHEN KNIFE DADA THROUGH THE LAST WEIMAR BEER-BELLY CULTURAL EPOCH IN GERMANY**
1919. Photomontage and collage with watercolor, 44⅞ × 35⅜″ (114 × 90 cm). Nationalgalerie, Staatliche Museen zu Berlin.

Credit: © 2016 Photo Scala, Florence/BPK, Bildargentur für Kunst, Kultur und Geschichte, Berlin.Photo Jörg P. Anders. © 2016 Artists Rights Society (ARS), New York/VG Bild-Kunst, Bonn

CULTURAL EPOCH IN GERMANY (FIG. 32-32), Höch combines images and words from the popular press, political posters, and photographs to create a complex and angry critique of the Weimar Republic in 1919. This photomontage includes portraits of androgynous Dada characters, such as herself and several other Berlin Dada artists, along with pictures of Marx and Lenin, asserting the artists' solidarity with revolutionaries in opposition to the anti-Dadaists whose images are gathered in the upper right corner.

Modernist Tendencies in America

When avant-garde Modern art was first widely exhibited in the United States, it received a cool welcome. While some American artists did work in abstract or Modernist ways, most preferred to work in a more naturalistic manner, at least until around 1915.

STIEGLITZ AND THE "291" GALLERY The chief proponent of European Modernism in the United States was the photographer Alfred Stieglitz (1864–1946). Born in New Jersey to a wealthy German immigrant family, Stieglitz studied photography in the 1880s at the Technische Hochschule in Berlin, quickly recognizing photography's artistic potential. In 1890, he began to photograph New York City street scenes. He promoted his views through an organization called the Photo-Secession, founded in 1902, and three years later opened a tiny gallery known as 291 on Fifth Avenue. Like Kahnweiler in Paris, he supported many of the early American Modernist artists in New York.

By 1910, the 291 gallery had become a focal point for both photographers and painters, with Stieglitz giving shows (sometimes their first) to artists such as Arthur Dove, John Marin, and Georgia O'Keeffe, and bringing to America the art of European artists such as Matisse, Braque, Cézanne, and Rodin. As a photographer himself, Stieglitz also sought to establish the legitimacy of photography as a fine art with these exhibitions.

In his own photographs, Stieglitz composed poetic images of romanticized urban scenes. In **THE FLATIRON BUILDING (FIG. 32-33)**, the tree trunk to the right is echoed by branches in the grove farther back and by the wedge-shaped Flatiron Building to the rear. The entire scene is suffused with a misty, wintery atmosphere, which the artist created by manipulating his viewpoint, exposure, and possibly both the negative and the print itself. Ironically, Stieglitz softens and romanticizes the Flatiron Building, one of New York's earliest skyscrapers and a symbol of the city's modernity. The magazine *Camera Work*, a high-quality photographic publication that Stieglitz edited, published a reproduction of this photograph in 1903; it

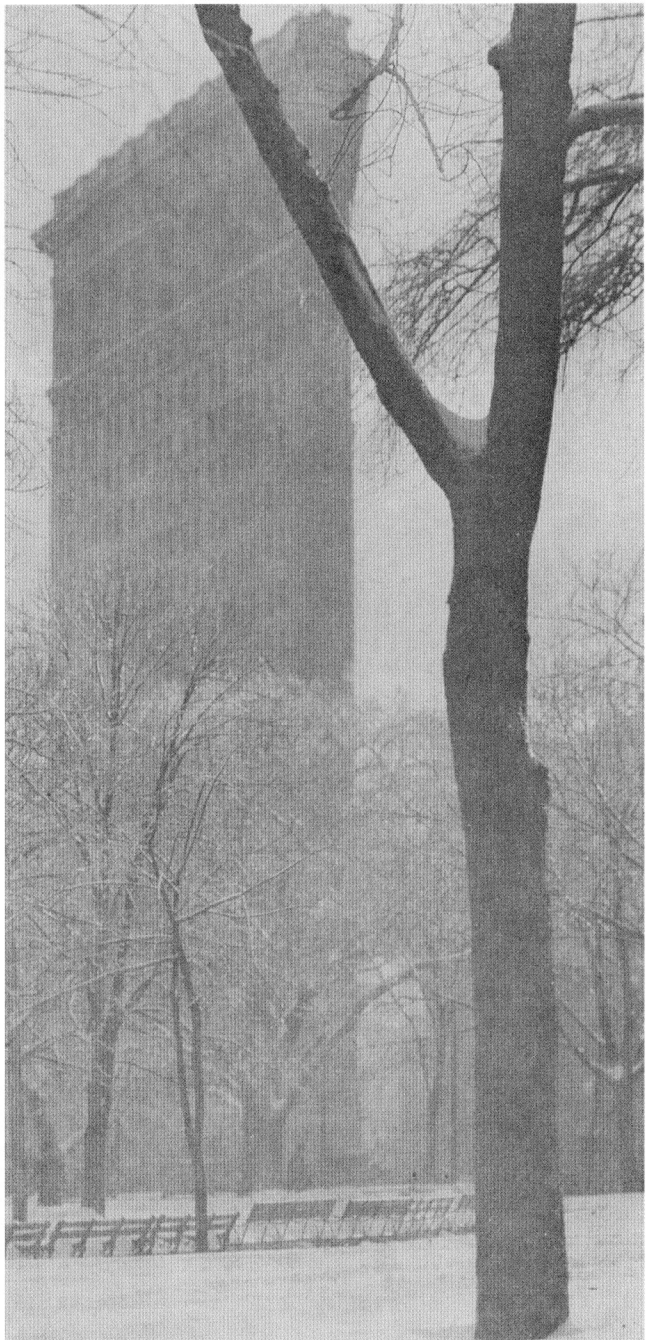

32–33 Alfred Stieglitz **THE FLATIRON BUILDING, NEW YORK**

1903. Photogravure, 6¹¹⁄₁₆ × 3⁵⁄₁₆″ (17 × 8.4 cm) mounted. Metropolitan Museum of Art, New York. Gift of J.B. Neumann, 1958 (58.577.37).

Credit: © 2016 Georgia O'Keeffe Museum/Artists Rights Society (ARS), New York. © 2016. Digital image, The Metropolitan Museum of Art, New York/Art Resource/Scala, Florence

also featured numerous images of American and European Modernist art as well as some important American Modernist art criticism.

THE ARMORY SHOW AND HOME-GROWN MODERNISM In 1913, Modernist art arrived in New York en masse with an enormous exhibition held in the drill hall of

the 69th Regiment Armory on Lexington Avenue between 25th and 26th Streets. Walt Kuhn (1877–1949) and Arthur B. Davies (1862–1928) were the principal organizers of the so-called Armory Show, which featured more than 1,600 works, a quarter of them by European artists. Most of the art, even the Modernist art, was well received and sold well, but the art of a few European Modernists, including Matisse and Duchamp in particular, caused a public outcry in which the artists were described as "cousins to the anarchists." When selected works from the exhibition traveled on to Chicago, a few faculty members and some students of the School of the Art Institute hanged Matisse in effigy, while civic leaders called for a morals commission to investigate the show. Yet the exhibition consolidated American Modernist art and inspired its artists, who later found more enthusiastic collectors and exhibition venues.

One of the most significant early American Modernists was Arthur Dove (1880–1946). Dove studied the work of the Fauves in Europe in 1907–1909 and even exhibited at the Autumn Salon. After returning home, he began painting abstract nature studies at about the same time as Kandinsky, although each was unaware of the other. Dove's **NATURE SYMBOLIZED NO. 2** (FIG. 32–34) is one of a remarkable series of small works that reveals his beliefs about the spiritual power of nature. But while Kandinsky's art focuses on a spiritual vision of nature, Dove's abstract paintings reflect his deeply felt experience of the landscape itself; he said that he had "no [artistic] background except perhaps the woods, running streams, hunting, fishing, camping, the sky." Dove supported himself by farming in rural Connecticut, but he exhibited his art in New York and was both well received by and well connected to the New York art community.

32–34 Arthur Dove **NATURE SYMBOLIZED NO. 2**

c. 1911. Pastel on paper, 18 × 21⅝″ (45.8 × 55 cm). The Art Institute of Chicago. Alfred Stieglitz Collection (1949.533).

Credit: Photo © The Art Institute of Chicago

A Closer Look

PORTRAIT OF A GERMAN OFFICER

While living in Berlin in 1914, Hartley fell in love with a young Prussian lieutenant, Karl von Freyburg, whom Hartley described as "in every way a perfect being—physically, spiritually, and mentally." Freyburg's death in World War I devastated Hartley, who memorialized this fallen warrior in a series of symbolic portraits.

Symbolic references to Freyburg include epaulettes, lance tips, and the Iron Cross he was awarded posthumously.

The black-and-white checkerboard patterns represent Freyburg's love of chess.

The blue-and-white diamond pattern comes from the Bavarian flag; the red, white, and black bands constitute the flag of the German Empire, adopted in 1871, and the black-and-white stripes are those of the historic flag of Prussia.

Freyburg's regiment number ("4") is shown at the center of the abstracted chest along with a red cursive *E*, which stands for "Edmund" (Hartley's given name). This places Hartley over Freyburg's heart.

The funereal black background heightens the intensity of the foreground colors.

Hartley identifies his subject with his initials ("Kv.F") in gold on red.

Freyburg's age ("24") is noted in gold on blue.

The red cross means injury or death and also refers to the International Red Cross, often seen in Berlin during the war.

32–35 Marsden Hartley **PORTRAIT OF A GERMAN OFFICER**
c. 1914. Oil on canvas, 68¼ × 41⅜" (1.78 × 1.05 m). Metropolitan Museum of Art, New York. Alfred Stieglitz Collection, 1949 (49.70.42).

Credit: © 2016. Image copyright The Metropolitan Museum of Art/Art Resource/Scala, Florence

Another pioneer of American Modernism who exhibited at the Armory Show was Marsden Hartley (1877–1943), who was also a regular exhibitor at 291. Between 1912 and 1915, Hartley lived mostly abroad, first in Paris, where he discovered Cubism, then in Berlin, where he began to paint colorful Expressionistic art. Around 1914, however, Hartley developed a powerfully original and intense style of his own in *Portrait of a German Officer* (see "Closer Look" opposite), a tightly arranged composition of boldly colored shapes and patterns interspersed with numbers, letters, and fragments of German military imagery that memorializes Karl von Freyburg, a German soldier with whom Hartley had fallen in love.

Stieglitz "discovered" Georgia O'Keeffe (1887–1986)—born in rural Wisconsin, and already studying and teaching art between 1905 and 1915—when a New York friend showed him some of her charcoal drawings. Stieglitz's reported response was "At last, a woman on paper!"

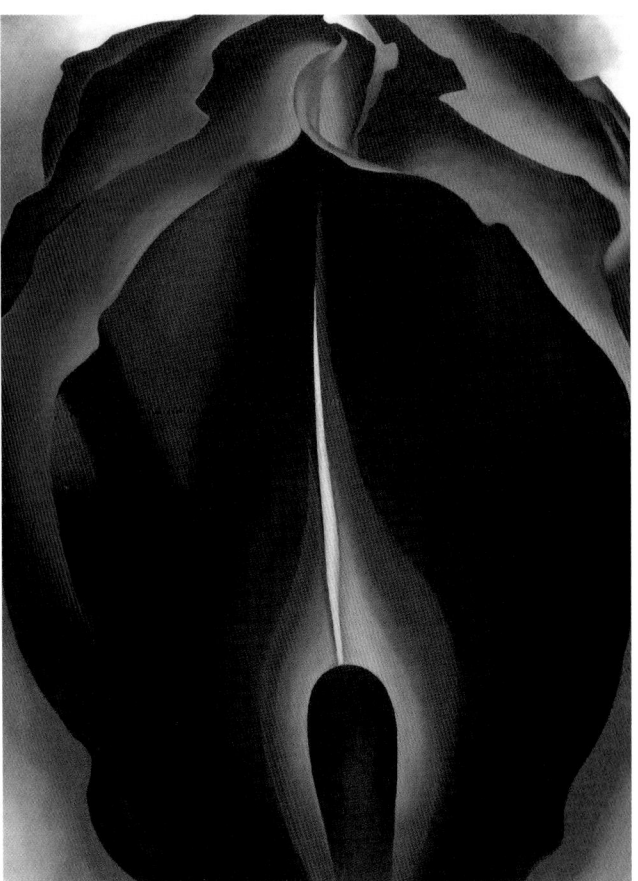

32–37 Georgia O'Keeffe **JACK-IN-THE-PULPIT, NO. IV**
1930. Oil on canvas, 40 × 30″ (101.6 × 76.2 cm). National Gallery of Art, Washington, DC. Alfred Stieglitz Collection, Bequest of Georgia O'Keeffe 1987.58.3.

Credit: © 2016 Georgia O'Keeffe Museum/Artists Rights Society (ARS), New York. Image courtesy the National Gallery of Art, Washington

32–36 Georgia O'Keeffe **CITY NIGHT**
1926. Oil on canvas, 48 × 30″ (123 × 76.9 cm). Minneapolis Institute of Arts. Gift of funds from the Regis Corporation, Mr. and Mrs. W. John Driscoll, the Beim Foundation, the Larsen Fund (80.28).

Credit: © 2016 Georgia O'Keeffe Museum/Artists Rights Society (ARS), New York. Bridgeman Images

In 1916, he included O'Keeffe's work in a group show at 291 and mounted her first solo exhibition the following year. O'Keeffe moved to New York in 1918 and married Stieglitz in 1924. In 1925, she began to paint New York skyscrapers, which were acclaimed at the time as embodiments of American inventiveness and energy. But paintings such as **CITY NIGHT** (**FIG. 32–36**) are not unambiguous celebrations of lofty buildings. She portrays the skyscrapers from a low vantage point so that they appear to loom ominously over the viewer; their dark tonalities, stark forms, and exaggerated perspective produce a sense of menace that also appears in the art of other American Modernists.

In 1925, O'Keeffe also began to exhibit a series of close-up paintings of flowers, which became her best-known subjects. In **JACK-IN-THE-PULPIT, NO. IV** (**FIG. 32–37**) of 1930, O'Keeffe brings the heart of the flower to the front and center of the picture plane, revealing its inner forms and surfaces. By painting the flower's hidden, organic aspects rather than the way it looks to a distant viewer, she creates from it a new abstract beauty, distilling the vigor of the plant's life force. Critics described O'Keeffe's flower paintings as elementally feminine and vaginal, and

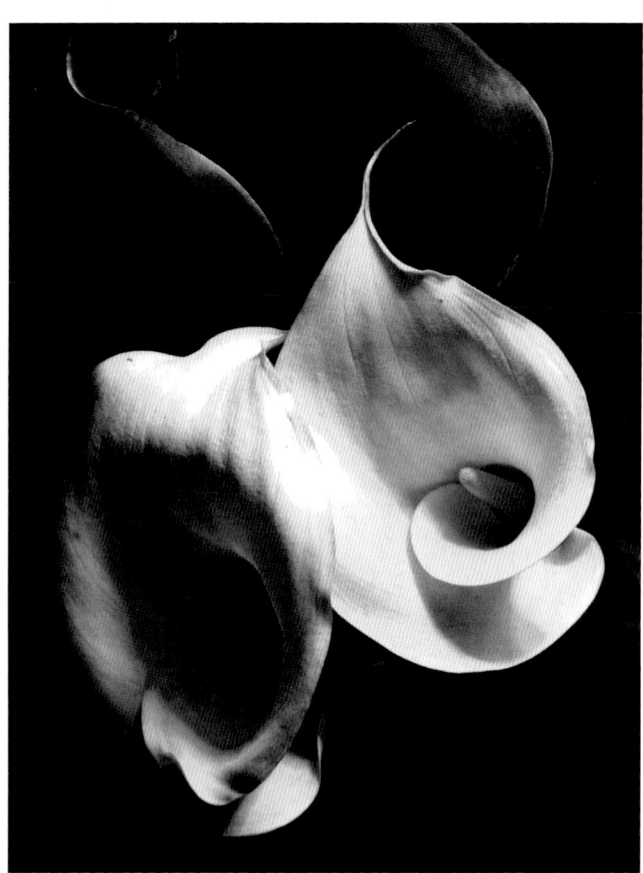

32–38 Imogen Cunningham **TWO CALLAS**
c.1925. Gelatin-silver print, 12 × 9½″ (30.4 × 24.1 cm).
Museum of Modern Art, New York.

Credit: © 2016 Imogen Cunningham Trust

Stieglitz did little to dissuade viewers from this reading. In fact, he promoted it—in spite of O'Keeffe's strong objections to this critical caricature and its implicit pigeonholing of her as a "woman artist." In 1929, O'Keeffe began spending summers in New Mexico; she moved there permanently in the 1940s, dedicating her art to evocative representations of the local landscape and culture.

Imogen Cunningham (1883–1976) followed in O'Keeffe's footsteps with a series of experimental photographs that emphasize the abstract patterns of plants by zooming in to extract them from their natural context. In her photograph of **TWO CALLAS** (**FIG. 32-38**), Cunningham uses straightforward camera work to capture the forms and textures of her subjects accurately, if drained of their color. But the artistic character of her photographic image depends not on the exacting detail recorded by the camera, but on the compositional choices and dramatic lighting controlled by the artist who used it.

32–39 Adolf Loos
STEINER HOUSE, VIENNA
1910.

Credit: Photo: Carlo Fumarola

32–40 Le Corbusier **VILLA SAVOYE, POISSY-SUR-SEINE**
France. 1929–1930.

Credit: © F.L.C./ADAGP, Paris/Artists Rights Society (ARS), New York 2016. © 2016. White Images/Scala, Florence.

Early Modern Architecture

New industrial materials and engineering innovations enabled twentieth-century architects to create buildings of unprecedented height that vastly increased the usable space in structures built on scarce and valuable city lots. At the same time that Modernist artists in Europe rejected the decorative in painting and sculpture, American architects increasingly embraced the plain, geometric shapes and undecorated surfaces of skyscraper architecture.

EUROPEAN MODERNISM In Europe, a stripped-down and severely geometric style of Modernist architecture developed partly in reaction to the natural organic lines of Art Nouveau. In Vienna, Adolf Loos (1870–1933), one of the pioneers of European architectural Modernism, insisted in his 1913 essay "Ornament and Crime" that "the evolution of a culture is synonymous with the removal of ornament from utilitarian objects." For Loos, ornament was a sign of cultural degeneracy. Thus his **STEINER HOUSE (FIG. 32–39)** is a stucco-covered, reinforced concrete construction without decorative embellishment. The rectangular windows, for instance, are completely plain, and they were arranged only in relation to the functional demands of interior spaces. Loos argued that the only purpose of a building's interior was to provide protection from the elements.

The most important French Modernist architect was Swiss-born Le Corbusier, whose **VILLA SAVOYE (FIG. 32–40)**, a private home outside Paris, became an icon of the International Style (discussed later in this chapter) and reflects his Purist ideals in its geometric design and lack of ornamentation. It is also one of the best expressions of his **domino construction** system, introduced in 1914, in which slabs of ferroconcrete (concrete reinforced with steel bars) rest on six free-standing steel posts placed at the positions of the six dots on a domino piece. Over the next decade Le Corbusier further explored the possibilities of the domino system and in 1926 published "The Five Points of a New Architecture," in which he proposed raising houses above the ground on pilotis (free-standing posts); using flat roofs as terraces; using movable partition walls slotted between supports on the interior and **curtain walls** (non-load-bearing walls) on the exterior to allow greater design flexibility; and using ribbon windows (which run the length of a wall). These became common features of Modernist architecture. Le Corbusier believed that a modern house should be "a machine for living in," meaning that it should be designed as rationally and functionally as an automobile or a machine. After World War I—like his fellow Modernist architects—Le Corbusier developed designs for mass-produced, standardized housing to help rebuild Europe's destroyed infrastructure.

32–41 Frank Lloyd Wright **FREDERICK C. ROBIE HOUSE, CHICAGO**
1906–1909. Chicago History Museum. (HB-19312A2).

Credit: © Universal Images Group North America LLC/DeAgostini/Alamy Stock Photo

AMERICAN MODERNISM   Frank Lloyd Wright (1867–1959) was not only America's most important Modernist architect, he was also one of the most influential architects in the world during the early twentieth century. After briefly studying engineering at the University of Wisconsin, Wright apprenticed to a Chicago architect, then spent five years with the firm of Dankmar Adler and Louis Sullivan (SEE FIG. 31–55), advancing to the post of chief drafter. In 1893, Wright established his own office, specializing in domestic architecture. Around 1900, he and several other architects in the Oak Park suburb of Chicago—together known as the Prairie School—began to design low, horizontal houses with flat roofs and heavy overhangs that echoed the flat plains of the prairie in the Midwest.

32–42 Frank Lloyd Wright **COLOR RECONSTRUCTION OF THE DINING ROOM, FREDERICK C. ROBIE HOUSE**

Credit: Courtesy of the Frank Lloyd Wright Trust. © 2016 Frank Lloyd Wright Foundation, Scottsdale, AZ/Artists Rights Society (ARS), NY

32-43 Frank Lloyd Wright **FALLINGWATER (EDGAR KAUFMANN HOUSE), MILL RUN**
Pennsylvania. 1937.

Credit: Thomas A Heinz, AIA, Photographer © Western Pennsulvania Conservancy 2007

The **FREDERICK C. ROBIE HOUSE** (FIG. **32-41**) is one of Wright's early **Prairie Style** masterpieces. A central chimney, above a fireplace that radiated heat throughout the house in the bitter Chicago winter, forms the center of the sprawling design. Low, flat overhanging roofs—dramatically cantilevered on both sides of the chimney—shade against the summer sun, and open porches provide places to sleep outside on cool summer nights. Low bands of windows—many with stained glass—surround the house, creating a colored screen between the interior and the outside world, while also inviting those inside to look through the windows into the garden beyond.

The main story is one long space divided into living and dining areas by a free-standing fireplace. There are no dividing walls. Wright had visited the Japanese exhibit at the 1893 Chicago World's Fair and was deeply influenced by the aesthetics of Japanese architecture, particularly its sense of space and screenlike windows (see "*Shoin* Design" in Chapter 26 on page 835). Wright's homes frequently featured built-in closets and bookcases, and he hid heating and lighting fixtures when possible. He also designed and arranged the furniture for his interiors (FIG. **32-42**). Here, machine-cut components create the chairs' modern geometric designs, while their high backs huddle around the table to form the intimate effect of a room within a room. Wright integrated lights and flower holders into posts near the table's corners so that there would be no need for lights or flowers on the table.

Wright had an uneasy relationship with European Modernist architecture; he was uninterested in the machine aesthetic of Le Corbusier. Although he routinely used new building materials such as ferroconcrete, plate glass, and steel, he tried to maintain a natural sensibility, connecting his buildings to their sites by using brick and local wood or stone. **FALLINGWATER** (FIG. **32-43**) in rural Pennsylvania is a prime example of this practice. It is also the most famous expression of Wright's conviction that buildings should not simply sit *on* the landscape but coordinate *with* it.

Fallingwater was commissioned by Edgar Kaufmann, a Pittsburgh department-store owner, to replace a family summer cottage on the site of a waterfall and a pool where his children played. To Kaufmann's surprise, Wright decided to build the new house right into the cliff and over the pool, allowing the waterfall to flow around and under the house. A large boulder where the family had sunbathed in the summers was used for the central hearthstone of the fireplace. In a dramatic move that engineers questioned (with reason, as subsequent sagging has shown), Wright used cantilevers to extend a series of broad concrete terraces out from the cliff to parallel the great slabs of natural rock below. Poured concrete forms the terraces, but Wright painted the material a soft earth tone. Long bands of windows and glass doors offer spectacular views uniting woods, water, and house. Such houses do not simply testify to the ideal of living in harmony with nature; they declare war on the modern city. When asked what could be done to improve city architecture, Wright responded: "Tear it down."

Mary Colter (1869–1958) expressed an even stronger connection to the landscape in her architecture. Born in Pittsburgh and educated at the California School of Design in San Francisco, she spent much of her career as architect and decorator for the Fred Harvey Company, a firm in the Southwest that catered to the tourist trade. Colter was an avid student of Native American arts, and her buildings quoted liberally from Puebloan traditions, notably in the use of exposed logs for structural supports. She designed several visitor facilities at Grand Canyon National Park, of which **LOOKOUT STUDIO** (**FIG. 32-44**) is the most dramatic. Built on the edge of the canyon's south rim, the building's foundation is in natural rock, its walls are built from local stone, and the roofline is deliberately irregular to echo the surrounding canyon wall. The only concession to modernity is a liberal use of glass windows and a smooth cement floor. Colter's designs for hotels and railroad stations throughout the region helped establish a distinctive Southwest style.

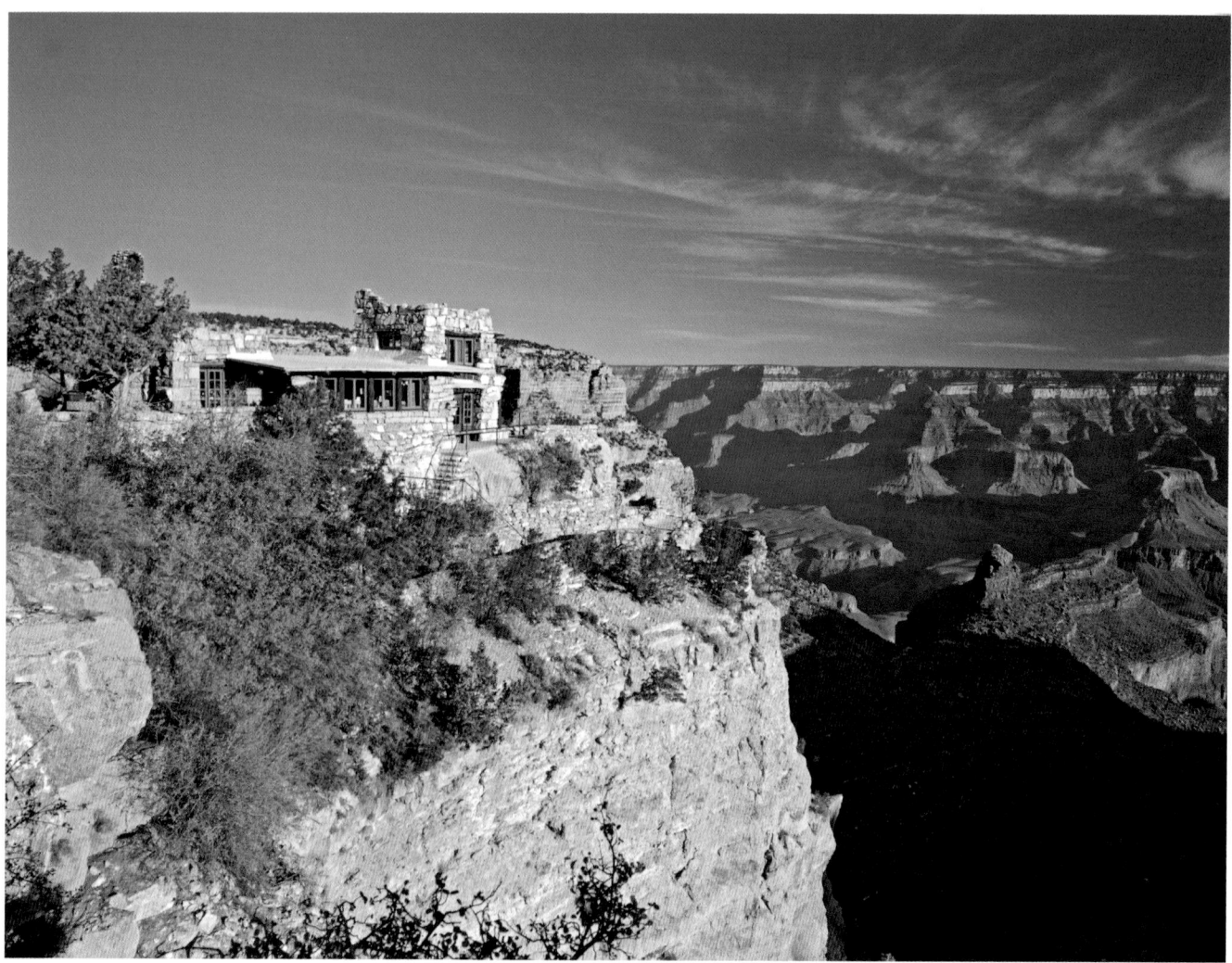

32-44 Mary Colter **LOOKOUT STUDIO, GRAND CANYON NATIONAL PARK**
Arizona. 1914. Grand Canyon National Park Museum Collection.

THE AMERICAN SKYSCRAPER   After 1900, New York City assumed a lead over Chicago in the development of the skyscraper, whose soaring height was made possible by the use of the steel-frame skeleton for structural support (see "The Skyscraper" below). New York clients, however, rejected the more utilitarian Chicago style of Louis Sullivan and others, preferring the historicizing approach then still popular on the east coast. The **WOOLWORTH BUILDING** (FIG. 32-45)

of 1911–1913, designed by the Minnesota-based firm of Cass Gilbert (1859–1934), was the world's tallest building at 792 feet and 55 floors when first completed. Its Gothic-style external details, inspired by the soaring towers of late medieval churches, gave the building a strong visual personality. In 1916, a prominent New York pastor christened this building as the "Cathedral of Commerce" to characterize its status as an ethical white-collar workplace.

Elements of Architecture

THE SKYSCRAPER

The development of the skyscraper design and aesthetic depended on several things: metal beams and girders for the structural-support skeleton; separation of the building-support structure from the enclosing wall layer (the cladding); fireproof materials and measures; elevators; and overall integration of plumbing, central heating, artificial lighting, and ventilation systems. The first generation of skyscrapers, built between about 1880 and 1900, were concentrated in the Midwest, chiefly in Chicago and St. Louis (SEE FIG. 31-55). Second-generation skyscrapers, mostly with over 20 stories, date from after 1895 and are found more frequently in New York. The first tall buildings were free-standing towers, sometimes with a base, such as the Woolworth Building of 1911–1913 (SEE FIG. 32-45). New York City's Building Zone Resolution of 1916 introduced mandatory setbacks—decreases in girth as the building rose—to ensure light and ventilation to adjacent sites. Built in 1931, the 1,250-foot setback form of the Empire State Building, diagrammed here, has a streamlined design. The Art Deco exterior cladding (see diagram inset) conceals the structural elements, and mechanisms such as elevators that make its great height possible. The Empire State Building was the tallest building in the world when it was built, and its distinctive profile ensures that it remains one of the most recognizable even today.

skyscraper

32–45 Cass Gilbert **WOOLWORTH BUILDING, NEW YORK** 1911–1913.

Credit: Photo © Andrew Garn

Art Between the Wars in Europe

What are the new developments in European Modernism between World Wars I and II?

World War I had a devastating effect on Europe's artists and architects. Many responded to the destruction and loss of a generation of young men by criticizing the European tradition, while others concentrated on rebuilding. Either way, much of the art created between 1919 and 1939 addressed the needs and concerns of a society in turmoil or transition.

Utilitarian Art Forms in Russia

In the 1917 Russian Revolution, the radical socialist Bolsheviks overthrew the tsar, withdrew Russia from World War I, and turned inward to fight a civil war that lasted until 1920 and led to the establishment of the U.S.S.R. (Union of Soviet Socialist Republics). Most Russian avant-garde artists enthusiastically supported the Bolsheviks, who initially in turn supported them.

The case of Vladimir Tatlin is fairly representative. In 1919, as part of his work on a committee to implement Russian leader Vladimir Lenin's Plan for Monumental Propaganda, Tatlin conceived the Monument to the Third International (**FIG. 32–46**), a 1,300-foot-tall building to house the organization devoted to the worldwide spread of communism. Tatlin's visionary plan combined the appearance of avant-garde sculpture with a fully utilitarian building, a new hybrid form as revolutionary as the politics it represented. In Tatlin's model, the steel structural support, a pair of leaning spirals connected by grillwork, is on the outside rather than the inside of the building. He combined the skeletal structure of the Eiffel Tower (SEE FIG. 31–1)—which his tower would dwarf—with the formal vocabulary of the Cubo-Futurists to convey the dynamism of what Lenin called the "permanent revolution" of communism. Inside the steel frame would be four separate spaces: a large cube to house conferences and congress meetings, a pyramid for executive committees, a cylinder for propaganda offices, and a hemisphere at the top, apparently meant for radio equipment. Each of these units would rotate at a different speed, from yearly at the bottom to hourly at the top. Although Russia lacked the resources to build Tatlin's monument, models displayed publicly were a symbolic affirmation of faith in what the country's science and technology would eventually achieve.

CONSTRUCTIVISM In 1921, one of Tatlin's associates, Aleksandr Rodchenko (1891–1956), helped launch a group known as the Constructivists, which was committed to leaving the studio and going "into the factory, where the

32–46 Vladimir Tatlin **MODEL FOR THE MONUMENT TO THE THIRD INTERNATIONAL**
1919–1920. Wood, iron, and glass. Destroyed.

Credit: © Vladimir Tatlin

real body of life is made"—renouncing painting as a selfish activity and condemning self-expression as weak, unproductive, and socially irresponsible. Instead of pleasing themselves, politically committed artists would create useful objects and promote the aims of the collective, seeing themselves as workers who literally "constructed" art for the people. After 1921, Rodchenko himself worked as a photographer producing posters, books, textiles, and theater sets to foster the goals of the new Soviet society.

In 1925, Rodchenko designed a model **WORKERS' CLUB** for the Soviet Pavilion at the Paris International Exposition of Modern Decorative and Industrial Arts (**FIG. 32–47**). He emphasized ease of use and simplicity of construction; the furniture was made of wood because Soviet industry was best equipped for mass production in wood. The high, straight backs of the chairs were meant to promote a physical and moral posture of uprightness among the workers.

32–47 Aleksandr Rodchenko **WORKERS' CLUB**
Exhibited at the International Exposition of Modern Decorative and Industrial Arts, Paris. 1925.

Credit: Art © Estate of Aleksandr Rodchenko/RAO, Moscow, VAGA, New York

32–48 El Lissitzky **PROUN SPACE**
Created for the Great Berlin Art Exhibition. 1923, reconstruction 1971. Collection Van Abbemuseum, Eindhoven, the Netherlands.

Credit: Photo: Peter Cox, Eindhoven, The Netherlands

Another artist active in early Soviet Russia was El Lissitzky (1890–1941). After the Revolution, he taught architecture and graphic arts at the Vitebsk School of Fine Arts, where Malevich also taught. By 1919, Lissitzky was both teaching and using a Constructivist vocabulary for propaganda posters and for artworks he called Prouns (pronounced "pro-oon"), thought to be an acronym for the Russian *proekt utverzhdenya novogo* ("project for the affirmation of the new"). Although most Prouns were paintings or prints, a few of them were early examples of **installation art** (**FIG. 32-48**)—artworks created for a specific site, arranged to create a total environment. Lissitzky rejected painting as too personal and imprecise, preferring to "construct" Prouns for the collective using the less personal instruments of mechanical drawing. Like many other Soviet artists of the late 1920s, Lissitzky also turned to more socially engaged projects such as architectural design, typography, photography, and photomontage for publication.

SOCIALIST REALISM In the mid-1920s, Soviet artists increasingly rejected abstraction in favor of a more widely understandable, and thus more politically useful, Socialist Realism that was ultimately established as official Soviet art. Many of Russia's pioneering Modernists and Constructivists made the change willingly because they were already committed to the national cause; others who refused to change were fired from public positions and lost public support.

The move to Socialist Realism was led by the Association of Artists of Revolutionary Russia (AKhRR), founded in 1922 to depict Russian workers, peasants, revolutionary activists, and the Red Army. AKhRR documented the history of the U.S.S.R. by promoting its leaders and goals. Artists were commissioned to create public paintings and sculptures as well as posters for mass distribution; their subjects were heroic or inspirational people and themes, and their style was an easily readable realism.

Vera Mukhina (1889–1953) was a member of AKhRR and is best known for her 78-foot-tall stainless-steel **WORKER AND COLLECTIVE FARM WOMAN** (**FIG. 32-49**), a powerfully built male factory worker and an equally powerful female farm laborer with hammer and sickle held high in the air—the same two tools that appeared on the Soviet flag. The figures stand as equals, partners in their common cause, striding into the future with determined faces, their windblown clothing billowing behind them.

32–49 Vera Mukhina **WORKER AND COLLECTIVE FARM WOMAN**
Sculpture for the Soviet Pavilion, Paris Universal Exposition. 1937.
Stainless steel, height approx. 78′ (23.8 m).

Credit: Art © Estate of Vera Mukhina/RAO, Moscow/VAGA, New York

De Stijl in the Netherlands

In the Netherlands after World War I, abstraction took a different turn from that in the U.S.S.R. The Dutch artist Piet Mondrian (1872–1944) encountered Cubism on a trip to Paris in 1912, where he began to abstract animals, trees, and landscapes, searching for their essential form. After his return to the Netherlands he met Theo van Doesburg (1883–1931), who in 1917 started a magazine named *De Stijl* ("The Style") that became a focal point for Dutch artists, architects, and designers after the war. Writing in the magazine, Van Doesburg argued that beauty took two distinct forms: sensual or subjective beauty and a higher, rational, universal beauty. He challenged De Stijl (note the term translates as "*The* Style" rather than "*A* Style") artists to aspire to universal beauty. Mondrian sought to accomplish this by eliminating everything sensual or subjective from his paintings, but he also followed M.H.J. Schoenmaekers's ideas about Theosophy as expressed in his 1915 book *New Image of the World*. Schoenmaekers argued that an inner visual construction of nature consisted of a balance between opposing forces, such as heat and cold, male and female, and order and disorder, and that artists might represent this inner construction in abstract paintings by using only horizontal and vertical lines and primary colors.

Mondrian's later paintings are visual embodiments of both Schoenmaekers's theory and De Stijl's artistic ideas. In **COMPOSITION WITH YELLOW, RED, AND BLUE** (FIG. 32–50), for example, Mondrian uses the three primary colors (red, yellow, and blue), two neutrals (white and black), and a grid of horizontal and vertical lines in his search for the essence of higher beauty and the balance of forces.

32–50 Piet Mondrian **COMPOSITION WITH YELLOW, RED, AND BLUE**
1927. Oil on canvas, 14⅞ × 13¾″
(37.8 × 34.9 cm). The Menil Collection, Houston.

32–51 Gerrit Rietveld **SCHRÖDER HOUSE, UTRECHT**
The Netherlands. 1925.

Credit: © Ger Bosma/Alamy Stock Photo

Mondrian's opposing lines and colors balance a harmony of opposites that he called a "dynamic equilibrium," which he achieved by carefully plotting an arrangement of colors, shapes, and visual weights grouped asymmetrically around the edges of a canvas, with the center acting as a blank white fulcrum. Mondrian hoped that De Stijl would have applications in the real world by creating an entirely new visual environment for living, designed according to the rules of a universal beauty that, when perfectly balanced, would bring equilibrium and purity to the world. Mondrian said that he hoped to be the world's last artist, because when universal beauty infused all aspects of life, there would no longer be a need for art.

32–52 Gerrit Rietveld **INTERIOR, SCHRÖDER HOUSE, WITH "RED-BLUE" CHAIR**
1925.

Credit: Photo: Jannes Linders. © 2016 Artists Rights Society (ARS), New York/c/o Pictoright Amsterdam

The architect and designer Gerrit Rietveld (1888–1964) applied Mondrian's principles of dynamic equilibrium and De Stijl's aesthetic theories to architecture and created one of the most important examples of the International Style. Interlocking gray and white planes of varying sizes, combined with horizontal and vertical accents in primary colors and black, create the radically asymmetrical exterior of the **SCHRÖDER HOUSE** in Utrecht (**FIG. 32-51**). Inside, the **"RED-BLUE" CHAIR** (**FIG. 32-52**) echoes this same arrangement. Sliding partitions allow modifications in the interior spaces used for sleeping, working, and entertaining. The patron of the house, Truus Schröder Schräder, wanted a home that suggested an elegant austerity with basic necessities sleekly integrated into a balanced and restrained whole.

The Bauhaus in Germany

In Germany, Walter Gropius (1883–1969) considered the strict geometric shapes and lines of Purism (SEE FIG. 32-40) and De Stijl too rigid and argued that a true German architecture and design should emerge organically. To help this occur, he founded the Bauhaus ("House of Building") in Weimar in 1919. At the Bauhaus, Gropius brought together German architects, designers, and craftspeople to create an integrated system of design and production based on German traditions and styles. Gropius believed that he could revive the spirit of collaboration of the medieval building guilds (*Bauhütten*) that had once erected Germany's cathedrals.

Although Gropius's "Bauhaus Manifesto" of 1919 declared that "the ultimate goal of all artistic activity is the building," the Bauhaus offered no formal training in architecture until 1927. Gropius only allowed his students to begin architectural training after they completed a mandatory foundation course and received full training in design and crafts in the Bauhaus workshops. These included pottery, metalwork, textiles, stained glass, furniture, wood carving, and wall paintings. In 1922, Gropius added a new emphasis on industrial design and the next year hired the Hungarian-born László Moholy-Nagy (1895–1946) to reorient the workshops toward more functional design suitable for mass production.

In 1925, when the Bauhaus moved to Dessau, Gropius designed its new building. Although the structure openly acknowledges its reinforced concrete, steel, and glass materials, there is also a balanced asymmetry to its three large cubic areas that was intended to convey the dynamism of modern life (**FIG. 32-53**). A glass-panel wall wraps around two sides of the workshop wing of the building to

32-53 Walter Gropius **BAUHAUS BUILDING, DESSAU**
Anhalt, Germany. 1925–1926. View from northwest.
Credit: © stockeurope/Alamy Stock Photo.

32–54 Marianne Brandt **COFFEE AND TEA SERVICE**

1924. Silver and ebony, with glass cover for sugar bowl. Tray, 13 × 20¼"
(33 × 51.5 cm). Bauhaus Archiv, Berlin.

Credit: © 2016 Artists Rights Society (ARS), New York/VG Bild-Kunst, Bonn

provide natural light for the workshops inside, while a parapet below demonstrates how modern engineering methods could create light, airy spaces. Both Moholy-Nagy and Gropius left the Bauhaus in 1928. The school eventually moved to Berlin in 1932, but lasted only one more year before the new German chancellor, Adolf Hitler, forced its closure. Hitler opposed Modernist art on two grounds: First, he believed it was cosmopolitan rather than nationalistic; second, he erroneously maintained that it was overly influenced by Jews.

Marianne Brandt's elegant **COFFEE AND TEA SERVICE** (FIG. 32-54)—a prototype handcrafted in silver for mass production in cheaper metals—is an example of the collaboration between design and industry at the Bauhaus. While the Bauhaus was in Dessau, Brandt (1893–1983) also designed lighting fixtures and table lamps for mass production, earning much-needed revenue for the school. After the departure of Moholy-Nagy and Gropius, Brandt took over the metal workshop for a year before she too left in 1929. As a woman in the otherwise all-male metal workshop, Brandt made an exceptional contribution to the Bauhaus.

Although the Bauhaus claimed that women were admitted on an equal basis with men, Gropius opposed their education as architects and channeled them into what he considered the more gender-appropriate workshops of pottery and textiles. Berlin-born Anni Albers (b. Annelise Fleischmann, 1899–1994) arrived at the school in 1922 and married the Bauhaus graduate and professor Josef Albers (1888–1976) in 1925. Obliged to enter the textiles workshop rather than the painting studio, Anni Albers

32–55 Anni Albers **WALL HANGING**

1926. Silk, three-ply weave, 5'11⁵⁄₁₆" × 3'11⁵⁄₈" (1.83 × 1.22 m). Harvard Art Museums/Busch-Reisinger Museum, Association Fund.

Credit: © 2016 The Josef and Anni Albers Foundation/Artists Rights Society (ARS), New York. Bridgeman Images made "pictorial" weavings and wall hangings (**FIG. 32–55**) that were so innovative that they actually replaced paintings on the walls of several modern buildings. Her decentralized, rectilinear designs refer to the aesthetics of De Stijl, but differ in their open acknowledgment of the natural process of weaving. Albers's goal was "to let threads be articulate … and find a form for themselves to no other end than their own orchestration."

THE INTERNATIONAL STYLE   After World War I, increased communication among Modernist architects led to the development of a common formal language transcending national boundaries, which came to be known as the International Style. The first concentrated manifestation of the movement was in 1927 at the Deutscher Werkbund's Weissenhofsiedlung exhibition in Stuttgart, Germany, directed by Ludwig Mies van der Rohe (1886–1969), an architect who, like Gropius, was associated with the Bauhaus in Germany. The purpose of this semipermanent show was to present a range of model homes that used new technologies and made no reference to historical styles. The buildings featured flat roofs, plain walls, off-center openings, and rectilinear designs by Mies, Gropius, Le Corbusier, and others.

The term "International Style" became well known as a result of a 1932 exhibition at the Museum of Modern Art in New York called "The International Style: Architecture since 1922," organized by architectural historian Henry-Russell Hitchcock and architect and curator Philip Johnson. Hitchcock and Johnson identified three fundamental principles of the style.

The first was "the conception of architecture as volume rather than mass." The use of a structural skeleton of steel and ferroconcrete made it possible to eliminate load-bearing walls on both the exterior and the interior. As a result, buildings could be wrapped in skins of glass, metal, or masonry, creating the effect of enclosed space (volume) rather than dense material (mass). Interiors featured open, free-flowing plans providing maximum flexibility in the organization of space.

The second was "regularity rather than symmetry as the chief means of ordering design." Regular distribution of structural supports and the use of standard building parts promoted rectangular regularity, not the balanced axial symmetry of Classical architecture. The avoidance of Classical balance also encouraged an asymmetrical arrangement of the building's components, including doors and windows.

The third was the rejection of "arbitrary applied decoration." The new architecture depended on the intrinsic elegance of its materials and the formal arrangement of its elements to produce harmonious aesthetic effects. The most extreme International Style buildings would be unadorned glass boxes.

According to Hitchcock and Johnson, the International Style originated in the Netherlands (De Stijl), France (Purism), and Germany (Bauhaus). After the 1932 exhibition, it spread to the United States. The conceptual clarity of the International Style allowed it to remain vital until the 1970s, especially in the United States, where many of its original European architects, such as Mies and Gropius, who had escaped Hitler and the rise of Nazism in Germany in the 1930s, practiced.

SUPPRESSION OF THE AVANT-GARDE IN NAZI GERMANY   In the 1930s, the avant-garde was increasingly criticized by Hitler and the rising Nazi Party, eventually leading to direct efforts to suppress it. One of the principal targets was the Bauhaus. Through much of the 1920s, important artists such as Mies, Kandinsky, Josef Albers, and Paul Klee taught classes there, but they struggled against an increasingly hostile political climate. As early as 1924, conservatives accused the Bauhaus of being not only educationally unsound, but also politically subversive. To avoid having the school shut down, Gropius moved it to Dessau in 1925 at the invitation of Dessau's liberal mayor. But the mayor left office soon after the relocation, and his successors faced increasing political pressure to close the school. The Bauhaus moved again in 1932, this time to Berlin.

After Adolf Hitler came to power in 1933, the Nazi Party mounted an even more aggressive campaign against Modern art. In his youth Hitler had been a mediocre landscape painter, and he developed an intense hatred of the avant-garde. During the first year of his regime, the Bauhaus was forced to close permanently. A number of its faculty—including Albers, Gropius, and Mies—fled to the United States.

The Nazis also attacked German Expressionist artists, whose depictions of German politics and the economic crisis after the war criticized the state and whose frequent caricatures of German facial features and body types undermined Nazi attempts to redraw Germans as idealized Aryans. Expressionist and avant-garde art was removed from museums and confiscated, and artists were forbidden to buy materials and subjected to public intimidation.

In 1937 the Nazi leadership organized an exhibition called "Degenerate Art" of the work they had confiscated from German museums and artists. In it, they described avant-garde Modernism as sick and degraded, presenting the paintings and sculptures as specimens of pathology and scrawling slogans and derisive commentaries on the exhibition's walls (**FIG. 32–56**). Ironically, in Munich as many as 2 million people viewed the four-month exhibition of 650 paintings, sculptures, prints, and books, and another 1 million visitors saw it on its three-year tour of German cities.

32–56 THE DADA WALL IN ROOM 3 OF THE "DEGENERATE ART" ("ENTARTETE KUNST") EXHIBITION
Munich. 1937.

Credit: Art © Estate of George Grosz/Licensed by VAGA, New York. Akademie der Künste/Archiv Bildende Kunst/George Grosz-Archiv

Large numbers of confiscated works officially destined for destruction were actually taken by Nazi officials and sold in Switzerland in exchange for foreign currency. The ownership of much of the surviving art is still in question. Many artists fled to neighboring countries or the United States, but some, like Ernst Ludwig Kirchner, whose *Street, Berlin* (SEE FIG. 32-13) appeared in the "Degenerate Art" exhibition, were driven to suicide by their loss. Even the work of artists sympathetic to the Nazi position was not safe. The works of Emil Nolde (SEE FIG. 32-12), who had joined the Nazi Party in 1932, were also confiscated.

Surrealism and the Mind

In France during the early 1930s, a group of artists and writers took a very different approach to Modernism in a revolt against logic and reason. Embracing irrational, disorderly, aberrant, and even violent social interventions, Surrealism emerged initially as an offshoot of Dada, born from the mind of poet André Breton (1896–1966). Breton trained in medicine and psychiatry and served in a neurological hospital during World War I where he used Freudian analysis on shell-shocked soldiers. By 1924, Breton, still drawn to the vagaries of the human mind, published the "Manifesto of Surrealism," reflecting Freud's conception of the human mind as a battleground where the

forces of the unconscious wage a constant war against the rational, orderly, and oppressive forces of the conscious. Breton sought to explore humanity's most base, irrational, and forbidden sexual desires, secret fantasies, and violent instincts by freeing the conscious mind from reason. As he wrote in 1934, "we still live under the rule of logic." To escape this restraint, he and other Surrealists developed strategies to liberate the unconscious using dream analysis, free association, automatic writing, word games, and hypnotic trances. Surrealists studied acts of "criminal madness" and the "female mind" in particular, believing the latter to be weaker and more irrational than the male mind. The only way to improve the war-sick society of the 1920s, Breton thought, was to discover the more intense "surreality" that transcended rational constraint.

AUTOMATISM Surrealist artists employed a variety of techniques, including **automatism**—releasing the unconscious to create the work of art without rational intervention—in order to produce surprising new imagery and forms. Max Ernst (1891–1976), a self-taught German artist who collaborated in Cologne Dada and later joined Breton's circle in Paris, developed the automatist technique of **frottage** in 1925. First he rubbed a pencil or crayon over a piece of paper placed on a textured surface, then he allowed the resulting image to stimulate his imagination, discovering

32–57 Max Ernst **THE HORDE**
1927. Oil on canvas, 44⅞ × 57½" (114 × 146.1 cm).
Stedelijk Museum, Amsterdam.

Credit: © 2016 Artists Rights Society (ARS), New York/ADAGP,
Paris. Collection Stedelijk Museum, Amsterdam

within it fantastic creatures, plants, and land-scapes that he articulated more clearly with additional drawing. In painting, Ernst called this new technique **grattage**, laying a painted canvas on a textured surface and then scraping the paint away, then "revealing" the imagery he saw in the paint with additional painting. **THE HORDE** (**FIG. 32–57**) of 1927 shows a nightmarish scene of monsters advancing against an unseen force. Surely the horrors of World War I that Ernst had experienced first-hand in the German army lie behind such frightening images.

UNEXPECTED JUXTAPOSITIONS The paintings of Salvador Dalí (1904–1989) include more recognizable forms, but they also reveal the visual wonders of an unconscious mind run wild. Dalí trained at the San Fernando Academy of Fine Arts in Madrid, where he mastered traditional methods of illusionistic representation, and traveled to Paris in 1928, where he met the Surrealists. Dalí's

contribution to Surrealist theory was the "paranoid-critical method," in which he cultivated the paranoid's ability to misread, mangle, and misconstrue ordinary appearances, thus liberating himself from conventional thought. Then he painted what he had imagined.

Dalí's paintings focus on a few key themes: sexuality, violence, and putrefaction. In the **BIRTH OF LIQUID DESIRES** (**FIG. 32–58**), we see a large yellow **biomorphic** form (an organic shape resembling a living organism)–

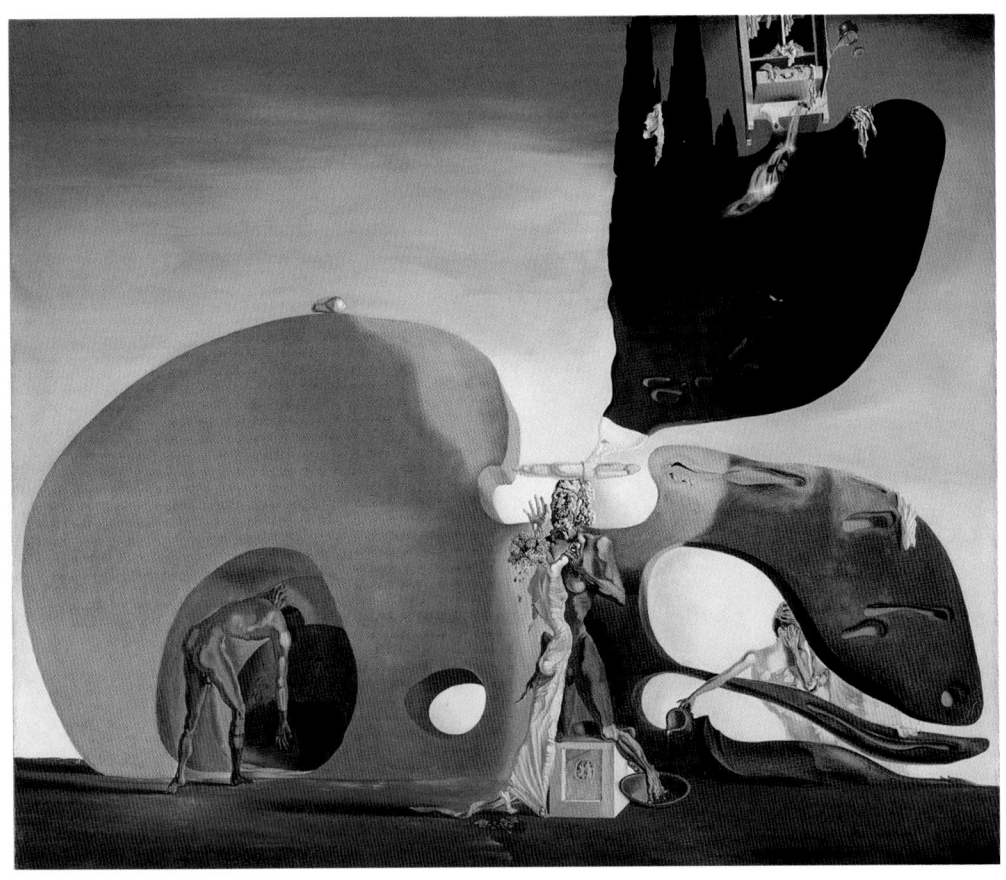

32–58 Salvador Dalí **BIRTH OF LIQUID DESIRES**
1931–1932. Oil and collage on canvas, 37⅞ × 44¼" (96.1 × 112.3 cm). The Solomon R. Guggenheim Foundation. Peggy Guggenheim Collection, Venice 1976 (76.2553 PG 100).

Credit: © Salvador Dalí, Fundació Gala-Salvador Dalí, Artists Rights Society (ARS), New York 2016. The Solomon R. Guggenheim Foundation/Art Resource, NY

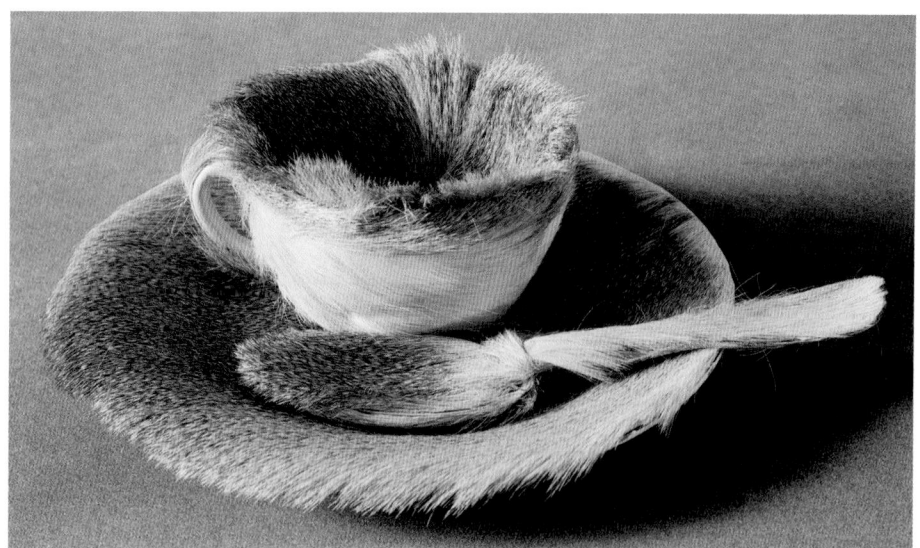

32–59 Meret Oppenheim **OBJECT (LUNCHEON IN FUR)**

1936. Fur-covered cup, diameter 4⅜″ (10.9 cm); fur-covered saucer, diameter 9⅜″ (23.7 cm); fur-covered spoon, length 8″ (20.2 cm); overall height, 2⅞″ (7.3 cm). Museum of Modern Art, New York.

Credit: © 2016 Artists Rights Society (ARS), New York/ProLitteris, Zurich. © 2016. Digital image, The Museum of Modern Art, New York/ Scala, Florence

looking like a monster's face, a painter's palette, or a woman's body—that serves as the backdrop for four figures. A woman in white embraces a hermaphroditic figure who stands with one foot in a bowl that is being filled with liquid by a third figure, partially hidden, while a fourth figure enters a cavernous hole to the left. A thick black cloud rises above the scene. Dalí claimed that he simply painted what his paranoid-critical mind had conjured up in his nightmares. His images are thus, as Breton advocated, "the true process of thought, free from the exercise of reason and from any aesthetic or moral purpose."

They defy rational interpretation, although they trigger fear, anxiety, and even regression in our empathetic minds. But that does not mean they are without subject matter. This painting refers to the legend of William Tell, which Dali related to his own sense of rejection by his father, an anxiety intensified after 1929 because his father disapproved of his relationship with Gala Éluard, whom he would marry in 1934. The famous apple on the head of William Tell's son is replaced here by a baguette perched on the head of the central and tallest figure, evidence of the castration anxiety Dali associated with Tell's famous feat of marksmanship.

32–60 Joan Miró **COMPOSITION**

1933. Oil on canvas, 51⅜ × 64⅛″ (130.49 × 162.88 cm). Wadsworth Athenaeum, Hartford, Connecticut. The Ella Gallup Sumner and Mary Catlin Sumner Collection Fund, 1934.40.

Credit: © Successió Miró/ Artists Rights Society (ARS), New York/ADAGP, Paris 2016. Photo: Allen Phillips/ Wadsworth Atheneum

Dalí's strangely compelling art also draws on the Surrealist interest in unexpected juxtapositions of disparate realities. Surrealists argued that by bringing together several disparate ordinary objects in strange new contexts artists could create uncanny surrealities. One of the most disturbingly exquisite and mockingly humorous examples is **OBJECT (LUNCHEON IN FUR)** (FIG. 32-59), by the Swiss artist Meret Oppenheim (1913–1985). Oppenheim was one of the few women invited to participate in the Surrealist movement; Surrealists generally treated women as their muses or as objects of study, but not their equals. This work was inspired by a conversation between Oppenheim, Picasso, and the photographer Dora Maar at a Parisian café. After admiring the fur trim on Oppenheim's bracelet, Picasso claimed that one could cover anything with fur, to which Oppenheim is said to have replied, "Even this cup and saucer." When Breton invited her to participate in the first Surrealist exhibition devoted to objects, she bought an actual cup, saucer, and spoon and covered them with the fur of a Chinese gazelle. The result removes two objects (a tea setting and gazelle fur) from their ordinary reality and recontextualizes them in an irrational new surreality— an uncanny object that is simultaneously desirable and deeply disturbing.

BIOMORPHIC ABSTRACTION The Catalan artist Joan Miró (1893–1983) exhibited regularly with the Surrealists but never formally joined the movement. Miró's biomorphic abstraction is also intended to free the mind from rationality, but in a more benign manner. His images seem to take shape before our eyes, but their identity is always in flux. In **COMPOSITION** (FIG. 32-60) of 1933, curving biomorphic primal or mythic shapes that seem arranged by chance emerge from the artist's mind uncensored, like doodles, to dance around the canvas. The Surrealists used the free association of doodling to relax the conscious mind so that images could bubble up from the unconscious; Miró reportedly doodled on many of his canvases as a first step of creation. This particular work was based on a collage assembled from advertisements cut from catalogs, magazines, and newspapers. Miró was also fascinated by children's art, which he thought of as spontaneous and expressive. Although he was a well-trained artist himself, he said that he wished he could learn to paint with the freedom of a child.

Unit One in England

In 1933, the English artists Barbara Hepworth (1903–1975), Henry Moore (1898–1986), and Paul Nash (1889–1946), along with the poet and critic Herbert Read (1893–1968), founded Unit One. Although short-lived, this group promoted the use of handcrafted, Surrealist-influenced biomorphic forms in sculpture, brought new energy to

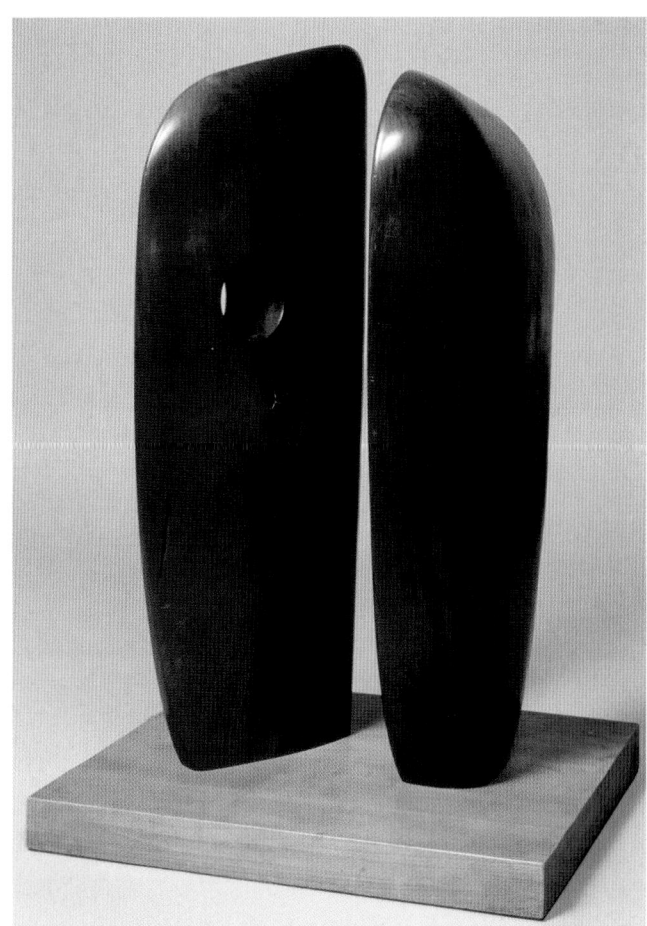

32-61 Barbara Hepworth **FORMS IN ECHELON**
1938. Wood, 42½ × 23⅔ × 28″ (108 × 60 × 71 cm). Tate, London. Presented by the artist 1964.

Credit: Works by Barbara Hepworth copyright Bowness. © Tate, London 2016

British art in the 1930s, and exerted a lasting impact on British sculpture.

Hepworth studied at the Leeds School of Art. She punctuated her exquisitely crafted sculptures with holes so that air and light could pass through them. Images seem to take shape before our eyes, but their identity is always in flux. Hepworth's **FORMS IN ECHELON** (FIG. 32-61) consists of two biomorphic shapes carved in highly polished wood. She hoped that viewers would allow their eyes to play around with these organic forms, so their imagination could generate changing associations and meanings.

Moore also carved punctured sculptural abstractions, although his works were more obviously based on the human form. He also studied at the Leeds School of Art and then at the Royal College of Art in London. The African, Oceanic, and Pre-Columbian sculpture that he saw at the British Museum, however, had a more powerful impact than his academic training on his developing aesthetic. He felt that artists beyond the Western tradition showed a greater respect for the inherent qualities of materials such as stone or wood than their Western counterparts did.

32–62 Henry Moore
RECUMBENT FIGURE

1938. Green Hornton stone, 35 × 52 × 29″ (88.9 × 132.7 × 73.7 cm). Tate, London.

Moore created this work to fulfill a commission from Russian-born British architect Serge Chermayeff, who installed it on the terrace of his modern home on the English South Downs.

The reclining female nude is the dominant theme of Moore's art. The massive, simplified body in **RECUMBENT FIGURE** (FIG. 32-62) refers to the *chacmool*, a reclining human form in Toltec and Maya art (SEE FIG. 13-15). Moore's sculptures also reveal his special sensitivity to the inherent qualities of his stone, which he sought out in remote quarries, always insisting that each of his works be labeled with the specific kind of stone he had used. While certain aspects of the human body are clearly described in this sculpture—the head, breasts, supporting elbow, and raised knee—other parts seem to flow together into an undulating mass suggestive of a hilly landscape. The cavity at the center inverts our expectations about the solid and void. In 1937, Moore wrote, "A hole can itself have as much shape-meaning as a solid mass."

Picasso's *Guernica*

In January 1937, as the Spanish Civil War between the Republicans and the Nationalists began to escalate, Picasso—a Spaniard who was then living in Paris—was commissioned to make a large painting for the Spanish

32–63 RUINS OF GUERNICA, SPAIN
April 1937.

Credit: © Bettmann/Corbis

Pavilion of the 1938 Paris Exposition, a direct descendant of the nineteenth-century World's Fairs that had resulted in the Crystal Palace and the Eiffel Tower. The 1938 Spanish Pavilion was the first Spanish national pavilion at any World's Fair.

As Picasso pondered what he might create, on April 26, 1937, Nationalist-supporting German bombers attacked the town of Guernica in the Basque region of Spain, killing and wounding 1,600 civilians. For more than three hours, 25 bombers dropped 100,000 pounds of explosives on the town, while more than 20 fighter planes strafed anyone caught in the streets trying to flee destroyed or burning buildings. Fires burned in Guernica for three days. By the end, one third of the town's population was killed or wounded and 75 percent of its buildings had been destroyed (FIG. 32-63). The cold-blooded, calculating nature of the attack shocked Europe. It seemed to serve no military purpose, other than to allow Franco's Nationalist forces to terrorize civilian populations, but the world's shock worsened with the revelation that the German commander had planned the massacre merely as a "training mission" for the German air force. Horrified, Picasso now had his subject for the Fair.

On May 1, 1 million protesters marched in Paris, and the following day Picasso made the first preliminary sketches for his visual response to this atrocity. Picasso had been trained in the traditions of academic painting, and he planned **GUERNICA** (FIG. 32-64) as a monumental history painting detailing the historic, and ignoble, events

32–64 Pablo Picasso GUERNICA
1937. Oil on canvas, 11'6" × 25'8" (3.5 × 7.8 m). Museo Nacional Centro de Arte Reina Sofía, Madrid. On permanent loan from the Museo del Prado, Madrid.

Credit: © 2016 Estate of Pablo Picasso/Artists Rights Society (ARS), New York of the attack. During ten days of intensive planning he made several sketches (*esquisses*) to develop the composition before moving on to canvas. He worked at the painting itself—changing figures and developing themes—for another month.

Guernica is a complex painting, layered with meaning. Picasso rarely used specific or obvious symbolism in his art, preferring to let individual viewers interpret details themselves. What is beyond question, however, is that *Guernica* is a scene of brutality, chaos, and suffering. Painted in black, white, and gray, the image resonates with anguish. It freezes figures in mid-movement in stark black and white as if caught by the flashbulb of a reporter's camera. Many of the subjects are clearly identifiable: an expressionistically reconfigured head of a bull in the upper left, a screeching wounded horse in the center, broken human forms scattered across the expanse, a giant lightbulb suggesting an all-seeing eye at the top, a lamp below it, and smoke and fire visible beyond the destroyed room in which the disjointed action takes place. These images have inspired a variety of interpretations. Some have seen in the bull and horse symbols of Nationalist and Republican forces, variously identified with one or the other. The lightbulb, javelin, dagger, lamp, and bird have also been assigned specific meanings. Picasso, however, refused to acknowledge any particular significance to any of these seeming symbols. *Guernica*, he claimed, is about the massacred victims of this atrocity—beyond that, its meaning remains fluid.

Guernica appeared in the Spanish Pavilion along with other works of art supporting the Republican cause, including works by painter Joan Miró, sculptor Alexander Calder, filmmaker Luis Buñuel, and others. Because Picasso refused to allow *Guernica* to be shown in Spain under the regime of Nationalist leader General Franco,

it hung in the Museum of Modern Art in New York for years, finally traveling to Spain for installation in the Reina Sofía in Madrid only in 1981, six years after Franco's death. Since 1985, a tapestry copy of *Guernica* has hung in the headquarters of the United Nations in New York as a powerful reminder of the brutal human cost of unrestrained warfare.

Art Between the Wars in the Americas

How does art develop in the Americas between World Wars I and II?

A need for a national visual identity emerged in American art between the wars, but since the United States was a large, diverse nation with multiple "identities," attempts to preserve a fiction of a single, essentially male, Anglo-Saxon national profile only heightened the visibility of the creative and experimental works of art by African Americans, immigrants, women, and others.

The Harlem Renaissance

Between 1910 and 1930, hundreds of thousands of African Americans migrated from the rural, mostly agricultural American South to the urban, industrialized North to escape racial oppression and find greater social and economic opportunities. This First Great Migration prompted the formation of the nationwide New Negro movement and the Harlem Renaissance in New York, which called for greater social and political activism among African Americans.

32–65 James Van Der Zee **COUPLE WEARING RACCOON COATS WITH A CADILLAC, TAKEN ON WEST 127TH STREET, HARLEM, NEW YORK**

1932. Gelatin-silver print.

Credit: © Donna Mussenden VanDerZee

32-66 Aaron Douglas **ASPECTS OF NEGRO LIFE: FROM SLAVERY THROUGH RECONSTRUCTION**
1934. Oil on canvas, 5' × 11'7" (1.5 × 3.5 m). Schomburg Center for Research in Black Culture, New York Public Library.

Credit: Art © Heirs of Aaron Douglas/Licensed by VAGA, New York, NY. Schomburg Center, NYPL/Art Resource, NY

Harlem's wealthy middle-class African-American community produced some of the nation's most talented artists of the 1920s and 1930s, such as the jazz musician Duke Ellington, the novelist Jean Toomer, and the poet Langston Hughes. The movement's intellectual leader was Alain Locke (1886–1954), a critic and philosophy professor who argued that black artists should seek their artistic roots in the traditional arts of Africa rather than assimilate within mainstream American or European artistic traditions.

James Van Der Zee (1886–1983), a studio photographer who took carefully crafted portraits of the Harlem upper-middle classes, opened his studio in 1916, working as both a news reporter and a society photographer. **COUPLE WEARING RACCOON COATS WITH A CADILLAC (FIG. 32-65)** captures a wealthy man and woman posing with their new car in 1932, at the height of the Great Depression. The photograph reveals the glamour of Harlem, then the center of African-American cultural life.

The painter Aaron Douglas (1898–1979) moved to New York City from Topeka, Kansas, in 1925. He developed a silhouette style that owes much to African art and had a lasting impact on later African-American artists (SEE FIG. 33-69). He painted **ASPECTS OF NEGRO LIFE: FROM SLAVERY THROUGH RECONSTRUCTION (FIG. 32-66)** for the Harlem branch of the New York Public Library under the sponsorship of the Depression-era Public Works of Art Project. To the right, slaves are celebrating the Emancipation Proclamation of 1863, from which radiate concentric circles of light. At the center, an orator gestures dramatically, pointing to the United States Capitol in the background as if to urge all African Americans, some of whom are still picking cotton in the foreground, to exercise their right to vote. To the left, Union soldiers leave the

South after Reconstruction, while Ku Klux Klan members, hooded and on horseback, charge in, reminding viewers that the fight for civil rights has only just begun.

The career of sculptor Augusta Savage (1892–1962) reflects the myriad difficulties faced by African Americans in the art world. Savage studied at Cooper Union in New York, but her 1923 application to study in Europe was turned down because of her race. In a letter of protest, she wrote, "Democracy is a strange thing. My brother was good enough to be accepted in one of the regiments that saw service in France during the war, but it seems his sister is not good enough to be a guest of the country for which he fought." Finally, in 1930, Savage was able to study in Paris. On her return to the United States, she sculpted portraits of several African-American leaders, including Marcus Garvey and W.E.B. DuBois. Inspired by the story of the Haitian Revolution in 1791 following the Slave Revolt (SEE FIG. 30-40), she portrayed a female figure of freedom in **LA CITADELLE: FREEDOM (FIG. 32-67)** raising her hand to the sky and balancing on the toes of one foot while she flies through the air. La Citadelle was the castle residence of one of Haiti's first leaders of African heritage. For Savage, it represented the possibility and promise of freedom and equality.

Savage established a small private art school in Harlem and received Federal funds under the Works Progress Administration to transform it into the Harlem Community Art Center. Hundreds of these centers were eventually established all over the country, but Savage's became an unofficial salon for Harlem artists, poets, composers, dancers, and historians.

One of the best-known artists to emerge from the Harlem Community Art Center was Jacob Lawrence (1917–2000). Lawrence's early works often depict

32–67 Augusta Savage **LA CITADELLE: FREEDOM**
1930. Bronze, 14½ × 7 × 6" (35.6 × 17.8 × 15.2 cm).
Howard University Gallery of Art, Washington, DC.

Credit: © Augusta Savage

African-American history in series of small narrative paintings, each accompanied by a text. His themes include the history of Harlem and the lives of Haitian revolutionary leader Toussaint L'Ouverture and American abolitionist John Brown. Lawrence created his most expansive series in 1940–1941. Entitled **THE MIGRATION SERIES**, 60 panels chronicle the Great Migration, a journey that had brought Lawrence's own parents from South Carolina to Atlantic City, New Jersey. In the first panel (**FIG. 32-68**), African-American migrants stream through the doors of a Southern train station on their way to Chicago, New York, or St. Louis. Lawrence's boldly abstracted silhouette style, with its flat, bright shapes and colors, draws consciously and directly—like that of Douglas—on African visual sources.

Rural America

Other artists, known collectively as the Regionalists, developed Midwestern themes during the 1930s. In 1930, at the height of the Depression, Grant Wood (1891–1942) painted **AMERICAN GOTHIC** (**FIG. 32-69**), which was purchased by the Art Institute of Chicago and established Wood's national fame. This picture embodied all that was good and bad about the heartland in the 1930s. Wood, who later taught at the University of Iowa, portrays an aging father standing with his unmarried daughter in front of their Gothic Revival framed house. Even for the time their clothes are old-fashioned. Wood's dentist and his sister Nan—wearing a homemade ricrac-edged apron and their mother's cameo—posed for the figures, and the building was modeled on a modest small-town home in Eldon, Iowa. The daughter's long, sad face echoes her father's; she is unmarried and likely to stay that way. In 1930, husbands were hard to come by in the Midwest because many young men had fled the farms for jobs in Chicago. With its tightly painted descriptive detail, this painting is a homage to the Flemish Renaissance painters that Wood admired.

FEDERAL PATRONAGE OF ART DURING THE GREAT DEPRESSION In the early 1930s during the Great Depression, President Franklin D. Roosevelt's New Deal established a series of programs to provide relief for the unemployed and to revive the nation's economy, including several initiatives to create work for American artists. The 1933 Public Works of Art Project (PWAP) lasted only five months but supplied employment to 4,000 artists, who produced more than 15,000 works. The Treasury Department established a Section of Painting and Sculpture in October 1934, which survived until 1943, commissioning murals and sculptures for public buildings. The Federal Art Project (FAP) of the Works Progress Administration (WPA), which ran from 1935 to 1943, succeeded the PWAP and was the most important work-relief agency of the Depression era. By 1943, it had employed more than 6 million workers in programs that included, in addition to the FAP, the Federal Theater Project and the Federal Writers' Project. About 10,000 artists participated in the FAP, producing a staggering 108,000 paintings, 18,000 sculptures, 2,500 murals, and thousands of prints, photographs, and posters, all of which became public property. Many of the murals and sculptures, commissioned for public buildings such as train stations, schools, hospitals, and post offices, survive today, but most easel paintings were later sold as "plumber's canvas" and destroyed.

To build public support for Federal assistance in rural America, the Resettlement Agency (RA) and Farm Security Administration (FSA) hired photographers to document the effects of the Depression across the country in photographs available to this day, copyright-free, to any newspaper, magazine, or publisher. San Francisco-based Dorothea

32-68 Jacob Lawrence **THE MIGRATION SERIES, PANEL NO. 1: DURING WORLD WAR I THERE WAS A GREAT MIGRATION NORTH BY SOUTHERN AFRICAN AMERICANS**

1940–1941. Tempera on masonite, 12 × 18″ (30.5 × 45.7 cm). The Phillips Collection, Washington, DC.

Credit: © 2016 The Jacob and Gwendolyn Knight Lawrence Foundation, Seattle/Artists Rights Society (ARS), New York

32-69 Grant Wood **AMERICAN GOTHIC**

1930. Oil on beaverboard, 29⅞ × 24⅞″ (74.3 × 62.4 cm). The Art Institute of Chicago. Friends of American Art Collection, 1930.934.

Credit: Art © Figge Art Museum, successors to the Estate of Nan Wood Graham/Licensed by VAGA, New York, NY. Photo © The Art Institute of Chicago

Lange (1895–1965), an RA/FSA photographer between 1935 and 1939, documented the plight of migrant farm laborers who fled the Dust Bowl conditions of the Great Plains and then crowded California looking for work.

MIGRANT MOTHER, NIPOMO, CALIFORNIA (**FIG. 32-70**) shows Florence Owens Thompson, a 32-year-old mother of seven, representative of the poverty suffered by thousands of migrant workers in California. Lange carefully constructed her photograph for maximum emotional impact. She zoomed in very close to the subject, focusing on the mother's worn expression and apparent resolve. The composition refers to images of the Virgin Mary holding the Child Jesus (SEE FIG. 21-6) or perhaps sorrowful

32-70 Dorothea Lange **MIGRANT MOTHER, NIPOMO, CALIFORNIA**

February 1936. Gelatin-silver print. Library of Congress, Washington, DC.

In 1960, Lange described the experience of taking this photograph, writing, "I saw and approached the hungry and desperate mother, as if drawn by a magnet. I do not remember how I explained my presence or my camera to her, but I do remember she asked me no questions. I made five exposures, working closer and closer from the same direction. I did not ask her name or her history. She told me her age, that she was thirty-two. She said that they had been living on frozen vegetables from the surrounding fields, and birds that the children killed. She had just sold the tires from her car to buy food. There she sat in that lean-to tent with her children huddled around her, and seemed to know that my pictures might help her, and so she helped me. There was a sort of equality about it." (*Popular Photography*, February 1960)

Credit: Courtesy the Library of Congress

scenes in which she contemplates his loss (SEE FIG. 21-14). Lange chose to eliminate from this photograph the makeshift tent in which the family was camped, the dirty dishes on a battered trunk, trash strewn around the campsite, and, most significant, Thompson's teenage daughter—all documented in her other photographs of the same scene. Lange decided to focus here on the purity and moral worth of her subject, for whom she sought Federal aid; she could not allude to the fact that Thompson had been a teenage mother or even that she was Cherokee. *Migrant Mother* (then unidentified by name) became the "poster child" of the Great Depression, and her powerfully sad, distant gaze still resonates with audiences today, demonstrating the propaganda power of the visual image.

During the Depression, the FAP paid a generous average salary of about $20 a week (a salesclerk at Woolworth's earned only about $11) for painters and sculptors to devote themselves full time to art. New York City's painters, in particular, developed a group identity, meeting in the bars and coffeehouses of Greenwich Village to discuss art. The FAP thus provided the financial grounds on which New York artists built a sense of community—a community that would produce the Abstract Expressionists and that allowed New York to supersede Paris as the center of the world of Modern art.

Canada

In the nineteenth century, Canadian artists, like their counterparts in the United States, began to assert independence from European art by painting Canada's great untamed wilderness. A number of Canadians, however, used the academic realism they learned in Paris to paint figurative subjects, while others painted the Canadian landscape through the lens of Impressionism.

LANDSCAPE AND IDENTITY   In the early 1910s, a young group of Toronto artists, many of whom worked for the same commercial art firm, began to sketch together, adopting the rugged landscape of the Canadian north as an expression of national identity.

A key figure in this movement was Tom Thomson (1877–1917), who, as of 1912, spent the warm months of each year in Algonquin Provincial Park, a large forest reserve 180 miles north of Toronto. He made many small, swiftly painted, oil-on-board sketches as the basis for the full-size paintings that he executed in his studio during the winter. One such sketch led to **THE WEST WIND** (**FIG. 32-71**). This tightly organized composition features a vibrant stylized tree rising from a rocky foreground and set against a luminous but more subdued background of lake, hills, and sky. The cropped, silhouetted form of a curvilinear tree set close to the viewer against a harmonious Canadian landscape in the distance was one of his favorite subjects.

32-71 Tom Thomson **THE WEST WIND**

1916–17. Oil on canvas, 45½ × 54″ (120.7 × 137.9 cm). Art Gallery of Ontario, Toronto. Gift of Canadian Club of Toronto, 1926 #784.

Credit: © akg-images

NATIVE AMERICAN INFLU-ENCE   Born in Victoria, British Columbia, the West Coast artist Emily Carr (1871–1945) studied art in San Francisco, England, and Paris. On a 1907 trip to Alaska she encountered the monumental carved poles of Northwest Coast Native peoples and resolved to document these "real art treasures of a passing race." Over the next 23 years, Carr visited more than 30 sites across British Columbia making drawings and watercolors as a basis for oil paintings. After a commercially unsuccessful exhibition of her Native subjects, Carr returned to Victoria in 1913, opened a boarding house, and painted very little for the next 15 years. In 1927, however, she was invited to participate in an exhibition of West Coast art at the National Gallery of Canada. On her trip east for the show's opening, Carr met members of the Group of Seven,

a group of landscape painters established in 1920 by some of Tom Thomson's former colleagues. They rekindled her interest in painting.

With the Group of Seven, Carr developed a dramatic and powerfully sculptural style full of dark, brooding energy. **BIG RAVEN** (**FIG. 32-72**), painted in 1931 from a 1912 watercolor, shows an abandoned village in the Queen Charlotte Islands where Carr found a carved raven on a pole, the surviving member of a pair that originally marked a mortuary house. In her autobiography Carr described the raven as "old and rotting," but in the painting she shows it as strong and majestic, thrusting dynamically above the swirling vegetation, a symbol of enduring spiritual power and national pride.

32-72 Emily Carr **BIG RAVEN**

1931. Oil on canvas, 34¼ × 44⅞″ (87 × 114 cm). Collection of the Vancouver Art Gallery, Emily Carr Trust.

Credit: Vancouver Art Gallery, Photo: Trevor Mills

Mexico, Brazil, and Cuba

The Mexican Revolution of 1910 overthrew the 35-year dictatorship of General Porfirio Díaz and initiated ten years of political instability. In 1920, reformist president Álvaro Obregón restored political order, and the leaders of his new government—as in the U.S.S.R.—engaged artists in the service of the people and state. Several Mexican artists received government commissions to decorate public buildings with murals celebrating the history, life, and work of the Mexican people. These artists painted in a naturalistic style because the new government believed that the public at large could not understand abstract art.

Diego Rivera (1886–1957) was prominent in the Mexican mural movement that developed from these commissions. He enrolled in Mexico City's Academia de San Carlos at age 11, and from 1911 to 1919, he lived in Paris where he met Picasso and David Siqueiros (1896–1974), another Mexican muralist. Both Rivera and Siqueiros sought to create a revolutionary art in the service of the people in their public murals. In 1920–1921, Rivera traveled to Italy to study Renaissance frescoes, and he also visited ancient Mexican sites to study indigenous mural paintings. In 1945, he painted **THE GREAT CITY OF TENOCHTITLAN** (FIG. **32-73**) as part of a mural cycle in the National Palace in Mexico City that used stylized forms and brilliant colors to portray the history of Mexico. Rivera also painted murals in the United States.

The art of Frida Kahlo (1907–1954) is more personal. Breton claimed Kahlo as a natural Surrealist, although she herself said, "I never painted dreams. I painted my own reality." That reality included her mixed heritage, born of a German father and Mexican mother. In a double self-portrait—**THE TWO FRIDAS** (FIG. **32-74**)—Kahlo presents an identity split into two ethnic selves: the European one in a Victorian dress and the Mexican one wearing traditional Mexican clothing. The painting also reflects her stormy relationship with Diego Rivera, whom she married in 1929 but was divorcing in 1939 while painting this picture. She told an art historian at the time that the Mexican image was the Frida whom Diego loved, and the European image was one he did not. The two Fridas join hands; the artery running between them begins at a miniature portrait of Rivera as a boy held by the Mexican Frida, travels through the exposed hearts of both Fridas, and ends in the lap of the European Frida, who attempts without success to stem the flow of blood. Kahlo had suffered a broken pelvis in an accident at age 17, and she endured a lifetime of surgeries. This work alludes to her constant pain, as well as to the Aztec custom of human sacrifice by heart removal.

BRAZIL Elsewhere in Latin America, art in the nineteenth century was often dominated by the academic tradition. Several nations had thriving academies and large art communities, and artists traveled in significant numbers to study in Paris. By 1914, artists in many Latin American countries used their own versions of Impressionism to paint national themes. After World War I, artists who studied abroad also brought home ideas drawn from Modernist art and the European avant-garde, which they translated into a specifically Latin American vision. For instance, in 1922, as Brazil marked the centenary of its independence from Portugal, the avant-garde in São Paulo celebrated with Modern Art Week, an event Brazilian artists used to declare their artistic independence from Europe. Modern Art Week brought avant-garde poets, dancers, musicians, and visual artists to São Paulo and took on

32-73 Diego Rivera
THE GREAT CITY OF TENOCHTITLAN (DETAIL)
Mural in patio corridor, National Palace, Mexico City. 1945. Fresco, 16′1¾″ × 31′10¼″ (4.92 × 9.71 m).

32–74 Frida Kahlo **THE TWO FRIDAS**
1939. Oil on canvas, 5'8½" × 5'8½"
(1.74 × 1.74 m). Museo de Arte Moderno,
Instituto Nacional de Bellas Artes,
Mexico City.

Credit: © 2016 Banco de México Diego Rivera Frida
Kahlo Museums Trust, Mexico, D.F./Artists Rights
Society (ARS), New York. © 2016. Photo Art Resource/
Bob Schalkwijk/Scala, Florence

a distinctly confrontational character. Poets derided their
elders in poetry, dancers enacted modern versions of traditional dances, and the composer Hector Villa-Lobos (1887–
1959) appeared on stage in a bathrobe and slippers to play
new music based on Afro-Brazilian rhythms.

In 1928, the São Paulo poet Oswald de Andrade, one
of Modern Art Week's organizers, wrote the "Anthropophagic Manifesto," proposing a tongue-in-cheek, if radical, solution to Brazil's seeming dependence on European
culture. He suggested that Brazilians imitate the ancient
Brazilians' response to Portuguese explorers arriving on
their shore—eat them. He mockingly described this relationship as anthropophagic or cannibalistic and proposed
that Brazilians gobble up European culture, digest it, let it
strengthen their Brazilianness, and then get rid of it.

The painter who most closely embodies this irreverent
attitude is Tarsila do Amaral (1887–1974), a daughter of the
coffee-planting aristocracy, who studied in Europe with
Fernand Léger (SEE FIG. 32–21), among others. Her painting **THE ONE WHO EATS (ABAPORÚ)** **(FIG. 32–75)** shows
an appreciation of the art of Léger and Brancusi (SEE FIG.
32–27), which Tarsila collected. But she also inserted several
"tropical" clichés—the abstracted forms of a cactus and a
lemon-slice sun. The subject is Andrade's irreverent cannibal, sitting in a caricatured Brazilian landscape, as if to
say: If Brazilians are caricatured abroad as cannibals, then
let us act like cannibals. As Andrade wrote in one of his

32–75 Tarsila do Amaral **THE ONE WHO EATS (ABAPORÚ)**
1928. Oil on canvas, 34 × 29" (86.4 × 73.7 cm). Museo de Arte
Latinoamericano, Buenos Aires. Courtesy of Guilherme Augusto do
Amaral/Malba-Coleccion Constantini, Buenos Aires.

Credit: © Tarsila do Amara. Collection of MALBA, Museo de Arte
Latinoamericano de Buenos Aires

manifestos, "Carnival in Rio is the religious outpouring of our race. Richard Wagner yields to the samba. Barbaric but ours. We have a dual heritage: The jungle and the school."

CUBA Cuba's 1920s avant-garde was one of the most interdisciplinary, consisting of anthropologists, poets, composers, and even a few scientists, who gathered in Havana and called themselves "The Minority." They issued a manifesto in 1927 repudiating government corruption, "Yankee imperialism," and dictatorship on any continent. "Minority" artists, they urged, should pursue a new, popular, Modern art rooted in Cuban soil.

Amelia Peláez (1896–1968) left Cuba for Paris shortly after this manifesto was issued. When she returned home, she joined the anthropologist Lydia Cabrera to study Cuban popular and folk arts. Her paintings focus on the woman's realm—the domestic interior—and national identity, as in **HIBISCUS (MARPACÍFICO)** (FIG. 32-76). Her visual language is Cubist, as seen in the flattened overlapping forms and compressed pictorial space, but it shows recognizable objects—a mirror, a tabletop, and local hibiscus flowers—whose heavy black outlines and pure color reflect the flat, fan-shaped stained-glass windows that decorate many Cuban homes.

32-76 Amelia Peláez **HIBISCUS (MARPACÍFICO)**
1943. Oil on canvas, 45½ × 35″ (115.6 × 88.9 cm).
Art Museum of the Americas, Washington, DC. Gift of IBM.
Credit: © Amelia Pelaez Foundation

Postwar Art in Europe and the Americas

What artistic trends emerged after World War II?

The horrors of World War II surpassed even those of World War I. The human loss was almost too profound and grotesque to comprehend. Between loss of life in action, those killed in work camps and death camps (concentration camps), those lost to starvation, and those lost in the bombing of civilian targets, more than 30 million people died and an estimated 40 million people were displaced. The unimaginable horror of the concentration camps and the awful impact of the dropping of nuclear bombs shook humanity to its core. Winston Churchill described the extent of the catastrophe when he said, "What is Europe now? A rubble heap, a charnel house, a breeding ground of pestilence and hate."

Figural Responses and Art Informel in Europe

Most European artists in the immediate postwar period tried to use their art to come to terms with what they had experienced, often debating about how best to do this: figuratively or abstractly.

In England, Francis Bacon (1909–1992) captured in his canvases the horrors that haunted him. Bacon was self-taught and produced very few pictures until the 1940s. He served as an air-raid warden during World War II and saw the bloody impact of the bombing of civilians in London firsthand. In **FIGURE WITH MEAT** (FIG. 32-77), Bacon presents an anguished and insubstantial man howling in a black void as two bloody sides of beef enclose him in a claustrophobic box that contains his screams and amplifies his terror. The painting was directly inspired by Velázquez's 1650 portrait of Pope Innocent X and by Rembrandt's paintings of dripping meat. Bacon wrote, "I hope to make the best human cry in painting … to remake the violence of reality itself."

One of the most distinctive postwar European art movements was Art Informel ("Formless Art"), which was also called *Tachisme* (*tache* is French for "spot" or "stain"). Art Informel was promoted by the French critic Michel Tapié (1909–1987), who suggested that art should express an authentic concept of postwar humanity through simple, honest marks.

The informal leader of Art Informel was Wolfgang Schulze, called Wols (1913–1951), who lived through the dislocation and devastation experienced by millions in Europe in the 1930s and 1940s. Born in Germany, Wols left his homeland in protest when Hitler came to power, first settling in Paris, where he worked as a photographer for *Vogue* and *Harper's Bazaar*. When the Germans occupied

32-77 Francis Bacon FIGURE WITH MEAT

1954. Oil on canvas, 50¾ × 48" (129 × 122 cm). The Art Institute of Chicago. Harriott A. Fox Fund (1956.1201).

France, he fled to Spain but was arrested, stripped of his passport, and deported to spend the rest of the war as a stateless person in a refugee camp in southern France. When the war ended, Wols returned to Paris and resumed painting, producing passionate pictures by applying paint with whatever came to hand, scraping his heavy surfaces with a knife and allowing the paint to drip and run. **PAINTING** (**FIG. 32-78**) represents a disease-ridden and violent world in which the semiabstracted forms resemble either infected cells or dark, muddy bacterial growths. Wols was temporarily supported by the French philosopher and novelist Jean-Paul Sartre, but died of food poisoning in 1951.

Experiments in Latin America

In Cuba, the abstract and Surrealist paintings of Wifredo Lam (1902–1980) embodied the violence and anguish of his country's struggle against colonialism. Lam was of mixed Chinese, Spanish, and African heritage and brought issues of identity and self-discovery to his art. He studied at the National Academy in Havana, moved to Paris, where he knew both Picasso and the Surrealists, and was forced to return to Cuba when the Nazis invaded France. He found himself on the same ship as the Surrealist leader Breton; Lam disembarked at Havana, while Breton traveled on to New York. Once home, Lam explored his African-Cuban heritage in the company of anthropologist Lydia Cabrera and novelist Alejo Carpentier. His work from the late 1940s reflects African-Cuban art and the polytheistic spiritual imagery of the African-Cuban religion Santería. The jagged, semiabstracted forms of **ZAMBEZIA, ZAMBEZIA** (**FIG. 32-79**) refer to European Modernism, but their source is in Santería religious ritual; the central figure is a composite Santería deity. "Zambezia" was the early colonial name for Zimbabwe in southeastern Africa, at this time a British colonial possession known as Rhodesia. Much earlier, Zambezia had been a source

32-78 Wols (Wolfgang Schulze) **PAINTING**

1944–1945. Oil on canvas, 31⅞ × 32" (81 × 81.1 cm). Museum of Modern Art, New York. Gift of D. and J. de Menil Fund (29.1956).

for slaves who were brought to Cuba. Lam said, "I wanted with all my heart to paint the drama of my country.... In this way I could act as a Trojan horse spewing forth hallucinating figures with the power to surprise, to disturb the dreams of the exploiters."

In Buenos Aires, two groups of avant-garde artists formed immediately after the war—Arte Concreto-Invención and Madí, even though Argentina's fascist leader Juan Perón (1895–1974) disliked Modern art profoundly. The best-known Latin American artist of the time was the Uruguayan Joaquín Torres-García (1874–1949), who established the "School of the South" in Montevideo, Uruguay's capital. Torres-García had spent 43 years in Europe before returning home after the war, but his art was deeply rooted in the indigenous art of the Inca (for example, see FIG. 27-10); he believed ancient Uruguayan culture to be a fertile soil in which to grow a new national and cultural visual identity. In **ABSTRACT ART IN FIVE TONES AND COMPLEMENTARIES** (FIG. 32-80), Torres-García fused European ideas of abstraction and Modernism with Inca imagery and masonry patterns in a style that he named Constructive Universalism.

Abstract Expressionism in New York

The United States recovered from World War II more quickly than Europe did. Its territory was spared the ravages of war, and the trauma it felt was limited to those Americans who were part of military action in Europe or the Pacific, to European refugees to the United States, and to Japanese-American citizens who had been held in camps within the United States. While the European art world was disrupted by the war and Paris lost avant-garde

32–79 Wifredo Lam **ZAMBEZIA, ZAMBEZIA**
1950. Oil on canvas, 49⅜ × 43⅝" (125 × 110 cm). Solomon R. Guggenheim Museum, New York. Gift, Mr. Joseph Cantor, 1974 (74.2095).

Credit: © 2016 Artists Rights Society (ARS), New York/ADAGP, Paris. The Solomon R. Guggenheim Foundation/Art Resource, NY.

momentum, New York served as a refuge for European artists and gradually developed into a vibrant and progressive urban art center.

32–80 Joaquín Torres-García
ABSTRACT ART IN FIVE TONES AND COMPLEMENTARIES
1943. Oil on board mounted on panel, 20½ × 26⅝" (52.1 × 67 cm). Albright Knox Art Gallery, Buffalo, New York. Gift of Mr. and Mrs. Armand J. Castellani, 1979.

Credit: Art Resource, NY

THE CENTER SHIFTS TO NEW YORK Many leading European artists and writers escaped to the United States during World War II. By 1941, Breton, Dalí, Léger, Mondrian, and Ernst were all living in New York, where they altered the character and artistic concerns of the art scene. American artists were most deeply affected by the work of the European Surrealist artists in New York, but ultimately artists developed their own uniquely American artistic identities by drawing from, but radically reimagining, European and American Modernism—coming to be known as Abstract Expressionists.

The term "Abstract Expressionism" describes the art of a fairly wide range of artists in New York in the 1940s and early 1950s. It was not a formally organized movement, but rather a loosely affiliated group of artists who worked in the city and were bound by a common purpose: to express their profound social alienation after World War II and make a new kind of art.

The influential **Formalist** (valuing form over content) critic Clement Greenberg urged the Abstract Expressionists to consider their paintings "autonomous" and completely self-referential objects. The best paintings, he argued, made no reference to the outside world, but had their own internal meaning and order. Some early Abstract Expressionist artists were also deeply influenced by the theories of the Swiss psychoanalyst Carl Jung (1875–1961), who described a collective unconscious of universal archetypes shared by all humans; many early Abstract Expressionists aspired to create works that embodied such universal symbolic forms. As the 1940s progressed, however, the symbolic content of some paintings became increasingly personal and abstract.

By referring to "primitive," mythic imagery and archaic, archetypal, and primal symbolism, some artists hoped to make a connection among all people through the collective unconscious; several used biomorphic forms or developed an individual symbolic language in their paintings; all made passionate and expressive statements on large canvases. The Abstract Expressionists felt destined to transform art history.

Though their paintings project a personal vision, the Abstract Expressionists shared a commitment to two major projects: (1) an interest in the traditional history of painting, but a desire to rebel against it, including the recent ideas of European Modernism and (2) a desire to treat the act of painting on canvas as a self-contained expressive, even heroic, exercise that would communicate universal ideas.

THE FORMATIVE PHASE Arshile Gorky (1904–1948) was born in Armenia and fled to Russia in 1915 with family members during the Ottoman Turkish genocide of the Armenian people. After his mother died of starvation in exile, Gorky escaped to the United States in 1920. The trauma of Gorky's loss of his mother fills the Surrealist paintings, where he threads idyllic images of his childhood home into visual memorials to the people and places he has lost.

A series of paintings in the early 1940s called **GARDEN IN SOCHI** (**FIG. 32-81**) transformed Gorky's memories of his father's garden in Khorkom, Armenia, into a mythical dreamscape. According to the artist, this garden was known locally as the Garden of Wish Fulfillment because it contained both a rock upon which village women, his mother included, rubbed their bared breasts when making

32-81 Arshile Gorky GARDEN IN SOCHI

c. 1943. Oil on canvas, 31 × 39″ (78.7 × 99.1 cm). Museum of Modern Art, New York. Acquired through the Lillie P. Bliss Bequest (492.1969).

Credit: © 2016 The Arshile Gorky Foundation/The Artists Rights Society (ARS), New York. © 2016. Digital image, The Museum of Modern Art, New York/ Scala, Florence.

32-82 Jackson Pollock **AUTUMN RHYTHM (NUMBER 30)**
1950. Oil on canvas, 8'9" × 17'3" (2.66 × 5.25 m). Metropolitan Museum of Art, New York. George A. Hearn Fund, 1957 (57.92).

Credit: © 2016 The Pollock-Krasner Foundation/Artists Rights Society (ARS), New York. © 2016. Image copyright The Metropolitan Museum of Art, New York/Art Resource/Scala, Florence

a wish, and a "Holy Tree" to which people tied strips of clothing. In this painting, the mythical garden floats on a dense white ground. Forms, shapes, and colors come together in a bare-breasted woman to the left and the Holy Tree to the center, as well as strips of clothing and "the beautiful Armenian slippers" that Gorky and his father wore in Khorkom. The painting suggests vital life forces, an ancient connection to the earth, and Gorky's vision of a lost world.

JACKSON POLLOCK AND ACTION PAINTING Jackson Pollock (1912–1956) is the most famous of the Abstract Expressionist. Born in Wyoming, Pollock moved to New York in 1930. By all accounts, he was self-destructive from an early age, developing a drinking problem by age 16, reading Jung by 22, and institutionalized for psychiatric problems and alcohol abuse at 26. Friends described two Pollocks—one shy and sober, the other obnoxious and drunk. When he entered Jungian psychotherapy in 1939, he already knew Jung's theory that visual images had the ability to tap into the primordial consciousness of viewers. Pollock remained free of alcohol from 1948–1950, supported emotionally by his lover, the artist Lee Krasner. This was when he created his most celebrated works.

Pollock's first solo exhibition was in 1943 at the heiress Peggy Guggenheim's gallery. He was propelled into stardom by the critic Clement Greenberg, who by 1947 described Pollock as "the most powerful painter

in contemporary America." Pollock pushed beyond the Surrealist strategy of automatic painting by placing raw, unstretched canvas on the floor and throwing, dripping, and dribbling paint onto it to create abstract networks of overlapping lines as the paint fell. In 1950 *Time* magazine

32-83 Rudolph Burckhardt **JACKSON POLLOCK PAINTING**
1950.

Credit: © 2016 Estate of Rudy Burckhardt and The Pollock - Krasner Foundation / Artists Rights Society (ARS), New York. © Sygma/Corbis described Pollock as "Jack the Dripper," and two years later, Rosenberg coined the term **Action painting** in an essay, "The American Action Painters." Describing the development and purpose of Action painting, Rosenberg wrote, "At a certain moment the canvas began to appear to one American painter after another as an arena in which to act—rather than a space in which to reproduce, redesign, analyze, or 'express' an object, actual or imagined."

In 1950, while Pollock painted **AUTUMN RHYTHM (NUMBER 30)** (**FIG. 32-82**), Hans Namuth filmed him and Rudolph Burkhardt photographed him (**FIG. 32-83**). Pollock worked in a renovated barn, where he could reach into the laid canvas from all four sides. The German expatriate artist Hans Hofmann (1880–1966) had poured and dripped paint before Pollock, but Pollock's unrestrained gestures transformed the idea of painting itself by moving around and within the canvas, dripping and scoring commercial-grade enamel paint (rather than specialist artist's paint) onto it using sticks and trowels. Some have described Pollock's arcs and whorls of paint as chaotic, but he saw them as labyrinths that led viewers along complex paths and into an organic, calligraphic web of natural and biomorphic forms. Pollock's compositions lack hierarchical arrangement, contain multiple focal points, and deny perspectival space. Art historians have referred to such paintings as "all-over compositions," because of the uniform treatment of the canvas from edge to edge and how this invites viewers to explore across the surface rather than to focus on one particular area. These self-contained paintings burst with anxious energy, ready to explode at any moment.

Autumn Rhythm is heroic in scale, almost 9 feet tall by over 17 feet wide. It engulfs the viewer's entire field of vision. According to Krasner, Pollock was a "jazz addict" who spent many hours listening to the explosively improvised bebop of Charlie Parker and Dizzy Gillespie. His interests extended to Native American art, which he associated with his western roots and which

enjoyed widespread coverage in popular and art magazines in the 1930s. Pollock was particularly intrigued by the images and processes of Navajo sand painters who demonstrated their work at the Natural History Museum in New York. He also drew on Jung's theories of the collective unconscious. But Pollock was more than the sum of his influences. His paintings communicate on a grand, Modernist, primal level. In a radio interview, he said that he was creating for "the age of the airplane, the atom bomb, and the radio."

KRASNER, DE KOONING, MITCHELL, RIOPELLE, AND FRANKENTHALER Lee Krasner (1908–1984) studied in New York with Hans Hofmann. She moved in with Pollock in 1942 and virtually stopped painting in order to take care of him. But when they moved to Long Island in 1945, she set up a small studio in a guest bedroom, where she produced small, tight, gestural paintings, arriving at fully nonrepresentational work with all-over compositions in 1946, at the same time as Pollock. After Pollock's death in an automobile crash in 1956, however, Krasner took over his studio and produced a series of large, dazzling gestural paintings that marked her re-emergence into the mainstream art world. Works such as **THE SEASONS** (**FIG. 32-84**) feature bold, sweeping curves that express not only a new sense of liberation but also her powerful identification with the forces of nature in bursting, rounded forms and springlike colors. Krasner explored that "Painting, for me, when it really 'happens' is as miraculous as any natural phenomenon."

In contrast, Willem de Kooning (1904–1997) wrote that "Art never seems to make me peaceful or pure" and remarked "I'm still working out of doubt." A 1926 immigrant from the Netherlands who settled in New York, De Kooning befriended several Modernist artists. His paintings were highly structured and controlled, and although aspects of his composition appear spontaneous, they are the result of much experiment and revision. De Kooning

32-84 Lee Krasner
THE SEASONS

1957. Oil on canvas, 7'8¾" × 16'11¾" (2.36 × 5.18 m). Whitney Museum of American Art, New York. Purchased with funds from Frances and Sydney Lewis (by exchange), the Mrs. Percy Uris Purchase Fund, and the Painting and Sculpture Committee (87.7).

Credit: © 2016 Pollock-Krasner Foundation/Artists Rights Society (ARS), New York

32–85 Willem de Kooning **WOMAN I**
1950–1952. Oil on canvas, 75⅞ × 58" (192.7 × 147.3 cm).
Museum of Modern Art, New York.

Credit: © 2016. Digital image, The Museum of Modern Art, New York/Scala,
Florence. © 2016 The Willem de Kooning Foundation/Artists Rights Society
(ARS), New York

applied paint, scraped it off, and repeated the process
until he achieved the effect he wanted. In 1953, he shocked
the art world by moving away from pure abstraction

with a series of figurative paintings of women. **WOMAN
I (FIG. 32–85)** took him two years to complete, and his
wife Elaine de Kooning estimated that he scraped and
repainted it about 200 times. The portrayal of the woman
appears to many as hostile, sexist, and powerfully sexual,
full of implied violence and intense passion. De Kooning
described his paintings of women as images of goddesses
like the *Woman from Willendorf* (SEE FIG. 1-7) and early Mesopotamian statuettes (SEE FIG. 2-5), or as a composite of stereotypes taken from the media and film. He explored both
figuration and abstraction throughout his career.

A second generation of Abstract Expressionist painters assembled in the Greenwich Village neighborhood of
New York during the 1950s, forming a close-knit community that organized discussion groups to share their ideas
and cooperative galleries to exhibit their work. Prominent
among them was Joan Mitchell (1925–1992), who moved to
New York after studying first at Smith College and then at
the School of the Art Institute in her native Chicago. After a
decade in New York, painting energetic but lyrical abstract
paintings that show the impact of Gorky and De Kooning
in particular, she moved permanently to France in 1959,
where she continued to develop her style untouched by
the Pop Art that transformed the New York scene during the 1960s. Mitchell painted in a personal adaptation
of Abstract Expressionism, visualizing her memories of
natural and urban landscapes and how they affected her.
In **LADYBUG (FIG. 32–86)**, she created energetic but controlled rhythms with gestural brushstrokes, setting the
lyrical complexity of her distinctive color palette against a
neutral ground in a seeming reference to the figure-and-
field relationship of traditional painting. She explained,
"The freedom in my work is quite controlled. I don't close
my eyes and hope for the best."

Abstract Expressionism
spread quickly to Canada. In
his native Montreal, the French
Canadian painter Jean-Paul Riopelle (1923–2002) worked with
Les Automatistes, a group of
artists using the Surrealist technique of automatism to create
abstract paintings. In 1947, Riopelle moved to Paris and in paintings such as **KNIGHT WATCH (FIG.
32–87)** during the early 1950s, he
began to squeeze paint directly

32–86 Joan Mitchell **LADYBUG**
1957. Oil on canvas, 6'7⅞" × 9'
(1.98 × 2.74 m). Museum of Modern Art,
New York. Purchase (385.1961).

Credit: © Estate of Joan Mitchell. © 2016.
Digital image, The Museum of Modern Art,
New York/Scala, Florence

32–87 Jean-Paul Riopelle **KNIGHT WATCH**

1953. Oil on canvas, 38 × 76⅝" (96.6 × 194.8 cm). National Gallery of Canada, Ottawa.

Credit: © 2016 Artists Rights Society (ARS), New York/SODRAC, Montreal. National Gallery of Canada

onto canvas before spreading it with a palette knife to create bright swatches of color traversed by networks of spidery lines.

Helen Frankenthaler (1928–2011) visited Pollock's studio in 1951 and began to create a more lyrical version of Action painting that had a significant impact on later artists. Like Pollock, she worked on the floor, but she poured paint onto unprimed canvas in thin washes so that it soaked into the fabric rather than sitting on its surface. Frankenthaler described her process as starting with an aesthetic question or image, which evolved as the self-expressive act of painting took over. She explained, "I will sometimes start a picture feeling, What will happen if I work with three blues … ? And very often midway through the picture I have to change the basis of the experience. Or I add and add to the canvas…. When I say gesture, my gesture, I mean what my mark is. I think there is something now that I am still working out in paint; it is a struggle for me to both discard and retain what is gestural and personal." In **MOUNTAINS AND SEA (FIG. 32–88)**, Frankenthaler outlined selected forms in charcoal and then poured several diluted colors onto the canvas. The result reminded her of the coast of Nova Scotia where she frequently went to sketch.

COLOR FIELD PAINTING AND SCULPTURE New York School artists used abstract means to express various kinds of emotional states, not all of them as urgent or improvisatory as those of the Action painters. The Color Field painters moved in a different direction, painting large, flat areas of color to produce more-contemplative moods.

Mark Rothko (1903–1970) had very little formal art training, but by 1940 he was already producing paintings deeply influenced by the European Surrealists and by Jung's archetypal imagery. By the mid-1940s, he began to paint very large canvases with rectangular shapes arranged in a vertical format in which he allowed the colors

32–88 Helen Frankenthaler **MOUNTAINS AND SEA**

1952. Oil and charcoal on canvas, 7'2¾" × 9'8¼" (2.2 × 2.95 m). Helen Frankenthaler Foundation, on loan to the National Gallery of Art, Washington, DC.

Credit: Image courtesy of the National Gallery of Art, Washington. © 2016 Helen Frankenthaler Foundation, Inc./Artists Rights Society (ARS), New York

32–89 Mark Rothko **UNTITLED (ROTHKO NUMBER 5068.49)**

1949. Oil on canvas, 6′9⅜″ × 5′6⅜″ (2.1 × 1.4 m). National Gallery of Art, Washington, DC.

Credit: © 1998 Kate Rothko Prizel & Christopher Rothko/Artists Rights Society (ARS), New York. Image courtesy the National Gallery of Art, Washington

together in series or rows, lit indirectly to evoke moods of transcendental meditation.

Barnett Newman (1905–1970) also addressed modern humanity's existential condition in very large canvases, some painted mostly in a single brilliant color divided by thin, jagged lines in another color that he called "zips." Newman claimed his art was about "[t]he self, terrible and constant." **VIR HEROICUS SUBLIMIS** (Latin for "Man, Heroic and Sublime") (**FIG. 32-90**) shows how Newman's total concentration on a single color focuses his meaning. The broad field of red does not describe any form; it presents an absolute state of sublime redness across a vast, heroic canvas, interrupted only by the zips of other colors that threaten, like a human flaw, to unbalance it. Newman wrote, "The present painter is concerned not with his own feelings or with the mystery of his own personality but with the penetration into the world mystery. His imagination is therefore attempting to dig into metaphysical secrets. To that extent his art is concerned with the sublime."

to bleed into one another. Paintings such as **UNTITLED (ROTHKO NUMBER 5068.49)** (**FIG. 32-89**) and *No. 3/No. 13 (Magenta, Black, Green on Orange)* (SEE FIG. Intro-1) are not simply arrangements of flat, geometric shapes on a canvas, nor are they atmospheric, archetypical landscapes. Rothko thought of his shapes as fundamental ideas expressed in rectangular form uninterrupted by a recognizable subject, which sit in front of a painted field (hence the name "Color Field painting"). He preferred to show his paintings

Sculpture tended to resist the kind of instantaneous gestural processes developed by painters, although some sculptors managed to communicate both abstractly and expressionistically in three dimensions. David Smith (1906–1965) learned to weld and rivet while working at an automobile plant in Indiana. He trained as a painter,

32–90 Barnett Newman **VIR HEROICUS SUBLIMIS**

1950–1951. Oil on canvas, 95⅜ × 213¼″ (242 × 541.7 cm). Museum of Modern Art, New York. Gift of Mr. and Mrs. Ben Heller.

Credit: © 2016 The Barnett Newman Foundation, New York / Artists Rights Society (ARS), New York. © 2016. Digital image, The Museum of Modern Art, New York/ Scala, Florence but became a sculptor after seeing reproductions of welded metal sculptures by artists such as Picasso. Smith avoided the precious materials of traditional sculpture and created works out of standard industrial materials. After World War II, he began to weld horizontally formatted sculptures that were like drawings in space. The forms of the **CUBI** series (**FIG. 32-91**) were created from precut pieces of stainless-steel sheets fabricated to the artist's specifications. The name for the series intentionally invokes the sculptures'

visual similarity to the Cubist paintings of Braque and Picasso. In photographs they sometimes look coldly industrial, but when observed outdoors as Smith intended, their highly burnished surfaces show the gestural marks made by the sculptor's tools and reflect the sun in different ways depending on the time of day, weather conditions, and the distance from which they are viewed. Vaguely humanoid, like giant totemic figures, the sculptures are surprisingly organic when seen at close range.

32-91 David Smith **CUBI**

"Cubi" series shown installed at Bolton Landing, New York, in 1965. *Cubi XVIII* (left), 1964. Stainless steel, 9′8″ (2.94 m). Museum of Fine Arts, Boston. *Cubi XVII* (center), 1963. Stainless steel, 9′2″ (2.79 m). Dallas Museum of Arts. *Cubi XIX* (right), 1964. Stainless steel, 9′5⅜″ (2.88 m). Tate, London.

Credit: Art © The Estate of David Smith/Licensed by VAGA, New York, NY

Think About It

1   Discuss the goals and interests of the painters associated with Abstract Expressionism. Characterize the role played by Surrealism and other early twentieth-century avant-garde art movements in the formation of this new direction in Modern art.

2   Explain the impact of the two world wars on the visual arts in Europe and North America. Use two works from this chapter—one European and one American—as the focus of your discussion.

3   Summarize the events of the Great Depression and discuss its impact on American art.

4   Explain how Dada and Surrealism changed the form, content, and concept of art. Which two works discussed in this chapter would you choose to represent these movements? Why?

Crosscurrents

Throughout the history of art, artists have created eloquent and moving expressions of the horrific violence of war and oppression. Discuss the political circumstances that led to the creation of these two examples and assess how they relate to the styles of these two artists and their time. Who were the audiences for these works?

FIG. 30–45

FIG. 32–64

33–1 Jasper Johns **TARGET WITH PLASTER CASTS**

1955. Encaustic and collage on canvas with objects, 51 × 44″ (129.5 × 111.8 cm). Collection Mr. and Mrs. Leo Castelli.

Chapter 33
The International Scene since the 1950s

 ## Learning Objectives

33.a Identify the visual hallmarks of art and architecture created since the 1950s for formal, technical, and expressive qualities.

33.b Interpret the meaning of works of art created since the 1950s based on their themes, subjects, and symbols.

33.c Relate artists and art created since the 1950s to their cultural, economic, and political contexts.

33.d Apply the vocabulary and concepts relevant to contemporary art, artists, and art history.

33.e Interpret a work of contemporary art using the art historical methods of observation, comparison, and inductive reasoning.

33.f Select visual and textual evidence in various media to support an argument or an interpretation of a work of contemporary art.

In the early 1950s, a new generation of artists emerged in New York who thought art should be firmly anchored in real life. At the time, Abstract Expressionism, championed by the powerful critic Clement Greenberg, dominated the art world. But younger artists like Robert Rauschenberg and Jasper Johns challenged Greenberg's belief that the best art was characterized by abstract imagery that conveyed transcendent meaning through an emphasis only on the formal effects of paint on a flat surface. Inspired by the expansive visual culture of postwar America, they resisted the emotional overtones of Abstract Expressionism and explored its conceptual implications through art that was ironic and intellectually demanding.

Johns pushed Greenbergian Formalism to its limit in **TARGET WITH PLASTER CASTS** (**FIG. 33-1**) by creating an object that is both sculpture and painting. Colorful casts of a foot, hand, penis, and other body parts sit in wooden boxes along the top, calling attention to the three-dimensionality of the stretched canvas and inviting the viewer to open or close the doors to the sculptures inside. The painted target below appeals to the viewer's tactile and visual senses. Johns used **encaustic**, an ancient technique in which pigment is suspended in molten beeswax that is applied in thin layers to build up an image. Unlike the Action paintings of Pollock or De Kooning, Johns's visible brushstrokes result from deliberate working of the medium and appear almost sculpted in the dense, waxy surface of the target. The concentric circles suggest an all-over abstract composition, but are also recognizable (and

functional) as an ordinary target, which raises the question: Is this a painting of a target or is it an actual target?

Unlike Abstract Expressionist paintings, Johns's art is emotionally cool and highly cerebral. Like many artists of his generation, he puts readily recognizable, real-world images and objects in purposefully unusual contexts in order to question art's form, appearance, content, and function. Thus, like much art after 1950, Johns's art demands the viewer's visual, physical, and intellectual engagement. A critical figure in art since 1950, Johns embodies themes that would become central later in the twentieth century: the ongoing desire of artists to cross boundaries separating real life from art, to investigate art's conceptual foundations, to use nontraditional materials, and to recognize art as a performative experience involving artist, viewer, and object.

The World since the 1950s

How does contemporary art challenge art history's study of period and regional styles?

As the world worked to overcome the trauma of World War II, the United States and the U.S.S.R. arose as major superpowers. The Soviet occupation and sponsorship of governments across Eastern and Central Europe and the emergence of communist dictatorships in the People's Republic of China and Cuba compelled the United States to try to contain further expansion of Soviet influence. This led to extended military actions in Korea and Vietnam and

MAP 33–1 THE WORLD SINCE 1950

International sites in the contemporary art world in the Americas, Europe, and Africa.

covert operations in Central America, intended to support regimes sympathetic to the U.S. In addition to these violent outbreaks, the United States and the U.S.S.R. each built large stockpiles of nuclear weapons, adopting a strategy of mutually assured destruction that prevented nuclear war by threatening complete destruction of both nations if either chose to strike first. This period, known as the Cold War, lasted from the 1950s until 1989, when the fall of the Berlin Wall signaled the end of the Soviet Union.

Although marked by fear of the threat of war and Soviet takeover, the postwar years were a time of extraordinary economic prosperity in the United States. A growing mass media propelled a new consumer society, selling the promise of the American dream through advertisements, glossy magazines, and television. But recognition that not everyone had the same access to this dream caused tensions around racial and social inequality and gave way to the politicized climate of the 1960s, which saw fights for African-American, gay, and women's rights and an increasing anti-establishment attitude that questioned existing political, economic, and social values.

In recent years, advancements in communication technology and the Internet continue to affect society in profound ways. Mobile devices, social networking sites, and the ability to connect with people across the globe have led to a wave of grassroots activism. The potential

for large-scale impact was realized in 2011 with the Arab Spring uprisings that spread across North Africa, giving way to revolutions in Tunisia and Egypt, and the Occupy Movement that began with a few protesters in New York's financial district and has grown into a worldwide effort to call attention to economic and social disparity.

While digital technology has bolstered humanitarian efforts around issues like worldwide poverty, social injustice, and the need for assistance in crisis, its pervasiveness has also brought new worries about religious and political extremism, violence and cultural terrorism, and tension between national security and individual privacy rights. Likewise, society's reliance on industry and technology has given rise to environmental concerns about the depletion of natural resources, global warming, and dramatic climate change.

The History of Art since the 1950s

Since the 1950s, artists have reconceptualized and reimagined art, producing radically new forms to express new ideas and content. Their art takes on complex social and political questions that lack a definitive solution and challenges us to consider own morality, behavior, and complacency. It sometimes assaults and accuses. It sometimes brings wonder, joy, and human insight. Artists today acknowledge viewers as active participants who make meaning through their individual interpretations and contribute to a work's cultural significance. While recent art may seem challenging at first, it demands we look longer and think harder—creating a catalyst for conversations about its meaning and our world.

The study of contemporary art presents a challenge to art historians whose goal is to bring historical perspective to the art of our present time. A key issue is the fundamental need to define the period of study. A historical marker exists in the aesthetic and philosophical shifts that gave rise to Pop Art, Minimalism, and Conceptual Art. In recent decades, scholars have exploded the apparent cohesion of these art historical movements to reveal a complex network of diverse but related styles, practices, philosophical concerns, and interdisciplinary interests that emerged in the 1950s and early 1960s. The inherent messiness of this period, characterized by creative thinkers in art, literature, music, dance, theater, science, and technology working together in experimental and ephemeral formats, defies traditions of art history and museums that privilege visual analysis of the material object, and continues to present challenges today.

The artistic production of these formative years anticipates the plurality of late twentieth-century art and offers the key to making sense of more recent contemporary developments. Growth in the variety of artistic formats, creative practices, and interdisciplinary collaborations today has been made even more complicated by extraordinary growth in the art market, private and public

museums, and popular interest in art of the post–World War II period. What we find is that contemporary art is a distinct field that is currently under construction. This issue has provoked a growing crisis in art history that questions how the increasing scholarly focus on contemporary works of art may impact the discipline's established values and practices, and what its effect may be on the future of art history itself. These ongoing debates offer a unique opportunity to consider the fluid and evolving nature of academic study in art history and other humanities, as well as the cultural institutions that support them.

The Expanding Art World

What key ideas and formative artistic practices develop in the generation after Abstract Expressionism?

The generation of artists who began to make art in the 1950s increasingly addressed the ordinary experiences of life. Drawing inspiration from Cubist and Dadaist artists of the early twentieth century, they incorporated everyday objects into real space and time and expanded the idea of painting to include characteristics traditionally associated with sculpture and other creative disciplines. The result was a proliferation of new formats and techniques that aimed to blur the distinctions between art and life, investigate the role of advertising and popular imagery in visual culture, and critique the insistence on art's autonomy and formalist interpretations of meaning.

Finding New Forms

Louise Nevelson (1899–1988) collected discarded packing boxes in which she would carefully arrange chair legs, broom handles, cabinet doors, spindles, and other wooden refuse. Reflecting a Cubist approach to assemblage, Nevelson unified the fragmented forms by painting her compositions matte black, white, or gold. These monochromatic schemes obscured the identity of the individual elements and evoked some sense of mood. She heightened this poetic element in her monumental assemblage **SKY CATHEDRAL** (**FIG. 33-2**) by displaying it bathed in soft blue light, recalling moonlight. While artists like Nevelson used assemblage for formal and expressive

33-2 Louise Nevelson **SKY CATHEDRAL**
1958. Assemblage of wood construction painted black,
11'3½" × 10'¼" × 18" (3.44 × 3.05 × 0.46 m).
Museum of Modern Art, New York.

33-3 Robert Rauschenberg **CANYON**

1959. Oil, pencil, paper, metal, photograph, fabric, wood on canvas, plus buttons, mirror, stuffed eagle, pillow tied with cord, and paint tube; 81¾ × 70 × 24" (2.08 × 1.78 × 0.61 m). Museum of Modern Art, New York. Gift of the family of Ileana Sonnabend.

Credit: Art © Robert Rauschenberg Foundation/Licensed by VAGA, New York, NY. @ 2016. Digital image, Museum of Modern Art/Scala, Florence

effect, others, influenced by Dada, saw that by integrating everyday objects into their art, they could challenge the artistic autonomy and high-minded intellectualism of Abstract Expressionism.

Inspired by the example of Marcel Duchamp (see Chapter 32), Jasper Johns combined assemblage with painting techniques in works like *Target with Plaster Casts* (SEE FIG. 33-1) to address formal and conceptual issues in art. Johns also raised psychological questions about perceptions of the self in the modern era. The fragmented body casts above the target lack any sense of the organic whole. Closing the lids on the boxes that contain the casts further depersonalizes the individual by obliterating all or a selective part of the human presence. The combination of fragmented and partially hidden body parts with the target takes on richer meaning when we consider that Johns was a gay artist in the restrictive climate of Cold War America.

RAUSCHENBERG, CAGE, AND BLACK MOUNTAIN COLLEGE Many of these ideas found new form at Black Mountain College in western North Carolina, founded to advance progressive education in the liberal arts within a communal living environment. For the short time it was open (1933–1956), Black Mountain College's experimental atmosphere drew creative thinkers in different fields and became a hub of avant-garde innovation. In the 1940s, the school was led by Josef Albers, who had taught at the Bauhaus, and figures such as Buckminster Fuller, Merce Cunningham, John Cage, M.C. Richards, Willem de Kooning, and Clement Greenberg served as faculty, many teaching in summer sessions when the arts were emphasized.

Raised in Texas, Robert Rauschenberg (1925–2008) studied painting in Paris after World War II before arriving at Black Mountain College in 1948. His desire "to act in the gap between [art and life]" explains his irreverent and often humorous approach to an art world dominated by Abstract Expressionism. To create *Erased De Kooning* of 1953, Rauschenberg asked Willem de Kooning for

a drawing that he could erase. Knowing Rauschenberg's intent, De Kooning relinquished one that included oil paint and crayon—so it took over a month for the younger artist to rub out its imagery. This work ironically underscores Rauschenberg's impulse to make his own creative work through an active process that negated De Kooning's expressive mark. Rauschenberg's oedipal act against the generation that had come before him signaled the transition from Abstract Expressionism to the radical ideas of a new generation of artists.

In 1955, Rauschenberg began a series of assemblages that he called **combines** because they blended features of both painting and sculpture. **CANYON** (FIG. 33-3) incorporates old family photos, a picture of the Statue of Liberty, bits of newsprint, and political posters alongside ordinary objects like a flattened steel drum adhered to the work's surface. Other elements, including a stuffed eagle and a dirty pillow suspended by a piece of wood, project into the real space of the viewer. Rauschenberg added dripping splashes of paint to his composition as well, an ironic reference to Abstract Expressionist Action painting. Similar to Johns's more conceptual approach, Rauschenberg combined imagery from popular culture and avant-garde painting to undermine the idea of an autonomous art.

John Cage (1912–1992) was born in Los Angeles and studied art, music, and poetry in Europe before returning to California, where he worked with composer Arnold Schoenberg. Strongly influenced by Eastern philosophy and the ideas of Marcel Duchamp, Cage explored how chance might be used to eliminate intention and personal taste in art making. Some of his experiments included altering pianos by inserting objects between the strings, playing 12 radios at once, and assigning musical notes to the random markings found on a sheet of paper. Cage first visited Black Mountain College in 1948 and taught regularly in the summer sessions. There, his exchanges with Rauschenberg were of particular importance. In the summer of 1951, Rauschenberg exhibited a series of entirely white paintings at the college. Devoid of representation, their brightly lit surface called attention to the dust particles and shadows cast on them. Cage described these paintings as "mirrors of the air," and they inspired him to produce 4′33″, a composition where the musician sits motionless for 4 minutes and 33 seconds while the audience listens. Like Rauschenberg's "blank" canvas, Cage used time to call attention to the ambient noises that take place even in what we usually consider to be silence.

In the summer of 1952, Cage organized *Theater Piece, No. 1* at Black Mountain College. Sometimes called the first "Happening" (a term discussed further later in this chapter), it took place in the dining hall and involved the simultaneous occurrence of unrelated activities including a lecture on Zen Buddhism read from atop a ladder, dancers and musicians moving around the audience, a dog interrupting the performance, and movies projected upside down on the wall. Rauschenberg, who played scratchy

records from a wind-up phonograph, hung his white paintings from the ceiling as a set for the performance, which ended when coffee was served. Like Duchamp, who claimed that the artist could choose an object to be art, Cage proposed that artists might use time to bracket ordinary life events in order to heighten our awareness of the experience and thus transform it into a work of art. Other Cage–Rauschenberg collaborations in the 1950s and 1960s, often including Johns and the dancer Merce Cunningham, continued to blur the line separating art from life and to challenge disciplinary boundaries that divided the visual arts from dance, music, and theatrical performance.

New Forms Abroad

Artists in other parts of the world conducted similar experiments in the 1950s, expanding painting to include performance and interactive exhibition formats. Rejecting the spontaneity and expressionism of Art Informel, many artists in Europe worked collaboratively to explore the conceptual implications of painting and the viewer's perception of space and time. Variously associated with Nouveau Réalism in France, Arte Povera in Italy, the German Zero Group, and the New Tendencies collectives in Eastern Europe, this network of avant-garde artists pushed the limits of painting to the breaking point and crossed into realms of assemblage, kinetic sculpture, performance, and electronic media.

In a career cut short by a heart attack at age 34, Yves Klein (1928–1962) stands out as both influential and provocative. An avid interest in judo and spiritual mysticism informed Klein's diverse artistic production and his goal of freeing the creative essence in art from its material form. This ambition led him to monochromatic paintings using a distinctive color that he associated with natural forces, which he named IKB (International Klein Blue); other "paintings" made by exposing his canvases to elements like rain and fire; and his series of *Anthropométries*, made by nude women that Klein described as "living brushes." In **ANTHROPOMÉTRIES OF THE BLUE PERIOD** (FIG. 33–4), presented in 1960 at the Galerie Internationale d'Art Contemporain, Klein, dressed in formal

33–4 Yves Klein **ANTHROPOMÉTRIES OF THE BLUE PERIOD**

1960. Performance at the Galerie Internationale d'Art Contemporain, Paris.

Credit: © Yves Klein/Artists Rights Society (ARS), New York/ADAGP, Paris 2016. Photo: Shunk - Kender @ J Paul Getty Trust. Getty Research Institute, LA. (2014.R.20)

33-5 Shozo Shimamoto
HURLING COLORS

1956. Performance at the second Gutai Exhibition, Tokyo.

Credit: Courtesy of Shozo Shimamoto

attire, orchestrated three women's movements as they covered themselves in paint and then imprinted parts of their bodies on large sheets of white paper. Klein explained, "It would never cross my mind to soil my hands with paint. Detached and distant, the work of art must be completed under my eyes and under my command." A small string orchestra accompanied the performance with Klein's *Monotone Symphony*, a single continuous sound played for the duration. The artist's self-aggrandizing quest for the immaterial—and flare for the theatrical—have led skeptics to see Klein as a charlatan, but his work remains an important precedent for those who move art beyond the confines of material objecthood and acknowledge creative forces in nature.

In Japan, Yoshihara Jirō founded the Gutai collective of artists in 1954 "to pursue the possibilities of pure and creative activity with great energy," as he explained in a manifesto of 1956. The Gutai (meaning "concrete" or "embodiment") organized outdoor installations, theatrical events, and dramatic performances intended to reveal art's relationship to viewers and the natural surroundings. These works highlighted the physical act of creating art through sometimes violent interactions with paint, mud, paper, electric lights, and industrial materials. At the second Gutai Exhibition in 1956, Shozo Shimamoto (1928–2013) performed **HURLING COLORS** (**FIG. 33-5**) by smashing bottles of paint against a canvas on the floor. Informed by Japanese philosophy, Shimamoto recognized his act of destruction to be one of creation as well, writing that "in this age, the boundary between the two no longer exists." The Gutai moved past Pollock's gestural influence to the point where the painting's production appeared as important as the object produced, if not more so.

Happenings and Fluxus

Emphasis on the artist's creative act gave rise to a performative impulse throughout the early 1960s, most clearly seen among artists involved with Happenings and Fluxus. These loosely formed groups owe a debt to Cage's ideas about chance methods of artistic production and the synthesis of art and life. The classes Cage taught at the New School in New York from 1956 to 1961 drew a mix of artists, musicians, performers, and writers and had a lasting influence on the avant-garde community in the United States and abroad. Variously described as assemblage, environments, dance, Happenings, and events, this type of art broke all boundaries by actively invading the viewer's space and often involving the audience—sometimes unknowingly— as participants in the artwork's production.

In the late 1950s, Allan Kaprow (1927–2006), who studied with Cage in New York, began to create Environments. These built on assemblage practices to extend the work of art into space surrounding the viewer. Trained as a painter, Kaprow found inspiration in Pollock, whose drip technique and large-scale compositions suggested to him new forms of art that rejected painting entirely. In his 1958 essay "The Legacy of Jackson Pollock," Kaprow concluded that artists "must become preoccupied with and even dazzled by the space and objects of our everyday life ... objects of every sort are materials for the new art." In **YARD** (**FIG. 33-6**) Kaprow filled the courtyard behind the Martha Jackson Gallery in Manhattan with used tires, tar paper, and barrels, and asked viewers to walk through it, thus positioning them as a part of the artwork itself. Different from a painting on the gallery wall, *Yard* called attention to the viewer's physical experience, stumbling amid detritus and smelling the dirty rubber and tar—features of the urban environment that might go unnoticed outside of the art gallery context.

33–6 Allan Kaprow **YARD**
1961. View of tires in court of Martha Jackson Gallery,
New York, 1961.

Credit: Photo: Ken Heyman

where it was filmed and photographed. Eight men and women first undressed one another, then danced, rolled on the floor ecstatically, and played with a mixture of raw fish, raw sausages, partially plucked raw and bloody chickens, wet paint, and scraps of paper. Schneemann wanted both performers and audience to experience the smell, taste, and feel of the body and its fluids. Critics described the piece variously as an erotic rite and a visceral celebration of flesh and blood. It countered the expectation that a work of art was something to be examined in the cool, detached space of an art gallery where the viewer remains passively in control and the artist remains invisible. *Meat Joy* forced the viewer to become complicit in the live event. Many feminist artists like Schneemann embraced Happenings and other forms of what was beginning to be called **performance art**, a term that distinguished such events from traditional theatrical presentation. These practices offered a powerful tool to challenge the objectification of women's bodies that had existed in art for centuries. Performance art enabled women to assert their own artistic agency by determining how their bodies were viewed and even confronting their audience who, in turn, had to acknowledge the woman's active presence.

HAPPENINGS   In contrast to Environments, which invited the viewers to interact with static installations, were works that Kaprow called **Happenings**: immersive, chance-based performances like Cage's *Theatre Piece No. 1.* These overwhelmed the audience with a barrage of unrelated activities that invoked a range of sensual and emotional responses. One example was **MEAT JOY** (**FIG. 33-7**) by Carolee Schneemann (b. 1939), enacted first at the Festival de la Libre Expression in Paris and then in New York,

FLUXUS   Whereas Happenings were visually stimulating and dynamic, Fluxus events were more conceptual and deliberate in their actions, which often focused on ordinary behaviors—like pouring water, cutting hair, or eating a meal—performed methodically and repeatedly, sometimes over extended periods of time. The ritualistic nature of these performances underscores the influence of Eastern religious practice, where deep contemplation of routine tasks may result in spiritual enlightenment. In spite of their aesthetic differences, Happenings and Fluxus artists often showed their work in the same galleries and other venues. One of

33–7 Carolee Schneemann
MEAT JOY
1964. Gelatin-silver print. Photograph
by Tony Ray-Jones, taken in Judson
Memorial Church in November 1964.

Credit: © 2016 Carolee Schneemann/
Artists Rights Society (ARS), New York.
© Tony Ray-Jones/National Media Museum/
Science & Society Picture Library

THREE AQUEOUS EVENTS

● ice

● water

● steam

Summer, 1961

33–8 George Brecht
**THREE AQUEOUS
EVENTS**
1961. Event score
from Water Yam edition,
1972. Plastic, paper.
Collection Walker Art
Center, Minneapolis.
Walker Special Purchase
Fund, 1989

Performance view,
Rutgers University, New
Jersey, 1963.

Credit: © 2016 Artists Rights
Society (ARS), New York/
VG Bild-Kunst, Bonn.
(far left) courtesy Walker Art
Center; (left) photo by Peter
Moore © Barbara Moore/
Licensed by VAGA, New
York, NY. Courtesy Paula
Cooper Gallery, New York

these, the AG Gallery, was owned by George Maciunas, who coined the name Fluxus in an attempt to codify and promote the diverse movement. As part of his efforts, Maciunas organized international festivals that helped to spread these ideas and connect the group with a broader network of avant-garde artists throughout the world.

Many Fluxus events were presented as written "scores," reflecting the importance of Cage and the broad reach of the movement to include musicians, writers, dancers, and visual artists. George Brecht's **THREE AQUEOUS EVENTS (FIG. 33–8)** is one of 69 cards with written instructions for activities that could be performed by the reader; the cards were collected, boxed, and published in editions. The ambiguous nature of Brecht's printed prompts reflects

the tendency of Fluxus artists to blur the boundaries between life, art, action, and object. Brecht's other scores included *Exit Event*, where the instructions were simply the word "Exit," and *Duration Event*, with only "Red" and "Green" appearing on the card. In each case, the reader is left to choose whether or not to follow the cue, how it might be realized, and even if they will acknowledge their action as a work of art.

After settling in New York, Yoko Ono (b. 1933) became involved with Fluxus in the early 1960s, and her loft at 112 Chambers Street became an important site for many avant-garde activities. In **CUT PIECE (FIG. 33–9)**, performed first in Japan in 1964 and the following year at New York's Carnegie Hall, Ono knelt passively on stage while members of the audience were invited to use sewing shears, which were provided next to her, to cut away bits of her clothing to take with them. This powerful work demonstrated key characteristics of Fluxus: its reliance on the audience to realize the event and the ritualistic nature of the performance, which suggested both self-sacrifice and desecration. The performance was charged with implicit violence and eroticism as the body of the young Japanese woman was slowly exposed by the deliberate action of each audience member who walked

33–9 Yoko Ono **CUT PIECE**
1965. Film still of performance at the Carnegie
Recital Hall, New York on March 21, 1965.
Film by Albert and David Maysles.

Credit: © Yoko Ono

33–10 Nam June Paik with Charlotte Moorman **TV BRA FOR LIVING SCULPTURE**

1969. Performance view. Gelatin silver print. Collection Walker Art Center. Minneapolis, T.B.Walker Acquisition Fund, 1991. Photograph by Peter Moore.

Credit: © Barbara Moore/Licensed by VAGA, New York, NY. Courtesy Paula Cooper Gallery, New York

up and chose to make the next cut. Although *Cut Piece* was not recognized as a feminist work of art at the time, Ono has since described it as "against ageism, against racism, against sexism, and against violence."

Often described as the father of video art, Korean artist Nam June Paik (1932–2006) came from a classical music background and was deeply influenced by Cage. Paik's interest in mass-media technology led to his early experiments altering broadcast images with magnets he attached to the top of television consoles. In the 1960s, Paik produced a number of works in collaboration with musician Charlotte Moorman (1933–1991) that were included as part of Fluxus festivals. **TV BRA FOR LIVING SCULPTURE** (**FIG. 33–10**) combined Paik's interest in sculpture, technology, music, and performance and demonstrated the humor and sexual content often seen in Fluxus works. Designed to be worn by Moorman while playing the cello, the device was wired so she could manipulate images broadcast on the screens with foot pedals and her musical technique. Paik described the work as an effort to humanize technology, but it also highlighted the fetish-like status afforded both women's breasts and television in a society dominated by mass media. Moorman's role as a "living sculpture" further suggested the human body as an object akin to sculpture, thus reflecting the Fluxus idea that life itself is art that we enact every day.

Fluxus festivals and performances helped connect avant-garde artists internationally. Joseph Beuys (1921–1986) contributed conceptual and performance-based

works that, along with his roles as teacher and political activist, made him one of the most influential artists of the period. Beuys created a personal mythology for himself based on his experience as a fighter pilot in the German Luftwaffe during World War II. He claimed to have been shot down over the Crimea and saved by Tatars who wrapped him in animal fat and felt, materials that held important symbolic value for Beuys and reappeared throughout his work. Beuys saw art as a means of social redemption and healing from the horrors and guilt left after the Holocaust. As an artist, he took on a mysterious, shaman-like persona, and many of his actions assumed the seriousness of sacred rituals with goals of spiritual renewal and transformation.

In **HOW TO EXPLAIN PICTURES TO A DEAD HARE** (**FIG. 33–11**), a performance staged at the opening of an exhibition of his drawings in Dusseldorf, Beuys initially sat visible on a chair in the gallery, which was closed to visitors

33–11 Joseph Beuys **HOW TO EXPLAIN PICTURES TO A DEAD HARE**

1965. Photograph of performance at the Schmela Gallery, Dusseldorf, November 26, 1965.

Credit: © Ute Klophaus © 2016 Artists Rights Society (ARS), New York/VG Bild-Kunst, Bonn. Courtesy Ronald Feldman Fine Arts, NY outside. His head was coated in honey and covered by a mask of gold leaf. In his lap he cradled a dead hare to which he muttered incomprehensibly. His left foot rested on felt, suggesting spiritual warmth, while his right foot rested on steel, symbolizing cold, hard reason. He carried the hare's corpse around the gallery for several hours, quietly explaining his pictures—implying a spiritual connection with the dead hare and underscoring the inadequacy of words to convey art's true meaning and potential for profound revelation. Beuys said, "Even a dead animal preserves more powers of intuition than some human beings."

Pop Art

Many artists focused their attention on the mid-century explosion in visual culture that was fueled by the growing mass media and the disposable income of the postwar generation. Pop Art originated in Britain in the years soon after World War II, but its primary development was in the United States in the early 1960s. First seen in the cool, slick aesthetic of New York artists like Andy Warhol and Roy Lichtenstein, variations of Pop Art soon emerged in Chicago and along the West Coast to reflect regional distinctions in consumer tastes and popular culture. Homes, automobiles, and luxury products reflected life as it appeared on television, in films, and in print advertising,

and the visible display of one's possessions was increasingly seen as an indication of personal identity and social standing. Pop artists seemed to both embrace and possibly critique the superficial fiction of a perfect life.

HAMILTON In the early 1950s, while the British government maintained that the country's postwar recovery depended on sustained consumption of domestic goods, an interdisciplinary collective of artists, architects, photographers, and writers came together in London as the Independent Group. One of its members, Richard Hamilton (1922–2011), argued that mass visual culture was fast replacing traditional art for the general public: Movies, television, and advertising, not high art, now defined standards of beauty. Society's idols were no longer politicians or military heroes, but international movie stars, and social status was now measured by what one bought and owned. To create a visual expression of this new world of excessive consumption, Hamilton created collages of images drawn from advertising. In **JUST WHAT IS IT THAT MAKES TODAY'S HOMES SO DIFFERENT, SO APPEALING?** (**FIG. 33-12**) from 1956, Hamilton critiques marketing strategies by imitating them. The title parodies an advertising slogan, while the collage itself shows two figures named Adam and Eve in a domestic setting. Like the biblical figures, these are almost naked, but the temptations to which they have given in are those of consumer culture. Adam is a bodybuilder and Eve a pin-up girl. In an attempt to recreate their lost Garden of Eden, the first couple has filled their home with all the best new products: a television, a tape recorder, a vacuum cleaner, and fashionable new furniture. Displayed on the wall is not high art but a poster advertising a romance novel, hung next to a traditional portrait of a stern-looking man. Adam holds a huge, suggestively placed Tootsie Pop, which the English critic Lawrence Alloway cited when he described this work as "Pop art," one possible source of the movement's name. Like assemblages in the United States, Hamilton's collage comments on the visual overload of popular

33-12 Richard Hamilton **JUST WHAT IS IT THAT MAKES TODAY'S HOMES SO DIFFERENT, SO APPEALING?**
1956. Collage, 10¼ × 9¾" (26 × 24.7 cm). Kunsthalle Tübingen, Collection Zundel.

33–13 Andy Warhol **MARILYN DIPTYCH**

1962. Oil, acrylic, and silkscreen on enamel on canvas; two panels, each 6'10" × 4'9" (2.05 × 1.44 m). Tate, London.

Credit: Marilyn Monroe LLC under license authorized by CMG Worldwide Inc., Indianapolis, In © 2016 The Andy Warhol Foundation for the Visual Arts, Inc./Artists Rights Society (ARS), New York. © Tate, London 2016

culture and on society's inability to differentiate between the advertising world and the real one.

By 1960, several American artists also began to incorporate images from popular mass culture into their art. Their reliance on everyday subject matter recalls the tendency among Rauschenberg and other artists to transgress boundaries between art and life. Pop Art, however, developed a slicker style that recalls the mass-production techniques of advertising and gives this work a flat, commercial feel that erases the presence of the hand of the individual artist. This cool, detached quality suggested both the glorification of popular culture, now raised to fine-art status, and an implicit critique of how consumer culture transformed all things—from movie stars to art itself—into commodities to be bought and sold.

WARHOL AND LICHTENSTEIN As Pop Art flourished in the United States, Andy Warhol (1928–1987) emerged as a dominant figure. Warhol created an immense body of work between 1960 and his death in 1987, including prints, paintings, sculptures, and films. He published *Interview* magazine and managed The Velvet Underground, a radical and hugely influential rock band. Since he trained as a commercial artist, Warhol knew advertising culture well,

and by 1962, he was incorporating images from American mass-media advertising in his art. He took as subjects popular consumer items such as Campbell's Soup cans and Coca-Cola bottles, reproducing them with the cheap industrial print method of **silkscreen** (in which a fine mesh fabric screen is used as a printing stencil), as well as in paintings and sculptures.

In 1962, movie star Marilyn Monroe was found dead in an apparent suicide. Warhol's **MARILYN DIPTYCH** (**FIG. 33-13**) is one of a series of silkscreens that he made immediately after the actress's death. Warhol memorializes the screen image of Monroe, using a famous publicity photograph transferred directly onto silkscreen, thus rendering it flat and bland so that Monroe's signature features—her bleach-blond hair, her ruby lips, and her sultry, blue-eyeshadowed eyes—stand out as a caricature of the actress. The face portrayed is not that of Norma Jeane (Monroe's real name) but of Marilyn, the celluloid sex symbol as made over by the movie industry. Warhol made multiple prints from this screen, aided—as he was in many of his works—by a host of assistants working with assembly-line efficiency. In 1965, Warhol ironically named his studio "The Factory," further highlighting the commercial aspect of his art.

The *Marilyn Diptych*, however, has deeper undertones. The diptych format carries religious connotations (see "Altars and Altarpieces" in Chapter 19 on page 579), perhaps implying that Monroe was a martyred saint or goddess in the pantheon of departed movie stars. In another print, Warhol surrounded her head with the gold background used in Orthodox religious icons. Additionally, the flat and undifferentiated Monroes on the colored left side of the diptych contrast with those in black and white on the right side, which fade progressively as they are printed and reprinted without re-inking the screen until all that remains of the original portrait is the ghostly image of a disappearing person.

Warhol was one of the first artists to exploit the realization that while the mass media—television in particular—seem to bring us closer to the world, they actually allow us to observe the world only as detached voyeurs, not real participants. We become desensitized to death and disaster by the constant repetition of images on television, which we are able literally to switch off at any time. While Warhol's *Marilyn Diptych* is similarly repetitive, superficial, and bland, it exploits these traits that, in the mass media, might desensitize us to the full impact of the actress's tragic life. Warhol, known for his quotable phrases, once said, "I am a deeply superficial person." But the apparent superficiality of his art seems shrewdly profound.

In 1964, in his first sculptural project, **BRILLO SOAP PADS BOXES** (**FIG. 33-14**), Warhol hired carpenters to create plywood boxes identical in size and shape to the

33-15 Roy Lichtenstein OH, JEFF... I LOVE YOU, TOO... BUT...

1964. Oil and Magna on canvas, 48 × 48″ (122 × 122 cm). Private collection.

Credit: © Estate of Roy Lichtenstein/DACS 2016

cardboard cartons used to ship boxes of Brillo soap pads to supermarkets. By silkscreening onto these boxes the logos and texts that appeared on the actual cartons, the artist created what were essentially useless replicas of commercial packaging. Stacking the fabricated boxes in piles, Warhol transformed the interior space of the Stable Gallery in New York into what looked like a grocery stockroom, simultaneously pointing to the commercial foundation of the art gallery system and critiquing the nature of art.

Roy Lichtenstein (1923–1997) also investigated the ways that popular imagery resonated with high art, imitating the format of comic books in his critique of mass-produced visual culture. In 1961, while teaching at Rutgers University with Allan Kaprow, Lichtenstein began to make paintings based on panels from war and romance comic books. He cropped and simplified the source images to focus on dramatic emotions or actions, simultaneously representing and parodying the flat, superficial ways in which comic books of the time graphically communicated with their readers. His use of heavy black outlines, flat primary colors, and hand-painted **Benday dots** like those used in commercial printing ironically replicate the mechanical character of cartoons. **OH, JEFF... I LOVE YOU TOO... BUT...** (**FIG. 33-15**) compresses into a single frame a romantic storyline involving a crisis threatening a love relationship. Lichtenstein plays a witty game: We know that comic books are often unrealistically melodramatic, yet he presents this overblown episode vividly, almost reverently, enshrined in a work of high art.

33-14 Andy Warhol BRILLO SOAP PADS BOX
1964. Silkscreen print on painted wood, 17 × 17 × 14″ (43.2 × 43.2 × 35.6 cm). Collection of the Andy Warhol Museum, Pittsburgh.

Credit: © 2016 The Andy Warhol Foundation for the Visual Arts, Inc./Artists Rights Society (ARS), New York

Minimalism

Around the same time Pop artists like Warhol and Lichtenstein were gaining notoriety, another group of New York artists began to produce spare, geometric objects in a style that soon became known as Minimalism. Although Minimalism shuns representational subject matter, it is similar to Pop Art in its lack of obvious content, reference to techniques of mass production, and literal presentation style. Dan Flavin's unaltered fluorescent lightbulbs, Carl Andre's rows of firebricks, and Sol LeWitt's gridlike cubes seemed simplified to the extreme and initially gave rise to names like "ABC Art" and "No-Art Nihilism." Frank Stella, a painter linked to the movement, wrote famously, "What you see is what you see." Stella's work of this period relied on the shape of the canvas to dictate his abstract imagery, echoing Warhol's imitation of advertising images—both used as strategies to reduce artistic subjectivity and expressionism, hallmarks of Abstract Expressionism, in art.

The group's most visible advocates were Donald Judd (1928–1994) and Robert Morris (b.1931), who produced sophisticated essays explaining their ideas. In 1965, Judd, who worked as an art critic as well as an artist, published "Specific Objects" in *Arts Yearbook*. Although he included such artists as Klein, Claes Oldenburg, and Kenneth Noland, the essay clearly articulates his own position and significantly influenced the critical response to Minimalism. Morris's series of essays entitled "Notes on Sculpture" appeared in *Artforum* from 1966 to 1969, staking out his artistic stance to provide an intellectual framework for the new sculptural aesthetic. The two artists' highly theoretical discourse signals an important shift in the history of art. In contrast to the Abstract Expressionists, many postwar artists were able to attend college on the GI Bill, a government program that paid veterans' educational expenses. Similar to early Modernists' publishing manifestos, this generation recognized language as an essential complement to their art, and they relied on it to communicate about and shape the public's understanding of their work.

The Minimalist creation of three-dimensional objects was a logical extension of the desire to eliminate illusionism in art, effectively moving it into the real space of the gallery. In "Specific Objects" Judd wrote, "The new work obviously resembles sculpture more than it does painting, but it is nearer to painting." He further rejected the gesture and emotion invested in the handcrafted object by hiring industrial fabricators to create his sculpture in materials such as Plexiglas and steel. Judd explained that this approach synthesized art's various component parts into a unified whole that could be valued for its formal and material qualities. This idea is evident in **UNTITLED** (**FIG. 33–16**) of 1969, consisting of ten rectangular units made of galvanized iron and tinted Plexiglas that are hung in a vertical row on the gallery wall. Although each unit remains

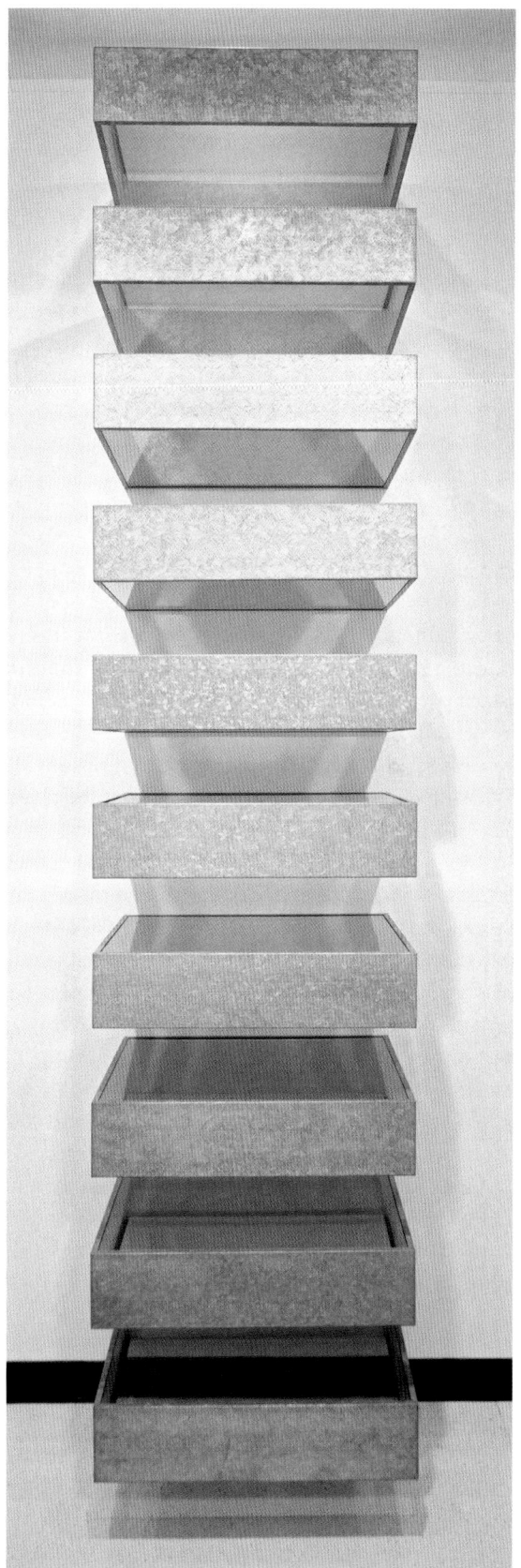

33–16 Donald Judd **UNTITLED**
1969. Galvanized iron and Plexiglas; 10 units, each 6 × 27⅛ × 24" (15.24 × 68.8 × 60.96 cm), overall 120 × 27⅛ × 24" (3.05 × 0.69 × 0.61 m). Albright-Knox Art Gallery, Buffalo, New York.

33-17 Robert Morris **UNTITLED (MIRRORED CUBES)**
1965–1971. Mirror, plate glass, and wood, 36 × 36 × 36″ (91.4 × 91.4 × 91.4 cm). Tate, London.

Credit: © 2016 Robert Morris/ Artists Rights Society (ARS), New York. © Tate, London 2016

discrete, the regular repetition of identical forms creates the impression of a single, large-scale structure. Judd's industrial production technique eliminates the expressionistic implications of brushwork to leave a smooth, even surface infused with subtle color. The arrangement avoids references to any imagined subject, allowing the objects to be seen only as themselves.

While characteristic of Minimalism's repeated geometric forms, industrial materials, and machine-made surfaces that lack the artist's touch, Morris's **UNTITLED (MIRRORED CUBES) (FIG. 33-17)** is different because the mirrors deflect the viewer's attention away from the boxes. Morris argued that Minimalist sculpture heightens psychological perceptions of an object in its spatial surroundings, forcing viewers to consider the art's relationship to their own bodily experience moving around the gallery and observing the work from many sides. This idea derived in part from Morris's involvement in dance and experimental performance with artists involved in Happenings and Fluxus, and contributed to critic Michael Fried's characterization of Minimalism as "theatrical" because it relied on space, time, and physical interaction with the viewer.

The Dematerialization of Art

What interests and ideas gave rise to alternative formats and art's "dematerialization" in the 1960s?

The experiments of the early 1960s marked a crucial turning point for new artistic formats that developed throughout the decade. Writing in 1968, art critics John R. Chandler and Lucy Lippard characterized the period by "the dematerialization of art" that resulted from a shift away from traditional painting and sculpture. Ephemeral, anti-aesthetic, and unskilled forms of art proliferated, emphasizing artistic concept over the material object of display. At the heart of this change was Duchamp's assertion that the idea motivating an artist to create a work of art could be separated from production of the artwork's final form, whose primary function was to communicate meaning to the viewer. Artists explored a range of media they felt could best represent their underlying concept and called attention to how they developed an idea to its final outcome. For this reason, conceptual works of art usually include a visual trace, such as a written text, photograph, or film, that serves as an artifact documenting the artist's process. Within the politicized context of the 1970s, artists' reliance on impermanent forms for their work resisted **commodification** (the treatment of art as merely something to be bought and sold) and carried an implicit—sometimes explicit—critique of the commercial galleries, museums, critics, and art historians who assign cultural and economic value to works of art.

Conceptual Art and Language

Conceptual Art found inspiration in both Fluxus and Minimalism, especially in art's relationship to systems of communication. Artists like Joseph Kosuth rejected traditional aesthetics and employed language itself as a medium for art. Drawing on the linguistic philosophy of Ludwig Wittgenstein and the study of semiotics, Kosuth explored the role of visual signs to communicate meaning in **ONE AND THREE CHAIRS (FIG. 33-18)**. He illustrated this idea by juxtaposing a wooden chair, a photograph of a chair, and a printed definition of the word "chair" in the dictionary. The installation showed the visual equivalence of three distinct forms to represent a singular abstract concept.

33–18 Joseph Kosuth **ONE AND THREE CHAIRS**
1965. Wooden folding chair, photograph of chair, and photographic
enlargement of dictionary definition of chair; chair 32⅜ × 14⅞ × 20⅞"
(82.2 × 37.8 × 53 cm), photo panel 36 × 24⅛" (91.4 × 61.3 cm),
text panel 24⅛ × 24½" (61.3 × 62.2 cm). Museum of Modern Art,
New York. Larry Aldrich Foundation Fund (383.1970 a–c).

Credit: © 2016 Joseph Kosuth/Artists Rights Society (ARS), New York. © 2016.
Digital image, The Museum of Modern Art/Scala, Florence

The title highlights the inherent ambiguity in systems of
communication: We can read this work as one chair represented three different ways or as three different chairs.
Kosuth's work may seem a philosophical exercise, but his
questions about words and what they represent encourage
more critical inquiry into the systems that endow art with
value and meaning.

New Media

Bruce Nauman (b. 1941) uses performance, video, and
other nontraditional media to explore the effects of physical, psychological, and intellectual experiences. Like
Kosuth, Nauman considers the role of language and visual
representation in demonstrating our individual identities. From 1966 to 1967, Nauman made a series of 11 color
photographs based on his reenactment of common words
and phrases. **SELF-PORTRAIT AS A FOUNTAIN** (FIG. **33–19**)
shows the bare-chested artist tipping his head back and
spurting water into the air. Cleverly pulling together
artistic identity, bodily experience, and visual communication, Nauman's photograph serves many functions. It
documents his physical transformation into "a fountain,"
resembling the nude statues that often work to fill a traditional public fountain's basin. It acts as a self-portrait that
represents the artist as his own work of art. And Nauman's
title also recalls Duchamp's *Fountain* (SEE FIG. 32–29), suggesting the young artist's authority to recreate the famous
readymade using his own body. Characteristically, Nauman uses humor and wit to engage the viewer and investigate challenging conceptual issues.

Known for her pioneering use of technology in art,
Laurie Anderson (b. 1947) crosses boundaries between
experimental music, performance art, traditional storytelling, and popular entertainment. One of her earliest performances, **DUETS ON ICE** (FIG. **33–20**), was presented in 1974
at five different locations throughout New York. For each,
Anderson alternated telling personal stories and playing the violin while wearing ice skates frozen in blocks of
ice until the ice melted to release the blades. Anderson's
piece dealt with issues of identity, physical experience,
and artistic expression, similar to Nauman's
work, but it did so through the mediating factors of technology and public performance.
Describing her violin as a ventriloquist
dummy or alter ego, Anderson modified
her instrument with technology in ways
that allowed her to pre-record audio, distort
sounds, or accompany her own live playing.
By manipulating her "voice," she challenges
the expressive authenticity of the artist's performance, an effect further highlighted by
any changes in her playing brought about by
the physical discomfort of standing in ice for
an extended time.

33–19 Bruce Nauman **SELF-PORTRAIT
AS A FOUNTAIN**
1966–1967. Color photograph, 19¾ × 23¾" (50.1 ×
60.3 cm). Courtesy Leo Castelli Gallery, New York.

Credit: Photo: Eric Pollitzer. © 2016 Bruce Nauman/Artists
Rights Society (ARS), New York

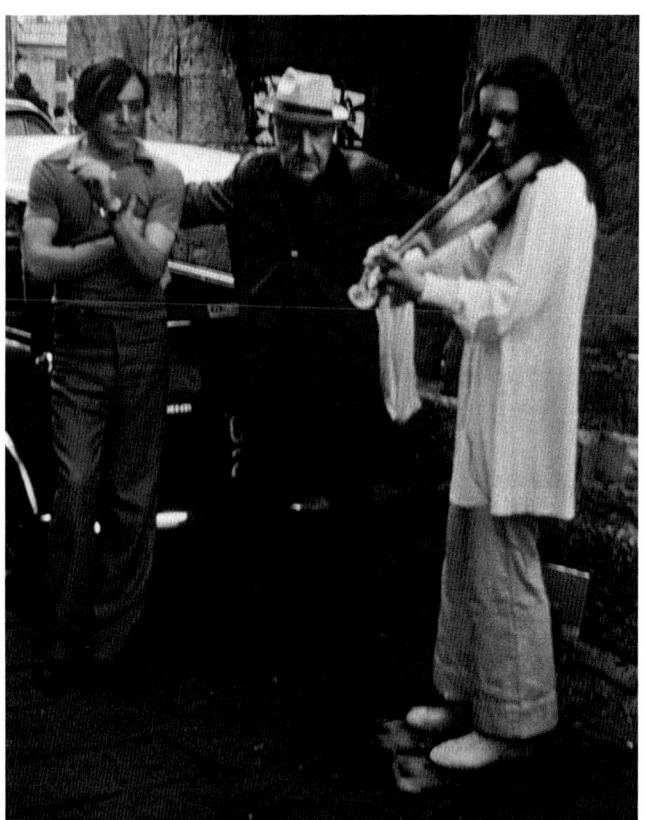

33-20 Laurie Anderson **DUETS ON ICE**
1974. Photograph of a performance in New York, 1975.

Credit: Courtesy the artist. Photo: Bob Bielecki

VIOLA AND PAIK   In 1996, the California video artist Bill Viola (b. 1951) created **THE CROSSING** (**FIG. 33-21**), which consists of two brilliantly colored videos projected simultaneously on opposite sides of a 16-foot screen. One side shows a man who slowly walks forward to fill the entire screen. A few drops of water start to fall, gradually becoming a downpour that obliterates the man's image and seems to wash him away. On the other side, a similar scenario unfolds. A man appears surrounded by small flames that escalate until a giant conflagration engulfs him entirely. Interested in how perception affects meaning, Viola supplies a soundtrack that fills the room with soft percussive noise that grows to a deafening roar. Synchronized to the natural elements as they intensify in each video, the sound remains ambiguous, but we perceive it as either fire or water depending on which scene we watch. Presented in a darkened room, the large scale of the projection and the surrounding sound overwhelm the viewer in an appeal to all the senses. Viola's use of fire and water evokes the elemental

33-21 Bill Viola **THE CROSSING**
1996. Two channels of color video projections from opposite sides of a large dark gallery onto two back-to-back screens suspended from the ceiling and mounted on the floor; four channels of amplified stereo sound, four speakers. Height 16′ (4.88 m).

Credit: Courtesy Bill Viola Studio LLC. Performer: Phil Esposito. Photo: Kira Perov

33-22 Nam June Paik **ELECTRONIC SUPERHIGHWAY: CONTINENTAL U.S.**
1995. Forty-seven-channel closed-circuit video installation with 313 monitors; neon, steel structure, color, and sound, approx. 15 × 32 × 4′ (4.57 × 9.75 × 1.2 m). Smithsonian American Art Museum, Washington, DC. Gift of the artist.

Credit: © Estate of Nam June Paik. Gift of the artist. Photograph © 2016 Photo Smithsonian American Art Museum/Art Resource/ Scala

symbolism of ritual, adding to the work's open-ended meaning and encouraging viewers to find personal significance in their experience.

In **ELECTRONIC SUPERHIGHWAY: CONTINENTAL U.S.** (**FIG. 33-22**), Nam June Paik (1931–1996) built on his early experiments with video and new media to comment on communication technology in the United States. A tribute to Paik's adopted country, the monumental sculpture refers to the intricate system of interstate highways across the United States, which were still new in 1964 when the Korean artist first arrived. Outlined in colorful neon lights, each of the 50 states is filled with television monitors—336 in the entire work—that flicker out moving images from popular entertainment, news broadcasts, and Paik's own video footage.

The artist chose imagery based on his associations with each state. Some, like scenes from the film *The Wizard of Oz* in Kansas, pictures of potatoes in Idaho, and Martin Luther King giving a speech in Alabama, reflect shared cultural knowledge; others are more personal, like Charlotte Moorman seen on screens in her home state of Arkansas in *TV Bra for Living Sculpture* (SEE FIG. 33-10), her collaborative performance with Paik. Paik also chose to involve the viewer in a witty way by placing a closed-circuit live feed of visitors looking at the work on the monitor in the District of Columbia, where the sculpture resides in the collection of the Smithsonian American Art Museum. The title *Electronic Superhighway* seems to predict the growth of the Internet, only beginning when Paik produced this sculpture in 1995, into a digital superhighway that increases the ability of mass media and social networking to connect people globally and create cultural identity through the proliferation of visual imagery.

Process and Materials

Some artists in the 1960s looked to art making itself as a source of conceptual investigation. Since the 1950s, artists inspired by Pollock's Action painting had sought new ways to bring together process and form. In their efforts to eliminate the expressionistic associations of the artist's hand, Pop and Minimalist artists emphasized the mass-produced "objecthood" of their work. In 1968, Robert Morris published "Anti-Form," expanding his earlier "Notes on Sculpture" to address the importance of materials to artistic process and sculptural form. Whereas the "well-built" cubes of Minimalism were the logical outcome of using rigid plywood, steel, and glass, Morris and other artists began to explore the variability of forms made with materials like molten lead, industrial fiber, and a variety of organic matter.

American artist Eva Hesse (1936–1970) adapted the formal vocabulary of abstraction in sculptures that highlight both process and tactility. Born in Hamburg and narrowly escaping the Holocaust as a child, she made evocative works full of personal history and meaning. For feminist critics such as Lucy Lippard, this type of "eccentric" abstraction suggested an alternative to the confrontational style of male-dominated Minimalism. **NO TITLE** (**FIG. 33-23**) exemplifies the organic quality of Hesse's sculpture. Like her Minimalist colleagues, Hesse often used industrial materials, but instead of steel and Plexiglas, she used latex, polyester resin, and fiberglass, giving her work a translucency and texture very different than the slick, machinelike surfaces of Minimalism. In *No Title* Hesse put knots in a long piece of rope before dipping it in liquid

33–23 Eva Hesse
NO TITLE

1969–1970. Latex over rope, string, and wire; two strands, dimensions variable. Whitney Museum of American Art, New York. Purchase, with funds from Eli and Edythe L. Broad, the Mrs. Percy Uris Purchase Fund, and the Painting and Sculpture Committee (88.17 a–b).

Credit: © The Estate of Eva Hesse. Hauser & Wirth. Whitney Museum of American Art, New York. Photo: Geoffrey Clement

latex and hanging it from the ceiling to dry. The resulting sculpture is a chaotic mass of looping, open webs and dense tangles, showing the pull of gravity on the heavy rope suspended from above. Hesse intended the sculpture to morph, shrink, expand, and look different each time it was exhibited, and this openness contributes to the work's impression of being alive: The unusual forms suggest internal organs or other bodily tissue; we can also imagine them as a literal representation of the expressive drips and lines of a Pollock painting. Hesse embraced the instability, irrationality, and emotive power of art, reflecting her own life and feelings in the work.

ARTE POVERA Italian critic and curator Germano Celant coined the term Arte Povera in 1967 to describe a range of international art practices incorporating everyday,

"poor," materials, but it is applied more narrowly today to describe the Italian artists involved in this activity. The group's emphasis on organic materials and physical interactions between natural and manmade objects links Arte Povera to other types of Process Art. Gilberto Zorio (b. 1944) created sculpture and performances using salt, acids, and other reactive compounds that altered the work's aesthetic and structural form. Inspired by the medieval practice of alchemy, Zorio saw the scientific process of metamorphosis as a visual metaphor for the power of art to effect social change. In **PINK-BLUE-PINK** (**FIG. 33-24**), he sliced an industrial pipe in half and filled it with a thick paste made from cobalt chloride. Highly sensitive to humidity, the chemical alternates between blue and pink depending on its surrounding environmental conditions. Measuring over 9 feet, the sculpture was long enough that

33–24 Gilberto Zorio
PINK-BLUE-PINK

1967. Semicylinder filled with cobalt chloride, $11\frac{7}{8} \times 112\frac{1}{4} \times 6''$ (30 × 285 × 15 cm). Galleria Civic D'Arte Moderna e Contemporanea, Torino, Italy. Purchased by the Fondazione Guido ed Ettore De Fornaris from Pier Luigi Pero, Turin, 1985.

Credit: © 2016 Artists Rights Society (ARS), New York/SIAE, Rome. Photo: Fotografico Studio Gonella, 2006

33-25 Robert Smithson
SPIRAL JETTY

1969–1970. Mud, precipitated salt crystals, rocks, and water; length 1,500' (457 m), width 15' (4.5 m). Great Salt Lake, Utah.

Smithson incorporated one of the few living organisms found in the otherwise dead lake into his work: an alga that turns a reddish color under certain conditions. *Spiral Jetty* is one vehicle wide: To create the work, earth was hauled out into the lake in a huge land-moving truck.

Credit: Photo Gianfranco Gorgoni. Courtesy James Cohan Gallery, New York. Art © Holt-Smithson Foundation/Licensed by VAGA, New York, NY

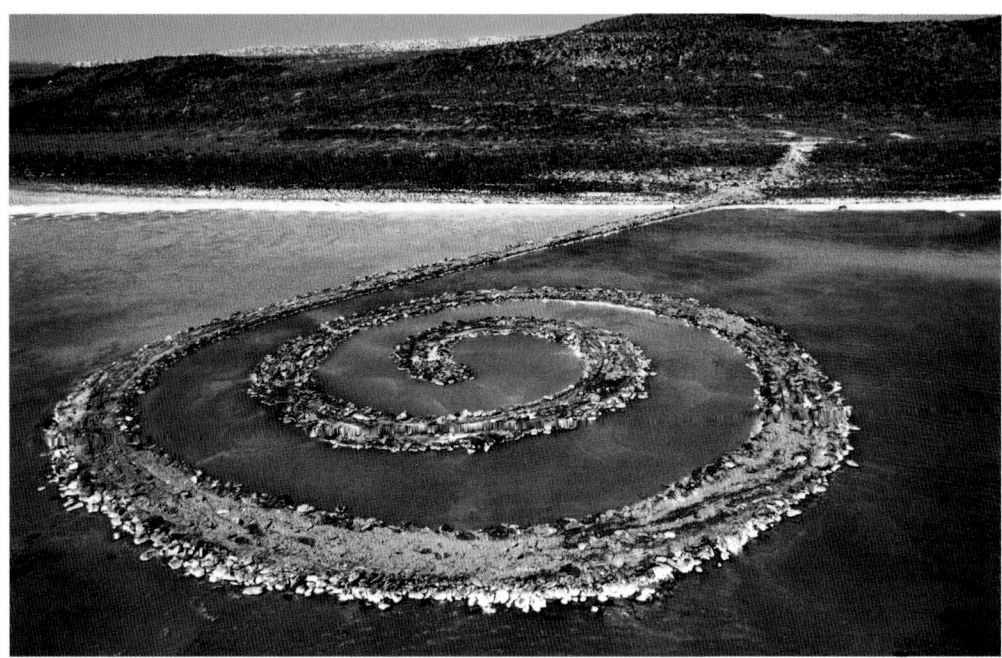

the humidity (and thus the color) might vary along different segments of the pipe. Like other conceptual artists of the period, Arte Povera artists intended the impermanence of their sculpture and performances as a way to prevent institutions from reducing art to symbols of wealth and status. Their work was evidence of a politically charged desire among many artists to see nature as an arcane source of power and beauty, well suited to countering the social ills brought on by industrial expansion.

Earthworks

Some artists, sharing this interest in nature and desire to operate outside the art market, chose to move entirely away from the confines of the gallery. They turned to the earth itself as a medium to manipulate, craft, and change. Some earthworks are vast sculptures that altered the landscape permanently, and others are ambitious temporary works that called attention to their environmental surroundings and the social conditions of their production. Like other ephemeral art practices, earthworks are often documented through photographs and film, which provide collectable objects other than the work itself. Many of these projects are in remote, difficult to access locations, making it a real effort for most viewers to visit. Part of these works, then, is the idea of pilgrimage, which likens the viewer's physical encounter with a unique work of art in its natural surroundings to a spiritual experience.

Robert Smithson (1938–1973) sought to illustrate what he called the "ongoing dialectic" in nature between the constructive forces that build and shape form and the destructive forces that destroy it. **SPIRAL JETTY** (**FIG. 33-25**) of 1970, a 1,500-foot stone-and-earth platform spiraling into the Great Salt Lake in Utah, reflects these

ideas. To Smithson, the salty water and algae of the lake suggested both the primordial ocean where life began and a dead sea that killed it; the abandoned oil rigs dotting the lake's shore reminded him of dinosaur skeletons and the remains of vanished civilizations. Smithson used the spiral because it is an archetypal shape—found throughout nature in galaxies, DNA molecules, seashells, as well as used for millennia in the art of different cultures. Although it recalls the geometry favored by Modernist artists, the spiral is a "dialectical" shape that endlessly curls and uncurls, suggesting growth and decay, creation and destruction, or, in Smithson's words, the perpetual "coming and going of things." He ordered that no maintenance be done on *Spiral Jetty* so that the work would be governed by the natural elements over time. Since its completion, the work has been changed by the varying environmental conditions of the lake, including years when it was completely submerged. Now covered with crystallized salt, it is visible to visitors at the site and as well as on Google Earth.

Christo Javacheff (b. 1935) and Jeanne-Claude de Guillebon (1935–2009), who use only their first names in their work as artists, are best known for monumental site-specific projects that temporarily alter their surroundings. In 1958, Christo emigrated from Bulgaria to Paris, where he met Jeanne-Claude; they moved to New York together in 1964. By using swathes of fabric to cover entire buildings and land masses, they transform familiar urban and rural settings into dramatic art installations that demand our attention. For example, they erected *Running Fence* across 24½ miles of farmland into Bodega Bay in Northern California in 1976, and "wrapped" the Reichstag (the building where the German Parliament meets) in Berlin 1995. Their work is political and interventionist in its references to capitalism and the packaging of consumer products.

33-26 Christo and Jeanne-Claude **THE GATES, CENTRAL PARK, NEW YORK, 1979–2005**
1979–2005. Shown here during its installation in 2005.

Credit: © 2016 Christo and Jeanne-Claude. Photo: Wolfgang Volz

The process of planning and overcoming government regulations is part of every piece, taking years to complete compared to the final project, which stays in place for a very short time.

THE GATES, CENTRAL PARK, NEW YORK, 1979–2005 (**FIG. 33-26**) took Christo and Jeanne-Claude 26 years to realize. The artists battled their way through various New York bureaucracies, meeting many obstacles and making changes to the work along the way. Working with an army of paid workers, they finally installed 7,503 saffron-colored nylon panels on "gates" along 23 miles of pathway in Central Park in February 2005. Lasting for only 16 days, the brightly colored flapping panels enlivened the frigid winter landscape and drew many visitors, becoming an enormous public success.

Feminist Art

What characterizes the work of feminist artists in the 1970s?

Rooted in the fight for civil rights and social activism of the 1960s, the women's liberation movement of the early 1970s paralleled a call in the art world for greater recognition of women artists both past and present. Art historical research revealed that although women had regularly contributed to the development of Western art, they were rarely mentioned in its written history. Feminist art historians began the process of recovering the legacies of these artists and expanding the canon to include their stories. Linda Nochlin pushed deeper in her groundbreaking essay of 1971, "Why Have There Been No Great Women Artists?," to show the lack of women in art's history as systemic within patriarchal society. Nochlin argued that women could not be described as "great" if the standard for greatness relied on a canon, or set of accepted "great works," that always favored men. She showed that throughout history, art institutions had denied women access to art education and opportunities readily available to men, effectively making competition on equal terms impossible. Thus, for women to be acknowledged as great artists, the conditions of the canon and the art system had to be changed.

Feminist artists drew on the experimental and politicized art forms that had emerged throughout 1960s. Performance and Conceptual Art offered alternatives to established traditions like painting and sculpture that had historically been dominated by men and in which women commonly appeared as passive objects of sexual desire, created by and for men. Some artists were influenced by essentialist ideas of feminism that defined female experience in terms of the biological differences between women and men. They created imagery based on female anatomy, explored taboo topics around menstruation and reproduction, and used their own bodies in performance. Looking to women's domestic roles as a source of empowerment, they took up traditions of craft and decorative arts that had historically employed women, but had previously been considered marginal to the fine arts. Others looked to constructivist theories that considered gender to be shaped by social demands and established codes of behavior; these artists adapted Conceptual Art practices to critique social, political, and art historical frameworks that maintained the systematic oppression of women.

Chicago and Schapiro

Born Judy Cohen and married as Judy Gerowitz, Judy Chicago (b. 1939) adopted the name of the city of her birth in order to free herself from "all names imposed upon her through male social dominance." Chicago used a Minimalist aesthetic in her early work, but in the late 1960s she began making abstracted images of female genitalia to challenge the male-dominated art world and to assert the value of the female experience. In 1970, she established a feminist studio art course at Fresno State College (now California State University, Fresno) and the next year moved to Los Angeles to join the painter Miriam Schapiro

(1923–2015) in establishing the Feminist Art Program at the California Institute of the Arts (CalArts).

In 1971–1972 Chicago, Schapiro, and 21 of their female students created *Womanhouse*, a collaborative art environment in a run-down Hollywood mansion that the artists renovated and filled with feminist installations. In collaboration with Sherry Brody, Schapiro's contribution to the project was *Dollhouse*, a mixed-media construction of several miniature rooms adorned with richly patterned fabrics. Schapiro subsequently began to incorporate pieces of fabric into her acrylic paintings, developing a type of work she called femmage (from "female" and "collage"). Characteristic of femmage, **PERSONAL APPEARANCE #3** (**FIG. 33-27**) celebrates traditional women's crafts with a formal and emotional richness that was meant to counter the male-dominated Minimalist aesthetic of the 1960s. Schapiro later returned to New York to lead the Pattern and Decoration movement, a group of female and male artists who merged the aesthetics of abstraction with ornamental motifs derived from women's craft, folk art, and art beyond the Western tradition in a nonhierarchical manner.

Chicago's **THE DINNER PARTY** (**FIG. 33-28**) is a large, complex, mixed-media installation dedicated to hundreds of women and women artists rescued from anonymity by early feminist artists and historians. It took six years of collaborative effort to make and drew on the assistance of hundreds of female and several male volunteers. At the center is a large, triangular table, each side stretching 48 feet; Chicago conceived of the equilateral triangle as a symbol of both the feminine and the equalized world sought by feminism. The table rests on a triangular platform of 2,304 triangular porcelain tiles comprising the "Heritage Floor" that bears the names of 999 notable women from myth, legend, and history. Along each side of the table are 13 place settings representing famous women—13 being the number of men at the Last Supper as well as the number of witches in a coven. Among the 39 women honored with individual place settings are the Egyptian ruler Hatshepsut (SEE FIG. 3-22), the Italian noblewoman Isabella d'Este (SEE FIG. 21-29), the Baroque painter Artemisia Gentileschi (SEE FIG. 23-13), the American abolitionist Sojourner Truth, and the American painter Georgia O'Keeffe (SEE FIGS. 32-36, 32-37).

33-27 Miriam Schapiro **PERSONAL APPEARANCE #3**

1973. Acrylic and fabric on canvas, 60 × 50″ (152.4 × 127 cm). Collection of Marilyn Stokstad.

Credit: Photo: Robert Hickerson

33–28A Judy Chicago **THE DINNER PARTY**
1974–1979. Overall installation view. White tile floor inscribed in gold with 999 women's names; triangular table with painted porcelain, sculpted porcelain plates, and needlework, each side 48 × 42 × 3′ (14.6 × 12.8 × 1 m). Brooklyn Museum, New York. Gift of the Elizabeth A. Sackler Foundation (2002.10).

Credit: Photo ©Donald Woodman/Through the Flower. © 2016 Judy Chicago/Artists Rights Society (ARS), New York

33–28B GEORGIA O'KEEFFE PLACE SETTING, DETAIL OF *THE DINNER PARTY*

Credit: Photo ©Donald Woodman/Through the Flower. © 2016 Judy Chicago/Artists Rights Society (ARS), New York

Each larger-than-life place setting includes a 14-inch-wide painted porcelain plate, ceramic flatware, a ceramic chalice with a gold interior, and an embroidered napkin, sitting upon an elaborately ornamented woven and stitched runner. Most of the plates feature abstract designs based on female genitalia because, as Chicago said, "that is all [these women] had in common.... They were from different periods, classes, ethnicities, geographies, experiences, but [that is] what kept them within the same confined historical space." The prominent place given to china painting and needlework in *The Dinner Party* celebrates traditional women's crafts and argues for their place in the pantheon of "high art," while at the same time informing the viewer about some of the unrecognized contributions that women have made to history.

ANA MENDIETA Ana Mendieta (1948–1985) was born in Cuba but sent to Iowa in 1961 as part of "Operation Peter Pan," which relocated 14,000 unaccompanied Cuban children after the 1959 revolution that brought Fidel Castro and communism to power in Cuba. Mendieta never fully recovered from the trauma of her removal. A sense of

33–29 Ana Mendieta **UNTITLED, FROM THE "TREE OF LIFE" SERIES**
1977. Color photograph, 20 × 13¼″ (50.8 × 33.7 cm).

Credit: © Estate of Ana Mendieta Collection, LLC. Courtesy Galerie Lelong, New York personal dislocation haunted her, and much of her work reveals a need to find deeper connection with her physical surroundings. Influenced by the work of Beuys and the African-Cuban religion of Santería, Mendieta produced ritualistic actions that invoked both spiritual redemption through communion with nature and the power of the feminine rooted in the earth. For the creation of her "Silhouettes," Mendieta enacted 200 private performances on location in Mexico and Iowa, which she documented in photographs and on film. Each involved the artist using materials such as mud, flowers, gunpowder, and fire to act upon the landscape, leaving a trace form or impression of her body. An image from her **TREE OF LIFE** series (**FIG. 33–29**) shows Mendieta with arms upraised, pressed against a tree and covered in mud, as if to invite the tree to absorb her and connect her to the earth as a maternal source of life.

MARY KELLY Produced over a six-year period by Mary Kelly (b. 1941), **POST-PARTUM DOCUMENT** (**FIG. 33–30**) is a monumental artwork that tracks the artist's changing relationship with her son after his birth. Kelly's pseudo-scientific approach draws on Marxism, feminist philosophy, and psychoanalytic theory to explore her experience as a woman, a professional, and a mother in a male-dominated society. Although she based *Post-Partum Document* on her own life, she describes it as "an interplay of voices—the mother's experience, feminist analysis, academic discussion, political debate." The work, which includes 135 objects, photographs, diagrams, charts, printed transcripts, handwritten notes, scribbles, and drawings, acts as both a personal record of her child's development and evidence of Kelly's rigorous art-making process. Each of its six parts focuses on key moments related to the child's acquisition of language and Kelly's feelings of loss and change as her son grows up. Although *Post-Partum Document* has only been exhibited once in its entirety, Kelly has also published the project as a book, underscoring how conceptual artists often rely on multiple formats to communicate their ideas.

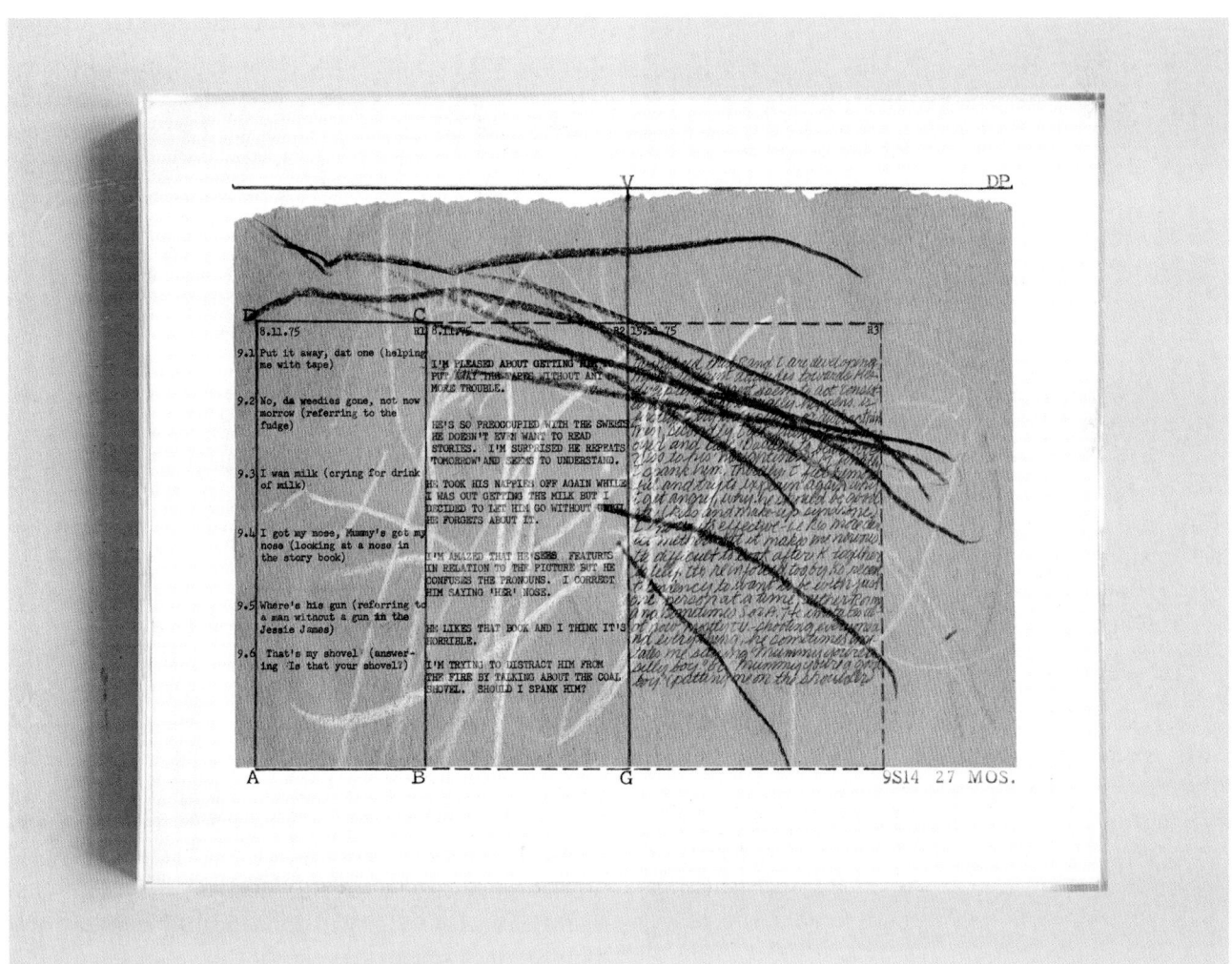

33–30 Mary Kelly **POST-PARTUM DOCUMENT**
1975. Documentation III, Analysed Markings and Diary-perspective Schema. Perspex unit, white card, sugar paper, crayon. 1 of 13 units, 14 × 11″ (35.3 × 28 cm).
Credit: Courtesy Susanne Vielmetter Los Angeles Projects

33–31 Ludwig Mies van der Rohe and Philip Johnson **SEAGRAM BUILDING, NEW YORK** 1954–1958.

Credit: Photo: Andrew Garn.

Architecture: Mid-Century Modernism to Postmodernism

What formal and technological changes occur in architecture in the mid-twentieth century?

The International Style, with its plainly visible structure and rejection of historicism, dominated new urban construction in much of the world after World War II, which meant that the utopian and revolutionary aspects of Modernist architecture settled into a form that largely came to stand for corporate power and wealth. Several major European International Style architects, such as Walter Gropius (SEE FIG. 32–53), migrated to the United States and assumed important positions in architecture schools, where they trained several generations of like-minded architects.

Mid-Century Modernist Architecture

Ludwig Mies van der Rohe (1886–1969) created the most extreme examples of postwar International Style buildings (see Chapter 32). A former Bauhaus teacher and a refugee from Nazi Germany, Mies designed the rectilinear glass towers that came to personify postwar capitalism. The crisp, clean lines of the **SEAGRAM BUILDING** in New York City (**FIG. 33–31**), designed with Philip Johnson, epitomize the standardization and impersonality that became synonymous with corporations in the postwar period. Such buildings, with their efficient construction methods and use of materials, allowed architects to pack an immense amount of office space into a building on a very small lot; they were also economical to construct. Although criticized for building relatively unadorned glass boxes, Mies advocated "Less is more." He did, however, use nonfunctional, decorative bronze beams on the outside of the Seagram Building to echo the functional beams inside and give the façade a sleek, rich, and dignified appearance.

Although the pared-down, rectilinear forms of the International Style dominated the urban skyline, other architects departed from its impersonal principles so that even in commercial architecture, expressive designs using new structural techniques and more materials also appeared. For instance, the **TRANS WORLD AIRLINES (TWA) TERMINAL** (**FIG. 33–32**) at John F. Kennedy Airport in New York City, by the Finnish-born American architect Eero Saarinen (1910–1961), dramatically breaks out of the box. Saarinen sought to evoke the thrill and glamour of air travel by giving the TWA Terminal's roof two broad, wing-like canopies of reinforced concrete that suggest a huge bird about to take flight. The interior consists of large, open, dramatically flowing spaces. Saarinen designed each

33–32 Eero Saarinen **TRANS WORLD AIRLINES (TWA) TERMINAL, JOHN F. KENNEDY AIRPORT, NEW YORK**

1956–1962.

Credit: Photo © Karen Johnson

detail of the interior—from ticket counters to telephone booths—to complement his gull-winged shell.

Frank Lloyd Wright (SEE FIGS. 32–41, 32–42, 32–43) transformed museum architecture with the **GUGGENHEIM MUSEUM** (**FIG. 33–33**) in New York, designed as a sculptural work of art in its own right. The Guggenheim was created to house Solomon Guggenheim's personal collection of Modern art and, like the TWA Terminal, took on an organic shape, in this case a spiral. The museum's galleries spiral downward from a glass ceiling, wrapping themselves around a spectacular five-story atrium. Wright intended visitors to begin by taking the elevator to the top floor and then walk down the sloping and increasingly widening ramp, enjoying paintings along the way. Today, the interior maintains the intended intimacy of a "living room," despite alterations by the museum's first directors.

33–33 Frank Lloyd Wright **SOLOMON R. GUGGENHEIM MUSEUM, NEW YORK**

1943–1959.

The large building behind the museum is a later addition designed in 1992 by Gwathmey Siegel and Associates.

Credit: Photo © Andrew Garn.

Wright wanted the building to contrast with skyscrapers like the Seagram Building and become a Manhattan landmark—and it remains one of the twentieth century's most distinctive museum spaces.

Postmodern Architecture

In the 1970s, architects began to move away from the sleek, glass-and-steel boxes of the International Style and add elements of past styles into their designs. Architectural historians trace the origins of this new Postmodern style to the work of Jane Jacobs (1916–2006), who wrote *The Death and Life of Great American Cities* (1961), as well as to Philadelphia architect Robert Venturi (b. 1925), who rejected the abstract purity of the International Style by incorporating elements drawn from vernacular (meaning popular, common, or ordinary) sources into his designs.

Venturi parodied Mies's aphorism "Less is more" with his own: "Less is a bore." He accused Mies and other Modernist architects of ignoring human needs in their quest for uniformity, purity, and abstraction and challenged

Postmodernism to address the complex, contradictory, and heterogeneous mixture of "high" and "low" architecture that comprised the modern city. Venturi encouraged new architecture to embrace eclecticism; he reintroduced references to past architectural styles into his own designs and began to apply decoration to his buildings.

While writing his treatise on Postmodernism—*Complexity and Contradiction in Architecture* (1966)—Venturi designed a house for his mother (**FIG. 33-34**) that put many of his new ideas into practice. The shape of the façade returns to the traditional Western "house" shape that Modernists (SEE FIGS. 32-39, 32-40, 32-51) had rejected because of its clichéd historical associations. Venturi's vocabulary of triangles and squares is arranged in a playful asymmetry that skews the staid harmonies of Modernist design, while the curved moldings are a purely decorative flourish—forbidden in the strict International Style. But the most disruptive element of the façade is the deep cleavage over the door, which opens to reveal a mysterious upper wall and chimney top. The interior is also complex and contradictory. The irregular floor plan, including

33-34A Robert Venturi **FAÇADE, VANNA VENTURI HOUSE, CHESTNUT HILL**
Philadelphia, Pennsylvania. 1961–1964.

Credit: Venturi, Scott Brown Collection. © The Architectual Archives, University of Pennsylvania. Photo: Matt Wargo

33-34B Robert Venturi **PLAN, VANNA VENTURI HOUSE, CHESTNUT HILL**
Philadelphia, Pennsylvania. 1961–1964.

Credit: Venturi, Scott Brown Collection. © The Architectual Archives, University of Pennsylvania.

an odd stairway leading up to the second floor, is further complicated by irregular ceiling levels that are partially covered by a barrel vault.

In the 1970s, Postmodern ideas were also applied to commercial architecture. One of the first examples was the **AT&T CORPORATE HEADQUARTERS** (now the Sony Building) in New York City (**FIG. 33-35**) by Philip Johnson (1906–2005) and John Burgee (b. 1933). This elegant, granite-clad skyscraper has 36 oversized stories, making it as tall as the average 60-story building. It mimics its International Style neighbors with its smooth, uncluttered skin, while its Classical window groupings set between vertical piers also echo nearby skyscrapers from much earlier in the century. But the overall profile of the building bears a whimsical resemblance to the shape of a Chippendale highboy, an eighteenth-century chest of drawers with a long-legged base and angled top—this seems to be an intended pun on the terms "highboy" and "high-rise." The round notch at the top of the building as well as the rounded entryway at its base suggest the coin slot and coin return of an old pay telephone in a clever reference to the building's client, the AT&T telephone company.

33-35 Philip Johnson and John Burgee **AT&T CORPORATE HEADQUARTERS, NEW YORK** 1978–1983.

Postmodernism

How do Postmodernism and changing attitudes around identity affect art after the 1970s?

Throughout the 1970s, Postmodernist ideas percolated throughout the Western art world, and by 1980 much of the art produced served as a clear illustration of theories set out by philosophers like Roland Barthes, Michel Foucault, and Jean Baudrillard. Rather than a distinctive style, Postmodernist art is best recognized by its attempt to undermine key principles of Modernism, especially its insistence on an art that was pure, autonomous, and universal. Just as Modernist art had heralded an industrial, technological society, the advent of Postmodernism signaled a shift toward a post-industrial, capitalist society living in an age of mass communication that required tolerance for difference and rapid change. The 1980s gave rise to the personal computer, music videos, and cable TV. Immersed in a vast visual culture that had now become commonplace, artists chose imagery from high-art and lowbrow sources, combining it in complex, contrary, and humorous ways that resisted formal unity and singular meaning. The effect was to crack the authoritative façade of Modernism and reveal that its truths were fiction, open to revision and interpretation.

Neo-Expressionism

Neo-Expressionism, one of the first international manifestations of Postmodernism, reintroduced large-scale representational paintings that brought back the luxury of the painted surface, but also employed Postmodernist strategies to layer meaning through eclectic imagery and expressive technique. The German artist Anselm Kiefer (b. 1945), born in the final weeks of World War II, builds on the style and political undertones of German Expressionism from the early twentieth century (see Chapter 32). Heavily worked with thick layers of paint and shellac, **HEATH OF THE BRANDENBURG MARCH** (**FIG. 33-36**) evokes the historical tradition of German landscape painting to confront his country's Nazi past. The linear perspective of the central road pulls the viewer into a scorched and barren countryside, alluding to centuries of past warfare in this region around Berlin. Scrawled on top of the desolate scene, the words of the Nazi marching song "Märkische Heide, märkische Sand" appear in the foreground. Kiefer's work resists being interpreted in only one way, but instead has layers of meaning when looked at through the varied lenses of artistic style, cultural heritage, and political association. Combining the influences of Postmodernism and Kiefer's teacher Beuys, Kiefer's art confronts Germany's rich—and at times horrific—historical past, perhaps suggesting an opportunity for national healing.

Brooklyn-born Jean-Michel Basquiat (1960–1988) grew up in middle-class comfort before leaving home as a teenager for New York's Lower East Side. As a street artist, he covered walls with short and witty philosophical texts signed with the tag "SAMO©." He gained critical attention in 1980 in the highly publicized "Times Square Show," which showcased many of the city's subway and graffiti artists. Basquiat's active brushwork,

33–36 Anselm Kiefer **HEATH OF THE BRANDENBURG MARCH**
1974. Oil, acrylic, and shellac on burlap, 3'10½" × 8'4" (1.18 × 2.54 m). Collection Van Abbemuseum, Eindhoven, the Netherlands.

33–37 Jean-Michel
Basquiat **HORN PLAYERS**

1983. Acrylic and oil paintstick on
canvas; three panels, overall 8′ × 6′5″
(2.44 × 1.91 m). Broad Art Foundation,
Santa Monica, California.

Credit: © The Estate of Jean-Michel
Basquiat/ADAGP, Paris/ARS, New York 2016

autobiographical elements, and personal iconography link him to Neo-Expressionism. **HORN PLAYERS** (**FIG. 33–37**) of 1983 references the triptych format to pay homage to musicians Charlie Parker (upper left) and Dizzy Gillespie (center right). A fan of jazz, Basquiat echoes the improvisational bebop style Parker made popular in the 1950s in his painting technique, and his expressive images and text offer a range of interpretative meanings. The painting underscores Basquiat's passionate determination to focus on African-American subjects in an unsentimental way. As he said, "Black people are never portrayed realistically, not even portrayed, in Modern art, and I'm glad to do that."

Appropriation, Identity, and Critique

Many Postmodern artists found appropriation a useful strategy with which to counter Modernist values. They borrowed imagery directly from the onslaught of mass visual culture, repositioning and recontextualizing it to twist and complicate its meaning. For artists known as the "Pictures" generation, photography was a conceptual tool to deconstruct Modernist beliefs about originality, patriarchal authority, and artistic identity. Their work exposes how consumer culture and the mass media bombard us with pictures of a life that is impossible to attain but made to seem real by the very images that present it to us.

Jeff Koons (b. 1955) capitalizes on the ambiguity of Pop Art to elevate and critique everyday subjects at the same time. He has made a career glorifying the banal and superficial in contemporary life with a knack for self-promotion that some critics believe surpasses his art. In the 1980s, Koons appropriated consumer goods such as basketballs and vacuum cleaners, exhibiting them in Plexiglas showcases similar to those in department stores—and in museums. The effect is to place the objects' artistic status directly alongside their value as products for sale, thus underscoring their dual role as commodities with economic and cultural worth. **PINK PANTHER** (**FIG. 33–38**) recalls Warhol's *Marilyn Diptych* (SEE FIG. 33–13) in its attention to celebrity culture, but Koons's work is closer to celebrity's kitschy imitation. The pin-up girl, based on B-movie star Jayne Mansfield, is caught striking a pose as she embraces the cuddly cartoon character in one hand while the other covers her exposed breast. The garish pastels and slickly textured finish heighten her artificial prettiness. Although the nearly life-size sculpture appears to elevate a tawdry subject, Koons hired European fabricators to produce the object in porcelain, a material better known for cheap knick-knacks than fine art in museums. Koons's work suggests

33–39 Sherrie Levine **AFTER WALKER EVANS: 4**
1981. Gelatin-silver print, 5¹⁄₁₆ × 3⁷⁄₈″ (12.8 × 9.8 cm). Metropolitan Museum of Art, New York. Gift of the artist, 1995.

Credit: © Sherrie Levine Courtesy Simon Lee Gallery. © Walker Evans Archive, The Metropolitan Museum of Art. © 2016. Image copyright The Metropolitan Museum of Art/Art Resource/Scala, Florence

33–38 Jeff Koons **PINK PANTHER**
1988. Porcelain, ed. 1/3. 41 × 20½ × 19″ (104.1 × 52.1 × 48.3 cm). Collection Museum of Contemporary Art, Chicago.

Credit: © Jeff Koons. Photography © Museum of Contemporary Art, Chicago

the influence of both Duchamp and Minimalist sculpture while also addressing key Postmodern themes. Yet his bland presentation style seems openly materialistic and shallow—inviting, and even welcoming, critical dissent.

Like Neo-Expressionist painting, the work of Sherrie Levine (b. 1947) and others of the Pictures generation signaled the return of image making after a decade dominated by dematerialized art forms. **AFTER WALKER EVANS: 4** (**FIG. 33–39**) is from a provocative series of photographs—actually reproductions of Depression-era photographs by Walker Evans—in which Levine questions the nature of artistic originality and authority. While working with the Farm Securities Administration in the 1930s, Evans produced images that were widely shown as evidence of poverty in the South. Levine's direct appropriation of Evans's work claims the legacy of a well-known male artist for herself, while seeming to indict his own appropriation of his destitute subjects for personal artistic and commercial gain. Furthermore, as exact copies of Evan's images, Levine's work highlights photography's resistance to how Modernism tends to value most highly the original work of art and forces us to consider the influence of mass media on cultural knowledge.

FEMINISM AND APPROPRIATION Barbara Kruger (b. 1945) appropriates advertising and marketing techniques to subvert the messages in mainstream mass media. Her early career, working as a designer and art director at *Mademoiselle*, *House and Garden*, and other popular magazines, informs the signature look of her work. She relies on her provocative juxtapositions of words and image to challenge expected meanings that come from our experience of popular advertising. **UNTITLED (YOUR GAZE HITS THE SIDE OF MY FACE) (FIG. 33–40)** is typical in the slightly nostalgic quality of the female mannequin's appearance and the graphic contrast that recalls the three-color printing once common in newspapers. By addressing the viewer directly, Kruger forces us to acknowledge the relationship usually kept hidden between the viewer and the viewed. Framed within an advertising context, the viewer is likened to the consumer who looks at an object of desire for purchase. Although Kruger's pronouns are ambiguous in terms of gender, they seem an implicit reference to the "male gaze" in art described by critics like Laura Mulvey and John Berger and much discussed in the 1970s and 1980s. Kruger's work, however, raises broad Postmodernist issues of power and the need to expose underlying social structures that oppress and subjugate others.

While women contributed significantly to artistic developments in the 1960s and 1970s, major museums and galleries continued to privilege work by male artists. In 1984 the Museum of Modern Art included only 13 women among 169 (mostly white) artists in "An International Survey of Painting and Sculpture," an exhibition claiming to highlight the period's most important art. In response, a group of feminist artists, curators, critics, and art historians in New York formed the Guerrilla Girls, an activist group that would function, in their words, as "the conscience of the art world." The group's mandate is to expose gender and racial inequities in the art world, demonstrate against discrimination, and fight for the rights of women and artists of color.

The Guerrilla Girls use the tactics of guerrilla warfare: acting covertly to strike at the enemy. Their first campaign was to paste posters on walls throughout New York's art districts, citing damning statistics of discrimination in the city's galleries and art museums. Members remain anonymous, but adopt the names of dead women artists as pseudonyms. This strategy protects them from reprisal and circumvents the art world's tendency to focus on individual instead of collective accomplishment. To protect their identities at protests and public events, they don gorilla masks, a play on the word "guerrilla" that reflects their use of humor to disarm critics and promote their message. The group produces sharp, witty posters that draw on the best advertising strategies. The posters are now collected by many of the institutions that they were made to critique.

33–40 Barbara Kruger **UNTITLED (YOUR GAZE HITS THE SIDE OF MY FACE)**
1981. Photograph, red painted frame, 55 × 41″ (140 × 104 cm). Mary Boone Gallery, New York.

Credit: © Barbara Kruger. Courtesy Mary Boone Gallery, New York

One of the most famous features Ingres's *Large Odalisque* wearing a gorilla mask with the headline "Do women have to be naked to get into the Met. Museum?" The poster, made in 1989, notes that while women represented less than 5 percent of the artists in the famous museum, they were 85 percent of the nudes on display. (The Guerrilla Girls repeated the survey in 2005 and found the number of women artists had decreased to only 3 percent—but pointed out with characteristic humor that at least there were more naked men.) **THE ADVANTAGES OF BEING A WOMAN ARTIST (FIG. 33–41)** delivers a clever, ironic, and sadly still accurate list of the treatment afforded women artists.

Cindy Sherman (b. 1954) also turned to photography as a way to engage in Postmodern critique. In her series "Untitled Film Stills," Sherman creates fictional narratives with herself in the starring role. Each of the black-and-white photographs resembles a publicity still from popular cinema of the early 1960s, in which Sherman appears, costumed and made-up, in settings that seem to quote from the plots of old movies. Although each untitled image stands alone, we recognize these women's stories. In **UNTITLED FILM STILL #21 (FIG. 33–42)**, for instance, Sherman assumes the part of "small-town girl" recently

33–41 Guerrilla Girls **THE ADVANTAGES OF BEING A WOMAN ARTIST**

1988. Offset print, 17 × 22" (43.2 × 55.9 cm). Collection of the artists.

Credit: © Guerrilla Girls www.guerrillagirls.com

THE ADVANTAGES OF BEING A WOMAN ARTIST:

Working without the pressure of success
Not having to be in shows with men
Having an escape from the art world in your 4 free-lance jobs
Knowing your career might pick up after you're eighty
Being reassured that whatever kind of art you make it will be labeled feminine
Not being stuck in a tenured teaching position
Seeing your ideas live on in the work of others
Having the opportunity to choose between career and motherhood
Not having to choke on those big cigars or paint in Italian suits
Having more time to work when your mate dumps you for someone younger
Being included in revised versions of art history
Not having to undergo the embarrassment of being called a genius
Getting your picture in the art magazines wearing a gorilla suit

A PUBLIC SERVICE MESSAGE FROM **GUERRILLA GIRLS** CONSCIENCE OF THE ART WORLD

arrived in the big city. Others show her as "the hardworking housewife," "the femme-fatale," "the teenage runaway," and other stereotypical personae. Part performance and part Conceptual Art, these works play on the documentary status we give the photograph and our familiarity with the cinematic narratives Sherman recreates. By forcing us to acknowledge the illusion of her own image, Sherman underscores the power of visual representation to construct female identity and alludes to the performances we enact every day in roles like "the best friend" or "the good student."

33–42 Cindy Sherman **UNTITLED FILM STILL #21**

1978. Black-and-white photograph, 8 × 10" (20.3 × 25.4 cm).

Credit: Courtesy the artist and Metro Pictures

Identity Politics and the Culture Wars

For some, Postmodernism's challenge to the status quo seemed a strike at Western culture's most fundamental values. Throughout the 1980s, tensions grew between factions with opposing beliefs about religion and politics, finally giving way around 1990 to what is sometimes called the "Culture Wars." This battle was pronounced in the art world, where conflicts raged over freedom of speech and public funding for the arts, particularly with regard to the right to make art that might be considered offensive or obscene by others. Building on the model of feminist artists asserting their identity, others made art addressing racial and ethnic difference and began to explore the topic of gender broadly to consider its relationship to sexual identity and orientation. Fueled by the emotion and urgency brought about by the AIDS crisis, individuals who had once stayed at the edges of society and the art establishment began to claim center stage by making work confronting issues of identity and unequal treatment based on gender, sexual orientation, race, or class.

James Luna (b. 1950) asks us to confront Native American stereotypes in **THE ARTIFACT PIECE** (**FIG. 33–43**), first staged in 1987 in a hall dedicated to a traditional ethnographic exhibition at the Museum of Man in San Diego. Luna lay almost naked in a glass display case filled with sand embedded with artifacts from his life, including his favorite music and books and personal legal papers. Museum-style labels pointed to marks and scars on his

33–43 James Luna
THE ARTIFACT PIECE

First staged in 1987 at the Museum of Man, San Diego. Luna also performed the piece for "The Decade Show," 1990, in New York.

Credit: Courtesy James Luna

body that he had acquired while drinking or fighting or in accidents. In this way, Luna turned his living body and his life into an ethnographic object for people to ogle and judge. By objectifying himself, he challenges our prejudices and assumptions about Native Americans and highlights the cultural role of institutions to perpetuate or counter such myths.

Using Postmodern strategies similar to Barbara Kruger and Cindy Sherman, Lorna Simpson (b. 1960) also addresses female stereotyping, but she expands the issue to include the question of race. In **STEREO STYLES** (**FIG. 33–44**), Simpson arranges ten Polaroid photographs in two rows. Each depicts an African-American woman wearing a plain white shift and photographed from behind to reveal her head and shoulders. The only key to her identity is the distinctive hairstyle in each image, described by words such as "Daring," "Boyish," "Magnetic," "Country Fresh," and "Sweet" written in cursive on a plaque between the

rows. Simpson's gridlike display of black-and-white images uses Conceptual Art's straightforward presentation of information, encouraging us to look more closely at the relationship of visual appearance to our perceptions of individual identity.

African-American artist Faith Ringgold (b. 1930) uses narrative structure and non-Western traditions to consider race and gender in society. Trained as an abstract painter in the 1950s, Ringgold—engaged by the civil rights and feminist movements—shifted to other formats like performance and craft-based practices in the 1960s. In the 1980s, she began making "story-quilts," which combine representational subject matter, African-American quilt making, and written text to create visual narratives richly layered with meaning. In **TAR BEACH** (**FIG. 33–45**) the narrator is 8-year-old Cassie Louise Lightfoot—although Ringgold draws on her own memories growing up in Harlem. "Tar Beach" refers to the roof of the apartment building where

33–44 Lorna Simpson **STEREO STYLES**
1988. Ten black-and-white Polaroid prints and ten engraved plastic plaques, 5′4″ × 9′8″ (1.63 × 2.95 m) overall. Private collection.

Credit: Courtesy of the artist

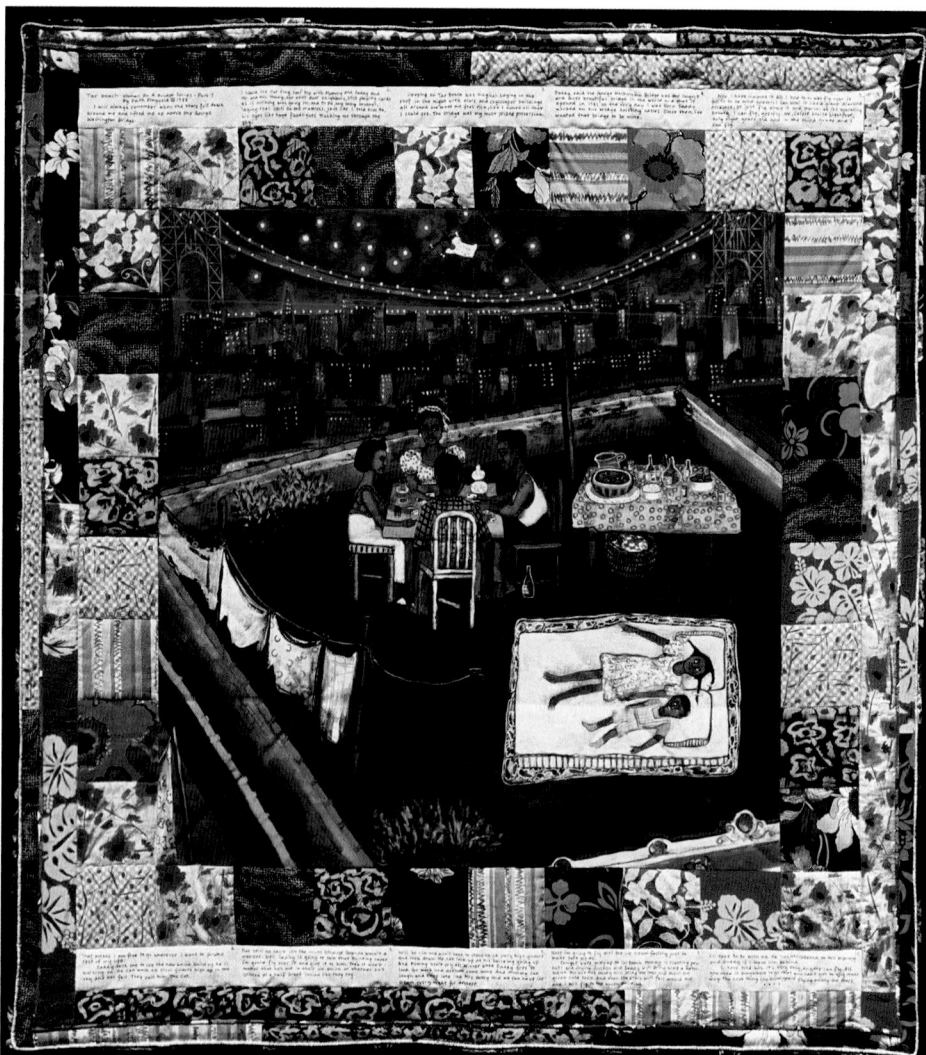

33–45 Faith Ringgold
TAR BEACH
Part I from the "Women on a Bridge" series. 1988. Acrylic on canvas, bordered with printed, painted, quilted, and pieced cloth, 74⅝ × 68½" (190.5 × 174 cm). Solomon R. Guggenheim Museum, New York. Gift of Mr. and Mrs. Gus and Judith Lieber.

Credit: © Faith Ringgold

Ringgold slept on hot summer nights and describes as a magical place. Surrounded by a colorful patchwork border, the central panel of the quilt shows Cassie on the roof with her brother, lying on a blanket while their parents and neighbors play cards. Hand-written on white horizontal panels stitched into the border are details of the story. Cassie tells of her dream that she can possess all the things she flies over: She claims the George Washington Bridge for herself; a new union-constructed building for her father, who as an African-American construction worker was not allowed to join the union; and an ice-cream factory for her mother. Cassie's fantasy is charming, but reminds viewers of the real social and economic prejudices facing African Americans. The popularity of *Tar Beach* inspired Ringgold to recreate the story-quilt as a children's picture book, which received a prestigious Caldecott Medal in 1992.

Controversies Over Funding in the Arts

Some of the most notorious battles in the Culture Wars revolved around public funding of the arts. At the center

was the National Endowment for the Arts (NEA), a federal agency established by Congress in 1965 to provide funding giving "Americans the opportunity to participate in the arts, exercise their imaginations, and develop their creative capacities." The controversy gained national attention in 1989 when Andres Serrano's photograph *Piss Christ* drew criticism from religious groups and conservative politicians. Although Serrano did not receive public money to produce the photograph, the Southeastern Center for Contemporary Art had paid Serrano a stipend to include the work in an exhibition organized with NEA support.

Created in 1987, two years before the NEA controversy, **PISS CHRIST** (**FIG. 33-46**) is one of many photographs Serrano (b. 1950) made that involve bodily fluids like blood, semen, and human milk. These function to highlight the tension between his images' aesthetic appeal and the abject undertones Serrano makes clear in the title. *Piss Christ* is an almost 2-foot-high, brilliantly colored Cibachrome photograph that shows a Christian crucifix bathed in a hazy, ethereal light. Serrano made the haunting image by submerging a small plastic crucifix in a Plexiglas container filled with his own urine. Serrano, who was raised a strict Catholic, has argued that the work addresses the physical death of Christ's body and critiques the commercialization of Christ's image.

Around the same time that the exhibition of *Piss Christ* was being challenged, another traveling exhibition funded by the NEA—this one a retrospective of photographer

Robert Mapplethorpe organized by Philadelphia's Institute of Contemporary Art—came under similar attack for the inclusion of several homoerotic and sadomasochistic images, including self-portraits of the artist, who had recently died of AIDS. A flurry of debate developed in Congress questioning the authority of the NEA to distribute taxpayers' money to support art that some members of the public found distasteful or obscene.

Succumbing to political pressure, the Corcoran Gallery of Art in Washington, DC cancelled the Mapplethorpe exhibition. When it was shown in Cincinnati in 1990, the show was shut down and the museum director arrested on charges of obscenity. That same year, the NEA rescinded grants awarded to four artists—who became known as the "NEA Four" (Karen Finley, John Fleck, Holly Hughes, and Tim Miller)—because their art included lesbian, gay, or radical feminist content. Although the artists sued and won back their grants in 1993, a so-called "obscenity clause" was added to NEA regulations requiring jurors to consider the "general standards of decency and respect

33–47 Chris Ofili **THE HOLY VIRGIN MARY**
1996. Acrylic, oil paint, polyester resin, paper collage, glitter, map pins, and elephant dung on linen, 7'11" × 5'11⅝16" (2.44 × 1.83 m). MONA, Museum of Old and New Art, Hobart, Tasmania, Australia.

Credit: © Chris Ofilli. Courtesy the Artist and Victoria Miro Gallery, London

33–46 Andres Serrano **PISS CHRIST**
1987. Cibachrome print mounted on Plexiglas, 23½ × 16" (59.7 × 40.6 cm).

Credit: © Andres Serrano/Courtesy of the artist and Yvon Lambert Paris, New York

for the diverse beliefs and values of the American public" when making awards. Over the next few years, the Republican-controlled House of Representatives, some of whose members wanted to eliminate the agency altogether, dramatically restructured the NEA, including cutting its budget by 40 percent.

Another controversy erupted in 1999 when the Brooklyn Museum exhibited "Sensation: Young British Artists from the Saatchi Collection." New York Mayor Rudolph Giuliani and Catholic leaders took particular offense to **THE HOLY VIRGIN MARY** (**FIG. 33–47**) by Nigerian-British artist Chris Ofili (b. 1968). The large, glittering canvas features a stylized African Madonna augmented with mixed-media elements of elephant dung and found pornographic photographs of women's buttocks. Ofili, who spent a year studying in Zimbabwe, explained that many African nations have a tradition of using found objects and materials in both popular and high art. He intended the painting as a contemporary, bicultural reinvention of the Western Madonna tradition, using elephant dung to reinforce this black Madonna's connection to the art and religion of Zimbabwe and to represent her fertility.

When the Brooklyn Museum refused Mayor Giuliani's demands to cancel the show, the mayor withheld the city's monthly maintenance payment to the museum of $497,554 and filed a suit in the state court to revoke its lease. In response, the museum filed for an injunction against Giuliani's actions on the grounds that they violated the First Amendment. A federal district court eventually barred Giuliani from punishing or retaliating against the museum in any way for mounting the exhibition. Giuliani had argued that Ofili's art fostered religious intolerance, but the court ruled that the government has "no legitimate interest in protecting any or all religions from views distasteful to them," adding that taxpayers "subsidize all manner of views with which they do not agree" and even those "they abhor."

Public Art

Debates over public funding of art do not always stem from moral outcry over artists' use of sexual or religious content. Many revolve around the art produced for public spaces. Throughout history, art has functioned as propaganda to reinforce cultural values, commemorate historical events, and celebrate individual accomplishments. Most controversies around public art today involve community response to a work's appearance and questions about its artistic and cultural value. Such concerns grow when tax dollars are used to finance projects that some find objectionable for reasons ranging from the costs involved to misperceptions or disagreement about the art's meaning. In the early 1980s, two such public projects gained a great deal of attention for the reaction and challenge brought by the public. A comparison reveals the contentiousness of contemporary art in the public realm and asks us to consider its place in the world today.

In 1981, Richard Serra (b. 1939) won a commission from the United States General Services Administration, which approved plans for **TILTED ARC** (**FIG. *33–48***), a curved and slightly angled Cor-Ten steel wall, 120 feet long, 12 feet tall, and 2½ inches thick, that would bisect the plaza in front of the Javits Federal Building in New York. After its installation, the sculpture began to draw criticism for its impact on the public space, because it forced people to detour as they crossed the plaza and made it impossible to hold concerts or performances. Over time, the steel weathered to a rusty brown and became covered with pigeon droppings and graffiti. Public outrage grew so intense that in 1986 Serra's sculpture was removed to a Brooklyn parking lot, an action that incited further furor, this time among artists and critics. Serra argued that moving *Tilted Arc* effectively

33–48 Richard Serra **TILTED ARC**
1981–1989. Jacob K. Javits Federal Plaza, New York. Steel. Destroyed.

Credit: © 2016 Richard Serra/Artists Rights Society (ARS), New York. Photo: David Aschkenas

33–49 Maya Lin **VIETNAM VETERANS MEMORIAL, WASHINGTON, DC**
1981–1983.

Credit: © Frank Fournier

destroyed the site-specific sculpture; he filed a lawsuit claiming censorship, but the federal district court found no legal merit in his case and denied his plea.

Around the same time of Serra's commission, a jury of architects, landscape architects, and sculptors awarded Maya Lin (b. 1959) the commission for the **VIETNAM VETERANS MEMORIAL** (**FIG. 33–49**), to be built near the National Mall in Washington, DC. A student at Yale University, Lin proposed a simple and dramatic memorial cut into the ground in a V shape like a scar, as a symbol of national healing over the divisive war. The sculpture is made of two highly polished black granite slabs that reach out from deep in the earth at the center. Each slab is 247 feet long, and they meet at a 130-degree angle where they are 10 feet tall. The names of 58,272 American soldiers killed or declared missing in action during the Vietnam War are listed chronologically in the order they died or were lost, beginning in 1956 at the shallowest point to the left and climaxing in 1968 at the tallest part of the sculpture, representing the year of highest casualties. The memorial serves both to commemorate the dead and missing and to provide a place where survivors can confront their own loss.

It is one of the best-known works of public art in the United States and has transformed the way the nation mourns its war dead.

Visitors often describe the *Vietnam Veterans Memorial* as a powerful and profound experience, but Lin's design was contested at the time of her commission. Opponents described it as a "black gash in the Mall," its color contrasting with the pervasive white marble of the surrounding memorials. Others saw Lin's use of abstraction as a departure from the representational monuments often used to honor war heroes. In response to the criticism, the Vietnam Veterans Memorial Fund commissioned Frederick Hart (1943–1999) in 1983 to create another, more naturalistic memorial depicting three soldiers, which was placed 120 feet from the wall; in 1993, a comparable sculpture of three nurses by Glenda Goodacre (b. 1939) was added 300 feet to the south to memorialize the contribution of women during the war.

While Serra and Lin's monuments appear similar, their distinctive qualities may explain the differing public responses to each. In addition to the spare geometric forms of the sculptures, both rely on their physical scale to heighten the viewer's perceptual awareness and suggest additional meaning. In *Tilted Arc*, this translates to a vaguely threatening feeling as the imposing structure looms ominously over viewers and forces them to alter their path walking across the plaza. By contrast, Lin's sculpture seems to grow in height, impressing visitors physically with the sheer magnitude of inscribed names as they walk the lengthy path. Instead of Serra's industrial steel, Lin employs polished granite, commonly used for tombstones, that reflects the faces of visitors as they read names of the dead and missing. The effect is both to humanize the written words and to implicate the viewer who now bears witness to the national tragedy of the war.

The examples of *Tilted Arc* and the *Vietnam Veterans Memorial* raise important questions about the rights and responsibilities of artists, as well as the obligations of those who commission public works of art. The case of *Tilted Arc* prompted changes in the commissioning of public sculpture. (In court, the artist had not attempted to defend his work on aesthetic grounds, but claimed the right to create the piece as planned and approved.) Today neighborhood groups and local officials meet with artists well in advance of public commissions, but rarely are all parties completely satisfied.

High Tech and Deconstructivist Architecture

What are some of the formal and technological changes affecting architecture since the 1980s?

Computer-aided design (CAD) programs with 3-D graphics transformed architecture and architectural practice in the 1980s and 1990s. These new tools enabled architects to design structures virtually, to calculate engineering stresses faster and more precisely, to experiment with advanced building technologies and materials, and to imagine new ways of composing a building's mass.

High Tech Architecture

The new technology let architects break out of the restrictive shape of the Modernist "glass box" (SEE FIG. 33–31) and experiment with dramatically designed engineering marvels. These buildings are characterized by a spectacular use of materials, equipment, and architectural components and frequently by a visible display of service systems such as heating and power.

The **HONG KONG & SHANGHAI BANK** (FIG. 33–50) by British architect Norman Foster (b. 1935) is among the most spectacular examples of High Tech architecture. Foster was invited to spare no expense in designing this

33–50 Norman Foster **HONG KONG & SHANGHAI BANK, HONG KONG**

1986.

Credit: © Arcaid Images/Alamy Stock Photo

futuristic 47-story skyscraper. The load-bearing steel skeleton, composed of giant masts and girders, is on the exterior. The individual stories hang from it, making possible the uninterrupted rows of windows that fill the building with natural light. Motorized "sunscoops" at the top of the structure track the sun's rays and channel them into the building, pouring additional daylight into a ten-story atrium space in the banking hall in the lower part of the building. The sole concession Foster makes to tradition in this design is his placement of two bronze lions taken from the bank's previous headquarters flanking the public entrance. Touching the lions before entering the bank is believed to bring good luck.

Deconstructivist Architecture

Deconstructivist architecture, more theory-based than High Tech, emerged in the early 1990s. Deconstructivist architects deliberately disturb traditional architectural assumptions about harmony, unity, and stability to create "decentered," skewed, and distorted designs. The aesthetic of Russian Suprematists and Constructivists (SEE FIG. 32–48) is an influence, as are the principles of Deconstruction as developed by French philosopher Jacques Derrida (1930–2004). Derridean Deconstruction claims that written texts possess no single, intrinsic meaning, that meaning is always "intertextual," a product of one text's relationship to other texts. As a result, meaning is always "decentered," "dispersed," or "diffused" through an infinite web of "signs," which themselves have unstable meanings. Deconstructivist architecture is likewise intertextual, in that it plays with meaning by mixing diverse architectural features, forms, and contexts; it is decentered by this diffusion as well as by its perceived instability of both meaning and form.

A good example of Deconstructivist architecture is the **VITRA FIRE STATION** in Weil-am-Rhein, Germany (**FIG. 33–51**), designed by Baghdad-born architect Zaha Hadid (b. 1950), who studied in London and established her practice there in 1979. Formally influenced by the paintings of Kazimir Malevich (SEE FIG. 32–25), the Vitra Fire Station features reinforced concrete walls that lean into one another, meet at unexpected angles, and jut out dramatically into space, denying a sense of visual unity or structural coherence but creating a feeling of immediacy, speed, and dynamism appropriate to the building's function.

The Toronto-born, California-based Frank O. Gehry (b. 1929) also creates dynamic Deconstructivist forms with curved, winglike shapes that extend far beyond the solid masses of his buildings. One of his most spectacular designs is the **GUGGENHEIM MUSEUM** in Bilbao, Spain (**FIG. 33–52**). In the 1990s, the designing of art museums became more and more spectacular as they increasingly came to define the visual landscape of cities. Gehry developed his asymmetrical design using a CATIA CAD program that enabled him to create a powerfully organic, sculptural structure. The complex steel skeleton is covered by a thin skin of silvery titanium that shimmers gold or silver depending on the time of day and the weather conditions. From the north the building resembles a living organism, while from other angles it looks like a giant ship, a reference to the industry on which Bilbao has traditionally depended, thereby identifying the museum with the city. Despite the sculptural beauty of the museum, however, the interior is a notoriously difficult space in which to display art, a characteristic this building shares with Wright's spiraling design of the New York Guggenheim (SEE FIG. 33–33), a notable forebear of Gehry's explorations of the sculptural potential of architecture.

33–51 Zaha Hadid
**VITRA FIRE
STATION,
WEIL-AM-RHEIN**
Germany. 1989–1993.

Credit: © F1 ONLINE/
SuperStock

33–52 Frank O. Gehry **GUGGENHEIM MUSEUM, BILBAO**
Spain. 1993–1997. Sculpture of spider in foreground: Louise Bourgeois (1911–2010), *Maman*, 1999.

Credit: © AAD Worldwide Travel Images/Alamy Stock Photo

Contemporary Art in an Expanding World

What are some ways that artists since the 1990s have synthesized aesthetic interests, social content, and political activism in their work?

Since the 1990s, the art world has mirrored the multiplicity and connectivity of today's global culture. Artists look to the alternative practices, ideas, and formats that emerged in the latter half of the twentieth century, as well as to traditional media like painting and photography, adapting them in many ways to produce new works that respond to a rapidly changing culture. The popularity of postwar art has exploded in recent years. New museums devoted to its display are on the rise; many, like the Broad in Los Angeles, have been opened by private collectors. In addition to long-held international exhibitions like the Venice Biennale and Documenta, in Kassel, West Germany, international exhibitions now occur regularly in places such as Sharjah in United Arab Emirates, Gwanju in China, and Havana, Cuba. These offer curators a global stage on which to explore broad themes and changing ideologies, and generate extensive—often contentious—critical response. A similar proliferation of art fairs like Art Basel in Switzerland allows artists, dealers, and collectors to gather throughout the year. All this has led to unprecedented growth in the international art market, which reached $53.9 billion in 2014, with Modern and contemporary art accounting for 48 percent of total sales. That this boom has occurred at a time when many people are experiencing financial and political hardship raises issues of art's continued elitism, with critics pointing to the relatively small number of artists and collectors who participate in these major events.

Globalization and the Art World

Globalization refers to the expanding economic, social, and cultural network that has developed through transnational trade agreements, economic unions, and advancements in digital communication since the 1990s. Postcolonial discourse has long warned of the excessive influence of industrialized nations on developing countries—and as the world becomes smaller, anxieties arise about the effects of globalization on national identity and cultural heritage. There are also increasing conflicts over religious differences and political control. Artists like Shirin Neshat and Yinka Shonibare (SEE FIG. 29–25) highlight the complexity of these issues, forcing us to acknowledge our cultural biases and to recognize our shared histories, entwined by the legacy of imperialism.

Born in Iran in 1957, Neshat moved to the United States in 1974. She returned to Iran for the first time in 1993 to see the country transformed by the fundamentalist regime that came to power with the 1979 Islamic Revolution. Soon afterward, Neshat began to create beautifully poetic photographs and films that explore complicated realities of gender, religion, and cultural difference. In her 1994 "Women of Allah" series, she exposes Western stereotypes of Muslim women, claiming their identities are more varied and complex than usually assumed. Typical of the series, **REBELLIOUS SILENCE** (FIG. 33-53) is a black-and-white photograph of a woman clad in a traditional chador. The woman's face is exposed, and Neshat has inscribed on the photograph, in Farsi, text from a twentieth-century Iranian female writer. A rifle barrel runs vertically through the composition, bisecting the woman's figure. Like the veil covering her body, the calligraphy and gun seem to protect the woman and show how little we understand her. She looks out to meet our gaze, challenging beliefs about submissive Muslim women and reinforcing fears of fundamentalist Islamic militarism. Produced for Western audiences, the image's meaning remains unclear as Neshat confronts our national prejudices and raises questions about the role of women in post-revolutionary Iran.

Wenda Gu (b. 1955) studied traditional ink painting at China's National Academy of Fine Arts before emigrating to the United States in 1987. In 1992, he began the ongoing project "United Nations Series" that now includes more than 20 "monuments," which highlight the histories and traditions of particular countries. These large-scale installations are constructed with transparent walls and screens of human hair collected from the floors of hairdressers around the world and woven to create lacelike patterns and pseudo-characters based on Chinese, English, Arabic, and Hindi languages. Although the text appears readable, closer scrutiny shows it to be Gu's own invented script. His point is that in a global society our understanding of one another may be fragmented, misunderstood, or incorrect.

Gu references an imperial altar from the Ming dynasty in **CHINA MONUMENT: TEMPLE OF HEAVEN** (FIG. 33-54),

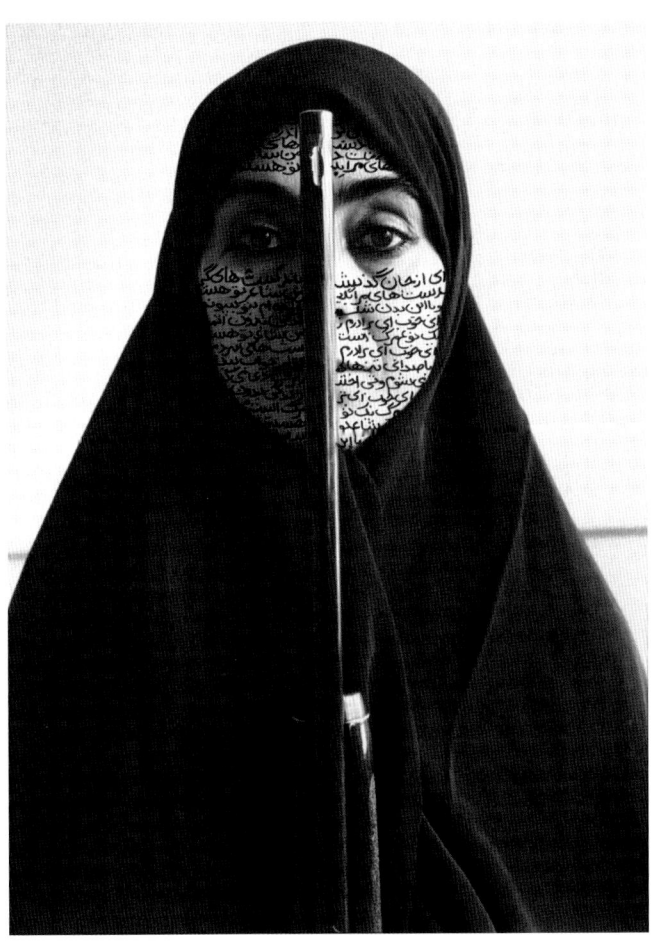

33-53 Shirin Neshat **REBELLIOUS SILENCE**
1994. Black-and-white RC print and ink (photograph by C. Preston), 11 × 14″ (27.9 × 35.6 cm). Barbara Gladstone Gallery, New York.

Credit: © Shirin Neshat. Courtesy Gladstone Gallery

33-54 Wenda Gu **CHINA MONUMENT: TEMPLE OF HEAVEN**

1998. Installation with screens of human hair, wooden chairs and tables, and video. Commissioned by the Asia Society. Permanent collection of the Hong Kong Museum of Art.

Credit: © Wenda Gu. Photo by Jiang Min

33–55 Felix Gonzalez-Torres "UNTITLED" (LOVERBOY)

1990. Blue paper, endless supply, at ideal height 7½ × 29 × 23″ (19.1 × 73.7 × 58.4 cm). Installation view at Andrea Rosen Gallery, New York, 1990.

Credit: © The Felix Gonzalez-Torres Foundation. Courtesy of Andrea Rosen Gallery, New York. Photo: Peter Muscato

commissioned in 1998 by the Asia Society in New York. Draped curtains, made from hair collected in China, New York's Chinatown, and other American cities, enclose the space around a meditation area. Video monitors in chairs project images of clouds and sky while music of ancient Chinese bells plays in the background. Gu's goal to bring all people together may seem utopian, but he feels his dream can be "fully realized in the art world."

The Body in Contemporary Art

An important theme throughout art history, the body was central to postwar artists who sought to demonstrate art's relationship to human life, experience, and identity. While such concerns remained prominent, they took on new dimensions in the wake of the AIDS epidemic. For many artists, the body offered a universal metaphor to explore the material, psychological, and philosophical questions inherent to the human condition. AIDS activists highlighted the physical effects of the disease, linking it to emotional pain and suffering felt by others, even those not personally afflicted. The Culture Wars had railed against artists who incorporated graphic imagery or used the body to explore gender and sexuality—but these strategies brought new attention to the body's material reality and physiological functions and led artists throughout the 1990s to address topics, traditionally suppressed by societal taboo, that delve deep into the psychological effects of our most basic instincts.

THE IMPACT OF AIDS ON ART In 1981, reports emerged about a mysterious disease that seemed to be affecting gay men. Over the next decade, society came to learn that the disease—named Acquired Immune Deficiency Syndrome in 1983—was caused by the human immunodeficiency virus (HIV), a blood-borne, sexually transmitted virus that could live for years in the carrier's body and be unknowingly passed to others, regardless of gender or sexual orientation. By the mid-1980s AIDS was declared a global epidemic, and by 1994 it was the leading cause of death among all Americans between 25 and 44. Throughout the 1980s, uncertainty about how it was spread led to paranoia among the general public, and the disproportionate impact of AIDS on the gay community, bolstered by preexisting stigmas about homosexuality, led some to disregard the seriousness of the epidemic. During this time, the rapid spread of AIDS, its physical effects on the body, and the loss of thousands of people—most in the prime of life—had a profound effect on the arts community. Many artists adapted activist strategies to educate the public about the disease and to call for government action. Others, inspired by their own suffering and loss, created artworks confronting human emotions such as anger, love, grief, and hope.

Felix Gonzales-Torres (1957–1996) infused Minimalism's preference for spare geometries, repetition, and mass-produced materials with deeply personal meaning in works that offer profound statements on human mortality. He created **"UNTITLED" (LOVERBOY)** (**FIG. 33–55**) in 1990 when his longtime partner, Ross Laycock, was dying from AIDS. The piece was deceptively simple: A stack of pale blue paper sat on the gallery floor with instructions for visitors to take a sheet with them. As the sheets were removed, the vertical stack gradually diminished in height, an allegory of the slowly disappearing body of Gonzalez-Torres's partner. Similarly, in *"Untitled"* of 1991 the artist created a mound of individually wrapped candies totalling 175 pounds—his partner's ideal weight—which viewers were invited to take away with them, thus realizing the meaning in the work and carrying with them a small reminder of its purpose. By involving the viewer as a participant, Gonzalez-Torres transformed a story of individual loss into a political act that called attention to the social impact of the AIDS epidemic, as well as a lasting memorial to those who had died. Gonzalez-Torres himself died of AIDS in 1996.

David Wojnarowicz (1955–1992), another artist lost to AIDS, found inspiration for his photographs, films, and books in the stories of people he met while living on the

33–56 David Wojnarowicz **UNTITLED (HANDS)**
1992. Silver print with silkscreened text, 38 × 26″
(96.5 × 66 cm). Courtesy of the estate of David
Wojnarowicz and PPOW Gallery, New York.

Credit: Courtesy of the estate of David Wojnarowicz and PPOW
Gallery, New York

streets after leaving an abusive home. His frequent combination of imagery with lengthy passages of texts suggests a need to give voice to those marginalized by society. Around 1987, when faced with the death of his lover, photographer Peter Hujar, and his own diagnosis as HIV-positive, Wojnarowicz began to focus his art on the feelings involved in watching a loved one die while facing one's own mortality. **UNTITLED (HANDS)** (FIG. 33–56) shows a black-and-white photograph of two outstretched hands, bound by white bandages that suggest human pain, suffering, and the need for compassion. Superimposed is an angry text in red type taken from Wojnarowicz's book *Memories That Smell Like Gasoline*, in which he describes himself hollowing out from the inside and becoming invisible as he dies. Wojnarowicz's work can often be disturbing in its graphic imagery and allusion to religious symbolism. A frequent target of critics during the Culture Wars of the 1990s, it remains controversial even today.

The **AIDS MEMORIAL QUILT** (FIG. 33–57) is an ongoing effort to address personal loss and political issues brought about by the AIDS epidemic. Quilts have historically served a

33–57 THE AIDS MEMORIAL QUILT
1987–present. Photograph taken at the Mall, Washington DC on October 12, 1996.

Credit: © Evan Agostini/ Getty Images

community purpose, often made collectively to mark life events like marriages and births and to preserve cultural history and beliefs. Growing out of the gay community in San Francisco, the *AIDS Memorial Quilt* builds on this tradition to educate the public and create a lasting tribute to thousands of individuals who have lost their lives to AIDS. Gay-rights activist Clive Jones began the *Quilt* in the mid-1980s. Each 3 by 6 foot panel is sewn by friends, families, and lovers to commemorate an individual lost to AIDS. The panels are then organized in 8-panel, 12-foot-square blocks that can be exhibited separately. An assembly of 1,920 panels was displayed on the National Mall in Washington, DC in 1987 as a visual demonstration of the scale of the epidemic and to incite a call for government action toward research and education preventing its spread. In 1989, the project was nominated for a Nobel Peace Prize. Today, the quilt includes 48,000 panels in remembrance of over 94,000 individuals, and it is still growing. The NAMES Project Foundation, an international nonprofit organization, continues this work by inviting participants to create new memorial panels, organizing exhibitions of the *Quilt* around the world, and maintaining an archive of each person's name in a searchable online database.

THE MATERIAL BODY   Kiki Smith (b. 1954), whose sister died of AIDS, focuses on the body's materiality and loss of physical control in **UNTITLED** (**FIG. 33–58**), in which two life-size, naked figures, female and male, hang limply side by side about a foot above the ground. Milk appears to drip from the woman's breasts and semen down the man's leg, as if both figures have lost control of bodily functions that were once a source of vitality and pleasure. Reflecting the influence of process-based artists like Hesse, the flesh-colored beeswax contributes a tactility that underscores Smith's visceral content. She points out that the societal demand that we conceal and control bodily functions makes our inability to maintain them when sick and dying humiliating and frightening. Acceptance of our body's reality generates a profound sense of loss, but also of release and liberation. Like essentialist feminists who gave voice to female experience by representing taboo subjects like menstruation, Smith calls attention to the body that cannot be controlled and asks us to consider the impact of this repression.

Along with Ofili, Damien Hirst (b. 1965) is one of the so-called "YBAs," or Young British Artists. Hirst first gained notoriety in the 1990s for his outrageous behavior

33–58 Kiki Smith **UNTITLED**
1990. Beeswax with microcrystalline wax figures on metal stands; female figure installed height 6'1½" (1.87 m), male figure 6'4¹⁵⁄₁₆" (1.95 m). Whitney Museum of American Art, New York.

Credit: © Kiki Smith, courtesy Pace Gallery. Photo: Jerry L. Thompson

33–59 Damien Hirst **MOTHER AND CHILD (DIVIDED), EXHIBITION COPY 2007 (ORIGINAL 1993)**
2007. Glass, painted stainless steel, silicone, acrylic, monofilament, stainless steel, cow, calf, and formaldehyde solution; two tanks at
82⅓ × 126⅞ × 43″ (209 × 322 × 109 cm), two tanks at 45 × 66½ × 24⅝″ (114 × 169 × 62.5 cm). Photo: Prudence Cuming Associates.

and shocking artwork that he continues to produce. An example is *For the Love of God* (2007), a diamond-encrusted human skull with an asking price of $100 million. Despite its sensationalism, the object speaks to Hirst's persistent interest in death and philosophical questions involving mortality and spiritual existence. Many of his works feature dead and preserved animals. In **MOTHER AND CHILD (DIVIDED)** (**FIG. 33–59**), Hirst bisected vertically and longitudinally the bodies of a cow and her calf and displayed them in glass cases filled with formaldehyde solution. This sculpture resembles a display in a natural history museum, but here viewers can walk around and between the cases. From the outside, the animals look amazingly lifelike (even their eyelashes and individual hairs are visible), preserved inside the brilliant blue formaldehyde solution, but once we see the cleavages in their bones, muscles, organs, and flesh on the "inside" sides of the cases, the reality of the dead carcasses is overwhelming. Hirst also plays on the art historical theme of the mother and child, iconic in Christian tradition, to symbolize the union of earthly and spiritual realms. *Mother and Child (Divided)* suggests that we are caught between the separation of life and death, between mother and child, and between scientific reality and our own fears and emotions.

Between 1994 and 2002, Matthew Barney (b. 1967) created a series of films entitled "The Cremaster Cycle" in which he developed an arcane sexual mythology drawing on Celtic legend, Masonic ritual, Mormonism, and the life of Harry Houdini. The concept of biological mutability dominates the narrative, which questions gender assignation and roles throughout. The cremaster muscle, for which the series is named, controls the ascent and descent of the testes, usually in response to changes in temperature but also in response to fear or sexual arousal. It also determines sexual differentiation in the human embryo. Barney uses a diagrammatic representation of the cremaster muscle as his visual emblem throughout the series.

Each film has its own complex narrative and catalog of multilayered symbols. *Cremaster 3* from 2002 describes the construction of the Chrysler Building in New York and features the artist Richard Serra as the architect. In one segment, the Solomon R. Guggenheim Museum in New York is the setting where Barney, playing Serra's apprentice, dressed in a peach-colored kilt and gagged, must accomplish a series of tasks to assert his supremacy over the master. Barney scales the walls of the rotunda to complete a task on each level before gaining enlightenment. Along the way he encounters a series of challenges—a line of Rockettes dressed as Masonic lambs; warring punk-rock bands; a leopard woman played by the double-amputee athlete; model, and speaker Aimee Mullins; and finally Serra, throwing molten wax down the museum's spiraling ramp in a nod to the sculptor's famous casting of process-based works out of lead in the 1960s. The settings and costumes are lavish, and the epic plot is complex and enigmatic.

33–60 Matthew Barney **CREMASTER 3: MAHABYN**
2002. 46½ × 54 × 1½″ (118 × 137 × 3.8 cm).

Credit: © Matthew Barney, courtesy Barbara Gladstone Gallery (Part of the Cremaster Cycle 1994–2002). Photo: Chris Winget

In **MAHABYN** (FIG. **33-60**), from *Cremaster 3*, Barney and the leopard woman transform by donning modified Masonic costumes. While the meaning remains ambiguous, the extravagant work seems to refer to a crisis among white, middle-class, heterosexual male artists in an era exploring difference and identity.

New Approaches to Painting and Photography

Gerhard Richter (b. 1932) studied art in Soviet-controlled Dresden before moving in 1961 to West Germany where he first learned about Pop Art and Fluxus. Although Richter consistently identifies as a painter, his work's underlying conceptualism characterizes much painting of the contemporary period. Rejecting the expectation that artists demonstrate only one "signature" style, Richter has worked throughout his career simultaneously in abstract and representational styles, often using photographic sources as the basis for his work. **MAN SHOT DOWN (1) ERSCHOSSENER (1) FROM OCTOBER 18, 1977** (FIG 33-61) is from Richter's 1988 series based on newspaper reports in 1977 about three members of the Red Army Faction, an anticapitalist terrorist group known as the Baader-Meinhof Gang, who were found dead in their prison cells. Although the deaths were ruled as suicides, suspicions arose about whether the German government had been responsible. In life-size paintings, Richter reproduces in blurry detail the grainy black-and-white photographs that appeared in the press. His direct reproduction questions the powerful role of the mass media to shape historical events, the ability of photography to create cultural and personal memories of the past, and the value of the hand of the artist, even when, as in this case, it is almost invisible.

33–61 Gerhard Richter **MAN SHOT DOWN (1) ERSCHOSSENER (1) FROM OCTOBER 18, 1977**
1988. Oil on canvas, 39½ × 55¼″ (100 × 140 cm). Museum of Modern Art, New York. The Sidney and Harriet Janis Collection, gift of Philip Johnson, and acquired through the Lillie P. Bliss Bequest (all by exchange); Enid A. Haupt Fund; Nina and Gordon Bunshaft Bequest Fund; and gift of Emily Rauh Pulitzer (169.1995.g.).

Credit: © Gerhard Richter

33–62 Jeff Wall **AFTER "INVISIBLE MAN" BY RALPH ELLISON, THE PREFACE**
1999–2001. Transparency in lightbox, 68½ × 98⅝" (174 × 250.5 cm).

Credit: Courtesy Marian Goodman Gallery

One of the Pictures generation of artists, Jeff Wall (b. 1946) uses multiple photographs and elaborate stage sets to create large-scale visual narratives that he compares to nineteenth-century history paintings. Wall exhibits these as brilliantly colored transparencies mounted in light-boxes—a format used in advertising that also recalls the cinema. He works like a movie director, carefully designing sets and posing actors to photograph, then digitally combining multiple images to create the final transparency. **AFTER "INVISIBLE MAN" BY RALPH ELLISON, THE PREFACE** (FIG. 33–62), is an elaborate composition; it took 18 months to design and construct the sets and 3 weeks to take the photographs. Basing the work on Ralph Ellison's 1951 novel about a young African-American man struggling to find recognition in a racially divided society, Wall depicts a scene from the book's prologue where the narrator explains that he's retreated to an underground cellar, lit by 1,369 lightbulbs, to write his story.

African-American painter Kerry James Marshall (b. 1955) also looks to narrative history painting to address contemporary issues of race, class, and poverty in the United States. **MANY MANSIONS** (FIG. 33–63) is one of Marshall's series of five paintings based on public housing projects. The work refers to Chicago's Stateway Gardens,

which was one of the largest and worst-maintained housing projects in America before its demolition in 2007. Playing on the irony of the development's name, Marshall depicts three well-dressed African-American men tending a garden of manicured topiary, flowerbeds, and cellophane-wrapped Easter baskets before the high-rise buildings in the background. The painting includes other biting elements, including the red ribbon at the top with the inscription "In my mother's house there are many mansions," twisting the gender of a biblical reference to God (John 14:2) and offering derisive commentary on the housing conditions. Adding to the fantasy are two blue-birds, like those in a Disney cartoon, which carry a light blue ribbon that reads "Bless our happy home" to place above the seal of the Chicago Housing Authority. Based on Géricault's *The Raft of the Medusa* (SEE FIG. 30–51), Marshall's triangular composition lends his subject the dramatic hero-ism of history painting. Similarly, the visible drips and patches of loosely applied paint refer to Abstract Expressionism, but here they look more like graffiti and white-washing done to mask urban blight.

Born in Ethiopia, Julie Mehretu (b. 1970) builds on the abstraction pioneered by Kandinsky and other early Modern artists to give visual form to complex systems and

33–63 Kerry James Marshall **MANY MANSIONS**
1994. Acrylic on paper mounted on canvas, 114¼ × 135⅛" (290 × 343 cm). The Art Institute of Chicago. Max V. Kohnstamm Fund (1995.147).

Credit: Image courtesy of the artist and Jack Shainman Gallery, NY. Photo © The Art Institute of Chicago

global networks. Her highly finished paintings, made from thinly applied layers of translucent paint built up and polished, have a smooth, waxy-looking surface. Working on a monumental scale, Mehretu employs a rich vocabulary from sources that include architectural drawings, maps, graffiti, and aerial photographs. One of a triptych of paintings created for the 2004–2005 Carnegie International, **STADIA II** (**FIG. 33-64**) captures the excitement and energy of major athletic events by layering fragmented architectural drawings of sports arenas from around the world. Mehretu uses the subject to address themes of national identity, commerce, entertainment, and conflict. Colorful geometric shapes suggest flags and banners denoting cultural and team alliances, and superimposed graphic elements unify the composition while also contributing dynamism and a sense of chaos.

33–64 Julie Mehretu **STADIA II**
2004. Ink and acrylic on canvas, 107⅜ × 140⅛ × 2¼" (272.73 × 355.92 × 5.71 cm). Gift of Jeanne Greenberg Rohatyn and Nicolas Rohatyn and A.W. Mellon Acquisition Endowment Fund.

Credit: © Julie Mehretu. Courtesy of the artist, Marian Goodman Gallery and White Cube. Photo by Richard Stoner

The New Formalism

During the 1990s, a new aesthetic emerged that is seen clearly in sculpture and large-scale installations. Different from Greenberg's reductive ideas, this contemporary tendency shows a renewed interest in the potential meanings associated with artists' materials and technical processes. Drawing on Process art and feminist appropriation of craft practices in the 1970s, artists today choose from a range of formal strategies to produce visual, tactile, and spatial sensations for the viewer—all of which work together to form the artwork's content. This desire to engage the viewer aesthetically makes these recent works different from their mid-twentieth-century predecessors, which adopted an anti-aesthetic stance to emphasize their conceptual underpinnings and prevent expressive readings.

Today, sculptors produce frankly beautiful works of art, like Anish Kapoor's *Cloud Gate* in Chicago's Millennium Park and Serra's breathtaking series of mammoth torqued ellipses and spirals. Others like Ann Hamilton and Olafur Eliasson offer joyous site-specific installations, commissioned to fill the large spaces museums have built to accommodate such ambitious projects. Likewise, artists like Martin Puryear, Cat Mazza, and El Anatsui (SEE FIG. 29-21) have redefined contemporary craft arts by exploring materials, production methods, conceptual practices, and modes of display that reject craft's once marginalized place in the world of fine art.

CRAFT AND CRAFTSMANSHIP Although the clarity and scale of Martin Puryear's abstract sculptures suggest a Minimalist influence, his emphasis on technique reflects ideas of Process art. But unlike these earlier movements, Puryear's art draws on vernacular craft traditions that value the handmade object and highly skilled workmanship. Puryear (b. 1941) learned woodworking from African carvers while in Sierra Leone with the Peace Corps. He later studied traditional furniture-making techniques used in Scandinavia and the United States before pursuing an MFA in sculpture at Yale University.

In **PLENTY'S BOAST** (FIG. 33-65), Puryear highlights the sculpture's visible joints and natural materials. He exploits the grain of the wood in the radiating lines inside the horn and spirals around the tail. His attention to detail is further revealed in the precision of his joining method, the irregular hand-finished surfaces on the mouth of the sculpture, and the binding of its tail. But Puryear's work diverges from traditional craft by lacking the practical function of furniture or a well-built cabinet. And while he wants viewers to appreciate the aesthetic qualities of his work, his forms create many allusions. The bell shape of *Plenty's Boast* may be seen as a musical horn, an old-fashioned gramophone horn, a flower's bell, or most likely, a cornucopia (horn of plenty) filled with the fruits of harvest and symbolizing abundance. Ironically, however, this cone is empty, implying an "empty boast"—a phrase suggested by the title.

A socially minded artist committed to working in the public realm, David Hammons (b. 1943) is an outspoken critic of the gallery system, arguing that art must intervene in society in order to resist commercialization and encourage action. In **UNTITLED** (FIG. 33-66), he makes a provocative statement asserting the place of African Americans within American culture. Traditionally sewn by hand, flags are deeply meaningful objects that publically proclaim national identity, political alliance, and ideological values through abstract forms and colors. Originally created in 1990 for the Studio Museum in Harlem, Hammon's flag responded to a controversy about the flying of the Confederate flag

33-65 Martin Puryear
PLENTY'S BOAST
1994–1995. Red cedar and pine. 68 × 83 × 118" (172.7 × 210.8 × 299.7 cm) The Nelson-Atkins Museum of Art, Kansas City, Missouri. Purchase of the Renee C. Crowell Trust (95-16 A-C).

Credit: © Martin Puryear. Courtesy Matthew Marks Gallery, New York under apartheid. In the film, the medical examination of Soho Eckstein—a greedy white businessman character in several of Kentridge's films—symbolizes white South Africans recognizing their responsibility for the suffering under apartheid. Kentridge describes drawing as an act of compassion and redemption. He explains that he finds sympathy for others through the extended contemplation and time spent studying his subjects, and that this process redeems his appropriation of their pain as the raw material for his art.

on public buildings in some states. By replacing the colors of the flag of the United States with those of the Pan-African Flag, adopted by the Universal Negro Improvement Association and African Communities League in 1920 as a symbol of liberation for all people of African descent, Hammons counters the racist implications of the Confederate emblem and suggests that African Americans are integrated into the very fabric of American society.

South African artist William Kentridge (b. 1955) explores difficult themes like violence, pain, and social justice in animated films made more affecting by his expressive drawing style and narrative structure. Kentridge creates each scene by filming a large charcoal drawing, which he erases and redraws to advance the narrative. This physical process is visible in the final film as trace markings appear and disappear throughout each scene. Created from 20 individual drawings, **HISTORY OF THE MAIN COMPLAINT** (**FIG. 33-67**) was made in 1996, soon after South Africa established the Truth and Reconciliation Commission to conduct public hearings of civil rights abuses that had taken place

IMMERSIVE INSTALLATION   The site-specific installations of Ann Hamilton (b. 1956) demonstrate the intersection of craft tradition, conceptual practice, and immersive experience in contemporary art. Hamilton uses sensual materials like horsehair, fabric, and audiovisual elements, as well as live animals and performers, to evoke a range of emotional and physical responses in viewers. Trained in textile design, she often uses sewing and weaving as metaphors for social interactions that she feels are rooted in the body. For example, her 2012 installation at New York's Park Avenue Armory, *In the Event of a Thread*, relied on visitors to raise and lower a billowing white curtain, set in motion by giant swings that controlled a web of strings and pulleys on the ceiling.

Hamilton's installations respond to the architectural conditions and social histories of their particular sites. **MYEIN** (**FIG. 33-68**), created for the 1999 Venice Biennale, was inspired by the Neoclassical building that housed the

33–67 William Kentridge **HISTORY OF THE MAIN COMPLAINT**
1996. Stills. Film, 35 mm, shown as video, projection, black and white, and sound (mono), 5 min. 50 sec. Courtesy Marion Goodman Gallery, New York.

33–68 Ann Hamilton **MYEIN**

1999. Installation at the United States Pavilion, 48th Venice Biennale, 1999.

Four skylights, glass and gridded steel wall [18 × 90′ (5.4 × 27.4 m)], wood table, white cloths, mirrored glass, vinyl powder, auger system, electronic controllers, plaster, recorded voice, digital audio, computer, 16 speakers.

Credit: © Ann Hamilton

United States Pavilion and by Hamilton's interest in the darker parts of American history that are invisible or unspoken, although we know they exist. This is reflected in her title, an ancient Greek word meaning "to close the eyes or mouth," which also refers to the practice of medieval cults keeping their initiation rites secret. For the installation, Hamilton surrounded the pavilion with a 90 by 16-foot glass wall that blurred the building's façade, suggesting movement and alluding to the perceptual distortions caused by the passage of time. Inside, words by the poet Charles Reznikoff describing human suffering and injustice in the United States were written in Braille on the white walls. Fine fuchsia powder fell from the perimeter of the ceiling, collecting on the raised Braille surfaces and pooling in bright areas on the floor. The installation also included a soundtrack in which Abraham Lincoln's second Inaugural Address was whispered in phonetic code to make the words indecipherable. The effect was haunting yet beautiful and reflected Hamilton's goal to call attention to unspoken histories that remain mysterious and cryptic.

Kara Walker (b. 1969) uses installation as a strategy to involve, and perhaps implicate, her viewers. She has said, "It's interesting that as soon as you start telling the story of racism you start reliving it." In **DARKYTOWN REBELLION** (**FIG. 33–69**) she depicts a story about slave revolt and massacre. Based on eighteenth-century craft tradition, Walker's large-scale silhouettes are cut out of black construction paper, then applied to gallery walls to tell an unfolding tale of horror. Like the nightlight in a child's room, beautiful yellow, pink, and blue lights swirl through the gallery, but they reveal nightmarish shadows dancing across the walls. As we walk around the space, we step in front of the light source, casting our own shadows that insert us into the narrative. Set in the antebellum American South, Walker's stories draw variously from slave narratives, minstrel shows, advertising

33–69 Kara Walker **DARKYTOWN REBELLION**

2001. Cut paper and projection on wall, 14 × 37′ (4.3 × 11.3 m) overall. Installation view of "Kara Walker: My Complement, My Enemy, My Oppressor, My Love", Walker Art Center, Minneapolis, 2007. Collection Musée d'Art Moderne Grand-Duc Jean (MUDAM), Luxembourg.

Credit: © Kara Walker/Courtesy of Sikkema Jenkins & Co., New York. Photo: Dave Sweeney

33-70 Olafur Eliasson **THE WEATHER PROJECT**
2004 installation, Turbine Hall, Tate Modern, London.

Credit: © Olafur Eliasson. Photo: Jens Ziehe. Courtesy of the artist; neugerriemschneider, Berlin; Tanya Bonaker Gallery, New York

memorabilia, and even Harlequin romance novels, blending fiction and fact to evoke a history of oppression and terrible violence. Her grotesque rendering of plantation life can be an uncomfortable experience, forcing us to confront racial stereotypes and fears, as well as our culpability in maintaining them.

The growing popularity—and scale—of contemporary art propelled a wave of expansive projects in museums around the world. When London's Tate Gallery decided to relocate its Modern and contemporary art collections into a refurbished power plant, they transformed the Turbine Hall, an enormous area where the building's electric generators once stood, into an impressive entry for the new museum. Measuring 115 by 375 feet, it provides an ideal site for monumental installations, and the Tate launched the Unilever Series, which commissions artists to create temporary works specifically for this vast open space. Projects have included a large crack that ran the length of the concrete floor (Doris Salcedo, *Shibboleth*, 2007) and choreographed encounters that encouraged conversations among strangers who crowd the hall (Tito Seghal, *These Associations*, 2012). In **THE WEATHER PROJECT** (**FIG. 33-70**), Danish artist Olafur Eliasson (b. 1967) covered the entire ceiling with foil mirrors to visually double the massive hall, which he filled with an artificially generated foglike mist. At one end of the hall, he placed a semicircular screen backlit by 200 mono-frequency lights that, when reflected in the mirrors, created the illusion of a giant yellow sun shining brilliantly in a darkened sky.

Eliasson based the project on his notion that weather is one of the few authentic ways that city dwellers interact with nature. His goal was to bring the city into the museum and to encourage visitors to take the memory of their experience back outside. Visitors were overwhelmed by the immense scale and simple beauty of the installation. People gathered, wandered around, and even lay down on the floor to enjoy the soft, golden light that permeated the space. While such reactions may recall the Romantic landscape painters' pursuit of the sublime, Eliasson instead hoped to highlight the artifice of the encounter imposed by the museum context. By exposing the wires and mechanical devices used to create the illusion, he asked viewers to question their experience, perhaps contrasting it to real moments they spent in nature.

Activist Strategies and Participatory Art

Like the AIDS activists discussed earlier, many contemporary artists assume an intentionally political stance, turning their attention to the shifting social causes and current issues that garner public concern. Activist art today relies on practices used by conceptual artists in the 1960s and 1970s for institutional critique and by collectives like the Art Workers' Coalition, formed in New York in 1969, and Situationist International, active throughout the 1960s. Their influence is especially apparent in projects that enlist viewers directly as agents of social protest and change. Sometimes called Social Practice, this art encompasses a range of participatory strategies that work outside traditional contexts to engage directly with the public, government, or other institutions to realize the artists' activist goals. One example is Conflict Kitchen, a take-out restaurant in Pittsburgh that serves food that is traditional in countries currently in conflict with the United States. Started in 2010 by Jon Rubin and Dawn Weleski, art professors at Carnegie Mellon University, the project builds on the dynamics of sharing a meal to encourage diners to converse and learn about these other cultures. The Internet and social media have also provided artists with a tool to

33–71 Krzysztof Wodiczko
HOMELESS VEHICLE
1988–1989. Aluminum and mixed media.
Variant 3 of 4, pictured at Trump Tower,
New York.

Credit: © Krzysztof Wodiczko. Courtesy Galerie
Lelong, New York

spread their message, as in the case of Chinese artist Ai Weiwei who, despite Chinese government restrictions on his travel from 2011 to 2015, was able to maintain contact with an international audience.

In the late 1980s, Polish-born Canadian artist Krzysztof Wodiczko (b. 1943) designed the **HOMELESS VEHICLE** (**FIG. 33–71**) in collaboration with homeless people in New York. The vehicle, shown in art exhibitions and prototyped on the streets, was intended to draw attention to the problem of homelessness in New York. Recalling Constructivist product design, the *Homeless Vehicle* includes an extendable metal pod for sleeping, washing, or toilet needs, baskets underneath to store belongings and cans that could be sold, and a brightly colored flag to signal approach. Wodiczko explains its use as "both communication and the transport; a vehicle that could articulate the real conditions of work and life and the resistance of this group" instead of the stolen grocery carts often linked to the homeless. Critics of his work say that the project undermines efforts to help homelessness because it does not address the systemic roots of the problem.

Another of the YBAs, sculptor Rachel Whiteread (b. 1963) made her reputation by casting the inside of ordinary objects like mattresses or book shelves, thus transforming overlooked negative spaces into poignant memorials alluding to absence and loss. Made with materials like rubber, resin, and plaster, Whiteread's work has the spare appearance of Minimalist sculpture, but visible details offer hints to its functional origins. Whiteread addressed the invisibility of the British working classes in **HOUSE** (**FIG. 33–72**). She sprayed liquid concrete on the inner walls of a three-story Victorian row house before it was carefully dismantled, leaving a ghostlike replica in its place. The project took place in the Grove Road area of London's East End, where the last row of the Victorian houses that had originally filled the area was slated to be demolished by developers. Over the years, similar projects had effectively erased all vestiges of the community by replacing the row houses with high-rise apartments and other structures. Like much of Whiteread's work, *House* is about the memories

33–72 Rachel Whiteread **HOUSE**
1993. Corner of Grove and Roman Roads, London. Concrete. Destroyed 1994. Commissioned by Artangel. Received the Turner Prize, Tate Britain, London. Photo: Sue Omerod.

Credit: © Rachel Whiteread; Courtesy of the artist, Luhring Augustine, New York, Lorcan O'Neill, Rome, and Gagosian Gallery. © Artangel. Photo: Sue Ormerod contained in places and times and how easily they can be lost. Whiteread intended *House* as a political statement about development practices in England and "the ludicrous policy of knocking down homes like this and building badly designed tower blocks which themselves have to be knocked down after 20 years." The publicity surrounding Whiteread's project, which occurred at the same time as she won the prestigious Turrner Prize, succeeded in bringing these critical issues to the public's attention.

American artist Patricia Cronin (b. 1963) employs many artistic formats for her politically charged subjects. Addressing themes of homosexuality, feminism, and art history, Cronin's work supports her goal of raising public awareness of these issues. **SHRINE FOR GIRLS** (FIG. **33-73**) presented in conjunction with the 2015 Venice Biennale, appeared at the sixteenth-century church of San Gallo. On the chapel's three marble altars, Cronin placed photographs of young girls next to mounds of clothing to suggest relics of religious martyrs. The monuments referred to incidents of violence against women around the world. Brilliantly colored saris on the central altar related to two Indian teenagers who were gang-raped, murdered, and found strung from trees in 2014. Muslim hijabs (head coverings) were on the altar to the left, representing 276 Nigerian schoolgirls kidnapped in 2014 by Boko Haram militants in Nigeria; the altar on the right displayed uniforms like those worn by women imprisoned and forced to work in Magdalene asylums across Europe and the United States throughout the nineteenth and into the twentieth century.

Cronin's installation exploited the aesthetic contrast of the rich, colorful fabrics and the stone architecture to contribute visual impact and iconographical meaning, and the photographs gave a human face to a problem that might seem far removed from our own experience. Cronin notes that the church context brought about a behavioral change in many visitors, who become quiet and respectful as they viewed *Shrine for Girls.* Cronin's installation was temporary, but she used the opportunity to enlist visitors to do something by creating a website suggesting ways to help end global violence toward women and listing organizations dedicated to this cause.

The Future of New Media

Since the mid twentieth century, artists have continued to explore intersections of scientific and technological innovations and artistic production. Since the 1990s, art has been made using biological and genetic components, robotics, augmented and virtual reality, data visualization, and other web-based platforms that encourage viewer interaction and widespread distribution. Today architects, designers, engineers, computer programmers, scientists, and artists are among the people exploring the creative use of new media, and its potential for growth is enormous. The ongoing expansion of new media presents a new challenge to the old question "What is art?"

Video games are an example of interactive technology that is gaining acceptance as art in museums. Since gaming's emergence in the 1970s, its technology, graphic effects, and popularity have increased exponentially. Advocates argue that, rooted in visual experience, video games are a new development in the way artists and viewers interact that is distinct from video, performance, and other time-based media. Paola Antonelli, senior curator in the Department of Architecture and Design at the Museum of Modern Art in New York, explains that in addition to a game's historical and cultural relevance, its "visual quality and aesthetic experience ... and the elegance of the coding to design viewer's behavior" are criteria for inclusion in that museum's collection.

While games like Tetris and Minecraft encourage geometrical problem-solving, **FLOWER** (FIG. **33-74**), created by Jenova Chen (b. 1981) and Kellee Santiago (b. 1979) of Thatgamecompany, allows the viewer to assume the

33-73 Patricia Cronin
SHRINE FOR GIRLS
2015. Installation at Chiesa di San Gallo, Campo San Gallo, solo Collateral Event at the 56th Venice Biennale.

33-74 Jenova Chen and Kellee Santiago **FLOWER**
2007. Video game for SONY PS3, color, sound. Smithsonian American Art Museum, Washington, DC. Gift of Thatgamecompany.

Credit: © 2016. Photo Smithsonian American Art Museum/Art Resource/Scala, Florence

game requires the player's interaction to demonstrate its full effects.

In *Flower*, we recognize ideas and themes that have emerged in art since 1950. The reliance on the viewer, the desire to blur the distinction between art and real life, and the synthesis of conceptual origins and aesthetic experience find new form in the intersection of computer animation and interactive design. As the world continues to evolve and develop in ways we cannot yet imagine, artists will certainly advance new theories and explore innovative formats that aim to communicate their interests and offer us alternative perspectives from which to consider the world and our place in it. Although art in the future will no doubt be different from contemporary art today, it will continue its historical tradition to reflect, critique, and document humanity's struggles and accomplishments and to inspire those who encounter it.

role of the wind and navigate through a lush and lyrical landscape, creating their own visual narrative as they are propelled along their path. Having grown up in the dense urban environment of Shanghai, Chen says his inspiration for the game was driving through rolling green hills and pastures on his first visit to California. The goal for *Flower* was to recreate that sensation by allowing the player to fly up and see the scale of the surrounding landscape. He explains, "[Games have] the sense of endlessness, the sense of freedom. You can go anywhere you want." While still images capture the saturated color and pleasing contours that make *Flower* so visually appealing, the

Think About It

1   How did the emergence of Pop Art and Minimalism in the early 1960s reflect cultural changes in the postwar United States? Compare and contrast works associated with each movement.
2   In what ways have artists built on the experimental art formats and practices that emerged in the 1950s and 1960s? Choose an example made after 1980 and discuss its relationship to an artistic development in the mid twentieth century.

3   Discuss the changing role of the viewer in art since the 1950s. Choose two examples from this chapter and compare how they engage the viewer.
4   Explain the effect of globalism on art today. What are some of the themes, styles, and characteristics that reflect this influence?

Crosscurrents

Distinguished twentieth-century architects designed private homes as well as large, commercial, religious, or public buildings. Discuss the circumstances that led to the creation of these two famous houses. How do these works fit into the careers of their architects and also engage with the larger concerns of architectural design at the moment when they were built? How is the physical context of each related to its design?

FIG. 32-43

FIG. 33-34A

Glossary

abacus (p. 110) The flat slab at the top of a **capital**, directly under the **entablature**.

abbey church (p. 226) An abbey is a monastic religious community headed by an abbot or abbess. An abbey church often has an especially large **choir** to provide space for the monks or nuns.

absolute dating (p. 12) A method, especially in archaeology, of assigning a precise historical date at which, or span of years during which, an object was made. Based on known and recorded events in the region, as well as technically extracted physical evidence (such as carbon-14 disintegration). See also **radiometric dating**, **relative dating**.

abstract (p. 8) Of art that does not attempt to describe the appearance of visible forms but rather to transform them into stylized patterns or to alter them in conformity to ideals.

academy (p. 942) An institution established for the training of artists. Academies date from the Renaissance and after; they were particularly powerful, state-run institutions in the seventeenth and eighteenth centuries. In general, academies replaced **guilds** as the venues where students learned the craft of art and were educated in art theory. Academies helped the recognition of artists as trained specialists, rather than craftspeople, and promoted their social status. An academician is an academy-trained artist.

acanthus (p. 111) A Mediterranean plant whose leaves are reproduced in Classical architectural ornament used on **moldings**, **friezes**, and **capitals**.

acroterion (*pl.* **acroteria**) (p. 111) An ornament at the corner or peak of a roof.

Action painting (p. 1091) Using broad gestures to drip or pour paint onto a pictorial surface. Associated with mid-twentieth-century American Abstract Expressionists, such as Jackson Pollock.

adobe (p. 404) Sun-baked blocks made of clay mixed with straw. Also: buildings made with this material.

aedicula (p. 622) A decorative architectural frame, usually found around a niche, door, or window. An aedicula is made up of a **pediment** and **entablature** supported by **columns** or **pilasters**.

aerial perspective (p. 633) See under **perspective**.

agora (p. 140) An open space in a Greek town used as a central gathering place or market. Compare **forum**.

aisle (p. 226) Passage or open corridor of a church, hall, or other building that parallels the main space, usually on both sides, and is delineated by a row, or **arcade**, of **columns** or

piers. Called side aisles when they flank the **nave** of a church.

akropolis (p. 131) The citadel of an ancient Greek city, located at its highest point and housing temples, a treasury, and sometimes a royal palace. The most famous is the Akropolis in Athens.

album (p. 810) A book consisting of a series of paintings or prints (album leaves) mounted into book form.

allegory (p. 635) In a work of art, an image (or images) that symbolizes an idea, concept, or principle, often moral or religious.

alloy (p. 24) A mixture of metals; different metals melted together.

altarpiece (p. xxxvi) A painted or carved panel or ensemble of panels placed at the back of or behind and above an altar. Contains religious imagery (often specific to the place of worship for which it was made) that viewers can look at during liturgical ceremonies (especially the **Eucharist**) or personal devotions.

amalaka (p. 306) In Hindu architecture, the circular or square-shaped element on top of a spire (*shikhara*), often crowned with a **finial**, symbolizing the cosmos.

ambulatory (p. 228) The passage (walkway) around the **apse** in a church, especially a **basilica**, or around the central space in a **central-plan building**.

amphora (*pl.* **amphorae**) (p. 103) An ancient Greek or Roman jar for storing oil or wine, with an egg-shaped body and two curved handles.

animal style (p. 445) Decoration made of interwoven animals or serpents, often found in early medieval Northern European art.

ankh (p. 51) A looped cross signifying life, used by ancient Egyptians.

apartheid (p. 435) A political system in South Africa that used race as grounds for the segregation, discrimination, and political disenfranchisement of nonwhite South Africans. It officially ended in 1994.

appropriation (p. xxiv) The practice of some Postmodern artists of adopting images in their entirety from other works of art or from visual culture for use in their own art. The act of recontextualizing the appropriated image allows the artist to critique both it and the time and place in which it was created.

apse (p. 192) A large semicircular or polygonal (and usually **vaulted**) recess on an end wall of a building. In a Christian church, it often contains the altar. "Apsidal" is the adjective describing the condition of having such a space.

arabesque (p. 270) European term for a type of linear surface decoration based on foliage and

calligraphic forms, thought by Europeans to be typical of Islamic art and usually characterized by flowing lines and swirling shapes.

arcade (p. 171) A series of **arches**, carried by **columns** or **piers** and supporting a common wall or **lintel**. In a **blind arcade**, the arches and supports are **engaged** and have a purely decorative function.

arch (p. 96) In architecture, a curved structural element that spans an open space. Built from wedge-shaped stone blocks called **voussoirs** placed together and held at the top by a trapezoidal **keystone**. It forms an effective space-spanning and weight-bearing unit, but requires **buttresses** at each side to contain the outward thrust caused by the weight of the structure. *Corbeled arch*: an arch or **vault** formed by **courses** of stones, each of which projects beyond the lower course until the space is enclosed; usually finished with a **capstone**. *Horseshoe arch*: an arch of more than a half-circle; typical of western Islamic architecture. *Round arch*: an arch that displaces most of its weight, or downward thrust, along its curving sides, transmitting that weight to adjacent supporting uprights (door or window **jambs**, **columns**, or **piers**). *Ogival arch*: a sharply pointed arch created by S curves. *Relieving arch*: an arch built into a heavy wall just above a **post-and-lintel** structure (such as a gate, door, or window) to help support the wall above by transferring the load to the side walls. *Transverse arch*: an arch that connects the wall **piers** on both sides of an interior space, up and over a stone **vault**.

Archaic smile (p. 117) The curved lips of ancient Greek statues in the period c. 600–480 BCE, usually interpreted as a way of animating facial features.

architrave (p. 110) The bottom element in an **entablature**, beneath the **frieze** and the **cornice**.

archivolt (p. 491) A band of **molding** framing an **arch**, or a series of stone blocks that form an arch resting directly on flanking **columns** or **piers**.

ashlar (p. 101) A highly finished, precisely cut block of stone. When laid in even **courses**, ashlar masonry creates a uniform face with fine joints. Often used as a facing on the visible exterior of a building, especially as a veneer for the **façade**. Also called **dressed stone**.

assemblage (p. 1040) Artwork created by gathering and manipulating two- and/or three-dimensional found objects.

astragal (p. 111) A thin convex decorative **molding**, often found on a Classical **entablature**, and usually decorated with a continuous row of beadlike circles.

atelier (p. 790) The studio or workshop of a master artist or craftsperson, often including junior associates and apprentices.

atmospheric perspective (p. 185) See under **perspective**.

atrial cross (p. 959) A cross placed in the **atrium** of a church. In Colonial America, used to mark a gathering and teaching place.

atrium (p. 160) An unroofed interior courtyard or room in a Roman house, sometimes having a pool or garden, sometimes surrounded by **columns**. Also: the open courtyard in front of a Christian church; or an entrance area in modern architecture.

automatism (p. 1072) A technique in which artists abandon the usual intellectual control over their brushes or pencils to allow the subconscious to create the artwork without rational interference.

avant-garde (p. 989) Term derived from the French military word meaning "before the group," or "vanguard." Avant-garde denotes those artists or concepts of a strikingly new, experimental, or radical nature for their time.

axis (p. xxviii) In pictures, an implied line around which elements are composed or arranged. In buildings, a dominant line around which parts of the structure are organized and along which human movement or attention is concentrated.

axis mundi (p. 305) A concept of an "axis of the world," which marks sacred sites and denotes a link between the human and celestial realms. For example, in South Asian art, the axis mundi can be marked by monumental free-standing decorative pillars.

baldacchino (p. 484) A canopy (whether suspended from the ceiling, projecting from a wall, or supported by columns) placed over an honorific or sacred space such as a throne or church altar.

bar tracery (p. 522) See under **tracery**.

barbarian (p. 152) A term used by the ancient Greeks and Romans to label all foreigners outside their cultural orbit (for example, Celts, Goths, Vikings). The word derives from an imitation of what the "barblings" of their language sounded like to those who could not understand it.

barrel vault (p. 190) See under **vault**.

bas-relief (p. 328) Another term for low relief ("bas" is the French word for "low"). See under **relief sculpture**.

basilica (p. 192) A large rectangular building. Often built with a **clerestory**, side **aisles** separated from the center **nave** by **colonnades**, and an **apse** at one or both ends. Originally Roman centers for administration, later adapted to Christian church use.

bay (p. 171) A unit of space defined by architectural elements such as **columns**, **piers**, and walls.

beehive tomb (p. 100) A **corbel-vaulted** tomb, conical in shape like a beehive, and covered by an earthen mound.

Benday dots (p. 1108) In modern printing and typesetting, the individual dots that, together with many others, make up lettering and images. Often machine- or computer-generated, the dots are very small and closely spaced to give the effect of density and richness of tone.

bilum (p. 880) Netted bags made mainly by women throughout the central highlands of New Guinea. The bags can be used for everyday purposes or even to carry the bones of the recently deceased as a sign of mourning.

biomorphic (p. 1073) Denoting the biologically or organically inspired shapes and forms that were routinely included in abstracted Modern art in the early twentieth century.

black-figure (p. 108) A technique of ancient Greek **ceramic** decoration in which black figures are painted on a red clay ground. Compare **red-figure**.

blackware (p. 869) A **ceramic** technique that produces pottery with a primarily black surface with **matte** and glossy patterns on the surface.

blind arcade (p. 794) See under **arcade**.

bodhisattva (p. 304) In Buddhism, a being who has attained enlightenment but chooses to remain in this world in order to help others advance spiritually. Also defined as a potential buddha.

Book of Hours (p. 562) A prayer book for private use, containing a calendar, services for the canonical hours, and sometimes special prayers.

boss (p. 450) A decorative knoblike element that can be found in many places, e.g. at the intersection of a Gothic **rib vault** or as a buttonlike projection on metalwork.

bracket, bracketing (p. 346) An architectural element that projects from a wall to support a horizontal part of a building, such as beams or the eaves of a roof.

buon fresco (p. 89) See under **fresco**.

burin (p. 602) A metal instrument used in **engraving** to cut lines into the metal plate. The sharp end of the burin is trimmed to give a diamond-shaped cutting point, while the other end is finished with a wooden handle that fits into the engraver's palm.

buttress, buttressing (p. 171) A projecting support built against an external wall, usually to counteract the lateral **thrust** of a **vault** or **arch** within. In Gothic church architecture, a **flying buttress** is an arched bridge above the **aisle** roof that extends from the upper **nave** wall, where the lateral thrust of the main vault is greatest, down to a solid **pier**.

cairn (p. 18) A pile of stones or earth and stones that served both as a prehistoric burial site and as a marker for underground tombs.

calligraphy (p. 279) Handwriting as an art form.

calotype (p. 987) The first photographic process utilizing negatives and paper positives; invented by William Henry Fox Talbot in the late 1830s.

calyx krater (p. 121) See under **krater**.

came (*pl.* **cames**) (p. 512) A lead strip used in the making of leaded or **stained-glass** windows. Cames have an indented groove on the sides into which individual pieces of glass are fitted to make the overall design.

cameo (p. 177) Gemstone, clay, glass, or shell having layers of color, carved in low relief (see under **relief sculpture**) to create an image and ground of different colors.

camera obscura (p. 762) An early cameralike device used in the Renaissance and later for recording images from the real world. It consists of a dark box (or room) with a hole in one side (sometimes fitted with a lens). The camera obscura operates when bright light shines through the hole, casting an upside-down image of an object outside onto the inside wall of the box.

canon of proportions (p. 52) A set of ideal mathematical ratios in art based on measurements, as in the proportional relationships between the basic elements of the human body.

canopic jar (p. 54) In ancient Egyptian culture, a special jar used to store the major organs of a body before embalming.

capital (p. 68) The sculpted block that tops a **column**. According to the **conventions** of the orders, capitals include different decorative elements (see **order**). A *historiated capital* is one displaying a figural composition and/or narrative scenes.

capriccio (*pl.* **capricci**) (p. 931) A painting or print of a fantastic, imaginary landscape, usually with architecture.

capstone (p. 18) The final, topmost stone in a **corbeled arch** or **vault**, which joins the sides and completes the structure.

cartoon (p. 512) A full-scale drawing of a design that will be executed in another **medium**, such as wall painting, **tapestry**, or **stained glass**.

cartouche (p. 189) A frame for a **hieroglyphic** inscription formed by a rope design surrounding an oval space. Used to signify a sacred or honored name. Also: in architecture, a decorative device or plaque, usually with a plain center used for inscriptions or epitaphs.

caryatid (p. 110) A sculpture of a draped female figure acting as a **column** supporting an **entablature**.

cassone (*pl.* **cassoni**) (p. 630) An Italian dowry chest, often highly decorated with carvings, paintings, inlaid designs, and gilt embellishments.

catacomb (p. 217) An underground cemetery consisting of tunnels on different levels, having niches for urns and **sarcophagi** and often incorporating rooms (*cubicula*).

cathedral (p. 222) The principal Christian church in a diocese, the bishop's administrative center and housing his throne (*cathedra*).

celadon (p. 362) A high-fired, transparent **glaze** of pale bluish-green hue whose principal coloring agent is an oxide of iron. In China and Korea, such glazes were typically applied over a pale gray **stoneware** body, though Chinese potters sometimes applied them over **porcelain** bodies during the Ming (1368–1644) and Qing (1644–1911) dynasties. Chinese potters invented celadon glazes and initiated the continuous production of celadon-glazed wares as early as the third century CE.

cella (p. 110) The principal interior room at the center of a Greek or Roman temple within which the cult statue was usually housed. Also called the **naos**.

celt (p. 387) A smooth, oblong stone or metal object, shaped like an axe-head.

cenotaph (p. 783) A funerary monument commemorating an individual or group buried elsewhere.

centering (p. 171) A temporary structure that supports a masonry **arch**, **vault**, or **dome** during construction until the mortar is fully dried and the masonry is self-sustaining.

central-plan building (p. 225) Any structure designed with a primary central space surrounded by symmetrical areas on each side, e.g., a **rotunda**.

ceramics (p. 20) A general term covering all types of wares made from fired clay.

chacmool (p. 400) In Maya sculpture, a half-reclining figure probably representing an offering bearer.

chaitya (p. 309) A type of Buddhist temple found in India. Often built in the form of a hall or **basilica**, a *chaitya* hall is highly decorated with sculpture and usually is carved from a cave or natural rock location. It houses a sacred shrine or **stupa** for worship.

chamfer (p. 793) The slanted surface produced when an angle is trimmed or beveled, common in building and metalwork.

chasing (p. 445) Ornamentation made on metal by incising or hammering the surface.

château (*pl.* **châteaux**) (p. 704) A French country house or residential castle. A *château fort* is a military castle incorporating defensive works such as towers and battlements.

chattri (p. 793) In Indian architecture, a decorative pavilion with an umbrella-shaped **dome**.

chevron (p. 360) A decorative or heraldic motif of repeated *V*s; a zigzag pattern.

chiaroscuro (p. 650) An Italian word designating the contrast of dark and light in a painting, drawing, or print. *Chiaroscuro* creates spatial depth and volumetric forms through gradations in the intensity of light and shadow.

choir (p. 454) The part of a church reserved for the clergy, monks, or nuns, either between the **transept** crossing and the **apse** or extending farther into the **nave**; separated from the rest of the church by screens or walls and fitted with stalls (seats).

cista (*pl.* **cistae**) (p. 159) Cylindrical containers used in antiquity by wealthy women as a case for toiletry articles such as a mirror.

clerestory (p. 59) In a **basilica**, the topmost zone of a wall with windows, extending above the **aisle** roofs. Provides direct light into the **nave**.

cloisonné (p. 262) An **enameling** technique in which artists affix wires or strips to a metal surface to delineate designs and create compartments (*cloisons*) that they subsequently fill with enamel.

cloister (p. 458) An enclosed space, open to the sky, especially within a monastery, surrounded by an **arcaded** walkway, often having a fountain and garden. Since the most important monastic buildings (e.g., dormitory, refectory, church) open off the cloister, it represents the center of the monastic world.

codex (*pl.* **codices**) (p. 249) A book, or a group of **manuscript** pages (folios), held together by stitching or other binding along one edge.

coffer (p. 198) A recessed decorative panel used to decorate ceilings or **vaults**. The use of coffers is called coffering.

coiling (p. 863) A technique in basketry. In coiled baskets a spiraling coil, braid, or rope of material is held in place by stitching or interweaving to create a permanent shape.

collage (p. 917) A composition made of cut and pasted scraps of materials, sometimes with lines or forms added by the artist.

colonnade (p. 69) A row of **columns**, supporting a straight **lintel** (as in a **porch** or **portico**) or a series of **arches** (an **arcade**).

colophon (p. 447) The data placed at the end of a book listing the book's author, publisher, illuminator, and other information related to its production. In East Asian **handscrolls**, the inscriptions which follow the painting are also called colophons.

column (p. 111) An architectural element used for support and/or decoration. Consists of a rounded or polygonal vertical **shaft** placed on a base and topped by a decorative **capital**. In Classical architecture, columns are built in accordance with the rules of one of the architectural **orders**. They can be free-standing or attached to a background wall (**engaged**).

combine (p. 1100) Term used by Robert Rauschenberg to describe his works that combined painting and nontraditional sculptural elements.

commodification (p. 1100) Treating goods, services, ideas, or art merely as things to be bought or sold.

complementary color (p. 1011) The primary and secondary colors across from each other on the color wheel (red and green, blue and orange, yellow and purple). When juxtaposed, the intensity of both colors increases. When mixed together, they negate each other to make a neutral gray–brown.

Composite order (p. 162) See under **order**.

composite pose or **image** (p. 11) Combining different viewpoints within a single representation.

composition (p. xxv) The overall arrangement, organizing design, or structure of a work of art.

conch (p. 239) A halfdome.

connoisseur (p. 294) A French word meaning "an expert," and signifying one who studies and evaluates art based primarily on formal, visual, and stylistic analysis. A connoisseur studies the style and technique of an object to assess its relative quality and identify its maker through visual comparison with other works of secure authorship. See also **Formalism**.

continuous narrative (p. 249) See under **narrative image**.

contrapposto (p. 124) Italian term meaning "set against," used to describe the Classical convention of representing human figures with opposing alternations of tension and relaxation on either side of a central **axis** to give figures a sense of the potential for movement.

convention (p. 31) A traditional way of representing forms.

corbel, corbeling (p. 18) An early roofing and arching technique in which each **course** of stone projects slightly beyond the previous layer (a corbel) until the uppermost corbels meet; see also under **arch**. Also: **brackets** that project from a wall.

corbeled vault (p. 101) See under **vault**.

Corinthian order (p. 110) See under **order**.

cornice (p. 111) The uppermost section of a Classical **entablature**. More generally, a horizontally projecting element found at the top of a building wall or **pedestal**. A *raking cornice* is formed by the junction of two slanted cornices, most often found in **pediments**.

course (p. 101) A horizontal layer of stone used in building.

crenellation, crenellated (p. 44) Alternating high and low sections of a wall, giving a notched appearance and creating permanent defensive shields on top of fortified buildings.

crocket (p. 598) A stylized leaf used as decoration along the outer angle of spires, pinnacles, gables, and around **capitals** in Gothic architecture.

cruciform (p. 233) Of anything that is cross-shaped, as in the cruciform plan of a church.

cubiculum (*pl.* **cubicula**) (p. 224) A small private room for burials in a **catacomb**.

cuneiform (p. 29) An early form of writing with wedge-shaped marks impressed into wet clay with a **stylus**, primarily used by ancient Mesopotamians.

curtain wall (p. 1059) A wall in a building that does not support any of the weight of the structure.

cyclopean (p. 96) A method of construction using huge blocks of rough-hewn stone. Any large-scale, monumental building project that impresses by sheer size. Named after the Cyclopes (sing. Cyclops), one-eyed giants of legendary strength in Greek myths.

cylinder seal (p. 34) A small cylindrical stone decorated with **incised** patterns. When rolled across soft clay or wax, the resulting raised pattern or design served in Mesopotamian and Indus Valley cultures as an identifying signature.

dado (*pl.* **dadoes**) (p. 162) The lower part of a wall, differentiated in some way (by a **molding** or different coloring or paneling) from the upper section.

daguerreotype (p. 986) An early photographic process that makes a positive print on a light-sensitized copperplate; invented and marketed in 1839 by Louis-Jacques-Mandé Daguerre.

dendrochronology (p. xxxiii) The dating of wood based on the patterns of the tree's growth rings.

desert varnish (p. 411) A naturally occurring coating that turns rock faces into dark surfaces. Artists would draw images by scraping through the dark surface and revealing the color of the underlying rock. Extensively used in southwest North America.

diptych (p. xxxiii) Two panels of equal size (usually decorated with paintings or reliefs) hinged together.

dogu (p. 366) Small human figurines made in Japan during the Jomon period. Shaped from clay, the figures have exaggerated expressions and are in contorted poses. They were probably used in religious rituals.

dolmen (p. 17) A prehistoric structure made up of two or more large upright stones supporting a large, flat, horizontal slab or slabs.

dome (p. 190) A rounded **vault**, usually over a circular space. Consists of curved masonry and can vary in shape from hemispherical to bulbous to ovoidal. May use a supporting vertical wall (**drum**), from which the vault springs, and may be crowned by an open space (**oculus**) and/or an exterior **lantern**. When a dome is built over a square space, an intermediate element is required to make the transition to a circular drum. There are two systems. A dome on **pendentives** incorporates arched, sloping intermediate sections of wall that carry the weight and **thrust** of the dome to heavily **buttressed** supporting **piers**. A dome on **squinches** uses an arch built into the wall (squinch) in the upper corners of the space to carry the weight of the dome across the corners of the square space below. A halfdome or **conch** may cover a semicircular space.

domino construction (p. 1059) System of building construction introduced by the architect Le Corbusier in which reinforced concrete floor slabs are floated on six free-standing posts placed as if at the positions of the six dots on a domino playing piece.

Doric order (p. 110) See **order**.

dressed stone (p. 87) Another term for **ashlar**.

drillwork (p. 190) The technique of using a drill for the creation of certain effects in sculpture.

drum (p. 111) The circular wall that supports a **dome**. Also: a segment of the circular **shaft** of a **column**.

drypoint (p. 759) An **intaglio** printmaking process by which a metal (usually copper) plate is directly inscribed with a pointed instrument (**stylus**). The resulting design of scratched lines is inked, wiped, and printed. Also: the print made by this process.

earthenware (p. 21) A low-fired, opaque **ceramic** ware, employing humble clays that are naturally heat-resistant and remain porous after firing unless **glazed**. Earthenware occurs in a range of earth-toned colors, from white and tan to gray and black, with tan predominating.

earthwork (p. 402) Usually very large-scale, outdoor artwork that is produced by altering the natural environment.

echinus (p. 111) A cushionlike circular element found below the **abacus** of a Doric **capital**. Also: a similarly shaped **molding** (usually with egg-and-dart motifs) underneath the **volutes** of an Ionic capital.

electronic spin resonance (p. 13) Method that uses magnetic field and microwave irradiation to date material such as tooth enamel and its surrounding soil.

elevation (p. 110) The arrangement, proportions, and details of any vertical side or face of a building. Also: an architectural drawing showing an exterior or interior wall of a building.

embroidery (p. 403) Stitches applied in a decorative pattern on top of an already-woven fabric ground.

en plein air (p. 1003) French term (meaning "in the open air") describing the Impressionist practice of painting outdoors so artists could have direct access to the fleeting effects of light and atmosphere while working.

enamel (p. 259) Powdered, then molten, glass applied to a metal surface, and used by artists to create designs. After firing, the glass forms an opaque or transparent substance that fuses to the metal background. Also: an object created by the enameling technique. See also *cloisonné*.

encaustic (p. 1097) A painting **medium** using pigments mixed with hot wax.

engaged (p. 172) Of an architectural feature, usually a **column**, attached to a wall.

engraving (p. 602) An **intaglio** printmaking process of inscribing an image, design, or letters onto a metal or wood surface from which a print is made. An engraving is usually drawn with a sharp implement (**burin**) directly onto the surface of the plate. Also: the print made from this process.

entablature (p. 110) In the Classical **orders**, the horizontal elements above the **columns** and **capitals**. The entablature consists of, from bottom to top, an **architrave**, a **frieze**, and a **cornice**.

entasis (p. 110) A slight swelling of the **shaft** of a Greek **column**. The optical illusion of entasis makes the column appear from a distance to be straight.

esquisse (p. 962) French for "sketch." A quickly executed drawing or painting conveying the overall idea for a finished painting.

etching (p. 759) An **intaglio** printmaking process in which a metal plate is coated with acid-resistant resin and then inscribed with a **stylus** in a design, revealing the plate below. The plate is then immersed in acid, and the exposed metal of the design is eaten away by the acid. The resin is removed, leaving the design etched permanently into the metal and the plate ready to be inked, wiped, and printed.

Eucharist (p. 222) The central rite of the Christian Church, from the Greek word for "thanksgiving." Also known as the Mass or Holy Communion, it reenacts Christ's sacrifice on the cross and commemorates the Last Supper. According to traditional Catholic Christian belief, consecrated bread and wine become the body and blood of Christ; in Protestant belief, bread and wine symbolize the body and blood.

exedra (*pl.* **exedrae**) (p. 198) In architecture, a semicircular niche. On a small scale, often used as decoration, whereas larger exedrae can form interior spaces (such as an **apse**).

expressionism (p. 153) Artistic styles in which aspects of works of art are exaggerated to evoke subjective emotions rather than to portray objective reality or elicit a rational response.

façade (p. 53) The face or front wall of a building.

faience (p. 89) Type of **ceramic** covered with colorful, opaque glazes that form a smooth, impermeable surface. First developed in ancient Egypt.

fang ding (p. 339) A square or rectangular bronze vessel with four legs. The *fang ding* was used for ritual offerings in ancient China during the Shang dynasty.

fête galante (p. 926) A subject in painting depicting well-dressed people at leisure in a park or country setting. It is most often associated with eighteenth-century French Rococo painting.

filigree (p. 93) Delicate, lacelike ornamental work.

fillet (p. 111) The flat ridge between the carved-out **flutes** of a **column shaft**.

finial (p. 306) A knoblike architectural decoration usually found at the top point of a spire, pinnacle, canopy, or gable. Also found on furniture. Also the ornamental top of a staff.

flutes (p. 111) In architecture, evenly spaced, rounded parallel vertical grooves incised on **shafts** of **columns** or on columnar elements such as **pilasters**.

flying buttress (p. 516) See under **buttress**.

flying gallop (p. 89) A non-naturalistic pose in which animals are depicted hovering above the ground with legs fully extended backward and forward to signify that they are running.

foreshortening (p. xxvii) The illusion created on a flat surface by which figures and objects appear to recede or project sharply into space. Accomplished according to the rules of **perspective**.

formal analysis (p. xxv) An exploration of the visual character that artists bring to their works through the expressive use of elements such as line, form, color, and light, and through its overall structure or composition.

Formalism (p. 1089) An approach to the understanding, appreciation, and valuation of art based almost solely on considerations of form. The Formalist's approach tends to regard an artwork as independent of its time and place of making.

forum (p. 178) A Roman town center; site of temples and administrative buildings and used as a market or gathering area for the citizens.

fresco (p. 83) A painting technique in which water-based pigments are applied to a plaster surface. If the plaster is painted when wet, the color is absorbed by the plaster, becoming a permanent part of the wall (*buon fresco*). *Fresco secco* is created by painting on dried plaster, and the color may eventually flake off. Murals made by both these techniques are called frescos.

frieze (p. 110) The middle element of an **entablature**, between the **architrave** and the **cornice**. Usually decorated with sculpture, painting, or **moldings**. Also: any continuous flat band with **relief sculpture** or painted decoration.

frottage (p. 1072) A design produced by laying a piece of paper over a textured surface and rubbing with charcoal or other soft **medium**.

fusuma (p. 834) Sliding doors covered with paper, used in traditional Japanese construction. *Fusuma* are often highly decorated with paintings and colored backgrounds.

gallery (p. 241) A roofed passageway with one or both of its long sides open to the air. In church architecture, the story found above the side **aisles** of a church or across the width at the end of the **nave** or **transepts**, usually open to and overlooking the area below. Also: a building or hall in which art is displayed or sold.

garbhagriha (p. 306) From the Sanskrit word meaning "womb chamber," a small room or shrine in a Hindu temple containing its principal holy image.

genre painting (p. 727) A term used to loosely categorize paintings depicting scenes of everyday life, including (among others) domestic interiors, parties, inn scenes, and street scenes.

geoglyph (p. 402) Earthen design on a colossal scale, often created in a landscape as if to be seen from an aerial viewpoint.

gesso (p. 556) A primer made from glue, gypsum, and/or chalk, used as the ground of a wood panel or the priming layer of a canvas. Provides a smooth surface for painting.

gilding (p. 91) The application of paper-thin gold leaf or gold pigment to an object made from another **medium** (for example, a sculpture or painting). Usually used as a decorative finishing detail.

giornata (*pl.* **giornate**) (p. 551) Adopted from the Italian term meaning "a day's work," a *giornata* is the section of a **fresco** plastered and painted in a single day.

glazing (p. 613) In **ceramics**, an outermost layer of vitreous liquid (**glaze**) that, upon firing, renders the ware waterproof and forms a decorative surface. In painting, a technique used with oil **media** in which a transparent layer of paint (glaze) is laid over another, usually lighter, painted or glazed area. In architecture, the process of filling openings in a building with windows of clear or **stained glass**.

gold leaf (p. 47) Paper-thin sheets of hammered gold that are used in **gilding**. In some cases (such as Byzantine **icons**), also used as a ground for paintings.

gopura (p. 787) The towering gateway to an Indian Hindu temple complex.

Grand Manner (p. 940) An elevated style of painting popular in the eighteenth century in which the artist looked to the ancients and to the Renaissance for inspiration; for portraits as well as history painting, the artist would adopt the poses, compositions, and attitudes of Renaissance and antique models.

Grand Tour (p. 929) Popular during the eighteenth and nineteenth centuries, an extended tour of cultural sites in France and Italy intended to finish the education of a young upper-class person primarily from Britain or North America.

granulation (p. 93) A technique of decoration in which metal granules, or tiny metal balls, are fused onto a metal surface.

graphic arts (p. 711) A term referring to those arts that are drawn or printed and that utilize paper as the primary support.

grattage (p. 1073) A pattern created by scraping off layers of paint from a canvas laid over a textured surface. Compare **frottage**.

grid (p. 65) A system of regularly spaced horizontally and vertically crossed lines that gives regularity to an architectural plan or in the composition of a work of art. Also: in painting, a grid is used to allow designs to be enlarged or transferred easily.

grisaille (p. 552) A style of monochromatic painting in shades of gray. Also: a painting made in this style.

groin vault (p. 190) See under **vault**.

grozing (p. 512) Chipping away at the edges of a piece of glass to achieve the precise shape needed for inclusion in the composition of a **stained-glass** window.

guild (p. 425) An association of artists or craftspeople. Medieval and Renaissance guilds had great economic power, as they controlled the marketing of their members' products and provided economic protection, political solidarity, and training in the craft to its members. The painters' guild was usually dedicated to St. Luke, their patron saint.

hall church (p. 532) A church with **nave** and **aisles** of the same height, giving the impression of a large, open hall.

halo (p. 217) A circle of light that surrounds and frames the heads of emperors and holy figures to signify their power and/or sanctity. Also known as a nimbus.

handscroll (p. 347) A long, narrow, horizontal painting or text (or combination thereof) common in Chinese and Japanese art and of a size intended for individual use. A handscroll is stored wrapped tightly around a wooden pin and is unrolled for viewing or reading.

hanging scroll (p. 810) In Chinese and Japanese art, a vertical painting or text mounted within sections of silk. At the top is a semicircular rod; at the bottom is a round dowel. Hanging scrolls are kept rolled and tied except for special occasions, when they are hung for display, contemplation, or commemoration.

haniwa (p. 366) Pottery forms, including cylinders, buildings, and human figures, that were placed on top of Japanese tombs or burial mounds during the Kofun period (300–552 C.E.).

Happening (p. 1103) Term coined by Allan Kaprow in the 1960s to describe artworks incorporating elements of performance, theater, and visual images. Organized without a specific narrative or intent and with audience participation, the event proceeded according to chance and individual improvisation.

hemicycle (p. 525) A semicircular interior space or structure.

henge (p. 18) A circular area enclosed by stones or wood posts set up by Neolithic peoples. It is usually bounded by a ditch and raised embankment.

hierarchic scale (p. 27) The use of differences in size to indicate relative importance. For example, with human figures, the larger the figure, the greater her or his importance.

hieratic (p. 495) Highly stylized, severe, and detached, often in relation to a strict religious tradition.

hieroglyph (p. 53) Picture writing; words and ideas rendered in the form of pictorial symbols.

high relief (p. 312) See under **relief sculpture**.

historiated capital (p. 497) See under **capital**.

historicism (p. 981) The strong consciousness of and attention to the institutions, themes, styles, and forms of the past, made accessible by historical research, textual study, and archaeology.

history paintings (p. 942) Paintings based on historical, mythological, or biblical narratives. Once considered the noblest form of art, history paintings generally convey a high moral or intellectual idea and are often painted in a grand pictorial style.

horizon line (p. 581) A horizontal "line" formed by the implied meeting point of earth and sky. In linear perspective (under **perspective**), the **vanishing point** or points are located on this "line."

horseshoe arch (p. 277) See under **arch**.

hue (p. 79) Pure color. The saturation or intensity of the hue depends on the purity of the color. Its value depends on its lightness or darkness.

hydria (p. 142) A large ancient Greek or Roman jar with three handles (horizontal ones at both sides and one vertical at the back), used for storing water.

hypostyle hall (p. 66) A large interior room characterized by many closely spaced **columns** that support its roof.

icon (p. 250) An image representing a sacred figure or event in the Byzantine (later the Orthodox) Church. Icons are venerated by the faithful, who believe their prayers are transmitted through them to God.

iconic image (p. 217) A picture that expresses or embodies an intangible concept or idea.

iconoclasm (p. 251) The banning and/or destruction of images, especially **icons** and religious art. Iconoclasm in eighth- and ninth-century Byzantium and sixteenth- and seventeenth-century Protestant territories arose from differing beliefs about the power, meaning, function, and purpose of imagery in religion.

iconography (p. xxix) Identifying and studying the subject matter and **conventional** symbols in works of art.

iconology (p. xxx) Interpreting works of art as embodiments of cultural situation by placing them within broad social, political, religious, and intellectual contexts.

iconophile (p. 251) From the Greek for "lover of images." In periods of **iconoclasm**, iconophiles advocate the continued use of sacred images.

idealization (p. 136) A process in art through which artists strive to make their forms and figures attain perfection, based on pervading cultural values and/or their own personal ideals.

illumination (p. 249) A painting on paper or parchment used as an illustration and/or decoration in a **manuscript** or **album**. Usually richly colored, often supplemented by gold and other precious materials. The artists are referred to as illuminators. Also: the technique of decorating manuscripts with such paintings.

impasto (p. 761) Thick applications of paint that give a painting a palpable surface texture.

impluvium (p. 180) A pool under a roof opening that collected rainwater in the **atrium** of a Roman house.

impost block (p. 171) A block of masonry imposed between the top of a **pier** or above the **capital** of a **column** in order to provide extra support at the springing of an **arch**.

incising (p. 120) A technique in which a design or inscription is cut into a hard surface with a sharp instrument. Such a surface is said to be incised.

ink painting (p. 826) A monochromatic style of painting developed in China, using black ink with gray washes.

inlay (p. 29) To set pieces of a material or materials into a surface to form a design. Also: material used in or decoration formed by this technique.

installation, installation art (p. 1066) Contemporary art created for a specific site, especially a gallery or outdoor area, that creates a complete and controlled environment.

intaglio (p. 602) A technique in which the design is carved out of the surface of an object, such as an engraved seal stone. In the **graphic arts**, intaglio includes **engraving**, **etching**, and **drypoint**—all processes in which ink transfers to paper from incised, ink-filled lines cut into a metal plate.

intarsia (p. 636) Technique of **inlay** decoration using variously colored woods.

intuitive perspective (p. 182) See under **perspective**.

Ionic order (p. 110) See under **order**.

iwan (p. 283) In Islamic architecture, a large, vaulted chamber with a monumental arched opening on one side.

jamb (p. 491) In architecture, the vertical element found on both sides of an opening in a wall, and supporting an **arch** or **lintel**.

Japonisme (p. 1010) A style in French and American nineteenth-century art that was highly influenced by Japanese art, especially prints.

jasperware (p. 935) A fine-grained, unglazed, white **ceramic** developed in the eighteenth century by Josiah Wedgwood, often with raised designs remaining white above a background surface colored by metallic oxides.

Jataka tales (p. 308) In Buddhism, stories associated with the previous lives of Shakyamuni, the historical Buddha.

joggled voussoirs (p. 279) Interlocking **voussoirs** in an **arch** or **lintel**, often of contrasting materials for colorful effect.

joined-block sculpture (p. 376) Large-scale wooden sculpture constructed by a method developed in Japan. The entire work is made from smaller hollow blocks, each individually carved, and assembled when complete. The joined-block technique allowed production of larger sculpture, as the multiple joints alleviate the problems of drying and cracking found with sculpture carved from a single block.

kantharos (p. 121) A type of ancient Greek goblet with two large handles and a wide mouth.

keep (p. 490) The innermost and strongest structure or central tower of a medieval castle, sometimes used as living quarters, as well as for defense. Also called a donjon.

kente (p. 898) A cloth made by the Asante peoples of Ghana. It is woven in long, narrow strips featuring complex, irregular, geometric patterns. The strips are then sewn together to make a large rectangular fabric, which is worn by wrapping it around the body under the arms with one end draped up over one shoulder.

key block (p. 843) The master block in the production of a colored **woodblock print**, which requires different blocks for each color. The key block is a flat piece of wood upon which the outlines for the entire design of the print were first drawn on its surface and then all but these outlines were carved away with a knife. These outlines serve as a guide for the accurate **registration** or alignment of the other blocks needed to add colors to specific parts of a print.

keystone (p. 171) The topmost **voussoir** at the center of an **arch**, and the last block to be placed. The pressure of this block holds the arch together. Often of a larger size and/or decorated.

kiln (p. 21) An oven designed to produce enough heat for the baking, or firing, of clay, for the melting of the glass used in **enamel** work, and for the fixing of vitreous paint on **stained glass**.

kiva (p. 409) A subterranean, circular room used as a ceremonial center in some Native American cultures.

kondo (p. 370) The main hall inside a Japanese Buddhist temple where the images of Buddha are housed.

korambo (p. 879) A ceremonial or spirit house in Pacific cultures, reserved for the men of a village and used as a meeting place as well as to hide religious artifacts from the uninitiated.

kore (*pl.* *korai*) (p. 116) An Archaic Greek statue of a young woman.

koru (p. 886) A design depicting a curling stalk with a bulb at the end that resembles a young tree fern; often found in Maori art.

kouros (*pl.* *kouroi*) (p. 116) An Archaic Greek statue of a young man or boy.

kowhaiwhai (p. 886) Painted curvilinear patterns often found in Maori art.

krater (p. 101) An ancient Greek vessel for mixing wine and water, with many subtypes that each have a distinctive shape. *Calyx krater:* a bell-shaped vessel with handles near the base that resembles a flower calyx. *Volute krater:* a krater with handles shaped like scrolls.

Kufic (p. 280) An ornamental, angular Arabic script.

kylix (p. 124) A shallow ancient Greek cup, used for drinking, with a wide mouth and small handles near the rim.

lacquer (p. 840) A type of hard, glossy surface varnish, originally developed for use on objects in East Asian cultures, made from the sap of the Asian sumac or from shellac, a resinous secretion from the lac insect. Lacquer can be layered and manipulated or combined with pigments and other materials for various decorative effects.

lakshana (p. 311) The 32 marks of the historical Buddha. The *lakshana* include, among others, the Buddha's golden body, his long arms, the wheel impressed on his palms and the soles of his feet, the *urna* between his eyes, and the *ushnisha* on his head.

lamassu (p. 41) Supernatural guardian-protector of ancient Near Eastern palaces and throne rooms, often represented sculpturally as a combination of the bearded head of a man, powerful body of a lion or bull, wings of an eagle, and the horned headdress of a god, usually possessing five legs.

lancet (p. 516) A tall, narrow window crowned by a sharply pointed arch, typically found in Gothic architecture.

lantern (p. 476) A turretlike structure situated on a roof, vault, or dome, with windows that allow light into the space below.

lekythos (*pl.* **lekythoi**) (p. 144) A slim ancient Greek oil vase with one handle and a narrow mouth.

linear perspective (p. 607) See under **perspective**.

linga **shrine** (p. 319) A place of worship centered on an object or representation in the form of a phallus or column (the *linga*), which symbolizes the power of the Hindu god Shiva.

lintel (p. 18) A horizontal element of any material carried by two or more vertical supports to form an opening.

literati painting (p. 807) A style of painting that reflects the taste of the educated class of East Asian intellectuals and scholars. Characteristics include an appreciation for the antique, small scale, and an intimate connection between maker and audience.

lithography (p. 969) Process of making a print (lithograph) from a design drawn on a flat stone block with greasy crayon. Ink is applied to the wet stone and adheres only to the greasy areas of the design.

loggia (p. 546) Italian term for a **gallery**. Often used as a corridor between buildings or around a courtyard, a loggia usually features an **arcade** or **colonnade**.

longitudinal-plan building (p. 225) Any structure designed with a rectangular shape and a longitudinal axis. In a cross-shaped building, the main arm of the building would be longer than any arms that cross it. For example, a **basilica**.

lost-wax casting (p. 36) A method of casting metal, such as bronze. A wax model is covered with clay and plaster, then fired, thus melting the model and leaving a hollow form. Molten metal is then poured into the hollow space and slowly cooled. When the hardened clay and plaster exterior shell is removed, a solid metal form remains to be smoothed and polished.

low relief (p. 40) See under **relief sculpture**.

lunette (p. 223) A semicircular wall area, framed by an **arch** over a door or window. Can be either plain or decorated.

lusterware (p. 281) Pottery decorated with metallic **glazes**.

madrasa (p. 283) An Islamic institution of higher learning, where teaching is focused on theology and law.

maenad (p. 105) In ancient Greece, a female devotee of the wine god Dionysos who participated in orgiastic rituals. Often depicted with swirling drapery to indicate wild movement or dance. Also called a Bacchante, after Bacchus, the Roman equivalent of Dionysos.

majolica (p. 585) Pottery painted with a tin **glaze** that, when fired, gives a lustrous and colorful surface.

mandala (p. 307) An image of the cosmos represented by an arrangement of circles or concentric geometric shapes containing diagrams or images. Used for meditation and contemplation by Buddhists.

mandapa (p. 306) In a Hindu temple, an open hall dedicated to ritual worship.

mandorla (p. 248) Light encircling, or emanating from, the entire figure of a sacred person.

manuscript (p. 248) A hand-written book or document.

maqsura (p. 277) An enclosure in a Muslim **mosque**, near the *mihrab*, designated for dignitaries.

martyrium (*pl.* **martyria**) (p. 242) A church, chapel, or shrine built over the grave of a Christian martyr.

mastaba (p. 54) A flat-topped, one-story structure with slanted walls built over an ancient Egyptian underground tomb.

matte (p. 585) Of a smooth surface that is without shine or luster.

mausoleum (p. 177) A monumental building used as a tomb. Named after the tomb of King Mausolos erected at Halikarnassos around 350 B.C.E.

medallion (p. 224) Any round ornament or decoration. Also: a large medal.

medium (*pl.* **media**) (p. xxv) The material from which a work of art is made.

megalith (*adj.* **megalithic**) (p. 17) A large stone used in some prehistoric architecture.

megaron (p. 95) The main hall of a Mycenaean palace or grand house.

memento mori (p. 925) From Latin for "remember that you must die." An object, such as a skull or extinguished candle, typically found in a *vanitas* image, symbolizing the transience of life.

menorah (p. 188) A Jewish lampstand with seven or nine branches; the nine-branched menorah is used during the celebration of Hanukkah. Representations of the seven-branched menorah, once used in the Temple of Jerusalem, became a symbol of Judaism.

metope (p. 111) The carved or painted rectangular panel between the **triglyphs** of a Doric **frieze**.

mihrab (p. 269) A recess or niche that distinguishes the wall oriented toward Mecca (*qibla*) in a **mosque**.

millefiori (p. 447) A glassmaking technique in which rods of differently colored glass are fused in a long bundle that is subsequently sliced to produce disks or beads with small-scale, multicolor patterns. The term derives from the Italian for "a thousand flowers."

minaret (p. 274) A tower on or near a **mosque** from which Muslims are called to prayer five times a day.

minbar (p. 269) A high platform or pulpit in a **mosque**.

miniature (p. 249) Anything small. In painting, miniatures may be illustrations within **albums** or **manuscripts** or intimate portraits.

mirador (p. 286) In Spanish and Islamic palace architecture, a very large window or room with windows, and sometimes balconies, providing views to interior courtyards or the exterior landscape.

mithuna (p. 310) The amorous male and female couples in Buddhist sculpture, usually found at the entrance to a sacred building. The *mithuna* symbolizes the harmony and fertility of life.

moai (p. 889) Statues found in Polynesia, carved from tufa, a yellowish brown volcanic stone, and depicting the human form. Nearly 1,000 of these statues have been found on the island of Rapa Nui but their significance has been a matter of speculation.

modeling (p. xxv) In painting, the process of creating the illusion of three-dimensionality on a two-dimensional surface by use of light and shade. In sculpture, the process of molding a three-dimensional form out of a malleable substance.

module (p. 351) A segment or portion of a repeated design. Also: a basic building block.

molding (p. 323) A shaped or sculpted strip with varying contours and patterns. Used as decoration on architecture, furniture, frames, and other objects.

mortise-and-tenon (p. 19) A method of joining two elements. A projecting pin (tenon) on one element fits snugly into a hole designed for it (mortise) on the other.

mosaic (p. 148) Image formed by arranging small colored stone or glass pieces (**tesserae**) and affixing them to a hard, stable surface.

mosque (p. 269) A building used for communal Islamic worship.

Mozarabic (p. 455) Of an eclectic style practiced in Christian medieval Spain when much of the Iberian peninsula was ruled by Islamic dynasties.

mudra (p. 312) A symbolic hand gesture in Buddhist art that denotes certain behaviors, actions, or feelings.

mullion (p. 522) A slender straight or curving bar that divides a window into subsidiary sections to create **tracery**.

muqarna (p. 286) In Islamic architecture, one of the nichelike components, often stacked in tiers to mark the transition between flat and rounded surfaces and often found on the **vault** of a **dome**.

naos (p. 241) The principal room in a temple or church. In ancient architecture, the **cella**. In a Byzantine church, the **nave** and **sanctuary**.

narrative image (p. 217) A picture that recounts an event drawn from a story, either factual (e.g. biographical) or fictional. In **continuous narrative**, multiple scenes from the same story appear within a single compositional frame.

narthex (p. 222) The vestibule or entrance porch of a church.

nave (p. 192) The central space of a church, two or three stories high and usually flanked by **aisles**.

ndop (p. 900) A Kikuba (Kuba) term meaning "statue." It is sculpted of wood to commemorate a Kuba king (*nyim*) and the role he serves in Kuba society.

necropolis (p. 54) A large cemetery or burial area; literally a "city of the dead."

nemes headdress (p. 51) The royal headdress of ancient Egypt.

niello (p. 93) A metal technique in which a black sulfur **alloy** is rubbed into fine lines engraved into metal (usually gold or silver). When heated, the alloy becomes fused with the surrounding metal and provides contrasting detail.

oculus (*pl.* **oculi**) (p. 190) In architecture, a circular opening. Usually found either as windows or at the apex of a **dome**. When at the top of a dome, an oculus is either open to the sky or covered by a decorative exterior **lantern**.

odalisque (p. 968) Turkish word for "harem slave girl" or "concubine."

oil paint (p. 585) Pigments suspended in a **medium** of oil and used for painting. Oil paint has particular properties that allow for greater ease of working: among others, a slow drying time (which allows for corrections), and a great range of relative opaqueness of paint layers (which permits a high degree of detail and luminescence).

oinochoe (p. 128) An ancient Greek jug used for wine.

olpe (p. 107) Any ancient Greek vessel without a spout.

one-point perspective (p. 264) See under **perspective**.

orant (p. 222) Of a standing figure represented praying with outstretched and upraised arms.

oratory (p. 233) A small chapel.

order (p. 111) A system of proportions in Classical architecture that includes every aspect of the building's plan, elevation, and decorative system. *Composite*: a combination of the Ionic and the Corinthian orders. The **capital** combines **acanthus** leaves with **volute** scrolls. *Corinthian*: the most ornate of the orders, the Corinthian includes a **base** and a **fluted column shaft** with a capital elaborately decorated with acanthus leaf carvings. Its **entablature** consists of an **architrave** decorated with **moldings**, a **frieze** often containing **relief sculpture**, and a **cornice** with **dentils**. *Doric*: the column shaft of the Doric order can be fluted or smooth-surfaced and has no base. The Doric capital consists of an undecorated **echinus** and **abacus**. The Doric entablature has a plain architrave, a frieze with **metopes**

and **triglyphs**, and a simple cornice. *Ionic*: the column of the Ionic order has a base, a fluted shaft, and a capital decorated with volutes. The Ionic entablature consists of an architrave of three panels and moldings, a frieze usually containing sculpted relief ornament, and a cornice with dentils. *Tuscan*: a variation of Doric characterized by a smooth-surfaced column shaft with a base, a plain architrave, and an undecorated frieze. *Colossal* or giant: any of the above built on a large scale, rising through two or more stories in height and often raised from the ground on a **pedestal**.

Orientalism (p. 982) A fascination with Middle Eastern cultures that inspired eclectic nineteenth-century European fantasies of exotic life that often formed the subject of paintings.

orthogonal (p. 141) Any line running back into the represented space of a picture perpendicular to the imagined **picture plane**. In **linear perspective**, all orthogonals converge at a single **vanishing point** in the picture and are the basis for a **grid** that maps out the internal space of the image. An orthogonal plan is any plan for a building or city that is based exclusively on right angles, such as the grid plan of many major cities.

pagoda (p. 352) An East Asian **reliquary** tower built with successively smaller, repeated stories. Each story is usually marked by an elaborate projecting roof.

painterly (p. 257) A style of painting which emphasizes the techniques and surface effects of brushwork (also color, light, and shade).

palace complex (p. 41) A group of buildings used for living and governing by a ruler and his or her supporters, usually fortified.

palazzo (p. 614) Italian term for palace, used for any large urban dwelling.

palette (p. 184) A hand-held support used by artists for arranging colors and mixing paint during the process of painting. Also: the choice of a range of colors used by an artist in a particular work, as typical of his or her style. In ancient Egypt, a flat stone used to grind and prepare makeup.

panel painting (p. xxxvii) Any painting executed on a wood support, usually planed to provide a smooth surface. A panel can consist of several boards joined together.

parchment (p. 249) A writing surface made from treated skins of animals. Very fine parchment is known as **vellum**.

parterre (p. 772) An ornamental, highly regimented flowerbed; especially as an element of the ornate gardens of a seventeenth-century palace or **château**.

passage grave (p. 18) A prehistoric tomb under a **cairn**, reached by a long, narrow, slab-lined access passageway or passageways.

pastel (p. 930) Dry pigment, chalk, and gum in stick or crayon form. Also: a work of art made with pastels.

pedestal (p. 110) A platform or base supporting a sculpture or other monument. Also: the block found below the base of a Classical **column** (or **colonnade**), serving to raise the entire element off the ground.

pediment (p. 110) A triangular gable found over major architectural elements such as Classical Greek **porticos**, windows, or doors. Formed by an **entablature** and the ends of a sloping roof or a raking **cornice**. A similar architectural element is often used decoratively above a door or window, sometimes with a curved upper **molding**. A *broken pediment* is a variation on the traditional pediment, with an open space at the center of the topmost angle and/or the horizontal cornice.

pendant (also **pendent**) (p. 652) One of a pair of artworks meant to be seen in relation to each other as a set.

pendentive (p. 241) The concave triangular section of a **vault** that forms the transition between a square or polygonal space and the circular base of a **dome**.

performance art (p. 1103) Works of art that are performed live by the artist and sometimes involve audience participation.

peristyle (p. 66) In Greek architecture, a surrounding **colonnade**. A peristyle building is surrounded on the exterior by a colonnade. Also: a peristyle court is an open colonnaded courtyard, often having a pool and garden.

perspective (p. xxiii) A system for representing three-dimensional space on a two-dimensional surface. *Atmospheric* or *aerial perspective*: a method of rendering the effect of spatial distance by subtle variations in color and clarity of representation. *Intuitive perspective*: a method of giving the impression of recession by visual instinct, not by the use of an overall system or program. *Oblique perspective*: an intuitive spatial system in which a building or room is placed with one corner in the **picture plane**, and the other parts of the structure recede to an imaginary **vanishing point** on its other side. Oblique perspective is not a comprehensive, mathematical system. *One-point* and multiple-point perspective (also called linear, scientific, or mathematical perspective): a method of creating the illusion of three-dimensional space on a two-dimensional surface by delineating a **horizon line** and multiple **orthogonal** lines. These recede to meet at one or more points on the horizon (vanishing point), giving the appearance of spatial depth. Called scientific or mathematical because its use requires some knowledge of geometry and mathematics, as well as optics. *Reverse perspective*: a Byzantine perspective theory in which the orthogonals or rays of sight do not converge on a vanishing point in the picture, but are thought to originate in the viewer's eye in front of the picture. Thus, in reverse perspective the image is constructed with orthogonals that diverge, giving a slightly tipped aspect to objects.

photomontage (p. 1053) A photographic work created from many smaller photographs arranged (and often overlapping) in a composition that is then rephotographed.

pictograph (p. 340) A highly stylized depiction serving as a symbol for a person or object. Also: a type of writing utilizing such symbols.

picture plane (p. 587) The theoretical plane corresponding with the actual surface of a painting, separating the spatial world evoked in the painting from the spatial world occupied by the viewer.

picturesque (p. 935) Of the taste for the familiar, the pleasant, and the agreeable, popular in the eighteenth and nineteenth centuries in Europe. Originally used to describe the "picturelike" qualities of some landscape scenes. When contrasted with the **sublime**, the picturesque stood for the interesting but ordinary domestic landscape.

piece-mold casting (p. 338) A casting technique in which the mold consists of several sections that are connected during the pouring of molten metal, usually bronze. After the cast form has hardened, the pieces of the mold are disassembled, leaving the completed object.

pier (p. 273) A masonry support made up of many stones, or rubble and concrete (in contrast to a column **shaft** which is formed from a single stone or a series of **drums**), often square or rectangular in plan, and capable of carrying very heavy architectural loads.

pietà (p. 231) A devotional subject in Christian religious art. After the Crucifixion the body of Jesus was laid across the lap of his grieving mother, Mary. When other mourners are present, the subject is called the Lamentation.

pietra serena (p. 613) A gray Tuscan sandstone used in Florentine architecture.

pilaster (p. 161) An **engaged** columnlike element that is rectangular in format and used for decoration in architecture.

pilgrimage church (p. 226) A church that attracts visitors wishing to venerate **relics** as well as attend religious services.

pinnacle (p. 517) In Gothic architecture, a steep pyramid decorating the top of another element such as a **buttress**. Also: the highest point.

plate tracery (p. 516) See under **tracery**.

plein air (p. 1003) See under *en plein air*.

plinth (p. 162) The slablike base or **pedestal** of a **column**, statue, wall, building, or piece of furniture.

podium (p. 141) A raised platform that acts as the foundation for a building, or as a platform for a speaker.

poesia (*pl.* **poesie**) (p. 668) Italian Renaissance paintings based on Classical themes, often with erotic overtones, notably in the mid-sixteenth-century works of the Venetian painter Titian.

polychromy (p. 537) Multicolored decoration applied to any part of a building, sculpture, or piece of furniture. This can be accomplished with paint or by the use of multicolored materials.

polyptych (p. xxxiii) An **altarpiece** constructed from multiple panels, sometimes with hinges to allow for movable wings.

porcelain (p. 20) A type of extremely hard and fine white **ceramic** first made by Chinese potters in the eighth century CE. Made from a mixture of kaolin and petuntse, porcelain is fired at a very high temperature, and the final product has a translucent surface.

porch (p. 110) The covered entrance on the exterior of a building. With a row of **columns** or **colonnade**, also called a **portico**.

portal (p. 40) A grand entrance, door, or gate, usually to an important public building, often decorated with sculpture.

portico (p. 63) In architecture, a projecting roof or porch supported by **columns**, often marking an entrance. See also **porch**.

post-and-lintel (p. 17) An architectural system of construction with two or more vertical elements (posts) supporting a horizontal element (**lintel**).

potassium-argon dating (p. 12) Archaeological method of **radiometric dating** that measures the decay of a radioactive potassium isotope into a stable isotope of argon, and inert gas.

potsherd (p. 21) A broken piece of **ceramic** ware.

poupou (p. 886) In Pacific cultures, a house panel, often carved with designs.

Prairie Style (p. 1061) Style developed by a group of Midwestern architects who worked together using the aesthetic of the prairie and indigenous prairie plants for landscape design to create mostly domestic homes and small public buildings.

predella (p. 557) The base of an **altarpiece**, often decorated with small scenes that are related in subject to that of the main panel or panels.

primitivism (p. 1037) The borrowing of subjects or forms, usually from non-European or prehistoric sources, by Western artists in an attempt to infuse work with expressive qualities attributed to other cultures, especially colonized cultures.

pronaos (p. 110) The enclosed vestibule of a Greek or Roman temple, found in front of the **cella** and marked by a row of **columns** at the entrance.

proscenium (p. 151) The stage of an ancient Greek or Roman theater. In a modern theater, the area of the stage in front of the curtain. Also: the framing **arch** that separates a stage from the audience.

psalter (p. 260) In Jewish and Christian scripture, a book of the Psalms (songs) attributed to King David.

psykter (p. 127) An ancient Greek vessel with an extended base to allow it to float in a larger **krater**; used to chill wine.

putto (*pl.* **putti**) (p. 228) A plump, naked little boy, often winged. In Classical art, called a cupid; in Christian art, a cherub.

pylon (p. 66) A massive gateway formed by a pair of tapering walls of oblong shape. Erected by ancient Egyptians to mark the entrance to a temple complex.

qibla (p. 274) The **mosque** wall oriented toward Mecca; indicated by the *mihrab*.

quatrefoil (p. 520) A four-lobed decorative pattern common in Gothic art and architecture.

quillwork (p. 861) A Native American technique in which the quills of porcupines and bird feathers are dyed and attached to materials in patterns.

radiometric dating (p. 12) Archaeological method of **absolute dating** by measuring the degree to which radioactive materials have degenerated over time. For dating organic (plant

or animal) materials, one radiometric method measures a carbon isotope called radiocarbon, or carbon-14.

raigo (p. 382) A painted image that depicts the Amida Buddha and other Buddhist deities welcoming the soul of a dying believer to paradise.

raku (p. 838) A type of **ceramic** made by hand, coated with a thick, dark **glaze**, and fired at a low heat. The resulting vessels are irregularly shaped and glazed and are highly prized for use in the Japanese tea ceremony.

readymade (p. 913) An object from popular or material culture presented without further manipulation as an artwork by the artist.

récupération (p. 913) A French term for the West African method of using found objects to make fine-art sculptures and installations.

red-figure (p. 120) A technique of ancient Greek **ceramic** decoration characterized by red clay-colored figures on a black background. The figures are reserved against a painted ground and details are drawn, not engraved; compare **black-figure**.

register (p. 30) A device used in systems of spatial definition. In painting, a register indicates the use of differing ground-lines to differentiate layers of space within an image. In **relief sculpture**, the placement of self-contained bands of reliefs in a vertical arrangement.

registration marks (p. 843) In Japanese **woodblock prints**, two marks carved on the blocks to indicate proper alignment of the paper during the printing process. In multicolor printing, which used a separate block for each color, these marks were essential for achieving the proper position or registration of the colors.

relative dating (p. 12) Archaeological process of determining relative chronological relationships among excavated objects. Compare **absolute dating**.

relic (p. 226) Venerated object or body part associated with a holy figure, such as a saint, and usually housed in a **reliquary**.

relief sculpture (p. 5) A three-dimensional image or design whose flat background surface is carved away to a certain depth, setting off the figure. Called *high* or *low (bas-) relief* depending upon the extent of projection of the image from the background. Called *sunken relief* when the image is carved below the original surface of the background, which is not cut away.

reliquary (p. 371) A container, often elaborate and made of precious materials, used as a repository for sacred relics.

repoussé (p. 93) A technique of pushing or hammering metal from the back to create a protruding image. Elaborate reliefs are created by pressing or hammering metal sheets against carved wooden forms.

rhyton (p. 90) A vessel in the shape of a figure or an animal, used for drinking or pouring liquids on special occasions.

rib vault (p. 511) See under **vault**.

ridgepole (p. 17) A longitudinal timber at the apex of a roof that supports the upper ends of the rafters.

roof comb (p. 396) In a Maya building, a masonry wall along the apex of a roof that is built above the level of the roof proper. Roof combs support the highly decorated false **façades** that rise above the height of the building at the front.

rose window (p. 516) A round window, often filled with stained glass set into tracery patterns in the form of wheel spokes, found in the **façades** of the **naves** and **transept**s of large Gothic churches.

rosette (p. 108) A round or oval ornament resembling a rose.

rotunda (p. 197) Any building (or part thereof) constructed in a circular (or sometimes polygonal) shape, usually producing a large open space crowned by a **dome**.

round arch (p. 171) See under **arch**.

roundel (p. 161) Any ornamental element with a circular format, often placed as a decoration on the exterior of a building.

rune stone (p. 452) In early medieval northern Europe, a stone used as a commemorative monument and carved or inscribed with runes, a writing system used by early Germanic peoples.

rustication (p. 614) In architecture, the rough, irregular, and unfinished effect deliberately given to the exterior facing of a stone edifice. Rusticated stones are often large and used for decorative emphasis around doors or windows, or across the entire lower floors of a building.

sacra conversazione (p. 642) Italian for "holy conversation." Refers to a type of religious painting developed in fifteenth-century Florence in which a central image of the Virgin and Child is flanked by standing saints of comparable size who stand within the same spatial setting and often acknowledge each other's presence.

salon (p. 923) A large room for entertaining guests or a periodic social or intellectual gathering, often of prominent people, held in such a room. Also: a hall or **gallery** for exhibiting works of art.

sanctuary (p. 105) A sacred or holy enclosure used for worship. In ancient Greece and Rome, consisted of one or more temples and an altar. In Christian architecture, the space around the altar in a church called the chancel or presbytery.

sarcophagus (*pl.* **sarcophagi**) (p. 49) A stone coffin. Often rectangular and decorated with **relief sculpture**.

scarab (p. 51) In ancient Egypt, a stylized dung beetle associated with the sun and the god Amun.

scarification (p. 413) Ornamental decoration applied to the surface of the body by cutting the skin for cultural and/or aesthetic reasons.

school of artists or **painting** (p. 288) An art historical term describing a group of artists, usually working at the same time and sharing similar styles, influences, and ideals. The artists in a particular school may not necessarily be directly associated with one another, unlike those in a workshop or **atelier**.

scriptorium (*pl.* **scriptoria**) (p. 248) A room in a monastery for writing or copying **manuscripts**.

scroll painting (p. 352) A painting executed on a flexible support with rollers at each end. The rollers permit the horizontal scroll to be unrolled as it is studied or the vertical scroll to be hung for contemplation or decoration.

sculpture in the round (p. 5) Three-dimensional sculpture that is carved free of any background or block. Compare **relief sculpture**.

serdab (p. 54) In ancient Egyptian tombs, the small room in which the *ka* statue was placed.

sfumato (p. 650) Italian term meaning "smoky," soft, and mellow. In painting, the effect of haze in an image. Resembling the color of the atmosphere at dusk, *sfumato* gives a smoky effect.

sgraffito (p. 615) Decoration made by incising or cutting away a surface layer of material to reveal a different color beneath.

shaft (p. 111) The main vertical section of a **column** between the **capital** and the base, usually circular in cross section.

shaft grave (p. 98) A deep pit used for burial.

shikhara (p. 306) In the architecture of northern India, a conical (or pyramidal) spire found atop a Hindu temple and often crowned with an *amalaka*.

shoin (p. 835) A term used to describe the various features found in the most formal room of upper-class Japanese residential architecture.

shoji (p. 835) A standing Japanese screen covered in translucent rice paper and used in interiors.

siapo (p. 889) A type of *tapa* cloth found in Samoa and still used as an important gift for ceremonial occasions.

silkscreen printing (p. 1107) A technique of printing in which paint or ink is pressed through a stencil and specially prepared cloth to reproduce a design in multiple copies.

silverpoint (p. 591) A drawing technique using a stylus with a sharp silver tip to produce very fine, precise lines.

sinopia (*pl.* *sinopie*) (p. 551) Italian word taken from Sinope, the ancient city in Asia Minor that was famous for its red-brick pigment. In **fresco** paintings, a full-sized, preliminary sketch done in this color on the first rough coat of plaster or *arriccio*.

site-specific (p. 895) Commissioned and/or designed for a particular location.

skeuomorph (p. 427) A decorative object or design that mimics elements from a predecessor object that were integral to the function or structure of the predecessor.

slip (p. 120) A mixture of clay and water applied to a **ceramic** object as a final decorative coat. Also: a solution that binds different parts of a vessel together, such as the handle and the main body.

spandrel (p. 171) The area of wall adjoining the exterior curve of an **arch** between its **springing** and the **keystone**, or the area between two arches, as in an **arcade**.

spolia (p. 227) Fragments of older architecture or sculpture reused in a secondary context. Latin for "hide stripped from an animal."

springing (p. 171) The point at which the curve of an **arch** or **vault** meets with and rises from its support.

squinch (p. 241) An **arch** or **lintel** built across the upper corners of a square space, allowing a circular or polygonal **dome** to be securely set above the walls.

stained glass (p. 293) Glass stained with color while molten, using metallic oxides. Stained glass is most often used in windows, for which small pieces of different colors are precisely cut and assembled into a design, held together by lead **cames**. Additional details may be added with vitreous paint.

stave church (p. 453) A Scandinavian wooden structure with four huge timbers (staves) at its core.

stele (*pl.* **stelai**), also **stela** (*pl.* **stelae**) (p. 27) A stone slab placed vertically and decorated with inscriptions or reliefs. Used as a grave marker or commemorative monument.

stereobate (p. 111) In Classical architecture, the foundation upon which a temple stands.

still life (*pl.* **still lifes**) (p. xxx) A type of painting that has as its subject inanimate objects (such as food and dishes) or fruit and flowers taken out of their natural contexts.

stoa (p. 109) In Greek architecture, a long roofed walkway, usually having **columns** on one long side and a wall on the other.

stoneware (p. 21) A high-fired, vitrified, but opaque **ceramic** ware that is fired in the range of 1,200 to 1,400 degrees Centigrade. At that temperature, particles of silica in the clay bodies fuse together so that the finished vessels are impervious to liquids, even without glaze. Stoneware pieces are glazed to enhance their aesthetic appeal and to aid in keeping them clean. Stoneware occurs in a range of earth-toned colors, from white and tan to gray and black, with light gray predominating. Chinese potters were the first in the world to produce stoneware, which they were able to make as early as the Shang dynasty.

stringcourse (p. 517) A continuous horizontal band, such as a **molding**, decorating the face of a wall.

stucco (p. 74) A mixture of lime, sand, and other ingredients made into a material that can easily be molded or modeled. When dry, it produces a durable surface used for covering walls or for architectural sculpture and decoration.

stupa (p. 306) In Buddhist architecture, a bell-shaped or dome-like religious monument, made of piled earth, brick, or stone, and containing sacred **relics**.

style (p. xxxiii) A particular manner, form, or character of representation, construction, or expression that is typical of an individual artist or of a certain place or period.

stylobate (p. 111) In Classical architecture, the stone foundation on which a temple **colonnade** stands.

stylus (p. 29) An instrument with a pointed end (used for writing and printmaking), which makes a delicate line or scratch. Also: a special writing tool for **cuneiform** writing with one pointed end and one triangular.

sublime (p. 973) Of a concept, thing, or state of greatness or vastness with high spiritual, moral,

intellectual, or emotional value; or something awe-inspiring. The sublime was a goal to which many nineteenth-century artists aspired in their artworks.

sunken relief (p. 73) See under **relief sculpture**.

symposium (p. 121) An elite gathering of wealthy and powerful men in ancient Greece that focused principally on wine, music, poetry, conversation, games, and love-making.

syncretism (p. 222) A process whereby artists assimilate and combine images and ideas from different cultural traditions, beliefs, and practices, giving them new meanings.

taotie (p. 338) A mask with a dragon- or animal-like face common as a decorative motif in Chinese art.

tapa (p. 889) A type of cloth used for various purposes in Pacific cultures, made from tree bark stripped and beaten, and often bearing subtle designs from the mallets used to work the bark.

tapestry (p. 295) Multicolored decorative weaving to be hung on a wall or placed on furniture. Pictorial or decorative motifs are woven directly into the supporting fabric, completely concealing it.

tatami (p. 835) Mats of woven straw used in Japanese houses as a floor covering.

temenos (p. 110) An enclosed sacred area reserved for worship in ancient Greece.

tempera (p. 144) A painting **medium** made by blending egg yolks with water, pigments, and occasionally other materials, such as glue.

tenebrism (p. 738) The use of strong *chiaroscuro* and artificially illuminated areas to create a dramatic contrast of light and dark in a painting.

terra cotta (p. 116) A **medium** made from clay fired over a low heat and sometimes left unglazed. Also: the orange–brown color typical of this medium.

tessera (*pl.* **tesserae**) (p. 148) A small piece of stone, glass, or other object that is pieced together with many others to create a **mosaic**.

thatch (p. 17) Plant material such as reeds or straw tied over a framework of poles to make a roof, shelter, or small building.

thermo-luminescence dating (p. 13) A method of **radiometric dating** that measures the irradiation of the crystal structure of material such as flint or pottery and the soil in which it is found, determined by how much a sample glows when it is heated.

tholos (p. 100) A small, round building. Sometimes built underground, as, for example, with a Mycenaean tomb.

thrust (p. 171) The outward pressure caused by the weight of a **vault** and supported by **buttressing**. See also under **arch**.

tondo (*pl.* **tondi**) (p. 128) A painting or **relief sculpture** of circular shape.

torana (p. 306) In Indian architecture, an ornamented gateway arch in a temple, usually leading to the **stupa**.

torc (p. 152) A circular neck ring worn by Celtic warriors.

toron (p. 425) In West African **mosque** architecture, one of the wooden beams that project from the walls. Torons are used as support for the scaffolding erected annually for the replastering of the building.

tracery (p. 517) Stonework or woodwork forming a pattern in the open space of windows or applied to wall surfaces. In *plate tracery*, a series of openings are cut through the wall. In *bar tracery*, **mullions** divide the space into segments to form decorative patterns

transept (p. 226) The arm of a **cruciform** church perpendicular to the **nave**. The point where the nave and transept intersect is called the crossing. Beyond the crossing lies the **sanctuary**, whether **apse**, **choir**, or chevet.

transverse arch (p. 475) See under **arch**.

trefoil (p. 302) An ornamental design made up of three rounded lobes placed adjacent to one another.

triforium (p. 516) The element of the interior elevation of a church found directly below the **clerestory** and consisting of a series of arched openings in front of a passageway within the thickness of the wall.

triglyph (p. 111) Rectangular block between the **metope**s of a Doric **frieze**. Identified by the three carved vertical grooves, which approximate the appearance of the end of wooden beams.

triptych (p. 579) An artwork made up of three panels. The panels may be hinged together in such a way that the side segments (wings) fold over the central area.

trompe l'oeil (p. 587) A manner of representation in which artists faithfully describe the appearance of natural space and forms with the express intention of fooling the eye of the viewer, who may be convinced momentarily that the subject actually exists as three-dimensional reality.

trumeau (p. 491) A **column**, **pier**, or post found at the center of a large **portal** or doorway, supporting the **lintel**.

tugra (p. 293) A calligraphic imperial monogram used in Ottoman courts.

tukutuku (p. 886) Lattice panels created by women from the Maori culture and used in architecture.

Tuscan order (p. 161) See under **order**.

twining (p. 863) A basketry technique in which short rods are sewn together vertically. The panels are then joined together to form a container or other object.

tympanum (p. 491) In medieval and later architecture, the area over a door enclosed by an **arch** and a **lintel**, often decorated with sculpture or mosaic.

ukiyo-e (p. 842) A Japanese term for a type of popular art that was favored from the sixteenth century, particularly in the form of color **woodblock prints**. *Ukiyo-e* prints often depicted the world of the common people in Japan, such as courtesans and actors, as well as landscapes and myths.

undercutting (p. 214) A technique in sculpture by which the material is cut back under the edges so that the remaining form projects strongly forward, casting deep shadows.

underglaze (p. 813) Color or decoration applied to a **ceramic** piece before glazing.

upeti (p. 890) In Pacific cultures, a carved wooden design tablet, used to create patterns in cloth by dragging the fabric across it.

uranium-thorium dating (p. 12) Technique used to date prehistoric cave paintings by measuring the decay of uranium into thorium in the deposits of calcium carbonate that cover the surfaces of cave walls, to determine the minimum age of the paintings under the crust.

urna (p. 311) In Buddhist art, the curl of hair on the forehead that is a characteristic mark of a buddha. The *urna* is a symbol of divine wisdom.

ushnisha (p. 311) In Asian art, a round cranial bump or bun of hair symbolizing royalty and, when worn by a buddha, enlightenment.

vanishing point (p. 623) In a **perspective** system, the point on the **horizon line** at which **orthogonals** meet. A complex system can have multiple vanishing points.

vanitas (p. xxxii) An image, especially popular in Europe during the seventeenth century, in which all the objects symbolize the transience of life. *Vanitas* paintings are usually of **still lifes** or genre subjects.

vault (p. 18) An arched masonry structure that spans an interior space. *Barrel* or *tunnel vault*: an elongated or continuous semicircular vault, shaped like a half-cylinder. *Corbeled vault*: a vault made by projecting **courses** of stone; see also under **corbel**. *Groin* or *cross vault*: a vault created by the intersection of two barrel vaults of equal size which creates four side compartments of identical size and shape. *Quadrant vault*: a half-barrel vault. *Rib vault*: a groin vault with ribs (extra masonry) demarcating the junctions. Ribs may function to reinforce the groins or may be purely decorative.

veduta (*pl.* **vedute**) (p. 931) Italian for "vista" or "view." Paintings, drawings, or prints, often of expansive city scenes or of harbors.

vellum (p. 249) A fine animal skin prepared for writing and painting. See also **parchment**.

verism (p. 169) Style in which artists concern themselves with describing the exterior likeness of an object or person, usually by rendering its visible details in a finely executed, meticulous manner.

vihara (p. 309) From the Sanskrit term meaning "for wanderers." A *vihara* is, in general, a Buddhist monastery in India. It also signifies monks' cells and gathering places in such a monastery.

volute (p. 111) A spiral scroll, as seen on an Ionic **capital**.

votive figure (p. 31) An image created as a devotional offering to a deity.

voussoir (p. 171) Wedge-shaped stone block used to build an **arch**. The topmost voussoir is called a **keystone**. See also **joggled voussoirs**.

warp (p. 295) The vertical threads in a weaver's loom. Warp threads make up a fixed framework that provides the structure for the entire piece of cloth, and are thus often thicker than **weft** threads.

wattle and daub (p. 17) A wall construction method combining upright branches, woven with twigs (wattles) and plastered or filled with clay or mud (daub).

wax print fabric (p. 918) Cotton fabric printed to look like Indonesian batik cloth. Originally made in the Netherlands and exported to African coastal nations during the fifteenth through twenty-first centuries, it is now manufactured around the world, including in many African countries.

weft (p. 295) The horizontal threads in a woven piece of cloth. Weft threads are woven at right angles to and through the **warp** threads to make up the bulk of the decorative pattern. In carpets, the weft is often completely covered or formed by the rows of trimmed knots that form the carpet's soft surface.

westwork (p. 457) The monumental, west-facing entrance section of a Carolingian, Ottonian, or Romanesque church. The exterior consists of multiple stories between two towers; the interior includes an entrance vestibule, a chapel, and a series of **galleries** overlooking the **nave**.

white-ground (p. 143) A type of ancient Greek pottery in which the background color of the object was painted with a **slip** that turns white in the firing process. Figures and details were added by painting on or incising into this slip. White-ground wares were popular in the Classical period as funerary objects.

woodblock print (p. 602) A print made from one or more carved wooden blocks. In Japan, woodblock prints were made using multiple blocks carved in relief, usually with a block for each color in the finished print. See also **woodcut**.

woodcut (p. 602) A type of print made by carving a design into a wooden block. The ink is applied to the block with a roller. As the ink touches only on the surface areas and lines remaining between the carved-away parts of the block, it is these areas that make the print when paper is pressed against the inked block, leaving the carved-away parts of the design to appear blank. Also: the process by which the woodcut is made.

yaksha, yakshi (p. 305) The male (*yaksha*) and female (*yakshi*) nature spirits associated with fertility and abundance. Their sculpted images are often found on Buddhist and Hindu temples and other sacred places, particularly at the entrances.

yamato-e (p. 377) A native style of Japanese painting developed during the twelfth and thirteenth centuries, distinguished from Japanese painting styles that emulated Chinese traditions.

ziggurat (p. 29) In ancient Mesopotamia, a tall stepped tower of earthen materials, often supporting a shrine.

Bibliography

This bibliography is composed of books in English that are suggested "further reading" titles. Most are available in good libraries, whether college, university, or public. Recently published works have been emphasized so that the research information would be current. There are three classifications of listings: general surveys and art history reference tools, including journals and Internet directories; surveys of large periods that encompass multiple chapters (ancient art in the Western tradition, European medieval art, European Renaissance through eighteenth-century art, Modern art in the West, Asian art, African and Oceanic art, and art of the Americas); and books for individual Chapters 1 through 33.

General Art History Surveys and Reference Tools

Adams, Laurie Schneider. *Art Across Time*. 4th ed. New York: McGraw-Hill, 2011.

Barnet, Sylvan. *A Short Guide to Writing about Art*. 11th ed. Upper Saddle River, NJ: Pearson/ Prentice Hall, 2010.

Bony, Anne. *Design: History, Main Trends, Main Figures*. Edinburgh: Chambers, 2005.

Boström, Antonia. *Encyclopedia of Sculpture*. 3 vols. New York: Fitzroy Dearborn, 2004.

Broude, Norma, and Mary D. Garrard, eds. *Feminism and Art History: Questioning the Litany*. Icon Editions. New York: Harper & Row, 1982.

Chadwick, Whitney. *Women, Art, and Society*. 4th ed. New York: Thames & Hudson, 2007.

Chilvers, Ian, ed. *The Oxford Dictionary of Art*. 4th ed. New York: Oxford Univ. Press, 2009.

Curl, James Stevens. *A Dictionary of Architecture and Landscape Architecture*. 2nd ed. Oxford: Oxford Univ. Press, 2006.

Davies, Penelope J.E., et al. *Janson's History of Art: The Western Tradition*. 8th ed. Upper Saddle River, NJ: Prentice Hall, 2010.

The Dictionary of Art. Ed. Jane Turner. 34 vols. New York: Grove's Dictionaries, 1996.

Frank, Patrick, Duane Preble, and Sarah Preble. *Prebles' Artforms*. 10th ed. Upper Saddle River, NJ: Pearson/ Prentice Hall, 2011.

Gaze, Delia, ed. *Dictionary of Women Artists*. 2 vols. London: Fitzroy Dearborn, 1997.

Griffiths, Antony. *Prints and Printmaking: An Introduction to the History and Techniques*. 2nd ed. London: British Museum Press, 1996.

Hadden, Peggy. *The Quotable Artist*. New York: Allworth Press, 2002.

Hall, James. *Dictionary of Subjects and Symbols in Art*. 2nd ed. Boulder, CO: Westview Press, 2008.

Holt, Elizabeth Gilmore, ed. *A Documentary History of Art*. 3 vols. New Haven: Yale Univ. Press, 1986.

Honour, Hugh, and John Fleming. *The Visual Arts: A History*. 7th ed. rev. Upper Saddle River, NJ: Pearson/ Prentice Hall, 2010.

Johnson, Paul. *Art: A New History*. New York: HarperCollins, 2003.

Kemp, Martin, ed. *The Oxford History of Western Art*. Oxford: Oxford Univ. Press, 2000.

Kleiner, Fred S. *Gardner's Art through the Ages*. Enhanced 15th ed. Belmont, CA: Thomson/ Wadsworth, 2011.

Kostof, Spiro. *A History of Architecture: Settings and Rituals*. 2nd ed. Revised Greg Castillo. New York: Oxford Univ. Press, 1995.

Levenson, Jay A., ed. *Circa 1492: Art in the Age of Exploration*. New Haven: Yale Univ. Press and the National Gallery of Art, Washington, DC, 1991.

MacGregor, Neil. *A History of the World in 100 Objects*. New York: Penguin Books, 2013.

Mackenzie, Lynn. *Non-Western Art: A Brief Guide*. 2nd ed. Upper Saddle River, NJ: Pearson/ Prentice Hall, 2001.

Marmor, Max, and Alex Ross, eds. *Guide to the Literature of Art History 2*. Chicago: American Library Association, 2005.

Onians, John, ed. *Atlas of World Art*. New York: Oxford Univ. Press, 2004.

Sayre, Henry M. *Writing about Art*. 6th ed. Upper Saddle River, NJ: Pearson/Prentice Hall, 2009.

Sed-Rajna, Gabrielle. *Jewish Art*. Trans. Sara Friedman and Mira Reich. New York: Abrams, 1997.

Slatkin, Wendy. *Women Artists in History: From Antiquity to the Present*. 4th ed. Upper Saddle River, NJ: Pearson/ Prentice Hall, 2001.

Sutton, Ian. *Western Architecture: From Ancient Greece to the Present*. World of Art. New York: Thames & Hudson, 1999.

Trachtenberg, Marvin, and Isabelle Hyman. *Architecture, from Prehistory to Postmodernity*. 2nd ed. Upper Saddle River, NJ: Pearson/ Prentice Hall, 2002.

Tucker, Amy. *Visual Literacy: Writing about Art*. Boston: McGraw-Hill, 2002.

Watkin, David. *A History of Western Architecture*. 4th ed. New York: Watson-Guptill, 2005.

Art History Journals: A Selected List of Current Titles

African Arts. Quarterly. Los Angeles: Univ. of California at Los Angeles, James S. Coleman African Studies Center, 1967–.

American Art: The Journal of the Smithsonian American Art Museum. 3/year. Chicago: Univ. of Chicago Press, 1987–.

American Journal of Archaeology. Quarterly. Boston: Archaeological Institute of America, 1885–.

Antiquity: A Periodical of Archaeology. Quarterly. Cambridge: Antiquity Publications Ltd., 1927–.

Apollo: The International Magazine of the Arts. Monthly. London: Apollo Magazine Ltd., 1925–.

Archaeology Magazine. Bimonthly. New York: Archaeological Institute of America, 1948–.

Architectural History. Annually. Farnham, UK: Society of Architectural Historians of Great Britain, 1958–.

Archives of American Art Journal. Quarterly. Washington, DC: Archives of American Art, Smithsonian Institution, 1960–.

Archives of Asian Art. Annually. New York: Asia Society, 1945–.

Ars Orientalis: The Arts of Asia, Southeast Asia, and Islam. Annually. Ann Arbor: Univ. of Michigan Dept. of Art History, 1954–.

Art Bulletin. Quarterly. New York: College Art Association, 1913–.

Art History: Journal of the Association of Art Historians. 5/year. Oxford: Blackwell Publishing Ltd., 1978–.

Art in America. Monthly. New York: Brant Publications Inc., 1913–.

Art Journal. Quarterly. New York: College Art Association, 1960–.

The Art Newspaper. Monthly. London and New York: The Art Newspaper, 1990–.

Art Nexus. Quarterly. Bogota, Colombia: Arte en Colombia Ltda, 1976–.

Art Papers Magazine. Bimonthly. Atlanta: Atlanta Art Papers Inc., 1976–.

Artforum International. 10/year. New York: Artforum International Magazine Inc., 1962–.

Artibus Asiae. Biannually. Zürich: Museum Rietberg, 1925–.

Artnews. 11/year. New York: Artnews LLC, 1902–.

Bulletin of the Metropolitan Museum of Art. Quarterly. New York: Metropolitan Museum of Art, 1905–.

The Burlington Magazine. Monthly. London: Burlington Magazine Publications Ltd., 1903–.

Dumbarton Oaks Papers. Annually. Locust Valley, NY: J.J. Augustin Inc., 1940–.

Flash Art International. Bimonthly. Trevi, Italy: Giancarlo Politi Editore, 1980–.

Gesta. Semiannually. New York: International Center of Medieval Art, 1963–.

History of Photography. Quarterly. Abingdon, UK: Taylor & Francis Ltd., 1976–.

International Review of African American Art. Quarterly. Hampton, VA: International Review of African American Art, 1976–.

Journal of the American Research Center in Egypt. Annually. San Antonio: The American Research Center in Egypt, 1962–.

Journal of Design History. Quarterly. Oxford: Oxford Univ. Press, 1988–.

Journal of Egyptian Archaeology. Annually. London: Egypt Exploration Society, 1914–.

Journal of Hellenic Studies. Annually. London: Society for the Promotion of Hellenic Studies, 1880–.

Journal of Roman Archaeology. Annually. Portsmouth, RI: Journal of Roman Archaeology LLC, 1988–.

Journal of the Society of Architectural Historians. Quarterly. Chicago: Society of Architectural Historians, 1940–.

Journal of the Warburg and Courtauld Institutes. Annually. London: Warburg Institute, 1937–.

Leonardo: Art, Science, and Technology. 6/year.

Cambridge, MA: MIT Press, 1968–.

Marg. Quarterly. Mumbai, India: Scientific Publishers, 1946–.

Master Drawings. Quarterly. New York: Master Drawings Association, 1963–.

Muqarnas. Annually. Cambridge, MA: E.J. Brill, 1983–.

October. Cambridge, MA: MIT Press, 1976–.

Oxford Art Journal. 3/year. Oxford: Oxford Univ. Press, 1978–.

Parkett. 3/year. Zürich, Switzerland: Parkett Verlag AG, 1984–.

Print Quarterly. Quarterly. London: Print Quarterly Publications, 1984–.

Simiolus: Netherlands Quarterly for the History of Art. Quarterly. Apeldoorn, Netherlands: Stichting voor Nederlandse Kunsthistorische Publicaties, 1966–.

Source: Notes in the History of Art. Quarterly. Chicago: Univ. of Chicago Press, 1981–.

Studies in Iconography. Annually. Kalamazoo: Medieval Institute Publications, Western Michigan Univ., 1993–.

Woman's Art Journal. Semiannually. Philadelphia: Old City Publishing Inc., 1980–.

Internet Directories for Art History Information: A Selected List

ALBERTI'S WINDOW: AN ART HISTORY BLOG,
http://albertis-window.com
Maintained by art historian Monica Bowen, this blog provides interesting and accessible posts for those curious about the history of art of various cultures and periods.

ARCHITECTURE AND BUILDING,
http://www.library.unlv.edu/arch/rsrce/webresources/
A directory of architecture websites collected by Jeanne Brown at the Univ. of Nevada at Las Vegas. Topical lists include architecture, building and construction, design, history, housing, planning, preservation, and landscape architecture. Most entries include a brief annotation and the last date the link was accessed by the compiler.

ART HISTORY RESOURCES ON THE WEB,
http://witcombe.sbc.edu/ARTHLinks.html
Authored by Professor Christopher L.C.E. Witcombe of Sweet Briar College in Virginia since 1995, the site includes an impressive number of links for various art historical eras as well as links to research resources, museums, and galleries. The content is frequently updated.

THE ART STORY,
http://www.theartstory.org
Dedicated to demonstrating the significance of modern and contemporary art, this site includes topic pages on the important artists, movements, and ideas from the mid nineteenth to the twenty-first century, as well as timelines and a blog with frequent posts examining a variety of related topics.

ART THROUGH TIME: A GLOBAL VIEW,
http://www.learner.org/courses/globalart/
Developed by Annenberg Learner, this 13-part series is a thematic and global overview of the history of art. The website makes use of videos, images, and text for each of the themes, which include the body, conflict, portraits, death, belief, cultures, dreams, history, ceremony, writing, domestic life, the natural world, and urban experience.

ART21,
http://www.art21.org/
Devoted to chronicling contemporary art and artists, this site provides access to films, articles, interviews, and other interpretive resources in order to introduce the public to contemporary art and the creative process.

ARTBABBLE,
http://www.artbabble.org/
An online community created by staff at the Indianapolis Museum of Art to showcase art-based video content, including interviews with artists and curators, original documentaries, and art installation videos. Partners and contributors to the project include ART21, Los Angeles County Museum of Art, the Museum of Modern Art, the New York Public Library, San Francisco Museum of Modern Art, and Smithsonian American Art Museum.

ARTCYCLOPEDIA: THE GUIDE TO GREAT ART ON THE INTERNET,
http://www.artcyclopedia.com
With more than 2,100 art sites and 75,000 links, this is one of the most comprehensive Web directories for artists and art topics. The primary search is by artist's name but access is also available by title of artwork, artistic movement, museum and gallery, nationality, period, and medium.

ARTSTOR,
http://www.artstor.org
Created by the Andrew W. Mellon Foundation, Artstor is a digital library of more than 1.9 million images for educational and research purposes gathered from institutions and databases around the world. The site also provides instructor resources, including curriculum and subject guides as well as tools for sharing and downloading images.

ARTSY,
https://www.artsy.net
With the goal of making the world's art accessible online, Artsy provides a rapidly expanding image database for works of art, design, and architecture from galleries, museums, estates, auctions, art fairs, and foundations. Especially strong in contemporary art and collecting, this site also continues to develop its pool of historical images and educational resources, including lesson plans.

EUROPEANA COLLECTIONS,
http://www.europeana.eu/portal/
Excellent for accessing more than 48 million European artworks, artifacts, videos, and books, this site offers compilations of collections by theme, period, location, or artist as well as online curated exhibitions, blog posts, and eBooks.

THE GETTY,
http://www.getty.edu/museum/index.html
The J. Paul Getty Museum's website is a great resource with access to the archived collection with thousands of downloadable images, art-historical research databases, and videos exploring works and themes related to the collection, conservation, and exhibitions.

GOOGLE ART PROJECT,
https://www.google.com/culturalinstitute/u/0/project/art-project
In 2011, Google launched this site in order to make the world's cultural heritage and objects more widely accessible for a global audience. Since then, they have compiled more than 700 digitized collections worldwide and have partnered with more than 850 institutions to provide access to high-resolution images and curated digital exhibitions.

HEILBRUNN TIMELINE OF ART HISTORY,
http://www.metmuseum.org/toah/
Illustrating the Metropolitan Museum of Art's collection, this resource compiles essays and images alongside chronologies to narrate the global history of art and culture. Includes the option to search for content by time period, region, or theme.

THE MODERN ART NOTES PODCAST,
https://manpodcast.com/
Hosted and produced by the historian and award-winning art critic Tyler Green, the MAN Podcast features hour-long interviews with artists, art historians, authors, curators, and conservators each week to discuss their work and topics current in the art world.

MoMA LEARNING,
http://www.moma.org/learn/moma_learning
The Museum of Modern Art's online resources for approaching modern and contemporary art. Organized by theme or artist, this site compiles lesson plans, PowerPoints, worksheets, and videos to engage students with the art in MoMA's collection.

MOTHER OF ALL ART AND ART HISTORY LINKS PAGES,
http://umich.edu/~motherha
Maintained by the Dept. of the History of Art at the Univ. of Michigan, this directory covers art history departments, art museums, and fine-arts schools and departments, as well as links to research resources. Each entry includes annotations.

VOICE OF THE SHUTTLE,
http://vos.ucsb.edu
Sponsored by Univ. of California, Santa Barbara, this directory includes more than 70 pages of links to humanities and humanities-related resources on the Internet. The structured guide includes specific subsections on architecture, on art (modern and contemporary), and on art history. Links usually include a one-sentence explanation, and the resource is frequently updated with new information.

Ancient Art in the Western Tradition, General

Amiet, Pierre. *Art in the Ancient World: A Handbook of Styles and Forms.* New York: Rizzoli, 1981.

Beard, Mary, and John Henderson. *Classical Art: From Greece to Rome.* Oxford History of Art. Oxford: Oxford Univ. Press, 2001.

Boardman, John. *Oxford History of Classical Art.* New York: Oxford Univ. Press, 2001.

Chitham, Robert. *The Classical Orders of Architecture.* 2nd ed. Boston: Elsevier/Architectural Press, 2005.

Ehrich, Robert W., ed. *Chronologies in Old World Archaeology.* 3rd ed. 2 vols. Chicago: Univ. of Chicago Press, 1992.

Gerster, Georg. *The Past from Above: Aerial Photographs of Archaeological Sites.* Ed. Charlotte Trümpler. Trans. Stewart Spencer. Los Angeles: J. Paul Getty Museum, 2005.

Groenewegen-Frankfort, H.A., and Bernard Ashmole. *Art of the Ancient World: Painting, Pottery, Sculpture, Architecture from Egypt, Mesopotamia, Crete, Greece, and Rome.* Library of Art History. Upper Saddle River, NJ: Prentice Hall, 1972.

Haywood, John. *The Penguin Historical Atlas of Ancient Civilizations*. New York: Penguin, 2005.

Milleker, Elizabeth J., ed. *The Year One: Art of the Ancient World East and West*. New York: Metropolitan Museum of Art, 2000.

Nagle, D. Brendan. *The Ancient World: A Social and Cultural History*. 7th ed. Upper Saddle River, NJ: Pearson/ Prentice Hall, 2010.

Saggs, H.W.F. *Civilization before Greece and Rome*. New Haven: Yale Univ. Press, 1989.

Smith, William Stevenson. *Interconnections in the Ancient Near East: A Study of the Relationships between the Arts of Egypt, the Aegean, and Western Asia*. New Haven: Yale Univ. Press, 1965.

Tadgell, Christopher. *Imperial Form: From Achaemenid Iran to Augustan Rome*. New York: Whitney Library of Design, 1998.

———. *Origins: Egypt, West Asia, and the Aegean*. New York: Whitney Library of Design, 1998.

Trigger, Bruce G. *Understanding Early Civilizations: A Comparative Study*. New York: Cambridge Univ. Press, 2003.

Woodford, Susan. *The Art of Greece and Rome*. 2nd ed. New York: Cambridge Univ. Press, 2004.

European Medieval Art, General

Backman, Clifford R. *The Worlds of Medieval Europe*. 2nd ed. New York: Oxford Univ. Press, 2009.

Bennett, Adelaide Louise, et al. *Medieval Mastery: Book Illumination from Charlemagne to Charles the Bold: 800– 1475*. Trans. Lee Preedy and Greta Arblaster-Holmer. Turnhout: Brepols, 2002.

Benton, Janetta R. *Art of the Middle Ages*. World of Art. New York: Thames & Hudson, 2002.

Binski, Paul. *Painters*. Medieval Craftsmen. London: British Museum Press, 1991.

Brown, Sarah, and David O'Connor. *Glass-painters*. Medieval Craftsmen. London: British Museum Press, 1991.

Calkins, Robert G. *Medieval Architecture in Western Europe: From A.D. 300 to 1500*. New York: Oxford Univ. Press, 1998.

Cherry, John F. *Goldsmiths*. Medieval Craftsmen. London: British Museum Press, 1992.

Clark, William W. *The Medieval Cathedrals*. Westport, CT: Greenwood Press, 2006.

Coldstream, Nicola. *Masons and Sculptors*. Medieval Craftsmen. London: British Museum Press, 1991.

———. *Medieval Architecture*. Oxford History of Art. Oxford: Oxford Univ. Press, 2002.

De Hamel, Christopher. *Scribes and Illuminators*. Medieval Craftsmen. London: British Museum Press, 1992.

Duby, Georges. *Art and Society in the Middle Ages*. Trans. Jean Birrell. Malden, MA: Blackwell, 2000.

Fossier, Robert, ed. *The Cambridge Illustrated History of the Middle Ages*. Trans. Janet Sondheimer and Sarah Hanbury Tenison. 3 vols. Cambridge: Cambridge Univ. Press, 1986–97.

Hoffman, Eva R., ed. *Late Antique and Medieval Art of the Mediterranean World*. Malden, MA: Blackwell Publishing Ltd., 2007.

Hürlimann, Martin, and Jean Bony. *French Cathedrals*. Rev. & enlarged ed. London: Thames & Hudson, 1967.

Jotischky, Andrew, and Caroline Susan Hull. *The Penguin Historical Atlas of the Medieval World*. New York: Penguin, 2005.

Kenyon, John. *Medieval Fortifications*. Leicester: Leicester Univ. Press, 1990.

Pfaffenbichler, Matthias. *Armourers*. Medieval Craftsmen. London: British Museum Press, 1992.

Rebold Benton, Janetta. *Art of the Middle Ages*. World of Art. New York: Thames & Hudson, 2002.

Rudolph, Conrad, ed. *A Companion to Medieval Art*. Blackwell Companions to Art History. Oxford: Blackwell, 2006.

Sekules, Veronica. *Medieval Art*. Oxford History of Art. New York: Oxford Univ. Press, 2001.

Snyder, James, Henry Luttikhuizen, and Dorothy Verkerk. *Art of the Middle Ages*. 2nd ed. Upper Saddle River, NJ: Pearson/Prentice Hall, 2006.

Staniland, Kay. *Embroiderers*. Medieval Craftsmen. London: British Museum Press, 1991.

Stokstad, Marilyn. *Medieval Art*. 2nd ed. Boulder, CO: Westview Press, 2004.

———. *Medieval Castles*. Greenwood Guides to Historic Events of the Medieval World. Westport, CT: Greenwood Press, 2005.

European Renaissance through Eighteenth-Century Art, General

Black, C.F., et al. *Cultural Atlas of the Renaissance*. New York: Prentice Hall, 1993.

Blunt, Anthony. *Art and Architecture in France, 1500–1700*. 5th ed. Revised Richard Beresford. Pelican History of Art. New Haven: Yale Univ. Press, 1999.

Brown, Jonathan. *Painting in Spain: 1500–1700*. Pelican History of Art. New Haven: Yale Univ. Press, 1998.

Campbell, Stephen J., and Michael W. Cole. *Italian Renaissance Art*. New York: Thames & Hudson, 2014.

Cole, Bruce. *Studies in the History of Italian Art, 1250–1550*. London: Pindar Press, 1996.

Graham-Dixon, Andrew. *Renaissance*. Berkeley: Univ. of California Press, 1999.

Harbison, Craig. *The Mirror of the Artist: Northern Renaissance Art in Its Historical Context*. Perspectives. New York: Abrams, 1995.

Harris, Ann Sutherland. *Seventeenth-Century Art & Architecture*. 2nd ed. Upper Saddle River, NJ: Pearson/ Prentice Hall, 2008.

Harrison, Charles, Paul Wood, and Jason Gaiger. *Art in Theory 1648–1815: An Anthology of Changing Ideas*. Oxford: Blackwell, 2000.

Hartt, Frederick, and David G. Wilkins. *History of Italian Renaissance Art: Painting, Sculpture, Architecture*. 7th ed. Upper Saddle River, NJ: Pearson/Prentice Hall, 2011.

Jestaz, Bertrand. *The Art of the Renaissance*. Trans. I. Mark Paris. New York: Abrams, 1994.

Minor, Vernon Hyde. *Baroque & Rococo: Art & Culture*. New York: Abrams, 1999.

Paoletti, John T., and Gary M. Radke. *Art in Renaissance Italy*. 3rd ed. Upper Saddle River, NJ: Pearson/Prentice Hall, 2005.

Smith, Jeffrey Chipps. *The Northern Renaissance*. Art & Ideas. London and New York: Phaidon Press, 2004.

Stechow, Wolfgang. *Northern Renaissance, 1400–1600: Sources and Documents*. Upper Saddle River, NJ: Pearson/ Prentice Hall, 1966.

Summerson, John. *Architecture in Britain, 1530– 1830*. 9th ed. Pelican History of Art. New Haven: Yale Univ. Press, 1993.

Waterhouse, Ellis K. *Painting in Britain, 1530–1790*. 5th ed. Pelican History of Art. New Haven: Yale Univ. Press, 1994.

Whinney, Margaret Dickens. *Sculpture in Britain: 1530– 1830*. 2nd ed. Revised John Physick. Pelican History of Art. London: Penguin, 1988.

Modern Art in the West, General

Arnason, H.H., and Elizabeth C. Mansfield. *History of Modern Art: Painting, Sculpture, Architecture, Photography*. 6th ed. Upper Saddle River, NJ: Pearson/Prentice Hall, 2009.

Ballantyne, Andrew, ed. *Architectures: Modernism and After*. New Interventions in Art History, 3. Malden, MA: Blackwell, 2004.

Barnitz, Jacqueline. *Twentieth-Century Art of Latin America*. Austin: Univ. of Texas Press, 2001.

Bjelajac, David. *American Art: A Cultural History*. Rev. and expanded ed. Upper Saddle River, NJ: Pearson/Prentice Hall, 2005.

Bowness, Alan. *Modern European Art*. World of Art. New York: Thames & Hudson, 1995.

Brettell, Richard R. *Modern Art, 1851 1929: Capitalism and Representation*. Oxford History of Art. Oxford: Oxford Univ. Press, 1999.

Chipp, Herschel B. *Theories of Modern Art: A Source Book by Artists and Critics*. California Studies in the History of Art, 11. Berkeley: Univ. of California Press, 1984.

Clarke, Graham. *The Photograph*. Oxford History of Art. Oxford: Oxford Univ. Press, 1997.

Craven, David. *Art and Revolution in Latin America, 1910–1990*. New Haven: Yale Univ. Press, 2002.

Craven, Wayne. *American Art: History and Culture*. 2nd ed. Boston: McGraw-Hill, 2003.

Doordan, Dennis P. *Twentieth-Century Architecture*. New York: Abrams, 2002.

Doss, Erika. *Twentieth-Century American Art*. Oxford History of Art. Oxford: Oxford Univ. Press, 2002.

Edwards, Steve, and Paul Wood, eds. *Art of the Avant-Gardes*. Art of the 20th Century. New Haven: Yale Univ. Press, 2004.

Foster, Hal, et al. *Art Since 1900: Modernism, Antimodernism, Postmodernism*. New York: Thames & Hudson, 2004.

Gaiger, Jason, ed. *Frameworks for Modern Art*. Art of the 20th Century. New Haven: Yale Univ. Press, 2003.

———, and Paul Wood, eds. *Art of the Twentieth Century: A Reader*. New Haven: Yale Univ. Press, 2003.

Hamilton, George Heard. *Painting and Sculpture in Europe, 1880–1940*. 6th ed. Pelican History of Art. New Haven: Yale Univ. Press, 1993.

Hammacher, A.M. *Modern Sculpture: Tradition and Innovation*. Enl. ed. New York: Abrams, 1988.

Harris, Ann Sutherland, and Linda Nochlin. *Women Artists: 1550–1950*. Los Angeles: Los Angeles County Museum of Art, 1976.

Harrison, Charles, and Paul Wood, eds. *Art in Theory: 1900–2000: An Anthology of Changing Ideas*. 2nd ed. Malden, MA: Blackwell, 2003.

Hunter, Sam, John Jacobus, and Daniel Wheeler. *Modern Art: Painting, Sculpture, Architecture, Photography*. 3rd rev. & exp. ed. Upper Saddle River, NJ: Pearson/Prentice Hall, 2004.

Krauss, Rosalind E. *Passages in Modern Sculpture*. Cambridge, MA: MIT Press, 1977.

Mancini, JoAnne Marie. *Pre-Modernism: Art-World Change and American Culture from the Civil War to the Armory Show*. Princeton, NJ: Princeton Univ. Press, 2005.

Marien, Mary Warner. *Photography: A Cultural History*. 3rd ed. Upper Saddle River, NJ: Pearson/Prentice Hall, 2011.

Meecham, Pam, and Julie Sheldon. *Modern Art: A Critical Introduction*. 2nd ed. New York: Routledge, 2005.

Newlands, Anne. *Canadian Art: From Its Beginnings to 2000*. Willowdale, Ont.: Firefly Books, 2000.

Phaidon Atlas of Contemporary World Architecture. London: Phaidon Press, 2004.

Powell, Richard J. *Black Art: A Cultural History*. World of Art. 2nd ed. New York: Thames & Hudson, 2003.

Rosenblum, Naomi. *A World History of Photography*. 4th ed. New York: Abbeville Press, 2007.

Ruhrberg, Karl. *Art of the 20th Century*. Ed. Ingo F. Walther. 2 vols. New York: Taschen, 1998.

Scully, Vincent Joseph. *Modern Architecture and Other Essays*. Princeton, NJ: Princeton Univ. Press, 2003.

Stiles, Kristine, and Peter Selz. *Theories and Documents of Contemporary Art: A Sourcebook of Artists' Writings*. California Studies in the History of Art, 35. Berkeley: Univ. of California Press, 1996.

Tafuri, Manfredo. *Modern Architecture*. History of World Architecture. 2 vols. New York: Electa/Rizzoli, 1986.

Upton, Dell. *Architecture in the United States*. Oxford History of Art. Oxford: Oxford Univ. Press, 1998.

Wood, Paul, ed. *Varieties of Modernism*. Art of the 20th Century. New Haven: Yale Univ. Press, 2004.

Woodham, Jonathan M. *Twentieth-Century Design*. Oxford History of Art. Oxford: Oxford Univ. Press, 1997.

Asian Art, General

Addiss, Stephen, Gerald Groemer, and J. Thomas Rimer, eds. *Traditional Japanese Arts and Culture: An Illustrated Sourcebook*. Honolulu: Univ. of Hawai'i Press, 2006.

Barnhart, Richard M. *Three Thousand Years of Chinese Painting*. New Haven: Yale Univ. Press, 1997.

Blunden, Caroline, and Mark Elvin. *Cultural Atlas of China*. 2nd ed. New York: Checkmark Books, 1998.

Brown, Kerry, ed. *Sikh Art and Literature*. New York: Routledge in collaboration with the Sikh Foundation, 1999.

Chang, Léon Long-Yien, and Peter Miller. *Four Thousand Years of Chinese Calligraphy*. Chicago: Univ. of Chicago Press, 1990.

Chang, Yang-mo. *Arts of Korea*. Ed. Judith G. Smith. New York: Metropolitan Museum of Art, 1998.

Clark, John. *Modern Asian Art*. Honolulu: Univ. of Hawai'i Press, 1998.

Clunas, Craig. *Art in China*. 2nd ed. Oxford History of Art. Oxford: Oxford Univ. Press, 2009.

Coaldrake, William H. *Architecture and Authority in Japan*. London: Routledge, 1996.

Collcutt, Martin, Marius Jansen, and Isao Kumakura. *Cultural Atlas of Japan*. New York: Facts on File, 1988.

Craven, Roy C. *Indian Art: A Concise History*. Rev. ed. World of Art. New York: Thames & Hudson, 1997.

Dehejia, Vidya. *Indian Art*. Art & Ideas. London: Phaidon Press, 1997.

Fisher, Robert E. *Buddhist Art and Architecture*. World of Art. New York: Thames & Hudson, 1993.

Fu, Xinian. *Chinese Architecture*. Ed. & exp. ed., Nancy S. Steinhardt. New Haven: Yale Univ. Press, 2002.

Hearn, Maxwell K., and Judith G. Smith, eds. *Arts of the Sung and Yüan: Papers Prepared for an International Symposium*. New York: Dept. of Asian Art, Metropolitan Museum of Art, 1996.

Heibonsha Survey of Japanese Art. 31 vols. New York: Weatherhill, 1972–80.

Hertz, Betti-Sue. *Past in Reverse: Contemporary Art of East Asia*. San Diego: San Diego Museum of Art, 2004.

Japanese Arts Library. 15 vols. New York: Kodansha International, 1977–87.

Kerlogue, Fiona. *Arts of Southeast Asia*. World of Art. New York: Thames & Hudson, 2004.

Khanna, Balraj, and George Michell. *Human and Divine: 2000 Years of Indian Sculpture*. London: Hayward Gallery, 2000.

Lee, Sherman E. *A History of Far Eastern Art*. 5th ed. Ed. Naomi Noble Richards. New York: Abrams, 1994.

———. *China, 5000 Years: Innovation and Transformation in the Arts*. New York: Solomon R. Guggenheim Museum, 1998.

Leidy, Denise Patry. *The Art of Buddhism: An Introduction to Its History and Meaning*. Boston: Shambhala Publications, 2008.

Liu, Cary Y., and Dora C.Y. Ching, eds. *Arts of the Sung and Yüan: Ritual, Ethnicity, and Style in Painting*. Princeton, NJ: Art Museum, Princeton Univ., 1999.

McArthur, Meher. *The Arts of Asia: Materials, Techniques, Styles*. New York: Thames & Hudson, 2005.

———. *Reading Buddhist Art: An Illustrated Guide to Buddhist Signs and Symbols*. New York: Thames & Hudson, 2002.

Mason, Penelope. *History of Japanese Art*. 2nd ed. Upper Saddle River, NJ: Pearson/Prentice Hall, 2005.

Michell, George. *Hindu Art and Architecture*. World of Art. London: Thames & Hudson, 2000.

———. *The Penguin Guide to the Monuments of India*. 2 vols. New York: Viking, 1989.

Mitter, Partha. *Indian Art*. Oxford History of Art. Oxford: Oxford Univ. Press, 2001.

Murase, Miyeko. *Bridge of Dreams: The Mary Griggs Burke Collection of Japanese Art*. New York: Metropolitan Museum of Art, 2000.

Nickel, Lukas, ed. *Return of the Buddha: The Qingzhou Discoveries*. London: Royal Academy of Arts, 2002.

Pak, Youngsook, and Roderick Whitfield. *Buddhist Sculpture: Handbook of Korean Art*. London: Laurence King Publishing, 2003.

Rawson, Philip. *The Art of Southeast Asia*. World of Art. London: Thames & Hudson, 1967.

Sullivan, Michael. *The Arts of China*. 5th ed., rev. & exp. Berkeley: Univ. of California Press, 2008.

Thorp, Robert L., and Richard Ellis Vinograd. *Chinese Art & Culture*. New York: Abrams, 2001.

Topsfield, Andrew, ed. *In the Realm of Gods and Kings: Arts of India*. London: Philip Wilson, 2004.

Tucker, Jonathan. *The Silk Road: Art and History*. Chicago: Art Media Resources, 2003.

Tregear, Mary. *Chinese Art*. Rev. ed. World of Art. New York: Thames & Hudson, 1997.

Vainker, S.J. *Chinese Pottery and Porcelain: From Prehistory to the Present*. New York: Braziller, 1991.

African and Oceanic Art and Art of the Americas, General

Anderson, Richard L., and Karen L. Field, eds. *Art in Small-Scale Societies: Contemporary Readings*. Upper Saddle River, NJ: Pearson/Prentice Hall, 1993.

Bassani, Ezio, ed. *Arts of Africa: 7000 Years of African Art*. Milan: Skira, 2005.

Benson, Elizabeth P. *Retratos: 2,000 Years of Latin American Portraits*. San Antonio, TX: San Antonio Museum of Art, 2004.

Berlo, Janet Catherine, and Lee Anne Wilson. *Arts of Africa, Oceania, and the Americas: Selected Readings*. Upper Saddle River, NJ: Prentice Hall, 1993.

Calloway, Colin G. *First Peoples: A Documentary Survey of American Indian History*. 3rd ed. Boston: Bedford/St. Martin's, 2008.

Coote, Jeremy, and Anthony Shelton, eds. *Anthropology, Art, and Aesthetics*. New York: Oxford Univ. Press, 1992.

Drewal, Henry, and John Pemberton III. *Yoruba: Nine Centuries of African Art and Thought*. New York: Center for African Art, 1989.

Evans, Susan Toby. *Ancient Mexico & Central America: Archaeology and Culture History*. 2nd ed. New York: Thames & Hudson, 2008.

———, and David L. Webster, eds. *Archaeology of Ancient Mexico and Central America: An Encyclopedia*. New York: Garland, 2001.

———, and Joanne Pillsbury, eds. *Palaces of the Ancient New World: A Symposium at Dumbarton Oaks, 10th and 11th October, 1998*. Washington, DC: Dumbarton Oaks Research Library and Collection, 2004.

Mack, John, ed. *Africa, Arts and Cultures*. London: British Museum Press, 2000.

Mexico: Splendors of Thirty Centuries. New York: Metropolitan Museum of Art, 1990.

Nunley, John W., and Cara McCarty. *Masks: Faces of Culture*. New York: Abrams in assoc. with the Saint Louis Art Museum, 1999.

Perani, Judith, and Fred T. Smith. *The Visual Arts of Africa: Gender, Power, and Life Cycle Rituals*. Upper Saddle River, NJ: Pearson/Prentice Hall, 1998.

Phillips, Tom, ed. *Africa: The Art of a Continent*. New York: Prestel, 1995.

Rabineau, Phyllis. *Feather Arts: Beauty, Wealth, and Spirit from Five Continents*. Chicago: Field Museum of Natural History, 1979.

Scott, John F. *Latin American Art: Ancient to Modern*. Gainesville: Univ. Press of Florida, 1999.

Stepan, Peter. *Africa*. Trans. John Gabriel and Elizabeth Schwaiger. London: Prestel, 2001.

Visonà, Monica Blackmun, et al. *A History of Art in Africa*. 2nd ed. Upper Saddle River, NJ: Pearson/Prentice Hall, 2008.

Introduction

Acton, Mary. *Learning to Look at Paintings*. 2nd ed. New York: Routledge, 2009.

Arnold, Dana. *Art History: A Very Short Introduction*. Oxford and New York: Oxford Univ. Press, 2004.

Baxandall, Michael. *Patterns of Intention: On the Historical Explanation of Pictures*. New Haven: Yale Univ. Press, 1985.

Clearwater, Bonnie. *The Rothko Book*. London: Tate Publishing, 2006.

Decoteau, Pamela Hibbs. *Clara Peeters, 1594–ca.1640 and the Development of Still-Life Painting in Northern Europe*. Lingen: Luca Verlag, 1992.

Geertz, Clifford. "Art as a Cultural System." *Modern Language Notes* 91 (1976): 1473–1499.

Hochstrasser, Julie Berger. *Still Life and Trade in the Dutch Golden Age*. New Haven: Yale Univ. Press, 2007.

Holstein, Jonathan. *The Pieced Quilt: An American Design Tradition*. New York: Galahad Books, 1973.

Jolly, Penny Howell. "Rogier van der Weyden's Escorial and Philadelphia Crucifixions and Their Relation to Fra Angelico at San Marco." *Oud Holland* 95 (1981): 113–126.

Mainardi, Patricia. "Quilts: The Great American Art." *The Feminist Art Journal* 2/1 (1973): 1, 18–23.

Miller, Angela L., et al. *American Encounters: Art, History, and Cultural Identity.* Upper Saddle River, NJ: Pearson/ Prentice Hall, 2008.

Minor, Vernon Hyde. *Art History's History.* Upper Saddle River, NJ: Pearson/Prentice Hall, 2001.

Nelson, Robert S., and Richard Shiff, eds. *Critical Terms for Art History.* 2nd ed. Chicago: Univ. of Chicago Press, 2003.

Panofsky, Erwin. *Studies in Iconology: Humanistic Themes in the Art of the Renaissance.* New York: Oxford Univ. Press, 1939.

———. *Meaning in the Visual Arts.* Phoenix ed. Chicago: Univ. of Chicago Press, 1982.

Preziosi, Donald, ed. *The Art of Art History: A Critical Anthology.* 2nd ed. Oxford and New York: Oxford Univ. Press, 2009.

Rothko, Mark. *Writings on Art.* Ed. Miguel López-Remiro. New Haven: Yale Univ. Press, 2006.

———. *The Artist's Reality: Philosophies of Art.* Ed. Christopher Rothko. New Haven: Yale Univ. Press, 2004.

Schapiro, Meyer. "The Apples of Cézanne: An Essay on the Meaning of Still Life." *Art News Annual* 34 (1968): 34–53. Reprinted in *Modern Art 19th & 20th Centuries: Selected Papers* 2. London: Chatto & Windus, 1978.

Sowers, Robert. *Rethinking the Forms of Visual Expression.* Berkeley: Univ. of California Press, 1990.

Taylor, Joshua. *Learning to Look: A Handbook for the Visual Arts.* 2nd ed. Chicago: Chicago Univ. Press, 1981.

Tucker, Mark. "Rogier van der Weyden's 'Philadelphia Crucifixion.'" *Burlington Magazine* 139 (1997): 676–683.

Wang, Fangyu, et al., eds. *Master of the Lotus Garden: The Life and Art of Bada Shanren* (1626–1705). New Haven: Yale Univ. Press, 1990.

Chapter 1 Prehistoric Art

Aujoulat, Norbert. *Lascaux: Movement, Space, and Time.* New York: Abrams, 2005.

Bahn, Paul G. *The Cambridge Illustrated History of Prehistoric Art.* Cambridge Illustrated History. Cambridge: Cambridge Univ. Press, 1998.

Bataille, Georges. *The Cradle of Humanity: Prehistoric Art and Culture.* Ed. Stuart Kendall. Trans. Michelle Kendall and Stuart Kendall. New York: Zone Books, 2005.

Berghaus, Gunter. *New Perspectives on Prehistoric Art.* Westport, CT: Praeger, 2004.

Chippindale, Christopher. *Stonehenge Complete.* 3rd ed. New York: Thames & Hudson, 2004.

Clottes, Jean. *Chauvet Cave: The Art of Earliest Times.* Salt Lake City: Univ. of Utah Press, 2003.

———. *World Rock Art.* Trans. Guy Bennett. Los Angeles: Getty Conservation Institute, 2002.

———, and J. David Lewis-Williams. *The Shamans of Prehistory: Trance and Magic in the Painted Caves.* Trans. Sophie Hawkes. New York: Abrams, 1998.

Connah, Graham. *African Civilizations: An Archaeological Perspective.* 2nd ed. Cambridge: Cambridge Univ. Press, 2001.

Coulson, David, and Alec Campbell. *African Rock Art: Painting and Engravings on Stone.* New York: Abrams, 2001.

Cunliffe, Barry W., ed. *The Oxford Illustrated History of Prehistoric Europe.* New York: Oxford Univ. Press, 2001.

Forte, Maurizio, and Alberto Siliotti. *Virtual Archaeology: Re- Creating Ancient Worlds.* New York: Abrams, 1997.

Freeman, Leslie G. *Altamira Revisited and Other Essays on Early Art.* Chicago: Institute for Prehistoric Investigation, 1987.

Garlake, Peter S. *The Hunter's Vision: The Prehistoric Art of Zimbabwe.* Seattle: Univ. of Washington Press, 1995.

Gowlett, John A.J. *Ascent to Civilization: The Archaeology of Early Humans.* 2nd ed. New York: McGraw-Hill, 1993.

Guthrie, R. Dale. *The Nature of Paleolithic Art.* Chicago: Univ. of Chicago Press, 2005.

Jope, E.M. *Early Celtic Art in the British Isles.* 2 vols. New York: Oxford Univ. Press, 2000.

Kenrick, Douglas M. *Jomon of Japan: The World's Oldest Pottery.* New York: Kegan Paul, 1995.

Le Quellec, Jean-Loïc. *Rock Art in Africa: Mythology and Legend.* Trans. Paul Bahn. Paris: Flammarion, 2004.

Leakey, Richard E., and Roger Lewin. *Origins Reconsidered: In Search of What Makes Us Human.* New York: Doubleday, 1992.

Leroi-Gourhan, André. *The Dawn of European Art: An Introduction to Paleolithic Cave Painting.* Trans. Sara Champion. Cambridge: Cambridge Univ. Press, 1982.

Lewis-Williams, J. David. *The Mind in the Cave: Consciousness and the Origins of Art.* New York: Thames & Hudson, 2002.

O'Kelly, Michael J. *Newgrange: Archaeology, Art, and Legend.* New Aspects of Antiquity. London: Thames & Hudson, 1982.

Price, T. Douglas. *Images of the Past.* 5th ed. Boston: McGraw-Hill, 2008.

Renfrew, Colin, ed. *The Megalithic Monuments of Western Europe.* London: Thames & Hudson, 1983.

Sandars, N.K. *Prehistoric Art in Europe.* 2nd ed. Pelican History of Art. New Haven: Yale Univ. Press, 1992.

Sieveking, Ann. *The Cave Artists.* Ancient People and Places, vol. 93. London: Thames & Hudson, 1979.

Sura Ramos, Pedro A. *The Cave of Altamira.* Gen. Ed. Antonio Beltran. New York: Abrams, 1999.

White, Randall. *Prehistoric Art: The Symbolic Journey of Mankind.* New York: Abrams, 2003.

Chapter 2 Art of the Ancient Near East

Akurgal, Ekrem. *Ancient Civilizations and Ruins of Turkey: From Prehistoric Times until the End of the Roman Empire.* 5th ed. London: Kegan Paul, 2002.

Aruz, Joan, et al., eds. *Beyond Babylon: Art, Trade, and Diplomacy in the Second Millennium B.C.* New Haven: Yale Univ. Press, and Metropolitan Museum of Art, 2008.

———, ed. *Art of the First Cities: The Third Millennium B.C. from the Mediterranean to the Indus.* New York: Metropolitan Museum of Art, 2003.

Bahrani, Zainab. *The Graven Image: Representation in Babylonia and Assyria.* Archaeology, Culture, and Society Series. Philadelphia: Univ. of Pennsylvania Press, 2003.

Boardman, John. *Persia and the West: An Archaeological Investigation of the Genesis of Achaemenid Art.* New York: Thames & Hudson, 2000.

Bottero, Jean. *Everyday Life in Ancient Mesopotamia.* Trans. Antonia Nevill. Baltimore, MD: Johns Hopkins Univ. Press, 2001.

Charvat, Petr. *Mesopotamia before History.* Rev. & updated ed. New York: Routledge, 2002.

Crawford, Harriet. *Sumer and the Sumerians.* 2nd ed. New York: Cambridge Univ. Press, 2004.

Curtis, John, and Nigel Tallis, eds. *Forgotten Empire: The World of Ancient Persia.* Berkeley: Univ. of California Press, 2005.

Ferrier, R.W., ed. *The Arts of Persia.* New Haven: Yale Univ. Press, 1989.

Frankfort, Henri. *The Art and Architecture of the Ancient Orient.* 5th ed. Pelican History of Art. New Haven: Yale Univ. Press, 1996.

Haywood, John. *Ancient Civilizations of the Near East and Mediterranean.* London: Cassell, 1997.

Meyers, Eric M., ed. *The Oxford Encyclopedia of Archaeology in the Near East.* 5 vols. New York: Oxford Univ. Press, 1997.

Moorey, P.R.S. *Idols of the People: Miniature Images of Clay in the Ancient Near East.* The Schweich Lectures of the British Academy, 2001. New York: Oxford Univ. Press, 2003.

Polk, Milbry, and Angela M.H. Schuster. *The Looting of the Iraq Museum, Baghdad: The Lost Legacy of Ancient Mesopotamia.* New York: Abrams, 2005.

Reade, Julian. *Assyrian Sculpture.* Cambridge, MA: Harvard Univ. Press, 1999.

Roaf, Michael. *Cultural Atlas of Mesopotamia and the Ancient Near East.* New York: Facts on File, 1990.

Roux, Georges. *Ancient Iraq.* 3rd ed. London: Penguin, 1992.

Winter, Irene. "Sex, Rhetoric, and the Public Monument: The Alluring Body of the Male Ruler." In *Sexuality in Ancient Art*, eds. Natalie Kampen and Bettina A. Bergmann. Cambridge: Cambridge Univ. Press, 1996: 11–26.

Zettler, Richard L., and Lee Horne, eds. *Treasures from the Royal Tombs of Ur.* Philadelphia: Univ. of Pennsylvania, Museum of Archaeology and Anthropology, 1998.

Chapter 3 Art of Ancient Egypt

Ancient Egyptian Literature: An Anthology. Trans. John L. Foster. Austin: Univ. of Texas Press, 2001.

Arnold, Dieter. *Temples of the Last Pharaohs.* New York: Oxford Univ. Press, 1999.

Baines, John, and Jaromír Málek. *Cultural Atlas of Ancient Egypt.* Rev. ed. New York: Facts on File, 2000.

Egyptian Art in the Age of the Pyramids. New York: Metropolitan Museum of Art, 1999.

The Egyptian Book of the Dead: The Book of Going Forth by Day: Being the Papyrus of Ani (Royal Scribe of the Divine Offerings). 2nd rev. ed. Trans. Raymond O. Faulkner. San Francisco: Chronicle, 2008.

Freed, Rita E., Sue D'Auria, and Yvonne J. Markowitz. *Pharaohs of the Sun: Akhenaten, Nefertiti, Tutankhamen.* Boston: Museum of Fine Arts in assoc. with Bulfinch Press/Little, Brown, 1999.

Hawass, Zahi A. *Tutankhamun and the Golden Age of the Pharaohs.* Washington, DC: National Geographic, 2005.

Ikram, Salima. *Death and Burial in Ancient Egypt.* Cairo: The American Univ. in Cairo Press, 2015.

Ikram, Salima, and Aidan Dodson. *The Mummy in Ancient Egypt: Equipping the Dead for Eternity.* London: Thames and Hudson, 1998.

Johnson, Paul. *The Civilization of Ancient Egypt.* Updated ed. New York: HarperCollins, 1999.

Kozloff, Arielle P. *Egypt's Dazzling Sun: Amenhotep III and His World.* Cleveland: Cleveland Museum of Art, 1992.

Lehner, Mark. *The Complete Pyramids.* New York: Thames & Hudson, 2008.

Málek, Jaromir. *Egypt: 4,000 Years of Art.* London: Phaidon Press, 2003.

Reeves, Nicholas, and Richard H. Wilkinson. *The Complete Valley of the Kings.* London: Thames and Hudson, 2008.

Robins, Gay. *The Art of Ancient Egypt.* Rev. ed. Cambridge, MA: Harvard Univ. Press, 2008.

Roehrig, Catharine H., Renee Dreyfus, and Cathleen A. Keller. *Hatshepsut, from Queen to Pharaoh.* New York: Metropolitan Museum of Art, 2005.

Russmann, Edna R. *Egyptian Sculpture: Cairo and Luxor.* Austin: Univ. of Texas Press, 1989.

Smith, Craig B. *How the Great Pyramid Was Built.* Washington, DC: Smithsonian Books, 2004.

Smith, William Stevenson. *The Art and Architecture of Ancient Egypt.* 3rd ed. Revised William Kelly Simpson. Pelican History of Art. New Haven: Yale Univ. Press, 1998.

Strouhal, Eugen. *Life of the Ancient Egyptians.* Trans. Deryck Viney. Norman: Univ. of Oklahoma Press, 1992.

Strudwick, Nigel, and Helen Strudwick. *Thebes in Egypt: A Guide to the Tombs and Temples of Ancient Luxor.* Ithaca, NY: Cornell Univ. Press, 1999.

Thomas, Thelma K. *Late Antique Egyptian Funerary Sculpture: Images for this World and for the Next.* Princeton, NJ: Princeton Univ. Press, 2000.

Tiradritti, Francesco. *Ancient Egypt: Art, Architecture and History.* Trans. Phil Goddard. London: British Museum Press, 2002.

The Treasures of Ancient Egypt: From the Egyptian Museum in Cairo. New York: Rizzoli, 2003.

Wilkinson, Richard H. *The Complete Temples of Ancient Egypt.* New York: Thames & Hudson, 2000.

———. *Reading Egyptian Art: A Hieroglyphic Guide to Ancient Egyptian Painting and Sculpture.* London: Thames & Hudson, 1992.

Winstone, H.V.F. *Howard Carter and the Discovery of the Tomb of Tutankhamen.* Rev. ed. Manchester: Barzan, 2006.

Ziegler, Cristiane, ed. *The Pharaohs.* New York: Rizzoli, 2002.

Zivie-Coche, Christiane. *Sphinx: History of a Monument.* Trans. David Lorton. Ithaca, NY: Cornell Univ. Press, 2002.

Chapter 4 Art of the Ancient Aegean

Castleden, Rodney. *The Knossos Labyrinth: A New View of the "Palace of Minos" at Knossos.* London: Routledge, 1990.

———. *Mycenaeans.* New York: Routledge, 2005.

Demargne, Pierre. *The Birth of Greek Art.* Trans. Stuart Gilbert and James Emmons. Arts of Mankind, vol. 6. New York: Golden, 1964.

Doumas, Christos. *The Wall-Paintings of Thera.* 2nd ed. Trans. Alex Doumas. Athens: Kapon Editions, 1999.

Fitton, J. Lesley. *Cycladic Art.* 2nd ed. London: British Museum Press, 1999.

Getz-Gentle, Pat. *Personal Styles in Early Cycladic Sculpture.* Madison: Univ. of Wisconsin Press, 2001.

Hamilakis, Yannis. ed. *Labyrinth Revisited: Rethinking "Minoan" Archaeology.* Oxford: Oxbow, 2002.

Hendrix, Elizabeth. "Painted Ladies of the Early Bronze Age." *The Metropolitan Museum of Art Bulletin New Series,* 55/3 (Winter 1997–1998): 4–15.

Higgins, Reynold A. *Minoan and Mycenean Art.* New. ed. World of Art. New York: Thames & Hudson, 1997.

Hitchcock, Louise. *Minoan Architecture: A Contextual Analysis.* Studies in Mediterranean Archaeology and Literature, Pocket-Book, 155. Jonsered: P. Åströms Förlag, 2000.

Hoffman, Gail L. "Painted Ladies: Early Cycladic II Mourning Figures?" *American Journal of Archaeology* 106/4 (October 2002): 525–550.

Immerwahr, Sara Anderson. *Aegean Painting in the Bronze Age.* University Park: Pennsylvania State Univ. Press, 1990.

Preziosi, Donald, and Louise Hitchcock. *Aegean Art and Architecture.* Oxford History of Art. Oxford: Oxford Univ. Press, 1999.

Shelmerdine, Cynthia W., ed. *The Cambridge Companion to the Aegean Bronze Age.* New York: Cambridge Univ. Press, 2008.

Strasser, Thomas F. "Location and Perspective in the Theran Flotilla Fresco." *Journal of Mediterranean Archaeology* 23/1 (2010): 3–26.

Chapter 5 Art of Ancient Greece

Barletta, Barbara A. *The Origins of the Greek Architectural Orders.* New York: Cambridge Univ. Press, 2001.

Beard, Mary. *The Parthenon.* Cambridge, MA: Harvard Univ. Press, 2003.

Belozerskaya, Marina, and Kenneth D.S. Lapatin. *Ancient Greece: Art, Architecture, and History.* Los Angeles: J. Paul Getty Museum, 2004.

Boardman, John. *Early Greek Vase Painting: 11th–6th Centuries B.C.: A Handbook.* World of Art. London: Thames & Hudson, 1998.

———. *Greek Sculpture: The Archaic Period: A Handbook.* World of Art. London: Thames & Hudson, 1991.

———. *Greek Sculpture: The Classical Period: A Handbook.* World of Art London: Thames & Hudson, 1985.

———. *Greek Sculpture: The Late Classical Period and Sculpture in Colonies and Overseas.* World of Art. New York: Thames & Hudson, 1995.

———. *The History of Greek Vases: Potters, Painters, and Pictures.* New York: Thames & Hudson, 2001.

Burn, Lucilla. *Hellenistic Art: From Alexander the Great to Augustus.* Los Angeles: J. Paul Getty Museum, 2004.

Clark, Andrew J., Maya Elston, and Mary Louise Hart. *Understanding Greek Vases: A Guide to Terms, Styles, and Techniques.* Los Angeles: J. Paul Getty Museum, 2002.

De Grummond, Nancy T. and Brunilde S. Ridgway. *From Pergamon to Sperlonga: Sculpture in Context.* Berkeley: Univ. of California Press, 2000.

Donohue, A.A. *Greek Sculpture and the Problem of Description.* New York: Cambridge Univ. Press, 2005.

Fullerton, Mark D. *Greek Art.* Cambridge: Cambridge Univ. Press, 2000.

Hard, Robin. *The Routledge Handbook of Greek Mythology:* Based on H.J. Rose's "Handbook of Greek Mythology." 7th ed. London: Routledge, 2008.

Hurwit, Jeffrey M. *The Acropolis in the Age of Pericles.* New York: Cambridge Univ. Press, 2004.

Karakasi, Katerina. *Archaic Korai.* Los Angeles: J. Paul Getty Museum, 2003.

Lawrence, A.W. *Greek Architecture.* 5th ed. Revised R.A. Tomlinson. Pelican History of Art. New Haven: Yale Univ. Press, 1996.

Martin, Roland. *Greek Architecture: Architecture of Crete, Greece, and the Greek World.* History of World Architecture. New York: Electa/Rizzoli, 1988.

Neils, Jenifer. *The British Museum Concise Introduction to Ancient Greece.* Ann Arbor: Univ. of Michigan, 2008.

Osborne, Robin. *Archaic and Classical Greek Art.* Oxford History of Art. Oxford: Oxford Univ. Press, 1998.

Palagia, Olga, ed. *Greek Sculpture: Function, Materials, and Techniques in the Archaic and Classical Periods.* New York: Cambridge Univ. Press, 2006.

———, and J.J. Pollitt, eds. *Personal Styles in Greek Sculpture.* Yale Classical Studies, vol. 30. Cambridge: Cambridge Univ. Press, 1996.

Pedley, John Griffiths. *Greek Art and Archaeology.* 5th ed. Upper Saddle River, NJ: Pearson/Prentice Hall, 2012.

Pollitt, J.J. *Art and Experience in Classical Greece.* Cambridge: Cambridge Univ. Press, 1972; reprinted 1999.

———. *The Art of Ancient Greece: Sources and Documents.* 2nd ed. rev. Cambridge: Cambridge Univ. Press, 2001.

Ridgway, Brunilde Sismondo. *The Archaic Style in Greek Sculpture.* 2nd ed. Chicago: Ares, 1993.

———. *Fifth Century Styles in Greek Sculpture.* Princeton, NJ: Princeton Univ. Press, 1981.

———. *Fourth Century Styles in Greek Sculpture.* Wisconsin Studies in Classics. Madison: Univ. of Wisconsin Press, 1997.

———. *Hellenistic Sculpture 1: The Styles of ca. 331–200 B.C.* Wisconsin Studies in Classics. Madison: Univ. of Wisconsin Press, 1990.

Stafford, Emma J. *Life, Myth, and Art in Ancient Greece.* Los Angeles: J. Paul Getty Museum, 2004.

Stewart, Andrew F. *Greek Sculpture: An Exploration.* 2 vols. New Haven: Yale Univ. Press, 1990.

Whitley, James. *The Archaeology of Ancient Greece.* New York: Cambridge Univ. Press, 2001.

Chapter 6 Etruscan and Roman Art

Bianchi Bandinelli, Ranuccio. *Rome: The Centre of Power: Roman Art to A.D. 200.* Trans. Peter Green. Arts of Mankind, 15. London: Thames & Hudson, 1971.

———. *Rome: The Late Empire: Roman Art A.D. 200–400.* Trans. Peter Green. Arts of Mankind, 17. New York: Braziller, 1971.

Borrelli, Federica. *The Etruscans: Art, Architecture, and History.* Ed. Stefano Peccatori and Stefano Zuffi. Trans. Thomas Michael Hartmann. Los Angeles: J. Paul Getty Museum, 2004.

Brendel, Otto J. *Prolegomena to the Study of Roman Art.* New Haven: Yale Univ. Press, 1979.

———. *Etruscan Art.* 2nd ed. Pelican History of Art. New Haven: Yale Univ. Press, 1995.

Conlin, Diane Atnally. *The Artists of the Ara Pacis: The Process of Hellenization in Roman Relief Sculpture.* Studies in the History of Greece & Rome. Chapel Hill: Univ. of North Carolina Press, 1997.

Cornell, Tim, and John Matthews. *Atlas of the Roman World.* New York: Facts on File, 1982.

D'Ambra, Eve. *Roman Art.* Cambridge: Cambridge Univ. Press, 1998.

Elsner, Jas. *Imperial Rome and Christian Triumph: The Art of the Roman Empire A.D. 100–450.* Oxford History of Art. Oxford: Oxford Univ. Press, 1998.

Gabucci, Ada. *Ancient Rome: Art, Architecture, and History.* Eds. Stefano Peccatori and Stephano Zuffi. Trans. T.M. Hartman. Los Angeles: J. Paul Getty Museum, 2002.

Haynes, Sybille. *Etruscan Civilization: A Cultural History.* Los Angeles: J. Paul Getty Museum, 2000.

Holloway, R. Ross. *Constantine & Rome.* New Haven: Yale Univ. Press, 2004.

Kleiner, Fred. S. *A History of Roman Art.* Belmont, CA: Thomson/Wadsworth, 2007.

MacDonald, William L. *The Architecture of the Roman Empire: An Introductory Study.* Rev. ed. 2 vols. Yale Publications in the History of Art, 17, 35. New Haven: Yale Univ. Press, 1982.

———. *The Pantheon: Design, Meaning, and Progeny.* New foreword by John Pinto. Cambridge, MA: Harvard Univ. Press, 2002.

Mattusch, Carol C. *Pompeii and the Roman Villa: Art and Culture around the Bay of Naples.* Washington, DC: National Gallery of Art, 2008.

Mazzoleni, Donatella. *Domus: Wall Painting in the Roman House.* Los Angeles: J. Paul Getty Museum, 2004.

Packer, James E. *The Forum of Trajan in Rome: A Study of the Monuments in Brief.* Berkeley: Univ. of California Press, 2001.

Pollitt, J.J. *The Art of Rome, c. 753 B.C.–337 A.D.: Sources and Documents.* Upper Saddle River, NJ: Pearson/Prentice Hall, 1966.

Polybius. *The Histories.* Trans. W.R. Paton. 6 vols. Loeb Classical Library. Cambridge, MA: Harvard Univ. Press, 2000.

Ramage, Nancy H., and Andrew Ramage. *Roman Art: Romulus to Constantine.* 5th ed. Upper Saddle River, NJ: Pearson/Prentice Hall, 2009.

Spivey, Nigel. *Etruscan Art.* World of Art. New York: Thames & Hudson, 1997.

Stamper, John W. *The Architecture of Roman Temples: The Republic to the Middle Empire.* New York: Cambridge Univ. Press, 2005.

Stewart, Peter. *Statues in Roman Society: Representation and Response.* Oxford Studies in Ancient Culture and Representation. New York: Oxford Univ. Press, 2003.

Strong, Donald. *Roman Art.* 2nd ed. rev. & annotated. Ed. Roger Ling. Pelican History of Art. New Haven: Yale Univ. Press, 1995.

Ward-Perkins, J.B. *Roman Architecture.* History of World Architecture. New York: Electa/Rizzoli, 1988.

———. *Roman Imperial Architecture.* Pelican History of Art. New Haven: Yale Univ. Press, 1981.

Wilson Jones, Mark. *Principles of Roman Architecture.* New Haven: Yale Univ. Press, 2000.

Chapter 7 Jewish and Early Christian Art

Age of Spirituality: Late Antique and Early Christian Art, Third to Seventh Century. New York: Metropolitan Museum of Art, 1979.

Beckwith, John. *Early Christian and Byzantine Art.* 2nd ed. Pelican History of Art. New Haven: Yale Univ. Press, 1986.

Bleiberg, Edward, ed. *Tree of Paradise: Jewish Mosaics from the Roman Empire.* Brooklyn: Brooklyn Museum, 2005.

Cioffarelli, Ada. *Guide to the Catacombs of Rome and its Surroundings.* Rome: Bonsignori, 2000.

Fine, Steven. *Art and Judaism in the Greco–Roman World: Toward a New Jewish Archaeology.* New York: Cambridge Univ. Press, 2005.

Hachlili, Rachel. *Ancient Mosaic Pavements: Themes, Issues, and Trends.* Leiden: Brill, 2009.

Jensen, Robin Margaret. *Understanding Early Christian Art.* New York: Routledge, 2000.

Krautheimer, Richard, and Slobodan Curcic. *Early Christian and Byzantine Architecture.* 4th ed. Pelican History of Art. New Haven: Yale Univ. Press, 1992.

Levine, Lee I., and Zeev Weiss, eds. *From Dura to Sepphoris: Studies in Jewish Art and Society in Late Antiquity.* Journal of Roman Archaeology: Supplementary Series, no. 40. Portsmouth, RI: Journal of Roman Archaeology, 2000.

Lowden, John. *Early Christian and Byzantine Art.* Art & Ideas. London: Phaidon Press, 1997.

Mathews, Thomas F. *The Clash of Gods: A Reinterpretation of Early Christian Art.* Rev. ed. Princeton, NJ: Princeton Univ. Press, 1999.

Olin, Margaret. *The Nation without Art: Examining Modern Discourses on Jewish Art.* Lincoln: Univ. of Nebraska Press, 2001.

Olsson, Birger, and Magnus Zetterholm, eds. *The Ancient Synagogue from Its Origins until 200 C.E.: Papers Presented at an International Conference at Lund University, October 14–17, 2001.* Coniectanea Biblica: New Testament Series, 39. Stockholm: Almqvist & Wiksell International, 2003.

Rutgers, Leonard V. *Subterranean Rome: In Search of the Roots of Christianity in the Catacombs of the Eternal City.* Leuven: Peeters, 2001.

Sed-Rajna, Gabrielle. *Jewish Art.* Trans. Sara Friedman and Mira Reich. New York: Abrams, 1997.

Spier, Jeffrey, ed. *Picturing the Bible: The Earliest Christian Art.* New Haven: Yale Univ. Press, 2007.

Tadgell, Christopher. *Imperial Space: Rome, Constantinople and the Early Church.* New York: Whitney Library of Design, 1998.

Webb, Matilda. *The Churches and Catacombs of Early Christian Rome: A Comprehensive Guide.* Brighton, UK: Sussex Academic Press, 2001.

Weitzmann, Kurt. *Late Antique and Early Christian Book Illumination.* New York: Braziller, 1977.

Wharton, Annabel Jane. *Refiguring the Post-Classical City: Dura Europos, Jerash, Jerusalem and Ravenna.* Cambridge: Cambridge Univ. Press, 1995.

White, L. Michael. *The Social Origins of Christian Architecture.* 2 vols. Baltimore, MD: Johns Hopkins Univ. Press, 1990.

Chapter 8 Byzantine Art

Beckwith, John. *Early Christian and Byzantine Art.* 2nd ed. Pelican History of Art. New Haven: Yale Univ. Press, 1986.

Cormack, Robin. *Byzantine Art.* Oxford: Oxford Univ. Press, 2000.

———, and Maria Vassilaki, eds. *Byzantium, 330–1453.* London: Royal Academy of Arts, 2008.

Cutler, Anthony. *The Hand of the Master: Craftsmanship, Ivory, and Society in Byzantium (9th–11th Centuries).* Princeton, NJ: Princeton Univ. Press, 1994.

Eastmond, Antony, and Liz James, eds. *Icon and Word: The Power of Images in Byzantium: Studies Presented to Robin Cormack.* Burlington, VT: Ashgate, 2003.

Evans, Helen C., ed. *Byzantium: Faith and Power (1261–1557).* New York: Metropolitan Museum of Art, 2004.

———, and William D. Wixom, eds. *The Glory of Byzantium: Art and Culture of the Middle Byzantine Era, A.D. 843–1261.* New York: Abrams, 1997.

Freely, John. *Byzantine Monuments of Istanbul.* Cambridge & New York: Cambridge Univ. Press, 2004.

Gerstel, Sharon. *Beholding the Sacred Mysteries: Programs of the Byzantine Sanctuary.* Seattle: College Art Association in association with Univ. of Washington Press, 1999.

———. *Rural Lives and Landscapes in Late Byzantium: Art, Archeology, and Ethnography.* Cambridge: Cambridge Univ. Press, 2015.

Gerstel, Sharon, and Robert Nelson. *Approaching the Holy Mountain: Art and Liturgy at St. Catherine's Monastery in the Sinai.* Turnhout: Brepols, 2010.

Grabar, André. *Byzantine Painting: Historical and Critical Study.* Trans. Stuart Gilbert. New York: Rizzoli, 1979.

Kitzinger, Ernst. *The Art of Byzantium and the Medieval West: Selected Studies.* Ed. W. Eugene Kleinbauer. Bloomington: Indiana Univ. Press, 1976.

———. *Byzantine Art in the Making: Main Lines of Stylistic Development in Mediterranean Art, 3rd–7th Century.* Cambridge, MA: Harvard Univ. Press, 1977.

Kleinbauer, W. Eugene. *Hagia Sophia.* London: Scala, 2004.

Krautheimer, Richard, and Slobodan Curcic. *Early Christian and Byzantine Architecture.* 4th ed. Pelican History of Art. New Haven: Yale Univ. Press, 1992.

Lowden, John. *Early Christian and Byzantine Art.* Art & Ideas. London: Phaidon Press, 1997.

Maguire, Henry. *The Icons of Their Bodies: Saints and Their Images in Byzantium.* Princeton, NJ: Princeton Univ. Press, 1996.

Mainstone, Rowland J. *Hagia Sophia: Architecture, Structure and Liturgy of Justinian's Great Church.* 2nd ed. New York: Thames & Hudson, 2001.

Mango, Cyril. *Art of the Byzantine Empire, 312–1453: Sources and Documents.* Upper Saddle River, NJ: Pearson/Prentice Hall, 1972.

Mathews, Thomas F. *Byzantium: From Antiquity to the Renaissance.* Perspectives. New York: Abrams, 1998.

Ousterhout, Robert. *Master Builders of Byzantium.* Princeton, NJ: Princeton Univ. Press, 1999.

Pentcheva, Bissera. *The Sensual Icon: Space, Ritual, and the Senses in Byzantium.* University Park: Pennsylvania State Univ. Press, 2010.

Procopius, with an English translation by H.B. Dewing. 7 vols. Loeb Classical Library. Cambridge, MA: Harvard Univ. Press, 1940.

Rodley, Lyn. *Byzantine Art and Architecture: An Introduction.* Cambridge: Cambridge Univ. Press, 1994.

Weitzmann, Kurt. *Place of Book Illumination in Byzantine Art.* Princeton, NJ: Art Museum, Princeton Univ., 1975.

Chapter 9 Islamic Art

Al-Faruqi, Isma'il R., and Lois Ibsen Al-Faruqi. *Cultural Atlas of Islam.* New York: Macmillan, 1986.

Atil, Esin. *The Age of Sultan Suleyman the Magnificent.* Washington, DC: National Gallery of Art, 1987.

Baker, Patricia L. *Islam and the Religious Arts.* London: Continuum, 2004.

Barry, Michael A. *Figurative Art in Medieval Islam and the Riddle of Bihzâd of Herât (1465–1535)*. Paris: Flammarion, 2004.

Blair, Sheila S., and Jonathan Bloom. *The Art and Architecture of Islam 1250–1800*. Pelican History of Art. New Haven: Yale Univ. Press, 1995.

Dodds, Jerrilynn D., ed. *Al-Andalus: The Art of Islamic Spain*. New York: Metropolitan Museum of Art, 1992.

Ecker, Heather. *Caliphs and Kings: The Art and Influence of Islamic Spain*. Washington, DC: Arthur M. Sackler Gallery, 2004.

Ettinghausen, Richard, Oleg Grabar, and Marilyn Jenkins-Madina. *Islamic Art and Architecture, 650–1250*. 2nd ed. Pelican History of Art. New Haven: Yale Univ. Press, 2001.

Frishman, Martin, and Hasan-Uddin Khan. *The Mosque: History, Architectural Development and Regional Diversity*. London: Thames & Hudson, 1994.

Grabar, Oleg. *The Formation of Islamic Art*. Rev. and enl. ed. New Haven: Yale Univ. Press, 1987.

———. *The Great Mosque of Isfahan*. New York: New York Univ. Press, 1990.

———. *Islamic Visual Culture, 1100–1800*. Burlington, VT: Ashgate, 2006.

———, *Mostly Miniatures: An Introduction to Persian Painting*. Princeton, NJ: Princeton Univ. Press, 2000.

———, Mohammad Al-Asad, Abeer Audeh, and Said Nuseibeh. *The Shape of the Holy: Early Islamic Jerusalem*. Princeton, NJ: Princeton Univ. Press, 1996.

Hillenbrand, Robert. *Islamic Art and Architecture*. World of Art. London: Thames & Hudson, 1999.

Irwin, Robert. *The Alhambra*. Cambridge, MA: Harvard Univ. Press, 2004.

Khalili, Nasser D. *Visions of Splendour in Islamic Art and Culture*. London: Worth Press, 2008.

Komaroff, Linda, and Stefano Carboni, eds. *The Legacy of Genghis Khan: Courtly Art and Culture in Western Asia, 1256–1353*. New York: Metropolitan Museum of Art, 2002.

Lentz, Thomas W., and Glenn D. Lowry. *Timur and the Princely Vision: Persian Art and Culture in the Fifteenth Century*. Los Angeles: Los Angeles County Museum of Art, 1989.

Necipolu, Gülru. *The Age of Sinan: Architectural Culture in the Ottoman Empire*. Princeton, NJ: Princeton Univ. Press, 2005.

Petruccioli, Attilio, and Khalil K. Pirani, eds. *Understanding Islamic Architecture*. New York: Routledge Curzon, 2002.

Roxburgh, David J., ed. *Turks: A Journey of a Thousand Years, 600–1600*. London: Royal Academy of Arts, 2005.

Sims, Eleanor, B.I. Marshak, and Ernst J. Grube. *Peerless Images: Persian Painting and Its Sources*. New Haven: Yale Univ. Press, 2002.

Stanley, Tim, Mariam Rosser-Owen, and Stephen Vernoit. *Palace and Mosque: Islamic Art from the Middle East*. London: V&A Publications, 2004.

Stierlin, Henri. *Islamic Art and Architecture*. New York: Thames & Hudson, 2002.

Tadgell, Christopher. *Four Caliphates: The Formation and Development of the Islamic Tradition*. London: Ellipsis, 1998.

Ward, R.M. *Islamic Metalwork*. New York: Thames & Hudson, 1993.

Watson, Oliver. *Ceramics from Islamic Lands*. New York: Thames & Hudson in assoc. with the al-Sabah Collection, Dar al-Athar al-Islamiyyah, Kuwait National Museum, 2004.

Chapter 10 Art of South and Southeast Asia before 1200

Atherton, Cynthia Packert. *The Sculpture of Early Medieval Rajasthan*. Studies in Asian Art and Archaeology, vol. 21. New York: Brill, 1997.

Behl, Benoy K. *The Ajanta Caves: Artistic Wonder of Ancient Buddhist India*. New York: Abrams, 1998.

Behrendt, Kurt A. *The Buddhist Architecture of Gandhara*. Handbook of Oriental Studies: Section Two: India, vol. 17. Boston: Brill, 2004.

Brown, Robert L., ed. *Art from Thailand*. Mumbai: Marg Publications, 1999.

Chakrabarti, Dilip K. *India, an Archaeological History: Palaeolithic Beginnings to Early Historic Foundations*. 2nd ed. New York: Oxford Univ. Press, 2009.

Craven, Roy C. *Indian Art: A Concise History*. Rev. ed. World of Art. New York: Thames & Hudson, 1997.

Czuma, Stanislaw J. *Kushan Sculpture: Images from Early India*. Cleveland: Cleveland Museum of Art, 1985.

Dehejia, Vidya. *Art of the Imperial Cholas*. New York: Columbia Univ. Press, 1990.

———. *The Sensuous and the Sacred: Chola Bronzes from South India*. New York: American Federation of Arts, 2002.

Dessai, Vishakha N., and Darielle Mason, eds. *Gods, Guardians, and Lovers: Temple Sculptures from North India, A.D. 700–1200*. New York: Asia Society Galleries, 1993.

Dhavalikar, Madhukar Keshav. *Ellora*. New York: Oxford Univ. Press, 2003.

Girard-Geslan, Maud. *Art of Southeast Asia*. Trans. J.A. Underwood. New York: Abrams, Inc., 1998.

Guy, John, ed. *Lost Kingdoms: Hindu-Buddhist Sculpture of Early Southeast Asia*. New Haven: Yale Univ. Press and Metropolitan Museum of Art, 2014.

Heller, Amy. *Early Himalayan Art*. Oxford: Ashmolean Museum, 2008.

Huntington, Susan L. *The Art of Ancient India: Buddhist, Hindu, Jain*. New York: Weatherhill, 1985.

———. *Leaves from the Bodhi Tree: The Art of Pala India (8th–12th Centuries) and Its International Legacy*. Dayton, OH: Dayton Art Institute, 1990.

Hutt, Michael. *Nepal: A Guide to the Art and Architecture of the Kathmandu Valley*. Boston: Shambhala, 1995.

Knox, Robert. *Amaravati: Buddhist Sculpture from the Great Stupa*. London: British Museum Press, 1992.

Khanna, Sucharita. *Dancing Divinities in Indian Art: 8th–12th Century A.D.* Delhi: Sharada Pub. House, 1999.

Kramrisch, Stella. *The Art of Nepal*. New York: Abrams, 1964.

———. *The Presence of Siva*. Princeton, NJ: Princeton Univ. Press, 1981.

Meister, Michael, ed. *Encyclopedia of Indian Temple Architecture*. 2 vols. in 7. Philadelphia: Univ. of Pennsylvania Press, 1983.

Michell, George. *Elephanta*. Bombay: India Book House, 2002.

———. *Hindu Art and Architecture*. World of Art. London: Thames & Hudson, 2000.

Mitter, Partha. *Indian Art*. Oxford History of Art. Oxford: Oxford Univ. Press, 2001.

Neumayer, Erwin. *Lines on Stone: The Prehistoric Rock Art of India*. New Delhi: Manohar, 1993.

Pal, Pratapaditya, ed. *The Ideal Image: The Gupta Sculptural Tradition and Its Influence*. New York: Asia Society, 1978.

Poster, Amy G. *From Indian Earth: 4,000 Years of Terracotta Art*. Brooklyn, NY: Brooklyn Museum, 1986.

Skelton, Robert, and Mark Francis. *Arts of Bengal: The Heritage of Bangladesh and Eastern India*. London: Whitechapel Art Gallery, 1979.

Stierlin, Henri. *Hindu India: From Khajuraho to the Temple City of Madurai*. Taschen's World Architecture. New York: Taschen, 1998.

Strachan, Paul. *Imperial Pagan: Art and Architecture of Old Burma*. Honolulu: Univ. of Hawai'i Press, 1990.

Tadgell, Christopher. *India and South-East Asia: The Buddhist and Hindu Tradition*. New York: Whitney Library of Design, 1998.

Williams, Joanna G. *Art of Gupta India, Empire and Province*. Princeton, NJ: Princeton Univ. Press, 1982.

Chapter 11 Chinese and Korean Art before 1279

Ciarla, Roberto, ed. *The Eternal Army: The Terracotta Soldiers of the First Chinese Emperor*. Vercelli: White Star, 2005.

Fong, Wen, ed. *Beyond Representation: Chinese Painting and Calligraphy, 8th–14th Century*. Princeton Monographs in Art and Archaeology, 48. New York: Metropolitan Museum of Art, 1992.

Fraser, Sarah Elizabeth. *Performing the Visual: The Practice of Buddhist Wall Painting in China and Central Asia, 618–960*. Stanford, CA: Stanford Univ. Press, 2004.

James, Jean M. *A Guide to the Tomb and Shrine Art of the Han Dynasty 206 B.C.–A.D. 220*. Chinese Studies, 2. Lewiston, NY: Mellen Press, 1996.

Karetzky, Patricia Eichenbaum. *Court Art of the Tang*. Lanham, MD: Univ. Press of America, 1996.

Kim, Kumja Paik. *Goryeo Dynasty: Korea's Age of Enlightenment, 918–1392*. San Francisco: Asian Art Museum—Chong-Moon Lee Center for Asian Art and Culture in cooperation with the National Museum of Korea and the Nara National Museum, 2003.

Ledderose, Lothar. *Ten Thousand Things: Module and Mass Production in Chinese Art*. Princeton: Princeton Univ. Press, 2000.

Li, Jian, ed. *The Glory of the Silk Road: Art from Ancient China*. Dayton, OH: Dayton Art Institute, 2003.

Little, Stephen, and Shawn Eichman. *Taoism and the Arts of China*. Chicago: Art Institute of Chicago, 2000.

Liu, Cary Y., Dora C.Y. Ching, and Judith G. Smith, eds. *Character & Context in Chinese Calligraphy*. Princeton, NJ: Art Museum, Princeton Univ., 1999.

Luo, Zhewen. *Ancient Pagodas in China*. Beijing, China: Foreign Languages Press, 1994.

Ma, Chengyuan. *Ancient Chinese Bronzes*. Ed. Hsio-Yen Shih. Hong Kong: Oxford Univ. Press, 1986.

Murck, Alfreda. *Poetry and Painting in Song China: The Subtle Art of Dissent*. Harvard-Yenching Institute Monograph Series. Cambridge, MA: Harvard Univ. Asia Center for the Harvard-Yenching Institute, 2000.

Ortiz, Valérie Malenfer. *Dreaming the Southern Song Landscape: The Power of Illusion in Chinese Painting*. Studies in Asian Art and Archaeology, vol. 22. Boston: Brill, 1999.

Paludan, Ann. *Chinese Tomb Figurines*. Hong Kong: Oxford Univ. Press, 1994.

Portal, Jane. *Korea: Art and Archaeology.* New York: Thames & Hudson, 2000.

Rawson, Jessica. *Mysteries of Ancient China: New Discoveries from the Early Dynasties.* London: British Museum Press, 1996.

Rhie, Marylin M. *Early Buddhist Art of China and Central Asia.* 2 vols in 3. Handbuch der Orientalistik. Vierte Abteilung; China, 12. Leiden: Brill, 1999.

Scarpari, Maurizio. *Splendours of Ancient China.* London: Thames & Hudson, 2000.

So, Jenny F., ed. *Noble Riders from Pines and Deserts: The Artistic Legacy of the Qidan.* Hong Kong: Art Museum, Chinese Univ. of Hong Kong, 2004.

Sturman, Peter Charles. *Mi Fu: Style and the Art of Calligraphy in Northern Song.* New Haven: Yale Univ. Press, 1997.

Wang, Eugene Y. *Shaping the Lotus Sutra: Buddhist Visual Culture in Medieval China.* Seattle: Univ. of Washington Press, 2005.

Watson, William. *The Arts of China to A.D. 900.* Pelican History of Art. New Haven: Yale Univ. Press, 1995.

———. *The Arts of China 900–1620.* Pelican History of Art. Reissue ed. 2003. New Haven: Yale Univ. Press, 2000.

Watt, James C.Y. *China: Dawn of a Golden Age, 200–750 A.D.* New York: Metropolitan Museum of Art, 2004.

Whitfield, Susan, and Ursula Sims-Williams, eds. *The Silk Road: Trade, Travel, War and Faith.* Chicago: Serindia Publications, 2004.

Wu Hung. *Monumentality in Early Chinese Art and Architecture.* Stanford, CA: Stanford Univ. Press, 1995.

Yang, Xiaoneng, ed. *The Golden Age of Chinese Archaeology: Celebrated Discoveries from the People's Republic of China.* Washington, DC: National Gallery of Art, 1999.

Chapter 12 Japanese Art before 1333

Cunningham, Michael R. *Buddhist Treasures from Nara.* Cleveland: Cleveland Museum of Art, 1998.

Gerhart, Karen. *The Material Culture of Death in Medieval Japan.* Honolulu: Univ. of Hawai'i Press, 2009.

Harris, Victor, ed. *Shinto: The Sacred Art of Ancient Japan.* London: British Museum Press, 2001.

Izutsu, Shinryu, and Shoryu Omori. *Sacred Treasures of Mount Koya: The Art of Japanese Shingon Buddhism.* Honolulu: Koyasan Reihokan Museum, 2002.

Kurata, Bunsaku. *Horyu-ji, Temple of the Exalted Law: Early Buddhist Art from Japan.* New York: Japan Society, 1981.

Levine, Gregory P.A., and Yukio Lippit. *Awakenings: Zen Figure Painting in Medieval Japan.* New York: Japan Society, 2007.

McCallum, Donald F. *The Four Great Temples: Buddhist Archaeology, Architecture, and Icons of Seventh-Century Japan.* Honolulu: Univ. of Hawai'i Press, 2009.

Mino, Yutaka. *The Great Eastern Temple: Treasures of Japanese Buddhist Art from Todai-ji.* Chicago: Art Institute of Chicago, 1986.

Mizoguchi, Koji. *An Archaeological History of Japan: 30,000 B.C. to A.D. 700.* Philadelphia: Univ. of Pennsylvania Press, 2002.

Murase, Miyeko. *The Tale of Genji: Legends and Paintings.* New York: Braziller, 2001.

Nishiwara, Kyotaro, and Emily J. Sano. *The Great Age of Japanese Buddhist Sculpture, A.D. 60–1300.* Fort Worth, TX: Kimbell Art Museum, 1982.

Pearson, Richard J. *Ancient Japan.* Washington, DC: Arthur M. Sackler Gallery, 1992.

Ten Grotenhuis, Elizabeth. *Japanese Mandalas: Representations of Sacred Geography.* Honolulu: Univ. of Hawai'i Press, 1999.

Washizuka, Hiromitsu, Park Youngbok, and Kang Woo-bang. *Transmitting the Forms of Divinity: Early Buddhist Art from Korea and Japan.* Ed. Naomi Noble Richard. New York: Japan Society, 2003.

Wong, Dorothy C., and Eric M. Field, eds. *Horyuji Reconsidered.* Newcastle: Cambridge Scholars, 2008.

Chapter 13 Art of the Americas before 1300

Benson, Elizabeth P., and Beatriz de la Fuente. *Olmec Art of Ancient Mexico.* Washington, DC: National Gallery of Art, 1996.

Berrin, Kathleen, ed. *Feathered Serpents and Flowering Trees: Reconstructing the Murals of Teotihuacan.* San Francisco: Fine Arts Museums of San Francisco, 1988.

Brody, J.J. *Anasazi and Pueblo Painting.* Albuquerque: Univ. of New Mexico Press, 1991.

Burger, Richard L. *Chavin and the Origins of Andean Civilization.* New York: Thames & Hudson, 1992.

Clark, John E., and Mary E. Pye, eds. *Olmec Art and Archaeology in Mesoamerica.* Studies in the History of Art, 58: Symposium Papers, 35. Washington, DC: National Gallery of Art, 2000.

Clayton, Lawrence A., Vernon J. Knight, and Edward Moore, eds. *The De Soto Chronicles: The Expedition of Hernando de Soto to North America, 1539–1543.* 2 vols. Tuscaloosa: Univ. of Alabama Press, 1993.

Coe, Michael D. and Rex Koontz. *Mexico: From the Olmecs to the Aztecs.* 5th ed. New York: Thames & Hudson, 2005.

———. *Breaking the Maya Code.* Rev. ed. New York: Thames & Hudson, 1999.

Donnan, Christopher. *Moche Portraits from Ancient Peru.* Austin: Univ. of Texas Press, 2003.

Fagan, Brian M. *Chaco Canyon: Archaeologists Explore the Lives of an Ancient Society.* New York: Oxford Univ. Press, 2005.

Hall, Robert L. *An Archaeology of the Soul: North American Indian Belief and Ritual.* Urbana: Univ. of Illinois Press, 1997.

Heyden, Doris, and Paul Gendrop. *Pre-Columbian Architecture of Mesoamerica.* Trans. Judith Stanton. History of World Architecture. New York: Electa/Rizzoli, 1988.

Korp, Maureen. *The Sacred Geography of the American Mound Builders.* Native American Studies. Lewiston, NY: Mellen Press, 1990.

Kubler, George. *The Art and Architecture of Ancient America: The Mexican, Maya, and Andean Peoples.* 3rd ed. with updated bib. Pelican History of Art. New Haven: Yale Univ. Press, 1993.

Labbé, Armand J. *Shamans, Gods, and Mythic Beasts: Colombian Gold and Ceramics in Antiquity.* New York: American Federation of Arts, 1998.

LeBlanc, Steven A. *Painted by a Distant Hand: Mimbres Pottery from the American Southwest.* Cambridge, MA: Peabody Museum Press, 2004.

Loendorf, Lawrence L., Christopher Chippindale, and David S. Whitley, eds. *Discovering North American Rock Art.* Tucson: Univ. of Arizona Press, 2005.

Martin, Simon, and Nikolai Grube. *Chronicle of the Maya Kings and Queens: Deciphering the Dynasties of the Ancient Maya.* 2nd ed. New York: Thames & Hudson, 2008.

Miller, Mary Ellen. *The Art of Mesoamerica: From Olmec to Aztec.* 4th ed. World of Art. London: Thames & Hudson, 2006.

———. *Maya Art and Architecture.* World of Art. London: Thames & Hudson, 1999.

———, and Simon Martin. *Courtly Art of the Ancient Maya.* San Francisco: Fine Arts Museums of San Francisco, 2004.

———, and Karl Taube. *The Gods and Symbols of Ancient Mexico and the Maya: An Illustrated Dictionary of Mesoamerican Religion.* London: Thames & Hudson, 1993.

Milner, George R. *The Moundbuilders: Ancient Peoples of Eastern North America.* Ancient Peoples and Places, 110. London: Thames & Hudson, 2004.

Noble, David Grant. *In Search of Chaco: New Approaches to an Archaeological Enigma.* Santa Fe, NM: School of American Research Press, 2004.

O'Connor, Mallory McCane. *Lost Cities of the Ancient Southeast.* Gainesville: Univ. Press of Florida, 1995.

Pasztory, Esther. *Teotihuacan: An Experiment in Living.* Norman: Univ. of Oklahoma Press, 1997.

Pillsbury, Joanne, ed. *Moche Art and Archaeology in Ancient Peru.* Studies in the History of Art: Center for Advanced Study in the Visual Arts, 63: Symposium Papers, 40. Washington, DC: National Gallery of Art, 2001.

Power, Susan C. *Early Art of the Southeastern Indians: Feathered Serpents & Winged Beings.* Athens: Univ. of Georgia Press, 2004.

Rohn, Arthur H., and William M. Ferguson. *Puebloan Ruins of the Southwest.* Albuquerque: Univ. of New Mexico Press, 2006.

Sharer, Robert J., and Loa P. Traxler. *The Ancient Maya.* 6th ed. Stanford, CA: Stanford Univ. Press, 2006.

Stierlin, Henri. *The Maya: Palaces and Pyramids of the Rainforest.* Cologne: Taschen, 2001.

Stone-Miller, Rebecca. *Art of the Andes: From Chavin to Inca.* 2nd ed. World of Art. New York: Thames & Hudson, 2002.

———. *To Weave for the Sun: Ancient Andean Textiles.* New York: Thames & Hudson 1994.

Townsend, Richard F., and Robert V. Sharp, eds. *Hero, Hawk, and Open Hand: American Indian Art of the Ancient Midwest and South.* Chicago: Art Institute of Chicago, 2004.

Von Hagen, Adriana, and Craig Morris. *The Cities of the Ancient Andes.* New York: Thames & Hudson, 1998.

Chapter 14 Arts of Africa to the Sixteenth Century

Bassani, Ezio, and M.D. McLeod. *African Art and Artefacts in European Collections: 1400–1800.* London: British Museum, 2000.

Blier, Suzanne Preston. *The Royal Arts of Africa: The Majesty of Form.* Perspectives. New York: Abrams, 1998.

Connah, Graham. *African Civilizations: An Archaeological Perspective,* 2nd ed. New York: Cambridge Univ. Press, 2001.

Gunsch, Kathryn Wysocki. *The Benin Plaques: A 16th Century Imperial Monument.* London: Ashgate, 2017 [in press].

LaGamma, Alisa. *"Ethiopia's Enduring Cultural Heritage."* Heilbrunn Timeline of Art History (September 2008). Accessed August 11, 2015. http://www.metmuseum.org/toah/hd/ethi/hd_ethi.htm.

Lamp, Frederick John. "Ancient Terracotta Figures from Northern Nigeria." *Yale University Art Gallery Bulletin* 53 (2011): 49–57.

Lewis-Williams, J. David. *San Rock Art. Ohio Short Histories of Africa.* Athens: Ohio Univ. Press, 2013.

Nelson, Steven. *From Cameroon to Paris: Mousgoum Architecture in and out of Africa.* Chicago and London: Univ. of Chicago Press, 2007.

Visonà, Monica Blackmun, Robin Poynor, and Herbert M. Cole. *A History of Art in Africa.* 2nd ed. Upper Saddle River, NJ: Pearson/ Prentice Hall, 2008.

Walters Art Museum. *"Ethiopian Gospels."* The Walters Art Museum. Last modified 2015. Accessed August 12, 2015. http://art.thewalters. org/detail/31912/ethiopian-gospels-3/

Chapter 15 Early Medieval Art in Europe

Alexander, J.J.G. *Medieval Illuminators and Their Methods of Work.* New ed. New Haven: Yale Univ. Press, 1994.

The Art of Medieval Spain, A.D. 500–1200. New York: Metropolitan Museum of Art, 1993.

Backhouse, Janet, D.H. Turner, and Leslie Webster, eds. *The Golden Age of Anglo-Saxon Art, 966–1066.* Bloomington: Indiana Univ. Press, 1984.

Bandmann, Günter. *Early Medieval Architecture as Bearer of Meaning.* New York: Columbia Univ. Press, 2005.

Brown, Michelle P. *The Lindisfarne Gospels: Society, Spirituality and the Scribe.* Toronto: Univ. of Toronto Press, 2003.

Calkins, Robert G. *Illuminated Books of the Middle Ages.* Ithaca, NY: Cornell Univ. Press, 1983.

Carver, Martin. *Sutton Hoo: A Seventh-Century Princely Burial Ground and Its Context.* London: British Museum Press, 2005.

Davis-Weyer, Caecilia. *Early Medieval Art, 300–1150: Sources and Documents.* Upper Saddle River, NJ: Pearson/ Prentice Hall, l971.

Diebold, William J. *Word and Image: An Introduction to Early Medieval Art.* Boulder, CO: Westview Press, 2000.

Dodwell, C.R. *Pictorial Arts of the West, 800–1200.* Pelican History of Art. New Haven: Yale Univ. Press, 1993.

Farley, Julia, and Fraser Hunter. *Celts: Art and Identity.* London: British Museum Press, 2015.

Farr, Carol. *The Book of Kells: Its Function and Audience.* London: British Library, 1997.

Fitzhugh, William W., and Elisabeth I. Ward, eds. *Vikings: The North Atlantic Saga.* Washington, DC: Smithsonian Institution Press, 2000.

Harbison, Peter. *The Golden Age of Irish Art: The Medieval Achievement, 600–1200.* London: Thames & Hudson, 1999.

Henderson, George. *From Durrow to Kells: The Insular Gospel-Books, 650–800.* London: Thames & Hudson, 1987.

Horn, Walter W., and Ernest Born. *Plan of Saint Gall: A Study of the Architecture and Economy of and Life in a Paradigmatic Carolingian Monastery.* California Studies in the History of Art, 19. 3 vols. Berkeley: Univ. of California Press, 1979.

Lasko, Peter. *Ars Sacra, 800–1200.* 2nd ed. Pelican History of Art. New Haven: Yale Univ. Press, 1994.

McClendon, Charles B. *The Origins of Medieval Architecture: Building in Europe, A.D. 600–900.* New Haven: Yale Univ. Press, 2005.

Mayr-Harting, Henry. *Ottonian Book Illumination: An Historical Study.* 2nd rev. ed. 2 vols. London: Harvey Miller, 1999.

Mentré, Mireille. *Illuminated Manuscripts of Medieval Spain.* New York: Thames & Hudson, 1996.

Nees, Lawrence. *Early Medieval Art.* Oxford History of Art. Oxford: Oxford Univ. Press, 2002.

Richardson, Hilary, and John Scarry. *An Introduction to Irish High Crosses.* Dublin: Mercier, 1990.

Schapiro, Meyer. *Language of Forms: Lectures on Insular Manuscript Art.* Ed. Jane Rosenthal. New York: Pierpont Morgan Library, 2006.

Stalley, R.A. *Early Medieval Architecture.* Oxford History of Art. Oxford: Oxford Univ. Press, 1999.

Wickham, Chris. *Framing the Early Middle Ages: Europe and the Mediterranean 400–800.* New York: Oxford Univ. Press, 2005.

Williams, John. *Early Spanish Manuscript Illumination.* New York: Braziller, 1977.

Wilson, David M. *Anglo-Saxon Art: From the Seventh Century to the Norman Conquest.* London: Thames & Hudson, 1984.

———, and Ole Klindt-Jensen. *Viking Art.* 2nd ed. Minneapolis: Univ. of Minnesota Press, 1980.

Chapter 16 Romanesque Art

Barral i Altet, Xavier. *The Romanesque: Towns, Cathedrals and Monasteries.* Taschen's World Architecture. New York: Taschen, 1998.

The Book of Sainte Foy. Ed. and trans. Pamela Sheingorn. Philadelphia: Univ. of Pennsylvania Press, 1995.

Cahn, Walter. *Romanesque Manuscripts: The Twelfth Century.* 2nd ed. 2 vols. A Survey of Manuscripts Illuminated in France. London: Harvey Miller, 1996.

Caviness, Madeline H. "Hildegard as Designer of the Illustrations to her Works." In *Hildegard of Bingen: The Context of her Thought and Art.* Ed. Charles Burnett and Peter Dronke. London: Warburg Institute, 1998: 29–63.

Davis-Weyer, Caecilia. *Early Medieval Art, 300–1150. Sources and Documents.* Upper Saddle River, NJ: Pearson/ Prentice Hall, 1971.

Dimier, Anselme. *Stones Laid before the Lord: A History of Monastic Architecture.* Trans. Gilchrist Lavigne. Cistercian Studies Series, no. 152. Kalamazoo, MI: Cistercian Publications, 1999.

Fergusson, Peter. *Architecture of Solitude: Cistercian Abbeys in Twelfth-Century England.* Princeton, NJ: Princeton Univ. Press, 1984.

Forsyth, Ilene H. *The Throne of Wisdom: Wood Sculptures of the Madonna in Romanesque France.* Princeton, NJ: Princeton Univ. Press, 1972.

Gaud, Henri, and Jean-François Leroux-Dhuys. *Cistercian Abbeys: History and Architecture.* Cologne: Könemann, 1998.

Gerson, Paula, ed. *The Pilgrim's Guide to Santiago de Compostela: A Critical Edition.* 2 vols. London: Harvey Miller, 1998.

Grivot, Denis, and George Zarnecki. *Gislebertus: Sculptor of Autun.* New York: Orion Press, 1961.

Hearn, M.F. *Romanesque Sculpture: The Revival of Monumental Stone Sculptures in the Eleventh and Twelfth Centuries.* Ithaca, NY: Cornell Univ. Press, 1981.

Hicks, Carola. *The Bayeux Tapestry: The Life Story of a Masterpiece.* London: Chatto & Windus, 2006.

Holt, Elizabeth Gilmore, ed. *A Documentary History of Art.* 2 vols. Princeton, NJ: Princeton Univ. Press, 1982–86.

Hourihane, Colum, ed. *Romanesque Art and Thought in the Twelfth Century: Essays in Honor of Walter Cahn.* The Index of Christian Art Occasional Papers 10. University Park, PA: Penn State Press, 2008.

Kubach, Hans E. *Romanesque Architecture.* History of World Architecture. New York: Electa/ Rizzoli, 1988.

Minne-Sève, Viviane, and Hervé Kergall. *Romanesque and Gothic France: Architecture and Sculpture.* Trans. Jack Hawkes and Lory Frankel. New York: Abrams, 2000.

Newman, Barbara. *Sister of Wisdom: St. Hildegard's Theology of the Feminine.* 2nd ed. Berkeley: Univ. of California Press, 1997.

Rudolph, Conrad. *The "Things of Greater Importance": Bernard of Clairvaux's Apologia and the Medieval Attitude Toward Art.* Philadelphia: Univ. of Pennsylvania Press, 1990.

Schapiro, Meyer. *Romanesque Art: Selected Papers.* New York: George Braziller, 1977.

———. *The Romanesque Sculpture of Moissac.* New York: Braziller, 1985.

———. *Romanesque Architectural Sculpture: The Charles Eliot Norton Lectures.* Ed. Linda Seidel. Chicago: Univ. of Chicago Press, 2006.

Seidel, Linda. *Legends in Limestone: Lazarus, Gislebertus, and the Cathedral of Autun.* Chicago: Univ. of Chicago Press, 1999.

Sundell, Michael G. *Mosaics in the Eternal City.* Tempe: Arizona Center for Medieval and Renaissance Studies, 2007.

Swanson, R.N. *The Twelfth-Century Renaissance.* Manchester: Manchester Univ. Press, 1999.

Theophilus. *On Divers Arts: The Foremost Medieval Treatise on Painting, Glassmaking, and Metalwork.* Trans. John G. Hawthorne and Cyril Stanley Smith. New York: Dover, 1979.

Toman, Rolf, ed. *Romanesque: Architecture, Sculpture, Painting.* Trans. Fiona Hulse and Ian Macmillan. Cologne: Könemann, 1997.

Wilson, David M. *The Bayeux Tapestry: The Complete Tapestry in Color.* London: Thames & Hudson and New York: Knopf, 2004.

Zarnecki, George, Janet Holt, and Tristram Holland, eds. *English Romanesque Art, 1066– 1200.* London: Weidenfeld and Nicolson, 1984.

Chapter 17 Gothic Art of the Twelfth and Thirteenth Centuries

Barnes, Carl F. *The Portfolio of Villard de Honnecourt: A New Critical Edition and Color Facsimile.* Burlington, VT: Ashgate, 2009.

Binding, Günther. *High Gothic: The Age of the Great Cathedrals.* Taschen's World Architecture. London: Taschen, 1999.

Binski, Paul. *Becket's Crown: Art and Imagination in Gothic England, 1170–1300.* New Haven: Yale Univ. Press, 2004.

Bony, Jean. *French Gothic Architecture of the 12th and 13th Centuries.* California Studies in the History of Art, 20. Berkeley: Univ. of California Press, 1983.

Camille, Michael. *Gothic Art: Glorious Visions.* Perspectives. New York: Abrams, 1996.

Coldstream, Nicola. *Masons and Sculptors.* Toronto & Buffalo, NY: Univ. of Toronto Press, 1991.

Crosby, Sumner M. *The Royal Abbey of Saint-Denis from Its Beginnings to the Death of Suger, 475–1151.* Yale Publications in the History of Art, 37. New Haven: Yale Univ. Press, 1987.

Erlande-Brandenburg, Alain. *Gothic Art.* Trans. I. Mark Paris. New York: Abrams, 1989.

Frankl, Paul. *Gothic Architecture.* Revised Paul Crossley. Pelican History of Art. New Haven: Yale Univ. Press, 2000.

Frisch, Teresa G. *Gothic Art, 1140–c.1450: Sources and Documents.* Upper Saddle River, NJ: Pearson/Prentice Hall, 1971.

Grodecki, Louis, and Catherine Brisac. *Gothic Stained Glass, 1200–1300.* Ithaca, NY: Cornell Univ. Press, 1985.

Jordan, Alyce A. *Visualizing Kingship in the Windows of the Sainte-Chapelle.* Turnhout: Brepols, 2002.

Moskowitz, Anita Fiderer. *Nicola & Giovanni Pisano: The Pulpits: Pious Devotion, Pious Diversion.* London: Harvey Miller, 2005.

Nussbaum, Norbert. *German Gothic Church Architecture.* Trans. Scott Kleager. New Haven: Yale Univ. Press, 2000.

Panofsky, Erwin. *Abbot Suger on the Abbey Church of St.- Denis and Its Art Treasures.* 2nd ed. Ed. Gerda Panofsky- Soergel. Princeton, NJ: Princeton Univ. Press, 1979.

Parry, Stan. *Great Gothic Cathedrals of France.* New York: Viking Studio, 2001.

Sauerländer, Willibald. *Gothic Sculpture in France, 1140–1270.* Trans. Janet Sandheimer. London: Thames & Hudson, 1972.

Scott, Robert A. *The Gothic Enterprise: A Guide to Understanding the Medieval Cathedral.* Berkeley: Univ. of California Press, 2003.

Simsom, Otto Georg von. *The Gothic Cathedral: Origins of Gothic Architecture and the Medieval Concept of Order.* 3rd ed. exp. Bollingen Series. Princeton, NJ: Princeton Univ. Press, 1988.

Suckale, Robert, and Matthias Weniger. *Painting of the Gothic Era.* Ed. Ingo F. Walther. New York: Taschen, 1999.

Williamson, Paul. *Gothic Sculpture, 1140–1300.* Pelican History of Art. New Haven: Yale Univ. Press, 1995.

Chapter 18 Fourteenth-Century Art in Europe

Alexander, Jonathan, and Paul Binski, eds. *Age of Chivalry: Art in Plantagenet England, 1200–1400.* London: Royal Academy of Arts, 1987.

Backhouse, Janet. *Illumination from Books of Hours.* London: British Library, 2004.

Boehm, Barbara Drake, and Jirí Fajt, eds. *Prague: The Crown of Bohemia, 1347–1437.* New York: Metropolitan Museum of Art, 2005.

Bony, Jean. *The English Decorated Style: Gothic Architecture Transformed, 1250–1350.* The Wrightsman Lecture, 10. Oxford: Phaidon Press, 1979.

Cennini, Cennino. *The Craftsman's Handbook "Il libro dell'arte."* Trans. D.V. Thompson, Jr. New York: Dover, 1960.

Derbes, Anne, and Mark Sandona, eds. *The Cambridge Companion to Giotto.* Cambridge and New York: Cambridge Univ. Press, 2003.

Fajt, Jirí, ed. *Magister Theodoricus, Court Painter to Emperor Charles IV: The Pictorial Decoration of the Shrines at Karlstejn Castle.* Prague: National Gallery, 1998.

Holt, Elizabeth Gilmore, ed. *A Documentary History of Art.* 2 vols. Princeton, NJ, Princeton Univ. Press, 1982–86.

Ladis, Andrew. ed, *The Arena Chapel and the Genius of Giotto: Padua.* Giotto and the World of Early Italian Art, 2. New York: Garland, 1998.

Meiss, Millard. *Painting in Florence and Siena after the Black Death: The Arts, Religion, and Society in the Mid-Fourteenth Century.* 2nd ed. Princeton, NJ: Princeton Univ. Press, 1978.

Moskowitz, Anita Fiderer. *Italian Gothic Sculpture: c. 1250–c. 1400.* New York: Cambridge Univ. Press, 2001.

Norman, Diana, ed. *Siena, Florence, and Padua: Art, Society, and Religion 1280–1400.* 2 vols. New Haven: Yale Univ. Press, 1995.

Poeschke, Joachim. *Italian Frescoes, the Age of Giotto, 1280–1400.* New York: Abbeville Press, 2005.

Schleif, Corine. "St. Hedwig's Personal Ivory Madonna: Women's Agency and the Powers of Possessing Portable Figures." *The Four Modes of Seeing: Approaches to Medieval Imagery in Honor of Madeline Harrison Caviness.* Ed. Evelyn Staudinger Lane, Elizabeth Carson Paston, and Ellen M. Shortell. Farnham, Surrey: Ashgate, 2009: 282–403.

Vasari, Giorgio. *The Lives of the Artists.* Trans. Julia Conaway Bondanella and Peter Bondanella. Oxford World's Classics. New York: Oxford Univ. Press, 2008.

Welch, Evelyn S. *Art in Renaissance Italy, 1350–1500.* New ed. Oxford History of Art. Oxford: Oxford Univ. Press, 2000.

White, John. *Art and Architecture in Italy, 1250 to 1400.* 3rd ed. Pelican History of Art. Harmondsworth, UK: Penguin, 1993.

Wieck, Roger S. *Time Sanctified: The Book of Hours in Medieval Art and Life.* 2nd ed. New York: Braziller, 2001.

Chapter 19 Fifteenth-Century Art in Northern Europe

Art from the Court of Burgundy: The Patronage of Philip the Bold and John the Fearless 1364–1419. Dijon: Musée des Beaux-Arts and Cleveland: Cleveland Museum of Art, 2004.

Baxandall, Michael. *The Limewood Sculptors of Renaissance Germany.* New Haven: Yale Univ. Press, 1980.

Blum, Shirley. *Early Netherlandish Triptychs: A Study in Patronage.* California Studies in the History of Art, 13. Berkeley: Univ. of California Press, 1969.

Borchert, Till-Holger. *Age of Van Eyck: The Mediterranean World and Early Netherlandish Painting, 1430–1530.* New York: Thames & Hudson, 2002.

Campbell, Lorne. *The Fifteenth-Century Netherlandish Schools.* National Gallery Catalogues. London: National Gallery, 1998.

Cavallo, Adolph S. *The Unicorn Tapestries at the Metropolitan Museum of Art.* New York: Metropolitan Museum of Art, 1998.

Chastel, Andrè. *French Art: The Renaissance, 1430–1620.* Paris: Flammarion, 1995.

Dhanens, Elisabeth. *Van Eyck: The Ghent Altarpiece.* New York: Viking Press, 1973.

Füssel, Stephan. *Gutenberg and the Impact of Printing.* Trans. Douglas Martin. Burlington, VT: Ashgate, 2005.

Koster, Margaret L. "The *Arnolfini Double Portrait*: A Simple Solution." *Apollo* 157 (September 2003): 3–14.

Lane, Barbara G. *The Altar and the Altarpiece: Sacramental Themes in Early Netherlandish Painting.* New York: Harper & Row, 1984.

Marks, Richard, and Paul Williamson, eds. *Gothic: Art for England 1400–1547.* London: V&A Publications, 2003.

Meiss, Millard. *French Painting in the Time of Jean de Berry: The Limbourgs and their Contemporaries.* 2 vols. New York: Braziller, 1974.

Müller, Theodor. *Sculpture in the Netherlands, Germany, France, and Spain: 1400–1500.* Trans. Elaine and William Robson Scott. Pelican History of Art. Harmondsworth, UK: Penguin, 1966.

Pächt, Otto. *Early Netherlandish Painting: From Rogier van der Weyden to Gerard David.* Ed. Monika Rosenauer. Trans. David Britt. London: Harvey Miller, 1997.

———. *Van Eyck and the Founders of Early Netherlandish Painting.* London: Miller, 1994.

Panofsky, Erwin. *Early Netherlandish Painting, Its Origins and Character.* 2 vols. Cambridge, MA: Harvard Univ. Press, 1966.

Parshall, Peter W., and Rainer Schoch. *Origins of European Printmaking: Fifteenth-Century Woodcuts and their Public.* Washington, DC: National Gallery of Art, 2005.

Plummer, John. *The Last Flowering: French Painting in Manuscripts, 1420–1530, from American Collections.* New York: Pierpont Morgan Library, 1982.

Seidel, Linda. *Jan van Eyck's Arnolfini Portrait: Stories of an Icon.* New York: Cambridge Univ. Press, 1993.

Smith, Jeffrey Chipps. *The Northern Renaissance.* London and New York: Phaidon Press, 2004.

Snyder, James. *Northern Renaissance Art: Painting, Sculpture, the Graphic Arts from 1350 to 1575.* 2nd ed. rev. Larry Silver and Henry Luttikhuizen. Upper Saddle River, NJ: Prentice Hall, 2005.

Vos, Dirk de. *The Flemish Primitives: The Masterpieces.* Princeton, NJ: Princeton Univ. Press, 2002.

Zuffi, Stefano. *European Art of the Fifteenth Century.* Trans. Brian D. Phillips. Art through the Centuries. Los Angeles: J. Paul Getty Museum, 2005.

Chapter 20 Renaissance Art in Fifteenth- Century Italy

Adams, Laurie Schneider. *Italian Renaissance Art.* Boulder, CO: Westview Press, 2001.

Ahl, Diane Cole, ed. *The Cambridge Companion to Masaccio.* New York: Cambridge Univ. Press, 2002.

Alberti, Leon Battista. *On Painting.* Trans. John R. Spencer. New Haven: Yale Univ. Press, 1966.

Ames-Lewis, Francis. *Drawing in Early Renaissance Italy.* 2nd ed. New Haven: Yale Univ. Press, 2000.

———. *The Intellectual Life of the Early Renaissance Artist.* New Haven: Yale Univ. Press, 2000.

Baxandall, Michael. *Painting and Experience in Fifteenth- Century Italy: A Primer in the Social History of Pictorial Style.* 2nd ed. Oxford: Oxford Univ. Press, 1988.

Boskovits, Miklós. *Italian Paintings of the Fifteenth Century.* The Collections of the National Gallery of Art. Washington, DC: National Gallery of Art, 2003.

Botticelli and Filippino: Passion and Grace in Fifteenth-Century Florentine Painting. Milan: Skira, 2004.

Brown, Patricia Fortini. *Art and Life in Renaissance Venice.* Perspectives. New York: Abrams, 1997. Reissue ed. Upper Saddle River, NJ: Pearson/ Prentice Hall, 2006.

Brucker, Gene. *Florence: The Golden Age, 1138– 1737.* Berkeley: Univ. of California Press, 1998.

Christiansen, Keith, Laurence B. Kanter, and Carl Brandon Strehlke. *Painting in Renaissance Siena, 1420–1500.* New York: Metropolitan Museum of Art, 1988.

Gilbert, Creighton, ed. *Italian Art, 1400–1500: Sources and Documents.* Evanston, IL: Northwestern Univ. Press, 1992.

Heydenreich, Ludwig Heinrich. *Architecture in Italy, 1400–1500.* Revised Paul Davies. Pelican History of Art. New Haven: Yale Univ. Press, 1996.

Hind, Arthur M. *An Introduction to a History of Woodcut.* New York: Dover, 1963.

Hyman, Timothy. *Sienese Painting: The Art of a City-Republic (1278–1477)*. World of Art. New York: Thames & Hudson, 2003.

King, Ross. *Brunelleschi's Dome: How a Renaissance Genius Reinvented Architecture*. New York: Walker, 2000.

Pächt, Otto. *Venetian Painting in the 15th Century: Jacopo, Gentile and Giovanni Bellini and Andrea Mantegna*. Ed. Margareta Vyoral-Tschapka and Michael Pächt. Trans. Fiona Elliott. London: Harvey Miller, 2003.

Partridge, Loren W. *The Art of Renaissance Rome, 1400–1600*. 2nd ed. Upper Saddle River, NJ: Pearson/Prentice Hall, 2006.

———. *Art of Renaissance Florence, 1400–1600*. Berkeley: Univ. of California Press, 2009.

de Pisan, Christine. *The Book of the City of Ladies*. Trans. Rosalind Brown-Grant. London: Penguin Books, 1999.

Poeschke, Joachim. *Donatello and His World: Sculpture of the Italian Renaissance*. Trans. Russell Stockman. New York: Abrams, 1993.

Pope-Hennessy, John. *Italian Renaissance Sculpture*. 4th ed. London: Phaidon Press, 1996.

Radke, Gary M., ed. *The Gates of Paradise: Lorenzo Ghiberti's Masterpiece*. New Haven: Yale Univ. Press, 2007.

Randolph, Adrian W.B., *Engaging Symbols: Gender, Politics, and Public Art in Fifteenth-Century Florence*. New Haven: Yale Univ. Press, 2002.

Troncelliti, Latifah. *The Two Parallel Realities of Alberti and Cennini: The Power of Writing* and *the Visual Arts in the Italian Quattrocento*. Studies in Italian Literature, vol. 14. Lewiston, NY: Mellen Press, 2004.

Turner, Richard. *Renaissance Florence: The Invention of a New Art*. Perspectives. New York: Abrams, 1997. Reissue ed. Upper Saddle River, NJ: Pearson/Prentice Hall, 2006.

Vasari, Giorgio. *The Lives of the Artists*. Trans. Julia Conaway Bondanella and Peter Bondanella. Oxford World's Classics. New York: Oxford Univ. Press, 2008.

Verdon, Timothy, and John Henderson, eds. *Christianity and the Renaissance: Image and Religious Imagination in the Quattrocento*. Syracuse, NY: Syracuse Univ. Press, 1990.

Walker, Paul Robert. *The Feud that Sparked the Renaissance: How Brunelleschi and Ghiberti Changed the Art World*. New York: William Morrow, 2002.

Welch, Evelyn S. *Art and Society in Italy, 1350–1500*. Oxford History of Art. Oxford: Oxford Univ. Press, 1997.

Chapter 21 Sixteenth-Century Art in Italy

Acidini Luchinat, Cristina, et al. *The Medici, Michelangelo, & the Art of Late Renaissance Florence*. New Haven: Yale Univ. Press, 2002.

Bambach, Carmen. *Drawing and Painting in the Italian Renaissance Workshop: Theory and Practice, 1330–1600*. Cambridge: Cambridge Univ. Press, 1999.

Barriault, Anne B., ed. *Reading Vasari*. London: Philip Wilson in assoc. with the Georgia Museum of Art, 2005.

Brambilla Barcilon, Pinin. *Leonardo: The Last Supper*. Chicago: Univ. of Chicago Press, 2001.

Brown, Patricia Fortini. *Art and Life in Renaissance Venice*. Perspectives. New York: Abrams, 1997.

Cellini, Benvenuto. *Autobiography*. Rev. ed. Trans. George Bull. Penguin Classics. New York: Penguin, 1998.

Chelazzi Dini, Giulietta, Alessandro Angelini, and Bernardina Sani. *Sienese Painting: From Duccio to the Birth of the Baroque*. New York: Abrams, 1998.

Clark, Kenneth. *Leonardo da Vinci*. Ed. Martin Kemp. London: Penguin, 2015.

Cole, Alison. *Virtue and Magnificence: Art of the Italian Renaissance Courts*. Perspectives. New York: Abrams, 1995. Reissue ed. as *Art of the Italian Courts*. Upper Saddle River, NJ: Pearson/Prentice Hall, 2006.

Franklin, David, ed. *Leonardo da Vinci, Michelangelo, and the Renaissance in Florence*. Ottawa: National Gallery of Canada in assoc. with Yale Univ. Press, 2005.

Freedberg, S.J. *Painting in Italy, 1500 to 1600*. 3rd ed. Pelican History of Art. New Haven: Yale Univ. Press, 1993.

Goffen, Rona. *Renaissance Rivals: Michelangelo, Leonardo, Raphael, Titian*. New Haven: Yale Univ. Press, 2002.

———. *Titian's Venus of Urbino*. Masterpieces of Western Painting. Cambridge: Cambridge Univ. Press, 1997.

———. *Titian's Women*. New Haven: Yale Univ. Press, 1997.

Hall, Marcia B. *After Raphael: Painting in Central Italy in the Sixteenth Century*. New York: Cambridge Univ. Press, 1999.

———, ed. *The Cambridge Companion to Raphael*. New York: Cambridge Univ. Press, 2005.

Hollingsworth, Mary. *Patronage in Sixteenth Century Italy*. London: John Murray, 1996.

Hopkins, Andrew. *Italian Architecture: From Michelangelo to Borromini*. World of Art. New York: Thames & Hudson, 2002.

Hughes, Anthony. *Michelangelo*. Art & Ideas. London: Phaidon Press, 1997.

Huse, Norbert, and Wolfgang Wolters. *Art of Renaissance Venice: Architecture, Sculpture, and Painting, 1460–1590*. Trans. Edmund Jephcott. Chicago: Univ. of Chicago Press, 1990.

Joannides, Paul. *Titian to 1518: The Assumption of Genius*. New Haven: Yale Univ. Press, 2001.

Klein, Robert, and Henri Zerner. *Italian Art, 1500–1600: Sources and Documents*. Upper Saddle River, NJ: Pearson/ Prentice Hall, 1966.

Kliemann, Julian-Matthias, and Michael Rohlmann. *Italian Frescoes: High Renaissance and Mannerism, 1510–1600*. Trans. Steven Lindberg. New York: Abbeville Press, 2004.

Landau, David, and Peter Parshall. *The Renaissance Print: 1470–1550*. New Haven: Yale Univ. Press, 1994.

Lieberman, Ralph. *Renaissance Architecture in Venice, 1450–1540*. New York: Abbeville Press, 1982.

Lotz, Wolfgang. *Architecture in Italy, 1500–1600*. Revised Deborah Howard. Pelican History of Art. New Haven: Yale Univ. Press, 1995.

Meilman, Patricia, ed. *The Cambridge Companion to Titian*. New York: Cambridge Univ. Press, 2004.

Mitrovic, Branko. *Learning from Palladio*. New York: Norton, 2004.

Murray, Linda. *The High Renaissance and Mannerism: Italy, the North and Spain, 1500–1600*. World of Art. London: Thames & Hudson, 1995.

Palladio, Andrea. *The Four Books on Architecture*. Trans. Robert Tavernor and Richard Schofield. Cambridge, MA: MIT Press, 1997.

Partridge, Loren W. *The Art of Renaissance Rome, 1400–1600*. 2nd ed. Upper Saddle River, NJ: Pearson/Prentice Hall, 2006.

———. *Art of Renaissance Florence, 1400–1600*. Berkeley: Univ. of California Press, 2009.

———. *Michelangelo, the Last Judgment: A Glorious Restoration*. New York: Abrams, 1997.

Pilliod, Elizabeth. *Pontormo, Bronzino, Allori: A Genealogy of Florentine Art*. New Haven: Yale Univ. Press, 2001.

Pope-Hennessy, John. *Italian High Renaissance and Baroque Sculpture*. 4th ed. London: Phaidon Press, 1996.

Rosand, David. *Painting in Cinquecento Venice: Titian, Veronese, Tintoretto*. Rev. ed. Cambridge: Cambridge Univ. Press, 1997.

Rowe, Colin, and Leon Satkowski. *Italian Architecture of the 16th Century*. New York: Princeton Architectural Press, 2002.

Rowland, Ingrid D. *The Culture of the High Renaissance: Ancients and Moderns in Sixteenth Century Rome*. Cambridge: Cambridge Univ. Press, 1998.

Shearman, John. *Mannerism*. Harmondsworth, UK: Penguin, 1967. Reissue ed. New York: Penguin, 1990.

Syson, Luke. *Leonardo da Vinci: Painter at the Court of Milan*. London and New Haven: Yale Univ. Press, 2011.

Vasari, Giorgio. *The Lives of the Artists*. Trans. Julia Conaway Bondanella and Peter Bondanella. Oxford World's Classics. New York: Oxford Univ. Press, 2008.

Verheyen, Egon. *The Paintings in the Studiolo of Isabella d'Este at Mantua*. Monographs on Archaeology and Fine Arts, 23. New York: New York Univ. Press, 1971.

Williams, Robert. *Art, Theory, and Culture in Sixteenth-Century Italy: From Techne to Metateche*. Cambridge: Cambridge Univ. Press, 1997.

Zöllner, Frank et al. *Michelangelo: Complete Works*. Cologne: Taschen, 2014.

Chapter 22 Sixteenth-Century Art in Northern Europe and the Iberian Peninsula

Bartrum, Giulia. *Albrecht Dürer and his Legacy: The Graphic Work of a Renaissance Artist*. London: British Museum Press, 2002.

———. *German Renaissance Prints 1490–1550*. London: British Museum Press, 1995.

Brown, Jonathan. *Painting in Spain, 1500–1700*. Pelican History of Art. New Haven: Yale Univ. Press, 1998.

Buck, Stephanie, and Jochen Sander. *Hans Holbein the Younger: Painter at the Court of Henry VIII*. Trans. Rachel Esner and Beverley Jackson. New York: Thames & Hudson, 2004.

Chapuis, Julien. *Tilman Riemenschneider: Master Sculptor of the Late Middle Ages*. Washington, DC: National Gallery of Art, 1999.

Davies, David, and John H. Elliott. *El Greco*. London: National Gallery, 2003.

Dixon, Laurinda. *Bosch*. Art & Ideas. New York: Phaidon Press, 2003.

Foister, Susan. *Holbein and England*. New Haven: Published for Paul Mellon Centre for Studies in British Art by Yale Univ. Press, 2004.

Harbison, Craig. *The Art of the Northern Renaissance*. London: Laurence King Publishing, 2012.

Hayum, Andrée. *The Isenheim Altarpiece: God's Medicine and the Painter's Vision*. Princeton Essays on the Arts, 18. Princeton, NJ: Princeton Univ. Press, 1989.

Hearn, Karen, ed. *Dynasties: Painting in Tudor and Jacobean England, 1530–1630*. New York: Rizzoli, 1996.

Koerner, Joseph Leo. *The Reformation of the Image*. Chicago: Univ. of Chicago Press, 2004.

———. *The Moment of Self-Portraiture in German Renaissance Art.* Chicago: Univ. of Chicago Press, 1996.

Kubler, George. *Building the Escorial.* Princeton, NJ: Princeton Univ. Press, 1982.

Nash, Susie. *Northern Renaissance Art.* Oxford History of Art. New York: Oxford Univ. Press, 2008.

Price, David Hotchkiss. *Albrecht Dürer's Renaissance: Humanism, Reformation, and the Art of Faith.* Studies in Medieval and Early Modern Civilization. Ann Arbor: Univ. of Michigan Press, 2003.

Roberts-Jones, Philippe, and Françoise Roberts-Jones. *Pieter Bruegel.* New York: Abrams, 2002.

Smith, Jeffrey Chipps. *Nuremberg, a Renaissance City, 1500–1618.* Austin: Huntington Art Gallery, Univ. of Texas, 1983.

———. *The Northern Renaissance.* London and New York: Phaidon Press, 2004.

———. *Durer.* London and New York: Phaidon, 2012.

Snyder, James. *Northern Renaissance Art: Painting, Sculpture, the Graphic Arts from 1350 to 1575.* 2nd ed. rev. Larry Silver and Henry Luttikhuizen. Upper Saddle River, NJ: Pearson/Prentice Hall, 2005.

Strong, Roy C. *Artists of the Tudor Court: The Portrait Miniature Rediscovered, 1520–1620.* London: V&A Publications, 1983.

Zerner, Henri. *Renaissance Art in France: The Invention of Classicism.* Paris: Flammarion, 2003.

Zorach, Rebecca. *Blood, Milk, Ink, Gold: Abundance and Excess in the French Renaissance.* Chicago: Univ. of Chicago Press, 2005.

Chapter 23 Seventeenth-Century Art in Europe

Adams, Laurie Schneider. *Key Monuments of the Baroque.* Boulder, CO: Westview Press, 2000.

Allen, Christopher. *French Painting in the Golden Age.* World of Art. New York: Thames & Hudson, 2003.

Alpers, Svetlana. *The Art of Describing: Dutch Art in the Seventeenth Century.* Chicago: Chicago Univ. Press, 1983.

———. *The Making of Rubens.* New Haven: Yale Univ. Press, 1995.

Blankert, Albert. *Rembrandt: A Genius and His Impact.* Melbourne: National Gallery of Victoria, 1997.

Belkin, Kristin Lohse. *Rubens. Art & Ideas.* London: Phaidon, 1998.

Boucher, Bruce. *Italian Baroque Sculpture.* World of Art. New York: Thames & Hudson, 1998.

Brown, Beverly Louise, ed. *The Genius of Rome, 1592–1623.* London: Royal Academy of Arts, 2001.

Brown, Jonathan. *Painting in Spain, 1500–1700.* Pelican History of Art. New Haven: Yale Univ. Press, 1998.

———, and Carmen Garrido. *Velásquez: The Technique of Genius.* New Haven: Yale Univ. Press, 2003.

Careri, Giovanni. *Baroques.* Tran. Alexandra Bonfante-Warren. Princeton: Princeton Univ. Press, 2003.

Chapman, H. Perry. *Rembrandt's Self-Portraits: A Study in 17th-Century Identity.* Princeton: Princeton Univ. Press, 1990.

Chong, Alan, and Wouter Kloek. *Still-Life Paintings from the Netherlands, 1550–1720.* Zwolle: Waanders, 1999.

Enggass, Robert, and Jonathan Brown. *Italian and Spanish Art, 1600–1750: Sources and Documents.* 2nd ed. Evanston, IL: Northwestern Univ. Press, 1992.

Franklin, David, and Sebastian Schütze. *Caravaggio and his Followers in Rome.* New Haven: Yale Univ. Press, 2011.

Frantis, Wayne E., ed. *The Cambridge Companion to Vermeer.* Cambridge: Cambridge Univ. Press, 2001.

———. *Dutch Seventeenth-Century Genre Painting: Its Stylistic and Thematic Evolution.* New Haven: Yale Univ. Press, 2004.

Harbison, Robert. *Reflections on Baroque.* Chicago: Univ. of Chicago Press, 2000.

Keazor, Henry. *Nicolas Poussin, 1594–1665.* Cologne & London: Taschen, 2007.

Kiers, Judikje, and Fieke Tissink. *Golden Age of Dutch Art: Painting, Sculpture, Decorative Art.* London: Thames & Hudson, 2000.

Lagerlöf, Margaretha Rossholm. *Ideal Landscape: Annibale Carracci, Nicolas Poussin, and Claude Lorrain.* New Haven: Yale Univ. Press, 1990.

Martin, John Rupert. *Baroque.* Boulder, CO: Westview Press, 1977.

McPhee, Sarah. *Bernini and the Bell Towers: Architecture and Politics at the Vatican.* New Haven: Yale Univ. Press, 2002.

Millon, Henry A., ed. *The Triumph of the Baroque: Architecture in Europe, 1600–1750.* 2nd ed. rev. New York: Rizzoli, 1999.

Morrissey, Jake. *The Genius in the Design: Bernini, Borromini, and the Rivalry that Transformed Rome.* New York: William Morrow, 2005.

Puttfarken (translation of Roger de Piles), referenced p727

Rand, Richard. *Claude Lorrain, the Painter as Draftsman: Drawings from the British Museum.* New Haven: Yale Univ. Press; Williamstown, MA: Clark Art Institute, 2006.

Slive, Seymour. *Dutch Painting 1600–1800.* Pelican History of Art. New Haven: Yale Univ. Press, 1995.

Summerson, John. *Inigo Jones.* New Haven: Published for the Paul Mellon Centre for Studies in British Art by Yale Univ. Press, 2000.

Tomlinson, Janis. *From El Greco to Goya: Painting in Spain, 1561–1828.* Perspectives. New York: Abrams, 1997.

Vlieghe, Hans. *Flemish Art and Architecture, 1585–1700.* Pelican History of Art. Reissue ed. 2004. New Haven: Yale Univ. Press, 1998.

Walker, Stefanie, and Frederick Hammond, eds. *Life and the Arts in the Baroque Palaces of Rome: Ambiente Barocco.* New Haven: Yale Univ. Press; for the Bard Graduate Center for Studies in the Decorative Arts, New York, 1999.

Westermann, Mariët. *Rembrandt. Art & Ideas.* London: Phaidon, 2000.

———. *A Worldly Art: The Dutch Republic, 1585–1718.* New Haven and London: Yale Univ. Press, 2004.

Wheelock Jr., Arthur K. *Flemish Paintings of the Seventeenth Century.* Washington, DC: National Gallery of Art, 2005.

Wittkower, Rudolf. *Art and Architecture in Italy, 1600–1750.* 3 vols. 6th ed. Revised Joseph Connors and Jennifer Montague. Pelican History of Art. New Haven: Yale Univ. Press, 1999.

Zega, Andrew, and Bernd H. Dams. *Palaces of the Sun King: Versailles, Trianon, Marly: The Châteaux of Louis XIV.* New York: Rizzoli, 2002.

Chapter 24 Art of South and Southeast Asia after 1200

Asher, Catherine B. *Architecture of Mughal India.* New York: Cambridge Univ. Press, 1992.

Beach, Milo Cleveland. *Mughal and Rajput Painting.* New York: Cambridge Univ. Press, 1992.

Brown, Rebecca M. *Art for a Modern India, 1947–1980.* Durham and London: Duke Univ. Press, 2009.

Guy, John, and Deborah Swallow, eds. *Arts of India, 1550–1900.* London: V&A Publications, 1990.

Khanna, Balraj, and Aziz Kurtha. *Art of Modern India.* London: Thames & Hudson, 1998.

Koch, Ebba. *Mughal Art and Imperial Ideology: Collected Essays.* New Delhi: Oxford Univ. Press, 2001.

Love Song of the Dark Lord: Jayadeva's Gitagovinda. Trans. Barbara Stoler Miller. New York: Columbia Univ. Press, 1977.

Michell, George. *Hindu Art and Architecture.* World of Art. London: Thames & Hudson, 2000.

Mitter, Partha. *Art and Nationalism in Colonial India, 1850–1922: Occidental Orientations.* Cambridge and New York: Cambridge Univ. Press, 1997.

Moynihan, Elizabeth B., ed. *The Moonlight Garden: New Discoveries at the Taj Mahal.* Asian Art & Culture. Washington, DC: Arthur M. Sackler Gallery, 2000.

Nou, Jean-Louis. *Taj Mahal.* Text by Amina Okada and M.C. Joshi. New York: Abbeville Press, 1993.

Pal, Pratapaditya. *Court Paintings of India, 16th–19th Centuries.* New York: Navin Kumar, 1983.

———. *The Peaceful Liberators: Jain Art from India.* New York: Thames & Hudson, 1994.

Rossi, Barbara. *From the Ocean of Painting: India's Popular Paintings, 1589 to the Present.* New York: Oxford Univ. Press, 1998.

Schimmel, Annemarie. *The Empire of the Great Mughals: History, Art and Culture.* Ed. Burzine K. Waghmar. Trans. Corinne Attwood. London: Reaktion Books, 2004.

Stronge, Susan. *Painting for the Mughal Emperor: The Art of the Book, 1560–1660.* London: V&A Publications, 2002.

Tillotson, G.H.R. *Mughal India.* Architectural Guides for Travelers. San Francisco: Chronicle Books, 1990.

———. *The Tradition of Indian Architecture: Continuity, Controversy, and Change since 1850.* New Haven: Yale Univ. Press, 1989.

Verma, Som Prakash. *Painting the Mughal Experience.* New York: Oxford Univ. Press, 2005.

Welch, Stuart Cary. *The Emperors' Album: Images of Mughal India.* New York: Metropolitan Museum of Art, 1987.

———. *India: Art and Culture 1300–1900.* New York: Metropolitan Museum of Art, 1985.

Chapter 25 Chinese and Korean Art after 1279

Andrews, Julia Frances, and Kuiyi Shen. *A Century in Crisis: Modernity and Tradition in the Art of Twentieth-Century China.* New York: Solomon R. Guggenheim Museum, 1998.

Barnhart, Richard M. *Painters of the Great Ming: The Imperial Court and the Zhe School.* Dallas: Dallas Museum of Art, 1993.

Barrass, Gordon S. *The Art of Calligraphy in Modern China.* London: British Museum Press, 2002.

Berger, Patricia Ann. *Empire of Emptiness: Buddhist Art and Political Authority in Qing China.* Honolulu: Univ. of Hawai'i Press, 2003.

Bickford, Maggie. *Ink Plum: The Making of a Chinese Scholar-Painting*. New York: Cambridge Univ. Press, 1996.

Billeter, Jean François. *The Chinese Art of Writing*. New York: Skira/Rizzoli, 1990.

Bush, Susan, and Hsio-yen Shih, eds. *Early Chinese Texts on Painting*. Cambridge, MA: Harvard Univ. Press, 1985.

Cahill, James. *The Distant Mountains: Chinese Painting in the Late Ming Dynasty, 1580–1644*. New York: Weatherhill, 1982.

———. *Hills Beyond a River: Chinese Painting of the Y'uan Dynasty, 1279–1368*. New York: Weatherhill, 1976.

———. *Parting at the Shore: Chinese Painting of the Early and Middle Ming Dynasty 1368–1580*. New York: Weatherhill, 1978.

Chaves, Jonathan (trans.). *The Chinese Painter as Poet*. New York: Art Media Resources, 2000.

Chung, Anita. *Drawing Boundaries: Architectural Images in Qing China*. Honolulu: Univ. of Hawai'i Press, 2004.

Clunas, Craig. *Pictures and Visuality in Early Modern China*. Princeton, NJ: Princeton Univ. Press, 1997.

Fang, Jing Pei. *Treasures of the Chinese Scholar: Form, Function, and Symbolism*. Ed. J. May Lee Barrett. New York: Weatherhill, 1997.

Fong, Wen C. *Between Two Cultures: Late-Nineteenth- and Twentieth-Century Chinese Paintings from the Robert H. Ellsworth Collection in the Metropolitan Museum of Art*. New York: Metropolitan Museum of Art, 2001.

Hearn, Maxwell K., and Judith G. Smith, eds. *Chinese Art: Modern Expressions*. New York: Dept. of Asian Art, Metropolitan Museum of Art, 2001.

Ho, Chuimei, and Bennet Bronson. *Splendors of China's Forbidden City: The Glorious Reign of Emperor Qianlong*. Chicago: Field Museum, 2004.

Ho, Wai-kam, ed. *The Century of Tung Ch'i-Ch'ang, 1555–1636*. 2 vols. Kansas City, MO: Nelson-Atkins Museum of Art, 1992.

Kim, Hongnam. *The Life of a Patron: Zhou Lianggong (1612– 1672) and the Painters of Seventeenth-Century China*. New York: China Institute in America, 1996.

Knapp, Ronald G. *China's Vernacular Architecture: House Form and Culture*. Honolulu: Univ. of Hawai'i Press, 1989.

Lee, Sherman, and Wai-Kam Ho. *Chinese Art Under the Mongols: The Y'uan Dynasty, 1279–1368*. Cleveland: Cleveland Museum of Art, 1968.

Lim, Lucy, ed. *Wu Guanzhong: A Contemporary Chinese Artist*. San Francisco: Chinese Culture Foundation, 1989.

Moss, Paul. *Escape from the Dusty World: Chinese Paintings and Literati Works of Art*. London: Sydney L. Moss, 1999.

Ng, So Kam. *Brushstrokes: Styles and Techniques of Chinese Painting*. San Francisco: Asian Art Museum of San Francisco, 1993.

The Poetry [of] Ink: The Korean Literati Tradition, 1392–1910. Paris: Réunion des Musées Nationaux: Musée National des Arts Asiatiques Guimet, 2005.

Smith, Karen. *Nine Lives: The Birth of Avant-Garde Art in New China*. Zürich: Scalo, 2006.

Till, Barry. *The Manchu Era (1644–1912), Arts of China's Last Imperial Dynasty*. Victoria, BC: Art Gallery of Greater Victoria, 2004.

Vainker, S.J. *Chinese Pottery and Porcelain: From Prehistory to the Present*. London: British Museum Press, 1991.

Watson, William. *The Arts of China 900–1620*. Pelican History of Art. New Haven: Yale Univ. Press, 2000.

Weidner, Marsha Smith. *Views from Jade Terrace: Chinese Women Artists, 1300–1912*. Indianapolis, IN: Indianapolis Museum of Art, 1988.

Xinian, Fu, et al. *Chinese Architecture*. Ed. Nancy S. Steinhardt. New Haven: Yale Univ. Press, 2002.

Chapter 26 Japanese Art after 1333

Addiss, Stephen. *The Art of Zen: Painting and Calligraphy by Japanese Monks, 1600–1925*. New York: Abrams, 1989.

Berthier, François. *Reading Zen in the Rocks: The Japanese Dry Landscape Garden*. Trans. & essay Graham Parkes. Chicago: Univ. of Chicago Press, 2000.

Calza, Gian Carlo. *Ukiyo-e*. New York: Phaidon Press, 2005.

Graham, Patricia J. *Faith and Power in Japanese Buddhist Art, 1600–2005*. Honolulu: Univ. of Hawai'i Press, 2007.

———. *Tea of the Sages: The Art of Sencha*. Honolulu: Univ. of Hawai'i Press, 1998.

Guth, Christine. *Art of Edo Japan: The Artist and the City 1615–1868*. Perspectives. New York: Abrams, 1996.

Hickman, Money L. *Japan's Golden Age: Momoyama*. New Haven: Yale Univ. Press, 1996.

Kobayashi, Tadashi, and Lisa Rotondo-McCord. *An Enduring Vision: 17th to 20th Century Japanese Painting from the Gitter-Yelen Collection*. New Orleans: New Orleans Museum of Art, 2003.

Lillehoji, Elizabeth, ed. *Critical Perspectives on Classicism in Japanese Painting, 1600–1700*. Honolulu: Univ. of Hawai'i Press, 2004.

McKelway, Matthew P. *Traditions Unbound: Groundbreaking Painters of Eighteenth-Century Kyoto*. San Francisco: Asian Art Museum–Chong-Moon Lee Center, 2005.

Meech, Julia, and Jane Oliver. *Designed for Pleasure: The World of Edo Japan in Prints and Paintings, 1680–1860*. Seattle: Univ. of Washington Press in association with the Asia Society and Japanese Art Society of America, New York, 2008.

Miyajima, Shin'ichi and Sato Yasuhiro. *Japanese Ink Painting*. Ed. George Kuwayama. Los Angeles: Los Angeles County Museum of Art, 1985.

Munroe, Alexandra. *Japanese Art after 1945: Scream Against the Sky*. New York: Abrams, 1994.

Murase, Miyeko, ed. *Turning Point: Oribe and the Arts of Sixteenth-Century Japan*. New York: Metropolitan Museum of Art, 2003.

Newland, Amy Reigle, ed. *The Hotei Encyclopedia of Japanese Woodblock Prints*. 2 vols. Amsterdam: Hotei Publishing, 2005.

Ohki, Sadako. *Tea Culture of Japan*. New Haven: Yale Univ. Press, 2009.

Rousmaniere, Nicole, ed. *Crafting Beauty in Modern Japan: Celebrating Fifty Years of the Japan Traditional Art Crafts Exhibition*. Seattle: Univ. of Washington Press, 2007.

Screech, Timon. *The Lens Within the Heart: The Western Scientific Gaze and Popular Imagery in Later Edo Japan*. 2nd ed. Honolulu: Univ. of Hawai'i Press, 2002.

Singer, Robert T., and John T. Carpenter. *Edo, Art in Japan 1615–1868*. Washington, DC: National Gallery of Art, 1998.

Chapter 27 Art of the Americas after 1300

Bauer, Brian S. *Ancient Cuzco: Heartland of the Inca*. Joe R. and Teresa Lozano Long Series in Latin American and Latino Art and Culture. Austin: Univ. of Texas Press, 2004.

Berlo, Janet Catherine, and Ruth B. Phillips. *Native North American Art*. Oxford History of Art. 2nd ed. Oxford: Oxford Univ. Press, 2014.

Bringhurst, Robert. *The Black Canoe: Bill Reid and the Spirit of Haida Gwaii*. Seattle: Univ. of Washington Press, l991.

Burger, Richard L., and Lucy C. Salazar, eds. *Machu Picchu: Unveiling the Mystery of the Incas*. New Haven: Yale Univ. Press, 2004.

Coe, Michael D. and Rex Koontz. *Mexico: From the Olmecs to the Aztecs*. 5th ed. New York: Thames & Hudson, 2005.

Fields, Virginia M., and Victor Zamudio-Taylor. *The Road to Aztlan: Art from a Mythic Homeland*. Los Angeles: Los Angeles County Museum of Art, 2001.

Griffin-Pierce, Trudy. *Earth is my Mother, Sky is my Father: Space, Time, and Astronomy in Navajo Sandpainting*. Albuquerque: Univ. of New Mexico Press, 1992.

Jonaitis, Aldona. *Art of the Northwest Coast*. Seattle: Univ. of Washington Press, 2006.

Kaufman, Alice, and Christopher Selser. *The Navajo Weaving Tradition: 1650 to the Present*. New York: Dutton, 1985.

Macnair, Peter L., Robert Joseph, and Bruce Grenville. *Down from the Shimmering Sky: Masks of the Northwest Coast*. Vancouver: Douglas & McIntyre, 1998.

Matos Moctezuma, Eduardo, and Felipe R. Solís Olguín. *Aztecs*. London: Royal Academy of Arts, 2002.

Matthews, Washington. "The Night Chant: A Navaho Ceremony." *Memoirs of the American Museum of Natural History*, vol. 6. New York, 1902.

Moseley, Michael E. *The Incas and Their Ancestors: The Archaeology of Peru*. Rev. ed. London: Thames & Hudson, 2001.

Nabokov, Peter, and Robert Easton. *Native American Architecture*. New York: Oxford Univ. Press, 1989.

Pasztory, Esther. *Aztec Art*. Norman: Univ. of Oklahoma Press, 2000.

Rushing III, W. Jackson, ed. *Native American Art in the Twentieth Century: Makers, Meanings, Histories*. New York: Routledge, 1999.

Shaw, George Everett. *Art of the Ancestors: Antique North American Indian Art*. Aspen, CO: Aspen Art Museum, 2004.

Taylor, Colin F. *Buckskin & Buffalo: The Artistry of the Plains Indians*. New York: Rizzoli, 1998.

Townsend, Richard F., ed. *The Aztecs*. 2nd rev. ed. Ancient Peoples and Places. London: Thames & Hudson, 2000.

Trimble, Stephen. *Talking with the Clay: The Art of Pueblo Pottery in the 21st Century*. 20th anniversary rev. ed. Santa Fe, NM: School for Advanced Research Press, 2007.

Wood, Nancy C. *Taos Pueblo*. New York: Knopf, 1989.

Chapter 28 Art of Pacific Cultures

Caruana, Wally. *Aboriginal Art*. 2nd ed. World of Art. New York: Thames & Hudson, 2003.

Craig, Barry, Bernie Kernot, and Christopher Anderson, eds. *Art and Performance in Oceania*. Honolulu: Univ. of Hawai'i Press, 1999.

D'Alleva, Anne. *Arts of the Pacific Islands*. Perspectives. New York: Abrams, 1998.

Herle, Anita, et al. *Pacific Art: Persistence, Change, and Meaning*. Honolulu: Univ. of Hawai'i Press, 2002.

Kaeppler, Adrienne Lois, Christian Kaufmann, and Douglas Newton. *Oceanic Art*. Trans. Nora Scott and Sabine Bouladon. New York: Abrams, 1997.

Kirch, Patrick Vinton. *The Lapita Peoples: Ancestors of the Oceanic World*. The Peoples of South-East Asia and the Pacific. Cambridge, MA: Blackwell, 1997.

Kjellgren, Eric. *Splendid Isolation: Art of Easter Island*. New York: Metropolitan Museum of Art, 2001.

———, and Carol Ivory. *Adorning the World: Art of the Marquesas Islands*. New Haven: Yale Univ. Press in assoc. with the Metropolitan Museum of Art, 2005.

Küchler, Susanne, and Graeme Were. *Pacific Pattern*. London: Thames & Hudson, 2005.

Lilley, Ian, ed. *Archaeology of Oceania: Australia and the Pacific Islands*. Malden, MA: Blackwell, 2006.

McCulloch, Susan. *Contemporary Aboriginal Art: A Guide to the Rebirth of an Ancient Culture*. Rev. ed. Crows Nest, NSW, Australia: Allen & Unwin, 2001.

Moore, Albert C. *Arts in the Religions of the Pacific: Symbols of Life*. Religion and the Arts Series. New York: Pinter, 1995.

Morphy, Howard. *Aboriginal Art*. London: Phaidon Press, 1998.

Morwood, M.J. *Visions from the Past: The Archaeology of Australian Aboriginal Art*. Washington, DC: Smithsonian Institution Press, 2002.

Neich, Roger, and Mick Pendergrast. *Traditional Tapa Textiles of the Pacific*. London: Thames & Hudson, 1997.

Newton, Douglas, ed. *Arts of the South Seas: Island Southeast Asia, Melanesia, Polynesia, Micronesia; The Collections of the Musée Barbier-Mueller*. Trans. David Radzinowicz Howell. New York: Prestel, 1999.

Rainbird, Paul. *The Archaeology of Micronesia*. Cambridge World Archaeology. New York: Cambridge Univ. Press, 2004.

Smidt, Dirk, ed. *Asmat Art: Woodcarvings of Southwest New Guinea*. New York: George Braziller in assoc. with Rijksmuseum voor Volkenkunde, Leiden, 1993.

Starzecka, D.C., ed. *Maori Art and Culture*. London: British Museum Press, 1996.

Taylor, Luke. *Seeing the Inside: Bark Painting in Western Arnhem Land*. Oxford Studies in Social and Cultural Anthropology. New York: Oxford Univ. Press, 1996.

Thomas, Nicholas. *Oceanic Art*. World of Art. New York: Thames & Hudson, 1995.

———, Anna Cole, and Bronwen Douglas, eds. *Tattoo: Bodies, Art, and Exchange in the Pacific and the West*. Durham, NC: Duke Univ. Press, 2005.

Chapter 29 Arts of Africa from the Sixteenth Century to the Present

Adewunmi, Bim. "Zanele Muholi: 'I Cannot Give Up Myself and My Soul Simply Because I Need Some Exposure.' The Photographer and Visual Activist Talks to Bim Adewunmi." *The New Statesman* (March 30, 2013). Accessed September 4, 2015. http://www.newstatesman.com/bim-adewunmi/2013/03/zanele-muholi-i-cannot-give-myself-and-my-soul-simply-because-i-need-some-expos.

Aronson, Lisa, and John S. Weber. *Environment and Object: Recent African Art*. Saratoga Springs, NY: Frances Young Tang Teaching Museum and Art Gallery at Skidmore College, 2012.

Dina, Jeanne. "The Hazomanga among the Masikoro of Southwest Madagascar: Identity and History." *Ethnohistory*, 48, no. 1/2 (Winter–Spring 2001): 13–30. http://www.jstor.org/stable/40280039.

Enwezor, Okwui, and Chika Okeke-Agulu. *Contemporary African Art Since 1980*. Bologna: Damiani, 2009.

Farrell, Laurie Ann, ed. *Looking Both Ways: Art of the Contemporary African Diaspora*. Gent: Snoeck Publishers and the Museum for African Art, New York, 2003.

Geary, Christraud. "Bamum Two-Figure Thrones: Additional Evidence." *African Arts* 16, no. 4 (August 1983): 46–53, 86–87. http://www.jstor.org/stable/3336034.

Jewsiewicki, Bogumil, D. Dibwe dia Mwembu, and Museum for African Art (New York). *A Congo Chronicle: Patrice Lumumba in Urban Art*. New York: Museum for African Art, 1999.

Martinez, Jessica Levin. "Ephemeral Fang Reliquaries: A Post-History." *African Arts* 43, no. 1 (Spring 2010): 28–43. http://www.jstor.org/stable/29546084.

Mutu, Wangechi, et al. *Wangechi Mutu: A Fantastic Journey*. Durham, NC: Nasher Museum of Art, Duke Univ. Press, 2013.

Chapter 30 European and America Art, 1715–1840

Bailey, Colin B., Philip Conisbee, and Thomas W. Gaehtgens. *The Age of Watteau, Chardin, and Fragonard: Masterpieces of French Genre Painting*. New Haven: Yale Univ. Press in assoc. with the National Gallery of Canada, Ottawa, 2003.

Boime, Albert. *Art in an Age of Bonapartism, 1800–1815*. Chicago: Univ. of Chicago Press, 1990.

———. *Art in an Age of Counterrevolution, 1815–1848*. Chicago: Univ. of Chicago Press, 2004.

———. *Art in an Age of Revolution, 1750–1800*. Chicago: Univ. of Chicago Press, 1987.

Bowron, Edgar Peters, and Joseph J. Rishel, eds. *Art in Rome in the Eighteenth Century*. London: Merrell in association with Philadelphia Museum of Art, 2000.

Brown, David Blayney. *Romanticism*. London: Phaidon Press, 2001.

Chinn, Celestine, and Kieran McCarty. *Bac: Where the Waters Gather*. Univ. of Arizona: Mission San Xavier Del Bac, 1977.

Craske, Matthew. *Art in Europe, 1700–1830: A History of the Visual Arts in an Era of Unprecedented Urban Economic Growth*. Oxford History of Art. Oxford: Oxford Univ. Press, 1997.

Denis, Rafael Cardoso, and Colin Trodd, eds. *Art and the Academy in the Nineteenth Century*. New Brunswick, NJ: Rutgers Univ. Press, 2000.

Goodman, Elise, ed. *Art and Culture in the Eighteenth Century: New Dimensions and Multiple Perspectives*. Studies in Eighteenth-Century Art and Culture. Newark: Univ. of Delaware Press, 2001.

Hofmann, Werner. *Goya: To Every Story There Belongs Another*. New York: Thames & Hudson, 2003.

Irwin, David G. *Neoclassicism*. Art & Ideas. London: Phaidon Press, 1997.

Jarrassé, Dominique. *18th-Century French Painting*. Trans. Murray Wyllie. Paris: Terrail, 1999.

Kalnein, Wend von. *Architecture in France in the Eighteenth Century*. Trans. David Britt. Pelican History of Art. New Haven: Yale Univ. Press, 1995.

Levey, Michael. *Painting in Eighteenth-Century Venice*. 3rd ed. New Haven: Yale Univ. Press, 1994.

Lewis, Michael J. *The Gothic Revival*. World of Art. New York: Thames & Hudson, 2002.

Lovell, Margaretta M. *Art in a Season of Revolution: Painters, Artisans, and Patrons in Early America*. Early American Studies. Philadelphia: Univ. of Pennsylvania Press, 2005.

Monneret, Sophie. *David and Neo-Classicism*. Trans. Chris Miller and Peter Snowdon. Paris: Terrail, 1999.

Natter, Tobias, ed. *Angelica Kauffman: A Woman of Immense Talent*. Ostfildern: Hatje Cantz, 2007.

Porterfield, Todd, and Susan L. Siegfried. *Staging Empire: Napoleon, Ingres, and David*. University Park: Pennsylvania State Univ. Press, 2006.

Poulet, Anne L. *Jean-Antoine Houdon: Sculptor of the Enlightenment*. Washington, DC: National Gallery of Art, 2003.

Summerson, John. *Architecture of the Eighteenth Century*. World of Art. New York: Thames & Hudson, 1986.

Wilton, Andrew, and Ilaria Bignamini, eds. *Grand Tour: The Lure of Italy in the Eighteenth Century*. London: Tate Gallery, 1996.

Chapter 31 Mid- to Late Nineteenth-Century Art in Europe and the United States

Adams, Steven. *The Barbizon School and the Origins of Impressionism*. London: Phaidon Press, 1994.

Bajac, Quentin. *The Invention of Photography*. Discoveries. New York: Abrams, 2002.

Barger, M. Susan, and William B. White. *The Daguerreotype: Nineteenth-Century Technology and Modern Science*. Washington, DC: Smithsonian Institution Press, 1991.

Benjamin, Roger. *Orientalist Aesthetics: Art, Colonialism, and French North Africa, 1880–1930*. Berkeley: Univ. of California Press, 2003.

Bergdoll, Barry. *European Architecture, 1750–1890*. Oxford History of Art. New York: Oxford Univ. Press, 2000.

Blühm, Andreas, and Louise Lippincott. *Light!: The Industrial Age 1750–1900: Art & Science, Technology & Society*. New York: Thames & Hudson, 2001.

Boime, Albert, *The Academy and French Painting in the Nineteenth Century*. 2nd ed. New Haven: Yale Univ. Press, 1986.

Butler, Ruth, and Suzanne G. Lindsay. *European Sculpture of the Nineteenth Century*. Washington, DC: National Gallery of Art, 2000.

Callen, Anthea. *The Art of Impressionism: Painting Technique & the Making of Modernity*. New Haven: Yale Univ. Press, 2000.

Chu, Petra ten-Doesschate. *Nineteenth Century European Art*. 3rd. ed. Upper Saddle River, NJ: Pearson/Prentice Hall, 2012.

Clark, T. J. *The Painting of Modern Life: Paris in the Art of Manet and His Followers*. Rev. ed. London: Thames & Hudson, 1999.

Conrads, Margaret C. *Winslow Homer and the Critics: Forging a National Art in the 1870s*. Princeton, NJ: Princeton Univ. Press in assoc. with the Nelson-Atkins Museum of Art, 2001.

Denis, Rafael Cardoso, and Colin Trodd. *Art and the Academy in the Nineteenth Century*. New Brunswick, NJ: Rutgers Univ. Press, 2000.

Eisenman, Stephen F. *Nineteenth Century Art: A Critical History*. 3rd ed. New York: Thames & Hudson, 2007.

Eitner, Lorenz. *Nineteenth Century European Painting: David to Cezanne.* Rev. ed. Boulder, CO: Westview Press, 2002.

Frazier, Nancy. *Louis Sullivan and the Chicago School.* New York: Knickerbocker Press, 1998.

Fried, Michael. *Manet's Modernism, or, The Face of Painting in the 1860s.* Chicago: Univ. of Chicago Press, 1996.

Gerdts, William H. *American Impressionism.* 2nd ed. New York: Abbeville Press, 2001.

Greenhalgh, Paul, ed. *Art Nouveau, 1890–1914.* London: V&A Publications, 2000.

Grigsby, Darcy Grimaldo. *Extremities: Painting Empire in Post-Revolutionary France.* New Haven: Yale Univ. Press, 2002.

Groseclose, Barbara. *Nineteenth-Century American Art.* Oxford History of Art. Oxford: Oxford Univ. Press, 2000.

Harrison, Charles, Paul Wood, and Jason Gaiger. *Art in Theory 1815–1900: An Anthology of Changing Ideas.* Oxford: Blackwell, 1998.

Herrmann, Luke. *Nineteenth Century British Painting.* London: Giles de la Mare, 2000.

Hirsh, Sharon L. *Symbolism and Modern Urban Society.* New York: Cambridge Univ. Press, 2004.

Kaplan, Wendy. *The Arts & Crafts Movement in Europe & America: Design for the Modern World.* New York: Thames & Hudson in assoc. with the Los Angeles County Museum of Art, 2004.

Kendall, Richard. *Degas: Beyond Impressionism.* London: National Gallery, 1996.

Lambourne, Lionel. *Japonisme: Cultural Crossings between Japan and the West.* New York: Phaidon Press, 2005.

Lemoine, Bertrand. *Architecture in France, 1800–1900.* Trans. Alexandra Bonfante-Warren. New York: Abrams, 1998.

Lewis, Mary Tompkins, ed. *Critical Readings in Impressionism and Post-Impressionism: An Anthology.* Berkeley: Univ. of California Press, 2007.

Lochnan, Katharine Jordan. *Turner Whistler Monet.* London: Tate Publishing in assoc. with the Art Gallery of Ontario, 2004.

Miller, Angela L., et al. *American Encounters: Art, History, and Cultural Identity.* Upper Saddle River, NJ: Pearson/ Prentice Hall, 2008.

Moffett, Charles S., et al. *The New Painting: Impressionism 1874–1886.* San Francisco: The Fine Arts Museums, 1986.

Nochlin, Linda. *Realism.* New York: Penguin Books, 1990.

——. *The Politics of Vision: Essays on Nineteenth-Century Art and Society.* New York: Harper and Row, 1989.

Noon, Patrick J. *Crossing the Channel: British and French Painting in the Age of Romanticism.* London: Tate Publishing, 2003.

Pissarro, Joachim. *Pioneering Modern Painting: Cézanne & Pissarro 1865–1885.* New York: Museum of Modern Art, 2005.

Rodner, William S. *J.M.W. Turner: Romantic Painter of the Industrial Revolution.* Berkeley: Univ. of California Press, 1997.

Rosenblum, Robert, and H.W. Janson. *19th Century Art.* Rev. & updated ed. Upper Saddle River, NJ: Pearson/ Prentice Hall, 2005.

Rubin, James H. *Impressionism. Art & Ideas.* London: Phaidon Press, 1999.

Rybczynski, Witold. *A Clearing in the Distance: Frederick Law Olmsted and America in the Nineteenth Century.* New York: Scribner, 1999.

Smith, Paul. *Seurat and the Avant-Garde.* New Haven: Yale Univ. Press, 1997.

Thomson, Belinda. *Impressionism: Origins, Practice, Reception.* World of Art. New York: Thames & Hudson, 2000.

Twyman, Michael. *Breaking the Mould: The First Hundred Years of Lithography.* The Panizzi Lectures, 2000. London: British Library, 2001.

Vaughan, William, and Francoise Cachin. *Arts of the 19th Century.* 2 vols. New York: Abrams, 1998.

Werner, Marcia. *Pre-Raphaelite Painting and Nineteenth- Century Realism.* New York: Cambridge Univ. Press, 2005.

Zemel, Carol M. *Van Gogh's Progress: Utopia, Modernity, and Late-Nineteenth-Century Art.* California Studies in the History of Art, 36. Berkeley: Univ. of California Press, 1997.

Chapter 32 Modern Art in Europe and the Americas, 1900–1950

Ades, Dawn, comp. *Art and Power: Europe under the Dictators, 1930–45.* Stuttgart, Germany: Oktagon in assoc. with Hayward Gallery, 1995.

Antliff, Mark, and Patricia Leighten. *Cubism and Culture.* World of Art. London: Thames & Hudson, 2001.

Bailey, David A. *Rhapsodies in Black: Art of the Harlem Renaissance.* London: Hayward Gallery, 1997.

Balken, Debra Bricker. *Debating American Modernism: Stieglitz, Duchamp, and the New York Avant-Garde.* New York: American Federation of Arts, 2003.

Barron, Stephanie, ed. *Degenerate Art: The Fate of the Avant-Garde in Nazi Germany.* Los Angeles: Los Angeles County Museum of Art, 1991.

——, and Wolf-Dieter Dube, eds. *German Expressionism: Art and Society.* New York: Rizzoli, 1997.

Bochner, Jay. *An American Lens: Scenes from Alfred Stieglitz's New York Secession.* Cambridge, MA: MIT Press, 2005.

Bohn, Willard. *The Rise of Surrealism: Cubism, Dada, and the Pursuit of the Marvelous.* Albany: State Univ. of New York Press, 2002.

Bowlt, John E., and Evgeniia Petrova, eds. *Painting Revolution: Kandinsky, Malevich and the Russian Avant-Garde.* Bethesda, MD: Foundation for International Arts and Education, 2000.

Bown, Matthew Cullerne. *Socialist Realist Painting.* New Haven: Yale Univ. Press, 1998.

Brown, Milton W. *Story of the Armory Show.* 2nd ed. New York: Abbeville Press, 1988.

Caws, Mary Ann. *Surrealism.* Themes and Movements. London: Phaidon, 2004.

Chassey, Eric de, ed. *American Art: 1908–1947, from Winslow Homer to Jackson Pollock.* Trans. Jane McDonald. Paris: Réunion des Musées Nationaux, 2001.

Corn, Wanda M. *The Great American Thing: Modern Art and National Identity, 1915–1935.* Berkeley: Univ. of California Press, 1999.

Curtis, Penelope. *Sculpture 1900–1945: After Rodin.* Oxford History of Art. Oxford: Oxford Univ. Press, 1999.

Dachy, Marc. *Dada: The Revolt of Art.* Trans. Liz Nash. New York: Abrams, 2006.

Dickerman, Leah, ed. *Dada: Zurich, Berlin, Hannover, Cologne, New York, Paris.* Washington, DC: National Gallery of Art, 2005.

Elger, Dietmar. *Expressionism: A Revolution in German Art.* Ed. Ingo F. Walther. Trans. Hugh Beyer. New York: Taschen, 1998.

Fer, Briony. *On Abstract Art.* New Haven: Yale Univ. Press, 1997.

Fletcher, Valerie J. *Crosscurrents of Modernism: Four Latin American Pioneers: Diego Rivera, Joaquín Torres-García, Wifredo Lam, Matta.* Washington, DC: Hirshhorn Museum and Sculpture Garden in assoc. with the Smithsonian Institution Press, 1992.

Folgarait, Leonard. *Mural Painting and Social Revolution in Mexico, 1920–1940: Art of the New Order.* New York: Cambridge Univ. Press, 1998.

Forgács, Eva. *The Bauhaus Idea and Bauhaus Politics.* Trans. John Bátki. New York: Central European Univ. Press, 1995.

Frampton, Kenneth. *Modern Architecture: A Critical History.* 4th ed. World of Art. London: Thames & Hudson, 2007.

Gooding, Mel. *Abstract Art.* Movements in Modern Art. Cambridge: Cambridge Univ. Press, 2001.

Grant, Kim. *Surrealism and the Visual Arts: Theory and Reception.* New York: Cambridge Univ. Press, 2005.

Gray, Camilla, and Marian Burleigh-Motley. *The Russian Experiment in Art, 1863–1922.* World of Art. New York: Thames and Hudson, 1986.

Green, Christopher. *Art in France: 1900–1940.* Pelican History of Art. New Haven: Yale Univ. Press, 2000.

Harris, Jonathan. *Federal Art and National Culture: The Politics of Identity in New Deal America.* Cambridge Studies in American Visual Culture. New York: Cambridge Univ. Press, 1995.

Harrison, Charles, Francis Frascina, and Gill Perry. *Primitivism, Cubism, Abstraction: The Early Twentieth Century.* New Haven: Yale Univ. Press, 1993.

Haskell, Barbara. *The American Century: Art & Culture, 1900–1950.* New York: Whitney Museum of American Art, 1999.

Herskovic, Marika, ed. *American Abstract Expressionism of the 1950s: An Illustrated Survey: With Artists' Statements, Artwork and Biographies.* New York: New York School Press, 2003.

Hill, Charles C. *The Group of Seven: Art for a Nation.* Ottawa: National Gallery of Canada, 1995.

James-Chakraborty, Kathleen, ed. *Bauhaus Culture: From Weimar to the Cold War.* Minneapolis: Univ. of Minnesota Press, 2006.

Karmel, Pepe. *Picasso and the Invention of Cubism.* New Haven: Yale Univ. Press, 2003.

Krauss, Rosalind. *The Originality of the Avant-Garde and Other Modernist Myths.* Cambridge, MA and London: MIT Press, 1986.

Kuenzli, Rudolf. *Dada. Themes and Movements.* London: Phaidon, 2006.

Lista, Giovanni. *Futurism.* Trans. Susan Wise. Paris: Terrail, 2001.

Lucie-Smith, Edward. *Latin American Art of the 20th Century.* 2nd ed. World of Art. London: Thames & Hudson, 2005.

McCarter, Robert, ed. *On and by Frank Lloyd Wright: A Primer of Architectural Principles.* New York: Phaidon Press, 2005.

Moudry, Roberta, ed. *The American Skyscraper: Cultural Histories.* New York: Cambridge Univ. Press, 2005.

Rickey, George. *Constructivism: Origins and Evolution.* Rev. ed. New York: Braziller, 1995.

Taylor, Brandon. *Collage: The Making of Modern Art.* London: Thames & Hudson, 2004.

Weston, Richard. *Modernism.* London: Phaidon Press, 1996.

White, Michael. *De Stijl and Dutch Modernism.* Critical Perspectives in Art History. New York: Manchester Univ. Press, 2003.

Whitfield, Sarah. *Fauvism*. World of Art. New York: Thames & Hudson, 1996.

Whitford, Frank. *The Bauhaus: Masters and Students by Themselves*. Woodstock, NY: Overlook Press, 1993.

Zurier, Rebecca, Robert W. Snyder, and Virginia M. Mecklenburg. *Metropolitan Lives: The Ashcan Artists and Their New York*. Washington, DC: National Museum of American Art, 1995.

Chapter 33 The International Scene since the 1950s

Alberro, Alexander, and Blake Stimson, eds. *Conceptual Art: A Critical Anthology*. Cambridge, MA: MIT Press, 1999.

Archer, Michael. *Art Since 1960*. 2nd ed. World of Art. New York: Thames & Hudson, 2002.

Atkins. Robert. *Artspeak: A Guide to Contemporary Ideas, Movements, and Buzzwords*. 2nd ed. New York: Abbeville Press, 1997.

Ault, Julie. *Art Matters: How the Culture Wars Changed America*. Ed. Brian Wallis, Marianne Weems, and Philip Yenawine. New York: New York Univ. Press, 1999.

Battcock, Gregory. *Minimal Art: A Critical Anthology*. Berkeley: Univ. of California Press, 1995.

Beardsley, John. *Earthworks and Beyond: Contemporary Art in the Landscape*. 4th ed. eBook. New York: Abbeville Press, 2006.

Bird, Jon, and Michael Newman, eds. *Rewriting Conceptual Art*. Critical Views. London: Reaktion Books, 1999.

Bishop, Claire. *Installation Art: A Critical History*. New York: Routledge, 2005.

Bishop, Claire. *Participation*. London: Whitechapel, 2006.

Blais, Joline, and Jon Ippolito. *At the Edge of Art*. London: Thames & Hudson, 2006.

Buchloh, Benjamin H.D. *Neo-Avantgarde and Culture Industry: Essays on European and American Art from 1955 to 1975*. Cambridge, MA: MIT Press, 2000.

Buszek, Maria Elena. *Extra/ordinary: Craft and Contemporary Art*. Durham, NC: Duke Univ. Press, 2011.

Causey, Andrew. *Sculpture Since 1945*. Oxford History of Art. Oxford: Oxford Univ. Press, 1998.

Corris, Michael, ed. *Conceptual Art: Theory, Myth, and Practice*. New York: Cambridge Univ. Press, 2004.

De Oliveira, Nicolas, Nicola Oxley, and Michael Petry. *Installation Art in the New Millennium: The Empire of the Senses*. New York: Thames & Hudson, 2003.

De Salvo, Donna, ed. *Open Systems: Rethinking Art c. 1970*. London: Tate Gallery, 2005.

Dumbadze, Alexander Blair, and Suzanne Perling Hudson. *Contemporary Art: 1989 to the Present*. Chichester, West Sussex: Wiley-Blackwell, 2013.

Fabozzi, Paul F. *Artists, Critics, Context: Readings In and Around American Art Since 1945*. Upper Saddle River, NJ: Pearson/Prentice Hall, 2002.

Fineberg, Jonathan. *Art Since 1940: Strategies of Being*. 3rd ed. Upper Saddle River, NJ: Pearson/Prentice Hall, 2011.

Flood, Richard, and Frances Morris. *Zero to Infinity: Arte Povera, 1962–1972*. Minneapolis, MN: Walker Art Center, 2001.

Fried, Michael. "Art and Objecthood." *Artforum* 5 (June 1967): 12–23.

Goldberg, RoseLee. *Performance Art: From Futurism to the Present*. Rev. and exp. ed. World of Art. London: Thames & Hudson, 2001.

Goldstein, Ann. *A Minimal Future? Art as Object 1958–1968*. Los Angeles: Museum of Contemporary Art, 2004.

Grande, John K. *Art Nature Dialogues: Interviews with Environmental Artists*. Albany: State Univ. of New York Press, 2004.

Grosenick, Uta, ed. *Women Artists in the 20th and 21st Century*. New York: Taschen, 2001.

Grunenberg, Christoph, ed. *Summer of Love: Art of the Psychedelic Era*. London: Tate Gallery, 2005.

Haskell Barbara, and John G. Hanhardt. *Blam! the Explosion of Pop, Minimalism, and Performance, 1958–1964*. New York: Whitney Museum of American Art in association with W.W. Norton & Co, 1984.

Heineman, David S. *Thinking about Video Games: Interviews with the Experts*. Bloomington: Indiana Univ. Press, 2015.

Higgins, Hannah. *Fluxus Experience*. Berkeley: Univ. of California Press, 2002.

Hitchcock, Henry Russell, and Philip Johnson. *The International Style*. New York: Norton, 1995.

Hopkins, David. *After Modern Art: 1945–2000*. Oxford History of Art. Oxford: Oxford Univ. Press, 2000.

Jencks, Charles. *The New Paradigm in Architecture: The Language of Post-Modernism*. New Haven: Yale Univ. Press, 2002.

Jodidio, Philip. *New Forms: Architecture in the 1990s*. Taschen's World Architecture. New York: Taschen, 2001.

Johnson, Deborah, and Wendy Oliver, eds. *Women Making Art: Women in the Visual, Literary, and Performing Arts Since 1960*. Eruptions, vol. 7. New York: Peter Lang, 2001.

Jones, Caroline A. *Machine in the Studio: Constructing the Postwar American Artist*. Chicago: Univ. of Chicago Press, 1996.

Joselit, David. *American Art Since 1945*. World of Art. London: Thames & Hudson, 2003.

Judd, Donald. "Specific Objects." *Arts Yearbook* 8 (1965): 74–82.

Kaprow, Allan. "The Legacy of Jackson Pollock." *Art News* 57, no. 6 (October 1958): 24–26, 55–57.

Legault, Réjean, and Sarah Williams Goldhagen, eds. *Anxious Modernisms: Experimentation in Postwar Architectural Culture*. Montréal: Canadian Centre for Architecture, 2000.

Lucie-Smith, Edward. *Movements in Art Since 1945*. New ed. World of Art. London: Thames & Hudson, 2001.

Madoff, Steven Henry, ed. *Pop Art: A Critical History*. The Documents of Twentieth-Century Art. Berkeley: Univ. of California Press, 1997.

Molesworth, Helen Anne, and Ruth Erickson. *Leap Before You Look: Black Mountain College, 1933–1957*. New Haven: Yale Univ. Press, 2015.

Meyer, James Sampson. *Minimalism: Art and Polemics in the Sixties*. New Haven: Yale Univ. Press, 2001.

Nochlin, Linda. "Why Have There Been No Great Women Artists?" *Art News* 69 (January 1972): 22–39.

Owens, Craig. "The Discourse of Others: Feminists and Postmodernism." *The Anti-Aesthetic: Essays on Postmodern Culture*, ed. Hal Foster. Seattle: Bay Press, 1983: 57–82.

Phillips, Lisa. *The American Century: Art and Culture, 1950–2000*. New York: Whitney Museum of American Art, 1999.

Pop Art: Contemporary Perspectives. Princeton, NJ: Princeton Univ. Art Museum, 2007.

Ratcliff, Carter. *The Fate of a Gesture: Jackson Pollock and Postwar American Art*. New York: Farrar, Straus, Giroux, 1996.

Reckitt, Helena, ed. *Art and Feminism*. Themes and Movements. London: Phaidon Press, 2001.

Robertson, Jean, and Craig McDaniel. *Themes of Contemporary Art: Visual Art after 1980*. 3rd ed. New York: Oxford Univ. Press, 2013.

Robinson, Hilary, ed. *Feminism-Art-Theory: An Anthology, 1968–2000*. Malden, MA: Blackwell, 2001.

Rorimer, Anne. *New Art in the 60s and 70s: Redefining Reality*. New York: Thames & Hudson, 2001.

Rush, Michael. *New Media in Late 20th-Century Art*. 2nd ed. World of Art. London: Thames & Hudson, 2005.

———. *Video Art*. 2nd ed. London: Thames & Hudson, 2007.

Sandler, Irving. *Art of the Postmodern Era: From the Late 1960s to the Early 1990s*. New York: Icon Editions, 1996.

Schimmel, Paul, and Kristine Stiles. *Out of Actions: Between Performance and the Object, 1949–1979*. Los Angeles: The Museum of Contemporary Art, 1998.

Shohat, Ella. *Talking Visions: Multicultural Feminism in a Transnational Age*. Documentary Sources in Contemporary Art, vol. 5. New York: New Museum of Contemporary Art, 1998.

Smith, Terry. *Contemporary Art: World Currents*. Upper Saddle River, NJ: Pearson/Prentice Hall, 2011.

Stiles, Kristine, and Peter Selz. *Theories and Documents of Contemporary Art: A Sourcebook of Artists' Writings*. California Studies in the History of Art, 35. 2nd ed. Berkeley: Univ. of California, 2012.

Sylvester, David. *About Modern Art*. 2nd ed. New Haven: Yale Univ. Press, 2001.

Varnedoe, Kirk, Paola Antonelli, and Joshua Siegel, eds. *Modern Contemporary: Art since 1980 at MoMA*. Rev. ed. New York: Museum of Modern Art, 2004.

Waldman, Diane. *Collage, Assemblage, and the Found Object*. New York: Abrams, 1992.

Weintraub, Linda, Arthur Danto, and Thomas McEvilley. *Art on the Edge and Over: Searching for Art's Meaning in Contemporary Society, 1970s–1990s*. Litchfield, CT: Art Insights, 1996.

Yoshihara, Jirō. "The Gutai Manifesto." *Genijutsu Shincho*. December, 1956. 821. Reprinted in Kristine Stiles and Peter Selz. *Theories and Documents of Contemporary Art*. 2nd ed. Berkeley: Univ. of California Press, 2012.

Text Credits

Index